COMPLETE JEWISH BIBLE

COMPLETE JEWISH BIBLE

An English Version of the *Tanakh* (Old Testament)
and *B'rit Hadashah* (New Testament)

David H. Stern

"For out of Tziyon will go forth *Torah*,
the Word of ADONAI from Yerushalayim."
—Yesha'yahu (Isaiah) 2:3

JEWISH NEW TESTAMENT PUBLICATIONS, INC.

Clarksville, Maryland USA   Jerusalem, Israel

Cover illustration by Mickey Klugman Caspi
Printed in the United States of America

09 08 07 06 05   9 8 7 6 5 4
Library of Congress Catalog Control Number: 98-66344

ISBN 965-359-018-9 (paperback)
ISBN 965-359-015-4 (hardback)
ISBN 965-359-019-7 (leather)

Published by
JEWISH NEW TESTAMENT PUBLICATIONS, INC.
Post Office Box 615
Clarksville, Maryland 21029

Distributed by
MESSIANIC JEWISH RESOURCES INTERNATIONAL
Order line: (800) 410-7367
E-mail: lederer@messianicjewish.net
Website: www.messianicjewish.net

ברוך אתה יהוה אלהינו מלך העולם אשר נותן תורת-אמת
ובשורת-ישועה לעמו ישראל ולכל העמים על-ידי בנו ישוע
המשיח אדוננו.

Praised are you, *Adonai* our God, King of the universe, who
gives the *Torah* of truth and the Good News of salvation to his
people Israel and to all the peoples through his son Yeshua the
Messiah, our Lord.

CONTENTS

CONTENTS

APPENDIXES

BOOKS OF THE *TANAKH*
Listed in Christian Old Testament Order

BOOKS OF THE BIBLE
Listed in Alphabetical Order
(Including both the Jewish and the Christian names for the books)

INTRODUCTION

Why is this Bible different from all other Bibles? Because it is the only English version of the Bible fully Jewish in style and presentation that includes both the *Tanakh* ("Old Testament") and the *B'rit Hadashah* (New Covenant, "New Testament"). Even its title, the *Complete Jewish Bible*, challenges both Jews and Christians to see that the whole Bible is Jewish, the *B'rit Hadashah* as well as the *Tanakh*. Jews are challenged by the implication that without it the *Tanakh* is an *in*complete Bible. Christians are challenged with the fact that they are joined to the Jewish people through faith in the Jewish Messiah, Yeshua (Jesus) — so that because Christianity can be rightly understood only from a Jewish perspective, anti-Semitism is condemned absolutely and forever. In short, the *Complete Jewish Bible* restores the Jewish unity of the Bible. Also for the first time the information needed for the synagogue readings from the *Torah* and the Prophets is completely integrated with similar use of the *B'rit Hadashah*.

I. HOW THE *COMPLETE JEWISH BIBLE* CAME TO BE

A bit of personal history will give the reader some insight as to why the *Complete Jewish Bible* exists. Bible introductions are usually more formal, eschewing the use of the first-person singular pronoun, because the seriousness of the Bible seems to call for it — a formal introduction reinforces the authority of the Bible itself. After all, the Bible is God's Word to humanity, the only completely reliable verbal communication God has given us. It is worthy of acceptance, belief, trust; it is his handbook for faith and practice.[1] Since this is so, the writer of an introduction to the Bible necessarily shoulders a heavy responsibility, one in which informality and focus on oneself seem out of place.

Nevertheless, there is another side: precisely because the Bible deals with such serious topics as sin, judgment, God's will, repentance and forgiveness, as well as the role in life and history of Yeshua the Messiah (whom Christians call Jesus Christ), readers of translations tend to forget that there is a very specific human input which does not date from Bible times and which both fosters and impedes their understanding of Scripture, namely, the translator. My choice of style for this Introduction, especially in Sections I and II, stems from my desire to have the translator's role in this Bible version and others better understood. Farther on, I will deal with the content of the Bible itself (Sections III–VIII), the specific features of the *Complete Jewish Bible* (Sections IX–XIV) and how to make the best use of this version (Sections XV–XVII). But here, I am presenting the translator's story.

I am Jewish, was raised in the Jewish religion by Jewish parents and did not come to faith in the Jewish Messiah, Yeshua, until I was thirty-seven years old. As a Messianic Jew (a Jew who honors Yeshua as the Messiah), I saw that the greatest schism in the world is the separation between the Church and the Jewish people; and I experienced it as God's will for my life that I do what I could to resolve this — it

---

[1] For a brief explanation and defense of these assertions, see Section VI below.

would be my contribution to *tikkun-ha'olam* (repairing the world). Although I had a doctorate in economics, I returned to school to learn more about both Christianity and Judaism — Fuller Theological Seminary for the Christian elements and the University of Judaism for the Jewish.

Thus equipped, I set out in 1977 to write a Messianic Jewish commentary on the New Testament; I wanted to produce a single book that would deal with all the "Jewish issues" I could think of in connection with the New Testament — questions Jews have about Yeshua, the New Testament, and Christianity; questions Christians have about Judaism and the Jewish roots of their own faith; and questions we Messianic Jews have about our own identity and role in the light of two thousand years of separation and conflict between the Church and the Jews. But I quickly discovered that much of what I was writing consisted of arguments with the translator of the English version I was using; they took the form, "Our English version says such-and-such, but what it *really* means is so-and-so." The idea came to me to attempt my own translation of the New Testament from the ancient Greek original; then, obviously, I would have a version I agreed with, so I could focus exclusively on the subject matter. I did a sample and was pleased with it. Thus was born the *Jewish New Testament (JNT)*, which was published in 1989.

I spent the next three years finishing up the *Jewish New Testament Commentary*. Meanwhile, the *JNT* had been well received by Messianic Jews and by Christians open to experiencing the Jewishness of their faith. Bible translation may not be known as a glamorous profession, but I have fans. My fans, who said that they appreciated my re-introduction of Jewishness into the New Testament and that they enjoyed my "informal yet respectful" style of writing, kept asking me, "When are you going to do the Old Testament?" They wanted to have a single book containing the entire Bible that they could bring to their congregational meetings, instead of having to carry the *Jewish New Testament* plus a second book containing the *Tanakh*.

I put them off for three more years but finally bowed to the inevitable and got to work. My delay was due to lack of incentive. In translating the *Jewish New Testament* I had had a strong and directed desire to show everyone, Jews and Christians alike, that the New Testament is a thoroughly Jewish book. But with the Old Testament I had no such motivation—everyone knows it's Jewish, so what's to prove? Moreover, at the age of sixty I didn't care to spend years and years and more years doing a translation from the original Hebrew. Even though I had been living in Israel and speaking Hebrew since 1979, I knew from observing my children that my level of competence in the language was approximately that of a native Israeli fifth-grader. I certainly had no special expertise in biblical Hebrew that would justify my trying to translate the *Tanakh*.

So I set myself a simpler task. Initially my thought was to acquire the rights to some modern translation of the *Tanakh* which would be stylistically compatible with my own English style in the *JNT*. I couldn't imagine that the owners of any copy-righted Jewish-sponsored translation would permit me to combine it with the New Testament in a single volume having my projected title, so I looked for suitable candidates among the Christian versions. My first choice was rejected by the copy-right holders, but my second choice was accepted. However, just as I was ready to move ahead, I realized that if this was to be the *Complete **Jewish** Bible*, I couldn't use any Christian Old Testament, because Christians modify the Masoretic text (the

Hebrew text of the *Tanakh* accepted by Judaism) with information gleaned from the Septuagint and other early versions.[2] Elation was replaced by gloom. Suddenly it occurred to me that the old Jewish Publication Society (JPS) version of the *Tanakh*, perhaps the best-known and most used Jewish translation in the English-speaking world, had just gone into the public domain — it had been published in 1917, and copyrights run 75 years. But although it had been published in 1917, for various sociological reasons it sounded as if it had been written in 1617! It was full of King James Bible English and was altogether incompatible with the modern English I had used in the *JNT*.

I tried having this old JPS edition scanned into a computer, with the object of modernizing its English by means of a few global-search-and-replace commands. I wanted to be able to press two buttons and have every "thou" turn into a "you" and "doeth" into "do"; "Abraham" into "Avraham" and "Isaac" into "Yitz'chak." It proved to be not that simple. Not only the words but the sentence structures were archaic. The more I fiddled with the JPS text the less satisfied I was. It was like restoring an old car with lots of dents. You fix the first three, and the fourth, fifth and sixth stand out. Repair them, and numbers 7, 8, 9 and 10 beg for attention. Eventually you repair all the big dents, and you have a car with thousands of little dents, so it still doesn't look right.

So I decided to paraphrase the entire JPS *Tanakh* into modern English, typing in the whole thing by hand, as I decided how to express each word, each phrase, each verse. Though a huge project, it would be much less demanding than a translation. And that is how much of this *Tanakh* came into existence.

However, there were many places where I questioned the JPS version's renderings. In such cases I translated the Hebrew of the Masoretic text myself. I also made use of other English versions to assist me in expressing certain verses in modern English. All Bible translators do this — the people who put together the *King James Version* did it too, acknowledging their debt to those who had gone before them in their famous subtitle, "and with the former translations diligently compared and revised." So the *Tanakh* you have in this book is something between a translation and a paraphrase; since it is partly one and partly the other, I refuse to define it as either and instead call it simply a "version." On the other hand, the books of the New Covenant are my translation from the original Greek.

II. TRANSLATIONS AND TRANSLATORS

Is There Such a Thing as a "Best" Translation of the Bible? While on the subject of the translation-and/or-paraphrasing process, I want to make some general remarks about translations. First, it is a common belief that there is such a thing as a "best" translation of a text from one language to another. I question that. Languages have different words, different syntaxes, different sentence structures, different semantics, different cultures out of which they arise and evolve, and many other differences; so that translation cannot be a simple, automated process. Moreover, readers differ. Some prefer a simple style with a modest vocabulary, while others respond to a more elegant or complex style with a larger vocabulary. Even the concept of accuracy is reader-dependent — what scholars might consider an accurate translation might fail

---

[2] See Section VIII.

to accurately communicate to less informed readers. If translators fail to consider who their readers are, aren't the translators responsible for the lack of communication? Clearly some translations are, by all reasonable standards, worse, while others are better. But because readers differ, no one version can be best for all.

Translations and Their Purposes. Therefore, one has to ask, "What is the purpose of a given translation, and does it accomplish its purpose well?" The *King James Version* is unmatched in the beauty of its language; moreover, English would not be what it is without it. But today not everyone can get the sense of the text from its archaic expressions, and, with advances in historical, archeological and linguistic studies, some scholars believe that a number of its renderings are wrong. The newer JPS translation of the *Tanakh*, from 1985, is particularly useful for noting phrases where the meaning of the original Hebrew is unclear; whereas in my version I have not provided that information. The *Today's English Version* ("Good News Bible") produced by the United Bible Societies makes use of a limited vocabulary so that those for whom English is a second language can understand it. The *New English Bible* has echoes of the great writers—Shakespeare, Milton—which makes it ideal for public reading in Anglican churches. Everett Fox's recent translation of the *Torah* is unique in giving a feel for Hebrew style and thought-forms, as well as the culture of Bible times. *The Living Bible*, originally prepared by Ken Taylor for his teenage children, conveys, at least to young Americans, an unmatched energy and presence. No one version could possibly serve all these purposes at once. The beauty of God's Word is that it can be translated in various ways that serve these purposes and others, without obscuring the Bible's own purpose — which is to show people the truth about God, themselves, relationships and the meaning of life, and to call forth the appropriate and necessary responses.

Purposes of This Version of the Bible. Therefore I owe it to my readers to state the purposes of the *Complete Jewish Bible (CJB)*.

1) My first purpose is, as I said, to restore the unified Jewishness of the Bible, and, particularly, to show that the books of the New Covenant are Jewish through and through.

2) The second aim of the *Complete Jewish Bible* is to express the Word of God—*Tanakh* and *B'rit Hadashah* together—in enjoyable modern English. I want the Bible to be accessible and easy to read, flowing easily from the page into the mind and heart, unimpeded as much as possible by the differences between the environment of the Bible and that of the present.

3) My third purpose is to make the *CJB* fully usable in a Messianic synagogue, where the *B'rit Hadashah* would be read in the service along with the *Torah* and the Prophets. (The *CJB* can be used to follow the readings in a non-Messianic synagogue as well.)

4) And finally, I am supplying at last what my fans have been asking me for — a single volume containing my version of the entire Bible.

With the above as background, there are three philosophical points raised in translation work that need to be addressed: (1) formal versus dynamic equivalence ("literal translations" versus "paraphrases"), (2) the degree to which a translator's interpretation of a text's meaning should be reflected in his translation, and (3) the pluses and minuses of a version produced by a single individual versus one produced by a translation team.

"Literal Translations" Versus "Paraphrases." There is a scale on which translations can be measured. At one end of the scale are "literal" translations, which reproduce in the receptor language (English) the grammatical forms of the source language (Hebrew, Aramaic, Greek); translators call these "formally equivalent translations." The *King James Version*, the *Revised Standard Version*, the *New American Standard Version* and the 1917 Jewish Publication Society version of the Hebrew Bible are examples; an interlinear version (or "pony"), which renders the original-language text word by word, is the ultimate literal translation. At the other end of the scale are "dynamically equivalent translations," which aim at reproducing in the receptor language not the grammatical forms of the source language but the meanings that the original readers would have understood. Popularly these are sometimes called "paraphrases," although that term ought to be reserved for documents in which the source and receptor languages are the same (for example, a paraphrase of the Gettysburg Address might begin, "Eighty-seven years ago the founders of our nation . . ."). The *Today's English Version* ("Good News Bible") and the *New Jerusalem Bible* (Roman Catholic) are examples of dynamically equivalent translations. The *New English Bible*, the *New International Version*, and the modern JPS edition fall somewhere between.

On this scale the *Complete Jewish Bible* tends toward the dynamically equivalent end of the scale. And at certain points especially related to Jewish issues, the New Covenant portion becomes militantly so. For example, the Greek phrase *upo nomon* (literally, "under law") is usually rendered "under the law." But because this phrase has become a buzzword in anti-*Torah* Christian theology, the *Jewish New Testament* and now the *Complete Jewish Bible* spell out the meaning of these two Greek words in thirteen English words: "in subjection to the system which results from perverting the *Torah* into legalism."[3]

The Translator and His Interpretations. This example raises the question of whether the translator should "inject his opinions" into his translation. I cautiously answer in the affirmative, on the ground that it inevitably happens anyhow; so that the translator who supposes he "maintains neutrality," merely channeling ideas from the source language to the receptor language without influencing the result, deludes both himself and his readers. For necessarily every decision as to how to render a word or phrase from another language into English expresses the translator's opinion. A translator ideologically committed to not intruding his opinions does so in spite of himself, but without taking responsibility for it.

Therefore, I believe a translator should decide what a word or phrase means — in his opinion — and then convey that meaning as clearly as possible. For example, in the case of *upo nomon*,[4] precisely because wrong meanings have been conveyed

---

[3]   For more on this topic, see Section XIII below.
[4]   Discussed above and in Section XIII.

in the past, I consider it my responsibility to convey what I believe to be the one and only correct meaning in as unmistakable a way as possible. Even when an expression in the original language seems vague, capable of more than one interpretation, I don't think a translator should transfer the ambiguity into English. Rather, he should decide on *one* of the possible interpretations and render that one well. In editions that supply alternative readings, ambiguities can be addressed in a marginal note. This edition does a little of that, but very little; that is not one of its major purposes. A commentary is the right place to deal with such matters fully, and that is one of my purposes in the *Jewish New Testament Commentary*.

On the other side of the picture, this approach lends itself to abuse. The fact that the translator's opinions will necessarily be reflected in his translation does not mean that he should exploit his role, attempting with a partisan rendering to sway his readers toward a partisan position.

Since this is my philosophy and my working rule, I caution readers who want to check whether a word or phrase means what the *CJB* says it means to look at other versions, to use concordances and other Bible helps, and to go back to the Hebrew/Aramaic and Greek originals. To expect that the *CJB* will render perfectly, and with all the necessary nuances for every reader, the sense of every word and phrase in the Bible to ask for more than it or any translation can do.

Lone Translator Versus Translation Team. A number of people have asked whether it would not have been better to have had a translation team produce the *Jewish New Testament*, and of course the same question can be raised about the *CJB*'s *Tanakh*. My answer is framed in terms of available resources, both human and financial. Certainly the best known Bible translations have been a team product, including the *King James Version*, the *Revised Standard Version*, the *New International Version*, both JPS versions, and others. Traditionally, even the first translation of the *Tanakh* into Greek, the Septuagint, was produced by a team of seventy (hence the name, which means "seventy") in the third century B.C.E.[5] A team allows for peer review, discussion of problematical texts, and style control; while a single translator may come up with a more unified product (provided he can remember how he translated similar passages). Frankly, I can admit that a team might have done a better job; but I have done the best I can. I hope readers will not be disappointed.[6]

III. THE BIBLE

The Central Message of the Bible. In telling about God, his people Israel, and his Messiah Yeshua, the Bible's constant theme is that human beings need to be saved, and that God provides salvation. The purpose of life and the meaning of history is that God will deliver humanity from the misery of sin and restore the conditions that enable individuals and peoples to relate rightly with him. Morality and happiness are inseparably linked with salvation.

---

5   The abbreviations "B.C.E." and "C.E.," which mean "Before the Common Era" and "Common Era" respectively, are used by the Jewish community in place of "B.C." and "A.D.," which signify "Before Christ" and "*Anno Domini*" (Latin for "in the year of our Lord").

6   More about the original-language texts used for the *CJB* will be found in Section VIII.

The *Tanakh*. For according to the *Tanakh*,[7] God created human beings in his image to be in intimate, loving and obedient fellowship with him.[8] But humanity rebelled — people chose their own way instead of God's[9] — and still do.[10] The name for such rebellion is sin, and the penalty for sin is death[11] — not only cessation of physical life but everlasting separation from God.[12] However, God, who is merciful as well as just, wills to save human beings from the eternal death they have earned and deserve. To this end God chose one person, Avraham, and through him brought forth a people, the Jews, commissioning them to "be a blessing" and "a light to the nations."[13] Through Moshe he gave them a *Torah* (literally, "teaching" or "instruction," though usually translated "law"), making known his standards for righteousness. Through judges, kings and prophets he encouraged them, disciplined them and promised that final salvation would come to them and the other peoples through an "anointed one" (Hebrew *mashiach*, which has come over into English as "messiah"; the Greek word for "*mashiach*" is "*christos*," which evolved into the English word "Christ").

The *B'rit Hadashah* and Yeshua. Continuing this chronicle, the books of the New Covenant proclaim that the Messiah of Israel prophesied in the *Tanakh* is Yeshua, a real, historical person who, like others, was born, lived and died. However, unlike others, he had no human father but was given birth by a virgin named Miryam (Mary). Also unlike others, he did not die simply because his life ended or because of his own sin (he had committed none), but in order to redeem us from our sins. Finally, again unlike others, he was resurrected from the dead, is alive now "at the right hand of God"[14] and will come a second time to rule as King of Israel and bring peace to the world. In explaining why he alone was qualified to be the final sacrifice for sins the *B'rit Hadashah* calls him both Son of Man and Son of God. The first term, taken from the *Tanakh*,[15] means that he is fully and ideally human, sinless, "a lamb without blemish."[16] Since he did not owe his life for his own sins, he could be "God's lamb. . .taking away the sin of the world."[17] The second term, hinted at in the *Tanakh*,[18] means not only that God's Holy Spirit (the *Ruach HaKodesh*), supernaturally caused Miryam to become pregnant,[19] but also that "in him, bodily, lives the fullness of all that God is";[20] so that he is uniquely able to express God's love to humanity.[21]

---

[7] The word *Tanakh* is an acronym made from the first letters of the three main divisions of the Hebrew Bible: *Torah* (the "Law," Pentateuch), *Nevi'im* (Prophets) and *K'tuvim* (Writings).

[8] Genesis 1:26–2:25

[9] Genesis 3:1–19

[10] 1 Kings 8:46; Ecclesiastes 7:20; Romans 3:23

[11] Genesis 2:17, 5:5; Romans 6:23

[12] Genesis 3:22–24; Isaiah 59:1–2

[13] Genesis 12:1–3; Isaiah 49:6

[14] Psalm 110:1; Acts 7:56; and throughout Messianic Jews (Hebrews)

[15] Daniel 7:13

[16] Exodus 12:5; Leviticus 1–6; 1 Peter 1:19

[17] John 1:29, 36

[18] Isaiah 9:5–6(6–7); Zechariah 12:10; Psalm 2:7; Proverbs 30:4

[19] Matthew 1:18–23

[20] Colossians 2:9

[21] John 3:16

The Messianic Community. The *B'rit Hadashah* also describes formative events among the early Jewish and Gentile followers of Yeshua and explains how this new Messianic Community or "Church" is related to the Jewish people. Unlike much Christian theology, the *B'rit Hadashah* does not say that the Messianic Community replaces the Jews as God's people. Nor does it say that the Messianic Community stands alongside the Jews as a second eternal people of God with a separate destiny and separate promises. Rather, the relationship is more complex: Gentiles are grafted as "wild olive branches" into a Jewish "cultivated olive tree," some of whose branches "fell off" but will one day be "grafted back into their own olive tree," so that in the end, "all Israel will be saved."[22] Thus the Jews are not, as many Christians think, and as many Jews fear, annihilated as a people by being "absorbed into the Church." On the contrary, as Yirmeyahu (Jeremiah) states — in the same passage as where he announces that God will make a New Covenant with the house of Isra'el and the house of Y'hudah — the Jews remain God's people forever, for as long as the sun, moon and stars give light to the earth.[23] But the Jews will become a people who honor the Messiah for whom they have hoped and waited so long: Yeshua. It is on this basis that unity will be restored between the Messianic Community and the Jewish people and the great schism finally healed.

Breadth of Vision. The Bible's concept of salvation is both individual and corporate, so that the *Tanakh* and *B'rit Hadashah* speak to the full range of human activity — family life, class struggle, social concerns, commerce, agriculture, the environment, national identity, government, justice, repentance, forgiveness, interpersonal relationships, personal identity, gender issues, worship, prayer, physical health, emotional well-being, the inner life of the spirit, death, the after-life and final judgment. In all of these areas the Bible informs us that right response to God's initiatives will bring salvation to every part of our lives — individually, socially, communally, nationally and universally.

Covenants and Testaments, Old and New. Christians call the *Tanakh* the Old Testament and the *B'rit Hadashah* the New Testament. But the English word "testament" reflects a tension between the Hebrew language of the *Tanakh* and the Greek of the *B'rit Hadashah*. The Hebrew word *b'rit* means "covenant, contract." The Greek word for "covenant" or "*b'rit*" is "*diathêkê*." But "*diathêkê*" can also mean "testament" in the sense of "will."[24] The Hebrew words "*b'rit hadashah*" can be translated only as "new covenant," but the equivalent Greek words can also be translated "new testament" — and usually are. So although Jeremiah foretold a new foundational "contract" between God and the Jewish people, not a "will" — a covenant, not a testament — the term "New Testament" has become standard terminology which obscures the meaning of the original Hebrew, "new covenant." For this reason, in this Introduction, I generally write about the *Tanakh* instead of the Old Testament and the *B'rit Hadashah* or "books of the New Covenant" instead of the New Testament.

---

[22] Romans 11:16–26
[23] Jeremiah 31:30–36(31–37)
[24] Hebrews 9:16–17 (The Greek text plays on the double meaning.)

Moreover, a "new" covenant implies an "old" one, in this case the Mosaic Covenant made by God with the Jewish people at Mount Sinai.[25] The *B'rit Hadashah* makes this explicit at Messianic Jews (Hebrews) 8:6–13, where, in context, "old" does not imply "bad" but merely "earlier." Since the books constituting the *Tanakh*, in which the Mosaic Covenant is pivotal, date from between 1500 and 300 B.C.E., Christians call it the Old Testament, distinguishing it from the first-century C.E. writings which constitute the New Testament.

Two "Testaments," One Bible. Nevertheless, the two parts of the Bible, the *Tanakh* and the *B'rit Hadashah*, form one Bible. These two parts deal with parallel material in complementary ways. History, having commenced with the creation of heaven and earth and the sinless paradise of 'Eden in the first two chapters of the *Tanakh*, ends with the sinless paradise of "a new heaven and a new earth"[26] in the last two chapters of the *B'rit Hadashah*. The *B'rit Hadashah*, continuing the salvation history set forth in the *Tanakh* on the basis of covenants made with Noach (Noah), Avraham (Abraham), Moshe (Moses) and David, presents itself as encompassing the "new covenant" which God promised in the *Tanakh* to make "with the house of Isra'el and the house of Y'hudah (Judah)"[27] and presents Yeshua as consummating the systems of kings, prophets, *cohanim* (priests) and sacrifices described therein, as well as being himself the sum and substance of the *Torah*. Thus the New Testament apart from the Old is heretical, and the Old Testament apart from the New is incomplete — two testaments, one Bible.

The *Complete Jewish Bible* Presents the Bible's Unity. The *Complete Jewish Bible* graphically presents this unity by eliminating all separation between the *Tanakh* and the *B'rit Hadashah*. Most Christian translations insert a special title page to divide the Old Testament from the New and even number the pages separately, so that the book of *Mattityahu* (Matthew) starts on the New Testament's own Page 1. The *Complete Jewish Bible* divides the entire Bible into seven sections: the *Torah*, the Prophets, the Writings, the Gospels, the Acts of the Emissaries, the Letters, and the Book of Revelation. Pagination is continuous. There is no need to collect the first three-quarters of the Bible into the "Old Testament" and the last quarter into the "New." Rather, the Bible is presented as a seamless whole, a unified Word of God, a complete Jewish Bible for all humanity.

IV. CONTENTS OF THE BIBLE

Of the seven sections of the Bible, the *Tanakh* consists of the first three, and the *B'rit Hadashah* the remaining four.

The *Torah*. The first five books of the Bible constitute the Pentateuch, the Five Books of Moshe (Moses), traditionally attributed to Moshe himself; some scholars believe that later writers modified what Moses wrote or even wrote the books themselves. *B'resheet* (Genesis) contains the creation narratives, the story of the Flood and the

---

25   Exodus 19–24
26   Isaiah 65:17; Revelation 21:1
27   Jeremiah 31:30–33(31–34)

prehistoric dispersion of the nations. With Genesis 12 commences the story of the Jewish People, first with the Patriarchs Avraham (Abraham), Yitz'chak (Isaac) and Ya'akov (Jacob), and finally with the story of Yosef (Joseph) in Egypt. *Sh'mot* (Exodus) tells of Moshe rescuing the Jewish people from slavery, of the ten plagues, of the exodus from Egypt through the Yam Suf (Red Sea) into the Sinai Desert, and of God, appearing on Mount Sinai, giving the Ten Words and other regulations. There follow God's instructions to Moses as to how the tabernacle was to be constructed. This is interrupted by the apostasy of the people through making the golden calf. Afterwards, the tabernacle is constructed and dedicated, and the system of *cohanim* (priests) is set up. *Vayikra* (Leviticus) gives instructions concerning the sacrificial system and other aspects of life. *B'midbar* (Numbers) describes the people's journeys through the desert for forty years, together with their rebellious ways, as God molds a people for himself. In *D'varim* (Deuteronomy), Moshe conveys additional laws in the context of reviewing the previous forty years of history. He appoints Y'hoshua (Joshua) his successor and concludes with a cautionary poem and blessings for the twelve tribes. The *Torah* ends with the death of Moshe at some point in the 15th to 13th centuries B.C.E. (scholars disagree over the dating).

The Prophets. The Prophets are generally divided into the Early Prophets (*Nevi'im Rishonim*) and the Later Prophets (*Nevi'im Acharonim*). The first group consists of the four books of *Y'hoshua* (Joshua), *Shof'tim* (Judges), *Sh'mu'el Alef* and *Bet* (1–2 Samuel) and *M'lakhim Alef* and *Bet* (1–2 Kings). The book of *Y'hoshua* tells of the people of Israel under Y'hoshua as they enter the Land of Israel, conquer it and divide it among the twelve tribes. *Shof'tim* tells of the next several centuries under various "judges," such as Gid'on (Gideon) and Shimshon (Samson). The last of these judges, Sh'mu'el (Samuel), has his name attached to 1–2 Samuel, which describes the rulership of the first two kings, Sha'ul (Saul) and David. Then 1–2 Kings recount the remaining history of the kingship, starting shortly after 1000 B.C.E. with Shlomo (Solomon); continuing with the dividing up of the territory he ruled into the Northern Kingdom, Isra'el, and the Southern Kingdom, Y'hudah (Judah); proceeding with the stories of the prophets Eliyahu (Elijah) and Elisha and a series of kings to the destruction by Ashur (Assyria) of the Northern Kingdom in 732 B.C.E. and on to the Babylonian conquest of Y'hudah in 586 B.C.E.

The Later Prophets also consists of four books — a book by each of the three "major prophets," *Yesha'yahu* (Isaiah), *Yirmeyahu* (Jeremiah) and *Yechezk'el* (Ezekiel), and a book containing the writings of the *Shneim-'Asar* (the Twelve), known also as the "minor prophets." These books contain warnings to the people of Isra'el and ethical advice. Often through these prophets God pleads with Israel to remain faithful to him, to turn away from false gods and wrong aims. Through them God often promises rewards for obedience and punishments for disobedience. How God's love is combined with his holiness is constantly displayed. While sometimes the Prophets make predictions, they are less foretellers than forth-tellers, boldly announcing God's word to people not always willing to hear it.

The Writings. The Writings include a variety of different forms. *Tehillim* (Psalms) consists of 150 poems or songs expressing the deepest spiritual yearnings and truths. *Mishlei* (Proverbs) falls in the category of "wisdom literature," in which wisdom is encapsulated in pithy sayings, as does *Kohelet* (Ecclesiastes). The book of *Iyov* (Job) addresses the question of why bad things happen to good people; its poetry is unsurpassed in any language. Its Hebrew is the most difficult in the *Tanakh*, because it contains a great many words that appear nowhere else. The five *Megillot* (Scrolls) are short books; each "whole *megillah*" is read on a particular holiday in the Jewish year — *Shir-HaShirim* (Song of Songs, called the Song of Solomon in Christian Bibles) at Passover; *Rut* (Ruth) at *Shavu'ot*, because it's a harvest festival; *Eikhah* (Lamentations) on the Ninth of Av, which is a day of fasting in memory of the destruction of both temples; *Kohelet* (Ecclesiastes) at *Sh'mini 'Atzeret*, the festival anticipating winter, which immediately follows *Sukkot*; and *Ester* (Esther) at *Purim*, since the book tells the story of that holiday. *Dani'el* and *'Ezra-Nechemyah* (Ezra-Nehemiah) evoke life in and after the Babylonian Exile, while *Divrei HaYamim Alef* and *Bet* (1–2 Chronicles) review from a priestly viewpoint the history detailed in *Sh'mu'el* (Samuel) and *M'lakhim* (Kings). The beginning of *'Ezra* and the end of 2 Chronicles show that *'Ezra* is the sequel to Chronicles.

The Gospels. The twenty-seven books of the *B'rit Hadashah* were written in the first century of the Common Era by at least eight authors.[28] Of these, the first four present four distinct views of Yeshua's life and purpose in "salvation history" (God's involvement in human history for the purpose of saving mankind). The first and fourth Gospels are understood to have been written by two of Yeshua's twelve *talmidim* (disciples), Mattityahu (Matthew) and Yochanan (John). The second is attributed to Mark, who accompanied another of Yeshua's *talmidim*, Kefa (Peter). The author of the third was Luke, an associate of Sha'ul (Saul/Paul).

The old English word "gospel" means "good news." Therefore, in a significant sense there are not four gospels but one, namely, the Good News of who Yeshua is and what he has done. But each of the four Gospels presents this Good News in its own way, just as four honest witnesses to an event will each have his own version of what happened. Broadly speaking, one may say that Mattityahu has a Jewish readership in mind, while it seems that Luke is writing for Gentiles.[29] Mark's version is fast-paced and filled with human-interest details. Yochanan's never loses sight of Yeshua's heavenly origin, portraying him clearly as not only Son of Man but Son of God.

The first three are known as the Synoptic Gospels (the word "synoptic" means "same viewpoint"), since many of the same incidents are reported in two or three of them, often in similar or even identical language. Scholars have attempted to explain the differences and similarities in the Synoptics, often by postulating that one writer copied from another, or, more sophisticatedly, that two or all three of them had direct or indirect access to some of the same oral or written sources.

The Acts of the Emissaries. Luke is also the author of "The Acts of the Emissaries," which could as well be called "Luke, Part II" (see the opening verses of both Luke

---

[28] The following material concerning the historicity of the events related in the *B'rit Hadashah* and the authorship and dating of its documents is based on mainstream conservative New Testament scholarship. See the discussion of tradition and scholarship below in Section V.

[29] His emphasis on the universality of salvation and his addressing his book to "Theophilos" (Greek for "lover of God") suggest that he is writing for the broadest possible audience.

and Acts). This book, in which Yeshua's emissaries ("apostles") Kefa and Sha'ul are the chief protagonists, describes the history of the early Messianic Community (that is, the Church) from about 30 C.E. to 65 C.E. The setting is first Yerushalayim, where believing in Yeshua was entirely an internal Jewish matter, and then, as the Gospel spread, "Y'hudah, Shomron, indeed . . . the ends of the earth,"[30] that is, Rome, the pagan antithesis of Yerushalayim. A major purpose of the book of Acts is to prove that Gentiles can become Messianic without converting to Judaism. It is ironic that today popular opinion requires a reverse application of the book of Acts to show that Jews can become Messianic without "converting" to what has become identified as an alien religion, Christianity.

The Letters. The rest of the B'rit Hadashah, except for the last book, consists of letters. The first thirteen are by Sha'ul, the "emissary to the Gentiles."[31] Five are to Messianic communities which he founded in Greece—two to Corinth, one to Philippi and two to Thessalonica (modern Salonika). Two are to communities he founded in what is now Turkey—Galatia and Ephesus; and two are to communities established by others—Colosse (near Ephesus), and Rome. These nine letters deal with issues of behavior and belief which arose in the several congregations. Of the remaining four, known as the Pastoral Letters, three are to his trainees Timothy (two) and Titus, and one, to Philemon, requests him to welcome back as a free brother a slave of his who ran away.

Next is "A Letter to a Group of Messianic Jews," otherwise known as "To the Hebrews." Though sometimes attributed to Sha'ul, Apollos or Priscilla and Aquila, its authorship is uncertain. Addressing a Messianic Jewish readership, it relates the new dispensation brought by Yeshua to the themes of the Tanakh. Following are a letter from Ya'akov (James), the brother of Yeshua and leader of the Messianic community in Yerushalayim; two letters from Kefa (Peter); three from Yochanan (John); and one from Y'hudah (Jude), another brother of Yeshua. As a group these are called the General Letters and are concerned with matters of faith and practice.

Revelation. The final book of the B'rit Hadashah is "The Revelation of Yeshua the Messiah to Yochanan," which contains descriptions of visions revealed by the resurrected and glorified Messiah to the emissary Yochanan (John), or, some believe, to a different Yochanan. It is also known as the Apocalypse, since it describes "apocalyptic" events, that is, end-time disasters and interventions of God in history connected with the final judgment of humankind. Containing over five hundred quotations from and allusions to the Tanakh, more than any other New Testament book, it resembles and draws on the visions of such writers as Yesha'yahu (Isaiah), Yechezk'el (Ezekiel), Z'kharyah (Zechariah) and Dani'el. Some consider it to be speaking of what today is still in the future, others regard it as describing the whole age of history which began two thousand years ago, and still others believe its primary reference is to first-century events. Its figurative language gives room for such different interpretive approaches or for a combination thereof.

---

[30] Acts 1:8
[31] Romans 11:13; Galatians 2:7–8

V. OTHER FEATURES OF THE BIBLE

Dating. Traditionally the *Torah* dates from the 15th to 13th centuries B.C.E., depending on when Moshe lived. The Early Prophets traditionally date from the 14th to 10th centuries B.C.E., the Later Prophets from the 9th to 4th centuries B.C.E., and the Writings from the 10th to 3rd centuries B.C.E. Many scholars accept later dates, up to the 2nd century B.C.E.

The earliest *B'rit Hadashah* books, such as Sha'ul's letters to the Galatians, Thessalonians and Corinthians, and probably the letter of Ya'akov, were written around 50 C.E., some twenty years after Yeshua's death and resurrection. Sha'ul's other letters date from the 50s and 60s, the Gospels and Acts in their essentially final form from between 65 and 85, and the other General Letters and Revelation from between 65 and 100. Some scholars believe that some New Testament books underwent final editing in the early second century C.E.

The Canon. Scholars agree that the canon of the *Torah* achieved its present form before the time of 'Ezra (around 445 B.C.E.), the Prophets later and the Writings last. But the final review of the canon was made by the Council of Yavneh (Jamnia) convened around 90 C.E. by Rabbi Yochanan Ben-Zakkai in the wake of the destruction of the temple by the Romans twenty years earlier. Several books now included in the *Tanakh* were questioned — Daniel and Ezekiel, because of their startling visions and experiences; Esther, because God is not mentioned in it; Song of Songs, because of its overtly sexual character; and Ecclesiastes, because of its depressed world-viewpoint (except for the last two verses, which redeemed it). Ecclesiasticus (not the same as Ecclesiastes) was rejected by the rabbis of Yavneh but is found in the Apocrypha, a collection of fifteen ancient Jewish books that include Tobit, Judith, 1–2 Maccabees and the Wisdom of Solomon. Catholic and Anglican Bibles include the Apocrypha. Some sixty other ancient books are collectively called the Pseudepigrapha. English-language editions of the Apocrypha[32] and the Pseudepigrapha[33] are available.

Besides the documents which now form the New Testament, there were written other versions of the Good News, other histories of events in the early Messianic Community, other discussions of doctrine and practice and other apocalypses.[34] It was the early Messianic Community which exercised the spiritual discernment necessary to decide which books truly brought God's message to humanity and which were lesser creations, perhaps of historical or spiritual value but not God-breathed. Quotations from *B'rit Hadashah* books are found already in the non-canonical "Teaching of the Apostles" (80–100 C.E.), but the first list including books of the *B'rit Hadashah* was made by the heretic Marcion around 150 C.E. This product of error surely stimulated the development of an orthodox canon, such as appears in the Muratorian Fragment at the end of the second century, while the earliest known enumeration of exactly the twenty-seven books constituting today's *B'rit Hadashah*, with neither additions nor

---

[32] For example, *The New Oxford Annotated Bible With the Apocrypha* (New York: Oxford University Press, 1973)

[33] See James H. Charlesworth, *The Old Testament Pseudepigrapha*, 2 volumes (Garden City, New York: Doubleday & Company, Inc., 1983).

[34] See Edgar Hennecke, *New Testament Apocrypha* (Philadelphia: The Westminster Press, 1965).

omissions, is in the Thirty-Ninth Paschal Letter of Athanasius (367 C.E.). Though the list is late, the books themselves were used in Messianic congregations from the time they were written, just as the books of the *Tanakh* were an integral part of Judaism centuries before its canon was authoritatively determined by the Council of Yavneh.

Tradition and Scholarship. The above introductory material reflects mainstream conservative Bible scholarship, which confirms most of the traditional views on these subjects. But during the past two centuries all the authorships have been challenged, likewise all the datings, and the historicity of most of the events.

The debate continues but ought to be confined within certain limits controlled by facts and aware of assumptions. For example, there are handwritten manuscripts of portions of the New Testament from as early as the first half of the second century, disproving the more extreme suggestions that the New Testament was written two, three or four hundred years after Yeshua. Also some of the criticism is based on presuppositions which are religious in character but in opposition to the Bible, thus determining a negative conclusion *a priori*, e.g., a world-view of doubt or "scientism" that precludes the possibility of such miracles as the crossing of the Yam Suf (Red Sea) on dry land,[35] or a disbelief in the ability of the ancient writers to distinguish between real and imaginary events, or a too willing confidence that the early Messianic communities altered reports to fit their agenda.

Although there is no lack of unanswered questions, many respected scholars nevertheless believe that the traditional authors are in fact the authors, that the early datings are correct, and, most importantly in the case of the *B'rit Hadashah*, that Yeshua really lived, "died for our sins, . . . and . . . was raised on the third day, in accordance with what the *Tanakh* says."[36]

VI. WHY THE BIBLE IS GOD'S WORD

In the first paragraph of Section I, I wrote that "the Bible is God's Word to humanity, the only completely reliable verbal communication God has given us. It is worthy of acceptance, belief, trust; it is his handbook for faith and practice." I owe readers who are not convinced of this an explanation of why I believe that behind the several authors of the Bible, the true Author is God; afterwards I will say why it makes a difference to think so.

Theologians call this topic the "divine inspiration of Scripture," where the word "inspiration" has its literal meaning, "breathing into." Thus in regarding God as the ultimate Author of the Bible, they do not mean that he dictated every word, so that the human "authors" were really only secretaries, but rather, that the authors often expressed what God had breathed into them through their own personalities in their own words. The alternative view is that the Bible may contain beautiful thoughts, high moral sentiments, wonderful stories and great literature, "inspired" in the ordinary, humanistic sense, "worthy of genius"; but that it is not God himself speaking, telling us about himself, about ourselves, and about how to live.

---

[35] Exodus 14–15
[36] 1 Corinthians 15:3– 4

There are three reasons for considering the Bible inspired by God, God-breathed: it claims to be, it seems to be, and it proves to be.

The Bible Claims to be God's Word. Over and over appear the words, "*Adonai* says," or, in the thunderous phrase from the King James Version, "Thus saith the Lord." These words are found in the Bible some 2,500 times, placed there by numerous authors over a period of more than a thousand years. By itself this claim proves nothing — anyone can write, "God says." But this claim is not made so very often; hence when it is made — and when many people believe it — it could be worth investigating to find out if it is true.

The Bible Seems to be God's Word. Its breadth of subject matter, its wisdom, its deeply felt honesty, its understanding of the human condition, its expressions of joy, wonder, sadness, anger and every other emotion, its way of dealing with history and politics all delineate as the character underlying the Bible an entity, a person, worthy of being called and honored as God, lover and creator of you and me and the universe. Some readers may find portions which seem less than divine or even contrary to their view of what God ought to say. I suggest that these readers consider changing their concept of God. For only in the Bible will one find the authoritative description of the God of the Bible, who he is and what he "ought" to be. It is there where one should look for the paradoxes to be resolved — and also where it becomes clear that some antinomies (contradictory elements that resist resolution) will not be fully resolved, at least not in this world (two examples: free will and predestination, and Job's problem — why bad things happen to good people).

The Bible Proves to be God's Word. While not every statement in the Bible can be scientifically verified, some can. Historical and archeological studies are repeatedly providing evidence that places, events and customs the Bible reports about were real. Since I moved to Israel in 1979, the newspapers have reported the discovery at Tel Dan, in the north of the country, of the first independent witness to the existence of King David, an ostracon from his time inscribed with that name (it proves, of course, only that the name existed, not the king). Another discovery was of one of the pomegranates that hung from the robe of the *cohen gadol* (high priest),[37] and a third was a seal from the sixth century B.C.E. having on it the tetragrammaton — the oldest such evidence. These do not prove the existence of God, but they demonstrate the reliability of the writers and suggest that what they say about the unverifiable might also be trustworthy.

Why It Makes a Difference to Believe that God "Wrote the Bible." On principle I would not give science the last word in determining truth, because I don't think faith should be relegated to a category of knowledge inferior to science. The philosophical underpinnings of the Western World are centered on two cities — Athens and Jerusalem. The Greeks developed philosophy in a rational manner, but largely at the expense of separating heart and head. Many psychological and spiritual ills stem from this separation (one can also speak of this separation as between body and soul). The Jews kept head and heart, body and soul, together, and the Bible reflects

---

[37] Exodus 28:33

this unitary view of human nature. The head has its way of knowing, and the heart has its way of knowing, and neither should be ignored. If head and heart are connected, there is the possibility that what the Bible claims, seems and proves to be will move the heart to respond in faith. If one believes that in the Bible God is speaking, one will be much more likely to take seriously its promises, threats, suggestions and commands; and the result, I propose, will be a better life for oneself and the others one meets.

VII. JEWISH *TANAKH* VERSUS CHRISTIAN OLD TESTAMENT

The title of this Section of the Introduction may perplex some readers, especially after the remarks in Section V, because it is usual to think of the Christian Old Testament and the Jewish *Tanakh* as the same. Actually, there are important differences; and for purposes of understanding the *Complete Jewish Bible*, these must now be addressed.

Different Order for the Books. The most obvious difference, clear from the Table of Contents, is that the books of the *Tanakh* appear in a different order than those of the Old Testament (OT), as any Christian looking for the book of Malachi at the end of the *Tanakh* will quickly discover. As the acronym *TaNaKh* reminds us, the Hebrew Bible is divided into three parts — *Torah* (Law, Teaching), *Nevi'im* (Prophets) and *K'tuvim* (Writings). But Christians divide the OT into four parts — Pentateuch, Historical Books, Writings and Prophets. Both OT and *Tanakh* have the five books of Moses first, whether one calls them the *Torah* or the Pentateuch. The Prophets section of the *Tanakh* is divided into the Early and Later Prophets. The Early Prophets correspond to the Historical Books of the OT minus the books of Ruth, 1–2 Chronicles, Ezra, Nehemiah, and Esther, which are placed with the Writings. The Later Prophets are the same as the "Prophets" section of the OT, except that the Hebrew Bible places Lamentations and Daniel with the Writings. The *Tanakh*'s "Writings" section is larger than that of the OT, because it includes the eight books which in the OT are located elsewhere. Finally, in the *Tanakh* the Later Prophets come immediately after the Early Prophets, but in the OT the Prophets come last.

Why these differences? Because the Christian OT follows the order found in the oldest manuscripts of the Septuagint, the translation of the *Tanakh* into Greek made by Greek-speaking Jews in Alexandria, Egypt, two or three centuries before Yeshua's birth; while the *Tanakh* sequence was finalized in the Land of Israel after the time of Ezra. This is the order Yeshua knew, as evidenced by his referring in Luke 24:44 to "the *Torah* of Moshe, the Prophets and the Psalms" (by "Psalms" he referred to the Writings section, which in the *Tanakh* begins with the book of Psalms, not Job, as in the OT).

Different Number of Books. A second difference is that by Jewish reckoning the *Tanakh* consists of twenty-four books, whereas Christians count thirty-nine in the Old Testament. This is because the *Tanakh* considers each of the following to be a single book: 1–2 Samuel, 1–2 Kings, the twelve Minor Prophets (so called because their books are short — Hosea, Joel, Amos, Obadiah, Jonah, Micah, Nahum, Habakkuk, Zephaniah, Haggai, Zechariah and Malachi), Ezra-Nehemiah, and 1–2 Chronicles. Thus what the OT counts as twenty books appears in the *Tanakh* as five.

Different Names for the Books. A third difference is in the names. Many of the *Tanakh* books are simply called by their first words. What the OT calls Genesis the *Tanakh* calls *B'resheet* ("In the beginning"); and Exodus (the book about the Jewish exodus from Egypt) is called *Sh'mot* ("Names"), because the books starts out, "These are the names. . . ." Leviticus (about the Levitical priesthood) is called *Vayikra* ("And he called"), from its initial words "And he [God] called to Moshe . . ." Lamentations is called *Eikhah* ("How"); it begins, "How lonely lies the city. . . ."

The reader wanting further clarification on these three points of difference should examine carefully the tables of contents; the main one lists the books of the Bible by both their Hebrew and usual English names in the order followed in Jewish Bibles and in the *Complete Jewish Bible*; the second lists the books of the *Tanakh* by their usual English names in the Old Testament/Septuagint order familiar to Christians; the third table of contents lists all the books of the Bible by all the names, in alphabetical order.

Why did I choose the Jewish order and names for the *CJB*? To emphasize the Jewish unity of the *Tanakh* and the *B'rit Hadashah* — not just the "unity," which all Christians recognize, but the "Jewish unity," the fact that both *Tanakh* and *B'rit Hadashah* are Jewish through and through. When the *Tanakh* is dissected, with its parts rearranged and renamed, its Jewishness is also being taken apart. This is, then, just one more way in which the *CJB* reminds Christians that their faith is Jewish.

At the same time, by presenting, as fully as the English language allows, the Jewishness of both *Tanakh* and *B'rit Hadashah* together in a single volume, I am placing the Jewishness of the *B'rit Hadashah* squarely in front of Jewish people who have absorbed the false idea that the New Testament is the Christian Bible and therefore has nothing to do with them as Jews. This is also why I wrote the *Jewish New Testament Commentary* — to deal with the various reservations about Yeshua, the New Testament and Christianity that have become an almost inseparable part of Jewish culture and thinking, and show that they are based on misunderstandings, so that Jewish people can hear what God has to say to them in both the *Tanakh* and the *B'rit Hadashah* — in the complete Jewish Bible.

Different Chapter and Verse Numbering. A fourth difference is in the numbering of chapters and verses. The Jewish and Christian chapter and verse numbers differ here and there throughout the *Tanakh*. My general rule is that where they are not the same I include both, the chapter and verse numbers found in the Hebrew Bible first, with the dissenting numberings in parentheses afterwards. Thus the reference, "Psalm 69:9(8)," means that what Hebrew Bibles call verse 9 of Psalm 69 is called verse 8 in at least *some* other Bibles. Similarly, "Joel 3:1–5(2:28–32)" is the consequence of the fact that the Hebrew Bible makes a separate Chapter 3 out of what the OT has as the last five verses of Chapter 2. A number of the Psalms have titles such as Psalm 21's, "For the leader. A psalm of David." The Hebrew Bible often considers them to be Verse 1, but the OT does not assign them verse numbers at all. In this case, the *CJB* assigns them "Christian" verse number zero: Psalm 21:1(0).

Different Endings for Four of the Books. A small detail which nevertheless epitomizes a characteristic of the Jewish approach to life is that in the case of the four books in the *Tanakh* with a negative-sounding last verse, it is customary to accentuate the positive by printing the next-to-last verse a second time at the end of the book. The *CJB* does this, using brackets and smaller type.

Different Underlying Texts. The final difference is that the *Tanakh* consists of the traditionally preserved "Masoretic Text" of the Hebrew Bible, while the Christian "Old Testament" draws on scholarly studies and other ancient texts of the Bible to arrive at a presumedly more accurate Hebrew text. The details are discussed in Section VIII below.

More Alike Than Different. In spite of these differences, the Christian Old Testament is much more like the *Tanakh* than different from it; and for this reason I will continue in this Introduction to use the terms *"Tanakh"* and "Old Testament" more or less interchangeably.

VIII. ORIGINAL-LANGUAGE TEXTS UNDERLYING THE *COMPLETE JEWISH BIBLE*

Hebrew/Aramaic Text Used for the *Tanakh*. Except for the Dead Sea Scrolls, which are more than two thousand years old, the oldest extant Hebrew and Aramaic manuscripts of the *Tanakh* date back to the 9th to 11th centuries C.E. The *Tanakh* was written originally with only consonants, and the *Torah* scrolls read today in the synagogue contain only consonants.

In the 6th to 9th centuries a group of scribes called the Masoretes (the word comes from Hebrew *masoret*, which means "tradition") developed a system of notation for recording the vowels traditionally used when reading the consonantal text of the *Tanakh*. Without these, the consonants of most Hebrew words could be pronounced in several ways and given several meanings. For example, if English were written with only consonants, how would you pronounce "st"? Would it be "sat," "set, "sit," "sot," "sate," "seat," "site," "soot" or "suit"? From context you would know. But there developed a need to make the meanings crystal-clear as Hebrew fell into disuse and not all contexts were understood. So the Masoretes recorded the traditional "vowel pointings," as they are called today; and printed editions of the *Tanakh* all have them. Moreover, Hebrew is taught with them; and while a modern Israeli reads his newspaper without vowel pointings, a new immigrant to Israel learns how to pronounce Hebrew with their aid. Moreover, they continue to be used in published editions of Hebrew poetry and in the Jewish prayerbooks.

In addition, the Masoretes codified a system of punctuation, also included in printed editions of the *Tanakh*. These "cantillation marks" are used when the *Torah* is chanted in the synagogue; but their more important use is to clarify which words of the text go together. For example, in a passage familiar to Christians as well as Jews, because the New Testament makes use of it, *Yesha'yahu* (Isaiah) 40:3 says, "A voice cries out: 'Clear a road through the desert for *ADONAI* [the LORD].'" But at *Mattityahu* (Matthew) 3:3 many translations have something like, "A voice cries out in the desert, 'Clear a road for *ADONAI*.'" However, the cantillation marks show that "in the desert" tells about the road, not the voice.

The Masoretes modified the written text (the *k'tiv*, pronounced *kuh-teev*) in a number of places, so that what is read aloud in the synagogue today (the *kere*, pronounced *keh-ray*) differs at these points from what appears in the *Torah* scroll. One example comes from Psalm 100:3. The *King James Version*, following the *k'tiv*, reads, "Know ye that the LORD, he is God; it is he who hath made us, and not we ourselves." But most other versions, Jewish and Christian alike, follow the *kere*; thus the *CJB* has, "it is he who made us; and we are his." If the Hebrew word *lo* in *lo anachnu* is spelled *lamed-alef* (לא), it means "not we," but if it's spelled *lamed-vav* (לו), it means "we are his." The Masoretes evidently concluded that the author had written "his," and a scribe had mis-copied the word.

From a Jewish religious point of view, the Masoretic alterations embodied in the *kere* are the only permitted changes to the received written consonantal text, the *k'tiv*. But Christian and non-Orthodox Jewish scholars are not constrained by this restriction. Thus they apply the criteria of historical and linguistic scholarship to the Masoretic text in determining its reliability. Moreover, from ancient versions such as the Greek Septuagint they can infer the existence of alternative underlying Hebrew texts, vowel-pointing or punctuation. Here is a well-known instance of how significant this can be.

In Psalm 22, verse 17 of Jewish versions reads, "Like a lion [at] my hands and feet," while the corresponding verse 16 of Christian versions says, "They pierced my hands and feet." If this passage prophesies Yeshua's crucifixion, as Messianic Jews and Christians believe it does, the prophecy is certainly clearer in the Christian versions, since the *B'rit Hadashah* reports that Yeshua's hands and feet were nailed to the execution-stake (as the *CJB* calls the cross), but says nothing about lions at his hands and feet. How can two such different meanings arise from the same text? They don't; the texts are different. The Masoretic text has the Hebrew word *k'ari* (כארי, "like a lion"); while the Christian versions make use of the Septuagint, where the Greek word implies an underlying Hebrew text with the word *karu* (כרו, "they pierced"). The differences — the presence in the Masoretic Hebrew of the letter *alef* (א), and of the letter *yud* (י) instead of *vav* (ו)— are both easily explainable as scribal errors (in one direction or the other). In this case, as in virtually all cases, the *CJB* adheres to the Masoretic text, but a footnote gives the alternative rendering and refers to this paragraph of the Introduction. There are hundreds of similar differences, although few are as important for Messianic understanding of the Bible. In general I have not indicated where these differences are, because that is outside the scope of my purposes in preparing the *Complete Jewish Bible*.

The scholars also use other early versions — Jerome's Latin Vulgate (430 C.E.), the Syriac, Targum Yonatan, and others dating from the fifth century C.E. or earlier. These offer still more readings which add to the possibilities and to the confusion. Scholars frequently find historical, archeological, literary, theological or logical justification for emending the text itself — that is, correcting it to what they believe it must have originally said. It may well be that the scholars often approach the Hebrew original more closely than the Masoretic text does. However, my choosing to render the Jewish *Tanakh* obligates me to use the Masoretic text; very rarely do I deviate from it.

The Greek of the *B'rit Hadashah*. While the *Tanakh* was written largely in Hebrew (portions of *'Ezra-Nechemyah* and *Dani'el* are in a related Semitic language,

Aramaic), most of the early manuscripts of the New Testament are in Greek — not the classical language of Homer or of Plato, but *koinê* ("common") Greek, the *lingua franca* of everyday affairs throughout the Eastern Mediterranean and Middle East during the first century.

Nevertheless, there is good reason to think that several of the books of the New Testament were written in either Hebrew or Aramaic, or drew upon source materials in those languages; this case has been made by one scholar or another for all four Gospels, Acts, Revelation and several of the General Letters. Moreover, Sha'ul, whose letters were composed in Greek, clearly drew on his native Jewish and Hebraic thought-forms when he wrote. In fact, some phrases in the New Testament manuscripts make no sense unless one reaches through the Greek to the underlying Hebrew expressions. Here is an example, only one of many.[38] Yeshua says in the Sermon on the Mount,[39] literally, "If your eye be evil, your whole body will be dark."[40] What is an evil eye? Someone not knowing the Jewish background might suppose Yeshua was talking about casting spells. However, in Hebrew, having an *'ayin ra'ah*, an "evil eye," means being stingy; while having an *'ayin tovah*, a "good eye," means being generous. Yeshua is simply urging generosity against stinginess. And this understanding fits with the surrounding verses: "Where your wealth is, there your heart will be also.... You can't be a slave to both God and money."[41]

Greek Text Used for the *B'rit Hadashah*. There are more than five thousand ancient manuscripts of all or part of the New Testament, more than for any other document from antiquity. Due to scribal errors and other factors, they do not agree with each other at every point. Textual criticism, which sets out to determine the correct reading of a text from disagreeing and imperfect sources, is far beyond the competence of most Bible translators, including me. Fortunately there exist critical editions of the Greek text of the New Testament, wherein specialists have investigated, compared and judged the accuracy of the differing textual readings found in the manuscripts. My translation of the *B'rit Hadashah* is based primarily on the United Bible Societies' *The Greek New Testament*;[42] but I also consulted a number of English and Hebrew versions and commentaries.

IX. POETRY IN THE *COMPLETE JEWISH BIBLE*

Frequency and Character of the Bible's Poetry. About thirty percent of the *Tanakh* is written in the form of poetry, mostly in the Later Prophets and in the Writings. This often surprises people, because many editions of the Bible hide the poetry by layout that doesn't show it. Because so much of the power, drama and nuance of what is being communicated is inseparable from the poetic form the writers

---

[38] For others, consult David Bivin and Roy Blizzard, Jr., *Understanding the Difficult Words of Jesus* (Austin, Texas: Center for Judaic-Christian Studies, 1984). See also the *Jewish New Testament Commentary* (Jewish New Testament Publications, Inc., 4th edition, 1996) and Section XI below.

[39] Matthew 5–7

[40] Matthew 6:23

[41] Matthew 6:21, 24

[42] 3rd Edition (New York: American Bible Society, 1975).

use, I have given high priority to making it as easy as possible for readers to see and feel the poetry in the Bible. (Apart from *Tanakh* citations, the *B'rit Hadashah* is at most one or two percent poetry, with the book of Revelation having the highest proportion.)

This is why I have chosen to typeset the *CJB* in one column rather than two — it makes it possible for each line of poetry to take only one line of type. When lines of poetry require two lines of type, the reader's attention is taken with determining where a line of poetry ends, leaving him less energy for scanning the line and finding its underlying rhythm. I know that for some the one-column format will make the prose reading more difficult, since the eye must follow a wider line of type across the page. But I decided in favor of easing the more difficult task of reading poetry.

Aids to Reading the Bible's Poetry. The key to Biblical Hebrew poetry is not primarily rhythm, but parallelism. The poetry is generally divided into two-line stanzas. The second line usually does one of three things: it expresses essentially the same idea as the first, or it presents a contrasting idea, or it adds to the first line's thought. The table below gives examples of all three.

However, English poetry is characterized by repeated rhythms (except for free verse), and this is what most English-speakers expect from poetry. To this end, I have tried to make it possible to scan every line of poetry into four beats. In the examples below I show where I understand the beats are by placing a superscript number before the emphasized syllable. Sometimes there will be silent beats; these are shown below by superscript-four at the end of the line; in fact these lines have three beats, but it makes the poetry read better to allow them four, with one of them silent. Occasionally you may find that there are too many syllables in a line to squeeze them comfortably into four beats; in this case, I suggest slowing the pace enough to find four main beats while allowing the words to be read without rushing. Moreover, keep in mind that there can be more than one right way to scan a line; for example, see the three ways of scanning Proverbs 2:21b below.

Verse	Type of Parallelism	Location of Beats in the Text
Psalm 38:22(21)	Thought	[1]Don't a[2]bandon me, [3]*ADO*[4]*NAI*!
	Same thought	My [1]God, [2]don't be [3]far from me! [4]
Proverbs 2:21	Thought	For the [1]upright will [2]live in the [3]land, [4]
	Same thought	the [1]pure-hearted [2]will re[3]main there; [4]
	(second scan)	the [1]pure-[2]hearted will re[3]main [4]there;
	(third scan)	the [1]pure-[2]hearted [3]will re[4]main there;
Proverbs 10:2	Thought	No [1]good [2]comes from [3]ill-gotten [4]wealth,
	Contrasting thought	but [1]righteousness [2]rescues from [3]death. [4]
Isaiah 54:10	Thought	For the [1]mountains may [2]leave and the [3]hills be re[4]moved,
	Contrasting thought	but my [1]grace will [2]never [3]leave you, [4]

Proverbs 23:29	Thought	[1]Who gets [2]bruised for [3]no good [4]reason?
	Addition to the thought	[1]Who has [2]bloodshot [3]eyes? [4]
Job 13:5	Thought	I [1]wish you would [2]just stay [3]silent; [4]
	Addition to the thought	for [1]you, [2]that would be [3]wisdom! [4]
Malachi 2:10	Thought #1	[1]Don't we [2]all have the [3]same [4]father?
	Same thought	[1]Didn't one [2]God cre[3]ate us [4]all?
	Thought #2	Then [1]why do [2]we break [3]faith with each [4]other,
	Addition to thought #2	pro[1]faning the [2]covenant of our [3]ancestors? [4]

Finally, although awareness of poetry's rhythm will enhance its reading, one should not let it degenerate into singsong that overwhelms the meaning of the text.

X. THE NAME OF GOD IN THE *COMPLETE JEWISH BIBLE*

The Basic Problem: God's Personal Name is Never Spoken. When Moshe turned aside in the wilderness of Midyan to see the bush that burned without being consumed, God revealed himself to him and told him his own personal Name. That Name in Hebrew consists of the four letters *Yud-Heh-Vav-Heh* (י-ה-ו-ה) and is therefore called the tetragrammaton (four-letter writing). The Bible makes it clear that this Name was not to be used casually. The third commandment prohibits taking God's Name in vain,[43] and the man who used it in a curse was put to death at God's explicit instruction.[44] Already by Yeshua's time, no one ever spoke God's name except the *cohen hagadol* (high priest) when he entered the Especially Holy Place in the temple to make atonement for the sins of Isra'el on *Yom Kippur*. So strictly was this rule enforced that when the Masoretes wrote down the vowel points for the *Torah*, they did not write the actual vowels to be used in pronouncing the tetragrammaton. By then, the word *Adonai*, which is a term for God found frequently in the Bible and which means "my Lord," was said instead of the Name whenever the *Torah* was read; so the Masoretes put the vowel pointing for "*Adonai*" under the letters *Yud-Heh-Vav-Heh*. To this day, when the *Torah* is read in the synagogue, "*Adonai*" is substituted for the Name. The English word "Jehovah" is an English representation of the Name (J-H-V-H) combined with the vowel sounds of "*Adonai*," a hybrid word without historical foundation. Most English translations represent the Name by "LORD," written as it is here, in large and small capital letters. More than six thousand times the *Complete Jewish Bible* uses the Hebrew word ADONAI also in large and small capital letters (and italicized, like other Hebrew words) to represent the tetragrammaton.

Other Problems. But a number of problems remain. First, there are places in the Bible where the Hebrew text reads, "*Adonai Yud-Heh-Vav-Heh*." To avoid having

---

[43]   Exodus 20:7; Deuteronomy 5:11
[44]   Leviticus 24:10–23

the word "*Adonai*" read twice in a row, the Jewish practice in these cases is to say, "*Adonai ELOHIM*"; and the *CJB* does the same in some 270 places. The word "*Elohim*" means "God" and is so translated elsewhere in the *CJB*, as in other Bible versions.

Second, there are three places in the Bible where, in my judgment, it is necessary to present the Name in a form as close to the original as possible — Exodus 3:13–17, 6:2–3, and 34:6–7. In these places the *CJB* has "*Yud-Heh-Vav-Heh.*" Otherwise the force of what is being communicated would be greatly compromised.

Third, Jewish religious practice, especially among the ultra-Orthodox, has withdrawn even from using such words as "*Adonai*" and "*Elohim*" except in specific religious settings. Euphemisms such as "*HaShem*" (the Name), "*Ado-shem*" (a combination of "*Adonai*" with "*HaShem*"), and "*Elokim*" (an intentional mispronunciation of "*Elohim*") are used instead; and if the tetragrammaton has to be spelled out, it is pronounced, "*Yud-kay-vav-kay.*" I considered using "*HaShem*" but eventually decided against it on the ground that the *CJB* constitutes a justifiable "religious setting." At the same time, I did not use "Yahweh" or "Yahveh," as some versions do, on the grounds, first, that Jews, as explained, don't pronounce the Name at all; second, that we don't really know if these are good representations of how the Name was pronounced; and, third, that these words sound too strange in the ears of most Jews, who are not accustomed to hearing them in any context. I avoided "the LORD," simply because English-speakers have become so used to this phrase in Bibles that, in my judgment, it no longer can be counted on to evoke the awareness and reverence for God that it should. But it won't hurt my feelings if others say for the Name something other than what the *CJB* has in print.

The Tetragrammaton in the New Testament. Finally, the problem of God's name takes on a further dimension of uncertainty in the *B'rit Hadashah*. There the Greek word *kurios* is frequently ambiguous. It can mean "sir," "lord" (as in "lord of the manor"), "Lord" (with divine overtones), and "*Yud-Heh-Vav-Heh.*" Most translations, by always rendering *kurios* "Lord," finesse the issue of when it means "*Yud-Heh-Vav-Heh.*" The *CJB* and the *Jewish New Testament* do not — in keeping with the principle stated in Section II above that translators should decide the true meaning of a word and render that meaning clearly, rather than transfer vagueness from one language to another, the word "*ADONAI*" is used in the *B'rit Hadashah* wherever I, as the translator, believe "*kurios*" is the Greek representation of the tetragrammaton.

In several places this approach brings into bold relief a key theological issue separating Messianic from traditional Judaism, namely, whether *ADONAI* can include Yeshua the Messiah and/or the Holy Spirit. Philippians 2:10–11 informs us that the day is coming when "every knee will bow . . . and every tongue will acknowledge that Yeshua the Messiah is *kurios.*" Since this passage quotes Isaiah 45:23, where it is explicit that every knee will bow to *ADONAI*, *kurios* is here translated "*ADONAI.*" At 2 Corinthians 3:16–18 Sha'ul (Paul) alludes to Exodus 34:34 in writing that "whenever someone turns to *ADONAI*, the veil is taken away"; then he explicitly points out that "'*ADONAI*' in this text means the Spirit," and uses the phrase, "*ADONAI* the Spirit."

XI. THE JEWISHNESS OF THE NEW TESTAMENT

So much for the differences between the *CJB*'s *Tanakh* and the Old Testament with which Christians are familiar. We turn now to the differences between the *CJB*'s *B'rit Hadashah* and other translations of the New Testament. Given that there were already literally hundreds of English versions of the New Testament in existence when the *Jewish New Testament* came out, why was another one needed? The reason is that my version was the first to express fully the New Testament's original and essential Jewishness; nearly all the other English translations of the New Testament presented its message in a Gentile-Christian linguistic, cultural and theological framework.[45]

And what was wrong with that? Nothing! For although the Gospel is Jewish in origin, it is not only for Jews but also for Gentiles. The New Testament itself could not be clearer about that,[46] so it is appropriate that its message be communicated to non-Jews in ways that impose on them a minimum of alien cultural baggage.[47] And this approach has been successful: millions of Gentiles have come to trust in the God of Avraham, Yitz'chak and Ya'akov and in the Jewish Messiah, Yeshua.[48]

The New Testament Is a Jewish Book. However, the time came for restoring the Jewishness of the New Testament. For the New Testament is in fact a Jewish book — by Jews, mostly about Jews, and for Jews as well as Gentiles. It is all very well to adapt a Jewish book for easier appreciation by non-Jews, but not at the cost of suppressing its inherent Jewishness. The *Jewish New Testament* expressed this Jewishness first of all in its very name, which, like the name of the evangelistic organization "Jews for Jesus," unites two ideas that some consider incompatible and would rather keep separate.

But such separation cannot be. For the central figure of the New Testament, Yeshua the Messiah, was a Jew who was born into a Jewish family in Beit-Lechem, grew up among Jews in Natzeret, ministered to Jews in the Galil, and died and rose from the grave in the Jewish capital, Yerushalayim — all in *Eretz-Yisra'el*, the land God gave the Jewish people. Moreover, Yeshua is still a Jew, since he is still alive; and nowhere does Scripture say or suggest that he has stopped being Jewish. His twelve closest followers were Jews. For years all his *talmidim* (disciples) were Jews, eventually numbering "tens of thousands" in Yerushalayim alone.[49] The New Testament was written entirely by Jews (Luke being, in all likelihood, a proselyte to

---

45 Exceptions in varying degrees: Sid Roth's *The Book of Life* (Nashville: Thomas Nelson, 1982) and David Bronstein, Jr.'s *The Living Bible: Messianic Edition* (Wheaton, Ilinois: Tyndale House, 1984); both are adaptations of existing English versions made by Messianic Jews. The *Original New Testament* (San Francisco: Harper & Row, 1985) is Hugh Schonfield's revision of his earlier translation, The *Authentic New Testament* (1955); Schonfield (1901–1988) accepted Yeshua as the Messiah in his youth but reneged in later years. *God's New Covenant: A New Testament Translation*, by the Messianic Jew, Heinz W. Cassirer (1903–1979), was published by William B. Eerdsman Publishing Company, Grand Rapids, Michigan, in 1989.

46 Romans 1:16, 3:29–30, 10:12

47 See 1 Corinthians 9:19–23.

48 These are the Hebrew names of Abraham, Isaac, Jacob and Jesus. For guidance in pronouncing Hebrew see Section XVI below and the Pronouncing Explanatory Glossary at the end of the book.

49 Acts 21:20

Judaism); and its message is directed "to the Jew especially, but equally to the Gentile."[50] It was Jews who brought the Gospel to non-Jews, not the other way round. Sha'ul ("also known as Paul"),[51] the chief emissary to the Gentiles, was a lifelong observant Jew, as is abundantly clear from evidence in the book of Acts.[52] Indeed the main issue in the early Messianic Community — that is, the "Church" — was not whether a Jew could believe in Yeshua, but whether a Gentile could become a Christian without converting to Judaism![53] The Messiah's vicarious atonement is rooted in the Jewish sacrificial system.[54] The Lord's Supper is rooted in the Jewish Passover. Immersion (baptism) is a Jewish practice. The New Covenant itself was promised by the Jewish prophet Yirmeyahu (Jeremiah).[55] The very concept of a Messiah is exclusively Jewish, and that Jewish Messiah taught that "salvation is from the Jews."[56] Indeed, as the name *Complete Jewish Bible* suggests, the *B'rit Hadashah* completes the *Tanakh*; so that the New Testament without the Old is as impossible as the second floor of a house without the first, and the Old without the New as unfinished as a house without a roof.

Moreover, much of what is written in the *B'rit Hadashah* is incomprehensible apart from its Jewish context. I gave one example in Section VIII above, in the paragraph on the Greek of the *B'rit Hadashah*, and here is another. At *Mattityahu* (Matthew) 1:21 an angel of *ADONAI* tells Yosef (Joseph) that Miryam (Mary), his betrothed, will give birth to a son, "and you are to name him Yeshua, because he will save his people from their sins." In English the reason explains nothing — why not name him "George, because he will save his people from their sins"? Likewise in Greek — the name *Iêsous* has nothing to do with *sotêr*, the Greek word for "save." Only in Hebrew or Aramaic does the explanation explain. The Hebrew name *Yeshua* (ישוע), which is the masculine form of the word *yeshu'ah* (ישועה — "salvation"), is based on the same root (*yud-shin-'ayin* — ע-ש-י) as *yoshia* (יושיע), which means "he will save."

But the best demonstration of the New Testament's Jewishness is also the most convincing proof of its truth, namely, the number of *Tanakh* prophecies, all of them centuries older than the New Testament events, which are fulfilled in the person of Yeshua from Natzeret. The probability that anyone could satisfy dozens of prophetic conditions by mere chance is infinitesimal. No pretender to Messiahship, such as Shim'on Bar-Kokhva,[57] Shabtai Tzvi[58] or, more recently, the late leader of the *HaBaD* Hasidic movement among ultra-Orthodox Jews, Menachem Schneerson[59] has fulfilled more than a few of them. Yeshua fulfilled every prophecy intended to be fulfilled at

---

[50] Romans 1:16
[51] The phrase is quoted from Acts 13:9. Some suppose that at this point God changed his name from Sha'ul to Paul as a sign that he "had stopped being a Jew and become a Christian." Nothing could be further from the truth. Like many Jews in the Diaspora both then and now, he had two names — one suited to the country in which he was living, and the other, his Hebrew name, given at his circumcision.
[52] See Acts 16:3, 17:2, 18:18, 20:16, 21:23–27, 23:5–6, 25:8, 28:17.
[53] See Acts 15:1–29 and the whole book of Galatians.
[54] See especially Leviticus 17:11.
[55] Jeremiah 31:30–33(31–34)
[56] John 4:22
[57] Died 135 C.E.
[58] 1626–1676
[59] 1902–1995

his first coming; Section XIV below lists fifty-four of them. The rest of the prophecies he will fulfill when he returns in glory.

Thus the *Jewish New Testament* began to make it normal to think of the New Testament as Jewish.

There are three additional areas in which the *Jewish New Testament* and the *Complete Jewish Bible* can aid in *tikkun-ha'olam* (fixing the world): Christian anti-Semitism, Jewish failure to receive the Gospel, and the split between the Church and the Jewish people.

Christian Anti-Semitism. First, a vicious circle of Christian anti-Semitism feeds on the New Testament. The New Testament itself contains no anti-Semitism; but since the early days of the Church, anti-Semitism has misused the New Testament to justify itself and infiltrate Christian theology. Translators of the New Testament, steeped in that anti-Semitic theology, produce anti-Jewish translations, even when they themselves are not anti-Semites. Readers of these translations absorb attitudes which are anti-Jewish and alien to Judaism. Some of these readers become theologians who refine and develop the anti-Semitic character of Christian theology (they may even be unaware of the built-in anti-Semitism); while others become anti-Semitic activists who persecute Jews, thinking that by so doing they are serving God. This vicious circle must be broken. The *Jewish New Testament*, by removing centuries-old anti-Semitic theological biases and positively stressing Jewishness, has contributed to doing so, and now the *Complete Jewish Bible* continues this effort.

Jewish Misgivings About the Gospel. Second, while there are between 100,000 and 500,000 Messianic Jews in the English-speaking countries (and possibly twice as many in the world — the figures are very uncertain because they depend on whom one counts as Jewish and whom one counts as Messianic), it is obvious that most of the world's 13-to-17 million Jewish people do not accept Yeshua as the Messiah. While the reasons include Christian persecution of Jews, secular worldviews that allow little place for either God or a Messiah, and, as with non-Jews, refusal to turn from sin, a major cause is the perception by Jews that the Gospel is irrelevant to them. This perceived irrelevancy arises partly from the way Christianity presents itself, but also from the alienation induced by most New Testament translations. With their Gentile Christian cultural trappings and their anti-Jewish theological underpinnings, they lead many Jews to see the New Testament as a Gentile book about a Gentile god. The Jesus portrayed therein seems to bear little relationship to Jewish life. It becomes hard for a Jew to experience Yeshua the Messiah as who he really is, namely, a friend to every Jewish heart. While the *Jewish New Testament* and the *Complete Jewish Bible* cannot eliminate all the barriers between every Jew and his faith in the Messiah, they do remove some of the linguistic, cultural and theological obstacles. A Jewish person reading the *JNT* or the *CJB* should be able to see clearly that Yeshua is indeed the Messiah promised by the *Tanakh* to the Jewish people, that the *B'rit Hadashah* is for Jews as much as for Gentiles, and that the message of the Bible as a whole, both testaments together, is true, important and worthy of acceptance, the key to both individual and Jewish national salvation.

The Split Between the Messianic Community and the Jewish People. Finally, centuries of Jewish rejection of Yeshua and Christian rejection of Jews has produced today's conventional wisdom that Christianity is Christianity, and Judaism is Judaism, and never the twain shall meet. Moreover, many Jews and Christians are perfectly satisfied with this arrangement. Most Jews accept the false assumption that receiving Yeshua as the Messiah implies ceasing to be a Jew, so that if Jews do this in significant numbers, it is equivalent to annihilation of themselves as a people and—as Jewish philosopher Emil Fackenheim put it—giving Hitler a posthumous victory. But it was never meant to be so, never God's will that for a Jew to believe in Yeshua meant that he could no longer be Jewish, and never God's will that there be two separate peoples of God, the Jews and the Christians. Yet only in the past two or three decades, with the emergence of Messianic Judaism and this movement's acceptance by significant parts of the Church, has there developed an effective institutional framework for preserving the identity of the Jewish people within the Messianic Community. Gentile Christians who recognize that they have *joined* Israel, not *replaced* it, and Messianic Jews who identify fully with *both* the Jewish people *and* the Jewish Messiah, Yeshua, are now working together to heal the split between the Church and the Jewish people. The *Complete Jewish Bible* with the *Jewish New Testament* are forwarding this great work by presenting Jews and Gentiles alike with the Jewish unity of the *Tanakh* and the *B'rit Hadashah*.

XII. HOW THE *COMPLETE JEWISH BIBLE* EXPRESSES THE *B'RIT HADASHAH*'S JEWISHNESS

Three Ways of Bringing Out the Jewishness of the *B'rit Hadashah*. This translation accomplishes its goal of bringing out the Jewishness of the *B'rit Hadashah* in three somewhat overlapping ways — cosmetically (or superficially), culturally and religiously, and theologically.

- **Cosmetically.** Cosmetic changes from the usual renderings are the most frequent and obvious. The names "Jesus," "John," "James" and "Peter" never appear, only "Yeshua," "Yochanan," "Ya'akov" and "Kefa." The terms "immersion," "emissary," "execution-stake" and "Messianic community" (or "congregation") replace "baptism," "apostle," "cross" and "church." Semitic terms which belong to "Jewish English" (see below) substitute for certain English words — for example, "*talmid*" instead of "disciple" and "do *tzedakah*" instead of "give to charity." Many of these alterations replace "church language," in which buzzwords produce automatic responses, with neutral terminology that encourages the reader to think. Although any one of these changes is superficial, the sheer quantity of them impresses on the reader that the *B'rit Hadashah* is indeed a Jewish book, and this true and genuine effect is not superficial.

- **Culturally and Religiously.** Cultural-religious changes strengthen the reader's awareness of the Jewish cultural or religious context in which events of the *B'rit Hadashah* took place. One example is at *Mattityahu* 9:20, where the lady seeking to be healed touches not merely the "fringe" or "edge" of Yeshua's robe, but his "*tzitzit*," the ritual tassel which the *Torah* instructs Jewish men to wear on the corners of their garments as a reminder to obey all of God's *mitzvot* (commandments).[60] Another is at Acts 20:7, where the evening meeting of Sha'ul with the believers in Ephesus on (literally) "the one of the week," usually rendered, "the first day of the week," was probably held not on Sunday but, reflecting the Jewish, biblical way of organizing the calendar, on "*Motza'ei-Shabbat*," that is, "the going-out of the Sabbath," which takes place Saturday night.

- **Theologically.** Theological changes are the most penetrating, since New Testament translating has been thoroughly permeated by Gentile Christian theologies which de-emphasize the Jews as still God's people, the *Torah* as still valid, and God as still One. An example of such a change is at Messianic Jews (Hebrews) 8:6, where the Greek word *nenomothetêtai* means not merely that the New Covenant "has been enacted" on the basis of better promises, but on those promises "has been made *Torah*." Another is at Romans 10:4, where the word *telos* does not mean that the Messiah terminates the Law, but that he is "the goal at which the *Torah* aims." Theological implications of these and some other *CJB* New Testament renderings are discussed in Section XIII below.

"Jewish English." Besides systematically using the original Semitic names for persons and places in and near the land of Israel the *Complete Jewish Bible*'s New Testament draws on what I call "Jewish English," defined as Hebrew and Yiddish expressions which many English-speaking Jews incorporate into everyday speech. While meant to bring the Jewishness of the *B'rit Hadashah* into clearer focus, some readers may find this aspect of the translation unfamiliar or anachronistic and therefore exhausting or jarring; or they may take exception to particular decisions — for example, to using the word "*shalom*" instead of "peace," or "*talmid*" instead of "disciple," or the Yiddish word "*tsuris*" instead of "troubles" — or to generally *not* using "*Mashiach*" in place of "Messiah." I expect such objections, because "Jewish English" is an *ad hoc* concept, so that each English-speaking Jew creates his own version of it. Some Jews are unaware of these speech patterns. Some regard certain phrases as second nature but are unacquainted with others. Some who know the expressions may find them uncongenial in a Bible, while others may tire from seeing too many unfamiliar terms scattered through the book. But since "Jewish English" in its manifold variety is widely used, I appeal for tolerance of those elements included in the *CJB*.

However, there are more Hebrew terms and more "Jewish English" in the *CJB*'s *B'rit Hadashah* than in its *Tanakh* because, as I indicated earlier, I don't need to stress the *Tanakh*'s Jewishness. True, all the names in the *Tanakh* are presented in their Hebrew form, more than three thousand of them; and this may be difficult for some readers. But it shouldn't be any harder to say "Achazyah" than "Ahaziah" or "Ya'akov" than "Jacob"; and it seems more authentic to point readers toward the actual Hebrew names than toward the English mispronunciations of them! To help

---

[60] Numbers 15:37–41

out, I have included Section XVI below on how to pronounce Hebrew; and at the
end is an Pronouncing Explanatory Glossary which defines the terms, in addition to
showing their pronunciation.

Jewish New Testament Commentary. I mentioned in Section I that I wrote the *Jewish
New Testament Commentary* as a companion volume to the *Jewish New Testament*.
This verse-by-verse commentary, which can be used with the *CJB*'s *B'rit Hadashah*,
defends controversial *B'rit Hadashah* renderings and provides background of interest to both Jews and Christians. Passages which are problematical from a Jewish
viewpoint are treated, such as *Mattityahu* 27:25 ("His blood is on us and on our
children!") and Yochanan's remarks in his gospel about "the Jews" (in my translation frequently "the Judeans"). Likewise, present-day points of friction between Jews
and Christians are discussed at some appropriate place — for instance, the issue
of whether evangelizing Jews is in principle unethical is treated in the context
of 2 Corinthians 4:2 ("We refuse to make use of shameful underhanded methods,
employing deception or distorting God's message."). Section XIII below deals briefly
with a few topics of this kind, providing a taste of what *Jewish New Testament
Commentary* readers can expect in its 930 pages.

**Minor Differences between the *Jewish New Testament* and the *Complete Jewish
Bible*'s *B'rit Hadashah*.** My "fans," the people who have come to know and like the
Jewish New Testament, may notice some minor differences between the *JNT* and the
CJB's *B'rit Hadashah*. Actually, there would have been more of them had I not felt
constrained to make as few modifications as possible for two reasons: (1) there may
be public reading at congregation meetings and Bible studies where some will have
this book and others will have the *JNT*, so that too many differences would cause
confusion; and (2) I want this book to be easily usable with the *Jewish New Testament
Commentary*, which is keyed to the *JNT*; again, differences might confuse *JNTC*
users. So I limited changes primarily to conforming the spelling of some words to
the pattern I decided on for the *CJB*'s *Tanakh*; in particular, no Hebrew names or
terms that begin with the Hebrew letter *het* start with "ch"; see Section XVI below.
The word "*Adonai*" is now printed in large and small capital letters, as explained in
Section X. I also re-formatted some of the poetry. There are a very few textual changes.

   This is also why I did not respond to the desire of a number of readers that I
reduce my use of Yiddish words in the text of the *B'rit Hadashah*. For them the Yiddish
did not enhance the New Testament's Jewishness but intruded an anachronistic
element — it made them think not of Bible times but of the Eastern European *shtetl*.
Also, because Yiddish often has a humorous valence for English-speakers, it
demeaned for them the seriousness of God's Word. Although there are only eleven
purely Yiddish words in the *JNT*, and most of them are used only once, they are
admittedly a strong spice. In their favor is the fact that they do convey the sense of
the Greek original as well as or better than equivalent English words.

   I also left unchanged the names which include the Hebrew words "Bar" and
"Ben" (son of) and "Bat" (daughter of), even though in the *Tanakh* I use the English
equivalents. I felt that there, because these words are used so often in the Hebrew
genealogies and elsewhere, too many "Bens" would overly disrupt the flow of
the English.

XIII. REASONS FOR CERTAIN *B'RIT HADASHAH* RENDERINGS

A number of the renderings in the *CJB*'s *B'rit Hadashah* differ from those found in most versions of the New Testament and have significant implications for theology. While there is not space in the *CJB* to defend all the controversial renderings and outline their theological implications, the following material is intended to demonstrate that such defenses exist, and it constitutes a sample of what is discussed more fully in the *Jewish New Testament Commentary*. Much of this material is presented topically in my *Messianic Jewish Manifesto*, or its abridgement, *Restoring the Jewishness of the Gospel: A Message for Christians.*[61]

Did Yeshua "Fill" or "Fulfill" the *Torah*? The common Greek word *plerôsai* means "to fill." At *Mattityahu* 5:17 most translations render it "to fulfill." The theological implication often drawn is that Yeshua fulfilled all the prophecies of the *Tanakh*, so that none remain today for the Jews, and that he obeyed every relevant *Torah* command, so that no one needs to observe the *Torah* today. But these conclusions do not follow logically, and in fact they contradict Yeshua's immediately preceding statement that he did *not* come to abolish (or destroy) the *Torah*. More fundamental, however, is the translation issue of whether *plerôsai* ought to be rendered "to fulfill" at all. My view[62] is that Yeshua came not to *fulfill*, but to *fill* the *Torah* and the ethical pronouncements of the Prophets *full* with their *complete meaning*, so that everyone can know all that obedience entails. For this reason the *CJB*'s *B'rit Hadashah* says that Yeshua came "not to abolish but to complete." In fact, this is the theme of the entire Sermon on the Mount;[63] and *Mattityahu* 5:17, understood in this way, is its theme sentence; for Yeshua goes on from there to give specifics. Interestingly, this understanding is concordant with Jewish tradition, which says that when the Messiah comes he will both explain obscure passages of *Torah* and actually change it.

Binding and Loosing: Who Has the Authority to Determine *Halakhah*? At *Mattityahu* 18:18 the Greek words usually rendered "bind" and "loose" are translated "prohibit" and "permit." This reflects the first-century Jewish application of these concepts to their leaders, who were understood as having authority from God to decide what practices should be followed by the community, i.e., to determine *halakhah* ("Jewish law," although this meaning dates from a later period). In verses 18–20 the Messiah transfers this power from the rabbis to his own *talmidim* (disciples). This authority was not assumed instantaneously,[64] nor was it assumed later when it should have been. But the fact that Messianic Jews and Gentiles have hitherto made little use of Yeshua's far-reaching grant of authority does not cancel it. Moreover, this understanding gives verses 19–20 a different meaning from what most Christians understand — they say that two or three Messianic Community leaders suffice to determine proper practice (Messianic *halakhah*). The usual Christian application is that when two or three believers pray together, God listens. Though true, it is not the point of these verses.

---

61   All these books are published by Jewish New Testament Publications, Inc.
62   See David H. Stern, *Messianic Jewish Manifesto* and *Restoring the Jewishness of the Gospel: A Message for Christians* (Clarksville, MD, Jewish New Testament Publications, Inc., 1997).
63   Matthew 5–7
64   See Matthew 23:2.

Does the Messiah Bring the *Torah* to an End, or Is He Its Goal? At Romans 10:4 the *King James Version* gives a translation typical of most versions: "For Christ is the end of the law for righteousness to everyone that believeth." But Greek *telos*, which gives us the English word "teleology," usually means "goal, purpose, consummation," not "termination." The Messiah did *not* bring the *Torah* to an end. Rather, as the *CJB*'s *B'rit Hadashah* renders it, "the goal at which the *Torah* aims is the Messiah, who offers righteousness to everyone who trusts." This is the point which Sha'ul is making in the entire passage, Romans 9:30–10:13. For this reason the Greek word *de* at the beginning of Romans 10:6 is rendered as a continuative, "moreover," rather than as an adversative, "but"; for the latter could imply that there are two paths to righteousness — through deeds (i.e., obeying the *Torah* apart from faith, verse 5) and through faith (verses 6–10). However, Sha'ul's point throughout the passage, and indeed throughout Romans, is that for Jews and Gentiles alike there has never been more than one route to righteousness, namely, trusting God; so that the *Torah* is built on trusting God and from beginning to end has always required faith.[65]

The New Testament Has Been Given as *Torah*. At Messianic Jews (Hebrews) 8:6 most translations inform us that the New Covenant has been "enacted" or "legislated" on the basis of better promises. This would be an adequate translation were the subject matter Athenian legislation or Roman decrees. But the Greek word used here, *nenomothetêtai*, is a compound of *nomos*, which can mean "law" generally but in the book of Messianic Jews always means the *Torah* specifically, and *tithêmi*, a common word meaning "put" or "place." The only other appearance of *nenomothetêtai* in the New Testament is a few verses earlier, at 7:11, where all agree that it refers to the giving of the *Torah* on Mount Sinai, as do the related words *nomothesia* (Romans 9:4) and *nomothetês* (Ya'akov 4:12).

Therefore the *CJB* says that the New Covenant "has been given as *Torah* on the basis of better promises." This not only strengthens the theological contention that the *Torah* remains in force, but makes it clear that the New Covenant given through Yeshua is *Torah* just as much as the Sinaitic Covenant given through Moshe.

"Works of the Law" and "Under the Law": Is the *Torah* Legalistic? The Greek phrases *erga nomou* and *upo nomon* were coined by Sha'ul and used by him in three of his letters — Romans, Galatians and 1 Corinthians; each appears ten times in the New Testament. They are usually translated "works of the law" and "under the law," respectively. This often causes the reader to infer that keeping the *Torah* is bad, and that being within the framework of *Torah*-observance is bad. The *CJB*'s *B'rit Hadashah*, following the lead of Cranfield,[66] takes these phrases as referring not to the *Torah* itself but to man's legalistic perversion of it. Therefore *erga nomou* is rendered, "legalistic observance of *Torah* commands," and *upo nomon*, "in subjection to the system which results from perverting the *Torah* into legalism." The reader can

---

[65] Romans 1:16–17. For more on this, see Daniel P. Fuller, *Gospel and Law: Contrast or Continuum?* (Grand Rapids, Michigan: Eerdmans, 1980), as well as Chapter V of my *Messianic Jewish Manifesto*, mentioned above.

[66] C. E. B. Cranfield, *International Critical Commentary: The Epistle to the Romans* (Edinburgh: T.& T. Clark, Ltd., 1979), p. 853.

then infer, correctly, that according to the New Testament teaching of Sha'ul, legalism — whether Jewish, Christian or other — is bad, but living according to God's *Torah* is good.

The Land of Israel in the New Covenant. The Greek phrase *ê gê* is usually translated "the earth," but eighteen times in the New Testament it refers to the land of Israel. Two are explicit—*Mattityahu* 2:20–21 calls the Holy Land *Eretz-Yisra'el* (the land of Isra'el). Four are citations from the *Tanakh*—*Mattityahu* 5:5 (Psalm 37:11), *Mattityahu* 24:30 and Revelation 1:7 (Zechariah 12:10–14), and Ephesians 6:3 (Deuteronomy 5:16). Five are based on the *Tanakh* — Luke 4:25 and *Ya'akov* 5:17–18 (1 Kings 17:1, 18:1, 41–45), Messianic Jews 11:9 (Genesis 12, 13, 15, 20, 23), and Revelation 20:9 (Ezekiel 38–39). The remaining eight are implied by the context— *Mattityahu* 5:13, 10:34, 27:45; Mark 15:33; Luke 12:51, 21:23, 23:44; and Revelation 11:10. In an age when many Christian theologians use "replacement theology" (which asserts that the Church has replaced the Jews as God's people) in an attempt to prove that the land of Isra'el is no longer promised by God to the Jewish people, it is important to see that the physical land of Israel plays a significant role in the New Testament's portrayals of God's plan for the Jews in particular and for humanity in general, past, present and future.

XIV. *TANAKH* PROPHECIES FULFILLED BY YESHUA THE MESSIAH

As noted in Section XI, the most convincing evidence of Yeshua's being Isra'el's Messiah is the number of prophecies in the *Tanakh* that he fulfilled at his first coming. Following is a partial list of these Messianic prophecies, along with the New Testament verses verifying Yeshua's fulfillment of them.

Space does not permit showing why each of these prophecies should be understood as referring to Yeshua the Messiah. Many books discuss this subject in detail, mentioning other *Tanakh* prophecies which point to Yeshua.[67]

Besides prophecies there are incidents in the *Tanakh* which function as pictures in advance, or "types," of Yeshua. What is known in Judaism as the *akedah* ("binding"), the near-sacrifice of Yitz'chak by Avraham, is explicitly called a type of Yeshua the Messiah at Messianic Jews (Hebrews) 11:17–19. The life of Yosef provides another example: his brothers tried to kill him, but in the end he saved them from death, even though they did not recognize him at first. This does not mean that Genesis 22 contains a "prophecy" that Yeshua would be raised from the dead, or that Genesis 37–45 states that the Jewish people, as a nation, would initially reject their Savior. Rather it shows that God's salvation plan unfolding itself in history has a unity determined by him from the beginning to be consummated in Yeshua the Messiah. Indeed Yeshua himself explained it this way to two of his *talmidim*.[68]

---

[67] See Appendix VII of *The Life and Times of Jesus the Messiah*, 2nd ed. (New York: Anson D. F. Randolph and Company, 1884), by the Messianic Jew Alfred Edersheim, in which a list of 456 *Tanakh* passages messianically applied in ancient rabbinic writings is supported by 558 quotations from those writings. Also see J. Barton Payne, *Encyclopedia of Biblical Prophecy* (New York: Harper & Row, 1973).

[68] Luke 24:25–27

PROPHECY: THE MESSIAH MUST. . .	SOURCE IN THE *TANAKH*	FULFILLMENT IN THE *B'RIT HADASHAH*
Be the "seed of the woman" that would "bruise" or "crush" the serpent's "head"	Genesis 3:15	Galatians 4:4; 1 Yochanan 3:8
Be the "seed of Avraham"	Genesis 12:3	Mattityahu 1:1; Acts 3:25; Galatians 3:16
Be the "seed of Yitz'chak"	Genesis 17:19; 21:12	Mattityahu 1:2; Luke 3:34; Messianic Jews 11:17–19
Be the "seed of Ya'akov" and the "star out of Ya'akov" who will "have dominion"	Genesis 28:14; Numbers 24:17, 19	Mattityahu 1:2; Luke 3:34; Revelation 22:16
Be a descendant of Y'hudah	Genesis 49:10	Mattityahu 1:2–3; Luke 3:33; Messianic Jews 7:14
Be a descendant of David and heir to his throne	2 Samuel 7:12–13; Isaiah 9:6(7); 11:1–5; Jeremiah 23:5	Mattityahu 1:1, 6; Acts 13:22–23; Romans 1:3
Have eternal existence	Micah 5:1(2)	Yochanan 1:1, 14; 8:58; Ephesians 1:3–4; Colossians 1:15–19; Revelation 1:18
Be the Son of God	Psalm 2:7; Proverbs 30:4	Mattityahu 3:17; Luke 1:32
Have God's own name, *Yud-Heh-Vav-Heh*, applied to him	Isaiah 9:5–6(6–7); Jeremiah 23:5–6	Romans 10:9; Philippians 2:9–11
Come 69 x 7 years (483 years) after the rebuilding of the wall of Yerushalayim	Daniel 9:24–26	Mattityahu 2:1, 16, 19; Luke 3:1, 23
Be born of a virgin[69]	Isaiah 7:14	Mattityahu 1:18–2:1; Luke 1:26–35

[69] The Hebrew word *'almah* in Isaiah 7:14 means "a young woman," and in the context of the *Tanakh* always "a young woman of unsullied reputation," which is why the Jewish translators of the Septuagint, the Greek version of the *Tanakh* prepared 200 years before Yeshua's birth, rendered this word into Greek as *parthenos*, "virgin"; this is the word used at *Mattityahu* 1:23.

PROPHECY: THE MESSIAH MUST. . .	SOURCE IN THE *TANAKH*	FULFILLMENT IN THE *B'RIT HADASHAH*
Be born in Beit-Lechem, in Y'hudah	Micah 5:1(2)	Mattityahu 2:1; Luke 2:4–7
Be adored by great persons	Psalm 72:10–11	Mattityahu 2:1–11
Be preceded by one who would announce him	Isaiah 40:3–5; Malachi 3:1	Mattityahu 3:1–3; Luke 1:17; 3:2–6
Be anointed with the Spirit of God	Isaiah 11:2, 61:1; Psalm 45:8(7)	Mattityahu 3:16; Yochanan 3:34; Acts 10:38
Be a prophet like Moshe	Deuteronomy 18:15, 18	Acts 3:20–22
Have a ministry of binding up the brokenhearted, proclaiming liberty to the captives and announcing the acceptable year of the Lord	Isaiah 61:1–2	Luke 4:18–19
Have a ministry of healing	Isaiah 35:5–6; 42:18	Mattityahu 11:5; throughout the Gospels
Have a ministry in the Galil	Isaiah 8:23–9:1(9:1–2)	Mattityahu 4:12–16
Be tender and compassionate	Isaiah 40:11; 42:3	Mattityahu 12:15, 20; Messianic Jews 4:15
Be meek and unostentatious	Isaiah 42:2	Mattityahu 12:15–16, 19
Be sinless and without guile	Isaiah 53:9	1 Kefa 2:22
Bear the reproaches due others	Isaiah 53:11–12; Psalm 69:10(9)	Romans 15:3
Be a priest	Psalm 110:4	Messianic Jews 5:5–6; 6:20; 7:15–17
Enter publicly into Yerushalayim on a donkey	Zechariah 9:9	Mattityahu 21:1–11; Mark 11:1–11
Enter the Temple with authority	Malachi 3:1	Mattityahu 21:12–24:1; Luke 2:27–38, 45–50; Yochanan 2:13–22

PROPHECY: THE MESSIAH MUST...	SOURCE IN THE *TANAKH*	FULFILLMENT IN THE *B'RIT HADASHAH*
Be hated without cause	Isaiah 49:7; Psalm 69:5(4)	Yochanan 15:24–25
Be undesired and rejected by his own people	Isaiah 53:2–3; 63:3, 5; Psalm 69:9(8)	Mark 6:3; Luke 9:58; Yochanan 1:11; 7:3–5
Be rejected by the Jewish leadership	Psalm 118:22	Mattityahu 21:42; Yochanan 7:48
Be plotted against by Jews and Gentiles together	Psalm 2:1–2	Acts 4:27
Be betrayed by a friend	Psalm 41:10(9); 55:13–15(12–14)	Mattityahu 26:21–25, 47–50; Yochanan 13:18–21; Acts 1:16–18
Be sold for 30 pieces of silver	Zechariah 11:12	Mattityahu 26:15
Have his price given for a potter's field	Zechariah 11:13	Mattityahu 27:6–7
Be forsaken by his *talmidim*	Zechariah 13:7	Mattityahu 26:31, 56
Be struck on the cheek	Micah 4:14(5:1)	Mattityahu 27:30
Be spat on	Isaiah 50:6	Mattityahu 26:67; 27:30
Be mocked	Psalm 22:8–9(7–8)	Mattityahu 26:67–68; 27:31, 39–44
Be beaten	Isaiah 50:6	Mattityahu 26:67; 27:26, 30
Be executed by crucifixion, by having his hands and feet pierced[70]	Psalm 22:17(16); Zechariah 12:10	Mattityahu 27:35; Luke 24:39; Yochanan 19:18, 34–37; 20:20–28; Revelation 1:7
Be thirsty during his execution	Psalm 22:16(15)	Yochanan 19:28

---

[70] The Septuagint (see footnote 69) has: "They pierced my hands and my feet," implying the Hebrew word *karu* (כרו) in its source text. The Masoretic Hebrew text, accepted as standard in traditional Judaism, has *k'ari* (כארי), and the line reads, "Like a lion, my hands and my feet." See Section VIII, paragraph 6.

PROPHECY: THE MESSIAH MUST...	SOURCE IN THE *TANAKH*	FULFILLMENT IN THE *B'RIT HADASHAH*
Be given vinegar to quench that thirst	Psalm 69:22(21)	Mattityahu 27:34
Be executed without having a bone broken	Exodus 12:46; Psalm 34:21(20)	Yochanan 19:33–36
Be considered a transgressor	Isaiah 53:12	Mattityahu 27:3
Be "cut off, but not for himself," 69 x 7 years after rebuilding of the wall of Jerusalem	Daniel 9:24–26	Romans 5:16; 1 Kefa 3:18
Be the one whose death would atone for sins of mankind	Isaiah 53:5–7, 12	Mark 10:45; Yochanan 1:29; 3:16; Acts 8:30–35
Be buried with the rich when dead	Isaiah 53:9	Mattityahu 27:57–60
Be raised from the dead	Isaiah 53:9–10; Psalm 2:7; 16:10	Mattityahu 28:1–20; Acts 2:23–36; 13:33–37; 1 Corinthians 15:4–6
Ascend to the right hand of God	Psalm 16:11; 68:19(18); 110:1	Luke 24:51; Acts 1:9–11; 7:55; Messianic Jews 1:3
Exercise his priestly office in heaven	Zechariah 6:13	Romans 8:34; Messianic Jews 7:25–8:2
Be the cornerstone of God's Messianic Community	Isaiah 28:16; Psalm 118:22–23	Mattityahu 21:42; Ephesians 2:20; 1 Kefa 2:5–7
Be sought after by Gentiles as well as Jews	Isaiah 11:10; 42:1	Acts 10:45–46; 13:46–48
Be accepted by the Gentiles	Isaiah 11:10; 42:1–4; 49:1–6	Mattityahu 12:18–21; Romans 9:30; 10:20; 11:11; 15:10
Be the king	Psalm 2:6	Yochanan 18:33, 37
Be seen by Israel as pierced[71]	Zechariah 12:10; Psalm 22:17(16)	Luke 24:39; Yochanan 19:34–37; Revelation 1:7

---

[71] See footnote 70.

XV. SYNAGOGUE USAGE OF THE *COMPLETE JEWISH BIBLE*

Reading in the Synagogue from the *Torah*, the Prophets and the *B'rit Hadashah*.
Every Saturday morning, in synagogues all over the world, *Torah* scrolls are
ceremoniously removed from arks, carried through the aisles to be touched reverently
by the congregants (the custom symbolizes devotion to the Word of God), and then
placed on the *bimah* (pulpit). Seven persons are called up to recite blessings before
and after they or more experienced readers read the sacred Hebrew text of the *Torah*
from the scroll. The practice of public reading from the *Torah* dates back at least to
the time of Ezra,[72] if not to King Y'hoshafat[73] or King Yoshiyahu;[74] and the *B'rit
Hadashah* attests it as well.[75] The portion (*parashah*) read each week, anywhere
between one and six chapters long, is not picked on the spur of the moment but
follows a prescribed sequence tied to the Jewish year. Fifty-four *parashot* are read in
order, commencing with *B'resheet* (Genesis) 1 on the autumn holiday *Simchat-
Torah* (Rejoicing of the *Torah*) and ending with *D'varim* (Deuteronomy) 34 on
Simchat-Torah the following year, when with great joy the scroll is immediately
re-rolled, and *B'resheet* 1 is read again.

Moreover, the reading from the Bible does not end with the *Torah* portion. After
the *Torah*, a related section from the Prophets is read; this is called the *haftarah*
(completion), since it completes the prescribed synagogue Scripture reading. The
B'rit Hadashah reports that in Natzeret (Nazareth) Yeshua was invited to read the
haftarah, which that week was from the book of Isaiah, and he daringly applied the
passage to himself.[76] In times past there was also a reading from the Writings section
of the Bible, but this custom has fallen away.

Being called up to the *bimah* for the *Torah* reading is an honor. The Hebrew
word for such an invitation is *'aliyah*; it means "going up." (The same word, *'aliyah*,
means "immigrating to Israel," since it is a spiritual "going up" for a Jew to return to
the land God gave to our people.) The first *'aliyah* is given to a *cohen* (priest) if one
is present, the second to a *Levi* (Levite) if present, and the rest to any Jew. The *'oleh*
(the person called up for an *'aliyah*) recites the blessing, stands at the *bimah* while
he or the *ba'al-kore* (pronounced *ba·'al ko·ray* — the master reader) reads from the
scroll; he then recites the closing blessing, remains standing there during the following
'aliyah, shakes hands all around, and then returns to his seat. In Orthodox Judaism only
men are given *'aliyot*; in Conservative and Reform Judaism both men and women
may be called up.

**How the *Complete Jewish Bible* Provides the Necessary Information for Public
Reading of the Bible in the Synagogue on *Shabbat*.** The *Complete Jewish
Bible* contains all the information (except Jewish calendar dates) that one needs
in order to organize or follow the synagogue readings from the *Torah* and the
Prophets. In addition, I have suggested readings from the *B'rit Hadashah* that

---

[72]   Nehemiah 8:1
[73]   2 Chronicles 17:9
[74]   2 Kings 22:8–23:3
[75]   Acts 13:14–15
[76]   Luke 4:16–30

are related to the *parashah* for each week. I chose them because they either quote or allude to a passage from the *parashah* or deal with the same subject matter. Since Messianic Judaism is in its formative stages and has not determined "prescribed readings," I have sometimes suggested more material than is needed. Congregations should choose a portion of appropriate length or substitute another passage if it seems more suitable.

At the beginning of each *parashah* the *CJB* gives its name and its included Bible verses. Like the books of the *Tanakh* themselves, each *parashah* is named for its first words (the English translation of these is supplied). At the end of each *parashah* are given its *haftarah* and *B'rit Hadashah* readings. The table starting on page 1616 summarizes this information for all 54 *Shabbats*.

Within each *Torah* portion are bold-face italicized Roman numerals from "*ii*" to "*vii*" indicating where each of the *'aliyot* begins (the first *'aliyah* begins at the start of the *parashah*). Near the end of the seventh *'aliyah* is the word "*Maftir*"; whoever is to read the *haftarah* starts by reading these final verses of the *Torah* portion from the scroll and then reads the Prophets portion from a printed edition of the Bible.

The prescribed readings differ somewhat between the Ashkenazic (European) and Sefardic (Middle Eastern and North African) Jewish communities; where necessary "*A*" and "*S*" indicate the differences.

The Jewish calendar also enters the picture. The Jewish calendar is unusual in that its months are lunar, but its year is solar. Since a lunar month is twenty-nine or thirty days long, twelve lunar months take about 354 days. To prevent the year from moving through the seasons (as the Muslim year does), there is a system for leap years; however, the leap year doesn't add merely a day, but a whole month. This happens seven years out of nineteen — every two or three years the month of "Second Adar" is added in early spring. Thus in leap years, there are four or five more *Shabbats* than in regular years; so in leap years each of the fifty-four *parashot* is read separately, but in regular years, with only about fifty *Shabbats*, some of them are read together. The necessary adjustments are indicated where needed by the abbreviations "*RY*" for regular years and "*LY*" for leap years.

Messianic adaptations. At the end of the second, forty-eighth and forty-ninth *parashot* I have included a "Messianic adaptation" of the prescribed *haftarah* reading. For reasons not conclusively known, although some have speculated that it was in order to avoid the passage in the *Tanakh* that most clearly prophesies Yeshua as the Messiah, the rabbis of old did not select *Yesha'yahu* (Isaiah) 52:13–53:12 to be a *haftarah* reading. The portions before and after are included, but this one is not. I can safely say that it expresses the will and spiritual discernment of the Messianic Jewish community that this passage should not be excluded from the *haftarot* in the synagogue.

Readings for Jewish Holidays. In addition, there are *Torah* and *haftarah* readings prescribed for each of the biblical holidays and for some other Jewish holidays and fast-days. The table starting on page 1616 lists these, along with suggested *B'rit Hadashah* readings, and with the same "Messianic adaptation" of two of the *haftarot*. Also it is suggested that the *Torah* readings for *Yom Kippur* add Leviticus 17 because of its verse 11, and that the *haftarah* for Tish'ah B'Av include Zechariah 12.

The number of *aliyot* is different on the Holidays. On *Yom Kippur* morning there are six (except that if it falls on *Shabbat*, there are seven). On *Rosh-HaShanah* and the three festivals (*Pesach*, *Shavu'ot*, and *Sukkot*) there are five. On *Rosh-Hodesh* (new moon, start of a month) and *Hol-HaMo'ed* (middle days of the *Sukkot* and *Pesach* festivals) there are four. On *Yom Kippur* afternoon there are two plus the *Maftir*.

Blessings Before and After Reading from the *B'rit Hadashah*. The blessings pronounced before and after the *Torah* and *haftarah* readings can be found in virtually any *siddur* (Jewish prayerbook). Following is a suggested pair of prayers for before and after reading from the *B'rit Hadashah*:

Before:

> *Barukh attah* ADONAI *Eloheinu melekh-ha'olam, asher natan lanu et Yeshua binkha k'meshichenu goalenu moshi'enu kapporatenu va'adonenu, ve'et sifrei B'rit heChadashah le 'amenu ulekhol ha'amim. Barukh attah* ADONAI *noten yeshu'ah b'Yeshua HaMashiach.*

Praised be you, O LORD our God, king of the universe, who has given us Yeshua your son as our Messiah, our redeemer, our savior, our atonement and our Lord, and the books of the New Covenant to our people and to all the peoples. Praised be you, O LORD, giver of salvation in Yeshua the Messiah.

After:

> *Barukh attah* ADONAI *Eloheinu melekh-ha'olam, asher natan et d'varkha haTanakh vaB'rit heChadashah lekhol b'nei-adam. Barukh attah* ADONAI *mevi et hago'el Yeshua l'ma'an sh'mo b'ahavah.*

Praised be you, O LORD our God, king of the universe, who has given your Word, the Hebrew Scriptures and the New Covenant, to all humanity. Praised be you, O LORD, who, for his own name's sake, in love, has brought the Redeemer, Yeshua.

XVI. HOW TO PRONOUNCE THE HEBREW NAMES AND TERMS

There is a "Pronouncing Explanatory Glossary" at the back of the book which shows how to pronounce and accent each Hebrew name and term, gives the usual English forms of all names, and translates all terms. Its first page gives a brief summary of how I transliterate Hebrew into English.

There is also a "Reverse Glossary" for some of the more common English names and terms, from which the reader can learn that the person he is used to calling Isaac is known in the *CJB* as Yitz'chak, that Mary is called Miryam and that "crucify" is rendered as "execute on a stake (as a criminal)."

But a number of people familiar with the *Jewish New Testament* have complained that they felt overwhelmed trying to cope with its Hebrew. Therefore in this

Section, I do what I can to help readers pronounce Hebrew correctly. I know that some will find it tedious, but others will appreciate my attention to the subject. It is the sort of thing one can safely skip and return to at one's convenience.

I transliterate Hebrew names and terms as most modern Israelis would pronounce them. There is a scholarly way to do this very accurately, but I haven't utilized it because it uses a number of signs that would look strange to most people, only adding to their confusion. Following is an explanation of my system.

Vowels. In my transliteration of Hebrew, the vowels are pronounced as follows:

Vowel	Pronunciation	Examples in Hebrew Words
a	as in "**father**" (fah-ther)	Adam (ah-**dahm**)
ai	as in "**aisle**," a long-i sound, like "high," "pie." Not a long-a sound	Haggai (hah-**guy**) El Shaddai (**el** shah-**die**)
e	as in "**bed**," a short-e sound "er" sounds like "air," not "ur"	Hesed (**heh**-sehd) Peretz (**peh**-retz) Gershon (gehr-**shone**)
ee	as in "**feed**," long-e	Sheetim (shee-**teem**)
ei	as in "**weigh**," a long-a sound like "day," "main." Not a long-i or long-e sound.	'Ein-Gedi ('ain-**geh**-dee) Beit-Lechem (bait-**leh**-chehm)
i	when accented: as in marine, long-e when not accented: as in "**invest**," short-i; in last syllable, even if not accented, long-e	cohanim (ko-hah-**neem**) Migdal (mig-**dahl**) Gershuni (gehr-**shoo**-nee)
o	as in "**so**," long-o, like "boat" or as in "**more**" an "aw"sound	Gat-Rimmon (gaht-rim-**moan**) Dor (door)
u	as in "**rule**," an "oo" sound, like "shoot"	Hizkiyahu (hiz-kee-**yah**-hoo) Beit-Tzur (bait-tzoor)
'		

I use the apostrophe in two ways — to represent the vowel *sh'va* (:) and the consonant *alef* (א—see next paragraph). The *sh'va* is an unaccented dull sort of vowel, an "uh" sound like the "a" in "above," the second "i" in "similarly," or the second "o" in "consonant." Thus Hebrew "G'rar" is pronounced "guh-**rahr**." The usual representation, Gerar, gets people to say "geh-**rahr**," which isn't quite right. Sometimes I represent a *sh'va* by nothing at all; but in this case, "Grar" doesn't get people to leave quite enough space between the "g" and the "rar." Similarly, "Y'hudah" should be pronounced somewhere between "yeh-hoo-**dah**" and "yoo-**dah**." I use the apostrophe to represent *sh'va* only when I feel it's needed to bring forth the right pronunciation; otherwise, I just leave it out; for example, I write "Gilgal," not "Gil'gal"; "Shimshon," not "Shim'shon." In some cases it's a hard call whether to stick in an apostrophe or not.

Consonants. The consonants are used and pronounced as follows:

'   As I said, the apostrophe represents the Hebrew letter *alef* (א) and the Hebrew vowel-sound *sh'va* (:). *Alef* is considered a consonant, but it's best described as a slight break in the flow of sound, like the break between the two "uh's" of "uh-uh," which people say when they mean "No," or the break between "umbrella" and "above" in "Put the umbrella above the table." So in the Hebrew word "Pa'ran," the apostrophe makes you separate the "Pa" from the "ran" instead of running the syllables together, which you would otherwise do (pah'-**rahn**, not par**rahn**). "Eli'el" is pronounced "elly-'**el**," not "elli**yell**." "Natan'el" is pronounced "nah-tan-**ell**," not "nah-tah-**nell**." When a word starts with *alef* I leave the apostrophe out; thus all transliterated Hebrew words that commence with English vowels start with *alef*; words commencing with a reverse apostrophe followed by an English vowel start with the Hebrew letter *'ayin* (ע—see next paragraph).

'   The reverse-apostrophe represents Hebrew letter *'ayin* (ע—pronounced **'ah**-yin), when it isn't signifying the start of a quote-within-a-quote. This is a glottal stop, a sound not found in English or other Western European languages. It's a sound produced deep in the throat, a kind of gagging sound. English sometimes represents this sound by the letter "g," as in "Gaza Strip" or "Gomorrah," but that's not really it. Arabic has it, but it's a hard sound for westerners to produce. However, if nothing else works, make the break-sound for *alef* described in the preceding paragraph, and that will pass. Many Israelis do no better.

h and   represent Hebrew letters *heh* (ה) and *het* (ח). The letter *heh* is always repre-
ch   sented by "h," since *heh* is the equivalent of English "h." At the end of a word it is usually silent, as in English "Hurrah!" and elsewhere it has the ordinary English "h" sound, as in "horse" or "greyhound." The Hebrew word *Halleluyah* has both kinds of *heh*. The *het* is what causes the problems. It has a guttural sound, like the "ch" in "Johann Sebastian Bach" and "Loch Lomond." If it occurs in the middle of a word, I represent it by "ch," as in "Beit-Lechem." At the beginning of a word, however, I represent it by "h." My reason is that otherwise, people may give it an English "ch" sound ("church") or a French one ("Chanel #5"). Thus the reader can't determine from the *Complete Jewish Bible* whether a Hebrew name starts with *heh* or *het*. This seems a small price to pay for assuring that no one will say that the Jewish wedding canopy (*hupah*) is a "tchoopah" or call the city of Hevron (Hebron) by the name of a gas station ("Chevron").

kh   represents Hebrew letter *kaf* (כ) when it's a "soft" *kaf*. It too has the sound of "ch" in "Bach."

k, c   The letter "k" represents the Hebrew letter *kuf* (ק) and the letter *kaf* (כ) when it's hard. I use the letter "c" for *kaf* in the word *cohen* (priest) because the name Cohen is so well known in English.

g   represents the Hebrew letter *gimel* (ג) and is always hard, never a j-sound. Thus the "g" in "Gezer" is pronounced as in "get," not as in "gem."

v, b   The letter "v" represents both *vav* (ו), when it's a consonant, and soft *bet* ("*vet*"—ב), while "b" represents hard "*bet*" (ב).

p, f   The letter "p" represents hard *peh* (פ), while "f" represents soft *peh* ("*feh*"—פ).

z and   The letter "z" represents zayin (ז); while the two letters "tz" represent *tzadeh*
tz   (צ), which has the sound of "ts" in "tsetse fly."

r   represents *resh* (ר), which ideally one should produce from the back of the mouth, somewhat as the French do, so that it sounds somewhere between "r" and hard "g." If this doesn't work for you, don't worry about it.

s   represents the letters *samekh* (ס) and *sin* (ש); both have the "s" sound.

sh   The two letters "sh" represent the Hebrew letter *shin* (ש).

d, l, m,   These represent, respectively, *dalet* (ד), *lamed* (ל), *mem* (מ), *nun* (נ), and
n, y   *yud* (י) and present no problems.

t   represents *tet* (ט) and *tav* (ת); both have the "t" sound. Ashkenazic pronunciation treats "*tav*" differently than Israeli (Sephardic) pronunciation — a "*tav*" at the end of a word will be pronounced "s" by Ashkenazim, who pronounce *Shabbat* **Shab**-bes, not Shab-**bat**.

Accentuation. The last example also highlights the fact that Ashkenazim often move the accent closer to the beginning of a word. For another example, the word *Torah* is pronounced "toe-**rah**" by Israelis, but Ashkenazim say "**toe**-rah," and some with Polish or other eastern European background say "**toy**-rah." The *CJB* glossary gives Israeli (Sephardic) accentings in nearly all cases; the exceptions are for words and names that are well-known among Jews in America, such as Moshe, which is pronounced "Mo-**she**" in Israel but "**Mo**-she" in America. In the glossary it appears as "**Mo**-she*"; the asterisk means, "If you want to say it the correct Israeli way, accent the last syllable."

XVII. USING THE *COMPLETE JEWISH BIBLE*

In this Section, I explain certain conventions I have adopted for the *CJB* and describe a number of reader's helps.

Semitic Terms and Names. Hebrew, Aramaic and Yiddish terms (including names of God) appear in italics (*bat-kol*, *El 'Elyon*), but Semitic names of persons and places do not (Shlomo, Ashdod). Thus *"Levi"* when it's a Levite and "Levi" when it's a person.

Textual Notes. In this edition of the *CJB* discussion of textual issues is kept to a minimum. About twenty passages in the *B'rit Hadashah* regarded as inauthentic by most scholars, none more than two verses in length, are absent from the text and placed in footnotes at the bottom of the page. Three passages — Mattityahu 6:13b, Mark 16:9–20 and Yochanan 7:53–8:11 — are included in the text but given a footnote briefly explaining the textual problem. In the *Tanakh* there are fewer issues of this kind; they too are dealt with in footnotes. This edition offers almost no textual variants or alternative readings.

Translator's Interpolations. Words in brackets are explanatory interpolations supplied by the translator and corresponding to nothing in the original text. There are more of these in the *Tanakh* than in the *B'rit Hadashah*; however, two examples from the *B'rit Hadashah* are at *Mattityahu* (Matthew) 1:21; 6:23. Words in parentheses are parenthetical remarks that are present in the original text; for an example, see *Mattityahu* 1:23. Certain words or phrases in the original language may be represented by "expanded" renderings[77] which for philosophical reasons[78] are not distinguished from the rest of the translation. Let me say here that there are places in the *CJB*, especially in the *Tanakh*, where some might consider the rendering so free that it should have been placed in brackets. On such things opinions differ; but in any case, the reader has been warned.

Other Features. Following is a summary of reader's helps to be found at the front and back of the book:

    Three Tables of Contents for the Books of the Bible (pages vii–xi). At the front of the book are three tables of contents to help readers with varying backgrounds to locate Bible books quickly. The first lists the books of the *Tanakh* in the Jewish order found in Hebrew Bibles and Jewish translations, and in the *CJB* itself. The second lists them in the order found in the Septuagint and seen in virtually all Christian translations. The third lists all the books of the Bible in alphabetical order by both English and Hebrew names.

    Pronouncing Explanatory Glossary (pages 1556–1604). At the back of the book are five items. The first is a comprehensive glossary of Hebrew, Aramaic and Yiddish words and names used in the *CJB*. Its first page summarizes rules of Hebrew pronunciation (Section XVI above deals with this in more detail). The definitions and explanations vary in length from one line to a paragraph. More information is provided for names and terms in the *B'rit Hadashah* than for those which appear only in the *Tanakh*; this is because these entries already existed in the *Jewish New Testament*, but I decided that providing similar entries for the names and terms in the *Tanakh* would make the Glossary too long.

    "Reverse" Glossary (pages 1605–1609). Readers acquainted with the Bible in other versions may wish to know what the *CJB* substitutes for names and terms

---

[77]   See, for example, the discussions of *upo nomon* and *erga nomou* in Sections II and XIII.
[78]   See Section II.

familiar to them. In the Reverse Glossary one may look up words such as "apostle" and "John" to find their *CJB* equivalents ("emissary" and "Yochanan").

Tanakh Passages Cited in the B'rit Hadashah (pages 1610–1615). In order to highlight the connection between the New Testament and the *Tanakh*, on which it builds, *Tanakh* verses cited in the *B'rit Hadashah* are printed there in **boldface** and their sources given in footnotes at the bottom of the page. The chapter-and-verse numberings and the order of the books of the *Tanakh* within a given footnote are those found in the *CJB*'s *Tanakh*. Where the Christian versions (and some Jewish ones) have a different chapter and verse, these are given afterwards in parentheses, e.g., Joel 3:1–5(2:28–32), Psalm 69:9(8).

The "Index of *Tanakh* Passages Cited in the *B'rit Hadashah*" lists every one of the 484 *Tanakh* verses cited in the text of the *B'rit Hadashah* and shows for each one all the verses in the *B'rit Hadashah* citing that *Tanakh* verse.

Scripture Readings (pages 1616–1623). As explained in Section XV above, these two tables list synagogue readings from the *Torah*, the Prophets and the *B'rit Hadashah* for the fifty-four *Shabbats* and for the festivals and fasts throughout the Jewish calendar year.

Maps and Map Indexes (pages 1624–1631). The Bible narratives are tied to particular places, but it is beyond the scope of the *CJB* to provide more than the limited geographical information found in the five maps of this section.

XVIII. ACKNOWEDGEMENTS

My wife Martha has been of inestimable value to me in preparing this version. Besides her encouragement and self-sacrifice in general, she checked the entire second draft of the *Tanakh* with me word for word, as I read it aloud from the computer screen. Ten years earlier she had similarly read the *Jewish New Testament* with me. She is truly an *eshet-chayil* ("a capable wife," Proverbs 31:10–31) and an *ezer k'negdi* ("a companion suitable for helping me," Genesis 2:18).

Barry and Steffi Rubin have been our friends for over twenty years. Barry, who directs Lederer/Messianic Jewish Communications, also manages Jewish New Testament Publications, Inc. Steffi, a fine artist, typeset the entire *Complete Jewish Bible*. We appreciate their work and friendship.

Paul Ellingworth, translation consultant for the United Bible Societies, spent three weeks with me reviewing an early version of the *Jewish New Testament*. His advice improved my translation and I thank him for it.

Many others have contributed in ways that have improved this version, and I thank them, too.

Finally, thanks to my God, the God of Avraham, Yitzchak and Ya'akov, and to his Messiah Yeshua, my and the Jewish people's Savior and Lord. *Barukh attah, Adonai Eloheynu, Melekh-ha'olam, shehecheyanu v'kimanu v'higianu lazman hazeh!* ("Praised be you, Lord our God, King of the universe, who has kept us alive, preserved us and enabled us to arrive at this point in time!")

May God bless you richly as you read from his Word in this version.

David H. Stern

Jerusalem, Israel
Passover 5758 (April 1998)

B'resheet
GENESIS

Parashah 1: B'resheet (In the beginning) 1:1–6:8

1 ¹ In the beginning God created the heavens and the earth. ² The earth was unformed and void, darkness was on the face of the deep, and the Spirit of God hovered over the surface of the water. ³ Then God said, "Let there be light"; and there was light. ⁴ God saw that the light was good, and God divided the light from the darkness. ⁵ God called the light Day, and the darkness he called Night. So there was evening, and there was morning, one day.

⁶ God said, "Let there be a dome in the middle of the water; let it divide the water from the water." ⁷ God made the dome and divided the water under the dome from the water above the dome; that is how it was, ⁸ and God called the dome Sky. So there was evening, and there was morning, a second day.

⁹ God said, "Let the water under the sky be gathered together into one place, and let dry land appear," and that is how it was. ¹⁰ God called the dry land Earth, the gathering together of the water he called Seas, and God saw that it was good.

¹¹ God said, "Let the earth put forth grass, seed-producing plants, and fruit trees, each yielding its own kind of seed-bearing fruit, on the earth"; and that is how it was. ¹² The earth brought forth grass, plants each yielding its own kind of seed, and trees each producing its own kind of seed-bearing fruit; and God saw that it was good. ¹³ So there was evening, and there was morning, a third day.

(A: ii) ¹⁴ God said, "Let there be lights in the dome of the sky to divide the day from the night; let them be for signs, seasons, days and years; ¹⁵ and let them be for lights in the dome of the sky to give light to the earth"; and that is how it was. ¹⁶ God made the two great lights — the larger light to rule the day and the smaller light to rule the night — and the stars. ¹⁷ God put them in the dome of the sky to give light to the earth, ¹⁸ to rule over the day and over the night, and to divide the light from the darkness; and God saw that it was good. ¹⁹ So there was evening, and there was morning, a fourth day.

²⁰ God said, "Let the water swarm with swarms of living creatures, and let birds fly above the earth in the open dome of the sky." ²¹ God created the great sea creatures and every living thing that creeps, so that the water swarmed with all kinds of them, and there was every kind of winged bird; and God saw that it was good. ²² Then God blessed them, saying, "Be fruitful, multiply and fill the water of the seas, and let birds multiply on the earth." ²³ So there was evening, and there was morning, a fifth day.

(A: iii) ²⁴ God said, "Let the earth bring forth each kind of living creature — each kind of livestock, crawling animal and wild beast"; and that is how it was.

²⁵ God made each kind of wild beast, each kind of livestock and every kind of animal that crawls along the ground; and God saw that it was good.

²⁶ Then God said, "Let us make humankind in our image, in the likeness of ourselves; and let them rule over the fish in the sea, the birds in the air, the animals, and over all the earth, and over every crawling creature that crawls on the earth."

²⁷   So God created humankind in his own image;
        in the image of God he created him:
        male and female he created them.

²⁸ God blessed them: God said to them, "Be fruitful, multiply, fill the earth and subdue it. Rule over the fish in the sea, the birds in the air and every living creature that crawls on the earth." ²⁹ Then God said, "Here! Throughout the whole earth I am giving you as food every seed-bearing plant and every tree with seed-bearing fruit. ³⁰ And to every wild animal, bird in the air and creature crawling on the earth, in which there is a living soul, I am giving as food every kind of green plant." And that is how it was. ³¹ God saw everything that he had made, and indeed it was very good. So there was evening, and there was morning, a sixth day.

2 ¹ Thus the heavens and the earth were finished, along with everything in them. ² On the seventh day God was finished with his work which he had made, so he rested on the seventh day from all his work which he had made. ³ God blessed the seventh day and separated it as holy; because on that day God rested from all his work which he had created, so that it itself could produce.

(A: iv, S: ii) ⁴ Here is the history of the heavens and the earth when they were created. On the day when ADONAI, God, made earth and heaven, ⁵ there was as yet no wild bush on the earth, and no wild plant had as yet sprung up; for ADONAI, God, had not caused it to rain on the earth, and there was no one to cultivate the ground. ⁶ Rather, a mist went up from the earth which watered the entire surface of the ground.

⁷ Then ADONAI, God, formed a person [Hebrew: *adam*] from the dust of the ground [Hebrew: *adamah*] and breathed into his nostrils the breath of life, so that he became a living being. ⁸ ADONAI, God, planted a garden toward the east, in 'Eden, and there he put the person whom he had formed. ⁹ Out of the ground ADONAI, God, caused to grow every tree pleasing in appearance and good for food, including the tree of life in the middle of the garden and the tree of the knowledge of good and evil.

¹⁰ A river went out of 'Eden to water the garden, and from there it divided into four streams. ¹¹ The name of the first is Pishon; it winds throughout the land of Havilah, where there is gold. ¹² The gold of that land is good; aromatic resin and onyx stone are also found there. ¹³ The name of the second river is Gichon; it winds throughout the land of Kush. ¹⁴ The name of the third river is Tigris; it is the one that flows toward the east of Ashur. The fourth river is the Euphrates.

¹⁵ ADONAI, God, took the person and put him in the garden of 'Eden to cultivate and care for it. ¹⁶ ADONAI, God, gave the person this order: "You may freely eat from every tree in the garden ¹⁷ except the tree of the knowledge of good and evil. You are not to eat from it, because on the day that you eat from it, it will become certain that you will die."

¹⁸ ADONAI, God, said, "It isn't good that the person should be alone. I will make for him a companion suitable for helping him." ¹⁹ So from the ground ADONAI, God, formed every wild animal and every bird that flies in the air, and he brought them to the person to see what he would call them. Whatever the person would call each living creature, that was to be its name. *(S: iii)* ²⁰ So the person gave names to all the livestock, to the birds in the air and to every wild animal. But for Adam there was not found a companion suitable for helping him.

²¹ Then God caused a deep sleep to fall upon the person; and while he was sleeping, he took one of his ribs and closed up the place from which he took it with flesh. ²² The rib which ADONAI, God, had taken from the person, he made a woman-person; and he brought her to the man-person. ²³ The man-person said, "At last! This is bone from my bones and flesh from my flesh. She is to be called Woman [Hebrew: *ishah*], because she was taken out of Man [Hebrew: *ish*]." ²⁴ This is why a man is to leave his father and mother and stick with his wife, and they are to be one flesh.

²⁵ They were both naked, the man and his wife, and they were not ashamed.

3 ¹ Now the serpent was more crafty than any wild animal which ADONAI, God, had made. He said to the woman, "Did God really say, 'You are not to eat from any tree in the garden'?" ² The woman answered the serpent, "We may eat from the fruit of the trees of the garden, ³ but about the fruit of the tree in the middle of the garden God said, 'You are neither to eat from it nor touch it, or you will die.'" ⁴ The serpent said to the woman, "It is not true that you will surely die; ⁵ because God knows that on the day you eat from it, your eyes will be opened, and you will be like God, knowing good and evil." ⁶ When the woman saw that the tree was good for food, that it had a pleasing appearance and that the tree was desirable for making one wise, she took some of its fruit and ate. She also gave some to her husband, who was with her; and he ate. ⁷ Then the eyes of both of them were opened, and they realized that they were naked. So they sewed fig leaves together to make themselves loincloths.

⁸ They heard the voice of ADONAI, God, walking in the garden at the time of the evening breeze, so the man and his wife hid themselves from the presence of ADONAI, God, among the trees in the garden. ⁹ ADONAI, God, called to the man, "Where are you?" ¹⁰ He answered, "I heard your voice in the garden, and I was afraid, because I was naked, so I hid myself." ¹¹ He said, "Who told you that you were naked? Have you eaten from the tree from which I ordered you not to eat?" ¹² The man replied, "The woman you gave to be with me — she gave me fruit from the tree, and I ate." ¹³ ADONAI, God, said to the woman, "What is this you have done?" The woman answered, "The serpent tricked me, so I ate."

¹⁴ ADONAI, God, said to the serpent, "Because you have done this, you are cursed more than all livestock and wild animals. You will crawl on your belly and eat dust as long as you live. ¹⁵ I will put animosity between you and the woman, and between your descendant and her descendant; he will bruise your head, and you will bruise his heel."

¹⁶ To the woman he said, "I will greatly increase your pain in childbirth. You will bring forth children in pain. Your desire will be toward your husband, but he will rule over you."

¹⁷ To Adam he said, "Because you listened to what your wife said and ate from the tree about which I gave you the order, 'You are not to eat from it,' the ground is

3

cursed on your account; you will work hard to eat from it as long as you live. ^{18} It will produce thorns and thistles for you, and you will eat field plants. ^{19} You will eat bread by the sweat of your forehead till you return to the ground — for you were taken out of it: you are dust, and you will return to dust."

^{20} The man called his wife Havah [life], because she was the mother of all living. ^{21} *ADONAI*, God, made garments of skin for Adam and his wife and clothed them.

(A: v, S: iv) ^{22} *ADONAI*, God, said, "See, the man has become like one of us, knowing good and evil. Now, to prevent his putting out his hand and taking also from the tree of life, eating, and living forever — " ^{23} therefore *ADONAI*, God, sent him out of the garden of 'Eden to cultivate the ground from which he was taken. ^{24} So he drove the man out, and he placed at the east of the garden of 'Eden the *k'ruvim* and a flaming sword which turned in every direction to guard the way to the tree of life.

4 ^{1} The man had sexual relations with Havah his wife; she conceived, gave birth to Kayin [acquisition] and said, "I have acquired a man from *ADONAI*." ^{2} In addition she gave birth to his brother Hevel. Hevel kept sheep, while Kayin worked the soil. ^{3} In the course of time Kayin brought an offering to *ADONAI* from the produce of the soil; ^{4} and Hevel too brought from the firstborn of his sheep, including their fat. *ADONAI* accepted Hevel and his offering ^{5} but did not accept Kayin and his offering. Kayin was very angry, and his face fell. ^{6} *ADONAI* said to Kayin, "Why are you angry? Why so downcast? ^{7} If you are doing what is good, shouldn't you hold your head high? And if you don't do what is good, sin is crouching at the door — it wants you, but you can rule over it." ^{8} Kayin had words with Hevel his brother; then one time, when they were in the field, Kayin turned on Hevel his brother and killed him.

^{9} *ADONAI* said to Kayin, "Where is Hevel your brother?" And he replied, "I don't know; am I my brother's guardian?" ^{10} He said, "What have you done? The voice of your brother's blood is crying out to me from the ground! ^{11} Now you are cursed from the ground, which has opened its mouth to receive your brother's blood at your hands. ^{12} When you farm the ground it will no longer yield its strength to you. You will be a fugitive, wandering the earth." ^{13} Kayin said to *ADONAI*, "My punishment is greater than I can bear. ^{14} You are banning me today from the land and from your presence. I will be a fugitive wandering the earth, and whoever finds me will kill me." ^{15} *ADONAI* answered him, "Therefore, whoever kills Kayin will receive vengeance sevenfold," and *ADONAI* put a sign on Kayin, so that no one who found him would kill him. ^{16} So Kayin left the presence of *ADONAI* and lived in the land of Nod [wandering], east of 'Eden.

^{17} Kayin had sexual relations with his wife; she conceived and gave birth to Hanokh. Kayin built a city and named the city after his son Hanokh. ^{18} To Hanokh was born 'Irad. 'Irad fathered Mechuya'el, Mechuya'el fathered Metusha'el, and Metusha'el fathered Lemekh.

(S: v) ^{19} Lemekh took himself two wives; the name of the one was 'Adah, while the name of the other was Tzilah. ^{20} 'Adah gave birth to Yaval; he was the ancestor of those who live in tents and have cattle. ^{21} His brother's name was Yuval; and he was the ancestor of all who play lyre and flute. ^{22} Tzilah gave birth to Tuval-Kayin, who forged all kinds of tools from brass and iron; the sister of Tuval-Kayin was Na'amah. ^{23} Lemekh said to his wives,

"'Adah and Tzilah, listen to me;
wives of Lemekh, hear what I say:
I killed a man for wounding me,
a young man who injured me.
24   If Kayin will be avenged sevenfold,
then Lemekh seventy-sevenfold!"

^{25} Adam again had sexual relations with his wife, and she gave birth to a son whom she named Shet [granted], "For God has granted me another seed in place of Hevel, since Kayin killed him." ^{26} To Shet too was born a son, whom he called Enosh. That is when people began to call on the name of ADONAI.

5 *(vi)* ^{1} Here is the genealogy of Adam. On the day that God created man he made him in the likeness of God; ^{2} he created them male and female; he blessed them and called them Adam [humankind, man] on the day they were created. ^{3} After Adam lived 130 years he fathered a son like himself and named him Shet. ^{4} After Shet was born, Adam lived another 800 years and had both sons and daughters. ^{5} In all, Adam lived 930 years, and then he died.

^{6} Shet lived 105 years and fathered Enosh. ^{7} After Enosh was born, Shet lived another 807 years and had sons and daughters. ^{8} In all, Shet lived 912 years; then he died.

^{9} Enosh lived ninety years and fathered Kenan. ^{10} After Kenan was born, Enosh lived another 815 years and had sons and daughters. ^{11} In all, Enosh lived 905 years; then he died.

^{12} Kenan lived seventy years and fathered Mahalal'el. ^{13} After Mahalal'el was born, Kenan lived another 840 years and had sons and daughters. ^{14} In all, Kenan lived 910 years; then he died.

^{15} Mahalal'el lived sixty-five years and fathered Yered. ^{16} After Yered was born, Mahalal'el lived another 830 years and had sons and daughters. ^{17} In all, Mahalal'el lived 895 years; then he died.

^{18} Yered lived 162 years and fathered Hanokh. ^{19} After Hanokh was born, Yered lived 800 years and had sons and daughters. ^{20} In all, Yered lived 962 years; then he died.

^{21} Hanokh lived sixty-five years and fathered Metushelach. ^{22} After Metushelach was born, Hanokh walked with God 300 years and had sons and daughters. ^{23} In all, Hanokh lived 365 years. ^{24} Hanokh walked with God, and then he wasn't there, because God took him.

(vii) ^{25} Metushelach lived 187 years and fathered Lemekh. ^{26} After Lemekh was born, Metushelach lived 782 years and had sons and daughters. ^{27} In all, Metushelach lived 969 years; then he died.

^{28} Lemekh lived 182 years and fathered a son, ^{29} whom he called Noach [restful]; for he said, "This one will comfort us in our labor, in the hard work we do with our hands [to get what comes] from the ground that ADONAI cursed." ^{30} After Noach was born, Lemekh lived 595 years and had sons and daughters. ^{31} In all, Lemekh lived 777 years; then he died.

^{32} Noach was 500 years old; and Noach fathered Shem, Ham and Yefet.

6 ^{1} In time, when men began to multiply on earth, and daughters were born to them, ^{2} the sons of God saw that the daughters of men were attractive; and they took wives for themselves, whomever they chose. ³ADONAI said, "My Spirit will not live in human beings forever, for they too are flesh; therefore their life span is to be 120 years." ⁴The N'filim were on the earth in those days, and also afterwards, when the sons of God came in to the daughters of men, and they bore children to them; these were the ancient heroes, men of renown.

(Maftir) ⁵ADONAI saw that the people on earth were very wicked, that all the imaginings of their hearts were always of evil only. ⁶ADONAI regretted that he had made humankind on the earth; it grieved his heart. ⁷ADONAI said, "I will wipe out humankind, whom I have created, from the whole earth; and not only human beings, but animals, creeping things and birds in the air; for I regret that I ever made them." ⁸But Noach found grace in the sight of ADONAI.

Haftarah B'resheet: Yesha'yahu (Isaiah) 42:5–43:10 (A); 42:5–21 (S)

B'rit Hadashah suggested readings for Parashah B'resheet: Mattityahu (Matthew) 1:1–17; 19:3–9; Mark 10:1–12; Luke 3:23–38; Yochanan (John) 1:1–18; 1 Corinthians 6:15–20; 15:35–58; Romans 5:12–21; Ephesians 5:21–32; Colossians 1:14–17; 1 Timothy 2:11–15; Messianic Jews (Hebrews) 1:1–3; 3:7–4:11; 10:28–39; 2 Kefa (2 Peter) 3:3–14; Revelation 21:1–5; 22:1–5

Parashah 2: Noach (Noah) 6:9–11:32

⁹Here is the history of Noach. In his generation, Noach was a man righteous and wholehearted; Noach walked with God. ¹⁰Noach fathered three sons, Shem, Ham and Yefet. ¹¹The earth was corrupt before God, the earth was filled with violence. ¹²God saw the earth, and, yes, it was corrupt; for all living beings had corrupted their ways on the earth.

¹³God said to Noach, "The end of all living beings has come before me, for because of them the earth is filled with violence. I will destroy them along with the earth. ¹⁴Make yourself an ark of *gofer*-wood; you are to make the ark with rooms and cover it with pitch both outside and inside. ¹⁵Here is how you are to build it: the length of the ark is to be 450 feet, its width seventy-five feet and its height forty-five feet. ¹⁶You are to make an opening for daylight in the ark eighteen inches below its roof. Put a door in its side; and build it with lower, second and third decks.

¹⁷"Then I myself will bring the flood of water over the earth to destroy from under heaven every living thing that breathes; everything on earth will be destroyed. ¹⁸But I will establish my covenant with you; you will come into the ark, you, your sons, your wife and your sons' wives with you.

¹⁹"From everything living, from each kind of living being, you are to bring two into the ark, to keep them alive with you; they are to be male and female. ²⁰Of each kind of bird, each kind of livestock, and each kind of animal creeping on the ground, two are to come to you, so that they can be kept alive. ²¹Also take from all the kinds of food that are eaten, and collect it for yourself; it is to be food for you and for them." ²²This is what Noach did; he did all that God ordered him to do.

7 *(ii)* ¹ A*DONAI* said to Noach, "Come into the ark, you and all your household; for I have seen that you alone in this generation are righteous before me. ² Of every clean animal you are to take seven couples, and of the animals that are not clean, one couple; ³ also of the birds in the air take seven couples — in order to preserve their species throughout the earth. ⁴ For in seven more days I will cause it to rain on the earth forty days and forty nights; I will wipe out every living thing that I have made from the face of the earth." ⁵ Noach did all that A*DONAI* ordered him to do.

⁶ Noach was 600 years old when the water flooded the earth. ⁷ Noach went into the ark with his sons, his wife and his sons' wives, because of the floodwaters. ⁸ Of clean animals, of animals that are not clean, of birds, and of everything that creeps on the ground, ⁹ couples, male and female, went in to Noach in the ark, as God had ordered Noach.

¹⁰ After seven days the water flooded the earth. ¹¹ On the seventeenth day of the second month of the 600th year of Noach's life all the fountains of the great deep were broken up, and the windows of the sky were opened. ¹² It rained on the earth forty days and forty nights.

¹³ On that same day Noach entered the ark with Shem, Ham and Yefet the sons of Noach, Noach's wife and the three wives of his sons accompanying them; ¹⁴ they, and every animal of every species, all the livestock of every species, every animal that creeps on the ground of every species, and every bird of every species — all sorts of winged creatures. ¹⁵ They went in to Noach in the ark, couples from every kind of living thing that breathes. ¹⁶ Those that entered went in, male and female, from every kind of living thing being, as God had ordered him; and A*DONAI* shut him inside.

(iii) ¹⁷ The flood was forty days on the earth; the water grew higher and floated the ark, so that it was lifted up off the earth. ¹⁸ The water overflowed the earth and grew deeper, until the ark floated on the surface of the water. ¹⁹ The water overpowered the earth mightily; all the high mountains under the entire sky were covered; ²⁰ the water covered the mountains by more than twenty-two-and-a-half feet. ²¹ All living beings that moved on the earth perished — birds, livestock, other animals, insects, and every human being, ²² everything in whose nostrils was the breath of the spirit of life; whatever was on dry land died. ²³ He wiped out every living thing on the surface of the ground — not only human beings, but livestock, creeping animals and birds in the air. They were wiped out from the earth; only Noach was left, along with those who were with him in the ark. ²⁴ The water held power over the earth for 150 days.

8 ¹ God remembered Noach, every living thing and all the livestock with him in the ark; so God caused a wind to pass over the earth, and the water began to go down. ² Also the fountains of the deep and the windows of the sky were stopped, the rain from the sky was restrained, ³ and the water came back from completely covering the earth. It was after 150 days that the water went down. ⁴ On the seventeenth day of the seventh month the ark came to rest on the mountains of Ararat. ⁵ The water kept going down until the tenth month; on the first day of the tenth month the tops of the mountains were seen.

⁶ After forty days Noach opened the window of the ark which he had built; ⁷ and he sent out a raven, which flew back and forth until the water had dried up from the earth.

⁸ Then he sent out a dove, to see if the water had gone from the surface of the ground. ⁹ But the dove found no place for her feet to rest, so she returned to him in the ark, because the water still covered the whole earth. He put out his hand, took her and brought her in to him in the ark. ¹⁰ He waited another seven days and again sent the dove out from the ark. ¹¹ The dove came in to him in the evening, and there in her mouth was a freshly plucked olive leaf, so Noach knew that the water had cleared from the earth. ¹² He waited yet another seven days and sent out the dove, and she didn't return to him any more.

¹³ By the first day of the first month of the 601ˢᵗ year the water had dried up from off the earth; so Noach removed the covering of the ark and looked; and, yes, the surface of the ground was dry. ¹⁴ It was on the twenty-seventh day of the second month that the earth was dry.

(iv) ¹⁵ God said to Noach, ¹⁶ "Go out from the ark, you, your wife, your sons and your son's wives with you. ¹⁷ Bring out with you every living thing you have with you — birds, livestock and every animal that creeps on the earth — so that they can swarm on the earth, be fruitful and multiply on the earth." ¹⁸ So Noach went out with his sons, his wife and his sons' wives; ¹⁹ every animal, every creeping thing and every bird, whatever moves on the earth, according to their families, went out of the ark.

²⁰ Noach built an altar to Adonai. Then he took from every clean animal and every clean bird, and he offered burnt offerings on the altar. ²¹ Adonai smelled the sweet aroma, and Adonai said in his heart, "I will never again curse the ground because of humankind, since the imaginings of a person's heart are evil from his youth; nor will I ever again destroy all living things, as I have done. ²² So long as the earth exists, sowing time and harvest, cold and heat, summer and winter, and day and night will not cease."

9 ¹ God blessed Noach and his sons and said to them, "Be fruitful, multiply and fill the earth. ² The fear and dread of you will be upon every wild animal, every bird in the air, every creature populating the ground, and all the fish in the sea; they have been handed over to you. ³ Every moving thing that lives will be food for you; just as I gave you green plants before, so now I give you everything — ⁴ only flesh with its life, which is its blood, you are not to eat. ⁵ I will certainly demand an accounting for the blood of your lives: I will demand it from every animal and from every human being. I will demand from every human being an accounting for the life of his fellow human being. ⁶ Whoever sheds human blood, by a human being will his own blood be shed; for God made human beings in his image. ⁷ And you people, be fruitful, multiply, swarm on the earth and multiply on it."

(v) ⁸ God spoke to Noach and his sons with him; he said, ⁹ "As for me — I am herewith establishing my covenant with you, with your descendants after you, ¹⁰ and with every living creature that is with you — the birds, the livestock and every wild animal with you, all going out of the ark, every animal on earth. ¹¹ I will establish my covenant with you that never again will all living beings be destroyed by the waters of a flood, and there will never again be a flood to destroy the earth." ¹² God added, "Here is the sign of the covenant I am making between myself and you and every living creature with you, for all generations to come: ¹³ I am putting my rainbow in the cloud — it will be there as a sign of the covenant between myself and the earth.

^{14} Whenever I bring clouds over the earth, and the rainbow is seen in the cloud; ^{15} I will remember my covenant which is between myself and you and every living creature of any kind; and the water will never again become a flood to destroy all living beings. ^{16} The rainbow will be in the cloud; so that when I look at it, I will remember the everlasting covenant between God and every living creature of any kind on the earth."

^{17} God said to Noach, "This is the sign of the covenant which I have established between myself and every living creature on the earth."

(vi) ^{18} The sons of Noach who went out from the ark were Shem, Ham and Yefet. Ham is the father of Kena'an. ^{19} These three were the sons of Noach, and the whole earth was populated by them.

^{20} Noach, a farmer, was the first to plant a vineyard. ^{21} He drank so much of the wine that he got drunk and lay uncovered in his tent. ^{22} Ham, the father of Kena'an, saw his father shamefully exposed, went out and told his two brothers. ^{23} Shem and Yefet took a cloak, put it over both their shoulders, and, walking backward, went in and covered their naked father. Their faces were turned away, so that they did not see their father lying there shamefully exposed.

^{24} When Noach awoke from his wine, he knew what his youngest son had done to him. ^{25} He said, "Cursed be Kena'an; he will be a servant of servants to his brothers." ^{26} Then he said, "Blessed be ADONAI, the God of Shem; Kena'an will be their servant. ^{27} May God enlarge Yefet; he will live in the tents of Shem, but Kena'an will be their servant."

^{28} After the flood Noach lived 350 years. ^{29} In all, Noach lived 950 years; then he died.

10 ^{1} Here is the genealogy of the sons of Noach — Shem, Ham and Yefet; sons were born to them after the flood.

^{2} The sons of Yefet were Gomer, Magog, Madai, Yavan, Tuval, Meshekh and Tiras. ^{3} The sons of Gomer were Ashkenaz, Rifat and Togarmah. ^{4} The sons of Yavan were Elishah, Tarshish, Kittim and Dodanim. ^{5} From these the islands of the nations were divided into their lands, each according to its language, according to their families, in their nations.

^{6} The sons of Ham were Kush, Mitzrayim, Put and Kena'an. ^{7} The sons of Kush were S'va, Havilah, Savta, Ra'mah and Savt'kha. The sons of Ra'mah were Sh'va and D'dan.

^{8} Kush fathered Nimrod, who was the first powerful ruler on earth. ^{9} He was a mighty hunter before ADONAI — this is why people say, "Like Nimrod, a mighty hunter before ADONAI." ^{10} His kingdom began with Bavel, Erekh, Akkad and Kalneh, in the land of Shin'ar. ^{11} Ashur went out from that land and built Ninveh, the city Rechovot, Kelach, ^{12} and Resen between Ninveh and Kelach — that one is the great city.

^{13} Mitzrayim fathered the Ludim, the 'Anamim, the L'havim, the Naftuchim, ^{14} the Patrusim, the Kasluchim (from whom came the P'lishtim) and the Kaftorim.

^{15} Kena'an fathered Tzidon his firstborn, Het, ^{16} the Y'vusi, the Emori, the Girgashi, ^{17} the Hivi, the 'Arki, the Sini, ^{18} the Arvadi, the Tz'mari and the Hamati. Afterwards, the families of the Kena'ani were dispersed. ^{19} The border of the Kena'ani was from Tzidon, as you go toward G'rar, to 'Azah; as you go toward S'dom, 'Amora, Admah and Tzvoyim, to Lesha.

²⁰ These were the descendants of Ham, according to their families and languages, in their lands and in their nations.

²¹ Children were also born to Shem, ancestor of all the descendants of 'Ever and older brother of Yefet. ²² The sons of Shem were 'Elam, Ashur, Arpakhshad, Lud and Aram. ²³ The sons of Aram were 'Utz, Hul, Geter and Mash. ²⁴ Arpakhshad fathered Shelach, and Shelach fathered 'Ever. ²⁵ To 'Ever were born two sons. One was given the name Peleg [division], because during his lifetime the earth was divided. His brother's name was Yoktan. ²⁶ Yoktan fathered Almodad, Shelef, Hatzar-Mavet, Yerach, ²⁷ Hadoram, Uzal, Diklah, ²⁸ 'Oval, Avima'el, Sheva, ²⁹ Ofir, Havilah and Yovav— all these were the sons of Yoktan. ³⁰ Their territory stretched from Mesha, as you go toward S'far, to the mountain in the east.

³¹ These were the descendants of Shem, according to their families and languages, in their lands and in their nations.

³² These were the families of the sons of Noach, according to their generations, in their nations. From these the nations of the earth were divided up after the flood.

11 *(S: vii)* ¹ The whole earth used the same language, the same words. ² It came about that as they traveled from the east, they found a plain in the land of Shin'ar and lived there. ³ They said to one another, "Come, let's make bricks and bake them in the fire." So they had bricks for building-stone and clay for mortar. ⁴ Then they said, "Come, let's build ourselves a city with a tower that has its top reaching up into heaven, so that we can make a name for ourselves and not be scattered all over the earth."

⁵ *ADONAI* came down to see the city and the tower the people were building. ⁶ *ADONAI* said, "Look, the people are united, they all have a single language, and see what they're starting to do! At this rate, nothing they set out to accomplish will be impossible for them! ⁷ Come, let's go down and confuse their language, so that they won't understand each other's speech." ⁸ So from there *ADONAI* scattered them all over the earth, and they stopped building the city. ⁹ For this reason it is called Bavel [confusion]— because there *ADONAI* confused the language of the whole earth, and from there *ADONAI* scattered them all over the earth.

¹⁰ Here is the genealogy of Shem. Shem was 100 years old when he fathered Arpakhshad two years after the flood. ¹¹ After Arpakhshad was born, Shem lived another 500 years and had sons and daughters.

¹² Arpakhshad lived thirty-five years and fathered Shelach. ¹³ After Shelach was born, Arpakhshad lived another 403 years and had sons and daughters.

¹⁴ Shelach lived thirty years and fathered 'Ever. ¹⁵ After 'Ever was born, Shelach lived another 403 years and had sons and daughters.

¹⁶ 'Ever lived thirty-four years and fathered Peleg. ¹⁷ After Peleg was born, 'Ever lived another 430 years and had sons and daughters.

¹⁸ Peleg lived thirty years and fathered Re'u. ¹⁹ After Re'u was born, Peleg lived another 209 years and had sons and daughters.

²⁰ Re'u lived thirty-two years and fathered S'rug. ²¹ After S'rug was born, Re'u lived another 207 years and had sons and daughters.

²² S'rug lived thirty years and fathered Nachor. ²³ After Nachor was born, S'rug lived another 200 years and had sons and daughters.

²⁴ Nachor lived twenty-nine years and fathered Terach. ²⁵ After Terach was born, Nachor lived another 119 years and had sons and daughters.
²⁶ Terach lived seventy years and fathered Avram, Nachor and Haran. ²⁷ Here is the genealogy of Terach. Terach fathered Avram, Nachor and Haran; and Haran fathered Lot. ²⁸ Haran died before his father Terach in the land where he was born, in Ur of the Kasdim.

(Maftir) ²⁹ Then Avram and Nachor took wives for themselves. The name of Avram's wife was Sarai, and the name of Nachor's wife was Milkah the daughter of Haran. He was the father of Milkah and of Yiskah. ³⁰ Sarai was barren— she had no child. ³¹ Terach took his son Avram, his son Haran's son Lot, and Sarai his daughter-in-law, his son Avram's wife; and they left Ur of the Kasdim to go to the land of Kena'an. But when they came to Haran, they stayed there. ³² Terach lived 205 years, and he died in Haran.

Haftarah Noach: Yesha'yahu (Isaiah) 54:1–55:5 (A); 54:1–10 (S)
[Messianic adaptation: commence the reading at 52:13]

B'rit Hadashah suggested readings for Parashah Noach: Mattityahu (Matthew) 24:36–44; Luke 17:26–37; Acts 2:1–16; 1 Kefa (1 Peter) 3:18–22; 2 Kefa (2 Peter) 2:5

Parashah 3: Lekh L'kha (Get yourself out) 12:1–17:27

12 ¹ Now ADONAI said to Avram, "Get yourself out of your country, away from your kinsmen and away from your father's house, and go to the land that I will show you. ² I will make of you a great nation, I will bless you, and I will make your name great; and you are to be a blessing. ³ I will bless those who bless you, but I will curse anyone who curses you; and by you all the families of the earth will be blessed."

⁴ So Avram went, as ADONAI had said to him, and Lot went with him. Avram was 75 years old when he left Haran. ⁵ Avram took his wife Sarai, his brother's son Lot, and all their possessions which they had accumulated, as well as the people they had acquired in Haran; then they set out for the land of Kena'an and entered the land of Kena'an.

⁶ Avram passed through the land to the place called Sh'khem, to the oak of Moreh. The Kena'ani were then in the land. ⁷ ADONAI appeared to Avram and said, "To your descendants I will give this land." So he built an altar there to ADONAI, who had appeared to him.

⁸ He left that place, went to the hill east of Beit-El and pitched his tent. With Beit-El to the west and 'Ai to the east, he built an altar there and called on the name of ADONAI. ⁹ Then Avram traveled on, continuing toward the Negev. ¹⁰ But there was a famine in the land, so Avram went down into Egypt to stay there, because the famine in the land was severe.

¹¹ When he came close to Egypt and was about to enter, he said to Sarai his wife, "Here now, I know that you are a good-looking woman; ¹² so that when the Egyptians see you, they will say, 'This is his wife,' and kill me but keep you alive. ¹³ Please say that you are my sister, so that it will go well with me for your sake, and so that I will stay alive because of you."

(ii) ¹⁴ When Avram entered Egypt, the Egyptians did notice that the woman was very beautiful. ¹⁵ Pharaoh's princes saw her and commended her to Pharaoh, so the woman was taken into Pharaoh's house. ¹⁶ He treated Avram well for her sake, giving him sheep, cattle, male and female donkeys, male and female slaves, and camels.

¹⁷ But ADONAI inflicted great plagues on Pharaoh and his household because of Sarai Avram's wife. ¹⁸ Pharaoh called Avram and said, "What is this that you have done to me? Why didn't you tell me that she was your wife? ¹⁹ Why did you say, 'She is my sister,' so that I took her to be my own wife? Now therefore, here is your wife! Take her, and go away!" ²⁰ So Pharaoh gave orders concerning him to his men, and they sent him on his way with his wife and everything he had.

13 ¹ Avram went up from Egypt — he, his wife and everything he had, and Lot with him — into the Negev. ² Avram became wealthy, with much cattle, silver and gold. ³ As he went on his travels from the Negev, he came to Beit-El, to the place where his tent had been at the beginning, between Beit-El and 'Ai, ⁴ where he had first built the altar; and there Avram called on the name of ADONAI.

(iii) ⁵ Lot, who was traveling with Avram, also had flocks, herds and tents. ⁶ But the land could not support their living together, because their possessions were too great for them to remain together. ⁷ Moreover, quarreling arose between Avram's and Lot's herdsmen. The Kena'ani and the P'rizi were then living in the land. ⁸ Avram said to Lot, "Please, let's not have quarreling between me and you, or between my herdsmen and yours, since we're kinsmen. ⁹ Isn't the whole land there in front of you? Please separate yourself from me — if you go to the left, I will go to the right; if you go to the right, I will go to the left." ¹⁰ Lot looked up and saw that the whole plain of the Yarden was well watered everywhere, before ADONAI destroyed S'dom and 'Amora, like the garden of ADONAI, like the land of Egypt in the direction of Tzo'ar. ¹¹ So Lot chose all the plain of the Yarden for himself, and Lot traveled eastward; thus they separated themselves from each other. ¹² Avram lived in the land of Kena'an; and Lot lived in the cities of the plain, setting up his tent near S'dom. ¹³ Now the men of S'dom were evil, committing great sins against ADONAI.

¹⁴ ADONAI said to Avram, after Lot had moved away from him, "Look all around you from where you are, to the north, the south, the east and the west. ¹⁵ All the land you see I will give to you and your descendants forever, ¹⁶ and I will make your descendants as numerous as the specks of dust on the earth — so that if a person can count the specks of dust on the earth, then your descendants can be counted. ¹⁷ Get up and walk through the length and breadth of the land, because I will give it to you." ¹⁸ Avram moved his tent and came to live by the oaks of Mamre, which are in Hevron. There he built an altar to ADONAI.

14 *(iv)* ¹ When Amrafel was king of Shin'ar, Aryokh king of Elasar, K'dorla'omer king of 'Elam and Tid'al king of Goyim; ² they made war together against Bera king of S'dom and against Birsha king of 'Amora, Shin'av king of Admah, Shem'ever king of Tzvoyim, and the king of Bela (which is the same as Tzo'ar). ³ All the latter kings joined forces in the Siddim Valley, where the Dead Sea is. ⁴ They had served K'dorla'omer twelve years, but in the thirteenth year they rebelled.

⁵ In the fourteenth year K'dorla'omer and the kings with him came and defeated the Refa'im in 'Asht'rot-Karnayim, the Zuzim in Ham, the Eimim in Shaveh-Kiryatayim ⁶ and the Hori at Se'ir, their mountain, all the way to Eil-Pa'ran by the desert. ⁷ Next they turned back, came to 'Ein-Mishpat (which is the same as Kadesh), and defeated all the country of the 'Amaleki, and also the Emori, who lived in Hatzatzon-Tamar. ⁸ Then the kings of S'dom, 'Amora, Admah, Tzvoyim and Bela (that is, Tzo'ar) came out and arrayed themselves for battle in the Siddim Valley ⁹ against K'dorla'omer king of 'Elam, Tid'al king of Goyim, Amrafel king of Admah and Aryokh king of Elasar, four kings against the five.

¹⁰ Now the Siddim Valley was full of clay pits; and when the kings of S'dom and 'Amora fled, some fell into them; while the rest fled to the hills. ¹¹ The victors took all the possessions of S'dom and 'Amora and all their food supply; then they left. ¹² But as they left, they took Lot, Avram's brother's son, and his possessions; since he was living in S'dom. ¹³ Someone who had escaped came and told Avram the Hebrew, who was living by the oaks of Mamre the Emori, brother of Eshkol and brother of 'Aner; all of them allies of Avram. ¹⁴ When Avram heard that his nephew had been taken captive, he led out his trained men, who had been born in his house, 318 of them, and went in pursuit as far as Dan. ¹⁵ During the night he and his servants divided his forces against them, then attacked and pursued them all the way to Hovah, north of Dammesek. ¹⁶ He recovered all the goods and brought back his nephew Lot with his goods, together with the women and the other people. ¹⁷ After his return from slaughtering K'dorla'omer and the kings with him, the king of S'dom went out to meet him in the Shaveh Valley, also known as the King's Valley.

¹⁸ Malki-Tzedek king of Shalem brought out bread and wine. He was *cohen* of *El 'Elyon* [God Most High], ¹⁹ so he blessed him with these words:

"Blessed be Avram by *El 'Elyon*,
    maker of heaven of earth.
²⁰   and blessed be *El 'Elyon*,
    who handed your enemies over to you."

Avram gave him a tenth of everything.

(*v*) ²¹ The king of S'dom said to Avram, "Give me the people, and keep the goods for yourself." ²² But Avram answered the king of S'dom, "I have raised my hand in an oath to ADONAI, *El 'Elyon*, maker of heaven and earth, ²³ that I will not take so much as a thread or a sandal thong of anything that is yours; so that you won't be able to say, 'I made Avram rich.' ²⁴ I will take only what my troops have eaten and the share of the spoil belonging to the men who came with me — 'Aner, Eshkol and Mamre; let them have their share."

15 ¹ Some time later the word of ADONAI came to Avram in a vision: "Don't be afraid, Avram. I am your protector; your reward will be very great." ² Avram replied, "ADONAI, God, what good will your gifts be to me if I continue childless; and Eli'ezer from Dammesek inherits my possessions? ³ You haven't given me a child," Avram continued, "so someone born in my house will be my heir." ⁴ But the word of ADONAI came to him: "This man will not be your heir. No, your heir will be a child from your own body." ⁵ Then he brought him outside and said, "Look up at the sky, and count the stars — if you can count them! Your descendants will be that many!" ⁶ He believed in Adonai, and he credited it to him as righteousness.

(vi) ⁷ Then he said to him, "I am Adonai, who brought you out from Ur-Kasdim to give you this land as your possession." ⁸ He replied, "Adonai, God, how am I to know that I will possess it?" ⁹ He answered him, "Bring me a three-year-old cow, a three-year-old female goat, a three-year-old ram, a dove and a young pigeon." ¹⁰ He brought him all these, cut the animals in two and placed the pieces opposite each other; but he didn't cut the birds in half. ¹¹ Birds of prey swooped down on the carcasses, but Avram drove them away.

¹² As the sun was about to set, a deep sleep fell on Avram; horror and great darkness came over him. ¹³ Adonai said to Avram, "Know this for certain: your descendants will be foreigners in a land that is not theirs. They will be slaves and held in oppression there four hundred years. ¹⁴ But I will also judge that nation, the one that makes them slaves. Afterwards, they will leave with many possessions. ¹⁵ As for you, you will join your ancestors in peace and be buried at a good old age. ¹⁶ Only in the fourth generation will your descendants come back here, because only then will the Emori be ripe for punishment."

¹⁷ After the sun had set and there was thick darkness, a smoking fire pot and a flaming torch appeared, which passed between these animal parts. ¹⁸ That day Adonai made a covenant with Avram: "I have given this land to your descendants — from the *Vadi* of Egypt to the great river, the Euphrates River — ¹⁹ the territory of the Keni, the K'nizi, the Kadmoni, ²⁰ the Hitti, the P'rizi, the Refa'im, ²¹ the Emori, the Kena'ani, the Girgashi and the Y'vusi."

16 ¹ Now Sarai Avram's wife had not borne him a child. But she had an Egyptian slave-girl named Hagar; ² so Sarai said to Avram, "Here now, Adonai has kept me from having children; so go in and sleep with my slave-girl. Maybe I'll be able to have children through her." Avram listened to what Sarai said.

³ It was after Avram had lived ten years in the land of Kena'an that Sarai Avram's wife took Hagar the Egyptian, her slave-girl, and gave her to Avram her husband to be his wife. ⁴ Avram had sexual relations with Hagar, and she conceived. But when she became aware that she was pregnant, she looked on her mistress with contempt. ⁵ Sarai said to Avram, "This outrage being done to me is your fault! True, I gave my slave-girl to you to sleep with; but when she saw that she was pregnant, she began holding me in contempt. May Adonai decide who is right — I or you!" ⁶ However, Avram answered Sarai, "Look, she's your slave-girl. Deal with her as you think fit." Then Sarai treated her so harshly that she ran away from her.

⁷ The angel of Adonai found her by a spring in the desert, the spring on the road to Shur, ⁸ and said, "Hagar! Sarai's slave-girl! Where have you come from, and where are you going?" She answered, "I'm running away from my mistress Sarai." ⁹ The angel of Adonai said to her, "Go back to your mistress, and submit to her authority." ¹⁰ The angel of Adonai said to her, "I will greatly increase your descendants; there will be so many that it will be impossible to count them." ¹¹ The angel of Adonai said to her, "Look, you are pregnant, and you will give birth to a son. You are to call him Yishma'el [God pays attention] because Adonai has paid attention to your misery. ¹² He will be a wild donkey of a man, with his hand against everyone and everyone's hand against him, living his life at odds with all his kinsmen."

¹³ So she named ADONAI who had spoken with her El Ro'i [God of seeing], because she said, "Have I really seen the One who sees me [and stayed alive]?" ¹⁴ This is why the well has been called Be'er-Lachai-Ro'i [well of the one who lives and sees]; it lies between Kadesh and Bered.

¹⁵ Hagar bore Avram a son, and Avram called the son whom Hagar had borne Yishma'el. ¹⁶ Avram was 86 years old when Hagar bore Yishma'el to Avram.

17 ¹ When Avram was 99 years old ADONAI appeared to Avram and said to him, "I am *El Shaddai* [God Almighty]. Walk in my presence and be pure-hearted. ² I will make my covenant between me and you, and I will increase your numbers greatly." ³ Avram fell on his face, and God continued speaking with him: ⁴ "As for me, this is my covenant with you: you will be the father of many nations. ⁵ Your name will no longer be Avram [exalted father], but your name will be Avraham [father of many], because I have made you the father of many nations. ⁶ I will cause you to be very fruitful. I will make nations of you, kings will descend from you.

(vii) ⁷ "I am establishing my covenant between me and you, along with your descendants after you, generation after generation, as an everlasting covenant, to be God for you and for your descendants after you. ⁸ I will give you and your descendants after you the land in which you are now foreigners, all the land of Kena'an, as a permanent possession; and I will be their God."

⁹ God said to Avraham, "As for you, you are to keep my covenant, you and your descendants after you, generation after generation. ¹⁰ Here is my covenant, which you are to keep, between me and you, along with your descendants after you: every male among you is to be circumcised. ¹¹ You are to be circumcised in the flesh of your foreskin; this will be the sign of the covenant between me and you. ¹² Generation after generation, every male among you who is eight days old is to be circumcised, including slaves born within your household and those bought from a foreigner not descended from you. ¹³ The slave born in your house and the person bought with your money must be circumcised; thus my covenant will be in your flesh as an everlasting covenant. ¹⁴ Any uncircumcised male who will not let himself be circumcised in the flesh of his foreskin — that person will be cut off from his people, because he has broken my covenant."

¹⁵ God said to Avraham, "As for Sarai your wife, you are not to call her Sarai [mockery]; her name is to be Sarah [princess]. ¹⁶ I will bless her; moreover, I will give you a son by her. Truly I will bless her: she will be a mother of nations; kings of peoples will come from her." ¹⁷ At this Avraham fell on his face and laughed — he thought to himself, "Will a child be born to a man a hundred years old? Will Sarah give birth at ninety?" ¹⁸ Avraham said to God, "If only Yishma'el could live in your presence!" ¹⁹ God answered, "No, but Sarah your wife will bear you a son, and you are to call him Yitz'chak [laughter]. I will establish my covenant with him as an everlasting covenant for his descendants after him. ²⁰ But as for Yishma'el, I have heard you. I have blessed him. I will make him fruitful and give him many descendants. He will father twelve princes, and I will make him a great nation. ²¹ But I will establish my covenant with Yitz'chak, whom Sarah will bear to you at this time next year." ²² With that, God finished speaking with Avraham and went up from him.

²³ Avraham took Yishma'el his son, all the slaves born in his house and all who had been bought with his money, every male among the people in Avraham's household, and circumcised the flesh of their foreskin that very day, just as God had said to him.

(Maftir) ²⁴ Avraham was ninety-nine years old when he was circumcised in the flesh of his foreskin, ²⁵ and Yishma'el his son was thirteen years old when he was circumcised in the flesh of his foreskin. ²⁶ Avraham and Yishma'el his son were circumcised on the same day; ²⁷ and all the men in his household, both slaves born in his house and those bought with money from a foreigner, were circumcised with him.

Haftarah Lekh L'kha: Yesha'yahu (Isaiah) 40:27–41:16

B'rit Hadashah suggested readings for Parashah Lekh L'kha: Acts 7:1–8; Romans 3:19–5:6; Galatians 3:15–18; 5:1–6; Colossians 2:11–15; Messianic Jews (Hebrews) 7:1–19; 11:8–12

Parashah 4: Vayera (He appeared) 18:1–22:24

18 ¹ ADONAI appeared to Avraham by the oaks of Mamre as he sat at the entrance to the tent during the heat of the day. ² He raised his eyes and looked, and there in front of him stood three men. On seeing them, he ran from the tent door to meet them, prostrated himself on the ground, ³ and said, "My lord, if I have found favor in your sight, please don't leave your servant. ⁴ Please let me send for some water, so that you can wash your feet; then rest under the tree, ⁵ and I will bring a piece of bread. Now that you have come to your servant, refresh yourselves before going on." "Very well," they replied, "do what you have said."

⁶ Avraham hurried into the tent to Sarah and said, "Quickly, three measures of the best flour! Knead it and make cakes." ⁷ Avraham ran to the herd, took a good, tender calf and gave it to the servant, who hurried to prepare it. ⁸ Then he took curds, milk and the calf which he had prepared, and set it all before the men; and he stood by them under the tree as they ate. ⁹ They said to him, "Where is Sarah your wife?" He said, "There, in the tent." ¹⁰ He said, "I will certainly return to you around this time next year, and Sarah your wife will have a son." Sarah heard him from the entrance of the tent, behind him. ¹¹ Avraham and Sarah were old, advanced in years; Sarah was past the age of childbearing. ¹² So Sarah laughed to herself, thinking, "I am old, and so is my lord; am I to have pleasure again?" ¹³ ADONAI said to Avraham, "Why did Sarah laugh and ask, 'Am I really going to bear a child when I am so old?' ¹⁴ Is anything too hard for ADONAI? At the time set for it, at this season next year, I will return to you; and Sarah will have a son." *(ii)* ¹⁵ Sarah denied it, saying, "I didn't either laugh," because she was afraid. He said, "Not so— you did laugh."

¹⁶ The men set out from there and looked over toward S'dom, and Avraham went with them to see them on their way. ¹⁷ ADONAI said, "Should I hide from Avraham what I am about to do, ¹⁸ inasmuch as Avraham is sure to become a great and strong nation, and all the nations of the earth will be blessed by him? ¹⁹ For I have made myself known to him, so that he will give orders to his children and to his household

after him to keep the way of *Adonai* and to do what is right and just, so that *Adonai* may bring about for Avraham what he has promised him." ²⁰ *Adonai* said, "The outcry against S'dom and 'Amora is so great and their sin so serious ²¹ that I will now go down and see whether their deeds warrant the outcry that has reached me; if not, I will know." ²² The men turned away from there and went toward S'dom, but Avraham remained standing before *Adonai*. ²³ Avraham approached and said, "Will you actually sweep away the righteous with the wicked? ²⁴ Maybe there are fifty righteous people in the city; will you actually sweep the place away, and not forgive it for the sake of the fifty righteous who are there? ²⁵ Far be it from you to do such a thing — to kill the righteous along with the wicked, so that the righteous and the wicked are treated alike! Far be it from you! Shouldn't the judge of all the earth do what is just?" ²⁶ *Adonai* said, "If I find in S'dom fifty who are righteous, then I will forgive the whole place for their sake."

²⁷ Avraham answered, "Here now, I, who am but dust and ashes, have taken it upon myself to speak to *Adonai*. ²⁸ What if there are five less than fifty righteous?" He said, "I won't destroy it if I find forty-five there."

²⁹ He spoke to him yet again: "What if forty are found there?" He said, "For the sake of the forty I won't do it."

³⁰ He said, "I hope *Adonai* won't be angry if I speak. What if thirty are found there?" He said, "I won't do it if I find thirty there."

³¹ He said, "Here now, I have taken it upon myself to speak to *Adonai*. What if twenty are found there?" He said, "For the sake of the twenty I won't destroy it."

³² He said, "I hope *Adonai* won't be angry if I speak just once more. What if ten are found there?" He said, "For the sake of the ten I won't destroy it." ³³ *Adonai* went on his way as soon as he had finished speaking to Avraham, and Avraham returned to his place.

19 *(iii)* ¹ The two angels came to S'dom that evening, when Lot was sitting at the gate of S'dom. Lot saw them, got up to greet them and prostrated himself on the ground. ² He said, "Here now, my lords, please come over to your servant's house. Spend the night, wash your feet, get up early, and go on your way." "No," they answered, "we'll stay in the square." ³ But he kept pressing them; so they went home with him; and he made them a meal, baking *matzah* for their supper, which they ate.

⁴ But before they could go to bed, the men of the city surrounded the house — young and old, everyone from every neighborhood of S'dom. ⁵ They called Lot and said to him, "Where are the men who came to stay with you tonight? Bring them out to us! We want to have sex with them!" ⁶ Lot went out to them and stood in the doorway, closing the door behind him, ⁷ and said, "Please, my brothers, don't do such a wicked thing. ⁸ Look here, I have two daughters who are virgins. Please, let me bring them out to you, and you can do with them what seems good to you; but don't do anything to these men, since they are guests in my house." ⁹ "Stand back!" they replied. "This guy came to live here, and now he's decided to play judge. For that we'll deal worse with you than with them!" Then they crowded in on Lot, in order to get close enough to break down the door. ¹⁰ But the men inside reached out their hands, brought Lot into the house

to them and shut the door. ¹¹ Then they struck the men at the door of the house with blindness, both small and great, so that they couldn't find the doorway.

¹² The men said to Lot, "Do you have any people here besides yourself? Whomever you have in the city — son-in-law, your sons, your daughters — bring them out of this place; ¹³ because we are going to destroy it. ADONAI has become aware of the great outcry against them, and ADONAI has sent us to destroy it." ¹⁴ Lot went out and spoke with his sons-in-law, who had married his daughters, and said, "Get up and leave this place, because ADONAI is going to destroy the city." But his sons-in-law didn't take him seriously.

¹⁵ When morning came, the angels told Lot to hurry. "Get up," they said, "and take your wife and your two daughters who are here; otherwise you will be swept away in the punishment of the city." ¹⁶ But he dallied, so the men took hold of his hand, his wife's hand and the hands of his two daughters — ADONAI was being merciful to him — and led them, leaving them outside the city. ¹⁷ When they had brought them out, he said, "Flee for your life! Don't look behind you, and don't stop anywhere in the plain, but escape to the hills! Otherwise you will be swept away." ¹⁸ Lot said to them, "Please, no, my lord! ¹⁹ Here, your servant has already found favor in your sight, and you have shown me even greater mercy by saving my life. But I can't escape to the hills, because I'm afraid the disaster will overtake me, and I will die. ²⁰ Look, there's a town nearby to flee to, and it's a small one. Please let me escape there — isn't it just a small one? — and that way I will stay alive."

(iv) ²¹ He replied, "All right, I agree to what you have asked. I won't overthrow the city of which you have spoken. ²² Hurry, and escape to that place, because I can't do anything until you arrive there." For this reason the city was named Tzo'ar [small].

²³ By the time Lot had come to Tzo'ar, the sun had risen over the land. ²⁴ Then ADONAI caused sulfur and fire to rain down upon S'dom and 'Amora from ADONAI out of the sky. ²⁵ He overthrew those cities, the entire plain, all the inhabitants of the cities and everything growing in the ground. ²⁶ But his wife looked back from behind him, and she became a column of salt.

²⁷ Avraham got up early in the morning, went to the place where he had stood before ADONAI, ²⁸ and looked out toward S'dom and 'Amora, scanning the entire plain. There before him the smoke was rising from the land like smoke from a furnace! ²⁹ But when God destroyed the cities of the plain, he remembered Avraham and sent Lot out, away from the destruction, when he overthrew the cities in which Lot lived.

³⁰ Lot went up from Tzo'ar and lived in the hills with his two daughters, because he was afraid to stay in Tzo'ar. He and his two daughters lived in a cave. ³¹ The firstborn said to the younger, "Our father is old, and there isn't a man on earth to come in to us in the manner customary in the world. ³² Come, let's have our father drink wine; then we'll sleep with him, and that way we'll enable our father to have descendants."

³³ So they plied their father with wine that night, and the older one went in and slept with her father; he didn't know when she lay down or when she got up. ³⁴ The following day, the older said to the younger, "Here, I slept last night with my father. Let's make him drink wine again tonight, and you go in and sleep with him, and that way we'll enable our father to have descendants." ³⁵ They plied their father with wine that night also, and the younger one got up and slept with him, and he didn't

know when she lay down or when she got up. ³⁶ Thus both the daughters of Lot became pregnant by their father.

³⁷ The older one gave birth to a son and called him Mo'av; he is the ancestor of Mo'av to this day. ³⁸ The younger also gave birth to a son, and she called him Ben-'Ammi; he is the ancestor of the people of 'Amon to this day.

20 ¹ Avraham traveled from there toward the Negev and lived between Kadesh and Shur. While living as an alien in G'rar, ² Avraham was saying of Sarah his wife, "She is my sister"; so Avimelekh king of G'rar sent and took Sarah. ³ But God came to Avimelekh in a dream one night and said to him, "You are about to die because of the woman you have taken, since she is someone's wife." ⁴ Now Avimelekh had not come near her; so he said, "Lord, will you kill even an upright nation? ⁵ Didn't he himself say to me, 'She is my sister'? And even she herself said, 'He is my brother.' In doing this, my heart has been pure and my hands innocent." ⁶ God said to him in the dream, "Yes, I know that in doing this, your heart has been pure; and I too have kept you from sinning against me. This is why I didn't let you touch her. ⁷ Therefore, return the man's wife to him now. He is a prophet, and he will pray for you, so that you will live. But if you don't return her, know that you will certainly die — you and all who belong to you."

⁸ Avimelekh got up early in the morning, called all his servants and told them these things; and the men became very afraid. ⁹ Then Avimelekh called Avraham and said to him, "What have you done to us? How have I sinned against you to cause you to bring on me and my kingdom a great sin? You have done things to me that are just not done." ¹⁰ Avimelekh went on, asking Avraham, "Whatever could have caused you to do such a thing?" ¹¹ Avraham replied, "It was because I thought, 'There could not possibly be any fear of God in this place, so they will kill me in order to get my wife.' ¹² But she actually is also my sister, the daughter of my father but not the daughter of my mother, and so she became my wife. ¹³ When God had me leave my father's house, I told her, 'Do me this favor: wherever we go, say about me, "He is my brother."'"

¹⁴ Avimelekh took sheep, cattle, and male and female slaves, and gave them to Avraham; and he returned to him Sarah his wife. ¹⁵ Then Avimelekh said, "Look, my country lies before you; live where you like." ¹⁶ To Sarah he said, "Here, I have given your brother a thousand pieces of silver. That will allay the suspicions of everyone who is with you. Before everyone you are cleared." ¹⁷ Avraham prayed to God, and God healed Avimelekh and his wife and slave-girls, so that they could have children. ¹⁸ For *Adonai* had made every woman in Avimelekh's household infertile on account of Sarah Avraham's wife.

21 ¹ *Adonai* remembered Sarah as he had said, and *Adonai* did for Sarah what he had promised. ² Sarah conceived and bore Avraham a son in his old age, at the very time God had said to him. ³ Avraham called his son, born to him, whom Sarah bore to him, Yitz'chak. ⁴ Avraham circumcised his son Yitz'chak when he was eight days old, as God had ordered him to do.

(v) ⁵ Avraham was one hundred years old when his son Yitz'chak [laughter] was born to him. ⁶ Sarah said, "God has given me good reason to laugh; now everyone who hears about it will laugh with me." ⁷ And she said, "Who would have said

to Avraham that Sarah would nurse children? Nevertheless, I have borne him a son in his old age!"

⁸ The child grew and was weaned, and Avraham gave a great banquet on the day that Yitz'chak was weaned. ⁹ But Sarah saw the son of Hagar the Egyptian, whom Hagar had borne to Avraham, making fun of Yitz'chak; ¹⁰ so Sarah said to Avraham, "Throw this slave-girl out! And her son! I will not have this slave-girl's son as your heir along with my son Yitz'chak!"

¹¹ Avraham became very distressed over this matter of his son. ¹² But God said to Avraham, "Don't be distressed because of the boy and your slave-girl. Listen to everything Sarah says to you, because it is your descendants through Yitz'chak who will be counted. ¹³ But I will also make a nation from the son of the slave-girl, since he is descended from you."

¹⁴ Avraham got up early in the morning, took bread and a skin of water and gave it to Hagar, putting it on her shoulder, and the child; then he sent her away. After leaving, she wandered in the desert around Be'er-Sheva. ¹⁵ When the water in the skin was gone, she left the child under a bush, ¹⁶ and went and sat down, looking the other way, about a bow-shot's distance from him; because she said, "I can't bear to watch my child die." So she sat there, looking the other way, crying out and weeping. ¹⁷ God heard the boy's voice, and the angel of God called to Hagar from heaven and said to her, "What's wrong with you, Hagar? Don't be afraid, because God has heard the voice of the boy in his present situation. ¹⁸ Get up, lift the boy up, and hold him tightly in your hand, because I am going to make him a great nation." ¹⁹ Then God opened her eyes, and she saw a well of water. So she went, filled the skin with water and gave the boy water to drink.

²⁰ God was with the boy, and he grew. He lived in the desert and became an archer. ²¹ He lived in the Pa'ran Desert, and his mother chose a wife for him from the land of Egypt.

(vi) ²² At that time Avimelekh and Pikhol the commander of his army spoke to Avraham. They said, "God is with you in everything you do. ²³ Therefore, swear to me here by God that you will never deal falsely with me or with my son or grandson; but according to the kindness with which I have treated you, you will treat me and the land in which you have lived as a foreigner. ²⁴ Avraham said, "I swear it."

²⁵ Now Avraham had complained to Avimelekh about a well which Avimelekh's servants had seized. ²⁶ Avimelekh answered, "I don't know who has done this. You didn't tell me, and I heard about it only today." ²⁷ Avraham took sheep and cattle and gave them to Avimelekh, and the two of them made a covenant. ²⁸ Avraham put seven female lambs from the flock by themselves. ²⁹ Avimelekh asked Avraham, "What is the meaning of these seven female lambs you have put by themselves?" ³⁰ He answered, "You are to accept these seven female lambs from me as witness that I dug this well." ³¹ This is why that place was called Be'er-Sheva [well of seven, well of an oath] — because they both swore an oath there. ³² When they made the covenant at Be'er-Sheva, Avimelekh departed with Pikhol the commander of his army and returned to the land of the P'lishtim. ³³ Avraham planted a tamarisk tree in Be'er-Sheva, and there he called on the name of *ADONAI*, the everlasting God. ³⁴ Avraham lived for a long time as a foreigner in the land of the P'lishtim.

22 *(vii)* [1] After these things, God tested Avraham. He said to him, "Avraham!" and he answered, "Here I am." [2] He said, "Take your son, your only son, whom you love, Yitz'chak; and go to the land of Moriyah. There you are to offer him as a burnt offering on a mountain that I will point out to you."

[3] Avraham got up early in the morning, saddled his donkey, and took two of his young men with him, together with Yitz'chak his son. He cut the wood for the burnt offering, departed and went toward the place God had told him about. [4] On the third day, Avraham raised his eyes and saw the place in the distance. [5] Avraham said to his young men, "Stay here with the donkey. I and the boy will go there, worship and return to you." [6] Avraham took the wood for the burnt offering and laid it on Yitz'chak his son. Then he took in his hand the fire and the knife, and they both went on together.

[7] Yitz'chak spoke to Avraham his father: "My father?" He answered, "Here I am, my son." He said, "I see the fire and the wood, but where is the lamb for a burnt offering?" [8] Avraham replied, "God will provide himself the lamb for a burnt offering, my son"; and they both went on together.

[9] They came to the place God had told him about; and Avraham built the altar there, set the wood in order, bound Yitz'chak his son and laid him on the altar, on the wood. [10] Then Avraham put out his hand and took the knife to kill his son. [11] But the angel of ADONAI called to him out of heaven: "Avraham? Avraham!" He answered, "Here I am." [12] He said, "Don't lay your hand on the boy! Don't do anything to him! For now I know that you are a man who fears God, because you have not withheld your son, your only son, from me." [13] Avraham raised his eyes and looked, and there behind him was a ram caught in the bushes by its horns. Avraham went and took the ram and offered it up as a burnt offering in place of his son. [14] Avraham called the place ADONAI Yir'eh [ADONAI will see (to it), ADONAI provides] — as it is said to this day, "On the mountain ADONAI is seen."

[15] The angel of ADONAI called to Avraham a second time out of heaven. [16] He said, "I have sworn by myself— says ADONAI— that because you have done this, because you haven't withheld your son, your only son, [17] I will most certainly bless you; and I will most certainly increase your descendants to as many as there are stars in the sky or grains of sand on the seashore. Your descendants will possess the cities of their enemies, [18] and by your descendants all the nations of the earth will be blessed— because you obeyed my order."

[19] So Avraham returned to his young men. They got up and went together to Be'er-Sheva, and Avraham settled in Be'er-Sheva.

(Maftir) [20] Afterwards, Avraham was told, "Milkah too has borne children, to your brother Nachor— [21] 'Utz his firstborn, Buz his brother, K'mu'el the father of Aram, [22] Kesed, Hazo, Pildash, Yidlaf and B'tu'el. [23] B'tu'el fathered Rivkah. These eight Milkah bore to Nachor Avraham's brother. [24] His concubine, whose name was Re'umah, bore children also: Tevach, Gacham, Tachash and Ma'akhah."

Haftarah Vayera: M'lakhim Bet (2 Kings) 4:1–37 (A); 4:1–23 (S)

B'rit Hadashah suggested readings for Parashah Vayera: Luke 17:26–37; Romans 9:6–9; Galatians 4:21–31; Messianic Jews (Hebrews) 6:13–20; 11:13–19; Ya'akov (James) 2:14–24; 2 Kefa (2 Peter) 2:4–10

Parashah 5: Hayyei-Sarah (Sarah's life) 23:1–25:18

23 ¹ Sarah lived to be 127 years old; these were the years of Sarah's life. ² Sarah died in Kiryat-Arba, also known as Hevron, in the land of Kena'an; and Avraham came to mourn Sarah and weep for her. ³ Then he got up from his dead one and said to the sons of Het, ⁴ "I am a foreigner living as an alien with you; let me have a burial site with you, so that I can bury my dead wife." ⁵ The sons of Het answered Avraham, ⁶ "Listen to us, my lord. You are a prince of God among us, so choose any of our tombs to bury your dead — not one of us would refuse you his tomb for burying your dead."

⁷ Avraham got up, bowed before the people of the land, the sons of Het, ⁸ and spoke with them. "If it is your desire to help me bury my dead, then listen to me: ask 'Efron the son of Tzochar ⁹ to give me the cave of Makhpelah, which he owns, the one at the end of his field. He should sell it to me in your presence at its full value; then I will have a burial site of my own."

¹⁰ 'Efron the Hitti was sitting among the sons of Het, and he gave Avraham his answer in the presence of the sons of Het who belonged to the ruling council of the city: ¹¹ "No, my lord, listen to me: I'm giving you the field, with its cave — I'm giving it to you. In the presence of my people I give it to you." ¹² Avraham bowed before the people of the land ¹³ and spoke to 'Efron in their hearing: "Please be good enough to listen to me. I will pay the price of the field; accept it from me, and I will bury my dead there." ¹⁴ But 'Efron answered Avraham, ¹⁵ "My lord, listen to me. A plot of land worth 400 silver *shekel*s — what is that between me and you? Just bury your dead." ¹⁶ Avraham got the point of what 'Efron had said, so he weighed out for 'Efron the amount of money he had specified in the presence of the sons of Het, 400 silver *shekel*s of the weight accepted among merchants [ten pounds].

(ii) ¹⁷ Thus the field of 'Efron in Makhpelah, which is by Mamre — the field, its cave and all the trees in and around it — were deeded ¹⁸ to Avraham as his possession in the presence of the sons of Het who belonged to the ruling council of the city.

¹⁹ Then Avraham buried Sarah his wife in the cave of the field of Makhpelah, by Mamre, also known as Hevron, in the land of Kena'an. ²⁰ The field and its cave had been purchased by Avraham from the sons of Het as a burial-site which would belong to him.

24 ¹ By now Avraham was old, advanced in years; and *ADONAI* had blessed Avraham in everything. ² Avraham said to the servant who had served him the longest, who was in charge of all he owned, "Put your hand under my thigh; ³ because I want you to swear by *ADONAI*, God of heaven and God of the earth, that you will not choose a wife for my son from among the women of the Kena'ani, among whom I am living; ⁴ but that you will go to my homeland, to my kinsmen, to choose a wife for my son Yitz'chak." ⁵ The servant replied, "Suppose the woman isn't willing to follow me to this land. Must I then bring your son back to the land from which you came?" ⁶ Avraham said to him, "See to it that you don't bring my son back there. ⁷ *ADONAI*, the God of heaven — who took me away from my father's house and away from the land I was born in, who spoke to me and swore to me, 'I will give this land to your descendants' — he will send his angel ahead of you; and you are to bring a wife for my son from there. ⁸ But if the woman is unwilling to follow you, then you are released from your obligation under my oath. Just don't bring my son back there."

⁹ The servant put his hand under the thigh of Avraham his master and swore to him concerning the matter.

(iii) ¹⁰ Then the servant took ten of his master's camels and all kinds of gifts from his master, got up and went to Aram-Naharayim, to Nachor's city. ¹¹ Toward evening, when the women go out to draw water, he had the camels kneel down outside the city by the well. ¹² He said, "ADONAI, God of my master Avraham, please let me succeed today; and show your grace to my master Avraham. ¹³ Here I am, standing by the spring, as the daughters of the townsfolk come out to draw water. ¹⁴ I will say to one of the girls, 'Please lower your jug, so that I can drink.' If she answers, 'Yes, drink; and I will water your camels as well,' then let her be the one you intend for your servant Yitz'chak. This is how I will know that you have shown grace to my master."

¹⁵ Before he had finished speaking, Rivkah the daughter of B'tu'el son of Milkah the wife of Nachor Avraham's brother, came out with her jug on her shoulder. ¹⁶ The girl was very beautiful, a virgin, never having had sexual relations with any man. She went down to the spring, filled her jug and came up. ¹⁷ The servant ran to meet her and said, "Please give me a sip of water from your jug to drink." ¹⁸ "Drink, my lord," she replied, and immediately lowered her jug onto her arm and let him drink. ¹⁹ When she was through letting him drink, she said, "I will also draw water for your camels until they have drunk their fill." ²⁰ She quickly emptied her jug into the trough, then ran again to the well to draw water, and kept on drawing water for all his camels. ²¹ The man gazed at her in silence, waiting to find out whether ADONAI had made his trip successful or not.

²² When the camels were done drinking, the man took a gold nose-ring weighing one-fifth of an ounce and two gold bracelets weighing four ounces ²³ and asked, "Whose daughter are you? Tell me, please. Is there room in your father's house for us to spend the night?" ²⁴ She answered, "I am the daughter of B'tu'el the son Milkah bore to Nachor," ²⁵ adding, "We have plenty of straw and fodder, and room for staying overnight." ²⁶ The man bowed his head and prostrated himself before ADONAI. *(iv)* ²⁷ Then he said, "Blessed be ADONAI, God of my master Avraham, who has not abandoned his faithful love for my master; because ADONAI has guided me to the house of my master's kinsmen." ²⁸ The girl ran off and told her mother's household what had happened.

²⁹⁻³⁰ Rivkah had a brother named Lavan. When he saw the nose-ring, and the bracelets on his sister's wrists besides, and when he heard his sister Rivkah's report of what the man had said to her, he ran out to the spring and found the man standing there by the camels. ³¹ "Come on in," he said, "you whom ADONAI has blessed! Why are you standing outside when I have made room in the house and prepared a place for the camels?" ³² So the man went inside, and while the camels were being unloaded and provided straw and fodder, water was brought for him to wash his feet and the feet of the men with him.

³³ But when a meal was set before him, he said, "I won't eat until I say what I have to say." Lavan said, "Speak." ³⁴ He said, "I am Avraham's servant. ³⁵ ADONAI has greatly blessed my master, so that he has grown wealthy. He has given him flocks and herds, silver and gold, male and female slaves, camels and donkeys. ³⁶ Sarah my master's wife bore my master a son when she was old, and he has given him everything he has. ³⁷ My master made me swear, saying, 'You are not to choose

a wife for my son from among the women of the Kena'ani, among whom I am living; [38] rather, you are to go to my father's house, to my kinsmen, to choose a wife for my son.' [39] I said to my master, 'Suppose the woman isn't willing to follow me.' [40] Avraham answered me, 'ADONAI, in whose presence I live, will send his angel with you to make your trip successful; and you are to pick a wife for my son from my kinsmen in my father's house; [41] this will release you from your obligation under my oath. But if, when you come to my kinsmen, they refuse to give her to you, this too will release you from my oath.'

[42] "So today, I came to the spring and said, 'ADONAI, God of my master Avraham, if you are causing my trip to succeed in its purpose, [43] then, here I am, standing by the spring. I will say to one of the girls coming out to draw water, "Let me have a sip of water from your jug." [44] If she answers, "Yes, drink; and I will water your camels as well," then let her be the woman you intend for my master's son.' [45] And even before I had finished speaking to my heart, there came Rivkah, going out with her jug on her shoulder; she went down to the spring and drew water. When I said to her, 'Please let me have a drink,' [46] she immediately lowered the jug from her shoulder and said, 'Drink, and I will water your camels as well.' So I drank, and she had the camels drink too.

[47] "I asked her, 'Whose daughter are you?' and she answered, 'The daughter of B'tu'el son of Nachor, whom Milkah bore to him.' Then I put the ring on her nose and the bracelets on her wrists, [48] bowed my head, prostrated myself before ADONAI and blessed ADONAI, God of my master Avraham, for having led me in the right way to obtain my master's brother's [grand]daughter for his son.

[49] "So now if you people intend to show grace and truth to my master, tell me. But if not, tell me, so that I can turn elsewhere."

[50] Lavan and B'tu'el replied, "Since this comes from ADONAI, we can't say anything to you either bad or good. [51] Rivkah is here in front of you; take her and go. Let her be your master's son's wife, as ADONAI has said." [52] When Avraham's servant heard what they said, he prostrated himself on the ground to ADONAI. (v) [53] Then the servant brought out silver and gold jewelry, together with clothing, and gave them to Rivkah. He also gave valuable gifts to her brother and mother. [54] He and his men then ate and drank and stayed the night.

In the morning they got up; and he said, "Send me off to my master." [55] Her brother and mother said, "Let the girl stay with us a few days, at least ten. After that, she will go." [56] He answered them, "Don't delay me, since ADONAI has made my trip successful, but let me go back to my master." [57] They said, "We will call the girl and see what she says." [58] They called Rivkah and asked her, "Will you go with this man?" and she replied, "I will."

[59] So they sent their sister Rivkah away, with her nurse, Avraham's servant and his men. [60] They blessed Rivkah with these words: "Our sister, may you be the mother of millions, and may your descendants possess the cities of those who hate them." [61] Then Rivkah and her maids mounted the camels and followed the man. So the servant took Rivkah and went on his way.

[62] Meanwhile, Yitz'chak, one evening after coming along the road from Be'er-Lachai-Ro'i — he was living in the Negev — [63] went out walking in the field; and as he looked up, he saw camels approaching. [64] Rivkah too looked up; and when she saw Yitz'chak, she quickly dismounted the camel. [65] She said to the servant, "Who is

this man walking in the field to meet us?" When the servant replied, "It's my master," she took her veil and covered herself. ⁶⁶ The servant told Yitz'chak everything he had done. ⁶⁷ Then Yitz'chak brought her into his mother Sarah's tent and took Rivkah, and she became his wife, and he loved her. Thus was Yitz'chak comforted for the loss of his mother.

25 *(vi)* ¹ Avraham took another wife, whose name was K'turah. ² She bore him Zimran, Yokshan, Medan, Midyan, Yishbak; and Shuach. ³ Yokshan fathered Sh'va and D'dan. The sons of D'dan were Ashurim, L'tushim and L'umim. ⁴ The sons of Midyan were 'Eifah, 'Efer, Hanokh, Avida and Elda'ah. All these were descendants of K'turah.

⁵ Avraham gave everything he owned to Yitz'chak. ⁶ But to the sons of the concubines he made grants while he was still living and sent them off to the east, to the land of Kedem, away from Yitz'chak his son.

⁷ This is how long Avraham lived: 175 years. ⁸ Then Avraham breathed his last, dying at a ripe old age, an old man full of years; and he was gathered to his people. ⁹ Yitz'chak and Yishma'el his sons buried him in the cave of Makhpelah, in the field of 'Efron the son of Tzochar the Hitti, by Mamre, ¹⁰ the field which Avraham purchased from the sons of Het. Avraham was buried there with Sarah his wife.

¹¹ After Avraham died, God blessed Yitz'chak his son, and Yitz'chak lived near Be'er-Lachai-Ro'i.

(vii) ¹² Here is the genealogy of Yishma'el, Avraham's son, whom Hagar the Egyptian woman bore to Avraham. ¹³ These are the names of the sons of Yishma'el, listed in the order of their birth. The firstborn of Yishma'el was N'vayot; followed by Kedar, Adbe'el, Mivsam, ¹⁴ Mishma, Dumah, Massa, ¹⁵ Hadad, Teima, Y'tur, Nafish and Kedmah. *(Maftir)* ¹⁶ These are the sons of Yishma'el, and these are their names, according to their settlements and camps, twelve tribal rulers.

¹⁷ This is how long Yishma'el lived: 137 years. Then he breathed his last, died and was gathered to his people.

¹⁸ Yishma'el's sons lived between Havilah and Shur, near Egypt as you go toward Ashur; he settled near all his kinsmen.

Haftarah Hayyei-Sarah: M'lakhim Alef (1 Kings) 1:1–31

B'rit Hadashah suggested readings for Parashah Hayyei-Sarah: Mattityahu (Matthew) 8:19–22; 27:3–10; Luke 9:57–62

Parashah 6: Tol'dot (History) 25:19–28:9

¹⁹ Here is the history of Yitz'chak, Avraham's son. Avraham fathered Yitz'chak. ²⁰ Yitz'chak was forty years old when he took Rivkah, the daughter of B'tu'el the Arami from Paddan-Aram and sister of Lavan the Arami, to be his wife. ²¹ Yitz'chak prayed to ADONAI on behalf of his wife, because she was childless. ADONAI heeded his prayer, and Rivkah became pregnant. ²² The children fought with each other inside her so much that she said, "If it's going to be like this, why go on living?" So she went to inquire of ADONAI, ²³ who answered her, "There

are two nations in your womb. From birth they will be two rival peoples. One of these peoples will be stronger than the other, and the older will serve the younger." ²⁴ When the time for her delivery came, there were twins in her womb. ²⁵ The first to come out was reddish and covered all over with hair, like a coat; so they named him 'Esav [completely formed, that is, having hair already]. ²⁶ Then his brother emerged, with his hand holding 'Esav's heel, so he was called Ya'akov [he catches by the heel, he supplants]. Yitz'chak was sixty years old when she bore them.

²⁷ The boys grew; and 'Esav became a skillful hunter, an outdoorsman; while Ya'akov was a quiet man who stayed in the tents. ²⁸ Yitz'chak favored 'Esav, because he had a taste for game; Rivkah favored Ya'akov.

²⁹ One day when Ya'akov had cooked some stew, 'Esav came in from the open country, exhausted, ³⁰ and said to Ya'akov, "Please! Let me gulp down some of that red stuff — that red stuff! I'm exhausted!" (This is why he was called Edom [red].) ³¹ Ya'akov answered, "First sell me your rights as the firstborn." ³² "Look, I'm about to die!" said 'Esav. "What use to me are my rights as the firstborn?" ³³ Ya'akov said, "First, swear to me!" So he swore to him, thus selling his birthright to Ya'akov. ³⁴ Then Ya'akov gave him bread and lentil stew; he ate and drank, got up and went on his way. Thus 'Esav showed how little he valued his birthright.

26 ¹ A famine came over the land, not the same as the first famine, which had taken place when Avraham was alive. Yitz'chak went to G'rar, to Avimelekh king of the P'lishtim. ² ADONAI appeared to him and said, "Don't go down into Egypt, but live where I tell you. ³ Stay in this land, and I will be with you and bless you, because I will give all these lands to you and to your descendants. I will fulfill the oath which I swore to Avraham your father — ⁴ I will make your descendants as numerous as the stars in the sky, I will give all these lands to your descendants, and by your descendants all the nations of the earth will bless themselves. ⁵ All this is because Avraham heeded what I said and did what I told him to do — he followed my *mitzvot*, my regulations and my teachings."

(ii) ⁶ So Yitz'chak settled in G'rar. ⁷ The men of the place asked him about his wife, and out of fear he said, "She is my sister." He thought, "If I tell them she's my wife, they might kill me in order to take Rivkah. After all, she is a beautiful woman." ⁸ But one day, after he had lived there a long time, Avimelekh king of the P'lishtim happened to be looking out of a window when he spotted Yitz'chak caressing Rivkah his wife. ⁹ Avimelekh summoned Yitz'chak and said, "So she is your wife, after all! How come you said, 'She is my sister'?" Yitz'chak responded, "Because I thought, 'I could get killed because of her.'" ¹⁰ Avimelekh said, "What is this you have done to us? One of the people could easily have slept with your wife, and you would have brought guilt on us!" ¹¹ Then Avimelekh warned all the people: "Whoever touches this man or his wife will certainly be put to death."

¹² Yitz'chak planted crops in that land and reaped that year a hundred times as much as he had sowed. ADONAI had blessed him.

(iii) ¹³ The man became rich and prospered more and more, until he had become very wealthy indeed. ¹⁴ He had flocks, cattle and a large household; and the P'lishtim envied him. ¹⁵ Now the P'lishtim had stopped up and filled with dirt all the wells his father's servants had dug during the lifetime of Avraham his father. ¹⁶ Avimelekh

said to Yitz'chak, "You must go away from us, because you have become much more powerful than we are." ¹⁷ So Yitz'chak left, set up camp in *Vadi* G'rar and lived there. ¹⁸ Yitz'chak reopened the wells which had been dug during the lifetime of Avraham his father, the ones the P'lishtim had stopped up after Avraham died, and called them by the names his father had used for them. ¹⁹ Yitz'chak's servants dug in the *vadi* and uncovered a spring of running water. ²⁰ But the herdsmen of G'rar quarreled with Yitz'chak's herdsmen, claiming, "That water is ours!" So he called the well 'Esek [quarrel], because they quarreled with him. ²¹ They dug another well and quarreled over that one too. So he called it Sitnah [enmity]. ²² He went away from there and dug another well, and over that one they didn't quarrel. So he called it Rechovot [wide open spaces] and said, "Because now *Adonai* has made room for us, and we will be productive in the land."

(iv) ²³ From there Yitz'chak went up to Be'er-Sheva. ²⁴ *Adonai* appeared to him that same night and said, "I am the God of Avraham your father. Don't be afraid, because I am with you; I will bless you and increase your descendants for the sake of my servant Avraham." ²⁵ There he built an altar and called on the name of *Adonai*. He pitched his tent there, and there Yitz'chak's servants dug a well.

²⁶ Then Avimelekh went to him from G'rar with his friend Achuzat and Pikhol the commander of his army. ²⁷ Yitz'chak said to them, "Why have you come to me, even though you were unfriendly to me and sent me away?" ²⁸ They answered, "We saw very clearly that *Adonai* has been with you; so we said, 'Let there be an oath between us: let's make a pact between ourselves and you ²⁹ that you will not harm us, just as we have not caused you offense but have done you nothing but good and sent you on your way in peace. Now you are blessed by *Adonai*.'"

(v) ³⁰ Yitz'chak prepared a banquet for them, and they ate and drank. ³¹ The next morning, they got up early and swore to each other. Then Yitz'chak sent them on their way, and they left him peacefully. ³² That very day Yitz'chak's servants came and told him about the well they had dug, "We have found water." ³³ So he called it Shiv'ah [oath, seven], and for this reason the name of the city is Be'er-Sheva [well of seven, well of an oath] to this day.

³⁴ When 'Esav was forty years old, he took as wives Y'hudit the daughter of Be'eri the Hitti and Basmat the daughter of Elon the Hitti. ³⁵ But they became a cause for embitterment of spirit to Yitz'chak and Rivkah.

27 ¹ In the course of time, after Yitz'chak had grown old and his eyes dim, so that he couldn't see, he called 'Esav his older son and said to him, "My son?" and he answered, "Here I am." ² "Look, I'm old now, I don't know when I will die. ³ Therefore, please take your hunting gear — your quiver of arrows and your bow; go out in the country, and get me some game. ⁴ Make it tasty, the way I like it; and bring it to me to eat. Then I will bless you [as firstborn], before I die."

⁵ Rivkah was listening when Yitz'chak spoke to his son 'Esav. So when 'Esav went out to the country to hunt for game and bring it back, ⁶ she said to her son Ya'akov, "Listen! I heard your father telling 'Esav your brother, ⁷ 'Bring me game, and make it tasty, so I can eat it. Then I will give you my blessing in the presence of *Adonai*, before my death.' ⁸ Now pay attention to me, my son; and do what I tell you. ⁹ Go to the flock, and bring me back two choice kids. I will make it tasty for your father, the way he likes it; ¹⁰ and you will bring it to your father to eat; so that he will

give his blessing to you before his death." ¹¹ Ya'akov answered Rivkah his mother, "Look, 'Esav is hairy, but I have smooth skin. ¹² Suppose my father touches me — he'll know I'm trying to trick him, and I'll bring a curse on myself, not a blessing!" ¹³ But his mother said, "Let your curse be on me. Just listen to me, and go get me the kids!" ¹⁴ So he went, got them and brought them to his mother; and his mother prepared them in the tasty way his father loved. ¹⁵ Next, Rivkah took 'Esav her older son's best clothes, which she had with her in the house, and put them on Ya'akov her younger son; ¹⁶ and she put the skins of the goats on his hands and on the smooth parts of his neck. ¹⁷ Then she gave the tasty food and the bread she had prepared to her son Ya'akov.

¹⁸ He went to his father and said, "My father?" He replied, "Here I am; who are you, my son?" ¹⁹ Ya'akov said to his father, "I am 'Esav your firstborn. I've done what you asked me to do. Get up now, sit down, eat the game, and then give me your blessing." ²⁰ Yitz'chak said to his son, "How did you find it so quickly, my son?" He answered, "*Adonai* your God made it happen that way." ²¹ Yitz'chak said to Ya'akov, "Come here, close to me, so I can touch you, my son, and know whether you are in fact my son 'Esav or not." ²² Ya'akov approached Yitz'chak his father, who touched him and said, "The voice is Ya'akov's voice, but the hands are 'Esav's hands." ²³ However, he didn't detect him; because his hands were hairy like his brother 'Esav's hands; so he gave him his blessing. ²⁴ He asked, "Are you really my son 'Esav?" And he replied, "I am." ²⁵ He said, "Bring it here to me, and I will eat my son's game, so that I can give you my blessing." So he brought it up to him, and he ate; he also brought him wine, and he drank. ²⁶ Then his father Yitz'chak said to him, "Come close now, and kiss me, my son." ²⁷ He approached and kissed him. Yitz'chak smelled his clothes and blessed Ya'akov with these words: "See, my son smells like a field which *Adonai* has blessed. *(vi)* ²⁸ So may God give you dew from heaven, the richness of the earth, and grain and wine in abundance. ²⁹ May peoples serve you and nations bow down to you. May you be lord over your kinsmen, let your mother's descendants bow down to you. Cursed be everyone who curses you, and blessed be everyone who blesses you!"

³⁰ But as soon as Yitz'chak had finished giving his blessing to Ya'akov, when Ya'akov had barely left his father's presence, 'Esav his brother came in from his hunting. ³¹ He too had prepared a tasty meal and brought it to his father, and now he said to his father, "Let my father get up and eat from his son's game, so that you may give me your blessing." ³² Yitz'chak his father said to him, "Who are you?" and he answered, "I am your son, your firstborn, 'Esav." ³³ Yitz'chak began trembling uncontrollably and said, "Then who was it that took game and brought it to me? I ate it all just before you came, and I gave my blessing to him. That's the truth, and the blessing must stand." ³⁴ When 'Esav heard his father's words he burst into loud, bitter sobbing. "Father, bless me too," he begged. ³⁵ He replied, "Your brother came deceitfully and took away your blessing." ³⁶ 'Esav said, "His name, Ya'akov [he supplants], really suits him — because he has supplanted me these two times: he took away my birthright, and here, now he has taken away my blessing!" Then he asked, "Haven't you saved a blessing for me?" ³⁷ Yitz'chak answered 'Esav, "Look, I have made him your lord, I have given him all his kinsmen as servants, and I have given him grain and wine to sustain him. What else is there that I can do for you, my son?" ³⁸ 'Esav said to his father, "Have you only one blessing, my father? Father, bless me too!" 'Esav wept aloud, ³⁹ and Yitz'chak his father answered him: "Here!

Your home will be of the richness of the earth and of the dew of heaven from above.
⁴⁰ You will live by your sword, and you will serve your brother. But when you break
loose, you will shake his yoke off your neck." ⁴¹ 'Esav hated his brother because of the blessing his father had given him. 'Esav
said to himself, "The time for mourning my father will soon come, and then I will
kill my brother Ya'akov." ⁴² But the words of 'Esav her older son were told to Rivkah.
She sent for Ya'akov her younger son and said to him, "Here, your brother 'Esav is
comforting himself over you by planning to kill you. ⁴³ Therefore, my son, listen to
me: get up and escape to Lavan my brother in Haran. ⁴⁴ Stay with him a little while,
until your brother's anger subsides. ⁴⁵ Your brother's anger will turn away from you,
and he will forget what you did to him. Then I'll send and bring you back from there.
Why should I lose both of you on the same day?"

⁴⁶ Rivkah said to Yitz'chak, "I'm sick to death of Hitti women! If Ya'akov marries
one of the Hitti women, like those who live here, my life won't be worth living."

28 ¹ So Yitz'chak called Ya'akov, and, after blessing him, charged him: "You are
not to choose a wife from the Hitti women. ² Go now to the home of B'tu'el your
mother's father, and choose a wife there from the daughters of Lavan your mother's
brother. ³ May *El Shaddai* bless you, make you fruitful and increase your
descendants, until they become a whole assembly of peoples. ⁴ And may he give
you the blessing which he gave Avraham, you and your descendants with you, so
that you will possess the land you will travel through, the land God gave to Avraham."

(vii) ⁵ So Yitz'chak sent Ya'akov away; and he went to Paddan-Aram, to Lavan,
son of B'tu'el the Arami, the brother of Rivkah Ya'akov's and 'Esav's mother. ⁶ Now
'Esav saw that Yitz'chak had blessed Ya'akov and sent him away to Paddan-Aram to
choose a wife from there, and that as he blessed him he charged him, "You are not to
choose a Kena'ani woman as your wife," *(Maftir)* ⁷ and that Ya'akov had listened to
his father and mother and gone to Paddan-Aram. ⁸ 'Esav also saw that the Kena'ani
women did not please Yitz'chak his father. ⁹ So 'Esav went to Yishma'el and took, in
addition to the wives he already had, Machalat the daughter of Yishma'el Avraham's
son, the sister of N'vayot, to be his wife.

Haftarah Tol'dot: Mal'akhi (Malachi) 1:1–2:7

*B'rit Hadashah suggested readings for Parashah Tol'dot: Romans 9:6–16;
Messianic Jews (Hebrews) 11:20; 12:14–17*

Parashah 7: Vayetze (He went out) 28:10–32:3(2)

¹⁰ Ya'akov went out from Be'er-Sheva and traveled toward Haran. ¹¹ He came to a
certain place and stayed the night there, because the sun had set. He took a stone
from the place, put it under his head and lay down there to sleep. ¹² He dreamt
that there before him was a ladder resting on the ground with its top reaching to
heaven, and the angels of *Adonai* were going up and down on it. ¹³ Then suddenly
Adonai was standing there next to him; and he said, "I am *Adonai*, the God of
Avraham your [grand]father and the God of Yitz'chak. The land on which you are

lying I will give to you and to your descendants. ¹⁴ Your descendants will be as numerous as the grains of dust on the earth. You will expand to the west and to the east, to the north and to the south. By you and your descendants all the families of the earth will be blessed. ¹⁵ Look, I am with you. I will guard you wherever you go, and I will bring you back into this land, because I won't leave you until I have done what I have promised you."

¹⁶ Ya'akov awoke from his sleep and said, "Truly, Aᴅᴏɴᴀɪ is in this place — and I didn't know it!" ¹⁷ Then he became afraid and said, "This place is fearsome! This has to be the house of God! This is the gate of heaven!" ¹⁸ Ya'akov got up early in the morning, took the stone he had put under his head, set it up as a standing-stone, poured olive oil on its top ¹⁹ and named the place Beit-El [house of God]; but the town had originally been called Luz.

²⁰ Ya'akov took this vow: "If God will be with me and will guard me on this road that I am traveling, giving me bread to eat and clothes to wear, ²¹ so that I return to my father's house in peace, then Aᴅᴏɴᴀɪ will be my God; ²² and this stone, which I have set up as a standing-stone, will be God's house; and of everything you give me, I will faithfully return one-tenth to you."

29 *(ii)* ¹ Continuing his journey, Ya'akov came to the land of the people of the east. ² As he looked, he saw a well in a field; and there were three flocks of sheep lying there next to it; because they watered the sheep from that well. The stone on the well's mouth was large, ³ and only when all the flocks had gathered there would they roll the stone away from the opening of the well and water the sheep. Then they would put the stone back in its place on the well's opening.

⁴ Ya'akov said to them, "My brothers, where are you from?" They answered, "We're from Haran." ⁵ He asked them, "Do you know Lavan the [grand]son of Nachor?" They said, "We do." ⁶ He asked them, "Are things going well with him?" "Yes," they answered, "and here comes his daughter Rachel with the sheep." ⁷ He said, "Look, there's still plenty of daylight left; and it isn't time to bring the animals home; so water the sheep; then go, and put them out to pasture." ⁸ They answered, "We can't, not until all the flocks have been gathered together, and they roll the stone away from the opening of the well. That's when we water the sheep."

⁹ While he was still speaking with them, Rachel came with her father's sheep, because she took care of them. ¹⁰ When Ya'akov saw Rachel the daughter of Lavan his mother's brother, and the sheep of Lavan his mother's brother, Ya'akov went up and rolled the stone away from the opening of the well and watered the flock of Lavan his mother's brother. ¹¹ Ya'akov kissed Rachel and wept aloud. ¹² Ya'akov told Rachel that he was her father's relative, and that he was Rivkah's son; and she ran and told her father. ¹³ When Lavan heard the news of Ya'akov his sister's son, he ran to meet him, hugged him and kissed him, and brought him to his house. Ya'akov told Lavan all that had happened. ¹⁴ Lavan said to him, "You are indeed my own flesh and blood."

After Ya'akov had stayed with him for a whole month, ¹⁵ Lavan said to him, "Why should you work for me for nothing, just because you are my relative? Tell me how much I should pay you." ¹⁶ Now Lavan had two daughters; the name of the older was Le'ah, and the name of the younger was Rachel. ¹⁷ Le'ah's eyes were weak; but Rachel was good-looking, with beautiful features.

(iii) [18] Ya'akov had fallen in love with Rachel and said, "I will work for you seven years in exchange for Rachel your younger daughter." [19] Lavan answered, "Better that I give her to you than to someone else; stay with me." [20] So Ya'akov worked seven years for Rachel, and it seemed only a few days to him, because he was so much in love with her.

[21] Ya'akov said to Lavan, "Give me my wife, since my time is finished, so that I can start living with her." [22] Lavan gathered all the men of the place and gave a banquet. [23] In the evening he took Le'ah his daughter and brought her to Ya'akov, and he went in and slept with her. [24] Lavan also gave his slave-girl Zilpah to his daughter Le'ah as her slave-girl.

[25] In the morning Ya'akov saw that he was with Le'ah, and he said to Lavan, "What kind of thing is this that you've done to me? Didn't I work for you for Rachel? Why have you deceived me?" [26] Lavan answered, "In our place that isn't how it's done, to give the younger daughter before the firstborn. [27] Finish the marriage week of this one, and we'll give you the other one also in exchange for the work you will do for me during yet another seven years." [28] Ya'akov agreed to this, so he finished her week, and Lavan gave him his daughter Rachel as his wife. [29] Lavan also gave to his daughter Rachel his slave-girl Bilhah as her slave-girl. [30] So not only did Ya'akov go in and sleep with Rachel, but he also loved Rachel more than Le'ah. Then he served Lavan another seven years.

[31] ADONAI saw that Le'ah was unloved, so he made her fertile, while Rachel remained childless. [32] Le'ah conceived and gave birth to a son, whom she named Re'uven [see, a son!], for she said, "It is because ADONAI has seen how humiliated I have been, but now my husband will love me." [33] She conceived again, gave birth to a son and said, "It is because ADONAI has heard that I am unloved; therefore he has given me this son also." So she named him Shim'on [hearing]. [34] Once more she conceived and had a son; and she said, "Now this time my husband will be joined to me, because I have borne him three sons." Therefore she named him Levi [joining]. [35] She conceived yet again, had a son and said, "This time I will praise ADONAI"; therefore she named him Y'hudah [praise]. Then she stopped having children.

30

[1] When Rachel saw that she was not bearing children for Ya'akov, she envied her sister and said to Ya'akov, "Give me children, or I will die!" [2] This made Ya'akov angry at Rachel; he answered, "Am I in God's place? He's the one who is denying you children." [3] She said, "Here is my maid Bilhah. Go, sleep with her, and let her give birth to a child that will be laid on my knees, so that through her I too can build a family." [4] So she gave him Bilhah her slave-girl as his wife, and Ya'akov went in and slept with her. [5] Bilhah conceived and bore Ya'akov a son. [6] Rachel said, "God has judged in my favor; indeed he has heard me and given me a son." Therefore she called him Dan [he judged].

[7] Bilhah Rachel's slave-girl conceived again and bore Ya'akov a second son. [8] Rachel said, "I have wrestled mightily with my sister and won," and called him Naftali [my wrestling].

[9] When Le'ah saw that she had stopped having children, she took Zilpah her slave-girl and gave her to Ya'akov as his wife. [10] Zilpah Le'ah's slave-girl bore Ya'akov a son; [11] and Le'ah said, "Good fortune has come," calling him Gad [good fortune].

¹² Zilpah Le'ah's slave-girl bore Ya'akov a second son; ¹³ and Le'ah said, "How happy I am! Women will say I am happy!" and called him Asher [happy].

(iv) ¹⁴ During the wheat harvest season Re'uven went and found mandrakes in the field and brought them to his mother Le'ah. Rachel said to Le'ah, "Please give me some of your son's mandrakes [so that I can be fertile]." ¹⁵ She answered, "Isn't it enough that you have taken away my husband? Do you have to take my son's mandrakes too?" Rachel said, "Very well; in exchange for your son's mandrakes, sleep with him tonight." ¹⁶ When Ya'akov came in from the field in the evening, Le'ah went out to meet him and said, "You have to come and sleep with me, because I've hired you with my son's mandrakes." So Ya'akov slept with her that night. ¹⁷ God listened to Le'ah, and she conceived and bore Ya'akov a fifth son. ¹⁸ Le'ah said, "God has given me my hire, because I gave my slave-girl to my husband." So she called him Yissakhar [hire, reward].

¹⁹ Le'ah conceived again and bore a sixth son to Ya'akov. ²⁰ Le'ah said, "God has given me a wonderful gift. Now at last my husband will live with me, since I have borne him six sons." And she called him Z'vulun [living together].

²¹ After this, she gave birth to a daughter and named her Dinah [controversy over rights].

²² Then God took note of Rachel, heeded her prayer and made her fertile. ²³ She conceived, had a son and said, "God has taken away my disgrace." ²⁴ She called him Yosef [may he add], saying, "May *ADONAI* add to me another son."

²⁵ After Rachel had given birth to Yosef, Ya'akov said to Lavan, "Send me on my way, so that I can return to my own place, to my own country. ²⁶ Let me take my wives, for whom I have served you, and my children; and let me go. You know very well how faithfully I have served you." ²⁷ Lavan answered him, "If you regard me favorably, then please listen: I have observed the signs that *ADONAI* has blessed me on account of you. *(v)* ²⁸ Name your wages," he said; "I will pay them." ²⁹ Ya'akov replied, "You know how faithfully I have served you and how your livestock have prospered under my care. ³⁰ The few you had before I came have increased substantially; *ADONAI* has blessed you wherever I went. But now, when will I provide for my own household?" ³¹ Lavan said, "What should I give you?" "Nothing," answered Ya'akov, "just do this one thing for me: once more I will pasture your flock and take care of it. ³² I will also go through the flock and pick out every speckled, spotted or brown sheep, and every speckled or spotted goat; these and their offspring will be my wages. ³³ And I will let my integrity stand as witness against me in the future: when you come to look over the animals constituting my wages, every goat that isn't speckled or spotted and every sheep that isn't brown will count as stolen by me." ³⁴ Lavan replied, "As you have said, so be it."

³⁵ That day Lavan removed the male goats that were streaked or spotted and all the female goats that were speckled or spotted, every one with white on it, and all the brown sheep; turned them over to his sons; ³⁶ and put three days' distance between himself and Ya'akov. Ya'akov fed the rest of Lavan's flocks.

³⁷ Ya'akov took fresh-cut branches from poplar, almond and plane trees and made white streaks on them by peeling off the bark. ³⁸ Then he set the rods he had peeled upright in the watering troughs, so that the animals would see them when they came to drink. And since they bred when they came to drink, ³⁹ the animals mated in sight of the rods and gave birth to streaked, speckled and spotted young.

⁴⁰ Ya'akov divided the lambs and had the animals mate with the streaked and the brown in the flock of Lavan. He also kept his own livestock separate and did not have them mix with Lavan's flock. ⁴¹ Whenever the hardier animals came into heat, Ya'akov would set up the rods in the watering troughs; so that the animals would see them and conceive in front of them; ⁴² but he didn't set up the rods in front of the weaker animals. Thus the more feeble were Lavan's and the stronger Ya'akov's. ⁴³ In this way the man became very rich and had large flocks, along with male and female slaves, camels and donkeys.

31 ¹ But then he heard what Lavan's sons were saying: "Ya'akov has taken away everything that our father once had. It's from what used to belong to our father that he has gotten so rich." ² He also saw that Lavan regarded him differently than before. ³ *Adonai* said to Ya'akov, "Return to the land of your ancestors, to your kinsmen; I will be with you." ⁴ So Ya'akov sent for Rachel and Le'ah and had them come to the field where his flock was. ⁵ He said to them, "I see by the way your father looks that he feels differently toward me than before; but the God of my father has been with me. ⁶ You know that I have served your father with all my strength, ⁷ and that your father has belittled me and has changed my wages ten times; but God did not allow him to do me any damage. ⁸ If he said, 'The speckled will be your wages,' then all the animals gave birth to speckled young; and if he said, 'The streaked will be your wages,' then all the animals gave birth to streaked young. ⁹ This is how God has taken away your father's animals and given them to me. ¹⁰ Once, when the animals were mating, I had a dream: I looked up and there in front of me the male goats which mated with the females were streaked, speckled and mottled. ¹¹ Then, in the dream, the angel of God said to me, 'Ya'akov!' and I replied, 'Here I am.' ¹² He continued, 'Raise your eyes now, and look: all the male goats mating with the females are streaked, speckled and mottled; for I have seen everything Lavan has been doing to you. ¹³ I am the God of Beit-El, where you anointed a standing-stone with oil, where you vowed your vow to me. Now get up, get out of this land, and return to the land where you were born.'" ¹⁴ Rachel and Le'ah answered him, "We no longer have any inheritance from our father's possessions; ¹⁵ and he considers us foreigners, since he has sold us; moreover, he has consumed everything he received in exchange for us. ¹⁶ Nevertheless, the wealth which God has taken away from our father has become ours and our children's anyway; so whatever God has told you to do, do."

(vi) ¹⁷ Then Ya'akov got up, put his sons and wives on the camels, ¹⁸ and carried off all his livestock, along with all the riches he had accumulated, the livestock in his possession which he had acquired in Paddan-Aram, to go to Yitz'chak his father in the land of Kena'an.

¹⁹ Now Lavan had gone to shear his sheep, so Rachel stole the household idols that belonged to her father, ²⁰ and Ya'akov outwitted Lavan the Arami by not telling him of his intended flight. ²¹ So he fled with everything he had: he departed, crossed the [Euphrates] River and set out for the hill-country of Gil'ad. ²² Not until the third day was Lavan told that Ya'akov had fled.

²³ Lavan took his kinsmen with him and spent the next seven days pursuing Ya'akov, overtaking him in the hill-country of Gil'ad. ²⁴ But God came to Lavan the Arami in a dream that night and said to him, "Be careful that you don't say anything to Ya'akov, either good or bad."

²⁵ When Lavan caught up with Ya'akov, Ya'akov had set up camp in the hill-country; so Lavan and his kinsmen set up camp in the hill-country of Gil'ad. ²⁶ Lavan said to Ya'akov, "What do you mean by deceiving me and carrying off my daughters as if they were captives taken in war? ²⁷ Why did you flee in secret and deceive me and not tell me? I would have sent you off with joy and singing to the music of tambourines and lyres. ²⁸ You didn't even let me kiss my sons and daughters good-bye! What a stupid thing to do! ²⁹ I have it in my power to do you harm; but the God of your father spoke to me last night and said, 'Be careful that you don't say anything to Ya'akov, either good or bad.' ³⁰ Granted that you had to leave, because you longed so deeply for your father's house; but why did you steal my gods?" ³¹ Ya'akov answered Lavan, "Because I was afraid. I said, 'Suppose you take your daughters away from me by force?' ³² But if you find your gods with someone, that person will not remain alive. So with our kinsmen to witness, if you spot anything that I have which belongs to you, take it back." Ya'akov did not know that Rachel had stolen them. ³³ Lavan went into Ya'akov's tent, then into Le'ah's tent and into the tent of the two slave-girls; but he did not find them. He left Le'ah's tent and entered Rachel's tent. ³⁴ Now Rachel had taken the household gods, put them in the saddle of the camel and was sitting on them. Lavan felt all around the tent but did not find them. ³⁵ She said to her father, "Please don't be angry that I'm not getting up in your presence, but it's the time of my period." So he searched, but he didn't find the household gods.

³⁶ Then Ya'akov became angry and started arguing with Lavan. "What have I done wrong?" he demanded. "What is my offense, that you have come after me in hot pursuit? ³⁷ You have felt around in all my stuff, but what have you found of all your household goods? Put it here, in front of my kinsmen and yours, so that they can render judgment between the two of us! ³⁸ I have been with you for these twenty years! Your female sheep and goats haven't aborted their young, and I haven't eaten the male animals in your flocks. ³⁹ If one of your flock was destroyed by a wild animal, I didn't bring the carcass to you but bore the loss myself. You demanded that I compensate you for any animal stolen, whether by day or by night. ⁴⁰ Here's how it was for me: during the day thirst consumed me, and at night the cold — my sleep fled from my eyes. ⁴¹ These twenty years I've been in your house — I served you fourteen years for your two daughters and six years for your flock; and you changed my wages ten times! ⁴² If the God of my father, the God of Avraham, the one whom Yitz'chak fears, had not been on my side, by now you would certainly have already sent me away with nothing! God has seen how distressed I've been and how hard I've worked, and last night he passed judgment in my favor."

(vii) ⁴³ Lavan answered Ya'akov, "The daughters are mine, the children are mine, the flocks are mine, and everything you see is mine! But what can I do today about these daughters of mine or the children they have borne? ⁴⁴ So now, come, let's make a covenant, I and you; and let it stand as a testimony between me and you." ⁴⁵ Ya'akov took a stone and set it upright as a standing-stone. ⁴⁶ Then Ya'akov said to his kinsmen, "Gather some stones"; and they took stones, made a pile of them and ate there by the pile of stones. ⁴⁷ Lavan called it Y'gar-Sahaduta ["pile of witness" in Aramaic], while Ya'akov called it Gal-'Ed ["pile of witness" in Hebrew].

⁴⁸ Lavan said, "This pile witnesses between me and you today." This is why it is called Gal-'Ed ⁴⁹ and also HaMitzpah [the watchtower], because he said, "May *Adonai* watch between me and you when we are apart from each other. ⁵⁰ If you cause pain to my daughters, or if you take wives in addition to my daughters, then, even if no one is there with us, still God is witness between me and you." ⁵¹ Lavan also said to Ya'akov, "Here is this pile, and here is this standing-stone, which I have set up between me and you. ⁵² May this pile be a witness, and may the standing-stone be a witness, that I will not pass beyond this pile to you, and you will not pass beyond this pile and this standing-stone to me, to cause harm. ⁵³ May the God of Avraham and also the god of Nachor, the god of their father, judge between us." But Ya'akov swore by the One his father Yitz'chak feared. ⁵⁴ Ya'akov offered a sacrifice on the mountain and invited his kinsmen to the meal. They ate the food and spent the whole night on the mountain.

32 *(Maftir)* ¹⁽³¹:⁵⁵⁾ Early in the morning Lavan got up, kissed his sons and daughters, and blessed them. Then Lavan left and returned to his own place. ²⁽¹⁾ Ya'akov went on his way, and the angels of God met him. ³⁽²⁾ When Ya'akov saw them, he said, "This is God's camp," and called that place Machanayim [two camps].

Haftarah Vayetze: Hoshea (Hosea) 12:13(12)–14:10(9) (A); 11:7–12:12(11) (S)

B'rit Hadashah suggested reading for Parashah Vayetze: Yochanan (John) 1:43–51

Parashah 8: Vayishlach (He sent) 32:4(3)–36:43

⁴⁽³⁾ Ya'akov sent messengers ahead of him to 'Esav his brother toward the land of Se'ir, the country of Edom, ⁵⁽⁴⁾ with these instructions: "Here is what you are to say to my lord 'Esav: 'Your servant Ya'akov says, "I have been living with Lavan and have stayed until now. ⁶⁽⁵⁾ I have cattle, donkeys and flocks, and male and female servants. I am sending to tell this news to my lord, in order to win your favor." ' " ⁷⁽⁶⁾ The messengers returned to Ya'akov saying, "We went to your brother 'Esav, and he is coming to meet you; with him are four hundred men."

⁸⁽⁷⁾ Ya'akov became greatly afraid and distressed. He divided the people, flocks, cattle and camels with him into two camps, ⁹⁽⁸⁾ saying, "If 'Esav comes to the one camp and attacks it, at least the camp that is left will escape." ¹⁰⁽⁹⁾ Then Ya'akov said, "God of my father Avraham and God of my father Yitz'chak, *Adonai*, who told me, 'Return to your country and your kinsmen, and I will do you good': ¹¹⁽¹⁰⁾ I'm not worthy of all the love and faithfulness you have shown your servant, since I crossed the Yarden with only my staff. But now I have become two camps. ¹²⁽¹¹⁾ Please! Rescue me from my brother 'Esav! I'm afraid of him, afraid he'll come and attack me, without regard for mothers or children. ¹³⁽¹²⁾ You said, 'I will certainly do you good and make your descendants as numerous as the grains of sand by the sea, which are so many they can't be counted.' "

(ii) ¹⁴⁽¹³⁾ He stayed there that night; then he chose from among his possessions the following as a present for 'Esav his brother: ¹⁵⁽¹⁴⁾ two hundred female goats and twenty males, two hundred female sheep and twenty males, ¹⁶⁽¹⁵⁾ thirty milk-camels and their colts, forty cows and ten bulls, twenty female donkeys and ten colts. ¹⁷⁽¹⁶⁾ He turned them over to his servants, every drove by itself, and said to his servants, "Cross over in front of me, and keep a space between each drove and the next one." ¹⁸⁽¹⁷⁾ He instructed the servant in front, "When 'Esav my brother meets you and asks you, 'Whose servant are you? Where are you going? And whose animals are these?' ¹⁹⁽¹⁸⁾ then you are to say, 'They belong to your servant Ya'akov, and they are a present he has sent to my lord 'Esav; and Ya'akov himself is just behind us.'" ²⁰⁽¹⁹⁾ He also instructed the second servant, and the third, and all that followed the droves, "When you encounter 'Esav, you are to speak to him in the same way, ²¹⁽²⁰⁾ and you are to add, 'And there, just behind us, is your servant Ya'akov.'" For he said, "I will appease him first with the present that goes ahead of me; then, after that, I will see him myself — and maybe he will be friendly toward me." ²²⁽²¹⁾ So the present crossed over ahead of him, and he himself stayed that night in the camp.

²³⁽²²⁾ He got up that night, took his two wives, his two slave-girls, and his eleven children, and forded the Yabok. ²⁴⁽²³⁾ He took them and sent them across the stream, then sent his possessions across; ²⁵⁽²⁴⁾ and Ya'akov was left alone. Then some man wrestled with him until daybreak. ²⁶⁽²⁵⁾ When he saw that he did not defeat Ya'akov, he struck Ya'akov's hip socket, so that his hip was dislocated while wrestling with him. ²⁷⁽²⁶⁾ The man said, "Let me go, because it's daybreak." But Ya'akov replied, "I won't let you go unless you bless me." ²⁸⁽²⁷⁾ The man asked, "What is your name?" and he answered, "Ya'akov." ²⁹⁽²⁸⁾ Then the man said, "From now on, you will no longer be called Ya'akov, but Isra'el; because you have shown your strength to both God and men and have prevailed." ³⁰⁽²⁹⁾ Ya'akov asked him, "Please tell me your name." But he answered, "Why are you asking about my name?" and blessed him there.

(iii) ³¹⁽³⁰⁾ Ya'akov called the place P'ni-El [face of God], "Because I have seen God face to face, yet my life is spared." ³²⁽³¹⁾ As the sun rose upon him he went on past P'ni-El, limping at the hip. ³³⁽³²⁾ This is why, to this day, the people of Isra'el do not eat the thigh muscle that passes along the hip socket — because the man struck Ya'akov's hip at its socket.

33 ¹ Ya'akov raised his eyes and looked out; and there was 'Esav coming, and four hundred men with him. So Ya'akov divided the children between Le'ah, Rachel and the two slave-girls, ² putting the slave-girls and their children first, Le'ah and her children second, and Rachel and Yosef last. ³ Then he himself passed on ahead of them and prostrated himself on the ground seven times before approaching his brother. ⁴ 'Esav ran to meet him, hugged him, threw his arms around his neck and kissed him; and they wept. ⁵ 'Esav looked up; on seeing the women and children, he asked, "Who are these with you?" Ya'akov answered, "The children God has graciously given to your servant."

(iv) ⁶ Then the slave-girls approached with their children, and they prostrated themselves; ⁷ Le'ah too and her children approached and prostrated themselves; and last came Yosef and Rachel; and they prostrated themselves. ⁸ 'Esav asked, "What was the meaning of this procession of droves I encountered?" and he answered, "It was

to win my lord's favor." ⁹ 'Esav replied, "I have plenty already; my brother, keep your possessions for yourself." ¹⁰ Ya'akov said, "No, please! If now I have won your favor, then accept my gift. Just seeing your face has been like seeing the face of God, now that you have received me. ¹¹ So please accept the gift I have brought you, for God has dealt kindly with me and I have enough." Thus he urged him, until he accepted it.

¹² 'Esav said, "Let's break camp and get going. I'll go first." ¹³ Ya'akov said to him, "My lord knows that the children are small, and the sheep and cattle suckling their young concern me, because if they overdrive them even one day, all the flocks will die. ¹⁴ Instead, please, let my lord go on ahead of his servant. I will travel more slowly, at the pace of the cattle ahead of me and at the pace of the children, until I come to my lord in Se'ir." ¹⁵ 'Esav replied, "Then let me leave with you some of the people I have with me." But Ya'akov said, "There's no need for my lord to be so kind to me." ¹⁶ So 'Esav left that day to return to Se'ir. ¹⁷ Ya'akov went on to Sukkot, where he built himself a house and put up shelters for his cattle. This is why the place is called Sukkot [shelters].

¹⁸ Having traveled from Paddan-Aram, Ya'akov arrived safely at the city of Sh'khem, in Kena'an, and set up camp near the city. ¹⁹ From the sons of Hamor Sh'khem's father he bought for one hundred pieces of silver the parcel of land where he had pitched his tent. ²⁰ There he put up an altar, which he called El-Elohei-Yisra'el [God, the God of Isra'el].

34 *(v)* ¹ One time Dinah the daughter of Le'ah, whom she had borne to Ya'akov, went out to visit the local girls; ² and Sh'khem the son of Hamor the Hivi, the local ruler, saw her, grabbed her, raped her and humiliated her. ³ But actually he was strongly attracted to Dinah the daughter of Ya'akov; he fell in love with the girl and tried to win her affection. ⁴ Sh'khem spoke with his father Hamor and said, "Get this girl for me; I want her to be my wife."

⁵ When Ya'akov heard that he had defiled Dinah his daughter, his sons were with his livestock in the field; so Ya'akov restrained himself until they came. ⁶ Hamor the father of Sh'khem went out to Ya'akov to speak with him ⁷ just as Ya'akov's sons were coming in from the field. When they heard what had happened, the men were saddened and were very angry at the outrage this man had committed against Isra'el by raping Ya'akov's daughter, something that is simply not done. ⁸ But Hamor said to them, "My son Sh'khem's heart is set on your daughter. Please give her to him as his wife; ⁹ and intermarry with us: give your daughters to us, and take our daughters for yourselves. ¹⁰ You will live with us, and the land will be available to you — you'll live, do business and acquire possessions here."

¹¹ Then Sh'khem said to her father and brothers, "Only accept me, and I will give whatever you tell me. ¹² Ask as large a bride-price as you like, I'll pay whatever you tell me. Just let me marry the girl." ¹³ The sons of Ya'akov answered Sh'khem and Hamor his father deceitfully, because he had defiled Dinah their sister. ¹⁴ They said to them, "We can't do it, because it would be a disgrace to give our sister to someone who hasn't been circumcised. ¹⁵ Only on this condition will we consent to what you are asking: that you become like us by having every male among you get circumcised. ¹⁶ Then we'll give our daughters to you, and we'll take your daughters for ourselves, and we'll live with you and become one people. ¹⁷ But if you won't do as we say and get circumcised, then we'll take our daughter and go away." ¹⁸ What

they said seemed fair to Hamor and Sh'khem the son of Hamor, ¹⁹ and the young man did not put off doing what was asked of him, even though he was the most respected member of his father's family, because he so much wanted Ya'akov' s daughter.

²⁰ Hamor and Sh'khem his son came to the entrance of their city and spoke with its leading men: ²¹ "These people are peaceful toward us; therefore let them live in the land and do business in it; for, as you can see, the land is large enough for them. Let us take their daughters as wives for ourselves, and we'll give them our daughters. ²² But the people will consent to live with us and become one people only on this condition: that every male among us gets circumcised, as they themselves are circumcised. ²³ Won't their cattle, their possessions and all their animals be ours? Only let's consent to do what they ask, and then they will live with us." ²⁴ Everyone going out the city's gate listened to Hamor and Sh'khem his son; so every male was circumcised, every one that went out the gate of the city.

²⁵ On the third day after the circumcision, when they were in pain, two of Ya'akov's sons, Shim'on and Levi, Dinah's brothers, took their swords, boldly descended on the city and slaughtered all the males. ²⁶ They killed Hamor and Sh'khem his son with their swords, took Dinah out of Sh'khem's house, and left. ²⁷ Then the sons of Ya'akov entered over the dead bodies of those who had been slaughtered and plundered the city in reprisal for defiling their sister. ²⁸ They took their flocks, cattle and donkeys, and everything else, whether in the city or in the field, ²⁹ everything they owned. Their children and wives they took captive, and they looted whatever was in the houses.

³⁰ But Ya'akov said to Shim'on and Levi, "You have caused me trouble by making me stink in the opinion of the local inhabitants, the Kena'ani and the P'rizi. Since I don't have many people, they'll align themselves together against me and attack me; and I will be destroyed, I and my household." ³¹ They replied, "Should we let our sister be treated like a whore?"

35 ¹ God said to Ya'akov, "Get up, go up to Beit-El and live there, and make there an altar to God, who appeared to you when you fled 'Esav your brother." ² Then Ya'akov said to his household and all the others with him, "Get rid of the foreign gods that you have with you, purify yourselves, and put on fresh clothes. ³ We're going to move on and go up to Beit-El. There I will build an altar to God, who answered me when I was in such distress and stayed with me wherever I went." ⁴ They gave Ya'akov all the foreign gods in their possession and the earrings they were wearing, and Ya'akov buried them under the pistachio tree near Sh'khem. ⁵ While they were traveling, a terror from God fell upon the cities around them, so that none of them pursued the sons of Ya'akov.

⁶ Ya'akov and all the people with him arrived at Luz (that is, Beit-El) in the land of Kena'an. ⁷ He built there an altar and called the place El-Beit-El [God of Beit-El], because it was there that God was revealed to him, at the time when he was fleeing from his brother.

⁸ Then D'vorah, Rivkah's nurse, died. She was buried below Beit-El under the oak, which was given the name Alon-Bakhut [oak of weeping].

⁹ After Ya'akov arrived from Paddan-Aram, God appeared to him again and blessed him. ¹⁰ God said to him, "Your name is Ya'akov, but you will be called Ya'akov no longer; your name will be Isra'el." Thus he named him Isra'el. ¹¹ God further said

to him, "I am *El Shaddai*. Be fruitful and multiply. A nation, indeed a group of nations, will come from you; kings will be descended from you. *(A: vi)* ¹² Moreover, the land which I gave to Avraham and Yitz'chak I will give to you, and I will give the land to your descendants after you." ¹³ Then God went up from him there where he had spoken with him. *(S: vi)* ¹⁴ Ya'akov set up a standing-stone in the place where he had spoken with him, a stone pillar. Then he poured out a drink offering on it and poured oil on it. ¹⁵ Ya'akov called the place where God spoke with him Beit-El.

¹⁶ Then they traveled on from Beit-El, and while there was still some distance to go before arriving in Efrat, Rachel went into labor, and she had great difficulty with it. ¹⁷ While she was undergoing this hard labor, the midwife said to her, "Don't worry, this is also a son for you." ¹⁸ But she died in childbirth. As she was dying she named her son Ben-Oni [son of my grief], but his father called him Binyamin [son of the right hand, son of the south]. ¹⁹ So Rachel died and was buried on the way to Efrat (that is, Beit-Lechem). ²⁰ Ya'akov set up a standing-stone on her grave; it is the standing-stone of Rachel's grave to this day.

²¹ Isra'el continued his travels and pitched his tent on the other side of Migdal-'Eder. ²² It was while Isra'el was living in that land that Re'uven went and slept with Bilhah his father's concubine, and Isra'el heard about it.

Ya'akov had twelve sons. ²³ The sons of Le'ah were Re'uven Ya'akov's firstborn, Shim'on, Levi, Y'hudah, Yissakhar and Z'vulun. ²⁴ The sons of Rachel were Yosef and Binyamin. ²⁵ The sons of Bilhah Rachel's slave-girl were Dan and Naftali. ²⁶ And the sons of Zilpah Le'ah's slave-girl were Gad and Asher. These were Ya'akov's sons, born to him in Paddan-Aram.

²⁷ Ya'akov came home to his father Yitz'chak at Mamre, near Kiryat-Arba (also known as Hevron), where Avraham and Yitz'chak had lived as foreigners. ²⁸ Yitz'chak lived to be 180 years old. ²⁹ Then he breathed his last, died and was gathered to his people, an old man full of years; and his sons 'Esav and Ya'akov buried him.

36 ¹ This is the genealogy of 'Esav (that is, Edom). ² 'Esav chose Kena'ani women as his wives: 'Adah the daughter of Eilon the Hitti; Oholivamah the daughter of 'Anah the daughter of Tziv'on the Hivi; ³ and Basmat Yishma'el's daughter, sister of N'vayot. ⁴ 'Adah bore to 'Esav Elifaz, Basmat bore Re'u'el, ⁵ and Oholivamah bore Ye'ush, Ya'lam and Korach. These were the sons of 'Esav born to him in the land of Kena'an.

⁶ 'Esav took his wives, his sons and daughters, the others in his household, his cattle and other animals and everything else he owned, which he had acquired in the land of Kena'an, and went off to a country distant from his brother Ya'akov. ⁷ For their possessions had become too great for them to live together, and the countryside through which they were traveling couldn't support so much livestock. ⁸ So 'Esav lived in the hill-country of Se'ir. ('Esav is Edom.)

⁹ This is the genealogy of 'Esav the father of Edom in the hill-country of Se'ir. ¹⁰ The names of 'Esav's sons were Elifaz, son of 'Adah the wife of 'Esav, and Re'u'el the son of Basmat the wife of 'Esav.

¹¹ The sons of Elifaz were Teman, Omar, Tzefo, Ga'tam and K'naz. ¹² Timnah was the concubine of Elifaz 'Esav's son, and she bore to Elifaz 'Amalek. These were the descendants of 'Adah 'Esav's wife.

¹³ The sons of Re'u'el were Nachat, Zerach, Shammah and Mizah. These were the sons of Basmat 'Esav's wife.

¹⁴ These were the sons of Oholivamah, the daughter of 'Anah the daughter of Tziv'on, 'Esav's wife: she bore to 'Esav Ye'ush, Ya'lam and Korach.

¹⁵ The chieftains of the sons of 'Esav were the sons of Elifaz the firstborn of 'Esav and the chieftains of Teman, Omar, Tzefo, K'naz, ¹⁶ Korach, Ga'tam and 'Amalek. These were the chieftains descended from Elifaz in Edom and from 'Adah.

¹⁷ The sons of Re'u'el 'Esav's son were the chieftains of Nachat, Zerach, Shammah and Mizah. These were the chieftains descended from Re'u'el in the land of Edom and from Basmat 'Esav's wife.

¹⁸ The sons of Oholivamah 'Esav's wife were the chieftains of Ye'ush, Ya'lam and Korach. These were the chieftains descended from Oholivamah the daughter of 'Anah, 'Esav's wife.

¹⁹ These were the descendants of 'Esav (that is, Edom), and these were their chieftains.

(vii) ²⁰ These were the descendants of Se'ir the Hori, the local inhabitants: Lotan, Shoval, Tziv'on, 'Anah, ²¹ Dishon, Etzer and Dishan. They were the chieftains descended from the Hori, the people of Se'ir in the land of Edom. ²² The sons of Lotan were Hori and Hemam; Lotan's sister was Timnah. ²³ The sons of Shoval were 'Alvan, Manachat, 'Eival, Sh'fo and Onam. ²⁴ The sons of Tziv'on were Ayah and 'Anah. This is the 'Anah who found the hot springs in the desert while pasturing his father Tziv'on's donkeys. ²⁵ The children of 'Anah were Dishon and Oholivamah the daughter of 'Anah. ²⁶ The sons of Dishon were Hemdan, Eshban, Yitran and K'ran. ²⁷ The sons of Etzer were Bilhan, Za'avan and 'Akan. ²⁸ The sons of Dishan were 'Utz and Aran. ²⁹ These were the chieftains descended from the Hori: the chieftains of Lotan, Shoval, Tziv'on, 'Anah, ³⁰ Dishon, Etzer and Dishan. They were the chieftains descended from the Hori by their clans in Se'ir.

³¹ Following are the kings who reigned in the land of Edom before any king had reigned over the people of Isra'el. ³² Bela the son of B'or reigned in Edom; the name of his city was Dinhavah. ³³ When Bela died, Yovav the son of Zerach from Botzrah reigned in his place. ³⁴ When Yovav died, Husham from the land of the Temani reigned in his place. ³⁵ When Husham died, Hadad the son of B'dad, who killed Midyan in the field of Mo'av, reigned in his place; the name of his city was 'Avit. ³⁶ When Hadad died, Samlah of Masrekah reigned in his place. ³⁷ When Samlah died, Sha'ul of Rechovot-by-the-River reigned in his place. ³⁸ When Sha'ul died, Ba'al-Chanan the son of 'Akhbor reigned in his place. ³⁹ When Ba'al-Chanan died, Hadar reigned in his place; the name of his city was Pa'u; and his wife's name was M'heitav'el the daughter of Matred the daughter of Mei-Zahav.

(Maftir) ⁴⁰ These are the names of the chieftains descended from 'Esav, according to their clans, places and names: the chieftains of Timna, 'Alvah, Y'tet, ⁴¹ Oholivamah, Elah, Pinon, ⁴² Kenaz, Teman, Mivtzar, ⁴³ Magdi'el and 'Iram. These were the chieftains of Edom according to their settlements in the land they owned. This is 'Esav the father of Edom.

Haftarah Vayishlach: Hoshea (Hosea) 11:7–12:12(11) (A); 'Ovadyah (Obadiah) 1–21 (S)

B'rit Hadashah suggested readings for Parashah Vayishlach: 1 Corinthians 5:1–13; Revelation 7:1–12

Parashah 9: Vayeshev (He continued living) 37:1–40:23

37 [1] Ya'akov continued living in the land where his father had lived as a foreigner, the land of Kena'an. [2] Here is the history of Ya'akov. When Yosef was seventeen years old he used to pasture the flock with his brothers, even though he was still a boy. Once when he was with the sons of Bilhah and the sons of Zilpah, his father's wives, he brought a bad report about them to their father. [3] Now Isra'el loved Yosef the most of all his children, because he was the son of his old age; and he made him a long-sleeved robe. [4] When his brothers saw that their father loved him more than all his brothers, they began to hate him and reached the point where they couldn't even talk with him in a civil manner.

[5] Yosef had a dream which he told his brothers, and that made them hate him all the more. [6] He said to them, "Listen while I tell you about this dream of mine. [7] We were tying up bundles of wheat in the field when suddenly my bundle got up by itself and stood upright; then your bundles came, gathered around mine and prostrated themselves before it." [8] His brothers retorted, "Yes, you will certainly be our king. You'll do a great job of bossing us around!" And they hated him still more for his dreams and for what he said.

[9] He had another dream which he told his brothers: "Here, I had another dream, and there were the sun, the moon and eleven stars prostrating themselves before me." [10] He told his father too, as well as his brothers, but his father rebuked him: "What is this dream you have had? Do you really expect me, your mother and your brothers to come and prostrate ourselves before you on the ground?" [11] His brothers were jealous of him, but his father kept the matter in mind.

(ii) [12] After this, when his brothers had gone to pasture their father's sheep in Sh'khem, [13] Isra'el asked Yosef, "Aren't your brothers pasturing the sheep in Sh'khem? Come, I will send you to them." He answered, "Here I am." [14] He said to him, "Go now, see whether things are going well with your brothers and with the sheep, and bring word back to me." So he sent him away from the Hevron Valley, and he went to Sh'khem, [15] where a man found him wandering around in the countryside. The man asked him, "What are you looking for?" [16] "I'm looking for my brothers," he answered. "Tell me, please, where are they pasturing the sheep?" [17] The man said, "They've left here; because I heard them say, 'Let's go to Dotan.'" Yosef went after his brothers and found them in Dotan.

[18] They spotted him in the distance, and before he had arrived where they were, they had already plotted to kill him. [19] They said to each other, "Look, this dreamer is coming! [20] So come now, let's kill him and throw him into one of these water cisterns here. Then we'll say some wild animal devoured him. We'll see then what becomes of his dreams!" [21] But when Re'uven heard this, he saved him from being destroyed by them. He said, "We shouldn't take his life. [22] Don't shed blood," Re'uven added. "Throw him into this cistern here in the wilds, but don't lay hands on him yourselves." He intended to rescue him from them later and restore him to his father.

(iii) [23] So it was that when Yosef arrived to be with his brothers, they stripped off his robe, the long-sleeved robe he was wearing, [24] and took him and threw him into the cistern (the cistern was empty; without any water in it). [25] Then they sat down to eat their meal; but as they looked up, they saw in front of them a caravan of Yishma'elim coming from Gil'ad, their camels loaded with aromatic gum, healing

41

resin and opium, on their way down to Egypt. ²⁶ Y'hudah said to his brothers, "What advantage is it to us if we kill our brother and cover up his blood? ²⁷ Come, let's sell him to the Yishma'elim, instead of putting him to death with our own hands. After all, he is our brother, our own flesh." His brothers paid attention to him. ²⁸ So when the Midyanim, merchants, passed by, they drew and lifted Yosef up out of the cistern and sold him for half a pound of silver *shekel*s to the Yishma'elim, who took Yosef on to Egypt.

²⁹ Re'uven returned to the cistern, and, upon seeing that Yosef wasn't in it, tore his clothes in mourning. ³⁰ He returned to his brothers and said, "The boy isn't there! Where can I go now?"

³¹ They took Yosef's robe, killed a male goat and dipped the robe in the blood. ³² Then they sent the long-sleeved robe and brought it to their father, saying, "We found this. Do you know if it's your son's robe or not?" ³³ He recognized it and cried, "It's my son's robe! Some wild animal has torn Yosef in pieces and eaten him!" ³⁴ Ya'akov tore his clothes and, putting sackcloth around his waist, mourned his son for many days. ³⁵ Though all his sons and daughters tried to comfort him, he refused all consolation, saying, "No, I will go down to the grave, to my son, mourning." And his father wept for him.

³⁶ In Egypt the Midyanim sold Yosef to Potifar, one of Pharaoh's officials, a captain of the guard.

38 *(iv)* ¹ It was at this time that Y'hudah went off from his brothers and settled near a man named Hirah who was an 'Adulami. ² There Y'hudah saw one of the daughters of a certain Kena'ani whose name was Shua, and he took her and slept with her. ³ She conceived and had a son, whom he named 'Er. ⁴ She conceived again and had a son, and she called him Onan. ⁵ Then she conceived yet again and had a son whom she called Shelah; he was in K'ziv when she gave birth to him.

⁶ Y'hudah took a wife for 'Er his firstborn, and her name was Tamar. ⁷ But 'Er, Y'hudah's firstborn, was evil from ADONAI's perspective, so ADONAI killed him. ⁸ Y'hudah said to Onan, "Go and sleep with your brother's wife — perform the duty of a husband's brother to her, and preserve your brother's line of descent." ⁹ However, Onan knew that the child would not count as his; so whenever he had intercourse with his brother's wife, he spilled the semen on the ground, so as not to give his brother offspring. ¹⁰ What he did was evil from ADONAI's perspective, so he killed him too.

¹¹ Then Y'hudah said to Tamar his daughter-in-law, "Stay a widow in your father's house until my son Shelah grows up"; for he thought, "I don't want him to die too, like his brothers." So Tamar went and lived at home with her father. ¹² In due time, Shua's daughter, the wife of Y'hudah, died. After Y'hudah had been comforted, he went up to be with his sheep-shearers in Timnah, he and his friend Hirah the 'Adulami. ¹³ Tamar was told, "Your father-in-law has gone up to Timnah to shear his sheep." ¹⁴ So she took off her widow's clothes, completely covered her face with her veil, and sat at the entrance to 'Einayim, which is on the way to Timnah. For she saw that Shelah had grown up, but she still was not being given to him as his wife. ¹⁵ When Y'hudah saw her, he thought she was a prostitute, because she had covered her face. ¹⁶ So he went over to her where she was sitting and said, not realizing that she was his daughter-in-law, "Come, let me sleep with you." She answered, "What will you pay to sleep with me?"

^{17} He said, "I will send you a kid from the flock of goats." She said, "Will you also give me something as a guarantee until you send it" ^{18} He answered, "What should I give you as a guarantee?" She said, "Your seal, with its cord, and the staff you're carrying in your hand." So he gave them to her, then went and slept with her; and she conceived by him. ^{19} She got up and went away, took off her veil and put on her widow's clothes.

^{20} Y'hudah sent the kid with his friend the 'Adulami to receive the guarantee items back from the woman, but he couldn't find her. ^{21} He asked the people near where she had been, "Where is the prostitute who was on the road at 'Einayim?" But they answered, "There hasn't been any prostitute here." ^{22} So he returned to Y'hudah and said, "I couldn't find her; also the people there said, 'There hasn't been any prostitute here.'" ^{23} Y'hudah said, "All right, let her keep the things, so that we won't be publicly shamed. I sent the kid, but you didn't find her."

^{24} About three months later Y'hudah was told, "Tamar your daughter-in-law has been acting like a whore; moreover, she is pregnant as a result of her prostitution." Y'hudah said, "Bring her out, and let her be burned alive!" ^{25} When she was brought out, she sent this message to her father-in-law: "I am pregnant by the man to whom these things belong. Determine, I beg you, whose these are — the signet, the cords and the staff." ^{26} Then Y'hudah acknowledged owning them. He said, "She is more righteous than I, because I didn't let her become the wife of my son Shelah." And he never slept with her again.

^{27} When she went into labor, it became evident that she was going to have twins. ^{28} As she was in labor, one of them put out his hand; and the midwife took his hand and tied a scarlet thread on it, saying, "This one came out first." ^{29} But then he withdrew his hand, and his brother came out; so she said, "How did you manage to break out first?" Therefore he was named Peretz [breaking out]. ^{30} Then out came his brother, with the scarlet thread on his hand, and he was given the name Zerach [scarlet].

39 *(v)* ^{1} Yosef was brought down to Egypt, and Potifar, an officer of Pharaoh's and captain of the guard, an Egyptian, bought him from the Yishma'elim who had brought him there. ^{2} ADONAI was with Yosef, and he became wealthy while he was in the household of his master the Egyptian. ^{3} His master saw how ADONAI was with him, that ADONAI prospered everything he did. ^{4} Yosef pleased him as he served him, and his master appointed him manager of his household; he entrusted all his possessions to Yosef. ^{5} From the time he appointed him manager of his household and all his possessions, ADONAI blessed the Egyptian's household for Yosef's sake; ADONAI's blessing was on all he owned, whether in the house or in the field. ^{6} So he left all his possessions in Yosef's care; and because he had him, he paid no attention to his affairs, except for the food he ate.

Now Yosef was well-built and handsome as well. *(vi)* ^{7} In time, the day came when his master's wife took a look at Yosef and said, "Sleep with me!" ^{8} But he refused, saying to his master's wife, "Look, because my master has me, he doesn't know what's going on in this house. He has put all his possessions in my charge. ^{9} In this house I am his equal; he hasn't withheld anything from me except yourself, because you are his wife. How then could I do such a wicked thing and sin against God?" ^{10} But she kept pressing him, day after day. Nevertheless, he didn't listen to her; he refused to sleep with her or even be with her.

¹¹ However, one day, when he went into the house to do his work, and none of the men living in the house was there indoors, ¹² she grabbed him by his robe and said, "Sleep with me!" But he fled, leaving his robe in her hand, and got himself outside. ¹³ When she saw that he had left his robe in her hand and had escaped, ¹⁴ she called the men of her house and said to them, "Look at this! My husband brought in a Hebrew to make fools of us. He came in and wanted to sleep with me, but I yelled out loudly. ¹⁵ When he heard me yelling like that, he left his robe with me and ran out." ¹⁶ She put the robe aside until his master came home. ¹⁷ Then she said to him, "This Hebrew slave you brought us came in to make a fool of me. ¹⁸ But when I yelled out, he left his robe with me and fled outside." ¹⁹ When his master heard what his wife said as she showed him, "Here's what your slave did to me," he became furious. ²⁰ Yosef's master took him and put him in prison, in the place where the king's prisoners were kept; and there he was in the prison.

²¹ But ADONAI was with Yosef, showing him grace and giving him favor in the sight of the prison warden. ²² The prison warden made Yosef supervisor of all the prisoners in the prison; so that whatever they did there, he was in charge of it. ²³ The prison warden paid no attention to anything Yosef did, because ADONAI was with him; and whatever he did, ADONAI prospered.

40 *(vii)* ¹ Some time later it came about that the Egyptian king's cupbearer and baker gave offense to their lord the king of Egypt. ² Pharaoh became angry with his two officers the chief cupbearer and the chief baker. ³ So he put them in custody in the house of the captain of the guard, in the prison, in the same place where Yosef was kept. ⁴ The captain of the guard charged Yosef to be with them, and he became their attendant while they remained in prison.

⁵ One night the two of them, the king of Egypt's cupbearer and his baker, there in prison, both had dreams, each dream with its own meaning. ⁶ Yosef came in to them in the morning and saw that they looked sad. ⁷ He asked Pharaoh's officers there with him in the prison of his master's house, "Why are you looking so sad today?" ⁸ They said to him, "We each had a dream, and there's no one around who can interpret it." Yosef said to them, "Don't interpretations belong to God? Tell it to me, please."

⁹ Then the chief cupbearer told Yosef his dream: "In my dream, there in front of me was a vine, ¹⁰ and the vine had three branches. The branches budded, then it suddenly began to blossom, and finally clusters of ripe grapes appeared. ¹¹ Pharaoh's cup was in my hand, so I took the grapes and pressed them into Pharaoh's cup, and gave the cup to Pharaoh." ¹² Yosef said to him, "Here is its interpretation: the three branches are three days. ¹³ Within three days Pharaoh will lift up your head and restore you to your office: you will be giving Pharaoh his cup as you used to when you were his cupbearer. ¹⁴ But remember me when it goes well with you; and show me kindness, please; and mention me to Pharaoh, so that he will release me from this prison. ¹⁵ For the truth is that I was kidnapped from the land of the Hebrews, and here too I have done nothing wrong that would justify putting me in this dungeon."

¹⁶ When the chief baker saw that the interpretation was favorable, he said to Yosef, "I too saw in my dream: there were three baskets of white bread on my head. ¹⁷ In the uppermost basket there were all kinds of baked goods for Pharaoh, but the

birds ate them out of the basket on my head." ¹⁸ Yosef answered, "Here is its interpretation: the three baskets are three days. ¹⁹ Within three days Pharaoh will lift up your head from off of you — he will hang you on a tree, and the birds will eat your flesh off you."

(Maftir) ²⁰ On the third day, which was Pharaoh's birthday, he gave a party for all his officials, and he lifted up the head of the chief cupbearer and the head of the chief baker among his officials. ²¹ He restored the chief cupbearer back to his position, so that he again gave Pharaoh his cup. ²² But he hanged the chief baker, as Yosef had interpreted to them. ²³ Nevertheless, the chief cupbearer didn't remember Yosef, but forgot him.

Haftarah Vayeshev: 'Amos (Amos) 2:6–3:8

B'rit Hadashah suggested reading for Parashah Vayeshev: Acts 7:9–16 (specifically vv. 9–10)

Parashah 10: Mikketz *(At the end) 41:1–44:17*

41 ¹ At the end of two years, Pharaoh had a dream: he was standing beside the Nile River; ² and there came up out of the river seven cows, sleek and fat; and they began feeding in swamp grass. ³ After them, there came up out of the river seven more cows, miserable-looking and lean; and they stood by the other cows at the edge of the river. ⁴ Then the miserable-looking and lean cows ate up the seven sleek, fat cows. At this point Pharaoh woke up. ⁵ But he went to sleep again and dreamt a second time: seven full, ripe ears of grain grew out of a single stalk. ⁶ After them, seven ears, thin and blasted by the east wind, sprang up. ⁷ And the thin ears swallowed up the seven full, ripe ears. Then Pharaoh woke up and realized it had been a dream.

⁸ In the morning he found himself so upset that he summoned all the magicians of Egypt and all its wise men. Pharaoh told them his dreams, but no one there could interpret them for him. ⁹ Then the chief cupbearer said to Pharaoh, "Today reminds me of something wherein I am at fault: ¹⁰ Pharaoh was angry with his officials and put me in the prison of the house of the captain of the guard, me and the chief baker. ¹¹ One night both I and he had dreams, and each man's dream had its own meaning. ¹² There was with us a young man, a Hebrew, a servant of the captain of the guard; and we told him our dreams, and he interpreted them for us — he interpreted each man's dream individually. ¹³ And it came about as he interpreted to us — I was restored to my office, and he was hanged."

¹⁴ Then Pharaoh summoned Yosef, and they brought him quickly out of the dungeon. He shaved himself, changed his clothes, and came in to Pharaoh. *(A: ii)* ¹⁵ Pharaoh said to Yosef, "I had a dream, and there is no one who can interpret it; but I've heard it said about you that when you hear a dream, you can interpret it." ¹⁶ Yosef answered Pharaoh, "It isn't in me. God will give Pharaoh an answer that will set his mind at peace." *(S: ii)* ¹⁷ Pharaoh said to Yosef, "In my dream, I stood at the edge of the river; ¹⁸ and there came up out of the river seven cows, fat and sleek; and they began feeding in the swamp grass. ¹⁹ After them, there came up out of the river seven more cows, poor, miserable-looking and lean — I've never seen such bad-looking cows in all the land of Egypt! ²⁰ Then the lean and miserable-

looking cows ate up the first seven fat cows. ²¹ But after they had eaten them up, one couldn't tell that they had eaten them; because they were as miserable-looking as before. At this point I woke up. ²² But I dreamed again and saw seven full, ripe ears of grain growing out of a single stalk. ²³ After them, seven ears, thin and blasted by the east wind, sprang up. ²⁴ And the thin ears swallowed up the seven ripe ears. I told this to the magicians, but none of them could explain it to me."

²⁵ Yosef said to Pharaoh, "The dreams of Pharaoh are the same: God has told Pharaoh what he is about to do. ²⁶ The seven good cows are seven years, and the seven good ears of grain are seven years — the dreams are the same. ²⁷ Likewise the seven lean and miserable-looking cows that came up after them are seven years, and also the seven empty ears blasted by the east wind — there will be seven years of famine. ²⁸ This is what I told Pharaoh: God has shown Pharaoh what he is about to do. ²⁹ Here it is: there will be seven years of abundance throughout the whole land of Egypt; ³⁰ but afterwards, there will come seven years of famine; and Egypt will forget all the abundance. The famine will consume the land, ³¹ and the abundance will not be known in the land because of the famine that will follow, because it will be truly terrible. ³² Why was the dream doubled for Pharaoh? Because the matter has been fixed by God, and God will shortly cause it to happen.

³³ "Therefore, Pharaoh should look for a man both discreet and wise to put in charge of the land of Egypt. ³⁴ Pharaoh should do this, and he should appoint supervisors over the land to receive a twenty percent tax on the produce of the land of Egypt during the seven years of abundance. ³⁵ They should gather all the food produced during these good years coming up and set aside grain under the supervision of Pharaoh to be used for food in the cities, and they should store it. ³⁶ This will be the land's food supply for the seven years of famine that will come over the land of Egypt, so that the land will not perish as a result of the famine."

³⁷ The proposal seemed good both to Pharaoh and to all his officials. ³⁸ Pharaoh said to his officials, "Can we find anyone else like him? The Spirit of God lives in him!" *(iii)* ³⁹ So Pharaoh said to Yosef, "Since God has shown you all this — there is no one as discerning and wise as you — ⁴⁰ you will be in charge of my household; all my people will be ruled by what you say. Only when I rule from my throne will I be greater than you." ⁴¹ Pharaoh said to Yosef, "Here, I place you in charge of the whole land of Egypt." ⁴² Pharaoh took his signet ring off his hand and put it on Yosef's hand, had him clothed in fine linen with a gold chain around his neck ⁴³ and had him ride in his second best chariot; and they cried before him, "Bow down!" Thus he placed him in charge of the whole land of Egypt. ⁴⁴ Pharaoh said to Yosef, "I, Pharaoh, decree that without your approval no one is to raise his hand or his foot in all the land of Egypt." ⁴⁵ Pharaoh called Yosef by the name Tzafnat-Pa'neach and gave him as his wife Osnat the daughter of Poti-Fera priest of On. Then Yosef went out through all the land of Egypt.

⁴⁶ Yosef was thirty years old when he stood before Pharaoh king of Egypt; then he left Pharaoh's presence and traveled through all the land of Egypt. ⁴⁷ During the seven years of abundance, the earth brought forth heaps of produce. ⁴⁸ He collected all the food of these seven years in the land of Egypt and stored it in the cities — the food grown in the fields outside each city he stored in that city. ⁴⁹ Yosef stored grain in quantities like the sand on the seashore, so much that they stopped counting, because it was beyond measure.

⁵⁰ Two sons were born to Yosef before the year of famine came; Osnat the daughter of Poti-Fera priest of On bore them to him. ⁵¹ Yosef called the firstborn M'nasheh [causing to forget], "Because God has caused me to forget all the troubles I suffered at the hands of my family." ⁵² The second he called Efrayim [fruit], "For God has made me fruitful in the land of my misfortune."

(iv) ⁵³ The seven years of abundance in the land of Egypt ended; ⁵⁴ and the seven years of famine began to come, just as Yosef had said. There was famine in all lands, but throughout the land of Egypt there was food. ⁵⁵ When the whole land of Egypt started feeling the famine, the people cried to Pharaoh for food, and Pharaoh said to all the Egyptians, "Go to Yosef, and do what he tells you to do." ⁵⁶ The famine was over all the earth, but then Yosef opened all the storehouses and sold food to the Egyptians, since the famine was severe in the land of Egypt. ⁵⁷ Moreover all countries came to Egypt to Yosef to buy grain, because the famine was severe throughout the earth.

42 ¹ Now Ya'akov saw that there was grain in Egypt; so Ya'akov said to his sons, "Why are you staring at each other? ² Look," he said, "I've heard that there's grain in Egypt. Go down there and buy some for us from there, so that we can stay alive and not die!" ³ Thus Yosef's ten brothers went down to buy grain from Egypt, ⁴ except for Binyamin, Yosef's brother. Ya'akov did not send him with his brothers, because he was afraid something might happen to him.

⁵ The sons of Isra'el came to buy along with the others that came, since the famine extended to the land of Kena'an. ⁶ Yosef was governor over the land; it was he who sold to all the people of the land. Now when Yosef's brothers came and prostrated themselves before him on the ground, ⁷ Yosef saw his brothers and recognized them; but he acted toward them as if he were a stranger and spoke harshly with them. He asked them, "Where are you from?" They answered, "From the land of Kena'an to buy food." ⁸ So Yosef recognized his brothers, but they didn't recognize him.

⁹ Remembering the dreams he had had about them, Yosef said to them, "You are spies! You've come to spot our country's weaknesses!" ¹⁰ "No, my lord," they replied, "your servants have come to buy food. ¹¹ We're all the sons of one man, we're upright men; your servants aren't spies." ¹² "No," he said to them, "you've come to spy out our country's weaknesses." ¹³ They said, "We, your servants, are twelve brothers, the sons of one man in the land of Kena'an; the youngest stayed with our father, and another one is gone." ¹⁴ "Just as I said," replied Yosef, "you're spies! ¹⁵ Here's how you can prove you're not lying: as Pharaoh lives, you will not leave here unless your youngest brother comes here. ¹⁶ Send one of you, and let him bring your brother. Meanwhile, you will be kept in custody. This will prove whether there is any truth in what you say. Otherwise, as Pharaoh lives, you are certainly spies." ¹⁷ Then he put all of them together in prison for three days.

¹⁸ On the third day, Yosef said to them, "Do what I say, and stay alive, for I fear God. *(v)* ¹⁹ If you are upright men, let one of your brothers remain incarcerated in the prison you're being kept in, while you go and carry grain back to relieve the famine in your homes. ²⁰ But bring your youngest brother to me. In this way your statements will be verified, and you won't die."

So they did it. ²¹ They said to each other, "We are in fact guilty concerning our brother. He was in distress and pleaded with us; we saw it and wouldn't listen. That's why this distress has come upon us now." ²² Re'uven answered them, "Didn't I tell you, 'Don't wrong the boy'? But you wouldn't hear of it. Now comes the reckoning for his blood!" ²³ They had no idea that Yosef understood them, since an interpreter was translating for them. ²⁴ Yosef turned away from them and wept; then he returned and spoke to them. He took Shim'on from among them and put him in prison before their eyes. ²⁵ Next he ordered that their containers be filled with grain, that every man's money be put back in his pack and that they be given provisions for the journey. When these things had been done for them, ²⁶ they loaded their grain on their donkeys and departed.

²⁷ But at camp that night, as one of them opened his pack to give fodder to his donkey, he noticed his money — there it was, just inside his pack. ²⁸ He said to his brothers, "My money has been restored — there it is, right in my pack!" At that, their hearts sank; they turned, trembling, to one another and said, "What is this that God has done to us?"

²⁹ They returned to Ya'akov their father in the land of Kena'an and told him all that had happened to them. ³⁰ "The man, the lord of the land, spoke harshly with us. He took us for spies in his country. ³¹ We said to him, 'We are upright men, we're not spies; ³² we are twelve brothers, sons of our father; one is gone, and the youngest stayed with our father in the land of Kena'an.' ³³ But the man, the lord of the land, said to us, 'Here is how I will know that you are upright men: leave one of your brothers with me, take grain to relieve the famine in your homes, and go on your way; ³⁴ but bring your youngest brother to me. By this I will know that you aren't spies, but are upright men; then I will return your brother to you; and you will do business in the land.'"

³⁵ Next, as they emptied their packs, there was each man's bag of money in his pack; and when they and their father saw their bags of money, they became afraid. ³⁶ Ya'akov their father said to them, "You have robbed me of my children! Yosef is gone, Shim'on is gone, now you're taking Binyamin away — it all falls on me!" ³⁷ Re'uven said to his father, "If I don't bring him back to you, you can kill my own two sons! Put him in my care; I will return him to you." ³⁸ But he replied, "My son will not go down with you. His brother is dead, and he alone is left. If anything were to happen to him while traveling with you, you would bring my gray hair down to Sh'ol with grief."

43 ¹ But the famine was severe in the land; ² so when they had eaten up the grain which they had brought out of Egypt, their father said to them, "Go again, buy us a little food." ³ Y'hudah said to him, "The man expressly warned us, 'You will not see my face unless your brother is with you.' ⁴ If you will send our brother with us, we will go down and buy you food; ⁵ but if you will not send him, we will not go down; for the man said to us, 'You will not see my face unless your brother is with you.'" ⁶ Isra'el said, "Why did you bring such trouble my way by telling the man you had another brother?" ⁷ They answered, "The man kept questioning us about ourselves and about our kinsmen. He asked, 'Is your father still alive?' 'Do you have another brother?' and we answered according to the literal meaning of his questions. How were we to know he would say, 'Bring your brother down'?"

[8] Y'hudah said to Isra'el his father, "Send the boy with me; and we will make preparations and leave; so that we may stay alive and not die, both we and you, and also our little ones. [9] I myself will guarantee his safety; you can hold me responsible. If I fail to bring him to you and present him to your face, let me bear the blame forever. [10] Except for our lengthy delay, we would have been there again by now."

[11] Their father Isra'el answered them, "If that's how it is, do this: take in your containers some of the land's best products, and bring the man a gift — some healing resin, a little honey, aromatic gum, opium, pistachio nuts and almonds. [12] Take twice the amount of money with you; and return the money that came back with you in your packs — it could have been an oversight. [13] Yes, and take your brother too; and get ready; and go again to the man. [14] May *El Shaddai* give you favor in the man's sight, so that he will release to you your other brother as well as Binyamin. As for me, if I must lose my children, lose them I will." [15] The men took that gift, and they took twice the money with them, and Binyamin; then they prepared, went down to Egypt and stood before Yosef.

(vi) [16] When Yosef saw Binyamin with them, he said to his household manager, "Take the men inside the house, kill the animals and prepare the meat. These men will dine with me at noon." [17] The man did as Yosef ordered and brought the men into Yosef's house.

[18] Upon being ushered inside Yosef's house, the men became fearful. They said, "It's because of the money that was returned in our packs the first time that we have been brought inside — so that he can use it as an excuse to attack us, take us as slaves and seize our donkeys too." [19] So they approached the manager of Yosef's household and spoke to him at the entrance of the house: [20] "Please, my lord, the first time we indeed came down to buy food; [21] but when we got to camp, we opened our packs, and there inside our packs was each man's money, the full amount. We have brought it back with us; [22] moreover, we have brought down other money to buy food. We have no idea who put our money in our packs." [23] "Stop worrying," he replied, "don't be afraid. Your God and the God of your father put treasure in your packs. As for your money — I was the one who received it." Then he brought Shim'on out to them.

[24] The man brought the men into Yosef's house and gave them water, and they washed their feet, and he provided fodder for their donkeys. [25] Then they got their gift ready for Yosef's arrival at noon, for they had heard that they were going to eat a meal there. [26] When Yosef arrived home, they went in the house and presented him with the gift they had brought with them, then prostrated themselves before him on the ground. [27] He asked them how they were and inquired, "Is your father well, the old man of whom you spoke? Is he still alive?" [28] They answered, "Your servant our father is well; yes, he is still alive," as they bowed in respect. [29] He looked up and saw Binyamin his brother, his mother's son, and said, "Is this your youngest brother, of whom you spoke to me?" and added, "May God be good to you, my son."

(vii) [30] Then Yosef hurried out, because his feelings toward his brother were so strong that he wanted to cry; he went into his bedroom and there he wept. [31] Then he washed his face and came out, but he controlled himself as he gave the order to serve the meal. [32] They served him by himself, the brothers by themselves, and the Egyptians included at the meal by themselves — Egyptians don't eat with Hebrews, because that is abhorrent to them. [33] So they sat there facing him, the firstborn in the place of honor,

the youngest in last place; and the men expressed their amazement to each other. ³⁴ Each was given his serving there in front of him, but Binyamin's portion was five times as large as any of theirs. So they drank and enjoyed themselves with him.

44 ¹ Then he ordered the manager of his household, "Fill the men's packs with food, as much as they can carry, and put each man's money just inside his pack. ² And put my goblet, the silver one, just inside the pack of the youngest, along with his grain money." He did what Yosef told him to do.

³ At daybreak the men were sent off with their donkeys; ⁴ but before they were far from the city Yosef said to his manager, "Up, go after the men; and when you overtake them, say to them, 'Why have you repaid good with evil? ⁵ Isn't this the goblet my lord drinks from, indeed the one he uses for divination? What you have done is evil!'" ⁶ So he caught up with them and said these words to them. ⁷ They replied, "Why does my lord speak this way? Heaven forbid that we should do such a thing! ⁸ Why, the money we found inside our packs we brought back to you from the land of Kena'an! So how would we steal silver or gold from your lord's house? ⁹ Whichever one of us the goblet is found with, let him be put to death — and the rest of us will be my lord's slaves!" ¹⁰ He replied, "Fine; let it be as you have said: whichever one it is found with will be my slave. But the rest of you will be blameless." ¹¹ Then each hurried to put his pack down on the ground, and each one opened his pack. ¹² He searched, starting with the oldest and ending with the youngest; and the goblet was found in the pack belonging to Binyamin. ¹³ At this, they tore their clothes from grief. Then each man loaded up his donkey and returned to the city.

(A: Maftir) ¹⁴ Y'hudah and his brothers arrived at Yosef's house. He was still there, and they fell down before him on the ground. *(S: Maftir)* ¹⁵ Yosef said to them, "How could you do such a thing? Don't you know that a man such as myself can learn the truth by divination?" ¹⁶ Y'hudah said, "There's nothing we can say to my lord! How can we speak? There's no way we can clear ourselves! God has revealed your servants' guilt; so here we are, my lord's slaves — both we and also the one in whose possession the cup was found." ¹⁷ But he replied, "Heaven forbid that I should act in such a way. The man in whose possession the goblet was found will be my slave; but as for you, go in peace to your father."

Haftarah Mikketz: M'lakhim Alef (1 Kings) 3:15–4:1

B'rit Hadashah suggested reading for Parashah Mikketz: Acts 7:9–16 (specifically vv. 11–12)

Parashah 11: Vayigash (He approached) 44:18–47:27

¹⁸ Then Y'hudah approached Yosef and said, "Please, my lord! Let your servant say something to you privately; and don't be angry with your servant, for you are like Pharaoh himself. ¹⁹ My lord asked his servants, 'Do you have a father? or a brother?' ²⁰ We answered my lord, 'We have a father who is an old man, and a child of his old age, a little one whose brother is dead; so that of his mother's children he alone is left; and his father loves him.' ²¹ But you said to your servants, 'Bring him down to

me, so that I can see him.' ²² We answered my lord, 'The boy can't leave his father; if he were to leave his father, his father would die.' ²³ You said to your servants, 'You will not see my face again unless your brother is with you.' ²⁴ We went up to your servant my father and told him what my lord had said; ²⁵ but when our father said, 'Go again, and buy us some food,' ²⁶ we answered, 'We can't go down. Only if our youngest brother is with us will we go down, because we can't see the man's face unless our youngest brother is with us.' ²⁷ Then your servant my father said to us, 'You know that my wife bore me two sons: ²⁸ the one went out from me, and I said, "Surely he has been torn to pieces," and I haven't seen him since. ²⁹ Now if you take this one away from me too, and something happens to him, you will bring my gray hair down to Sh'ol with grief.' ³⁰ So now if I go to your servant my father, and the boy isn't with us — seeing how his heart is bound up with the boy's heart — *(ii)* ³¹ when he sees that the boy isn't with us, he will die; and your servants will bring the gray hair of your servant our father down to Sh'ol with grief. ³² For your servant himself guaranteed his safety; I said, 'If I fail to bring him to you, then I will bear the blame before my father forever.' ³³ Therefore, I beg you, let your servant stay as a slave to my lord instead of the boy, and let the boy go up with his brothers. ³⁴ For how can I go up to my father if the boy isn't with me? I couldn't bear to see my father so overwhelmed by anguish."

45 ¹ At last Yosef could no longer control his feelings in front of his attendants and cried, "Get everybody away from me!" So no one else was with him when Yosef revealed to his brothers who he was. ² He wept aloud, and the Egyptians heard, and Pharaoh's household heard. ³ Yosef said to his brothers, "I am Yosef! Is it true that my father is still alive?" His brothers couldn't answer him, they were so dumbfounded at seeing him. ⁴ Yosef said to his brothers, "Please! Come closer." And they came closer. He said, "I am Yosef, your brother, whom you sold into Egypt. ⁵ But don't be sad that you sold me into slavery here or angry at yourselves, because it was God who sent me ahead of you to preserve life. ⁶ The famine has been over the land for the last two years, and for yet another five years there will be neither plowing nor harvest. ⁷ God sent me ahead of you to ensure that you will have descendants on earth and to save your lives in a great deliverance. *(iii)* ⁸ So it was not you who sent me here, but God; and he has made me a father to Pharaoh, lord of all his household and ruler over the whole land of Egypt. ⁹ Hurry, go up to my father, and tell him, 'Here is what your son Yosef says: "God has made me lord of all Egypt! Come down to me, don't delay! ¹⁰ You will live in the land of Goshen and be near me — you, your children, your grandchildren, flocks, herds, everything you own. ¹¹ I will provide for you there, so that you won't become poverty-stricken, you, your household and all that you have; because five years of famine are yet to come."' ¹² Here! Your own eyes see, and the eyes of my brother Binyamin, that it is my own mouth speaking to you. ¹³ Tell my father how honored I am in Egypt and everything you have seen, and quickly bring my father down here!" ¹⁴ Then he embraced his brother Binyamin and wept, and Binyamin wept on his neck, ¹⁵ and he kissed all his brothers and wept on them. After that, his brothers talked with him.

¹⁶ The report of this reached Pharaoh's house: "Yosef's brothers have come"; and Pharaoh and his servants were pleased. ¹⁷ Pharaoh said to Yosef, "Tell your

brothers, 'Here is what you are to do. Load up your animals, go to the land of Kena'an, ¹⁸ take your father and your families, and come back to me. I will give you good property in Egypt, and you will eat the fat of the land.

(iv) ¹⁹ "'Moreover— and this is an order— do this: take wagons from the land of Egypt to carry your little ones and your wives, and bring your father, and come. ²⁰ Don't worry about your stuff, because everything good in the land of Egypt is yours.'"

²¹ The sons of Isra'el acted accordingly; and Yosef gave them wagons, as Pharaoh had ordered, and gave them provisions for their journey. ²² To each of them he gave a set of new clothes; but to Binyamin he gave seven-and-a-half pounds of silver and five sets of new clothes. ²³ Likewise, to his father he sent ten donkeys loaded with the finest goods Egypt produced, as well as ten female donkeys loaded with grain, bread and food for his father to eat on the return journey. ²⁴ Thus he sent his brothers on their way, and they left; he said to them, "Don't quarrel among yourselves while you're traveling!"

²⁵ So they went up out of Egypt, entered the land of Kena'an and came to Ya'akov their father. ²⁶ They told him, "Yosef is still alive! He is ruler over the whole land of Egypt!" He was stunned at the news; he couldn't believe them. ²⁷ So they reported to him everything Yosef had said to them; but it was only when he saw the wagons which Yosef had sent to carry him that the spirit of Ya'akov their father began to revive. *(v)* ²⁸ Isra'el said, "Enough! My son Yosef is still alive! I must go and see him before I die."

46 ¹ Isra'el took everything he owned with him on his journey. He arrived at Be'er-Sheva and offered sacrifices to the God of his father Yitz'chak. ² In a vision at night God called to Isra'el, "Ya'akov! Ya'akov!" He answered, "Here I am." ³ He said, "I am God, the God of your father. Don't be afraid to go down to Egypt. It is there that I will make you into a great nation. ⁴ Not only will I go down with you to Egypt; but I will also bring you back here again, after Yosef has closed your eyes."

⁵ So Ya'akov left Be'er-Sheva; the sons of Isra'el brought Ya'akov their father, their little ones and their wives in the wagons Pharaoh had sent to carry them. ⁶ They took their cattle and their possessions which they had acquired in the land of Kena'an and arrived in Egypt, Ya'akov and all his descendants with him — ⁷ his sons, grandsons, daughters, granddaughters and all his descendants he brought with him into Egypt.

⁸ These are the names of Isra'el's children who came into Egypt, Ya'akov and his sons: Re'uven Ya'akov's firstborn; ⁹ and the sons of Re'uven — Hanokh, Pallu, Hetzron and Karmi.

¹⁰ The sons of Shim'on: Y'mu'el, Yamin, Ohad, Yakhin, Tzochar and Sha'ul the son of a Kena'ani woman.

¹¹ The sons of Levi: Gershon, K'hat and M'rari.

¹² The sons of Y'hudah: 'Er, Onan, Shelah, Peretz and Zerach; but 'Er and Onan died in the land of Kena'an. The sons of Peretz were Hetzron and Hamul.

¹³ The sons of Yissakhar: Tola, Puvah, Yov and Shimron.

¹⁴ The sons of Z'vulun: Sered, Elon and Yachle'el.

¹⁵ These were the children of Le'ah whom she bore to Ya'akov in Paddan-Aram, with his daughter Dinah. In sum, his sons and daughters numbered thirty-three.

^{16} The sons of Gad: Tzifyon, Haggi, Shuni, Etzbon, 'Eri, Arodi and Ar'eli.

^{17} The children of Asher: Yimnah, Yishvah, Yishvi, B'ri'ah, and their sister Serach. The sons of B'ri'ah were Hever and Malki'el.

^{18} These were the children of Zilpah, whom Lavan gave to Le'ah his daughter; she bore them to Ya'akov — sixteen people.

^{19} The sons of Rachel Ya'akov's wife: Yosef and Binyamin.

^{20} To Yosef in the land of Egypt were born M'nasheh and Efrayim, whom Osnat the daughter of Poti-Fera priest of On bore to him.

^{21} The sons of Binyamin: Bela, Bekher, Ashbel, Gera, Na'aman, Echi, Rosh, Mupim, Hupim and Ard.

^{22} These were the children of Rachel who were born to Ya'akov — in sum, fourteen people.

^{23} The sons of Dan: Hushim.

^{24} The sons of Naftali: Yachtze'el, Guni, Yetzer and Shillem.

^{25} These were the sons of Bilhah, whom Lavan gave to Rachel his daughter; she bore them to Ya'akov — in sum, seven people.

^{26} All the people belonging to Ya'akov coming into Egypt, his direct descendants (not counting Ya'akov's sons' wives), totaled sixty-six. ^{27} The sons of Yosef, born to him in Egypt, were two in number. Thus all the people in Ya'akov's family who entered Egypt numbered seventy.

(vi) ^{28} Ya'akov sent Y'hudah ahead of him to Yosef, so that the latter might guide him on the road to Goshen; thus they arrived in the land of Goshen. ^{29} Yosef prepared his chariot and went up to Goshen to meet Isra'el his father. He presented himself to him, embraced him and wept on his neck for a long time. ^{30} Then Isra'el said to Yosef, "Now I can die, because I have seen your face and seen that you are still alive."

^{31} Yosef said to his brothers and his father's family, "I'm going up to tell Pharaoh. I'll say to him, 'My brothers and my father's family, who were in the land of Kena'an, have come to me. ^{32} The men are shepherds and keepers of livestock; they have brought their flocks, their herds and all their possessions.' ^{33} Now when Pharaoh summons you and asks, 'What is your occupation?' ^{34} tell him, 'Your servants have been keepers of livestock from our youth until now, both we and our ancestors.' This will ensure that you will live in the land of Goshen — for any shepherd is abhorrent to the Egyptians."

47 ^{1} Then Yosef went in and told Pharaoh, "My father and brothers have come from the land of Kena'an with their flocks, livestock and all their possessions; right now they are in the land of Goshen." ^{2} He took five of his brothers and presented them to Pharaoh. ^{3} Pharaoh said to his brothers, "What is your occupation?" They answered Pharaoh, "Your servants are shepherds, both we and our ancestors," ^{4} and added, "We have come to live in the land, because in the land of Kena'an there is no place to pasture your servant's flocks, the famine is so severe there. Therefore, please, let your servants live in the land of Goshen." ^{5} Pharaoh said to Yosef, "Your father and brothers have come to you, ^{6} and the land of Egypt lies before you. Have your father and brothers live on the best property in the country — let them live in the land of Goshen. Moreover, if you know that some of them are particularly competent, put them in charge of my livestock."

^{7} Yosef then brought in Ya'akov his father and presented him to Pharaoh, and Ya'akov blessed Pharaoh. ^{8} Pharaoh asked Ya'akov, "How old are you?" ^{9} and Ya'akov replied, "The time of my stay on earth has been 130 years; they have been few and difficult, fewer than the years my ancestors lived." [10] Then Ya'akov blessed Pharaoh and left his presence.

(vii) [11] Yosef found a place for his father and brothers and gave them property in the land of Egypt, in the best region of the country, in the land of Ra'amses, as Pharaoh had ordered. [12] Yosef provided food for his father, his brothers and all his father's household, taking full care of even the youngest.

[13] There was no food anywhere, for the famine was very severe, so that both Egypt and Kena'an grew weak from hunger. [14] Yosef collected all the money there was in Egypt and Kena'an in exchange for the grain they bought, and put the money in Pharaoh's treasury. [15] When all the money in Egypt had been spent, and likewise in Kena'an, all the Egyptians approached Yosef and said, "Give us something to eat, even though we have no money; why should we die before your eyes?" [16] Yosef replied, "Give me your livestock. If you don't have money, I will give you food in exchange for your livestock." [17] So they brought Yosef their livestock; and Yosef gave them food in exchange for the horses, flocks, cattle and donkeys — all that year he provided them with food in exchange for all their livestock.

[18] When that year was over, they approached Yosef again and said to him, "We won't hide from my lord that all our money is spent, and the herds of livestock belong to my lord. We have nothing left, as my lord can see, but our bodies and our land. [19] Why should we die before your eyes, both we and our land? Buy us and our land for food, and we and our land will be enslaved to Pharaoh. But also give us seed to plant, so that we can stay alive and not die, and so that the land won't become barren." [20] So Yosef acquired all the land in Egypt for Pharaoh, as one by one the Egyptians sold their fields, because the famine weighed on them so severely. Thus the land became the property of Pharaoh. [21] As for the people, he reduced them to serfdom city by city, from one end of Egypt's territory to the other. [22] Only the priests' land did he not acquire, because the priests were entitled to provisions from Pharaoh, and they ate from what Pharaoh provided them; therefore they did not sell their land.

[23] Then Yosef said to the people, "As of today I have acquired you and your land for Pharaoh. Here is seed for you to sow the land. [24] When harvest time comes, you are to give twenty percent to Pharaoh; eighty percent will be yours to keep for seed to plant in the fields, as well as for your food and for that of your households and your little ones."

(Maftir) [25] They replied, "You have saved our lives! So if it pleases my lord, we will be Pharaoh's slaves." [26] Yosef made it a law for the country of Egypt, valid to this day, that Pharaoh should have twenty percent. Only the property belonging to the priests did not become Pharaoh's.

[27] Isra'el lived in the land of Egypt seventeen years. They acquired possessions in it and were productive, and their numbers multiplied greatly.

Haftarah Vayigash: Yechezk'el (Ezekiel) 37:15–28

B'rit Hadashah suggested reading for Parashah Vayigash: Acts 7:9–16 (specifically vv. 13–15)

Parashah 12: Vayechi (He lived) 47:28–50:26

²⁸ Ya'akov lived in the land of Egypt seventeen years; thus Ya'akov lived to be 147 years old. ²⁹ The time came when Isra'el was approaching death; so he called for his son Yosef and said to him, "If you truly love me, please put your hand under my thigh and pledge that, out of consideration for me, you will not bury me in Egypt. ³⁰ Rather, when I sleep with my fathers, you are to carry me out of Egypt and bury me where they are buried." He replied, "I will do as you have said." ³¹ He said, "Swear it to me," and he swore to him. Then Isra'el bowed down at the head of his bed.

48 ¹ Awhile later someone told Yosef that his father was ill. He took with him his two sons, M'nasheh and Efrayim. ² Ya'akov was told, "Here comes your son Yosef." Isra'el gathered his strength and sat up in bed. ³ Ya'akov said to Yosef, "*El Shaddai* appeared to me at Luz in the land of Kena'an and blessed me, ⁴ saying to me, 'I will make you fruitful and numerous. I will make of you a group of peoples; and I will give this land to your descendants to possess forever.' ⁵ Now your two sons, who were born to you in the land of Egypt before I came to you in Egypt, are mine; Efrayim and M'nasheh will be as much mine as Re'uven and Shim'on are. ⁶ The children born to you after them will be yours, but for purposes of inheritance they are to be counted with their older brothers.

⁷ "Now as for me, when I came from Paddan, Rachel died suddenly, as we were traveling through the land of Kena'an, while we were still some distance from Efrat; so I buried her there on the way to Efrat (also known as Beit-Lechem)."

⁸ Then Isra'el noticed Yosef's sons and asked, "Whose are these?" ⁹ Yosef answered his father, "They are my sons, whom God has given me here." Ya'akov replied, "I want you to bring them here to me, so that I can bless them." *(ii)* ¹⁰ Now Isra'el's eyes were dim with age, so that he could not see. Yosef brought his sons near to him, and he kissed them and embraced them. ¹¹ Isra'el said to Yosef, "I never expected to see even you again, but God has allowed me to see your children too!" ¹² Yosef brought them out from between his legs and prostrated himself on the ground. ¹³ Then Yosef took them both, Efrayim in his right hand toward Isra'el's left hand and M'nasheh in his left hand toward Isra'el's right hand, and brought them near to him. ¹⁴ But Isra'el put out his right hand and laid it on the head of the younger one, Efrayim, and put his left hand on the head of M'nasheh — he intentionally crossed his hands, even though M'nasheh was the firstborn. ¹⁵ Then he blessed Yosef: "The God in whose presence my fathers Avraham and Yitz'chak lived, the God who has been my own shepherd all my life long to this day, ¹⁶ the angel who has rescued me from all harm, bless these boys. May they remember who I am and what I stand for, and likewise my fathers Avraham and Yitz'chak, who they were and what they stood for. And may they grow into teeming multitudes on the earth."

(iii) ¹⁷ When Yosef saw that his father was laying his right hand on Efrayim's head, it displeased him, and he lifted up his father's hand to remove it from Efrayim's head and place it instead on M'nasheh's head. ¹⁸ Yosef said to his father, "Don't do it that way, my father; for this one is the firstborn. Put your right hand on his head." ¹⁹ But his father refused and said, "I know that, my son, I know it. He too will become a people, and he too will be great; nevertheless his younger brother will be greater than he, and his descendants will grow into many nations." ²⁰ Then he added this blessing on them

that day: "Isra'el will speak of you in their own blessings by saying, 'May God make you like Efrayim and M'nasheh.'" Thus he put Efrayim ahead of M'nasheh.

²¹ Isra'el then said to Yosef, "You see that I am dying, but God will be with you and will bring you back to the land of your ancestors. ²² Moreover, I am giving to you a *sh'khem* [shoulder, ridge, share, city of Sh'khem] more than to your brothers; I captured it from the Emori with my sword and bow."

49 *(iv)* ¹ Then Ya'akov called for his sons and said,

> "Gather yourselves together, and I will tell you
> what will happen to you in the *acharit-hayamim*.

² Assemble yourselves and listen, sons of Ya'akov;
pay attention to Isra'el your father.

³ "Re'uven, you are my firstborn,
my strength, the firstfruits of my manhood.

⁴ Though superior in vigor and power
you are unstable as water, so your superiority will end,
because you climbed into your father's bed
and defiled it — he climbed onto my concubine's couch!

⁵ "Shim'on and Levi are brothers,
related by weapons of violence.

⁶ Let me not enter their council,
let my honor not be connected with their people;
for in their anger they killed men,
and at their whim they maimed cattle.

⁷ Cursed be their anger, for it has been fierce;
their fury, for it has been cruel.
I will divide them in Ya'akov
and scatter them in Isra'el.

⁸ "Y'hudah, your brothers will acknowledge you,
your hand will be on the neck of your enemies,
your father's sons will bow down before you.

⁹ Y'hudah is a lion's cub;
my son, you stand over the prey.
He crouches down and stretches like a lion;
like a lioness, who dares to provoke him?

¹⁰ The scepter will not pass from Y'hudah,
nor the ruler's staff from between his legs,
until he comes to whom [obedience] belongs; *
and it is he whom the peoples will obey.

¹¹ Tying his donkey to the vine,

---

* or: until Shiloh comes

his donkey's colt to the choice grapevine,
he washes his clothes in wine,
his robes in the blood of grapes.

12 His eyes will be darker than wine,
his teeth whiter than milk.

13 "Z'vulun will live at the seashore,
with ships anchoring along his coast
and his border at Tzidon.

14 "Yissakhar is a strong donkey
lying down in the sheep sheds.

15 On seeing how good is settled life
and how pleasant the country,
he will bend his back to the burden,
and submit to forced labor.

16 "Dan will judge his people
as one of the tribes of Isra'el.

17 Dan will be a viper on the road,
a horned snake in the path
that bites the horse's heels
so its rider falls off backward.

18 I wait for your deliverance, ADONAI.

(v) 19 "Gad [troop]— a troop will troop on him,
but he will troop on their heel.

20 "Asher's food is rich —
he will provide food fit for a king.

21 "Naftali is a doe set free
that bears beautiful fawns. *

22 "Yosef is a fruitful plant,
a fruitful plant by a spring,
with branches climbing over the wall.

23 The archers attacked him fiercely,
shooting at him and pressing him hard;

24 but his bow remained taut;
and his arms were made nimble
by the hands of the Mighty One of Ya'akov,
from there, from the Shepherd, the Stone of Isra'el,

25 by the God of your father, who will help you,
by El Shaddai, who will bless you
with blessings from heaven above,

---

* or: that says beautiful words.

blessings from the deep, lying below,
blessings from the breasts and the womb.
²⁶ The blessings of your father are more powerful
than the blessings of my parents,
extending to the farthest of the everlasting hills;
they will be on the head of Yosef,
on the brow of the prince among his brothers.

(vi) ²⁷ "Binyamin is a ravenous wolf,
in the morning devouring the prey,
in the evening still dividing the spoil."

²⁸ All these are the twelve tribes of Isra'el, and this is how their father spoke to them and blessed them, giving each his own individual blessing.

²⁹ Then he charged them as follows: "I am to be gathered to my people. Bury me with my ancestors in the cave that is in the field of 'Efron the Hitti, ³⁰ the cave in the field of Makhpelah, by Mamre, in the land of Kena'an, which Avraham bought together with the field from 'Efron the Hitti as a burial-place belonging to him — ³¹ there they buried Avraham and his wife Sarah, there they buried Yitz'chak and his wife Rivkah, and there I buried Le'ah — ³² the field and the cave in it, which was purchased from the sons of Het."

³³ When Ya'akov had finished charging his sons, he drew his legs up into the bed, breathed his last and was gathered to his people.

50 ¹ Yosef fell on his father's face, wept over him and kissed him. ² Then Yosef ordered the physicians in his service to embalm his father. So the physicians embalmed Isra'el. ³ Forty days were spent at this, the normal amount of time for embalming. Then the Egyptians mourned for him seventy days.

⁴ When the period of mourning was over, Yosef addressed to the household of Pharaoh: "I would like to ask a favor. Tell Pharaoh, ⁵ 'My father had me swear an oath. He said, "I am going to die. You are to bury me in my grave, which I dug for myself in the land of Kena'an." Therefore, I beg you, let me go up and bury my father; I will return.'" ⁶ Pharaoh responded, "Go up and bury your father, as he made you swear."

⁷ So Yosef went up to bury his father. With him went all Pharaoh's servants, the leaders of his household and the leaders of the land of Egypt, ⁸ along with the entire household of Yosef, his brothers and his father's household; only their little ones, their flocks and their cattle did they leave in the land of Goshen. ⁹ Moreover, there went up with him both chariots and horsemen — it was a very large caravan.

¹⁰ When they arrived at the threshing-floor in Atad, beyond the Yarden, they raised a loud and bitter lamentation, mourning for his father seven days. ¹¹ When the local inhabitants, the Kena'ani, saw the mourning on the floor of Atad they said, "How bitterly the Egyptians are mourning!" This is why the place was given the name Avel-Mitzrayim [mourning of Egypt], there beyond the Yarden.

¹² His sons did to him as he had ordered them to do — ¹³ they carried him into the land of Kena'an and buried him in the cave in the field of Makhpelah, which Avraham had bought, along with the field, as a burial-place belonging to him, from 'Efron the Hitti, by Mamre.

[14] Then, after burying his father, Yosef returned to Egypt, he, his brothers and all who had gone up with him to bury his father. [15] Realizing that their father was dead, Yosef's brothers said, "Yosef may hate us now and pay us back in full for all the suffering we caused him." [16] So they sent a message to Yosef which said, "Your father gave this order before he died: [17] 'Say to Yosef, "I beg you now, please forgive your brothers' crime and wickedness in doing you harm."' So now, we beg of you, forgive the crime of the servants of the God of your father." Yosef wept when they spoke to him; [18] and his brothers too came, prostrated themselves before him and said, "Here, we are your slaves." [19] But Yosef said to them, "Don't be afraid! Am I in the place of God? [20] You meant to do me harm, but God meant it for good — so that it would come about as it is today, with many people's lives being saved. *(vii)* [21] So don't be afraid — I will provide for you and your little ones." In this way he comforted them, speaking kindly to them.

[22] Yosef continued living in Egypt, he and his father's household. Yosef lived 110 years. *(Maftir)* [23] Yosef lived to see Efrayim's great-grandchildren, and the children of M'nasheh's son Makhir were born on Yosef's knees.

[24] Yosef said to his brothers, "I am dying. But God will surely remember you and bring you up out of this land to the land which he swore to Avraham, Yitz'chak and Ya'akov." [25] Then Yosef took an oath from the sons of Isra'el: "God will surely remember you, and you are to carry my bones up from here." [26] So Yosef died at the age of 110, and they embalmed him and put him in a coffin in Egypt.

Haftarah Vayechi: M'lakhim Alef (1 Kings) 2:1–12

B'rit Hadashah suggested readings for Parashah Vayechi: Acts 7:9–16 (specifically vv. 15–16); Messianic Jews (Hebrews) 11:21–22; 1 Kefa (1 Peter) 1:3–9; 2:11–17

Hazak, hazak, v'nit'chazek!
Be strong, be strong, and let us be strengthened!

Sh'mot
EXODUS

Parashah 13: Sh'mot (Names) 1:1– 6:1

1 ¹ These are the names of the sons of Isra'el who came into Egypt with Ya'akov; each man came with his household: ² Re'uven, Shim'on, Levi, Y'hudah, ³ Yissakhar, Z'vulun, Binyamin, ⁴ Dan, Naftali, Gad and Asher. ⁵ All told, there were seventy descendants of Ya'akov; Yosef was already in Egypt.

⁶ Yosef died, as did all his brothers and all that generation. ⁷ The descendants of Isra'el were fruitful, increased abundantly, multiplied and grew very powerful; the land became filled with them.

⁸ Now there arose a new king over Egypt. He knew nothing about Yosef ⁹ but said to his people, "Look, the descendants of Isra'el have become a people too numerous and powerful for us. ¹⁰ Come, let's use wisdom in dealing with them. Otherwise, they'll continue to multiply; and in the event of war they might ally themselves with our enemies, fight against us and leave the land altogether."

¹¹ So they put slavemasters over them to oppress them with forced labor, and they built for Pharaoh the storage cities of Pitom and Ra'amses. ¹² But the more the Egyptians oppressed them, the more they multiplied and expanded, until the Egyptians came to dread the people of Isra'el ¹³ and worked them relentlessly, ¹⁴ making their lives bitter with hard labor — digging clay, making bricks, all kinds of field work; and in all this toil they were shown no mercy.

¹⁵ Moreover, the king of Egypt spoke to the Hebrew midwives, one of whom was called Shifrah and the other Pu'ah. ¹⁶ "When you attend the Hebrew women and see them giving birth," he said, "if it's a boy, kill him; but if it's a girl, let her live." ¹⁷ However, the midwives were God-fearing women, so they didn't do as the king of Egypt ordered but let the boys live. *(ii)* ¹⁸ The king of Egypt summoned the midwives and demanded of them, "Why have you done this and let the boys live?" ¹⁹ The midwives answered Pharaoh, "It's because the Hebrew women aren't like the Egyptian women — they go into labor and give birth before the midwife arrives." ²⁰ Therefore God prospered the midwives, and the people continued to multiply and grow very powerful. ²¹ Indeed, because the midwives feared God, he made them founders of families. ²² Then Pharaoh gave this order to all his people: "Every boy that is born, throw in the river; but let all the girls live."

2 ¹ A man from the family of Levi took a woman also descended from Levi as his wife. ² When she conceived and had a son, upon seeing what a fine child he was, she hid him for three months. ³ When she could no longer hide him, she took a papyrus basket, coated it with clay and tar, put the child in it and placed it among the reeds on the riverbank. ⁴ His sister stood at a distance to see what would happen to him.

⁵ The daughter of Pharaoh came down to bathe in the river while her maids-in-attendance walked along the riverside. Spotting the basket among the reeds, she sent her slave-girl to get it. ⁶ She opened it and looked inside, and there in front of her was a crying baby boy! Moved with pity, she said, "This must be one of the Hebrews' children." ⁷ At this point, his sister said to Pharaoh's daughter, "Would you like me to go and find you one of the Hebrew women to nurse the baby for you?" ⁸ Pharaoh's daughter answered, "Yes, go." So the girl went and called the baby's own mother. ⁹ Pharaoh's daughter told her, "Take this child away, and nurse it for me, and I will pay you for doing it." So the woman took the child and nursed it. ¹⁰ Then, when the child had grown some, she brought him to Pharaoh's daughter; and she began to raise him as her son. She called him Moshe [pull out], explaining, "Because I pulled him out of the water."

(iii) ¹¹ One day, when Moshe was a grown man, he went out to visit his kinsmen; and he watched them struggling at forced labor. He saw an Egyptian strike a Hebrew, one of his kinsmen. ¹² He looked this way and that; and when he saw that no one was around, he killed the Egyptian and hid his body in the sand. ¹³ The next day, he went out and saw two Hebrew men fighting with each other. To the one in the wrong he said, "Why are you hitting your companion?" ¹⁴ He retorted, "Who appointed you ruler and judge over us? Do you intend to kill me the way you killed the Egyptian?" Moshe became frightened. "Clearly," he thought, "the matter has become known." ¹⁵ When Pharaoh heard of it, he tried to have Moshe put to death. But Moshe fled from Pharaoh to live in the land of Midyan.

One day, as he was sitting by a well, ¹⁶ the seven daughters of the priest of Midyan came to draw water. They had filled the troughs to water their father's sheep, ¹⁷ when the shepherds came and tried to drive them away. But Moshe got up and defended them; then he watered their sheep. ¹⁸ When they came to Re'u'el their father, he said, "How come you're back so soon today?" ¹⁹ They answered, "An Egyptian rescued us from the shepherds; more than that, he drew water for us and watered the sheep." ²⁰ He asked his daughters, "Where is he? Why did you leave the man there? Invite him to have something to eat."

²¹ Moshe was glad to stay on with the man, and he gave Moshe his daughter Tzipporah in marriage. ²² She gave birth to a son, and he named him Gershom [foreigner there], for he said, "I have been a foreigner in a foreign land."

²³ Sometime during those many years the king of Egypt died, but the people of Isra'el still groaned under the yoke of slavery, and they cried out, and their cry for rescue from slavery came up to God. ²⁴ God heard their groaning, and God remembered his covenant with Avraham, Yitz'chak and Ya'akov. ²⁵ God saw the people of Isra'el, and God acknowledged them.

3 (iv) ¹ Now Moshe was tending the sheep of Yitro his father-in-law, the priest of Midyan. Leading the flock to the far side of the desert, he came to the mountain of God, to Horev. ² The angel of ADONAI appeared to him in a fire blazing from the middle of a bush. He looked and saw that although the bush was flaming with fire, yet the bush was not being burned up. ³ Moshe said, "I'm going to go over and see this amazing sight and find out why the bush isn't being burned up." ⁴When *ADONAI* saw that he had gone over to see, God called to him from the middle of the bush, "Moshe! Moshe!" He answered, "Here I am." ⁵He said, "Don't come any closer! Take your sandals off your feet, because the place where you are standing is holy ground. ⁶I am the God of your father," he continued, "the God of Avraham, the God of Yitz'chak and the God of Ya'akov." Moshe covered his face, because he was afraid to look at God. ⁷*ADONAI* said, "I have seen how my people are being oppressed in Egypt and heard their cry for release from their slavemasters, because I know their pain. ⁸I have come down to rescue them from the Egyptians and to bring them up out of that country to a good and spacious land, a land flowing with milk and honey, the place of the Kena'ani, Hitti, Emori, P'rizi, Hivi and Y'vusi. ⁹Yes, the cry of the people of Isra'el has come to me, and I have seen how terribly the Egyptians oppress them. ¹⁰Therefore, now, come; and I will send you to Pharaoh; so that you can lead my people, the descendants of Isra'el, out of Egypt."

¹¹Moshe said to God, "Who am I, that I should go to Pharaoh and lead the people of Isra'el out of Egypt?" ¹²He replied, "I will surely be with you. Your sign that I have sent you will be that when you have led the people out of Egypt, you will worship God on this mountain."

¹³Moshe said to God, "Look, when I appear before the people of Isra'el and say to them, 'The God of your ancestors has sent me to you'; and they ask me, 'What is his name?' what am I to tell them?" ¹⁴God said to Moshe, "*Ehyeh Asher Ehyeh* [I am/will be what I am/will be]," and added, "Here is what to say to the people of Isra'el: '*Ehyeh* [I Am *or* I Will Be] has sent me to you.'" ¹⁵God said further to Moshe, "Say this to the people of Isra'el: '*Yud-Heh-Vav-Heh* [*ADONAI*], the God of your fathers, the God of Avraham, the God of Yitz'chak and the God of Ya'akov, has sent me to you.' This is my name forever; this is how I am to be remembered generation after generation. *(v)* ¹⁶Go, gather the leaders of Isra'el together, and say to them, '*ADONAI*, the God of your fathers, the God of Avraham, Yitz'chak and Ya'akov, has appeared to me and said, "I have been paying close attention to you and have seen what is being done to you in Egypt; ¹⁷and I have said that I will lead you up out of the misery of Egypt to the land of the Kena'ani, Hitti, Emori, P'rizi, Hivi and Y'vusi, to a land flowing with milk and honey."' ¹⁸They will heed what you say. Then you will come, you and the leaders of Isra'el, before the king of Egypt; and you will tell him, '*ADONAI*, the God of the Hebrews, has met with us. Now, please, let us go three days' journey into the desert; so that we can sacrifice to *ADONAI* our God.' ¹⁹I know that the king of Egypt will not let you leave unless he is forced to do so. ²⁰But I will reach out my hand and strike Egypt with all my wonders that I will do there. After that, he will let you go. ²¹Moreover, I will make the Egyptians so well-disposed toward this people that when you go, you won't go empty-handed. ²²Rather, all the women will ask their neighbors and house guests for silver and gold jewelry and clothing, with which you will dress your own sons and daughters. In this way you will plunder the Egyptians."

4 ¹Moshe replied, "But I'm certain they won't believe me, and they won't listen to what I say, because they'll say, '*ADONAI* did not appear to you.'" ²*ADONAI* answered him, "What is that in your hand?" and he said, "A staff." ³ He said, "Throw it on the ground!" and he threw it on the ground. It turned into a snake, and Moshe recoiled from it. ⁴ Then *Adonai* said to Moshe, "Put your hand out and take it by the tail." He reached out with his hand and took hold of it, and it became a staff in his hand. ⁵ "This is so that they will believe that *Adonai*, the God of their fathers, the God of Avraham, the God of Yitz'chak and the God of Ya'akov, has appeared to you!"

⁶ Furthermore *Adonai* said to him, "Now put your hand inside your coat." He put his hand in his coat; and when he took it out his hand was leprous, as white as snow. ⁷ Then God said, "Now put your hand back in your coat." He put his hand back in his coat; and when he took it out, it was as healthy as the rest of his body. ⁸ "If they won't believe you or heed the evidence of the first sign, they will be convinced by the second. ⁹ But if they aren't persuaded even by both these signs and still won't listen to what you say, then take some water from the river, and pour it on the ground. The water you take from the river will turn into blood on the dry land."

¹⁰ Moshe said to *Adonai*, "Oh, *Adonai*, I'm a terrible speaker. I always have been, and I'm no better now, even after you've spoken to your servant! My words come slowly, my tongue moves slowly." ¹¹ *Adonai* answered him, "Who gives a person a mouth? Who makes a person dumb or deaf, keen-sighted or blind? Isn't it I, *Adonai*? ¹² Now, therefore, go; and I will be with your mouth and will teach you what to say."

¹³ But he replied, "Please, Lord, send someone else — anyone you want!" ¹⁴ At this, *Adonai*'s anger blazed up against Moshe; he said, "Don't you have a brother, Aharon the *Levi*? I know that he's a good speaker. In fact, here he is now, coming out to meet you; and he'll be happy to see you. ¹⁵ You will speak to him and put the words in his mouth; and I will be with your mouth and his, teaching you both what to do. ¹⁶ Thus he will be your spokesman to the people, in effect; for you, he will be a mouth; and for him, you will be like God. ¹⁷ Now take this staff in your hand, because you need it to perform the signs."

(vi) ¹⁸ Moshe left, returned to Yitro his father-in-law and said to him, "I beg you to let me go and return to my kinsmen in Egypt, to see if they are still alive." Yitro said to Moshe, "Go in peace." ¹⁹ *Adonai* said to Moshe in Midyan, "Go on back to Egypt, because all the men who wanted to kill you are dead." ²⁰ So Moshe took his wife and sons, put them on a donkey, and started out for Egypt. Moshe took God's staff in his hand. ²¹ *Adonai* said to Moshe, "When you get back to Egypt, make sure that you do before Pharaoh every one of the wonders I have enabled you to do. Nevertheless, I am going to make him hardhearted, and he will refuse to let the people go. ²² Then you are to tell Pharaoh: '*Adonai* says, "Isra'el is my firstborn son. ²³ I have told you to let my son go in order to worship me, but you have refused to let him go. Well, then, I will kill your firstborn son!"'"

²⁴ At a lodging-place on the way, *Adonai* met Moshe and would have killed him, ²⁵ had not Tzipporah taken a flintstone and cut off the foreskin of her son. She threw it at his feet, saying, "What a bloody bridegroom you are for me!" ²⁶ But then, God let Moshe be. She added, "A bloody bridegroom because of the circumcision!"

²⁷ *Adonai* said to Aharon, "Go into the desert to meet Moshe." He went, met him at the mountain of God and kissed him. ²⁸ Moshe told him everything *Adonai* had said in sending him, including all the signs he had ordered him to perform. ²⁹ Then

Moshe and Aharon went and gathered together all the leaders of the people of Isra'el. ³⁰ Aharon said everything ADONAI had told Moshe, who then performed the signs for the people to see. ³¹ The people believed; when they heard that ADONAI had remembered the people of Isra'el and seen how they were oppressed, they bowed their heads and worshipped.

5 *(vii)* ¹ After that, Moshe and Aharon came and said to Pharaoh, "Here is what ADONAI, the God of Isra'el, says: 'Let my people go, so that they can celebrate a festival in the desert to honor me.'" ² But Pharaoh replied, "Who is ADONAI, that I should obey when he says to let Isra'el go? I don't know ADONAI, and I also won't let Isra'el go." ³ They said, "The God of the Hebrews has met with us. Please let us go three days' journey into the desert, so that we can sacrifice to ADONAI our God. Otherwise, he may strike us with a plague or with the sword." ⁴ The king of Egypt answered them, "Moshe and Aharon, what do you mean by taking the people away from their work? Get back to your labor! ⁵ Look!" Pharaoh added, "the population of the land has grown, yet you are trying to have them stop working!"

⁶ That same day Pharaoh ordered the slavemasters and the people's foremen, ⁷ "You are no longer to provide straw for the bricks the people are making, as you did before. Let them go and gather straw for themselves. ⁸ But you will require them to produce the same quantity of bricks as before, don't reduce it, because they're lazing around. This is why they're crying, 'Let us go and sacrifice to our God.' ⁹ Give these people harder work to do. That will keep them too busy to pay attention to speeches full of lies."

¹⁰ The people's slavemasters went out, their foremen too, and said to the people, "Here is what Pharaoh says: 'I will no longer give you straw. ¹¹ You go, yourselves, and get straw wherever you can find it. But your output is not to be reduced.'" ¹² So the people were dispersed throughout all the land of Egypt to gather stubble for straw. ¹³ The slavemasters kept pressing them. "Keep working! Make your daily quota, just as when straw was provided." ¹⁴ The foremen of the people of Isra'el, whom Pharaoh's slavemasters had appointed to be over them, were flogged and asked, "Why haven't you fulfilled your quota of bricks yesterday and today, as you did formerly?"

¹⁵ Then the foremen of the people of Isra'el came and complained to Pharaoh: "Why are you treating your servants this way? ¹⁶ No straw is given to your servants, yet they keep telling us to make bricks. And now your servants are being flogged, but the fault lies with your own people." ¹⁷ "Lazy!" he retorted, "You're just lazy! That's why you say, 'Let us go and sacrifice to ADONAI.' ¹⁸ Get going now, and get back to work! No straw will be given to you, and you will still deliver the full amount of bricks." ¹⁹ When they said, "You are not to reduce your daily production quota of bricks," the foremen of the people of Isra'el could see that they were in deep trouble.

²⁰ As they were leaving Pharaoh, they encountered Moshe and Aharon standing by the road; ²¹ and they said to them, "May ADONAI look at you and judge accordingly, because you have made us utterly abhorrent in the view of Pharaoh and his servants, and you have put a sword in their hands to kill us!" *(Maftir)* ²² Moshe returned to ADONAI and said, "ADONAI, why have you treated this people

so terribly? What has been the value of sending me? ²³ For ever since I came to Pharaoh to speak in your name, he has dealt terribly with this people! And you haven't rescued your people at all!"

6 ¹ ADONAI said to Moshe, "Now you will see what I am going to do to Pharaoh. With a mighty hand he will send them off; with force he will drive them from the land!"

Haftarah Sh'mot: Yesha'yahu (Isaiah) 27:6–28:13; 29:22–23 (A);
Yirmeyahu (Jeremiah) 1:1–2:3 (S)

B'rit Hadashah suggested readings for Parashah Sh'mot: Mattityahu
(Matthew) 22:23–33; 41–46; Mark 12:18–27; 35–37; Luke 20:27–44;
Acts 3:12–15; 5:27–32; 7:17–36; 22:12–16; 24:14–16; Messianic Jews
(Hebrews) 11:23–26

Parashah 14: Va'era (I appeared) 6:2–9:35

² God spoke to Moshe; he said to him, "I am ADONAI. ³ I appeared to Avraham, Yitz'chak and Ya'akov as *El Shaddai*, although I did not make myself known to them by my name, *Yud-Heh-Vav-Heh* [ADONAI]. ⁴ Also with them I established my covenant to give them the land of Kena'an, the land where they wandered about and lived as foreigners. ⁵ Moreover, I have heard the groaning of the people of Isra'el, whom the Egyptians are keeping in slavery; and I have remembered my covenant.

⁶ "Therefore, say to the people of Isra'el: 'I am ADONAI. I will free you from the forced labor of the Egyptians, rescue you from their oppression, and redeem you with an outstretched arm and with great judgments. ⁷ I will take you as my people, and I will be your God. Then you will know that I am ADONAI your God, who freed you from the forced labor of the Egyptians. ⁸ I will bring you into the land which I swore to give to Avraham, Yitz'chak and Ya'akov — I will give it to you as your inheritance. I am ADONAI.'"

⁹ Moshe said this to the people of Isra'el. But they wouldn't listen to him, because they were so discouraged, and their slavery was so cruel.

¹⁰ ADONAI said to Moshe, ¹¹ "Go in; and tell Pharaoh, king of Egypt, to let the people of Isra'el leave his land." ¹² Moshe said to ADONAI, "Look, the people of Isra'el haven't listened to me; so how will Pharaoh listen to me, poor speaker that I am?" ¹³ But ADONAI spoke to Moshe and Aharon and gave them orders concerning both the people of Isra'el and Pharaoh, king of Egypt, to bring the people of Isra'el out of the land of Egypt.

(ii) ¹⁴ These were the heads of their families: the sons of Re'uven the firstborn of Isra'el were Hanokh, Pallu, Hetzron and Karmi. These were the families of Re'uven. ¹⁵ The sons of Shim'on were Y'mu'el, Yamin, Ohad, Yakhin, Tzochar and Sha'ul the son of a Kena'ani woman. These were the families of Shim'on.

¹⁶ These are the names of the sons of Levi with their descendants: Gershon, K'hat and M'rari. Levi lived to be 137 years old. ¹⁷ The sons of Gershon were Livni and Shim'i, with their families. ¹⁸ The sons of K'hat were 'Amram, Yitz'har, Hevron and 'Uzi'el. K'hat lived to be 133 years old. ¹⁹ The sons of M'rari were Machli and Mushi. These were the families of Levi with their descendants.

²⁰ 'Amram married Yokheved his father's sister, and she bore him Aharon and Moshe. 'Amram lived to be 137 years old. ²¹ The sons of Yitz'har were Korach, Nefeg and Zikhri. ²² The sons of 'Uzi'el were Misha'el, Eltzafan and Sitri. ²³ Aharon married Elisheva daughter of 'Amminadav and sister of Nachshon, and she bore him Nadav, Avihu, El'azar and Itamar. ²⁴ The sons of Korach were Asir, Elkanah and Avi'asaf. These were the Korchi families. ²⁵ El'azar the son of Aharon married one of the daughters of Puti'el, and she bore him Pinchas. These were the heads of the families of Levi, family by family.

²⁶ These are the Aharon and Moshe to whom ADONAI said, "Bring the people of Isra'el out of the land of Egypt, division by division," ²⁷ and who told Pharaoh king of Egypt, to let the people of Isra'el leave Egypt. These are the same Moshe and Aharon.

²⁸ On the day when ADONAI spoke to Moshe in the land of Egypt, *(iii)* ²⁹ he said, "I am ADONAI. Tell Pharaoh, king of Egypt, everything I say to you."

³⁰ Moshe answered ADONAI, "Look, I'm such a poor speaker that Pharaoh won't listen to me."

7 ¹ But ADONAI said to Moshe, "I have put you in the place of God to Pharaoh, and Aharon your brother will be your prophet. ² You are to say everything I order you, and Aharon your brother is to speak to Pharaoh and tell him to let the people of Isra'el leave his land. ³ But I will make him hardhearted. Even though I will increase my signs and wonders in the land of Egypt, ⁴ Pharaoh will not listen to you. Then I will lay my hand on Egypt and bring my armies, my people the sons of Isra'el, out of the land of Egypt with great acts of judgment. ⁵ Then, when I stretch out my hand over Egypt and bring the people of Isra'el out from among them, the Egyptians will know that I am ADONAI."

⁶ Moshe and Aharon did exactly what ADONAI ordered them to do. ⁷ Moshe was eighty years old and Aharon eighty-three when they spoke to Pharaoh.

(iv) ⁸ ADONAI said to Moshe and Aharon, ⁹ "When Pharaoh says to you, 'Perform a miracle,' tell Aharon to take his staff and throw it down in front of Pharaoh, so that it can become a snake." ¹⁰ Moshe and Aharon went in to Pharaoh and did this, as ADONAI had ordered — Aharon threw down his staff in front of Pharaoh and his servants, and it turned into a snake. ¹¹ But Pharaoh in turn called for the sages and sorcerers; and they too, the magicians of Egypt, did the same thing, making use of their secret arts. ¹² Each one threw his staff down, and they turned into snakes. But Aharon's staff swallowed up theirs. ¹³ Nevertheless, Pharaoh was made hardhearted; and he didn't listen to them, as ADONAI had said would happen.

¹⁴ ADONAI said to Moshe, "Pharaoh is stubborn. He refuses to let the people go. ¹⁵ Go to Pharaoh in the morning when he goes out to the water. Stand on the riverbank to confront him, take in your hand the staff which was turned into a snake, ¹⁶ and say to him, 'ADONAI, the God of the Hebrews, sent me to you to say: "Let my people go, so that they can worship me in the desert." But until now you haven't listened; ¹⁷ so ADONAI says, "This will let you know that I am ADONAI": I will take the staff in my hand and strike the water in the river, and it will be turned into blood. ¹⁸ The fish in the river will die, the river will stink and the Egyptians won't want to drink water from the river.'"

¹⁹ ADONAI said to Moshe, "Say to Aharon, 'Take your staff, reach out your hand over the waters of Egypt, over their rivers, canals, ponds and all their reservoirs, so

that they can turn into blood. There will be blood throughout the whole land of Egypt, even in the wooden buckets and stone jars.'" ²⁰ Moshe and Aharon did exactly what ADONAI had ordered. He raised the staff and, in the sight of Pharaoh and his servants, struck the water in the river; and all the water in the river was turned into blood. ²¹ The fish in the river died, and the river stank so badly that the Egyptians couldn't drink its water. There was blood throughout all the land of Egypt.

²² But the magicians of Egypt did the same with their secret arts, so that Pharaoh was made hardhearted and didn't listen to them, as ADONAI had said would happen. ²³ Pharaoh just turned and went back to his palace, without taking any of this to heart. ²⁴ All the Egyptians dug around the river for water to drink, because they couldn't drink the river water.

²⁵ Seven days after ADONAI had struck the river, ²⁶⁽⁸:¹⁾ ADONAI said to Moshe, "Go in to Pharaoh and say to him, 'Here is what ADONAI says: "Let my people go, so that they can worship me. ²⁷⁽⁸:²⁾ If you refuse to let them go, I will strike all your territory with frogs. ²⁸⁽⁸:³⁾ The river will swarm with frogs. They will go up, enter your palace and go into your bedroom, onto your bed. They will enter the houses of your servants and your people and go into your ovens and kneading bowls. ²⁹⁽⁸:⁴⁾ The frogs will climb all over you, your people and your servants."'"

8 ¹⁽⁵⁾ ADONAI said to Moshe, "Say to Aharon, 'Reach out your hand with your staff over the rivers, canals and ponds; and cause frogs to come up onto the land of Egypt.'" ²⁽⁶⁾ Aharon put out his hand over the waters of Egypt, and the frogs came up and covered the land of Egypt. ³⁽⁷⁾ But the magicians did the same with their secret arts and brought up frogs onto the land of Egypt.

⁴⁽⁸⁾ Then Pharaoh summoned Moshe and Aharon and said, "Intercede with ADONAI to take the frogs away from me and my people, and I will let the people go and sacrifice to ADONAI." ⁵⁽⁹⁾ Moshe said to Pharaoh, "Not only that, but you can have the honor of naming the time when I will pray for you, your servants and your people to be rid of the frogs, both yourselves and your homes, and that they stay only in the river." ⁶⁽¹⁰⁾ He answered, "Tomorrow." Moshe said, "It will be as you have said, and from this you will learn that ADONAI our God has no equal. *(v)* ⁷⁽¹¹⁾ The frogs will leave you and your homes, also your servants and your people; they will stay in the river only." ⁸⁽¹²⁾ Moshe and Aharon left Pharaoh's presence, and Moshe cried to ADONAI about the frogs he had brought on Pharaoh. ⁹⁽¹³⁾ ADONAI did as Moshe had asked — the frogs died in the houses, courtyards and fields; ¹⁰⁽¹⁴⁾ they gathered them in heaps till the land stank. ¹¹⁽¹⁵⁾ But when Pharaoh saw that he had been given some relief, he made himself hardhearted and would not listen to them, just as ADONAI had said would happen.

¹²⁽¹⁶⁾ ADONAI said to Moshe, "Say to Aharon: 'Reach out with your staff and strike the dust on the ground; it will become lice throughout all the land of Egypt.'" ¹³⁽¹⁷⁾ They did it — Aharon reached out his hand with his staff and struck the dust on the ground, and there were lice on people and animals; all the dust on the ground became lice throughout the whole land of Egypt. ¹⁴⁽¹⁸⁾ The magicians tried with their secret arts to produce lice, but they couldn't. There were lice on people and animals. ¹⁵⁽¹⁹⁾ Then the magicians said to Pharaoh, "This is the finger of God." But Pharaoh was made hardhearted, so that he didn't listen to them, just as ADONAI had said would happen.

$^{16(20)}$ *Adonai* said to Moshe, "Get up early in the morning, stand before Pharaoh when he goes out to the water and say to him, 'Here is what *Adonai* says: "Let my people go, so that they can worship me. $^{17(21)}$ Otherwise, if you won't let my people go, I will send swarms of insects on you, your servants and your people, and into your houses. The houses of the Egyptians will be full of swarms of insects, and likewise the ground they stand on. $^{18(22)}$ But I will set apart the land of Goshen, where my people live — no swarms of insects will be there — so that you can realize that I am *Adonai*, right here in the land. *(vi)* $^{19(23)}$ Yes, I will distinguish between my people and your people, and this sign will happen by tomorrow."'" $^{20(24)}$ *Adonai* did it: terrible swarms of insects went into Pharaoh's palace and into all his servants' houses — the insects ruined the entire land of Egypt.

$^{21(25)}$ Pharaoh summoned Moshe and Aharon and said, "Go, and sacrifice to your God here in the land." $^{22(26)}$ But Moshe replied, "It would be inappropriate for us to do that, because the animal we sacrifice to *Adonai* our God is an abomination to the Egyptians. Won't the Egyptians stone us to death if before their very eyes we sacrifice what they consider an abomination? $^{23(27)}$ No, we will go three days' journey into the desert and sacrifice to *Adonai* our God, as he has ordered us to do." $^{24(28)}$ Pharaoh said, "I will let you go, so that you can sacrifice to *Adonai* your God in the desert. Only you are not to go very far away. Intercede on my behalf." $^{25(29)}$ Moshe said, "All right, I am going away from you, and I will intercede with *Adonai*; so that tomorrow, the swarms of insects will leave Pharaoh, his servants and his people. Just make sure that Pharaoh stops playing games with the people by preventing them from going and sacrificing to *Adonai*."

$^{26(30)}$ Moshe left Pharaoh and interceded with *Adonai*, $^{27(31)}$ and *Adonai* did what Moshe had asked: he removed the swarms of insects from Pharaoh, his servants and his people — not one remained. $^{28(32)}$ But this time, too, Pharaoh made himself stubborn and didn't let the people go.

9 ^{1} Then *Adonai* said to Moshe, "Go to Pharaoh, and tell him, 'Here is what *Adonai*, the God of the Hebrews, says: "Let my people go, so that they can worship me. ^{2} If you refuse to let them go and persist in holding on to them, ^{3} the hand of *Adonai* is on your livestock in the field — on the horses, donkeys, camels, cattle and flocks — and will make them suffer a devastating illness. ^{4} But *Adonai* will distinguish between Egypt's and Isra'el's livestock — nothing belonging to the people of Isra'el will die."'" ^{5} *Adonai* determined the exact time by saying, "Tomorrow *Adonai* will do this in the land." ^{6} The following day, *Adonai* did it — all the livestock of Egypt died; but not one of the animals belonging to the people of Isra'el died. ^{7} Pharaoh investigated and found that not even one of the animals of the people of Isra'el had died. Nevertheless, Pharaoh's heart remained stubborn, and he didn't let the people go.

^{8} *Adonai* said to Moshe and Aharon, "Take handfuls of ashes from a kiln, and let Moshe throw them in the air before Pharaoh's eyes. ^{9} They will turn into fine dust over all the land of Egypt and become infected sores on men and animals throughout Egypt." ^{10} So they took ashes from a kiln, stood in front of Pharaoh and threw them in the air; and they became infected sores on men and animals. ^{11} The magicians couldn't even stand in Moshe's presence because of the sores, which were on them as well as on the other Egyptians. ^{12} But *Adonai* made Pharaoh hardhearted, so that he didn't listen to them — just as *Adonai* had said to Moshe.

¹³ ADONAI said to Moshe, "Get up early in the morning, stand before Pharaoh, and say to him, 'Here is what ADONAI says: "Let my people go, so that they can worship me. ¹⁴ For this time, I will inflict my plagues on you, yourself, and on your officials and your people; so that you will realize that I am without equal in all the earth. ¹⁵ By now I could have stretched out my hand and struck you and your people with such severe plagues that you would have been wiped off the earth. ¹⁶ But it is for this very reason that I have kept you alive — to show you my power, and so that my name may resound throughout the whole earth. *(vii)* ¹⁷ Since you are still setting yourself up against my people and not letting them go, ¹⁸ tomorrow, about this time, I will cause a hailstorm so heavy that Egypt has had nothing like it from the day it was founded until now. ¹⁹ Therefore, send and hurry to bring indoors all your livestock and everything else you have in the field. For hail will fall on every human being and animal left in the field that hasn't been brought home, and they will die."'"

²⁰ Whoever among Pharaoh's servants feared what ADONAI had said had his slaves and livestock escape into the houses; ²¹ but those who had no regard for what ADONAI had said left their slaves and livestock in the field.

²² ADONAI said to Moshe, "Reach out your hand toward the sky, so that there will be hail in all the land of Egypt, falling on people, animals and everything growing in the field, throughout the land of Egypt." ²³ Moshe reached out with his staff toward the sky, and ADONAI sent thunder and hail, and fire ran down to the earth. ADONAI caused it to hail on the land of Egypt — ²⁴ it hailed, and fire flashed up with the hail; it was terrible, worse than any hailstorm in all of Egypt since it became a nation. ²⁵ Throughout all the land of Egypt, the hail struck everything in the field, people and animals; and the hail struck every plant growing in the field and broke every tree there. ²⁶ But in the land of Goshen, where the people of Isra'el were, there was no hail.

²⁷ Pharaoh summoned Moshe and Aharon and said to them, "This time I have sinned: ADONAI is in the right; I and my people are in the wrong. ²⁸ Intercede with ADONAI — we can't take any more of this terrible thunder and hail; and I will let you go, you will stay no longer." ²⁹ Moshe said to him, "As soon as I have gone out of the city, I will spread out my hands to ADONAI; the thunder will end, and there won't be any more hail — so that you can know that the earth belongs to ADONAI. ³⁰ But you and your servants, I know you still won't fear ADONAI, God." ³¹ The flax and barley were ruined, because the barley was ripe and the flax in bud. ³² But the wheat and buckwheat were not ruined, because they come up later. *(Maftir)* ³³ Moshe went out of the city, away from Pharaoh, and spread out his hands to ADONAI. The thunder and hail ended, and the rain stopped pouring down on the earth. ³⁴ When Pharaoh saw that the rain, hail and thunder had ended, he sinned still more by making himself hardhearted, he and his servants. ³⁵ Pharaoh was made hardhearted, and he didn't let the people of Isra'el go, just as ADONAI had said through Moshe.

Haftarah Va'era: Yechezk'el (Ezekiel) 28:25–29:21

B'rit Hadashah suggested readings for Parashah Va'era: Romans 9:14–17; 2 Corinthians 6:14–7:1

Parashah 15: Bo (Go) 10:1–13:16

10 ¹ ADONAI said to Moshe, "Go to Pharaoh, for I have made him and his servants hardhearted, so that I can demonstrate these signs of mine among them, ² so that you can tell your son and grandson about what I did to Egypt and about my signs that I demonstrated among them, and so that you will all know that I am ADONAI." ³ Moshe and Aharon went in to Pharaoh and said to him, "Here is what ADONAI, God of the Hebrews, says: 'How much longer will you refuse to submit to me? Let my people go, so that they can worship me. ⁴ Otherwise, if you refuse to let my people go, tomorrow I will bring locusts into your territory. ⁵ One won't be able to see the ground, so completely will the locusts cover it. They will eat anything you still have that escaped the hail, including every tree you have growing in the field. ⁶ They will fill your houses and those of your servants and of all the Egyptians. It will be like nothing your fathers or their fathers have ever seen since the day they were born until today.'" Then he turned his back and left.

⁷ Pharaoh's servants said to him, "How much longer must this fellow be a snare for us? Let the people go and worship ADONAI their God. Don't you understand yet that Egypt is being destroyed?" ⁸ So Moshe and Aharon were brought to Pharaoh again, and he said to them, "Go, worship ADONAI your God. But who exactly is going?" ⁹ Moshe answered, "We will go with our young and our old, our sons and our daughters; and we will go with our flocks and herds; for we must celebrate a feast to ADONAI." ¹⁰ Pharaoh said to them, "ADONAI certainly will be with you if I ever let you go with your children! It's clear that you are up to no good. ¹¹ Nothing doing! Just the men among you may go and worship ADONAI. That's what you want, isn't it?" And they were driven out of Pharaoh's presence.

(ii) ¹² ADONAI said to Moshe, "Reach out your hand over the land of Egypt, so that locusts will invade the land and eat every plant that the hail has left." ¹³ Moshe reached out with his staff over the land of Egypt, and ADONAI caused an east wind to blow on the land all day and all night; and in the morning the east wind brought the locusts. ¹⁴ The locusts went up over all the land of Egypt and settled throughout Egypt's territory. It was an invasion more severe than there had ever been before or will ever be again. ¹⁵ They completely covered the ground, so that the ground looked black. They ate every plant growing from the ground and all the fruit of the trees left by the hail. Not one green thing remained, not a tree and not a plant in the field, in all the land of Egypt.

¹⁶ Pharaoh hurried to summon Moshe and Aharon and said, "I have sinned against ADONAI your God and against you. ¹⁷ Now, therefore, please forgive my sin just this once; and intercede with ADONAI your God, so that he will at least take away from me this deadly plague!" ¹⁸ He went out from Pharaoh and interceded with ADONAI. ¹⁹ ADONAI reversed the wind and made it blow very strongly from the west. It took up the locusts and drove them into the Sea of Suf; not one locust remained on Egyptian soil. ²⁰ But ADONAI made Pharaoh hardhearted, and he didn't let the people of Isra'el go.

²¹ ADONAI said to Moshe, "Reach out your hand toward the sky, and there will be darkness over the land of Egypt, darkness so thick it can be felt!" ²² Moshe reached out his hand toward the sky, and there was a thick darkness in the entire land of

Egypt for three days. ²³ People couldn't see each other, and no one went anywhere for three days. But all the people of Isra'el had light in their homes.

(iii) ²⁴ Pharaoh summoned Moshe and said, "Go, worship ADONAI; only leave your flocks and herds behind — your children may go with you." ²⁵ Moshe answered, "You must also see to it that we have sacrifices and burnt offerings, so that we can sacrifice to ADONAI our God. ²⁶ Our livestock will also go with us — not a hoof will be left behind — because we must choose some of them to worship ADONAI our God, and we don't know which ones we will need to worship ADONAI until we get there." ²⁷ But ADONAI made Pharaoh hardhearted, and he would not let them go. ²⁸ Pharaoh said to them, "Get away from me! And you had better not see my face again, because the day you see my face, you will die!" ²⁹ Moshe answered, "Well spoken! I will see your face no more."

11 ¹ ADONAI said to Moshe, "I'm going to bring still one more plague on Pharaoh and Egypt, and after that he will let you leave here. When he does let you go, he will throw you out completely! ² Now tell the people that every man is to ask his neighbor and every woman her neighbor for gold and silver jewelry." ³ ADONAI made the Egyptians favorably disposed toward the people. Moreover, Moshe was regarded by Pharaoh's servants and the people as a very great man in the land of Egypt.

(iv) ⁴ Moshe said, "Here is what ADONAI says: 'About midnight I will go out into Egypt, ⁵ and all the firstborn in the land of Egypt will die, from the firstborn of Pharaoh sitting on his throne to the firstborn of the slave-girl at the handmill, and all the firstborn of the livestock. ⁶ There will be a horrendous wailing throughout all the land of Egypt — there has never been another like it, and there never will be again. ⁷ But not even a dog's growl will be heard against any of the people of Isra'el, neither against people nor against animals. In this way you will realize that ADONAI distinguishes between Egyptians and Isra'el. ⁸ All your servants will come down to me, prostrate themselves before me and say, "Get out! — you and all the people who follow you!" and after that, I will go out!' " And he went out from Pharaoh in the heat of anger. ⁹ ADONAI said to Moshe, "Pharaoh will not listen to you, so that still more of my wonders will be shown in the land of Egypt."

¹⁰ Moshe and Aharon did all these wonders before Pharaoh, but ADONAI had made Pharaoh hardhearted, and he didn't let the people of Isra'el leave his land.

12 ¹ ADONAI spoke to Moshe and Aharon in the land of Egypt; he said, ² "You are to begin your calendar with this month; it will be the first month of the year for you. ³ Speak to all the assembly of Isra'el and say, 'On the tenth day of this month, each man is to take a lamb or kid for his family, one per household — ⁴ except that if the household is too small for a whole lamb or kid, then he and his next-door neighbor should share one, dividing it in proportion to the number of people eating it. ⁵ Your animal must be without defect, a male in its first year, and you may choose it from either the sheep or the goats.

⁶ "'You are to keep it until the fourteenth day of the month, and then the entire assembly of the community of Isra'el will slaughter it at dusk. ⁷ They are to take some of the blood and smear it on the two sides and top of the door-frame at the entrance of the house in which they eat it. ⁸ That night, they are to eat the meat, roasted

in the fire; they are to eat it with *matzah* and *maror.* ⁹Don't eat it raw or boiled, but roasted in the fire, with its head, the lower parts of its legs and its inner organs. ¹⁰Let nothing of it remain till morning; if any of it does remain, burn it up completely.

¹¹ "'Here is how you are to eat it: with your belt fastened, your shoes on your feet and your staff in your hand; and you are to eat it hurriedly. It is ADONAI's *Pesach* [Passover]. ¹²For that night, I will pass through the land of Egypt and kill all the firstborn in the land of Egypt, both men and animals; and I will execute judgment against all the gods of Egypt; I am ADONAI. ¹³The blood will serve you as a sign marking the houses where you are; when I see the blood, I will pass over [Hebrew: *pasach*] you — when I strike the land of Egypt, the death blow will not strike you.

¹⁴ "'This will be a day for you to remember and celebrate as a festival to ADONAI; from generation to generation you are to celebrate it by a perpetual regulation.

¹⁵ "'For seven days you are to eat *matzah* — on the first day remove the leaven from your houses. For whoever eats *hametz* [leavened bread] from the first to the seventh day is to be cut off from Isra'el. ¹⁶On the first and seventh days, you are to have an assembly set aside for God. On these days no work is to be done, except what each must do to prepare his food; you may do only that. ¹⁷You are to observe the festival of *matzah*, for on this very day I brought your divisions out of the land of Egypt. Therefore, you are to observe this day from generation to generation by a perpetual regulation. ¹⁸From the evening of the fourteenth day of the first month until the evening of the twenty-first day, you are to eat *matzah*. ¹⁹During those seven days, no leaven is to be found in your houses. Whoever eats food with *hametz* in it is to be cut off from the community of Isra'el — it doesn't matter whether he is a foreigner or a citizen of the land. ²⁰Eat nothing with *hametz* in it. Wherever you live, eat *matzah*.'"

*(v)*²¹ Then Moshe called for all the leaders of Isra'el and said, "Select and take lambs for your families, and slaughter the *Pesach* lamb. ²²Take a bunch of hyssop leaves and dip it in the blood which is in the basin, and smear it on the two sides and top of the door-frame. Then, none of you is to go out the door of his house until morning. ²³For ADONAI will pass through to kill the Egyptians; but when he sees the blood on the top and on the two sides, ADONAI will pass over the door and will not allow the Slaughterer to enter your houses and kill you. ²⁴You are to observe this as a law, you and your descendants forever.

²⁵ "When you come to the land which ADONAI will give you, as he has promised, you are to observe this ceremony. ²⁶When your children ask you, 'What do you mean by this ceremony?' ²⁷say, 'It is the sacrifice of ADONAI's *Pesach* [Passover], because [ADONAI] passed over the houses of the people of Isra'el in Egypt, when he killed the Egyptians but spared our houses.'" The people of Isra'el bowed their heads and worshipped. ²⁸Then the people of Isra'el went and did as ADONAI had ordered Moshe and Aharon — that is what they did.

(vi) ²⁹ At midnight ADONAI killed all the firstborn in the land of Egypt, from the firstborn of Pharaoh sitting on his throne to the firstborn of the prisoner in the dungeon, and all the firstborn of livestock. ³⁰Pharaoh got up in the night, he, all his servants and all the Egyptians; and there was horrendous wailing in Egypt; for there wasn't a single house without someone dead in it. ³¹He summoned Moshe and Aharon by night and said, "Up and leave my people, both you and the people of Isra'el; and go, serve ADONAI as you said. ³²Take both your flocks and your herds, as you said; and get out of here! But bless me, too."

³³ The Egyptians pressed to send the people out of the land quickly, because they said, "Otherwise we'll all be dead!" ³⁴ The people took their dough before it had become leavened and wrapped their kneading bowls in their clothes on their shoulders. ³⁵ The people of Isra'el had done what Moshe had said — they had asked the Egyptians to give them silver and gold jewelry and clothing; ³⁶ and ADONAI had made the Egyptians so favorably disposed toward the people that they had let them have whatever they requested. Thus they plundered the Egyptians.

³⁷ The people of Isra'el traveled from Ra'amses to Sukkot, some six hundred thousand men on foot, not counting children. ³⁸ A mixed crowd also went up with them, as well as livestock in large numbers, both flocks and herds. ³⁹ They baked *matzah* loaves from the dough they had brought out of Egypt, since it was unleavened; because they had been driven out of Egypt without time to prepare supplies for themselves.

⁴⁰ The time the people of Isra'el lived in Egypt was 430 years. ⁴¹ At the end of 430 years to the day, all the divisions of ADONAI left the land of Egypt. ⁴² This was a night when ADONAI kept vigil to bring them out of the land of Egypt, and this same night continues to be a night when ADONAI keeps vigil for all the people of Isra'el through all their generations.

⁴³ ADONAI said to Moshe and Aharon, "This is the regulation for the *Pesach* lamb: no foreigner is to eat it. ⁴⁴ But if anyone has a slave he bought for money, when you have circumcised him, he may eat it. ⁴⁵ Neither a traveler nor a hired servant may eat it. ⁴⁶ It is to be eaten in one house. You are not to take any of the meat outside the house, and you are not to break any of its bones. ⁴⁷ The whole community of Isra'el is to keep it. ⁴⁸ If a foreigner staying with you wants to observe ADONAI's *Pesach*, all his males must be circumcised. Then he may take part and observe it; he will be like a citizen of the land. But no uncircumcised person is to eat it. ⁴⁹ The same teaching is to apply equally to the citizen and to the foreigner living among you."

⁵⁰ All the people of Isra'el did just as ADONAI had ordered Moshe and Aharon. ⁵¹ On that very day, ADONAI brought the people of Isra'el out of the land of Egypt by their divisions.

13 *(vii)* ¹ ADONAI said to Moshe, ² "Set aside for me all the firstborn. Whatever is first from the womb among the people of Isra'el, both of humans and of animals, belongs to me." ³ Moshe said to the people, "Remember this day, on which you left Egypt, the abode of slavery; because ADONAI, by the strength of his hand, has brought you out of this place. Do not eat *hametz*. ⁴ You are leaving today, in the month of Aviv. ⁵ When ADONAI brings you into the land of the Kena'ani, Hitti, Emori, Hivi and Y'vusi, which he swore to your ancestors to give you, a land flowing with milk and honey, you are to observe this ceremony in this month. ⁶ For seven days you are to eat *matzah*, and the seventh day is to be a festival for ADONAI. ⁷ *Matzah* is to be eaten throughout the seven days; neither *hametz* nor leavening agents are to be seen with you throughout your territory. ⁸ On that day you are to tell your son, 'It is because of what ADONAI did for me when I left Egypt.'

⁹ "Moreover, it will serve you as a sign on your hand and as a reminder between your eyes, so that ADONAI's *Torah* may be on your lips; because with a strong hand ADONAI brought you out of Egypt. ¹⁰ Therefore you are to observe this regulation at its proper time, year after year. ¹¹ When ADONAI brings you into the land of the Kena'ani,

as he swore to you and your ancestors, and gives it to you, ¹²you are to set apart for ADONAI everything that is first from the womb. Every firstborn male animal will belong to ADONAI. ¹³Every firstborn from a donkey, you are to redeem with a lamb; but if you choose not to redeem it, you must break its neck. But from people, you are to redeem every firstborn son. *(Maftir)* ¹⁴When, at some future time, your son asks you, 'What is this?' then say to him, 'With a strong hand ADONAI brought us out of Egypt, out of the abode of slavery. ¹⁵When Pharaoh was unwilling to let us go, ADONAI killed all the firstborn males in the land of Egypt, both the firstborn of humans and the firstborn of animals. This is why I sacrifice to ADONAI any male that is first from the womb of an animal, but all the firstborn of my sons I redeem.' ¹⁶This will serve as a sign on your hand and at the front of a headband around your forehead that with a strong hand ADONAI brought us out of Egypt."

> *Haftarah Bo: Yirmeyahu (Jeremiah) 46:13–28*

> *B'rit Hadashah suggested readings for Parashah Bo: Luke 2:22–24;*
> *Yochanan (John) 19:31–37; Acts 13:16–17; Revelation 8:6–9:12; 16:1–21*

Parashah 16: B'shallach (After he had let go) 13:17–17:16

¹⁷After Pharaoh had let the people go, God did not guide them to the highway that goes through the land of the P'lishtim, because it was close by—God thought that the people, upon seeing war, might change their minds and return to Egypt. ¹⁸Rather, God led the people by a roundabout route, through the desert by the Sea of Suf. The people of Isra'el went up from the land of Egypt fully armed.

¹⁹Moshe took the bones of Yosef with him, for Yosef had made the people of Isra'el swear an oath when he said, "God will certainly remember you; and you are to carry my bones up with you, away from here."

²⁰They traveled from Sukkot and set up camp in Etam, at the edge of the desert. ²¹ADONAI went ahead of them in a column of cloud during the daytime to lead them on their way, and at night in a column of fire to give them light; thus they could travel both by day and by night. ²²Neither the column of cloud by day nor the column of fire at night went away from in front of the people.

14 ¹ADONAI said to Moshe, ²"Tell the people of Isra'el to turn around and set up camp in front of Pi-Hachirot, between Migdol and the sea, in front of Ba'al-Tz'fon; camp opposite it, by the sea. ³Then Pharaoh will say that the people of Isra'el are wandering aimlessly in the countryside, the desert has closed in on them. ⁴I will make Pharaoh so hardhearted that he will pursue them; thus I will win glory for myself at the expense of Pharaoh and all his army, and the Egyptians will realize at last that I am ADONAI." The people did as ordered.

⁵When the king of Egypt was told that the people had fled, Pharaoh and his servants had a change of heart toward the people. They said, "What have we done, letting Isra'el stop being our slaves?" ⁶So he prepared his chariots and took his people with him — ⁷he took 600 first-quality chariots, as well as all the other chariots in Egypt, along with their commanders. ⁸ADONAI made Pharaoh hardhearted, and he

pursued the people of Isra'el, as they left boldly. *(ii)* ⁹ The Egyptians went after them, all the horses and chariots of Pharaoh, with his cavalry and army, and overtook them as they were encamped by the sea, by Pi-Hachirot, in front of Ba'al-Tz'fon. ¹⁰ As Pharaoh approached, the people of Isra'el looked up and saw the Egyptians right there, coming after them. In great fear the people of Isra'el cried out to ADONAI ¹¹ and said to Moshe, "Was it because there weren't enough graves in Egypt that you brought us out to die in the desert? Why have you done this to us, bringing us out of Egypt? ¹² Didn't we tell you in Egypt to let us alone, we'll just go on being slaves for the Egyptians? It would be better for us to be the Egyptians' slaves than to die in the desert!" ¹³ Moshe answered the people, "Stop being so fearful! Remain steady, and you will see how ADONAI is going to save you. He will do it today — today you have seen the Egyptians, but you will never see them again! ¹⁴ ADONAI will do battle for you. Just calm yourselves down!"

(A: iii) ¹⁵ ADONAI asked Moshe, "Why are you crying to me? Tell the people of Isra'el to go forward! ¹⁶ Lift your staff, reach out with your hand over the sea, and divide it in two. The people of Isra'el will advance into the sea on dry ground. ¹⁷ As for me, I will make the Egyptians hardhearted; and they will march in after them; thus I will win glory for myself at the expense of Pharaoh and all his army, chariots and cavalry. ¹⁸ Then the Egyptians will realize that I am ADONAI, when I have won myself glory at the expense of Pharaoh, his chariots and his cavalry."

¹⁹ Next, the angel of God, who was going ahead of the camp of Isra'el, moved away and went behind them; and the column of cloud moved away from in front of them and stood behind them. ²⁰ It stationed itself between the camp of Egypt and the camp of Isra'el — there was cloud and darkness here, but light by night there; so that the one did not come near the other all night long.

²¹ Moshe reached his hand out over the sea, and ADONAI caused the sea to go back before a strong east wind all night. He made the sea become dry land, and its water was divided in two. ²² Then the people of Isra'el went into the sea on the dry ground, with the water walled up for them on their right and on their left.

²³ The Egyptians continued their pursuit, going after them into the sea — all Pharaoh's horses, chariots and cavalry. ²⁴ Just before dawn, ADONAI looked out on the Egyptian army through the column of fire and cloud and threw them into a panic. ²⁵ He caused the wheels of their chariots to break off, so that they could move only with difficulty. The Egyptians said, "ADONAI is fighting for Isra'el against the Egyptians! Let's get away from them!"

(A: iv, S: iii) ²⁶ ADONAI said to Moshe, "Reach your hand out over the sea, and the water will return and cover the Egyptians with their chariots and cavalry." ²⁷ Moshe reached his hand out over the sea, and by dawn the sea had returned to its former depth. The Egyptians tried to flee, but ADONAI swept them into the sea. ²⁸ The water came back and covered all the chariots and cavalry of Pharaoh's army who had followed them into the sea — not even one of them was left. ²⁹ But the people of Isra'el walked on dry ground in the sea, with the water walled up for them on their right and on their left.

³⁰ On that day, ADONAI saved Isra'el from the Egyptians; Isra'el saw the Egyptians dead on the shore. ³¹ When Isra'el saw the mighty deed that ADONAI had performed against the Egyptians, the people feared ADONAI, and they believed in ADONAI and in his servant Moshe.

15 ¹ Then Moshe and the people of Isra'el sang this song to *Adonai*:

"I will sing to *Adonai*, for he is highly exalted:
the horse and its rider he threw in the sea.

2 *Yah* is my strength and my song,
and he has become my salvation.
This is my God: I will glorify him;
my father's God: I will exalt him.

3 *Adonai* is a warrior;
Adonai is his name.

4 Pharaoh's chariots and his army
he hurled into the sea.
His elite commanders
were drowned in the Sea of Suf.

5 The deep waters covered them;
they sank to the depths like a stone.

6 Your right hand, *Adonai*, is sublimely powerful;
your right hand, *Adonai*, shatters the foe.

7 By your great majesty you bring down your enemies;
you send out your wrath to consume them like stubble.

8 With a blast from your nostrils the waters piled up —
the waters stood up like a wall,
the depths of the sea became firm ground.

9 The enemy said, 'I will pursue and overtake,
divide the spoil and gorge myself on them.
I will draw my sword; my hand will destroy them.'

10 You blew with your wind, the sea covered them,
they sank like lead in the mighty waters.

11 Who is like you, *Adonai*, among the mighty?
Who is like you, sublime in holiness,
awesome in praises, working wonders?

12 You reached out with your right hand:
the earth swallowed them.

13 In your love, you led the people you redeemed;
in your strength, you guided them to your holy abode.

14 The peoples have heard, and they tremble;
anguish takes hold of those living in P'leshet;

15 then the chiefs of Edom are dismayed;
trepidation seizes the heads of Mo'av;
all those living in Kena'an are melted away.

16   Terror and dread fall on them;
        by the might of your arm they are still as stone
        until your people pass over, ADONAI,
        till the people you purchased pass over.

17   You will bring them in and plant them
        on the mountain which is your heritage,
        the place, ADONAI, that you made your abode,
        the sanctuary, Adonai, which your hands established.

18   ADONAI will reign forever and ever.

19   For the horses of Pharaoh went with his chariots
        and with his cavalry into the sea,
        but ADONAI brought the sea waters back upon them,
        while the people of Isra'el walked on dry land
        in the midst of the sea!"

^{20} Also Miryam the prophet, sister of Aharon, took a tambourine in her hand; and all the women went out after her with tambourines, dancing, ^{21} as Miryam sang to them:

        "Sing to ADONAI, for he is highly exalted!
        The horse and its rider he threw in the sea!"

^{22} Moshe led Isra'el onward from the Sea of Suf. They went out into the Shur Desert; but after traveling three days in the desert, they had found no water. ^{23} They arrived at Marah but couldn't drink the water there, because it was bitter. This is why they called it Marah [bitterness]. ^{24} The people grumbled against Moshe and asked, "What are we to drink?" ^{25} Moshe cried to ADONAI; and ADONAI showed him a certain piece of wood, which, when he threw it into the water, made the water taste good. There ADONAI made laws and rules of life for them, and there he tested them. ^{26} He said, "If you will listen intently to the voice of ADONAI your God, do what he considers right, pay attention to his *mitzvot* and observe his laws, I will not afflict you with any of the diseases I brought on the Egyptians; because I am ADONAI your healer."

(A: v, S: iv) ^{27} They came to Eilim, where there were twelve springs and seventy palm trees, and camped there by the water.

16 ^{1} They traveled on from Eilim, and the whole community of the people of Isra'el arrived at the Seen Desert, between Eilim and Sinai, on the fifteenth day of the second month after leaving the land of Egypt. ^{2} There in the desert the whole community of the people of Isra'el grumbled against Moshe and Aharon. ^{3} The people of Isra'el said to them, "We wish ADONAI had used his own hand to kill us off in Egypt! There we used to sit around the pots with the meat boiling, and we had as much food as we wanted. But you have taken us out into this desert to let this whole assembly starve to death!"

⁴ADONAI said to Moshe, "Here, I will cause bread to rain down from heaven for you. The people are to go out and gather a day's ration every day. By this I will test whether they will observe my *Torah* or not. ⁵On the sixth day, when they prepare what they have brought in, it will turn out to be twice as much as they gather on the other days." ⁶Moshe and Aharon said to all the people of Isra'el, "This evening, you will realize that it has been ADONAI who brought you out of Egypt; ⁷and in the morning, you will see ADONAI's glory. For he has listened to your grumblings against ADONAI — what are we that you should grumble against us?" ⁸Moshe added, "What I have said will happen when ADONAI gives you meat to eat this evening and your fill of bread tomorrow morning. ADONAI has listened to your complaints and grumblings against him — what are we? Your grumblings are not against us but against ADONAI."

⁹Moshe said to Aharon, "Say to the whole community of Isra'el, 'Come close, into the presence of ADONAI, for he has heard your grumblings.'" ¹⁰As Aharon spoke to the whole community of the people of Isra'el, they looked toward the desert; and there before them the glory of ADONAI appeared in the cloud; *(A: vi, S: v)* ¹¹and ADONAI said to Moshe, ¹²"I have heard the grumblings of the people of Isra'el. Say to them: 'At dusk you will be eating meat, and in the morning you will have your fill of bread. Then you will realize that I am ADONAI your God.'"

¹³That evening, quails came up and covered the camp; while in the morning there was a layer of dew all around the camp. ¹⁴When the dew had evaporated, there on the surface of the desert was a fine flaky substance, as fine as frost on the ground. ¹⁵When the people of Isra'el saw it, they asked each other, "*Man hu?* [What is it?]" because they didn't know what it was. Moshe answered them, "It is the bread which ADONAI has given you to eat. ¹⁶Here is what ADONAI has ordered: each man is to gather according to his appetite — each is to take an '*omer* [two quarts] per person for everyone in his tent." ¹⁷The people of Isra'el did this. Some gathered more, some less; ¹⁸but when they put it in an '*omer*-measure, whoever had gathered much had no excess; and whoever had gathered little had no shortage; nevertheless each person had gathered according to his appetite.

¹⁹Moshe told them, "No one is to leave any of it till morning." ²⁰But they didn't pay attention to Moshe, and some kept the leftovers until morning. It bred worms and rotted, which made Moshe angry at them. ²¹So they gathered it morning after morning, each person according to his appetite; but as the sun grew hot, it melted.

²²On the sixth day they gathered twice as much bread, two '*omer*s per person; and all the community leaders came and reported to Moshe. ²³He told them, "This is what ADONAI has said: 'Tomorrow is a holy *Shabbat* for ADONAI. Bake what you want to bake; boil what you want to boil; and whatever is left over, set aside and keep for the morning.'" ²⁴They set it aside till morning, as Moshe had ordered; and it didn't rot or have worms. ²⁵Moshe said, "Today, eat that; because today is a *Shabbat* for ADONAI — today you won't find it in the field. ²⁶Gather it six days, but the seventh day is the *Shabbat* — on that day there won't be any." ²⁷However, on the seventh day, some of the people went out to gather and found none.

²⁸ADONAI said to Moshe, "How long will you refuse to observe my *mitzvot* and teachings? ²⁹Look, ADONAI has given you the *Shabbat*. This is why he is providing bread for two days on the sixth day. Each of you, stay where you are; no one is to leave his place on the seventh day." *(S: vi)* ³⁰So the people rested on the seventh day.

³¹ The people called the food *man*. It was like coriander seed, white; and it tasted like honey cakes. ³² Moshe said, "Here is what ADONAI has ordered: 'Let two quarts of *man* be kept through all your generations, so that they will be able to see the bread which I fed you in the desert when I brought you out of Egypt.'" ³³ Moshe said to Aharon, "Take a jar, put in it two quarts of *man*, and set it aside before ADONAI to be kept through all your generations." ³⁴ Just as ADONAI ordered Moshe, Aharon set it aside before the testimony to be kept. ³⁵ The people of Isra'el ate *man* for forty years, until they came to an inhabited land. They ate *man* until they arrived at the borders of the land of Kena'an. ³⁶ (An *'omer* is one-tenth of an *eifah* [which is a bushel dry-measure].)

17 *(vii)* ¹ The whole community of the people of Isra'el left the Seen Desert, traveling in stages, as ADONAI had ordered, and camped at Refidim; but there was no water for the people to drink. ² The people quarreled with Moshe, demanding, "Give us water to drink!" But Moshe replied, "Why pick a fight with me? Why are you testing ADONAI?" ³ However, the people were thirsty for water there and grumbled against Moshe, "For what did you bring us up from Egypt? To kill us, our children and our livestock with thirst?"

⁴ Moshe cried out to ADONAI, "What am I to do with these people? They're ready to stone me!" ⁵ ADONAI answered Moshe, "Go on ahead of the people, and bring with you the leaders of Isra'el. Take your staff in your hand, the one you used to strike the river; and go. ⁶ I will stand in front of you there on the rock in Horev. You are to strike the rock, and water will come out of it, so the people can drink." Moshe did this in the sight of the leaders of Isra'el. ⁷ The place was named Massah [testing] and M'rivah [quarreling] because of the quarreling of the people of Isra'el and because they tested ADONAI by asking, "Is ADONAI with us or not?"

⁸ Then 'Amalek came and fought with Isra'el at Refidim. ⁹ Moshe said to Y'hoshua, "Choose men for us, go out, and fight with 'Amalek. Tomorrow I will stand on top of the hill with God's staff in my hand." ¹⁰ Y'hoshua did as Moshe had told him and fought with 'Amalek. Then Moshe, Aharon and Hur went up to the top of the hill. ¹¹ When Moshe raised his hand, Isra'el prevailed; but when he let it down, 'Amalek prevailed. ¹² However, Moshe's hands grew heavy; so they took a stone and put it under him, and he sat on it. Aharon and Hur held up his hands, the one on the one side and the other on the other; so that his hands stayed steady until sunset. ¹³ Thus Y'hoshua defeated 'Amalek, putting their people to the sword.

(Maftir) ¹⁴ ADONAI said to Moshe, "Write this in a book to be remembered, and tell it to Y'hoshua: I will completely blot out any memory of 'Amalek from under heaven." ¹⁵ Moshe built an altar, called it ADONAI Nissi [ADONAI is my banner/miracle], ¹⁶ and said, "Because their hand was against the throne of *Yah*, ADONAI will fight 'Amalek generation after generation."

Haftarah B'shallach: Shof'tim (Judges) 4:4–5:31 (A); 5:1–31 (S)

B'rit Hadashah suggested readings for Parashah B'shallach: Luke 2:22–24; Yochanan (John) 6:25–35; 19:31–37; 1 Corinthians 10:1–13; 2 Corinthians 8:1–15; Revelation 15:1–4

Parashah 17: Yitro (Jethro) 18:1–20:23(26)

18 ¹ Now Yitro the priest of Midyan, Moshe's father-in-law, heard about all that God had done for Moshe and for Isra'el his people, how *ADONAI* had brought Isra'el out of Egypt. ² After Moshe had sent away his wife Tzipporah and her two sons, Yitro Moshe's father-in-law had taken them back. ³ The name of the one son was Gershom [a foreigner there], for Moshe had said, "I have been a foreigner in a foreign land." ⁴ The name of the other was Eli'ezer [my God helps], "because the God of my father helped me by rescuing me from Pharaoh's sword." ⁵ Yitro Moshe's father-in-law brought Moshe's sons and wife to him in the desert where he was encamped, at the mountain of God. ⁶ He sent word to Moshe, "I, your father-in-law Yitro, am coming to you with your wife and her two sons."

⁷ Moshe went out to meet his father-in-law, prostrated himself and kissed him. Then, after inquiring of each other's welfare, they entered the tent. ⁸ Moshe told his father-in-law all that *ADONAI* had done to Pharaoh and the Egyptians for Isra'el's sake, all the hardships they had suffered while traveling and how *ADONAI* had rescued them. ⁹ Yitro rejoiced over all the good that *ADONAI* had done for Isra'el by rescuing them from the Egyptians. ¹⁰ Yitro said, "Blessed be *ADONAI*, who has rescued you from the Egyptians and from Pharaoh, who has rescued the people from the harsh hand of the Egyptians. ¹¹ Now I know that *ADONAI* is greater than all other gods, because he rescued those who were treated so arrogantly." ¹² Yitro Moshe's father-in-law brought a burnt offering and sacrifices to God, and Aharon came with all the leaders of Isra'el to share the meal before God with Moshe's father-in-law.

(ii) ¹³ The following day Moshe sat to settle disputes for the people, while the people stood around Moshe from morning till evening. ¹⁴ When Moshe's father-in-law saw all that he was doing to the people, he said, "What is this that you are doing to the people? Why do you sit there alone, with all the people standing around you from morning till evening?" ¹⁵ Moshe answered his father-in-law, "It's because the people come to me seeking God's guidance. ¹⁶ Whenever they have a dispute, it comes to me; I judge between one person and another, and I explain to them God's laws and teachings."

¹⁷ Moshe's father-in-law said to him, "What you are doing isn't good. ¹⁸ You will certainly wear yourself out — and not only yourself, but these people here with you as well. It's too much for you — you can't do it alone, by yourself. ¹⁹ So listen now to what I have to say. I will give you some advice, and God will be with you. You should represent the people before God, and you should bring their cases to God. ²⁰ You should also teach them the laws and the teachings, and show them how to live their lives and what work they should do. ²¹ But you should choose from among all the people competent men who are God-fearing, honest and incorruptible to be their leaders, in charge of thousands, hundreds, fifties and tens. ²² Normally, they will settle the people's disputes. They should bring you the difficult cases; but ordinary matters they should decide themselves. In this way, they will make it easier for you and share the load with you. ²³ If you do this — and God is directing you to do it — you will be able to endure; and all these people too will arrive at their destination peacefully."

(iii) ²⁴ Moshe paid attention to his father-in-law's counsel and did everything he said. ²⁵ Moshe chose competent men from all Isra'el and made them heads

over the people, in charge of thousands, hundreds, fifties and tens. ²⁶ As a general rule, they settled the people's disputes — the difficult cases they brought to Moshe, but every simple matter they decided themselves. ²⁷ Then Moshe let his father-in-law leave, and he went off to his own country.

19 *(iv)* ¹ In the third month after the people of Isra'el had left the land of Egypt, the same day they came to the Sinai Desert. ² After setting out from Refidim and arriving at the Sinai Desert, they set up camp in the desert; there in front of the mountain, Isra'el set up camp.

³ Moshe went up to God, and *ADONAI* called to him from the mountain: "Here is what you are to say to the household of Ya'akov, to tell the people of Isra'el: ⁴ 'You have seen what I did to the Egyptians, and how I carried you on eagles' wings and brought you to myself. ⁵ Now if you will pay careful attention to what I say and keep my covenant, then you will be my own treasure from among all the peoples, for all the earth is mine; ⁶ and you will be a kingdom of *cohanim* for me, a nation set apart.' These are the words you are to speak to the people of Isra'el."

(v) ⁷ Moshe came, summoned the leaders of the people and presented them with all these words which *ADONAI* had ordered him to say. ⁸ All the people answered as one, "Everything *ADONAI* has said, we will do." Moshe reported the words of the people to *ADONAI*. ⁹ *ADONAI* said to Moshe, "See, I am coming to you in a thick cloud, so that the people will be able to hear when I speak with you and also to trust in you forever." Moshe had told *ADONAI* what the people had said; ¹⁰ so *ADONAI* said to Moshe, "Go to the people; today and tomorrow separate them for me by having them wash their clothing; ¹¹ and prepare for the third day. For on the third day, *ADONAI* will come down on Mount Sinai before the eyes of all the people. ¹² You are to set limits for the people all around; and say, 'Be careful not to go up on the mountain or even touch its base; whoever touches the mountain will surely be put to death. ¹³ No hand is to touch him; for he must be stoned or shot by arrows; neither animal nor human will be allowed to live.' When the *shofar* sounds, they may go up on the mountain."

(S: vi) ¹⁴ Moshe went down from the mountain to the people and separated the people for God, and they washed their clothing. ¹⁵ He said to the people, "Prepare for the third day; don't approach a woman."

¹⁶ On the morning of the third day, there was thunder, lightning and a thick cloud on the mountain. Then a *shofar* blast sounded so loudly that all the people in the camp trembled. ¹⁷ Moshe brought the people out of the camp to meet God; they stood near the base of the mountain. ¹⁸ Mount Sinai was enveloped in smoke, because *ADONAI* descended onto it in fire — its smoke went up like the smoke from a furnace, and the whole mountain shook violently. ¹⁹ As the sound of the *shofar* grew louder and louder, Moshe spoke; and God answered him with a voice.

(A: vi, S: vii) ²⁰ *ADONAI* came down onto Mount Sinai, to the top of the mountain; then *ADONAI* called Moshe to the top of the mountain; and Moshe went up. ²¹ *ADONAI* said to Moshe, "Go down and warn the people not to force their way through to *ADONAI* to see him; if they do, many of them will perish. ²² Even the *cohanim*, who are allowed to approach *ADONAI*, must keep themselves holy; otherwise, *ADONAI* may break out against them." ²³ Moshe said to *ADONAI*, "The people can't come up to Mount Sinai, because you ordered us to set limits around the mountain and separate it." ²⁴ But *ADONAI* answered him, "Go, get down! Then come back up, you and Aharon

with you. But don't let the *cohanim* and the people force their way through to come up to A*DONAI*, or he will break out against them." ²⁵ So Moshe went down to the people and told them.

20 ¹ Then God said all these words:

א ² "I am A*DONAI* your God, who brought you out of the land of Egypt, out of the abode of slavery.

ב ³ "You are to have no other gods before me. ⁴ You are not to make for yourselves a carved image or any kind of representation of anything in heaven above, on the earth beneath or in the water below the shoreline. ⁵ You are not to bow down to them or serve them; for I, A*DONAI* your God, am a jealous God, punishing the children for the sins of the parents to the third and fourth generation of those who hate me, ⁶ but displaying grace to the thousandth generation of those who love me and obey my *mitzvot*.

ג ⁷ "You are not to use lightly the name of A*DONAI* your God, because A*DONAI* will not leave unpunished someone who uses his name lightly.

ד ⁸ "Remember the day, *Shabbat*, to set it apart for God. ⁹ You have six days to labor and do all your work, ¹⁰ but the seventh day is a *Shabbat* for A*DONAI* your God. On it, you are not to do any kind of work — not you, your son or your daughter, not your male or female slave, not your livestock, and not the foreigner staying with you inside the gates to your property. ¹¹ For in six days, A*DONAI* made heaven and earth, the sea and everything in them; but on the seventh day he rested. This is why A*DONAI* blessed the day, *Shabbat*, and separated it for himself.

ה ¹² "Honor your father and mother, so that you may live long in the land which A*DONAI* your God is giving you.

ו ¹³ "Do not murder.

ז ⁽¹⁴⁾ "Do not commit adultery.

ח ⁽¹⁵⁾ "Do not steal.

ט ⁽¹⁶⁾ "Do not give false evidence against your neighbor.

י ¹⁴⁽¹⁷⁾ "Do not covet your neighbor's house; do not covet your neighbor's wife, his male or female slave, his ox, his donkey or anything that belongs to your neighbor."

(A: vii) ¹⁵⁽¹⁸⁾ All the people experienced the thunder, the lightning, the sound of the *shofar*, and the mountain smoking. When the people saw it, they trembled. Standing at a distance, ¹⁶⁽¹⁹⁾ they said to Moshe, "You, speak with us; and we will listen. But don't let God speak with us, or we will die." ¹⁷⁽²⁰⁾ Moshe answered the people, "Don't

be afraid, because God has come only to test you and make you fear him, so that you won't commit sins." [18(21)] So the people stood at a distance, but Moshe approached the thick darkness where God was.

(A: Maftir) [19(22)] ADONAI said to Moshe, "Here is what you are to say to the people of Isra'el: 'You yourselves have seen that I spoke with you from heaven. [20(23)] You are not to make with me gods of silver, nor are you to make gods of gold for yourselves. *(S: Maftir)* [21(24)] For me you need make only an altar of earth; on it you will sacrifice your burnt offerings, peace offerings, sheep, goats and cattle. In every place where I cause my name to be mentioned, I will come to you and bless you. [22(25)] If you do make me an altar of stone, you are not to build it of cut stones; for if you use a tool on it, you profane it. [23(26)] Likewise, you are not to use steps to go up to my altar; so that you won't be indecently uncovered.'"

Haftarah Yitro: Yesha'yahu (Isaiah) 6:1–7:6; 9:5(6)–6(7) (A); 6:1–13 (S)

B'rit Hadashah suggested readings for Parashah Yitro: Mattityahu (Matthew) 5:21–30; 15:1–11; 19:16–30; Mark 7:5–15; 10:17–31; Luke 18:18–30; Acts 6:1–7; Romans 2:17–29; 7:7–12; 13:8–10; Ephesians 6:1–3; 1 Timothy 3:1–14; 2 Timothy 2:2; Titus 1:5–9; Messianic Jews (Hebrews) 12:18–29; Ya'akov (James) 2:8–13; 1 Kefa (1 Peter) 2:9–10

Parashah 18: Mishpatim (Rulings) 21:1–24:18

21 ^1 "These are the rulings you are to present to them:

^2 "If you purchase a Hebrew slave, he is to work six years; but in the seventh, he is to be given his freedom without having to pay anything. ^3 If he came single, he is to leave single; if he was married when he came, his wife is to go with him when he leaves. ^4 But if his master gave him a wife, and she bore him sons or daughters, then the wife and her children will belong to her master, and he will leave by himself. ^5 Nevertheless, if the slave declares, 'I love my master, my wife and my children, so I don't want to go free,' ^6 then his master is to bring him before God; and there at the door or doorpost, his master is to pierce his ear with an awl; and the man will be his slave for life.

^7 "If a man sells his daughter as a slave, she is not to go free like the men-slaves. ^8 If her master married her but decides she no longer pleases him, then he is to allow her to be redeemed. He is not allowed to sell her to a foreign people, because he has treated her unfairly. ^9 If he has her marry his son, then he is to treat her like a daughter. ^10 If he marries another wife, he is not to reduce her food, clothing or marital rights. ^11 If he fails to provide her with these three things, she is to be given her freedom without having to pay anything.

^12 "Whoever attacks a person and causes his death must be put to death. ^13 If it was not premeditated but an act of God, then I will designate for you a place to which he can flee. ^14 But if someone willfully kills another after deliberate planning, you are to take him even from my altar and put him to death.

^15 "Whoever attacks his father or mother must be put to death.

¹⁶ "Whoever kidnaps someone must be put to death, regardless of whether he has already sold him or the person is found still in his possession.

¹⁷ "Whoever curses his father or mother must be put to death.

¹⁸ "If two people fight, and one hits the other with a stone or with his fist, and the injured party doesn't die but is confined to his bed; ¹⁹ then, if he recovers enough to be able to walk around outside, even if with a cane, the attacker will be free of liability, except to compensate him for his loss of time and take responsibility for his care until his recovery is complete.

(ii) ²⁰ "If a person beats his male or female slave with a stick so severely that he dies, he is to be punished; ²¹ except that if the slave lives for a day or two, he is not to be punished, since the slave is his property.

²² "If people are fighting with each other and happen to hurt a pregnant woman so badly that her unborn child dies, then, even if no other harm follows, he must be fined. He must pay the amount set by the woman's husband and confirmed by judges. ²³ But if any harm follows, then you are to give life for life, ²⁴ eye for eye, tooth for tooth, hand for hand, foot for foot, ²⁵ burn for burn, wound for wound and bruise for bruise.

²⁶ "If a person hits his male or female slave's eye and destroys it, he must let him go free in compensation for his eye. ²⁷ If he knocks out his male or female slave's tooth, he must let him go free in compensation for his tooth.

²⁸ "If an ox gores a man or a woman to death, the ox is to be stoned and its flesh not eaten, but the owner of the ox will have no further liability. ²⁹ However, if the ox was in the habit of goring in the past, and the owner was warned but did not confine it, so that it ended up killing a man or a woman; then the ox is to be stoned, and its owner too is to be put to death. ³⁰ However, a ransom may be imposed on him; and the death penalty will be commuted if he pays the amount imposed. ³¹ If the ox gores a son or daughter, the same rule applies. ³² If the ox gores a male or female slave, its owner must give their master twelve ounces of silver; and the ox is to be stoned to death.

³³ "If someone removes the cover from a cistern or digs one and fails to cover it, and an ox or donkey falls in, ³⁴ the owner of the cistern must make good the loss by compensating the animal's owner; but the dead animal will be his.

³⁵ "If one person's ox hurts another's, so that it dies, they are to sell the live ox and divide the revenue from the sale; and they are also to divide the dead animal. ³⁶ But if it is known that the ox was in the habit of goring in the past, and the owner did not confine it; he must pay ox for ox, but the dead animal will be his.

³⁷⁽²²:¹⁾ "If someone steals an ox or a sheep and slaughters or sells it, he is to pay five oxen for an ox and four sheep for a sheep.

22 ¹⁽²⁾ "If a thief caught in the act of breaking in is beaten to death, it is not murder; ²⁽³⁾ unless it happens after sunrise, in which case it is murder. A thief must make restitution; so if he has nothing, he himself is to be sold to make good the loss from the theft. ³⁽⁴⁾ If what he stole is found alive in his possession, he is to pay double, no matter whether it is an ox, a donkey or a sheep.

(iii) ⁴⁽⁵⁾ "If a person causes a field or vineyard to be grazed over or lets his animal loose to graze in someone else's field, he is to make restitution from the best produce of his own field and vineyard.

$^{5(6)}$ "If a fire is started and spreads to thorns, so that stacked grain, standing grain or a field is destroyed, the person who lit it must make restitution.

$^{6(7)}$ "If a person entrusts a neighbor with money or goods, and they are stolen from the trustee's house, then, if the thief is found, he must pay double. $^{7(8)}$ But if the thief is not found, then the trustee must state before God that he did not take the person's goods himself. $^{8(9)}$ In every case of dispute over ownership, whether of an ox, a donkey, a sheep, clothing, or any missing property, where one person says, 'This is mine,' both parties are to come before God; and the one whom God condemns must pay the other one double.

$^{9(10)}$ "If a person trusts a neighbor to look after a donkey, ox, sheep or any animal, and it dies, is injured or is driven away unseen, $^{10(11)}$ then the neighbor's oath before *Adonai* that he has not taken the goods will settle the matter between them — the owner is to accept it without the neighbor's making restitution. $^{11(12)}$ But if it was stolen from the neighbor, he must make restitution to the owner. $^{12(13)}$ If it was torn to pieces by an animal, the neighbor must bring it as evidence, and then he doesn't need to make good the loss.

$^{13(14)}$ "If someone borrows something from his neighbor, and it gets injured or dies with the owner not present, he must make restitution. $^{14(15)}$ If the owner was present, he need not make good the loss. If the owner hired it out, the loss is covered by the hiring fee.

$^{15(16)}$ "If a man seduces a virgin who is not engaged to be married and sleeps with her, he must pay the bride-price for her to be his wife. $^{16(17)}$ But if her father refuses to give her to him, he must pay a sum equivalent to the bride-price for virgins.

$^{17(18)}$ "You are not to permit a sorceress to live.

$^{18(19)}$ "Whoever has sexual relations with an animal must be put to death.

$^{19(20)}$ "Anyone who sacrifices to any god other than *Adonai* alone is to be completely destroyed.

$^{20(21)}$ "You must neither wrong nor oppress a foreigner living among you, for you yourselves were foreigners in the land of Egypt.

$^{21(22)}$ "You are not to abuse any widow or orphan. $^{22(23)}$ If you do abuse them in any way, and they cry to me, I will certainly heed their cry. $^{23(24)}$ My anger will burn, and I will kill you with the sword — your own wives will be widows and your own children fatherless.

$^{24(25)}$ "If you loan money to one of my people who is poor, you are not to deal with him as would a creditor; and you are not to charge him interest. $^{25(26)}$ If you take your neighbor's coat as collateral, you are to restore it to him by sundown, $^{26(27)}$ because it is his only garment — he needs it to wrap his body; what else does he have in which to sleep? Moreover, if he cries out to me, I will listen; because I am compassionate.

(iv) $^{27(28)}$ "You are not to curse God, and you are not to curse a leader of your people.

$^{28(29)}$ "You are not to delay offering from your harvest of grain, olive oil or wine.

"The firstborn of your sons you are to give to me. $^{29(30)}$ You are to do the same with your oxen and your sheep — it is to stay with its mother seven days, and on the eighth day you are to give it to me.

$^{30(31)}$ "You are to be my specially separated people. Therefore you are not to eat any flesh torn by wild animals in the countryside; rather, throw it out for the dogs.

23 ¹ "You are not to repeat false rumors; do not join hands with the wicked by offering perjured testimony. ²Do not follow the crowd when it does what is wrong; and don't allow the popular view to sway you into offering testimony for any cause if the effect will be to pervert justice. ³On the other hand, don't favor a person's lawsuit simply because he is poor.

⁴ "If you come upon your enemy's ox or donkey straying, you must return it to him. ⁵If you see the donkey which belongs to someone who hates you lying down helpless under its load, you are not to pass him by but to go and help him free it.

*(v)*⁶ "Do not deny anyone justice in his lawsuit simply because he is poor. ⁷ Keep away from fraud, and do not cause the death of the innocent and righteous; for I will not justify the wicked. ⁸ You are not to receive a bribe, for a bribe blinds the clearsighted and subverts the cause of the righteous.

⁹ "You are not to oppress a foreigner, for you know how a foreigner feels, since you were foreigners in the land of Egypt.

¹⁰ "For six years, you are to sow your land with seed and gather in its harvest. ¹¹ But the seventh year, you are to let it rest and lie fallow, so that the poor among your people can eat; and what they leave, the wild animals in the countryside can eat. Do the same with your vineyard and olive grove.

¹² "For six days, you are to work. But on the seventh day, you are to rest, so that your ox and donkey can rest, and your slave-girl's son and the foreigner be renewed. ¹³ "Pay attention to everything I have said to you; do not invoke the names of other gods or even let them be heard crossing your lips.

¹⁴ "Three times a year, you are to observe a festival for me. ¹⁵ Keep the festival of *matzah*: for seven days, as I ordered you, you are to eat *matzah* at the time determined in the month of Aviv; for it was in that month that you left Egypt. No one is to appear before me empty-handed. ¹⁶ Next, the festival of harvest, the firstfruits of your efforts sowing in the field; and last, the festival of ingathering, at the end of the year, when you gather in from the fields the results of your efforts. ¹⁷ Three times a year all your men are to appear before the Lord, *ADONAI*.

¹⁸ "You are not to offer the blood of my sacrifice with leavened bread, nor is the fat of my festival to remain all night until morning. ¹⁹ "You are to bring the best firstfruits of your land into the house of *ADONAI* your God.

"You are not to boil a young animal in its mother's milk.

(vi) ²⁰ "I am sending an angel ahead of you to guard you on the way and bring you to the place I have prepared. ²¹ Pay attention to him, listen to what he says and do not rebel against him; because he will not forgive any wrongdoing of yours, since my name resides in him. ²² But if you listen to what he says and do everything I tell you, then I will be an enemy to your enemies and a foe to your foes. ²³ When my angel goes ahead of you and brings you to the Emori, Hitti, P'rizi, Kena'ani, Hivi and Y'vusi, I will make an end of them. ²⁴ You are not to worship their gods, serve them or follow their practices; rather, you are to demolish them completely and smash their standing-stones to pieces.

²⁵ "You are to serve *ADONAI* your God; and he will bless your food and water. I will take sickness away from among you. *(vii)* ²⁶ In your land your women will not miscarry or be barren, and you will live out the full span of your lives. ²⁷ I will send terror of me ahead of you, throwing into confusion all the people to whom you

come; and I will make all your enemies turn their backs on you. ²⁸ I will send hornets ahead of you to drive out the Hivi, Kena'ani and Hitti from before you. ²⁹ I will not drive them out from before you in one year, which would cause the land to become desolate and the wild animals too many for you. ³⁰ I will drive them out from before you gradually, until you have grown in number and can take possession of the land. ³¹ I will set your boundaries from the Sea of Suf to the sea of the P'lishtim and from the desert to the [Euphrates] River, for I will hand the inhabitants of the land over to you, and you will drive them out from before you. ³² You are not to make a covenant with them or with their gods. ³³ They are not to live in your land; otherwise they will make you sin against me by ensnaring you to serve their gods."

24 ¹ To Moshe [*Adonai*] said, "Come up to *Adonai*—you, Aharon, Nadav, Avihu, and seventy of the leaders of Isra'el. Prostrate yourselves at a distance, ² while Moshe alone approaches *Adonai*—the others are not to approach, and the people are not to go up with him." ³ Moshe came and told the people everything *Adonai* had said, including all the rulings. The people answered with one voice: "We will obey every word *Adonai* has spoken."

⁴ Moshe wrote down all the words of *Adonai*. He rose early in the morning, built an altar at the base of the mountain and set upright twelve large stones to represent the twelve tribes of Isra'el. ⁵ He sent the young men of the people of Isra'el to offer burnt offerings and sacrifice peace offerings of oxen to *Adonai*. ⁶ Moshe took half of the blood and put it in basins; the other half of the blood he splashed against the altar. ⁷ Then he took the book of the covenant and read it aloud, so that the people could hear; and they responded, "Everything that *Adonai* has spoken, we will do and obey." ⁸ Moshe took the blood, sprinkled it on the people and said, "This is the blood of the covenant which *Adonai* has made with you in accordance with all these words."

⁹ Moshe, Aharon, Nadav, Avihu and seventy of the leaders went up; ¹⁰ and they saw the God of Isra'el. Under his feet was something like a sapphire stone pavement as clear as the sky itself. ¹¹ He did not reach out his hand against these notables of Isra'el; on the contrary, they saw God, even as they were eating and drinking.

¹² *Adonai* said to Moshe, "Come up to me on the mountain, and stay there. I will give you the stone tablets with the *Torah* and the *mitzvot* I have written on them, so that you can teach them." ¹³ Moshe got up, also Y'hoshua his assistant; and Moshe went up onto the mountain of God. ¹⁴ To the leaders he said, "Stay here for us, until we come back to you. See, Aharon and Hur are with you; whoever has a problem should turn to them." *(S: Maftir)* ¹⁵ Moshe went up onto the mountain, and the cloud covered the mountain. *(A: Maftir)* ¹⁶ The glory of *Adonai* stayed on Mount Sinai, and the cloud covered it for six days. On the seventh day he called to Moshe out of the cloud. ¹⁷ To the people of Isra'el the glory of *Adonai* looked like a raging fire on the top of the mountain. ¹⁸ Moshe entered the cloud and went up on the mountain; he was on the mountain forty days and nights.

Haftarah Mishpatim: Yirmeyahu (Jeremiah) 34:8–22; 33:25–26

B'rit Hadashah suggested readings for Parashah Mishpatim: Mattityahu (Matthew) 5:38–42; 15:1–20; Mark 7:1–23; Acts 23:1–11; Messianic Jews (Hebrews) 9:15–22; 10:28–39

Parashah 19: T'rumah (Contribution) 25:1–27:19

25 ¹ ADONAI said to Moshe, ² "Tell the people of Isra'el to take up a collection for me — accept a contribution from anyone who wholeheartedly wants to give. ³ The contribution you are to take from them is to consist of gold, silver and bronze; ⁴ blue, purple and scarlet yarn; fine linen, goat's hair, ⁵ tanned ram skins and fine leather; acacia-wood; ⁶ oil for the light, spices for the anointing oil and for the fragrant incense; ⁷ onyx stones and other stones to be set, for the ritual vest and breastplate.

⁸ "They are to make me a sanctuary, so that I may live among them. ⁹ You are to make it according to everything I show you — the design of the tabernacle and the design of its furnishings. This is how you are to make it.

¹⁰ "They are to make an ark of acacia-wood three-and-three-quarters feet long, two-and-a-quarter feet wide and two-and-a-quarter feet high. ¹¹ You are to overlay it with pure gold — overlay it both inside and outside — and put a molding of gold around the top of it. ¹² Cast four gold rings for it, and attach them to its four feet, two rings on each side. ¹³ Make poles of acacia-wood, and overlay them with gold. ¹⁴ Put the poles into the rings on the sides of the ark; you will use them to carry the ark. ¹⁵ The poles are to remain in the rings of the ark; they are not to be removed from it. ¹⁶ Into the ark you are to put the testimony which I am about to give you.

(ii) ¹⁷ "You are to make a cover for the ark out of pure gold; it is to be three-and-three-quarters feet long and two-and-a-quarter feet high. ¹⁸ You are to make two *k'ruvim* of gold. Make them of hammered work for the two ends of the ark-cover. ¹⁹ Make one *keruv* for one end and one *keruv* for the other end; make the *k'ruvim* of one piece with the ark-cover at its two ends. ²⁰ The *k'ruvim* will have their wings spread out above, so that their wings cover the ark, and their faces are toward each other and toward the ark-cover. ²¹ You are to put the ark-cover on top of the ark.

"Inside the ark you will put the testimony that I am about to give you. ²² There I will meet with you. I will speak with you from above the ark-cover, from between the two *k'ruvim* which are on the ark for the testimony, about all the orders I am giving you for the people of Isra'el.

²³ "You are to make a table of acacia-wood three feet long, eighteen inches wide and eighteen inches high. ²⁴ Overlay it with pure gold, and put a molding of gold around the top of it. ²⁵ Make around it a rim a handbreadth wide, and put a molding of gold around the rim. ²⁶ Make four gold rings for it, and attach the rings to the four corners, near its four legs. ²⁷ The rings to hold the poles used to carry the table are to be placed close to the rim. ²⁸ Make the poles of acacia-wood, overlay them with gold, and use them to carry the table.

²⁹ "Make its dishes, pans, bowls and pitchers of pure gold. ³⁰ On the table you are to place the bread of the presence in my presence always.

(S: iii) ³¹ "You are to make a *menorah* of pure gold. It is to be made of hammered work; its base, shaft, cups, ring of outer leaves and petals are to be of one piece with it. ³² It is to have six branches extending from its sides, three branches of the *menorah* on one side of it and three on the other. ³³ On one branch are to be three cups shaped like almond blossoms, each with a ring of outer leaves and petals; likewise on the opposite branch three cups shaped like almond blossoms, each with a ring of outer leaves and petals; and similarly for

all six branches extending from the *menorah*. ³⁴ On the central shaft of the *menorah* are to be four cups shaped like almond blossoms, each with its ring of outer leaves and petals. ³⁵ Where each pair of branches joins the central shaft is to be a ring of outer leaves of one piece with the pair of branches — thus for all six branches. ³⁶ The rings of outer leaves and their branches are to be of one piece with the shaft. Thus the whole *menorah* is to be a single piece of hammered work made of pure gold.

³⁷ "Make seven lamps for the *menorah*, and mount them so as to give light to the space in front of it. ³⁸ Its tongs and trays are to be of pure gold. ³⁹ The *menorah* and its utensils are to be made of sixty-six pounds of pure gold. ⁴⁰ See that you make them according to the design being shown you on the mountain.

26 *(A: iii)* ¹ "You are to make the tabernacle with ten sheets of finely woven linen and with blue, purple and scarlet yarn. You are to make them with *k'ruvim* worked in, that have been crafted by a skilled artisan. ² Each one is to be forty-two feet long and six feet wide; all the sheets are to be the same size. ³ Five sheets are to be joined one to another, and the other five sheets are to be joined one to another. ⁴ Make loops of blue on the edge of the outermost sheet in the first set, and do the same on the edge of the outermost sheet in the second set. ⁵ Make fifty loops on the one sheet, and make fifty loops on the edge of the sheet in the second set; the loops are to be opposite one another. ⁶ Make fifty fasteners of gold, and couple the sheets to each other with the fasteners, so that the tabernacle forms a single unit.

⁷ "You are to make sheets of goat's hair to be used as a tent covering the tabernacle; make eleven sheets. ⁸ Each sheet is to be forty-five feet long and six feet wide — all eleven sheets are to be the same size. ⁹ Join five sheets together and six sheets together, and fold the sixth sheet double at the front of the tent. ¹⁰ Make fifty loops on the edge of the outermost sheet in the first set and fifty loops on the edge of the outermost sheet in the second set. ¹¹ Make fifty fasteners of bronze, put the fasteners in the loops, and join the tent together, so that it forms a single unit. ¹² As for the overhanging part that remains of the sheets forming the tent, the half-sheet remaining is to hang over the back of the tabernacle; ¹³ and the eighteen inches on the one side and the eighteen inches on the other side of that remaining in the length of the sheets forming the tent is to hang over the tabernacle to cover it on each side.

¹⁴ "You are to make a covering for the tent of tanned ram skins and an outer covering of fine leather.

(iv) ¹⁵ "Make the upright planks for the tabernacle out of acacia-wood. ¹⁶ Each plank is to be fifteen feet long and two-and-a-quarter feet wide. ¹⁷ There are to be two projections on each plank, and the planks are to be joined one to another. That is how you are to make all the planks for the tabernacle.

¹⁸ "Make the planks for the tabernacle as follows: twenty planks for the south side, facing southward. ¹⁹ Make forty silver sockets under the twenty planks, two sockets under one plank for its two projections and two sockets under another plank for its two projections. ²⁰ "For the second side of the tabernacle, to the north, make twenty planks ²¹ and their forty silver sockets, two sockets under one plank and two under another. ²² "For the rear part of the tabernacle, toward the west, make six planks.

²³ For the corners of the tabernacle in the rear, make two planks; ²⁴ these are to be double from the bottom all the way to the top but joined at a single ring. Do the same with both of them; they are to form the two corners. ²⁵ Thus there will be eight planks with their silver sockets, sixteen sockets, two sockets under one plank and two under another.

²⁶ "Make crossbars of acacia-wood, five for the planks of the one side of the tabernacle, ²⁷ five crossbars for the planks of the other side of the tabernacle, and five crossbars for the planks at the side of the tabernacle at the rear toward the west. ²⁸ The middle crossbar, halfway up the planks, is to extend from end to end. ²⁹ Overlay the planks with gold, make gold rings for them through which the crossbars will pass, and overlay the crossbars with gold.

³⁰ "You are to erect the tabernacle according to the design you have been shown on the mountain.

(v) ³¹ "You are to make a curtain of blue, purple and scarlet yarn and finely woven linen. Make it with *k'ruvim* worked in, that have been crafted by a skilled artisan. ³² Hang it with gold hooks on four acacia-wood posts overlaid with gold and standing in four silver sockets. ³³ Hang the curtain below the fasteners. Then bring the ark for the testimony inside the curtain; the curtain will be the divider for you between the Holy Place and the Especially Holy Place. ³⁴ You are to put the ark-cover on the ark for the testimony in the Especially Holy Place.

³⁵ "You are to put the table outside the curtain and the *menorah* opposite the table on the side of the tabernacle toward the south; put the table on the north side.

³⁶ "For the entrance to the tent, make a screen of blue, purple and scarlet yarn and finely woven linen; it should be in colors, the work of a weaver. ³⁷ For the screen, make five posts of acacia-wood; overlay them with gold; and cast for them five sockets of bronze.

27 *(vi)* ¹ "You are to make the altar of acacia-wood, seven-and-a-half feet long and seven-and-a-half feet wide — the altar is to be square and four-and-a-half feet high. ² Make horns for it on its four corners; the horns are to be of one piece with it; and you are to overlay it with bronze.

³ "Make its pots for removing ashes, and its shovels, basins, meat-hooks and fire pans; all its utensils you are to make of bronze. ⁴ Make for it a grate of bronze netting; and on the four corners of the netting, make four bronze rings. ⁵ Put it under the rim of the altar, so that the netting reaches halfway up the altar. ⁶ Make poles of acacia-wood for the altar and overlay them with bronze. ⁷ Its poles are to be put into the rings; the poles are to be on both sides of the altar for carrying it. ⁸ The altar is to be made of planks and hollow inside. They are to make it just as you were shown on the mountain.

(vii) ⁹ "Here is how you are to make the courtyard of the tabernacle. On the south side, facing southward, are to be tapestries for the courtyard made of finely woven linen, 150 feet for one side, ¹⁰ supported on twenty posts in twenty bronze sockets; the hooks on the posts and the attached rings for hanging are to be of silver. ¹¹ Likewise, along the north side are to be tapestries 150 feet long, hung on twenty posts in twenty bronze sockets, with silver hooks and rings for the posts. ¹² Across the width of the courtyard on the west side are to be tapestries seventy-five feet long, hung on ten posts in ten sockets. ¹³ The width of the

courtyard on the east side, facing east, will be seventy-five feet. ¹⁴ The tapestries for one side [of the gateway] will be twenty-two-and-a-half feet long, hung on three posts in three sockets; ¹⁵ for the other side there will be tapestries twenty-two-and-a-half feet long on three posts in three sockets.

¹⁶ "For the gateway of the courtyard there is to be a screen thirty feet long made of blue, purple and scarlet yarn and finely woven linen. It should be in colors, the work of a weaver. It is to be on four posts in four sockets. *(Maftir)* ¹⁷ All the posts all the way around the courtyard are to be banded with silver and to stand in sockets of bronze. ¹⁸ The length of the courtyard is to be 150 feet and the width seventy-five feet everywhere; with the height seven-and-a-half feet. The tapestries and screen are to be of finely woven linen, and the sockets are to be of bronze.

¹⁹ "All the equipment needed for every kind of service in the tabernacle, as well as the tent pegs for the tabernacle and for the courtyard, are to be of bronze.

Haftarah T'rumah: M'lakhim Alef (1 Kings) 5:26(12)–6:13

B'rit Hadashah suggested readings for Parashah T'rumah: Messianic Jews (Hebrews) 8:1–6; 9:23–24; 10:1

Parashah 20: Tetzaveh (You are to order) 27:20–30:10

²⁰ "You are to order the people of Isra'el to bring you pure oil of pounded olives for the light, and to keep a lamp burning continually. ²¹ Aharon and his sons are to put it in the tent of meeting, outside the curtain in front of the testimony, and keep it burning from evening until morning before ADONAI. This is to be a permanent regulation through all the generations of the people of Isra'el.

28 ¹ "You are to summon your brother Aharon and his sons to come from among the people of Isra'el to you, so that they can serve me as *cohanim* — Aharon and his sons Nadav, Avihu, El'azar and Itamar. ² You are to make for your brother Aharon garments set apart for serving God, expressing dignity and splendor. ³ Speak to all the craftsmen to whom I have given the spirit of wisdom, and have them make Aharon's garments to set him apart for me, so that he can serve me in the office of *cohen*.

⁴ "The garments they are to make are these: a breastplate, a ritual vest, a robe, a checkered tunic, a turban and a sash. They are to make holy garments for your brother Aharon and his sons, so that he can serve me in the office of *cohen*. ⁵ They are to use gold; blue, purple and scarlet yarn; and fine linen.

⁶ "They are to make the ritual vest of gold, of blue, purple and scarlet yarn, and of finely woven linen, crafted by a skilled artisan. ⁷ Attached to its front and back edges are to be two shoulder-pieces that can be fastened together. ⁸ Its decorated belt is to be of the same workmanship and materials — gold; blue, purple and scarlet yarn; and finely woven linen. ⁹ Take two onyx stones and engrave on them the names of the sons of Isra'el — ¹⁰ six of their names on one stone and the six remaining names on the other, in the order of their birth. ¹¹ An engraver should engrave the names of the sons of Isra'el on the two stones as he would engrave a seal. Mount the

stones in gold settings, ¹² and put the two stones on the shoulder-pieces of the vest as stones calling to mind the sons of Isra'el. Aharon is to carry their names before ADONAI on his two shoulders as a reminder.

(ii) ¹³ "Make gold squares ¹⁴ and two chains of pure gold, twisted like cords; attach the cord-like chains to the squares.

¹⁵ "Make a breastplate for judging. Have it crafted by a skilled artisan; make it like the work of the ritual vest — make it of gold; blue, purple and scarlet yarn; and finely woven linen. ¹⁶ When folded double it is to be square — a hand-span by a hand-span. ¹⁷ Put on it settings of stones, four rows of stones: the first row is to be a carnelian, a topaz and an emerald; ¹⁸ the second row a green feldspar, a sapphire and a diamond; ¹⁹ the third row an orange zircon, an agate and an amethyst; ²⁰ and the fourth row a beryl, an onyx and a jasper. They are to be mounted in their gold settings. ²¹ The stones will correspond to the names of the twelve sons of Isra'el; they are to be engraved with their names as a seal would be engraved, to represent the twelve tribes.

²² "On the breastplate, make two pure gold chains twisted like cords. ²³ Also for the breastplate, make two gold rings; and put the gold rings on the two ends of the breastplate. ²⁴ Put the two twisted gold chains in the two rings at the two ends of the breastplate; ²⁵ attach the other two ends of the twisted chains to the front of the shoulder-pieces of the ritual vest. ²⁶ Make two gold rings and put them on the two ends of the breastplate, at its edge, on the side facing in toward the vest. ²⁷ Also make two gold rings and attach them low on the front part of the vest's shoulder-pieces, near the join, above the vest's decorated belt. ²⁸ Then bind the breastplate by its rings to the rings of the vest with a blue cord, so that it can be on the vest's decorated belt, and so that the breastplate won't swing loose from the vest. ²⁹ Aharon will carry the names of the sons of Isra'el on the breastplate for judging, over his heart, when he enters the Holy Place, as a continual reminder before ADONAI. ³⁰ You are to put the *urim* and the *tumim* in the breastplate for judging; they will be over Aharon's heart when he goes into the presence of ADONAI. Thus Aharon will always have the means for making decisions for the people of Isra'el over his heart when he is in the presence of ADONAI.

(iii) ³¹ "You are to make the robe for the ritual vest entirely of blue. ³² It is to have an opening for the head in the middle. Around the opening is to be a border woven like the neck of a coat of mail, so that it won't tear. ³³ On its bottom hem make pomegranates of blue, purple and scarlet; and put them all the way around, with gold bells between them all the way around — ³⁴ gold bell, pomegranate, gold bell, pomegranate, all the way around the hem of the robe. ³⁵ Aharon is to wear it when he ministers, and its sound will be heard whenever he enters the Holy Place before ADONAI and when he leaves, so that he won't die.

³⁶ "You are to make an ornament of pure gold and engrave on it as on a seal, 'Set apart for ADONAI.' ³⁷ Fasten it to the turban with a blue cord, on the front of the turban, ³⁸ over Aharon's forehead. Because Aharon bears the guilt for any errors committed by the people of Isra'el in consecrating their holy gifts, this ornament is always to be on his forehead, so that the gifts for ADONAI will be accepted by him.

³⁹ "You are to weave the checkered tunic of fine linen, make a turban of fine linen, and make a belt, the work of a weaver in colors. ⁴⁰ Likewise for Aharon's sons make tunics, sashes and headgear expressing dignity and splendor. ⁴¹ With them clothe

your brother Aharon and his sons. Then anoint them, inaugurate them, and consecrate them, so that they will be able to serve me in the office of *cohen*. ⁴² Also make
for them linen shorts reaching from waist to thigh, to cover their bare flesh. ⁴³ Aharon
and his sons are to wear them when they go into the tent of meeting and when they
approach the altar to minister in the Holy Place, so that they won't incur guilt and
die. This is to be a perpetual regulation, both for him and for his descendants.

29 *(iv)* ¹ "Here is what you are to do to consecrate them for ministry to me in the
office of *cohen*. Take one young bull and two rams without defect, ² also *matzah*,
matzah cakes mixed with olive oil, and *matzah* wafers spread with oil — all made
from fine wheat flour; ³ put them together in a basket, and present them in the basket,
along with the bull and the two rams.

⁴ "Bring Aharon and his sons to the entrance of the tent of meeting, and wash
them with water. ⁵ Take the garments, and put on Aharon the tunic, the robe for the
ritual vest, the vest itself, and the breastplate. Fasten the vest on him with its belt.
⁶ Put the turban on his head and attach the holy ornament to the turban. ⁷ Then take
the anointing oil, and anoint him by pouring it on his head. ⁸ Bring his sons; put
tunics on them; ⁹ wrap sashes around them, Aharon and his sons; and put the headgear on their heads. The office of *cohen* is to be theirs by a permanent regulation.
Thus you will consecrate Aharon and his sons.

¹⁰ "Bring the young bull to the front of the tent of meeting. Aharon and his sons
are to lay their hands on the bull's head, ¹¹ and you are to slaughter the bull in the
presence of ADONAI at the entrance to the tent of meeting. ¹² Take some of the bull's
blood, and put it on the horns of the altar with your finger; pour out all the rest of the
blood at the base of the altar. ¹³ Take all the fat that covers the inner organs, the
covering of the liver and the two kidneys with their fat, and offer them up in smoke
on the altar. ¹⁴ But the bull's flesh, skin and dung you are to destroy by fire outside
the camp; it is a sin offering.

¹⁵ "Take one of the rams: Aharon and his sons are to lay their hands on the ram's
head; ¹⁶ and you are to slaughter the ram, take its blood, and splash it on all sides of
the altar. ¹⁷ Quarter the ram, wash the inner organs and the lower parts of the legs,
and put them with the quarters and the head. ¹⁸ Then offer up the whole ram in smoke
on the altar. It is a burnt offering for ADONAI, a pleasing aroma, an offering made to
ADONAI by fire.

(v) ¹⁹ "Take the other ram: Aharon and his sons are to lay their hands on the
ram's head; ²⁰ and you are to slaughter the ram, take some of its blood, and put it on
the lobe of Aharon's right ear, on the lobes of his sons' right ears, on the thumbs of
their right hands and on the big toes of their right feet. Take the rest of the blood and
splash it on all sides of the altar. ²¹ Then take some of the blood that is on the altar and
some of the anointing oil, and sprinkle it on Aharon and his clothing and on his sons
and the clothing of his sons with him; so that he and his clothing will be consecrated,
and with him his sons and his sons' clothing. ²² Also take the fat from the ram, the fat
tail, the fat that covers the inner organs, the two kidneys, the fat covering them and
the right thigh — for it is a ram of consecration — ²³ along with one loaf of bread,
one cake of oiled bread and one wafer from the basket of *matzah* which is before
ADONAI — ²⁴ and put it all in the hands of Aharon and his sons. They are to wave them
as a wave offering in the presence of ADONAI. ²⁵ Then take them back; and burn them

up in smoke on the altar, on top of the burnt offering, to be a pleasing aroma before
Adonai; it is an offering made to *Adonai* by fire.

²⁶ "Take the breast of the ram for Aharon's consecration, and wave it as a wave
offering before *Adonai*; it will be your share. ²⁷ Consecrate the breast of the wave
offering and the thigh of any contribution that has been waved and raised up, whether
from the ram of consecration, or from anything else meant for Aharon or his sons;
²⁸ this will belong to Aharon and his sons as their share perpetually due from the
people of Isra'el — it will be a contribution from the people of Isra'el from their
peace offerings, their contribution to *Adonai*.

²⁹ "The holy garments of Aharon will be used by his sons after him; they will be
anointed and consecrated in them. ³⁰ The son who becomes *cohen* in his place, who
comes into the tent of meeting to serve in the Holy Place, is to wear them for seven
days. ³¹ Take the ram of consecration, and boil its meat in a holy place. ³² Aharon and
his sons will eat the ram's meat and the bread in the basket at the entrance to the tent
of meeting. ³³ They are to eat the things with which atonement was made for them, to
inaugurate and consecrate them; no one else may eat this food, because it is holy. ³⁴ If
any of the meat for the consecration or any of the bread remains until morning, burn
up what remains; it is not to be eaten, because it is holy. ³⁵ Carry out all these orders
I have given you concerning Aharon and his sons. You are to spend seven days
consecrating them.

³⁶ "Each day, offer a young bull as a sin offering, besides the other offerings of
atonement; offer the sin offering on the altar as your atonement for it; then anoint it
to consecrate it. ³⁷ Seven days you will make atonement on the altar and consecrate it;
thus the altar will be especially holy, and whatever touches the altar will become holy.

(vi) ³⁸ "Now this is what you are to offer on the altar: two lambs a year old,
regularly, every day. ³⁹ The one lamb you are to offer in the morning and the other
lamb at dusk. ⁴⁰ With the one lamb offer two quarts of finely ground flour mixed with
one quart of oil from pressed olives; along with one quart of wine as a drink offering.
⁴¹ The other lamb you are to offer at dusk; do with it as with the morning grain and
drink offerings — it will be a pleasing aroma, an offering made to *Adonai* by fire.
⁴² Through all your generations this is to be the regular burnt offering at the entrance
to the tent of meeting before *Adonai*. There is where I will meet with you to speak
with you. ⁴³ There I will meet with the people of Isra'el; and the place will be
consecrated by my glory. ⁴⁴ I will consecrate the tent of meeting and the altar,
likewise I will consecrate Aharon and his sons to serve me in the office of *cohen*.
⁴⁵ Then I will live with the people of Isra'el and be their God: ⁴⁶ they will know that
I am *Adonai* their God, who brought them out of the land of Egypt in order to live
with them. I am *Adonai* their God.

30 *(vii)* ¹ "You are to make an altar on which to burn incense; make it of acacia-
wood. ² It is to be eighteen inches square and three feet high; its horns are to be of
one piece with it. ³ Overlay it with pure gold — its top, all around its sides, and its
horns; and put around it a molding of gold. ⁴ Make two gold rings for it under its
molding at the two corners on both sides; this is where the carrying-poles will go.
⁵ Make the poles of acacia-wood, and overlay them with gold.

⁶ "Place it in front of the curtain by the ark for the testimony, in front of the ark-
cover that is over the testimony, where I will meet with you. ⁷ Aharon will burn

fragrant incense on it as a pleasing aroma every morning; he is to burn it when he prepares the lamps. *(Maftir)* ⁸ Aharon is also to burn it when he lights the lamps at dusk; this is the regular burning of incense before ADONAI through all your generations. ⁹ You are not to offer unauthorized incense on it, or a burnt offering or a grain offering; and you are not to pour a drink offering on it. ¹⁰ Aharon is to make atonement on its horns once a year — with the blood of the sin offering of atonement he is to make atonement for it once a year through all your generations; it is especially holy to ADONAI."

Haftarah Tetzaveh: Yechezk'el (Ezekiel) 43:10–27

B'rit Hadashah suggested reading for Parashah Tetzaveh: Philippians 4:10–20

Parashah 21: Ki Tissa (When you take) 30:11–34:35

¹¹ ADONAI said to Moshe, ¹² "When you take a census of the people of Isra'el and register them, each, upon registration, is to pay a ransom for his life to ADONAI, to avoid any breakout of plague among them during the time of the census. ¹³ Everyone subject to the census is to pay as an offering to ADONAI half a *shekel* [one-fifth of an ounce of silver]— by the standard of the sanctuary *shekel* (a *shekel* equals twenty *gerah*s). ¹⁴ Everyone over twenty years of age who is subject to the census is to give this offering to ADONAI — ¹⁵ the rich is not to give more or the poor less than the half-*shekel* when giving ADONAI's offering to atone for your lives. ¹⁶ You are to take the atonement money from the people of Isra'el and use it for the service in the tent of meeting, so that it will be a reminder of the people of Isra'el before ADONAI to atone for your lives."

¹⁷ ADONAI said to Moshe, ¹⁸ "You are to make a basin of bronze, with a base of bronze, for washing. Place it between the tent of meeting and the altar, and put water in it. ¹⁹ Aharon and his sons will wash their hands and feet there ²⁰ when they enter the tent of meeting — they are to wash with water, so that they won't die. Also when they approach the altar to minister by burning an offering for ADONAI, ²¹ they are to wash their hands and feet, so that they won't die. This is to be a perpetual law for them through all their generations."

²² ADONAI said to Moshe, ²³ "Take the best spices — 500 *shekel*s of myrrh [12¹/₂ pounds], half this amount (250 *shekel*s) of aromatic cinnamon [6¹/₄ pounds], 250 *shekel*s of aromatic cane, ²⁴ 500 *shekel*s of cassia (use the sanctuary standard), and one gallon of olive oil — ²⁵ and make them into a holy anointing oil; blend it and perfume it as would an expert perfume-maker; it will be a holy anointing oil. ²⁶ Use it to anoint the tent of meeting, the ark for the testimony, ²⁷ the table and all its utensils, the *menorah* and all its utensils, the incense altar, ²⁸ the altar for burnt offerings and all its utensils, and the basin with its base. ²⁹ You are to consecrate them — they will be especially holy, and whatever touches them will be holy. ³⁰ Then you are to anoint Aharon and his sons — you are to consecrate them to serve me in the office of *cohen*.

³¹ "Tell the people of Isra'el, 'This is to be a holy anointing oil for me through all your generations. ³² It is not to be used for anointing a person's body; and you are

not to make any like it, with the same composition of ingredients — it is holy, and you are to treat it as holy. ^{33} Whoever makes any like it or uses it on any unauthorized person is to be cut off from his people.'"

^{34} ADONAI said to Moshe, "Take aromatic plant substances — balsam resin, sweet onycha root and bitter galbanum gum — these spices along with frankincense, all in equal quantities; ^{35} and make incense, blended and perfumed as would an expert perfume-maker, salted, pure and holy. ^{36} You are to grind up some of it very finely and put it in front of the testimony in the tent of meeting where I will meet with you; you are to regard it as especially holy. ^{37} You are not to make for your own use any incense like it, with the same composition of ingredients — you are to treat it as holy, for ADONAI. ^{38} Whoever makes up any like it to use as perfume is to be cut off from his people."

31 ^{1} ADONAI said to Moshe, ^{2} "I have singled out B'tzal'el the son of Uri the son of Hur, of the tribe of Y'hudah. ^{3} I have filled him with the Spirit of God — with wisdom, understanding and knowledge concerning every kind of artisanry. ^{4} He is a master of design in gold, silver, bronze, ^{5} cutting precious stones to be set, woodcarving and every other craft.

^{6} "I have also appointed as his assistant Oholi'av the son of Achisamakh, of the tribe of Dan. Moreover, I have endowed all the craftsmen with the wisdom to make everything I have ordered you — ^{7} the tent of meeting, the ark for the testimony, the ark-cover above it, all the furnishings of the tent, ^{8} the table and its utensils, the pure *menorah* and all its utensils, the incense altar, ^{9} the altar for burnt offerings and all its utensils, the basin and its base, ^{10} the garments for officiating, the holy garments for Aharon the *cohen* and the garments for his sons, so that they can serve in the office of *cohen*, ^{11} the anointing oil and the incense of aromatic spices for the Holy Place: they are to make everything just as I have ordered you."

^{12} ADONAI said to Moshe, ^{13} "Tell the people of Isra'el, 'You are to observe my *Shabbat*s; for this is a sign between me and you through all your generations; so that you will know that I am ADONAI, who sets you apart for me. ^{14} Therefore you are to keep my *Shabbat*, because it is set apart for you. Everyone who treats it as ordinary must be put to death; for whoever does any work on it is to be cut off from his people. ^{15} On six days work will get done; but the seventh day is *Shabbat*, for complete rest, set apart for ADONAI. Whoever does any work on the day of *Shabbat* must be put to death. ^{16} The people of Isra'el are to keep the *Shabbat*, to observe *Shabbat* through all their generations as a perpetual covenant. ^{17} It is a sign between me and the people of Isra'el forever; for in six days ADONAI made heaven and earth, but on the seventh day he stopped working and rested.'"

(ii) ^{18} When he had finished speaking with Moshe on Mount Sinai, ADONAI gave him the two tablets of the testimony, tablets of stone inscribed by the finger of God.

32 ^{1} When the people saw that Moshe was taking a long time to come down from the mountain, they gathered around Aharon and said to him, "Get busy; and make us gods to go ahead of us; because this Moshe, the man that brought us up from the land of Egypt — we don't know what has become of him." ^{2} Aharon said to them, "Have your wives, sons and daughters strip off their gold earrings; and bring them to me." ^{3} The people stripped off their gold earrings and brought them to Aharon.

⁴ He received what they gave him, melted it down, and made it into the shape of a calf. They said, "Isra'el! Here is your god, who brought you up from the land of Egypt!" ⁵ On seeing this, Aharon built an altar in front of it and proclaimed, "Tomorrow is to be a feast for *ADONAI*." ⁶ Early the next morning they got up and offered burnt offerings and presented peace offerings. Afterwards, the people sat down to eat and drink; then they got up to indulge in revelry.

⁷ *ADONAI* said to Moshe, "Go down! Hurry! Your people, whom you brought up from the land of Egypt, have become corrupt! ⁸ So quickly they have turned aside from the way I ordered them to follow! They have cast a metal statue of a calf, worshipped it, sacrificed to it and said, 'Isra'el! Here is your god, who brought you up from the land of Egypt!'" ⁹ *ADONAI* continued speaking to Moshe: "I have been watching these people; and you can see how stiffnecked they are. ¹⁰ Now leave me alone, so that my anger can blaze against them, and I can put an end to them! I will make a great nation out of you instead."

¹¹ Moshe pleaded with *ADONAI* his God. He said, "*ADONAI*, why must your anger blaze against your own people, whom you brought out of the land of Egypt with great power and a strong hand? ¹² Why let the Egyptians say, 'It was with evil intentions that he led them out, to slaughter them in the hills and wipe them off the face of the earth'? Turn from your fierce anger! Relent! Don't bring such disaster on your people! ¹³ Remember Avraham, Yitz'chak and Isra'el, your servants, to whom you swore by your very self. You promised them, 'I will make your descendants as many as the stars in the sky; and I will give all this land I have spoken about to your descendants; and they will possess it forever.'" ¹⁴ *ADONAI* then changed his mind about the disaster he had planned for his people.

¹⁵ Moshe turned and went down from the mountain with the two tablets of the testimony in his hand, tablets inscribed on both sides, on the front and on the back. ¹⁶ The tablets were the work of God; and the writing was the writing of God, engraved on the tablets. ¹⁷ When Y'hoshua heard the noise of the people shouting he said to Moshe, "It sounds like war in the camp!" ¹⁸ He answered, "That is neither the clamor of victory nor the wailings of defeat; what I hear is the sound of people singing."

¹⁹ But the moment Moshe got near the camp, when he saw the calf and the dancing, his own anger blazed up. He threw down the tablets he had been holding and shattered them at the base of the mountain. ²⁰ Seizing the calf they had made, he melted it in the fire and ground it to powder, which he scattered on the water. Then he made the people of Isra'el drink it.

²¹ Moshe said to Aharon, "What did these people do to you to make you lead them into such a terrible sin?" ²² Aharon replied, "My lord shouldn't be so angry. You know what these people are like, that they are determined to do evil. ²³ So they said to me, 'Make us gods to go ahead of us; because this Moshe, the man that brought us up from the land of Egypt — we don't know what has become of him.' ²⁴ I answered them, 'Anyone with gold, strip it off!' So they gave it to me. I threw it in the fire, and out came this calf!"

²⁵ When Moshe saw that the people had gotten out of control — because Aharon had allowed them to get out of control, to the derision of their enemies — ²⁶ Moshe stood at the entrance to the camp and shouted, "Whoever is for *ADONAI*, come to me!" All the descendants of Levi rallied around him. ²⁷ He told them, "Here is what *ADONAI*, the God of Isra'el, says: 'Each of you, put his sword on his side; and go up and down

the camp, from gate to gate; and every man is to kill his own kinsman, his own friend and his own neighbor!" ²⁸ The sons of Levi did what Moshe said, and that day three thousand of the people died. ²⁹ Moshe said, "You have consecrated yourselves today to ADONAI, because every one of you has been against his own son and against his own kinsman, in order to bring a blessing on yourselves today."

³⁰ The next day Moshe said to the people, "You have committed a terrible sin. Now I will go up to ADONAI; maybe I will be able to atone for your sin." ³¹ Moshe went back to ADONAI and said, "Please! These people have committed a terrible sin: they have made themselves a god out of gold. ³² Now, if you will just forgive their sin! But if you won't, then, I beg you, blot me out of your book which you have written!" ³³ ADONAI answered Moshe, "Those who have sinned against me are the ones I will blot out of my book. ³⁴ Now go and lead the people to the place I told you about; my angel will go ahead of you. Nevertheless, the time for punishment will come; and then I will punish them for their sin." ³⁵ ADONAI struck the people with a plague because they had made the calf, the one Aharon made.

33 ¹ ADONAI said to Moshe, "Leave, you and the people you brought up from the land of Egypt; and move on from here toward the land of which I swore to Avraham, Yitz'chak and Ya'akov, 'I will give it to your descendants.' ² I will send an angel ahead of you; and I will drive out the Kena'ani, Emori, Hitti, P'rizi, Hivi and Y'vusi. ³ You will go to a land flowing with milk and honey; but I myself will not go with you, because you are such a stiffnecked people that I might destroy you on the way." ⁴ When the people heard this bad news, they went into mourning; and no one wore his ornaments. ⁵ ADONAI said to Moshe, "Tell the people of Isra'el, 'You are a stiffnecked people! If I were to go up with you for even one moment, I would exterminate you! Now, keep your ornaments off; then I will decide what to do to you.'" ⁶ So from Mount Horev onward, the people of Isra'el stripped themselves of their ornaments.

⁷ Moshe would take the tent and pitch it outside the camp, far away from the camp. He called it the tent of meeting. Everyone who wanted to consult ADONAI would go out to the tent of meeting, outside the camp. ⁸ Whenever Moshe went out to the tent, all the people would get up and stand, each man at his tent door, and look at Moshe until he had gone into the tent. ⁹ Whenever Moshe entered the tent, the column of cloud would descend and station itself at the entrance to the tent; and ADONAI would speak with Moshe. ¹⁰ When all the people saw the column of cloud stationed at the entrance to the tent, they would get up and prostrate themselves, each man at his tent door. ¹¹ ADONAI would speak to Moshe face to face, as a man speaks to his friend. Then he would return to the camp; but the young man who was his assistant, Y'hoshua the son of Nun, never left the inside of the tent.

(iii) ¹² Moshe said to ADONAI, "Look, you say to me, 'Make these people move on!' But you haven't let me know whom you will be sending with me. Nevertheless you have said, 'I know you by name,' and also, 'You have found favor in my sight.' ¹³ Now, please, if it is really the case that I have found favor in your sight, show me your ways; so that I will understand you and continue finding favor in your sight. Moreover, keep on seeing this nation as your people." ¹⁴ He answered, "Set your mind at rest — my presence will go with you, after all." ¹⁵ Moshe replied, "If your

presence doesn't go with us, don't make us go on from here. ¹⁶ For how else is it to be known that I have found favor in your sight, I and your people, other than by your going with us? That is what distinguishes us, me and your people, from all the other peoples on earth."

(iv) ¹⁷ ADONAI said to Moshe, "I will also do what you have asked me to do, because you have found favor in my sight, and I know you by name." ¹⁸ But Moshe said, "I beg you to show me your glory!" ¹⁹ He replied, "I will cause all my goodness to pass before you, and in your presence I will pronounce the name of ADONAI. Moreover, I show favor to whomever I will, and I display mercy to whomever I will. ²⁰ But my face," he continued, "you cannot see, because a human being cannot look at me and remain alive. ²¹ Here," he said, "is a place near me; stand on the rock. ²² When my glory passes by, I will put you inside a crevice in the rock and cover you with my hand, until I have passed by. ²³ Then I will remove my hand, and you will see my back, but my face is not to be seen."

34 *(v)*¹ ADONAI said to Moshe, "Cut yourself two tablets of stone like the first ones; and I will inscribe on the tablets the words that were on the first tablets, which you broke. ² Be ready by morning; in the morning you are to ascend Mount Sinai and present yourself to me on the top of the mountain. ³ No one is to come up with you, and no one is to be seen anywhere on the mountain; don't even let the flocks or herds feed in front of this mountain." ⁴ Moshe cut two stone tablets like the first. Then he got up early in the morning and, with the two stone tablets in his hands, ascended Mount Sinai, as ADONAI had ordered him to do.

⁵ ADONAI descended in the cloud, stood with him there and pronounced the name of ADONAI. ⁶ ADONAI passed before him and proclaimed: "*YUD-HEH-VAV-HEH*!!! *Yud-Heh-Vav-Heh* [ADONAI] is God, merciful and compassionate, slow to anger, rich in grace and truth; ⁷ showing grace to the thousandth generation, forgiving offenses, crimes and sins; yet not exonerating the guilty, but causing the negative effects of the parents' offenses to be experienced by their children and grandchildren, and even by the third and fourth generations." ⁸ At once Moshe bowed his head to the ground, prostrated himself ⁹ and said, "If I have now found favor in your view, *Adonai*, then please let *Adonai* go with us, even though they are a stiffnecked people; and pardon our offenses and our sin; and take us as your possession."

(vi) ¹⁰ He said, "Here, I am making a covenant; in front of all your people I will do wonders such as have not been created anywhere on earth or in any nation. All the people around you will see the work of ADONAI. What I am going to do through you will be awesome! ¹¹ Observe what I am ordering you to do today. Here! I am driving out ahead of you the Emori, Kena'ani, Hitti, P'rizi, Hivi and Y'vusi. ¹² Be careful not to make a covenant with the people living in the land where you are going, so that they won't become a snare within your own borders. ¹³ Rather, you are to demolish their altars, smash their standing-stones and cut down their sacred poles; ¹⁴ because you are not to bow down to any other god; since ADONAI — whose very name is Jealous — is a jealous God. ¹⁵ Do not make a covenant with the people living in the land. It will cause you to go astray after their gods and sacrifice to their gods. Then they will invite you to join them in eating their sacrifices, ¹⁶ and you will take their daughters as wives for your sons. Their daughters will prostitute themselves to their own gods and make your sons do the same!

^{17}"Do not cast metal gods for yourselves.

^{18}"Keep the festival of *matzah* by eating *matzah*, as I ordered you, for seven days during the month of Aviv; for it was in the month of Aviv that you came out from Egypt.

^{19}"Everything that is first from the womb is mine. Of all your livestock, you are to set aside for me the males, the firstborn of cattle and flock. ^{20}The firstborn of a donkey you must redeem with a lamb; if you won't redeem it, break its neck. All the firstborn of your sons you are to redeem, and no one is to appear before me empty-handed.

^{21}"Six days you will work, but on the seventh day you are to rest — even in plowing time and harvest season you are to rest.

^{22}"Observe the festival of *Shavu'ot* with the first-gathered produce of the wheat harvest, and the festival of ingathering at the turn of the year. ^{23}Three times a year all your men are to appear before the Lord, A*DONAI*, the God of Isra'el. ^{24}For I am going to expel nations ahead of you and expand your territory, and no one will even covet your land when you go up to appear before A*DONAI* your God three times a year. ^{25}You are not to offer the blood of my sacrifice with leavened bread, and the sacrifice of the feast of *Pesach* is not to be left until morning. ^{26}You are to bring the best firstfruits of your land into the house of A*DONAI* your God.

"You are not to boil a young goat in its mother's milk."

(vii) ^{27}A*DONAI* said to Moshe, "Write these words down, because they are the terms of the covenant I have made with you and with Isra'el." ^{28}Moshe was there with A*DONAI* forty days and forty nights, during which time he neither ate food nor drank water. [A*DONAI*] wrote on the tablets the words of the covenant, the Ten Words.

^{29}When Moshe came down from Mount Sinai with the two tablets of the testimony in his hand, he didn't realize that the skin of his face was sending out rays of light as a result of his talking with [A*DONAI*]. ^{30}When Aharon and the people of Isra'el saw Moshe, the skin of his face was shining; and they were afraid to approach him. ^{31}But Moshe called to them; then Aharon and all the community leaders came back to him, and Moshe spoke to them. ^{32}Afterwards, all the people of Isra'el came near; and he passed on to them all the orders that A*DONAI* had told him on Mount Sinai.

(Maftir) ^{33}Once Moshe had finished speaking with them, he put a veil on his face. ^{34}But when he went in before A*DONAI* for him to speak, he would take the veil off until he came out; then, when he came out, he would tell the people of Isra'el what he had been ordered. ^{35}But when the people of Isra'el saw Moshe's face, that the skin of Moshe's face shone, he would put the veil back over his face until he went in again to speak with [A*DONAI*].

Haftarah Ki Tissa: M'lakhim Alef (1 Kings) 18:1–39 (A); 18:20–39 (S)

B'rit Hadashah suggested reading for Parashah Ki Tissa: Luke 11:14–20; Acts 7:35–8:1; 1 Corinthians 10:1–13; 2 Corinthians 3:1–18

Parashah 22: Vayak'hel (He assembled) 35:1–38:20
[In regular years read with Parashah 23, in leap years read separately]

35 ¹ Moshe assembled the whole community of the people of Isra'el and said to them, "These are the things which ADONAI has ordered you to do. ² On six days work is to be done, but the seventh day is to be a holy day for you, a *Shabbat* of complete rest in honor of ADONAI. Whoever does any work on it is to be put to death. ³ You are not to kindle a fire in any of your homes on *Shabbat.*"

⁴ Moshe said to the whole community of the people of Isra'el, "Here is what ADONAI has ordered: ⁵ 'Take up a collection for ADONAI from among yourselves — anyone whose heart makes him willing is to bring the offering for ADONAI: gold, silver and bronze; ⁶ blue, purple and scarlet yarn; fine linen, goat's hair, ⁷ tanned ram skins and fine leather; acacia-wood; ⁸ oil for the light, spices for the anointing oil and for the fragrant incense; ⁹ onyx stones and stones to be set, for the ritual vest and the breastplate.

¹⁰ "'Then let all the craftsmen among you come and make everything ADONAI has ordered: ¹¹ the tabernacle with its tent, covering, fasteners, planks, crossbars, posts and sockets; ¹² the ark with its poles, ark-cover and the curtain to screen it; ¹³ the table with its poles, all its utensils and the showbread; ¹⁴ the *menorah* for the light, with its utensils and lamps, and the oil for the light; ¹⁵ the incense altar with its poles; the anointing oil; the fragrant incense; the screen for the entranceway at the entrance to the tabernacle; ¹⁶ the altar for burnt offerings, with its poles and all its utensils; the basin with its base; ¹⁷ the tapestries for the courtyard, with their posts and sockets; the screen for the gateway of the courtyard; ¹⁸ the tent pegs for the tabernacle; the tent pegs for the courtyard, with their ropes; ¹⁹ the garments for officiating, for serving in the Holy Place; and the holy garments for Aharon the *cohen* and the garments for his sons, so that they can serve in the office of *cohen.*'"

²⁰ Then the whole community of the people of Isra'el withdrew from Moshe's presence; *(LY: ii)* ²¹ and they came, everyone whose heart stirred him and everyone whose spirit made him willing, and brought ADONAI's offering for the work on the tent of meeting, for the service in it and for the holy garments. ²² Both men and women came, as many as had willing hearts; they brought nose-rings, earrings, signet-rings, belts, all kinds of gold jewelry — everyone bringing an offering of gold to ADONAI. ²³ Everyone who had blue, purple or scarlet yarn; fine linen; tanned ram skins or fine leather brought them. ²⁴ Everyone contributing silver or bronze brought his offering for ADONAI, and everyone who had acacia-wood suitable for any of the work brought it. ²⁵ All the women who were skilled at spinning got to work and brought what they had spun, the blue, purple and scarlet yarn and the fine linen. ²⁶ Likewise the women whose heart stirred them to use their skill spun the goat's hair. ²⁷ The leaders brought the onyx stones and the stones to be set, for the ritual vest and the breasplate; ²⁸ the spices; and the oil for the light, for the anointing oil and for the fragrant incense. ²⁹ Thus every man and woman of the people of Isra'el whose heart impelled him to contribute to any of the work ADONAI had ordered through Moshe brought it to ADONAI as a voluntary offering.

(RY: ii, LY: iii) ³⁰ Moshe said to the people of Isra'el, "See, ADONAI has singled out B'tzal'el the son of Uri, the son of Hur, of the tribe of Y'hudah. ³¹ He has filled him with the Spirit of God — with wisdom, understanding and knowledge

concerning every kind of artisanry. ³²He is a master of design in gold, silver, bronze, ³³cutting precious stones to be set, woodcarving and every other craft. ³⁴[ADONAI] has also given him and Oholi'av the son of Achisamakh, of the tribe of Dan, the ability to teach others. ³⁵He has filled them with the skill needed for every kind of work, whether done by an artisan, a designer, an embroiderer using blue, purple and scarlet yarn, and fine linen, or a weaver — they have the skill for every kind of work and design.

36 ¹"B'tzal'el and Oholi'av, along with all the craftsmen whom ADONAI has endowed with the wisdom and skill necessary to carry out the work needed for the sanctuary, are to do exactly according to everything ADONAI has ordered."

²Moshe summoned B'tzal'el, Oholi'av and every craftsman to whom ADONAI had given wisdom, everyone whose heart stirred him, to come and take part in the work. ³They received from Moshe all the offering which the people of Isra'el had brought for the work of building the sanctuary. But they still kept bringing voluntary offerings every morning, ⁴until all the craftsmen doing the work for the sanctuary left the work they were involved with ⁵to tell Moshe, "The people are bringing far more than is needed to do the work ADONAI has ordered done." ⁶So Moshe gave an order which was proclaimed throughout the camp: "Neither men nor women are to make any further efforts for the sanctuary offering." In this way, the people were restrained from making additional contributions. ⁷For what they had already was not only sufficient for doing all the work, but too much!

(LY: iv) ⁸With all the skilled men who were carrying out the work, B'tzal'el made the tabernacle, using ten sheets of finely woven linen and of blue, purple and scarlet yarn. He made them with *k'ruvim* worked in that had been crafted by a skilled artisan. ⁹Each sheet was forty-two feet long and six feet wide; all the sheets were the same size. ¹⁰He joined five sheets one to another, and the other five sheets he joined one to another. ¹¹He made loops of blue on the edge of the outermost sheet in the first set and did the same on the edge of the outermost sheet in the second set. ¹²He made fifty loops on the one sheet, and he made fifty loops on the edge of the sheet in the second set; the loops were opposite one another. ¹³He made fifty fasteners of gold and coupled the sheets to each other with the fasteners, so that the tabernacle formed a single unit.

¹⁴He made sheets of goat's hair to be used as a tent covering the tabernacle; he made eleven sheets. ¹⁵Each sheet was forty-five feet long and six feet wide; all eleven sheets were the same size. ¹⁶He joined five sheets together and six sheets together. ¹⁷He made fifty loops on the edge of the outermost sheet in the first set and fifty loops on the outermost sheet in the second set. ¹⁸He made fifty fasteners of bronze to join the tent together, so that it would be a single unit.

¹⁹He made a covering for the tent of tanned ram skins and an outer covering of fine leather.

(LY: v) ²⁰He made the upright planks of acacia-wood for the tabernacle. ²¹Each plank was fifteen feet long and two-and-a-quarter feet wide. ²²There were two projections on each plank, and the planks were joined one to another. This is how he made all the planks for the tabernacle.

²³He made the planks for the tabernacle as follows: twenty planks for the south side, facing southward. ²⁴He made forty silver sockets under the twenty planks, two sockets under one plank for its two projections and two sockets

under another plank for its two projections. ²⁵ For the second side of the tabernacle, to the north, he made twenty planks ²⁶ and their forty silver sockets, two sockets under one plank and two under another. ²⁷ For the rear part of the tabernacle, toward the west, he made six planks. ²⁸ For the corners of the tabernacle in the rear he made two planks, ²⁹ double from the bottom all the way to the top but joined at a single ring. He did the same with both of them at the two corners. ³⁰ Thus there were eight planks with their silver sockets, sixteen sockets, two sockets under each plank.

³¹ He made crossbars of acacia-wood, five for the planks of the one side of the tabernacle, ³² five crossbars for the planks of the other side of the tabernacle, and five crossbars for the planks at the side of the tabernacle at the rear toward the west. ³³ He made the middle crossbar so that it extended from one end of the planks to the other, halfway up. ³⁴ He overlaid the planks with gold, made gold rings for them through which the crossbars could pass and overlaid the crossbars with gold.

³⁵ He made the curtain of blue, purple and scarlet yarn and finely woven linen. He made them with k'ruvim worked in that had been crafted by a skilled artisan. ³⁶ He made for it four posts of acacia-wood and overlaid them with gold, and gold hooks; and cast for them four silver sockets.

³⁷ For the entrance to the tent he made a screen of blue, purple and scarlet yarn and finely woven linen, in colors, the work of a weaver; ³⁸ with its five posts and their hooks. He overlaid their capitals and their attached rings for hanging with gold, while their five sockets were of bronze.

37 ¹ B'tzal'el made the ark of acacia-wood three-and-three-quarters feet long, two-and-a-quarter feet wide and two-and-a-quarter feet high. ² He overlaid it with pure gold inside and outside and put a molding of gold for it around the top. ³ He cast four gold rings for it at its four feet, two rings on each side. ⁴ He made poles of acacia-wood and overlaid them with gold. ⁵ He put the carrying-poles for the ark in the rings on the sides of the ark.

⁶ He made a cover for the ark of pure gold, three-and-three-quarters feet long and two-and-a-quarter feet wide. ⁷ He made two k'ruvim of gold; he made them of hammered work for the two ends of the ark-cover — ⁸ one keruv for one end and one keruv for the other end; he made the k'ruvim of one piece with the ark-cover at its two ends. ⁹ The k'ruvim had their wings spread out above, so that their wings covered the ark; their faces were toward each other and toward the ark-cover.

¹⁰ He made the table of acacia-wood, three feet long, eighteen inches wide and eighteen inches high. ¹¹ He overlaid it with pure gold and put a molding of gold around the top of it. ¹² He made around it a rim a handbreadth wide and put a molding of gold around the rim. ¹³ He cast for it four gold rings and attached the rings to the four corners, near its four legs. ¹⁴ The rings to hold the carrying-poles for the table were placed close to the rim. ¹⁵ He made the carrying-poles for the table of acacia-wood and overlaid them with gold. ¹⁶ He made the utensils to be put on the table — its dishes, pans, bowls and pitchers — of pure gold.

(RY: iii, LY: vi) ¹⁷ He made the *menorah* of pure gold. He made it of hammered work; its base, shaft, cups, rings of outer leaves and flowers were a single unit. ¹⁸ There were six branches extending from its sides, three branches of the *menorah* on one side of it and three on the other. ¹⁹ On one branch were three cups shaped like

almond blossoms, a ring of outer leaves and petals; likewise on the opposite branch three cups shaped like almond blossoms, a ring of outer leaves and petals; and similarly for all six branches extending from the *menorah*. ²⁰ On the central shaft of the *menorah* were four cups shaped like almond blossoms, each with its ring of outer leaves and petals. ²¹ Where each pair of branches joined the central shaft was a ring of outer leaves of one piece with the pair of branches — thus for all six branches. ²² Their rings of outer leaves and their branches were of one piece with the shaft. Thus the whole *menorah* was one piece of hammered work made of pure gold. ²³ He made its seven lamps, its tongs and its trays of pure gold. ²⁴ The *menorah* and its utensils were made of sixty-six pounds of pure gold.

²⁵ He made the altar on which to burn incense of acacia-wood, eighteen inches square and three feet high; its horns were a single unit. ²⁶ He overlaid it with pure gold — its top, all around its sides and its horns; and he put around it a molding of gold. ²⁷ He made two gold rings for it under its molding at the two corners on both sides, to hold the carrying-poles. ²⁸ He made the poles of acacia-wood and overlaid them with gold.

²⁹ He made the holy anointing oil and the pure incense of aromatic plant substances as would an expert perfume-maker.

38 *(RY: iv, LY: vii)* ¹ He made the altar for burnt offerings of acacia-wood, seven-and-a-half feet long and seven-and-a-half feet wide — it was square — and four-and-a-half feet high. ² He made horns for it on its four corners, the horns were of one piece with it, and he overlaid it with bronze.

³ He made all the utensils for the altar — its pots, shovels, basins, meat-hooks and fire pans; all its utensils he made of bronze. ⁴ He made for the altar a grate of bronze netting, under its rim, reaching halfway up the altar. ⁵ He cast four rings for the four ends of the bronze grate to hold the poles. ⁶ He made the poles of acacia-wood and overlaid them with bronze. ⁷ He put the carrying-poles into the rings on the sides of the altar; he made it of planks and hollow inside.

⁸ He made the basin of bronze with its base of bronze from the mirrors of the women serving at the entrance to the tent of meeting.

⁹ He made the courtyard. On the south side, facing southward, the tapestries for the courtyard were made of finely woven linen, 150 feet long, ¹⁰ supported on twenty posts in twenty bronze sockets; the hooks on the posts and the attached rings for hanging were of silver. ¹¹ On the north side they were 150 feet long, hung on twenty posts in twenty bronze sockets, with the hooks on the posts and their rings of silver. ¹² On the west side were tapestries seventy-five feet long, hung on ten posts in ten sockets, with the hooks on the posts and their rings of silver. ¹³ On the east side were tapestries seventy-five feet long. ¹⁴ The tapestries for the one side [of the gateway] were twenty-two-and-a-half feet long, hung on three posts in three sockets; ¹⁵ likewise for the other side — on either side [of the gate] were tapestries twenty-two-and-a-half feet long on three posts in three sockets. ¹⁶ All the tapestries for the courtyard, all the way around, were of finely woven linen; ¹⁷ the sockets for the posts were of bronze; the hooks on the posts and their rings were of silver; the capitals of the posts were overlaid with silver; and all the posts of the courtyard were banded with silver.

(LY: Maftir) ¹⁸ The screen for the gateway to the courtyard was the work of a weaver in colors, of blue, purple and scarlet yarn and finely woven linen. Its length

was thirty feet and its height seven-and-a-half feet all the way along, like the tapestries of the courtyard. [19] It had four posts in four bronze sockets, with silver hooks, capitals overlaid with silver and silver fasteners. [20] The tent pegs for the tabernacle and for the courtyard around it were of bronze.

Haftarah Vayak'hel: M'lakhim Alef (1 Kings) 7:40–50 (A); 7:13–26 (S)

B'rit Hadashah suggested readings for Parashah Vayak'hel: 2 Corinthians 9:1–15; Messianic Jews (Hebrews) 9:1–14; Revelation 11:1–13

Parashah 23: P'kudei (Accounts) 38:21–40:38
[In regular years read with Parashah 22, in leap years read separately]

[21] These are the accounts of the tabernacle, the tabernacle of the testimony, recorded, as Moshe ordered, by the *L'vi'im* under the direction of Itamar the son of Aharon, the *cohen.* [22] B'tzal'el the son of Uri, the son of Hur, of the tribe of Y'hudah, made everything that ADONAI ordered Moshe to make. [23] Assisting him was Oholi'av the son of Achisamakh, of the tribe of Dan, who was an engraver, a designer and a weaver in colors — in blue, purple and scarlet yarn and in fine linen. [24] All the gold used for the work in everything needed for the sanctuary, the gold of the offering, weighed 29 talents 730 *shekels* [1,930 pounds], using the sanctuary *shekel.* [25] The silver given by the community weighed 100 talents 1,775 *shekels* [6,650 pounds], using the sanctuary *shekel.* [26] This was a *beka* per person, that is, half a *shekel* [one-fifth of an ounce], using the sanctuary *shekel,* for everyone twenty years old or older counted in the census, 603,550 men. [27] The hundred talents of silver were used to cast the sockets for the sanctuary and the sockets for the curtain — one hundred sockets made from the hundred talents, one talent [sixty-six pounds] per socket. [28] The 1,775 *shekels* [fifty pounds] he used to make hooks for the posts, to overlay their capitals and to make fasteners for them. [29] The bronze in the offering came to 4,680 pounds. [30] He used it to make the sockets for the entrance to the tent of meeting, the bronze altar, its bronze grate, all the utensils for the altar, [31] the sockets for the courtyard around it, the sockets for the gateway to the courtyard, all the tent pegs for the tabernacle and all the tent pegs for the courtyard around it.

39 [1] From the blue, purple and scarlet yarn they made the garments for officiating, for serving in the Holy Place; and they made the holy garments for Aharon, as ADONAI had ordered Moshe. *(RY: v, LY: ii)* [2] He made the ritual vest of gold, of blue, purple and scarlet yarn, and of finely woven linen. [3] They hammered the gold into thin plates and cut them into threads in order to work it into the blue, purple and scarlet yarn and the fine linen crafted by the skilled artisan. [4] They made shoulder-pieces for it, joined together; they were joined together at the two ends. [5] The decorated belt on the vest, used to fasten it, was of the same workmanship and materials — gold; blue, purple and scarlet yarn; and finely twined linen — as ADONAI had ordered Moshe. [6] They worked the onyx stones, mounted in gold settings, engraving them with the names of the sons of Isra'el as they would be engraved on a seal. ⁷ Then he put them on the shoulder-pieces of the vest to be stones calling to mind the sons of Isra'el, as *ADONAI* had ordered Moshe.

⁸ He made the breastplate; it was crafted by a skilled artisan and made like the work of the ritual vest — of gold; blue, purple and scarlet yarn; and finely woven linen. ⁹ When folded double, the breastplate was square — doubled, it was a hand-span by a hand-span. ¹⁰ They put on it four rows of stones: the first row was a carnelian, a topaz and an emerald; ¹¹ the second row a green feldspar, a sapphire and a diamond; ¹² the third row an orange zircon, an agate and an amethyst; ¹³ and the fourth row a beryl, an onyx and a jasper. They were mounted in settings of gold. ¹⁴ The stones corresponded to the names of the twelve sons of Isra'el; they were engraved with their names as a seal would be engraved, each name representing one of the twelve tribes.

¹⁵ On the breastplate they made two pure gold chains, twisted like cords. ¹⁶ Also for the breastplate they made two settings of gold and two gold rings, and they put the two rings at the two ends of the breastplate. ¹⁷ They put the two twisted gold chains in the two rings at the ends of the breastplate ¹⁸ and attached the other two ends of the twisted chains to the front of the shoulder-pieces of the ritual vest. ¹⁹ They also made two gold rings and put them on the two ends of the breastplate, at its edge, on the side facing in toward the vest. ²⁰ Also they made two gold rings and attached them low on the front part of the vest's shoulder-pieces, near the join, above the vest's decorated belt. ²¹ Then they bound the breastplate by its rings to the rings of the vest with a blue cord, so that it could be on the vest's decorated belt, and so that the breastplate would not swing loose from the vest — as *ADONAI* had ordered Moshe.

(RY: vi, LY: iii) ²² He made the robe for the ritual vest; it was woven entirely of blue, ²³ with its opening in the middle, like that of a coat of mail, and with a border around the opening, so that it wouldn't tear. ²⁴ On the bottom hem they made pomegranates of blue, purple and scarlet, and woven linen; ²⁵ and they made bells of pure gold, and put the bells between the pomegranates all the way around the hem of the robe — between the pomegranates, ²⁶ that is, bell, pomegranate, bell, pomegranate, all the way around the hem of the robe for service — as *ADONAI* had ordered Moshe.

²⁷ They made the tunics of finely woven linen for Aharon and his sons, ²⁸ the turban of fine linen, the splendid headgear of fine linen, the linen shorts, ²⁹ and the sash of finely woven linen and blue, purple and scarlet yarn, the work of a weaver in colors — as *ADONAI* had ordered Moshe.

³⁰ They made the ornament for the holy turban of pure gold; wrote on it the words, "Set apart for *ADONAI*," like the engraving on a seal; ³¹ and tied a blue cord on it to fasten it to the front of the turban — as *ADONAI* had ordered Moshe.

³² Thus all the work for the tabernacle, the tent of meeting, was finished, with the people of Isra'el doing everything exactly as *ADONAI* had ordered Moshe.

(LY: iv) ³³ Then they brought the tabernacle to Moshe — the tent and all its furnishings, clasps, planks, crossbars, posts and sockets; ³⁴ the covering of tanned ram skins, the covering of fine leather and the curtain for the screen; ³⁵ the ark for the testimony, its poles and the ark-cover; ³⁶ the table, all its utensils and the showbread; ³⁷ the pure *menorah*, its lamps and their arrangement for display, its accessories and the oil for the light; ³⁸ the gold altar; the anointing oil; the fragrant incense; the screen

for the entrance to the tent; ^{39} the bronze altar with its bronze grate, poles and all its utensils; the basin with its base; ^{40} the tapestries for the courtyard, with their posts and sockets; the screen for the entrance to the courtyard, with its ropes and tent pegs; all the utensils for the service in the tabernacle, the tent of meeting; ^{41} the garments for officiating, for serving in the Holy Place; the holy garments for Aharon the *cohen*; and the garments for his sons to serve in the office of *cohen.*

^{42} The people of Isra'el did all the work just as A*DONAI* had ordered Moshe. ^{43} Moshe saw all the work, and — there it was! — they had done it! Exactly as A*DONAI* had ordered, they had done it. And Moshe blessed them.

40 *(RY: vii, LY: v)* ^{1} A*DONAI* said to Moshe, ^{2} "On the first day of the first month, you are to set up the tabernacle, the tent of meeting. ^{3} Put in it the ark for the testimony, and conceal the ark with the curtain. ^{4} Bring in the table, and arrange its display. Bring in the *menorah*, and light its lamps. ^{5} Set the gold altar for incense in front of the ark for the testimony, and set up the screen at the entrance to the tabernacle. ^{6} Place the altar for burnt offerings in front of the entrance to the tabernacle, the tent of meeting. ^{7} Set the basin between the tent of meeting and the altar, and put water in it. ^{8} Set up the courtyard all the way around, and hang up the screen for the entrance to the courtyard.

^{9} "Take the anointing oil, and anoint the tabernacle and everything in it — consecrate it with all its furnishings; then it will be holy. ^{10} Anoint the altar for burnt offerings with all its utensils — consecrate the altar; then the altar will be especially holy. ^{11} Anoint the basin and its base, and consecrate it.

^{12} "Then bring Aharon and his sons to the entrance of the tent of meeting and wash them with water. ^{13} Put the holy garments on Aharon, anoint him, and consecrate him, so that he can serve me in the office of *cohen.* ^{14} Bring his sons, put tunics on them, ^{15} and anoint them as you anointed their father, so that they can serve me in the office of *cohen.* Their anointing will signify that the office of *cohen* is theirs through all their generations."

^{16} Moshe did this — he acted in accordance with everything A*DONAI* had ordered him to do.

(LY: vi) ^{17} On the first day of the first month of the second year, the tabernacle was set up. ^{18} Moshe erected the tabernacle, put its sockets in place, put up its planks, put in its crossbars and set up its posts. ^{19} He spread the tent over the tabernacle and put the covering of the tent above it, as A*DONAI* had ordered Moshe. ^{20} He took and put the testimony inside the ark, put the poles on the ark, and set the ark-cover above, on the ark. ^{21} Then he brought the ark into the tabernacle, set up the curtain as a screen and concealed the ark for the testimony, as A*DONAI* had ordered Moshe.

^{22} He put the table in the tent of meeting on the side of the tabernacle facing north, outside the curtain. ^{23} He arranged a row of bread on it before A*DONAI*, as A*DONAI* had ordered Moshe.

^{24} He put the *menorah* in the tent of meeting across from the table, on the side of the tabernacle facing south. ^{25} Then he lit the lamps before A*DONAI*, as A*DONAI* had ordered Moshe.

^{26} He set the gold altar in the tent of meeting in front of the curtain ^{27} and burned on it incense made from aromatic spices, as A*DONAI* had ordered Moshe.

(LY: vii) ²⁸ He set up the screen at the entrance to the tabernacle. ²⁹ The altar for burnt offerings he placed at the entrance to the tabernacle, the tent of meeting, and offered on it the burnt offering and the grain offering, as Adonai had ordered Moshe.

³⁰ He set the basin between the tent of meeting and the altar and put water in it for washing, ³¹ so that Moshe and Aharon and his sons could wash their hands and feet there — ³² so that they could wash when entering the tent of meeting and when approaching the altar, as Adonai had ordered Moshe.

³³ Finally, he erected the courtyard around the tabernacle and the altar and set up the screen for the entrance to the courtyard.

(Maftir) ³⁴ Then the cloud covered the tent of meeting, and the glory of Adonai filled the tabernacle. ³⁵ Moshe was unable to enter the tent of meeting, because the cloud remained on it, and the glory of Adonai filled the tabernacle.

³⁶ Whenever the cloud was taken up from over the tabernacle, the people of Isra'el continued with all their travels. ³⁷ But if the cloud was not taken up, then they did not travel onward until the day when it was taken up. ³⁸ For the cloud of Adonai was above the tabernacle during the day, and fire was in [the cloud] at night, so that all the house of Isra'el could see it throughout all their travels.

Haftarah P'kudei: M'lakhim Alef (1 Kings) 7:51–8:21 (A); 7:40–50 (S)

B'rit Hadashah suggested reading for Parashah P'kudei: Revelation 15:5–8

Hazak, hazak, v'nit'chazek!
Be strong, be strong, and let us be strengthened!

Vayikra
LEVITICUS

Parashah 24: Vayikra (He called) 1:1–5:26(6:7)

1 ¹ *ADONAI* called to Moshe and spoke to him from the tent of meeting. He said, ² "Speak to the people of Isra'el; say to them, 'When any of you brings an offering to *ADONAI*, you may bring your animal offering either from the herd or from the flock. ³ If his offering is a burnt offering from the herd, he must offer a male without defect. He is to bring it to the entrance of the tent of meeting, so that it can be accepted by *ADONAI*. ⁴ He is to lay his hand upon the head of the burnt offering, and it will be accepted on his behalf to make atonement for him. ⁵ He is to slaughter the young bull before *ADONAI*; and the sons of Aharon, the *cohanim*, are to present the blood. They are to splash the blood against all sides of the altar, which is by the entrance to the tent of meeting. ⁶ He is to skin the burnt offering and cut it in pieces. ⁷ The descendants of Aharon the *cohen* are to put fire on the altar and arrange wood on the fire. ⁸ The sons of Aharon, the *cohanim*, are to arrange the pieces, the head and the fat on the wood which is on the fire on the altar. ⁹ He is to wash the entrails and lower parts of the legs with water, and the *cohen* is to cause all of it to go up in smoke on the altar as a burnt offering; it is an offering made by fire, a fragrant aroma for *ADONAI*.

¹⁰ "'If his offering is from the flock, whether from the sheep or from the goats, for a burnt offering, he must offer a male without defect. ¹¹ He is to slaughter it on the north side of the altar before *ADONAI*; and the sons of Aharon, the *cohanim*, are to splash its blood against all sides of the altar. ¹² He is to cut it into pieces, and the *cohen* is to arrange them with the head and fat on the wood which is on the fire on the altar. ¹³ He is to wash the entrails and lower parts of the legs with water; and the *cohen* is to offer it all and make it go up in smoke on the altar as a burnt offering; it is an offering made by fire, a fragrant aroma for *ADONAI*.

(ii) ¹⁴ "'If his offering to *ADONAI* is a burnt offering of birds, he must offer a dove or a young pigeon. ¹⁵ The *cohen* is to bring it to the altar, snap off its head and make it go up in smoke on the altar; its blood is to be drained out on the side of the altar. ¹⁶ He is to remove the food pouch and its feathers from its neck and discard it on the pile of ashes just east of the altar. ¹⁷ He is to pull it open with a wing on each side, but without tearing it in half. The *cohen* is to make it go up in smoke on the altar, on the wood which is on the fire, as a burnt offering; it is an offering made by fire, a fragrant aroma for *ADONAI*.

2 ¹ "Anyone who brings a grain offering to *ADONAI* is to make his offering of fine flour; he is to pour olive oil on it and put frankincense on it. ² He is to bring it to the sons of Aharon, the *cohanim*. The *cohen* is to take a handful of fine flour from it, together with its olive oil and all its frankincense, and make this reminder portion go up in smoke on the altar as an offering made by fire, a fragrant aroma for ADONAI. ³ But the rest of the grain offering will belong to Aharon and his sons; it is an especially holy part of the offerings for ADONAI made by fire.

⁴ "'When you bring a grain offering which has been baked in the oven, it is to consist of either unleavened cakes made of fine flour mixed with olive oil or *matzah* spread with olive oil. ⁵ If your offering is a grain offering cooked on a griddle, it is to consist of unleavened fine flour mixed with olive oil; ⁶ you are to break it in pieces and pour olive oil on it — it is a grain offering. *(iii)* ⁷ If your offering is a grain offering cooked in a pot, it is to consist of fine flour with olive oil.

⁸ "'You are to bring the grain offering prepared in any of these ways to ADONAI; it is to be presented to the *cohen*, and he is to bring it to the altar. ⁹ The *cohen* is to remove the reminder portion of the grain offering and make it go up in smoke on the altar as an offering made by fire, a fragrant aroma for ADONAI. ¹⁰ But the rest of the grain offering will belong to Aharon and his sons; it is an especially holy part of the offerings for ADONAI made by fire.

¹¹ "'No grain offering that you bring to ADONAI is to be made with leaven, because you are not to cause any leaven or honey to go up in smoke as an offering made by fire to ADONAI. ¹² As an offering of firstfruits you may bring these to ADONAI, but they are not to be brought up onto the altar to make a fragrant aroma. ¹³ You are to season every grain offering of yours with salt — do not omit from your grain offering the salt of the covenant with your God, but offer salt with all your offerings.

¹⁴ "'If you bring a grain offering of firstfruits to ADONAI, you are to bring as the grain offering from your firstfruits kernels of grain from fresh ears, dry-roasted with fire. ¹⁵ Put olive oil on it, and lay frankincense on it; it is a grain offering. ¹⁶ The *cohen* is to cause the reminder portion of it, its grits and olive oil, with all its frankincense, to go up in smoke; it is an offering made by fire for ADONAI.

3 *(iv)* ¹ "'If his offering is a sacrifice of peace offerings, then, if he offers before ADONAI an animal from the herd, then, no matter whether it is male or female, it must be without defect. ² He is to lay his hand on the head of his offering and slaughter it at the entrance to the tent of meeting; and the sons of Aharon, the *cohanim*, are to splash the blood against all sides of the altar. ³ He is to present the sacrifice of the peace offerings as an offering made by fire to ADONAI; it is to consist of the fat covering the inner organs, all the fat above the inner organs, ⁴ the two kidneys, the fat on them near the flanks, and the covering of the liver, which he will remove with the kidneys. ⁵ Aharon's sons will make it go up in smoke on the altar on top of the burnt offering which is on the wood on the fire; it is an offering made by fire, a fragrant aroma for ADONAI.

⁶ "'If his offering for a sacrifice of peace offerings to ADONAI is from the flock, then, when he offers it, no matter whether it is male or female, it must be without defect. ⁷ If he brings a lamb for his offering, then he is to present it before ADONAI. ⁸ He is to lay his hand on the head of his offering and slaughter it at the entrance to the tent of meeting, and the sons of Aharon are to splash its blood against all sides of the altar. ⁹ From the sacrifices made as peace offerings, he is to present ADONAI with an offering made by fire; it is to consist of its fat, the entire fat tail, which he will remove close to the lower backbone, the fat covering the inner organs, all the fat above the inner organs, ¹⁰ the two kidneys, the fat on them near the flanks, and the

covering of the liver, which he will remove with the kidneys. [11] The *cohen* will make it go up in smoke on the altar; it is food, an offering made by fire to ADONAI.

[12] "'If his offering is a goat, then he is to present it before ADONAI. [13] He is to lay his hand on its head and slaughter it in front of the tent of meeting, and the sons of Aharon are to splash its blood against all sides of the altar. [14] He is to present from it his offering, an offering made by fire to ADONAI; it is to consist of the fat covering the inner organs, all the fat above the inner organs, [15] the two kidneys, the fat on them near the flanks, and the covering of the liver, which he will remove with the kidneys. [16] The *cohen* will make them go up in smoke on the altar; it is food, an offering made by fire to be a fragrant aroma; all the fat belongs to ADONAI. [17] It is to be a permanent regulation through all your generations wherever you live that you will eat neither fat nor blood.'"

4 (*v*) [1] ADONAI said to Moshe, [2] "Tell the people of Isra'el: 'If anyone sins inadvertently against any of the *mitzvot* of ADONAI concerning things which should not be done, if he does any one of them, [3] then, if it is the anointed *cohen* who sinned and thus brought guilt on the people, he is to offer ADONAI a young bull without defect as a sin offering for the sin he committed. [4] He must bring the bull to the entrance of the tent of meeting before ADONAI, lay his hand on the bull's head and slaughter the bull in the presence of ADONAI. [5] The anointed *cohen* is to take some of the bull's blood and bring it to the tent of meeting. [6] The *cohen* is to dip his finger in the blood and sprinkle some of the blood seven times in the presence of ADONAI in front of the curtain of the sanctuary. [7] The *cohen* is to put some of the blood on the horns of the altar for fragrant incense before ADONAI there in the tent of meeting. All the remaining blood of the bull he is to pour out at the base of the altar for burnt offerings, which is at the entrance to the tent of meeting. [8] He is to remove from the bull for the sin offering all of its fat — the fat covering the inner organs, all the fat above the inner organs, [9] the two kidneys, the fat on them near the flanks, and the covering of the liver, which he will remove with the kidneys [10] as it is removed from an ox sacrificed as a peace offering; and the *cohen* is to make these parts go up in smoke on the altar for burnt offerings. [11] But the bull's hide and all its flesh, with its head, the lower parts of its legs, its inner organs and dung — [12] in other words, the entire bull — he is to bring outside the camp to a clean place, where the ashes are emptied out. There he is to burn it on wood with fire; there, where the ashes are emptied out, it is to be burned up.

[13] "'If the entire community of Isra'el inadvertently makes a mistake, with the assembly being unaware of the matter, and they do something against any of the *mitzvot* of ADONAI concerning things which should not be done, they are guilty. [14] When the sin they have committed becomes known, then the assembly is to offer a young bull as a sin offering and bring it before the tent of meeting. [15] The leaders of the community are to lay their hands on the bull's head and slaughter the bull in the presence of ADONAI. [16] The anointed *cohen* is to bring some of the bull's blood to the tent of meeting. [17] The *cohen* is to dip his finger in the blood and sprinkle it seven times in the presence of ADONAI in front of the curtain. [18] He is to put some of the blood on the horns of the altar before ADONAI, there in the tent of meeting. All the remaining blood he is to pour out at the base of the altar for burnt offerings, which is at the entrance to the tent of meeting. [19] He is to remove all its fat and make it go up in smoke on the altar. [20] This is what he is to do with the bull — he must do the same with this bull as he does with the one for the sin offering. Thus the *cohen* will make

atonement for them, and they will be forgiven. ²¹ He is to bring the bull outside the camp and burn it as he burned the first bull; it is the sin offering for the assembly.

²² "'When a leader sins and inadvertently does something against any of the *mitzvot* of ADONAI concerning things which should not be done, he is guilty. ²³ If the sin which he committed becomes known to him, he is to bring as his offering a male goat without defect, ²⁴ lay his hand on the goat's head and slaughter it in the place where they slaughter the burnt offering in the presence of ADONAI; it is a sin offering. ²⁵ The *cohen* is to take some of the blood of the sin offering with his finger and put it on the horns of the altar for burnt offerings. Its remaining blood he is to pour out at the base of the altar for burnt offerings. ²⁶ All its fat he is to make go up in smoke on the altar, like the fat of the sacrifice for peace offerings; thus the *cohen* will make atonement for him in regard to his sin, and he will be forgiven.

(vi) ²⁷ "'If an individual among the people commits a sin inadvertently, doing something against any of the *mitzvot* of ADONAI concerning things which should not be done, he is guilty. ²⁸ If the sin he committed becomes known to him, he is to bring as his offering a female goat without defect for the sin he committed, ²⁹ lay his hand on the head of the sin offering and slaughter the sin offering in the place of burnt offerings. ³⁰ The *cohen* is to take some of its blood with his finger and put it on the horns of the altar for burnt offerings. All its remaining blood he is to pour out at the base of the altar. ³¹ All its fat he is to remove, as the fat is removed from the sacrifice for peace offerings; and the *cohen* is to make it go up in smoke on the altar as a fragrant aroma for ADONAI. Thus the *cohen* will make atonement for him, and he will be forgiven.

³² "'If he brings a lamb as his sin offering, he is to bring a female without defect, ³³ lay his hand on the head of the sin offering and slaughter it as a sin offering in the place where they slaughter burnt offerings. ³⁴ The *cohen* is to take some of the blood of the sin offering with his finger and put it on the horns of the altar for burnt offerings. All its remaining blood he is to pour out at the base of the altar. ³⁵ All its fat he is to remove, as the fat of a lamb is removed from the sacrifice for peace offerings; and the *cohen* is to make it go up in smoke on the altar on top of the offerings for ADONAI made by fire. Thus the *cohen* will make atonement for him in regard to the sin he committed, and he will be forgiven.

5 ¹ "'If a person who is a witness, sworn to testify, sins by refusing to tell what he has seen or heard about the matter, he must bear the consequences. ² If a person touches something unclean, whether the carcass of an unclean wild animal, a domestic animal or a reptile, he is guilty, even though he may not be aware that he is unclean. ³ If he touches some human uncleanness, no matter what the source of his uncleanness is, and is unaware of it, then, when he learns of it, he is guilty. ⁴ If someone allows to slip from his mouth an oath to do evil or to do good, and he doesn't remember that he clearly spoke this oath, then, no matter what it was about, when he learns of it, he is guilty. ⁵ A person guilty of any of these things is to confess in what manner he sinned ⁶ and bring his guilt offering to ADONAI for the sin he committed; it is to be a female from the flock, either a lamb or a goat, as a sin offering; and the *cohen* will make atonement for him in regard to his sin.

⁷ "'If he can't afford a lamb, he is to bring as his guilt offering for the sin he committed two doves or two young pigeons for ADONAI — the one as a sin offering

and the other as a burnt offering. [8] He is to bring them to the *cohen*, who will offer the one for a sin offering first. He is to wring its neck but not remove the head, [9] sprinkle some of the blood of the sin offering on the side of the altar and drain out the rest of the blood at the base of the altar; it is a sin offering. [10] He is to prepare the second as a burnt offering in the manner prescribed. Thus the *cohen* will make atonement for him in regard to the sin which he committed, and he will be forgiven.

(vii) [11] "'But if his means are insufficient even for two doves or two young pigeons, then he is to bring as his offering for the sin he committed two quarts of fine flour for a sin offering; he is not to put any olive oil or frankincense on it, because it is a sin offering. [12] He is to bring it to the *cohen*, and the *cohen* is to take a handful of it as its reminder portion and make it go up in smoke on the altar on top of the offerings for ADONAI made by fire; it is a sin offering. [13] Thus the *cohen* will make atonement for him in regard to the sin he committed concerning any of these things, and he will be forgiven. The rest will belong to the *cohanim*, as with a grain offering.'"

[14] ADONAI said to Moshe, [15] "If anyone acts improperly and inadvertently sins in regard to the holy things of ADONAI, he is to bring as his guilt offering for ADONAI a ram without defect from the flock or its equivalent in silver *shekels* (using the sanctuary *shekel* as the standard), according to your appraisal of its value; it is a guilt offering. [16] In addition, he is to make restitution for whatever he did wrong in regard to the holy thing; moreover, he is to add to that one-fifth and give it to the *cohen*. Then the *cohen* will make atonement with the ram of the guilt offering, and he will be forgiven.

[17] "If someone sins by doing something against any of the *mitzvot* of ADONAI concerning things which should not be done, he is guilty, even if he is unaware of it; and he bears the consequences of his wrongdoing. [18] He must bring a ram without defect from the flock, or its equivalent according to your appraisal, to the *cohen* for a guilt offering; the *cohen* will make atonement concerning the error which he committed, even though he was unaware of it; and he will be forgiven. [19] It is a guilt offering — he is certainly guilty before ADONAI."

[20(6:1)] ADONAI said to Moshe, [21(6:2)] "If someone sins and acts perversely against ADONAI by dealing falsely with his neighbor in regard to a deposit or security entrusted to him, by stealing from him, by extorting him, [22(6:3)] or by dealing falsely in regard to a lost object he has found, or by swearing to a lie — if a person commits any of these sins, [23(6:4)] then, if he sinned and is guilty, he is to restore whatever it was he stole or obtained by extortion, or whatever was deposited with him, or the lost object which he found, *(Maftir)* [24(6:5)] or anything about which he has sworn falsely. He is to restore it in full plus an additional one-fifth; he must return it to the person who owns it, on the day when he presents his guilt offering. [25(6:6)] He is to bring as his guilt offering to ADONAI a ram without defect from the flock, or its equivalent according to your appraisal, to the *cohen*; it is a guilt offering. [26(6:7)] Thus the *cohen* will make atonement for him before ADONAI, and he will be forgiven in regard to whatever it was he did that made him guilty.

Haftarah Vayikra: Yesha'yahu (Isaiah) 43:21–44:23

B'rit Hadashah suggested readings for Parashah Vayikra: Romans 8:1–13; Messianic Jews (Hebrews) 10:1–14; 13:10–16

Parashah 25: Tzav (Give an order) 6:1(8)–8:36

6 $^{1(8)}$ *ADONAI* said to Moshe, $^{2(9)}$ "Give this order to Aharon and his sons: 'This is the law for the burnt offering [Hebrew: *'olah*]: it is what goes up [Hebrew: *'olah*] on its firewood upon the altar all night long, until morning; in this way the fire of the altar will be kept burning. $^{3(10)}$ When the fire has consumed the burnt offering on the altar, the *cohen*, having put on his linen garment and covered himself with his linen shorts, is to remove the ashes and put them beside the altar. $^{4(11)}$ Then he is to remove those garments and put on others, before carrying the ashes outside the camp to a clean place. $^{5(12)}$ In this way, the fire on the altar will be kept burning and not be allowed to go out. Each morning, the *cohen* is to kindle wood on it, arrange the burnt offering and make the fat of the peace offerings go up in smoke. $^{6(13)}$ Fire is to be kept burning on the altar continually; it is not to go out.

$^{7(14)}$ "'This is the law for the grain offering: the sons of Aharon are to offer it before *ADONAI* in front of the altar. $^{8(15)}$ He is to take from the grain offering a handful of its fine flour, some of its olive oil and all of the frankincense which is on the grain offering; and he is to make this reminder portion of it go up in smoke on the altar as a fragrant aroma for *ADONAI*. $^{9(16)}$ The rest of it Aharon and his sons are to eat; it is to be eaten without leaven in a holy place — they are to eat it in the courtyard of the tent of meeting. $^{10(17)}$ It is not to be baked with leaven. I have given it as their portion of my offerings made by fire; like the sin offering and the guilt offering, it is especially holy. $^{11(18)}$ Every male descendant of Aharon may eat from it; it is his share of the offerings for *ADONAI* made by fire forever through all your generations. Whatever touches those offerings will become holy.'"

(ii) $^{12(19)}$ *ADONAI* said to Moshe, $^{13(20)}$ "This is the offering for *ADONAI* that Aharon and his sons are to offer on the day he is anointed: two quarts of fine flour, half of it in the morning and half in the evening, as a grain offering from then on. $^{14(21)}$ It is to be well mixed with olive oil and fried on a griddle; then bring it in, break it in pieces and offer the grain offering as a fragrant aroma for *ADONAI*. $^{15(22)}$ The anointed *cohen* who will take Aharon's place from among his descendants will offer it; it is a perpetual obligation. It must be entirely made to go up in smoke for *ADONAI*; $^{16(23)}$ every grain offering of the *cohen* is to be entirely made to go up in smoke — it is not to be eaten."

$^{17(24)}$ *ADONAI* said to Moshe, $^{18(25)}$ "Tell Aharon and his sons, 'This is the law for the sin offering: the sin offering is to be slaughtered before *ADONAI* in the place where the burnt offering is slaughtered; it is especially holy. $^{19(26)}$ The *cohen* who offers it for sin is to eat it — it is to be eaten in a holy place, in the courtyard of the tent of meeting. $^{20(27)}$ Whatever touches its flesh will become holy; if any of its blood splashes on any item of clothing, you are to wash it in a holy place. $^{21(28)}$ The clay pot in which it is cooked must be broken; if it is cooked in a bronze pot, it must be scoured and rinsed in water. $^{22(29)}$ Any male from a family of *cohanim* may eat the sin offering; it is especially holy. $^{23(30)}$ But no sin offering which has had any of its blood brought into the tent of meeting to make atonement in the Holy Place is to be eaten; it is to be burned up completely.

7 ^{1} "'This is the law for the guilt offering: it is especially holy. ^{2} They are to slaughter the guilt offering in the place where they slaughter the burnt offering, and its blood is to be splashed against all sides of the altar. ^{3} He is to offer all its fat — the fat tail, the fat covering the inner organs, ⁴ the two kidneys, the fat on them near the flanks, and the covering of the liver, which he will remove with the kidneys. ⁵ The *cohen* will make them go up in smoke on the altar as an offering made by fire to ADONAI; it is a guilt offering. ⁶ Every male from a family of *cohanim* may eat it; it is to be eaten in a holy place; it is especially holy. ⁷ The guilt offering is like the sin offering; the same law governs them — it will belong to the *cohen* who uses it to make atonement.

⁸ "'The *cohen* who offers someone's burnt offering will possess the hide of the burnt offering which he has offered.

⁹ "'Every grain offering baked in the oven, cooked in a pot or fried on a griddle will belong to the *cohen* who offers it. ¹⁰ But every grain offering which is mixed with olive oil or is dry will belong to all the sons of Aharon equally.

(iii) ¹¹ "'This is the law for sacrificing peace offerings offered to ADONAI: ¹² If a person offers it for giving thanks, he is to offer it with the thanksgiving sacrifice of unleavened cakes mixed with olive oil, *matzah* spread with olive oil, and cakes made of fine flour mixed with olive oil and fried. ¹³ With cakes of leavened bread he is to present his offering together with the sacrifice of his peace offerings for giving thanks. ¹⁴ From each kind of offering he is to present one as a gift for ADONAI; it will belong to the *cohen* who splashes the blood of the peace offerings against the altar. ¹⁵ The meat of the sacrifice of his peace offerings for giving thanks is to be eaten on the day of his offering; he is not to leave any of it until morning. ¹⁶ But if the sacrifice connected with his offering is for a vow or is a voluntary offering, then, while it is to be eaten on the day he offers his sacrifice, what remains of it may be eaten the next day. ¹⁷ However, what remains of the meat of the sacrifice on the third day is to be burned up completely. ¹⁸ If any of the meat of the sacrifice of his peace offerings is eaten on the third day, the sacrifice will neither be accepted nor credited to the person offering it; rather, it will have become a disgusting thing, and whoever eats it will bear the consequences of his wrongdoing. ¹⁹ Meat which touches something unclean is not to be eaten but burned up completely. As for the meat, everyone who is clean may eat it; ²⁰ but a person in a state of uncleanness who eats any meat from the sacrifice of peace offerings made to ADONAI will be cut off from his people. ²¹ Anyone who touches something unclean — whether the uncleanness be from a person, from an unclean animal or from some other unclean detestable thing — and then eats the meat from the sacrifice of peace offerings for ADONAI, that person will be cut off from his people.'"

²² ADONAI said to Moshe, ²³ "Say to the people of Isra'el, 'You are not to eat the fat of bulls, sheep or goats. ²⁴ The fat of animals that die of themselves or are killed by wild animals may be used for any other purpose, but under no circumstances are you to eat it. ²⁵ For whoever eats the fat of animals of the kind used in presenting an offering made by fire to ADONAI will be cut off from his people. ²⁶ You are not to eat any kind of blood, whether from birds or animals, in any of your homes. ²⁷ Whoever eats any blood will be cut off from his people.'"

²⁸ ADONAI said to Moshe, ²⁹ "Say to the people of Isra'el, 'A person who offers his sacrifice of peace offerings to ADONAI is to bring part of his sacrifice of peace offerings as his offering for ADONAI. ³⁰ He is to bring with his own hands the offerings for ADONAI made by fire— he is to bring the breast with its fat. The breast is to be waved as a wave offering before ADONAI. ³¹ The *cohen* is to make the fat go up in

smoke on the altar, but the breast will belong to Aharon and his descendants. ³² You are to give the right thigh from your sacrifices of peace offerings to the *cohen* as a contribution. ³³ The descendant of Aharon who offers the blood of the peace offerings is to have the right thigh as his share. ³⁴ For the breast that has been waved and the thigh that has been contributed I have taken from the people of Isra'el out of their sacrifices of peace offerings and given them to Aharon the *cohen* and to his descendants as their share forever from the people of Isra'el.'"

³⁵ On the day when Aharon and his sons were presented to serve *Adonai* in the office of *cohen*, this portion was set aside for him and his descendants from the offerings for *Adonai* made by fire. ³⁶ On the day they were anointed, *Adonai* ordered that this be given to them by the people of Isra'el. It is their share forever through all their generations.

³⁷ This is the law for the burnt offering, the grain offering, the sin offering, the guilt offering, the consecration offering and the sacrifice of peace offerings ³⁸ which *Adonai* ordered Moshe on Mount Sinai on the day he ordered the people of Isra'el to present their offerings to *Adonai*, in the Sinai Desert.

8 *(iv)* ¹ *Adonai* said to Moshe, ² "Take Aharon and his sons with him, the garments, the anointing oil, the bull for the sin offering, the two rams and the basket of *matzah*; ³ and assemble the entire community at the entrance to the tent of meeting." ⁴ Moshe did as *Adonai* ordered him, and the community was assembled at the entrance to the tent of meeting. ⁵ Moshe said to the community, "This is what *Adonai* has ordered to be done."

⁶ Moshe brought Aharon and his sons, washed them with water, ⁷ put the tunic on him, wrapped the sash around him, clothed him with the robe, put the ritual vest on him, wrapped around him the decorated belt and fastened the vest to him with it. ⁸ He put the breastplate on him, and into the breastplate he put the *urim* and *tumim*. ⁹ He set the turban on his head, and on the front of the turban he affixed the gold plate, the holy ornament, as *Adonai* had ordered Moshe. ¹⁰ Then Moshe took the anointing oil and anointed the tabernacle and everything in it, thus consecrating them. ¹¹ He sprinkled some on the altar seven times, anointing the altar with all its utensils and the basin with its base, to consecrate them. ¹² He poured some of the anointing oil on Aharon's head and anointed him, to consecrate him. ¹³ Moshe brought Aharon's sons, clothed them with tunics, wrapped sashes on them and put headgear on them, as *Adonai* had ordered Moshe.

(v) ¹⁴ Then the young bull for the sin offering was brought, and Aharon and his sons laid their hands on the head of the bull for the sin offering. ¹⁵ After it had been slaughtered, Moshe took the blood and put it on the horns of the altar all the way around with his finger, thus purifying the altar. The remaining blood he poured out at the base of the altar and consecrated it, to make atonement for it. ¹⁶ Moshe took all the fat on the inner organs, the covering of the liver, the two kidneys and their fat, and made it go up in smoke on the altar. ¹⁷ But the bull, its hide, its flesh and its dung were taken outside the camp and burned up completely, as *Adonai* had ordered Moshe.

¹⁸ Next, the ram for the burnt offering was presented. Aharon and his sons laid their hands on the head of the ram; ¹⁹ and after it had been slaughtered, Moshe splashed the blood on all sides of the altar. ²⁰ When the ram had been cut in pieces, Moshe made the head, the pieces and the fat go up in smoke. ²¹ When the inner organs and the lower parts of the legs had been washed with water, Moshe made the entire ram

go up in smoke on the altar; it was a burnt offering giving a fragrant aroma, an offering made by fire to *Adonai* — as *Adonai* had ordered Moshe.

(vi) ²² Then the other ram was presented, the ram of consecration; Aharon and his sons laid their hands on the head of the ram. ²³ After it had been slaughtered, Moshe took some of its blood and put it on the tip of Aharon's right ear, on the thumb of his right hand, and on the big toe of his right foot. ²⁴ Next Aharon's sons were brought, and Moshe put some of the blood on the tips of their right ears, on the thumbs of their right hands, and on the big toes of their right feet; then Moshe splashed the blood on all sides of the altar. ²⁵ He took the fat, the fat tail, all the fat covering the inner organs, the covering of the liver, the two kidneys with their fat, and the right thigh. ²⁶ From the basket of *matzah* that was before *Adonai* he took one piece of *matzah*, one cake of oiled bread, and one wafer, and placed them on the fat and on the right thigh. ²⁷ Then he put it all in Aharon's hands and in the hands of his sons and waved them as a wave offering before *Adonai*. ²⁸ Moshe took them out of their hands and made them go up in smoke on the altar on top of the burnt offering; they were a consecration offering giving a fragrant aroma; an offering made by fire to *Adonai*. ²⁹ Moshe took the breast and waved it as a wave offering before *Adonai*; it was Moshe's portion of the ram of consecration — as *Adonai* had ordered Moshe.

(vii) ³⁰ Moshe took some of the anointing oil and some of the blood which was on the altar and sprinkled it on Aharon and his clothing, and on his sons with him and their clothing, and consecrated Aharon and his clothing together with his sons and their clothing.

³¹ Moshe said to Aharon and his sons, "Boil the meat at the door of the tent of meeting; and eat it there with the bread that is in the basket of consecration, as I ordered when I said that Aharon and his sons are to eat it. ³² Whatever is left over of the meat and bread you are to burn up completely. *(Maftir)* ³³ You are not to go out from the entrance to the tent of meeting for seven days, until the days of your consecration are over; since *Adonai* will be consecrating you for seven days. ³⁴ He ordered done what has been done today, in order to make atonement for you. ³⁵ You are to remain at the entrance to the tent of meeting day and night for seven days, thereby obeying what *Adonai* ordered done, so that you may not die. For this is what I was ordered." ³⁶ Aharon and his sons did all the things which *Adonai* ordered through Moshe.

Haftarah Tzav: Yirmeyahu (Jeremiah) 7:21–8:3; 9:22(23)–23(24)

Suggested readings for Parashah Tzav from the B'rit Hadashah: Mark 12:28–34; Romans 12:1–2; 1 Corinthians 10:14–23

Parashah 26: Sh'mini (Eighth) 9:1–11:47

9 ¹ On the eighth day, Moshe called Aharon, his sons and the leaders of Isra'el, ² and said to Aharon, "Take a male calf for a sin offering and a ram for a burnt offering, both without defect, and offer them before *Adonai*. ³ Then tell the people of Isra'el, 'Take a male goat for a sin offering and a calf and a lamb, both a year old and without defect, for a burnt offering, ⁴ and an ox and a ram for peace offerings, to sacrifice before *Adonai*; also a grain offering mixed with olive oil — because today *Adonai* is going to appear to you.'" ⁵ They brought what Moshe had ordered before the tent of meeting, and the whole community approached and stood before ADONAI.

⁶ Moshe said, "This is what ADONAI has ordered you to do, so that the glory of ADONAI will appear to you." ⁷ Moshe told Aharon, "Approach the altar, offer your sin offering and burnt offering, and make atonement for yourself and the people. Then present the offering of the people and make atonement for them, as ADONAI ordered." ⁸ So Aharon approached the altar and slaughtered the calf of the sin offering which was for himself. ⁹ The sons of Aharon presented the blood to him; and he dipped his finger in the blood and put it on the horns of the altar; then he poured out the blood at the base of the altar. ¹⁰ But the fat, the kidneys and the covering of the liver of the sin offering he made go up in smoke on the altar, as ADONAI had ordered Moshe. ¹¹ The meat and the skin were burned up completely outside the camp.

¹² Next he slaughtered the burnt offering; Aharon's sons brought him the blood, and he splashed it against all sides of the altar. ¹³ They brought him the burnt offering, piece by piece, and the head; and he made them go up in smoke on the altar. ¹⁴ He washed the inner organs and the lower parts of the legs and made them go up in smoke on top of the burnt offering on the altar.

¹⁵ Then the people's offering was presented. He took the goat of the sin offering which was for the people, slaughtered it and offered it for sin, like the earlier sin offering. ¹⁶ The burnt offering was presented, and he offered it in the prescribed manner. *(ii)* ¹⁷ The grain offering was presented; he took a handful of it and made it go up in smoke on the altar, in addition to the morning's burnt offering. ¹⁸ He slaughtered the ox and the ram, the people's sacrifice as peace offerings; Aharon's sons brought him the blood, which he splashed against all sides of the altar, ¹⁹ and the fat of the ox and of the ram — the fat tail, the fat which covers the inner organs, the kidneys and the covering of the liver. ²⁰ They put the fat on the breasts, and he made the fat go up in smoke on the altar. ²¹ The breasts and right thigh Aharon waved as a wave offering before ADONAI, as Moshe had ordered.

²² Aharon raised his hands toward the people, blessed them and came down from offering the sin offering, the burnt offering and the peace offerings. ²³ Moshe and Aharon entered the tent of meeting, came out and blessed the people. Then the glory of ADONAI appeared to all the people! *(iii)* ²⁴ Fire came forth from the presence of ADONAI, consuming the burnt offering and the fat on the altar. When all the people saw it, they shouted and fell on their faces.

10 ¹ But Nadav and Avihu, sons of Aharon, each took his censer, put fire in it, laid incense on it, and offered unauthorized fire before ADONAI, something he had not ordered them to do. ² At this, fire came forth from the presence of ADONAI and consumed them, so that they died in the presence of ADONAI. ³ Moshe said to Aharon, "This is what ADONAI said:

'Through those who are near me I will be consecrated,
    and before all the people I will be glorified.'"

Aharon kept silent.

⁴ Moshe called Misha'el and Eltzafan, sons of 'Uzi'el Aharon's uncle, and told them, "Come here, and carry your cousins away from in front of the sanctuary to a

place outside the camp." ⁵ They approached and carried them in their tunics out of the camp, as Moshe had said.

⁶ Then Moshe told Aharon and his sons El'azar and Itamar, "Don't unbind your hair or tear your clothes in mourning, so that you won't die and so that ADONAI won't be angry with the entire community. Rather, let your kinsmen — the whole house of Isra'el — mourn, because of the destruction ADONAI brought about with his fire. ⁷ Moreover, don't leave the entrance to the tent of meeting, or you will die, because ADONAI's anointing oil is on you."

⁸ ADONAI said to Aharon, ⁹ "Don't drink any wine or other intoxicating liquor, neither you nor your sons with you, when you enter the tent of meeting, so that you will not die. This is to be a permanent regulation through all your generations, ¹⁰ so that you will distinguish between the holy and the common, and between the unclean and the clean; ¹¹ and so that you will teach the people of Isra'el all the laws ADONAI has told them through Moshe."

(iv) ¹² Moshe said to Aharon and to El'azar and Itamar, his remaining sons, "Take the grain offering left from the offerings for ADONAI made by fire, and eat it without leaven next to the altar, because it is especially holy. ¹³ Eat it in a holy place, because it is your and your sons' share of the offerings for ADONAI made by fire; for this is what I have been ordered. ¹⁴ The breast that was waved and the thigh that was raised you are to eat in a clean place — you, your sons and your daughters with you; for these are given as your and your children's share of the sacrifices of the peace offerings presented by the people of Isra'el. ¹⁵ They are to bring the raised thigh and the waved breast, along with the offerings of fat made by fire, and wave it as a wave offering before ADONAI; then it will belong to you and your descendants with you as your perpetual share, as ADONAI has ordered."

(v) ¹⁶ Then Moshe carefully investigated what had happened to the goat of the sin offering and discovered that it had been burned up. He became angry with El'azar and Itamar, the remaining sons of Aharon, and asked, ¹⁷ "Why didn't you eat the sin offering in the area of the sanctuary, since it is especially holy? He gave it to you to take away the guilt of the community, to make atonement for them before ADONAI. ¹⁸ Look! Its blood wasn't brought into the sanctuary! You should have eaten it there in the sanctuary, as I ordered." ¹⁹ Aharon answered Moshe, "Even though they offered their sin offering and burnt offering today, things like these have happened to me! If I had eaten the sin offering today, would it have pleased ADONAI?" ²⁰ On hearing this reply, Moshe was satisfied.

11 *(vi)* ¹ ADONAI said to Moshe and Aharon, ² "Tell the people of Isra'el, 'These are the living creatures which you may eat among all the land animals: ³ any that has a separate hoof which is completely divided and chews the cud — these animals you may eat. ⁴⁻⁶ But you are not to eat those that only chew the cud or only have a separate hoof. For example, the camel, the coney and the hare are unclean for you, because they chew the cud but don't have a separate hoof; ⁷ while the pig is unclean for you, because, although it has a separate and completely divided hoof, it doesn't chew the cud. ⁸ You are not to eat meat from these or touch their carcasses; they are unclean for you.

⁹ "'Of all the things that live in the water, you may eat these: anything in the water that has fins and scales, whether in seas or in rivers — these you may eat.

[10] But everything in the seas and rivers without both fins and scales, of all the small water-creatures and of all the living creatures in the water, is a detestable thing for you. [11] Yes, these will be detestable for you — you are not to eat their meat, and you are to detest their carcasses. [12] Whatever lacks fins and scales in the water is a detestable thing for you.

[13] "'The following creatures of the air are to be detestable for you — they are not to be eaten, they are a detestable thing: the eagle, the vulture, the osprey, [14] the kite, the various kinds of buzzards, [15] the various kinds of ravens, [16] the ostrich, the screech-owl, the seagull, the various kinds of hawks, [17] the little owl, the cormorant, the great owl, [18] the horned owl, the pelican, the barn owl, [19] the stork, the various kinds of herons, the hoopoe and the bat.

[20] "'All winged swarming creatures that go on all fours are a detestable thing for you; [21] except that of all winged swarming creatures that go on all fours, you may eat those that have jointed legs above their feet, enabling them to jump off the ground. [22] Specifically, of these you may eat the various kinds of locusts, grasshoppers, katydids and crickets. [23] But other than that, all winged swarming creatures having four feet are a detestable thing for you.

[24] "'The following will make you unclean; whoever touches the carcass of them will be unclean until evening, [25] and whoever picks up any part of their carcass is to wash his clothes and be unclean until evening: [26] every animal that has a separate but incompletely divided hoof or that doesn't chew the cud is unclean for you; anyone who touches them will become unclean. [27] Whatever goes on its paws, among all animals that go on all fours, is unclean for you; whoever touches its carcass will be unclean until evening; [28] and whoever picks up its carcass is to wash his clothes and be unclean until evening — these are unclean for you.

[29] "'The following are unclean for you among the small creatures that swarm on the ground: the weasel, the mouse, the various kinds of lizards, [30] the gecko, the land crocodile, the skink, the sand-lizard and the chameleon. [31] They are unclean crawling creatures; whoever touches them when they are dead will be unclean until evening. [32] Anything on which one of them falls when dead will become unclean — wooden utensil, article of clothing, leather, sacking — any utensil used for work; it must be put in water, and it will be unclean until evening; then it will be clean. *(vii)* [33] If one of them falls into a clay pot, whatever is in it will become unclean, and you are to break the pot. [34] Any food permitted to be eaten that water from such a vessel gets on will become unclean, and any permitted liquid in such a vessel will become unclean. [35] Everything on which any carcass-part of theirs falls will become unclean, whether oven or stove; it is to be broken in pieces — they are unclean and will be unclean for you; [36] although a spring or cistern for collecting water remains clean. But anyone who touches one of their carcasses will become unclean. [37] If any carcass-part of theirs falls on any kind of seed to be sown, it is clean; [38] but if water is put on the seed and a carcass-part of theirs falls on it, it is unclean for you.

[39] "'If an animal of a kind that you are permitted to eat dies, whoever touches its carcass will be unclean until evening. [40] A person who eats meat from its carcass or carries its carcass is to wash his clothes; he will be unclean until evening.

[41] "'Any creature that swarms on the ground is a detestable thing; it is not to be eaten — [42] whatever moves on its stomach, goes on all fours, or has many legs —

all creatures that swarm on the ground; you are not to eat them, because they are a detestable thing. ⁴³ You are not to make yourselves detestable with any of these swarming, crawling creatures; do not make yourselves unclean with them, do not defile yourselves with them. ⁴⁴ For I am *ADONAI* your God; therefore, consecrate yourselves and be holy, for I am holy; and do not defile yourselves with any kind of swarming creature that moves along the ground. *(Maftir)* ⁴⁵ For I am *ADONAI*, who brought you up out of the land of Egypt to be your God. Therefore you are to be holy, because I am holy.

⁴⁶ "'Such, then, is the law concerning animals, flying creatures, all living creatures that move about in the water, and all creatures that swarm on the ground. ⁴⁷ Its purpose is to distinguish between the unclean and the clean, and between the creatures that may be eaten and those that may not be eaten.'"

Haftarah Sh'mini: Sh'mu'el Bet (2 Samuel) 6:1–7:17 (A); 6:1–19 (S)

Suggested readings for Parashah Sh'mini from the B'rit Hadashah: Mark 7:1–23; Acts 5:1–11; 10:1–35; 2 Corinthians 6:14–7:1; Galatians 2:11–16; 1 Kefa (1 Peter) 1:14–16

Parashah 27: Tazria (She conceives) 12:1–13:59
[In regular years read with Parashah 28, in leap years read separately]

12 ¹ *ADONAI* said to Moshe, ² "Tell the people of Isra'el: 'If a woman conceives and gives birth to a boy, she will be unclean for seven days with the same uncleanness as in *niddah*, when she is having her menstrual period. ³ On the eighth day, the baby's foreskin is to be circumcised. ⁴ She is to wait an additional thirty-three days to be purified from her blood; she is not to touch any holy thing or come into the sanctuary until the time of her purification is over. ⁵ But if she gives birth to a girl, she will be unclean for two weeks, as in her *niddah*; and she is to wait another sixty-six days to be purified from her blood.

⁶ "'When the days of her purification are over, whether for a son or for a daughter, she is to bring a lamb in its first year for a burnt offering and a young pigeon or dove for a sin offering to the entrance of the tent of meeting, to the *cohen*. ⁷ He will offer it before *ADONAI* and make atonement for her; thus she will be purified from her discharge of blood. Such is the law for a woman who gives birth, whether to a boy or to a girl. ⁸ If she can't afford a lamb, she is to take two doves or two young pigeons, the one for a burnt offering and the other for a sin offering; the *cohen* will make atonement for her, and she will be clean.'"

13 ¹ *ADONAI* said to Moshe and Aharon, ² "If someone develops on his skin a swelling, scab or bright spot which could develop into the disease *tzara'at*, he is to be brought to Aharon the *cohen* or to one of his sons who are *cohanim*. ³ The *cohen* is to examine the sore on his skin; if the hair in the sore has turned white, and the sore appears to go deep into the skin, it is *tzara'at*, and after examining him the *cohen* is to declare him unclean. ⁴ If the bright spot on his skin is white, but it does not appear to go deep into the skin, and its hair has not turned white, then the *cohen* is to isolate him for seven days. ⁵ On the seventh day the *cohen* is to examine him again, and if the sore appears the same as before and has not spread on the skin, then the *cohen* is to isolate him for seven more days. *(LY: ii)* ⁶ On the seventh day the *cohen* is to examine him again, and if the sore has faded and hasn't spread on the skin, then the *cohen* is to declare him clean — it is only a scab, so he is to wash his clothes and be clean. ⁷ But if the scab spreads further on the skin after he has been examined by the *cohen* and declared clean, he is to let himself be examined yet again by the *cohen*. ⁸ The *cohen* will examine him, and if he sees that the scab has spread on his skin, then the *cohen* will declare him unclean; it is *tzara'at*.

⁹ "If a person has *tzara'at*, he is to be brought to the *cohen*. ¹⁰ The *cohen* is to examine him, and if he sees that there is a white swelling in the skin which has turned the hair white and inflamed flesh in the swelling, ¹¹ then it is chronic *tzara'at* on his skin, and the *cohen* is to declare him unclean; he is not to isolate him, because it is already clear that he is unclean. ¹² If the *tzara'at* breaks out all over the skin, so that, as far as the *cohen* can see, the person with *tzara'at* has sores everywhere on his body, from his head to his feet; ¹³ then the *cohen* is to examine him, and if he sees that the *tzara'at* has covered his entire body, he is to pronounce the person with the sores clean — it has all turned white, and he is clean. ¹⁴ But if one day inflamed flesh appears on him, he will be unclean. ¹⁵ The *cohen* will examine the inflamed flesh and declare him unclean; the inflamed flesh is unclean; it is *tzara'at*. ¹⁶ However, if the inflamed flesh again turns white, he is to come to the *cohen*. ¹⁷ The *cohen* will examine him, and if he sees that the sores have turned white, then the *cohen* is to declare clean the person with the sores; he is clean.

(LY: iii) ¹⁸ "If a person has on his skin a boil that heals ¹⁹ in such a way that in place of the boil there is a white swelling or a reddish-white bright spot, it is to be shown to the *cohen*. ²⁰ The *cohen* is to examine it; if he sees that it appears to be more than skin-deep, and its hair has turned white, then the *cohen* is to pronounce him unclean — the disease of *tzara'at* has broken out in the boil. ²¹ But if the *cohen* looks at it and doesn't see any white hairs in it, and it isn't more than skin-deep but appears faded, the *cohen* is to isolate him for seven days. ²² If it spreads on the skin, the *cohen* is to declare him unclean; it is the disease. ²³ But if the bright spot stays where it was and has not spread, it is the scar of the boil; and the *cohen* is to declare him clean.

(RY: ii, LY: iv) ²⁴ "Or if someone has on his skin a burn caused by fire; and the inflamed flesh where it was burned has become a bright spot, reddish-white or white, ²⁵ then the *cohen* is to examine it; and if he sees that the hair in the bright spot has turned white and that it appears to be deeper than the skin around it, it is *tzara'at*; it has broken out in the burn, and the *cohen* is to declare him unclean; it is a sore from *tzara'at*. ²⁶ But if the *cohen* examines it and sees no white hair in the bright spot, and it is no more than skin-deep but looks faded, then the *cohen* is to isolate him for seven days. ²⁷ On the seventh day the *cohen* is to examine him; if it has spread on the skin, then the *cohen* is to declare him unclean; it is a sore from *tzara'at*. ²⁸ But if the bright spot stays where it was and has not spread on the skin but appears faded, it is a swelling due to the burn; and the *cohen* is to declare him clean; because it is only a scar from the burn.

(LY: v) ²⁹ "If a man or woman has a sore on the head or a man in his beard, ³⁰ then the *cohen* is to examine the sore; if he sees that it appears to be deeper than the

skin around it, with yellow, thin hair in it, then the *cohen* is to declare him unclean; it is a crusted area, a *tzara'at* of the head or beard. ^{31} If the *cohen* examines the diseased crusted area and sees that it appears not to be deeper than the skin around it, and without any black hair in it, then the *cohen* is to isolate for seven days the person with the diseased crusted area. ^{32} On the seventh day the *cohen* is to examine the sore, and if he sees that the crusted area hasn't spread, that it has no yellow hair in it, and that the crusted area is not deeper than the skin around it; ^{33} then the person is to be shaved, except for the crusted area itself, and the *cohen* is to isolate him for seven more days. ^{34} On the seventh day the *cohen* is to examine the crusted area; and if he sees that the crusted area has not spread on the skin and does not appear to be deeper than the skin around it, then the *cohen* is to declare him clean; he is to wash his clothes and be clean. ^{35} But if the crusted area spreads after his purification, ^{36} then the *cohen* is to examine him; and if he sees that the crusted area has spread on the skin, the *cohen* is not to look for yellow hair; he is unclean. ^{37} But if the crusted area's appearance doesn't change, and black hair grows up in it, then the crusted area is healed; he is clean; and the *cohen* is to declare him clean.

(RY: iii, LY: vi) ^{38} "If a man or woman has bright spots on his skin, bright white spots; ^{39} then the *cohen* is to examine them. If he sees that the bright spots on the skin are dull white, it is only a rash that has broken out on the skin; he is clean.

^{40} "If a man's hair has fallen from his scalp, he is bald; but he is clean. ^{41} If his hair has fallen off the front part of his head, he is forehead-bald; but he is clean. ^{42} But if on the bald scalp or forehead there is a reddish-white sore, it is *tzara'at* breaking out on his bald scalp or forehead. ^{43} Then the *cohen* is to examine him; if he sees that there is a reddish-white swelling on his bald scalp or forehead, appearing like *tzara'at* on the rest of the body, ^{44} he is a person with *tzara'at*; he is unclean; the *cohen* must declare him unclean; the sore is on his head.

^{45} "Everyone who has *tzara'at* sores is to wear torn clothes and unbound hair, cover his upper lip and cry, 'Unclean! Unclean!' ^{46} As long as he has sores, he will be unclean; since he is unclean, he must live in isolation; he must live outside the camp.

^{47} "When *tzara'at* infects an article of clothing, whether it be a woolen or a linen garment, ^{48} on the threads or the woven-in parts of either linen or wool, or on a hide or item made of leather; ^{49} then if the stain on the garment, hide, threads, woven-in parts or leather item is greenish or reddish, it is an infection of *tzara'at* and is to be shown to the *cohen*. ^{50} The *cohen* is to examine the stain and isolate the article that has the infection for seven days. ^{51} On the seventh day he is to examine the stain; if the stain has spread on the garment, threads, woven-in parts or leather, whatever its use, the infection is a contagious *tzara'at*; the garment is unclean. ^{52} He is to burn the garment, threads, woven-in parts of either wool or linen, or item of leather having the infection; for it is a contagious *tzara'at*; it must be burned up completely. ^{53} But if, when the *cohen* examines it, he sees that the infection has not spread on the garment or in the threads, woven-in parts or leather item, ^{54} then the *cohen* is to order that the article having the infection be washed and isolated for seven more days. *(RY: iv, LY: vii)* ^{55} The *cohen* is to examine it after the stain has been washed, and if he sees that the stain has not changed color, then, even though the stain has not spread, it is unclean; you are to burn it up completely — it is rotten, no matter whether the spot is on the outside or on the inside. ^{56} If the *cohen* examines it and sees that the stain has faded after being washed, then he is to tear the stain out of the garment, leather, threads or woven-in parts. *(LY: Maftir)* ⁵⁷ If it appears again in the garment, threads, woven-in parts or leather item, it is contagious, and you are to burn up completely the article that had the stain. ⁵⁸ But if the infection is gone from the garment, threads, woven-in parts or leather item that you washed, then it is to be washed a second time, and it will be clean. ⁵⁹ This is the law concerning infections of *tzara'at* in a garment of wool or linen, or in the threads or the woven-in parts, or in any leather item — when to declare it clean and when to declare it unclean.

Haftarah Tazria: M'lakhim Bet (2 Kings) 4:42–5:19

B'rit Hadashah suggested readings for Parashah Tazria: Mattityahu (Matthew) 8:1–4, 11:2–6; Mark 1:40–45; Luke 2:22–24; 5:12–16; 7:18–23

Parashah 28: M'tzora (Person afflicted with tzara'at) 14:1–15:33
[In regular years read with Parashah 27, in leap years read separately]

14 ¹ ADONAI said to Moshe, ² "This is to be the law concerning the person afflicted with *tzara'at* on the day of his purification. He is to be brought to the *cohen*, ³ and the *cohen* is to go outside the camp and examine him there. If he sees that the *tzara'at* sores have been healed in the afflicted person, ⁴ then the *cohen* will order that two living clean birds be taken for the one to be purified, along with cedar-wood, scarlet yarn and hyssop leaves. ⁵ The *cohen* is to order one of the birds slaughtered in a clay pot over running water. ⁶ As for the live bird, he is to take it with the cedar-wood, scarlet yarn and hyssop and dip them and the living bird in the blood of the bird slaughtered over running water, ⁷ and sprinkle the person to be purified from the *tzara'at* seven times. Next he is to set the live bird free in an open field. ⁸ He who is to be purified must wash his clothes, shave off all his hair and bathe himself in water. Then he will be clean; and after that, he may enter the camp; but he must live outside his tent for seven days. ⁹ On the seventh day he is to shave all the hair off his head, also his beard and eyebrows — he must shave off all his hair; and he is to wash his clothes and bathe his body in water; and he will be clean.

¹⁰ "On the eighth day he is to take two male lambs without defect, one female lamb in its first year without defect and six-and-a-half quarts of fine flour for a grain offering, mixed with olive oil, and two-thirds of a pint of olive oil. ¹¹ The *cohen* purifying him is to place the person being purified with these items before ADONAI at the entrance to the tent of meeting. ¹² The *cohen* is to take one of the male lambs and offer it as a guilt offering with the two-thirds-pint of olive oil, then wave them as a wave offering before ADONAI. *(LY: ii)* ¹³ He is to slaughter the male lamb at the place in the sanctuary for slaughtering sin offerings and burnt offerings, because the guilt offering belongs to the *cohen*, just like the sin offering; it is especially holy. ¹⁴ The *cohen* is to take some of the blood of the guilt offering and put it on the tip of the right ear of the person being purified, on the thumb of his right hand and on the big toe of his right foot. ¹⁵ Next, the *cohen* is to take some of the two-thirds-pint of olive oil and pour it into the palm of his own left hand, ¹⁶ dip his right finger in the oil that is in his left hand and sprinkle from the oil with his finger seven times before ADONAI. ¹⁷ Then the

cohen is to put some of the remaining oil in his hand on the tip of the right ear of the person being purified, on the thumb of his right hand, on the big toe of his right foot and on the blood of the guilt offering. ¹⁸ Finally, the *cohen* is to put the rest of the oil in his hand on the head of the person being purified; and the *cohen* will make atonement for him before A*DONAI*. ¹⁹ The *cohen* is to offer the sin offering and make atonement for the person being purified because of his uncleanness; afterwards, he is to slaughter the burnt offering. ²⁰ The *cohen* is to offer the burnt offering and the grain offering on the altar; thus the *cohen* will make atonement for him; and he will be clean.

(RY: v, LY: iii) ²¹ "If he is poor, so that he can't afford to do otherwise, he is to take one male lamb as a guilt offering to be waved, to make atonement for him; two quarts of fine flour mixed with olive oil for a grain offering; two-thirds of a pint of olive oil; ²² and two doves or two young pigeons, such as he can afford, the one for a sin offering and the other for a burnt offering. ²³ On the eighth day, he will bring them to the *cohen* for his purification, to the entrance of the tent of meeting before A*DONAI*. ²⁴ The *cohen* is to take the lamb of the guilt offering and the two-thirds of a pint of olive oil and wave them as a wave offering before A*DONAI*. ²⁵ He is to slaughter the lamb of the guilt offering; and the *cohen* is to take some of the blood of the guilt offering and put it on the tip of the right ear of the person being purified, on the thumb of his right hand and on the big toe of his right foot. ²⁶ The *cohen* is to take some of the olive oil and pour it into the palm of his own left hand, ²⁷ and sprinkle with his right hand some of the oil that is in his left hand seven times before A*DONAI*. ²⁸ The *cohen* is to put some of the oil in his hand on the tip of the right ear of the person being purified, on the thumb of his right hand, on the big toe of his right foot — in the same place as the blood of the guilt offering. ²⁹ Finally, the *cohen* is to put the rest of the oil in his hand on the head of the person being purified, to make atonement for him before A*DONAI*. ³⁰ He is to offer one of the doves or young pigeons, such as the person can afford, ³¹ whatever his means suffice for — the one as a sin offering and the other as a burnt offering — with the grain offering; thus the *cohen* will make atonement before A*DONAI* for the person being purified. ³² Such is the law for the person who has *tzara'at* sores if he cannot afford the usual elements used for his purification."

(RY: vi, LY: iv) ³³ A*DONAI* said to Moshe and Aharon, ³⁴ "When you have entered the land of Kena'an which I am giving you as a possession, and I put an infection of *tzara'at* in a house in the land that you possess, ³⁵ then the owner of the house is to come and tell the *cohen*, 'It seems to me that there may be an infection in the house.' ³⁶ The *cohen* is to order the house emptied before he goes in to inspect the infection, so that everything in the house won't be made unclean; afterwards, the *cohen* is to enter and inspect the house. ³⁷ He will examine the infection; and if he sees that the infection is in the walls of the house, with greenish or reddish depressions that seem to go in deeper than the surface of the wall, ³⁸ he is to go out of the house to its door and seal up the house for seven days. ³⁹ The *cohen* will come again on the seventh day and examine the house; if he sees that the infection has spread over its walls, ⁴⁰ he is to order them to remove the infected stones and throw them into some unclean place outside the city. ⁴¹ Next, he is to have the inside of the house thoroughly scraped, and the scraped-off plaster

is to be discarded outside the city in an unclean place. ⁴²Finally, other stones must be set in the place of the first stones and other plaster used to replaster the house. ⁴³If the infection returns and breaks out in the house after the stones have been removed and the house scraped and plastered; ⁴⁴then the *cohen* is to enter and examine it. If he sees that the infection has spread in the house, it is a contagious *tzara'at* in the house; it is unclean. ⁴⁵He must break down the house and take its stones, timber and plaster out of the city to an unclean place. ⁴⁶Moreover, whoever enters the house at any time while it is sealed up will be unclean until evening. ⁴⁷Whoever lies down or eats in the house must wash his clothes. ⁴⁸If the *cohen* enters, examines and sees that the infection has not spread in the house since it was plastered; then he is to declare the house clean; because the infection is cured.

⁴⁹"To purify the house, he is to take two birds, cedar-wood, scarlet yarn and hyssop leaves. ⁵⁰He is to slaughter one of the birds in a clay pot over running water. ⁵¹He is to take the cedar-wood, the hyssop, the scarlet yarn and the live bird and dip them in the blood of the slaughtered bird and in the running water, and sprinkle the house seven times. ⁵²He will purify the house with the blood of the bird, the running water, the live bird, the cedar-wood, the hyssop and the scarlet yarn. ⁵³But he is to set the live bird free outside the city in an open field; thus will he make atonement for the house; and it will be clean.

(LY: v) ⁵⁴"Such is the law for all kinds of *tzara'at* sores, for a crusted area, ⁵⁵for *tzara'at* in a garment, for a house, ⁵⁶for a swelling, for a scab and for a bright spot, ⁵⁷to determine when it is clean and when it is unclean. This is the law concerning *tzara'at*."

15 ¹A𝐷𝑂𝑁𝐴𝐼 said to Moshe and Aharon, ²"Tell the people of Isra'el, 'When any man has a discharge from his body, the discharge is unclean. ³The discharge is unclean no matter whether it continues flowing or has stopped; it is still his uncleanness. ⁴Every bed which the person with the discharge lies on is unclean, and everything he sits on is unclean. ⁵Whoever touches his bed is to wash his clothes and bathe himself in water; he will be unclean until evening. ⁶Whoever sits on anything the person with the discharge sat on is to wash his clothes and bathe himself in water; he will be unclean until evening. ⁷Anyone who touches the body of the person with the discharge is to wash his clothes and bathe himself in water; he will be unclean until evening. ⁸If the person with the discharge spits on someone who is clean, the latter is to wash his clothes and bathe himself in water; he will be unclean until evening. ⁹Any saddle that the person with the discharge rides on will be unclean. ¹⁰Whoever touches anything that was under him will be unclean until evening; he who carries those things is to wash his clothes and bathe himself in water; he will be unclean until evening. ¹¹If the person with the discharge fails to rinse his hands in water before touching someone, that person is to wash his clothes and bathe himself in water; he will be unclean until evening. ¹²If the person with the discharge touches a clay pot, it must be broken; if he touches a wooden utensil, it must be rinsed in water.

¹³"'When a person with a discharge has become free of it, he is to count seven days for his purification. Then he is to wash his clothes and bathe his body in running water; after that, he will be clean. ¹⁴On the eighth day, he is to take for himself

two doves or two young pigeons, come before A*DONAI* to the entrance of the tent of meeting and give them to the *cohen*. [15] The *cohen* is to offer them, the one as a sin offering and the other as a burnt offering; thus the *cohen* will make atonement for him on account of his discharge before A*DONAI*.

(RY: vii, LY: vi) [16] "'If a man has a seminal emission, he is to bathe his entire body in water; he will be unclean until evening. [17] Any clothing or leather on which there is any semen is to be washed with water; it will be unclean until evening. [18] If a man goes to bed with a woman and has sexual relations, both are to bathe themselves in water; they will be unclean until evening.

[19] "'If a woman has a discharge, and the discharge from her body is blood, she will be in her state of *niddah* for seven days. Whoever touches her will be unclean until evening. [20] Everything she lies on or sits on in her state of *niddah* will be unclean. [21] Whoever touches her bed is to wash his clothes and bathe himself in water; he will be unclean until evening. [22] Whoever touches anything she sits on is to wash his clothes and bathe himself in water; he will be unclean until evening. [23] As soon as he touches the bed or something she sat on, he will be unclean until evening. [24] If a man goes to bed with her, and her menstrual flow touches him, he will be unclean seven days; and every bed he lies on will be unclean.

[25] "'If a woman has a discharge of blood for many days not during her period, or if her discharge lasts beyond the normal end of her period, then throughout the time she is having an unclean discharge she will be as when she is in *niddah* — she is unclean. [26] Every bed she lies on at any time while she is having her discharge will be for her like the bed she uses during her time of *niddah*; and everything she sits on will be unclean with uncleanness like that of her time of *niddah*. [27] Whoever touches those things will be unclean; he is to wash his clothes and bathe himself in water; he will be unclean until evening.

[28] "'If she has become free of her discharge, she is to count seven days; after that, she will be clean. *(LY: vii)* [29] On the eighth day, she is to take for herself two doves or two young pigeons and bring them to the *cohen* at the entrance to the tent of meeting. [30] The *cohen* is to offer the one as a sin offering and the other as a burnt offering; thus the *cohen* will make atonement for her before A*DONAI* on account of her unclean discharge.

(Maftir) [31] "'In this way you will separate the people of Isra'el from their uncleanness, so that they will not die in a state of uncleanness for defiling my tabernacle which is there with them.

[32] "'Such is the law for the person who has a discharge; for the man who has a seminal emission that makes him unclean; [33] for the woman in *niddah* during her menstrual period; for the person, man or woman, with a discharge; and for the man who has sexual relations with a woman who is unclean.

Haftarah M'tzora: M'lakhim Bet (2 Kings) 7:3–20

B'rit Hadashah suggested readings for Parashah M'tzora: Mattityahu (Matthew) 9:20–26; Mark 5:24b–34; Luke 8:42b–48; Messianic Jews (Hebrews) 13:4

Parashah 29: Acharei Mot (After the death) 16:1–18:30
[In regular years read with Parashah 30, in leap years read separately]

16 ¹ ADONAI spoke with Moshe after the death of Aharon's two sons, when they tried to sacrifice before ADONAI and died; ² ADONAI said to Moshe, "Tell your brother Aharon not to come at just any time into the Holy Place beyond the curtain, in front of the ark-cover which is on the ark, so that he will not die; because I appear in the cloud over the ark-cover.

³ "Here is how Aharon is to enter the Holy Place: with a young bull as a sin offering and a ram as a burnt offering. ⁴ He is to put on the holy linen tunic, have the linen shorts next to his bare flesh, have the linen sash wrapped around him, and be wearing the linen turban — they are the holy garments. He is to bathe his body in water and put them on.

⁵ "He is to take from the community of the people of Isra'el two male goats for a sin offering and one ram for a burnt offering. ⁶ Aharon is to present the bull for the sin offering which is for himself and make atonement for himself and his household. ⁷ He is to take the two goats and place them before ADONAI at the entrance to the tent of meeting. ⁸ Then Aharon is to cast lots for the two goats, one lot for ADONAI and the other for 'Az'azel. ⁹ Aharon is to present the goat whose lot fell to ADONAI and offer it as a sin offering. ¹⁰ But the goat whose lot fell to 'Az'azel is to be presented alive to ADONAI to be used for making atonement over it by sending it away into the desert for 'Az'azel.

¹¹ "Aharon is to present the bull of the sin offering for himself; he will make atonement for himself and his household; he is to slaughter the bull of the sin offering which is for himself. ¹² He is to take a censer full of burning coals from the altar before ADONAI and, with his hands full of ground, fragrant incense, bring it inside the curtain. ¹³ He is to put the incense on the fire before ADONAI, so that the cloud from the incense will cover the ark-cover which is over the testimony, in order that he not die. ¹⁴ He is to take some of the bull's blood and sprinkle it with his finger on the ark-cover toward the east; and in front of the ark-cover he is to sprinkle some of the blood with his finger seven times.

¹⁵ "Next, he is to slaughter the goat of the sin offering which is for the people, bring its blood inside the curtain and do with its blood as he did with the bull's blood, sprinkling it on the ark-cover and in front of the ark-cover. ¹⁶ He will make atonement for the Holy Place because of the uncleannesses of the people of Isra'el and because of their transgressions — all their sins; and he is to do the same for the tent of meeting which is there with them right in the middle of their uncleannesses. ¹⁷ No one is to be present in the tent of meeting from the time he enters the Holy Place to make atonement until the time he comes out, having made atonement for himself, for his household and for the entire community of Isra'el. *(LY: ii)* ¹⁸ Then he is to go out to the altar that is before ADONAI and make atonement for it; he is to take some of the bull's blood and some of the goat's blood and put it on all the horns of the altar. ¹⁹ He is to sprinkle some of the blood on it with his finger seven times, thus purifying it and setting it apart from the uncleannesses of the people of Isra'el.

²⁰ "When he has finished atoning for the Holy Place, the tent of meeting and the altar, he is to present the live goat. ²¹ Aharon is to lay both his hands on the head of the live goat and confess over it all the transgressions, crimes and sins of the people

of Isra'el; he is to put them on the head of the goat and then send it away into the desert with a man appointed for the purpose. ²² The goat will bear all their transgressions away to some isolated place, and he is to let the goat go in the desert.

²³ "Aharon is to go back into the tent of meeting, where he is to remove the linen garments he put on when he entered the Holy Place, and he is to leave them there. ²⁴ Then he is to bathe his body in water in a holy place, put on his other clothes, come out and offer his burnt offering and the burnt offering of the people, thus making atonement for himself and for the people. *(RY: ii, LY: iii)* ²⁵ He is to make the fat of the sin offering go up in smoke on the altar.

²⁶ "The man who let go the goat for 'Az'azel is to wash his clothes and bathe his body in water; afterwards, he may return to the camp.

²⁷ "The bull for the sin offering and the goat for the sin offering, whose blood was brought in to make atonement in the Holy Place, is to be carried outside the camp; there they are to burn up completely their hides, meat and dung. ²⁸ The person burning them is to wash his clothes and bathe his body in water; afterwards, he may return to the camp.

²⁹ "It is to be a permanent regulation for you that on the tenth day of the seventh month you are to deny yourselves and not do any kind of work, both the citizen and the foreigner living with you. ³⁰ For on this day, atonement will be made for you to purify you; you will be clean before *Adonai* from all your sins. ³¹ It is a *Shabbat* of complete rest for you, and you are to deny yourselves.

"This is a permanent regulation. ³² The *cohen* anointed and consecrated to be *cohen* in his father's place will make the atonement; he will put on the linen garments, the holy garments; ³³ he will make atonement for the Especially Holy Place; he will make atonement for the tent of meeting and the altar; and he will make atonement for the *cohanim* and for all the people of the community. ³⁴ This is a permanent regulation for you, to make atonement for the people of Isra'el because of all their sins once a year." Moshe did as *Adonai* had ordered him.

17 *(LY: iv)* ¹ *Adonai* said to Moshe, ² "Speak to Aharon and his sons and to all the people of Isra'el. Tell them that this is what *Adonai* has ordered: ³ 'When someone from the community of Isra'el slaughters an ox, lamb or goat inside or outside the camp ⁴ without bringing it to the entrance of the tent of meeting to present it as an offering to *Adonai* before the tabernacle of *Adonai*, he is to be charged with blood — he has shed blood, and that person is to be cut off from his people. ⁵ The reason for this is so that the people of Isra'el will bring their sacrifices that they sacrifice out in the field — so that they will bring them to *Adonai*, to the entrance of the tent of meeting, to the *cohen*, and sacrifice them as peace offerings to *Adonai*. ⁶ The *cohen* will splash the blood against the altar of *Adonai* at the entrance to the tent of meeting and make the fat go up in smoke as a pleasing aroma for *Adonai*. ⁷ No longer will they offer sacrifices to the goat-demons, before whom they prostitute themselves! This is a permanent regulation for them through all their generations.'

(RY: iii, LY: v) ⁸ "Also tell them, 'When someone from the community of Isra'el or one of the foreigners living with you offers a burnt offering or sacrifice ⁹ without bringing it to the entrance of the tent of meeting to sacrifice it to *Adonai*, that person is to be cut off from his people. ¹⁰ When someone from the community of Isra'el or

one of the foreigners living with you eats any kind of blood, I will set myself against that person who eats blood and cut him off from his people. ^{11} For the life of a creature is in the blood, and I have given it to you on the altar to make atonement for yourselves; for it is the blood that makes atonement because of the life.' ^{12} This is why I told the people of Isra'el, 'None of you is to eat blood, nor is any foreigner living with you to eat blood.'

^{13} "When someone from the community of Isra'el or one of the foreigners living with you hunts and catches game, whether animal or bird that may be eaten, he is to pour out its blood and cover it with earth. ^{14} For the life of every creature — its blood is its life. Therefore I said to the people of Isra'el, 'You are not to eat the blood of any creature, because the life of every creature is its blood. Whoever eats it will be cut off.'

^{15} "Anyone eating an animal that dies naturally or is torn to death by wild animals, whether he is a citizen or a foreigner, is to wash his clothes and bathe himself in water; he will be unclean until evening; then he will be clean. ^{16} But if he doesn't wash them or bathe his body, he will bear the consequences of his wrongdoing."

18 ^{1} ADONAI said to Moshe, ^{2} "Speak to the people of Isra'el; tell them, 'I am ADONAI your God. ^{3} You are not to engage in the activities found in the land of Egypt, where you used to live; and you are not to engage in the activities found in the land of Kena'an, where I am bringing you; nor are you to live by their laws. ^{4} You are to obey my rulings and laws and live accordingly; I am ADONAI your God. ^{5} You are to observe my laws and rulings; if a person does them, he will have life through them; I am ADONAI.

(LY: vi) ^{6} "'None of you is to approach anyone who is a close relative in order to have sexual relations; I am ADONAI. ^{7} You are not to have sexual relations with your father, and you are not to have sexual relations with your mother. She is your mother — do not have sexual relations with her. ^{8} You are not to have sexual relations with your father's wife; that is your father's prerogative. ^{9} You are not to have sexual relations with your sister, the daughter of your father or the daughter of your mother, whether born at home or elsewhere. Do not have sexual relations with them. ^{10} You are not to have sexual relations with your son's daughter or with your daughter's daughter. Do not have sexual relations with them, because their sexual disgrace will be your own. ^{11} You are not to have sexual relations with your father's wife's daughter, born to your father, because she is your sister; do not have sexual relations with her. ^{12} You are not to have sexual relations with your father's sister, because she is your father's close relative. ^{13} You are not to have sexual relations with your mother's sister, because she is your mother's close relative. ^{14} You are not to disgrace your father's brother by having sexual relations with his wife, because she is your aunt. ^{15} You are not to have sexual relations with your daughter-in-law; because she is your son's wife. Do not have sexual relations with her. ^{16} You are not to have sexual relations with your brother's wife, because this is your brother's prerogative.

^{17} "'You are not to have sexual relations with both a woman and her daughter, nor are you to have sexual relations with her son's daughter or her daughter's daughter; they are close relatives of hers, and it would be shameful. ^{18} You are not to take a woman to be a rival with her sister and have sexual relations with her while her sister is still alive. ¹⁹ You are not to approach a woman in order to have sexual relations with her when she is unclean from her time of *niddah*. ²⁰ You are not to go to bed with your neighbor's wife and thus become unclean with her.

²¹ "'You are not to let any of your children be sacrificed to Molekh, thereby profaning the name of your God; I am ADONAI.

(RY: iv, LY: vii) ²² "'You are not to go to bed with a man as with a woman; it is an abomination.

²³ "'You are not to have sexual relations with any kind of animal and thus become unclean with it; nor is any woman to present herself to an animal to have sexual relations with it; it is perversion.

²⁴ "'Do not make yourselves unclean by any of these things, because all the nations which I am expelling ahead of you are defiled with them. ²⁵ The land has become unclean, and this is why I am punishing it — the land itself will vomit out its inhabitants. ²⁶ But you are to keep my laws and rulings and not engage in any of these disgusting practices, neither the citizen nor the foreigner living with you; *(LY: Maftir)* ²⁷ for the people of the land have committed all these abominations, and the land is now defiled. ²⁸ If you make the land unclean, it will vomit you out too, just as it is vomiting out the nation that was there before you. ²⁹ For those who engage in any of these disgusting practices, whoever they may be, will be cut off from their people. ³⁰ So keep my charge not to follow any of these abominable customs that others before you have followed and thus defile yourselves by doing them. I am ADONAI your God.'"

Haftarah Acharei Mot: Yechezk'el (Ezekiel) 22:1–19 (A); 22:1–16 (S)

B'rit Hadashah suggested readings for Parashah Acharei Mot: Romans 3:19–28; 9:30–10:13; 1 Corinthians 5:1–13 with 2 Corinthians 2:1–11; Galatians 3:10–14; Messianic Jews (Hebrews) 7:23–10:25

Parashah 30: K'doshim (Holy people) 19:1–20:27
[In regular years read with Parashah 29, in leap years read separately]

19 ¹ ADONAI said to Moshe, ² "Speak to the entire community of Isra'el; tell them, 'You people are to be holy because I, ADONAI your God, am holy.

³ "'Every one of you is to revere his father and mother, and you are to keep my *Shabbats*; I am ADONAI your God.

⁴ "'Do not turn to idols, and do not cast metal gods for yourselves; I am ADONAI your God.

⁵ "'When you offer a sacrifice of peace offerings to ADONAI, offer it in a way that will make you accepted. ⁶ It is to be eaten the same day you offer it and the following day; but if any of it remains until the third day, it is to be burned up completely. ⁷ If any of it is eaten on the third day, it will have become a disgusting thing and will not be accepted; ⁸ moreover, everyone who eats it will bear the consequences of profaning something holy meant for ADONAI — that person will be cut off from his people.

[9] "'When you harvest the ripe crops produced in your land, don't harvest all the way to corners of your field, and don't gather the ears of grain left by the harvesters. [10] Likewise, don't gather the grapes left on the vine or fallen on the ground after harvest; leave them for the poor and the foreigner; I am ADONAI your God.

[11] "'Do not steal from, defraud or lie to each other. [12] Do not swear by my name falsely, which would be profaning the name of your God; I am ADONAI. [13] Do not oppress or rob your neighbor; specifically, you are not to keep back the wages of a hired worker all night until morning.

[14] "'Do not speak a curse against a deaf person or place an obstacle in the way of a blind person; rather, fear your God; I am ADONAI.

(RY: v, LY: ii) [15] "'Do not be unjust in judging — show neither partiality to the poor nor deference to the mighty, but with justice judge your neighbor.

[16] "'Do not go around spreading slander among your people, but also don't stand idly by when your neighbor's life is at stake; I am ADONAI.

[17] "'Do not hate your brother in your heart, but rebuke your neighbor frankly, so that you won't carry sin because of him. [18] Don't take vengeance on or bear a grudge against any of your people; rather, love your neighbor as yourself; I am ADONAI.

[19] "'Observe my regulations.

"'Don't let your livestock mate with those of another kind, don't sow your field with two different kinds of grain, and don't wear a garment of cloth made with two different kinds of thread.

[20] "'If a man has sexual relations with a woman who is a slave intended for another man, and she has neither been redeemed nor given her freedom, there is to be an investigation. They are not to be put to death, because she was not free. [21] In reparation he is to bring a ram as a guilt offering for himself to the entrance of the tent of meeting. [22] The *cohen* will make atonement for him with the ram of the guilt offering before ADONAI for the sin he committed, and he will be forgiven for the sin he committed.

(LY: iii) [23] "'When you enter the land and plant various kinds of fruit trees, you are to regard its fruit as forbidden — for three years it will be forbidden to you and not eaten. [24] In the fourth year all its fruit will be holy, for praising ADONAI. [25] But in the fifth year you may eat its fruit, so that it will produce even more for you; I am ADONAI your God.

[26] "'Do not eat anything with blood. Do not practice divination or fortune-telling. [27] Don't round your hair at the temples or mar the edges of your beard. [28] Don't cut gashes in your flesh when someone dies or tattoo yourselves; I am ADONAI.

[29] "'Do not debase your daughter by making her a prostitute, so that the land will not fall into prostitution and become full of shame.

[30] "'Keep my *Shabbat*s, and revere my sanctuary; I am ADONAI.

[31] "'Do not turn to spirit-mediums or sorcerers; don't seek them out, to be defiled by them; I am ADONAI your God.

[32] "'Stand up in the presence of a person with gray hair, show respect for the old; you are to fear your God; I am ADONAI.

(RY: vi, LY: iv) [33] "'If a foreigner stays with you in your land, do not do him wrong. [34] Rather, treat the foreigner staying with you like the native-born among you — you are to love him as yourself, for you were foreigners in the land of Egypt; I am ADONAI your God.

³⁵ "'Don't be dishonest when measuring length, weight or capacity. ³⁶ Rather, use an honest balance-scale, honest weights, an honest bushel dry-measure and an honest gallon liquid-measure; I am A*DONAI* your God, who brought you out of the land of Egypt. ³⁷ Observe all my regulations and rulings, and do them; I am A*DONAI*.'"

20 *(LY: v)* ¹ A*DONAI* said to Moshe, ² "Say to the people of Isra'el, 'If someone from the people of Isra'el or one of the foreigners living in Isra'el sacrifices one of his children to Molekh, he must be put to death; the people of the land are to stone him to death. ³ I too will set myself against him and cut him off from his people, because he has sacrificed his child to Molekh, defiling my sanctuary and profaning my holy name. ⁴ If the people of the land look the other way when that man sacrifices his child to Molekh and fail to put him to death, ⁵ then I will set myself against him, his family and everyone who follows him to go fornicating after Molekh, and cut them off from their people.

⁶ "'The person who turns to spirit-mediums and sorcerers to go fornicating after them — I will set myself against him and cut him off from his people. ⁷ Therefore consecrate yourselves — you people must be holy, because I am A*DONAI* your God. *(RY: vii, LY: vi)* ⁸ Observe my regulations, and obey them; I am A*DONAI*, who sets you apart to be holy.

⁹ "'A person who curses his father or mother must be put to death; having cursed his father or his mother, his blood is on him.

¹⁰ "'If a man commits adultery with another man's wife, that is, with the wife of a fellow countryman, both the adulterer and the adulteress must be put to death. ¹¹ The man who goes to bed with his father's wife has disgraced his father sexually, and both of them must be put to death; their blood is on them. ¹² If a man goes to bed with his daughter-in-law, both of them must be put to death; they have committed a perversion, and their blood is on them. ¹³ If a man goes to bed with a man as with a woman, both of them have committed an abomination; they must be put to death; their blood is on them. ¹⁴ If a man marries a woman and her mother, it is depravity; they are to be put to death by fire, both he and they, so that there will not be depravity among you. ¹⁵ If a man has sexual relations with an animal, he must be put to death, and you are to kill the animal. ¹⁶ If a woman approaches an animal and has sexual relations with it, you are to kill the woman and the animal; their blood will be on them. ¹⁷ If a man takes his sister, his father's daughter or his mother's daughter, and has sexual relations with her, and she consents, it is a shameful thing; they are to be cut off publicly — he has had sexual relations with his sister, and he will bear the consequences of their wrongdoing. ¹⁸ If a man goes to bed with a woman in her menstrual period and has sexual relations with her, he has exposed the source of her blood, and she has exposed the source of her blood; both of them are to be cut off from their people. ¹⁹ You are not to have sexual relations with your mother's sister or your father's sister; a person who does this has had sexual relations with his close relative; they will bear the consequences of their wrongdoing. ²⁰ If a man goes to bed with his uncle's wife, he has disgraced his uncle sexually; they will bear the consequences of their sin and die childless. ²¹ If a man takes his brother's wife, it is uncleanness; he has disgraced his brother sexually; they will be childless.

²² "'You are to observe all my regulations and rulings and act on them, so that the land to which I am bringing you will not vomit you out. *(LY: vii)* ²³ Do not live by

the regulations of the nation which I am expelling ahead of you; because they did all these things, which is why I detested them. ²⁴ But to you I have said, "You will inherit their land; I will give it to you as a possession, a land flowing with milk and honey." I am Adonai your God, who has set you apart from other peoples. *(Maftir)* ²⁵ Therefore you are to distinguish between clean and unclean animals and between clean and unclean birds; do not make yourselves detestable with an animal, bird or reptile that I have set apart for you to regard as unclean. ²⁶ Rather, you people are to be holy for me; because I, Adonai, am holy; and I have set you apart from the other peoples, so that you can belong to me.

²⁷ "'A man or woman who is a spirit-medium or sorcerer must be put to death; they are to stone them to death; their blood will be on them.'"

Haftarah K'doshim: 'Amos 9:7–15 (A); Yechezk'el (Ezekiel) 20:2–20 (S)

B'rit Hadashah suggested readings for Parashah K'doshim: Mattityahu (Matthew) 5:33–37; 5:43–48; 15:1–11; 19:16–30; 22:33–40; Mark 7:1–23; 12:28–34; Luke 10:25–37; Romans 13:8–10; Galatians 5:13–26; Ya'akov (James) 2:1–9; 1 Kefa (1 Peter) 1:13–21

Parashah 31: Emor (Speak) 21:1–24:23

21 ¹ Adonai said to Moshe, "Speak to the *cohanim*, the sons of Aharon; tell them: 'No *cohen* is to make himself unclean for any of his people who dies, ² except for his close relatives—his mother, father, son, daughter and brother; ³ he may also make himself unclean for his virgin sister who has never married and is therefore dependent on him. ⁴ He may not make himself unclean, because he is a leader among his people; doing so would profane him. ⁵ *Cohanim* are not to make bald spots on their heads, mar the edges of their beards or cut gashes in their flesh. ⁶ Rather, they are to be holy for their God and not profane the name of their God. For they are the ones who present Adonai with offerings made by fire, the bread of their God; therefore they must be holy.

⁷ "'A *cohen* is not to marry a woman who is a prostitute, who has been profaned or who has been divorced; because he is holy for his God. ⁸ Rather, you are to set him apart as holy, because he offers the bread of your God; he is to be holy for you, because I, Adonai, who makes you holy, am holy. ⁹ The daughter of a *cohen* who profanes herself by prostitution profanes her father; she is to be put to death by fire.

¹⁰ "'The *cohen* who is ranked highest among his brothers, the one on whose head the anointing oil is poured and who is consecrated to put on the garments, is not to stop grooming his hair, tear his clothes, ¹¹ go in to where any dead body is or make himself unclean, even when his father or mother dies. ¹² He may not leave the sanctuary then or profane the sanctuary of his God, because the consecration of the anointing oil of his God is on him; I am Adonai.

¹³ "'He is to marry a virgin; ¹⁴ he may not marry a widow, divorcee, profaned woman or prostitute; but he must marry a virgin from among his own people ¹⁵ and not disqualify his descendants among his people; because I am Adonai, who makes him holy.'"

(ii) ¹⁶ A<small>DONAI</small> said to Moshe, ¹⁷ "Tell Aharon, 'None of your descendants who has a defect may approach to offer the bread of his God. ¹⁸ No one with a defect may approach — no one blind, lame, with a mutilated face or a limb too long, ¹⁹ a broken foot or a broken arm, ²⁰ a hunched back, stunted growth, a cataract in his eye, festering or running sores, or damaged testicles — ²¹ no one descended from Aharon the *cohen* who has such a defect may approach to present the offerings for A<small>DONAI</small> made by fire; he has a defect and is not to approach to offer the bread of his God. ²² He may eat the bread of his God, both the especially holy and the holy; ²³ only he is not to go in to the curtain or approach the altar, because he has a defect — so that he will not profane my holy places, because I am A<small>DONAI</small>, who makes them holy.'"
²⁴ Moshe said these things to Aharon, his sons and all the people of Isra'el.

22 ¹ A<small>DONAI</small> said to Moshe, ² "Tell Aharon and his sons to separate themselves from the holy things of the people of Isra'el which they set apart as holy for me, so that they will not profane my holy name; I am A<small>DONAI</small>. ³ Tell them, 'Any descendant of yours through all your generations who approaches the holy things that the people of Isra'el consecrate to A<small>DONAI</small> and is unclean will be cut off from before me; I am A<small>DONAI</small>.

⁴ "'Any descendant of Aharon with *tzara'at* or a discharge is not to eat the holy things until he is clean. Anyone who has touched a person made unclean by a dead body, or who has had a seminal emission, ⁵ or who has touched a reptile or insect that can make him unclean, or a man who is unclean for any reason and who can transmit to him his uncleanness — ⁶ the person who touches any of these will be unclean until evening and is not to eat the holy things unless he bathes his body in water. ⁷ After sunset he will be clean; and afterwards, he may eat the holy things; because they are his food. ⁸ But he is not to eat anything that dies naturally or is torn to death by wild animals and thereby make himself unclean; I am A<small>DONAI</small>. ⁹ The *cohanim* must observe this charge of mine; otherwise, if they profane it, they will bear the consequences of their sin for doing so and die in it; I am A<small>DONAI</small>, who makes them holy.

¹⁰ "'No one who is not a *cohen* may eat anything holy, nor may a tenant or employee of a *cohen* eat anything holy. ¹¹ But if a *cohen* acquires a slave, either through purchase or through his being born in his household, he may share his food. ¹² If the daughter of a *cohen* is married to a man who is not a *cohen*, she is not to have a share of the food set aside from the holy things. ¹³ But if the daughter of a *cohen* is a widow or divorcee and has no child, and she is sent back to her father's house as when she was young, she may share in her father's food; but no one not a *cohen* is to share in it. ¹⁴ If a person eats holy food by mistake, he must add one-fifth to it and give the holy food to the *cohen*. ¹⁵ They are not to profane the holy things of the people of Isra'el that they have set apart for A<small>DONAI</small> ¹⁶ and thus cause them to bear guilt requiring a guilt offering, by eating their holy things; because I am A<small>DONAI</small>, who makes them holy.'"

(iii) ¹⁷ A<small>DONAI</small> said to Moshe, ¹⁸ "Speak to Aharon and his sons and to the entire people of Isra'el; tell them: 'When anyone, whether a member of the house of Isra'el or a foreigner living in Isra'el, brings his offering, either in connection with a vow or as a voluntary offering, and brings it to A<small>DONAI</small> as a burnt offering, ¹⁹ in order for you to be accepted, you must bring a male without defect from the cattle, the sheep or the goats. ²⁰ You are not to bring anything with a defect, because it will not be accepted from you. ²¹ Whoever brings a sacrifice of peace offerings to A<small>DONAI</small> in fulfillment of

a vow or as a voluntary offering, whether it come from the herd or from the flock, it must be unblemished and without defect in order to be accepted. ²² If it is blind, injured, mutilated, has an abnormal growth or has festering or running sores, you are not to offer it to ADONAI or make such an offering by fire on the altar to ADONAI. ²³ If a bull or lamb has a limb which is too long or short, you may offer it as a voluntary offering; but for a vow it will not be accepted. ²⁴ An animal with bruised, crushed, torn or cut genitals you are not to offer to ADONAI. You are not to do these things in your land, ²⁵ and you are not to receive any of these from a foreigner for you to offer as bread for your God, because their deformity is a defect in them — they will not be accepted from you.'"

²⁶ ADONAI said to Moshe, ²⁷ "When a bull, sheep or goat is born, it is to stay with its mother for seven days; but from the eighth day on, it may be accepted for an offering made by fire to ADONAI. ²⁸ However, no animal is to be slaughtered together with its young on the same day, neither cow nor ewe.

²⁹ "When you offer a sacrifice of thanksgiving to ADONAI, you must do it in a way such that you will be accepted. ³⁰ It must be eaten on the same day it is offered; leave none of it till morning; I am ADONAI.

³¹ "You are to keep my *mitzvot* and obey them; I am ADONAI. ³² You are not to profane my holy name; on the contrary, I am to be regarded as holy among the people of Isra'el; I am ADONAI, who makes you holy, ³³ who brought you out of the land of Egypt to be your God; I am ADONAI."

23 *(iv)* ¹ ADONAI said to Moshe, ² "Tell the people of Isra'el: 'The designated times of ADONAI which you are to proclaim as holy convocations are my designated times.

³ "'Work is to be done on six days; but the seventh day is a *Shabbat* of complete rest, a holy convocation; you are not to do any kind of work; it is a *Shabbat* for ADONAI, even in your homes.

⁴ "'These are the designated times of ADONAI, the holy convocations you are to proclaim at their designated times.

⁵ "'In the first month, on the fourteenth day of the month, between sundown and complete darkness, comes *Pesach* for ADONAI. ⁶ On the fifteenth day of the same month is the festival of *matzah*; for seven days you are to eat *matzah*. ⁷ On the first day you are to have a holy convocation; don't do any kind of ordinary work. ⁸ Bring an offering made by fire to ADONAI for seven days. On the seventh day is a holy convocation; do not do any kind of ordinary work.'"

⁹ ADONAI said to Moshe, ¹⁰ "Tell the people of Isra'el, 'After you enter the land I am giving you and harvest its ripe crops, you are to bring a sheaf of the firstfruits of your harvest to the *cohen*. ¹¹ He is to wave the sheaf before ADONAI, so that you will be accepted; the *cohen* is to wave it on the day after the *Shabbat*. ¹² On the day that you wave the sheaf, you are to offer a male lamb without defect, in its first year, as a burnt offering for ADONAI. ¹³ Its grain offering is to be one gallon of fine flour mixed with olive oil, an offering made by fire to ADONAI as a fragrant aroma; its drink offering is to be of wine, one quart. ¹⁴ You are not to eat bread, dried grain or fresh grain until the day you bring the offering for your God; this is a permanent regulation through all your generations, no matter where you live.

¹⁵ "'From the day after the day of rest — that is, from the day you bring the sheaf for waving — you are to count seven full weeks, ¹⁶ until the day after the

seventh week; you are to count fifty days; and then you are to present a new grain offering to ADONAI. ¹⁷ You must bring bread from your homes for waving — two loaves made with one gallon of fine flour, baked with leaven — as firstfruits for ADONAI. ¹⁸ Along with the bread, present seven lambs without defect one year old, one young bull and two rams; these will be a burnt offering for ADONAI, with their grain and drink offerings, an offering made by fire as a fragrant aroma for ADONAI. ¹⁹ Offer one male goat as a sin offering and two male lambs one year old as a sacrifice of peace offerings. ²⁰ The *cohen* will wave them with the bread of the firstfruits as a wave offering before ADONAI, with the two lambs; these will be holy for ADONAI for the *cohen*. ²¹ On the same day, you are to call a holy convocation; do not do any kind of ordinary work; this is a permanent regulation through all your generations, no matter where you live.

²² "'When you harvest the ripe crops produced in your land, don't harvest all the way to the corners of your field, and don't gather the ears of grain left by the harvesters; leave them for the poor and the foreigner; I am ADONAI your God.'"

(v) ²³ ADONAI said to Moshe, ²⁴ "Tell the people of Isra'el, 'In the seventh month, the first of the month is to be for you a day of complete rest for remembering, a holy convocation announced with blasts on the *shofar.* ²⁵ Do not do any kind of ordinary work, and bring an offering made by fire to ADONAI.'"

²⁶ ADONAI said to Moshe, ²⁷ "The tenth day of this seventh month is *Yom-Kippur*; you are to have a holy convocation, you are to deny yourselves, and you are to bring an offering made by fire to ADONAI. ²⁸ You are not to do any kind of work on that day, because it is *Yom-Kippur*, to make atonement for you before ADONAI your God. ²⁹ Anyone who does not deny himself on that day is to be cut off from his people; ³⁰ and anyone who does any kind of work on that day, I will destroy from among his people. ³¹ You are not to do any kind of work; it is a permanent regulation through all your generations, no matter where you live. ³² It will be for you a *Shabbat* of complete rest, and you are to deny yourselves; you are to rest on your *Shabbat* from evening the ninth day of the month until the following evening."

(vi) ³³ ADONAI said to Moshe, ³⁴ "Tell the people of Isra'el, 'On the fifteenth day of this seventh month is the feast of *Sukkot* for seven days to ADONAI. ³⁵ On the first day there is to be a holy convocation; do not do any kind of ordinary work. ³⁶ For seven days you are to bring an offering made by fire to ADONAI; on the eighth day you are to have a holy convocation and bring an offering made by fire to ADONAI; it is a day of public assembly; do not do any kind of ordinary work.

³⁷ "'These are the designated times of ADONAI that you are to proclaim as holy convocations and bring an offering made by fire to ADONAI — a burnt offering, a grain offering, a sacrifice and drink offerings, each on its own day — ³⁸ besides the *Shabbat*s of ADONAI, your gifts, all your vows and all your voluntary offerings that you give to ADONAI.

³⁹ "'But on the fifteenth day of the seventh month, when you have gathered the produce of the land, you are to observe the festival of ADONAI seven days; the first day is to be a complete rest and the eighth day is to be a complete rest. ⁴⁰ On the first day you are to take choice fruit, palm fronds, thick branches and river-willows, and celebrate in the presence of ADONAI your God for seven days. ⁴¹ You are to observe it as a feast to ADONAI seven days in the year; it is a permanent regulation, generation after generation; keep it in the seventh month. ⁴² You are to live in *sukkot* for seven

days; every citizen of Isra'el is to live in a *sukkah*, ⁴³ so that generation after generation of you will know that I made the people of Isra'el live in *sukkot* when I brought them out of the land of Egypt; I am A*DONAI* your God.'"

⁴⁴ Thus Moshe announced to the people of Isra'el the designated times of A*DONAI*.

24 *(vii)* ¹ A*DONAI* said to Moshe, ² "Order the people of Isra'el to bring you pure oil from crushed olives for the light, to keep lamps burning always. ³ Outside the curtain of the testimony in the tent of meeting, Aharon is to arrange for the light to be kept burning always from evening until morning before A*DONAI*; this is to be a permanent regulation through all your generations. ⁴ He is always to keep in order the lamps on the pure *menorah* before A*DONAI*.

⁵ "You are to take fine flour and use it to bake twelve loaves, one gallon per loaf. ⁶ Arrange them in two rows, six in a row, on the pure table before A*DONAI*. ⁷ Put frankincense with each row to be an offering made by fire to A*DONAI* in place of the bread and as a reminder of it. ⁸ Regularly, every *Shabbat*, he is to arrange them before A*DONAI*; they are from the people of Isra'el, as a covenant forever. ⁹ They will belong to Aharon and his sons; and they are to eat them in a holy place; because for him they are, of the offerings for A*DONAI* made by fire, especially holy. This is a permanent law."

¹⁰ There was a man who was the son of a woman of Isra'el and an Egyptian father. He went out among the people of Isra'el, and this son of a woman of Isra'el had a fight in the camp with a man of Isra'el, ¹¹ in the course of which the son of the woman of Isra'el uttered the Name [*Yud-Heh-Vav-Heh*] in a curse. So they brought him to Moshe. (His mother's name was Shlomit the daughter of Dibri, of the tribe of Dan.) ¹² They put him under guard until A*DONAI* would tell them what to do. ¹³ A*DONAI* said to Moshe, ¹⁴ "Take the man who cursed outside the camp, have everyone who heard him lay their hands on his head, and have the entire community stone him. ¹⁵ Then tell the people of Isra'el, 'Whoever curses his God will bear the consequences of his sin; ¹⁶ and whoever blasphemes the name of A*DONAI* must be put to death; the entire community must stone him. The foreigner as well as the citizen is to be put to death if he blasphemes the Name.

¹⁷ "'Anyone who strikes another person and kills him must be put to death. ¹⁸ Anyone who strikes an animal and kills it is to make restitution, life for life. ¹⁹ If someone injures his neighbor, what he did is to be done to him — ²⁰ break for break, eye for eye, tooth for tooth — whatever injury he has caused the other person is to be rendered to him in return. *(Maftir)* ²¹ He who kills an animal is to make restitution, but he who kills another person is to be put to death. ²² You are to apply the same standard of judgment to the foreigner as to the citizen, because I am A*DONAI* your God."

²³ So Moshe spoke to the people of Isra'el, and they took the man who had cursed outside the camp and stoned him to death. Thus the people of Isra'el did as A*DONAI* had ordered Moshe.

Haftarah Emor: Yechezk'el (Ezekiel) 44:15–31

B'rit Hadashah suggested readings for Parashah Emor: Mattityahu
(Matthew) 5:38–42; Galatians 3:26–29 [In connection with the feasts,
see readings for Parashah 41]

Parashah 32: B'har (On Mount) 25:1–26:2
[In regular years read with Parashah 33, in leap years read separately]

25 [1] *Adonai* spoke to Moshe on Mount Sinai; he said, [2] "Tell the people of Isra'el, 'When you enter the land I am giving you, the land itself is to observe a *Shabbat* rest for *Adonai*. [3] Six years you will sow your field; six years you will prune your grapevines and gather their produce. [4] But in the seventh year is to be a *Shabbat* of complete rest for the land, a *Shabbat* for *Adonai*; you will neither sow your field nor prune your grapevines. [5] You are not to harvest what grows by itself from the seeds left by your previous harvest, and you are not to gather the grapes of your untended vine; it is to be a year of complete rest for the land. [6] But what the land produces during the year of *Shabbat* will be food for all of you — you, your servant, your maid, your employee, anyone living near you, [7] your livestock and the wild animals on your land; everything the land produces may be used for food.

[8] "'You are to count seven *Shabbat*s of years, seven times seven years, that is, forty-nine years. [9] Then, on the tenth day of the seventh month, on *Yom-Kippur*, you are to sound a blast on the *shofar*; you are to sound the *shofar* all through your land; [10] and you are to consecrate the fiftieth year, proclaiming freedom throughout the land to all its inhabitants. It will be a *yovel* for you; you will return everyone to the land he owns, and everyone is to return to his family. [11] That fiftieth year will be a *yovel* for you; in that year you are not to sow, harvest what grows by itself or gather the grapes of untended vines; [12] because it is a *yovel*. It will be holy for you; whatever the fields produce will be food for all of you. [13] In this year of *yovel*, every one of you is to return to the land he owns.

(LY: ii) [14] "'If you sell anything to your neighbor or buy anything from him, neither of you is to exploit the other. [15] Rather, you are to take into account the number of years after the *yovel* when you buy land from your neighbor, and he is to sell to you according to the number of years crops will be raised. [16] If the number of years remaining is large, you will raise the price; if few years remain, you will lower it; because what he is really selling you is the number of crops to be produced. [17] Thus you are not to take advantage of each other, but you are to fear your God; for I am *Adonai* your God.

[18] "'Rather, you are to keep my regulations and rulings and act accordingly. If you do, you will live securely in the land. *(RY: ii, LY: iii)* [19] The land will yield its produce, you will eat until you have enough, and you will live there securely.

[20] "'If you ask, "If we aren't allowed to sow seed or harvest what our land produces, what are we going to eat the seventh year?" [21] then I will order my blessing on you during the sixth year, so that the land brings forth enough produce for all three years. [22] The eighth year you will sow seed, but eat the old, stored produce until the ninth year; that is, until the produce of the eighth year comes in, you will eat the old, stored food.

[23] "'The land is not to be sold in perpetuity, because the land belongs to me — you are only foreigners and temporary residents with me. [24] Therefore, when you sell your property, you must include the right of redemption. *(LY: iv)* [25] That is, if one of you becomes poor and sells some of his property, his next-of-kin can come and buy back what his relative sold. [26] If the seller has no one to redeem it but becomes rich enough to redeem it himself, [27] he will calculate the number of years the land was

sold for, refund the excess to its buyer, and return to his property. ²⁸ If he hasn't sufficient means to get it back himself, then what he sold will remain in the hands of the buyer until the year of *yovel*; in the *yovel* the buyer will vacate it and the seller return to his property.

(RY: iii, LY: v) ²⁹ "'If someone sells a dwelling in a walled city, he has one year after the date of sale in which to redeem it. For a full year he will have the right of redemption; ³⁰ but if he has not redeemed the dwelling in the walled city within the year, then title in perpetuity passes to the buyer through all his generations; it will not revert in the *yovel*. ³¹ However, houses in villages not surrounded by walls are to be dealt with like the fields in the countryside — they may be redeemed [before the *yovel*], and they revert in the *yovel*.

³² "'Concerning the cities of the *L'vi'im* and the houses in the cities they possess, the *L'vi'im* are to have a permanent right of redemption. ³³ If someone purchases a house from one of the *L'vi'im*, then the house he sold in the city where he owns property will still revert to him in the *yovel*; because the houses in the cities of the *L'vi'im* are their tribe's possession among the people of Isra'el. ³⁴ The fields in the open land around their cities may not be sold, because that is their permanent possession.

³⁵ "'If a member of your people has become poor, so that he can't support himself among you, you are to assist him as you would a foreigner or a temporary resident, so that he can continue living with you. ³⁶ Do not charge him interest or otherwise profit from him, but fear your God, so that your brother can continue living with you. ³⁷ Do not take interest when you loan him money or take a profit when you sell him food. ³⁸ I am *ADONAI* your God, who brought you out of the land of Egypt in order to give you the land of Kena'an and be your God.

(RY: iv, LY: vi) ³⁹ "'If a member of your people has become poor among you and sells himself to you, do not make him do the work of a slave. ⁴⁰ Rather, you are to treat him like an employee or a tenant; he will work for you until the year of *yovel*. ⁴¹ Then he will leave you, he and his children with him, and return to his own family and regain possession of his ancestral land. ⁴² For they are my slaves, whom I brought out of the land of Egypt; therefore they are not to be sold as slaves. ⁴³ Do not treat him harshly, but fear your God.

⁴⁴ "'Concerning the men and women you may have as slaves: you are to buy men- and women-slaves from the nations surrounding you. ⁴⁵ You may also buy the children of foreigners living with you and members of their families born in your land; you may own these. ⁴⁶ You may also bequeath them to your children to own; from these groups you may take your slaves forever. But as far as your brothers the people of Isra'el are concerned, you are not to treat each other harshly.

(LY: vii) ⁴⁷ "'If a foreigner living with you has grown rich, and a member of your people has become poor and sells himself to this foreigner living with you or to a member of the foreigner's family, ⁴⁸ he may be redeemed after he has been sold. One of his brothers may redeem him; ⁴⁹ or his uncle or his uncle's son may redeem him; or any near relative of his may redeem him; or, if he becomes rich, he may redeem himself. ⁵⁰ He will calculate with the person who bought him the time from the year he sold himself to him to the year of *yovel*; and the amount to be paid will be according to the number of years and his time at an employee's wage. ⁵¹ If many years remain, according to them will he refund the amount for his redemption from

the amount he was bought for. [52] If there remain only a few years until the year of *yovel*, then he will calculate with him; according to his years will he refund the amount for his redemption. [53] He will be like a worker hired year by year. You will see to it that he is not treated harshly.

[54] "'If he has not been redeemed by any of these procedures, nevertheless he will go free in the year of *yovel* — he and his children with him. *(LY: Maftir)* [55] For to me the people of Isra'el are slaves; they are my slaves whom I brought out of the land of Egypt; I am A*DONAI* your God.

26 [1] "'You are not to make yourselves any idols, erect a carved statue or a standing-stone, or place any carved stone anywhere in your land in order to bow down to it. I am A*DONAI* your God.

[2] "'Keep my *Shabbat*s, and revere my sanctuary; I am A*DONAI.*

Haftarah B'har: Yirmeyahu (Jeremiah) 32:6–27

B'rit Hadashah suggested readings for Parashah B'har: Luke 4:16–21;
1 Corinthians 7:21–24; Galatians 6:7–10

Parashah 33: B'chukkotai (By my regulations) 26:3–27:34
[In regular years read with Parashah 32, in leap years read separately]

[3] "'If you live by my regulations, observe my *mitzvot* and obey them; [4] then I will provide the rain you need in its season, the land will yield its produce, and the trees in the field will yield their fruit. [5] Your threshing time will extend until the grape harvest, and your grape harvesting will extend until the time for sowing seed. You will eat as much food as you want and live securely in your land.

(LY: ii) [6] "'I will give *shalom* in the land — you will lie down to sleep unafraid of anyone. I will rid the land of wild animals. The sword will not go through your land. [7] You will pursue your enemies, and they will fall before your sword. [8] Five of you will chase a hundred, and a hundred of you will chase ten thousand — your enemies will fall before your sword.

[9] "'I will turn toward you, make you productive, increase your numbers and uphold my covenant with you. *(RY: v, LY: iii)* [10] You will eat all you want from last year's harvest and throw out what remains of the old to make room for the new. [11] I will put my tabernacle among you, and I will not reject you, [12] but I will walk among you and be your God, and you will be my people. [13] I am A*DONAI* your God, who brought you out of the land of Egypt, so that you would not be their slaves. I have broken the bars of your yoke, so that you can walk upright.

[14] "'But if you will not listen to me and obey all these *mitzvot*, [15] if you loathe my regulations and reject my rulings, in order not to obey all my *mitzvot* but cancel my covenant; [16] then I, for my part, will do this to you: I will bring terror upon you — wasting disease and chronic fever to dim your sight and sap your strength. You will sow your seed for nothing, because your enemies will eat the crops. [17] I will set my face against you — your enemies will defeat you, those who hate you will hound you, and you will flee when no one is pursuing you.

¹⁸ If these things don't make you listen to me, then I will discipline you seven times over for your sins. ¹⁹ I will break the pride you have in your own power. I will make your sky like iron, your soil like bronze — ²⁰ you will spend your strength in vain, because the land will not yield its produce or the trees in the field their fruit.

²¹ "'Yes, if you go against me and don't listen to me, I will increase your calamities sevenfold, according to your sins. ²² I will send wild animals among you; they will rob you of your children, destroy your livestock and reduce your numbers, until your roads are deserted.

²³ "'If, in spite of all this, you refuse my correction and still go against me; ²⁴ then I too will go against you; and I, yes I, will strike you seven times over for your sins. ²⁵ I will bring a sword against you which will execute the vengeance of the covenant. You will be huddled inside your cities, I will send sickness among you, and you will be handed over to the power of the enemy. ²⁶ I will cut off your supply of bread, so that ten women will bake your bread in one oven and dole out your bread by weight, and you will eat but not be satisfied.

²⁷ "'And if, for all this, you still will not listen to me, but go against me; ²⁸ then I will go against you furiously, and I also will chastise you yet seven times more for your sins. ²⁹ You will eat the flesh of your own sons, you will eat the flesh of your own daughters. ³⁰ I will destroy your high places, cut down your pillars for sun-worship, and throw your carcasses on the carcasses of your idols; and I will detest you. ³¹ I will lay waste to your cities and make your sanctuaries desolate, so as not to smell your fragrant aromas. ³² I will desolate the land, so that your enemies living in it will be astounded by it. ³³ You I will disperse among the nations, and I will draw out the sword in pursuit after you; your land will be a desolation and your cities a wasteland. ³⁴ Then, at last, the land will be paid its *Shabbat*s. As long as it lies desolate and you are in the lands of your enemies, the land will rest and be repaid its *Shabbat*s. ³⁵ Yes, as long as it lies desolate it will have rest, the rest it did not have during your *Shabbat*s, when you lived there. ³⁶ As for those of you who are left, I will fill their hearts with anxiety in the lands of their enemies. The sound of a driven leaf will frighten them, so that they will flee as one flees from the sword and fall when no one is pursuing. ³⁷ Yes, with no one pursuing they will stumble over each other as if fleeing the sword — you will have no power to stand before your enemies. ³⁸ And among the nations you will perish; the land of your enemies will devour you.

³⁹ Those of you who remain will pine away in the lands of your enemies from guilt over your misdeeds and those of your ancestors. ⁴⁰ Then they will confess their misdeeds and those of their ancestors which they committed against me in their rebellion; they will admit that they went against me. ⁴¹ At that time I will be going against them, bringing them into the lands of their enemies. But if their uncircumcised hearts will grow humble, and they are paid the punishment for their misdeeds; ⁴² then I will remember my covenant with Ya'akov, also my covenant with Yitz'chak and my covenant with Avraham; and I will remember the land. ⁴³ For the land will lie abandoned without them, and it will be paid its *Shabbat*s while it lies desolate without them; and they will be paid the punishment for their misdeeds, because they rejected my rulings and loathed my regulations. ⁴⁴ Yet, in spite of all that, I will not reject them when they are in the lands of their enemies, nor will I loathe them to the point of utterly destroying them and thus break my covenant with them, because I am *ADONAI* their God. ⁴⁵ Rather, for their sakes, I will remember the covenant of their

ancestors whom I brought out of the land of Egypt—with the nations watching—so that I might be their God; I am A*DONAI*.'"

⁴⁶ These are the laws, rulings and teachings that A*DONAI* himself gave to the people of Isra'el on Mount Sinai through Moshe.

27 *(RY: vi; LY: iv)* ¹ A*DONAI* said to Moshe, ² "Tell the people of Isra'el, 'If someone makes a clearly defined vow to A*DONAI* to give him an amount equal to the value of a human being, ³ the value you are to assign to a man between the ages of twenty and sixty years is to be fifty *shekel*s of silver [one-and-a-quarter pounds], with the sanctuary *shekel* being the standard, ⁴ if a woman, thirty *shekel*s. ⁵ If it is a child five to twenty years old, assign a value of twenty *shekel*s for a boy and ten for a girl; ⁶ if a baby one month to five years of age, five *shekel*s for a boy and three for a girl; ⁷ if a person past sixty, fifteen *shekel*s for a man and ten for a woman. ⁸ If the person is too poor to be evaluated, set him before the *cohen*, who will assign him a value in keeping with the means of the person who made the vow.

⁹ "'If the vow is for the value of an animal of the kind used when people bring an offering to A*DONAI*, all that a person gives of such animals to A*DONAI* will be holy. ¹⁰ He is not to exchange or replace it by substituting a good animal for a bad one or vice versa; if he does make such a substitution, both the original animal and the one replacing it will be holy. ¹¹ If the animal is an unclean one, such as may not be used in an offering to A*DONAI*, he must set it before the *cohen*; ¹² and the *cohen* is to set a value on it in relation to its good and bad points; the value set by you the *cohen* will stand. ¹³ But if the person making the vow wishes to redeem the animal, he must add one-fifth to your valuation.

¹⁴ "'When a person consecrates his house to be holy for A*DONAI*, the *cohen* is to set a value on it in relation to its good and bad points; the value set by the *cohen* will stand. ¹⁵ If the consecrator wishes to redeem his house, he must add one-fifth to the value you have set on it; and it will revert to him.

(RY: vii, LY: v) ¹⁶ "'If a person consecrates to A*DONAI* part of a field belonging to his tribe's possession, you are to value it according to its production, with five bushels of barley being valued at fifty *shekel*s of silver [one-and-a-quarter pounds]. ¹⁷ If he consecrates his field during the year of *yovel*, this valuation will stand. ¹⁸ But if he consecrates his field after the *yovel*, then the *cohen* is to calculate the price according to the years remaining till the next *yovel*, with a corresponding reduction from your valuation. ¹⁹ If the one consecrating the field wishes to redeem it, he must add one-fifth to your valuation, and the field will be set aside to revert to him. ²⁰ If the seller does not wish to redeem the field, or if [the treasurer for the *cohanim*] has already sold the field to someone else, it can no longer be redeemed. ²¹ But when the purchaser has to vacate the field in the *yovel*, it will become holy to A*DONAI*, like a field unconditionally consecrated; it will belong to the *cohanim*.

(LY: vi) ²² "'If he consecrates to A*DONAI* a field which he has bought, a field which is not part of his tribe's possession, ²³ then the *cohen* is to calculate its value according to the years remaining until the year of *yovel*; and the man will on that same day pay this amount; since it is holy to A*DONAI*. ²⁴ In the year of *yovel* the field will revert to the person from whom it was bought, that is, to the person to whose tribal possession it belongs.

²⁵ "'All your valuations are to be according to the sanctuary *shekel* [two-fifths of an ounce], twenty *gerah*s to the *shekel.* ²⁶ "'However, the firstborn among animals, since it is already born as a firstborn for ADONAI, no one can consecrate — neither ox nor sheep — since it belongs to ADONAI already. ²⁷ But if it is an unclean animal, he may redeem it at the price at which you value it and add one-fifth; or if he does not redeem it, it is to be sold at the price at which you value it. ²⁸ However, nothing consecrated unconditionally which a person may consecrate to ADONAI out of all he owns — person, animal or field he possesses — is to be sold or redeemed; because everything consecrated unconditionally is especially holy to ADONAI. *(LY: vii)* ²⁹ No person who has been sentenced to die, and thus unconditionally consecrated, can be redeemed; he must be put to death.

³⁰ "'All the tenth given from the land, whether from planted seed or fruit from trees, belongs to ADONAI; it is holy to ADONAI. ³¹ If someone wants to redeem any of his tenth, he must add to it one-fifth.

(Maftir) ³² "'All the tenth from the herd or the flock, whatever passes under the shepherd's crook, the tenth one will be holy to ADONAI. ³³ The owner is not to inquire whether the animal is good or bad, and he cannot exchange it; if he does exchange it, both it and the one he substituted for it will be holy; it cannot be redeemed.'"

³⁴ These are the *mitzvot* which ADONAI gave to Moshe for the people of Isra'el on Mount Sinai.

Haftarah B'chukkotai: Yirmeyahu (Jeremiah) 16:19–17:14

B'rit Hadashah suggested readings for Parashah B'chukkotai: Yochanan (John) 14:15–21; 15:10–12; 1 Yochanan (1 John)

Hazak, hazak, v'nit'chazek!
Be strong, be strong, and let us be strengthened!

B'midbar
NUMBERS

Parashah 34: B'midbar (In the desert) 1:1–4:20

1¹ ADONAI spoke to Moshe in the Sinai Desert, in the tent of meeting, on the first day of the second month of the second year after they had left the land of Egypt. He said, ² "Take a census of the entire assembly of the people of Isra'el, by clans and families. Record the names of all the men ³ twenty years old and over who are subject to military service in Isra'el. You and Aharon are to enumerate them company by company.

⁴ Take with you from each tribe someone who is head of a clan. ⁵ These are the men to take with you:

	From Re'uven, Elitzur the son of Sh'de'ur;
6	From Shim'on, Shlumi'el the son of Tzurishaddai;
7	From Y'hudah, Nachshon the son of 'Amminadav;
8	From Yissakhar, N'tan'el the son of Tzu'ar;
9	From Z'vulun, Eli'av the son of Helon.
10	Of the children of Yosef:
	From Efrayim, Elishama the son of 'Ammihud;
	From M'nasheh, Gamli'el the son of P'dahtzur.
11	From Binyamin, Avidan the son of Gid'oni;
12	From Dan, Achi'ezer the son of 'Ammishaddai;
13	From Asher, Pag'i'el the son of 'Okhran;
14	From Gad, Elyasaf the son of De'u'el;
15	From Naftali, Achira the son of 'Enan."

¹⁶ These were the ones called from the assembly, the chiefs of their fathers' clans and heads of thousands in Isra'el. ¹⁷ So Moshe and Aharon took these men who had been designated by name; ¹⁸ and, on the first day of the second month, they gathered the whole assembly to state their genealogies by families and clans and recorded the names of all those twenty years old and over, as well as their total numbers. ¹⁹ Moshe counted them in the Sinai Desert, just as ADONAI had ordered him.

(ii) ²⁰ The men twenty years old and over who were subject to military service were recorded by name, family and clan, starting with the descendants of Re'uven, Isra'el's firstborn. Here are the totals:

145

21	Descendants of Re'uven	46,500
22-23	Descendants of Shim'on	59,300
24-25	Descendants of Gad	45,650
26-27	Descendants of Y'hudah	74,600
28-29	Descendants of Yissakhar	54,400
30-31	Descendants of Z'vulun	57,400
32-33	Descendants of Efrayim	40,500
34-35	Descendants of M'nasheh	32,200
36-37	Descendants of Binyamin	35,400
38-39	Descendants of Dan	62,700
40-41	Descendants of Asher	41,500
42-43	Descendants of Naftali	53,400

⁴⁴ Moshe, Aharon and the twelve leaders of Isra'el, each from a clan, ⁴⁵ counted the people of Isra'el by their clans, those twenty years old and over, eligible for military service in Isra'el; ⁴⁶ and the grand total came to 603,550.

⁴⁷ But those who were *L'vi'im*, according to the clan of their fathers, were not counted in this census; ⁴⁸ because *ADONAI* had told Moshe, ⁴⁹ "Do not include the clan of Levi when you take the census of the people of Isra'el. ⁵⁰ Instead, give the *L'vi'im* charge over the tabernacle of the testimony, its equipment and everything else connected with it. They are to carry the tabernacle and all its equipment, serve in it and set up their camp around it. ⁵¹ When the tabernacle is to be moved onward, it is the *L'vi'im* who are to take it down and set it up in the new location; anyone else who involves himself is to be put to death. ⁵² The rest of Isra'el are to set up camp, company by company, each man with his own banner. ⁵³ But the *L'vi'im* are to camp around the tabernacle of the testimony, so that no anger will come upon the assembly of the people of Isra'el. The *L'vi'im* are to be in charge of the tabernacle of the testimony."

⁵⁴ This is what the people of Isra'el did — they did everything that *ADONAI* had ordered Moshe.

2 *(iii)* ¹ *ADONAI* said to Moshe and Aharon, ² "The people of Isra'el are to set up camp by clans, each man with his own banner and under his clan's symbol; they are to camp around the tent of meeting, but at a distance.

³⁻⁹ "Those camping on the east side toward the sunrise are to be under the banner of the camp of Y'hudah; they are to camp according to companies; by tribe and leader they are as follows:

Tribe	Chief	Number
Y'hudah	Nachshon the son of 'Amminadav	74,600
Yissakhar	N'tan'el the son of Tzu'ar	54,400
Z'vulun	Eli'av the son of Helon	57,400
Total		186,400

"This group is to set out first.

¹⁰⁻¹⁶ "Those camping on the south are to be under the banner of the camp of Re'uven; they are to camp according to companies; by tribe and leader they are as follows:

Tribe	Chief	Number
Re'uven	Elitzur the son of Sh'de'ur	46,500
Shim'on	Shlumi'el the son of Tzurishaddai	59,300
Gad	Elyasaf the son of Re'u'el	45,650
Total		151,450

"This group is to set out second.

¹⁷ "Then the tent of meeting, with the camp of the *L'vi'im*, will set out, with the other camps in front and behind. They will go in the same order as their camps are set up — each man will go forward in his position, under his banner.

¹⁸⁻²⁴ "Those camping on the west are to be under the banner of the camp of Efrayim; they are to camp according to companies; by tribe and leader they are as follows:

Tribe	Chief	Number
Efrayim	Elishama the son of 'Ammihud	40,500
M'nasheh	Gamli'el the son of P'dahtzur	32,200
Binyamin	Avidan the son of Gid'oni	35,400
Total		108,100

"This group is to set out third.

²⁵⁻³¹ "Those camping on the north are to be under the banner of the camp of Dan; they are to camp according to companies; by tribe and leader they are as follows:

Tribe	Chief	Number
Dan	Achi'ezer the son of 'Ammishaddai	62,700
Asher	Pag'i'el the son of 'Okhran	41,500
Naftali	Achira the son of 'Enan	53,400
Total		157,600

"This group is to set out last with their banners."

³² These are the ones counted from the people of Isra'el by clans; the total number recorded in the camps, company by company, was 603,550. ³³ But, as ADONAI ordered Moshe, the *L'vi'im* were not counted with the rest of Isra'el.

³⁴ The people of Isra'el did everything ADONAI had ordered Moshe: they set up camp under their banners, and they set out, each according to his family and clan.

3 *(iv)* ¹ These are the descendants of Aharon and Moshe as of the day when ADONAI spoke with Moshe on Mount Sinai. ² The names of the sons of Aharon are: Nadav the firstborn, Avihu, El'azar and Itamar. ³ These were the names of the sons of Aharon the *cohen*, whom he anointed and ordained as *cohanim*. ⁴ But Nadav and Avihu died in the presence of ADONAI when they offered unauthorized fire before ADONAI in the Sinai Desert, and they had no children; El'azar and Itamar served as *cohanim* in the presence of Aharon their father.

⁵ ADONAI said to Moshe, ⁶ "Summon the tribe of Levi, and assign them to Aharon the *cohen*, so that they can help him. ⁷ They are to carry out his duties and the duties of the whole community before the tent of meeting in performing the service of the tabernacle. ⁸ They are to be in charge of all the furnishings of the tent of meeting and to carry out all the duties of the people of Isra'el connected with the service of the tabernacle. ⁹ Assign the *L'vi'im* to Aharon and his sons; their one responsibility in regard to the people of Isra'el is to serve him. ¹⁰ You are to appoint Aharon and his sons to carry out the duties of *cohanim*; anyone else who involves himself is to be put to death."

¹¹ ADONAI said to Moshe, ¹² "I have taken the *L'vi'im* from among the people of Isra'el in lieu of every firstborn male that is first from the womb among the people of Isra'el; the *L'vi'im* are to be mine. ¹³ All the firstborn males belong to me, because on the day that I killed all the firstborn males in the land of Egypt, I separated for myself all the firstborn males in Isra'el, both human and animal. They are mine; I am ADONAI."

(v) ¹⁴ ADONAI said to Moshe in the Sinai Desert, ¹⁵ "Take a census of the tribe of Levi by clans and families. Count every male a month old or over." ¹⁶ Moshe counted them in the manner ADONAI had said, as he had been ordered. ¹⁷ The names of the sons of Levi were Gershon, K'hat and M'rari. ¹⁸ The names of the sons of Gershon were Livni and Shim'i; they fathered their respective clans; ¹⁹ likewise the sons of K'hat — 'Amram, Yitz'har, Hevron and 'Uzi'el — ²⁰ and the sons of M'rari — Machli and Mushi. These fathered the clans of the *L'vi'im*.

²¹ Gershon fathered the clans of Livni and Shim'i; these were the Gershon clans. ²² Of them, 7,500 males a month old and over were counted. ²³ The Gershon clans were to camp behind the tabernacle, toward the west. ²⁴ The chief of the Gershon clan was Elyasaf, the son of La'el. ²⁵ In connection with the tent of meeting, the descendants of Gershon were to be in charge of the following: the tabernacle itself, its inner and outer coverings, the screen for the entrance of the tent of meeting, ²⁶ the curtains surrounding the courtyard, the screen for the entrance of the courtyard surrounding the tabernacle and the altar, all the fixtures and ropes for these items, and their maintenance.

²⁷ K'hat fathered the clans of 'Amram, Yitz'har, Hevron and 'Uzi'el; these were the K'hat clans. ²⁸ Of them, 8,600 males a month old and over were counted; they were in charge of the Holy Place. ²⁹ The K'hat clans were to camp next to the tabernacle, toward the south. ³⁰ The chief of the K'hat clan was Elitzafan the son of 'Uzi'el. ³¹ They were responsible for the ark, the table, the *menorah*, the altars, the utensils the *cohanim* use when they serve in the Holy Place, the curtain, and everything involved with the maintenance of these things. ³² El'azar the son of Aharon the *cohen* was first among the chiefs of the *L'vi'im* and supervised those in charge of the Holy Place.

³³ M'rari fathered the clans of Machli and Mushi; these were the M'rari clans. ³⁴ Of them, 6,200 males a month old and over were counted. ³⁵ The chief of the M'rari clan was Tzuri'el the son of Avichayil. They were to camp next to the tabernacle, toward the north. ³⁶ The M'rari clans were assigned responsibility for the frames of

the tabernacle, along with its crossbars, posts, sockets and fittings, together with their maintenance; ³⁷ also the posts of the surrounding courtyard, with their sockets, pegs and ropes.

³⁸ Those who were to camp in front of the tabernacle on the east, in front of the tent of meeting toward the sunrise, were Moshe, Aharon and his sons who were in charge of the Holy Place. They carried out their responsibility on behalf of the people of Isra'el, and anyone else who involved himself was to be put to death.

³⁹ The total number of *L'vi'im* whom Moshe and Aharon counted by their clans, all the males a month old and over, was 22,000.

(vi) ⁴⁰ ADONAI said to Moshe, "Register all the firstborn males of the people of Isra'el a month old and over, and determine how many there are. ⁴¹ Then you are to take the *L'vi'im* for me, ADONAI, in place of all the firstborn among the people of Isra'el, and the cattle of the *L'vi'im* in place of the firstborn of the cattle belonging to the people of Isra'el." ⁴² Moshe counted, as ADONAI had ordered him, all the firstborn among the people of Isra'el. ⁴³ The total number of firstborn males registered, a month old and over, of those who were counted, was 22,273.

⁴⁴ ADONAI said to Moshe, ⁴⁵ "Take the *L'vi'im* in place of all the firstborn among the people of Isra'el, and the cattle of the *L'vi'im* in place of their cattle; the *L'vi'im* are to belong to me, ADONAI. ⁴⁶ Since there were 273 more firstborn males from Isra'el than male *L'vi'im*, in order to redeem them, ⁴⁷ you are to take five *shekels* [two ounces] for each of these (use the sanctuary *shekel*, which is equal to twenty *gerahs*). ⁴⁸ Give the redemption money for these extra people to Aharon and his sons." ⁴⁹ Moshe took the redemption money from those who were over and above those redeemed by the *L'vi'im*; ⁵⁰ the amount of money he took from the firstborn of the people of Isra'el was 1,365 *shekels*, using the sanctuary *shekel*. ⁵¹ Moshe gave the redemption-money to Aharon and his sons, in keeping with what ADONAI had said, as ADONAI had ordered Moshe.

4 *(vii)* ¹ ADONAI said to Moshe and Aharon, ² "Take a census of the descendants of K'hat, who are among the descendants of Levi, by clans and families, ³ all those from thirty to fifty years old; these will enter the corps doing the work in the tent of meeting.

⁴ "Here is how the descendants of K'hat are to serve in the tent of meeting and deal with the especially holy things: ⁵ when the time comes to break camp, Aharon is to go in with his sons, take down the curtain which serves as a screen, and cover the ark of the testimony with it. ⁶ On that they are to place a covering of fine leather, and on top of that spread an all-blue cloth. Then they are to insert the carrying-poles. ⁷ On the table of showbread they are to spread a blue cloth and place on it the dishes, incense pans, offering bowls and pitchers. The perpetual bread is to remain on the table. ⁸ They are to spread on these things a scarlet cloth, cover them with a covering of fine leather and insert the poles. ⁹ They are to take a blue cloth and cover the *menorah* for the light, its lamps, its tongs, its trays and the jars used to add oil to it. ¹⁰ They are to wrap it and all its accessories in fine leather and place them on a carrying-frame. ¹¹ On the gold altar they are to spread a blue cloth, cover it with a covering of fine leather and insert its carrying-poles. ¹² They are to take all the utensils they use when serving in the sanctuary and put them in a blue cloth, cover them with fine leather and place them on a carrying-frame. ¹³ After removing the greasy ashes from the altar, they are to spread a purple

cloth over it ¹⁴ and place on it all the utensils required for their altar service — the fire pans, meat-hooks, shovels, basins and other utensils for the altar. Then they are to spread over it a fine leather covering and insert its carrying-poles. ¹⁵ When Aharon and his sons have finished covering the holy furnishings and all the holy utensils, when the camp is about to move forward, then the descendants of K'hat are to come and carry them. But they are not to touch the holy things, so that they won't die. These things are the responsibility of the descendants of K'hat in the tent of meeting.

¹⁶ "El'azar the son of Aharon the *cohen* is to be responsible for the oil for the light, the fragrant incense, the continuing grain offering and the anointing oil. He is to be in charge of the entire tabernacle and everything in it, including the sanctuary and its furnishings."

(Maftir) ¹⁷ A*donai* said to Moshe and Aharon, ¹⁸ "Do not cut off the clan of K'hat from among the *L'vi'im*; ¹⁹ rather, do this for them, so that they will live and not die: when they approach the especially holy things, Aharon and his sons are to go in — and you are to assign each one his task; ²⁰ but the descendants of K'hat are not to go in and look at the holy things as they are being covered; if they do, they will die."

Haftarah B'midbar: Hoshea (Hosea) 2:1(1:10)–2:22(20)

B'rit Hadashah suggested readings for Parashah B'midbar: Luke 2:1–7;
1 Corinthians 12:12–31

Parashah 35: Naso (Take) 4:21–7:89

²¹ A*donai* said to Moshe, ²² "Take a census of the descendants of Gershon also, by clans and families; ²³ count all those between thirty and fifty years old, all who will enter the corps doing the work of serving in the tent of meeting.

²⁴ "The Gershon families are to be responsible for serving and for transporting loads. ²⁵ They are to carry the curtains of the tabernacle, the tent of meeting, its covering, the fine leather covering above it, the screen for the entrance to the tent of meeting, ²⁶ the tapestries for the courtyard, and the screen for the entrance to the courtyard by the tabernacle and around the altar, along with the ropes and all the utensils they need for their service; and they are to do the work connected with these things. ²⁷ Aharon and his sons are to supervise all the work of the Gershon clan in transporting loads and serving, and to assign them who is to carry what. ²⁸ This is how the Gershon families are to serve in the tent of meeting, and they are to be under the direction of Itamar the son of Aharon the *cohen*.

²⁹ "As for the descendants of M'rari, take a census by clans and families ³⁰ of all those between thirty and fifty years old, all who will be in the corps doing the work of serving in the tent of meeting.

³¹ "Their service for the tent of meeting will be to carry the frames, crossbars, posts and sockets of the tabernacle; ³² also the posts for the surrounding courtyard, with their sockets, tent pegs, ropes and other accessories, and everything having to do with their service. You are to assign particular loads to specific persons by name. ³³ This is how the M'rari families are to serve in the tent of meeting, directed by Itamar the son of Aharon the *cohen*."

(S: ii) ³⁴ Moshe, Aharon and the community leaders took a census of the descendants of K'hat by their clans and families, ³⁵ all those between thirty and fifty years old who were part of the corps serving in the tent of meeting. ³⁶ Registered by their families, they numbered 2,750. ³⁷ These are the ones counted from the K'hat families of all those serving in the tent of meeting, whom Moshe and Aharon enumerated, in keeping with the order given by ADONAI through Moshe.

(A: ii) ³⁸ The census of the descendants of Gershon, by their clans and families, ³⁹ all those between thirty and fifty years old who were part of the corps serving in the tent of meeting, ⁴⁰ yielded 2,630, registered by their clans and families. ⁴¹ These are the ones counted from the families of the descendants of Gershon of all those serving in the tent of meeting, whom Moshe and Aharon enumerated, in keeping with the order given by ADONAI.

⁴² The census of the families of the descendants of M'rari, by their clans and families, ⁴³ all those between thirty and fifty years old who were part of the corps serving in the tent of meeting, ⁴⁴ yielded 3,200, registered by their families. ⁴⁵ These are the ones counted from the families of the descendants of M'rari, whom Moshe and Aharon enumerated, in keeping with the order given by ADONAI through Moshe.

⁴⁶ The census of the L'vi'im, whom Moshe, Aharon and the leaders of Isra'el enumerated by their clans and families, ⁴⁷ all those between thirty and fifty years old who were part of those working to serve and working to carry loads in the tent of meeting, ⁴⁸ yielded a total of 8,580 persons.

⁴⁹ According to ADONAI's order they were appointed by Moshe, each one to his specific service or work. They were also enumerated, as ADONAI had ordered Moshe.

5 *(iii)* ¹ ADONAI said to Moshe, ² "Order the people of Isra'el to expel from the camp everyone with *tzara'at*, everyone with a discharge and whoever is unclean because of touching a corpse. ³ Both male and female you must expel; put them outside the camp; so that they won't defile their camp, where I live among you." ⁴ The people of Isra'el did this and put them outside the camp — the people of Isra'el did what ADONAI had said to Moshe.

⁵ ADONAI said to Moshe, ⁶ "Tell the people of Isra'el, 'When a man or woman commits any kind of sin against another person and thus breaks faith with ADONAI, he incurs guilt. ⁷ He must confess the sin which he has committed; and he must make full restitution for his guilt, add twenty percent and give it to the victim of his sin. ⁸ But if the person has no relative to whom restitution can be made for the guilt, then what is given in restitution for guilt will belong to ADONAI, that is, to the *cohen* — in addition to the ram of atonement through which atonement is made for him.

⁹ "'Every contribution which the people of Isra'el consecrate and present to the *cohen* will belong to him. ¹⁰ Anything an individual consecrates will be his own [to allocate among the *cohanim*], but what a person gives to the *cohen* will belong to him.'"

(A: iv) ¹¹ ADONAI said to Moshe, ¹² "Tell the people of Isra'el, 'If a man's wife goes astray and is unfaithful to him; ¹³ that is, if another man goes to bed with her without her husband's knowledge, so that she becomes impure secretly, and there is no witness against her, and she was not caught in the act; ¹⁴ then, if a spirit of jealousy comes over him, and he is jealous of his wife, and she has become impure — or, for that matter, if the spirit of jealousy comes over him, and he is jealous of his wife, and she has not become impure — ¹⁵ he is to bring his wife to

the *cohen*, along with the offering for her, two quarts of barley flour on which he has not poured olive oil or put frankincense, because it is a grain offering for jealousy, a grain offering for remembering, for recalling guilt to mind. [16] The *cohen* will bring her forward and place her before *Adonai*. [17] The *cohen* will put holy water in a clay pot, and then the *cohen* will take some of the dust on the floor of the tabernacle and put it in the water. [18] The *cohen* will place the woman before *Adonai*, unbind the woman's hair and put the grain offering for remembering in her hands, the grain offering for jealousy; while the *cohen* has in his hand the water of embitterment and cursing. [19] The *cohen* will make her swear by saying to her, "If no man has gone to bed with you, if you have not gone astray to make yourself unclean while under your husband's authority, then be free from this water of embitterment and cursing. [20] But if you have in fact gone astray while under your husband's authority and become unclean, because some man other than your husband has gone to bed with you . . ." [21] then the *cohen* is to make the woman swear with an oath that includes a curse; the *cohen* will say to the woman, ". . .may *Adonai* make you an object of cursing and condemnation among your people by making your private parts shrivel and your abdomen swell up! [22] May this water that causes the curse go into your inner parts and make your abdomen swell and your private parts shrivel up!" — and the woman is to respond, "Amen! Amen!" [23] The *cohen* is to write these curses on a scroll, wash them off into the water of embitterment [24] and make the woman drink the water of embitterment and cursing — the water of cursing will enter her and become bitter. [25] Then the *cohen* is to remove the grain offering for jealousy from the woman's hand, wave the grain offering before *Adonai* and bring it to the altar. [26] The *cohen* is to take a handful of the grain offering as its reminder portion and make it go up in smoke on the altar; afterwards, he is to make the woman drink the water. [27] When he has made her drink the water, then, if she is unclean and has been unfaithful to her husband, the water that causes the curse will enter her and become bitter, so that her abdomen swells and her private parts shrivel up; and the woman will become an object of cursing among her people. [28] But if the woman is not unclean but clean, then she will be innocent and will have children. [29] This is the law for jealousy: when either a wife under her husband's authority goes astray and becomes unclean, [30] or the spirit of jealousy comes over a husband and he becomes jealous of his wife, then he is to place the woman before *Adonai*, and the *cohen* is to deal with her in accordance with all of this law. [31] The husband will be clear of guilt, but the wife will bear the consequences of her guilt.'"

6 [1] *Adonai* said to Moshe, [2] "Tell the people of Isra'el, 'When either a man or a woman makes a special kind of vow, the vow of a *nazir*, consecrating himself to *Adonai*; [3] he is to abstain from wine and other intoxicating liquor, he is not to drink vinegar from either source, he is not to drink grape juice, and he is not to eat grapes or raisins. [4] As long as he remains a *nazir* he is to eat nothing derived from the grapevine, not even the grape-skins or the seeds.

[5] "'Throughout the period of his vow as a *nazir*, he is not to shave his head. Until the end of the time for which he has consecrated himself to *Adonai* he is to be holy: he is to let the hair on his head grow long.

⁶ "'Throughout the period for which he has consecrated himself to *Adonai*, he is not to approach a corpse. ⁷ He is not to make himself unclean for his father, mother, brother or sister when they die, since his consecration to God is on his head. ⁸ Throughout the time of his being a *nazir* he is holy for *Adonai*.

⁹ "'If someone next to him dies very suddenly, so that he defiles his consecrated head, then he is to shave his head on the day of his purification; he is to shave it on the seventh day. ¹⁰ On the eighth day he is to bring two doves or two young pigeons to the *cohen* at the entrance to the tent of meeting. ¹¹ The *cohen* is to prepare one as a sin offering and the other as a burnt offering and thus make atonement for him, inasmuch as he sinned because of the dead person. That same day he is to re-consecrate his head; ¹² he is to consecrate to *Adonai* the full period of his being a *nazir* by bringing a male lamb in its first year as a guilt offering. The previous days will not be counted, because his consecration became defiled.

¹³ "'This is the law for the *nazir* when his period of consecration is over: he is to be brought to the entrance of the tent of meeting, ¹⁴ where he will present his offering to *Adonai* — one male lamb in its first year without defect as a burnt offering, one female lamb in its first year without defect as a sin offering, one ram without defect as peace offerings, ¹⁵ a basket of *matzah*, loaves made of fine flour mixed with olive oil, unleavened wafers spread with olive oil, their grain offering and their drink offerings. ¹⁶ The *cohen* is to bring them before *Adonai*, offer his sin offering, his burnt offering, ¹⁷ and his ram as a sacrifice of peace offerings to *Adonai*, with the basket of *matzah*. The *cohen* will also offer the grain offering and drink offering that go with the peace offering. ¹⁸ The *nazir* will shave his consecrated head at the entrance to the tent of meeting, take the hair removed from his consecrated head and put it on the fire under the sacrifice of peace offerings. ¹⁹ When the ram has been boiled, the *cohen* is to take its shoulder, one loaf of *matzah* from the basket and one unleavened wafer, and place them in the hands of the *nazir*, after he has shaved his consecrated head. ²⁰ The *cohen* is to wave them as a wave offering before *Adonai*; this is set aside for the *cohen*, along with the breast for waving and the raised-up thigh. Following that, the *nazir* may drink wine.

²¹ "'This is the law for the *nazir* who makes a vow and for his offering to *Adonai* for his being a *nazir* — in addition to anything more for which he has sufficient means. In keeping with whatever vow he makes, he must do it according to the law for the *nazir*.'"

²² *Adonai* said to Moshe, ²³ "Speak to Aharon and his sons, and tell them that this is how you are to bless the people of Isra'el: you are to say to them,

²⁴   '*Y'varekh'kha Adonai v'yishmerekha.*
       [May *Adonai* bless you and keep you.]
²⁵   *Ya'er Adonai panav eleikha vichunekka.*
       [May *Adonai* make his face shine on you and show you his favor.]
²⁶   *Yissa Adonai panav eleikha v'yasem l'kha shalom.*
       [May *Adonai* lift up his face toward you and give you peace.]'

²⁷ "In this way they are to put my name on the people of Isra'el, so that I will bless them."

7 *(A: v, S: iv)* [1] On the day Moshe finished putting up the tabernacle, he anointed and consecrated it, all its furnishings, and the altar with its utensils. After anointing and consecrating them, [2] the leaders of Isra'el, who were heads of their father's clans, made an offering. These were the tribal leaders in charge of those counted in the census. [3] They brought their offering before ADONAI, six covered wagons and twelve oxen — a wagon for every two leaders and for each an ox — and presented them in front of the tabernacle.

[4] ADONAI said to Moshe, [5] "Receive these from them; they are to be used for the service in the tent of meeting. Give them to the *L'vi'im*, to each as needed for his duties." [6] So Moshe took the wagons and oxen and gave them to the *L'vi'im*. [7] He gave two wagons and four oxen to the descendants of Gershon, in keeping with the needs of their duties. [8] Four wagons and eight oxen he gave to the descendants of M'rari, in keeping with the needs of their duties, directed by Itamar the son of Aharon the *cohen*. [9] But to the descendants of K'hat he gave none, because their duties involved the holy articles, which they carried on their own shoulders.

[10] The leaders brought the offering for dedicating the altar on the day it was anointed. The leaders brought their offering before the altar, [11] and ADONAI said to Moshe, "They are to present their offerings to dedicate the altar, each leader on his own day."

(S: v) [12] Nachshon the son of 'Amminadav, from the tribe of Y'hudah, presented his offering on the first day. [13] He offered one silver dish weighing 130 *shekels* [three-and-a-quarter pounds] and one silver basin of seventy *shekels* (using the sanctuary *shekel*) [one-and-three-quarters pounds], both full of fine flour mixed with olive oil for a grain offering; [14] one gold pan of ten *shekels* [one-quarter pound], full of incense; [15] one young bull, one ram, one male lamb in its first year as a burnt offering, [16] one male goat as a sin offering, [17] and, for the sacrifice of peace offerings, two oxen, five rams, five male goats and five male lambs in their first year. This was the offering of Nachshon the son of 'Amminadav.

[18] On the second day N'tan'el the son of Tzu'ar, leader of Yissakhar, presented his offering. [19] He offered one silver dish weighing 130 *shekels* [three-and-a-quarter pounds] and one silver basin of seventy *shekels* (using the sanctuary *shekel*) [one-and-three-quarters pounds], both full of fine flour mixed with olive oil for a grain offering; [20] one gold pan of ten *shekels* [one-quarter pound], full of incense; [21] one young bull, one ram, one male lamb in its first year as a burnt offering, [22] one male goat as a sin offering, [23] and, for the sacrifice of peace offerings, two oxen, five rams, five male goats and five male lambs in their first year. This was the offering of N'tan'el the son of Tzu'ar.

[24] On the third day Eli'av the son of Helon, leader of Z'vulun, presented his offering. [25] He offered one silver dish weighing 130 *shekels* [three-and-a-quarter pounds] and one silver basin of seventy *shekels* (using the sanctuary *shekel*) [one-and-three-quarters pounds], both full of fine flour mixed with olive oil for a grain offering; [26] one gold pan of ten *shekels* [one-quarter pound], full of incense; [27] one young bull, one ram, one male lamb in its first year as a burnt offering, [28] one male goat as a sin offering, [29] and, for the sacrifice of peace offerings, two oxen, five rams, five male goats and five male lambs in their first year. This was the offering of Eli'av the son of Helon.

[30] On the fourth day was Elitzur the son of Sh'de'ur, leader of the descendants of Re'uven. [31] He offered one silver dish weighing 130 *shekel*s [three-and-a-quarter pounds] and one silver basin of seventy *shekel*s (using the sanctuary *shekel*) [one-and-three-quarters pounds], both full of fine flour mixed with olive oil for a grain offering; [32] one gold pan of ten *shekel*s [one-quarter pound], full of incense; [33] one young bull, one ram, one male lamb in its first year as a burnt offering, [34] one male goat as a sin offering, [35] and, for the sacrifice of peace offerings, two oxen, five rams, five male goats and five male lambs in their first year. This was the offering of Elitzur the son of Sh'de'ur.

[36] On the fifth day was Shlumi'el the son of Tzurishaddai, leader of the descendants of Shim'on. [37] He offered one silver dish weighing 130 *shekel*s [three-and-a-quarter pounds] and one silver basin of seventy *shekel*s (using the sanctuary *shekel*) [one-and-three-quarters pounds], both full of fine flour mixed with olive oil for a grain offering; [38] one gold pan of ten *shekel*s [one-quarter pound], full of incense; [39] one young bull, one ram, one male lamb in its first year as a burnt offering, [40] one male goat as a sin offering, [41] and, for the sacrifice of peace offerings, two oxen, five rams, five male goats and five male lambs in their first year. This was the offering of Shlumi'el the son of Tzurishaddai.

(vi) [42] On the sixth day was Elyasaf the son of De'u'el, leader of the descendants of Gad. [43] He offered one silver dish weighing 130 *shekel*s [three-and-a-quarter pounds] and one silver basin of seventy *shekel*s (using the sanctuary *shekel*) [one-and-three-quarters pounds], both full of fine flour mixed with olive oil for a grain offering; [44] one gold pan of ten *shekel*s [one-quarter pound], full of incense; [45] one young bull, one ram, one male lamb in its first year as a burnt offering, [46] one male goat as a sin offering, [47] and, for the sacrifice of peace offerings, two oxen, five rams, five male goats and five male lambs in their first year. This was the offering of Elyasaf the son of De'u'el.

[48] On the seventh day was Elishama the son of 'Ammihud, leader of the descendants of Efrayim. [49] He offered one silver dish weighing 130 *shekel*s [three-and-a-quarter pounds] and one silver basin of seventy *shekel*s (using the sanctuary *shekel*) [one-and-three-quarters pounds], both full of fine flour mixed with olive oil for a grain offering; [50] one gold pan of ten *shekel*s [one-quarter pound], full of incense; [51] one young bull, one ram, one male lamb in its first year as a burnt offering, [52] one male goat as a sin offering, [53] and, for the sacrifice of peace offerings, two oxen, five rams, five male goats and five male lambs in their first year. This was the offering of Elishama the son of 'Ammihud.

[54] On the eighth day was Gamli'el the son of P'dahtzur, leader of the descendants of M'nasheh. [55] He offered one silver dish weighing 130 *shekel*s [three-and-a-quarter pounds] and one silver basin of seventy *shekel*s (using the sanctuary *shekel*) [one-and-three-quarters pounds], both full of fine flour mixed with olive oil for a grain offering; [56] one gold pan of ten *shekel*s [one-quarter pound], full of incense; [57] one young bull, one ram, one male lamb in its first year as a burnt offering, [58] one male goat as a sin offering, [59] and, for the sacrifice of peace offerings, two oxen, five rams, five male goats and five male lambs in their first year. This was the offering of Gamli'el the son of P'dahtzur.

[60] On the ninth day was Avidan the son of Gid'oni, leader of the descendants of Binyamin. [61] He offered one silver dish weighing 130 *shekel*s [three-and-a-quarter

pounds] and one silver basin of seventy *shekels* (using the sanctuary *shekel*) [one-and-three-quarters pounds], both full of fine flour mixed with olive oil for a grain offering; ⁶²one gold pan of ten *shekels* [one-quarter pound], full of incense; ⁶³one young bull, one ram, one male lamb in its first year as a burnt offering, ⁶⁴one male goat as a sin offering, ⁶⁵and, for the sacrifice of peace offerings, two oxen, five rams, five male goats and five male lambs in their first year. This was the offering of Avidan the son of Gid'oni.

⁶⁶On the tenth day was Achi'ezer the son of 'Ammishaddai, leader of the descendants of Dan. ⁶⁷He offered one silver dish weighing 130 *shekels* [three-and-a-quarter pounds] and one silver basin of seventy *shekels* (using the sanctuary *shekel*) [one-and-three-quarters pounds], both full of fine flour mixed with olive oil for a grain offering; ⁶⁸one gold pan of ten *shekels* [one-quarter pound], full of incense; ⁶⁹one young bull, one ram, one male lamb in its first year as a burnt offering, ⁷⁰one male goat as a sin offering, ⁷¹and, for the sacrifice of peace offerings, two oxen, five rams, five male goats and five male lambs in their first year. This was the offering of Achi'ezer the son of 'Ammishaddai.

(vii) ⁷²On the eleventh day was Pag'i'el the son of 'Okhran, leader of the descendants of Asher. ⁷³He offered one silver dish weighing 130 *shekels* [three-and-a-quarter pounds] and one silver basin of seventy *shekels* (using the sanctuary *shekel*) [one-and-three-quarters pounds], both full of fine flour mixed with olive oil for a grain offering; ⁷⁴one gold pan of ten *shekels* [one-quarter pound], full of incense; ⁷⁵one young bull, one ram, one male lamb in its first year as a burnt offering, ⁷⁶one male goat as a sin offering, ⁷⁷and, for the sacrifice of peace offerings, two oxen, five rams, five male goats and five male lambs in their first year. This was the offering of Pag'i'el the son of 'Okhran.

⁷⁸On the twelfth day was Achira the son of 'Enan, leader of the descendants of Naftali. ⁷⁹He offered one silver dish weighing 130 *shekels* [three-and-a-quarter pounds] and one silver basin of seventy *shekels* (using the sanctuary *shekel*) [one-and-three-quarters pounds], both full of fine flour mixed with olive oil for a grain offering; ⁸⁰one gold pan of ten *shekels* [one-quarter pound], full of incense; ⁸¹one young bull, one ram, one male lamb in its first year as a burnt offering, ⁸²one male goat as a sin offering, ⁸³and, for the sacrifice of peace offerings, two oxen, five rams, five male goats and five male lambs in their first year. This was the offering of Achira the son of 'Enan.

⁸⁴This was the offering for dedicating the altar which was given by the leaders of Isra'el on the day of its anointing: twelve silver dishes, twelve silver basins and twelve gold pans. ⁸⁵Each silver dish weighed 130 *shekels* [three-and-a-quarter pounds] and each basin seventy shekels [one-and-three-quarters pounds]; all the silver of the vessels weighed 2,400 *shekels* (using the sanctuary *shekel*) [just over sixty pounds]. ⁸⁶The twelve gold pans, full of incense, weighed ten *shekels* apiece (using the sanctuary *shekel*) [one-quarter pound]; all the gold of the pans weighed 120 *shekels* [three pounds]. *(Maftir)* ⁸⁷The livestock for the burnt offering consisted of twelve bulls, twelve rams and twelve male lambs in their first year, with their grain offering. There were twelve male goats for a sin offering. ⁸⁸The livestock for the sacrifice of peace offerings consisted of twenty-four bulls, sixty rams, sixty male goats and sixty male lambs in their first year. This was the offering for dedicating the altar after it had been anointed.

⁸⁹ When Moshe went into the tent of meeting in order to speak with ADONAI, he heard the voice speaking to him from above the ark-cover on the ark for the testimony, from between the two *k'ruvim*; and he spoke to him.

Haftarah Naso: Shof'tim (Judges) 13:2–25

B'rit Hadashah suggested readings for Parashah Naso: Yochanan (John) 7:53–8:11; Acts 21:17–32

Parashah 36: B'ha'alotkha (When you set up) 8:1–12:16

8 ¹ ADONAI said to Moshe, ² "Tell Aharon, 'When you set up the lamps, the seven lamps are to cast their light forward, in front of the *menorah*.'" ³ Aharon did this: he lit its lamps so as to give light in front of the *menorah*, as ADONAI had ordered Moshe. ⁴ Here is how the *menorah* was made: it was hammered gold from its base to its flowers, hammered work, following the pattern ADONAI had shown Moshe. This is how he made the *menorah*.

⁵ ADONAI said to Moshe, ⁶ "Take the *L'vi'im* from among the people of Isra'el and cleanse them. ⁷ Here is how you are to cleanse them: sprinkle the purification water on them, have them shave their whole body with a razor, and have them wash their clothes and cleanse themselves. ⁸ Then they are to take a young bull with its grain offering, which is to be fine flour mixed with olive oil; while you take another bull for a sin offering. ⁹ You are to present the *L'vi'im* in front of the tent of meeting, and assemble the entire community of the people of Isra'el. ¹⁰ You will present the *L'vi'im* before ADONAI, the people of Isra'el will lay their hands on the *L'vi'im*, ¹¹ and Aharon will offer the *L'vi'im* before ADONAI as a wave offering from the people of Isra'el, so that they may do ADONAI's service. ¹² The *L'vi'im* will lay their hands on the heads of the bulls; the one you will offer as a sin offering and the other as a burnt offering to ADONAI to make atonement for the *L'vi'im*. ¹³ You are to place the *L'vi'im* before Aharon and his sons, and offer them as a wave offering to ADONAI. ¹⁴ In this way you will separate the *L'vi'im* from the people of Isra'el, and the *L'vi'im* will belong to me.

(ii) ¹⁵ "After that, the *L'vi'im* will enter and do the service of the tent of meeting. You will cleanse them and offer them as a wave offering, ¹⁶ because they are entirely given to me from among the people of Isra'el; I have taken them for myself in place of all those who come first out of the womb, that is, the firstborn males of the people of Isra'el. ¹⁷ For all the firstborn among the people of Isra'el are mine, both humans and animals; on the day I struck all the firstborn in the land of Egypt, I set them apart for myself. ¹⁸ But I have taken the *L'vi'im* in place of all the firstborn among the people of Isra'el, ¹⁹ and I have given the *L'vi'im* to Aharon and his sons from among the people of Isra'el to do the service of the people of Isra'el in the tent of meeting and to make atonement for the people of Isra'el, so that no plague will fall on the people of Isra'el in consequence of their coming too close to the sanctuary."

²⁰ This is what Moshe, Aharon and all the community of the people of Isra'el did to the *L'vi'im*. The people of Isra'el acted in accordance with everything that ADONAI had ordered Moshe in regard to the *L'vi'im*. ²¹ The *L'vi'im* purified themselves and

washed their clothes. Then Aharon offered them as a holy gift before ADONAI and made atonement for them in order to cleanse them. ²² After that, the *L'vi'im* came to do their service in the tent of meeting in front of Aharon and his sons; they acted in accordance with ADONAI's orders to Moshe in regard to the *L'vi'im*.

²³ ADONAI said to Moshe, ²⁴ "Here are instructions concerning the *L'vi'im*: when they reach the age of twenty-five, they are to begin performing their duties serving in the tent of meeting; ²⁵ and when they reach the age of fifty, they are to stop performing this work and not serve any longer. ²⁶ They will assist their brothers who are performing their duties in the tent of meeting, but they themselves will not do any of the work. This is what you are to do with the *L'vi'im* in regard to their duties."

9 *(iii)* ¹ ADONAI spoke to Moshe in the Sinai Desert in the first month of the second year after they had left the land of Egypt; he said, ² "Let the people of Isra'el observe *Pesach* at its designated time. ³ On the fourteenth day of this month, at dusk, you are to observe it — at its designated time. You are to observe it according to all its regulations and rules." ⁴ Moshe told the people of Isra'el to observe *Pesach*. ⁵ So they observed *Pesach* at dusk on the fourteenth day of the month in the Sinai Desert; the people of Isra'el acted in accordance with all that ADONAI had ordered Moshe.

⁶ But there were certain people who had become unclean because of someone's corpse, so that they could not observe *Pesach* on that day. So they came before Moshe and Aharon that day ⁷ and said to him, "We are unclean because of someone's corpse; but why must we be kept from bringing the offering for ADONAI at the time designated for the people of Isra'el?" ⁸ Moshe answered them, "Wait, so that I can hear what ADONAI will order concerning you." ⁹ ADONAI said to Moshe, ¹⁰ "Tell the people of Isra'el, 'If any of you now or in future generations is unclean because of a corpse, or if he is on a trip abroad, nevertheless he is to observe *Pesach*. ¹¹ But he will observe it in the second month on the fourteenth day at dusk. They are to eat it with *matzah* and *maror*, ¹² they are to leave none of it until morning, and they are not to break any of its bones — they are to observe it according to all the regulations of *Pesach*. ¹³ But the person who is clean and not on a trip who fails to observe *Pesach* will be cut off from his people; because he did not bring the offering for ADONAI at its designated time, that person will bear the consequences of his sin. ¹⁴ If a foreigner is staying with you and wants to observe *Pesach* for ADONAI, he is to do it according to the regulations and rules of *Pesach* — you are to have the same law for the foreigner as for the citizen of the land.'"

(iv) ¹⁵ On the day the tabernacle was put up, the cloud covered the tabernacle, that is, the tent of the testimony; and in the evening, over the tabernacle was what appeared to be fire, which remained until morning. ¹⁶ So the cloud always covered it, and it looked like fire at night. ¹⁷ Whenever the cloud was taken up from above the tent, the people of Isra'el continued their travels; and they camped wherever the cloud stopped. ¹⁸ At the order of ADONAI, the people of Isra'el traveled; at the order of ADONAI, they camped; and as long as the cloud stayed over the tabernacle, they stayed in camp. ¹⁹ Even when the cloud remained on the tabernacle for a long time, the people of Isra'el did what ADONAI had charged them to do and did not travel. ²⁰ Sometimes the cloud was a few days over the tabernacle; according to ADONAI's order, they remained in camp; and according to ADONAI's order, they traveled.

²¹ Sometimes the cloud was there only from evening until morning; so that when the cloud was taken up in the morning, they traveled. Or even if it continued up both day and night, when the cloud was up, they traveled. ²² Whether it was two days, a month or a year that the cloud remained over the tabernacle, staying on it, the people of Isra'el remained in camp and did not travel; but as soon as it was taken up, they traveled. ²³ At ADONAI's order, they camped; and at ADONAI's order, they traveled — they did what ADONAI had charged them to do through Moshe.

10 ¹ADONAI said to Moshe, ² "Make two trumpets; make them of hammered silver. Use them for summoning the community and for sounding the call to break camp and move on. ³ When they are sounded, the entire community is to assemble before you at the entrance to the tent of meeting. ⁴ If only one is sounded, then just the leaders, the heads of the clans of Isra'el, are to assemble before you.

⁵ "When you sound an alarm, the camps to the east will commence traveling. ⁶ When you sound a second alarm, the camps to the south will set out; they will sound alarms to announce when to travel. ⁷ However, when the community is to be assembled, you are to sound; but don't sound an alarm. ⁸ It will be the sons of Aharon, the *cohanim*, who are to sound the trumpets; this will be a permanent regulation for you through all your generations.

⁹ "When you go to war in your land against an adversary who is oppressing you, you are to sound an alarm with the trumpets; then you will be remembered before ADONAI your God, and you will be saved from your enemies.

¹⁰ "Also on your days of rejoicing, at your designated times and on *Rosh-Hodesh*, you are to sound the trumpets over your burnt offerings and over the sacrifices of your peace offerings; these will be your reminder before your God. I am ADONAI your God."

(*v*) ¹¹ On the twentieth day of the second month of the second year, the cloud was taken up from over the tabernacle of the testimony; ¹² and the people of Isra'el moved out in stages from the Sinai Desert. The cloud stopped in the Pa'ran Desert. ¹³ So they set out on their first journey, in keeping with ADONAI's order through Moshe. ¹⁴ In the lead was the banner of the camp of the descendants of Y'hudah, whose companies moved forward; over his company was Nachshon the son of 'Amminadav. ¹⁵ Over the company of the tribe of the descendants of Yissakhar was N'tan'el the son of Tzu'ar. ¹⁶ Over the company of the descendants of Z'vulun was Eli'av the son of Helon.

¹⁷ Then the tabernacle was taken down; and the descendants of Gershon and the descendants of M'rari set out, carrying the tabernacle.

¹⁸ Next, the banner of the camp of Re'uven moved forward by companies; over his company was Elitzur the son of Sh'de'ur. ¹⁹ Over the company of the tribe of the descendants of Shim'on was Shlumi'el the son of Tzurishaddai. ²⁰ Over the company of the descendants of Gad was Elyasaf the son of De'u'el.

²¹ Then the descendants of K'hat set out, carrying the sanctuary, so that [at the next camp] the tabernacle could be set up before they arrived.

²² The banner of the camp of the descendants of Efrayim moved forward by companies; over his company was Elishama the son of 'Ammihud. ²³ Over the company of the tribe of the descendants of M'nasheh was Gamli'el the son of P'dahtzur. ²⁴ Over the company of the descendants of Binyamin was Avidan the son of Gid'oni.

^{25} The banner of the camp of the descendants of Dan, forming the rearguard for all the camps, moved forward by companies; over his company was Achi'ezer the son of 'Ammishaddai. ^{26} Over the company of the tribe of the descendants of Asher was Pag'i'el the son of 'Okhran. ^{27} Over the company of the descendants of Naftali was Achira the son of 'Enan.

^{28} This is how the people of Isra'el traveled by companies; thus they moved forward.

(S: vi) ^{29} Moshe said to Hovav the son of Re'u'el the Midyani, Moshe's father-in-law, "We are traveling to the place about which ADONAI said, 'I will give it to you.' Come with us, and we will treat you well, because ADONAI has promised good things to Isra'el." ^{30} But he replied, "I will not go; I would rather go back to my own country and my own kinsmen." ^{31} Moshe continued, "Please don't leave us, because you know that we have to camp in the desert, and you can serve as our eyes. ^{32} If you do go with us, then whatever good ADONAI does for us, we will do the same for you."

^{33} So they set out from ADONAI's mountain and traveled for three days. Ahead of them on this three-day journey went the ark of ADONAI's covenant, searching for a new place to stop. ^{34} The cloud of ADONAI was over them during the day as they set out from the camp. *(A: vi)* ^{35} When the ark moved forward, Moshe said,

> "Arise, ADONAI! May your enemies be scattered!
> Let those who hate you flee before you!"

^{36} When it stopped, he said,

> "Return, ADONAI of the many, many
> thousands of Isra'el!"

11 ^{1} But the people began complaining about their hardships to ADONAI. When ADONAI heard it, his anger flared up, so that fire from ADONAI broke out against them and consumed the outskirts of the camp. ^{2} Then the people cried to Moshe, Moshe prayed to ADONAI, and the fire abated. ^{3} That place was called Tav'erah [burning] because ADONAI's fire broke out against them.

^{4} Next, the mixed crowd that was with them grew greedy for an easier life; while the people of Isra'el, for their part, also renewed their weeping and said, "If only we had meat to eat! ^{5} We remember the fish we used to eat in Egypt — it cost us nothing! — and the cucumbers, the melons, the leeks, the onions, the garlic! ^{6} But now we're withering away, we have nothing to look at but this *man*."

^{7} The *man*, by the way, was like coriander seed and white like gum resin. ^{8} The people would go around gathering it and would grind it up in mills or pound it to paste with mortar and pestle. Then they would cook it in pots and make it into loaves that tasted like cakes baked with olive oil. ^{9} When the dew settled on the camp during the night, the *man* came with it.

^{10} Moshe heard the people crying, family after family, each person at the entrance to his tent; the anger of ADONAI flared up violently; and Moshe too was displeased. ^{11} Moshe asked ADONAI, "Why are you treating your servant so badly? Why haven't I found favor in your sight, so that you put the burden of this entire people on me? ^{12} Did I conceive this people? Was I their father, so that you tell me, 'Carry them in your arms, like a nurse carrying a baby, to the land you swore to their ancestors?'

¹³ Where am I going to get meat to give to this entire people? — because they keep bothering me with their crying and saying, 'Give us meat to eat!' ¹⁴ I can't carry this entire people by myself alone — it's too much for me! ¹⁵ If you are going to treat me this way, then just kill me outright! — please, if you have any mercy toward me! — and don't let me go on being this miserable!"

¹⁶ Adonai said to Moshe, "Bring me seventy of the leaders of Isra'el, people you recognize as leaders of the people and officers of theirs. Bring them to the tent of meeting, and have them stand there with you. ¹⁷ I will come down and speak with you there, and I will take some of the Spirit which rests on you and put it on them. Then they will carry the burden of the people along with you, so that you won't carry it yourself alone.

¹⁸ "Tell the people, 'Consecrate yourselves for tomorrow, and you will eat meat; because you cried in the ears of Adonai, "If only we had meat to eat! We had the good life in Egypt!" All right, Adonai is going to give you meat, and you will eat it. ¹⁹ You won't eat it just one day, or two days, or five, or ten, or twenty days, ²⁰ but a whole month! — until it comes out of your nose and you hate it! — because you have rejected Adonai, who is here with you, and distressed him with your crying and asking, "Why did we ever leave Egypt?"'"

²¹ But Moshe said, "Here I am with six hundred thousand men on foot, and yet you say, 'I will give them meat to eat for a whole month!' ²² If whole flocks and herds were slaughtered for them, would it be enough? If all the fish in the sea were collected for them, would even that be enough?" ²³ Adonai answered Moshe, "Has Adonai's arm grown short? Now you will see whether what I said will happen or not!"

²⁴ Moshe went out and told the people what Adonai had said. Then he collected seventy of the leaders of the people and placed them all around the tent. ²⁵ Adonai came down in the cloud, spoke to him, took some of the Spirit that was on him and put it on the seventy leaders. When the Spirit came to rest on them, they prophesied — then but not afterwards.

²⁶ There were two men who stayed in the camp, one named Eldad and the other Medad, and the Spirit came to rest on them. They were among those listed to go out to the tent, but they hadn't done so, and they prophesied in the camp. ²⁷ A young man ran and told Moshe, "Eldad and Medad are prophesying in the camp!" ²⁸ Y'hoshua, the son of Nun, who from his youth up had been Moshe's assistant, answered, "My lord, Moshe, stop them!" ²⁹ But Moshe replied, "Are you so zealous to protect me? I wish all of Adonai's people were prophets! I wish Adonai would put his Spirit on all of them!"

(vii) ³⁰ Moshe and the leaders of Isra'el went back into the camp; ³¹ and Adonai sent out a wind which brought quails from across the sea and let them fall near the camp, about a day's trip away on each side of the camp and all around it, covering the ground to a depth of three feet. ³² The people stayed up all that day, all night and all the next day gathering the quails — the person gathering the least collected ten heaps; then they spread them out for themselves all around the camp. ³³ But while the meat was still in their mouth, before they had chewed it up, the anger of Adonai flared up against the people, and Adonai struck the people with a terrible plague. ³⁴ Therefore that place was named Kivrot-HaTa'avah [graves of greed], because there they buried the people who were so greedy.

³⁵ From Kivrot-HaTa'avah the people traveled to Hatzerot, and they stayed at Hatzerot.

12 ¹ Miryam and Aharon began criticizing Moshe on account of the Ethiopian woman he had married, for he had in fact married an Ethiopian woman. ² They said, "Is it true that ADONAI has spoken only with Moshe? Hasn't he spoken with us too?" ADONAI heard them. ³ Now this man Moshe was very humble, more so than anyone on earth. ⁴ Suddenly ADONAI told Moshe, Aharon and Miryam, "Come out, you three, to the tent of meeting." The three of them went out.

⁵ ADONAI came down in a column of cloud and stood at the entrance to the tent. He summoned Aharon and Miryam, and they both went forward. ⁶ He said, "Listen to what I say: when there is a prophet among you, I, ADONAI, make myself known to him in a vision, I speak with him in a dream. ⁷ But it isn't that way with my servant Moshe. He is the only one who is faithful in my entire household. ⁸ With him I speak face to face and clearly, not in riddles; he sees the image of ADONAI. So why weren't you afraid to criticize my servant Moshe?" ⁹ The anger of ADONAI flared up against them, and he left.

¹⁰ But when the cloud was removed from above the tent, Miryam had *tzara'at*, as white as snow. Aharon looked at Miryam, and she was as white as snow. ¹¹ Aharon said to Moshe, "Oh, my lord, please don't punish us for this sin we committed so foolishly. ¹² Please don't let her be like a stillborn baby, with its body half eaten away when it comes out of its mother's womb!" ¹³ Moshe cried to ADONAI, "Oh God, I beg you, please, heal her!" *(Maftir)* ¹⁴ ADONAI answered Moshe, "If her father had merely spit in her face, wouldn't she hide herself in shame for seven days? So let her be shut out of the camp for seven days; after that, she can be brought back in." ¹⁵ Miryam was shut out of the camp seven days, and the people did not travel until she was brought back in. ¹⁶ Afterwards, the people went on from Hatzerot and camped in the Pa'ran Desert.

Haftarah B'ha'alotkha: Z'kharyah (Zechariah) 2:14–4:7

B'rit Hadashah suggested readings for Parashah B'ha'alotkha: Yochanan (John) 19:31–37; Messianic Jews (Hebrews) 3:1–6

Parashah 37: Shlach L'kha (Send on your behalf) 13:1–15:41

13 ¹ ADONAI said to Moshe, ² "Send men on your behalf to reconnoiter the land of Kena'an, which I am giving to the people of Isra'el. From each ancestral tribe send someone who is a leader in his tribe." ³ Moshe dispatched them from the Pa'ran Desert as ADONAI had ordered; all of them were leading men among the people of Isra'el. ⁴ Here are their names:

	from the tribe of Re'uven, Shamua the son of Zakur;
⁵	from the tribe of Shim'on, Shafat the son of Hori;
⁶	from the tribe of Y'hudah, Kalev the son of Y'funeh;
⁷	from the tribe of Yissakhar, Yig'al the son of Yosef;
⁸	from the tribe of Efrayim, Hoshea the son of Nun;
⁹	from the tribe of Binyamin, Palti the son of Rafu;
¹⁰	from the tribe of Z'vulun, Gadi'el the son of Sodi;
¹¹	from the tribe of Yosef, that is, from the tribe of M'nasheh, Gadi the son of Susi;
¹²	from the tribe of Dan, 'Ammi'el the son of G'malli;

¹³ from the tribe of Asher, S'tur the son of Mikha'el;

¹⁴ from the tribe of Naftali, Nachbi the son of Vofsi; and

¹⁵ from the tribe of Gad, Ge'u'el the son of Makhi.

¹⁶ These are the names of the men Moshe sent out to reconnoiter the land. Moshe gave to Hoshea the son of Nun the name Y'hoshua.

¹⁷ Moshe sent them to reconnoiter the land of Kena'an, instructing them, "Go on up to the Negev and into the hills, ¹⁸ and see what the land is like. Notice the people living there, whether they are strong or weak, few or many; ¹⁹ and what kind of country they live in, whether it is good or bad; and what kind of cities they live in, open or fortified. ²⁰ See whether the land is fertile or unproductive and whether there is wood in it or not. Finally, be bold enough to bring back some of the fruit of the land."

When they left it was the season for the first grapes to ripen. *(ii)* ²¹ They went up and reconnoitered the land from the Tzin Desert to Rechov near the entrance to Hamat. ²² They went up into the Negev and arrived at Hevron; Achiman, Sheshai and Talmai, the 'Anakim, lived there. (Hevron was built seven years before Tzo'an in Egypt.) ²³ They came to the Eshkol Valley; and there they cut off a branch bearing one cluster of grapes, which they carried on a pole between two of them; they also took pomegranates and figs. ²⁴ That place was called the Valley of Eshkol [cluster], because of the cluster which the people of Isra'el cut down there.

²⁵ Forty days later, they returned from reconnoitering the land ²⁶ and went to Moshe, Aharon and the entire community of the people of Isra'el at Kadesh in the Pa'ran Desert, where they brought back word to them and to the entire community and showed them the fruit of the land. ²⁷ What they told him was this: "We entered the land where you sent us, and indeed it does flow with milk and honey — here is its fruit! ²⁸ However the people living in the land are fierce, and the cities are fortified and very large. Moreover, we saw the 'Anakim there. ²⁹ 'Amalek lives in the area of the Negev; the Hitti, the Y'vusi and the Emori live in the hills; and the Kena'ani live by the sea and alongside the Yarden."

³⁰ Kalev silenced the people around Moshe and said, "We ought to go up immediately and take possession of it; there is no question that we can conquer it." ³¹ But the men who had gone with him said, "We can't attack those people, because they are stronger than we are"; ³² and they spread a negative report about the land they had reconnoitered for the people of Isra'el by saying, "The land we passed through in order to spy it out is a land that devours its inhabitants. All the people we saw there were giant! ³³ We saw the N'filim, the descendants of 'Anak, who was from the N'filim; to ourselves we looked like grasshoppers by comparison, and we looked that way to them too!"

14 ¹ At this all the people of Isra'el cried out in dismay and wept all night long. ² Moreover, all the people of Isra'el began grumbling against Moshe and Aharon; the whole community told them, "We wish we had died in the land of Egypt! or that we had died here in the desert! ³ Why is ADONAI bringing us to this land, where we will die by the sword? Our wives and our little ones will be taken as booty! Wouldn't it be better for us to return to Egypt?" ⁴ And they said to each other, "Let's appoint a leader and return to Egypt!"

⁵ Moshe and Aharon fell on their faces before the entire assembled community of the people of Isra'el. ⁶ Y'hoshua the son of Nun and Kalev the son of Y'funeh, from the detachment that had reconnoitered the land, tore their clothes ⁷ and said to the whole community of Isra'el, "The land we passed through in order to spy it out is an outstandingly good land! *(iii)* ⁸ If *Adonai* is pleased with us, then he will bring us into this land and give it to us — a land flowing with milk and honey. ⁹ Just don't rebel against *Adonai*. And don't be afraid of the people living in the land — we'll eat them up! Their defense has been taken away from them, and *Adonai* is with us! Don't be afraid of them!"

¹⁰ But just as the whole community were saying they should be stoned to death, the glory of *Adonai* appeared in the tent of meeting to all the people of Isra'el. ¹¹ *Adonai* said to Moshe, "How much longer is this people going to treat me with contempt? How much longer will they not trust me, especially considering all the signs I have performed among them? ¹² I am going to strike them with sickness, destroy them and make from you a nation greater and stronger than they are!"

¹³ However, Moshe replied to *Adonai*, "When the Egyptians hear about this — [and they will,] because it was from among them that you, by your strength, brought this people up — ¹⁴ they will tell the people living in this land. They have heard that you, *Adonai*, are with this people; that you, *Adonai*, are seen face to face; that your cloud stands over them; that you go ahead of them in a column of cloud by day and a column of fire by night. ¹⁵ If you kill off this people at a single stroke, then the nations that have heard of your reputation will say ¹⁶ that the reason *Adonai* slaughtered this people in the desert is that he wasn't able to bring them into the land which he swore to give them. ¹⁷ So now, please, let *Adonai*'s power be as great as when you said, ¹⁸ '*Adonai* is slow to anger, rich in grace, forgiving offenses and crimes; yet not exonerating the guilty, but causing the negative effects of the parents' offenses to be experienced by their children and even by the third and fourth generations.' ¹⁹ Please! Forgive the offense of this people according to the greatness of your grace, just as you have borne with this people from Egypt until now."

²⁰ *Adonai* answered, "I have forgiven, as you have asked. ²¹ But as sure as I live, and that the whole earth is filled with the glory of *Adonai*, ²² none of the people who saw my glory and the signs I did in Egypt and in the desert, yet tested me these ten times and did not listen to my voice, ²³ will see the land I swore to their ancestors! None of those who treated me with contempt will see it. ²⁴ But my servant Kalev, because he had a different Spirit with him and has fully followed me — him I will bring into the land he entered, and it will belong to his descendants.

²⁵ "Now, since the 'Amaleki and the Kena'ani are living in the valley, tomorrow turn around and get yourselves into the desert along the way to the Sea of *Suf*."

(iv) ²⁶ *Adonai* said to Moshe and Aharon, ²⁷ "How long am I to put up with this evil community who keep grumbling about me? I have heard the complaints of the people of Isra'el, which they continue to raise against me. ²⁸ Tell them this: 'As surely as I live, *Adonai* swears, as surely as you have spoken in my ears, I will do this to you: ²⁹ your carcasses will fall in this desert! Every single one of you who were included in the census over the age of twenty, you who have complained against me,

³⁰ will certainly not enter the land about which I raised my hand to swear that I would have you live in it — except for Kalev the son of Y'funeh and Y'hoshua the son of Nun. ³¹ But your little ones, who you said would be taken as booty — them I will bring in. They will know the land you have rejected. ³² But you, your carcasses will fall in this desert; ³³ and your children will wander about in the desert for forty years bearing the consequences of your prostitutions until the desert eats up your carcasses. ³⁴ It will be a year for every day you spent reconnoitering the land that you will bear the consequences of your offenses — forty days, forty years. Then you will know what it means to oppose me! ³⁵ I, ADONAI, have spoken.' I will certainly do this to this whole evil community who have assembled together against me — they will be destroyed in this desert and die there."

³⁶ The men whom Moshe had sent to reconnoiter the land and who, when they returned, made the entire community complain against him by giving an unfavorable report about the land — ³⁷ those men who gave the unfavorable report about the land died by the plague in the presence of ADONAI. ³⁸ Of the men who went to reconnoiter the land, only Y'hoshua the son of Nun and Kalev the son of Y'funeh remained alive.

³⁹ When Moshe told these things to all the people of Isra'el, the people felt great remorse. ⁴⁰ They arose early the next morning, came up to the top of the mountain and said, "Here we are, and we did sin, but now we'll go up to the place ADONAI promised." ⁴¹ Moshe answered, "Why are you opposing what ADONAI said? You won't succeed! ⁴² Don't go up there, because ADONAI isn't with you. If you do, your enemies will defeat you. ⁴³ The 'Amalekim and the Kena'anim are there ahead of you, and you will be struck down by the sword. The reason will be that you have turned away from following ADONAI, so that ADONAI won't be with you."

⁴⁴ But they were presumptuous and went on up toward the high parts of the hill-country, even though the ark for the covenant of ADONAI — and Moshe — stayed in the camp. ⁴⁵ So the 'Amalekim and the Kena'anim living in that hill-country descended, struck them down and beat them back all the way to Hormah.

15 ¹ ADONAI said to Moshe, ² "Tell the people of Isra'el, 'When you have come into the land where you are going to live, which I am giving to you, ³ and want to make an offering by fire to ADONAI — a burnt offering or sacrifice to fulfill a special vow, or to be a voluntary offering, or at your designated times, to make a fragrant aroma for ADONAI — then, whether it comes from the herd or from the flock, ⁴ the person bringing the offering is to present ADONAI with a grain offering consisting of two quarts of fine flour mixed with one quart of olive oil, ⁵ and one quart of wine for the drink offering. This is what you are to prepare with the burnt offering or for each lamb sacrificed.

⁶ "'For a ram, prepare one gallon of fine flour mixed with one-and-one-third quarts of olive oil; ⁷ while for the drink offering, you are to present one-and-one-third quarts of wine as a fragrant aroma for ADONAI.

(v) ⁸ "'When you prepare a bull as a burnt offering, as a sacrifice to fulfill a special vow or as peace offerings for ADONAI, ⁹ there is to be presented with the bull a grain offering of one-and-a-half gallons of fine flour mixed with two quarts of olive oil. ¹⁰ For the drink offering, present two quarts of wine for an offering made by fire, a fragant aroma for ADONAI.

^{11} "'Do it this way for each bull, ram, male lamb or kid. ^{12} For as many animals as you prepare, do this for each one, regardless of how many animals there are.

^{13} "'Every citizen is to do these things in this way when presenting an offering made by fire as a fragrant aroma for ADONAI. ^{14} If a foreigner stays with you — or whoever may be with you, through all your generations — and he wants to bring an offering made by fire as a fragrant aroma for ADONAI, he is to do the same as you. ^{15} For this community there will be the same law for you as for the foreigner living with you; this is a permanent regulation through all your generations; the foreigner is to be treated the same way before ADONAI as yourselves. ^{16} The same *Torah* and standard of judgment will apply to both you and the foreigner living with you.'"

(vi) ^{17} ADONAI said to Moshe, ^{18} "Speak to the people of Isra'el; tell them, 'When you enter the land where I am bringing you ^{19} and eat bread produced in the land, you are to set aside a portion as a gift for ADONAI. ^{20} Set aside from your first dough a cake as a gift; set it aside as you would set aside a portion of the grain from the threshing-floor. ^{21} From your first dough you will give ADONAI a portion as a gift through all your generations.

^{22} "'If by mistake you fail to observe all these *mitzvot* that ADONAI has spoken to Moshe, ^{23} yes, everything that ADONAI has ordered you to do through Moshe, from the day ADONAI gave the order and onward through all your generations, ^{24} then, if it was done by mistake by the community and was not known to them, the whole community is to offer one young bull for a burnt offering as a fragrant aroma to ADONAI, with its grain and drink offerings, in keeping with the rule, and one male goat as a sin offering. ^{25} The *cohen* is to make atonement for the whole community of the people of Isra'el; and they will be forgiven; because it was a mistake; and they have brought their offering, an offering made by fire, to ADONAI, and their sin offering before ADONAI for their mistake. ^{26} The whole community of the people of Isra'el will be forgiven, likewise the foreigner staying with them; because for all the people it was a mistake.

(vii) ^{27} "'If an individual sins by mistake, he is to offer a female goat in its first year as a sin offering. ^{28} The *cohen* will make atonement before ADONAI for the person who makes a mistake by sinning inadvertently; he will make atonement for him, and he will be forgiven — ^{29} no matter whether he is a citizen of Isra'el or a foreigner living with them. You are to have one law for whoever it is that does something wrong by mistake.

^{30} "'But an individual who does something wrong intentionally, whether a citizen or a foreigner, is blaspheming ADONAI. That person will be cut off from his people. ^{31} Because he has had contempt for the word of ADONAI and has disobeyed his command, that person will be cut off completely; his offense will remain with him.'"

^{32} While the people of Isra'el were in the desert, they found a man gathering wood on *Shabbat*. ^{33} Those who found him gathering wood brought him to Moshe, Aharon and the whole congregation. ^{34} They kept him in custody, because it had not yet been decided what to do to him. ^{35} Then ADONAI said to Moshe, "This man must be put to death; the entire community is to stone him to death outside the camp." ^{36} So the whole community brought him outside the camp and threw stones at him until he died, as ADONAI had ordered Moshe.

(Maftir) ³⁷ A*DONAI* said to Moshe, ³⁸ "Speak to the people of Isra'el, instructing them to make, through all their generations, *tzitziyot* on the corners of their garments, and to put with the *tzitzit* on each corner a blue thread. ³⁹ It is to be a *tzitzit* for you to look at and thereby remember all of A*DONAI*'s *mitzvot* and obey them, so that you won't go around wherever your own heart and eyes lead you to prostitute yourselves; ⁴⁰ but it will help you remember and obey all my *mitzvot* and be holy for your God. ⁴¹ I am A*DONAI* your God, who brought you out of the land of Egypt in order to be your God. I am A*DONAI* your God."

Haftarah Shlach L'kha: Y'hoshua (Joshua) 2:1–24

B'rit Hadashah suggested reading for Parashah Shlach L'kha: Messianic Jews (Hebrews) 3:7–19

Parashah 38: Korach (Korah) 16:1–18:32

16 ¹ Now Korach the son of Yitz'har, the son of K'hat, the son of Levi, along with Datan and Aviram, the sons of Eli'av, and On, the son of Pelet, descendants of Re'uven, took men and ² rebelled against Moshe. Siding with them were 250 men of Isra'el, leaders of the community, key members of the council, men of reputation. ³ They assembled themselves against Moshe and Aharon and said to them, "You take too much on yourselves! After all, the entire community is holy, every one of them, and A*DONAI* is among them. So why do you lift yourselves up above A*DONAI*'s assembly?"

⁴ When Moshe heard this he fell on his face. ⁵ Then he said to Korach and his whole group, "In the morning, A*DONAI* will show who are his and who is the holy person he will allow to approach him. Yes, he will bring whomever he chooses near to himself. ⁶ Do this: take censers, Korach and all your group; ⁷ put fire in them; and put incense in them before A*DONAI* tomorrow. The one whom A*DONAI* chooses will be the one who is holy! It is you, you sons of Levi, who are taking too much on yourselves!"

⁸ Then Moshe said to Korach, "Listen here, you sons of Levi! ⁹ Is it for you a mere trifle that the God of Isra'el has separated you from the community of Isra'el to bring you close to himself, so that you can do the work in the tabernacle of A*DONAI* and stand before the community serving them? ¹⁰ He has brought you close and all your brothers the sons of Levi with you. Now you want the office of *cohen* too! ¹¹ That's why you and your group have gathered together against A*DONAI*! After all, what is Aharon that you complain against him?"

¹² Then Moshe sent to summon Datan and Aviram, the sons of Eli'av. But they replied, "We won't come up! ¹³ Is it such a mere trifle, bringing us up from a land flowing with milk and honey to kill us in the desert, that now you arrogate to yourself the role of dictator over us? *(ii)* ¹⁴ You haven't at all brought us into a land flowing with milk and honey, and you haven't put us in possession of fields and vineyards. Do you think you can gouge out these men's eyes and blind them? We won't come up!"

¹⁵ Moshe was very angry and said to A*DONAI*, "Don't accept their grain offering! I haven't taken one donkey from them, I've done nothing wrong to any of them."

¹⁶ Moshe said to Korach, "You and your group, be there before ADONAI tomorrow — you, they and Aharon. ¹⁷ Each of you take his fire pan and put incense in it; every one of you, bring before ADONAI his fire pan, 250 fire pans, you too, and Aharon — each one his fire pan."

¹⁸ Each man took his fire pan, put fire in it, laid incense on it and stood at the entrance to the tent of meeting with Moshe and Aharon. ¹⁹ Korach assembled all the group who were against them at the entrance to the tent of meeting. Then the glory of ADONAI appeared to the whole assembly.

(iii) ²⁰ ADONAI said to Moshe and Aharon, ²¹ "Separate yourselves from this assembly; I'm going to destroy them right now!" ²² They fell on their faces and said, "Oh God, God of the spirits of all humankind, if one person sins, are you going to be angry with the entire assembly?" ²³ ADONAI answered Moshe, ²⁴ "Tell the assembly to move away from the homes of Korach, Datan and Aviram." ²⁵ Moshe got up and went to Datan and Aviram, and the leaders of Isra'el followed him. ²⁶ There he said to the assembly, "Leave the tents of these wicked men! Don't touch anything that belongs to them, or you may be swept away in all their sins." ²⁷ So they moved away from all around the area where Korach, Datan and Aviram lived.

Then Datan and Aviram came out and stood at the entrance to their tents with their wives, sons and little ones. ²⁸ Moshe said, "Here is how you will know that ADONAI has sent me to do all these things and that I haven't done them out of my own ambition: ²⁹ if these men die a natural death like other people, only sharing the fate common to all humanity, then ADONAI has not sent me. ³⁰ But if ADONAI does something new — if the ground opens up and swallows them with everything they own, and they go down alive to Sh'ol — then you will understand that these men have had contempt for ADONAI."

³¹ The moment he finished speaking, the ground under them split apart — ³² the earth opened its mouth and swallowed them up with their households, all the people who had sided with Korach and everything they owned. ³³ So they and everything they owned went down alive into Sh'ol, the earth closed over them and their existence in the community ceased. ³⁴ All Isra'el around them fled at their shrieks, shouting, "The earth might swallow us too!" ³⁵ Then fire came out from ADONAI and destroyed the 250 men who had offered the incense.

17 ¹⁽¹⁶:³⁶⁾ ADONAI said to Moshe, ²⁽¹⁶:³⁷⁾ "Tell El'azar the son of Aharon the *cohen* to remove the fire pans from the fire, and scatter the smoldering coals at a distance, because they have become holy. ³⁽¹⁶:³⁸⁾ Also the fire pans of these men, whose sin cost them their lives, have become holy, because they were offered before ADONAI. Therefore, have them hammered into plates to cover the altar. This will be a sign for the people of Isra'el."

⁴⁽¹⁶:³⁹⁾ El'azar the *cohen* took the brass fire pans which the men who had been burned to death had offered, and they hammered them into a covering for the altar, ⁵⁽¹⁶:⁴⁰⁾ to remind the people of Isra'el that an ordinary person, not descended from Aharon, is not to approach and burn incense before ADONAI, if he wants to avoid the fate of Korach and his group — as ADONAI had said to him through Moshe.

⁶⁽¹⁶:⁴¹⁾ But the very next day, the whole community of the people of Isra'el complained against Moshe and Aharon: "You have killed ADONAI's people!" ⁷⁽¹⁶:⁴²⁾ However, as the community was assembling against Moshe and Aharon, they looked in

the direction of the tent of meeting and saw the cloud cover it and the glory of ADONAI appear. ⁸⁽¹⁶:⁴³⁾ Moshe and Aharon came to the front of the tent of meeting.

(iv) ⁹⁽¹⁶:⁴⁴⁾ ADONAI said to Moshe, ¹⁰⁽¹⁶:⁴⁵⁾ "Get away from this assembly, and I will destroy them at once!" But they fell on their faces. ¹¹⁽¹⁶:⁴⁶⁾ Moshe said to Aharon, "Take your fire pan, put fire from the altar in it, lay incense on it, and hurry with it to the assembly to make atonement for them, because anger has gone out from ADONAI, and the plague has already begun!" ¹²⁽¹⁶:⁴⁷⁾ Aharon took it, as Moshe had said, and ran into the middle of the assembly. There the plague had already begun among the people, but he added the incense and made atonement for the people. ¹³⁽¹⁶:⁴⁸⁾ He stood between the dead and the living, and the plague was stopped. ¹⁴⁽¹⁶:⁴⁹⁾ Those dying from the plague numbered 14,700 — besides those who died in the Korach incident. ¹⁵⁽¹⁶:⁵⁰⁾ Aharon returned to Moshe at the entrance to the tent of meeting, and the plague was stopped.

(v) ¹⁶⁽¹⁾ ADONAI said to Moshe, ¹⁷⁽²⁾ "Speak to the people of Isra'el, and take from them staffs, one for each ancestral tribe from each leader of a tribe, twelve staffs. Write each man's name on his staff; ¹⁸⁽³⁾ and write Aharon's name on the staff of Levi, for each tribe's leader is to have one staff. ¹⁹⁽⁴⁾ Put them in the tent of meeting in front of the testimony, where I meet with you. ²⁰⁽⁵⁾ The staff of the man I am going to choose will sprout buds — in this way I will put a stop to the complaints the people of Isra'el keep making against you."

²¹⁽⁶⁾ Moshe spoke to the people of Isra'el, and all their leaders gave him staffs, one for each leader, according to their ancestral tribes, twelve staffs. Aharon's staff was among their staffs. ²²⁽⁷⁾ Moshe put the staffs before ADONAI in the tent of the testimony. ²³⁽⁸⁾ The next day Moshe went into the tent of the testimony, and there he saw that Aharon's staff for the house of Levi had budded — it had sprouted not only buds but flowers and ripe almonds as well. ²⁴⁽⁹⁾ Moshe brought out all the staffs from before ADONAI to all the people of Isra'el, and they looked, and each man took back his staff.

(vi) ²⁵⁽¹⁰⁾ ADONAI said to Moshe, "Return Aharon's staff to its place in front of the testimony. It is to be kept there as a sign to the rebels, so that they will stop grumbling against me and thus not die." ²⁶⁽¹¹⁾ Moshe did this; he did as ADONAI had ordered him.

²⁷⁽¹²⁾ But the people of Isra'el said to Moshe, "Oh no! We're dead men! Lost! We're all lost! ²⁸⁽¹³⁾ Whenever anyone approaches the tabernacle of ADONAI, he dies! Will we all perish?"

18 ¹ ADONAI said to Aharon, "You, your sons and your father's family line will be responsible for anything that goes wrong in the sanctuary. You and your sons with you will be responsible for anything wrong in your service as *cohanim*. ² But you are to bring your kinsmen, the tribe of Levi, along with yourselves, to work together with you and help you — you and your sons with you — when you are there before the tent of meeting. ³ They are to be at your disposal and perform all kinds of tasks related to the tent; only they are not to come near the holy furnishings or the altar, so that neither they nor you will die. ⁴ They will work together with you in your duties related to the tent of meeting, whatever the service in the tent may be; but an unauthorized person is not to come near you. ⁵ You will take charge of all the holy things and the altar, so that there will no longer be anger against the people of Isra'el. ⁶ I myself have taken your kinsmen the *L'vi'im* from among the people of Isra'el;

they have been given as a gift to ADONAI for you, so that you can perform the service in the tent of meeting. ⁷ You and your sons with you will exercise your prerogatives and duties as *cohanim* in regard to everything having to do with the altar and within the curtain. I entrust the service required of *cohanim* to you; the unauthorized person who tries to perform it is to be put to death."

⁸ ADONAI said to Aharon, "I myself have put you in charge of the contributions given to me. Everything consecrated by the people of Isra'el I have given and set aside for you and your sons; this is a perpetual law. ⁹ Here is what is to be yours of the especially holy things taken from the fire: every offering they make — that is, every grain offering, sin offering and guilt offering of theirs that they turn over to me — will be especially holy for you and your sons. ¹⁰ You are to eat it in an especially holy place; every male may eat it; it will be set apart for you.

¹¹ "Also yours is the contribution the people of Isra'el give in the form of wave offerings. I have given these to you, your sons and your daughters with you; this is a perpetual law. Everyone in your family who is clean may eat it. ¹² All the best of the olive oil, wine and grain, the first portion of what they give to ADONAI, I have given to you. ¹³ The first produce to turn ripe of all that is in their land, which they bring to ADONAI, is to be yours; every clean person in your family may eat it.

¹⁴ "Everything in Isra'el which has been consecrated unconditionally is to be yours.

¹⁵ "Everything that comes first out of the womb, of all living things which they offer to ADONAI, whether human or animal, will be yours. However, the firstborn of a human being you must redeem, and the firstborn of an unclean beast you are to redeem. ¹⁶ The sum to be paid for redeeming anyone a month old or over is to be five *shekel*s of silver [two ounces], as you value it, using the sanctuary *shekel* (this is the same as twenty *gerah*s). ¹⁷ But the firstborn of an ox, sheep or goat you are not to redeem; they are holy — you are to splash their blood against the altar and make their fat go up in smoke as an offering made by fire, as a fragrant aroma for ADONAI. ¹⁸ Their meat will be yours, like the breast that is waved and the right thigh — they will be yours. ¹⁹ All the contributions of holy things which the people of Isra'el offer to ADONAI I have given to you, your sons and your daughters with you; this is a perpetual law, an eternal covenant of salt before ADONAI for you and your descendants with you."

²⁰ ADONAI said to Aharon, "You are not to have any inheritance or portion in their land; I am your portion and inheritance among the people of Isra'el.

(vii) ²¹ "To the descendants of Levi I have given the entire tenth of the produce collected in Isra'el. It is their inheritance in payment for the service they render in the tent of meeting. ²² From now on, the people of Isra'el are not to approach the tent of meeting, so that they will not bear the consequences of their sin and die. ²³ Only the *L'vi'im* are to perform the service in the tent of meeting, and they will be responsible for whatever they do wrong. This is to be a permanent regulation through all your generations. They are to have no inheritance among the people of Isra'el, ²⁴ because I have given to the *L'vi'im* as their inheritance the tenths of the produce which the people of Isra'el set aside as a gift for ADONAI. This is why I have said to them that they are to have no inheritance among the people of Isra'el."

²⁵ ADONAI said to Moshe, ²⁶ "Tell the *L'vi'im*, 'When you take from the people of Isra'el the tenth of the produce which I have given you from them as your inheritance, you are to set aside from it a gift for ADONAI, one tenth of the tenth.

²⁷ The gift you set aside will be accounted to you as if it were grain from the thresh-ing-floor and grape juice from the wine vat. ²⁸ In this way you will set aside a gift for ADONAI from all your tenths that you receive from the people of Isra'el, and from these tenths you are to give to Aharon the *cohen* the gift set aside for ADONAI. ²⁹ From everything given to you, you are to set aside all that is due ADONAI, the best part of it, its holy portion.'

(Maftir) ³⁰ "Therefore you are to tell them, 'When you set aside from it its best part, it will be accounted to the *L'vi'im* as if it were grain from the threshing-floor and grape juice from the wine vat. ³¹ You may eat it anywhere, you and your house-holds; because it is your payment in return for your service in the tent of meeting. ³² Moreover, because you will have set aside from it its best parts, you will not be committing any sin because of it; for you are not to profane the holy things of the people of Isra'el, or you will die.'"

Haftarah Korach: Sh'mu'el Alef (1 Samuel) 11:14–12:22

B'rit Hadashah suggested readings for Parashah Korach: 2 Timothy 2:8–21; Y'hudah (Jude) 1–25

Parashah 39: Hukkat (Regulation) 19:1–22:1
[In regular years read with Parashah 40, in leap years read separately]

19 ¹ ADONAI said to Moshe and Aharon, ² "This is the regulation from the *Torah* which ADONAI has commanded. Tell the people of Isra'el to bring you a young red female cow without fault or defect and which has never borne a yoke. ³ You are to give it to El'azar the *cohen*; it is to be brought outside the camp and slaughtered in front of him. ⁴ El'azar the *cohen* is to take some of its blood with his finger and sprinkle this blood toward the front of the tent of meeting seven times. ⁵ The heifer is to be burned to ashes before his eyes—its skin, meat, blood and dung is to be burned to ashes. ⁶ The *cohen* is to take cedar-wood, hyssop and scarlet yarn and throw them onto the heifer as it is burning up. ⁷ Then the *cohen* is to wash his clothes and himself in water, after which he may re-enter the camp; but the *cohen* will remain unclean until evening. ⁸ The person who burned up the heifer is to wash his clothes and himself in water, but he will remain unclean until evening. ⁹ A man who is clean is to collect the ashes of the heifer and store them outside the camp in a clean place. They are to be kept for the community of the people of Isra'el to prepare water for purification from sin. ¹⁰ The one who collected the ashes of the heifer is to wash his clothes and be unclean until evening. For the people of Isra'el and for the foreigner staying with them this will be a permanent regulation.

¹¹ "Anyone who touches a corpse, no matter whose dead body it is, will be unclean for seven days. ¹² He must purify himself with [these ashes] on the third and seventh days; then he will be clean. But if he does not purify himself the third and seventh days, he will not be clean. ¹³ Anyone who touches a corpse, no matter whose dead body it is, and does not purify himself has defiled the tabernacle of ADONAI. That person will be cut off from Isra'el, because the water for purification was not sprinkled on him. He will be unclean; his uncleanness is still on him.

¹⁴ "This is the law: when a person dies in a tent, everyone who enters the tent and everything in the tent will be unclean for seven days. ¹⁵ Every open container without a cover closely attached is unclean. ¹⁶ Also whoever is in an open field and touches a corpse, whether of someone killed by a weapon or of someone who died naturally, or the bone of a person, or a grave, will be unclean for seven days.

¹⁷ "For the unclean person they are to take some of the ashes of the animal burned up as a purification from sin and add them to fresh water in a container. *(LY: ii)* ¹⁸ A clean person is to take a bunch of hyssop leaves, dip it in the water and sprinkle it on the tent, on all the containers, on the people who were there, and on the person who touched the bone or the person killed or the one who died naturally or the grave. ¹⁹ The clean person will sprinkle the unclean person on the third and seventh days. On the seventh day he will purify him; then he will wash his clothes and himself in water; and he will be clean at evening. ²⁰ The person who remains unclean and does not purify himself will be cut off from the community because he has defiled the sanctuary of ADONAI. The water for purification has not been sprinkled on him; he is unclean. ²¹ This is to be a permanent regulation for them. The person who sprinkles the water for purification is to wash his clothes. Whoever touches the water for purification will be unclean until evening. ²² Anything the unclean person touches will be unclean, and anyone who touches him will be unclean until evening."

20 ¹ The people of Isra'el, the whole community, entered the Tzin Desert in the first month, and they stayed in Kadesh. There Miryam died, and there she was buried.

² Because the community had no water, they assembled themselves against Moshe and Aharon. ³ The people quarreled with Moshe and said, "We wish we had died when our brothers died before ADONAI. ⁴ Why did you bring ADONAI's community into this desert? To die there, we and our livestock? ⁵ Why did you make us leave Egypt? To bring us to this terrible place without seed, figs, grapevines, pomegranates or even water to drink?" ⁶ Moshe and Aharon left the assembly, went to the entrance of the tent of meeting and fell on their faces; and the glory of ADONAI appeared to them.

(RY: ii, LY: iii) ⁷ ADONAI said to Moshe, ⁸ "Take the staff, assemble the community, you and Aharon your brother; and before their eyes, tell the rock to produce its water. You will bring them water out of the rock and thus enable the community and their livestock to drink." ⁹ Moshe took the staff from the presence of ADONAI, as he had ordered him. ¹⁰ But after Moshe and Aharon had assembled the community in front of the rock, he said to them, "Listen here, you rebels! Are we supposed to bring you water from this rock?" ¹¹ Then Moshe raised his hand and hit the rock twice with his staff. Water flowed out in abundance, and the community and their livestock drank.

¹² But ADONAI said to Moshe and Aharon, "Because you did not trust in me, so as to cause me to be regarded as holy by the people of Isra'el, you will not bring this community into the land I have given them." ¹³ This is M'rivah Spring [Disputation Spring], where the people of Isra'el disputed with ADONAI, and he was caused to be regarded as holy by them.

(LY: iv) ¹⁴ Moshe sent messengers from Kadesh to the king of Edom: "This is what your brother Isra'el says: you know all the troubles we have gone through — ¹⁵ that our ancestors went down into Egypt, we lived in Egypt a long time, and the Egyptians treated us and our ancestors badly. ¹⁶ But when we cried out to ADONAI, he heard us, sent an angel and brought us out of Egypt. Now here we are in Kadesh, a

city at the edge of your territory. ^{17} Please let us pass through your land. We will not go through fields or vineyards, and we won't drink any water from the wells. We will go along the King's Highway, not turning aside either to the right or to the left until we have left your territory."

^{18} But Edom answered, "You are not to pass through my land; if you do, I will come out against you with the sword." ^{19} The people of Isra'el replied, "We will keep to the highway; if we do drink the water, either we or our livestock, we will pay for it. Just let us pass through on foot — it's nothing." ^{20} But he said, "You are not to pass through"; and Edom came out against them with many people and much force. ^{21} Thus Edom refused to allow Isra'el passage through its territory, so Isra'el turned away.

(RY: iii, LY: v) ^{22} They traveled on from Kadesh; and the people of Isra'el, the whole community, arrived at Mount Hor. ^{23} At Mount Hor, by the border of the land of Edom, ADONAI said to Moshe and Aharon, ^{24} "Aharon is about to be gathered to his people, because he is not to enter the land I have given to the people of Isra'el, inasmuch as you rebelled against what I said at the M'rivah Spring. ^{25} Take Aharon and El'azar his son, bring them up to Mount Hor, ^{26} remove the garments from Aharon and put them on El'azar his son. Aharon will be gathered to his people — he will die there." ^{27} Moshe did as ADONAI had ordered. They went up onto Mount Hor before the eyes of the whole community. ^{28} Moshe removed the garments from Aharon, and put them on El'azar his son, and Aharon died there on the top of the mountain. Then Moshe and El'azar came down the mountain. ^{29} When the entire community saw that Aharon was dead, they mourned Aharon thirty days, the whole house of Isra'el.

21 ^{1} Then the king of 'Arad, a Kena'ani who lived in the Negev, heard that Isra'el was approaching by way of Atarim, so he attacked Isra'el and took some of them captive. ^{2} Isra'el made a vow to ADONAI, "If you will hand this people over to me, I will completely destroy their cities." ^{3} ADONAI listened to what Isra'el said and handed over the Kena'anim, so they completely destroyed them and their cities and named the place Hormah [complete destruction].

^{4} Then they traveled from Mount Hor on the road toward the Sea of Suf in order to go around the land of Edom; but the people's tempers grew short because of the detour. ^{5} The people spoke against God and against Moshe: "Why did you bring us up out of Egypt? To die in the desert? There's no real food, there's no water, and we're sick of this miserable stuff we're eating!"

(LY: vi) ^{6} In response, ADONAI sent poisonous snakes among the people; they bit the people, and many of Isra'el's people died. ^{7} The people came to Moshe and said, "We sinned by speaking against ADONAI and against you. Pray to ADONAI that he rid us of these snakes." Moshe prayed for the people, ^{8} and ADONAI answered Moshe: "Make a poisonous snake and put it on a pole. When anyone who has been bitten sees it, he will live." ^{9} Moshe made a bronze snake and put it on the pole; if a snake had bitten someone, then, when he looked toward the bronze snake, he stayed alive.

^{10} The people of Isra'el traveled on and camped at Ovot. ^{11} From Ovot they traveled and camped at 'Iyei-Ha'avarim, in the desert fronting Mo'av on the east. ^{12} From there they traveled and camped in *Vadi* Zered. ^{13} From there they traveled and camped on the other side of the Arnon, in the desert; this river comes out of the territory of the Emori; for the Arnon is the boundary between Mo'av and the Emori. ^{14} This is why it says, in the Book of the Wars of ADONAI, ". . . Vahev at Sufah, the *vadi*s of Arnon,

¹⁵ and the slope of the *vadi*s extending as far as the site of 'Ar, which lie next to the territory of Mo'av."

¹⁶ From there they went on to Be'er [well]; that is the well about which ADONAI said to Moshe, "Assemble the people, and I will give them water." ¹⁷ Then Isra'el sang this song:

> "Spring up, oh well!
> Sing to the well
> ¹⁸ sunk by the princes,
> dug by the people's leaders
> with the scepter,
> with their staffs!"

From the desert they went to Mattanah, ¹⁹ from Mattanah to Nachali'el, from Nachali'el to Bamot, ²⁰ and from Bamot to the valley by the plain of Mo'av at the start of the Pisgah range, where it overlooks the desert.

(RY: iv, LY: vii) ²¹ Isra'el sent messengers to Sichon, king of the Emori, with this message: ²² "Let me pass through your land. We won't turn aside into fields or vineyards, and we won't drink any water from the wells. We will go along the King's Highway until we have left your territory." ²³ But Sichon would not allow Isra'el to pass through his territory. Instead, Sichon mustered all his people and went out into the desert to fight Isra'el. On reaching Yachatz, he fought Isra'el. ²⁴ Isra'el defeated him by force of arms and took control of his land from the Arnon to the Yabok River, but only as far as the people of 'Amon, because the territory of the people of 'Amon was well defended. ²⁵ Isra'el took all these cities — Isra'el lived in all the cities of the Emori, in Heshbon and all its surrounding towns. ²⁶ Heshbon was the city of Sichon, the king of the Emori, who had fought against the former king of Mo'av and conquered all his land up to the Arnon. ²⁷ This is why the storytellers say,

> "Come to Heshbon! Let it be rebuilt!
> Let Sichon's city be restored!
> ²⁸ "For fire burst out of Heshbon,
> a flame from the city of Sichon.
> It consumed 'Ar of Mo'av,
> the lords of Arnon's high places.
> ²⁹ "Woe to you, Mo'av!
> You are destroyed, people of K'mosh!
> He let his sons be fugitives and his daughters captives
> of Sichon, king of the Emori.
> ³⁰ "We shot them down; Heshbon is destroyed,
> all the way to Divon.
> We even laid waste to Nofach,
> which extends as far as Meidva."

³¹ Thus Isra'el lived in the land of the Emori. ³² Moshe sent men to reconnoiter Ya'zer; they captured its towns and drove out the Emori who were there. ³³ Then they turned and went up along the road to Bashan; and 'Og, the king of Bashan, marched out against them, he with all his people, to fight at Edre'i. *(LY: Maftir)* ³⁴ A_DONAI_ said to Moshe, "Don't be afraid of him, for I have handed him over to you with all his people and his land. You will treat him just as you did Sichon, king of the Emori, who lived at Heshbon." ³⁵ So they struck him down, with his sons and all his people, until there was no one left alive; and then they took control of his land.

22 ¹ Then the people of Isra'el traveled on and camped in the plains of Mo'av beyond the Yarden River, opposite Yericho.

Haftarah Hukkat: Shof'tim (Judges) 11:1–33

B'rit Hadashah suggested readings for Parashah Hukkat: Yochanan (John) 3:9–21; 4:3–30; 12:27–50

Parashah 40: Balak 22:2–25:9
[In regular years read with Parashah 39, in leap years read separately]

² Now Balak the son of Tzippor saw all that Isra'el had done to the Emori. ³ Mo'av was very afraid of the people, because there were so many of them; Mo'av was overcome with dread because of the people of Isra'el. ⁴ So Mo'av said to the leaders of Midyan, "This horde will lick up everything around us, the way an ox licks up grass in the field."

Balak the son of Tzippor was king of Mo'av at that time. ⁵ He sent messengers to Bil'am the son of B'or, at P'tor by the [Euphrates] River in his native land, to tell him, "Listen, a people has come out of Egypt, spread over all the land and settled down next to me. ⁶ Therefore, please come, and curse this people for me, because they are stronger than I am. Maybe I will be able to strike them down and drive them out of the land, for I know that whomever you bless is in fact blessed, and whomever you curse is in fact cursed." ⁷ The leaders of Mo'av and Midyan left, taking with them the payment for divining, came to Bil'am and spoke to him the words of Balak. ⁸ He said to them, "Stay here tonight, and I will bring you back whatever answer A_DONAI_ tells me." So the princes of Mo'av stayed with Bil'am.

⁹ God came to Bil'am and said, "Who are these men with you?" ¹⁰ Bil'am said to God, "Balak the son of Tzippor, king of Mo'av, has sent me this message: ¹¹ 'The people who came out of Egypt have spread over the land; now, come and curse them for me; maybe I will be able to fight against them and drive them out.'" ¹² God answered Bil'am, "You are not to go with them; you are not to curse the people, because they are blessed."

(RY: v; LY: ii) ¹³ Bil'am got up in the morning and said to the princes of Balak, "Return to your own land, because A_DONAI_ refuses to give me permission to

go with you." ^{14} The princes of Mo'av got up, returned to Balak and said, "Bil'am refuses to come with us."

^{15} Balak again sent princes, more of them and of higher status than the first group. ^{16} They went to Bil'am and said to him, "Here is what Balak the son of Tzippor says: 'Please don't let anything keep you from coming to me. ^{17} I will reward you very well, and whatever you say to me I will do. So please come, and curse this people for me.'" ^{18} Bil'am answered the servants of Balak, "Even if Balak were to give me his palace filled with silver and gold, I cannot go beyond the word of ADONAI my God to do anything, great or small. ^{19} Now, please, you too, stay here tonight; so that I may find out what else ADONAI will say to me." ^{20} God came to Bil'am during the night and said to him, "If the men have come to summon you, get up and go with them; but do only what I tell you."

(LY: iii) ^{21} So Bil'am got up in the morning, saddled his donkey and went with the princes of Mo'av. ^{22} But God's anger flared up because he went, and the angel of ADONAI stationed himself on the path to bar his way. He was riding on his donkey, and his two servants were with him. ^{23} The donkey saw the angel of ADONAI standing on the road, drawn sword in hand; so the donkey turned off the road into the field; and Bil'am had to beat the donkey to get it back on the road. ^{24} Then the angel of ADONAI stood on the road where it became narrow as it passed among the vineyards and had stone walls on both sides. ^{25} The donkey saw the angel of ADONAI and pushed up against the wall, crushing Bil'am's foot against the wall. So he beat it again. ^{26} The angel of ADONAI moved ahead and stood in a place so tight that there was no room to turn either right or left. ^{27} Again the donkey saw the angel of ADONAI and lay down under Bil'am, which made him so angry that he hit the donkey with his stick. ^{28} But ADONAI enabled the donkey to speak, and it said to Bil'am, "What have I done to you to make you beat me these three times?" ^{29} Bil'am said to the donkey, "It's because you've been making a fool of me! I wish I had a sword in my hand; I would kill you on the spot!" ^{30} The donkey said to Bil'am, "I'm your donkey, right? You've ridden me all your life, right? Have I ever treated you like this before?" "No," he admitted. ^{31} Then ADONAI opened Bil'am's eyes, so that he could see the angel of ADONAI standing in the way with his drawn sword in his hand, and he bowed his head and fell on his face. ^{32} The angel of ADONAI said to him, "Why did you hit your donkey three times like that? I have come out here to bar your way, because you are rushing to oppose me. ^{33} The donkey saw me and turned aside these three times; and indeed, if she hadn't turned away from me, I would have killed you by now and saved it alive!" ^{34} Bil'am said to the angel of ADONAI, "I have sinned. I didn't know that you were standing on the road to block me. Now, therefore, if what I am doing displeases you, I will go back." ^{35} But the angel of ADONAI said to Bil'am, "No, go on with the men; but you are to say only what I tell you to say." So Bil'am went along with the princes of Balak.

^{36} When Balak heard that Bil'am had come, he went out to meet him in the city of Mo'av at the Arnon border, in the farthest reaches of the territory. ^{37} Balak said to Bil'am, "I sent more than once to summon you! Why didn't you come to me? Did you think I couldn't pay you enough?" ^{38} Bil'am replied to Balak, "Here, I've come to you! But I have no power of my own to say anything. The word that God puts in my mouth is what I will say."

(RY: vi, LY: iv) ³⁹ Bil'am went with Balak. When they arrived at Kiryat-Hutzot, ⁴⁰ Balak sacrificed cattle and sheep, then sent to Bil'am and the princes with him. ⁴¹ In the morning Balak took Bil'am and brought him up to the high places of Ba'al; from there he could see a portion of the people.

23 ¹ Bil'am said to Balak, "Build me seven altars here, and prepare me seven bulls and seven rams here." ² Balak did as Bil'am said; then Balak and Bil'am offered a bull and a ram on each altar. ³ Bil'am said to Balak, "Stand by your burnt offering while I go off; maybe ADONAI will come and meet me; and whatever he shows me I will tell you." He went off to a bare hill. ⁴ God met Bil'am, who said to him, "I prepared the seven altars and offered a bull and a ram on each altar." ⁵ Then ADONAI put a word in Bil'am's mouth and said, "Go on back to Balak, and speak as I tell you." ⁶ He went back to him, and there, standing by his burnt offering, he with all the princes of Mo'av, ⁷ he made his pronouncement:

> "Balak, the king of Mo'av,
> brings me from Aram, from the eastern hills, saying,
> 'Come, curse Ya'akov for me;
> come and denounce Isra'el.'

⁸
> "How am I to curse
> those whom God has not cursed?
> How am I to denounce
> those whom ADONAI has not denounced?

⁹
> "From the top of the rocks I see them,
> from the hills I behold them —
> yes, a people that will dwell alone
> and not think itself one of the nations.

¹⁰
> "Who has counted the dust of Ya'akov
> or numbered the ashes of Isra'el?
> May I die as the righteous die!
> May my end be like theirs!"

¹¹ Balak said to Bil'am, "What have you done to me?! To curse my enemies is why I brought you; and, here, you have totally blessed them!" ¹² He answered, "Mustn't I take care to say just what ADONAI puts in my mouth?"

(LY: v) ¹³ Balak said to him, "All right, come with me to another place where you can see them. You will see only some of them, not all; but you can curse them for me from there." ¹⁴ He took him through the field of Tzofim to the top of the Pisgah Range, built seven altars and offered a bull and a ram on each altar. ¹⁵ Bil'am said to Balak, "Stand here by your burnt offering, while I go over there for a meeting." ¹⁶ ADONAI met Bil'am, put a word in his mouth and said, "Go on back to Balak, and speak as I tell you." ¹⁷ He came to him and stood by his burnt offering, with all the princes of Mo'av. Balak asked him, "What did ADONAI say?" ¹⁸ Then Bil'am made his pronouncement:

"Get up, Balak, and listen!
Turn your ears to me, son of Tzippor!

19 "God is not a human who lies
or a mortal who changes his mind.
When he says something, he will do it;
when he makes a promise, he will fulfill it.

20 Look, I am ordered to bless;
when he blesses, I can't reverse it.

21 "No one has seen guilt in Ya'akov,
or perceived perversity in Isra'el;
ADONAI their God is with them
and acclaimed as king among them.

22 "God, who brought them out of Egypt,
gives them the strength of a wild ox;
23 thus one can't put a spell on Ya'akov,
no magic will work against Isra'el.
It can now be said of Ya'akov and Isra'el,
'What is this that God has done?!'

24 "Here is a people rising up like a lioness;
like a lion he rears himself up —
he will not lie down till he eats up the prey
and drinks the blood of the slain."

^{25} Balak said to Bil'am, "Obviously, you won't curse them. But at least don't bless them!" ^{26} However, Bil'am answered Balak, "Didn't I warn you that I must do everything ADONAI says?"

(RY: vii, LY: vi) ^{27} Balak said to Bil'am, "Come, I will take you now to another place; maybe it will please God for you to curse them for me from there." ^{28} Balak took Bil'am to the top of P'or, overlooking the desert. ^{29} Bil'am said to Balak, "Build me seven altars here, and prepare me seven bulls and seven rams." ^{30} Balak did as Bil'am said and offered a bull and a ram on each altar.

24 ^{1} When Bil'am saw that it pleased ADONAI to bless Isra'el, he didn't go, as at the other times, to make use of divination, but looked out toward the desert. ^{2} Bil'am raised his eyes and saw Isra'el encamped tribe by tribe. Then the Spirit of God came upon him, ^{3} and he made his pronouncement:

"This is the speech of Bil'am, son of B'or;
the speech of the man whose eyes have been opened;
4 the speech of him who hears God's words;
who sees what *Shaddai* sees,
who has fallen, yet has open eyes:

5   "How lovely are your tents, Ya'akov;
        your encampments, Isra'el!
6   They spread out like valleys,
        like gardens by the riverside,
        like succulent aloes planted by ADONAI,
        like cedar trees next to the water.

7   "Water will flow from their branches,
        their seed will have water aplenty.
        Their king will be higher than Agag
        and his kingdom lifted high.
8   God, who brought them out of Egypt,
        gives them the strength of a wild ox.
        They will devour the nations opposing them,
        break their bones, pierce them with their arrows.

9   "When they lie down they crouch like a lion,
        or like a lioness — who dares to rouse it?
        Blessed be all who bless you!
        Cursed be all who curse you!"

10 Balak blazed with fury against Bil'am. He struck his hands together and said to Bil'am, "I summoned you to curse my enemies. But here, you have done nothing but bless them — three times already! 11 Now you had better escape to your own place! I had planned to reward you very well, but now ADONAI has deprived you of payment."

12 Bil'am answered Balak, "Didn't I tell the messengers you sent me 13 that even if Balak would give me his palace full of silver and gold, I could not of my own accord go beyond the word of ADONAI to do either good or bad? that what ADONAI said is what I would say? *(LY: vii)* 14 But now that I am going back to my own people, come, I will warn you what this people will do to your people in the *acharit-hayamim*. 15 So he made his pronouncement:

    "This is the speech of Bil'am, son of B'or;
        the speech of the man whose eyes have been opened;
16   the speech of him who hears God's words;
        who knows what *'Elyon* knows,
        who sees what *Shaddai* sees,
        who has fallen, yet has open eyes:

17   "I see him, but not now;
        I behold him, but not soon —
        a star will step forth from Ya'akov,
        a scepter will arise from Isra'el,
        to crush the corners of Mo'av
        and destroy all descendants of Shet.
18   His enemies will be his possessions —

Edom and Se'ir, possessions.
Isra'el will do valiantly,

19   From Ya'akov will come someone who will rule,
and he will destroy what is left of the city."

²⁰ He saw 'Amalek and made this pronouncement:

"First among nations was 'Amalek,
but destruction will be its end."

²¹ He saw the Keini and made this pronouncement:

"Though your dwelling is firm,
your nest set on rock,

22   Kayin will be wasted
while captive to Ashur."

²³ Finally, he made this pronouncement:

"Oh no! Who can live when God does this?

24   But ships will come from the coast of Kittim
to subdue Ashur and subdue 'Ever,
but they too will come to destruction."

²⁵ Then Bil'am got up, left and returned to his home; and Balak too went his way.

25 ¹ Isra'el stayed at Sheetim, and there the people began whoring with the women of Mo'av. ² These women invited the people to the sacrifices of their gods, where the people ate and bowed down to their gods. ³ With Isra'el thus joined to Ba'al-P'or, the anger of ADONAI blazed up against Isra'el.

⁴ ADONAI said to Moshe, "Take all the chiefs of the people, and hang them facing the sun before ADONAI, so that the raging fury of ADONAI will turn away from Isra'el." ⁵ Moshe said to the judges of Isra'el, "Each of you is to put to death those in his tribe who have joined themselves to Ba'al-P'or."

⁶ Just then, in the sight of Moshe and the whole community of Isra'el, as they were weeping at the entrance to the tent of meeting, a man from Isra'el came by, bringing to his family a woman from Midyan. *(Maftir)* ⁷ When Pinchas the son of El'azar, the son of Aharon the *cohen*, saw it, he got up from the middle of the crowd, took a spear in his hand, ⁸ and pursued the man from Isra'el right into the inner part of the tent, where he thrust his spear through both of them—the man from Isra'el and the woman through her stomach. Thus was the plague among the people of Isra'el stopped; ⁹ nevertheless, 24,000 died in the plague.

Haftarah Balak: Mikhah (Micah) 5:6(7)–6:8

*B'rit Hadashah suggested readings for Parashah Balak: 2 Kefa (2 Peter)
2:1–22; Y'hudah (Jude) 11; Revelation 2:14–15*

Parashah 41: Pinchas (Phinehas) 25:10–30:1(29:40)

¹⁰ *ADONAI* said to Moshe, ¹¹ "Pinchas the son of El'azar, the son of Aharon the *cohen*, has deflected my anger from the people of Isra'el by being as zealous as I am, so that I didn't destroy them in my own zeal. ¹² Therefore say, 'I am giving him my covenant of *shalom*, ¹³ making a covenant with him and his descendants after him that the office of *cohen* will be theirs forever.' This is because he was zealous on behalf of his God and made atonement for the people of Isra'el."

¹⁴ The name of the man from Isra'el who was killed, put to death with the woman from Midyan, was Zimri the son of Salu, leader of one of the clans from the tribe of Shim'on. ¹⁵ The name of the woman from Midyan who was killed was Kozbi the daughter of Tzur, and he was head of the people in one of the clans of Midyan.

¹⁶ *ADONAI* said to Moshe, ¹⁷ "Treat the Midyanim as enemies and attack them; ¹⁸ because they are treating you as enemies by the trickery they used to deceive you in the P'or incident and in the affair of their sister Kozbi, the daughter of the leader from Midyan, the woman who was killed on the day of the plague in the P'or incident."

¹⁹⁽²⁶:¹⁾ After the plague,

26 ¹ *ADONAI* said to Moshe and El'azar, the son of Aharon the *cohen*, ² "Take a census of the entire assembly of the people of Isra'el twenty years old and over, by their ancestral clans, all who are subject to military service in Isra'el." ³ Moshe and El'azar the *cohen* spoke with them on the plains of Mo'av by the Yarden across from Yericho, explaining, ⁴ "Those twenty years old and over who came out of the land of Egypt, as *ADONAI* ordered Moshe and the people of Isra'el."

(ii) ⁵ [The census results begin with] Re'uven, the firstborn of Isra'el. The descendants of Re'uven were: of Hanokh, the family of the Hanokhi; of Pallu, the family of the Pallu'i; ⁶ of Hetzron, the family of the Hetzroni; and of Karmi the family of the Karmi. ⁷ These were the the families of the Re'uveni; of them were counted 43,730. ⁸ The sons of Pallu: Eli'av; ⁹ and the sons of Eli'av: N'mu'el, Datan and Aviram. These are the same Datan and Aviram, men of reputation in the community, who rebelled against Moshe and Aharon in Korach's group, when they rebelled against *ADONAI*; ¹⁰ and the earth opened its mouth and swallowed them up together with Korach when that group died, and the fire consumed 250 men, and they became a warning sign. ¹¹ (However, the sons of Korach did not die.)

¹² The descendants of Shim'on, by their families, were: of N'mu'el, the family of the N'mu'eli; of Yamin, the family of the Yamini; of Yakhin, the family of the Yakhini; ¹³ of Zerach, the family of the Zarchi; and of Sha'ul, the family of the Sha'uli. ¹⁴ These were the families of the Shim'oni, 22,200.

¹⁵ The descendants of Gad, by their families, were: of Tz'fon, the family of the Tz'foni; of Haggi, the family of the Haggi; of Shuni, the family of the Shuni; ¹⁶ of Ozni, the family of the Ozni; of 'Eri, the family of the 'Eri; ¹⁷ of Arod, the family of the Arodi; and of Ar'eli, the family of the Ar'eli. ¹⁸ These were the families of the sons of Gad, according to those counted of them, 40,500.

¹⁹ The sons of Y'hudah: First 'Er and Onan, but 'Er and Onan died in the land of Kena'an. ²⁰ The sons of Y'hudah who had descendants were: of Shelah, the family of the Shelani; of Peretz, the family of the Partzi; and of Zerach, the family of the Zarchi. ²¹ The sons of Peretz were: of Hetzron, the family of the Hetzroni; and of

Hamul, the family of the Hamuli. ²² These were the families of Y'hudah, according to those counted of them, 76,500.

²³ The descendants of Yissakhar, by their families, were: of Tola, the family of the Tola'i; of Puvah, the family of the Puni; ²⁴ of Yashuv, the family of the Yashuvi; and of Shimron, the family of the Shimroni. ²⁵ These were the families of Yissakhar, according to those counted of them, 64,300.

²⁶ The descendants of Z'vulun, by their families, were: of Sered, the family of the Sardi; of Elon, the family of the Eloni; and of Yachle'el, the family of the Yachle'eli. ²⁷ These were the families of the Z'vuloni, according to those counted of them, 60,500.

²⁸ The sons of Yosef, by their families, were M'nasheh and Efrayim. ²⁹ The descendants of M'nasheh were: of Makhir, the family of the Makhiri. Makhir was the father of Gil'ad; of Gil'ad, the family of the Gil'adi. ³⁰ These are the descendants of Gil'ad: of I'ezer, the family of the I'ezri; of Helek, the family of the Helki; ³¹ of Asri'el, the family of the Asri'eli; of Sh'khem, the family of the Shikhmi; ³² of Sh'mida, the family of the Sh'mida'i; and of Hefer, the family of the Hefri. ³³ Tz'lof'chad the son of Hefer had no sons but daughters; the names of the daughters of Tz'lof'chad were Machlah, No'ah, Hoglah, Milkah and Tirtzah. ³⁴ These were the families of M'nasheh; of them were counted 52,700.

³⁵ These are the descendants of Efrayim, by their families: of Shutelach, the family of the Shutalchi; of Bekher, the family of the Bakhri; and of Tachan, the family of the Tachani. ³⁶ These are the descendants of Shutelach: of 'Eran, the family of the 'Erani. ³⁷ These were the families of the descendants of Efrayim, according to those of them that were counted, 32,500. These were the descendants of Yosef, by their families.

³⁸ The descendants of Binyamin, by their families were: of Bela, the family of the Bal'i; of Ashbel, the family of the Ashbeli; of Achiram, the family of the Achirami; ³⁹ of Sh'fufam, the family of the Shufami; and of Hufam, the family of the Hufami. ⁴⁰ The sons of Bela were Ard and Na'aman; [of Ard,] the family of the Ardi; and of Na'aman, the family of the Na'ami. ⁴¹ These were the descendants of Binyamin, by their families; of them were counted 45,600.

⁴² The descendants of Dan, by their families, were: of Shucham, the family of the Shuchami. These are the families of Dan, by their families. ⁴³ All the families of the Shuchami, according to those of them that were counted, were 64,400.

⁴⁴ The descendants of Asher, by their families: of Yimnah, the family of the Yimnah; of Yishvi, the family of the Yishvi; and of B'ri'ah, the family of the B'ri'i. ⁴⁵ Of the descendants of B'ri'ah: of Hever, the family of the Hevri; and of Malki'el, the family of the Malki'eli. ⁴⁶ The name of Asher's daughter was Serach. ⁴⁷ These were the families of the descendants of Asher, according to those of them that were counted, 53,400.

⁴⁸ The descendants of Naftali, by their families: of Yachtze'el, the families of the Yachtze'eli; of Guni, the family of the Guni; ⁴⁹ of Yetzer, the family of the Yitzri; and of Shillem, the family of the Shillemi. ⁵⁰ These are the families of Naftali according to their families; those of them that were counted were 45,400.

⁵¹ Thus those who were counted of the people of Isra'el numbered 601,730.

(iii) ⁵² ADONAI said to Moshe, ⁵³ "The land is to be parceled out among these as a possession to be inherited, according to the number of names. ⁵⁴ To those families

with more persons you are to give a greater inheritance, and to those with fewer you are to give a smaller inheritance — each family's inheritance is to be given according to the number counted in it. ⁵⁵ However, the land is to be awarded by lot. They will inherit according to the names of the tribes of their ancestors, ⁵⁶ but the inheritance is to be parceled out by lot between the families with more and those with fewer."

⁵⁷ Those counted among the Levi, by their families, were: of Gershon, the family of the Gershuni, of K'hat, the family of the K'hati; and of M'rari, the family of the M'rari. ⁵⁸ These are the families of Levi: the family of the Livni, the family of the Hevroni, the family of the Machli, the family of the Mushi and the family of the Korchi. K'hat was the father of 'Amram. ⁵⁹ The name of 'Amram's wife was Yokheved the daughter of Levi, who was born to Levi in Egypt; and she bore to 'Amram Aharon, Moshe and their sister Miryam. ⁶⁰ To Aharon were born Nadav, Avihu, El'azar and Itamar; ⁶¹ but Nadav and Avihu died when they offered unauthorized fire before ADONAI. ⁶² Those males one month old or more counted of the Levi were 23,000. These were not included in the census of the people of Isra'el, because no land for inheritance was given to them among the people of Isra'el.

⁶³ These are the ones counted by Moshe and El'azar the *cohen*, who took a census of the people of Isra'el in the plains of Mo'av by the Yarden across from Yericho. ⁶⁴ But there was not a man among them who had also been included in the census of Moshe and Aharon the *cohen* when they enumerated the people of Isra'el in the Sinai Desert; ⁶⁵ because ADONAI had said of them, "They will surely die in the desert." So there was not left even one of them, except Kalev the son of Y'funeh and Y'hoshua the son of Nun.

27 ¹ Then the daughters of Tz'lof'chad the son of Hefer, the son of Gil'ad, the son of Machir, the son of M'nasheh, of the families of M'nasheh, the son of Yosef, approached. These were the names of his daughters: Machlah, No'ah, Hoglah, Milkah and Tirtzah. ² They stood in front of Moshe, El'azar the *cohen*, the leaders and the whole community at the entrance to the tent of meeting and said, ³ "Our father died in the desert. He wasn't part of the group who assembled themselves to rebel against ADONAI in Korach's group, but he died in his own sin, and he had no sons. ⁴ Why should the name of our father be eliminated from his family just because he didn't have a son? Give us property to possess along with the brothers of our father." ⁵ Moshe brought their cause before ADONAI.

(iv) ⁶ ADONAI answered Moshe, ⁷ "The daughters of Tz'lof'chad are right in what they say. You must give them property to be inherited along with that of their father's brothers; have what their father would have inherited pass to them. ⁸ Moreover, say to the people of Isra'el, 'If a man dies and does not have a son, you are to have his inheritance pass to his daughter. ⁹ If he doesn't have a daughter, give his inheritance to his brothers. ¹⁰ If he has no brothers, give his inheritance to his father's brothers. ¹¹ If his father doesn't have brothers, give his inheritance to the closest relative in his family, and he will possess it. This will be the standard for judgment to be used by the people of Isra'el, as ADONAI ordered Moshe.'"

¹² ADONAI said to Moshe, "Climb this mountain in the 'Avarim Range, and look out at the land which I have given the people of Isra'el. ¹³ After you have seen it, you too will be gathered to your people, just as Aharon your brother was gathered; ¹⁴ because in the Tzin Desert, when the community was disputing with me, you

rebelled against my order to uphold my holiness by means of the water, with them looking on." (This was M'rivat-Kadesh Spring, in the Tzin Desert.)

¹⁵ Moshe said to ADONAI, ¹⁶ "Let ADONAI, God of the spirits of all human beings, appoint a man to be over the community, ¹⁷ to go out and come in ahead of them, to lead them out and bring them in, so that ADONAI's community will not be like sheep without a shepherd."

¹⁸ ADONAI said to Moshe, "Take Y'hoshua the son of Nun, a spiritual man, and lay your hand on him. ¹⁹ Put him in front of El'azar the *cohen* and the whole community, and commission him in their sight. ²⁰ Delegate to him some of your authority, so that the entire community of Isra'el will obey him. ²¹ He is to present himself to El'azar the *cohen*, who is to find out by means of the *urim* what ADONAI's will is for Y'hoshua's decisions. Then, at his word they will go out, and at his word they will come in, both he and all the people of Isra'el with him, the whole community."

²² Moshe did as ADONAI had ordered him. He took Y'hoshua, put him before El'azar the *cohen* and the whole community, ²³ laid his hands on him, and commissioned him, as ADONAI had said through Moshe.

28 (v) ¹ ADONAI said to Moshe, ² "Give an order to the people of Isra'el. Tell them, 'You are to take care to offer me at the proper time the food presented to me as offerings made by fire, providing a fragrant aroma for me.' ³ Tell them, 'This is the offering made by fire that you are to bring to ADONAI: male lambs in their first year and without defect, two daily as a regular burnt offering. ⁴ Offer the one lamb in the morning and the other lamb at dusk, ⁵ along with two quarts of fine flour as a grain offering, mixed with one quart of oil from pressed olives. ⁶ It is the regular burnt offering, the same as was offered on Mount Sinai to give a fragrant aroma, an offering made by fire for ADONAI. ⁷ Its drink offering is to be one-quarter *hin* for one lamb; in the Holy Place you are to pour out a drink offering of intoxicating liquor to ADONAI. ⁸ The other lamb you are to present at dusk; present it with the same kind of grain offering and drink offering as in the morning; it is an offering made by fire, with a fragrant aroma for ADONAI.

⁹ "'On *Shabbat* offer two male lambs in their first year and without defect, with one gallon of fine flour as a grain offering, mixed with olive oil, and its drink offering. ¹⁰ This is the burnt offering for every *Shabbat*, in addition to the regular burnt offering and its drink offering.

¹¹ "'At each *Rosh-Hodesh* of yours, you are to present a burnt offering to ADONAI consisting of two young bulls, one ram and seven male lambs in their first year and without defect; ¹² with six quarts of fine flour mixed with olive oil as a grain offering for for each bull, four quarts of fine flour mixed with olive oil as a grain offering for the one ram, ¹³ and two quarts of fine flour mixed with olive oil as a grain offering for each lamb. This will be the burnt offering giving a fragrant aroma, an offering made by fire for ADONAI. ¹⁴ Their drink offerings will be two quarts of wine for a bull, one-and-one-third quarts for the ram, and one quart for each lamb. This is the burnt offering for every *Rosh-Hodesh* throughout the months of the year. ¹⁵ Also a male goat is to be offered as a sin offering to ADONAI, in addition to the regular burnt offering and its drink offering.

(vi) ¹⁶ "'In the first month, on the fourteenth day of the month, is ADONAI's *Pesach*. ¹⁷ On the fifteenth day of the month is to be a feast. *Matzah* is to be eaten for seven days. ¹⁸ The first day is to be a holy convocation: do not do any kind of ordinary work; ¹⁹ but present an offering made by fire, a burnt offering, to ADONAI, consisting of two young bulls, one ram, and seven male lambs in their first year (they are to be without defect for you) ²⁰ with their grain offering, fine flour mixed with olive oil. Offer six quarts for a bull, four quarts for the ram, ²¹ and two quarts for each of the seven lambs; ²² also a male goat as a sin offering, to make atonement for you. ²³ You are to offer these in addition to the morning burnt offering, which is the regular burnt offering. ²⁴ In this fashion you are to offer daily, for seven days, the food of the offering made by fire, making a fragrant aroma for ADONAI; it is to be offered in addition to the regular burnt offering and its drink offering. ²⁵ On the seventh day you are to have a holy convocation; do not do any kind of ordinary work.

²⁶ "'On the day of the firstfruits, when you bring a new grain offering to ADONAI in your feast of *Shavu'ot*, you are to have a holy convocation; do not do any kind of ordinary work; ²⁷ but present a burnt offering as a fragrant aroma for ADONAI, consisting of two young bulls, one ram, seven male lambs in their first year, ²⁸ and their grain offering — fine flour mixed with olive oil, six quarts for each bull, four quarts for the one ram, ²⁹ and two quarts for each of the seven lambs — ³⁰ plus a male goat to make atonement for you. ³¹ You are to offer these in addition to the regular burnt offering and its grain offering (they are to be without defect for you), with their drink offerings.

29 ¹ "'In the seventh month, on the first day of the month, you are to have a holy convocation; do not do any kind of ordinary work; it is a day of blowing the *shofar* for you. ² Prepare a burnt offering to make a fragrant aroma for ADONAI — one young bull, one ram and seven male lambs in their first year and without defect — ³ with their grain offering, consisting of fine flour mixed with olive oil — six quarts for the bull, four quarts for the ram, ⁴ and two quarts for each of the seven lambs — ⁵ also one male goat as a sin offering to make atonement for you. ⁶ This is to be in addition to the burnt offering for *Rosh-Hodesh* with its grain offering, the regular burnt offering with its grain offering, and their drink offerings, according to the rule for them; this will be a fragrant aroma, an offering made by fire to ADONAI.

⁷ "'On the tenth day of this seventh month you are to have a holy convocation. You are to deny yourselves, and you are not to do any kind of work; ⁸ but you are to present a burnt offering to ADONAI to make a fragrant aroma: one young bull, one ram, and seven male lambs in their first year (they are to be without defect for you), ⁹ with their grain offering, fine flour mixed with olive oil, six quarts for the bull, four quarts for the one ram, ¹⁰ and two quarts for each of the seven lambs; ¹¹ also one male goat as a sin offering; in addition to the sin offering for atonement and the regular burnt offering with its grain offering, and their drink offerings.

(vii) ¹² "'On the fifteenth day of the seventh month you are to have a holy convocation. You are not to do any kind of ordinary work, and you are to observe a feast to ADONAI seven days. ¹³ You are to present a burnt offering, an offering made by fire, bringing a fragrant aroma to ADONAI. It is to consist of thirteen young bulls, two rams, fourteen male lambs in their first year (they are to be without defect), ¹⁴ with their grain offering — fine flour mixed with olive oil, six quarts for each of the thirteen bulls, four quarts for each of the two rams, ¹⁵ and two quarts for each of the fourteen lambs; ¹⁶ also one male goat as a sin offering; in addition to the regular burnt offering with its grain and drink offerings.

^{17} "'On the second day you are to present twelve young bulls, two rams, fourteen male lambs in their first year, without defect; ^{18} with the grain and drink offerings for the bulls, rams and lambs, according to their number, in keeping with the rule; ^{19} also one male goat as a sin offering; in addition to the regular burnt offering, its grain offering and their drink offerings.

^{20} "'On the third day eleven bulls, two rams, fourteen male lambs in their first year, without defect; ^{21} with the grain and drink offerings for the bulls, rams and lambs, according to their number, in keeping with the rule; ^{22} also one male goat as a sin offering; in addition to the regular burnt offering with its grain and drink offerings.

^{23} "'On the fourth day ten bulls, two rams, fourteen male lambs in their first year, without defect; ^{24} with the grain and drink offerings for the bulls, rams and lambs, according to their number, in keeping with the rule; ^{25} also one male goat as a sin offering; in addition to the regular burnt offering with its grain and drink offerings.

^{26} "'On the fifth day nine bulls, two rams, fourteen male lambs in their first year, without defect; ^{27} with the grain and drink offerings for the bulls, rams and lambs, according to their number, in keeping with the rule; ^{28} also one male goat as a sin offering; in addition to the regular burnt offering with its grain and drink offerings.

^{29} "'On the sixth day eight bulls, two rams, fourteen male lambs in their first year, without defect; ^{30} with the grain and drink offerings for the bulls, rams and lambs, according to their number, in keeping with the rule; ^{31} also one male goat as a sin offering; in addition to the regular burnt offering with its grain and drink offerings.

^{32} "'On the seventh day seven bulls, two rams, fourteen male lambs in their first year, without defect; ^{33} with the grain and drink offerings for the bulls, rams and lambs, according to their number, in keeping with the rule; ^{34} also one male goat as a sin offering; in addition to the regular burnt offering with its grain offering and drink offerings.

(Maftir) ^{35} "'On the eighth day you are to have a festive assembly: you are not to do any kind of ordinary work; ^{36} but you are to present a burnt offering, an offering made by fire, giving a fragrant aroma to ADONAI — one bull, one ram, seven male lambs in their first year, without defect; ^{37} with the grain and drink offerings for the bull, the ram and the lambs, according to their number, in keeping with the rule; ^{38} also one male goat as a sin offering; in addition to the regular burnt offering with its grain and drink offerings.

^{39} "'You are to offer these to ADONAI at your designated times in addition to your vows and voluntary offerings — whether these are your burnt offerings, grain offerings, drink offerings or peace offerings.'"

30 $^{1(29:40)}$ Moshe told the people of Isra'el everything, just as ADONAI had ordered Moshe.

Haftarah Pinchas: M'lakhim Alef (1 Kings) 18:46–19:21

B'rit Hadashah suggested readings for Parashah Pinchas: Mattityahu (Matthew) 26:1–30; Mark 14:1–26; Luke 22:1–20; Yochanan (John) 2:13–22; 7:1–13, 37–39; 11:55–12:1; 13:1; 18:28, 39; 19:14; Acts 2:1–21; 12:3–4; 20:5–6, 16; 27:9–11; 1 Corinthians 5:6–8; 16:8; Messianic Jews (Hebrews) 11:28

Parashah 42: Mattot (Tribes) 30:2(1)–32:42
[In regular years read with Parashah 43, in leap years read separately]

²⁽¹⁾ Then Moshe spoke to the heads of the tribes of the people of Isra'el. He said, "Here is what *ADONAI* has ordered: ³⁽²⁾ when a man makes a vow to *ADONAI* or formally obligates himself by swearing an oath, he is not to break his word but is to do everything he said he would do.

⁴⁽³⁾ "When a woman makes a vow to *ADONAI*, formally obligating herself, while she is a minor living in her father's house; ⁵⁽⁴⁾ then, if her father has heard what she vowed or obligated herself to do and holds his peace, then all her vows remain binding — every obligation she has bound herself to will stand. ⁶⁽⁵⁾ But if on the day her father hears it, he expresses his disapproval, then none of her vows or obligations she has bound herself to will stand; and *ADONAI* will forgive her, because her father expressed his disapproval.

⁷⁽⁶⁾ "If, having made vows or rashly committed herself to an obligation, she gets married; ⁸⁽⁷⁾ and her husband hears but holds his peace with her on the day he learns of it, then her vows and obligations she has bound herself to will stand. ⁹⁽⁸⁾ But if her husband expresses his disapproval on the day he hears it, he will void the vow which is on her and the obligation to which she has bound herself; and *ADONAI* will forgive her.

¹⁰⁽⁹⁾ "The vow of a widow, however, or of a divorcee, including everything to which she has obligated herself, will stand against her.

¹¹⁽¹⁰⁾ "If a woman vowed in her husband's house or obligated herself with an oath; ¹²⁽¹¹⁾ and her husband heard it but held his peace with her and did not express disapproval, then all her vows and obligations will stand. ¹³⁽¹²⁾ But if her husband makes them null and void on the day he hears them, then whatever she said, vows or binding obligation, will not stand; her husband has voided them; and *ADONAI* will forgive her. ¹⁴⁽¹³⁾ Her husband may let every vow and every binding obligation stand, or he may void it. ¹⁵⁽¹⁴⁾ But if her husband entirely holds his peace with her day after day, then he confirms all her vows and obligations; he must let them stand, because he held his peace with her on the day he heard them. ¹⁶⁽¹⁵⁾ If he makes them null and void after he has heard them, then he will bear the consequent guilt."

¹⁷⁽¹⁶⁾ These are the laws which *ADONAI* ordered Moshe between a man and his wife, and between a father and his daughter, if she is a minor living in her father's house.

31 *(LY: ii)* ¹ *ADONAI* said to Moshe, ² "On behalf of the people of Isra'el, take vengeance on the Midyanim. After that, you will be gathered to your people."

³ Moshe said to the people, "Equip men from among yourselves for war. They are to go and fight Midyan, in order to carry out *ADONAI*'s vengeance on Midyan. ⁴ You are to send to the war a thousand men from every one of Isra'el's tribes." ⁵ So out of the thousands of people in Isra'el, a thousand armed men from each tribe, 12,000 altogether, were mustered for war. ⁶ Moshe sent them, a thousand from each tribe, to the war; he sent them and Pinchas the son of El'azar the *cohen* to the war, with the holy utensils and the trumpets for sounding the alarm in his care.

⁷ They fought against Midyan, as *ADONAI* had ordered Moshe, and killed every male. ⁸ They killed the kings of Midyan along with the others who were slain — Evi, Rekem, Tzur, Hur and Reva, the five kings of Midyan. They also killed Bil'am the son of B'or with the sword. ⁹ The people of Isra'el took captive the women of Midyan

and their little ones, and they took as booty all their cattle, flocks and other goods. ¹⁰ They set fire to all their cities in the areas where they lived and all their camps. ¹¹ They took all the booty, all the people and animals they had captured, ¹² and brought the captives, booty and spoil to Moshe, El'azar the *cohen* and the community of Isra'el in the camp on the plains of Mo'av by the Yarden across from Yericho.

(RY: ii, LY: iii) ¹³ Moshe, El'azar the *cohen* and all the community leaders went to meet them outside the camp. ¹⁴ But Moshe was angry with the army officers, the commanders of thousands and the commanders of hundreds coming in from the battlefield. ¹⁵ Moshe asked them, "You let the women live? ¹⁶ Why, these are the ones who — because of Bil'am's advice — caused the people of Isra'el to rebel, breaking faith with Adonai in the P'or incident, so that the plague broke out among Adonai's community! ¹⁷ Now kill every male among the little ones, and kill every woman who has ever slept with a man. ¹⁸ But the young girls who have never slept with a man, keep alive for yourselves. ¹⁹ Pitch your tents outside the camp for seven days. Whoever has killed a person or touched the corpse of someone slain, purify yourselves on the third and seventh days, you and your captives. ²⁰ Also purify every garment, whether of skin or goat's hair, and everything made of wood."

²¹ El'azar the *cohen* said to the soldiers who had gone to the front, "This is the regulation from the *Torah* which Adonai has ordered Moshe. ²² Even though gold, silver, brass, iron, tin and lead ²³ can all withstand fire, so that you are indeed to purify everything made of these materials by having them pass through fire; nevertheless they must also be purified with the water for purification. Everything that can't withstand fire you are to have go through the water. ²⁴ On the seventh day you are to wash your clothes, and you will be clean; after that you may enter the camp."

(LY: iv) ²⁵ Adonai said to Moshe, ²⁶ "Take all the booty, both people and animals, you, El'azar the *cohen* and the leaders of clans in the community; ²⁷ and divide the booty into two parts: half for the experienced soldiers who went out to battle, and half for the rest of the community. ²⁸ From the portion of the soldiers who went out to battle, levy a tax for Adonai consisting of one-five-hundredth of the persons, cattle, donkeys and sheep; ²⁹ take it from their half and give it to El'azar the *cohen* as a portion set apart for Adonai. ³⁰ From the half that goes to the people of Isra'el, you are to take one-fiftieth of the persons, and of the cattle, donkeys and sheep, that is, of all the livestock; and give them to the *L'vi'im* taking care of the tabernacle of Adonai." ³¹ Moshe and El'azar the *cohen* did as Adonai had ordered Moshe.

³² The booty, over and above the portion which the soldiers took, came to 675,000 sheep, ³³ 72,000 cattle, ³⁴ 61,000 donkeys, ³⁵ and 32,000 persons in all, consisting of the women who had never slept with a man.

³⁶ The half which was the portion of the soldiers who went out to fight, numbered 337,500 sheep, ³⁷ of which Adonai's tribute was 675; ³⁸ 36,000 cattle, of which Adonai's tribute was seventy-two; ³⁹ 30,500 donkeys, of which Adonai's tribute was sixty-one; ⁴⁰ and 16,000 persons, of whom Adonai's tribute was thirty-two persons. ⁴¹ Moshe gave the tribute set apart for Adonai to El'azar the *cohen*, as Adonai had ordered Moshe.

(LY: v) ⁴² From the half that went to people of Isra'el, which Moshe separated from that of the men who had gone to fight — ⁴³ now the community's half consisted of 337,500 sheep, ⁴⁴ 36,000 cattle, ⁴⁵ 30,500 donkeys ⁴⁶ and 16,000 persons —

⁴⁷ from the people of Isra'el's half, Moshe took one-fiftieth of the persons and animals and gave them to the *L'vi'im* taking care of the tabernacle of ADONAI, as ADONAI had ordered Moshe.

⁴⁸ The officers in charge of the thousands who fought, the commanders of thousands and the commanders of hundreds, approached Moshe ⁴⁹ and said to him, "Your servants have counted all the soldiers under our command, and not one of us is missing. ⁵⁰ We have brought an offering for ADONAI, what every man has obtained in the way of gold jewelry — armlets, bracelets, signet rings, earrings and belts — to make atonement for ourselves before ADONAI."

⁵¹ Moshe and El'azar the *cohen* accepted their gold, all the jewelry. ⁵² All the gold in this gift which the commanders of thousands and the commanders of hundreds set apart for ADONAI weighed 420 pounds. ⁵³ For the soldiers had taken booty, every man for himself. ⁵⁴ Moshe and El'azar the *cohen* took the gold from the commanders of thousands and of hundreds and brought it into the tent of meeting as a reminder for the people of Isra'el before ADONAI.

32 *(RY: iii; LY: vi)* ¹ The descendants of Re'uven and the descendants of Gad had vast quantities of livestock. When they saw that the land of Ya'zer and the land of Gil'ad were good for livestock, ² the descendants of Gad and of Re'uven came and spoke to Moshe, El'azar the *cohen* and the community leaders. They said, ³ "'Atarot, Divon, Ya'zer, Nimrah, Heshbon, El'aleh, S'vam, N'vo and Be'on, ⁴ the country that ADONAI conquered before the community of Isra'el, is livestock country; and your servants have livestock. ⁵ If you regard us favorably," they went on, "let this land be given to your servants as their possession; and don't have us cross the Yarden."

⁶ Moshe answered the descendants of Gad and of Re'uven: "Are your brothers to go to war while you stay here? ⁷ Besides, why are you trying to discourage the people of Isra'el from crossing into the land ADONAI gave them? ⁸ This is what your fathers did when I sent them from Kadesh-Barnea to see the land. ⁹ For when they went up to the Eshkol Valley and saw the land, they disheartened the people of Isra'el, so that they wouldn't enter the land ADONAI had given them. ¹⁰ ADONAI's anger blazed up on that day; and he swore, ¹¹ 'None of the people aged twenty or more who came out of Egypt will see the land I swore to Avraham, Yitz'chak and Ya'akov; because they haven't followed me unreservedly — ¹² except Kalev the son of Y'funeh the K'nizi and Y'hoshua the son of Nun, because they have followed ADONAI unreservedly.' ¹³ Thus ADONAI's anger blazed against Isra'el, so that he made them wander here and there in the desert forty years, until all the generation that had done evil in the sight of ADONAI had died out. ¹⁴ Now you, another brood of sinners, have arisen in your fathers' place to increase still more the fierce anger of ADONAI toward Isra'el! ¹⁵ For if you turn away from him, he will leave them in the desert again, and thus you will cause the destruction of all these people!"

¹⁶ But they came up to him and said, "Here we will build enclosures for our livestock and cities for our little ones, ¹⁷ but we ourselves will be armed and ready for action to march at the head of the people of Isra'el, until we have brought them to their place. Our little ones will stay in the fortified cities here because of the people now living in the land. ¹⁸ However, we will not return to our own homes until every man in Isra'el has taken possession of his land for

inheritance. ^{19} We will not have an inheritance with them on the other side of the Yarden, westward; because our inheritance has fallen to us on this side of the Yarden, eastward."

(RY: iv, LY: vii) ^{20} Moshe said to them, "If you will do this — if you will arm yourselves to go before ADONAI to the war, ^{21} and if every one of your soldiers will cross the Yarden before ADONAI, until he has driven out his enemies ahead of him, ^{22} and if the land has been conquered before ADONAI, and only after that do you return — then you will be clear before ADONAI and before Isra'el, and this land here will be yours to possess before ADONAI. ^{23} But if you will not do this, then you have sinned against ADONAI, and you must understand that your sin will find you out. ^{24} Build cities for your little ones and enclosures for your sheep; then do what you said you would do."

^{25} The descendants of Gad and the descendants of Re'uven said to Moshe, "Your servants will do as my lord orders. ^{26} Our little ones, wives, flocks and all our livestock will be there in the cities of Gil'ad; ^{27} but your servants will cross over, every man armed for war, before ADONAI to do battle, as my lord says."

^{28} So Moshe gave orders concerning them to El'azar the *cohen*, Y'hoshua the son of Nun and the clan leaders of the tribes of the people of Isra'el. ^{29} Moshe said to them, "If the descendants of Gad and of Re'uven cross over the Yarden with you, every man armed for battle, before ADONAI; and if the land is conquered before you, then you are to give them the land of Gil'ad as theirs to possess. ^{30} But if they do not cross with you armed, they are to possess land along with you in Kena'an."

^{31} The descendants of Gad and of Re'uven answered, "We will do as ADONAI has said to your servants. ^{32} We will cross over into the land of Kena'an armed before ADONAI, and the land we will possess for inheritance will be on this side of the Yarden."

^{33} So Moshe gave the descendants of Gad and of Re'uven, and also to the half-tribe of M'nasheh the son of Yosef, the kingdom of Sichon king of the Emori and the kingdom of 'Og king of Bashan — the country and its cities within its borders, along with their surrounding towns. ^{34} The descendants of Gad built Divon, 'Atarot, 'Aro'er, ^{35} 'Atrot-Shofan, Ya'zer, Yogbehah, ^{36} Beit-Nimrah and Beit-Haran — fortified cities; and also enclosures for sheep. ^{37} The descendants of Re'uven built Heshbon, El'aleh, Kiryatayim, ^{38} N'vo, Ba'al-M'on (these names have been changed) and Sivmah; they renamed the cities they built.

(LY: Maftir) ^{39} The descendants of Machir the son of M'nasheh went to Gil'ad and conquered it, dispossessing the Emori who were there. ^{40} Moshe gave Gil'ad to Machir the son of M'nasheh, and he lived in it. ^{41} Ya'ir the son of M'nasheh went and captured its villages and called them Havot-Ya'ir [villages of Ya'ir]. ^{42} Novach went and captured K'nat with its villages and named it Novach after himself.

Haftarah Mattot: Yirmeyahu (Jeremiah) 1:1–2:3

B'rit Hadashah suggested reading for Parashah Mattot: Mattityahu (Matthew) 5:33–37

Parashah 43: Masa'ei (Stages) 33:1–36:13
[In regular years read with Parashah 42, in leap years read separately]

33 ¹ These are the stages in the journey of the people of Isra'el as they left the land of Egypt divided into groups under the leadership of Moshe and Aharon. ² Moshe recorded each of the stages of their journey by order of *Adonai*; here are the starting-points of each stage:

³ They began their journey from Ram'ses in the first month. On the fifteenth day of the first month, the morning after the *Pesach*, the people of Isra'el left proudly in view of all the Egyptians; ⁴ while the Egyptians were burying those among them whom *Adonai* had killed, all their firstborn; *Adonai* had also executed judgment on their gods. ⁵ The people of Isra'el moved on from Ram'ses and camped at Sukkot.
⁶ They moved on from Sukkot and camped at Etam, by the edge of the desert.
⁷ They moved on from Etam and turned back to Pi-Hachirot, in front of Ba'al-Tz'fon, and camped before Migdol. ⁸ They moved on from P'nei-Hachirot, passed through the sea to the desert, continued three days' journey into the Etam Desert and camped at Marah. ⁹ They moved on from Marah and came to Eilim; in Eilim were twelve springs and seventy palm trees, so they camped there. ¹⁰ They moved on from Eilim and camped by the Sea of Suf.

(LY: ii) ¹¹ They moved on from the Sea of Suf and camped in the Seen Desert.
¹² They moved on from the Seen Desert and camped at Dofkah. ¹³ They moved on from Dofkah and camped at Alush. ¹⁴ They moved on from Alush and camped at Refidim, where there was no water for the people to drink. ¹⁵ They moved on from Refidim and camped in the Sinai Desert. ¹⁶ They moved on from the Sinai Desert and camped at Kivrot-HaTa'avah. ¹⁷ They moved on from Kivrot-HaTa'avah and camped in Hatzerot. ¹⁸ They moved on from Hatzerot and camped at Ritmah. ¹⁹ They moved on from Ritmah and camped at Rimmon-Peretz. ²⁰ They moved on from Rimmon-Peretz and camped at Livnah. ²¹ They moved on from Livnah and camped at Rissah. ²² They moved on from Rissah and camped at K'helah. ²³ They moved on from K'helah and camped at Mount Shefer. ²⁴ They moved on from Mount Shefer and camped at Haradah. ²⁵ They moved on from Haradah and camped at Mak'helot. ²⁶ They moved on from Mak'helot and camped at Tachat. ²⁷ They moved on from Tachat and camped at Terach. ²⁸ They moved on from Terach and camped at Mitkah. ²⁹ They moved on from Mitkah and camped at HaShmonah. ³⁰ They moved on from HaShmonah and camped at Moserot. ³¹ They moved on from Moserot and camped at B'nei-Ya'akan. ³² They moved on from B'nei-Ya'akan and camped at Hor-HaGidgad. ³³ They moved on from Hor-HaGidgad and camped at Yotvatah. ³⁴ They moved on from Yotvatah and camped at Avronah. ³⁵ They moved on from Avronah and camped at 'Etzyon-Gever. ³⁶ They moved on from 'Etzyon-Gever and camped in the Tzin Desert, that is, Kadesh.

³⁷ They moved on from Kadesh and camped at Mount Hor, at the border of the land of Edom. ³⁸ At *Adonai*'s order Aharon the *cohen* went up on Mount Hor, and he died there on the first day of the fifth month of the fortieth year after the people of Isra'el had left the land of Egypt. ³⁹ Aharon was 123 years old when he died on Mount Hor. ⁴⁰ The Kena'ani king of 'Arad, who lived in the Negev in the land of Kena'an, had heard that the people of Isra'el were coming; ⁴¹ so they moved on from Mount Hor and camped at Tzalmonah.

⁴² They moved on from Tzalmonah and camped at Punon. ⁴³ They moved on from Punon and camped at Ovot. ⁴⁴ They moved on from Ovot and camped at 'Iyei-Ha'Avarim, by the border of Mo'av. ⁴⁵ They moved on from 'Iyim and camped at Divon-Gad. ⁴⁶ They moved on from Divon-Gad and camped at 'Almon-Divlatayim. ⁴⁷ They moved on from Almon-Divlatayim and camped in the 'Avarim Range, in front of N'vo. ⁴⁸ They moved on from the 'Avarim Range and camped in the plains of Mo'av by the Yarden, across from Yericho. ⁴⁹ Their camp by the Yarden extended from Beit-HaYeshimot all the way to Avel-HaSheetim in the plains of Mo'av.

(RY: v; LY: iii) ⁵⁰ ADONAI spoke to Moshe in the plains of Mo'av by the Yarden, across from Yericho. He said ⁵¹ to tell the people of Isra'el, "When you cross the Yarden into the land of Kena'an, ⁵² you are to expel all the people living in the land from in front of you. Destroy all their stone figures, destroy all their metal statues and demolish all their high places. ⁵³ Drive out the inhabitants of the land, and live in it, for I have given the land to you to possess. ⁵⁴ You will inherit the land by lot according to your families. You are to give more land to the larger families and less to the smaller ones. Wherever the lot falls to any particular person, that will be his property. You will inherit according to the tribes of your ancestors. ⁵⁵ But if you don't drive out the inhabitants of the land from in front of you, then those you allow to remain will become like thorns in your eyes and stings in your sides — they will harass you in the land where you are living. ⁵⁶ And in this event, I will do to you what I intended to do to them."

34 ¹ ADONAI told Moshe ² to give this order to the people of Isra'el: "When you enter the land of Kena'an, it will become your land to pass on as an inheritance, the land of Kena'an as defined by these borders.

³ "Your southern portion will extend from the Tzin Desert close to the border of Edom. The eastern terminus of your southern border is at the end of the Dead Sea. ⁴ From there your border turns, goes south of the 'Akrabbim Ascent and passes on to Tzin. From there it goes south of Kadesh-Barnea, on to Hatzar-Adar, and on to 'Atzmon. ⁵ Then the border turns and goes from 'Atzmon to the *Vadi* of Egypt and along it to the Sea.

⁶ "Your western border will be the Great Sea.

⁷ "Your northern border will be as follows: from the Great Sea mark a line to Mount Hor, ⁸ and from Mount Hor mark a line to the entrance of Hamat. The border goes out to Tz'dad. ⁹ Then the border goes to Zifron and finally to Hatzar-'Einan; this is your northern border.

¹⁰ "For the eastern border mark your line from Hatzar-'Einan to Sh'fam. ¹¹ Then the border goes down from Sh'fam to Rivlah, on the east side of 'Ayin, then down until it hits the slope east of Lake Kinneret. ¹² From there it goes down the Yarden River till it flows into the Dead Sea. These will be the borders of your land."

¹³ Moshe gave this order to the people of Isra'el: "This is the land in which you will receive inheritances by lot, which ADONAI has ordered to give to the nine tribes and the half-tribe. ¹⁴ The tribe of the descendants of Re'uven have already received their land for inheritance according to their clans, and so have the descendants of Gad and the half-tribe of M'nasheh. ¹⁵ These two-and-a-half tribes have received their inheritance on this side of the Yarden, across from Yericho and eastward, toward the sunrise."

(RY: vi; LY: iv) ¹⁶ A*DONAI* said to Moshe, ¹⁷ "These are the names of the men who will take possession of the land for you: El'azar the *cohen* and Y'hoshua the son of Nun. ¹⁸ Also appoint one leader from each tribe to take possession of the land. ¹⁹ The names of these men are:

> from the tribe of Y'hudah, Kalev the son of Y'funeh;
> ²⁰ from the tribe of the descendants of Shim'on, Sh'mu'el the son of 'Ammihud;
> ²¹ from the tribe of Binyamin, Elidad the son of Kislon;
> ²² from the tribe of the descendants of Dan, a leader, Buki the son of Yogli;
> ²³ from the descendants of Yosef:
> from the tribe of the descendants of M'nasheh, a leader, Hani'el the son of Efod;
> ²⁴ from the tribe of the descendants of Efrayim, a leader, K'mu'el the son of Shiftan;
> ²⁵ from the tribe of the descendants of Z'vulun, a leader, Elitzafan the son of Parnakh;
> ²⁶ from the tribe of the descendants of Yissakhar, a leader, Palti'el the son of 'Azan;
> ²⁷ from the tribe of the descendants of Asher, a leader, Achihud the son of Shlomi;
> ²⁸ from the tribe of the descendants of Naftali, a leader, P'dah'el the son of 'Ammihud."

²⁹ These are the ones whom A*DONAI* ordered to divide the inheritance among the people of Isra'el in the land of Kena'an.

35 *(LY: v)* ¹ In the plains of Mo'av by the Yarden, across from Yericho, A*DONAI* said to Moshe, ² "Order the people of Isra'el to give to the *L'vi'im* cities to live in from the heritage they will possess, and you are also to give the *L'vi'im* some of the open land surrounding the cities. ³ They are to have the cities to live in, while their open land will be for their livestock, for growing crops and for all their animals. ⁴ The open land around the cities you give to the *L'vi'im* is to commence at a line drawn around the city wall 1,500 feet outside it and is to extend outward from there. ⁵ Measure 3,000 feet outward from the city wall to the east, south, west and north, with the city in the center. The space between the 1,500-foot line and the 3,000-foot line will be their open land around the cities. ⁶ The cities you give to the *L'vi'im* are to be the six cities of refuge to which you permit the person who kills someone to flee to; plus an additional forty-two cities. ⁷ Thus you will give the *L'vi'im* forty-eight cities, with their surrounding open land. ⁸ As to the cities you will give from those the people of Isra'el possess, from the many you will take many, and from the few you will take few — each tribe will contribute from its cities to the *L'vi'im* in accordance with the size of its inheritance."

(RY: vii, LY: vi) ⁹ A*DONAI* said to Moshe, ¹⁰ "Tell the people of Isra'el, 'When you cross the Yarden into the land of Kena'an, ¹¹ you are to designate for yourselves cities that will be cities of refuge for you, to which anyone who kills someone by mistake can flee. ¹² These cities are to be a refuge for you from the dead person's next-of-kin, who might otherwise avenge his kinsman's death by slaying the killer prior to his standing trial before the community. ¹³ In regard to the cities you are to give, there are to be six cities of refuge for you. ¹⁴ You are to give three cities east of the Yarden and three cities in the land of Kena'an; they will be cities of refuge. ¹⁵ These six cities will serve as refuge for the people of Isra'el, as well as for the foreigner and resident alien with them; so that anyone who kills someone by mistake may flee there.

^{16} "'However, if he hits him with an iron implement and thus causes his death, he is a murderer; the murderer must be put to death. ^{17} Or if he hits him with a stone in his hand big enough to kill someone, and he dies, he is a murderer; the murderer must be put to death. ^{18} Or if he hits him with a wood utensil in his hand capable of killing someone, and he dies, he is a murderer; the murderer must be put to death. ^{19} The next-of-kin avenger is to put the murderer to death himself — upon meeting him, he is to put him to death. ^{20} Likewise, if he shoves him out of hatred; or intentionally throws something at him, causing his death; ^{21} or out of hostility strikes him with his hand, so that he dies; then the one who struck him must be put to death; he is a murderer; and the next-of-kin avenger is to put the murderer to death upon meeting him.

^{22} "'But suppose he shoves him suddenly, but without hostility; or he throws something at him unintentionally; ^{23} or, without seeing him, being his enemy or seeking to harm him, he throws a stone big enough to cause death; and the person dies. ^{24} Then the community is to judge between the one who struck him and the next-of-kin avenger in accordance with these rules; ^{25} and the community is to save the killer from the next-of-kin avenger. The community is to return him to the city of refuge to which he fled, and he is to live there until the *cohen hagadol*, who was anointed with the holy oil, dies. ^{26} But if the killer ever goes beyond the limits of the city of refuge he fled to, ^{27} and the next-of-kin avenger finds him outside the limits of his city of refuge, and the avenger kills the killer, he will not be guilty of the man's blood; ^{28} because he must stay in his city of refuge until the death of the *cohen hagadol*. But after the death of the *cohen hagadol* the killer may return to the land he owns. ^{29} These things shall constitute your standard for judgment through all your generations, wherever you live.

^{30} "'If anyone kills someone, the murderer is to be put to death upon the testimony of witnesses; but the testimony of only one witness will not suffice to cause a person to be put to death. ^{31} Also, you are not to accept a ransom in lieu of the life of a murderer condemned to death; rather, he must be put to death. ^{32} Likewise, you are not to accept for someone who has fled to his city of refuge a ransom that would allow him to return to his land before the death of the *cohen*. ^{33} In this way you will not defile the land in which you are living. For blood defiles the land, and in this land no atonement can be made for the blood shed in it except the blood of him who shed it. ^{34} No, you are not to defile the land in which you live and in which I live; for I, ADONAI, live among the people of Isra'el.'"

36 *(LY: vii)* ^{1} The leaders of the clans of the family of the descendants of Gil'ad, the son of Machir, the son of M'nasheh, of the families of the descendants of Yosef, approached and addressed Moshe and the leaders, the heads of the clans of the people of Isra'el. ^{2} They said, "ADONAI ordered my lord to give by lot the land to be inherited by the people of Isra'el, and my lord was ordered by ADONAI to give the inheritance of our kinsman Tz'lof'chad to his daughters. ^{3} But if they get married to anyone belonging to another of the tribes of the people of Isra'el, then their inheritance will be taken away from the inheritance of our ancestors and be added to the inheritance of the tribe they will then belong to; thus it will be taken away from the sum total of our inheritance. ^{4} And when the *yovel* of the people of Isra'el comes, their inheritance will be added to the land possessed by the tribe they will then belong to and be subtracted from the inheritance belonging to the tribe of our ancestors."

⁵ Moshe gave this order to the people of Isra'el, in keeping with the word of ADONAI: "The tribe of the descendants of Yosef is right in what it says. ⁶ Here is what ADONAI has ordered concerning the daughters of Tz'lof'chad: 'Let them be married to whomever they think best, but they must marry only into a family from their father's tribe. ⁷ In this way no inheritance of the people of Isra'el will move from one tribe to another; for each of the people of Isra'el is to hold on to the land for inheritance belonging to his father's tribe. ⁸ Every daughter who possesses an inheritance in any tribe of the people of Isra'el is to become the wife of someone from the family of her father's tribe, so that every one of the people of Isra'el will stay in possession of his ancestors' inheritance. ⁹ Thus no inheritance will move from one tribe to another, for each of the tribes of the people of Isra'el will hold on to its own inheritance."

(Maftir) ¹⁰ The daughters of Tz'lof'chad did as ADONAI had ordered Moshe. ¹¹ Machlah, Tirtzah, Hoglah, Milkah and No'ah all got married to sons of their father's brothers. ¹² They were married into the families of the descendants of M'nasheh the son of Yosef, and their inheritance remained in the tribe of their father's family.

¹³ These are the *mitzvot* and rulings which ADONAI gave through Moshe to the people of Isra'el in the plains of Mo'av by the Yarden, across from Yericho.

Haftarah Masa'ei: Yirmeyahu (Jeremiah) 2:4–28; 3:4 (A); 2:4–28; 4:1–2 (S)

B'rit Hadashah suggested reading for Parashah Mattot: Ya'akov (James) 4:1–12

Hazak, hazak, v'nit'chazek!
Be strong, be strong, and let us be strengthened!

D'varim

DEUTERONOMY

Parashah 44: D'varim (Words) 1:1–3:22

1 ¹ These are the words Moshe spoke to all Isra'el on the far side of the Yarden River, in the desert, in the 'Aravah, across from Suf, between Pa'ran and Tofel, Lavan, Hatzerot and Di-Zahav. ² It is eleven days' journey from Horev to Kadesh-Barnea by way of Mount Se'ir.

³ On the first day of the eleventh month of the fortieth year, Moshe spoke to the people of Isra'el, reviewing everything ADONAI had ordered him to tell them. ⁴ This was after he had defeated Sichon, king of the Emori, who lived in Heshbon, and 'Og, king of Bashan, who lived in 'Ashtarot, at Edre'i. ⁵ There, beyond the Yarden, in the land of Mo'av, Moshe took it upon himself to expound this *Torah* and said:

⁶ "ADONAI spoke to us in Horev. He said, 'You have lived long enough by this mountain. ⁷ Turn, get moving and go to the hill-country of the Emori and all the places near there in the 'Aravah, the hill-country, the Sh'felah, the Negev and by the seashore — the land of the Kena'ani, and the L'vanon, as far as the great river, the Euphrates River. ⁸ I have set the land before you! Go in, and take possession of the land ADONAI swore to give to your ancestors Avraham, Yitz'chak and Ya'akov, and their descendants after them.'

⁹ "At that time I told you, 'You are too heavy a burden for me to carry alone. ¹⁰ ADONAI your God has multiplied your numbers, so that there are as many of you today as there are stars in the sky. ¹¹ May ADONAI, the God of your ancestors, increase you yet a thousandfold and bless you, as he has promised you! *(ii)* ¹² But you are burdensome, bothersome and quarrelsome! How can I bear it by myself alone? ¹³ Pick for yourselves from each of your tribes men who are wise, understanding and knowledgeable; and I will make them heads over you.'

¹⁴ "You answered me, 'What you have said would be a good thing for us to do.' ¹⁵ So I took the heads of your tribes, men wise and knowledgable, and made them heads over you — leaders in charge of thousands, of hundreds, of fifties and of tens, and officers, tribe by tribe. ¹⁶ At that time I commissioned your judges, 'Hear the cases that arise between your brothers; and judge fairly between a man and his brother, and the foreigner who is with him. ¹⁷ You are not to show favoritism when judging, but give equal attention to the small and to the great. No matter how a person presents himself, don't be afraid of him; because the decision is God's. The case that is too hard for you, bring to me and I will hear it.' ¹⁸ I also gave you orders at that time concerning all the things you were to do.

¹⁹ "So we left Horev and went through all that vast and fearsome desert which you saw on the way to the hill-country of the Emori, as *Adonai* our God ordered us; and we arrived at Kadesh-Barnea. ²⁰ There I said to you, 'You have come to the hill-country of the Emori, which *Adonai* our God is giving to us. ²¹ Look! *Adonai* your God has placed the land before you. Go up, take possession, as *Adonai*, the God of your ancestors, has told you. Don't be afraid, don't be dismayed.'

(iii) ²² "You approached me, every one of you, and said, 'Let's send men ahead of us to explore the country for us and bring back word concerning what route we should use in going up and what the cities we will encounter are like.' ²³ The idea seemed good to me, so I took twelve of your men, one from each tribe; ²⁴ and they set out, went up into the hills, came to the Eshkol Valley and reconnoitered it. ²⁵ They took some of the produce of the land and brought it down to us; they also brought back word to us — 'The land *Adonai* our God is giving to us is good.'

²⁶ "But you would not go up. Instead you rebelled against the order of *Adonai* your God; ²⁷ and in your tents you complained, 'It's because *Adonai* hated us that he has brought us out of the land of Egypt, only to hand us over to the Emori to destroy us. ²⁸ What sort of place is it that we're heading for? Our brothers made our courage fail when they said, "The people are bigger and taller than we are; the cities are great and fortified up to the sky; and finally, we have seen 'Anakim there."'

²⁹ "I answered you, 'Don't be fearful, don't be afraid of them. ³⁰ *Adonai* your God, who is going ahead of you, will fight on your behalf, just as he accomplished all those things for you in Egypt before your eyes, ³¹ and likewise in the desert, where you saw how *Adonai* your God carried you, like a man carries his child, along the entire way you traveled until you arrived at this place. ³² Yet in this matter you don't trust *Adonai* your God, ³³ even though he went ahead of you, seeking out places for you to pitch your tents and showing you which way to go, by fire at night and by a cloud during the day.'

³⁴ "*Adonai* heard what you were saying, became angry and swore, ³⁵ 'Not a single one of these people, this whole evil generation, will see the good land I swore to give to your ancestors, ³⁶ except Kalev the son of Y'funeh — he will see it; I will give him and his descendants the land he walked on, because he has fully followed *Adonai*.'

³⁷ "Also, because of you *Adonai* was angry with me and said, 'You too will not go in there. ³⁸ Y'hoshua the son of Nun, your assistant — he will go in there. So encourage him, because he will enable Isra'el to take possession of it. *(iv)* ³⁹ Moreover, your little ones, who you said would be taken as booty, and your children who don't yet know good from bad — they will go in there; I will give it to them, and they will have possession of it. ⁴⁰ But as for yourselves, turn around and head into the desert by the road to the Sea of Suf.'

⁴¹ "Then you answered me, 'We have sinned against *Adonai*. Now we will go up and fight, in accordance with everything *Adonai* our God ordered us.' And every man among you put on his arms, considering it an easy matter to go up into the hill-country. ⁴² But *Adonai* said to me, 'Tell them, "Don't go up, and don't fight, because I am not there with you; if you do, your enemies will defeat you."' ⁴³ So I told you, but you wouldn't listen. Instead, you rebelled against *Adonai*'s order, took matters into your own hands and went up into the hill-country;

⁴⁴ where the Emori living in that hill-country came out against you like bees, defeated you in Se'ir and chased you back all the way to Hormah. ⁴⁵ You returned and cried before ADONAI, but ADONAI neither listened to what you said nor paid you any attention. ⁴⁶ This is why you had to stay in Kadesh as long as you did.

2 ¹ "Then we turned and began traveling into the desert along the road to the Sea of Suf, as ADONAI had said to me; and we skirted Mount Se'ir for a long time. *(v)* ² Finally ADONAI said to me, ³ 'You have been going around this mountain long enough! Head north, ⁴ and give this order to the people: "You are to pass through the territory of your kinsmen the descendants of 'Esav who live in Se'ir. They will be afraid of you, so be very cautious, ⁵ and don't get into disputes with them; for I am not going to give you any of their land, no, not even enough for one foot to stand on; inasmuch as I have given Mount Se'ir to 'Esav as his possession. ⁶ Pay them money for the food you eat, and pay them money for the water you drink. ⁷ For ADONAI your God has blessed you in everything your hands have produced. He knows that you have been traveling through this vast desert; these forty years ADONAI your God has been with you; and you have lacked nothing.'

⁸ "So we went on past our kinsmen the descendants of 'Esav living in Se'ir, left the road through the 'Aravah from Eilat and 'Etzyon-Gever, and turned to pass along the road through the desert of Mo'av. ⁹ ADONAI said to me, 'Don't be hostile toward Mo'av or fight with them, because I will not give you any of their land to possess, since I have already given 'Ar to the descendants of Lot as their territory.'" ¹⁰ (The Emim used to live there, a great and numerous people as tall as the 'Anakim. ¹¹ They are also considered Refa'im, as are the 'Anakim, but the Mo'avim call them Emim. ¹² In Se'ir the Horim used to live, but the descendants of 'Esav dispossessed and destroyed them, settling in their place. Isra'el did similarly in the land it came to possess, which ADONAI gave to them.) ¹³ "'Now get going, and cross *Vadi* Zered!'

"So we crossed *Vadi* Zered. ¹⁴ The time between our leaving Kadesh-Barnea and our crossing *Vadi* Zered was thirty-eight years — until the whole generation of men capable of bearing arms had been eliminated from the camp, as ADONAI had sworn they would be. ¹⁵ Moreover, ADONAI's hand was against them to root them out of the camp until the last of them was gone. ¹⁶ When all the men who were able to bear arms had died and were no longer part of the people, ¹⁷ ADONAI said to me, ¹⁸ 'Today you are to cross the border of Mo'av at 'Ar. ¹⁹ When you approach the descendants of 'Amon, don't bother them or fight with them, for I will not give you any of the territory of the people of 'Amon to possess, since I have given it to the descendants of Lot as their territory.'"

²⁰ (This too is considered a land of the Refa'im: Refa'im, whom the Emori call Zamzumim, used to live there. ²¹ They were a large, numerous people, as tall as the 'Anakim; but ADONAI destroyed them as the people of 'Amon advanced and settled in their place — ²² just as he destroyed the Horim as descendants of 'Esav advanced into Se'ir and settled in their place, where they live to this day. ²³ It was the same with the 'Avim, who lived in villages as far away as 'Azah — the Kaftorim, coming from Kaftor, destroyed them and settled in their place.)

²⁴ "'Get up, get moving, and cross the Arnon Valley! Here, I have put in your hands Sichon the Emori, king of Heshbon, and his land; commence the conquest,

begin the battle! ²⁵ Today I will start putting the fear and dread of you into all the peoples under heaven, so that the mere mention of your name will make them quake and tremble before you.'

²⁶ "I sent envoys from the K'demot Desert to Sichon king of Heshbon with a peaceable message, ²⁷ 'Let me pass through your land. I will keep to the road, turning neither right nor left. ²⁸ You will sell me food to eat for money and give me water to drink for money. I only want to pass through. ²⁹ Do as the people of 'Esav living in Se'ir and the Mo'avim living in 'Ar did with me, until I cross the Yarden into the land ADONAI our God is giving us.'

³⁰ "But Sichon king of Heshbon would not let us pass through his territory, because ADONAI your God had hardened his spirit and made him stubborn, so that he could hand him over to you, as is the case today. *(vi)* ³¹ ADONAI said to me, 'See, I have begun handing over Sichon and his territory before you; start taking possession of his land.' ³² Then Sichon came out against us, he and all his people, to fight at Yahatz; ³³ and ADONAI our God handed him over to us, so that we defeated him, his sons and all his people. ³⁴ At that time we captured all his cities and completely destroyed every city — men, women, little ones — we left none of them. ³⁵ As booty for ourselves we took only the cattle, along with the spoil from the cities we had captured. ³⁶ From 'Aro'er, on the edge of the Arnon Valley, and from the city in the valley, all the way to Gil'ad, there was not one city too well fortified for us to capture — ADONAI our God gave all of them to us. ³⁷ The only land you didn't approach was that of the descendants of 'Amon — the region around the Yabok River, the cities in the hills and wherever else ADONAI our God forbade us to go.

3 ¹ "Then we turned and went up the road to Bashan, and 'Og the king of Bashan came out against us with all his people to fight at Edre'i. ² ADONAI said to me, 'Don't be afraid of him; for I have handed him, all his people and his territory over to you; you will do to him as you did to Sichon king of the Emori, who lived at Heshbon.' ³ So ADONAI our God also handed over to us 'Og the king of Bashan with all his people, and we defeated him until he had no one left. ⁴ At that time we captured all his cities; there was not one city of theirs that we didn't capture. There were sixty cities, all the region of Argov, the kingdom of 'Og in Bashan; ⁵ all of them fortified cities with high walls, gates and bars — in addition to a great number of unwalled towns. ⁶ We completely destroyed them, as we did with Sichon king of Heshbon, annihilating every city —men, women and little ones. ⁷ But we took all the livestock, along with the spoil from the cities, as booty for ourselves.

⁸ "At that time we captured the territory of the two kings of the Emori east of the Yarden between the Arnon Valley and Mount Hermon," ⁹ the Hermon which the Tzidonim call Siryon and the Emori call S'nir, ¹⁰ "all the cities of the plain, all Gil'ad and all Bashan, as far as Salkhah and Edre'i, cities of the kingdom of 'Og in Bashan." ¹¹ 'Og king of Bashan was the last survivor of the Refa'im. His bed was made of iron; it is still in Rabbah with the people of 'Amon. It was nine cubits long and four cubits wide, using the normal cubit [thirteen-and-a-half by six feet].

¹² "Of this land that we took possession of then, I assigned to the Re'uveni and the Gadi the territory extending from 'Aro'er along the Arnon Valley together with half the hill-country of Gil'ad, including its cities. ¹³ The rest of Gil'ad and all Bashan, the kingdom of 'Og, I gave to the half-tribe of M'nasheh."

The whole region of Argov together with all of Bashan form what is called the land of Refa'im. ¹⁴ Ya'ir the son of M'nasheh took all the region of Argov, as far as the border with the G'shuri and the Ma'akhati; he named this whole area, including Bashan, after himself — it remains Havot-Ya'ir to this day.

(vii) ¹⁵ "I gave Gil'ad to Machir; ¹⁶ and to the Re'uveni and the Gadi I gave the territory from Gil'ad to the Arnon Valley, with the middle of the valley as the border, as far as the Yabok River, which is the border with the people of 'Amon; ¹⁷ the 'Aravah too, the Yarden being its border, from Kinneret to the Sea of the 'Aravah, the Dead Sea, at the foot of the slopes of Pisgah to the east.

¹⁸ "At that time I gave you this order: 'ADONAI your God has given you this land to possess. But all of you who are fit to fight must cross over, armed, ahead of your brothers the people of Isra'el. ¹⁹ Your wives, your little ones and your livestock — I know you have much livestock — will stay in your cities which I have given you, *(Maftir)* ²⁰ until ADONAI allows your brothers to rest, as he has allowed you; and they too take possession of the land ADONAI your God is giving them on the west side of the Yarden. At that point you will return, each man to his own possession which I have given you.'

²¹ "Also at that time I gave this order to Y'hoshua: 'Your eyes have seen everything that ADONAI your God has done to these two kings. ADONAI will do the same to all the kingdoms you encounter when you cross over. ²² Don't be afraid of them, because ADONAI your God will fight on your behalf.'

Haftarah D'varim: Yesha'yahu (Isaiah) 1:1–27

B'rit Hadashah suggested readings for Parashah D'varim: Yochanan (John) 15:1–11; Messianic Jews (Hebrews) 3:7–4:11

Parashah 45: Va'etchanan (I pleaded) 3:23–7:11

²³ "Then I pleaded with ADONAI, ²⁴ 'Adonai ELOHIM, you have begun to reveal your greatness to your servant, and your strong hand — for what other god is there in heaven or on earth that can do the works and mighty deeds that you do? ²⁵ Please! Let me go across and see the good land on the other side of the Yarden, that wonderful hill-country and the L'vanon!' ²⁶ But ADONAI was angry with me on account of you, and he didn't listen to me. ADONAI said to me, 'Enough from you! Don't say another word to me about this matter! ²⁷ Climb up to the top of Pisgah and look out to the west, north, south and east. Look with your eyes — but you will not go across this Yarden. ²⁸ However, commission Y'hoshua, encourage him and strengthen him; for he will lead this people across and enable them to inherit the land that you will see.' ²⁹ So we stayed in the valley across from Beit-P'or.

4 ¹ "Now, Isra'el, listen to the laws and rulings I am teaching you, in order to follow them, so that you will live; then you will go in and take possession of the land that ADONAI, the God of your fathers, is giving you. ² In order to obey the *mitzvot* of ADONAI your God which I am giving you, do not add to what I am saying, and do not subtract from it. ³ You saw with your own eyes what ADONAI did at Ba'al-P'or, that A*DONAI* destroyed from among you all the men who followed Ba'al-P'or; ⁴ but you who stuck with A*DONAI* your God are still alive today, every one of you. *(ii)* ⁵ Look, I have taught you laws and rulings, just as A*DONAI* my God ordered me, so that you can behave accordingly in the land where you are going in order to take possession of it. ⁶ Therefore, observe them; and follow them; for then all peoples will see you as having wisdom and understanding. When they hear of all these laws, they will say, 'This great nation is surely a wise and understanding people.' ⁷ For what great nation is there that has God as close to them as A*DONAI* our God is, whenever we call on him? ⁸ What great nation is there that has laws and rulings as just as this entire *Torah* which I am setting before you today? ⁹ Only be careful, and watch yourselves diligently as long as you live, so that you won't forget what you saw with your own eyes, so that these things won't vanish from your hearts. Rather, make them known to your children and grandchildren — ¹⁰ the day you stood before A*DONAI* your God at Horev, when A*DONAI* said to me, 'Gather the people to me, and I will make them hear my very words, so that they will learn to hold me in awe as long as they live on earth, and so that they will teach their children.' ¹¹ You approached and stood at the foot of the mountain; and the mountain blazed with fire to the heart of heaven, with darkness, clouds and thick mist. ¹² Then A*DONAI* spoke to you out of the fire! You heard the sound of words but saw no shape, there was only a voice. ¹³ He proclaimed his covenant to you, which he ordered you to obey, the Ten Words; and he wrote them on two stone tablets. ¹⁴ At that time A*DONAI* ordered me to teach you laws and rulings, so that you would live by them in the land you are entering in order to take possession of it.

¹⁵ "Therefore, watch out for yourselves! Since you did not see a shape of any kind on the day A*DONAI* spoke to you in Horev from the fire, ¹⁶ do not become corrupt and make yourselves a carved image having the shape of any figure — not a representation of a human being, male or female, ¹⁷ or a representation of any animal on earth, or a representation of any bird that flies in the air, ¹⁸ or a representation of anything that creeps along on the ground, or a representation of any fish in the water below the shoreline. ¹⁹ For the same reason, do not look up at the sky, at the sun, moon, stars and everything in the sky, and be drawn away to worship and serve them; A*DONAI* your God has allotted these to all the peoples under the entire sky. ²⁰ No, you A*DONAI* has taken and brought out of the smelting furnace, out of Egypt, to be a people of inheritance for him, as you are today.

²¹ "But A*DONAI* was angry with me on account of you and swore that I would not cross the Yarden and go into that good land, which A*DONAI* your God is giving you to inherit. ²² Rather, I must die in this land and not cross the Yarden; but you are to cross and take possession of that good land. ²³ Watch out for yourselves, so that you won't forget the covenant of A*DONAI* your God, which he made with you, and make yourself a carved image, a representation of anything forbidden to you by A*DONAI* your God. ²⁴ For A*DONAI* your God is a consuming fire, a jealous God.

²⁵ "When you have had children and grandchildren, lived a long time in the land, become corrupt and made a carved image, a representation of something, and thus done what is evil in the sight of A*DONAI* your God and provoked him; ²⁶ I call on the sky and the earth to witness against you today that you will quickly disappear from the land that you are crossing the Yarden to possess. You will not prolong your days there but will be completely destroyed. ²⁷ A*DONAI* will scatter you among the

peoples; and among the nations to which ADONAI will lead you away, you will be left few in number. ²⁸ There you will serve gods which are the product of human hands, made of wood and stone, which can't see, hear, eat or smell. ²⁹ However, from there you will seek ADONAI your God; and you will find him if you search after him with all your heart and being. ³⁰ In your distress, when all these things have come upon you, in the *acharit-hayamim*, you will return to ADONAI your God and listen to what he says; ³¹ for ADONAI your God is a merciful God. He will not fail you, destroy you, or forget the covenant with your ancestors which he swore to them.

³² "Indeed, inquire about the past, before you were born: since the day God created human beings on the earth, from one end of heaven to the other, has there ever been anything as wonderful as this? Has anyone heard anything like it? ³³ Did any other people ever hear the voice of God speaking out of a fire, as you have heard, and stay alive? ³⁴ Or has God ever tried to go and take for himself a nation from the very bowels of another nation, by means of ordeals, signs, wonders, war, a mighty hand, an outstretched arm and great terrors — like all that ADONAI your God did for you in Egypt before your very eyes? ³⁵ This was shown to you, so that you would know that ADONAI is God, and there is no other beside him. ³⁶ From heaven he caused you to hear his voice, in order to instruct you; and on earth he caused you to see his great fire; and you heard his very words coming out from the fire. ³⁷ Because he loved your ancestors, chose their descendants after them and brought you out of Egypt with his presence and great power, ³⁸ in order to drive out ahead of you nations greater and stronger than you, so that he could bring you in and give you their land as an inheritance, as is the case today; ³⁹ know today, and establish it in your heart, that ADONAI is God in heaven above and on earth below — there is no other. ⁴⁰ Therefore, you are to keep his laws and *mitzvot* which I am giving you today, so that it will go well with you and with your children after you, and so that you will prolong your days in the land ADONAI your God is giving you forever."

(A: iii) ⁴¹ Then Moshe separated three cities on the east side of the Yarden, toward the sunrise, ⁴² to which a killer might flee, that is, someone who kills by mistake a person whom he did not previously hate, and upon fleeing to one of these cities might live there. ⁴³ The cities were Betzer in the desert, in the flatland, for the Re'uveni; Ramot in Gil'ad for the Gadi; and Golan in Bashan for the M'nashi.

⁴⁴ This is the *Torah* which Moshe placed before the people of Isra'el — ⁴⁵ these are the instructions, laws and rulings which Moshe presented to the people of Isra'el after they had come out of Egypt — ⁴⁶ beyond the Yarden River, in the valley across from Beit-P'or, in the land of Sichon king of the Emori, who lived at Heshbon, whom Moshe and the people of Isra'el defeated when they came out of Egypt; ⁴⁷ and they took possession of his land and the land of 'Og king of Bashan, the two kings of the Emori, who were beyond the Yarden toward the sunrise; ⁴⁸ from 'Aro'er on the edge of the Arnon Valley to Mount Si'on," that is, Mount Hermon, ⁴⁹ "with all the 'Aravah beyond the Yarden eastward, all the way to the Dead Sea at the foot of the slopes of Pisgah.

5 *(A: iv, S: iii)* ¹ Then Moshe called to all Isra'el and said to them, "Listen, Isra'el, to the laws and rulings which I am announcing in your hearing today, so that you will learn them and take care to obey them. ² ADONAI our God made a covenant with us at Horev. ³ ADONAI did not make this covenant with our fathers, but with us — with us, who are all of us here alive today. ⁴ ADONAI spoke with you face to face from the fire on the mountain. ⁵ At that time I stood between *Adonai* and you in order to tell you what *Adonai* was saying; because, on account of the fire, you were afraid and wouldn't go up onto the mountain. He said,

א ⁶ "'I am *Adonai* your God, who brought you out of the land of Egypt, where you lived as slaves.

ב ⁷ "'You are to have no other gods before me. ⁸ You are not to make for yourselves a carved image or any kind of representation of anything in heaven above, on the earth beneath or in the water below the shoreline — ⁹ you are not to bow down to them or serve them; for I, *Adonai* your God, am a jealous God, punishing the children for the sins of the parents, also the third and fourth generation of those who hate me, ¹⁰ but displaying grace to the thousandth generation of those who love me and obey my *mitzvot*.

ג ¹¹ "'You are not to misuse the name of *Adonai* your God, because *Adonai* will not leave unpunished someone who misuses his name.

ד ¹² "'Observe the day of *Shabbat*, to set it apart as holy, as *Adonai* your God ordered you to do. ¹³ You have six days to labor and do all your work, ¹⁴ but the seventh day is a *Shabbat* for *Adonai* your God. On it you are not to do any kind of work — not you, your son or your daughter, not your male or female slave, not your ox, your donkey or any of your other livestock, and not the foreigner staying with you inside the gates to your property — so that your male and female servants can rest just as you do. ¹⁵ You are to remember that you were a slave in the land of Egypt, and *Adonai* your God brought you out from there with a strong hand and an outstretched arm. Therefore *Adonai* your God has ordered you to keep the day of *Shabbat*.

ה ¹⁶ "'Honor your father and mother, as *Adonai* your God ordered you to do, so that you will live long and have things go well with you in the land *Adonai* your God is giving you.

ו ¹⁷ "'Do not murder.

ז ⁽¹⁸⁾ "'Do not commit adultery.

ח ⁽¹⁹⁾ "'Do not steal.

ט ⁽²⁰⁾ "'Do not give false evidence against your neighbor.

י ¹⁸⁽²¹⁾ "'Do not covet your neighbor's wife; do not covet your neighbor's house, his field, his male or female slave, his ox, his donkey or anything that belongs to your neighbor.'

(A: v, S: iv) ¹⁹⁽²²⁾ "These words *Adonai* spoke to your entire gathering at the mountain from fire, cloud and thick mist, in a loud voice; then it ceased. But he wrote them on two stone tablets, which he gave to me. $^{20(23)}$ When you heard the voice coming out of the darkness, as the mountain blazed with fire, you came to me, all the heads of your tribes and your leaders, $^{21(24)}$ and said, 'Here, ADONAI our God has shown us his glory and his greatness! We have heard his voice coming from the fire, and we have seen today that God does speak with human beings, and they stay alive. $^{22(25)}$ But why should we keep risking death? This great fire will consume us! If we hear the voice of ADONAI our God any more, we will die! $^{23(26)}$ For who is there of all humanity that has heard the voice of the living God speaking from the fire, as we have, and stayed alive? $^{24(27)}$ You, go near; and hear everything ADONAI our God says. Then you will tell us everything ADONAI our God says to you; and we will listen to it and do it.'

$^{25(28)}$ "ADONAI heard what you were saying when you spoke to me, and ADONAI said to me, 'I have heard what this people has said when speaking to you, and everything they have said is good. $^{26(29)}$ Oh, how I wish their hearts would stay like this always, that they would fear me and obey all my *mitzvot*; so that it would go well with them and their children forever. $^{27(30)}$ Go, tell them to return to their tents. $^{28(31)}$ But you, stand here by me; and I will tell you all the *mitzvot*, laws and rulings which you are to teach them, so that they can obey them in the land I am giving them as their possession.'

$^{29(32)}$ "Therefore you are to be careful to do as ADONAI your God has ordered you; you are not to deviate either to the right or the left. $^{30(33)}$ You are to follow the entire way which ADONAI your God has ordered you; so that you will live, things will go well with you, and you will live long in the land you are about to possess.

6 ^{1} "Now this is the *mitzvah*, the laws and rulings which ADONAI your God ordered me to teach you for you to obey in the land you are crossing over to possess, ^{2} so that you will fear ADONAI your God and observe all his regulations and *mitzvot* that I am giving you — you, your child and your grandchild — as long as you live, and so that you will have long life. ^{3} Therefore listen, Isra'el, and take care to obey, so that things will go well with you, and so that you will increase greatly, as ADONAI, the God of your ancestors, promised you by giving you a land flowing with milk and honey.

(A:vi, S: v) ^{4} "*Sh'ma, Yisra'el! ADONAI Eloheinu, ADONAI echad* [Hear, Isra'el! ADONAI our God, ADONAI is one]; ^{5} and you are to love ADONAI your God with all your heart, all your being and all your resources. ^{6} These words, which I am ordering you today, are to be on your heart; ^{7} and you are to teach them carefully to your children. You are to talk about them when you sit at home, when you are traveling on the road, when you lie down and when you get up. ^{8} Tie them on your hand as a sign, put them at the front of a headband around your forehead, ^{9} and write them on the door-frames of your house and on your gates.

(S: vi) ^{10} "When ADONAI your God has brought you into the land he swore to your ancestors Avraham, Yitz'chak and Ya'akov that he would give you — cities great and prosperous, which you didn't build; ^{11} houses full of all sorts of good things, which you didn't fill; water cisterns dug out, which you didn't dig; vineyards and olive trees, which you didn't plant — and you have eaten your fill; ^{12} then be careful not to forget ADONAI, who brought you out of the land of Egypt, where you lived as slaves. ^{13} You are to fear ADONAI your God, serve him and swear by his name. ^{14} You are not to follow other gods, chosen from the gods of the peoples around you; ^{15} because ADONAI, your God, who is here with you, is a jealous God. If you do, the anger of ADONAI your God will flare up against you and he will destroy you from the face of the earth.

¹⁶ Do not put *Adonai* your God to the test, as you tested him at Massah [testing]. ¹⁷ Observe diligently the *mitzvot* of *Adonai* your God, and his instructions and laws which he has given you. ¹⁸ You are to do what is right and good in the sight of *Adonai*, so that things will go well with you, and you will enter and possess the good land *Adonai* swore to your ancestors, ¹⁹ expelling all your enemies ahead of you, as *Adonai* said.

²⁰ "Some day your child will ask you, 'What is the meaning of the instructions, laws and rulings which *Adonai* our God has laid down for you?' ²¹ Then you will tell your child, 'We were slaves to Pharaoh in Egypt, and *Adonai* brought us out of Egypt with a strong hand. ²² *Adonai* worked great and terrible signs and wonders against Egypt, Pharaoh and all his household, before our very eyes. ²³ He brought us out from there in order to bring us to the land he had sworn to our ancestors that he would give us. ²⁴ *Adonai* ordered us to observe all these laws, to fear *Adonai* our God, always for our own good, so that he might keep us alive, as we are today. ²⁵ It will be righteousness for us if we are careful to obey all these *mitzvot* before *Adonai* our God, just as he ordered us to do.'"

7 *(vii)* ¹ "*Adonai* your God is going to bring you into the land you will enter in order to take possession of it, and he will expel many nations ahead of you — the Hitti, Girgashi, Emori, Kena'ani, P'rizi, Hivi and Y'vusi, seven nations bigger and stronger than you. ² When he does this, when *Adonai* your God hands them over ahead of you, and you defeat them, you are to destroy them completely! Do not make any covenant with them. Show them no mercy. ³ Don't intermarry with them — don't give your daughter to his son, and don't take his daughter for your son. ⁴ For he will turn your children away from following me in order to serve other gods. If this happens, the anger of *Adonai* will flare up against you, and he will quickly destroy you. ⁵ No, treat them this way: break down their altars, smash their standing-stones to pieces, cut down their sacred poles and burn up their carved images completely. ⁶ For you are a people set apart as holy for *Adonai* your God. *Adonai* your God has chosen you out of all the peoples on the face of the earth to be his own unique treasure. ⁷ *Adonai* didn't set his heart on you or choose you because you numbered more than any other people — on the contrary, you were the fewest of all peoples. ⁸ Rather, it was because *Adonai* loved you, and because he wanted to keep the oath which he had sworn to your ancestors, that *Adonai* brought you out with a strong hand and redeemed you from a life of slavery under the hand of Pharaoh king of Egypt. *(Maftir)* ⁹ From this you can know that *Adonai* your God is indeed God, the faithful God, who keeps his covenant and extends grace to those who love him and observe his *mitzvot*, to a thousand generations. ¹⁰ But he repays those who hate him to their face and destroys them. He will not be slow to deal with someone who hates him; he will repay him to his face. ¹¹ Therefore, you are to keep the *mitzvot*, laws and rulings which I am giving you today, and obey them.

Haftarah Va'etchanan: Yesha'yahu (Isaiah) 40:1–26

B'rit Hadashah suggested readings for Parashah Va'etchanan: Mattityahu (Matthew) 4:1–11; 22:33–40; Mark 12:28–34; Luke 4:1–13; 10:25–37; Acts 13:13–43; Romans 3:27–31; 1 Timothy 2:4–6; Ya'akov (James) 2:14–26; and all the readings for Parashah 17

Parashah 46: 'Ekev (Because) 7:12–11:25

[12] "Because you are listening to these rulings, keeping and obeying them, ADONAI your God will keep with you the covenant and mercy that he swore to your ancestors. [13] He will love you, bless you and increase your numbers; he will also bless the fruit of your body and the fruit of your ground — your grain, wine, olive oil and the young of your cattle and sheep — in the land he swore to your ancestors that he would give you. [14] You will be blessed more than all other peoples; there will not be a sterile male or female among you, and the same with your livestock. [15] ADONAI will remove all illness from you — he will not afflict you with any of Egypt's dreadful diseases, which you have known; instead, he will lay them on those who hate you. [16] You are to devour all the peoples that ADONAI your God hands over to you — show them no pity, and do not serve their gods, because that will become a trap for you. [17] If you think to yourselves, 'These nations outnumber us; how can we dispossess them?' [18] nevertheless, you are not to be afraid of them; you are to remember well what ADONAI your God did to Pharaoh and all of Egypt — [19] the great ordeals which you yourself saw, and the signs, wonders, strong hand and outstretched arm by which ADONAI your God brought you out. ADONAI will do the same to all the peoples of whom you are afraid. [20] Moreover, ADONAI your God will send the hornet among them until those who are left and those who hide themselves perish ahead of you. [21] You are not to be frightened of them, because ADONAI your God is there with you, a God great and fearsome. [22] ADONAI your God will expel those nations ahead of you little by little; you can't put an end to them all at once, or the wild animals will become too numerous for you. [23] Nevertheless, ADONAI your God will give them over to you, sending one disaster after another upon them until they have been destroyed. [24] He will hand their kings over to you, and you will wipe out their name from under heaven; none of them will be able to stand against you until you have destroyed them. [25] You are to burn up completely the carved statues of their gods. Don't be greedy for the silver or gold on them; don't take it with you, or you will be trapped by it; for it is abhorrent to ADONAI your God. [26] Don't bring something abhorrent into your house, or you will share in the curse that is on it; instead, you are to detest it completely, loathe it utterly; for it is set apart for destruction.

8 [1] "All the *mitzvot* I am giving you today you are to take care to obey, so that you will live, increase your numbers, enter and take possession of the land ADONAI swore about to your ancestors. [2] You are to remember everything of the way in which ADONAI led you these forty years in the desert, humbling and testing you in order to know what was in your heart — whether you would obey his *mitzvot* or not. [3] He humbled you, allowing you to become hungry, and then fed you with *man*, which neither you nor your ancestors had ever known, to make you understand that a person does not live on food alone but on everything that comes from the mouth of ADONAI. [4] During these forty years the clothing you were wearing didn't grow old, and your feet didn't swell up. [5] Think deeply about it: ADONAI was disciplining you, just as a man disciplines his child. [6] So obey the *mitzvot* of ADONAI your God, living as he directs and fearing him. [7] For ADONAI your God is bringing you into a good land, a land with streams, springs and water welling up from the depths in valleys and on hillsides. ⁸ It is a land of wheat and barley, grapevines, fig trees and pomegranates; a land of olive oil and honey; ⁹ a land where you will eat food in abundance and lack nothing in it; a land where the stones contain iron and the hills can be mined for copper. ¹⁰ So you will eat and be satisfied, and you will bless *Adonai* your God for the good land he has given you.

(ii) ¹¹ "Be careful not to forget *Adonai* your God by not obeying his *mitzvot*, rulings and regulations that I am giving you today. ¹² Otherwise, after you have eaten and are satisfied, built fine houses and lived in them, ¹³ and increased your herds, flocks, silver, gold and everything else you own, ¹⁴ you will become proud-hearted. Forgetting *Adonai* your God — who brought you out of the land of Egypt, where you lived as slaves; ¹⁵ who led you through the vast and fearsome desert, with its poisonous snakes, scorpions and waterless, thirsty ground; who brought water out of flint rock for you; ¹⁶ who fed you in the desert with *man*, unknown to your ancestors; all the while humbling and testing you in order to do you good in the end — ¹⁷ you will think to yourself, 'My own power and the strength of my own hand have gotten me this wealth.' ¹⁸ No, you are to remember *Adonai* your God, because it is he who is giving you the power to get wealth, in order to confirm his covenant, which he swore to your ancestors, as is happening even today. ¹⁹ If you forget *Adonai* your God, follow other gods and serve and worship them, I am warning you in advance today that you will certainly perish. ²⁰ You will perish just like the nations that *Adonai* is causing to perish ahead of you, because you will not have heeded the voice of *Adonai* your God."

9 ¹ "Listen, Isra'el! You are to cross the Yarden today, to go in and dispossess nations greater and stronger than you, great cities fortified up to the sky; ² a people great and tall, the 'Anakim, whom you know about and of whom you have heard it said, 'Who can stand before the descendants of 'Anak?' ³ Therefore understand today that *Adonai* your God will himself cross ahead of you as a devouring fire; he will destroy them and bring them down before you. Thus will you drive them out and cause them to perish quickly, as *Adonai* has said to you.

(iii) ⁴ "Don't think to yourself, after your God has pushed them out ahead of you, 'It is to reward my righteousness that *Adonai* has brought me in to take possession of this land.' No, it is because these nations have been so wicked that *Adonai* is driving them out ahead of you. ⁵ It is not because of your righteousness, or because your heart is so upright, that you go in to take possession of their land; but to punish the wickedness of these nations that *Adonai* your God is driving them out ahead of you, and also to confirm the word which *Adonai* swore to your ancestors, Avraham, Yitz'chak and Ya'akov. ⁶ Therefore, understand that it is not for your righteousness that *Adonai* your God is giving you this good land to possess.

"For you are a stiffnecked people! ⁷ Remember, don't forget, how you made *Adonai* your God angry in the desert. From the day you left the land of Egypt till you arrived at this place, you have been rebelling against *Adonai*. ⁸ Also in Horev you made *Adonai* angry — *Adonai* was angry enough with you to destroy you! ⁹ I had gone up the mountain to receive the stone tablets, the tablets on which was written the covenant *Adonai* had made with you. I stayed on the mountain forty days and nights without eating food or drinking water. ¹⁰ Then *Adonai* gave me the two stone tablets inscribed by the finger of God; and on them was written every word *Adonai* had said to you from the fire on the mountain the day of the assembly. ¹¹ Yes, after forty days and nights ADONAI gave me the two stone tablets, the tablets of the covenant. ¹² Then ADONAI said to me, 'Get up, and hurry down from here, because your people, whom you led out of Egypt, have become corrupt. So quickly have they turned aside from the way I ordered them to follow! They have made themselves a metal image!' ¹³ Moreover, ADONAI said to me, 'I have seen this people, and what a stiffnecked people they are! ¹⁴ Let me alone, so that I can put an end to them and blot out their name from under heaven! I will make out of you a nation bigger and stronger than they.' ¹⁵ I came down from the mountain. The mountain was blazing fire, and the two tablets of the covenant were in my two hands. ¹⁶ I looked, and there, you had sinned against ADONAI your God! You had made yourselves a metal calf, you had turned aside quickly from the way ADONAI had ordered you to follow. ¹⁷ I seized the two tablets, threw them out of my two hands and broke them before your eyes. ¹⁸ Then I fell down before ADONAI, as I had the first time, for forty days and nights, during which time I neither ate food nor drank water, all because of the sin you committed by doing what was evil in the sight of ADONAI and thus provoking him. ¹⁹ I was terrified that because of how angry ADONAI was at you, of how heatedly displeased he was, that he would destroy you. But ADONAI listened to me that time too. ²⁰ In addition, ADONAI was very angry with Aharon and would have destroyed him; but I prayed for Aharon also at the same time. ²¹ I took your sin, the calf you had made, and burned it up in the fire, beat it to pieces, and ground it up still smaller, until it was as fine as dust; then I threw its dust into the stream coming down from the mountain.

²² "Again at Tav'erah, Massah and Kivrot-HaTa'avah you made ADONAI angry; ²³ and when ADONAI sent you off from Kadesh-Barnea by saying, 'Go up and take possession of the land I have given you,' you rebelled against the order of ADONAI your God — you neither trusted him nor heeded what he said. ²⁴ You have been rebelling against ADONAI from the day I first knew you!

²⁵ "So I fell down before ADONAI for those forty days and nights; and I lay there; because ADONAI had said he would destroy you. ²⁶ I prayed to ADONAI; I said, '*Adonai Elohim!* Don't destroy your people, your inheritance! You redeemed them through your greatness, you brought them out of Egypt with a strong hand! ²⁷ Remember your servants Avraham, Yitz'chak and Ya'akov! Don't focus on the stubbornness of this people, or on their wickedness or on their sin. ²⁸ Otherwise, the land you brought us out of will say, "It is because ADONAI wasn't able to bring them into the land he promised them and because he hated them that he has brought them out to kill them in the desert." ²⁹ But in fact they are your people, your inheritance, whom you brought out by your great power and your outstretched arm.'

10 *(iv)* ¹ "At that time ADONAI said to me, 'Cut yourself two stone tablets like the first ones, come up to me on the mountain, and make yourself an ark of wood. ² I will inscribe on the tablets the words that were on the first tablets, which you broke; and you are to put them in the ark.' ³ So I made an ark of acacia-wood and cut two stone tablets like the first, then climbed the mountain with the two tablets in my hand. ⁴ He inscribed the tablets with the same inscription as before, the Ten Words which ADONAI proclaimed to you from the fire on the mountain the day of the assembly; and ADONAI gave them to me. ⁵ I turned, came down the mountain and put the tablets in the ark I had made; and there they remain; as ADONAI ordered me.

⁶ "The people of Isra'el traveled from the wells of B'nei-Ya'akan to Moserah, where Aharon died and was buried; and El'azar his son took his place, serving in the office of *cohen*. ⁷ From there they traveled to Gudgod, and from Gudgod to Yotvatah, a region with running streams. ⁸ At that time ADONAI set apart the tribe of Levi to carry the ark for the covenant of ADONAI and to stand before ADONAI to serve him and to bless in his name, as they still do today. ⁹ This is why Levi has no share or inheritance with his brothers; ADONAI is his inheritance, as ADONAI your God had said to him.

¹⁰ "I stayed on the mountain forty days and nights, as previously; and ADONAI listened to me that time too — ADONAI would not destroy you. ¹¹ Then ADONAI said to me, 'Get up, and go on your way at the head of the people, so that they can enter and take possession of the land I swore to their ancestors that I would give them.'

(v) ¹² "So now, Isra'el, all that ADONAI your God asks from you is to fear ADONAI your God, follow all his ways, love him and serve ADONAI your God with all your heart and all your being; ¹³ to obey, for your own good, the *mitzvot* and regulations of ADONAI which I am giving you today. ¹⁴ See, the sky, the heaven beyond the sky, the earth and everything on it all belong to ADONAI your God. ¹⁵ Only ADONAI took enough pleasure in your ancestors to love them and choose their descendants after them — yourselves — above all peoples, as he still does today. ¹⁶ Therefore, circumcise the foreskin of your heart; and don't be stiffnecked any longer! ¹⁷ For ADONAI your God is God of gods and Lord of lords, the great, mighty and awesome God, who has no favorites and accepts no bribes. ¹⁸ He secures justice for the orphan and the widow; he loves the foreigner, giving him food and clothing. ¹⁹ Therefore you are to love the foreigner, since you were foreigners in the land of Egypt. ²⁰ You are to fear ADONAI your God, serve him, cling to him and swear by his name. ²¹ He is your praise, and he is your God, who has done for you these great and awesome things, which you have seen with your own eyes. ²² Your ancestors went down into Egypt with only seventy people, but now ADONAI your God has made your numbers as many as the stars in the sky!

11 ¹ "Therefore, you are to love ADONAI your God and always obey his commission, regulations, rulings and *mitzvot*. ² Today it is you I am addressing — not your children, who haven't known or experienced the discipline of ADONAI your God, his greatness, his strong hand, his outstretched arm, ³ his signs and his actions which he did in Egypt to Pharaoh the king of Egypt and to his entire country. ⁴ They didn't experience what he did to Egypt's army, horses and chariots — how ADONAI overwhelmed them with the water of the Sea of Suf as they were pursuing you, so that they remain destroyed to this day. ⁵ They didn't experience what he kept doing for you in the desert until you arrived at this place; ⁶ or what he did to Datan and Aviram, the sons of Eli'av the descendant of Re'uven — how the earth opened its mouth and swallowed them up, along with their households, tents and every living thing in their company, there in front of all Isra'el. ⁷ But you have seen with your own eyes all these great deeds of ADONAI. ⁸ Therefore, you are to keep every *mitzvah* I am giving you today; so that you will be strong enough to go in and take possession of the land you are crossing over to conquer; ⁹ and so that you will live long in the land ADONAI swore to give to your ancestors and their descendants, a land flowing with milk and honey.

(vi) ¹⁰ "For the land you are entering in order to take possession of it isn't like the land of Egypt. There you would sow your seed and had to use your feet to

operate its irrigation system, as in a vegetable garden. ¹¹ But the land you are crossing over to take possession of is a land of hills and valleys, which soaks up water when rain falls from the sky. ¹² It is a land ADONAI your God cares for. The eyes of ADONAI your God are always on it, from the beginning of the year to the end of the year.

¹³ "So if you listen carefully to my *mitzvot* which I am giving you today, to love ADONAI your God and serve him with all your heart and all your being; ¹⁴ then, [says ADONAI,] 'I will give your land its rain at the right seasons, including the early fall rains and the late spring rains; so that you can gather in your wheat, new wine and olive oil; ¹⁵ and I will give your fields grass for your livestock; with the result that you will eat and be satisfied.' ¹⁶ But be careful not to let yourselves be seduced, so that you turn aside, serving other gods and worshipping them. ¹⁷ If you do, the anger of ADONAI will blaze up against you. He will shut up the sky, so that there will be no rain. The ground will not yield its produce, and you will quickly pass away from the good land ADONAI is giving you. ¹⁸ Therefore, you are to store up these words of mine in your heart and in all your being; tie them on your hand as a sign; put them at the front of a headband around your forehead; ¹⁹ teach them carefully to your children, talking about them when you sit at home, when you are traveling on the road, when you lie down and when you get up; ²⁰ and write them on the door-frames of your house and on your gates — ²¹ so that you and your children will live long on the land ADONAI swore to your ancestors that he would give them for as long as there is sky above the earth.

(vii & Maftir) ²² "For if you will take care to obey all these *mitzvot* I am giving you, to do them, to love ADONAI your God, to follow all his ways and to cling to him, ²³ then ADONAI will expel all these nations ahead of you; and you will dispossess nations bigger and stronger than you are. ²⁴ Wherever the sole of your foot steps will be yours; your territory will extend from the desert to the L'vanon and from the River, the Euphrates River, to the Western Sea. ²⁵ No one will be able to withstand you; ADONAI your God will place the fear and dread of you on all the land you step on, as he told you.

Haftarah 'Ekev: Yesha'yahu (Isaiah) 49:14–51:3

B'rit Hadashah suggested readings for Parashah 'Ekev: Mattityahu (Matthew) 4:1–11; Luke 4:1–13; Ya'akov (James) 5:7–11

Parashah 47: Re'eh (See) 11:26–16:17

²⁶ "See, I am setting before you today a blessing and a curse — ²⁷ the blessing, if you listen to the *mitzvot* of ADONAI your God that I am giving you today; ²⁸ and the curse, if you don't listen to the *mitzvot* of ADONAI your God, but turn aside from the way I am ordering you today and follow other gods that you have not known.

²⁹ "When ADONAI your God brings you into the land you are entering in order to take possession of it, you are to put the blessing on Mount G'rizim and the curse on Mount 'Eival. ³⁰ Both are west of the Yarden, in the direction of the sunset, in the land of the Kena'ani living in the 'Aravah, across from Gilgal, near the pistachio trees of Moreh. ³¹ For you are to cross the Yarden to enter and take possession of the land ADONAI your God is giving you; you are to own it and live in it. ³² And you are to take care to follow all the laws and rulings I am setting before you today.

12 ^{1} Here are the laws and rulings you are to observe and obey in the land ADONAI, the God of your ancestors, has given you to possess as long as you live on earth. ^{2} You must destroy all the places where the nations you are dispossessing served their gods, whether on high mountains, on hills, or under some leafy tree. ^{3} Break down their altars, smash their standing-stones to pieces, burn up their sacred poles completely and cut down the carved images of their gods. Exterminate their name from that place. ^{4} "But you are not to treat ADONAI your God this way. ^{5} Rather, you are to come to the place where ADONAI your God will put his name. He will choose it from all your tribes; and you will seek out that place, which is where he will live, and go there. ^{6} You will bring there your burnt offerings, your sacrifices, your tenths [that you set aside for ADONAI], the offerings that you give, the offerings you have vowed, your voluntary offerings, and the firstborn of your cattle and sheep. ^{7} There you will eat in the presence of ADONAI your God; and you will rejoice over everything you set out to do, you and your households, in which ADONAI your God has blessed you. ^{8} You will not do things the way we do them here today, where everyone does whatever in his own opinion seems right; ^{9} because you haven't yet arrived at the rest and inheritance which ADONAI your God is giving you. ^{10} But when you cross the Yarden and live in the land ADONAI your God is having you inherit, and he gives you rest from all your surrounding enemies, so that you are living in safety; *(ii)* ^{11} then you will bring all that I am ordering you to the place ADONAI your God chooses to have his name live — your burnt offerings, sacrifices, tenths, the offering from your hand, and all your best possessions that you dedicate to ADONAI; ^{12} and you will rejoice in the presence of ADONAI your God — you, your sons and daughters, your male and female slaves and the *Levi* staying with you, inasmuch as he has no share or inheritance with you.

^{13} "Be careful not to offer your burnt offerings just anywhere you see, ^{14} but do it in the place ADONAI will choose in one of your tribal territories; there is where you are to offer your burnt offerings and do everything I order you to do. ^{15} However, you may slaughter and eat meat wherever you live and whenever you want, in keeping with the degree to which ADONAI your God has blessed you. The unclean and the clean may eat it, as if it were gazelle or deer. ^{16} But don't eat the blood; pour it out on the ground like water.

^{17} "You are not to eat on your own property the tenth of your grain, new wine or olive oil [that you set aside for ADONAI], or the firstborn of your cattle or sheep, or any offering you have vowed, or your voluntary offering, or the offering from your hand. ^{18} No, you are to eat these in the presence of ADONAI your God in the place ADONAI your God will choose — you and your sons, daughters, male and female slaves, and the *Levi* who is your guest; and you are to rejoice before ADONAI your God in everything you undertake to do. ^{19} As long as you are living on your property, take care not to abandon the *Levi*.

^{20} "When ADONAI your God expands your territory, as he has promised you, and you say, 'I want to eat meat,' simply because you want to eat meat, then you may eat meat, as much as you want. ^{21} If the place which ADONAI your God chooses to place his name is too far away from you; then you are to slaughter animals from your cattle or sheep, which ADONAI has given you; and eat on your own property, as much as you want. ^{22} Eat it as you would gazelle or deer; the unclean and clean alike may eat it. ^{23} Just take care not to eat the blood, for the blood is the life, and you are not to eat the life with the meat. ^{24} Don't eat it, but pour it out on the ground like water. ^{25} Do not eat it, so that things will go well with you and with your children after you, as you do what ADONAI sees as right. ²⁶ Only the things set aside for God which you have, and the vows you have vowed to make, you must take and go to the place which ADONAI will choose. ²⁷ There you will offer your burnt offerings, the meat and the blood, on the altar of ADONAI your God. The blood of your sacrifices is to be poured out on the altar of ADONAI your God, and you will eat the meat. ²⁸ Obey and pay attention to everything I am ordering you to do, so that things will go well with you and with your descendants after you forever, as you do what ADONAI sees as good and right.

(iii) ²⁹ "When ADONAI your God has cut off ahead of you the nations you are entering in order to dispossess, and when you have dispossessed them and are living in their land; ³⁰ be careful, after they have been destroyed ahead of you, not to be trapped into following them; so that you inquire after their gods and ask, 'How did these nations serve their gods? I want to do the same.' ³¹ You must not do this to ADONAI your God! For they have done to their gods all the abominations that ADONAI hates! They even burn up their sons and daughters in the fire for their gods!

13 ¹⁽¹²:³²⁾ "Everything I am commanding you, you are to take care to do. Do not add to it or subtract from it.

²⁽¹⁾ "If a prophet or someone who gets messages while dreaming arises among you and he gives you a sign or wonder, ³⁽²⁾ and the sign or wonder comes about as he predicted when he said, 'Let's follow other gods, which you have not known; and let us serve them,' ⁴⁽³⁾ you are not to listen to what that prophet or dreamer says. For ADONAI your God is testing you, in order to find out whether you really do love ADONAI your God with all your heart and being. ⁵⁽⁴⁾ You are to follow ADONAI your God, fear him, obey his *mitzvot*, listen to what he says, serve him and cling to him; ⁶⁽⁵⁾ and that prophet or dreamer is to be put to death; because he urged rebellion against ADONAI your God, who brought you out of the land of Egypt and redeemed you from a life of slavery; in order to seduce you away from the path ADONAI your God ordered you to follow. This is how you are to rid your community of this wickedness.

⁷⁽⁶⁾ "If your brother the son of your mother, or your son, or your daughter, or your wife whom you love, or your friend who means as much to you as yourself, secretly tries to entice you to go and serve other gods, which you haven't known, neither you nor your ancestors — ⁸⁽⁷⁾ gods of the peoples surrounding you, whether near or far away from you, anywhere in the world — ⁹⁽⁸⁾ you are not to consent, and you are not to listen to him; and you must not pity him or spare him; and you may not conceal him. ¹⁰⁽⁹⁾ Rather, you must kill him! Your own hand must be the first one on him in putting him to death, and afterwards the hands of all the people. ¹¹⁽¹⁰⁾ You are to stone him to death; because he has tried to draw you away from ADONAI your God, who brought you out of the land of Egypt, out of a life of slavery. ¹²⁽¹¹⁾ Then all Isra'el will hear about it and be afraid, so that they will stop doing such wickedness as this among themselves.

¹³⁽¹²⁾ "If you hear it told that in one of your cities which ADONAI your God is giving you to live in, ¹⁴⁽¹³⁾ certain scoundrels have sprung up among you and have drawn away the inhabitants of their city by saying, 'Let's go and serve other gods, which you haven't known,' ¹⁵⁽¹⁴⁾ then you are to investigate the matter, inquiring and searching diligently. If the rumor is true, if it is confirmed that such detestable things are being done among you, ¹⁶⁽¹⁵⁾ you must put the inhabitants of that city to death

with the sword, destroying it completely with the sword, everything in it, including its livestock. ¹⁷⁽¹⁶⁾ Heap all its spoils in an open space, and burn the city with its spoils to the ground for ADONAI your God; it will remain a *tel* forever and not be built again — ¹⁸⁽¹⁷⁾ none of what has been set apart for destruction is to stay in your hands. Then ADONAI will turn from his fierce anger and show you mercy, have compassion on you and increase your numbers, as he swore to your ancestors — ¹⁹⁽¹⁸⁾ provided you listen to what ADONAI says and obey all his *mitzvot* that I am giving you today, thus doing what ADONAI your God sees as right.

14 *(iv)* ¹ "You are the people of ADONAI your God. You are not to gash yourselves or shave the hair above your foreheads in mourning for the dead, ² because you are a people set apart as holy for ADONAI your God. ADONAI your God has chosen you to be his own unique treasure out of all the peoples on the face of the earth.

³ "You are not to eat anything disgusting. ⁴ The animals which you may eat are: ox, sheep, goat, ⁵ deer, gazelle, roebuck, ibex, antelope, oryx and mountain sheep. ⁶ Any animal that has a separate hoof that is completely divided and also chews the cud, these animals you may eat. ⁷ But you are not to eat those that only chew the cud or only have a divided hoof. For example, the camel, the hare and the coney are unclean for you because they chew the cud but don't have a separate hoof; ⁸ while the pig is unclean for you because, although it has a separate hoof, it doesn't chew the cud. You are not to eat meat from these or touch their carcasses.

⁹ "Of all that lives in the water, you may eat these: anything in the water that has fins and scales, these you may eat. ¹⁰ But whatever lacks fins and scales you are not to eat; it is unclean for you.

¹¹ "You may eat any clean bird; ¹² but these you are not to eat: eagles, vultures, ospreys, ¹³ kites, any kind of buzzard, ¹⁴ any kind of raven, ¹⁵ ostriches, screech-owls, seagulls, any kind of hawk, ¹⁶ little owls, great owls, horned owls, ¹⁷ pelicans, barn owls, cormorants, ¹⁸ storks, any kind of heron, hoopoes and bats.

¹⁹ "All winged swarming creatures are unclean for you; they are not to be eaten; ²⁰ but all clean flying creatures you may eat.

²¹ "You are not to eat any animal that dies naturally; although you may let a stranger staying with you eat it, or sell it to a foreigner; because you are a holy people for ADONAI your God.

"You are not to boil a young animal in its mother's milk.

(v) ²² "Every year you must take one tenth of everything your seed produces in the field, ²³ and eat it in the presence of ADONAI your God. In the place where he chooses to have his name live you will eat the tenth of your grain, new wine and olive oil, and the firstborn of your cattle and sheep, so that you will learn to fear ADONAI your God always. ²⁴ But if the distance is too great for you, so that you are unable to transport it, because the place where ADONAI chooses to put his name is too far away from you; then, when ADONAI your God prospers you, ²⁵ you are to convert it into money, take the money with you, go to the place which ADONAI your God will choose, ²⁶ and exchange the money for anything you want — cattle, sheep, wine, other intoxicating liquor, or anything you please — and you are to eat there in the presence of ADONAI your God, and enjoy yourselves, you and your household.

²⁷ "But don't neglect the *Levi* staying with you, because he has no share or inheritance like yours. ²⁸ At the end of every three years you are to take all the tenths

of your produce from that year and store it in your towns. ²⁹ Then the *Levi*, because he has no share or inheritance like yours, along with the foreigner, the orphan and the widow living in your towns, will come, eat and be satisfied — so that A*DONAI* your God will bless you in everything your hands produce.

15 *(vi)* ¹ "At the end of every seven years you are to have a *sh'mittah*. ² Here is how the *sh'mittah* is to be done: every creditor is to give up what he has loaned to his fellow member of the community — he is not to force his neighbor or relative to repay it, because A*DONAI*'s time of remission has been proclaimed. ³ You may demand that a foreigner repay his debt, but you are to release your claim on whatever your brother owes you. ⁴ In spite of this, there will be no one needy among you; because A*DONAI* will certainly bless you in the land which A*DONAI* your God is giving you as an inheritance to possess — ⁵ if only you will listen carefully to what A*DONAI* your God says and take care to obey all these *mitzvot* I am giving you today. ⁶ Yes, A*DONAI* your God will bless you, as he promised you — you will lend money to many nations without having to borrow, and you will rule over many nations without their ruling over you.

⁷ "If someone among you is needy, one of your brothers, in any of your towns in your land which A*DONAI* your God is giving you, you are not to harden your heart or shut your hand from giving to your needy brother. ⁸ No, you must open your hand to him and lend him enough to meet his need and enable him to obtain what he wants. ⁹ Guard yourself against allowing your heart to entertain the mean-spirited thought that because the seventh year, the year of *sh'mittah* is at hand, you would be stingy toward your needy brother and not give him anything; for then he may cry out to A*DONAI* against you, and it will be your sin. ¹⁰ Rather, you must give to him; and you are not to be grudging when you give to him. If you do this, A*DONAI* your God will bless you in all your work, in everything you undertake — ¹¹ for there will always be poor people in the land. That is why I am giving you this order, 'You must open your hand to your poor and needy brother in your land.'

¹² "If your kinsman, a Hebrew man or woman, is sold to you, he is to serve you for six years; but in the seventh year, you are to set him free. ¹³ Moreover, when you set him free, don't let him leave empty-handed; ¹⁴ but supply him generously from your flock, threshing-floor and winepress; from what A*DONAI* your God has blessed you with, you are to give to him. ¹⁵ Remember that you were a slave in the land of Egypt, and A*DONAI* your God redeemed you; that is why I am giving you this order today. ¹⁶ But if he says to you, 'I don't want to leave you,' because he loves you and your household, and because his life with you is a good one; ¹⁷ then take an awl, and pierce his ear through, right into the door; and he will be your slave forever. Do the same with your female slave. ¹⁸ Don't resent it when you set him free, since during his six years of service he has been worth twice as much as a hired employee. Then A*DONAI* your God will bless you in everything you do.

(vii) ¹⁹ "All the firstborn males in your herd of cattle and in your flock you are to set aside for A*DONAI* your God; you are not to do any work with a firstborn from your herd or shear a firstborn sheep. ²⁰ Each year you and your household are to eat it in the presence of A*DONAI* your God in the place which A*DONAI* will choose. ²¹ But if it has a defect, is lame or blind, or has some other kind of fault, you are not to sacrifice it to

ADONAI your God; ²² rather, eat it on your own property; the unclean and the clean alike may eat it, like the gazelle or the deer. ²³ Just don't eat its blood, but pour it out on the ground like water.

16 ¹ "Observe the month of Aviv, and keep *Pesach* to ADONAI your God; for in the month of Aviv, ADONAI your God brought you out of Egypt at night. ² You are to sacrifice the *Pesach* offering from flock and herd to ADONAI your God in the place where ADONAI will choose to have his name live. ³ You are not to eat any *hametz* with it; for seven days you are to eat with it *matzah*, the bread of affliction; for you came out of the land of Egypt in haste. Thus you will remember the day you left the land of Egypt as long as you live. ⁴ No leaven is to be seen with you anywhere in your territory for seven days. None of the meat from your sacrifice on the first day in the evening is to remain all night until morning. ⁵ You may not sacrifice the *Pesach* offering in just any of the towns that ADONAI your God is giving you; ⁶ but at the place where ADONAI your God will choose to have his name live — there is where you are to sacrifice the *Pesach* offering, in the evening, when the sun sets, at the time of year that you came out of Egypt. ⁷ You are to roast it and eat it in the place ADONAI your God will choose; in the morning you will return and go to your tents. ⁸ For six days you are to eat *matzah*; on the seventh day there is to be a festive assembly for ADONAI your God; do not do any kind of work.

⁹ "You are to count seven weeks; you are to begin counting seven weeks from the time you first put your sickle to the standing grain. ¹⁰ You are to observe the festival of *Shavu'ot* [weeks] for ADONAI your God with a voluntary offering, which you are to give in accordance with the degree to which ADONAI your God has prospered you. ¹¹ You are to rejoice in the presence of ADONAI your God — you, your sons and daughters, your male and female slaves, the *L'vi'im* living in your towns, and the foreigners, orphans and widows living among you — in the place where ADONAI your God will choose to have his name live. ¹² Remember that you were a slave in Egypt; then you will keep and obey these laws.

(Maftir) ¹³ "You are to keep the festival of *Sukkot* for seven days after you have gathered the produce of your threshing-floor and winepress. ¹⁴ Rejoice at your festival — you, your sons and daughters, your male and female slaves, the *L'vi'im*, and the foreigners, orphans and widows living among you. ¹⁵ Seven days you are to keep the festival for ADONAI your God in the place ADONAI your God will choose, because ADONAI your God will bless you in all your crops and in all your work, so you are to be full of joy!

¹⁶ "Three times a year all your men are to appear in the presence of ADONAI your God in the place which he will choose — at the festival of *matzah*, at the festival of *Shavu'ot* and at the festival of *Sukkot*. They are not to show up before ADONAI empty-handed, ¹⁷ but every man is to give what he can, in accordance with the blessing ADONAI your God has given you.

Haftarah Re'eh: Yesha'yahu (Isaiah) 54:11–55:5

B'rit Hadashah suggested readings for Parashah Re'eh: 1 Corinthians 5:9–13; 1 Yochanan (1 John) 4:1–6

Parashah 48: Shof'tim (Judges) 16:18–21:9

¹⁸ "You are to appoint judges and officers for all your gates [in the cities] ADONAI your God is giving you, tribe by tribe; and they are to judge the people with righteous judgment. ¹⁹ You are not to distort justice or show favoritism, and you are not to accept a bribe, for a gift blinds the eyes of the wise and twists the words of even the upright. ²⁰ Justice, only justice, you must pursue; so that you will live and inherit the land ADONAI your God is giving you.

²¹ "You are not to plant any sort of tree as a sacred pole beside the altar of ADONAI your God that you will make for yourselves. ²² Likewise, do not set up a standing-stone; ADONAI your God hates such things.

17 ¹ "You are not to sacrifice to ADONAI your God a cow or sheep that has a defect or anything wrong with it; that would be an abomination to ADONAI your God.

² "If there is found among you, within any of your gates [in any city] that ADONAI your God gives you, a man or woman who does what ADONAI your God sees as wicked, transgressing his covenant ³ by going and serving other gods and worshipping them, the sun, the moon, or anything in the sky — something I have forbidden — ⁴ and it is told to you, or you hear about it; then you are to investigate the matter diligently. If it is true, if it is confirmed that such detestable things are being done in Isra'el; ⁵ then you are to bring the man or woman who has done this wicked thing to your city gates, and stone that man or woman to death. ⁶ The death sentence is to be carried out only if there was testimony from two or three witnesses; he may not be sentenced to death on the testimony of only one witness. ⁷ The witnesses are to be the first to stone him to death; afterwards, all the people are to stone him. Thus you will put an end to this wickedness among you.

⁸ "If a case comes before you at your city gate which is too difficult for you to judge, concerning bloodshed, civil suit, personal injury or any other controversial issue; you are to get up, go to the place which ADONAI your God will choose, ⁹ and appear before the *cohanim*, who are *L'vi'im*, and the judge in office at the time. Seek their opinion, and they will render a verdict for you. ¹⁰ You will then act according to what they have told you there in that place which ADONAI will choose; you are to take care to act according to all their instructions. ¹¹ In accordance with the *Torah* they teach you, you are to carry out the judgment they render, not turning aside to the right or the left from the verdict they declare to you. ¹² Anyone presumptuous enough not to pay attention to the *cohen* appointed there to serve ADONAI your God or to the judge — that person must die. Thus you will exterminate such wickedness from Isra'el — ¹³ all the people will hear about it and be afraid to continue acting presumptuously.

(ii) ¹⁴ "When you have entered the land ADONAI your God is giving you, have taken possession of it and are living there, you may say, 'I want to have a king over me, like all the other nations around me.' ¹⁵ In that event, you must appoint as king the one whom ADONAI your God will choose. He must be one of your kinsmen, this king you appoint over you — you are forbidden to appoint a foreigner over you who is not your kinsman. ¹⁶ However, he is not to acquire many horses for himself or have the people return to Egypt to obtain more horses, inasmuch as ADONAI told you never to go back that way again. ¹⁷ Likewise, he is not to acquire many wives for himself, so that his heart will not turn away; and he is not to acquire excessive quantities of silver and gold.

¹⁸ "When he has come to occupy the throne of his kingdom, he is to write a copy of this *Torah* for himself in a scroll, from the one the *cohanim* and *L'vi'im* use. ¹⁹ It is to remain with him, and he is to read in it every day, as long as he lives; so that he will learn to fear A<small>DONAI</small> his God and keep all the words of this *Torah* and these laws and obey them; ²⁰ so that he will not think he is better than his kinsmen; and so that he will not turn aside either to the right or to the left from the *mitzvah*. In this way he will prolong his own reign and that of his children in Isra'el.

18 *(iii)* ¹ The *cohanim*, who are *L'vi'im*, and indeed the whole tribe of Levi, is not to have a share or an inheritance with Isra'el. Instead, their support will come from the food offered by fire to A<small>DONAI</small> and from whatever else becomes his. ² They will have no inheritance with their brothers, because A<small>DONAI</small> is their inheritance — as he has said to them.

³ "The *cohanim* will have the right to receive from the people, from those offering a sacrifice, whether ox or sheep, the shoulder, the jowls and the stomach. ⁴ You will also give him the firstfruits of your grain, new wine and olive oil, and the first of the fleece of your sheep. ⁵ For A<small>DONAI</small> your God has chosen him from all your tribes to stand and serve in the name of A<small>DONAI</small>, him and his sons forever.

(iv) ⁶ "If a *Levi* from one of your towns anywhere in Isra'el where he is living comes, highly motivated, to the place which A<small>DONAI</small> will choose, ⁷ then he will serve there in the name of A<small>DONAI</small> his God, just like his kinsmen the *L'vi'im* who stand and serve in the presence of A<small>DONAI</small>. ⁸ Such a *Levi* will receive the same share as they do, in addition to what he may receive from selling his inherited ancestral property.

⁹ "When you enter the land A<small>DONAI</small> your God is giving you, you are not to learn how to follow the abominable practices of those nations. ¹⁰ There must not be found among you anyone who makes his son or daughter pass through fire, a diviner, a soothsayer, an enchanter, a sorcerer, ¹¹ a spell-caster, a consulter of ghosts or spirits, or a necromancer. ¹² For whoever does these things is detestable to A<small>DONAI</small>, and because of these abominations A<small>DONAI</small> your God is driving them out ahead of you. ¹³ You must be wholehearted with A<small>DONAI</small> your God. *(v)* ¹⁴ For these nations, which you are about to dispossess, listen to soothsayers and diviners; but you, A<small>DONAI</small> your God does not allow you to do this.

¹⁵ "A<small>DONAI</small> will raise up for you a prophet like me from among yourselves, from your own kinsmen. You are to pay attention to him, ¹⁶ just as when you were assembled at Horev and requested A<small>DONAI</small> your God, 'Don't let me hear the voice of A<small>DONAI</small> my God any more, or let me see this great fire ever again; if I do, I will die!' ¹⁷ On that occasion A<small>DONAI</small> said to me, 'They are right in what they are saying. ¹⁸ I will raise up for them a prophet like you from among their kinsmen. I will put my words in his mouth, and he will tell them everything I order him. ¹⁹ Whoever doesn't listen to my words, which he will speak in my name, will have to account for himself to me.

²⁰ "'But if a prophet presumptuously speaks a word in my name which I didn't order him to say, or if he speaks in the name of other gods, then that prophet must die.' ²¹ You may be wondering, 'How are we to know if a word has not been spoken by A<small>DONAI</small>?' ²² When a prophet speaks in the name of A<small>DONAI</small>, and the prediction does not come true — that is, the word is not fulfilled — then A<small>DONAI</small> did not speak that word. The prophet who said it spoke presumptuously; you have nothing to fear from him.

19 ¹ "When *Adonai* your God cuts off the nations whose land *Adonai* your God is giving you, and you take their place and settle in their cities and houses, ² you are to set aside three cities for yourselves in your land that *Adonai* your God is giving you to possess. ³ Divide the territory of your land, which *Adonai* your God is having you inherit, into three parts; and prepare the roads, so that any killer can flee to these cities. ⁴ The killer who will live if he flees there is someone who has killed his fellow member of the community by mistake, who did not hate him in the past. ⁵ An example would be if a man goes into the forest with his neighbor to cut wood and takes a stroke with the axe to fell a tree, but the head of the axe flies off the handle, hits his neighbor and kills him. Then he is to flee to one of these cities and live there. ⁶ Otherwise the next-of-kin avenger, in the heat of his anger, may pursue the killer, overtake him because the distance [to the city of refuge] is long, and strike him dead — even though he didn't deserve to die, inasmuch as he hadn't hated him in the past. ⁷ This is why I am ordering you to set aside for yourselves three cities.

⁸ "If *Adonai* your God expands your territory, as he swore to your ancestors that he would, and gives you all the land he promised to give to your ancestors — ⁹ provided you keep and observe all these *mitzvot* I am giving you today, loving *Adonai* your God and always following his ways — then you are to add three more cities for yourselves, besides these three; ¹⁰ so that innocent blood will not be shed in the land *Adonai* your God is giving you as an inheritance, and thus blood guilt be on you.

¹¹ "However, if someone hates his fellow member of the community, lies in wait for him, attacks him, strikes him a death blow, and then flees into one of these cities; ¹² then the leaders of his own town are to send and bring him back from there and hand him over to the next-of-kin avenger, to be put to death. ¹³ You are not to pity him. Rather, you must put an end to the shedding of innocent blood in Isra'el. Then things will go well with you.

(vi) ¹⁴ "You are not to move your neighbor's boundary marker from the place where people put it long ago, in the inheritance soon to be yours in the land *Adonai* your God is giving you to possess.

¹⁵ "One witness alone will not be sufficient to convict a person of any offense or sin of any kind; the matter will be established only if there are two or three witnesses testifying against him.

¹⁶ "If a malicious witness comes forward and gives false testimony against someone, ¹⁷ then both the men involved in the controversy are to stand before *Adonai*, before the *cohanim* and the judges in office at the time. ¹⁸ The judges are to investigate carefully. If they find that the witness is lying and has given false testimony against his brother, ¹⁹ you are to do to him what he intended to do to his brother. In this way, you will put an end to such wickedness among you. ²⁰ Those who remain will hear about it, be afraid and no longer commit such wickedness among you. ²¹ Show no pity: life for life, eye for eye, tooth for tooth, hand for hand, foot for foot.

20 ¹ "When you go out to fight your enemies and see horses, chariots and a force larger than yours, you are not to be afraid of them; because *Adonai* your God, who brought you up from the land of Egypt, is with you. ² When you are about to go into battle, the *cohen* is to come forward and address the people. ³ He should tell them, 'Listen, Isra'el! You are about to do battle against your enemies.

Don't be fainthearted or afraid; don't be alarmed or frightened by them; ⁴ because ADONAI your God is going with you to fight on your behalf against your enemies and give you victory.'

⁵ "Then the officials will speak to the soldiers. They are to say, 'Is there a man here who has built a new house, but hasn't dedicated it yet? He should go back home now; otherwise he may die fighting, and another man will dedicate it.

⁶ "'Is there a man here who has planted a vineyard, but hasn't yet made use of its fruit? He should go back home; otherwise he may die fighting, and another man will use it.

⁷ "'Is there a man here who is engaged to a woman, but hasn't married her yet? He should go back home; otherwise he may die fighting, and another man will marry her.'

⁸ "The officials will then add to what they have said to the soldiers: 'Is there a man here who is afraid and fainthearted? He should go back home; otherwise his fear may demoralize his comrades as well.' ⁹ When the officials have finished speaking with the soldiers, commanders are to be appointed to lead the army.

(vii) ¹⁰ "When you advance on a town to attack it, first offer it terms for peace. ¹¹ If it accepts the terms for peace and opens its gates to you, then all the people there are to be put to forced labor and work for you. ¹² However, if they refuse to make peace with you but prefer to make war against you, you are to put it under siege. ¹³ When ADONAI your God hands it over to you, you are to put every male to the sword. ¹⁴ However, you are to take as booty for yourself the women, the little ones, the livestock, and everything in the city — all its spoil. Yes, you will feed on your enemies' spoil, which ADONAI your God has given you. ¹⁵ This is what you are to do to all the towns which are at a great distance from you, which are not the towns of these nations.

¹⁶ "As for the towns of these peoples, which ADONAI your God is giving you as your inheritance, you are not to allow anything that breathes to live. ¹⁷ Rather you must destroy them completely — the Hitti, the Emori, the Kena'ani, the P'rizi, the Hivi and the Y'vusi — as ADONAI your God has ordered you; ¹⁸ so that they won't teach you to follow their abominable practices, which they do for their gods, thus causing you to sin against ADONAI your God.

¹⁹ "When, in making war against a town in order to capture it, you lay siege to it for a long time, you are not to destroy its trees, cutting them down with an axe. You can eat their fruit, so don't cut them down. After all, are the trees in the field human beings, so that you have to besiege them too? ²⁰ However, if you know that certain trees provide no food, you may destroy them and cut them down, in order to build siege-works against the town making war with you, until it falls.

21 ¹ "If, in the land ADONAI your God is giving you to possess, a murder victim is found lying in the countryside; and the perpetrator of the murder is not known; ² then your leaders and judges are to go out and measure the distance between it and the surrounding towns. ³ After it has been determined which town is the closest, the leaders of that town are to take a young female cow that has never been put to work or yoked for use as a draft animal. ⁴ The leaders of that town are to bring the heifer down to a *vadi* with a stream in it that never dries up, to a place that is neither plowed nor sown; and they are to break the cow's neck there in the *vadi*. ⁵ Then the *cohanim*, who are *L'vi'im*, are to approach; for A*DONAI* your God has chosen them to serve him and to pronounce blessings in the name of A*DONAI*; they will decide the outcome of every dispute and matter involving violence. ⁶ All the leaders of the town nearest the murder victim are to wash their hands over the cow whose neck was broken in the *vadi*. *(Maftir)* ⁷ Then they are to speak up and say, 'This blood was not shed by our hands, nor have we seen who did it. ⁸ A*DONAI*, forgive your people Isra'el, whom you redeemed; do not allow innocent blood to be shed among your people Isra'el.' And they will be forgiven this bloodshed. ⁹ Thus you will banish the shedding of innocent blood from among you, by doing what A*DONAI* sees as right.

> *Haftarah Shof'tim: Yesha'yahu (Isaiah) 51:12–52:12 [Messianic adaptation: conclude the reading at 53:12]*

> *B'rit Hadashah suggested readings for Parashah Shof'tim: Mattityahu (Matthew) 5:38–42; 18:15–20; Acts 3:13–26; 7:35–53; 1 Corinthians 5:9–13; 1 Timothy 5:17–22; Messianic Jews (Hebrews) 10:28–31*

Parashah 49: Ki Tetze (When you go out) 21:10–25:19

¹⁰ "When you go out to war against your enemies, and A*DONAI* your God hands them over to you, and you take prisoners, ¹¹ and you see among the prisoners a woman who looks good to you, and you feel attracted to her and want her as your wife; ¹² you are to bring her home to your house, where she will shave her head, cut her fingernails ¹³ and remove her prison clothing. She will stay there in your house, mourning her father and mother for a full month; after which you may go in to have sexual relations with her and be her husband, and she will be your wife. ¹⁴ In the event that you lose interest in her, you are to let her go wherever she wishes; but you may not sell her for money or treat her like a slave, because you humiliated her.

¹⁵ "If a man has two wives, the one loved and the other unloved, and both the loved and unloved wives have borne him children, and if the firstborn son is the child of the unloved wife; ¹⁶ then, when it comes time for him to pass his inheritance on to his sons, he may not give the inheritance due the firstborn to the son of the loved wife in place of the son of the unloved one, who is in fact the firstborn. ¹⁷ No, he must acknowledge as firstborn the son of the unloved wife by giving him a double portion of everything he owns, for he is the firstfruits of his manhood, and the right of the firstborn is his.

¹⁸ "If a man has a stubborn, rebellious son who will not obey what his father or mother says, and even after they discipline him he still refuses to pay attention to them; ¹⁹ then his father and mother are to take hold of him and bring him out to the leaders of his town, at the gate of that place, ²⁰ and say to the leaders of his town, 'This son of ours is stubborn and rebellious, he doesn't pay attention to us, lives wildly, gets drunk.' ²¹ Then all the men of his town are to stone him to death; in this way you will put an end to such wickedness among you, and all Isra'el will hear about it and be afraid.

(ii) ²² "If someone has committed a capital crime and is put to death, then hung on a tree, ²³ his body is not to remain all night on the tree, but you must bury him the

same day, because a person who has been hanged has been cursed by God — so that you will not defile your land, which ADONAI your God is giving you to inherit.

22 ¹ "You are not to watch your brother's ox or sheep straying and behave as if you hadn't seen it; you must bring it back to your brother. ² If your brother is not close by, or you don't know who the owner is, you are to bring it home to your house; and it will remain with you until your brother asks for it; then you are to give it back to him. ³ You are to do the same with his donkey, his coat or anything else of your brother's that he loses. If you find something he lost, you must not ignore it.

⁴ "If you see your brother's donkey or ox collapsed on the road, you may not behave as if you hadn't seen it; you must help him get it up on its feet again.

⁵ "A woman is not to wear men's clothing, and a man is not to put on women's clothing, for whoever does these things is detestable to ADONAI your God.

⁶ "If, as you are walking along, you happen to see a bird's nest in a tree or on the ground with chicks or eggs, and the mother bird is sitting on the chicks or the eggs, you are not to take the mother with the chicks. ⁷ You must let the mother go, but you may take the chicks for yourself; so that things will go well with you, and you will prolong your life.

(iii) ⁸ "When you build a new house, you must build a low wall around your roof; otherwise someone may fall from it, and you will be responsible for his death.

⁹ "You are not to sow two kinds of seed between your rows of vines; if you do, both the two harvested crops and the yield from the vines must be forfeited. ¹⁰ You are not to plow with an ox and a donkey together. ¹¹ You are not to wear clothing woven with two kinds of thread, wool and linen together.

¹² "You are to make for yourself twisted cords on the four corners of the garment you wrap around yourself.

¹³ "If a man marries a woman, has sexual relations with her and then, having come to dislike her, ¹⁴ brings false charges against her and defames her character by saying, 'I married this woman, but when I had intercourse with her I did not find evidence that she was a virgin'; ¹⁵ then the girl's father and mother are to take the evidence of the girl's virginity to the leaders of the town at the gate. ¹⁶ The girl's father will say to the leaders, 'I let my daughter marry this man, but he hates her, ¹⁷ so he has brought false charges that he didn't find evidence of her virginity; yet here is the evidence of my daughter's virginity' — ⁽¹⁸⁾ and they will lay the cloth before the town leaders. ¹⁸⁽¹⁹⁾ The leaders of that town are to take the man, punish him, ¹⁹ and fine him two-and-a-half pounds of silver *shekel*s, which they will give to the girl's father, because he has publicly defamed a virgin of Isra'el. She will remain his wife, and he is forbidden from divorcing her as long as he lives.

²⁰ "But if the charge is substantiated that evidence for the girl's virginity could not be found; ²¹ then they are to lead the girl to the door of her father's house, and the men of her town will stone her to death, because she has committed in Isra'el the disgraceful act of being a prostitute while still in her father's house. In this way you will put an end to such wickedness among you.

²² "If a man is found sleeping with a woman who has a husband, both of them must die — the man who went to bed with the woman and the woman too. In this way you will expel such wickedness from Isra'el.

²³ "If a girl who is a virgin is engaged to a man, and another man comes upon her in the town and has sexual relations with her; ²⁴ you are to bring them both out to the gate of the city and stone them to death — the girl because she didn't cry out for help, there in the city, and the man because he has humiliated his neighbor's wife. In this way you will put an end to such wickedness among you.

²⁵ "But if the man comes upon the engaged girl out in the countryside, and the man grabs her and has sexual relations with her, then only the man who had intercourse with her is to die. ²⁶ You will do nothing to the girl, because she has done nothing deserving of death. The situation is like the case of the man who attacks his neighbor and kills him. ²⁷ For he found her in the countryside, and the engaged girl cried out, but there was no one to save her.

²⁸ "If a man comes upon a girl who is a virgin but who is not engaged, and he grabs her and has sexual relations with her, and they are caught in the act, ²⁹ then the man who had intercourse with her must give to the girl's father one-and-a-quarter pounds of silver *shekels*, and she will become his wife, because he humiliated her; he may not divorce her as long as he lives.

23 ¹⁽²²:³⁰⁾ "A man is not to take his father's wife, thus violating his father's rights.

²⁽¹⁾ "A man with crushed or damaged private parts may not enter the assembly of ADONAI.

³⁽²⁾ "A *mamzer* may not enter the assembly of ADONAI, nor may his descendants down to the tenth generation enter the assembly of ADONAI.

⁴⁽³⁾ "No 'Amoni or Mo'avi may enter the assembly of ADONAI, nor may any of his descendants down to the tenth generation ever enter the assembly of ADONAI, ⁵⁽⁴⁾ because they did not supply you with food and water when you were on the road after leaving Egypt, and because they hired Bil'am the son of B'or from P'tor in Aram-Naharayim to put a curse on you. ⁶⁽⁵⁾ But ADONAI your God would not listen to Bil'am; rather, ADONAI your God turned the curse into a blessing for you; because ADONAI your God loved you. ⁷⁽⁶⁾ So you are never to seek their peace or well being, as long as you live.

(iv) ⁸⁽⁷⁾ "But you are not to detest an Edomi, because he is your brother; and you are not to detest an Egyptian, because you lived as a foreigner in his land. ⁹⁽⁸⁾ The third generation of children born to them may enter the assembly of ADONAI.

¹⁰⁽⁹⁾ "When you are in camp, at war with your enemies, you are to guard yourself against anything bad. ¹¹⁽¹⁰⁾ If there is a man among you who is unclean because of a nocturnal emission, he is to go outside the camp; he is not to enter the camp. ¹²⁽¹¹⁾ When evening arrives he is to bathe himself in water, and after sunset he may enter the camp. ¹³⁽¹²⁾ Also you are to have an area outside the camp to use as a latrine. ¹⁴⁽¹³⁾ You must include a trowel with your equipment, and when you relieve yourself, you are to dig a hole first and afterwards cover your excrement. ¹⁵⁽¹⁴⁾ For ADONAI your God moves about in your camp to rescue you and to hand over your enemies to you. Therefore your camp must be a holy place. [ADONAI] should not see anything indecent among you, or he will turn away from you.

¹⁶⁽¹⁵⁾ "If a slave has escaped from his master and taken refuge with you, you are not to hand him back to his master. ¹⁷⁽¹⁶⁾ Allow him to stay with you, in whichever place suits him best among your settlements; do not mistreat him.

$^{18(17)}$ "No woman of Isra'el is to engage in ritual prostitution, and no man of Isra'el is to engage in ritual homosexual prostitution. $^{19(18)}$ Nothing earned through heterosexual or homosexual prostitution is to be brought into the house of ADONAI your God in fulfillment of any vow, for both of these are abhorrent to ADONAI your God.

$^{20(19)}$ "You are not to lend at interest to your brother, no matter whether the loan is of money, food or anything else that can earn interest. $^{21(20)}$ To an outsider you may lend at interest, but to your brother you are not to lend at interest, so that ADONAI your God will prosper you in everything you set out to do in the land you are entering in order to take possession of it.

$^{22(21)}$ "When you make a vow to ADONAI your God, you are not to delay in fulfilling it, for ADONAI your God will certainly demand it of you, and your failure to do so will be your sin. $^{23(22)}$ If you choose not to make a vow at all, that will not be a sin for you; $^{24(23)}$ but if a vow passes your lips, you must take care to perform it according to what you voluntarily vowed to ADONAI your God, what you promised in words spoken aloud.

(v) $^{25(24)}$ "When you enter your neighbor's vineyard, you may eat enough grapes to satisfy your appetite; but you are not to put any in your basket. $^{26(25)}$ When you enter your neighbor's field of growing grain, you may pluck ears with your hand; but you are not to put a sickle to your neighbor's grain.

24 ^{1} "Suppose a man marries a woman and consummates the marriage but later finds her displeasing, because he has found her offensive in some respect. He writes her a divorce document, gives it to her and sends her away from his house. ^{2} She leaves his house, goes and becomes another man's wife; ^{3} but the second husband dislikes her and writes her a *get*, gives it to her and sends her away from his house; or the second husband whom she married dies. ^{4} In such a case her first husband, who sent her away, may not take her again as his wife, because she is now defiled. It would be detestable to ADONAI, and you are not to bring about sin in the land ADONAI your God is giving you as your inheritance.

(vi) ^{5} "If a man has recently married his wife, he is not to be subject to military service; he is to be free of external obligations and left at home for one year to make his new wife happy.

^{6} "No one may take a mill or even an upper millstone as collateral for a loan, because that would be taking as collateral the debtor's very means of sustenance.

^{7} "If a man kidnaps any of his brothers, fellow members of the community of Isra'el, and makes him his slave or sells him, that kidnapper must die; in this way you will put an end to such wickedness among you.

^{8} "When there is an outbreak of *tzara'at*, be careful to observe and do just what the *cohanim*, who are *L'vi'im*, teach you. Take care to do as I ordered them. ^{9} Remember what ADONAI your God did to Miryam on the road after you left Egypt.

^{10} "When you make any kind of loan to your neighbor, you are not to enter his house to take his collateral. ^{11} You must stand outside, and the borrower will bring the collateral outside to you. ^{12} If he is poor, you are not to go to bed with what he gave as collateral in your possession; ^{13} rather, you must restore the pledged item at sunset; then he will go to sleep wearing his garment and bless you. This will be an upright deed of yours before ADONAI your God.

(vii) ¹⁴ "You are not to exploit a hired worker who is poor and needy, whether one of your brothers or a foreigner living in your land in your town. ¹⁵ You are to pay him his wages the day he earns them, before sunset; for he is poor and looks forward to being paid. Otherwise he will cry out against you to A*DONAI*, and it will be your sin.

¹⁶ "Fathers are not to be executed for the children, nor are children to be executed for the fathers; every person will be executed for his own sin.

¹⁷ "You are not to deprive the foreigner or the orphan of the justice which is his due, and you are not to take a widow's clothing as collateral for a loan. ¹⁸ Rather, remember that you were a slave in Egypt; and A*DONAI* your God redeemed you from there. That is why I am ordering you to do this.

¹⁹ "When harvesting the grain in your field, if you forgot a sheaf of grain there, you are not to go back and get it; it will remain there for the foreigner, the orphan and the widow, so that A*DONAI* your God will bless you in all the work you do. ²⁰ When you beat your olive tree, you are not to go back over the branches again; the olives that are left will be for the foreigner, the orphan and the widow. ²¹ When you gather the grapes from your vineyard, you are not to return and pick grapes a second time; what is left will be for the foreigner, the orphan and the widow. ²² Remember that you were a slave in the land of Egypt. That is why I am ordering you to do this.

25 ¹ "If people have a dispute, seek its resolution in court, and the judges render a decision in favor of the righteous one and condemning the wicked one; ² then, if the wicked one deserves to be flogged, the judge is to have him lie down and be flogged in his presence. The number of strokes is to be proportionate to his offense; ³ but the maximum number is forty. He is not to exceed this; if he goes over this limit and beats him more than this, your brother will be humiliated before your eyes.

⁴ "You are not to muzzle an ox when it is treading out the grain.

⁵ "If brothers live together, and one of them dies childless, his widow is not to marry someone unrelated to him; her husband's brother is to go to her and perform the duty of a brother-in-law by marrying her. ⁶ The first child she bears will succeed to the name of his dead brother, so that his name will not be eliminated from Isra'el. ⁷ If the man does not wish to marry his brother's widow, then his brother's widow is to go up to the gate, to the leaders, and say, 'My brother-in-law refuses to raise up for his brother a name in Isra'el; he will not perform the duty of a husband's brother for me.' ⁸ The leaders of his town are to summon him and speak to him. If, on appearing before them, he continues to say, 'I don't want to marry her,' ⁹ then his brother's widow is to approach him in the presence of the leaders, pull his sandal off his foot, spit in his face and say, 'This is what is done to the man who refuses to build up his brother's family.' ¹⁰ From that time on, his family is to be known in Isra'el as 'the family of the man who had his sandal pulled off.'

¹¹ "If men are fighting with each other, and the wife of one comes up to help her husband get away from the man attacking him by grabbing the attacker's private parts with her hand, ¹² you are to cut off her hand; show no pity.

¹³ "You are not to have in your pack two sets of weights, one heavy, the other light. ¹⁴ You are not to have in your house two sets of measures, one big, the other small.

¹⁵ You are to have a correct and fair weight, and you are to have a correct and fair measure, so that you will prolong your days in the land *Adonai* your God is giving you. ¹⁶ For all who do such things, all who deal dishonestly, are destestable to *Adonai* your God.

(Maftir) ¹⁷ "Remember what 'Amalek did to you on the road as you were coming out of Egypt, ¹⁸ how he met you by the road, attacked those in the rear, those who were exhausted and straggling behind when you were tired and weary. He did not fear God. ¹⁹ Therefore, when *Adonai* your God has given you rest from all your surrounding enemies in the land *Adonai* your God is giving you as your inheritance to possess, you are to blot out all memory of 'Amalek from under heaven. Don't forget!

Haftarah Ki Tetze: Yesha'yahu (Isaiah) 54:1–10 [Messianic adaptation: commence the reading at 52:13]

B'rit Hadashah suggested readings for Parashah Ki Tetze: Mattityahu (Matthew) 5:31–32; 19:3–12; 22:23–32; Mark 10:2–12; 12:18–27; Luke 20:27–38; 1 Corinthians 9:4–18; Galatians 3:9–14; 1 Timothy 5:17–18

Parashah 50: Ki Tavo (When you come) 26:1–29:8(9)

26 ¹ "When you have come to the land *Adonai* your God is giving you as your inheritance, taken possession of it and settled there; ² you are to take the firstfruits of all the crops the ground yields, which you will harvest from your land that *Adonai* your God is giving you, put them in a basket and go to the place where *Adonai* your God will choose to have his name live. ³ You will approach the *cohen* holding office at the time and say to him, 'Today I declare to *Adonai* your God that I have come to the land *Adonai* swore to our ancestors that he would give us.' ⁴ The *cohen* will take the basket from your hand and put it down in front of the altar of *Adonai* your God.

⁵ "Then, in the presence of *Adonai* your God, you are to say, 'My ancestor was a nomad from Aram. He went down into Egypt few in number and stayed. There he became a great, strong, populous nation. ⁶ But the Egyptians treated us badly; they oppressed us and imposed harsh slavery on us. ⁷ So we cried out to *Adonai*, the God of our ancestors. *Adonai* heard us and saw our misery, toil and oppression; ⁸ and *Adonai* brought us out of Egypt with a strong hand and a stretched-out arm, with great terror, and with signs and wonders. ⁹ Now he has brought us to this place and given us this land, a land flowing with milk and honey. ¹⁰ Therefore, as you see, I have now brought the firstfruits of the land which you, *Adonai*, have given me.' You are then to put the basket down before *Adonai* your God, prostrate yourself before *Adonai* your God, ¹¹ and take joy in all the good that *Adonai* your God has given you, your household, the *Levi* and the foreigner living with you.

(ii) ¹² "After you have separated a tenth of the crops yielded in the third year, the year of separating a tenth, and have given it to the *Levi*, the foreigner, the orphan and the widow, so that they can have enough food to satisfy them while staying with you; ¹³ you are to say, in the presence of *Adonai* your God, 'I have rid my house of the things set aside for God and given them to the *Levi*, the foreigner, the orphan and the

widow, in keeping with every one of the *mitzvot* you gave me. I haven't disobeyed any of your *mitzvot* or forgotten them. ¹⁴ I haven't eaten any of this food when mourning, I haven't put any of it aside when unclean, nor have I given any of it for the dead. I have listened to what A*DONAI* my God has said, and I have done everything you ordered me to do. ¹⁵ Look out from your holy dwelling-place, from heaven; and bless your people Isra'el and the land you gave us, as you swore to our ancestors, a land flowing with milk and honey.'

(iii) ¹⁶ "Today A*DONAI* your God orders you to obey these laws and rulings. Therefore, you are to observe and obey them with all your heart and all your being. ¹⁷ You are agreeing today that A*DONAI* is your God and that you will follow his ways; observe his laws, *mitzvot* and rulings; and do what he says. ¹⁸ In turn A*DONAI* is agreeing today that you are his own unique treasure, as he promised you; that you are to observe all his *mitzvot*; ¹⁹ and that he will raise you high above all the nations he has made, in praise, reputation and glory; and that, as he said, you will be a holy people for A*DONAI* your God."

27 *(iv)* ¹ Then Moshe and all the leaders of Isra'el gave orders to the people. They said, "Observe all the *mitzvot* I am giving you today. ² When you cross the Yarden to the land A*DONAI* your God is giving you, you are to set up large stones, put plaster on them, ³ and, after crossing over, write this *Torah* on them, every word — so that you can enter the land A*DONAI* your God is giving you, a land flowing with milk and honey, as A*DONAI*, the God of your ancestors, promised you. ⁴ When you have crossed the Yarden, you are to set up these stones, as I am ordering you today, on Mount 'Eival; and put plaster on them. ⁵ There you are to erect an altar to A*DONAI* your God, an altar made of stones. You are not to use any iron tool on them, ⁶ but are to build the altar of A*DONAI* your God of uncut stones; and you are to offer burnt offerings on it to A*DONAI* your God. ⁷ Also you are to sacrifice peace offerings, eat there and be joyful in the presence of A*DONAI* your God. ⁸ You are to write on the stones all the words of this *Torah* very clearly."

⁹ Next Moshe and the *cohanim*, who are *L'vi'im*, spoke to all Isra'el. They said, "Be quiet; and listen, Isra'el! Today you have become the people of A*DONAI* your God. ¹⁰ Therefore you are to listen to what A*DONAI* your God says and obey his *mitzvot* and laws, which I am giving you today."

(v) ¹¹ That same day Moshe commissioned the people as follows: ¹² "These are the ones who are to stand on Mount G'rizim and bless the people after you have crossed the Yarden: Shim'on, Levi, Y'hudah, Yissakhar, Yosef and Binyamin; ¹³ while these are to stand on Mount 'Eival for the curse: Re'uven, Gad, Asher, Z'vulun, Dan and Naftali. ¹⁴ The *L'vi'im*, speaking loudly, will proclaim to every man of Isra'el:

¹⁵ "'A curse on anyone who makes a carved or metal image, something A*DONAI* detests, the handiwork of a craftsman, and sets it up in secret!' All the people are to respond by saying, 'Amen!'

¹⁶ "'A curse on anyone who dishonors his father or mother.' All the people are to say, 'Amen!'

¹⁷ "'A curse on anyone who moves his neighbor's boundary marker.' All the people are to say, 'Amen!'

¹⁸ "'A curse on anyone who causes a blind person to lose his way on the road.' All the people are to say, 'Amen!'

¹⁹ "'A curse on anyone who interferes with justice for the foreigner, orphan or widow.' All the people are to say, 'Amen!'

²⁰ "'A curse on anyone who has sexual relations with his father's wife, because he has violated his father's rights.' All the people are to say, 'Amen!'

²¹ "'A curse on anyone who has sexual relations with any kind of animal.' All the people are to say, 'Amen!'

²² "'A curse on anyone who has sexual relations with his sister, no matter whether she is the daughter of his father or of his mother.' All the people are to say, 'Amen!'

²³ "'A curse on anyone who has sexual relations with his mother-in-law.' All the people are to say, 'Amen!'

²⁴ "'A curse on anyone who secretly attacks a fellow member of the community.' All the people are to say, 'Amen!'

²⁵ "'A curse on anyone who accepts a bribe to kill an innocent person.' All the people are to say, 'Amen!'

²⁶ "'A curse on anyone who does not confirm the words of this *Torah* by putting them into practice.' All the people are to say, 'Amen!'

28 ¹ "If you listen closely to what ADONAI your God says, observing and obeying all his *mitzvot* which I am giving you today, ADONAI your God will raise you high above all the nations on earth; ² and all the following blessings will be yours in abundance — if you will do what ADONAI your God says:

³ "A blessing on you in the city, and a blessing on you in the countryside.

⁴ "A blessing on the fruit of your body, the fruit of your land and the fruit of your livestock — the young of your cattle and flocks.

⁵ "A blessing on your grain-basket and kneading-bowl.

⁶ "A blessing on you when you go out, and a blessing on you when you come in.

(vi) ⁷ "ADONAI will cause your enemies attacking you to be defeated before you; they will advance on you one way and flee before you seven ways.

⁸ "ADONAI will order a blessing to be with you in your barns and in everything you undertake; he will bless you in the land ADONAI your God is giving you.

⁹ "ADONAI will establish you as a people separated out for himself, as he has sworn to you — if you will observe the *mitzvot* of ADONAI your God and follow his ways. ¹⁰ Then all the peoples on earth will see that ADONAI's name, his presence, is with you; so that they will be afraid of you.

¹¹ "ADONAI will give you great abundance of good things — of the fruit of your body, the fruit of your livestock and the fruit of your land in the land ADONAI swore to your ancestors to give you. ¹² ADONAI will open for you his good treasure, the sky, to give your land its rain at the right seasons and to bless everything you undertake. You will lend to many nations and not borrow; ¹³ ADONAI will make you the head and not the tail; and you will be only above, never below — if you will listen to, observe and obey the *mitzvot* of ADONAI your God ¹⁴ and not turn away from any of the words I am ordering you today, neither to the right nor to the left, to follow after other gods and serve them.

¹⁵ "But if you refuse to pay attention to what ADONAI your God says, and do not observe and obey all his *mitzvot* and regulations which I am giving you today, then all the following curses will be yours in abundance:

¹⁶ "A curse on you in the city, and a curse on you in the countryside.

[17] "A curse on your grain-basket and kneading-bowl.

[18] "A curse on the fruit of your body, the fruit of your land and the young of your cattle and flocks.

[19] "A curse on you when you come in, and a curse on you when you go out.

[20] "*Adonai* will send on you curses, disasters and frustration in everything you set out to do, until you are destroyed and quickly perish, because of your evil actions in abandoning me.

[21] "*Adonai* will bring on you a plague that will stay with you until he has exterminated you from the land you are entering in order to take possession of it. [22] *Adonai* will strike you down with wasting diseases, fever, inflammation, fiery heat, drought, blasting winds and mildew; and they will pursue you until you perish.

[23] "The sky over your head will be brass and the earth under you iron. [24] *Adonai* will turn the rain your land needs into powder and dust that will fall on you from the sky until you are destroyed.

[25] "*Adonai* your God will cause you to be defeated before your enemies; you will advance on them one way and flee before them seven. You will become an object of horror to every kingdom on earth. [26] Your carcasses will become food for all the birds in the air and the wild animals, and there will be no one to scare them away.

[27] *Adonai* will strike you down with the boils that broke out on the Egyptians, tumors, skin lesions and itching, all incurable. [28] *Adonai* will strike you with insanity, blindness and utter confusion. [29] You will grope about at noon like a blind person groping in the dark, unable to find your way.

"You will be continually oppressed and robbed, and there will be no one to save you. [30] You will get engaged to a woman, but another man will marry her. You will build a house but not live in it. You will plant a vineyard but not use its fruit. [31] Your ox will be slaughtered before your eyes, but you won't eat any of its meat. Your donkey will be taken away from you by force as you watch, and you won't get it back. Your sheep will be given to your enemies, and there will be no one to help you. [32] Your sons and daughters will be handed over to another people; you will watch for them longingly all day but not see them; and there will be nothing you can do about it. [33] A nation unknown to you will eat the fruit of your land and labor. Yes, you will be continually oppressed and crushed, [34] till you go crazy from what your eyes have to see. [35] *Adonai* will strike you down in the knees and legs with painful and incurable boils; they will spread from the sole of your foot to the crown of your head. [36] *Adonai* will bring you and your king whom you have put over yourselves to a nation you have not known, neither you nor your ancestors; and there you will serve other gods made of wood and stone. [37] You will be so devastated as to become a proverb and a laughingstock among all the peoples to which *Adonai* will drive you.

[38] "You will carry much seed out to the field but gather little in, because locusts will devour it. [39] You will plant vineyards and dress them but neither drink the wine nor gather the grapes, because worms will eat them. [40] You will have olive trees throughout your territory but not anoint yourself with the oil, because your olives will fall off unripe. [41] You will father sons and daughters, but they won't belong to you, because they will go into captivity. [42] The bugs will inherit all your trees and the produce of your land.

⁴³ "The foreigner living with you will rise higher and higher while you sink lower and lower. ⁴⁴ He will lend to you, but you will not lend to him; he will be the head and you the tail.

⁴⁵ "All these curses will come on you, pursuing you and overtaking you until you are destroyed, because you didn't pay attention to what ADONAI your God said, observing his *mitzvot* and regulations that he gave you. ⁴⁶ These curses will be on you and your descendants as a sign and a wonder forever. ⁴⁷ Because you didn't serve ADONAI your God with joy and gladness in your heart when you had such an abundance of everything; ⁴⁸ ADONAI will send your enemy against you; and you will serve him when you are hungry, thirsty, poorly clothed and lacking everything; he will put a yoke of iron on your neck until he destroys you. ⁴⁹ Yes, ADONAI will bring against you a nation from far away that will swoop down on you from the end of the earth like a vulture, a nation whose language you don't understand, ⁵⁰ a nation grim in appearance, whose people neither respect the old nor pity the young. ⁵¹ They will devour the offspring of your livestock and the produce of your soil, until you have been destroyed. They will leave you without grain, wine, olive oil, or your young cattle and sheep — until they have caused you to perish. ⁵² They will besiege all your towns until your high, fortified walls, in which you trusted, collapse everywhere in your land, which ADONAI your God gave you. ⁵³ Then, because of the severity of the siege and distress that your enemies are inflicting on you, you will eat the offspring of your own body, the flesh of your own sons and daughters, whom ADONAI your God has given you. ⁵⁴ Even the most gentle and sensitive man among you will be without pity for his brother, his beloved wife or his surviving children, ⁵⁵ to the degree that he will refuse to share with any of them the flesh of his children whom he is eating; because if he did, he would have nothing left for himself — in the severity of the siege and distress your enemies are inflicting on you in all your towns. ⁵⁶ The most delicate and sensitive woman among you, so sensitive and delicate that she wouldn't think of touching the sole of her foot to the ground, will so begrudge her own beloved husband, son and daughter ⁵⁷ that she will secretly eat the afterbirth that comes out of her and even her own children as she bears them — so desperately hungry will she be in the severity of the siege and distress your enemies are inflicting on you in your towns.

⁵⁸ "If you will not observe and obey all the words of this *Torah* that are written in this book, so that you will fear this glorious and awesome name, ADONAI your God; ⁵⁹ then ADONAI will strike down you and your descendants with extraordinary plagues and severe sicknesses that go on and on. ⁶⁰ He will bring back upon you all the diseases the Egyptians had, which you were in dread of; and they will cling to you. ⁶¹ Not only that, but ADONAI will bring upon you all the sicknesses and plagues that are not written in this book of the *Torah* — until you are destroyed. ⁶² You will be left few in number, whereas you were once as numerous as the stars in the sky — because you did not pay attention to the voice of ADONAI your God.

⁶³ "Thus it will come about that just as once ADONAI took joy in seeking to do you good and increase your numbers, so now ADONAI will take joy in causing you to perish and be destroyed, and you will be plucked off the land you are entering in order to take possession of it. ⁶⁴ ADONAI will scatter you among all peoples from one end of the earth to the other, and there you will serve other gods, made of wood and

stone, which neither you nor your ancestors have known. ⁶⁵ Among these nations you will not find repose, and there will be no rest for the sole of your foot; rather ADONAI will give you there anguish of heart, dimness of eyes and apathy of spirit. ⁶⁶ Your life will hang in doubt before you; you will be afraid night and day and have no assurance that you will stay alive. ⁶⁷ In the morning you will say, 'Oh, how I wish it were evening!' and in the evening you will say, 'Oh, how I wish it were morning!' — because of the fear overwhelming your heart and the sights your eyes will see. ⁶⁸ Finally, ADONAI will bring you back in ships to Egypt, the place of which I said to you, 'You will never ever see it again'; and there you will try to sell yourselves as slaves to your enemies, but no one will buy you."

⁶⁹⁽²⁹:¹⁾ These are the words of the covenant which ADONAI ordered Moshe to make with the people of Isra'el in the land of Mo'av, in addition to the covenant which he made with them in Horev.

29 *(vii)* ¹⁽²⁾ Then Moshe summoned all Isra'el and said to them, "You saw everything ADONAI did before your eyes in the land of Egypt to Pharaoh, to all his servants and to all his land; ²⁽³⁾ the great testings which you saw with your own eyes, and the signs and those great wonders. ³⁽⁴⁾ Nevertheless, to this day ADONAI has not given you a heart to understand, eyes to see or ears to hear! ⁴⁽⁵⁾ I led you forty years in the desert. Neither the clothes on your body nor the shoes on your feet wore out. ⁵⁽⁶⁾ You didn't eat bread, and you didn't drink wine or other intoxicating liquor; this was so that you would know that 'I am ADONAI your God.' *(Maftir)* ⁶⁽⁷⁾ When you arrived at this place, Sichon the king of Heshbon and 'Og the king of Bashan advanced against us in battle, and we defeated them, ⁷⁽⁸⁾ took their land and gave it as an inheritance to the Re'uveni, the Gadi and the M'nashi. ⁸⁽⁹⁾ Therefore, observe the words of this covenant and obey them; so that you can make everything you do prosper.

Haftarah Ki Tavo: Yesha'yahu (Isaiah) 60:1–22

B'rit Hadashah suggested readings for Parashah Ki Tavo: Mattityahu (Matthew) 13:1–23; Luke 21:1–4; Acts 28:17–31; Romans 11:1–15

Parashah 51: Nitzavim (Standing) 29:9(10)–30:20
[In regular years read with Parashah 52, in leap years read separately]

⁹⁽¹⁰⁾ "Today you are standing, all of you, before ADONAI your God — your heads, your tribes, your leaders and your officers — all the men of Isra'el, ¹⁰⁽¹¹⁾ along with your little ones, your wives and your foreigners here with you in your camp, from the one who chops your wood to the one who draws your water. ¹¹⁽¹²⁾ The purpose is that you should enter into the covenant of ADONAI your God and into his oath which ADONAI your God is making with you today, *(LY: ii)* ¹²⁽¹³⁾ so that he can establish you today for himself as a people, and so that for you he will be God — as he said to you and as he swore to your ancestors, to Avraham, Yitz'chak and Ya'akov.

¹³⁽¹⁴⁾ "But I am not making this covenant and this oath only with you. ¹⁴⁽¹⁵⁾ Rather, I am making it both with him who is standing here with us today before ADONAI our God and also with him who is not here with us today. *(LY: iii)* ¹⁵⁽¹⁶⁾ For you know

how we lived in the land of Egypt and how we came directly through the nations you passed through; ¹⁶⁽¹⁷⁾ and you saw their detestable things and their idols of wood, stone, silver and gold that they had with them. ¹⁷⁽¹⁸⁾ So let there not be among you a man, woman, family or tribe whose heart turns away today from ADONAI our God to go and serve the gods of those nations. Let there not be among you a root bearing such bitter poison and wormwood. ¹⁸⁽¹⁹⁾ If there is such a person, when he hears the words of this curse, he will bless himself secretly, saying to himself, 'I will be all right, even though I will stubbornly keep doing whatever I feel like doing; so that I, although "dry," [sinful,] will be added to the "watered" [righteous].' ¹⁹⁽²⁰⁾ But ADONAI will not forgive him. Rather, the anger and jealousy of ADONAI will blaze up against that person. Every curse written in this book will be upon him. ADONAI will blot out his name from under heaven. ²⁰⁽²¹⁾ ADONAI will single him out from all the tribes of Isra'el to experience what is bad in all the curses of the covenant written in this book of the *Torah*.

²¹⁽²²⁾ "When the next generation, your children who will grow up after you, and the foreigner who arrives from a distant land, see the plagues of that land and the diseases with which ADONAI has made it sick, ²²⁽²³⁾ and that the whole land has become burning sulfur and salt, that it isn't being sown or bearing crops or even producing grass — like the overthrow of S'dom, 'Amora, Admah and Tzvoyim, which ADONAI overthrew in his furious anger — ²³⁽²⁴⁾ then all the nations will ask, 'Why did ADONAI do this to this land? What is the meaning of such frenzied, furious anger?' ²⁴⁽²⁵⁾ People will answer, 'It's because they abandoned the covenant of ADONAI, the God of their fathers, which he made with them when he brought them out of the land of Egypt. ²⁵⁽²⁶⁾ They went and served other gods, prostrating themselves before them, gods they had not known and which he had not assigned them. ²⁶⁽²⁷⁾ For this reason, the anger of ADONAI blazed up against this land and brought upon it every curse written in this book; ²⁷⁽²⁸⁾ and ADONAI, in anger, fury and incensed with indignation, uprooted them from their land and threw them out into another land — as it is today.'

²⁸⁽²⁹⁾ "Things which are hidden belong to ADONAI our God. But the things that have been revealed belong to us and our children forever, so that we can observe all the words of this *Torah*.

30 *(RY: ii, LY: iv)* ¹ "When the time arrives that all these things have come upon you, both the blessing and the curse which I have presented to you; and you are there among the nations to which ADONAI your God has driven you; then, at last, you will start thinking about what has happened to you; ² and you will return to ADONAI your God and pay attention to what he has said, which will be exactly what I am ordering you to do today — you and your children, with all your heart and all your being. ³ At that point, ADONAI your God will reverse your exile and show you mercy; he will return and gather you from all the peoples to which ADONAI your God scattered you. ⁴ If one of yours was scattered to the far end of the sky, ADONAI your God will gather you even from there; he will go there and get you. ⁵ ADONAI your God will bring you back into the land your ancestors possessed, and you will possess it; he will make you prosper there, and you will become even more numerous than your ancestors. ⁶ Then ADONAI your God will circumcise your hearts and the hearts of your children, so that you will love ADONAI your God with all your heart and all your being, and thus you will live. *(RY: iii, LY: v)* ⁷ ADONAI your God will put all these curses on your enemies, on those who hated and persecuted you; ⁸ but you will return and pay attention to what ADONAI says and obey all his *mitzvot* which I am giving you today. ⁹ Then ADONAI your God will give you more than enough in everything you set out to do — the fruit of your body, the fruit of your livestock, and the fruit of your land will all do well; for ADONAI will once again rejoice to see you do well, just as he rejoiced in your ancestors.

¹⁰ "However, all this will happen only if you pay attention to what ADONAI your God says, so that you obey his *mitzvot* and regulations which are written in this book of the *Torah*, if you turn to ADONAI your God with all your heart and all your being. *(LY: vi)* ¹¹ For this *mitzvah* which I am giving you today is not too hard for you, it is not beyond your reach. ¹² It isn't in the sky, so that you need to ask, 'Who will go up into the sky for us, bring it to us and make us hear it, so that we can obey it?' ¹³ Likewise, it isn't beyond the sea, so that you need to ask, 'Who will cross the sea for us, bring it to us and make us hear it, so that we can obey it?' ¹⁴ On the contrary, the word is very close to you — in your mouth, even in your heart; therefore, you can do it!

(RY: iv, LY: vii) ¹⁵ "Look! I am presenting you today with, on the one hand, life and good; and on the other, death and evil — ¹⁶ in that I am ordering you today to love ADONAI your God, to follow his ways, and to obey his *mitzvot*, regulations and rulings ; for if you do, you will live and increase your numbers; and ADONAI your God will bless you in the land you are entering in order to take possession of it. ¹⁷ But if your heart turns away, if you refuse to listen, if you are drawn away to prostrate yourselves before other gods and serve them; *(LY: Maftir)* ¹⁸ I am announcing to you today that you will certainly perish; you will not live long in the land you are crossing the Yarden to enter and possess.

¹⁹ "I call on heaven and earth to witness against you today that I have presented you with life and death, the blessing and the curse. Therefore, choose life, so that you will live, you and your descendants, ²⁰ loving ADONAI your God, paying attention to what he says and clinging to him — for that is the purpose of your life! On this depends the length of time you will live in the land ADONAI swore he would give to your ancestors Avraham, Yitz'chak and Ya'akov."

Haftarah Nitzavim: Yesha'yahu (Isaiah) 61:10–63:9

B'rit Hadashah suggested readings for Parashah Nitzavim: Romans 9:30–10:13; Messianic Jews (Hebrews) 12:14–15

Parashah 52: Vayelekh (He went) 31:1–30
[In regular years read with Parashah 51, in leap years read separately]

31 ¹ Moshe went and spoke the following words to all Isra'el: ² "I am 120 years old today. I can't get around any longer; moreover, ADONAI has said to me, 'You will not cross this Yarden.' ³ ADONAI your God — he will cross over ahead of you. He will destroy these nations ahead of you, and you will dispossess them. Y'hoshua — he will cross over ahead of you, as ADONAI has said. *(LY: ii)* ⁴ ADONAI will do to them what he did to Sichon and 'Og, the kings of the Emori, and to their land — he destroyed them. [5]ADONAI will defeat them ahead of you, and you are to do to them just as I have ordered you to do. [6]Be strong, be bold, don't be afraid or frightened of them, for ADONAI your God is going with you. He will neither fail you nor abandon you."

(RY: v, LY: iii) [7]Next Moshe summoned Y'hoshua and, in the sight of all Isra'el, said to him, "Be strong, be bold, for you are going with this people into the land ADONAI swore to their ancestors he would give them. You will be the one causing them to inherit it. [8]But ADONAI — it is he who will go ahead of you. He will be with you. He will neither fail you nor abandon you, so don't be afraid or downhearted."

[9]Then Moshe wrote down this *Torah* and gave it to the *cohanim*, the descendants of Levi who carried the ark with the covenant of ADONAI, and to all the leaders of Isra'el. *(LY: iv)* [10]Moshe gave them these orders: "At the end of every seven years, during the festival of *Sukkot* in the year of *sh'mittah*, [11]when all Isra'el have come to appear in the presence of ADONAI at the place he will choose, you are to read this *Torah* before all Isra'el, so that they can hear it. [12]Assemble the people — the men, the women, the little ones and the foreigners you have in your towns — so that they can hear, learn, fear ADONAI your God and take care to obey all the words of this *Torah*; [13]and so that their children, who have not known, can hear and learn to fear ADONAI your God, for as long as you live in the land you are crossing the Yarden to possess."

(RY: vi, LY: v) [14]ADONAI said to Moshe, "The time is coming for you to die. Summon Y'hoshua, and present yourselves in the tent of meeting, so that I can commission him." Moshe and Y'hoshua went and presented themselves in the tent of meeting. [15]ADONAI appeared in the tent in a column of cloud; the column of cloud stood above the entrance to the tent. [16]ADONAI said to Moshe, "You are about to sleep with your ancestors. But this people will get up and offer themselves as prostitutes to the foreign gods of the land where they are going. When they are with those gods, they will abandon me and break my covenant which I have made with them. [17]Then my anger will flare up, and I will abandon them and hide my face from them. They will be devoured, and many calamities and troubles will come upon them. Then they will ask, 'Haven't these calamities come upon us because our God isn't here with us?' [18]But I will be hiding my face from them because of all the evil they will have done in turning to other gods.

[19]"Therefore, write this song for yourselves, and teach it to the people of Isra'el. Have them learn it by heart, so that this song can be a witness for me against the people of Isra'el. *(RY: vii, LY: vi)* [20]For when I have brought them into the land I swore to their ancestors, flowing with milk and honey; and they have eaten their fill, grown fat and turned to other gods, serving them and despising me, and broken my covenant; [21]then, after many calamities and troubles have come upon them, this song will testify before them as a witness, because their descendants will still be reciting it and will not have forgotten it. For I know how they think even now, even before I have brought them into the land about which I swore." [22]So Moshe wrote this song that same day and taught it to the people of Isra'el.

[23]ADONAI also commissioned Y'hoshua the son of Nun with these words: "Be strong and full of courage; for you are to bring the people of Isra'el into the land about which I swore to them; and I will be with you."

[24]Moshe kept writing the words of this *Torah* in a book until he was done. When he had finished, *(LY: vii)* [25]Moshe gave these orders to the *L'vi'im* who

carried the ark with the covenant of ADONAI. ²⁶ "Take this book of the *Torah* and put it next to the ark with the covenant of ADONAI your God, so that it can be there to witness against you. ²⁷ For I know how rebellious and stiffnecked you are! Here, even while I am still alive with you today, you have rebelled against ADONAI; so how much more will you do so after my death? *(Maftir)* ²⁸ Assemble for me all the leaders of your tribes and your officials, so that I can say these things in their hearing, calling heaven and earth to witness against them — ²⁹ because I know that after my death you will become very corrupt and turn aside from the way that I have ordered you, and that disaster will come upon you in the *acharit-hayamim*, because you will do what ADONAI sees as evil and provoke him by your deeds."

³⁰ Then Moshe spoke in the hearing of the whole assembly of Isra'el the words of this song, from beginning to end:

Haftarah Vayelekh: Hoshea (Hosea) 14:2(1)–10(9); Mikhah (Micah) 7:18–20; Yo'el (Joel) 2:15–27

B'rit Hadashah suggested reading for Parashah Vayelekh: Messianic Jews (Hebrews) 13:5–8

Parashah 53: Ha'azinu (Hear) 32:1–52

32¹   "Hear, oh heavens, as I speak!
Listen, earth, to the words from my mouth!
²   May my teaching fall like rain.
May my speech condense like dew,
like light rain on blades of grass,
or showers on growing plants.

³   "For I will proclaim the name of ADONAI.
Come, declare the greatness of our God!
⁴   The Rock! His work is perfect,
for all his ways are just.
A trustworthy God who does no wrong,
he is righteous and straight.

⁵   "He is not corrupt; the defect is in his children,
a crooked and perverted generation.
⁶   You foolish people, so lacking in wisdom,
is this how you repay ADONAI?
He is your father, who made you his!
It was he who formed and prepared you!

*(ii)*⁷   "Remember how the old days were;
think of the years through all the ages.
Ask your father — he will tell you;
your leaders too — they will inform you.

8   "When *Elyon* gave each nation its heritage,
when he divided the human race,
he assigned the boundaries of peoples
according to Isra'el's population;

9   but *Adonai*'s share was his own people,
Ya'akov his allotted heritage.

10   "He found his people in desert country,
in a howling, wasted wilderness.
He protected him and cared for him,
guarded him like the pupil of his eye,

11   like an eagle that stirs up her nest,
hovers over her young,
spreads out her wings, takes them
and carries them as she flies.

12   "*Adonai* alone led his people;
no alien god was with him.

(iii)[13]   He made them ride on the heights of the earth.
They ate the produce of the fields.
He had them suck honey from the rocks
and olive oil from the crags,

14   curds from the cows and milk from the sheep,
with lamb fat, rams from Bashan and goats,
with the finest wheat flour;
and you drank sparkling wine from the blood of grapes.

15   "But Yeshurun grew fat and kicked
(you grew fat, thick, gross!).
He abandoned God his Maker;
he scorned the Rock, his salvation.

16   They roused him to jealousy with alien gods,
provoked him with abominations.

17   They sacrificed to demons, non-gods,
gods that they had never known,
new gods that had come up lately,
which your ancestors had not feared.

18   You ignored the Rock who fathered you,
you forgot God, who gave you birth.

(iv)[19]   "*Adonai* saw and was filled with scorn
at his sons' and daughters' provocation.

20   He said, 'I will hide my face from them
and see what will become of them;
for they are a perverse generation,
untrustworthy children.

21   They aroused my jealousy with a non-god
       and provoked me with their vanities;
       I will arouse their jealousy with a non-people
       and provoke them with a vile nation.

22   "'For my anger has been fired up.
       It burns to the depths of Sh'ol,
       devouring the earth and its crops,
       kindling the very roots of the hills.
23   I will heap disasters on them
       and use up all my arrows against them.

24   "'Fatigued by hunger, they will be
       consumed by fever and bitter defeat;
       I will send them the fangs of wild beasts,
       and the poison of reptiles crawling in the dust.
25   Outside, the sword makes parents childless;
       inside, there is panic,
       as young men and girls alike are slain,
       sucklings and graybeards together.

26   "'I considered putting an end to them,
       erasing their memory from the human race;
27   but I feared the insolence of their enemy,
       feared that their foes would mistakenly think,
       "We ourselves accomplished this;
       ADONAI had nothing to do with it."

28   "'They are a nation without common sense,
       utterly lacking in discernment.
(v)²⁹ If they were wise they could figure it out
       and understand their destiny.
30   After all, how can one chase a thousand
       and two put ten thousand to rout,
       unless their Rock sells them to their enemies,
       unless ADONAI hands them over?
31   For our enemies have no rock like our Rock —
       even they can see that!

32   "'Rather, their vine is from the vine of S'dom,
       from the fields of 'Amora —
       their grapes are poisonous,
       their clusters are bitter;
33   their wine is snake poison,
       the cruel venom of vipers.

34   "'Isn't this hidden with me,
        sealed in my storehouses?

35   Vengeance and payback are mine
        for the time when their foot slips;
        for the day of their calamity is coming soon,
        their doom is rushing upon them.'

36   "Yes, ADONAI will judge his people,
        taking pity on his servants,
        when he sees that their strength is gone,
        that no one is left, slave or free.

37   Then he will ask, 'Where are their gods,
        the rock in whom they trusted?

38   Who ate the fat of their sacrifices
        and drank the wine of their drink offering?
        Let him get up and help you,
        let him protect you!

39   See now that I, yes, I, am he;
        and there is no god beside me.
        I put to death, and I make alive;
        I wound, and I heal;
        no one saves anyone from my hand!

(vi)⁴⁰   "'For I lift up my hand to heaven and swear,
        "As surely as I am alive forever,

41   if I sharpen my flashing sword
        and set my hand to judgment,
        I will render vengeance to my foes,
        repay those who hate me.

42   I will make my arrows drunk with blood,
        my sword will devour flesh —
        the blood of the slain and the captives,
        flesh from the wild-haired heads of the enemy."'

43   "Sing out, you nations, about his people!
        For he will avenge the blood of his servants.
        He will render vengeance to his adversaries
        and make atonement for the land of his people."

(vii) ⁴⁴ Moshe came and proclaimed all the words of this song in the hearing of the people and of Hoshea the son of Nun.

⁴⁵ When he had finished speaking all these words to all Isra'el, ⁴⁶ he said to them, "Take to heart all the words of my testimony against you today, so that you can use them in charging your children to be careful to obey all the words of this *Torah*. ⁴⁷ For this is not a trivial matter for you; on the contrary, it is your life! Through it you will live long in the land you are crossing the Yarden to possess."

(Maftir) [48] That same day A*DONAI* said to Moshe, [49] "Go up into the 'Avarim Range, to Mount N'vo, in the land of Mo'av across from Yericho; and look out over the land of Kena'an, which I am giving the people of Isra'el as a possession. [50] On the mountain you are ascending you will die and be gathered to your people, just as Aharon your brother died on Mount Hor and was gathered to his people. [51] The reason for this is that both of you broke faith with me there among the people of Isra'el at the M'rivat-Kadesh Spring, in the Tzin Desert; you failed to demonstrate my holiness there among the people of Isra'el. [52] So you will see the land from a distance, but you will not enter the land I am giving to the people of Isra'el."

Haftarah Ha'azinu: Sh'mu'el Bet (2 Samuel) 22:1–51

B'rit Hadashah suggested readings for Parashah Ha'azinu: Romans 10:14–21; 12:14–21; Messianic Jews (Hebrews) 12:28–29

Parashah 54: V'Zot HaBrachah (This is the blessing) 33:1–34:12

33 [1] This is the blessing that Moshe, the man of God, spoke over the people of Isra'el before his death:

[2] "A*DONAI* came from Sinai;
from Se'ir he dawned on his people,
shone forth from Mount Pa'ran;
and with him were myriads of holy ones;
at his right hand
was a fiery law for them.

[3] He truly loves the peoples —
all his holy ones are in your hand;
sitting at your feet,
they receive your instruction,

[4] the *Torah* Moshe commanded us
as an inheritance for the community of Ya'akov.

[5] Then a king arose in Yeshurun
when the leaders of the people were gathered,
all the tribes of Isra'el together.

[6] "Let Re'uven live and not die out,
even though his numbers grow few."

[7] Of Y'hudah he said:

 "Hear, A*DONAI*, the cry of Y'hudah!
Bring him in to his people,
let his own hands defend him;
but you, help him against his enemies."

(ii) [8] Of Levi he said:

>"Let your *tumim* and *urim*
>be with your pious one,
>whom you tested at Massah,
>with whom you struggled at M'rivah Spring.

[9]
>Of his father and mother he said, 'I don't know them';
>he didn't acknowledge his brothers or children.
>For he observed your word,
>and he kept your covenant.

[10]
>They will teach Ya'akov your rulings,
>Isra'el your *Torah*.
>They will set incense before you
>and whole burnt offerings on your altar.

[11]
>*ADONAI*, bless his possessions,
>accept the work he does;
>but crush his enemies hip and thigh;
>may those who hate him rise no more."

[12] Of Binyamin he said:

>"*ADONAI*'s beloved lives securely.
>He protects him day after day.
>He lives between his shoulders."

(iii) [13] Of Yosef he said:

>"May *ADONAI* bless his land
>with the best from the sky, for the dew,
>and for what comes from the deep beneath,

[14]
>with the best of what the sun makes grow,
>with the best of what comes up each month,

[15]
>with the best from the mountains of old,
>with the best from the eternal hills,

[16]
>with the best from the earth and all that fills it,
>and the favor of him who lived in the [burning] bush.
>May blessing come on the head of Yosef,
>on the brow of the prince among his brothers.

[17]
>His firstborn bull — glory is his;
>his horns are those of a wild ox;
>With them he will gore the peoples,
>all of them, to the ends of the earth.
>These are the myriads of Efrayim;
>these are the thousands of M'nasheh."

(iv) [18] Of Z'vulun he said:

>"Rejoice, Z'vulun, as you go forth,
>and you, Yissakhar, in your tents.

¹⁹
They will summon peoples to the mountain
and there offer righteous sacrifices;
for they will draw from the abundance of the seas
and from the hidden treasures of the sand."

²⁰ Of Gad he said:

"Blessed is he who makes Gad so large;
he lies there like a lion,
tearing arm and scalp.
²¹
He chose the best for himself
when the princely portion was assigned.
When the leaders of the people came,
he carried out ADONAI's justice
and his rulings concerning Isra'el."

(v) ²² Of Dan he said:

"Dan is a lion cub
leaping forth from Bashan."

²³ Of Naftali he said:

"You, Naftali, satisfied with favor
and full of blessing from ADONAI,
take possession of the sea and the south."

²⁴ Of Asher he said:

"May Asher be most blessed of sons,
may he be the favorite among his brothers
and bathe his feet in oil.
²⁵
May your bolts be of iron and bronze
and your strength last as long as you live.

²⁶
"Yeshurun, there is no one like God,
riding through the heavens to help you,
riding on the clouds in his majesty.
(vi) ²⁷
The God of old is a dwelling-place,
with everlasting arms beneath.
He expelled the enemy before you
and he said, 'Destroy!'
²⁸
So Isra'el lives in security;
the fountain of Ya'akov is alone
in a land of grain and new wine,
where the skies drip with dew.
²⁹
Happy are you, Isra'el!

"Who is like you, a people saved by *Adonai*,
your defender helping you
and your sword of triumph?
Your enemies will cringe before you,
but you will trample down their high places."

34 *(vii)* ¹ Moshe ascended from the plains of Mo'av to Mount N'vo, to the summit of Pisgah, across from Yericho. There *Adonai* showed him all the land — Gil'ad as far as Dan, ² all Naftali, the land of Efrayim and M'nasheh, the land of Y'hudah all the way to the sea beyond, ³ the Negev and the plain, including the valley where Yericho the City of Date-Palms is, as far away as Tzo'ar. ⁴ *Adonai* said to him, "This is the land concerning which I swore to Avraham, Yitz'chak and Ya'akov, 'I will give it to your descendants.' I have let you see it with your eyes, but you will not cross over there."

⁵ So Moshe, the servant of *Adonai*, died there in the land of Mo'av, as *Adonai* had said. ⁶ He was buried in the valley across from Beit-P'or in the land of Mo'av, but to this day no one knows where his grave is.

⁷ Moshe was 120 years old when he died, with eyes undimmed and vigor undiminished. ⁸ The people of Isra'el mourned Moshe on the plains of Mo'av for thirty days; after this, the days of crying and mourning for Moshe ended.

⁹ Y'hoshua the son of Nun was full of the Spirit of wisdom, for Moshe had laid his hands on him, and the people of Isra'el heeded him and did what *Adonai* had ordered Moshe.

¹⁰ Since that time there has not arisen in Isra'el a prophet like Moshe, whom *Adonai* knew face to face. ¹¹ What signs and wonders *Adonai* sent him to perform in the land of Egypt upon Pharaoh, all his servants and all his land! ¹² What might was in his hand! What great terror he evoked before the eyes of all Isra'el!

Haftarah V'zot HaBrachah: Y'hoshua (Joshua) 1:1–18 (A); 1:1–9 (S)

B'rit Hadashah suggested readings for Parashah V'zot HaBrachah: Mattityahu (Matthew) 17:1–9; Mark 9:2–10; Luke 9:28–36; Y'hudah (Jude) 3–4, 8–10

Hazak, hazak, v'nit'chazek!
Be strong, be strong, and let us be strengthened!

Y'hoshua
JOSHUA

1 ¹ After the death of Moshe the servant of ADONAI, ADONAI said to Y'hoshua the son of Nun, Moshe's assistant, ² "Moshe my servant is dead. So now, get up and cross over this Yarden, you and all the people, to the land I am giving to them, the people of Isra'el. ³ I am giving you every place you will step on with the sole of your foot, as I said to Moshe. ⁴ All the land from the desert and the L'vanon to the great river, the Euphrates River — all the land of the Hitti — and on to the Great Sea in the west will be your territory. ⁵ No one will be able to withstand you as long as you live. Just as I was with Moshe, so I will be with you. I will neither fail you nor abandon you.

⁶ "Be strong, be bold; for you will cause this people to inherit the land I swore to their fathers I would give them. ⁷ Only be strong and very bold in taking care to follow all the *Torah* which Moshe my servant ordered you to follow; do not turn from it either to the right or to the left; then you will succeed wherever you go. ⁸ Yes, keep this book of the *Torah* on your lips, and meditate on it day and night, so that you will take care to act according to everything written in it. Then your undertakings will prosper, and you will succeed. ⁹ Haven't I ordered you, 'Be strong, be bold'? So don't be afraid or downhearted, because ADONAI your God is with you wherever you go."

¹⁰ Y'hoshua instructed the officials of the people ¹¹ to go through the camp and order the people, "Prepare provisions, because in three days you will cross this Yarden to go in and take possession of the land ADONAI your God is giving you."

¹² To the Re'uveni, the Gadi and the half-tribe of M'nasheh Y'hoshua said, ¹³ "Remember what Moshe the servant of ADONAI ordered you: 'ADONAI your God has let you rest and will give you this land.' ¹⁴ Your wives, your little ones and your livestock will stay in the land Moshe gave you on the east side of the Yarden; but you are to cross over armed as a fighting force ahead of your brothers, to help them; ¹⁵ until ADONAI allows your brothers to rest, as he has allowed you; and they too have taken possession of the land ADONAI your God is giving them. At that point, you will return to the land which is yours and possess it, the land Moshe the servant of ADONAI gave you in 'Ever-HaYarden to the east, toward the sunrise."

¹⁶ They answered Y'hoshua, "We will do everything you have ordered us to do, and we will go wherever you send us. ¹⁷ Just as we listened to everything Moshe said, so will we listen to you. Only may ADONAI your God be with you as he was with Moshe. ¹⁸ If anyone rebels against your order and doesn't heed what you say in every detail of your order, he will be put to death. Just be strong, be bold!"

2 ¹ Y'hoshua the son of Nun secretly sent two spies from Sheetim with these instructions: "Go, inspect the land and Yericho." They left and came to the house of a prostitute named Rachav, where they spent the night. ² The king of Yericho was told about it — "Tonight some men from Isra'el came here to reconnoiter the land." ³ The king of Yericho sent a message to Rachav, "Bring out the men who came to you and are staying in your house, because they have come to reconnoiter all the land." ⁴ However, the woman, after taking the two men and hiding them, replied, "Yes, the men did come to me; but I didn't know where they had come from. ⁵ The men left around the time when they shut the gate, when it was dark. Where they went I don't know; but if you chase after them quickly, you will overtake them." ⁶ Actually she had brought them up to the roof and hidden them under some stalks of flax she had spread out there. ⁷ The men pursued them all the way to the fords at the Yarden; as soon as the pursuit party had left, the gate was shut.

⁸ The two men had not yet lain down when she returned to the roof ⁹ and said to them, "I know that ADONAI has given you the land. Fear of you has fallen on us; everyone in the land is terrified at the thought of you. ¹⁰ We've heard how ADONAI dried up the water in the Sea of Suf ahead of you, when you left Egypt; and what you did to the two kings of the Emori on the other side of the Yarden, Sichon and 'Og, that you completely destroyed them. ¹¹ As soon as we heard it, our hearts failed us. Because of you, everyone is in a state of depression. For ADONAI your God — he is God in heaven above and on the earth below. ¹² So, please, swear to me by ADONAI that, since I have been kind to you, you will also be kind to my father's family. Give me some evidence of your good faith, ¹³ that you will spare the lives of my father, mother, brothers and sisters and all who are theirs, so that we won't be killed." ¹⁴ The men replied to her, "Our lives are certainly worth yours, provided you don't betray our mission. So when ADONAI gives us the land, we will treat you kindly and in good faith."

¹⁵ Then she lowered them by a rope through the window; since her house abutted the city wall, indeed was actually built into it. ¹⁶ She told them, "Head for the hills, so that the pursuit party won't get their hands on you; and hide yourselves there for three days, until the pursuers have returned. After that, you can go on your way." ¹⁷ The men said to her, "We will not be guilty of violating the oath you made us swear, provided that ¹⁸ when we enter the land, you tie this piece of scarlet cord in the window you let us down from; and you gather together in your house your father, mother, brothers, and your father's entire household. ¹⁹ If anyone goes out the doors of your house into the street, he will be responsible for his own blood, and we will be guiltless. But everyone who stays with you in the house — we will be responsible for his blood if anyone lays a hand on him. ²⁰ However, if you say a word about this business of ours, then we will be free of your oath that you made us swear." ²¹ "According to your words, so be it," she said, and sent them away. As they departed, she tied the scarlet cord in the window.

²² They left, arrived in the hills, and stayed there three days, until the pursuers had returned. The pursuers had searched for them all the way but hadn't found them. ²³ Then the two men returned. Descending from the hills they crossed over and came to Y'hoshua the son of Nun, and reported everything that had happened to them. ²⁴ "Truly ADONAI has handed over all the land to us," they told Y'hoshua. "Everyone in the land is terrified that we're coming."

3 ¹ Y'hoshua got up early in the morning, and they left Sheetim and came to the Yarden, he with all the people of Isra'el; they camped there before crossing. ² After three days, the officials circulated through the camp ³ and gave the people these orders: "When you see the ark for the covenant of ADONAI your God and the *cohanim*, who are *L'vi'im*, carrying it, you are to leave your position and follow it. ⁴ But keep a distance between yourelves and it of about a thousand yards — don't come any closer, so that you will understand which way to go, because you haven't gone this way before."

⁵ Y'hoshua said to the people, "Consecrate yourselves, because tomorrow ADONAI is going to work wonders among you." ⁶ Then Y'hoshua said to the *cohanim*, "Take the ark for the covenant, and go on ahead of the people." They took the ark for the covenant and went ahead of the people.

⁷ ADONAI said to Y'hoshua, "Starting today, I will make you great in full view of all Isra'el; so that they will know that just as I was with Moshe, so I will be with you. ⁸ Now you are to order the *cohanim* carrying the ark for the covenant as follows: 'When you come to the edge of the Yarden River, you are to stop in the Yarden itself.'"

⁹ Y'hoshua said to the people of Isra'el, "Come here, and listen to the words of ADONAI your God." ¹⁰ Then Y'hoshua said, "Here is how you will know that the living God is here with you and that, without fail, he will drive out from before you the Kena'ani, the Hitti, the Hivi, the P'rizi, the Girgashi, the Emori and the Y'vusi: ¹¹ the ark for the covenant of the Lord of all the earth is going on ahead of you across the Yarden. ¹² Now choose yourselves twelve men out of the tribes of Isra'el, one man for each tribe. ¹³ As soon as the *cohanim* carrying the ark of ADONAI, the Lord of all the earth, put the soles of their feet in the water of the Yarden, the water of the Yarden will be cut off upstream and stand piled up like an embankment."

¹⁴ So the people left their tents to cross the Yarden, with the *cohanim* carrying the ark for the covenant ahead of the people. ¹⁵ When those carrying the ark had come to the Yarden, and the *cohanim* carrying the ark had waded into the water (for throughout harvest season the Yarden overflows its banks), ¹⁶ the water upstream stood piled up like an embankment for a great distance at Adam, the city next to Tzartan; so that the water flowing downstream toward the Sea of the 'Aravah, the Dead Sea, was completely cut off; and the people crossed over right by Yericho. ¹⁷ The *cohanim* carrying the ark for the covenant of ADONAI stood fast on dry ground in the middle of the Yarden, while all Isra'el crossed on dry ground, until the entire nation had finished crossing the Yarden.

4 ¹ After the whole nation had finished crossing the Yarden, ADONAI said to Y'hoshua, ² "Take for yourselves from the people twelve men, a man from every tribe; ³ and give them this order: 'Take twelve stones from the middle of the Yarden riverbed, where the *cohanim* are standing, carry them over with you and set them down in the place where you will camp tonight.'" ⁴ Y'hoshua called the twelve men whom he had chosen from the people of Isra'el, a man from every tribe, ⁵ and said to them, "Go on ahead of the ark of ADONAI your God into the riverbed of the Yarden. Then, each of you take a stone on his shoulder, corresponding to the number of tribes of the people of Isra'el. ⁶ This will be a sign for you. In the future, when your children ask, 'What do you mean by these stones?' ⁷ you will answer them, 'It's because the water in the Yarden was cut off before the ark for the covenant of ADONAI; when it crossed the Yarden, the water in the Yarden was cut off; and these stones are to be a reminder for the people of Isra'el forever.'"

⁸ The people of Isra'el did just as Y'hoshua had ordered. They took twelve stones out of the Yarden riverbed, as ADONAI had said to Y'hoshua, corresponding to the number of the tribes of the people of Isra'el, carried them over with them to the place where they were camping, and set them down there. ⁹ Y'hoshua also set up twelve stones in the Yarden River itself, in the place where the feet of the *cohanim* carrying the ark for the covenant had stood. They are there to this day. ¹⁰ The *cohanim* carrying the ark stood in the Yarden riverbed until Y'hoshua had finished saying to the people everything that ADONAI had ordered him to say, in keeping with everything that Moshe had ordered Y'hoshua; then the people hurried across. ¹¹ When all the people had finished crossing, the ark of ADONAI passed on, and the *cohanim*, ahead of the people. ¹² The descendants of Re'uven, the descendants of Gad and the half-tribe of M'nasheh went on, armed, ahead of the people of Isra'el, as Moshe had said to them; ¹³ some 40,000 armed soldiers ready for battle crossed in the presence of ADONAI to the plains of Yericho.

¹⁴ That day ADONAI made Y'hoshua great in full view of all Isra'el. They were in awe of him, just as they had been in awe of Moshe all his life.

¹⁵ ADONAI said to Y'hoshua, ¹⁶ "Order the *cohanim* carrying the ark for the testimony to come up out of the Yarden." ¹⁷ So Y'hoshua ordered the *cohanim*, "Come up out of the Yarden!" ¹⁸ The *cohanim* carrying the ark for the covenant of ADONAI came up from the Yarden riverbed, and as soon as the soles of the feet of the *cohanim* touched dry ground, the water of the Yarden returned to its place and the river overflowed its banks as it had before.

¹⁹ The people came up out of the Yarden on the tenth day of the first month and camped at Gilgal, by the eastern boundary of Yericho. ²⁰ Those twelve stones which they took out of the Yarden, Y'hoshua piled up at Gilgal. ²¹ Then he said to the people of Isra'el, "In the future, when your children ask their fathers what these stones mean, ²² you are to explain it to them by saying, 'Isra'el came over this Yarden on dry land. ²³ For ADONAI your God dried up the water in the Yarden from in front of you, until you had crossed, just as ADONAI your God did to the Sea of Suf, which he dried up from in front of us, until we had crossed. ²⁴ From this all the peoples of the earth can know that the hand of ADONAI is strong, and you can fear ADONAI your God forever.'"

5 ¹ When all the kings of the Emori on the west side of the Yarden and all the kings of the Kena'ani near the sea heard how ADONAI had dried up the Yarden River ahead of the people of Isra'el until they had crossed it, their hearts failed them, and they fell into depression because of the people of Isra'el.

² It was at that time that ADONAI said to Y'hoshua, "Make yourself knives of flint, and circumcise the people of Isra'el again, a second time. ³ So Y'hoshua made himself knives of flint and circumcised the people of Isra'el at Giv'at-Ha'Aralot [the hill of foreskins]. ⁴ The reason Y'hoshua circumcised was that all the people who had left Egypt who were males, all the fighting men, had died in the desert along the way after leaving Egypt. ⁵ For although all the people who left Egypt had been circumcised, all those who had been born in the desert on the way as they went on from Egypt had not been circumcised; ⁶ because the people of Isra'el walked forty years in the desert until the whole nation, that is, the fighting men who had left

Egypt, had died out; because they had not heeded what *Adonai* said. *Adonai* had sworn that he would not allow them to see the land which *Adonai* swore to their ancestors that he would give us, a land flowing with milk and honey. ⁷ So he raised up their children to take their place, and it was these whom Y'hoshua circumcised; till then they had been uncircumcised, because they had not been circumcised while traveling.

⁸ When all the nation had been circumcised, every one of them, they stayed where they were in camp until they had healed. ⁹ *Adonai* said to Y'hoshua, "Today I have rolled off from you the stigma of Egypt." This is why the place has been called Gilgal [rolling] ever since. ¹⁰ The people of Isra'el camped at Gilgal, and they observed *Pesach* on the fourteenth day of the month, there on the plains of Yericho. ¹¹ The day after *Pesach* they ate what the land produced, *matzah* and roasted ears of grain that day. ¹² The following day, after they had eaten food produced in the land, the *man* ended. From then on the people of Isra'el no longer had *man*; instead, that year, they ate the produce of the land of Kena'an.

¹³ One day, when Y'hoshua was there by Yericho, he raised his eyes and looked; and in front of him stood a man with his drawn sword in his hand. Y'hoshua went over to him and asked him, "Are you on our side or on the side of our enemies?" ¹⁴ "No," he replied, "but I am the commander of *Adonai*'s army; I have come just now." Y'hoshua fell down with his face to the ground and worshiped him, then asked, "What does my lord have to say to his servant?" ¹⁵ The commander of *Adonai*'s army answered Y'hoshua, "Take your sandals off your feet, because the place where you are standing is holy." And Y'hoshua did so.

6 ¹ Yericho had completely barricaded its gates against the people of Isra'el — no one left, and no one entered. ² *Adonai* said to Y'hoshua, "I have handed Yericho over to you, including its king and his warriors. ³ You are to encircle the city with all your soldiers and march around it once. Do this for six days. ⁴ Seven *cohanim* are to carry seven *shofar*s in front of the ark. On the seventh day you are to march around the city seven times, and the *cohanim* will blow the *shofar*s. ⁵ Then they are to blow a long blast on the *shofar*. On hearing the sound of the *shofar*, all the people are to shout as loudly as they can; and the wall of the city will fall down flat. Then the people are to go up into the city, each one straight from where he stands."

⁶ Y'hoshua the son of Nun called the *cohanim* and told them, "Take up the ark for the covenant, and have seven *cohanim* carry seven *shofar*s ahead of the ark of *Adonai*." ⁷ To the people he said, "Move on, encircle the city, and have the army march ahead of the ark of *Adonai*." ⁸ When Y'hoshua had spoken to the people, the seven *cohanim* carrying the seven *shofar*s before *Adonai* passed on and blew on the *shofar*s, with the ark for the covenant of *Adonai* following them. ⁹ The fighting men went ahead of the *cohanim* blowing the *shofar*s, while the rearguard marched after the ark, with incessant blowing on the *shofar*s. ¹⁰ Y'hoshua gave this order to the people: "Don't shout, don't let your voice be heard, don't let a single word out of your mouth until the day I tell you to shout; then you will shout."

¹¹ So he had the ark of *Adonai* make a circle around the city, going around it once; then they returned to camp and stayed in the camp. ¹² The next morning Y'hoshua got up early, and the *cohanim* took up the ark of *Adonai*. ¹³ The seven *cohanim* carrying the seven *shofar*s ahead of the ark of *Adonai* went on, continually blowing on their *shofar*s, with the fighting men marching ahead of them and the rearguard

following after the ark of *Adonai*; all the while the blowing on the *shofars* was incessant. ^{14} The second day, they went around the city once and returned to camp. They did the same for six days.

^{15} On the seventh day, they got up early, at sunrise, and went around the city in the same way seven times. That was the only day they encircled the city seven times. ^{16} The seventh time, when the *cohanim* blew on their *shofars*, Y'hoshua said to the people, "Shout! because *Adonai* has given you the city! ^{17} But the city and everything in it is to be set aside for *Adonai* and therefore to be destroyed completely; only Rachav the prostitute is to be spared, she and everyone with her in her house, because she hid the messengers we sent. ^{18} So you, keep clear of everything reserved for destruction. If you bring a curse on yourselves by taking anything set aside to be destroyed, you will bring a curse on the whole camp of Isra'el and cause great distress there. ^{19} All the silver and gold, and all the brass and iron utensils are to be separated out for *Adonai* and added to the treasury of *Adonai*."

^{20} So the people shouted, with the *shofars* blowing. When the people heard the sound of the *shofars*, the people let out a great shout; and the wall fell down flat; so that the people went up into the city, each one straight ahead of him; and they captured the city. ^{21} They completely destroyed everything in the city with the sword — men and women, young and old, cattle, sheep and donkeys.

^{22} Y'hoshua said to the two men who had reconnoitered the land, "Go into the prostitute's house and bring the woman out with all that she has, as you swore to her." ^{23} The young men, the spies, went in and brought out Rachav with her father, mother, brothers and all she had; they brought out all her relatives and put them safely outside the camp of Isra'el.

^{24} Then they burned the city to ashes with everything in it, except for the silver, the gold and the brass and iron utensils, which they put in the treasury of the house of *Adonai*. ^{25} But Y'hoshua spared Rachav the prostitute, her father's household and everything she had; and she has continued living with Isra'el from then until now; because she hid the messengers Y'hoshua had sent to reconnoiter Yericho. ^{26} Y'hoshua then made the people take this oath: "A curse before *Adonai* on anyone who rises up and rebuilds this city of Yericho: he will lay its foundation with the loss of his first-born son and set up its gates with the loss of his youngest son." ^{27} So *Adonai* was with Y'hoshua, and people heard about him throughout the land.

7 ^{1} But the people of Isra'el misappropriated some of the goods set aside to be destroyed; for 'Akhan, the son of Karmi, the son of Zavdi, the son of Zerach, of the tribe of Y'hudah, took some of the things reserved for destruction. In consequence, the anger of *Adonai* blazed up against the people of Isra'el.

^{2} Y'hoshua sent men from Yericho to 'Ai, which is next to Beit-Aven, east of Beit-El, telling them to go up and spy out the land. So the men went up, reconnoitered 'Ai, ^{3} returned to Y'hoshua and told him, "Don't have all the people go up; but let perhaps two or three thousand men go up and attack 'Ai. There's no point in making all the people exert themselves to get there, because there are only a few of them." ^{4} So from the people about three thousand men went up there, but they were routed by the men of 'Ai. ^{5} The men of 'Ai killed some thirty-six of them and chased them from before their gate all the way to Sh'varim, attacking them on the descent. The hearts of the people melted and turned to water.

^{6} Y'hoshua tore his clothes and fell to his face on the ground before the ark of ADONAI until evening, he and the leaders of Isra'el, and they put dust on their heads. ^{7} Y'hoshua said, "Oh, *Adonai ELOHIM*! Why did you take the trouble to bring this people across the Yarden if you meant to hand us over to the Emori and have us perish? We should have been satisfied to live on the other side of the Yarden! ^{8} Oh, ADONAI! What can I say, after Isra'el has turned their backs and retreated before their enemies? ^{9} For when the Kena'ani and the other people living in the land hear about it, they will surround us and wipe us off the face of the earth. What will you do then to save the honor of your great name?"

^{10} ADONAI said to Y'hoshua, "Stand up! Why are you lying there face down? ^{11} Isra'el has sinned. Yes, they have violated my covenant, which I commanded them. They have taken some of what was to have been set aside for destruction. They have stolen it, lied about it and put it with their own things. ^{12} This is why the people of Isra'el cannot stand before their enemies. They turn their backs on their enemies, because they have come under a curse. I won't be with you any more unless you destroy the things meant for destruction that you have with you. ^{13} So get up, consecrate the people, and say, 'Consecrate yourselves in preparation for tomorrow; for here is what ADONAI the God of Isra'el says: "Isra'el, you have things under the curse of destruction among you; and you will not be able to stand before your enemies until you remove the things that were to have been destroyed from among you." ^{14} Therefore, tomorrow morning you are to come forward, one tribe at a time; the tribe ADONAI takes is to come forward, one family at a time; the family ADONAI takes is to come forward, one household at a time; and the household ADONAI takes is to come forward, one person at a time. ^{15} The person who is caught with things in his possession that were reserved for destruction is to be burned to ashes, he and everything he has, because he has violated the covenant of ADONAI and has committed a shameful deed in Isra'el.'"

^{16} So Y'hoshua got up early in the morning and had Isra'el come forward, one tribe at a time; and the tribe of Y'hudah was taken. ^{17} He had the families of Y'hudah come forward and took the family of the Zarchi. He had the Zarchi family come forward by household leaders, and Zavdi was taken. ^{18} He had his household come forward, one person at a time; and 'Akhan the son of Karmi, the son of Zavdi, the son of Zerach, of the tribe of Y'hudah, was taken.

^{19} Y'hoshua said to 'Akhan, "My son, swear to ADONAI, the God of Isra'el, that you will tell the truth and confess to him. Tell me, now, what did you do? Don't hide anything from me." ^{20} 'Akhan answered Y'hoshua, "It is true: I have sinned against ADONAI, the God of Isra'el. Here is exactly what I did: ^{21} when I saw there with the spoil a beautiful robe from Shin'ar, five pounds of silver *shekel*s and a one-and-a-quarter-pound wedge of gold, I really wanted them. So I took them. You will find them hidden in the ground inside my tent, with the silver underneath." ^{22} Y'hoshua sent messengers, who ran to the tent. It was all there, hidden in his tent, including the silver underneath. ^{23} They took the things from inside the tent, brought them to Y'hoshua and all the people of Isra'el, and put them down before ADONAI.

^{24} Y'hoshua, together with all Isra'el, took 'Akhan, the son of Zerach, with the silver, the robe, the gold wedge, his sons, his daughters, his cattle, his donkeys, his sheep, his tent, and everything he had, and brought them up to the Akhor Valley. ^{25} Y'hoshua said, "Why have you brought trouble on us? Today ADONAI will bring trouble on you!" Then all Isra'el stoned him to death; they burned them to ashes and stoned them. ²⁶ Over him they piled a great mound of stones, which is there to this day. Finally ADONAI turned away from his fierce anger. And this is why that place is called the Valley of Akhor [trouble] to this day.

8 ¹ ADONAI said to Y'hoshua, "Don't be afraid or fall into despair! Take all the people who can fight with you, set out, and go up to 'Ai; because now I have handed over to you the king of 'Ai, his people, his city and his land. ²Do to 'Ai and its king as you did to Yericho and its king; but this time, take its spoil and cattle as booty for yourselves. Ambush the city from behind."

³ So Y'hoshua set out for 'Ai with all the people who could fight. Y'hoshua chose 30,000 men, the most courageous of his troops, and sent them out by night. ⁴He instructed them, "You are to lie in wait to ambush the city from behind. Stay close to the city; and all of you, be ready. ⁵I and all the troops with me will approach the city; and when they come out to attack us, as they did before, we will run away from them. ⁶They will chase after us until we have drawn them away from the city; because they will say, 'They're running away from us, as they did before'; so we'll run away from them. ⁷Then you will jump up from your ambush position and take possession of the city, for ADONAI your God will hand it over to you. ⁸When you have captured the city, you are to set it on fire; do according to what ADONAI has said. Those are your orders."

⁹ Y'hoshua sent them out; and they went to the place for the ambush, staying between Beit-El and 'Ai, to the west of 'Ai; while Y'hoshua camped that night with the people. ¹⁰Y'hoshua got up early in the morning, mustered his men and went up to 'Ai ahead of the people, he and the leaders of Isra'el . ¹¹ All the troops marching with him went up, advanced, arrived in front of the city and camped on the north side of 'Ai, with a valley between him and 'Ai. ¹²Then he took about 5,000 men and set them in ambush between Beit-El and 'Ai, to the west of 'Ai. ¹³Thus the people arrayed themselves, with all the army to the north of the city, and their rearguard lying in wait to the west of the city. Y'hoshua spent that night in the valley.

¹⁴The king of 'Ai saw this, so the men in the city hurried out early in the morning to battle against Isra'el, he and all his people, at a meeting-place facing the 'Aravah. But he was unaware that behind the city an ambush had been laid against him. ¹⁵Y'hoshua and all Isra'el made as if they had been defeated before them and ran off on the road to the desert. ¹⁶All the people in 'Ai were summoned together to pursue them, so they chased Y'hoshua and were drawn away from the city. ¹⁷Not a man was left in 'Ai or Beit-El who had not gone after Isra'el; pursuing Isra'el, they left the city wide open.

¹⁸ Then ADONAI said to Y'hoshua, "Point the spear in your hand toward 'Ai, because I will hand it over to you." Y'hoshua pointed the spear in his hand toward the city. ¹⁹ The men in ambush jumped up quickly from their place; the moment he stretched out his hand, they ran, entered the city and captured it; and they hurried to set the city on fire. ²⁰ When the men of 'Ai looked behind them, they saw it — there was the smoke from the city, rising to the sky; and they had no power to flee this way or that — at which point the people who had run off toward the desert turned back on the pursuers. ²¹ When Y'hoshua and all Isra'el saw that the ambush had captured the city and that the smoke of the city was going up, they turned back and slaughtered

the men of 'Ai; ²² while the others came out of the city against them too; so that they were surrounded by Isra'el with some on this side and some on that side. They attacked them, allowing none to remain or escape. ²³ But they took the king of 'Ai alive and brought him to Y'hoshua.

²⁴ When Isra'el had finished slaughtering all the inhabitants of 'Ai in the countryside, in the desert where they had pursued them, and they had all fallen, consumed by the sword, then all Isra'el returned to 'Ai and defeated it with the sword. ²⁵ Twelve thousand men and women fell that day, everyone in 'Ai. ²⁶ For Y'hoshua did not withdraw his hand, which he had used to point the spear, until he had utterly destroyed all the inhabitants of 'Ai. ²⁷ Only the livestock and the spoil of that city did Isra'el take as booty for themselves, in keeping with the order ADONAI had given Y'hoshua. ²⁸ So Y'hoshua burned down 'Ai and turned it into a *tel* forever, so that it remains a ruin to this day. ²⁹ The king of 'Ai he hanged on a tree until evening; at sundown Y'hoshua gave an order, so they took his carcass down from the tree, threw it at the entrance of the city gate and piled on it a big heap of stones, which is there to this day.

³⁰ Then Y'hoshua built an altar to ADONAI, the God of Isra'el, on Mount 'Eival, ³¹ as Moshe the servant of ADONAI had ordered the people of Isra'el to do (this is written in the book of the *Torah* of Moshe), an altar of uncut stones that no one had touched with an iron tool. On it they offered burnt offerings to ADONAI and sacrificed peace offerings. ³² He wrote there on the stones a copy of the *Torah* of Moshe, inscribing it in the presence of the people of Isra'el. ³³ Then all Isra'el, including their leaders, officials and judges, stood on either side of the ark in front of the *cohanim*, who were *L'vi'im* and who carried the ark for the covenant of ADONAI. The foreigners were there along with the citizens. Half of the people were in front of Mount G'rizim and half of them in front of Mount 'Eival, as Moshe the servant of ADONAI had ordered them earlier in connection with blessing the people of Isra'el. ³⁴ After this, he read all the words of the *Torah*, the blessing and the curse, according to everything written in the book of the *Torah*. ³⁵ There was not a word of everything Moshe had ordered that Y'hoshua did not read before all Isra'el assembled, including the women, the little ones and the foreigners living with them.

9 ¹ When all the kings on the west side of the Yarden in the hills, in the Sh'felah and all along the shore of the Great Sea that fronts the L'vanon — the Hitti, Emori, Kena'ani, P'rizi, Hivi and Y'vusi — heard what had happened, ² they joined forces to fight together against Y'hoshua and Isra'el. ³ But when the inhabitants of Giv'ah heard what Y'hoshua had done to Yericho and 'Ai, ⁴ they developed a clever deception: they made themselves look as if they had been on a long journey by putting old sacks on their donkeys and taking used wineskins that had burst and been mended back together. ⁵ They put old, patched sandals on their feet and dressed in worn-out clothes; and took as provisions nothing but dried-up bread that was crumbling to pieces. ⁶ Then they went to Y'hoshua in the camp at Gilgal and said to him and the men of Isra'el, "We have come from a country far away. Now, make a covenant with us." ⁷ The men of Isra'el said to the Hivi, "How do we know that you don't live here among us? If you do, we don't want to make a covenant with you." ⁸ But they answered Y'hoshua, "We are your servants." Y'hoshua asked, "Who are you, and where do you come from?" ⁹ They answered him, "Your servants have come from a very distant country because of the reputation of ADONAI your God. We have heard reports about him — everything he did in Egypt, ¹⁰ and everything he did to the two kings of the Emori across the Yarden, Sichon king of Heshbon and 'Og king of Bashan at 'Ashtarot. ¹¹ So our leaders and all the people living in our country said to us, "Take provisions with you for the journey, go to meet them, and say to them, 'We are your servants, and now make a covenant with us.' ¹² Here is the bread which we took for our provisions. It was still warm when we took it out of our homes the day we left to come to you. Now look at it! It's dry and turned to crumbs! ¹³ And these wineskins were new when we filled them, but look, now they're torn. Likewise these clothes of ours and our shoes are worn out because of the very long journey."

¹⁴ The men sampled some of their food but didn't seek the advice of ADONAI, ¹⁵ so Y'hoshua made peace with them and made a covenant with them to spare their lives, and the leading officials of the community swore to them. ¹⁶ But three days later, after they had made the covenant with them, they heard that they were their neighbors, that they lived there with them.

¹⁷ The people of Isra'el traveled and arrived at their cities on the third day. Their cities were Giv'on, K'firah, Be'erot and Kiryat-Ye'arim. ¹⁸ The people of Isra'el did not attack them, because the leading officials of the community had sworn to them by ADONAI, the God of Isra'el; but all the community grumbled against the leaders. ¹⁹ However, the leaders replied to the whole community, "We have sworn to them by ADONAI, the God of Isra'el; so we can't touch them. ²⁰ Here is what we will do to them: we will let them live, so that God's anger will not be on us because of the oath we swore to them. ²¹ Yes, let them live," the leaders continued, "but let them chop wood and draw water for the whole community." This is what the leaders said.

²² Y'hoshua summoned them and said this to them: "Why have you deceived us by saying, 'We come from a place very far away,' when in fact you are living right here with us? ²³ Now you have a curse on you: you will be slaves forever, supplying people to chop wood and draw water for the house of my God." ²⁴ They answered Y'hoshua, "It is because we heard the reports that ADONAI your God had ordered his servant Moshe to give you all the land and to destroy all the inhabitants of the land from ahead of you. So we were terrified for our lives on account of you; that's why we did this. ²⁵ Now, as you see, we are in your hands; do to us whatever seems good and right to you." ²⁶ So Y'hoshua did exactly that: he saved them from the power of the people of Isra'el, so that they didn't kill them. ²⁷ But he did that same day make them choppers of wood and drawers of water for the community and for the altar of ADONAI in the place which he would choose; and they remain so to this day.

10 ¹ When Adoni-Tzedek king of Yerushalayim heard how Y'hoshua had taken 'Ai and utterly destroyed it — he had done the same to 'Ai and its king as he had done to Yericho and its king — and how the inhabitants of Giv'on had made peace with Isra'el and were living among them, ² his people became greatly alarmed; because Giv'on was as large as one of the royal cities, larger than 'Ai, and all its men were courageous. ³ So Adoni-Tzedek king of Yerushalayim sent this message to Hoham king of Hevron, Pir'am king of Yarmut, Yafia king of Lakhish and D'vir king of 'Eglon: ⁴ "Come up and help me, and we'll attack Giv'on, because it has made peace with Y'hoshua and the people of Isra'el." ⁵ So the five kings of the Emori — the kings of Yerushalayim, Hevron, Yarmut, Lakhish and 'Eglon — got together, went up with all their armies, pitched camp against Giv'on and made war against it.

⁶ The people of Giv'on sent a message to Y'hoshua at their camp in Gilgal that said, "Don't ignore your servants! Come up to us quickly, and save us! Help us, because all the kings of the Emori living in the hills have gotten together to fight us." ⁷ Y'hoshua went up from Gilgal, he and all the fighting men with him, including all the bravest ones. ⁸ ADONAI said to Y'hoshua, "Don't be afraid of them, for I have handed them over to you; not one of their men will stand against you." ⁹ Having spent the entire night marching up from Gilgal, Y'hoshua fell upon them, taking them by surprise. ¹⁰ ADONAI threw them into confusion before Isra'el and defeated them in a great slaughter at Giv'on, pursuing them along the road that goes up from Beit-Horon, and beating them back to 'Azekah and all the way to Makkedah. ¹¹ As they fled before Isra'el down the road to Beit-Horon, ADONAI threw huge hailstones down on them all the way to 'Azekah, and they died; more died because of the hail than because Isra'el had killed them with the sword.

¹² Then, on the day ADONAI handed over the Emori to the people of Isra'el, Y'hoshua spoke to ADONAI; in the sight of Isra'el he said,

"Sun, stand motionless over Giv'on!
Moon, you too, over Ayalon Valley!"

¹³ So the sun stood still and the moon stayed put,
till Isra'el took vengeance on their enemies.

This is written in the book of Yashar. The sun stood still in the sky and was in no rush to set for nearly a whole day. ¹⁴ There has never been a day like that before or since, when ADONAI listened to the voice of a man; it happened because ADONAI was fighting on Isra'el's behalf.

¹⁵ Y'hoshua returned with all Isra'el to the camp at Gilgal. ¹⁶ But those five kings fled and hid themselves in the cave at Makkedah, ¹⁷ and it was reported to Y'hoshua that the five kings had been found hiding in the cave at Makkedah. ¹⁸ Y'hoshua said, "Roll big stones to the mouth of the cave, and put men there to guard them. ¹⁹ However, you, don't wait, but keep chasing your enemies, and attack those farthest in the rear. Don't allow them to return to their cities, because ADONAI has handed them over to you." ²⁰ After Y'hoshua and the people of Isra'el had finished killing them off in a very great slaughter, till they had been destroyed, and the remaining remnant had entered the fortified cities, ²¹ all the people returned safely to Y'hoshua at the camp in Makkedah; and no one said a word against any of the people of Isra'el.

²² Then Y'hoshua said, "Open up the mouth of the cave, and bring those five kings out of the cave to me. ²³ They did it; they brought the five kings out to him — the kings of Yerushalayim, Hevron, Yarmut, Lakhish and 'Eglon. ²⁴ After they had brought the five kings to Y'hoshua, he summoned all the men of Isra'el and said to the commanders of the soldiers who had gone with him, "Come here and put your feet on the necks of these kings." They came and put their feet on their necks. ²⁵ Y'hoshua said to them, "Don't be afraid or confused, but be strong and bold, because this is what ADONAI will do to all your enemies that you fight against." ²⁶ With that, Y'hoshua struck them and put them to death, hanging them on five trees, where they remained hanging until evening. ²⁷ At sunset Y'hoshua

gave an order, and they lowered them from the trees and threw them into the cave where they had hidden themselves, then laid big stones at the mouth of the cave; and there they remain to this day. ²⁸ Y'hoshua captured Makkedah that day, defeating it and its king by the sword. He completely destroyed them, everyone there — he left no one; and he did to the king of Makkedah what he had done to the king of Yericho.

²⁹ Y'hoshua went on from Makkedah, and all Isra'el with him, to Livnah; and he fought against Livnah. ³⁰ ADONAI also handed it and its king over to Isra'el. He defeated it with the sword, everyone there — he left no one, and he did to its king what he had done to the king of Yericho.

³¹ Y'hoshua went on from Livnah, and all Isra'el with him, to Lakhish; and he pitched camp against it and fought against it. ³² ADONAI handed it over to Isra'el; he captured it the second day. He defeated it with the sword, everyone there, exactly as he had done to Livnah. ³³ But then Horam king of Gezer came up to help Lakhish; so Y'hoshua attacked him and his people, until he had no one left with him.

³⁴ Y'hoshua went on from Lakhish, and all Isra'el with him, to 'Eglon; and he pitched camp against it and fought against it. ³⁵ They captured it that very day. He defeated it with the sword, completely destroying everyone there, exactly as he had done to Lakhish.

³⁶ Y'hoshua went up from 'Eglon, and all Isra'el with him, to Hevron; and they fought against it. ³⁷ They captured it, defeating it with the sword, including its king, its villages and everyone there; he left no one, exactly as he had done to 'Eglon; but he completely destroyed it and everyone there.

³⁸ Y'hoshua turned back, and all Isra'el with him, to D'vir and fought against it. ³⁹ They captured it, its king and all its villages, defeating them with the sword and utterly destroying everyone there; he left no one. He did to D'vir and it king as he had done to Hevron and as he had done to Livnah and its king.

⁴⁰ So Y'hoshua attacked all the land — the hills, the Negev, the Sh'felah and the mountain slopes — and all their kings; he left none but completely destroyed everything that breathed, as ADONAI the God of Isra'el had ordered. ⁴¹ Y'hoshua attacked them from Kadesh-Barnea to 'Azah and all the land of Goshen, as far as Giv'on. ⁴² Y'hoshua captured all these kings and their land all at the same time, because ADONAI the God of Isra'el fought on Isra'el's behalf. ⁴³ Then Y'hoshua returned, and all Isra'el with him, to the camp at Gilgal.

11 ¹ When Yavin king of Hatzor heard of it, he informed Yovav king of Madon; the king of Shimron; the king of Akhshaf; ² the kings to the north, in the hills, in the 'Aravah south of Kinn'rot, in the Sh'felah and in the regions of Dor on the west; ³ the Kena'ani to east and west; the Emori, Hitti, P'rizi and Y'vusi in the hills; and the Hivi at the foot of Hermon in the land of Mitzpah. ⁴ So they set out, they and all their armies, many people, in number like the sand at the seashore, with very many horses and chariots. ⁵ All these kings met together, then came and pitched camp together at the Merom Spring, to fight Isra'el.

⁶ ADONAI said to Y'hoshua, "Don't be afraid on their account; because at this time tomorrow I will hand them over, all of them dead, before Isra'el. You are to hamstring their horses and burn up their chariots." ⁷ So Y'hoshua came against them suddenly with all his fighting men and fell on them at the Merom Spring.

^{8} *ADONAI* handed them over to Isra'el — they attacked and chased them to Greater Tzidon, Misrefot-Mayim and eastward to the Mitzpeh Valley; they attacked them until none of them was left. ^{9} Y'hoshua did to them what *ADONAI* had ordered — he hamstrung their horses and burned up their chariots. ^{10} Then Y'hoshua turned back and captured Hatzor, striking its king dead with the sword; for in time past Hatzor had been the head of all those kingdoms. ^{11} They put everyone there to death with the sword, completely destroying them; there was nothing left that breathed; and he burned Hatzor to the ground. ^{12} Y'hoshua captured all the cities of those kings and the kings as well; he defeated them with the sword and completely destroyed them, as Moshe the servant of *ADONAI* had ordered. ^{13} But as for the cities built on their *tels*, Isra'el burned none of them except Hatzor; Y'hoshua did burn that one. ^{14} All the spoil of these cities and the livestock the people of Isra'el took as booty for themselves; but every human being they put to death with the sword, until they had destroyed them — they left no one breathing. ^{15} Moshe had given orders to Y'hoshua, just as *ADONAI* had given orders to Moshe his servant, and Y'hoshua acted accordingly — he did everything *ADONAI* had ordered Moshe.

^{16} So Y'hoshua captured all that land, the hills, the Negev, all the land of Goshen, the Sh'felah, the 'Aravah and the Isra'el hills and Sh'felah, ^{17} from the bare mountain that goes up to Se'ir to Ba'al-Gad in the L'vanon Valley under Mount Hermon; and he took all their kings, struck them and put them to death. ^{18} Y'hoshua made war with all those kings for a long time. ^{19} Not one city made peace with the people of Isra'el, except for the Hivi living in Giv'on; they took everything in battle. ^{20} For it was *ADONAI* who caused them to harden their hearts and come against Isra'el in battle, so that they would be utterly destroyed, so that they would not find favor but be destroyed, in keeping with the orders *ADONAI* had given Moshe.

^{21} Y'hoshua at that time came and cut off the 'Anakim from the land — from Hevron, D'vir, 'Anav and from all the hill-country of Y'hudah and Isra'el; Y'hoshua utterly destroyed them and their cities. ^{22} No 'Anakim were left in the land of the people of Isra'el — only in 'Azah, Gat and Ashdod did some remain. ^{23} Y'hoshua took the whole land, in keeping with all that *ADONAI* had said to Moshe and to Isra'el according to their divisions into tribes. Then the land rested from war.

12 ^{1} These are the kings of the land whom the people of Isra'el defeated and of whose land they took possession, across the Yarden toward the east, from the Arnon Valley to Mount Hermon and all the 'Aravah eastward:

^{2} Sichon king of the Emori, who lived in Heshbon and ruled the territory that includes 'Aro'er, at the edge of the Arnon Valley; the middle of the valley; half of Gil'ad, to the Yabok River, which forms the border with the people of 'Amon; ^{3} the 'Aravah to Lake Kinneret eastward and to the sea of the 'Aravah, the Dead Sea, eastward by way of Beit-Yeshimot and on the south under the slopes of Pisgah.

^{4} There was also the territory of 'Og king of Bashan, who belonged to the remnant of the Refa'im. He lived at 'Ashtarot and at Edre'i; ^{5} and he ruled Mount Hermon; Salkhah; all Bashan, to the border with the G'shuri and the Ma'akhati; and half of Gil'ad, to its border with Sichon king of Heshbon.

^{6} Moshe the servant of *ADONAI*, with the people of Isra'el, defeated them; and Moshe the servant of *ADONAI* gave it to the Re'uveni, the Gadi and the half-tribe of M'nasheh as their possession.

⁷⁻⁸ Following are the kings of the land whom Y'hoshua, with the people of Isra'el, defeated in the area west of the Yarden, between Ba'al-Gad in the L'vanon Valley and the bare mountain that goes up to Se'ir. Y'hoshua gave this land, inhabited by the Hitti, Emori, Kena'ani, P'rizi, Hivi and Y'vusi, to the tribes of Isra'el to possess, according to their divisions, in the hills, the Sh'felah, the 'Aravah, the mountain slopes, the desert and the Negev:

⁹   the king of Yericho,
     the king of 'Ai, by Beit-El,
¹⁰   the king of Yerushalayim,
     the king of Hevron,
¹¹   the king of Yarmut,
     the king of Lakhish,
¹²   the king of 'Eglon,
     the king of Gezer,
¹³   the king of D'vir,
     the king of Geder,
¹⁴   the king of Hormah,
     the king of 'Arad,
¹⁵   the king of Livnah,
     the king of 'Adulam,
¹⁶   the king of Makkedah,
     the king of Beit-El,
¹⁷   the king of Tapuach,
     the king of Hefer,
¹⁸   the king of Afek,
     the king of Sharon,
¹⁹   the king of Madon,
     the king of Hatzor,
²⁰   the king of Shimron-M'ron,
     the king of Akhshaf,
²¹   the king of Ta'anakh,
     the king of Megiddo,
²²   the king of Kedesh,
     the king of Yokne'am in Karmel,
²³   the king of Dor in the region of Dor,
     the king of Goyim in the Gilgal, and
²⁴   the king of Tirtzah —

making a total of thirty-one kings.

13 ¹ Now Y'hoshua was old; the years had taken their toll. ADONAI said to him, "You are old, and the years have taken their toll; but there is yet a great deal of land to be possessed.

² "This is the land that still remains: all the regions of the P'lishtim and all the G'shuri, ³ from the Shichor which fronts Egypt, to the border of 'Ekron (northward from there the land is considered as belonging to the Kena'ani)—that is, the territory of

the rulers of the P'lishtim in 'Azah, Ashdod, Ashkelon, Gat and 'Ekron; also the 'Avim ⁴to the south; all the land of the Kena'ani; Me'arah, which belongs to the Tzidonim, as far as Afek and on to the border with the Emori; ⁵the land of the Givli; all the L'vanon eastward, from Ba'al-Gad at the foot of Mount Hermon to the entrance of Hamat.

⁶ "As for the inhabitants of the hills between the L'vanon and Misrefot-Mayim, that is, all the Tzidonim, I myself will expel them ahead of the people of Isra'el; all you have to do is assign it to Isra'el as an inheritance, as I have ordered you. ⁷ So now, divide this land as an inheritance for the nine tribes and the half-tribe of M'nasheh."

⁸ With the half-tribe of M'nasheh, the Re'uveni and the Gadi received their inheritance, which Moshe had given them, beyond the Yarden eastward, just as Moshe the servant of ADONAI had given them — ⁹ from 'Aro'er on the edge of the Arnon Valley, the city in the middle of the valley, all the plateau between Meidva and Divon, ¹⁰ and all the cities of Sichon king of the Emori who ruled in Heshbon to the border with the people of 'Amon; ¹¹ and Gil'ad, the territory of the G'shuri and Ma'akhati, all Mount Hermon, all Bashan as far as Salkhah — ¹² that is, all the kingdom of 'Og in Bashan, who ruled in 'Ashtarot and Edre'i. 'Og was one of those remaining from the Refa'im, whom Moshe defeated and expelled. ¹³ However, the people of Isra'el expelled neither the G'shuri nor the Ma'akhati, with the consequence that G'shur and Ma'akhat have lived among Isra'el to this day.

¹⁴ Only to the tribe of Levi did Moshe give no inheritance; because the offerings made by fire for ADONAI the God of Isra'el are its inheritance; as [ADONAI] had said to Moshe.

¹⁵ Moshe gave land to the tribe of the descendants of Re'uven by clans. ¹⁶ Their territory included 'Aro'er on the edge of the Arnon Valley, the city in the middle of the valley, all the plateau near Meidva, ¹⁷ Heshbon and its villages on the plateau, Divon, Bamot-Ba'al, Beit-Ba'al-M'on, ¹⁸ Yahatz, K'demot, Mefa'at, ¹⁹ Kiryatayim, Sivmah, Tzeret-Shachar at the top of the valley, ²⁰ Beit-P'or, the slopes of Pisgah, Beit-Yeshimot, ²¹ all the cities of the plateau — all the kingdom of Sichon king of the Emori, who ruled in Heshbon. Moshe defeated him with the chiefs of Midyan, along with Evi, Rekem, Tzur, Hur and Reva the princes of Sichon who lived in the land. ²² Along with the others the people of Isra'el killed with the sword, they also struck down Bil'am the son of B'or, who practiced divination. ²³ The Yarden formed the border for the descendants of Re'uven. This was the inheritance of the descendants of Re'uven by clans, with its cities and villages.

²⁴ Moshe gave land to the tribe of Gad, to the descendants of Gad by clans. ²⁵ Their territory included Ya'zer; all the cities of Gil'ad; half the land of the people of 'Amon, as far as 'Aro'er fronting Rabbah — ²⁶ that is, from Heshbon to Ramot-Mitzpeh and B'tonim; and from Machanayim to the border of Lidvir; ²⁷ while in the valley it included Beit-Haram, Beit-Nimrah, Sukkot and Tzafon — in other words, the rest of the kingdom of Sichon king of Heshbon; with the Yarden to the far end of Lake Kinneret as its border, their territory extended eastward. ²⁸ This is the inheritance of the descendants of Gad by clans, with its cities and villages.

²⁹ Moshe gave an inheritance to the half-tribe of M'nasheh; it was for the half-tribe of the descendants of M'nasheh by clans. ³⁰ Their territory included Machanayim and all of Bashan — that is, all the kingdom of 'Og king of Bashan; all the villages of Ya'ir in Bashan, sixty cities; ³¹ half of Gil'ad; and 'Ashtarot and Edre'i,

the cities of the kingdom of 'Og in Bashan. All this was for the descendants of Makhir the son of M'nasheh, or, rather, for half of the descendants of Makhir, by clans. ³²These are the inheritances which Moshe distributed in the plains of Mo'av, beyond the Yarden and Yericho, eastward. ³³But to the tribe of Levi Moshe gave no inheritance; ADONAI the God of Isra'el is their inheritance — as he told them.

14 ¹These are the inheritances which the people of Isra'el took in the land of Kena'an, which El'azar the *cohen*, Y'hoshua the son of Nun and the heads of the ancestral clans of the tribes of the people of Isra'el distributed to them ²by lot for them to inherit, as ADONAI ordered through Moshe, for the nine tribes and the half-tribe. ³Moshe had already given the inheritances to the two tribes and the half-tribe beyond the Yarden; to the *L'vi'im* he gave no inheritance among them. ⁴The descendants of Yosef constituted two tribes, M'nasheh and Efrayim; and they gave no portion of the land to the *L'vi'im* except cities to live in, with the open land surrounding them for their livestock and crops. ⁵As ADONAI had ordered Moshe, so the people of Isra'el did — they divided the land.

⁶The descendants of Y'hudah approached Y'hoshua in Gilgal, and Kalev the son of Y'funeh the K'nizi said to him, "You know what ADONAI told Moshe the man of God about me and you in Kadesh-Barnea. ⁷I was forty years old when Moshe the servant of ADONAI sent me from Kadesh-Barnea to reconnoiter the land, and I brought back to him an honest report. ⁸My brothers who went up with me discouraged the people, but I followed ADONAI my God completely. ⁹On that day Moshe swore, 'Surely the land where your foot has been will be the inheritance for you and your descendants forever, because you have followed ADONAI my God completely.' ¹⁰Now, look: ADONAI has kept me alive these forty-five years, as he said he would, from the time ADONAI said this to Moshe, when Isra'el was going through the desert. Today I am eighty-five years old, ¹¹but I am as strong today as on the day Moshe sent me — I'm as strong now as I was then, whether for war or simply for going here and there. ¹²Therefore, give me this hill, the one ADONAI spoke about on that day; for on that day you heard how the 'Anakim were there with great, fortified cities; perhaps ADONAI will be with me, and I will drive them away, as ADONAI said."

¹³Y'hoshua blessed him and gave Hevron to Kalev the son of Y'funeh as his inheritance. ¹⁴So Hevron became the inheritance of Kalev the son of Y'funeh the K'nizi, as it is to this day; because he followed ADONAI the God of Isra'el completely. ¹⁵(Hevron was formerly called Kiryat-Arba; this Arba was the greatest man among the 'Anakim.) Then the land had rest from war.

15 ¹The territory chosen by lot for the tribe of the descendants of Y'hudah according to their families extended to the border of Edom in the Tzin Desert, toward the Negev in the far south.

²Their southern border began at the far shore of the Dead Sea, from the bay facing southward, ³and went out south of the Scorpion Ascent, passed toward Tzin, went up south of Kadesh-Barnea, passed Hetzron, went up toward Adar, turned toward Karka, ⁴passed toward 'Atzmon, and went out at the *Vadi* of Egypt, with the border ending at the sea; this will be your southern border. ⁵The eastern border was the Dead Sea to where the Yarden entered it.

The northern border began at the bay of the sea at the end of the Yarden; ⁶then the border went up to Beit-Hoglah and passed north of Beit-'Aravah; next the border went up to the Stone of Bohan the son of Re'uven; ⁷then the border went up to D'vir from the Akhor Valley, then northward facing Gilgal (that is, across from Ma'alei-Adumim, which is on the south side of the *vadi*); next the border passed to the 'Ein-Shemesh Spring and went out at 'Ein-Rogel. ⁸Then the border went up the Ben-Hinnom Valley to the south side of the Y'vusi (that is, Yerushalayim), and the border continued up to the top of the hill in front of the Hinnom Valley on the west (which is also at the northernmost end of the Refa'im Valley) ⁹From this hilltop the border was drawn to the source of the Neftoach Spring and continued out to the cities of Mount 'Efron; next the border was drawn to Ba'alah (that is, Kiryat-Ye'arim). ¹⁰Then the border turned from Ba'al westward to Mount Se'ir, passed the spur of Mount Ye'arim (also called K'salon) on the north, went down to Beit-Shemesh and passed Timnah. ¹¹Next the border went out toward the side of 'Ekron northward; and finally, the border was drawn to Shikron, passed Mount Ba'alah, and went out at Yavne'el, with the border ending at the sea.

¹²As for the west border, the Great Sea was its border. These were the borders of the territory of the descendants of Y'hudah, by clans.

¹³To Kalev the son of Y'funeh he gave a portion with the descendants of Y'hudah, as ADONAI had ordered Y'hoshua, namely, Kiryat-Arba (Arba was the father of the 'Anak), also called Hevron. ¹⁴Kalev expelled from there three descendants of 'Anak — Sheshai, Achiman and Talmai, children of 'Anak. ¹⁵From there he went up to fight the inhabitants of D'vir (D'vir was formerly called Kiryat-Sefer). ¹⁶Kalev said, "To whoever overpowers Kiryat-Sefer and captures it I will give my daughter Akhsah as his wife." ¹⁷'Otni'el the son of K'naz, Kalev's brother, captured it; so he gave him 'Akhsah his daughter as his wife. ¹⁸After becoming his wife, she persuaded him to ask her father to give them a field; when she got off her donkey, Kalev asked her, "What do you want?" ¹⁹She said to him: "Give me a blessing: since you gave me land in the Negev, also give me sources of water." So Kalev gave her the Upper Springs and the Lower Springs.

²⁰This is the inheritance of the tribe of the descendants of Y'hudah, by clans.

²¹The cities at the outer part of the tribe of Y'hudah toward the border with Edom in the south were: Kavtze'el, 'Eder, Yagur, ²²Kinah, Dimonah, 'Ad'adah, ²³Kedesh, Hatzor, Yitnan, ²⁴Zif, Telem, Be'alot, ²⁵Hatzor, Hadatah, K'riot, Hetzron (which is Hatzor), ²⁶Amam, Sh'ma, Moladah, ²⁷Hatzar-Gadah, Heshmon, Beit-Pelet, ²⁸Hatzar-Shu'al, Be'er-Sheva, Bizyot-Yah, ²⁹Ba'alah, 'Iyim, 'Etzem, ³⁰El-Tolad, K'sil, Hormah, ³¹Ziklag, Madmanah, Sansanah, ³²L'va'ot, Shilchim, 'Ayin and Rimmon — twenty-nine cities in all, together with their villages.

³³In the Sh'felah: Eshta'ol, Tzor'ah, Ashnah, ³⁴Zanoach, 'Ein-Ganim, Tapuach, 'Enam, ³⁵Yarmut, 'Adulam, Sokhoh, 'Azekah, ³⁶Sh'arim, 'Aditayim, G'derah and G'derotayim — fourteen cities, together with their villages. ³⁷Tz'nan, Hadashah, Migdal-Gad, ³⁸Dil'an, Mitzpeh, Yokte'el, ³⁹Lakhish, Bozkat, 'Eglon, ⁴⁰Kabon, Lachmas, Kitlish, ⁴¹G'derot, Beit-Dagon, Na'amah and Makkedah — sixteen cities, together with their villages. ⁴²Livnah, 'Eter, 'Ashan, ⁴³Yiftach, Ashnah, N'tziv, ⁴⁴Ke'ilah, Akhziv and Mareshah — nine cities, together with their villages. ⁴⁵'Ekron, with its towns and villages — ⁴⁶from 'Ekron to the sea; all those near Ashdod, with

their villages; ⁴⁷ Ashdod, with its towns and villages; 'Azah, with its towns and villages, to the *Vadi* of Egypt, with the Great Sea as its border.

⁴⁸ In the hills: Shamir, Yatir, Sokhoh, ⁴⁹ Danah, Kiryat-Sanna (that is, D'vir), ⁵⁰ 'Anav, Esht'moh, 'Anim, ⁵¹ Goshen, Holon and Giloh — eleven cities, together with their villages. ⁵² Arav, Dumah, Esh'an, ⁵³ Yanum, Beit-Tapuach, Afekah, ⁵⁴ Humtah, Kiryat-Arba (that is, Hevron) and Tzi'or — nine cities, together with their villages. ⁵⁵ Ma'on, Karmel, Zif, Yutah, ⁵⁶ Yizre'el, Yokde'am, Zanoach, ⁵⁷ Kayin, Giv'ah and Timnah — ten cities, together with their villages. ⁵⁸ Halchul, Beit-Tzur, G'dor, ⁵⁹ Ma'arat, Beit-'Anot, Elt'kon — six cities, together with their villages. ⁶⁰ Kiryat-Ba'al (that is, Kiryat-Ye'arim) and Rabbah — two cities, together with their villages.

⁶¹ In the desert: Beit-'Aravah, Middin, S'khakhah, ⁶² Nivshan, 'Ir-Hamelach and 'Ein-Gedi — six cities, together with their villages.

⁶³ As for the Y'vusi, who lived in Yerushalayim, the descendants of Y'hudah could not drive them out; so the Y'vusi live with the descendants of Y'hudah in Yerushalayim to this day.

16 ¹ The border of the territory chosen by lot for the descendants of Yosef began from the Yarden at Yericho, at the spring of Yericho on the east, went up from Yericho through the hills and desert to Beit-El, ² went out from Beit-El to Luz, passed on to the border with the Arki to 'Atarot, ³ went down westward to the border with the Yafleti, to the border of Lower Beit-Horon, on to Gezer and ending at the sea. ⁴ So the descendants of Yosef, M'nasheh and Efrayim took the inheritance.

⁵ The border of the descendants of Efrayim according to their families was as follows: the eastern border of their inheritance began at 'Atrot-Adar and went to Upper Beit-Horon; ⁶ then the border extended westward, with Mikhm'tat on the north; next the border turned eastward to Ta'anat-Shiloh and passed by it to the east of Yanochah; ⁷ then it went down from Yanochah to 'Atarot, went to Na'arah, extended to Yericho and ended at the Yarden. ⁸ From Tapuach the border went westward to *Vadi* Kanah and ended at the sea. This is the inheritance of the tribe of the descendants of Efrayim according to their families, ⁹ together with the cities set aside for the descendants of Efrayim inside the territory to be inherited by the descendants of M'nasheh, all the cities with their villages. ¹⁰ They did not drive out the Kena'ani living in Gezer, so the Kena'ani live together with Efrayim to this day, having become slaves to do the heavy work.

17 ¹ This was the territory chosen by lot for the tribe of M'nasheh, for he was the firstborn of Yosef. As for Makhir the firstborn of M'nasheh, the father of Gil'ad, because he was a warrior he got Gil'ad and Bashan. ² So the lot was drawn for the other descendants of M'nasheh according to their families — for the descendants of Avi'ezer, Helek, Asri'el, Sh'khem, Hefer and Sh'mida; these were the male descendants of M'nasheh according to their families.

³ But Tz'lof'chad the son of Hefer, the son of Gil'ad, the son of Makhir, the son of M'nasheh, had no sons, only daughters; these are the names of his daughters: Machlah, No'ah, Hoglah, Milkah and Tirtzah. ⁴ They approached El'azar the *cohen*, Y'hoshua the son of Nun and the leaders and said, "A*DONAI* ordered Moshe to give us an inheritance together with our kinsmen." Therefore, in keeping with A*DONAI*'s order, he gave them an inheritance together with the kinsmen of their father. ⁵ Thus ten parts fell

to M'nasheh, in addition to the land of Gil'ad and Bashan beyond the Yarden, ⁶ because the daughters of M'nasheh had an inheritance along with his descendants; but the land of Gil'ad belonged to the rest of the descendants of M'nasheh.

⁷ The border of M'nasheh began at Asher and went to Mikhm'tat, which is across from Sh'khem; next the border went along to the right, to the people of 'Ein-Tapuach. ⁸ The land of Tapuach belonged to M'nasheh, but Tapuach on the border of M'nasheh belonged to the descendants of Efrayim. ⁹ The border descended to *Vadi* Kanah, south of the *vadi*, by cities which belonged to Efrayim among the cities of M'nasheh; but the border with M'nasheh was on the north side of the *vadi*, and it ended at the sea. ¹⁰ Southward it was Efrayim's, northward it was M'nasheh's, and the sea was its border; while to the north they extended to Asher, and on the east to Yissakhar.

¹¹ In Asher and Yissakhar, M'nasheh had Beit-Sh'an and its villages; Yivle'am and its villages; and the inhabitants of Dor and its villages, of 'Ein-Dor and its villages, of Ta'anakh and its villages, and of Megiddo and its villages — three districts in all. ¹² But the descendants of M'nasheh could not drive out the inhabitants of those cities; the Kena'ani wanted to stay in that land. ¹³ After the people of Isra'el had become strong, they made the Kena'ani do heavy labor but didn't completely drive them out.

¹⁴ Then the descendants of Yosef spoke to Y'hoshua; they said, "Why have you given me only one lot and only one portion to inherit? After all, I am a great people, since *ADONAI* has blessed me so." ¹⁵ Y'hoshua answered them, "If you are a great people, go up to the forest, and clear land for yourself there in the territory of the P'rizi and the Refa'im — since the hills of Efrayim don't give you enough space." ¹⁶ The descendants of Yosef replied, "The hills won't be enough for us; and all the Kena'ani living in the valleys have iron chariots — both those in Beit-Sh'an and its villages and those in the Yizre'el Valley." ¹⁷ Then Y'hoshua said to the house of Yosef, to both Efrayim and M'nasheh, "You are a great people with much power; you will not have only one lot, ¹⁸ but the hills too will be yours. Although it is a forest, you will clear it, and the resulting open land will be yours. You will drive out the Kena'ani, even though they have iron chariots and are strong."

18 ¹ The entire community of the people of Isra'el assembled themselves together at Shiloh and set up the tent of meeting there, after the land had been subdued before them. ² There still remained among the people of Isra'el seven tribes that had not yet received their inheritance. ³ Y'hoshua said to the people of Isra'el, "How long will you delay going in to take possession of the land which *ADONAI* the God of your ancestors has given you? ⁴ Appoint three men for each tribe; I will commission them; and they are to set out, go through the land and describe it according to their inheritance; then they are to come back to me. ⁵ They are to divide it into seven portions, with Y'hudah remaining in its territory to the south and the house of Yosef in their territory to the north. ⁶ You will describe seven portions of land and bring the descriptions here to me; then I will cast lots for you here before *ADONAI* our God. ⁷ But the *L'vi'im* have no share with you, because the office of *cohen* to *ADONAI* is their inheritance; and Gad and Re'uven and the half-tribe of M'nasheh have received their inheritance beyond the Yarden to the east, which Moshe the servant of *ADONAI* gave them."

⁸ So the men got up and went. Y'hoshua gave them this commission as they left to describe the land: "Go; walk through the land; and describe it; then come back to me,

and I will cast lots for you here before *Adonai* in Shiloh." ⁹ The men went and passed through the land, surveying it by cities, dividing it into seven regions and writing the results on a scroll. Then they came to Y'hoshua in the camp at Shiloh. ¹⁰ Y'hoshua cast lots for them in Shiloh before *Adonai*, and there Y'hoshua divided the land among the people of Isra'el according to their regions.

¹¹ The lot for the tribe of the descendants of Binyamin came up according to their families. The border of their territory chosen by lot was between the descendants of Y'hudah and the descendants of Yosef.

¹² On the north side, their border began at the Yarden, went up alongside Yericho on the north, continued up through the hills westward and arrived at the Beit-Aven Desert. ¹³ From there the border passed on to Luz, to the south side of Luz (that is, Beit-El); then the border went down to 'Atrot-Adar, by the hill on the south side of Lower Beit-Horon.

¹⁴ The border was delineated as turning at the western corner and heading south-ward, from the hill located in front of Beit-Horon on the south; and it ended at Kiryat-Ba'al (that is, Kiryat-Ye'arim), a city belonging to the descendants of Y'hudah; this was the west side.

¹⁵ On the south the border extended westward from the most distant part of Kiryat-Ye'arim, going out to the source of the Neftoach Spring. ¹⁶ Then the border went down to the farthest part of the hill located in front of the Ben-Hinnom Valley, north of the Refa'im Valley, south of the Y'vusi; and continued down to 'Ein-Rogel, ¹⁷ where it was drawn to the north; then it went on to 'Ein-Shemesh; continued to G'lilot, which is across from Ma'alei-Adumim; went down to the Stone of Bohan the son of Re'uven; ¹⁸ passed alongside the 'Aravah, heading north; and went down to the 'Aravah. ¹⁹ Then the border passed alongside Beit-Hoglah, heading north; and the border ended at the north bay of the Dead Sea, at the south end of the Yarden; this was the south border.

²⁰ The Yarden was to be its border on the east side.

This was the inheritance of the descendants of Binyamin, defined by its surrounding borders, according to their families.

²¹ The cities of the tribe of the descendants of Binyamin according to their families were: Yericho, Beit-Hoglah, 'Emek-K'tzitz, ²² Beit-'Aravah, Tz'marayim, Beit-El, ²³ 'Avim, Parah, 'Ofrah, ²⁴ K'far-Ha'amonah, 'Ofni and Geva — twelve cities, together with their villages. ²⁵ Giv'on, Ramah, Be'erot, ²⁶ Mitzpeh, K'firah, Motzah, ²⁷ Rekem, Yirpe'el, Tar'alah, ²⁸ Tzela, Elef, Y'vusi (that is, Yerushalayim), Giv'at and Kiryat — fourteen cities, together with their villages.

This is the inheritance of the descendants of Binyamin according to their families.

19 ¹ The second lot came out for Shim'on, for the tribe of the descendants of Shim'on according to their families. Their inheritance was inside the inheritance of the descendants of Y'hudah. ² For their inheritance they had Be'er-Sheva, Sheva, Moladah, ³ Hatzar-Shu'al, Balah, 'Etzem, ⁴ El-Tolad, B'tul, Hormah, ⁵ Ziklag, Beit-Markavot, Hatzar-Susah, ⁶ Beit-L'va'ot and Sharuchen — thirteen cities, together with their villages; ⁷ 'Ayin, Rimmon, 'Eter and 'Ashan — four cities, together with their villages; ⁸ and all the villages surrounding these cities, as far as Ba'alat-Be'er, Ramah of the Negev. This is the inheritance of the tribe of the descendants of Shim'on according to their families. ⁹ The inheritance of the descendants of Shim'on was taken out of the allotment for the descendants of Y'hudah, because the portion given to the descendants of Y'hudah was too much for them, so the descendants of Shim'on had an inheritance inside the descendants of Y'hudah.

¹⁰ The third lot came up for the descendants of Z'vulun according to their families. The border of their inheritance began at Sarid. ¹¹ Then their border went up westward to Mar'alah, extended to Dabeshet and on to the *vadi* fronting Yokne'am. ¹² Also from Sarid it turned toward the sunrise to the east to the border of Kislot-Tavor, went on to Dovrat and up to Yafia. ¹³ From there it passed eastward to Gat-Hefer, on to 'Et-Katzin, went out at Rimmon and reached to Ne'ah. ¹⁴ Then the border turned on the north side to Hanaton, ending in the Yiftach'el Valley. ¹⁵ Also Katat, Nahalal, Shimron, Yid'alah and Beit-Lechem—twelve cities, together with their villages. ¹⁶ This is the inheritance of the descendants of Z'vulun according to their families, these cities with their villages.

¹⁷ The fourth lot came out for Yissakhar, for the descendants of Yissakhar according to their families. ¹⁸ Their territory included Yizre'el, K'sulot, Shunem, ¹⁹ Hafarayim, Shi'on, Anacharat, ²⁰ Rabit, Kishyon, Evetz, ²¹ Remet, 'Ein-Ganim, 'Ein-Hadah and Beit-Patzetz. ²² Their territory extended to Tavor, Shachatzimah and Beit-Shemesh; and their territory ended at the Yarden— sixteen cities, together with their villages. ²³ This is the inheritance of the tribe of the descendants of Yissakhar according to their families, the cities, with their villages.

²⁴ The fifth lot came out for the tribe of the descendants of Asher according to their families. ²⁵ Their territory included Helkat, Hali, Beten, Akhshaf, ²⁶ Alamelekh, 'Am'ad and Mish'al. It extended to the Karmel on the west and to Shichor-Livnat. ²⁷ The border turned eastward to Beit-Dagon, reached to Z'vulun and the Yiftach'el Valley on its north, then Beit-'Emek and Ne'i'el, went out to Kavul on the left, ²⁸ then 'Evron, Rechov, Hamon, Kanah and on to greater Tzidon. ²⁹ The border turned toward Ramah and the fortified city of Tzor; next the border turned to Hosah; and it ended at the sea from Hevel to Akhziv. ³⁰ Also included were 'Umah, Afek and Rechov — twenty cities, together with their villages. ³¹ This is the inheritance of the tribe of the descendants of Asher according to their families, these cities with their villages.

³² The sixth lot came out for the descendants of Naftali, for the descendants of Naftali according to their families. ³³ Their border went from Helef and the oak in Tza'ananim, included Adami-Nekev and Yavne'el, went on to Lakum and ended at the Yarden. ³⁴ Westward the border turned to Aznot-Tavor and went out from there to Hukok, reaching to Z'vulun on the south, Asher on the west and Y'hudah at the Yarden toward the east. ³⁵ The fortified cities were Tzidim, Tzer, Hamat, Rakat, Kinneret, ³⁶ Adamah, Ramah, Hatzor, ³⁷ Kedesh, Edre'i, 'Ein-Hatzor, ³⁸ Yir'on, Migdal-El, Horem, Beit-'Anat and Beit-Shemesh— nineteen cities, together with their villages. ³⁹ This is the inheritance of the tribe of the descendants of Naftali according to their families, the cities with their villages.

⁴⁰ The seventh lot came out for the tribe of the descendants of Dan according to their families. ⁴¹ The territory of their inheritance included Tzor'ah, Eshta'ol, 'Ir-Shemesh, ⁴² Sha'alabin, Ayalon, Yitlah, ⁴³ Eilon, Timnah, 'Ekron, ⁴⁴ Elt'keh, Gib'ton, Ba'alat, ⁴⁵ Y'hud, B'nei-Brak, Gat-Rimmon, ⁴⁶ Yarkon Springs and Rakon, with the border fronting Yafo. ⁴⁷ The territory of the descendants of Dan was too small for them, so the descendants of Dan went up and fought against Leshem, captured it, defeated it by the sword, took possession of it and lived there, calling Leshem "Dan"

after Dan their ancestor. ⁴⁸ This is the inheritance of the tribe of the descendants of Dan according to their families, these cities with their villages.

⁴⁹ When they had finished distributing the land for inheritance according to its borders, the people of Isra'el gave an inheritance within their territory to Y'hoshua the son of Nun. ⁵⁰ According to ADONAI's order they gave him the city he had asked for, Timnat-Serach in the hills of Efrayim; so he built up the city and lived in it.

⁵¹ These are the inheritances which El'azar the *cohen*, Y'hoshua the son of Nun and the leaders of the ancestral clans of the tribes of the people of Isra'el distributed for inheritance by lot in Shiloh before ADONAI at the door of the tent of meeting. Thus they finished dividing up the land.

20 ¹ ADONAI said to Y'hoshua, ² "Tell the people of Isra'el, 'Select the cities of refuge about which I spoke to you through Moshe; ³ so that anyone who kills someone by mistake and unknowingly may escape there; they will serve as refuges for you from the next-of-kin avenger. ⁴ He is to flee to one of those cities, stand at the entrance to the city gate and state his cause to the city leaders. Then they will bring him into the city with them and give him a place, so that he may live among them. ⁵ If the next-of-kin avenger pursues him, they are not to hand over the killer to him; because he struck his fellow community member unknowingly and had not hated him previously. ⁶ So he will live in that city until he stands trial before the community, until the death of the *cohen hagadol* who is in office at the time. When that time comes, the killer may return to his own city and his own house, to the city from which he fled.'"

⁷ So they set apart Kedesh in the Galil, in the hills of Naftali; Sh'khem in the hills of Efrayim; and Kiryat-Arba (that is, Hevron) in the hills of Y'hudah. ⁸ Beyond the Yarden east of Yericho they selected Betzer in the desert, on the plateau, out of the tribe of Re'uven; Ramot in Gil'ad out of the tribe of Gad, and Golan in Bashan out of the tribe of M'nasheh.

⁹ These were the cities selected for all the people of Isra'el and for the foreigner living among them, so that anyone who kills any person by mistake could flee there and not die at the hand of the next-of-kin avenger prior to standing trial before the community.

21 ¹ Then the leaders of the ancestral clans of the *L'vi'im* approached El'azar the *cohen*, Y'hoshua the son of Nun and the leaders of the ancestral clans of the tribes of the people of Isra'el. ² It was at Shiloh in the land of Kena'an that they spoke to them; they said, "ADONAI ordered through Moshe that we be given cities to live in, with the surrounding open land for our livestock." ³ So out of their inheritance the people of Isra'el gave the *L'vi'im* the following cities with the surrounding open land:

⁴ The lot came out for the families of the K'hati. The descendants of Aharon the *cohen*, who were of the *L'vi'im*, received by lot thirteen cities from the tribes of Y'hudah, Shim'on and Binyamin. ⁵ The rest of the descendants of K'hat received by lot ten cities from the families of the tribes of Efrayim and Dan and the half-tribe of M'nasheh. ⁶ The descendants of Gershon received by lot thirteen cities from the families of the tribes of Yissakhar, Asher, Naftali and the half-tribe of M'nasheh in Bashan. ⁷ The descendants of M'rari according to their families received twelve

cities from the tribes of Re'uven, Gad and Z'vulun. ⁸ The people of Isra'el gave by lot to the *L'vi'im* these cities with the surrounding open land, as ADONAI had ordered through Moshe.

⁹ They gave from the tribe of the descendants of Y'hudah and from the tribe of the descendants of Shim'on these cities here mentioned by name; ¹⁰ they were for the descendants of Aharon, of the families of the K'hati, who were among the descendants of Levi; because theirs was the first lot. ¹¹ They gave them: Kiryat-Arba— this Arba was the father of 'Anak — (that is, Hevron), in the hills of Y'hudah, with the surrounding open land; ¹² but the fields and villages of the city they gave to Kalev the son of Y'funeh as his possession. ¹³ Thus to the descendants of Aharon the *cohen* they gave: Hevron with its surrounding open land, already a city of refuge for the killer; Livnah with its surrounding open land; ¹⁴ Yatir with its surrounding open land; Esht'moa with its surrounding open land; ¹⁵ Holon with its surrounding open land; D'vir with its surrounding open land; ¹⁶ 'Ayin with its surrounding open land, Yutah with its surrounding open land and Beit-Shemesh with its surrounding open land— nine cities out of these two tribes. ¹⁷ Out of the tribe of Binyamin: Giv'on with its surrounding open land, Geva with its surrounding open land, ¹⁸ 'Anatot with its surrounding open land and 'Almon with its surrounding open land— four cities. ¹⁹ All the cities of the descendants of Aharon, the *cohanim*, numbered thirteen cities with their surrounding open land.

²⁰ The families of the descendants of K'hat, who were *L'vi'im*, that is, the rest of the descendants of K'hat, received the cities of their lot. Out of the tribe of Efrayim ²¹ they gave them: Sh'khem with its surrounding open land, in the hills of Efrayim, the city of refuge for the killer; Gezer with its surrounding open land; ²² Kivtzayim with its surrounding open land and Beit-Horon with its surrounding open land— four cities. ²³ Out of the tribe of Dan: Elt'ke with its surrounding open land, Gib'ton with its surrounding open land, ²⁴ Ayalon with its surrounding open land and Gat-Rimmon with its surrounding open land — four cities. ²⁵ Out of the half-tribe of M'nasheh: Ta'nakh with its surrounding open land and Gat-Rimmon with its surrounding open land — two cities. ²⁶ All the cities of the families of the rest of the descendants of K'hat numbered ten with their surrounding open land.

²⁷ To the descendants of Gershon, of the families of the *L'vi'im*, out of the half-tribe of M'nasheh they gave: Golan in Bashan with its surrounding open land, the city of refuge for the killer; and B'esht'rah with its surrounding open land— two cities. ²⁸ Out of the tribe of Yissakhar: Kishyon with its surrounding open land, Dovrat with its surrounding open land, ²⁹ Yarmut with its surrounding open land and 'Ein-Ganim with its surrounding open land— four cities. ³⁰ Out of the tribe of Asher: Mishal with its surrounding open land, 'Avdon with its surrounding open land, ³¹ Helkat with its surrounding open land and Rechov with its surrounding open land — four cities. ³² Out of the tribe of Naftali: Kedesh in the Galil with its surrounding open land, the city of refuge for the killer; Hammot-Dor with its surrounding open land; and Kartan with its surrounding open land— three cities. ³³ All the cities of the Gershuni according to their families were thirteen cities with their surrounding open land.

³⁴ To the families of the descendants of M'rari, the rest of the *L'vi'im*, out of the tribe of Z'vulun: Yokne'am with its surrounding open land, Kartah with its surrounding open land, ³⁵ Dimnah with its surrounding open land and Nahalal with its surrounding open land— four cities. {⁽³⁶⁾ Out of the tribe of Re'uven: Betzer with its

surrounding open land, Yachtzah with its surrounding open land, ^(37) K'demot with its surrounding open land and Mefa'at with its surrounding open land— four cities.}*
^36(38) Out of the tribe of Gad: Ramot in Gil'ad with its surrounding open land, the city of refuge for the killer; Machanayim with its surrounding open land; ^37(39) Heshbon with its surrounding open land and Ya'zer with its surrounding open land— four cities in all.
^38(40) All these were the cities of the descendants of M'rari according to their families, the rest of the families of the L'vi'im; their lot totaled twelve cities.

^39(41) All the cities of the L'vi'im, forty-eight cities with their surrounding open land, are to be in among the lands possessed by the people of Isra'el— ^40(42) these cities, each with its surrounding open land; thus is it to be with all these cities.

^41(43) So ADONAI gave Isra'el all the land which he swore to give to their ancestors, and they took possession of it and lived in it. ^42(44) Then ADONAI gave them rest all around, according to everything he had sworn to their ancestors. Not a man from all their enemies stood against them; ADONAI handed all their enemies over to them. ^43(45) Not one good thing that ADONAI had spoken of to the household of Isra'el failed to happen; it all took place.

22 ^1 Then Y'hoshua called the Re'uveni, the Gadi and the half-tribe of M'nasheh, ^2 and said to them, "You have done everything Moshe the servant of ADONAI ordered you to do and heeded what I said in all the orders I gave you. ^3 All this time you have not abandoned your kinsmen but have obeyed your commission, as ADONAI your God ordered. ^4 Now ADONAI your God has given rest to your kinsmen, as he told them he would. So you too, return to your tents in the land which is your possession, which Moshe the servant of ADONAI gave you beyond the Yarden. ^5 Only take great care to obey the *mitzvah* and the *Torah* which Moshe the servant of ADONAI gave you — to love ADONAI your God, follow all his ways, observe his *mitzvot*, cling to him, and serve him with all your heart and being." ^6 Then Y'hoshua blessed them and sent them away, and they went to their tents. ^7 (To the one half-tribe of M'nasheh, Moshe had given an inheritance in Bashan; but to the other half, Y'hoshua gave one among their kinsmen on the west side of the Yarden.) When Y'hoshua sent them away to their tents he blessed them, ^8 saying, "Return with great riches to your tents — with very much livestock, with silver, gold, bronze, iron and with great quantities of clothing; share the spoil of your enemies with your kinsmen."

^9 So the descendants of Re'uven, the descendants of Gad and the half-tribe of M'nasheh returned; they left the people of Isra'el in Shiloh, in the land of Kena'an, to go to the land of Gil'ad, to the land they were to possess and which they already did possess — according to the order of ADONAI through Moshe. ^10 When the descendants of Re'uven, the descendants of Gad and the half-tribe arrived in the area of the land of Kena'an near the Yarden, they built an altar there by the Yarden, a large, impressive altar. ^11 The people of Isra'el heard of it and said, "Look! The descendants of Re'uven, the descendants of Gad and the half-tribe of M'nasheh have built an altar by the frontier of the land of Kena'an, in the area by the Yarden, on the side that belongs to the people of Isra'el."

---

*These verses do not appear in the Masoretic text; they are usually included with the Masoretic text, accompanied by a note stating that they are taken from the parallel description at 1 Chronicles 6:63–64.

¹² When the people of Isra'el heard of it, the entire community of Isra'el gathered together in Shiloh to wage war against them. ¹³ The people of Isra'el sent Pinchas the son of El'azar the *cohen* into the land of Gil'ad to the descendants of Re'uven, the descendants of Gad and the half-tribe of M'nasheh. ¹⁴ With him were ten leaders, one leader of an ancestral clan for each of the tribes of Isra'el; each one was a head of his ancestral clan among the thousands of Isra'el. ¹⁵ They came to the descendants of Re'uven, the descendants of Gad and the half-tribe of M'nasheh in the land of Gil'ad and spoke with them; they said, ¹⁶ "Here is what the whole community of ADONAI is saying: 'What is this treachery that you have committed against the God of Isra'el, turning away today from following ADONAI, in that you have built yourselves an altar, thus rebelling today against ADONAI? ¹⁷ Is the guilt we incurred at P'or not enough for us? We haven't cleansed ourselves from it to this day, even though a plague came on the community of ADONAI. ¹⁸ Is this why you have to turn away today from following ADONAI? If you rebel against ADONAI today, he will be angry tomorrow with the whole community of Isra'el. ¹⁹ If the land you have taken possession of is unclean, then cross back over into the land which belongs to ADONAI, where the tabernacle of ADONAI is located, and take a possession among us. But don't rebel against ADONAI, and don't rebel against us, by building yourselves an altar other than the altar of ADONAI our God. ²⁰ Didn't Achan the son of Zerach commit a sin in regard to things set aside for destruction, and God's anger fell on the whole community of Isra'el? He was not the only one who died for his crime.'"

²¹ Then the descendants of Re'uven, the descendants of Gad and the half-tribe of M'nasheh answered the leaders of the thousands of Isra'el: ²² "The Mighty One, God, is ADONAI! He knows, and Isra'el will know — if we acted in rebellion or treachery against ADONAI, don't vindicate us today! ²³ We haven't built an altar in order to turn away from following ADONAI or to offer on it burnt offerings, grain offerings or sacrifices as peace offerings. If we have, let ADONAI himself require us to atone for it. ²⁴ Rather, we did this out of anxiety, because we thought, 'Sometime in the future, your descendants might say to our descendants, "You don't have anything to do with ADONAI, the God of Isra'el, ²⁵ because ADONAI made the Yarden the border between us and you, so you descendants of Re'uven and Gad have no share in ADONAI.'" In this way your descendants could make our descendants stop fearing ADONAI. ²⁶ So we said, 'Let us now make preparations and build ourselves an altar, not for burnt offerings or sacrifices, ²⁷ but as a witness between us and you, and between our generations who will come after us, so that we may perform the service for ADONAI in his presence with our burnt offerings, sacrifices and peace offerings — so that your descendants will not say to our descendants at some future time, "You have no share in ADONAI.'" ²⁸ For this reason we said, 'When they accuse us or future generations in this way, we will say, "Look! Here is a replica of the altar of ADONAI which our ancestors made, not for burnt offerings or sacrifices, but as a witness between us and you.'" ²⁹ Far be it from us that we should rebel against ADONAI and turn away today from following ADONAI by building an altar for burnt offerings, grain offerings or sacrifices other than the altar of ADONAI our God which stands in front of his tabernacle!"

³⁰ When Pinchas the *cohen* and the leaders of the community, the heads of the thousands of Isra'el who were with him, heard what the descendants of Re'uven, the descendants of Gad and the descendants of M'nasheh said, it satisfied them. ³¹ Pinchas the son of El'azar the *cohen* said to the descendants of Re'uven, the descendants of

Gad and the descendants of M'nasheh, "Today we know that ADONAI is here with us, because you have not committed this treasonous act against ADONAI. Now you have saved the people of Isra'el from the anger of ADONAI." ³² So Pinchas the son of El'azar the *cohen* and the leaders returned from the descendants of Re'uven and Gad, from the land of Gil'ad to the land of Kena'an and the people of Isra'el, bringing word back to them. ³³ What they said satisfied the people of Isra'el. The people of Isra'el blessed God and said no more about going to wage war against the descendants of Re'uven and Gad and destroying the land where they lived. ³⁴ The descendants of Re'uven and Gad called the altar "'*Ed* [a witness]" between us that ADONAI is God.

23 ¹ A long time afterwards, when ADONAI had given Isra'el rest from all their surrounding enemies, and Y'hoshua was old, with age taking its toll, ² Y'hoshua summoned all Isra'el — their leaders, heads, judges and officials — and said to them, "I am old; age is taking its toll. ³ You have seen everything that ADONAI your God has done to all these nations because of you, for it is ADONAI your God who has fought on your behalf. ⁴ Here, I have allotted to you land for inheritance according to your tribes between the Yarden and the Great Sea to the west; it includes the land of the nations I have destroyed and the nations which remain. ⁵ ADONAI your God will thrust them out ahead of you and drive them out of your sight, so that you will possess their land, as ADONAI your God told you.

⁶ "Therefore be very firm about keeping and doing everything written in the book of the *Torah* of Moshe and not turning aside from it either to the right or to the left. ⁷ Then you won't become like those nations remaining among you. Don't even mention the name of their gods, let alone have people swear by them, serve them or worship them; ⁸ but cling to ADONAI your God, as you have done to this day. ⁹ This is why ADONAI has driven out great, strong nations ahead of you; and it explains why no one has prevailed against you to this day, ¹⁰ why one man of you has chased a thousand — it is because ADONAI your God has fought on your behalf, as he said to you.

¹¹ "Therefore take great care to love ADONAI your God. ¹² Otherwise, if you retreat and cling to the remnant of these other nations remaining among you, if you make marriages with them and have children with them and they with you, ¹³ know for certain that ADONAI your God will stop driving out these nations from your sight. Instead, they will become a snare and a trap for you, whipping your sides and pricking your eyes, until you perish from this good land which ADONAI your God has given you.

¹⁴ "Today I am going the way of all the earth. Therefore consider in all your heart and being that not one of all the good things ADONAI your God said concerning you has failed to happen; it has all come to pass; nothing of it has failed. ¹⁵ Nevertheless, just as all the good things ADONAI your God promised you have come upon you, likewise ADONAI will bring upon you all the bad things too, until he has destroyed you from this good land which ADONAI your God has given you. ¹⁶ When you violate the covenant of ADONAI your God, which he ordered you to obey, and go and serve other gods and worship them, then the anger of ADONAI will blaze up against you; and you will perish quickly from the good land which he has given you!"

24 ¹ Y'hoshua gathered all the tribes of Isra'el to Sh'khem; he summoned the leaders, heads, judges and officials of Isra'el; and they presented themselves before God. ² Y'hoshua said to all the people, "This is what ADONAI the God of Isra'el says:

²In antiquity your ancestors lived on the other side of the [Euphrates] River—Terach the father of Avraham and Nachor—and they served other gods. ³I took your ancestor Avraham from beyond the River, led him through all the land of Kena'an, increased his descendants and gave him Yitz'chak. ⁴I gave to Yitz'chak Ya'akov and 'Esav. To 'Esav I gave Mount Se'ir as his possession, but Ya'akov and his children went down into Egypt. ⁵I sent Moshe and Aharon, I inflicted plagues on Egypt in accordance with what I did among them, and afterwards I brought you out. ⁶Yes, I brought your fathers out of Egypt: you arrived at the sea, and the Egyptians were pursuing your ancestors with chariots and horsemen to the Sea of Suf. ⁷But when they cried out to ADONAI, he put darkness between you and the Egyptians, overwhelmed them with the sea and drowned them. Your eyes saw what I did in Egypt, and then you lived in the desert for a long time. ⁸I brought you into the land of the Emori living beyond the Yarden; they fought against you, but I handed them over to you. You took possession of their land, and I destroyed them ahead of you. ⁹Then Balak the son of Tzippor, king of Mo'av, rose up and fought against Isra'el. He sent and summoned Bil'am the son of B'or to put a curse on you. ¹⁰But I refused to listen to Bil'am, and he actually blessed you. In this way I rescued you from him. ¹¹Next you crossed the Yarden and came to Yericho. The men of Yericho fought against you—the Emori, P'rizi, Kena'ani, Hitti, Girgashi, Hivi and Y'vusi—and I handed them over to you. ¹²I sent the hornet ahead of you, driving them out from ahead of you, the two kings of the Emori—it wasn't by your sword or your bow. ¹³Then I gave you a land where you had not worked and cities you had not built, and you live there. You eat fruit from vineyards and olive groves which you did not plant.'

¹⁴"Therefore fear ADONAI, and serve him truly and sincerely. Put away the gods your ancestors served beyond the [Euphrates]River and in Egypt, and serve ADONAI! ¹⁵If it seems bad to you to serve ADONAI, then choose today whom you are going to serve! Will it be the gods your ancestors served beyond the River? or the gods of the Emori, in whose land you are living? As for me and my household, we will serve ADONAI!"

¹⁶The people answered, "Far be it from us that we would abandon ADONAI to serve other gods; ¹⁷because it is ADONAI our God who brought us and our fathers up out of the land of Egypt, from a life of slavery, and did those great signs before our eyes, and preserved us all along the way we traveled and among all the peoples we passed through; ¹⁸and it was ADONAI who drove out from ahead of us all the peoples, the Emori living in the land. Therefore we too will serve ADONAI, for he is our God."

¹⁹Y'hoshua said to the people, "You can't serve ADONAI; because he is a holy God, a jealous God, and he will not forgive your crimes and sins. ²⁰If you abandon ADONAI and serve foreign gods, he will turn, doing you harm and destroying you after he has done you good."

²¹But the people said to Y'hoshua, "No, but we will serve ADONAI."

²²Y'hoshua said to the people, "You are witnesses against yourselves that you have chosen ADONAI, to serve him."

They answered, "We are witnesses."

²³"Now," Y'hoshua urged, "put away the foreign gods you have among you, and turn your hearts to ADONAI, the God of Isra'el."

²⁴The people answered Y'hoshua, "We will serve ADONAI our God; we will pay attention to what he says."

[25] So Y'hoshua made a covenant with the people that day, laying down for them laws and rulings there in Sh'khem. [26] Y'hoshua wrote these words in the book of the *Torah* of God. Then he took a big stone and set it up there under the oak next to the sanctuary of ADONAI. [27] Y'hoshua said to all the people, "See, this stone will be a witness against us; because it has heard all the words of ADONAI which he said to us; therefore it will be a witness against you, in case you deny your God." [28] Then Y'hoshua sent the people away, every man to his inheritance.

[29] After this, Y'hoshua the son of Nun, the servant of ADONAI, died; he was 110 years old. [30] They buried him on his property in Timnat-Serach, which is in the hills of Efrayim, north of Mount Ga'ash.

[31] Isra'el served ADONAI throughout Y'hoshua's lifetime and throughout the lifetimes of the leaders who outlived Y'hoshua and had known all the deeds that ADONAI had done on behalf of Isra'el.

[32] The bones of Yosef, which the people of Isra'el had brought up from Egypt, they buried in Sh'khem, in the parcel of ground which Ya'akov had bought from the sons of Hamor the father of Sh'khem for a hundred pieces of silver; and they became a possession of the descendants of Yosef.

[33] Finally, El'azar the son of Aharon died; and they buried him on the hill belonging to Pinchas his son, which had been given to him in the hills of Efrayim.

Shof'tim
JUDGES

1 ¹ After the death of Y'hoshua, the people of Isra'el asked *Adonai*, "Who will go up for us first to fight against the Kena'ani?" ² *Adonai* said: "Y'hudah will go up; here, I have handed the land over to him." ³ Y'hudah said to his brother Shim'on, "Come up with me into my assigned territory, so that we can fight against the Kena'ani; and I likewise will go with you into your territory." So Shim'on went with him. ⁴ Y'hudah went up; and *Adonai* gave the Kena'ani and the P'rizi into their hands; of those in Bezek they killed ten thousand men. ⁵ They found Adoni-Bezek in Bezek; and they fought against him. They killed the Kena'ani and the P'rizi, ⁶ but Adoni-Bezek fled. They pursued him, caught him, and cut off his thumbs and big toes. ⁷ Adoni-Bezek said: "Seventy kings, with their thumbs and their big toes cut off, gathered food under my table; God has paid me back in accordance with what I did." They brought him to Yerushalayim, and he died there.

⁸ Then the people of Y'hudah fought against Yerushalayim, captured it, overpowered it with the sword, and set the city on fire. ⁹ Afterwards, the people of Y'hudah went down to fight against the Kena'ani who lived in the hill-country, in the Negev, and in the Sh'felah. ¹⁰ Y'hudah also attacked the Kena'ani living in Hevron (formerly called Kiryat-Arba), and they overpowered Sheshai, Achiman and Talmai.

¹¹ From there they attacked the inhabitants of D'vir (D'vir was formerly called Kiryat-Sefer). ¹² Kalev said: "To whoever overpowers Kiryat-Sefer and captures it I will give my daughter 'Akhsah as his wife." ¹³ 'Otni'el the son of K'naz, Kalev's younger brother, captured it; so he gave him 'Akhsah his daughter as his wife. ¹⁴ After becoming his wife, she persuaded him to ask her father to give them a field; when she got off her donkey, Kalev asked her, "What do you want?" ¹⁵ She said to him: "Give me a blessing: since you gave me land in the Negev, also give me sources of water." So Kalev gave her the Upper Springs and the Lower Springs.

¹⁶ Next, the descendants of the Keini, Moshe's father-in-law, went up out of the City of Date-Palms with the people of Y'hudah into the Y'hudah Desert south of 'Arad; and they came and settled with the people.

¹⁷ Y'hudah went with Shim'on his brother; they overpowered the Kena'ani who inhabited Tz'fat, and completely destroyed it. The name of the city was called Hormah. ¹⁸ Y'hudah also took 'Azah with its territory, Ashkelon with its territory and 'Ekron with its territory. ¹⁹ *Adonai* was with Y'hudah, and they took possession of the hill-country, because they could not drive out the inhabitants of the valley, since they had iron chariots.

²⁰ They gave Hevron to Kalev, as Moshe had said to do; and he drove out from there the three sons of 'Anak.

²¹ The people of Binyamin did not drive out the Y'vusi who inhabited Yerushalayim; rather, the Y'vusi continued living with the people of Binyamin in Yerushalayim, as they do to this day. ²² The house of Yosef likewise attacked Beit-El; and ADONAI was with them. ²³ The house of Yosef sent spies to Beit-El (the city was formerly called Luz). ²⁴ The spies saw a man coming out of the city and said to him: "Please show us the way to enter the city, and we will treat you kindly." ²⁵ So he showed them the way into the city, and they overpowered the city with the sword, but they let the man and all his family go free. ²⁶ He went into the land of the Hittim, built a city and called it Luz, which is its name to this day.

²⁷ M'nasheh did not drive out the inhabitants of Beit-Sh'an and its villages, Ta'anakh and its villages, Dor and its villages, Yivle'am and its villages or Megiddo and its villages; so that the Kena'ani managed to keep on living in that land. ²⁸ In time, when Isra'el had grown strong, they did put the Kena'ani to forced labor but failed to drive them out completely.

²⁹ Efrayim did not drive out the Kena'ani living in Gezer; so the Kena'ani continued living in Gezer along with them.

³⁰ Z'vulun did not drive out the inhabitants of Kitron or Nahalol; so the Kena'ani continued to live among them but became subject to forced labor.

³¹ Asher did not drive out the inhabitants of 'Akko, Tzidon, Achlav, Akhziv, Helbah, Afik or Rechov; ³² so the Asheri lived among the Kena'ani who were living in the land, because they didn't drive them out.

³³ Naftali did not drive out the inhabitants of Beit-Shemesh or Beit-'Anat but lived among the Kena'ani living in the land; however, the inhabitants of Beit-Shemesh and Beit-'Anat became forced labor for them.

³⁴ The Emori forced the people of Dan into the hills; for they would not let them come down to the valley. ³⁵ The Emori had resolved to live in the Heres Hills, in Ayalon and in Sha'alvim; but when the power of the house of Yosef grew greater, they became subject to forced labor. ³⁶ So the territory of the Emori was from the Scorpion Ascent and the Rock upward.

2 ¹ Now the angel of ADONAI came up from Gilgal to Bokhim and said, "I brought you up out of Egypt, led you to the land I swore to your fathers and said, 'I will never break my covenant with you; ² you, for your part, are not to make any covenant with the inhabitants of this land but must tear down their altars.' However, you have paid no attention to what I said. What is this you have done? ³ This is why I also said, 'I will not drive them out before you; but they will be on your flanks, and their gods will become a snare for you.'" ⁴ When the angel of ADONAI spoke these words to all the people of Isra'el, they began crying and wailing at the top of their voices. ⁵ So they called the name of that place Bokhim [crying] and sacrificed there to ADONAI.

⁶ When Y'hoshua had sent the people away, the people of Isra'el had gone each one to his assigned property in order to take possession of the land. ⁷ The people served ADONAI throughout Y'hoshua's life and throughout the lives of all the older men who outlived Y'hoshua and who had seen all the great work of ADONAI which he had done for Isra'el. ⁸ When Y'hoshua the son of Nun, the servant of ADONAI, died, he was 110 years old; ⁹ and they buried him near the boundary of his property in Timnat-Heres, in the hills of Efrayim, north of Mount Ga'ash.

¹⁰ When that entire generation had been gathered to their ancestors, another generation arose that knew neither ADONAI nor the work he had done for Isra'el. ¹¹ Then the people of Isra'el did what was evil from ADONAI's perspective and served the ba'alim. ¹² They abandoned ADONAI, the God of their fathers, who had brought them out of the land of Egypt, and followed other gods, selected from the gods of the peoples around them, and worshipped them; this made ADONAI angry. ¹³ They abandoned ADONAI and served Ba'al and the 'ashtarot. ¹⁴ The anger of ADONAI blazed against Isra'el; and he handed them over to pillagers, who plundered them, and to their enemies around them; so that they could no longer resist their enemies. ¹⁵ Whenever they launched an attack, the power of ADONAI was against them, so that things turned out badly — just as ADONAI had said would happen and had sworn to them. They were in dire distress.

¹⁶ But then ADONAI raised up judges, who rescued them from the power of those who were plundering them. ¹⁷ Yet they did not pay attention to their judges, but made whores of themselves to other gods and worshipped them; they quickly turned away from the path on which their ancestors had walked, the way of obeying ADONAI's mitzvot — they failed to do this. ¹⁸ When ADONAI raised up judges for them, ADONAI was with the judge and delivered them from the hands of their enemies throughout the lifetime of the judge; for ADONAI was moved to pity by their groaning under those oppressing and crushing them. ¹⁹ But after the judge died, they would relapse into worse behavior than that of their ancestors, following other gods to serve and worship them; they abandoned none of their practices or stubborn ways. ²⁰ So the anger of ADONAI blazed against Isra'el; he said, "Because this nation violates my covenant, which I ordered their fathers to obey; and they don't pay attention to what I say; ²¹ in the future, I will not expel ahead of them any of the nations that Y'hoshua left when he died. ²² This is how I will test Isra'el, to see whether or not they will keep the way of ADONAI, living according to it, as their ancestors did." ²³ So ADONAI allowed those nations to remain where they were, without quickly driving them out; he did not hand them over to Y'hoshua.

3 ¹ These are the nations which ADONAI allowed to remain, in order to put to the test all the people of Isra'el who had not known any of the wars with Kena'an. ² This was only so that the generations of Isra'el who had previously known nothing of war might learn about it. ³ These nations consisted of the five chiefs of the P'lishtim, all the Kena'ani, the Tzidoni, and the Hivi who lived in the hills of the L'vanon between Mount Ba'al-Hermon and the entrance to Hamat. ⁴ They stayed there to test whether Isra'el would pay attention to the mitzvot of ADONAI, which, through Moshe, he had ordered their ancestors to obey. ⁵ So the people of Isra'el lived among the Kena'ani, Hitti, Emori, P'rizi, Hivi and Y'vusi; ⁶ taking their daughters as their wives, giving their own daughters to their sons and serving their gods.

⁷ Thus the people of Isra'el did what was evil from ADONAI's perspective, forgot ADONAI their God, and served the ba'alim and asherim. ⁸ Therefore the anger of ADONAI blazed against Isra'el, and he gave them over into the hands of Kushan-Rish'atayim king of Aram-Naharayim; and the people of Isra'el served Kushan-Rish'atayim eight years. ⁹ But when the people of Isra'el cried out to ADONAI, ADONAI raised up a savior for the people of Isra'el; and he rescued them; this was 'Otni'el, the son of Kalev's younger brother K'naz. ¹⁰ The spirit of ADONAI came upon him, and he judged Isra'el.

Then he went out to war, and *ADONAI* gave Kushan-Rish'atayim king of Aram into his hands; his power prevailed against Kushan-Rish'atayim. [11] So the land had rest for forty years, until 'Otni'el the son of K'naz died.

[12] But the people of Isra'el again did what was evil from *ADONAI*'s perspective, so *ADONAI* strengthened 'Eglon the king of Mo'av against Isra'el, because they had done what was evil from *ADONAI*'s perspective. [13] In confederation with the people of 'Amon and 'Amalek, 'Eglon went out and defeated Isra'el, capturing the City of Date-Palms;[14] and the people of Isra'el served 'Eglon the king of Mo'av eighteen years.

[15] But when the people of Isra'el cried out to *ADONAI*, *ADONAI* raised up for them a savior, Ehud the son of Gera, from the tribe of Binyamin, a left-handed man. The people of Isra'el appointed him to take their tribute to 'Eglon the king of Mo'av. [16] Ehud made himself a double-edged sword eighteen inches long and strapped it to his right thigh under his clothes. [17] Then he presented the tribute to 'Eglon king of Mo'av. Now 'Eglon was a very fat man. [18] When he had finished presenting the tribute, he dismissed the people who had brought it. [19] But he himself, after reaching the quarries at Gilgal, went back and said, "King, I have a secret message for you." The king commanded silence, and all his attendants withdrew. [20] Ehud came to him; he was sitting alone by himself in his upstairs room, where it was cool. Ehud said: "I have a message from God for you." As the king arose from his seat, [21] Ehud reached out with his left hand, took the sword from his right thigh, and thrust it into the king's belly. [22] The hilt too went in after the blade, and the fat closed around the blade, for he did not draw the sword out of his belly, so that it came out behind. [23] Then Ehud went out onto the porch, shut the doors of the upstairs room behind him and locked them. [24] After Ehud had left, the king's servants came. Seeing that the doors of the upper room were locked, they said, "He must be relieving himself in the inner part of the cool room." [25] They waited until they became embarrassed, but he still didn't open the doors of the upstairs room. So they took the key and opened them; and there before them lay their master, dead on the ground.

[26] But while they were delaying, Ehud escaped — he passed beyond the quarries and arrived safely in Se'irah. [27] Upon arrival in the hills of Efrayim, he began sounding the call on the *shofar*; and the people of Isra'el went down with him from the hill-country; he himself took the lead. [28] He said to them: "Follow me, because *ADONAI* has given your enemy Mo'av into your hands. They went down after him, seized the fords of the Yarden opposite Mo'av and permitted no one to cross. [29] On that occasion they defeated Mo'av, some ten thousand men, all tough, experienced soldiers; not one of them escaped. [30] Thus was Mo'av subdued that day under the power of Isra'el. Then the land had rest for eighty years.

[31] After Ehud came Shamgar the son of 'Anat, who killed 600 P'lishtim with an oxgoad; and he too rescued Isra'el.

4 [1] But after Ehud had died, the people of Isra'el again did what was evil from *ADONAI*'s perspective. [2] So *ADONAI* handed them over to Yavin king of Kena'an. He ruled from Hatzor; and the commander of his army was Sisra, who lived in Haroshet-HaGoyim. [3] The people of Isra'el cried out to *ADONAI*, because he had 900 iron chariots, and for twenty years he cruelly oppressed the people of Isra'el.

⁴ Now D'vorah, a woman and a prophet, the wife of Lapidot, was judging Isra'el at that time. ⁵ She used to sit under D'vorah's Palm between Ramah and Beit-El, in the hills of Efrayim; and the people of Isra'el would come to her for judgment. ⁶ She sent for Barak the son of Avino'am, from Kedesh in Naftali, and said to him: "*Adonai* has given you this order: 'Go, march to Mount Tavor, and take with you 10,000 men from the people of Naftali and Z'vulun. ⁷ I will cause Sisra, the commander of Yavin's army, to encounter you at the Kishon River with his chariots and troops; and I will hand him over to you.'"

⁸ Barak answered her: "If you go with me, I'll go; but if you won't go with me, I won't go." ⁹ She replied, "Yes, I will gladly go with you; but the way you are doing it will bring you no glory; because *Adonai* will hand Sisra over to a woman." Then D'vorah set out and went with Barak to Kedesh. ¹⁰ Barak summoned Z'vulun and Naftali to come to Kedesh. Ten thousand men followed him, and D'vorah went up with him.

¹¹ Now Hever the Keini had cut himself off from the rest of Kayin, the descendants of Hovav Moshe's father-in-law; he had pitched his tent near the oak at Tza'ananim, which is close to Kedesh. ¹² Sisra was informed that Barak the son of Avino'am had gone up to Mount Tavor. ¹³ So Sisra rallied his chariots, all 900 iron chariots, and all the troops he had with him, from Haroshet-HaGoyim to the Kishon River.

¹⁴ D'vorah said to Barak: "Get going! This is the day when *Adonai* will hand Sisra over to you! *Adonai* has gone out ahead of you!" So Barak went down from Mount Tavor with 10,000 men following him; ¹⁵ and *Adonai* threw Sisra, all his chariots and his entire army into a panic before Barak's sword; so that Sisra got down from his chariot and fled on foot. ¹⁶ But Barak pursued the chariots and the army all the way to Haroshet-HaGoyim. Sisra's entire army was put to the sword; not one man was left.

¹⁷ However, Sisra ran on foot to the tent of Ya'el the wife of Hever the Keini, because there was peace between Yavin the king of Hatzor and the family of Hever the Keini. ¹⁸ Ya'el went out to meet Sisra and said to him, "Come in, my lord; stay here with me; and don't be afraid." So he went into her tent, and she covered him with a blanket. ¹⁹ He said to her, "Please give me a little water to drink — I'm thirsty." She opened a goatskin of milk, gave him some to drink, and covered him up again. ²⁰ He said to her, "Stand at the entrance to the tent; and if anyone asks you if somebody is here, say, 'No.'" ²¹ But when he was deeply asleep, Ya'el the wife of Hever took a tent peg and a hammer in her hand, crept in to him quietly and drove the tent peg into his temple, right through to the ground; so that he died without waking up. ²² So here is Barak pursuing Sisra, and Ya'el steps out to meet him and says, "Come, I will show you the man you are looking for." He goes into her tent; and there is Sisra, lying dead with the tent peg through his temple.

²³ Thus God on that day defeated Yavin the king of Kena'an in the presence of the people of Isra'el. ²⁴ The hand of the people of Isra'el came down more and more heavily against Yavin the king of Kena'an, until they had completely destroyed Yavin the king of Kena'an.

5 ¹ On that day D'vorah and Barak the son of Avino'am sang this song:

²   "When leaders in Isra'el dedicate themselves,
          and the people volunteer,
          you should all bless *Adonai*.

3   Hear, kings; listen, princes;
       I will sing to ADONAI!
       I will sing praise to ADONAI
       the God of Isra'el.

4   "ADONAI, when you went out from Se'ir,
       when you marched out from the field of Edom,
       the earth quaked, and the sky shook;
       yes, the clouds poured down torrents.
5   The mountains melted at the presence of ADONAI,
       at Sinai, before ADONAI the God of Isra'el.

6   "In the days of Shamgar the son of 'Anat,
       in the days of Ya'el, the main roads were deserted;
       travelers walked the byways.
7   The rulers ceased in Isra'el, they ceased,
       until you arose, D'vorah,
       arose a mother in Isra'el.

8   "They chose new gods when war was at the gates.
       Was there a shield or spear to be seen
       among Isra'el's forty thousand men?
9   My heart goes out to Isra'el's leaders
       and to those among the people who volunteer.
       All of you, bless ADONAI.

10   "You who ride white donkeys,
       sitting on soft saddle-blankets,
       and you walking on the road,
       talk about it!
11   Louder than the sound of archers at the watering-holes
       will they sound as they retell
       the righteous acts of ADONAI,
       the righteous acts of his rulers in Isra'el.

       "Then ADONAI's people marched down to the gates.

12   "Awake, awake, D'vorah!
       Awake, awake, break into song!
       Arise, Barak! Lead away your captives,
       son of Avino'am!

13   "Then a remnant of the nobles marched down;
       the people of ADONAI marched down to me like warriors.
14   From Efrayim came those rooted in 'Amalek.
       Behind you, Binyamin is with your peoples.
       From Makhir the commanders marched down,

¹⁵ and from Z'vulun those holding the musterer's staff.
The princes of Yissakhar were with D'vorah,
Yissakhar, along with Barak;
into the valley they rushed forth behind him.
Among the divisions of Re'uven
they made great resolutions in their hearts.

¹⁶ But why did you stay at the pens for the sheep,
and listen to the shepherd's flute playing for the flocks?
Concerning the divisions of Re'uven
there were great searchings of heart.

¹⁷ Gil'ad lives beyond the Yarden.
Dan — why does he stay by the ships?
Asher stayed by the shore of the sea,
remaining near its bays.

¹⁸ The people of Z'vulun risked their lives,
Naftali too, on the open heights.

¹⁹ "Kings came; they fought.
Yes, the kings of Kena'an fought
at Ta'anakh, by the waters of Megiddo;
but they took no spoil of silver.

²⁰ They fought from heaven, the stars in their courses;
yes, they fought against Sisra.

²¹ The Kishon River swept them away,
that ancient river, the Kishon River.
O my soul, march on with strength!

²² Then the horses' hoofs pounded the ground,
their mighty steeds galloping at full speed.

²³ "'Curse Meroz!' said the angel of ADONAI,
'Curse the people living there with a bitter punishment
for not coming to help ADONAI,
to help ADONAI against the mighty warriors.'

²⁴ "Ya'el will be blessed more than all women.
The wife of Hever the Keini
will be blessed more than any woman in the tent.

²⁵ He asked for water, and she gave him milk;
In an elegant bowl she brought him curds.

²⁶ Then she took a tent peg in her left hand
and a workman's hammer in her right;
with the hammer she struck Sisra, pierced his skull,
yes, she shattered and crushed his temple.

²⁷ He sank down at her feet, he fell and lay there;
he sank at her feet, he fell —
where he sank down, there he fell dead.

28   "Sisra's mother looks out the window;
            peering out through the lattice she wonders,
            'Why is his chariot so long in coming?
            Why are his horses so slow to return?'
29   The wisest of her ladies answer her,
            and she repeats it to herself,
30   'Of course! They're collecting and dividing the spoil —
            a girl, two girls for every warrior,
            for Sisra booty of dyed clothing,
            a plunder of colorfully embroidered garments,
            two embroidered scarves for every soldier's neck.'

31   "May all your enemies perish like this, ADONAI;
            but may those who love him be like the sun
            going forth in its glory!"

Then the land had rest for forty years.

6 ¹ But the people of Isra'el did what was evil from ADONAI's perspective, so ADONAI handed them over to Midyan for seven years. ² Midyan exercised its power harshly against Isra'el, and because of Midyan the people of Isra'el hid themselves in mountains, in caves and in other safe places. ³ One time, after Isra'el's sowing season, Midyan, with 'Amalek and others from the east, attacked them. ⁴ They set up camp by them and destroyed the produce of the country all the way to 'Azah; they left nothing for people to live on, no sheep, no oxen, no donkeys. ⁵ For they came up with their cattle and tents, and they came in as thick as locusts; both they and their camels were beyond numbering, and they came into the land to destroy it. ⁶ Isra'el became very discouraged because of Midyan, and the people of Isra'el cried out to ADONAI.

⁷ When the people of Isra'el cried out to ADONAI because of Midyan, ⁸ ADONAI sent a prophet to the people of Isra'el, who said to them: "ADONAI the God of Isra'el says, 'I brought you up from Egypt, out of a life of slavery. ⁹ I delivered you from the power of the Egyptians and from the power of all your oppressors. I drove them out ahead of you and gave you their land. ¹⁰ And I said to you: "I am ADONAI your God; you are not to be afraid of the gods of the Emori in whose land you are living." But you paid no attention to what I said!'"

¹¹ Then the angel of ADONAI came and sat under the pistachio tree in 'Ofrah that belonged to Yo'ash the Avi'ezri. His son Gid'on was threshing wheat in the winepress, in order to hide it from Midyan. ¹² The angel of ADONAI appeared to him and said to him: "You valiant hero! ADONAI is with you!" ¹³ "Excuse me, sir," answered Gid'on, "but if ADONAI is with us, then why is all this happening to us? And where are all his miracles our ancestors told us about when they said, 'Didn't ADONAI bring us up from Egypt?' For now ADONAI has abandoned us and handed us over to Midyan." ¹⁴ ADONAI turned to him and said, "Go in this strength of yours and save Isra'el from the hands of Midyan. Haven't I sent you?" ¹⁵ But Gid'on answered him, "Forgive me, my Lord, but with what am I to save Isra'el? Why, my family is the poorest in M'nasheh, and I'm the youngest person in my father's house!" ¹⁶ ADONAI said to him, "Because I will be with you, you will strike down Midyan as easily as if they were just one man."

¹⁷ Gid'on replied, "If indeed you favor me, would you mind giving me a sign that it is really you talking with me? ¹⁸ Please don't leave until I go and return with a gift and present it to you." He replied, "I'll wait till you come back."

¹⁹ Gid'on went in, cooked a young goat and made *matzot* from a bushel of flour. He put the meat in a basket and the broth in a pot, brought them out to him under the pistachio tree and presented them. ²⁰ The angel of God said to him, "Take the meat and *matzot*, lay them on this rock, and pour out the broth." Gid'on did so. ²¹ Then the angel of ADONAI reached out with the stick he was holding, touched the meat and *matzot*, and fire shot up out of the rock and burned up the meat and *matzot*. Then the angel of ADONAI disappeared before his eyes. ²² Gid'on realized that he was the angel of ADONAI and said, "Oh no! My Lord! ADONAI! Because I've seen the angel of ADONAI face-to-face!" ²³ But ADONAI reassured him, "Shalom to you, don't be afraid, you won't die!" ²⁴ Then Gid'on built an altar there to ADONAI and called it "ADONAI-Shalom"; to this day it remains in 'Ofrah of the Avi'ezri.

²⁵ That very night ADONAI said to him, "Take your father's bull and the other bull, the seven-year-old. Destroy the altar to Ba'al that belongs to your father, cut down the sacred pole next to it, ²⁶ and build a proper altar to ADONAI your God on top of this strong-point. Then take the second bull; and offer it as a burnt offering, using the wood of the sacred pole you cut down." ²⁷ Gid'on took ten of his servants and did what ADONAI had told him to do. He didn't do it by day, because he was afraid of the men in his father's household and those from the city, so he did it at night. ²⁸ When the men of the city got up the next morning, there was the altar of Ba'al destroyed, the sacred pole cut down, and the second bull a burnt offering on the newly built altar. ²⁹ They asked each other, "Who could have done this?" But after investigating, they concluded that Gid'on the son of Yo'ash had done it. ³⁰ "Bring out your son," the men of the city demanded of Yo'ash, "so that he may die, because he destroyed the altar of Ba'al and cut down the sacred pole next to it!" ³¹ But Yo'ash said to all those crowding around him, "You're defending Ba'al, are you? It's your job to save him? Anyone who defends Ba'al will be put to death before morning! If he's a god, let him defend himself! After all, somebody destroyed his altar!" ³² Therefore on that day Gid'on was given the name Yeruba'al [let Ba'al defend], because they said, "Let Ba'al defend himself against him, since he destroyed his altar."

³³ Now all Midyan, 'Amalek and the others from the east joined forces, crossed the Yarden, and set up camp in the Yizre'el Valley. ³⁴ But the Spirit of ADONAI covered Gid'on. He sounded the call on the *shofar*, and Avi'ezer rallied behind him. ³⁵ He sent messengers throughout all M'nasheh, and they too rallied behind him. He also sent messengers to Asher, Z'vulun and Naftali; and they came up to join them.

³⁶ Gid'on said to God, "If you are going to save Isra'el through me, as you said you would, ³⁷ then, here: I will lay a wool fleece on the threshing-floor; if there is dew on the fleece only, while all the ground stays dry, I will be convinced that you will save Isra'el through me, as you said you would." ³⁸ And it happened! He got up early in the morning, pressed the fleece together and wrung dew out of it, a bowlful of water. ³⁹ But Gid'on said to God, "Don't be angry with me because I am asking one more thing, let me make one more test, please: this time let it be dry only on the fleece, with dew all over the ground." ⁴⁰ And that is what God did that night — it was dry only on the fleece, even though there was dew all over the ground.

7 ¹ Then Yeruba'al, that is, Gid'on, and all the people with him, got up early and set up camp by 'Ein-Harod; the camp of Midyan was north of them, by Giv'at-Moreh, in the valley. ² *ADONAI* said to Gid'on, "There are too many people with you for me to hand Midyan over to them, because I don't want Isra'el to be able to boast against me, 'We saved ourselves by our own strength.' ³ Therefore, proclaim to the people 'Anyone who is anxious or afraid should go back home, while we stay here on Mount Gil'ad.'" Twenty-two thousand returned, but ten thousand remained.

⁴ *ADONAI* said to Gid'on, "There are still too many people. Have them come down to the water, and there I will screen them for you. If I say of anyone, 'This one is for you,' he will go with you; and if I say, 'This one is not for you,' he won't go with you." ⁵ So he brought the people down to the water, and *ADONAI* said to Gid'on, "Put to one side everyone who laps up water with his tongue the way a dog does, and put to the other side everyone who gets down on his knees to drink." ⁶ Three hundred lapped, putting their hand to their mouth; all the rest of the men got down on their knees to drink water. ⁷ *ADONAI* said to Gid'on, "I will use the three hundred men who lapped the water to save you; I will hand Midyan over to you. Let all these others go back home." ⁸ So they took the provisions and the *shofar*s of the people; then he sent all the men of Isra'el away, each to his tent. But the three hundred men he kept.

The camp of Midyan was in the valley below him. ⁹ That night *ADONAI* said to him, "Get up and attack the camp, because I have handed it over to you. ¹⁰ But if you are afraid to attack, go down with your servant Purah; ¹¹ and after you hear what they are saying, you will have the courage to attack the camp." So with his servant Purah he went down to the outposts of the camp. ¹² Now Midyan, 'Amalek and all the others from the east had settled in the valley as thick as locusts; their camels too were beyond counting, like the sand on the seashore. ¹³ Gid'on got there just as a man was telling a comrade about a dream he had had: "I just now dreamt that a loaf of barley bread fell into the camp of Midyan, came to the tent and struck it so hard that it overturned the tent and knocked it flat." ¹⁴ His comrade answered, "This can only be the sword of Gid'on son of Yo'ash, a man of Isra'el. God has given Midyan and all its army into his hands."

¹⁵ When Gid'on heard the dream and its interpretation, he fell on his knees in worship. Then he returned to the camp of Isra'el and said, "Get up! because *ADONAI* has handed Midyan's army over to you." ¹⁶ He divided the three hundred men into three companies. He put in the hands of all of them *shofar*s and empty pitchers with torches in them. ¹⁷ Then he said to them, "Watch me, and do what I do. When I get to the edge of the camp, whatever I do, you do the same. ¹⁸ When I and everyone with me blow the *shofar*, then you blow your *shofar*s all around the whole camp, and shout, "For *ADONAI* and for Gid'on!"

¹⁹ Gid'on and the hundred men with him arrived at the edge of the camp a little before midnight, just after they had changed the guard. They blew the *shofar*s and broke in pieces the pitchers that were in their hands. ²⁰ All three companies blew the *shofar*s, broke the pitchers and held the torches in their left hands, keeping their right hands free for the *shofar*s they were blowing; and they shouted, "The sword for *ADONAI* and for Gid'on!" ²¹ Then, as every man stood still in place around the camp, the whole camp was thrown into panic, with everyone screaming and trying to escape. ²² Gid'on's men blew their 300 *shofar*s, and *ADONAI* caused everyone in the camp to

attack his comrades; and the enemy fled beyond Beit-Sheetah near Tz'rerah, as far as the border of Avel-M'cholah, by Tabat. ²³ Then men of Isra'el were summoned from Naftali, Asher, and both regions of M'nasheh; and they pursued Midyan. ²⁴ Gid'on sent messengers through all the hills of Efrayim, with the message, "Come down and attack Midyan; and capture the rivers before they get there, as far as Beit-Barah, and also the Yarden." So all the men of Efrayim came together and seized the rivers as far as Beit-Barah and the Yarden. ²⁵ They also captured two chiefs of Midyan, 'Orev and Ze'ev. They put 'Orev to death at the Rock of 'Orev and Ze'ev at Ze'ev's Winepress; then, as they kept pursuing Midyan, they brought the heads of Orev and Ze'ev to Gid'on, who had crossed to the far side of the Yarden.

8 ¹ But the men of Efrayim complained to Gid'on, "Why didn't you call on us when you went to fight Midyan? Why did you treat us this way?" They were sharp in their criticism. ² He answered by saying to them, "How can what I have done be compared with what you have done? Aren't the grapes Efrayim leaves on the vines better than the ones Avi'ezer harvests? ³ God handed over to you Midyan's chiefs, 'Orev and Ze'ev. What could I do that matches what you did?" By saying that, he appeased their anger at him.

⁴ By now Gid'on and his three hundred men had come to the Yarden and crossed over. They were exhausted but were still pursuing the enemy. ⁵ In Sukkot he asked the people there, "Please give some loaves of bread to the men following me, because they are exhausted, and I am pursuing Zevach and Tzalmuna the kings of Midyan." ⁶ But the chiefs of Sukkot said, "You haven't captured Zevach and Tzalmuna yet, so why should we give bread to your army?" ⁷ Gid'on said: "If that's your answer, then after ADONAI has put Zevach and Tzalmuna in my hands, I will tear your flesh apart with desert thorns and thistles!"

⁸ From there he went up to P'nu'el and made the same request, and the people of P'nu'el gave the same answer as those of Sukkot. ⁹ So he answered the people of P'nu'el similarly, "When I return safe and sound, I will break down this tower!"

¹⁰ Now Zevach and Tzalmuna were in Karkor with their army, about 15,000 men, all that remained of the entire army of the people from the east; since 120,000 arms-bearing soldiers had fallen. ¹¹ Gid'on went up, using the route of the nomads east of Novach and Yogbehah, and struck down the army when they thought they were safe. ¹² Zevach and Tzalmuna fled, but Gid'on pursued them. Thus he captured the two kings of Midyan, Zevach and Tzalmuna, and routed their whole army in panic. ¹³ When Gid'on the son of Yo'ash returned from the battle by way of the Heres Pass, ¹⁴ he captured a young man from Sukkot and asked him about the chiefs and leaders of Sukkot; he wrote down for him the names of seventy-seven of them. ¹⁵ Then he came to the people of Sukkot and said: "You insulted me when you said, 'You haven't captured Zevach and Tzalmuna yet, so why should we give bread to your exhausted men?' Well, here are Zevach and Tzalmuna!" ¹⁶ And he took the leaders of the city and desert thorns and thistles, and used them to teach the people of Sukkot a lesson! ¹⁷ He also broke down the tower of P'nu'el and put the men of the city to death.

¹⁸ Then he said to Zevach and Tzalmuna, "Tell me about the men you killed at Tavor." They answered, "They looked like you, like a king's sons." ¹⁹ Gid'on replied, "They were my brothers, my mother's sons. As surely as ADONAI is alive, I swear that

if you had spared them, I would not kill you." ²⁰ Then he ordered his oldest son, Yeter, "Get up, and kill them!" But the boy didn't draw his sword; being still a boy, he was afraid. ²¹ Then Zevach and Tzalmuna said, "You, do it. You, kill us. Let a grown man do what takes a grown man's strength." So Gid'on got up and killed Zevach and Tzalmuna; then he took the ornamental crescents from around their camels' necks.

²² The men of Isra'el said to Gid'on: "Rule over us, you, your son and your grandson, because you saved us from the power of Midyan. ²³ Gid'on replied, "Neither I nor my son will rule over you; ADONAI will rule over you." ²⁴ Then he added, "But I have this request to make of you, that each of you would give me the earrings from the booty you have taken." For the enemy soldiers had worn gold earrings, like all the other tribes descended from Yishma'el. ²⁵ They replied, "We're glad to give them to you." They spread out a robe, and each man threw in the earrings from his booty. ²⁶ The gold earrings he requested weighed more than forty-two pounds; and this doesn't include the crescents, pendants and purple cloth worn by the kings of Midyan and the chains around their camels' necks. ²⁷ Out of these things Gid'on made a ritual vest, which he located in his city, 'Ofrah. But all Isra'el turned it into an idol there, and it thus became a snare to Gid'on and his family.

²⁸ This is how Midyan was defeated by Isra'el, so that they ceased to be a threat. The land had rest forty years during the lifetime of Gid'on; ²⁹ Yeruba'al the son of Yo'ash returned to his home and stayed there.

³⁰ Gid'on became the father of seventy sons, because he had many wives. ³¹ He also had a concubine in Sh'khem, and she too bore him a son, whom he called Avimelekh. ³² Gid'on the son of Yo'ash died at a ripe old age and was buried in the tomb of his father Yo'ash, in 'Ofrah of the Avi'ezri.

³³ But as soon as Gid'on was dead, the people of Isra'el again went astray after the ba'alim and made Ba'al-B'rit their god. ³⁴ They forgot ADONAI their God, who had saved them from the power of all their enemies on every side; ³⁵ and they showed no kindness toward the family of Yeruba'al, that is, Gid'on, to repay them for all the good he had done for Isra'el.

9 ¹ Avimelekh the son of Yeruba'al went to Sh'khem, to his mother's brothers, and spoke with them and with the whole clan of his maternal grandfather. He said, ² "Please ask all the men of Sh'khem, 'Which is better for you — that all seventy sons of Yeruba'al rule over you, or that one person rule over you? And remember that I am your blood relative.'" ³ His mother's brothers spoke to all the men of Sh'khem and said all this about him, so that they followed their feelings and supported Avimelekh, arguing, "After all, he's our brother." ⁴ They also gave him seventy pieces of silver from the temple of Ba'al-B'rit; and he used these to pay good-for-nothing thugs to follow him. ⁵ He went back to his father's house in 'Ofrah and killed his brothers the sons of Yeruba'al, all seventy of them, on a single rock, except for Yotam Yeruba'al's youngest son, who stayed alive because he hid himself.

⁶ All the men of Sh'khem and all Beit-Millo got together and went and made Avimelekh king at the oak by the cult-pillar in Sh'khem. ⁷ When they told this to Yotam, he went and stood on top of Mount G'rizim and shouted, "Listen to me, you leaders of Sh'khem; then God will listen to you! ⁸ Once the trees went out to choose a king to rule them. They said to the olive tree, 'Rule over us!' ⁹ But the olive tree replied, 'Am I supposed to leave my oil, which is used to honor both God and humanity,

just to go and hold sway over the trees?' ¹⁰ So the trees said to the fig tree, 'You, come and rule over us!' ¹¹ But the fig tree replied, 'Am I supposed to leave my sweetness and my good fruit just to go and hold sway over the trees?' ¹² So the trees said to the grapevine, 'You, come and rule over us!' ¹³ But the grapevine replied, 'Am I supposed to leave my wine, which gives cheer to God and humanity, just to go and hold sway over the trees?' ¹⁴ Finally, all the trees said to the thorn bush, 'You, come and rule over us!' ¹⁵ The thorn bush replied, 'If you really make me king over you, then come and take shelter in my shade. But if not, let fire come out of the thorn bush and burn down the cedars of the L'vanon!'

¹⁶ "Here's the point. Have you been honest and straightforward in making Avimelekh king? Have you been fair with Yeruba'al and his household and treated him as he deserves? ¹⁷ My father fought on your behalf, risking his life, and rescued you from the power of Midyan; ¹⁸ and now you are rebelling against my father's household. You've killed his seventy sons on a single stone and made Avimelekh, the son of his slave-girl, king over the men of Sh'khem, because he's your brother. ¹⁹ I say this: if you are dealing honestly and righteously with Yeruba'al and his household today, then may you enjoy Avimelekh and may he enjoy you! ²⁰ But if not, let fire come out from Avimelekh and burn up the men of Sh'khem and Beit-Millo; and let fire come out from the men of Sh'khem and Beit-Millo and burn up Avimelekh!" ²¹ Then Yotam fled, making his way to Be'er, and he lived there for fear of Avimelekh his brother.

²² Avimelekh was chief over Isra'el for three years. ²³ But God sent a spirit of discord between Avimelekh and the men of Sh'khem, so that the men of Sh'khem dealt treacherously with Avimelekh. ²⁴ This came about so that the crime against the seventy sons of Yeruba'al might be avenged and the responsibility for their bloody death be placed on Avimelekh their brother, who murdered them, and on the men of Sh'khem, who helped him kill his brothers. ²⁵ So the men of Sh'khem sent out men to ambush him on the mountaintops. They robbed everyone who went past them, and Avimelekh was told about it.

²⁶ Ga'al the son of a slave came with his brothers and went on to Sh'khem, and the men of Sh'khem put their trust in him. ²⁷ They went out into the field, gathered their grapes and pressed the juice out of them. Then they held a feast and went into the house of their god to eat and drink, and there they insulted Avimelekh. ²⁸ Ga'al the son of a slave said, "Who is Avimelekh? Think of the contrast with Sh'khem! Why should we serve Avimelekh? Isn't he the son of Yeruba'al? Isn't Z'vul his officer? Serve the men of Hamor the father of Sh'khem! Why should we serve Avimelekh? ²⁹ If I were in control of this people, I'd get rid of Avimelekh!" Then, addressing his words to Avimelekh, he said, "Come out and fight! I don't care if you make your army even larger!"

³⁰ When Z'vul the ruler of the city heard the words of Ga'al the son of a slave, he was enraged. ³¹ He sent messengers to Avimelekh in Tormah with this message: "Ga'al the son of a slave and his brothers have come to Sh'khem, and they're inciting the city against you. ³² You and the men with you should come up now at night and lie in wait in the field. ³³ In the morning, get up early, as soon as the sun rises; and attack the city. Then, when Ga'al and the men with him come out to fight you, do whatever you can to them."

³⁴ Avimelekh and all the men with him came up by night and lay in wait against Sh'khem in four groups. ³⁵ Ga'al the son of a slave went out and stationed himself at

the entrance to the city gate. Then Avimelekh and his men rose from their ambush. ³⁶ When Ga'al saw the men, he said to Z'vul, "Look, there are men coming down from the mountaintops." Z'vul answered, "You're seeing the shadows of the mountains as if they were men." ³⁷ Ga'al said again, "Look, there are men coming down from the main hill in the land, and one group is coming on the road from the Fortune-teller's Oak. ³⁸ Z'vul said to him, "Where's your mouth now? You said, 'Who is Avimelekh? Why should we serve him?' Aren't these the people you despise? Go on out and fight them!" ³⁹ So Ga'al went out, leading the men of Sh'khem, and fought Avimelekh. ⁴⁰ But Avimelekh gave chase, and Ga'al took to flight; many fell wounded, strewn all along the way to the city gate.

⁴¹ Then Avimelekh took up residence in Arumah, and Z'vul drove out Ga'al and his brothers, so that they could not live in Sh'khem. ⁴² But the very next day, the people went out into the field, and Avimelekh was told about it. ⁴³ He took his men, divided them into three groups, and lay in wait in the field. When he saw the people going out of the city, he came out of hiding and slaughtered them. ⁴⁴ Avimelekh and his group rushed forward and occupied the entrance to the city gate, while the other two groups attacked all those in the field and killed them. ⁴⁵ Avimelekh fought against the city all that day; captured it, killed its people, destroyed its buildings and sowed its land with salt.

⁴⁶ When all the men in the fortress at Sh'khem heard about this, they took refuge in the stronghold of the temple of El-B'rit. ⁴⁷ Avimelekh was told that all the men from the Sh'khem fortress had gathered together; ⁴⁸ so he led all his men up to Mount Tzalmon, where he took an axe in his hand, cut a branch off a tree, and laid it on his shoulder. Then he said to those with him, "Quick! Do just what you saw me do!" ⁴⁹ They all did likewise, each man cutting off his branch; and they followed Avimelekh. They put the branches up against the stronghold, set them on fire, and burned down the stronghold; so that all the people from the Sh'khem fortress died, about a thousand men and women.

⁵⁰ Then Avimelekh went to Tevetz, set up camp against Tevetz and captured it. ⁵¹ But there was a fortified tower inside the city; and all the men and women took refuge in it, everyone in the city. They shut themselves inside and went up onto the roof of the tower. ⁵² However, when Avimelekh approached the tower, attacked it, and then came up close to the tower's door in order to burn it down, ⁵³ a woman dropped an upper millstone on Avimelekh's head, cracking his skull. ⁵⁴ He quickly called out to the young man holding his armor, "Draw your sword, and finish me off, so that people won't say a woman killed me." So his attendant ran him through, and he died. ⁵⁵ When the men of Isra'el saw that Avimelekh was dead, they all went back home.

⁵⁶ This is how God paid back Avimelekh for the wrong he did to his father in murdering his seventy brothers. ⁵⁷ God also repaid the men of Sh'khem for all the wrong they had done; on them came the curse of Yotam the son of Yeruba'al.

10 ¹ After Avimelekh there arose to save Isra'el Tola the son of Pu'ah, the son of Dodo, from the tribe of Yissakhar. He lived in Shamir, in the hills of Efrayim. ² He judged Isra'el twenty-three years, and when he died he was buried in Shamir.

³ After him arose Ya'ir, from Gil'ad. He judged Isra'el twenty-two years. ⁴ He had thirty sons who rode on thirty young donkeys. They owned thirty cities which are called Havot-Ya'ir to this day; they are in the territory of Gil'ad. ⁵ When Ya'ir died, he was buried in Kamon.

⁶ Again the people of Isra'el did what was evil from ADONAI's perspective — they served the *ba'alim*, the *'ashtarot*, the gods of Aram, the gods of Tzidon, the gods of Mo'av, the gods of the people of 'Amon and the gods of the P'lishtim. They abandoned ADONAI and did not serve him; ⁷ so the anger of ADONAI blazed against Isra'el, and he handed them over to the P'lishtim and the people of 'Amon. ⁸ For eighteen years, starting that year, they oppressed and persecuted all the people of Isra'el who lived beyond the Yarden, in the territory of the Emorim, in Gil'ad. ⁹ The people of 'Amon also crossed the Yarden to fight Y'hudah, Binyamin and the house of Efrayim; so that Isra'el was greatly distressed.

¹⁰ Then the people of Isra'el cried to ADONAI, "We have sinned against you by forsaking our God and serving the *ba'alim*." ¹¹ ADONAI said to the people of Isra'el, "I saved you from the Egyptians, the Emorim, the people of 'Amon, and the P'lishtim, didn't I? ¹² Likewise, when the people of Tzidon, 'Amalek and Ma'on oppressed you, you cried out to me; and I rescued you from their power. ¹³ Yet you abandoned me and served other gods; therefore I will not rescue you any more. ¹⁴ Go and cry to the gods you chose; let them rescue you when you're in trouble!" ¹⁵ The people of Isra'el said to ADONAI, "We have sinned! Treat us in whatever way seems good to you, but save us today, please!" ¹⁶ They got rid of their foreign gods and served ADONAI, and he became troubled by Isra'el's misery.

¹⁷ Then the people of 'Amon gathered together and set up camp in Gil'ad, while the people of Isra'el assembled and camped at Mitzpah. ¹⁸ The people, the chiefs of Gil'ad, said to each other, "Whoever leads the battle against the army of 'Amon will be head over everyone living in Gil'ad."

11 ¹ Now Yiftach, a brave soldier from Gil'ad, was the son of a prostitute. His father, Gil'ad, ² had other sons by his wife; and when his wife's sons grew up, they drove Yiftach away and told him, "You will not inherit from our father, because you are another woman's son." ³ Then Yiftach fled from his brothers and lived in the territory of Tov, where he enlisted a gang of rowdies who would go out raiding with him.

⁴ After a while the people of 'Amon made war against Isra'el. ⁵ When the army of 'Amon attacked Isra'el, the leaders of Gil'ad went to fetch Yiftach from the territory of Tov ⁶ and said to him, "Come and be our chief, so that we can fight the army of 'Amon." ⁷ Yiftach answered the leaders of Gil'ad, "Didn't you hate me so much that you forced me out of my father's house? Why are you coming to me now, when you're in trouble?" ⁸ The leaders of Gil'ad replied, "Here is why we've come back to you now: if you lead us in war with the people of 'Amon, you will be head over everyone living in Gil'ad." ⁹ Yiftach answered them, "If you bring me back home to fight the army of 'Amon, and ADONAI defeats them for me, I will be your head." ¹⁰ The leaders of Gil'ad said to Yiftach, "ADONAI is witness that we promise to do what you have said." ¹¹ Then Yiftach went with the leaders of Gil'ad, and the people made him head and chief over them. Yiftach repeated all these conditions at Mitzpah in the presence of ADONAI.

¹² Yiftach sent messengers to the king of the people of 'Amon to say, "What's your problem with us? Why are you invading our territory?" ¹³ The king of 'Amon answered the messengers of Yiftach, "Because Isra'el took away my territory when they came up from Egypt. They took everything from the Arnon to the Yabok and the Yarden. Now, restore it peacefully." ¹⁴ Yiftach sent messengers again to the king

of the people of 'Amon [15] with this response, "Here is what Yiftach has to say: 'Isra'el captured neither the territory of Mo'av nor the territory of the people of 'Amon. [16] But when Isra'el came up from Egypt, walked through the desert to the Red Sea and arrived at Kadesh, [17] then Isra'el sent messengers to the king of Edom, to say, "Please let us pass through your land." But the king of Edom wouldn't let them. He sent a similar message to the king of Mo'av, but neither would he, so Isra'el stayed at Kadesh. [18] Then they walked through the desert, around the territory of Edom and the territory of Mo'av, past the east border of the territory of Mo'av, and pitched camp on the other side of the Arnon; but they did not cross the border into Mo'av, for the Arnon was the border of Mo'av. [19] Isra'el sent messengers to Sichon king of the Emori and king of Heshbon with this message, "Please let us pass through your land to our own place." [20] But Sichon did not trust that Isra'el would only pass through his land, so he gathered all his people together, pitched camp in Yahatz and fought against Isra'el. [21] Adonai the God of Isra'el handed Sichon and all his people over to Isra'el, and they killed them. Thus Isra'el possessed all the territory of the Emori who lived there. [22] They took possession of all the territory of the Emori from the Arnon to the Yabok and from the desert to the Yarden. [23] So now that Adonai the God of Isra'el has expelled the Emori before his people Isra'el, do you think that you will expel us? [24] You should just keep the territory your god K'mosh has given you; while we, for our part, will hold onto whatever Adonai our God has given us of the lands that belonged to others before us. [25] Really, are you better than Balak the son of Tzippor, king of Mo'av? Did he ever pick a quarrel with Isra'el or fight with us? [26] Isra'el lived in Heshbon and its villages, in 'Aro'er and its villages and in all the cities on the banks of the Arnon for three hundred years. Why didn't you take them back during that time? [27] No, I have done you no wrong. But you are doing me wrong to war against me. May Adonai the Judge be judge today between the people of Isra'el and the people of 'Amon.'" [28] But the king of the people of 'Amon paid no attention to the message Yiftach sent him.

[29] Then the spirit of Adonai came upon Yiftach; and he passed through Gil'ad and M'nasheh, on through Mitzpeh of Gil'ad, and from there over to the people of 'Amon. [30] Yiftach made a vow to Adonai: "If you will hand the people of 'Amon over to me, [31] then whatever comes out the doors of my house to meet me when I return in peace from the people of 'Amon will belong to Adonai; I will sacrifice it as a burnt offering." [32] So Yiftach crossed over to fight the people of 'Amon, and Adonai handed them over to him. [33] He killed them from 'Aro'er until you reach Minnit, twenty cities, all the way to Avel-K'ramim; it was a massacre. So the people of 'Amon were defeated before the people of Isra'el.

[34] As Yiftach was returning to his house in Mitzpah, his daughter came dancing out to meet him with tambourines. She was his only child; he had no other son or daughter. [35] When he saw her, he tore his clothes and said, "Oh, no, my daughter! You're breaking my heart! Why must you be the cause of such pain to me? I made a vow to Adonai, and I can't go back on my word." [36] She said to him, "Father, you made a vow to Adonai; so do whatever you said you would do to me; because Adonai did take vengeance on your enemies the people of 'Amon." [37] Then she said to her father, "Just do this one thing for me — let me be alone for two months. I'll go away into the mountains with my friends and mourn, because I will die without getting married." [38] "You may go," he answered, and

he sent her away for two months. She left, she and her friends, and mourned in the mountains that she would die unmarried. ³⁹ After two months she returned to her father, and he did with her what he had vowed; she had remained a virgin. So it became a law in Isra'el ⁴⁰ that the women of Isra'el would go every year for four days to lament the daughter of Yiftach from Gil'ad.

12 ¹ The men of Efrayim assembled, crossed into Tzafon and said to Yiftach, "Why didn't you call us to go with you when you went over to fight the people of 'Amon? We're ready to burn down your house with you in it!" ² Yiftach answered, "When my people and I were in a serious dispute with the people of 'Amon, I called you; and you didn't rescue me from their power. ³ When I saw that you weren't rescuing me, I put my life in my own hands and went over to attack the people of 'Amon; and ADONAI gave them over into my power. So why have you come up today to fight me?" ⁴ Then Yiftach gathered together all the men of Gil'ad and fought with Efrayim, and the men of Gil'ad defeated Efrayim; because they were saying, "You Gil'ad men who live in Efrayim and M'nasheh have deserted Efrayim!" ⁵ The men of Gil'ad cut off Efrayim from the crossings over the Yarden, and whenever anyone from Efrayim tried to escape and said, "Let me go across," the men of Gil'ad would ask him, "Are you from Efrayim?" and if he said, "No," ⁶ they would tell him to say "*Shibbolet.*" If he said, "*Sibbolet,*" because he could not make his mouth pronounce it right, they took hold of him and killed him on the spot at the Yarden crossing; at that time 42,000 men of Efrayim died.

⁷ Yiftach judged Isra'el for six years. Then Yiftach from Gil'ad died, and he was buried in one of the cities of Gil'ad.

⁸ After him Ibtzan of Beit-Lechem judged Isra'el. ⁹ He had thirty sons, and he had thirty daughters whom he sent abroad; he brought thirty women from abroad in to marry his sons. He judged Isra'el for seven years. ¹⁰ Then Ibtzan died and was buried at Beit-Lechem.

¹¹ After him Elon from Z'vulun judged Isra'el; he judged Isra'el for ten years. ¹² Then Elon from Z'vulun died and was buried at Ayalon, in the territory of Z'vulun.

¹³ After him Avdon the son of Hillel from Pir'aton judged Isra'el. ¹⁴ He had forty sons and thirty grandsons who rode on seventy young donkeys. He judged Isra'el for eight years. ¹⁵ Then Avdon the son of Hillel from Pir'aton died and was buried at Pir'aton in the territory of Efrayim, in the 'Amalek hills.

13 ¹ Again the people of Isra'el did what was evil from ADONAI's perspective, and ADONAI handed them over to the P'lishtim for forty years.

² There was a man from Tzor'ah from the family of Dan, whose name was Manoach; his wife was barren, childless. ³ The angel of ADONAI appeared to the woman and said to her, "Listen! You are barren, you haven't had a child, but you will conceive and bear a son. ⁴ Now, therefore, be careful not to drink any wine or other intoxicating liquor, and don't eat anything unclean. ⁵ For indeed you will conceive and bear a son. No razor is to touch his head, because the child will be a *nazir* for God from the womb. Moreover, he will begin to rescue Isra'el from the power of the P'lishtim."

⁶ The woman came and told her husband; she said, "A man of God came to me; his face was fearsome, like that of the angel of God. I didn't ask him where he came from, and he didn't tell me his name. ⁷ But he said to me, 'Listen! You will conceive

and bear a son, so now don't drink any wine or other intoxicating liquor, and don't eat anything unclean, because the child will be a *nazir* for God from the womb until the day he dies.'" ⁸ Then Manoach prayed to ADONAI, "Please, *Adonai*, let the man of God you sent come again to us and teach us what we should do for the child who will be born." ⁹ God paid attention to what Manoach said, and the angel of God came again to the woman as she sat in the field, but her husband Manoach wasn't with her. ¹⁰ The woman hurried and ran to tell her husband, "Here! That man, the one who came to me the other day, he's come again!" ¹¹ Manoach got up, followed his wife, went to the man and said to him, "Are you the man who spoke to the woman?" He answered, "I am." ¹² Manoach asked, "Now, when what you said comes true, what are the guidelines for raising the child? What should be done for him?" ¹³ The angel of ADONAI said to Manoach, "The woman should take care to do everything I said to her. ¹⁴ She shouldn't eat anything that comes from a grapevine, she shouldn't drink wine or other intoxicating liquor, and she shouldn't eat anything unclean. She should do everything I ordered her to do."

¹⁵ Manoach said to the angel of ADONAI, "Please stay with us a bit longer, so that we can cook a young goat for you." ¹⁶ The angel of ADONAI said to Manoach, "Even if I do stay, I won't eat your food; and if you prepare a burnt offering, you must offer it to ADONAI." For Manoach did not know that he was the angel of ADONAI. ¹⁷ Manoach said to the angel of ADONAI, "Tell us your name, so that when your words come true we can honor you." ¹⁸ The angel of ADONAI answered him, "Why are you asking about my name? It is wonderful." ¹⁹ Manoach took the kid and the grain offering and offered them on the rock to ADONAI. Then, with Manoach and his wife looking on, the angel did something wonderful — ²⁰ as the flame went up toward the sky from the altar, the angel of ADONAI went up in the flame from the altar. When Manoach and his wife saw it, they fell to the ground on their faces. ²¹ But the angel of ADONAI did not appear again to Manoach or his wife. Then Manoach realized it had been the angel of ADONAI. ²² Manoach said to his wife, "We will surely die, because we have seen God!" ²³ But his wife said to him, "If ADONAI had wanted to kill us, he wouldn't have accepted a burnt offering and a grain offering from us, and he wouldn't have shown us all this or told us such things at this time."

²⁴ The woman bore a son and called him Shimshon. The child grew, and ADONAI blessed him. ²⁵ The Spirit of ADONAI began to stir him when he was in the Camp of Dan, between Tzor'ah and Eshta'ol.

14 ¹ Shimshon went down to Timnah, and in Timnah he saw a woman who was one of the P'lishtim. ² He came up and told his father and mother, "I saw a woman in Timnah, one of the P'lishtim. Now get her for me to be my wife." ³ His father and mother replied, "Isn't there any woman from the daughters of your kinsmen or among all my people? Must you go to the uncircumcised P'lishtim to find a wife?" Shimshon said to his father, "Get her for me. I like her." ⁴ His father and mother didn't know that all this came from ADONAI, who was seeking grounds for a quarrel with the P'lishtim. (At that time the P'lishtim were ruling Isra'el.)

⁵ Shimshon went down with his father and mother to Timnah. When they came to the vineyards of Timnah, a young lion roared at him. ⁶ The Spirit of ADONAI came powerfully upon Shimshon, and barehanded he tore the lion to pieces as easily as if

it had been a young goat. But he didn't tell his father or mother what he had done. ⁷ Then he went down and talked with the woman and found he still liked her.

⁸ Awhile later, as he was returning to claim his bride, he turned aside to look at the carcass of the lion and saw that there was now a swarm of bees in the body of the lion, and honey. ⁹ He scraped the honey out into his hands and went on, eating as he went; and when he came to his father and mother, he gave them some; and they ate too. But he didn't tell them that he had scraped the honey out of the body of the lion.

¹⁰ His father went down to the woman, and there Shimshon gave a banquet — this is what the young men used to do. ¹¹ When the P'lishtim saw him, they provided thirty companions to be with him. ¹² Shimshon said to them, "Let me present you with a riddle. If you can solve it within the seven days of the banquet and tell me the solution, I will give you thirty linen shirts and thirty changes of good clothes. ¹³ But if you can't solve it, you give me thirty linen shirts and thirty changes of good clothes." They answered, "Tell us the riddle, we want to hear it." ¹⁴ So he said to them,

> "Out of the eater came food;
> out of the strong came sweetness."

Three days passed, and they couldn't solve the riddle. ¹⁵ On the seventh day, they said to Shimshon's wife, "Coax your husband into telling us the solution to the riddle. Otherwise we'll burn down your father's house and you with it. You two called us here to turn us into paupers, didn't you?" ¹⁶ Shimshon's wife went to him in tears and said, "You don't love me, you hate me! You told a riddle to my fellow countrymen, and you haven't told me the answer." He said to her, "Look, I haven't even told it to my father and mother! Should I tell you?" ¹⁷ But she had been crying throughout the seven days of the banquet; so on the seventh day, because she had kept pressing him, he told her the solution; and she passed it on to her people. ¹⁸ Then, before sundown on the seventh day, the men of the city said to him,

> "What is sweeter than honey?
> and what is stronger than a lion?"

Shimshon answered,

> "If you hadn't plowed with my young cow,
> you wouldn't have solved my riddle now."

¹⁹ Then the Spirit of ADONAI came over him powerfully. He went down to Ashkelon, killed thirty of their men, took their good clothes, and gave them to the men who had "solved" the riddle. He was boiling with rage, so he went straight up to his father's house, ²⁰ and his wife was given to the companion who had been best man at the wedding.

15 ¹ But after a while, during the wheat-harvest season, Shimshon went to see his wife. He brought a young goat for her and said to her father, "I want to go to my wife in her room." But he wouldn't let him. ² Her father said, "I really thought you hated her altogether, so I gave her to your best man. But her younger sister — isn't she even prettier? Why not take her instead?" ³ Shimshon said to them, "This time I'm through with the P'lishtim! I'm going to do something terrible to them!" ⁴ So Shimshon went and caught three hundred foxes. Then he took torches, tied pairs of foxes to each other by their tails, and put a torch in the knot of every pair of tails. ⁵ Then he set the torches on fire and let the foxes loose in wheat fields of the P'lishtim. In this way he burned up the harvested wheat along with the grain waiting to be harvested, and the olive orchards as well. ⁶ The P'lishtim asked, "Who did this?" They answered, "Shimshon the son-in-law of the man from Timnah, because he took Shimshon's wife and gave her to his best man." Then the P'lishtim came up and burned both her and her father to death. ⁷ Shimshon said to them, "I will certainly have my revenge on you for doing such a thing; but after I do, I'll stop." ⁸ Infuriated, he began killing them right and left; it was a massacre. Then he went down and stayed in the cave at the 'Eitam Rock.

⁹ The P'lishtim went up, pitched camp in Y'hudah and attacked Lechi. ¹⁰ The men of Y'hudah said, "Why are you attacking us?" They replied, "To arrest Shimshon, that's why — to treat him the way he treated us." ¹¹ Then 3,000 men from Y'hudah went down to the cave at the Eitam Rock and said to Shimshon, "Don't you know that the P'lishtim are our rulers? What are you doing to us?" He answered, "I've only treated them the way they treated me." ¹² They said to him, "We've come down to arrest you and hand you over to the P'lishtim." Shimshon replied, "Swear to me that you won't fall on me yourselves." ¹³ They said to him, "No, but we will tie you up and hand you over to them. However, we promise not to kill you." So they tied him up with two new ropes and brought him up from the rock. ¹⁴ When he got to Lechi, the P'lishtim came running and shouting at him; and the Spirit of ADONAI came on him powerfully. The ropes on his arms became as weak as burnt flax and fell from his arms. ¹⁵ He found a fresh donkey jawbone, took it in his hand, and with it he struck down a thousand men. ¹⁶ Shimshon said,

"With the jawbone of a donkey I left heaps piled on heaps!
With the jawbone of a donkey I killed a thousand men!"

¹⁷ After he finished speaking he threw the jawbone away, and the place came to be called Ramat-Lechi [jawbone heights].

¹⁸ Then he felt very thirsty, so he called on ADONAI, saying, "You accomplished this great rescue through your servant. But am I now to die from thirst and fall into the hands of the uncircumcised?" ¹⁹ Then God made a gash in the crater at Lechi, and water came out. When he had drunk, his spirit came back; and he revived. This is why the place was called 'Ein-HaKorei [the spring of him who called], and it is there in Lechi until now. ²⁰ He judged Isra'el in the period of the P'lishtim for twenty years.

16 ¹ Shimshon went to 'Azah, where he saw a prostitute and went in to spend the night with her. ² The people in 'Azah were told that Shimshon had come, so they surrounded the place where he was and also set an ambush for him all night at the city gate. Their plan was to do nothing at night, but to wait until morning and then kill him. ³ However, Shimshon stayed in bed until midnight; then he got up, took hold of the doors of the city gate and the two posts as well, pulled them up, bar and all, hoisted them on his shoulders, and carried them up to the top of the hill overlooking Hevron.

⁴ After this, he fell in love with a woman who lived in the Sorek Valley, whose name was D'lilah. ⁵ The chiefs of the P'lishtim went up to her and said, "Coax him into telling you where his great strength comes from and how we can overcome him, so that we can tie him up and subdue him. If you do, each of us will give you 1,100 pieces of silver." ⁶ D'lilah said to Shimshon, "Please tell me what it is that makes you so strong, and how someone could tie you up and subdue you." ⁷ Shimshon replied, "If they tie me up with seven fresh bowstrings that have never been dried, I will become as weak as any other man." ⁸ The chiefs of the P'lishtim brought up to her seven fresh bowstrings which had not been dried, and she tied him up with them. ⁹ Now she had people lying in wait in the inside room. So she said to him, "Shimshon! The P'lishtim have come for you!" But he snapped the bowstrings as easily as a piece of straw breaks when it touches fire, and the source of his strength remained unknown.

¹⁰ D'lilah said to Shimshon, "You're making fun of me, telling me lies. Now, come on, tell me what it takes to tie you up." ¹¹ "All it takes," he answered, "is to tie me up with new ropes that haven't been used. Then I'll become weak and be like anyone else." ¹² So D'lilah took new ropes, tied him up, and said to him, "Shimshon! The P'lishtim have come for you!" (The people lying in wait were in the inside room.) But he broke the ropes from off his arms like a thread.

¹³ D'lilah said to Shimshon, "Till now you've been making fun of me and telling me lies. Tell me what it takes to tie you up." He said, "If you weave the seven locks of my hair across thread on a loom." ¹⁴ So she fastened her cloth work in the loom with a pin and wove his hair in, then said to him, "Shimshon! The P'lishtim have come for you!" He awoke from his sleep and pulled away the loom pin and the interwoven cloth. ¹⁵ She said to him, "How can you say you love me when your heart isn't with me? Three times you've made fun of me, and you haven't told me the source of your great strength."

¹⁶ Every day she kept nagging at him and pressing at him, till it bothered him to death, ¹⁷ so that he finally told her everything. He said to her, "No razor has ever touched my head, because I have been a *nazir* of God since I was born. If someone shaves me, then my strength will leave me; and I will be like any other man." ¹⁸ When D'lilah saw that he had really confided in her, she sent and summoned the chiefs of the P'lishtim with the message, "Come up this one last time, because he has finally told me the truth." The chiefs of the P'lishtim went up to her and brought the money with them. ¹⁹ She had him go to sleep in her lap and called for a man to shave off his seven locks of hair. Then she began tormenting him, but his strength had gone away. ²⁰ She said, "Shimshon! The P'lishtim have come for you!" He awoke from his sleep and said, "I'll get out this time, just as I shook myself loose before." But he didn't know that *Adonai* had left him. ²¹ So the P'lishtim seized him, gouged out his eyes and took him down to 'Azah. There they bound him with two bronze chains and put him to work grinding grain at the mill in the prison. ²² However, after the hair on his head had been cut off, it began growing back again.

²³ The chiefs of the P'lishtim assembled to offer a great sacrifice to their god Dagon. As they celebrated they sang,

> "Our god has handed over to us
> our enemy Shimshon."

²⁴ Upon seeing him, the people praised their god:

"Our god has handed over to us
our enemy, who destroyed our land
and killed so many of us."

²⁵ When they were in high spirits they said, "Summon Shimshon to amuse us." So they called Shimshon out of the prison, and he amused them. When they put him between the columns, ²⁶ Shimshon said to the boy holding him by the hand, "Let me feel the columns supporting the building, so that I can lean on them." ²⁷ The building was full of men and women; and all the chiefs of the P'lishtim were there; in addition to them, there were about three thousand men and women on the roof, watching, as Shimshon performed. ²⁸ Shimshon called to ADONAI, "Adonai ELOHIM, just this once, please, think of me, and please, give me strength, so that I can take revenge on the P'lishtim for at least one of my two eyes." ²⁹ Shimshon got a good hold on the two middle columns supporting the building and leaned on them, on one with his right hand and on the other with his left. ³⁰ Then, crying, "Let me die with the P'lishtim!" he pushed with all his might; and the building collapsed on the chiefs and on all the people inside. So he killed more at his death than he had killed during his life.

³¹ His brothers and all his father's family came down, took him, brought him up and buried him between Tzor'ah and Eshta'ol, in the tomb of his father Manoach. He had judged Isra'el twenty years.

17 ¹ There was a man from the hills of Efrayim named Mikhay'hu. ² He said to his mother, "You know the 1,100 pieces of silver that were taken from you — you pronounced a curse about it, and you told me about it? Well, the money is with me. I took it." His mother said, "May ADONAI bless my son," ³ as he restored the 1,100 pieces of silver to his mother. Then his mother said, "I solemnly dedicate this money of mine to ADONAI, in order for my son to make a carved image overlaid with silver. So now I'm giving it back to you." ⁴ But he returned the money to his mother, and she took 200 pieces of silver and gave them to the metalworker, who made a carved image overlaid with silver which was put in Mikhay'hu's house. ⁵ This man Mikhah owned a house of God; so he made a ritual vest and household gods and consecrated one of his sons, who became his *cohen*. ⁶ At that time there was no king in Isra'el; a man simply did whatever he thought was right.

⁷ There was a young man from Beit-Lechem in Y'hudah, from the family of Y'hudah, who was a *Levi*. He had been staying ⁸ in Beit-Lechem, but he left there to find another place to live and came to the hills of Efrayim, where eventually he made his way to the house of Mikhah. ⁹ Mikhah asked him, "Where are you coming from?" He answered, "I am a *Levi* from Beit-Lechem in Y'hudah, and I'm looking for a place to live." ¹⁰ Mikhah replied, "Stay with me, and be a father and *cohen* for me; I will give you ten pieces of silver a year, in addition to your clothing and food." So the *Levi* went in ¹¹ and agreed to stay with the man; the young man became like one of his sons. ¹² After Mikhah consecrated the *Levi*, the young man became his *cohen* and stayed there in Mikhah's house. ¹³ Mikhah said, "Now I know that ADONAI will treat me well, because I have a *Levi* for a *cohen*.

18 ¹ At that time there was no king in Isra'el, and it was also at that time that the tribe of Dan was looking for a place to claim ownership of and settle in, since they had not yet been given any land of their own among the tribes of Isra'el. ² The people of Dan sent five leading men from Tzor'ah and Eshta'ol, representing their whole tribe, to spy out and explore the land. They instructed them, "Go, and explore the land." They came to the hills of Efrayim, to the house of Mikhah, and stayed there. ³ While they were at Mikhah's house they recognized the accent of the young man, the *Levi*, so they approached him and said, "Who brought you here? What are you doing in this place? What is there for you here?" ⁴ He answered, "Here's the arrangement Mikhah has made with me: he pays me a wage, and I serve as his *cohen*." ⁵ They said to him, "Please ask God whether our journey will be successful." ⁶ The *cohen* replied, "Don't worry. ADONAI is with you on this journey."

⁷ The five men left, came to Layish and saw the people there living securely according to the customs of the Tzidonim, quietly and securely; since no one in the land was exercising authority that might shame them in any respect; moreover, they were far away from the Tzidonim and had no dealings with other peoples. ⁸ When they returned to their kinsmen in Tzor'ah and Eshta'ol, they asked them what they had to report. ⁹ They said, "Let's go up and attack them. We've seen the land, and it's excellent. Don't delay; start moving! Go in, and take the land! ¹⁰ When you go, you will come to a people who feel safe. There's plenty of land, the place lacks nothing, it has everything there is on earth, and God has given it to you."

¹¹ So from the tribe of Dan 600 men equipped for war set out from there, from Tzor'ah and Eshta'ol. ¹² They went up and camped at Kiryat-Ye'arim, in Y'hudah, which is why that place is called Machaneh-Dan [the camp of Dan] to this day (actually, it's behind Kiryat-Ye'arim). ¹³ From there they passed on into the hills of Efrayim and came to Mikhah's house. ¹⁴ The men who had gone to spy out the land of Layish then said to their kinsmen, "Are you aware that in these buildings there is a ritual vest, household gods and a carved image overlaid with silver? Decide what you ought to do." ¹⁵ They turned off the road and went to the house of the young *Levi*, that is, to Mikhah's house, and asked how he was doing. ¹⁶ The 600 soldiers from Dan stayed at the gate, ¹⁷ while the five who had spied out the land went in and took the idol overlaid with silver, the vest and the household gods. The *cohen* had stayed with the 600 soldiers by the gate. ¹⁸ But when they went into Mikhah's house and took the silver-covered image, the vest and the household gods, the *cohen* asked them, "What are you doing?" ¹⁹ They replied, "Be quiet, keep your mouth shut, and come with us. Be a father and a *cohen* for us. Which is better? To be a *cohen* in the house of one man or to be *cohen* to a whole tribe and family in Isra'el?" ²⁰ This made the *cohen* feel very good; so he took the ritual vest, the household gods and the image and went off with the people. ²¹ So they turned and left, with their children, cattle and belongings going ahead of them.

²² When they were a good distance from Mikhah's house, the men who lived in the houses near his got together [with him], overtook the people from Dan ²³ and began shouting at them. The people from Dan turned and said to Mikhah, "What's wrong with you, that you've gathered such a crowd?" ²⁴ He answered, "You've taken away my god, which I made, and gone off with the *cohen*! What more have I got? How can you ask me, 'What's wrong with you?'" ²⁵ The men from Dan replied, "You had best say no more to us, because some of us might get angry and attack you. You

could lose your life, and so might the others in your household." ²⁶ Then the people from Dan went their way; and when Mikhah saw that they were too strong for him, he turned and went back to his house. ²⁷ So they took what Mikhah had made and his *cohen*. They came to Layish, to a quiet and trusting people. They attacked, killed them and burned down the city. ²⁸ No one came to rescue them, because it was far from Tzidon, and they had no dealings with other peoples. This was in the valley near Beit-Rechov.

Then the people of Dan rebuilt the city and settled there. ²⁹ They named the city Dan, after Dan their ancestor, who was born to Isra'el; although the city had previously been called Layish. ³⁰ The people of Dan set up the image for themselves. Y'honatan the son of Gershom, the son of M'nasheh, and his sons were *cohanim* for the tribe of the people of Dan until the day of the exile from the land. ³¹ Thus they erected for themselves Mikhah's idol which he had made, and it remained there as long as the house of God was in Shiloh.

19 ¹ In those days, when there was no king in Isra'el, there was a certain *Levi* living on the far side of the Efrayim hills who took a woman from Beit-Lechem in Y'hudah to be his concubine. ² But his concubine was unfaithful to him and left him to go to her father's house at Beit-Lechem in Y'hudah, where she stayed for some time, four months. ³ Then her husband went after her to persuade her to return; he had his servant with him and a pair of donkeys. She brought him into her father's house; and when the girl's father saw him, he was glad to meet him. ⁴ His father-in-law, the girl's father, kept him there; so he remained with him three days; they ate, drank and stayed there. ⁵ On the fourth day they got up early in the morning, and he prepared to leave. But the girl's father said to his son-in-law, "You'll feel better if you have a bite of food before you leave." ⁶ So the two of them sat down and ate and drank together. Then the girl's father said to the man, "Please stay one more night, and have a good time." ⁷ The man rose to leave, but his father-in-law pressed him, so he stayed there again. ⁸ The morning of the fifth day, he got up early to leave; but the girl's father said, "Why don't you have something to eat, and leave this afternoon?" So the two men ate. ⁹ When the man got up to leave with his concubine and servant, his father-in-law, the girl's father, said to him, "Look, it's almost evening. Please stay the night — you see that it's getting late. Stay on, enjoy yourself, and tomorrow get going early on your way home." ¹⁰ But the man wouldn't stay that night; so he got up and left with his concubine and his two saddled donkeys; and they arrived at Y'vus, also known as Yerushalayim.

¹¹ By the time they arrived at Y'vus it was nearly evening; and the servant said to his master, "Why don't we go on into this city of the Y'vusi and stay there?" ¹² But his master said to him, "We won't go into a city of foreigners which doesn't belong to the people of Isra'el. We'll go on across to Giv'ah." ¹³ He said to his servant, "Let's go, and we'll get to one of those places; we'll stay in Giv'ah or Ramah." ¹⁴ So they went on and kept traveling, until the sun set on them near Giv'ah, which belongs to Binyamin. ¹⁵ There they turned off the road to go and stay in Giv'ah. He went in and sat down in the city's open space, since no one had offered his home for them to spend the night.

¹⁶ In time, at nightfall, an old man came from his work in the field. He was from the Efrayim hills and was staying in Giv'ah, although the residents were of Binyamin.

¹⁷ The old man looked up, saw the traveler in the city's open space and said, "Where are you going, and where are you coming from?" ¹⁸ He replied, "We're crossing from Beit-Lechem in Y'hudah to the far side of the Efrayim hills. That's where I'm from. I went to Beit-Lechem in Y'hudah, and now I'm going to the house of *Adonai*; but there's no one here who will let me spend the night in his home. ¹⁹ We have straw and food for our donkeys, also bread and wine for me, my concubine and the boy there with your servants; we don't need anything else." ²⁰ The old man said, "You're welcome to stay with me. I'll take care of anything you lack; just don't spend the night out in the open." ²¹ So he brought him home and gave food to the donkeys. Then they washed their feet, and ate and drank.

²² They were relaxing, when suddenly some men from the city, good-for-nothings, surrounded the house and began beating at the door. "Send out the man who came home with you!" they demanded of the old man whose house it was. "We want to have sex with him!" ²³ The man whose house it was went out and said to them, "No, my brothers, please don't do anything as wrong as this. Look, he's just a guest in my house; don't do this degrading thing. ²⁴ Here's my daughter, who's a virgin, and his concubine. I'll bring them out. Mistreat them, do what you want to them, but don't do such a degrading thing to this man." ²⁵ However, the men wouldn't listen to him; so the man took hold of his concubine and brought her out to them. They raped her and abused her all night long; only at dawn did they let her go. ²⁶ At daybreak the woman came and fell down at the door of the man's house where her husband was, and she was still there when it grew light. ²⁷ When her husband got up, opened the doors of the house, and went out to go on his way, he saw the woman lying there with her hands stretched out toward the door. ²⁸ He said to her, "Get up! Let's go!" But there was no answer. So he loaded her body on the donkey and began his trip home. ²⁹ On arrival at his house, he got a knife, took hold of his concubine's body, cut her up into twelve pieces, and sent them to all the regions of Isra'el. ³⁰ Everyone who saw it said, "From the day the people of Isra'el came up from Egypt until now, never has such a thing happened or been seen. What are we going to do about it? Talk it over and decide."

20 ¹ All the people of Isra'el came out, from Dan to Be'er-sheva, including Gil'ad; the community assembled with one accord before *Adonai* at Mitzpah. ² The leaders of all the tribes of Isra'el presented themselves in the assembly of the people of God, 400,000 foot soldiers armed with swords. ³ Now the people of Binyamin heard that the people of Isra'el had gone up to Mitzpah. The people of Isra'el said, "Tell us, how was this crime committed?" ⁴ The *Levi*, the husband of the murdered woman, answered, "I came to Giv'ah, which belongs to Binyamin, I and my concubine, to stay the night; ⁵ and the men in Giv'ah attacked me and surrounded the house I was staying in at night. They wanted to kill me, but instead they raped my concubine to death. ⁶ I took my concubine's body, cut it into pieces and sent them throughout all the territories belonging to Isra'el; because they committed a shockingly obscene and degrading crime in Isra'el. ⁷ Look, you are all people of Isra'el. So discuss what to do, and give your advice here and now."

⁸ All the people stood up in agreement and said, "None of us will go home to his tent or his house. ⁹ What we will do now to Giv'ah is this: we'll draw lots, ¹⁰ we'll take ten men out of each hundred throughout all the tribes of Isra'el, and a hundred

out of a thousand, and a thousand out of ten thousand to collect food for the others. When these come to Giv'ah in Binyamin, they will avenge the crime that was committed." [11] Thus all the men of Isra'el, joined together in complete agreement, assembled to attack the city.

[12] The tribes of Isra'el sent men throughout all the tribe of Binyamin with this message: "What is this crime committed by some of your people? [13] Turn over these good-for-nothings who are in Giv'ah at once, so that we can execute them and rid Isra'el of such evil." But the people of Binyamin refused to obey the order of their kinsmen the people of Isra'el. [14] Instead the people of Binyamin gathered themselves together from their cities and went to Giv'ah to fight the people of Isra'el. [15] On that day there were 26,000 men from Binyamin armed with swords, besides the inhabitants of Giv'ah, who numbered 700 specially chosen men. [16] All of these 700 specially picked men were left-handed, and every one could sling a stone at a hair and not miss.

[17] The army of Isra'el, apart from Binyamin, numbered 400,000 men with swords; they were all experienced soldiers. [18] The army of Isra'el began by going up to Beit-El, where they asked God, "Who should go up first to attack the army of Binyamin?" ADONAI said, "Y'hudah first." [19] So the army of Isra'el got up in the morning and set up their camp near Giv'ah. [20] Then the army of Isra'el went out to attack Binyamin and set up their battle line in front of Giv'ah. [21] But the army of Binyamin came out of Giv'ah and slaughtered the army of Isra'el; on that day 22,000 men fell. [22] The people, the men of Isra'el, restored their morale and again positioned themselves for battle where they had been the first day. [23] Then the army of Isra'el went up and cried before ADONAI until evening. They asked ADONAI, "Should we attack our kinsmen the people of Binyamin again? ADONAI answered, "Attack them."

[24] So the army of Isra'el went out to attack the army of Binyamin the second day. [25] But Binyamin went out against them from Giv'ah the second day and slaughtered the army of Isra'el; 18,000 men armed with swords fell. [26] Then the whole army of Isra'el, all the people, went up to Beit-El and cried and sat there in the presence of ADONAI. They fasted that day until evening, offered burnt offerings and peace offerings to ADONAI, [27] and asked ADONAI what to do. The ark for the covenant of God was there at that time; [28] and Pinchas the son of El'azar, the son of Aharon, stood before it at that time. They asked, "Should we still go out to battle again against our kinsmen the people of Binyamin, or should we stop?" ADONAI answered, "Attack, because tomorrow I will hand them over to you."

[29] Isra'el hid some men around Giv'ah, [30] and on the third day Isra'el attacked the army of Binyamin and took a position against Giv'ah as they had the other times. [31] Again the army of Binyamin went out against the people. Lured away from the city, they began attacking and killing some of the people, as they had the other times — they killed about thirty men of Isra'el in the countryside and on the roads, one of which goes up to Beit-El and the other to Giv'ah. [32] The army of Binyamin said, "They're defeated, just as before." But the army of Isra'el said, "Let's run off and draw them away from the city onto the roads." [33] All the men of Isra'el left their places and took up a battle position at Ba'al-Tamar, while the other Isra'el men burst out of their hiding places at Ma'areh-Geva. [34] Ten thousand men chosen out of all Isra'el came over to attack Giv'ah, and the combat was intense. But the army of Binyamin didn't know that they were about to be defeated. [35] For ADONAI routed Binyamin in Isra'el's presence; that day the army of Isra'el destroyed 25,100

men of Binyamin, all of whom carried swords; ³⁶ and the people of Binyamin realized that they had been beaten.

The men of Isra'el, trusting the ones they had put in place to ambush Binyamin, gave ground to the men of Binyamin. ³⁷ Then the men who had been lying in wait rushed in on Giv'ah, drew their swords and destroyed the city. ³⁸ The army of Isra'el and the ambushers had agreed that as a signal they would make a huge cloud of smoke rise from the city, ³⁹ at which time the men of Isra'el would turn back. When this happened, Binyamin began to attack. They killed about thirty of Isra'el's men and said, "Clearly we're defeating them again, as in the first battle." ⁴⁰ But when the smoke signal began rising from the city, the men of Binyamin looked behind them and saw the whole city going up to the sky in smoke. ⁴¹ Then, as the men of Isra'el reversed direction, those of Binyamin were overcome with terror. When they saw that disaster had come upon them, ⁴² they turned their backs on the men of Isra'el and made for the road to the desert. But the battle followed them, and those who came out of the city destroyed them from the rear. ⁴³ They surrounded the men of Binyamin, chased them and trampled them down across from Giv'ah on the east. ⁴⁴ Eighteen thousand men of Binyamin fell, all of them experienced soldiers. ⁴⁵ They turned and fled toward the desert to the Rock of Rimmon; and 5,000 of them were killed on the roads. They followed them to Gid'om and killed another 2,000. ⁴⁶ Thus the total number from Binyamin who fell that day was 25,000 experienced, sword-bearing soldiers. ⁴⁷ But 600 turned and fled toward the desert to the Rock of Rimmon, and lived there four months. ⁴⁸ The men of Isra'el turned back on the people of Binyamin and killed them with the sword, the entire city, the cattle and everything they found. Moreover, they set on fire all the cities they encountered.

21 ¹ The men of Isra'el had sworn in Mitzpah that none of them would let his daughter marry a man from Binyamin. ² The people came to Beit-El and stayed there before God till evening crying out and weeping. ³ They said: "ADONAI, why has this come about in Isra'el? Why should there be today in Isra'el one tribe missing?" ⁴ The next day the people got up early, built an altar and offered burnt offerings and peace offerings. ⁵ The people of Isra'el asked, "Who among the tribes of Isra'el did not come up to assemble before ADONAI? For they had made a great oath to put to death whoever didn't come up to ADONAI at Mitzpah. ⁶ The people of Isra'el became sorry for Binyamin their brother and said, "Today one tribe has been cut off from Isra'el. ⁷ How are we going to obtain wives for those who remain alive, since we've sworn by ADONAI that we won't let our daughters marry them?"

⁸ Then they asked who from the tribes of Isra'el had not come up to ADONAI at Mitzpah and found that none had come from Yavesh-Gil'ad to the camp where the assembly was; ⁹ since when the people were counted, none of the inhabitants of Yavesh-Gil'ad were found there. ¹⁰ So the gathering sent 12,000 warriors there and ordered them, "Go, and put the people who live in Yavesh-Gil'ad to death with the sword, including women and children. ¹¹ Completely destroy every man and every woman who has had sex with a man." ¹² Among the inhabitants of Yavesh-Gil'ad they found 400 young virgins who had not known a man by lying with him, and they brought them to the camp at Shiloh, which is in the land of Kena'an.

¹³ Then the whole gathering sent a message proclaiming peace to the people of Binyamin who were at the Rock of Rimmon. ¹⁴ So Binyamin returned at that time,

and the people of Isra'el gave them the women they had kept alive of the women from Yavesh-Gil'ad. But those weren't enough for them. [15] The people were still sorry for Binyamin because ADONAI had made a division among the tribes of Isra'el.

[16] The leaders of the assembly asked, "What are we to do for those who still don't have wives, inasmuch as all the women of Binyamin have been killed?" [17] They said, "There has to be a way to help the survivors preserve Binyamin's inheritance, so that a tribe will not be eliminated from Isra'el. [18] Yet we can't give them our daughters as wives." For the people of Isra'el had sworn, "Cursed be whoever gives a wife to Binyamin."

[19] Then they said, "Look, each year there's a festival in honor of ADONAI in Shiloh, north of Beit-El, on the east side of the road that goes up from Beit-El to Sh'khem, and south of Levonah." [20] They ordered the men of Binyamin, "Go, hide in the vineyards, [21] and keep watch. If the girls of Shiloh come out to do their dances, then come out of the vineyards, and each of you catch for himself a wife from the Shiloh girls, and go on to the land of Binyamin. [22] When their fathers or brothers come to complain to us, we will say to them, 'Give them as a personal favor to us, because we didn't take wives for each of them in battle. You didn't give them to them; that would have made you guilty of breaking your oath.'" [23] So the men of Binyamin did this — they took wives for themselves from the girls who were dancing, as many as they needed. They carried them off, went back to the land of their inheritance, rebuilt the cities and lived in them. [24] The people of Isra'el then left that place, each man returned to his tribe and family, and each man went out from there to the land he had inherited.

[25] At that time there was no king in Isra'el; a man simply did whatever he thought was right.

Sh'mu'el Alef
1 SAMUEL

1 ¹ There was a man from Ramatayim-Tzofim, in the hills of Efrayim, whose name was Elkanah the son of Yerocham, the son of Elihu, the son of Tochu, the son of Tzuf, from Efrat. ² He had two wives, one named Hannah and the other P'ninah. P'ninah had children, but Hannah had no children. ³ This man went up from his city every year to worship and sacrifice to ADONAI-Tzva'ot in Shiloh. The two sons of 'Eli, Hofni and Pinchas, were *cohanim* of ADONAI there.

⁴ One day, when Elkanah was sacrificing, he gave a portion of the sacrifice to his wife P'ninah and portions to each of her sons and daughters; ⁵ but to Hannah he gave a double portion, because he loved Hannah, even though ADONAI had kept her from having children. ⁶ Her rival taunted her and made her feel bad, because ADONAI had kept her from having children; ⁷ He did the same every year; and each time she went up to the house of ADONAI, she taunted her so much that she would cry and not eat. ⁸ Her husband Elkanah said to her, "Hannah, why are you crying, and why aren't you eating? Why be so sad? Am I not better to you than ten sons?" ⁹ So Hannah got up after they had finished eating and drinking in Shiloh. 'Eli the *cohen* was sitting on his seat by the doorpost of the temple of ADONAI. ¹⁰ In deep depression she prayed to ADONAI and cried. ¹¹ Then she took a vow; she said, "ADONAI-Tzva'ot, if you will notice how humiliated your servant is, if you will remember me and not forget your servant but will give your servant a male child, then I will give him to ADONAI for as long as he lives; and no razor will ever come on his head." ¹² She prayed for a long time before ADONAI; and as she did so, 'Eli was watching her mouth. ¹³ Hannah was speaking in her heart — her lips moved, but her voice could not be heard — so 'Eli thought she was drunk. ¹⁴ 'Eli said to her, "How long are you going to stay drunk? Stop drinking your wine!" ¹⁵ But Hannah answered, "No, my lord, I am a very unhappy woman. I have not drunk either wine or other strong liquor; rather, I've been pouring out my soul before ADONAI. ¹⁶ Don't think of your servant as a worthless woman; because I have been speaking from the depth of my distress and anger." ¹⁷ Then 'Eli replied, "Go in peace. May the God of Isra'el grant what you have asked of him." ¹⁸ She replied, "May your servant find favor in your sight." So the woman went on her way, and she ate, and her face was no longer sad. ¹⁹ They got up early in the morning and worshipped before ADONAI, then returned and came to their house in Ramah.

Elkanah had sexual relations with Hannah his wife, and ADONAI remembered her. ²⁰ She conceived; and in due time she gave birth to a son, whom she named Sh'mu'el, "because I asked ADONAI for him." *

---

* "Sh'mu'el" is derived from *shem El*, "name of God," but sounds like *sha'ul me'el*, "asked from God."

²¹ The husband, Elkanah, went up with all his household to offer the yearly sacrifice to ADONAI and fulfill his vow. ²² But Hannah did not go up, explaining to her husband, "Not till the child has been weaned. Then I will bring him, so that he can appear before ADONAI and live there forever." ²³ Her husband Elkanah answered her, "Do what seems good to you; stay here until you have weaned him. Only may ADONAI bring about what he said." So the woman stayed behind and nursed the child, until she weaned him. ²⁴ After weaning him, she took him up with her, along with three young bulls, a bushel of flour and a skin of wine, and brought him to the house of ADONAI in Shiloh, even though he was just a child. ²⁵ After the bull had been slaughtered, the child was brought to 'Eli; ²⁶ and she said, "My lord, as surely as you live, my lord, I am the woman who stood here near you, praying to ADONAI. ²⁷ I prayed for this child, and ADONAI has granted the request I asked of him. ²⁸ Therefore, I too have loaned him to ADONAI — as long as he lives, he is on loan to ADONAI." And he prostrated himself there before ADONAI.

2 ¹ Then Hannah prayed; she said:

> "My heart exults in ADONAI!
> My dignity has been restored by ADONAI!
> I can gloat over my enemies,
> because of my joy at your saving me.

²   "No one is as holy as ADONAI,
> because there is none to compare with you,
> no rock like our God.

³   "Stop your proud boasting!
> Don't let arrogance come from your mouth!
> For ADONAI is a God of knowledge,
> and he appraises actions.

⁴   The bows of the mighty are broken,
> while the feeble are armed with strength.

⁵   The well-fed hire themselves for bread,
> while those who were hungry hunger no more.
> The barren woman has borne seven,
> while the mother of many wastes away.

⁶   "ADONAI kills and makes alive;
> he brings down to the grave, and he brings up.

⁷   ADONAI makes poor, and he makes rich;
> he humbles, and he exalts.

⁸   He raises the poor from the dust,
> lifts up the needy from the trash pile;
> he gives them a place with leaders
> and assigns them seats of honor.

"For the earth's pillars belong to ADONAI;
    on them he has placed the world.
9 He will guard the steps of his faithful,
    but the wicked will be silenced in darkness.
    For it is not by strength that a person prevails —
10 those who fight ADONAI will be shattered;
    he will thunder against them in heaven —
    ADONAI will judge the ends of the earth.
    He will strengthen his king
    and enhance the power of his anointed."

¹¹ Elkanah went home to Ramah, while the child began ministering to ADONAI under the direction of 'Eli the *cohen.*

¹² 'Eli's sons were scoundrels who had no regard for ADONAI. ¹³ The rule these *cohanim* followed in dealing with the people was that when anyone offered a sacrifice, the *cohen*'s servant would come, while the meat was stewing, with a three-pronged fork in his hand. ¹⁴ He would stick it in the pan, kettle, caldron or pot; and the *cohen* would take for himself whatever the fork brought up. This is how they dealt with all the people of Isra'el who came there to Shiloh. ¹⁵ The *cohen*'s servant would actually come before the fat had burned to smoke and say to the man who was sacrificing, "Give the *cohen* meat he can roast; because he doesn't want your meat stewed, but raw." ¹⁶ If the man answered, "First let the fat burn to smoke, then take as much as you want," he would say, "No, give it to me now, or I'll take it by force." ¹⁷ The sin of these young men was very serious in ADONAI's view, because they treated offerings made to ADONAI with contempt.

¹⁸ But Sh'mu'el ministered in the presence of ADONAI, wearing a linen ritual vest even though he was only a child. ¹⁹ Each year his mother would make him a little coat and bring it when she came up with her husband to offer the annual sacrifice. ²⁰ 'Eli would bless Elkanah and his wife and say, "May ADONAI give you children from this woman because of the boy you have loaned to ADONAI"; then they would go home. ²¹ So ADONAI took notice of Hannah, and she conceived and bore three more sons and two daughters. Meanwhile, the boy Sh'mu'el grew in the presence of ADONAI.

²² When 'Eli was very old, he heard about everything his sons were doing to all Isra'el, and that they were having sex with the women doing service at the door of the tent of meeting. ²³ He asked them, "Why are you doing things like this? I am hearing bad reports about you from all these people. ²⁴ No, my sons, I don't hear ADONAI's people spreading a single good report! ²⁵ If a person commits a sin against another person, the judges can mediate between them. But if a person commits a sin against ADONAI, who can intercede for him?" However, they wouldn't pay attention to what their father said, because ADONAI had decided to kill them.

²⁶ The child Sh'mu'el kept growing and gaining favor both with ADONAI and with people.

²⁷ A man of God came to 'Eli and told him, "Here is what ADONAI says: 'Didn't I reveal myself to your ancestor's clan when they were in Egypt, serving as slaves in Pharaoh's household? ²⁸ Didn't I choose him out of all the tribes of Isra'el to be my *cohen*, go up to my altar, burn incense and wear a ritual vest in my presence? Didn't I assign to your ancestor's clan all the offerings of the

people of Isra'el made by fire? ²⁹ So why are you showing such disrespect for my sacrifices and offerings, which I ordered to be made at my dwelling? Why do you show more honor to your sons than to me, making yourselves fat with the choicest parts of all the offerings of Isra'el my people?'

³⁰ "Therefore ADONAI the God of Isra'el says, 'I did indeed say that your family and your father's family would walk in my presence forever.' But now ADONAI says, 'Forget it! I respect those who respect me, but those who despise me will meet with contempt. ³¹ The day is coming when I will break your strength and the strength of your father's family, so that no one in your family will live to old age. ³² At a time when Isra'el is prospering, you will see a rival in my Dwelling; and never will anyone in your family live to old age. ³³ Still, I won't cut off every one of your men from my altar; because that would make your eyes grow dim, and you would waste away. Nevertheless, all your descendants will die young. ³⁴ Your sign that this will occur will be what happens to your two sons Hofni and Pinchas — they will both die on the same day. ³⁵ I will raise up for myself a faithful *cohen* who will do what I want and what I intend. I will make his family faithful, and he will serve in the presence of my anointed one forever. ³⁶ Everyone left in your family will come, prostrate himself before him for a silver coin or a loaf of bread, and say, "Please, won't you give me some work as a *cohen*, so I can have a scrap of bread to eat?"'"

3 ¹ The child Sh'mu'el continued ministering to ADONAI under 'Eli's direction. Now, in those days ADONAI rarely spoke, and visions were few. ² Once, during that period, 'Eli had gone to bed — his eyes had begun to grow dim, so that it was hard for him to see. ³ The lamp of God had not yet gone out; and Sh'mu'el had lain down to sleep in the sanctuary of ADONAI, where the ark of God was.

⁴ ADONAI called, "Sh'mu'el!" and he answered, "Here I am." ⁵ Then he ran to 'Eli and said, "Here I am — you called me?" But he said, "I didn't call you; go back, and lie down." So he went and lay down. ⁶ ADONAI called a second time, "Sh'mu'el!" Sh'mu'el got up, went to 'Eli and said, "Here I am — you called me." He answered, "I didn't call, my son; lie down again." ⁷ Now Sh'mu'el didn't yet know ADONAI; the word of ADONAI had not yet been revealed to him. ⁸ ADONAI called, "Sh'mu'el!" again, a third time. He got up, went to 'Eli and said, "Here I am — you called me." At last 'Eli realized it was ADONAI calling the child. ⁹ So 'Eli said to Sh'mu'el, "Go, and lie down. If you are called again, say, 'Speak, ADONAI; your servant is listening.'" Sh'mu'el went and lay down in his place.

¹⁰ ADONAI came and stood, then spoke as at the other times: "Sh'mu'el! Sh'mu'el!" Then Sh'mu'el said, "Speak; your servant is listening." ¹¹ ADONAI said to Sh'mu'el, "Look! I am going to do something in Isra'el that will make both ears of everyone who hears about it tingle. ¹² On that day I will do against 'Eli everything I have said with regard to his family, from beginning to end. ¹³ For I have told him that I will execute judgment against his family forever, because of his wickedness in not rebuking his sons, even though he knew that they had brought a curse on themselves. ¹⁴ Therefore I have sworn to the family of 'Eli that the wickedness of 'Eli's family will never be atoned for by any sacrifice or offering."

¹⁵ Sh'mu'el lay there until morning; then he opened the doors of the house of ADONAI. But Sh'mu'el was afraid to tell 'Eli the vision. ¹⁶ Then 'Eli called Sh'mu'el: "Sh'mu'el, my son!" He answered, "Here I am." ¹⁷ 'Eli said, "What did he say to you?

Please, don't hide it from me; may God do to you whatever he said and worse, if you hide from me anything he said to you." [18] So Sh'mu'el told him every word and hid nothing. 'Eli replied, "It is *Adonai*; let him do what seems good to him."

[19] Sh'mu'el kept growing, *Adonai* was with him, and he let none of his words fall to the ground. [20] All Isra'el from Dan to Be'er-Sheva became aware that Sh'mu'el had been confirmed as a prophet of *Adonai*. [21] *Adonai* continued appearing in Shiloh, for *Adonai* revealed himself to Sh'mu'el in Shiloh by the word of *Adonai*.

4 [1] So the word of Sh'mu'el came to all Isra'el.

Isra'el went out to fight against the P'lishtim, setting up camp at Even-'Ezer, while the P'lishtim camped at Afek. [2] The P'lishtim drew up in battle formation against Isra'el. The battle was fierce, and Isra'el was beaten by the P'lishtim — they killed about four thousand soldiers on the battlefield. [3] When the army had returned to camp, the leaders of Isra'el asked, "Why has *Adonai* defeated us today before the P'lishtim? Let's bring the ark for the covenant of *Adonai* from Shiloh to us, so that he will come among us and save us from our enemies." [4] So the people sent to Shiloh and brought from there the ark for the covenant of *Adonai-Tzva'ot*, who is present above the *k'ruvim*. The two sons of 'Eli, Hofni and Pinchas, were there with the ark for the covenant of God.

[5] When the ark for the covenant of *Adonai* entered the camp, all Isra'el gave a mighty shout that resounded through the land. [6] On hearing the shout, the P'lishtim asked, "What does this great shout in the Hebrews' camp mean?" Then they realized that the ark of *Adonai* had arrived in the camp, [7] and the P'lishtim became afraid. They said, "God has entered the camp! We're lost! There was no such thing yesterday or the day before. [8] We're lost! Who will rescue us from the power of these mighty gods? These are the gods that completely overthrew the Egyptians in the desert. [9] Be strong; and behave like men, you P'lishtim; so that you won't become slaves to the Hebrews, as they have been to you. Behave like men, and fight!"

[10] The P'lishtim fought, Isra'el was defeated, and every man fled to his tent. It was a terrible slaughter — 30,000 of Isra'el's foot soldiers fell. [11] Moreover, the ark of God was captured; and the two sons of 'Eli, Hofni and Pinchas, died. [12] One of the soldiers, a man from Binyamin, ran and came to Shiloh the same day with his clothes torn and earth on his head [as a sign of mourning]. [13] As he arrived, 'Eli was sitting on his seat by the road, watching; because he was trembling with anxiety over the ark of God. When the man entered the city and told the news, the whole city began crying out. [14] On hearing the cries, 'Eli asked, "What does this uproar mean?" So the man hurried, came to 'Eli and told him. [15] 'Eli was ninety-eight years old, and his gaze was fixed, because he was blind. [16] The man said to 'Eli, "I'm the soldier that came; I escaped today from the battlefield." He asked, "How did things go, my son?" [17] The one who had come with the news answered, "Isra'el fled before the P'lishtim, and there was a terrible slaughter among the people. Your two sons, Hofni and Pinchas, also are dead; and the ark of God was captured. [18] As soon as he mentioned what had happened to the ark of God, 'Eli fell backward off his seat next to the gate, broke his neck and died; for he was an old man, and heavy. He had judged Isra'el forty years.

[19] His daughter-in-law, Pinchas's wife, was pregnant and near delivery-time. When she heard the news that the ark of God had been captured and that her

father-in-law and husband were dead, she went into abnormal labor, bent over and gave birth. ²⁰ As she was dying, the women standing by her said to her, "Don't be afraid, because you have given birth to a son." But she didn't answer or show any sign of recognition. ²¹ She named the child I-Khavod [without glory], saying, "The glory has departed from Isra'el"; because the ark of God had been captured, and because of her father-in-law and husband. ²² She said, "The glory of Isra'el has gone into exile, because the ark of God has been captured."

5 ¹ The P'lishtim had captured the ark of God and brought it from Even-'Ezer to Ashdod. ² Then the P'lishtim took the ark of God, brought it to the temple of Dagon and set it next to Dagon. ³ But early the next morning, when the people of Ashdod got up, there was Dagon, fallen down with his face to the ground before the ark of ADONAI. They took Dagon and set him in his place again; ⁴ but early the following morning, when they got up, Dagon was again fallen down with his face to the ground before the ark of ADONAI; this time, the head of Dagon and both hands lay there, severed, on the threshold; all that was left of Dagon was his torso. ⁵ This is why, to this day, the priests of Dagon and those entering his temple never walk on the threshold of Dagon in Ashdod.

⁶ ADONAI began oppressing the people of Ashdod; he ravaged them, striking Ashdod and its surrounding area with tumors. ⁷ When the people of Ashdod came to understand what was happening, they said, "The ark of the God of Isra'el can't remain with us, because he is oppressing us and our god Dagon." ⁸ They summoned all the leaders of the P'lishtim and asked, "What are we to do with the ark of the God of Isra'el?" They answered, "Have the ark of the God of Isra'el carried to Gat."

So they carried the ark of the God of Isra'el to Gat. ⁹ But after it arrived there, ADONAI oppressed that city, causing terrible panic. He struck the people of the city, great and small alike; tumors broke out on them.

¹⁰ Next they sent the ark of God to 'Ekron; but when the ark of God arrived in 'Ekron the 'Ekronim shouted, "Now they've brought the ark of the God of Isra'el to us, to kill us and our people!" ¹¹ So they summoned all the leaders of the P'lishtim and said, "Send the ark of the God of Isra'el away! Let it go back to its own place, so that it won't kill us and our people!" — because death and panic pervaded the whole city; God's oppression was very heavy there. ¹² The people who didn't die were struck with the tumors; and the city's cries for help reached the skies.

6 ¹ The ark of ADONAI was in the country of the P'lishtim for seven months. ² The P'lishtim summoned the priests and soothsayers and asked them, "What are we to do with the ark of ADONAI? Tell us how to send it back where it belongs." ³ They said, "If you do send off the ark of the God of Isra'el, don't send it back empty, but return it with some sort of guilt offering for him. Then you will be cured, and you will learn why he has not stopped oppressing you." ⁴ They asked, "What kind of guilt offering should we send him?" and they replied, "Five gold models of tumors and five gold rats, because that's how many leaders the P'lishtim have, and you and your leaders all had the same illness. ⁵ So make models of your tumors and models of your rats that are infesting your land, and show respect to the God of Isra'el. Maybe he will stop oppressing you, your gods and your land. ⁶ Why be obstinate like the Egyptians and Pharaoh were? When he had done his work among them, didn't they let the people go? — and they left. ⁷ Now take and prepare yourselves a new cart and two milk-cows that have never been under a yoke. Harness the cows to the cart, but put their calves back in the shed. ⁸ Then take the ark of ADONAI and lay it on the cart. In a box next to it, put the gold objects you are sending back to him as a guilt offering. Then send it away to go off by itself, ⁹ but watch to see if it goes up the road to Beit-Shemesh in its own territory. If it does, he is responsible for this great tragedy; if not, we will know that it is not his oppression which has been over us, but that what has been happening to us has been only by chance."

¹⁰ The men did it. They took two milk-cows, harnessed them to the cart and confined their calves to the shed. ¹¹ Then they put the ark on the cart, along with the box containing the gold rats and the models of their tumors. ¹² The cows made straight for the road to Beit-Shemesh and took that route, mooing as they went and turning off neither to the right nor to the left. The leaders of the P'lishtim followed them as far as the border of Beit-Shemesh.

¹³ The people of Beit-Shemesh were harvesting their wheat in the valley when they looked up and saw the ark. They were so happy to see it! ¹⁴ The cart entered the field of Y'hoshua the Beit-Shimshi and stood there by a big rock. They cut up the wood of the cart and offered up the cows as a burnt offering to ADONAI. ¹⁵ Then the L'vi'im removed the ark of ADONAI and the box that was with it, which contained the gold objects, and put them on the big rock. That same day the men of Beit-Shemesh offered burnt offerings and sacrifices to ADONAI. ¹⁶ Upon seeing this, the five leaders of the P'lishtim returned that day to 'Ekron.

¹⁷ The gold tumors which the P'lishtim sent back as a guilt offering for ADONAI were one each for Ashdod, 'Azah, Ashkelon, Gat and 'Ekron; ¹⁸ and the gold rats also corresponded to the number of all the cities of the P'lishtim that belonged to the five leaders — fortified cities and country villages. [The rock] is a witness to this day of the great mourning [which resulted from] putting the ark of ADONAI on it in the field of Y'hoshua the Beit-Shimshi; ¹⁹ for [ADONAI] struck the people of Beit-Shemesh for looking at the ark of ADONAI. He killed 50,070 of the people; the people mourned because ADONAI had struck them with such a terrible slaughter. ²⁰ The people of Beit-Shemesh asked, "Who can stand before ADONAI, this holy God? To whom can we send it, to get it away from us?"

²¹ They sent messengers to the people living in Kiryat-Ye'arim with this message: "The P'lishtim have returned the ark of ADONAI. Come down and bring it back up with you."

7 ¹ So the men of Kiryat-Ye'arim came and brought back the ark of ADONAI. They took it to the home of Avinadav on the hill and appointed his son El'azar to guard the ark of ADONAI. ² From the day that the ark arrived in Kiryat-Ye'arim a long time elapsed, twenty years; and all the people of Isra'el yearned for ADONAI.

³ Sh'mu'el addressed all the people of Isra'el; he said: "If you are returning to ADONAI with all your heart, then be done with the foreign gods and 'ashtarot that you have with you, and direct your hearts to ADONAI. If you will serve only him, he will rescue you from the power of the P'lishtim." ⁴ So the people of Isra'el banished the ba'alim and the 'ashtarot and served only ADONAI.

⁵ Sh'mu'el said, "Gather all Isra'el to Mitzpah, and I will pray for you to ADONAI." ⁶ So they gathered together at Mitzpah, drew water and poured it out before ADONAI,

fasted that day, and said there, "We have sinned against ADONAI." Sh'mu'el began serving as judge over the people of Isra'el at Mitzpah.

⁷ When the P'lishtim heard that the people of Isra'el had gathered together at Mitzpah, the leaders of the P'lishtim marched up against Isra'el; and when the people of Isra'el heard about this, they were afraid of the P'lishtim. ⁸ The people of Isra'el said to Sh'mu'el, "Don't stop crying out to ADONAI our God for us, to save us from the power of the P'lishtim." ⁹ Sh'mu'el took a baby lamb and offered it as a whole burnt offering to ADONAI. Then Sh'mu'el cried to ADONAI for Isra'el, and ADONAI answered him. ¹⁰ As Sh'mu'el was presenting the burnt offering, the P'lishtim advanced to attack Isra'el. But this time, ADONAI thundered violently over the P'lishtim, throwing them into such confusion that they were struck down before Isra'el. ¹¹ The men of Isra'el went out from Mitzpah, pursuing the P'lishtim and attacking them all the way to Beit-Kar.

¹² Sh'mu'el took a stone, placed it between Mitzpah and Shen, and gave it the name Even-'Ezer [stone of help], explaining, "ADONAI has helped us until now." ¹³ Thus the P'lishtim were humbled, so that they no longer entered Isra'el's territory; and the hand of ADONAI was against the P'lishtim as long as Sh'mu'el lived. ¹⁴ The cities between 'Ekron and Gat which the P'lishtim had captured from Isra'el were restored to Isra'el, and Isra'el rescued all this territory from the power of the P'lishtim. There was also peace between Isra'el and the Emori.

¹⁵ Sh'mu'el continued in office as judge of Isra'el as long as he lived. ¹⁶ Year by year he would travel in a circuit that included Beit-El, Gilgal and Mitzpah; and in all these places he served as judge over Isra'el. ¹⁷ Then he would return to Ramah, because that's where his home was, and he would judge Isra'el there too. He also built an altar there to ADONAI.

8 ¹ When Sh'mu'el grew old, he appointed his sons as judges over Isra'el. ² His firstborn was named Yo'el, while his second son was named Aviyah; they were judges in Be'er-Sheva. ³ However, his sons did not follow his way of life; they turned off it to pursue riches, so that they would take bribes to distort justice. ⁴ All the leaders of Isra'el gathered themselves together, approached Sh'mu'el in Ramah ⁵ and said to him, "Look, you have grown old, and your sons are not following your ways. Now make us a king to judge us like all the nations." ⁶ Sh'mu'el was not pleased to hear them say, "Give us a king to judge us"; so he prayed to ADONAI. ⁷ ADONAI said to Sh'mu'el, "Listen to the people, to everything they say to you; for it is not you they are rejecting; they are rejecting me; they don't want me to be king over them. ⁸ They are doing to you exactly what they have been doing to me, from the day I brought them out of Egypt until today, by abandoning me and serving other gods. ⁹ So do what they say, but give them a sober warning, telling them what kinds of rulings their king will make."

¹⁰ Sh'mu'el reported everything ADONAI had said to the people asking him for a king. ¹¹ He said, "Here is the kind of rulings your king will make: he will draft your sons and assign them to take care of his chariots, be his horsemen and be bodyguards running ahead of his chariots. ¹² He will appoint them to serve him as officers in charge of a thousand or of fifty, plowing his fields, gathering his harvest, and making his weapons and the equipment for his chariots. ¹³ He will take your daughters and have them be perfume-makers, cooks and bakers. ¹⁴ He will expropriate your fields, vineyards and olive groves — the very best of them! — and hand them over to his servants. ¹⁵ He will take the ten-percent tax of your crops and vineyards and give it to

his officers and servants. ¹⁶ He will take your male and female servants, your best young men and your donkeys, and make them work for him. ¹⁷ He will take the ten-percent tax of your flocks, and you will become his servants. ¹⁸ When that happens, you will cry out on account of your king, whom you yourselves chose. But when that happens, ADONAI will not answer you!"

¹⁹ However, the people refused to listen to what Sh'mu'el told them, and they said, "No! We want a king over us, ²⁰ so that we can be like all the nations, with our king to judge us, lead us and fight our battles." ²¹ Sh'mu'el heard everything the people said and repeated them for ADONAI to hear. ²² ADONAI said to Sh'mu'el, "Do what they ask, and set up a king for them." So Sh'mu'el told the men of Isra'el, "Each of you, return to his city."

9 ¹ There was a man from Binyamin named Kish the son of Avi'el, the son of Tz'ror, the son of B'khorat, the son of Afiach, the son of a man from Binyamin. He was a man of substance and brave as well. ² He had a son named Sha'ul who was young and good-looking; among the people of Isra'el there was no one better-looking than he; he stood head and shoulders taller than anyone else in Isra'el.

³ Once the donkeys belonging to Kish Sha'ul's father got lost. Kish said to his son Sha'ul, "Please take one of the servants with you, go out, and look for the donkeys." ⁴ He went through the hills of Efrayim and the territory of Shalishah, but they didn't find them. Then they went through the territory of Sha'alim, but they weren't there. They went through the territory of Binyamin but didn't find them there either. ⁵ On reaching the territory of Tzuf, Sha'ul said to his servant with him, "Come, let's go back; otherwise my father will stop thinking about the donkeys and start worrying about us." ⁶ His servant replied, "Here now, there's a man of God in this city, a man who is highly respected, and everything he says proves true. Let's go to him; maybe he can tell us something about where we should go." ⁷ "But look," Sha'ul said to his servant, "if we go to the man, what can we bring him? We've used up all the bread in our packs, and there's nothing for us to give the man of God — what do we have left?" ⁸ The servant replied again to Sha'ul: "See, I have here in my hand a silver quarter-*shekel* [one-tenth of an ounce]. I will give it to the man of God to tell us which way to go." ⁹ (In Isra'el, back in the old days, when someone went to consult God, he would say, "Come, let's go to the seer"; because a person now called a prophet used to be called a seer.) ¹⁰ "Well said," Sha'ul answered his servant. "Come on, let's go."

So they went to the city where the man of God was. ¹¹ Ascending the slope to the town they found girls going out to draw water and asked them, "Is the seer here?" ¹² The girls answered them, "He's here, he's right ahead of you. Hurry now, he just came into the city today, because the people are sacrificing today at the high place. ¹³ Find him as soon as you enter the city, before he goes up to the high place to eat; because the people won't eat until he comes and blesses the sacrifice. Afterwards, the ones invited will eat. So go on up, because this is when you will find him."

¹⁴ They went up to the city; and as they entered the city, there was Sh'mu'el coming out toward them to go up to the high place. ¹⁵ The day before Sha'ul arrived, ADONAI had given Sh'mu'el a revelation: ¹⁶ "Tomorrow at about this time I will send you a man from the territory of Binyamin. You are to anoint him prince over my people Isra'el. He will save my people from the power of the P'lishtim, because I have seen my people's situation, and their cry of distress has come to me."

^{17} When Sh'mu'el saw Sha'ul, Adonai said to him, "Here is the man I told you about, the one who is going to govern my people." ^{18} Sha'ul approached Sh'mu'el in the gateway and said, "Please tell me where the seer's house is." ^{19} Sh'mu'el answered Sha'ul, "I'm the seer. Go up ahead of me to the high place, because you are going to dine with me today. In the morning, I will let you leave; and I will tell you everything that is on your heart. ^{20} As for your donkeys that got lost three days ago, don't worry about them; they've been found. Now, who is it that all Isra'el wants? Isn't it you, and all your father's household?" ^{21} Sha'ul replied, "I'm only a man from Binyamin, the smallest tribe in Isra'el; and my family is the least important of all the families in the tribe of Binyamin! Why are you saying such a thing to me?"

^{22} Sh'mu'el took Sha'ul and his servant, brought them into the room and had them sit in the place reserved for the most important of the invited guests, who numbered about thirty persons. ^{23} Sh'mu'el instructed the cook, "Serve the portion I gave you and told you to set aside." ^{24} The cook took the thigh and the adjoining meat and served it to Sha'ul. Sh'mu'el said, "Here, this is what remains! Put it in front of you and eat — it was kept especially for you until the right time; because I said, 'I have invited the people.'" So Sha'ul dined with Sh'mu'el that day. ^{25} On coming down from the high place to the city, he spoke with Sha'ul on the roof. ^{26} They got up early. About daybreak, Sh'mu'el called out to Sha'ul on the roof, "Get up, so I can send you on your way." Sha'ul got up, and both of them — he and Sh'mu'el — went out. ^{27} As they were going down, at the edge of the city, Sh'mu'el said to Sha'ul, "Tell the servant to go on ahead"; so the servant went on. "But you, stand still now, because I want you to hear what God has said."

10 ^{1} Then Sh'mu'el took a flask of oil he had prepared and poured it on Sha'ul's head. He kissed him and said, "Adonai has anointed you to be prince over his inheritance. ^{2} After you leave me today, you will find two men by Rachel's Tomb, in the territory of Binyamin at Tzeltzah. They will tell you that the donkeys you were searching for have been found, and that your father has stopped thinking about the donkeys and is anxious over you and asking, 'What am I to do about my son?'" ^{3} Go on from there, and you will come to the Oak of Tavor. Three men will meet you there on their way up to God at Beit-El. One of them will be carrying three kids, another three loaves of bread and the third a skin of wine. ^{4} They will greet you and give you two loaves of bread, which you are to accept from them. ^{5} After that, you will come to Giv'ah of God, where the P'lishtim are garrisoned. On arrival at the city there, you will meet a group of prophets coming down from the high place, preceded by lutes, tambourines, flutes and lyres; and they will be prophesying. ^{6} Then the Spirit of Adonai will fall on you; you will prophesy with them and be turned into another man! ^{7} When these signs come over you, just do whatever you feel like doing, because God is with you. ^{8} Then you are to go down ahead of me to Gilgal, and there I will come down to you to offer burnt offerings and present sacrifices as peace offerings. Wait there seven days, until I come to you and tell you what to do."

^{9} As it happened, as soon as he had turned his back to leave Sh'mu'el, God gave him another heart; and all those signs took place that day. ^{10} When they arrived at the hill, and there in front of him was a group of prophets, the Spirit

of God fell on him and he prophesied along with them. ¹¹When those who knew
him from before saw him there, prophesying with the prophets, they asked each
other, "What's happened to Kish's son? Is Sha'ul a prophet, too?" ¹² Someone in the
crowd answered, "Must prophets' fathers be special?" So it became an expression —
"Is Sha'ul a prophet, too?"

¹³ When he had finished prophesying, he arrived at the high place. ¹⁴ Sha'ul's
uncle said to him and his servant, "Where did you go?" He answered, "To look for
the donkeys. When we saw that they hadn't been found, we went to Sh'mu'el."
¹⁵ "Tell me, please," said Sha'ul's uncle, "what Sh'mu'el said to you." ¹⁶ Sha'ul
answered his uncle, "He told us that the donkeys had been found," but said nothing
to him about the matter of his being made king.

¹⁷ Sh'mu'el summoned the people to ADONAI in Mitzpah. ¹⁸ He said to the
people of Isra'el, "Here is what ADONAI the God of Isra'el says: 'I brought Isra'el
up from Egypt. I rescued you from the power of the Egyptians and from the
power of all the kingdoms that oppressed you.' ¹⁹ But today you have rejected
your God, who himself saves you from all your disasters and distress. You have
said to him, 'No! Put a king over us!' So now, present yourselves before ADONAI
by your tribes and families." ²⁰ So Sh'mu'el had all the tribes come forward,
and the tribe of Binyamin was chosen. ²¹ He had the tribe of Binyamin come
forward by families, and the family of the Matri was chosen, and Sha'ul the son
of Kish was chosen. But when they looked for him, he couldn't be found. ²² They
asked ADONAI, "Has the man come here?" ADONAI answered, "There he is, hiding, in
among the equipment." ²³ They ran and brought him from there, and when he
stood among the people he was head and shoulders taller than anyone around.
²⁴ Sh'mu'el said to all the people, "Do you see the man ADONAI has chosen, that
there is no one like him among all the people?" Then all the people shouted,
"Long live the king!"

²⁵ Sh'mu'el told the people what kinds of rulings should be made in the
kingdom, then wrote it on a scroll and set it down before ADONAI. After that, he
sent all the people away, everyone to his own home. ²⁶ Sha'ul too went home to
Giv'ah, accompanied by warriors whose hearts God had touched. ²⁷ True, there were
some scoundrels who said, "How can this man save us?" They showed him no
respect and brought him no gift, but he held his peace.

11 ¹ Then Nachash the 'Amoni came up and set up camp to fight Yavesh-Gil'ad. All
the men of Yavesh said to Nachash, "If you will make a treaty with us, we will be
your subjects." ² Nachash the 'Amoni replied, "I'll do it on this condition: that all
your right eyes be gouged out and thus bring disgrace on all of Isra'el." ³ The leaders
of Yavesh answered him, "Give us seven days' grace to send messengers throughout
Isra'el's territory; then, if no one will rescue us, we will surrender to you."

⁴ The messengers came to Giv'ah, where Sha'ul lived, and said these words
in the hearing of the people; and all the people cried out and wept. ⁵ As this was
going on, Sha'ul came, following the oxen out of the field. Sha'ul asked, "What's
wrong with the people to make them cry like that?" They told him what the men
from Yavesh had said. ⁶ The Spirit of God fell on Sha'ul when he heard this;
blazing furiously with anger, ⁷ he seized a pair of oxen and cut them in pieces;
then he sent them throughout the territory of Isra'el with messengers saying,

"Anyone who doesn't come and follow Sha'ul and Sh'mu'el, this is what will be done to his oxen!" The fear of *ADONAI* fell on the people, and they came out with united hearts. ⁸ He reviewed them in Bezek; there were 300,000 from the people of Isra'el; the men of Y'hudah numbered 30,000. ⁹ To the messengers that had come they said, "Tell the men of Yavesh-Gil'ad, 'Tomorrow, by the time the sun is hot, you will have been rescued.'" The messengers returned and told the men of Yavesh; they were overjoyed. ¹⁰ Then the men of Yavesh said [to Nachash], "Tomorrow we will surrender to you, and you can do with us whatever you like."

¹¹ The next day Sha'ul divided the people into three companies. Then they entered the camp of the 'Amoni during the morning watch and kept attacking until the heat of the day, until those who remained were so scattered that no two of them were left together. ¹² The people said to Sh'mu'el, "Who are the men who said, 'Is Sha'ul to rule over us?' Hand them over to us, so we can put them to death." ¹³ But Sha'ul said, "No one will be put to death today, because today *ADONAI* has rescued Isra'el."

¹⁴ Then Sh'mu'el said to the people, "Come, let's go to Gilgal and inaugurate the kingship there. ¹⁵ So all the people went to Gilgal; and there in Gilgal, before *ADONAI*, they made Sha'ul king. They presented sacrifices as peace offerings before *ADONAI* there, and there Sha'ul and all the people of Isra'el celebrated with great joy.

12 ¹ Sh'mu'el said to all Isra'el, "Here, I have done everything you asked me to do— I have made a king over you. ² There is the king, walking ahead of you; but I am old and gray-headed. There are my sons with you, and I have walked at your head from when I was a boy until today. ³ So here I am; now is the time to witness against me before *ADONAI* and before his anointed king. Does any of you think I have taken your ox or donkey, defrauded or oppressed you, or accepted a bribe to deprive you of justice? Tell me, and I will restore it to you." ⁴ They answered, "You haven't defrauded or oppressed us, and you have accepted nothing from anyone." ⁵ He said, "*ADONAI* is witness against you, and his anointed king is witness against you today, that you have found nothing in my hands?" They replied, "He is witness."

⁶ Sh'mu'el said to the people, "It was *ADONAI* who appointed Moshe and Aharon and who brought your ancestors up from the land of Egypt. ⁷ Now, hold still; because I am going to enter into judgment with you before *ADONAI* regarding all the righteous acts of *ADONAI* that he did for you and your ancestors.

⁸ "After Ya'akov had entered Egypt, your ancestors cried to *ADONAI*; and *ADONAI* sent Moshe and Aharon, who brought your ancestors out of Egypt and had them live here in this place. ⁹ But they forgot *ADONAI* their God; so he handed them over to Sisra, commander of the army of Hatzor, and to the P'lishtim, and to the king of Mo'av; and they fought against them. ¹⁰ But they cried to *ADONAI* and said, 'We sinned by abandoning *ADONAI* and serving the *ba'alim* and *'ashtarot*. But now, if you rescue us from the power of our enemies, we will serve you.' ¹¹ So *ADONAI* sent Yeruba'al, B'dan, Yiftach and Sh'mu'el and rescued you from the power of your enemies on every side, and you lived securely. ¹² When you saw that Nachash the king of the people of 'Amon was attacking you, you said to me, "No, we want a king to rule over us"— when *ADONAI* your God was your king. ¹³ Now, here's the king you have chosen, the one you asked for. See, *ADONAI* has put a king over you. ¹⁴ If you will fear *ADONAI*, serve him, obey what he says and not rebel against *ADONAI*'s orders— if both

you and the king ruling you remain followers of ADONAI your God — [then things will go well for you.] ¹⁵ But if you refuse to obey what ADONAI says and rebel against ADONAI's orders, then ADONAI will oppress both you and your leaders.

¹⁶ "Now therefore, hold still; and see the great deed which ADONAI will perform before your very eyes. ¹⁷ Now is wheat harvest time, isn't it? I am going to call on ADONAI to send thunder and rain. Then you will understand and see how wicked from ADONAI's viewpoint is the thing you have done in asking for a king." ¹⁸ Sh'mu'el called to ADONAI, and ADONAI sent thunder and rain that day. Then all the people became very much afraid of ADONAI and Sh'mu'el. ¹⁹ All the people said to Sh'mu'el, "Pray to ADONAI your God for your servants, so that we won't die; because to all our other sins now we've added this evil as well, asking for a king over us." ²⁰ Sh'mu'el answered the people, "Don't be afraid. You have indeed done all this evil; yet now, just don't turn away from following ADONAI; but serve ADONAI with all your heart. ²¹ Don't turn to the side; because then you would go after useless things that can neither help nor rescue, they are so futile. ²² For the sake of his great reputation, ADONAI will not abandon his people; because it has pleased ADONAI to make you a people for himself. ²³ As for me, far be it from me to sin against ADONAI by ceasing to pray for you! Rather, I will continue instructing you in the good and right way. ²⁴ Only fear ADONAI, and serve him faithfully with all your heart; for think what great things he has done for you! ²⁵ However, if you insist on doing wicked things, you will be swept away — both you and your king!"

13 ¹ Sha'ul was — years old* when he began his reign, and he had ruled Isra'el for two years, ² when he chose three thousand of Isra'el's men. Two thousand of them were with Sha'ul in Mikhmas and in the hills of Beit-El, and a thousand were with Y'honatan in Giv'at-Binyamin. The rest of the people he sent back to their respective tents.

³ Y'honatan assassinated the governor of the P'lishtim in Geva. The P'lishtim heard of it; so Sha'ul had the *shofar* sounded throughout the land, saying, "Let the Hebrews hear!" ⁴ All Isra'el heard that Sha'ul had assassinated the governor of the P'lishtim and thus made Isra'el a stench in the nostrils of the P'lishtim. So the people rallied behind Sha'ul in Gilgal; ⁵ while the P'lishtim assembled themselves together to make war on Isra'el — 30,000 chariots, 6,000 horsemen and an army as large as the number of sand grains on the seashore. They came up and pitched camp at Mikhmas, east of Beit-Aven. ⁶ The men of Isra'el saw that their options were limited and that the people felt so hard pressed that they were hiding themselves in caves, thickets, crevices, watchtowers and cisterns; ⁷ while some of the Hebrews crossed the Yarden to the territory of Gad and Gil'ad. But Sha'ul was still in Gilgal, where all the people were eager to follow him. ⁸ He waited seven days, as Sh'mu'el had instructed; but Sh'mu'el didn't come to Gilgal; so the army began to drift away from him. ⁹ Sha'ul said, "Bring me the burnt offering and the peace offerings," and he offered the burnt offering. ¹⁰ As soon as he had finished sacrificing the burnt offering, there was Sh'mu'el — he had come, and Sha'ul went out to meet and greet him.

¹¹ Sh'mu'el said, "What have you done?" Sha'ul answered, "I saw that the army was drifting away from me, that you hadn't come during the time appointed

---

* The Hebrew text lacks the number.

and that the P'lishtim had assembled at Mikhmas. ¹² I said, 'Now the P'lishtim will fall on me at Gilgal, and I haven't asked the favor of ADONAI,' so I forced myself and offered the burnt offering." ¹³ Sh'mu'el said to Sha'ul, "You did a foolish thing. You didn't observe the *mitzvah* of ADONAI, which he gave you. If you had, ADONAI would have set up your kingship over Isra'el forever. ¹⁴ But as it is, your kingship will not be established. ADONAI has sought for himself a man after his own heart, and ADONAI has appointed him to be prince over his people, because you did not observe what ADONAI ordered you to do." ¹⁵ Then Sh'mu'el left Gilgal and went up to Giv'at-Binyamin.

Sha'ul counted how many were still there with him, about 600 men. ¹⁶ Sha'ul, Y'honatan his son and the men with him took up quarters at Giv'at-Binyamin, while the P'lishtim remained in camp at Mikhmas. ¹⁷ Then raiding parties began coming out from the camp of the P'lishtim, three of them: one group turned toward the road leading to 'Ofrah in the territory of Shu'al; ¹⁸ another group took the road toward Beit-Horon; and another company took the road toward the desert through the territory overlooking *Vadi* Tzvo'im.

¹⁹ Now there was no metalsmith to be found anywhere in all the land of Isra'el, because the P'lishtim had said, "We don't want the Hebrews making themselves swords or spears." ²⁰ So whenever any of the people of Isra'el wanted to sharpen his hoe, plowshare, axe or pick, he had to go down to the P'lishtim, ²¹ where the exorbitant prices were two-thirds of a *shekel* for filing a pick or plowshare and one-third of a *shekel* for filing an axe or setting an oxgoad in its handle. ²² Thus when the time came to fight, no one in the army of Sha'ul and Y'honatan was equipped with either sword or spear; although Sha'ul and Y'honatan his son did have them. ²³ A garrison of the P'lishtim had gone out to the pass of Mikhmas.

14 ¹ One day Y'honatan the son of Sha'ul said to the young man carrying his armor, "Come, let's go across to the garrison of the P'lishtim on the other side. But he didn't tell his father. ² Sha'ul was waiting at the far edge of Giv'ah under the pomegranate tree in Migron; the force with him numbered about 600 men. ³ Achiyah the son of Achituv, I-Khavod's brother, the son of Pinchas the son of 'Eli, the *cohen* of ADONAI in Shiloh, was carrying a ritual vest. No one knew that Y'honatan had gone.

⁴ Between the passes by which Y'honatan was trying to cross to the garrison of the P'lishtim, there was a rocky spur on one side and another rocky spur on the other side; the name of the one was Botzetz, and of the other, Seneh. ⁵ The one spur rose up on the north, in front of Mikhmas, and the other on the south, in front of Geva. ⁶ Y'honatan said to his armor-bearer, "Come on, let's go across to the garrison of these uncircumcised people. Maybe ADONAI will do something for us, since ADONAI can rescue with a few people as easily as with many." ⁷ His armor-bearer replied, "Do everything you think you should; I'm with you, whatever you decide." ⁸ Y'honatan said, "Here, we'll cross over to those men and let them know we're there. ⁹ If they say, 'Wait till we come to you,' we'll stand still where we are and not go up to them. ¹⁰ But if they say, 'Come up to us,' we'll go on up; and that will be the sign that ADONAI has given us victory over them."

¹¹ So both of them let their presence be known to the garrison of the P'lishtim; and the P'lishtim said, "Look, some Hebrews coming out of the holes they've been

hiding in!" ¹²Then the men of the garrison said to Y'honatan and his armor-bearer, "Come up to us; we want to show you something." Y'honatan told his armor-bearer, "Come on up after me, for ADONAI has handed them over to Isra'el." ¹³Y'honatan climbed up, using his hands as well as his feet, with his armor-bearer behind him. The P'lishtim fell before Y'honatan, and his armor-bearer following him finished them off. ¹⁴That first slaughter, of about twenty men, was accomplished by Y'honatan and his armor bearer in a space only half as long as one side of the area a pair of oxen could plow in a day [about 200 yards].

¹⁵There was panic in the field camp among all the P'lishtim; likewise, the garrison and the raiding party panicked. Besides all this, there was an earthquake; thus it grew into panic caused by God. ¹⁶Sha'ul's men on watch in Giv'at-Binyamin could see the enemy camp scattering and running in all directions. ¹⁷Sha'ul ordered the forces with him to call the roll and see who was missing. So they called the roll, and found Y'honatan and his armor-bearer not present. ¹⁸Sha'ul told Achiyah, "Bring the ark of God here"; for at that time the ark of God was with the people of Isra'el. ¹⁹But while Sha'ul was talking to the *cohen*, the uproar in the camp of the P'lishtim continued and kept getting louder. Sha'ul said to the *cohen*, "Put your hand down." ²⁰Sha'ul and the entire force with him assembled and went to battle, but they found the P'lishtim all fighting each other in utter confusion. ²¹The Hebrews from the surrounding countryside who had previously been with the P'lishtim and had gone up with them into the camp deserted and went over to Isra'el with Sha'ul and Y'honatan. ²²Likewise, on hearing that the P'lishtim were fleeing, all the men of Isra'el who had hidden themselves in the hills of Efrayim pursued them in battle. ²³So ADONAI saved Isra'el that day, and the battle spread as far as Beit-Aven.

²⁴Isra'el's soldiers had been driven to exhaustion that day; but Sha'ul issued this warning to the people: "A curse on any man who eats any food until evening, when I will have finished taking vengeance on my enemies." So none of the people even tasted food. ²⁵Now the people came to a forest where there was a honeycomb on the ground. ²⁶When the people had entered the forest, they saw there the honeycomb with honey dripping out; but no one put his hand to his mouth, because the people feared the oath. ²⁷But Y'honatan hadn't heard his father charging the people with the oath, so he put out the end of the staff in his hand, dipped it in the honeycomb and raised it to his mouth; whereupon his eyes lit up. ²⁸But one of the people said in response, "Your father strictly charged the people with an oath, 'A curse on any man who eats any food today'; even though the people are fainting with hunger." ²⁹Y'honatan answered, "My father has brought trouble to the land. Just look how my eyes have lit up because I tasted a little of this honey. ³⁰How much greater would the slaughter of the P'lishtim have been today, then, if the people had eaten freely of the spoil they found with their enemies!"

³¹That day they had attacked the P'lishtim from Mikhmas to Ayalon; but the people were very exhausted. ³²So the people rushed at the spoil, seizing sheep, cows and calves, slaughtering them on the ground, and eating the flesh with the blood. ³³Sha'ul was told, "Look how the people are sinning against ADONAI, eating with the blood." He said, "You have not kept faith! Roll a big stone to me immediately!" ³⁴Now," Sha'ul said, "go around among the people and tell them, 'Each of you is to bring his cow and his sheep and slaughter them here. Then eat. Don't sin against

ADONAI by eating with the blood." So each person brought his animal with him that evening and killed it there. ³⁵ Sha'ul erected an altar to ADONAI; it was the first altar that he erected to ADONAI.

³⁶ Sha'ul said, "Let's go after the P'lishtim by night. We'll plunder them until dawn; we won't leave one of them alive." They answered, "Do whatever seems good to you." But the *cohen* said, "Let's approach God here." ³⁷ Sha'ul consulted God: "Should I go down in pursuit of the P'lishtim? Will you hand them over to Isra'el?" But he didn't answer him that day. ³⁸ Sha'ul said, "Come here, all you heads of the people. Think carefully: who has committed this sin today? ³⁹ For, as ADONAI Isra'el's deliverer lives, even if it proves to be Y'honatan my son, he must be put to death." But no one among all the people answered him. ⁴⁰ Then he said to all Isra'el, "You be on one side, and I and Y'honatan my son will be on the other side." The people replied to Sha'ul, "Do what seems good to you." ⁴¹ Sha'ul said to ADONAI the God of Isra'el, "Who is right?" Y'honatan and Sha'ul were chosen by lot, and the people went free. ⁴² Sha'ul said, "Cast lots between me and Y'honatan my son." Y'honatan was chosen. ⁴³ Then Sha'ul said to Y'honatan, "Tell me what you did." Y'honatan told him, "Yes, I tasted a little honey with the end of the staff in my hand. Here I am; I'm ready to die." ⁴⁴ Sha'ul said, "May God do the same to me and more also if you are not put to death, Y'honatan!" ⁴⁵ But the people said to Sha'ul, "Must Y'honatan die, who has accomplished this great deliverance in Isra'el? Heaven forbid! As ADONAI lives, not one hair of his head will fall to the ground; because he worked with God today!" In this way the people rescued Y'honatan, so that he didn't die. ⁴⁶ Then Sha'ul stopped pursuing the P'lishtim, and the P'lishtim returned to their own territory.

⁴⁷ So Sha'ul took over the rulership of Isra'el. He fought against all his enemies on every side — against Mo'av, the people of 'Amon, Edom, the kings of Tzovah and the P'lishtim. No matter which way he turned, he defeated them. ⁴⁸ He demonstrated his strength by attacking 'Amalek, and he saved Isra'el from the power of those who were plundering them.

⁴⁹ The sons of Sha'ul were Y'honatan, Yishvi and Malkishua, while the names of his two daughters were these: the name of the older, Merav, and of the younger, Mikhal. ⁵⁰ Sha'ul's wife was named Achino'am the daughter of Achima'atz; the commander of his army was named Avner the son of Ner, Sha'ul's uncle. ⁵¹ Kish was the father of Sha'ul, and Ner the father of Avner was the son of Avi'el.

⁵² As long as Sha'ul lived there was bitter war against the P'lishtim. Whenever Sha'ul saw any strong or courageous man, he recruited him into his service.

15 ¹ Sh'mu'el said to Sha'ul, "ADONAI sent me to anoint you king over his people, over Isra'el. Now listen to what ADONAI has to say. ² Here is what ADONAI-Tzva'ot says: 'I remember what 'Amalek did to Isra'el, how they fought against Isra'el when they were coming up from Egypt. ³ Now go and attack 'Amalek, and completely destroy everything they have. Don't spare them, but kill men and women, children and babies, cows and sheep, camels and donkeys.'"

⁴ Sha'ul summoned the people and reviewed them in T'la'im — 200,000 foot soldiers, with another 10,000 men from Y'hudah. ⁵ Sha'ul arrived at the city of 'Amalek and lay in wait in the valley. ⁶ Sha'ul said to the Keni, "Go away, withdraw, leave your homes there with the 'Amaleki. Otherwise, I might destroy you along

with them, even though you were kind to all the people of Isra'el when they came out of Egypt." So the Keni went away from among the 'Amaleki. ⁷Then Sha'ul attacked 'Amalek, starting at Havilah and continuing toward Shur, at the border of Egypt. ⁸He took Agag the king of 'Amalek alive; but he completely destroyed the people, putting them to the sword. ⁹However, Sha'ul and the people spared Agag, along with the best of the sheep and cattle, and even the second best, also the lambs, and everything that was good — they weren't inclined to destroy these things. But everything that was worthless or weak they completely destroyed.

¹⁰Then the word of ADONAI came to Sh'mu'el: ¹¹"I regret setting up Sha'ul as king, because he has turned back from following me and hasn't obeyed my orders." This made Sh'mu'el very sad, so that he cried to ADONAI all night. ¹²Sh'mu'el got up early in the morning to meet Sha'ul; however, Sh'mu'el was told, "Sha'ul came to Karmel to set up a monument for himself there, but now he has left and is on his way down to Gilgal." ¹³Sh'mu'el went to Sha'ul; Sha'ul said to him, "May ADONAI bless you! I have done what ADONAI ordered." ¹⁴But Sh'mu'el answered, "If so, why do I hear sheep bleating and cows mooing?" ¹⁵Sha'ul said, "They brought them from the 'Amaleki, because the people spared the best of the sheep and cattle to sacrifice to ADONAI your God. But we completely destroyed the rest." ¹⁶Then Sh'mu'el said to Sha'ul, "Stop! I'm going to tell you what ADONAI said to me last night." He said, "Speak." ¹⁷Sh'mu'el then said, "You may be small in your own sight, but you are head of the tribes of Isra'el — ADONAI anointed you king over Isra'el! ¹⁸Now ADONAI sent you on a mission and told you, 'Go and completely destroy 'Amalek, those sinners; keep making war on them until they have been exterminated.' ¹⁹Why did you seize the spoil instead of paying attention to what ADONAI said? From ADONAI's viewpoint, you have done an evil thing." ²⁰Sha'ul said to Sh'mu'el, "I did too pay attention to what ADONAI said, and I carried out the mission on which ADONAI sent me. I brought back Agag the king of 'Amalek, and I completely destroyed 'Amalek. ²¹But the people took some of the spoil, the best of the sheep and cattle set aside for destruction, to sacrifice to ADONAI your God in Gilgal." ²²Sh'mu'el said,

> "Does ADONAI take as much pleasure
> in burnt offerings and sacrifices
> as in obeying what ADONAI says?
> Surely obeying is better than sacrifice,
> and heeding orders than the fat of rams.

²³
> "For rebellion is like the sin of sorcery,
> stubbornness like the crime of idolatry.
> Because you have rejected the word of ADONAI,
> he too has rejected you as king."

²⁴Sha'ul said to Sh'mu'el, "I have sinned. I violated the order of ADONAI and your words too, because I was afraid of the people and listened to what they said. ²⁵Now, please, pardon my sin; and come back with me, so that I can worship ADONAI." ²⁶But Sh'mu'el said to Sha'ul, "I will not go back with you, because you have rejected the word of ADONAI, and ADONAI has rejected you as king over Isra'el." ²⁷As Sh'mu'el was turning around to leave, he took hold of the hem of his cloak, and it tore.

²⁸ Sh'mu'el said to him, "*ADONAI* has torn the kingdom of Isra'el away from you today and given it to a fellow countryman of yours who is better than you. ²⁹ Moreover, the Eternal One of Isra'el will not lie or change his mind, because he isn't a mere human being subject to changing his mind." ³⁰ Then Sha'ul said, "I have sinned; but in spite of that, please show me respect now before the leaders of my people and before Isra'el by coming back with me, so that I can worship *ADONAI* your God." ³¹ So Sh'mu'el followed Sha'ul back, and Sha'ul worshipped *ADONAI*.

³² Then Sh'mu'el said, "Bring Agag the king of 'Amalek here to me. Agag came to him in chains and said, "Without doubt, mine will be a bitter death." ³³ Sh'mu'el said,

"Just as your sword has left women childless,
so will your mother be left childless among women."

Then Sh'mu'el cut Agag in pieces before *ADONAI* in Gilgal.

³⁴ Sh'mu'el returned to Ramah, and Sha'ul went up to his house in Giv'at-Sha'ul. ³⁵ Never again did Sh'mu'el see Sha'ul, until the day he died. But Sh'mu'el grieved over Sha'ul, and *ADONAI* regretted that he had made Sha'ul king over Isra'el.

16 ¹ *ADONAI* said to Sh'mu'el, "How much longer are you going to go on grieving for Sha'ul, now that I have rejected him as king over Isra'el? Fill your horn with oil, and set out; I will send you to Yishai the Beit-Lachmi, because I have chosen myself a king from among his sons." ² Sh'mu'el said, "How can I go? If Sha'ul hears of it, he will have me killed." *ADONAI* said, "Take a female cow with you and say, 'I have come to sacrifice to *ADONAI*.' ³ Summon Yishai to the sacrifice. I will tell you what to do, and you are to anoint for me the person I point out to you."

⁴ Sh'mu'el did what *ADONAI* said and arrived at Beit-Lechem. The leaders of the city came trembling to meet him and asked, "Are you coming in peace?" ⁵ He answered, "In peace. I have come to sacrifice to *ADONAI*. Consecrate yourselves, and come with me to the sacrifice." He consecrated Yishai and his sons and summoned them to the sacrifice. ⁶ When they had come, he looked at Eli'av and said, "This has to be *ADONAI*'s anointed one, here before him." ⁷ But *ADONAI* said to Sh'mu'el, "Don't pay attention to how he looks or how tall he is, because I have rejected him. *ADONAI* doesn't see the way humans see — humans look at the outward appearance, but *ADONAI* looks at the heart." ⁸ Then Yishai called Avinadav and presented him to Sh'mu'el; but he said, "*ADONAI* hasn't chosen this one either." ⁹ Yishai presented Shammah; again Sh'mu'el said, "*ADONAI* hasn't chosen this one either." ¹⁰ Yishai presented seven of his sons to Sh'mu'el; but Sh'mu'el told Yishai, "*ADONAI* has not chosen these. ¹¹ Are all your sons here?" Sh'mu'el asked Yishai. He replied, "There is still the youngest; he's out there tending the sheep." Sh'mu'el said to Yishai, "Send and bring him back, because we won't sit down to eat until he gets here." ¹² He sent and brought him in. With ruddy cheeks, red hair and bright eyes, he was a good-looking fellow. *ADONAI* said, "Stand up and anoint him; he's the one." ¹³ Sh'mu'el took the horn of oil and anointed him there in his brothers' presence. From that day on, the Spirit of *ADONAI* would fall upon David with power. So Sh'mu'el set out and went to Ramah.

¹⁴ Now the Spirit of *ADONAI* had left Sha'ul; instead, an evil spirit from *ADONAI* would suddenly come over him. ¹⁵ Sha'ul's servants said to him, "Do you notice that there's an evil spirit from God that suddenly comes over you? ¹⁶ Let our lord now

command your servants who are here with you to look for a man who knows how to play the lyre. Then, if the evil spirit from God comes over you, he will play; and it will do you good." ¹⁷ Sha'ul said to his servants, "Find me a man who can play well, and bring him to me." ¹⁸ One of the young men answered, "Here, I've seen one of the sons of Yishai the Beit-Lachmi who knows how to play. He's a brave soldier, he can fight, he chooses his words carefully and he's pleasant-looking. Besides, ADONAI is with him." ¹⁹ So Sha'ul sent messengers to Yishai saying, "Send me David your son, who is out with the sheep." ²⁰ Yishai took a donkey, loaded it with bread, a skin of wine and a kid, and sent them with David his son to Sha'ul. ²¹ David came to Sha'ul and presented himself to him. Sha'ul took a great liking to him and made him his armor-bearer. ²² Sha'ul sent a message to Yishai: "Please let David stay in my service, because I'm pleased with him." ²³ So it was that whenever the [evil] spirit from God came over Sha'ul, David would take the lyre and play it, with the result that Sha'ul would find relief and feel better, as the evil spirit left him.

17 ¹ The P'lishtim rallied their troops for war, assembling at Sokhoh in Y'hudah and setting up camp between Sokhoh and 'Azekah in Efes-Damim. ² Sha'ul and the men of Isra'el assembled, set up camp in the Elah Valley and drew up their battle line opposite the P'lishtim. ³ The P'lishtim occupied a position on one hill and Isra'el a position on another hill, with a valley between them.

⁴ There came out a champion from the camp of the P'lishtim named Golyat, from Gat, who was nine feet nine inches tall. ⁵ He had a bronze helmet on his head, and he wore a bronze armor plate weighing 120 pounds. ⁶ He had bronze armor protecting his legs and a bronze javelin between his shoulders. ⁷ The shaft of his spear was as big as a weaver's beam, and the iron spearhead weighed fifteen pounds. His shield-bearer went ahead of him. ⁸ He stood and yelled at the armies of Isra'el, "Why come out and draw up a battle line? I'm a P'lishti, and you are servants of Sha'ul, so choose a man for yourselves, and let him come down to me. ⁹ If he can fight me and kill me, we'll be your slaves; but if I beat him and kill him, you will become slaves and serve us." ¹⁰ The P'lishti added, "I challenge Isra'el's armies today — give me a man, and we'll fight it out!" ¹¹ When Sha'ul and all Isra'el heard those words of the P'lishti, they were shaken and terrified.

¹² Now David was the son of that Efrati from Beit-Lechem in Y'hudah named Yishai. He had eight sons; and in the time of Sha'ul he was old — the years had taken their toll. ¹³ Yishai's three oldest sons had followed Sha'ul to battle; the names of his three sons who went to battle were Eli'av the firstborn, next to him Avinadav, and the third Shammah. ¹⁴ David was the youngest; the three oldest followed Sha'ul. ¹⁵ David went back and forth from Sha'ul to pasture his father's sheep at Beit-Lechem. ¹⁶ Meanwhile, the P'lishti approached with his challenge every morning and evening for forty days.

¹⁷ Yishai said to David his son, "Please take your brothers five bushels of this roasted grain and these ten loaves of bread; hurry, and carry them to your brothers at the camp. ¹⁸ Also bring these ten cheeses to their field officer. Find out if your brothers are well, and bring back some token from them. ¹⁹ Sha'ul and your brothers, with all the army of Isra'el, are in the Elah Valley, fighting the P'lishtim."

²⁰ David got up early in the morning, left the sheep with a helper, took his load and set out, as Yishai had ordered him. He arrived at the barricade of the camp just as

the troops were going out to their battle stations and shouting the war cry. ^{21} Isra'el and the P'lishtim had set up their battle lines facing each other. ^{22} David left his equipment in charge of the equipment guard, ran to the troops, went to his brothers and asked if they were well. ^{23} As he was talking with them, there came the champion, the P'lishti from Gat named Golyat, from the ranks of the P'lishtim, saying the same words as before; and David heard them. ^{24} When the soldiers from Isra'el saw the man, they all ran away from him, terrified. ^{25} The soldiers from Isra'el said [to each other], "You saw that man who just came up? He has come to challenge Isra'el. To whoever kills him, the king will give a rich reward; he'll also give him his daughter and exempt his father's family from all service and taxes in Isra'el." ^{26} David said to the men standing with him, "What reward will be given to the man who kills this P'lishti and removes this disgrace from Isra'el? Who is this uncircumcised P'lishti anyway, that he challenges the armies of the living God?" ^{27} The people answered with what they had been saying, adding, "That's what will be done for the man who kills him." ^{28} Eli'av his oldest brother heard when David spoke to the men, and it made Eli'av angry at him. He asked, "Why did you come down here? With whom did you leave those few sheep in the desert? I know how conceited you are and how wicked your heart is! You just came down to watch the fighting." ^{29} David said, "What have I done now? I only asked a question." ^{30} He turned away from him to someone else and asked the same question, and the people gave him the same answer.

^{31} David's words were overheard and told to Sha'ul, who summoned him. ^{32} David said to Sha'ul, "No one should lose heart because of him; your servant will go and fight this P'lishti." ^{33} Sha'ul said to David, "You can't go to fight this P'lishti — you're just a boy, and he has been a warrior from his youth!" ^{34} David answered Sha'ul, "Your servant used to guard his father's sheep. When a lion or a bear would come and grab a lamb from the flock, ^{35} I would go after it, hit it, and snatch the lamb from its mouth; and if it turned on me, I would catch it by the jaw, smack it and kill it. ^{36} Your servant has defeated both lions and bears, and this uncircumcised P'lishti will be like one of them, because he has challenged the armies of the living God." ^{37} Then David said, "ADONAI, who rescued me from the paw of the lion and from the paw of the bear, will rescue me from the paw of this P'lishti!" Sha'ul said to David, "Go; may ADONAI be with you."

^{38} Sha'ul dressed David in his own armor — he put a bronze helmet on his head and gave him armor plate to wear. ^{39} David buckled his sword on his armor and tried to walk, but he wasn't used to such equipment. David said to Sha'ul, "I can't move wearing these things, because I'm not used to them." So David took them off. ^{40} Then he took his stick in his hand and picked five smooth stones from the riverbed, putting them in his shepherd's bag, in his pouch. Then, with his sling in his hand, he approached the P'lishti. ^{41} The P'lishti, with his shield-bearer ahead of him, came nearer and nearer to David. ^{42} The P'lishti looked David up and down and had nothing but scorn for what he saw — a boy with ruddy cheeks, red hair and good looks. ^{43} The P'lishti said to David, "Am I a dog? Is that why you're coming at me with sticks?" — and the P'lishti cursed David by his god. ^{44} Then the P'lishti said to David, "Come here to me, so I can give your flesh to the birds in the air and the wild animals." ^{45} David answered the P'lishti, "You're coming at me with a sword, a spear and a javelin. But I'm coming at you in the name of ADONAI-Tzva'ot, the God of the armies of Isra'el, whom you have challenged. ^{46} Today ADONAI will hand you over to me. I will attack you, lop your head off, and give the carcasses of the army of the P'lishtim to the birds in the air and the animals in the land. Then all the land will know that there is a God in Isra'el, ⁴⁷ and everyone assembled here will know that ADONAI does not save by sword or spear. For this is ADONAI's battle, and he will hand you over to us." ⁴⁸ When the P'lishti got up, approached and came close to meet David, David hurried and ran toward the army to meet the P'lishti. ⁴⁹ David put his hand in his bag, took out a stone, and hurled it with his sling. It struck the P'lishti in his forehead and buried itself in his forehead, so that he fell face down on the ground. ⁵⁰ Thus David defeated the P'lishti with a sling and a stone, striking the P'lishti and killing him; but David had no sword in his hand. ⁵¹ Then David ran and stood over the P'lishti, took his sword, drew it out of its sheath, and finished killing him, cutting off his head with it.

When the P'lishtim saw that their hero was dead, they fled. ⁵² The men of Isra'el and Y'hudah got up, shouting, and pursued the P'lishtim all the way to Gat and the gates of 'Ekron. The wounded P'lishtim fell down all along the road from Sha'arayim to Gat and 'Ekron. ⁵³ After chasing the P'lishtim, the army of Isra'el returned and plundered their camp.

⁵⁴ David took the head of the P'lishti and brought it to Yerushalayim, but he put the armor of the P'lishti in his tent.

⁵⁵ When Sha'ul saw David go out to fight the P'lishti, he said to Avner, the army's commander, "Avner, whose son is this boy?" "By your life, O king," Avner replied, "I don't know." ⁵⁶ The king said, "Find out whose son this boy is." ⁵⁷ As David returned from killing the P'lishti, Avner took him and brought him to Sha'ul with the head of the P'lishti in his hand. ⁵⁸ Sha'ul asked him, "Young man, whose son are you?" David answered, "I am the son of your servant Yishai the Beit-Lachmi."

18 ¹ By the time David had finished speaking to Sha'ul, Y'honatan found himself inwardly drawn by David's character, so that Y'honatan loved him as he did himself. ² That day, Sha'ul took David into his service and would not let him go home to his father's house any more. ³ Y'honatan made a covenant with David, because he loved him as he did himself. ⁴ Y'honatan removed the cloak he was wearing and gave it to David, his armor too, including his sword, bow and belt. ⁵ David would go out, and no matter where Sha'ul sent him, he was successful. Sha'ul put him in charge of the fighting men; all the people thought it good, and so did Sha'ul's servants.

⁶ As David and the others were returning from the slaughter of the P'lishti, the women came out of all the cities of Isra'el to meet King Sha'ul, singing and dancing joyfully with tambourines and three-stringed instruments. ⁷ In their merrymaking the women sang,

"Sha'ul has killed his thousands,
but David his tens of thousands."

⁸ Sha'ul became very angry, because this song displeased him. He said, "They give David credit for tens of thousands, but me they give credit for only thousands. Now all he lacks is the kingdom!" ⁹ From that day on, Sha'ul viewed David with suspicion.

¹⁰ The following day an evil spirit from God came powerfully over Sha'ul, so that he fell into a frenzy in the house. David was there, playing his lyre as on other

occasions. This time Sha'ul had his spear in his hand; ¹¹ and he threw the spear, thinking, "I will pin David to the wall!" But David dodged out of the way twice. ¹² Sha'ul became afraid of David, because ADONAI was with him and had left Sha'ul. ¹³ Therefore Sha'ul put him at a distance from himself by making him commander over a thousand; his goings and comings became public knowledge. ¹⁴ David had great success in all his ways; ADONAI was with him. ¹⁵ When Sha'ul saw how very successful he was, he became afraid of him. ¹⁶ But all Isra'el and Y'hudah loved David, because they knew about all his campaigns.

¹⁷ Sha'ul said to David, "Here is my older daughter Merav. I will give her to you as your wife; only continue displaying your courage for me, and fight ADONAI's battles." Sha'ul was thinking, "I don't dare touch him, so let the P'lishtim do away with him." ¹⁸ David's response to Sha'ul was, "Who am I, that I should become the king's son-in-law? I don't have any kind of a life, and my father's family has no rank in Isra'el." ¹⁹ However, when it was time for Merav Sha'ul's daughter to be given to David, she was given to Adri'el the Mecholati as his wife. ²⁰ But Mikhal Sha'ul's daughter fell in love with David. They told Sha'ul, and it pleased him. ²¹ Sha'ul said, "I'll give her to him, so that she can entrap him, and the P'lishtim can do away with him." So Sha'ul said to David, "Today you will become my son-in-law through the second [daughter]." ²² Sha'ul ordered his servants to speak privately with David and say, "Look, the king is pleased with you, and all his servants like you; so become the king's son-in-law." ²³ Sha'ul's servants said this to David; but David replied, "Do you think being the king's son-in-law is something to be treated so casually, given that I'm a poor man without social standing?" ²⁴ Sha'ul's servants reported back to him how David had responded. ²⁵ Sha'ul said, "Here's what you are to say to David: 'The king doesn't want any dowry; he wants a hundred foreskins of the P'lishtim, so that he can have vengeance on the king's enemies.'" For Sha'ul was hoping to have David killed by the P'lishtim. ²⁶ When his servants said these words to David, it pleased David to become the king's son-in-law. Even before the time [for him to be married], ²⁷ David got up and set out, he and his men, and killed two hundred men of the P'lishtim. He brought their foreskins and gave all of them to the king in order to become the king's son-in-law. Then Sha'ul gave him Mikhal his daughter as his wife.

²⁸ Sha'ul saw and understood that ADONAI was with David and that Mikhal Sha'ul's daughter loved him. ²⁹ This only made Sha'ul the more afraid of David, so that Sha'ul became David's enemy for the rest of his life.

³⁰ The leaders of the P'lishtim would attack; but whenever they attacked, David was more successful than any of Sha'ul's servants; so that David acquired a great reputation.

19 ¹ Sha'ul told Y'honatan his son and all his servants that they should have David killed. But because Y'honatan was very fond of David, ² he told him, "My father Sha'ul is out to have you killed. Therefore you must be very cautious tomorrow morning. Find a well-concealed place to hide in. ³ I will go out and stand next to my father in the countryside where you're hiding. I will talk with my father about you; and if I learn anything, I'll tell you."

⁴ Y'honatan spoke well of David to Sha'ul his father and said to him, "The king shouldn't sin against his servant David, because he hasn't sinned against you. On the

contrary, his work for you has been very good indeed. ⁵ He put his life in his hands to attack the P'lishtim, and ADONAI accomplished a great victory for all Isra'el. You yourself saw it, and you were happy about it. So why do you want to sin against innocent blood by killing David without any reason?" ⁶ Sha'ul heeded Y'honatan's advice and swore, "As ADONAI lives, he will not be put to death." ⁷ Y'honatan called David and told him all these things. Then Y'honatan brought David to Sha'ul to be in attendance on the king, as before.

⁸ War broke out again, and David went and fought the P'lishtim. He defeated them with a great slaughter, and they fled before him. ⁹ Then an evil spirit from ADONAI came upon Sha'ul, as he sat in his house with his spear in his hand. David was playing his lyre, ¹⁰ when Sha'ul tried to pin David to the wall with the spear. But he dodged it and moved out of Sha'ul's way, so that the spear stuck in the wall. David fled, so that night he escaped.

¹¹ But Sha'ul sent messengers to David's house to watch for him and kill him in the morning. Mikhal David's wife told him, "If you don't save your life tonight, tomorrow you'll be dead." ¹² So Mikhal let David down through the window; and he left, fled and escaped. ¹³ Mikhal took the household idol, laid it on the bed, put a goat's-hair quilt at its head and covered it with a cloth. ¹⁴ When Sha'ul sent messengers to capture David, she said, "He's ill." ¹⁵ Sha'ul sent the messengers to see David with the order, "Bring him up to me, bed and all, so that I can kill him." ¹⁶ But when the messengers entered, there before them was the household idol in the bed, with the goat's-hair quilt at its head. ¹⁷ Sha'ul asked Mikhal, "Why did you deceive me this way and let my enemy go and escape?" Mikhal answered Sha'ul, "He threatened me, 'Let me go, or I'll kill you.'"

¹⁸ David fled and escaped, then came to Sh'mu'el in Ramah and told him everything Sha'ul had done to him. So he and Sh'mu'el went and stayed in the prophets' dormitory. ¹⁹ The news reached Sha'ul that David had been seen at the prophets' dormitory in Ramah. ²⁰ Sha'ul sent messengers to capture David. But when they saw the group of prophets prophesying, with Sh'mu'el standing and leading them, the Spirit of God fell on Sha'ul's messengers; and they too began prophesying. ²¹ When Sha'ul was told, he sent other messengers; but they too began prophesying. Sha'ul sent messengers a third time, and they also prophesied. ²² Then he himself went to Ramah. When he arrived at the big cistern in Sekhu, he asked, "Where are Sh'mu'el and David?" Someone answered, "They're at the prophets' dormitory in Ramah." ²³ While on his way to the prophets' dormitory in Ramah, the Spirit of God fell on him too; and he went on, prophesying, until he arrived at the prophets' dormitory in Ramah. ²⁴ He also stripped off his clothes, prophesied in Sh'mu'el's presence and lay there naked all that day and all that night. Hence it continues to be an expression, "Is Sha'ul a prophet, too?"

20 ¹ David fled from the prophets' dormitory in Ramah, returned to Y'honatan and said, "What have I done? Where have I gone wrong? What sin have I committed that makes your father want to take my life?" ² Y'honatan replied, "Heaven forbid! You're not going to die! Look, my father does nothing important or unimportant without telling me first; so why should my father hide this from me? It just won't happen!" ³ In response David swore, "Your father knows very well that you have made me your friend. This is why he will say, 'Y'honatan must not know this, or he will be unhappy.' As truly as *Adonai* lives, and as truly as you are alive, there is only a step between me and death." ⁴ Y'honatan said to David, "Anything you want me to do for you, I'll do." ⁵ David answered Y'honatan, "Look, tomorrow is *Rosh-Hodesh*, and I ought to be dining with the king. Instead, let me go and hide myself in the countryside until evening of the third day. ⁶ If your father misses me at all, say, 'David begged me to let him hurry to Beit-Lechem, his city; because it's the annual sacrifice there for his whole family.' ⁷ If he says, 'Very good,' then your servant will be all right. But if he gets angry, you will know that he has planned something bad. ⁸ Therefore show kindness to your servant, for you bound your servant to yourself by a covenant before *Adonai*. But if I have done something wrong, kill me yourself! Why turn me over to your father?" ⁹ Y'honatan said, "Heaven forbid! If I ever were to learn that my father had definitely decided to do you harm, wouldn't I tell you?" ¹⁰ Then David asked Y'honatan, "Who will tell me in the event your father gives you a harsh answer?" ¹¹ Y'honatan said to David, "Come, let's go out in the countryside."

They went out, both of them, to the countryside. ¹² Y'honatan said to David, "*Adonai*, the God of Isra'el [is witness]: after I have sounded out my father, about this time tomorrow, or the third day, then, if things look good for David, I will send and let you know. ¹³ But if my father intends to do you harm, may *Adonai* do as much and more to me if I don't let you know and send you away, so that you can go in peace. And may *Adonai* be with you, just as he used to be with my father. ¹⁴ However, you are to show me *Adonai*'s kindness not only while I am alive, so that I do not die; ¹⁵ but also, after *Adonai* has eliminated every one of David's enemies from the face of the earth, you are to continue showing kindness to my family forever." ¹⁶ Thus Y'honatan made a covenant with the family of David, adding, "May *Adonai* seek its fulfillment even through David's enemies." ¹⁷ Y'honatan had David swear it again, because of the love he had for him — he loved him as he loved himself. ¹⁸ Y'honatan said to him, "Tomorrow is *Rosh-Hodesh*, and you will be missed, because your seat will be empty. ¹⁹ The third day, hide yourself well in the same place as you did before; stay by the Departure Stone. ²⁰ I will shoot three arrows to one side, as if I were shooting at a target. ²¹ Then I will send my boy to recover them. If I tell the boy, 'They're here on this side of you, take them,' then come — it means that everything is peaceful for you; as *Adonai* lives, there's nothing wrong. ²² But if I tell the boy, 'The arrows are out there, beyond you,' then get going, because *Adonai* is sending you away. ²³ As for the matter we discussed earlier, *Adonai* is between you and me forever."

²⁴ So David hid himself in the countryside. When *Rosh-Hodesh* came, the king sat down to eat his meal. ²⁵ The king sat at his usual place by the wall. Y'honatan stood up, and Avner sat next to Sha'ul, but David's place was empty. ²⁶ However, Sha'ul didn't say anything that day; because he thought, "Something has happened to him, he is unclean. Yes, that's it, he isn't clean." ²⁷ The day after *Rosh-Hodesh*, the second day, David's place was empty; and Sha'ul said to Y'honatan his son, "Why hasn't Yishai's son come to the meal either yesterday or today?" ²⁸ Y'honatan answered Sha'ul, "David begged me to let him go to Beit-Lechem. ²⁹ He said, 'Please let me go, because our family has a sacrifice in the city, and my brother demanded that I come. So now, if you look on me favorably, please let me get away and see my brothers.' That's why he hasn't come to the king's table." ³⁰ At that Sha'ul flew into a rage at Y'honatan and said, "You crooked rebel! Don't I know that you've made this son of Yishai your best friend? You don't care that you're shaming yourself and

dishonoring your mother, do you? ³¹ Because as long as the son of Yishai lives on this earth, neither you nor your kingdom will be secure. Now send and bring him here to me — he deserves to die." ³² Y'honatan answered Sha'ul his father, "Why should he be put to death? What has he done?" ³³ But Sha'ul threw his spear at him, aiming to kill; Y'honatan could no longer doubt that his father was determined to put David to death. ³⁴ Y'honatan got up from the table in a fury, and he ate no food the second day of the month, both because he was upset over David and because his father had put him to shame.

³⁵ The next morning Y'honatan went out into the country at the time he had arranged with David, taking with him a young boy. ³⁶ He told the boy, "Now run and find the arrows I'm about to shoot." As the boy ran, he shot an arrow beyond him. ³⁷ When the boy reached the place where the arrow was that Y'honatan had shot, Y'honatan shouted at the boy, "Isn't the arrow beyond you?" ³⁸ Y'honatan continued shouting after the boy, "Quick! Hurry! Don't just stand there!" Y'honatan's boy gathered the arrows and returned to his master, ³⁹ but the boy didn't understand anything about the matter — only Y'honatan and David understood. ⁴⁰ Y'honatan gave his weapons to his boy and said to him, "Go, carry them to the city."

⁴¹ As soon as the boy had gone, David got up from a place south of the stone, fell face down on the ground and prostrated himself three times; and they kissed one another and wept each with the other until it became too much for David. ⁴² Y'honatan said to David, "Go in peace; because we have sworn, both of us, in the name of ADONAI, that ADONAI will be between me and you, and between my descendants and yours, forever."

21 ¹⁽²⁰:⁴²ᵇ⁾ So David got up and left, and Y'honatan went back to the city.

²⁽¹⁾ David went to see Achimelekh the *cohen* in Nov. Achimelekh came trembling to meet David and asked, "Why are you alone? Why is no one with you?" ³⁽²⁾ David said to Achimelekh the *cohen*, "The king has sent me on a mission and told me not to let anyone know its purpose or what I've been ordered to do. I've arranged a place where the guards are to meet me. ⁴⁽³⁾ Now, what do you have on hand? If you can spare five loaves of bread, give them to me, or whatever there is." ⁵⁽⁴⁾ The *cohen* answered David, "I don't have any regular bread; however, there is consecrated bread — but only if the guards have abstained from women. ⁶⁽⁵⁾ David answered the *cohen*, "Of course women have been kept away from us, as on previous campaigns. Whenever I go out on campaign, the men's gear is clean, even if it's an ordinary trip. How much more, then, today, when they will be putting something consecrated in their packs!" ⁷⁽⁶⁾ So the *cohen* gave him consecrated bread, because there was no bread there other than the showbread that had been removed from before ADONAI to be replaced by freshly baked bread on the day the old bread was removed.

⁸⁽⁷⁾ One of the servants of Sha'ul happened to be there that day, detained before ADONAI. His name was Do'eg the Edomi, the head of Sha'ul's shepherds. ⁹⁽⁸⁾ David said to Achimelekh, "Perhaps you have here with you a spear or a sword? I brought neither my sword nor my other weapons, because the king's mission was urgent." ¹⁰⁽⁹⁾ The *cohen* said, "The sword of Golyat the P'lishti you killed in the Elah Valley, is over there behind the ritual vest, wrapped in a cloth. If you want it, take it; it's the only one here." David said, "There's nothing like it; give it to me."

¹¹⁽¹⁰⁾The same day, David took flight from Sha'ul and went to Akhish king of Gat. ¹²⁽¹¹⁾The servants of Akhish said to him, "Isn't this David, king of the land? Weren't they dancing and singing to each other,

'Sha'ul has killed his thousands,
but David his tens of thousands'?"

¹³⁽¹²⁾These remarks were not lost on David, and he became very much afraid of Akhish king of Gat. ¹⁴⁽¹³⁾So, as they were watching, he changed his behavior and acted like a madman when they had hold of him, scratching marks on the doors of the city gate and drooling down his beard. ¹⁵⁽¹⁴⁾Akhish said to his servants, "Here, you see that the man is *meshugga*; why bring him to me? ¹⁶⁽¹⁵⁾Am I short of *meshugga'im*? Is that why you've brought this one to go crazy on me? Must I have this one in my house?"

22 ¹David left there and took refuge in the Cave of 'Adulam. When his brothers and the rest of his father's family heard of it, they went down to see him there. ²Then all the people in distress, in debt or embittered began gathering around him, and he became their leader; there were about four hundred with him.

³David went from there to Mitzpeh of Mo'av and said to the king of Mo'av, "Please let my father and mother come and stay with you until I know what God will do for me." ⁴He presented them to the king of Mo'av, and they lived with him as long as David remained in his stronghold. ⁵But the prophet Gad said to David, "Don't stay in the stronghold. Leave, and go to the land of Y'hudah." So David left and went to the Forest of Heret.

⁶Sha'ul heard that David and the men with him had been located. Sha'ul was sitting in Giv'ah, under the tamarisk tree on the hill, with his spear in his hand and all his servants standing around him. ⁷Sha'ul said to his servants standing around him, "Listen, you men of Binyamin! Is Yishai's son going to give any of you fields and vineyards? Is he going to make you all commanders of thousands and hundreds? ⁸Is this why you have all conspired against me, why none of you told me when my son went in league with Yishai's son? None of you is concerned about me! Otherwise you would have told me that my son had incited my servant to become my enemy, as he is now."

⁹Then Do'eg the Edomi, who had been put in charge of Sha'ul's servants, answered, "I saw Yishai's son come to Nov, to Achimelekh the son of Achituv. ¹⁰He consulted ADONAI for him, gave him food and gave him the sword of Golyat the P'lishti." ¹¹The king sent to summon Achimelekh the *cohen* the son of Achituv, along with all his father's family, the *cohanim* in Nov; and all of them went to the king. ¹²Sha'ul said, "Listen here, you son of Achituv!" He answered, "Here I am, my lord." ¹³Sha'ul said to him, "Why did you conspire against me, you and Yishai's son? By giving him bread and a sword and consulting God for him, you helped him rebel against me and become my enemy, which he now is!" ¹⁴Achimelekh answered the king, "Is there anyone among all your servants more trustworthy than David? He's the king's son-in-law, he carries out your every request, your household honors him. ¹⁵I didn't start consulting God for him just today. Heaven forbid! The king shouldn't accuse me or my father's family of anything! Your servant knows nothing at all about any of this!" ¹⁶But the king said, "You must die, you and your father's

whole family." ¹⁷ Then the king told the guards standing around him, "Go around, and kill the *cohanim* of A_DONAI_, because they are siding with David, and because they knew he was escaping, yet they didn't tell me." But the king's servants refused to lift their hands against the *cohanim* of A_DONAI_. ¹⁸ So the king said to Do'eg, "You go around and kill the *cohanim*!" Do'eg the Edomi went around and fell on the *cohanim*; that day he killed eighty-five persons wearing linen ritual vests. ¹⁹ He also attacked Nov, the city of the *cohanim*, with the sword; he put to the sword both men and women, children and babies, cattle, donkeys and sheep.

²⁰ One of the sons of Achimelekh the son of Achituv, named Avyatar, escaped and fled to join David. ²¹ Avyatar told David that Sha'ul had killed the *cohanim* of A_DONAI_. ²² David said to Avyatar, "I knew it! That day, when Do'eg the Edomi was there, I knew he would tell Sha'ul. I caused the death of every person in your father's family. ²³ Stay with me; don't be afraid; because the one who is seeking my life seeks yours too. You'll be safe with me."

23 ¹ David was told, "The P'lishtim are fighting Ke'ilah and plundering the threshing-floors." ² David consulted A_DONAI_, asking, "Should I go and attack these P'lishtim?" A_DONAI_ answered David, "Go, and attack the P'lishtim, and save Ke'ilah." ³ David's men said to him, "Look, we're already afraid here in Y'hudah. How much more, then, if we go to Ke'ilah to fight the armies of the P'lishtim!" ⁴ David consulted A_DONAI_ again; and A_DONAI_ answered him, "Set out, and go down to Ke'ilah, because I will hand the P'lishtim over to you." ⁵ David and his men went to Ke'ilah and fought the P'lishtim. They defeated them in a great slaughter and led away their livestock. Thus David saved the inhabitants of Ke'ilah.

⁶ When Avyatar the son of Achimelekh fled to David in Ke'ilah, he had brought a ritual vest with him. ⁷ Now Sha'ul, on being informed that David had gone to Ke'ilah, had said, "God has put him into my hands. He's trapped himself by entering a town with gates and bars." ⁸ So Sha'ul summoned all the people to war, to go down to Ke'ilah and besiege David and his men. ⁹ David knew that Sha'ul was plotting something against him, so he told Avyatar the *cohen*, "Bring the ritual vest here." ¹⁰ Then David said, "A_DONAI_ God of Isra'el, your servant has certainly heard that Sha'ul intends to come to Ke'ilah and destroy the city just to get me. ¹¹ Will the men of Ke'ilah turn me over to him? Will Sha'ul come down, as your servant has heard? A_DONAI_ God of Isra'el, please tell your servant!" A_DONAI_ said, "He will come down." ¹² Then David asked, "Will the men of Ke'ilah hand me and my men over to Sha'ul?" A_DONAI_ said, "They will hand you over." ¹³ So David and his men, now around six hundred, got up, left Ke'ilah and went wherever they could. It was told Sha'ul that David had escaped from Ke'ilah, so he called off the expedition. ¹⁴ David stayed in the desert strongholds, remaining in the hills of the Zif Desert. Sha'ul kept trying to find him, but God did not hand him over to him.

¹⁵ David saw that Sha'ul had mounted another expedition to seek his life. David was then at Horesh in the Zif Desert. ¹⁶ Y'honatan Sha'ul's son set out and went to David at Horesh to encourage him in God. ¹⁷ He said to him, "Don't be afraid, because my father's forces will not find you; you will be king over Isra'el, and I will be second to you. Sha'ul my father knows this, too." ¹⁸ Then the two of them made a covenant in the presence of A_DONAI_, after which David stayed at Horesh and Y'honatan returned home.

¹⁹ The people of Zif came to Sha'ul in Giv'ah and said, "David is hiding himself with us in the strongholds at Horesh, on Hakhilah Hill, south of Yeshimon. ²⁰ So now, king, since you've wanted so much to come down, come down! Our part will be to turn him over to you." ²¹ Sha'ul said, "May ADONAI bless you for showing me compassion! ²² Please go and make still more certain exactly where he is and who has seen him there, because I've been told that he's very tricky. ²³ So look closely, find out where all his hiding-places are, and come back when you're sure. Then I will go with you, and if he is there in that territory, I'll search till I find him among all the thousands of Y'hudah."

²⁴ They set out and went to Zif before Sha'ul. But David and his men had gone on to the Ma'on Desert, in the 'Aravah south of Yeshimon. ²⁵ Sha'ul and his men went searching for him. David was told, so he came down to the rock and stayed in the Ma'on Desert. When Sha'ul heard that, he pursued David in the Ma'on Desert. ²⁶ Sha'ul went along one side of the mountain, while David and his men went along the other. David was hurrying to get away from Sha'ul, while Sha'ul and his men were trying to surround David and his men in order to capture them. ²⁷ But then a messenger came to Sha'ul, saying, "Hurry, come, because the P'lishtim are invading the country!" ²⁸ So Sha'ul stopped chasing David and went to fight the P'lishtim. Therefore they called that place Sela-Hamachlekot [rock of divisions].

24 ¹⁽²³:²⁹⁾ From there David went up and lived in the strongholds of 'Ein-Gedi. ²⁽¹⁾ When Sha'ul returned from pursuing the P'lishtim, he was told that David was in the desert at 'Ein-Gedi. ³⁽²⁾ Sha'ul took three thousand men chosen from all Isra'el and went searching for David and his men on the cliffs where the mountain goats are. ⁴⁽³⁾ Near some sheep pens along the way was a cave, and Sha'ul went inside to relieve himself. It happened that David and his men were sitting in the recesses at the back of the cave; ⁵⁽⁴⁾ and David's men said to him, "Look! The day has come that ADONAI told you about when he said to you, 'I will turn your enemy over to you, and you will do to him whatever seems good to you.'" Then David stole over unobserved and cut off the corner of Sha'ul's cloak. ⁶⁽⁵⁾ But after doing this, David felt remorse over cutting Sha'ul's garment. ⁷⁽⁶⁾ He said to his men, "ADONAI forbid that I should do such a thing to my lord, ADONAI's anointed, as raise my hand against him! After all, he is ADONAI's anointed." ⁸⁽⁷⁾ By saying this, David stopped his men and would not let them do anything to Sha'ul. Sha'ul got up, left the cave and went on his way.

⁹⁽⁸⁾ Then David too got up and went outside the cave, where he called after Sha'ul, "My lord the king!" When Sha'ul looked behind him, David bowed with his face to the ground and prostrated himself. ¹⁰⁽⁹⁾ David said to Sha'ul, "Why do you listen to people who say, 'David is out to harm you?' ¹¹⁽¹⁰⁾ Here, today you have seen with your own eyes that ADONAI put you in my power there in the cave. Some of my men said I should kill you, but I spared you; I said, 'I won't raise my hand against my lord, because he is ADONAI's anointed.' ¹²⁽¹¹⁾ Moreover, my father, look! Here in my hand you see the corner of your cloak. By the fact that I only cut off a piece of your cloak and didn't kill you, you can see and understand that I have no plan to do harm or rebel, and that I haven't sinned against you — even though you are seeking every chance you get to take my life. ¹³⁽¹²⁾ May ADONAI judge between you and me, and may ADONAI avenge me on you! But I

will not lay a hand on you — ¹⁴⁽¹³⁾ as the old saying has it, 'Out of the wicked comes wickedness, but I will not lay a hand on you.' ¹⁵⁽¹⁴⁾ The king of Isra'el has come on a campaign — after whom? Whom are you chasing? A dead dog! A single flea! ¹⁶⁽¹⁵⁾ ADONAI be the judge; let him decide between you and me. May he take my side and rescue me from your power!"

¹⁷⁽¹⁶⁾ After David had finished speaking to Sha'ul, Sha'ul said, "Is that your voice, my son David?" Then Sha'ul cried out and wept; ¹⁸⁽¹⁷⁾ and he said to David, "You are more righteous than I, because you have treated me well, while I have been treating you badly. ¹⁹⁽¹⁸⁾ You have made it clear to me today that you have done me good; for when ADONAI put my fate in your hands, you didn't kill me. ²⁰⁽¹⁹⁾ A man finds his enemy and lets him go unharmed?! May ADONAI reward you well for what you did to me today. ²¹⁽²⁰⁾ Now I'm certain that you will indeed become king, and that the kingship of Isra'el will be established in your hands. ²²⁽²¹⁾ So swear to me by ADONAI that you will not kill my descendants after I die or blot out my name from my father's family." ²³⁽²²⁾ David swore to Sha'ul, and Sha'ul went home, but David and his men went back up to the stronghold.

25 ¹ Sh'mu'el died. All of Isra'el assembled to mourn him and bury him at his home in Ramah.

Then David set out and went down to the Pa'ran Desert. ² Now there was a man in Ma'on who had property in Karmel. He was very rich, having three thousand sheep and a thousand goats; and he was shearing his sheep in Karmel. ³ The man's name was Naval, and his wife was named Avigayil. The woman was intelligent and attractive, but the man was surly and mean in his actions; he belonged to the clan of Kalev. ⁴ David, there in the desert, heard that Naval was shearing his sheep. ⁵ David sent off ten young men with these orders: "Go up to Naval in Karmel, and bring him greetings from me. ⁶ Say, 'Long life and *shalom* to you, *shalom* to your household, and *shalom* to everything that is yours! ⁷ I've heard that you now have shearers. Your shepherds were with us [for a while], we did them no harm, and they found nothing missing all the time they were in Karmel. ⁸ Ask your own men; they'll tell you. Therefore, receive my men favorably, since we have come on a festive day. Please give what you can to your servants and to your son David.'"

⁹ On arrival, David's men said all these things to Naval in David's name. When they had finished, ¹⁰ Naval answered David's servants, "Who is David? Who is the son of Yishai? There are many servants nowadays running away from their masters. ¹¹ Am I supposed to take my bread, my water and my meat that I slaughtered for my shearers and give it to men coming from who knows where?" ¹² So David's men turned around, went back and came and told him everything Naval had said. ¹³ David said to his men, "Buckle your swords on, all of you!" Each one buckled on his sword, David too; and there went up after David about four hundred men, while two hundred stayed with the equipment.

¹⁴ But one of Naval's men told Avigayil his wife, "David sent messengers from the desert to greet our master, and he flew on them in a rage, ¹⁵ even though the men had been very good to us — they didn't harm us, and we found nothing missing during the entire time we went with them, while we were out in the countryside. ¹⁶ They served as a wall protecting us day and night all the time we were with them caring for the sheep.

¹⁷ So now decide what you are going to do, for clearly harm is on its way to our master and all his household, but he's so mean that no one can tell him anything."

¹⁸ Avigayil wasted no time in taking 200 loaves of bread, two skins of wine, five sheep already prepared, six quarts of roasted grain, a hundred clusters of raisins and 200 fig cakes, and having them loaded on donkeys. ¹⁹ Then she said to her young men, "Go on ahead of me, and I'll come along after you." But she didn't tell her husband Naval.

²⁰ She was riding her donkey down past the hiding-place in the mountain, when David and his men descended toward her, and she met them. ²¹ David had said, "What a waste it has been guarding everything this fellow has in the desert, so that nothing of his was missing! He has repaid me bad for good!" ²² Then he swore, "May God do the same and more to David's enemies if I leave alive even one male of everything he owns."

²³ When Avigayil saw David, she hurried to dismount from her donkey, fell on her face in front of David and bowed down to the ground. ²⁴ Having fallen at his feet, she said, "It's all my fault, my lord, all my fault! Please let your servant speak in your ears, and listen to what your servant says. ²⁵ Please! My lord shouldn't pay any attention to this worthless fellow Naval, because he's just like his name — 'Naval' means 'boor,' and his boorishness stays with him. But I, your servant, did not see my lord's men, whom you sent. ²⁶ Therefore, my lord, as ADONAI lives, and as you live, inasmuch as ADONAI has kept you from the guilt of shedding blood and from taking vengeance into your own hands — therefore, may your enemies and anyone seeking your harm be [as worthless] as Naval. ²⁷ Meanwhile, let this present which your servant has brought to my lord be given to the men in my lord's service. ²⁸ And please forgive the offense your servant has caused; because ADONAI will certainly establish my lord's dynasty, for my lord fights ADONAI's battles, and nothing bad has been found in you all your life long. ²⁹ Even if someone comes along searching for you and seeking your life, your life will be bound in the bundle of life with ADONAI your God. But the lives of your enemies he will fling away as if from the pouch of a slingshot. ³⁰ Then, when ADONAI has done all the good to my lord that he has said about you and made you ruler over Isra'el, ³¹ what happens here will not have become an obstacle to you or a cause for remorse to my lord, neither that you shed blood without cause nor that my lord took vengeance into his own hands. Finally, when ADONAI has dealt well with my lord, then remember your servant."

³² David said to Avigayil, "Blessed be ADONAI the God of Isra'el, who sent you today to meet me; ³³ and blessed be your tactfulness, and blessed be yourself for having kept me today from the guilt of shedding blood and taking vengeance into my own hands. ³⁴ For as ADONAI the God of Isra'el, lives, who has kept me from harming you, if you hadn't rushed to meet me, not even one male would have been left to Naval by morning!" ³⁵ So David received from her what she had brought him, then said to her, "Go up in peace to your home. I have listened to what you said and granted your request."

³⁶ Avigayil came to Naval; there he was in his house, holding a feast fit for a king. He was in high spirits, because he was very drunk. So she told him nothing whatever until the next morning. ³⁷ In the morning, when he was sober and his wife

told him what had happened, he had a stroke and became as motionless as a stone. ³⁸ Some ten days later ADONAI struck Naval, and he died.

³⁹ When David heard that Naval was dead, he said, "Blessed be ADONAI for having taken my side in the matter of Naval's insult and for having prevented his servant from doing anything bad. On the contrary, ADONAI has caused Naval's bad deeds to return on his own head." Then David sent a message that he wanted to make Avigayil his own wife. ⁴⁰ When David's servants reached Avigayil in Karmel, they said to her, "David has sent us to you to bring you to him to be his wife." ⁴¹ She got up, bowed with her face to the ground, and said, "Your servant is here to serve you, to wash the feet of my lord's servants." ⁴² Avigayil then hurried, set out and rode off on a donkey, with five of her female servants following her; she went after David's messengers; and she became his wife. ⁴³ David also took Achino'am of Yizre'el; both of them became his wives.

⁴⁴ Meanwhile, Sha'ul had given Mikhal his daughter, David's wife, to Palti the son of Layish, who came from Gallim.

26 ¹ The people from Zif went to Sha'ul in Giv'ah and said, "David is hiding himself on Hakhilah Hill, across from Yeshimon." ² Then Sha'ul set out and went down to the Zif Desert with three thousand men chosen from Isra'el, to search for David in the Zif Desert. ³ Sha'ul pitched camp on Hakhilah Hill, across from Yeshimon, near the road. David was staying in the desert, and he saw that Sha'ul was coming into the desert after him. ⁴ So David dispatched spies and determined that Sha'ul had definitely come.

⁵ David set out and went to where Sha'ul had pitched his camp. He saw where Sha'ul and Avner the son of Ner, the commander of his army, were sleeping. Sha'ul was lying inside the barricade with the troops asleep all around him. ⁶ David said to Achimelekh the Hitti and Avishai the son of Tz'ruyah, Yo'av's brother, "Who will go down with me to Sha'ul in the camp?" Avishai said, "I will go down with you." ⁷ So David and Avishai went to the soldiers by night. Sha'ul was lying there asleep inside the barricade. His spear was stuck in the ground next to his head, with Avner and the troops asleep all around him. ⁸ Avishai said to David, "God has handed your enemy over to you today; so now, please, let me pin him to the ground with just one stroke of the spear. I won't strike him a second time." ⁹ But David said to Avishai, "Don't destroy him! Nobody can raise his hand against ADONAI's anointed without becoming guilty!" ¹⁰ David then added, "As ADONAI lives, ADONAI will strike him down, or the day will come for him to die, or he will go down to battle and be swept away. ¹¹ ADONAI forbid that I should raise my hand against ADONAI's anointed! But now, we'll take the spear by his head and the jug of water, and get out of here." ¹² So David took the spear and the water jug from Sha'ul's head and got away. Nobody saw or knew about it, and no one awoke, because they were all asleep—a deep sleep from ADONAI had fallen over them.

¹³ David crossed to the other side and climbed to the top of the distant ridge, leaving a considerable space between them. ¹⁴ Then David called out to the troops and to Avner the son of Ner. "Avner! Aren't you going to answer?" Avner answered, "Who are you, calling to the king?" ¹⁵ David said to Avner, "Aren't you the brave one! Who is there in Isra'el to compare with you? So why haven't you kept watch over your lord the king? Someone came in to kill the king, your lord! ¹⁶ It's not good, what you've done! As ADONAI lives, you deserve to die; because you didn't keep

watch over your lord, ADONAI's anointed. And now, see where the king's spear is, and the jug of water that was next to his head!" ^{17} Sha'ul recognized David's voice and said, "Is that your voice, my son David?" David said, "It is my voice, my lord king!" ^{18} and continued, "Why is my lord chasing his servant? What have I done? What evil am I planning? ^{19} Please, now, may my lord the king hear what his servant is saying. If it is ADONAI who has stirred you up against me, let him receive an offering. But if it's human beings, then a curse on them before ADONAI! — because, as things stand today, they have driven me out, so that I can no longer share in ADONAI's inheritance — they've said, 'Go, serve other gods!' ^{20} Now don't let my blood fall on the ground away from the presence of ADONAI. The king of Isra'el has gone out in search of a single flea, as if he were hunting partridge in the mountains!"

^{21} Then Sha'ul said, "I have sinned. Come back, my son David. I won't harm you any longer, because you regarded my life as precious today. Yes, I have behaved like a fool. I was altogether in the wrong." ^{22} David answered, "Here is the king's spear. Send one of the men over to bring it back. ^{23} ADONAI will give every person a reward suited to his uprightness and faithfulness. ADONAI put you in my power today, but I would not raise my hand against ADONAI's anointed. ^{24} Look: just as I put great value on your life today, so may my life be given great value by ADONAI. May he deliver me from every kind of trouble!" ^{25} Sha'ul answered David, "Blessings on you, my son David! No question that you will accomplish everything you set out to do!" So David went on his way, and Sha'ul returned to his place.

27 ^{1} But David said to himself, "One day Sha'ul will sweep me away. The best thing for me to do is to escape into the territory of the P'lishtim. Then Sha'ul will give up trying to find me here or there in Isra'el's territory, and at last I'll be free of him." ^{2} So David set out with his six hundred men and passed on to Akhish the son of Ma'okh, king of Gat. ^{3} David lived with Akhish, he and his men, each man with his household — including David with his two wives Achino'am from Yizre'el and Avigayil from Karmel, Naval's widow. ^{4} Sha'ul was told that David had escaped to Gat, whereupon he stopped searching for him.

^{5} David said to Akhish, "If you are now favorably disposed toward me, let me have a place to live in one of the cities in the countryside. Why should your servant live in the royal city with you?" ^{6} That very day Akhish gave him Ziklag, and that's why to this day Ziklag belongs to the kings of Y'hudah.

^{7} After David had been living in the country of the P'lishtim for a year and four months, ^{8} he and his men began going up and raiding the G'shuri, the Gizri and the 'Amaleki (from ancient times these people had lived in the land in the direction of Shur, all the way to Egypt). ^{9} David would attack the land, leaving alive neither men nor women, but taking the sheep, cattle, donkeys, camels and clothing. Then he would return and go to Akhish. ^{10} Akhish would ask, "Where were you raiding today?" and David would answer, "Against the Negev of Y'hudah," or "Against the Negev of the Yerachme'eli," or "Against the Negev of the Keni." ^{11} The reason David spared neither men nor women to be brought to Gat is that he thought, "We don't want them telling on us, saying, 'David did so-and-so.'" That's how he conducted his raids for as long as he lived in the country of the P'lishtim. ^{12} And Akhish believed him; he said, "David has caused his own people Isra'el to despise him utterly; he will be my servant forever."

28 [1] In due time the P'lishtim assembled their armies for war against Isra'el. Akhish told David, "You know, of course, that you and your men will join me and the army in battle." [2] David answered Akhish, "I see that you already know what your servant will do." Akhish said to David, "For that answer, I am making you my personal bodyguard for life."

[3] Now Sh'mu'el was dead; all Isra'el had mourned him and buried him in his city, Ramah. Also Sha'ul had expelled from the land those who tell the future by communicating with the dead or with a demonic spirit.

[4] The P'lishtim assembled; then they went and pitched camp at Shunem; while Sha'ul gathered all Isra'el together and pitched camp at Gilboa. [5] When Sha'ul saw the army of the P'lishtim, he became afraid — it struck terror in his heart. [6] But when he consulted ADONAI, ADONAI didn't answer him — not by dreams, not by *urim* and not by prophets.

[7] Then Sha'ul said to his servants, "Try to find a woman who tells the future by communicating with the dead; I want to go and consult with her." His servants answered him, "Yes, there's a woman in 'Ein-Dor who tells the future by communicating with the dead." [8] So Sha'ul disguised himself by wearing different clothing, went with two men, came to the woman by night and said, "Tell me the future, please. Bring up from the dead the person I name to you." [9] The woman answered, "Here, you know what Sha'ul did, how he expelled from the land those who tell the future by communicating with the dead or with a demonic spirit. Why are you trying to entrap me into causing my own death?" [10] But Sha'ul swore to her by ADONAI, "As ADONAI lives, you will not be punished for doing this." [11] Then the woman asked, "Whom should I bring up for you?" He said, "Bring up for me Sh'mu'el." [12] When the woman saw Sh'mu'el, she let out a shriek. Then the woman said to Sha'ul, "Why have you deceived me? You yourself are Sha'ul!" [13] The king replied, "Don't be afraid. Just tell me what you see." The woman said to Sha'ul, "I see a god-like being coming up out of the earth." [14] He asked her, "What does he look like?" She said, "An old man is coming up; he's wearing a cloak." Sha'ul realized it was Sh'mu'el, so he bowed with his face to the ground and prostrated himself.

[15] Sh'mu'el asked Sha'ul, "Why have you disturbed me and brought me up?" Sha'ul answered, "I'm very upset; because the P'lishtim are making war against me; and God has left me and doesn't answer me any more, neither by prophets nor by dreams. This is why I've called you, so that you can let me know what to do." [16] Sh'mu'el said, "Why ask me, if ADONAI has left you and become your enemy? [17] ADONAI has done for himself what he foretold through me — ADONAI has torn the kingdom out of your hands and given it to your fellow countryman David, [18] because you didn't obey what ADONAI said and execute his furious anger toward 'Amalek. That's why ADONAI is doing this to you today. [19] ADONAI is giving Isra'el as well as yourself over into the power of the P'lishtim, and tomorrow you and your sons will be with me. ADONAI will hand over Isra'el's army to the power of the P'lishtim."

[20] Sha'ul immediately fell full length on the ground and became terribly frightened because of what Sh'mu'el had said. He had no strength left in him, for he had eaten nothing all that day and night. [21] The woman approached Sha'ul, saw that he was panic-stricken and said to him, "Here, your servant listened to

what you said; I put my life in my hands and did what you requested me to do. ²² Now therefore, please, you listen to what your servant says: let me put a little food in front of you; then eat, so you will have some strength when you go on your way." ²³ But he refused and said, "I won't eat." Then his servants, together with the woman, urged him; and he heeded what they said. He got up off the ground and sat on the bed. ²⁴ The woman had a fattened calf in the house; she hurried to slaughter it; then she took flour, kneaded it and baked *matzah* with it. ²⁵ She served it to Sha'ul and his servants, and they ate. Afterwards, they got up; and they went away that night.

29 ¹ The P'lishtim gathered all their army together at Afek, while Isra'el's army pitched camp by the spring in Yizre'el. ² The leaders of the P'lishtim were passing by with their hundreds and thousands; David and his men were bringing up the rear with Akhish. ³ The chiefs of the P'lishtim asked, "What are these Hebrews doing here?" Akhish answered the chiefs of the P'lishtim, "This is David, who was a servant of Sha'ul, king of Isra'el. He's been with me now for well over a year, and I haven't found anything wrong with him between the time he deserted to me and now." ⁴ But the chiefs of the P'lishtim became angry and said to him, "Have the man return and go back to the place you set aside for him. Don't let him go into battle with us, because on the battlefield he might become our enemy. What better way could there be for him to get reconciled with his lord than by [cutting off] the heads of our men? ⁵ This is David! They used to dance and sing about him,

'Sha'ul has killed his thousands,
but David his tens of thousands'!"

⁶ So Akhish summoned David and said to him, "As ADONAI lives, you have been upright; and I myself would be more than pleased to have you go on campaign with me; because I haven't found anything wrong with you between the day you arrived and now. However, the chiefs don't trust you. ⁷ Therefore, now, go on back; and go in peace, so as not to do what appears bad to the chiefs of the P'lishtim. ⁸ David said to Akhish, "But what have I done? What have you found in your servant during the time I've been with you that disqualifies me from going and fighting against the enemies of my lord the king?" ⁹ Akhish answered David, "I know that you are as good, from my point of view, as an angel of God. Nevertheless, the chiefs of the P'lishtim have said, 'He is not to go up with us to the battlefield.' ¹⁰ So get up early in the morning with the servants of your lord who came with you; and as soon as you are up and it gets light, leave." ¹¹ David got up early in the morning, he and his men, to leave and go back into the land of the P'lishtim; while the P'lishtim continued up to Yizre'el.

30 ¹ Three days later, when David and his men arrived in Ziklag, they found that the 'Amaleki had raided the Negev and Ziklag. They had sacked Ziklag and burned it down; ² and they had taken captive the women and everyone there, great and small. They hadn't killed anyone but had carried them off as they went on their way. ³ So when David and his men arrived at the city, there it was, burned down, with their wives, sons and daughters taken captive. ⁴ Then David and the people with him cried aloud until they had no more power to cry. ⁵ David's two wives had been taken captive — Achino'am from Yizre'el and Avigayil the widow of Naval from Karmel.

⁶ David was in serious trouble: the people were talking about stoning him to death, because all the people were in such deep grief, each man over his sons and daughters. But David strengthened himself in ADONAI his God. ⁷ David said to Avyatar the *cohen*, the son of Achimelekh, "Please bring the ritual vest here to me." Avyatar brought the vest to David. ⁸ Then David consulted ADONAI. He asked, "Should I go in pursuit of these raiders? Will I catch up with them?" And [ADONAI] answered him, "Go in pursuit, because you will overtake them and recover everyone and everything." ⁹ So David went, he and the six hundred men with him. They came to *Vadi* B'sor, where those who were to stay behind waited. ¹⁰ Then David continued in pursuit with four hundred men, while two hundred too exhausted to cross *Vadi* B'sor stayed behind.

¹¹ They found an Egyptian in the countryside and brought him to David. They gave him some bread to eat and water to drink; ¹² they also gave him a lump of dried figs and two bunches of raisins. After eating, he revived; because he hadn't eaten anything or drunk any water for three days and nights. ¹³ David asked him, "To whom do you belong, and where are you from?" He answered, "I'm an Egyptian boy, the slave of an 'Amaleki. My master abandoned me three days ago, because I got sick. ¹⁴ We raided the Negev of the K'reti, the Negev of Y'hudah and the Negev of Kalev; and we burned down Ziklag." ¹⁵ David asked him, "Will you lead me down to this raiding party?" He said, "If you will swear by God to me that you won't kill me or hand me back to my master, I will lead you down to the raiders." ¹⁶ He led them down, and there they were, spread out all over the ground, eating, drinking and celebrating how much spoil they had taken from the territory of the P'lishtim and the territory of Y'hudah. ¹⁷ David attacked them from dawn until the evening of the next day. Not one of them escaped, except for 400 young men who jumped on camels and got away. ¹⁸ David recovered all that the 'Amaleki had taken; he also rescued his two wives. ¹⁹ They found nothing missing, big or little — not sons, not daughters, not plundered goods or anything else they had taken — David brought it all back. ²⁰ David took all the flocks and herds and drove them ahead of their own livestock, announcing, "This is David's spoil."

²¹ David came to where the two hundred men were who had been too exhausted to follow him, whom they had let stay at *Vadi* B'sor. They came out to meet David and the people with him. When David approached them he greeted them. ²² But some of the men who had gone with David were evil men, scoundrels; and they said, "They didn't go with us, so we're not giving them any of the property we've recovered. Each man can take his wife and children and leave." ²³ Then David said, "No, my brothers, don't do this with the goods ADONAI has given us. He protected us, and he handed the raiding party over to us. ²⁴ Anyhow, no one agrees with you about this. No, the share of someone who stays with the equipment will be the same as the share of someone who goes out and fights — they will share equally." ²⁵ It has been that way from that day on; he established it as a ruling for Isra'el to this day.

²⁶ When David came to Ziklag, he sent some of the spoil to the leaders of Y'hudah who were his friends with a note, "Here is a present for you from the spoil of the enemies of ADONAI." ²⁷ He sent such gifts

to those in Beit-El,
to those in Ramot,
to those in Yatir,
²⁸ to those in 'Aro'er,
to those in Sifmot,
to those in Esht'moa,
²⁹ to those in Rakhal,
to those in Yerachme'eli,
to those in the cities of the Keni,
³⁰ to those in Hormah,
to those in Kor-'Ashan,
to those in 'Atakh,
³¹ to those in Hevron,

and to all the places where David and his men had frequently visited.

31 ¹ Now the P'lishtim pressed their attack on Isra'el. The men of Isra'el fled before the P'lishtim, leaving their dead on Mount Gilboa. ² The P'lishtim pursued and overtook Sha'ul and his sons; and the P'lishtim killed Y'honatan, Avinadav and Malkishua, the sons of Sha'ul. ³ The fighting went hard against Sha'ul; then the archers overtook and wounded him, so that he was in agony. ⁴ Sha'ul said to his armor-bearer, "Draw your sword and run me through with it. Otherwise these uncircumcised men will come, run me through and make sport of me." But his armor-bearer refused, he was too frightened. So Sha'ul took his sword and fell on it. ⁵ When his armor-bearer saw that Sha'ul was dead, he too fell on his own sword and died with him. ⁶ Thus Sha'ul, his three sons, his armor-bearer and all his men died that same day together.

⁷ When the men of Isra'el who were on the other side of the valley and those who were on the far side of the Yarden saw that the men of Isra'el had fled and that Sha'ul and his sons were dead, they abandoned the cities and fled; then the P'lishtim came and lived in them.

⁸ The following day, when the P'lishtim came to strip the dead, they found Sha'ul and his three sons lying dead on Mount Gilboa. ⁹ They cut off his head, stripped off his armor and sent these all over the territory of the P'lishtim to carry the news to the temples of their idols and to the people. ¹⁰ Then they put his armor in the temple for the 'ashtarot and fastened his body to the wall of Beit-Sh'an.

¹¹ When the people living in Yavesh-Gil'ad heard what the P'lishtim had done to Sha'ul, ¹² all their warriors set out, traveling all night. They took the body of Sha'ul and the bodies of his sons off the wall of Beit-Sh'an, returned to Yavesh and burned them there. ¹³ Then they took their bones, buried them under the tamarisk tree in Yavesh and fasted seven days.

Sh'mu'el Bet
2 SAMUEL

1 ¹ Sha'ul had died, and David had been two days in Ziklag after returning from the slaughter of the 'Amaleki. ² On the third day, there came a man from Sha'ul's camp with his clothes torn and earth on his head. He approached David, fell to the ground and prostrated himself. ³ David said to him, "Where are you coming from?" "I escaped from the camp of Isra'el," he replied. ⁴ "Tell me, please, how did things go?" asked David. "The people have fled the battle," he answered, "and many of them are wounded or dead. Sha'ul and Y'honatan his son are dead too." ⁵ David asked the young man who had told him this, "How do you know that Sha'ul and Y'honatan his son are dead?" ⁶ The young man who had told him said, "I happened to be on Mount Gilboa when I saw Sha'ul leaning on his spear. The chariots and cavalry were bearing down on him. ⁷ He looked behind him, saw me and called to me. I answered, 'Here I am.' ⁸ He said to me, 'Who are you?' and I answered, 'I'm an 'Amaleki' ⁹ He said to me, 'I'm in agony, and I'm going to die, but I'm still alive. So please, stand next to me; and kill me.' ¹⁰ So I stood next to him and killed him, because I was sure he was so badly wounded that he couldn't live. I took the crown that was on his head and the bracelet on his arm and have brought them here to my lord."

¹¹ Then David took hold of his clothes and tore them, and likewise all the men who were with him. ¹² They wailed and cried, and they fasted until evening for Sha'ul, for Y'honatan his son, for Adonai's people and for the house of Isra'el; because they had fallen by the sword.

¹³ David said to the young man who had told him, "Where are you from?" He answered, "I'm the son of a [resident] foreigner, an 'Amaleki." ¹⁴ David asked him, "How is it that you weren't afraid to raise your hand to destroy Adonai's anointed?" ¹⁵ David called one of his young men and said, "Go over to him, and kill him." The man struck him down, and he died. ¹⁶ David said to him, "Your blood is on your own head. Your own mouth convicted you when you said, 'I killed Adonai's anointed.'"

¹⁷ Then David pronounced this lament over Sha'ul and over Y'honatan his son, ¹⁸ in order to teach the people of Y'hudah [not to underestimate] archery (the lament has been written down in the book of Yashar):

¹⁹   "Your glory, Isra'el, lies dead on your high places!
        How the heroes have fallen!
²⁰   Don't speak of it in Gat;
        don't proclaim it in the streets of Ashkelon;
        then the daughters of the P'lishtim won't rejoice,
        the daughters of the uncircumcised won't gloat.

²¹   "Mountains of Gilboa — may there be on you
        no dew, no rain, no fields with good crops;

because there the shields of the heroes were dishonored,
the shield of Sha'ul was no longer rubbed with oil.

²² "From the blood of the dead, from the flesh of heroes,
the bow of Y'honatan did not retreat
or the sword of Sha'ul return unsatisfied.

²³ Sha'ul and Y'honatan, loved and gracious while alive,
were not separated even in death;
they were swifter than eagles, stronger than lions.

²⁴ "Daughters of Isra'el, weep over Sha'ul!
He clothed you luxuriously in scarlet
and put gold jewelry on your clothing.

²⁵ "How the heroes have fallen in the heat of battle,
Y'honatan killed on your high places!

²⁶ I grieve for you, my brother Y'honatan,
you meant so much to me!
Your love for me was deeper
than the love of women.

²⁷ How the heroes have fallen
and the weapons of war perished"

2 ¹ After this, David consulted ADONAI; he asked, "Should I go up into any of the cities of Y'hudah?" ADONAI said to him, "Go up." David asked, "Where should I go up?" He said, "To Hevron." ² So David went up there with his two wives Achino'am from Yizre'el and Avigayil the widow of Naval from Karmel. ³ David brought the men up with him, each with his household; and they lived in the cities of Hevron. ⁴ Then the men of Y'hudah came, and there they anointed David king over the house of Y'hudah. They informed David that the men of Yavesh-Gil'ad were the ones who had buried Sha'ul. ⁵ So David sent messengers to the men of Yavesh-Gil'ad with this message: "May you be blessed by ADONAI, because you showed this kindness to your lord, Sha'ul, and buried him. ⁶ Now may ADONAI show kindness and truth to you; and I too will show you favor because you have done this. ⁷ Be strong, and be brave. Sha'ul your lord is dead, but the house of Y'hudah have anointed me king over them."

⁸ Avner the son of Ner, commander of Sha'ul's army, had taken Ish-Boshet the son of Sha'ul, brought him over to Machanayim, ⁹ and made him king over Gil'ad, the Ashuri, Yizre'el, Efrayim, Binyamin and all Isra'el. ¹⁰ Ish-Boshet the son of Sha'ul was forty years old when he began to rule over Isra'el, and he ruled for two years. But the house of Y'hudah followed David. ¹¹ David was king in Hevron over the house of Y'hudah for seven years and six months.

¹² Avner the son of Ner and the servants of Ish-Boshet the son of Sha'ul went out from Machanayim to Giv'on; ¹³ while Yo'av the son of Tz'ruyah and David's servants also went out; and they met together by the pool at Giv'on. One group sat down on one side of the pool and the other on the other side. ¹⁴ Avner said to Yo'av, "If it's all right with you, let's have the young men get up and fight it out between

themselves, while we watch." Yo'av said, "Yes, let them." ¹⁵ So they got up and paired off, twelve for Binyamin and Ish-Boshet the son of Sha'ul, and twelve of David's servants. ¹⁶ Each one grabbed his partner by the head and drove his sword into his side, so that they fell down together. For this reason that place was named Helkat-Hatzurim [field of blades]; it is in Giv'on. ¹⁷ The battle that day was very fierce; Avner and the men of Isra'el were beaten by David's servants.

¹⁸ The three sons of Tz'ruyah were there, Yo'av, Avishai and 'Asah'el. 'Asah'el was as fleet-footed as a gazelle in an open field. ¹⁹ 'Asah'el chased Avner, going straight for him, veering neither right nor left. ²⁰ Avner looked behind him and asked, "Is that you, 'Asah'el?" "Yes, it is," he answered. ²¹ Avner said to him, "Turn off to your right or your left, catch one of the young men and take his armor." But 'Asah'el wouldn't turn aside and kept following him. ²² Avner said again to 'Asah'el, "Turn aside and stop following me! Why should I kill you? If I did, how could I look your brother Yo'av in the eye?" ²³ But he still refused to turn aside; so Avner stabbed him in the groin with the back end of the spear, so that the shaft protruded behind him. He fell down and died on the spot. Everyone who came to the place where 'Asah'el lay dead stopped there.

²⁴ Yo'av and Avishai continued in pursuit of Avner; the sun went down when they arrived at Amah Hill, across from Giach along the Giv'on Desert road. ²⁵ The people of Binyamin gathered themselves together into a phalanx behind Avner and stood on top of a hill. ²⁶ Then Avner called out to Yo'av, "Must the sword go on devouring forever? Don't you know that in the end it can produce only bitterness? How long will it be, then, before you tell the people to quit pursuing their brothers?" ²⁷ Yo'av said, "As God lives, if you hadn't said something, there is no doubt that the people would have kept following their brothers all night long." ²⁸ Then Yo'av sounded the *shofar*, and with that the people halted. They stopped pursuing Isra'el, and they stopped fighting.

²⁹ Avner and his men went through the 'Aravah all that night; they crossed the Yarden, went through all of Bitron and arrived at Machanayim. ³⁰ Yo'av returned from following Avner. When he brought the troops together for review, nineteen of David's servants were missing, along with 'Asah'el. ³¹ But David's servants had killed 360 of Avner's men of Binyamin. ³² They took 'Asah'el and buried him in his father's tomb in Beit-Lechem. Then Yo'av and his men marched all night, so that they reached Hevron at daybreak.

3 ¹ The war between the house of Sha'ul and the house of David dragged on, but David grew stronger, while the house of Sha'ul became weaker.

² Sons were born to David in Hevron. His firstborn was Amnon, whose mother was Achino'am from Yizre'el; ³ his second, Kil'av, whose mother was Avigayil the widow of Naval from Karmel; the third, Avshalom, whose mother was Ma'akhah the daughter of Talmai king of G'shur; ⁴ the fourth, Adoniyah the son of Haggit; the fifth, Sh'fatyah the son of Avital; ⁵ and the sixth, Yitre'am, whose mother was 'Eglah David's wife. These were born to David in Hevron.

⁶ During the war that was going on between the house of Sha'ul and the house of David, Avner strengthened his position in the house of Sha'ul. ⁷ Sha'ul had had a concubine named Ritzpah, the daughter of Ayah; and [Ish-Boshet] challenged Avner: "Why did you go and sleep with my father's concubine?" ⁸ These words

of Ish-Boshet's enraged Avner. "What am I," he shouted, "[that you treat me with such contempt]? A dog's head in Y'hudah? Till this moment I have shown only kindness to the house of Sha'ul your father, and to his brothers and to his friends; and I haven't handed you over to David. Yet you choose today to pick a fight with me over this woman! ⁹ May God bring terrible curses on Avner and worse ones yet if I don't accomplish what ADONAI swore to David— ¹⁰ to transfer the kingdom from the house of Sha'ul and set up the throne of David over Isra'el and Y'hudah, from Dan all the way to Be'er-Sheva!" ¹¹ Ish-Boshet couldn't answer Avner a word, because he was afraid of him.

¹² Avner immediately sent envoys to David with this message: "Who is going to control the land? If you make yourself my ally, I will use my power to bring all Isra'el over to you." ¹³ David sent this reply: "Very well, I will be your ally— on one condition: you will not come into my presence unless at the same time you bring with you Mikhal Sha'ul's daughter." ¹⁴ David sent messengers to say to Ish-Boshet the son of Sha'ul, "Give me back my wife Mikhal. I betrothed her to myself for 100 foreskins of the P'lishtim." ¹⁵ Ish-Boshet sent and took her from her husband Palti'el the son of Layish. ¹⁶ Her husband went with her, crying as he went, and followed her to Bachurim. But when Avner told him, "Go back," he returned.

¹⁷ Then Avner conferred with the leaders of Isra'el. He said, "In the past, you wanted David to be king over you. ¹⁸ So now, do it. For ADONAI has said of David, 'Through my servant David I will rescue my people Isra'el from the power of the P'lishtim and from the power of all their enemies.'" ¹⁹ Avner also spoke with the people of Binyamin.

Then Avner went to Hevron and reported to David everything that had been agreed to by Isra'el and the house of Binyamin. ²⁰ When Avner came to David in Hevron he brought twenty men with him. David held a feast for Avner and his men. ²¹ Avner said to David, "I must get up and go to gather all Isra'el to my lord the king, so that they can make a covenant with you. Then you will be able to rule over everything your heart desires." David sent Avner off, giving him safe conduct.

²² Just then David's men and Yo'av returned from a raid, bringing a lot of plunder with them. But Avner was not with David in Hevron, because he had sent him off under safe conduct. ²³ When Yo'av and all his army had arrived, Yo'av was told, "Avner the son of Ner came to the king, but he sent him off, and he has left under safe conduct." ²⁴ Yo'av went to the king and said, "What have you done? Here, Avner came to you, and you sent him away, and now he's gone! Why? ²⁵ You know Avner the son of Ner — he came only to deceive you, to learn what campaigns you're planning and to find out everything you're doing!"

²⁶ After leaving David, Yo'av sent messengers after Avner, and they brought him back from the water cistern at Sirah without David's knowledge. ²⁷ Upon Avner's return to Hevron, Yo'av took him aside into the space between the outer and inner city gates as if to speak with him privately; and there he struck him in the groin, so that he died— thus avenging the death of 'Asah'el his brother.

²⁸ Afterwards, when David heard of it, he said, "I and my kingdom are forever innocent of the death of Avner the son of Ner. ²⁹ Let it fall on the head of Yo'av and all his father's family. May Yo'av's family always have someone with a hemorrhage or tzara'at, or who has to walk with a cane, or who dies by the sword or who lacks food." ³⁰ Thus Yo'av and Avishai his brother killed Avner, because he had killed their brother 'Asah'el during the battle in Giv'on. ³¹ But David said to Yo'av and all those with him,

"Tear your clothes, put on sackcloth, and mourn over Avner." King David himself walked behind the body as it was carried. ³² They buried Avner at Hevron; the king wept aloud at Avner's grave, and all the people wept. ³³ The king sang this lament over Avner:

> "Should Avner have died like a thug?
³⁴   Your hands weren't tied, your feet weren't fettered;
>   you fell like one who falls at the hands
>   of criminals."

Then all the people wept over him more than ever.

³⁵ All the people came to David and tried to make him eat some bread while it was still daytime; but David swore, "May God bring terrible curses on me and worse ones yet if I taste bread or anything else until the sun goes down." ³⁶ All the people took note of this, and it pleased them; whatever the king did pleased all the people. ³⁷ So that day, all the people and all Isra'el understood that the king had had no part in the killing of Avner the son of Ner. ³⁸ The king said to his servants, "You realize that a leader, a great man, has fallen today in Isra'el. ³⁹ Even though I have just been anointed king, I feel weak today; and these men, the sons of Tz'ruyah, are too brutal for me. May ADONAI repay the criminal as his crime deserves!"

4 ¹ When Ish-Boshet the son of Sha'ul heard that Avner had died in Hevron, his courage failed; and all Isra'el became alarmed. ² Sha'ul's son had two men who were captains of raiding parties, one called Ba'anah and the other Rekhav, sons of Rimmon the Be'eroti, of the people of Binyamin (for Be'erot is counted as part of Binyamin, ³ even though the Be'erotim fled to Gittayim and have lived as foreigners there to this day). ⁴ Now Y'honatan the son of Sha'ul's had a son, and he was lame in both legs. He had been five years old when the news about Sha'ul and Y'honatan came from Yizre'el. His nurse had gathered him up and fled; but as she was hurrying to get away, he fell and became lame. His name was M'fivoshet. ⁵ The sons of Rimmon the Be'eroti, Rekhav and Ba'anah went and arrived during the heat of the day at the home of Ish-Boshet as he was taking his afternoon rest. ⁶ They went right into the house, as if they were coming to get wheat, and stabbed him in the groin; then Rekhav and Ba'anah his brother escaped. ⁷ They entered the house as he lay on his bed in his bedroom, stabbed him and killed him; then they beheaded him, took his head and fled all night along the road through the 'Aravah. ⁸ They brought the head of Ish-Boshet to David in Hevron and said to the king, "Here is the head of Ish-Boshet the son of Sha'ul your enemy, who wanted to take your life. Today ADONAI has taken revenge on Sha'ul and his son for the sake of my lord the king."

⁹ But David answered Rekhav and Ba'anah his brother, the sons of Rimmon the Be'eroti, "As ADONAI lives, who has rescued me from every kind of difficulty, ¹⁰ when someone told me, 'Here, Sha'ul is dead,' thinking to himself that he was bringing good news, I didn't reward him for his news but seized him and killed him in Ziklag. ¹¹ How much more, when criminals have killed an innocent man in his own house on his own bed, shouldn't I hold you responsible for his death and rid the earth of you?" ¹² David then gave the order to his men, and they put them to death, cutting off their hands and feet and hanging them up next to the pool at Hevron. But they took the head of Ish-Boshet and buried it in Avner's grave at Hevron.

5 ^{1} Then all the tribes of Isra'el came to David in Hevron and said, "Here, we are your own flesh and bone. ^{2} In the past, when Sha'ul was king over us, it was you who led Isra'el's military campaigns; and A*DONAI* said to you, 'You will shepherd my people Isra'el, and you will be chief over Isra'el.'" ^{3} So all the leaders of Isra'el came to the king in Hevron, and King David made a covenant with them in Hevron in the presence of A*DONAI*. Then they anointed David king over Isra'el. ^{4} David was thirty years old when he began his rule, and he ruled forty years. ^{5} In Hevron he ruled over Y'hudah seven years and six months; then in Yerushalayim he ruled thirty-three years over all Isra'el and Y'hudah.

^{6} The king and his men went to Yerushalayim to attack the Y'vusi, the inhabitants of that region. They taunted David, "You won't get in here! Even the blind and the lame could fend you off!" — in other words, they were thinking, "David will never get in here." ^{7} Nevertheless, David captured the stronghold of Tziyon, also known [now] as the City of David. ^{8} What David said on that day was, "In order to attack the Y'vusi, you have to climb up [from the spring outside the city] through the water tunnel. Then you can do away with those [so-called] 'lame and blind'" (whom David despises — hence the expression, "The 'blind and lame' keep him from entering the house").

^{9} David lived in the stronghold and called it the City of David. Then David built up the city around it, starting at the Millo [earth rampart] and working inward. ^{10} David grew greater and greater, because A*DONAI* the God of Armies was with him. ^{11} Hiram king of Tzor sent envoys to David with cedar logs, and with them were carpenters and stonemasons; and they built David a palace. ^{12} David then knew that A*DONAI* had set him up as king over Isra'el and increased his royal power for the sake of his people.

^{13} David took for himself more concubines and wives in Yerushalayim after coming from Hevron, so that still more sons and daughters were born to David. ^{14} Here are the names of those born to him in Yerushalayim: Shamua, Shovav, Natan, Shlomo, ^{15} Yivchar, Elishua, Nefeg, Yafia, ^{16} Elishama, Elyada and Elifelet.

^{17} When the P'lishtim heard that David had been anointed king over Isra'el, all the P'lishtim went up in search of David. On learning of it, David went down to the stronghold. ^{18} The P'lishtim came and deployed in the Refa'im Valley. ^{19} David consulted A*DONAI*, asking, "Should I attack the P'lishtim? Will you hand them over to me?" A*DONAI* answered David, "Attack; I will certainly hand the P'lishtim over to you." ^{20} So David went to Ba'al-P'ratzim and defeated them there. He said, "A*DONAI* has broken through my enemies for me like a river breaking through its banks." This is why he called the place Ba'al-P'ratzim [Lord of breaking through]. ^{21} The P'lishtim had left their idols there, so David and his men took them away.

^{22} The P'lishtim came up again and deployed in the Refa'im Valley. ^{23} When David consulted A*DONAI*, he said, "Don't attack! Circle behind them, and engage them opposite the balsam trees. ^{24} When you hear the sound of marching in the tops of the balsam trees, advance; because then A*DONAI* has gone out ahead of you to defeat the army of the P'lishtim." ^{25} David did exactly as A*DONAI* had ordered him to do and pursued his attack on the P'lishtim from Geva all the way to Gezer.

6 ^{1} Again David summoned all the picked troops of Isra'el, 30,000 men. ^{2} Then David, taking along the entire force he had with him then, set out for Ba'alei-Y'hudah to bring up from there the ark of God, which bears the Name, the name of A*DONAI*-

Tzva'ot enthroned above the *k'ruvim*. ³ They set the ark of God on a new cart and brought it out of the house of Avinadav on the hill, with 'Uzah and Achyo, the sons of Avinadav, driving the new cart. ⁴ They led it from the house of Avinadav on the hill, with the ark of God; Achyo walked in front of the ark. ⁵ David and the whole house of Isra'el celebrated in the presence of ADONAI with all kinds of musical instruments made of cypress-wood, including lyres, lutes, tambourines, rattles and cymbals.

⁶ When they arrived at Nakhon's threshing-floor, the oxen stumbled; and 'Uzah put out his hand to steady the ark of God. ⁷ But ADONAI's anger blazed up against 'Uzah, and God struck him down on the spot for his offense, so that he died there by the ark of God. ⁸ It upset David that ADONAI had broken out against 'Uzah; that place has been called Peretz-'Uzah [breaking-out of 'Uzah] ever since. ⁹ David was frightened of ADONAI that day; he asked, "How can the ark of ADONAI come to me?" ¹⁰ So David would not bring the ark of ADONAI into the City of David; rather, David took it over to the house of 'Oved-Edom the Gitti. ¹¹ The ark of ADONAI stayed in the house of 'Oved-Edom the Gitti for three months; and ADONAI blessed 'Oved-Edom and all his household.

¹² King David was told, "ADONAI has blessed the house of 'Oved-Edom and everyone who belongs to him, thanks to the ark of God." So David went and joyously brought the ark of God up from the house of 'Oved-Edom into the City of David. ¹³ When those bearing the ark of ADONAI had gone only six paces, he sacrificed an ox and a fattened sheep. ¹⁴ Then David danced and spun around with abandon before ADONAI, wearing a linen ritual vest. ¹⁵ So David and all the house of Isra'el brought up the ark of ADONAI with shouting and the sound of the *shofar*. ¹⁶ As the ark of ADONAI entered the City of David, Mikhal the daughter of Sha'ul, watching from the window, saw King David leaping and spinning before ADONAI; and she was filled with contempt for him.

¹⁷ They brought the ark of ADONAI in and put it in its place inside the tent that David had set up for it. David offered burnt offerings and peace offerings before ADONAI. ¹⁸ When David had finished offering the burnt offering and peace offerings, he blessed the people in the name of ADONAI-Tzva'ot. ¹⁹ Then he distributed to all the people of Isra'el, to everyone there, both men and women, a loaf of bread, a portion of meat and a raisin cake, after which the people all left for their homes.

²⁰ When David returned to bless his household, Mikhal the daughter of Sha'ul came out to meet him and said, "Such honor the king of Isra'el earned for himself today — exposing himself before his servants' slave-girls like some vulgar exhibitionist!" ²¹ David answered Mikhal, "In the presence of ADONAI— who chose me over your father and over everyone in his family to make me chief over ADONAI's people, over Isra'el — I will celebrate in the presence of ADONAI! ²² I will make myself still more contemptible than that, and I will be humiliated in my own eyes, but those slave-girls you mentioned will honor me!" ²³ Mikhal the daughter of Sha'ul remained childless until the day she died.

7 ¹ After the king had been living in his palace awhile and ADONAI had given him rest from all his surrounding enemies, ² the king said to Natan the prophet, "Here, I'm living in a cedar-wood palace; but the ark of God is kept in a tent!" ³ Natan said to the king, "Go, do everything that is in your heart, for ADONAI is with you."

[4] But that same night the word of *Adonai* came to Natan: [5] "Go and tell my servant David that this is what *Adonai* says: 'You are going to build me a house to live in? [6] Since the day I brought the people of Isra'el out of Egypt until today, I never lived in a house; rather, I traveled in a tent and a tabernacle. [7] Everywhere I traveled with all the people of Isra'el, did I ever speak a word to any of the tribes of Isra'el, whom I ordered to shepherd my people Isra'el, asking, "Why haven't you built me a cedar-wood house?"'

[8] "Therefore say this to my servant David that this is what *Adonai-Tzva'ot* says: 'I took you from the sheep-yards, from following the sheep, to make you chief over my people, over Isra'el. [9] I have been with you wherever you went; I have destroyed all your enemies ahead of you; and I am making your reputation great, like the reputations of the greatest people on earth. [10] I will assign a place to my people Isra'el; I will plant them there, so that they can live in their own place without being disturbed any more. The wicked will no longer oppress them, as they did at the beginning, [11] and as they did from the time I ordered judges to be over my people Isra'el; instead, I will give you rest from all your enemies.

"'Moreover, *Adonai* tells you that *Adonai* will make you a house. [12] When your days come to an end and you sleep with your ancestors, I will establish one of your descendants to succeed you, one of your own flesh and blood; and I will set up his rulership. [13] He will build a house for my name, and I will establish his royal throne forever. [14] I will be a father for him, and he will be a son for me. If he does something wrong, I will punish him with a rod and blows, just as everyone gets punished; [15] nevertheless, my grace will not leave him, as I took it away from Sha'ul, whom I removed from before you. [16] Thus your house and your kingdom will be made secure forever before you; your throne will be set up forever.'" [17] Natan told David all of these words and described this entire vision.

[18] Then David went in, sat before *Adonai* and said, "Who am I, *Adonai Elohim*; and what is my family, that has caused you to bring me this far? [19] Yet in your view, *Adonai Elohim*, even this was too small a thing; so you have even said that your servant's dynasty will continue on into the distant future. This is [indeed] a teaching for a man, *Adonai Elohim* — [20] what more can David say to you? For you know your servant intimately, *Adonai Elohim*. [21] It is for the sake of your word and in accordance with your own heart that you have done all this greatness and revealed it to your servant. [22] Therefore, you are great, *Adonai*, God; for there is no one like you, and there is no God besides you — everything we have heard confirms that. [23] Who can be compared with your people, with Isra'el? What other nation on earth did God set out to redeem and make into a people for himself? You made yourself a reputation by doing for your land things that even for you are great and terrifying, for the sake of your people whom you redeemed for yourself from Egypt and from other nations and from their gods. [24] You set up your people for yourself as your people forever; and you, *Adonai*, became their God. [25] So now, *Adonai*, God, establish forever the word you have spoken to your servant and his house; do what you have promised. [26] May your name be magnified forever, so that it will be said, '*Adonai-Tzva'ot* is God over Isra'el, and the dynasty of your servant David will be set up in your presence.' [27] You, *Adonai-Tzva'ot*, God of Isra'el, have disclosed to your servant, 'I will build you a house.' This is why your servant has the courage to pray this prayer to you. [28] Now, *Adonai Elohim*, you alone are God; your words are truth; and you have made this wonderful promise to your servant.

²⁹ So may it please you to bless the family of your servant and thereby cause it to continue forever in your presence. For you, *Adonai Elohim*, have said it. May your servant's family be blessed forever by your blessing."

8 ¹ Some time afterwards, David attacked the P'lishtim and subdued them; David took Meteg-Amah out of the hands of the P'lishtim. ² He also defeated Mo'av; making them lie down on the ground, he measured them with a length of cord; for every two lengths to be put to death he designated one length to be kept alive. The people of Mo'av became subjects of David and paid tribute. ³ David, on his way to establish his dominion as far as the Euphrates River, also defeated Hadad'ezer the son of Rechov king of Tzovah. ⁴ David captured 1,700 horsemen and 20,000 foot soldiers. He reserved enough horses for 100 chariots and disabled the rest. ⁵ When people of Aram from Dammesek came to the aid of Hadad'ezer king of Tzovah, David killed 22,000 men of Aram. ⁶ Then David put garrisons among the people of Aram in Dammesek; Aram became subject to David and paid tribute. *Adonai* gave victory to David wherever he went. ⁷ David took the gold shields which Hadad'ezer's servants were wearing and brought them to Yerushalayim. ⁸ From Betach and Berotai, cities of Hadad'ezer, King David took a great quantity of bronze.

⁹ When To'i king of Hamat heard that David had defeated Hadad'ezer's entire army, ¹⁰ To'i sent Yoram his son to King David to greet and congratulate him on fighting and defeating Hadad'ezer, for Hadad'ezer had been at war with To'i. Yoram brought with him articles of silver, articles of gold and articles of bronze, ¹¹ which King David dedicated to *Adonai*, along with the silver and gold that he dedicated from all the nations he conquered — ¹² Aram, Mo'av, the people of 'Amon, the P'lishtim, 'Amalek, and the spoil taken from Hadad'ezer son of Rechov, king of Tzovah. ¹³ David gained more fame on returning from killing 18,000 men from Aram in the Salt Valley. ¹⁴ David stationed garrisons in Edom; he put garrisons throughout all of Edom, and all the people of Edom became subject to him. *Adonai* gave victory to David wherever he went.

¹⁵ David ruled over all Isra'el; David administered law and justice for all his people. ¹⁶ Yo'av the son of Tz'ruyah was commander of the army, Y'hoshafat the son of Achilud was chief adviser, ¹⁷ Tzadok the son of Achituv and Achimelekh the son of Evyatar were *cohanim*, S'rayah was secretary, ¹⁸ B'nayahu the son of Y'hoyada was in charge of the K'reti and P'leti [serving as the king's bodyguards], and David's sons were *cohanim*.

9 ¹ David inquired, "Is there anyone still alive from the family of Sha'ul, to whom, for Y'honatan's sake, I can show kindness?" ² In Sha'ul's household there had been a servant named Tziva, and they summoned him to David. The king asked him, "Are you Tziva?" and he answered, "At your service." ³ The king said, "Is there anyone still alive from the family of Sha'ul, to whom I can show God's grace?" Tziva said to the king, "There is still Y'honatan's son with the lame legs." ⁴ The king said to him, "Where is he?" and Tziva answered, "He's there in the house of Makhir the son of 'Ammi'el, in Lo-D'var." ⁵ King David sent and took him from the house of Makhir the son of 'Ammi'el in Lo-D'var. ⁶ M'fivoshet the son of Y'honatan, the son of Sha'ul, came to David, fell on his face and prostrated himself. David said, "M'fivoshet!" and he answered, "Here is your servant!" ⁷ David said to him, "Don't be afraid, for I am determined to be kind to you for the sake of Y'honatan your father. I will restore to you all the land of Sha'ul your [grand]father, and you will always eat at my table." ⁸ He prostrated himself and said, "What is your servant that makes you pay such attention to a dead dog like me?" ⁹ The king called to Tziva, Sha'ul's servant, and said to him, "I have given everything Sha'ul and his family owned to your master's [grand]son. ¹⁰ You are to work the land for him, you, your sons and your slaves. Harvest the crops, so that your master's [grand]son will have food to feed his family; but M'fivoshet your master's [grand]son will always eat at my table." Tziva had fifteen sons and twenty slaves. ¹¹ Tziva said to the king, "Your servant will do everything my lord the king commands his servant, although M'fivoshet has been eating at my table as one of the king's descendants." ¹² M'fivoshet had a young son whose name was Mikha. Everyone living in Tziva's house was a servant of M'fivoshet. ¹³ But M'fivoshet lived in Yerushalayim; he always ate at the king's table, and he was lame in both legs.

10 ¹ Some time later, when the king of the people of 'Amon died, his son Hanun became king in his place. ² David said, "I will show grace to Hanun the son of Nachash, as his father showed grace to me." So David sent his servants to pass him a message of comfort concerning his father.

David's servants entered the territory of the people of 'Amon; ³ but the leaders of the people of 'Amon said to Hanun their lord, "Do you really think David is honoring your father by sending people to comfort you? Hasn't David actually sent his servants to you in order to look the city over, reconnoiter it and overthrow it?" ⁴ So Hanun took David's servants, shaved off half their beards, cut off their clothes halfway up, at their buttocks, and then sent them away. ⁵ On hearing how they had been treated, David sent a delegation to meet them, because the men had been deeply humiliated. The king said, "Stay in Yericho until your beards have grown back, and then return."

⁶ Aware that they were utterly abhorrent to David, the people of 'Amon sent and hired 20,000 Aram foot soldiers from Beit-Rechov and Tzovah, the king of Ma'akhah with 1,000 men, and 12,000 soldiers from Tov. ⁷ When David heard of it, he sent Yo'av with his entire army of trained soldiers.

⁸ The army of 'Amon came out and went into battle formation at the entrance to the city gate; the men of Aram from Tzovah and Rechov and the men of Tov and Ma'akhah were by themselves in the open countryside. ⁹ When Yo'av saw that he would be fighting on two fronts, ahead and behind, he chose the best troops of Isra'el to deploy against Aram; ¹⁰ while the rest of the army he put under the command of Avishai his brother to deploy against the army of 'Amon. ¹¹ He said, "If Aram is too strong for me, you help me; but if the army of 'Amon is too strong for you, then I will come and help you. ¹² Take courage, and let's be strong for the sake of our people and the cities of our God. May ADONAI do what seems good to him."

¹³ So Yo'av and the people with him went to battle Aram, and they fled before him. ¹⁴ When the people of 'Amon saw that Aram had fled, they likewise fled before Avishai and retreated into the city. Yo'av returned from the people of 'Amon and went to Yerushalayim.

¹⁵ When Aram saw that Isra'el had gotten the better of them, they gathered themselves together. ¹⁶ Hadad'ezer sent and brought out the people of Aram who lived beyond the [Euphrates] River. They came to Heilam with Shovakh the commander

of Hadad'ezer's army at their head. ^{17} It was reported to David; so he gathered all Isra'el together, crossed the Yarden and came to Heilam. Aram deployed themselves against David and fought him. ^{18} But Aram fled before Isra'el; David killed 700 chariot-drivers and 40,000 horsemen from Aram, and he struck Shovakh the commander of their army, so that he died there. ^{19} When all Hadad'ezer's vassal kings saw that they had been defeated by Isra'el, they made peace with Isra'el and became their subjects. So Aram was afraid to help the people of 'Amon any more.

11 ^{1} In the spring, at the time when kings go out to war, David sent out Yo'av, his servants who were with him and all Isra'el. They ravaged the people of 'Amon and laid siege to Rabbah. But David stayed in Yerushalayim. ^{2} Once, after his afternoon nap, David got up from his bed and went strolling on the roof of the king's palace. From the roof he saw a woman bathing, who was very beautiful. ^{3} David made inquiries about the woman and was told that she was Bat-Sheva the daughter of Eli'am, the wife of Uriyah the Hitti. ^{4} David sent messengers to get her, and she came to him, and he went to bed with her (for she had been purified from her uncleanness). Then she returned to her house. ^{5} The woman conceived; and she sent a message to David, "I am pregnant."

^{6} David sent this order to Yo'av: "Send me Uriyah the Hitti." Yo'av sent Uriyah to David. ^{7} When Uriyah had come to him, David asked him how Yo'av was doing, how the people were feeling and how the war was going. ^{8} Then David said to Uriyah, "Go down to your house and wash your feet." Uriyah left the king's palace and was followed by a present of food from the king. ^{9} But Uriyah slept at the door of the king's palace with all the servants of his lord and didn't go down to his house. ^{10} When they told David, "Uriyah didn't go down to his house," David said to Uriyah, "Haven't you just arrived from a journey? Why didn't you go down to your house?" ^{11} Uriyah answered David, "The ark, Isra'el and Y'hudah stay in tents; and my lord Yo'av and the servants of my lord are camping in the countryside. So should I go into my house to eat and drink and go to bed with my wife? As surely as you live, I will not do such a thing!" ^{12} David said to Uriyah, "Stay here today also; tomorrow I will let you leave." So Uriyah stayed in Yerushalayim that day and the following day. ^{13} David summoned him, ate and drank with him, and got him drunk. But in the evening he went out and lay on his bed with his lord's servants and did not go down to his house.

^{14} In the morning David wrote a letter to Yo'av and sent it with Uriyah. ^{15} In the letter he wrote, "Put Uriyah on the front lines of the fiercest fighting; then pull back from him, so that he will be wounded and killed." ^{16} So while Yo'av had the city under siege, he assigned Uriyah to the place where he knew the toughest defenders were. ^{17} The men of the city went out and fought Yo'av; a number of people fell, including some of David's servants, with Uriyah the Hitti among the dead.

^{18} Yo'av sent a message to David reporting all the news concerning the war, ^{19} and he instructed the messenger, "When you have finished telling the king all the news about the war, ^{20} he may become angry and ask you, 'Why did you get so close to the city to fight? Didn't you know they would shoot from the wall? ^{21} Didn't you think about the person who struck Avimelekh the son of Yerubeshet, that a woman threw an upper millstone down on him from the wall, so that he died at Tevetz? Why did you go so near the wall?' If he says this, tell him, 'Your servant Uriyah is dead also.'" ^{22} So the messenger left, and on arrival he told David all that Yo'av had sent him to say. ²³ The messenger said to David, "The men were overpowering us and came out after us into the countryside. But we chased them back all the way to the entrance of the city gate. ²⁴ The archers shot at your servants from the wall; some of the king's servants are dead; also your servant Uriyah the Hitti is dead." ²⁵ David said to the messenger, "Tell Yo'av, 'Don't let this matter get you down — the sword devours in one way or another. Intensify your battle against the city, and overthrow it.' And encourage him."

²⁶ When the wife of Uriyah heard that Uriyah her husband was dead, she mourned her husband. ²⁷ When the mourning was over, David sent and took her home to his palace, and she became his wife and bore him a son.

But ADONAI saw what David had done as evil.

12 ¹ ADONAI sent Natan to David. He came and said to him, "In a certain city there were two men, one rich, the other poor. ² The rich man had vast flocks and herds; ³ but the poor man had nothing, except for one little ewe lamb, which he had bought and reared. It had grown up with him and his children; it ate from his plate, drank from his cup, lay on his chest — it was like a daughter to him. ⁴ One day a traveler visited the rich man, and instead of picking an animal from his own flock or herd to cook for his visitor, he took the poor man's lamb and cooked it for the man who had come to him."

⁵ David exploded with anger against the man and said to Natan, "As ADONAI lives, the man who did this deserves to die! ⁶ For doing such a thing, he has to pay back four times the value of the lamb — and also because he had no pity."

⁷ Natan said to David, "You are the man.

"Here is what ADONAI, the God of Isra'el says: 'I anointed you king over Isra'el. I rescued you from the power of Sha'ul. ⁸ I gave you your master's house and your master's wives to embrace. I gave you the house of Isra'el and the house of Y'hudah. And if that had been too little, I would have added to you a lot more.

⁹ "'So why have you shown such contempt for the word of ADONAI and done what I see as evil? You murdered Uriyah the Hitti with the sword and took his wife as your own wife; you put him to death with the sword of the people of 'Amon.

¹⁰ Now therefore, the sword will never leave your house — because you have shown contempt for me and taken the wife of Uriyah the Hitti as your own wife.' ¹¹ Here is what ADONAI says: 'I will generate evil against you out of your own household. I will take your wives before your very eyes and give them to your neighbor; he will go to bed with your wives, and everyone will know about it. ¹² For you did it secretly, but I will do this before all Isra'el in broad daylight.'"

¹³ David said to Natan, "I have sinned against ADONAI."

Natan said to David, "ADONAI also has taken away your sin. You will not die. ¹⁴ However, because by this act you have so greatly blasphemed ADONAI, the child born to you must die." ¹⁵ Then Natan returned to his house.

ADONAI struck the child that Uriyah's wife had borne to David, and it became very ill. ¹⁶ David prayed to God on behalf of the child; David fasted, then came and lay all night on the ground. ¹⁷ The court officials got up and stood next to him trying to get him off the ground, but he refused, and he wouldn't eat food with them. ¹⁸ On the seventh day, the child died. The servants of David were afraid to tell him that the child was dead, because they said, "While the child was still alive, we spoke to him, and he didn't listen to us; if we tell him now that the child is dead, he may do himself some harm." ¹⁹ But when David saw his servants whispering to each other, he suspected that the child was dead. David asked his servants, "Is the child dead?" and they answered, "He is dead."

²⁰ Then David got up off the ground, washed, anointed himself and changed his clothes. He went into the house of ADONAI and worshipped; then he went to his own palace; and when he asked for food, they served it to him; and he ate. ²¹ His servants asked him, "What are you doing? You fasted and wept for the child while it was alive; but now that the child is dead, you get up and eat food!" ²² He answered, "While the child was still alive, I fasted and wept; because I thought, 'Maybe ADONAI will show his grace to me and let the child live.' ²³ But now that he's dead, why should I fast? Can I bring him back again? I will go to him, but he will not return to me."

²⁴ David comforted his wife Bat-Sheva, came to her and went to bed with her; she gave birth to a son and named him Shlomo. ADONAI loved him ²⁵ and sent through Natan the prophet to have him named Y'didyah [loved by God], for ADONAI's sake.

²⁶ Yo'av fought against Rabbah of the people of 'Amon and took the royal city. ²⁷ Yo'av sent people to David with this message: "I have fought against Rabbah and captured its water supply. ²⁸ Therefore, assemble the rest of the people; lay siege to the city; and capture it. Otherwise, I will capture the city; and it will be named after me!" ²⁹ David assembled all the people, went to Rabbah, fought against it and captured it. ³⁰ He took the crown off Malkam's head; it weighed sixty-six pounds, with its gold and precious stones; and it was placed on David's head. He carried off great quantities of spoil from the city. ³¹ In addition, he expelled the people who were in it and set them to work with saws, iron harrows and iron axes, or had them cross over to work in the brick factory. This is what he did to all the cities of the people of 'Amon. Then David and all the people returned to Yerushalayim.

13 ¹ Now Avshalom the son of David had a beautiful sister named Tamar. Some time after the previous events, Amnon the son of David fell in love with her. ² Amnon became so obsessed with his sister Tamar that he became ill, for she was a virgin, and Amnon thought it would be impossible to approach her. ³ But Amnon had a friend named Yonadav the son of Shim'ah David's brother; and Yonadav was a very shrewd fellow. ⁴ He asked him, "Why, son of the king, are you growing thinner every day? Won't you tell me?" Amnon answered him, "I'm in love with Tamar, my brother Avshalom's sister." ⁵ Yonadav said to him, "Lie down on your bed, and pretend you're sick. When your father comes to see you, say to him, 'Please let my sister Tamar come and give me food to eat, and have her prepare the food where I can watch. I'll eat what she serves me.'" ⁶ So Amnon lay down and pretended he was sick. When the king came to see him, Amnon said to the king, "Please let my sister Tamar come and make me a couple of cakes here where I can watch, and I'll eat what she serves me." ⁷ David sent this instruction home to Tamar: "Go now to your brother Amnon's house, and prepare him some food." ⁸ So Tamar went to her brother Amnon's house; he was lying down. She took dough, kneaded it, made cakes while he watched, and baked the cakes. ⁹ Then she took the pan and turned them out in front of him, but he refused to eat. Amnon said, "Have everyone leave me"; and everyone left him. ¹⁰ Amnon said to Tamar, "Bring the food into the room, so that I can have you serve me. Tamar took the cakes she had made and brought them into the room to Amnon her brother.

[11] But when she brought them near, so that he could eat, he grabbed her and said to her, "Come to bed with me, my sister." [12] "No, my brother," she answered him, "don't force me! Things like this aren't done in Isra'el; don't behave so disgracefully! [13] Where could I go with such shame? And as for you, you will be regarded as one of Isra'el's vulgar brutes. Now therefore, please! Speak to the king, because he won't keep me from you." [14] However, he wouldn't listen to her; and since he was stronger than she, he overpowered her and raped her. [15] But then he was filled with utter revulsion for her — his hatred of her was even greater than the love he had had for her before. Amnon said to her, "Get up, and get out of here!" [16] "No," she objected, "because throwing me out like this is an even worse thing than what you've already done to me!" But he wouldn't listen to her; [17] he called his personal servant and said, "Get rid of this woman for me! Throw her out, and lock the door after her!" [18] She was wearing a long-sleeved robe (this was how they used to dress the king's daughters who were virgins). His servant took her out and locked the door after her. [19] Tamar put ashes on her head, tore her long-sleeved robe that she was wearing, laid her hand on her head and went off, crying aloud as she went.

[20] Avshalom her brother said to her, "Has Amnon your brother been with you? But now, my sister, keep quiet; because he's your brother. Don't take the matter to heart." But Tamar remained desolate in her brother Avshalom's house.

[21] When King David heard about all these things, he became very angry. [22] As for Avshalom, he refused to say a word to Amnon, either good or bad; for Avshalom hated Amnon for having raped his sister Tamar.

[23] Two years later, when Avshalom had sheep-shearers in Ba'al-Hatzor, near Efrayim, Avshalom invited all the king's sons. [24] Avshalom went to the king and said, "Your servant has sheep-shearers; please let the king and his servants come along with your servant." [25] The king replied to Avshalom, "No, my son, let's not all go — we don't want to be a burden to you." Avshalom pressed him, but he wouldn't go; however he gave him his blessing. [26] Then Avshalom said, "If you won't go, then please let my brother Amnon go with us." The king said to him, "Why should he go with you?" [27] But Avshalom kept pressing him, so he let Amnon and all the king's sons go with him.

[28] Avshalom ordered his servants, "Pay close attention: when Amnon is in high spirits from drinking wine, and I say to you, 'Kill Amnon,' then strike him down. Don't be afraid — I'm the one ordering you to do it — but take courage, and be bold." [29] Avshalom's servants did to Amnon as Avshalom had ordered. At this, all the king's sons jumped up, mounted their mules and fled.

[30] While they were on their way, the news came to David that Avshalom had killed all the king's sons, and not one of them was left alive. [31] The king got up, tore his clothes and lay on the ground, while all his servants stood by with their clothes torn too. [32] But then Yonadav, the son of Shim'ah, David's brother, spoke up; he said, "My lord shouldn't think they have killed all the young men, the king's sons. Only Amnon is dead; for Avshalom has meant to do this ever since the day he raped his sister Tamar. [33] So my lord the king shouldn't take it as seriously as if all the king's sons are dead; only Amnon is dead."

[34] However, Avshalom took flight. The young man keeping watch looked up and saw many people coming along the road behind him on the hillside. [35] Yonadav said to the king, "Here, the king's sons have come; it's just as your servant said."

³⁶ The moment he finished speaking, the king's sons came, cried out and wept; and the king too, with all his servants, cried out in great pain. ³⁷ Avshalom fled and went to Talmai the son of 'Ammihud, king of G'shur. David mourned for his son every day. ³⁸ So Avshalom fled, went to G'shur and stayed there three years. ³⁹ But as King David became reconciled to the death of his son Amnon, he was increasingly filled with longing to see Avshalom.

14 ¹ Yo'av the son of Tz'ruyah perceived that the king missed Avshalom; ² so Yo'av sent to T'koa, brought from there a clever woman and said to her, "Please, pretend you're a mourner. Put on mourning clothes, and don't anoint yourself with oil, but appear to be a woman who has mourned for the dead a long time. ³ Go in to the king and speak to him in this fashion—" and then Yo'av told her just what to say. ⁴ When the woman of T'koa spoke to the king, she fell down with her face to the ground, prostrating herself, and said, "King, help!" ⁵ The king said to her, "What's the trouble?" She answered, "I'm a widow. After my husband died, ⁶ my two sons were out in the field; and they got into a fight with each other. There was no one to separate them, and one hit the other and killed him. ⁷ Now the whole family has come against me, your servant; they're saying, 'Hand over the one who hit his brother, so that we can put him to death for killing his brother.' They want to destroy the heir as well and thus quench my one remaining coal; then my husband will have neither name nor survivor anywhere on earth."

⁸ The king said to the woman, "Go back home; I myself will decide what to do about you." ⁹ The woman of T'koa said to the king, "My lord, king, let the guilt be on me and my father's family; the king and his throne be guiltless." ¹⁰ The king answered, "If anyone says anything to you, bring him to me; and he won't bother you any more." ¹¹ "Please," she said, "let the king swear by ADONAI your God that the blood avengers won't do any more destroying, so they won't destroy my son." He said, "As ADONAI lives, not one of your son's hairs will fall to the ground."

¹² Then the woman said, "Please allow your servant to say something else to my lord the king." "Go on," he replied. ¹³ The woman said, "Why is it, then, that you have produced a situation exactly like this against God's people? By saying what you have said, the king has virtually incriminated himself—in that the king does not bring home again the son he banished. ¹⁴ For we will all die someday; we'll be like water spilled on the ground that can't be gathered up again; and God makes no exception for anyone. The king should think of some way to keep the son he banished from being forever an outcast. ¹⁵ Now the reason I came to speak about this matter to my lord the king is that the people were intimidating me; so your servant said, 'I will speak now to the king; maybe the king will do what his servant is asking. ¹⁶ For the king will listen and rescue his servant from the hands of those who would destroy me and my son together from our share of God's inheritance.' ¹⁷ Then your servant said, 'Please let my lord the king say something that will give me relief; for my lord the king is like an angel of God in discerning good from bad—and may ADONAI your God be with you.'"

¹⁸ The king then answered the woman: "I'm going to ask you a question, and please don't hide anything from me." The woman said, "Let my lord the king now speak." ¹⁹ The king asked, "Did Yo'av put you up to this?" The woman answered, "As you live, my lord the king, when my lord the king speaks, no one can avoid the

issue by turning either right or left. Yes, it was your servant Yo'av who had me do this, and he put in my mouth every word you have heard your servant say. ^{20} Your servant Yo'av did this in order to bring about some change in the situation. But my lord is wise, he has the wisdom of an angel of God when it comes to understanding anything going on in the land."

^{21} The king said to Yo'av, "All right, I am granting this request. Go, and bring back young Avshalom." ^{22} Yo'av fell to the ground on his face, prostrating himself, and blessed the king; Yo'av said, "Today your servant knows that I have won your favor, my lord, king, because the king has done what your servant requested." ^{23} Then Yo'av got up, went to G'shur and brought Avshalom to Yerushalayim. ^{24} However, the king said, "Let him return to his own house, but he is not to appear in my presence." So Avshalom returned to his own house and did not appear before the king.

^{25} Now in all Isra'el there was no one more praised for his beauty than Avshalom — there was no defect on him from the sole of his foot to the crown of his head. ^{26} He would cut his hair only once a year, at the end of the year; and the only reason he cut it then was because it weighed him down. He weighed the hair from his head at 200 *shekel*s (using the royal weight) [about five pounds]. ^{27} To Avshalom were born three sons and one daughter, whose name was Tamar; she was a beautiful woman.

^{28} Avshalom lived two years in Yerushalayim without appearing before the king. ^{29} Then Avshalom summoned Yo'av, planning to send him to the king; but he refused to come to him. He summoned him a second time, but he still wouldn't come. ^{30} So he said to his servants, "See, Yo'av's field is close to mine, and he has barley there; go, and set it on fire." Avshalom's servants set the field on fire. ^{31} Then Yo'av got up, went to Avshalom at his house and asked him, "Why did your servants set my field on fire?" ^{32} Avshalom answered Yo'av, "Look, I sent a message to you to come here, so that I could send you to the king to ask, 'Why did I come from G'shur? It would have been better for me if I had stayed there. So now, let me appear before the king; and if I'm guilty of anything, he can kill me.'"

^{33} Yo'av went to the king and told him; and when he had called for Avshalom, he went to the king and prostrated himself with his face to the ground before the king. Then the king kissed Avshalom.

15 ^{1} Some time later, Avshalom prepared himself a chariot and horses, with fifty men to run ahead of him. ^{2} He would get up early and stand by the road leading to the city gate; and if someone had a case that was to come before the king for judgment, Avshalom would call to him and ask, "What city are you from?" and he would answer, "Your servant is from the such-and-such tribe in Isra'el." ^{3} Avshalom would say to him, "Look, your cause is good and just; but the king hasn't deputized anyone to hear your case." ^{4} Then Avshalom would continue, "Now if I were made judge in the land, anyone with a suit or other cause could come to me, and I would see that he gets justice!" ^{5} Moreover, whenever any man came close to prostrate himself before him, he would put out his hand, take hold of him and kiss him. ^{6} This is how Avshalom behaved toward anyone in Isra'el who came to the king for judgment, and in this way Avshalom stole the hearts of the people of Isra'el.

^{7} At the end of forty years, Avshalom said to the king, "Please let me go to Hevron and fulfill the vow I made to Adonai. ^{8} Your servant made a vow while I was staying at G'shur in Aram to the effect that if Adonai would bring me back to

Yerushalayim, then I would serve ADONAI." ⁹ The king said to him, "Go in peace." So he set out and went to Hevron.

¹⁰ But Avshalom sent spies through all the tribes of Isra'el to say, "The moment you hear the sound of the *shofar*, then start proclaiming, 'Avshalom is king in Hevron.'" ¹¹ With Avshalom went 200 men from Yerushalayim who had been invited; they went innocently, knowing nothing about the scheme. ¹² Avshalom sent for Achitofel the Giloni, David's counselor, to come from his town Giloh and be with him while offering the sacrifices. The conspiracy grew strong, because the number of people favoring Avshalom kept increasing.

¹³ A messenger came to David saying, "The men of Isra'el have aligned themselves with Avshalom." ¹⁴ David said to all his servants with him in Yerushalayim, "Get up! We must flee! Otherwise none of us will escape from Avshalom. Hurry, and leave; or he will soon overtake us, attack us and put the city to the sword." ¹⁵ The king's servants said to the king, "Here, your servants are ready to do whatever my lord the king decides." ¹⁶ So the king set out, and all his household after him. The king left ten women who were concubines to care for the palace. ¹⁷ The king set out with all the people after him, but they waited at the last house ¹⁸ for all his servants to pass by him in review; all the K'reti and P'leti and all the Gittim (600 men who had accompanied him from Gat) passed in review before the king.

¹⁹ Then the king said to Ittai the Gitti, "You too? Why are you going with us? Go back, and stay with your king, since you are both a foreigner and in exile from your own place. ²⁰ You arrived only yesterday; should I ask you to wander around with us? There's no telling where I may go. Return, and take your kinsmen back with you. Grace and truth be with you." ²¹ But Ittai answered the king, "As ADONAI lives, and as my lord the king lives, wherever my lord the king may be, whether for death or for life, your servant will be there too." ²² "Go, move along," said David to Ittai; and Ittai the Gitti moved on, accompanied by all his men and the little ones with him.

²³ The whole country wept and wailed as all the people left. When the king crossed *Vadi* Kidron, all the people crossed, too, heading toward the desert road. ²⁴ Tzadok also came, accompanied by all the *L'vi'im* bearing the ark for the covenant of God. They set the ark of God down, but Evyatar went up until all the people had finished leaving the city. ²⁵ The king said to Tzadok, "Carry the ark of God back into the city. If I find favor in ADONAI's sight, he will bring me back and show me both it and the place where it is kept. ²⁶ But if he says, 'I am displeased with you,' then — here I am; let him do to me whatever seems good to him." ²⁷ The king then said to Tzadok the *cohen*, "Do you see? Return to the city in peace, your two sons with you — Achima'atz your own son and Y'honatan the son of Evyatar. ²⁸ I will wait on the desert plains until a message with new information comes from you." ²⁹ So Tzadok and Evyatar carried the ark of God back to Yerushalayim and stayed there.

³⁰ David continued up the road to the Mount of Olives, weeping as he went up, head covered and barefoot; and all the people with him had their heads covered and wept as they went up. ³¹ One of them told David, "Achitofel is among the conspirators with Avshalom." David said, "ADONAI, please! Turn Achitofel's advice into foolishness!"

³² When David reached the top of the ascent, where it was customary to worship God, Hushai the Arki came to meet him with his tunic torn and earth on his head. ³³ David said to him, "If you go on with me, you will become a burden to me.

³⁴ But if you go back to the city and tell Avshalom, 'King, I will be your servant; just as I was your father's servant in the past, so I will now be your servant' — then you will be able to frustrate Achitofel's advice for me. ³⁵ You have Tzadok and Evyatar the *cohanim* there with you. So whatever you hear from the king's house, you tell to Tzadok and Evyatar the *cohanim*. ³⁶ Their two sons, Achima'atz the son of Tzadok and Y'honatan the son of Evyatar, are there with them; through them send me everything you hear." ³⁷ So Hushai David's friend came into the city when Avshalom was about to enter Yerushalayim.

16 ¹ When David had gone a little past the summit, there was Tziva, the servant of M'fivoshet, who met him with a pair of donkeys saddled and on them 200 loaves of bread, 100 bunches of raisins, 100 pieces of summer fruit and a skin of wine. ² The king said to Tziva, "What do you mean by these?" Tziva replied, "The donkeys are for the king's household to ride on; the bread and summer fruit are for the young men to eat; and the wine is for those who collapse in the desert to drink." ³ The king asked, "Where is your master's [grand]son?" Tziva answered the king, "He's staying in Yerushalayim, because he said, 'Today the house of Isra'el will restore my father's kingship to me.'" ⁴ The king said to Tziva, "Everything that belongs to M'fivoshet is now yours." Tziva answered, "I bow down before you; may I find favor in your sight, my lord, king."

⁵ When King David arrived at Bachurim, there came out from there a man from Sha'ul's family named Shim'i the son of Gera; and he came out pronouncing curses ⁶ and throwing stones at David and all King David's servants; even though all the people, including his bodyguard, surrounded him right and left. ⁷ When Shim'i cursed, he said, "Get out of here! Get out of here, you killer, you good-for-nothing! ⁸ ADONAI has brought back on you all the blood of the house of Sha'ul. You usurped his kingship, but ADONAI has handed over the kingdom to Avshalom your son. Now your own evil has overtaken you, because you are a man of blood!"

⁹ Avishai the son of Tz'ruyah said to the king, "Why allow this dead dog to curse my lord the king? Just let me go over and remove his head!" ¹⁰ The king said, "Do you sons of Tz'ruyah and I have anything in common? Let him curse. If ADONAI tells him, 'Curse David,' who has the right to ask, 'Why are you doing it?'" ¹¹ David then said to Avishai and all his servants, "Look, my own son, who came from my own body, seeks my life. So how much more now this Binyamini! Let him alone; and let him curse, if ADONAI told him to. ¹² Maybe ADONAI will notice how I'm treating him, and ADONAI will reward me with good instead of his curses." ¹³ So David and his men went on their way, while on the opposite hillside Shim'i kept pace with him, cursing, throwing stones and flinging dust as he went. ¹⁴ The king and all the people with him arrived exhausted, so he rested there.

¹⁵ Meanwhile Avshalom and all the people, the men of Isra'el, came to Yerushalayim; Achitofel was with him. ¹⁶ Hushai the Arki, David's friend, came to Avshalom and said to him, "Long live the king! Long live the king!" ¹⁷ Avshalom asked Hushai, "Is this how you show kindness to your friend? Why didn't you go with your friend?" ¹⁸ Hushai replied, "No, but whomever ADONAI and this people and all the men of Isra'el choose, his I will be; and with him I will stay. ¹⁹ Moreover, whom should I serve? Shouldn't I serve in the presence of his son? Just as I have served in your father's presence, so will I be in your presence."

²⁰ Avshalom said to Achitofel, "Give your advice as to what we should do." ²¹ Achitofel answered Avshalom, "Go in, and sleep with your father's concubines, the ones he left to take care of the palace. All Isra'el will hear that your father utterly despises you, and this will strengthen the position of all those who are on your side." ²² So they set up a tent for Avshalom on the roof of the palace; and Avshalom went in to sleep with his father's concubines in the sight of all Isra'el. ²³ In those days Achitofel's advice was regarded as highly as if someone had sought out the word of God; it was this way with Achitofel's advice both to David and to Avshalom.

17 ¹ Achitofel said to Avshalom, "Let me now choose 12,000 men, and I will pursue David tonight. ² I'll fall on him unexpectedly when he's tired and powerless. I'll frighten him, all the people with him will flee, and I'll attack only the king. ³ Then I will bring back to you all the people; and when they have all returned, except the one you are seeking, all the people will be at peace." ⁴ What he said pleased Avshalom and all the leaders of Isra'el.

⁵ Then Avshalom said, "Now call also Hushai the Arki, and let's give equal hearing to what he has to say." ⁶ When Hushai appeared before Avshalom, Avshalom said to him, "Achitofel has said such-and-such. Should we do what he says? If not, you tell us." ⁷ Hushai said to Avshalom, "The advice Achitofel has given this time is not good. ⁸ You know," continued Hushai, "that your father and his men are powerful men, and that they are as bitter as a bear deprived of her cubs in the wild. Moreover, your father is a military man, and he won't camp with the rest of the people — ⁹ right now he's hidden in a pit or somewhere. So what will happen is this: when they begin their attack, and whoever hears about it says, 'A slaughter is taking place among Avshalom's followers,' ¹⁰ then even the strongest among them, someone whose courage is that of a lion, will completely collapse! For all Isra'el knows that your father is a powerful man, and those with him are powerful men. ¹¹ Rather, I advise that you summon all Isra'el to come to you, from Dan to Be'er-Sheva, numbering as many as sand grains on the seashore; and then you go to battle, yourself. ¹² In this way we'll come upon him wherever he is, and we'll fall on him as the dew falls on the ground; of him and all the men with him we won't leave even one alive. ¹³ If he withdraws into a city, then all Isra'el will bring up ropes to that city, and we will drag it into the riverbed until not even a pebble is left." ¹⁴ Avshalom and all the men of Isra'el said, "The advice of Hushai the Arki is better than the advice of Achitofel" — for ADONAI had determined to frustrate the good advice of Achitofel, so that ADONAI could bring disaster on Avshalom.

¹⁵ Then Hushai said to Tzadok and Evyatar the *cohanim*, "Achitofel gave such-and-such advice to Avshalom and the leaders of Isra'el, but I advised so and so. ¹⁶ Now therefore send quickly and tell David, "Don't stay tonight in the desert plains; but, whatever it takes, move on from there! Otherwise, the king and all the people with him will be engulfed." ¹⁷ Y'honatan and Achima'atz were staying at 'Ein-Rogel; a female servant was to go and tell them, and they in turn were to go and tell King David — for it would not do to have them seen entering the city. ¹⁸ But a boy saw them and told Avshalom; so both of them took off quickly and came to the house of a man in Bachurim who had a cistern in his courtyard; and they went down into it. ¹⁹ His wife spread a covering over the cistern's opening and scattered drying grain on it, so that nothing showed. ²⁰ Avshalom's servants came to the woman at the

house and asked, "Where are Achima'atz and Y'honatan?" The woman answered them, "They've crossed the stream." After searching and not finding them, they returned to Yerushalayim. ²¹ After they had left, the two climbed out of the cistern and went and told King David, "Get up and cross the river, because Achitofel has given such-and-such advice against you." ²² David and all the people with him got up and crossed the Yarden; by dawn every one of them had crossed the Yarden. ²³ When Achitofel saw that his advice was not being followed, he saddled his donkey, set out, and went home to his own city. After setting his house in order, he hanged himself; he died and was buried in his father's tomb. ²⁴ David had reached Machanayim by the time Avshalom and all the men of Isra'el crossed the Yarden. ²⁵ Avshalom had put 'Amasa in charge of the army in place of Yo'av. 'Amasa was the son of a man whose name was Yitra the Isra'eli, who had had sexual relations with Avigal the daughter of Nachash, Tz'ruyah's sister and Yo'av's mother. ²⁶ Isra'el and Avshalom pitched camp in the land of Gil'ad.

²⁷ After David had arrived in Machanayim, Shovi the son of Nachash, from Rabbah of the people of 'Amon; Machir the son of 'Ammi'el from Lo-D'var and Barzillai the Gil'adi from Roglim ²⁸ brought beds, basins, clay pots, wheat, barley, flour, roasted grain, beans, lentils, roasted millet, ²⁹ honey, curdled milk, sheep and cheese made of cow's milk for David and the people with him to eat; because they said, "These people are hungry, tired and thirsty from the desert."

18 ¹ David took a census of the people who were with him and appointed over them commanders of thousands and of hundreds. ² Then David dispatched the people, a third of them under the command of Yo'av, a third under Avishai the son of Tz'ruyah, Yo'av's brother, and a third under Ittai the Gitti; and the king said to the people, "I will also go out with you, myself." ³ But the people replied, "Don't go out; because if we flee, they won't care about us. Even if half of us die, they won't care about us. But you are worth ten thousand of us; so it is better now that you stay in the city and be ready if we need help." ⁴ The king answered them, "I will do whatever you think best." So the king stood at the side of the gate, while all the people went out by hundreds and by thousands. ⁵ The king gave orders to Yo'av, Avishai and Ittai, "For my sake, deal gently with young Avshalom." All the people were listening when the king gave all the commanders this order concerning Avshalom.

⁶ So the people went out into the field against Isra'el; the battle took place in the forest of Efrayim. ⁷ The people of Isra'el were defeated there by David's servants; there was a terrible slaughter that day of 20,000 men. ⁸ For the battle there was spread all over the countryside; the forest devoured more people that day than did the sword.

⁹ Avshalom happened to meet some of David's servants. Avshalom was riding his mule, and as the mule walked under the thick branches of a big terebinth tree, his head got caught in the terebinth, so that he was left hanging between earth and sky, as the mule went on from under him. ¹⁰ Someone saw it and told Yo'av, "I saw Avshalom hanging in a terebinth." ¹¹ Yo'av asked the man who told him, "Here now, you saw it; so why didn't you strike him to the ground then and there? I would have had to give you ten pieces of silver and a belt besides." ¹² The man replied to Yo'av, "Even if I were to get a thousand pieces of silver, I still wouldn't raise my hand against the son of the king! After all, while we were listening, the king ordered you,

Avishai and Ittai, 'Be careful that no one touches young Avshalom.' ¹³ Or, if I had pretended that I didn't know, the king would have known otherwise anyway; and you wouldn't have interceded for me either." ¹⁴ Yo'av said, "I can't waste time arguing with you!" He took three darts in his hand and rammed them through Avshalom's heart while he was still alive, hanging from the terebinth. ¹⁵ Then Yo'av's ten young armor-bearers surrounded Avshalom, struck him and killed him.

¹⁶ Yo'av sounded the *shofar*, and the people returned from pursuing Isra'el, because Yo'av held back the troops. ¹⁷ They took Avshalom and threw him into a big pit in the forest and piled a big heap of stones over him. All Isra'el fled, each one to his tent. ¹⁸ In his own lifetime Avshalom had taken and raised for himself the pillar which stands in the King's Valley; because he said, "I don't have a son to preserve the memory of my name." So he named the pillar after himself, and it's called Avshalom's Monument to this day.

¹⁹ Then Achima'atz the son of Tzadok said, "Let me run now and bring news to the king that ADONAI has judged in his favor by releasing him from his enemies." ²⁰ Yo'av said to him, "You are not to be the one to bring the news today; you can convey news another day; but today you will not bring news, because the king's son is dead." ²¹ Then Yo'av said to the Ethiopian, "Go, tell the king what you saw." The Ethiopian bowed to Yo'av, then ran off. ²² But Achima'atz the son of Tzadok said again to Yo'av, "Come what may, please let me also run after the Ethiopian." Yo'av answered, "Why do you want to run, my son? You won't receive any reward for bringing the news." ²³ "I don't care — whatever happens, I want to run." So he said to him, "Run." Then Achima'atz ran by the road through the desert flats and outran the Ethiopian.

²⁴ David was sitting between the two gates. A watchman went up to the roof of the gate and out onto the wall, raised his eyes, looked, and saw there a man running by himself. ²⁵ The watchman cried out and told the king. The king said, "If he's alone, he has good news to tell." As he ran along and came close, ²⁶ the watchman saw another man running and called to the gatekeeper, "There's another man running by himself." The king said, "He too must have good news." ²⁷ The watchman said, "The first one runs like Achima'atz the son of Tzadok." The king said, "He's a good man, he comes with good news."

²⁸ Achima'atz called to the king, "*Shalom*," prostrated himself before the king with his face to the ground and said, "Blessed be ADONAI your God, who has handed over the men who rebelled against my lord the king." ²⁹ The king asked, "Is everything all right with young Avshalom?" Achima'atz answered, "When Yo'av sent the king's servant and me your servant, I saw a big commotion; but I didn't know what it was." ³⁰ The king said, "Go, and stand over there." So he went and stood there. ³¹ Then up came the Ethiopian, and the Ethiopian said, "There's good news for my lord the king, for ADONAI has judged in your favor and rid you of all those who rebelled against you." ³² The king asked the Ethiopian, "Is everything all right with young Avshalom?" The Ethiopian answered, "May the enemies of my lord the king and all who rebel against you in order to harm you be as that young man is."

19 ¹⁽¹⁸:³³⁾ Trembling, the king went up to the room over the gate, weeping and crying, "Oh, my son Avshalom! My son! My son Avshalom! If only I had died instead of you! Oh, Avshalom, my son, my son!"

²⁽¹⁾ Yo'av was told, "The king is weeping, mourning for Avshalom." ³⁽²⁾ Thus the victory that day was turned into mourning for all the people, for the people heard it said that day that the king was grieving for his son; ⁴⁽³⁾ so that the people entered the city furtively that day, the way that people who are ashamed creep away when fleeing a battlefield. ⁵⁽⁴⁾ Meanwhile, the king covered his face and cried aloud, "Oh, my son Avshalom! Oh, Avshalom, my son, my son!"

⁶⁽⁵⁾ Yo'av went inside to the king and said, "Today you made all your servants feel ashamed. They saved your life today, and the lives of your sons, daughters, wives and concubines. ⁷⁽⁶⁾ But you love those who hate you and hate those who love you. Today you said that princes and servants mean nothing to you — for I can see today that it would have pleased you more if Avshalom had lived today, and we had all died! ⁸⁽⁷⁾ Now get up, go out and speak heart-to-heart with your servants. For I swear by *ADONAI* that if you don't go out, not one man will stay here with you tonight — and that will be worse for you than all the misfortunes you have suffered from your youth until now." ⁹⁽⁸⁾ So the king got up and sat in the city gateway; and when all the people were told, "Now the king is sitting in the gate," they came before the king.

Meanwhile, Isra'el had fled, each man to his tent; ¹⁰⁽⁹⁾ and throughout all the tribes of Isra'el there was dissension among all the people. They were saying, "The king delivered us from the power of our enemies, and he saved us from the power of the P'lishtim; but now he has fled the land to escape Avshalom. ¹¹⁽¹⁰⁾ However, Avshalom, whom we anointed to rule us, is dead in battle. So now, why doesn't anyone suggest bringing the king back?"

¹²⁽¹¹⁾ King David sent this message to Tzadok and Evyatar the *cohanim*: "Ask the leaders of Y'hudah, 'Why are you the last to bring the king back to his palace? The king has already heard that all Isra'el wants to return him to his palace. ¹³⁽¹²⁾ You are my kinsmen, my flesh and bone; so why are you the last to bring back the king?' ¹⁴⁽¹³⁾ Also tell 'Amasa, 'You are my flesh and bone. May God bring terrible curses on me and worse ones yet if from now on you are not permanent commander of my army instead of Yo'av.'" ¹⁵⁽¹⁴⁾ Thus he turned the hearts of all the men of Y'hudah around as if they were one man, so that they sent a message to the king, "Come back, you and all your servants!"

¹⁶⁽¹⁵⁾ The king started back and arrived at the Yarden, while Y'hudah came to Gilgal in order to meet the king and bring the king over the Yarden. ¹⁷⁽¹⁶⁾ Shim'i the son of Gera, the Binyamini from Bachurim, hurried and came down with the men of Y'hudah to meet King David. ¹⁸⁽¹⁷⁾ There were a thousand men of Binyamin with him, also Tziva the servant of the house of Sha'ul with his fifteen sons and twenty servants; and they rushed into the Yarden ahead of the king ¹⁹⁽¹⁸⁾ to ferry the king's household across and do whatever else the king wanted done. Shim'i the son of Gera fell down before the king when he was ready to cross the Yarden ²⁰⁽¹⁹⁾ and said to the king, "May my lord not hold me guilty of a crime. Don't remember the wrong your servant did on the day my lord the king left Yerushalayim. May the king not take it to heart! ²¹⁽²⁰⁾ For your servant knows that I have sinned. Therefore, look — I am the first one of all the house of Yosef to come today and go down to meet my lord the king."

²²⁽²¹⁾ Avishai the son of Tz'ruyah answered, "Shouldn't Shim'i be put to death for this? After all, he cursed *ADONAI*'s anointed ruler!" ²³⁽²²⁾ But David said, "What do I have in common with you, you sons of Tz'ruyah? Why have you become my adversaries today? Should anyone in Isra'el be put to death today? Don't I know that

today I am king over Isra'el?" ²⁴⁽²³⁾ Then the king said to Shim'i, "You will not be put to death," and the king swore it to him.

²⁵⁽²⁴⁾ M'fivoshet the son of Sha'ul came down to meet the king. He hadn't cared for his legs, trimmed his beard or washed his clothes from the day the king had left until the day he came home in peace. ²⁶⁽²⁵⁾ When he came to Yerushalayim to meet the king, the king said to him, "Why didn't you go with me, M'fivoshet?" ²⁷⁽²⁶⁾ He answered, "My lord king, my servant deceived me. I your servant had said, 'I will saddle a donkey for myself to ride on and go with the king,' since your servant is lame. ²⁸⁽²⁷⁾ But he slandered me your servant to my lord the king. However, my lord the king is like an angel of God; so do whatever seems right to you. ²⁹⁽²⁸⁾ For all my father's household deserved death at the hand of my lord the king; nevertheless you placed your servant with those who eat at your own table. I deserve nothing more; so why should I come crying any more to the king?" ³⁰⁽²⁹⁾ The king said to him, "Why speak any more about these matters of yours? I say: you and Tziva, divide the land." ³¹⁽³⁰⁾ M'fivoshet said to the king, "Indeed, let him take it all; for me it's enough that my lord the king has come home in peace."

³²⁽³¹⁾ Barzillai the Gil'adi had come down from Roglim and passed on to the Yarden with the king to bring him across the Yarden. ³³⁽³²⁾ Barzillai was a very old man, eighty years old; he had provided for the king's needs when he was staying at Machanayim; for he was a wealthy man. ³⁴⁽³³⁾ The king said to Barzillai, "Come on across with me, and I will provide for your needs with me in Yerushalayim." ³⁵⁽³⁴⁾ Barzillai said to the king, "How much longer can I live, that I should go up with the king to Yerushalayim? ³⁶⁽³⁵⁾ I am now eighty years old. Can I tell good from bad? Can your servant even taste what he eats or drinks? Can I hear the voice of men and women singing any more? Why should your servant burden my lord the king? ³⁷⁽³⁶⁾ Your servant only wants to cross the Yarden with the king; why should the king reward this so generously? ³⁸⁽³⁷⁾ Please, just let your servant go back and die in my own city, near the grave of my father and mother. But here is your servant Khimham; let him cross with my lord the king; and do for him whatever seems good to you." ³⁹⁽³⁸⁾ The king answered, "Khimham will cross with me, and I will do for him whatever seems good to you. Whatever you ask of me, I will do for you." ⁴⁰⁽³⁹⁾ So all the people crossed the Yarden; and the king crossed too. The king kissed Barzillai and blessed him; then he returned to his home. ⁴¹⁽⁴⁰⁾ The king crossed over to Gilgal, and Khimham crossed with him. All the people of Y'hudah brought the king across, as did half the people of Isra'el.

⁴²⁽⁴¹⁾ Now all the men of Isra'el came to the king and said to him, "Why have our kinsmen, the men of Y'hudah, stolen you away and brought the king and his household across the Yarden, and all David's men with him?" ⁴³⁽⁴²⁾ All the men of Y'hudah answered the men of Isra'el, "Because the king is our close relative. Why are you angry about this? Have we eaten anything at the king's expense? Has any gift been given to us?"

⁴⁴⁽⁴³⁾ The men of Isra'el answered the men of Y'hudah, "We have ten shares in the king; also we have more right in David than you. So why did you despise us? Weren't we the first to suggest bringing our king back?" But the men of Y'hudah spoke more vehemently than the men of Isra'el.

20 [1] There happened to be there a scoundrel whose name was Sheva the son of Bikhri, a Binyamini. He sounded the *shofar* and said, "We have no share in David, no inheritance in the son of Yishai; so, Isra'el, every man to his tent!" [2] All the men of Isra'el left off following David and went after Sheva the son of Bikhri. But the men of Y'hudah stuck with their king, from the Yarden to Yerushalayim.

[3] When David arrived at his palace in Yerushalayim, the king took the ten women who were his concubines, whom he had left to care for the palace, and put them under guard. He provided for their needs but never slept with them again. They were kept in confinement until the day of their death, living like widows with their husband still alive.

[4] The king said to 'Amasa, "Summon the men of Y'hudah to come to me within three days; and you, be here too." [5] 'Amasa went to summon the men of Y'hudah but took longer than the time he had been given. [6] David said to Avishai, "Sheva the son of Bikhri is going to do us more harm than Avshalom. Take your lord's servants and pursue him, so that he won't take over fortified cities and escape us." [7] With him went Yo'av's men, the K'reti, the P'leti and all the experienced soldiers; they left Yerushalayim in pursuit of Sheva the son of Bikhri.

[8] On arrival at the big rock in Giv'on, 'Amasa came to meet them. Yo'av was wearing his battle clothes, over which he had girded a belt with a sheathed sword; but as he came forward it fell out. [9] Yo'av said to 'Amasa, "Is it going well with you, my brother? Then, with his right hand, Yo'av took 'Amasa by the beard to kiss him. [10] 'Amasa took no notice of the sword in Yo'av's hand, so Yo'av stabbed him in the groin. His insides poured out on the ground, and he died without being stabbed a second time.

Yo'av and Avishai his brother continued in pursuit of Sheva the son of Bikhri. [11] One of Yo'av's young men standing by Yo'av said, "Whoever is on Yo'av's side, whoever is for David — let him follow Yo'av." [12] 'Amasa lay wallowing in his blood in the middle of the road; so that as the troops came up, they all halted there. When the man saw that all the people were standing still, he dragged 'Amasa off the road into the field and threw a cloak over him. [13] Once he had been removed from the road, all the troops went on after Yo'av, to pursue Sheva the son of Bikhri.

[14] Sheva went through all the tribes of Isra'el, to Avel and Beit-Ma'akhah, and to all the Berim; they assembled and followed him. [15] Yo'av's troops came and put him under siege in Avel of Beit-Ma'akhah — they put up a ramp in the moat against the city wall; and all the people with Yo'av battered the wall in order to bring it down. [16] Then a wise woman in the city shouted, "Listen! Listen! Please tell Yo'av, 'Come over here, so that I can speak with you.'" [17] He approached her, and the woman asked, "Are you Yo'av?" He answered, "I am." She said to him, "Listen to what your servant has to say." He answered, "I'm listening." [18] Then she said, "In the old days they used to say, 'They will ask advice at Avel'; and that would end the discussion. [19] We are among those in Isra'el who are peaceful and faithful. Why are you destroying a city and a mother in Isra'el? Why swallow up the inheritance of *ADONAI*?" [20] Yo'av answered, "Heaven forbid! Heaven forbid that I should swallow or destroy anything! [21] That's not how it is. Rather, a man from the hills of Efrayim, Sheva the son of Bikhri, has raised his hand against the king, against David. Just turn him over to me, and I will leave the city." The

woman said to Yo'av, "All right, his head will be thrown to you over the wall." ²² Then the woman went to all the people with her wise plan. They cut off the head of Sheva the son of Bikhri and threw it out to Yo'av. So he sounded the *shofar*, and they left the city, sending each man to his tent; while Yo'av returned to the king in Yerushalayim.

²³ Once again Yo'av was commander over the whole army of Isra'el, while B'nayah the son of Y'hoyada was over the K'reti and P'leti, ²⁴ Adoram was in charge of forced labor, Y'hoshafat the son of Achilud was secretary of state, ²⁵ Sh'va was recorder, Tzadok and Evyatar were *cohanim*, ²⁶ and 'Ira the Ya'iri was David's *cohen*.

21 ¹ In David's time there was a famine that lasted three years, and David consulted ADONAI. ADONAI said, "It is because of Sha'ul and his bloodstained house, because he put to death the people of Giv'on." ² The king summoned the Giv'onim and said to them— these Giv'onim were not part of the people of Isra'el but from the remnant of the Emori; and the people of Isra'el had sworn to them; but Sha'ul, in his zeal for the people of Isra'el and Y'hudah, had sought to exterminate them— ³ David said to the Giv'onim, "What should I do for you? With what should I make atonement, so that you will be able to bless ADONAI's heritage?" ⁴ The Giv'onim said to him, "Our dispute with Sha'ul can't be resolved with silver or gold; and we don't have the right to put anyone in Isra'el to death." He said, "So, what do you say that I should do for you?" ⁵ They answered the king, "The man who ruined us, who schemed against us so that we would cease to exist anywhere in Isra'el's territory— ⁶ have seven of his male descendants handed over to us, and we will put them to death by hanging before ADONAI in Giv'ah of Sha'ul, whom ADONAI chose." The king said, "I will hand them over." ⁷ But the king spared M'fivoshet, the son of Y'honatan the son of Sha'ul, because of the oath before ADONAI between David and Y'honatan the son of Sha'ul. ⁸ The king took the two sons of Ritzpah the daughter of Ayah, whom she bore to Sha'ul, Armoni and M'fivoshet; and the five sons of Mikhal the daughter of Sha'ul, whom she bore to Adri'el the son of Barzillai the Mecholati; ⁹ and handed them over to the Giv'onim, who hanged them on the hill before ADONAI. All seven died; they were put to death during the first days of the harvest season, at the beginning of the barley harvest. ¹⁰ Ritzpah the daughter of Ayah took sackcloth, spread it out toward a cliff for herself and stayed there from the beginning of the harvest until water was poured out on the bodies from the sky, not letting the birds land on them during the day or the wild animals at night.

¹¹ David was told what Ritzpah the daughter of Ayah, the concubine of Sha'ul, had done. ¹² So David went and took the bones of Sha'ul and the bones of Y'honatan his son from the men of Yavesh-Gil'ad, who had stolen them from the open square of Beit-Sh'an, where the P'lishtim had hanged them at the time the P'lishtim had killed Sha'ul at Gilboa; ¹³ and he brought up from there the bones of Sha'ul and the bones of Y'honatan his son. They also gathered the bones of those who had been hanged. ¹⁴ Then they buried the bones of Sha'ul and Y'honatan his son in the territory of Binyamin in Tzela, in the tomb of Kish his father; they did everything the king ordered. Only after that was God prevailed on to show mercy to the land.

^{15} Once again the P'lishtim made war on Isra'el. David went down with his servants and fought against the P'lishtim, but David began to get tired. ^{16} Yishbi-B'nov, one of the sons of the giant, said that he would kill David; his spear weighed seven pounds, and he was wearing new armor. ^{17} But Avishai the son of Tz'ruyah came to David's rescue by striking the P'lishti and killing him. Then David's men swore to him, "You must no longer go out with us to battle, in order not to quench the lamp of Isra'el." ^{18} A while after this there was again war with the P'lishtim, at Gov. Sibkhai the Hushati killed Saf, one of the sons of the giant. ^{19} There was more war with the P'lishtim at Gov; and Elchanan the son of Ya'arei-Orgim, the Beit-Lachmi, killed Golyat the Gitti, who had a spear with a shaft like a weaver's beam. ^{20} There was again war at Gat, where there was a belligerent man with six fingers on each hand and six toes on each foot — twenty-four in all — and he too was a son of the giant. ^{21} When he mocked Isra'el, Y'honatan the son of Shim'ah David's brother killed him. ^{22} These four were sons of the giant in Gat; they fell at the hands of David and his servants.

22 ^{1} David said the words of this song to A*DONAI* on the day A*DONAI* delivered him from the power of all his enemies and from the power of Sha'ul. ^{2} He said:

"A*DONAI* is my Rock, my fortress and deliverer,
3   the God who is my Rock, in whom I find shelter,
      my shield, the power that saves me,
      my stronghold and my refuge.
      My savior, you have saved me from violence.
4   I call on A*DONAI*, who is worthy of praise;
      and I am saved from my enemies.

5   "For death's breakers were closing over me,
      the floods of B'liya'al terrified me,
6   the ropes of Sh'ol were wrapped around me,
      the snares of death lay there before me.
7   In my distress I called to A*DONAI*;
      yes, I called to my God.
      Out of his temple he heard my voice,
      and my cry entered his ears.

8   "Then the earth quaked and shook,
      the foundations of heaven trembled.
      They were shaken because he was angry.
9   Smoke arose in his nostrils;
      and from his mouth, devouring fire,
      with coals blazing from it.
10   He lowered heaven and came down
      with thick darkness under his feet.
11   He rode on a *keruv* and flew,
      he was seen on the wings of the wind.
12   He made darkness his canopy around him,
      thick clouds in the skies dense with water.

13   From the brightness before him,
        fiery coals flamed out.

14   "*ADONAI* thundered from heaven,
        Ha'Elyon sounded his voice.
15   He sent out arrows and scattered them;
        with lightning he routed them.
16   The channels of the sea appeared,
        the foundations of the world were exposed
        at *ADONAI*'s rebuke,
        at the blast of breath from his nostrils.

17   "He sent from on high, he took me
        and pulled me out of deep water;
18   he rescued me from my powerful enemy,
        from those who hated me, for they were stronger than I.
19   They came against me on my day of calamity,
        but *ADONAI* was my support.

20   "He brought me out to an open place;
        he rescued me, because he took pleasure in me.
21   *ADONAI* rewarded me for my uprightness,
        he repaid me because my hands were clean.

22   "For I have kept the ways of *ADONAI*,
        I have not done evil by leaving my God;
23   for all his rulings were before me,
        I did not depart from his regulations.
24   I was pure-hearted toward him
        and kept myself from my sin.

25   "Hence *ADONAI* repaid me for my uprightness,
        according to my purity in his view.
26   With the merciful, you are merciful;
        with the champion of purity, you are pure;
27   with the honest, you are honest;
        but with the crooked you are cunning.
28   People afflicted, you save;
        but when your eyes are on the haughty, you humble them.

29   "For you, *ADONAI*, are my lamp;
        ADONAI lights up my darkness.
30   With you I can run through a whole troop of men,
        with my God I can leap a wall.

31   "As for God, his way is perfect,
        the word of *ADONAI* has been tested by fire;

he shields all who take refuge in him.

32 For who is God but *ADONAI*,
and who is a Rock but our God?

33 "God is my strength and protection;
he makes my way go straight.

34 He makes me swift and sure-footed as a deer
and enables me to stand on my high places.

35 He trains my hands for war
until my arms can bend a bow of bronze;

36 You give me your shield, which is salvation;
your answers make me great.

37 You lengthen the steps I can take,
yet my ankles do not turn.

38 "I pursued my enemies and wiped them out,
without turning back until they were destroyed.

39 I destroyed them, crushed them; they can't get up;
they have fallen under my feet.

40 "For you braced me with strength for the battle
and bent down my adversaries beneath me.

41 You made my enemies turn their backs in flight,
so that I could destroy those who hate me.

42 "They looked, but there was no one to help,
even to *ADONAI*, but he didn't answer.

43 I pulverized them like dust on the ground,
pounded and stamped on them like mud in the streets.

44 "You also freed me from the quarrels of my people.
You kept me to be the head of the nations;
a people I did not know now serve me.

45 Foreigners come cringing to me;
the moment they hear of me, they obey me.

46 Foreigners lose heart as they stagger from their fortresses.

47 "*ADONAI* is alive! Blessed is my Rock!
Exalted be God, the Rock of my salvation,

48 the God who gives me vengeance
and makes peoples submit to me.

49 He brings me out from my enemies.
You raise me over those who rebel against me,
you rescue me from violent men.

50 "So I give thanks to you, *ADONAI*, among the nations;
I sing praises to your name.

51 He is a tower of salvation for his king;
he displays grace to his anointed,
to David and his descendants forever."

23 ¹ Here are David's last words:

"This is the speech of David the son of Yishai,
the speech of the man who has been raised up,
the one anointed by the God of Ya'akov,
the sweet singer of Isra'el.

2 "The Spirit of ADONAI spoke through me,
his word was on my tongue.

3 The God of Isra'el spoke;
the Rock of Isra'el said to me,
'A ruler over people must be upright,
ruling in the fear of God;

4 like the morning light at sunrise
on a cloudless day
that makes the grass on the earth
sparkle after a rain.'

5 "For my house stands firm with God —
he made an everlasting covenant with me.
It is in order, fully assured,
that he will bring to full growth
all my salvation and every desire.

6 "But the ungodly are like thorn bushes
to be pushed aside, every one of them.
They cannot be taken in one's hand;

7 To touch them one uses pitchfork or spear-shaft,
and then only to burn them where they lie."

⁸ Following are the names of David's warrior-heroes:

Yoshev-Bashevet the Tach'kmoni, chief of the three, also known as 'Adino the 'Etzni; he is the one who came against 800 men, whom he killed in a single encounter.

⁹ After him was El'azar the son of Dodo the son of Achochi, one of the three warriors with David when they put their lives in jeopardy against the P'lishtim who were there assembled for battle, while the men of Isra'el had gone away. ¹⁰ He stood firm and attacked the P'lishtim until his hand went into spasm, so that he couldn't let go of his sword. ADONAI accomplished a great victory that day; but the people didn't return until he had finished, and then only to plunder the bodies of the dead.

¹¹ After him was Shammah the son of Age the Harari. The P'lishtim had assembled at Lechi, where there was a plot of ground full of lentils; and the people fled from the P'lishtim. ¹² But he stood in the middle of the plot and defended it, killing the P'lishtim; and ADONAI brought about a great victory.

¹³ During harvest season three of the thirty leaders went down and came to David at the cave of 'Adulam when a company of P'lishtim had set up camp in the Refa'im Valley. ¹⁴ At that time David was in the fortress, and the garrison of the P'lishtim was in Beit-Lechem. ¹⁵ David had a craving and said, "I wish someone could give me water to drink from the well by the gate of Beit-Lechem!" ¹⁶ The three warrior-heroes broke through the army of the P'lishtim, drew water from the well by the gate of Beit-Lechem, took it and brought it to David. But he wouldn't drink it. Instead, he poured it out to ADONAI ¹⁷ and said, "ADONAI! Heaven forbid that I should do such a thing! Am I to drink the blood of men who went and put their lives in jeopardy?"— and he would not consent to drink it. These are the things the three warrior-heroes did. ¹⁸ Avishai the brother of Yo'av, the son of Tz'ruyah, was chief of these three. He raised his spear against 300 men and killed them; thus he had a reputation even among the three. ¹⁹ He had the most honor of these three and was therefore made their leader; however, he did not achieve the status of the first three.

²⁰ B'nayah the son of Y'hoyada, the son of a valiant man of Kavtze'el, was a man of many exploits. He struck down two lion-hearted men of Mo'av. One day when it was snowing, he went down into a pit and killed a lion. ²¹ Here is how he killed an Egyptian, a man of intimidating appearance: the Egyptian had a spear in his hand, and he went down to him with only a stick, seized the spear from the Egyptian's hand and killed him with his own spear. ²² These are things that B'nayah the son of Y'hoyada did that earned him a name among the three warrior-heroes. ²³ He had more honor than the thirty, but he did not achieve the status of the first three. David put him in command of his personal guard.

²⁴   'Asah'el the brother of Yo'av was one of the thirty,
    Elchanan the son of Dodo of Beit-Lechem,
²⁵   Shammah the Harodi,
    Elika the Harodi,
²⁶   Heletz the Palti,
    'Ira son of 'Ikesh from T'koa,
²⁷   Avi'ezer from 'Anatot,
    M'vunai the Hushati,
²⁸   Tzalmon the Achochi,
    Mahrai the N'tofati,
²⁹   Helev the son of Ba'anah the N'tofati,
    Ittai the son of Rivai from Giv'ah, of the people of Binyamin,
³⁰   B'nayahu from Pir'aton,
    Hiddai from the *vadi*s of Ga'ash,
³¹   Avi-'Alvon the 'Arvati,
    'Azmavet the Barchumi,
³²   Elyachba the Sha'alvoni, of the sons of Yashen,
    Y'honatan,
³³   Shammah the Harari,
    Achi'am the son of Sharar the Arari,
³⁴   Elifelet the son of Achasbai the son of the Ma'akhati,
    Eli'am the son of Achitofel from Giloh,

³⁵ Hetzrai from Karmel,
Pa'arai the Arbi,
³⁶ Yig'al the son of Natan of Tzovah,
Bani the Gadi,
³⁷ Tzelek the 'Amoni,
Nachrai the Be'eroti, armor-bearer for Yo'av the son of Tz'ruyah,
³⁸ 'Ira the Yitri,
Garev the Yitri, and
³⁹ Uriyah the Hitti —

thirty-seven in all.

24 ¹The anger of ADONAI blazed up against Isra'el, so he moved David to act against them by saying, "Go, take a census of Isra'el and Y'hudah." ²The king said to Yo'av the commander of the army, who was with him, "Go systematically through all the tribes of Isra'el, from Dan to Be'er-Sheva; and take a census of the population; so that I can know how many people there are." ³Yo'av said to the king, "May ADONAI your God add to the people a hundredfold, no matter how many there are; and may the eyes of my lord the king see it. But why does my lord the king take pleasure in doing this?" ⁴However, the king's word prevailed against Yo'av and the army officers. So Yo'av and the army officers went out from the king's presence to take a census of the people of Isra'el.

⁵They crossed the Yarden and pitched camp in 'Aro'er, to the south of the city in the *Vadi* of Gad; went on to Ya'zer; ⁶came to Gil'ad and continued to the land of Tachtim-Hodshi. Then they arrived at Dan-Ya'an, went around to Tzidon ⁷and came to the stronghold of Tzor. They went on to the cities of the Hivi and of the Kena'ani, and finished in the south of Y'hudah, at Be'er-Sheva. ⁸When they were done going through all the land, they came back to Yerushalayim; it had taken nine months and twenty days. ⁹Yo'av reported the results of the census to the king: there were in Isra'el 800,000 valiant men who could handle a sword, while the men of Y'hudah numbered 500,000.

¹⁰But after he had taken the census, David was conscience-stricken. David said to ADONAI, "I have greatly sinned in what I have done. But now, ADONAI, please! Put aside your servant's sin, for I have done a very foolish thing." ¹¹When David got up in the morning, this word of ADONAI came to the prophet Gad, David's seer: ¹²"Go and say to David that this is what ADONAI says: 'I am giving you a choice of three punishments. Choose one of them, and I will execute it against you.'" ¹³Gad came to David and told him; he said: "Do you want seven years of famine in your land? or do you want to flee before your enemies for three months while they pursue you? or do you want three days of plague in your land? Think about it, and tell me what to answer the one who sent me."

¹⁴David said to Gad, "This is very hard for me. Let us fall into the hand of ADONAI, because his mercies are great, rather than have me fall into the hand of man." ¹⁵So ADONAI sent a plague on Isra'el from that morning until the end of the specified time; 70,000 of the people died between Dan and Be'er-Sheva. ¹⁶But when the angel stretched out his hand toward Yerushalayim to destroy it, ADONAI changed his mind about causing such distress and said to the angel destroying the people,

"Enough! Now withdraw your hand." The angel of ADONAI was at the threshing-floor of Aravnah the Y'vusi.

[17] David spoke to ADONAI when he saw the angel striking the people; he said, "Here, I have sinned, I have done wrong. But these sheep, what have they done? Please! Let your hand be against me and against my father's family!"

[18] Gad came to David that day and said to him, "Go, set up an altar to ADONAI on the threshing-floor of Aravnah the Y'vusi." [19] David went up and did what Gad had said, as ADONAI had ordered. [20] Aravnah looked out and saw the king and his servants coming toward him. Aravnah went out and prostrated himself before the king with his face to the ground. [21] Then Aravnah said, "Why has my lord the king come to his servant?" David said, "To buy your threshing-floor, in order to build an altar to ADONAI, so that the plague will be lifted from the people." [22] Aravnah said to David, "Let my lord the king take and offer up anything that seems good to him. Here are the oxen for the burnt offering; you can use the threshing-sledges and the yokes for the oxen as firewood. [23] All this, O king, Aravnah gives to the king." Then Aravnah said to the king, "May ADONAI your God accept you."

[24] But the king said to Aravnah, "No; I insist on buying it from you at a price. I refuse to offer to ADONAI my God burnt offerings that cost me nothing." So David bought the threshing-floor and the oxen for one-and-a-quarter pounds of silver shekels. [25] Then David built an altar to ADONAI there and offered burnt offerings and peace offerings. After this, ADONAI took pity on the land and lifted the plague from Isra'el.

M'lakhim Alef
1 KINGS

1 ¹ King David grew old, the years took their toll, and he couldn't get warm even when they covered him with bedclothes. ² His servants said to him, "Let us try to find a young virgin for my lord the king. She can wait on the king and be a companion for him, and she can lie next to you, so that my lord the king will get some heat." ³ After looking through all of Isra'el's territory for a beautiful girl, they found Avishag the Shunamit and brought her to the king. ⁴ The girl was very beautiful and became a companion for the king. She took care of him, but the king did not have sexual relations with her.

⁵ Adoniyah the son of Haggit was beginning to claim that he would be king; to this end he organized chariots and horsemen, with fifty men to run ahead of him. ⁶ (His father had never in his life confronted him by asking, "Why are you behaving this way?" Moreover, he was a very handsome man; he was born next after Avshalom.) ⁷ He conferred with Yo'av the son of Tz'ruyah and Evyatar the *cohen*; and they both supported Adoniyah. ⁸ But Tzadok the *cohen*, B'nayah the son of Y'hoyada, Natan the prophet, Shim'i, Re'i and David's elite guard were not on Adoniyah's side.

⁹ One day Adoniyah killed sheep, oxen and fattened calves at the Stone of Zochelet, by 'Ein-Rogel. He summoned all his brothers the king's sons, and all the men of Y'hudah the king's servants; ¹⁰ but he did not summon Natan the prophet, B'nayah, the elite guard or Shlomo his brother.

¹¹ Natan went to Bat-Sheva the mother of Shlomo and said, "Haven't you heard that Adoniyah the son of Haggit has become king without the knowledge of David our lord? ¹² Now, come, please let me give you advice, so that you can save both your own life and that of your son Shlomo. ¹³ Go, get in to see King David, and say to him, 'My lord, king, didn't you swear to your servant, "Your son Shlomo will be king after me; he will sit on my throne"? So why is Adoniyah king?' ¹⁴ Right then, while you are still talking with the king, I will also come in after you and confirm what you are saying."

¹⁵ Bat-Sheva went in to the king in his room. (The king was very old; Avishag the Shunamit was in attendance on the king.) ¹⁶ Bat-Sheva bowed, prostrating herself to the king. The king asked, "What do you want?" ¹⁷ She answered him, "My lord, you swore by ADONAI your God to your servant, 'Your son Shlomo will be king after me; he will sit on my throne.' ¹⁸ But now, here is Adoniyah ruling as king; and you, my lord the king, don't know anything about it. ¹⁹ He has killed oxen, fattened calves and sheep in great numbers; and he has summoned all the sons of the king, Evyatar the *cohen* and Yo'av the commander of the army; but he didn't summon Shlomo your servant. ²⁰ As for you, my lord the king, all Isra'el is watching you; they are waiting for you to tell them who is to sit on the throne

of my lord the king after him. ²¹ If you don't, then, when my lord the king sleeps with his ancestors, I and my son Shlomo will be considered criminals."

²² Right then, while she was still talking with the king, Natan the prophet entered. ²³ They told the king, "Natan the prophet is here." After coming into the king's presence, he prostrated himself before the king with his face to the ground. ²⁴ Natan said, "My lord king, did you say, 'Adoniyah is to be king after me; he will sit on my throne'? ²⁵ For he has gone down today and killed oxen, fattened calves and sheep in great numbers; and he has summoned all the king's sons, the commanders of the army and Evyatar the *cohen*; right now they are eating and drinking in his presence and proclaiming, 'Long live King Adoniyah!' ²⁶ But he didn't summon me your servant, or Tzadok the *cohen*, or B'nayah the son of Y'hoyada or your servant Shlomo. ²⁷ Is this authorized by my lord the king without your having told your servant who would sit on the throne of my lord the king after him?"

²⁸ King David answered by saying, "Summon Bat-Sheva to me." She entered the king's presence and stood before the king. ²⁹ Then the king swore an oath: "As ADONAI lives, who has delivered me from all adversity, ³⁰ as I swore to you by ADONAI the God of Isra'el, 'Your son Shlomo will be king after me; he will sit on my throne in my place,' so will I do today." ³¹ Bat-Sheva bowed with her face to the ground, prostrating herself to the king, and said, "Let my lord King David live forever."

³² King David said, "Summon Tzadok the *cohen*, Natan the prophet and B'nayah the son of Y'hoyada." They came before the king. ³³ The king said to them, "Take with you the servants of your lord, have Shlomo my son ride on my own mule and bring him down to Gichon. ³⁴ There Tzadok the *cohen* and Natan the prophet are to anoint him king over Isra'el. Sound the *shofar* and say, 'Long live King Shlomo!' ³⁵ Then escort him back; he is to come and sit on my throne; for he is to take my place as king. I have appointed him to rule over Isra'el and Y'hudah." ³⁶ B'nayah responded to the king by saying, "*Amen!* May ADONAI, the God of my lord the king, confirm it! ³⁷ Just as ADONAI has been with my lord the king, so may he be with Shlomo and make his throne even greater than the throne of my lord King David!"

³⁸ So Tzadok the *cohen*, Natan the prophet, B'nayah the son of Y'hoyada and the K'reti and P'leti went down, had Shlomo ride on King David's mule and brought him to Gichon. ³⁹ Tzadok the *cohen* took the horn of olive oil out of the tent and anointed Shlomo. They sounded the *shofar*, and all the people shouted, "Long live King Shlomo!" ⁴⁰ All the people escorted him back, playing flutes and rejoicing greatly, so that the earth shook with the sound.

⁴¹ Adoniyah and all his guests heard it while they were finishing their meal; but it was Yo'av who, when he heard the blast on the *shofar*, asked, "That noise — what's the meaning of this uproar in the city?" ⁴² While he was still speaking, there came Yonatan the son of Evyatar the *cohen*. Adoniyah said, "Come in! You're a worthy man, so you must be bringing good news!" ⁴³ Yonatan answered Adoniyah, "The truth is, our lord King David has made Shlomo king. ⁴⁴ Moreover, the king sent with him Tzadok the *cohen*, Natan the prophet, B'nayah the son of Y'hoyada and the K'reti and P'leti; they had him ride on the king's mule; ⁴⁵ and Tzadok the *cohen* and Natan the prophet anointed him king in Gichon. Then they escorted him back from there rejoicing, so that the city is in an uproar; this is the noise you've been hearing. ⁴⁶ Moreover, Shlomo is now sitting on the throne of the kingdom. ⁴⁷ More than that, the king's servants came and blessed our lord King David with these words: 'May

God make the name of Shlomo better than your name and his throne greater than your throne,' after which the king bowed down on the bed. ⁴⁸ Finally, the king said, 'Blessed be ADONAI the God of Isra'el, who has given someone to sit on my throne today, when my own eyes can see it.'"

⁴⁹ At this all Adoniyah's guests grew frightened; they got up, everyone going his own way. ⁵⁰ Adoniyah too was afraid because of Shlomo; he got up, went and took hold of the horns of the altar. ⁵¹ Shlomo was told, "Here, Adoniyah is terrified of King Shlomo; he has grabbed hold of the horns of the altar and is saying, 'First let King Shlomo swear to me that he will not have his servant executed.'" ⁵² Shlomo said, "If he will demonstrate that he is a worthy man, not a hair of his will fall to the earth. But if he is found making trouble, he will die." ⁵³ So King Shlomo sent, and they brought him down from the altar. He came and prostrated himself before King Shlomo; and Shlomo said to him, 'Go on home.'"

2 ¹ The time came near for David to die; so he commissioned Shlomo his son as follows: ² "I am going the way of all the earth. Therefore, be strong; show yourself a man. ³ Observe the charge of ADONAI your God to go in his ways and keep his regulations, *mitzvot*, rulings and instructions in accordance with what is written in the *Torah* of Moshe; so that you will succeed in all you do and wherever you go. ⁴ If you do, ADONAI will fulfill what he promised me when he said, 'If your children pay attention to how they live, conducting themselves before me honestly with all their heart and being, you will never lack a man on the throne of Isra'el.'

⁵ "Moreover, you are aware of what Yo'av the son of Tz'ruyah did to me, that is, what he did to the two commanders of the armies of Isra'el, Avner the son of Ner and 'Amasa the son of Yeter — he killed them, shedding the blood of war in peacetime, putting the blood of war on the belt around his waist and the shoes on his feet. ⁶ Therefore, act according to your wisdom; don't let his gray head go down to the grave in peace.

⁷ "But show kindness to the sons of Barzillai the Gil'adi. Include them with those who eat at your table, because they came and stood with me when I was fleeing from Avshalom your brother.

⁸ "Finally, you have with you Shim'i the son of Gera the Binyamini, from Bachurim. He laid a terrible curse on me when I was on my way to Machanayim; but he came down to meet me at the Yarden; so I swore to him by ADONAI that I would not have him put to death with the sword. ⁹ Now, however, you should not let him go unpunished. You are a wise man, and you will know what you should do to him — you will bring his gray head down to the grave with blood."

¹⁰ Then David slept with his ancestors and was buried in the City of David. ¹¹ David had ruled Isra'el for forty years — seven years in Hevron and thirty-three years in Yerushalayim.

¹² Shlomo sat on the throne of David his father; and his rule had become firmly established, ¹³ when Adoniyah the son of Haggit came to Bat-Sheva the mother of Shlomo. She asked, "Have you come as a friend?" He answered, "Yes, as a friend." ¹⁴ Then he continued, "I have something to say to you." She said, "Go on." ¹⁵ He said, "You know that the kingdom should have been mine, that all Isra'el was looking to me to be their ruler. No matter; the kingdom has turned around and become my brother's, because ADONAI gave it to him. ¹⁶ But now I ask one favor of you; don't

deny me." "Go on," she said. [17] He said, "Please speak to Shlomo the king — for he won't say 'No' to you — and ask him to give me Avishag the Shunamit as my wife." [18] Bat-Sheva said, "All right, I will speak to the king on your behalf."

[19] So Bat-Sheva went to King Shlomo to speak to him on behalf of Adoniyah. The king rose to meet her and bowed down to her. Then he sat down on his throne and had a throne set up for the king's mother, so that she sat at his right. [20] She said, "I am asking one small favor of you; don't deny me." The king said to her, "Ask, mother; I won't deny you." [21] She said, "Let Avishag the Shunamit be given to Adoniyah your brother as his wife." [22] King Shlomo answered his mother, "Why are you asking Avishag the Shunamit for Adoniyah? Ask the kingdom for him too! After all, he's my older brother! Yes, for him, and for Evyatar the *cohen* and for Yo'av the son of Tz'ruyah!" [23] Then King Shlomo swore by ADONAI, "May God do terrible things to me and worse if Adoniyah hasn't condemned himself to death with this request! [24] Now therefore, as ADONAI lives, who has established me, put me on the throne of David my father and set up a dynasty for me, as he promised, Adoniyah will certainly be put to death today." [25] King Shlomo commissioned B'nayah the son of Y'hoyada, and he struck him down, so that he died.

[26] To Evyatar the *cohen* the king said, "You, get yourself to 'Anatot, to your own fields. You deserve to die; but I won't put you to death just now; since you did carry the ark of *Adonai* ELOHIM before David my father; and you suffered together with my father in everything he suffered." [27] So Shlomo forced Evyatar out of his task as *cohen* to ADONAI, so that what ADONAI had said in Shiloh about the family of 'Eli might be fulfilled.

[28] When the news came to Yo'av, he fled to the tent of ADONAI and took hold of the horns of the altar; for Yo'av had given his support to Adoniyah, even though he had not supported Avshalom. [29] King Shlomo was told, "Yo'av has fled to the tent of ADONAI; he's there by the altar." Shlomo sent B'nayah the son of Y'hoyada with the order, "Go, strike him down." [30] B'nayah came to the tent of ADONAI and said to him, "The king says: leave!" He answered, "No, I'd rather die here." B'nayah brought the message back to the king, "This is what Yo'av said to me." [31] The king answered him, "Do what he said — strike him down, and bury him. In this way you will take away from me and my father's family the blood which Yo'av shed for no reason. [32] ADONAI will bring his blood back on his own head, because he struck down two men more righteous and better than he — he killed them with the sword without my father David's awareness: Avner the son of Ner, commander of the army of Isra'el, and 'Amasa the son of Yeter, commander of the army of Y'hudah. [33] In this way their blood will return on the head of Yo'av and his descendants forever; but for David, his descendants, his family and his throne there will be peace forever from ADONAI." [34] So B'nayah the son of Y'hoyada went up, struck him down and killed him; he was buried in his own house in the desert. [35] The king put B'nayah the son of Y'hoyada in charge of the army instead of him, and the king replaced Evyatar with Tzadok the *cohen*.

[36] The king summoned Shim'i and said to him, "Build yourself a house in Yerushalayim, and live there; don't go outside the city walls. [37] Know for a fact that on the day you go out and cross *Vadi* Kidron, you will certainly die; your blood will be on your own head." [38] Shim'i answered the king, "What you have said is good; as my lord the king has said, so will your servant do." So Shim'i lived in Yerushalayim for a long time.

[39] But after three years, two of Shim'i's slaves ran away and went to Akhish son of Ma'akhah, king of Gat. They told Shim'i, "Your slaves are in Gat." [40] So Shim'i set out, saddled his donkey and went to Akhish in Gat to look for his slaves; then Shim'i returned, bringing his slaves from Gat. [41] Shlomo was told that Shim'i had gone from Yerushalayim to Gat and back. [42] The king summoned Shim'i and said to him, "Didn't I have you swear by ADONAI and forewarn you by telling you, 'Know for a fact that on the day you leave and go anywhere outside the city, you will certainly die'? and you answered me, 'What you're saying is good; I hear it.' [43] Why, then, haven't you kept the oath of ADONAI and the *mitzvah* I charged you with?" [44] Moreover, the king said to Shim'i, "You know in your own heart all the terrible things you did to David my father; therefore ADONAI will bring back your wickedness on your own head. [45] But King Shlomo will be blessed, and the throne of David will be established before ADONAI forever." [46] So the king gave the order to B'nayah the son of Y'hoyada, and he went out and struck him down, so that he died.

Thus the kingdom was established in Shlomo's hands.

3 [1] Shlomo formed an alliance with Pharaoh king of Egypt by marrying Pharaoh's daughter. He brought her into the City of David, [where she lived] until he had finished building his own palace, the house of ADONAI and the wall around Yerushalayim. [2] The people, however, were still sacrificing on the high places, because no house had yet been built for the name of ADONAI. [3] Shlomo loved ADONAI, living according to the regulations set forth by David his father; nevertheless, he sacrificed and made offerings on the high places.

[4] One time the king went to Giv'on to sacrifice there, because that was the main high place. Shlomo offered a thousand burnt offerings on the altar there. [5] At Giv'on ADONAI appeared to Shlomo in a dream at night; God said, "Tell me what I should give you." [6] Shlomo said, "You showed your servant David my father much grace, as he lived before you honestly and righteously, having an upright heart with you. You preserved this great grace for him by giving him a son to sit on his throne, as is the case today. [7] So now, ADONAI my God, you have made your servant king in the place of David my father; but I am a mere child — I don't know how to lead! [8] Moreover your servant is among your people, whom you chose, a great people so numerous that they cannot be counted. [9] Therefore, give your servant an understanding heart able to administer justice to your people, so that I can discern between good and bad — for who is equal to judging this great people of yours?"

[10] What Shlomo had said in making this request pleased ADONAI. [11] God said to him, "Because you have made this request instead of asking long life or riches for yourself, or your enemies' death, but rather asked for yourself understanding to discern justice; [12] I am doing what you requested. I am giving you a wise and understanding heart, so that there has never been anyone like you, nor will there ever again be anyone like you. [13] I am also giving you what you didn't ask for, riches and honor greater than that of any other king throughout your life. [14] More than that, if you will live according to my ways, obeying my laws and *mitzvot* like your father David, I will give you a long life." [15] Shlomo awoke and found it had been a dream. But he went to Yerushalayim, stood before the ark for the covenant of ADONAI and offered up burnt offerings and peace offerings. He also made a feast for all his servants.

^{16} After this, there came to the king two women who were prostitutes. After presenting themselves to him, ^{17} one of the women said, "My lord, I and this woman live in the same house; and when she was in the house, I gave birth to a baby. ^{18} Three days after I gave birth, this woman also gave birth. We were there together; there was no one else with us in the house except the two of us. ^{19} During the night this woman's child died, because she rolled over on top of it. ^{20} So she got up in the middle of the night and took my son from next to me, while your servant was sleeping, and put it in her arms; and she laid her dead child in my arms. ^{21} When I awoke in the morning to feed my child from my breast, there it was, dead. But when I took a closer look later in the morning, why, it wasn't my son at all — not the one I gave birth to!" ^{22} The other woman broke in, "No! The living one is my son, and the dead one is your son!" The first one said, "No! The dead one is your son and the living one is my son!" This is how they spoke in the presence of the king.

^{23} Then the king said, "This woman says, 'The living one is my son; your son is the dead one'; while the other says, 'No, the dead one is your son, and the living one is my son.' ^{24} Bring me a sword," said the king. They brought a sword to the king. ^{25} The king said, "Cut the living child in two; give half to the one and half to the other." ^{26} At this, the woman to whom the living child belonged addressed the king, because she felt so strongly toward her son: "Oh, my lord, give her the living child; you mustn't kill it!" But the other one said, "It will be neither yours nor mine. Divide it up!" ^{27} Then the king answered, "Give the living child to the first woman, don't kill it, because she is its mother." ^{28} All Isra'el heard of the decision the king had made and held the king in awe, for they saw that God's wisdom was in him, enabling him to render justice properly.

4 ^{1} King Shlomo was king over all Isra'el, ^{2} and these were his high officials:

'Azaryah the son of Tzadok, the *cohen*;

^{3} Elichoref and Achiyah the sons of Shisha, secretaries;
Y'hoshafat the son of Achilud, secretary of state;

^{4} B'nayah the son of Y'hoyada, commander of the army;
Tzadok and Evyatar, *cohanim*;

^{5} 'Azaryah the son of Natan, chief administrator;
Zavud the son of Natan, the king's trusted counselor;

^{6} Achishar, in charge of the palace;
Adoniram the son of 'Avda, in charge of forced labor.

^{7} Shlomo had twelve officers over all Isra'el who were in charge of providing food and supplies for the king and his household; each one was in charge of provisions for one month out of the year. ^{8} They were:

the son of Hur, in the hills of Efrayim;

^{9} the son of Deker, in Makatz, Sha'albim, Beit-Shemesh and Eilon-Beit-Hanan;

^{10} the son of Hesed, in Arubot; he also had charge of Sokhoh and all the territory of Hefer;

^{11} the son of Avinadav, in all the area of Dor; he had Tafat the daughter of Shlomo as his wife;

¹²   Ba'ana the son of Achilud, in Ta'anakh, Megiddo, and all Beit-Sh'an by
        Tzartan below Yizre'el, from Beit-Sh'an to Avel-M'cholah, as far as
        beyond Yokme'am;
¹³   the son of Gever, in Ramot-Gil'ad; he was in charge of the villages of Ya'ir
        the son of M'nasheh in Gil'ad and in charge of the region of Argov in
        Bashan, sixty large cities with walls and bronze bars;
¹⁴   Achinadav the son of 'Iddo, in Machanayim;
¹⁵   Achima'atz, in Naftali; he also took Basmat the daughter of Shlomo
        as his wife;
¹⁶   Ba'ana the son of Hushai, in Asher and in Alot;
¹⁷   Y'hoshafat the son of Paruach, in Yissakhar;
¹⁸   Shim'i the son of Ela, in Binyamin; and
¹⁹   Gever the son of Uri, in the land of Gil'ad, the country of Sichon king of
        the Emori and 'Og king of Bashan.

Over all these, there was one administrator in the land.

²⁰ Y'hudah and Isra'el were as numerous as sand grains on the seashore; they
ate, drank and enjoyed themselves.

5 ^{1(4:21)} Shlomo ruled over all the kingdoms from the [Euphrates] River through the
land of the P'lishtim to the border of Egypt; they paid tribute and served Shlomo as
long as he lived. ^{2(4:22)} Shlomo's provisions for one day consisted of 150 bushels of
fine flour, 310 bushels of meal, ^{3(4:23)} ten fattened oxen, twenty pasture-fed oxen and
one hundred sheep, in addition to deer, gazelles, roebucks and fattened poultry.
^{4(4:24)} For he ruled all the area this side of the [Euphrates] River, from Tifsach to 'Azah.
He was over all the kings on this side of the River; and he had peace all around him,
on every side. ^{5(4:25)} From Dan to Be'er-Sheva, Y'hudah and Isra'el lived securely,
every man under his vine and fig tree, throughout the lifetime of Shlomo. ^{6(4:26)} Shlomo
also had 40,000 stalls for the horses used with his chariots and 12,000 horsemen.

^{7(4:27)} Those officers [named above] supplied food and other materials for King
Shlomo and for everyone for whom Shlomo provided. Each was responsible for his
month's supplies; they saw to it that nothing was lacking. ^{8(4:28)} They also made sure
there was barley and straw where it was needed for the horses and draft animals;
each filled his quota.

^{9(4:29)} God gave Shlomo exceptional wisdom and understanding, as well as a
heart as vast as the sandy beach by the sea. ^{10(4:30)} Shlomo's wisdom surpassed the
wisdom of the people from the east and all the wisdom of Egypt. ^{11(4:31)} For he was
wiser than everyone— wiser than Eitan the Ezrachi and wiser than Heiman, Kalkol
and Darda the sons of Machol; so that his fame spread to all the surrounding nations.
^{12(4:32)} He composed 3,000 proverbs and 1,005 songs. ^{13(4:33)} He could discuss trees,
from the cedar in the L'vanon to the hyssop growing out of the wall; he could discuss
wild animals, poultry, reptiles and fish. ^{14(4:34)} People from all nations came to hear
the wisdom of Shlomo, including kings from all over the earth who had heard of
his wisdom.

¹⁵⁽¹⁾ Hiram king of Tzor sent his servants to Shlomo, because he had heard that
they had anointed him king in his father's place, and Hiram had always loved David.
¹⁶⁽²⁾ Shlomo returned this message to Hiram: ¹⁷⁽³⁾ "You know that David my father

wasn't able to build a house for the name of ADONAI his God, because of the wars that beset him from every side, until ADONAI put his enemies under the soles of my feet. $^{18(4)}$ But now ADONAI my God has given me rest on every side; there is neither adversary nor calamity. $^{19(5)}$ So now I intend to build a house for the name of ADONAI my God, in keeping with what ADONAI said to David my father, 'Your son, whom I will put on your throne in your place, will be the one to build the house for my name.' $^{20(6)}$ Therefore, order your people to cut down cedar trees from the L'vanon for me. My servants will be with your servants. I will pay your servants according to everything you say; for you know that we have no one among us as skilled in felling trees as the Tzidonim."

$^{21(7)}$ When Hiram heard Shlomo's message, he was very happy and said, "Blessed be ADONAI today, who has given David a wise son to rule this great people." $^{22(8)}$ Then Hiram sent Shlomo this message: "I have heard the message you sent me, and I will do everything you want concerning cedar logs and cypress logs. $^{23(9)}$ My servants will bring them down from the L'vanon to the sea. I will make them into rafts to go by sea to whatever place you tell me and will have them broken up there, and you will receive them. You will compensate me by providing food for my household."

$^{24(10)}$ So Hiram gave Shlomo all the cedar logs and cypress logs he wanted; $^{25(11)}$ and Shlomo gave Hiram 100,000 bushels of wheat as food for his household and a thousand gallons of oil from pressed olives — this is what Shlomo gave Hiram each year. $^{26(12)}$ ADONAI gave Shlomo wisdom, as he had promised him; and there was peace between Hiram and Shlomo — the two of them formed an alliance together.

$^{27(13)}$ King Shlomo conscripted 30,000 men from all Isra'el for forced labor. $^{28(14)}$ He sent them to the L'vanon in monthly relays of 10,000; they would stay a month in the L'vanon and two months at home. Adoniram was in charge of the forced labor.

$^{29(15)}$ Shlomo had 70,000 men to carry loads and another 80,000 stonecutters in the hills, $^{30(16)}$ besides Shlomo's 3,300 supervisors who were in charge of the people doing the work. $^{31(17)}$ The king gave orders; and they quarried large stones, expensive stones, to lay the foundation of the house with cut stone. $^{32(18)}$ Shlomo's and Hiram's builders, along with the men from G'val, worked the stones and prepared the timber and stones for building the house.

6 ^{1} It was in the 480th year after the people of Isra'el had left the land of Egypt, in the fourth year of Shlomo's reign over Isra'el, in the month of Ziv, which is the second month, that he began to build the house of ADONAI. ^{2} The house which King Shlomo built for ADONAI was 105 feet long, thirty-five feet wide and fifty-two-and-a-half feet high. ^{3} The hall fronting the temple of the house was thirty-five feet long, the same as the width of the house itself, so that its seventeen-and-a-half-foot width extended frontward from the house. ^{4} The windows he made for the house were wide on the inside and narrow on the outside. ^{5} Against the wall of the house he built an annex all the way around; it went all the way around the walls of the house, including both the temple and the sanctuary. ^{6} The lowest floor of the annex was eight-and-three-quarters feet wide, the middle floor ten-and-a-half feet wide and the third floor twelve-and-a-quarter feet wide; for he had made the outer part of the wall of the house step-shaped, so that the beams of the annex would not have to be attached to the house walls. ^{7} For the house, when under construction, was built of stone prepared at the quarry; so that no hammer, chisel or iron tool of any kind was heard in the house while it was being built.

⁸ The entrance to the lowest floor was on the south side of the house; a spiral staircase went up to the middle floor and on to the third. ⁹ So he built the house, and after finishing it, he put its roof on — cedar planks over beams. ¹⁰ Each floor of the annex surrounding the house was eight-and-three-quarters feet high and was attached to the house with beams of cedar.

¹¹ Then this word of ADONAI came to Shlomo: ¹² "Concerning this house which you are building: if you will live according to my regulations, follow my rulings and observe all my *mitzvot* and live by them, then I will establish with you my promise that I made to David your father — ¹³ I will live in it among the people of Isra'el, and I will not abandon my people Isra'el."

¹⁴ So Shlomo finished building the house. ¹⁵ The insides of the walls of the house he built with boards of cedar: from the floor of the house to the joists of the ceiling he covered them on the inside with wood, and he covered the floor of the house with boards of cypress. ¹⁶ The thirty-five-foot back portion of the house he built with boards of cedar from the floor to the joists and reserved this part of the house to be a sanctuary, the Especially Holy Place; ¹⁷ while the rest of the house, that is, the temple in front, was seventy feet long. ¹⁸ The cedar covering the house was carved with gourds and open flowers; all was cedar; no stone was visible. ¹⁹ In the inner part of the house he set up the sanctuary, so that the ark for the covenant of ADONAI could be placed there. ²⁰ This sanctuary was thirty-five feet long, wide and high; and it was overlaid with pure gold. In front of it he set an altar, which he covered with cedar. ²¹ Shlomo overlaid the interior of the house with pure gold and had chains of gold placed before the sanctuary, which itself he overlaid with gold. ²² The entire house he overlaid with gold until it was completely covered with it. He also overlaid with gold the entire altar that belonged to the sanctuary.

²³ Inside the sanctuary he made two *k'ruvim* of olive-wood, each seventeen-and-a-half feet high. ²⁴ Each of the two wings of one of the *k'ruvim* was eight-and-three quarters feet long, so that the distance from the end of one wing to the end of the other was seventeen-and-a-half feet. ²⁵ Likewise the [wingspread of the] other *keruv* was seventeen-and-a-half feet; both *k'ruvim* were identical in shape and size. ²⁶ The height of the one *keruv* was seventeen-and-a-half feet, likewise that of the other. ²⁷ He set the *k'ruvim* in the inner house; the wings of the *k'ruvim* were stretched out, so that the wing of the one touched the one wall, and the wing of the other *keruv* touched the other wall; their wings touched each other in the middle of the house. ²⁸ He overlaid the *k'ruvim* with gold. ²⁹ All around the walls of the house, both inside the sanctuary and outside it, he carved figures of *k'ruvim*, palm trees and open flowers. ³⁰ He overlaid the floor of the house with gold, both inside the sanctuary and outside it.

³¹ For the entrance to the sanctuary he made doors of olive-wood, set within a five-sided door-frame. ³² On the two olive-wood doors he carved figures of *k'ruvim*, palm trees and open flowers. He overlaid the doors with gold, forcing the gold into the shapes of the *k'ruvim* and palm trees as well. ³³ For the entrance to the temple he also made doorposts of olive-wood, set within a rectangular door-frame, ³⁴ and two doors of cypress-wood; the two leaves of the one door were folding, as were the two leaves of the other. ³⁵ On them he carved *k'ruvim*, palm trees and open flowers, overlaying them with gold fitted to the carved work. ³⁶ He built the inner courtyard with three rows of cut stone and a row of cedar beams.

³⁷ The foundation of the house of ADONAI was laid in the fourth year, in the month of Ziv. ³⁸ In the eleventh year, in the month of Bul, which is the eighth month, all parts of the house were completed exactly as designed. Thus he was seven years building it.

7 ¹ Shlomo built a palace for himself, taking thirteen years to finish it. ² For he built the House of the L'vanon Forest 175 feet long, eighty-seven-and-a-half feet wide and fifty-two-and-a-half feet high, on four rows of cedar posts, with cedar beams on the posts. ³ It had a roof made of cedar and supported by beams lying on forty-five posts, fifteen in a row. ⁴ There were three rows of window openings, placed so that the windows on facing walls were opposite each other at all three levels. ⁵ All the doors and doorways were rectangular and opposite each other at all three levels.

⁶ He made the columned hall eighty-seven-and-a-half feet long and fifty-two-and-a-half feet wide, with a columned, corniced porch in front of it.

⁷ He made the Hall of the Throne his place for dispensing justice, that is, the Hall of Judgment; it was covered with cedar from floor to ceiling.

⁸ His own living quarters, in the other courtyard, set back from the Hall, were similarly designed. He also made a house like this Hall for Pharaoh's daughter, whom Shlomo had taken as his wife.

⁹ All these buildings were made of expensive stone blocks, cut to measure and finished by saws on the inner surfaces as well as the outer ones. These stones were used from the foundation to the eaves and outward from the buildings all the way to the Great Courtyard. ¹⁰ The foundation was of expensive stone blocks, very large ones — stones fourteen to eighteen feet long. ¹¹ Above these were costly stones, cut to measure, and cedar-wood. ¹² The surrounding Great Courtyard had three rows of cut stone and a row of cedar beams like the inner courtyard of the house of ADONAI and the courtyard by the hall of the house.

¹³ King Shlomo sent for Hiram and brought him from Tzor. ¹⁴ He was the son of a widow from the tribe of Naftali, but his father was from Tzor, a bronze-worker filled with wisdom, understanding and skill for all kinds of bronze craftsmanship. He came to King Shlomo and did all his bronzework. ¹⁵ He made the two bronze columns, each one thirty-one-and-a-half feet high and twenty-one feet in circumference. ¹⁶ He made two capitals of melted bronze to set on the tops of the columns; each capital was eight-and-three-quarters feet high; ¹⁷ he also made checker-work nets and chained wreaths, seven for the top of each capital. ¹⁸ When he made the columns, he made two rows of pomegranates to put at the top of each column around the netting covering its capital. ¹⁹ The capitals on the columns in the hall had shapes like lilies and were seven feet high. ²⁰ As for the capitals on the two columns, there were 200 pomegranates in rows around each capital near the molding by the netting. ²¹ He erected the columns in the hall of the temple; on erecting the right column he gave it the name "Yakhin," and on erecting the left column he named it "Bo'az." ²² On the tops of the columns were shapes like lilies; thus the work of the columns was finished.

²³ He made the cast metal "Sea" circular, seventeen-and-a-half feet from rim to rim, eight-and-three quarter feet high and fifty-two-and-a-half feet in circumference. ²⁴ Under its rim, three hundred gourds encircled it in two rows; they were cast when the Sea was cast. ²⁵ It rested on twelve oxen, three looking north, three looking west,

three looking south and three looking east, all with their hindquarters toward the center. The Sea was set on top of them. ²⁶ It was a handbreadth thick, its rim was made like the rim of a cup, like the flower of a lily; and its capacity was 11,000 gallons.

²⁷ He made ten bronze trolleys, each one seven feet long, seven feet wide, and five-and-a-quarter feet high. ²⁸ They were designed with panels that were set between the corner-posts, ²⁹ and on the panels between the corner-posts were lions, oxen and k'ruvim. The corner-posts above were similarly designed. Below the lions and oxen were wreaths of hammered work. ³⁰ Every trolley had four bronze wheels and bronze axles, and its four legs each had cast supports which were under the basin, with wreaths next to each. ³¹ The opening of the stand into which the basin was inserted was eighteen inches high; the stand was round, resembling a pedestal, and it was two-and-a-half feet in diameter. On the stand were carvings, and the outside was square, not round. ³² The four wheels were under the panels, and the axles for the wheels were attached to the trolleys; each wheel was two-and-a-half feet in diameter. ³³ The wheels were made like chariot wheels; their axles, rims, spokes and hubs were all cast metal. ³⁴ There were four supports at the four corners of each trolley; the supports were attached to the trolley itself. ³⁵ In the top of the trolley was a circular support ten-and-a-half inches high, and the trolley's corner-posts and panels were attached to its top. ³⁶ On the sides of the panels and on its corners he carved k'ruvim, lions and palm trees, according to the amount of space each required, with wreaths surrounding. ³⁷ According to this design he made the ten trolleys; all of them were cast from a single mold, so that they had the same size and shape.

³⁸ He made ten bronze basins; each basin's capacity was 220 gallons and had a diameter of seven feet; there was a basin for each of the ten trolleys. ³⁹ He arranged five of the trolleys on the right side of the house and five on the left side. The Sea he placed on the right side of the house, toward the southeast.

⁴⁰ Hiram made the ash pots, shovels and sprinkling basins. With that, Hiram completed all the work he had done for King Shlomo in the house of ADONAI — ⁴¹ the two columns, the two moldings of the capitals on top of the columns, the two nettings covering the two moldings of the capitals atop the columns, ⁴² the 400 pomegranates for the two nettings, two rows of pomegranates for each netting, to cover the two moldings of the capitals atop the columns, ⁴³ the ten trolleys, the ten basins on the trolleys, ⁴⁴ the one Sea, the twelve oxen under the Sea, ⁴⁵ the ash pots, the shovels and the sprinkling basins. All these articles that Hiram made for King Shlomo in the house of ADONAI were of burnished bronze. ⁴⁶ The king cast them in the plain of the Yarden, in the clay ground between Sukkot and Tzartan. ⁴⁷ Shlomo did not weigh any of these objects, because there were so many of them; thus the total weight of the bronze could not be determined.

⁴⁸ Shlomo made all the objects that were inside the house of ADONAI: the gold altar; the table of gold on which the showbread was displayed; ⁴⁹ the menorahs — five on the right and five on the left in front of the sanctuary — of pure gold; the flowers, lamps and tongs of gold; ⁵⁰ the cups, snuffers, basins, incense pans and fire pans of pure gold; and the hinges of gold, both those for the doors of the inner house, the Especially Holy Place, and those for the doors of the house, that is, of the temple.

⁵¹ Thus all the work that King Shlomo did in the house of ADONAI was finished. After this, Shlomo brought in the gifts which David his father had dedicated — the silver, the gold and the utensils — and put them in the treasuries of the house of ADONAI.

8 ¹ Then Shlomo assembled all the leaders of Isra'el, all the heads of the tribes and the chiefs of the paternal clans of the people of Isra'el, to King Shlomo in Yerushalayim, to bring the ark for the covenant of ADONAI out of the City of David, also known as Tziyon. ² All the men of Isra'el assembled before King Shlomo at the festival in the month of Etanim, the seventh month. ³ All the leaders of Isra'el came. The *cohanim* took the ark ⁴ and brought up the ark of ADONAI, the tent of meeting and all the holy utensils that were in the tent; these are what the *cohanim* and *L'vi'im* brought up. ⁵ King Shlomo and the whole community of Isra'el assembled in his presence were with him in front of the ark, sacrificing sheep and oxen in numbers beyond counting or recording.

⁶ The *cohanim* brought the ark for the covenant of ADONAI in to its place inside the sanctuary of the house, to the Especially Holy Place, under the wings of the *k'ruvim*. ⁷ For the *k'ruvim* spread out their wings over the place for the ark, covering the ark and its poles from above. ⁸ The poles were so long that their ends could be seen from the Holy Place in front of the sanctuary, but they could not be seen from outside; they are there to this day. ⁹ There was nothing in the ark except the two tablets of stone which Moshe put there at Horev, when ADONAI made the covenant with the people of Isra'el at the time of their leaving the land of Egypt.

¹⁰ When the *cohanim* came out of the Holy Place, the cloud filled the house of ADONAI, ¹¹ so that, because of the cloud, the *cohanim* could not stand up to perform their service; for the glory of ADONAI filled the house of ADONAI.

¹² Shlomo said, "ADONAI said he would live in thick darkness. ¹³ But I have built you a magnificent house, a place where you can live forever."

¹⁴ Then the king turned around and blessed the whole community of Isra'el. The whole community of Isra'el stood ¹⁵ as he said: "Blessed be ADONAI, the God of Isra'el, who spoke to my father David with his mouth and fulfilled his promise with his hand. He said, ¹⁶ 'Since the day I brought my people Isra'el out of Egypt, I chose no city from any of the tribes of Isra'el in which to build a house, so that my name might be there; but I did choose David to be over my people Isra'el.' ¹⁷ Now it was in the heart of David my father to build a house for the name of ADONAI the God of Isra'el; ¹⁸ but ADONAI said to David my father, 'Although it was in your heart to build a house for my name, and you did well that it was in your heart, ¹⁹ nevertheless you will not build the house. Rather, you will father a son, and it will be he who will build the house for my name.' ²⁰ Now ADONAI has fulfilled this spoken word of his; for I have succeeded my father and sit on the throne of Isra'el, as ADONAI promised; and I have built the house for the name of ADONAI the God of Isra'el. ²¹ And there I have made a place for the ark containing the covenant of ADONAI, which he made with our ancestors when he brought them out of the land of Egypt."

²² Then Shlomo stood before the altar of ADONAI in the presence of the whole community of Isra'el, spread out his hands toward heaven, ²³ and said, "ADONAI, God of Isra'el, there is no God like you in heaven above or on earth below. You keep covenant with your servants and show them grace, provided they live in your presence with all their heart. ²⁴ You have kept your promise to your servant David, my father; you spoke with your mouth and fulfilled it with your hand; so it is today. ²⁵ Now therefore, ADONAI, God of Isra'el, keep what you promised to your servant David, my father, when you said, 'You will never lack a man in my presence to

sit on the throne of Isra'el, if only your children are careful about what they do, so that they live in my presence, just as you have lived in my presence.' ²⁶ Now therefore, God of Isra'el, please let your word, which you spoke to your servant David, my father, be confirmed.

²⁷ "But can God actually live on the earth? Why, heaven itself, even the heaven of heavens, cannot contain you; so how much less this house I have built? ²⁸ Even so, Adonai my God, pay attention to your servant's prayer and plea, listen to the cry and prayer that your servant is praying before you today, ²⁹ that your eyes will be open toward this house night and day — toward the place concerning which you said, 'My name will be there' — to listen to the prayer your servant will pray toward this place. ³⁰ Yes, listen to the plea of your servant, and also that of your people Isra'el when they pray toward this place. Hear in heaven where you live; and when you hear, forgive!

³¹ "If a person sins against a fellow member of the community, and he is made to swear under oath, and he comes and swears before your altar in this house; ³² then hear in heaven, act, and judge your servants, condemning the wicked, so that his way of life devolves on his own head, and vindicating the one who is right, giving him what his righteousness deserves.

³³ "When your people Isra'el sin against you and in consequence are defeated by an enemy; then if they turn back to you, acknowledge your name, and pray and make their plea to you in this house; ³⁴ hear in heaven, forgive the sin of your people Isra'el, and bring them back to the land you gave to their ancestors.

³⁵ "When they sin against you, and in consequence the sky is shut, so that there is no rain; then, if they pray toward this place, acknowledge your name and turn from their sin when you have brought them low; ³⁶ hear in heaven, forgive the sin of your servants and of your people Isra'el — since you keep teaching them the good way by which they should live — and send down rain on your land, which you have given your people as their inheritance.

³⁷ "If there is famine in the land, or blight, windstorm, mildew, locusts or shearer-worms; or if their enemy comes to the land and besieges them in any of their cities — no matter what kind of plague or sickness it is; ³⁸ then, regardless of what prayer or plea anyone among all your people Isra'el makes — for each individual will know what is plagueing his own conscience — and the person spreads out his hands toward this house; ³⁹ hear in heaven where you live, and forgive, and act, and, since you know what is in each one's heart, give each person what his conduct deserves (because you, and only you, know all human hearts), ⁴⁰ so that they will fear you throughout the time they live in the land you gave our ancestors.

⁴¹ "Also the foreigner who does not belong to your people Isra'el — when he comes from a distant country because of your reputation ⁴² (for they will hear of your great reputation, your mighty hand and your outstretched arm), when he comes and prays toward this house; ⁴³ then hear in heaven where you live, and act in accordance with everything about which the foreigner is calling to you; so that all the peoples of the earth will know your name and fear you, as does your people Isra'el, and so that they will know that this house which I have built bears your name.

⁴⁴ "If your people go out to fight against their enemy, no matter by which way you send them, and they pray to Adonai toward the city you chose, toward the house I built for your name; ⁴⁵ then, in heaven, hear their prayer and plea, and uphold their cause.

⁴⁶ "If they sin against you — for there is no one who doesn't sin — and you are angry with them and hand them over to the enemy, so that they carry them off captive to the land of their enemy, whether far away or nearby; ⁴⁷ then, if they come to their senses in the land where they have been carried away captive, turn back and make their plea to you in the land of those who carried them off captive, saying, 'We sinned, we acted wrongly, we behaved wickedly,' ⁴⁸ if, in the land of their enemies who carried them off captive, they return to you with all their heart and being and pray to you toward their own land, which you gave to their ancestors, toward the city you chose and toward the house I have built for your name; ⁴⁹ then, in heaven where you live, hear their prayer and plea, uphold their cause, ⁵⁰ and forgive your people who have sinned against you — forgive their transgressions which they have committed against you, and give them compassion in the sight of their captors, so that they will show compassion toward them; ⁵¹ for they are your people, your inheritance, whom you brought out of Egypt, out of the flames of the iron furnace.

⁵² "May your eyes be open to the plea of your servant and to the plea of your people Isra'el, so that you will hear them whenever they cry out to you. ⁵³ For you made a distinction between them and all the peoples of the earth by making them your inheritance, as you said through Moshe your servant when you brought our ancestors out of Egypt, *Adonai ELOHIM.*"

⁵⁴ When Shlomo had finished praying all this prayer and plea to ADONAI, he got up from in front of the altar of ADONAI, where he had been kneeling with his hands spread out toward heaven, ⁵⁵ stood up, and raised his voice to bless the whole community of Isra'el. He said, ⁵⁶ "Blessed be ADONAI, who has given rest to his people Isra'el, in accordance with everything he promised. Not one word has failed of his good promise, which he made through Moshe his servant. ⁵⁷ May ADONAI our God be with us, as he was with our ancestors. May he never leave us or abandon us. ⁵⁸ In this way he will incline our hearts toward him, so that we will live according to his ways and observe his *mitzvot,* laws and rulings which he ordered our fathers to obey. ⁵⁹ May these words of mine, which I have used in my plea before ADONAI, be present with ADONAI our God day and night, so that he will uphold the cause of his servant and the cause of his people Isra'el day by day. ⁶⁰ Then all the peoples of the earth will know that ADONAI is God; there is no other. ⁶¹ So be wholehearted with ADONAI our God, living by his laws and observing his *mitzvot,* as you are doing today."

⁶² Then the king, together with all Isra'el, offered sacrifices before ADONAI. ⁶³ For the sacrifice of peace offerings which Shlomo offered to ADONAI, he offered 22,000 oxen and 120,000 sheep. Thus the king and all the people of Isra'el dedicated the house of ADONAI.

⁶⁴ The same day, the king consecrated the center of the courtyard in front of the house of ADONAI, because he had to offer the burnt offering, the grain offering and the fat of the peace offerings there. For the bronze altar before ADONAI was too small to receive the burnt offering, the grain offering and the fat of the peace offerings.

⁶⁵ So Shlomo celebrated the festival at that time. All Isra'el, a huge gathering [that had come all the way] from the entrance of Hamat to the *Vadi* [of Egypt], celebrated with him before ADONAI our God for seven days and then for seven

more days — fourteen days in all. ⁶⁶ On the eighth day he sent the people away. They blessed the king and returned to their tents full of joy and glad of heart for all the goodness ADONAI had shown to David his servant and to Isra'el his people.

9 ¹ After Shlomo had finished building the house of ADONAI, the royal palace and everything else he wanted to build for himself, ² ADONAI appeared to Shlomo a second time, as he had appeared to him in Giv'on. ³ ADONAI said to him, "I have heard your prayer and your plea that you made before me: I am consecrating this house which you built and placing my name there forever; my eyes and heart will always be there. ⁴ As for you, if you will live in my presence, as did David your father, in pureness of heart and uprightness, doing everything I have ordered you to do, and observing my laws and rulings; ⁵ then I will establish the throne of your rulership over Isra'el forever, just as I promised David your father when I said, 'You will never lack a man on the throne of Isra'el.' ⁶ But if you turn away from following me, you or your children, and do not observe my *mitzvot* and regulations which I have set before you, and go and serve other gods, worshipping them; ⁷ then I will cut off Isra'el from the land I have given them. This house, which I consecrated for my name, I will eject from my sight; and Isra'el will become an example to avoid and an object of scorn among all peoples. ⁸ This house, now so exalted — everyone passing by will gasp in shock at the sight of it and will ask, 'Why has ADONAI done this to this land and to this house?' ⁹ But the answer will be, 'It's because they abandoned ADONAI their God, who brought their ancestors out of the land of Egypt, and took hold of other gods, worshipping and serving them; this is why ADONAI brought all these calamities on them.'"

¹⁰ At the end of twenty years, during which time Shlomo had built the two buildings, the house of ADONAI and the royal palace, ¹¹ King Shlomo gave Hiram twenty cities in the land of the Galil (recall that Hiram the king of Tzor had supplied Shlomo with cedar and cypress logs and with all the gold Shlomo wanted). ¹² Hiram came over from Tzor to see the cities Shlomo had given him, but he was not satisfied with them. ¹³ He said, "What kind of cities are these which you have given me, my brother?" So they have been called the land of Kabul [good for nothing] till this day. ¹⁴ (Hiram had sent the king four tons of gold.)

¹⁵ Following is the account of the forced labor levied by King Shlomo for building the house of ADONAI, his own palace, the Millo, the wall of Yerushalayim, and the cities of Hatzor, Megiddo and Gezer. ¹⁶ Pharaoh king of Egypt had gone up, taken Gezer, burned it to the ground and killed the Kena'ani living in the city; then he had given it as a dowry for his daughter, Shlomo's wife. ¹⁷ So Shlomo rebuilt Gezer; he also built Lower Beit-Horon, ¹⁸ Ba'alat, Tadmor in the desert, in the land, ¹⁹ as well as all the cities that Shlomo had for storing supplies, the cities for his chariots, the cities for his horsemen, and the other buildings Shlomo wanted to build for himself in Yerushalayim, in the L'vanon and throughout the land he ruled. ²⁰ All the people still left from the Emori, Hitti, P'rizi, Hivi, and Y'vusi, who were not part of the people of Isra'el, ²¹ that is, their descendants remaining after them in the land, whom the people of Isra'el were not able to destroy completely — from them Shlomo levied his forced laborers; as it is to this day. ²² But Shlomo did not raise any of his forced labor from the people of Isra'el; rather, they were the soldiers, his servants, administrators and commanders, and

the officials in charge of his chariots and horsemen. ²³ There were 550 chief officers over Shlomo's work, in charge of the workers.

²⁴ Pharaoh's daughter came up from the City of David to her house, which Shlomo had built for her. After that he built the Millo.

²⁵ Three times a year Shlomo offered burnt offerings and peace offerings on the altar which he had built for ADONAI, offering incense with them on the altar before ADONAI. So he finished the house.

²⁶ King Shlomo built a fleet of ships in 'Etzyon-Gever, by Elot on the shore of the Sea of Suf in the land of Edom. ²⁷ Hiram sent some of his own servants, experienced sailors who understood the sea, to serve with Shlomo's servants. ²⁸ They went to Ofir and took from there gold, fourteen tons of it, which they brought back to King Shlomo.

10 ¹ When the queen of Sh'va heard what was being said about Shlomo because of the name of ADONAI, she came to test him with difficult questions. ² She arrived in Yerushalayim accompanied by a very great retinue, including camels bearing spices and gold in great abundance, and precious stones. When she appeared before Shlomo she spoke with him about everything on her heart, ³ and Shlomo answered all her questions; nothing was hidden from the king that he could not explain to her. ⁴ After the queen of Sh'va had seen all Shlomo's wisdom, the palace he had built, ⁵ the food at his table, the manner of seating his officials, the manner in which his staff served him, how they were dressed, his personal servants and his burnt offering which he offered in the house of ADONAI, it left her breathless. ⁶ She said to the king, "What I heard in my own country about your deeds and your wisdom is true, ⁷ but I couldn't believe the report until I came and saw for myself. Actually, they didn't tell me even the half of it — your wisdom and prosperity surpass the reports I heard. ⁸ How happy your people must be, how happy these servants of yours who are always here attending you and get to hear your wisdom! ⁹ Blessed be ADONAI your God, who took pleasure in you to put you on the throne of Isra'el. Because of ADONAI's eternal love for Isra'el, he has made you king, to administer judgment and justice fairly." ¹⁰ Then she gave the king four tons of gold, a huge amount of spices, and precious stones; never again did there arrive such an abundance of spices as those the queen of Sh'va gave to King Shlomo.

¹¹ Hiram's fleet which had brought gold from Ofir now brought in from Ofir a large quantity of sandalwood and precious stones. ¹² The king used the sandalwood to make columns for the house of ADONAI and for the royal palace, and also lyres and lutes for the singers. No sandalwood like it has come or been seen to this day.

¹³ King Shlomo gave the queen of Sh'va everything she wanted, whatever she asked, in addition to the presents he gave her on his own initiative. After this, she returned and went back to her own country, she and her servants.

¹⁴ The weight of the gold Shlomo received annually came to twenty-two tons of gold, ¹⁵ besides that which came from sales taxes, customs duties and assessments collected by all the kings of the mixed peoples and by the district governors. ¹⁶ King Shlomo made 200 large shields of hammered gold; fifteen pounds of gold went into one shield. ¹⁷ He made 300 more shields of hammered gold, with three-and-three-quarters pounds going into one shield; the king put these in the House of the L'vanon Forest.

^{18} The king also made a large throne of ivory and overlaid it with the finest gold. ^{19} The throne had six steps, a back with a rounded top, arms on either side of the seat, two lions standing beside the arms, ^{20} and twelve more lions standing on each side of the six steps. Nothing like it had ever been made in any kingdom.

^{21} All King Shlomo's drinking vessels were of gold; and all the utensils in the House of the L'vanon Forest were of pure gold; none was of silver, for in Shlomo's time it was regarded as having little value. ^{22} The king had a fleet of large "Tarshish" ships along with Hiram's fleet; once every three years the "Tarshish" fleet came in, bringing gold, silver, ivory, apes and peacocks.

^{23} So King Shlomo surpassed all the kings on earth in both wealth and wisdom. ^{24} All the earth sought to have an audience with Shlomo, in order to hear his wisdom, which God had put in his heart. ^{25} Each one brought his present — articles of silver, articles of gold, clothing, armor, spices, horses and mules; and this continued year after year.

^{26} Shlomo amassed chariots and horsemen; he had 1,400 chariots and 12,000 horsemen; he assigned them to the chariot cities and to the king in Yerushalayim. ^{27} The king made silver in Yerushalayim as common as stones, and he made cedars as abundant as sycamore-fig trees are in the Sh'felah. ^{28} Shlomo's horses had been brought from Egypt and from Keveh, with the king's agents having bought them from the dealers in Keveh at the going price. ^{29} A chariot from Egypt cost fifteen pounds of silver *shekel*s and a horse three-and-three quarters pounds [of *shekel*s]; all the kings of the Hittim and the kings of Aram purchased them at these prices through Shlomo's agents.

11 ^{1} King Shlomo loved many foreign women besides the daughter of Pharaoh. There were women from the Mo'avi, 'Amoni, Edomi, Tzidoni and Hitti — ^{2} nations about which *Adonai* had said to the people of Isra'el, "You are not to go among them or they among you, because they will turn your hearts away toward their gods." But Shlomo was deeply attached to them by his love. ^{3} He had 700 wives, all princesses, and 300 concubines; and his wives turned his heart away. ^{4} For when Shlomo became old, his wives turned his heart away toward other gods; so that he was not wholehearted with *Adonai* his God, as David his father had been. ^{5} For Shlomo followed 'Ashtoret the goddess of the Tzidoni and Milkom the abomination of the 'Amoni. ^{6} Thus Shlomo did what was evil in *Adonai*'s view and did not fully follow *Adonai*, as David his father had done. ^{7} Shlomo built a high place for K'mosh the abomination of Mo'av on the hill in front of Yerushalayim, and another for Molekh the abomination of the people of 'Amon. ^{8} This is what he did for all his foreign wives, who then offered and sacrificed to their gods. ^{9} So *Adonai* grew angry with Shlomo, because his heart had turned away from *Adonai* the God of Isra'el, who had appeared to him twice ^{10} and given him orders concerning this matter that he should not follow other gods. But he didn't obey *Adonai*'s orders.

^{11} So *Adonai* said to Shlomo, "Since this is what has been in your mind, and you haven't kept my covenant and my regulations which I ordered you to obey, I will tear the kingdom from you and give it to your servant. ^{12} However, for David your father's sake I won't do it while you are alive, but I will tear it away from your son. ^{13} Even then, I won't tear away all the kingdom; I will give one tribe to your son for the sake of David my servant and for the sake of Yerushalayim, which I have chosen."

[14] Then *ADONAI* raised up an adversary against Shlomo, Hadad the Edomi, of the royal line of Edom. [15] Back when David had been in Edom, and Yo'av the commander of the army had gone up to bury the dead, having killed every male in Edom [16] (for Yo'av and all Isra'el had stayed there six months, until he had eliminated every male in Edom), [17] Hadad had fled, he and a number of Edomi servants of his father's with him, and gone into Egypt; at the time Hadad had been but a small boy. [18] On their way, they passed through Midyan and arrived in Pa'ran, took with them men from Pa'ran, and went on into Egypt, to Pharaoh king of Egypt. He gave Hadad a house, saw to it that he had food and gave him land. [19] Hadad became a great favorite of Pharaoh, so that he gave him his own wife's sister in marriage, that is, the sister of Tachp'neis the queen. [20] The sister of Tachp'neis bore him G'nuvat his son, and Tachp'neis brought him up in Pharaoh's own house, so that G'nuvat was in Pharaoh's house along with Pharaoh's sons. [21] When Hadad in Egypt heard that David slept with his ancestors and Yo'av the commander of the army was dead, Hadad said to Pharaoh, "Let me leave, so that I can return to my own country." [22] Pharaoh asked him, "But what have you lacked with me that makes you want just now to go to your own country?" "Nothing in particular," he replied, "but let me leave, anyway."

[23] God raised up another adversary against Shlomo, Rezon the son of Elyada, who had fled from his lord Hadad'ezer king of Tzovah [24] when David killed the men from Tzovah. Rezon rallied men to himself and became the leader of a band of marauders; they went to Dammesek and settled there, while he became king of Dammesek. [25] He remained an adversary as long as Shlomo lived, causing difficulties in addition to those of Hadad. He detested Isra'el and ruled Aram.

[26] Also Yarov'am the son of N'vat, an Efrati from Tz'redah, whose mother's name was Tz'ru'ah, one of Shlomo's servants, rebelled against the king. [27] Here is the reason he rebelled against the king: Shlomo was building the Millo and closing the breach in [the wall of] the City of David his father. [28] Now this Yarov'am was a strong, energetic man; and Shlomo, seeing how serious the young man was, made him supervisor over all the work being done by the tribe of Yosef. [29] Once, during this period, when Yarov'am had gone out of Yerushalayim, the prophet Achiyah from Shiloh spotted him traveling. Achiyah was wearing a new cloak, and the two of them were alone in open country. [30] Achiyah took hold of his new cloak that he was wearing and tore it into twelve pieces. [31] Then he said to Yarov'am, "Take ten pieces for yourself! For here is what *ADONAI* the God of Isra'el says: 'I am going to tear the kingdom out of Shlomo's hand, and I will give ten tribes to you. [32] But he will keep one tribe for the sake of my servant David and for the sake of Yerushalayim, the city I have chosen from all the tribes of Isra'el. [33] I will do this because they have abandoned me and worshipped 'Ashtoret the goddess of the Tzidoni, K'mosh the god of Mo'av and Milkom the god of the people of 'Amon. They haven't lived according to my ways, so that they could do what was right in my view and obey my regulations and rulings, as did David his father. [34] Nevertheless, I will not take the entire kingdom away from him; but I will make him prince as long as he lives, for the sake of David my servant, whom I chose, because he obeyed my *mitzvot* and regulations. [35] However, I will take the kingdom away from his son and give ten tribes of it to you. [36] To his son I will give one tribe, so that David my servant

will always have a light burning before me in Yerushalayim, the city I chose for myself as the place to put my name. ³⁷ I will take you, and you will rule over everything you want; you will be king over Isra'el. ³⁸ Now if you will listen to all that I order you, live according to my ways and do what is right in my view, so that you observe my regulations and *mitzvot*, as David my servant did; then I will be with you, and I will build you a lasting dynasty, as I built for David; and I will give Isra'el to you. ³⁹ For this [offense] I will trouble David's descendants, but not forever." ⁴⁰ Because of this Shlomo tried to kill Yarov'am; but Yarov'am roused himself, fled to Egypt, to Shishak king of Egypt, and stayed in Egypt until the death of Shlomo.

⁴¹ Other activities of Shlomo, all he accomplished and his wisdom are recorded in the Annals of Shlomo. ⁴² The length of Shlomo's reign in Yerushalayim over all Isra'el was forty years. ⁴³ Then Shlomo slept with his ancestors and was buried in the City of David his father, and Rechav'am his son became king in his place.

12 ¹ Rechav'am went to Sh'khem, where all Isra'el had come to proclaim him king. ² When Yarov'am the son of N'vat heard of it — for he was still in Egypt, where he had fled from Shlomo; so Yarov'am was living in Egypt; ³ but they sent and summoned him — Yarov'am and the whole community of Isra'el came and said to Rechav'am, ⁴ "Your father laid a harsh yoke on us. But if you will lighten the harsh service we had to render your father and ease his heavy yoke that he put on us, we will serve you." ⁵ He said to them, "Leave me alone for three days, then come back to me." So the people left.

⁶ King Rechav'am consulted the older men who had been in attendance on Shlomo his father during his lifetime and asked, "What advice would you give me as to how to answer these people?" ⁷ They said to him, "If you will start today being a servant to these people — if you will serve them, be responsive to them and give them favorable consideration, then they will be your servants forever." ⁸ But he didn't take the advice the older men gave him; instead he consulted the young men he had grown up with, who were now his attendants. ⁹ He asked them, "What advice would you give me, so that we can give an answer to these people who said to me, 'Lighten the yoke that your father laid on us'?" ¹⁰ The young men he had grown up with said to him, "These people who said to you, 'Your father made our yoke heavy; but you, make it lighter for us' — here's the answer you should give them: 'My little finger is thicker than my father's waist! ¹¹ Yes, my father burdened you with a heavy yoke, but I will make it heavier! My father controlled you with whips, but I will control you with scorpions!'"

¹² So Yarov'am and all the people came to Rechav'am the third day, as the king had requested by saying, "Come to me again the third day"; ¹³ and the king answered the people harshly. Abandoning the advice the older men had given him, ¹⁴ he addressed them according to the advice of the young men and said, "My father made your yoke heavy, but I will add to your yoke! My father controlled you with whips, but I will control you with scorpions!" ¹⁵ So the king didn't listen to the people; and that was something *Adonai* brought about, so that he could fulfill his word, which *Adonai* had spoken through Achiyah from Shiloh to Yarov'am the son of N'vat.

¹⁶ When all Isra'el saw that the king wasn't listening to them, the people answered the king,

"Do we have any share in David?
We have no heritage in the son of Yishai!
Go to your tents, Isra'el!
Care for your own house, David!"

So Isra'el left for their tents. ¹⁷ But as for the people of Isra'el living in the cities of Y'hudah, Rechav'am ruled over them. ¹⁸ King Rechav'am then sent Adoram, who was in charge of forced labor; but all Isra'el stoned him to death. King Rechav'am managed to mount his chariot and flee to Yerushalayim. ¹⁹ Isra'el has been in rebellion against the dynasty of David to this day.

²⁰ On hearing that Yarov'am had returned, all Isra'el summoned him to the assembly and proclaimed him king over all Isra'el. No one followed the dynasty of David except the tribe of Y'hudah.

²¹ When Rechav'am arrived in Yerushalayim, he assembled all the house of Y'hudah and the tribe of Binyamin, 180,000 select soldiers, to fight the house of Isra'el and bring the rulership back to Rechav'am the son of Shlomo. ²² But this word from God came to Sh'ma'yah the man of God: ²³ "Speak to Rechav'am the son of Shlomo, king of Y'hudah, to all the house of Y'hudah and Binyamin and to the rest of the people; tell them ²⁴ that this is what ADONAI says: 'You are not to go up and fight your brothers the people of Isra'el! Every man is to go back home, because this is my doing.'" They paid attention to the word of ADONAI and turned back, as ADONAI had told them to do.

²⁵ Then Yarov'am built up Sh'khem in the hills of Efrayim and lived there. After that, he left and built up P'nu'el. ²⁶ Nevertheless Yarov'am said to himself, "Now the rulership will return to the house of David. ²⁷ For if these people continue going up to offer sacrifices in the house of ADONAI in Yerushalayim, their hearts will turn back to their lord, Rechav'am king of Y'hudah. Then they will kill me and return to Rechav'am king of Y'hudah." ²⁸ After seeking advice, the king made two calves of gold and said to the people, "You have been going up to Yerushalayim long enough! Here are your gods, Isra'el, who brought you out of the land of Egypt!" ²⁹ He placed one in Beit-El and the other in Dan, ³⁰ and the affair became a sin, for the people went to worship before the one [in Beit-El and] all the way to Dan [to worship the other]. ³¹ He also set up temples on the high places and made *cohanim* from among all the people, even though they were not descended from Levi.

³² Yarov'am instituted a festival in the eighth month, on the fifteenth day of the month, similar to the festival held in Y'hudah; he went up to the altar in Beit-El to sacrifice to the calves he had made; and he placed in Beit-El the *cohanim* he had appointed for the high places. ³³ He went up to the altar which he had set up in Beit-El on the fifteenth day of the eighth month, in the month which he had chosen on his own, and instituted a festival for the people of Isra'el; he went up to the altar to burn incense.

13 ¹ Just then, as Yarov'am was standing by the altar to burn incense, a man of God came out of Y'hudah, directed to Beit-El by a word from ADONAI. ² And by the word from ADONAI he cried out against the altar: "Altar, altar, here is what ADONAI says: 'A son will be born to the house of David; his name will be Yoshiyahu; and on you he will sacrifice the *cohanim* of the high places who burn incense on you! They will burn human bones on you!'" ³ That same day he also gave a sign: "Here is the sign which A*DONAI* has decreed:

> "'The altar will be split apart;
> the ashes on it will be scattered about.'"

⁴ When the king heard what the man of God said, how he denounced the altar in Beit-El, Yarov'am took his hand away from the altar and said, "Seize him!" But his hand, the one he had stretched out against him, shriveled up; so that he could not draw it back to himself. ⁵ Also the altar was split apart, and the ashes scattered from the altar, according to the sign which the man of God had given by the word of A*DONAI*. ⁶ The king then responded to the man of God. "Ask now the favor of A*DONAI* your God," he said, "and pray for me, that my hand will be restored to me." The man of God prayed to A*DONAI*, and the king's hand was restored to him and became as it had been before. ⁷ The king then said to the man of God, "Come home with me, and refresh yourself, and I will give you a reward. ⁸ But the man of God replied to the king, "Even if you give me half your household, I will not accept your hospitality; nor will I eat food or drink water in this place. ⁹ For this is the order I received through the word of A*DONAI*: 'Don't eat food or drink water, and don't return by the road you took when you came.'" ¹⁰ So he went another way and did not return by the road by which he had come to Beit-El.

¹¹ Now there lived an old prophet in Beit-El; and one of his sons came and told him all the things the man of God had done that day in Beit-El; also they told their father what he had said to the king. ¹² Their father asked them, "Which way did he go?" For his sons had seen what road the man of God from Y'hudah had taken. ¹³ He then said to his sons, "Saddle the donkey for me." So they saddled the donkey for him; and, riding on it, ¹⁴ he went after the man of God. He found him sitting under a pistachio tree and said to him, "Are you the man of God who came from Y'hudah?" He answered, "I am." ¹⁵ Then he said to him, "Come home with me and eat some food." ¹⁶ He replied, "I cannot return with you or partake of your hospitality, nor will I eat food or drink water with you in this place; ¹⁷ because it was said to me by the word of A*DONAI*, 'You are not to eat food or drink water there, and you are not to go back by the way you came.'" ¹⁸ The other said to him, "I too am a prophet, just like you; and an angel spoke to me by the word of A*DONAI* and said, 'Bring him back with you to your house, so that he can eat food and drink water.'" But he was lying to him. ¹⁹ So he went back with him and did eat food and drink water in his house. ²⁰ As they were sitting at the table, the word of A*DONAI* came to the prophet who had brought him back; ²¹ and he cried to the man of God who had come from Y'hudah, "Here is what A*DONAI* says: 'Since you rebelled against the word of A*DONAI* and didn't obey the *mitzvah* A*DONAI* your God gave you, ²² but came back and ate food and drank water in the place where he warned you not to eat food or drink water, your corpse will not arrive at the tomb of your ancestors.'" ²³ After he had eaten food and drunk, he saddled the donkey for the prophet he had brought back. ²⁴ But after he had gone, a lion encountered the man of God on the road and killed him. His corpse lay there in the road, with the donkey and the lion standing next to it. ²⁵ In time, people passed by and saw the corpse lying in the road with the lion standing next to it; and they came and told about it in the city where the old prophet lived.

²⁶ When the prophet who had brought him back from the road heard about it, he said, "It is the man of God who rebelled against the word of ADONAI; this is why ADONAI handed him over to the lion to tear him to pieces and kill him, in keeping with the word ADONAI spoke to him." ²⁷ To his sons he said, "Saddle the donkey for me," and they saddled it. ²⁸ He went and found his corpse lying in the road, with the donkey and the lion standing next to the corpse; the lion had neither eaten the corpse nor attacked the donkey. ²⁹ The prophet picked up the corpse of the man of God, laid it on the donkey and brought it back to the city where he lived, to mourn and bury him. ³⁰ He laid the corpse in his own burial cave, and they mourned him— "Oh! My brother!" ³¹ After burying him he said to his sons, "When I die, put me in the burial cave where the man of God is buried; lay my bones next to his bones. ³² For the thing he cried by the word of ADONAI against the altar in Beit-El and against all the temples on the high places near the cities of Shomron will surely happen."

³³ After this, Yarov'am did not turn back from his evil way but continued appointing *cohanim* for the high places from among all the people; he consecrated anyone who wanted to be a *cohen* of the high places. ³⁴ This brought sin to the house of Yarov'am that would eventually cut it off and destroy it from the face of the earth.

14 ¹ At this time, Aviyah the son of Yarov'am fell ill. ² Yarov'am said to his wife, "Please come, and disguise yourself, so that you won't be recognized as Yarov'am's wife, and go to Shiloh. Achiyah the prophet is there, the one who said that I would be king over these people. ³ Take with you ten loaves of bread, some cakes and a jug of honey; and go to him. He will tell you what will happen to the boy."

⁴ Yarov'am's wife did this; she set out, went to Shiloh and arrived at the house of Achiyah. Now Achiyah could not see, because his eyes were dim with age. ⁵ ADONAI had told Achiyah, "Yarov'am's wife is on her way to you to ask about her son, who is ill. You are to tell her thus and thus; moreover, when she comes, she will be pretending she is another woman."

⁶ When Achiyah heard the sound of her feet as she came in the door, he said, "Enter, wife of Yarov'am! Why pretend you are someone else? I've been given bad news for you. ⁷ Go, tell Yarov'am that this is what ADONAI says: 'I raised you up from among the people, made you prince over my people Isra'el, ⁸ tore the kingdom away from the dynasty of David and gave it to you. In spite of this, you have not been like my servant David, who obeyed my *mitzvot* and followed me with all his heart, so that he could do only what I regarded as right. ⁹ Rather, you have committed more evil than anyone before you! You went and made other gods for yourself and images of cast metal to make me angry, but me you shoved behind your back! ¹⁰ Therefore, I will now bring disaster on the house of Yarov'am. I will cut off every male of Yarov'am's line, whether a slave or free in Isra'el; I will sweep away the house of Yarov'am as completely as when someone sweeps away dung until it's all gone. ¹¹ If someone from the line of Yarov'am dies in the city, the dogs will eat him; if he dies in the countryside, the vultures will eat him. For ADONAI has said it.' ¹² So get up and go home; when your feet enter the city, the boy will die. ¹³ All Isra'el will mourn him, and they will bury him; he is the only one of Yarov'am's line who will lie in a grave, because he alone in the house of Yarov'am has in him an element of good toward ADONAI the God of Isra'el. ¹⁴ Moreover, ADONAI will raise up for himself a king

over Isra'el who at that time will cut off the house of Yarov'am. And what will God do now? [15] ADONAI will strike Isra'el until it shakes like a reed in the water; he will uproot Isra'el from this good land, which he gave to their ancestors, and scatter them beyond the [Euphrates] River; because they made sacred poles for themselves, thus making ADONAI angry. [16] He will give up on Isra'el because of the sins of Yarov'am, which he committed himself, and with which he made Isra'el sin as well."

[17] Yarov'am's wife got up, left and went to Tirtzah. The moment she reached the threshold of the house, the boy died. [18] All Isra'el buried him and mourned him, in keeping with the word of ADONAI spoken through his servant Achiyah the prophet.

[19] Other activities of Yarov'am, how he fought and how he ruled are recorded in the Annals of the Kings of Isra'el. [20] Yarov'am's reign lasted twenty-two years; then he slept with his ancestors, and Nadav his son became king in his place.

[21] Rechav'am the son of Shlomo was reigning in Y'hudah. Rechav'am was forty-one years old when he began to rule; and he ruled seventeen years in Yerushalayim, the city ADONAI had chosen from all the tribes of Isra'el to bear his name; his mother's name was Na'amah the 'Amonit.

[22] Y'hudah did what was evil from ADONAI's perspective; they made him angry because of their sins, which were worse than any their ancestors had committed. [23] For they erected high places, standing-stones and sacred poles on every high hill and under every green tree. [24] Also there were male and female cult-prostitutes in the land attached to these shrines, doing all the disgusting things which the nations did that ADONAI had expelled ahead of the people of Isra'el.

[25] In the fifth year of King Rechav'am, Shishak king of Egypt attacked Yerushalayim. [26] He took the treasures in the house of ADONAI and the treasures in the royal palace — he took everything, including all the gold shields Shlomo had made. [27] To replace them, King Rechav'am made shields of bronze, which he entrusted to the commanders of the contingent guarding the gate to the royal palace. [28] Whenever the king went to the house of ADONAI, the guard would get the shields; later they would return them to the guardroom.

[29] Other activities of Rechav'am and all his accomplishments are recorded in the Annals of the Kings of Y'hudah. [30] But there was continual war between Rechav'am and Yarov'am. [31] Rechav'am slept with his ancestors and was buried with his ancestors in the City of David; his mother's name was Na'amah the 'Amonit. Then Aviyam his son became king in his place.

15 [1] It was in the eighteenth year of King Yarov'am the son of N'vat that Aviyam began his reign over Y'hudah. [2] He ruled three years in Yerushalayim; his mother's name was Ma'akhah the daughter of Avishalom. [3] He committed all the sins his father had committed before him; he was not wholehearted with ADONAI his God, as David his forefather had been. [4] Nevertheless, for David's sake ADONAI his God gave him a lamp burning in Yerushalayim by establishing his son after him and making Yerushalayim secure. [5] For David had done what was right from ADONAI's perspective; he had not turned away from anything he had ordered him to do, as long as he lived, except in the matter of Uriyah the Hitti.

[6] There was war between Rechav'am and Yarov'am as long as he lived.

[7] Other activities of Aviyam and all his accomplishments are recorded in the Annals of the Kings of Y'hudah. But there was war between Aviyam and Yarov'am.

⁸ Aviyam slept with his ancestors, and they buried him in the City of David. Then Asa his son became king in his place.

⁹ It was in the twentieth year of Yarov'am king of Isra'el that Asa began his reign over Y'hudah. ¹⁰ He ruled forty-one years in Yerushalayim; his [grand]mother's name was Ma'akhah the daughter of Avishalom. ¹¹ Asa did what was right from the perspective of ADONAI, as David his ancestor had done. ¹² He rid the land of cult-prostitutes and removed all the idols his ancestors had made. ¹³ He also deposed Ma'akhah from her position as queen mother, because she had made a disgusting image as an *asherah*. Asa cut down this image of hers and burned it in *Vadi* Kidron. ¹⁴ But the high places were not removed. Nevertheless, Asa was wholehearted with ADONAI throughout his life. ¹⁵ He brought into the house of ADONAI all the articles his father had consecrated, also the things he himself had consecrated — silver, gold and utensils.

¹⁶ There was war between Asa and Ba'sha king of Isra'el as long as they both lived. ¹⁷ Ba'sha attacked Y'hudah, and he fortified Ramah to prevent anyone's leaving or entering the territory of Asa king of Y'hudah. ¹⁸ Then Asa took all the silver and gold left among the treasures of the house of ADONAI and among the treasures of the royal palace; and, entrusting them to his servants, King Asa sent them to Ben-Hadad the son of Tavrimmon, the son of Hezyon, king of Aram, who lived in Dammesek, with this message: ¹⁹ "There is a covenant between me and you, which existed already between my father and your father. Here, I am sending you a present of silver and gold; go, and break your covenant with Ba'sha king of Isra'el, so that he will leave me alone." ²⁰ Ben-Hadad did as King Asa asked — he sent the commanders of his armies against the cities of Isra'el, attacking 'Iyon, Dan, Avel-Beit-Ma'akhah, all of Kinn'rot and all the land of Naftali. ²¹ As soon as Ba'sha heard of it, he stopped building Ramah and stayed in Tirtzah. ²² King Asa then issued a proclamation requiring every man in Y'hudah, with no exception, to come and carry off the stones and timber Ba'sha had used to fortify Ramah. With them King Asa fortified Geva of Binyamin and Mitzpah.

²³ The other activities of Asa, all his power, all his accomplishments and the cities he fortified are recorded in the Annals of the Kings of Y'hudah. But in his old age he suffered from a disease in his legs. ²⁴ Asa slept with his ancestors and was buried with his ancestors in the City of David his ancestor. Then Y'hoshafat his son became king in his place.

²⁵ It was in the second year of Asa king of Y'hudah that Nadav the son of Yarov'am began his reign over Isra'el, and he ruled Isra'el two years. ²⁶ He did what was evil from ADONAI's perspective, following the example of his father and the sin through which he had made Isra'el sin.

²⁷ Ba'sha the son of Achiyah, from the descendants of Yissakhar, conspired against him; and Ba'sha attacked him at Gib'ton, which belonged to the P'lishtim; for at the time Nadav and all Isra'el were besieging Gib'ton. ²⁸ It was in the third year of Asa king of Y'hudah that Ba'sha killed Nadav and became king in his place.

²⁹ As soon as he had become king he killed off the entire house of Yarov'am, destroying every living soul and leaving not one survivor. This was in keeping with what ADONAI had said through his servant Achiyah from Shiloh; ³⁰ it was the punishment for the sins Yarov'am had committed and through which he had made Isra'el sin, thereby angering ADONAI the God of Isra'el.

³¹ Other activities of Nadav and all his accomplishments are recorded in the Annals of the Kings of Isra'el. ³² There was war between Asa and Ba'sha king of Isra'el as long as they both lived.

³³ It was in the third year of Asa king of Y'hudah that Ba'sha the son of Achiyah began his reign over all Isra'el in Tirtzah, and his rule lasted twenty-four years. ³⁴ He did what was wrong from *Adonai*'s perspective, following the example of Yarov'am and committing the sin through which he had made Isra'el sin.

16 ¹ The word of *Adonai* came to Yehu the son of Hanani against Ba'sha: ² "I raised you up out of the dust and made you prince over my people Isra'el. But you have lived in the same way as Yarov'am and caused my people Isra'el to sin, so that their sinning has made me angry. ³ Therefore I will sweep away Ba'sha and his house completely; I will make your house like the house of Yarov'am the son of N'vat. ⁴ If someone from the line of Ba'sha dies in the city, the dogs will eat him; if he dies in the countryside, the vultures will eat him."

⁵ Other activities of Ba'sha, his accomplishments and his power are recorded in the Annals of the Kings of Isra'el. ⁶ Ba'sha slept with his ancestors, and Elah his son became king in his place. ⁷ Through the prophet Yehu the son of Hanani the word of *Adonai* was proclaimed against Ba'sha and his house both because he did so much evil from *Adonai*'s perspective, angering him with his actions and becoming like the house of Yarov'am, and because he killed [Nadav].

⁸ It was in the twenty-sixth year of Asa king of Y'hudah that Elah the son of Ba'sha began his reign over all Isra'el in Tirtzah, and he ruled for two years. ⁹ His servant Zimri, commander of half of his chariots, plotted against him. Finally, one time when Elah was in Tirtzah, drinking himself senseless in the house of Artza, administrator of the palace in Tirtzah, ¹⁰ Zimri entered, struck him down and killed him. This was in the twenty-seventh year of Asa king of Y'hudah; Zimri then took Elah's place as king.

¹¹ At the beginning of his reign, as soon as he took over the throne, he killed off the entire house of Ba'sha; he left not a single male, neither of his relatives nor of his friends. ¹² Thus Zimri eliminated all the house of Ba'sha, in keeping with the word of *Adonai* spoken against Ba'sha through Yehu the prophet. This word had been spoken ¹³ because of all of Ba'sha's sins and the sins of Elah his son, which they committed and with which they made Isra'el sin, thereby angering *Adonai* the God of Isra'el with their worthless idols. ¹⁴ Other activities of Elah and all his accomplishments are recorded in the Annals of the Kings of Isra'el.

¹⁵ It was in the twenty-seventh year of Asa king of Y'hudah that Zimri ruled for seven days in Tirtzah. At that time, the army was besieging Gib'ton, which belonged to the P'lishtim. ¹⁶ The troops in their camp heard it said that Zimri had plotted and killed the king, whereupon that same day, there in the camp, all Isra'el made 'Omri, the commander of the army, king over Isra'el. ¹⁷ 'Omri and all Isra'el with him withdrew from Gib'ton and besieged Tirtzah. ¹⁸ When Zimri saw that the city had been captured, he went into the citadel of the royal palace and burned down the royal palace over him, so that he died. ¹⁹ This came about because of the sins he committed in doing what was evil from *Adonai*'s perspective, in living as Yarov'am had lived, and in sinning by making Isra'el sin. ²⁰ Other activities of Zimri and his conspiracy are recorded in the Annals of the Kings of Isra'el.

²¹ At this point the people of Isra'el divided into two factions. Half of the people went after Tivni the son of Ginat to make him king, while the other half followed 'Omri. ²² But the faction supporting 'Omri won out over that of Tivni the son of Ginat; so Tivni died, and 'Omri became king.

²³ It was in the thirty-first year of Asa king of Y'hudah that 'Omri began his reign over Isra'el, and he ruled for twelve years, six of them in Tirtzah. ²⁴ He bought Mount Shomron from Shemer for 132 pounds of silver. On the mountain he built a city, which he named Shomron after Shemer, who had owned the mountain.

²⁵ 'Omri did what was evil from ADONAI's perspective, outdoing all his predecessors in wickedness; ²⁶ for he lived entirely in the manner of Yarov'am the son of N'vat, committing the sins with which he made Isra'el sin, thereby angering ADONAI the God of Isra'el with their worthless idols. ²⁷ Other activities of 'Omri and the power he demonstrated are recorded in the Annals of the Kings of Isra'el. ²⁸ Then 'Omri slept with his ancestors and was buried in Shomron, and Ach'av his son became king in his place.

²⁹ It was in the thirty-eighth year of Asa king of Y'hudah that Ach'av the son of 'Omri began his rule over Isra'el; Ach'av the son of 'Omri ruled twenty-two years over Isra'el in Shomron. ³⁰ Ach'av the son of 'Omri did what was evil from ADONAI's perspective, outdoing all his predecessors [in wickedness]. ³¹ But then, as if it had been a trifling thing for him to commit the sins of Yarov'am the son of N'vat, he took as his wife Izevel the daughter of Etba'al king of the Tzidonim, and went and served Ba'al and worshipped him. ³² He erected an altar for Ba'al in the house of Ba'al, which he had built in Shomron. ³³ Ach'av also set up the *asherah*; indeed, Ach'av did more to anger ADONAI the God of Isra'el, than all the kings of Isra'el preceding him. ³⁴ It was during his time that Hi'el of Beit-El rebuilt Yericho. He laid its foundation at the cost of his firstborn son Aviram and erected its gates at the cost of his youngest son S'guv. This was in keeping with the word of ADONAI spoken through Y'hoshua the son of Nun.

17 ¹ Eliyahu from Tishbe, an inhabitant of Gil'ad, said to Ach'av, "As ADONAI the God of Isra'el lives, before whom I stand, there will be neither rain nor dew in the years ahead unless I say so." ² Then the word of ADONAI came to him: ³ "Leave here, turn to the east, and hide in *Vadi* K'rit near the Yarden. ⁴ You are to drink from the stream, and I have ordered the ravens to feed you there." ⁵ So he went and acted according to the word of ADONAI— he went and lived in *Vadi* K'rit near the Yarden. ⁶ The ravens brought him bread and meat in the morning, and bread and meat in the evening; and he drank from the stream. ⁷ After a while the stream dried up, because there was no rain in the land.

⁸ Then this word of ADONAI came to him: ⁹ "Get up; go to Tzarfat, a village in Tzidon; and live there. I have ordered a widow there to provide for you." ¹⁰ So he set out and went to Tzarfat. On reaching the gate of the city, he saw a widow there gathering sticks. He called out to her, "Please bring a little water in a container for me to drink." ¹¹ As she was going to get it, he called after her, "Please bring me a piece of bread in your hand." ¹² She answered, "As ADONAI your God lives, I have nothing baked, only a handful of meal in a pot and a little oil in the jug. Here I am, gathering a couple sticks of wood, so that I can go and cook it for myself and my son. After we have eaten that, we will die." ¹³ Eliyahu said to her, "Don't be afraid. Go; and do what you said; but first, use a little of it to make me a small loaf of bread; and

bring it out to me. After that, make food for yourself and your son. ¹⁴ For this is what ADONAI the God of Isra'el, says: 'The pot of meal will not get used up, nor will there fail to be oil in the jug, until the day ADONAI sends rain down on the land.'" ¹⁵ She went and acted according to what Eliyahu had said; and she, he and her household had food to eat for a long time. ¹⁶ The pot of meal did not get used up, nor did there fail to be oil in the jug, in fulfillment of the word of ADONAI spoken through Eliyahu.

¹⁷ A while later, the son of the woman whose house it was fell ill; his illness grew increasingly serious until his breathing stopped. ¹⁸ She said to Eliyahu, "What do you have against me, you man of God? Did you come to me just to remind me how sinful I am by killing my son?" ¹⁹ "Give me your son," he said to her. Taking him from her lap, he carried him into the room upstairs where he was staying and laid him on his own bed. ²⁰ Then he cried out to ADONAI: "ADONAI my God! Have you brought also this misery on the widow I'm staying with by killing her son?" ²¹ He stretched himself out on the child three times and cried out to ADONAI: "ADONAI my God, please! Let this child's soul come back into him!" ²² ADONAI heard Eliyahu's cry, the child's soul came back into him, and he revived. ²³ Eliyahu took the child, brought him down from the upstairs room into the house and gave him to his mother; and Eliyahu said, "See? Your son is alive." ²⁴ The woman replied to Eliyahu, "Now I know that you are a man of God and that the word of ADONAI that you speak is the truth."

18 ¹ A long time passed. Then, in the third year, the word of ADONAI came to Eliyahu: "Go, present yourself to Ach'av, and I will send rain down on the land." ² When Eliyahu went to present himself to Ach'av, the famine in Shomron had become severe. ³ Ach'av called 'Ovadyah, who was in charge of the palace. Now 'Ovadyah greatly revered ADONAI; ⁴ for example, when Izevel was murdering ADONAI's prophets, 'Ovadyah took a hundred prophets, hid them in two caves, fifty in each, and supplied them with food and water. ⁵ Ach'av said to 'Ovadyah, "Go throughout the land, and check all the springs and vadis; maybe we can find grass somewhere, so that we can keep the horses and mules alive and not lose all the animals." ⁶ So they divided between them the territory to be visited; Ach'av went one way by himself, and 'Ovadyah went another way by himself.

⁷ 'Ovadyah was on the road when suddenly Eliyahu encountered him. 'Ovadyah recognized him, fell on his face and said, "Is it really you, my lord Eliyahu?" ⁸ He answered, "Yes, it is I; go, tell your master, 'Eliyahu is here.'" ⁹ 'Ovadyah replied, "How have I sinned, that you would hand your servant over to Ach'av to kill me? ¹⁰ As ADONAI your God lives, there can't be a single nation or kingdom where my master hasn't sent to search you out; and in each kingdom or nation where they said, 'He isn't here,' he made them take an oath that they hadn't found you. ¹¹ Now you say, 'Go tell your master, "Eliyahu is here."' ¹² But as soon as I leave you, the Spirit of ADONAI will carry you off to I don't know where; so that when I come and tell Ach'av, and he can't find you, he will kill me. But I your servant have revered ADONAI from my youth — ¹³ wasn't my lord told what I did when Izevel killed ADONAI's prophets, how I hid a hundred of ADONAI's prophets by fifties in caves and supplied their food and water? ¹⁴ Now you say, 'Go tell your master, "Look, Eliyahu is here."' Why, he'll kill me!" ¹⁵ Eliyahu said, "As ADONAI-Tzva'ot lives, before whom I stand, I will present myself to him today."

¹⁶ So 'Ovadyah went, found Ach'av and told him; and Ach'av went to meet Eliyahu. ¹⁷ When Ach'av saw Eliyahu, Ach'av said to him, "Is it really you, you troubler of Isra'el?" ¹⁸ He answered, "I haven't troubled Isra'el, you have, you and your father's house, by abandoning ADONAI's *mitzvot* and following the *ba'alim*. ¹⁹ Now order all Isra'el to assemble before me on Mount Karmel, along with the 450 prophets of Ba'al and the 400 prophets of the *asherah* who eat at Izevel's table."

²⁰ Ach'av sent word to all the people of Isra'el and assembled the prophets together on Mount Karmel. ²¹ Eliyahu stepped forward before all the people and said, "How long are you going to jump back and forth between two positions? If ADONAI is God, follow him; but if it's Ba'al, follow him!" The people answered him not a word. ²² Then Eliyahu said to the people, "I, I alone, am the only prophet of ADONAI who is left, while Ba'al's prophets number 450. ²³ Let them give us two young bulls, and they can choose the bull they want for themselves. Then let them cut it in pieces and lay it on the wood but put no fire under it. I will prepare the other bull, lay it on the wood and put no fire under it. ²⁴ Then, you, call on the name of your god; and I will call on the name of ADONAI; and the God who answers with fire, let him be God!" All the people answered, "Good idea! Agreed!"

²⁵ Then Eliyahu said to the prophets of Ba'al, "Choose one bull for yourselves, and prepare it first; because there are many of you. Then call on the name of your god, but put no fire under it." ²⁶ They took the bull that was given to them, prepared it and called on the name of Ba'al from morning till noon — "Ba'al! Answer us!" But no voice was heard; and no one answered, as they jumped around on the altar they had made. ²⁷ Around noon Eliyahu began ridiculing them: "Shout louder! After all, he's a god, isn't he? Maybe he's daydreaming, or he's on the potty, or he's away on a trip. Maybe he's asleep, and you have to wake him up." ²⁸ So they shouted louder and slashed themselves with swords and knives, as their custom was, until blood gushed out all over them. ²⁹ By now it was afternoon, and they went on ranting and raving until it was time for the evening offering. But no voice came, no one answered, no one paid any attention.

³⁰ Then Eliyahu said to all the people, "Come here to me." All the people came up to him, as he set about repairing the altar of ADONAI that had been broken down. ³¹ Eliyahu took twelve stones, in keeping with the number of tribes of the sons of Ya'akov, to whom the word of ADONAI had come, saying, "Your name is to be Isra'el." ³² With the stones he built an altar in the name of ADONAI. Then he dug a trench around the altar large enough for half a bushel of grain. ³³ He arranged the wood, cut up the bull and laid it on the wood. ³⁴ Then he said, "Fill four pots with water, and pour it on the burnt offering and on the wood." They did it. "Do it again," he said, and they did it again. "Do it a third time," he said, and they did it a third time. ³⁵ By now the water was flowing around the altar, and it had filled the trench. ³⁶ Then, when it came time for offering the evening offering, Eliyahu the prophet approached and said, "ADONAI, God of Avraham, Yitz'chak and Isra'el, let it be known today that you are God in Isra'el, and that I am your servant, and that I have done all these things at your word. ³⁷ Hear me, ADONAI, hear me, so that this people may know that you, ADONAI, are God, and that you are turning their hearts back to you."

³⁸ Then the fire of ADONAI fell. It consumed the burnt offering, the wood, the stones and the dust; and it licked up the water in the trench. ³⁹ When all the people

saw it, they fell on their faces and said, "ADONAI is God! ADONAI is God!" ⁴⁰ Eliyahu said to them, "Seize the prophets of Ba'al! Don't let one of them escape!" They seized them; and Eliyahu brought them down to *Vadi* Kishon and killed them there.

⁴¹ Then Eliyahu said to Ach'av, "Get up, eat, and drink, because I hear the sound of heavy rain." ⁴² Ach'av went up to eat and drink, while Eliyahu went up to the top of the Karmel. He bowed down to the ground and put his face between his knees. ⁴³ "Now," he said to his servant, "go up, and look out toward the sea." He went up, looked, and said, "There's nothing there." Seven times he said, "Go again." ⁴⁴ The seventh time, the servant said, "Now there's a cloud coming up out of the sea, no bigger than a man's hand." Eliyahu said, "Go up, and say to Ach'av, 'Prepare your chariot, and get down the mountain before the rain stops you!'" ⁴⁵ A little later, the sky grew black with clouds and wind; and heavy rain began falling; as Ach'av, riding in his chariot, made for Yizre'el. ⁴⁶ The hand of ADONAI was on Eliyahu; he tucked up his clothing and ran ahead of Ach'av to the entrance of Yizre'el.

19 ¹ Ach'av told Izevel everything Eliyahu had done and how he had put all the prophets to the sword. ² Then Izevel sent a messenger to say to Eliyahu, "May the gods do terrible things to me and worse ones besides if by this time tomorrow I haven't taken your life, just as you took theirs!" ³ On seeing that, he got up and fled for his life.

When he arrived in Be'er-Sheva, in Y'hudah, he left his servant there; ⁴ but he himself went a day farther into the desert, until he came to a broom tree. He sat down under it and prayed for his own death. "Enough!" he said. "Now, ADONAI, take my life. I'm no better than my ancestors." ⁵ Then he lay down under the broom tree and went to sleep. Suddenly, an angel touched him and said to him, "Get up and eat!" ⁶ He looked, and there by his head was a cake baked on the hot stones and a jug of water. He ate and drank, then lay down again. ⁷ The angel came again, a second time, touched him and said, "Get up and eat, or the journey will be too much for you." ⁸ He got up, ate and drank, and, on the strength of that meal, traveled forty days and nights until he reached Horev the mountain of God.

⁹ There he went into a cave and spent the night. Then the word of ADONAI came to him; he said to him, "What are you doing here, Eliyahu?" ¹⁰ He answered, "I have been very zealous for ADONAI the God of armies, because the people of Isra'el have abandoned your covenant, broken down your altars and killed your prophets with the sword. Now I'm the only one left, and they're coming after me to kill me too." ¹¹ He said, "Go outside, and stand on the mountain before ADONAI"; and right then and there, ADONAI went past. A mighty blast of wind tore the mountains apart and broke the rocks in pieces before ADONAI, but ADONAI was not in the wind. After the wind came an earthquake, but ADONAI was not in the earthquake. ¹² After the earthquake, fire broke out; but ADONAI was not in the fire. And after the fire came a quiet, subdued voice. ¹³ When Eliyahu heard it, he covered his face with his cloak, stepped out and stood at the entrance to the cave. Then a voice came to him and said, "What are you doing here, Eliyahu?" ¹⁴ He answered, "I have been very zealous for ADONAI the God of armies; because the people of Isra'el have abandoned your covenant, broken down your altars and killed your prophets with the sword. Now I'm the only one left, and they're after me to kill me too."

¹⁵ ADONAI said to him, "Go back by way of the Dammesek Desert. When you get there, anoint Haza'el to be king over Aram. ¹⁶ Also anoint Yehu the son of Nimshi to be king over Isra'el, and anoint Elisha the son of Shafat of Avel-M'cholah to be prophet after you. ¹⁷ Yehu will kill whoever escapes the sword of Haza'el, and Elisha will kill whoever escapes the sword of Yehu. ¹⁸ Still, I will spare seven thousand in Isra'el, every knee that hasn't bent down before Ba'al and every mouth that has not kissed him."

¹⁹ So he left and found Elisha the son of Shafat. He was plowing with twelve yoke of oxen; he himself was behind the twelfth. Eliyahu went over to him and threw his cloak on him. ²⁰ He left the oxen, ran after Eliyahu and said, "Please let me kiss my father and mother good-bye; then I will follow you." He answered, "Go; but return, because of what I did to you." ²¹ Elisha stopped following him. Then he took the yoke of oxen, slaughtered them, cooked their meat over the wooden yokes of the oxen and gave it to the people to eat. Then he got up, went after Eliyahu and became his servant.

20 ¹ Now Ben-Hadad the king of Aram rallied his whole army; with him were thirty-two kings, besides horses and chariots. Then he marched on Shomron and laid siege to it. ² He sent messengers inside the city to Ach'av king of Isra'el ³ to say to him, "Here is the message from Ben-Hadad: 'Your silver and gold are mine, also your wives and your best children are mine.'" ⁴ The king of Isra'el answered, "Just as you say, my lord, king; I am yours, along with everything I own."

⁵ The messengers returned and said, "Here is Ben-Hadad's response: 'I sent you a message to hand over your silver, gold, wives and children to me. ⁶ But I am going to send my servants to you tomorrow around this time; they will ransack your house and the houses of your servants; and whatever they see that they like they will seize and remove.'" ⁷ Then the king of Isra'el summoned all the leaders of the land and said, "Please take notice! Do you see how this man is trying to make trouble? First he demanded my wives, children, silver and gold; and I denied him nothing." ⁸ All the leaders and all the people said to him, "Don't listen, and don't agree." ⁹ So he said to Ben-Hadad's messengers, "Tell my lord the king, 'I will do all that you asked of me the first time, but this I cannot do.'" The messengers left and brought word back to him.

¹⁰ Ben-Hadad then sent this message to him: "May the gods do terrible things to me and worse ones as well if there's enough dust in Shomron to give each of my followers a handful!" ¹¹ The king of Isra'el answered, "Tell him: 'He who is putting on his armor shouldn't boast as if he were taking it off!'" ¹² It happened that Ben-Hadad received this message when he was drinking, he and his kings, in the field-barracks. He ordered his servants: "Take up your battle positions!" So they got ready to attack the city.

¹³ At that moment a prophet approached Ach'av king of Isra'el and said, "Here is what ADONAI says: 'Have you seen this vast army? I am going to give you victory over them today. Then you will know that I am ADONAI!'" ¹⁴ Ach'av asked, "Who will defeat them?" He answered, "This is what ADONAI says: 'The young men who serve the district governors.'" He asked, "Who will start the fighting?" and he answered, "You will." ¹⁵ He counted the district governors' young men; there were 232. After that, he counted all the people, all the people of Isra'el; there were 7,000.

¹⁶ They set out at noon. Ben-Hadad was drinking himself senseless in the field-barracks, he and the kings, the thirty-two kings who were his allies. ¹⁷ The district governors' men went out first. Ben-Hadad sent for information, and they reported, "Men have come out from Shomron." ¹⁸ He said, "Whether they have come out for peace or for war, take them alive." ¹⁹ So the district governors' men left the city, followed by the army; ²⁰ and each one killed his man. Aram fled, and Isra'el pursued them. Ben-Hadad king of Aram escaped on horseback with some of the cavalry. ²¹ The king of Isra'el went out and attacked the horses and chariots, inflicting a massive defeat on Aram.

²² Afterwards, the prophet approached the king of Isra'el and said to him, "Go, regroup your forces, and think carefully what to do, for next year at this time the king of Aram will renew his attack." ²³ Meanwhile, the servants of the king of Aram said to him, "Their God is a God of the hills; that's why they were stronger than we were. But if we fight them on level ground, we will certainly be stronger than they are. ²⁴ Also do this: remove all the kings from their commands, and put professional officers in their place. ²⁵ Then recruit an army as big as the army you lost, horse for horse and chariot for chariot. We will attack them on level ground, and we will certainly be stronger than they." He heeded what they said and acted accordingly.

²⁶ At the same time the following year, Ben-Hadad mustered the army of Aram and went up to Afek to attack Isra'el. ²⁷ The army of Isra'el, already mobilized and supplied, went to meet them; but the army of Isra'el, encamped opposite them, looked like two herds of goats; while Aram filled the land.

²⁸ At this point, a man of God approached and said to the king of Isra'el, "Here is what Adonai says: 'Because Aram said that Adonai is a God of the hills but not a God of the valleys, I will hand over to you this entire huge army. Then you will know that I am Adonai.'"

²⁹ They remained in camp opposite each other for seven days. On the seventh day, the battle began; and the people of Isra'el killed 100,000 soldiers of Aram in a single day. ³⁰ The rest fled to Afek, into the city; and the wall fell on 27,000 of the men who were left. Ben-Hadad fled into the city and took refuge in an inside room. ³¹ His servants said to him, "Here now, we have heard that the kings of the house of Isra'el are merciful kings. If it's all right with you, let's put sackcloth around our waists and ropes on our heads, and go out to the king of Isra'el. Maybe he will spare your life." ³² So they put sackcloth around their waists and ropes on their heads, went to the king of Isra'el and said, "Your servant Ben-Hadad says, 'Please spare my life.'" And he answered, "He's still alive? He is my brother." ³³ The men took this as a promising indication and seized on it to say, "Yes, Ben-Hadad is your brother." Then Ach'av said, "Go, and bring him here." Ben-Hadad went out to him, and Ach'av had him climb up into his chariot. ³⁴ Ben-Hadad said to him, "I will return the cities my father took from your father. Also you can set up markets for trade in Dammesek, as my father did in Shomron." "If you put this covenant in writing," said Ach'av, "I will set you free." So he made a covenant with him and set him free.

³⁵ One of the members of the prophets' guild said to another one, by the word of Adonai, "Hit me!" But the man refused to hit him. ³⁶ Then he said to him, "Because you didn't listen to the voice of Adonai, the moment you leave me, a lion will kill you." No sooner had he left him than a lion found him and killed him. ³⁷ The prophet went to another man and said, "Hit me!" The man struck him a blow and wounded him.

³⁸ The prophet left and waited for the king by the road, disguising himself with a bandage over his eyes. ³⁹ As the king passed by, he called out to the king and said, "Your servant was on his way into the thick of the fighting when someone turned, brought a man to me and said, 'Guard this man! If he is missing, you will pay for his life with yours; or else you will pay sixty-six pounds of silver.' ⁴⁰ But while your servant was busy with one thing and another, he disappeared." The king of Isra'el said to him, "So that is your sentence; you have pronounced it on yourself." ⁴¹ Quickly he removed the bandage from his eyes, and the king of Isra'el recognized him as one of the prophets. ⁴² Then he said to the king, "Here is what ADONAI says: 'Because you have let escape the man I had given over to be destroyed, you will pay with your life for his life and with your people for his people.'" ⁴³ The king of Isra'el returned home to Shomron resentful and depressed.

21 ¹ A while later, an incident occurred involving Navot the Yizre'eli. He owned a vineyard in Yizre'el, right next to the palace of Ach'av king of Shomron. ² Ach'av spoke to Navot and said, "Give me your vineyard, so that I can have it as my vegetable garden, because it's close to my palace. In exchange I will give you a better vineyard; or, if you prefer, I will give you its monetary value." ³ But Navot said to Ach'av, "ADONAI forbid that I should give you my ancestral heritage!" ⁴ Ach'av went home resentful and depressed at what Navot the Yizre'eli had said to him, since he had said, "I won't give you my ancestral heritage." He lay down on his bed, turned his face away and refused to eat. ⁵ Izevel his wife went and said to him, "Why are you so depressed that you refuse to eat?" ⁶ He answered her, "Because I spoke to Navot the Yizre'eli and said to him, 'Sell me your vineyard for money; or else, if you prefer, I will give you another vineyard for it'; but he answered, 'I won't give you my vineyard.'" ⁷ "Are you the king of Isra'el or not?" asked his wife Izevel. "Get up, eat some food, and cheer up! I will give you the vineyard of Navot the Yizre'eli."

⁸ So she wrote letters in Ach'av's name, sealed them with his seal and sent the letters to the leaders and notables of the city where Navot lived. ⁹ In the letters she wrote, "Proclaim a fast, and give Navot the seat of honor among the people. ¹⁰ Have two good-for-nothing men sit opposite him, and have them accuse him publicly of cursing God and the king. Then take him outside and stone him to death."

¹¹ The leaders and notables of the city he lived in did as Izevel had written in the letters she sent to them. ¹² They proclaimed a fast and gave Navot the seat of honor among the people. ¹³ The two good-for-nothing men came in and sat opposite him, and these scoundrels publicly accused Navot, saying, "Navot cursed God and the king." So they took him outside the city and stoned him to death, ¹⁴ then sent a message to Izevel, "Navot has been stoned to death."

¹⁵ When Izevel heard that Navot had been stoned to death, she said to Ach'av, "Get up, and take possession of the vineyard that Navot the Yizre'eli refused to sell you, because Navot is no longer alive; he is dead." ¹⁶ When Ach'av heard that Navot was dead, he set out to go down to the vineyard of Navot the Yizre'eli, to take possession of it.

¹⁷ But the word of ADONAI came to Eliyahu from Tishbe: ¹⁸ "Get up, go down to meet Ach'av king of Isra'el, who lives in Shomron. Right now he is in the vineyard of Navot; he has gone down there to take possession of it. ¹⁹ This is what you are to say to him: 'Here is what ADONAI says: "You have committed murder, and now

you are stealing the victim's property!"' Also say to him, 'Here is what ADONAI says: "In the very place where dogs licked up the blood of Navot, dogs will lick up your blood — yours!"'"

²⁰ Ach'av said to Eliyahu, "My enemy! You've found me!" He answered, "Yes, I have found you; because you have given yourself over to do what is evil from ADONAI's perspective. ²¹ 'Here,' [says ADONAI,] 'I am bringing disaster on you! I will sweep you away completely; I will cut off from Ach'av every male, whether a slave or free in Isra'el. ²² I will make your house like the house of Yarov'am the son of N'vat and like the house of Ba'sha the son of Achiyah for provoking my anger and leading Isra'el into sin.' ²³ ADONAI also said this about Izevel: 'The dogs will eat Izevel by the wall around Yizre'el. ²⁴ If someone from the line of Ach'av dies in the city, the dogs will eat him; if he dies in the country-side, the vultures will eat him.'"

²⁵ Truly, there was never anyone like Ach'av. Stirred up by his wife Izevel, he gave himself over to do what is evil from ADONAI's perspective. ²⁶ His behavior in following idols was grossly abominable; he did everything the Emori had done, whom ADONAI expelled ahead of the people of Isra'el.

²⁷ Ach'av, on hearing these words, tore his clothes, put sackcloth on himself and fasted. He slept in the sackcloth and went about dejectedly. ²⁸ Then the word of ADONAI came to Eliyahu from Tishbe: ²⁹ "Do you see how Ach'av has humbled him-self before me? Since he has humbled himself before me, I will not bring this evil during his lifetime; but during his son's lifetime I will bring the evil on his house."

22 ¹ For three years there was no war between Aram and Isra'el. ² Then, in the third year, Y'hoshafat the king of Y'hudah came down to the king of Isra'el. ³ The king of Isra'el said to his servants, "Are you aware that Ramot-Gil'ad belongs to us; yet, we're doing nothing to recover it from the king of Aram?" ⁴ He said to Y'hoshafat, "Will you go with me to attack Ramot-Gil'ad?" Y'hoshafat answered the king of Isra'el, "I'm with you all the way; think of my troops and horses as yours." ⁵ But Y'hoshafat said to the king of Isra'el, "First, we should seek the word of ADONAI."

⁶ So the king of Isra'el assembled the prophets, about 400 men. "Should I attack Ramot-Gil'ad?" he asked them, "Or should I hold off?" They said, "Attack! Adonai will hand it over to the king." ⁷ But Y'hoshafat said, "Besides these, isn't there a prophet of ADONAI here that we can consult?" ⁸ The king of Isra'el said to Y'hoshafat, "Yes, there is still one man through whom we can consult ADONAI, Mikhay'hu the son of Yimlah; but I hate him, because he doesn't proph-esy good things for me, but bad!" Y'hoshafat replied, "The king shouldn't say such a thing."

⁹ Then the king of Isra'el called an officer and said, "Quickly! Bring Mikhay'hu the son of Yimlah." ¹⁰ Now the king of Isra'el and Y'hoshafat the king of Y'hudah were each sitting on his throne, dressed in their royal robes, on a threshing-floor at the entrance to the gate of Shomron; and all the prophets were there, prophesying in their presence. ¹¹ Tzidkiyah the son of Kena'anah had made himself some horns out of iron and said, "This is what ADONAI says: 'With these you will gore Aram until they are destroyed.'" ¹² All the prophets prophesied the same thing: "Go up and attack Ramot-Gil'ad. You will succeed, for ADONAI will hand it over to the king."

¹³ The messenger who had gone to call Mikhay'hu said to him, "Here, now, the prophets are unanimously predicting success for the king. Please let your word be like the word of one of them — say something good." ¹⁴ But Mikhay'hu answered, "As ADONAI lives, whatever ADONAI says to me is what I will say."

¹⁵ When he reached the king, the king asked him, "Mikhay'hu, should we go up and attack Ramot-Gil'ad; or should we hold off?" He answered, "Go up, you will succeed, ADONAI will hand it over to the king." ¹⁶ The king said to him, "How many times do I have to warn you to tell me nothing but the truth in the name of ADONAI?" ¹⁷ Then he said, "I saw all Isra'el scattered over the hills like sheep without a shepherd; and ADONAI said, 'These men have no leader; let everyone go home in peace.'" ¹⁸ The king of Isra'el said to Y'hoshafat, "Didn't I tell you that he wouldn't prophesy good things about me, but bad?"

¹⁹ Mikhay'hu continued: "Therefore hear the word of ADONAI. I saw ADONAI sitting on his throne with the whole army of heaven standing by him on his right and on his left. ²⁰ ADONAI asked, 'Who will entice Ach'av to go up to his death at Ramot-Gil'ad?' One of them said, 'Do it this way,' and another, 'Do it that way.' ²¹ Then a spirit stepped up, stood in front of ADONAI and said, 'I will entice him.' ²² ADONAI asked, 'How?' and he answered, 'I will go and be a deceiving spirit in the mouths of all his prophets.' ADONAI said, 'You will succeed in enticing him. Go, and do it.' ²³ So now ADONAI has put a deceiving spirit in the mouths of all these prophets of yours; meanwhile, ADONAI has ordained disaster for you."

²⁴ Then Tzidkiyah the son of Kena'anah came up, slapped Mikhay'hu in the face and said, "And how did the Spirit of ADONAI leave me to speak to you?" ²⁵ Mikhay'hu said, "You'll find out the day you go into an inside room, trying to hide."

²⁶ The king of Isra'el said, "Seize Mikhay'hu, and take him back to Amon the governor of the city and Yo'ash the king's son. ²⁷ Say, 'The king says to put this man in prison; and feed him only bread and water, and not much of that, until I return in peace.'" ²⁸ Mikhay'hu said, "If you return in peace at all, ADONAI has not spoken through me!" Then he added, "Did you hear me, you peoples, all of you?"

²⁹ So the king of Isra'el and Y'hoshafat the king of Y'hudah went up to Ramot-Gil'ad. ³⁰ The king of Isra'el said to Y'hoshafat, "I will disguise myself and go into battle; but you, put on your robes." So the king of Isra'el disguised himself and went into battle. ³¹ Now the king of Aram had ordered the thirty-two chariot commanders, "Don't attack anyone of either high or low rank, only the king of Isra'el." ³² So when the chariot commanders saw Y'hoshafat they said, "This must be the king of Isra'el," and turned to attack him. But Y'hoshafat gave a yell, ³³ so that the chariot commanders saw that he wasn't the king of Isra'el and stopped pursuing him. ³⁴ However, one soldier shot an arrow at random and struck the king of Isra'el between his lower armor and his breastplate. So the king said to his chariot-driver, "Turn the reins, and take me out of the fighting; I'm collapsing from my wounds." ³⁵ But the fighting grew fiercer that day; and they propped the king upright in his chariot facing Aram until he died, in the evening, with the blood streaming from his wound onto the floor of the chariot. ³⁶ Around sundown, a cry spread through the ranks: "Every man to his own town! Every man to his own land!" ³⁷ So the king died and was brought to Shomron, and they buried the king in Shomron. ³⁸ They washed the chariot at the Pool of Shomron where the prostitutes bathed, and the dogs licked up his blood, in keeping with the word ADONAI had spoken.

³⁹ Other activities of Ach'av's reign, all his accomplishments, the ivory palace he built and all the cities he built are recorded in the Annals of the Kings of Isra'el. ⁴⁰ So Ach'av slept with his ancestors, and Achazyah his son became king in his place.

⁴¹ Y'hoshafat the son of Asa began his reign over Y'hudah in the fourth year of Ach'av king of Isra'el. ⁴² Y'hoshafat was thirty-five years old when he began to rule, and he ruled twenty-five years in Yerushalayim. His mother's name was 'Azuvah the daughter of Shilchi.

⁴³ He lived in the manner of Asa his father and did not turn away from it, doing what was right from ADONAI's perspective; ⁴⁴(⁴³b) although the high places were not taken away — the people still sacrificed and presented offerings on the high places. ⁴⁵(⁴⁴) Y'hoshafat made peace with the king of Isra'el.

⁴⁶(⁴⁵) Other activities of Y'hoshafat, all his power that he demonstrated and how he made war are recorded in the Annals of the Kings of Y'hudah.

⁴⁷(⁴⁶) He rid the land of the male and female cult-prostitutes remaining from the time of his father Asa.

⁴⁸(⁴⁷) There had previously been no king in Edom, but now a deputy was made king. ⁴⁹(⁴⁸) Y'hoshafat built some large "Tarshish" ships to go to Ofir for gold, but they didn't make the voyage, because they were wrecked at 'Etzyon-Gever. ⁵⁰(⁴⁹) Achazyah the son of Ach'av suggested to Y'hoshafat that his men should go to sea with Y'hoshafat's men, but Y'hoshafat would not agree.

⁵¹(⁵⁰) So Y'hoshafat slept with his ancestors and was buried with his ancestors in the City of David his ancestor, and Y'horam his son became king in his place.

⁵²(⁵¹) Achazyah the son of Ach'av began his reign over Isra'el in Shomron in the seventeenth year of Y'hoshafat king of Y'hudah, and he ruled two years over Isra'el. ⁵³(⁵²) He did what was evil from ADONAI's perspective, living in the manner of his father, his mother and Yarov'am the son of N'vat, by which he led Isra'el into sin. ⁵⁴(⁵³) He also served Ba'al and worshipped him; and he made ADONAI the God of Isra'el angry, in keeping with everything his father had done.

M'lakhim Bet
2 KINGS

1 ¹ After Ach'av's death Mo'av rebelled against Isra'el.

² When Achazyah fell through a latticed window of his upper room in Shomron and lay injured, he sent messengers and said to them, "Go, consult Ba'al-Z'vuv the god of 'Ekron, and ask whether I will recover from this injury." ³ But an angel of ADONAI said to Eliyahu from Tishbe, "Get up, and intercept the messengers of the king of Shomron, and ask them, 'Is it because there's no God in Isra'el that you're on your way to consult Ba'al-Z'vuv the god of 'Ekron? ⁴ Therefore ADONAI says, "You will never leave the bed you are lying on; you will certainly die."'" Then Eliyahu left. ⁵ The messengers returned to Achazyah, and he asked them, "Why have you

come back?" ⁶ They answered him, "A man came to meet us. He told us to go and
return to the king who sent us, and tell him, 'Here is what ADONAI says: "Is it because
there's no God in Isra'el that you're sending to consult Ba'al-Z'vuv the god of 'Ekron?
Therefore you will never leave the bed you are lying on; you will certainly die.""'
⁷ He asked them, "The man who came to meet you and told you these things, what
kind of a man was he?" ⁸ "He was a hairy man," they answered him, "with a leather
belt around his waist." He said, "It was Eliyahu from Tishbe."

⁹ Then the king sent a commander of fifty to Eliyahu, together with his fifty
men. Eliyahu was sitting at the top of a hill. The commander climbed up to him and
said, "Man of God, the king says to come down." ¹⁰ Eliyahu answered the commander of fifty, "If I am in fact a man of God, let fire come down from heaven and
burn you up, along with your fifty men." Fire came down from heaven, and it burned
up him and his fifty men. ¹¹ The king sent him another commander of fifty, together
with his fifty men. He said to him, "Man of God, the king says, 'Come down immediately!'" ¹² Eliyahu answered them, "If I am in fact a man of God, let fire come
down from heaven and burn you up, along with your fifty men." Fire came down
from heaven, and it burned up him and his fifty men. ¹³ The king sent a third
commander of fifty, with his fifty men. The third commander of fifty climbed
up, approached Eliyahu and fell on his knees before him. He pleaded with him:
"Man of God, please! Have some regard for my life and the lives of these fifty
servants of yours! ¹⁴ I know that fire came down from heaven and burned up the two
other commanders with their fifty men; but now, have some regard for my life."
¹⁵ The angel of ADONAI said to Eliyahu, "Go down with him; don't be afraid of him."
So he got up and went down with him to the king.

¹⁶ Eliyahu said to the king, "Here is what ADONAI says: 'You sent messengers to
consult Ba'al-Z'vuv the god of 'Ekron. Is it because there's no God in Isra'el you can
consult? Therefore, you will never leave the bed you are lying on; you will certainly
die.'" ¹⁷ So he died, in keeping with the word of ADONAI spoken through Eliyahu.

Y'horam began to rule in place of him during the second year of Y'horam the
son of Y'hoshafat king of Y'hudah, because he had no son. ¹⁸ Other activities of
Achazyah are recorded in the Annals of the Kings of Isra'el.

2 ¹ The time came for ADONAI to take Eliyahu up into heaven in a whirlwind. Eliyahu
and Elisha were on their way from Gilgal, ² when Eliyahu said to Elisha, "Please
wait here, because ADONAI has sent me all the way to Beit-El." But Elisha said, "As
ADONAI lives, and as you live, I will not leave you." So they went down to Beit-El.
³ The guild prophets of Beit-El came out to Elisha and said to him, "Do you know
that ADONAI is taking your master away from you today?" "Yes, I know," he
answered; "say no more."

⁴ Eliyahu said to him, "Elisha, please wait here, because ADONAI has sent me to
Yericho." He replied, "As ADONAI lives, and as you live, I will not leave you." So
they came to Yericho. ⁵ The guild prophets of Yericho approached Elisha and said to
him, "Do you know that ADONAI is taking your master away from you today?" "Yes,
I know," he answered; "say no more."

⁶ Eliyahu said to him, "Please wait here, because ADONAI has sent me to the
Yarden." He replied, "As ADONAI lives, and as you live, I will not leave you." So the
two of them went on. ⁷ Fifty of the guild prophets went and stood watching them

from a distance, while they stood by the Yarden. ⁸ Then Eliyahu took his cloak, rolled it up and struck the water with it; and the water divided itself to the left and to the right; so that they crossed on dry ground. ⁹ After they had crossed, Eliyahu said to Elisha, "Tell me what I can do for you before I am taken away from you." Elisha said, "Please! Let a double share of your spirit be on me!" ¹⁰ He replied, "You have requested a hard thing. Nevertheless, if you see me when I am taken from you, you will get what you asked for; but if not, you won't."

¹¹ Suddenly, as they were walking on and talking, there appeared a fiery chariot with horses of fire; and as it separated the two of them from each other, Eliyahu went up into heaven in a whirlwind. ¹² Elisha saw it and cried out, "My father! My father! The chariots and horsemen of Isra'el!" Then he lost sight of him. Seizing his clothes, he tore them in half. ¹³ Then he picked up Eliyahu's cloak, which had fallen off him. Standing on the bank of the Yarden, ¹⁴ he took the cloak that had fallen off Eliyahu, struck the water and said, "Where is ADONAI, the God of Eliyahu?" But when he actually did strike the water, it divided itself to the left and to the right; then Elisha crossed over.

¹⁵ When the guild prophets of Yericho saw him in the distance, they said, "The spirit of Eliyahu does rest on Elisha." Advancing to meet him, they prostrated themselves on the ground before him ¹⁶ and said to him, "Here now, your servants include fifty strong men. Please let them go and look for your master, in the event that the Spirit of ADONAI has taken him up and set him down on some mountain or in some valley." He answered, "Don't send them." ¹⁷ But they kept pressing him until finally, embarrassed, he said to send them. So they sent fifty men. For three days they searched, but they didn't find him. ¹⁸ On returning to him where he was waiting in Yericho, he said to them, "I told you not to go, didn't I?"

¹⁹ The men of the city said to Elisha, "My lord can see that this is a pleasant city to live in; but the water is bad, so that the ground is causing miscarriages." ²⁰ "Bring me a new jug," he said, "and put salt in it." They brought it to him. ²¹ He went out to the source of the water, threw salt into it and said, "This is what ADONAI says: 'I have healed this water; it will no longer cause death or miscarrying.'" ²² The water was healed and has remained healed to this day, in keeping with Elisha's spoken word.

²³ Elisha left to go up to Beit-El. As he was on his way up the road, some boys came out of the town and began making fun of him. "Go on up, baldy! Go on up, baldy!" ²⁴ He looked behind him, saw them and put a curse on them in the name of ADONAI; whereupon two female bears came out of the woods and mauled forty-two of the boys. ²⁵ He went on from there to Mount Karmel and then returned to Shomron.

3 ¹ Y'horam the son of Ach'av began his reign over Isra'el in Shomron during the eighteenth year of Y'hoshafat king of Y'hudah, and he ruled for twelve years. ² He did what was evil from ADONAI's perspective; but he was not as bad as his father and mother, because he got rid of Ba'al's standing-stone which his father had made. ³ Nevertheless, he clung to the sins of Yarov'am the son of N'vat, with which he had led Isra'el into sin; he never turned away from them.

⁴ Mesha king of Mo'av was a sheep-breeder, and he used to send the king of Isra'el the wool of 100,000 lambs and of 100,000 rams as tribute. ⁵ But after Ach'av died, the king of Mo'av rebelled against the king of Isra'el. ⁶ Y'horam left Shomron and mustered all Isra'el. ⁷ He also went and sent this word to Y'hoshafat king of Y'hudah: "The king of Mo'av has rebelled against me. Will you join me in attacking

Mo'av?" He answered, "I will join in the attack — I'm with you all the way; think of my people and horses as yours. ⁸ Which route should we take?" he added. "The road through the desert of Edom," answered Y'horam.

⁹ So the king of Isra'el set out, along with the king of Y'hudah and the king of Edom. After a roundabout journey of seven days, there was no water for either the army or the animals following them. ¹⁰ "This is terrible!" exclaimed the king of Isra'el. "Has ADONAI called these three kings together only to hand them over to Mo'av?" ¹¹ But Y'hoshafat said, "Isn't there a prophet of ADONAI here through whom we can consult ADONAI?" One of the servants of the king of Isra'el answered, "Elisha the son of Shafat is here, the one who used to pour water on Eliyahu's hands." ¹² Y'hoshafat said, "The word of ADONAI is with him." So the king of Isra'el, Y'hoshafat and the king of Edom went down to consult him.

¹³ Elisha said to the king of Isra'el, "What do you and I have in common? Go, consult your father's prophets and your mother's prophets!" But the king of Isra'el answered him, "No, because ADONAI has called these three kings together to hand them over to Mo'av." ¹⁴ Elisha said, "As ADONAI-Tzva'ot lives, before whom I stand, if I didn't respect the fact that Y'hoshafat the king of Y'hudah is here, I wouldn't even look in your direction or take notice of you. ¹⁵ But now, bring me a musician." As the musician played, the hand of ADONAI fell on Elisha; ¹⁶ and he said, "ADONAI says to dig until this valley is full of trenches. ¹⁷ For here is what ADONAI says: 'You won't see wind, and you won't see rain. Nevertheless the valley will be filled with water; and you will drink — you, your cattle and your other animals. ¹⁸ That's an easy thing to do, from ADONAI's perspective. He will also hand Mo'av over to you. ¹⁹ You will conquer every fortified city and every choice town, you will chop down every good tree, stop up every well and ruin every good field with stones.'" ²⁰ The next morning, around the time for making the offering, water came from the direction of Edom, and the countryside was filled with water.

²¹ When all Mo'av heard that the kings had come up to attack them, every man was summoned, from the youngest capable of bearing arms to older ones, and stationed on the border. ²² They rose early in the morning, when the sun was shining on the water. Mo'av, when they saw the water in the distance looking as red as blood, ²³ said, "That's blood! The kings must have quarreled, and their soldiers killed each other. Mo'av! To the plunder!"

²⁴ When they arrived at the camp of Isra'el, Isra'el launched an attack, so that Mo'av fled before them. But they advanced on Mo'av and struck it. ²⁵ They made ruins of the cities. Each man threw his stone on every good field, covering it. They stopped up all the wells. They chopped down all the good trees. Finally, all that remained was Kir-Hareset behind its stone wall, with the slingers surrounding and attacking it. ²⁶ When the king of Mo'av saw that the fighting was too much for him, he took with him 700 men armed with swords and tried to break through to the king of Edom; but they couldn't do it. ²⁷ Then he took his firstborn son, who was to have succeeded him as king, and offered him as a burnt offering on the wall. Following this, such great anger came upon Isra'el that they left him and went back to their own land.

4 ¹ The wife of one of the guild prophets complained to Elisha. "Your servant my husband died," she said, "and you know that he feared ADONAI. Now a creditor has come to take my two children as his slaves." ² Elisha asked her, "What should I do for you? Tell me, what do you have in the house?" She answered, "Your servant has nothing in the house but a flask of oil." ³ Then he said, "Go, and borrow containers from all your neighbors, empty containers; and don't borrow just a few! ⁴ Then go in; shut the door, with you and your sons inside; and pour oil into all those containers; and as they are filled, put them aside." ⁵ So she left him and shut the door on herself and her sons. They brought her the containers while she poured. ⁶ When the containers were full, she said to her son, "Bring me another container"; but he answered, "There isn't another container." Then the oil stopped flowing. ⁷ She came and told the man of God; and he said, "Go, sell the oil, and pay your debt; then you and your sons can live on what's left."

⁸ One day Elisha visited Shunem, and a well-to-do woman living there pressed him to stay and eat a meal. After this, whenever he came through, he stopped there for a meal. ⁹ She said to her husband, "I can see that this is a holy man of God who keeps stopping at our place. ¹⁰ Please, let's build him a little room on the roof. We'll put a bed and a table in it for him, and a stool and a candlestick. Then, whenever he comes to visit us, he can stay there."

¹¹ One day Elisha came to visit there, and he went into the upper room to lie down. ¹² He said to Geichazi his servant, "Call this Shunamit." He called her; and when she arrived, ¹³ he said to him, "Tell her this: 'You have shown us so much hospitality! What can I do to show my appreciation? Do you want me to say anything to the king for you? or to the commander of the army?" She answered, "I'm happy living as I do, among my own people." ¹⁴ He said, "What, then, is to be done for her?" Geichazi answered, "There's one thing — she doesn't have a son; and her husband is old. ¹⁵ Elisha said, "Call her." After he called her, she stood in the doorway. ¹⁶ He said, "Next year, when the season comes around, you will be holding a son." "No, my lord," she answered. "Man of God, don't lie to your servant!" ¹⁷ But the woman conceived and gave birth to a son the following year when the season came around, just as Elisha had said to her.

¹⁸ When the child was old enough, he went out one day to be with his father, who was with the reapers. ¹⁹ Suddenly he cried out to his father, "My head! My head hurts!" He said to his servant, "Carry him back to his mother." ²⁰ When he had taken him and brought him to his mother, he lay on her lap until noon; and then he died. ²¹ She went up and laid him on the bed of the man of God, shut the door on him and went out. ²² She called to her husband and said, "Please send me one of the servants with a donkey. I must get to the man of God as fast as I can; I'll come straight back." ²³ He asked, "Why are you going to him today? It isn't *Rosh-Hodesh* and it isn't *Shabbat*." She said, "It's all right." ²⁴ Then she saddled the donkey and ordered her servant, "Drive as fast as you can; don't slow down for me unless I say so."

²⁵ She set out and came to the man of God on Mount Karmel. When the man of God saw her in the distance, he said to Geichazi his servant, "Look, here comes that Shunamit. ²⁶ Run now to meet her, and ask her, "Is everything all right with you? with your husband? with the child?" She answered, "Everything is all right." ²⁷ But when she reached the man of God on the hill, she grabbed his feet. Geichazi came up to push her away, but the man of God said, "Leave her alone. She is in great distress, but ADONAI has hidden from me what it is, he hasn't told me." ²⁸ Then she said, "Did I ask my lord for a son? Didn't I say not to deceive me?" ²⁹ Then Elisha said to Geichazi, "Get dressed for action, take my staff in your hand, and be on your way. If

you meet anyone, don't greet him; if anyone greets you, don't answer; and lay my staff on the child's face." ³⁰ The mother of the child said, "As ADONAI lives, and as you live, I will not leave you." He got up and followed her. ³¹ Geichazi went on ahead of them and laid the staff on the child's face, but there was no sound or sign of life. So he went back to Elisha and told him, "The child didn't wake up."

³² When Elisha reached the house, there the child was, dead and laid on the bed. ³³ He went in, shut the door on the two of them and prayed to ADONAI. ³⁴ Then he got up on the bed and lay on top of the child, putting his mouth on his mouth, his eyes on his eyes and his hands on his hands. As he stretched himself out on the child, its flesh began to grow warm. ³⁵ Then he went down, walked around in the house awhile, went back up and stretched himself out on the child again. The child sneezed seven times, then opened his eyes. ³⁶ Elisha called Geichazi and said, "Call this Shunamit." So he called her; and when she came in to him, he said, "Pick up your son." ³⁷ She entered, fell at his feet and prostrated herself on the floor. Then she picked up her son and went out.

³⁸ Elisha went back to Gilgal. At the time, there was a famine in the land. The guild prophets were sitting before him, and he said to his servant, "Put the big pot on the fire, and boil some soup for the prophets." ³⁹ One of them went out to the field to gather vegetables and came upon a wild vine, from which he filled the front of his cloak with wild squash. On returning he cut them up and put them into the stew; they didn't know what they were. ⁴⁰ Then they poured it out for the men to eat; but on tasting it, they cried, "Man of God! There's death in that pot!" And they couldn't eat it. ⁴¹ But he said, "Bring some flour." He threw it in the pot, then said, "Pour it out for the people to eat." This time there was nothing harmful in the pot.

⁴² A man came from Ba'al-Shalishah bringing the man of God twenty loaves of bread made from the barley firstfruits and fresh ears of grain in his sack. Elisha said, "Give this to the people to eat." ⁴³ His servant said, "How am I to serve this to a hundred men?" But he said, "Give it to the people to eat; for ADONAI says that they will eat and have some left over." ⁴⁴ So he served them, and they ate and had some left over, as ADONAI had said.

5 ¹ Na'aman, commander of the king of Aram's army, was highly respected and esteemed by his master; because through him ADONAI had brought victory to Aram. But although he was a brave warrior, he also suffered from *tzara'at*. ² Now on one of their raids into Isra'el's territory, Aram carried away captive a little girl, who became a servant for Na'aman's wife. ³ She said to her mistress, "I wish my lord could go to the prophet in Shomron! He could heal his *tzara'at*. ⁴ Na'aman went in and told his lord, "The girl from the land of Isra'el said such-and-such." ⁵ The king of Aram said, "Go now, and I will send a letter to the king of Isra'el."

He set out, taking with him 660 pounds of silver, 6,000 pieces of gold and ten changes of clothes. ⁶ He brought the king of Isra'el the letter, which said, "When this letter reaches you, you will see that I have sent my servant Na'aman to you, so that you can heal his *tzara'at*." ⁷ When the king of Isra'el finished reading the letter, he tore his clothes. "Am I God, able to kill and make alive," he asked, "so that he sends me a man to heal of *tzara'at*? You can see that he is only seeking an excuse to quarrel with me." ⁸ But when Elisha the man of God heard that the king of Isra'el had torn his clothes, he sent a message to the king: "Why did you tear your clothes? Just have him come to me, and he will know that there is a prophet in Isra'el."

⁹ So Na'aman came with his horses and chariots and stood at the door of Elisha's house. ¹⁰ Elisha sent a messenger to him, who said, "Go, and bathe in the Yarden seven times. Your skin will become as it was, and you will be clean." ¹¹ But Na'aman became angry and left, saying, "Here now! I thought for certain that he would come out personally, that he would stand, call on the name of ADONAI his God and wave his hand over the diseased place and thus heal the person with *tzara'at*. ¹² Aren't Amanah and Parpar, the rivers of Dammesek, better than all the water in Isra'el? Why can't I bathe in them and be clean?" So he turned and went off in a rage. ¹³ But his servants approached him and said, "My father! If the prophet had asked you to do something really difficult, wouldn't you have done it? So, doesn't it make even more sense to do what he says, when it's only, 'Bathe, and be clean'?" ¹⁴ So he went down and immersed himself seven times in the Yarden, as the man of God had said to do; and his skin was restored and became like the skin of a child; and he became clean.

¹⁵ Then, with his whole retinue, he returned to the man of God, went and stood before him, and said, "Well, I've learned that there is no God in all the earth except in Isra'el; therefore, please accept a present from your servant." ¹⁶ But Elisha answered, "As ADONAI lives, before whom I stand, I will not accept it." And despite his urging him to take it, he refused. ¹⁷ So Na'aman said, "If you won't take it, then please let your servant be given as much earth as two mules can carry; because from now on, your servant will offer neither burnt offerings nor sacrifices to other gods, but only to ADONAI. ¹⁸ Except this, and may ADONAI forgive your servant for it: when my master goes into the temple of Rimmon to worship there, and he leans on my hand, and I bow down in the temple of Rimmon — when I bow down, may ADONAI forgive your servant for this." ¹⁹ Elisha said to him, "Go in peace."

Na'aman had gone only a short distance from him, ²⁰ when Geichazi, the servant of Elisha the man of God, said to himself, "Here, my master has made it easy on this Arami Na'aman by not accepting from him what he brought. As ADONAI lives, I'll run after him and get at least something from him." ²¹ So Geichazi hurried off after Na'aman. When Na'aman saw someone running after him, he got down from his chariot to meet him and asked, "Is everything all right?" ²² "Yes," he replied. "My master sent me with this message: 'Two young men have just now come to me, guild prophets from the hills of Efrayim. Would you be kind enough to give them a talent of silver [sixty-six pounds] and two changes of clothes?" ²³ "By all means, take two talents!" said Na'aman, pressing him. He tied up the two talents of silver in two bags and gave them, with the two changes of clothes, to two of his servants, who carried them ahead of Geichazi. ²⁴ On reaching the hill, he took the bags from them and put them away in the house. Then he let the men go, and they left. ²⁵ He went in and stood before his master. Elisha asked, "Where have you been, Geichazi?" "Your servant hasn't gone anywhere," he said. ²⁶ Elisha said to him, "Wasn't my heart there with you when the man left his chariot to meet you? Is this a time to receive silver and clothing — and olive groves and vineyards and sheep and oxen and male and female slaves? ²⁷ Therefore Na'aman's *tzara'at* will cling to you and your descendants forever." He left Elisha's presence with *tzara'at* as white as snow.

6 ¹ The guild prophets said to Elisha, "As you can see, the place where we are living in order to be with you is too small for us. ² Please allow us to go to the Yarden; each of us will collect a log there, and we'll build a place there for us to live." He answered, "Go ahead." ³ But one of them said, "Please, won't you come with your servants?" He answered, "All right, I will"; ⁴ so he went with them. When they arrived at the Yarden, they cut down trees; ⁵ but as one was felling a tree trunk, the head of his axe fell in the water. "Oh, no!" he cried. "My master, it was a borrowed one!" ⁶ The man of God asked, "Where did it fall?" He showed him the place. Then Elisha cut a stick, threw it in there, and the iron axe-head floated to the surface. ⁷ "Lift it out," he said. So he put out his hand and took it.

⁸ Now the king of Aram went to war against Isra'el; and in consulting his servants he said, "I'll set up my ambush camp in such-and-such a place." ⁹ The man of God sent this message to the king of Isra'el: "Be careful not to go past such-and-such a place, because Aram will attack there." ¹⁰ So the king of Isra'el sent men to the place the man of God had told him and warned him about, and he took special precautions there. This happened more than once or twice, ¹¹ and it greatly upset the king of Aram. He called his servants and said to them, "Tell me which of you is betraying us to the king of Isra'el?" ¹² One of his servants replied, "It's not that, my lord, king. Rather, Elisha, the prophet who is in Isra'el, tells the king of Isra'el the words you speak privately in your own bedroom!" ¹³ He said, "Go and see where he is, so that I can send and bring him here." They told him, "He's in Dotan."

¹⁴ So he sent horses, chariots and a large army there; they came by night and surrounded the city. ¹⁵ The servant of the man of God got up early in the morning; on going outside, he saw an army with horses and chariots surrounding the city. His servant said to him, "Oh, my master, this is terrible! What are we going to do?" ¹⁶ He answered, "Don't be afraid— those who are with us outnumber those who are with them!" ¹⁷ Elisha prayed, "ADONAI, I ask you to open his eyes, so that he can see." Then ADONAI opened the young man's eyes, and he saw: there before him, all around Elisha, the mountain was covered with horses and fiery chariots. ¹⁸ When they came down to him, Elisha prayed to ADONAI, "Please strike these people blind"; and he struck them blind, as Elisha had asked. ¹⁹ Next, Elisha told them, "You've lost your way, and this isn't even the right city. Follow me, and I'll take you to the man you're looking for." Then he led them to Shomron. ²⁰ On their arrival in Shomron, Elisha said, "ADONAI, open the eyes of these men, so that they can see." ADONAI opened their eyes, and they saw: there they were, in the middle of Shomron.

²¹ When the king of Isra'el saw them, he asked Elisha, "My father, should I attack them? Should I attack them?" ²² He answered, "Don't attack them! You wouldn't even attack prisoners you had captured with your own sword and bow, would you? So give them food to eat and water to drink, and let them return to their master." ²³ So he provided well for them; and after they had eaten and drunk, he sent them away; and they returned to their master. After that, no more raiding parties entered the land of Isra'el from Aram.

²⁴ But some time afterwards, Ben-Hadad king of Aram gathered all his army, went up and laid siege to Shomron. ²⁵ At the time, there was a severe famine in Shomron; and they maintained their siege until a donkey's head sold for eighty pieces of silver and half a pint of doves' dung for five pieces of silver. ²⁶ As the king of Isra'el was passing by on the wall, a woman cried out to him, "Help, my lord, king!" ²⁷ He said, "If ADONAI isn't helping you, how do you expect me to help you? There isn't any grain, and there isn't any wine." ²⁸ Then the king asked her, "What's troubling you?" She answered, "This woman said to me, 'Give me your son, so that

we can eat him today; and we'll eat my son tomorrow.' ²⁹ So we boiled my son and ate him. The next day I said to her, 'Give your son, so that we can eat him,' but she has hidden her son." ³⁰ When the king heard what the woman said, he tore his clothes. At the time, he was passing by on the wall; and when the people looked, they saw him there with sackcloth against his skin. ³¹ Then he said, "May God do terrible things to me, and worse ones too, if the head of Elisha the son of Shafat remains on his body by day's end." ³² Elisha was sitting in his house, and the leaders were sitting there with him. The king sent a messenger ahead, but before he arrived, Elisha said to the leaders, "Do you see how this son of a murderer has sent someone to remove my head? Look, when the messenger comes, close the door and keep it shut against him. You can hear his master's footsteps following right behind him!" ³³ While he was still speaking, the messenger arrived with this message from the king: "Here, this evil is from ADONAI. Why should I wait for ADONAI any longer?"

7 ¹ Elisha answered, "Listen to the word of ADONAI. Here is what ADONAI says: 'Tomorrow, by this time, six quarts of fine flour will sell for only a *shekel*, and half a bushel of barley for a *shekel* [in the market] at the gate to Shomron.'" ² The servant on whose arm the king was leaning answered the man of God: "Why, this couldn't happen even if ADONAI made windows in heaven!" Elisha answered, "All right, you yourself will see it with your own eyes; but you won't eat any of it!"

³ Now there were four men with *tzara'at* at the entrance to the city gate, and they said to each other, "Why should we sit here till we die? ⁴ If we say, 'We'll enter the city, then the city has been struck by the famine, so we'll die there. And if we sit still here, we'll also die. So let's go and surrender to the army of Aram; if they spare our lives, we will live; and if they kill us, we'll only die." ⁵ They got up during the twilight to go to the camp of Aram. But when they reached the outskirts of the camp of Aram, they saw no one! ⁶ For ADONAI had caused the army of Aram to hear the sound of chariots and horses; it sounded like a huge army; and they said to each other, "The king of Isra'el must have hired the kings of the Hitti and the kings of the Egyptians to attack us." ⁷ So they jumped up and fled in the twilight, leaving their tents, horses, donkeys and the whole camp just as it was, and ran for their lives. ⁸ When these men with *tzara'at* reached the outskirts of the camp, they entered one of the tents, ate and drank; then took some silver, gold and clothing; and went and hid it. Next they returned and entered another tent, took stuff from there, and went and hid it. ⁹ But finally they said to each other, "What we are doing is wrong. At a time of good news like this, we shouldn't keep it to ourselves. If we wait even till morning, we will earn only punishment; so come on, let's go and tell the king's household." ¹⁰ So they came and shouted to the gatekeepers of the city and told them the news: "We went to the camp of Aram, and no one was there, no human voice — just the horses and donkeys tied up, and the tents left in place." ¹¹ The gatekeepers called and told it to the king's household inside. ¹² Then the king got up in the night; he said to his servants, "I'll tell you what Aram has done to us. They know that we're hungry, so they've gone outside the camp and hidden in the countryside, saying, 'When they come out of the city, we'll take them alive and then get inside the city.'" ¹³ One of his servants answered, "I suggest letting some men take five of the remaining horses that are left in the city — they're like everything else in Isra'el that remains, like everything else in Isra'el, practically finished — and we'll send and see." ¹⁴ So they

took two chariots with horses, and the king sent after the army of Aram, saying, "Go, and see." ¹⁵ They went after them all the way to the Yarden, and found the entire distance strewn with clothing and other articles Aram had thrown away in their haste. The messengers returned and told the king. ¹⁶ Then the people went out and ransacked the camp of Aram — with the result that six quarts of fine flour was sold for only a *shekel* and half a bushel of barley for a *shekel*, in keeping with what ADONAI had said.

¹⁷ The king put the servant on whose arm he had leaned in charge of the gate, and the people trampled him down in the gateway, so that he died, as the man of God had said he would, who spoke when the king came to him. ¹⁸ For the man of God had said to the king, "Tomorrow by this time six quarts of barley will sell for only a *shekel* and half a bushel of fine flour for a *shekel* [in the market] at the gate of Shomron"; ¹⁹ the servant had answered the man of God, "Why, this couldn't happen even if ADONAI made windows in heaven!" and Elisha had said, "All right, you yourself will see it with your own eyes; but you won't eat any of it!" ²⁰ That is exactly what happened to him, because the people trampled him down in the gateway, so that he died.

8 ¹ Now Elisha had said to the woman whose son he had restored to life, "Move away, you and your household, and stay wherever you can; because ADONAI has called for a famine; and it will be on the land for seven years." ² The woman acted at once and did as the man of God had said — she went with her household and stayed in the land of the P'lishtim for seven years. ³ At the end of seven years the woman returned from the land of the P'lishtim and sought an audience with the king to claim her house and land. ⁴ The king was talking with Geichazi the servant of the man of God. "Tell me," he said, "all the great things Elisha has done." ⁵ Just as he was telling the king how he had restored a dead person to life, at that very moment the woman whose son he had restored to life came to the king with her claim for her house and land. Geichazi said, "My lord, king, this is the woman; and this is her son, the one Elisha restored to life." ⁶ On being asked by the king, the woman verified it. At this, the king appointed a special officer and charged him, "Restore everything that belongs to her, including the income her fields have produced from the day she left them until now."

⁷ Elisha went to Dammesek. Ben-Hadad the king of Aram was ill; and he was told, "The man of God has come here." ⁸ The king said to Haza'el, "Take with you a gift, go meet the man of God and consult ADONAI through him; ask if I will recover from this illness." ⁹ Haza'el went to meet him, taking with him a gift that included everything good Dammesek had, forty camel-loads. He came, stood before him and said, "Your son Ben-Hadad king of Aram has sent me to you; he asks, 'Will I recover from this illness?'" ¹⁰ Elisha answered, "Go and say to him, 'You will surely recover' — even though ADONAI has shown me that he will surely die." ¹¹ Then the man of God fixed his gaze on him for so long that Haza'el became embarrassed; finally Elisha began to cry. ¹² Haza'el asked, "Why is my lord crying?" He answered, "Because I know the disasters you will bring on the people of Isra'el — you will set their fortresses on fire, you will kill their young men with the sword, you will dash their little ones to pieces and rip their pregnant women apart." ¹³ Haza'el said, "But what is your servant? Nothing but a dog! How could he do anything of such magnitude?" Elisha answered, "ADONAI has shown me that you will be king over Aram."

¹⁴ Then he left Elisha and returned to his master, who asked him, "What did Elisha say to you?" "He told me you would surely recover." ¹⁵ The next day he took a blanket, dipped it in water and spread it on his face, so that he died; and Haza'el took his place as king.

¹⁶ It was when Yoram the son of Ach'av king of Isra'el was in the fifth year of his reign that Y'horam the son of Y'hoshafat began his rule over Y'hudah. ¹⁷ He was thirty-two years old when he began to rule, and he ruled eight years in Yerushalayim. ¹⁸ He lived after the example of the kings of Isra'el, as did the house of Ach'av; because he had married Ach'av's daughter; he did what was evil from ADONAI's perspective. ¹⁹ However, ADONAI was unwilling to destroy Y'hudah, because of his servant David; inasmuch as he had promised to give him and his children a lamp that would burn forever.

²⁰ During his time Edom revolted against Y'hudah and set up its own king. ²¹ In response, Yoram crossed to Tza'ir with all his chariots. At night he and his chariot commanders set out and attacked Edom who had surrounded him; then the people fled to their tents. ²² Nevertheless, since that day Edom has remained free of Y'hudah's domination. Livnah revolted at the same time. ²³ Other activities of Yoram and all his accomplishments are recorded in the Annals of the Kings of Y'hudah. ²⁴ Yoram slept with his ancestors and was buried with his ancestors in the City of David, and Achazyah his son took his place as king.

²⁵ It was in the twelfth year of Yoram the son of Ach'av king of Isra'el that Achazyah the son of Y'horam king of Y'hudah began his reign. ²⁶ Achazyah was twenty-two years old when he began to rule, and he ruled for one year in Yerushalayim. His mother's name was 'Atalyahu the daughter of 'Omri king of Isra'el. ²⁷ He lived after the example of the house of Ach'av; he did what was evil from ADONAI's perspective, as had the house of Ach'av; for he was a son-in-law in the house of Ach'av.

²⁸ With Yoram the son of Ach'av he went to war against Haza'el king of Aram at Ramot-Gil'ad, and the Aramim wounded Yoram. ²⁹ King Yoram returned to Yizre'el to be healed of the wounds which the Aramim had inflicted on him at Ramah while fighting Haza'el king of Aram. Achazyah the son of Y'horam, king of Y'hudah, went down to visit Yoram the son of Ach'av in Yizre'el, because he was not feeling well.

9 ¹ Elisha the prophet summoned one of the guild prophets and said to him, "Prepare for traveling, take this flask of oil in your hand and go to Ramot-Gil'ad. ² When you get there, look for Yehu the son of Y'hoshafat, the son of Nimshi. Enter, have him step away from his companions, and take him to an inside room. ³ Then take the flask of oil, pour it on his head, and say, 'This is what ADONAI says: "I have anointed you king over Isra'el."' After that, open the door; and get away from there as fast as you can."

⁴ So the young prophet left for Ramot-Gil'ad. ⁵ When he arrived, he found the senior army officers sitting there. He said, "I have a message for you, commander." Yehu asked, "For which one of us?" "For you, commander," he said. ⁶ Yehu got up and went into the house. Then the prophet poured the oil on his head and said to him, "This is what ADONAI the God of Isra'el says: 'I have anointed you king over the people of ADONAI, over Isra'el. ⁷ You will attack the house of Ach'av your master, so that I can avenge the blood of my servants the prophets and of all the servants of ADONAI, blood shed by Izevel. ⁸ The entire house of Ach'av will perish; I will cut off

from Ach'av every male, whether a slave or free in Isra'el. ⁹I will make the house of Ach'av like the house of Yarov'am the son of N'vat and like the house of Ba'sha the son of Achiyah. ¹⁰ Moreover, the dogs will eat Izevel in the dumping-ground of Yizre'el, and there will be no one to bury her.'" Then he opened the door and fled.

¹¹ Yehu returned to the servants of his lord, and one of them said to him, "Is everything all right? Why did this *meshugga* come to you?" He answered them, "You know the kind and how they babble." ¹²They said, "You're being evasive. Come on, tell us the truth." Then he said, "This is exactly what he said to me and how he said it: 'Here is what ADONAI says: "I have anointed you king over Isra'el."'"
¹³ At this, they hurried each one to take his cloak and put it under Yehu at the top of the stairs. Then they blew the *shofar* and proclaimed, "Yehu is king!"

¹⁴Yehu the son of Y'hoshafat, the son of Nimshi, formed a conspiracy against Yoram. (At the time, Yoram was guarding Ramot-Gil'ad, he and all Isra'el, because of Haza'el king of Aram; ¹⁵but Yoram himself had returned to Yizre'el to recover from the wounds Aram had inflicted on him when fighting Haza'el king of Aram.) "If you agree," said Yehu, "then don't allow anyone to leave town and take the news to Yizre'el." ¹⁶So Yehu, riding in a chariot, went to Yizre'el, for Yoram was laid up there. Achazyah king of Y'hudah had come down to visit Yoram.

¹⁷ The lookout standing on the watchtower in Yizre'el saw Yehu's troops approaching and said, "I see some troops coming." Yoram said, "Have a horseman go to meet him and ask, "Are you coming in peace?" ¹⁸ So a man on horseback went to meet him and said, "The king asks if you are coming in peace." Yehu answered, "Peace? What business is that of yours? Turn around, and get behind me!" The watchman reported, "The messenger reached them, but he isn't coming back." ¹⁹ So he sent out a second man on horseback, who, on coming to him, said, "The king asks if you are coming in peace." Yehu answered, "Peace? What business is that of yours? Turn around, and get behind me!" ²⁰ The watchman reported, "He reached them, but he isn't coming back. Also, it looks like the driving of Yehu Nimshi's [grand]son — he's driving like a maniac!" ²¹ "Harness my chariot!" ordered Yoram. They got it ready. Then Yoram king of Isra'el and Achazyah king of Y'hudah, each in his chariot, went out to meet Yehu. They met him in the field of Navot the Yizre'eli.

²² When Yoram saw Yehu he said, "Are you coming in peace, Yehu?" He answered, "Peace? With your mother Izevel continuing all her cult prostitution and witchcraft? What a question!" ²³ Yoram wheeled around and fled, shouting, "Treachery, Achazyah!" ²⁴ Yehu drew his bow with all his strength and struck Yoram between the shoulder-blades; the arrow went through his heart, and he collapsed in his chariot. ²⁵ "Pick him up," said Yehu to Bidkar his servant, "and throw him into the field of Navot the Yizre'eli; for remember how, when you and I were riding together after Ach'av his father, ADONAI pronounced this sentence against him: ²⁶ 'ADONAI says: "Yesterday I saw the blood of Navot and the blood of his sons." ADONAI also says: "I will pay you back in this field."' Therefore, pick him up; and throw him into the field, in keeping with what ADONAI said."

²⁷ But when Achazyah the king of Y'hudah saw this, he fled on the road past Beit-HaGan. Yehu pursued him and ordered, "Strike him too in his chariot!" [So they struck him] at the Gur ascent, near Yivle'am. He fled to Megiddo, but there he died. ²⁸ His servants carried him in a chariot to Yerushalayim and buried him in his tomb with his ancestors in the City of David.

²⁹ It was in the eleventh year of Yoram the son of Ach'av that Achazyah had begun his rule over Y'hudah.

³⁰ When Yehu reached Yizre'el, and Izevel heard of it, she put on eye make-up, fixed her hair and looked out the window. ³¹ As Yehu came through the city gate, she asked, "Are you here in peace, you Zimri, you murderer of your master?" ³² Looking up at the window he said, "Who is on my side? Who?" Two or three officers looked out toward him. ³³ He said, "Throw her down!" So they threw her down. Some of her blood splashed onto the wall and the horses, and she was trampled underfoot. ³⁴ He went in, ate and drank, and then said, "Deal with this accursed woman — bury her, because she's a king's daughter." ³⁵ They went to bury her but found no more of her than her skull, feet and hands. ³⁶ So they came back and told him. He said, "This is what ADONAI said through his servant Eliyahu from Tishbe: 'In the field of Yizre'el the dogs will eat the flesh of Izevel; ³⁷ Izevel's corpse in the field of Yizre'el will be like dung on the ground, unrecognizable as Izevel.'"

10 ¹ There were seventy descendants of Ach'av in Shomron. Yehu wrote letters and sent them to Shomron to the rulers of Yizre'el, to the leaders, and to the guardians of Ach'av's sons. The letters said, ² "You have with you your master's sons, also chariots and horses, as well as fortified cities and armor. So, as soon as this letter reaches you, ³ choose the best and most suitable of your master's sons, set him on his father's throne and fight for your master's dynasty." ⁴ They were panic-stricken and said, "If the other two kings couldn't withstand him, how will we?" ⁵ So the administrator of the palace, the governor of the city, the leaders and the children's guardians sent this message to Yehu: "We are your servants. We will do everything you ask us to; we won't appoint anyone king. Do as you see fit."

⁶ He wrote a second letter to them, which said, "If you are on my side, and if you are ready to obey my orders, then bring the heads of your master's sons to me in Yizre'el by this time tomorrow." Now the seventy sons of the king were with the prominent men who had raised them. ⁷ When the letter reached them, they seized the king's sons and killed them, all seventy of them, put their heads in baskets and sent them to Yehu in Yizre'el. ⁸ A messenger came and told him, "They have brought the heads of the king's sons." He said, "Leave them in two piles at the entrance of the city gate until morning." ⁹ When morning came, he went out, stood before the people and said, "You are not responsible [for the deaths of these men]. Yes, I conspired against my master and killed him. But who killed all these? ¹⁰ Understand, then, that no part of ADONAI's word which ADONAI spoke concerning the dynasty of Ach'av falls to the ground; because ADONAI has done what he said through his servant Eliyahu." ¹¹ So Yehu killed everyone who remained from the house of Ach'av in Yizre'el, all his leading men, his close friends and his *cohanim*, until not one of them was left alive. ¹² Then he set out and went to Shomron.

On the way he reached a shearing shed for shepherds, ¹³ where he encountered relatives of Achazyah king of Y'hudah. "Who are you?" he asked. "We're relatives of Achazyah," they answered, "and we're going down to pay our respects to the families of the king and of the queen mother." ¹⁴ "Take them alive," said Yehu. They took them alive, forty-two men, slaughtered them and threw them into the shearing shed's pit; he spared not one of them.

¹⁵ On leaving there, he happened upon Y'honadav the son of Rekhav coming toward him. He greeted him and said to him, "Are you wholeheartedly with me, as I am with you?" "Yes," answered Y'honadav. "If so, give me your hand." He gave him his hand, and Yehu took him up into the chariot. ¹⁶ He said, "Come with me, and see how zealous I am for ADONAI." So they had him ride in his chariot.

¹⁷ On arriving in Shomron he put to death everyone that Ach'av still had in Shomron, until he had destroyed him, in keeping with the word of ADONAI which he had spoken to Eliyahu.

¹⁸ Next, Yehu assembled all the people and said to them, "Ach'av served Ba'al in limited measure, but Yehu will serve him with full zeal. ¹⁹ Therefore summon all the prophets of Ba'al to me, all his worshippers and all his priests. None of them is to be missing, because I am going to offer a great sacrifice to Ba'al; whoever is missing will not remain alive." But Yehu was setting a trap, in order to destroy the worshippers of Ba'al. ²⁰ Yehu said, "Proclaim a solemn assembly for Ba'al," and they did so. ²¹ Yehu sent throughout all Isra'el, and all the worshippers of Ba'al came, so that there was not one man left that didn't come. They entered the temple of Ba'al, and the temple of Ba'al was filled from one end to the other. ²² To the man in charge of the wardrobe he said, "Bring out robes for all the worshippers of Ba'al"; and he brought them clothes. ²³ Yehu and Y'honadav the son of Rekhav entered the house of Ba'al and said to the worshippers of Ba'al, "Search to see that none of the servants of ADONAI is here with you, only worshippers of Ba'al." ²⁴ Then they went in to offer sacrifices and burnt offerings.

But Yehu had chosen eighty men to remain outside. He said, "If any of the men I am about to put in your hands escapes, it will be your life for his." ²⁵ As soon as he had finished offering the burnt offering, Yehu said to the guards and officers, "Go in, and kill them; don't let one of them get out." So they killed them with the sword; then, after the guards and officers had thrown their bodies outside, they went into temple of Ba'al's inner shrine, ²⁶ brought out the pillars in the temple of Ba'al and burned them. ²⁷ Finally, they broke down Ba'al's standing-stone and demolished the temple of Ba'al, converting it into a latrine, which it still is today. ²⁸ Thus Yehu rid Isra'el of Ba'al.

²⁹ However, Yehu did not turn away from the sins of Yarov'am the son of N'vat, with which he had led Isra'el into sin, the gold calves that were in Beit-El and Dan. ³⁰ ADONAI said to Yehu, "Because you did well in accomplishing what is right from my perspective, and have done to the house of Ach'av everything that was in my heart, your descendants down to the fourth generation will sit on the throne of Isra'el." ³¹ But Yehu made no effort to live wholeheartedly according to the Torah of ADONAI the God of Isra'el and did not turn away from the sins of Yarov'am, with which he had led Isra'el into sin.

³² It was during that period that ADONAI began to dismember Isra'el. Haza'el attacked them throughout the territory of Isra'el ³³ east of the Yarden — all the land of Gil'ad, the Gadi, Re'uveni and M'nashi, from 'Aro'er by the Arnon River, including Gil'ad and Bashan.

³⁴ Other activities of Yehu, all his accomplishments and all his power are recorded in the Annals of the Kings of Isra'el. ³⁵ Yehu slept with his ancestors, and they buried him in Shomron. Then Y'ho'achaz his son became king in his place. ³⁶ Yehu ruled over Isra'el in Shomron for twenty-eight years.

413

11 ¹ When 'Atalyah the mother of Achazyah saw that her son was dead, she set about destroying the entire royal family. ² But Y'hosheva the daughter of King Yoram, sister of Achazyah, took Yo'ash the son of Achazyah and stole him away from among the princes who were being slaughtered. She took him and his nurse, sequestered them in a bedroom, and hid them from 'Atalyah, so that he was not killed. ³ He remained hidden with his nurse in the house of ADONAI for six years; during this time 'Atalyah ruled the land. ⁴ In the seventh year Y'hoyada summoned the captains of hundred-man platoons, of both the Kari and the guard. He brought them into the house of ADONAI, made an agreement with them and had them swear to it in the house of ADONAI. Then he showed them the king's son ⁵ and gave them this instruction: "Here is what you are to do: of you who come on duty on *Shabbat*, a third [normally] guards the royal palace, ⁶ a third is at the Sur Gate and a third is at the gate behind the guards. [The first third] is to continue guarding the palace and serve as a barrier, ⁷ while the other two groups of you who come on duty on *Shabbat* will guard the house of ADONAI, where the king is. ⁸ You are to surround the king, each man with his weapons in his hand. Anyone who penetrates the ranks is to be killed. Stay with the king whenever he leaves or enters."

⁹ The captains over hundreds did exactly as Y'hoyada the *cohen* ordered. Each took his men, those coming on duty on *Shabbat* and those going off duty on *Shabbat*, and came to Y'hoyada the *cohen*. ¹⁰ The *cohen* issued to the captains of hundreds the spears and shields that had been King David's and were kept in the house of ADONAI. ¹¹ The guards then took positions, each man with his weapons in his hand, from the right side of the house to the left side of the house, alongside the altar, alongside [the exterior of] the house and around the king. ¹² Then he brought out the king's son, crowned him, gave him [a copy of] the testimony and thus made him king; they anointed him, clapped their hands and shouted, "Long live the king!"

¹³ When 'Atalyah heard the shouting of the guard and the people, she entered the house of ADONAI where the people were, ¹⁴ looked and saw the king standing there on the platform, in keeping with the rule, with the leaders and trumpeters next to the king. All the people of the land were celebrating and blowing the trumpets. At this 'Atalyah tore her clothes and cried, "Treason! Treason!" ¹⁵ Y'hoyada the *cohen* ordered the captains of hundreds, the army officers, "Escort her out past the ranks [of guards]; but anyone who follows her, kill with the sword." For the *cohen* had said, "She must not be put to death in the house of ADONAI." ¹⁶ So they took her by force and led her through the horses' entry to the royal palace, and there she was put to death.

¹⁷ Y'hoyada made a covenant between ADONAI, the king and the people, that they would be ADONAI's people, and [a covenant] between the king and the people. ¹⁸ Then all the people of the land went to the house of Ba'al and broke it down; they completely smashed its altars and images and killed Mattan the priest of Ba'al in front of the altars.

Next, the *cohen* appointed officers over the house of ADONAI. ¹⁹ He took the captains of hundreds, the Kari, the guards and all the people of the land; and they brought the king down from the house of ADONAI, going by way of the gate of the guards to the royal palace. There he sat on the throne of the kings. ²⁰ All the people of the land celebrated, and at last the city was quiet. That is how they killed 'Atalyah with the sword at the royal palace.

12 ^{1(11:21)} Y'ho'ash was seven years old when he began his reign. ²⁽¹⁾ It was in the seventh year of Yehu that Y'ho'ash began to rule, and he ruled forty years in Yerushalayim. His mother's name was Tzivyah, from Be'er-Sheva. ³⁽²⁾ Y'ho'ash did what was right from ADONAI's perspective throughout the lifetime of Y'hoyada the *cohen*, who instructed him. ⁴⁽³⁾ Nevertheless the high places were not taken away; the people still sacrificed and presented offerings on the high places.

⁵⁽⁴⁾ Y'ho'ash said to the *cohanim*, "All the funds for sacred purposes which are brought to the house of ADONAI— the half-*shekel* tax, the taxes on persons in a man's household, and all the offerings anyone voluntarily brings to the house of ADONAI— ⁶⁽⁵⁾ the *cohanim* are to receive from whoever personally makes contributions to them; and they are to use these funds to repair the damaged parts of the house, wherever damage is found. ⁷⁽⁶⁾ But twenty-three years into the reign of King Y'ho'ash, the *cohanim* had still not repaired the damaged places in the house. ⁸⁽⁷⁾ So King Y'ho'ash summoned Y'hoyada the *cohen* and the other *cohanim* and said to them, "Why aren't you repairing the damaged places in the house? Therefore, you are no longer to take money from those who contribute it personally to you; you must hand it over to be used for repairing the damage in the house." ⁹⁽⁸⁾ The *cohanim* agreed not to receive money from the people, and they would no longer be responsible for repairing the damage to the house.

¹⁰⁽⁹⁾ Then Y'hoyada the *cohen* took a chest, drilled a hole in its lid and set it by the altar, on the right, as one enters the house of ADONAI; and the *cohanim* in charge of the entry put in it all the money brought into the house of ADONAI. ¹¹⁽¹⁰⁾ When they saw that there was a large amount of money in the chest, the king's secretary and the *cohen hagadol* would come up, count the money found in the house of ADONAI and put it in bags. ¹²⁽¹¹⁾ Then they would give the weighed-out money to those supervising the work in the house of ADONAI, who would use it to pay the carpenters and construction-workers doing the work in the house of ADONAI, ¹³⁽¹²⁾ on masons, stoneworkers, timber, worked stone and everything else needed for repairing the damaged places in the house of ADONAI. ¹⁴⁽¹³⁾ But none of the money brought into the house of ADONAI was used to make silver cups, snuffers, bowls, trumpets or other articles of gold or silver for the house of ADONAI; ¹⁵⁽¹⁴⁾ because they gave the money to those doing the work, thus restricting its use to repairing the damage in the house of ADONAI. ¹⁶⁽¹⁵⁾ Moreover, they did not require an accounting from the supervisors given the money to pay the workers, because they dealt honestly. ¹⁷⁽¹⁶⁾ Money from guilt offerings and sin offerings, however, was not brought into the house of ADONAI; it went to the *cohanim*.

¹⁸⁽¹⁷⁾ Haza'el king of Aram went up and fought against Gat; and after capturing it, Haza'el made his decision to attack Yerushalayim. ¹⁹⁽¹⁸⁾ Y'ho'ash king of Y'hudah took all the consecrated articles that Y'hoshafat, Y'horam and Achazyah, his ancestors, kings of Y'hudah, had dedicated, as well as his own consecrated articles and all the gold found in the treasuries of the house of ADONAI and of the royal palace, and sent them to Haza'el king of Aram, who then withdrew from Yerushalayim.

²⁰⁽¹⁹⁾ Other activities of Yo'ash and all his accomplishments are recorded in the Annals of the Kings of Y'hudah.

²¹⁽²⁰⁾ Then his servants got together, formed a conspiracy and murdered Yo'ash at Beit-Millo on the way down to Sila. ²²⁽²¹⁾ His servants Yozakhar the son of Shim'at and Y'hozavad the son of Shomer struck him, so that he died. They buried him with his ancestors in the City of David, and Amatzyah his son took his place as king.

13 ¹ It was in the twenty-third year of Yo'ash the son of Achazyah, king of Y'hudah, that Y'ho'achaz the son of Yehu began his reign over Isra'el in Shomron; he ruled for seventeen years. ² He did what was evil from ADONAI's perspective; he followed the sins of Yarov'am the son of N'vat, who made Isra'el sin; and he never ceased committing those sins. ³ ADONAI's anger burned against Isra'el, and he kept handing them over to Haza'el king of Aram and Ben-Hadad the son of Haza'el. ⁴ But Y'ho'achaz pleaded to ADONAI, and ADONAI listened to him, because he saw the oppression the king of Aram was inflicting on Isra'el. ⁵ So ADONAI gave Isra'el a savior who freed them from the grip of Aram, so that the people of Isra'el could live in their tents, as they had before. ⁶ Despite that, instead of turning from the sins of the house of Yarov'am, who made Isra'el sin, they continued to live in this sinful way. Moreover, the *asherah* continued to stand in Shomron. ⁷ The king of Aram destroyed Y'ho'achaz's army, making them like chaff when grain is threshed, except for fifty horsemen, ten chariots and 10,000 foot soldiers.

⁸ Other activities of Y'ho'achaz, all his accomplishments and his power are recorded in the Annals of the Kings of Isra'el. ⁹ Y'ho'achaz slept with his ancestors, and they buried him in Shomron. Then Yo'ash his son took his place as king.

¹⁰ It was in the thirty-seventh year of Yo'ash king of Y'hudah that Yo'ash the son of Y'ho'achaz began his rule over Isra'el in Shomron; he ruled for sixteen years. ¹¹ He did what was evil from ADONAI's perspective and did not turn from all the sins of Yarov'am the son of N'vat, who made Isra'el sin; on the contrary, he lived in this sinful way.

¹² Other activities of Yo'ash, all his accomplishments and his power in fighting Amatzyah king of Y'hudah are recorded in the Annals of the Kings of Isra'el. ¹³ Yo'ash slept with his ancestors, and Yarov'am occupied his throne. Yo'ash was buried in Shomron with the kings of Isra'el.

¹⁴ Elisha was now ill with the disease from which he would eventually die. Yo'ash the king of Isra'el came down to visit him and wept over him; he said, "My father! My father! The chariots and horsemen of Isra'el!" ¹⁵ Elisha said to him, "Bring a bow and arrows"; and he brought him a bow and arrows. ¹⁶ He said to the king of Isra'el, "Put your hand on the bow"; and he put his hand on it. Then Elisha laid his hands on the king's hands ¹⁷ and said, "Open the east window." He opened it. Elisha said, "Shoot"; and he shot. He said, "ADONAI's arrow of victory, the arrow of victory against Aram! You will defeat Aram completely at Afek!" ¹⁸ He said, "Take the arrows"; and he took them. He told the king of Isra'el, "Strike the ground." He struck three times, then stopped. ¹⁹ The man of God became angry with him; he said, "You should have struck five or six times; then you would have defeated Aram completely. As it is, you will defeat Aram only three times."

²⁰ Elisha died, and they placed him in a burial cave. Now the raiding parties of Mo'av used to make yearly incursions into the land at the start of the year. ²¹ Once it happened that just as they were burying a man, they spotted a raiding party; so they threw the man's body into Elisha's burial cave; and the moment the man touched the bones of Elisha, he revived and stood on his feet.

²² Haza'el king of Aram oppressed Isra'el throughout the lifetime of Y'ho'achaz; ²³ but ADONAI was gracious, took pity on them and looked on them with favor, because of his covenant with Avraham, Yitz'chak and Ya'akov. He was not willing to destroy them, and to this day he has not banished them from his presence.

²⁴ Haza'el king of Aram died, and Ben-Hadad his son took his place as king. ²⁵ Then Y'ho'ash the son of Y'ho'achaz captured from Ben-Hadad the son of Haza'el the cities which he had captured in war from Y'ho'achaz his father. Three times Yo'ash defeated him, thus recovering the cities of Isra'el.

14 ¹ It was in the second year of Yo'ash son of Y'ho'achaz king of Isra'el that Amatzyah the son of Yo'ash king of Y'hudah began his reign. ² He was twenty-five years old when he began to rule, and he ruled for twenty-nine years in Yerushalayim. His mother's name was Y'ho'adan, from Yerushalayim. ³ He did what was right from ADONAI's perspective, although not like David his ancestor; he lived the same way as his father Yo'ash. ⁴ However, the high places were not removed; the people still sacrificed and offered on the high places.

⁵ As soon as he had the kingdom firmly under his control, he put to death the servants of his who had murdered the king his father. ⁶ But he did not put the children of the murderers to death, because of what is written in the scroll of the *Torah* of Moshe, as ADONAI ordered when he said, "Fathers are not to be executed for the children, nor are children to be executed for the fathers; every person will be executed for his own sin."

⁷ He slaughtered 10,000 men of Edom in the Salt Valley and captured Sela in the war, renaming it Yokte'el, as it is today. ⁸ Then Amatzyah sent messengers to Y'ho'ash the son of Y'ho'achaz, son of Yehu, king of Isra'el, with this challenge: "Come on, let's have it out face-to-face." ⁹ Y'ho'ash the king of Isra'el sent this reply to Amatzyah king of Y'hudah: "Once, in the L'vanon, the thistle sent a message to the cedar: 'Give your daughter to my son in marriage.' But a wild animal passed by the thistle and squashed it. ¹⁰ True, you have defeated Edom, and now you're ambitious. So enjoy the glory, but stay home! Why provoke calamity, to your own ruin, yours and Y'hudah's too?" ¹¹ But Amatzyah wouldn't listen. So Y'ho'ash king of Isra'el went up; and he and Amatzyah king of Y'hudah had it out face-to-face at Beit-Shemesh, which belongs to Y'hudah. ¹² Y'hudah was defeated by Isra'el, and every man fled to his tent. ¹³ Y'ho'ash king of Isra'el took Amatzyah king of Y'hudah, the son of Y'ho'ash the son of Achazyah, prisoner at Beit-Shemesh. Then he went to Yerushalayim and demolished the wall of Yerushalayim between the Gate of Efrayim and the Corner Gate, a section 600 feet long. ¹⁴ He took all the gold and silver, all the articles he could find in the house of ADONAI and in the treasuries of the royal palace, and hostages; then he returned to Shomron.

¹⁵ Other activities of Y'ho'ash that he did, his power and how he fought Amatzyah king of Y'hudah are recorded in the Annals of the Kings of Isra'el. ¹⁶ Y'ho'ash slept with his ancestors and was buried in Shomron with the kings of Isra'el. Then Yarov'am took his place as king.

¹⁷ Amatzyah the son of Yo'ash king of Y'hudah lived another fifteen years after the death of Y'ho'ash son of Y'ho'achaz, king of Isra'el. ¹⁸ Other activities of Amatzyah are recorded in the Annals of the Kings of Y'hudah.

¹⁹ Because of a conspiracy formed against him in Yerushalayim, Amatzyah fled to Lakhish; but they followed him to Lakhish and killed him there. ²⁰ They brought his body back on horses, and he was buried in Yerushalayim with his ancestors in the City of David. ²¹ Then all the people of Y'hudah took 'Azaryah at the age of sixteen and made him king in place of his father Amatzyah.

²² 'Azaryah recovered Eilat for Y'hudah and rebuilt it; after that the king [Amatzyahu] slept with his ancestors. ²³ It was in the fifteenth year of Amatzyah the son of Yo'ash, king of Y'hudah, that Yarov'am the son of Yo'ash, king of Isra'el, began to reign in Shomron; and he ruled for forty-one years. ²⁴ He did what was evil from ADONAI's perspective; he did not turn from all the sins of Yarov'am the son of N'vat, who made Isra'el sin.

²⁵ He recovered the territory of Isra'el between the entrance of Hamat and the sea of the 'Aravah, in keeping with the word of ADONAI the God of Isra'el, which he spoke through his servant Yonah the son of Amitai, the prophet from Gat-Hefer. ²⁶ For ADONAI saw how bitterly Isra'el had suffered, with no one left, either slave or free, and no one coming to Isra'el's aid. ²⁷ ADONAI did not threaten to blot out the name of Isra'el from under heaven, but saved them through Yarov'am the son of Yo'ash.

²⁸ Other activities of Yarov'am, all his accomplishments, all his power, how he conducted war and how he recovered Dammesek and Hamat for Y'hudah in Isra'el are recorded in the Annals of the Kings of Isra'el. ²⁹ Yarov'am slept with his ancestors the kings of Isra'el, and Z'kharyah took his place as king.

15 ¹ It was in the twenty-seventh year of Yarov'am king of Isra'el that 'Azaryah the son of Amatzyah, king of Y'hudah, began his reign. ² He was sixteen years old when he began to rule, and he ruled for fifty-two years in Yerushalayim. His mother's name was Y'kholyahu, from Yerushalayim. ³ He did what was right from ADONAI's perspective, following the example of everything his father Amatzyah had done. ⁴ However, the high places were not taken away; the people still sacrificed and offered on the high places.

⁵ ADONAI struck the king, so that he had *tzara'at* until his dying day, so that he lived in a separate house, while Yotam the king's son ran the king's household and was regent over the people of the land.

⁶ Other activities of 'Azaryah and all his accomplishments are recorded in the Annals of the Kings of Y'hudah. ⁷ So 'Azaryah slept with his ancestors the kings of Isra'el, and they buried him with his ancestors in the City of David. Then Yotam his son took his place as king.

⁸ It was in the thirty-eighth year of 'Azaryah king of Y'hudah that Z'kharyah the son of Yarov'am began his reign over Isra'el in Shomron; he ruled for six months. ⁹ He did what was evil from ADONAI's perspective, just as his ancestors had done; he did not turn from all the sins of Yarov'am the son of N'vat, who made Isra'el sin.

¹⁰ Shalum the son of Yavesh formed a conspiracy against him. He struck him in the presence of the people and killed him; then he took his place as king. ¹¹ Other activities of Z'kharyah are recorded in the Annals of the Kings of Isra'el. ¹² The word of ADONAI which he had spoken to Yehu was, "Your descendants down to the fourth generation will sit on the throne of Isra'el"; and that is exactly what happened.

¹³ Shalum the son of Yavesh began his reign in the thirty-ninth year of 'Uziyah king of Y'hudah; he ruled in Shomron for only a month. ¹⁴ Menachem the son of Gadi went up from Tirtzah, came to Shomron, struck Shalum the son of Yavesh in Shomron and killed him. Then he took his place as king.

¹⁵ Other activities of Shalum and the conspiracy he formed are recorded in the Annals of the Kings of Isra'el

¹⁶ From Tirtzah Menachem attacked Tifsach, all the people in it and its territory, because they had not opened their gates to him. So he sacked the city and ripped apart all its pregnant women.

¹⁷ It was in the thirty-ninth year of 'Azaryah king of Y'hudah that Menachem the son of Gadi began his reign over Isra'el; he ruled ten years in Shomron. ¹⁸ He did what was evil from ADONAI's perspective; throughout his life he did not turn from the sins of Yarov'am the son of N'vat, who made Isra'el sin.

¹⁹ Pul the king of Ashur invaded the land. Menachem gave Pul thirty-three tons of silver, so that he would confirm Menachem's hold on the kingdom. ²⁰ He did this by taxing the wealthy men in Isra'el; from each he required one-and-a-quarter pounds of silver to give to the king of Ashur. Then the king of Ashur turned around and left the land.

²¹ Other activities of Menachem and all his accomplishments are recorded in the Annals of the Kings of Isra'el. ²² Menachem slept with his ancestors, and P'kachyah his son took his place as king.

²³ It was in the fiftieth year of 'Azaryah king of Y'hudah that P'kachyah the son of Menachem began his reign over Isra'el in Shomron; he ruled for two years. ²⁴ He did what was evil from ADONAI's perspective; he did not turn from the sins of Yarov'am the son of N'vat, who made Isra'el sin.

²⁵ Pekach the son of Remalyahu, one of his commanders, conspired against him. With Argov, Aryeh and fifty men from Gil'ad, he assassinated him in the palace stronghold in Shomron. After killing him, he took his place as king.

²⁶ Other activities of P'kachyah and all his accomplishments are recorded in the Annals of the Kings of Isra'el.

²⁷ It was in the fifty-second year of 'Azaryah king of Y'hudah that Pekach the son of Remalyah began to reign over Isra'el in Shomron; his reign lasted twenty years. ²⁸ He did what was evil from ADONAI's perspective; he did not turn from the sins of Yarov'am the son of N'vat, who made Isra'el sin.

²⁹ During the time of Pekach king of Isra'el, Tiglat-Pil'eser king of Ashur came and conquered 'Iyon, Avel-Beit-Ma'akhah, Yanoach, Kedesh, Hatzor, Gil'ad, and the Galil — all the land of Naftali — and took them captive to Ashur.

³⁰ Hoshea the son of Elah conspired against Pekach the son of Remalyah, struck him, killed him and took his place as king in the twentieth year of Yotam the son of 'Uziyah.

³¹ Other activities of Pekach and all his accomplishments are recorded in the Annals of the Kings of Isra'el.

³² It was in the second year of Pekach the son of Remalyah, king of Isra'el, that Yotam the son of 'Uziyah king of Y'hudah began his reign. ³³ He was twenty-five years old when he began his reign, and he ruled for sixteen years in Yerushalayim. His mother's name was Yerusha the daughter of Tzadok. ³⁴ He did what was right from ADONAI's perspective, following the example of everything his father 'Uziyah had done. ³⁵ However, the high places were not taken away; and the people still sacrificed and offered on the high places.

He built the Upper Gate of the house of ADONAI.

³⁶ Other activities of Yotam and all his accomplishments are recorded in the Annals of the Kings of Y'hudah.

³⁷ It was during this period that ADONAI began sending against Y'hudah Retzin the king of Aram and Pekach the son of Remalyah. ³⁸ Yotam slept with his ancestors and was buried with his ancestors in the City of David his ancestor. Then Achaz his son took his place as king.

16 ¹ It was in the seventeenth year of Pekach the son of Remalyah that Achaz the son of Yotam king of Y'hudah began his reign. ² Achaz was twenty years old when he began to rule, and he reigned sixteen years in Yerushalayim. But he did not do what was right from the perspective of ADONAI his God, as David his ancestor had done. ³ Rather, he lived in the manner of the kings of Isra'el; he even made his son pass through fire [as a sacrifice], in keeping with the abominable practices of the pagans, whom ADONAI had thrown out ahead of the people of Isra'el. ⁴ He also sacrificed and offered on the high places, on the hills and under any green tree.

⁵ Then Retzin king of Aram and Pekach son of Remalyah, king of Isra'el, came up to fight against Yerushalayim. They put Achaz under siege, but they could not overcome him. ⁶ It was at that time that Retzin king of Aram recovered Eilat for Aram and drove the Judeans from Eilat; whereupon people from Edom came to Eilat to live, as they do to this day. ⁷ Then Achaz sent messengers to Tiglat-Pil'eser king of Ashur with this message: "I am your servant and your son. Come up, and save me from the king of Aram and the king of Isra'el, who are attacking me." ⁸ Achaz took the silver and gold that was in the house of ADONAI and in the treasuries of the royal palace and sent it as a present to the king of Ashur. ⁹ The king of Ashur heeded him— the king of Ashur attacked Dammesek and captured it; then he carried its people captive to Kir and killed Retzin.

¹⁰ When King Achaz went to Dammesek to meet Tiglat-Pil'eser king of Ashur and saw the altar that was in Dammesek, he sent a drawing and model of the altar to Uriyah the *cohen*, with details of its construction and decoration. ¹¹ Then Uriyah the *cohen* built an altar exactly according to the design King Achaz had sent from Dammesek; Uriyah the *cohen* had it ready by the time King Achaz returned from Dammesek. ¹² When the king arrived from Dammesek he saw the altar, and the king approached the altar and offered on it. ¹³ He offered his burnt offering and his grain offering, poured out his drink offering and splashed the blood of his peace offerings on the altar. ¹⁴ The bronze altar, which was before ADONAI, he brought from in front of the house, from between his own altar and the house of ADONAI, and put it on the north side of his own altar. ¹⁵ Then King Achaz instructed Uriyah the *cohen* as follows: "Henceforth, it is on the large altar that you are to offer the morning burnt offering, the evening grain offering, the king's burnt offering and his grain offering, together with the burnt offering of all the people of the land, their grain offering and their drink offerings; and you are to splash all the blood of the burnt offering against it and all the blood of the sacrifice. As for the bronze altar, I will take care of that." ¹⁶ Uriyah the *cohen* acted in accordance with everything King Achaz ordered. ¹⁷ King Achaz removed the panels of the trolleys and took the basins off them; he took the Sea off the bronze oxen supporting it and set it on the stone pavement; ¹⁸ and, because of the king of Ashur, he removed from the house of ADONAI the colonnade used on *Shabbat* that had been built for it and the king's entranceway outside it.

¹⁹Other activities of Achaz and all his accomplishments are recorded in the Annals of the Kings of Y'hudah. ²⁰Achaz slept with his ancestors and was buried with his ancestors in the City of David. Then Hizkiyahu his son took his place as king.

17 ¹It was in the twelfth year of Achaz king of Y'hudah that Hoshea the son of Elah began his reign over Isra'el in Shomron; he ruled for nine years. ²He did what was evil from ADONAI's perspective, although he wasn't as bad as the kings of Isra'el who had preceded him.

³Shalman'eser king of Ashur advanced against Hoshea, and Hoshea became his vassal and paid him tribute. ⁴But the king of Ashur found that Hoshea was conspiring [against him] — he had sent messengers to So the king of Egypt and not paid his tribute to the king of Ashur, as he had previously done every year. For this the king of Ashur imprisoned him, putting him in chains. ⁵Then the king of Ashur invaded all the land, advanced on Shomron and put it under siege for three years. ⁶In the ninth year of Hoshea, the king of Ashur captured Shomron. He carried Isra'el away captive to Ashur, resettling them in Halach, in Havor on the Gozan River and in the cities of the Medes.

⁷This came about because the people of Isra'el had sinned against ADONAI their God, who had brought them out of the land of Egypt, out from under the domination of Pharaoh king of Egypt. They feared other gods ⁸and lived by the customs of the nations that ADONAI had expelled ahead of the people of Isra'el and by those of the kings of Isra'el. ⁹The people of Isra'el secretly did things that were not right, according to ADONAI their God. They built high places for themselves wherever they lived, from the watchtower to the fortified city. ¹⁰They set up standing-stones and sacred poles for themselves on any high hill and under any green tree. ¹¹Then they would make offerings on all the high places, like the nations ADONAI had expelled ahead of them, and would do wicked things to provoke the anger of ADONAI; ¹²moreover, they served idols, something ADONAI had expressly told them not to do. ¹³ADONAI had warned Isra'el and Y'hudah in advance through every prophet and seer, "Turn from your evil ways; and obey my *mitzvot* and regulations, in accordance with the entire *Torah* which I ordered your ancestors to keep and which I sent to you through my servants the prophets." ¹⁴Nevertheless, they refused to listen but made themselves as stubborn as their ancestors, who did not put their trust in ADONAI their God. ¹⁵Thus they rejected his laws; his covenant, which he had made with their ancestors; and the solemn warnings he had given them. Instead they pursued worthless things and became worthless themselves, imitating the nations around them, whom ADONAI had ordered them not to emulate. ¹⁶They abandoned all the *mitzvot* of ADONAI their God. They made cast metal images for themselves, two calves. They made an *asherah*. They worshipped the whole army of heaven. They served Ba'al. ¹⁷They had their sons and daughters pass through fire [as a sacrifice]. They used divination and magic spells. And they gave themselves over to do what was evil from ADONAI's perspective, thereby provoking him; ¹⁸so that ADONAI, by now very angry with Isra'el, removed them from his sight. None was left except the tribe of Y'hudah alone. ¹⁹(However, neither did Y'hudah obey the *mitzvot* of ADONAI their God; rather they lived according to the customs of Isra'el.)

²⁰ Yes, *ADONAI* came to despise all the descendants of Isra'el. He caused them trouble and handed them over to plunderers, until finally he threw them out of his sight. ²¹ He tore Isra'el away from the house of David. They made Yarov'am the son of N'vat king; and Yarov'am drew Isra'el away from following *ADONAI* and made them commit a great sin. ²² The people of Isra'el followed the example of all the sins that Yarov'am had committed and did not turn away from them, ²³ until *ADONAI* removed Isra'el out of his sight, as he had said he would through all his servants the prophets. Thus Isra'el was carried away captive from their own land to Ashur, and it remains so to this day.

²⁴ The king of Ashur brought people from Bavel, Kutah, 'Ava, Hamat and S'farvayim and settled them in the cities of Shomron in place of the people of Isra'el; they took possession of Shomron and lived in its cities. ²⁵ When they first came to live there, they did not fear *ADONAI*. Therefore *ADONAI* sent lions among them, which killed some of them. ²⁶ So they said to the king of Ashur, "The nations you carried away and settled in the cities of Shomron are not familiar with the rules for worshipping the God of the land. Therefore he has sent lions among them; and they are there, killing them; because they're not familiar with the rules for worshipping the God of the land." ²⁷ In response, the king of Ashur gave this order: "Take back one of the *cohanim* you brought from there. Have him go and live there, and have him teach them the rules for worshipping the God of the land." ²⁸ So one of the *cohanim* they had carried away captive from Shomron came and lived in Beit-El, and he taught them how they should fear *ADONAI*.

²⁹ Nevertheless, every nation made gods of their own and put them in the temples on the high places which the Shomronim had made, every nation in the cities where they lived. ³⁰ Thus the people from Bavel made Sukkot-B'not, those from Kutah made Nergal, those from Hamat made Ashima, ³¹ the 'Avim made Nivchaz and Tartak, and the S'farvim burned up their children in the fire as sacrifices to Adramelekh and 'Anamelekh the gods of S'farvayim. ³² So they feared *ADONAI*, while at the same time they appointed for themselves priests from among themselves to preside at the high places, and they would sacrifice for them in the temples on the high places. ³³ They both feared *ADONAI* and served their own gods in the manner customary among the nations from which they had been taken away. ³⁴ To this day they continue to follow their former [pagan] customs. They do not fear *ADONAI*. They do not follow the regulations, rulings, *Torah* or *mitzvah* which *ADONAI* ordered the descendants of Ya'akov, to whom he gave the name Isra'el, ³⁵ with whom *ADONAI* had made a covenant and charged them, "Do not fear other gods or bow down to them, serve them or sacrifice to them. ³⁶ On the contrary, you are to fear *ADONAI*, who brought you out of the land of Egypt with great power and an outstretched arm. Worship him, and sacrifice to him. ³⁷ You are to observe forever the laws, rulings, *Torah* and *mitzvah* which he wrote for you. You are not to fear other gods, ³⁸ and you are not to forget the covenant I made with you. No, you must not fear other gods ³⁹ but must fear *ADONAI* your God; then he will rescue you from the power of all your enemies." ⁴⁰ However, they didn't listen, but followed their old [pagan] practices. ⁴¹ So these nations mixed fearing *ADONAI* with serving their carved idols; likewise their children; and to this day, their descendants do the same as their ancestors did.

18 ¹ It was in the third year of Hoshea the son of Elah, king of Isra'el, that Hizkiyahu the son of Achaz, king of Y'hudah, began his reign. ² He was twenty-five years old when he began his reign, and he ruled for twenty-nine years in Yerushalayim. His mother's name was Avi the daughter of Z'kharyah. ³ He did what was right from ADONAI's perspective, following the example of everything David his ancestor had done. ⁴ He removed the high places, smashed the standing-stones, cut down the *asherah* and broke in pieces the bronze serpent that Moshe had made; because in those days the people of Isra'el were making offerings to it, calling it N'chushtan.* ⁵ He put his trust in ADONAI the God of Isra'el; after him there was no one like him among all the kings of Y'hudah, nor had there been among those before him. ⁶ For he clung to ADONAI and did not leave off following him, but obeyed his *mitzvot*, which ADONAI had given Moshe. ⁷ So ADONAI was with him. Wherever he went out to battle, he did well. He rebelled against the king of Ashur and refused to be his vassal. ⁸ He drove the P'lishtim back to 'Azah and laid waste to their territory from the watchtower to the fortified city.

⁹ It was in the fourth year of King Hizkiyahu, which was the seventh year of Hoshea son of Elah, king of Isra'el, that Shalman'eser king of Ashur advanced against Shomron and laid siege to it. ¹⁰ At the end of three years they captured it — that is, Shomron was captured in the sixth year of Hizkiyahu, which was the ninth year of Hoshea king of Isra'el. ¹¹ The king of Ashur carried Isra'el away captive to Ashur and settled them in Halach, in Havor on the Gozan River and in the cities of the Medes. ¹² This happened because they did not heed the voice of ADONAI their God, but violated his covenant, everything that Moshe the servant of ADONAI had ordered them to do, and would neither hear it nor do it.

¹³ In the fourteenth year of King Hizkiyahu, Sancheriv king of Ashur advanced against all the fortified cities of Y'hudah and captured them. ¹⁴ Hizkiyahu king of Y'hudah sent this message to the king of Ashur at Lakhish: "I have done wrong. If you will go away from me, I will pay whatever penalty you impose on me." The king of Ashur imposed on Hizkiyahu a penalty of ten tons of silver and a ton of gold. ¹⁵ Hizkiyahu gave him all the silver that could be found in the house of ADONAI and in the treasuries of the royal palace. ¹⁶ It was at that time that Hizkiyahu stripped the gold from the doors of the sanctuary of ADONAI and from the doorposts which Hizkiyahu king of Y'hudah himself had overlaid, and gave it to the king of Ashur.

¹⁷ From Lakhish the king of Ashur sent Tartan, Rav-Saris and Rav-Shakeh to King Hizkiyahu in Yerushalayim with a large army. They advanced and came to Yerushalayim. Upon arrival, they came and positioned themselves by the aqueduct from the Upper Pool, which is by the road to the Launderers' Field. ¹⁸ They summoned the king, but those answering the call were Elyakim the son of Hilkiyahu, who was in charge of the household, Shevnah the general secretary and Yo'ach the son of Asaf the foreign minister. ¹⁹ Rav-Shakeh addressed them: "Tell Hizkiyahu: 'Here is what the great king, the king of Ashur, says: "What makes you so confident? ²⁰ Do you think that mere spoken words constitute strategy and strength for battle? In whom, then, are you trusting when you rebel against me like this? ²¹ Now look! Relying on Egypt is like using a broken stick as a staff — when you lean on it, it

---

* Hebrew *nachash* means "serpent," and *n'choshet* means "bronze."

punctures your hand. That's what Pharaoh king of Egypt is like for anyone who puts his trust in him. ²² But if you tell me, 'We trust in ADONAI our God,' then isn't he the one whose high places and altars Hizkiyahu has removed, telling Y'hudah and Yerushalayim, 'You must worship before this altar in Yerushalayim'? ²³ All right, then, make a wager with my lord the king of Ashur: I will give you two thousand horses if you can find enough riders for them. ²⁴ How then can you repulse even one of my master's lowest-ranked army officers? Yet you are relying on Egypt for chariots and riders! ²⁵ Do you think I have come up to this place to destroy it without ADONAI's approval? ADONAI said to me, 'Attack this land, and destroy it'!'"

²⁶ Elyakim the son of Hilkiyahu, Shevnah and Yo'ach said to Rav-Shakeh, "Please speak to your servants in Aramaic, since we understand it; don't speak with us in Hebrew while the people on the wall are listening." ²⁷ But Rav-Shakeh answered them, "Did my master send me to deliver my message just to your master and yourselves? Didn't he send me to address the men sitting on the wall, who, like you, are going to eat their own dung and drink their own urine?" ²⁸ Then Rav-Shakeh stood up and, speaking loudly in Hebrew, said: "Hear what the great king, the king of Ashur, says! ²⁹ This is what the king says: 'Don't let Hizkiyahu deceive you, because he won't be able to save you from the power of the king of Ashur. ³⁰ And don't let Hizkiyahu make you trust in ADONAI by saying, "ADONAI will surely save us; this city will not be given over to the king of Ashur." ³¹ Don't listen to Hizkiyahu.' For this is what the king of Ashur says: 'Make peace with me, surrender to me. Then every one of you can eat from his vine and fig tree and drink the water in his own cistern; ³² until I come and take you away to a land like your own land, a land with grain and wine, a land with bread and vineyards, a land with olive trees and honey; so that you can live and not die. So don't listen to Hizkiyahu; he is only deluding you when he says, "ADONAI will save us." ³³ Has any god of any nation ever saved his land from the power of the king of Ashur? ³⁴ Where are the gods of Hamat and Arpad? Where are the gods of S'farvayim, Hena and 'Ivah? Did they save Shomron from my power? ³⁵ Where is the god of any country that has saved its country from my power, so that ADONAI might be able to save Yerushalayim from my power?'" ³⁶ But the people kept still and didn't answer him so much as a word; for the king's order was, "Don't answer him."

³⁷ Then Elyakim the son of Hilkiyah, who was in charge of the household, Shevnah the general secretary and Yo'ach the son of Asaf the foreign minister went to Hizkiyahu with their clothes torn and reported to him what Rav-Shakeh had said.

19 ¹ On hearing it, King Hizkiyahu tore his clothes, covered himself with sackcloth and entered the house of ADONAI. ² He sent Elyakim, who was in charge of the household, Shevnah the general secretary and the leading *cohanim*, covered with sackcloth, to Yesha'yahu the prophet, the son of Amotz. ³ They said to him, "This is what Hizkiyahu says: 'Today is a day of trouble, rebuke and disgrace. Children are ready to be born, but there is no strength to bring them to birth. ⁴ Maybe ADONAI your God will hear all the words of Rav-Shakeh, whom his master the king of Ashur has sent to taunt the living God, and will rebuke the message which ADONAI your God has heard. So pray for the remnant that is left.'"

⁵ When King Hizkiyahu's servants came to Yesha'yahu, ⁶ he said to them, "Tell your master that this is what ADONAI says: 'Don't be afraid of the words you heard the servants of the king of Ashur use to insult me. ⁷ I will put a spirit in him that will make him hear a rumor and return to his own land; then I will cause him to die by the sword in his own land.'"

⁸ Rav-Shakeh returned and, having heard that the king of Ashur had left Lakhish, found him making war with Livnah. ⁹ Then, on hearing it said that Tirhakah king of Ethiopia was on his way to fight him, the king of Ashur sent messengers to Hizkiyahu, telling them, ¹⁰ "This is what you are to say to Hizkiyahu king of Y'hudah: 'Don't let your God in whom you trust deceive you by saying, "Yerushalayim will not be handed over to the power of the king of Ashur." ¹¹ You have heard what the kings of Ashur have done to all lands — they have completely destroyed them. So how will you be delivered? ¹² Have the gods of the nations delivered them? No, my ancestors destroyed them — Gozan, Haran, Retzef and the people of 'Eden who were in Tel'asar. ¹³ Where is the king of Hamat? the king of Arpad? the king of the city of S'farvayim, of Hena and 'Ivah?'"

¹⁴ Hizkiyahu took the letter from the messengers' hands and read it. Then Hizkiyahu went up to the house of ADONAI and spread it out before ADONAI. ¹⁵ Hizkiyahu prayed as follows in the presence of ADONAI: "ADONAI God of Isra'el, who dwells above the k'ruvim! You alone are God of all the kingdoms on earth. You made heaven and earth. ¹⁶ Turn your ear, ADONAI, and hear! Open your eyes, ADONAI, and see! Hear the words that Sancheriv sent to taunt the living God. ¹⁷ It is true, ADONAI, that the kings of Ashur have laid waste the nations and their lands ¹⁸ and have thrown their gods into the fire. For those were non-gods, merely the product of people's hands, wood and stone; this is why they could destroy them. ¹⁹ Now therefore, ADONAI our God, please save us from his power — so that all the kingdoms on earth will know that you are ADONAI, God — you only."

²⁰ Then Yesha'yahu the son of Amotz sent this message to Hizkiyahu: "ADONAI the God of Isra'el says: 'You prayed to me against Sancheriv king of Ashur, and I have heard you.' ²¹ Here is ADONAI's answer concerning him:

'The virgin daughter of Tziyon
despises you; she laughs you to scorn.
The daughter of Yerushalayim
shakes her head at you.

²² Whom have you taunted and insulted?
Against whom have you raised your voice
and haughtily lifted your eyes?
The Holy One of Isra'el!

²³ "'Through your messengers you taunted *Adonai*.
You said, "With my many chariots
I have ascended the mountain heights
even in the far reaches of the L'vanon.
I cut down its tall cedars
and its best cypresses.
I reached its remotest corners

²⁴ and its best forests.
I dug [wells] in foreign lands,
and I drank the water.
The soles of my [soldiers'] feet
dried up all the rivers of Egypt.'

²⁵ "'Haven't you heard? Long ago I made it;
in antiquity I produced it;
and now I am making it happen:
you are turning fortified cities
into heaps of ruins;
²⁶ while their inhabitants, shorn of power,
are disheartened and ashamed,
weak as grass, frail as plants,
like grass on the rooftops
or grain scorched by the east wind.

²⁷ "'But I know when you sit, when you leave,
when you enter — and when you rage against me.
²⁸ And because of your rage against me,
because of your pride that has reached my ears,
I am putting my hook in your nose
and my bridle on your lips;
and I will make you return
by the way on which you came.'

²⁹ "'This will be the sign for you: this year, you will eat the grain that grows of itself;
the second year, you will eat what grows from that; but in the third year, you will
sow, reap, plant vineyards and eat their fruit.

³⁰ "'Meanwhile, the remnant
of the house of Y'hudah that has escaped
will again take root downward
and bear fruit upward;
³¹ for a remnant will go out from Yerushalayim,
those escaping will go out from Mount Tziyon.
The zeal of ADONAI-Tzva'ot
will accomplish this.'

³² "Therefore this is what ADONAI says concerning the king of Ashur:

'He will not come to this city
or even shoot an arrow there;
he will not confront it with a shield
or erect earthworks against it.
³³ By the way he came he will return;
he will not come to this city,'

426

says *Adonai*. ³⁴ 'For I will defend this city and save it, both for my own sake and for my servant David's sake.'"

³⁵ That night the angel of *Adonai* went out and struck down 185,000 men in the camp of Ashur. Early the next morning, there they were, all of them, corpses — dead. ³⁶ So Sancheriv king of Ashur left, went and returned to live in Ninveh.

³⁷ One day, as he was worshipping in the temple of Nisrokh his god, [his sons] Adramelekh and Shar'etzer struck him with the sword and escaped into the land of Ararat. So his son Esar-Hadon took his place as king.

20 ¹ Around this time, Hizkiyahu became ill to the point of death. Yesha'yahu the prophet, the son of Amotz, came and said to him, "Here is what *Adonai* says: 'Put your house in order, because you are going to die; you will not live.'" ² Hizkiyahu turned his face toward the wall and prayed to *Adonai*: ³ "I plead with you, *Adonai*, remember now how I have lived before you truly and wholeheartedly, and how I have done what you see as good." And he cried bitter tears.

⁴ Before Yesha'yahu had left the city's middle courtyard, the word of *Adonai* came to him: ⁵ "Go back, and tell Hizkiyahu the prince of my people, that this is what *Adonai*, the God of David your ancestor, says: 'I have heard your prayer and seen your tears, and I will heal you. On the third day, you are to go up to the house of *Adonai*. ⁶ I will add fifteen years to your life. Also I will rescue you and this city from the power of the king of Ashur; I will defend this city for my own sake and for my servant David's sake.'" ⁷ Then Yesha'yahu said, "Prepare a fig-plaster." They brought it and laid it on the inflammation, so that he would recover.

⁸ Hizkiyahu said to Yesha'yahu, "What sign will there be that *Adonai* will heal me and that I will be able to go up to the house of *Adonai* on the third day?" ⁹ Yesha'yahu said, "Here is the sign for you from *Adonai* that *Adonai* will do what he said: do you want the shadow [of the sundial] to go forward ten intervals or backward ten intervals? ¹⁰ Hizkiyahu answered, "It's easy for the shadow to go down ten intervals. No, let the shadow return backward ten intervals." ¹¹ Yesha'yahu called out to *Adonai*, and he brought the shadow on the sundial of Achaz ten intervals backward after it had gone down that far.

¹² B'rodakh-Bal'adan the son of Bal'adan, king of Bavel, heard that Hizkiyahu had been ill, so he sent a letter and a gift to him. ¹³ Hizkiyahu listened to [the messengers] and showed them the building where he kept his treasures, including the silver, gold, spices and precious oils; also the building where he kept his armor; and everything in his treasury — there was nothing in his palace or in his entire domain that Hizkiyahu did not show them. ¹⁴ Then Yesha'yahu the prophet came to King Hizkiyahu and asked him, "What did these men say? Where did they come from?" Hizkiyahu answered, "They came from a distant country, Bavel." ¹⁵ Yesha'yahu asked, "What have they seen in your palace?" "They have seen everything in my palace," said Hizkiyahu. "There isn't a thing among my treasures that I haven't shown them." ¹⁶ Yesha'yahu said to Hizkiyahu, "Hear what *Adonai* says: ¹⁷ 'The day will come when everything in your palace, along with everything your ancestors stored up until today, will be carried off to Bavel. Nothing will be left,' says *Adonai*. ¹⁸ 'They will carry off some of your descendants, your own offspring; and they will be made eunuchs serving in the palace of the king of Bavel.'" ¹⁹ Hizkiyahu said to Yesha'yahu,

"The word of ADONAI which you have just told me is good." He thought, "Isn't it, though, if peace and truth continue at least through my lifetime?" ^{20} Other activities of Hizkiyahu, his power and how he built the pool and aqueduct to bring water into the city are recorded in the Annals of the Kings of Y'hudah. ^{21} Then Hizkiyahu slept with his ancestors, and M'nasheh his son took his place as king.

21 ^{1} M'nasheh was twelve years old when he began his reign, and he ruled for fifty-five years in Yerushalayim. His mother's name was Heftzibah. ^{2} He did what was evil from ADONAI's perspective, following the disgusting practices of the nations whom ADONAI had expelled ahead of the people of Isra'el. ^{3} For he rebuilt the high places Hizkiyahu his father had destroyed; he erected altars for Ba'al and made an *asherah*, as had Ach'av king of Isra'el; and he worshipped all the army of heaven and served them. ^{4} He erected altars in the house of ADONAI, about which ADONAI had said, "In Yerushalayim I will put my name." ^{5} He erected altars for all the army of heaven in the two courtyards of the house of ADONAI. ^{6} He made his son pass through the fire [as a sacrifice]. He practiced soothsaying and divination and appointed mediums and persons who used spirit guides. He did much that was evil from ADONAI's perspective, thus provoking him to anger. ^{7} He set the carved image for the *asherah* he had made in the house concerning which ADONAI had told David and Shlomo his son, "In this house and in Yerushalayim, which I have chosen out of all the tribes of Isra'el, I will put my name forever. ^{8} Also I will not have the feet of Isra'el wander any longer out of the land which I gave their ancestors — if only they will take heed to obey every order I have given them and live in accordance with all the *Torah* that my servant Moshe ordered them to obey." ^{9} But they did not take heed; and M'nasheh misled them into doing even worse things than the nations ADONAI had destroyed ahead of the people of Isra'el.

^{10} ADONAI spoke this message through his servants the prophets: ^{11} "Because M'nasheh king of Y'hudah has done these disgusting things; because he has done things more wicked than anything the Emori, who were there before him, did; also because with his idols he made Y'hudah sin; ^{12} therefore here is what ADONAI the God of Isra'el, says: 'I am going to bring such calamity on Yerushalayim and Y'hudah that the ears of all who hear of it will tingle. ^{13} I will measure Yerushalayim with the same measuring cord that I used over Shomron, the same plumbline as for the house of Ach'av. I will scour Yerushalayim clean just as one scours a plate, scouring it and then turning it upside down. ^{14} I will abandon the remnant of my heritage, delivering them into the power of their enemies — they will become prey and plunder for all their enemies; ^{15} because they have done what is evil from my perspective and have provoked me to anger from the day their ancestors came out of Egypt to this very day.'"

^{16} Moreover, M'nasheh shed so much innocent blood that he flooded Yerushalayim from one end to the other — this in addition to his sin through which he caused Y'hudah to sin by doing what is evil from ADONAI's perspective.

^{17} Other activities of M'nasheh, all his accomplishments and the sin he committed are recorded in the Annals of the Kings of Y'hudah. ^{18} Then M'nasheh slept with his ancestors and was buried in the garden of his own house, the Garden of 'Uza; and Amon his son took his place as king.

¹⁹ Amon was twenty-two years old when he began his reign, and he ruled for two years in Yerushalayim. His mother's name was Meshulemet the daughter of Harutz from Yotvah. ²⁰ He did what was evil from *Adonai*'s perspective, as had M'nasheh his father. ²¹ He followed entirely the manner of life of his father, serving the idols that his father served and worshipping them. ²² He abandoned *Adonai*, the God of his ancestors, and did not live in *Adonai*'s way.

²³ Amon's servants conspired against him and put the king to death in his own palace. ²⁴ But the people of the land put to death all those who had been part of the conspiracy against King Amon. Then the people of the land made Yoshiyahu his son king in place of him.

²⁵ Other activities of Amon and all he acomplished are recorded in the Annals of the Kings of Y'hudah. ²⁶ Amon was buried in his tomb in the Garden of Uza, and Yoshiyahu his son took his place as king.

22 ¹ Yoshiyahu was eight years old when he began his reign, and he ruled for thirty-one years in Yerushalayim. His mother's name was Y'didah the daughter of 'Adayah from Botzkat. ² He did what was right from *Adonai*'s perspective, living entirely in the manner of David his ancestor and turning away neither to the right nor to the left.

³ In the eighteenth year of King Yoshiyahu, the king sent Shafan the son of Atzalyahu, the son of Meshulam, the secretary, to the house of *Adonai* after instructing him, ⁴ "Go up to Hilkiyahu the *cohen hagadol*, and have him total the money that has been brought into the house of *Adonai*, which the doorkeepers have collected from the people. ⁵ Then have them give it to the supervisors of the work being done in the house of *Adonai*; they in turn are to use it to pay the laborers in the house of *Adonai* to repair damaged places in the building — ⁶ the carpenters, construction-workers and stonemasons — and to purchase timber and worked stone for doing the repairs on the building." ⁷ However, they did not require an accounting from the supervisors given the money to spend, because they dealt honestly.

⁸ Hilkiyahu the *cohen hagadol* said to Shafan the secretary, "I have found the scroll of the *Torah* in the house of *Adonai*." Hilkiyah gave the scroll to Shafan, who read it. ⁹ Then Shafan the secretary went back to the king and gave the king this report: "Your servants have poured out the money found in the house and handed it over to the people supervising the work in the house of *Adonai*." ¹⁰ Shafan the secretary also told the king, "Hilkiyah the *cohen hagadol* gave me a scroll." Then Shafan read it aloud before the king. ¹¹ After the king had heard what was written in the scroll of the *Torah*, he tore his clothes. ¹² Then the king issued this order to Hilkiyah the *cohen*, Achikam the son of Shafan, 'Akhbor the son of Mikhayah, Shafan the secretary and 'Asayah the king's servant: ¹³ "Go; and consult *Adonai* for me, for the people and for all Y'hudah in regard to what is written in this scroll which has been found. For *Adonai* must be furious at us, since our ancestors did not listen to the words written in this scroll and didn't do everything written there that concerns us." ¹⁴ So Hilkiyahu the *cohen*, Achikam, Akhbor, Shafan and 'Asayah went to Huldah the prophet, the wife of Shalum the son of Tikvah, the son of Harchas, keeper of the wardrobe — she lived in the Second Quarter of Yerushalayim — and spoke with her. ¹⁵ She told them, "*Adonai* the God of Isra'el says to tell the man who sent you to me ¹⁶ that *Adonai* says this: 'I am going to bring calamity on this place and on its inhabitants, every word in the scroll the king of Y'hudah has read; ¹⁷ because they have abandoned me and

offered to other gods, in order to provoke me with everything they do. Therefore my anger will burn against this place and will not be quenched.' ¹⁸ But you are to tell the king of Y'hudah, who sent you to consult ADONAI, that ADONAI the God of Isra'el also says this: 'In regard to the words you have heard, ¹⁹ because your heart was tender, and you humbled yourself before ADONAI when you heard what I said against this place and its inhabitants — that they would become an object of astonishment and cursing — and have torn your clothes and cried before me, I have also heard you, says ADONAI. ²⁰ Therefore I will gather you to your ancestors, you will go to your grave in peace, and your eyes will not see all the calamity I am going to bring on this place.'" So they brought word back to the king.

23 ¹ Then the king summoned all the leaders of Y'hudah and Yerushalayim, and they assembled with him. ² The king went up to the house of ADONAI with all the men of Y'hudah, all those living in Yerushalayim, the *cohanim*, the prophets and all the people, both small and great; and he read in their hearing everything written in the scroll of the covenant that had been found in the house of ADONAI. ³ The king stood on the platform and made a covenant in the presence of ADONAI to live following ADONAI, observing his *mitzvot*, instructions and regulations wholeheartedly and with all his being, so as to confirm the words of the covenant written in this scroll. All the people stood, pledging themselves to keep the covenant.

⁴ Then the king ordered Hilkiyahu the *cohen hagadol*, the *cohanim* of the second rank and the doorkeepers to remove from the sanctuary of ADONAI all the articles that had been made for Ba'al, for the *asherah* and for the entire army of heaven; and he burned them up outside Yerushalayim in the fields of Kidron and carried their ashes to Beit-El.

⁵ He deposed the idolatrous priests the kings of Y'hudah had ordained to offer on the high places by the cities of Y'hudah and in the places surrounding Yerushalayim; he also deposed those who offered to Ba'al, the sun, the moon, the constellations and the whole army of heaven.

⁶ He took the *asherah* from the house of ADONAI to Vadi Kidron outside Yerushalayim and burned it in Vadi Kidron, stamped the ashes to powder and threw the powder onto the burial-ground for the common people.

⁷ He smashed the houses of the cult prostitutes that were in the house of ADONAI, where the women also wove garments for the *asherah*.

⁸ He removed the *cohanim* from the cities of Y'hudah; then, from Geva to Be'er-Sheva, he desecrated the high places where the *cohanim* had been making offerings. He also smashed the High Places of the Gates that were at the entrance of the Gate of Y'hoshua the governor of the city, on the left as one enters the city. ⁹ But although the *cohanim* who had been at the high places did not come up to the altar of ADONAI in Yerushalayim, nevertheless they did share *matzah* with their kinsmen.

¹⁰ He desecrated the Tofet fire pit in the Ben-Hinnom Valley, so that no one could cause his son or daughter to pass through fire [as a sacrifice] to Molekh.

¹¹ He confiscated the horses which the kings of Y'hudah had given to the sun, at the entrance to the house of ADONAI near the room of the officer N'tan-Melekh, in the side-courtyard; and he burned up the chariots of the sun.

¹² The king smashed the altars on the roof of the upper room of Achaz, which the kings of Y'hudah had made, and the altars which M'nasheh had made in the two

courtyards of the house of *ADONAI*. He broke them into pieces and threw the rubble into *Vadi* Kidron.

¹³ The king desecrated the high places facing Yerushalayim south of the Mount of Destruction, which Shlomo the king of Isra'el had built for 'Ashtoret the abomination of the Tzidonim, K'mosh the abomination of Mo'av and Milkom the abomination of the people of 'Amon. ¹⁴ He smashed the standing-stones, chopped down the sacred poles and covered their remains with human bones.

¹⁵ He smashed the altar that was at Beit-El and the high place made by Yarov'am the son of N'vat, who caused Isra'el to sin. Yes, he smashed that altar and the high place; he burned the high place, stamped the ashes to powder, and burned up the *asherah*. ¹⁶ Then, as Yoshiyahu was turning around, he noticed the burial caves that were there on the mountain; so he sent and had the bones taken out of the burial caves and burned them on the altar, thus desecrating it, in keeping with the word of *ADONAI* which the man of God had proclaimed, foretelling that these things would happen. ¹⁷ Then he asked, "This monument here that I'm looking at, what is it?" The men of the city told him, "It marks the burial cave of the man of God who came from Y'hudah and foretold the very things you have done to the altar of Beit-El." ¹⁸ He replied, "Let him be; no one is to move his bones." So they left his bones undisturbed, along with the bones of the prophet who had come from Shomron.

¹⁹ Yoshiyahu also removed all the shrines of the high places in the cities of Shomron, which the kings of Isra'el had made in order to provoke [*ADONAI*] to anger, and treated them the same as in Beit-El. ²⁰ He put to death all the priests of those high places on the altars there, then burned human bones on them. Finally he returned to Yerushalayim.

²¹ The king issued this order to all the people: "Observe *Pesach* to *ADONAI* your God, as written in this scroll of the covenant." ²² For *Pesach* had not been so observed since the days when the judges ruled Isra'el — not during the times of any of the kings of Isra'el or of the kings of Y'hudah. ²³ But in the eighteenth year of King Yoshiyahu this *Pesach* was observed to *ADONAI* in Yerushalayim.

²⁴ Yoshiyahu got rid of the mediums and the people using spirit guides, as well as the household gods, the idols and all the disgusting things spotted anywhere in Y'hudah and Yerushalayim. He did this in order to establish the words of the *Torah* written in the scroll Hilkiyahu the *cohen* had found in the house of *ADONAI*.

²⁵ No previous king was like him; because he turned to *ADONAI* with all his heart, with all his being and with all his power, in accordance with all the *Torah* of Moshe; nor did any king like him arise afterwards. ²⁶ Nevertheless, *ADONAI* did not turn away from his fiercely raging, furious anger that burned against Y'hudah because of all the things M'nasheh had done to provoke him. ²⁷ *ADONAI* said, "Just as I removed Isra'el, I will also remove Y'hudah out of my sight; and I will reject this city, which I chose, Yerushalayim, and the house concerning which I said, 'My name will be there.'"

²⁸ Other activities of Yoshiyahu and all his accomplishments are recorded in the Annals of the Kings of Y'hudah.

²⁹ During his time Pharaoh N'khoh king of Egypt went up toward the Euphrates River to attack the king of Ashur. King Yoshiyahu went out to oppose him; but at Megiddo, Pharaoh spotted Yoshiyahu and killed him. ³⁰ His servants carried his dead body from Megiddo to Yerushalayim in a chariot and buried

him in his own tomb. The people of the land took Y'ho'achaz the son of Yoshiyahu, anointed him, and made him king in his father's place. ³¹ Y'ho'achaz was twenty-three years old when he began his reign, and he ruled for three months in Yerushalayim. His mother's name was Hamutal the daughter of Yirmeyahu from Livnah. ³² He did what was evil from ADONAI's perspective, following the example of everything his ancestors had done. ³³ Pharaoh N'khoh imprisoned him at Rivlah in the land of Hamat, so that he would not be able to rule in Yerushalayim. He also imposed a penalty on the land of three-and-a-quarter tons of silver and sixty-six pounds of gold. ³⁴ Then Pharaoh N'khoh made Elyakim the son of Yoshiyahu king in place of Yoshiyahu his father and changed his name to Y'hoyakim. He also carried Y'ho'achaz off to Egypt, where he died. ³⁵ Y'hoyakim remitted the silver and gold to Pharaoh; but in order to pay the money Pharaoh demanded, he had to levy a tax on the land. He taxed the people of the land, each according to his means, to pay the silver and gold to Pharaoh N'khoh.

³⁶ Y'hoyakim was twenty-five years old when he began his reign, and he ruled for eleven years in Yerushalayim. His mother's name was Z'vudah the daughter of P'dayah, from Rumah. ³⁷ He did what was evil from the perspective of ADONAI, following the example of everything his ancestors had done.

24 ¹ It was in Y'hoyakim's time that N'vukhadnetzar king of Bavel invaded. Y'hoyakim became his vassal for three years, but then he turned against him and rebelled. ² ADONAI sent against him raiding parties from the Kasdim, Aram, Mo'av and the people of 'Amon; he sent them against Y'hudah to destroy it, in keeping with the word of ADONAI which he had spoken through his servants the prophets. ³ Yes, it was at ADONAI's order that this happened to Y'hudah, in order to remove them from his sight because of the sins of M'nasheh and all he had done, ⁴ and also because of the innocent blood he had shed — for he had flooded Yerushalayim with innocent blood, and ADONAI was unwilling to forgive.

⁵ Other activities of Y'hoyakim and all his accomplishments are recorded in the Annals of the Kings of Y'hudah. ⁶ Then Y'hoyakim slept with his ancestors, and Y'hoyakhin his son took his place as king.

⁷ The king of Egypt did not leave his own land any more, because the king of Bavel had captured all the territory of the king of Egypt between the Vadi of Egypt and the Euphrates River.

⁸ Y'hoyakhin was eighteen years old when he began his reign, and he ruled in Yerushalayim for three months. His mother's name was N'chushta the daughter of Elnatan, from Yerushalayim. ⁹ He did what was evil from ADONAI's perspective, following the example of everything his father had done.

¹⁰ It was then that the officers of N'vukhadnetzar king of Bavel marched on Yerushalayim and laid siege to the city. ¹¹ N'vukhadnetzar king of Bavel himself went to the city while it was under siege; ¹² and Y'hoyakhin king of Y'hudah went out to meet the king of Bavel — he, his mother, and his servants, princes and officers; and the king of Bavel took him captive in the eighth year of his reign. ¹³ He also carried away from there all the treasures in the house of ADONAI and the treasures in the royal palace. He cut in pieces all the articles of gold which Shlomo king of Isra'el had made in the temple of ADONAI, as ADONAI had said would happen.

¹⁴ He carried all Yerushalayim away captive — all the princes, all the bravest soldiers — 10,000 captives; also all the craftsmen and metalworkers. No one was left but the poorest people of the land.

¹⁵ Y'hoyakhin he carried off to Bavel; likewise he carried off the king's mother, the king's wives, his officers and the main leaders of the land from Yerushalayim into captivity in Bavel. ¹⁶ All the strong men — 7,000 of them, as well as 1,000 craftsmen and metalsmiths, all of them strong and trained for war — the king of Bavel brought captive to Bavel.

¹⁷ The king of Bavel made Matanyah, Y'hoyakhin's father's brother, king in place of Y'hoyakhin and changed his name to Tzidkiyahu. ¹⁸ Tzidkiyahu was twenty-one years old when he began to rule, and he ruled for eleven years in Yerushalayim. His mother's name was Hamutal the daughter of Yirmeyahu, from Livnah. ¹⁹ He did what was evil from the perspective of ADONAI, following the example of everything Y'hoyakim had done. ²⁰ And it was because of ADONAI's anger that all these things happened to Yerushalayim and Y'hudah, until he had thrown them out of his presence.

Tzidkiyahu rebelled against the king of Bavel;

25 ¹ so in the ninth year of his reign, in the tenth month, on the tenth day of the month, N'vukhadnetzar king of Bavel marched against Yerushalayim with his entire army. He set up camp against it and built siege towers against it on every side. ² The city remained under siege into the eleventh year of King Tzidkiyahu.

³ On the ninth day of the [fourth] month, when the famine in the city was so severe that there was no food for the people of the land, ⁴ they broke through into the city. All the soldiers [fled] by night through the gate between the two walls, near the king's garden. Because the Kasdim were surrounding the city, the king took the route through the 'Aravah. ⁵ But the army of the Kasdim went in pursuit of the king and overtook him on the plains near Yericho; all his troops deserted him. ⁶ Then they took the king and brought him up to the king of Bavel in Rivlah, where they passed judgment on him. ⁷ They slaughtered his sons before his eyes. Then they put out Tzidkiyahu's eyes, bound him in chains and carried him off to Bavel.

⁸ In the fifth month, on the seventh day of the month, which was also the nineteenth year of King N'vukhadnetzar, king of Bavel, N'vuzar'adan, the commander of the guard and an officer of the king of Bavel, entered Yerushalayim. ⁹ He burned down the house of ADONAI, the royal palace and all the houses in Yerushalayim — every notable person's house he burned to the ground. ¹⁰ The whole army of the Kasdim, who were with the commander of the guard, broke down the walls of Yerushalayim on every side. ¹¹ N'vuzar'adan the commander of the guard then deported the remaining population of the city, the deserters who had defected to the king of Bavel and the rest of the common people. ¹² But the commander of the guard left behind some of the poor people of the land to be vineyard-workers and farmers.

¹³ The Kasdim smashed the bronze columns in the house of ADONAI, also the trolleys and bronze Sea that were in the house of ADONAI, and carried their bronze to Bavel. ¹⁴ They also took away the pots, shovels, snuffers, pans, and all the bronze articles that had been used for worship. ¹⁵ The commander of the guard took the censers, the sprinkling bowls, everything made of gold and everything made of silver. ¹⁶ The bronze in the two columns, the one Sea and the bases, all of which Shlomo

had made for the house of ADONAI, was more than could be weighed. ¹⁷ The height of one column was thirty-one-and-a-half feet; on it was a capital of bronze five-and-a-quarter feet high, with netting and pomegranates all around the capital, all of bronze; the second column was similar, also with netting.

¹⁸ The commander of the guard took [prisoner] S'rayah the chief *cohen*, Z'kharyah the second-ranking *cohen* and three doorkeepers. ¹⁹ From the city he took an official in charge of the soldiers, five close associates of the king who had been found in the city, the army commander's secretary in charge of military conscription, and sixty of the common people found in the city. ²⁰ N'vuzar'adan the commander of the guard took them and brought them to the king of Bavel in Rivlah. ²¹ There in Rivlah, in the land of Hamat, the king of Bavel had them put to death. Thus Y'hudah was carried away captive out of his land.

²² N'vukhadnetzar king of Babylon appointed G'dalyahu the son of Achikam, the son of Shafan, governor over the people remaining behind in the land of Y'hudah after he left. ²³ When all the army officers and their men heard that the king of Bavel had made G'dalyahu governor, they came to G'dalyahu in Mitzpah — Yishma'el the son of N'tanyah, Yochanan the son of Kareach, S'rayah the son of Tanchumet the N'tofati and Ya'azanyahu the son of the Ma'akhati — they and their men. ²⁴ Taking an oath, G'dalyahu said to them, "Don't be afraid of the servants of the Kasdim. Just live in the land and serve the king of Bavel, and things will go well for you." ²⁵ But in the seventh month Yishma'el the son of N'tanyah, the son of Elishama, of royal blood, came with ten men and assassinated G'dalyah and the Judeans and Kasdim who were with him in Mitzpah. ²⁶ In the wake of this, all kinds of people, great and small, as well as the army officers, set out and went to Egypt; because they were afraid of the Kasdim.

²⁷ In the thirty-seventh year of the captivity of Y'hoyakhin king of Y'hudah, in the twelfth month, on the twenty-seventh day of the month, Eveel-M'rodakh began his reign as king of Bavel; and in his first year he commuted the sentence of Y'hoyakhin king of Y'hudah and released him from prison. ²⁸ He treated him with kindness and gave him a throne higher than those of the other kings there with him in Bavel. ²⁹ So Y'hoyakhin no longer had to wear prison clothes; moreover, he was provided with food as long as he lived; ³⁰ and he was granted a daily allowance by the king to spend on his other needs for as long as he lived.

Yesha'yahu
ISAIAH

1 ¹ This is the vision of Yesha'yahu the son of Amotz, which he saw concerning Y'hudah and Yerushalayim during the days of 'Uziyahu, Yotam, Achaz and Y'chizkiyahu, kings of Y'hudah:

²   "Hear, heaven! Listen, earth!
    For ADONAI is speaking.

    "I raised and brought up children,
    but they rebelled against me.
³   An ox knows its owner
    and a donkey its master's stall,
    but Isra'el does not know,
    my people do not reflect.

⁴   "Oh, sinful nation,
    a people weighed down by iniquity,
    descendants of evildoers,
    immoral children!
    They have abandoned ADONAI,
    spurned the Holy One of Isra'el,
    turned their backs on him!

⁵   "Where should I strike you next,
    as you persist in rebelling?
    The whole head is sick,
    the whole heart diseased.
⁶   From the sole of the foot to the head
    there is nothing healthy,
    only wounds, bruises and festering sores
    that haven't been dressed or bandaged
    or softened up with oil.

⁷   "Your land is desolate,
    your cities are burned to the ground;
    foreigners devour your land in your presence;
    it's as desolate as if overwhelmed by floods.

8   The daughter of Tziyon is left
     like a shack in a vineyard,
     like a shed in a cucumber field,
     like a city under siege."

9   If ADONAI-Tzva'ot had not left us
     a tiny, tiny remnant,
     we would have become like S'dom,
     we would have resembled 'Amora.

10   Hear what ADONAI says,
     you rulers of S'dom!
     Listen to God's Torah,
     you people of 'Amora!

11   "Why are all those sacrifices
     offered to me?" asks ADONAI.
     "I'm fed up with burnt offerings of rams
     and the fat of fattened animals!
     I get no pleasure from the blood
     of bulls, lambs and goats!

12   Yes, you come to appear in my presence;
     but who asked you to do this,
     to trample through my courtyards?

13   Stop bringing worthless grain offerings!
     They are like disgusting incense to me!
     Rosh-Hodesh, Shabbat, calling convocations —
     I can't stand evil together with your assemblies!

14   Everything in me hates your Rosh-Hodesh
     and your festivals;
     they are a burden to me —
     I'm tired of putting up with them!

15   "When you spread out your hands,
     I will hide my eyes from you;
     no matter how much you pray,
     I won't be listening;
     because your hands are covered with blood.

16   "Wash yourselves clean!
     Get your evil deeds out of my sight!
     Stop doing evil, [17] learn to do good!
     Seek justice, relieve the oppressed,
     defend orphans, plead for the widow.

18   "Come now," says ADONAI,
     "let's talk this over together.
     Even if your sins are like scarlet,

436

they will be white as snow;
even if they are red as crimson,
they will be like wool.

19 If you are willing and obedient,
you will eat the good of the land;

20 but if you refuse and rebel,
you will be eaten by the sword";
for the mouth of ADONAI has spoken.

21 How the faithful city has become a whore!
Once she was filled with justice,
righteousness lodged in her;
but now murderers!

22 Your silver is no longer pure,
your wine is watered down.

23 Your leaders are rebels, friends of thieves.
They all love bribes and run after gifts.
They give no justice to orphans,
the widow's complaint doesn't catch their attention.

24 "Therefore," says the Lord, ADONAI-Tzva'ot,
the Mighty One of Isra'el,
"I will free myself of my adversaries,
I will take vengeance on my enemies.

25 But I will also turn my hand against you!
I will cleanse your impurities as with lye
and remove all your alloyed base metal.

26 I will restore your judges as at first
and your advisers as at the beginning.
After that, you will be called
the City of Righteousness, Faithful City.

27 Tziyon will be redeemed by justice;
and those in her who repent, by righteousness.

28 "Rebels and sinners together will be broken
and those who abandon ADONAI will be consumed.

29 You will be ashamed of the sacred oaks you desired,
you will blush at the gardens you chose;

30 for you will be like an oak whose leaf fades,
like a garden without any water.

31 The strong will be like tinder
and [the idol's] maker like a spark;
both will burn together,
and no one will put them out."

2 ¹ This is the word that Yesha'yahu the son of Amotz saw concerning Y'hudah and Yerushalayim:

2 In the *acharit-hayamim*
the mountain of ADONAI's house
will be established as the most important mountain.
It will be regarded more highly than the other hills,
and all the *Goyim* will stream there.

3 Many peoples will go and say,
"Come, let's go up to the mountain of ADONAI,
to the house of the God of Ya'akov!
He will teach us about his ways,
and we will walk in his paths."
For out of Tziyon will go forth *Torah*,
the word of ADONAI from Yerushalayim.

4 He will judge between the nations
and arbitrate for many peoples.
Then they will hammer their swords into plow-blades
and their spears into pruning-knives;
nations will not raise swords at each other,
and they will no longer learn war.

5 Descendants of Ya'akov, come!
Let's live in the light of ADONAI!

6 For you have abandoned your people
the house of Ya'akov.
Now they are filled from the east,
full of sorcerers, like the P'lishtim;
even the children of foreigners
are enough for them!

7 Their land is full of silver and gold;
They have no end of treasures.
Their land is full of horses;
They have no end of chariots.

8 Their land is full of idols;
everyone worships the work of his hands,
what his own fingers have made.

9 A person bows down, a man lowers himself —
don't forgive them!

10 Come into the rock, hide in the dust
to escape the terror of ADONAI
and the glory of his majesty.

11 The proud looks of man will be humiliated;
the arrogance of men will be bowed down;
and when that day comes,
ADONAI alone will be exalted.

12 Yes, ADONAI-*Tzva'ot* has a day in store
for all who are proud and lofty,

13 for all who are lifted high to be humiliated;
for all cedars of the L'vanon that are high and lifted up,
for all the oaks of the Bashan;
14 for all the high mountains,
for all the hills that are lifted up;
15 for every high tower,
for every fortified wall;
16 for every "Tarshish" ship,
for every luxurious vessel.
17 The pride of man will be bowed down,
the arrogance of men will be humiliated,
and when that day comes,
ADONAI alone will be exalted.
18 The idols will be completely abolished.
19 People will enter cracks in the rocks
and holes in the ground
to escape the terror of ADONAI
and his glorious majesty,
when he sets out to convulse the earth.

20 On that day a man will take hold
of his idols of silver and idols of gold,
which they made for themselves to worship,
and fling them away to the moles and bats!
21 Then they will enter the cracks in the rocks
and the crevices in the cliffs
to escape the terror of ADONAI
and his glorious majesty,
when he sets out to convulse the earth.

22 Stop relying on man,
in whose nostrils is a mere breath —
after all, he doesn't count for much,
does he?

3¹ For see! The Lord, ADONAI-*Tzva'ot*,
will remove from Yerushalayim and Y'hudah
every kind of support —
all reserves of food and water;
2 heroes and warriors, judges and prophets,
diviners and leaders, ³ captains of fifty,
men of rank and advisers,
skillful magicians and expert enchanters.
4 I will put children in authority;
capriciousness will govern them.
5 People will oppress each other —
everyone his friend, everyone his neighbor.

The young will be insolent toward their elders,
the insignificant arrogant toward the respected.
6 A man will take hold of his brother
in his father's house and say,
"You have a coat, so rule us!
Take charge of this ruin!"
7 But on that day, he will protest,
"I don't have a remedy,
I lack food and clothing for my own house;
don't put me in charge of people!"

8 For Yerushalayim is ruined,
and Y'hudah has fallen;
because their words and deeds defy ADONAI,
in open provocation of his glory.
9 Their very look witnesses against them!
They parade their sin, like S'dom;
they don't even try to hide it —
all the worse for them! —
they bring evil on themselves.
10 Say that it will go well with the righteous,
that they will enjoy the fruit of their actions;
11 but woe to the wicked, it will go badly with him;
for what he has done will be done to him.
12 My people — children oppress them,
and women are ruling over them.
My people! Your guides lead you astray
and obliterate the paths you should follow.
13 ADONAI rises to accuse,
he stands to judge the peoples.
14 ADONAI presents the indictment
against the leaders and officers of his people:
"It is you who devour the vineyard;
in your houses is plunder taken from the poor.
15 What do you mean by crushing my people
and grinding down the faces of the poor?"
says Adonai ELOHIM-Tzva'ot.

16 Moreover ADONAI says:
"Because Tziyon's women are so proud,
walking with their heads in the air
and throwing seductive glances,
moving with mincing steps
and jingling their anklets —
17 Adonai will strike the crown of the heads
of Tziyon's women with sores,
and ADONAI will expose their private parts."

^{18} On that day *Adonai* will take away their finery — their anklets, medallions and crescents, ^{19} their pendants, bracelets and veils; ^{20} their headbands, armlets, sashes, perfume bottles, amulets, ^{21} rings and nose-jewels; ^{22} their fine dresses, wraps, shawls, handbags, ^{23} gauze scarves, linen underclothes, turbans and capes. ^{24} Then, there will be

> instead of perfume, a stench;
> instead of a belt, a rope;
> instead of well-set hair, a shaved scalp;
> instead of a rich robe, a sackcloth skirt;
> and a slave-brand instead of beauty.

^{25} Your men will fall by the sword
> and your warriors in battle.

^{26} Her gates will lament and mourn;
> ravaged, she will sit on the ground.

4 ^{1} On that day, seven women will grab hold of one man and say,

> "We will supply our own food
> and wear our own clothes.
> Just let us bear your name;
> take away our disgrace."

^{2} On that day, *Adonai*'s plant will be beautiful and glorious; and the fruit of the land will be the pride and splendor of Isra'el's survivors. ^{3} Those left in Tziyon and remaining in Yerushalayim will be called holy, and everyone in Yerushalayim written down for life.

^{4} When *Adonai* washes away the filth of the women of Tziyon and cleanses Yerushalayim from the blood shed in it with a blast of searing judgment, ^{5} *Adonai* will create over the whole site of Mount Tziyon and over those who assemble there a smoking cloud by day and a shining, flaming fire by night; for the Glory will be over everything like a *hupah*. ^{6} A *sukkah* will give shade by day from the heat; it will also provide refuge and cover from storm and rain.

5 ^{1} I want to sing a song for someone I love,
> a song about my loved one and his vineyard.
> My loved one had a vineyard
> on a very fertile hill.

^{2} He dug up its stones and cleared them away,
> planted it with the choicest vines,
> built a watchtower in the middle of it,
> and carved out in its rock a winepress.
> He expected it to produce good grapes,
> but it produced only sour, wild grapes.

^{3} "Now, citizens of Yerushalayim and people of Y'hudah,
> judge between me and my vineyard.

4 What more could I have done for my vineyard
that I haven't already done in it?
So why, when I expected good grapes,
did it produce sour, wild grapes?

5 "Now come, I will tell you
what I will do to my vineyard:
I will remove its hedge,
and [its grapes] will be eaten up;
I will break through its fence,
and [its vines] will be trampled down.
6 I will let it go to waste:
it will be neither pruned nor hoed,
but overgrown with briars and thorns.
I will also order the clouds
not to let rain fall on it."

7 Now the vineyard of *ADONAI-Tzva'ot*
is the house of Isra'el,
and the men of Y'hudah
are the plant he delighted in.
So he expected justice,
but look — bloodshed! —
and righteousness, but listen —
cries of distress!

8 Woe to those who add house to house
and join field to field,
until there's no room for anyone else,
and you live in splendor alone on your land.
9 *ADONAI-Tzva'ot* said in my ears,
"Many houses will be brought to ruin,
large, magnificent ones left empty;
10 for a ten-acre vineyard will produce
only five gallons of wine,
and seed from five bushels of grain
will yield but half a bushel."

11 Woe to those who get up early
to pursue intoxicating liquor;
who stay up late at night,
until wine inflames them.
12 They have lutes and lyres, drums and flutes,
and wine at their parties;
but they pay no attention to how *ADONAI* works
and never look at what his hands have made.
13 For such lack of knowledge

442

my people go into exile;
this is also why their respected men starve
and their masses are parched from thirst.

14 Therefore Sh'ol has enlarged itself
and opened its limitless jaws —
and down go their nobles and masses,
along with their noise and revels.

15 The masses are lowered, the nobles are humbled —
proud looks will be brought down.

16 But *Adonai-Tzva'ot* is exalted through justice,
God the Holy One is consecrated through righteousness.

17 Then lambs will be able to feed
as if they were in their own pasture,
and those wandering through will eat
from the ruined fields of the overfed.

18 Woe to those who begin by pulling
at transgression with a thread,
but end by dragging sin along
as if with a cart rope.

19 They say, "We want God to speed up his work,
to hurry it along, so we can see it!
We want the Holy One of Isra'el's plan
to come true right now, so we can be sure of it!"

20 Woe to those who call evil good
and good evil,
who change darkness into light
and light into darkness,
who change bitter into sweet
and sweet into bitter!

21 Woe to those seeing themselves as wise,
esteeming themselves as clever.

22 Woe to those who are heroes at drinking wine,
men whose power goes to mixing strong drinks,

23 who acquit the guilty for bribes
but deny justice to the righteous!

24 Therefore, as fire licks up the stubble,
and the chaff is consumed in the flame;
so their root will rot,
and their flowers scatter like dust;
because they have rejected the *Torah*
of *Adonai-Tzva'ot*,
they have despised the word
of the Holy One of Isra'el.

25   This is why ADONAI's anger blazed up against his people,
why he stretched out his hand against them and struck them
[so hard that] the hills shook,
and corpses lay like trash in the streets.

Even after all this, his anger remains,
his upraised hand still threatens.

26   He will give a signal to faraway nations,
he will whistle for them to come
from the ends of the earth;
and here they come, so fast! —

27   none of them tired or stumbling,
none of them sleeping or drowsy,
none with a loose belt,
none with a broken sandal-strap.

28   Their arrows are sharp,
all their bows are strung,
their horses' hoofs are like flint,
and their [chariot] wheels like a whirlwind.

29   They will roar like lions —
yes, roaring like young lions,
they growl and seize the prey
and carry it off, with no one to rescue.

30   On that day they will growl at them,
like the sea when it growls —
and when one looks toward land,
one sees darkness closing in;
the light is dissipated
in the obscuring overcast.

6 ¹ In the year of King 'Uziyahu's death I saw *Adonai* sitting on a high, lofty throne! The hem of his robe filled the temple. ² *S'rafim* stood over him, each with six wings — two for covering his face, two for covering his feet and two for flying. ³ They were crying out to each other,

"More holy than the holiest holiness
is ADONAI-*Tzva'ot*!
The whole earth is filled
with his glory!"

⁴ The doorposts shook at the sound of their shouting, and the house was filled with smoke. ⁵ Then I said,

"Woe to me! I [too] am doomed! —
because I, a man with unclean lips,
living among a people with unclean lips,

have seen with my own eyes
the King, ADONAI-Tzva'ot!"

⁶ One of the s'rafim flew to me with a glowing coal in his hand, which he had taken
with tongs from the altar. ⁷ He touched my mouth with it and said,

"Here! This has touched your lips.
Your iniquity is gone,
your sin is atoned for."

⁸ Then I heard the voice of Adonai saying,

"Whom should I send?
Who will go for us?"

I answered, "I'm here, send me!" ⁹ He said, "Go and tell this people:

'Yes, you hear, but you don't understand.
You certainly see, but you don't get the point!'

¹⁰ "Make the heart of this people [sluggish with] fat,
stop up their ears, and shut their eyes.
Otherwise, seeing with their eyes,
and hearing with their ears,
then understanding with their hearts,
they might repent and be healed!"

¹¹ I asked, "Adonai, how long?" and he answered,

"Until cities become uninhabited ruins,
houses without human presence,
the land utterly wasted;
¹² until ADONAI drives the people far away,
and the land is one vast desolation.
¹³ If even a tenth [of the people] remain,
it will again be devoured.

"But like a pistachio tree or an oak,
whose trunk remains alive
after its leaves fall off,
the holy seed will be its trunk."

7 ¹ During the days of Achaz the son of Yotam, the son of 'Uziyahu, king of Y'hudah,
Retzin the king of Aram and Pekach the son of Remalyah, king of Isra'el, advanced
on Yerushalayim to attack it but were unable to conquer it. ² It was told to the house
of David that Aram and Efrayim had become allies. Achaz's heart began to tremble,
as did the hearts of his people, like forest trees shaken by the wind.

³ Then ADONAI said to Yesha'yahu, "Go out now to meet Achaz, you and your son Sh'ar Yashuv, at the end of the aqueduct from the Upper Pool, on the road to the Launderers' Field; ⁴ and say to him, 'Take care to stay calm and unafraid; don't be demoralized by these two smoldering stumps of firewood, by the blazing anger of Retzin and Aram or the son of Remalyah; ⁵ or because Aram, Efrayim and the son of Remalyah have been plotting against you, thinking, ⁶ "We will invade Y'hudah, tear it apart, divide it among ourselves and appoint the son of Tav'el as king there."

7 "'This is what Adonai ELOHIM says:
"It won't occur, it won't happen.
8 For the head of Aram is Dammesek,
and the head of Dammesek Retzin.
In sixty-five years Efrayim will be broken
and will cease to be a people.
9 The head of Efrayim is Shomron,
and the head of Shomron is the son of Remalyah.
Without firm faith,
you will not be firmly established."'"

¹⁰ ADONAI spoke again to Achaz; he said, ¹¹ "Ask ADONAI your God to give you a sign. Ask it anywhere, from the depths of Sh'ol to the heights above." ¹² But Achaz answered, "I won't ask, I won't test ADONAI."

¹³ Then [the prophet] said,

"Listen here, house of David!
Is trying people's patience
such a small thing for you
that you must try the patience
of my God as well?
14 Therefore Adonai himself
will give you people a sign:
the young woman* will become pregnant,
bear a son and name him 'Immanu El [God is with us].
15 By the time he knows enough
to refuse evil and choose good,
he will [have to] eat
curdled milk and [wild] honey.
16 Yes, before the child knows enough
to refuse evil and choose good,
the land whose two kings you dread
will be left abandoned.
17 ADONAI will bring the king of Ashur
on you, your people and your father's house.
These will be days worse than any you've known
since Efrayim broke loose from Y'hudah."

*Or: "the virgin." See Introduction, Section XIV, footnote 69.

18 Yes, when that day comes,
    ADONAI will whistle for the fly
    in the farthest streams of the Nile in Egypt
    and for the bee in the land of Ashur.
19 They will come and settle, all of them,
    in steep *vadis* and holes in the rocks
    and on all thorn bushes and brambles.

20 When that day comes, *Adonai* will shave—
    with a razor hired beyond the [Euphrates] River,
    that is, with the king of Ashur—
    the head and the hair between the legs,
    and get rid of the beard as well.

21 When that day comes, a man will raise
    a young cow and two sheep.
22 Will they produce in abundance?
    No, he will [have to] eat curdled milk.
    Indeed, everyone left in the land
    will eat curdled milk and [wild] honey.

23 When that day comes,
    wherever there once were a thousand grapevines,
    worth a thousand pieces of silver,
    there will be only briars and thorns.
24 One will go there [to hunt] with bow and arrow,
    because all the land will be briars and thorns.
25 You won't visit hills once worked with a hoe,
    for fear of the briars and thorns;
    it will be good only for pasturing cattle
    and being trampled down by sheep.

8 ¹ADONAI said to me, "Take a large tablet, and write on it in easily readable letters; '*Maher shalal, hash baz* [the spoil hurries, the prey speeds along].'" ² I had it witnessed for me by reliable witnesses—Uriyah the *cohen* and Z'kharyahu the son of Y'verekhyahu. ³ Then I had sexual relations with my wife; she became pregnant and gave birth to a son; and ADONAI said to me, "Name him Maher Shalal Hash Baz; ⁴ because before the child knows how to cry, '*Abba!*' and '*Eema!*', the riches of Dammesek and the spoil of Shomron will be carried off and given to the king of Ashur." ⁵ ADONAI went on speaking and said more to me:

6   "Since this people has rejected
    the gently flowing waters from Shilo'ach
    and takes joy in Retzin and the son of Remalyah;
7   now *Adonai* will bring upon them
    the mighty floodwaters of the [Euphrates] River—
    that is, the king of Ashur and his power.

447

It will rise above all its channels
and overflow all its banks.
8 It will sweep through Y'hudah,
flooding everything and passing on.
It will reach even up to the neck,
and its outspread wings
will fill the whole expanse of the land."

God is with us! [Hebrew: *'immanu El*]
9 You may make an uproar, peoples;
but you will be shattered.
Listen, all of you from distant lands:
arm yourselves, but you will be shattered;
yes, arm yourselves,
but you will be shattered;
10 devise a plan, but it will come to nothing;
say anything you like, but it won't happen;
because God is with us [Hebrew: *'immanu El*].

11 For this is what ADONAI said to me, speaking with a strong hand, warning me not to live the way this people does:

12 "Don't regard as alliance what this people calls alliance,
and don't fear what they fear or be awestruck by it;
13 but ADONAI-Tzva'ot — consecrate him!
Let him be the object of your fear and awe!
14 He is there to be a sanctuary.
But for both the houses of Isra'el
he will be a stone to stumble over,
a rock obstructing their way;
a trap and a snare
for the inhabitants of Yerushalayim.
15 Many of them will stumble and fall,
be broken and trapped and captured.

16 "Wrap up this document, and confine its teaching to those I have instructed."

17 I will wait for ADONAI,
who is hiding his face
from the house of Ya'akov;
yes, I will look for him.
18 Meanwhile, I and the children
whom ADONAI has given me
will become for Isra'el
signs and wonders
from ADONAI-Tzva'ot
living on Mount Tziyon.

19 So when they tell you to consult
those squeaking, squawking mediums and fortune-tellers;
[you are to answer],
"Shouldn't a people seek their God?
Must the living ask the dead
20 for teaching and instruction?"
For they will indeed give you
this unenlightened suggestion.

21 Distressed and hungry
they will pass through the land;
and because of their hunger they will grow angry
and curse by their king and by their God.
But whether they look up [to God]
22 or [down] at the earth,
they will see only trouble and darkness,
anguished gloom and pervasive darkness.

23(9:1) But there will be no more gloom
for those who are now in anguish.
In the past the land of Z'vulun
and the land of Naftali were regarded lightly;
but in the future he will honor the way to the lake,
beyond the Yarden, Galil-of-the-*Goyim*.

9 1(2) The people living in darkness
have seen a great light;
upon those living in the land that lies
in the shadow of death, light has dawned.

2(3) You have enlarged the nation
and increased their joy;
they rejoice in your presence
as if rejoicing at harvest time,
the way men rejoice
when dividing up the spoil.

3(4) For the yoke that weighed them down,
the bar across their shoulders,
and their driver's goad
you have broken as on the day of Midyan['s defeat].

4(5) For all the boots of soldiers marching
and every cloak rolled in blood
is destined for burning,
fuel for the fire.

5(6) For a child is born to us,
a son is given to us;
dominion will rest on his shoulders,
and he will be given the name

449

Pele-Yo'etz El Gibbor
Avi-'Ad Sar-Shalom
[Wonder of a Counselor, Mighty God,
Father of Eternity, Prince of Peace],

6(7)   in order to extend the dominion
and perpetuate the peace
of the throne and kingdom of David,
to secure it and sustain it
through justice and righteousness
henceforth and forever.
The zeal of *Adonai-Tzva'ot*
will accomplish this.

7(8)   *Adonai* sent a word to Ya'akov,
and it has fallen on Isra'el.

8(9)   All the people know it,
Efrayim and the inhabitants of Shomron.
But they say in pride,
in the arrogance of their hearts,

9(10)   "The bricks have fallen,
but we will rebuild with cut stone;
the sycamore-fig trees have been chopped down,
but we will replace them with cedars."

10(11)   So *Adonai* has raised up Retzin's foes against him
and spurred on his enemies —

11(12)   Aram from the east, P'lishtim from the west;
and they devour Isra'el with an open mouth.

Even after all this, his anger remains,
his upraised hand still threatens.

12(13)   Yet the people do not turn to the one striking them,
they don't seek *Adonai-Tzva'ot*.

13(14)   Therefore *Adonai* will cut off
Isra'el's head and tail,
[tall] palm frond and [lowly] reed in a single day.

14(15)   The old and the honored are the head,
while prophets teaching lies are the tail.

15(16)   For those leading this people lead them astray,
and those led by them are destroyed.

16(17)   Therefore *Adonai* takes no joy in their young men
and has no compassion on their orphans and widows;
for everyone is ungodly and does evil,
every mouth speaks foolishly.

Even after all this, his anger remains,
his upraised hand still threatens.

17(18)	For wickedness burns like fire,
	it devours briars and thorns;
	it sets the forest underbrush ablaze,
	with clouds of smoke whirling upward.
18(19)	The anger of ADONAI-Tzva'ot
	is burning up the land;
	the people, too, are fuel for the fire —
	no one spares even his brother.
19(20)	The one on the right grabs but stays hungry,
	the one on the left eats but is unfilled.
	Everyone devours his own arm's flesh —
20(21)	M'nasheh devours Efrayim;
	and Efrayim, M'nasheh;
	while together they oppose Y'hudah.

Even after all this, his anger remains,
his upraised hand still threatens.

10 1 Woe to those who enact unjust decrees
and draft oppressive legislation
2 to deprive the impoverished of justice
and rob my people's poor of their rights,
looting widows and preying on orphans!
3 What will you do on the day of punishment,
when calamity comes from afar?
To whom will you flee for help?
Where will you leave your wealth,
4 so as not to squat among the prisoners
or fall among the slain?

Even after all this, his anger remains,
his upraised hand still threatens.

5 "Oh Ashur, the rod expressing my anger!
The club in their hands is my fury!
6 I am sending him against a hypocritical nation,
ordering him to march against a people who enrage me,
to take the spoil and the plunder
and trample them down like mud in the street.
7 That is not what Ashur intends,
that is not what they think;
rather, they mean to destroy,
to cut down nation after nation.
8 For [their king] says,
'Aren't all my commanders kings?
9 Hasn't Kalno [suffered] like Kark'mish,
Hamat like Arpad, Shomron like Dammesek?

10   Just as my hand reached the kingdoms of non-gods,
       with more images than in Yerushalayim and Shomron;
11   so won't I do to Yerushalayim and her non-gods
       what I did to Shomron and her idols?'"

¹² Therefore when *Adonai* has done everything he intends to do to Mount Tziyon and Yerushalayim, "I will punish the king of Ashur for the boasting that comes from his proud heart and from reveling in his arrogant looks. ¹³ For he says,

    "'With my own strong arm I have done this,
    and with my wisdom, because I'm so clever!
    I erased the boundaries between peoples,
    I plundered their stores for the future;
    as a mighty man, I subjugated the inhabitants.
14   My hand found the riches of the peoples like a nest;
    and as one gathers abandoned eggs,
    I gathered the whole earth!
    Not one wing fluttered,
    not one beak opened or let out a chirp!'"

15   Should the axe glorify itself
    over the one who chops with it?
    Should the saw magnify itself
    over the one who moves it?
    It's as if a stick could wave
    the hand that raises it up,
    or as if a wooden staff could lift
    [a person, who is] not made of wood.
16   Therefore the Lord, *Adonai-Tzva'ot*,
    will send leanness to his well-fed ones;
    and in place of his glory,
    a fire will be kindled that will burn and burn.
17   The light of Isra'el will become a fire
    and his Holy One a flame,
    burning and devouring
    his thorns and briars in a single day.
18   The glory of his forest
    and of his fertile land
    he will consume body and soul,
    like an invalid wasting away.
19   So few forest trees will remain
    that a child could list them.

20   On that day the remnant of Isra'el,
    those of the house of Ya'akov who escaped,
    will no longer rely
    on the man who struck them down,

but will truly rely on *ADONAI*,
the Holy One of Isra'el.

21 A remnant will return,
the remnant of Ya'akov,
to the mighty God.

22 For, although your people, Isra'el,
are like the sand of the sea,
only a remnant of them will return.
Destruction is decreed, overflowing with justice.

23 *Adonai ELOHIM-Tzva'ot*
will bring about this decreed destruction
throughout all the land.

24 Therefore *Adonai ELOHIM-Tzva'ot* says:

"My people living in Tziyon,
don't be afraid of Ashur,
even when he strikes you with a stick
and raises his staff against you,
the way it was in Egypt.

25 For in but a little while, my fury will end;
and my anger will have destroyed them."

26 *ADONAI-Tzva'ot* will wield a whip against them, as he did when striking Midyan at the Rock of 'Orev; as his staff was over the sea, he will raise it, the way it was in Egypt.

27 On that day his burden will fall from your shoulders
and his yoke from your neck;
the yoke will be destroyed
by your prosperity.

28 He has come to 'Ayat
and passed through Migron.
He has stored his equipment at Mikhmas.

29 They have crossed the pass,
then lodged at Geva.
Ramah is shaking,
Giv'at-Sha'ul has fled.

30 Cry, shriek, Bat-Gallim!
Listen, Layish! Poor 'Anatot!

31 Madmenah is in flight,
The people of Gevim take cover.

32 This very day he will stop at Nov;
and he will shake his fist
at the mountain of the daughter of Tziyon,
at the hill of Yerushalayim.

33 See how *Adonai ELOHIM-Tzva'ot*

lops off the branches with terrible violence!
The ones standing highest are chopped down,
the lofty are laid low.

34 He will hack down the forest underbrush with an axe,
and the L'vanon in its splendor falls.

11 1 But a branch will emerge from the trunk of Yishai,
a shoot will grow from his roots.

2 The Spirit of *Adonai* will rest on him,
the Spirit of wisdom and understanding,
the Spirit of counsel and power,
the Spirit of knowledge and fearing *Adonai* —

3 he will be inspired by fearing *Adonai*.
He will not judge by what his eyes see
or decide by what his ears hear,

4 but he will judge the impoverished justly;
he will decide fairly for the humble of the land.
He will strike the land with a rod from his mouth
and slay the wicked with a breath from his lips.

5 Justice will be the belt around his waist,
faithfulness the sash around his hips.

6 The wolf will live with the lamb;
the leopard lie down with the kid;
calf, young lion and fattened lamb together,
with a little child to lead them.

7 Cow and bear will feed together,
their young will lie down together,
and the lion will eat straw like the ox.

8 An infant will play on a cobra's hole,
a toddler put his hand in a viper's nest.

9 They will not hurt or destroy
anywhere on my holy mountain,
for the earth will be as full
of the knowledge of *Adonai*
as water covering the sea.

10 On that day the root of Yishai,
which stands as a banner for the peoples —
the *Goyim* will seek him out,
and the place where he rests will be glorious.

11 On that day *Adonai* will raise his hand
again, a second time,
to reclaim the remnant of his people who remain
from Ashur, Egypt, Patros,
Ethiopia, 'Eilam, Shin'ar,
Hamat and the islands in the sea.

12 He will hoist a banner for the *Goyim*,
    assemble the dispersed of Isra'el,
    and gather the scattered of Y'hudah
    from the four corners of the earth.

13 Efrayim's jealousy will cease —
    those who harass Y'hudah will be cut off,
    Efrayim will stop envying Y'hudah,
    and Y'hudah will stop provoking Efrayim.

14 They will swoop down on the flank of the P'lishtim to the west.
    Together they will pillage the people to the east —
    they will put out their hand over Edom and Mo'av,
    and the people of 'Amon will obey them.

15 ADONAI will dry up the gulf
    of the Egyptian Sea.
    He will shake his hand over the [Euphrates] River
    to bring a scorching wind,
    dividing it into seven streams
    and enabling people to cross dryshod.

16 There will be a highway for the remnant of his people
    who are still left from Ashur,
    just as there was for Isra'el
    when he came out from the land of Egypt.

12 ¹ On that day you will say:

    "I thank you, ADONAI,
    because, although you were angry at me,
    your anger is now turned away;
    and you are comforting me.

2   "See! God is my salvation.
    I am confident and unafraid;
    for *Yah* ADONAI is my strength and my song,
    and he has become my salvation!"

3   Then you will joyfully draw water
    from the springs of salvation.

4   On that day you will say,
    "Give thanks to ADONAI! Call on his name!
    Make his deeds known among the peoples,
    declare how exalted is his name.

5   Sing to ADONAI, for he has triumphed —
    this is being made known throughout the earth.

6   Shout and sing for joy,
    you who live in Tziyon;
    for the Holy One of Isra'el
    is with you in his greatness!"

13 ^{1} This is a prophecy about Bavel, which Yesha'yahu the son of Amotz saw:

^{2} Hoist a banner on a high mountain,
shout to [the invaders];
beckon them to enter the Nobles' Gate.

^{3} "I have ordered my holy ones,
summoned my heroes, eager and bold,
to execute my anger."

^{4} Listen! A tumult on the mountains —
it sounds like a vast multitude!
Listen! The uproar of the kingdoms
of the nations gathering together!
ADONAI-Tzva'ot is mustering
an army for war.

^{5} They come from a distant land,
from beyond the horizon.
It's ADONAI, with the weapons of his rage,
to lay waste to all the earth.

^{6} Howl! for the Day of ADONAI is at hand,
destruction coming from Shaddai.

^{7} This is why every arm will hang limp
and everyone's courage melt away.

^{8} They will be gripped by panic,
seized with pain and agony,
writhing like a woman in labor,
looking aghast at each other, faces aflame.

^{9} Here comes the Day of ADONAI,
full of cruelty, rage and hot fury,
to desolate the earth
and destroy the sinners in it.

^{10} For the stars, the constellations in the sky,
will no longer give their light;
the sun will be dark when it rises;
and the moon will no longer shine.

^{11} "I will punish the world for its evil
and the wicked for their iniquity.
I will end the arrogance of the proud
and humble the insolence of tyrants.

^{12} I will make humans rarer than gold,
scarcer than Ofir's pure gold.

^{13} This is why I will make the heavens tremble,
and the earth will be shaken from its place
at the wrath of ADONAI-Tzva'ot
on the day of his fierce anger.

^{14} Then, like a hunted gazelle,
like sheep with no one to gather them,

everyone will head back to his own people;
everyone will flee to his own land.
15 Anyone found will be pierced through;
anyone caught will fall by the sword,
16 their babies dashed to pieces before their eyes,
their houses looted, their wives raped.
17 I will stir up against them the Medes,
who cannot be tempted by silver
or bought off with gold.
18 Their bows will tear young men to pieces,
they will have no pity on the fruit of the womb,
their eye will not spare children."

19 Thus Bavel, that jewel of kingdoms,
the pride and glory of the Kasdim,
will be like S'dom and 'Amora
when overthrown by God.
20 It will never again be inhabited,
never lived in through all generations.
Arabs will not pitch tents there
nor shepherds bring their flocks.
21 But wildcats will lie there,
their houses will be full of owls,
ostriches will live there,
and wild goats will dance there.
22 Jackals will howl in their palaces
and wild dogs in their temples of delight.
Its time is close at hand,
its days will not last long.

14 ¹ For *ADONAI* will have compassion on Ya'akov — he will once again choose Isra'el and resettle them in their own land, where foreigners will join them, attaching themselves to the house of Ya'akov. ² Peoples will take and escort them to their homeland, and the house of Isra'el will possess them in the land of *ADONAI* as male and female slaves. They will take their captors captive and rule over their oppressors. ³ Then, when *ADONAI* gives you rest from your suffering and trouble and from the hard service imposed on you, ⁴ you will take up this taunt-song against the king of Bavel:

"At last the oppressor is stilled,
his arrogance is ended!
5 *ADONAI* has broken the staff of the wicked,
the scepter of the rulers,
6 which furiously struck down peoples
with unceasing blows,
angrily beating down nations
with relentless persecution.

7   The whole earth is at rest and quiet.
    They break into song.

8   The cypresses rejoice over you,
    with the cedars of the L'vanon —
    'Now that you are laid low,
    no one comes to cut us down.'

9   "Sh'ol below is stirred up
    to meet you when you come.
    It awakens for you the ghosts of the dead
    who were leaders on earth;
    it makes all the kings of the nations
    arise from their thrones.

10 They all greet you with these words:
    'Now you are as weak as we are,
    you have become like us!

11 Your pride has been brought down to Sh'ol
    with the music of your lyres,
    under you a mattress of maggots,
    over you a blanket of worms.'

12 "How did you come to fall from the heavens,
    morning star, son of the dawn?
    How did you come to be cut to the ground,
    conqueror of nations?

13 You thought to yourself, 'I will scale the heavens,
    I will raise my throne above God's stars.
    I will sit on the Mount of Assembly
    far away in the north.

14 I will rise past the tops of the clouds,
    I will make myself like the Most High.'

15 "Instead you are brought down to Sh'ol,
    to the uttermost depths of the pit.

16 Those who see you will stare at you,
    reflecting on what has become of you:
    'Is this the man who shook the earth,
    who made kingdoms tremble,

17 who made the world a desert,
    who destroyed its cities,
    who would not set his prisoners free?'

18 "All other kings of the nations, all of them,
    lie in glory, each in his tomb.

19 But you are discarded, unburied,
    like a loathed branch,
    clothed like the slain who were pierced by the sword,

then fall to the stones inside a pit,
like a corpse to be trampled underfoot.

20 You will not be joined with those kings in the grave,
because you destroyed your own land,
you have brought death to your own people.
The descendants of evildoers will be utterly forgotten.

21 Get ready to slaughter his sons
for the iniquity of their fathers;
so they won't arise, take over the earth
and cover the world with their cities."

22 "I will arise against them,"
says ADONAI-Tzva'ot.
"I will cut off from Bavel name and remnant,
offshoot and offspring," says ADONAI.

23 "I will make it a haunt for hedgehogs,
it will become a swampy waste,
I will sweep it with the broom of destruction,"
says ADONAI-Tzva'ot.

24 ADONAI-Tzva'ot has sworn,
"Just as I thought it, it will occur;
just as I planned it, so it will be.

25 I will break Ashur in my land,
I will trample him down on my mountains.
Then his yoke will fall off them,
his burden be removed from their shoulders."

26 This is the program planned for all the earth,
this is the hand stretched out over all the nations.

27 ADONAI-Tzva'ot has made his decision.
Who is there that can stop him?
He has stretched out his hand.
Who can turn it back?

28 In the year that King Achaz died, this prophecy came:

29 Do not rejoice, P'leshet, any of you,
that the rod which struck you is broken;
for out of the snake's root will come a viper,
and his offspring will be a flying fiery serpent.

30 While the firstborn of the poor graze
and the needy lie down in safety,
I will kill off your root with famine
and slaughter the rest of you.

31 Howl, gate! Cry, city!
Melt away, P'leshet, all of you!

For a smoke is coming from the north,
with not a straggler in its ranks.

32 And what is one to answer
the messengers of the nation?
That ADONAI founded Tziyon,
and there the poor of his people will find refuge.

15 ¹ This is a prophecy about Mo'av:

The night 'Ar is sacked, Mo'av is ruined.
The night Kir is sacked, Mo'av is ruined.

2 He went up to the temple,
to Dibon and to the high places, to weep.
On N'vo and Meidva Mo'av is howling,
every head shaved bald, every beard cut off.

3 In the streets they wear sackcloth;
on their roofs and in their squares,
everyone howls and weeps profusely.

4 Heshbon and El'aleh cry out,
they are heard as far as Yachatz.
Mo'av's best troops cry aloud,
as their courage faints away.

5 My heart cries out for Mo'av!
Its fugitives flee to Tzo'ar,
a calf three years old.
They ascend the slope of Luchit,
weeping as they go;
on their way to Horonayim,
they utter heartrending cries.

6 The waters of Nimrim are desolate,
the grass is dried up, the new growth fails,
nothing green is left.

7 Therefore they carry away their wealth,
everything they have put aside,
across the *Vadi* of the Willows.

8 For the cry has circulated
throughout Mo'av's territory —
its howling has reached Eglayim,
its howling has reached Be'er-Elim.

9 For the waters of Dimon are full of blood,
yet I have worse in store for Dimon —
a lion for those who escape from Mo'av
and for those who remain in its land.

16 ¹ Send lambs for the ruler of the land
from the crags toward the desert
to the mountain of the daughter of Tziyon.

2   The daughters of Mo'av at the fords of the Arnon
are like fluttering birds pushed from the nest.
3   "Give [us] counsel! Decide [to help]!
Make your shadow [over us]
like night in the middle of noonday.
Hide [our] outcasts! Don't betray [our] fugitives!
4   Let our outcasts live with you!
Protect Mo'av from the attacks of robbers!"

For when the extorting ends, the spoiling ceases,
and those trampling on the land are destroyed,
5   a throne will be set up by grace,
and on it, in the tent of David,
will sit an honest judge,
seeking justice and pursuing righteousness.

6   We have heard about Mo'av's pride,
how very proud they are;
about their haughty arrogance,
their insolence and bravado.
7   Therefore Mo'av will wail for Mo'av —
they will all wail!
You will sigh, stricken by grief,
for the raisin-cakes of Kir-Hareset.
8   For the grainfields of Heshbon are withering,
also the vineyards of Sibmah,
whose red grapes overpowered rulers of nations —
once they reached as far as Ya'zer
and trailed out into the desert;
their spreading branches even crossed the sea.
9   Therefore I will weep for Sibmah's vine
as I weep for Ya'zer;
I will water you with my tears,
Heshbon and El'aleh;
because the shouts of battle are falling
on your summer fruits and harvest;
10   gladness and joy are removed
from the fruitful fields.
No revelry in the vineyards,
no happy shouting,
no one treading grapes in the wine presses —
I have silenced the vintage-cheers.
11   This is why my heart throbs
like a lyre for Mo'av,
and everything in me
for Kir-Heres.
12   Even when Mo'av is seen growing weary

of worshipping on the high places
and entering their sanctuaries to pray,
they will have accomplished nothing.

¹³ This is the word ADONAI spoke against Mo'av in the past. ¹⁴ But now ADONAI has said, "Within three years [and not a day more], as if a hired worker were keeping track of the time, the glory of Mo'av will be brought into contempt, despite its large population; and the surviving remnant will be few and feeble."

17 ¹ This is a prophecy about Dammesek:

"Dammesek will soon stop being a city;
it will become a heap of ruins.
²   The cities of 'Aro'er will be abandoned,
given over to flocks lying down undisturbed.
³   Efrayim will have no defenses,
Dammesek will cease to rule,
and Aram's survivors will share the fate
of Isra'el's finest sons,"

says ADONAI-Tzva'ot.

⁴   "When that day comes, Ya'akov's glory will wane,
and his full body grow thin,
⁵   as when the harvester collects the standing grain,
reaping the ears of grain with his arm;
yes, as when they glean the grain
in the Refa'im Valley.
⁶   Yet gleanings will be left,
as when beating an olive tree —
two or three olives at the very top,
four or five on its fruitful branches,"

says ADONAI, the God of Isra'el.

⁷   On that day, a person will heed his Maker
and turn his eyes toward the Holy One of Isra'el.
⁸   He will pay no heed to the altars
made with his own hands,
he will not turn toward what his fingers made,
the sacred poles and standing-stones for sun-worship.
⁹   When that day comes, his strong cities,
which others abandoned when Isra'el advanced,
will be like abandoned woods and forests;
they will be laid waste.
¹⁰   For you have forgotten the God who saved you,
failed to remember the Rock of your strength;

so you plant pagan-style gardens
and set out vine-cuttings for a foreign god.

11 Though you make them grow on the day you plant them,
and in the morning your seedlings flower;
the crop will vanish the day disease comes,
a day of incurable pain.

12 Oh, the terror-stricken uproar of many peoples,
roaring like the roar of the seas,
and the rushing about of nations,
rushing and surging like wild, wild waters!

13 Yes, the nations will roar like the mighty ocean,
but he will rebuke them, and far will they flee,
driven like chaff by a mountain wind,
like whirling dust in advance of the storm.

14 As evening falls, you can see terror;
before sunrise, they have ceased to be.
This is the lot of those who plunder us,
the fate of those who prey on us.

18 1 Woe to the land of whirring wings
beyond the rivers of Ethiopia;

2 they send ambassadors by sea,
across the water in papyrus-reed boats!
Go, swift messengers, to a nation tall and bronzed,
to a people feared far and near,
to a strong and conquering nation
whose land is divided by rivers!

3 All you inhabitants of the world,
you who live on the earth:
when a banner is hoisted on the mountains, look!
When the *shofar* is blown, listen!

4 For *Adonai* has said this to me:
"I will look on from my place and do nothing,
like heat shimmering in the sun,
like a cloud of dew in the heat of harvest."

5 For before the harvest, when the flowering is over,
and the bud becomes a ripening grape,
he will cut off the branches with pruning-knives,
lop off the twigs and take them away.

6 They will all be left to the vultures in the mountains
and to the wild animals in the fields;
the vultures will feed on them in summer,
and the wild animals of the fields in winter.

7 At that time tribute will be brought
to *Adonai-Tzva'ot*

from a nation tall and bronzed,
from a people feared far and near,
from a strong and conquering nation
whose land is divided by rivers,
to the place where the name of ADONAI-Tzva'ot
lives, Mount Tziyon.

19 ¹ This is a prophecy about Egypt:

Look! ADONAI is riding a swift cloud,
on his way to Egypt.
Before him Egypt's idols tremble,
Egypt's courage melts within them.

² "I will incite Egypt against Egypt,
brother will fight against brother,
friend against friend, city against city,
kingdom against kingdom.

³ The courage of Egypt will ebb away within it,
I will reduce its counsel to confusion.
They will consult idols and mediums,
ghosts and spirits.

⁴ I will hand over the Egyptians to a cruel master.
A harsh king will rule them,"

says the Lord, ADONAI-Tzva'ot.

⁵ The water will ebb from the sea,
the river will be drained dry.

⁶ The rivers will become foul,
the canals of Egypt's Nile will dwindle and dry up,
the reeds and rushes will wither.

⁷ The river-plants on the banks of the Nile
and everything sown near the Nile
will dry up, blow away and be no more.

⁸ Fishermen too will lament,
all who cast hooks in the Nile will mourn,
those who spread nets on the water lose heart.

⁹ The linen-workers will be in despair,
along with the weavers of white cotton;

¹⁰ the spinners will be crushed,
the hired workers dejected.

¹¹ The princes of Tzo'an are utter fools,
Pharaoh's wisest counselors give stupid advice.
How can you say to Pharaoh,
"I'm a sage, descended from kings of old."

¹²   Where are they, then, those sages of yours?
Let them tell you, so all can know
what ADONAI-Tzva'ot has planned against Egypt!
¹³   The princes of Tzo'an have been fooled,
the princes of Nof have been duped,
Egypt's clan chiefs have led her astray.
¹⁴   ADONAI has mixed up their minds
with a spirit that distorts judgment,
so they make Egypt stagger in whatever she does,
like a drunk staggering in his vomit.
¹⁵   Nobody in Egypt
will find work to do —
neither head nor tail,
neither [tall] palm frond nor [lowly] reed.

¹⁶ On that day Egypt will be like women trembling with fear, because ADONAI-Tzva'ot is shaking his fist at them. ¹⁷ Just mentioning the land of Y'hudah to the Egyptians will throw them into panic; they will be afraid because of what ADONAI-Tzva'ot has planned for them.

¹⁸ On that day there will be five cities in the land of Egypt that speak the language of Kena'an and swear loyalty to ADONAI-Tzva'ot; one of them will be called the City of Destruction.*

¹⁹ On that day there will be an altar to ADONAI in the middle of the land of Egypt, as well as a standing-stone for ADONAI at its border. ²⁰ It will be a sign and witness to ADONAI-Tzva'ot in the land of Egypt; so that when they cry out to ADONAI for help because of the oppressors, he will send them a savior to defend and rescue them.

²¹   ADONAI will make himself known to Egypt;
on that day, the Egyptians will know ADONAI.
They will worship him with sacrifices and offerings,
they will make vows to ADONAI and keep them.
²²   Yet ADONAI will strike Egypt, both striking and healing,
so they will return to ADONAI.
He will listen to their prayers,
and he will heal them.

²³   On that day there will be a highway
from Egypt to Ashur.
Ashur will come to Egypt and Egypt to Ashur,
and Egypt will worship with Ashur.
²⁴   On that day Isra'el will be a third partner
with Egypt and Ashur, a blessing here on earth;
²⁵   for ADONAI-Tzva'ot has blessed him:
"Blessed be Egypt my people,
Ashur the work of my hands
and Isra'el my heritage."

---

* Hebrew 'ir haheres, parodying 'ir hacheres, "City of the Sun," i.e., Heliopolis

20 ¹ In the year that Sargon the king of Ashur sent his commander-in-chief to attack Ashdod, he captured it. ² It was at that time that ADONAI, speaking through Yesha'yahu the son of Amotz, said, "Go and unwind the sackcloth from around your waist, and take your sandals off your feet." So he did it, going about unclothed and barefoot. ³ In time, ADONAI said,

> "Just as my servant Yesha'yahu
> has gone about unclothed and barefoot
> for three years as a sign and portent
> against Egypt and Ethiopia,
⁴
> so will the king of Ashur lead away
> the captives of Egypt and the exiles of Ethiopia,
> young and old, unclothed and barefoot,
> with their buttocks exposed, to the shame of Egypt.
⁵
> They will be dismayed and ashamed
> because of Ethiopia their hope and Egypt their pride.
⁶
> On that day, the people living
> along this coast will say,
> 'Look what happened to the people
> to whom we fled for help,
> hoping they would rescue us
> from the king of Ashur!
> How will we escape now?'"

21 ¹ A prophecy about the coastal desert:

> Like whirlwinds sweeping over the Negev,
> it comes from the desert, from a fearsome land.
²
> A dire vision has been shown to me:
> the betrayer betrays, and the spoiler spoils.
> 'Eilam, advance! Madai, lay siege!
> I will end all groaning.
³
> This is why my insides are racked with pain;
> I am seized by pangs, like a woman in labor;
> wrenched by what I hear,
> aghast at what I see.
⁴
> My mind reels, shuddering assails me.
> The twilight I longed for terrifies me.
⁵
> They set the table, light the lamps,
> eat and drink —
> "Get going, princes! Oil the shields!"
⁶
> For this is what *Adonai* said to me:
> "Go, post a watchman to report what he sees!
⁷
> If he sees the cavalry, horsemen in pairs,
> riders on donkeys, riders on camels,
> he must be on alert, on full alert!"
⁸
> He calls out like a lion: "My lord,

I stand on the watchtower all day long,
I stay at my post all night."

9 Then, as they appeared — the cavalry,
horsemen in pairs — he spoke these words:
"She has fallen! She has fallen — Bavel!
All the carved images of her gods
lie shattered on the ground."

10 My people, who have been threshed,
grain trodden down on my threshing-floor:
I am telling you what I have heard
from *ADONAI-Tzva'ot*, the God of Isra'el.

11 A prophecy about Dumah:

Someone is calling to me from Se'ir:
"Watchman, how much longer is it night?
Watchman, how much longer is it night?"

12 The watchman answers:
"Morning is coming, but also the night.
If you want to ask, ask! Come back again!"

13 A prophecy about Arabia:

You caravans of D'danim will camp
in the desert growth of Arabia.

14 Bring water to the thirsty, you who live in Teima,
greet the fugitives with food;

15 because they are fleeing the sword, the drawn sword,
the bent bow and the press of battle.

16 For this is what *Adonai* has told me: "Within a year [and not a day more], as if a hired worker were keeping track of the time, the glory of Kedar will come to an end. 17 Few of Kedar's valiant archers will be left. " *ADONAI* the God of Isra'el has spoken.

22 1 A prophecy about the Valley of Vision:

Tell me what is wrong with you,
that you have all gone up on the roofs.

2 You city full of noise, confusion
and boisterous excitement,
your slain did not fall to the sword,
nor did they die in battle.

3 All your leaders fled together
and were captured without the use of a bow;
all from you who were found were captured,
even though they had fled far away.

4 This is why I said, "Don't look at me,

leave me alone to weep bitterly,
don't try to comfort me
over the destruction of my people."
5 For it is a day of panic,
trampling and confusion
from *Adonai ELOHIM-Tzva'ot*
in the Valley of Vision.
With walls crashing down,
they cry for help to the mountains.
6 'Eilam picks up the quivers,
with cavalry and horsemen,
and Kir uncovers the shields.
7 In time, your choicest valleys
are overrun by chariots,
and the cavalry take their posts by the gate;
8 thus is Y'hudah's protection removed.

That day you looked for the armor
in the House of the Forest.
9 You saw how many breaches there were
in the City of David,
you collected water from the lower pool,
10 you surveyed the houses in Yerushalayim,
tearing some down to fortify the wall.
11 You also built a reservoir between the two walls
for the water from the Old Pool;
but you didn't look to Him who made these things;
you had no respect for Him who fashioned them long ago.

12 That day *Adonai ELOHIM-Tzva'ot*
called on you to weep and mourn,
to shave your heads and wear sackcloth;
13 but instead, one sees joy and celebrating,
killing of oxen, slaughtering of sheep,
eating of meat, drinking of wine —
"Let's eat and drink now,
because tomorrow we'll be dead!"

¹⁴ Then *ADONAI-Tzva'ot* revealed himself in my ears: "You will not atone for this iniquity until you die." This is what *Adonai ELOHIM-Tzva'ot* says.

¹⁵ Thus says *Adonai ELOHIM-Tzva'ot*: "Go and find that steward, Shevna, administrator of the palace, and ask him:

16 'What do you own here,
and who gave you the right
to cut yourself a tomb here?
Why do you get such an eminent tomb?

Why are you carving a resting-place
for yourself in the rock?'"

¹⁷ Look, strong man! *ADONAI* is about
to throw you out! He will grab you,
¹⁸ roll you up, and toss you around
like a ball in the open country.
There you will die, with your fancy chariots,
you disgrace to your master's palace!

¹⁹ "I will remove you from your office,
I will snatch you from your post.
²⁰ When that day comes, I will summon
my servant Elyakim the son of Hilkiyahu.
²¹ I will dress him in your robe,
gird him with your sash of office,
and invest him with your authority.
He will be a father to the people
living in Yerushalayim
and to the house of Y'hudah.
²² I will place the key of David's house
on his shoulder;
no one will shut what he opens;
no one will open what he shuts.

²³ "I will fasten him firmly in place like a peg, so that he will become a seat of honor for his clan. ²⁴ They will hang on him all the weight of his clan, descendants and offspring, as well as all the vessels of small capacity, from pitchers to cups. ²⁵ When that day comes, the peg fastened firmly in place will give way; it will be cut down and fall, and the weight that was on it will be cut off." For *ADONAI* has said it.

23¹ A prophecy about Tzor:

Howl, you "Tarshish" ships,
because the harbor is destroyed!
On returning from Kittim,
they discover they cannot enter it.
² Silence, you who live on the coast,
you who have been enriched
by the merchants of Tzidon crossing the sea.
³ By the great water the grain of Shichor,
the harvest of the Nile, brought you profits.
She was marketplace for the nations.
⁴ Shame, Tzidon, for the sea speaks;
the fortress of the sea says,
"I no longer have labor pains or bear children,
yet I have raised neither boys nor girls."

5   When the report reaches Egypt,
they will be in anguish at the fate of Tzor.

6   Cross over to Tarshish!
Howl, you who live on the coast!

7   Is this your boisterous city,
whose feet long ago in antiquity
carried her off to found distant colonies?

8   Who planned this against Tzor,
the city that once bestowed crowns,
whose merchants are princes,
whose traders are honored throughout the earth?

9   ADONAI-Tzva'ot planned it
to break the pride of all the arrogant,
to humiliate all those who are honored
everywhere on earth.

10   People of Tarshish!
Nothing restricts you now.
You can flow freely over your land
just like the Nile River.

11   He has stretched out his hand against the sea,
he has shaken kingdoms;
ADONAI has ordered that Kena'an's
fortresses be destroyed.

12   He has said, "Exult no more,
oppressed virgin daughter of Tzidon.
Arise, cross to Kittim;
even there you will find no rest."

13   Look at the land of the Kasdim!
This was the people who did not exist
when Ashur destined it for desert creatures.
They erected their siege towers
and tore down her palaces,
so that it has been made a ruin.

14   Howl, you "Tarshish" ships,
because your fortress is destroyed.

15 When that day comes, Tzor will be forgotten for seventy years, the lifetime of a king. After seventy years, its fate will be the same as that of the prostitute in this song:

16   "Take a lyre, walk the city,
you poor, forgotten whore!
Play sweetly, sing all your songs,
so that they will remember you!"

¹⁷ After seventy years are over ADONAI will remember Tzor. She will receive her wages again and prostitute herself to all the world's kingdoms on the face of the earth. ¹⁸ But her merchandise and profits will be dedicated to ADONAI; they will not be stored up or hoarded, because her profits will be for those living in ADONAI's presence, so that they can eat their fill and wear fine clothing.

24 ¹ Look! ADONAI is stripping
and destroying the land,
turning it upside down
and scattering its inhabitants —
² *cohen* and commoner, slave and master,
maid and mistress, buyer and seller,
lender and borrower, creditor and debtor.
³ The land will be completely stripped,
completely plundered,
for ADONAI has spoken this word.
⁴ The land fades and withers,
the world wilts and withers,
the exalted of the land languish.
⁵ The land lies defiled under its inhabitants;
because they have transgressed the teachings,
changed the law
and broken the everlasting covenant.
⁶ Therefore a curse is devouring the land,
and its inhabitants are punished for their guilt.
It is why those living there waste away,
and the people left are few.
⁷ The new wine fails, the vines wilt,
all the revelers sigh,
⁸ the happy sound of tambourines ceases,
the shouts of merrymakers are stilled,
the joy of the lyre ends.
⁹ They no longer sing as they drink their wine,
strong liquor tastes bitter to those drinking it.
¹⁰ The city of chaos is shattered,
every house closed up; no one can enter.
¹¹ In the streets they are crying over the wine;
all joy has faded, cheer has left the land.
¹² In the city, only desolation,
its gates are battered beyond repair.

¹³ Around the earth, among the peoples,
it will be as when beating an olive tree,
as when gleaning the grapes at the end of the harvest.
¹⁴ They lift their voices, singing for joy,
shouting from the west to honor ADONAI.
¹⁵ So in the east, honor ADONAI;

in the coastlands, honor the name of ADONAI,
the God of Isra'el.

16 From the farthest part of the earth
we have heard them sing,
"Glory to the Righteous One!"

But, I say, I'm wasting away,
I am wasting away!
Woe to me! Traitors betray!
Oh, how the traitors betray and betray!

17 Terror, pit and trap are upon you,
you who are living on earth.

18 He who flees at the sound of terror
will fall into the pit.
He who climbs up out of the pit
will be caught in the trap.
For the windows above have been opened,
and the earth's foundations shake.

19 The earth cracks and breaks open,
the earth crumbles to pieces,
the earth trembles and totters.

20 The earth staggers to and fro like a drunk,
sways back and forth like a watchman's shelter;
its transgression weighs heavy upon it;
it will fall and not rise again.

21 When that day comes, ADONAI will punish
the armies of the high heaven on high,
and the kings of the earth here on earth.

22 They will be assembled like prisoners in a dungeon
and shut up in prison to be punished many years.

23 Then the moon will be confused and the sun ashamed,
for ADONAI-Tzva'ot will rule on Mount Tziyon
and in Yerushalayim,
with his glory manifest to the rulers of his people.

25 1 ADONAI, you are my God.
I exalt you, I praise your name.
For you have accomplished marvels,
[fulfilled] ancient plans faithfully and truly.

2 For you have made a city a heap of stones,
turned a fortified city into rubble,
made the foreigners' fortress
a city that will never be rebuilt.

3 Therefore mighty peoples glorify you,
the city of ruthless nations fears you.

4 For you have been a refuge for the poor,

472

a refuge for the needy in distress,
shelter from the storm,
shade from the heat —
for the blast from the ruthless
was like a storm that could destroy a wall.

5   Like desert heat, you subdue
the foreigners' uproar;
like heat subdued by a cloud's shadow,
the song of the ruthless dies away.

6   On this mountain ADONAI-*Tzva'ot*
will make for all peoples
a feast of rich food and superb wines,
delicious, rich food and superb, elegant wines.

7   On this mountain he will destroy
the veil which covers the face of all peoples,
the veil enshrouding all the nations.

8   He will swallow up death forever.
Adonai ELOHIM will wipe away
the tears from every face,
and he will remove from all the earth
the disgrace his people suffer.
For ADONAI has spoken.

9   On that day they will say,
"See! This is our God!
We waited for him to save us.
This is ADONAI; we put our hope in him.
We are full of joy, so glad he saved us!"

10   For on this mountain
the hand of ADONAI will rest.

But Mo'av will be trampled down where they are,
like straw trampled into a pile of manure.

11   They will spread out their hands in Mo'av,
like a swimmer using his hands to tread water;
but their pride will be humbled and sunk,
no matter how clever the strokes of their hands.

12   Your high, fortified walls he will level,
strike to the ground, lay in the dust.

26 1   On that day this song will be sung
in the land of Y'hudah:
"We have a strong city!
He has built walls and ramparts for our safety.

2   Open the gates! Let the righteous nation enter,
a nation that keeps faith!

3   "A person whose desire rests on you
      you preserve in perfect peace,
      because he trusts in you.
4   Trust in *Adonai* forever,
      because in *Yah Adonai*
      is a Rock of Ages."

5   For he has humbled those in high places,
      levelling the lofty city,
      levelling it to the ground,
      laying it in the dust.
6   It is trampled underfoot by the feet of the poor,
      by the footsteps of the needy.

7   The way of the righteous is level;
      Righteous One, you smooth the path for the righteous.
8   Following the way of your judgments,
      we put our hope in you.
      The desire of all our soul
      is to remember you and your name.
9   My soul desires you at night,
      my spirit in me seeks you at dawn;
      for when your judgments are here on earth,
      the people in the world learn what righteousness is.
10   Even if pity is shown to the wicked,
      he still doesn't learn what righteousness is.
      In a land of uprightness he will still act wrongly
      and fail to see the majesty of *Adonai*.
11   *Adonai*, you raised your hand,
      but they still didn't see.
      Yet with shame they will see your zeal for the people.
      Yes, fire will destroy your enemies.
12   *Adonai*, you will grant us peace;
      because all we have done, you have done for us.
13   *Adonai* our God, other lords
      besides you have ruled us,
      but only you do we invoke
      by name.
14   The dead will not live again,
      the ghosts will not rise again;
      for you punished and destroyed them,
      wiped out all memory of them.
15   You enlarged the nation, *Adonai*,
      you enlarged the nation;
      and thus you glorified yourself;
      you extended all the frontiers of the country.
16   *Adonai*, when they were troubled,

they sought you.
When you chastened them,
they poured out a silent prayer.

17 As a pregnant woman about to give birth
cries out and writhes in her labor pains,
so we have been at your presence, ADONAI —
18 we have been pregnant and been in pain.
But we, as it were, have given birth to wind;
we have not brought salvation to the land,
and those inhabiting the world have not come to life.
19 Your dead will live, my corpse will rise;
awake and sing, you who dwell in the dust;
for your dew is like the morning dew,
and the earth will bring the ghosts to life.

20 Come, my people, enter your rooms,
and shut your doors behind you.
Hide yourselves for a little while
until the wrath is past.
21 For see! ADONAI emerges from his place
to punish those on earth for their sin.
Then the earth will reveal the blood shed on it
and no longer conceal its slain.

27 1 On that day ADONAI,
with his great, strong, relentless sword,
will punish Livyatan the fleeing serpent,
the twisting serpent Livyatan;
he will slay the sea monster.

2 On that day, a pleasant vineyard —
sing about it!

3 "I, ADONAI, guard it.
Moment by moment I water it.
So that no harm will come to it,
I guard it night and day.
4 I have no anger in me.
If it gives me briars and thorns,
then, as in war, I will trample it down
and burn it up at once;
5 unless it takes hold of my strength,
in order to make peace with me,
yes, to make peace with me."

6 The time is coming when Ya'akov will take root;
Isra'el will bud and flower,

and fill the whole world with a harvest.

7 [ADONAI] will not strike Isra'el,
as he did others who struck Isra'el;
he will not kill them,
as he did the others.

8 Your controversy with her is fully resolved
by sending her [into exile].
He removes her with a rough gust of wind
on a day when it's blowing from the east.

9 So the iniquity of Ya'akov is atoned for by this,
and removing his sin produces this result:
he chops up all the altar stones like chalk —
sacred poles and sun-pillars stand no more.

10 For the fortified city is alone,
abandoned and deserted, like the desert.
Calves graze and lie down there,
stripping its branches bare.

11 When its harvest dries up, it is broken off;
women come and set it on fire.
For this is a people without understanding.
Therefore he who made them will not pity them,
he who formed them will show them no mercy.

12 On that day ADONAI will beat out the grain
between the Euphrates River and the *Vadi* of Egypt;
and you will be gathered, one by one,
people of Isra'el!

13 On that day a great *shofar* will sound.
Those lost in the land of Ashur will come,
also those scattered through the land of Egypt;
and they will worship ADONAI
on the holy mountain in Yerushalayim.

28 1 Woe to the haughty crown of Efrayim's drunks,
to the fading flower of its proud splendor,
located at the head of the rich valley
belonging to people overcome by wine!

2 *Adonai* has someone strong and powerful.
He comes like a hailstorm, a destructive tempest,
like a flood of water, rushing, overwhelming;
with his hand he hurls them to the ground.

3 The haughty crown of Efrayim's drunks
is trampled underfoot;

4 and the fading flower of its proud splendor,
located at the head of the rich valley,
is like the first ripe fig of summer —

5 whoever sees it picks and eats it.
On that day, ADONAI-Tzva'ot
will be a glorious crown,
a brilliant diadem
for the remnant of his people.

6 He will also be a spirit of justice
for whoever sits as a judge,
and a source of strength for those
repelling enemy attacks at the gate.

7 But there are others reeling from wine,
staggering about because of strong liquor;
cohen and prophet reel from strong liquor,
they are confused by wine.
Led astray by strong liquor,
they err in their visions and stumble when judging.

8 All tables are covered with vomit and feces,
not a single place is clean.

9 Can no one be taught anything?
Can no one understand the message?
Must one teach barely weaned toddlers,
babies just taken from the breast,

10 so that [one has to use nursery rhymes]? —
Tzav la-tzav, tzav la-tzav,
kav la-kav, kav la-kav
z'eir sham, z'eir sham
[Precept by precept, precept by precept,
line by line, line by line,
a little here, a little there].

11 So with stammering lips, in a foreign accent,
[ADONAI] will speak to this people.

12 He once told this people, "It's time to rest,
the exhausted can rest, now you can relax" —
but they wouldn't listen.

13 So now the word of ADONAI for them comes
"precept by precept, precept by precept,
line by line, line by line,
a little here, a little there,"
so that when they walk, they stumble backward,
and are broken, trapped and captured!

14 So listen to the word of ADONAI, you scoffers,
composing taunts for this people in Yerushalayim:

15 Because you said, "We made a covenant with death,
we made a contract with Sh'ol.
When the raging flood passes through,
it will not touch us.

For we have made lies our refuge
and hid ourselves in falsehoods" —

[16] therefore here is what *Adonai ELOHIM* says:

"Look, I am laying in Tziyon
a tested stone, a costly cornerstone,
a firm foundation-stone;
he who trusts will not rush here and there.

[17] I will make justice the plumbline
and righteousness the plumb-bob;
hail will sweep away the refuge of lies,
water will overflow the hiding place,

[18] your covenant with death will be annulled,
and your contract with Sh'ol will not stand.
When the raging flood passes through,
you will be trampled down by it.

[19] As often as it passes through, it will take you,
for it will pass through every morning,
day after day, night after night;
understanding the message will be sheer terror."

[20] For, [as the saying goes,]
"The bed is too short for a person to stretch,
and the blanket too narrow [to protect him from cold]
even if he crams himself in."

[21] For *ADONAI* will arise, as at Mount P'ratzim,
and storm with rage, as in the Giv'on Valley;
so he can do his deed, his strange deed,
and perform his task, his alien task.

[22] Therefore, now, stop your scoffing,
or your bonds will be further tightened;
for I have heard from *Adonai ELOHIM-Tzva'ot*
that destruction is decreed for the whole land.

[23] Listen and hear my voice;
pay attention, and hear what I say:

[24] Does a farmer sowing keep plowing forever?
Does he never stop breaking up and harrowing his land?

[25] No — when he finishes levelling it,
he scatters his dill-seed, sows his cumin,
puts wheat in rows, barley where it belongs,
and plants buckwheat around the edges;

[26] because his God has taught him this,
has given him instruction.

[27] Dill must not be threshed with a sledge
or cartwheels driven over cumin;

rather, dill one beats with a stick
and cumin with a flail.

28 When crushing grain for bread,
one doesn't thresh it forever;
one drives the horse and cart wheels over it
but doesn't crush it to powder.

29 This too comes from *Adonai-Tzva'ot* —
his counsel is wonderful, his wisdom great.

29 ¹ Woe to Ari'el [fireplace on God's altar, lion of God] —
Ari'el, the city where David encamped!
Celebrate the feasts for a few more years,

² but then I will bring trouble to Ari'el.
There will be mourning and moaning,
as she becomes truly an *ari'el* for me.

³ I will encamp all around you, besiege you with towers
and mount siege-works against you.

⁴ Prostrate, you will speak from the ground;
your words will be stifled by the dust;
your voice will sound like a ghost in the ground,
your words like squeaks in the dust.

⁵ But your many foes will become like fine powder,
the horde of tyrants like blowing chaff,
and it will happen very suddenly.

⁶ You will be visited by *Adonai-Tzva'ot*
with thunder, earthquakes and loud noises,
whirlwinds, tempests, flaming firestorms.

⁷ Then, all the nations fighting Ari'el,
every one at war with her,
the ramparts around her, the people that trouble her
will fade like a dream, like a vision in the night.

⁸ It will be like a hungry man dreaming he's eating;
but when he wakes up, his stomach is empty;
or like a thirsty man dreaming he's drinking;
but when he wakes up, he is dry and exhausted —
it will be like this for the horde of all nations
fighting against Mount Tziyon.

⁹ If you make yourselves stupid, you will stay stupid!
If you blind yourselves, you will stay blind!
You are drunk, but not from wine;
you are staggering, but not from strong liquor.

¹⁰ For *Adonai* has poured over you a spirit of lethargy;
he has closed your eyes (that is, the prophets)
and covered your heads (that is, the seers).

11   For you this whole prophetic vision
        has become like the message in a sealed-up scroll.
        When one gives it to someone who can read and says,
        "Please read this," he answers, "I can't, because it's sealed."
12   If the scroll is given to someone who can't read
        with the request, "Please read this," he says, "I can't read."

13 Then *Adonai* said:

        "Because these people approach me with empty words,
        and the honor they bestow on me is mere lip-service;
        while in fact they have distanced their hearts from me,
        and their 'fear of me' is just a *mitzvah* of human origin —
14   therefore, I will have to keep shocking these people
        with astounding and amazing things,
        until the 'wisdom' of their 'wise ones' vanishes,
        and the 'discernment' of their 'discerning ones' is hidden away."

15   Woe to those who burrow down deep
        to hide their plans from A*donai*!
        They work in the dark and say to themselves,
        "Nobody sees us, nobody knows us."
16   How you turn things upside down! —
        Is the potter not better than the clay,
        Does something made say of its maker,
        "He didn't make me"?
        Does the product say of its producer,
        "He has no discernment"?

17   In but a little while the L'vanon
        will be turned into a fruitful field,
        and the fruitful field regarded as a forest.
18   On that day the deaf
        will hear the words of a book,
        and out of gloom and darkness
        the eyes of the blind will see.
19   The humble will again rejoice in A*donai*
        and the poor exult in the Holy One of Isra'el,
20   for the tyrant is now nothing, the scoffer is finished,
        and all alert to do evil are cut off —
21   those whose words make a man out to be a sinner,
        those who set traps for the arbitrator at the city gate,
        and those who groundlessly deny justice
        to the one in the right.

22 Therefore, here are the words of A*donai*, who redeemed Avraham, concerning the
house of Ya'akov:

"Ya‘akov will no longer be ashamed,
no longer will his face grow pale.

23 When his descendants see the work of my hands
among them, they will consecrate my name.
Yes, they will consecrate the Holy one of Ya‘akov
and stand in awe of the God of Isra’el.

24 Those whose spirits stray will come to understand,
and those who complain will learn their lesson.

30 1 "Woe to the rebellious children," says ADONAI.
"They make plans, but the plans are not mine;
they develop alliances, but not from my Spirit,
in order to pile sin upon sin.

2 They go down to Egypt but don't consult me,
seeking refuge in Pharaoh's protection,
seeking shelter in Egypt's shadow.

3 But Pharaoh's protection will bring you shame,
shelter in Egypt's shadow will lead to disgrace.

4 Though his princes are at Tzo‘an,
and his envoys have reached Hannes,

5 they all are disappointed
with a people that doesn't help them,
who give no assistance and no advantage,
only disappointment and disgrace."

6 A prophecy about the animals in the Negev:

In a land of trouble and anguish,
of lionesses and roaring lions,
of vipers and poisonous flying serpents,
they carry their riches on donkeys' backs
and their treasures on camels' humps
to a people who will not help them.

7 For Egypt's help is worthless, pointless;
so I call her "Arrogance Doing Nothing."

8 Now go, inscribe it on a tablet,
write it for them in a scroll,
so that on the final day it will be
a witness forever and ever.

9 For this is a rebellious people;
they are lying children,
children who refuse to hear
the *Torah* of ADONAI.

10 They say to the seers, "Do not see!"
to those who have visions, "Do not tell us
the visions you have as they really are;
but flatter us, fabricate illusions!

11   Get out of the way! Leave the path!
        Rid us of the Holy One of Isra'el!"

12 Therefore here is what the Holy One of Isra'el says:

        "Because you reject this word,
        trust in extortion and rely on deceit,
13   this sin will become for you
        a crack bulging out high on a wall,
        showing signs it is ready to fall;
        then suddenly, all at once, it breaks."

14   He will break it like a clay pot,
        ruthlessly shattering it into pieces
        so tiny not even a potsherd remains
        for taking fire from the fireplace
        or scooping water from the cistern.
15   For this is what *Adonai ELOHIM*,
        the Holy One of Isra'el, says:
        "Returning and resting is what will save you;
        calmness and confidence will make you strong —
        but you want none of this!
16   'No!' you say, 'We will flee on horseback!'
        Therefore you will surely flee.
        And, 'We will ride on swift ones!'
        So your pursuers will be swift.
17   A thousand will flee at the threat of one,
        you all will flee at the threat of five,
        until you are left isolated,
        like a flagstaff on a mountaintop,
        like a banner on a hill."

18   Yet *ADONAI* is just waiting to show you favor,
        he will have pity on you from on high;
        for *ADONAI* is a God of justice;
        happy are all who wait for him!
19   People in Tziyon, who live in Yerushalayim,
        you will weep no more.
        At the sound of your cry, he will show you his grace;
        on hearing it, he will answer you.
20   Though *Adonai* may give you but bread and water,
        and not very much of that;
        your teacher will no longer hide himself,
        but with your own eyes you will see your teacher.
21   With your ears you will hear a word from behind you:
        "This is the way; stay on it,
        whether you go to the right or the left."

22   You will treat as unclean your silver-covered idols
    and your cast metal images plated with gold;
    you will throw them away, like menstrual cloths;
    you will say to them, "Get out of here!"

23   Then he will give you rain for the seed
    you use to sow your land;
    and the food that comes from the ground
    will be rich and abundant.
    When that day comes, your cattle
    will graze in spacious pastures.

24   The oxen and donkeys that work the land
    will eat a tasty mixture,
    winnowed free of chaff,
    spread by pitchfork and shovel.

25   On every high mountain and lofty hill
    will be streams and flowing brooks,
    on a day of great slaughter,
    when the towers fall.

26   Moreover, the light of the moon will be
    as bright as the light of the sun;
    and the light of the sun will be seven times stronger,
    like the light of seven days [in one],
    on the day ADONAI binds up the wounds of his people
    and heals the bruise caused by the blow.

27   Here comes the name of ADONAI from afar,
    his anger burning, in thick rising smoke.
    His lips are full to the brim with fury,
    his tongue a consuming fire.

28   His breath is like a racing torrent
    that rises up to the neck,
    to sift the nations with the sieve of destruction,
    and put a bridle in the peoples' mouths to lead them astray.

29   Your song will be like one that is sung
    on a night when a holy feast is kept,
    and your hearts will be happy,
    as if walking to the sound of the flute,
    to the mountain of ADONAI,
    to the Rock of Isra'el.

30   ADONAI will make his glorious voice heard,
    and he will reveal his arm descending
    with furious anger in a flaming firestorm,
    with cloudbursts, tempests and hailstones.

31   For ADONAI's voice will terrify Ashur,
    as with his scepter he strikes them down.

32   Every sweep of the punishing rod

that *ADONAI* imposes on him
will be to tambourines and lyres,
as he brandishes his arm against them in battle.

33 For the Tofet fire pit has long been ready,
prepared for the king, made large and deep,
with plenty of wood and blazing with fire;
like a stream of sulfur, *ADONAI*'s breath sets it aflame.

31 1 Woe to those going down to Egypt
expecting help — relying on horses;
trusting in chariots, because they have many,
and in the strength of their cavalrymen —
but not looking to the Holy One of Isra'el,
not consulting *ADONAI*.

2 But he too is wise and can bring disaster,
and he does not take back his words;
he will rise against the house of evildoers
and against the help of those who do wrong.

3 Now the Egyptians are men and not God,
and their horses flesh and not spirit.
So when *ADONAI* stretches out his hand,
both he who helps will stumble,
and he who is helped will fall;
both will perish together.

4 For here is what *ADONAI* says to me:
"As a lion or lion cub growls at its prey
and isn't frightened away by the shouts
of hordes of shepherds called out against him —
their voices do not upset him —
so likewise *ADONAI-Tzva'ot* will descend
to fight on Mount Tziyon, on its hill.

5 Like hovering birds, *ADONAI-Tzva'ot*
will protect Yerushalayim.
In protecting it, he will rescue it;
in sparing it, he will save it.

6 People of Isra'el! Return to him
to whom you have been so deeply disloyal!

7 For on that day everyone will discard
his idols of silver and idols of gold,
which you made for yourselves
with your own sinful hands.

8 Then Ashur will fall by a sword not of mortals,
a sword, not of humans, will devour him;
he will flee before the sword,
and his young men will be put to forced labor.

9 His rock, out of terror, will pass away,
and his panicked officers will desert the standard."

So says *ADONAI*, whose fire is in Tziyon,
whose furnace is in Yerushalayim.

32 ¹ There is coming a king who will reign justly
and princes who will rule uprightly.

² A man will be like a refuge from the wind,
like protection from a storm,
like streams of water on arid ground,
like a rock cliff shading a weary land.

³ The eyes of those seeing will not be closed,
the ears of those hearing will pay close attention.

⁴ The minds of the impetuous will learn to weigh carefully,
the tongues of the stutterers will speak readily and clearly.

⁵ The mean person will no longer be called generous,
or the miserly said to be noble;

⁶ for the mean person will speak meanness,
his heart planning evil, so that he can act godlessly,
spreading error concerning *ADONAI*,
as he lets the hungry go on starving
and deprives the thirsty of drink.

⁷ The mean person's means are mean —
he devises wicked devices
to ruin the poor and needy with lies,
even when their cause is just.

⁸ But the generous person devises generous things,
and his generosity will keep him standing.

⁹ You women who are so complacent, listen to me!
Overconfident women, pay attention to my words!

¹⁰ In a year and a few days more,
you overconfident women will shudder,
because the vintage will fail,
the harvest will not come.

¹¹ Tremble, you complacent women!
Shudder, you overconfident women!
Strip bare, wear sackcloth to cover yourselves.

¹² Beat your breasts in mourning
for the pleasant fields and fruitful vines,

¹³ for the land of my people, producing thorns and briars,
for all the happy homes in the joyful city.

¹⁴ For the palace will be abandoned,
the crowded city deserted,
'Ofel and fortress wastelands forever,
a delight for wild donkeys and a pasture for flocks —

¹⁵ till the Spirit is poured out on us from above,
and the desert becomes a fertile field,

with the fertile field regarded as a forest.

16 Then justice will dwell in the desert,
and righteousness abide in the fertile field.

17 The effect of righteousness will be peace;
the result of righteousness, quiet trust forever.

18 My people will live in a peaceful place,
in secure neighborhoods and tranquil dwellings.

19 Just as the forest will surely come down,
the city will surely be laid low.

20 Happy are you who sow by all streams,
letting oxen and donkeys roam freely.

33 1 Woe, destroyer, yourself undestroyed!
Woe, betrayer, yourself unbetrayed!
When you stop destroying, you will be destroyed;
when you tire of betraying, they will betray you.

2 *ADONAI*, show us mercy;
we have waited for you.
Be their arm every morning,
and our salvation in time of trouble.

3 At the sound of the tumult, the peoples wander off;
when you exalt yourself, the nations are scattered.

4 Your spoil is gathered as if stripped by shearer-worms;
they run over it like a swarm of locusts.

5 *ADONAI* is exalted, for he dwells on high;
he has filled Tziyon with justice and right.

6 He will be the stability of your times,
a wealth of salvation, wisdom and knowledge,
and fear of *ADONAI*, which is his treasure.

7 Hear their brave men crying out for help!
The envoys of peace weep bitterly.

8 The highways are deserted, there are no travelers.
He has broken the covenant, despised the cities;
he has no regard for human life.

9 The land is mourning and wilting away.
The L'vanon is withering with shame.
The Sharon has become like the 'Aravah.
Bashan and Karmel have been shaken bare.

10 "Now I will arise," says *ADONAI*,
"Now I will exalt and lift myself up.

11 You conceive chaff and give birth to stubble,
your breath is a fire devouring you.

12 The peoples will be as if burned into lime,

like thorns cut off to burn in the fire.

13 You living far off, hear what I have done!
You who are near, acknowledge my strength!"

14 The sinners in Tziyon are frightened;
trembling has seized the ungodly.
"Who of us can live with the devouring fire?
Who of us can live with eternal burning?"

15 He whose life is right and whose speech is straight,
he who scorns getting rich by extortion,
he who shakes his hands free of bribes,
stops his ears against talk of bloodshed
and shuts his eyes against looking at evil.

16 Such a person will live on the heights,
his refuge a fortress among the cliffs,
his food and water in steady supply.

17 Your eyes will see the king in his beauty,
they will gaze on a land stretching into the distance.

18 Your mind will meditate on the terror:
"Where is the man who did the counting?
Where is the man who did the weighing?
Where is the man who numbered the towers?"

19 You will not see the intransigent people,
that people whose language is so obscure,
whose stuttering speech you cannot understand.

20 Look at Tziyon, the city of our festivals;
your eyes will see Yerushalayim a secure abode,
a tent that will not be removed,
whose pegs will never be pulled out
and whose guy-ropes will not be cut.

21 But there in his splendor ADONAI will be with us,
in a place of rivers and broad streams.
But no boat with oars will go there,
no majestic ship will pass by.

22 For ADONAI is our judge, ADONAI is our lawgiver,
ADONAI is our king. He will save us.

23 For your ropes are hanging loose,
not holding the mast, not spreading the sail.
Then the plunder shared out is so huge
that even the lame get part of the spoil.

24 No inhabitant will say, "I am ill";
the people living there will be forgiven their sin.

34 1 Come close, you nations, and listen!
Pay close attention, you peoples!

Let the earth hear, and everything in it;
the world, with all it produces.

2 For ADONAI is angry at every nation,
furious with all their armies;
he has completely destroyed them,
handed them over to slaughter.

3 Their slain will be thrown out,
the stench will rise from their corpses,
the mountains will flow with their blood.

4 The whole host of heaven will decompose,
the heavens themselves be rolled up like a scroll;
all their array will wither away
like a withering grape-leaf that falls from a vine
or a withered fig from a fig tree.

5 "For my sword has drunk its fill in heaven;
now it descends on Edom to judge them,
the people I have doomed to destruction."

6 There is a sword that belongs to ADONAI.
It is filled with blood, gorged with fat,
filled with the blood of lambs and goats,
gorged with the fat of the kidneys of rams.
For ADONAI has a sacrifice in Botzrah,
a great slaughter in the land of Edom.

7 The wild oxen will fall with them,
the young bulls with the strong, mature ones.
Their land will be drunk with blood
and their dust made greasy with fat.

8 For ADONAI has a day of vengeance,
a year of requital for fighting with Tziyon.

9 Its streams will be changed to tar,
its dust to sulfur, its land burning tar

10 that will not be quenched night or day;
its smoke will rise forever.
In all generations it will lie waste;
no one will pass through it ever again.

11 Horned owl and hawk will possess it,
screech owl and raven will live there;
he will stretch over it the measuring line of confusion
and the plumbline of the empty void.

12 Of its nobles, none will be called to be king,
and all its princes will be nothing.

13 Thorns will overgrow its palaces,
nettles and thistles its fortresses;
it will become a lair for jackals,
an enclosure for ostriches.

14 Wildcats and hyenas will meet there;

and billy-goats call to each other;
Lilit [the night monster] will lurk there
and find herself a place to rest.

15 There the hoot owl will nest, lay her eggs,
hatch and gather her young in its shade.
There the vultures will assemble,
every one with its mate.

16 Consult the book of ADONAI and read it:
not one of these will be missing,
none will be lacking a mate.
For by his own mouth he gave the order,
and by his Spirit he brought them together.

17 It is he who cast the lot for them,
his hand measured out their shares.
They will possess it forever,
and live there through all generations.

35 1 The desert and the dry land will be glad;
the 'Aravah will rejoice and blossom like the lily.

2 It will burst into flower,
will rejoice with joy and singing,
will be given the glory of the L'vanon,
the splendor of Karmel and the Sharon.
They will see the glory of ADONAI,
the splendor of our God.

3 Strengthen your drooping arms,
and steady your tottering knees.

4 Say to the fainthearted, "Be strong and unafraid!
Here is your God; he will come with vengeance;
with God's retribution he will come and save you."

5 Then the eyes of the blind will be opened,
and the ears of the deaf will be unstopped;

6 then the lame man will leap like a deer,
and the mute person's tongue will sing.
For in the desert, springs will burst forth,
streams of water in the 'Aravah;

7 the sandy mirage will become a pool,
the thirsty ground springs of water.
The haunts where jackals lie down will become
a marsh filled with reeds and papyrus.

8 A highway will be there, a way,
called the Way of Holiness.
The unclean will not pass over it,
but it will be for those whom he guides —

⁹ fools will not stray along it.
No lion or other beast of prey
will be there, traveling on it.
They will not be found there,
but the redeemed will go there.

¹⁰ Those ransomed by ADONAI will return
and come with singing to Tziyon,
on their heads will be everlasting joy.
They will acquire gladness and joy,
while sorrow and sighing will flee.

36 ¹ It was in the fourteenth year of King Hizkiyahu that Sancheriv king of Ashur advanced against all the fortified cities of Y'hudah and captured them. ² From Lakhish the king of Ashur sent Rav-Shakeh to Hizkiyahu in Yerushalayim with a large army. He positioned himself by the aqueduct from the Upper Pool, which is by the road to the Launderers' Field. ³ Elyakim the son of Hilkiyahu, who was in charge of the household, Shevnah the general secretary and Yo'ach the son of Asaf the foreign minister went out to meet him.

⁴ Rav-Shakeh addressed them: "Tell Hizkiyahu: 'Here is what the great king, the king of Ashur, says: "What makes you so confident? ⁵ I say: do mere words constitute strategy and strength for battle? In whom, then, are you trusting when you rebel against me like this? ⁶ Look! Relying on Egypt is like using a broken stick as a staff — when you lean on it, it punctures your hand. That's what Pharaoh king of Egypt is like for anyone who puts his trust in him. ⁷ But if you tell me, 'We trust in ADONAI our God,' then isn't he the one whose high places and altars Hizkiyahu has removed, telling Y'hudah and Yerushalayim, 'You must worship before this altar'? ⁸ All right, then, make a wager with my lord the king of Ashur: I will give you two thousand horses if you can find enough riders for them. ⁹ How then can you repulse even one of my master's lowest-ranked army officers? Yet you are relying on Egypt for chariots and riders! ¹⁰ Do you think I have come up to this land to destroy it without ADONAI's approval? ADONAI said to me, 'Go up against this land and destroy it!'"'"

¹¹ Elyakim, Shevnah and Yo'ach said to Rav-Shakeh, "Please speak to your servants in Aramaic, since we understand it; don't speak to us in Hebrew while the people on the wall are listening." ¹² But Rav-Shakeh answered, "Did my master send me to deliver my message just to your master and yourselves? Didn't he send me to address the men sitting on the wall, who, like you, are going to eat their own dung and drink their own urine?" ¹³ Then Rav-Shakeh stood up and, speaking loudly in Hebrew, said: "Hear what the great king, the king of Ashur, says! ¹⁴ This is what the king says: 'Don't let Hizkiyahu deceive you, because he won't be able to save you. ¹⁵ And don't let Hizkiyahu make you trust in ADONAI by saying, "ADONAI will surely save us; this city will not be given over to the king of Ashur." ¹⁶ Don't listen to Hizkiyahu.' For this is what the king says: 'Make peace with me, surrender to me. Then every one of you can eat from his vine and fig tree and drink the water in his own cistern, ¹⁷ until I come and take you away to a land like your own land, a land with grain and wine, a land with bread and vineyards. ¹⁸ Beware of Hizkiyahu; he is only deluding you when he says, "ADONAI will save us." Has any god of any nation ever saved his land from the power of the king of Ashur? ¹⁹ Where are the gods of

Hamat and Arpad? Where are the gods of S'farvayim? Did they save Shomron from my power? [20] Where is the god of any of these countries that has saved its country from my power, so that ADONAI might be able to save Yerushalayim from my power?'" [21] But they kept still and didn't answer him so much as a word, for the king's order was, "Don't answer him."

[22] Then Elyakim the son of Hilkiyahu, who was in charge of the household, Shevnah the general secretary and Yo'ach the son of Asaf the foreign minister went to Hizkiyahu with their clothes torn and reported to him what Rav-Shakeh had said.

37 [1] On hearing it, King Hizkiyahu tore his clothes, covered himself with sackcloth and entered the house of ADONAI. [2] He sent Elyakim, who was in charge of the household, Shevnah the general secretary and the leading *cohanim*, covered with sackcloth, to Yesha'yahu the prophet, the son of Amotz. [3] They said to him, "This is what Hizkiyahu says: 'Today is a day of trouble, rebuke and disgrace. Children are ready to be born, but there is no strength to bring them to birth. [4] Maybe ADONAI your God will hear the words of Rav-Shakeh, whom his master the king of Ashur has sent to taunt the living God, and will rebuke the message which ADONAI your God has heard. So pray for the remnant that is left.'"

[5] When King Hizkiyahu's servants came to Yesha'yahu, [6] he said to them, "Tell your master that this is what ADONAI says: 'Don't be afraid of the words you heard the servants of the king of Ashur use to insult me. [7] I will put a spirit in him that will make him hear a rumor and return to his own land; then I will cause him to die by the sword in his own land.'"

[8] Rav-Shakeh returned and, having heard that the king of Ashur had left Lakhish, found him making war with Livnah. [9] Then he heard it said that Tirhakah king of Ethiopia was on his way to fight him. On hearing this, the king of Ashur sent messengers to Hizkiyahu, after ordering them, [10] "This is what you are to say to Hizkiyahu king of Y'hudah: 'Don't let your God in whom you trust deceive you by saying, "Yerushalayim will not be handed over to the power of the king of Ashur." [11] You have heard what the kings of Ashur have done to all lands — they have completely destroyed them. So how will you be delivered? [12] Have the gods of the nations delivered them? No, my ancestors destroyed them — Gozan, Haran, Retzef and the people of 'Eden who were in Tel'asar. [13] Where is the king of Hamat? the king of Arpad? the king of the city of S'farvayim, of Hena and 'Ivah?'" [14] Hizkiyahu took the letter from the messengers' hands and read it. Then Hizkiyahu went up to the house of ADONAI and spread it out before ADONAI. [15] This is the prayer that Hizkiyahu prayed to ADONAI: [16] "ADONAI-Tzva'ot, God of Isra'el, who dwells above the k'ruvim! You alone are God of all the kingdoms on earth. You made heaven and earth. [17] Turn your ear, ADONAI, and hear! Open your eyes, ADONAI, and see! Hear all the words that Sancheriv sent to taunt the living God. [18] It is true that the kings of Ashur have laid waste all the countries and their lands [19] and have thrown their gods into the fire. For those were nongods, merely the products of people's hands, wood and stone; this is why they could destroy them. [20] Now therefore, ADONAI our God, save us from his power — so that all the kingdoms on earth will know that you are ADONAI — you only."

[21] Then Yesha'yahu the son of Amotz sent this message to Hizkiyahu: "ADONAI the God of Isra'el says: 'You prayed to me against Sancheriv king of Ashur.' [22] Here is ADONAI's answer concerning him:

"'The virgin daughter of Tziyon
despises you; she laughs you to scorn.
The daughter of Yerushalayim
shakes her head at you.

23   Whom have you taunted and insulted?
Against whom have you raised your voice
and haughtily lifted your eyes?
The Holy One of Isra'el!

24   "'Through your servants you taunted *Adonai*.
You said, "With my many chariots
I have ascended the mountain heights
even in the far reaches of the L'vanon.
I cut down its tall cedars
and its best cypress trees.
I reached its remotest heights
and its best forests.

25   I dug [wells] and drank the water.
The soles of my [soldiers'] feet
dried up all the rivers of Egypt."

26   "'Haven't you heard? Long ago I made it;
in antiquity I produced it;
and now I am making it happen:
you are turning fortified cities
into heaps of ruins,

27   while their inhabitants, shorn of power,
are disheartened and ashamed,
weak as grass, frail as plants,
like grass on the rooftops
or grain scorched by the east wind.

28   "'But I know when you sit, when you leave,
when you enter — and when you rage against me.

29   And because of your rage against me,
because of your pride that has reached my ears,
I am putting my hook in your nose
and my bridle on your lips;
and I will make you return
by the way on which you came.'

30 "'This will be the sign for you [people of Isra'el]: this year, you will eat the grain that grows of itself; the second year, you will eat what grows from that; but in the third year, you will sow, reap, plant vineyards and eat their fruit.

31   "'Meanwhile, the remnant
of the house of Y'hudah that has escaped

492

will again take root downward
and bear fruit upward;

32   for a remnant will go out from Yerushalayim,
those escaping will go out from Mount Tziyon.
The zeal of *ADONAI-Tzva'ot*
will accomplish this.'

³³ "Therefore this is what *ADONAI* says concerning the king of Ashur:

" 'He will not come to this city
or even shoot an arrow there;
he will not confront it with a shield
or erect earthworks against it.

34   " 'By the way he came he will return;
he will not come to this city,'

says *ADONAI*. ³⁵ 'For I will defend this city and save it, both for my own sake and for my servant David's sake.' "

³⁶ Then the angel of *ADONAI* went out and struck down 185,000 men in the camp of Ashur. Early the next morning, there they were, all of them, corpses — dead. ³⁷ So Sancheriv king of Ashur left, went and returned to live in Ninveh.

³⁸ One day, as he was worshipping in the temple of Nisrokh his god, his sons Adramelekh and Shar'etzer struck him with the sword and escaped into the land of Ararat. So his son Esar-Hadon took his place as king.

38 ¹ Around this time Hizkiyahu became ill to the point of death. Yesha'yahu the prophet, the son of Amotz, came and said to him, "Here is what *ADONAI* says: 'Put your house in order, because you are going to die; you will not live.' " ² Hizkiyahu turned his face toward the wall and prayed to *ADONAI*: ³ "I plead with you, *ADONAI*, remember now how I have lived before you truly and wholeheartedly, and how I have done what you see as good." And he cried bitter tears.

⁴ Then the word of *ADONAI* came to Yesha'yahu: ⁵ "Go and tell Hizkiyahu that this is what *ADONAI*, the God of David your ancestor, says: 'I have heard your prayer and seen your tears; therefore I will add fifteen years to your life. ⁶ Also I will rescue you and this city from the power of the king of Ashur; I will defend this city. ⁷ The sign for you from *ADONAI* that *ADONAI* will do what he said is ⁸ that I will cause the shadow of the sundial, which has started going down on the sundial of Achaz, to go backward ten intervals.' " So the sun went back ten intervals of the distance it had already gone down.

⁹ After Hizkiyahu king of Y'hudah had been ill and had recovered, he wrote the following:

10   "I once said: 'In the prime of life
I am going off to the gates of Sh'ol.
I am being deprived of living out
the full span of my life.'

493

11 "I said, 'I will never again see *Yah*,
  Yah in the land of the living;
  I will look on human beings no more
  or be with those who live in this world.
12 My home is uprooted and taken away
  from me like a shepherd's tent.
  Like a weaver, I have rolled up my life;
  he cuts me off from the loom.
  Between day and night you could finish me off.
13 I try to be strong like a lion till morning,
  but still my illness breaks all my bones —
  between day and night you could finish me off.
14 I make little chattering sounds like a swallow,
  I moan aloud like a dove,
  My eyes are weary with looking upward.
  Adonai, I am overwhelmed; guarantee my life!'

15 "What is there that I can say?
  He has spoken to me and acted!
  I will go humbly all my years,
  remembering how bitter I was.
16 *Adonai*, by these things people live;
  in all these is the life of my spirit.
  You're restoring my health and giving me life —
17 though instead of peace, I felt very bitter.
  You desired my life and preserved it
  from the nothingness pit;
  for you threw all my sins behind your back.

18 "Sh'ol cannot thank you, death cannot praise you;
  those descending to the pit cannot hope for your truth.
19 The living, the living — they can thank you,
  as I do today;
  fathers will make their children know
  about your faithfulness.
20 *Adonai* is ready to save me;
  hence we will make our stringed instruments sound
  all the days of our life
  in the house of *Adonai*."

21 Then Yesha'yahu said, "Have them take a fig-plaster and apply it to the inflammation, and he will recover." 22 Hizkiyahu asked, "What sign will there be that I will be able to go up to the house of *Adonai*?"

39 1 M'rodakh-Bal'adan the son of Bal'adan, king of Bavel, heard that Hizkiyahu had been ill and had recovered, so he sent a letter and a gift to him. 2 Hizkiyahu was pleased with the gifts and showed the messengers all of the building where he kept his treasures, including the silver, gold, spices and precious oils; also all of the building where he kept his armor; and everything in his treasury — there was nothing in his palace or in his entire domain that Hizkiyahu did not show them. ³ Then Yesha'yahu the prophet came to King Hizkiyahu and asked him, "What did these men say? Where did they come from?" Hizkiyahu answered, "They came to me from a distant country, Bavel." ⁴ Yesha'yahu asked, "What have they seen in your palace?" "They have seen everything in my palace," said Hizkiyahu. "There isn't a thing among my treasures that I haven't shown them." ⁵ Yesha'yahu said to Hizkiyahu, "Hear what ADONAI-*Tzva'ot* says: ⁶ 'The day will come when everything in your palace, along with everything your ancestors stored up until today, will be carried off to Bavel. Nothing will be left,' says ADONAI. ⁷ 'They will carry off some of your descendants, your own offspring; and they will be made eunuchs serving in the palace of the king of Bavel." ⁸ Hizkiyahu said to Yesha'yahu, "The word of ADONAI which you have just told me is good"; because he thought, "At least peace and truth will continue during my lifetime."

40 ¹ "Comfort and keep comforting my people," says your God.

² "Tell Yerushalayim to take heart; proclaim to her
that she has completed her time of service,
that her guilt has been paid off,
that she has received at the hand of ADONAI
double for all her sins."

³ A voice cries out:

"Clear a road through the desert for ADONAI!
Level a highway in the 'Aravah for our God!
⁴ Let every valley be filled in,
every mountain and hill lowered,
the bumpy places made level
and the crags become a plain.
⁵ Then the glory of ADONAI will be revealed;
all humankind together will see it,
for the mouth of ADONAI has spoken."

⁶ A voice says, "Proclaim!"
And I answer, "What should I proclaim?"
"All humanity is merely grass,
all its kindness like wildflowers:
⁷ the grass dries up, the flower fades,
when a wind from ADONAI blows on it.
Surely the people are grass!
⁸ The grass dries up, the flower fades;
but the word of our God will stand forever."

⁹ You who bring good news to Tziyon,
get yourself up on a high mountain;

you who bring good news to Yerushalayim,
cry out at the top of your voice!
Don't be afraid to shout out loud!
Say to the cities of Y'hudah,
"Here is your God!

10 Here comes *Adonai Elohim* with power,
and his arm will rule for him.
Look! His reward is with him,
and his recompense is before him.

11 He is like a shepherd feeding his flock,
gathering his lambs with his arm,
carrying them against his chest,
gently leading the mother sheep."

12 Who has counted the handfuls of water in the sea,
measured off the sky with a ruler,
gauged how much dust there is on the earth,
weighed the mountains on scales, or the hills in a balance?

13 Who has measured the Spirit of *Adonai*?
Who has been his counselor, instructing him?

14 Whom did he consult, to gain understanding?
Who taught him how to judge,
taught him what he needed to know,
showed him how to discern?

15 The nations are like a drop in a bucket,
they count like a grain of dust on the scales.
The islands weigh as little as specks of dust.

16 The L'vanon would not suffice for fuel
or its animals be enough for burnt offerings.

17 Before him all the nations are like nothing.
He regards them as less than nothing.

18 With whom, then, will you compare God?
By what standard will you evaluate him?

19 An image made by a craftsman,
which a goldsmith overlays with gold,
for which he then casts silver chains?

20 A man too poor to afford an offering
chooses a piece of wood that won't rot,
then seeks out a skilled artisan
to prepare an image that won't fall over.

21 Don't you know? Don't you hear?
Haven't you been told from the start?
Don't you understand how the earth is set up?

22 He who sits above the circle of the earth—

for whom its inhabitants appear like grasshoppers —
stretches out the heavens like a curtain,
spreads them out like a tent to live in.

23 He reduces princes to nothing,
the rulers of the earth to emptiness.

24 Scarcely are they planted, scarcely sown,
scarcely their stem taken root in the ground,
when he blows on them, they dry up,
and the whirlwind carries them off like straw.

25 "With whom, then, will you compare me?
With whom am I equal?" asks the Holy One.

26 Turn your eyes to the heavens!
See who created these things!
He brings out the army of them in sequence,
summoning each by name.
Through his great might and his massive strength,
not one of them is missing.

27 Why do you complain, Ya'akov;
why do you say, Isra'el,
"My way is hidden from ADONAI,
my rights are ignored by my God"?

28 Haven't you known, haven't you heard
that the everlasting God, ADONAI,
the Creator of the ends of the earth,
does not grow tired or weary?
His understanding cannot be fathomed.

29 He invigorates the exhausted,
he gives strength to the powerless.

30 Young men may grow tired and weary,
even the fittest may stumble and fall;

31 but those who hope in ADONAI will renew their strength,
they will soar aloft as with eagles' wings;
when they are running they won't grow weary,
when they are walking they won't get tired.

41 1 "Keep silence before me, coastlands!
Let the peoples replenish their strength!
Let them approach; then let them speak.
Let us assemble for judgment."

2 Who has raised from the east one who is just
and called him to be in his service?
He hands nations over to him
and subjects kings to him;
his sword reduces them to dust,
his bow to driven straw.

3   He pursues them, passing on unscathed,
    hardly touching the path with his feet.
4   Whose work is this? Who has brought it about?
    He who called the generations from the beginning,
    "I, ADONAI, am the first;
    and I am the same with those who are last."
5   The coastlands have seen and became afraid.
    The ends of the earth have trembled.
    They have approached, and now they have come.

6   Every one helps his fellow workman,
    everyone says to his brother, "Be strong!"
7   The woodworker encourages the goldsmith,
    the polisher encourages the hammerer;
    he says of the soldering, "Yes, that's good,"
    then puts nails in [the idol] to keep it from moving.

8   "But you, Isra'el, my servant;
    Ya'akov, whom I have chosen,
    descendants of Avraham my friend,
9   I have taken you from the ends of the earth,
    summoned you from its most distant parts
    and said to you, 'You are my servant' —
    I have chosen you, not rejected you.
10 Don't be afraid, for I am with you;
    don't be distressed, for I am your God.
    I give you strength, I give you help,
    I support you with my victorious right hand.
11 All those who were angry with you
    will be disgraced, put to shame;
    those who fought against you
    will be destroyed, brought to nothing.
12 You will seek them but not find them,
    those who contended with you;
    yes, those who made war with you
    will be brought to nothing, nothing at all.
13 For I, ADONAI, your God,
    say to you, as I hold your right hand,
    'Have no fear; I will help you.
14 Have no fear, Ya'akov, you worm,
    you men of Isra'el!'
    I will help you," says ADONAI;
    "Your redeemer is the Holy One of Isra'el.

15 "I will make you into a threshing-sledge,
    new, with sharp, pointed teeth,
    to thresh the mountains and crush them to dust,

16 to reduce the hills to chaff.
As you fan them, the wind will carry them off,
and the whirlwind will scatter them.
Then you will rejoice in ADONAI,
you will glory in the Holy One of Isra'el.

17 "The poor and needy look for water in vain;
their tongues are parched with thirst.
I, ADONAI, will answer them.
I, the God of Isra'el, will not leave them.

18 I will open up rivers on the barren hills
and wells down in the broad valleys.
I will turn the desert into a lake
and dry ground into springs.

19 I will plant the desert with cedars,
acacias, myrtles and olive trees;
In the 'Aravah I will put cypresses
together with elm trees and larches.

20 Then the people will see and know,
together observe and understand
that the hand of ADONAI has done this,
that the Holy One of Isra'el created it.

21 "Present your case," says ADONAI,
"Produce your arguments," says Ya'akov's king.

22 Bring out those idols!
Have them foretell the future for us,
tell us about past events,
so that we can reflect on them
and understand their consequences.
Or tell us about events yet to come,

23 state what will happen in the future,
so that we can know you are gods.
At least, do something, either good or bad —
anything, to make us awestruck and fearful!

24 You can't! — because you are less than nothing.
Whoever chooses you is an abomination!

25 "I roused someone from the north,
and he has come from the rising sun;
he will call on my name.
He will trample on rulers as if they were mud,
like a potter treading clay."

26 Who said this at the start, so we could know,
or foretold it, so we could say, "He's right"?

499

In fact, no one said it; no one foretold it —
the fact is, nobody hears what you say.

27 I am the first to declare it to Tziyon,
to send Yerushalayim a messenger with good news.

28 But when I look around, there is no one —
not a single one can give counsel,
who, when I ask, can give an answer.

29 Look at them all! What they do is nothing!
Their idols are so much wind and waste.

42 1 "Here is my servant, whom I support,
my chosen one, in whom I take pleasure.
I have put my Spirit on him;
he will bring justice to the *Goyim*.

2 He will not cry or shout;
no one will hear his voice in the streets.

3 He will not snap off a broken reed
or snuff out a smoldering wick.
He will bring forth justice according to truth;

4 he will not weaken or be crushed
until he has established justice on the earth,
and the coastlands wait for his *Torah*."

5 Thus says God, ADONAI,
who created the heavens and spread them out,
who stretched out the earth and all that grows from it,
who gives breath to the people on it
and spirit to those who walk on it:

6 "I, ADONAI, called you righteously,
I took hold of you by the hand,
I shaped you and made you a covenant for the people,
to be a light for the *Goyim*,

7 so that you can open blind eyes,
free the prisoners from confinement,
those living in darkness from the dungeon.

8 I am ADONAI; that is my name.
I yield my glory to no one else,
nor my praise to any idol.

9 See how the former predictions come true;
and now new things do I declare —
before they sprout I tell you about them."

10 Sing to ADONAI a new song!
Let his praise be sung from the ends of the earth
by those sailing the sea and by everything in it,
by the coastlands and those living there.

11 Let the desert and its cities raise their voices,

the villages where Kedar lives;
let those living in Sela shout for joy;
let them cry out from the mountaintops!

12 Let them give glory to ADONAI
and proclaim his praise in the coastlands.

13 ADONAI will go out like a soldier,
like a soldier roused to the fury of battle;
he will shout, yes, he raises the battle cry;
as he triumphs over his foes.

14 "For a long time I have held my peace,
I have been silent, restrained myself.
Now I will shriek like a woman in labor,
panting and gasping for air.

15 I will devastate mountains and hills,
wither all their vegetation,
turn the rivers into islands
and dry up the lakes.

16 The blind I will lead on a road they don't know,
on roads they don't know I will lead them;
I will turn darkness to light before them,
and straighten their twisted paths.
These are things I will do without fail.

17 Those who trust in idols,
who say to statues, 'You are our gods,'
will be repulsed in utter shame.

18 Listen, you deaf! Look, you blind! —
so that you will see!

19 Who is as blind as my servant,
or as deaf as the messenger I send?
Who is as blind as the one I rewarded,
as blind as the servant of ADONAI?"

20 You see much but don't pay attention;
you open your ears, but you don't listen.

21 ADONAI was pleased, for his righteousness' sake,
to make the *Torah* great and glorious.

22 But this is a people pillaged and plundered,
all trapped in holes and sequestered in prisons.
They are there to be plundered, with no one to rescue them;
there to be pillaged, and no one says, "Return them!"

23 Which of you will listen to this?
Who will hear and give heed in the times to come?

24 Who gave Ya'akov to be pillaged,
Isra'el to the plunderers?
Didn't ADONAI, against whom we have sinned,
in whose ways they refused to walk,

he whose *Torah* they did not obey?

25   This is why he poured on him his blazing anger
as well as the fury of battle—
it wrapped him in flames, yet he learned nothing;
it burned him, yet he did not take it to heart.

43 ¹   But now this is what ADONAI says,
he who created you, Ya'akov,
he who formed you, Isra'el:
"Don't be afraid, for I have redeemed you;
I am calling you by your name; you are mine.

2   When you pass through water, I will be with you;
when you pass through rivers, they will not overwhelm you;
when you walk through fire, you will not be scorched—
the flame will not burn you.

3   For I am ADONAI, your God,
the Holy One of Isra'el, your Savior—
I have given Egypt as your ransom,
Ethiopia and S'va for you.

4   Because I regard you as valued and honored,
and because I love you.
For you I will give people,
nations in exchange for your life.

5   Don't be afraid, for I am with you.
I will bring your descendants from the east,
and I will gather you from the west;

6   I will say to the north, 'Give them up!'
and to the south, 'Don't hold them back!
Bring my sons from far away,
and my daughters from the ends of the earth,

7   everyone who bears my name,
whom I created for my glory—
I formed him, yes, I made him.'"

8   Bring forward the people who are blind but have eyes,
also the deaf who have ears.

9   All the nations are gathered together,
and the peoples are assembled.
Who among them can proclaim this
and reveal what happened in the past?
Let them bring their witnesses to justify themselves,
so that others, on hearing, can say, "That's true."

10   "You are my witnesses," says ADONAI,
"and my servant whom I have chosen,
so that you can know and trust me
and understand that I am he—

no god was produced before me,
nor will any be after me.

11 I, yes I, am *Adonai*;
besides me there is no deliverer.

12 I have declared, saved and proclaimed —
not some alien god among you.
Therefore you are my witnesses,"
says *Adonai*. "I am God.

13 Since days began, I have been he.
No one can deliver from my hand.
When I act, who can reverse it?"

14 Here is what *Adonai*, your redeemer,
the Holy One of Isra'el, says:
"For your sake I have sent [an army] to Bavel
and knocked down the fleeing Kasdim, all of them;
their songs of triumph are now lamentations.

15 I am *Adonai*, your Holy One,
the Creator of Isra'el, your King."

16 Here is what *Adonai* says,
who made a way in the sea,
a path through the raging waves;

17 who led out chariot and horse,
the army in its strength—
they lay down, never to rise again,
snuffed out and quenched like a wick:

18 "Stop dwelling on past events
and brooding over times gone by;

19 I am doing something new;
it's springing up—can't you see it?
I am making a road in the desert,
rivers in the wasteland.

20 The wild animals will honor me,
the jackals and the ostriches;
because I put water in the desert,
rivers in the wasteland,
for my chosen people to drink,

21 the people I formed for myself,
so that they would proclaim my praise.

22 But you haven't called on me, Ya'akov;
because you have grown weary of me, Isra'el.

23 You have not brought me sheep for your burnt offerings,
you have not honored me with your sacrifices.
I didn't burden you by requiring grain offerings.
or weary you by demanding frankincense.

24 You have not spent money to buy me sweet cane

or filled me with the fat of your sacrifices.
Instead, you have burdened me with your sins
and wearied me with your crimes.

25 I, yes I, am the one who blots out
your offenses for my own sake;
I will not remember your sins.

26 Remind me when we're in court together —
tell your side, make the case that you are right.

27 Your first father sinned,
and your spokesmen rebelled against me.

28 Therefore I repudiated the officials of the sanctuary,
delivered Ya'akov to the curse of destruction,
and subjected Isra'el to scorn.

44 1 "Now listen, Ya'akov my servant,
Isra'el whom I have chosen:

2 Thus says ADONAI, who made you,
formed you in the womb, and will help you:
'Don't be afraid, Ya'akov my servant,
Yeshurun, whom I have chosen.

3 For I will pour water on the thirsty land
and streams on the dry ground;
I will pour my Spirit on your descendants,
my blessing on your offspring.

4 They will spring up among the grass
like willows on the riverbanks.

5 One will say, "I belong to ADONAI."
Another will be called by the name of Ya'akov.
Yet another will write that he belongs to ADONAI.
and adopt the surname Isra'el.'"

6 Thus says ADONAI, Isra'el's King
and Redeemer, ADONAI-Tzva'ot:
"I am the first, and I am the last;
besides me there is no God.

7 Who is like me? Let him speak out!
Let him show me clearly what has been happening
since I set up the eternal people;
let him foretell future signs and events.

8 Don't be frightened, don't be afraid.
Didn't I tell you this long ago?
I foretold it, and you are my witnesses.
Is there any God besides me?
There is no other Rock — I know of none."

9 All idol-makers amount to nothing;
their precious productions profit no one;

and their witnesses, to their own shame,
neither see nor understand.

10 Who would fashion a god or cast an image
that profits no one anything?

11 All involved will be ashamed,
but more than anyone else, the people who made them.
Let them all be assembled, let them stand up;
let them fear and be shamed together.

12 A blacksmith makes a tool over burning coals;
with his strong arm he shapes it with hammers.
But when he gets hungry, his strength fails;
if he doesn't drink water, he grows tired.

13 A carpenter takes his measurements,
sketches the shape with a stylus,
planes the wood, checks it with calipers,
and carves it into the shape of a man;
and, since it is honored like a man,
of course it has to live in a house.

14 He goes to chop down cedars;
he takes an evergreen and an oak;
he especially tends one tree in the forest,
plants a pine for the rain to nourish.

15 In time, when it's ready for use as fuel,
he takes some of it to keep himself warm
and burns some more to bake bread.
Then he makes a god and worships it,
carves it into an idol and falls down before it.

16 So half of it he burns in the fire;
with that half he roasts meat and eats his fill;
he warms himself; says, "It feels so good,
getting warm while watching the flames!"

17 With the rest of the log he fashions a god,
a carved image, then falls down before it;
he worships it and prays to it.
"Save me," he says, "for you are my god!"

18 Such people know nothing, understand nothing.
Their eyes are sealed shut, so that they can't see;
their hearts too, so they can't understand.

19 Not one thinks to himself or has the knowledge
or the discernment to say,
"I burned half of it in the fire,
baked bread on its coals, roasted meat and ate it.
Should I now make the rest an abomination?
Should I prostrate myself to a tree trunk?"

20   He is relying on ashes!
      A deceived heart has led him astray;
      so that now he won't save himself, just won't say,
      "This thing in my hand is a fraud!"

21   "Keep these matters in mind, Ya'akov,
      for you, Isra'el, are my servant.
      I formed you, you are my own servant;
      Isra'el, don't forget me.
22   Like a thick cloud, I wipe away your offenses;
      like a cloud, your sins.
      Come back to me, for I have redeemed you."

23   Sing, you heavens, for ADONAI has done it!
      Shout, you depths of the earth!
      Mountains, break out into song,
      along with every tree in the forest!
      For ADONAI has redeemed Ya'akov;
      he glorifies himself in Isra'el.

24   Here is what ADONAI says, your Redeemer,
      he who formed you in the womb:
      "I am ADONAI, who makes all things,
      who stretched out the heavens all alone,
      who spread out the earth all by myself.
25   I frustrate false prophets and their omens,
      I make fools of diviners,
      I drive back the sages
      and make their wisdom look silly.
26   I confirm my servants' prophecies
      and make my messengers' plans succeed.
      I say of Yerushalayim: 'She will be lived in,'
      of the cities of Y'hudah, 'They will be rebuilt;
      I will restore their ruins.'
27   I say to the deep sea, 'Dry up!
      I will make your streams run dry.'
28   I say of Koresh, 'He is my shepherd,
      he will do everything I want.
      He will say of Yerushalayim,
      "You will be rebuilt,"
      and of the temple,
      "Your foundation will be laid."'"

45 ¹   Thus says ADONAI to Koresh, his anointed,
      whose right hand he has grasped,
      so that he subdues nations before him
      and strips kings of their robes,

506

so that doors open in front of him,
and no gates are barred:

2   "I will go ahead of you,
levelling the hills,
shattering the bronze gates,
smashing the iron bars.

3   I will give you treasures
hoarded in the dark,
secret riches hidden away,
so that you will know that I, ADONAI,
calling you by your name,
am the God of Isra'el.

4   It is for the sake of Ya'akov my servant,
yes, for Isra'el my elect,
that I call you by your name
and give you a title, although you don't know me.

5   I am ADONAI; there is no other;
besides me there is no God.
I am arming you, although you don't know me,

6   so that those from the east and those from the west
will know that there is none besides me —
I am ADONAI; there is no other.

7   I form light, I create darkness;
I make well-being, I create woe;
I, ADONAI, do all these things.

8   "Heavens above, rain down justice;
let the clouds pour it down.
Let the earth open,
so that salvation springs up,
and justice sprouts with it.
I, ADONAI, have created it."

9   Woe to anyone who argues with his maker,
like potsherds lying on the ground!
Does the clay ask the potter, "What are you doing?"
or, "What's this you're making, that has no hands?"

10   Woe to him who asks a father,
"Of what are you the father?"
or who asks a woman,
"To what are you giving birth?"

11   Thus says ADONAI,
the Holy One of Isra'el, his Maker:
"You ask for signs concerning my children?
You give orders concerning the work of my hands?

12   I am the one who made the earth!

I created human beings on it!
I — my hands — stretched out the heavens,
and directed all their number.

13 I am stirring up Koresh to righteousness,
I am smoothing out all his paths.
He will rebuild my city;
and he will free my exiles,
taking neither ransom nor bribe,"
says ADONAI-Tzva'ot.

14 Here is what ADONAI says:
"The earnings of Egypt, the commerce of Ethiopia,
and men of stature from S'va
will come over to you and become yours;
they will come in chains and follow you.
They will prostrate themselves before you;
they will pray to you:
'Surely God is with you; there is no other,
other gods are nothing.'"

15 Truly, you are a God who hides himself,
God of Isra'el, Savior!

16 The idol-makers will be ashamed,
disgraced, all of them;
they will go dishonored together.

17 But Isra'el, saved by ADONAI
with an everlasting salvation,
you will never, ever, be ashamed or disgraced.

18 For thus says ADONAI, who created the heavens,
God, who shaped and made the earth,
who established and created it not to be chaos,
but formed it to be lived in:
"I am ADONAI; there is no other.

19 I did not speak in secret, in a land of darkness.
I did not say to the descendants of Ya'akov,
'It is in vain that you will seek me.'
I, ADONAI, speak rightly; I say what is true.

20 Assemble, come and gather together,
you refugees from the nations!
Those carrying their wooden idols are ignorant,
they pray to a god that cannot save.

21 Let them stand and present their case!
Indeed, let them take counsel together.
Who foretold this long ago,
announced it in times gone by?
Wasn't it I, ADONAI?

²²
There is no other God besides me,
a just God and a Savior;
there is none besides me.
Look to me, and be saved,
all the ends of the earth!
For I am God;
there is no other.

²³
In the name of myself I have sworn,
from my mouth has rightly gone out,
a word that will not return —
that to me every knee will bow
and every tongue will swear ²⁴ about me
that only in ADONAI
are justice and strength."

All who rage against him
will come to him ashamed,

²⁵
but all the descendants of Isra'el
will find justice and glory in ADONAI.

46 ¹
Bel bows down, N'vo stoops low;
their idols are borne by animals, beasts of burden.
The loads you yourselves were carrying
are now burdening tired animals.

²
They stoop and bow down together;
they cannot save the burden,
but themselves go into captivity.

³
"Listen to me, house of Ya'akov,
all who remain of the house of Isra'el:
I have borne you from birth,
carried you since the womb.

⁴
Till your old age I will be the same —
I will carry you until your hair is white.
I have made you, and I will bear you;
yes, I will carry and save you.

⁵
To whom will you liken me and equate me?
With whom will you compare me, as if we were similar?"

⁶
They squander the gold from their bags
and weigh silver on a scale;
they hire a goldsmith to make a god,
before which they fall down and worship!

⁷
It is borne on shoulders and carried,
then set in its place; and there it stands.
From its place it does not move.
If one cries to it, it cannot answer

8   or save anyone from his troubles.
Remember this, and stand firm.
Keep it in mind, you rebels.

9   "Remember things that happened
at the beginning, long ago —
that I am God, and there is no other;
I am God, and there is none like me.

10   At the beginning I announce the end,
proclaim in advance things not yet done;
and I say that my plan will hold,
I will do everything I please to do.

11   I call a bird of prey from the east,
the man I intended, from a distant country.
I have spoken and will bring it about;
I have made a plan, and I will fulfill it.

12   Listen to me, you stubborn people,
so far from righteousness:

13   I am bringing my justice nearer,
it is not far away;
my salvation will not be delayed,
I will place my salvation in Tziyon
for Isra'el my glory.

47 ¹   "Come down, and sit in the dust,
you virgin daughter of Bavel!
Sit on the ground, not on a throne,
daughter of the Kasdim!
No longer are you to be called
dainty and delicate.

2   Take the millstones, and grind meal;
take off your veil, strip off your skirt,
uncover your legs, wade through the streams.

3   Your private parts will be exposed;
yes, your shame will be seen.
I am going to take vengeance,
and no one will stand in my way."

4   Our Redeemer! *ADONAI-Tzva'ot* is his name,
the Holy One of Isra'el!

5   "Sit there speechless, go into darkness,
you daughter of the Kasdim!
For you will no longer be called
the mistress of kingdoms.

6   I was angry with my people,
I desecrated my own possession

and gave them over to you.
But you showed them no mercy;
you made your yoke very heavy,
even upon the aged.

7 You said, 'I will be mistress forever.'
so you didn't consider these things
or think about the consequences.

8 Now hear this, you lover of luxuries,
lolling at ease and saying to yourself,
'I am important, and no one else!
I will never be a widow
or know the loss of children.'

9 But both will come over you in an instant,
in a single day loss of children and widowhood;
they will utterly overwhelm you,
despite your many occult practices
and powerful spells to prevent it."

10 You were at ease in your wickedness,
you thought, "No one sees me."
Your "wisdom" and "knowledge" perverted you,
as you thought to yourself,
"I am important, and no one else."

11 Yet disaster will befall you,
and you won't know how to charm it away;
calamity will come upon you,
and you won't be able to turn it aside;
ruin will overcome you,
suddenly, before you know it.

12 So for now, keep on with your powerful spells
and your many occult practices;
from childhood you have been working at them;
maybe they will do you some good,
maybe you will inspire terror!

13 You are worn out with all your consultations —
so let the astrologers and stargazers,
the monthly horoscope-makers,
come forward now and save you
from the things that will come upon you!

14 Look, they will be like straw!
The fire will consume them.
They will not save even themselves
from the power of the flame.
It will not be coals for warming oneself,
not a fire to sit beside!

15 So much for your [wizards],
with whom you have worked all your life!

Each will wander off in his own direction,
and nobody will save you.

48 1 Listen to this, house of Ya'akov,
called by the name of Isra'el,
who have come from the spring of Y'hudah,
who swear by the name of A*DONAI*
and invoke the God of Isra'el! —
it is not sincerely or justifiably
2 that they call themselves people of the holy city
or rely on the God of Isra'el —
A*DONAI*-*Tzva'ot* is his name:

3 "I announced things that happened at the beginning, long ago;
they issued from my mouth, I proclaimed them.
Then suddenly I acted, and they occurred.
4 Because I knew that you were stubborn,
your neck an iron sinew, your forehead bronze,
5 I announced it to you long ago;
before it occurred, I proclaimed it to you;
so that you could not say, 'My idol did it;
my carved image, my statue, gave the order for it.'
6 You have heard and seen all this,
so why won't you admit it?

"Now I am announcing new things to you,
secret things you have not known,
7 created now, not long ago;
before today, you did not hear them:
so you can't say, 'I already know about them.'
8 No, you haven't heard, and you haven't known;
these things have not reached your ears before.
For I knew how treacherous you were —
you were called a rebel from the womb.
9 Yet for the sake of my own reputation
I am deferring my anger;
for the sake of my praise I am patient with you,
so as not to cut you off.

10 "Look, I have refined you,
but not [as severely] as silver;
[rather] I have tested you
in the furnace of affliction.
11 For my sake I will do it,
for my own sake.
I will not let [my reputation] be tarnished;
I will not yield my glory to anyone else.

¹² "Listen to me, Ya‘akov;
Isra'el, whom I have called:
I am he who is first;
I am also the last.

¹³ My hand laid the foundation of the earth,
my right hand spread out the heavens;
when I summoned them,
at once they rose into being.

¹⁴ "All of you, assemble and listen:
which of you has foretold what is coming?
ADONAI's friend will do his will against Bavel,
using his arm against the Kasdim.

¹⁵ It is I who have spoken,
I have summoned him,
I have brought him,
and he will succeed.

¹⁶ "Come close to me, and listen to this:
since the beginning I have not spoken in secret,
since the time things began to be, I have been there;
and now Adonai ELOHIM has sent me and his Spirit."

¹⁷ Thus says ADONAI, your Redeemer,
the Holy One of Isra'el:
"I am ADONAI, your God,
who teaches you for your own good,
who guides you on the path you should take.

¹⁸ If only you would heed my mitzvot!
Then your peace would flow on like a river,
and your righteousness like the waves of the sea.

¹⁹ Your descendants would be numerous as the sand,
your offspring countless as its grains.
Their name would never be cut off
or destroyed from my presence."

²⁰ Get out of Bavel! Flee the Kasdim!
With shouts of joy announce it, proclaim it!
Send the news out to the ends of the earth!
Say, "ADONAI has redeemed his servant Ya‘akov."

²¹ They weren't thirsty when he led them through the deserts,
he made water flow from the rock for them —
he split the rock, and out gushed the water.

²² But there is no peace, says ADONAI, for the wicked.

49 ¹ Coastlands, listen to me;
listen, you peoples far away:

ADONAI called me from the womb;
before I was born, he had spoken my name.

2   He has made my mouth like a sharp sword
while hiding me in the shadow of his hand;
he has made me like a sharpened arrow
while concealing me in his quiver.

3   He said to me, "You are my servant,
Isra'el, through whom I will show my glory."

4   But I said, "I have toiled in vain,
spent my strength for nothing, futility."
Yet my cause is with ADONAI,
my reward is with my God.

5   So now ADONAI says —
he formed me in the womb to be his servant,
to bring Ya'akov back to him,
to have Isra'el gathered to him,
so that I will be honored in the sight of ADONAI,
my God having become my strength —

6   he has said, "It is not enough
that you are merely my servant
to raise up the tribes of Ya'akov
and restore the offspring of Isra'el.
I will also make you a light to the nations,
so my salvation can spread to the ends of the earth."

7   Here is what ADONAI,
the Redeemer of Isra'el,
his Holy One, says to the one despised,
whom the nations detest, to the servant of tyrants:
"When kings see you, they will stand up;
princes too will prostrate themselves,
because of ADONAI, who is faithful,
the Holy One of Isra'el, who has chosen you."

8   Here is what ADONAI says:
"At the time when I choose, I will answer you;
on the day of salvation, I will help you.
I have preserved you, and I have appointed you
to be the covenant for a people,
to restore the land and distribute again
its ruined inheritances to their owners,

9   to say to the prisoners, 'Come out!'
to those in darkness, 'Show yourselves!'
They will feed along the paths,
and all the high hills will be their pastures.

10 They will be neither hungry nor thirsty;

neither scorching wind nor sun will strike them;
for he who has mercy on them will lead them
and guide them to springs of water.

11 I will turn all my mountains into a road,
my highways will be raised up.

12 There they come, some from far away,
some from the north, some from the west,
and some from the land of Sinim."

13 Sing, heaven! Rejoice, earth!
Break out in song, you mountains!
For ADONAI is comforting his people,
having mercy on his own who have suffered.

14 "But Tziyon says, 'ADONAI has abandoned me,
Adonai has forgotten me.'

15 Can a woman forget her child at the breast,
not show pity on the child from her womb?
Even if these were to forget,
I would not forget you.

16 I have engraved you on the palms of my hands,
your walls are always before me."

17 Your children are coming quickly,
your destroyers and plunderers are leaving and going.

18 Raise your eyes, and look around:
they are all gathering and coming to you.
ADONAI swears: "As surely as I am alive,
you will wear them all like jewels,
adorn yourself with them like a bride."

19 For your desolate places and ruins
and your devastated land
will be too cramped for those living in it;
your devourers will be far away.

20 The day will come when the children born
when you were mourning will say to you,
"This place is too cramped for me!
Give me room, so I can live!"

21 Then you will ask yourself,
"Who fathered these for me?
I've been mourning my children, alone,
as an exile, wandering to and fro;
so who has raised these?
I was left alone, so where have these come from?"

22 Adonai ELOHIM answers:
"I am beckoning to the nations,

515

raising my banner for the peoples.
They will bring your sons in their arms
and carry your daughters on their shoulders.

23 Kings will be your foster-fathers,
their princesses your nurses.
They will bow to you, face toward the earth,
and lick the dust on your feet.
Then you will know that I am ADONAI —
those who wait for me will not be sorry."

24 But can booty be wrested from a warrior?
Can a victor's captives be freed?

25 Here is ADONAI's answer:
"Even a warrior's captives will be snatched away,
and the booty of the fearful will be freed.
I will fight those who fight you,
and I will save your children.

26 I will feed those oppressing you with their own flesh;
they will be drunk on their own blood as with wine.
Then everyone will know that I, ADONAI, am your Savior
and your Redeemer, the Mighty One of Ya'akov."

50 ¹ADONAI says:

"Where is your mother's divorce document
which I gave her when I divorced her?
Or: to which of my creditors
did I sell you?
You were sold because of your sins;
because of your crimes was your mother divorced.

2 Why was no one here when I came?
Why, when I called, did nobody answer?
Is my arm too short to redeem?
Have I too little power to save?
With my rebuke I dry up the sea;
I turn rivers into desert,
their fish rot for lack of water
and they die of thirst;

3 I dress the heavens in black to mourn
and make their covering sackcloth."

4 *Adonai ELOHIM* has given me
the ability to speak as a man well taught,
so that I, with my words,
know how to sustain the weary.
Each morning he awakens my ear

516

to hear like those who are taught.
5 *Adonai ELOHIM* has opened my ear,
and I neither rebelled nor turned away.
6 I offered my back to those who struck me,
my cheeks to those who plucked out my beard;
I did not hide my face
from insult and spitting.
7 For *Adonai ELOHIM* will help.
This is why no insult can wound me.
This is why I have set my face like flint,
knowing I will not be put to shame.
8 My vindicator is close by;
let whoever dares to accuse me
appear with me in court!
Let whoever has a case against me step forward!
9 Look, if *Adonai ELOHIM* helps me,
who will dare to condemn me?
Here, they are all falling apart
like old, moth-eaten clothes.

10 "Who among you fears *ADONAI*?
Who obeys what his servant says?
Even when he walks in the dark,
without any light,
he will trust in *ADONAI*'s reputation
and rely on his God.
11 But all of you who are lighting fires
and arming yourselves with firebrands:
go, walk in the flame of your own fire,
among the firebrands you lit!
From my hands this [fate] awaits you:
you will lie down in torment.

51 ¹ "Listen to me, you pursuers of justice,
you who seek *ADONAI*:
consider the rock from which you were cut,
the quarry from which you were dug —
2 consider Avraham your father
and Sarah, who gave birth to you;
in that I called him when he was only one person,
then blessed him and made him many.
3 For *ADONAI* will comfort Tziyon,
will comfort all her ruined places,
will make her desert like 'Eden,
her 'Aravah like the garden of *ADONAI*.
Joy and gladness will be there,
thanksgiving and the sound of music.

4   "Pay attention to me, my people!
My nation, listen to me!
For *Torah* will go out from me;
I will calm them with my justice
as a light for the peoples.

5   My righteousness is at hand,
my salvation goes out,
my arms will judge the peoples.
The coastlands are putting their hope in me,
trusting in my arm.

6   "Raise your eyes toward the skies,
look at the earth below.
The skies will vanish like smoke,
the earth will wear out like clothing.
Those living on it will die like flies;
but my salvation will be forever,
and my justice will never end.

7   "Listen to me, you who know justice,
you people who have my *Torah* in your heart:
don't be afraid of people's taunts,
don't be upset by their insults.

8   For the moth will eat them up like clothing,
the worm will eat them like wool;
but my justice will be forever,
and my salvation for all generations."

9   Awake! Awake! Arm of ADONAI,
clothe yourself with strength!
Awake, as in days of old,
as in ancient generations!
Wasn't it you who hacked Rahav to pieces,
you who pierced the sea monster?*

10   Wasn't it you who dried up the sea,
the waters of the great deep;
you who made the sea bottom a road
for the redeemed to cross?

11   Those ransomed by ADONAI will return
and come with singing to Tziyon;
on their heads will be everlasting joy.
They will acquire gladness and joy,
while sorrow and sighing will flee.

---

* Rahav symbolizes Egypt; the sea monster symbolizes Pharaoh

12   "I, yes I, am the one who comforts you!
    Why are you afraid of a man, who must die;
    of a human being, who will wither like grass?

13   You have forgotten ADONAI, your maker,
    who stretched out the heavens
    and laid the foundations of the earth.
    Instead, you are in constant fear all day
    because of the oppressor's rage,
    as he prepares to destroy!
    But where is the oppressor's rage?

14   The captive will soon be set free;
    he will not die and go down to Sh'ol;
    on the contrary, his food supply will be secure.

15   For I am ADONAI your God,
    who stirs up the sea, who makes its waves roar —
    ADONAI-Tzva'ot is my name.

16   I have put my words in your mouth
    and covered you with the shadow of my hand,
    in order to plant the skies [anew],
    lay the foundations of the earth [anew]
    and say to Tziyon, 'You are my people.'"

17   Awake! Awake! Stand up, Yerushalayim!
    At ADONAI's hand you drank the cup of his fury;
    you have drained to the dregs
    the goblet of drunkenness.

18   There is no one to guide her
    among all the sons she has borne.
    Not one of all the children she raised
    is taking her by the hand.

19   These two disasters have overcome you —
    yet who will grieve with you? —
    plunder and destruction, famine and sword;
    by whom can I comfort you?

20   Your children lie helpless at every street corner,
    like an antelope trapped in a net;
    they are full of ADONAI's fury,
    the rebuke of your God.

21   Therefore, please hear this in your affliction,
    you who are drunk, but not with wine;

22   this is what your Lord ADONAI says,
    your God, who defends his people:
    "Here, I have removed from your hand
    the cup of drunkenness,
    the goblet of my fury.
    You will never drink it again.

23   I will put it in the hands of your tormentors,

who said to you, 'Bend down, so we can trample you,'
and you flattened your back on the ground
like a street for them to walk on."

52 ¹ Awake! Awake, Tziyon!
Clothe yourself with your strength!
Dress in your splendid garments,
Yerushalayim, the holy city!
For the uncircumcised and the unclean
will enter you no more.

² Shake off the dust! Arise!
Be enthroned, Yerushalayim!
Loosen the chains on your neck,
captive daughter of Tziyon!

³ For thus says ADONAI:
"You were sold for nothing,
and you will be redeemed without money."

⁴ For thus says Adonai ELOHIM:
"Long ago my people went down to Egypt
to live there as aliens,
and Ashur oppressed them for no reason.

⁵ So now, what should I do here," asks ADONAI,
"since my people were carried off for nothing?
Their oppressors are howling," says ADONAI,
"and my name is always being insulted, daily.

⁶ Therefore my people will know my name;
therefore on that day they will know
that I, the one speaking — here I am!"

⁷ How beautiful on the mountains
are the feet of him who brings good news,
proclaiming *shalom*, bringing good news
of good things, announcing salvation
and saying to Tziyon, "Your God is King!"

⁸ Listen! Your watchmen are raising their voices,
shouting for joy together.
For they will see, before their own eyes,
ADONAI returning to Tziyon.

⁹ Break out into joy! Sing together,
you ruins of Yerushalayim!
For ADONAI has comforted his people,
he has redeemed Yerushalayim!

¹⁰ ADONAI has bared his holy arm
in the sight of every nation,
and all the ends of the earth will see
the salvation of our God.

11   Leave! Leave! Get out of there!
      Don't touch anything unclean!
      Get out from inside it, and be clean,
      you who carry ADONAI's temple equipment.

12   You need not leave in haste,
      you do not have to flee;
      for ADONAI will go ahead of you,
      and the God of Isra'el will also be behind you.

13   "See how my servant will succeed!
      He will be raised up, exalted, highly honored!

14   Just as many were appalled at him,
      because he was so disfigured
      that he didn't even seem human
      and simply no longer looked like a man,

15   so now he will startle many nations;
      because of him, kings will be speechless.
      For they will see what they had not been told,
      they will ponder things they had never heard."

53[1]   Who believes our report?
      To whom is the arm of ADONAI revealed?

2   For before him he grew up like a young plant,
      like a root out of dry ground.
      He was not well-formed or especially handsome;
      we saw him, but his appearance did not attract us.

3   People despised and avoided him,
      a man of pains, well acquainted with illness.
      Like someone from whom people turn their faces,
      he was despised; we did not value him.

4   In fact, it was our diseases he bore,
      our pains from which he suffered;
      yet we regarded him as punished,
      stricken and afflicted by God.

5   But he was wounded because of our crimes,
      crushed because of our sins;
      the disciplining that makes us whole fell on him,
      and by his bruises* we are healed.

6   We all, like sheep, went astray;
      we turned, each one, to his own way;
      yet ADONAI laid on him
      the guilt of all of us.

---

* Or: and in fellowship with him

7   Though mistreated, he was submissive —
    he did not open his mouth.
    Like a lamb led to be slaughtered,
    like a sheep silent before its shearers,
    he did not open his mouth.

8   After forcible arrest and sentencing,
    he was taken away;
    and none of his generation protested
    his being cut off from the land of the living
    for the crimes of my people,
    who deserved the punishment themselves.

9   He was given a grave among the wicked;
    in his death he was with a rich man.

    Although he had done no violence
    and had said nothing deceptive,

10   yet it pleased ADONAI to crush him with illness,
    to see if he would present himself as a guilt offering.
    If he does, he will see his offspring;
    and he will prolong his days;
    and at his hand ADONAI's desire
    will be accomplished.

11   After this ordeal, he will see satisfaction.
    "By his knowing [pain and sacrifice],
    my righteous servant makes many righteous;
    it is for their sins that he suffers.

12   Therefore I will assign him a share with the great,
    he will divide the spoil with the mighty,
    for having exposed himself to death
    and being counted among the sinners,
    while actually bearing the sin of many
    and interceding for the offenders."

54 1   "Sing, barren woman who has never had a child!
    Burst into song, shout for joy,
    you who have never been in labor!
    For the deserted wife will have more children
    than the woman who is living with her husband," says ADONAI.

2   Enlarge the space for your tent,
    extend the curtains of your dwelling;
    do not hold back, lengthen your cords,
    make your tent pegs firm.

3   For you will spread out to the right and the left,
    your descendants will possess the nations
    and inhabit the desolated cities.

4   Don't be afraid, for you won't be ashamed;
    don't be discouraged, for you won't be disgraced.

You will forget the shame of your youth,
no longer remember the dishonor of being widowed.
5 For your husband is your Maker,
ADONAI-*Tzva'ot* is his name.
The Holy One of Isra'el is your Redeemer.
He will be called the God of all the earth.
6 For ADONAI has called you back
like a wife abandoned and grief-stricken;
"A wife married in her youth
cannot be rejected," says your God.
7 "Briefly I abandoned you,
but with great compassion I am taking you back.
8 I was angry for a moment
and hid my face from you;
but with everlasting grace
I will have compassion on you,"
says ADONAI your Redeemer.
9 "For me this is like Noach's flood.
Just as I swore that no flood like Noach's
would ever again cover the earth,
so now I swear that never again
will I be angry with you or rebuke you.
10 For the mountains may leave and the hills be removed,
but my grace will never leave you,
and my covenant of peace will not be removed,"
says ADONAI, who has compassion on you.

11 "Storm-ravaged [city], unconsoled,
I will set your stones in the finest way,
lay your foundations with sapphires,
12 make your windows shine with rubies,
your gates with garnet, your walls with gemstones.
13 All your children will be taught by ADONAI;
your children will have great peace.
14 In righteousness you will be established,
far from oppression, with nothing to fear;
far from ruin, for it will not come near you.
15 Any alliance that forms against you
will not be my doing;
whoever tries to form such an alliance
will fall because of you.
16 It is I who created the craftsman
who blows on the coals and forges weapons
suited to their purpose;
I also created the destroyer to work havoc.
17 No weapon made will prevail against you.
In court you will refute every accusation.

The servants of *Adonai* inherit all this;
the reward for their righteousness is from me,"

says *Adonai*.

55 ¹ "All you who are thirsty, come to the water!
You without money, come, buy, and eat!
Yes, come! Buy wine and milk
without money — it's free!

² Why spend money for what isn't food,
your wages for what doesn't satisfy?
Listen carefully to me, and you will eat well,
you will enjoy the fat of the land.

³ Open your ears, and come to me;
listen well, and you will live —
I will make an everlasting covenant with you,
the grace I assured David.

⁴ I have given him as a witness to the peoples,
a leader and lawgiver for the peoples.

⁵ You will summon a nation you do not know,
and a nation that doesn't know you will run to you,
for the sake of *Adonai* your God,
the Holy One of Isra'el, who will glorify you."

⁶ Seek *Adonai* while he is available,
call on him while he is still nearby.

⁷ Let the wicked person abandon his way
and the evil person his thoughts;
let him return to *Adonai*,
and he will have mercy on him;
let him return to our God,
for he will freely forgive.

⁸ "For my thoughts are not your thoughts,
and your ways are not my ways," says *Adonai*.

⁹ "As high as the sky is above the earth
are my ways higher than your ways,
and my thoughts than your thoughts.

¹⁰ For just as rain and snow fall from the sky
and do not return there, but water the earth,
causing it to bud and produce,
giving seed to the sower and bread to the eater;

¹¹ so is my word that goes out from my mouth —
it will not return to me unfulfilled;
but it will accomplish what I intend,
and cause to succeed what I sent it to do."

¹² Yes, you will go out with joy,
you will be led forth in peace.
As you come, the mountains and hills
will burst out into song,
and all the trees in the countryside
will clap their hands.

¹³ Cypresses will grow in place of thorns,
myrtles will grow instead of briars.
This will bring fame to ADONAI
as an eternal, imperishable sign.

56 ¹ Here is what ADONAI says:

"Observe justice, do what is right,
for my salvation is close to coming,
my righteousness to being revealed."

² Happy is the person who does this,
anyone who grasps it firmly,
who keeps *Shabbat* and does not profane it,
and keeps himself from doing any evil.

³ A foreigner joining ADONAI should not say,
"ADONAI will separate me from his people";
likewise the eunuch should not say,
"I am only a dried-up tree."

⁴ For here is what ADONAI says:
"As for the eunuchs who keep my *Shabbat*s,
who choose what pleases me
and hold fast to my covenant:

⁵ in my house, within my walls,
I will give them power and a name
greater than sons and daughters;
I will give him an everlasting name
that will not be cut off.

⁶ "And the foreigners who join themselves to ADONAI
to serve him, to love the name of ADONAI,
and to be his workers,
all who keep *Shabbat* and do not profane it,
and hold fast to my covenant,

⁷ I will bring them to my holy mountain
and make them joyful in my house of prayer;
their burnt offerings and sacrifices
will be accepted on my altar;
for my house will be called
a house of prayer for all peoples."

8   *Adonai* E*LOHIM* says,
he who gathers Isra'el's exiles:
"There are yet others I will gather,
besides those gathered already."

9   All you wild animals, come and devour,
yes, all you animals in the forest!

10   [Isra'el's] watchmen are, all of them, blind;
they don't know anything.
They are all dumb dogs, unable to bark,
lying there dreaming, loving to sleep.

11   Greedy dogs, never satisfied —
such are the shepherds, unable to understand;
they all turn to their own way,
each one intent on his own gain:

12   "Come, I'll get some wine,
we'll fill up on good, strong liquor!
Tomorrow will be like today;
in fact, it will be even better!"

57 1   The righteous person perishes,
and nobody gives it a thought.
Godly men are taken away,
and no one understands
that the righteous person is taken away
from the evil yet to come.

2   Yes, those who live uprightly
will have peace as they rest on their couches.

3   "But you, you witches' children, come here,
you spawn of adulterers and whores!

4   Whom are you making fun of?
At whom are you laughing and sticking out your tongue?
Aren't you rebellious children,
just a brood of liars?

5   You go into heat among the oak trees,
under every spreading tree.
You kill the children in the valleys
under the cracks in the rocks.

6   Your place is among the smooth stones in the *vadi*;
these, these are what you deserve;
you pour out drink offerings to them,
you offer grain offerings to them.
Should I calmly ignore these things?

7   You set up your bed on a high, lofty mountain;
you also went up there to offer sacrifices.

8   Behind door and doorpost

you set up your [lewd] memorial;
then, far from me, you uncovered your bed,
climbed up on it and opened it wide,
made an agreement with some of them,
whose bed you loved when you saw their hand beckoning.

9 You went to the king with scented oil;
you added to your perfumes;
you sent your envoys far away,
even down to Sh'ol.

10 Though worn out by so much travel,
you did not say, 'All hope is gone';
rather, finding your strength renewed,
you did not grow weak.

11 Of whom have you been so afraid,
so fearful that you lied?
But me you don't remember,
you don't give me a thought!
I have held my peace so long
that you no longer fear me.

12 I will expose your [so-called] 'righteousness';
and what you have done won't help you.

13 When you cry, will those [idols] you gathered rescue you?
The wind will carry them all away,
a puff of air will take them off.
But whoever takes refuge in me will possess
the land and inherit my holy mountain."

14 Then he will say,

"Keep building! Keep building! Clear the way!
Remove everything blocking my people's path!"

15 For thus says the High, Exalted One
who lives forever, whose name is Holy:
"I live in the high and holy place
but also with the broken and humble,
in order to revive the spirit of the humble
and revive the hearts of the broken ones.

16 For I will not fight them forever
or always nurse my anger;
otherwise their spirits would faint before me,
the creatures I myself have made.

17 It was because of their flagrant greed
that I was angry and struck them;
I hid myself and was angry,
but they continued on their own rebellious way.

18 I have seen their ways, and I will heal them;
I will lead them and give comfort

to them and to those who mourn for them —

19 I will create the right words:
'*Shalom shalom* to those far off
and to those nearby!' says ADONAI;
'I will heal them!'"

20 But the wicked are like the restless sea —
unable to be still,
its waters toss up mud and dirt.

21 There is no *shalom*, says my God,
for the wicked.

58 1 Shout out loud! Don't hold back!
Raise your voice like a *shofar*!
Proclaim to my people what rebels they are,
to the house of Ya'akov their sins.

2 "Oh yes, they seek me day after day
and [claim to] delight in knowing my ways.
As if they were an upright nation
that had not abandoned the rulings of their God,
they ask me for just rulings
and [claim] to take pleasure in closeness to God,

3 [asking,] 'Why should we fast, if you don't see?
Why mortify ourselves, if you don't notice?'

"Here is my answer: when you fast,
you go about doing whatever you like,
while keeping your laborers hard at work.

4 Your fasts lead to quarreling and fighting,
to lashing out with violent blows.
On a day like today, fasting like yours
will not make your voice heard on high.

5 "Is this the sort of fast I want,
a day when a person mortifies himself?
Is the object to hang your head like a reed
and spread sackcloth and ashes under yourself?
Is this what you call a fast,
a day that pleases ADONAI?

6 "Here is the sort of fast I want —
releasing those unjustly bound,
untying the thongs of the yoke,
letting the oppressed go free,
breaking every yoke,

7 sharing your food with the hungry,

taking the homeless poor into your house,
clothing the naked when you see them,
fulfilling your duty to your kinsmen!"

8 Then your light will burst forth like the morning,
your new skin will quickly grow over your wound;
your righteousness will precede you,
and *Adonai*'s glory will follow you.

9 Then you will call, and *Adonai* will answer;
you will cry, and he will say, "Here I am."
If you will remove the yoke from among you,
stop false accusation and slander,

10 generously offer food to the hungry
and meet the needs of the person in trouble;
then your light will rise in the darkness,
and your gloom become like noon.

11 *Adonai* will always guide you;
he will satisfy your needs in the desert,
he will renew the strength in your limbs;
so that you will be like a watered garden,
like a spring whose water never fails.

12 You will rebuild the ancient ruins,
raise foundations from ages past,
and be called "Repairer of broken walls,
Restorer of streets to live in."

13 "If you hold back your foot on *Shabbat*
from pursuing your own interests on my holy day;
if you call *Shabbat* a delight,
Adonai's holy day, worth honoring;
then honor it by not doing your usual things
or pursuing your interests or speaking about them.

14 If you do, you will find delight in *Adonai* —
I will make you ride on the heights of the land
and feed you with the heritage of your ancestor Ya‘akov,
for the mouth of *Adonai* has spoken."

59 1 *Adonai*'s arm is not too short to save,
nor is his ear too dull to hear.

2 Rather, it is your own crimes
that separate you from your God;
your sins have hidden his face from you,
so that he doesn't hear.

3 For your hands are stained with blood
and your fingers with crime;
your lips speak lies,
your tongues utter wicked things.

4   No one sues with just cause,
    no one pleads honestly in court,
    they trust in empty words
    and say worthless things;
    they conceive trouble
    and give birth to evil.

5   They hatch viper eggs
    and spin spiderwebs;
    whoever eats their eggs dies,
    and the crushed egg hatches a snake.

6   Their webs are useless as clothing,
    their deeds are useless for wearing;
    their deeds are deeds of wickedness,
    their hands produce violence.

7   Their feet run to evil,
    they rush to shed innocent blood,
    their thoughts are thoughts of wickedness,
    their paths lead to havoc and ruin.

8   The way of *shalom* they do not know,
    their goings-about obey no law,
    they make devious paths for themselves;
    no one treading them will ever know *shalom.*

9   This is why justice is far from us,
    and righteousness doesn't catch up with us;
    we look for light, but see only darkness,
    for brightness, but we walk in gloom.

10   We grope for the wall like the blind;
    like people without eyes we feel our way;
    we stumble at noonday as if it were dusk,
    we are in dark places like the dead.

11   We growl, all of us, like bears
    and moan pitifully like doves;
    we look for justice, but there is none;
    for salvation, but it is far from us.

12   For our crimes multiply before you,
    our sins testify against us;
    for our crimes are present with us;
    and our sins, we know them well:

13   rebelling and denying ADONAI,
    turning away from following our God,
    talking about oppression and revolt,
    uttering lies which our hearts have conceived.

14   Thus justice is repelled,
    righteousness stands apart, at a distance;

for truth stumbles in the public court,
and uprightness cannot enter.

15 Honesty is lacking,
he who leaves evil becomes a target.

ADONAI saw it, and it displeased him
that there was no justice.

16 He saw that there was no one,
was amazed that no one interceded.
Therefore his own arm brought him salvation,
and his own righteousness sustained him.

17 He put on righteousness as his breastplate,
salvation as a helmet on his head;
he clothed himself with garments of vengeance
and wrapped himself in a mantle of zeal.

18 He repays according to their deeds —
fury to his foes, reprisal to his enemies;
to the coastlands he will repay their due;

19 in the west they will fear the name of ADONAI,
and likewise, in the east, his glory.

For he will come like a pent-up stream,
impelled by the Spirit of ADONAI.

20 "Then a Redeemer will come to Tziyon,
to those in Ya‘akov who turn from rebellion."
So says ADONAI.

21 "And as for me," says ADONAI,
"this is my covenant with them:
my Spirit, who rests on you,
and my words which I put in your mouth
will not depart from your mouth
or from the mouth of your children,
or from the mouth of your children's children,
now or ever," says ADONAI.

60 1 "Arise, shine [Yerushalayim],
for your light has come,
the glory of ADONAI
has risen over you.

2 For although darkness covers the earth
and thick darkness the peoples;
on you ADONAI will rise;
over you will be seen his glory.

3 Nations will go toward your light
and kings toward your shining splendor.

4 Raise your eyes and look around:
they are all assembling and coming to you;

your sons are coming from far off,
your daughters being carried on their nurses' hips.

5   Then you will see and be radiant,
your heart will throb and swell with delight;
for the riches of the seas will be brought to you,
the wealth of nations will come to you.

6   Caravans of camels will cover your land,
young camels from Midyan and 'Eifah,
all of them coming from Sh'va,
bringing gold and frankincense,
and proclaiming the praises of ADONAI.

7   All the flocks of Kedar will be gathered for you,
the rams of N'vayot will be at your service;
they will come up and be received on my altar,
as I glorify my glorious house.

8   "Who are these, flying along like clouds,
like doves to their dovecotes?

9   The coastlands are putting their hope in me,
with the 'Tarshish' ships in the lead,
to bring your children from far away,
and with them their silver and gold,
for the sake of ADONAI your God,
the Holy One of Isra'el, who glorifies you.

10   Foreigners will rebuild your walls,
their kings will be at your service;
for in my anger I struck you,
but in my mercy I pity you.

11   Your gates will always be open,
they will not be shut by day or by night,
so that people can bring you the wealth of nations,
with their kings led in procession.

12   For the nation or kingdom that won't serve you will perish;
yes, those nations will be utterly destroyed.

13   "The glory of the L'vanon will come to you,
cypresses together with elm trees and larches,
to beautify the site of my sanctuary —
I will glorify the place where I stand.

14   The children of your oppressors will come
and bow low before you,
all who despised you will fall at your feet,
calling you the city of ADONAI,
Tziyon of the Holy One of Isra'el.

15   "In the past you were abandoned and hated,
so that no one would even pass through you;

but now I will make you the pride of the ages,
a joy for many generations.

16 You will drink the milk of nations,
you will nurse at royal breasts
and know that I, ADONAI, am your Savior,
your Redeemer, the Mighty One of Ya'akov.

17 "For bronze I will bring you gold,
for iron I will bring you silver,
bronze in place of wood,
and iron in place of stones.
I will make *shalom* your governor
and righteousness your taskmaster.

18 Violence will no longer be heard in your land,
desolation or destruction within your borders;
instead, you will call your walls Salvation
and your gates Praise.

19 "No more will the sun be your light by day,
nor will moonlight shine on you;
instead ADONAI will be your light forever
and your God your glory.

20 No longer will your sun go down;
your moon will no longer wane;
for ADONAI will be your light forever;
your days of mourning will end.

21 All your people will be *tzaddikim*;
they will inherit the land forever;
they will be the branch I planted,
my handiwork, in which I take pride.

22 The smallest will grow to a thousand,
the weakest will become a mighty nation.
I, ADONAI, when the right time comes,
will quickly bring it about."

61 1 The Spirit of *Adonai* ELOHIM is upon me,
because ADONAI has anointed me
to announce good news to the poor.
He has sent me to heal the brokenhearted;
to proclaim freedom to the captives,
to let out into light those bound in the dark;

2 to proclaim the year of the favor of ADONAI
and the day of vengeance of our God;
to comfort all who mourn,

3 yes, provide for those in Tziyon who mourn,
giving them garlands instead of ashes,
the oil of gladness instead of mourning,

a cloak of praise instead of a heavy spirit,
so that they will be called oaks of righteousness
planted by ADONAI, in which he takes pride.

4 They will rebuild the ancient ruins,
restore sites long destroyed;
they will renew the ruined cities,
destroyed many generations ago.

5 Strangers will stand and feed your flocks,
foreigners plow your land and tend your vines;

6 but you will be called *cohanim* of ADONAI,
spoken of as ministers to our God.
You will feed on the wealth of nations,
and revel in their riches.

7 Because of your shame, which was doubled,
and because they cried, "They deserve disgrace,"
therefore in their land what they own will be doubled,
and joy forever will be theirs.

8 "For I, ADONAI, love justice;
I hate robbery for burnt offerings.
So I will be faithful to reward them
and make an eternal covenant with them."

9 Their descendants will be known among the nations,
their offspring among the peoples;
all who see them will acknowledge
that they are the seed ADONAI has blessed.

10 I am so joyful in ADONAI!
My soul rejoices in my God,
for he has clothed me in salvation,
dressed me with a robe of triumph,
like a bridegroom wearing a festive turban,
like a bride adorned with her jewels.

11 For just as the earth brings forth its plants,
or a garden makes its plants spring up,
so ADONAI, God, will cause victory and glory
to spring up before all nations.

62 1 For Tziyon's sake I will not be silent,
for Yerushalayim's sake I will not rest,
until her vindication shines out brightly
and her salvation like a blazing torch.

2 The nations will see your vindication
and all kings your glory.
Then you will be called by a new name
which ADONAI himself will pronounce.

3 You will be a glorious crown in the hand of ADONAI,
a royal diadem held by your God.

⁴ You will no longer be spoken of as 'Azuvah [Abandoned]
or your land be spoken of as 'Sh'mamah [Desolate];
rather, you will be called Heftzi-Vah [My-Delight-Is-In-Her]
and your land Be'ulah [Married].
For ADONAI delights in you,
and your land will be married —
⁵ as a young man marries a young woman,
your sons will marry you;
as a bridegroom rejoices over the bride,
your God will rejoice over you.

⁶ I have posted watchmen
on your walls, Yerushalayim;
they will never fall silent,
neither by day nor by night.
You who call on ADONAI,
give yourselves no rest;
⁷ and give him no rest till he restores Yerushalayim
and makes it a praise on earth.
⁸ ADONAI has sworn by his right hand
and by his mighty arm:
"Never again will I give your grain
to your enemies as food;
nor will strangers drink your wine,
for which you worked so hard;
⁹ but those who harvest the grain will eat it
with praises to ADONAI;
those who gathered the wine will drink it
in the courtyards of my sanctuary."

¹⁰ Go on through, go on through the gates,
clear the way for the people!
Build up a highway, build it up!
Clear away the stones!
Raise a banner for the peoples!
¹¹ ADONAI has proclaimed to the end of the earth,
"Say to the daughter of Tziyon,
'Here, your Salvation is coming!
Here, his reward is with him,
and his recompense is before him.'"
¹² They will call them The Holy People,
The Redeemed of ADONAI.
You will be called D'rushah [Sought-After],
'Ir Lo Ne'ezvah [City-No-Longer-Abandoned].

63 ¹ Who is this, coming from Edom,
from Botzrah with clothing stained crimson,

so magnificently dressed,
so stately in his great strength?

"It is I, who speak victoriously,
I, well able to save."

2 Why is your apparel red,
your clothes like someone treading a winepress?

3 "I have trodden the winepress alone;
from the peoples, not one was with me.
So I trod them in my anger,
trampled them in my fury;
so their lifeblood spurted out on my clothing,
and I have stained all my garments;

4 for the day of vengeance that was in my heart
and my year of redemption have come.

5 I looked, but there was no one to help,
and I was appalled that no one upheld me.
Therefore my own arm brought me salvation,
and my own fury upheld me.

6 In my anger I trod down the peoples,
made them drunk with my fury,
then poured out their lifeblood on the earth."

7 I will recall the grace of ADONAI
and the praises of ADONAI,
because of all that ADONAI has granted us
and his great goodness toward the house of Isra'el,
which he bestowed on them in keeping with his mercy,
in keeping with the greatness of his grace.

8 For he said, "They are indeed my people,
children who are not disloyal."
So he became their Savior.

9 In all their troubles he was troubled;
then the Angel of His Presence saved them;
in his love and pity he redeemed them.

He had lifted them up and carried them
throughout the days of old.

10 However, they rebelled,
they grieved his Holy Spirit;
so he became their enemy
and himself fought against them.

11 But then his people remembered
the days of old, the days of Moshe:

"Where is he who brought them up from the sea
with the shepherds of his flock?
Where is he who put his Holy Spirit
right there among them,
12   who caused his glorious arm to go
at Moshe's right hand?
He divided the water ahead of them,
to make himself an eternal name;
13   he led them through the deep
like a sure-footed horse through the desert;
14   like cattle going down into a valley
the Spirit of ADONAI had them rest.
This is how you led your people,
to make yourself a glorious name."

15   Look down from heaven; and see
from your holy, glorious dwelling.
Where are your zeal and your mighty deeds,
your inner concern and compassion?
Don't hold back, ¹⁶ for you are our father.
Even if Avraham were not to know us,
and Isra'el were not to acknowledge us,
you, ADONAI, are our father,
Our Redeemer of Old is your name.

17   ADONAI, why do you let us wander from your ways
and harden our hearts, so that we do not fear you?
Return, for the sake of your servants,
the tribes who are your possession.
18   Your holy people held your sanctuary such a short time,
before our adversaries trampled it down.
19   For so long we have been like those you never ruled,
like those who were not called by your name!

(64:1)   We wish you would tear open heaven and come down,
so the mountains would shake at your presence!

64 ¹⁽²⁾   It would be like fire kindling the brush,
and the fire then makes the water boil.
Then your enemies would know your name,
the nations would tremble before you!
2(3)   When you did tremendous things
that we were not expecting,
we wished that you would come down,
so that the mountains would shake at your presence!
3(4)   No one has ever heard,
no ear perceived, no eye seen,

any God but you.
You work for him who waits for you.

4(5) You favored those who were glad to do justice,
those who remembered you in your ways.
When you were angry, we kept sinning;
but if we keep your ancient ways, we will be saved.

5(6) All of us are like someone unclean,
all our righteous deeds like menstrual rags;
we wither, all of us, like leaves;
and our misdeeds blow us away like the wind.

6(7) No one calls on your name
or bestirs himself to take hold of you,
for you have hidden your face from us
and caused our misdeeds to destroy us.

7(8) But now, ADONAI, you are our father;
we are the clay, you are our potter;
and we are all the work of your hands.

8(9) Do not be so very angry, ADONAI!
Don't remember crime forever.
Look, please, we are all your people.

9(10) Your holy cities have become a desert,
Tziyon a desert, Yerushalayim a ruin.

10(11) Our holy, beautiful house,
where our ancestors used to praise you,
has been burned to the ground;
all we cherished has been ruined.

11(12) ADONAI, after all this,
will you still hold back?
Will you still stay silent
and punish us past endurance?

65 ¹ "I made myself accessible
to those who didn't ask for me,
I let myself be found
by those who didn't seek me.
I said, 'Here I am! Here I am!'
to a nation not called by my name.

2 I spread out my hands all day long
to a rebellious people
who live in a way that is not good,
who follow their own inclinations;

3 a people who provoke me to my face all the time,
sacrificing in gardens and burning incense on bricks.

4 They sit among the graves
and spend the night in caverns;
they eat pig meat

and their pots hold soup made from disgusting things.

5 They say, 'Keep your distance, don't come near me,
because I am holier than you.'
These are smoke in my nose,
a fire that burns all day!

6 See, it is written before me;
I will not be silent until I repay them;
I will repay them to the full,

7 your own crimes and those of your ancestors together,"

says ADONAI.

"They offered incense on the mountains
and insulted me on the hills.
First I will measure out their wages
and then repay them in full."

8 Here is what ADONAI says:
"As when juice is found in a cluster of grapes,
and people say, 'Don't destroy it,
there is still some good in it,'
so I will do likewise for the sake of my servants,
and not destroy them all.

9 I will bring forth descendants from Ya'akov,
heirs of my mountains from Y'hudah;
my chosen ones will possess them,
and my servants will live there.

10 The Sharon will be a pasture for flocks,
the Akhor Valley a place for cattle to rest,
for my people who have sought me.

11 "But as for you who abandon ADONAI,
who forget my holy mountain,
who prepare a table for Gad, a god of luck,
and fill bowls of mixed wine for Meni, a god of destiny —

12 I will destine you to the sword,
you will all bow down to be slaughtered;
because when I called, you did not answer;
when I spoke, you did not hear,
but did what was evil from my point of view
and chose what did not please me."

13 Therefore this is what Adonai ELOHIM says:

"My servants will eat, while you go hungry;
my servants will drink, while you go thirsty.
My servants will rejoice,

while you will be ashamed.
14 Yes, my servants will sing for joy from their hearts,
but you will cry out from the pain in your heart
and howl from an anguished spirit.
15 My chosen will use your name as a curse —
'May *Adonai Elohim* strike you dead!'
But to his servants he will give another name.
16 Thus someone on earth who blesses himself
will bless himself by the God of truth,
and someone on earth who swears an oath
will swear by the God of truth;
for past troubles will be forgotten,
hidden from my eyes.

17 "For, look! I create new heavens
and a new earth;
past things will not be remembered,
they will no more come to mind.
18 So be glad and rejoice forever
in what I am creating;
for look! I am making Yerushalayim a joy,
and her people a delight.
19 I will rejoice in Yerushalayim
and take joy in my people.
The sound of weeping will no longer be heard in it,
no longer the sound of crying.
20 No more will babies die in infancy,
no more will an old man die short of his days —
he who dies at a hundred will be thought young,
and at less than a hundred thought cursed.
21 They will build houses and live in them,
they will plant vineyards and eat their fruit.
22 They will not build and others live there,
they will not plant and others eat;
for the days of my people
will be like the days of a tree,
and my chosen will themselves enjoy
the use of what they make.
23 They will not toil in vain
or raise children to be destroyed,
for they are the seed blessed by *Adonai*;
and their offspring with them.
24 Before they call, I will answer;
while they are still speaking, I will hear.
25 The wolf and the lamb will feed together,
and the lion eat straw like an ox
(but the serpent — its food will be dust).

They will not hurt or destroy
anywhere on my holy mountain,"

says ADONAI.

66 ¹ "Heaven is my throne," says ADONAI,
"and the earth is my footstool.
What kind of house could you build for me?
What sort of place could you devise for my rest?
² Didn't I myself make all these things?
This is how they all came to be,"

says ADONAI.

"The kind of person on whom I look with favor
is one with a poor and humble spirit,
who trembles at my word.
³ Those others might as well kill a person as an ox,
as well break a dog's neck as sacrifice a lamb,
as well offer pig's blood as offer a grain offering,
as well bless an idol as burn incense.
Just as these have chosen their ways
and enjoy their disgusting practices,
⁴ so I will enjoy making fools of them,
and bring on them the very things they fear.
For when I called, no one answered;
when I spoke, they did not hear.
Instead they did what was evil in my sight
and chose what did not please me."

⁵ Hear the word of ADONAI,
you who tremble at his word:
"Your brothers, who hate you and reject you
because of my name, have said:
'Let ADONAI be glorified,
so we can see your joy.'
But they will be put to shame."
⁶ That uproar in the city,
that sound from the temple,
is the sound of ADONAI repaying
his foes what they deserve.

⁷ Before going into labor, she gave birth;
before her pains came, she delivered a male child.
⁸ Who ever heard of such a thing?
Who has ever seen such things?
Is a country born in one day?

Is a nation brought forth all at once?
For as soon as Tziyon went into labor,
she brought forth her children.

9 "Would I let the baby break through
and not be born?" asks ADONAI.
"Would I, who cause the birth,
shut the womb?" asks your God.

10 Rejoice with Yerushalayim!
Be glad with her, all you who love her!
Rejoice, rejoice with her,
all of you who mourned for her;

11 so that you nurse and are satisfied
by her comforting breast,
drinking deeply and delighting
in the overflow of her glory.

12 For ADONAI says, "I will spread *shalom*
over her like a river,
and the wealth of nations
like a flooding stream;
you will nurse and be carried in her arm
and cuddled in her lap.

13 Like someone comforted by his mother,
I will comfort you;
in Yerushalayim
you will be comforted."

14 Your heart will rejoice at the sight,
your bodies will flourish like newly sprouted grass.
It will be known that the hand of ADONAI
is with his servants; but with his enemies, his fury.

15 For — look! — ADONAI will come in fire,
and his chariots will be like the whirlwind,
to render his anger furiously,
his rebuke with blazing fire.

16 For ADONAI will judge all humanity
with fire and with the sword,
and those slain by ADONAI will be many.

17 "Those who consecrate and purify themselves
in order to enter the gardens,
then follow the one who was already there,
eating pig meat, reptiles and mice,
will all be destroyed together," says ADONAI.

18 "For I [know] their deeds and their thoughts.

542

"[The time] is coming when I will gather together all nations and languages. They will come and see my glory, ¹⁹ and I will give them a sign. I will send some of their survivors to the nations of Tarshish, Pul, Lud (these are archers), Tuval, Greece and more distant coasts, where they have neither heard of my fame nor seen my glory. They will proclaim my glory in these nations; ²⁰ and they will bring all your kinsmen out of all the nations as an offering to ADONAI — on horses, in chariots, in wagons, on mules, on camels — to my holy mountain Yerushalayim," says ADONAI, "just as the people of Isra'el themselves bring their offerings in clean vessels to the house of ADONAI. ²¹ I will also take *cohanim* and *L'vi'im* from them," says ADONAI.

²² "For just as the new heavens and the new earth that I am making will continue in my presence," says ADONAI, "so will your descendants and your name continue.

²³ "Every month on *Rosh-Hodesh*
and every week on *Shabbat*,
everyone living will come
to worship in my presence," says ADONAI.
²⁴ "As they leave, they will look on the corpses
of the people who rebelled against me.
For their worm will never die,
and their fire will never be quenched;
but they will be abhorrent
to all humanity."

["Every month on *Rosh-Hodesh*
and every week on *Shabbat*,
everyone living will come
to worship in my presence," says ADONAI.]

Yirmeyahu
JEREMIAH

1 ¹ These are the words of Yirmeyahu the son of Hilkiyahu, one of the *cohanim* living in 'Anatot, in the territory of Binyamin. ² The word of ADONAI came to him during the days of Yoshiyahu the son of Amon, king of Y'hudah, in the thirteenth year of his reign. ³ It also came during the days of Y'hoyakim the son of Yoshiyahu, king of Y'hudah, continuing until the eleventh year of Tzidkiyahu the son of Yoshiyahu, king of Y'hudah, right up until the time Yerushalayim was carried away captive, in the fifth month.

⁴ Here is the word of ADONAI that came to me:

⁵   "Before I formed you in the womb, I knew you;
      before you were born, I separated you for myself.
      I have appointed you to be a prophet to the nations."

⁶ I said, "Oh, *Adonai ELOHIM*, I don't even know how to speak! I'm just a child!" ⁷ But ADONAI said to me, "Don't say, 'I'm just a child.'

      "For you will go to whomever I send you,
      and you will speak whatever I order you.
⁸   Do not be afraid of them,
      for I am with you, says ADONAI,
      to rescue you."

⁹ Then ADONAI put out his hand and touched my mouth, and ADONAI said to me,

      "There! I have put my words in your mouth.
¹⁰   Today I have placed you over nations and kingdoms
      to uproot and to tear down,
      to destroy and to demolish,
      to build and to plant."

¹¹ The word of ADONAI came to me, asking, "Yirmeyahu, what do you see?" I answered, "I see a branch from an almond tree [Hebrew: *shaked*]. ¹² Then ADONAI said to me, "You have seen well, because I am watching [Hebrew: *shoked*] to fulfill my word."

¹³ A second time the word of ADONAI came to me, asking, "What do you see?" I answered, "I see a caldron tilted away from the north, over a fire fanned by the wind." ¹⁴ Then ADONAI said to me, "From the north calamity will boil over onto

everyone living in the land, ¹⁵ because I will summon all the families in the kingdoms of the north," says ADONAI,

> "and they will come and sit, each one, on his throne
> at the entrance to the gates of Yerushalayim,
> opposite its walls, all the way around,
> and opposite all the cities of Y'hudah.

¹⁶
> I will pronounce my judgments against them
> for all their wickedness in abandoning me,
> offering incense to other gods
> and worshipping what their own hands made.

¹⁷
> "But you, dress for action; stand up and tell them
> everything I order you to say.
> When you confront them, don't break down;
> or I will break you down in front of them!

¹⁸
> For today, you see, I have made you into
> a fortified city, a pillar of iron,
> a wall of bronze against the whole land —
> against the kings of Y'hudah, against its princes,
> against its *cohanim* and the people of the land.

¹⁹
> They will fight against you,
> but they will not overcome you,
> for I am with you," says ADONAI,
> "to rescue you."

2 ¹ The word of ADONAI came to me: ² "Go and shout in the ears of Yerushalayim that this is what ADONAI says:

> 'I remember your devotion when you were young;
> how, as a bride, you loved me;
> how you followed me through the desert,
> through a land not sown.

³
> "'Isra'el is set aside for ADONAI,
> the firstfruits of his harvest;
> all who devour him will incur guilt;
> evil will befall them," says ADONAI.

⁴
> Hear the word of ADONAI, house of Ya'akov
⁵
> and all families in the house of Isra'el;
> here is what ADONAI says:

> "What did your ancestors find wrong with me
> to make them go so far away from me,
> to make them go after nothings
> and become themselves nothings?

6   They didn't ask, 'Where is *Adonai*,
     who brought us out of the land of Egypt,
     who led us through the desert,
     through a land of wastes and ravines,
     through a land of drought and death-dark shadows,
     through a land where no one travels
     and where no one ever lived?'

7   I brought you into a fertile land
     to enjoy its fruit and all its good things;
     but when you entered, you defiled my land
     and made my heritage loathsome.

8   The *cohanim* didn't ask, 'Where is *Adonai*?'
     Those who deal with the *Torah* did not know me,
     the people's shepherds rebelled against me;
     the prophets prophesied by Ba'al
     and went after things of no value.

9   "So again I state my case against you," says *Adonai*,
     "and state it against your grandchildren too.

10   Cross to the coasts of the Kitti'im and look;
     send to Kedar and observe closely;
     see if anything like this has happened before:

11   has a nation ever exchanged its gods
     (and theirs are not gods at all!)?
     Yet my people have exchanged their Glory
     for something without value.

12   Be aghast at this, you heavens!
     Shudder in absolute horror!" says *Adonai*.

13   "For my people have committed two evils:
     they have abandoned me,
     the fountain of living water,
     and dug themselves cisterns, broken cisterns,
     that can hold no water!

14   "Is Isra'el a slave, born into serfdom?
     If not, why has he become plunder?

15   The young lions are roaring at him —
     how loudly they are roaring!
     They desolate his country,
     demolishing and depopulating his cities.

16   The people of Nof and Tachpanches
     feed on the crown of your head.

17   "Haven't you brought this on yourself
     by abandoning *Adonai* your God
     when he led you along the way?

18   If you go to Egypt, what's in it for you?

Drinking water from the Nile?
If you go to Ashur, what's in it for you?
Drinking water from the [Euphrates] River?

19   Your own wickedness will correct you,
your own backslidings will convict you;
you will know and see how bad and bitter
it was to abandon *Adonai* your God,
and how fear of me is not in you,"
says *Adonai Elohim-Tzva'ot*.

20   "For long ago I broke your yoke;
when I snapped your chains, you said, 'I won't sin.'
Yet on every high hill, under every green tree,
you sprawled and prostituted yourself.

21   But I planted you as a choice vine
of seed fully tested and true.
How did you degenerate
into a wild vine for me?

22   Even if you scrub yourself
with soda and plenty of soap,
the stain of your guilt is still there before me,"
says *Adonai Elohim*.

23   "How can you say, 'I am not defiled,
I have not pursued the *ba'alim*'?
Look at your conduct in the valley,
understand what you have done.
You are a restive young female camel,
running here and there,

24   wild, accustomed to the desert,
sniffing the wind in her lust —
who can control her when she's in heat?
Males seeking her need not weary themselves,
for at mating season they will find her.

25   "Stop before your shoes wear out,
and your throat is dry from thirst!
But you say, 'No, it's hopeless!
I love these strangers, and I'm going after them.'

26   Just as a thief is ashamed when caught,
so is the house of Isra'el ashamed —
they, their kings, their leaders,
their *cohanim* and their prophets,

27   who say to a log, 'You are my father,'
and to a stone, 'You gave us birth.'
For they have turned their backs to me
instead of their faces.

But when trouble comes, they will plead,
'Rouse yourself and save us!'
28 Where are your gods that you made for yourselves?
Let them rouse themselves,
if they can save you when trouble comes.
Y'hudah, you have as many gods
as you have cities!
29 Why argue with me? You have all
rebelled against me!" says ADONAI.

30 "In vain have I struck down your people.
They would not receive correction.
Your own sword has devoured your prophets
like a marauding lion.
31 You of this generation,
look at the word of ADONAI:
Have I been a desert to Isra'el?
or a land of oppressive darkness?
Why do my people say, 'We're free to roam,
we will no longer come to you'?
32 Does a girl forget her jewellery,
or a bride her wedding sash?
Yet my people have forgotten me,
days beyond numbering.
33 You are so clever in your search for love
that the worst of women can learn from you!
34 Right there on your clothing
is the blood of the innocent poor,
although you never caught them breaking and entering.
Yet concerning all these things,
35 you say, 'I am innocent;
surely he's no longer angry at me.'
Here, I am passing sentence on you,
because you say, 'I have done nothing wrong.'
36 You cheapen yourself
when you change course so often —
you will be disappointed by Egypt too,
just as you were disappointed by Ashur.
37 Yes, you will leave him too,
with your hands on your heads [in shame].
For ADONAI rejects those in whom you trust;
from them you will gain nothing."

3 ¹ [ADONAI] says:

"If a man divorces his wife,
and she leaves him and marries another man,

then if the first one marries her again,
that land will be completely defiled.
But you prostituted yourself to many lovers,
yet you want to return to me?" says ADONAI.

2 "Raise your eyes to the bare hills, take a look:
where have you not had sex?
You sat by the roadsides waiting for them
like a nomad in the desert.
You have defiled the land
with your prostitution and wickedness.

3 For this reason the showers have been withheld,
there has been no rain in the spring;
still you maintain a whore's brazen look
and refuse to be ashamed.

4 Didn't you just now cry to me,
'My father, you are my friend from my youth'? —

5 [thinking,] 'He won't bear a grudge forever, will he?
He wouldn't maintain it right to the end.'
You say this, but you keep doing evil things,
you just do whatever you want.'"

⁶ In the days of Yoshiyahu the king, ADONAI asked me, "Have you seen the things that backsliding Isra'el has been doing? She goes up on every bare hill and under every green tree and prostitutes herself there. ⁷ I said that after she had done all these things, she would return to me; but she hasn't returned. Meanwhile, her unfaithful sister Y'hudah has been watching. ⁸ I saw that even though backsliding Isra'el had committed adultery, so that I had sent her away and given her a divorce document, unfaithful Y'hudah her sister was not moved to fear — instead she too went and prostituted herself. ⁹ The ease with which Isra'el prostituted herself defiled the land, as she committed adultery with stones and with logs. ¹⁰ Yet in spite of all this, her unfaithful sister Y'hudah has not returned to me wholeheartedly; she only makes a pretense of it," said ADONAI.

¹¹ Then ADONAI said to me, "Backsliding Isra'el has proved herself more righteous than unfaithful Y'hudah. ¹² Go and proclaim these words toward the north:

'"Return, backsliding Isra'el," says ADONAI.
"I will not frown on you, for I am merciful," says ADONAI.
"I will not bear a grudge forever.

13 Only acknowledge your guilt,
that you have committed crimes
against ADONAI your God,
that you were promiscuous with strangers
under every green tree,
and that you have not paid attention
to my voice," says ADONAI.

14 "Return, backsliding children," says ADONAI;
"for I am your master.

I will take you, one from a city,
two from a family, and bring you to Tziyon.

15   I will give you shepherds
after my own heart,
and they will feed you
with knowledge and understanding.

16 "'And," says ADONAI, "in those days, when your numbers have increased in the land, people will no longer talk about the ark for the covenant of ADONAI — they won't think about it, they won't miss it, and they won't make another one. 17 When that time comes, they will call Yerushalayim the throne of ADONAI. All the nations will be gathered there to the name of ADONAI, to Yerushalayim. No longer will they live according to their stubbornly evil hearts. 18 In those days, the house of Y'hudah will live together with the house of Isra'el; they will come together from the lands in the north to the land I gave your ancestors as their heritage.

19 "'I thought that I would like to put you among the sons [with inheritance rights] and give you a pleasant land, the best heritage of all the nations. I thought that you would call me 'My father' and never stop following me. 20 But like a faithless woman who betrays her husband, you, house of Isra'el, have betrayed me," says ADONAI.'"

21   A sound is heard on the heights,
the house of Isra'el crying, pleading for mercy,
because they have perverted their way
and forgotten ADONAI their God.

22   "Return, backsliding children,
and I will heal your backsliding."

"Here we are, we are coming to you,
for you are ADONAI our God.

23   Indeed the hills have proved a delusion,
likewise the orgies on the mountains.
Truly the salvation of Isra'el
is in ADONAI our God.

24   But from our youth the shameful thing [idolatry]
has devoured the fruit of our ancestors' work,
their flocks and herds, their sons and daughters.

25   Let us lie down in our shame,
let our disgrace cover us,
for we have sinned against ADONAI our God,
both we and our ancestors,
from our youth until today;
we have not paid attention
to the voice of ADONAI our God."

4 1   "Isra'el, if you will return," says ADONAI,
"yes, return to me; and if you will banish

your abominations from my presence
without wandering astray again;

2 and if you will swear, 'As ADONAI lives,'
in truth, justice and righteousness;
then the nations will bless themselves by him,
and in him will they glory."

3 For here is what ADONAI says
to the people of Y'hudah and Yerushalayim:
"Break up your ground that hasn't been plowed,
and do not sow among thorns."

4 "People of Y'hudah and inhabitants of Yerushalayim,
circumcise yourselves for ADONAI,
remove the foreskins of your heart!
Otherwise my fury will lash out like fire,
burning so hot that no one can quench it,
because of how evil your actions are.

5 "Announce in Y'hudah, proclaim in Yerushalayim;
say: 'Blow the *shofar* in the land!'
Shout the message aloud: 'Assemble!
Let us go to the fortified cities!'

6 Set up a signal toward Tziyon,
head for cover without delay.
For I will bring disaster from the north,
yes, dire destruction.

7 A lion has risen from his lair,
a destroyer of nations has set out,
left his own place to ruin your land,
to demolish and depopulate your cities."

8 So wrap yourselves in sackcloth,
lament and wail, for ADONAI's fierce anger
has not turned away from us.

9 "When that day comes," says ADONAI,
"the king's heart will fail him,
likewise the princes';
the *cohanim* will be appalled
and the prophets stupefied."

10 Then I said, "Oh, Adonai ELOHIM! Surely you have sadly deceived this people and Yerushalayim by saying, 'You will have peace,' when the sword is at our very throats!"

11 "At that time it will be said
of this people and of Yerushalayim:

'A scorching wind from the desert heights
is sweeping down on my people.'
It is not coming to winnow or cleanse;

12 this wind of mine is too strong for that.
Now I will pass sentence on them."

13 Here he comes, like the clouds,
his chariots like the whirlwind,
his horses faster than eagles!
Woe to us, we are doomed!

14 Wash the evil from your heart, Yerushalayim,
so that you can be saved.
How long will you harbor within yourselves
your evil thoughts?

15 For a voice is announcing the news from Dan,
proclaiming disaster from the hills of Efrayim:

16 "Report it to the nations,
proclaim about Yerushalayim:
'[Enemies] are coming from a distant country,
watching and shouting their war cry
against the cities of Y'hudah.'

17 Like guards in a field they surround her,
because she has rebelled against me," says ADONAI.

18 "Your own ways and your actions
have brought these things on yourselves.
This is your wickedness, so bitter!
It has reached your very heart."

19 My guts! My guts! I'm writhing in pain!
My heart! It beats wildly — I can't stay still! —
because I have heard the *shofar* sound;
it's the call to war.

20 The news is disaster after disaster!
All the land is ruined!
My tents are suddenly destroyed,
my tent curtains in an instant.

21 How long must I see that signal
and hear the *shofar* sound?

22 "It is because my people are foolish —
they do not know me; they are stupid children,
without understanding, wise when doing evil;
but they don't know how to do good."

23 I looked at the land — it was unformed and void —
and at the sky — it had no light.

552

24 I looked at the mountains, and they shook —
all the hills moved back and forth.

25 I looked, and there was no human being;
all the birds in the air had fled.

26 I looked, and the fertile fields were a desert,
all the land's cities were razed to the ground
at the presence of ADONAI,
before his burning anger.

27 For here is what ADONAI says:

"The whole land will be desolate
(although I will not destroy it completely).

28 Because of this, the land will mourn
and the sky above be black;
for I have spoken, I have decided,
I will not change my mind, I will not turn back."

29 At the noise of the horsemen and archers,
the entire city flees —
some plunge into thickets; others climb rocks;
all cities are deserted; no one lives there.

30 And you, who are doomed to be plundered,
what do you mean by putting on crimson,
decking yourselves with jewels and gold,
enlarging your eyes with eye make-up?
You beautify yourself in vain —
your lovers despise you, they seek your life!

31 For I have heard a sound like a woman in labor,
in anguish giving birth to her first child.
It is the sound of the daughter of Tziyon
gasping for breath as she spreads her hands:
"Woe to me! Everything in me
is so weary before the killers."

5 1 "Roam the streets of Yerushalayim
look around, observe and ask in its open spaces:
if you can find anyone (if there is anyone!)
who acts with justice and seeks the truth,
I will pardon her.

2 And though they say, 'As ADONAI lives,'
the fact is that they are swearing falsely."

3 ADONAI, your eyes look for truth.
You struck them, but they weren't affected;
you [nearly] destroyed them,
but they refused correction.

They made their faces harder than rock,
refusing to repent.

4   My reaction was, "These must be the poor,
the foolish, not knowing the way of ADONAI
or the rulings of their God.

5   I will go to the prominent men,
and I will speak to them;
for they know the way of ADONAI
and the rulings of their God."
But these had completely broken the yoke
and torn the harness off.

6   This is why a forest lion kills them,
why a desert wolf can plunder them,
why a leopard guards their cities —
all who leave are torn to pieces —
because their crimes are many,
their backslidings keep increasing.

7   "Why should I forgive you?
Your people have abandoned me
and sworn by non-gods.
When I fed them to the full,
they committed adultery,
thronging to the brothels.

8   They have become like well-fed horses,
lusty stallions, each one neighing
after his neighbor's wife.

9   Should I not punish for this?" asks ADONAI.
"Should I not be avenged on a nation like this?"

10   Go through her rows [of vines], and destroy them
(but don't destroy them completely):
strip away her branches,
they do not belong to ADONAI.

11   "For the house of Isra'el
and the house of Y'hudah
have thoroughly betrayed me," says ADONAI.

12   They have denied ADONAI,
they have said, "He won't do anything,
calamity will not strike us,
we will see neither sword nor famine.

13   The prophets are merely wind,
they do not have the word;
the things that they are predicting
will happen only to them."

¹⁴ Therefore *ADONAI Elohei-Tzva'ot* says:

> "Because you people speak this way,
> I will make my words fire in your mouth, [Yirmeyahu,]
> and this people wood;
> so that it will devour them.

¹⁵ I will bring on you, house of Isra'el,
> a distant nation," says *ADONAI*,
> "an enduring nation, an ancient nation,
> a nation whose language you do not know —
> you will not understand what they are saying.

¹⁶ Their quiver is like an open grave,
> they are all mighty warriors.

¹⁷ They will eat up your harvest and your bread,
> they will eat up your sons and your daughters,
> they will eat up your flocks and your herds,
> they will eat up your vines and your fig trees;
> with the sword they will beat down
> your fortified cities, in which you trust.

¹⁸ But even in those days," says *ADONAI*,
> "I will not completely destroy you.

¹⁹ And when your people ask, 'Why has *ADONAI*
> our God done all these things to us?'
> you are to give them this answer:
> 'Just as you abandoned me
> and served strange gods in your own land,
> so likewise you will serve strangers
> in a land that is not your own.'

²⁰ Announce this in the house of Ya'akov,
> proclaim it in Y'hudah; say:

²¹ 'Hear this, stupid, brainless people,
> who have eyes but do not see,
> who have ears but do not hear:

²² Don't you fear me? — says *ADONAI*.
> Won't you tremble at my presence?
> I made the shore the limit for the sea;
> by eternal decree it cannot pass.
> Its waves may toss, but to no avail;
> although they roar, they cannot cross it.

²³ But this people has a rebellious, defiant heart;
> they have rebelled and gone!

²⁴ They don't say to themselves,
> "Let's fear *ADONAI* our God,
> who gives the fall and spring rains in season,
> who reserves us the weeks assigned for harvest."

²⁵ Your crimes have overturned nature's rules,
> your sins have kept back good from you.'

555

26   "For among my people there are wicked men,
who, like fowlers, lie in wait and set traps
to catch their fellow human beings.

27   Their houses are as full of fraud
as a cage full of birds.
They grow rich and great, ²⁸ sleek and bloated;
they excel in acts of wickedness
but do not plead on behalf of the orphan,
thus enabling his cause to succeed;
nor do they judge in favor of the poor.

29   "Should I not punish for this?" asks ADONAI.
"Should I not be avenged on a nation like this?

30   A shocking and horrifying thing
has happened in the land:

31   The prophets prophesy lies,
the *cohanim* obey the prophets,
and my people love it that way.
But what will you do at the end of it all?

6 ¹   "Head for cover, people of Binyamin,
get out of Yerushalayim!
Blow the *shofar* in T'koa,
light the beacon on Beit-Hakerem.
For disaster threatens from the north,
with great destruction.

2   Although she is beautiful and delicate,
I am cutting off the daughter of Tziyon."

3   Shepherds advance on her with their flocks;
all around her they pitch their tents,
each grazing his own plot of pasture.

4   "Prepare for war against her!
Get up! Let's attack at noon!"
"Woe to us! for the day is waning,
evening shadows are lengthening."

5   "Get up! Let's attack at night!
Let's destroy her palaces!"

⁶ For ADONAI-*Tzva'ot* says this:

"Cut down her trees, and raise a siege-ramp
against Yerushalayim!
This is the city to be punished;
in her there is nothing but oppression.

7   Just as a cistern keeps its water fresh,
so she keeps her wickedness fresh!

Violence and destruction are heard within her,
always before me sickness and wounds.

8 Accept correction, Yerushalayim,
or I will be estranged from you
and turn you into a desolate waste,
a land without inhabitants."

9 Thus says ADONAI-Tzva'ot:

"They will glean the remnant of Isra'el
as thoroughly as in a vineyard —
one last time, like a grape-picker,
pass your hand over the vines."

10 To whom should I speak? Whom should I warn?
Who will listen to me?
Their ears are dull, they can't pay attention.
For them the word of ADONAI has become
unattractive, an object of scorn.

11 This is why I am full of ADONAI's fury;
I am weary of holding it back.

"Pour it out on the children in the street
and on the groups of young men gathered;
for husbands and wives will be taken together,
seniors as well as the very old.

12 Their homes will be turned over to others,
their fields together with their wives.
Yes, I will stretch out my hand against those
who are living in the land," says ADONAI.

13 "For from the least to the greatest of them,
all are greedy for gains;
prophets and cohanim alike,
they all practice fraud —

14 they dress the wound of my people,
but only superficially,
saying, 'There is perfect shalom,'
when there is no shalom.

15 "They should be ashamed
of their detestable deeds,
but they are not ashamed at all;
they don't know how to blush.
Therefore when others fall,
they too will fall;
when I punish them,
they will stumble," says ADONAI.

¹⁶ Here is what *Adonai* says:

> "Stand at the crossroads and look;
> ask about the ancient paths,
> 'Which one is the good way?'
> Take it, and you will find rest for your souls.
> But they said, 'We will not take it.'
¹⁷
> I appointed sentinels to direct them:
> 'Listen for the sound of the *shofar*.'
> But they said, 'We will not listen.'
¹⁸
> So hear, you nations; know, you assembly,
> what there is against them.
¹⁹
> Hear, oh earth! I am going
> to bring disaster on this people;
> it is the consequence
> of their own way of thinking;
> for they pay no attention to my words;
> and as for my *Torah*, they reject it.
²⁰
> What do I care about incense from Sh'va
> or sweet cane from a distant land?
> Your burnt offerings are unacceptable,
> your sacrifices don't please me."

²¹ Therefore thus says *Adonai*:

> "I will put obstacles in the way of this people
> that they will stumble over —
> fathers and sons, neighbors and friends,
> all will perish together."

²² Here is what *Adonai* says:

> "A people is coming from the land of the north,
> a great nation will be aroused from the ends of the earth.
²³
> They will take hold of bow and spear;
> they are cruel; they have no compassion:
> their noise as they ride on horses
> is like the roaring sea;
> and they are equipped for battle
> against you, daughter of Tziyon.
²⁴
> 'We have heard the news,
> and our hands fall limp;
> anguish has seized us,
> pain like a mother's in childbirth.'"

²⁵
> Don't go into the countryside,
> don't walk out on the road;

for the sword of the enemy is spreading
terror in every direction.

26   Daughter of my people,
put on sackcloth, roll in ashes;
mourn as if for an only son,
wail most bitterly;
for suddenly the destroyer
will come upon us.

27   "I have made you a refiner and tester of my people,
to know and test how they behave.

28   All of them are total rebels,
spreading slanderous gossip;
they are bronze and iron, [inferior metals,]
all of them corrupt.

29   The bellows blast away;
and though the lead is consumed by the fire,
in vain has the smelter refined,
for the wicked have not been separated.

30   They are called 'rejected silver,'
because ADONAI has rejected them."

7 ¹ This word came to Yirmeyahu from ADONAI: ² "Stand at the gate of the house of ADONAI and proclaim this word: 'Listen to the word of ADONAI, all you from Y'hudah who enter these gates to worship ADONAI! ³ Here is what ADONAI-Tzva'ot, the God of Isra'el, says: "Improve your ways and actions, and I will let you stay in this place. ⁴ Don't rely on that deceitful slogan, 'The temple of ADONAI, the temple of ADONAI — these [buildings] are the temple of ADONAI.' ⁵ No, but if you really improve your ways and actions; if you really administer justice between people; ⁶ if you stop oppressing foreigners, orphans and widows; if you stop shedding innocent blood in this place; and if you stop following other gods, to your own harm; ⁷ then I will let you stay in this place, in the land I gave to your ancestors forever and ever. ⁸ Look! You are relying on deceitful words that can't do you any good. ⁹ First you steal, murder, commit adultery, swear falsely, offer to Ba'al and go after other gods that you haven't known. ¹⁰ Then you come and stand before me in this house that bears my name and say, 'We are saved' — so that you can go on doing these abominations! ¹¹ Do you regard this house, which bears my name, as a cave for bandits? I can see for myself what's going on," says ADONAI. ¹² "Go to the place in Shiloh that used to be mine, that used to bear my name, and see what I did to it because of the wickedness of my people Isra'el. ¹³ I spoke to you again and again, but you wouldn't listen. I called you, but you wouldn't answer. Now," says ADONAI, "because you have done all these things, ¹⁴ I will do to the house that bears my name, on which you rely, and to the place I gave you and your ancestors, what I did to Shiloh; ¹⁵ and I will drive you out of my presence, just as I drove out all your kinsmen, all the descendants of Efrayim.'"

[16] "So you, [Yirmeyahu,] don't pray for this people! Don't cry, pray or intercede on their behalf with me; because I won't listen to you. [17] Don't you see what they are doing in the cities of Y'hudah and in the streets of Yerushalayim? [18] The children gather the wood, the fathers light the fire, and the women knead the dough to make cakes for the queen of heaven; and, just to provoke me, they pour out drink offerings to other gods! [19] Are they really provoking me," asks ADONAI, "or are they provoking themselves, to their own ruin?"

[20] Therefore, here is what Adonai ELOHIM says: "My anger and fury will be poured out on this place, on men, animals, trees in the fields and produce growing from the ground; and it will burn without being quenched."

[21] Thus says ADONAI-Tzva'ot, the God of Isra'el: "You may as well eat the meat of your burnt offerings along with that of your sacrifices. [22] For I didn't speak to your ancestors or give them orders concerning burnt offerings or sacrifices when I brought them out of the land of Egypt. [23] Rather, what I did order them was this: 'Pay attention to what I say. Then I will be your God, and you will be my people. In everything, live according to the way that I order you, so that things will go well for you.' [24] But they neither listened nor paid attention, but lived according to their own plans, in the stubbornness of their evil hearts, thus going backward and not forward. [25] You have done this from the day your ancestors came out of Egypt until today. Even though I sent you all my servants the prophets, sending them time after time, [26] they would not listen or pay attention to me, but stiffened their necks; they did worse than their ancestors. [27] So tell them all this; but they won't listen to you; likewise, call to them; but they won't answer you. [28] Therefore, say to them,

'This is the nation that has not listened
to the voice of ADONAI their God.
They won't take correction; faithfulness has perished;
it has vanished from their mouths.'

[29] Cut off your hair, and throw it away,
take up a lament on the bare hills,
for ADONAI has rejected and abandoned
the generation that rouses his anger.'

[30] "For the people of Y'hudah have done what is evil from my perspective," says ADONAI; "they have set up their detestable things in the house which bears my name, to defile it. [31] They have built the high places of Tofet in the Ben-Hinnom Valley, to burn their sons and daughters in the fire, something I never ordered; in fact, such a thing never even entered my mind! [32] Therefore, the days are coming," says ADONAI, "when it will no longer be called either Tofet or the Ben-Hinnom Valley, but the Valley of Slaughter — they will put the dead in Tofet, because there will be no space left [anywhere else]. [33] The corpses of this people will become food for the birds in the air and the wild animals; no one will frighten them away. [34] Then in the cities of Y'hudah and the streets of Yerushalayim I will silence the sounds of joy and gladness and the voices of bridegroom and bride; because the land will be reduced to ruins.

8 ^{1} "At that time," says ADONAI, "[these enemies] will remove the bones of the kings of Y'hudah, the bones of his princes, the bones of the *cohanim*, the bones of the prophets and the bones of the inhabitants of Yerushalayim from their graves. ^{2} They will spread them out, exposed to the sun, the moon and the entire army of heaven, whom they loved, served, walked after, sought after and worshipped. The bones will not be collected or reburied but will be left lying on the ground like dung. ^{3} All the survivors of this evil family who remain wherever I have driven them will prefer death to life," says ADONAI-*Tzva'ot*. ^{4} "You are to tell them that ADONAI says:

'If a person falls, doesn't he get up again?
If someone goes astray, doesn't he turn back?
5   Why do these people keep backsliding?
Why is their backsliding so persistent?
They cling to deceit and refuse to return!
6   I listened attentively but they spoke nothing right.
No one repents of his wickedness,
saying, "What have I done!"
Each runs off in his own direction,
like a horse plunging headlong into battle.
7   Storks in the sky know their seasons;
doves, swallows and cranes their migration times;
but my people do not know
the rulings of ADONAI!

8   "'How can you say, "We are wise;
ADONAI's *Torah* is with us,"
when in fact the lying pen of the scribes
has turned it into falsehood?
9   The wise are put to shame,
alarmed, entrapped.
They have rejected the word of ADONAI,
so what wisdom do they have?

10   "'Therefore I will give their wives to others,
and their fields to those who take them over;
for from the least to the greatest,
all are greedy for gains;
prophets and *cohanim* alike
all practice fraud —
11   they dress the wound of the daughter of my people,
but only superficially,
saying, "There is perfect *shalom*,"
when there is no *shalom*.
12   They should be ashamed
of their detestable deeds,
but they are not ashamed at all,
they don't know how to blush.

So when others fall, they too will fall;
when I punish them, they will stumble,'
says ADONAI.

¹³ "'I will put an end to them,' says ADONAI.
'There are no grapes on the vine,
and no figs on the fig tree;
the leaf has withered; and what I have given them
will pass from their possession.'"

¹⁴ "Why are we sitting still? Assemble!
Let's enter the fortified cities
and meet our doom there!
For ADONAI our God has doomed us;
he has given us bitter water to drink,
because we have sinned against ADONAI.

¹⁵ When we look for peace, nothing good comes;
when we seek a time of healing, instead there is terror."

¹⁶ From Dan can be heard the snorting of his horses;
when his stallions neigh, the whole land trembles.
For they come devouring the land and all in it,
the city and those who dwell there.

¹⁷ "Yes, now I am sending snakes among you,
vipers that no one can charm,
and they will bite you," says ADONAI.

¹⁸ My grief has no cure, I am sick at heart.

¹⁹ Listen to my people's cry of distress
out of a distant land:
"Is ADONAI no longer in Tziyon?
Is her king no longer there?"

"Why do they provoke me with their idols
and their futile foreign gods?"

²⁰ "The harvest has passed, the summer is over,
and still we are not saved."

²¹ The daughter of my people is broken,
and it's tearing me to pieces;
everything looks dark to me,
horror seizes me.

²² Has Gil'ad exhausted its healing resin?
Is no physician there?
If there is, then why is the daughter of my people

562

so slow to recover her health?

23(9:1)   I wish my head were made of water
and my eyes were a fountain of tears,
so that I could cry day and night
over the slain of the daughter of my people!

9 1(2)   I wish I were out in the desert,
in some travelers' lodge —
then I could get away from my people
and distance myself from them!

"Indeed they are all adulterers,
a band of traitors is what they are.

2(3)   They bend their tongues, their 'bow' of falsehood,
and hold sway in the land, but not for truth.
For they go from evil to evil,
and me they do not know,"

says ADONAI.

3(4)   Everyone, be on guard against your neighbor,
don't trust even a brother;
for every brother is out to trick you,
and every neighbor goes around gossiping.

4(5)   Everyone deceives his neighbor,
no one speaks the truth;
they have taught their tongues to lie,
they wear themselves out with sinning.

5(6)   "You inhabit a world of deceit;
deceitfully they refuse to know me,"

says ADONAI.

6(7)   "Therefore," says ADONAI-Tzva'ot,
"I will refine them and test them.
What else can I do with the daughter of my people?

7(8)   Their tongues are sharpened arrows;
with their mouths they speak deceit —
they say nice words to their neighbors,
while inwardly plotting against them.

8(9)   Should I not punish them for these things?" asks ADONAI.
"Should I not take vengeance on such a nation?"

9(10)   I weep and wail for the mountains
and lament over the desert pastures,
because they have been burned up;

no one passes through;
they no longer hear the sound of cattle;
the birds and wild animals have fled, are gone.

10(11)   "I will make Yerushalayim a heap of ruins,
turn it into a lair for jackals,
and make the cities of Y'hudah desolate,
with no one living there."

11(12)   Who is wise enough to understand this?
To whom has the mouth of ADONAI spoken,
so that he can proclaim it?
Why has the land perished
and been laid waste like a desert,
so that no one passes through?

12(13) ADONAI answers:

"Because they abandoned my *Torah*,
which I set before them,
and neither listened to what I said
nor lived accordingly,
13(14)   but have lived by their own hearts' stubbornness
and by the *ba'alim*, as their ancestors taught them —
14(15)   therefore," says ADONAI-*Tzva'ot*,
the God of Isra'el:
"I will feed this people bitter wormwood
and give them poisonous water to drink.
15(16)   I will scatter them among nations
that neither they nor their ancestors have known.
I will send the sword after them
until I have wiped them out."

16(17) Thus says ADONAI-*Tzva'ot*:

"Mark this, then summon the mourning women,
so that they will come;
send for those who are best [at mourning],
so that they will come:
17(18)   'Have them hurry and wail for us,
so our eyes will be wet from crying,
and our eyelids gush with tears.'
18(19)   For the sound of wailing is heard from Tziyon:
'We are utterly ruined,
we are completely ashamed,
because we have left the land,
and our homes have been torn down!'"

19(20) You women, hear the word of *Adonai*!
Let your ears receive the words from his mouth.
Teach your daughters how to wail,
have each teach her friend how to lament:

20(21) "Death has come up through our windows,
it has entered our palaces,
it has cut down children in the streets
and young people in the public places."

21(22) Say: "Here is what *Adonai* says:
'The corpses of people are scattered
like dung in an open field,
like sheaves left behind by the reaper
with no one to gather them.'"

22(23) Here is what *Adonai* says:

"The wise man should not boast of his wisdom,
the powerful should not boast of his power,
the wealthy should not boast of his wealth;

23(24) instead, let the boaster boast about this:
that he understands and knows me —
that I am *Adonai*, practicing grace,
justice and righteousness in the land;
for in these things I take pleasure," says *Adonai*.

24(25) "The days are coming," says *Adonai*, "when I will punish all those who
have been circumcised in their uncircumcision — 25(26) Egypt, Y'hudah, Edom,
the people of 'Amon and Mo'av, and all those living in the desert who cut the
edges [of their beard]:

"For although all the *Goyim* are uncircumcised,
all the house of Isra'el have uncircumcised hearts."

10 1 Hear the word *Adonai* speaks to you,
house of Isra'el!

2 Here is what *Adonai* says:
"Don't learn the way of the *Goyim*,
don't be frightened by astrological signs,
even if the *Goyim* are afraid of them;

3 for the customs of the peoples are nothing.
They cut down a tree in the forest;
a craftsman works it with his axe;

4 they deck it with silver and gold.
They fix it with hammer and nails,
so that it won't move.

5 Like a scarecrow in a cucumber patch,
it cannot speak.

It has to be carried,
because it cannot walk.
Do not be afraid of it —
it can do nothing bad;
likewise it is unable
to do anything good!"

6   There is no one like you, ADONAI!
    You are great, and your name is great and mighty.
7   Who would not fear you, king of the nations?
    For it is your due! —
    since among all the wise of the nations
    and among all their royalty,
    there is no one like you.
8   One and all they are boorish and stupid;
    the teaching of their nothings is a piece of wood!
9   Silver is beaten into plates,
    then imported from Tarshish.
    Gold from Ufaz is worked by a craftsman
    and shaped by the hands of a goldsmith.
    They are clothed in blue and purple,
    all the work of skillful men.
10 But ADONAI, God, is the true God,
    the living God, the everlasting king.
    At his anger, the earth trembles;
    the nations cannot endure his fury.
11 "This is what you must say to them:
    'The gods that did not make heaven and earth
    will perish from earth and from under heaven.'"

12 God made the earth by his power,
    established the world by his wisdom
    spread out the sky by his understanding.
13 When he thunders, the waters in heaven roar,
    he raises clouds from the ends of the earth,
    he makes the lightning flash in the rain
    and brings the wind out from his storehouses.
14 At this, everyone is proved stupid, ignorant,
    every goldsmith put to shame by his idol!
    The figures he casts are a fraud;
    there is no breath in them;
15 they are nothings, ridiculous objects;
    when the day for their punishment comes, they will perish.

16 Ya'akov's portion is not like these,
    for he is the one who formed all things.

Isra'el is the tribe he claims as his heritage;
ADONAI-*Tzva'ot* is his name.

17 You who are living under the siege,
gather your belongings off the ground,
18 for here is what ADONAI says:
"At this time I am slinging away
the inhabitants of the land;
I will distress them,
so that they will feel it."

19 Woe to me because of my wound!
My injury is incurable!
I used to say, "It's only an illness,
and I can bear it."
20 But now my tent is ruined,
all its cords are severed;
my children have left me and are no more;
there is no one to set up my tent again,
no one to raise its curtains.
21 The shepherds have become stupid,
they have not consulted ADONAI.
This is why they have not prospered,
and all their flocks are scattered.
22 Listen! A noise! It's coming closer!
A great uproar from the land to the north,
to make the cities of Y'hudah desolate,
a place for jackals to live.
23 ADONAI, I know that the way of humans
is not in their control,
humans are not able
to direct their steps as they walk.
24 ADONAI, correct me, but in moderation,
not in your anger, or you'll reduce me to nothing.
25 Pour out your anger on the nations
that do not acknowledge you,
also on the families
that do not call on your name.
For they have consumed Ya'akov —
consumed him and finished him off,
and laid waste to his home.

11 ¹ Here is the word that came to Yirmeyahu from ADONAI: ² "Listen to the words of this covenant; then speak to the people of Y'hudah and the inhabitants of Yerushalayim; ³ tell them that ADONAI the God of Isra'el says: 'A curse on anyone who does not pay attention to the words of this covenant, ⁴ which I enjoined on your ancestors at the time that I brought them out of the land of Egypt, out of that iron-smelter. I said,

> "Listen to my voice,
> and carry out all my orders;
> then you will be my people,
> and I will be your God;
> 5   so that I can fulfill the oath
> that I swore to your ancestors,
> to give them a land flowing with milk and honey,
> as it is today.""'"

Then I responded, "*Amen*, ADONAI."

⁶ ADONAI said to me, "Proclaim all these words in the cities of Y'hudah and in the streets of Yerushalayim: 'Listen to the words of this covenant, and obey them. ⁷ For I solemnly warned your ancestors at the time when I brought them out of the land of Egypt; and until this day I have frequently warned them, "Listen to my voice!" ⁸ But they have not listened or paid attention; instead, each one has lived according to the stubbornness of his own evil heart. For this reason I have brought upon them all the words of this covenant, which I ordered them to obey, but which they did not obey.'"

⁹ Then ADONAI said to me, "The men of Y'hudah and the people living in Yerushalayim have formed a conspiracy. ¹⁰ They have returned to the sins of their ancestors, who refused to hear my words, and they have gone after other gods to serve them. The house of Isra'el and the house of Y'hudah have broken my covenant which I made with their ancestors." ¹¹ Therefore ADONAI says, "I am going to bring on them a disaster which they will not be able to escape; and even if they cry to me, I will not listen to them. ¹² Then the cities of Y'hudah and the people living in Yerushalayim will go and cry to the gods to whom they are making offerings; but they will not save them at all in their time of trouble. ¹³ For you have as many gods, Y'hudah, as you have towns; and you have erected as many altars for sacrificing to that shameful thing, Ba'al, as there are streets in Yerushalayim.

¹⁴ "So you, [Yirmeyahu,] don't pray for this people! Don't cry or pray on their behalf, because I won't listen to them when they cry to me because of their troubles. ¹⁵ What right does my beloved have to be in my house, when she has behaved so shamelessly with so many? Offerings of consecrated meat can no longer help, because it is when you are doing evil that you are happy."

> 16   ADONAI once called you an olive tree,
> beautiful, full of leaves and good fruit.
> Now with the roar of a violent storm,
> he has set it on fire;
> and its branches will be consumed.

> 17   For ADONAI-*Tzva'ot*, who planted you,
> has decreed evil for you.

"It is because of the evil which the house of Isra'el and the house of Y'hudah did to themselves, provoking me with their offerings of incense to Ba'al."

18 ADONAI made this known to me, and then I knew —
you showed me what they were doing.

19 But I was like a tame lamb
led to be slaughtered;
I did not know that they were plotting
schemes against me —
"Let's destroy the tree with its fruit,
we'll cut him off from the land of the living,
so that his name will be forgotten."

20 ADONAI-Tzva'ot, righteous judge,
tester of motives and thoughts,
I have committed my cause to you;
so let me see your vengeance on them.

²¹ Therefore, here is what ADONAI says concerning the men from 'Anatot who seek
your life and who tell you, "Stop prophesying in the name of ADONAI, or we will kill
you ourselves" — ²² this is what ADONAI-Tzva'ot says: "I will punish them. Their
young men will die by the sword, their sons and daughters will die by famine.
²³ None of them will remain, for I will bring disaster on the men from 'Anatot when
the year comes for them to be punished."

12 ¹ ADONAI, although you would be in the right
if I were to dispute with you,
nevertheless I want to discuss
some points of justice with you:
Why do the wicked prosper?
Why do the treacherous all thrive?

2 You planted them, and they took root;
they grow, and they bear fruit.
You are near in their mouths,
though far from their hearts.

3 But, ADONAI, you know me and see me;
you test my devotion to you;
drag them away like sheep to be slaughtered,
and set them apart for the day of slaughter.

4 How long must the land mourn
and the grass in all the fields wither?
The wild animals and birds are consumed
because of the wickedness of those who live there;
for they say, "He will not see how we end up."

5 If racing men on foot exhausts you,
how will you compete against horses?
You may feel secure in a land at peace,
but how will you do in the Yarden's thick brush?

6 For even your own brothers
and your father's family are betraying you;

they are in full cry after you.
Despite all their nice speech, don't believe them.

7   "I have abandoned my house,
I have rejected my heritage,
I have given my heart's beloved
over to the hands of her foes.

8   For me, my heritage has become
like a lion in the forest —
she roared out against me;
so now I hate her.

9   For me, my heritage is like a speckled bird of prey —
other birds of prey surround her and attack her.
Go, gather all the wild animals,
and bring them to devour her.

10   Many shepherds have destroyed my vineyard,
they have trampled my plot of land,
they have turned my desirable property
into a desert waste.

11   Yes, they have made it a waste;
wasted, it mourns to me;
the whole land is wasted,
because nobody really cares."

12   On all the desert's bare hills
plunderers have come;
yes, the sword of ADONAI devours the land
from one end to the other;
nothing alive is safe.

13   They sowed wheat and reaped thorns,
they wore themselves out and gained nothing.
So be ashamed of your [tiny] harvest,
the result of ADONAI's fierce anger.

¹⁴ Here is what ADONAI says: "As for all my evil neighbors who encroach on the
heritage I gave to my people Isra'el as their possession, I will uproot them from
their own land, and I will uproot Y'hudah from among them. ¹⁵ Then, after I
have uprooted them, I will take pity on them again and bring them back, each
one to his inheritance, each one to his own land. ¹⁶ Then, if they will carefully
learn my people's ways, swearing by my name, 'As ADONAI lives,' just as they
taught my people to swear by Ba'al, they will be built up among my people.
¹⁷ But if they refuse to listen, then I will uproot that nation, uproot and destroy
it," says ADONAI.

13 ¹ ADONAI said to me, "Go, buy yourself a linen loincloth, and wrap it around
your body; but don't soften it in water." ² So I bought a loincloth, as ADONAI had
said, and put it on.

³ Then the word of *Adonai* came to me a second time: ⁴ "Take the loincloth you bought and are wearing, get up, go to Parah, and hide it there in a hole in the rock." ⁵ So I went and hid it in Parah, as *Adonai* had ordered me.

⁶ A long time afterwards, *Adonai* said to me, "Get up, go to Parah, and recover the loincloth I ordered you to hide there." ⁷ So I went to Parah and dug up the loincloth; but when I took it from the place where I had hidden it, I saw that it was ruined and useless for anything. ⁸ Then the word of *Adonai* came to me: ⁹ "Here is what *Adonai* says: 'This is how I will ruin what makes Y'hudah so proud and Yerushalayim so very proud: ¹⁰ I will ruin this evil people, who refuse to hear my words and live according to their own stubborn inclinations, who go after other gods to serve and worship them. They will be like this loincloth, which is useless for anything. ¹¹ For just as a loincloth clings to a man's body, I made the whole house of Isra'el and the whole house of Y'hudah cling to me,' says *Adonai*, 'so that they could be my people, building me a name and becoming for me a source of praise and honor. But they would not listen. ¹² So you are to tell them, "This is what *Adonai* the God of Isra'el says: 'Every bottle is filled with wine.'" Then when they ask you, "Don't we already know that every bottle is filled with wine?" ¹³ you are to answer them, "This is what *Adonai* says: 'I am going to fill all the inhabitants of this land — including the kings sitting on the throne of David, the *cohanim*, the prophets and the inhabitants of Yerushalayim — with drunkenness. ¹⁴ Then I will smash them one against another, even fathers and sons together,' says *Adonai* 'I will show neither pity nor compassion, but I will destroy them relentlessly.'"'"

15   Listen and pay attention; don't be proud!
        For *Adonai* has spoken.

16   Give glory to *Adonai* your God
        before the darkness falls,
        before your feet stumble
        on the mountains in the twilight,
        and, while you are seeking light,
        he turns it into deathlike shadows
        and makes it completely dark.

17   But if you will not hear this warning,
        I will weep secretly because of your pride;
        my eyes will weep bitterly, streaming with tears,
        because *Adonai*'s flock is carried away captive.

18   Tell the king and the queen mother,
        "Come down from your thrones,
        for your magnificent crowns
        are falling from your heads."

19   The cities of the Negev are besieged,
        and no one can relieve them;
        all of Y'hudah is carried into exile,
        completely swept into exile.

20   Raise your eyes, and you will see them
        coming from the north.
        Where is the flock once entrusted to you,

the sheep that were your pride?

21 When he sets over you as rulers
those you trained to be allies,
what will you say? Won't pains seize you
like those of a woman in labor?

22 And if you ask yourself,
"Why have these things happened to me?"
it is because of your many sins
that your skirts are pulled up and you have been violated.

23 Can an Ethiopian change his skin?
or a leopard its spots?
If they can, then you can do good,
who are so accustomed to doing evil.

24 "So I will scatter them like chaff
that flies away in the desert wind.

25 This is what you get," says ADONAI,
"the portion I measure out to you,
because you have forgotten me
and trusted in the lie.

26 I myself will lift your skirts above your face,
and your privates will be exposed.

27 On the hills and in the fields,
I have seen your abominations —
your adulteries, your lustful neighings
your shameless prostitution.
Woe to you, Yerushalayim!
You refuse to be purified!
Won't you ever allow it?"

14 ¹ The word of ADONAI that came to Yirmeyahu concerning the drought:

2 "Y'hudah is mourning, her gates are languishing;
they sit on the ground in gloom;
Yerushalayim sends up a cry of anguish.

3 Her nobles send their servants for water;
they go to the cisterns but find no water,
so they return with empty jars.
Ashamed and dismayed, they cover their heads.

4 Because of the ground, which is cracked,
since it has not rained in the land,
the farmers are ashamed;
they cover their heads.

5 The doe in the countryside, giving birth,
abandons her young for lack of grass.

6 The wild donkeys standing on the bare heights
gasp for air like jackals;

their eyes grow dim from trying to spot
any vegetation."

7 Although our crimes witness against us,
take action, ADONAI, for your name's sake;
for our backslidings are many;
we have sinned against you.

8 You, hope of Isra'el,
its savior in time of trouble,
why should you be like a stranger in the land,
like a traveler turning aside for the night?

9 Why should you be like a man in shock,
like a champion unable to save?
You, ADONAI, are right here with us;
we bear your name — don't leave us!

10 Here is what ADONAI says to this people:
"They so love to wander,
they don't restrain their feet;
so ADONAI does not want them.
Now he will remember their crimes,
and he will punish their sins."

¹¹ Then ADONAI said to me, "Don't pray for this people or for their welfare. ¹² When they fast, I will not hear their cry; when they offer burnt offerings and grain offerings, I will not accept them. Rather, I will destroy them with war, famine and disease." ¹³ Then I said, "ADONAI, God! The prophets are telling them, 'You won't see war, and you won't have famine; but I will give you secure peace in this place.'"
¹⁴ ADONAI replied, "The prophets are prophesying lies in my name. I didn't send them, order them or speak to them. They are prophesying false visions to you, worthless divinations, the delusions of their own minds. ¹⁵ Therefore," ADONAI says, "concerning the prophets who prophesy in my name, whom I did not send, yet they say, 'There will be neither war nor famine in this land' — it will be war and famine that will destroy those prophets. ¹⁶ And the people to whom they are prophesying will be thrown out into the streets of Yerushalayim because of the famine and war, with no one to bury them — them, or their wives, or their sons, or their daughters — because I will pour their own wickedness out upon them.
¹⁷ You are to give them this message:

'Let my eyes stream with tears
night and day, unceasingly,
because the virgin daughter of my people
has been severely broken;
she has been dealt a crushing blow.

18 If I go out in the field,
I see those slain with the sword.
If I enter the city,

I see the victims of famine.
Meanwhile, prophets and *cohanim*
ply their trade in the land, knowing nothing.'"

19   Have you rejected Y'hudah completely?
Is Tziyon loathsome to you?
Why have you struck us irreparably?
We looked for peace, but to no avail;
for a time of healing, but instead found terror!

20   We confess our rebellion, ADONAI,
also the crimes of our ancestors;
yes, we have sinned against you.

21   For your name's sake, do not spurn us;
do not dishonor your glorious throne.
Remember your covenant with us;
do not break it.

22   Among the nations' idols,
can any make it rain?
Can the skies, of themselves,
send showers?
Aren't you the one,
ADONAI, our God?
Don't we look to you?
For you do all these things.

15 [1] Then ADONAI said to me, "Even if Moshe and Sh'mu'el were standing in front of me, my heart would not turn toward this people! Drive them out of my sight, get them out of here! [2] And when they ask you where they should go, tell them that this is what ADONAI says:

'Those destined for death — to death!
Those destined for the sword — to the sword!
Those destined for famine — to famine!
Those destined for captivity — to captivity!'

[3] "I will assign them four kinds [of scourges]," says ADONAI, "the sword to kill, dogs to drag away, birds in the air and wild animals to devour and destroy. [4] I will make them an object of horror to all the kingdoms of the earth, because of M'nasheh the son of Hizkiyahu king of Y'hudah, because of what he did in Yerushalayim.

5   "Who will take pity on you, Yerushalayim?
Who will grieve for you?
Who will turn aside
to ask about your welfare?

6   You have rejected me," says ADONAI.
"You are heading backward.
So I am stretching out my hand against you;

tired of sparing you, I am destroying you.

7 With a winnowing fork I am scattering them
to the wind at the gates of the land;
I am bereaving them, destroying my people,
because they will not return from their ways.

8 Their widows increase in number
more than the sand of the seas;
At midday I am bringing the destroyer
on the mothers of young men,
causing anguish and terror
suddenly to fall upon her.

9 The mother of seven sons grows faint,
panting in despair;
her sun has gone down while it's still daytime;
she is left disgraced and bewildered.
And the rest of them I will give to the sword,
to their enemies," says ADONAI.

10 Woe to me, mother, that you gave me birth,
a man who is the object of strife
and controversy throughout the land!
I neither lend nor borrow,
yet all of them curse me.

¹¹ ADONAI said, "I promise to release you for good, I promise to make your enemies
appeal to you when calamity and trouble come.
¹² "Can iron break iron and bronze from the north? ¹³ I will give away your
wealth and your treasures as plunder, and you will not be paid for them, because of
all your sins throughout your territory; ¹⁴ and I will make you pass together with your
enemies into a land you do not know. For my anger has become a blazing fire, and it
will flare up against you."

15 ADONAI, you know. Remember me, think of me,
and take vengeance for me on my persecutors.
Because you are patient, don't banish me;
know that for your sake I suffer insults.

16 When I found your words, I devoured them;
your words made me glad, they gave me joy;
because, ADONAI-Tzva'ot,
you had me bear your name.

17 I have never kept company with merrymakers,
I could not celebrate;
with your hand on me I sat by myself,
for you filled me with indignation.

18 Why is my pain unending,
my wound incurable, refusing to be healed?

Will you be for me like a deceptive *vadi,*
which is only sometimes filled with water?

¹⁹ This is ADONAI's answer:

"If you return — if I bring you back —
you will stand before me.
If you separate the precious from the base,
you will be my spokesman.
It will then be they who turn to you,
not you who turn to them.

²⁰ Toward this people I will make you
a fortified wall of bronze —
they will fight against you
but not prevail against you;
for I am with you to save you
and rescue you," says ADONAI.

²¹ "I will free you from the grasp of the wicked
and redeem you from the clutches of the ruthless."

16 ¹ This word of ADONAI came to me: ² "You are not to marry or have sons and daughters in this place. ³ For this is what ADONAI says concerning the sons and daughters born here, as well as their mothers who gave birth to them and their fathers who conceived them in this land: ⁴ 'They will die terrible deaths without being mourned or buried; they will be left on the ground like dung. They will die by the sword and by famine, and their corpses will be food for the birds in the air and the wild animals.'

⁵ "For here is what ADONAI says: 'Do not enter any house where there is mourning; don't lament them, and don't grieve for them; for I have removed my *shalom* from this people, as well as my grace and compassion,' says ADONAI. ⁶ 'Great and small alike will die in this land; they will not be buried, people will not lament them; nor will they cut their flesh or shave their heads for them. ⁷ No one will prepare a meal for those in mourning, to comfort them for the dead; and no one will give them a cup to drink, to console them for their father or mother.' ⁸ And you are not to go into any house where there is celebrating to sit with them, eating and drinking. ⁹ For here is what ADONAI-*Tzva'ot,* the God of Isra'el, says: 'In this place, while you are still alive, before your very eyes, I will put an end to the sounds of joy and gladness and to the voices of bridegroom and bride.'

¹⁰ "When you tell this people all that I have said, and they ask you, 'Why has ADONAI decreed all this terrible disaster against us? What is our iniquity, what is our sin, that we have committed against ADONAI our God?' ¹¹ then you are to say to them, 'It is because your ancestors abandoned me, says ADONAI, and went after other gods, serving and worshipping them, but abandoned me and did not keep my *Torah.* ¹² And you have done worse than your ancestors, for — look! — each of you lives according to the stubbornness of his own evil heart, so that you don't listen to me. ¹³ Therefore I am thrusting you out of this

land into a land you have not known, neither you nor your ancestors; and there you will serve other gods day and night; for I will show you no favor.'

¹⁴ "'Therefore,' says ADONAI, 'the day will come when people will no longer swear, "As ADONAI lives, who brought the people of Isra'el out of the land of Egypt," ¹⁵ but, "As ADONAI lives, who brought the people of Isra'el out of the land to the north and out of all the countries where he drove them"; for I will bring them back to their own land, which I gave to their ancestors.

¹⁶ "'Look,' says ADONAI, 'I will send for many fishermen, and they will fish for them. Afterwards, I will send for many hunters; and they will hunt them from every mountain and hill and out of caves in the rocks. ¹⁷ For I see all their ways; they are not hidden from me; their crimes are not concealed from my eyes. ¹⁸ First, I will pay them back double for their crimes and sins; because they have defiled the land which is mine; they have filled my heritage with the corpses of their horrors and abominations.'"

<blockquote>

19   ADONAI, my strength, my fortress,
    my refuge in time of trouble,
    the nations will come to you
    from the ends of the earth, saying,
    "Our ancestors inherited nothing but lies,
    futile idols, completely useless."

20   Can a person make himself gods?
    (In fact they aren't gods at all.)

21   "Therefore, I will make them know,
    once and for all, I will make them know
    my power and my might.
    Then they will know that my name is ADONAI.

</blockquote>

17 ¹ "Y'hudah's sin is written with an iron pen;
    with a diamond point it is engraved
    on the tablet of their hearts
    and on the horns of your altars.

2   As they remember their children,
    so they remember their altars
    and their sacred poles by the green trees
    on the high hills.

3   My mountain in the field, your wealth
    and all your treasures will be plundered;
    because of the sin of your high places
    throughout your territory.

4   You will relinquish your hold
    on your heritage which I gave you.
    I will make you serve your enemies
    in a land you do not know.
    For you have kindled my fiery anger,
    and it will burn forever."

⁵ Here is what *Adonai* says:

> "A curse on the person who trusts in humans,
> who relies on merely human strength,
> whose heart turns away from *Adonai*.

⁶
> He will be like a tamarisk in the 'Aravah —
> when relief comes, it is unaffected;
> for it lives in the sun-baked desert,
> in salty, uninhabited land.

⁷
> Blessed is the man who trusts in *Adonai*;
> *Adonai* will be his security.

⁸
> He will be like a tree planted near water;
> it spreads out its roots by the river;
> it does not notice when heat comes;
> and its foliage is luxuriant;
> it is not anxious in a year of drought
> but keeps on yielding fruit.

⁹
> "The heart is more deceitful than anything else
> and mortally sick. Who can fathom it?

¹⁰
> I, *Adonai*, search the heart;
> I test inner motivations;
> in order to give to everyone
> what his actions and conduct deserve."

¹¹
> A partridge hatches eggs it did not lay;
> like this are those who get rich unjustly:
> in the prime of life their wealth will desert them;
> in the end they will prove to be fools.

¹²
> Throne of Glory,
> exalted from the beginning!
> Our Holy Sanctuary,

¹³
> Hope of Isra'el, *Adonai*!
> All who abandon you will be ashamed,
> those who leave you will be inscribed in the dust,
> because they have abandoned *Adonai*,
> the source of living water.

¹⁴
> Heal me, *Adonai*, and I will be healed;
> save me, and I will be saved,
> for you are my praise.

¹⁵
> They keep asking me,
> "Where is the word of *Adonai*?
> Let it come now."

¹⁶
> As for me, I have not run away
> from being a shepherd who follows you;

578

> you know I didn't want this fatal day;
> what came from my lips has been clear to you.

17 So do not be my ruin,
> you, my refuge on the day of disaster.

18 Let my persecutors be ashamed, not me;
> let them be terrified, not me.
> Bring on them the day of disaster,
> destroy them with double destruction.

¹⁹ Then ADONAI said this to me: "Go, and stand at the People's Gate, where the kings of Y'hudah go in and out, and at all the gates of Yerushalayim; ²⁰ and say to them: 'Kings of Y'hudah, all Y'hudah and all living in Yerushalayim who enter through these gates, hear the word of ADONAI! ²¹ Here is what ADONAI says: "If you value your lives, don't carry anything on Shabbat or bring it in through the gates of Yerushalayim; ²² don't carry anything out of your houses on Shabbat; and don't do any work. Instead, make Shabbat a holy day. I ordered your ancestors to do this, ²³ but they neither listened nor paid attention; rather, they stiffened their necks, so that they wouldn't have to hear or receive instruction. ²⁴ However, if you will pay careful heed to me," says ADONAI "and carry nothing through the gates of this city on Shabbat, but instead make Shabbat a day which is holy and not for doing work; ²⁵ then kings and princes occupying the throne of David will enter through the gates of this city, riding in chariots and on horses. They, their princes, the people of Y'hudah and the inhabitants of Yerushalayim will enter; and this city will be inhabited forever. ²⁶ They will come from the cities of Y'hudah, from the places surrounding Yerushalayim, from the land of Binyamin, from the Sh'felah, from the hills and from the Negev, bringing burnt offerings, sacrifices, grain offerings, frankincense and thanksgiving sacrifices to the house of ADONAI. ²⁷ But if you will not obey me and make Shabbat a holy day and not carry loads through the gates of Yerushalayim on Shabbat, then I will set its gates on fire; it will burn up the palaces of Yerushalayim and not be quenched."'"

18 ¹ This word came to Yirmeyahu from ADONAI: ² "Get up, and go down to the potter's house; there I will tell you more." ³ So I went down to the house of the potter; and there he was, working at the wheels. ⁴ Whenever a pot he made came out imperfect, the potter took the clay and made another pot with it, in whatever shape suited him.

⁵ Then the word of ADONAI came to me: ⁶ "House of Isra'el, can't I deal with you as the potter deals with his clay? — says ADONAI. Look! You, house of Isra'el, are the same in my hand as the clay in the potter's hand. ⁷ At one time, I may speak about uprooting, breaking down and destroying a nation or kingdom; ⁸ but if that nation turns from their evil, which prompted me to speak against it, then I relent concerning the disaster I had planned to inflict on it. ⁹ Similarly, at another time, I may speak about building and planting a nation or kingdom; ¹⁰ but if it behaves wickedly from my perspective and doesn't listen to what I say, then I change my mind and don't do the good I said I would do that would have helped it.

¹¹ "So now, tell the people of Y'hudah and those living in Yerushalayim that this is what ADONAI says:

'I am designing disaster for you,
working out my plan against you.
Turn, each of you, from his evil ways;
improve your conduct and actions.'

12 "But they will answer, 'It's hopeless!
We will stick to our own plans;
each of us will stubbornly follow
his own evil desires!'

13 "Therefore, ADONAI says this:
'Ask among the nations
who has heard anything like this.
The virgin Isra'el has done
a most horrible thing.

14 Does the snow of the L'vanon
disappear from the mountain crags?
Do the cold waters of foreign lands
ever run dry?

15 No, but my people have forgotten me
and offer incense to nothings.
This causes them to stumble
as they walk the ancient paths;
they leave the highway
to walk on side-trails.

16 Thus they make their land an object of horror
and ongoing ridicule.
Passers-by shake their heads,
appalled, every one.

17 Like a strong east wind, I will scatter them
before the enemy.
I will see their back, not their face,
on their day of disaster.'"

18 Then they said, "Let's develop a plan for dealing with Yirmeyahu. *Torah* won't be lost from the *cohanim*, or counsel from the wise, or words from the prophets. So come, let's destroy him with slander; and meanwhile, we won't pay attention to anything he says."

19 Pay attention to me, ADONAI!
Listen to what my opponents are saying!

20 Is good to be repaid with evil?
For they have dug a pit [to trap] me.
Remember how I stood before you
and spoke well of them,
in order to turn your anger
away from them?

²¹ Therefore, hand their sons over to famine,
hurl them into the power of the sword,
let their wives be made childless and widows,
let their husbands be slain by disease,
let their young men be slain by the sword in battle,
²² let screams be heard from their houses
when you bring raiders on them without warning.
For they have dug a pit to catch me
and have laid snares for my feet.
²³ Nevertheless, ADONAI, you know
all their plans against me to stop me.
Do not forgive their crime,
do not blot out their sin from your sight;
but let them be made to stumble before you;
deal with them when you are angry.

19 ¹ ADONAI then said, "Go; buy a clay jar from the potter; take some of the people's leaders and some of the leading *cohanim*; ² and go out into the Ben-Hinnom Valley, by the entry to the Potsherd Gate. There you are to proclaim the words I am about to tell you. ³ Say: 'Hear the word of ADONAI, kings of Y'hudah and inhabitants of Yerushalayim! This is what ADONAI-Tzva'ot, the God of Isra'el, says: "I am about to bring disaster on this place that will make the ears of whoever hears about it ring. ⁴ This is because they have abandoned me and alienated this place. In it they have offered to other gods that neither they nor their ancestors have known, nor the kings of Y'hudah. They have filled this place with the blood of innocent people. ⁵ They have built the high places of Ba'al, in order to burn up their children in the fire as burnt offerings to Ba'al — something I never ordered or said; it never even entered my mind.

⁶ "'"Therefore the time is coming," says ADONAI, "when this place will no longer be called either Tofet or the Ben-Hinnom Valley, but the Valley of Slaughter. ⁷ I will nullify the plans of Y'hudah and Yerushalayim in this place. I will have them fall by the sword before their enemies and at the hand of those seeking their lives, and I will give their corpses as food for the birds in the air and the wild animals. ⁸ I will make this city an object of horror and ridicule; everyone passing by will be horrified and will ridicule it because of all its wounds. ⁹ I will cause them to eat the flesh of their own sons and daughters; everyone will be eating the flesh of his friends during the siege, because of the shortage imposed on them by their enemies and those set on killing them.'"

¹⁰ "Then you are to smash the jar in front of the people who went with you, ¹¹ and say to them, 'ADONAI-Tzva'ot says that this is how I will break this people and this city, just as one smashes a potter's vessel beyond the possibility of repair. The dead will be buried in Tofet, because there will be no space left for burial [anywhere else]. ¹² That is what I will do to this place,' says ADONAI 'and to its inhabitants; I will make it like Tofet. ¹³ The houses of Yerushalayim and those of the kings of Y'hudah will be defiled like this place Tofet — yes, all the houses on whose roofs they have offered to all the stars in heaven and poured out drink offerings to other gods.'"

¹⁴ Then Yirmeyahu returned from Tofet, where ADONAI had sent him to prophesy, stood in the courtyard of ADONAI's house and said to all the people, ¹⁵ "This is what

ADONAI-Tzva'ot, the God of Isra'el, says: 'I am bringing on this city and all its surrounding villages all the disaster I have pronounced against it; because they have stiffened their necks and refused to pay attention to my words.'"

20 ¹ Now when the *cohen* Pash'chur son of Immer, chief official in the house of *ADONAI*, heard Yirmeyahu prophesying these things, ² he had him flogged and put him in the stocks at the Upper Binyamin Gate of the house of *ADONAI*. ³ The following morning, when Pash'chur led Yirmeyahu out of the stocks, Yirmeyahu said to him, "*ADONAI* no longer calls you Pash'chur but Magor-Missaviv [terror on every side]. ⁴ For this is what *ADONAI* says: 'I will make you a terror to yourself and to all your friends. They will fall by the sword of their enemies, while you watch. I will hand over all of Y'hudah to the king of Bavel, and he will carry them off captive to Bavel and put them to the sword. ⁵ Moreover, I will hand over everything stored in this city, all its valuables, all its wealth, indeed all the treasures of the kings of Y'hudah, to their enemies, who will plunder them, take them and carry them to Bavel. ⁶ And you, Pash'chur, along with your entire household, will go into captivity; you will go to Bavel, where you will die and be buried — you and all your friends to whom you have prophesied lies.'"

7   You fooled me, *ADONAI*; I have been your dupe.
    You overpowered me, and you have prevailed.
    All day long I'm a laughingstock;
    everyone makes fun of me.
8   Whenever I speak, I have to cry out;
    I shout, "Violence!" and "Destruction!"
    Thus the word of *ADONAI* becomes for me
    the cause of reproach and derision all day!
9   But if I say, "I won't think about him,
    I won't speak in his name any more,"
    then it seems as though a fire
    is burning in my heart,
    imprisoned in my bones;
    I wear myself out
    trying to hold it in,
    but I just can't do it.
10   I have heard many whispering their plot:
    "'Terror in every direction'?
    Denounce him! Let's denounce him!"
    Even all my close friends
    are watching for me to make a false step —
    "Maybe he can be tricked,
    then we'll get the better of him,
    then we'll take our revenge on him."
11   But *ADONAI* is with me like a dreaded warrior;
    so my persecutors will stumble, defeated,
    greatly ashamed because of their failure;

their lasting disgrace will not be forgotten.

12   *ADONAI-Tzva'ot*, you who test the righteous
and see people's hearts and thoughts,
let me see you take vengeance on them,
for I have committed my cause to you.

13   Sing to *ADONAI*! Praise *ADONAI*!
For he rescues those in need
from the clutches of evildoers.

14   A curse on the day I was born!
The day my mother gave birth to me —
let it not be blessed!

15   A curse on the man who brought the news
to my father, "A son has been born to you!" —
thus making him very happy.

16   Let that man be like the cities
ADONAI overthrew without mercy!
Let him hear cries of alarm in the morning
and the sound of battle at noon,

17   because God did not put me to death in the womb
and let my mother become my grave,
her womb forever filled with me.

18   Why did I have to emerge from the womb,
just to see toil and sorrow,
and end my days in shame?

21 ¹ This is the word that came to Yirmeyahu from *ADONAI* when King Tzidkiyahu sent to him Pash'chur the son of Malkiyah and Tz'fanyah the son of Ma'aseiyah with this message: ² "Please consult *ADONAI* for us, because N'vukhadretzar king of Bavel is making war on us. Maybe *ADONAI* will perform a miracle for us and cause him to withdraw."

³ Yirmeyahu answered them, "Here is what you are to tell Tzidkiyahu: ⁴ 'This is what *ADONAI*, the God of Isra'el, says: "I will make the weapons of war that you have in your hands ineffectual in your fight against the king of Bavel and the Kasdim who are outside the walls besieging you. Instead, I will gather them inside this city; ⁵ and I myself will fight against you with my hand stretched out and with a strong arm, in anger, rage and great fury. ⁶ I will strike the inhabitants of this city, humans and animals alike, and they will die of a terrible plague. ⁷ Afterwards," says *ADONAI* "I will hand over Tzidkiyahu king of Y'hudah, his servants, the people, and anyone remaining alive in this city after the plague, war and famine, to N'vukhadretzar king of Bavel and to their enemies, to those who seek their lives; and he will put them to the sword. He will not spare them; he will have no pity, no compassion."'

⁸ "And here is what you are to tell this people: '*ADONAI* says: "Look! I am presenting you with the way of life and the way of death. ⁹ Anyone who stays in this city will die by sword, famine and plague. But he who leaves and surrenders to the Kasdim besieging you will stay alive; his own life will be his only 'spoils of war.' ¹⁰ For I

have determined absolutely that this city will have evil, not good," says *Adonai*. "It is going to be handed over to the king of Bavel, and he will burn it to the ground.'"

¹¹ "To the royal house of Y'hudah say: 'Hear the word of *Adonai*; ¹² house of David, this is what *Adonai* says:

> "Judge fairly every morning,
> rescue the wronged from their oppressors;
> or my fury will lash out like fire,
> burning so hot that no one can quench it,
> because of how evil your actions are."

13
> *Adonai* says, "I am against you, [Yerushalayim,]
> situated in a valley like a rock on a plain.
> You who say, 'Who can come down against us?
> Who can enter our lairs?' —

14
> I will punish you," says *Adonai*,
> "as your deeds deserve.
> I will set its forest on fire,
> and it will devour everything around it.""'

22 ¹ *Adonai* said, "Go down to the house of the king of Y'hudah and there speak this word: ² 'King of Y'hudah occupying David's throne, hear the word of *Adonai* — you, your servants and your people who enter through these gates. ³ This is what *Adonai* says:

> "Do what is right and just;
> rescue the wronged from their oppressors;
> do nothing wrong or violent
> to the stranger, orphan or widow;
> don't shed innocent blood in this place.

⁴ """If you are careful to do this, then future kings occupying David's throne will enter these palace gates riding in chariots and on horses — he, his servants and his people. ⁵ But if you will not pay attention to these words, then I swear by myself," says *Adonai*, "that this palace will become a ruin.""

⁶ "For here is what *Adonai* says concerning the palace of the king of Y'hudah:

> 'You are like Gil'ad to me,
> like the peak of the L'vanon;
> yet I will turn you into a desert,
> uninhabited cities.

7
> I will designate men to destroy you,
> each one with his weapons;
> they will chop down your choice cedars
> and throw them in the fire.'

⁸ "Many nations will pass by this city, and they will say to one another, 'Why has *Adonai* done such a thing to this great city?' ⁹ The answer will be, 'Because they abandoned the covenant of *Adonai* their God and worshipped other gods, serving them.'"

¹⁰ Do not weep for [the king] who has died,
do not mourn for him [Yoshiyahu].
But weep for him who departs [to Egypt],
for he will never return
or see his native land again.

¹¹ For this is what ADONAI says about Shalum the son of Yoshiyahu, king of Y'hudah,
who succeeded Yoshiyahu his father as king: "He has left this place, never to return;
¹² but he will die in the place where they have led him captive, without seeing this
land again.

¹³ "Woe to him who builds his palace unfairly,
its upper rooms by injustice;
who makes his neighbor work for free
and will not give him his wages;
¹⁴ who says, 'I will build me a spacious palace
with airy upper rooms,'
then makes windows and cedar panels
painted with vermilion!
¹⁵ Your cedar may be excellent,
but that doesn't make you a better king.
True, your father ate and drank,
but he also did what was right and just,
so things went well with him.
¹⁶ He upheld the cause of the poor and the weak,
so everything went well.
Isn't that what knowing me
is all about?" says ADONAI.
¹⁷ "In contrast, your eyes and heart
are controlled entirely by your greed,
your desire for shedding innocent blood,
oppressing and extorting."

¹⁸ Therefore here is what ADONAI says concerning Y'hoyakim the son of Yoshiyahu,
king of Y'hudah:

"There will be no one to mourn for him,
'Oh! My brother!' or 'Oh! My sister!'
There will be no one to mourn for him,
'Oh! My master!' or 'Oh! His glory!'
¹⁹ He will be given a donkey's 'burial' —
dragged out the gates of Yerushalayim
and thrown away [to rot].
²⁰ Climb up to the L'vanon and cry out,
raise your voice in Bashan,
cry out from 'Avarim,
for all your lovers are broken.

21   I spoke to you in your times of prosperity,
      but you said, 'I won't listen.'
      This has been your pattern since you were young —
      you pay no attention to what I say.

22   The wind will shepherd all your shepherds away,
      and your lovers will go into captivity.
      Then you will be ashamed and disgraced
      for all your wicked deeds.

23   You who live in the L'vanon,
      nesting in the cedars,
      how gracious will you be
      when pains come on you like a woman in labor?

²⁴ "As I live," says ADONAI, "even if Koniyahu the son of Y'hoyakim king of Y'hudah were the signet ring on my right hand, I would pull you off ²⁵ and hand you over to those who seek your life, to those you fear, N'vukhadretzar king of Bavel and the Kasdim. ²⁶ I will hurl you and the mother who gave birth to you into a country different from the one you were born in, and you will die there. ²⁷ They will not return to the country to which they long to return."

28   Is this man Koniyahu
      a despised, broken pot,
      an instrument nobody wants?
      Why are they being thrown out?
      Why are he and his offspring thrown out
      into a country they do not know?

29   Oh, land, land, land!
      Hear the word of ADONAI!

30   This what ADONAI says:
      "List this man as childless;
      he is a lifetime failure —
      none of his offspring will succeed,
      none will sit on David's throne
      or rule again in Y'hudah."

23 ¹ "Oh no! The shepherds are destroying and scattering the sheep in my pasture!" says ADONAI. ² Therefore this is what ADONAI, the God of Isra'el, says against the shepherds who shepherd my people: "You have scattered my flock, driven them away and not taken care of them. So I will 'take care of' you because of your evil deeds," says ADONAI. ³ "I myself will gather what remains of my flock from all the countries where I have driven them and bring them back to their homes, and they will be fruitful and increase their numbers. ⁴ I will appoint shepherds over them who will shepherd them; then they will no longer be afraid or disgraced; and none will be missing," says ADONAI.

5   "The days are coming," says ADONAI
      when I will raise a righteous Branch for David.

> He will reign as king and succeed,
> he will do what is just and right in the land.
> In his days Y'hudah will be saved,
> Isra'el will live in safety,
> and the name given to him will be
> ADONAI *Tzidkenu* [ADONAI our righteousness].

6

7 "Therefore," says ADONAI, "the day will come when people no longer swear, 'As ADONAI lives, who brought the people of Isra'el out of the land of Egypt,' 8 but, 'As ADONAI lives, who brought the descendants of the house of Isra'el up from the land to the north' and from all the countries where I drove them. Then they will live in their own land."

9 Concerning the prophets:

> My heart within me is broken,
> all my bones are shaking;
> I am like a drunk,
> like a man overcome by wine,
> because of ADONAI,
> because of his holy words.
> For the land is full of adulterers;
> because of a curse the land is in mourning —
> the desert pastures have dried up.
> Their course is evil, their power misused.
> "Both prophet and *cohen* are godless;
> In my own house I find their wickedness," says ADONAI.
> "Therefore their way will be slippery for them;
> they will be driven into darkness and fall there.
> For I will bring disaster upon them,
> their year of punishment," says ADONAI.
> "I have seen inappropriate conduct
> in the prophets of Shomron —
> they prophesied by Ba'al
> and led my people Isra'el astray.
> But in the prophets of Yerushalayim
> I have seen a horrible thing —
> they commit adultery, live in lies,
> so encouraging evildoers
> that none returns from his sin.
> For me they have all become like S'dom,
> its inhabitants like 'Amora."

10

11

12

13

14

15 Therefore, this is what ADONAI-*Tzva'ot* says concerning the prophets:

> "I will feed them bitter wormwood
> and make them drink poisonous water,
> for ungodliness has spread through all the land
> from the prophets of Yerushalayim."

¹⁶ *ADONAI-Tzva'ot* says:

> "Don't listen to the words of the prophets
> who are prophesying to you.
> They are making you act foolishly,
> telling you visions from their own minds
> and not from the mouth of *ADONAI.*

¹⁷ They keep reassuring those who despise me,
'*ADONAI* says you will be safe and secure,'
and saying to all living by their own stubborn hearts,
'Nothing bad will happen to you.'

¹⁸ But which of them has been present at the council
of *ADONAI* to see and hear his word?
Who has paid attention to
his word enough to hear it?"

¹⁹ Look! The storm of *ADONAI,*
bursting out in fury,
a whirling storm, whirling down
upon the heads of the wicked!

²⁰ *ADONAI*'s anger will not abate
till he fully accomplishes the purpose in his heart.
In the *acharit-hayamim,*
you will understand everything.

²¹ "I did not send these prophets; yet they ran.
I did not speak to them; yet they prophesied.

²² If they have been present at my council,
they should let my people hear my words
and turn them from their evil way
and the evil of their actions.

²³ Am I God only when near," asks *ADONAI,*
"and not when far away?

²⁴ Can anyone hide in a place so secret
that I won't see him?" asks *ADONAI.*
ADONAI says, "Do I not
fill heaven and earth?

²⁵ "I have heard what these prophets prophesying lies in my name are saying: 'I've had a dream! I've had a dream!' ²⁶ How long will this go on? Is [my word] in the hearts of prophets who are prophesying lies, who are prophesying the deceit of their own minds? ²⁷ With their dreams that they keep telling each other, they hope to cause my people to forget my name; just as their ancestors forgot my name when they worshipped Ba'al.

²⁸ "If a prophet has a dream,
let him tell it as a dream.

But someone who has my word
should speak my word faithfully.
What do chaff and wheat
have in common?" asks ADONAI.

²⁹ "Isn't my word like fire," asks ADONAI,
"like a hammer shattering rocks?

³⁰ So, I am against the prophets," says ADONAI,
"who steal my words from each other.

³¹ Yes, I am against the prophets," says ADONAI,
"who speak their own words, then add, 'He says.'

³² "I am against those who concoct prophecies out of fake dreams," says ADONAI. "They tell them, and by their lies and arrogance they lead my people astray. I didn't send them, I didn't commission them, and they don't do this people any good at all," says ADONAI.

³³ "When [someone from] this people, a prophet or a *cohen* asks you, 'What is the burden of ADONAI?' you are to answer them, 'What burden? I am throwing you off,' says ADONAI. ³⁴ As for a prophet, *cohen* or [someone else from] this people who speaks about 'the burden of ADONAI,' I will punish him and his household."

³⁵ So, when you speak with your neighbor or brother, ask, "What answer has ADONAI given?" or "What has ADONAI said?" ³⁶ Don't use the expression, "burden of ADONAI" any more; for every person's own word will be his burden. Must you twist the words of the living God, of ADONAI-*Tzva'ot*, our God? ³⁷ So, when speaking to a prophet, ask, "What answer has ADONAI given you?" or "What did ADONAI say?" ³⁸ But if you talk about "the burden of ADONAI," then here is what ADONAI says: "Because you use this expression, 'the burden of ADONAI,' after I have already sent you the order not to say, 'the burden of ADONAI,' ³⁹ I will lift you up, burden that you are, and throw you off, away from my presence — you and the city I gave you and your ancestors. ⁴⁰ Then I will subject you to everlasting disgrace — eternal, unforgettable shame."

24 ¹ It was after N'vukhadretzar king of Bavel had carried Y'khanyahu the son of Y'hoyakim, king of Y'hudah, along with the leaders of Y'hudah, the artisans and the skilled workers into exile from Yerushalayim and brought them to Bavel, that ADONAI gave me a vision. There, in front of the temple of ADONAI, two baskets of figs were placed. ² One of the baskets had in it very good figs, like those that ripen first; while the other basket had very bad figs, so bad that they were inedible. ³ Then ADONAI asked me, "Yirmeyahu, what do you see?" I answered, "Figs — the good figs are very good; but the bad ones are very bad, so bad they are inedible." ⁴ The word of ADONAI came to me: ⁵ "Here is what ADONAI the God of Isra'el says: 'I will regard the exiles from Y'hudah, whom I sent away from this place to the land of the Kasdim, as good, just as I do these good figs.

⁶ "'I will look after them for their good,
I will bring them back to this land;
I will build them up and not tear them down,
plant them and not pull them up.

⁷ I will give them a heart to know me

that I am *ADONAI.*
They will be my people,
and I will be their God;
for they will return to me
with all their heart.'

⁸ "But concerning the bad figs that are so bad as to be inedible, *ADONAI* says: 'I will make Tzidkiyahu the king of Y'hudah and his leaders resemble them, likewise the rest of Yerushalayim remaining in this land and those living in the land of Egypt. ⁹ Everywhere I drive them I will make them an object of horror, repulsive to all the kingdoms of the earth, a disgrace, a byword, a laughingstock and a curse; ¹⁰ and I will send sword, famine and plague among them until they have disappeared from the land I gave them and their ancestors.'"

25 ¹ This is the word that came to Yirmeyahu concerning all the people of Y'hudah in the fourth year of Y'hoyakim the son of Yoshiyahu, king of Y'hudah; this was also the first year of N'vukhadretzar king of Bavel. ² Yirmeyahu the prophet proclaimed it before all the people of Y'hudah and all the inhabitants of Yerushalayim: ³ "For twenty-three years, since the thirteenth year of Yoshiyahu the son of Amon, king of Y'hudah, until today, the word of *ADONAI* has come to me; and I have proclaimed it to you on numerous occasions; but you haven't listened. ⁴ Moreover, *ADONAI* sent you all his servants the prophets — again, on numerous occasions — but you didn't listen or pay attention. ⁵ The message was always: 'Every one of you, turn back from his evil way, from the evil of your actions. Then you will live in the land *ADONAI* gave you and your ancestors forever and ever. ⁶ Don't follow other gods by serving and worshipping them. "Don't provoke my anger with things your own hands have made; then I will do you no harm.' ⁷ But you wouldn't listen to me," says *ADONAI*, "so that you could provoke me with the products of your hands, to your own harm."

⁸ "Therefore, here is what *ADONAI-Tzva'ot* says: 'Because you haven't paid attention to what I've been saying, ⁹ I'm going to send for all the families of the north,' says *ADONAI*, 'and for my servant N'vukhadretzar the king of Bavel, and bring them against this land, against its inhabitants and against all the surrounding nations. I will completely destroy them, making them an object of horror and ridicule, a perpetual ruin. ¹⁰ Moreover, I will silence among them the sounds of joy and gladness, the voices of bridegroom and bride, the grinding of millstones and the light of lamps. ¹¹ This entire land will become a ruin, a waste; and these nations will serve the king of Bavel for seventy years. ¹² But when the seventy years are over, I will punish the king of Bavel and that nation for their sin,' says *ADONAI*, 'and I will turn the land of the Kasdim into everlasting ruins. ¹³ I will inflict on that land all my words that I have decreed against it, everything written in this book, in which Yirmeyahu has prophesied against all the nations. ¹⁴ For they too will become slaves to many nations and to powerful kings; I will pay them back according to their deeds and the work of their own hands.'

¹⁵ "For here is what *ADONAI* the God of Isra'el says to me: 'Take this cup of the wine of fury from my hand, and make all the nations where I am sending you drink it. ¹⁶ They will drink, stagger to and fro and behave like crazy people because of the sword that I will send among them.'"

¹⁷ Then I took the cup from *Adonai*'s hand and made all the nations drink, where *Adonai* had sent me — ¹⁸ Yerushalayim and the cities of Y'hudah, along with their kings and leaders, to make them a ruin and an object of horror, ridicule and cursing, as it is today; ¹⁹ Pharaoh king of Egypt, with his servants and leaders and all his people, both native ²⁰ and foreign; all the kings of the land of 'Utz; all the kings of the land of the P'lishtim, Ashkelon, 'Azah, 'Ekron and those remaining in Ashdod; ²¹ Edom, Mo'av, and the people of 'Amon; ²² all the kings of Tzor, of Tzidon and of the coastlands across the sea; ²³ D'dan, Teima, Buz and all who cut the corners of their beards; ²⁴ all the kings of Arabia and of the mixed peoples living in the desert; ²⁵ all the kings of Zimri, of 'Eilam and of the Medes; ²⁶ and all the kings of the north, far and near, one after another — indeed, all the kingdoms of the world that there are on the surface of the earth. And the king of Sheshakh will drink last of all.

²⁷ "You are to say to them, 'Here is what *Adonai-Tzva'ot*, the God of Isra'el, says: Drink until you're so drunk that you throw up, fall down, and never get up again, because of the sword I am sending among you!' ²⁸ If they refuse to take the cup from your hand and drink it, then say to them, 'Here is what *Adonai-Tzva'ot* says: You must drink! ²⁹ For, look! — if I am bringing disaster on the city that bears my own name, do you expect to go unpunished? Yes, I will summon a sword for all the inhabitants of the earth,' says *Adonai*.

³⁰ "As for you, [Yirmeyahu,] prophesy all these words against them; say to them,

'*Adonai* is roaring from on high,
raising his voice from his holy dwelling,
roaring with might against his own habitation,
shouting out loud, like those who tread grapes,
against everyone living on earth.

31   The sound resounds to the ends of the earth,
for *Adonai* is indicting the nations,
about to pass judgment on all humankind;
the wicked he has handed over to the sword,'

says *Adonai*." ³² Thus says *Adonai-Tzva'ot*:

"Disaster is spreading from nation to nation,
a mighty tempest is being unleashed
from the farthest ends of the earth."

33   On that day, those killed by *Adonai* will be strewn
from one end of the earth to the other;
they will not be mourned or gathered or buried,
but will lie on the ground like dung.

34   "Wail, shepherds! Cry!
Wallow in the dust, you lords of the flock!
For the days for your slaughter have come.
I will break you in pieces,
and like a prized vase you will fall."

35   The shepherds have no way to flee,
      the lords of the flock no way to escape.
36   Hear the cry of the shepherds,
      the wails of the lords of the flock!
      For ADONAI is destroying their pasture,
37   the peaceful grazing grounds are silenced,
      because of ADONAI's fierce anger.
38   Like a lion, he has abandoned his lair;
      for their land has become desolate
      because of the oppressor's fierce sword
      and because of ADONAI's fierce anger.

26 ¹ At the beginning of the reign of Y'hoyakim the son of Yoshiyahu, king of Y'hudah, this word came from ADONAI: ² "ADONAI says: 'Stand in the courtyard of ADONAI's house and speak to the people from all the cities in Y'hudah who come to worship at ADONAI's house; say everything I order you to say to them, and don't leave out a word. ³ Maybe they will listen, and each of them turn from his evil way; then I will be able to relent from the disaster I intend to bring on them because of how evil their deeds are. ⁴ So tell them that this is what ADONAI says: "If you will not pay attention to me and live according to my *Torah*, which I have given you, ⁵ and listen to what my servants the prophets, whom I send to you, say — I have sent them frequently, but you haven't listened — ⁶ then I will make this house like Shiloh, and I will make this city an object of cursing for all the nations of the earth."'"

⁷ The *cohanim*, the prophets and all the people heard Yirmeyahu speaking these words in the house of ADONAI. ⁸ When Yirmeyahu had finished saying everything ADONAI had ordered him to say to all the people, the *cohanim*, prophets and all the people seized him, shouting, "You will die for this! ⁹ Why have you prophesied in the name of ADONAI, 'This house will become like Shiloh,' and, 'This city will become uninhabited ruins'?" The people all crowded in on Yirmeyahu in ADONAI's house.

¹⁰ When the officials of Y'hudah heard about it, they came up from the king's palace to ADONAI's house and sat at the entrance to the New Gate of ADONAI's house. ¹¹ The *cohanim* and prophets said to the officials and all the people, "This man deserves a death sentence, because he has prophesied against this city; you have heard it with your own ears." ¹² Then Yirmeyahu said to the officials and all the people, "ADONAI sent me to prophesy against this house and against this city all the words you have heard. ¹³ Therefore now, improve your ways and your doings; and listen to the voice of ADONAI your God; then ADONAI will relent from the disaster he has decreed against you. ¹⁴ But as for me, here, I am in your hands; do with me whatever seems good and right to you. ¹⁵ Only know for certain that if you put me to death, you will bring innocent blood on yourselves, on this city and on its inhabitants; because the fact is that ADONAI sent me to you to speak all these words, so that you could hear them."

¹⁶ The officials and all the people then said to the *cohanim* and prophets, "This man does not deserve a death sentence, because he has spoken to us in the name of ADONAI our God." ¹⁷ At this point some of the leaders of the land stood up and addressed all the people assembled: ¹⁸ "Back in the time of Hizkiyahu king of Y'hudah, Mikhah from Moreshet was a prophet. He told all the people of Y'hudah, 'ADONAI-Tzva'ot says,

"Tziyon will be plowed under like a field,
Yerushalayim will become heaps of ruins,
and the mountain of the house like a forested height.'"

¹⁹ "Did Hizkiyahu king of Y'hudah and all Y'hudah put him to death? Not at all. Rather, he feared ADONAI, and prayed for ADONAI's favor; and ADONAI relented from the disaster he had pronounced against them. So [if we put Yirmeyahu to death,] we might bring great disaster on ourselves."

²⁰ On the other hand, there was also a man who prophesied in the name of ADONAI, Uriyahu the son of Sh'ma'yahu from Kiryat-Ye'arim, who prophesied against this city and against this land exactly what Yirmeyahu is saying. ²¹ When Y'hoyakim the king, with all his military men and other officials, heard what he was saying, the king wanted to have him killed. On hearing of this, Uriyahu became frightened, fled and went to Egypt. ²² Y'hoyakim the king sent men to Egypt — Elnatan the son of 'Akhbor and some others. ²³ They brought Uriyahu back from Egypt and took him to Y'hoyakim the king, who put him to the sword and threw his corpse into the burial-ground of the common people.

²⁴ But in this situation concerning Yirmeyahu, Achikam the son of Shafan used his influence to help him, so that he was not handed over to the people to be put to death.

27 ¹ At the beginning of the reign of Y'hoyakim the son of Yoshiyahu, king of Y'hudah, this word came to Yirmeyahu from ADONAI: ² "ADONAI says this to me: 'Make yourself a yoke of straps and crossbars, and put it on your neck. ³ Send [similar yokes] to the kings of Edom, of Mo'av, of the people of 'Amon, of Tzor, and of Tzidon by means of the envoys they send to Yerushalayim, and to Tzidkiyahu king of Y'hudah. ⁴ Give them this message for their masters by telling their envoys that ADONAI-Tzva'ot, the God of Isra'el, says for them to tell their masters:

⁵ "'"I made the earth, humankind, and the animals on the earth by my great power and my outstretched arm; and I give it to whom it seems right to me. ⁶ For now, I have given over all these lands to my servant N'vukhadnetzar the king of Bavel; I have also given him the wild animals to serve him. ⁷ All the nations will serve him, his son and his grandson, until his own country gets its turn — at which time many nations and great kings will make him their slave. ⁸ The nation and kingdom that refuses to serve this N'vukhadnetzar king of Bavel, that will not put their necks under the yoke of the king of Bavel, I will punish," says ADONAI "with sword, famine and plague, until I have put an end to them through him.

⁹ "'"You, therefore, don't listen to your prophets, diviners, dreamers, magicians or sorcerers, when they tell you that you won't be subject to the king of Bavel; ¹⁰ for they are prophesying lies to you that will result in your being removed far from your land, with my driving you out, so that you perish. ¹¹ But the nation that puts its neck under the yoke of the king of Bavel and serves him, that nation I will allow to remain on their own soil," says ADONAI. "They will farm it and live there."'"

¹² Then I spoke to Tzidkiyahu king of Y'hudah in just the same way: "Put your necks under the yoke of the king of Bavel, serve him and his people, and you will live. ¹³ Why would you want to die, you and your people, by sword, famine and plague — which is what ADONAI has decreed for the nation that will not serve the king of Bavel? ¹⁴ Don't listen to the words of the prophets who say to you, 'You will

not serve the king of Bavel'; because they are prophesying lies to you. ¹⁵ 'For I have not sent them,' says ADONAI, 'and they are prophesying falsely in my name, with the result that I will drive you out, and you will perish — you and the prophets prophesying to you.'"

¹⁶ I also spoke to the *cohanim* and to all this people; I said, "This is what ADONAI says: 'Don't listen to the words of the prophets prophesying to you that the articles from ADONAI's house will soon be returned from Bavel; because they are prophesying lies to you. ¹⁷ Don't listen to them. Serve the king of Bavel, and stay alive; why should this city become a ruin?' ¹⁸ But if they are in fact prophets, and if the word of ADONAI is with them, then let them now intercede with ADONAI-*Tzva'ot* that the articles still remaining in the house of ADONAI and in the palace of the king of Y'hudah will not go off to Bavel. ¹⁹ For this is what ADONAI-*Tzva'ot* says concerning the columns, the Sea, the bases and the rest of the articles still here in this city, ²⁰ that N'vukhadnetzar, king of Bavel did not seize when he carried off captive Y'khanyahu the son of Y'hoyakim, king of Y'hudah, from Yerushalayim to Bavel, along with all the leading men of Y'hudah and Yerushalayim — ²¹ yes, this is what ADONAI *Shaddai*, the God of Isra'el, says about the things remaining in the house of ADONAI, in the palace of the king of Y'hudah and in Yerushalayim: ²² 'They will be carried to Bavel; and there they will stay until the day I remember them, bring them back and restore them to this place,' says ADONAI."

28 ¹ That same year, at the beginning of the reign of Tzidkiyahu king of Y'hudah, in the fifth month of the fourth year, Hananyah the son of 'Azur the prophet, from Giv'on, spoke to me in ADONAI's house in front of the *cohanim* and all the people, saying, ² "This is what ADONAI-*Tzva'ot*, the God of Isra'el, says: 'I have broken the yoke of the king of Bavel. ³ Within two years I will restore to this place all the articles from ADONAI's house that N'vukhadnetzar king of Bavel removed from this place and carried to Bavel. ⁴ Also I will bring back here Y'khanyah the son of Y'hoyakim, king of Y'hudah, along with all those from Y'hudah who were taken captive to Bavel,' says ADONAI, 'for I will break the yoke of the king of Bavel.'"

⁵ Then the prophet Yirmeyahu said to the prophet Hananyah in front of the *cohanim* and all the people standing in ADONAI's house — ⁶ the prophet Yirmeyahu said, "*Amen*! May ADONAI do it! May ADONAI fulfill the words you have prophesied and bring back from Bavel to this place the articles from ADONAI's house and all the people who were carried away captive! ⁷ Nevertheless, listen now to this word that I am speaking for you to hear and for all the people to hear. ⁸ The prophets who were here before me and before you prophesied in times past against many countries and against great kingdoms about war, disaster and plagues. ⁹ As for a prophet who prophesies peace — when the word of that prophet is fulfilled, it will be evident concerning that prophet that ADONAI indeed did send him."

¹⁰ At this point Hananyah the prophet took the crossbar off the prophet Yirmeyahu's neck and broke it. ¹¹ Then Hananyah, in front of all the people, said, "Thus says ADONAI: 'In just this way will I break off the yoke of N'vukhadnetzar king of Bavel from the necks of all the nations within two years.'"

The prophet Yirmeyahu left them; ¹² but then this word of ADONAI came to Yirmeyahu, after Hananyah the prophet had broken off the crossbar from the neck of the prophet Yirmeyahu: ¹³ "Go and tell Hananyah that ADONAI says, 'You have broken the crossbars of wood, but you will make in their place crossbars of iron. ^{14} For here is what ADONAI-Tzva'ot, the God of Isra'el, says: "I have put a yoke of iron on the necks of all these nations, so that they can serve N'vukhadnetzar king of Bavel; and they will serve him; and I have given him the wild animals too."'" ^{15} Then the prophet Yirmeyahu said to Hananyah the prophet, "Listen here, Hananyah! ADONAI has not sent you! You are making these people trust in a lie! ^{16} Therefore, here is what ADONAI says: 'I am about to send you away from the face of the earth — this year you will die, because you have preached rebellion against ADONAI.'" ^{17} Hananyah the prophet died that same year, in the seventh month.

29 ^{1} Following is the text of the letter Yirmeyahu the prophet sent from Yerushalayim to the leaders remaining in exile, as well as to the *cohanim*, the prophets and all the people N'vukhadnetzar had carried off captive from Yerushalayim to Bavel. ^{2} This was after Y'khanyah the king, the queen mother, the officers, the leaders of Y'hudah and Yerushalayim, and the artisans and skilled workers had left Yerushalayim. ^{3} The letter was entrusted to El'asah the son of Shafan and G'maryah the son of Hilkiyah; Tzidkiyah king of Y'hudah sent them to Bavel, to N'vukhadnetzar king of Bavel. The letter said:

^{4} "Here is what ADONAI-Tzva'ot, the God of Isra'el, says to all those in exile, whom I have caused to be carried off captive from Yerushalayim to Bavel: ^{5} 'Build yourselves houses, and live in them. Plant gardens, and eat what they produce. ^{6} Choose women to marry, and have sons and daughters. Choose wives for your sons, and give your daughters in marriage to men, so that they can have sons and daughters — increase your numbers there, don't decrease. ^{7} Seek the welfare of the city to which I have caused you to go in exile, and pray to ADONAI on its behalf; for your welfare is bound up in its welfare.' ^{8} For this is what ADONAI-Tzva'ot, the God of Isra'el, says: 'Don't let your prophets who are living among you and your diviners deceive you, and don't pay attention to the dreams you urge them to dream. ^{9} For they are prophesying falsely in my name; I have not sent them,' says ADONAI.

^{10} "For here is what ADONAI says: 'After Bavel's seventy years are over, I will remember you and fulfill my good promise to you by bringing you back to this place. ^{11} For I know what plans I have in mind for you,' says ADONAI, 'plans for well-being, not for bad things; so that you can have hope and a future. ^{12} When you call to me and pray to me, I will listen to you. ^{13} When you seek me, you will find me, provided you seek for me wholeheartedly; ^{14} and I will let you find me,' says ADONAI. 'Then I will reverse your exile. I will gather you from all the nations and places where I have driven you,' says ADONAI, 'and bring you back to the place from which I exiled you.'

^{15} "You say that ADONAI has raised up prophets for you in Bavel. ^{16} But here is what ADONAI says about the king occupying David's throne and about all the people living in this city, your kinsmen who did not go into exile with you — ^{17} thus says ADONAI-Tzva'ot: 'I will attack them with sword, famine and plague; I will make them like bad figs, so bad they are inedible. ^{18} I will pursue them with sword, famine and plague and make them an object of horror to all the kingdoms of the earth; and they will bring on themselves cursing, astonishment, ridicule and reproach among all the nations where I have driven them; [19] because they have not paid attention to my words,' says *ADONAI*, 'which I sent to them through my servants the prophets. I sent them frequently, but you refused to listen,' says *ADONAI*.

[20]   "So pay attention now to the word of *ADONAI*, all of you in exile, whom I sent away from Yerushalayim to Bavel. [21] Here is what *ADONAI-Tzva'ot*, the God of Isra'el, says about Ach'av the son of Kolayah and Tzidkiyahu the son of Ma'aseiyah, who prophesy lies to you in my name: 'I will hand them over to N'vukhadretzar king of Bavel, and he will put them to death before your eyes. [22] In fact, all those exiled from Y'hudah who are in Bavel will take up this formula for cursing: "May *ADONAI* make you like Tzidkiyahu and Ach'av, whom the king of Bavel roasted in the fire!" [23] because they have done vile things in Isra'el, committing adultery with their neighbors' wives and speaking words in my name, falsely, which I did not order them to say. For I am he who knows; I am witness to this,' says *ADONAI*.

[24]   "To Sh'ma'yah the Nechelami you are to communicate this message: [25] 'This is a word from *ADONAI-Tzva'ot*, the God of Isra'el, because of the letters you sent in your own name to all the people in Yerushalayim, including Tz'fanyah the son of Ma'aseiyah the *cohen* and all the *cohanim*. [26] Your letter said, "*ADONAI* has made you *cohen* in place of Y'hoyada the *cohen*, in order to have officials in *ADONAI*'s house who will arrest any crazy person who makes himself out to be a prophet, so that you can restrain him in stocks and collar. [27] So why haven't you rebuked Yirmeyahu of 'Anatot, who makes himself out to be a prophet for you? [28] He even sends word to us in Bavel saying that the exile will last a long time; so build houses and live in them, plant gardens and eat what they produce." [29] Tz'fanyah the *cohen* read this letter to Yirmeyahu the prophet, and afterwards [30] the word of *ADONAI* came to Yirmeyahu, [31] instructing him to send to all those in exile this message: "Here is what *ADONAI* says about Sh'ma'yah the Nechelami: 'This Sh'ma'yah has prophesied to you, even though I did not send him, and has caused you to put your trust in a lie. [32] Because of this,' *ADONAI* says, 'I will punish Sh'ma'yah the Nechelami and his offspring. He will not have a man to live among this people, and he will not see the good I am planning to do for my people,' says *ADONAI*, 'because he has preached rebellion against *ADONAI*.'"'"

30 [1] This word came to Yirmeyahu from *ADONAI*: [2] "This is what *ADONAI* the God of Isra'el says: 'Write all the words I have spoken to you in a scroll. [3] For the day is coming,' says *ADONAI*, 'when I will reverse the exile of my people Isra'el and Y'hudah,' says *ADONAI*. 'I will cause them to return to the land I gave their ancestors, and they will take possession of it.'"

[4] These are the words *ADONAI* spoke concerning Isra'el and Y'hudah: [5] Here is what *ADONAI* says:

"We have heard a cry of terror,
of fear and not of peace.

6 Ask now and see:
can men give birth to children?
Why, then, do I see all the men
with their hands on their stomachs like women in labor,
with every face turned pale?

7 How dreadful that day will be! —
there has never been one like it:
a time of trouble for Ya'akov,
but out of it he will be saved.

8 "On that day," says ADONAI-*Tzva'ot*,
"I will break his yoke from off your neck,
I will snap your chains.
Foreigners will no longer enslave him.

9 Instead, they will serve ADONAI their God
and David their king, whom I will raise up for them.

10 "So don't be afraid, Ya'akov my servant,"
says ADONAI, "or be alarmed, Isra'el;
for I will return you from far away
and your offspring from their country of exile.
Ya'akov will again be quiet, at rest;
and no one will make him afraid.

11 "For I am with you to save you," says ADONAI,
"I will finish off all the nations
where I have scattered you.
However, you I will not finish off,
but will discipline only as you deserve;
I will not completely destroy you."

12 For here is what ADONAI says:

"Your wound is past healing,
your injury most severe;

13 no one thinks your wound can be bandaged;
you have no medicines that can heal you.

14 All your friends have forgotten you,
they no longer seek you out.
I have struck you down as an enemy would,
punished as a cruel man would,
because of your great wickedness,
because of your many sins.

15 Why cry that your wound and pain are past healing?
I have done these things to you

because of your great wickedness,
because of your many sins.

16 "But all who devour you will be devoured,
all your enemies will go into exile,
those who plunder you will be plundered,
those who pillage you will be pillaged.

17 For I will restore your health,
I will heal you of your wounds," says A*DONAI*,
"because they called you an outcast,
Tziyon, with no one who cares about her."

18 Thus says A*DONAI*:

"I will return Ya'akov's captives to their tents;
I will take pity on his dwellings.
Cities will be rebuilt on their own *tel*s,
with palaces where they're supposed to be.

19 From them will come thanksgiving
and the sound of people celebrating.
I will increase them; they will not be decreased;
I will honor them; they will not be despised.

20 Their children will be as they used to be,
their community confirmed in my presence;
and I will punish everyone
who oppresses them.

21 Their leader will be one of their own,
their ruler will come from among them.
I will cause him to come close
and let him approach me;
for, otherwise, who would guarantee his heart
enough to approach me?" says A*DONAI*.

22 "You will be my people,
and I will be your God."

23 Look! The storm of A*DONAI*,
bursting out in fury,
a sweeping storm, whirling down
upon the heads of the wicked!

24 A*DONAI*'s fierce anger will not abate
till he accomplishes the purpose in his heart.
In the *acharit-hayamim*,
you will understand.

25(31:1) "When that time comes," says A*DONAI*,
"I will be God of all the clans of Isra'el,
and they will be my people."

31 ¹⁽²⁾ Here is what ADONAI says:

> "The people escaping the sword
> found favor in the desert —
> I have brought Isra'el to its rest."

²⁽³⁾ From a distance ADONAI appeared to me, [saying,]
"I love you with an everlasting love;
this is why in my grace I draw you to me.
³⁽⁴⁾ Once again, I will build you; you will be rebuilt,
virgin of Isra'el.
Once again, equipped with your tambourines,
you will go out and dance with the merrymakers.
⁴⁽⁵⁾ Once again, you will plant vineyards on the hills of Shomron,
and those doing the planting will have the use of its fruit.
⁵⁽⁶⁾ For a day will come when the watchmen
on Mount Efrayim will call,
'Come, let's go up to Tziyon,
to ADONAI our God.'"

⁶⁽⁷⁾ For here is what ADONAI says:
"Sing with joy for Ya'akov!
shout for the chief of the nations!
Proclaim your praise, and say:
'ADONAI! You have saved your people,
the remnant of Isra'el!'
⁷⁽⁸⁾ Look! I am bringing them from the land in the north,
gathering them from the far ends of the earth;
among them are the blind and lame,
women with children, women in labor,
all together, a vast throng
returning here.
⁸⁽⁹⁾ They will come weeping and praying
as I bring them back.
I will lead them by streams of water
on smooth paths, so that they won't stumble.
For I am a father to Isra'el,
and Efrayim is my firstborn son."

⁹⁽¹⁰⁾ Nations, hear the word of ADONAI!
Proclaim it in the coastlands far away. Say:
"He who scattered Isra'el is gathering him,
guarding him like a shepherd his flock."
¹⁰⁽¹¹⁾ For ADONAI has ransomed Ya'akov,
redeemed him from hands too strong for him.
¹¹⁽¹²⁾ They will come and sing on the heights of Tziyon,
streaming to the goodness of Adonai,

to the grain, the wine, the olive oil,
and the young of the flock and the herd.
They themselves will be like a well-watered garden,
never to languish again.

12(13) "Then the virgin will dance for joy,
young men and old men together;
for I will turn their mourning into joy,
comfort and gladden them after their sorrow.

13(14) I will give the *cohanim* their fill of rich food,
and my people will be satisfied with my bounty," says ADONAI.

14(15) This is what ADONAI says:
"A voice is heard in Ramah,
lamenting and bitter weeping.
It is Rachel weeping for her children,
refusing to be comforted for her children,
because they are no longer alive."

15(16) This is what ADONAI says:
"Stop your weeping, and dry your eyes,
for your work will be rewarded," says ADONAI.
"They will return from the enemy's land;

16(17) so there is hope for your future," says ADONAI.
"Your children will return
to their own territory.

17(18) "I hear Efrayim bemoaning himself:
'You disciplined me, and I took your discipline
like a young ox not used to a yoke.
Let me return, and I will return,
for you are ADONAI, my God.

18(19) Yes, I turned away;
but later I repented.
When I had been made to understand,
I struck my thigh in shame and remorse,
bearing the weight of the disgrace
acquired when I was young.'

19(20) "Isn't Efrayim my very dear son,
a child who delights me so?
I speak about him all the time,
I can't help but recall him to mind.
In sum, I deeply yearn for him;
I will surely show him favor," says ADONAI.

20(21) Set up road signs, erect guideposts,
pay attention to the highway,
the path on which you traveled.

Come back, virgin Isra'el,
come back to these cities of yours!

21(22)   How long will you hesitate,
you unruly daughter?
For ADONAI has created something new on earth:
a woman with the strengths of a man.

22(23)   Here is what ADONAI-Tzva'ot,
the God of Isra'el, says:
"This expression will be used again
in the land of Y'hudah and its cities
after I have returned their exiles:
'May ADONAI bless you,
home of justice, holy mountain!'

23(24)   In it will live together
Y'hudah and all its cities,
the farmer and those who lead the flocks.

24(25)   For I have satisfied the weary
and filled the needs of all in distress."

25(26) At this point I woke up and looked around, but I had enjoyed my sleep.

26(27) "Here, the days are coming," says ADONAI, "when I will sow the house of Isra'el and the house of Y'hudah with the seed of humans and the seed of animals. 27(28) At that time, just as I used to watch over them with the intent to uproot, break down, overthrow, destroy and do harm; so then I will watch over them to build and plant," says ADONAI. 28(29) "When those days come they will no longer say,

'The fathers have eaten sour grapes,
and the children's teeth are set on edge.'

29(30)   Rather, each will die for his own sin;
every one who eats sour grapes,
his own teeth will be set on edge.

30(31) "Here, the days are coming," says ADONAI, "when I will make a new covenant with the house of Isra'el and with the house of Y'hudah. 31(32) It will not be like the covenant I made with their fathers on the day I took them by their hand and brought them out of the land of Egypt; because they, for their part, violated my covenant, even though I, for my part, was a husband to them," says ADONAI. 32(33) "For this is the covenant I will make with the house of Isra'el after those days," says ADONAI: "I will put my Torah within them and write it on their hearts; I will be their God, and they will be my people. 33(34) No longer will any of them teach his fellow community member or his brother, 'Know ADONAI'; for all will know me, from the least of them to the greatest; because I will forgive their wickednesses and remember their sins no more."

34(35)   This is what ADONAI says,
who gives the sun as light for the day,
who ordained the laws for the moon and stars

to provide light for the night,
who stirs up the sea until its waves roar —
ADONAI-*Tzva'ot* is his name:

³⁵⁽³⁶⁾ "If these laws leave my presence," says ADONAI,
"then the offspring of Isra'el will stop being
a nation in my presence forever."

³⁶⁽³⁷⁾ This is what ADONAI says:
"If the sky above can be measured
and the foundations of the earth be fathomed,
then I will reject all the offspring of Isra'el
for all that they have done," says ADONAI.

³⁷⁽³⁸⁾ "Look, the days are coming," says ADONAI, "when the city will be rebuilt for ADONAI from the Tower of Hanan'el to the Corner Gate. ³⁸⁽³⁹⁾ The measuring line will be stretched straight to Garev Hill, then turn to Go'ah. ³⁹⁽⁴⁰⁾ The whole valley of corpses and ashes, including all the fields as far as *Vadi* Kidron, and on to the corner of the Horse Gate to the east, will be separated out for ADONAI; it will never be uprooted or destroyed again."

32 ¹ This is the word that came to Yirmeyahu from ADONAI in the tenth year of Tzidkiyahu king of Y'hudah, which was the eighteenth year of N'vukhadretzar. ² At that time the army of the king of Bavel was besieging Yerushalayim; and Yirmeyahu the prophet was imprisoned in the guards' quarters attached to the king of Y'hudah's palace, ³ where Tzidkiyahu king of Y'hudah had imprisoned him after demanding, "How dare you prophesy that ADONAI says, 'I will hand this city over to the king of Bavel, and he will capture it; ⁴ Tzidkiyahu king of Y'hudah will not escape from the Kasdim but will certainly be handed over to the king of Bavel, who will address him face to face, with their eyes meeting; ⁵ and he will lead Tzidkiyahu to Bavel, where he will stay until I remember him,' says ADONAI, 'and even if you fight the Kasdim, you will fail'?"

⁶ Yirmeyahu said, "This word of ADONAI came to me: ⁷ 'Hanam'el, the son of your uncle Shalum, will approach you and say, "Buy my field at 'Anatot; you have next-of-kin's right to redeem it; so buy it."'" ⁸ As ADONAI had said, my cousin Hanam'el came to me in the guards' quarters and said, "Please buy my field at 'Anatot, in the territory of Binyamin; because you will inherit it, and you have next-of-kin's right to redeem it, so buy it for yourself." Then I was certain that this was ADONAI's word.

⁹ So I bought the field at 'Anatot which belonged to my cousin Hanam'el and weighed out the money for him, seven ounces of silver *shekels*. ¹⁰ I signed on the purchase contract, sealed it, called witnesses and weighed out the money for him on a balance scale. ¹¹ I took the purchase contract, both the sealed copy with the terms and conditions, and the unsealed copy, ¹² and gave the purchase contract to Barukh the son of Neriyah, the son of Machseyah, in the presence of my cousin Hanam'el, the witnesses who had signed the purchase contract and the people from Y'hudah sitting by the guards' quarters. ¹³ In their presence I instructed Barukh as follows: ¹⁴ "Here is what ADONAI-*Tzva'ot*, the God of Isra'el, says: 'Take these contracts, both the sealed and unsealed copies, and place them in a clay jar, so that they can be

preserved for a long time.' ¹⁵ For *Adonai-Tzva'ot*, the God of Isra'el, says that one day homes, fields and vineyards will again be bought in this land."

¹⁶ After giving the purchase contract to Barukh son of Neriyah, I prayed to *Adonai*: ¹⁷ "*Adonai*, God! You made heaven and earth by your great power and outstretched arm; nothing is too hard for you. ¹⁸ You display your grace to thousands but also repay the guilt of the fathers into the lap of their children who follow them. Great, powerful God, whose name is *Adonai-Tzva'ot*, ¹⁹ great in counsel, mighty in deed! Your eyes are open to all the ways of human beings in order to repay each one according to his ways, according to the consequences of what he does. ²⁰ You gave signs and performed miracles in the land of Egypt which continue to this day, also in Isra'el and among other people; thus you made yourself the reputation you have today. ²¹ You brought your people of Isra'el out of the land of Egypt with signs and miracles, with a strong hand and an outstretched arm and with great terror. ²² Then you gave them this land, which you had sworn to their ancestors that you would give them, a land flowing with milk and honey. ²³ They entered and took possession of it; but they did not pay attention to your voice, did not live according to your *Torah*, and did nothing of all you ordered them to do. Therefore you made this complete disaster befall them — ²⁴ the siege-works are already there; they have come to the city to capture it; and the city, by means of sword, famine and plague, is being handed over to the Kasdim fighting against it. What you foretold is being fulfilled; here, you see it, yourself. ²⁵ Yet you, *Adonai*, God, have said to me, 'Buy the field for money, and call witnesses; even as the city is being turned over to the Kasdim!'"

²⁶ Then this word of *Adonai* came to Yirmeyahu: ²⁷ "Look, I am *Adonai*, the God of every living creature; is there anything too hard for me? ²⁸ Therefore, here is what *Adonai* says: 'I will hand this city over to the Kasdim and to N'vukhadretzar king of Bavel; and he will capture it. ²⁹ The Kasdim who are fighting against this city will enter and set this city on fire; they will burn it down, including its houses, on whose roofs they offered to Ba'al and poured out drink offerings to other gods, in order to make me angry. ³⁰ For from their youth, the people of Isra'el and the people of Y'hudah have done only what is evil from my perspective; the people of Isra'el have done nothing but provoke me with what their hands make,' says *Adonai*. ³¹ 'This city has so provoked my anger and fury from the day they built it to this day that I ought to remove it from my presence, ³² because of all the evil that the people of Isra'el and the people of Y'hudah have done in order to make me angry — they, their kings, their leaders, their *cohanim*, their prophets, the men of Y'hudah and the inhabitants of Yerushalayim. ³³ They have turned their backs on me, not their faces; and although I taught them, taught them frequently, they have not listened so as to receive instruction. ³⁴ Instead they put their detestable idols in the house that bears my name, to defile it; ³⁵ and they built the high places for Ba'al which are in the Ben-Hinnom Valley, to burn alive their sons and daughters to Molekh — something I did not order them to do, it never even entered my mind that they would do such an abominable thing — and thus they caused Y'hudah to sin.'

³⁶ "Therefore, thus says *Adonai* the God of Isra'el concerning this city, of which you say that it is handed over to the king of Bavel by sword, famine and plague: ³⁷ 'I will gather them out of all the countries where I drove them in my anger, fury and great wrath; and I will bring them back to this place and have them live here in safety. ³⁸ They will be my people, and I will be their God. ³⁹ I will give them

singleness of heart and singleness of purpose, so that they will fear me forever — this will be for their own good and for the good of their children after them. ⁴⁰ I will make with them an everlasting covenant not to turn away from them, but to do them good; I will put fear of me in their hearts, so that they will not leave me. ⁴¹ I will take joy in them, so as to do them good. I will plant them in this land truly, with my whole heart and being.' ⁴² For here is what ADONAI says: 'Just as I have brought this complete disaster on this people, so likewise I will bring on them all the good I have promised them. ⁴³ Fields will be bought in this land, even though you say about it that it is desolate, devoid of human beings or animals, and given over to the Kasdim. ⁴⁴ Yes, people will buy fields for money, sign the purchase contracts, seal them and call witnesses, in the territory of Binyamin, in the areas around Yerushalayim, in the cities of Y'hudah, in the cities of the hill-country, in the cities of the Sh'felah and in the cities of the Negev. For I will cause their exiles to return,' says ADONAI."

33 ¹ The word of ADONAI came to Yirmeyahu a second time while he was still imprisoned in the guards' quarters:

² "Thus says ADONAI the maker,
   ADONAI who formed [the universe]
   so as to keep directing it —
   ADONAI is his name:
³ 'Call out to me,
   and I will answer you —
   I will tell you great things,
   hidden things of which you are unaware.'"

⁴ For here is what ADONAI the God of Isra'el says concerning the houses of this city and the palaces of the kings of Y'hudah which are about to be destroyed and used as siege-works and ramparts, ⁵ where they will come to fight the Kasdim: "These places will eventually be filled with the corpses of people whom I am striking down in my anger and fury, everyone whose wickedness has caused me to hide my face from this city. ⁶ However, I will bring it health and healing; I will heal them and reveal to them peace and truth in plenty. ⁷ I will cause the captives of Y'hudah and the captives of Isra'el to return; and I will build them up as I did at first. ⁸ I will cleanse them from all their sins, through which they offended me; and I will pardon all their sins, through which they offended and rebelled against me. ⁹ Then the name of this city will bring me joy, praise and glory before all the nations of the earth that hear about all the good I am doing for them; they will be overcome with fear and trembling at all the good and peace I am securing for it."

¹⁰ Here is what ADONAI says: "You say that this place is a wasteland, with neither people nor animals in the cities of Y'hudah, and that the streets of Yerushalayim are desolate, without people or animals — no inhabitants. Yet there will again be heard here ¹¹ the sounds of joy and gladness and the voices of bridegroom and bride, the voices of those who sing, 'Give thanks to ADONAI-Tzva'ot, for ADONAI is good, for his grace continues forever,' as they bring offerings of thanksgiving into the house of ADONAI. For I will cause those captured from the land to return, as before," says ADONAI.

¹² *Adonai-Tzva'ot* says, "In this place, which is a wasteland without people or animals, and in all its cities, there will once again be pasture-lands where shepherds can let their flocks rest. ¹³ In the cities of the hill-country, in the cities of the Sh'felah, in the cities of the Negev, in the territory of Binyamin, in the areas around Yerushalayim and in the cities of Y'hudah flocks will again pass under the hands of the one who counts them," says *Adonai*.

¹⁴ "Here, the days are coming," says *Adonai*, "when I will fulfill this good promise which I have proclaimed for the house of Isra'el and the house of Y'hudah.

¹⁵ When those days come, at that time,
I will cause to spring up for David
a Branch of Righteousness.
He will do what is just and right in the land.
¹⁶ When those days come, Y'hudah will be saved,
Yerushalayim will live in safety,
and the name given to her will be
Adonai Tzidkenu [*Adonai* our Righteousness]."

¹⁷ For this is what *Adonai* says: "There will never be cut off from David a man to occupy the throne of the house of Isra'el. ¹⁸ Nor will there ever be cut off from the *cohanim* who are *L'vi'im* a man before me to offer burnt offerings, burn grain offerings and offer sacrifices every day."

¹⁹ This word of *Adonai* came to Yirmeyahu: ²⁰ "Here is what *Adonai* says:

'If you can break my covenant with the day
and my covenant with the night,
so that daytime and nighttime no longer come
when they are supposed to,
²¹ then my covenant with my servant David
also can be broken,
so that he will not have a descendant
to reign from his throne
or *L'vi'im* who are *cohanim*
to minister to me.
²² To the degree that the armies of heaven are past counting
and the sand by the sea past measuring,
I will increase the descendants of my servant David
and the *L'vi'im* ministering to me.'"

²³ This word of *Adonai* came to Yirmeyahu: ²⁴ "Haven't you noticed that these people are saying, '*Adonai* has rejected the two families he chose'? Hence they despise my people and no longer look at them as a nation. ²⁵ Here is what *Adonai* says: 'If I have not established my covenant with day and night and fixed the laws for sky and earth, ²⁶ then I will also reject the descendants of Ya'akov and of my servant David, not choosing from his descendants people to rule over the descendants of Avraham, Yis'chak and Ya'akov. For I will cause their captives to come back, and I will show them compassion.'"

34 ^{1} This word came to Yirmeyahu from *ADONAI* when N'vukhadretzar king of Bavel, his whole army, all his vassal kingdoms and all the peoples fought against Yerushalayim and all its cities: ^{2} "*ADONAI* the God of Isra'el says to go and speak to Tzidkiyahu king of Y'hudah. Tell him that *ADONAI* says: 'I am going to hand this city over to the king of Bavel, and he will burn it to the ground. ^{3} You will not escape but will surely be captured and handed over to him; your eyes will see the eyes of the king of Bavel, he will speak with you face to face, and you will go to Bavel.' ^{4} Nevertheless, Tzidkiyahu king of Y'hudah, hear the word of *ADONAI*. *ADONAI* says this about you: 'You will not be put to the sword ^{5} but will die peacefully; and just as they burned spices for your ancestors, the earlier kings who preceded you, so they will burn spices for you and mourn you, "Oh! Master!" For I have spoken the word,' says *ADONAI*." ^{6} Yirmeyahu the prophet said all these words to Tzidkiyahu king of Y'hudah in Yerushalayim ^{7} at the time when the king of Bavel's army was fighting against Yerushalayim and against all the cities of Y'hudah that were left — that is, against Lakhish and 'Azekah, since only these remained of the fortified cities of Y'hudah.

^{8} This word came to Yirmeyahu from *ADONAI* after King Tzidkiyahu had made a covenant with all the people in Yerushalayim to emancipate them. ^{9} Everyone who had a male or female slave who was Hebrew was to let him go free; none was to keep as his slave a fellow Jew. ^{10} All the leaders and all the people listened who had entered into the covenant, wherein everyone was to free his male and female slaves and not keep them in bondage any longer. They listened, and they let them go. ^{11} But afterwards, they changed their minds; they made the male and female slaves, whom they had freed, return; and they brought them back into subjection as slaves. ^{12} Therefore this word of *ADONAI* came to Yirmeyahu from *ADONAI*: ^{13} "Here is what *ADONAI* the God of Isra'el says: 'When I brought your ancestors out of the land of Egypt, where they lived as slaves, I made this covenant with them: ^{14} "At the end of seven years every one of you is to set free his brother Hebrew who has been sold to you and has served you six years. You are to let him go free from you." But your ancestors did not listen to me or pay any attention. ^{15} Now you repented, you did what is right from my viewpoint when each of you proclaimed freedom to his fellow; and you made a covenant before me in the house bearing my name. ^{16} But then you changed your minds. You profaned my name when each of you took back his male and female slaves, whom you had set free to live as they wished, and brought them back into subjection as your slaves.' ^{17} Therefore here is what *ADONAI* says: 'You did not heed me and proclaim freedom, each to his brother and each to his neighbor; so now I proclaim for you a freedom,' says *ADONAI*, 'for sword, plague and famine. I will make you an object of horror to all the kingdoms on earth. ^{18} As for the men who violated my covenant by not living up to the conditions of the covenant which they made in my presence when they cut the calf in two and passed between its parts — ^{19} the leaders of Y'hudah, the leaders of Yerushalayim, the officials, the *cohanim* and all the people of the land who passed between the parts of the calf; ^{20} I will hand them over to their enemies, hand them over to those who seek their lives; and their corpses will become food for birds in the air and wild animals. ^{21} Tzidkiyahu king of Y'hudah and his officials I will hand over to their enemies, to those who seek their lives and to the army of the king of Bavel, which has withdrawn. ^{22} I will give the order,' says *ADONAI*, 'and cause them to return to this city. They will attack it, capture it and burn it to the ground; and I will make the cities of Y'hudah desolate and uninhabited.'"

35 ¹ This word came to Yirmeyahu from *ADONAI* during the time of Y'hoyakim the son of Yoshiyahu, king of Y'hudah: ² "Go to the Rekhavim, speak to them, bring them to one of the rooms in the house of *ADONAI*, and give them some wine to drink." ³ So I took Ya'azanyah the son of Yirmeyahu, the son of Havatzinyah, and his brothers, all his sons and all the Rekhavim, ⁴ and took them into the house of *ADONAI*, to the room of the sons of Hanan the son of Yigdalyahu, a man of God. It was by the room of the officials, which was above the room of Ma'aseiyah the son of Shalum, the gatekeeper. ⁵ There I set in front of the members of the clan of the Rekhavim pitchers full of wine and cups, and said to them, "Drink some wine." ⁶ But they said, "We will not drink any wine; because Yonadav the son of Rekhav, our ancestor, gave us this order: 'You are not to drink wine, neither you nor your descendants, forever. ⁷ Also you are not to build houses, sow seed, or plant or own vineyards. Rather, you are always to live in tents; so that you may live a long time in the land, in which you are not citizens.' ⁸ We have heeded the words of Yonadav the son of Rekhav, our ancestor, in all that he instructed us to do: not to drink wine as long as we live — we, our wives, our sons and our daughters; ⁹ not to build houses for ourselves to live in; and not to have vineyards, fields or seed. ¹⁰ We have lived in tents, and we have heeded Yonadav our ancestor and done everything he ordered us to do. ¹¹ But when N'vukhadretzar king of Bavel came up to attack the land, we said, 'Come, let's go up to Yerushalayim,' because we were afraid of the army of the Kasdim and the army of Aram; hence we are living in Yerushalayim."

¹² Then the word of *ADONAI* came to Yirmeyahu: ¹³ "*ADONAI-Tzva'ot* the God of Isra'el says to go to the men of Y'hudah and the inhabitants of Yerushalayim and say: 'Won't you ever learn to listen to my words?' says *ADONAI*. ¹⁴ 'The words of Yonadav the son of Rekhav which he ordered his offspring, not to drink wine, are obeyed; so to this day they don't drink any; because they heed their ancestor's order. But I have spoken to you, spoken frequently, and you have not listened to me. ¹⁵ I have also sent you all my servants the prophets, sent them frequently, with the message, "Every one of you should turn back now from his evil way, improve your actions and not follow other gods in order to serve them. Then you will live in the land I gave you and your ancestors. But you have not paid attention or listened to me. ¹⁶ Because the descendants of Yonadav the son of Rekhav have obeyed the order of their ancestor, which he ordered them; but this people has not listened to me; ¹⁷ therefore — " here is what *ADONAI Elohei-Tzva'ot*, the God of Isra'el, says: "I will inflict on Y'hudah and all the inhabitants of Yerushalayim all the disaster I have decreed against them; because I have spoken to them, but they have not listened; and I have called out to them, but they have not answered.""'

¹⁸ Then to the clan of the Rekhavim Yirmeyahu said, "Here is what *ADONAI-Tzva'ot*, the God of Isra'el, says: 'Because you have heeded the order of Yonadav your ancestor, observed all his commands and done what he ordered you to do; ¹⁹ therefore *ADONAI-Tzva'ot*, the God of Isra'el, says this: "Yonadav the son of Rekhav will never lack a descendant to stand before me.""'

36 ¹ In the fourth year of Y'hoyakim the son of Yoshiyahu, king of Y'hudah, this word came to Yirmeyahu from ADONAI: ² "Take a scroll and write on it all the words I have spoken to you against Isra'el, Y'hudah and all the other nations, from the day I started speaking to you, back in the time of Yoshiyahu, until today. ³ Perhaps the house of Y'hudah will listen to all the disaster I intend to bring on them, and turn back, each person from his evil way; then I will forgive their wickedness and sin."

⁴ So Yirmeyahu summoned Barukh the son of Neriyah; and Barukh wrote down on a scroll, at Yirmeyahu's dictation, all the words that ADONAI had said to him. ⁵ Then Yirmeyahu gave this order to Barukh: "I am not allowed to enter the house of ADONAI. ⁶ Therefore, you take the scroll which you wrote at my dictation, go into the house of ADONAI on a fast-day, and read from it the words of ADONAI in the hearing of the people; also read them to all Y'hudah as they exit their cities. ⁷ Perhaps they will turn to ADONAI in prayer and will return, each one, from his evil way. For the anger and fury which ADONAI has decreed against this people is great."

⁸ Barukh the son of Neriyah obeyed everything Yirmeyahu the prophet ordered him to do, reading the words of ADONAI from the scroll in ADONAI's house. ⁹ A fast was proclaimed in the ninth month of the fifth year of Y'hoyakim the son of Yoshiyahu, king of Y'hudah, for all the people in Yerushalayim and all the people who came from the cities of Y'hudah to Yerushalayim. ¹⁰ It was then that Barukh read from the scroll the words of Yirmeyahu in the house of ADONAI, in the chamber of G'maryahu the son of Shafan the secretary, in the upper courtyard, at the entry to the New Gate of ADONAI's house, for all the people to hear. ¹¹ When Mikhay'hu the son of G'maryahu, the son of Shafan, had heard from the scroll all the words of ADONAI, ¹² he went down to the king's palace, into the secretary's room. All the officials were there — Elishama the secretary, D'layahu the son of Sh'ma'yahu, Elnatan the son of 'Akhbor, G'maryah the son of Shafan, Tzidkiyahu the son of Hananyahu and all the [other] officials. ¹³ Mikhay'hu told them all the words he had heard when Barukh read the scroll in the people's hearing; ¹⁴ whereupon all the officials sent Y'hudi the son of N'tanyahu, the son of Shelemyahu, the son of Kushi, to Barukh to say, "Take in your hand the scroll from which you read in the hearing of the people, and come." So Barukh the son of Neriyah took the scroll in his hand and went to them. ¹⁵ They said to him, "Sit down, please, and read it to us." Barukh read it to them. ¹⁶ After they had heard all the words, they turned in fear to each other and said to Barukh, "We will certainly tell the king about all these words." ¹⁷ Then they asked Barukh, "Tell us now, how did you write all these words? At his dictation?" ¹⁸ Barukh answered them, "He said all these words to me with his mouth, and I wrote them with ink in the scroll." ¹⁹ At this, the officials said to Barukh, "Go and hide yourselves, you and Yirmeyahu; don't let anyone know where you are." ²⁰ After depositing the scroll in the room of Elishama the secretary, they went in to the courtyard and told everything to the king.

²¹ The king sent Y'hudi to bring the scroll, and he took it from the room of Elishama the secretary. Y'hudi read it to the king and all the officials standing near the king. ²² The king was sitting in his winter house; and since it was the ninth month, he had a fire burning in the stove in front of him. ²³ After Y'hudi had read three or four columns from the scroll, he would cut off that portion with a knife and throw it into the fire that was burning in the stove, until the entire scroll had been consumed by the fire in the stove. ²⁴ But even though they heard all these words, neither the king nor any of his servants grew afraid or tore their clothes. ²⁵ Elnatan, D'layahu

and G'maryahu had begged the king not to burn the scroll; but he wouldn't listen to them. ²⁶ Then the king ordered Yerachme'el the king's son, S'rayahu the son of 'Azri'el and Shelemyahu the son of 'Avde'el to arrest Barukh the scribe and Yirmeyahu the prophet; but ADONAI hid them.

²⁷ Then this word of ADONAI came to Yirmeyahu after the king had burned the scroll with the words Barukh had written at Yirmeyahu's dictation: ²⁸ "Take another scroll, and write on it all the words that were on the first scroll, which Y'hoyakim the king of Y'hudah burned up. ²⁹ And as far as Y'hoyakim king of Y'hudah is concerned, you are to say that ADONAI says, 'You burned this scroll, asking, "Why did you write in it that the king of Bavel will certainly come and destroy this land and leave it without either humans or animals?" ³⁰ Therefore ADONAI says this about Y'hoyakim king of Y'hudah: "He will have no one to occupy David's throne; and his dead body will be thrown out to lie in the heat by day and in the frost by night. ³¹ Moreover, I will punish him, his offspring and his officials for their wickedness; and I will bring on them, the inhabitants of Yerushalayim and the people of Y'hudah all the disaster I have decreed against them, to which they have paid no attention."'"

³² Then Yirmeyahu took another scroll and gave it to Barukh the scribe, the son of Neriyah. At Yirmeyahu's dictation he wrote in it all the words of the scroll which Y'hoyakim king of Y'hudah had burned up in the fire, and to those he added many similar words.

37 ¹ Tzidkiyahu the son of Yoshiyahu became king, succeeding Koniyahu the son of Y'hoyakim, whom N'vukhadretzar king of Bavel had made king over the land of Y'hudah. ² But neither he, his servants nor the people of the land paid attention to the words of ADONAI, which he spoke through the prophet Yirmeyahu.

³ Tzidkiyahu the king sent Y'hukhal the son of Shelemyahu and Tz'fanyahu the son of Ma'aseiyah, the *cohen*, to the prophet Yirmeyahu with the message, "Please pray to ADONAI our God for us." ⁴ At that time Yirmeyahu was mixing freely with the people, because they had not yet put him in prison. ⁵ At the same time Pharaoh's army marched out of Egypt; and when the Kasdim besieging Yerushalayim heard about them, they lifted the siege from Yerushalayim.

⁶ Then this word of ADONAI came to the prophet Yirmeyahu: ⁷ "ADONAI the God of Isra'el says to tell the king of Y'hudah, who sent you to me to consult me: 'Pharaoh's army has marched out to assist you; but they will return to Egypt, to their own country. ⁸ The Kasdim will return, attack this city, capture it and burn it to the ground.' ⁹ Here is what ADONAI says: 'Don't deceive yourselves by thinking that the Kasdim must withdraw from you, because they will not withdraw. ¹⁰ Even if you were to strike the entire army of the Kasdim fighting against you, to the degree that only their wounded were left, they would still rise up every man from his tent and burn this city to the ground.'"

¹¹ Then, at the time when the army of the Kasdim had lifted the siege of Yerushalayim out of fear of Pharaoh's army, ¹² Yirmeyahu left Yerushalayim to go to the territory of Binyamin to receive his share of an inheritance there. He was passing through the crowds ¹³ and had reached the gate leading toward Binyamin when a guard commander there named Yir'iyah the son of Shelemyah, the son of Hananyah, seized Yirmeyahu the prophet, shouting, "You're deserting to the Kasdim!" ¹⁴ Yirmeyahu answered, "That is a lie! I am not deserting to the Kasdim";

but Yir'iyah wouldn't listen to him. So he arrested Yirmeyahu and brought him to the officials. ¹⁵ The officials, furious with Yirmeyahu, had him beaten and jailed in the house of Y'honatan the secretary, which had been made over into a prison. ¹⁶ The cistern had been made into a dungeon, and Yirmeyahu was put in one of its cells; there he remained for a long time.

¹⁷ Then Tzidkiyahu the king sent and had him brought; and the king asked him secretly, in his palace, "Is there any word from ADONAI?" "There is," Yirmeyahu said. "You will be handed over to the king of Bavel." ¹⁸ Yirmeyahu asked King Tzidkiyahu, "In what way have I sinned against you or against your officials or against this people, that has caused you to put me in prison? ¹⁹ Where are your prophets now, the ones who prophesied to you that the king of Bavel wouldn't attack you or this land? ²⁰ So now, please listen, my lord king! I beg you, approve my request — don't make me return to the house of Y'honatan the secretary, or I will die there." ²¹ At that, Tzidkiyahu the king gave the order, at which they committed Yirmeyahu to the guards' quarters and gave him daily a loaf of bread from the Bakers' Street, until all the bread in the city had been used up. Thus Yirmeyahu remained in the guards' quarters.

38 ¹ But Sh'fatyah the son of Mattan, G'dalyahu the son of Pash'chur, Yukhal the son of Shelemyahu and Pash'chur the son of Malkiyah heard these words which Yirmeyahu had said to all the people, ² "Here is what ADONAI says: whoever remains in this city will die by sword, famine and plague; but whoever leaves and surrenders to the Kasdim will stay alive; his own life will be his only 'spoils of war,' but he will stay alive. ³ ADONAI says that this city will certainly be handed over to the army of the king of Bavel, and he will capture it." ⁴ The leaders said to the king, "Please let this man be put to death; because by speaking such words to the soldiers left in this city and to all the people, he is demoralizing them. This man is seeking not to benefit this people, but to harm them." ⁵ Tzidkiyahu the king said, "All right, he is in your hands; for the king can't prevent you from doing as you please."

⁶ Then they took Yirmeyahu and threw him into the cistern of Malkiyahu the king's son, which was in the guards' quarters; they let down Yirmeyahu into it with ropes. In the pit there was no water, but there was mud; and Yirmeyahu sank into the mud. ⁷ 'Eved-Melekh the Ethiopian, an officer in the king's house, heard that they had put Yirmeyahu in the cistern. When the king was sitting at the gate leading toward Binyamin, ⁸ 'Eved-Melekh left the palace and said to the king, ⁹ "My lord, king! What these men have done to Yirmeyahu the prophet is evil. They have thrown him into the cistern; and he is likely to die there where he is, because of the famine; for there is no more food in the city." ¹⁰ Then the king ordered 'Eved-Melekh the Ethiopian, "Take thirty men with you from here, and bring Yirmeyahu the prophet up out of the cistern before he dies." ¹¹ So 'Eved-Melekh took the men with him and entered a storeroom under the treasury in the king's palace, from which he took some old clothes and rags. These he let down with ropes to Yirmeyahu in the cistern. ¹² 'Eved-Melekh the Ethiopian then said to Yirmeyahu, "Use these old clothes and rags as padding between your armpits and the ropes." After Yirmeyahu had done this, ¹³ they pulled Yirmeyahu up with the ropes and took him out of the cistern. Yirmeyahu remained in the guards' quarters.

¹⁴ Tzidkiyahu summoned and had Yirmeyahu brought to him through the third entry in the house of ADONAI. Then the king said to Yirmeyahu, "I want to ask you

something; don't hide anything from me." ¹⁵ Yirmeyahu said to Tzidkiyahu, "If I do say it to you, won't you have me put to death? And if I give you counsel, you won't listen to me." ¹⁶ So Tzidkiyahu swore secretly to Yirmeyahu, "As ADONAI lives, who gave us our lives, I will not put you to death; nor will I hand you over to these men who want you put to death."

¹⁷ Then Yirmeyahu said to Tzidkiyahu, "Here is what ADONAI-Tzva'ot, the God of Isra'el, says: 'If you will go out and surrender to the king of Bavel's officers, then you will stay alive — this city will not be burned down; and you and your family will live. ¹⁸ But if you will not go out to the king of Bavel's officers, then this city will be handed over to the Kasdim; they will burn it to the ground; and you will not escape from them.'" ¹⁹ Tzidkiyahu the king said to Yirmeyahu, "I am afraid of the Judeans who deserted to the Kasdim. The Kasdim might hand me over to them, and they would mistreat me." ²⁰ Yirmeyahu answered, "They won't hand you over. I beg you, listen to the voice of ADONAI concerning what I'm telling you about; then it will go well with you, and you will live. ²¹ But if you refuse to surrender, then this is the word ADONAI has shown me: ²² all the women remaining in the king of Y'hudah's palace will be brought out to the king of Bavel's officers, and those women will taunt you:

'Your own close friends misled you
and took advantage of you.
Now that your feet are stuck in the mud,
they have abandoned you.'

²³ They will bring all your women and children out to the Kasdim, and you will not escape from them. Rather, you will be captured by the king of Bavel, and you will cause this city to be burned to the ground."

²⁴ Tzidkiyahu said to Yirmeyahu, "Don't tell anyone what you just said, or you will die. ²⁵ If the officials hear that I have talked with you, and they come to you and say, 'Tell us now what you said to the king; don't hide it from us, or we will put you to death, and also what the king said to you,' ²⁶ then tell them, 'I presented my request to the king that he would not make me return to Y'honatan's house, to die there.'" ²⁷ All the officials did come to Yirmeyahu and asked him, and he told them everything the king had ordered him to say. So they stopped speaking with him, since the matter had not been reported.

²⁸ Yirmeyahu remained in the guards' quarters until the day Yerushalayim was captured; he was there when Yerushalayim was captured.

39 ¹ In the ninth year of Tzidkiyahu king of Y'hudah, in the tenth month, N'vukhadretzar king of Bavel marched against Yerushalayim with his entire army and began to lay siege against it. ² On the ninth day of the fourth month of the eleventh year of Tzidkiyahu, they broke through into the city. ³ All the officers of the king of Bavel entered and sat at the Middle Gate — Nergal-Sar'etzer, Samgar-N'vo, Sars'khim the Rav-Saris, Nergal-Sar'etzer the Rav-Mag and all the other officers of the king of Bavel. ⁴ When Tzidkiyahu the king of Y'hudah and all the soldiers saw them, they fled, leaving the city by night through the king's garden, exiting from the gate between the two walls, and continuing out by the route through the 'Aravah.

⁵ But the army of the Kasdim went in pursuit of them and overtook Tzidkiyahu on the plains near Yericho. Upon capturing him, they brought him up to N'vukhadretzar king of Bavel at Rivlah, in the land of Hamat, where he passed judgment on him. ⁶ The king of Bavel slaughtered the sons of Tzidkiyahu before his eyes in Rivlah; the king of Bavel also slaughtered all the leading men of Y'hudah. ⁷ Then he put out Tzidkiyahu's eyes and bound him in chains to be carried off to Bavel. ⁸ The Kasdim burned down the royal palace and the people's houses, and they broke down the walls of Yerushalayim. ⁹ N'vuzar'adan commander of the guard then deported to Bavel the remaining population of the city, the deserters who had defected to him, and the rest of the people remaining. ¹⁰ But N'vuzar'adan the commander of the guard left behind in the territory of Y'hudah some of the poor people, those who had nothing, and at the same time gave them vineyards and fields.

¹¹ Concerning Yirmeyahu, N'vukhadretzar king of Bavel gave N'vuzar'adan the commander of the guard this order: ¹² "Take him, look after him well, and do him no harm, but treat him as he tells you." ¹³ So N'vuzar'adan the commander of the guard, N'vushazban the Rav-Saris, Nergal-Sar'etzer the Rav-Mag, and all the chief officers of the king of Bavel ¹⁴ sent to have Yirmeyahu taken out of the guards' quarters; they committed him to the care of G'dalyahu the son of Achikam, the son of Shafan, to be brought home. There he lived among the people.

¹⁵ This word of ADONAI came to Yirmeyahu while he was imprisoned in the guards' quarters: ¹⁶ "Go and tell 'Eved-Melekh the Ethiopian that ADONAI-Tzva'ot, the God of Isra'el, says: '"I am about to fulfill my words about this city for disaster, not for good; when the day arrives, they will come true before your eyes. ¹⁷ But at that time I will rescue you," says ADONAI, "and I will not hand you over to the men you fear. ¹⁸ Yes, I will keep you safe; you will not fall by the sword, but you will escape with your life, because you have put your trust in me," says ADONAI.'"

40 ¹ This word came to Yirmeyahu from ADONAI after N'vuzar'adan the commander of the guard had let him leave Ramah, after having taken him, bound in chains, with all the captives from Yerushalayim and Y'hudah that had been carried off to Bavel. ² The commander of the guard took Yirmeyahu and said to him, "ADONAI your God decreed this disaster for this place, ³ and ADONAI has brought it about; he has done what he said he would do, because you people sinned against ADONAI and did not listen to what he said; that is why this has come upon you. ⁴ Now, today, I am freeing you from the chains on your hand. If it seems good to you to come with me to Bavel, come; and I will look after you well. But if it seems not good to you to come with me to Bavel, then don't — the entire land is in front of you: wherever it seems good and right for you to go, go there." ⁵ Before Yirmeyahu could answer, [N'vuzar'adan said,] "Go back then to G'dalyahu the son of Achikam, the son of Shafan, whom the king of Bavel has made governor over the cities of Y'hudah, and live with him among the people; or go wherever it seems right for you to go." The commander of the guard gave him provisions and a gift, and dismissed him. ⁶ Yirmeyahu then went to G'dalyahu the son of Achikam in Mitzpah and lived with him among the people who were left in the land.

⁷ Now when all the field force commanders and their men heard that the king of Bavel had made G'dalyahu the son of Achikam governor in the land and had committed to his care men, women, children and some of the poorest people in the

land of those who had not been carried captive to Bavel; ⁸ they approached G'dalyahu in Mitzpah — in particular, Yishma'el the son of N'tanyahu, Yochanan and Yonatan the sons of Kareach, S'rayah the son of Tanchumet, the sons of 'Efai the N'tofati and Y'zanyahu the son of the Ma'akhati, they and their men. ⁹ G'dalyahu the son of Achikam, the son of Shafan, swore to them and their men, "Don't be afraid to serve the Kasdim. Live in the land, serve the king of Bavel; and things will go well with you. ¹⁰ As for me, I will live in Mitzpah and be responsible to the Kasdim who come to us. But you — harvest wine, summer fruits and olive oil; put them in your containers; and live in your cities that you have taken over."

¹¹ Likewise, when all the Judeans who were in Mo'av, in Edom, among the people of 'Amon, and in all the other countries heard that the king of Bavel had left a remnant in Y'hudah and had appointed G'dalyahu the son of Achikam, the son of Shafan, to govern them; ¹² then all the Judeans returned from all the places where they had been driven and came to the land of Y'hudah, to G'dalyahu in Mitzpah, and harvested wine and summer fruit in great abundance.

¹³ Yochanan the son of Kareach and all the field force commanders came to G'dalyahu in Mitzpah ¹⁴ and said to him, "Are you aware that Ba'alis the king of the people of 'Amon has sent Yishma'el the son of N'tanyahu to take your life?" But G'dalyahu the son of Achikam did not believe them. ¹⁵ Then Yochanan the son of Kareach spoke privately with G'dalyahu in Mitzpah: "Please, let me go, and I will kill Yishma'el the son of N'tanyahu; no one will know. Why let him assassinate you? Moreover, if he does, all the Judeans gathered around you will scatter; and the remnant of Y'hudah will perish." ¹⁶ But G'dalyahu the son of Achikam said to Yochanan the son of Kareach, "Don't do it. What you are saying about Yishma'el is not true."

41 ¹ In the seventh month Yishma'el the son of N'tanyahu, the son of Elishama, of royal blood and one of the chief officials of the king, came with ten men to G'dalyahu in Mitzpah. While eating a meal together there in Mitzpah, ² Yishma'el and the ten men with him rose and attacked G'dalyahu the son of Achikam, the son of Shafan, struck him with their swords, and assassinated the man whom the king of Bavel had appointed governor of the land. ³ Yishma'el also murdered all the Judeans who were with G'dalyahu at Mitzpah, as well as the Kasdim soldiers they found there.

⁴ The next day, before his assassination of G'dalyahu had become known, ⁵ eighty men from Sh'khem, Shiloh and Shomron came with beards shaved off, clothes torn and gashes on their bodies; they had grain offerings and frankincense with them to present in the house of ADONAI. ⁶ Yishma'el the son of N'tanyahu went out from Mitzpah to meet them, weeping all along the way; on meeting them, he said to them, "Come to G'dalyahu the son of Achikam." ⁷ But once they were inside the city, Yishma'el the son of N'tanyahu and the men with him slaughtered them and threw them into the cistern. ⁸ However, ten of them said to Yishma'el, "Don't kill us, for we have stores of wheat, barley, olive oil and honey hidden in the field." So he relented, and did not kill them along with their comrades. ⁹ The cistern in which Yishma'el threw the corpses of the men he had murdered with G'dalyahu was the one Asa the king had made in fear of Ba'asha king of Isra'el; it was this cistern that Yishma'el the son of N'tanyahu filled with the slaughtered men. ¹⁰ Then Yishma'el carried off captive the rest of the people in Mitzpah — the king's daughters and all the people

left in Mitzpah, whom N'vuzar'adan the commander of the guard had committed to the care of G'dalyahu the son of Achikam. Yishma'el the son of N'tanyahu carried them off captive and left to cross over to the people of 'Amon.

¹¹ When Yochanan the son of Kareach and all the military commanders with him heard of all the crimes committed by Yishma'el the son of N'tanyahu, ¹² they took all the men and went to attack Yishma'el the son of N'tanyahu. They found him by the big pool in Giv'on. ¹³ When all Yishma'el's captives saw Yochanan the son of Kareach and all the military commanders with him, they were overjoyed. ¹⁴ So all the people Yishma'el had carried off captive from Mitzpah turned and joined Yochanan the son of Kareach. ¹⁵ But Yishma'el the son of N'tanyahu escaped from Yochanan with eight men and went on to the people of 'Amon. ¹⁶ Yochanan the son of Kareach and the military commanders with him then took all the rest of the people he had freed from Yishma'el the son of N'tanyahu, those Yishma'el had taken from Mitzpah after assassinating G'dalyahu the son of Achikam — the heroes, the soldiers, the women, the children and the officers he had brought back from Giv'on — ¹⁷ and they left there to stay at Kimham's Lodge, near Beit-Lechem, intending to go on to Egypt ¹⁸ and thus escape the Kasdim. They were afraid of them, because Yishma'el the son of N'tanyahu had murdered G'dalyahu the son of Achikam, whom the king of Bavel had appointed governor of the land.

42 ¹ Then all the military commanders, Yochanan the son of Kareach, Y'zanyah the son of Hosha'yah and all the people, from the least to the greatest, approached ² and said to Yirmeyahu the prophet, "I beg you, approve our request: pray for us to ADONAI your God for all of this remnant. For, while once we were numerous, only a few of us are left, as you can see. ³ Pray that ADONAI your God will tell us what direction to take and what to do."

⁴ Yirmeyahu the prophet said to them: "I hear you. All right, I will pray to ADONAI your God, as you have asked. And whatever ADONAI answers you, I will tell you; I will withhold nothing from you." ⁵ They said to Yirmeyahu, "May ADONAI be a true and faithful witness against us if we fail to do any part of what ADONAI your God gives you to tell us. ⁶ Whether it be good or bad, we will listen to what ADONAI our God says. We are dispatching you to him so that things will go well with us, as we heed what ADONAI our God says."

⁷ Ten days later the word of ADONAI came to Yirmeyahu. ⁸ So he called Yochanan the son of Kareach, all the military commanders with him and all the people, from the least to the greatest, ⁹ and said to them, "You sent me to present your request to ADONAI the God of Isra'el. This is what he says: ¹⁰ 'If you will stay in this land, then I will build you up, not pull you down; I will plant you and not uproot you; for I am relenting from the calamity I inflicted on you. ¹¹ Don't be afraid of the king of Bavel — of whom you are afraid. Don't be afraid of him,' says ADONAI, 'for I am with you to save you and to rescue you from his power. ¹² I will take pity on you, so that he will take pity on you and cause you to return to your own land.

¹³ "But if you say, 'We will not stay in this land,' thereby not heeding what ADONAI your God is saying, ¹⁴ and instead say, 'No, we will go to the land of Egypt; because there we will not see war or hear the *shofar* sounding its alarm or be short of food; so we'll stay there'; ¹⁵ then hear what ADONAI says, remnant of Y'hudah — this is what ADONAI-Tzva'ot, the God of Isra'el, says: 'If you are determined to go to Egypt and stay there,

¹⁶ the sword, of which you are afraid, will overtake you there in the land of Egypt; and the famine, of which you are afraid, will pursue you relentlessly there in Egypt; and there you will die. ¹⁷ This is how it will be for all the people determined to go to Egypt and stay there — they will die by sword, famine and plague; none of them will remain or escape the disaster that I will bring upon them.' ¹⁸ For here is what ADONAI-Tzva'ot, the God of Isra'el, says: 'Just as my anger and fury were poured out on the inhabitants of Yerushalayim, so likewise my fury will be poured out on you if you go to Egypt; so that you will become an object of condemnation, astonishment, cursing and reproach; and you will see this place no more.'

¹⁹ "ADONAI has spoken concerning you, remnant of Y'hudah! Don't go to Egypt! You know for a fact that I have given you fair warning today. ²⁰ For you have been behaving deceitfully, against your own interests. You sent me to ADONAI your God, saying, 'Pray for us to ADONAI our God; tell us everything ADONAI our God says, and we will do it.' ²¹ Today I have told it to you, but you haven't heeded any part of what ADONAI your God gave me to tell you. ²² Therefore, know for a fact that you will die by sword, famine and plague in the place where you want to go and live."

43 ¹ When Yirmeyahu had finished telling all the people everything ADONAI their God had said, which ADONAI their God had sent him to tell them, the entire speech cited above, ² then 'Azaryah the son of Hosha'yah, Yochanan the son of Kareach and all the men with him had the effrontery to say to Yirmeyahu, "You are lying! ADONAI our God did not send you to say, 'Don't go to Egypt and live there'! ³ Rather, Barukh the son of Neriyah is inciting you against us, so that we can be handed over to the Kasdim to be put to death or carried off as captives to Bavel."

⁴ So Yochanan the son of Kareach, all the military commanders and all the people did not heed what ADONAI said, to live in the land of Y'hudah. ⁵ Instead, Yochanan the son of Kareach and all the military commanders took all the remnant of Y'hudah who had returned from all the nations where they had been driven to live in the land of Y'hudah — ⁶ the men, the women, the children, the king's daughters, everyone N'vuzar'adan the commander of the guard had committed to G'dalyahu the son of Achikam, the son of Shafan, and Yirmeyahu the prophet and Barukh the son of Neriyah — ⁷ and went to the land of Egypt; for they did not heed what ADONAI had said; and they arrived in Tachpanches.

⁸ Then this word of ADONAI came to Yirmeyahu in Tachpanches: ⁹ "With the men of Y'hudah watching, take some big stones, and set them with mortar in the pavement at the entry to Pharaoh's palace in Tachpanches. ¹⁰ Tell them: 'This is what ADONAI-Tzva'ot, the God of Isra'el, says: "I will summon N'vukhadretzar the king of Bavel, my servant, take him and set his throne on these stones I laid here; he will come and spread his royal canopy over them. ¹¹ He will come and attack the land of Egypt.

> Those destined for death — to death!
> Those destined for captivity — to captivity!
> Those destined for the sword — to the sword!

¹² I will light a fire in the temples of the gods of Egypt, and he will burn [those gods] or take them captive. He will fold up the land of Egypt like a shepherd folding up his cloak, and leave there victorious. ¹³ He will also break the standing-stones of

the temple of the sun in the land of Egypt and burn to the ground the temples of the gods of Egypt.""'

44 ¹ This word came to Yirmeyahu concerning all the people from Y'hudah living in the land of Egypt — in Migdol, Tachpanches, Nof and the land of Patros: ² "Here is what A*DONAI-Tzva'ot*, the God of Isra'el, says: 'You have seen all the disaster I inflicted on Yerushalayim and all the cities of Y'hudah; there they are today, ruined, with no one living in them. ³ It came about because of the wicked things they did to make me angry — sacrificing to and serving other gods, whom they did not know, neither they, nor you nor your ancestors. ⁴ I had sent you all my servants the prophets, sent them frequently, with the message, "Don't do this horrible thing which I hate!" ⁵ But they neither listened nor obeyed, so as to turn from their wickedness and stop offering to other gods. ⁶ Hence my fury and anger were poured out and ignited in the cities of Y'hudah and the streets of Yerushalayim; so that they became waste and desolate, as they are today.'

⁷ "Therefore now, A*DONAI-Tzva'ot*, the God of Isra'el, says this: 'Why are you committing this great sin against yourselves? The result can only be to cut you off from Y'hudah — men, women, children and babies — so that none of you remain. ⁸ For you continue provoking me with the products of your own hands, offering to other gods in the land of Egypt, where you have gone to live as aliens. It will lead only to your destruction and becoming an object of curses and reproaches among all the nations of the earth. ⁹ Have you forgotten the wicked deeds of your ancestors, the wicked deeds of the kings of Y'hudah, the wicked deeds of their wives, your own wicked deeds, and the wicked deeds of your wives, which they committed in the land of Y'hudah and in the streets of Yerushalayim? ¹⁰ To this day they remain unhumbled; they have not been afraid, and they have not lived according to my *Torah* or my regulations that I presented to you and your ancestors.'

¹¹ "Therefore here is what A*DONAI-Tzva'ot*, the God of Isra'el, says: 'I will decree disaster for you and destroy all of Y'hudah. ¹² I will take the remnant of Y'hudah, who determined to go to Egypt and live there as aliens, and they will all perish — in the land of Egypt they will fall and perish by sword and famine. They will die, from the least to the greatest, by sword and famine; and they will become an object of condemnation, astonishment, cursing and reproach. ¹³ Yes, I will punish those living in the land of Egypt, as I punished Yerushalayim, by sword, famine and plague; ¹⁴ so that none of the remnant of Y'hudah who went into the land of Egypt to live as aliens will escape or remain, to be able to return to the land of Y'hudah. They long to return and live there, but none will return except a few refugees.'"

¹⁵ Then all the men who knew that their wives were offering incense to other gods, along with all the women standing by, a huge crowd, all the people living in Patros in the land of Egypt, answered Yirmeyahu: ¹⁶ "As for the word you have just spoken to us in the name of A*DONAI*, we will not listen to you. ¹⁷ Instead, we will certainly continue to fulfill every word our mouths have spoken: we will offer incense to the queen of heaven and pour out drink offerings to her, as we have done, we and our ancestors, our kings and our leaders, in the cities of Y'hudah and the streets of Yerushalayim. For then we had plenty of food; everything was fine, we didn't experience anything unpleasant. ¹⁸ But since we stopped offering to the queen of heaven and pouring out drink offerings to her, we have lacked everything, and we

have been destroyed by sword and famine." ^{19} [Then the wives added,] "Are we the ones who offer incense to the queen of heaven? Do we pour out drink offerings to her? And did we make cakes marked with her image for her and pour out drink offerings to her without our husbands' consent?"

^{20} Then Yirmeyahu said to all the people — to the men, the women, and all the people who had answered him back: ^{21} "The incense you offered in the cities of Y'hudah and in the streets of Yerushalayim — you, your ancestors, your kings, your leaders and the people of the land — ADONAI kept remembering and taking note of this [insult], ^{22} until ADONAI could no longer bear it, so evil and so detestable were your deeds. This is why your land has become a wasteland, an object for astonishment and cursing, uninhabited, as it is today. ^{23} It is because you offered incense, sinned against ADONAI, didn't listen to what ADONAI said, and didn't live by his *Torah*, regulations and instructions that this disaster has befallen you, as it is today."

^{24} In addition, Yirmeyahu said to all the people, but especially the women: "Hear the word of ADONAI, all Y'hudah who are in the land of Egypt; ^{25} this is what ADONAI-*Tzva'ot*, the God of Isra'el, says: 'You and your wives stated your intentions with your mouths and performed them with your hands — you said, "We will certainly fulfill our vows that we made to offer incense to the queen of heaven and pour out drink offerings to her."' Without doubt, you will indeed fulfill every point of your vows. ^{26} Therefore hear the word of ADONAI, all Y'hudah living in the land of Egypt: 'I swear by my own great name,' says ADONAI, 'that no man of Y'hudah will speak my name again in the land of Egypt, swearing, "As ADONAI, God, lives." ^{27} I am watching over them for harm, not for good. All the men of Y'hudah in the land of Egypt will be destroyed by sword and famine, until none of them is left. ^{28} Those who escape the sword will return from the land of Egypt to the land of Y'hudah few in number; and all the remnant of Y'hudah who went into the land of Egypt to live will know whose word will stand — mine or theirs! ^{29} Moreover, here is a sign for you,' says ADONAI, 'that I will punish you in this place, so that you can know that my threats of disaster against you will come true.' ^{30} ADONAI says, 'I will hand over Pharaoh Hofra king of Egypt to his enemies, to those seeking his life — just as I handed Tzidkiyahu king of Y'hudah over to N'vukhadretzar king of Bavel, his enemy, who sought his life.'"

45 ^{1} Here is what Yirmeyahu said to Barukh the son of Neriyah when he wrote these words in a book at Yirmeyahu's dictation, in the fourth year of Y'hoyakim the son of Yoshiyahu, king of Y'hudah: ^{2} "This is what Adonai the God of Isra'el says concerning you, Barukh. You said,

^{3} 'Woe to me now!
         ADONAI has compounded my pain with sorrow,
         I am weary from groaning,
         and I can find no relief!'

^{4} "Tell him that ADONAI says:

         'I will tear down what I built up,
         I will uproot what I planted,
         and this throughout the land.

⁵ Are you seeking great things for yourself? Don't! For I am bringing disaster on every-thing living,' says *Adonai.* 'But wherever you go, you will escape with your life.'"

46 ¹ This is the word of *Adonai* that came to Yirmeyahu the prophet concerning the nations. ² Concerning Egypt, against the army of Pharaoh N'kho, king of Egypt, stationed by the Euphrates River in Kark'mish, which N'vukhadretzar king of Bavel attacked in the fourth year of Y'hoyakim son of Yoshiyahu, king of Y'hudah:

³   "Prepare breastplate and shield! Advance to battle!
⁴   Harness the horses! Riders, mount!
        [Troops,] fall in! Helmets in place!
        Polish the spears! Coats of mail on!

⁵   "Why do I see them retreating in panic,
        their heroes routed, fleeing headlong,
        not looking back, terror all around?"

asks *Adonai.*

⁶   "The swift cannot flee, nor the heroes escape.
        In the north, by the Euphrates River,
        they have stumbled and fallen."

⁷   Who is this, rising up like the Nile,
        like rivers whose waters surge out in flood?
⁸   It is Egypt, rising up like the Nile,
        like rivers whose waters surge out in flood,
        saying, "I will surge out and cover the earth,
        destroying the city along with its people."

⁹   Charge, horses! Full speed ahead, chariots!
        Let the warriors attack! —
        Kush and Put, bearing their shields,
        and the Ludim, strung bows in hand.

¹⁰   For on that day *Adonai Elohei-Tzva'ot*
        will have a day of vengeance
        for avenging himself on his enemies.
        The sword will destroy, have its fill,
        be made drunk on their blood.
        Yes, *Adonai Elohei-Tzva'ot*
        decrees slaughter in the land to the north
        by the Euphrates River.

¹¹   Go up to Gil'ad for its healing resin,
        virgin daughter of Egypt.
        You try many medicines, all in vain;

for you there is no cure.

12 The nations have heard about your disgrace;
your shrieks fill the earth
as warrior trips over warrior,
both falling down together.

13 This word ADONAI spoke to Yirmeyahu the prophet concerning how N'vukhadretzar king of Bavel would come and attack the land of Egypt:

14 "Proclaim in Egypt, announce in Migdol,
announce in Nof and Tachpanches;
say: 'Take your stand! Get ready!
For all around you the sword is destroying.

15 Why has your strong one been overthrown?
He failed to stand because ADONAI pushed him down.

16 He caused many to trip;
yes, they fell all over each other.'"

Then they said, "Let's get up,
let's return to our own people,
back to the land where we were born,
away from the sword that destroys."

17 They cried there, "Pharaoh king of Egypt makes noise,
but he lets the right time [for action] slip by."

18 "As I live," says the king,
whose name is ADONAI-Tzva'ot,
"when he comes, he will be [as mighty]
as Tavor among the mountains,
as Karmel next to the sea.

19 "Daughter living in Egypt,
prepare what you need for exile;
for Nof will become a ruin,
laid waste, without inhabitant.

20 Egypt is a beautiful female calf;
but a horsefly from the north has come to attack her.

21 Her mercenaries too, that she had with her,
were like well-fed calves in a stable;
but they too have withdrawn in retreat,
they all ran away without standing their ground.
For their day of disaster has come over them,
the time for them to be punished.

22 Egypt hisses like a snake,
as the enemy's army marches ahead,
attacking her with their axes
like lumbermen chopping trees.

²³ They cut down her forest," says ADONAI,
"for they cannot be numbered;
yes, there are more of them than locusts,
far too many to count.
²⁴ The daughter of Egypt is put to shame,
handed over to the people from the north."

²⁵ ADONAI-*Tzva'ot*, the God of Isra'el, says: "I will punish Amon from No, Pharaoh, and Egypt with her gods and kings — that is, Pharaoh and those who trust in him; ²⁶ I will hand them over to those who seek their lives, to N'vukhadretzar king of Bavel and to his servants. But afterwards, Egypt will be inhabited, as in the past," says ADONAI.

²⁷ "Yet don't be afraid, Ya'akov my servant;
don't be distressed, Isra'el.
For I will save you from faraway places,
and your offspring from the lands where they are held captive.
Ya'akov will return and be at peace,
quiet, with no one to make him afraid.
²⁸ Don't be afraid, Ya'akov my servant,"
says ADONAI, "for I am with you.
I will finish off all the nations
where I have scattered you.
However, you I will not finish off,
I will discipline you as you deserve,
but not completely destroy you."

47 ¹ This word of ADONAI came to Yirmeyahu the prophet concerning the P'lishtim before Pharaoh attacked 'Azah: ² "Here is what ADONAI says:

'Water is rising out of the north;
it will become a flooding stream,
flooding the land and all that is in it,
the city and its inhabitants.
The people are crying out in alarm,
everyone in the land is weeping
³ at the thunderous pounding of his stallions' hoofs,
at his rattling chariots' rumbling wheels.
Fathers fail to turn back for their children;
instead, their hands hang limp,
⁴ because the day has come
for destroying all the P'lishtim,
for cutting off from Tzor and Tzidon
the last of their allies;
for ADONAI is destroying the P'lishtim,
the remnant from the island of Kaftor.
⁵ 'Azah is shaved bald,
Ashkelon reduced to silence.

Those of you who remain in their valley,
how long will you go on gashing yourselves?'"

6 Oh, sword of ADONAI,
how long till you can be quiet?
Put yourself back in your scabbard!
Stop! Be still!
7 But how can you be still?
For ADONAI has given it orders
against Ashkelon, against the seacoast;
he has assigned it its task there.

48 ¹ Concerning Mo'av, this is what ADONAI-Tzva'ot, the God of Isra'el, says:

"Woe to N'vo, for it is ravaged;
Kiryatayim disgraced and captured.
Misgav is put to shame, distressed.

2 "In Mo'av, nothing is left to praise.
At Heshbon they plotted her downfall:
'Come, we'll cut her off as a nation.'
You too, Madmein, will be silenced;
the sword pursues behind you.
3 An agonized cry from Horonayim,
ruin, terrible devastation!
4 Mo'av has been shattered;
the cries of her young ones are heard,
5 as they ascend the slopes of Luchit,
weeping bitterly as they climb.
On the road down to Horonayim
shrieks of destruction ring out."

6 Flee! Save your lives!
Be strong, like a tamarisk in the desert.
7 Because you trust in your deeds and your wealth,
you too will be captured.
Together with his priests and princes,
K'mosh will go into exile.
8 A destroyer will descend on every city,
no city will escape.
The valley too will perish,
the plain will be laid waste,
as ADONAI has said.

9 Give Mo'av wings,
so it can fly and get away.
Its cities will become ruins,

10   with no one to live in them.
          A curse on him who does the work
          of ADONAI carelessly!
          A curse on him who withholds his sword
          from blood!

11   Mo'av has lived at ease from his youth;
          he is [wine] settled on its dregs,
          not decanted from jar to jar —
          he has not gone into exile.
          Therefore it retains its own [bad] taste,
          its aroma remains unchanged.

12 "So the days are coming," says ADONAI, "when I will send people to tilt him; they
will tilt his jars, emptying them and shattering the wine-flasks to pieces. 13 Mo'av
will be disappointed by K'mosh then, just as the house of Isra'el was disappointed
by Beit-El, a god in whom they had put their trust.

14   "How can you say, 'We are heroes,
          warriors valiant in battle'?
15   They are ravaging Mo'av, attacking its cities;
          its best young men go down to be slaughtered,"
          says the king, whose name is ADONAI-Tzva'ot.

16   Mo'av's ruin is coming soon,
          its disaster speeds on swiftly.
17   Pity him, all of you who are near him,
          all of you who know his name;
          say, "How the mighty scepter is shattered,
          that splendid staff!"
18   Descend from your glory, and sit in thirst,
          daughter living in Divon;
          for Mo'av's destroyer advances on you;
          he has destroyed your strongholds.
19   Stand by the road and watch,
          inhabitant of 'Aro'er;
          ask the man fleeing and the woman escaping,
          "What is going on?"

20   Mo'av is disgraced, indeed, destroyed.
          Wail aloud! Shriek!
          Proclaim it by the Arnon
          that Mo'av has been laid waste.

21 Judgment has come on the Plain — on Holon, Yachtzah, Mefa'at, 22 Divon, N'vo,
Beit-Diblatayim, 23 Kiryatayim, Beit-Gamul, Beit-M'on, 24 K'riot, Botzrah and all
the cities in the land of Mo'av, far and near.

25   "Mo'av's strength is cut down,
        his arm is broken," says ADONAI.

²⁶ Because Mo'av boasted against ADONAI, make him so drunk that he wallows in his
own vomit and becomes a laughingstock. ²⁷ After all, Isra'el was a laughingstock for
you. He didn't associate with thieves; nevertheless, whenever you spoke of him, you
shook your head.

28   You who live in Mo'av,
        leave the cities, and live on the rocks;
        be like the dove who makes her nest
        in a hole in the rock at the mouth of a cave.

29   We have heard of the pride of Mo'av:
        so very proud he is! —
        presumptuous, proud, conceited;
        so haughty his heart!

30   "I know what meager ground he has
        for his arrogance," says ADONAI.
        "His boasting has nothing behind it,
        and it hasn't accomplished a thing."

31   Therefore I wail for Mo'av;
        for all Mo'av I cry;
        for the people of Kir-Heres I lament.
32   I will weep for you, vineyard of Sivmah,
        more than I wept for Ya'zer.
        Your branches spread to the sea,
        reaching as far as the sea of Ya'zer.
        On your summer fruits and on your vintage
        the destroyer has fallen.
33   Gladness and joy have been removed
        from productive fields and the land of Mo'av.
        "I have stopped the flow of wine from the vats
        and the shouts of those who tread the grapes —
        those shouts of joy are stilled."

34   The cries from Heshbon to El'aleh
        are heard as far away as Yachatz;
        those from Tzo'ar to Horonayim
        are heard in 'Eglat-Shlishiyah;
        for even the waters of Nimrim
        have become a desolate waste.

35   "Moreover," says ADONAI,
        "in Mo'av I will put an end

to anyone sacrificing on a high place
or offering incense to his gods."

36 This is why my heart is moaning
for Mo'av like funeral flutes,
why my heart moans for the men
of Kir-Heres like funeral flutes;
for the wealth they produced has vanished.

37 Every head has been shaved bald,
every beard has been clipped short,
gashes are on every hand,
sackcloth around every waist.

38 On all the housetops of Mo'av
and in its open places —
lamentation everywhere!

"For I have broken Mo'av like a pot
that nobody wants," says ADONAI.

39 Wail, "How shattered is Mo'av!
How shamefully in retreat!"
Thus will Mo'av become an object
of ridicule and distress to all its neighbors.

40 For here is what ADONAI says:
"Look! Down he swoops like a vulture,
spreading his wings against Mo'av —

41 the cities are captured, the strongholds are seized.
On that day the hearts of Mo'av's warriors
will be like the heart of a woman in labor.

42 Mo'av will be destroyed as a people,
because he boasted against ADONAI.

43 Terror, pit and trap are upon you,
people of Mo'av," says ADONAI.

44 "Whoever flees from the terror
will fall into the pit;
and he who climbs up out of the pit
will be caught in the trap.
For I will bring on her, on Mo'av,
the year for her punishment," says ADONAI.

45 "In the shadow of Heshbon
the fugitives stop, exhausted.
For fire breaks out from Heshbon,
a flame from inside Sichon,
consuming the sides and tops of the heads
of Mo'av's noisy boasters.

46   Woe to you, Mo'av!
      K'mosh's people are doomed!
      For your sons have been taken captive,
      and your daughters led into captivity.
47   Yet I will end Mo'av's exile
      in the *acharit-hayamim*," says A*DONAI*.

This is the judgment on Mo'av.

49 ¹ Concerning the people of 'Amon, here is what A*DONAI* says:

      "Has Isra'el no sons?
      Has he no heir?
      Then why has Malkam inherited Gad,
      with his people settled in its cities?
2   Therefore," says A*DONAI*, "the days are coming
      when I will sound the battle alarm
      against Rabbah and the people of 'Amon;
      it will become a *tel* of ruins,
      her villages burned to the ground.
      Then Isra'el will inherit from them
      who disinherited him," says A*DONAI*.
3   "Wail, Heshbon, for 'Ai is doomed!
      Cry out, daughters of Rabbah!
      Wear sackcloth and mourn,
      running here and there among the sheep pens.
      For Malkam will go into exile,
      together with his priests and officers.
4   Why do you take such pride in the valleys,
      your well-watered valleys, rebellious daughter?
      You trusted in your riches
      and thought, 'Who can attack me?'
5   I am bringing terror on you,"
      says Adonai E*LOHEI*-*Tzva'ot*, "from every side.
      Each of you will be driven out headlong,
      with no one to gather the fugitives.
6   But afterwards, I will bring back
      the exiles of 'Amon," says A*DONAI*.

⁷ Concerning Edom, this is what A*DONAI*-*Tzva'ot* says:

      "Is there no wisdom left in Teman?
      Have her wise men forgotten how to counsel?
      Has their wisdom vanished?
8   Flee! Turn back! Hide yourselves well,
      you who live in D'dan;
      for I am bringing calamity on 'Esav,

when the time for me to punish him comes.

9   If grape-pickers came to you,
they would leave no grapes for gleaning.
If thieves came at night,
they would destroy until they were satisfied.

10   So I, for my part, have stripped 'Esav bare,
I have exposed his hiding-places;
he will not be able to hide himself.
He is doomed — sons, brothers and neighbors —
so that he is no more.

11   Leave your orphans; I will keep them alive;
let your widows trust in me."

12 For this is what ADONAI says: "Those who do not deserve to drink from this cup will have to drink it anyway, so should you go unpunished? No, you will not go unpunished; you will certainly drink it. 13 For I have sworn by myself," says ADONAI, "that Botzrah will become a ruin and an object of astonishment, reproach and cursing; all its cities will be ruins forever."

14   I have heard a message from ADONAI:
"A messenger is sent among the nations, saying:
'Gather together, and march against her!
Prepare for battle!'

15   Here! I will make you least among nations,
the most despised of people.

16   Your capacity to terrorize
has deceived you and made you arrogant.
You make your home in the rocky crags
and seize the top of the mountain;
but even if you build your nest high as an eagle's,
from there I will drag you down," says ADONAI.

17   Edom will become an object of horror;
everyone passing by will whistle
in astonishment at all its disasters.

18   It will be like the overthrow of S'dom,
'Amora and their neighboring towns," says ADONAI.
"No one will settle there any more,
no human being will live there again.

19   It will be like a lion coming up from the thickets
of the Yarden against a strong settlement:
in an instant I will chase him away
and appoint over it whomever I choose.
For who is like me? Who can call me to account?
What shepherd can stand up to me?"

20   So hear the plan of ADONAI
that he has devised against Edom,

and his purpose that he will accomplish
against those who live in Teman:
the least of the flock will drag them away;
their own pasture will be in shock at them.

21 The earth quakes at the sound of their fall;
their cry can be heard at the Sea of Suf.

22 Like a vulture he will soar, swoop down
and spread out his wings against Botzrah.
On that day the hearts of Edom's warriors
will be like the heart of a woman in labor.

²³ Concerning Dammesek:

"Hamat and Arpad are confused;
having heard bad news, they dissolve in fear,
like the churning sea, which cannot calm itself.

24 Dammesek, weakened, turns to flee;
trembling has seized her;
anguish and pain take hold of her
like the pains of a woman in labor.

25 How can a city so praised be deserted,
a city that gave me such joy?

26 Therefore her young men will fall in her squares,
and all her warriors be silenced on that day,"
says ADONAI-Tzva'ot.

27 "I will light a fire inside Dammesek's walls
which will consume the palaces of Ben-Hadad."

²⁸ Concerning Kedar and the kingdoms of Hatzor, which N'vukhadretzar king of
Bavel struck, ADONAI says:

"Set out! March against Kedar!
Plunder the people of the east!

29 They will seize their tents and their flocks,
their tent curtains and all their equipment;
their camels too they will take for themselves
and shout at them, 'Terror in every direction!'

30 Flee! Leave your homes! Hide yourselves well,
you who live in Hatzor," says ADONAI;
"for N'vukhadretzar king of Bavel
has devised a plan against you;
he has formed a scheme against you.

31 Get up! March on a nation at ease,
that lives secure," says ADONAI.
"They have neither gates nor bars;
they live in isolation.

32 Their camels will be booty,

their many cattle a spoil.
I will scatter to the winds
those who shave the sides of their heads;
From every direction I will bring
their disaster on them," says ADONAI.

33 "Hatzor will be a place for jackals to live,
desolate forever;
no one will settle there any more,
no human being will live there again."

³⁴ This is the word of ADONAI that came to Yirmeyahu the prophet concerning 'Eilam at the beginning of the reign of Tzidkiyahu king of Y'hudah: ³⁵ "ADONAI-Tzva'ot says:

'I will break 'Eilam's bow,
the mainstay of their might.

36 I will bring against 'Eilam the four winds
from the four quarters of the sky
and scatter them to all those winds.
There will not be one nation to which
the dispersed of 'Eilam will not come.

37 I will break 'Eilam before their foes,
before those who seek their lives;
I will bring disaster on them,
my burning anger,' says ADONAI.
'I will send the sword to pursue them
until I have finished them off.

38 I will put my throne in 'Eilam
and destroy their king and leaders,' says ADONAI.

39 'But in the *acharit-hayamim*,
I will bring back the exiles of 'Eilam,' says ADONAI."

50 ¹ This is the word which ADONAI spoke concerning Bavel, concerning the land of the Kasdim, through Yirmeyahu the prophet:

2 "Declare it among the nations, proclaim it!
Hoist a banner, proclaim it, don't hide it!
Say: 'Bavel is captured.
Bel is shamed, M'rodakh disgraced,
her images shamed, her idols disgraced.'

3 For from the north a nation is marching against her
that will desolate her land.
No one will live there —
both humans and animals have fled and gone.

4 In those days, at that time," says ADONAI,
"the people of Isra'el will come,
together with the people of Y'hudah.
They will weep as they go their way,

seeking *Adonai* their God.

5 They will ask the way to Tziyon;
and, turning their faces toward it, will say,
'Come, join yourselves to *Adonai*
by an everlasting covenant never to be forgotten.'

6 My people have been lost sheep.
My shepherds made them go astray,
turning them loose in the mountains.
As they wandered from mountain to hill,
they lost track of where their home is.

7 Everyone finding them ate them up.
Their enemies said, 'We aren't guilty;
for they sinned against *Adonai*,
the resting place of justice;
yes, against *Adonai*, their ancestors' hope.'

8 Flee from Bavel! Leave the land of the Kasdim!
Be like male goats leading the flock;

9 for I will stir up and bring against Bavel
an alliance of great nations from the country to the north.
They will array themselves against her;
from there she will be captured.
Their arrows are like those of a death-dealing warrior;
none will return in vain.

10 The land of the Kasdim will be plundered;
all who plunder it will get enough," says *Adonai*.

11 "Because you are glad, because you exult,
you plunderers of my heritage;
because you frisk like a calf in the grass
and neigh like stallions;

12 your mother will be utterly shamed,
she who bore you will be disgraced.
Here she is! — last among the nations,
a desert, parched and barren.

13 Because of the anger of *Adonai*,
no one will live there any more;
all of it will be desolate.
Everyone passing Bavel will whistle
in shock at all her plagues.

14 "Take your positions surrounding Bavel,
all you whose bows are strung;
shoot at her, spare no arrows;
because she sinned against *Adonai*.

15 From all sides raise the war cry against her!
Now she surrenders!
Her buttresses fall, her walls are thrown down,

for this is the vengeance of *Adonai*.
Avenge yourself on her!
As she has done, do to her!

16 Cut off the sower from Bavel
and the reaper with sickle at harvest-time.
For fear of the destroying sword
everyone returns to his own people,
each one flees to his own land.

17 "Isra'el is a stray lamb,
driven away by lions.
First to devour him was Ashur's king;
and the last to break his bones
is this N'vukhadretzar king of Bavel."

18 Therefore *Adonai-Tzva'ot*,
the God of Isra'el, says:
"I will punish the king of Bavel and his land
as I punished the king of Ashur.

19 I will bring Isra'el back to his pasture,
to graze on the Karmel and the Bashan,
on the hills of Efrayim and in Gil'ad
until he has his fill.

20 In those days, at that time," says *Adonai*,
"Isra'el's guilt will be sought,
but there will be none,
and Y'hudah's sins,
but they won't be found;
for I will pardon the remnant I leave.

21 "Attack the land of Meratayim;
attack it and those living in P'kod.
Waste them, utterly destroy them;
do all I have ordered you," says *Adonai*.

22 "The sound of battle is heard in the land,
with great destruction!

23 How the hammer of the whole earth
lies hacked apart and shattered!
What an object of horror among the nations
Bavel has become!

24 I set a trap and caught you,
Bavel, before you knew it.
You were discovered and seized,
because you challenged *Adonai*.

25 *Adonai* has opened his store of arms
and brought out the weapons of his wrath;
for Adonai *Elohei-Tzva'ot* has work
to do in the land of the Kasdim.

26 Attack her from every direction!
    Open her stores of grain!
    Pile her up like heaps of grain;
    destroy her completely; leave nothing!
27 Kill all her bulls!
    let them go down to be slaughtered!
    Woe to them! for their day has come,
    the time for them to be punished."

28 Hear the sound of the fugitives,
    of those escaping from Bavel,
    coming to proclaim in Tziyon
    the vengeance of ADONAI our God,
    vengeance over his temple.

29 "Call up archers against Bavel,
    all whose bows are strung.
    Besiege her from every side,
    let no one escape.
    Repay her for her deeds;
    as she has done, do to her.
    For she insulted ADONAI,
    the Holy One of Isra'el.
30 This is why her young men will fall
    in her open places,
    why all her warriors will be silenced
    on that day," says ADONAI.
31 "I am against you, arrogant [nation],"
    says Adonai ELOHEI-Tzva'ot.
    "For your day has come,
    the time for you to be punished.
32 The arrogant [nation] will stumble and fall,
    and no one will lift him up again.
    I will set his cities on fire,
    and it will devour everything around him."

³³ Thus says ADONAI-Tzva'ot:

    "The people of Isra'el are oppressed,
    and so are the people of Y'hudah.
    Those who took them captive hold them fast;
    they refuse to let them go.
34 But their redeemer is strong;
    ADONAI-Tzva'ot is his name.
    He will thoroughly plead their cause,
    so that he can give rest to the land
    but unrest to those who live in Bavel.

³⁵ ADONAI says,

> "A sword hangs over the Kasdim,
> and over those who live in Bavel,
> over her leaders and over her sages.

³⁶ A sword hangs over the lying diviners;
> they will become fools.
> A sword hangs over her warriors;
> they will be disgraced.

³⁷ A sword hangs over their horses,
> also over their chariots,
> also over the foreigners within her;
> they will become like women.
> A sword hangs over her treasures;
> they will be robbed.

³⁸ A drought hangs over her waters;
> they will be dried up.
> For this is a land of idols;
> they go mad over these horrors of theirs.

³⁹ "Therefore wildcats and jackals will live there,
> and ostriches will settle there.
> It will never again be peopled,
> it will be uninhabited age after age;

⁴⁰ as when God overthrew S'dom,
> 'Amora and their neighboring towns," says ADONAI.
> "No one will settle there any more,
> no human being will live there again.

⁴¹ "Look! A people is coming from the north;
> a great nation and many kings
> are being stirred up from the ends of the earth.

⁴² They are armed with bow and spear;
> they are cruel, without compassion;
> their sound is like the roaring sea,
> as they ride forth on horses.
> Their men take their battle positions
> against you, daughter of Bavel.

⁴³ The king of Bavel has heard news of them;
> his hands droop, helpless.
> Anguish seizes hold of him
> and pain, like a woman in labor.

⁴⁴ "It will be like a lion coming up from the thickets
> of the Yarden against a strong settlement;
> in an instant I will chase him away
> and appoint over it whomever I choose.

For who is like me? Who can call me to account?
What shepherd can stand up to me?"

45 So hear the plan of ADONAI
that he has devised against Bavel,
and his goals that he will accomplish
against the land of the Kasdim:
the least of the flock will drag them away;
their own pasture will be in shock at them.

46 At the sound of Bavel's capture the earth quakes;
their cry is heard throughout the nations.

51 ¹ ADONAI says this:

"Against Bavel and those living in Lev-Kamai
I will stir up a destructive wind.

2 Against Bavel I will send foreigners
to winnow her and leave her land empty.
They will besiege her from every side
on the day of disaster.

3 Let the archer draw his bow,
let him flaunt his coat of mail;
do not spare her young men,
completely destroy her whole army.

4 In the land of the Kasdim the slain will fall,
those thrust through [by the sword] in her streets.

5 Isra'el and Y'hudah are not left widowed
of their God, ADONAI-Tzva'ot;
but the land of [the Kasdim] is full of guilt
before the Holy One of Isra'el."

6 Flee from Bavel, let each one save his life!
Don't perish because of her guilt.
For the time has come for the vengeance of ADONAI;
he will repay her what she deserves.

7 Bavel was a gold cup in the hands of ADONAI;
it made the whole earth drunk —
the nations drank her wine;
this is why the nations have lost their senses.

8 Bavel has suddenly fallen.
She is broken; wail for her.
Bring healing ointment for her wounds;
perhaps she can be healed.

9 "We tried to heal Bavel,
but she cannot be healed.
So leave her alone, and each of us
will return to his own country."

For the judgment against her rises to the skies
and reaches even the clouds.

10 ADONAI has brought forth our victory.
Come, let us proclaim in Tziyon
the work of ADONAI our God!

11 Sharpen the arrows! Fill the quivers!
ADONAI roused the spirit of the kings of the Medes,
because he plans to destroy Bavel.
This is the vengeance of ADONAI
vengeance over his temple.

12 Raise a standard against the walls of Bavel!
Strengthen the guard! Post the sentries!
Prepare ambushes! For ADONAI
has both planned and accomplished
what he promised to do to those living in Bavel.

13 You who live near plenty of water,
so rich in treasure — your end has come,
your time for being cut off!

14 ADONAI-Tzva'ot has sworn by himself,
"I will fill you with men as numerous as grasshoppers;
they will raise over you a shout of triumph."

15 He made the earth by his power,
established the world by his wisdom
spread out the sky by his understanding.

16 When he thunders, the waters in heaven roar,
he raises clouds from the ends of the earth,
he makes the lightning flash in the rain
and brings the wind out from his storehouses.

17 At this, everyone is proved stupid, ignorant,
every goldsmith put to shame by his idol!
The figures he casts are a fraud,
there is no breath in them,

18 they are nothings, ridiculous objects;
when the day for their punishment comes, they will perish.

19 Ya'akov's portion is not like these,
for he is the one who formed all things,
including the tribe he claims as his heritage.
ADONAI-Tzva'ot is his name.

20 "[Bavel] you are my war club and weapons of war —
with you I shatter nations;
with you I destroy kingdoms;

21 with you I shatter horses and their riders;
with you I shatter chariots and their drivers;

22 with you I shatter husbands and wives;

with you I shatter old and young;
with you I shatter young men and virgins;
23   with you I shatter shepherds and their flocks;
with you I shatter farmers and their teams;
with you I shatter governors and deputies.

24   "But I will repay Bavel and all living
in the land of the Kasdim for all the evil
they did in Tziyon," says ADONAI,
"before your eyes [Y'hudah]."

25   "I am against you, destructive mountain,
destroying all the earth," says ADONAI.
"I will stretch out my hand against you,
to send you tumbling down from the crags
and make you a burned-out mountain.
26   No one will make cornerstones
or foundation-stones from you again;
but you will be desolate
forever," says ADONAI.

27   Raise up a banner in the land,
blow the *shofar* among the nations.
Prepare the nations for war against her.
Summon kingdoms against her —
Ararat, Minni and Ashkenaz.
Appoint an officer against her;
bring up horses like bristling grasshoppers.
28   Prepare the nations against her,
the kings of the Medes, his governors and deputies,
and all the land he controls.

29   The earth quakes and writhes,
as ADONAI's designs against Bavel are fulfilled,
to make the land of Bavel a ruin,
with no one living there.
30   Bavel's warriors have given up fighting;
they remain in their fortresses;
their courage has failed; they are now like women.
Her homes are on fire, her gate-bars broken.
31   One runner runs to meet another,
messenger to meet messenger,
to report to the king of Bavel
that every part of his city is taken,
32   the fords have been occupied,
and the swamp thickets set on fire,
while the warriors are seized with panic.

33 For here is what *ADONAI-Tzva'ot*,
the God of Isra'el, says:
"The daughter of Bavel is like
a threshing-floor at treading-time.
Just a little while longer,
and the time for harvesting her will come."

34 N'vukhadretzar king of Bavel
has devoured me, crushed me.
He left me like an empty pot.
Like a monster, he swallowed me whole.
With my delicacies he stuffed his belly;
then he rinsed me out.

35 But one who lives in Tziyon will say,
"May my torn flesh be avenged on Bavel";
and Yerushalayim will say,
"May my blood be avenged on the Kasdim."

36 Therefore here is what *ADONAI* says:
"I will plead your cause.
I will take vengeance for you.
I will dry up her river
and make her water sources dry.

37 Bavel will become a heap of ruins,
a place for jackals to live,
an object of horror and hissing,
with no one living there.

38 Together they roar like young lions,
growl like lion cubs.

39 When they are hot with desire,
I will prepare them a drink.
I will make them so drunk
they will have convulsions,
sleep forever and never wake up,"
says *ADONAI*.

40 "I will drag them down like lambs to be slaughtered,
like rams and male goats."

41 Sheshakh has been captured,
the pride of the whole earth seized!
Bavel has become an object of horror
throughout the nations!

42 The sea has flooded Bavel,
overwhelmed her with its raging waves.

43 Her cities have become desolate —
parched, arid land,
a land where no one lives;
nobody even passes through.

44 "I will punish Bel in Bavel
and make him disgorge what he swallowed.
The nations will no longer flow to him.
Bavel's wall will fall.

45 Get out of her, my people!
Each one, save yourself
from ADONAI's furious anger!

46 Don't be fainthearted, don't be afraid
of the rumors spreading abroad in the land.
One year one rumor comes,
the next year another one,
rumors of violence in the land
and rulers fighting rulers.

47 Therefore, listen! The days are coming
when I will pass judgment on Bavel's idols.
Her whole land will be put to shame,
as all her slain fall on home soil.

48 Then heaven and earth and all that is in them
will sing for joy over Bavel;
for the plunderers from the north
are coming to her," says ADONAI.

49 Just as Bavel caused
the slain of Isra'el to fall,
so at Bavel will fall
the slain of all the land.

50 You who escaped the sword,
go! Don't stand still!
Remember ADONAI from afar,
let Yerushalayim come into your minds.

51 "The reproaches we have heard have put us to shame,
disgrace covers our faces;
because foreigners have entered
the sanctuaries of ADONAI's house."

52 "Therefore," says ADONAI, "the days are coming
when I will pass judgment on her idols,
and the wounded will groan throughout her land.

53 Even if Bavel scales the heavens
or reinforces her lofty stronghold,
plunderers will come to her
from me," says ADONAI.

54 An agonized cry is heard from Bavel!
Great destruction in the land of the Kasdim!

55 For ADONAI is plundering Bavel
and silencing her noisy din —

their waves roar like the raging ocean,
their clamor sounds and resounds.

56   Yes, the plunderer has fallen upon her,
fallen on Bavel.
Her warriors are captured, their bows are broken.
For Adonai is a God of retribution;
he will surely repay.

57   "I will intoxicate her leaders and sages,
her governors, deputies and warriors.
They will sleep forever and never wake up,"
says the king, whose name is Adonai-Tzva'ot.

58   Thus says Adonai-Tzva'ot:
"The wide walls of Bavel will be razed to the ground,
her lofty gates will be set on fire.
The peoples are toiling for nothing,
the nation's labor goes up in flames,
and everyone is exhausted."

^{59} This is the order which Yirmeyahu the prophet gave to S'rayah the son of Neriyah, the son of Machseyah, when he went to Bavel with Tzidkiyahu the king of Y'hudah in the fourth year of his reign. S'rayah was quartermaster. ^{60} Yirmeyahu had written on a separate scroll all the above words describing the disaster that was to befall Bavel. ^{61} Yirmeyahu said to S'rayah, "See to it that when you arrive in Bavel you read all these words aloud. Then say, ^{62} 'Adonai, you have promised to destroy this place, that no one will live here, neither human nor animal, but that it will be desolate forever.' ^{63} When you finish reading this scroll, tie a rock to it, throw it into the middle of the Euphrates, ^{64} and say, 'Like this, Bavel will sink, never to rise again, because of the disaster I am bringing on her; and they will grow weary.'"

(Up to here, these have been the words of Yirmeyahu.)

52 ^{1} Tzidkiyahu was twenty-one years old when he began to rule, and he ruled for eleven years in Yerushalayim. His mother's name was Hamutal the daughter of Yirmeyahu, from Livnah. ^{2} He did what was evil from Adonai's perspective, following the example of everything Y'hoyakim had done. ^{3} And it was because of Adonai's anger that all these things happened to Yerushalayim and Y'hudah, until he had thrown them out of his presence.

Tzidkiyahu rebelled against the king of Bavel; ^{4} so in the ninth year of his reign, in the tenth month, on the tenth day of the month, N'vukhadretzar king of Bavel marched against Yerushalayim with his entire army. He set up camp against it and built siege towers against it on every side. ^{5} The city remained under siege into the eleventh year of King Tzidkiyahu.

^{6} On the ninth day of the fourth month, when the famine in the city was so severe that there was no food for the people of the land, ^{7} they broke through into the city. All the soldiers fled and left the city by night through the gate between the two walls, near the king's garden. Because the Kasdim were surrounding the city, they took the route through the 'Aravah. [8] But the army of the Kasdim went in pursuit of the king and overtook Tzidkiyahu on the plains near Yericho; all his troops deserted him. [9] Then they took the king and brought him up to the king of Bavel in Rivlah, in the land of Hamat, where he passed judgment on him. [10] The king of Bavel slaughtered his sons before his eyes; he also slaughtered all the leading men of Y'hudah in Rivlah. [11] Then the king of Bavel put out Tzidkiyahu's eyes, bound him in chains, carried him off to Bavel and kept him in prison until the day of his death.

[12] In the fifth month, on the tenth day of the month, which was also the nineteenth year of King N'vukhadretzar, king of Bavel, N'vuzar'adan, the commander of the guard and a close associate of the king of Bavel, entered Yerushalayim. [13] He burned down the house of ADONAI, the royal palace and all the houses in Yerushalayim — every notable person's house he burned to the ground. [14] The whole army of the Kasdim, who were with the commander of the guard, broke down all the walls of Yerushalayim on every side. [15] N'vuzar'adan the commander of the guard then deported some of the poor people, the remaining population of the city, the deserters who had defected to the king of Bavel and the rest of the common people. [16] But N'vuzar'adan the commander of the guard left behind some of the poor people of the land to be vineyard-workers and farmers.

[17] The Kasdim smashed the bronze columns of the house of ADONAI, also the trolleys and bronze Sea that were in the house of ADONAI, and carried their bronze to Bavel. [18] They also took away the pots, shovels, snuffers, basins, pans, and all the bronze articles they had used in worship. [19] The commander of the guard took the cups, censers, sprinkling bowls, pots, menorahs, pans and bowls — everything made of gold and everything made of silver. [20] The bronze in the two columns, the one Sea, and the twelve bronze bulls under the bases, all of which Shlomo had made for the house of ADONAI, was more than could be weighed. [21] As for the columns, the height of one column was thirty-one-and-a-half feet; it took a twenty-one-foot measuring line to go around it; and its thickness was four fingers — it was hollow. [22] On it was a capital of brass eight-and-three quarters feet high, with netting and pomegranates all around the capital, all of bronze; the second column was similar, also with pomegranates. [23] There were ninety-six pomegranates on the outside; while the total number of pomegranates in the netting was one hundred.

[24] The commander of the guard took [prisoner] S'rayah the chief cohen, Tz'fanyah the second-ranking cohen, and three doorkeepers. [25] From the city he took an official in charge of the soldiers, seven close associates of the king who had been found in the city, the army commander's secretary in charge of military conscription, and sixty of the common people found inside the city. [26] N'vuzar'adan the commander of the guard took them and brought them to the king of Bavel in Rivlah. [27] There in Rivlah, in the land of Hamat, the king of Bavel had them put to death. Thus Y'hudah was carried away captive out of his land.

[28] The numbers of people deported by N'vukhadretzar were as follows: in the seventh year, 3,023 persons from Y'hudah; [29] in the eighteenth year of N'vukhadretzar, 832 persons from Yerushalayim; [30] and in the twenty-third year of N'vukhadretzar, N'vuzar'adan the commander of the guard deported 745 persons from Y'hudah; the total comes to 4,600 persons.

[31] In the thirty-seventh year of the captivity of Y'hoyakhin king of Y'hudah, in the twelfth month, on the twenty-fifth day of the month, Eveel-M'rodakh began his

reign as king of Bavel; and in his first year, he commuted the sentence of Y'hoyakhin king of Y'hudah and released him from prison. ³² He treated him with kindness and gave him a throne higher than those of the other kings there with him in Bavel. ³³ So Y'hoyakhin no longer had to wear prison clothes; moreover, he was provided with food as long as he lived, ³⁴ and he was granted a daily allowance by the king of Bavel to spend on his other needs for as long as he lived, until the day of his death.

Yechezk'el
EZEKIEL

1 ¹ In the thirtieth year, on the fifth day of the fourth month, while I was among the exiles by the K'var River, the heavens were opened, and I saw visions of God. ² On the fifth day of the month, which was during the fifth year of King Y'hoyakhin's exile, ³ the word of ADONAI came to the *cohen* Yechezk'el son of Buzi, in the land of the Kasdim by the K'var River; there the hand of ADONAI was on him.

⁴ I looked and saw a windy storm approaching from the north and a huge cloud with flashing fire, glowing brightly all around with the color of gleaming amber from within the fire. ⁵ Inside, there appeared to be four living creatures that looked like human beings; ⁶ but each one had four faces and four wings. ⁷ Their legs were straight, with feet like calves' hoofs. They glittered like burnished bronze. ⁸ Beneath their wings they had human hands on their four sides. The four of them had faces and wings as follows: ⁹ they touched one another with their wings; they did not turn when they moved, but each one moved straight forward; ¹⁰ as for the appearance of their faces, they had human faces [in front], each of the four had a lion's face on the right, each of the four had a bull's face on the left, and each of the four had an eagle's face [toward the rear] — ¹¹ thus their faces. As for their wings, each had two that stretched upward and touched those of its neighbors, and two more that covered its body. ¹² Each [living creature] moved in the direction of any of its faces; in whichever direction the spirit wanted to go, they went, without turning as they moved — ¹³ thus the appearance of the living creatures.

With them was something that looked like fiery coals burning the way torches do, with the fire flashing here and there between the living creatures; the fire had a brilliance, and out of the fire went lightning. ¹⁴ The living creatures kept speeding here and there like flashes of lightning.

¹⁵ As I gazed at the living creatures, I saw wheels on the ground, one next to each of the four-faced living creatures. ¹⁶ All four wheels looked the same: their inner parts gleamed like beryl, and their structure seemed to be that of a wheel inside a wheel. ¹⁷ When they moved, they could go in any of the four directions without turning as they moved. ¹⁸ Their rims were tall and fearsome, because the rims of all four were full of eyes all around. ¹⁹ When the living creatures moved, the wheels moved along with them; and when the creatures were lifted off the ground, the wheels went with them. ²⁰ Wherever the spirit was to go, they went, in the direction the spirit wanted to go. The wheels were lifted up next to them, because the spirit of the living creatures was in the wheels. ²¹ When [the living creatures] moved, [the wheels] moved; when the former stood still, the latter stood still; and when the former were lifted off the ground, the wheels were lifted up next to them; because the spirit of the living creatures was in the wheels.

²² Over the heads of the living creatures was what appeared to be a dome glittering like ice; it was awesome, spread out over their heads, above them. ²³ Under the dome each had a pair of wings spread out straight toward those of others, and each had a pair which covered his body. ²⁴ I heard the sound of their wings when they moved; it was like the sound of rushing water, like the voice of *Shaddai*, like the noise of a tumultuous crowd or army. When they stopped, they lowered their wings. ²⁵ Whenever there was a sound from above the dome over their heads, they stopped and lowered their wings.

²⁶ Above the dome that was over their heads was something like a throne that looked like a sapphire. On it, above it, was what appeared to be a person. ²⁷ I saw what looked like gleaming, amber-colored fire radiating from what appeared to be his waist upward. Downward from what appeared to be his waist, I saw what looked like fire, giving a brilliant light all around him. ²⁸ This brilliance around him looked like a rainbow in a cloud on a rainy day. This was how the appearance of the glory of *Adonai* looked. When I saw it, I fell on my face, and I heard the voice of someone speaking.

2 ¹ He said to me, "Human being! Stand up! I want to speak with you!" ² As he spoke to me, a spirit entered me and put me on my feet, and I heard him who was speaking to me. ³ He said, "Human being! I am sending you to the people of Isra'el, that nation of rebels who have rebelled against me — they and their ancestors have been transgressing against me to this very day. ⁴ Because they are defiant, hardhearted children, I am sending you; and you are to tell them, 'Here is what *Adonai Elohim* says.' ⁵ Whether they listen or not, this rebellious house will still know that a prophet has been among them!

⁶ "As for you, human being, don't be afraid of them or their words, even if briars and thorns surround you, and you sit among scorpions. Don't be afraid of their words or be upset by their looks, for they are a rebellious house. ⁷ You are to speak my words to them, whether they listen or not, for they are very rebellious. ⁸ But you, human being, hear what I am telling you: don't you be rebellious like that rebellious house. Open your mouth, and eat what I am about to give you."

⁹ When I looked, there was a hand stretched out to me, holding a scroll. ¹⁰ He spread it out in front of me, and it was covered with writing front and back. Written on it were laments, dirges and woes.

3 ¹ He said to me, "Human being, eat what you see in front of you; eat this scroll. Then go and speak to the house of Isra'el." ² So I opened my mouth, and he gave me the scroll to eat, ³ as he said, "Human being, eat this scroll I am giving you; fill your insides with it." When I ate it, it tasted as sweet as honey.

⁴ "Human being," he said to me, "go to the house of Isra'el, and speak my words to them. ⁵ For you are not being sent to a people with a difficult language and unintelligible speech, but to the house of Isra'el — ⁶ not to many peoples with difficult languages and unintelligible speech, whose words you can't understand when you hear them. Without doubt, if I sent you to them, they would listen to you. ⁷ But the house of Isra'el will not be willing to listen to you, because they aren't willing to listen to me; since all the house of Isra'el are obstinate and hardhearted. ⁸ However, I am making you as defiant and obstinate as they are. ⁹ Yes, I am making your

resoluteness harder than flint, as hard as a diamond. So don't be afraid of them or depressed by how they look at you, because they are a rebellious house." ¹⁰ Then he said to me, "Human being, receive in your heart and hear with your ears all my words that I speak to you. ¹¹ Then go to the exiles, to your countrymen; and speak to them. Tell them, 'Here is what *Adonai* E*lohim*, says,' whether they listen or not."

¹² A spirit lifted me up, and I heard behind me a very loud sound — blessed be the glory of A*donai* from his place! ¹³ It was the sound of the wings of the living creatures as they beat against each other, and the sound of the wheels next to them, a very loud sound. ¹⁴ So a spirit lifted me up and took me away. I went in bitterness and the heat of my spirit, with the hand of A*donai* strong on me.

¹⁵ I went to the exiles who were living in Tel-Aviv, by the K'var River and stayed with them there in a stupefied state for seven days. ¹⁶ After seven days the word of A*donai* came to me: ¹⁷ "Human being, I have appointed you to be a watchman for the house of Isra'el. When you hear a word from my mouth, you are to warn them for me. ¹⁸ If I say to a wicked person, 'You will certainly die'; and you fail to warn him, to speak and warn the wicked person to leave his wicked way and save his life; then that wicked person will die guilty; and I will hold you responsible for his death. ¹⁹ On the other hand, if you warn the wicked person, and he doesn't turn from his wickedness or his wicked way, then he will still die guilty; but you will have saved your own life. ²⁰ Similarly, when a righteous person turns away from his righteousness and commits wickedness, I will place a stumbling block before him — he will die; because you failed to warn him, he will die in his sin; his righteous acts which he did will not be remembered; and I will hold you responsible for his death. ²¹ But if you warn the righteous person that a righteous person should not sin, and he doesn't sin; then he will certainly live, because he took the warning; and you too will have saved your life."

²² The hand of A*donai* came on me there, and he said to me, "Get up, go out to the valley, and I will speak with you there." ²³ So I got up and went out to the valley. The glory of A*donai* was there, like the glory I had seen by the K'var River; and I fell on my face. ²⁴ A spirit entered me and put me on my feet. Then he spoke with me and said to me, "Go, shut yourself inside your house. ²⁵ Human being, you are going to be bound with ropes, unable to go out among the people. ²⁶ I will make your tongue stick to the roof of your mouth, so that you will be mute, unable to reprove them; for they are a rebellious house. ²⁷ But when I speak with you, I will open your mouth; and you will say to them, 'This is what *Adonai* E*lohim* says.' Whoever is inclined to listen will listen, and whoever is inclined to refuse will refuse, because they are a rebellious house.

4 ¹ "As for you, human being, take a clay slab, lay it down in front of you, and draw on it the city of Yerushalayim. ² Show it under siege — build towers against it, raise earthworks against it, set up camps against it, and surround it with battering rams. ³ Then take an iron griddle and put it in place as a wall of iron between yourself and the city, and fix your gaze on it — the city is under siege, and you are the one besieging it. This will be a sign for the house of Isra'el.

⁴ "Next, you are to lie on your left side, and have it bear the guilt of the house of Isra'el — for as many days as you lie on your side, you will bear their guilt. ⁵ For I

am assigning you one day for each year of their guilt; thus you are to bear the guilt of the house of Isra'el for 390 days. ⁶ Then, when you have finished that, you are to lie on your right side and bear the guilt of the house of Y'hudah for forty days, each day corresponding to a year; this is what I am assigning you. ⁷ You are to fix your gaze on the siege of Yerushalayim, and, with your arm bared, prophesy against it. ⁸ I am tying you down with ropes, and you are not to turn from one side to the other until you have completed the days of your siege.

⁹ "Take wheat, barley, beans, lentils, millet and buckwheat; put them together in one bowl; and make bread from it. For as long as you lie on your side, 390 days, this is what you are to eat. ¹⁰ Each day the food you eat must weigh only three-quarters of a pound; you may eat it from time to time [during the day]. ¹¹ You are also to drink a limited amount of water, two-thirds of a quart; you may drink it from time to time [during the day]. ¹² [The bread] you eat is to be baked like barley cakes; you are to bake it before their eyes, using human dung as fuel." ¹³ ADONAI said, "This is how the people of Isra'el will eat their food — unclean — in the nations where I am driving them." ¹⁴ I objected: "No, *Adonai ELOHIM*! I have never defiled myself — from my youth until now I have never eaten anything that died by itself or was killed by wild animals; no such disgusting food has ever entered my mouth." ¹⁵ He answered, "All right, I will give you cow dung to use instead of human dung, and you can prepare your bread on it."

¹⁶ He then said to me, "Human being, I am going to cut off the supply of bread in Yerushalayim, so that they will anxiously weigh out bread to eat, and, horrified, ration water to drink. ¹⁷ Finally, due to lack of bread and water, they will stare at each other in shock, wasting away because of their guilt."

5 ¹ "Now you, human being, take a sharp sword; and use it like a barber's razor to shave your head and beard. Then weigh the hair on a balance-scale, and divide it up. ² A third of it you are to burn in the city when the days of the siege are over. Take another third, and hit it with your sword all around the city. Scatter the last third to the wind, and I will pursue them with drawn sword. ³ Also take a few hairs and tie them up in the folds of your garment. ⁴ Again, of these take some; throw them in the fire, and burn them up; from there a fire will come out against the entire house of Isra'el.

⁵ "Here is what *Adonai ELOHIM*, says:

'This is Yerushalayim!
I have placed her in the middle of the nations;
countries can be found all around her.

⁶ But she has rebelled against my rulings
and committed wickedness more than the nations,
against my laws more than the countries around her;
because they have rejected my rulings
and not lived according to my laws.'

⁷ "Therefore here is what *Adonai ELOHIM*, says: 'Because you have outdone the nations around you by not living according to my laws or following my rulings or even following the rules of the nations around you,' ⁸ therefore here is what *Adonai*

ELOHIM, says: 'I too am against you, yes, I; and I will execute judgments among you while all the nations look on. ⁹ Moreover, because of all your disgusting practices, I will do things to you that I have never done before; and I will never do such things again. ¹⁰ Parents among you will eat their children, and children will eat their parents! I will execute judgments among you and scatter to all the winds those of you who remain. ¹¹ For, as I live,' says *Adonai ELOHIM*, 'because you defiled my sanctuary with all your detestable things and disgusting practices, therefore I swear that I will cut you off — my eye will not spare, I will have no pity. ¹² A third of you will die from plague or be consumed by famine inside [Yerushalayim]; a third will fall by the sword all around [Yerushalayim]; and a third I will scatter to all the winds and pursue with the sword.' ¹³ In this way my anger will spend itself, my fury against them will die down, and I will be satisfied. Then, when I have spent my fury on them, they will know that I, *ADONAI*, have spoken out of my zeal. ¹⁴ 'I will make you a ruin and an object of reproach among the nations around you, in the sight of all passing by. ¹⁵ When I execute judgments and furious punishments among you in anger and fury, [Yerushalayim] will be an object of reproach, derision and horror, and a lesson to warn the nations around you. I, *ADONAI*, have announced it. ¹⁶ I will send upon them the deadly, destructive arrows of famine, which I will send to destroy you. I will make the famine worse for you by cutting off your food supply. ¹⁷ Yes, I will send famine and savage beasts upon you to leave you without children; plague and bloodshed will sweep through you; and I will bring the sword upon you. I, *ADONAI*, have spoken it.'"

6 ¹ The word of *ADONAI* came to me: ² "Human being, face toward the mountains of Isra'el, and prophesy against them: ³ 'Mountains of Isra'el, hear the word of *Adonai ELOHIM*: here is what *Adonai ELOHIM* says about the mountains, hills, ravines and valleys: "I myself will bring a sword against you and destroy your high places. ⁴ Your altars will be wrecked and your pillars for sun-worship broken, and I will throw down your slain ones in front of your idols. ⁵ I will lay the corpses of the people of Isra'el in front of their idols and scatter your bones all around your altars. ⁶ Everywhere you live, the cities will be destroyed and the high places wrecked; so that your altars can be destroyed and wrecked, your idols broken and abolished, your pillars for sun-worship cut down and the things you have made wiped out. ⁷ The slain will fall among you; then you will know that I am *ADONAI*.

⁸ ""Nevertheless, I will leave a remnant, some who will escape the sword among the nations, when you have been scattered throughout the countries. ⁹ Those of you who escape will remember me among the nations where they have been exiled. How broken I have been over their whoring hearts that left me, and over their eyes that went whoring after their idols! They are going to loathe themselves for all the evils they committed in their disgusting practices. ¹⁰ Then they will know that I am *ADONAI*; it isn't for nothing that I said I would bring this calamity upon them.""

¹¹ "Here is what *Adonai ELOHIM* says: 'Strike with your hand, and stamp with your foot, and bemoan all the terrible disgusting practices of the house of Isra'el. For they will fall by sword, famine and plague. ¹² Those far away will die from the plague, those nearby will fall by the sword, and whoever stays and is besieged will die from famine. This is how I will spend my fury on them. ¹³ You will know that I am *ADONAI* when their slain men are lying among their idols around their altars on every high

hill, on every mountaintop, under every green tree, under every thick pistachio tree, wherever they offered sweet-smelling sacrifices to appease their idols. ¹⁴ I will stretch out my hand over them and make the land wherever they live into a desolate waste worse than the Divlah Desert. Then they will know that I am ADONAI.'"

7 ¹ The word of ADONAI came to me: ² "As for you, human being, here is what *Adonai ELOHIM* says about the land of Isra'el:

'The end! The end is coming
to the four corners of the land!
³ Now the end is upon you!
I will send my anger upon you,
I will judge you according to your ways.
I will bring on you all your disgusting practices.
⁴ My eye will not spare you, I will have no pity,
but I will bring your ways upon you,
and your disgusting practices will be done among you.
Then you will know that I am ADONAI.'

⁵ "Here is what *Adonai ELOHIM* says:

'Disaster, unique disaster — here it comes!
⁶ The end is coming! The end is coming!
It rouses itself against you — here it comes!
⁷ Doom has come to you,
you who live in the land!
The time has come, the day is near,
for tumult, not joyful shouts on the mountains.
⁸ Now, soon, I will pour out my fury on you,
I will spend my anger on you;
I will judge you according to your ways
I will bring on you all your disgusting practices.
⁹ My eye will not spare you, I will have no pity;
but will bring upon you what your ways deserve;
and your disgusting practices will be among you.
Then you will know it is I, ADONAI, striking you.

¹⁰ "'Here is the day! Here it comes!
Doom has gone out, the rod has blossomed,
arrogance has budded. ¹¹ Violence has grown
into a rod of wickedness.
Nothing is left of them,
nothing of their crowds,
nothing of their wealth —
there is nothing of importance in them.
¹² The time has come, the day has arrived;
let neither buyer rejoice nor seller regret;

for wrath is coming to all her many people.

13 For the seller will not return to what he sold,
even if he is still alive;
for though the vision was brought to all her many people,
nobody repented.
Each kept living his own wicked life;
they weren't strong enough [to repent].

14 The *shofar* has sounded, everything is ready,
but no one goes out to the battle,
for my wrath is coming to all her many people.

15 "'Outside is the sword, inside plague and famine.
Those in the country will die by the sword.
And as for those in the city,
plague and famine will eat them up.

16 But if any of them manage to escape,
they will head for the mountains
like doves from the valleys,
all of them moaning, each for his sin.

17 All hands will droop, all knees turn to water.

18 They will put on sackcloth;
horror will cover them;
every face will be ashamed,
every head shaved bald.

19 They will throw their silver into the streets;
their gold will be like something unclean.
On the day of ADONAI's wrath their silver and gold
won't be able to rescue them.
These things won't satisfy their hunger,
these things won't fill their stomachs,
because these are what caused them to sin.

20 From their beautiful jewellery,
in which they took such pride,
they made their abominable idols
and their other detestable things;
therefore, for them I have caused it
to be like something unclean.

21 I will hand it over to foreigners as booty,
to the wicked of the earth as spoil,
and they will profane it.

22 I will turn my face away from them;
then [Bavel] will profane my secret place,
robbers will enter and profane it.

23 "'Forge a chain,
for the land is full of capital crimes
and the city full of violence.

647

24 Therefore I will bring the worst of the nations
to take possession of their homes;
I will end the arrogance of the strong;
and their holy places will be profaned.

25 When horror comes, they will seek peace;
but there will be none.

26 Calamity will follow calamity,
rumor will follow rumor;
they will seek a vision from the prophet,
but *Torah* will perish from the *cohen*
and advice from the leaders.

27 The king will go into mourning,
the prince will be clothed with fright,
and the hands of the people of the land
will tremble in terror.
I will treat them as their way of life deserves
and judge them as they have judged others.
Then they will know
that I am ADONAI.'"

8 ¹ On the fifth day of the sixth month of the sixth year, as I was sitting in my house, and the leaders of Y'hudah were sitting there with me, the hand of *Adonai ELOHIM* fell on me. ² I looked and saw what seemed like a man made of fire. From what appeared to be his waist downward was fire, and from his waist upward was what appeared to be a gleaming amber-colored brilliance. ³ The form of a hand was put out, which took me by a lock of my hair; and a spirit lifted me up between earth and heaven and brought me, in these visions from God, to Yerushalayim, to the entrance of the inner [courtyard] gate that faces north. There stood the idol that [arouses God's] jealousy and provokes [his] zealous indignation. ⁴ There before me was the glory of the God of Isra'el, as in the vision I had seen in the valley.

⁵ Then he said to me, "Human being, raise your eyes toward the north." I raised my eyes toward the north and saw, north of the Altar Gate, this image that [arouses God's] jealousy in the entryway. ⁶ He asked me, "Human being, do you see what they are doing, the horribly disgusting practices that the house of Isra'el is committing here, so that I must distance myself from my own sanctuary? But you will see even worse abominations."

⁷ He brought me to the entrance of the courtyard; and when I looked, I saw a hole in the wall. ⁸ He said to me, "Human being, dig into the wall." After digging in the wall, I saw a door. ⁹ "Go in," he said, "and see the wicked practices they are engaged in here." ¹⁰ So I went in and looked, and there, carved on the walls all around, were every kind of reptile and repulsive animal, along with all the idols of the house of Isra'el. ¹¹ Standing in front of them were seventy of the leading men of the house of Isra'el — in the center stood Ya'azanyahu the son of Shafan. Each man had his incense-burner in his hand, and a thick cloud of incense went up. ¹² Then he said to me, "Human being, did you see what the leaders of the house of Isra'el are doing in the dark, each one in the room of his own carved image, because they say, 'ADONAI can't see us; ADONAI has left the land.'?" ¹³ He also said to me, "You will see even worse abominations that they are doing."

[14] He brought me to the entrance of the north gate to ADONAI's house; and there before me were women weeping for Tammuz. [15] "Human being," he asked me, "have you seen this? You will see practices even more disgusting than these." [16] He brought me into the inner courtyard of ADONAI's house; and there, at the entrance to the temple of ADONAI, between the porch and the altar, were about twenty-five men with their backs toward the temple of ADONAI and their faces toward the east; and they were worshipping the sun toward the east. [17] He asked me, "Human being, have you seen this? Does the house of Y'hudah consider it a casual matter that they commit the disgusting practices they are committing here, thus filling the land with violence, provoking me still more? Look! They are even putting the branch to their nose! [18] Therefore I will act in fury, my eye will not spare, I will have no pity. Even if they cry loudly right in my ears, I will not listen to them."

9 [1] Then he cried loudly right in my ears: "Summon the commanders of the city, each holding his weapon of destruction." [2] At once, six men approached on the path from the upper gate, to the north, each man holding his weapon of destruction. Among them was a man clothed in linen, with a scribe's writing equipment at his waist. They entered and stood by the bronze altar. [3] Then the glory of the God of Isra'el was made to go up from over the *keruv*, where it had been, to the threshold of the house. He called to the man clothed in linen, who had the scribe's writing equipment at his waist. [4] ADONAI said to him, "Go throughout the city, through all Yerushalayim, and put a mark on the foreheads of the men who are sighing and crying over all the disgusting practices that are being committed in it." [5] To the others I heard him say, "Go through the city after him and strike! Don't let your eye spare; have no pity! [6] Kill old men, young men, girls, little children, women — slaughter them all! But don't go near anyone with the mark. Begin at my sanctuary." They began with the leaders in front of the house. [7] Then he said to them, "Defile the house! Fill the courtyards with corpses! Get going!" So they went out, spreading death in the city. [8] While the killing was going on, I was left alone. I fell on my face, cried, and said, "Oh, *Adonai ELOHIM*! In pouring out your fury on Yerushalayim, are you going to destroy everyone left in Isra'el?" [9] Then he said to me, "The wickedness of the house of Isra'el and Y'hudah is enormous, the land is full of blood, and the city is full of justice denied; because they say, 'ADONAI has left the land, ADONAI doesn't see.' [10] But as far as I am concerned, my eye will not spare, and I will have no pity, but I will bring [the consequences of] their ways on their own heads."

[11] At this point the man clothed in linen with the writing equipment at his waist returned and reported, "I have done everything you ordered me to do."

10 [1] Then I looked, and suddenly, on the dome over the heads of the *k'ruvim*, there appeared above them something like sapphire that seemed to take the form of a throne. [2] He spoke to the man clothed in linen; he said, "Go in between the wheels under the *k'ruvim*, fill both your hands with fiery coals from between the *k'ruvim*, and throw them on the city." As I watched, he went. [3] Now the *k'ruvim* were standing to the right of the house when the man entered, and the cloud filled the inner courtyard. [4] The glory of ADONAI rose from above the *keruv* to the threshold of the house, leaving the house filled with the cloud and the courtyard full of the brilliance of ADONAI's glory. [5] The sound of the wings of the *k'ruvim* could be heard even in the outer courtyard sounding like the voice of God, *Shaddai*, when he speaks. ⁶ When he ordered the man clothed in linen to take fire from between the wheels, from between the *k'ruvim*, he went in and stood next to a wheel; ⁷ and a *keruv* put out his hand from between the *k'ruvim* into the fire between the *k'ruvim*, took some of it, and put it in the hands of the one clothed in linen, who took it and went out. ⁸ Now there appeared among the *k'ruvim* the form of a man's hand under their wings. ⁹ I looked and saw four wheels next to the *k'ruvim*, one wheel next to one *keruv* and another wheel next to another *keruv*: the wheels had the color of beryl. ¹⁰ Their shape was the same for all four, like a wheel inside a wheel. ¹¹ When they moved, they could go in any of the four directions without turning as they moved; rather, wherever the head looked, they followed without turning as they moved. ¹² Their whole bodies, including their backs, hands and wings, and also the wheels, were full of eyes all around — even the wheels of the four *k'ruvim*. ¹³ As for the wheels, I heard them called "the wheel apparatus." ¹⁴ Every one [of the *k'ruvim*] had four faces: the first face was the face of a *keruv*, the second face was the face of a man, the third the face of a lion and the fourth the face of an eagle. ¹⁵ Then the *k'ruvim* rose. These were the living creatures I had seen by the K'var River. ¹⁶ When the *k'ruvim* moved, the wheels went with them; and when the *k'ruvim* lifted their wings to rise off the ground, these wheels did not stop going with them. ¹⁷ When [the *k'ruvim*] stood still, [the wheels] stood still; and when the former rose, the latter rose with them; because the spirit of the living creatures was in them.

¹⁸ Now the glory of *Adonai* left the threshold of the house and halted above the *k'ruvim*. ¹⁹ The *k'ruvim* lifted their wings and rose off the earth — I was watching as they went off with the wheels next to them. They paused at the entrance to the east gate of *Adonai*'s house, with the glory of the God of Isra'el over them, from above. ²⁰ This was the living creature I had seen beneath the God of Isra'el by the K'var River, so I knew they were *k'ruvim*. ²¹ Each of the four had four faces, and each had four wings, and what looked like a man's hands was under their wings. ²² As for how their faces looked, they were the faces I had seen by the K'var River, identical in appearance. Each one moved straight ahead.

11 ¹ Then a spirit lifted me up and brought me to the east gate of *Adonai*'s house, the gate that faces eastward. At the entrance of the gate I saw twenty-five men; among them were Ya'azanyah the son of 'Azur and P'latyahu the son of B'nayahu, leaders of the people. ² He said to me, "Human being, these are the men who make evil plans and give wicked advice in this city. ³ They say, 'The time hasn't come to build houses. This city is the cooking pot, and we're the meat!' ⁴ Therefore prophesy against them, human being, prophesy!" ⁵ The Spirit of *Adonai* fell on me, and he said to me, "Say, 'Here is what *Adonai* says: "What you are saying is correct, house of Isra'el; because I know how your minds work. ⁶ You have killed many in this city, you have filled its streets with the dead." ⁷ Therefore *Adonai Elohim* says this: "Those you have killed and strewn all over it, they are the meat; and this city is indeed the cooking pot; but you will be removed from it. ⁸ You are afraid of the sword, but I will bring the sword upon you," says *Adonai Elohim*. ⁹ "I will bring you out of it, hand you over to foreigners and execute judgments among you. ¹⁰ You will die by the sword; I will judge you at the border of Isra'el; and you will know that I am *Adonai*.

¹¹ This city will not be your cooking pot, but you will be the meat in it — I will judge you at Isra'el's frontier; ¹² and you will know that I am ADONAI. For you have not lived by my laws or obeyed my rulings but have acted according to the rules of the nations surrounding you.'"'

¹³ As I was prophesying, P'latyahu the son of B'nayah died. I fell down on my face and cried out, "Oh, *Adonai ELOHIM*! Are you going to destroy completely those of Isra'el who are left?" ¹⁴ Then the word of ADONAI came to me: ¹⁵ "Human being, it is to your kinsmen — your brothers, your relatives and the whole house of Isra'el — that the people living in Yerushalayim have said, 'Get away from ADONAI! This land has been given to us to possess!' ¹⁶ Therefore, say that *Adonai ELOHIM* says this: 'True, I removed them far away among the nations and scattered them among the countries; nevertheless, I have been a little sanctuary for them in the countries to which they have gone.' ¹⁷ Therefore, say that *Adonai ELOHIM* says this: "'I will gather you from the peoples and collect you from the countries where you have been scattered, and I will give the land of Isra'el to you." ¹⁸ Then they will go there and remove all its loathsome things and disgusting practices, ¹⁹ and I will give them unity of heart. "I will put a new spirit among you." I will remove from their bodies the hearts of stone and give them hearts of flesh; ²⁰ so that they will live by my regulations, obey my rulings and act by them. Then they will be my people, and I will be their God. ²¹ But as for those whose hearts go after the heart of their loathsome things and disgusting practices, I will bring [the consequences of] their ways on their own heads,' says *Adonai ELOHIM*."

²² The *k'ruvim* lifted their wings, and the wheels were next to them, with the glory of the God of Isra'el over them, above. ²³ Next, the glory of ADONAI rose from within the city and stood over the mountain which is on the east side of the city. ²⁴ Then a spirit lifted me up and brought me, in the vision, by the Spirit of God, to the exiles in the land of the Kasdim; after which the vision I had seen left me. ²⁵ So I told the exiles everything ADONAI had shown me.

12 ¹ The word of ADONAI came to me: ² "Human being, you are living among a rebellious people. They have eyes that can see, but they don't take notice; and they have ears that can hear, but they don't pay attention; because they are a rebellious people. ³ So you, human being, prepare supplies for exile; and during the daytime, as they watch, go away as if you were going into exile — leave your place, and go somewhere else as they watch. Perhaps they will take notice, even though they are a rebellious house. ⁴ Bring out your belongings during the day while they watch, as supplies for exile; and you yourself, while they watch, are to leave as people do who are going into exile. ⁵ Dig a hole through the wall while they watch, and carry [your belongings] out through it. ⁶ While they watch, you are to shoulder your pack and carry it out into the dark, with your face covered, so that you can't see the ground; for I am making you a sign for the house of Isra'el."

⁷ So I did as I had been ordered — I brought out my belongings during the day as supplies for exile, and in the evening I dug a hole through the wall with my hand; then I carried my pack out on my shoulder in the dark as they watched.

⁸ In the morning the word of ADONAI came to me: ⁹ "Human being, the house of Isra'el, that rebellious house, has asked you what you are doing. ¹⁰ Tell them that *Adonai ELOHIM* says this prophecy concerns the prince in Yerushalayim and all the

house of Isra'el there. ¹¹ Say: 'I am a sign for you. As I have done, so will it be done to them — they will go into exile, into captivity. ¹² The prince who is with them will shoulder his pack and leave in the dark. They will dig holes through the wall to carry out their supplies. He will cover his face, so that he won't be able to see the ground with his eyes. ¹³ I will spread my net over him, and he will be caught in my snare. Then I will bring him to Bavel, to the land of the Kasdim. But he will not see it, even though he is going to die there. ¹⁴ I will scatter to every wind all who are in attendance on him to help him, along with all his troops; and I will pursue them with the sword. ¹⁵ They will know that I am ADONAI when I scatter them among the nations and disperse them among the countries. ¹⁶ But I will spare a few of them from sword, famine and plague; so that they can tell about all their disgusting practices among the nations where they go; thus they too will know that I am ADONAI.'"

¹⁷ The word of ADONAI came to me: ¹⁸ "Human being, shake as you eat your food; tremble anxiously as you drink your water; ¹⁹ and say to the people of the land, 'Here is what Adonai ELOHIM says concerning those living in Yerushalayim in the land of Isra'el: "They will eat their bread in anxiety and drink their water in horror; because the land will be desolated from everything that fills it, due to the violence of those living there. ²⁰ The inhabited cities will be laid waste, the land will be desolate, and you will know that I am ADONAI.'"'"

²¹ The word of ADONAI came to me: ²² "Human being, don't you have this proverb in the land of Isra'el, 'Time keeps passing, and none of the visions are fulfilled'? ²³ Therefore tell them that Adonai ELOHIM says, 'I will put an end to that proverb; never again will they use it as a proverb in Isra'el.' Tell them, 'The time has come for the fulfillment of every vision. ²⁴ There will no longer be empty visions or falsely optimistic divinations in the house of Isra'el, ²⁵ because I am ADONAI. I will speak; and whatever statement I make, it will be accomplished. It will no longer be delayed; for in your days, you rebellious house, I will speak the word and accomplish it,' says Adonai ELOHIM."

²⁶ Again, the word of ADONAI came to me: ²⁷ "Human being, look! People from the house of Isra'el are saying, 'The vision he sees concerns the distant future; he is prophesying about a time far off.' ²⁸ Therefore, say to them that Adonai ELOHIM says, 'None of my words will be delayed any more, but the word that I speak will be accomplished,' says Adonai ELOHIM."

13 ¹ The word of ADONAI came to me: ² "Human being, prophesy against the prophets of Isra'el who prophesy. Tell those prophesying out of their own thoughts, 'Listen to what ADONAI says! ³ Adonai ELOHIM says: "Woe to the vile prophets who follow their own spirits and things which they have not seen! ⁴ Isra'el, your prophets have been like jackals among ruins. ⁵ You [prophets] have not gone up to the breaks in the barricade or repaired it for the house of Isra'el, so that they can stand fast in battle on the day of ADONAI. ⁶ Their visions are futile and their divination is false; they say, 'ADONAI says,' when ADONAI has not sent them; yet they hope that the word will be confirmed. ⁷ Haven't you had a futile vision and spoken a false divination when you say, 'ADONAI says,' and I have not spoken? ⁸ Therefore here is what Adonai ELOHIM does say: 'Because you have spoken futilities and seen falsehoods, therefore I am against you,' says Adonai ELOHIM.

⁹ "'"My hand will be against the prophets who have futile visions and produce false divinations; they will not be allowed into the council of my people, or be

written in the register of the house of Isra'el, or enter the land of Isra'el. Then you will know that I am *Adonai Elohim*. ¹⁰ They deserve this, because they have led my people astray by saying there is peace when there is no peace. If someone builds a wall without mortar, they 'plaster' it with whitewash [to make it appear strong]. ¹¹ Tell these 'plasterers' that a cloudburst is coming, with huge hailstones and gale-force winds; ¹² and the wall will fall down. Then people will ask you, 'Where is the whitewash you used to "plaster" it?'" ¹³ Therefore *Adonai Elohim* says: "In my rage I will cause gale-force winds to break out, and in my anger there will come a cloudburst, with huge hailstones to consume it in fury. ¹⁴ This is how I will break down the wall you covered with whitewash — I will smash it to the ground, so that its foundation will be revealed. The wall will fall down, and you will be consumed with it. Then you will know that I am *Adonai*. ¹⁵ In this way I will spend my fury on the wall and on those who covered it with whitewash; and I will say to you, 'The wall is gone, and so are those who "plastered" it,' ¹⁶ that is, the prophets of Isra'el who prophesy about Yerushalayim and see visions of peace for her when there is no peace," says *Adonai Elohim*.'

¹⁷ "You, human being, turn your face against the daughters of your people who prophesy out of their own thoughts. Prophesy against them; ¹⁸ tell them that *Adonai Elohim* says, 'Woe to the women who sew magic pads for all arm joints and put veils over people of all sizes, in order to hunt human lives! Will you hunt down the lives of my people while you keep your own lives safe? ¹⁹ You dishonor me before my people for a few handfuls of barley and crumbs of bread, killing people who should not die and sparing those who should not live, by your lying to my people, who love hearing lies.' ²⁰ Therefore here is what *Adonai Elohim* says: 'I am against your pads, with which you hunt human lives like birds; I will tear them from your arms and let the lives go, yes, the human lives that you hunt like birds. ²¹ I will also tear your veils and rescue my people from your clutches, so that they will no longer be in your power for you to hunt. Then you will know that I am *Adonai*. ²² Because you have disheartened the righteous with your lies when I was not trying to cause them pain and have encouraged the wicked not to turn from their wicked ways and thus be saved, ²³ therefore you will have no more futile visions, and you will produce no more divinations. I will rescue my people from your clutches, and you will know that I am *Adonai*.'"

14 ¹ Then certain of Isra'el's leaders came to me; and while they were sitting with me, ² the word of *Adonai* came to me: ³ "Human being, these men have taken their idols into their hearts, thus setting in front of themselves the stumbling block that leads to sin. Should I let them consult me at all? ⁴ Therefore speak to them, and tell them that *Adonai Elohim* says, 'Everyone in the house of Isra'el who takes his idols into his heart, thus setting in front of himself the stumbling block that leads to sin, and then comes to the prophet, I myself, *Adonai*, will answer him in a manner suited to his many idols, ⁵ in order to grab hold of the house of Isra'el in their hearts; since, through their idols, they have all fallen away from me.'

⁶ "Therefore say to the house of Isra'el that *Adonai Elohim* says, 'Repent! Turn yourselves away from your idols, turn your faces away from all your disgusting practices! ⁷ For everyone, whether from the house of Isra'el or a foreigner living in Isra'el, who separates himself from me and takes his idols into his heart, thus setting in front of himself the stumbling block that leads to sin, and then comes to the prophet,

asking him to consult me for him, I myself, ADONAI, will answer him. ⁸ I will set my face against that person, make him a warning sign and an example, and cut him off from my people. Then you will know that I am ADONAI.

⁹ "'Now, whenever a prophet is enticed into speaking a word, it will be I, ADONAI, who will have enticed that prophet. I will stretch out my hand over him and destroy him from among my people Isra'el. ¹⁰ The prophets will bear the guilt for their sins — the sin of the prophet will be the same as the sin of the inquirer — ¹¹ so that the house of Isra'el will no longer wander away from me or defile themselves with all their crimes; rather, they will be my people and I will be their God,' says Adonai ELOHIM."

¹² The word of ADONAI came to me: ¹³ "Human being, when a land sins against me by dealing treacherously with me, so that I stretch out my hand over it and break off its food supply, sending it famine and eliminating both its humans and its animals; ¹⁴ even if these three men were in it — Noach, Dani'el and Iyov — they would by their righteousness save only themselves," says Adonai ELOHIM.

¹⁵ "If I unleash wild beasts on the land, and they kill its children and desolate it, so that no one can pass through because of the animals; ¹⁶ even if these three men were in it, as I live," says Adonai ELOHIM, "they would save neither sons nor daughters; only they themselves would be saved, and the land would remain barren.

¹⁷ "Or if I bring the sword down on that land, saying, 'Let the sword pass through the land,' so that I eliminate both its humans and its animals; ¹⁸ even if these three men were in it, as I live," says Adonai ELOHIM, "they would save neither sons nor daughters; only they themselves would be saved.

¹⁹ "Or if I bring a plague into that land and pour out my fury on it in bloodshed, so that I eliminate both its humans and its animals; ²⁰ even if Noach, Dani'el and Iyov were in it, as I live," says Adonai ELOHIM, "they would save neither a son nor a daughter; they would save only themselves by their righteousness."

²¹ For here is what Adonai ELOHIM says: "Even if I inflict my four dreadful judgments on Yerushalayim — sword, famine, wild animals and plagues — to eliminate both its humans and its animals; ²² there will still be left a remnant in it to be brought out, including both sons and daughters. When they come out to you, and you see their way of life and how they act, then you will be consoled over the calamity I have brought upon Yerushalayim, over everything I have done to it. ²³ Yes, they will console you when you see their way of life and how they act; and you will understand that it was not without good reason that I did what I did in [Yerushalayim]," says Adonai ELOHIM.

15 ¹ The word of ADONAI came to me:

²   "Human being, why should wood from a grapevine be better
    than some other kind of wood,
    than some branch that one might find
    among the trees of the forest?
³   Its wood can't be used to make anything,
    not even a pin on which to hang a pot.
⁴   So now it is thrown in the fire as fuel,
    the fire consumes both ends of it,

and the middle of it is singed —
is it useful now for making something?

5   When it was whole, it was good for nothing;
    so how much less, when the fire
    has consumed it, and it is singed,
    will it be useful for making something!

6   "So *Adonai* ELOHIM says this:
    'Like wood from the vine among the trees of the forest,
    which I consign to the fire as fuel,
    so I give those living in Yerushalayim.

7   I will set my face against them —
    they may have escaped one fire,
    but the fire will consume them yet.
    When I set my face against them,
    you will know that I am ADONAI.

8   I will make the land desolate
    because they have dealt so treacherously,'
    says *Adonai* ELOHIM."

16 ¹ The word of ADONAI came to me: ² "Human being, make Yerushalayim realize how disgusting her practices are. ³ Say that *Adonai* ELOHIM is telling Yerushalayim, 'By origin and birth you are of the land of the Kena'ani — your father was an Emori, and your mother was a Hitti. ⁴ As for your birth — on the day you were born nobody cut your umbilical cord, washed you in water to clean you off, rubbed salt on you or wrapped you in cloth. ⁵ No one seeing you had enough pity on you to do any of these things for you — no one had any compassion on you. Instead, you were thrown into an open field in your own filth on the day you were born.

⁶ "'I passed by and saw you there, wallowing in your own blood; and as you lay in your blood I said to you, "Live!" Yes, I said to you, as you lay in your blood, "Live! ⁷ I will increase your numbers just like plants growing in the field." And you did increase, you developed, you reached puberty, your breasts appeared, and your hair grew long; but you were naked and exposed.

⁸ "'Again I passed by you, looked at you and saw that your time had come, the time for love. So I spread my cloak over you to cover your private parts and entered into a covenant with you,' says *Adonai* ELOHIM, 'and you became mine. ⁹ Then I bathed you in water, washed the blood off you, and anointed you with oil. ¹⁰ I also clothed you with an embroidered gown, gave you fine leather sandals to wear, put a fine linen headband on your head and covered you with silk. ¹¹ I gave you jewelry to wear, brace-lets for your hands, a necklace for your neck, ¹² a ring for your nose, earrings for your ears and a beautiful crown for your head. ¹³ Thus you were decked out in gold and silver; your clothing was of fine linen, silk and richly embroidered cloth; you ate the finest flour, honey and olive oil. You grew increasingly beautiful — you were fit to be queen. ¹⁴ Your fame spread among the nations because of your beauty, because it was perfect, due to my having bestowed my own splendor on you' says *Adonai* ELOHIM.

¹⁵ "'But you put your trust in your own beauty and began prostituting yourself because of your fame, soliciting everyone passing by and accepting all comers.

¹⁶ You took your clothes and used them to decorate with bright colors the high places you made for yourself, and there you continued prostituting yourself. Such things shouldn't happen, and in the future they won't. ¹⁷ You also took your beautiful jewels made of my gold and my silver, which I had given you, and made for yourself male images, with which you continued to prostitute yourself. ¹⁸ You took your embroidered clothing and covered them; you set my olive oil and my incense in front of them; ¹⁹ and you took my food, which I had given you — my fine flour, olive oil and honey, that I had given you to eat — and set it in front of them to give a pleasant aroma. That is how it was,' says *Adonai Elohim*.

²⁰ "'Moreover, your sons and daughters, whom you bore me, you took and sacrificed for them to devour. Were these fornications of yours a casual matter? — ²¹ killing my children, handing them over and setting them apart for [these idols]? ²² In all your disgusting practices and fornications you never remembered the condition you were in when you were young — naked, exposed and wallowing in your own blood.

²³ "'So, after all this wickedness of yours — woe, woe to you!' says *Adonai Elohim* — ²⁴ 'you built platforms and made yourself high places in every open space. ²⁵ You built your high places at every streetcorner, turning your beauty into an abomination, spreading your legs for every passer-by, and multiplying your acts of fornication. ²⁶ You had sex with your big-membered Egyptian neighbors and engaged in fornication over and over, just to provoke me. ²⁷ So now I have stretched out my hand over you, diminished your ration of food and put you at the mercy of those who hate you, the daughters of the P'lishtim, who find your lewd behavior revolting.

²⁸ "'Still unsatisfied, you acted like a whore also with the people of Ashur; yes, you fornicated with them and were still not satisfied. ²⁹ You multiplied your acts of fornication with the land of traders, the Kasdim, and still weren't satisfied.

³⁰ "'You are so weak-willed!' says *Adonai Elohim*. 'You do all these things, behaving like a shameless whore, ³¹ building your platforms on every streetcorner, making your high places in every open space — and yet you aren't like a whore, because you scorn getting paid. ³² Here is a wife who commits adultery, who goes to bed with strangers instead of her husband; ³³ but also instead of receiving gifts like every other prostitute, you give gifts to all your lovers, you bribe them to come to you from all over the place and have sex with you! ³⁴ You are the opposite of other women — you solicit the fornication, you aren't solicited; and you pay them, they don't pay you — you're the opposite!

³⁵ "'All right, you whore, listen to the word of *Adonai*!' ³⁶ *Adonai Elohim* says: 'Because your filth has been poured out and your privates exposed through your acts of fornication with your lovers, and because of all the idols of your disgusting practices, and because of the blood of your children, which you gave them, ³⁷ therefore, look! I am going to gather all your lovers, to whom you have been so very nice, all the ones you hate right along with all the ones you love — I will gather them against you from all over the place and expose your private parts to them, so that they will see you completely naked. ³⁸ I will pronounce on you the sentence that applies to women who commit adultery and murder; I will bring on you the death [decreed for] furious jealousy. ³⁹ Yes, I will hand you over to them; and they will make a ruin of your platforms, tear down your high places, strip you of your clothes, take away your jewels, and leave you naked and exposed. ⁴⁰ They will also bring up a mob against you, who will stone you to death and hack you to pieces with their swords.

[41] They will burn your houses to the ground and execute judgments against you in the presence of many women. I will make you stop fornicating, and you will never again pay for a lover.

[42] "'Yes, I will satisfy my fury against you. But after that, my jealousy will leave you; and I will calm down and no longer be angry.

[43] "'Because you didn't remember the condition you were in when you were young, but enraged me with all these things, therefore I will bring [the consequences of] your ways on your own head' says *Adonai ELOHIM*.

"'You committed these obscenities in addition to all your other disgusting practices! [44] Everyone who quotes proverbs will quote this proverb against you, "Like mother, like daughter." [45] Yes, you are your mother's daughter, who despises her husband and children; you are the sister of your sisters, who despise their husbands and children; your mother was a Hitti and your father an Emori. [46] Moreover, your older sister is Shomron, who lives at your left, she and her daughters; and your younger sister, living at your right, is S'dom with her daughters. [47] You didn't merely live by their ways and act according to their disgusting practices, but in a very short time you acted more corruptly than they in all your ways.

[48] "'As I live' says *Adonai ELOHIM*, 'your sister S'dom has not done, neither she nor her daughters, [as much evil] as you have done, you and your daughters. [49] The crimes of your sister S'dom were pride and gluttony; she and her daughters were careless and complacent, so that they did nothing to help the poor and needy. [50] They were arrogant and committed disgusting acts before me; so that when I saw it, I swept them away. [51] Shomron did not commit even half as many sins as you did. You committed many more disgusting acts than your sisters; in fact, in comparison with all the disgusting acts you have committed, they seem innocent! [52] But you too must bear your disgrace; for by your passing judgment that your sisters were innocent, through your having committed sins worse than theirs, they are shown to be more righteous than you. So be ashamed, and bear the disgrace you deserve for making your [guilty] sisters seem innocent!

[53] "'I will end their exile — the exile of S'dom and her daughters, the exile of Shomron and her daughters, and the exile of your captives there among them; [54] so that you can bear your own shame and experience the disgrace you deserve for all you have done to shield them from feeling their own guilt. [55] Your sisters, S'dom with her daughters and Shomron with her daughters, will return to their previous condition; and you with your daughters will return to your previous condition. [56] When you were so proud, you spoke with contempt about your sister S'dom, [57] before your own wickedness was exposed. But now the daughters of Aram mock you, as do her neighbors; and the daughters of the P'lishtim on every side are repulsed by you. [58] You have brought it all on yourself with your depravities and disgusting practices,' says *Adonai*.

[59] "For here is what *Adonai ELOHIM* says: 'I will do to you as you have done — you treated the oath with contempt by breaking the covenant. [60] Nevertheless, I will remember the covenant I made with you when you were a girl and will establish an everlasting covenant with you. [61] Then you will remember your behavior and be ashamed of it as you receive your older and younger sisters and make them your daughters, even though the covenant with you does not cover that; [62] and I will re-establish my covenant with you. Then you will know that I am *Adonai*;

⁶³ so that you will remember and be so ashamed that you will never open your mouth again, so ashamed will you be when I have forgiven you all that you have done,' says *Adonai ELOHIM*."

17 ¹ The word of *ADONAI* came to me: ² "Human being, propound this riddle, tell the house of Isra'el this allegory, ³ say that *Adonai ELOHIM* says this: 'A big eagle having great wings and long pinions full of varicolored feathers came to the L'vanon and took over the top of the cedar. ⁴ He cropped off the topmost of its young twigs, carried them to a land of traders and set them down in a city of merchants. ⁵ He also took some of the seed in the land and planted it in fertile soil, placing it where there was abundant water, as one would a willow. ⁶ It grew to become a fruitful vine sprawling over the ground; its branches turned toward him, and its roots were under him — thus it became a vine, sprouting branches and putting forth shoots.

⁷ "'There was another big eagle with great wings and many feathers; and the vine bent its roots toward him and put forth its branches toward him, so that he might water it more than in the bed where it was planted. ⁸ It had been planted in good soil, near plenty of water, so that it would produce branches, bear fruit and become a noble vine.'

⁹ "Say that *Adonai ELOHIM* asks: 'Will it succeed? Won't he pull it up by the roots and cut off its fruit; so that it dries up; and all its sprouting leaves wither? There will be no great power and few people there when it is plucked up by the roots. ¹⁰ Will it thrive just because it was planted? Won't it wither altogether when the east wind strikes it? Yes, it will wither right there in the beds where it was growing.'"

¹¹ The word of *ADONAI* came to me: ¹² "Say to the rebellious house: 'Don't you know what these things mean?' Tell them: 'Here, the king of Bavel came to Yerushalayim, took its king and princes and brought them to himself in Bavel. ¹³ Then he took a member of the royal family and made a covenant with him, putting him under oath. He removed the powerful leaders of the land, ¹⁴ so that this kingdom of his would stay humble and not develop aspirations of its own; rather, it would keep his covenant and live accordingly. ¹⁵ But this man rebelled and sent representatives to Egypt, in order to obtain horses and a sizeable army. Can he succeed? Can someone who does such things escape punishment? Can he break the covenant and still escape punishment?

¹⁶ "'As I live,' says *Adonai ELOHIM*, 'in the place where the king who gave him his throne lives, whose oath he despised and whose covenant he broke, there with him in Bavel I swear that he will die. ¹⁷ Pharaoh with his mighty army and numerous troops will give him no help in the war, when they raise siege-works and build fortified towers to destroy many people; ¹⁸ because he despised the oath by breaking the covenant to which he had sworn allegiance; having done all these things, he will not escape unpunished.' ¹⁹ Therefore *Adonai ELOHIM* says: 'As I live, I swear that it is my oath he has despised and my covenant he has broken, and I will bring this on his own head. ²⁰ I will spread my net over him, and he will be caught in my snare; I will bring him to Bavel and bring him to judgment there for breaking faith with me. ²¹ The elite troops among his forces will die by the sword, and those who survive will be scattered to every wind. Then you will know that I, *ADONAI*, said it.'

²² "*Adonai ELOHIM* says, 'From the top of this tall cedar, from its highest branch, I will take a shoot and plant it myself on a high and prominent mountain. ²³ I will

plant it on the highest mountain in Isra'el, where it will put out branches, bear fruit, and become a noble cedar. Under it will live all kinds of birds; winged creatures of every description will live there in the shadow of its branches. ²⁴ Then all the trees of the field will know that I, ADONAI, bring down the tall tree and raise up the low tree, wither the green tree and make the withered tree bear fruit. I, ADONAI, have spoken; and I will do it.'"

18 ¹ The word of ADONAI came to me: ² "What does it mean, that you keep quoting this proverb in the land of Isra'el —

'When parents eat sour grapes,
their children's teeth are set on edge'?

³ "As I live," says Adonai ELOHIM, "I swear that you will never again quote this proverb in Isra'el. ⁴ Look, all lives belong to me — both the parent's life and the child's life are equally mine — so it is the person who sins, himself, who must die.

⁵ "Consider someone who is righteous, who does what is lawful and right. ⁶ He doesn't eat on the mountains or raise his eyes toward the idols of the house of Isra'el; he doesn't defile his neighbor's wife or touch a woman during her time of menstrual impurity; ⁷ he doesn't wrong anyone; he returns any pledged property a debtor has given as collateral for a loan; he takes nothing by robbery, but gives his food to the hungry and clothing to those who need it; ⁸ he neither demands nor accepts interest on a loan; he refrains from what is evil; and he judges honestly between one person and another. ⁹ In short, he lives according to my laws and observes my rulings, so as to act faithfully. Such a person is righteous, and he will certainly live," says Adonai ELOHIM.

¹⁰ "Now suppose he is the father of a son who is a robber, a murderer, or who does any of these things to a brother — ¹¹ whereas the father himself does none of them. He eats on the mountains, defiles his neighbor's wife, ¹² wrongs the poor and needy, takes by robbery, doesn't restore pledged property, raises his eyes toward the idols, engages in disgusting practices, ¹³ demands and accepts interest. Should he live? He will not live, because he has engaged in all these disgusting practices — he must be put to death; his blood is on him.

¹⁴ "But now suppose he has a son who sees all the sins his father committed, thinks about them, and behaves differently. ¹⁵ He doesn't eat on the mountains, raise his eyes to the idols of the house of Isra'el, defile his neighbor's wife, ¹⁶ wrong others, keep pledged property or take by robbery, but gives his food to the hungry and clothing to those in need of it; ¹⁷ he refrains from oppressing the poor; and he neither demands nor accepts interest. He obeys my rulings and lives according to my laws. So he will not die for his father's sins but will certainly live. ¹⁸ Yet his father, because he oppressed so cruelly, committed robbery against his brother and never did anything good among his people — he will die for his sins.

¹⁹ "You ask, 'Why doesn't the son bear his father's guilt?' When the son has done what is lawful and right, has kept all my laws and obeyed them, he will certainly live. ²⁰ The person who sins is the one that will die — a son is not to bear his father's guilt with him, nor is the father to bear his son's guilt with him; but the righteousness of the righteous will be his own, and the wickedness of the wicked will be his own.

²¹ "However, if the wicked person repents of all the sins he committed, keeps my laws and does what is lawful and right; then he will certainly live, he will not die. ²² None of the transgressions he has committed will be remembered against him; for the righteousness that he has done, he will live. ²³ Do I take any pleasure at all in having the wicked person die?" asks *Adonai ELOHIM.* "Wouldn't I prefer that he turn from his ways and live?

²⁴ "On the other hand, when the righteous person turns away from his righteousness and commits wickedness by acting in accordance with all the disgusting practices that the wicked person does, will he live? None of the righteous deeds he has done will be remembered; for the trespasses and sins he has committed, he will die.

²⁵ "So now you say, '*ADONAI*'s way isn't fair.' Listen, house of Isra'el! Is it my way that is unfair? or your ways that are unfair? ²⁶ When the righteous person turns away from his righteousness and commits wickedness, he will die for it — for the wickedness he commits he will die. ²⁷ And when the wicked person turns away from all the wickedness he has committed and does what is lawful and right, he will save his life. ²⁸ Because he thinks it over and repents of all the transgressions he committed, he will certainly live, not die. ²⁹ Yet the house of Isra'el says, '*ADONAI*'s way isn't fair.' House of Isra'el, is it my ways that are unfair, or your ways that are unfair? ³⁰ Therefore, house of Isra'el, I will judge each of you according to his ways," says *Adonai ELOHIM.* "Repent, and turn yourselves away from all your transgressions, so that they will not be a stumbling block that brings guilt upon you. ³¹ Throw far away from yourselves all your crimes that you committed, and make yourselves a new heart and a new spirit; for why should you die, house of Isra'el? ³² I take no pleasure in the death of anyone who dies," says *Adonai ELOHIM,* "so turn yourselves around, and live!

19 ¹ "Moreover, raise a lament for the leaders of Isra'el; ² say:

> 'What a mother you had —
> a lioness among lions!
> She lay down among young lions
> and reared her cubs.
³   One of her cubs she singled out:
> he became a young lion,
> he learned to seize his prey,
> he became a man-eater.
⁴   The nations sounded an alarm against him;
> and he was caught in their pit.
> With hooks they dragged him off
> to the land of Egypt.
⁵   When she saw that she had been thwarted,
> that her hope was lost,
> she took another of her cubs
> and made a young lion of him.
⁶   He prowled among the lions,
> grew to be a young lion,
> learned to seize his prey

and became a man-eater.

7　　He raped their widows
　　　and destroyed their cities;
　　　the land and all in it were appalled
　　　at the sound of his roaring.

8　　The nations set a snare for him
　　　from the provinces all around,
　　　they spread their net over him,
　　　and he was caught in their pit.

9　　With hooks they put him in a cage
　　　and brought him to the king of Bavel
　　　to imprison him in a fortress,
　　　so that his roar would be heard no more
　　　on the mountains of Isra'el.

10　　"'Your mother was like a strong grapevine
　　　planted by the water.
　　　It was fruitful and luxuriant
　　　because of the abundant water.

11　　It had strong branches
　　　to be used as scepters by rulers;
　　　besides having thick foliage,
　　　it grew taller and taller,
　　　until its height was noticed,
　　　with its mass of branches.

12　　But it was torn up in fury
　　　and flung on the ground.
　　　An east wind withered her fruit,
　　　her strong branches were broken off;
　　　they dried up; and fire consumed the vine.

13　　It has been transplanted to the desert,
　　　to a dry, thirsty land.

14　　Fire has gone out from its own branches,
　　　burning up its fruit,
　　　so that now it has no strong branch
　　　to be a ruler's scepter.'"

This lamentation became very well known.

20 ¹ On the tenth day of the fifth month of the seventh year, some of Isra'el's leaders came to consult *Adonai* and sat with me; ² and the word of *Adonai* came to me: ³ "Human being, speak to Isra'el's leaders; tell them that *Adonai Elohim* asks, 'Have you come to consult me? As I live,' says *Adonai Elohim*, 'I swear that I will not let you consult me.'

⁴ "Are you going to judge them? Human being, are you going to judge them? Then have them realize how disgusting their ancestors' practices were. ⁵ Tell them that *Adonai Elohim* says this: 'Back on the day when I chose Isra'el, I raised my

hand to the descendants of the house of Ya'akov. I revealed myself to them in the land of Egypt when I raised my hand to them and said, "I am ADONAI your God." ⁶On the day I raised my hand to them, pledging to bring them out of the land of Egypt into a land I had reconnoitered for them, a land flowing with milk and honey, the most beautiful of all lands, ⁷I told them, "Each of you is to throw away the detestable things that draw your eyes. Do not defile yourselves with the idols of Egypt. I am ADONAI your God."

⁸ "'But they rebelled against me and wouldn't listen to me; they did not, each of them, throw away the detestable things that drew their eyes; and they did not abandon the idols of Egypt. Then I said I would pour out my fury on them and spend my anger on them there in the land of Egypt. ⁹But concern for my own reputation kept me from letting it be profaned in the sight of the nations among whom they were living, in the sight of whom I had made myself known to them, in order to bring them out of the land of Egypt. ¹⁰So I had them leave the land of Egypt and brought them into the desert. ¹¹I gave them my laws and showed them my rulings; if a person obeys them, he will have life through them. ¹²I gave them my *shabbat*s as a sign between me and them, so that they would know that I, ADONAI, am the one who makes them holy.

¹³ "'But the house of Isra'el rebelled against me in the desert. They did not live by my laws; and they rejected my rulings, which, if a person does, he will have life through them; moreover, they greatly profaned my *shabbat*s. Then I said I would pour out my fury on them in the desert, in order to destroy them. ¹⁴But concern for my own reputation kept me from letting it be profaned in the sight of the nations who had seen when I brought them out. ¹⁵Yet I also raised my hand and swore to them in the desert that I would not bring them into the land I was giving them, a land flowing with milk and honey, the most beautiful of all lands; ¹⁶because they had rejected my rulings, did not live by my laws and profaned my *shabbat*s; since their hearts went after their idols. ¹⁷However, I spared them from complete destruction; I did not completely finish them off in the desert.

¹⁸ "'I said to their children in the desert, "Don't live by the laws of your fathers, observe their rulings or defile yourselves with their idols. ¹⁹I am ADONAI your God; live by my laws, observe my rulings, and obey them, ²⁰and keep my *shabbat*s holy; and they will be a sign between me and you, so that you will know that I am ADONAI your God."

²¹ "'But the children too rebelled against me. They did not live by my laws or observe my rulings, to obey them, which, if a person does, he will have life by them; and they profaned my *shabbat*s. Then I said I would pour out my fury on them and spend my anger on them in the desert. ²²Nevertheless, I withdrew my hand and allowed concern for my own reputation to keep me from letting it be profaned in the sight of the nations who had seen when I brought them out.

²³ "'I also raised my hand and swore to them in the desert that I would scatter them among the nations and disperse them through the countries; ²⁴because they hadn't obeyed my rulings but had rejected my laws and profaned my *shabbat*s, and their eyes had turned toward their fathers' idols. ²⁵I also gave them laws which did them no good and rulings by which they did not live; ²⁶and I let them become defiled by their own gifts, in that they offered up their firstborn sons, so that I could fill them with revulsion, so that they would [finally] realize that I am ADONAI.'

²⁷ "Therefore, human being, speak to the house of Isra'el; tell them that *Adonai ELOHIM* says, 'Moreover, your ancestors blasphemed me by breaking faith with me in still another way: ²⁸ for after I had brought them into the land, which I had raised my hand in pledge to give them, they noted all its high hills and leafy trees and offered there their sacrifices; there they made offerings that provoked my anger, there they set out their sweet aromas, and there they poured out their drink offerings. ²⁹ When I asked them, "This high place where you go, what is the meaning of it?" they gave it the name Bamah* which it retains to this day.'

³⁰ "So tell the house of Isra'el that *Adonai ELOHIM* says, 'You are defiling yourselves in the same way as your ancestors, following their abominations and fornicating with them; ³¹ and when offering your gifts, you make your children pass through the fire and defile yourselves with all your idols — to this day. So, am I supposed to allow you to consult me, house of Isra'el? As I live,' says *Adonai ELOHIM*, 'I swear that I won't have you consult me, ³² and that what you have in mind when you say, "We will be like the *Goyim*, like the families of the other countries, serving wood and stone," will certainly not happen. ³³ As I live,' says *Adonai ELOHIM*, 'I swear that surely with a mighty hand, with a stretched-out arm and with poured-out fury I myself will be king over you. ³⁴ I will bring you out from the peoples and gather you out of the countries where you were scattered, with a mighty hand, with a stretched-out arm and with poured-out fury; ³⁵ then I will bring you into the desert of the peoples and judge you face to face. ³⁶ Just as I judged your ancestors in the desert of the land of Egypt, so will I judge you,' says *Adonai ELOHIM*. ³⁷ 'I will make you pass under the crook and bring you into the obligations of the covenant.³⁸ I will rid you of the rebels who are in revolt against me — I will bring them out from the land where they are living, but they will not enter the land of Isra'el; then you will know that I am *ADONAI*.'

³⁹ "As for you, house of Isra'el, here is what *Adonai ELOHIM* says: 'Go on serving your idols, every one of you! But afterwards, [I swear that] you will listen to me, and you will no longer profane my holy name with your gifts and with your idols. ⁴⁰ For on my holy mountain, the high mountain of Isra'el,' says *Adonai ELOHIM*, 'the whole house of Isra'el, all of them, will serve me in the land. I will accept them there, and there I will require your contributions, your best gifts and all your consecrated things. ⁴¹ I will accept you with your sweet aroma when I bring you out from the peoples and gather you out of the countries where you were scattered; and through you I will manifest my holiness in the sight of the nations.

⁴² "'You will know that I am *ADONAI* when I bring you into the land of Isra'el, into the country which I pledged, by raising my hand, to give to your ancestors. ⁴³ There you will remember your behavior and all the things you did by which you defiled yourselves, and you will loathe yourselves for all the evils you committed. ⁴⁴ You will know that I am *ADONAI* when I have dealt with you in a manner that preserves my reputation, and not according to your evil ways and corrupt actions, house of Isra'el' says *Adonai ELOHIM*."

---

* The Hebrew word *bamah* means "high place"; the etymology suggested here relates it to Hebrew *ba* ("go") and *mah* ("what").

21 ¹⁽²⁰ᐟ⁴⁵⁾ The word of *Adonai* came to me: ²⁽²⁰ᐟ⁴⁶⁾ "Human being, turn your face southward, preach to the south and prophesy to the scrublands of the Negev; ³⁽²⁰ᐟ⁴⁷⁾ say to the Negev forest: 'Hear the word of *Adonai*. *Adonai Elohim* says, "I will light a fire in you; it will devour every tree in you, green and dry alike; a blazing, unquenchable flame that will scorch every face from the Negev to the north. ⁴⁽²⁰ᐟ⁴⁸⁾ All humanity will see that I, *Adonai*, lit it; it will not be put out."'" ⁵⁽²⁰ᐟ⁴⁹⁾ I said, "Oh, *Adonai Elohim*! They complain that I speak only in parables."

⁶⁽¹⁾ Then the word of *Adonai* came to me: ⁷⁽²⁾ "Human being, turn your face toward Yerushalayim, preach to the sanctuaries and prophesy to the land of Isra'el; ⁸⁽³⁾ tell the land of Isra'el that *Adonai Elohim* says, 'I am against you. I will draw my sword from its scabbard and cut off from you the righteous and the wicked. ⁹⁽⁴⁾ Since I am going to rid you of both righteous and evildoers, my sword will also go out of its scabbard against everyone, from the Negev to the north. ¹⁰⁽⁵⁾ Everyone alive will know that I, *Adonai*, drew my sword from its scabbard; it will not be sheathed again.'

¹¹⁽⁶⁾ "Therefore, human being, groan! Groan bitterly, as if your heart would break, as they watch. ¹²⁽⁷⁾ Then, when they ask you, 'Why are you groaning?' you will answer, 'Because of the news, because it's coming. All hearts will melt, all hands hang limp, all spirits faint and all knees turn to water; here, it's coming, it will happen,' says *Adonai Elohim*."

¹³⁽⁸⁾ The word of *Adonai* came to me: ¹⁴⁽⁹⁾ "Human being, prophesy. Say that *Adonai Elohim* says to say this:

¹⁵⁽¹⁰⁾
'A sword, a sword has been sharpened and polished,
sharpened in order to slaughter and slaughter,
polished to flash like lightning.
But how can we rejoice?
My son rejects the rod
and every other stick.

¹⁶⁽¹¹⁾
The sword was given to be polished,
so that it could be wielded;
it was sharpened and polished
to be placed in the slaughterer's hand.'

¹⁷⁽¹²⁾ "Shout and wail, human being, because it's coming upon my people, upon all the leaders of Isra'el — they will be victims of the sword along with my people. Strike your thigh in remorse! ¹⁸⁽¹³⁾ For a test is coming, and what if he rejects the rod again then? He will cease to exist," says *Adonai Elohim*.

¹⁹⁽¹⁴⁾ "Therefore, human being, prophesy and clap your hands together. Then the sword will strike twice, three times, the sword for victims, the sword for a great slaughter, coming from every direction. ²⁰⁽¹⁵⁾ So that their hearts will melt, and many will stumble and fall, I have posted the point of the sword at every one of their gates. See how it flashes, sharpened for the kill!

²¹⁽¹⁶⁾
"Sword!
Slash to the right; destroy to the left,
whichever way your edge is aimed!

²²⁽¹⁷⁾   I too will clap my hands together
and satisfy my fury.

I, ADONAI, have spoken."

²³⁽¹⁸⁾ The word of ADONAI came to me: ²⁴⁽¹⁹⁾ "Now, human being, designate two roads for the sword of the king of Bavel to follow, both coming out of one country. Put up a signpost at the start of the road leading to the city. ²⁵⁽²⁰⁾ Make a road, so that the sword can come to Rabbah of the people of 'Amon and to Y'hudah in fortified Yerushalayim. ²⁶⁽²¹⁾ For the king of Bavel is standing at the fork in the road, where the two roads separate, about to use divination — he is shaking the arrows, consulting the household gods, examining the liver. ²⁷⁽²²⁾ Into his right hand comes the lot for Yerushalayim, to set up battering rams, give the order for slaughter, raise a shout, set battering rams against the gates, build siege ramps and erect watchtowers. ²⁸⁽²³⁾ The inhabitants will believe this is a false divination because of the oaths upon oaths [that their false prophets have sworn to the contrary]. But it will cause [God] to remember their guilt and thus ensure their capture.

²⁹⁽²⁴⁾ "Therefore this is what Adonai ELOHIM says: 'Because you have caused your guilt to be remembered, with your misdeeds revealed and the sins in all your actions evident — since you have been remembered, you will be captured.' ³⁰⁽²⁵⁾ As for you, you wicked prince of Isra'el, due to be killed, whose day has come, at the time of final punishment, ³¹⁽²⁶⁾ here is what Adonai ELOHIM says:

'Remove the turban, take off the crown!
Everything is being changed.
What was low will be raised up,
and what was high will be brought down.
³²⁽²⁷⁾   Ruin! Ruin!
I will leave it a ruin
such as there has never been,
and it will stay that way
until the rightful ruler comes,
and I give it to him.'

³³⁽²⁸⁾ "You, human being, prophesy! Say that Adonai ELOHIM says this about the people of 'Amon and their insults:

'A sword, a sword, is drawn for slaughter,
polished to the utmost, to flash like lightning —
³⁴⁽²⁹⁾   while [your prophets] produce false visions for you,
while they divine lies for you —
to lay you out upon the necks
of the wicked who are to be killed,
whose day has come,
at the time of final punishment.
³⁵⁽³⁰⁾   Cause it to return to its scabbard!
I will judge you in the place

where you were created,
in the land of your origin.

36(31) I will pour my fury out on you,
breathe on you with the fire of my rage,
and hand you over to barbarous men
highly skilled in destruction.

37(32) You will be fuel for the fire,
your blood will flow through the land,
you will be remembered no more;
for I, ADONAI, have spoken.'"

22 ¹ The word of ADONAI came to me: ² "Now, human being, are you prepared to judge? Are you prepared to judge the city drenched in blood? Then make her realize how disgusting all her practices are! ³ Say that Adonai ELOHIM says, 'City that sheds blood within yourself, thus speeding your own doom, and that makes idols for yourself that defile you: ⁴ you are guilty because of the blood you have shed, you are defiled by your idols that you have made. You have shortened your days, you have completed your years; therefore I have made you an object of scorn for the nations and a laughingstock for every country. ⁵ Those close by and those far off will taunt you, you who have such a defiled reputation and such great disorder.

⁶ "'The leaders of Isra'el in you all use their power in order to shed blood. ⁷ In you, they make light of fathers and mothers, they oppress foreigners, they wrong orphans and widows. ⁸ You treat my holy things with contempt, you profane my *shabbat*s. ⁹ In you, people gossip to the point of inciting bloodshed; in you are those who go to eat on the mountains; in you, they commit lewd acts; ¹⁰ in you, they commit incest; in you, they force themselves on women during their menstrual impurity. ¹¹ In you, one commits an abomination with his neighbor's wife; another commits some lewd act defiling his daughter-in-law; still another humbles his sister, his own father's daughter. ¹² In you, people take bribes to shed blood; you demand and accept interest on loans; in greed you make profits off your neighbors by extorting them; and you have forgotten me,' says Adonai ELOHIM.

¹³ "'Therefore, I am clapping my hands together because of your ill-gotten gains and the blood shed in you. ¹⁴ Can your courage last, can your strength continue during the days when I deal with you? I, ADONAI, have spoken it; and I will do it. ¹⁵ I will scatter you among the *Goyim* and disperse you throughout the countries; thus I will remove your defilement from you, ¹⁶ and you will cause yourselves to be profaned in full view of the *Goyim*. Then you will know that I am ADONAI.'"

¹⁷ The word of ADONAI came to me: ¹⁸ "Human being, the house of Isra'el has become an alloy of base metals for me; they are all copper, tin, iron and lead mixed together in the crucible, the dross left over from the silver. ¹⁹ Therefore Adonai ELOHIM says this: 'Because you have all become dross, I will collect all of you inside Yerushalayim. ²⁰ Then, just as they collect silver, copper, iron, lead and tin into a crucible and blow fire on it to melt it down; so likewise I will collect you in my anger and fury, throw you in there, and melt you down. ²¹ Yes, I will collect you and blow on you with the fire of my rage, and you will be melted down in it. ²² As silver is melted down in a crucible, so will you be melted down in [Yerushalayim]. Then you will know that it is I, ADONAI, who have poured out my fury on you.'"

²³ The word of *Adonai* came to me: ²⁴ "Human being, tell her this: 'You are a land that is neither cleansed nor rained on in the day of fury. ²⁵ There is a conspiracy of prophets in it like a roaring lion tearing up the prey; they have devoured people, seized wealth and valuables, and widowed many in it. ²⁶ Her *cohanim* have done violence to my *Torah*, profaned my holy things, made no difference between the holy and the common, not distinguished between unclean and clean, hidden their eyes from my *shabbat*s, and profaned me among themselves. ²⁷ Her leaders in it are like wolves tearing up the prey to shed blood and destroy people, in order to benefit unjustly. ²⁸ Her prophets have "plastered" for them with whitewash, seeing false visions and divining lies for them, saying, "Thus says *Adonai Elohim*," when *Adonai* has not spoken. ²⁹ The people of the land have extorted, robbed, wronged the poor and needy and unjustly oppressed foreigners.

³⁰ "'I sought for a man among them who could build a barricade or stand in the break to oppose me on behalf of the land, so that I would not destroy it; but I found no one. ³¹ Therefore I am pouring out my fury on them, consuming them with the fire of my rage, bringing their own ways on their own heads,' says *Adonai Elohim*."

23 ¹ The word of *Adonai* came to me: ² "Human being! There were two women, daughters of the same mother, ³ who were whores in Egypt — even as young girls they were whores. There they let their breasts be caressed, and there their virgin nipples were fondled. ⁴ Their names were Oholah, the older one, and Oholivah, her sister. They belonged to me, and they gave birth to sons and daughters. As for their names, Shomron is Oholah, and Yerushalayim is Oholivah.

⁵ "Even when she belonged to me, Oholah prostituted herself; she lusted after her lovers from Ashur — warriors ⁶ dressed in blue, governors, rulers, all of them good-looking young men riding on horseback. ⁷ She gave herself as a whore to them, all of them the elite of Ashur; and she defiled herself with all the idols of everyone she lusted after. ⁸ She did not give up the whoring she had begun in Egypt, where men had sex with her, fondled her virgin nipples and flooded her with their fornication.

⁹ "So I handed her over to her lovers, the men of Ashur she lusted after. ¹⁰ They exposed her private parts, took her sons and daughters, and put her to death with the sword; so that she became notorious among women for the judgments executed against her.

¹¹ "Her sister Oholivah saw this; nevertheless she was worse than her sister in lusting and likewise in whoring. ¹² She lusted after the men from Ashur, governors and rulers, warriors dressed to perfection, skilled horsemen, all of them good-looking young men. ¹³ I saw that she had defiled herself; both sisters had gone down the same path. ¹⁴ She prostituted herself more than ever; because she saw wall-carvings of men, depicting the Kasdim in vermilion, ¹⁵ with sashes wrapped around their waists and flowing turbans on their heads, all of them looking like military men, the very image of men of Bavel born in the land of the Kasdim. ¹⁶ The moment she saw them, she lusted after them and sent messengers to them in the land of the Kasdim; ¹⁷ and the men of Bavel climbed into her "love bed" and defiled her with their lust. She was defiled by them, and then filled with revulsion at them. ¹⁸ Thus did she reveal her fornication and expose her private parts. When this happened, I was filled with revulsion at her, just as I had been filled with revulsion at her sister. ¹⁹ Still she kept increasing her whoring, remembering the days when she was young, fornicating in

the land of Egypt. ²⁰ Yes, she lusted after their male prostitutes, whose members are like those of donkeys and who ejaculate like stallions. ²¹ You yearned for the lewdness of your girlhood, when the Egyptians used to fondle your nipples and caress your young breasts.

²² "Therefore, Oholivah, here is what *Adonai ELOHIM* says: 'I will raise up your lovers against you, the ones who fill you with revulsion, and bring them against you from every side — ²³ the men of Bavel and all the Kasdim, P'kod, Shoa and Koa, and with them all the men of Ashur, good-looking young men, all of them governors and rulers, commanders and officers, all on horseback. ²⁴ They will advance on you armed with chariots, wagons and with an army drawn from many peoples; they will array themselves against you from every side with breastplates, shields and helmets. I will give them the authority to judge, and they will judge you as they see fit. ²⁵ I will direct my jealousy against you, so that they will deal with you in fury — they will cut off your nose and ears, and what is left of you will die by the sword; they will seize your sons and daughters, and those who remain of you will be consumed by the fire. ²⁶ They will strip you of your clothes and seize your fine jewels. ²⁷ Thus I will put an end to your lewdness and your fornication brought from the land of Egypt, so that you will no longer raise your eyes toward them or remember Egypt any more.' ²⁸ For this is what *Adonai ELOHIM* says: 'I am about to hand you over to those you hate, to those who fill you with revulsion; ²⁹ and they will deal with you in hatred, seize everything you have worked for, and leave you naked and exposed — the full shame of your whoring will be exposed, your lewdness and your fornicating. ³⁰ These things will be done to you because you have gone fornicating with the *Goyim*, and because you are defiled with their idols. ³¹ You walked down your sister's path, so I will put her cup in your hand.'
³² *Adonai ELOHIM* says:

> 'You will drink from your sister's cup,
> a cup both deep and wide,
> full right up to the brim
> with scorn and derision,
³³
> filling you with drunkenness and sorrow,
> a cup of horror and devastation —
> the cup of your sister Shomron.
³⁴
> You will drink it, you will drain it,
> and then you will gnaw it to shreds
> and tear out your own breasts!
> For I have spoken it'

says *Adonai ELOHIM*.

³⁵ "Therefore this is what *Adonai ELOHIM* says: 'Because you forgot me and flung me behind your back, you will bear the guilt of your lewdness and whoring.'"

³⁶ Then *ADONAI* said to me, "Human being, are you ready to judge Oholah and Oholivah? Then confront them with their disgusting practices. ³⁷ For they committed adultery, and their hands are dripping with blood. They committed adultery with their idols; and they offered their sons, whom they bore to me, for these idols to eat. ³⁸ Moreover, they have done this to me as well: they defiled my

sanctuary on the same day, and they profaned my *shabbat*s. ³⁹ For after killing their children for their idols, they came the same day into my sanctuary to profane it; this they did in my house.

⁴⁰ "Worse still, you sent a messenger summoning men to come from a distance; and they came. For them you washed yourself, painted your eyes, decked yourself with your finery, ⁴¹ and sat on a sumptuous bed, with a table arranged before it, on which you put my incense and my olive oil. ⁴² The noise of a carefree crowd could be heard there; many of the men were brought in drunk from the desert. They put bracelets on their hands and magnificent crowns on their heads. ⁴³ I thought, 'That woman! She's worn out from all her adulteries, but they still go to fornicate with her!' ⁴⁴ For every one went in to her; just as men go in to a prostitute, so they went in to Oholah and Oholivah, those debauched women. ⁴⁵ Nevertheless, there are righteous men who will judge them as adulterers and murderers are supposed to be judged; because they are adulterers, and blood is dripping from their hands. ⁴⁶ For here is what *Adonai Elohim* says:

> 'Summon an assembly to punish them;
> give them over to terror and plunder.
⁴⁷   Let the assembly stone them to death,
> dispatch them with their swords,
> kill their sons and daughters
> and burn their houses to the ground.

⁴⁸ "'Thus I will put an end to lewdness in the land, so that all women may be taught not to imitate your lewdness. ⁴⁹ You will receive the punishment your lewdness deserves, and you will pay the penalty for your idolatries. Then you will know that I am *Adonai Elohim*.'"

24 ¹ The word of *Adonai* came to me on the tenth day of the tenth month of the ninth year: ² "Human being, write down today's date; because on this very day the king of Bavel has begun his attack on Yerushalayim. ³ And tell this allegory to these rebels; say that *Adonai Elohim* says:

> 'Put a pot on the fire;
> put it there, pour water in it;
⁴   Put in it pieces of meat,
> all the best parts — the thigh, the shoulder;
> fill it with the choicest cuts,
⁵   taken from the pick of the flock,
> and pile the bones underneath.
> Bring it to a rolling boil,
> till it's all cooked, even the bones.'

⁶ "Therefore *Adonai Elohim* says:

> 'Woe to the city drenched with blood,
> to the pot whose scum is in it,

and whose scum has not been removed.
Empty it piece by piece,
without troubling to draw lots.

7   For her blood is still in her;
    she poured it on bare rock;
    she did not pour it on the ground,
    to cover it with dust.

8   So in order to rouse my fury
    and excite my vengeance,
    I have fixed her blood there on the bare rock,
    where it will not be covered.'

9 "Therefore *Adonai* E*lohim* says this:

    'Woe to the city drenched with blood!
    I myself will make a huge bonfire,
10   heap on the wood, light it,
    cook the meat and add the spices —
    the bones can just be burned.
11   Put the empty pot on the coals,
    heat it till its copper bottom glows,
    till its impurity melts inside it,
    and its scum is burned away.
12   But the effort is in vain:
    its layers of scum will not leave it;
    so into the fire with its scum!
13   Because of your filthy lewdness,
    because you refused to be purified
    when I wanted to purify you;
    now you will not be purified from your filth
    until I have satisfied my fury on you.

14 "'I, A*donai*, have spoken it, and it will happen. I will do it, I will not turn back, I will not refrain or spare or relent. They will judge you as your ways and deeds deserve,' says *Adonai* E*lohim*."

15 The word of A*donai* came to me: 16 "Human being, with a single blow I am about to deprive you of the delight of your eyes. But you are not to lament, weep or let your tears run down. 17 Sigh silently, don't observe mourning for the dead, bind your turban on your head, put your sandals on your feet, don't cover your upper lip, and don't eat the food people prepare for mourners." 18 I spoke to the people in the morning, and that evening my wife died. So I did the following morning as I had been ordered. 19 The people asked me, "Won't you tell us what these actions of yours mean for us?" 20 I answered them, "The word of A*donai* came to me, telling me 21 to speak to the house of Isra'el and say that this is what *Adonai* E*lohim* says: 'I am about to profane my sanctuary, the pride of your strength, the delight of your eyes and your heart's desire. Your sons and daughters whom you have left behind will die by the sword. 22 But you are to do as I have done — not cover your upper lips, not eat

the food people prepare for mourners, ²³ put your turbans on your heads and your sandals on your feet, and neither observe mourning nor cry. Rather, because of your crimes you will pine away and groan to one another. ²⁴ Thus Yechezk'el will be a sign for you; you will do just what he has done; and when this happens, you will know that I am *Adonai ELOHIM*.'

²⁵ "As for you, human being, on the day when I take away from them their stronghold, their crowning joy, the delight of their eyes, their heart's desire, their sons and daughters — ²⁶ on that day a fugitive will come and bring you the news; ²⁷ and on that day your mouth will be opened for you to speak to the survivor and no longer be silent. In this way you will be a sign to them, and they will know that I am *ADONAI*."

25 ¹ The word of *ADONAI* came to me: ² "Human being, turn your face toward the people of 'Amon and prophesy against them; ³ say to the people of 'Amon, 'Hear the word of *Adonai ELOHIM*. *Adonai ELOHIM* says, "Because you gloated when my sanctuary was profaned, when the land of Isra'el was laid waste, and when the house of Y'hudah went into exile; ⁴ I will let the people from the east take possession of you. They will set up camps and build their homes among you; they will eat your fruit and drink your milk. ⁵ I will turn Rabbah into a camel pasture and 'Amon into a sheep-yard. Then you will know that I am *ADONAI*." ⁶ For here is what *Adonai ELOHIM* says: "Because you clapped your hands and stamped your feet, full of malicious joy over the land of Isra'el; ⁷ I am going to stretch out my hand over you and deliver you as plunder to the nations; I will cut you off from being a people and cause you to cease from being a nation; I will destroy you. Then you will know that I am *ADONAI*."'

⁸ "*Adonai ELOHIM* says: 'Because Mo'av and Se'ir say, "The house of Y'hudah is like all the other nations," ⁹ I will expose the flank of Mo'av, with all its cities — that is, all the cities on its frontier, the glory of the land, Beit-Yeshimot, Ba'al-M'on and Kiryatayim — ¹⁰ together with the people of 'Amon, to the people from the east, whom I will let take possession of them. Thus the people of 'Amon will not be remembered as being one of the nations; ¹¹ and I will execute judgments on Mo'av. Then they will know that I am *ADONAI*.'

¹² "*Adonai ELOHIM* says: 'Because Edom has taken severe vengeance against the house of Y'hudah, incurring much guilt by its acts of vengeance against them, ¹³ therefore,' *Adonai ELOHIM* says, 'I will stretch my hand out over Edom and eliminate both its humans and its animals. I will make it a ruin; from Teman to D'dan they will die by the sword. ¹⁴ Moreover, I will lay my vengeance on Edom through my people Isra'el; they will treat Edom in accordance with my anger and my fury; and they will know my vengeance' says *Adonai ELOHIM*.

¹⁵ "*Adonai ELOHIM* says, 'Because the P'lishtim have acted out of vengeance, taking revenge and destroying with malice of heart, due to their long-standing hatred; ¹⁶ therefore,' *Adonai ELOHIM* says, 'I will stretch out my hand over the P'lishtim, eliminate the K'reti and destroy the rest of the seacoast peoples. ¹⁷ I will execute great vengeance on them with furious punishments; and they will know that I am *ADONAI* when I lay my vengeance on them.'"

26 ¹ On the first day of the month in the eleventh year, the word of *ADONAI* came to me: ² "Human being, since Tzor has said against Yerushalayim,

'Ha! She is shattered,
the gateway of the peoples.
Now that she is ruined,
her riches will be mine';

³ therefore, *Adonai E*LOHIM* says,

'Look, Tzor! I am against you.
Just as the sea churns up its waves,
I will churn up many nations against you.
4   They will destroy the walls of Tzor,
they will demolish her towers.
I will scrape its soil from her
and reduce her to bare rock.
5   With the sea all around her, she will be
a place for drying fish nets
and a plunder for the nations.
I have spoken,' says *Adonai E*LOHIM*.
6   'Her daughters on the mainland
will be put to death with the sword;
then they will know
that I am A*DONAI*.'

⁷ "For here is what *Adonai E*LOHIM* says: 'I will bring upon Tzor, from the north,
N'vukhadretzar king of Bavel, king of kings, with horses, chariots, cavalry, and a
great and powerful army.

8   "'Your daughters on the mainland
he will put to death with the sword.
He will build siege-towers against you,
he will build a ramp against you
and raise a screen of shields against you.
9   He will pound your walls with his battering-rams
and break down your towers with his axes.
10   His horses are so many that their dust will cover you.
The thunder of cavalry, wagons and chariots
will shake your walls, as he enters your gates,
like men storming a city through a breach.
11   With the hoofs of his horses he will trample your streets.
He will put your people to the sword
and pull to the ground your massive standing-stones.
12   They will seize your wealth, loot your wares,
break down your walls, destroy your fine houses;
then they will throw your stones and timber
and even your dust into the sea.
13   I will put an end to your singing,
the sound of your lyres will be heard no more.

¹⁴ I will reduce you to bare rock,
you will be a place for drying fish nets,
you will never be built again,
for I, ADONAI, have spoken,'
says Adonai ELOHIM."

¹⁵ To Tzor Adonai ELOHIM says:

"How the coastlands will shake
at the sound of your fall,
when the wounded groan,
when the slaughter takes place in you!
¹⁶ Then all the princes of the sea
will step down from their thrones;
they will put aside their robes
and strip off their embroidered garments.
They will clothe themselves with trembling;
they will sit on the ground,
trembling all the time,
appalled at your condition.
¹⁷ Then they will raise this lament for you:
"'How you have been destroyed,
you who were peopled from the seas,
city so renowned, once so strong at sea,
you and your inhabitants, who used to spread terror
over all [the mainland's] inhabitants!
¹⁸ Now the coastlands tremble
on the day of your downfall,
and the islands in the sea
are in shock at your end.'

¹⁹ "For here is what Adonai ELOHIM says:

'When I make you a ruined city,
like other uninhabited cities;
when I bring the deep sea over you,
and its mighty waters cover you;
²⁰ then I will bring you down
with those who descend to the pit,
to the people of long ago,
and make you live in underworld places
like those who were ruined long ago,
with those who descend to the pit,
so that you will be uninhabited
when I give glory to the land of the living.
²¹ I will make you horrible;
you will cease to exist.

People will seek you but never more find you,'
says *Adonai Elohim*."

27 ¹ The word of *Adonai* came to me: ² "You, human being, raise this lament for
Tzor; ³ say to Tzor, located at the gateways to the sea, merchant for peoples to many
coastlands, that *Adonai Elohim* says:

'Tzor, you have said,
"My beauty is perfect."

⁴ Your borders are in the heart of the sea,
your builders perfected your beauty.

⁵ They used cypress logs from S'nir
to fashion all your planking.
They took cedars from the L'vanon
to make masts for you.

⁶ Out of oaks from Bashan
they made your oars.
Your deck they made of ivory
inlaid in larch from the coasts of Kittim.

⁷ Richly woven linen from Egypt
was used for your sail, which was also your banner.
Blue and purple from the coasts of Elishah
was used to cover your deck-tent.

⁸ The people of Tzidon and Arvad
served as your oarsmen.
Your own skilled men, Tzor,
were there as your pilots.

⁹ The leaders and craftsmen of G'val
sealed the cracks between your boards.

"'Every seagoing ship and its crew
came to you to trade in your wares.

¹⁰ Men from Paras, Lud and Put
were [mercenaries] in your army;
hanging shield and helmet on you,
they showed off your splendor.

¹¹ Men from Arvad and your own army
were posted around on your walls.
The Gamadim were in your towers;
they hung their shields all around your walls,
making your beauty perfect.

¹² "'Tarshish did business with you because of the quantity and variety of your
resources; they exchanged silver, iron, tin and lead for your goods. ¹³ Greece,
Tuval and Meshekh traded with you, exchanging slaves and articles of bronze
for your wares. ¹⁴ The people of Togarmah traded for your merchandise with
horses, horsemen and mules. ¹⁵ The men of D'dan traded with you. Many coastlands

were your customers, giving you ivory tusks and ebony in payment. ¹⁶ Aram traded with you, because you were so wealthy; for your goods they exchanged green feldspar, purple stuff, embroidery, fine linen, coral and rubies. ¹⁷ Y'hudah and the land of Isra'el also traded with you, exchanging for your goods wheat from Minnit, millet, honey, olive oil and resin for healing. ¹⁸ Because you were so wealthy, with such a variety of valuable merchandise, Dammesek traded wine from Helbon and white wool with you. ¹⁹ V'dan and Yavan from Uzal traded ironwork, cassia and aromatic cane for your goods. ²⁰ D'dan traded with you for riding gear. ²¹ Arabia and all the princes of K'dar were your customers; for your goods they traded lambs, rams and goats. ²² The traders of Sh'va and Ra'mah exchanged the best quality spices, all kinds of precious stones and gold for your goods. ²³ The merchants of Haran, Kaneh and 'Eden, who traded also with Sh'va, Ashur and Kilmad, ²⁴ brought you in exchange for your goods rich clothes, cloaks made of blue material and embroidery, and cedar-lined chests filled with multicolored clothing and bound with cords. ²⁵ "Tarshish" ships transported your imports and exports.

"'So you were full, loaded down,
surrounded by the sea.

26   Your oarsmen brought you
through heavy seas.
But the east wind will break you
surrounded by the sea.

27   Your riches, your goods, your merchandise,
your crew, your pilots, your ship-sealers,
your traders, all your warriors aboard,
and all the others in the ship with you
will sink surrounded by the sea
on the day of your shipwreck.

28   When they hear the cries of your pilots,
the mainland coasts will tremble.

29   The oarsmen, crew and pilots
will disembark and stand on shore,

30   mourning aloud at your fate,
crying bitterly,
throwing dust on their heads,
rolling in the ashes,

31   shaving their heads bald for you,
wrapping themselves in sackcloth,
with heartfelt bitterness weeping for you
in bitter lamentation.

32   Wailing, they will raise a lament for you;
this will be their lament for you:

""""Who anywhere in the sea
has ever been silenced like Tzor?

33   When your wares came forth from the seas,
you satisfied many peoples;

with your vast wealth and variety of goods
you enriched the kings of the earth.

34 But now you have been wrecked by the waves,
sunk in the watery depths;
your merchandise and all your people
have gone down with you.

35 All who live along the coasts
are aghast at you;
their kings are horribly afraid,
their faces are convulsed;

36 the merchants among the peoples
are gasping at your fate;
you are an object of terror,
and you will cease to exist.""'"

28 ¹ The word of ADONAI came to me: ² "Human being, tell the prince of Tzor that *Adonai ELOHIM* says:

'Because you are so proud
and have said, "I am a god;
I sit on the throne of God,
surrounded by the sea";
yet you are a man, not God,
even though you think that you think like God.

3 Sure, you are wiser than Dani'el!
No secret can be hidden from you!

4 By your wisdom and discernment
you have acquired wealth,
you have gathered gold and silver
into your treasuries.

5 By your great skill in trading
you have increased your wealth,
and it is because of your wealth
that you have become so proud.

6 "Therefore *Adonai ELOHIM* says,
'Because you think that you think like God,

7 I will bring foreigners against you,
the most barbarous of the nations,
to draw their swords against your fine wisdom
and defile your splendor.

8 They will lower you into the pit to die
a violent death surrounded by the sea.

9 Will you still say, "I am God,"
to them who are about to kill you?
You are a man, you are not God,
in the hands of those who defile you.

¹⁰   You will die the deaths of the uncircumcised
at the hands of foreigners.
For I have spoken,'
says *Adonai ELOHIM*."

¹¹ The word of *ADONAI* came to me: ¹² "Human being, raise a lament for the king of
Tzor, and tell him that *Adonai ELOHIM* says:

> 'You put the seal on perfection;
> you were full of wisdom and perfect in beauty;
¹³   you were in 'Eden, the garden of God;
> covered with all kinds of precious stones —
> carnelians, topaz, diamonds,
> beryl, onyx, jasper,
> sapphires, green feldspar, emeralds;
> your pendants and jewels were made of gold,
> prepared the day you were created.
¹⁴   You were a *keruv*, protecting a large region;
> I placed you on God's holy mountain.
> You walked back and forth
> among stones of fire.
¹⁵   You were perfect in your ways
> from the day you were created,
> until unrighteousness
> was found in you.

¹⁶   "'When your commerce grew,
> you became filled with violence;
> and in this way you sinned.
> Therefore I have thrown you out, defiled,
> from the mountain of God;
> I have destroyed you, protecting *keruv*,
> from among the stones of fire.
¹⁷   Your heart grew proud because of your beauty,
> you corrupted your wisdom for the sake of your splendor.
> But I have thrown you on the ground;
> before kings I have made you a spectacle.
¹⁸   By your many crimes in dishonest trading,
> you have profaned your sanctuaries;
> therefore I brought forth fire from within you,
> and it has devoured you;
> I reduced you into ashes on the ground
> in the sight of all who can see you.
¹⁹   All who know you among the peoples
> will be aghast at you.
> You are an object of terror,
> and you will cease to exist.'"

²⁰ The word of *Adonai* came to me: ²¹ "Human being, turn your face toward Tzidon, and prophesy against it. ²² Say that *Adonai Elohim* says:

'I am against you, Tzidon;
but I will be glorified in you.
They will know that I am *Adonai*,
once I execute judgments in her
and show my holiness in her.

²³ For I will send plagues into her,
and blood will flow in her streets;
attacked from all sides by the sword,
the wounded will fall within her.
Then they will know that I am *Adonai*.

²⁴ "'The house of Isra'el will no longer have a briar pricking away at them, no longer will any of its contemptuous neighbors be a thorn to stab them. Then they will know that I am *Adonai Elohim*.'

²⁵ "*Adonai Elohim* says, 'Once I have gathered the house of Isra'el from the peoples among whom they are scattered, once I have shown my holiness in them as the *Goyim* watch, then they will live in their own land, which I gave to my servant Ya'akov. ²⁶ They will have security when they live there, building houses and planting vineyards; yes, they will live in safety, once I have executed judgments against all their contemptuous neighbors. Then they will know that I am *Adonai* their God.'"

29 ¹ On the twelfth day of the tenth month of the twelfth year, the word of *Adonai* came to me: ² "Human being, turn your face against Pharaoh king of Egypt; prophesy against him and against all Egypt; ³ speak out; and say that *Adonai Elohim* says:

'I am against you,
Pharaoh king of Egypt,
you big crocodile
lying in the streams of the Nile!
You say, "My Nile is mine;
I made it for myself."

⁴ But I will put hooks in your jaws
and make your Nile fish stick to your scales.
Yes, I will bring you up from your Nile,
with all your Nile fish sticking to your scales,

⁵ and leave you in the desert,
you and all your Nile fish.
You will fall in the open field
and not be gathered or buried;
but I will give you as food
to wild animals and birds.

⁶ Then all who live in Egypt
will know that I am *Adonai*,

because they have been a support made of straw
for the house of Isra'el.

7 When they grasped you in hand, you splintered
and threw all their shoulders out of joint;
when they leaned on you, you broke
and made them all wrench their backs.'

8 "Therefore *Adonai* E_LOHIM_ says, 'I will bring the sword against you and eliminate both your people and your animals. 9 The land of Egypt will become a desolate waste, and they will know that I am A_DONAI_; because he said, "The Nile is mine; I made it." 10 So I am against you and your Nile; and I will make the land of Egypt a totally desolate waste from Migdol to S'venah, all the way to the border of Ethiopia. 11 No human foot will pass through it, and no animal foot will pass through it; it will be uninhabited for forty years. 12 Yes, I will make the land of Egypt desolate, even when compared with other desolate countries, likewise her cities in comparison with other ruined cities; they will be desolate forty years. I will scatter the Egyptians among the nations and disperse them through the countries.'

13 "For this is what *Adonai* E_LOHIM_ says: 'At the end of forty years I will gather the Egyptians from the peoples where they were scattered — 14 I will restore the fortunes of Egypt and cause them to return to the land of their origin, Patros. But there they will be a humble kingdom, 15 the humblest of kingdoms. It will never again dominate other nations; I will reduce them, so that they never again rule other nations. 16 Moreover, they will no longer be a source of confidence for Isra'el to turn to; rather, it will only bring to mind their guilt in having turned to them before. Then they will know that I am *Adonai* E_LOHIM_.'"

17 On the first day of the first month of the twenty-seventh year, the word of A_DONAI_ came to me: 18 "Human being, N'vukhadretzar king of Bavel had his army mount a massive expedition against Tzor; [the loads of dirt they carried] made every head bald and every shoulder raw; yet neither he nor his army derived any benefit from Tzor out of this expedition against it. 19 Therefore *Adonai* E_LOHIM_ says, 'I will give the land of Egypt to N'vukhadretzar king of Bavel. He will carry off its riches, take its spoil and its prey; and these will be the wages for his army. 20 I am giving him the land of Egypt as his wages for which he worked, because they were working for me,' says *Adonai* E_LOHIM_. 21 'When that day comes I will cause power to return to the house of Isra'el, and I will enable you [Yechezk'el] to open your mouth among them. Then they will know that I am A_DONAI_.'"

30 1 The word of A_DONAI_ came to me: 2 "Human being, prophesy; say that *Adonai* E_LOHIM_ says,

'Wail, "Oh no! It's today!"
3 For the day is near,
the Day of A_DONAI_, a day of clouds,
the time of the *Goyim*.
4 The sword will come against Egypt,
and Ethiopia will be in anguish,
when the slain fall in Egypt,

when they take away her wealth,
and her foundations are torn down.

5 Ethiopia, Put and Lud,
all the mixed population and Kuv,
and the people of allied lands
will die by the sword with them.'

6 "ADONAI says this:

'Those supporting Egypt will fall;
its arrogant power will be brought down;
from Migdol to S'venah they will die by the sword,'
says Adonai ELOHIM.

7 "They will be desolate even when compared with other desolate countries, likewise her cities in comparison with other ruined cities. 8 They will know that I am ADONAI when I set fire to Egypt, and those supporting it are destroyed. 9 When that day comes, I will send out messengers in ships to terrify the unsuspecting Ethiopians; and anguish will overcome them on the day of Egypt. Yes, here it comes!

10 "Adonai ELOHIM says:

'I will destroy the hordes of Egypt
through N'vukhadretzar king of Bavel.
11 He and his people, the most barbarous of the nations,
will be brought in to ravage the land.
They will unsheathe their swords against Egypt
and fill the land with corpses.
12 I will dry up the streams of the Nile
and sell the land to the wicked.
Through the power of foreigners I will make the land
and all that is in it desolate.
I, ADONAI, have spoken.'

13 "Here is what Adonai ELOHIM says:

'I will destroy the idols,
make the false gods in Nof cease to exist.
No longer will there be a prince from the land of Egypt;
I will put fear in the land of Egypt,
14 desolate Patros, set fire to Tzo'an,
execute judgements in No,
15 pour my fury on Seen the stronghold of Egypt,
and destroy the hordes of No.
16 Yes, I will set fire to Egypt;
Seen will writhe in anguish;
No will be torn apart;
enemies will attack Nof in broad daylight.

17   The young men of On and Pi-Veset
will die by the sword,
while the cities themselves
will go into captivity.

18   At T'chafn'ches the day will grow dark
when I break the yokes of Egypt there,
and the pride she takes in her power ceases.
A cloud will cover her,
and her daughters will go into captivity.

19   Thus will I execute judgments on Egypt.
Then they will know that I am ADONAI.'"

²⁰ On the seventh day of the first month of the eleventh year, the word of ADONAI came to me: ²¹ "Human being, I have broken the arm of Pharaoh king of Egypt; it has not been bound up with dressings and bandages, so that it can heal and become strong enough again to wield the sword. ²² Therefore Adonai ELOHIM says this: 'I am against Pharaoh king of Egypt. I will break his arms, both the sound one and the broken one, and I will make the sword fall from his hand. ²³ I will scatter the Egyptians among the nations and disperse them throughout the countries. ²⁴ I will strengthen the arms of the king of Bavel and put my sword in his hand; but I will break the arms of Pharaoh; he will groan like a man mortally wounded. ²⁵ Yes, I will hold up the arms of the king of Bavel; but the arms of Pharaoh will droop. They will know that I am ADONAI when I put my sword in the hand of the king of Bavel, and he stretches it out over the land of Egypt. ²⁶ Yes, I will scatter the Egyptians among the nations and disperse them throughout the countries; and they will know that I am ADONAI.'"

31 ¹ On the first day of third month of the eleventh year, the word of ADONAI came to me: ² "Human being, say to Pharaoh king of Egypt and to his hordes:

'Whom are you like in your greatness?

3   Like Ashur, a cedar in the L'vanon.
It had beautiful branches, dense foliage,
its tall crown surrounded by leafy boughs.

4   The water nourished it; the deep made it grow,
sending its rivers round the place where it was planted,
sending its streams to all the trees in the fields.

5   So it grew taller than any other tree,
its branches grew in number and spread far and wide,
for it had plenty of water to make them grow.

6   In its boughs all the birds of the air had their nests,
beneath its branches all the wild animals gave birth to their young,
and all great nations lived in its shade.

7   It was beautiful in its greatness and the length of its branches,
because its roots went down to plenty of water.

8   No cedar in God's garden was like it,
no cypress tree could compare with its boughs,
no chestnut tree could rival its branches,

no tree in God's garden could match its beauty.
⁹   I made it so beautiful, with its many branches;
all the trees in 'Eden, God's garden, envied it.'

¹⁰ "Therefore here is what *Adonai ELOHIM* says: 'Because you are so tall, because he has lifted his crown above the leafy boughs, because he has grown so arrogant about his height, ¹¹ I am handing him over to the mightiest of the nations, who will certainly deal with him as his wickedness deserves; I reject him. ¹² Foreigners, the most barbarous of the nations, will destroy him and leave him lying where he is. His branches will lie fallen on the mountains and in the valleys, his boughs will lie broken in all the rivers of the land, and all the peoples of the earth will withdraw from his shade and leave him. ¹³ All the birds will settle on his fallen trunk, and all the wild animals will be on his branches. ¹⁴ This is to warn all the trees growing near water not to grow so tall, not to lift their crowns above the leafy boughs, and all that take up water not to reach up in their height.

For they are all given over to death,
to the depths of the underworld,
along with human beings,
with those who descend to the pit.'

¹⁵ "Here is what *Adonai ELOHIM* says:

'On the day he descended to Sh'ol,
I caused the abyss to mourn
and cover itself for him;
I held back its rivers,
so that its deep waters were stopped.
I made the L'vanon mourn for him,
and all the field trees withered because of him.
¹⁶   At the sound of his fall
I made the nations shake,
when I hurled him down to Sh'ol
with those who descend to the pit.
All the trees of 'Eden,
the pick of the best in the L'vanon,
all that take up water,
were consoled in the underworld.
¹⁷   They descended with him to Sh'ol
to those who were killed by the sword,
to those who were his fighting arm,
those among the nations who lived in his shade.
¹⁸   Which of the trees of 'Eden
was your equal in glory or size?
Yet you will be brought down to the underworld
along with the trees of 'Eden.
You will lie there among the uncircumcised,

with those killed by the sword.
This is Pharaoh and his hordes,'

says *Adonai ELOHIM*."

32 ¹ On the first day of the twelfth month of the twelfth year, the word of *ADONAI* came to me: ² "Human being, raise a lament for Pharaoh king of Egypt; say to him,

'You compared yourself to a lion among the nations;
In fact, you are more like a crocodile in the lakes.
You burst out of your streams,
churn the water with your feet
and foul their streams.'

³ "So here is what *Adonai ELOHIM* says:

'With many nations assembled,
I will spread my net over you,
and they will haul you up in my dragnet.
⁴ Then I will throw you on the shore,
hurl you into an open field,
make all the birds in the air settle on you
and let the animals of the whole earth eat their fill of you.
⁵ I will leave your flesh on the mountains
and fill the valleys with your rotting carcass.
⁶ I will drench the land in which you swim
with your blood, as far as the mountains;
the waterways will be full of you.
⁷ When I extinguish you, I will cover the sky
and make its stars black;
I will cover the sun with a cloud,
and the moon will not give its light.
⁸ All the shining lights in the sky
I will darken above you;
I will spread darkness over your land,'
says *Adonai ELOHIM*.

⁹ "'I will anger many peoples
when I bring your destroyed ones
in among the nations,
into countries you have not known.
¹⁰ I will make many peoples aghast at you;
their kings will shudder in horror over you
when I brandish my sword before them.
On the day of your downfall
they will tremble continuously,
each man in fear of his life.'

¹¹ "For *Adonai ELOHIM* says this:

> 'The sword of the king of Bavel
> will come against you.
¹² With the swords of the warriors
> I will cause your hordes to fall.
> They are all the most barbarous of the nations,
> and they will shatter the glory of Egypt —
> all its hordes will be destroyed.
¹³ I will destroy all her cattle
> beside her plentiful waters.
> No human foot will trouble them again,
> nor the hoof of any animal.
¹⁴ Then I will make their water clear
> and cause their streams to flow like oil,'
> says *Adonai ELOHIM*.
¹⁵ 'When I make the land of Egypt a ruined waste,
> a land stripped of all that filled it;
> when I strike all those who live there;
> they will know that I am *ADONAI*.
¹⁶ This is the lament that they will raise;
> the daughters of the nations will use it to mourn;
> they will chant it for Egypt and all its hordes,'
> says *Adonai ELOHIM*."

¹⁷ On the fifteenth day of the month in the twelfth year, the word of *ADONAI* came to me:

¹⁸ "Human being, wail for the hordes of Egypt;
> send them with the daughters of mighty nations
> down to the underworld,
> with those who descend to the pit.
¹⁹ Are you more beautiful than the others?
> Go down, lie with the uncircumcised dead!
²⁰ They will fall among those killed by the sword;
> she is given to the sword; pull her down with her hordes.
²¹ From the depths of Sh'ol the mightiest warriors
> will speak of him with those who helped him.
> They went down; they lie still,
> the uncircumcised, killed by the sword.

²² "Ashur is there with her hordes;
> their graves are all around them,
> all of them slain, killed by the sword.
²³ Their graves are in the deepest parts of the pit,
> her hordes are all around her grave,
> all of them slain, killed by the sword,
> those who terrorized the land of the living.

24   "'Eilam is there, with her hordes around her grave,
      all of them slain, killed by the sword,
      descended uncircumcised to the underworld,
      those who terrorized the land of the living;
      they bear their shame together with those
      who descended to the pit.
25   They have given her a bed among the slain with her hordes;
      her graves are all around them,
      all of them uncircumcised, killed by the sword,
      because they terrorized the land of the living;
      they bear their shame with those who descended to the pit;
      they are put among those who were slain.

26   "Meshekh and Tuval with her horde is there,
      her graves are all around them,
      all of them uncircumcised, killed by the sword,
      because they terrorized the land of the living.
27   They do not lie with the fallen warriors
      of the uncircumcised who descended to Sh'ol
      with their weapons of war,
      their swords laid under their heads,
      and their crimes upon their bones;
      because these warriors terrorized the land of the living.
28   But you will lie broken among the uncircumcised,
      with those who were killed by the sword.

29   "There is Edom, her kings and all her princes,
      who, despite all their power, are laid with those
      who were killed by the sword, with the uncircumcised,
      with those who descended to the pit.

30   "There are all the princes of the north, all of them,
      and the Tzidoni, who descended with the slain,
      ashamed of all the terror they caused by their power;
      they lie uncircumcised with those killed by the sword,
      bearing their shame with those who descended to the pit.

31   "All of these Pharaoh will see,
      and he will be consoled about his hordes,
      Pharaoh and all his army, slain by the sword,"
      says *Adonai ELOHIM.*
32   "For I have put my terror in the land of the living,
      and he will lie among the uncircumcised,
      with those killed by the sword,
      Pharaoh and all his hordes,"

says *Adonai ELOHIM.*

33 ¹ The word of *ADONAI* came to me: ² "Human being, speak to your people; say to them, 'Suppose I bring the sword on a country, and the people of that country take one of their men and appoint him their watchman. ³ Now if, upon seeing the sword coming against that country, he blows the *shofar* and warns the people; ⁴ then, if the sword comes and takes away someone who heard the sound of the *shofar* but paid no attention to it, the responsibility for that person's death will be his own — ⁵ he heard the *shofar* but paid no attention, so the responsibility for his death is his own; whereas if he had paid attention, he would have saved his life. ⁶ But if the watchman sees the sword coming and does not blow the *shofar*, so that the people are not warned; and then the sword comes and takes any one of them, that one is indeed taken away in his guilt, but I will hold the watchman responsible for his death.'

⁷ "Likewise you, human being — I have appointed you as watchman for the house of Isra'el. Therefore, when you hear the word from my mouth, warn them for me. ⁸ When I tell the wicked person, 'Wicked person, you will certainly die'; and you fail to speak and warn the wicked person to leave his way; then that wicked person will die guilty; and I will hold you responsible for his death. ⁹ On the other hand, if you warn the wicked to turn from his way, and he doesn't turn from his way; then he will still die guilty, but you will have saved your own life.

¹⁰ "Therefore, you, human being, say to the house of Isra'el: 'You say, "Our crimes and sins are weighing us down, we're pining away because of them, how can we even stay alive?"' ¹¹ Say to them, 'As I live,' swears *Adonai ELOHIM*, 'I take no pleasure in having the wicked person die, but in having the wicked person turn from his way and live. So repent! Turn from your evil ways! For why should you die, house of Isra'el?'

¹² "Next, you, human being, say to your people: 'The righteousness of the righteous person will not save him, once he starts committing crimes; and likewise, the wickedness of the wicked person will not cause him to fall, once he turns from his wickedness. No, the righteous person cannot live by virtue of [his former righteousness], once he starts sinning. ¹³ So if, after I tell the righteous person that he will surely live, he begins trusting in his own [former] righteousness and starts committing crimes; then none of his [former] righteous actions will be remembered; on the contrary, he will die for the evil deeds he has committed. ¹⁴ Likewise, if, after I tell the wicked person, "You must die," he turns from his sin and does what is lawful and right — ¹⁵ if the wicked person restores pledged property and returns what he stole, so that he lives by the laws that give life and does not commit evil deeds; then he will live, he will not die. ¹⁶ None of the sins he committed will be remembered against him; he has done what is lawful and right; he will surely live.'

¹⁷ "Now your people say, '*Adonai's* way isn't fair!' But it is their way, theirs, that isn't fair! ¹⁸ When the righteous person turns away from his righteousness and commits wickedness, he will die because of it. ¹⁹ And when the wicked person turns from his wickedness and does what is lawful and right, he will live because of it. ²⁰ Yet you say, '*Adonai's* way isn't fair!' House of Isra'el, I will judge each of you according to his ways."

²¹ In the twelfth year of our exile, on the fifth day of the tenth month, a fugitive from Yerushalayim came to me with the news, "The city has been struck." ²² Now the hand of *ADONAI* had been on me that evening, before the fugitive arrived — he had opened my mouth prior to his coming to me in the morning, so my mouth was

open, and I was no longer mute. ²³ Then the word of ADONAI came to me: ²⁴ "Human being, those living in the desolate parts of the land of Isra'el are saying, 'Avraham was only one, and he inherited the land. But we are many, so [how much more] is the land given to us to inherit!' ²⁵ Therefore, tell them that Adonai ELOHIM says, 'You eat [flesh] with the blood, you raise your eyes to your idols, and you shed blood — and you still expect to possess the land? ²⁶ You depend on your swords, you commit disgusting practices, and each of you defiles his neighbor's wife — and you still expect to possess the land?' ²⁷ Tell them that Adonai ELOHIM swears, 'As I live, those living in the ruins will fall by the sword, those in the countryside I will give to the wild animals to eat, and those in the fortresses and caves will die of the plague. ²⁸ Moreover, I will utterly desolate the land; it will cease taking pride in its power; and the mountains of Isra'el will be so desolate that no one will pass through.' ²⁹ Then they will know that I am ADONAI, when I have made the land utterly desolate, because of all the disgusting practices they have committed.

³⁰ "Now you, human being, your people are gathering and talking about you by the walls and in the doorways of houses. They're saying to each other, each one telling his brother, 'Come, let's go and hear the latest word coming from ADONAI.' ³¹ So then they come to you, as people do, sit in front of you as my people, and hear your words; but they don't act on them. For with their mouths they flatter you, but their hearts are set on their own self-interest; ³² so for them you are like a love-song sung by someone with a nice voice who can play an instrument well — they hear your words, but they don't act on them. ³³ So when all this comes true, then, at last, they will realize that a prophet has been there with them."

34 ¹ The word of ADONAI came to me: ² "Human being, prophesy against the shepherds of Isra'el. Prophesy! Tell them, the shepherds, that Adonai ELOHIM says this: 'Woe to the shepherds of Isra'el who feed themselves! Shouldn't the shepherds feed the sheep? ³ You eat the choice meat, you clothe yourselves with the wool, and you slaughter the best of the herd; but you don't feed the sheep! ⁴ You don't strengthen the weak, heal the sick, bandage the broken, bring back the outcasts or seek the lost; on the contrary, you tyrannize them with crushing force. ⁵ So they were scattered, without a shepherd, and became food for every wild animal — they were scattered. ⁶ My sheep wandered around aimlessly on every mountain and hill; yes, my sheep were scattered all over the land, with no one to search for them or look after them.

⁷ "'Therefore, shepherds, hear the word of ADONAI: ⁸ "As I live," Adonai ELOHIM swears, "because my sheep have become prey, my sheep have become food for every wild animal, since there was no shepherd, since my shepherds didn't look for my sheep, and instead my shepherds fed themselves but not my sheep," ⁹ therefore, shepherds, hear the word of ADONAI! ¹⁰ Adonai ELOHIM says, "I am against the shepherds. I demand that they hand my sheep back to me. I will not allow them to feed the sheep, and they won't feed themselves either. I will rescue my sheep from their mouths; they will be food for them no longer."

¹¹ "'For here is what Adonai ELOHIM says: "I am taking over! I will search for my sheep and look after them, myself. ¹² Just as a shepherd looks after his flock when he finds himself among his scattered sheep, so I will look after my sheep. I will rescue them from all the places where they were scattered when it was cloudy and dark. ¹³ I will bring them back from those peoples, gather them from those countries and

return them to their own land. Then I will let them feed on the mountains of Isra'el, by the streams and in all the livable places of the land. ¹⁴ I will have them feed in good pastures; their grazing ground will be on the high mountains of Isra'el. They will rest in good grazing grounds and feed in rich pastures on Isra'el's mountains. ¹⁵ Yes, I will pasture my sheep; and I will let them rest" says *Adonai ELOHIM*. ¹⁶ "I will seek the lost, bring back the outcasts, bandage the broken, and strengthen the sick. But the fat and the strong I will destroy — I will feed them with judgment."

¹⁷ "'As for you, my flock,' *Adonai ELOHIM* says this: 'I will judge between sheep and other sheep, between rams and billy-goats. ¹⁸ Wasn't it enough for you to feed on the best pasture and drink from the clearest water? Did you have to trample the rest of the pasture and foul the remaining water with your feet? ¹⁹ So now my sheep eat what you have trampled with your feet and drink water fouled by your feet.' ²⁰ Therefore here is what *Adonai ELOHIM* says to them: 'I will judge between the fat sheep and the thin sheep. ²¹ Because you push them with your flanks and shoulders and butt all the weak ones with your horns, till you scatter them in every direction; ²² therefore I will save my flock; they will no longer be prey; and I will judge between sheep and other sheep.

²³ "'I will raise up one shepherd to be in charge of them, and he will let them feed — my servant David. He will pasture them and be their shepherd. ²⁴ I, *ADONAI*, will be their God; and my servant David will be prince among them. I, *ADONAI*, have spoken. ²⁵ I will make a covenant of peace with them; I will rid the land of wild animals; and they will live securely in the desert and sleep in the forests. ²⁶ I will make them and the places around my hill a blessing, and I will cause the rain to fall when it should — there will be showers of blessing. ²⁷ The trees in the field will bear their fruit and the soil its produce, and they will be secure in their land. Then they will know that I am *ADONAI*, when I break the bars of their yoke and rescue them from the power of those who turned them into slaves. ²⁸ No longer will they be prey for the *Goyim*, nor will the wild animals devour them; but they will live securely, with no one to make them afraid. ²⁹ I will make the productivity of their crops famous, and they will no longer be consumed by hunger in the land or bear the shame of the *Goyim* any more. ³⁰ They will know that I, *ADONAI* their God, am with them, and that they, the house of Isra'el, are my people,' says *Adonai ELOHIM*. ³¹ 'You, my sheep, the sheep in my pasture, are human beings; and I am your God,' says *Adonai ELOHIM*."

35 ¹ The word of *ADONAI* came to me: ² "Human being, turn your face against Mount Se'ir; prophesy against it, ³ and say that *Adonai ELOHIM* says, 'I am against you, Mount Se'ir. I will stretch out my hand against you and make you utterly desolate. ⁴ I will make your cities ruins and make you an utter waste, and you will know that I am *ADONAI*. ⁵ Because of your long-standing hatred, you put the people of Isra'el to the sword at their time of calamity, at the time of final iniquity. ⁶ Therefore, as I live,' *Adonai ELOHIM* swears, 'I will prepare you for blood. Blood will pursue you. You intensely hate your own blood [relatives]; therefore blood will pursue you. ⁷ Yes, I will make Mount Se'ir utterly desolate, cutting off from it anyone passing through or returning. ⁸ I will fill his mountains with his slain; in your hills and valleys and in all your ravines will fall those slain by the sword. ⁹ I will turn you into perpetual ruins; your cities will not return; and you will know that I am *ADONAI*.

¹⁰ "'Because you say, "These two nations, these two countries, will be mine; we will take possession of them," even though *Adonai* is there; ¹¹ therefore, as I live,' swears *Adonai Elohim*, 'I will deal with you as your anger and envy arising from your hatred deserve; and I will make myself known among them when I judge you. ¹² You will know that I, *Adonai*, have heard all your blasphemous talk against the mountains of Isra'el, such as, "They are desolated, they are given to us to devour." ¹³ Moreover, you have boasted against me with your mouths, speaking more and more against me — I have heard it.' ¹⁴ Here is what *Adonai Elohim* says: 'To the joy of all the land, I will desolate you. ¹⁵ Since you rejoiced over possessing the house of Isra'el, because it was desolate, that is what I will do to you — you will be desolate, Mount Se'ir and all Edom, all of it. Then they will know that I am *Adonai*.'

36 ¹ "Now you, human being, prophesy to the mountains of Isra'el. Say: 'Mountains of Isra'el, hear the message from *Adonai*. ² *Adonai Elohim* says: "The enemy is boasting over you, 'Ha! Even the ancient high places are ours now!' " ' ³ Therefore prophesy, and say that *Adonai Elohim* says, 'Because they desolated you and swallowed you up from every side, so that the other nations could take possession of you; and now people are gossiping about you and slandering you; ⁴ therefore, mountains of Isra'el, hear the message of *Adonai Elohim* — this is what *Adonai Elohim* says to the mountains and hills, the streams and valleys, the desolate wastes and the abandoned cities, now preyed on and derided by the other surrounding nations — ⁵ therefore this is what *Adonai Elohim* says: "In the heat of my jealousy I speak against the other nations and all of Edom, since, rejoicing with all their heart, they have arrogated my land to themselves as a possession and, with utter contempt, seized it as prey."'

⁶ "Therefore prophesy concerning the land of Isra'el, and say to the mountains, the hills, the streams and the valleys that *Adonai Elohim* says this: 'I speak in my jealousy and fury, because you have endured being shamed by the nations. ⁷ Therefore thus says *Adonai Elohim*: "I have raised my hand and sworn that the nations surrounding you will bear their shame. ⁸ But you, mountains of Isra'el, you will sprout your branches and bear your fruit for my people Isra'el, who will soon return. ⁹ I am here for you, and I will turn toward you; then you will be tilled and sown; ¹⁰ and I will multiply your population, all the house of Isra'el, all of it. The cities will be inhabited and the ruins rebuilt. ¹¹ I will multiply both the human and animal populations, they will increase and be productive; and I will cause you to be inhabited as you were before — indeed, I will do you more good than before; and you will know that I am *Adonai*. ¹² I will cause people to walk on you, my people Isra'el; they will possess you, and you will be their inheritance; never again will you make them childless." ¹³ *Adonai Elohim* says, "Because they say to you, 'Land, you devour people and make your nations childless,' ¹⁴ therefore you will no longer devour people, and you will not make your nations childless any more," says *Adonai Elohim*. ¹⁵ "I will not permit the nations to shame you, or the peoples to reproach you any longer; and you will no more cause your nations to stumble," says *Adonai Elohim*.'"

¹⁶ The word of *Adonai* came to me: ¹⁷ "Human being, when the house of Isra'el lived in their own land, they defiled it by their manner of life and their actions; their way before me was like the uncleanness of *niddah*. ¹⁸ Therefore I poured out my fury on them, because of the blood they had shed in the land and because they defiled it with their idols. ¹⁹ I scattered them among the nations and dispersed them throughout

the countries; I judged them in keeping with their manner of life and actions. [20] When they came to the nations they were going to, they profaned my holy name; so that people said of them, 'These are ADONAI's people, who have been exiled from his land.' [21] But I am concerned about my holy name, which the house of Isra'el is profaning among the nations where they have gone.

[22] "Therefore tell the house of Isra'el that Adonai ELOHIM says this: 'I am not going to do this for your sake, house of Isra'el, but for the sake of my holy name, which you have been profaning among the nations where you went. [23] I will set apart my great name to be regarded as holy, since it has been profaned in the nations — you profaned it among them. The nations will know that I am ADONAI,' says Adonai ELOHIM, 'when, before their eyes, I am set apart through you to be regarded as holy.

[24] For I will take you from among the nations,
gather you from all the countries,
and return you to your own soil.

[25] Then I will sprinkle clean water on you,
and you will be clean;
I will cleanse you from all your uncleanness
and from all your idols.

[26] I will give you a new heart
and put a new spirit inside you;
I will take the stony heart out of your flesh
and give you a heart of flesh.

[27] I will put my Spirit inside you
and cause you to live by my laws,
respect my rulings and obey them.

[28] You will live in the land I gave to your ancestors.
You will be my people,
and I will be your God.

[29] I will save you from all your uncleanliness.
I will summon the grain and increase it,
and not send famine against you.

[30] I will multiply the yield of fruit from the trees
and increase production in the fields,
so that you never again suffer the reproach
of famine among the nations.

[31] Then you will remember your evil ways
and your actions that were not good;
as you look at yourselves, you will loathe yourselves
for your guilt and disgusting practices.

[32] Understand,' says Adonai ELOHIM,
'that I am not doing this for your sake.
Instead, be ashamed and dismayed for your ways,
house of Isra'el.'

[33] "Adonai ELOHIM says, 'When the day comes for me to cleanse you from all your guilt, I will cause the cities to be inhabited and the ruins to be rebuilt. [34] The land that

was desolate will be tilled, whereas formerly it lay desolate for all passing by to see. ³⁵ Then they will say, "The land that used to be desolate has become like Gan-'Eden, and the cities formerly ruined, abandoned and wasted have been fortified and are inhabited!" ³⁶ Then the nations around you that remain will know that I, ADONAI, have rebuilt the ruins and replanted what was abandoned. I, ADONAI, have spoken; and I will do it.'

³⁷ "Adonai ELOHIM says, 'In addition, I will let the house of Isra'el pray to me to do this for them: to increase their numbers like sheep — ³⁸ like flocks of sheep for sacrifices, like the flocks of sheep in Yerushalayim at its designated times, in this degree will the ruined cities be filled with flocks of people. Then they will know that I am ADONAI.'"

37 ¹ With the hand of ADONAI upon me, ADONAI carried me out by his Spirit and set me down in the middle of the valley, and it was full of bones. ² He had me pass by all around them — there were so many bones lying in the valley, and they were so dry! ³ He asked me, "Human being, can these bones live?" I answered, "Adonai ELOHIM! Only you know that!" ⁴ Then he said to me, "Prophesy over these bones! Say to them, 'Dry bones! Hear what ADONAI has to say! ⁵ To these bones Adonai ELOHIM says, "I will make breath enter you, and you will live. ⁶ I will attach ligaments to you, make flesh grow on you, cover you with skin and put breath in you. You will live, and you will know that I am ADONAI."'"

⁷ So I prophesied as ordered; and while I was prophesying, there was a noise, a rattling sound; it was the bones coming together, each bone in its proper place. ⁸ As I watched, ligaments grew on them, flesh appeared and skin covered them; but there was no breath in them. ⁹ Next he said to me, "Prophesy to the breath! Prophesy, human being! Say to the breath that Adonai ELOHIM says, 'Come from the four winds, breath; and breathe on these slain, so that they can live.'"

¹⁰ So I prophesied as ordered, and the breath came into them, and they were alive! They stood up on their feet, a huge army! ¹¹ Then he said to me, "Human being! These bones are the whole house of Isra'el; and they are saying, 'Our bones have dried up, our hope is gone, and we are completely cut off.' ¹² Therefore prophesy; say to them that Adonai ELOHIM says, 'My people! I will open your graves and make you get up out of your graves, and I will bring you into the land of Isra'el. ¹³ Then you will know that I am ADONAI — when I have opened your graves and made you get up out of your graves, my people! ¹⁴ I will put my Spirit in you; and you will be alive. Then I will place you in your own land; and you will know that I, ADONAI, have spoken, and that I have done it,' says ADONAI."

¹⁵ The word of ADONAI came to me: ¹⁶ "You, human being, take one stick and write on it, 'For Y'hudah and those joined with him [among] the people of Isra'el.' Next, take another stick and write on it, 'For Yosef, the stick of Efrayim, and all the house of Isra'el who are joined with him.' ¹⁷ Finally, bring them together into a single stick, so that they become one in your hand. ¹⁸ When your people ask you what all this means, ¹⁹ tell them that Adonai ELOHIM says this: 'I will take the stick of Yosef, which is in the hand of Efrayim, together with the tribes of Isra'el who are joined with him, and put them together with the stick of Y'hudah and make them a single stick, so that they become one in my hand.' ²⁰ The sticks on which you write are to be in your hand as they watch. ²¹ Then say to them that Adonai ELOHIM says: 'I will take

the people of Isra'el from among the nations where they have gone and gather them from every side and bring them back to their own land. ²² I will make them one nation in the land, on the mountains of Isra'el; and one king will be king for all of them. They will no longer be two nations, and they will never again be divided into two kingdoms.

²³ "'They will never again defile themselves with their idols, their detestable things, or any of their transgressions; but I will save them from all the places where they have been living and sinning; and I will cleanse them, so that they will be my people, and I will be their God. ²⁴ My servant David will be king over them, and all of them will have one shepherd; they will live by my rulings and keep and observe my regulations. ²⁵ They will live in the land I gave to Ya'akov my servant, where your ancestors lived; they will live there — they, their children, and their grandchildren, forever; and David my servant will be their leader forever. ²⁶ I will make a covenant of peace with them, an everlasting covenant. I will give to them, increase their numbers, and set my sanctuary among them forever. ²⁷ My home will be with them; I will be their God, and they will be my people. ²⁸ The nations will know that I am ADONAI, who sets Isra'el apart as holy, when my sanctuary is with them forever.'"

38 ¹ The word of ADONAI came to me: ² "Human being, turn your face toward Gog (of the land of Magog), chief prince of Meshekh and Tuval; and prophesy against him. ³ Say that Adonai ELOHIM says, 'I am against you, Gog, chief prince of Meshekh and Tuval. ⁴ I will turn you around, put hooks in your jaws and bring you out with all your army, horses and horsemen, all completely equipped, a great horde with breastplates and shields, all wielding swords. ⁵ Paras, Ethiopia and Put are with them, all with breastplates and helmets; ⁶ Gomer with all its troops; the house of Togarmah in the far reaches of the north, with all its troops — many peoples are with you. ⁷ Prepare yourself, get ready, you and all your crowd gathered around you; and take charge of them. ⁸ After many days have passed, you will be mustered for service; in later years you will invade the land which has been brought back from the sword, gathered out of many peoples, the mountains of Isra'el. They had been lying in ruins for a long time, but now Isra'el has been extracted from the peoples and all of them are living there securely. ⁹ You will come up like a storm, you will be like a cloud covering the land — you and all your troops, and many other peoples with you.'

¹⁰ "Adonai ELOHIM says: 'When that day comes, thoughts will well up in your mind, and you will devise a sinister scheme. ¹¹ You will say, "I am going to invade this land of unwalled villages; I will take by surprise these people who are at peace, living securely, all in places without walls, bars or gates. ¹² I will seize the spoil and take the plunder." You will attack the former ruins that are now inhabited and come against the people gathered from the nations, who have acquired livestock and other wealth and are living in the central parts of the land. ¹³ Sh'va, D'dan and all the leading merchants of Tarshish will ask you, "Have you come to seize spoil? Have you assembled your hordes to loot; to carry off silver, gold, livestock and other wealth; to take much plunder?"'

¹⁴ "Therefore, human being, prophesy! Tell Gog that Adonai ELOHIM says this: 'Won't you be aware of it when my people Isra'el are living in security? ¹⁵ You will choose just that time to come from your place in the far reaches of the north, you and many peoples with you, all of them on horseback, a huge horde, a mighty army;

¹⁶ and you will invade my people Isra'el like a cloud covering the land. This will be in the *acharit-hayamim*; and I will bring you against my land, so that the *Goyim* will know me when, before their eyes, I am set apart as holy through you, Gog.'
¹⁷ "*Adonai ELOHIM* says: 'I spoke of you long ago through my servants the prophets of Isra'el. Back then, they prophesied for many years that I would have you invade them. ¹⁸ When that day comes, when Gog invades the land of Isra'el,' says *Adonai ELOHIM*, 'my furious anger will boil up. ¹⁹ In my jealousy, in my heated fury I speak: when that day comes there will be a great earthquake in the land of Isra'el; ²⁰ so that the fish in the sea, the birds in the air, the wild beasts, all the reptiles creeping on the ground and every human being there in the land will tremble before me. Mountains will fall, cliffs crumble and every wall crash to the ground. ²¹ I will summon a sword against him throughout all my mountains,' says *Adonai ELOHIM*; 'every man will wield his sword against his brother. ²² I will judge him with plague and with blood. I will cause torrential rain to fall on him, his troops and the many peoples with him, along with huge hailstones, fire and sulfur. ²³ I will show my greatness and holiness, making myself known in the sight of many nations; then they will know that I am *ADONAI*.'

39 ¹ "So you, human being, prophesy against Gog; say that *Adonai ELOHIM* says: 'I am against you, Gog, chief prince of Meshekh and Tuval. ² I will turn you around, lead you on and bring you from the far reaches of the north against the mountains of Isra'el. ³ But then I will knock your bow out of your left hand and make your arrows drop from your right hand. ⁴ You will fall on the mountains of Isra'el, you, your troops and all the peoples with you; I will give you to be eaten up by all kinds of birds of prey and by wild animals. ⁵ You will fall in the open field, for I have spoken,' says *Adonai ELOHIM*.

⁶ "'I will also send fire against Magog and against those living securely in the coastlands; then they will know that I am *ADONAI*. ⁷ I will make my holy name known among my people Isra'el; I will not allow my holy name to be profaned any longer. Then the *Goyim* will know that I am *ADONAI*, the Holy One in Isra'el. ⁸ Yes, this is coming, and it will be done,' says *Adonai ELOHIM*; 'this is the day about which I have spoken.

⁹ "'Those living in Isra'el's cities will go out and set fire to the weapons, to use as fuel — the shields, breastplates, bows, arrows, clubs and spears; they will use them for fire seven years; ¹⁰ so that they will not need to gather wood from the fields or cut down any from the forests; because they will use the weapons for fire. Thus they will plunder those who plundered them and rob those who robbed them,' says *Adonai ELOHIM*.

¹¹ "'When that day comes, I will give Gog a place there in Isra'el for graves, the Travelers' Valley, east of the sea; and it will block the travelers' passage. There they will bury Gog and all his horde, and they will rename it the Valley of Hamon-Gog [horde of Gog]. ¹² It will take the house of Isra'el seven months to bury them, in order to cleanse the land. ¹³ Yes, all the people of the land will be burying them; they will become famous for it. It will be a day for me to be glorified,' says *Adonai ELOHIM*. ¹⁴ 'They will then pick men for the continual duty of going through the land and burying with the travelers the corpses still lying out on the ground, in order to cleanse it; they will begin their search after the seven months. ¹⁵ As they go through the land, if anyone sees a human bone, he will put a marker next to it until the

gravediggers have buried it in the Valley of Hamon-Gog. ¹⁶ Moreover, "Hamonah" [its horde] will be the name of a city. Thus will they cleanse the land.'

¹⁷ "As for you, human, *Adonai Elohim* says that you are to speak to all kinds of birds and to every wild animal as follows: 'Assemble yourselves and come, gather yourselves from all around for the sacrifice I am preparing for you, a great sacrifice on the mountains of Isra'el, where you can eat flesh and drink blood! ¹⁸ You will eat the flesh of heroes and drink the blood of the earth's princes — rams, lambs, goats and bulls, fattened in Bashan, all of them. ¹⁹ You will eat fat till you are gorged and drink blood till you are drunk at the sacrifice I have prepared for you. ²⁰ At my table you will be satiated with horses, horsemen, heroes and every kind of warrior,' says *Adonai Elohim.*

²¹ "'Thus will I display my glory among the nations, so that all the nations will see my judgment when I execute it and my hand when I lay it on them. ²² From that day on, the house of Isra'el will know that I am *Adonai* their God; ²³ while the *Goyim* will know that the house of Isra'el went into exile because of their guilt, because they broke faith with me; so that I hid my face from them and handed them over to their adversaries; and they fell by the sword, all of them. ²⁴ Yes, I treated them as their uncleanness and crimes deserved; and I hid my face from them.'

²⁵ "Therefore *Adonai Elohim* says this: 'Now I will restore the fortunes of Ya'akov and have compassion on the entire house of Isra'el, and I will be jealous for my holy name. ²⁶ They will bear their shame and all their [guilt from] breaking faith with me, once they are living securely in their land, with no one to make them afraid. ²⁷ This will be after I have brought them back from the peoples and gathered them out of their enemies' lands, thereby being consecrated through them in the sight of many nations. ²⁸ Then they will know that I am *Adonai* their God, since it was I who caused them to go into exile among the nations, and it was I who regathered them to their own land. I will leave none of them there any more, ²⁹ and I will no longer hide my face from them, for I have poured out my Spirit on the house of Isra'el,' says *Adonai Elohim.*"

40 ¹ In the twenty-fifth year of our exile, at the beginning of the year, on the tenth day of the month — this was the fourteenth year after the city [of Yerushalayim] was struck — it was on that very day that the hand of *Adonai* was on me, and he took me there. ² In visions God brought me into the land of Isra'el and put me down on a very high mountain; on it, toward the south, it seemed that a city was being built. ³ That is where he took me, and there in front of me was a man whose appearance was like bronze. He had a flax cord and a measuring rod in his hand, and he stood in the gateway. ⁴ The man said to me, "Human being, look with your eyes, hear with your ears, and pay attention to all the things I am showing you; because the reason you were brought here is so that I could show them to you. Tell everything you see to the house of Isra'el."

⁵ There was a wall surrounding the house. The man had in his hand a measuring rod six cubits long [ten-and-a-half feet], each cubit [twenty-one inches] being a normal cubit [eighteen inches] plus a handbreadth [three inches]. He measured the wall's width at ten-and-a-half feet and its height ten-and-a-half feet. ⁶ He went to the east gate, climbed its steps and measured one of the gate's doorposts at ten-and-a-half feet wide and the other one the same. ⁷ There were guardrooms, each ten-and-a-half feet square; the distance between the guardrooms was eight-and-three-quarters feet.

The threshold of the gate adjoining the gate's entranceway facing the house measured ten-and-a-half feet. [8] He measured the gate's entranceway facing the house at ten-and-a-half feet. [9] Then he measured the gate's entranceway itself, fourteen feet, and its supports, three-and-a-half feet; the gate's entranceway was on the side facing the house. [10] There were three guardrooms on each side of the east gate, all the same size; and on each side the supports [between the guardrooms] were also all the same size. [11] He measured the width of the opening to the gateway at seventeen-and-a-half feet and the width of the passage through the gateway at twenty-two-and-three-quarters feet. [12] There was a partition in front of the guardrooms [on one side] twenty-one inches [wide] and a partition on the other side twenty-one inches [wide], with the guardrooms themselves being ten-and-a-half feet square. [13] He measured [inside] the gate from the back wall of one guardroom to the back wall of the other a distance of forty-three-and-three-quarters feet, the openings [to the guardrooms] being opposite each other. [14] He made the posts 105 feet, likewise the posts of the other gates around the courtyard. [15] The distance along the passage from the outer opening of the gateway to the far side of the entranceway at the inner end of the gateway was eighty-seven-and-a-half feet. [16] There were narrow windows to the guardrooms and to their supports facing inward all along the gate; also the vestibules had windows all around facing inward. On each side support were [carvings of] palm trees.

[17] Then he brought me into the outer courtyard. There I saw rooms and paved mosaic flooring made for the courtyard all around its perimeter, and thirty rooms facing the flooring. [18] The flooring was alongside the gates and corresponded to the length of the gates [from outside to inside], this lower flooring. [19] He measured at 175 feet the distance from inside this lower gate that faced east to the outside of the inner courtyard, and he did the same for the gate that faced north.

[20] Next he measured the length and width of the outer courtyard gate that faced north. [21] It had three guardrooms on each side, and its supports and vestibule were the same size as those at the first gate; its length was eighty-seven-and-a-half feet and its width forty-three-and-three-quarters feet. [22] Its windows, vestibule and palm trees were the same size as those at the east gate. Seven steps led up to it [from the outside], while its vestibule was toward the inside.

[23] There were gates to the inner courtyard across from the gates to the north and east; he measured 175 feet from each outer gate to its corresponding inner gate.

[24] He led me toward the south, and there I saw a gate that faced south. He measured its supports and vestibule; they were the same size as the others. [25] There were windows in it and all around its vestibule like the other windows; the length was eighty-seven-and-a-half feet and the width forty-three-and-three-quarters feet. [26] Seven steps led up to it [from the outside], while its vestibule was toward the inside. It had palm trees, one on each side, on its supports. [27] The inner courtyard had a gate on the south; he measured from gate to gate toward the south 175 feet.

[28] He brought me to the inner courtyard through its south gate. He measured this south gate as being the same size; [29] its guardrooms, supports and vestibule were the same size; it had windows and a vestibule surrounding it; it was eighty-seven-and-a-half feet long and forty-three-and-three-quarters feet wide. [30] There was a vestibule around it forty-three-and-three-quarters feet long and eight-and-three-quarters feet wide; [31] this vestibule faced the outer courtyard, palm trees were on its supports, and it had eight steps leading up to it.

[32] He brought me into the inner courtyard, went toward the east and measured that gate as being the same size; [33] its guardrooms, supports and vestibule were the same size; it had windows and a vestibule surrounding it; it was eighty-seven-and-a-half feet long and forty-three-and-three-quarters feet wide. [34] Its vestibule faced the outer courtyard, palm trees were on its supports, both on the one side and on the other; and it had eight steps leading up to it.

[35] He brought me over to the north gate and measured it as being the same size; [36] it had guardrooms, supports and a vestibule with windows all around; the length was eighty-seven-and-a-half feet and the width forty-three-and-three-quarters feet. [37] Its supports faced the outer courtyard; palm trees were on its supports, both on the one side and on the other; and it had eight steps leading up to it.

[38] There was a room with its entry by the supports at the gates where the burnt offerings were washed. [39] In the entranceway to the gate were two tables on the one side and two on the other, on which to slaughter the burnt offerings, sin offerings and guilt offerings. [40] On the outside, as one goes up to the entry of the north gate, were two tables; and on the other side of the entranceway to the gate were two tables. [41] So there were four tables on the one side and four on the other side, by the gate — eight tables on which to slaughter sacrifices. [42] There were four tables of cut stone for the burnt offering, thirty-one-and-a-half inches square and twenty-one inches high, on which to lay the instruments for slaughtering the burnt offerings and other sacrifices. [43] Hooks a handbreadth long were fastened all around the inside of the room; the flesh of the offerings was to be placed on the tables.

[44] Outside the inner gate, in the inner courtyard, were rooms for the singers, one facing south alongside the north gate, and one facing north alongside the east gate. [45] He said to me, "This room facing south is for the *cohanim* in charge of the house; [46] while the room facing north is for the *cohanim* in charge of the altar; these are the descendants of Tzadok, who are the descendants of Levi designated to approach *Adonai* and serve him."

[47] Then he measured the courtyard at 175 feet long and 175 feet wide — it was square. The altar was in front of the house.

[48] He brought me to the vestibule of the house and measured at eight-and-three-quarters feet the thickness of the walls on either side of its entrance. On each side, these walls extended five-and-a-quarter feet from the side-walls of the vestibule. [49] The length of the vestibule was thirty-five feet and the width nineteen-and-a-quarter feet; steps led up to it. There were columns on each side of the entrance.

41 [1] He brought me to the sanctuary and measured at ten-and-a-half feet the thickness of the walls on either side of its entrance, which was [also] the thickness of [the walls surrounding] the "tent" [that is, the sanctuary together with the Especially Holy Place]. [2] The width of the entrance was seventeen-and-a-half feet. The sides of the entrance were eight-and-three-quarters feet on the one side and the same on the other. He measured its length at seventy feet and its width at thirty-five feet.

[3] Next, he went farther in [to the entranceway leading to the Especially Holy Place] and measured at three-and-a-half feet [the thickness of] each entrance support. He measured at ten-and-a-half feet the total thickness of the walls on either side of the entrance; and he measured at twelve-and-a-quarter feet the width of the entrance. [4] [Continuing into the inner room,] he said to me, "This is the Especially Holy Place."

He measured its length at thirty-five feet and its width at thirty-five feet along the wall nearest the sanctuary. [5][On his way out,] he measured the thickness of the wall of the house at ten-and-a-half feet [at ground level], and the width of all the side-rooms surrounding the house, seven feet [at ground level]. [6]There were three floors of side-rooms, thirty on each floor; and the wall around the house was terraced, so that the side-rooms rested on the terraces and were not supported on [the vertical parts of] the wall. [7]The higher side-rooms surrounding the house were wider than the lower ones, as were the passageways next to the side-rooms on each floor; thus the width of the side-rooms plus that of the passageways increased as one went up from floor to floor. The ascent from the lowest floor to the highest was [by a ramp] through the middle floor.

[8]I saw that the house had a raised pavement all around it which extended outward a full rod of ten-and-a-half feet from where the foundations of the side-rooms joined it.

[9]The outer wall of the side-rooms was eight-and-three-quarters feet thick [at ground level], likewise the empty space left [between] the structure containing the side-rooms [and the house itself also measured eight-and-three quarters feet wide]. [10]On all sides around the house itself was a space thirty-five feet wide between it and the [block of] rooms [for the *cohanim*]. [11]The doors of the side-rooms opened toward an empty space, one door facing north and the other facing south; the empty space was eight-and-three-quarters feet [wide] all around.

[12]The building on the west facing the separated yard had a[n interior] width of 122½ feet, a[n interior] length of 157½ feet and exterior walls eight-and-three-quarters feet thick all the way around.

[13]He measured the length of the house at 175 feet; then a distance that included [the width of] the separated yard, [the interior width of] the building and [the thickness of] its [front and back exterior] walls, at 175 feet. [14]The distance along the facade of the house on the east through the separated yard[s to the north and south] was 175 feet. [15]He measured the length of the building facing the separated yard behind [the house], together with its galleries on both sides, at 175 feet.

The sanctuary, the inner place and the vestibules [leading from the house] to the courtyard, [16]as well as the thresholds, narrow windows and galleries around these three, had wood panelling around them as far as the thresholds and from the ground up to the windows; and the windows were covered. [17]From the area above the entrance to the interior of the house, as well as outside, and on the entire wall all the way around, both inside and outside, was a pattern [18]consisting of *k'ruvim* and palm trees, with a palm tree between every two *k'ruvim*. Every *keruv* had two faces; [19]so that there was the face of a man toward the palm tree on its one side and the face of a young lion toward the palm tree on its other side — this was the pattern all the way around the house. [20]The *k'ruvim* and palm trees ran from the ground to above the door, and likewise on the wall of the sanctuary. [21]As for the sanctuary, the door-frames were squared, and the appearance of the [Especially] Holy Place was like the appearance [I saw at the K'var River]. [22]The altar was of wood, five-and-a-quarter feet high and three-and-a-half feet long; its length and walls were also of wood. He said to me, "This is the table which is in the presence of *Adonai*."

²³ The sanctuary had two doors, and the [Especially] Holy Place ²⁴ had two doors. The doors had two swinging leaves each — two leaves for the one door and two for the other. ²⁵ On them, that is, on the doors of the sanctuary, were carved *k'ruvim* and palm trees like those on the walls; and on the exterior facade of the outside entrance were thick beams of wood. ²⁶ There were narrow windows flanked by palm trees on both sides of the entrance; the side-rooms of the house and the thick beams also [had palm trees].

42 ¹ Then he led me into the outer courtyard — the route went north — and brought me to the [block of] rooms opposite the separated yard and opposite the building to the north. ² The length of the front was 175 feet on the north side, where the door was; the width was eighty-seven-and-a-half feet. ³ It was located between the inner courtyard, which was thirty-five feet wide, and the flooring of the outer courtyard. It had galleries, one above the other, on three floors. ⁴ In front of the [block of] rooms was a walkway seventeen-and-a-half feet wide and a path twenty-one inches [wide]; their doors faced north.

⁵ The upper rooms were shorter, because the galleries took up some of their space, more than from the [rooms on the] lower and middle [floors] of the building. ⁶ For the rooms were on three floors, and they didn't have columns like those in the courtyards; therefore space was taken away from the [rooms on the] lower and middle [floors], in comparison with the ground. ⁷ The length of the wall outside, next to the rooms, toward the outer courtyard in front of the rooms, was eighty-seven-and-a-half feet. ⁸ For the length of the rooms toward the outer courtyard was eighty-seven-and-a-half feet, whereas [the length of] the side facing the sanctuary was 175 feet. ⁹ Under these rooms was the entrance to the east side, leading in from the outer courtyard.

¹⁰ In the width of the courtyard wall on the east, facing the separated yard and facing the building, there were rooms, ¹¹ with a passageway in front of them, similar to the rooms on the north. They were the same length and width and had similarly made exits and entrances.

¹² By the entrances of the rooms on the south there was an entrance at the end of the passage, the passageway right in front of the wall, toward the eastern entrances.

¹³ Then he said to me, "The north and south [blocks of] rooms in front of the separated yard are the holy rooms where the *cohanim* who approach A*DONAI* will eat the especially holy things. This is where they will put the especially holy things — the grain offerings, sin offerings and guilt offerings; for the place is holy. ¹⁴ When the *cohanim* come, they will not go out of the [Especially] Holy Place into the outer courtyard; rather, they will leave [in these rooms] the clothes they use when ministering, because they are holy. They will put on other clothes and only then approach the areas permitted to the people."

¹⁵ After he had finished measuring the inner house, he brought me out by way of the gate facing east and measured the whole area. ¹⁶ He measured the east side with the measuring rod; it was 875 feet by the measuring rod. ¹⁷ He measured the north side; it was 875 feet by the measuring rod. ¹⁸ He measured the south side; it was 875 feet by the measuring rod. ¹⁹ He turned to the west side and measured 875 feet with the measuring rod. ²⁰ He measured its four sides; it had a wall around it; and it was 875 [feet] long and 875 [feet] wide. Thus a division was made between what was holy and what was common.

43 ¹ After this, he brought me to the gate facing east. ² There I saw the glory of the God of Isra'el approaching from the east. His voice was like the sound of rushing water, and the earth shone with his glory. ³ The vision seemed like the vision I had seen when I came to destroy the city; also the visions were like the vision I had seen by the K'var River; and I fell on my face. ⁴ ADONAI's glory entered the house through the gate facing east.

⁵ Next, a spirit took me up and brought me into the inner courtyard, and I saw ADONAI's glory fill the house. ⁶ I heard someone speaking to me from the house, and a man was standing by me. ⁷ He said, "Human being, this is the place for my throne, the place for the soles of my feet, where I will live among the people of Isra'el forever. The house of Isra'el, both they and their kings, will never again defile my holy name by their prostitution, by [burying] the corpses of their kings [on] their high places, ⁸ or by placing their threshold next to my threshold and their door-frames next to my door-frames, with only a common wall between me and them. Yes, they defiled my holy name by the disgusting practices they committed; which is why I destroyed them in my anger. ⁹ So now, they should put their prostitution at a distance and the corpses of their kings far away from me; then I will live among them forever.

¹⁰ "You, human being, describe this house to the house of Isra'el, so that they will be ashamed of their crimes. And let them measure accurately. ¹¹ If they become ashamed of all they have done, show them the elevation and plan of the house, its exits and entrances, all its details and decorations, and all its specifications, its design and its *Torah*. Sketch it for them to see, so that they can observe the entire design with its specifications, and carry them out. ¹² This is *Torah* for the house: the whole surrounding area on the mountaintop will be especially holy. This is *Torah* for the house."

¹³ These are the measurements of the altar in cubits (a cubit here is defined as a normal cubit [eighteen inches] plus a handbreadth [three inches]): the base, one cubit [twenty-one inches] deep and one cubit wide; with the molding surrounding it at its rim about a hand-span [nine inches] in width. The height of the altar is thus: ¹⁴ from the base on the ground to the lower ledge, three-and-a-half feet, with the width twenty-one inches; from the lower ledge to the upper ledge, seven feet, with the width again twenty-one inches. ¹⁵ The hearth measures seven feet [high], with four horns on top of the hearth. ¹⁶ The hearth is a square twenty-one feet on each of its four sides. ¹⁷ The ledge measures a square twenty-four-and-a-half feet on each of its four sides; the molding around it ten-and-a-half inches [across]; and its base twenty-one inches [larger than the rest, all the way] around. Its steps face east.

¹⁸ He said to me, "Human being, Adonai ELOHIM says, 'These are the regulations for the altar when the time comes to construct it, offer burnt offerings on it and splash the blood against it: ¹⁹ you are to give to the *cohanim*, who are L'vi'im descended from Tzadok and who approach to serve me,' says Adonai ELOHIM, 'a young bull as a sin offering. ²⁰ You are to take its blood and put it on the four horns of the altar, on the four corners of the ledge and on the molding all the way around; this is how you will purify it and make atonement for it. ²¹ You are also to take the bull which is the sin offering and have it burned up at the designated place [on the grounds] of the house, outside the sanctuary. ²² On the second day you are to offer a male goat without defect as a sin offering, and they are to purify the altar as they purified it with the bull. ²³ When you have finished purifying it, you are to offer a young bull

without defect and a ram from the flock without defect. ²⁴ You are to present them before *Adonai*, and the *cohanim* will throw salt on them and offer them as a burnt offering to *Adonai*. ²⁵ Every day, for seven days, you are to prepare a goat as a sin offering; they are also to prepare a young bull and a ram from the flock without defect. ²⁶ For seven days, they are to make atonement for the altar and cleanse it; in this way they are to consecrate it. ²⁷ When these days are over, then, on the eighth day and afterwards, the *cohanim* will present your burnt offerings on the altar and your peace offerings; and I will accept you,' says *Adonai Elohim*."

44 ¹ Then he brought me back by way of the outer gate of the sanctuary, the one facing east; and it was shut. ² *Adonai* said to me, "This gate will remain shut; it will not be opened, and no one will go through it; because *Adonai*, the God of Isra'el, has gone through it. Therefore, it is to be kept shut. ³ Only the prince, since he is a prince, is to sit there to eat his meal before *Adonai*; he is to enter through the vestibule of the gate and leave the same way."

⁴ Then he brought me through the north gate to the front of the house. I looked, saw *Adonai*'s glory filling the house of *Adonai*, and fell on my face. ⁵ *Adonai* said to me, "Human being, pay attention; see with your eyes and hear with your ears everything I tell you about all the regulations of *Adonai*'s house and about all its *Torah*; pay attention to who can enter the house and who must be excluded from the sanctuary. ⁶ You are to tell the rebels, the house of Isra'el, that this is what *Adonai Elohim* says: 'House of Isra'el, enough of all your disgusting practices! ⁷ You brought in foreigners, uncircumcised in both heart and flesh, to be in my sanctuary and profane it — yes, my house — when you offered my food, the fat and the blood; thus in addition to all your disgusting practices, they broke my covenant. ⁸ Instead of taking care of my holy things yourselves, you have put these people in charge of my sanctuary.' ⁹ Here is what *Adonai Elohim* says: 'No foreigner, uncircumcised in both heart and flesh, is to enter my sanctuary — no foreigner living among the people of Isra'el.

¹⁰ "'Rather, the *L'vi'im*, who went far away from me when Isra'el went astray, going astray after their idols — they will bear the consequences of their guilt, ¹¹ but they are to serve in my sanctuary. They will have charge of the gates of the house and of serving in the house; they will slaughter the burnt offering and the sacrifice for the people; and they will attend and serve them. ¹² Because they served them in the presence of their idols and became an occasion of sin for the house of Isra'el, I am raising my hand against them,' says *Adonai Elohim*, 'and they will bear the consequences of their guilt. ¹³ They will not approach me to serve me in the office of *cohen* or approach any of the holy things or the especially holy things; but they will bear their shame for the disgusting practices they committed. ¹⁴ Yet I will put them in charge of the house and all its maintenance and everything to be done in it.

¹⁵ "'However, the *cohanim*, who are *L'vi'im* and descendants of Tzadok, who took care of my sanctuary when the people of Isra'el went astray from me — they are the ones who will approach me and serve me; it is they who will attend me and offer me the fat and the blood,' says *Adonai Elohim*. ¹⁶ 'They will enter my sanctuary, approach my table to minister to me and perform my service.

¹⁷ "'Once they enter the gates of the inner courtyard, they are to wear linen clothing; they are not to wear any wool while serving at the gates of the inner courtyard or inside it. ¹⁸ They are to wear linen turbans on their heads and linen

underclothes on their bodies, and they are not to wear anything that makes them sweat. [19] Before going out to the people in the outer courtyard, they are to remove the clothes in which they minister, lay them in the holy rooms, and put on other clothes; so that they won't transmit holiness to the people by means of their clothing. [20] They are not to shave their heads or let their hair grow long, but must keep their hair carefully trimmed. [21] No *cohen* is to drink wine when he enters the inner courtyard. [22] They may not marry a widow or a divorcee but must marry virgins descended from the house of Isra'el or a widow whose deceased husband was a *cohen*.

[23] "'They are to teach my people the difference between holy and common and enable them to distinguish between clean and unclean. [24] They are to be judges in controversies, and they are to render decisions in keeping with my rulings. At all my designated festivals they are to keep my laws and regulations, and they are to keep my *shabbat*s holy. [25] They are not to come to any dead person, because this would make them unclean; however, for father, mother, son, daughter, brother or sister who has had no husband they may make themselves unclean. [26] After a *cohen* has been purified, he is to wait seven days. [27] Then, on the day he enters the sanctuary, when he goes into the inner courtyard to minister in the sanctuary, he is to offer his sin offering,' says *Adonai* ELOHIM.

[28] "'Their inheritance is to be this: I myself am their inheritance. You are not to grant them any possession in Isra'el — I myself am their possession. [29] They are to eat the grain offerings, sin offerings and guilt offerings; and everything in Isra'el devoted [to God] will be theirs. [30] The first of all the firstfruits of everything, and every voluntary contribution of everything, from all your offerings, will be for the *cohanim*. You are also to give the *cohen* the first of your dough, so that a blessing will rest on your house. [31] The *cohanim* are not to eat anything, bird or animal, that dies naturally or is torn to death.

45 [1] "'When you divide the land by lot for inheritance, you are to set aside an offering for *Adonai*, a holy portion of the land. Its length is to be 25,000 [cubits, that is, eight miles] and its width 10,000 [three miles]; this entire region is to be holy. [2] Of this there is to be reserved for the holy place an area 875 [feet] square, with eighty-seven-and-a-half feet for open land around it. [3] Alongside this region you are to measure a length of eight [miles] and a width of three [miles]; in it is to be the sanctuary, which will be especially holy. [4] It is a holy portion of the land; it is for the *cohanim* who serve in the sanctuary, who approach to minister to *Adonai*; there will be a place for their houses and a place set aside for the sanctuary. [5] A portion eight by three [miles] will be owned by the *L'vi'im* who serve in the house; it will also have twenty [gatekeepers'] rooms. [6] You are to give the city possession of an area, alongside the offering of the holy portion, one-and-a-half by eight [miles]; it will be for the whole house of Isra'el.

[7] "'The prince is to have the territory on both sides of the holy offering and the city's holding; it will extend westward to the western border of the land and eastward to its eastern border; and the length [from the far side of one] of its two parts [to the far side of the other] will be the same as the length of one of the [tribal] portions. [8] His possession in Isra'el will be limited to this, and henceforth my princes will not wrong my people but will give the land to the house of Isra'el according to their tribes.' [9] *Adonai* ELOHIM says this: 'Princes of Isra'el, that should be enough for you!

701

Get rid of violence and looting, do what is right and just, and stop evicting my people from their land!' says *Adonai* ELOHIM.

¹⁰ "'You are to have honest balance-scales, an honest *eifah* [a one-bushel dry-measure] and an honest *bat* [a five-gallon liquid-measure]. ¹¹ The *eifah* and the *bat* are to contain the same volume — the *bat* is to contain one-tenth of a *homer*, and the *eifah* is to contain one-tenth of a *homer*; the *homer* is to set the standard for measurement. ¹² Also the *shekel* is to be twenty *gerah*s; your *maneh* will be the sum of a twenty-*shekel* piece, a twenty-five-*shekel* piece and a fifteen-*shekel* piece.

¹³ "'This is the offering you are to make: one-sixth of a bushel from every ten bushels of wheat, and you are to give one-sixth of a bushel from every ten bushels of barley. ¹⁴ The law for olive oil is to be half a gallon from every fifty gallons, which is the same as ten *bat*s or one *homer*, since ten *bat*s equal a *homer*. ¹⁵ From the flock, take one sheep from every two hundred being pastured in Isra'el; [all these are to be used] for grain offerings, burnt offerings and peace offerings, to make atonement for them,' says *Adonai* ELOHIM. ¹⁶ 'All the people in the land are to present this offering to the prince in Isra'el. ¹⁷ The prince's obligation will be to present the burnt offerings, grain offerings and drink offerings at the feasts, on *Rosh-Hodesh*, and on *Shabbat* — at all the designated times of the house of Isra'el. He is to prepare the sin offerings, grain offerings, burnt offerings and peace offerings to make atonement for the house of Isra'el.'

¹⁸ "*Adonai* ELOHIM says this: 'On the first day of the first month you are to take a young bull without defect and purify the sanctuary. ¹⁹ The *cohen* will take some of the blood from the sin offering and put it on the door-frames of the house, on the four corners of the altar's ledge and on the supports of the gate of the inner courtyard. ²⁰ You are also to do this on the seventh day of the month for everyone who has sinned inadvertently or through ignorance. Thus you will make atonement for the house.

²¹ "'On the fourteenth day of the first month you are to have the *Pesach*, a feast seven days long; *matzah* will be eaten. ²² On that day the prince will provide, for himself and for all the people of the land, a young bull as a sin offering. ²³ On the seven days of the feast he is to provide a burnt offering for *Adonai*, seven young bulls and seven rams without defect daily for the seven days, and a male goat daily as a sin offering. ²⁴ He is to provide as a grain offering a bushel [of grain] for a young bull and a bushel for a ram, and for each bushel [of grain] a gallon of olive oil.

²⁵ "'On the fifteenth day of the seventh month, during the feast [of Sukkot] he is to do the same thing for those seven days in regard to the sin offerings, burnt offerings, grain offerings and olive oil.'

46 ¹ "This is what *Adonai* ELOHIM says: 'The east gate of the inner courtyard is to be shut on the six working days, but on *Shabbat* it is to be opened, and on *Rosh-Hodesh* it is to be opened. ² The prince is to enter by way of the outer vestibule of the gate and stand by the support of the gate. The *cohanim* are to prepare his burnt offering and peace offerings. Then he is to prostrate himself in worship at the threshold of the gate, after which he is to leave; but the gate is not to be shut until evening. ³ The people of the land are also to prostrate themselves in worship before *Adonai* at the entrance to that gate on *Shabbat* and on *Rosh-Hodesh*.

⁴ "'The burnt offering the prince is to offer *Adonai* on *Shabbat* is to consist of six lambs without defect and a ram without defect. ⁵ The grain offering is to be a bushel for the ram, while for the lambs it can be as much as he wants to give; with a gallon

of olive oil per *eifah*. ⁶ On *Rosh-Hodesh* it is to be a young bull, six lambs and a ram, all without defect. ⁷ He is to prepare a grain offering consisting of a bushel for the bull, a bushel for the ram, and for the lambs as his means allow; with a gallon of olive oil per bushel.

⁸ "'When the prince enters, he is to go in by way of the vestibule of the gate, and he is to leave the same way. ⁹ But when the people of the land come before A*DONAI* at the designated times, whoever comes in to worship by way of the north gate is to leave by way of the south gate, and whoever comes in by way of the south gate is to leave by way of the north gate; he is not to go back out through the gate by which he entered but is to exit straight ahead of him. ¹⁰ [On these occasions,] the prince is to be among them when they enter; and when they leave, they are to leave together.

¹¹ "'At the festivals and at designated times, the grain offering is to be a bushel for a young bull and a bushel for a ram, while for the lambs it can be as much as he wants to give, with a gallon of olive oil per bushel.

¹² "'When the prince provides a voluntary offering, whether it is a burnt offering or peace offerings that he offers voluntarily to A*DONAI*, someone is to open the east gate for him; and he is to provide his burnt offering and peace offerings as he does on *Shabbat*. Then he will leave; and after he leaves, the gate is to be shut.

¹³ "'You are to provide a lamb in its first year that has no defect for a daily burnt offering to A*DONAI*; do this each morning. ¹⁴ Also each morning, provide with it a grain offering, one-sixth of a bushel, and one-third of a gallon of olive oil to moisten the fine flour; this is the ongoing grain offering for A*DONAI*, by a permanent regulation. ¹⁵ Thus they will offer a lamb, a grain offering and oil each morning as the ongoing burnt offering.'

¹⁶ "*Adonai* E*LOHIM* says this: 'If the prince turns over part of his hereditary property to one of his sons, it is his inheritance; it will belong to his sons; it is their possession by inheritance. ¹⁷ But if he gives part of his hereditary property to one of his slaves, it will be his until the year of freedom, at which time it will revert to the prince, so that the prince's heritage will go to his sons. ¹⁸ The prince is not to take over any of the people's inheritance, thereby evicting them wrongfully from their property; he is to give his sons an inheritance out of his own property, so that none of my people will be driven off their property.'"

¹⁹ Next, he brought me through the entry at the side of the gate into the holy rooms facing north that were for the *cohanim*. At their far west end I saw a place ²⁰ about which he said to me, "This is the place where the *cohanim* will boil the guilt offerings and sin offerings and bake the grain offerings. In this way they won't have to bring them into the outer courtyard and risk transmitting holiness to the people." ²¹ He took me into the outer courtyard and had me pass by the four corners of the courtyard, and there in each corner of the courtyard was another courtyard — ²² in the four corners of the courtyard were enclosed courtyards seventy feet long and fifty-two-and-a-half feet; the four courtyards in the corners were the same size. ²³ There was a wall around each of the four, with open stoves all around the bases of the walls. ²⁴ He said to me, "These are the stoves where those serving in the house will boil the people's sacrifices."

47 ¹ Then he brought me back to the entrance of the house, and I saw water flowing eastward from under the threshold of the house, for the house faced east. The water flowed down from under the right side of the house, south of the altar. [2] Next he led me out through the north gate and took me around outside to the outer gate, by way of the east gate, where I saw water trickling from the south side. [3] With a line in his hand the man went out toward the east and measured a thousand cubits [one-third of a mile] and had me wade across the stream; the water came up to my ankles. [4] He measured another thousand and had me wade through the water, which reached my knees. He measured another thousand and had me wade through water up to my waist. [5] Finally he measured a thousand, and it was a river I couldn't cross on foot, because the water was so deep one would have to swim across; it was a river that could not be waded through. [6] He asked me, "Human being, have you seen this?" Then, guiding me, he got me back to the riverbank. [7] After being returned, I saw on the bank of the river a great number of trees on the one side and on the other. [8] He said to me, "This water flows toward the eastern region and continues down to the 'Aravah. When it enters the sea, the sea of stagnant water, [the Dead Sea,] its water will become fresh. [9] When this happens, swarms of all kinds of living creatures will be able to live in it wherever the streams flow; so that there will be a vast number of fish; for this water is flowing there, so that, wherever the river goes, everything will be restored and able to live. [10] Then fishermen will stand on its shores spreading their nets all the way from 'Ein-Gedi to 'Ein-'Eglayim. There will be as many kinds of fish there as in the Great Sea, [the Mediterranean,] a great variety. [11] However, its mud flats and marshes will not become fresh but will remain salty. [12] On both riverbanks will grow all kinds of trees for food; their leaves will not dry up, nor will their fruit fail. There will be a different kind of fruit each month, because the water flows from the sanctuary, so that this fruit will be edible, and the leaves will have healing properties."

[13] "*Adonai Elohim* says this: 'These are the borders of the land you are to distribute for inheritance by the twelve tribes of Isra'el, with Yosef receiving two portions. [14] For inheritance you will each have equal shares. I swore to your ancestors that I would give them this land, and now it falls to you to inherit it.

[15] "'The borders of the land will be as follows: on the north, from the Great Sea through Hetlon to the entrance of Tz'dad, [16] Hamat, Berotah, Sibrayim (which is between the border of Dammesek and the border of Hamat), Hatzer-Hatikhon (which is toward the border of Havran). [17] The border from the sea will be Hatzar-'Einon (at the border of Dammesek); while on the north, northward, is the border of Hamat. This is the north side.

[18] "'On the east side, measure between Havran and Dammesek, Gil'ad and the land of Isra'el by the Yarden, from the border to the eastern sea. This is the east side.

[19] "'On the side of the Negev toward the south it will be from Tamar as far as the waters of M'rivot-Kadesh, then to the *Vadi* [of Egypt] and on to the Great Sea. This is the south side toward the Negev.

[20] "'The west side will be the Great Sea, as far as across from the entrance to Hamat. This is the west side.

[21] "'This is the territory you are to divide among the tribes of Isra'el. [22] You are to divide it by lot as an inheritance both to you and to the foreigners living among you who give birth to children living among you; for you they are to be no different from the native-born among the people of Isra'el — they are to have an inheritance with you among the tribes of Isra'el. [23] You are to give the foreigner an inheritance in the territory of the tribe with whom he is living,' says *Adonai Elohim*.

48 ¹ "'Following is the list of tribes:

"'This is Dan's territory: from the north end, through Hetlon to the entrance of Hamat, Hatzar-'Einan (at the border of Dammesek), northward, next to Hamat; and they will have their sides east and west.

² "'Asher's territory will run alongside the territory of Dan from east to west.

³ "'Naftali's territory will run alongside the territory of Asher from east to west.

⁴ "'M'nasheh's territory will run alongside the territory of Naftali from east to west.

⁵ "'Efrayim's territory will run alongside the territory of M'nasheh from east to west.

⁶ "'Re'uven's territory will run alongside the territory of Efrayim from east to west.

⁷ "'Y'hudah's territory will run alongside the territory of Re'uven from east to west.

⁸ "'Alongside the territory of Y'hudah, from east to west, will be the offering you are to set aside, 25,000 [cubits] wide [eight miles], and in length equal to distance between the east and west boundaries of one of the portions, with the sanctuary inside it. ⁹ The offering you are to set aside for ADONAI is to be eight [miles] long and three wide. ¹⁰ This holy offering will be for the *cohanim*; it will be eight [miles] in length along its north and south sides and three in width along its west and east sides; ADONAI's sanctuary will be inside it. ¹¹ The portion set aside as holy will be for the *cohanim* who are descendants of Tzadok that remained faithful to my commission and did not go astray when the people of Isra'el and the *L'vi'im* went astray. ¹² It is to be an especially holy portion set apart for them and taken from the offering of the land, next to the border of the *L'vi'im*.

¹³ "'Alongside the territory for the *cohanim*, the *L'vi'im* are to have a portion eight [miles] long and three wide — its total length will be eight and its width three. ¹⁴ They may not sell, exchange or alienate any of this choice land; because it is holy, for ADONAI.

¹⁵ "'The 5,000 [cubits, that is, the one-and-a-half miles] that are left of the width is to be for the common use of the city, for housing and for open fields. The city will be inside it. ¹⁶ and will measure 4,500 cubits [just under one-and-a-half miles] along each of its sides — north, south, east and west. ¹⁷ The city is to have outside it a border of land 440 feet wide on each side — north, south, east and west. ¹⁸ A strip next to the holy offering extending three [miles] to the east and three to the west is to be left. This area by the holy offering is to be used to grow food for those serving the city. ¹⁹ The people from all the tribes of Isra'el who serve in the city will farm it. ²⁰ The entire offering will be eight [miles] square, including the section for the city.

²¹ "'What remains will be for the prince — the land on the two sides of the holy offering and section for the city, that is, the portion eastward from the eight [miles] of the offering's eastern border to the land's eastern border and the portion westward from the eight [miles] of the offering's western border to the land's western border — this land adjacent to the [tribal] portions will be for the prince, with the holy offering and the sanctuary of the house inside it. ²² Thus the land belonging to the *L'vi'im* and the section for the city will be inside that which belongs to the prince.

"'The territory belonging to the prince will be between the territory of Y'hudah and the territory of Binyamin — ²³ which brings us to the rest of the tribes:

"'Binyamin's territory will run from east to west.

²⁴ "'Shim'on's territory will run alongside the territory of Binyamin from east to west.

²⁵ "'Yissakhar's territory will run alongside the territory of Shim'on from east to west.

²⁶ "'Z'vulun's territory will run alongside the territory of Yissakhar from east to west.

²⁷ "'Gad's territory will run alongside the territory of Z'vulun from east to west.

²⁸ "'Alongside the territory of Gad, from the Negev southward, the border will run from Tamar to the water at M'rivat-Kadesh, then to the *Vadi* [of Egypt], and on to the Great Sea. ²⁹ This is the land you are to distribute by lot to the tribes of Isra'el for inheritance, and these are their portions,' says *Adonai Elohim*.

³⁰⁻³⁴ "These are the city exits; they are to be named after the tribes of Isra'el, three gates on each of the four sides; the four sides each measure just under one-and-a-half [miles]: on the north, gates named after Re'uven, Y'hudah and Levi; on the east, gates named after Yosef, Binyamin and Dan; on the south, gates named after Shim'on, Yissakhar and Z'vulun; and on the west, gates named after Gad, Asher and Naftali.

³⁵ "'The perimeter of [the city] will be just under six [miles] long. And from that day on the name of the city will be *Adonai* Shamah [*Adonai* is there].'"

Hoshea
HOSEA

1 ¹ This is the word of ADONAI that came to Hoshea the son of Be'eri during the reigns of 'Uziyah, Yotam, Achaz and Y'chizkiyah, kings of Y'hudah, and during the reign of Yarov'am the son of Yo'ash, king of Isra'el. ² ADONAI's opening words in speaking to Hoshea were to instruct Hoshea,

> "Go, marry a whore,
> and have children with this whore;
> for the land is engaged in flagrant whoring,
> whoring away from ADONAI."

³ So he went and married Gomer the daughter of Divlayim, and she conceived and bore him a son. ⁴ ADONAI said to him, "Call him Yizre'el, because in only a short time I will punish the house of Yehu for having shed blood at Yizre'el; I will put an end to the kingdom of the house of Isra'el. ⁵ When that day comes, I will break the bow of Isra'el in the Yizre'el Valley."

⁶ She conceived again and bore a daughter. ADONAI said to him, "Name her Lo-Ruchamah [unpitied], for I will no longer have pity on the house of Isra'el. By no means will I forgive them. ⁷ But I will pity the house of Y'hudah; I will save them not by bow, sword, battle, horses or cavalry, but by ADONAI their God."

⁸ After weaning Lo-Ruchamah, she conceived and bore a son. ⁹ ADONAI said, "Name him Lo-'Ammi [not-my-people], because you are not my people, and I will not be your [God].

2 ¹⁽¹:¹⁰⁾ "Nevertheless, the people of Isra'el will number as many as the grains of sand by the sea, which cannot be measured or counted; so that the time will come when, instead of being told, 'You are not my people,' it will be said to them, 'You are the children of the living God.' ²⁽¹:¹¹⁾ Then the people of Y'hudah and the people of Isra'el will be gathered together; they will appoint for themselves one leader; and they will go up out of the land; for that will be a great day, [the day] of Yizre'el.

³⁽¹⁾ "Say to your brothers, '*Ammi* [My People]!'
and to your sisters, '*Ruchamah* [Pitied]!'

⁴⁽²⁾ Rebuke your mother, rebuke her;
for she isn't my wife, and I'm not her husband.
She must remove her whoring from her face,

and her adulteries from between her breasts.

5(3)
Otherwise, I will strip her naked
and place her as she was the day she was born,
make her like a desert, place her like a dry land
and kill her with thirst.

6(4)
I will have no pity on her children,
for they are children of whoring —

7(5)
their mother prostituted herself,
she who conceived them behaved shamelessly;
she said, 'I will pursue my lovers,
who give me my food and water,
wool, flax, olive oil and wine.'

8(6)
Therefore, I will block her way with thorns
and put up a hedge so she can't find her paths.

9(7)
She will pursue her lovers but not catch them.
She will seek them but won't find them.
Then she will say, 'I will go
and return to my first husband;
because things were better for me then
than they are now.'

10(8)
For she doesn't know it was I who gave her
the grain, the wine and the oil;
I who increased her silver and gold,
which they used for Ba'al.

11(9)
So I will take back my grain at harvest-time
and my wine in its season;
I will snatch away my wool and flax,
given to cover her naked body.

12(10)
Now I will uncover her shame,
while her lovers watch;
and no one will save her from me.

13(11)
I will end her happiness,
her festivals, *Rosh-Hodesh*, and *shabbat*s,
and all her designated times.

14(12)
I will ravage her vines and fig trees,
of which she says, 'These are my wages
that my lovers have given me.'
But I will turn them into a forest,
and wild animals will eat them.

15(13)
I will punish her for offering incense
on the feast days of the *ba'alim*,
when she decked herself with her earrings and jewels,
pursuing her lovers and forgetting me," says ADONAI.

16(14)
"But now I am going to woo her —
I will bring her out to the desert
and I will speak to her heart.

17(15)
I will give her her vineyards from there

and the Akhor Valley as a gateway to hope.
She will respond there as she did when young,
as she did when she came up from Egypt.

18(16) "On that day," says ADONAI
"you will call me *Ishi* [My Husband];
you will no longer call me *Ba'ali* [My Master].

19(17) For I will remove the names
of the *ba'alim* from her mouth;
they will never again be mentioned by name.

20(18) When that day comes, I will make
a covenant for them
with the wild animals, the birds in the air
and the creeping things of the earth.
I will break bow and sword,
sweep battle from the land,
and make them lie down securely.

21(19) I will betroth you to me forever;
yes, I will betroth you to me
in righteousness, in justice,
in grace and in compassion;

22(20) I will betroth you to me in faithfulness,
and you will know ADONAI.

23(21) When that day comes,
I will answer," says ADONAI
"I will answer the sky,
and it will answer the earth;

24(22) the earth will answer the corn, wine and oil,
and they will answer *Yizre'el* [God will sow].

25(23) I will sow her for me in the land.
I will have pity on *Lo-Ruchamah* [Unpitied];
I will say to *Lo-'Ammi* [Not-My-People], 'You are my people';
and they will say, 'You are my God.'"

3 ¹ ADONAI said to me, "Go once more, and show love to [this] wife [of yours]
who has been loved by her boyfriend, to this adulteress — just as ADONAI loves
the people of Isra'el, even though they turn to other gods and love the raisin cakes
[offered to them]."

² So I bought her back for myself with fifteen pieces of silver and eight bushels
of barley . ³ Then I told her, "You are to remain in seclusion for a long time and be
mine. You are not to be a prostitute, and you are not to be with any other man; and I
won't come in to have sex with you either." ⁴ For the people of Isra'el are going to be
in seclusion for a long time without a king, prince, sacrifice, standing-stone, ritual
vest or household gods. ⁵ Afterwards, the people of Isra'el will repent and seek ADONAI
their God and David their king; they will come trembling to ADONAI and his goodness
in the *acharit-hayamim*.

4 [1]   Hear the word of *ADONAI*,
    people of Isra'el!
    For *ADONAI* has a grievance
    against the inhabitants of the land:
    there is no truth, no faithful love
    or knowledge of God in the land;
[2]   only swearing and lying, killing and stealing
    and committing adultery!
    They break all bounds, with one blood crime
    following another.
[3]   Therefore the land mourns,
    and everyone living there languishes,
    wild animals too, and the birds in the air;
    even the fish in the sea are removed.
[4]   But no one should quarrel or rebuke,
    because your people are having to quarrel with the *cohen*.
[5]   Therefore you will stumble by day,
    and the prophet will stumble with you at night.

    "I will destroy your mother.
[6]   My people are destroyed for want of knowledge.
    Because you rejected knowledge,
    I will also reject you as *cohen* for me.
    Because you forgot the *Torah* of your God,
    I will also forget your children.
[7]   The more they increased in number,
    the more they sinned against me.
    I will change their glory into shame.
[8]   They feed on the sin of my people
    and are greedy for their crimes.
[9]   But the *cohen* will fare
    no better than the people;
    I will punish him for his ways
    and pay him back for his deeds.
[10]   They will eat but not have enough
    and consort with whores but have no children,
    because they stopped listening to *ADONAI*.
[11]   Whoring and wine, both old and new,
    take away my people's wits.
[12]   My people consult their piece of wood,
    their diviner's wand speaks to them;
    for the spirit of whoring makes them err,
    they go off whoring, deserting their God.
[13]   They sacrifice on the mountain peaks
    and offer incense on the hills
    under oaks, poplars and pistachio trees;
    because they give good shade.

Therefore your daughters behave like whores,
And your daughters-in-law commit adultery.
¹⁴ I won't punish your daughters when they act like whores,
or your daughters-in-law when they commit adultery;
because the men are themselves going off with whores
and sacrificing with prostitutes.
Yes, a people without understanding
will come to ruin."

¹⁵ If you, Isra'el, prostitute yourself,
still Y'hudah has no need to incur such guilt.
Don't go to Gilgal or up to Beit-Aven,
and don't swear, "As ADONAI lives."
¹⁶ For Isra'el is stubborn as a stubborn cow;
will ADONAI now feed them like a lamb in a big pasture?
¹⁷ Efrayim is joined to idols;
let him alone!
¹⁸ When they finish carousing, they start their whoring;
their rulers deeply love dishonor.
¹⁹ The wind will carry them off in its wings
and their sacrifices bring them nothing but shame.

5 ¹ "Hear this, *cohanim!*
Pay attention, house of Isra'el!
Listen, house of the king!
For judgment is coming to you.
You have become a snare for Mitzpah
and a net spread on Tavor.
² The rebels have deepened their slaughter,
and I am rejected by all of them.

³ "I know Efrayim;
Isra'el is not hidden from me;
for now, Efrayim, you are a whore;
Isra'el is defiled."

⁴ Their deeds will not allow them
to return to their God,
for the spirit of whoring is in them,
and they don't know ADONAI.
⁵ Isra'el's arrogance will testify in his face;
Isra'el and Efrayim will stumble in their crimes;
Y'hudah too will stumble with them.
⁶ With their flocks and herds
they will go in search of ADONAI.
But they won't find him;
he has withdrawn from them.

7 They have betrayed ADONAI,
by fathering foreign children.
Now within the month the invaders
will devour their lands.

8 "Blow the *shofar* in Giv'ah,
a trumpet at Ramah;
sound an alarm at Beit-Aven:
'Behind you, Binyamin!'

9 Efrayim will be laid waste
when the day for punishment comes;
I am announcing to the tribes of Isra'el
what will surely happen.

10 The leaders of Y'hudah are like men
who move boundary stones;
I will pour my fury out
upon them like water.

11 Efrayim is oppressed, crushed by the judgment,
because he deliberately sought out futility.

12 Therefore I am like a moth to Efrayim
and like rottenness to the house of Y'hudah.

13 When Efrayim saw his sickness
and Y'hudah his wound,
Efrayim went to Ashur
and sent envoys to a warring king;
but he can't heal you
or cure your wound.

14 For to Efrayim I will be like a lion,
and like a young lion to the house of Y'hudah —
I will tear them up and go away;
I will carry them off, and no one will rescue.

15 I will go and return to my place,
till they admit their guilt and search for me,
seeking me eagerly in their distress."

6 1 Come, let us return to ADONAI;
for he has torn, and he will heal us;
he has struck, and he will bind our wounds.

2 After two days, he will revive us;
on the third day, he will raise us up;
and we will live in his presence.

3 Let us know, let us strive to know ADONAI.
That he will come is as certain as morning;
he will come to us like the rain,
like the spring rains that water the earth.

4 "Efrayim, what should I do to you?
Y'hudah, what should I do to you?

For your 'faithful love' is like a morning cloud,
like dew that disappears quickly.

5   This is why I have cut them to pieces by the prophets,
slaughtered them with the words from my mouth —
the judgment on you shines out like light.

6   For what I desire is mercy, not sacrifices,
knowledge of God more than burnt offerings.

7   "But they, just like men, have broken the covenant,
they have been faithless in dealing with me.

8   Gil'ad is a city of criminals,
covered with bloody footprints;

9   just as bands of robbers wait to ambush someone,
so does a gang of *cohanim.*
They commit murder on the road to Sh'khem!
Their conduct is an outrage!

10   In the house of Isra'el
I have seen a horrible thing;
whoring is found there in Efrayim,
Isra'el is defiled.

11   For you, too, Y'hudah,
a harvest will come!

7 1   "When I restore the fortunes of my people,
when I am ready to heal Isra'el,
the crimes of Efrayim confront me,
along with the wickedness of Shomron.
For they keep practicing deceit;
thieves break in, bands of robbers raid outside.

2   They never say to themselves
that I remember all their evil.
Now their own deeds surround them;
they are right in front of me.

3   They make the king glad with their wickedness,
and the leaders with their lies.

4   They are all adulterers,
like an oven heated by the baker,
who doesn't stoke the fire
from kneading time till the dough has risen.

5   "On their king's special day
the leaders inflame him with wine,
and he joins hands with scorners,

6   who ready themselves like an oven
while they wait for their chance.
Their baker sleeps through the night;
then in the morning it bursts into flame.

7 They are all as hot as an oven,
and they devour their judges.
All their kings have fallen;
not one of them calls out to me.

8 "Efrayim mixes himself with the peoples,
Efrayim has become a half-baked cake.

9 Foreigners have eaten up his strength,
but he doesn't know it;
yes, gray hairs appear on him here and there,
but he doesn't know it.

10 The pride of Isra'el testifies in his face,
but in spite of all this they haven't returned
to ADONAI their God or sought him.

11 Efrayim behaves like a silly, foolish dove —
going to Egypt, then to Ashur for help.

12 Even as they go, I will spread my net over them;
I will bring them down like birds from the sky;
I will discipline them, as their assembly was told.

13 Woe to them! for they have strayed from me.
Destruction to them! for they have wronged me.
Am I supposed to redeem them,
when they have spoken lies against me?

14 They have not cried out to me from their hearts,
even though they wail on their beds.
They assemble themselves for grain and wine,
yet turn away from me.

15 It was I who trained and strengthened their arms,
yet they plot evil against me.

16 They return, but not upward;
they are like an unreliable bow.
Their leaders will die by the sword
because of their angry talk.
They will become a laughingstock
in the land of Egypt.

8 1 "Put the *shofar* to your lips!
Like a vulture [he swoops down] on the house of ADONAI,
because they have violated my covenant
and sinned intentionally against my *Torah*.

2 Will they cry out to me,
'We are Isra'el, God, we know you'?

3 Isra'el has thrown away what is good;
the enemy will pursue him.

4 They make kings, but without my authority;
they appoint leaders, but without my knowledge.
With their silver and gold they make themselves idols,
but these can lead only to their own destruction.

714

5   Your calf, Shomron, has been thrown away;
    my fury burns against them.
    How long will it be until they are able
    to make themselves clean?

6   Here is what Isra'el produces:
    a craftsman makes something — it's a non-god;
    the calf of Shomron will be broken to pieces.

7   For they sow the wind,
    so they will reap the whirlwind.
    The standing grain has no ears,
    so it will yield no flour;
    and if it does yield any,
    foreigners will swallow it up.

8   Isra'el is swallowed up;
    now they are among the *Goyim*
    like a vessel nobody wants.

9   For they have gone up to Ashur;
    like a wild donkey, alone by itself,
    Efrayim has bargained for lovers.

10 But even if they bargain among the *Goyim*,
    now I will round them up.
    Soon they will start to feel the burden
    of these kings and leaders.

11 For Efrayim keeps building altars for sin;
    yes, altars are sinful for him.

12 I write him so many things from my *Torah*,
    yet he considers them foreign.

13 They offer me sacrifices of flesh and eat them,
    but *Adonai* does not accept them.
    Now he will recall their crimes and punish their sins —
    they will return to Egypt.

14 For Isra'el forgot his maker and built palaces;
    and Y'hudah made more fortified cities;
    but I will send fire on his cities,
    and it will consume their strongholds."

9 1 Don't rejoice, Isra'el!
    Don't enjoy yourselves as other peoples do;
    for you have gone whoring away from your God,
    you love being hired as a whore on every grain-floor.

2   Threshing-floor and winepress won't feed them,
    and new wine will disappoint her.

3   They won't remain in the land of *Adonai*;
    instead, Efrayim will return to Egypt,
    and they will eat unclean food in Ashur.

4   They will not pour out wine offerings to *Adonai*;
    they will not be pleasing to him.

Their sacrifices will be for them like mourners' food —
everyone eating it will be polluted.
For their food will be merely to satisfy their appetite;
it will not come into the house of ADONAI.

5   What will you do at a designated time,
on a day which is a festival for ADONAI?
6   For suppose they escape the destruction —
Egypt will round them up,
Memphis will bury them.
And their precious treasures of silver?
Nettles will possess them,
thorns will be in their tents.
7   The days of punishment have come,
the days of retribution are here,
and Isra'el knows it.
[Yet they cry,] "The prophet is a fool,
the man of the spirit has gone crazy!"
Because your iniquity is so great,
the hostility [against you] is great.
8   The watchman of Efrayim is with my God,
but a prophet has a fowler's snare set on all his paths
and hostility even in the house of his God.
9   They have deeply corrupted themselves,
as in the days of Giv'ah.
He will remember their guilt,
and he will punish their sins.

10   "When I found Isra'el, it was like finding
grapes in the desert;
when I saw your ancestors, it was like seeing
a fig tree's first figs in its first season.
But as soon as they came to Ba'al-P'or,
they dedicated themselves to something shameful;
they became as loathsome
as the thing they loved.
11   The glory of Efrayim will fly away like a bird —
no birth, no pregnancy, no conception.
12   Even if they raise their children,
I will destroy them till none is left —
and woe to them when I leave them, too!"

13   Efrayim, as I see it, is like Tzor,
planted in a pleasant place;
but Efrayim will bring out his children
to the slaughterer.
14   ADONAI, give them — what will you give?
Give them wombs that miscarry and dried-up breasts!

15 "All their wickedness was already there in Gilgal;
that's where I came to hate them.
Because of the wickedness of their deeds
I will expel them from my house,
I will love them no more;
all their leaders are rebels.

16 Efrayim has been struck down,
their root has been dried up,
they will bear no fruit.
Even if they do give birth,
I will kill their cherished offspring."

17 My God will cast them aside,
because they wouldn't listen to him,
and they will become wanderers
among the *Goyim*.

10 1 Isra'el was a luxuriant vine,
freely putting forth fruit.
As his fruit increased,
he increased his altars;
as his land got better,
he improved his standing-stones.

2 Their heart is divided;
now they will bear their guilt.
He will break down their altars
and destroy their standing-stones.

3 For now they will say,
"We have no king,
because we didn't fear A*DONAI* —
and what could a king do for us, anyway?"

4 They mouth words,
swearing falsely, making treaties.
Thus judgment spreads like poisonous weeds
in the furrows of a field.

5 The inhabitants of Shomron are frightened
of the calf-gods of Beit-Aven.
Its people mourn over it;
its priests tremble over it,
over its glory, which has left it.

6 It will be carried to Ashur
as a present for a warring king.
Efrayim will be put to shame,
and Isra'el be ashamed of his own advice.

7 Shomron's king will perish
like foam on the surface of the water.

8 Destruction will come to the high places of Aven,
  that is, to the sin of Isra'el.
  Thorns and thistles will grow over their altars;
  and they will say to the mountains, "Cover us!"
  and to the hills, "Fall on us!"

9 "Since the days of Giv'ah you have sinned, Isra'el.
  There they took their stand.
  For these arrogant people at Giv'ah,
  war was insufficient punishment.

10 When I wish to, I will discipline them;
  and the peoples will be gathered against them
  to discipline them for their two crimes."

11 Efrayim is a well-taught cow —
  it loves to tread the grain,
  and I have spared her fair neck.
  But I will put Efrayim in harness,
  Y'hudah will have to plow,
  Ya'akov will harrow his own land.

12 If you sow righteousness for yourselves,
  you will reap according to grace.
  Break up unused ground for yourselves,
  because it is time to seek ADONAI,
  till he comes and rains down
  righteousness upon you.

13 You have plowed wickedness, reaped iniquity
  and eaten the fruit of lies.
  Because you trusted in your own way,
  in your large numbers of warriors,

14 turmoil will erupt among your peoples,
  and all your fortresses will be destroyed;
  just as Shalman destroyed Beit-Arbel
  on the day of battle,
  when mothers were dashed to pieces
  right along with their children.

15 Thus will be done to you, Beit-El,
  because of your great wickedness;
  at dawn the king of Isra'el
  will be completely cut off.

11 1 "When Isra'el was a child, I loved him;
  and out of Egypt I called my son.

2 But the more [the prophets] called them,
  the farther they went from them.
  They sacrificed to the *ba'alim*
  and offered incense to idols.

3   "Yet it was I who taught Efrayim to walk;
    I took them by their arms.
    But they did not know that it was I
    who was healing them,
4   who was guiding them on through human means
    with reins made of love.
    With them I was like someone removing
    the yoke from their jaws,
    and I bent down to feed them.
5   He will not return to the land of Egypt,
    but Ashur will be his king,
    because they refused to repent.
6   The sword will fall on his cities,
    destroying the bars of his gates,
    because they follow their own advice.
7   My people are hanging in suspense
    about returning to me;
    and though they call them upwards,
    nobody makes a move.
8   Efrayim, how can I give you up,
    or surrender you, Isra'el?
    How could I treat you like Admah
    or make you like Tzvoyim?
    My heart recoils at the idea,
    as compassion warms within me.
9   I will not give vent to the fierceness of my rage,
    I will not return to destroy Efrayim;
    for I am God, not a human being,
    the Holy One among you;
    so I will not come in fury.
10   They will go after ADONAI,
    who will roar like a lion;
    for he will roar, and the children will come
    trembling from the west.
11   They will tremble like a bird as they come from Egypt,
    like a dove as they come from the land of Ashur;
    and I will resettle them in their own houses,

says ADONAI.

12 ¹⁽¹¹:¹²⁾ "Efrayim surrounds me with lies
    and the house of Isra'el with deceit.
    Y'hudah still rules with God
    and is faithful with holy ones.
2(1)   Efrayim is chasing the wind,
    pursuing the wind from the east.
    All day he piles up lies and desolation —

they make a covenant with Ashur,
while sending olive oil to Egypt.

3(2)   *Adonai* also has a grievance against Y'hudah;
he will punish Ya'akov according to his ways
and pay him back for his misdeeds.

4(3)   In the womb he took his brother by the heel;
in the strength of his manhood he fought with God.

5(4)   Yes, he fought with an angel and won;
he wept and pleaded with him.
Then at Beit-El he found him,
and there he would [later] speak with us —

6(5)   Adonai *Elohei-Tzva'ot*;
Adonai is his name!

7(6)   So you, return to your God;
hold fast to grace and justice;
and always put your hope in your God.

8(7)   "A huckster keeps false scales,
and he loves to cheat.

9(8)   Efrayim says, 'I have gotten so rich!
I have made me a fortune!
And in all my profits no one will find
anything wrong or sinful.'

10(9)   "But I am *Adonai* your God,
from the land of Egypt.
Again I will make you live in tents,
as in the days of the established festival.

11(10)   I have spoken to the prophets;
it was I who gave vision after vision;
through the prophets I gave examples
to show what it would all be like.

12(11)   Is Gil'ad given to iniquity?
Yes, they have become worthless.
In Gilgal they sacrifice to bulls;
therefore their altars are like piles of stones
in a plowed field."

13(12)   Ya'akov fled to the land of Aram.
There Isra'el slaved to win a wife;
for a wife he tended sheep.

14(13)   By a prophet *Adonai* brought Isra'el up from Egypt,
and by a prophet he was protected.

15(14)   Efrayim has given bitter provocation,
so the penalty for his bloodshed will be thrown down on him,
and his Lord will repay him for his insult.

13 ¹ "When Efrayim spoke, there was trembling;
he was a power in Isra'el.
But when he incurred guilt through Ba'al,
he died.

² So now they keep adding sin to sin,
casting images from their silver;
idols they invent for themselves,
all of them the work of craftsmen.
'Sacrifice to them,' they say.
Men give kisses to calves!

³ Therefore they will be like a morning cloud,
like the dew that disappears early,
like chaff blown by wind from the threshing-floor,
or like smoke that goes out the window.

⁴ Still, I am *ADONAI* your God,
from the land of Egypt;
and you don't know any God but me
or, other than me, any Savior.

⁵ I knew you in the desert,
in a land of terrible drought.

⁶ When they were fed, they were satisfied;
when satisfied, they became proud.
Therefore they forgot me.

⁷ So now I have become like a lion to them;
like a leopard I will lurk by the road;

⁸ I will meet them like a bear
whose cubs have been taken away.
I will tear their hearts from their bodies.
I will devour them there like a lion,
like a wild animal ripping them up.

⁹ It is your destruction, Isra'el,
although your help is in me.

¹⁰ So now, where is your king,
to save you in all your cities?
Where are your judges, of whom you said,
'Give me a king and leaders'?

¹¹ I gave you a king in my anger;
and in my fury I took him away.

¹² "Efrayim's guilt has been wrapped up,
his sin is stored away.

¹³ The pain of being born will come to him;
but he is an unwise son.
The time has come; and he shouldn't delay,
there at the mouth of the womb.

¹⁴ Should I ransom them from the power of Sh'ol?
Should I redeem them from death?

Where are your plagues, death;
where is your destruction, Sh'ol?
My eyes are closed to compassion.
15 For though he flourishes among the reeds,
an east wind will come, a wind from ADONAI,
blowing up from the desert.
Then his water source will dry up,
then his spring will fail —
it will plunder his treasury,
removing every precious thing."

14 1(13:16) Shomron will bear her guilt,
for she has rebelled against her God.
They will fall by the sword,
their little ones will be dashed to pieces
and their pregnant women ripped open.

2(1) Return, Isra'el, to ADONAI your God,
for your guilt has made you stumble.

3(2) Take words with you, and return to ADONAI;
say to him, "Forgive all guilt,
and accept what is good;
we will pay instead of bulls
[the offerings of] our lips.

4(3) Ashur will not save us,
we will not ride on horses,
and we will no longer call
what we made with our hands our gods.
For it is only in you
that the fatherless can find mercy."

5(4) "I will heal their disloyalty,
I will love them freely;
for my anger has turned from him.

6(5) I will be like dew to Isra'el;
he will blossom like a lily
and strike roots like the L'vanon.

7(6) His branches will spread out,
his beauty be like an olive tree
and his fragrance like the L'vanon.

8(7) Again they will live in his shade and raise grain;
they will blossom like a vine,
and its aroma will be
like the wine of the L'vanon.

9(8) Efrayim [will say], 'What have I
to do any more with idols?'
And I, I answer and affirm him;

I am like a fresh, green cypress tree;
your fruitfulness comes from me."

10(9) Let the wise understand these things,
and let the discerning know them.
For the ways of ADONAI are straight,
And the righteous walk in them,
but in them sinners stumble.

Yo'el
JOEL

1 1 The word of ADONAI that came to Yo'el the son of P'tu'el:

2 "Hear this, you leaders!
Listen, all who live in the land!
Has anything like this ever happened in your days,
or in your ancestors' days?

3 Tell your children about it,
and have them tell it to theirs,
and have them tell the next generation.

4 What the cutter-worms left, the locusts ate;
what the locusts left, the grasshoppers ate;
what the grasshoppers left, the shearer-worms ate.

5 Wake up, drunkards, and weep!
wail, all you who drink wine,
because the juice of the grape
will be withheld from your mouth.

6 For a mighty and numberless nation
has invaded my land.
His teeth are lion's teeth;
his fangs are those of a lioness.

7 He has reduced my vines to waste,
my fig trees to splinters —
he plucked them bare, stripped their bark
and left their branches white."

8 Lament like a virgin wearing sackcloth
for the husband of her youth!

9 Grain offering and drink offering are cut off
from the house of ADONAI.
The *cohanim* are mourning,
those who are serving ADONAI.

723

10   The fields are ruined, the ground is grieving;
for the grain is ruined, the new wine dried up,
and the olive oil is wretched.

11   Despair, you farmers; lament, vinedressers,
over the wheat and the barley —
the harvest from the fields is lost.

12   The vines have withered, the fig trees wilted,
also the pomegranate, date-palm and apple tree —
all the trees in the fields have withered,
and the people's joy has withered away.

13   *Cohanim*, put on sackcloth, and weep!
Wail, you who serve at the altar!
Come, lie in sackcloth all night long,
you who serve my God!
For the grain offering and drink offering are withheld
from the house of your God.

14   Proclaim a holy fast,
call for a solemn assembly,
gather the leaders
and all who live in the land
to the house of *Adonai* your God,
and cry out to *Adonai*,

15   "Oh no! The Day!
The Day of *Adonai* is upon us!
As destruction from *Shaddai*
it is coming!

16   The food is cut off before our very eyes,
also joy and gladness from the house of our God.

17   The seed-grain is rotting in its furrows;
the granaries are deserted, the barns in ruins;
because the grain has withered.

18   How the animals groan!
The herds of cattle are perplexed,
because they have no pasture.
The flocks of sheep bear the punishment, too.

19   *Adonai*, I cry out to you!
For the fire has consumed the pastures in the desert,
and the flame set ablaze all the trees in the fields.

20   Even the wild animals
come to you, panting,
because the streambeds have dried up,
and fire has consumed the pastures in the desert."

2 ¹   "Blow the *shofar* in Tziyon!
Sound an alarm on my holy mountain!"

724

Let all living in the land tremble,
for the Day of *Adonai* is coming! It's upon us! —

2 a day of darkness and gloom,
a day of clouds and thick fog;
a great and mighty horde is spreading
like blackness over the mountains.
There has never been anything like it,
nor will there ever be again,
not even after the years
of many generations.

3 Ahead of them a fire devours,
behind them a flame consumes;
ahead the land is like Gan-'Eden,
behind them a desert waste.
From them there is no escape.

4 They look like horses,
and like cavalry they charge.

5 With a rumble like that of chariots
they leap over the mountaintops,
like crackling flames devouring stubble,
like a mighty horde in battle array.

6 At their presence the peoples writhe in anguish,
every face is drained of color.

7 Like warriors they charge,
they scale the wall like soldiers.
Each one keeps to his own course,
without getting in the other's way.

8 They don't jostle each other,
but stay on their own paths;
they burst through defenses unharmed,
without even breaking rank.

9 They rush into the city,
they run along the wall,
they climb up into the houses,
entering like a thief through the windows.

10 At their advance the earth quakes,
and the sky shakes,
the sun and moon turn black,
and the stars stop shining.

11 *Adonai* shouts orders to his forces —
his army is immense, mighty,
and it does what he says.
For great is the Day of *Adonai*, fearsome,
terrifying! Who can endure it?

12 "Yet even now," says *Adonai*,
"turn to me with all your heart,

13 with fasting, weeping and lamenting."
Tear your heart, not your garments;
and turn to ADONAI your God.
For he is merciful and compassionate,
slow to anger, rich in grace,
and willing to change his mind about disaster.

14 Who knows? He may turn, change his mind
and leave a blessing behind him,
[enough for] grain offerings and drink offerings
to present to ADONAI your God.

15 "Blow the *shofar* in Tziyon!
Proclaim a holy fast,
call for a solemn assembly."

16 Gather the people; consecrate the congregation;
assemble the leaders; gather the children,
even infants sucking at the breast;
let the bridegroom leave his room
and the bride the bridal chamber.

17 Let the *cohanim*, who serve ADONAI,
stand weeping between the vestibule and the altar.
Let them say, "Spare your people, ADONAI!
Don't expose your heritage to mockery,
or make them a byward among the *Goyim*.
Why should the peoples say, 'Where is their God?'"

18 Then ADONAI will become jealous for his land
and have pity on his people.

19 Here is how ADONAI will answer his people:
"I will send you grain, wine and olive oil,
enough to satisfy you;
and no longer will I make you
a mockery among the *Goyim*.

20 No, I will take the northerner away,
far away from you,
and drive him to a land
that is waste and barren;
with his vanguard toward the eastern sea
and his rearguard toward the western sea,
his stench and his rottenness will rise,
because he has done great things."

21 Don't fear, O soil; be glad! rejoice!
for ADONAI has done great things.

22 Don't be afraid, wild animals;
for the desert pastures are green,

the trees are putting out their fruit,
the fig tree and vine are giving full yield.

23 Be glad, people of Tziyon!
rejoice in ADONAI your God!
For he is giving you
the right amount of rain in the fall,
he makes the rain come down for you,
the fall and spring rains — this is what he does first.

24 Then the floors will be full of grain
and the vats overflow with wine and olive oil.

25 "I will restore to you the years that the locusts ate,
the grasshoppers, shearer-worms and cutter-worms,
my great army that I sent against you.

26 You will eat until you are satisfied
and will praise the name of ADONAI your God,
who has done with you such wonders.
Then my people will never again be shamed.

27 You will know that I am with Isra'el
and that I am ADONAI your God,
and that there is no other.
Then my people will never again be shamed.

3 1(2:28) "After this, I will pour out
my Spirit on all humanity.
Your sons and daughters will prophesy,
your old men will dream dreams, your young men will see visions;

2(2:29) and also on male and female slaves
in those days I will pour out my Spirit.

3(2:30) I will show wonders in the sky and on earth —
blood, fire and columns of smoke.

4(2:31) The sun will be turned into darkness
and the moon into blood
before the coming of the great
and terrible Day of ADONAI."

5(2:32) At that time, whoever calls
on the name of ADONAI will be saved.
For in Mount Tziyon and Yerushalayim
there will be those who escape,
as ADONAI has promised;
among the survivors will be those
whom ADONAI has called.

4(3) 1 "For then, at that time, when I restore
the fortunes of Y'hudah and Yerushalayim,

2 I will gather all nations and bring them down

to the Valley of Y'hoshafat [ADONAI judges].
I will enter into judgment there
for my people, my heritage Isra'el,
whom they scattered among the nations;
then they divided my land.

3 They drew lots for my people,
traded boys for whores,
sold girls for wine to drink.

4 "Moreover, what have you against me,
Tzor, Tzidon, all parts of P'leshet?
Are you paying me back for something I did?
If you're paying me back for something I did,
then easily, quickly, I'll pay you back
right on your own head.

5 You took my silver and gold.
You brought my good treasures into your temples.

6 The people of Y'hudah and Yerushalayim
you sold to the Greeks, so that you could remove them
far away from their land.

7 I will rouse them from the place where you sold them
and pay you back right on your own head —

8 I will sell your sons and daughters
to the people of Y'hudah;
and they will sell them to the men of Sh'va,
a nation far off; for ADONAI has spoken.

9 "Proclaim this among the nations:
'Prepare for war! Rouse the warriors!
Let all the fighting men approach and attack.'

10 Hammer your plow-blades into swords
and your pruning-knives into spears.
Let the weak say, 'I am strong.'

11 Hurry, come, you surrounding nations,
gather yourselves together!"

Bring your warriors down, ADONAI!

12 "Let the nations be roused and come up
to the Valley of Y'hoshafat [ADONAI judges].
For there I will sit to judge
all the surrounding nations."

13 Swing the sickle, for the harvest is ripe;
come, and tread, for the winepress is full.
The vats are overflowing,
for their wickedness is great.

14 Such enormous crowds
in the Valley of Decision!
For the Day of ADONAI is upon us
in the Valley of Decision!

15 The sun and moon have grown black,
and the stars have stopped shining.

16 ADONAI will roar from Tziyon,
he will thunder from Yerushalayim,
the sky and the earth will shake.

But ADONAI will be a refuge for his people,
a stronghold for the people of Isra'el.

17 "You will know that I am ADONAI your God,
living on Tziyon my holy mountain."

Then Yerushalayim will be holy,
and foreigners will pass through her no more.

18 Then, when that time comes,
the mountains will drip with sweet wine,
the hills will flow with milk,
all the streambeds of Y'hudah will run with water,
and a spring will flow from the house of ADONAI
to water the Sheetim Valley.

19 But Egypt will be desolate
and Edom a desert waste,
because of the violence done to the people of Y'hudah,
because they shed innocent blood in their land.

20 Y'hudah will be inhabited forever,
Yerushalayim through all generations.

21 "I will cleanse them of bloodguilt
which I have not yet cleansed,"
for ADONAI is living in Tziyon.

'Amos
AMOS

1 [1] The words of 'Amos, one of the sheep owners in T'koa, which he saw concerning Isra'el in the days of 'Uziyah king of Y'hudah and Yarov'am the son of Yo'ash, king of Isra'el, two years before the earthquake; [2] he said:

ADONAI is roaring from Tziyon
thundering from Yerushalayim;
the shepherds' pastures will mourn,
and Mount Karmel's summit will wither.

³ Here is what ADONAI says:

"For Dammesek's three crimes,
no, four — I will not reverse it —
because they threshed Gil'ad
with an iron-spiked threshing-sledge;
⁴ I will send fire to the house of Haza'el,
and it will consume the palaces of Ben-Hadad.
⁵ I will break the bars of Dammesek's gates.
I will cut off the inhabitants from Bik'at-Aven,
and him who holds the scepter from Beit-'Eden.
Then the people of Aram will go into exile
in Kir," says ADONAI.

⁶ Here is what ADONAI says:

"For 'Azah's three crimes,
no, four — I will not reverse it —
because they exiled a whole population
and handed them over to Edom;
⁷ I will send fire to the wall of 'Azah,
and it will consume its palaces.
⁸ I will cut off the inhabitant from Ashdod,
and him who holds the scepter from Ashkelon.
I will turn my hand against 'Ekron,
and the rest of the P'lishtim will perish,"
says ADONAI, God.

⁹ Here is what ADONAI says:

"For Tzor's three crimes,
no, four — I will not reverse it —
because they exiled a whole population to Edom
and did not remember the covenant with kinsmen;
¹⁰ I will send fire to the wall of Tzor,
and it will consume its palaces."

¹¹ Here is what ADONAI says:

"For Edom's three crimes,
no, four — I will not reverse it —
because with sword he pursued his kinsman

and threw aside all pity,
constantly nursing his anger,
forever fomenting his fury;
¹² I will send fire on Teman,
and it will consume the palaces of Botzrah."

¹³ Here is what ADONAI says:

"For the people of 'Amon's three crimes,
no, four — I will not reverse it —
because they ripped apart pregnant women
just to expand their territory,
¹⁴ I will set fire to the wall of Rabbah,
and it will consume its palaces
amid shouts on the day of battle,
amid a storm on the day of the whirlwind.
¹⁵ Their king will go into exile,
he and his princes together," says ADONAI.

2 ¹ Here is what ADONAI says:

"For Mo'av's three crimes,
no, four — I will not reverse it —
because he burned the bones of the king of Edom,
turning them into lime;
² I will send fire on Mo'av,
and it will consume the palaces of K'riot.
Mo'av will die with turmoil and shouting,
along with the sound of the *shofar*.
³ I will cut off the judge from among them
and kill all his princes with him," says ADONAI.

⁴ Here is what ADONAI says:

"For Y'hudah's three crimes,
no, four — I will not reverse it —
because they rejected ADONAI's *Torah*
and haven't observed his laws,
and their lies caused them to fall into error
and live the way their ancestors did;
⁵ I will send fire on Y'hudah,
and it will consume the palaces of Yerushalayim.

⁶ Here is what ADONAI says:

"For Isra'el's three crimes,
no, four — I will not reverse it —

because they sell the upright for silver
and the poor for a pair of shoes,

7 grinding the heads of the poor in the dust
and pushing the lowly out of the way;
father and son sleep with the same girl,
profaning my holy name;

8 lying down beside any altar
on clothes taken in pledge;
drinking wine in the house of their God
bought with fines they imposed.

9 "I destroyed the Emori before them;
though tall as cedars and strong as oaks,
I destroyed their fruit above
and their root below.

10 More than that, I brought you up from Egypt,
led you forty years in the desert,
so that you could have the Emori's land.

11 I raised up some of your sons to be prophets,
other young men of yours to be n'zirim.
People of Isra'el!
Isn't that true?" asks ADONAI.

12 But you gave the n'zirim wine to drink
and ordered the prophets, 'Don't prophesy!'

13 "Enough! I will make all this crush you,
just as a cart overloaded with grain
crushes what's under it.

14 Even the swift won't be able to flee;
the strong won't be able to use their strength,
the warriors won't save themselves.

15 Archers won't be able to stand,
the fastest runners won't save themselves,
those on horses won't save themselves.

16 On that day even the bravest warriors
will throw off their weapons and flee," says ADONAI.

3 ¹ "Listen to this word which ADONAI has spoken against you, people of Isra'el,
against the entire family that I brought up from the land of Egypt:

2 "Of all the families on earth,
only you have I intimately known.
This is why I will punish you
for all your crimes."

3 Do two people travel together
without having so agreed?

4 Does a lion roar in the forest
when it has no prey?

Does a young lion growl in his lair
if it has caught nothing?

5 Does a bird get caught in a trap on the ground
if it hasn't been baited?
Does a trap spring up from the ground
when it has taken nothing?

6 When the *shofar* is blown in the city,
don't the people tremble?
Can disaster befall a city
without ADONAI's having done it?

7 ADONAI, God, does nothing without
revealing his plan to his servants the prophets.

8 The lion has roared. Who will not fear?
ADONAI, God, has spoken. Who will not prophesy?

9 "Proclaim it on the palaces in Ashdod
and on the palaces in the land of Egypt; say:
'Assemble yourselves on the hills of Shomron!
See what great tumult is seething within it,
how much oppression is being done there.'

10 For they don't know how to do right," says ADONAI.
"They store up violence and robbery in their palaces."

11 Therefore, here is what *Adonai ELOHIM* says:

"An enemy will surround the land.
He will strip you of your strength,
and plunder your palaces."

12 This is what ADONAI says:

13 "As a shepherd rescues from the mouth of a lion
a couple of leg bones or a piece of an ear;
so the people of Isra'el in Shomron will be rescued,
huddled under cushions in the corners of their beds.

"Hear, and testify against the house of Ya'akov,"
says *Adonai ELOHIM Elohei-Tzva'ot.*

14 "For when I punish Isra'el's crimes,
I will also punish the altars of Beit-El.
The horns of the altar will be cut off,
and they will fall to the ground.

15 I will tear down winter houses
as well as summer houses;
houses adorned with ivory will be destroyed;
the mansions will be no more," says ADONAI.

4 1   "Listen, you [lovely] cows of Bashan,
who live on Mount Shomron,
who oppress the poor and grind down the needy,
who say to their husbands, 'Bring something to drink':
2   *Adonai* ELOHIM has sworn by his holiness
that your time is surely coming.

"You will be dragged away with hooks,
the last of you with fishhooks.
3   You will leave through breaks in the wall,
each woman right behind the next,
and be sent off to Harmonah," says ADONAI.

4   "Come to Beit-El, and commit crimes;
to Gilgal, and commit more crimes!
Bring your sacrifices in the morning
and your tithes after three days;
5   burn leavened bread as a thank offering;
brag in public about your voluntary offerings;
because that's what you love to do, Isra'el!"
says *Adonai* ELOHIM.

6   "I made your teeth clean of food in all your cities,
left you nothing to eat in all your villages;
still you haven't returned to me," says ADONAI.

7   "I withheld the rain from you
three months before the harvest.
I made it rain on one city
and not on another —
one field had rain,
while another with no rain dried up;
8   from two or three cities they would stagger to one city
for water to drink, but there wasn't enough;
still you haven't returned to me," says ADONAI.

9   "I struck your crops with hot winds and blight,
your many gardens and vineyards;
the cutter-worms devoured
your fig and olive trees;
still you haven't returned to me," says ADONAI.

10   "I sent a plague on you like that of Egypt,
put your young men to death with the sword;
let your horses be captured;
and filled your nostrils with the stench of your camps;
still you haven't returned to me," says ADONAI.

¹¹ "I overthrew some of you,
as when God overthrew S'dom and 'Amora;
you were like a burning stick snatched from the fire;
still you haven't returned to me," says ADONAI.

¹² "This is why I will deal with you in this way, Isra'el;
and because I will deal with you in this way,
prepare to meet your God, Isra'el —
¹³ him who forms mountains and creates wind,
who declares to humankind his thoughts,
who turns the morning to darkness
and strides on the heights of the earth —
Adonai ELOHEI-Tzva'ot is his name."

5 ¹ Hear this word that I take up against you
in lament, house of Isra'el:

² The virgin of Isra'el has fallen;
she will not rise again.
She lies abandoned on her own soil
with no one to lift her up.

³ For thus says *Adonai ELOHIM*:
"The city from which a thousand marched
will be left with a hundred,
and the one from which a hundred marched
will be left with ten
from the house of Isra'el."

⁴ For here is what ADONAI says
to the house of Isra'el:
"If you seek me, you will survive;
⁵ but don't seek Beit-El, or enter Gilgal
or pass on into Be'er-Sheva;
for Gilgal will certainly go into exile,
and Beit-El will come to nothing."

⁶ If you seek ADONAI, you will survive.
Otherwise, he will break out against
the house of Yosef like fire,
devouring Beit-El,
with no one to quench the flames.

⁷ You who turn justice to bitter wormwood
and throw righteousness to the ground!
⁸ He who made the Pleiades and Orion,
who brings deathlike shadows over the morning,

who darkens the day into night,
who calls for the water in the sea
and with it floods the earth —
ADONAI is his name —

9   he flashes destruction on the strong,
so that destruction overcomes the fortress.

10   They hate anyone promoting justice
at the city gate,
they detest anyone who speaks the truth.

11   Therefore, because you trample on the poor
and extort from them levies of grain;
although you have built houses of cut stone,
you will not live in them;
and though you have planted pleasant vineyards,
you will not drink their wine.

12   For I know how numerous are your crimes
and how outrageous your sins —
bullying the innocent, extorting ransoms
pushing the poor aside at the gate.

13   At times like these a prudent person stays silent,
for it is an evil time.

14   Seek good and not evil, so that you will survive.
Then *Adonai ELOHEI-Tzva'ot* will be with you,
as you say he is.

15   Hate evil, love good, and uphold justice at the gate.
Maybe *Adonai ELOHEI-Tzva'ot*
will take pity on the survivors of Yosef.

¹⁶ Therefore thus says *Adonai ELOHEI-Tzva'ot, Adonai*:

"In all public squares there will be lamentation,
in all the streets they will cry, 'Oh, no!'
They will summon farmers to mourn
and professional mourners to wail.

17   There will be wailing in every vineyard,
for I will pass through among you," says *ADONAI*.

18   Woe to you who want the Day of *ADONAI*!
Why do you want it, this Day of *ADONAI*?
It is darkness, not light;

19   as if someone were to run from a lion,
just to be met by a bear;
as if he entered a house, put his hand on the wall,
just to be bitten by a snake.

20 Won't the Day of *Adonai* be darkness, not light,
completely dark, with no brightness at all?

21 "I hate, I utterly loathe your festivals;
I take no pleasure in your solemn assemblies.

22 If you offer me burnt offerings and grain offerings,
I will not accept them;
nor will I consider the peace offerings
of your stall-fed cattle.

23 Spare me the noise of your songs!
I don't want to hear the strumming of your lutes!

24 Instead, let justice well up like water,
and righteousness like an ever-flowing stream.

25 Did you bring me sacrifices and offerings
in the desert forty years, house of Isra'el?

26 No, but now you will bear Sikkut as your king
and Kiyun, your images,
the star of your god, which you made for yourselves;

27 as I exile you beyond Dammesek,"
says *Adonai Elohei-Tzva'ot* —
that is his name.

6 1 Woe to those living at ease in Tziyon
and to those who feel complacent on the hills of Shomron,
renowned men in this foremost of nations,
to whom the rest of Isra'el come.

2 Travel to Kalneh and see;
from there go on to Hamat the great;
then go down to Gat of the P'lishtim.
Are you better than these kingdoms?
Is their territory larger than yours?

3 You put off all thought of the evil day
but hasten the reign of violence.

4 You lie on beds of ivory
and lounge sprawled out on your couches,
dining on meat from lambs in the flock
and from calves fattened in stalls.

5 You make up wild songs at your parties,
playing the lute and inventing other instruments —
[imagining that you're] like David!

6 You drink wine by the bowlful
and anoint yourselves with the finest oils,
but feel no grief at the ruin of Yosef.

7 Therefore now they will be the first
to go into exile with those being exiled,
and the revelry of those who lounged,
sprawling, will pass away.

8 "*Adonai Elohim* swears by himself,"

says *Adonai ELOHEI-Tzva'ot,*
"I detest that Ya'akov is so proud,
and I hate his palaces.
I will hand over the city,
along with everything in it."

⁹ When that day comes, if ten men remain in one house, they will die. ¹⁰ And if a [dead] man's uncle, coming to bring the corpse out of the house and burn it, finds a survivor hidden in the inmost recesses of the house and asks, "Is anyone else there with you?" — then, when he receives the answer, "No," he will say, "Don't say any more, because we mustn't mention the name of *ADONAI.*"

¹¹ For when *ADONAI* gives the order,
great houses will be shattered
and small houses reduced to rubble.
¹² Do horses run on rock?
Does one plow there with oxen?
Yet you have turned justice into poison
and the fruit of righteousness into bitter wormwood.
¹³ You take pleasure in worthless things.
You think your power comes from your own strength.

¹⁴ "But I will raise up a nation against you, house of Isra'el," says *Adonai ELOHEI-Tzva'ot,* "and they will oppress you from the entrance of Hamat to the *Vadi* of the 'Aravah."

7 ¹ Here is what *Adonai ELOHIM* showed me: he was forming a swarm of locusts as the late crop was starting to come up, the late crop after the hay had been cut to pay the king's tribute. ² While they were finishing up eating all the vegetation in the land, I said,

"*Adonai ELOHIM,* forgive — please!
How will tiny Ya'akov survive?"

³ So *ADONAI* changed his mind about this. "It won't happen," *ADONAI* said.

⁴ Next *Adonai ELOHIM* showed me this: *Adonai ELOHIM* was summoning a blazing fire to consume the great abyss, and it would have devoured the land too. ⁵ But I said,

"*Adonai ELOHIM,* stop — please!
How will tiny Ya'akov survive?"

⁶ *ADONAI* changed his mind about it. "This too won't happen," said *Adonai ELOHIM.*

⁷ Then he showed me this: *Adonai* was standing by a wall made with a plumbline, and he had a plumbline in his hand. ⁸ *ADONAI* asked me, "'Amos, what do you see?" I answered, "A plumbline." Then *Adonai* said,

"I am going to put a plumbline in
among my people Isra'el;

I will never again overlook their offenses.
9   The high places of Yitz'chak will be desolate,
     Isra'el's sanctuaries will be destroyed,
     and I will attack the house
     of Yarov'am with the sword."

¹⁰ Then Amatzyah the priest of Beit-El sent this message to Yarov'am king of Isra'el, "'Amos is conspiring against you there among the people of Isra'el, and the land can't bear all that he's saying. ¹¹ For 'Amos says: 'Yarov'am will die by the sword, and Isra'el will be led away from their land into exile.'" ¹² Amatzyah also said to 'Amos, "Go away, seer! Go back to the land of Y'hudah! Earn your living there; and prophesy there; ¹³ but don't prophesy any more at Beit-El; for this is the king's sanctuary, a royal temple."

¹⁴ 'Amos gave this answer to Amatzyah: "I am not trained as a prophet, and I'm not one of the guild prophets — I own sheep and grow figs. ¹⁵ But ADONAI took me away from following the flock, and ADONAI said to me, 'Go, prophesy to my people Isra'el.' ¹⁶ So now, hear what ADONAI says: 'You say, "Don't prophesy against Isra'el, don't lecture the people of Yitz'chak."' ¹⁷ Therefore ADONAI says this:

'Your wife will become a whore in the city,
your sons and daughters will die by the sword,
your land will be parcelled out with a measuring line,
you yourself will die in an unclean land,
and Isra'el will certainly be exiled from their land.'"

8 ¹ Here is what *Adonai ELOHIM* showed me: there in front of me was a basket of summer fruit. ² He asked, "'Amos, what do you see?" I answered, "A basket of summer [Hebrew: *kayitz*] fruit." Then ADONAI said to me,

"The end [Hebrew: *ketz*] has come for my people,
I will never again overlook their offenses.
3   When that time comes, the songs in the temple
     will be wailings," says *Adonai ELOHIM*.
"There will be many dead bodies;
everywhere silence will reign."

4   Listen, you who swallow the needy
     and destroy the poor of the land!
5   You say, "When will *Rosh-Hodesh* be over,
     so we can market our grain?
     and *Shabbat*, so we can sell wheat?"
     You measure the grain in a small *eifah*,
     but the silver in heavy *shekel*s,
     fixing the scales, so that you can cheat,
6   buying the needy for money
     and the poor for a pair of shoes,
     and sweeping up the refuse of the wheat to sell!"

7   *Adonai* swears by Ya'akov's pride,
"I will forget none of their deeds, ever.

8   Won't the land tremble for this,
and everyone mourn, who lives in the land?
It will all rise, just like the Nile,
be in turmoil and subside, like the Nile in Egypt.

9   "When that time comes," says *Adonai ELOHIM*,
"I will make the sun go down at noon
and darken the earth in broad daylight.

10   I will turn your festivals into mourning
and all your songs into wailing;
I will make you all put sackcloth around your waists
and shave your heads bald in grief.
I will make it like mourning for an only son
and its end like a bitter day.

11   "The time is coming," says *Adonai ELOHIM*,
"when I will send famine over the land,
not a famine of bread or a thirst for water,
but of hearing the words of *Adonai*.

12   People will stagger from sea to sea
and from north to east, running back and forth,
seeking the word of *Adonai*;
but they will not find it.

13   When that time comes, young women and men
will faint from thirst.

14   Those who swear by the sin of Shomron,
who say, 'As your god, Dan, lives,'
and, 'As the way of Be'er-Sheva lives' —
they will fall and never get up again."

9 ¹ I saw *Adonai* standing beside the altar, and he said,

"Strike the tops of the columns until the thresholds shake!
Smash them to pieces on the heads of all the people!
Those who remain I will kill with the sword;
not one of them will succeed in fleeing,
not one of them will escape.

2   If they dig down to Sh'ol,
my hand will haul them out;
if they climb up to heaven,
I will bring them down.

3   If they hide themselves on the top of the Karmel,
I will search them out and capture them there;
If they hide from me at the bottom of the sea,
I will order the serpent to bite them there.

4   If their enemies herd them into exile,
I will order the sword to kill them there.
I will fix my gaze on them
for harm and not for good."

5   For *Adonai ELOHIM-Tzva'ot*
is the one who can melt the earth with his touch,
and make all who live on it mourn.
It will all rise, just like the Nile,
and then subside, like the Nile in Egypt.

6   He builds his upper rooms in heaven
and establishes his sky-vault over the earth.
He summons the waters of the sea
and pours them out over the earth.
ADONAI is his name.

7   "People of Isra'el, are you any different
from the Ethiopians to me?" asks *ADONAI*.
"True, I brought Isra'el up from Egypt,
but I also brought the P'lishtim from Kaftor,
and Aram from Kir.

8   Look, the eyes of *Adonai ELOHIM*
are on the sinful kingdom.
I will wipe it off the face of the earth,
yet I will not completely destroy
the house of Ya'akov," says *ADONAI*.

9   "For when I give the order,
I will shake the house of Isra'el,
there among all the *Goyim*,
as one shakes with a sieve,
letting no grain fall to the ground.

10   All the sinners among my people
who say, 'Disaster will never overtake us
or confront us,' will die by the sword.

11   "When that day comes, I will raise up
the fallen *sukkah* of David.
I will close up its gaps, raise up its ruins
and rebuild it as it used to be,

12   so that Isra'el can possess
what is left of Edom
and of all the nations bearing my name,"
says *ADONAI*, who is doing this.

13   "The days will come," says *ADONAI*,
"when the plowman will overtake the reaper
and the one treading grapes the one sowing seed.
Sweet wine will drip down the mountains,

and all the hills will flow with it.

14 I will restore the fortunes of my people Isra'el;
they will rebuild and inhabit the ruined cities;
they will plant vineyards and drink their wine,
cultivate gardens and eat their fruit.

15 I will plant them on their own soil,
no more to be uprooted
from their land, which I gave them,"
says ADONAI your God.

'Ovadyah
OBADIAH

¹ This is the vision of 'Ovadyah. Here is what *Adonai ELOHIM* says about Edom. As a messenger was being sent among the nations saying, "Come on, let's attack her," we heard a message from *ADONAI*:

2 "I am making you the least of all nations,
you will be beneath contempt.

3 Your proud heart has deceived you,
you whose homes are caves in the cliffs,
who live on the heights and say to yourselves,
'Who can bring me down to the ground?'

4 If you make your nest as high as an eagle's,
even if you place it among the stars,
I will bring you down from there." says ADONAI.

5 If thieves were to come to you,
or if robbers by night
(Oh, how destroyed you are!),
wouldn't they stop when they'd stolen enough?
If grape-pickers came to you,
Wouldn't they leave some grapes for gleaning?

6 But see how 'Esav has been looted,
their secret treasures searched out!

7 Your allies went with you only to the border,
those at peace with you deceived and defeated you,
those who ate your food set a trap for you,
and you couldn't discern it.

8 "When that Day comes," says ADONAI,
"won't I destroy all the wise men of Edom

and leave no discernment on Mount 'Esav?

9   Your warriors, Teman, will be so distraught
that everyone on Mount 'Esav will be slaughtered.

10   For the violence done to your kinsman Ya'akov,
shame will cover you;
and you will be forever cut off.

11   On that day you stood aside,
while strangers carried off his treasure,
and foreigners entered his gates
to cast lots for Yerushalayim —
you were no different from them.

12   You shouldn't have gloated over your kinsman
on their day of disaster
or rejoiced over the people of Y'hudah
on their day of destruction.
You shouldn't have spoken arrogantly
on a day of trouble

13   or entered the gate of my people
on their day of calamity —
no, you shouldn't have gloated over their suffering
on their day of calamity
or laid hands on their treasure
on their day of calamity.

14   You shouldn't have stood at the crossroads
to cut down their fugitives
or handed over their survivors
on a day of trouble."

15   For the Day of *Adonai* is near for all nations;
as you did, it will be done to you;
your dealings will come back on your own head.

16   For just as you have drunk on my holy mountain,
so will all the nations drink in turn;
yes, they will drink and gulp it down
and be as if they had never existed.

17   But on Mount Tziyon there will be
a holy remnant who will escape,
and the house of Ya'akov will repossess
their rightful inheritance.

18   The house of Ya'akov will be a fire
and the house of Yosef a flame,
setting aflame and consuming
the stubble which is the house of 'Esav.
None of the house of 'Esav will remain,
for *Adonai* has spoken.

19   Those in the Negev will repossess

the mountain of 'Esav,
and those in the Sh'felah
the land of the P'lishtim;
they will repossess the field of Efrayim
and the field of Shomron,
and Binyamin will occupy Gil'ad.

20 Those from this army of the people of Isra'el
exiled among the Kena'anim as far away as Tzarfat,
and the exiles from Yerushalayim in S'farad,
will repossess the cities in the Negev.

21 Then the victorious will ascend Mount Tziyon
to rule over Mount 'Esav,
but the kingship will belong to ADONAI.

Yonah
JONAH

1 ¹ The word of ADONAI came to Yonah the son of Amitai: ² "Set out for the great city of Ninveh, and proclaim to it that their wickedness has come to my attention."

³ But Yonah, in order to get away from ADONAI, prepared to escape to Tarshish. He went down to Yafo, found a ship headed for Tarshish, paid the fare and went aboard, intending to travel with them to Tarshish and get away from ADONAI. ⁴ However, ADONAI let loose over the sea a violent wind, which created such stormy conditions that the ship threatened to break to pieces. ⁵ The sailors were frightened, and each cried out to his god. They threw the cargo overboard to make the ship easier for them to control.

Meanwhile, Yonah had gone down below into the hold, where he lay, fast asleep. ⁶ The ship's captain found him and said to him, "What do you mean by sleeping? Get up! Call on your god! Maybe the god will remember us, and we won't die."

⁷ Then they said to each other, "Come, let's draw lots to find out who is to blame for this calamity." They drew lots, and Yonah was singled out. ⁸ They said to him, "Tell us now, why has this calamity come upon us? What work do you do? Where are you from? What is your country? Which is your people?" ⁹ He answered them, "I am a Hebrew; and I fear ADONAI, the God of heaven, who made both the sea and the dry land." ¹⁰ At this the men grew very afraid and said to him, "What is this that you have done?" For the men knew he was trying to get away from ADONAI, since he had told them. ¹¹ They asked him, "What should we do to you, so that the sea will be calm for us?" — for the sea was getting rougher all the time. ¹² "Pick me up," he told them, "and throw me into the sea. Then the sea will be calm for you; because I know it's my fault that this terrible storm has come over you."

[13] Nevertheless, the men rowed hard, trying to reach the shore. But they couldn't, because the sea kept growing wilder against them. [14] Finally they cried to ADONAI, "Please, ADONAI, please! Don't let us perish for causing the death of this man, and don't hold us to account for shedding innocent blood; because you, ADONAI, have done what you saw fit." [15] Then they picked up Yonah and threw him into the sea, and the sea stopped raging. [16] Seized with great fear of ADONAI, they offered a sacrifice to ADONAI and made vows.

2 [1(1:17)] ADONAI prepared a huge fish to swallow Yonah; and Yonah was in the belly of the fish for three days and three nights. [2(1)] From the belly of the fish Yonah prayed to ADONAI his God; [3(2)] he said,

> "Out of my distress I called to ADONAI,
> and he answered me;
> from the belly of Sh'ol I cried,
> and you heard my voice.

[4(3)]
> For you threw me into the deep,
> into the heart of the seas;
> and the flood enveloped me;
> all your surging waves passed over me.

[5(4)]
> I thought, 'I have been banished from your sight.'
> But I will again look at your holy temple.

[6(5)]
> The water surrounded me, threatened my life;
> the deep closed over me, seaweed twined around my head.

[7(6)]
> I was going down to the bottoms of the mountains,
> to a land whose bars would close me in forever;
> but you brought me up alive from the pit,
> ADONAI, my God!

[8(7)]
> As my life was ebbing away,
> I remembered ADONAI;
> and my prayer came in to you,
> into your holy temple.

[9(8)]
> "Those who worship vain idols
> give up their source of mercy;

[10(9)]
> but I, speaking my thanks aloud,
> will sacrifice to you;
> what I have vowed, I will pay.
> Salvation comes from ADONAI!"

[11(10)] Then ADONAI spoke to the fish, and it vomited Yonah out onto dry land.

3 [1] The word of ADONAI came to Yonah a second time: [2] "Set out for the great city of Ninveh, and proclaim to it the message I will give you." [3] So Yonah set out and went to Ninveh, as ADONAI had said. Now Ninveh was such a large city that it took three days just to cross it. [4] Yonah began his entry into the city and had finished only his first day of proclaiming, 'In forty days Ninveh will be overthrown,' [5] when the people of Ninveh believed God. They proclaimed a fast and put on sackcloth, from the greatest of them to the least. ⁶ When the news reached the king of Ninveh, he got up from his throne, took off his robe, put on sackcloth and sat in ashes. ⁷ He then had this proclamation made throughout Ninveh: "By decree of the king and his nobles, no person or animal, herd or flock, is to put anything in his mouth; they are neither to eat nor drink water. ⁸ They must be covered with sackcloth, both people and animals; and they are to cry out to God with all their might — let each of them turn from his evil way and from the violence they practice. ⁹ Who knows? Maybe God will change his mind, relent and turn from his fierce anger; and then we won't perish."

¹⁰ When God saw by their deeds that they had turned from their evil way, he relented and did not bring on them the punishment he had threatened.

4 ¹ But this was very displeasing to Yonah, and he became angry. ² He prayed to ADONAI, "Now, ADONAI, didn't I say this would happen, when I was still in my own country? That's why I tried to get away to Tarshish ahead of time! I knew you were a God who is merciful and compassionate, slow to anger and rich in grace, and that you relent from inflicting punishment. ³ Therefore, ADONAI, please, just take my life away from me; it's better for me to be dead than alive!" ⁴ ADONAI asked, "Is it right for you to be so angry?"

⁵ Yonah left the city and found a place east of the city, where he made himself a shelter and sat down under it, in its shade, to see what would happen to the city. ⁶ ADONAI, God, prepared a castor-bean plant and made it grow up over Yonah to shade his head and relieve his discomfort. So Yonah was delighted with the castor-bean plant. ⁷ But at dawn the next day God prepared a worm, which attacked the castor-bean plant, so that it dried up. ⁸ Then, when the sun rose, God prepared a scorching east wind; and the sun beat down on Yonah's head so hard that he grew faint and begged that he could die, saying, "I would be better off dead than alive."

⁹ God asked Yonah, "Is it right for you to be so angry about the castor-bean plant?" He answered, "Yes, it's right for me to be so angry that I could die!" ¹⁰ ADONAI said, "You're concerned over the castor-bean plant, which cost you no effort; you didn't make it grow; it came up in a night and perished in a night. ¹¹ So shouldn't I be concerned about the great city of Ninveh, in which there are more than 120,000 people who don't know their right hand from their left — not to mention all the animals?"

Mikhah
MICAH

1 ¹ This is the word of ADONAI that came to Mikhah the Morashti during the days of Yotam, Achaz and Y'chizkiyah, kings of Y'hudah, which he saw concerning Shomron and Yerushalayim:

2   Listen, peoples, all of you!
     Pay attention, earth, and everything in it!
     Adonai Elohim will witness against you,
     Adonai, from his holy temple.

3   For — look! — *Adonai* is coming out of his place,
     coming down to tread on the high places of the land.

4   Beneath him the mountains will melt,
     the valleys split open like wax before fire,
     like water poured down a steep slope.

5   All this is because of the crime of Ya'akov
     and the sins of the house of Isra'el.
     What is the crime of Ya'akov?
     Isn't it Shomron?
     And what are the high places of Y'hudah?
     Aren't they Yerushalayim?

6   "So I will make Shomron a heap in the countryside,
     a place for planting vineyards;
     I will pour her stones down into the valley,
     laying bare her foundations.

7   All her carved images will be smashed to pieces,
     all she earned consumed by fire;
     and I will reduce her idols to rubble.
     She amassed them from a whore's wages,
     and as a whore's wages they will be spent again."

8   This is why I howl and wail,
     why I go barefoot and stripped,
     why I howl like the jackals
     and mourn like the ostriches.

9   For her wound cannot be healed,
     and now it is coming to Y'hudah as well;
     it reaches even to the gate of my people,
     to Yerushalayim itself.

10   Don't tell about it in Gat,
     don't shed any tears.
     At Beit-L'afrah [house of dust]
     roll yourself in the dust.

11   Inhabitants of Shafir, pass on your way
     in nakedness and shame.
     The inhabitants of Tza'anan
     have not left yet.
     The wailing of Beit-Ha'etzel
     will remove from you their support.

12   The inhabitants of Marot
     have no hope of anything good;
     for *Adonai* has sent down disaster

to the very gate of Yerushalayim.

13 Harness the chariots to the fastest horses,
inhabitants of Lakhish;
she was the beginning of sin
for the daughter of Tziyon;
for the crimes of Isra'el
are traceable to you.

14 Therefore you must bestow parting gifts
upon Moreshet-Gat.
The houses of Akhziv will disappoint
the kings of Isra'el.

15 Inhabitants of Mareshah,
I have yet to bring you
the one who will [invade and] possess you.
The glory of Isra'el will come to 'Adulam.

16 Shave the hair from your head as you mourn
for the children who were your delight;
make yourselves as bald as vultures,
for they have gone from you into exile.

2 1 Woe to those who think up evil
and plan wickedness as they lie in bed.
When morning comes, they do it,
since they have it in their power.

2 They covet fields and seize them;
they take over houses as well,
doing violence to both owner and house,
to people and their inherited land.

3 Therefore this is what ADONAI says:

"Against this family I am planning an evil
from which you will not withdraw your necks;
nor will you walk with your heads held high,
for it will be an evil time."

4 On that day they will take up a dirge for you;
sadly lamenting, they will wail,
"We are completely ruined!
Our people's land has changed hands.
Our fields are taken away from us;
instead of restoring them, he parcels them out."

5 Therefore, you will have no one
in the assembly of ADONAI
to stretch out a measuring line and restore
the land assigned by lot.

6 "Don't preach!" — thus they preach!

"They shouldn't preach about these things.
Shame will not overtake us" —

7   is this what the house of Ya'akov says?

Adonai has not grown impatient,
and these things are not his doings.
"Rather, my words do only good
to anyone living uprightly.

8   But lately my people behave like an enemy,
stripping both cloaks and tunics
from travelers who thought they were secure,
so that they become like war refugees.

9   You throw my people's women
out of the homes they love.
You deprive their children
of my glory forever.

10   Get up and go! You can't stay here!
Because [the land] is now unclean,
it will destroy you
with a grievous destruction."

11   If a man who walks in wind and falsehood
tells this lie: "I will preach to you
of [how good it is to drink] wine and strong liquor" —
this people will accept him as their preacher!

12   "I will assemble all of you, Ya'akov;
I will gather the remnant of Isra'el,
I will put them together like sheep in a pen,
like a herd in its pasture —
it will hum with the sounds of people."

13   The one breaking through went up before them;
they broke through, passed the gate and went out.
Their king passed on before them;
Adonai was leading them.

3 1   "I said, 'Please listen, leaders of Ya'akov,
rulers of the house of Isra'el:
Shouldn't you know what justice is?

2   Yet you hate what is good and love what is bad.
You strip off their skin from them
and their flesh from their bones,

3   you eat the flesh of my people,
skin them alive, break their bones;
yes, they chop them in pieces,
like flesh in a caldron, like meat in a pot.'"

4   Then they will call to ADONAI,
     but he will not answer them;
     when that time comes, he will hide his face from them,
     because their deeds were so wicked.

5 Here is what ADONAI says in regard to the prophets who cause my people to go
astray, who cry, "Peace" as soon as they are given food to eat but prepare war against
anyone who fails to put something in their mouths:

6   "Therefore you will have night, not vision,
     darkness and not divination;
     the sun will go down on the prophets,
     over them the day will be black."

7   The seers will be put to shame,
     the diviners will be disgraced.
     They will have to cover their mouths,
     because there will be no answer from God.
8   On the other hand, I am full of power
     by the Spirit of ADONAI,
     full of justice and full of might,
     to declare to Ya'akov his crime,
     to Isra'el his sin.
9   Hear this, please, leaders of the house of Ya'akov,
     rulers of the house of Isra'el,
     you who abhor what is just
     and pervert anything that is right,
10   who build up Tziyon with blood
     and Yerushalayim with wickedness.
11   Her leaders sell verdicts for bribes,
     her cohanim teach for a price,
     her prophets divine for money —
     yet they claim to rely on ADONAI!
     "Isn't ADONAI here with us?" they say.
     "No evil can come upon us."
12   Therefore, because of you,
     Tziyon will be plowed under like a field,
     Yerushalayim will become heaps of ruins,
     and the mountain of the house like a forested height.

4 ¹ But in the acharit-hayamim it will come about
     that the mountain of ADONAI's house
     will be established as the most important mountain.
     It will be regarded more highly than the other hills,
     and peoples will stream there.
2   Many Gentiles will go and say,
     "Come, let's go up to the mountain of ADONAI,

to the house of the God of Ya'akov!
He will teach us about his ways,
and we will walk in his paths."
For out of Tziyon will go forth *Torah*,
the word of ADONAI from Yerushalayim.

3   He will judge between many peoples
and arbitrate for many nations far away.
Then they will hammer their swords into plow-blades
and their spears into pruning-knives;
nations will not raise swords at each other,
and they will no longer learn war.

4   Instead, each person will sit under his vine
and fig tree, with no one to upset him,
for the mouth of ADONAI-*Tzva'ot*
has spoken.

5   For all the peoples will walk,
each in the name of its god;
but we will walk in the name of ADONAI
our God forever and ever.

6   "When that day comes," says ADONAI,
"I will assemble the lame
and gather those who were dispersed,
along with those I afflicted.

7   I will make the lame a remnant
and those who were driven off a strong nation."

ADONAI will rule them on Mount Tziyon
from that time forth and forever.

8   You, tower of the flock,
hill of the daughter of Tziyon,
to you your former sovereignty will return,
the royal power of the daughter of Yerushalayim.

9   Why are you now crying out?
Don't you have a king?
Has your counselor been destroyed,
that you are seized with pain like a woman in labor?

10   Be in pain! Work to give birth
like a woman in labor, daughter of Tziyon!
For now you will go out of the city
and live in the wilds till you reach Bavel.
There you will be rescued;
there ADONAI will redeem you
from the power of your enemies.

11   Now many nations have gathered against you;
they say, "Let her be defiled,
let's gloat over Tziyon."

12 But they don't know the thoughts of Adonai,
they don't understand his plan;
for he has gathered them like sheaves
on the threshing-floor.

13 Get up! Start threshing, daughter of Tziyon!
"For I will make your horns like iron
and your hoofs like bronze."
You will crush many peoples
and devote their plunder to Adonai,
their wealth to the Lord of all the earth.

14(5:1) Now gather yourself in troops,
you who are accustomed to being in troops;
they have laid siege to us.
They are striking the judge of Isra'el
on the cheek with a stick.

5 1(2) But you, Beit-Lechem near Efrat,
so small among the clans of Y'hudah,
out of you will come forth to me
the future ruler of Isra'el,
whose origins are far in the past,
back in ancient times.

2(3) Therefore he will give up [Isra'el]
only until she who is in labor gives birth.
Then the rest of his kinsmen
will return to the people of Isra'el.

3(4) He will stand and feed his flock
in the strength of Adonai,
in the majesty of the name
of Adonai his God;
and they will stay put, as he grows great
to the very ends of the earth;

4(5) and this will be peace.
If Ashur invades our land,
if he overruns our fortresses,
we will raise seven shepherds against him,
eight leaders of men.

5(6) They will shepherd the land of Ashur with the sword,
the land of Nimrod at its gates;
and he will rescue us from Ashur
when he invades our land,
when he overruns our borders.

6(7) Then the remnant of Ya'akov,
surrounded by many peoples,
will be like dew from Adonai,
like showers on the grass,

which doesn't wait for a man
or expect anything from mortals.

7(8)   The remnant of Ya'akov among the nations,
surrounded by many peoples,
will be like a lion among forest animals,
like a young lion among flocks of sheep —
if it passes through, tramples and tears to pieces,
there is no one to rescue them.

8(9)   Your hand will be raised over your enemies;
all your adversaries will be destroyed.

9(10)   "When that day comes," says ADONAI,
"I will cut off your horses from among you
and destroy your chariots.

10(11) I will cut off the cities of your land
and lay waste your strongholds.

11(12) I will cut off sorceries from your land;
you will no longer have soothsayers.

12(13) I will cut off your carved images
and standing-stones from among you;
no longer will you worship
what your own hands have made.

13(14) I will pull up your sacred poles from among you
and destroy your enemies.

14(15) I will wreak vengeance in anger and fury
on the nations, because they would not listen."

6 ¹   So listen now to what ADONAI says:
"Stand up and state your case to the mountains,
let the hills hear what you have to say."

²   Listen, mountains, to ADONAI's case;
also you enduring rocks that support the earth!
ADONAI has a case against his people;
he wants to argue it out with Isra'el:

³   "My people, what have I done to you?
How have I wearied you? Answer me!

⁴   I brought you up from the land of Egypt.
I redeemed you from a life of slavery.
I sent Moshe, Aharon
and Miryam to lead you.

⁵   My people, just remember what Balak
the king of Mo'av had planned,
what Bil'am the son of B'or answered him,
[and what happened] between Sheetim and Gilgal —
so that you will understand
the saving deeds of ADONAI."

⁶   "With what can I come before ADONAI

to bow down before God on high?
Should I come before him with burnt offerings?
with calves in their first year?

7   Would *ADONAI* take delight in thousands of rams
with ten thousand rivers of olive oil?
Could I give my firstborn to pay for my crimes,
the fruit of my body for the sin of my soul?"

8   Human being, you have already been told
what is good, what *ADONAI* demands of you —
no more than to act justly, love grace
and walk in purity with your God.

9   The voice of *ADONAI*! He calls to the city —
and it is wisdom to fear your name —
"Listen to the rod and to him who commissioned it.

10   Are there still ill-gotten gains in the house of the wicked?
still the detestable short *eifah*-measure?

11   Should I declare innocent wicked scales
and a bag of fraudulent weights?

12   The rich men there are full of violence,
the inhabitants tell lies,
with tongues of deceit in their mouths.

13   "Therefore, I am starting to strike you down,
to destroy you because of your sins.

14   You will eat but not be satisfied,
with hunger gnawing inside you.
You will conceive but not give birth;
if you do give birth, I will give him to the sword.

15   You will sow but will not reap,
you will press olives but not rub yourself with oil,
likewise you will press grapes but not drink the wine.

16   For you keep the regulations of 'Omri
and all the practices of the house of Ach'av,
modeling yourselves on their advice.
Therefore I will make you an object of horror,
the inhabitants of this city a cause for contempt;
you will suffer the insults aimed at my people."

7 ¹   Woe to me! for I have become
like the leavings of summer fruit,
like the gleanings when the vintage is finished —
there isn't a cluster worth eating,
no early-ripened fig that appeals to me.

2   The godly have been destroyed from the land,
there is no one upright among humankind.

They all lie in wait for blood,
each hunts his brother with a net.
3 Their hands do evil well.
The prince makes his request,
the judge grants it for a price,
and the great man expresses his evil desires —
thus they weave it together.
4 The best of them is a briar,
the most upright worse than a thorn hedge.
The time of your watchmen — of your punishment — has come;
now they will be confused.
5 Don't trust in your neighbor;
don't put confidence in a close friend;
shut the gates of your mouth even from [your wife],
lying there with you in bed.
6 For a son insults his father,
a daughter rises against her mother,
daughter-in-law against her mother-in-law —
a person's enemies are the members of his own household.

7 But as for me, I will look to ADONAI,
I will wait for the God of my salvation;
my God will hear me.
8 Enemies of mine, don't gloat over me!
Although I have fallen, I will rise;
though I live in the dark, ADONAI is my light.
9 I will endure ADONAI's rage,
because I sinned against him;
until he pleads my cause
and judges in my favor.
Then he will bring me out to the light,
and I will see his justice.
10 My enemies will see it too,
and shame will cover those
who said to me, "Where is ADONAI your God?"
I will gloat over them,
as they are trampled underfoot
like mud in the streets.

11 That will be the day for rebuilding your walls,
a day for expanding your territory,
12 a day when [your] people will come [back] to you
from Ashur and from the cities of Egypt,
from Egypt and from as far as the Euphrates River,
and from sea to sea, and from mountain to mountain.
13 The earth will be desolate for those living in it,
as a result of their deeds.

¹⁴ Shepherd your people with your staff,
the flock that belongs to you,
who live alone, like a forest
in the middle of a fertile pasture.
Let them feed in Bashan and Gil'ad,
as they did in days of old.

¹⁵ "As in the days when you came out of Egypt,
I will show them wonders."

¹⁶ The nations will see and be put to shame,
in spite of all their power.
They will cover their mouths with their hands,
and their ears will be deafened.

¹⁷ They will lick the dust like snakes;
they will emerge from their fortresses trembling
like reptiles that crawl about on the earth;
they will come with fear to ADONAI our God,
afraid because of you.

¹⁸ Who is a God like you,
pardoning the sin and overlooking the crimes
of the remnant of his heritage?
He does not retain his anger forever,
because he delights in grace.

¹⁹ He will again have compassion on us,
he will subdue our iniquities.
You will throw all their sins
into the depths of the sea.

²⁰ You will show truth to Ya'akov
and grace to Avraham,
as you have sworn to our ancestors
since days of long ago.

Nachum
NAHUM

1 ¹ This is a prophecy about Ninveh, the book of the vision of Nachum the Elkoshi:

² ADONAI is a jealous and vengeful God.
ADONAI avenges; he knows how to be angry.

ADONAI takes vengeance on his foes
and stores up wrath for his enemies.

3 ADONAI is slow to anger, but great in power;
and he does not leave the guilty unpunished.
ADONAI's path is in the whirlwind and storm,
and the clouds are the dust of his feet.

4 He rebukes the sea and leaves it dry,
he dries up all the rivers.
Bashan and the Karmel languish;
the flower of the L'vanon withers.

5 The mountains quake before him,
and the hills dissolve;
the earth collapses in his presence,
the world and everyone living in it.

6 Who can withstand his fury?
Who can endure his fierce anger?
His wrath is poured out like fire,
the rocks broken to pieces before him.

7 ADONAI is good,
a stronghold in time of trouble;
he takes care of those
who take refuge in him.

8 But with an overwhelming flood
he will make an end of [Ninveh's] place,
and darkness will pursue his enemies.

9 What are you planning against ADONAI?
He is making an end [of it];
trouble will not arise a second time.

10 For like men drunk with liquor,
they will be burned up like tangled thorns,
like straw completely dry.

11 Out of you, [Ninveh,] he came,
one who plots evil against ADONAI,
who counsels wickedness.

12 Here is what ADONAI says:
"Though they be many and strong,
they will be cut down, they will pass;
and though I have made you suffer,
I will make you suffer no more.

13 Now I will break his yoke from your necks
and snap the chains that bind you.

14 ADONAI gave this order concerning you:
you will have no descendants to bear your name;

from the house of your god I will cut off
carved image and cast metal image;
I will prepare your grave,
because you are worthless."

2 1(1:15)   Look! On the mountains are the feet
of him who brings good news, proclaiming *shalom.*
Keep your festivals, Y'hudah, fulfill your vows;
for B'liya'al will never pass through you again;
he has been completely destroyed.

2(1)   A destroyer has risen in front of your face;
guard the ramparts, keep watch on the road,
brace yourselves, marshall all your strength.

3(2)   For ADONAI is restoring the pride of Ya'akov,
along with the pride of Isra'el;
because plunderers have plundered them
and ravaged their vines.

4(3)   The shields of [Ninveh's] warriors are [dyed] red;
the soldiers are wearing scarlet.
The steel of the chariots flashes like fire
as they prepare for battle.
The cypress [spears] are poisoned.

5(4)   The chariots rush madly about in the streets,
jostling each other in the open places;
their appearance is like torches,
they run here and there like lightning.

6(5)   [The king of Ninveh] assigns his officers;
they stumble as they march;
they hurry to its wall and set up shields
to protect the battering ram.

7(6)   The gates of the rivers are opened,
and the palace melts away.

8(7)   Its mistress is stripped and carried away;
her handmaids moan, they sound like doves,
as they beat their breasts.

9(8)   Ninveh is like a pool whose water ebbs away.
"Stop! Stop!" But none of it goes back.

10(9)   Plunder the silver! Plunder the gold!
There is no end to the treasure,
weighed down with precious things.

11(10)   She is void, vacant; she is made bare.
Hearts are melting, knees are knocking;
every stomach is churning,
every face is drained of color.

12(11)   What has become of the lion's den,
          the cave where the young lions fed,
          where lion and lioness walked with their cubs,
          and no one made them afraid?
13(12)   The lion would tear up food for his cubs
          and strangle prey for his lionesses;
          he used to fill his caves with prey,
          his lairs with torn flesh.

14(13)   "I am against you," says ADONAI-Tzva'ot.
          "Her chariots I will send up in smoke,
          the sword will consume your lion cubs,
          I will destroy your prey from the earth,
          and your envoys' voices will be heard no more."

3 1   Woe to the city of blood, steeped in lies,
          full of prey, with no end to the plunder!
2   The crack of the whip! The rattle of wheels!
          Galloping horses, jolting chariots,
3   cavalry charging, swords flashing,
          spears glittering —
          and hosts of slain, heaps of bodies;
          there is no end to the corpses;
          they stumble over their corpses.

4   "Because of the continual whoring of this whore,
          this alluring mistress of sorcery,
          who sells nations with her whoring
          and families with her sorcery;
5   I am against you," says ADONAI-Tzva'ot.
          "I will uncover your skirts on your face;
          I will show the nations your private parts
          and the kingdoms your shame.
6   I will pelt you with disgusting filth,
          disgrace you and make a spectacle of you.
7   Then all who see you will recoil from you;
          they will say, 'Ninveh is destroyed!'
          Who will mourn for her?
          Where can I find people to comfort you?"

8   Are you any better than No-Amon,
          located among the streams of the Nile,
          with water all around her,
          the flood her wall of defense?
9   Ethiopia and Egypt gave her boundless strength,
          Put and Luvim were there to help you.
10   Still she went captive into exile,

her infants torn to pieces at every streetcorner.
Lots were drawn for her nobles,
and all her great men were bound in chains.

11 You too, [Ninveh,] will be drunk;
your senses completely overcome.
You too will seek a refuge
from the enemy.

12 All your fortifications will be
like fig trees with early ripening figs;
the moment they are shaken, they fall
into the mouth of the eater.

13 Look at your troops! They behave like women!
Your country's gates are wide open to your foes;
fire has consumed their bars.

14 Draw water for the siege!
Strengthen your fortifications!
Go down in the clay, tread the mortar,
Take hold of the mold for bricks!

15 There the fire will burn you up;
and the sword will cut you down;
it will devour you like grasshoppers.

Make yourselves as many as grasshoppers,
Make yourselves as many as locusts!

16 You had more merchants than stars in the sky.
The locust sheds its skin and flies away.

17 Your guards are like grasshoppers,
your marshals like swarms of locusts,
which settle on the walls on a cold day,
but when the sun rises they fly away;
they vanish to no one knows where.

18 Your shepherds are slumbering, king of Ashur.
Your leaders are asleep.
Your people are scattered all over the mountains,
with no one to round them up.

19 Your wound cannot be healed.
Your injury is fatal.
Everyone hearing the news about you
claps his hands in joy over you.
For who has not been overwhelmed
by your relentless cruelty?

Havakuk
HABAKKUK

1 ¹ This is the prophecy which Havakuk the prophet saw:

² *ADONAI*, how long must I cry
without your hearing?
"Violence!" I cry to you,
but you don't save.

³ Why do you make me see wrongdoing,
why do you permit oppression?
Pillage and cruelty confront me,
so that strife and discord prevail.

⁴ Therefore *Torah* is not followed;
justice never gets rendered,
because the wicked fence in the righteous.
This is why justice comes out perverted.

⁵ "Look around among the nations!
What you see will completely astound you!
For what is going to be done in your days
you will not believe, even when you are told.

⁶ I am raising up the Kasdim,
that bitter and impetuous nation,
who march far and wide over the earth
to seize homes that are not their own.

⁷ Fearsome and dreadful they are;
their rules and strength come from themselves.

⁸ Their horses are swifter than leopards,
fiercer than wolves at night.
Their cavalry gallop in from afar,
flying like vultures rushing to feed.

⁹ All of them come for violence,
their faces set eagerly forward,
scooping up captives like sand.

¹⁰ They scoff at kings;
princes they deride.
They laugh at any fortress;
they pile up earth and take it.

¹¹ Then they sweep on like the wind,
but they become guilty,
because they make their strength their god."

12   *ADONAI*, haven't you existed forever?
My God, my holy one, we will not die.
ADONAI, you appointed them to execute judgment.
Rock, you commissioned them to correct us.

13   Your eyes are too pure to see evil,
you cannot countenance oppression.
So why do you countenance traitors?
Why are you silent when evil people
swallow up those more righteous than they?

14   You make people like fish in the sea,
like reptiles that have no ruler.

15   The evil haul them all up with their hooks,
catch them in their fish net,
or gather them in their dragnet.
Then they rejoice and make merry,

16   offering sacrifices to their fishnet
and burning incense to their dragnet;
because through them they live in luxury,
with plenty of food to eat.

17   Should they, therefore, keep emptying their nets?
Should they keep slaughtering the nations without pity?

2 ¹   I will stand at my watchpost;
I will station myself on the rampart.
I will look to see what [God] will say through me
and what I will answer when I am reproved.

² Then *ADONAI* answered me; he said,

    "Write down the vision clearly on tablets,
so that even a runner can read it.

3   For the vision is meant for its appointed time;
it speaks of the end, and it does not lie.
It may take a while, but wait for it;
it will surely come, it will not delay.

4   "Look at the proud: he is inwardly not upright;
but the righteous will attain life through trusting faithfulness.

5   Truly, wine is treacherous;
the arrogant will not live at peace
but keeps expanding his desires like Sh'ol;
like death, he can never be satisfied;
he keeps collecting all the nations for himself,
rallying to himself all the peoples.

6   Won't all these take up taunting him
and say about him, in mocking riddles,

'Woe to him who amasses other people's wealth! —
how long must it go on? —
and to him who adds to himself the weight
of goods taken in pledge!

7 Won't your own creditors suddenly stand,
won't those who make you tremble wake up?
You will become their spoil.

8 Because you plundered many nations,
all the rest of the peoples will plunder you;
because of the bloodshed and violence done
to the land, the city and all who live there.

9 "'Woe to him who seeks unjust gain for his household,
putting his nest on the heights,
in order to be safe from the reach of harm.

10 By scheming to destroy many peoples,
you have brought shame to your house
and forfeited your life.

11 For the very stones will cry out from the wall,
and a beam in the framework will answer them.

12 "'Woe to him who builds a city with blood
and founds a town on injustice,

13 so that people toil for what will be burned up,
and nations exhaust themselves to no purpose.
Isn't all this from ADONAI-Tzva'ot?

14 For the earth will be as full
of the knowledge of ADONAI's glory
as water covering the sea.

15 "'Woe to him who has his neighbor drink,
adds his own poison and makes him drunk,
in order to see him naked.

16 You are filled with shame, not glory.
You, drink too, and stagger!
The cup of ADONAI's right hand
will be turned against you;
your shame will exceed your glory.

17 For the violence done to the L'vanon
will overwhelm you,
and the destruction of the wild animals
will terrify you;
because of the bloodshed and violence done
to the land, the city and all who live there.'"

18 What good is an idol, once its maker has shaped it,
a cast metal image and a teacher of lies,

that its maker puts his trust in it,
and goes on making non-gods, unable to talk?
19 Woe to him who tells a piece of wood, "Wake up!"
or a speechless stone, "Rouse yourself!"
Can this thing teach? Why, it's covered with gold and silver,
without the slightest breath in it!
20 But ADONAI is in his holy temple;
let all the earth be silent before him.

3 ¹ This is a prayer of Havakuk the prophet (on musical instruments called *shigyonot*).

2 ADONAI, I have heard the report about you.
ADONAI, I am awed by your deeds.
Bring your work to life in our own age,
make it known in our own time;
but in anger, remember compassion.
3 God comes from Teman,
the Holy One from Mount Pa'ran.   (*Selah*)
His splendor covers the sky,
and his praise fills the earth.
4 His brightness is like the sun,
rays come forth from his hand —
that is where his power is concealed.
5 Before him goes pestilence,
and close behind, the plague.
6 When he stands up, the earth shakes;
when he looks, the nations tremble,
the eternal mountains are smashed to pieces,
the ancient hills sink down;
the ancient paths are his.
7 I saw trouble in the tents of Kushan
and the tent hangings shaking in the land of Midyan.

8 ADONAI, is it against the rivers,
against the rivers that your anger is inflamed?
Is your fury directed at the sea?
Is that why you ride on your horses,
and drive your chariots to victory?
9 You brandish your naked bow
and order it filled with arrows.   (*Selah*)
You split the earth with rivers.
10 The mountains see you and tremble;
a torrent of water streams by;
the deep thunders forth,
as it raises enormous waves.
11 The sun and moon stand still in the sky
at the light of your arrows speeding by,

at the gleam of your glittering spear.
12 In fury you stride across the land,
in anger you trample the nations.
13 You come out to save your people,
to save your anointed one;
you crush the head of the house of the wicked,
uncovering its foundation all the way to the neck.
14 With their own rods you pierce the head of their warriors,
who come like a whirlwind to scatter us,
who rejoice at the prospect
of devouring the poor in secret.
15 You tread down the sea with your horses,
churning up the mighty waters.

16 When I heard, my whole body trembled,
my lips shook at the sound;
weakness overcame my limbs,
my legs gave way beneath me.
But I wait calmly for the day of trouble,
when it comes upon our assailants.
17 For even if the fig tree doesn't blossom,
and no fruit is on the vines,
even if the olive tree fails to produce,
and the fields yield no food at all,
even if the sheep vanish from the sheep pen,
and there are no cows in the stalls;
18 still, I will rejoice in ADONAI,
I will take joy in the God of my salvation.
19 ELOHIM Adonai is my strength!
He makes me swift and sure-footed as a deer
and enables me to stride over my high places.

For the leader. With my stringed instruments.

Tz'fanyah
ZEPHANIAH

1 ¹ This is the word of ADONAI that came to Tz'fanyah the son of Kushi, the son of G'dalyah, the son of Amaryah, the son of Hizkiyah, during the reign of Yoshiyahu the son of Amon, king of Y'hudah:

2 "I will completely sweep away everything
off the face of the land," says ADONAI.

3 "I will sweep away humans and animals,
the birds in the air and the fish in the sea,
also the wicked and what makes them stumble;
I will wipe humanity off the land," says ADONAI.

4 "I will stretch out my hand over Y'hudah
and all those living in Yerushalayim.
I will wipe every remnant of Ba'al from this place,
the idol-serving priests and even their names,

5 those worshipping heaven's army on the roofs,
also those who worship and swear by ADONAI
but swear by Malkam as well,

6 those who turned away from following ADONAI,
and those who haven't sought ADONAI
or consulted him at all."

7 Keep silent before Adonai ELOHIM,
for the Day of ADONAI is near.
ADONAI has prepared a sacrifice;
he has set apart those he invited.

8 When the time comes for ADONAI's sacrifice —
"I will punish the leaders
and the sons of the king,
also those who dress in foreign clothes.

9 On the same day I will also punish
all who jump over the threshold
to fill the house of their master
with violence and deceit.

10 Also on that day," says ADONAI,
"a cry will be heard from the Fish Gate,
wailing from the city's Second Quarter
and a loud crash from the hills.

11 Wail, you who live down in the hollow,
because all the merchants are destroyed,
all who trade with silver are ruined.

12 When that time comes, I will search
Yerushalayim with lamps
and punish those who are [smug and thick,
like wine] left too long on its dregs,
who say to themselves, 'ADONAI will do nothing —
neither good nor bad.'

13 For this, their wealth will be plundered;
and their houses will be destroyed.
Yes, they will build houses but not live in them;
they will plant vineyards but not drink the wine."

14   The great Day of ADONAI is near,
near and coming very quickly;
Hear the sound of the Day of ADONAI!
When it's here, even a warrior will cry bitterly.

15   That Day is a Day of fury,
a Day of trouble and distress,
a Day of waste and desolation,
a Day of darkness and gloom,
a Day of clouds and thick fog,

16   a Day of the *shofar* and battle-cry
against the fortified cities
and against the high towers [on the city walls].

17   "I will bring such distress on people
that they will grope their way like the blind,
because they have sinned against ADONAI.
Their blood will be poured out like dust
and their bowels like dung.

18   Neither their silver nor their gold
will be able to save them.
On the day of ADONAI's fury,
the whole land will be destroyed
in the fire of his jealousy.
For he will make an end, a horrible end,
of all those living in the land."

2 1   Gather together, gather yourselves,
nation devoid of shame;

2   before the decree takes effect,
and the day comes when one passes like chaff;
before ADONAI's fierce anger
comes on you,
before the day of ADONAI's anger
comes on you.

3   Seek ADONAI, all you humble in the land,
you who exercise his justice;
seek righteousness, seek humility —
you might be hidden
on the day of ADONAI's anger.

4   For 'Azah will be abandoned,
Ashkelon will be desolate,
they will evacuate Ashdod at noon,
and 'Ekron will be uprooted.

5   Woe to the inhabitants of the seacoast,
the nation of the K'reti!
The word of ADONAI is against you,

Kena'an, land of the P'lishtim:
"I will destroy you; no one will be left."

6   The seacoast will be reduced to pastures,
meadows for shepherds, pens for sheep;

7   and the coast will belong to the remnant
of the house of Y'hudah.
They will pasture their flocks there
and in the evening lie down
in the houses of Ashkelon.
For ADONAI their God will remember them
and restore their fortunes.

8   "I have heard the insults of Mo'av
and the taunts of the people of 'Amon,
how they reviled my people
and boasted of expanding their territory.

9   Therefore, as I live," says ADONAI-Tzva'ot,
the God of Isra'el,
"Mo'av will become like S'dom
and the people of 'Amon like 'Amora,
a land covered with nettles and salt pits,
desolate forever.
The remnant of my people will plunder them,
the survivors in my nation will inherit them."

10   This is what they will earn for their pride,
for having reviled and boasted against
the people of ADONAI-Tzva'ot.

11   ADONAI will be fearsome against them,
for he will make all the earth's gods waste away.
Then all the coasts and islands of the nations
will worship him, each from its place.

12   "You too, Ethiopians,
will be put to death by my sword."

13   He will stretch out his hand against the north;
he will destroy Ashur;
he will make Ninveh desolate,
as dry as the desert.

14   Herds will lie down in it,
and all kinds of wild animals too —
jackdaws and owls will roost on her columns,
voices screeching in the windows,
desolation on the doorsteps,
for its cedarwork is stripped bare.

15   This is the city, once so joyful,
whose people felt themselves secure,

who used to say to herself,
"I am [the greatest]! I have no rival."
What a ruin she has become —
a place for wild animals to lie down!
Everyone passing by her
hisses and shakes his fist!

3 ¹   Woe to her who is filthy, defiled;
woe to the tyrant city!

²   She wouldn't listen to the voice,
wouldn't receive correction;
she didn't trust in ADONAI,
didn't draw close to her God.

³   Her leaders there with her are roaring lions,
her judges desert wolves,
who don't leave even a bone for tomorrow.

⁴   Her prophets are reckless, treacherous men;
her *cohanim* profane the holy
and do violence to *Torah*.

⁵   ADONAI, who is righteous, is there among them;
he never does anything wrong.
Every morning he renders his judgment,
every morning, without fail;
yet the wrongdoer knows no shame.

⁶   "I have cut off nations,
their battlements are ruined;
I have made their streets ruins,
no one walks in them.
Their cities are destroyed,
abandoned, unpeopled.

⁷   I said, 'Surely now you will fear me,
you will receive correction';
so that her place will not be cut off
by all the punishments I brought on her.
But no, they only grew all the more eager
to be corrupt in all that they do.

⁸   Therefore, wait for me," says ADONAI,
"for the day when I rise to witness against you,
when I decide to assemble nations,
to gather kingdoms together,
to pour on them my indignation,
all my furious anger;
for all the earth will be consumed
in the fire of my passion.

⁹   For then I will change the peoples,
so that they will have pure lips,

to call on the name of *Adonai*, all of them,
and serve him with one accord.

10 Even from beyond Ethiopia's rivers
they will bring those who petition me,
the daughter of my dispersed as my offering.

11 When that day comes, you will not be ashamed
of everything you have done,
committing wrongs against me;
for then I will remove from among you
those of you who take joy in arrogance;
you will no longer be full of pride
on my holy mountain.

12 I will leave among you
a poor and afflicted people,
who will find their refuge
in the name of *Adonai*."

13 The remnant of Isra'el will not do wrong,
nor will they speak lies,
nor will there be found in their mouths
a tongue given over to deceit;
for they will be able to graze and lie down,
with no one to disturb them.

14 Sing, daughter of Tziyon!
Shout, Isra'el!
Be glad and rejoice with all your heart,
daughter of Yerushalayim!

15 *Adonai* has removed the judgments against you,
he has expelled your enemy;
the king of Isra'el, *Adonai*,
is right there with you.
You no longer need to fear
that anything bad will happen.

16 On that day, it will be said
to Yerushalayim,
"Do not fear, Tziyon!
don't let your hands droop down.

17 *Adonai* your God is right there with you,
as a mighty savior.
He will rejoice over you and be glad,
he will be silent in his love,
he will shout over you with joy."

18 "I will gather those of yours
who grieve over the appointed feasts
and bear the burden of reproach
[because they cannot keep them].

¹⁹ When that time comes, I will deal
with all those who oppress you.
I will save her who is lame,
gather her who was driven away,
and make them whose shame spread over the earth
the object of praise and renown.

²⁰ When that time comes, I will bring you in;
when that time comes, I will gather you
and make you the object of fame and praise
among all the peoples of the earth —
when I restore your fortunes
before your very eyes," says ADONAI.

Hagai
HAGGAI

1 ¹ In the second year of Daryavesh the king, on the first day of the sixth month, the following word of ADONAI came through Hagai the prophet to Z'rubavel the son of Sh'alti'el, governor of Y'hudah, and to Y'hoshua the son of Y'hotzadak, the *cohen hagadol*; ² "Here is what ADONAI-*Tzva'ot* says: 'This people is saying that now isn't the time — the time hasn't yet arrived for ADONAI's house to be rebuilt.'"

³ Then this word of ADONAI came through Hagai the prophet: ⁴ "So is now the time for you to be living in your own paneled houses, while this house lies in ruins? ⁵ Therefore here is what ADONAI-*Tzva'ot* says:

'Think about your life!

⁶ You sow much but bring in little;
you eat but aren't satisfied;
you drink but never have enough;
you clothe yourselves, but no one is warm;
and he who works for a living earns wages
that are put in a bag full of holes.'"

⁷ "Here is what ADONAI-*Tzva'ot* says: 'Think about your life! ⁸ Go up into the hills, get wood, and rebuild the house. I will be pleased with that, and then I will be glorified,' says ADONAI. ⁹ 'You looked for much, but it came to little; and when you brought it home, I blew it away. Why?' asks ADONAI-*Tzva'ot*. 'Because my house lies in ruins, while every one of you runs to take care of his own house. ¹⁰ This is why the sky above you has withheld the dew, so that there is none, and the land withholds its yield. ¹¹ In fact, I called for a drought on the land and on the hills, on the grain, the

771

wine and the olive oil, on what the ground brings up, on men, animals and on all that hands produce.'"

^{12} Then Z'rubavel the son of Sh'alti'el and Y'hoshua the son of Y'hotzadak, the *cohen hagadol*, with all the rest of the people, paid attention to what ADONAI their God had said and to the words of Hagai the prophet; since ADONAI their God had sent him; and the people were filled with fear in the presence of ADONAI. ^{13} Hagai the messenger of ADONAI conveyed this message of ADONAI to the people: "'I am with you,' says ADONAI."

^{14} ADONAI roused the spirit of Z'rubavel the son of Sh'alti'el, governor of Y'hudah, and the spirit of Y'hoshua the son of Y'hotzadak, the *cohen hagadol*, and the spirits of all the rest of the people; so that they came and began to work on the house of ADONAI-Tzva'ot their God. ^{15} This was on the twenty-fourth day of the sixth month of the second year of Daryavesh the king.

2 ^{1} On the twenty-first day of the seventh month, this word of ADONAI came through Hagai the prophet: ^{2} "Speak now to Z'rubavel the son of Sh'alti'el, governor of Y'hudah, and to Y'hoshua the son of Y'hotzadak, the *cohen hagadol*, and to the rest of the people; say this to them: ^{3} "'Who among you is left that saw this house in its former glory? And how does it look to you now? It seems like nothing to you, doesn't it? ^{4} Nevertheless, Z'rubavel, take courage now," says ADONAI; "and take courage, Y'hoshua the son of Y'hotzadak, the *cohen hagadol*; and take courage, all you people of the land," says ADONAI; "and get to work! For I am with you," says ADONAI-Tzva'ot. ^{5} "This is in keeping with the word that I promised in a covenant with you when you came out of Egypt, and my Spirit remains with you, so don't be afraid!" ^{6} For this is what ADONAI-Tzva'ot says: "It won't be long before one more time I will shake the heavens and the earth, the sea and the dry land; ^{7} and I will shake all the nations, so that the treasures of all the nations will flow in; and I will fill this house with glory," says ADONAI-Tzva'ot. ^{8} "The silver is mine, and the gold is mine," says ADONAI-Tzva'ot. ^{9} "The glory of this new house will surpass that of the old," says ADONAI-Tzva'ot, "and in this place I will grant *shalom*," says ADONAI-Tzva'ot.'"

^{10} On the twenty-fourth day of the ninth month in the second year of Daryavesh, this word of ADONAI came through Hagai the prophet: ^{11} "Here is what ADONAI-Tzva'ot says: 'Ask the *cohanim* what the *Torah* says about this: ^{12} if someone carries meat that has been set aside as holy in a fold of his cloak; and then he lets his cloak touch bread, stew, wine, olive oil or any other food; does that food become holy too?'" The *cohanim* answered, "No." ^{13} Then Hagai asked, "If someone who is unclean from having had contact with a corpse touches any of these [food items], will they become unclean?" The *cohanim* answered, "They become unclean." ^{14} Hagai then said, "'That is the condition of this people, that is the condition of this nation before me,' says ADONAI, 'and that is the condition of everything their hands produce; so that anything they offer there is unclean. ^{15} Now, please, from this day on, keep this in mind: before you began laying stones on each other to rebuild the temple of ADONAI, ^{16} throughout that whole time, when someone approached a twenty-measure pile [of grain], he found only ten; and when he came to the winepress to draw out fifty measures, there were only twenty. ^{17} I struck you with blasting winds, mildew and hail on everything your hands produced; but you still wouldn't return to me,' says ADONAI. ^{18} 'So please keep this in mind, from this day on, from the twenty-fourth day of the ninth month, from the day the foundation of ADONAI's temple was laid, consider this: ¹⁹ there's no longer any seed in the barn, is there? and the vine, fig tree, pomegranate tree and olive tree have produced nothing yet, right? However, from this day on, I will bless you.'"

²⁰ The word of ADONAI came a second time to Hagai on the twenty-fourth day of the month, as follows: ²¹ "Tell Z'rubavel, governor of Y'hudah, 'I will shake the heavens and the earth, ²² I will overturn the thrones of kingdoms, I will destroy the strength of the kingdoms of the nations, and I will overturn the chariots and the people riding in them; the horses and their riders will fall, each by the sword of his brother. ²³ When that day comes,' says ADONAI-Tzva'ot, 'I will take you, Z'rubavel, my servant, the son of Sh'alti'el,' says ADONAI, 'and wear you like a signet ring; for I have chosen you,' says ADONAI-Tzva'ot."

Z'kharyah
ZECHARIAH

1 ¹ In the eighth month of the second year of Daryavesh, the following message from ADONAI came to Z'kharyah the son of Berekhyah, the son of 'Iddo, the prophet: ² "ADONAI was extremely angry with your ancestors. ³ Therefore, tell them that ADONAI-Tzva'ot says this: "'Return to me,'" says ADONAI-Tzva'ot, "'and I will return to you,'" says ADONAI-Tzva'ot. ⁴ "Don't be like your ancestors. The earlier prophets proclaimed to them, 'ADONAI-Tzva'ot says to turn back now from your evil ways and deeds'; but they didn't listen or pay attention to me," says ADONAI. ⁵ "Your ancestors, where are they? And the prophets, do they live forever? ⁶ But my words and my laws, which I ordered my servants the prophets, overtook your ancestors, didn't they? Then they turned and said, 'ADONAI has dealt with us according to our ways and deeds, just as he intended to do.'"'"

⁷ On the twenty-fourth day of the eleventh month, the month of Sh'vat, in the second year of Daryavesh, this message from ADONAI came to Z'kharyah the son of Berekhyah, the son of 'Iddo, the prophet: ⁸ It was night, and I saw there before me a man riding on a russet-colored horse. He stood among the myrtle bushes in the valley; and behind him were other horses, russet, chestnut-colored and white. ⁹ I asked, "What are these, my Lord?" The angel speaking with me said to me, "I will show you what these are." ¹⁰ The man standing among the myrtles said, "These are those whom ADONAI has sent to wander throughout the earth." ¹¹ Then they themselves answered the angel of ADONAI standing among the myrtles, "We have been wandering throughout the earth, and the whole world is quiet and at peace." ¹² The angel of ADONAI said, "ADONAI-Tzva'ot, how long will you keep withholding mercy from Yerushalayim and the cities of Y'hudah? You've been angry with them for the past seventy years!" ¹³ ADONAI replied with kind and comforting words to the angel who was speaking with me. ¹⁴ The angel speaking with me then said to me, "Here is what ADONAI-

Tzva'ot says: 'I am extremely jealous on behalf of Yerushalayim and Tziyon; ¹⁵ and [to the same degree] I am extremely angry with the nations that are so self-satisfied; because I was only a little angry [at Yerushalayim and Tziyon], but they made the suffering worse.' ¹⁶ Therefore *ADONAI* says, 'I will return to Yerushalayim with merciful deeds. My house will be rebuilt there,' says *ADONAI-Tzva'ot*; 'yes, a measuring line will be stretched out over Yerushalayim.' ¹⁷ In addition, proclaim that *ADONAI-Tzva'ot* says, 'My cities will again overflow with prosperity.' *ADONAI* will again comfort Tziyon, and he will again make Yerushalayim the city of his choice."

2 ¹⁽¹:¹⁸⁾ Then I looked up and saw four horns. ²⁽¹:¹⁹⁾ I asked the angel who was speaking to me, "What are these?" He answered, "These are the horns that scattered Y'hudah, Isra'el and Yerushalayim."

³⁽¹:²⁰⁾ Next, *ADONAI* showed me four artisans. ⁴⁽¹:²¹⁾ I asked, "What are these coming to do?" He said, "Those horns that scattered Y'hudah so completely that no one could even raise his head — well, these men have come to terrify them, to overthrow the nations that raised their horns against the land of Y'hudah to scatter it."

⁵⁽¹⁾ I looked up and saw a man with a measuring line in his hand. ⁶⁽²⁾ I asked, "Where are you going?" He said to me, "To measure Yerushalayim, to determine its width and length."

⁷⁽³⁾ Here the angel who was speaking to me went forward, and another angel went out, met him ⁸⁽⁴⁾ and said to him, "Run and tell this young man, 'Yerushalayim will be inhabited without walls, because there will be so many people and animals; ⁹⁽⁵⁾ for," says *ADONAI*, "I will be for her a wall of fire surrounding her; and I will be the glory within her. ¹⁰⁽⁶⁾ Up!" says *ADONAI*, "Move! Flee the land of the north! For I scattered you like the four winds of the sky," says *ADONAI*. ¹¹⁽⁷⁾ "Move, Tziyon! You who are living with the daughter of Bavel, escape!" ¹²⁽⁸⁾ For *ADONAI-Tzva'ot* has sent me on a glorious mission to the nations that plundered you, and this is what he says: "Anyone who injures you injures the very pupil of my eye. ¹³⁽⁹⁾ But I will shake my hand over them, and they will be plundered by those who were formerly their slaves." Then you will know that *ADONAI-Tzva'ot* sent me. ¹⁴⁽¹⁰⁾ "Sing, daughter of Tziyon; rejoice! For, here, I am coming; and I will live among you," says *ADONAI*. ¹⁵⁽¹¹⁾ When that time comes, many nations will join themselves to *ADONAI*. "They will be my people, and I will live among you." Then you will know that it was *ADONAI-Tzva'ot* who sent me to you. ¹⁶⁽¹²⁾ *ADONAI* will take possession of Y'hudah as his portion in the holy land, and he will again make Yerushalayim his choice. ¹⁷⁽¹³⁾ Be silent, all humanity, before *ADONAI*; for he has been roused from his holy dwelling.'"

3 ¹ He showed me Y'hoshua the *cohen hagadol* standing before the angel of *ADONAI*, with the Accuser [Hebrew: *Satan*] standing at his right to accuse him. ² *ADONAI* said to the Accuser, "May *ADONAI* rebuke you, Accuser! Indeed, may *ADONAI*, who has made Yerushalayim his choice, rebuke you! Isn't this man a burning stick snatched from the fire?" ³ Y'hoshua was clothed in garments covered with dung; and he was standing before the angel, ⁴ who said to those standing in front of him, "Take those filthy garments off of him." Then to him he said, "See, I am taking your guilt away. I will clothe you in fine robes." ⁵ I said, "They should put a clean turban on his head." So they put a clean turban on his head and gave him fine robes to wear, while the angel of *ADONAI* stood by. ⁶ Then the angel of *ADONAI* gave Y'hoshua this warning:

⁷ "*ADONAI-Tzva'ot* says this: 'If you will walk in my ways, obey my commission, judge my house and guard my courtyards; then I will give you free access among these who are standing here. ⁸ Listen, *cohen gadol* Y'hoshua, both you and your colleagues seated here before you, because these men are a sign that I am going to bring my servant Tzemach [Sprout]. ⁹ For look at the stone I have put in front of Y'hoshua: on one stone are seven eyes; I will engrave what is to be written on it,' says *ADONAI-Tzva'ot*; 'and I will remove the guilt of this land in one day. ¹⁰ When that time comes,' says *ADONAI-Tzva'ot*, 'you will all invite each other to join you under your vines and fig trees.'"

4 ¹ Then the angel that had been speaking with me returned and roused me, as if he were waking someone up from being asleep, ² and asked me, "What do you see?" I answered, "I've been looking at a *menorah*; it's all of gold, with a bowl at its top, seven lamps on it, and seven tubes leading to the lamps at its top. ³ Next to it are two olive trees, one on the right side of the bowl and the other on its left." ⁴ I then asked the angel speaking with me, "What are these, my Lord?" The angel speaking with me said, ⁵ "Don't you know what these are?" I said, "No, my Lord." ⁶ Then he answered me, "This is the word of *ADONAI* to Z'rubavel: 'Not by force, and not by power, but by my Spirit,' says *ADONAI-Tzva'ot*. ⁷ 'What are you, you big mountain? Before Z'rubavel you will become a plain; and he will put the capstone in place, as everyone shouts, "It's beautiful! Beautiful!"'" ⁸ This message from *ADONAI* came to me: ⁹ 'The hands of Z'rubavel have laid the foundation of this house, and his hands will also finish it.' Then you will know that *ADONAI-Tzva'ot* sent me to you. ¹⁰ For even someone who doesn't think much of a day when such minor events take place will rejoice at seeing the plumbline in the hand of Z'rubavel. So these seven are the eyes of *ADONAI* that range about over all the earth."

¹¹ I replied by asking him, "What are those two olive trees on the right and left sides of the *menorah*?" ¹² Then I asked the question again: "What are those two olive branches discharging gold[-colored oil] through the two gold spouts?" ¹³ He replied, "Don't you know what they are?" I answered, "No, my Lord." ¹⁴ He said, "Those are the two who have been anointed with oil; they are standing with the Lord of all the land."

5 ¹ Again I raised my eyes, and I saw in front of me a flying scroll. ² He said to me, "What do you see?" I replied, "I see a flying scroll thirty feet long and fifteen feet wide. ³ Then he said to me, "This is the curse that goes out over the face of all the land; for [according to what is written] on one side, everyone who steals will be swept away; and [according to what is written] on the other side, everyone who swears will be swept away. ⁴ 'I will release it,' says *ADONAI-Tzva'ot*, 'and it will enter the house of the thief and the house of anyone who swears falsely by my name; it will stay there inside the house and consume it completely, even its timbers and stones.'"

⁵ Then the angel speaking with me went forward and said to me, "Now raise your eyes, and see what this thing is, passing by." ⁶ I asked, "What is it?" He said, "This is the *eifah*-measure [a one-bushel dry-measure] passing by." Then he added, "This is their eye in all the land." ⁷ Next I saw a lead disc lifted up to reveal a woman sitting in the *eifah*. ⁸ He said, "This is Evil." He threw her down into the *eifah* and pressed the lead weight over its opening. ⁹ I raised my eyes and saw two women

coming with the wind in their wings; for they had wings like those of a stork. They lifted the *eifah* up between the earth and the sky. ¹⁰ I asked the angel speaking with me, "Where are they taking the *eifah*?" ¹¹ He answered me, "To build it a shrine in the land of Shin'ar. When it's ready, [the *eifah*] will be set down there on its base."

6 ¹ Again I raised my eyes, and I saw in front of me four chariots coming out from between two mountains, and the mountains were mountains of bronze. ² The first chariot had red horses; the second chariot, black horses; ³ the third chariot, white horses; and the fourth chariot, spotted gray horses. ⁴ I asked the angel speaking with me, "What are these, my Lord?" ⁵ The angel answered me, "These are the four winds of the sky that go out, after presenting themselves before the Lord of all the land. ⁶ The one with the black horses is going out toward the land in the north, the white [horses] have gone out after them, and the spotted have gone out toward the land in the south." ⁷ Then the gray ones went out and were seeking to go and wander throughout the whole earth, when he said, "Wander throughout the whole earth"; and they did wander throughout the whole earth. ⁸ Then he called out to me and said, "Look! The ones going to the land in the north have given my Spirit rest in the north country."

⁹ This message from ADONAI came to me: ¹⁰ "Take [gifts] from the exiles of Heldai, Toviyah, and Y'da'yah, who have arrived from Bavel; then you, go to the house of Yoshiyah the son of Tz'fanyah. ¹¹ Take silver and gold; make crowns; put one on the head of Y'hoshua the son of Y'hotzadak, the *cohen hagadol*; ¹² and tell him, 'ADONAI-Tzva'ot says: "There is coming a man whose name is Tzemach [Sprout]. He will sprout up from his place and rebuild the temple of ADONAI. ¹³ Yes, he will rebuild the temple of ADONAI; and he will take up royal splendor, sitting and ruling from his throne. There will be a *cohen* before his throne; and they will accept each other's advice in complete harmony. ¹⁴ The other crowns will be for Helem, Toviyah, Y'da'yah and Hen the son of Tz'fanyah; then [they are to be kept] as a memorial in the temple of ADONAI. ¹⁵ Those who are now far away will come and help rebuild the temple of ADONAI." Then you will know that it is ADONAI-Tzva'ot who sent me to you. And it will all come about, provided you heed carefully what ADONAI your God says.'"

7 ¹ In the fourth year of King Daryavesh, on the fourth day of the ninth month, Kislev, a message from ADONAI came to Z'kharyah. ² He sent Sar'etzer and Regem-Melekh with his men to Beit-El in order to ask ADONAI's favor, ³ as they inquired of the *cohanim* of the house of ADONAI-Tzva'ot and the prophets, "Should we go into mourning and abstain from pleasure during the fifth month, as we have been doing for all these years?" ⁴ It was then that this message came to me from ADONAI-Tzva'ot: ⁵ "Speak to all the people of the land and to the *cohanim*. Tell them, 'When you fasted and mourned in the fifth and seventh months throughout these seventy years, were you really fasting for me? Was it for me? ⁶ Rather, when you eat and drink, it's just to please yourselves, isn't it? ⁷ Isn't this just what ADONAI proclaimed through the earlier prophets, when Yerushalayim was inhabited and prosperous, as were the cities around her; and the Negev and the Sh'felah were inhabited?'"

⁸ Then this message from ADONAI came to Z'kharyah: ⁹ "In the past ADONAI-Tzva'ot said, 'Administer true justice. Let everyone show mercy and compassion to his brother. ¹⁰ Don't oppress widows, orphans, foreigners or poor people. Don't plot evil against each other.' ¹¹ But they wouldn't listen, they stubbornly turned their shoulder away

and stopped up their ears, so that they wouldn't have to hear it. [12] Yes, they made their hearts as hard as a diamond, so that they wouldn't hear the *Torah* and the messages that *ADONAI-Tzva'ot* had sent by his Spirit through the earlier prophets. This is why great anger came from *ADONAI-Tzva'ot*; [13] and it came about that just as they hadn't listened when he called, so *ADONAI-Tzva'ot* said, 'I won't listen when they call; [14] but with the power of a whirlwind I will disperse them among all the nations which they have not known.' Thus the land was left desolate after them, so that no one came or went. They had turned a pleasant land into a desert."

8 [1] A message came from *ADONAI-Tzva'ot*: [2] "*ADONAI-Tzva'ot* says, 'I am extremely jealous on Tziyon's behalf, and I am jealous for her with great fury.' [3] *ADONAI* says, 'I am returning to Tziyon, and I will live in Yerushalayim. Then Yerushalayim will be called Truth City, *ADONAI-Tzva'ot*'s Mountain, the Mountain of the Holy One. [4] *ADONAI-Tzva'ot* says, 'Old men and old women will once again sit in the open places of Yerushalayim, each one with his cane in his hand, because of their great age. [5] The city's open places will also be full of boys and girls playing there.' [6] *ADONAI-Tzva'ot* says, 'This may seem amazing to the survivors in those days, but must it also seem amazing to me?' says *ADONAI-Tzva'ot*. [7] *ADONAI-Tzva'ot* says, 'I will save my people from lands east and west; [8] I will bring them back, and they will live in Yerushalayim. They will be my people; and I will be their God, with faithfulness and justice.'

[9] "*ADONAI-Tzva'ot* says, 'Take courage, you who are hearing only now, in these days, these words spoken by the prophets when the foundation was being laid for rebuilding the temple, the house of *ADONAI-Tzva'ot*. [10] For prior to that time, there were wages neither for people nor for animals; moreover, it was unsafe for anyone to go out or come in, because of the enemy; for I set all people each against the other. [11] But from now on, I will not treat the remnant of this people as I did before,' says *ADONAI-Tzva'ot*. [12] 'Now they will sow in peace, the vine will give its fruit, the ground will produce its yield, the sky will give its dew, and I will cause the remnant of this people to possess all these things. [13] House of Y'hudah and house of Isra'el, just as you were formerly a curse among the nations, so now I will save you; and you will be a blessing. Don't be afraid, but take courage!'

[14] "For *ADONAI-Tzva'ot* says, 'Just as I resolved to do you harm when your forefathers provoked me,' *ADONAI-Tzva'ot* says, 'and I did not relent; [15] so now, I resolve to do good to Yerushalayim and to the house of Y'hudah. Don't be afraid! [16] These are the things you are to do: speak the truth to each other; in your courts, administer justice that is true and conducive to peace; [17] don't plot harm against each other; and don't love perjury; for all these are things I hate,' says *ADONAI*."

[18] This word of *ADONAI-Tzva'ot* came to me: [19] "*ADONAI-Tzva'ot* says, 'The fast days of the fourth, fifth, seventh and tenth months are to become times of joy, gladness and cheer for the house of Y'hudah. Therefore, love truth and peace.'

[20] "*ADONAI-Tzva'ot* says, 'In the future, peoples and inhabitants of many cities will come; [21] the inhabitants of one city will travel to another and say, "We must go to ask *ADONAI*'s favor and consult *ADONAI-Tzva'ot*. I'll go too." [22] Yes, many peoples and powerful nations will come to consult *ADONAI-Tzva'ot* in Yerushalayim and to ask *ADONAI*'s favor.' [23] *ADONAI-Tzva'ot* says, 'When that time comes, ten men will take hold — speaking all the languages of the nations — will grab hold of the cloak of a Jew and say, "We want to go with you, because we have heard that God is with you."'"

9 [1] A prophecy, the word of *ADONAI*:

In the land of Hadrakh and Dammesek
is where [God] comes to rest,
for the eyes of humankind are directed toward *ADONAI*,
as are those of all the tribes of Isra'el,
[2] also Hamat at its border,
Tzor and Tzidon, for she is very wise.

[3] Tzor built herself a fortified tower,
heaping up silver as if it were dust
and fine gold as if it were mud in the streets.
[4] But *Adonai* will dispossess her
and break her power at sea,
while the city itself
will be destroyed by fire.
[5] On seeing this, Ashkelon will be terrified;
'Azah too will writhe in pain;
likewise 'Ekron, as her hopes are dashed.

"The king will vanish from 'Azah,
Ashkelon will be without people,
[6] and a mixed people will live in Ashdod,
as I destroy the pride of the P'lishtim.
[7] I will end their eating meat with its blood still in it,
snatching the disgusting things from between their teeth."

But the surviving remnant will belong to our God;
it will be like a clan in Y'hudah;
and 'Ekron will be like a Y'vusi.

[8] "Then I will guard my house against armies,
so that none will march through or return.
No oppressor will ever again overrun them,
for now I am watching with my own eyes.
[9] Rejoice with all your heart, daughter of Tziyon!
Shout out loud, daughter of Yerushalayim!
Look! Your king is coming to you.
He is righteous, and he is victorious.
Yet he is humble — he's riding on a donkey,
yes, on a lowly donkey's colt.
[10] I will banish chariots from Efrayim
and war-horses from Yerushalayim."
The warrior's bow will be banished,
and he will proclaim peace to the nations.
He will rule from sea to sea,
and from the [Euphrates] River to the ends of the earth.

11 "Also you, by the blood of your covenant,
I release your prisoners from [the dungeon,]
the cistern that has no water in it.

12 Return to the stronghold,
you prisoners with hope!
This day I declare to you
that I will grant you double reparation.

13 For I have bent Y'hudah as my bow
and made Efrayim its arrow.
I will rouse your sons, Tziyon,
and make you like a warrior's sword
against your sons, Greece."

14 ADONAI will appear over them,
and his arrow will flash like lightning.
Adonai ELOHIM will blow the *shofar*
and go out in the whirlwinds of the south.

15 ADONAI-Tzva'ot will defend them;
they will devour and trample the sling-stones.
They will drink and roar
as if they had drunk wine;
they will be filled, like basins
and like the corners of the altar.

16 On that day ADONAI their God
will save them as the flock of his people;
for they will be like gems in a crown,
sparkling over his countryside.

17 What wealth is theirs, what beauty!
Grain will make the young men thrive,
and new wine the young women.

10 1 Ask ADONAI for rain in the spring,
ADONAI who makes the rain clouds;
and he will give them showers of rain,
grass in the field to each one.

2 For the household gods talk nonsense,
the diviners have seen a lie;
their dreams convey delusions,
and the comfort they offer is in vain.
Therefore they go their way like sheep
in distress from lack of a shepherd.

3 "My anger burns against the shepherds,
and I will vent it on the leaders of the flock."
For ADONAI-Tzva'ot will care for his flock,
the people of Y'hudah;
he will make them like his royal war-horse.

⁴ From them come cornerstone and tent peg,
from them the bow for battle,
from them all the rulers together.
⁵ They will be like warriors
trampling the mud of the streets in battle.
They will fight, because ADONAI is with them;
they will rout even those on horseback.

⁶ "I will strengthen the house of Y'hudah
and save the house of Yosef.
I will bring them back in my compassion for them;
they will be as if I hadn't driven them out;
for I am ADONAI their God,
and I will answer them.
⁷ Efrayim's men will be like warriors;
their hearts will be cheered as if from wine.
Their children will see it and rejoice,
their hearts will be glad in ADONAI.

⁸ "I will whistle for them and gather them,
because I have redeemed them;
they will be as numerous
as they were before;
⁹ and I will sow them among the peoples.
In distant lands they will remember me;
they will rear their children and then return.
¹⁰ I will bring them back from the land of Egypt
and gather them out of Ashur.
I will bring them into Gil'ad and the L'vanon,
until there is no more room for them.

¹¹ "Trouble will pass over the sea
and stir up waves in the sea;
all the depths of the Nile will be dried up,
the pride of Ashur will be brought down,
and the scepter of Egypt will leave.
¹² But I will strengthen [Isra'el] in ADONAI;
they will travel here and there in his name,"

says ADONAI.

11 ¹ Open your doors, L'vanon,
so that fire can consume your cedars.
² Wail, cypress, because the cedar has fallen,
those splendid trees are ruined.
Wail, oaks of Bashan,
because the thick forest has been felled.

³ Listen to the wail of the shepherds,
because their glory is spoiled.
Listen to the roaring of young lions,
because the Yarden's thickets are plundered.

⁴ ADONAI my God says this: "Shepherd the flock for slaughter. ⁵ Their buyers kill them and go unpunished; while those who sell them say, 'Barukh ADONAI! Now I'm rich!' Even their own shepherds show them no pity. ⁶ I will no longer show pity to the inhabitants of the land," says ADONAI. "No, I will hand every one of them over to the power of a neighbor and to the power of his king; they will crush the land; and I won't rescue them from their power."

⁷ So I shepherded the flock for slaughter, truly the most miserable of the sheep; and I took two staffs for myself. I called the one No'am [pleasantness], the other I called Hovalim [bound together], and I shepherded the flock. ⁸ "In a single month I got rid of three shepherds, because I grew impatient with them; and besides, they detested me. ⁹ I said, 'I'm not going to shepherd you. Whichever one is going to die, let it die; whichever is going to be destroyed, let it be destroyed; and the rest can all devour each other.'"

¹⁰ I took my staff No'am and snapped it in two, "in order to break my covenant, which I made with all the peoples." ¹¹ On that day when it was broken, the most miserable of the sheep who paid attention to me knew that this was indeed a message from ADONAI. ¹² I said to them, "If it seems good to you, give me my wages; if not, don't." So they weighed out my wages, thirty silver [shekels, that is, twelve ounces]. ¹³ Concerning that "princely sum" at which they valued me, ADONAI said, "Throw it into the treasury!" So I took the thirty silver [shekels] and threw them into the treasury in the house of ADONAI.

¹⁴ Then I snapped in two my other staff Hovalim [bound together], in order to break up the brotherhood between Y'hudah and Isra'el. ¹⁵ ADONAI said to me, "This time, take the equipment of a worthless shepherd. ¹⁶ For I am going to raise up a shepherd in the land who won't bother about the ones who have been destroyed, won't seek out the young, won't heal the broken and won't feed those standing still; on the contrary, he will eat the meat of the fat ones and break their hoofs in pieces.

¹⁷ "Woe to the worthless shepherd
who abandons the sheep!
May a sword strike his arm
and his right eye.
May his arm be completely withered
and his right eye totally blinded."

12 ¹ A prophecy, the word of ADONAI concerning Isra'el — here is the message from ADONAI, who stretched out the heavens, laid the foundation of the earth and formed the spirit inside human beings:

² "I will make Yerushalayim a cup
that will stagger the surrounding peoples.

Even Y'hudah will be caught up
in the siege against Yerushalayim.

3 When that day comes, I will make Yerushalayim
a heavy stone for all the peoples.
All who try to lift it will hurt themselves,
and all the earth's nations will be massed against her.

4 When that day comes," says ADONAI,
"I will strike all the horses with panic
and their riders with madness;
I will keep watch over Y'hudah,
but I will strike blind all the horses of the peoples.

5 The leaders of Y'hudah will say to themselves,
'Those living in Yerushalayim are my strength
through ADONAI-Tzva'ot their God.'

6 When that day comes,
I will make the leaders of Y'hudah
like a blazing fire pan in a pile of wood,
like a fiery torch among sheaves of grain;
they will devour all the surrounding peoples,
on the right and on the left.
Yerushalayim will be inhabited
in her own place, Yerushalayim.

7 ADONAI will save the tents of Y'hudah first,
so that the glory of the house of David
and the glory of those living in Yerushalayim
will not appear greater than that of Y'hudah.

8 When that day comes, ADONAI will defend
those living in Yerushalayim.
On that day, even someone who stumbles
will be like David;
and the house of David will be like God,
like the angel of ADONAI before them.

9 "When that day comes, I will seek to destroy
all nations attacking Yerushalayim;

10 and I will pour out on the house of David
and on those living in Yerushalayim
a spirit of grace and prayer;
and they will look to me, whom they pierced."

They will mourn for him
as one mourns for an only son;
they will be in bitterness on his behalf
like the bitterness for a firstborn son.

11 When that day comes, there will be
great mourning in Yerushalayim,
mourning like that for Hadad-Rimmon

in the Megiddo Valley.

12 Then the land will mourn,
each family by itself —
the family of the house of David by itself,
and their wives by themselves;
the family of the house of Natan by itself,
and their wives by themselves;

13 the family of the house of Levi by itself,
and their wives by themselves;
the family of the Shim'i by itself,
and their wives by themselves;

14 all the remaining families, each by itself,
and their wives by themselves.

13 ¹ When that day comes, a spring will be opened up for the house of David and the people living in Yerushalayim to cleanse them from sin and impurity. ² "When that day comes," says ADONAI-*Tzva'ot*, "I will cut off the very names of the idols from the land, so that no one even remembers them any more. I will also expel the [false] prophets and the spirit of uncleanness from the land; ³ so that if anyone continues to prophesy, his own father and mother who brought him into the world will tell him, 'You cannot continue to live, because you are speaking lies in the name of ADONAI'; then his own father and mother who brought him into the world will stab him to death. ⁴ When that day comes, each one of the prophets will be shamed by his vision when he prophesies. He will stop wearing a hair cloak to deceive people; ⁵ and instead, he will say, 'I'm no prophet, I just work the soil; since my youth I've only wanted to be an ordinary man.' ⁶ If someone asks him, 'Then what are these gashes between your shoulders?' he will answer, 'I got hurt at my friends' house.'

7 "Awake, sword, against my shepherd,
against the man who is close to me,"
says ADONAI-*Tzva'ot*.
"Strike the shepherd, and the sheep will be scattered;
I will turn my hand against the young ones.

8 In time, throughout that land," says ADONAI,
"two-thirds of those in it will be destroyed —
they will die, but one-third will remain.

9 That third part I will bring through the fire;
I will refine them as silver is refined,
I will test them as gold is tested.
They will call on my name,
and I will answer them.
I will say, 'This is my people'
and they will say, 'ADONAI is my God.'"

14 ¹ Look, a day is coming for ADONAI
when your plunder, [Yerushalayim], will be divided
right there within you.

2   "For I will gather all the nations
    against Yerushalayim for war.
    The city will be taken,
    the houses will be rifled,
    the women will be raped,
    and half the city will go into exile;
    but the rest of the people
    will not be cut off from the city."

3   Then ADONAI will go out
    and fight against those nations,
    fighting as on a day of battle.

4   On that day his feet will stand
    on the Mount of Olives,
    which lies to the east of Yerushalayim;
    and the Mount of Olives will be split in half
    from east to west, to make a huge valley.
    Half of the mountain will move toward the north,
    and half of it toward the south.

5   You will flee to the valley in the mountains,
    for the valley in the mountains will reach to Atzel.
    You will flee, just as you fled before the earthquake
    in the days of 'Uziyah king of Y'hudah.
    Then ADONAI my God will come
    to you with all the holy ones.

6   On that day, there will be
    neither bright light nor thick darkness;

7   and one day, known to ADONAI,
    will be neither day nor night,
    although by evening there will be light.

8   On that day, fresh water will flow
    out from Yerushalayim,
    half toward the eastern sea
    and half toward the western sea,
    both summer and winter.

9   Then ADONAI will be king
    over the whole world.
    On that day ADONAI will be the only one,
    and his name will be the only name.

¹⁰ All the land will be made like the 'Aravah, from Geva to Rimmon in the Negev. Yerushalayim will be raised up and inhabited where she is, from Binyamin's Gate to the place where the earlier gate stood, and on to the Corner Gate, and from the Tower of Hanan'el to the king's winepresses. ¹¹ People will live there, the curse will be broken, and Yerushalayim will live in safety.

¹² ADONAI will strike all the peoples who made war against Yerushalayim with a plague in which their flesh rots away while they are standing on their feet, their eyes

rot away in their sockets, and their tongues rot away in their mouths. [13] When that day comes, there will be among them great panic, sent by ADONAI, so that everyone lays hands on his neighbor, who in turn attacks him. [14] Y'hudah too will fight against Yerushalayim; and the wealth of all the nations will be assembled — gold, silver and clothing in great abundance. [15] A plague like this plague will also affect the horses, mules, camels, donkeys and all the other animals in those camps.

[16] Finally, everyone remaining from all the nations that came to attack Yerushalayim will go up every year to worship the king, ADONAI-Tzva'ot, and to keep the festival of Sukkot. [17] If any of the families of the earth does not go up to Yerushalayim to worship the king, ADONAI-Tzva'ot, no rain will fall on them. [18] If the family of Egypt doesn't go up, if they refuse to come, they will have no [annual] overflow [from the Nile]; moreover, there will be the plague with which ADONAI will strike the nations that don't go up to keep the festival of Sukkot. [19] This will be Egypt's punishment and the punishment of all the nations that don't go up to keep the festival of Sukkot.

[20] When that day comes, this will be written on the bells worn by the horses: "Consecrated to ADONAI"; and the cooking pots in the house of ADONAI will be [as holy] as the sprinkling bowls before the altar. [21] Yes, every cooking pot in Yerushalayim and Y'hudah will be consecrated to ADONAI-Tzva'ot. Everyone who offers sacrifices will come, take them and use them to stew the meat. When that day comes, there will no longer be merchants in the house of ADONAI-Tzva'ot.

Mal'akhi
MALACHI

1 [1] A prophecy, the word of ADONAI to Isra'el through Mal'akhi:

2   "I love you," says ADONAI.
But you ask, "How do you show us your love?"
ADONAI answers, "'Esav was Ya'akov's brother.
Yet I loved Ya'akov [3] but hated 'Esav.
I made his mountains desolate
and gave his territory to desert jackals."

4   Edom says, "We are beaten down now,
but we will come back and rebuild the ruins."
ADONAI-Tzva'ot answers, "They can build,
but I will demolish.
They will be called the Land of Wickedness,
the people with whom ADONAI is permanently angry.

5   You will see it and say, 'ADONAI is great,
even beyond the borders of Isra'el.'"

⁶"A son honors his father and a servant his master. But if I'm a father, where is the honor due me? and if I'm a master, where is the respect due me? — says *Adonai-Tzva'ot* to you *cohanim* who despise my name. You ask, 'How are we despising your name?' ⁷By offering polluted food on my altar! Now you ask, 'How are we polluting you?' By saying that the table of *Adonai* doesn't deserve respect; ⁸so that there's nothing wrong with offering a blind animal as a sacrifice, nothing wrong with offering an animal that's lame or sick. Try offering such an animal to your governor, and see if he will be pleased with you! Would he even receive you?" asks *Adonai-Tzva'ot*. ⁹So if you pray now that God will show us favor, what your actions have accomplished is that *Adonai-Tzva'ot* asks, "Will he receive any of you? ¹⁰Why doesn't even one of you shut the doors and thus stop this useless lighting of fires on my altar? I take no pleasure in you," says *Adonai-Tzva'ot*, "and I will not receive an offering from you. ¹¹For from farthest east to farthest west my name is great among the nations. Offerings are presented to my name everywhere, pure gifts; for my name is great among the nations," says *Adonai-Tzva'ot*. ¹²"But you profane it by saying that the table of *Adonai* is polluted, so that the fruit and food offered deserve contempt. ¹³You also say, 'It's all so tiresome!' and sniff scornfully at it," says *Adonai-Tzva'ot*. "Then you bring animals that were taken by violence, or they are lame or sick. This is the sort of offering you bring. Am I supposed to accept this from you?" asks *Adonai*. ¹⁴"Moreover, cursed is the deceiver who has a male animal in his flock that is damaged, but vows and sacrifices to *Adonai* anyway. For I am a great king," says *Adonai-Tzva'ot*, "and my name is respected among the nations.

2 ¹ "Now, *cohanim*, this command is for you.
² If you won't listen, if you won't pay attention
to honoring my name,"
says *Adonai-Tzva'ot*,
"then I will send the curse on you;
I will turn your blessings into curses.
Yes, I will curse them,
because you pay no attention.
³ I will reject your seed;
I will throw dung in your faces,
the dung from your festival offerings;
and you will be carted off with it.
⁴ Then you will know that I sent you this command
to affirm my covenant with Levi,"
says *Adonai-Tzva'ot*.
⁵ "My covenant with him was one of life and peace,
and I gave him these things.
It was also one of fear, and he feared me;
he was in awe of my name.
⁶ The true *Torah* was in his mouth,
and no dishonesty was found on his lips;
he walked with me in peace and uprightness
and turned many away from sin.

7   A *cohen*'s lips should safeguard knowledge,
    and people should seek *Torah* from his mouth,
    because he is the messenger
    of *Adonai-Tzva'ot*.
8   But you turned away from the path,
    you caused many to fail in the *Torah*,
    you corrupted the covenant of Levi,"
    says *Adonai-Tzva'ot*.
9   "Therefore I have in turn made you
    contemptible and vile before all the people,
    because you did not keep my ways
    but were partial in applying the *Torah*."

10   Don't we all have the same father?
    Didn't one God create us all?
    Then why do we break faith with each other,
    profaning the covenant of our ancestors?
11   Y'hudah has broken faith;
    an abomination has been committed
    in Isra'el and Yerushalayim.
    For Y'hudah has profaned the sanctuary
    of *Adonai*, which he loves,
    by marrying the daughter of a foreign god.
12   If a man does this and presents an offering
    to *Adonai-Tzva'ot*, may *Adonai* cut him off
    from the tents of Ya'akov,
    whether initiator or follower.

13   Here is something else you do:
    you cover *Adonai*'s altar with tears,
    with weeping and with sighing,
    because he no longer looks at the offering
    or receives your gift with favor.
14   Nevertheless, you ask, "Why is this?"
    Because *Adonai* is witness
    between you and the wife of your youth
    that you have broken faith with her,
    though she is your companion, your wife by covenant.
15   And hasn't he made [them] one [flesh]
    in order to have spiritual blood-relatives?
    For what the one [flesh] seeks
    is a seed from God.
    Therefore, take heed to your spirit,
    and don't break faith with the wife of your youth.
16   "For I hate divorce,"
    says *Adonai* the God of Isra'el,

"and him who covers his clothing with violence,"
says ADONAI-Tzva'ot.
Therefore take heed to your spirit,
and don't break faith.

17 You have wearied ADONAI with your words.
Yet you ask, "How have we wearied him?"
By saying that anyone who does wrong
is good from ADONAI's perspective,
and that he is delighted with them;
or by asking, "Where is the God of justice?"

3 1 "Look! I am sending my messenger
to clear the way before me;
and the Lord, whom you seek,
will suddenly come to his temple.
Yes, the messenger of the covenant,
in whom you take such delight —
look! Here he comes,"
says ADONAI-Tzva'ot.

2 But who can endure the day when he comes?
Who can stand when he appears?
For he will be like a refiner's fire,
like the soapmaker's lye.

3 He will sit, testing and purifying the silver;
he will purify the sons of Levi,
refining them like gold and silver,
so that they can bring offerings to ADONAI uprightly.

4 Then the offering of Y'hudah and Yerushalayim
will be pleasing to ADONAI,
as it was in the days of old,
as in years gone by.

5 "Then I will approach you for judgment;
and I will be quick to witness
against sorcerers, adulterers and perjurers;
against those who take advantage
of wage-earners, widows and orphans;
against those who rob the foreigner of his rights
and don't fear me,"
says ADONAI-Tzva'ot.

6 "But because I, ADONAI, do not change,
you sons of Ya'akov will not be destroyed.

7 Since the days of your forefathers
you have turned from my laws and have not kept them.
Return to me, and I will return to you,"
says ADONAI-Tzva'ot.
"But you ask, 'In respect to what

8   are we supposed to return?'
     Can a person rob God?
     Yet you rob me.
     But you ask, 'How have we robbed you?'
     In tenths and voluntary contributions.
9   A curse is on you, on your whole nation,
     because you rob me.
10   Bring the whole tenth into the storehouse,
     so that there will be food in my house,
     and put me to the test,"
     says ADONAI-Tzva'ot.
     "See if I won't open for you
     the floodgates of heaven
     and pour out for you a blessing
     far beyond your needs.
11   For your sakes I will forbid the devourer
     to destroy the yield from your soil;
     and your vine will not lose its fruit
     before harvest-time,"
     says ADONAI-Tzva'ot.
12   "All nations will call you happy,
     for you will be a land of delights,"
     says ADONAI-Tzva'ot.

13   "You have spoken strongly against me," says ADONAI.
     "Yet you say, 'How have we spoken against you?'
14   By saying, 'There is no point in serving God.
     What good is it to obey his orders
     or to walk about as mourners
     before ADONAI-Tzva'ot?
15   We consider the arrogant happy;
     also evildoers prosper;
     they put God to the test;
     nevertheless, they escape.'"
16   Then those who feared ADONAI spoke together;
     and ADONAI listened and heard.
     A record book was written in his presence
     for those who feared ADONAI
     and had respect for his name.
17   "They will be mine," says ADONAI-Tzva'ot,
     "on the day when I compose my own special treasure.
     I will spare them as a man spares
     his own son who serves him.
18   Then once again you will see the difference
     between the righteous and the wicked,
     between the person who serves God
     and one that doesn't serve him.

19(4:1)   For the day is coming, burning like a furnace,
when all the proud and evildoers will be stubble;
the day that is coming will set them ablaze,"
says *Adonai-Tzva'ot*,
"and leave them neither root nor branch.

20(4:2)   But to you who fear my name,
the sun of righteousness will rise
with healing in its wings;
and you will break out leaping,
like calves released from the stall.

21(4:3)   You will trample the wicked,
they will be ashes under the soles of your feet
on the day when I take action,"
says *Adonai-Tzva'ot*.

22(4:4)   "Remember the *Torah* of Moshe my servant,
which I enjoined on him at Horev,
laws and rulings for all Isra'el.

23(4:5)   Look, I will send to you
Eliyahu the prophet
before the coming of the great
and terrible Day of *Adonai*.

24(4:6)   He will turn the hearts of the fathers to the children
and the hearts of the children to their fathers;
otherwise I will come and strike the land
with complete destruction."

[Look, I will send to you
Eliyahu the prophet
before the coming of the great
and terrible Day of *Adonai*.]

Tehillim
PSALMS

Book I: Psalms 1–41

1 ¹ How blessed are those
who reject the advice of the wicked,
don't stand on the way of sinners
or sit where scoffers sit!
² Their delight
is in ADONAI's *Torah*;
on his *Torah* they meditate
day and night.
³ They are like trees planted by streams —
they bear their fruit in season,
their leaves never wither,
everything they do succeeds.

⁴ Not so the wicked,
who are like chaff driven by the wind.
⁵ For this reason the wicked
won't stand up to the judgment,
nor will sinners
at the gathering of the righteous.
⁶ For ADONAI watches over
the way of the righteous,
but the way of the wicked
is doomed.

2 ¹ Why are the nations in an uproar,
the peoples grumbling in vain?
² The earth's kings are taking positions,
leaders conspiring together,
against ADONAI
and his anointed.
³ They cry, "Let's break their fetters!
Let's throw off their chains!"

⁴ He who sits in heaven laughs;
Adonai looks at them in derision.

⁵ Then in his anger he rebukes them,
terrifies them in his fury.

⁶ "I myself have installed my king
on Tziyon, my holy mountain."

⁷ "I will proclaim the decree:
ADONAI said to me,
'You are my son;
today I became your father.

⁸ Ask of me, and I will make
the nations your inheritance;
the whole wide world
will be your possession.

⁹ You will break them with an iron rod,
shatter them like a clay pot.'"

¹⁰ Therefore, kings, be wise;
be warned, you judges of the earth.

¹¹ Serve *ADONAI* with fear;
rejoice, but with trembling.

¹² Kiss the son*, lest he be angry,
and you perish along the way,
when suddenly his anger blazes.
How blessed are all who take refuge in him.

3 ¹⁽⁰⁾ A psalm of David, when he fled from Avshalom his son:

²⁽¹⁾ *ADONAI*, how many enemies I have!
How countless are those attacking me;

³⁽²⁾ how countless those who say of me,
"There is no salvation for him in God."   (*Selah*)

⁴⁽³⁾ But you, *ADONAI*, are a shield for me;
you are my glory, you lift my head high.

⁵⁽⁴⁾ With my voice I call out to *ADONAI*,
and he answers me from his holy hill.   (*Selah*)

⁶⁽⁵⁾ I lie down and sleep, then wake up again,
because *ADONAI* sustains me.

⁷⁽⁶⁾ I am not afraid of the tens of thousands
set against me on every side.

---

* or: Kiss purely

792

8(7)   Rise up, *ADONAI*!
    Save me, my God!
    For you slap all my enemies in the face,
    you smash the teeth of the wicked.

9(8)   Victory comes from *ADONAI*;
    may your blessing rest on your people.   (*Selah*)

4 1(0) For the leader. With stringed instruments. A psalm of David:

2(1)   O God, my vindicator!
    Answer me when I call!
    When I was distressed, you set me free;
    now have mercy on me, and hear my prayer.

3(2)   Men of rank, how long will you shame my honor,
    love what is vain, chase after lies?   (*Selah*)

4(3)   Understand that *ADONAI* sets apart
    the godly person for himself;
    ADONAI will hear when I call to him.

5(4)   You can be angry, but do not sin!
    Think about this as you lie in bed,
    and calm down.   (*Selah*)

6(5)   Offer sacrifices rightly,
    and put your trust in *ADONAI*.

7(6)   Many ask, "Who can show us some good?"
    ADONAI, lift the light of your face over us!

8(7)   You have filled my heart with more joy
    than all their grain and new wine.

9(8)   I will lie down and sleep in peace;
    for, *ADONAI*, you alone make me live securely.

5 1(0) For the leader. On wind instruments. A psalm of David:

2(1)   Give ear to my words, *ADONAI*,
    consider my inmost thoughts.

3(2)   Listen to my cry for help,
    my king and my God, for I pray to you.

4(3)   *ADONAI*, in the morning you will hear my voice;
    in the morning I lay my needs before you
    and wait expectantly.

5(4)   For you are not a God
    who takes pleasure in wickedness;
    evil cannot remain with you.

6(5)   Those who brag cannot stand before your eyes,
        you hate all who do evil,
7(6)   you destroy those who tell lies,
        ADONAI detests men of blood and deceivers.

8(7)   But I can enter your house
        because of your great grace and love;
        I will bow down toward your holy temple
        in reverence for you.
9(8)   Lead me, ADONAI, in your righteousness
        because of those lying in wait for me;
        make your way straight before me.
10(9)   For in their mouths there is nothing sincere,
        within them are calamities,
        their throats are open tombs,
        they flatter with their tongues.
11(10)   God, declare them guilty!
        Let them fall through their own intrigues,
        For their many crimes, throw them down;
        since they have rebelled against you.

12(11)   But let all who take refuge in you rejoice,
        let them forever shout for joy!
        Shelter them; and they will be glad,
        those who love your name.
13(12)   For you, ADONAI, bless the righteous;
        you surround them with favor like a shield.

6 ¹⁽⁰⁾ For the leader. With stringed instruments. On *sh'minit* [low-pitched musical instruments?]. A psalm of David:

2(1)   ADONAI, don't rebuke me in your anger,
        don't discipline me in the heat of your fury.
3(2)   Be gracious to me, ADONAI,
        because I am withering away;
        heal me, ADONAI,
        because my bones are shaking;
4(3)   I am completely terrified;
        and you, ADONAI — how long?
5(4)   Come back, ADONAI, and rescue me!
        Save me for the sake of your grace;
6(5)   for in death, no one remembers you;
        in Sh'ol, who will praise you?

7(6)   I am worn out with groaning;
        all night I drench my bed with tears,

	flooding my couch till it swims.
8(7)	My vision is darkened with anger;
	it grows weak because of all my foes.
9(8)	Get away from me, all you workers of evil!
	For *Adonai* has heard the sound of my weeping,
10(9)	*Adonai* has heard my pleading,
	Adonai will accept my prayer.
11(10)	All my enemies will be confounded,
	completely terrified;
	they will turn back
	and be suddenly put to shame.

7 ¹⁽⁰⁾ A *shiggayon* of David, which he sang to *Adonai* because of Kush the Ben-Y'mini:

2(1)	*Adonai* my God, in you I take refuge.
	Save me from all my pursuers, and rescue me;
3(2)	otherwise, they will maul me like a lion
	and tear me apart, with no rescuer present.
4(3)	*Adonai* my God, if I have caused this,
	if there is guilt on my hands,
5(4)	if I paid back evil to him who was at peace with me,
	when I even spared those who opposed me without cause;
6(5)	then let the enemy pursue me
	until he overtakes me
	and tramples my life down into the earth;
	yes, let him lay my honor in the dust. (*Selah*)
7(6)	Rise up, *Adonai*, in your anger!
	Arouse yourself against the fury of my foes.
	Wake up for me; you commanded justice.
8(7)	May the assembly of the peoples surround you;
	may you return to rule over them from on high.
9(8)	*Adonai*, who dispenses judgment to the peoples,
	judge me, *Adonai*, according to my righteousness
	and as my integrity deserves.
10(9)	Let the evil of the wicked come to an end,
	and establish the righteous;
	since you, righteous God,
	test hearts and minds.
11(10)	My shield is God,
	who saves the upright in heart.
12(11)	God is a righteous judge,
	a God whose anger is present every day.

13(12) If a person will not repent,
he sharpens his sword.
He has bent his bow, made it ready;
14(13) he has also prepared for him
weapons of death, his arrows,
which he has made into burning shafts.

15(14) Look how the wicked is pregnant with evil;
he conceives trouble, gives birth to lies.
16(15) He makes a pit, digs it deep,
and falls into the hole he made.
17(16) His mischief will return onto his own head,
his violence will recoil onto his own skull.

18(17) I thank ADONAI for his righteousness
and sing praise to the name of ADONAI 'Elyon.

8 $^{1(0)}$ For the leader. On the *gittit*. A psalm of David:

2(1) ADONAI! Our Lord! How glorious
is your name throughout the earth!
The fame of your majesty
spreads even above the heavens!

3(2) From the mouths of babies and infants at the breast
you established strength because of your foes,
in order that you might silence
the enemy and the avenger.

4(3) When I look at your heavens, the work of your fingers,
the moon and stars that you set in place —
5(4) what are mere mortals, that you concern yourself with them;
humans, that you watch over them with such care?

6(5) You made him but little lower than the angels,
you crowned him with glory and honor,
7(6) you had him rule what your hands made,
you put everything under his feet —
8(7) sheep and oxen, all of them,
also the animals in the wilds,
9(8) the birds in the air, the fish in the sea,
whatever passes through the paths of the seas.

10(9) ADONAI! Our Lord! How glorious
is your name throughout the earth!

9 1(0) For the leader. On the death of Labben. A psalm of David:

2(1)   I give thanks to ADONAI with all my heart.
    I will tell about all your wonderful deeds.
3(2)   I will be glad and exult in you.
    I will sing praise to your name, 'Elyon.

4(3)   When my enemies turn back,
    they stumble and perish before you.
5(4)   For you upheld my cause as just,
    sitting on the throne as the righteous judge.

6(5)   You rebuked the nations, destroyed the wicked,
    blotted out their name forever and ever.
7(6)   The enemy is finished, in ruins forever;
    you destroyed their cities; all memory of them is lost.

8(7)   But ADONAI is enthroned forever;
    he has set up his throne for judgment.
9(8)   He will judge the world in righteousness;
    he will judge the peoples fairly.

10(9)   ADONAI is a stronghold for the oppressed,
    a tower of strength in times of trouble.
11(10)   Those who know your name put their trust in you,
    for you have not abandoned those who seek you, ADONAI.

12(11)   Sing praises to ADONAI, who lives in Tziyon;
    proclaim his deeds among the peoples.
13(12)   For the avenger of blood remembers them,
    he does not ignore the cry of the afflicted:

14(13)   "Have mercy on me, ADONAI!
    See how I suffer from those who hate me;
    you raise me from the gates of death,
15(14)   so that I can proclaim all your praises
    at the gates of the daughter of Tziyon
    and rejoice in this deliverance of yours."

16(15)   The nations have drowned in the pit they dug,
    caught their own feet in the net they hid.
17(16)   ADONAI made himself known and executed judgment;
    the wicked are ensnared in the work of their own hands. (*Higgayon*; *Selah*)

18(17)   The wicked will return to Sh'ol,
    all the nations that forget God.

19(18)   For the poor will not always be forgotten
or the hope of the needy perish forever.

20(19)   Arise, ADONAI! Don't let mortals prevail!
Let the nations be judged in your presence.

21(20)   Strike them with terror, ADONAI!
Let the nations know they are only human.   (*Selah*)

10 ¹   Why, ADONAI, do you stand at a distance?
Why do you hide yourself in times of trouble?

²   The wicked in their arrogance hunt down the poor,
who get caught in the schemes they think up.

³   For the wicked boasts about his lusts;
he blesses greed and despises ADONAI.

⁴   Every scheme of the wicked in his arrogance [says],
"There is no God, [so] it won't be held against me."

⁵   His ways prosper at all times.
Your judgments are way up there,
so he takes no notice.
His adversaries? He scoffs at them all.

⁶   In his heart he thinks, "I will never be shaken;
I won't meet trouble, not now or ever."

⁷   His mouth is full of curses, deceit, oppression;
under his tongue, mischief and injustice.

⁸   He waits near settlements in ambush
and kills an innocent man in secret;
his eyes are on the hunt for the helpless.

⁹   Lurking unseen like a lion in his lair,
he lies in wait to pounce on the poor,
then seizes the poor and drags him off in his net.

¹⁰   Yes, he stoops, crouches down low;
and the helpless wretch falls into his clutches.

¹¹   He says in his heart, "God forgets,
he hides his face, he will never see."

¹²   Arise, ADONAI! God, raise your hand!
Don't forget the humble!

¹³   Why does the wicked despise God
and say in his heart, "It won't be held against me"?

¹⁴   You have seen; for you look at mischief and grief,
so that you can take the matter in hand.
The helpless commits himself to you;
you help the fatherless.

¹⁵   Break the arm of the wicked!
As for the evil man,

search out his wickedness
until there is none left.

16 *Adonai* is king forever and ever!
The nations have vanished from his land.

17 *Adonai*, you have heard what the humble want;
you encourage them and listen to them,

18 to give justice to the fatherless and oppressed,
so that no one on earth will strike terror again.

11 ¹⁽⁰⁾ For the leader. By David:

(1) In *Adonai* I find refuge.
So how can you say to me,
"Flee like a bird to the mountains!

2 See how the wicked are drawing their bows
and setting their arrows on the string,
to shoot from the shadows at honest men.

3 If the foundations are destroyed,
what can the righteous do?"

4 *Adonai* is in his holy temple.
Adonai, his throne is in heaven.
His eyes see and test humankind.

5 *Adonai* tests the righteous;
but he hates the wicked and the lover of violence.

6 He will rain hot coals down on the wicked,
fire, sulfur and scorching wind
will be what they get to drink.

7 For *Adonai* is righteous;
he loves righteousness;
the upright will see his face.

12 ¹⁽⁰⁾ For the leader. On *sh'minit* [low-pitched musical instruments?]. A psalm
of David:

2(1) Help, *Adonai*! For no one godly is left;
the faithful have vanished from humankind.

3(2) They all tell lies to each other,
flattering with their lips, but speaking from divided hearts.

4(3) May *Adonai* cut off all flattering lips
and the tongue that speaks so proudly,

5(4) those who say, "By our tongues, we will prevail;
our lips are with us. Who can master us?"

6(5)   "Because the poor are oppressed,
    because the needy are groaning,
    I will now rise up," says ADONAI,
    "and grant security to those whom they scorn."
7(6)   The words of ADONAI are pure words,
    silver in a melting-pot set in the earth,
    refined and purified seven times over.

8(7)   You, ADONAI, protect us;
    guard us forever from this generation —
9(8)   the wicked strut about everywhere
    when vileness is held in general esteem.

13 ¹⁽⁰⁾ For the leader. A psalm of David:

2(1)   How long, ADONAI?
    Will you forget me forever?
    How long will you hide your face from me?
3(2)   How long must I keep asking myself what to do,
    with sorrow in my heart every day?
    How long must my enemy dominate me?

4(3)   Look, and answer me, ADONAI my God!
    Give light to my eyes, or I will sleep the sleep of death.
5(4)   Then my enemy would say, "I was able to beat him";
    and my adversaries would rejoice at my downfall.

6(5)   But I trust in your grace,
    my heart rejoices as you bring me to safety.
(6)   I will sing to ADONAI, because he gives me
    even more than I need.

14 ¹⁽⁰⁾ For the leader. By David:

(1)   Fools say in their hearts,
    "There is no God."
    They deal corruptly, their deeds are vile,
    not one does what is right.

2   From heaven ADONAI observes humankind
    to see if anyone has understanding,
    if anyone seeks God.
3   But all turn aside, all alike are corrupt;
    no one does what is right,
    not a single one.

⁴ Don't they ever learn,
all those evildoers,
who eat up my people as if eating bread
and never call on ADONAI?
⁵ There they are, utterly terrified;
for God is with those who are righteous.
⁶ You may mock the plans of the poor,
but their refuge is ADONAI.

⁷ How I wish Isra'el's salvation
would come out of Tziyon!
When ADONAI restores his people's fortunes,
Ya'akov will rejoice, Isra'el will be glad!

15 ¹⁽⁰⁾ A psalm of David:

⁽¹⁾ ADONAI, who can rest in your tent?
Who can live on your holy mountain?

² Those who live a blameless life,
who behave uprightly,
who speak truth from their hearts
³ and keep their tongues from slander;
who never do harm to others
or seek to discredit neighbors;
⁴ who look with scorn on the vile,
but honor those who fear ADONAI;
who hold to an oath, no matter the cost;
⁵ who refuse usury when they lend money
and refuse a bribe to damage the innocent.

Those who do these things
never will be moved.

16 ¹⁽⁰⁾ Mikhtam. By David:

⁽¹⁾ Protect me, God,
for you are my refuge.
² I said to ADONAI, "You are my Lord;
I have nothing good outside of you."
³ The holy people in the land are the ones
who are worthy of honor; all my pleasure is in them.

⁴ Those who run after another god
multiply their sorrows.

To such gods I will not offer
drink offerings of blood
or take their names on my lips.

5   ADONAI, my assigned portion, my cup:
you safeguard my share.

6   Pleasant places were measured out for me;
I am content with my heritage.

7   I bless ADONAI, my counselor;
at night my inmost being instructs me.

8   I always set ADONAI before me;
with him at my right hand, I can never be moved;

9   so my heart is glad, my glory rejoices,
and my body too rests in safety;

10   for you will not abandon me to Sh'ol,
you will not let your faithful one see the Abyss.

11   You make me know the path of life;
in your presence is unbounded joy,
in your right hand eternal delight.

17 ¹⁽⁰⁾ A prayer of David:

(1)   Hear a just cause, ADONAI, heed my cry;
listen to my prayer from honest lips.

2   Let my vindication come from you,
let your eyes see what is right.

3   You probed my heart,
you visited me at night,
and you assayed me without finding evil thoughts
that should not pass my lips.

4   As for what others do, by words from your lips
I have kept myself from the ways of the violent;

5   my steps hold steadily to your paths,
my feet do not slip.

6   Now I call on you, God, for you will answer me.
Turn your ear to me, hear my words.

7   Show how wonderful is your grace,
savior of those who seek at your right hand
refuge from their foes.

8   Protect me like the pupil of your eye,
hide me in the shadow of your wings

9   from the wicked, who are assailing me,
from my deadly enemies, who are all around me.

10   They close their hearts to compassion;
    they speak arrogantly with their mouths;

11   they track me down, they surround me;
    they watch for a chance to bring me to the ground.

12   They are like lions eager to tear the prey,
    like young lions crouching in ambush.

13   Arise, ADONAI, confront them! Bring them down!
    With your sword deliver me from the wicked,

14   with your hand, ADONAI, from human beings,
    from people whose portion in life is this world.
    You fill their stomachs with your treasure,
    their children will be satisfied too
    and will leave their wealth to their little ones.

15   But my prayer, in righteousness, is to see your face;
    on waking, may I be satisfied with a vision of you.

18 ¹⁽⁰⁾ For the leader. By David the servant of ADONAI, who addressed the words of this song to ADONAI on the day when ADONAI delivered him from the power of all his enemies, including from the power of Sha'ul. ² He said:

(1)   "I love you, ADONAI, my strength!

3(2)   "ADONAI is my Rock, my fortress and deliverer,
    my God, my Rock, in whom I find shelter,
    my shield, the power that saves me,
    my stronghold.

4(3)   I call on ADONAI, who is worthy of praise;
    and I am saved from my enemies.

5(4)   "For the cords of death surrounded me,
    the floods of B'liya'al terrified me,

6(5)   the ropes of Sh'ol were wrapped around me,
    the snares of death lay there before me.

7(6)   In my distress I called to ADONAI;
    I cried out to my God.
    Out of his temple he heard my voice;
    my cry reached his ears.

8(7)   "Then the earth quaked and shook,
    the foundations of the mountains trembled.
    They were shaken because he was angry.

9(8)   Smoke arose in his nostrils;
    out of his mouth came devouring fire;
    sparks blazed forth from him.

10(9)   He lowered heaven and came down
with thick darkness under his feet.

11(10)   He rode on a *keruv*; he flew,
swooping down on the wings of the wind.

12(11)   He made darkness his hiding-place,
his canopy thick clouds dark with water.

13(12)   From the brightness before him,
there broke through his thick clouds
hailstones and fiery coals.

14(13)   "*ADONAI* also thundered in heaven,
Ha'Elyon sounded his voice —
hailstones and fiery coals.

15(14)   He sent out arrows and scattered them,
shot out lightning and routed them.

16(15)   The channels of water appeared,
the foundations of the world were exposed
at your rebuke, *ADONAI*,
at the blast of breath from your nostrils.

17(16)   "He sent from on high, he took me
and pulled me out of deep water;

18(17)   he rescued me from my powerful enemy,
from those who hated me,
for they were stronger than I.

19(18)   They came against me on my day of disaster,
but *ADONAI* was my support.

20(19)   He brought me out to an open place;
he rescued me, because he took pleasure in me.

21(20)   *ADONAI* rewarded me for my uprightness,
he repaid me because my hands were clean.

22(21)   "For I have kept the ways of *ADONAI*,
I have not done evil by leaving my God;

23(22)   for all his rulings were before me,
I did not distance his regulations from me.

24(23)   I was pure-hearted with him
and kept myself from my sin.

25(24)   "Hence *ADONAI* repaid me for my uprightness,
according to the purity of my hands in his view.

26(25)   With the merciful, you are merciful;
with a man who is sincere, you are sincere;

27(26)   with the pure, you are pure;
but with the crooked you are cunning.

28(27)   People afflicted, you save;
but haughty eyes, you humble.

29(28) "For you, *Adonai*, light my lamp;
    Adonai, my God, lights up my darkness.
30(29) With you I can run through a whole troop of men,
    with my God I can leap a wall.

31(30) "As for God, his way is perfect,
    the word of *Adonai* has been tested by fire;
    he shields all who take refuge in him.

32(31) "For who is God but *Adonai*?
    Who is a Rock but our God?

33(32) "It is God who girds me with strength;
    he makes my way go straight.
34(33) He makes me swift, sure-footed as a deer,
    and enables me to stand on my high places.
35(34) He trains my hands for war
    until my arms can bend a bow of bronze;

36(35) "You give me your shield, which is salvation,
    your right hand holds me up,
    your humility makes me great.
37(36) You lengthen the steps I can take,
    yet my ankles do not turn.

38(37) "I pursued my enemies and overtook them,
    without turning back until they were destroyed.
39(38) I crushed them, so that they can't get up;
    they have fallen under my feet.

40(39) "For you braced me with strength for the battle
    and bent down my adversaries beneath me.
41(40) You made my enemies turn their backs in flight,
    and I destroyed those who hated me.

42(41) "They cried out, but there was no one to help,
    even to *Adonai*, but he didn't answer.
43(42) I pulverized them like dust in the wind,
    threw them out like mud in the streets.

44(43) "You also freed me from the quarrels of my people.
    You made me head of the nations;
    a people I did not know now serve me —
45(44) the moment they hear of me, they obey me,
    foreigners come cringing to me.
46(45) Foreigners lose heart
    as they come trembling from their fortresses.

47(46) "*Adonai* is alive! Blessed is my Rock!
Exalted be the God of my salvation,

48(47) the God who avenges me
and subdues peoples under me.

49(48) He delivers me from my enemies.
You lift me high above my enemies,
you rescue me from violent men.

50(49) "So I give thanks to you, *Adonai*, among the nations;
I sing praises to your name.

51(50) Great salvation he gives to his king;
he displays grace to his anointed,
to David and his descendants forever."

19 ¹⁽⁰⁾ For the leader. A psalm of David:

2(1) The heavens declare the glory of God,
the dome of the sky speaks the work of his hands.

3(2) Every day it utters speech,
every night it reveals knowledge.

4(3) Without speech, without a word,
without their voices being heard,

5(4) their line goes out through all the earth
and their words to the end of the world.

In them he places a tent for the sun,

6(5) which comes out like a bridegroom from the bridal chamber,
with delight like an athlete to run his race.

7(6) It rises at one side of the sky,
circles around to the other side,
and nothing escapes its heat.

8(7) The *Torah* of *Adonai* is perfect,
restoring the inner person.
The instruction of *Adonai* is sure,
making wise the thoughtless.

9(8) The precepts of *Adonai* are right,
rejoicing the heart.
The *mitzvah* of *Adonai* is pure,
enlightening the eyes.

10(9) The fear of *Adonai* is clean,
enduring forever.
The rulings of *Adonai* are true,
they are righteous altogether,

11(10) more desirable than gold,
than much fine gold,

also sweeter than honey
or drippings from the honeycomb.

12(11) Through them your servant is warned;
in obeying them there is great reward.

13(12) Who can discern unintentional sins?
Cleanse me from hidden faults.

14(13) Also keep your servant from presumptuous sins,
so that they won't control me.
Then I will be blameless
and free of great offense.

15(14) May the words of my mouth
and the thoughts of my heart
be acceptable in your presence,
ADONAI, my Rock and Redeemer.

20 ¹⁽⁰⁾ For the leader. A psalm of David:

2(1) May ADONAI answer you in times of distress,
may the name of the God of Ya'akov protect you.

3(2) May he send you help from the sanctuary
and give you support from Tziyon.

4(3) May he be reminded by all your grain offerings
and accept the fat of your burnt offerings.   (*Selah*)

5(4) May he grant you your heart's desire
and bring all your plans to success.

6(5) Then we will shout for joy at your victory
and fly our flags in the name of our God.
May ADONAI fulfill all your requests.

7(6) Now I know that ADONAI
gives victory to his anointed one —
he will answer him from his holy heaven
with mighty victories by his right hand.

8(7) Some trust in chariots and some in horses,
but we praise the name of ADONAI our God.

9(8) They will crumple and fall,
but we will arise and stand erect.

10(9) Give victory, ADONAI!
Let the King answer us the day we call.

21 $^{1(0)}$ For the leader. A psalm of David:

$^{2(1)}$ ADONAI, the king finds joy in your strength;
        what great joy he displays in your victory!

$^{3(2)}$ You give him his heart's desire;
        you don't refuse the prayer from his lips.   (*Selah*)

$^{4(3)}$ For you come to meet him with the best blessings,
        you place a crown of fine gold on his head.

$^{5(4)}$ He asks you for life; you give it to him,
        years and years forever and ever.

$^{6(5)}$ Your victory brings him great glory;
        you confer on him splendor and honor.

$^{7(6)}$ For you bestow on him everlasting blessings,
        you make him glad with the joy of your presence.

$^{8(7)}$ For the king puts his trust in ADONAI,
        in the grace of '*Elyon*; he will not be moved.

$^{9(8)}$ Your hand will find all your enemies;
        your right hand will overtake those who hate you.

$^{10(9)}$ At your appearing,
        you will make them like a fiery furnace.
        ADONAI will swallow them up in his anger;
        fire will consume them.

$^{11(10)}$ You will destroy from the earth their descendants,
        rid humankind of their posterity;

$^{12(11)}$ for they intended evil against you;
        but despite their scheme, they won't succeed.

$^{13(12)}$ For you will make them turn their back
        by aiming your bow at their faces.

$^{14(13)}$ Arise, ADONAI, in your strength;
        and we will sing and praise your power.

22 $^{1(0)}$ For the leader. Set to "Sunrise." A psalm of David:

$^{2(1)}$ My God! My God!
        Why have you abandoned me?
        Why so far from helping me,
        so far from my anguished cries?

$^{3(2)}$ My God, by day I call to you,
        but you don't answer;
        likewise at night,
        but I get no relief.

4(3) Nevertheless, you are holy,
enthroned on the praises of Isra'el.

5(4) In you our ancestors put their trust;
they trusted, and you rescued them.

6(5) They cried to you and escaped;
they trusted in you and were not disappointed.

7(6) But I am a worm, not a man,
scorned by everyone, despised by the people.

8(7) All who see me jeer at me;
they sneer and shake their heads:

9(8) "He committed himself to Adonai,
so let him rescue him!
Let him set him free
if he takes such delight in him!"

10(9) But you are the one who took me from the womb,
you made me trust when I was on my mother's breasts.

11(10) Since my birth I've been thrown on you;
you are my God from my mother's womb.

12(11) Don't stay far from me, for trouble is near;
and there is no one to help.

13(12) Many bulls surround me,
wild bulls of Bashan close in on me.

14(13) They open their mouths wide against me,
like ravening, roaring lions.

15(14) I am poured out like water;
all my bones are out of joint;
my heart has become like wax —
it melts inside me;

16(15) my mouth is as dry as a fragment of a pot,
my tongue sticks to my palate;
you lay me down in the dust of death.

17(16) Dogs are all around me,
a pack of villains closes in on me
like a lion [at] my hands and feet.*

18(17) I can count every one of my bones,
while they gaze at me and gloat.

19(18) They divide my garments among themselves;
for my clothing they throw dice.

20(19) But you, Adonai, don't stay far away!
My strength, come quickly to help me!

21(20) Rescue me from the sword,

---

*Or: "They pierced my hands and feet." See Introduction, Section VIII, paragraph 6, and Section XIV, footnote 70.

22(21) my life from the power of the dogs.
Save me from the lion's mouth!

23(22) You have answered me from the wild bulls' horns.
I will proclaim your name to my kinsmen;
right there in the assembly I will praise you:

24(23) "You who fear ADONAI, praise him!
All descendants of Ya'akov, glorify him!
All descendants of Isra'el, stand in awe of him!

25(24) For he has not despised or abhorred
the poverty of the poor;
he did not hide his face from him
but listened to his cry."

26(25) Because of you
I give praise in the great assembly;
I will fulfill my vows
in the sight of those who fear him.

27(26) The poor will eat and be satisfied;
those who seek ADONAI will praise him;
Your hearts will enjoy life forever.

28(27) All the ends of the earth
will remember and turn to ADONAI;
all the clans of the nations
will worship in your presence.

29(28) For the kingdom belongs to ADONAI,
and he rules the nations.

30(29) All who prosper on the earth
will eat and worship;
all who go down to the dust
will kneel before him,
including him who can't keep himself alive.

31(30) A descendant will serve him;
the next generation will be told of *Adonai.*

32(31) They will come and proclaim
his righteousness
to a people yet unborn,
that he is the one who did it.

23 ¹(⁰) A psalm of David:

(1) ADONAI is my shepherd; I lack nothing.

2 He has me lie down in grassy pastures,
he leads me by quiet water,

3 he restores my inner person.

810

He guides me in right paths
for the sake of his own name.

4 Even if I pass through death-dark ravines,
I will fear no disaster; for you are with me;
your rod and staff reassure me.

5 You prepare a table for me,
even as my enemies watch;
you anoint my head with oil
from an overflowing cup.

6 Goodness and grace will pursue me
every day of my life;
and I will live in the house of ADONAI
for years and years to come.

24 ¹⁽⁰⁾ By David. A psalm:

⁽¹⁾ The earth is ADONAI's, with all that is in it,
the world and those who live there;

2 for he set its foundations on the seas
and established it on the rivers.

3 Who may go up to the mountain of ADONAI?
Who can stand in his holy place?

4 Those with clean hands and pure hearts,
who don't make vanities the purpose of their lives
or swear oaths just to deceive.

5 They will receive a blessing from ADONAI
and justice from God, who saves them.

6 Such is the character of those who seek him,
of Ya'akov, who seeks your face. (*Selah*)

7 Lift up your heads, you gates!
Lift them up, everlasting doors,
so that the glorious king can enter!

8 Who is he, this glorious king?
ADONAI, strong and mighty,
ADONAI, mighty in battle.

9 Lift up your heads, you gates!
Lift them up, everlasting doors,
so that the glorious king can enter!

10 Who is he, this glorious king?
ADONAI-Tzva'ot —
he is the glorious king. (*Selah*)

25 ¹⁽⁰⁾ By David:

⁽¹⁾   I lift my inner being to you, ADONAI;
²   I trust you, my God.
    Don't let me be disgraced,
    don't let my enemies gloat over me.
³   No one waiting for you will be disgraced;
    disgrace awaits those who break faith for no reason.

⁴   Make me know your ways, ADONAI,
    teach me your paths.
⁵   Guide me in your truth, and teach me;
    for you are the God who saves me,
    my hope is in you all day long.
⁶   Remember your compassion and grace, ADONAI;
    for these are ages old.
⁷   Don't remember my youthful sins or transgressions;
    but remember me according to your grace
    for the sake of your goodness, ADONAI.

⁸   ADONAI is good, and he is fair;
    this is why he teaches sinners the way [to live],
⁹   leads the humble to do what is right
    and teaches the humble [to live] his way.
¹⁰   All ADONAI's paths are grace and truth
    to those who keep his covenant and instructions.
¹¹   For the sake of your name, ADONAI,
    forgive my wickedness, great though it is.

¹²   Who is the person who fears ADONAI?
    He will teach him the way to choose.
¹³   He will remain prosperous,
    and his descendants will inherit the land.
¹⁴   ADONAI relates intimately with those who fear him;
    he makes them know his covenant.

¹⁵   My eyes are always directed toward ADONAI,
    for he will free my feet from the net.
¹⁶   Turn to me, and show me your favor;
    for I am alone and oppressed.
¹⁷   The troubles of my heart are growing and growing;
    bring me out of my distress.
¹⁸   See my affliction and suffering,
    and take all my sins away.

¹⁹   Consider my enemies, how many there are
    and how cruelly they hate me.

20   Protect me and rescue me;
     don't let me be disgraced,
     for I take refuge in you.

21   Let integrity and uprightness preserve me,
     because my hope is in you.

22   God! Redeem Isra'el
     from all their troubles!

26 ¹⁽⁰⁾ By David:

(1)   Vindicate me, ADONAI,
     for I have lived a blameless life;
     unwaveringly I trust in ADONAI.

2   Examine me, ADONAI, test me,
     search my mind and heart.

3   For your grace is there before my eyes,
     and I live my life by your truth.

4   I have not sat with worthless folks,
     I won't consort with hypocrites,

5   I hate the company of evildoers,
     I will not sit with the wicked.

6   I will wash my hands in innocence
     and walk around your altar, ADONAI,

7   lifting my voice in thanks
     and proclaiming all your wonders.

8   ADONAI, I love the house where you live,
     the place where your glory abides.

9   Don't include me with sinners
     or my life with the bloodthirsty.

10   In their hands are evil schemes;
     their right hands are full of bribes.

11   As for me, I will live a blameless life.
     Redeem me and show me favor.

12   My feet are planted on level ground;
     in the assemblies I will bless ADONAI.

27 ¹⁽⁰⁾ By David:

(1)   ADONAI is my light and salvation;
     whom do I need to fear?
     ADONAI is the stronghold of my life;
     of whom should I be afraid?

2   When evildoers assailed me
     to devour my flesh,
     my adversaries and foes,
     they stumbled and fell.
3   If an army encamps against me,
     my heart will not fear;
     if war breaks out against me,
     even then I will keep trusting.

4   Just one thing have I asked of ADONAI;
     only this will I seek:
     to live in the house of ADONAI
     all the days of my life,
     to see the beauty of ADONAI
     and visit in his temple.
5   For he will conceal me in his shelter
     on the day of trouble,
     he will hide me in the folds of his tent,
     he will set me high on a rock.
6   Then my head will be lifted up
     above my surrounding foes,
     and I will offer in his tent
     sacrifices with shouts of joy;
     I will sing, sing praises to ADONAI.

7   Listen, ADONAI, to my voice when I cry;
     show favor to me; and answer me.
8   "My heart said of you, 'Seek my face.'"
     Your face, ADONAI, I will seek.
9   Do not hide your face from me,
     don't turn your servant away in anger.
     You are my help; don't abandon me;
     don't leave me, God my savior.
10   Even though my father and mother have left me,
     ADONAI will care for me.
11   Teach me your way, ADONAI;
     lead me on a level path
     because of my enemies —
12   don't give me up to the whims of my foes;
     for false witnesses have risen against me,
     also those who are breathing violence.

13   If I hadn't believed that I would see
     ADONAI's goodness in the land of the living, . . .
14   Put your hope in ADONAI, be strong,
     and let your heart take courage!
     Yes, put your hope in ADONAI!

28 $^{1(0)}$ By David:

$^{(1)}$ ADONAI, I am calling to you;
my Rock, don't be deaf to my cry.
For if you answer me with silence,
I will be like those who fall in a pit.

^{2} Hear the sound of my prayers
when I cry to you,
when I lift my hands
toward your holy sanctuary.

^{3} Don't drag me off with the wicked,
with those whose deeds are evil;
they speak words of peace to their fellowmen,
but evil is in their hearts.

^{4} Pay them back for their deeds,
as befits their evil acts;
repay them for what they have done,
give them what they deserve.

^{5} For they don't understand the deeds of ADONAI
or what he has done.
He will break them down;
he will not build them up.

^{6} Blessed be ADONAI,
for he heard my voice as I prayed for mercy.

^{7} ADONAI is my strength and shield;
in him my heart trusted, and I have been helped.
Therefore my heart is filled with joy,
and I will sing praises to him.

^{8} ADONAI is strength for [his people],
a stronghold of salvation to his anointed.

^{9} Save your people! Bless your heritage!
Shepherd them, and carry them forever!

29 $^{1(0)}$ A psalm of David:

$^{(1)}$ Give ADONAI his due, you who are godly;
give ADONAI his due of glory and strength;

^{2} give ADONAI the glory due his name;
worship ADONAI in holy splendor.

^{3} The voice of ADONAI is over the waters;
the God of glory thunders,
ADONAI over rushing waters,

4   the voice of *Adonai* in power,
    the voice of *Adonai* in splendor.

5   The voice of *Adonai* cracks the cedars;
    Adonai splinters the cedars of the L'vanon
6   and makes the L'vanon skip like a calf,
    Siryon like a young wild ox.

7   The voice of *Adonai* flashes fiery flames;
8   the voice of *Adonai* rocks the desert,
    Adonai convulses the Kadesh Desert.
9   The voice of *Adonai* causes deer to give birth
    and strips the forests bare —
    while in his temple, all cry, "Glory!"
10 *Adonai* sits enthroned above the flood!
    Adonai sits enthroned as king forever!
11 May *Adonai* give strength to his people!
    May *Adonai* bless his people with *shalom!*

30 ¹⁽⁰⁾ A psalm. A song for the dedication of the house. By David:

2(1) I will exalt you, *Adonai*, because you drew me up;
      you didn't let my enemies rejoice over me.
3(2) *Adonai* my God, I cried out to you,
      and you provided healing for me.
4(3) *Adonai*, you lifted me up from Sh'ol;
      you kept me alive when I was sinking into a pit.

5(4) Sing praise to *Adonai*, you faithful of his;
      and give thanks on recalling his holiness.
6(5) For his anger is momentary,
      but his favor lasts a lifetime.
      Tears may linger for the night,
      but with dawn come cries of joy.

7(6) Once I was prosperous and used to say
      that nothing could ever shake me —
8(7) when you showed me favor, *Adonai*,
      I was firm as a mighty mountain.
      But when you hid your face,
      I was struck with terror.

9(8) I called to you, *Adonai*;
      to *Adonai* I pleaded for mercy:
10(9) "What advantage is there in my death,
      in my going down to the pit?

Can the dust praise you?
Can it proclaim your truth?

11(10) Hear me, ADONAI, and show me your favor!
ADONAI, be my helper!"

12(11) You turned my mourning into dancing!
You removed my sackcloth and clothed me with joy,

13(12) so that my well-being can praise you and not be silent;
ADONAI my God, I will thank you forever!

31 ¹⁽⁰⁾ For the leader. A psalm of David:

2(1) In you, ADONAI, I take refuge;
let me never be put to shame;
in your justice, save me!

3(2) Turn your ear toward me,
come quickly to my rescue,
be for me a rock of strength,
a fortress to keep me safe.

4(3) Since you are my rock and fortress,
lead me and guide me for your name's sake.

5(4) Free me from the net they have hidden to catch me,
because you are my strength.

6(5) Into your hand I commit my spirit;
you will redeem me, ADONAI, God of truth.

7(6) I hate those who serve worthless idols;
as for me, I trust in ADONAI.

8(7) I will rejoice and be glad in your grace,
for you see my affliction,
you know how distressed I am.

9(8) You did not hand me over to the enemy;
you set my feet where I can move freely.

10(9) Show me favor, ADONAI, for I am in trouble.
My eyes grow dim with anger,
my soul and body as well.

11(10) For my life is worn out with sorrow
and my years with sighing;
my strength gives out under my guilt,
and my bones are wasting away.

12(11) I am scorned by all my adversaries,
and even more by my neighbors;
even to acquaintances
I am an object of fear —

	when they see me in the street, they turn away from me.
13(12)	Like a dead man, I have passed from their minds; I have become like a broken pot.
14(13)	All I hear is whispering, terror is all around me; they plot together against me, scheming to take my life.
15(14)	But I, I trust in you, ADONAI; I say, "You are my God."
16(15)	My times are in your hand; rescue me from my enemies' power, from those who persecute me.
17(16)	Make your face shine on your servant; in your grace, save me.
18(17)	ADONAI, don't let me be put to shame, for I have called on you; let the wicked be put to shame, let them be silenced in Sh'ol.
19(18)	May lying lips be struck dumb, that speak insolently against the righteous with such pride and contempt.
20(19)	But oh, how great is your goodness, which you have stored up for those who fear you, which you do for those who take refuge in you, before people's very eyes!
21(20)	In the shelter of your presence you hide them from human plots, you conceal them in your shelter, safe from contentious tongues.
22(21)	Blessed be ADONAI! For he has shown me his amazing grace when I was in a city under siege.
23(22)	As for me, in my alarm I said, "I have been cut off from your sight!" Nevertheless, you heard my pleas when I cried out to you.
24(23)	Love ADONAI, you faithful of his. ADONAI preserves the loyal, but the proud he repays in full.
25(24)	Be strong, and fill your hearts with courage, all of you who hope in ADONAI.

32 ¹⁽⁰⁾ By David. A *maskil*:

(1) How blessed are those whose offense is forgiven,
those whose sin is covered!

2 How blessed those to whom ADONAI imputes no guilt,
in whose spirit is no deceit!

3 When I kept silent, my bones wasted away
because of my groaning all day long;

4 day and night your hand was heavy on me;
the sap in me dried up as in a summer drought. (*Selah*)

5 When I acknowledged my sin to you,
when I stopped concealing my guilt,
and said, "I will confess my offenses to ADONAI";
then you, you forgave the guilt of my sin. (*Selah*)

6 This is what everyone faithful should pray
at a time when you can be found.
Then, when the floodwaters are raging,
they will not reach to him.

7 You are a hiding-place for me,
you will keep me from distress;
you will surround me
with songs of deliverance. (*Selah*)

8 "I will instruct and teach you
in this way that you are to go;
I will give you counsel;
my eyes will be watching you."

9 Don't be like a horse or mule
that has no understanding,
that has to be curbed with bit and bridle,
or else it won't come near you.

10 Many are the torments of the wicked,
but grace surrounds those who trust in ADONAI.

11 Be glad in ADONAI; rejoice, you righteous!
Shout for joy, all you upright in heart!

33 ¹ Rejoice in ADONAI, you righteous!
Praise is well-suited to the upright.

2 Give thanks to ADONAI with the lyre,
sing praises to him with a ten-stringed harp.

3   Sing to him a new song,
make music at your best among shouts of joy.

4   For the word of ADONAI is true,
and all his work is trustworthy.

5   He loves righteousness and justice;
the earth is full of the grace of ADONAI.

6   By the word of ADONAI the heavens were made,
and their whole host by a breath from his mouth.

7   He collects the sea waters together in a heap;
he puts the deeps in storehouses.

8   Let all the earth fear ADONAI!
Let all living in the world stand in awe of him.

9   For he spoke, and there it was;
he commanded, and there it stood.

10   ADONAI brings to nothing the plans of nations,
he foils the plans of the peoples.

11   But the counsel of ADONAI stands forever,
his heart's plans are for all generations.

12   How blessed is the nation whose God is ADONAI,
the people he chose as his heritage!

13   ADONAI looks out from heaven;
he sees every human being;

14   from the place where he lives
he watches everyone living on earth,

15   he who fashioned the hearts of them all
and understands all they do.

16   A king is not saved by the size of his army,
a strong man not delivered by his great strength.

17   To rely on a horse for safety is vain,
nor does its great power assure escape.

18   But ADONAI's eyes watch over those who fear him,
over those who wait for his grace

19   to rescue them from death
and keep them alive in famine.

20   We are waiting for ADONAI;
he is our help and shield.

21   For in him our hearts rejoice,
because we trust in his holy name.

22   May your mercy, ADONAI, be over us,
because we put our hope in you.

34 ¹⁽⁰⁾ By David, when he pretended to be insane before Avimelekh, who then drove him away; so he left:

²⁽¹⁾   I will bless ADONAI at all times;
        his praise will always be in my mouth.
³⁽²⁾   When I boast, it will be about ADONAI;
        the humble will hear of it and be glad.

⁴⁽³⁾   Proclaim with me the greatness of ADONAI;
        let us exalt his name together.
⁵⁽⁴⁾   I sought ADONAI, and he answered me;
        he rescued me from everything I feared.

⁶⁽⁵⁾   They looked to him and grew radiant;
        their faces will never blush for shame.
⁷⁽⁶⁾   This poor man cried; ADONAI heard
        and saved him from all his troubles.
⁸⁽⁷⁾   The angel of ADONAI, who encamps
        around those who fear him, delivers them.

⁹⁽⁸⁾   Taste, and see that ADONAI is good.
        How blessed are those who take refuge in him!
¹⁰⁽⁹⁾   Fear ADONAI, you holy ones of his,
        for those who fear him lack nothing.
¹¹⁽¹⁰⁾   Young lions can be needy, they can go hungry,
        but those who seek ADONAI lack nothing good.

¹²⁽¹¹⁾   Come, children, listen to me;
        I will teach you the fear of ADONAI.
¹³⁽¹²⁾   Which of you takes pleasure in living?
        Who wants a long life to see good things?
¹⁴⁽¹³⁾   [If you do,] keep your tongue from evil
        and your lips from deceiving talk;
¹⁵⁽¹⁴⁾   turn from evil, and do good;
        seek peace, go after it!

¹⁶⁽¹⁵⁾   The eyes of ADONAI watch over the righteous,
        and his ears are open to their cry.
¹⁷⁽¹⁶⁾   But the face of ADONAI opposes those who do evil,
        to cut off all memory of them from the earth.

¹⁸⁽¹⁷⁾   [The righteous] cried out, and ADONAI heard,
        and he saved them from all their troubles.
¹⁹⁽¹⁸⁾   ADONAI is near those with broken hearts;
        he saves those whose spirit is crushed.
²⁰⁽¹⁹⁾   The righteous person suffers many evils,
        but ADONAI rescues him out of them all.

²¹⁽²⁰⁾ He protects all his bones;
not one of them gets broken.

²²⁽²¹⁾ Evil will kill the wicked,
and those who hate the righteous will be condemned.
²³⁽²²⁾ But ADONAI redeems his servants;
no one who takes refuge in him will be condemned.

35 ¹⁽⁰⁾ By David:

⁽¹⁾ ADONAI, oppose those who oppose me;
fight against those who fight against me.
² Grasp your shield and protective gear,
and rise to my defense.
³ Brandish spear and battle-axe
against my pursuers;
let me hear you say,
"I am your salvation."

⁴ May those who seek my life
be disgraced and put to confusion;
may those who are plotting harm for me
be repulsed and put to shame.
⁵ May they be like chaff before the wind,
with the angel of ADONAI to drive them on.
⁶ May their way be dark and slippery,
with the angel of ADONAI to pursue them.
⁷ For unprovoked, they hid their net over a pit;
unprovoked, they dug it for me.
⁸ May destruction come over him unawares.
May the net he concealed catch himself;
may he fall into it and be destroyed.

⁹ Then I will be joyful in ADONAI,
I will rejoice in his salvation.
¹⁰ All my bones will say,
"Who is like you?
Who can rescue the weak
from those stronger than they,
the poor and needy
from those who exploit them?"

¹¹ Malicious witnesses come forward,
asking me things about which I know nothing.
¹² They repay me evil for good;
it makes me feel desolate as a parent bereaved.

13 But I, when they were ill, wore sackcloth;
I put myself out and fasted;
I can pray that what I prayed for them
might also happen to me.

14 I behaved as I would for my friend or my brother;
I bent down in sorrow as if mourning my mother.

15 But when I stumble, they gather in glee;
they gather against me and strike me unawares;
they tear me apart unceasingly.

16 With ungodly mocking and grimacing,
they grind their teeth at me.

17 *Adonai*, how much longer will you look on?
Rescue me from their assaults,
save the one life I have from the lions!

18 I will give you thanks in the great assembly,
I will give you praise among huge crowds of people.

19 Don't let those who are wrongfully my enemies
gloat over me;
and those who hate me unprovoked —
don't let them smirk at me.

20 For they don't speak words of peace
but devise ways to deceive
the peaceful of the land.

21 They shout to accuse me, "Aha! Aha!
we saw you with our own eyes!"

22 You saw them, *Adonai*; don't stay silent.
Adonai, don't stay far away from me.

23 Wake up! Get up, my God, my Lord!
Defend me and my cause!

24 Give judgment for me, *Adonai*, my God,
as your righteousness demands.

Don't let them gloat over me.

25 Don't let them say to themselves,
"Aha! We got what we wanted!"
or say, "We swallowed them up!"

26 May those who gloat over my distress
be disgraced and humiliated.
May those who aggrandize themselves at my expense
be covered with shame and confusion.

27 But may those who delight in my righteousness
shout for joy and be glad!

> Let them say always, "How great is ADONAI,
> who delights in the peace of his servant!"
> 28 Then my tongue will tell of your righteousness
> and praise you all day long.

36 ¹⁽⁰⁾ For the leader. By David, the servant of ADONAI:

> ²⁽¹⁾ Crime speaks to the wicked.
> I perceive this in my heart;
> before his eyes there is no fear
> of God.
> ³⁽²⁾ For, the way he sees it,
> crime makes his life easy —
> that is, until his wrongs are discovered;
> then, he is hated.
> ⁴⁽³⁾ His words are wrong and deceitful;
> he has stopped being wise and doing good.
> ⁵⁽⁴⁾ He devises trouble as he lies in bed;
> so set is he on his own bad way
> that he doesn't hate evil.

> ⁶⁽⁵⁾ ADONAI, in the heavens is your grace;
> your faithfulness reaches to the skies.
> ⁷⁽⁶⁾ Your righteousness is like the mountains of God,
> your judgments are like the great deep.
> You save man and beast, ADONAI.
> ⁸⁽⁷⁾ How precious, God, is your grace!
> People take refuge in the shadow of your wings,
> ⁹⁽⁸⁾ they feast on the rich bounty of your house,
> and you have them drink from the stream of your delights.
> ¹⁰⁽⁹⁾ For with you is the fountain of life;
> in your light we see light.
> ¹¹⁽¹⁰⁾ Continue your grace to those who know you
> and your righteousness to the upright in heart.
> ¹²⁽¹¹⁾ Don't let the foot of the proud tread on me
> or the hands of the wicked drive me away.
> ¹³⁽¹²⁾ There they lie fallen, those evildoers,
> flung down and unable to rise.

37 ¹⁽⁰⁾ By David:

> ⁽¹⁾ Don't be upset by evildoers
> or envious of those who do wrong,
> ² for soon they will wither like grass
> and fade like the green in the fields.

3   Trust in *Adonai*, and do good;
       settle in the land, and feed on faithfulness.
4   Then you will delight yourself in *Adonai*,
       and he will give you your heart's desire.

5   Commit your way to *Adonai*;
       trust in him, and he will act.
6   He will make your vindication shine forth like light,
       the justice of your cause like the noonday sun.

7   Be still before *Adonai*;
       wait patiently till he comes.
       Don't be upset by those whose way
       succeeds because of their wicked plans.
8   Stop being angry, put aside rage,
       and don't be upset — it leads to evil.

9   For evildoers will be cut off,
       but those hoping in *Adonai* will inherit the land.
10   Soon the wicked will be no more;
       you will look for his place, and he won't be there.
11   But the meek will inherit the land
       and delight themselves in abundant peace.

12   The wicked plots against the righteous
       and grinds his teeth at him;
13   but *Adonai* laughs at the wicked,
       knowing his day will come.
14   The wicked have unsheathed their swords,
       they have strung their bows
       to bring down the poor and needy,
       to slaughter those whose way is upright.
15   But their swords will pierce their own hearts,
       and their bows will be broken.

16   Better the little that the righteous has
       than the wealth of all the wicked.
17   For the arms of the wicked will be broken,
       but *Adonai* upholds the righteous.
18   *Adonai* knows what the wholehearted suffer,
       but their inheritance lasts forever.
19   They will not be distressed when times are hard;
       when famine comes, they will have plenty.

20   For the wicked will perish;
       Adonai's enemies will be like sheep fat,
       ending up as smoke, finished.

21	The wicked borrows and doesn't repay,
	but the righteous is generous and gives.
22	For those blessed by [ADONAI] will inherit the land,
	but those cursed by him will be cut off.

23 ADONAI directs a person's steps,
and he delights in his way.

24 He may stumble, but he won't fall headlong,
for ADONAI holds him by the hand.

25 I have been young; now I am old;
yet not once have I seen the righteous abandoned
or his descendants begging for bread.

26 All day long he is generous and lends,
and his descendants are blessed.

27 If you turn from evil and do good,
you will live safely forever.

28 For ADONAI loves justice
and will not abandon his faithful;
they are preserved forever.
But the descendants of the wicked will be cut off.

29 The righteous will inherit the land
and live in it forever.

30 The mouth of the righteous articulates wisdom,
his tongue speaks justice.

31 The Torah of his God is in his heart;
his footsteps do not falter.

32 The wicked keeps his eye on the righteous,
seeking a chance to kill him.

33 But ADONAI will not leave him in his power
or let him be condemned when judged.

34 Put your hope in ADONAI, keep to his way,
and he will raise you up to inherit the land.
When the wicked are cut off, you will see it.

35 I have seen a wicked man wielding great power,
flourishing like a shade tree in its native soil.

36 But I passed by again, and he was no longer there;
I looked for him, but he could not be found.

37 Observe the pure person, consider the upright;
for the peaceful person will have posterity.

38 But transgressors will all be destroyed;
the posterity of the wicked will be cut off.

39   *ADONAI* is the one who saves the righteous;
     he is their stronghold in time of trouble.
40   *ADONAI* helps them and rescues them,
     rescues them from the wicked and saves them;
     because they take refuge in him.

38 ¹⁽⁰⁾ A psalm of David, serving as a reminder:

2(1)   *ADONAI*, don't rebuke me when you are angry
     or discipline me when you are enraged,
3(2)   for your arrows penetrate me deeply,
     and your hand is pressing me down.

4(3)   Your indignation left no part of me intact;
     my sin made my whole body sick;
5(4)   for my iniquities loom high over my head
     as a heavy burden, too heavy for me.

6(5)   I have stinking, festering wounds
     because of my foolishness.
7(6)   I am bent down, prostrate completely;
     I go about mourning all day long.

8(7)   For my insides burn with fever,
     and my whole body is sick.
9(8)   I am numb, completely crushed;
     my anguished heart makes me groan aloud.

10(9)   *Adonai*, all my longing is known to you;
     my sighing is not hidden from you.
11(10)   My heart is throbbing, my strength is gone,
     and the light in my eyes has left me.

12(11)   My friends and companions shun my disease;
     even the closest keep their distance.
13(12)   Those seeking my life lay snares for me,
     those seeking to harm me speak of disaster
     and think up deceptions all day long.

14(13)   But I'm like a deaf man — I don't hear it;
     and, like a mute, I don't say a word.
15(14)   Yes, I've become like a man who doesn't hear
     and in whose mouth are no defenses.

16(15)   For it is in you, *ADONAI*, that I hope.
     You will answer, *Adonai* my God.

17(16)   I said, "Don't let them gloat over me
or boast against me when my foot slips."

18(17)   For I am about to fall,
and my pain is always with me.
19(18)   I acknowledge my guilt,
I am anxious because of my sin.

20(19)   But my enemies are alive and well,
those who wrongfully hate me increase their numbers;
21(20)   and, since they repay good with evil,
they oppose me because I pursue good.

22(21)   Don't abandon me, ADONAI!
My God, don't be far from me!
23(22)   Come quickly to help me,
Adonai, my salvation!

39 1(0) For the leader. Set in the style of Y'dutun. A psalm of David:

2(1)   I said, "I will watch how I behave,
so that I won't sin with my tongue;
I will put a muzzle on my mouth
whenever the wicked confront me."

3(2)   I was silent, said nothing, not even good;
but my pain kept being stirred up.
4(3)   My heart grew hot within me;
whenever I thought of it, the fire burned.
Then, [at last,] I let my tongue speak:

5(4)   "Make me grasp, ADONAI, what my end must be,
what it means that my days are numbered;
let me know what a transient creature I am.
6(5)   You have made my days like handbreadths;
for you, the length of my life is like nothing."

Yes, everyone, no matter how firmly he stands,
is merely a puff of wind.   (Selah)
7(6)   Humans go about like shadows;
their turmoil is all for nothing.
They accumulate wealth, not knowing
who will enjoy its benefits.

8(7)   Now, Adonai, what am I waiting for?
You are my only hope.

9(8)   Rescue me from all my transgressions;
        don't make me the butt of fools.

10(9)   I am silent, I keep my mouth shut,
        because it is you who have done it.

11(10) Stop raining blows on me;
        the pounding of your fist is wearing me down.

12(11) With rebukes you discipline people for their guilt;
        like a moth, you destroy what makes them attractive;
        yes, everyone is merely a puff of wind.   (*Selah*)

13(12) Hear my prayer, ADONAI, listen to my cry,
        don't be deaf to my weeping;
        for with you, I am just a traveler
        passing through, like all my ancestors.

14(13) Turn your gaze from me, so I can smile again
        before I depart and cease to exist.

40 ¹⁽⁰⁾ For the leader. A psalm of David:

2(1)   I waited patiently for ADONAI,
        till he turned toward me and heard my cry.

3(2)   He brought me up from the roaring pit,
        up from the muddy ooze,
        and set my feet on a rock,
        making my footing firm.

4(3)   He put a new song in my mouth,
        a song of praise to our God.
        Many will look on in awe
        and put their trust in ADONAI.

5(4)   How blessed the man who trusts in ADONAI
        and does not look to the arrogant
        or to those who rely on things that are false.

6(5)   How much you have done, ADONAI my God!
        Your wonders and your thoughts toward us —
        none can compare with you!
        I would proclaim them, I would speak about them;
        but there's too much to tell!

7(6)   Sacrifices and grain offerings you don't want;
        burnt offerings and sin offerings you don't demand.
        Instead, you have given me open ears;

8(7)   so then I said, "Here I am! I'm coming!
        In the scroll of a book it is written about me.

9(8) Doing your will, my God, is my joy;
     your *Torah* is in my inmost being.

10(9) I have proclaimed what is right in the great assembly;
     I did not restrain my lips, ADONAI, as you know.

11(10) I did not hide your righteousness in my heart
     but declared your faithfulness and salvation;
     I did not conceal your grace and truth
     from the great assembly."

12(11) ADONAI, don't withhold your mercy from me.
     Let your grace and truth preserve me always.

13(12) For numberless evils surround me;
     my iniquities engulf me — I can't even see;
     there are more of them than hairs on my head,
     so that my courage fails me.

14(13) Be pleased, ADONAI, to rescue me!
     ADONAI, hurry and help me!

15(14) May those who seek to sweep me away
     be disgraced and humiliated together.
     May those who take pleasure in doing me harm
     be turned back and put to confusion.

16(15) May those who jeer at me, "Aha! Aha!"
     be aghast because of their shame.

17(16) But may all those who seek you
     be glad and take joy in you.
     May those who love your salvation say always,
     "ADONAI is great and glorious!"

18(17) But I am poor and needy;
     may *Adonai* think of me.
     You are my helper and rescuer;
     my God, don't delay!

41 ¹⁽⁰⁾ For the leader. A psalm of David:

2(1) How blessed are those who care for the poor!
     When calamity comes, ADONAI will save them.

3(2) ADONAI will preserve them, keep them alive,
     and make them happy in the land.
     You will not hand them over
     to the whims of their enemies.

4(3) ADONAI sustains them on their sickbed;
     when they lie ill, you make them recover.

5(4) I said, "ADONAI, have pity on me!
     Heal me, for I have sinned against you!"

6(5)	My enemies say the worst about me: "When will he die and his name disappear?"
7(6)	When they come to see me they speak insincerely, their hearts meanwhile gathering falsehoods; then they go out and spread bad reports.
8(7)	All who hate me whisper together against me, imagining the worst about me.
9(8)	"A fatal disease has attached itself to him; now that he lies ill, he will never get up."
10(9)	Even my close friend, on whom I relied, who shared my table, has turned against me.
11(10)	But you, ADONAI, have pity on me, put me on my feet, so I can pay them back.
12(11)	I will know you are pleased with me if my enemy doesn't defeat me.
13(12)	You uphold me because of my innocence you establish me in your presence forever.
14(13)	Blessed be ADONAI the God of Isra'el from eternity past to eternity future.

Amen. Amen.

Book II: Psalms 42–72

42 ¹⁽⁰⁾ For the leader. *A maskil* of the descendants of Korach:

2(1)	Just as a deer longs for running streams, God, I long for you.
3(2)	I am thirsty for God, for the living God! When can I come and appear before God?
4(3)	My tears are my food, day and night, while all day people ask me, "Where is your God?"
5(4)	I recall, as my feelings well up within me, how I'd go with the crowd to the house of God, with sounds of joy and praise from the throngs observing the festival.
6(5)	My soul, why are you so downcast? Why are you groaning inside me? Hope in God, since I will praise him again for the salvation that comes from his presence.

7(6)   My God, when I feel so downcast,
       I remind myself of you
       from the land of Yarden, from the peaks of Hermon,
       from the hill Mizar.

8(7)   Deep is calling to deep
       at the thunder of your waterfalls;
       all your surging rapids and waves
       are sweeping over me.

9(8)   By day ADONAI commands his grace,
       and at night his song is with me
       as a prayer to the God of my life.

10(9) I say to God my Rock,
       "Why have you forgotten me?
       Why must I go about mourning,
       under pressure by the enemy?

11(10) My adversaries' taunts make me feel
       as if my bones were crushed,
       as they ask me all day long,
       'Where is your God?' "

12(11) My soul, why are you so downcast?
       Why are you groaning inside me?
       Hope in God, since I will praise him again
       for being my Savior and God.

43 1 Judge me, God, and plead my cause
          against a faithless nation.
          Rescue me from those who deceive
          and from those who are unjust.

2   For you are the God of my strength;
          why have you thrust me aside?
          Why must I go about mourning,
          under pressure by the enemy?

3   Send out your light and your truth;
          let them be my guide;
          let them lead me to your holy mountain,
          to the places where you live.

4   Then I will go to the altar of God,
          to God, my joy and delight;
          I will praise you on the lyre,
          God, my God.

5   My soul, why are you so downcast?
          Why are you groaning inside me?
          Hope in God, since I will praise him again
          for being my Savior and God.

44 $^{1(0)}$ For the leader. By the descendants of Korach. A *maskil:*

$^{2(1)}$ God, we heard it with our ears;
our fathers told us about it —
a deed which you did in their days,
back in days of old.

$^{3(2)}$ With your hand you drove out nations
to plant them in [the land],
you crushed peoples
to make room for them.

$^{4(3)}$ For not by their own swords
did they conquer the land,
nor did their own arm
give them victory;
rather, it was your right hand,
your arm and the light of your face;
because you favored them.

$^{5(4)}$ God, you are my king;
command complete victory for Ya'akov.

$^{6(5)}$ Through you we pushed away our foes,
through your name we trampled down our assailants.

$^{7(6)}$ For I don't rely on my bow,
nor can my sword give me victory.

$^{8(7)}$ No, you saved us from our adversaries;
you put to shame those who hate us.

$^{9(8)}$ We will boast in our God all day
and give thanks to your name forever. (*Selah*)

$^{10(9)}$ Yet now you have thrust us aside and disgraced us;
you don't march out with our armies.

$^{11(10)}$ You make us retreat from the adversary,
and those who hate us plunder us at will.

$^{12(11)}$ You have handed us over like sheep to be eaten
and scattered us among the nations.

$^{13(12)}$ You sell your people for a pittance,
you don't even profit on the sale.

$^{14(13)}$ You make us an object for our neighbors to mock,
one of scorn and derision to those around us.

$^{15(14)}$ You make us a byword among the nations;
the peoples jeer at us, shaking their heads.

$^{16(15)}$ All day long my disgrace is on my mind,
and shame has covered my face

$^{17(16)}$ at the sound of those who revile and insult,
at the sight of the enemy bent on revenge.

18(17) Though all this came on us, we did not forget you;
we have not been false to your covenant;

19(18) our hearts have not turned back;
and our steps did not turn away from your path,

20(19) though you pressed us into a lair of jackals
and covered us with death-dark gloom.

21(20) If we had forgotten the name of our God
or spread out our hands to a foreign god,

22(21) wouldn't God have discovered this,
since he knows the secrets of the heart?

23(22) For your sake we are put to death all day long,
we are considered sheep to be slaughtered.

24(23) Wake up, *Adonai*! Why are you asleep?
Rouse yourself! Don't thrust us off forever.

25(24) Why are you turning your face away,
forgetting our pain and misery?

26(25) For we are lying flat in the dust,
our bodies cling to the ground.

27(26) Get up, and come to help us!
For the sake of your grace, redeem us!

45 1(0) For the leader. Set to "Lilies." By the descendants of Korach. A *maskil*.
A lovesong:

2(1) My heart is stirred by a noble theme;
I address my verses to the king;
my tongue is the pen of an expert scribe.

3(2) You are the most handsome of men;
gracious speech flows from your lips.
For God has blessed you forever.

4(3) Warrior, strap your sword at your thigh;
[gird on] your splendor and majesty.

5(4) In your majesty, succeed, ride on
in the cause of truth, meekness and righteousness.
May your right hand teach you awesome things.

6(5) Your arrows are sharp. The people fall under you,
as they penetrate the hearts of the king's enemies.

7(6) Your throne, God, will last forever and ever;
you rule your kingdom with a scepter of equity.

8(7) You have loved righteousness and hated wickedness.
Therefore God, your God, has anointed you
with the oil of joy in preference to your companions.

9(8) Your robes are all fragrant with myrrh, aloes and cassia;
from ivory palaces stringed instruments bring you joy.

10(9)   Daughters of kings are among your favorites;
         at your right stands the queen in gold from Ofir.

11(10)   Listen, daughter! Think, pay attention!
         Forget your own people and your father's house,
12(11)   and the king will desire your beauty;
         for he is your lord, so honor him.
13(12)   Then the daughter of Tzor, the richest of peoples,
         will court your favor with gifts.

14(13)   Inside [the palace], the king's daughter looks splendid,
         attired in checker-work embroidered with gold.
15(14)   In brocade, she will be led to the king,
         to you, with the virgins in her retinue.
16(15)   They will be led in with gladness and joy,
         they will enter the king's palace.
17(16)   You will have sons to succeed your ancestors;
         you will make them princes in all the land.
18(17)   I will make your name known through all generations;
         thus the peoples will praise you forever and ever.

46 $^{1(0)}$ For the leader. By the descendants of Korach. On *'alamot* [high-pitched musical instruments?]. A song:

2(1)   God is our refuge and strength,
        an ever-present help in trouble.
3(2)   Therefore we are unafraid,
        even if the earth gives way,
        even if the mountains tumble
        into the depths of the sea,
4(3)   even if its waters rage and foam,
        and mountains shake at its turbulence.   (*Selah*)

5(4)   There is a river whose streams
        gladden the city of God,
        the holy habitation of *'Elyon* —
6(5)   God is in the city.
        It will not be moved —
        when daybreak comes, God will help it.
7(6)   Nations were in turmoil,
        kingdoms were moved;
        his voice thundered forth,
        and the earth melted away.

8(7)   *Adonai-Tzva'ot* is with us,
        our fortress, the God of Ya'akov.   (*Selah*)

835

9(8)   Come and see the works of ADONAI,
the astounding deeds he has done on the earth.

10(9)   To the ends of the earth he makes wars cease —
he breaks the bow, snaps the spear,
burns the shields in the fire.

11(10)   "Desist, and learn that I am God,
supreme over the nations,
supreme over the earth."

12(11)   ADONAI-*Tzva'ot* is with us,
our fortress, the God of Ya'akov.   *(Selah)*

47 ¹⁽⁰⁾ For the leader. A psalm of the descendants of Korach:

2(1)   Clap your hands, all you peoples!
Shout to God with cries of joy!

3(2)   For ADONAI *'Elyon* is awesome,
a great king over all the earth.

4(3)   He makes peoples subject to us,
puts nations under our feet.

5(4)   He chooses our heritage for us,
the pride of Ya'akov, whom he loves.   *(Selah)*

6(5)   God goes up to shouts of acclaim,
ADONAI to a blast on the *shofar.*

7(6)   Sing praises to God, sing praises!
Sing praises to our king, sing praises!

8(7)   For God is king of all the earth;
sing praises in a *maskil.*

9(8)   God rules the nations;
God sits on his holy throne.

10(9)   The leaders of the people gather together,
the people of the God of Avraham;
for the rulers of the earth belong to God,
who is exalted on high.

48 ¹⁽⁰⁾ A song. A psalm of the descendants of Korach:

2(1)   Great is ADONAI
and greatly to be praised,
in the city of our God,
his holy mountain,

3(2)   beautiful in its elevation,
the joy of all the earth,
Mount Tziyon, in the far north,
the city of the great king.

4(3)   In its citadels God
has been revealed as a strong defense.
5(4)   For the kings met by agreement;
together they advanced.
6(5)   They saw and were filled with consternation;
terrified, they took to flight.
7(6)   Trembling took hold of them,
pains like those of a woman in labor,
8(7)   as when the wind out of the east
wrecks the "Tarshish" ships.
9(8)   We heard it, and now we see for ourselves
in the city of ADONAI-Tzva'ot,
in the city of our God.
May God establish it forever.   (Selah)

10(9)   God, within your temple
we meditate on your grace.
11(10) God, your praise, like your name,
extends to the ends of the earth.
Your right hand is filled with righteousness.
12(11) Let Mount Tziyon rejoice,
let the daughters of Y'hudah be glad,
because of your judgment [on the enemy].

13(12) Walk through Tziyon, go all around it;
count how many towers it has.
14(13) Note its ramparts, pass through its citadels,
so that you can tell generations to come
15(14) that such is God, our God forever;
he will guide us eternally.

49 ¹⁽⁰⁾ For the leader. A psalm of the descendants of Korach:

2(1)   Hear this, all you peoples!
Listen, everyone living on earth,
3(2)   regardless of whether low or high,
regardless of whether rich or poor!
4(3)   My mouth is about to speak wisdom;
my heart's deepest thoughts will give understanding.
5(4)   I will listen with care to [God's] parable,
I will set my enigma to the music of the lyre.

6(5)   Why should I fear when the days bring trouble,
when the evil of my pursuers surrounds me,
7(6)   the evil of those who rely on their wealth
and boast how rich they are?

8(7)	No one can ever redeem his brother
	or give God a ransom for him,
9(8)	because the price for him is too high
	(leave the idea completely alone!)
10(9)	to have him live on eternally
	and never see the pit.
11(10)	For he can see that wise men will die,
	likewise the fool and the brute will perish
	and leave their wealth to others.
12(11)	They think their homes will last forever,
	their dwellings through all generations;
	they give their own names to their estates.
13(12)	But people, even rich ones, will live only briefly;
	then, like animals, they will die.
14(13)	This is the manner of life of the foolish
	and those who come after, approving their words. *(Selah)*
15(14)	Like sheep, they are destined for Sh'ol;
	death will be their shepherd.
	The upright will rule them in the morning;
	and their forms will waste away in Sh'ol,
	until they need no dwelling.
16(15)	But God will redeem me from Sh'ol's control,
	because he will receive me. *(Selah)*
17(16)	Don't be afraid when someone gets rich,
	when the wealth of his family grows.
18(17)	For when he dies, he won't take it with him;
	his wealth will not go down after him.
19(18)	True, while he lived, he thought himself happy —
	people praise you when you do well for yourself —
20(19)	but he will join his ancestors' generations
	and never again see light.
21(20)	People, even rich ones, can fail to grasp
	that, like animals, they will die.

50 ^1(0) A psalm of Asaf:

(1)	The Mighty One, God, ADONAI, is speaking,
	summoning the world from east to west.
2	Out of Tziyon, the perfection of beauty,
	God is shining forth.
3	Our God is coming and not staying silent.
	With a fire devouring ahead of him
	and a great storm raging around him,
4	he calls to the heavens above and to earth,
	in order to judge his people.

5 "Gather to me my faithful,
those who made a covenant with me by sacrifice."

6 The heavens proclaim his righteousness,
for God himself is judge. (*Selah*)

7 "Listen, my people, I am speaking:
Isra'el, I am testifying against you,
I, God, your God.

8 I am not rebuking you for your sacrifices;
your burnt offerings are always before me.

9 I have no need for a bull from your farm
or for male goats from your pens;

10 for all forest creatures are mine already,
as are the animals on a thousand hills;

11 I know all the birds in the mountains;
whatever moves in the fields is mine.

12 If I were hungry, I would not tell you;
for the world is mine, and everything in it.

13 Do I eat the flesh of bulls
or drink the blood of goats?

14 Offer thanksgiving as your sacrifice to God,
pay your vows to the Most High,

15 and call on me when you are in trouble;
I will deliver you, and you will honor me."

16 But to the wicked God says:
"What right do you have to proclaim my laws
or take my covenant on your lips,

17 when you so hate to receive instruction
and fling my words behind you?

18 When you see a thief, you join up with him,
you throw in your lot with adulterers,

19 you give your mouth free rein for evil
and harness your tongue to deceit;

20 you sit and speak against your kinsman,
you slander your own mother's son.

21 When you do such things, should I stay silent?
You may have thought I was just like you;
but I will rebuke and indict you to your face.

22 Consider this, you who forget God,
or I will tear you to pieces, with no one to save you.

23 "Whoever offers thanksgiving
as his sacrifice honors me;
and to him who goes the right way
I will show the salvation of God."

51 $^{1(0)}$ For the leader. A psalm of David, ^{2} when Natan the prophet came to him after his affair with Bat-Sheva:

$^{3(1)}$ God, in your grace, have mercy on me;
in your great compassion, blot out my crimes.
$^{4(2)}$ Wash me completely from my guilt,
and cleanse me from my sin.
$^{5(3)}$ For I know my crimes,
my sin confronts me all the time.

$^{6(4)}$ Against you, you only, have I sinned
and done what is evil from your perspective;
so that you are right in accusing me
and justified in passing sentence.

$^{7(5)}$ True, I was born guilty,
was a sinner from the moment my mother conceived me.
$^{8(6)}$ Still, you want truth in the inner person;
so make me know wisdom in my inmost heart.

$^{9(7)}$ Sprinkle me with hyssop, and I will be clean;
wash me, and I will be whiter than snow.
$^{10(8)}$ Let me hear the sound of joy and gladness,
so that the bones you crushed can rejoice.
$^{11(9)}$ Turn away your face from my sins,
and blot out all my crimes.

$^{12(10)}$ Create in me a clean heart, God;
renew in me a resolute spirit.
$^{13(11)}$ Don't thrust me away from your presence,
don't take your *Ruach Kodesh* away from me.
$^{14(12)}$ Restore my joy in your salvation,
and let a willing spirit uphold me.
$^{15(13)}$ Then I will teach the wicked your ways,
and sinners will return to you.

$^{16(14)}$ Rescue me from the guilt of shedding blood,
God, God of my salvation!
Then my tongue will sing
about your righteousness —
$^{17(15)}$ *Adonai*, open my lips;
then my mouth will praise you.

$^{18(16)}$ For you don't want sacrifices, or I would give them;
you don't take pleasure in burnt offerings.
$^{19(17)}$ My sacrifice to God is a broken spirit;
God, you won't spurn a broken, chastened heart.

20(18)	In your good pleasure, make Tziyon prosper; rebuild the walls of Yerushalayim.
21(19)	Then you will delight in righteous sacrifices, in burnt offerings and whole burnt offerings; then they will offer bulls on your altar.

52 ¹⁽⁰⁾ For the leader. A *maskil* of David, ² when Do'eg from Edom came and told Sha'ul, "David has arrived at the house of Achimelekh":

3(1)	Why do you boast of your evil, you tyrant, when God's mercy is present every day?
4(2)	Your tongue, as sharp as a razor, plots destruction and works deception.
5(3)	You love evil more than good, lies rather than speaking uprightly. (*Selah*)
6(4)	You love all words that eat people up, you deceitful tongue!
7(5)	This is why God will strike you down, seize you, pluck you from your tent and uproot you from the land of the living. (*Selah*)
8(6)	The righteous will see and be awestruck; they will jeer at him, saying,
9(7)	"This fellow would not make God his refuge, but trusted in his own great wealth, relying on his evil plots."
10(8)	But I am like a leafy olive tree in the house of God; I put my trust in the grace of God forever and ever.
11(9)	I will praise you forever for what you have done, and I will put my hope in your name; for this is what is good in the presence of your faithful.

53 ¹⁽⁰⁾ For the leader. On *machalat*. A *maskil* of David:

2(1)	A brutish fool tells himself, "There isn't any God." Such people are depraved, all their deeds are vile, not one of them does what is good.

3(2)   God looks out from heaven
        upon the human race
        to see if even one is wise,
        if even one seeks God.

4(3)   Every one of them is unclean,
        altogether corrupt;
        not one of them does what is good,
        not a single one.

5(4)   Won't these evildoers ever learn?
        They devour my people
        as if they were eating bread,
        and they never call on God!

6(5)   They will be gripped with terror,
        even though now they are not afraid;
        for God will scatter the bones
        of him who is besieging you.
        You are putting them to shame,
        because God has rejected them.

7(6)   If only salvation for Isra'el
        would come out of Tziyon!
        When God restores his people's fortunes,
        what joy for Ya'akov! what gladness for Isra'el!

54 ¹⁽⁰⁾ For the leader. With stringed instruments. A *maskil* of David, ² when the
Zifim came and told Sha'ul, "David is hiding with us":

3(1)   God, deliver me by your name;
        in your power, vindicate me.

4(2)   God, hear my prayer;
        listen to the words from my mouth.

5(3)   For foreigners are rising against me,
        violent men are seeking my life;
        they give no thought to God.   (*Selah*)

6(4)   But God is helping me;
        Adonai is my support.

7(5)   May he repay the evil
        to those who are lying in wait for me.
        In your faithfulness, destroy them!

8(6)   Then I will generously sacrifice to you;
        I will praise your name, ADONAI,
        because it is good,

9(7)   because he rescued me from all trouble,
        and my eyes look with triumph at my enemies.

55 ¹⁽⁰⁾ For the leader. With stringed instruments. A *maskil* of David:

²⁽¹⁾ Listen, God, to my prayer!
Don't hide yourself from my plea!
³⁽²⁾ Pay attention to me, and answer me!

I am panic-stricken as I make my complaint,
I shudder ⁴⁽³⁾ at how the enemy shouts,
at how the wicked oppress;
for they keep heaping trouble on me
and angrily tormenting me.
⁵⁽⁴⁾ My heart within me is pounding in anguish,
the terrors of death press down on me,
⁶⁽⁵⁾ fear and trembling overwhelm me,
horror covers me.

⁷⁽⁶⁾ I said, "I wish I had wings like a dove!
Then I could fly away and be at rest.
⁸⁽⁷⁾ Yes, I would flee to a place far off,
I would stay in the desert. *(Selah)*
⁹⁽⁸⁾ I would quickly find me a shelter
from the raging wind and storm."

¹⁰⁽⁹⁾ Confuse, *Adonai*, confound their speech!
For I see violence and fighting in the city.
¹¹⁽¹⁰⁾ Day and night they go about its walls;
within are malice and mischief.
¹²⁽¹¹⁾ Ruin is rife within it,
oppression and fraud never leave its streets.

¹³⁽¹²⁾ For it was not an enemy who insulted me;
if it had been, I could have borne it.
It was not my adversary who treated me with scorn;
if it had been, I could have hidden myself.
¹⁴⁽¹³⁾ But it was you, a man of my own kind,
my companion, whom I knew well.

¹⁵⁽¹⁴⁾ We used to share our hearts with each other;
in the house of God we walked with the crowd.

¹⁶⁽¹⁵⁾ May he put death on them;
let them go down alive to Sh'ol;
for evil is in their homes
and also in their hearts.

¹⁷⁽¹⁶⁾ But I will call on God,
and *Adonai* will save me.

18(17) Evening, morning and noon I complain
        and moan; but he hears my voice.
19(18) He redeems me and gives me peace,
        so that no one can come near me.
        For there were many who fought me.
20(19) God will hear and will humble them,
        yes, he who has sat on his throne from the start.   (*Selah*)
        For they never change,
        and they don't fear God.

21(20) [My companion] attacked those
        who were at peace with him;
        he broke his solemn word.
22(21) What he said sounded smoother than butter,
        but his heart was at war.
        His words seemed more soothing than oil,
        but in fact they were sharp swords.

23(22) Unload your burden on ADONAI,
        and he will sustain you.
        He will never permit
        the righteous to be moved.

24(23) But you will bring them down, God,
        into the deepest pit.
        Those men, so bloodthirsty and treacherous,
        will not live out half their days.

        But for my part, [ADONAI,]
        I put my trust in you.

56 ¹⁽⁰⁾ For the leader. Set to "The Silent Dove in the Distance." By David; a *mikhtam*,
when the P'lishtim captured him in Gat:

2(1)   Show me favor, God;
       for people are trampling me down —
       all day they fight and press on me.
3(2)   Those who are lying in wait for me
       would trample on me all day.
       For those fighting against me are many.

       Most High, ⁴⁽³⁾ when I am afraid,
       I put my trust in you.
5(4)   In God — I praise his word —
       in God I trust; I have no fear;
       what can human power do to me?

6(5)	All day long they twist my words; their only thought is to harm me.
7(6)	They gather together and hide themselves, spying on my movements, hoping to kill me.
8(7)	Because of their crime, they cannot escape; in anger, God, strike down the peoples.
9(8)	You have kept count of my wanderings; store my tears in your water-skin — aren't they already recorded in your book?
10(9)	Then my enemies will turn back on the day when I call; this I know: that God is for me.
11(10)	In God — I praise his word — in *Adonai* — I praise his word —
12(11)	in God I trust; I have no fear; what can mere humans do to me?
13(12)	God, I have made vows to you; I will fulfill them with thank offerings to you.
14(13)	For you rescued me from death, you kept my feet from stumbling, so that I can walk in God's presence, in the light of life.

57 ¹⁽⁰⁾ For the leader. Set to "Do Not Destroy." By David, a *mikhtam*, when he fled from Sha'ul into the cave:

2(1)	Show me favor, God, show me favor; for in you I have taken refuge. Yes, I will find refuge in the shadow of your wings until the storms have passed.
3(2)	I call to God, the Most High, to God, who is accomplishing his purpose for me.
4(3)	He will send from heaven and save me when those who would trample me down mock me. (*Selah*) God will send his grace and his truth.
5(4)	I am surrounded by lions, I am lying down among people breathing fire, men whose teeth are spears and arrows and their tongues sharp-edged swords.
6(5)	Be exalted, God, above heaven! May your glory be over all the earth!

7(6)
They prepared a snare for my feet,
but I am bending over [to avoid it].
They dug a pit ahead of me,
but they fell into it themselves.   (Selah)

8(7)
My heart is steadfast, God, steadfast.
I will sing and make music.

9(8)
Awake, my glory! Awake, lyre and lute!
I will awaken the dawn.

10(9)
I will thank you, *Adonai*, among the peoples;
I will make music to you among the nations.

11(10)
For your grace is great, all the way to heaven,
and your truth, all the way to the skies.

12(11)
Be exalted, God, above heaven!
May your glory be over all the earth!

58 1(0) For the leader. Set to "Do Not Destroy." By David, a *mikhtam*:

2(1)
[Rulers,] does your silence really speak justice?
Are you judging people fairly?

3(2)
[No!] In your hearts you devise wrongs,
your hands dispense violence in the land.

4(3)
From the womb, the wicked are estranged,
liars on the wrong path since birth.

5(4)
Their venom is like snake's venom;
they are like a serpent that stops its ears,

6(5)
so as not to hear the voice of the charmer,
no matter how well he plays.

7(6)
God, break their teeth in their mouth!
Shatter the fangs of these lions, *Adonai*!

8(7)
May they vanish like water that drains away.
May their arrows be blunted when they aim their bows.

9(8)
May they be like a slug that melts as it moves,
like a stillborn baby that never sees the sun.

10(9)
Before your cook-pots feel the heat of the burning thorns,
may he blow them away, green and blazing alike.

11(10)
The righteous will rejoice to see vengeance done,
they will wash their feet in the blood of the wicked;

12(11)
and people will say, "Yes, the righteous are rewarded;
there is, after all, a God who judges the earth."

59 ¹⁽⁰⁾ For the leader. Set to "Do Not Destroy." By David; a *mikhtam*, when Sha'ul sent men to keep watch on David's house in order to kill him:

2(1)   My God, rescue me from my enemies!
       Lift me up, out of reach of my foes!
3(2)   Rescue me from evildoers,
       save me from bloodthirsty men.
4(3)   For there they are, lying in wait to kill me.
       Openly they gather themselves against me,
       and not because I committed a crime
       or sinned, ADONAI.
5(4)   For no fault of mine, they run and prepare.
       Awaken to help me, and see!
6(5)   You, ADONAI *Elohei-Tzva'ot*,
       God of Isra'el,
       arouse yourself to punish all the nations;
       spare none of those wicked traitors.   (*Selah*)

7(6)   They return at nightfall, snarling like dogs
       as they go around the city.
8(7)   Look what pours out of their mouth,
       what swords are on their lips,
       [as they say to themselves,]
       "No one is listening, anyway."
9(8)   But you, ADONAI, laugh at them,
       you mock all the nations.

10(9) My Strength, I will watch for you,
       for God is my fortress.
11(10) God, who gives me grace, will come to me;
       God will let me gaze in triumph at my foes.

12(11) Don't kill them, or my people will forget;
       instead, by your power, make them wander to and fro;
       but bring them down, *Adonai* our Shield,
13(12) for the sins their mouths make with each word from their lips.
       Let them be trapped by their pride
       for the curses and falsehoods they utter.
14(13) Finish them off in wrath,
       finish them off, put an end to them,
       and let them know to the ends of the earth
       that God is Ruler in Ya'akov.   (*Selah*)

15(14) They return at nightfall, snarling like dogs
       as they go around the city.
16(15) They roam about, looking for food,
       prowling all night if they don't get their fill.

17(16)　But as for me, I will sing of your strength;
　　　　in the morning I will sing aloud of your grace.
　　　　For you are my fortress,
　　　　a refuge when I am in trouble.
18(17)　My Strength, I will sing praises to you,
　　　　for God is my fortress, God, who gives me grace.

60 ¹⁽⁰⁾ For the leader. Set to "Lily of Testimony." A *mikhtam* of David for teaching about ² when he fought with Aram-Naharayim and with Aram-Tzovah, and Yo'av returned and killed 12,000 from Edom in the Salt Valley:

3(1)　God, you rejected us; you crushed us;
　　　　you were angry; but now revive us.
4(2)　You made the land shake, split it apart;
　　　　now repair the rifts, for it is collapsing.
5(3)　You made your people suffer hard times,
　　　　had us drink a wine that made us stagger.

6(4)　To those who fear you because of the truth
　　　　you gave a banner to rally around,　　　　　　　*(Selah)*
7(5)　so that those you love could be rescued;
　　　　so save with your right hand, and answer us!

8(6)　God in his holiness spoke,
　　　　and I took joy [in his promise]:
　　　　"I will divide Sh'khem
　　　　and determine the shares in the Sukkot Valley.
9(7)　Gil'ad is mine and M'nasheh mine,
　　　　Efrayim my helmet, Y'hudah my scepter.
10(8)　Mo'av is my washpot; on Edom I throw my shoe;
　　　　P'leshet, be crushed because of me!"

11(9)　Who will bring me into the fortified city?
　　　　Who will lead me to Edom?
12(10)　God, have you rejected us?
　　　　You don't go out with our armies, God.
13(11)　Help us against our enemy,
　　　　for human help is worthless.
14(12)　With God's help we will fight valiantly,
　　　　for he will trample our enemies.

61 ¹⁽⁰⁾ For the leader. With stringed instruments. By David:

2(1)　Hear my cry, God;
　　　　listen to my prayer.

³⁽²⁾ From the end of the earth, with fainting heart,
I call out to you.
Set me down on a rock
far above where I am now.

⁴⁽³⁾ For you have been a refuge for me,
a tower of strength in the face of the foe.

⁵⁽⁴⁾ I will live in your tent forever
and find refuge in the shelter of your wings. *(Selah)*

⁶⁽⁵⁾ For you, God, have heard my vows;
you have given me the heritage of those who fear your name.

⁷⁽⁶⁾ Prolong the life of the king!
May his years go on for many generations.

⁸⁽⁷⁾ May he be enthroned in God's presence forever!
Appoint grace and truth to preserve him!

⁹⁽⁸⁾ Then I will sing praise to your name forever,
as day after day I fulfill my vows.

62 ¹⁽⁰⁾ For the leader. Set in the style of Y'dutun. A psalm of David:

²⁽¹⁾ My soul waits in silence for God alone;
my salvation comes from him.

³⁽²⁾ He alone is my rock and salvation,
my stronghold; I won't be greatly moved.

⁴⁽³⁾ How long will you assail a person
in order to murder him, all of you,
as if he were a sagging wall
or a shaky fence?

⁵⁽⁴⁾ They only want to shake him from his height,
they take delight in lying —
with their mouths they bless,
but inwardly they curse. *(Selah)*

⁶⁽⁵⁾ My soul, wait in silence for God alone,
because my hope comes from him.

⁷⁽⁶⁾ He alone is my rock and salvation,
my stronghold; I won't be moved.

⁸⁽⁷⁾ My safety and honor rest on God.
My strong rock and refuge are in God.

⁹⁽⁸⁾ Trust in him, people, at all times;
pour out your heart before him;
God is a refuge for us. *(Selah)*

10(9)   Ordinary folks are merely a breath
and important people a sham;
if you lay them on a balance-scale, they go up —
both together are lighter than nothing.

11(10)   Don't put your trust in extortion,
don't put false hopes in robbery;
even if wealth increases,
don't set your heart on it.

12(11)   God has spoken once, I have heard it twice:
strength belongs to God.

13(12)   Also to you, *Adonai*, belongs grace;
for you reward all as their deeds deserve.

63 $^{1(0)}$ A psalm of David, when he was in the desert of Y'hudah:

2(1)   O God, you are my God;
I will seek you eagerly.
My heart thirsts for you,
my body longs for you
in a land parched and exhausted,
where no water can be found.

3(2)   I used to contemplate you in the sanctuary,
seeing your power and glory;

4(3)   for your grace is better than life.
My lips will worship you.

5(4)   Yes, I will bless you as long as I live;
in your name I will lift up my hands.

6(5)   I am as satisfied as with rich food;
my mouth praises you with joy on my lips

7(6)   when I remember you on my bed
and meditate on you in the night watches.

8(7)   For you have been my help;
in the shadow of your wings I rejoice;

9(8)   my heart clings to you;
your right hand supports me.

10(9)   But those who seek to destroy my life —
may they go to the lowest parts of the earth.

11(10)   May they be given over to the power of the sword;
may they become prey for jackals.

12(11)   But the king will rejoice in God.
Everyone who swears by him will exult,
for the mouths of liars will be silenced.

64 $^{1(0)}$ For the leader. A psalm of David:

$^{2(1)}$ Hear my voice, God, as I plead:
preserve my life from fear of the enemy.

$^{3(2)}$ Hide me from the secret intrigues of the wicked
and the open insurrection of evildoers.

$^{4(3)}$ They sharpen their tongues like a sword;
they aim their arrows, poisoned words,

$^{5(4)}$ in order to shoot from cover at the innocent,
shooting suddenly and fearing nothing.

$^{6(5)}$ They support each other's evil plans;
they talk of hiding snares
and ask, "Who would see them?"

$^{7(6)}$ They search for ways to commit crimes,
bringing their diligent search to completion
when each of them has thought it through
in the depth of his heart.

$^{8(7)}$ Suddenly God shoots them down with an arrow,
leaving them with wounds;

$^{9(8)}$ their own tongues make them stumble.
All who see them shake their heads.

$^{10(9)}$ Everyone is awestruck —
they acknowledge that it is God at work,
they understand what he has done.

$^{11(10)}$ The righteous will rejoice in ADONAI;
they will take refuge in him;
all the upright in heart will exult.

65 $^{1(0)}$ For the leader. A psalm of David. A song:

$^{2(1)}$ To you, God, in Tziyon, silence is praise;
and vows to you are to be fulfilled.

$^{3(2)}$ You who listen to prayer,
to you all living creatures come.

$^{4(3)}$ When deeds of wickedness overwhelm me,
you will atone for our crimes.

$^{5(4)}$ How blessed are those you choose and bring near,
so that they can remain in your courtyards!
We will be satisfied with the goodness of your house,
the Holy Place of your temple.

$^{6(5)}$ It is just that you answer us with awesome deeds,
God of our salvation,
you in whom all put their trust,
to the ends of the earth and on distant seas.

7(6) By your strength you set up the mountains.
      You are clothed with power.

8(7) You still the roaring of the seas,
      their crashing waves, and the peoples' turmoil.

9(8) This is why those living at the ends of the earth
      stand in awe of your signs.
      The places where the sun rises and sets
      you cause to sing for joy.

10(9) You care for the earth and water it,
      you enrich it greatly;
      with the river of God, full of water,
      you provide them grain and prepare the ground.

11(10) Soaking its furrows and settling its soil,
      you soften it with showers and bless its growth.

12(11) You crown the year with your goodness,
      your tracks overflow with richness.

13(12) The desert pastures drip water,
      the hills are wrapped with joy,

14(13) the meadows are clothed with flocks
      and the valleys blanketed with grain,
      so they shout for joy and break into song.

66 ¹⁽⁰⁾ For the leader. A song. A psalm:

(1)   Shout to God, all the earth!

2   Sing the glory of his name,
      make his praise glorious.

3   Tell God, "How awesome are your deeds!
      At your great power, your enemies cringe.

4   All the earth bows down to you,
      sings praises to you, sings praises to your name."   (*Selah*)

5   Come and see what God has done,
      his awesome dealings with humankind.

6   He turned the sea into dry land.
      They passed through the river on foot;
      there we rejoiced in him.

7   With his power he rules forever;
      his eyes keep watch on the nations.
      Let no rebel arise to challenge him.   (*Selah*)

8   Bless our God, you peoples!
      Let the sound of his praise be heard!

9   He preserves our lives
      and keeps our feet from stumbling.

10   For you, God, have tested us,
       refined us as silver is refined.
11   You brought us into the net
       and bound our bodies fast.
12   You made men ride over our heads;
       we went through fire and water.
       But you brought us out
       to a place of plenty.

13   I will come into your house with burnt offerings,
       I will fulfill my vows to you,
14   those my lips pronounced and my mouth spoke
       when I was in distress.
15   I will offer you burnt offerings of fattened animals,
       along with the sweet smoke of rams;
       I will offer bulls and goats.   *(Selah)*

16   Come and listen, all you who fear God,
       and I will tell what he has done for me.
17   I cried out to him with my mouth,
       his praise was on my tongue.
18   Had I cherished evil thoughts,
       Adonai would not have listened.
19   But in fact, God did listen;
       he paid attention to my prayer.
20   Blessed be God, who did not reject my prayer
       or turn his grace away from me.

67 ¹⁽⁰⁾ For the leader. With stringed instruments. A psalm. A song:

2(1)   God, be gracious to us, and bless us.
       May he make his face shine toward us,   *(Selah)*
3(2)   so that your way may be known on earth,
       your salvation among all nations.

4(3)   Let the peoples give thanks to you, God;
       let the peoples give thanks to you, all of them.
5(4)   Let the nations be glad and shout for joy,
       for you will judge the peoples fairly
       and guide the nations on earth.   *(Selah)*

6(5)   Let the peoples give thanks to you, God;
       let the peoples give thanks to you, all of them.
7(6)   The earth has yielded its harvest;
       may God, our God, bless us.
8(7)   May God continue to bless us,
       so that all the ends of the earth will fear him.

68 1(0) For the leader. A psalm of David. A song:

2(1) Let God arise, let his enemies be scattered;
let those who hate him flee from his presence.

3(2) Drive them away as smoke is driven away;
like wax melting in the presence of a fire,
let the wicked perish in the presence of God.

4(3) But let the righteous rejoice and be glad in God's presence;
yes, let them exult and rejoice.

5(4) Sing to God, sing praises to his name;
extol him who rides on the clouds
by his name, *Yah*;
and be glad in his presence.

6(5) God, in his holy dwelling,
is a father to orphans and defender of widows.

7(6) God gives homes to those who are alone
and leads prisoners out into prosperity.
But rebels must live in a parched wasteland.

8(7) God, when you went out at the head of your people,
when you marched out through the wilderness,   (*Selah*)

9(8) the earth quaked, and rain poured from the sky,
at the presence of God.
Even Sinai [shook] at the presence of God,
the God of Isra'el.

10(9) You rained down showers in plenty, God;
when your heritage was weary, you restored it.

11(10) Your flock settled in it;
in your goodness, God, you provided for the poor.

12(11) *Adonai* gives the command;
the women with the good news are a mighty army.

13(12) Kings and their armies are fleeing, fleeing,
while the women at home divide the spoil.

14(13) Even if you lie among the animal stalls,
there are wings of a dove covered with silver
and its plumes with yellow gold.

15(14) When *Shaddai* scatters kings there,
snow falls on Tzalmon.

16(15) You mighty mountain, Mount Bashan!
You rugged mountain, Mount Bashan!

17(16) You rugged mountain, why look with envy
at the mountain God wants for his place to live?
Truly, *Adonai* will live there forever.

18(17) God's chariots are myriads, repeated thousands;
Adonai is among them as in Sinai, in holiness.

19(18) After you went up into the heights,
you led captivity captive,
you took gifts among mankind,
yes, even among the rebels,
so that Yah, God, might live there.

20(19) Blessed be Adonai!
Every day he bears our burden,
does God, our salvation. (Selah)

21(20) Our God is a God who saves;
from ADONAI Adonai comes escape from death.

22(21) God will surely crush the heads of his enemies,
the hairy crowns of those who continue in their guilt.

23(22) Adonai said, "I will bring them back from Bashan,
I will fetch [those rebels] even from the depths of the sea;

24(23) so that you can wash your feet in their blood,
and your dogs' tongues too can get their share from your foes.

25(24) They see your processions, God,
the processions of my God, my king, in holiness.

26(25) The singers are in front, the musicians last,
in the middle are girls playing tambourines.

27(26) "In choruses, bless God, Adonai,
you whose source is Isra'el."

28(27) There is Binyamin, the youngest, at the head;
the princes of Y'hudah, crowding along;
the princes of Z'vulun; the princes of Naftali.

29(28) God, summon your strength!
Use your strength, God, as you did for us before,

30(29) from your temple in Yerushalayim,
where kings will bring tribute to you.

31(30) Rebuke the wild beast of the reeds,
that herd of bulls with their calves, the peoples,
who ingratiate themselves with bars of silver;
let him scatter the peoples who take pleasure in fighting.

32(31) Let envoys come from Egypt,
Let Ethiopia stretch out its hands to God.

33(32) Sing to God, kingdoms of the earth!
Sing praises to Adonai, (Selah)

34(33) to him who rides on the most ancient heavens.
Listen, as he utters his voice, a mighty voice!

35(34) Acknowledge that strength belongs to God,
with his majesty over Isra'el and his strength in the skies.

36(35) How awe-inspiring you are, God,
        from your holy places,
        the God of Isra'el, who gives strength
        and power to the people.
        Blessed be God!

69 ¹⁽⁰⁾ For the leader. Set to "Lilies." By David:

2(1) Save me, God!
      For the water threatens my life.
3(2) I am sinking down in the mud,
      and there is no foothold;
      I have come into deep water;
      the flood is sweeping over me.
4(3) I am exhausted from crying,
      my throat is dry and sore,
      my eyes are worn out
      with looking for my God.

5(4) Those who hate me for no reason
      outnumber the hairs on my head.
      My persecutors are powerful,
      my enemies accuse me falsely.
      Am I expected to return
      things I didn't steal?

6(5) God, you know how foolish I am;
      my guilt is not hidden from you.
7(6) Let those who put their hope in you,
      Adonai ELOHIM-Tzva'ot,
      not be put to shame through me;
      let those who are seeking you,
      God of Isra'el,
      not be disgraced through me.

8(7) For your sake I suffer insults,
      shame covers my face.
9(8) I am estranged from my brothers,
      an alien to my mother's children,
10(9) because zeal for your house is eating me up,
      and on me are falling the insults
      of those insulting you.
11(10) I weep bitterly, and I fast,
      but that too occasions insults.
12(11) I clothe myself with sackcloth
      and become an object of scorn,

13(12)   the gossip of those sitting by the town gate,
the theme of drunkards' songs.

14(13)   As for me, ADONAI, let my prayer to you
come at an acceptable time;
In your great grace, God, answer me
with the truth of your salvation.

15(14)   Rescue me from the mud!
Don't let me sink!
Let me be rescued from those who hate me
and from the deep water.

16(15)   Don't let the floodwaters overwhelm me,
don't let the deep swallow me up,
don't let the pit close its mouth over me.

17(16)   Answer me, ADONAI, for your grace is good;
in your great mercy, turn to me.

18(17)   Don't hide your face from your servant,
for I am in trouble; answer me quickly.

19(18)   Come near to me, and redeem me;
ransom me because of my enemies.

20(19)   You know how I am insulted,
shamed and disgraced;
before you stand all my foes.

21(20)   Insults have broken my heart
to the point that I could die.
I hoped that someone would show compassion,
but nobody did;
and that there would be comforters,
but I found none.

22(21)   They put poison in my food;
in my thirst, they gave me vinegar to drink.

23(22)   Let their dining table
before them become a snare;
when they are at peace,
let it become a trap;

24(23)   let their eyes be darkened,
so that they can't see,
and let their bodies
always be stumbling.

25(24)   Pour out your fury on them,
let your fierce anger overtake them.

26(25)   Let the place where they live be desolate,
with no one to live in their tents,

27(26)   for persecuting someone you had already stricken,
for adding to the pain of those you wounded.

28(27)   Add guilt to their guilt,
         don't let them enter your righteousness.
29(28)   Erase them from the book of life,
         let them not be written with the righteous.

30(29)   Meanwhile, I am afflicted and hurting;
         God, let your saving power raise me up.
31(30)   I will praise God's name with a song
         and extol him with thanksgiving.

32(31)   This will please ADONAI more than a bull,
         with its horns and hoofs.
33(32)   The afflicted will see it and rejoice;
         you seeking after God, let your heart revive.
34(33)   For ADONAI pays attention to the needy
         and doesn't scorn his captive people.

35(34)   Let heaven and earth praise him,
         the seas and whatever moves in them.
36(35)   For God will save Tziyon,
         he will build the cities of Y'hudah.
         [His people] will settle there and possess it.
37(36)   The descendants of his servants will inherit it,
         and those who love his name will live there.

70 ¹⁽⁰⁾ For the leader. By David. As a reminder:

2(1)   God, rescue me!
        ADONAI, hurry and help me!

3(2)   May those who seek my life
        be disgraced and humiliated.
        May those who take pleasure in doing me harm
        be turned back and put to confusion.
4(3)   May those who jeer, "Aha! Aha!"
        withdraw because of their shame.

5(4)   But may all those who seek you
        be glad and take joy in you.
        May those who love your salvation say always,
        "God is great and glorious!"

6(5)   But I am poor and needy;
        God, hurry for me.
        You are my helper and rescuer;
        ADONAI, don't delay!

71 ¹ In you, ADONAI, I have taken refuge;
    let me never be put to shame.

² In your righteousness, rescue me;
    and help me to escape.
    Turn your ear toward me,
    and deliver me.

³ Be for me a sheltering rock,
    where I can always come.
    You have determined to save me,
    because you are my bedrock and stronghold.

⁴ My God, help me escape from the power of the wicked,
    from the grasp of the unjust and ruthless.

⁵ For you are my hope, Adonai ELOHIM,
    in whom I have trusted since I was young.

⁶ From birth I have relied on you;
    it was you who took me from my mother's womb.

⁷ To many, I am an amazing example;
    but you are strong protection for me.

⁸ My mouth is full of praise for you,
    filled with your glory all day long.

⁹ Don't reject me when I grow old;
    when my strength fails, don't abandon me.

¹⁰ For my enemies are talking about me,
    those seeking my life are plotting together.

¹¹ They say, "God has abandoned him;
    go after him, and seize him,
    because no one will save him."

¹² God, don't distance yourself from me!
    My God, hurry to help me!

¹³ May those who are opposed to me
    be put to shame and ruin;
    may those who seek to harm me
    be covered with scorn and disgrace.

¹⁴ But I, I will always hope
    and keep adding to your praise.

¹⁵ All day long my mouth will tell
    of your righteous deeds and acts of salvation,
    though their number is past my knowing.

¹⁶ I will come in the power of Adonai ELOHIM
    and recall your righteousness, yours alone.

¹⁷ God, you have taught me since I was young,
    and I still proclaim your wonderful works.

18 So now that I'm old, and my hair is gray,
don't abandon me, God, till I have proclaimed
your strength to the next generation,
your power to all who will come,

19 your righteousness too, God,
which reaches to the heights.
God, you have done great things;
who is there like you?

20 You have made me see much trouble and hardship,
but you will revive me again
and bring me up from the depths of the earth.

21 You will increase my honor;
turn and comfort me.

22 As for me, I will praise you with a lyre
for your faithfulness, my God.
I will sing praises to you with a lute,
Holy One of Isra'el.

23 My lips will shout for joy;
I will sing your praise, because you have redeemed me.

24 All day long my tongue
will speak of your righteousness.
For those who are seeking to harm me
will be put to shame and disgraced.

72 [(0)] By Shlomo:

(1) God, give the king your fairness in judgment,
endow this son of kings with your righteousness,

2 so that he can govern your people rightly
and your poor with justice.

3 May mountains and hills provide your people
with peace through righteousness.

4 May he defend the oppressed among the people,
save the needy and crush the oppressor.

5 May they fear you as long as the sun endures
and as long as the moon, through all generations.

6 May he be like rain falling on mown grass,
like showers watering the land.

7 In his days, let the righteous flourish
and peace abound, till the moon is no more.

8 May his empire stretch from sea to sea,
from the [Euphrates] River to the ends of the earth.

9 May desert-dwellers bow before him;
may his enemies lick the dust.

10   The kings of Tarshish and the coasts will pay him tribute;
     the kings of Sh'va and S'va will offer gifts.
11   Yes, all kings will prostrate themselves before him;
     all nations will serve him.

12   For he will rescue the needy when they cry,
     the poor too and those with none to help them.
13   He will have pity on the poor and needy;
     and the lives of the needy he will save.
14   He will redeem them from oppression and violence;
     their blood will be precious in his view.

15   May [the king] live long!
     May they give him gold from the land of Sh'va!
     May they pray for him continually;
     yes, bless him all day long.
16   May there be an abundance of grain in the land,
     all the way to the tops of the mountains.
     May its crops rustle like the L'vanon.
     May people blossom in the city like the grasses in the fields.
17   May his name endure forever,
     his name, Yinnon, as long as the sun.*
     May people bless themselves in him,
     may all nations call him happy.

18   Blessed be ADONAI, God,
     the God of Isra'el,
     who alone works wonders.
19   Blessed be his glorious name forever,
     and may the whole earth be filled with his glory.
     Amen. Amen.

20 This completes the prayers of David the son of Yishai.

Book III: Psalms 73–89

73 ¹⁽⁰⁾ A psalm of Asaf:

(1)   How good God is to Isra'el,
      to those who are pure in heart!
2   But as for me, I lost my balance,
      my feet nearly slipped,

---

* Or: "May his name flourish/propagate as long as the sun." Jewish tradition considers Yinnon a name of the Messiah.

3   when I grew envious of the arrogant
and saw how the wicked prosper.

4   For when their death comes, it is painless;
and meanwhile, their bodies are healthy;

5   they don't have ordinary people's troubles,
they aren't plagued like others.

6   So for them, pride is a necklace;
and violence clothes them like a robe.

7   Their eyes peep out through folds of fat;
evil thoughts overflow from their hearts.

8   They scoff and speak with malice,
they loftily utter threats.

9   They set their mouths against heaven;
their tongues swagger through the earth.

10   Therefore his people return here
and [thoughtlessly] suck up that whole cup of water.

11   Then they ask, "How does God know?
Does the Most High really have knowledge?"

12   Yes, this is what the wicked are like;
those free of misfortune keep increasing their wealth.

13   It's all for nothing that I've kept my heart clean
and washed my hands, staying free of guilt;

14   for all day long I am plagued;
my punishment comes every morning.

15   If I had said, "I will talk like them,"
I would have betrayed a generation of your children.

16   When I tried to understand all this,
I found it too hard for me —

17   until I went into the sanctuaries of God
and grasped what their destiny would be.

18   Indeed, you place them on a slippery slope
and make them fall to their ruin.

19   How suddenly they are destroyed,
swept away by terrors!

20   They are like a dream when one awakens;
Adonai, when you rouse yourself,
you will despise their phantoms.

21   When I had a sour attitude
and felt stung by pained emotions,

22   I was too stupid to understand;
I was like a brute beast with you.

23 Nevertheless, I am always with you;
you hold my right hand.
24 You will guide me with your advice;
and afterwards, you will receive me with honor.

25 Whom do I have in heaven but you?
And with you, I lack nothing on earth.
26 My mind and body may fail; but God
is the rock for my mind and my portion forever.

27 Those who are far from you will perish;
you destroy all who adulterously leave you.
28 But for me, the nearness of God is my good;
I have made *Adonai Elohim* my refuge,
so that I can tell of all your works.

74 ¹⁽⁰⁾ A *maskil* of Asaf:

(1) Why have you rejected us forever, God,
with your anger smoking against the sheep you once pastured?
2 Remember your community, which you acquired long ago,
the tribe you redeemed to be your very own.
Remember Mount Tziyon, where you came to live.
3 Hurry your steps to these endless ruins,
to the sanctuary devastated by the enemy.

4 The roar of your foes filled your meeting-place;
they raised their own banners as a sign of their conquest.
5 The place seemed like a thicket of trees
when lumbermen hack away with their axes.
6 With hatchet and hammer they banged away,
smashing all the carved woodwork.
7 They set your sanctuary on fire,
tore down and profaned the abode of your name.
8 They said to themselves, "We will oppress them completely."
They have burned down all God's meeting-places in the land.

9 We see no signs, there is no prophet any more;
none of us knows how long it will last.
10 How much longer, God, will the foe jeer at us?
Will the enemy insult your name forever?
11 Why do you hold back your hand?
Draw your right hand from your coat, and finish them off!

12 God has been my king from earliest times,
acting to save throughout all the earth.

13 By your strength you split the sea in two,
    in the water you smashed sea monsters' heads,
14 you crushed the heads of Livyatan
    and gave it as food to the creatures of the desert.
15 You cut channels for springs and streams,
    you dried up rivers that had never failed.
16 The day is yours, and the night is yours;
    it was you who established light and sun.
17 It was you who fixed all the limits of the earth,
    you made summer and winter.

18 Remember how the enemy scoffs at ADONAI,
    how a brutish people insults your name.
19 Don't hand over the soul of your dove to wild beasts,
    don't forget forever the life of your poor.

20 Look to the covenant, for the land's dark places
    are full of the haunts of violence.
21 Don't let the oppressed retreat in confusion;
    let the poor and needy praise your name.

22 Arise, God, and defend your cause;
    remember how brutish men insult you all day.
23 Don't forget what your foes are saying,
    the ever-rising uproar of your adversaries.

75 ¹⁽⁰⁾ For the leader. Set to "Do Not Destroy!" A psalm of Asaf. A song:

2(1) We give thanks to you, God, we give thanks;
      your name is near, people tell of your wonders.

3(2) "At the time of my own choice,
      I will dispense justice fairly.
4(3) When the earth quakes, with all living on it,
      it is I who hold its support-pillars firm."   *(Selah)*

5(4) To the boastful I say, "Do not boast!"
      and to the wicked, "Don't flaunt your strength!
6(5) Don't flaunt your strength so proudly;
      don't speak arrogantly, with your nose in the air!
7(6) For you will not be raised to power
      by those in the east, the west or the desert;
8(7) since God is the judge; and it is he
      who puts down one and lifts up another.
9(8) In ADONAI's hand there is a cup of wine,
      foaming, richly spiced;

when he pours it out, all the wicked of the earth
will drain it, drinking it to the dregs."

10(9) But I will always speak out,
singing praises to the God of Ya'akov.

11(10) I will break down the strength of the wicked,
but the strength of the righteous will be raised up.

76 1(0) For the leader. With string music. A psalm of Asaf. A song:

2(1) In Y'hudah God is known;
his name is great in Isra'el.

3(2) His tent is in Shalem,
his place is in Tziyon.

4(3) There he broke the flashing arrows,
the shield, the sword, and the weapons of war. *(Selah)*

5(4) You are glorious, majestic,
more so than mountains of prey.

6(5) The bravest have been stripped of their spoil
and now are sleeping their final sleep;
not one of these courageous men
finds strength to raise his hands.

7(6) At your rebuke, God of Ya'akov,
riders and horses lie stunned.

8(7) You are fearsome! When once you are angry,
who can stand in your presence?

9(8) You pronounce sentence from heaven;
the earth grows silent with fear

10(9) when God arises to judge,
to save all the humble of the earth. *(Selah)*

11(10) Human wrath serves only to praise you;
what remains of this wrath you wear as an ornament.

12(11) Make vows to ADONAI your God, and keep them;
all who are around him must bring presents to the one who should be feared.

13(12) He curbs the spirit of princes;
he is fearsome to the kings of the earth.

77 1(0) For the leader. For Y'dutun. A psalm of Asaf:

2(1) I cry aloud to God,
aloud to God; and he hears me.

3(2) On the day of my distress I am seeking *Adonai*;
my hands are lifted up;

my tears flow all night without ceasing;
my heart refuses comfort.

4(3) When remembering God, I moan;
when I ponder, my spirit fails. *(Selah)*

5(4) You hold my eyelids [and keep me from sleeping];
I am too troubled to speak.

6(5) I think about the days of old,
the years of long ago;

7(6) in the night I remember my song,
I commune with myself, my spirit inquires:

8(7) "Will *Adonai* reject forever?
will he never show his favor again?

9(8) Has his grace permanently disappeared?
Is his word to all generations done away?

10(9) Has God forgotten to be compassionate?
Has he in anger withheld his mercy?" *(Selah)*

11(10) Then I add, "That's my weakness —
[supposing] the Most High's right hand could change."

12(11) So I will remind myself of *Yah*'s doings;
yes, I will remember your wonders of old.

13(12) I will meditate on your work
and think about what you have done.

14(13) God, your way is in holiness.
What god is as great as God?

15(14) You are the God who does wonders,
you revealed your strength to the peoples.

16(15) With your arm you redeemed your people,
the descendants of Ya'akov and Yosef. *(Selah)*

17(16) The water saw you, God;
the water saw you and writhed in anguish,
agitated to its depths.

18(17) The clouds poured water, the skies thundered,
and your arrows flashed here and there.

19(18) The sound of your thunder was in the whirlwind,
the lightning flashes lit up the world,
the earth trembled and shook.

20(19) Your way went through the sea,
your path through the turbulent waters;
but your footsteps could not be traced.

21(20) You led your people like a flock
under the care of Moshe and Aharon.

866

78 ¹⁽⁰⁾ A *maskil* of Asaf:

(1)   Listen, my people, to my teaching;
      turn your ears to the words from my mouth.
2   I will speak to you in parables
      and explain mysteries from days of old.

3   The things which we have heard and known,
      and which our fathers told us
4   we will not hide from their descendants;
      we will tell the generation to come
      the praises of ADONAI and his strength,
      the wonders that he has performed.

5   He raised up a testimony in Ya'akov
      and established a *Torah* in Isra'el.
      He commanded our ancestors
      to make this known to their children,
6   so that the next generation would know it,
      the children not yet born,
      who would themselves arise
      and tell their own children,
7   who could then put their confidence in God,
      not forgetting God's deeds,
      but obeying his *mitzvot*.
8   Then they would not be like their ancestors,
      a stubborn, rebellious generation,
      a generation with unprepared hearts,
      with spirits unfaithful to God.

9   The people of Efrayim, though armed with bows and arrows,
      turned their backs on the day of battle.
10   They did not keep the covenant of God
      and refused to live by his *Torah*.
11   They forgot what he had done,
      his wonders which he had shown them.

12   He had done wonderful things
      in the presence of their ancestors
      in the land of Egypt,
      in the region of Tzo'an.
13   He split the sea and made them pass through,
      he made the waters stand up like a wall.
14   He also led them by day with a cloud
      and all night long with light from a fire.
15   He broke apart the rocks in the desert
      and let them drink as if from boundless depths;

16   yes, he brought streams out of the rock,
    making the water flow down like rivers.

17   Yet they sinned still more against him,
    rebelling in the wilderness against the Most High;
18   in their hearts they tested God
    by demanding food that would satisfy their cravings.
19   Yes, they spoke against God by asking,
    "Can God spread a table in the desert?
20   True, he struck the rock, and water gushed out,
    until the *vadi*s overflowed;
    but what about bread? Can he give that?
    Can he provide meat for his people?"

21   Therefore, when ADONAI heard, he was angry;
    fire blazed up against Ya'akov;
    his anger mounted against Isra'el;
22   because they had no faith in God,
    no trust in his power to save.

23   So he commanded the skies above
    and opened the doors of heaven.
24   He rained down *man* on them as food;
    he gave them grain from heaven —
25   mortals ate the bread of angels;
    he provided for them to the full.

26   He stirred up the east wind in heaven,
    brought on the south wind by his power,
27   and rained down meat on them like dust,
    birds flying thick as the sand on the seashore.
28   He let them fall in the middle of their camp,
    all around their tents.
29   So they ate till they were satisfied;
    he gave them what they craved.
30   They were still fulfilling their craving,
    the food was still in their mouths,
31   when the anger of God rose up against them
    and slaughtered their strongest men,
    laying low the young men of Isra'el.

32   Still, they kept on sinning
    and put no faith in his wonders.
33   Therefore, he ended their days in futility
    and their years in terror.
34   When he brought death among them, they would seek him;
    they would repent and seek God eagerly,

35   remembering that God was their Rock,
     El 'Elyon their Redeemer.

36   But they tried to deceive him with their words,
     they lied to him with their tongues;
37   for their hearts were not right with him,
     and they were unfaithful to his covenant.
38   Yet he, because he is full of compassion,
     forgave their sin and did not destroy;
     many times he turned away his anger
     and didn't rouse all his wrath.
39   So he remembered that they were but flesh,
     a wind that blows past and does not return.

40   How often they rebelled against him in the desert
     and grieved him in the wastelands!
41   Repeatedly they challenged God
     and pained the Holy One of Isra'el.
42   They didn't remember how he used his hand
     on the day he redeemed them from their enemy,
43   how he displayed his signs in Egypt,
     his wonders in the region of Tzo'an.

44   He turned their rivers into blood,
     so they couldn't drink from their streams.
45   He sent swarms of flies, which devoured them,
     and frogs, which destroyed them.
46   He gave their harvest to shearer-worms,
     the fruit of their labor to locusts.
47   He destroyed their vineyards with hail
     and their sycamore-figs with frost.
48   Their cattle too he gave over to the hail
     and their flocks to lightning bolts.

49   He sent over them his fierce anger,
     fury, indignation and trouble,
     with a company of destroying angels
50   to clear a path for his wrath.
     He did not spare them from death,
     but gave them over to the plague,
51   striking all the firstborn in Egypt,
     the firstfruits of their strength in the tents of Ham.

52   But his own people he led out like sheep,
     guiding them like a flock in the desert.
53   He led them safely, and they weren't afraid,
     even when the sea overwhelmed their foes.

54 He brought them to his holy land,
to the hill-country won by his right hand.
55 He expelled nations before them,
apportioned them property to inherit
and made Isra'el's tribes live in their tents.

56 Yet they tested *El 'Elyon*
and rebelled against him,
refusing to obey his instructions.
57 They turned away and were faithless, like their fathers;
they were unreliable, like a bow without tension.
58 They provoked him with their high places
and made him jealous with their idols.

59 God heard, and he was angry;
he came to detest Isra'el completely.
60 He abandoned the tabernacle at Shiloh,
the tent he had made where he could live among people.
61 He gave his strength into exile,
his pride to the power of the foe.
62 He gave his people over to the sword
and grew angry with his own heritage.
63 Fire consumed their young men,
their virgins had no wedding-song,
64 their *cohanim* fell by the sword,
and their widows could not weep.

65 Then *Adonai* awoke, as if from sleep,
like a warrior shouting for joy from wine.
66 He struck his foes, driving them back
and putting them to perpetual shame.

67 Rejecting the tents of Yosef
and passing over the tribe of Efrayim,
68 he chose the tribe of Y'hudah,
Mount Tziyon, which he loved.
69 He built his sanctuary like the heights;
like the earth, he made it to last forever.

70 He chose David to be his servant,
taking him from the sheep-yards;
71 from tending nursing ewes he brought him
to shepherd Ya'akov his people,
Isra'el his heritage.
72 With upright heart he shepherded them
and guided them with skillful hands.

79 ¹⁽⁰⁾ A psalm of Asaf:

(1)   God, the pagans have entered your heritage.
          They have defiled your holy temple
          and turned Yerushalayim into rubble.

2   They have given the corpses of your servants
          as food for the birds in the air,
          yes, the flesh of those faithful to you
          for the wild animals of the earth.

3   All around Yerushalayim
          they have shed their blood like water,
          and no one is left to bury them.

4   We suffer the taunts of our neighbors,
          we are mocked and scorned by those around us.

5   How long, ADONAI?
          Will you be angry forever?
          How long will your jealousy burn like fire?

6   Pour out your wrath on the nations that don't know you,
          on the kingdoms that don't call out your name;

7   for they have devoured Ya'akov
          and left his home a waste.

8   Don't count past iniquities against us,
          but let your compassion come quickly to meet us,
          for we have been brought very low.

9   Help us, God of our salvation,
          for the sake of the glory of your name.
          Deliver us, forgive our sins,
          for your name's sake.

10   Why should the nations ask,
          "Where is their God?"

          Let the vengeance taken on your servants' shed blood
          be known among the nations before our eyes.

11   Let the groaning of the captives come before you;
          by your great strength save those condemned to death.

12   Repay our neighbors sevenfold where they can feel it
          for the insults they inflicted on you, Adonai.

13   Then we, your people and the flock in your pasture,
          will give you thanks forever.
          From generation to generation
          we will proclaim your praise.

80 $^{1(0)}$ For the leader. Set to "Lilies." A testimony. A psalm of Asaf:

$^{2(1)}$ Shepherd of Isra'el, listen!
You who lead Yosef like a flock,
you whose throne is on the *k'ruvim*,
shine out!

$^{3(2)}$ Before Efrayim, Binyamin and M'nasheh,
rouse your power; and come to save us.

$^{4(3)}$ God, restore us!
Make your face shine, and we will be saved.

$^{5(4)}$ ADONAI, God of armies, how long
will you be angry with your people's prayers?

$^{6(5)}$ You have fed them tears as their bread
and made them drink tears in abundance.

$^{7(6)}$ You make our neighbors fight over us,
and our enemies mock us.

$^{8(7)}$ God of armies, restore us!
Make your face shine, and we will be saved.

$^{9(8)}$ You brought a vine out of Egypt,
you expelled the nations and planted it,

$^{10(9)}$ you cleared a space for it;
then it took root firmly and filled the land.

$^{11(10)}$ The mountains were covered with its shade,
the mighty cedars with its branches —

$^{12(11)}$ it put out branches as far as the sea
and shoots to the [Euphrates] River.

$^{13(12)}$ Why did you break down [the vineyard's] wall,
so that all passing by can pluck [its fruit]?

$^{14(13)}$ The boar from the forest tears it apart;
wild creatures from the fields feed on it.

$^{15(14)}$ God of armies, please come back!
Look from heaven, see, and tend this vine!

$^{16(15)}$ Protect what your right hand planted,
the son you made strong for yourself.

$^{17(16)}$ It is burned by fire, it is cut down;
they perish at your frown of rebuke.

$^{18(17)}$ Help the man at your right hand,
the son of man you made strong for yourself.

$^{19(18)}$ Then we won't turn away from you —
if you revive us, we will call on your name.

$^{20(19)}$ ADONAI, God of armies, restore us!
Make your face shine, and we will be saved.

81 ¹⁽⁰⁾ For the Leader. On the *gittit*. By Asaf:

2(1) Sing for joy to God our strength!
Shout to the God of Ya'akov!

3(2) Start the music! Beat the drum!
Play the sweet lyre and the lute!

4(3) Sound the *shofar* at *Rosh-Hodesh*
and at full moon for the pilgrim feast,

5(4) because this is a law for Isra'el,
a ruling of the God of Ya'akov.

6(5) He placed it as a testimony in Y'hosef
when he went out against the land of Egypt.

I heard an unfamiliar voice say,

7(6) "I lifted the load from his shoulder;
his hands were freed from the [laborer's] basket.

8(7) You called out when you were in trouble,
and I rescued you;
I answered you from the thundercloud;
I tested you at the M'rivah Spring [by saying,]   (*Selah*)

9(8) "'Hear, my people, while I give you warning!
Isra'el, if you would only listen to me!

10(9) There is not to be with you any foreign god;
you are not to worship an alien god.

11(10) I am ADONAI your God,
who brought you up from the land of Egypt.
Open your mouth, and I will fill it.'

12(11) "But my people did not listen to my voice;
Isra'el would have none of me.

13(12) So I gave them over to their stubborn hearts,
to live by their own plans.

14(13) How I wish my people would listen to me,
that Isra'el would live by my ways!

15(14) I would quickly subdue their enemies
and turn my hand against their foes.

16(15) Those who hate ADONAI would cringe before him,
while [Isra'el's] time would last forever.

17(16) They would be fed with the finest wheat,
and I would satisfy you with honey from the rocks."

82 ¹⁽⁰⁾ A psalm of Asaf:

(1) *Elohim* [God] stands in the divine assembly;
there with the *elohim* [judges], he judges:

2   "How long will you go on judging unfairly,
           favoring the wicked?   *(Selah)*

3   Give justice to the weak and fatherless!
           Uphold the rights of the wretched and poor!

4   Rescue the destitute and needy;
           deliver them from the power of the wicked!"

5   They don't know, they don't understand,
           they wander about in darkness;
           meanwhile, all the foundations of the earth
           are being undermined.

6   "My decree is: 'You are *elohim* [gods, judges],
           sons of the Most High all of you.

7   Nevertheless, you will die like mortals;
           like any prince, you will fall.'"

8   Rise up, *Elohim*, and judge the earth;
           for all the nations are yours.

83 ¹⁽⁰⁾ A song. A psalm of Asaf:

2(1)   God, don't remain silent!
           Don't stay quiet, God, or still;

3(2)   because here are your enemies, causing an uproar;
           those who hate you are raising their heads,

4(3)   craftily conspiring against your people,
           consulting together against those you treasure.

5(4)   They say, "Come, let's wipe them out as a nation;
           let the name of Isra'el be remembered no more!"

6(5)   With one mind they plot their schemes;
           the covenant they have made is against you —

7(6)   the tents of Edom and the Yishma'elim,
           Mo'av and the Hagrim,

8(7)   G'val, 'Amon and 'Amalek,
           P'leshet with those living in Tzor;   *(Selah)*

9(8)   Ashur too is allied with them,
           to reinforce the descendants of Lot.

10(9)   Do to them as you did to Midyan,
           to Sisra and Yavin at *Vadi* Kishon —

11(10)   they were destroyed at 'Ein-Dor
           and became manure for the ground.

12(11)   Make their leaders like 'Orev and Ze'ev,
           all their princes like Zevach and Tzalmuna,

13(12) who said, "Let's take possession
of God's meadows for ourselves."

14(13) My God, make them like whirling dust,
like chaff driven by the wind.

15(14) Like fire burning up the forest,
like a flame that sets the mountains ablaze,

16(15) drive them away with your storm,
terrify them with your tempest.

17(16) Fill their faces with shame,
so that they will seek your name, ADONAI.

18(17) Let them be ashamed and fearful forever;
yes, let them perish in disgrace.

19(18) Let them know that you alone,
whose name is ADONAI,
are the Most High over all the earth.

84 ¹⁽⁰⁾ For the leader. On the *gittit*. A psalm of the sons of Korach:

2(1) How deeply loved are your dwelling-places,
ADONAI-Tzva'ot!

3(2) My soul yearns, yes, faints with longing
for the courtyards of ADONAI;
my heart and body cry for joy
to the living God.

4(3) As the sparrow finds herself a home
and the swallow her nest, where she lays her young,
[so my resting-place is] by your altars,
ADONAI-Tzva'ot, my king and my God.

5(4) How happy are those who live in your house;
they never cease to praise you!   (*Selah*)

6(5) How happy the man whose strength is in you,
in whose heart are [pilgrim] highways.

7(6) Passing through the [dry] Baka Valley,
they make it a place of springs,
and the early rain clothes it with blessings.

8(7) They go from strength to strength
and appear before God in Tziyon.

9(8) ADONAI, God of armies, hear my prayer;
listen, God of Ya'akov.   (*Selah*)

10(9) God, see our shield [the king];
look at the face of your anointed.

¹¹⁽¹⁰⁾ Better a day in your courtyards
than a thousand [days elsewhere].
Better just standing at the door of my God's house
than living in the tents of the wicked.

¹²⁽¹¹⁾ For *Adonai*, God, is a sun and a shield;
Adonai bestows favor and honor;
he will not withhold anything good
from those whose lives are pure.

¹³⁽¹²⁾ *Adonai-Tzva'ot*,
how happy is anyone who trusts in you!

85 ¹⁽⁰⁾ For the leader. A psalm of the sons of Korach:

²⁽¹⁾ *Adonai*, you have shown favor to your land;
you have restored the fortunes of Ya'akov,

³⁽²⁾ taken away the guilt of your people,
pardoned all their sin,   (*Selah*)

⁴⁽³⁾ withdrawn all your wrath,
turned from your fierce anger.

⁵⁽⁴⁾ Restore us, God of our salvation,
renounce your displeasure with us.

⁶⁽⁵⁾ Are you to stay angry with us forever?
Will your fury last through all generations?

⁷⁽⁶⁾ Won't you revive us again,
so your people can rejoice in you?

⁸⁽⁷⁾ Show us your grace, *Adonai*;
grant us your salvation.

⁹⁽⁸⁾ I am listening. What will God, *Adonai*, say?
For he will speak peace to his people,
to his holy ones —
but only if they don't relapse into folly.

¹⁰⁽⁹⁾ His salvation is near for those who fear him,
so that glory will be in our land.

¹¹⁽¹⁰⁾ Grace and truth have met together;
justice and peace have kissed each other.

¹²⁽¹¹⁾ Truth springs up from the earth,
and justice looks down from heaven.

¹³⁽¹²⁾ *Adonai* will also grant prosperity;
our land will yield its harvest.

¹⁴⁽¹³⁾ Justice will walk before him
and make his footsteps a path.

86$^{1(0)}$ A prayer of David:

$^{(1)}$ Listen, ADONAI, and answer me,
for I am poor and needy.

^{2} Preserve my life, for I am faithful;
save your servant,
who puts his trust in you
because you are my God.

^{3} Take pity on me, Adonai,
for I cry to you all day.

^{4} Fill your servant's heart with joy,
for to you, Adonai, I lift my heart.

^{5} Adonai, you are kind and forgiving,
full of grace toward all who call on you.

^{6} Listen, ADONAI, to my prayer;
pay attention to my pleading cry.

^{7} On the day of my trouble I am calling on you,
for you will answer me.

^{8} There is none like you among the gods, Adonai;
no deeds compare with yours.

^{9} All the nations you have made
will come and bow before you, Adonai;
they will honor your name.

^{10} For you are great, and you do wonders;
you alone are God.

^{11} ADONAI, teach me your way,
so that I can live by your truth;
make me single-hearted,
so that I can fear your name.

^{12} I will thank you, Adonai my God,
with my whole heart;
and I will glorify your name forever.

^{13} For your grace toward me is so great!
You have rescued me from the lowest part of Sh'ol.

^{14} God, arrogant men are rising against me,
a gang of brutes is seeking my life,
and to you they pay no attention.

^{15} But you, Adonai,
are a merciful, compassionate God,
slow to anger
and rich in grace and truth.

^{16} Turn to me, and show me your favor;
strengthen your servant, save your slave-girl's son.

17   Give me a sign of your favor,
     so that those who hate me
     will see it and be ashamed,
     because you, ADONAI,
     have helped and comforted me.

87 ¹⁽⁰⁾ A psalm of the sons of Korach. A song:

(1)   On the holy mountains is [the city's] foundation.
2   ADONAI loves the gates of Tziyon
      more than all the dwellings in Ya'akov.
3   Glorious things are said about you,
      city of God.   (*Selah*)

4   I count Rahav and Bavel
      among those who know me.
      Of P'leshet, Tzor and Ethiopia [they will say],
      "This one was born there."
5   But of Tziyon it will be said,
      "This one and that was born in it,
      for the Most High himself establishes it."
6   When he registers the peoples, ADONAI will record,
      "This one was born there."   (*Selah*)

7   Singers and dancers alike say,
      "For me, you are the source of everything."

88 ¹⁽⁰⁾ A song. A psalm of the sons of Korach. For the leader. Set to "Sickness that Causes Suffering." A *maskil* of Heiman the Ezrachi.

2(1)   ADONAI, God of my salvation,
       when I cry out to you in the night,
3(2)   let my prayer come before you,
       turn your ear to my cry for help!
4(3)   For I am oversupplied with troubles,
       which have brought me to the brink of Sh'ol.
5(4)   I am counted among those going down to the pit,
       like a man who is beyond help,
6(5)   left by myself among the dead,
       like the slain who lie in the grave —
       you no longer remember them;
       they are cut off from your care.

7(6)   You plunged me into the bottom of the pit,
       into dark places, into the depths.

8(7) Your wrath lies heavily on me;
      your waves crashing over me keep me down.   (*Selah*)
9(8) You separated me from my close friends,
      made me repulsive to them;
      I am caged in, with no escape;
10(9) my eyes grow dim from suffering.

      I call on you, ADONAI, every day;
      I spread out my hands to you.
11(10) Will you perform wonders for the dead?
      Can the ghosts of the dead rise up and praise you?   (*Selah*)
12(11) Will your grace be declared in the grave,
      or your faithfulness in Abaddon?
13(12) Will your wonders be known in the dark,
      or your righteousness in the land of oblivion?

14(13) But I cry out to you, ADONAI;
      my prayer comes before you in the morning.
15(14) So why, ADONAI, do you reject me?
      Why do you hide your face from me?

16(15) Since my youth I have been miserable, close to death;
      I am numb from bearing these terrors of yours.
17(16) Your fierce anger has overwhelmed me,
      your terrors have shriveled me up.
18(17) They surge around me all day like a flood,
      from all sides they close in on me.
19(18) You have made friends and companions shun me;
      the people I know are hidden from me.

89¹⁽⁰⁾ A *maskil* of Eitan the Ezrachi:

2(1) I will sing about ADONAI's acts of grace forever,
      with my mouth proclaim your faithfulness to all generations;
3(2) because I said, "Grace is built to last forever;
      in the heavens themselves you established your faithfulness."

4(3) You said, "I made a covenant with the one I chose,
      I swore to my servant David,
5(4) 'I will establish your dynasty forever,
      build up your throne through all generations.'"   (*Selah*)

6(5) Let the heavens praise your wonders, ADONAI,
      your faithfulness in the assembly of the angels.
7(6) For who in the skies can be compared with ADONAI?
      Which of these gods can rival ADONAI,

8(7)   a God dreaded in the great assembly of the holy ones
    and feared by all around him?

9(8)   *ADONAI Elohei-Tzva'ot!*
    Who is as mighty as you, *Yah?*
    Your faithfulness surrounds you.

10(9)   You control the raging of the sea;
    when its waves rear up, you calm them.

11(10)   You crushed Rahav like a carcass;
    with your strong arm you scattered your foes.

12(11)   The heavens are yours, and the earth is yours;
    you founded the world and everything in it.

13(12)   You created north and south;
    Tavor and Hermon take joy in your name.

14(13)   Your arm is mighty, your hand is strong,
    your right hand is lifted high.

15(14)   Righteousness and justice are the foundation of your throne;
    grace and truth attend you.

16(15)   How happy are the people who know the joyful shout!
    They walk in the light of your presence, *ADONAI.*

17(16)   They rejoice in your name all day
    and are lifted up by your righteousness,

18(17)   for you yourself are the strength in which they glory.
    Our power grows by pleasing you,

19(18)   for our shield comes from *ADONAI* —
    our king is from the Holy One of Isra'el.

20(19)   There was a time when you spoke in a vision;
    you declared to your loyal [prophets],
    "I have given help to a warrior,
    I have raised up someone chosen from the people.

21(20)   I have found David my servant
    and anointed him with my holy oil.

22(21)   My hand will always be with him,
    and my arm will give him strength.

23(22)   No enemy will outwit him,
    no wicked man overcome him.

24(23)   I will crush his foes before him
    and strike down those who hate him.

25(24)   My faithfulness and grace will be with him;
    through my name his power will grow.

26(25)   I will put his hand on the sea
    and his right hand on the rivers.

27(26)   He will call to me, 'You are my father,
    my God, the Rock of my salvation.'

28(27)	I will give him the position of firstborn, the highest of the kings of the earth.
29(28)	I will keep my grace for him forever, and in my covenant be faithful with him.
30(29)	I will establish his dynasty forever, and his throne as long as the heavens last.

31(30)	"If his descendants abandon my *Torah* and fail to live by my rulings,
32(31)	if they profane my regulations and don't obey my *mitzvot*,
33(32)	I will punish their disobedience with the rod and their guilt with lashes.
34(33)	But I won't withdraw my grace from him or be false to my faithfulness.
35(34)	I will not profane my covenant or change what my lips have spoken.
36(35)	I have sworn by my holiness once and for all; I will not lie to David —
37(36)	his dynasty will last forever, his throne like the sun before me.
38(37)	It will be established forever, like the moon, which remains a faithful witness in the sky."	(*Selah*)

39(38)	But you spurned your anointed one, rejected and vented your rage on him.
40(39)	You renounced the covenant with your servant and defiled his crown in the dust.
41(40)	You broke through all his defenses and left his strongholds in ruins.
42(41)	All who pass by plunder him; he is an object of scorn to his neighbors.
43(42)	You raised up the right hand of his foes and made all his enemies rejoice.
44(43)	You drive back his drawn sword and fail to support him in battle.
45(44)	You brought an end to his splendor and hurled his throne to the ground.
46(45)	You cut short the days of his youth and covered him with shame.	(*Selah*)

47(46)	How long, *ADONAI*? Will you hide yourself forever? How long will your fury burn like fire?
48(47)	Remember how little time I have! Was it for no purpose that you created all humanity?
49(48)	Who can live and not see death? Who can save himself from the power of the grave?	(*Selah*)

50(49)	Where, *Adonai*, are the acts of grace you once did, those which, in your faithfulness, you swore to David?
51(50)	Remember, *Adonai*, the taunts hurled at your servants, which I carry in my heart [from] so many peoples!
52(51)	Your enemies, ADONAI, have flung their taunts, flung them in the footsteps of your anointed one.
53(52)	Blessed be ADONAI forever. Amen. Amen.

Book IV: Psalms 90–106

90 ¹⁽⁰⁾ A prayer of Moshe the man of God:

(1)   *Adonai*, you have been our dwelling place
in every generation.

2   Before the mountains were born,
before you had formed the earth and the world,
from eternity past to eternity future
you are God.

3   You bring frail mortals to the point of being crushed,
then say, "People, repent!"

4   For from your viewpoint a thousand years
are merely like yesterday or a night watch.

5   When you sweep them away, they become like sleep;
by morning they are like growing grass,

6   growing and flowering in the morning,
but by evening cut down and dried up.

7   For we are destroyed by your anger,
overwhelmed by your wrath.

8   You have placed our faults before you,
our secret sins in the full light of your presence.

9   All our days ebb away under your wrath;
our years die away like a sigh.

10   The span of our life is seventy years,
or if we are strong, eighty;
yet at best it is toil and sorrow,
over in a moment, and then we are gone.

11   Who grasps the power of your anger and wrath
to the degree that the fear due you should inspire?

12 So teach us to count our days,
    so that we will become wise.

13 Return, *ADONAI*! How long must it go on?
    Take pity on your servants!

14 Fill us at daybreak with your love,
    so that we can sing for joy as long as we live.

15 Let our joy last as long as the time you made us suffer,
    for as many years as we experienced trouble.

16 Show your deeds to your servants
    and your glory to their children.

17 May the favor of *Adonai* our God be on us,
    prosper for us all the work that we do —
    yes, prosper the work that we do.

91 1 You who live in the shelter of *'Elyon*,
    who spend your nights in the shadow of *Shaddai*,

2   who say to *ADONAI*, "My refuge! My fortress!
    My God, in whom I trust!" —

3   he will rescue you from the trap of the hunter
    and from the plague of calamities;

4   he will cover you with his pinions,
    and under his wings you will find refuge;
    his truth is a shield and protection.

5   You will not fear the terrors of night
    or the arrow that flies by day,

6   or the plague that roams in the dark,
    or the scourge that wreaks havoc at noon.

7   A thousand may fall at your side,
    ten thousand at your right hand;
    but it won't come near you.

8   Only keep your eyes open,
    and you will see how the wicked are punished.

9   For you have made *ADONAI*, the Most High,
    who is my refuge, your dwelling-place.

10 No disaster will happen to you,
    no calamity will come near your tent;

11 for he will order his angels to care for you
    and guard you wherever you go.

12 They will carry you in their hands,
    so that you won't trip on a stone.

13 You will tread down lions and snakes,
    young lions and serpents you will trample underfoot.

14 "Because he loves me, I will rescue him;
because he knows my name, I will protect him.
15 He will call on me, and I will answer him.
I will be with him when he is in trouble.
I will extricate him and bring him honor.
16 I will satisfy him with long life
and show him my salvation."

92 ¹⁽⁰⁾ A psalm. A song for *Shabbat*:

2(1) It is good to give thanks to ADONAI
and sing praises to your name, '*Elyon*,
3(2) to tell in the morning about your grace
and at night about your faithfulness,
4(3) to the music of a ten-stringed [harp] and a lute,
with the melody sounding on a lyre.

5(4) For, ADONAI, what you do makes me happy;
I take joy in what your hands have made.
6(5) How great are your deeds, ADONAI!
How very deep your thoughts!

7(6) Stupid people can't know,
fools don't understand,
8(7) that when the wicked sprout like grass,
and all who do evil prosper,
it is so that they can be eternally destroyed,
9(8) while you, ADONAI, are exalted forever.

10(9) For your enemies, ADONAI,
your enemies will perish;
all evildoers will be scattered.
11(10) But you have given me
the strength of a wild bull;
you anoint me with fresh olive oil.
12(11) My eyes have gazed with pleasure on my enemies' ruin,
my ears have delighted in the fall of my foes.

13(12) The righteous will flourish like a palm tree,
they will grow like a cedar in the L'vanon.
14(13) Planted in the house of ADONAI,
they will flourish in the courtyards of our God.
15(14) Even in old age they will be vigorous,
still full of sap, still bearing fruit,
16(15) proclaiming that ADONAI is upright,
my Rock, in whom there is no wrong.

93 ¹ ADONAI is king, robed in majesty;
ADONAI is robed, girded with strength.
The world is well established;
it cannot be moved.
² Your throne was established long ago;
you have existed forever.
³ ADONAI, the deep is raising up,
the deep is raising up its voice,
the deep is raising its crashing waves.
⁴ More than the sound of rushing waters
or the mighty breakers of the sea,
ADONAI on high is mighty.
⁵ Your instructions are very sure;
holiness befits your house,
ADONAI, for all time to come.

94 ¹ God of vengeance, ADONAI!
God of vengeance, appear!
² Assert yourself as judge of the earth!
Pay back the proud as they deserve!

³ How long are the wicked, ADONAI,
how long are the wicked to triumph?
⁴ They pour out insolent words,
they go on bragging, all these evildoers.

⁵ They crush your people, ADONAI,
they oppress your heritage.
⁶ They kill widows and strangers
and murder the fatherless.

⁷ They say, "Yah isn't looking;
the God of Ya'akov won't notice."
⁸ Take notice, yourselves, you boors among the people!
You fools, when will you understand?
⁹ Will the one who planted the ear not hear?
Will the one who formed the eye not see?
¹⁰ Will the one who disciplines nations not correct them?
Will the teacher of humanity not know?
¹¹ ADONAI understands that people's thoughts
are merely a puff of wind.

¹² How happy the man whom you correct, Yah,
whom you teach from your Torah,
¹³ giving him respite from days of trouble,
till a pit is dug for the wicked!

14 For ADONAI will not desert his people,
he will not abandon his heritage.
15 Justice will once again become righteous,
and all the upright in heart will follow it.

16 Who will champion my cause against the wicked?
Who will stand up for me against evildoers?

17 If ADONAI hadn't helped me,
I would soon have dwelt in the land of silence.
18 When I said, "My foot is slipping!"
your grace, ADONAI, supported me.
19 When my cares within me are many,
your comforts cheer me up.

20 Can unjust judges be allied with you,
those producing wrong in the name of law?
21 They band together against the righteous
and condemn the innocent to death.

22 But ADONAI has become my stronghold,
my God is my rock of refuge.
23 But he repays them as their guilt deserves;
he will cut them off with their own evil;
ADONAI our God will cut them off.

95 1 Come, let's sing to ADONAI!
Let's shout for joy to the Rock of our salvation!
2 Let's come into his presence with thanksgiving;
let's shout for joy to him with songs of praise.

3 For ADONAI is a great God,
a great king greater than all gods.
4 He holds the depths of the earth in his hands;
the mountain peaks too belong to him.
5 The sea is his — he made it —
and his hands shaped the dry land.

6 Come, let's bow down and worship;
let's kneel before ADONAI who made us.
7 For he is our God, and we are the people
in his pasture, the sheep in his care.

If only today you would listen to his voice:
8 "Don't harden your hearts, as you did at M'rivah,
as you did on that day at Massah in the desert,

9   when your fathers put me to the test;
    they challenged me, even though they saw my work.
10   For forty years I loathed that generation;
    I said, 'This is a people whose hearts go astray,
    they don't understand how I do things.'
11   Therefore I swore in my anger
    that they would not enter my rest."

96 1   Sing to *Adonai* a new song!
    Sing to *Adonai*, all the earth!
2   Sing to *Adonai*, bless his name!
    Proclaim his victory day after day!
3   Declare his glory among the nations,
    his wonders among all peoples!

4   For *Adonai* is great, and greatly to be praised;
    he is to be feared more than all gods.
5   For all the gods of the peoples are idols,
    but *Adonai* made the heavens.
6   In his presence are honor and majesty;
    in his sanctuary, strength and splendor.

7   Give *Adonai* his due, you families from the peoples;
    give *Adonai* his due of glory and strength;
8   give *Adonai* the glory due to his name;
    bring an offering, and enter his courtyards.
9   Worship *Adonai* in holy splendor;
    tremble before him, all the earth!
10   Say among the nations, "*Adonai* is king!"
    The world is firmly established, immovable.
    He will judge the peoples fairly.

11   Let the heavens rejoice; let the earth be glad;
    let the sea roar, and everything in it;
12   let the fields exult and all that is in them.
    Then all the trees in the forest will sing
13   before *Adonai*, because he has come,
    he has come to judge the earth;
    he will judge the world rightly
    and the peoples with his faithfulness.

97 1   *Adonai* is king, let the earth rejoice,
    let the many coasts and islands be glad.
2   Clouds and thick darkness surround him;
    righteousness and justice are the foundation of his throne.

3 Fire goes before him,
setting ablaze his foes on every side.
4 His flashes of lightning light up the world;
the earth sees it and trembles.
5 The mountains melt like wax at the presence of *ADONAI*,
at the presence of the Lord of all the earth.
6 The heavens declare his righteousness,
and all the peoples see his glory.

7 All who worship images will be put to shame,
those who make their boast in worthless idols.
Bow down to him, all you gods!
8 Tziyon hears and is glad, *ADONAI*;
the daughters of Y'hudah rejoice at your rulings.
9 For you, *ADONAI*, most high over all the earth,
you are exalted far above all gods.

10 You who love *ADONAI*, hate evil!
He keeps his faithful servants safe.
He rescues them from the power of the wicked.
11 Light is sown for the righteous
and joy for the upright in heart.
12 Rejoice in *ADONAI*, you righteous;
and give thanks on recalling his holiness.

98 ¹⁽⁰⁾ A psalm:

⁽¹⁾ Sing a new song to *ADONAI*,
because he has done wonders.
His right hand, his holy arm
have won him victory.
2 *ADONAI* has made known his victory;
revealed his vindication in full view of the nations,
3 remembered his grace and faithfulness
to the house of Isra'el.
All the ends of the earth have seen
the victory of our God.

4 Shout for joy to *ADONAI*, all the earth!
Break forth, sing for joy, sing praises!
5 Sing praises to *ADONAI* with the lyre,
with the lyre and melodious music!
6 With trumpets and the sound of the *shofar*,
shout for joy before the king, *ADONAI*!
7 Let the sea roar, and everything in it;
the world, and those living in it.

8   Let the floods clap their hands;
    let the mountains sing together for joy
9   before ADONAI, for he has come to judge the earth;
    he will judge the world rightly and the peoples fairly.

99 1 ADONAI is king; let the peoples tremble.
    He sits enthroned on the *k'ruvim*; let the earth shake!
2   ADONAI is great in Tziyon;
    he is high above all the peoples.

3   Let them praise your great and fearsome name (he is holy):
4   "Mighty king who loves justice, you established
    fairness, justice and righteousness in Ya'akov."

5   Exalt ADONAI our God!
    Prostrate yourselves at his footstool (he is holy).

6   Moshe and Aharon among his *cohanim*
    and Sh'mu'el among those who call on his name
    called on ADONAI, and he answered them.
7   He spoke to them in the column of cloud;
    they kept his instructions and the law that he gave them.
8   ADONAI our God, you answered them.
    To them you were a forgiving God,
    although you took vengeance on their wrongdoings.

9   Exalt ADONAI our God,
    bow down toward his holy mountain,
    for ADONAI our God is holy!

100 1(0) A psalm of thanksgiving:

(1) Shout for joy to ADONAI, all the earth!
2   Serve ADONAI with gladness.
    Enter his presence with joyful songs.

3   Be aware that ADONAI is God;
    it is he who made us; and we are his,
    his people, the flock in his pasture.

4   Enter his gates with thanksgiving,
    enter his courtyards with praise;
    give thanks to him, and bless his name.
5   For ADONAI is good, his grace continues forever,
    and his faithfulness lasts through all generations.

101 ⁽⁰⁾ A psalm of David:

(1)   I am singing of grace and justice;
    I am singing to you, ADONAI.

2   I will follow the path of integrity;
    when will you come to me?
    I will run my life with a sincere heart
    inside my own house.

3   I will not allow before my eyes
    any shameful thing.
    I hate those who act crookedly;
    what they do does not attract me.

4   Deviousness will depart from me;
    I will not tolerate evil.

5   If someone slanders another in secret,
    I will cut him off.
    Haughty eyes and proud hearts
    I cannot abide.

6   I look to the faithful of the land,
    so that they can be my companions;
    those who live lives of integrity
    can be servants of mine.

7   No deceitful person can live in my house;
    no liar can be my advisor.

8   Every morning I will destroy
    all the wicked of the land,
    cutting off all evildoers
    from the city of ADONAI.

102 ⁽⁰⁾ Prayer of a sufferer overcome by weakness and pouring out his complaint before ADONAI:

2(1)   ADONAI, hear my prayer!
    Let my cry for help reach you!

3(2)   Don't hide your face from me
    when I am in such distress!
    Turn your ear toward me;
    when I call, be quick to reply!

4(3)   For my days are vanishing like smoke,
    my bones are burning like a furnace.

5(4)   I am stricken and withered like grass;
    I forget to eat my food.

6(5)   Because of my loud groaning,
    I am just skin and bones.

7(6)   I am like a great owl in the desert,
I've become like an owl in the ruins.

8(7)   I lie awake and become
like a bird alone on the roof.

9(8)   My enemies taunt me all day long;
mad with rage, they make my name a curse.

10(9)   For I have been eating ashes like bread
and mingling tears with my drink

11(10)   because of your furious anger,
since you picked me up just to toss me aside.

12(11)   My days decline like an evening shadow;
I am drying up like grass.

13(12)   But you, ADONAI, are enthroned forever;
your renown will endure through all generations.

14(13)   You will arise and take pity on Tziyon,
for the time has come to have mercy on her;
the time determined has come.

15(14)   For your servants love her very stones;
they take pity even on her dust.

16(15)   The nations will fear the name of ADONAI
and all the kings on earth your glory,

17(16)   when ADONAI has rebuilt Tziyon,
and shows himself in his glory,

18(17)   when he has heeded the plea of the poor
and not despised their prayer.

19(18)   May this be put on record for a future generation;
may a people yet to be created praise ADONAI.

20(19)   For he has looked down from the height of his sanctuary;
from heaven ADONAI surveys the earth

21(20)   to listen to the sighing of the prisoner,
to set free those who are sentenced to death,

22(21)   to proclaim the name of ADONAI in Tziyon
and his praise in Yerushalayim

23(22)   when peoples and kingdoms have been gathered together
to serve ADONAI.

24(23)   He has broken my strength in midcourse,
he has cut short my days.

25(24)   I plead, "God, your years last through all generations;
so don't take me away when my life is half over!

26(25)   In the beginning, you laid the foundations of the earth;
heaven is the work of your hands.

27(26) They will vanish, but you will remain;
        like clothing, they will all grow old;
        yes, you will change them like clothing,
        and they will pass away.
28(27) But you remain the same,
        and your years will never end.
29(28) The children of your servants will live securely
        and their descendants be established in your presence."

103 ¹⁽⁰⁾ By David:

(1)   Bless ADONAI, my soul!
        Everything in me, bless his holy name!
2   Bless ADONAI, my soul,
        and forget none of his benefits!

3   He forgives all your offenses,
        he heals all your diseases,
4   he redeems your life from the pit,
        he surrounds you with grace and compassion,
5   he contents you with good as long as you live,
        so that your youth is renewed like an eagle's.

6   ADONAI brings vindication and justice
        to all who are oppressed.
7   He made his ways known to Moshe,
        his mighty deeds to the people of Isra'el.
8   ADONAI is merciful and compassionate,
        slow to anger and rich in grace.
9   He will not always accuse,
        he will not keep his anger forever.
10   He has not treated us as our sins deserve
        or paid us back for our offenses,
11   because his mercy toward those who fear him
        is as far above earth as heaven.
12   He has removed our sins from us
        as far as the east is from the west.

13   Just as a father has compassion on his children,
        ADONAI has compassion on those who fear him.
14   For he understands how we are made,
        he remembers that we are dust.
15   Yes, a human being's days are like grass,
        he sprouts like a flower in the countryside —
16   but when the wind sweeps over, it's gone;
        and its place knows it no more.

17 But the mercy of *Adonai* on those who fear him
is from eternity past to eternity future,
and his righteousness extends
to his children's children,
18 provided they keep his covenant
and remember to follow his precepts.

19 *Adonai* has established his throne in heaven;
his kingly power rules everything.
20 Bless *Adonai*, you angels of his,
you mighty warriors who obey his word,
who carry out his orders!
21 Bless *Adonai*, all his troops,
who serve him and do what he wants!
22 Bless *Adonai*, all his works,
in every place where he rules!
Bless *Adonai*, my soul!

104 1 Bless *Adonai*, my soul!
Adonai, my God, you are very great;
you are clothed with glory and majesty,
2 wrapped in light as with a robe.
You spread out the heavens like a curtain,
3 you laid the beams of your palace on the water.
You make the clouds your chariot,
you ride on the wings of the wind.
4 You make winds your messengers,
fiery flames your servants.

5 You fixed the earth on its foundations,
never to be moved.
6 You covered it with the deep like a garment;
the waters stood above the mountains.
7 At your rebuke they fled;
at the sound of your thunder they rushed away,
8 flowing over hills, pouring into valleys,
down to the place you had fixed for them.
9 You determined a boundary they could not cross;
they were never to cover the earth again.

10 You make springs gush forth in the *vadi*s;
they flow between the hills,
11 supplying water to all the wild animals;
the wild donkeys quench their thirst.
12 On their banks the birds of the air build their nests;
among the branches they sing.

13 You water the mountains from your palace;
the earth is satisfied with how you provide —
14 you grow grass for the cattle;
and for people you grow the plants they need
to bring forth bread from the earth,
15 wine that gladdens the human heart,
oil to make faces glow,
and food to sustain their strength.

16 *ADONAI*'s trees are satisfied —
the cedars of the L'vanon, which he has planted.
17 In them sparrows build their nests,
while storks live in the fir trees.
18 For the wild goats there are the high mountains,
while the coneys find refuge in the rocks.

19 You made the moon to mark the seasons,
and the sun knows when to set.
20 You bring darkness, and it is night,
the time when all forest animals prowl.
21 The young lions roar after their prey
and seek their food from God.
22 The sun rises, they slink away
and lie down to rest in their dens;
23 while people go out to their work,
laboring on till evening.

24 What variety there is in your works, *ADONAI*!
How many [of them there are]!
In wisdom you have made them all;
the earth is full of your creations.

25 Look at the sea, so great, so wide!
It teems with countless creatures,
living beings, both large and small.
26 The ships are there, sailing to and fro;
Livyatan, which you formed to play there.

27 All of them look to you
to give them their food when they need it.
28 When you give it to them, they gather it;
when you open your hand, they are well satisfied.
29 If you hide your face, they vanish;
if you hold back their breath, they perish
and return to their dust.
30 If you send out your breath, they are created,
and you renew the face of the earth.

31 May the glory of *ADONAI* last forever!
May *ADONAI* rejoice in his works!
32 When he looks at the earth, it trembles;
when he touches the mountains, they pour out smoke.
33 I will sing to *ADONAI* as long as I live,
sing praise to my God all my life.
34 May my musings be pleasing to him;
I will rejoice in *ADONAI*.
35 May sinners vanish from the earth
and the wicked be no more!
Bless *ADONAI*, my soul!

Halleluyah!

105 1 Give thanks to *ADONAI*! Call on his name!
Make his deeds known among the peoples.
2 Sing to him, sing praises to him,
talk about all his wonders.
3 Glory in his holy name;
let those seeking *ADONAI* have joyful hearts.
4 Seek *ADONAI* and his strength;
always seek his presence.
5 Remember the wonders he has done,
his signs and his spoken rulings.

6 You descendants of Avraham his servant,
you offspring of Ya'akov, his chosen ones,
7 he is *ADONAI* our God!
His rulings are everywhere on earth.
8 He remembers his covenant forever,
the word he commanded to a thousand generations,
9 the covenant he made with Avraham,
the oath he swore to Yitz'chak,
10 and established as a law for Ya'akov,
for Isra'el as an everlasting covenant:
11 "To you I will give the land of Kena'an
as your allotted heritage."

12 When they were but few in number,
and not only few, but aliens there too,
13 wandering from nation to nation,
from this kingdom to that people,
14 he allowed no one to oppress them.
Yes, for their sakes he rebuked even kings:
15 "Don't touch my anointed ones
or do my prophets harm!"

16 He called down famine on the land,
   broke off all their food supply,
17 but sent a man ahead of them —
   Yosef, who was sold as a slave.
18 They shackled his feet with chains,
   and they bound him in irons;
19 until the time when his word proved true,
   God's utterance kept testing him.
20 The king sent and had him released,
   the ruler of peoples set him free;
21 he made him lord of his household,
   in charge of all he owned,
22 correcting his officers as he saw fit
   and teaching his counselors wisdom.

23 Then Isra'el too came into Egypt,
   Ya'akov lived as an alien in the land of Ham.
24 There God made his people very fruitful,
   made them too numerous for their foes,
25 whose hearts he turned to hate his people,
   and treat his servants unfairly.

26 He sent his servant Moshe
   and Aharon, whom he had chosen.
27 They worked his signs among them,
   his wonders in the land of Ham.

28 He sent darkness, and the land grew dark;
   they did not defy his word.

29 He turned their water into blood
   and caused their fish to die.

30 Their land swarmed with frogs,
   even in the royal chambers.

31 He spoke, and there came swarms of insects
   and lice throughout their land.

32 He gave them hail instead of rain,
   with fiery [lightning] throughout their land.
33 He struck their vines and fig trees,
   shattering trees all over their country.

34 He spoke, and locusts came,
   also grasshoppers without number;
35 they ate up everything green in their land,
   devoured the fruit of their ground.

36 He struck down all the firstborn in their land,
the firstfruits of all their strength.

37 Then he led his people out,
laden with silver and gold;
among his tribes not one stumbled.

38 Egypt was happy to have them leave,
because fear of [Isra'el] had seized them.

39 He spread out a cloud to screen them off
and fire to give them light at night.

40 When they asked, he brought them quails
and satisfied them with food from heaven.

41 He split a rock, and water gushed out,
flowing as a river over the dry ground,

42 for he remembered his holy promise
to his servant Avraham.

43 He led out his people with joy,
his chosen ones with singing.

44 Then he gave them the lands of the nations,
and they possessed what peoples had toiled to produce,

45 in order to obey his laws
and follow his teachings.

Halleluyah!

106 1 *Halleluyah!*

Give thanks to ADONAI; for he is good,
for his grace continues forever.

2 Who can express ADONAI's mighty doings
or proclaim in full his praise?

3 How happy are those who act justly,
who always do what is right!

4 Remember me, ADONAI, when you show favor to your people,
keep me in mind when you save them;

5 so I can see how well things are going
with those whom you have chosen,
so that I can rejoice in your nation's joy,
and glory in your heritage.

6 Together with our ancestors, we have sinned,
done wrong, acted wickedly.

7   Our ancestors in Egypt failed to grasp
the meaning of your wonders.
They didn't keep in mind your great deeds of grace
but rebelled at the sea, at the Sea of Suf.

8   Yet he saved them for his own name's sake,
to make known his mighty power.

9   He rebuked the Sea of Suf, and it dried up;
he led them through its depths as through a desert.

10   He saved them from hostile hands,
redeemed them from the power of the foe.

11   The water closed over their adversaries;
not one of them was left.

12   Then they believed his words,
and they sang his praise.

13   But soon they forgot his deeds
and wouldn't wait for his counsel.

14   In the desert they gave way to insatiable greed;
in the wastelands they put God to the test.

15   He gave them what they wanted
but sent meagerness into their souls.

16   In the camp they were jealous of Moshe
and Aharon, ADONAI's holy one.

17   The earth opened up and swallowed Datan
and closed over Aviram's allies.

18   A fire blazed out against that group,
the flames consumed the wicked.

19   In Horev they fashioned a calf,
they worshipped a cast metal image.

20   Thus they exchanged their Glory
for the image of an ox that eats grass!

21   They forgot God, who had saved them,
who had done great things in Egypt,

22   wonders in the land of Ham,
fearsome deeds by the Sea of Suf.

23   Therefore he said that he would destroy them,
[and he would have,] had not Moshe his chosen one
stood before him in the breach
to turn back his destroying fury.

24   Next, they rejected the beautiful land,
they didn't trust his promise;

25   and they complained in their tents,
they didn't obey ADONAI.

26 Therefore, raising his hand, he swore to them
that he would strike them down in the desert
27 and strike down their descendants among the nations,
dispersing them in foreign lands.

28 Now they joined themselves to Ba'al-P'or
and ate meat sacrificed to dead things.
29 Thus they provoked him to anger with their deeds,
so that a plague broke out among them.
30 Then Pinchas stood up and executed judgment;
so the plague was checked.
31 That was credited to him as righteousness,
through all generations forever.

32 They angered him at the M'rivah Spring,
and Moshe suffered on their account;
33 for when they embittered his spirit,
[Moshe] spoke up without thinking.

34 They failed to destroy the peoples,
as ADONAI had ordered them to do,
35 but mingled with the nations
and learned to follow their ways.
36 They went on to serve their idols,
which became a snare for them.
37 They even sacrificed their sons
and their daughters to demons.
38 Yes, they shed innocent blood,
the blood of their own sons and daughters,
whom they sacrificed to Kena'an's false gods,
polluting the land with blood.
39 Thus they were defiled by their deeds;
they prostituted themselves by their actions.

40 For this ADONAI's fury blazed up against his people,
and he detested his heritage.
41 He handed them over to the power of the nations,
and those who hated them ruled over them.
42 Their enemies oppressed them
and kept them in subjection to their power.
43 Many times [God] rescued them,
but they kept making plans to rebel.
Thus they were brought low
by their own wrongdoing.

44 Still he took pity on their distress
whenever he heard their cry.

⁴⁵ For their sakes he kept in mind his covenant
and in his limitless grace relented,
⁴⁶ causing them to be treated with compassion
by all who had taken them captive.

⁴⁷ Save us, ADONAI our God!
Gather us from among the nations,
so that we can thank your holy name
and glory in praising you.

⁴⁸ Blessed be ADONAI, the God of Isra'el,
from eternity past to eternity future.
Now let all the people say,
"Amen! Halleluyah!"

Book V: Psalms 107–150

107 ¹ Give thanks to ADONAI; for he is good,
for his grace continues forever.
² Let those redeemed by ADONAI say it,
those he redeemed from the power of the foe.
³ He gathered them from the lands,
from the east and from the west,
from the north and from the sea.

⁴ They wandered in the desert, on paths through the wastes,
without finding any inhabited city.
⁵ They were hungry and thirsty,
their life was ebbing away.

⁶ In their trouble they cried to ADONAI,
and he rescued them from their distress.
⁷ He led them by a direct path
to a city where they could live.

⁸ Let them give thanks to ADONAI for his grace,
for his wonders bestowed on humanity!
⁹ For he has satisfied the hungry,
filled the starving with that which is good.

¹⁰ Some lived in darkness, in death-dark gloom,
bound in misery and iron chains,
¹¹ because they defied God's word,
scorned the counsel of the Most High.

12 So he humbled their hearts by hard labor;
when they stumbled, no one came to their aid.

13 In their trouble they cried to *ADONAI*,
and he rescued them from their distress.

14 He led them from darkness, from death-dark gloom,
shattering their chains.

15 Let them give thanks to *ADONAI* for his grace,
for his wonders bestowed on humanity!

16 For he shattered bronze doors
and cut through iron bars.

17 There were foolish people who suffered affliction
because of their crimes and sins;

18 they couldn't stand to eat anything;
they were near the gates of death.

19 In their trouble they cried to *ADONAI*,
and he rescued them from their distress;

20 he sent his word and healed them,
he delivered them from destruction.

21 Let them give thanks to *ADONAI* for his grace,
for his wonders bestowed on humanity!

22 Let them offer sacrifices of thanksgiving
and proclaim his great deeds with songs of joy.

23 Those who go down to the sea in ships,
plying their trade on the great ocean,

24 saw the works of *ADONAI*,
his wonders in the deep.

25 For at his word the storm-wind arose,
lifting up towering waves.

26 The sailors were raised up to the sky,
then plunged into the depths.
At the danger, their courage failed them,

27 they reeled and staggered like drunk men,
and all their skill was swallowed up.

28 In their trouble they cried to *ADONAI*,
and he rescued them from their distress.

29 He silenced the storm and stilled its waves,

30 and they rejoiced as the sea grew calm.
Then he brought them safely
to their desired port.

³¹   Let them give thanks to ADONAI for his grace,
    for his wonders bestowed on humanity!
³²   Let them extol him in the assembly of the people
    and praise him in the leaders' council.

³³   He turns rivers into desert,
    flowing springs into thirsty ground,
³⁴   productive land into salt flats,
    because the people living there are so wicked.

³⁵   But he also turns desert into pools of water,
    dry land into flowing springs;
³⁶   there he gives the hungry a home,
    and they build a city to live in;
³⁷   there they sow fields and plant vineyards,
    which yield an abundant harvest.

³⁸   He blesses them, their numbers grow,
    and he doesn't let their livestock decrease.
³⁹   When their numbers fall, and they grow weak,
    because of oppression, disaster and sorrow,
⁴⁰   he pours contempt on princes
    and leaves them to wander in trackless wastes.

⁴¹   But the needy he raises up from their distress
    and increases their families like sheep.
⁴²   When the upright see this, they rejoice;
    while the wicked are reduced to silence.
⁴³   Let whoever is wise observe these things
    and consider ADONAI's loving deeds.

108 ¹⁽⁰⁾ A song. A psalm of David:

²⁽¹⁾   My heart is steadfast, God.
    I will sing and make music with my glory.
³⁽²⁾   Awake, lute and lyre!
    I will awaken the dawn.
⁴⁽³⁾   I will thank you, ADONAI, among the peoples;
    I will make music to you among the nations.
⁵⁽⁴⁾   For your grace is great, above heaven,
    and your truth, all the way to the skies.

⁶⁽⁵⁾   Be exalted, God, above heaven!
    May your glory be over all the earth,
⁷⁽⁶⁾   in order that those you love can be rescued;
    so save with your right hand, and answer me!

8(7) God in his holiness spoke,
and I took joy [in his promise]:
"I will divide Sh'khem
and determine the shares in the Sukkot Valley.

9(8) Gil'ad is mine and M'nasheh mine,
Efrayim my helmet, Y'hudah my scepter.

10(9) Mo'av is my washpot; on Edom I throw my shoe;
Over P'leshet I shout in triumph."

11(10) Who will bring me into the fortified city?
Who will lead me to Edom?

12(11) God, have you rejected us?
You don't go out with our armies, God.

13(12) Help us against our enemy,
for human help is worthless.

14(13) With God's help we will fight valiantly,
for he will trample our enemies.

109 1(0) For the leader. A psalm of David:

(1) God, whom I praise, don't remain silent!

2 For wicked and deceitful men
have opened their mouths against me,
spoken against me with lying tongues,

3 surrounded me with hateful words,
and attacked me without cause.

4 In return for my love they became my accusers,
even though I prayed for them.

5 They repay me evil for good
and hatred for my love.

6 [They say,] "Appoint a wicked man over him,
may an accuser stand at his right.

7 When he is tried, let him be found guilty,
may even his plea be counted a sin.

8 May his days be few,
may someone else take his position.

9 May his children be fatherless
and his wife a widow.

10 May his children be wandering beggars,
foraging for food from their ruined homes.

11 May creditors seize all he owns
and strangers make off with his earnings.

12 May no one treat him kindly,
and may no one take pity on his orphaned children.

13 May his posterity be cut off;
  may his name be erased within a generation.
14 May the wrongs of his ancestors be remembered by *ADONAI*,
  and may the sin of his mother not be erased;
15 may they always be before *ADONAI*,
  so he can cut off all memory of them from the earth.
16 For he did not remember to show kindness
  but hounded the downtrodden, the poor
  and the brokenhearted to death.
17 He loved cursing; may it recoil on him!
  He didn't like blessing; may it stay far from him!
18 He clothed himself with cursing
  as routinely as with his coat;
  may it enter inside him as easily as water,
  as easily as oil into his bones.
19 May it cling to him like the coat he wears,
  like the belt he wraps around himself."

20 This is what my adversaries want *ADONAI* to do,
  those who speak evil against me.
21 But you, God, *ADONAI*,
  treat me as your name demands;
  rescue me, because your grace is good.
22 For I am poor and needy,
  and my heart within me is wounded.
23 Like a lengthening evening shadow, I am gone;
  I am shaken off like a locust.
24 My knees are weak from lack of food,
  my flesh wastes away for lack of nourishment.
25 I have become the object of their taunts;
  when they see me, they shake their heads.

26 Help me, *ADONAI*, my God!
  Save me, in keeping with your grace;
27 so that they will know that this comes from your hand,
  that you, *ADONAI*, have done it.
28 Let them go on cursing;
  but you, bless!
  When they attack, let them be put to shame;
  but let your servant rejoice.
29 Let my adversaries be clothed with confusion,
  let them wear their own shame like a robe.

30 I will eagerly thank *ADONAI* with my mouth,
  I will praise him right there in the crowd,
31 because he stands alongside a needy person
  to defend him from unjust accusers.

110 $^{1(0)}$ A psalm of David:

(1)   ADONAI says to my Lord,
        "Sit at my right hand,
        until I make your enemies
        your footstool."

2   ADONAI will send your powerful scepter
        out from Tziyon,
        so that you will rule over
        your enemies around you.

3   On the day your forces mobilize,
        your people willingly offer themselves
        in holy splendors from the womb of the dawn;
        the dew of your youth is yours.

4   ADONAI has sworn it,
        and he will never retract —
        "You are a *cohen* forever,
        to be compared with Malki-Tzedek."

5   Adonai at your right hand
        will shatter kings on the day of his anger.

6   He will pass judgment among the nations,
        filling it with dead bodies;
        he will shatter heads
        throughout an extensive territory.

7   He will drink from a stream as he goes on his way;
        therefore he will hold his head high.

111 ^{1} *Halleluyah!*

        I will wholeheartedly give thanks to ADONAI
        in the council of the upright and in the assembly.

2   The deeds of ADONAI are great,
        greatly desired by all who enjoy them.

3   His work is full of majesty and splendor,
        and his righteousness continues forever.

4   He has gained renown for his wonders.
        ADONAI is merciful and compassionate.

5   He gives food to those who fear him.
        He remembers his covenant forever.

6   He shows his people how powerfully he works
        by giving them the nations as their heritage.

7   The works of his hands are truth and justice;
        all his precepts can be trusted.

8 They have been established forever and ever,
   to be carried out truly and honestly.
9 He sent redemption to his people
   and decreed that his covenant should last forever.
10 His name is holy and fearsome —
   the first and foremost point of wisdom is the fear of ADONAI;
   all those living by it gain good common sense.
   His praise stands forever.

112 1 *Halleluyah!*

How happy is anyone who fears ADONAI,
   who greatly delights in his *mitzvot.*
2 His descendants will be powerful on earth,
   a blessed generation of upright people.
3 Wealth and riches are in his house,
   and his righteousness stands forever.

4 To the upright he shines like a light in the dark,
   merciful, compassionate and righteous.
5 Things go well with the person who is merciful and lends,
   who conducts his affairs with fairness;
6 for he will never be moved.
   The righteous will be remembered forever.

7 He will not be frightened by bad news;
   he remains steady, trusting in ADONAI.
8 His heart is set firm, he will not be afraid,
   till finally he looks in triumph at his enemies.
9 He distributes freely, he gives to the poor;
   his righteousness stands forever.

   His power will be increased honorably.
10 The wicked will be angry when they see this;
   they will gnash their teeth and waste away,
   the desires of the wicked will come to nothing.

113 1 *Halleluyah!*

Servants of ADONAI, give praise!
   Give praise to the name of ADONAI!
2 Blessed be the name of ADONAI
   from this moment on and forever!
3 From sunrise until sunset
   ADONAI's name is to be praised.

4   *Adonai* is high above all nations,
      his glory above the heavens.
5   Who is like *Adonai* our God,
      seated in the heights,
6   humbling himself to look
      on heaven and on earth.

7   He raises the poor from the dust,
      lifts the needy from the rubbish heap,
8   in order to give him a place among princes,
      among the princes of his people.

9   He causes the childless woman
      to live at home happily as a mother of children.

      Halleluyah!

114 1   When Isra'el came out of Egypt,
      the house of Ya'akov from a people of foreign speech,
2   Y'hudah became [God's] sanctuary,
      Isra'el his domain.

3   The sea saw this and fled;
      the Yarden turned back;
4   the mountains skipped like rams,
      the hills like young sheep.

5   Why is it, sea, that you flee?
      Why, Yarden, do you turn back?
6   Why, mountains, do you skip like rams;
      and you hills like young sheep?

7   Tremble, earth, at the presence of the Lord,
      at the presence of the God of Ya'akov,
8   who turned the rock into a pool of water,
      flint into flowing spring.

115 1   Not to us, *Adonai*, not to us,
      but to your name give glory,
      because of your grace and truth.

2   Why should the nations ask,
      "Where is their God?"
3   Our God is in heaven;
      he does whatever pleases him.

907

4 Their idols are mere silver and gold,
made by human hands.
5 They have mouths, but they can't speak;
they have eyes, but they can't see;
6 they have ears, but they can't hear;
they have noses, but they can't smell;
7 they have hands, but they can't feel;
they have feet, but they can't walk;
with their throats they can't make a sound.
8 The people who make them will become like them,
along with everyone who trusts in them.

9 Isra'el, trust in ADONAI!
He is their help and shield.
10 House of Aharon, trust in ADONAI!
He is their help and shield.
11 You who fear ADONAI, trust in ADONAI!
He is their help and shield.
12 ADONAI has kept us in mind,
and he will bless.
He will bless the house of Isra'el;
he will bless the house of Aharon;
13 he will bless those who fear ADONAI,
great and small alike.

14 May ADONAI increase your numbers,
both yours and those of your children.
15 May you be blessed by ADONAI,
the maker of heaven and earth.
16 Heaven belongs to ADONAI,
but the earth he has given to humankind.

17 The dead can't praise ADONAI,
not those who sink down into silence.
18 But we will bless ADONAI
from now on and forever.

Halleluyah!

116 1 I love that ADONAI heard
my voice when I prayed;
2 because he turned his ear to me,
I will call on him as long as I live.

3 The cords of death were all around me,
Sh'ol's constrictions held me fast;

I was finding only distress and anguish.
4   But I called on the name of ADONAI:
"Please, ADONAI! Save me!"

5   ADONAI is merciful and righteous;
yes, our God is compassionate.
6   ADONAI preserves the thoughtless;
when I was brought low, he saved me.
7   My soul, return to your rest!
For ADONAI has been generous toward you.
8   Yes, you have rescued me from death,
my eyes from tears and my feet from falling.
9   I will go on walking in the presence of ADONAI
in the lands of the living.
10   I will keep on trusting even when I say,
"I am utterly miserable,"
11   even when, in my panic, I declare,
"Everything human is deceptive."

12   How can I repay ADONAI
for all his generous dealings with me?
13   I will raise the cup of salvation
and call on the name of ADONAI.
14   I will pay my vows to ADONAI
in the presence of all his people.

15   From ADONAI's point of view,
the death of those faithful to him is costly.
16   Oh, ADONAI! I am your slave;
I am your slave, the son of your slave-girl;
you have removed my fetters.
17   I will offer a sacrifice of thanks to you
and will call on the name of ADONAI.
18   I will pay my vows to ADONAI
in the presence of all his people,
19   in the courtyards of ADONAI's house,
there in your very heart, Yerushalayim.

Halleluyah!

117 ¹ Praise ADONAI, all you nations!
Worship him, all you peoples!
2   For his grace has overcome us,
and ADONAI's truth continues forever.

Halleluyah!

118 ¹ Give thanks to ADONAI; for he is good,
for his grace continues forever.

² Now let Isra'el say,
"His grace continues forever."

³ Now let the house of Aharon say,
"His grace continues forever."

⁴ Now let those who fear ADONAI say,
"His grace continues forever."

⁵ From my being hemmed in I called on *Yah*;
he answered and gave me more room.

⁶ With ADONAI on my side, I fear nothing —
what can human beings do to me?

⁷ With ADONAI on my side as my help,
I will look with triumph at those who hate me.

⁸ It is better to take refuge in ADONAI
than to trust in human beings;

⁹ better to take refuge in ADONAI
than to put one's trust in princes.

¹⁰ The nations all surrounded me;
in the name of ADONAI I cut them down.

¹¹ They surrounded me on every side
in the name of ADONAI I cut them down.

¹² They surrounded me like bees
but were extinguished [as quickly] as a fire in thorns;
in the name of ADONAI I cut them down.

¹³ You pushed me hard to make me fall,
but ADONAI helped me.

¹⁴ *Yah* is my strength and my song,
and he has become my salvation.

¹⁵ The sound of rejoicing and victory
is heard in the tents of the righteous:
"ADONAI's right hand struck powerfully!

¹⁶ ADONAI's right hand is raised in triumph!
ADONAI's right hand struck powerfully!"

¹⁷ I will not die; no, I will live
and proclaim the great deeds of *Yah*!

¹⁸ *Yah* disciplined me severely,
but did not hand me over to death.

¹⁹ Open the gates of righteousness for me;
I will enter them and thank *Yah*.

20 This is the gate of *Adonai*;
the righteous can enter it.

21 I am thanking you because you answered me;
you became my salvation.

22 The very rock that the builders rejected
has become the cornerstone!

23 This has come from *Adonai*,
and in our eyes it is amazing.

24 This is the day *Adonai* has made,
a day for us to rejoice and be glad.

25 Please, *Adonai*! Save us!
Please, *Adonai*! Rescue us!

26 Blessed is he who comes in the name of *Adonai*.
We bless you from the house of *Adonai*.

27 *Adonai* is God, and he gives us light.
Join in the pilgrim festival with branches
all the way to the horns of the altar.

28 You are my God, and I thank you.
You are my God; I exalt you.

29 Give thanks to *Adonai*; for he is good,
for his grace continues forever.

119

א *(Alef)*

1 How happy are those whose way of life is blameless,
who live by the *Torah* of *Adonai*!

2 How happy are those who observe his instruction,
who seek him wholeheartedly!

3 They do nothing wrong
but live by his ways.

4 You laid down your precepts
for us to observe with care.

5 May my ways be steady
in observing your laws.

6 Then I will not be put to shame,
since I will have fixed my sight on all your *mitzvot*.

7 I thank you with a sincere heart
as I learn your righteous rulings.

8 I will observe your laws;
don't completely abandon me!

ב (*Bet*)

9   How can a young man keep his way pure?
    By guarding it according to your word.

10 I seek you with all my heart;
    don't let me stray from your *mitzvot*.

11 I treasure your word in my heart,
    so that I won't sin against you.

12 Blessed are you, ADONAI!
    Teach me your laws.

13 I proclaim with my mouth
    all the rulings you have spoken.

14 I rejoice in the way of your instruction
    more than in any kind of wealth.

15 I will meditate on your precepts
    and keep my eyes on your ways.

16 I will find my delight in your regulations.
    I will not forget your word.

ג (*Gimel*)

17 Deal generously with your servant;
    then I will live and observe your word.

18 Open my eyes, so that I will see
    wonders from your *Torah*.

19 Though I'm just a wanderer on the earth,
    don't hide your *mitzvot* from me.

20 I am continually consumed
    with longing for your rulings.

21 You rebuke the proud, the cursed,
    who stray from your *mitzvot*.

22 Remove scorn and contempt from me,
    because I observe your instruction.

23 Even when princes sit and plot against me,
    your servant meditates on your laws.

24 Also your instructions are my delight;
    they are my counselors.

ד (*Dalet*)

25 I lie prostrate in the dust;
    revive me, in keeping with your word.

26 I told you of my ways, and you answered me;
    teach me your laws.

27 Make me understand the way of your precepts,
    and I will meditate on your wonders.

28 I am melting away from anxiety and grief;
    renew my strength, in keeping with your word.

29   Keep deceitful ways far from me,
       and favor me with your *Torah*.

30   I choose the way of trust;
       I set your rulings [before me].

31   I cling to your instruction;
       ADONAI, don't let me be put to shame!

32   I will run the way of your *mitzvot*,
       for you have broadened my understanding.

ה *(Heh)*

33   Teach me, ADONAI, the way of your laws;
       keeping them will be its own reward for me.

34   Give me understanding; then I will keep your *Torah*;
       I will observe it with all my heart.

35   Guide me on the path of your *mitzvot*,
       for I take pleasure in it.

36   Bend my heart toward your instructions
       and not toward selfish gain.

37   Turn my eyes away from worthless things;
       with your ways, give me life.

38   Fulfill your promise, which you made to your servant,
       which you made to those who fear you.

39   Avert the disgrace which I dread,
       for your rulings are good.

40   See how I long for your precepts;
       in your righteousness, give me life!

ו *(Vav)*

41   May your grace come to me, ADONAI,
       your salvation, as you promised;

42   then I will have an answer for those who taunt me;
       for I trust in your word.

43   Don't take away completely my power to speak the truth;
       for I put my hope in your rulings;

44   and I will keep your *Torah* always,
       forever and ever.

45   I will go wherever I like,
       for I have sought your precepts.

46   I will speak of your instructions even to kings
       without being ashamed.

47   I will delight myself in your *mitzvot*,
       which I have loved.

48   I will lift my hands to your *mitzvot*, which I love;
       and I will meditate on your laws.

ז (*Zayin*)

49 Remember your promise to your servant,
through which you have given me hope.

50 In my distress my comfort is this:
that your promise gives me life.

51 Though the arrogant scorn me completely,
I have not turned away from your *Torah*.

52 ADONAI, I keep in mind your age-old rulings;
in them I take comfort.

53 Fury seizes me when I think of the wicked,
because they abandon your *Torah*.

54 Your laws have become my songs
wherever I make my home.

55 I remember your name, ADONAI, at night;
and I observe your *Torah*.

56 This [comfort] has come to me,
because I observe your precepts.

ח (*Het*)

57 ADONAI, I say that my task
is to observe your words.

58 I beg your favor with my whole heart;
show pity to me, in keeping with your promise.

59 I thought about my ways
and turned my feet toward your instruction.

60 I hurry, I don't delay,
to observe your *mitzvot*.

61 Even when the cords of the wicked close around me,
I don't forget your *Torah*.

62 At midnight I rise to give you thanks
because of your righteous rulings.

63 I am a friend of all who fear you,
of those who observe your precepts.

64 The earth, ADONAI, is full of your grace;
teach me your laws.

ט (*Tet*)

65 You have treated your servant well,
ADONAI, in keeping with your word.

66 Teach me good judgment and knowledge,
because I trust in your *mitzvot*.

67 Before I was humbled, I used to go astray;
but now I observe your word.

68 You are good, and you do good;
teach me your laws.

69   The arrogant are slandering me,
      but I will wholeheartedly keep your precepts.
70   Their hearts are as thick as fat,
      but I take delight in your *Torah*.
71   It is for my good that I have been humbled;
      it was so that I would learn your laws.
72   The *Torah* you have spoken means more to me
      than a fortune in gold and silver.

י (*Yud*)

73   Your hands made and formed me;
      give me understanding, so I can learn your *mitzvot*.
74   Those who fear you rejoice at the sight of me,
      because I put my hope in your word.
75   I know, ADONAI, that your rulings are righteous,
      that even when you humble me you are faithful.
76   Let your grace comfort me,
      in keeping with your promise to your servant.
77   Show me pity, and I will live,
      for your *Torah* is my delight.
78   Let the proud be ashamed, because they wrong me with lies;
      as for me, I will meditate on your precepts.
79   Let those who fear you turn to me,
      along with those who know your instruction.
80   Let my heart be pure in your laws,
      so that I won't be put to shame.

כ (*Kaf*)

81   I am dying to know your salvation;
      my hope is in your word.
82   My eyes fail from watching for your promise;
      I ask, "When will you comfort me?"
83   For I have shriveled like a wineskin in a smoky room;
      still, I don't forget your laws.
84   How long can your servant stay alive?
      When will you bring judgment on my persecutors?
85   The arrogant have dug pits for me to fall in;
      this is not in keeping with your *Torah*!
86   All your *mitzvot* [show your] faithfulness;
      they are hounding me with lies; help me!
87   They have nearly ended my life on earth,
      but I have not abandoned your precepts.
88   In keeping with your grace, revive me;
      and I will observe your spoken instructions.

ל (Lamed)

⁸⁹ Your word continues forever, ADONAI,
firmly fixed in heaven;

⁹⁰ your faithfulness through all generations;
you established the earth, and it stands.

⁹¹ Yes, it stands today, in keeping with your rulings;
for all things are your servants.

⁹² If your *Torah* had not been my delight,
I would have perished in my distress.

⁹³ I will never forget your precepts,
for with them you have made me alive.

⁹⁴ I am yours; save me
because I seek your precepts.

⁹⁵ The wicked hope to destroy me,
but I focus on your instruction.

⁹⁶ I see the limits of all perfection,
but your *mitzvah* has no bounds.

מ (Mem)

⁹⁷ How I love your *Torah*!
I meditate on it all day.

⁹⁸ I am wiser than my foes,
because your *mitzvot* are mine forever.

⁹⁹ I have more understanding than all my teachers,
because I meditate on your instruction.

¹⁰⁰ I understand more than my elders,
because I keep your precepts.

¹⁰¹ I keep my feet from every evil way,
in order to observe your word.

¹⁰² I don't turn away from your rulings,
because you have instructed me.

¹⁰³ How sweet to my tongue is your promise,
truly sweeter than honey in my mouth!

¹⁰⁴ From your precepts I gain understanding;
this is why I hate every false way.

נ (Nun)

¹⁰⁵ Your word is a lamp for my foot
and light on my path.

¹⁰⁶ I have sworn an oath and confirmed it,
that I will observe your righteous rulings.

¹⁰⁷ I am very much distressed;
ADONAI, give me life, in keeping with your word.

¹⁰⁸ Please accept my mouth's voluntary offerings, ADONAI;
and teach me your rulings.

109 I am continually taking my life in my hands,
yet I haven't forgotten your *Torah*.

110 The wicked have set a trap for me,
yet I haven't strayed from your precepts.

111 I take your instruction as a permanent heritage,
because it is the joy of my heart.

112 I have resolved to obey your laws
forever, at every step.

ס (*Samekh*)

113 I hate doubleminded people,
but I love your *Torah*.

114 You are my hiding-place and shield;
I put my hope in your word.

115 Leave me alone, you evildoers,
so that I can keep my God's *mitzvot*.

116 Uphold me, as you promised; and I will live;
don't disappoint me in my hope.

117 Support me; and I will be saved,
always putting my attention on your laws.

118 You reject all who stray from your laws,
for what they deceive themselves with is false.

119 You discard the wicked of the earth like slag;
this is why I love your instruction.

120 My body trembles for fear of you;
your rulings make me afraid.

ע ('*Ayin*)

121 I have done what is just and right;
don't abandon me to my oppressors.

122 Guarantee your servant's well-being;
don't let the arrogant oppress me.

123 My eyes fail from watching for your salvation
and for [the fulfillment of] your righteous promise.

124 Deal with your servant in accordance with your grace,
and teach me your laws.

125 I am your servant; give me understanding,
so that I can know your instruction.

126 The time has come for *Adonai* to act,
because they are breaking your *Torah*.

127 Therefore I love your *mitzvot*
more than gold, more than fine gold.

128 Thus I direct my steps by [your] precepts;
every false way I hate.

פ *(Peh)*

129 Your instruction is a wonder;
this is why I follow it.

130 Your words are a doorway that lets in light,
giving understanding to the thoughtless.

131 My mouth is wide open, as I pant
with longing for your *mitzvot*.

132 Turn to me, and show me your favor;
in keeping with [your] judgment for those who love your name.

133 Guide my footsteps by your word;
don't let any kind of sin rule me.

134 Redeem me from human oppression,
and I will observe your precepts.

135 Make your face shine on your servant,
and teach me your laws.

136 Rivers of tears flow down from my eyes,
because they don't observe your *Torah*.

צ *(Tzadeh)*

137 You are righteous, ADONAI;
and your rulings are upright.

138 You have commanded your instructions
in righteousness and great faithfulness.

139 My zeal is destroying me,
because my foes have forgotten your words.

140 Your word is refined to complete purity,
and your servant loves it.

141 I may be small and despised,
but I do not forget your precepts.

142 Your righteousness is eternal righteousness,
and your *Torah* is truth.

143 Trouble and distress have overtaken me,
but your *mitzvot* are my delight.

144 Your instruction is righteous forever;
give me understanding, and I will live.

ק *(Kuf)*

145 Wholeheartedly I am calling on you;
answer me, ADONAI; I will keep your laws.

146 I am calling on you; save me;
and I will observe your instruction.

147 I rise before dawn and cry for help;
I put my hope in your word.

148 My eyes are open before the night watches,
so that I can meditate on your promise.

149	In your grace, hear my voice;
	ADONAI, in keeping with your justice, revive me.
150	The pursuers of carnality are getting close;
	they are distancing themselves from your *Torah*.
151	You are close by, ADONAI;
	and all your *mitzvot* are truth.
152	Long ago I learned from your instruction
	that you established it forever.

ר (*Resh*)

153	Look at my distress, and rescue me,
	for I do not forget your *Torah*.
154	Plead my cause, and redeem me;
	in keeping with your promise, revive me.
155	Salvation is far away from the wicked,
	because they don't seek your laws.
156	Great is your compassion, ADONAI;
	in keeping with your rulings, revive me.
157	Although my persecutors and foes are many,
	I have not turned away from your instruction.
158	I look at traitors with disgust,
	because they don't keep your word.
159	See how I love your precepts, ADONAI;
	in keeping with your grace, revive me.
160	The main thing about your word is that it's true;
	and all your just rulings last forever.

ש (*Shin*)

161	Princes persecute me for no reason,
	but my heart stands in awe of your words.
162	I take joy in your promise,
	like someone who finds much booty.
163	I hate falsehood, I detest it;
	but I love your *Torah*.
164	I praise you seven times a day
	because of your righteous rulings.
165	Those who love your *Torah* have great peace;
	nothing makes them stumble.
166	I hope for your deliverance, ADONAI;
	I obey your *mitzvot*.
167	My soul observes your instruction,
	and I love it so much!
168	I observe your precepts and instruction,
	for all my ways lie open before you.

ת (*Tav*)

169 Let my cry come before you, ADONAI;
in keeping with your word, give me understanding.
170 Let my prayer come before you;
in keeping with your promise, rescue me.
171 Let my lips speak praise,
because you teach me your laws.
172 Let my tongue sing of your promise,
because all your *mitzvot* are righteous.
173 Let your hand be ready to help me,
because I choose your precepts.
174 I long for your deliverance, ADONAI;
and your *Torah* is my delight.
175 Let me live, and I will praise you;
let your rulings help me.
176 I strayed like a lost sheep; seek out your servant;
for I do not forget your *mitzvot*.

120 [1(0)] A song of ascents:

(1) I called to ADONAI in my distress,
and he answered me.
2 Rescue me, ADONAI, from lips that tell lies,
from a tongue full of deceit.

3 What has he in store for you, deceitful tongue?
What more will he do to you?
4 A warrior's sharp arrows,
with red-hot coals from a broom tree.

5 How wretched I am, that I'm an alien in Meshekh,
that I must live among the tents of Keidar!
6 I have had to live far too long
with those who hate peace.
7 I am all for peace;
but when I speak, they are for war.

121 [1(0)] A song of ascents:

(1) If I raise my eyes to the hills,
from where will my help come?
2 My help comes from ADONAI,
the maker of heaven and earth.

3 He will not let your foot slip —
    your guardian is not asleep.
4 No, the guardian of Isra'el
    never slumbers or sleeps.

5 *ADONAI* is your guardian; at your right hand
    ADONAI provides you with shade —
6 the sun can't strike you during the day
    or even the moon at night.

7 *ADONAI* will guard you against all harm;
    he will guard your life.
8 *ADONAI* will guard your coming and going
    from now on and forever.

122 ¹⁽⁰⁾ A song of ascents. By David:

⁽¹⁾ I was glad when they said to me,
    "The house of *ADONAI*! Let's go!"
2   Our feet were already standing
    at your gates, Yerushalayim.

3   Yerushalayim, built as a city
    fostering friendship and unity.

4   The tribes have gone up there, the tribes of *ADONAI*,
    as a witness to Isra'el,
    to give thanks to the name of *ADONAI*.
5   For there the thrones of justice were set up,
    the thrones of the house of David.

6   Pray for *shalom* in Yerushalayim;
    may those who love you prosper.
7   May *shalom* be within your ramparts,
    prosperity in your palaces.

8   For the sake of my family and friends, I say,
    "*Shalom* be within you!"
9   For the sake of the house of *ADONAI* our God,
    I will seek your well-being.

123 ¹⁽⁰⁾ A song of ascents:

⁽¹⁾ I raise my eyes to you,
    whose throne is in heaven.

2   As a servant looks to the hand of his master,
       or a slave-girl to the hand of her mistress,
       so our eyes turn to ADONAI our God,
       until he has mercy on us.

3   Have mercy on us, ADONAI, have mercy;
       for we have had our fill of contempt,
4   more than our fill of scorn from the complacent
       and contempt from the arrogant.

124 ¹⁽⁰⁾ A song of ascents. By David:

⁽¹⁾   If ADONAI hadn't been for us —
       let Isra'el repeat it —
2   If ADONAI hadn't been for us
       when people rose to attack us,
3   then, when their anger blazed against us,
       they would have swallowed us alive!
4   Then the water would have engulfed us,
       the torrent would have swept over us.
5   Yes, the raging water
       would have swept right over us.

6   Blessed be ADONAI, who did not leave us
       to be a prey for their teeth!
7   We escaped like a bird from the hunter's trap;
       the trap is broken, and we have escaped.

8   Our help is in the name of ADONAI,
       the maker of heaven and earth.

125 ¹⁽⁰⁾ A song of ascents:

⁽¹⁾   Those who trust in ADONAI
       are like Mount Tziyon,
       which cannot be moved
       but remains forever.

2   Yerushalayim!
       Mountains all around it!
       Thus ADONAI is around his people
       henceforth and forever.

3   For the scepter of wickedness
       will not rule the inheritance of the righteous,

so that the righteous will not themselves
turn their hands to evil.

4   Do good, *Adonai*, to the good,
to those upright in their hearts.

5   But as for those who turn aside
to their own crooked ways,
may *Adonai* turn them away,
along with those who do evil.

Shalom on Isra'el!

126 ¹⁽⁰⁾ A song of ascents:

(1)   When *Adonai* restored Tziyon's fortunes,
we thought we were dreaming.

2   Our mouths were full of laughter,
and our tongues shouted for joy.

Among the nations it was said,
"*Adonai* has done great things for them!"
Adonai did do great things with us;
and we are overjoyed.

3

4   Return our people from exile, *Adonai*,
as streams fill *vadi*s in the Negev.

5   Those who sow in tears
will reap with cries of joy.

6   He who goes out weeping
as he carries his sack of seed
will come home with cries of joy
as he carries his sheaves of grain.

127 ¹⁽⁰⁾ A song of ascents. By Shlomo:

(1)   Unless *Adonai* builds the house,
its builders work in vain.
Unless *Adonai* guards the city,
the guard keeps watch in vain.

2   In vain do you get up early
and put off going to bed,
working hard to earn a living;
for he provides for his beloved,
even when they sleep.

³   Children too are a gift from ADONAI;
    the fruit of the womb is a reward.
⁴   The children born when one is young.
    are like arrows in the hand of a warrior.
⁵   How blessed is the man
    who has filled his quiver with them;
    he will not have to be embarrassed
    when contending with foes at the city gate.

128 ¹⁽⁰⁾ A song of ascents:

⁽¹⁾   How happy is everyone who fears ADONAI,
    who lives by his ways.

²   You will eat what your hands have produced;
    you will be happy and prosperous.
³   Your wife will be like a fruitful vine
    in the inner parts of your house.
    Your children around the table will be
    like shoots from an olive tree.

⁴   This is the kind of blessing that will fall
    on him who fears ADONAI.

⁵   May ADONAI bless you from Tziyon!
    May you see Yerushalayim prosper
    all the days of your life,
⁶   and may you live to see your children's children!

    Shalom on Isra'el.

129 ¹⁽⁰⁾ A song of ascents:

⁽¹⁾   Since I was young they have often attacked me —
    let Isra'el repeat it —
²   since I was young they have often attacked me,
    but they haven't overcome me.

³   The plowmen plowed on my back;
    wounding me with long furrows.
⁴   But ADONAI is righteous;
    he cuts me free from the yoke of the wicked.

⁵   Let all who hate Tziyon
    be thrown back in confusion.

6   Let them be like grass on the roof,
    which dries out before it grows up
7   and never fills the reaper's hands
    or the arms of the one who binds sheaves,
8   so that no passer-by says,
    "ADONAI's blessing on you!
    We bless you in the name of ADONAI!"

130 ¹⁽⁰⁾ A song of ascents. By David:

(1)   ADONAI, I call to you from the depths;
2   hear my cry, *Adonai!*
    Let your ears pay attention
    to the sound of my pleading.

3   *Yah,* if you kept a record of sins,
    who, *Adonai,* could stand?
4   But with you there is forgiveness,
    so that you will be feared.

5   I wait longingly for *ADONAI;*
    I put my hope in his word.
6   Everything in me waits for *Adonai*
    more than guards on watch wait for morning,
    more than guards on watch wait for morning.

7   Isra'el, put your hope in *ADONAI!*
    For grace is found with *ADONAI,*
    and with him is unlimited redemption.
8   He will redeem Isra'el
    from all their wrongdoings.

131 ¹⁽⁰⁾ A song of ascents. By David:

(1)   ADONAI, my heart isn't proud;
    I don't set my sight too high,
    I don't take part in great affairs
    or in wonders far beyond me.
2   No, I keep myself calm and quiet,
    like a little child on its mother's lap —
    I keep myself like a little child.

3   Isra'el, put your hope in *ADONAI*
    from now on and forever!

132 [1(0)] A song of ascents:

[1] Adonai, remember in David's favor
all the hardships he endured,
[2] how he swore to Adonai,
vowed to the Mighty One of Ya'akov,

[3] "I will not enter the house where I live
or get into my bed,
[4] I will not allow myself to sleep
or even close my eyes,
[5] until I find a place for Adonai,
a dwelling for the Mighty One of Ya'akov."

[6] We heard about it in Efrat,
we found it in the Fields of Ya'ar.
[7] Let's go into his dwelling
and prostrate ourselves at his footstool.

[8] Go up, Adonai, to your resting-place,
you and the ark through which you give strength.
[9] May your *cohanim* be clothed with righteousness;
may those loyal to you shout for joy.
[10] For the sake of your servant David,
don't turn away the face of your anointed one.

[11] Adonai swore an oath to David,
an oath he will not break:
"One of the sons from your own body
I will set on your throne.
[12] If your sons keep my covenant
and my instruction, which I will teach them,
then their descendants too, forever,
will sit on your throne."

[13] For Adonai has chosen Tziyon,
he has wanted it as his home.
[14] "This is my resting-place forever,
I will live here because I so much want to.
[15] I will bless it with plenty of meat,
I will give its poor their fill of food.
[16] Its *cohanim* I will clothe with salvation,
and its faithful will shout for joy.
[17] I will make a king sprout there from David's line
and prepare a lamp for my anointed one.
[18] His enemies I will clothe with shame,
but on him there will be a shining crown."

133 ¹⁽⁰⁾ A song of ascents. By David:

(1)   Oh, how good, how pleasant it is
            for brothers to live together in harmony.

2   It is like fragrant oil on the head
            that runs down over the beard,
            over the beard of Aharon,
            and flows down on the collar of his robes.

3   It is like the dew of Hermon
            that settles on the mountains of Tziyon.
            For it was there that ADONAI ordained
            the blessing of everlasting life.

134 ¹⁽⁰⁾ A song of ascents:

(1)   Come, bless ADONAI, all you servants of ADONAI,
            who serve each night in the house of ADONAI.
2   Lift your hands toward the sanctuary,
            and bless ADONAI.
3   May ADONAI, the maker of heaven and earth,
            bless you from Tziyon.

135 ¹⁽⁰⁾ *Halleluyah!*

(1)   Give praise to the name of ADONAI!
            Servants of ADONAI, give praise!
2   You who stand in the house of ADONAI,
            in the courtyards of the house of our God,
3   praise *Yah*, for ADONAI is good;
            sing to his name, because it is pleasant.

4   For *Yah* chose Ya'akov for himself,
            Isra'el as his own unique treasure.
5   I know that ADONAI is great,
            that our Lord is above all gods.
6   ADONAI does whatever pleases him,
            in heaven, on earth, in the seas, in all the depths.
7   He raises clouds from the ends of the earth,
            he makes the lightning flash in the rain
            and brings the wind out from his storehouses.

8   He struck down Egypt's firstborn,
            humans and animals alike.

927

9 He sent signs and wonders among you, Egypt,
   against Pharaoh and all his subjects.
10 He struck many nations,
   and slaughtered mighty kings —
11 Sichon king of the Emori,
   'Og king of Bashan,
   and all the kingdoms of Kena'an.
12 Then he gave their land as a heritage,
   to be possessed by Isra'el his people.

13 ADONAI, your name continues forever,
   your renown, ADONAI, through all generations.
14 For ADONAI will vindicate his people,
   he will take pity on his servants.

15 The idols of the nations are mere silver and gold,
   made by human hands.
16 They have mouths, but they can't speak;
   they have eyes, but they can't see;
17 they have ears, but they can't listen;
   and they have no breath in their mouths;
18 The people who make them will become like them,
   along with everyone who trusts in them.

19 House of Isra'el, bless ADONAI!
   House of Aharon, bless ADONAI!
20 House of Levi, bless ADONAI!
   You who fear ADONAI, bless ADONAI!
21 Blessed be ADONAI out of Tziyon,
   he who dwells in Yerushalayim!

   Halleluyah!

136 1 Give thanks to ADONAI, for he is good,
   for his grace continues forever.
2 Give thanks to the God of gods,
   for his grace continues forever.
3 Give thanks to the Lord of lords,
   for his grace continues forever;

4 to him who alone has done great wonders,
   for his grace continues forever;
5 to him who skillfully made the heavens,
   for his grace continues forever;
6 to him who spread out the earth on the water,
   for his grace continues forever;

7   to him who made the great lights,
    for his grace continues forever;
8   the sun to rule the day,
    for his grace continues forever;
9   the moon and stars to rule the night,
    for his grace continues forever;

10 to him who struck down Egypt's firstborn,
    for his grace continues forever;
11 and brought Isra'el out from among them,
    for his grace continues forever;
12 with a mighty hand and an outstretched arm,
    for his grace continues forever;

13 to him who split apart the Sea of Suf,
    for his grace continues forever;
14 and made Isra'el cross right through it,
    for his grace continues forever;
15 but swept Pharaoh and his army into the Sea of Suf,
    for his grace continues forever;

16 to him who led his people through the desert,
    for his grace continues forever;
17 to him who struck down great kings,
    for his grace continues forever;
18 yes, he slaughtered powerful kings,
    for his grace continues forever;
19 Sichon king of the Emori,
    for his grace continues forever;
20 and 'Og king of Bashan,
    for his grace continues forever;

21 then he gave their land as a heritage,
    for his grace continues forever;
22 to be possessed by Isra'el his servant,
    for his grace continues forever;

23 who remembers us whenever we are brought low,
    for his grace continues forever;
24 and rescues us from our enemies,
    for his grace continues forever;

25 who provides food for every living creature,
    for his grace continues forever.

26 Give thanks to the God of heaven,
    for his grace continues forever.

137 ¹ By the rivers of Bavel we sat down and wept
as we remembered Tziyon.

² We had hung up our lyres
on the willows that were there,

³ when those who had taken us captive
asked us to sing them a song;
our tormentors demanded joy from us —
"Sing us one of the songs from Tziyon!"

⁴ How can we sing a song about ADONAI
here on foreign soil?

⁵ If I forget you, Yerushalayim,
may my right hand wither away!

⁶ May my tongue stick to the roof of my mouth
if I fail to remember you,
if I fail to count Yerushalayim
the greatest of all my joys.

⁷ Remember, ADONAI, against the people of Edom
the day of Yerushalayim's fall,
how they cried, "Tear it down! Tear it down!
Raze it to the ground!"

⁸ Daughter of Bavel, you will be destroyed!
A blessing on anyone who pays you back
for the way you treated us!

⁹ A blessing on anyone who seizes your babies
and smashes them against a rock!

138 ¹⁽⁰⁾ By David:

⁽¹⁾ I give you thanks with all my heart.
Not to idols, but to you I sing praise.

² I bow down toward your holy temple
and give thanks to your name for your grace and truth;
for you have made your word [even] greater
than the whole of your reputation.

³ When I called, you answered me,
you made me bold and strong.

⁴ All the kings of the earth will thank you, ADONAI,
when they hear the words you have spoken.

⁵ They will sing about ADONAI's ways,
"Great is the glory of ADONAI!"

⁶ For though ADONAI is high, he cares for the lowly;
while the proud he perceives from afar.

⁷ You keep me alive when surrounded by danger;
you put out your hand when my enemies rage;

8

with your right hand you save me.
ADONAI will fulfill his purpose for me.
Your grace, ADONAI, continues forever.
Don't abandon the work of your hands!

139 ¹⁽⁰⁾ For the leader. A psalm of David:

⁽¹⁾

ADONAI, you have probed me, and you know me.

2

You know when I sit and when I stand up,
you discern my inclinations from afar,

3

you scrutinize my daily activities.
You are so familiar with all my ways

4

that before I speak even a word, ADONAI,
you know all about it already.

5

You have hemmed me in both behind and in front
and laid your hand on me.

6

Such wonderful knowledge is beyond me,
far too high for me to reach.

7

Where can I go to escape your Spirit?
Where can I flee from your presence?

8

If I climb up to heaven, you are there;
if I lie down in Sh'ol, you are there.

9

If I fly away with the wings of the dawn
and land beyond the sea,

10

even there your hand would lead me,
your right hand would hold me fast.

11

If I say, "Let darkness surround me,
let the light around me be night,"

12

even darkness like this
is not too dark for you;
rather, night is as clear as day,
darkness and light are the same.

13

For you fashioned my inmost being,
you knit me together in my mother's womb.

14

I thank you because I am awesomely made,
wonderfully; your works are wonders —
I know this very well.

15

My bones were not hidden from you
when I was being made in secret,
intricately woven in the depths of the earth.

16

Your eyes could see me as an embryo,
but in your book all my days were already written;
my days had been shaped
before any of them existed.

17   God, how I prize your thoughts!
      How many of them there are!
18   If I count them, there are more than grains of sand;
      if I finish the count, I am still with you.

19   God, if only you would kill off the wicked!
      Men of blood, get away from me!
20   They invoke your name for their crafty schemes;
      yes, your enemies misuse it.
21   ADONAI, how I hate those who hate you!
      I feel such disgust with those who defy you!
22   I hate them with unlimited hatred!
      They have become my enemies too.

23   Examine me, God, and know my heart;
      test me, and know my thoughts.
24   See if there is in me any hurtful way,
      and lead me along the eternal way.

140 ¹⁽⁰⁾ For the leader. A psalm of David:

2(1) Rescue me, ADONAI, from evil people,
      protect me from violent people.
3(2) They plan evil things in their hearts —
      they continually stir up bitter strife.
4(3) They have made their tongues as sharp as a snake's;
      viper's venom is under their lips.   (Selah)

5(4) Keep me, ADONAI, from the hands of the wicked,
      protect me from violent people
      who are trying to trip me up.
6(5) The arrogant hide snares for me;
      they spread nets by the side of the road,
      hoping to trap me there.   (Selah)

7(6) I said to ADONAI, "You are my God;
      listen, ADONAI, to my plea for mercy."
8(7) ADONAI, Adonai, my saving strength,
      my helmet shielding my head in battle,
9(8) ADONAI, don't grant the wicked their wishes;
      make their plot fail, so they won't grow proud.   (Selah)
10(9) May the heads of those who surround me
      be engulfed in the evil they spoke of, themselves.
11(10) May burning coals rain down on them,
      may they be flung into the fire,
      flung into deep pits,
      never to rise again.

932

12(11)	Let slanderers find no place in the land; let the violent and evil be hunted relentlessly.
13(12)	I know that ADONAI gives justice to the poor and maintains the rights of the needy.
14(13)	The righteous will surely give thanks to your name; the upright will live in your presence.

141 ¹⁽⁰⁾ A psalm of David:

(1)	ADONAI, I have called you; come to me quickly! Listen to my plea when I call to you.
2	Let my prayer be like incense set before you, my uplifted hands like an evening sacrifice.
3	Set a guard, ADONAI, over my mouth; keep watch at the door of my lips.
4	Don't let my heart turn to anything evil or allow me to act wickedly with men who are evildoers; keep me from eating their delicacies.
5	Let the righteous strike me, let him correct me; it will be an act of love. Let my head not refuse such choice oil, for I will keep on praying about their wickedness.
6	When their rulers are thrown down from the cliff, [the wicked] will hear that my words were fitting.
7	As when one plows and breaks the ground into clods, our bones are strewn at the mouth of Sh'ol.
8	For my eyes, ADONAI, Adonai, are on you; in you I take refuge; don't pour out my life.
9	Keep me from the trap they have set for me, from the snares of evildoers.
10	Let the wicked fall into their own nets, while I pass by in safety.

142 ¹⁽⁰⁾ A *maskil* of David, when he was in the cave. A prayer:

2(1)	With my voice I cry to ADONAI, with my voice I plead to ADONAI for mercy.
3(2)	Before him I pour out my complaint, before him I tell my trouble.
4(3)	When my spirit faints within me, you watch over my path.

By the road that I am walking
they have hidden a snare for me.

5(4) Look to my right, and see
that no one recognizes me.
I have no way of escape;
nobody cares for me.

6(5) I cried out to you, ADONAI;
I said, "You are my refuge,
my portion in the land of the living."

7(6) Listen to my cry,
for I have been brought very low.

Rescue me from my persecutors,
for they are too strong for me.

8(7) Lead me out of prison,
so that I can give thanks to your name;
in me the righteous will be crowning themselves,
because you will have treated me generously.

143 ¹⁽⁰⁾ A psalm of David:

(1) ADONAI, hear my prayer;
listen to my pleas for mercy.
In your faithfulness, answer me,
and in your righteousness.

2 Don't bring your servant to trial,
since in your sight no one alive
would be considered righteous.

3 For an enemy is pursuing me;
he has crushed my life into the ground
and left me to live in darkness,
like those who have been long dead.

4 My spirit faints within me;
my heart is appalled within me.

5 I remember the days of old,
reflecting on all your deeds,
thinking about the work of your hands.

6 I spread out my hands to you,
I long for you like a thirsty land.   (*Selah*)

7 Answer me quickly, ADONAI,
because my spirit is fainting.
Don't hide your face from me,
or I'll be like those who drop down into a pit.

8 Make me hear of your love in the morning,
   because I rely on you.
   Make me know the way I should walk,
   because I entrust myself to you.

9 ADONAI, rescue me from my enemies;
   I have hidden myself with you.

10 Teach me to do your will,
   because you are my God.
   Let your good Spirit guide me
   on ground that is level.

11 For your name's sake, ADONAI, preserve my life;
   in your righteousness, bring me out of distress.

12 In your grace, cut off my enemies;
   destroy all those harassing me;
   because I am your servant.

144 $^{1(0)}$ By David:

(1) Blessed be ADONAI, my rock,
    who trains my hands for war
    and my fingers for battle.

2 He shows me grace; and he is my fortress,
   my stronghold, in whom I find shelter,
   my shield, in whom I take refuge,
   who subdues my people under me.

3 ADONAI, what are mere mortals,
   that you notice them at all;
   humans, that you think about them?

4 Man is like a puff of wind,
   his days like a fleeting shadow.

5 ADONAI, lower the heavens, and come down;
   touch the mountains, make them pour out smoke.

6 Shoot out lightning, and scatter them;
   send out your arrows, and rout them.

7 Reach out your hands from on high;
   rescue me; save me out of deep water,
   out of the power of strangers,

8 whose mouths speak worthless words
   and whose right hands swear false oaths.

9 God, I will sing a new song to you;
   sing praises to you with a ten-stringed harp.

10 You give kings their victories;
   you save your servant David from the cruel sword.

11 Rescue me, save me from the power of strangers,
whose mouths speak worthless words
and whose right hands swear false oaths.

12 Our sons in their youth will be
like full-grown saplings,
our daughters will be like sculptured pillars
fit for the corner of a palace.

13 Our barns are full with crops of every kind;
the sheep in our fields number thousands, tens of thousands.

14 our oxen are well-fed,
our city walls have no breach,
our people are not taken captive,
and there are no cries of protest in our cities' open places.

15 How happy the people who live in such conditions!
How happy the people whose God is ADONAI!

145 ¹⁽⁰⁾ Praise. By David:

⁽¹⁾ I will praise you to the heights, my God, the king;
I will bless your name forever and ever.

2 Every day I will bless you;
I will praise your name forever and ever.

3 Great is ADONAI and greatly to be praised;
his greatness is beyond all searching out.

4 Each generation will praise your works to the next
and proclaim your mighty acts.

5 I will meditate on the glorious splendor
of your majesty and on the story of your wonders.

6 People will speak of your awesome power,
and I will tell of your great deeds.

7 They will gush forth the fame of your abounding goodness,
and they will sing of your righteousness.

8 ADONAI is merciful and compassionate,
slow to anger and great in grace.

9 ADONAI is good to all;
his compassion rests on all his creatures.

10 All your creatures will thank you, ADONAI,
and your faithful servants will bless you.

11 They will speak of the glory of your kingship,
and they will tell about your might;

12 to let everyone know of your mighty acts
and the glorious majesty of your kingship.

13 Your kingship is an everlasting kingship,
your reign continues through all generations.

14 ADONAI supports all who fall
and lifts up all who are bent over.

15 The eyes of all are looking to you;
you give them their food at the right time.
16 You open your hand
and satisfy the desire of every living thing.
17 ADONAI is righteous in all his ways,
full of grace in all he does.
18 ADONAI is close to all who call on him,
to all who sincerely call on him.
19 He fulfills the desire of those who fear him;
he hears their cry and saves them.
20 ADONAI protects all who love him,
but all the wicked he destroys.
21 My mouth will proclaim the praise of ADONAI;
all people will bless his holy name forever and ever.

146 1 *Halleluyah!*

Praise ADONAI, my soul!
2 I will praise ADONAI as long as I live.
I will sing praise to my God all my life.

3 Don't put your trust in princes
or in mortals, who cannot help.
4 When they breathe their last, they return to dust;
on that very day all their plans are gone.

5 Happy is he whose help is Ya'akov's God,
whose hope is in ADONAI his God.
6 He made heaven and earth,
the sea and everything in them;
he keeps faith forever.

7 He secures justice for the oppressed,
he gives food to the hungry.
ADONAI sets prisoners free,
8 ADONAI opens the eyes of the blind,
ADONAI lifts up those who are bent over.
ADONAI loves the righteous.
9 ADONAI watches over strangers,
he sustains the fatherless and widows;
but the way of the wicked he twists.

10 ADONAI will reign forever,
your God, Tziyon, through all generations.

Halleluyah!

147 ¹ *Halleluyah!*

How good it is to sing praises to our God!
How sweet, how fitting to praise him!

² ADONAI is rebuilding Yerushalayim,
gathering the dispersed of Isra'el.

³ He heals the brokenhearted
and binds up their wounds.

⁴ He determines how many stars there are
and calls them all by name.

⁵ Our Lord is great, his power is vast,
his wisdom beyond all telling.

⁶ ADONAI sustains the humble
but brings the wicked down to the ground.

⁷ Sing to ADONAI with thanks,
sing praises on the lyre to our God.

⁸ He veils the sky with clouds;
he provides the earth with rain;
he makes grass grow on the hills;

⁹ he gives food to the animals,
even to the young ravens when they cry.

¹⁰ He takes no delight in the strength of a horse,
no pleasure in a runner's speed.

¹¹ ADONAI takes pleasure in those who fear him,
in those who wait for his grace.

¹² Glorify ADONAI, Yerushalayim!
Praise your God, Tziyon!

¹³ For he strengthens the bars of your gates,
he blesses your children within you,

¹⁴ he brings peace within your borders,
he gives you your fill of the finest wheat.

¹⁵ He sends his word out over the earth,
his command runs swiftly.

¹⁶ Thus he gives snow like wool,
scatters hoarfrost like ashes,

¹⁷ sends crystals of ice like crumbs of bread —
who can withstand such cold?

¹⁸ Then he sends his word out and melts them;
he makes the winds blow, and the water flows.

¹⁹ He reveals his words to Ya'akov,
his laws and rulings to Isra'el.

20 He has not done this for other nations;
they do not know his rulings.

Halleluyah!

148 1 *Halleluyah!*

Praise ADONAI from the heavens!
Praise him in the heights!
2 Praise him, all his angels!
Praise him, all his armies!

3 Praise him, sun and moon!
Praise him, all shining stars!
4 Praise him, highest heaven,
and waters above the heavens!

5 Let them praise the name of ADONAI;
for he commanded, and they were created.
6 He established them forever and ever;
he has given a law to which they must conform.

7 Praise ADONAI from the earth,
sea monsters and watery depths,
8 fire and hail, snow and mist,
storm-winds that obey his word,
9 mountains and every hill,
fruit trees and all cedars,
10 wild animals and all livestock,
creeping reptiles, flying birds,
11 kings of the earth and all peoples,
princes and all rulers on earth,
12 young men and women alike,
old men and children.

13 Let them praise the name of ADONAI,
for his name alone is exalted;
his glory is above both earth and heaven.

14 He has increased the power of his people,
granted praise to all his faithful,
to the descendants of Isra'el,
a people close to him.

Halleluyah!

149 ¹ *Halleluyah!*

Sing to ADONAI a new song,
his praise in the assembly of the faithful.
² Let Isra'el rejoice in their maker,
let Tziyon's children take joy in their king.
³ Let them praise his name with dancing,
make melody to him with tambourine and lyre;
⁴ for ADONAI takes delight in his people,
he crowns the humble with salvation.
⁵ Let the faithful exult gloriously,
let them sing for joy on their beds.

⁶ Let the high praises of God be in their throats,
but a two-edged sword in their hands
⁷ to carry out vengeance on the nations
and punishment on the peoples,
⁸ to bind their kings with chains
and put their nobles in irons,
⁹ to execute the judgments decreed for them;
for this will glorify all his faithful.

Halleluyah!

150 ¹ *Halleluyah!*

Praise God in his holy place!
Praise him in the heavenly dome of his power!
² Praise him for his mighty deeds!
Praise him for his surpassing greatness!

³ Praise him with a blast on the *shofar!*
Praise him with lute and lyre!
⁴ Praise him with tambourines and dancing!
Praise him with flutes and strings!
⁵ Praise him with clanging cymbals!
Praise him with loud crashing cymbals!
⁶ Let everything that has breath praise ADONAI!

Halleluyah!

Mishlei
PROVERBS

1 ¹ The proverbs of Shlomo the son of David,
king of Isra'el,

² are for learning about wisdom and discipline;
for understanding words expressing deep insight;

³ for gaining an intelligently disciplined life,
doing what is right, just and fair;

⁴ for endowing with caution those who don't think
and the young person with knowledge and discretion.

⁵ Someone who is already wise
will hear and learn still more;
someone who already understands
will gain the ability to counsel well;

⁶ he will understand proverbs, obscure expressions,
the sayings and riddles of the wise.

⁷ The fear of *Adonai* is the beginning of knowledge,
but fools despise wisdom and discipline.

⁸ My son, heed the discipline of your father,
and do not abandon the teaching of your mother;

⁹ they will be a garland to grace your head,
a medal of honor for your neck.

¹⁰ My son, if sinners entice you,
don't go along with them.

¹¹ Suppose they say, "Come with us:
we'll ambush somebody and kill him,
we'll waylay some harmless soul, just for fun;

¹² we'll swallow him alive, like Sh'ol,
whole, like those who descend to the pit;

¹³ we'll find everything he has of value,
we'll fill our homes with loot!

¹⁴ Throw in your lot with us;
we'll share a common purse" —

¹⁵ my son, don't go along with them,
don't set foot on their path;

16   their feet run to evil,
    they rush to shed blood.

17   For in vain is the net baited
    if any bird can see it;

18   rather, they are ambushing themselves
    to shed their own blood, waylaying themselves.

19   So are the ways of all greedy for gain —
    it takes the lives of those who get it.

20   Wisdom calls aloud in the open air
    and raises her voice in the public places;

21   she calls out at streetcorners
    and speaks out at entrances to city gates:

22   "How long, you whose lives have no purpose,
    will you love thoughtless living?
    How long will scorners find pleasure in mocking?
    How long will fools hate knowledge?

23   Repent when I reprove —
    I will pour out my spirit to you,
    I will make my words known to you.

24   Because you refused when I called,
    and no one paid attention when I put out my hand,

25   but instead you neglected my counsel
    and would not accept my reproof;

26   I, in turn, will laugh at your distress,
    and mock when terror comes over you —

27   yes, when terror overtakes you like a storm
    and your disaster approaches like a whirlwind,
    when distress and trouble assail you.

28   Then they will call me, but I won't answer;
    they will seek me earnestly, but they won't find me.

29   Because they hated knowledge
    and did not choose the fear of ADONAI,

30   they refused my counsel
    and despised my reproof.

31   So they will bear the consequences of their own way
    and be overfilled with their own schemes.

32   For the aimless wandering of the thoughtless will kill them,
    and the smug overconfidence of fools will destroy them;

33   but those who pay attention to me will live securely,
    untroubled by fear of misfortune."

2 1   My son, if you will receive my words
    and store my commands inside you,

2   paying attention to wisdom
    inclining your mind toward understanding —

3   yes, if you will call for insight
       and raise your voice for discernment,
4   if you seek it as you would silver
       and search for it as for hidden treasure —
5   then you will understand the fear of *ADONAI*
       and find knowledge of God.

6   For *ADONAI* gives wisdom;
       from his mouth comes knowledge and understanding.
7   He stores up common sense for the upright,
       is a shield to those whose conduct is blameless,
8   in order to guard the courses of justice
       and preserve the way of those faithful to him.
9   Then you will understand righteousness, justice,
       fairness and every good path.
10   For wisdom will enter your heart,
       knowledge will be enjoyable for you,
11   discretion will watch over you,
       and discernment will guard you.

12   They will save you from the way of evil
       and from those who speak deceitfully,
13   who leave the paths of honesty
       to walk the ways of darkness,
14   who delight in doing evil
       and take joy in being stubbornly deceitful,
15   from those whose tracks are twisted
       and whose paths are perverse.

16   They will save you from a woman who is a stranger,
       from a loose woman with smooth talk,
17   who abandons the ruler she had in her youth
       and forgets the covenant of her God.
18   Her house is sinking toward death,
       her paths lead to the dead.
19   None who go to her return;
       they never regain the path to life.
20   Thus you will walk on the way of good people
       and keep to the paths of the righteous.
21   For the upright will live in the land,
       the pure-hearted will remain there;
22   but the wicked will be cut off from the land,
       the unfaithful rooted out of it.

3 ¹   My son, don't forget my teaching,
       keep my commands in your heart;

2   for they will add to you many days,
years of life and peace.

3   Do not let grace and truth leave you —
bind them around your neck;
write them on the tablet of your heart.

4   Then you will win favor and esteem
in the sight of God and of people.

5   Trust in ADONAI with all your heart;
do not rely on your own understanding.

6   In all your ways acknowledge him;
then he will level your paths.

7   Don't be conceited about your own wisdom;
but fear ADONAI, and turn from evil.

8   This will bring health to your body
and give strength to your bones.

9   Honor ADONAI with your wealth
and with the firstfruits of all your income.

10   Then your granaries will be filled
and your vats overflow with new wine.

11   My son, don't despise ADONAI's discipline
or resent his reproof;

12   for ADONAI corrects those he loves
like a father who delights in his son.

13   Happy the person who finds wisdom,
the person who acquires understanding;

14   for her profit exceeds that of silver,
gaining her is better than gold,

15   she is more precious than pearls —
nothing you want can compare with her.

16   Long life is in her right hand,
riches and honor in her left.

17   Her ways are pleasant ways,
and all her paths are peace.

18   She is a tree of life to those who grasp her;
whoever holds fast to her will be made happy.

19   ADONAI by wisdom founded the earth,
by understanding he established the heavens,

20   by his knowledge the deep [springs] burst open
and the dew condenses from the sky.

21 My son, don't let these slip from your sight;
   preserve common sense and discretion;
22 they will be life for your being
   and grace for your neck.
23 Then you will walk your way securely,
   without hurting your foot.
24 When you lie down, you will not be afraid;
   when you lie down, your sleep will be sweet.

25 Don't be afraid of sudden terror or destruction
   caused by the wicked, when it comes;
26 for you can rely on ADONAI;
   he will keep your foot from being caught in a trap.

27 Don't withhold good from someone entitled to it
   when you have in hand the power to do it.
28 Don't tell your neighbor, "Go away! Come another time;
   I'll give it to you tomorrow," when you have it now.
29 Don't plan harm against your neighbor
   who lives beside you trustingly.
30 Don't quarrel with someone for no reason,
   if he has done you no harm.
31 Don't envy a man of violence,
   don't choose any of his ways;
32 for the perverse is an abomination to ADONAI,
   but he shares his secret counsel with the upright.
33 ADONAI's curse is in the house of the wicked,
   but he blesses the home of the righteous.
34 The scornful he scorns,
   but gives grace to the humble.
35 The wise win honor,
   but fools win shame.

4 1 Listen, children, to a father's instruction;
   pay attention, in order to gain insight;
2 for I am giving you good advice;
   so don't abandon my teaching.
3 For I too was once a child to my father;
   and my mother, too, thought of me as her special darling.
4 He too taught me; he said to me,
   "Let your heart treasure my words;
   keep my commands, and live;
5 gain wisdom, gain insight;
   don't forget or turn from the words I am saying.
6 Don't abandon [wisdom]; then she will preserve you;
   love her, and she will protect you.

7   The beginning of wisdom is: get wisdom!
And along with all your getting, get insight!

8   Cherish her, and she will exalt you;
embrace her, and she will bring you honor;

9   she will give your head a garland of grace,
bestow on you a crown of glory."

10   Listen, my son, receive what I say,
and the years of your life will be many.

11   I'm directing you on the way of wisdom,
guiding you in paths of uprightness;

12   when you walk, your step won't be hindered;
and if you run, you won't stumble.

13   Hold fast to discipline, don't let it go;
guard it, for it is your life.

14   Don't follow the path of the wicked
or walk on the way of evildoers.

15   Avoid it, don't go on it,
turn away from it, and pass on.

16   For they can't sleep if they haven't done evil,
they are robbed of sleep unless they make someone fall.

17   For they eat the bread of wickedness
and drink the wine of violence.

18   But the path of the righteous is like the light of dawn,
shining ever brighter until full daylight.

19   The way of the wicked is like darkness;
they don't even know what makes them stumble.

20   My son, pay attention to what I am saying;
incline your ear to my words.

21   Don't let them out of your sight,
keep them deep in your heart;

22   for they are life to those who find them
and health to their whole being.

23   Above everything else, guard your heart;
for it is the source of life's consequences.

24   Keep crooked speech out of your mouth,
banish deceit from your lips.

25   Let your eyes look straight ahead,
fix your gaze on what lies in front of you.

26   Level the path for your feet,
let all your ways be properly prepared;

27   then deviate neither right nor left;
and keep your foot far from evil.

5 1 My son, pay attention to my wisdom;
incline your ear to my understanding;

2 so that you will preserve discretion
and your lips keep watch over knowledge.

3 For the lips of a woman who is a stranger drop honey,
her mouth is smoother than oil;

4 but in the end she is as bitter as wormwood,
sharp as a double-edged sword.

5 Her feet go down to death,
her steps lead straight to Sh'ol;

6 she doesn't walk the level path of life —
her course wanders all over, but she doesn't know it.

7 So now, children, listen to me;
don't turn away from what I am saying:

8 distance your way from her,
stay far from the door of her house;

9 so that you won't give your vigor to others
and your years to someone who is cruel,

10 so strangers won't be filled with your strength
and what you worked for go to a foreign house.

11 Then, when your flesh and bones have shrunk,
at the end of your life, you would moan,

12 "How I hated discipline!
My whole being despised reproof,

13 I ignored what my teachers said,
I didn't listen to my instructors.

14 I took part in almost every kind of evil,
and the whole community knew it."

15 Drink the water from your own cistern,
fresh water from your own well.

16 Let what your springs produce be dispersed outside,
streams of water flowing in the streets;

17 but let them be for you alone
and not for strangers with you.

18 Let your fountain, the wife of your youth,
be blessed; find joy in her —

19 a lovely deer, a graceful fawn;
let her breasts satisfy you at all times,
always be infatuated with her love.

20 My son, why be infatuated with an unknown woman?
Why embrace the body of a loose woman?

21 For ADONAI is watching a man's ways;
he surveys all his paths.

22 A wicked person's own crimes will trap him,
he will be held fast by the ropes of his sin.

23   He will die from lack of discipline;
     the magnitude of his folly will make him totter and fall.

6 ¹   My son, if you have put up security for your friend,
     if you committed yourself on behalf of another;
2   you have been snared by the words of your mouth,
     caught by the words of your own mouth.
3   Do this now, my son, and extricate yourself,
     since you put yourself in your friend's power:
     go, humble yourself, and pester your friend;
4   give your eyes no sleep,
     give your eyelids no rest;
5   break free, like a gazelle from the [hunter's] trap,
     like a bird from the grip of the fowler.

6   Go to the ant, you lazybones!
     Consider its ways, and be wise.
7   It has no chief, overseer or ruler;
8   yet it provides its food in summer
     and gathers its supplies at harvest-time.
9   Lazybones! How long will you lie there in bed?
     When will you get up from your sleep?
10   "I'll just lie here a bit, rest a little longer,
     just fold my hands for a little more sleep" —
11   and poverty comes marching in on you,
     scarcity hits you like an invading soldier.

12   A scoundrel, a vicious man,
     lives by crooked speech,
13   winking his eyes, shuffling his feet,
     pointing with his fingers.
14   With deceit in his heart,
     he is always plotting evil and sowing discord.
15   Therefore disaster suddenly overcomes him;
     unexpectedly, he is broken beyond repair.

16   There are six things ADONAI hates,
     seven which he detests:
17   a haughty look, a lying tongue,
     hands that shed innocent blood,
18   a heart that plots wicked schemes,
     feet swift in running to do evil,
19   a false witness who lies with every breath,
     and him who sows strife among brothers.

20   My son, obey your father's command,
     and don't abandon your mother's teaching.

21   Bind them always on your heart,
       tie them around your neck.

22   When you walk, they will lead you;
       when you lie down, they will watch over you;
       and when you wake up, they will talk with you.

23   For the *mitzvah* is a lamp, *Torah* is light,
       and reproofs that discipline are the way to life.

24   They keep you from an evil woman,
       from a loose woman's seductive tongue.

25   Don't let your heart lust after her beauty
       or allow her glance to captivate you.

26   The price of a whore is a loaf of bread,
       but the adulteress is hunting for a precious life.

27   Can a man carry fire inside his shirt
       without burning his clothes?

28   Can a man walk [barefoot] on hot coals
       without scorching his feet?

29   So is he who has sex with his neighbor's wife;
       anyone touching her will be punished.

30   A thief is not despised if he steals
       only to satisfy his appetite when hungry;

31   but even he, if caught, must pay back sevenfold;
       he may have to give up all the wealth that he owns.

32   He who commits adultery lacks sense;
       he who does it destroys himself.

33   He will get nothing but blows and contempt,
       and his disgrace will not be wiped away.

34   For jealousy drives a man into a rage;
       he will show no mercy when he takes revenge;

35   he will not accept compensation;
       he'll refuse every bribe, no matter how large.

7 ¹   My son, keep my words,
       store up my commands with you.

2   Obey my commands, and live;
       guard my teaching like the pupil of your eye.

3   Bind them on your fingers;
       write them on the tablet of your heart.

4   Say to wisdom, "You are my sister";
       call understanding your kinswoman;

5   so that they can keep you from unknown women,
       from loose women with their seductive talk.

6   For I was at the window of my house,
       glancing out through the lattice,

7   when I saw among the young men there,
among those who don't think for themselves,
a young fellow devoid of all sense.

8   He crosses the street near her corner
and continues on toward her house.

9   Dusk turns into evening,
and finally night, dark and black.

10   Then a woman approaches him,
dressed as a prostitute, wily of heart.

11   She's the coarse, impulsive type,
whose feet don't stay at home;

12   rather, she stalks the streets and squares,
lurking at every streetcorner.

13   She grabs him, gives him a kiss,
and, brazen-faced, she says to him,

14   "I had to offer peace sacrifices,
and I fulfilled my vows today.

15   This is why I came out to meet you,
to look for you; now I've found you.

16   I've spread quilts on my couch
made of colored Egyptian linen.

17   I've perfumed my bed
with myrrh, aloes and cinnamon.

18   Come on, let's make love till morning;
we'll enjoy making love.

19   My husband isn't at home,
he's gone on a long trip;

20   he took a bag of money with him
and won't be back till the moon is full."

21   With all her sweet talk she convinces him,
enticing him with her seductive words.

22   At once he follows her
like an ox on its way to be slaughtered;
like a fool to be punished in the stocks;

23   or like a bird rushing into a trap,
not knowing its life is at stake
till an arrow pierces its liver.

24   So now, children, listen to me;
pay attention to what I am saying.

25   Don't let your heart turn to her ways;
don't stray onto her paths.

26   For many are those she has struck down dead,
numerous those she has killed.

27   Her house is the way to Sh'ol;
it leads down to the halls of death.

8^{1} Wisdom is calling!
Understanding is raising her voice!

^{2} On the heights along the road,
where the paths meet, she is standing;

^{3} by the gates leading into the city,
at the entrances, she cries aloud:

^{4} "People, I am calling you,
raising my voice to all mankind.

^{5} You who don't direct your lives,
understand caution;
as for you, you fools,
get some common sense!

^{6} "Listen! I will say worthwhile things;
when I speak, my words are right.

^{7} My mouth says what is true,
because my lips detest evil.

^{8} All the words from my mouth are righteous;
nothing false or crooked is in them.

^{9} They are all clear to those who understand
and straightforward to those who gain knowledge.

^{10} Receive my instruction, rather than silver;
knowledge, rather than the finest gold.

^{11} For wisdom is better than pearls;
nothing you want can compare with her.

^{12} "I, wisdom, live together with caution;
I attain knowledge and discretion.

^{13} The fear of *ADONAI* is hatred of evil.
I hate pride and arrogance,
evil ways and duplicitous speech.

^{14} Good advice is mine, and common sense;
I am insight, power is mine.

^{15} By me kings reign,
and princes make just laws.

^{16} By me princes govern,
nobles too, and all the earth's rulers.

^{17} I love those who love me;
and those who seek me will find me.

^{18} Riches and honor are with me,
lasting wealth and righteousness.

^{19} My fruit is better than gold, fine gold,
my produce better than the finest silver.

^{20} I follow the course of righteousness
along the paths of justice,

^{21} to endow with wealth those who love me
and fill their treasuries.

22   "*Adonai* made me as the beginning of his way,
the first of his ancient works.

23   I was appointed before the world,
before the start, before the earth's beginnings.

24   When I was brought forth, there were no ocean depths,
no springs brimming with water.

25   I was brought forth before the hills,
before the mountains had settled in place;

26   he had not yet made the earth, the fields,
or even the earth's first grains of dust.

27   When he established the heavens, I was there.
When he drew the horizon's circle on the deep,

28   when he set the skies above in place,
when the fountains of the deep poured forth,

29   when he prescribed boundaries for the sea,
so that its water would not transgress his command,
when he marked out the foundations of the earth,

30   I was with him as someone he could trust.
For me, every day was pure delight,
as I played in his presence all the time,

31   playing everywhere on his earth,
and delighting to be with humankind.

32   "Therefore, children, listen to me:
happy are those who keep my ways.

33   Hear instruction, and grow wise;
do not refuse it.

34   How happy the person who listens to me,
who watches daily at my gates
and waits outside my doors.

35   For he who finds me finds life
and obtains the favor of *Adonai*.

36   But he who misses me harms himself;
all who hate me love death."

9 1   Wisdom has built herself a house;
she has carved her seven pillars.

2   She has prepared her food, spiced her wine,
and she has set her table.

3   She has sent out her young girls [with invitations];
she calls from the heights of the city,

4   "Whoever is unsure of himself, turn in here!"
To someone weak-willed she says,

5   "Come and eat my food!
Drink the wine I have mixed!

6   Don't stay unsure of yourself, but live!
Walk in the way of understanding!"

7 "He who corrects a scoffer only gets insulted;
reproving a wicked man becomes his blemish.

8 If you reprove a scoffer, he will hate you;
if you reprove a wise man, he will love you.

9 Give to a wise man, and he grows still wiser;
teach a righteous man, and he will learn still more.

10 The fear of ADONAI is the beginning of wisdom,
and knowledge of holy ones is understanding.

11 For with me, your days will be increased;
years will be added to your life.

12 If you are wise, your wisdom helps you;
but if you scoff, you bear the consequences alone."

13 The foolish woman is coarse;
she doesn't think, and she doesn't know a thing.

14 She sits at the door of her house
or on a seat at the heights of the city,

15 calling to those who pass by,
to those going straight along their ways,

16 "Whoever is unsure of himself, turn in here!"
To someone weak-willed she says,

17 "Stolen water is sweet;
food eaten in secret is pleasant."

18 But he doesn't realize
that the dead are there,
and that those who accept her invitation
are in the depths of Sh'ol.

10 ¹ The proverbs of Shlomo:

A wise son is a joy to his father,
but a foolish son is a grief to his mother.

2 No good comes from ill-gotten wealth,
but righteousness rescues from death.

3 ADONAI does not let the righteous go hungry,
but he thwarts the craving of the wicked.

4 Idle hands bring poverty;
diligent hands bring wealth.

5 A sensible person gathers in summer,
but he who sleeps during harvest is an embarrassment.

6 Blessings are for the head of the righteous,
but the speech of the wicked is a cover for violence.

7 The memory of the righteous will be for a blessing,
but the reputation of the wicked will rot.

8   Wise-hearted people take orders,
         but a babbling fool will have trouble.

9   He who walks purely walks securely,
         but he who walks in crooked ways will be found out.

10   He who winks his eye [instead of rebuking] causes pain,
         yet a babbling fool will have trouble.

11   The speech of the righteous is a fountain of life,
         but the speech of the wicked is a cover for violence.

12   Hate stirs up disputes,
         but love covers all kinds of transgressions.

13   On the lips of the intelligent is found wisdom,
         but a stick is in store for the back of a fool.
14   Wise people hide their knowledge,
         but when a fool speaks, ruin is imminent.

15   The wealth of the rich is his fortified city;
         the ruin of the poor is their poverty.

16   The activity of the righteous is for life;
         the income of the wicked is for sin.

17   He who observes discipline is on the way to life;
         but he who ignores correction is making a mistake.

18   He who covers up hate has lips that lie,
         and anyone who slanders is a fool.
19   When words are many, sin is not lacking;
         so he who controls his speech is wise.
20   The tongue of the righteous is like pure silver,
         but the mind of the wicked is worth little.
21   The lips of the righteous feed many,
         but fools die for lack of sense.

22   The blessing of *Adonai* is what makes people rich,
         and he doesn't mix sorrow with it.

23   To a fool, vileness is like a game,
         as is wisdom to a person of discernment.

24   What a fool dreads will overtake him,
         but the righteous will be given his desire.
25   When the storm has passed, the wicked are gone;
         but the righteous are firmly established forever.

26   Like vinegar to the teeth and smoke to the eyes
          is a lazy person to his employer.

27   The fear of *Adonai* adds length to life,
          but the years of the wicked are cut short.
28   What the righteous hope for will end in joy;
          what the wicked expect will come to nothing.
29   The way of *Adonai* is a stronghold to the upright
          but ruin to those who do evil.
30   The righteous will never be moved,
          but the wicked will not remain in the land.

31   The mouth of the righteous brings forth wisdom,
          but the perverse tongue will be cut off.
32   The lips of the righteous know what is wanted,
          but the mouth of the wicked [knows] deceit.

11 ¹   False scales are an abomination to *Adonai*,
          but accurate weights please him.

2   First comes pride, then disgrace;
          but with the humble is wisdom.

3   The integrity of the upright guides them,
          but the duplicity of the treacherous destroys them.

4   On the day of wrath, wealth doesn't help;
          but righteousness rescues from death.

5   The righteousness of the innocent levels their way,
          but the wickedness of the wicked makes them fall.
6   The righteousness of the upright rescues them,
          but the treacherous are trapped by their own intrigues.
7   When a wicked man dies, his hope perishes;
          what he hopes for from evil comes to nothing.
8   The righteous is delivered from trouble,
          and the wicked comes to take his place.
9   With his mouth the hypocrite can ruin his neighbor,
          but by knowledge the righteous are delivered.
10   When the righteous prosper, the city rejoices;
          and when the wicked perish, there is joy.
11   By the blessing of the upright, a city is raised up;
          but the words of the wicked tear it down.

12   He who belittles another lacks good sense,
          whereas a person of discernment stays silent.

13   A gossip goes around revealing secrets,
            but a trustworthy person keeps a confidence.

14   Without clever tactics an army is defeated,
            and victory comes from much planning.

15   He who guarantees a loan for a stranger will suffer,
            but refusing to underwrite is safe.

16   A gracious woman obtains honor;
            aggressive men obtain wealth.

17   A man who is kind does himself good,
            but the cruel does harm to himself.

18   The profits of the wicked are illusory;
            but those who sow righteousness gain a true reward.

19   Genuine righteousness leads to life,
            but the pursuer of evil goes to his own death.

20   The crooked-hearted are an abomination to ADONAI,
            but those sincere in their ways are his delight.

21   Depend on it: the evil will not go unpunished;
            but the offspring of the righteous will escape.

22   Like a gold ring in the snout of a pig
            is a beautiful woman who lacks good sense.

23   The righteous desire only good,
            but what the wicked hope for brings wrath.

24   Some give freely and still get richer,
            while others are stingy but grow still poorer.

25   The person who blesses others will prosper;
            he who satisfies others will be satisfied himself.

26   The people will curse him who withholds grain;
            but if he sells it, blessings will be on his head.

27   He who strives for good obtains favor,
            but he who searches for evil — it comes to him!

28   He who trusts in his riches will fall,
            but the righteous will flourish like sprouting leaves.

29   Those who trouble their families inherit the wind,
            and the fool becomes slave to the wise.

30   The fruit of the righteous is a tree of life,
            and he who is wise wins souls.

31   If the righteous are paid what they deserve here on earth,
       how much more the wicked and the sinner!

12 1   He who loves knowledge loves discipline,
       but he who hates correction is a boor.

2   A good man obtains ADONAI's favor,
       but the schemer his condemnation.

3   No one is made secure by wickedness,
       but the roots of the righteous will never be moved.

4   A capable wife is a crown for her husband,
       but a shameful one is like rot in his bones.

5   The plans of the righteous are just,
       but the schemes of the wicked are deceitful.
6   The words of the wicked are a deadly ambush,
       but the speech of the upright rescues them.
7   Once the wicked are down, it's the end of them;
       but the house of the upright endures.

8   A person wins praise in keeping with his common sense,
       but a person with a warped mind is treated with contempt.

9   Better to be despised and have a servant
       than to boast of one's status but have nothing to eat.

10   A righteous man takes care of his animal,
       but the wicked? Even his compassion is cruel.

11   He who farms his land will have plenty of food,
       but he who follows futilities has no sense.

12   The wicked covet the loot of evil men,
       but the root of the righteous gives forth of itself.
13   The wicked is trapped by his own sinful speech,
       but the righteous finds a way out of trouble.

14   One can be filled with good as the result of one's words,
       and one gets the reward one's deeds deserve.

15   Fools suppose their way is straight,
       but the wise pay attention to advice.
16   A fool's anger is known at once,
       but a cautious person slighted conceals his feelings.

17   He who tells the truth furthers justice,
      but a false witness furthers deceit.

18   Idle talk can pierce like a sword,
      but the tongue of the wise can heal.
19   Truthful words will stand forever,
      lying speech but a moment.

20   Deceit is in the hearts of those who plot evil,
      but for those advising peace there is joy.
21   No harm can come to the righteous,
      but the wicked are overwhelmed with disaster.

22   Lying lips are an abomination to Adonai,
      but those who deal faithfully are his delight.
23   A cautious person conceals knowledge,
      but the heart of a fool blurts out folly.

24   The diligent will rule,
      while the lazy will be put to forced labor.

25   Anxiety in a person's heart weighs him down,
      but a kind word cheers him up.

26   The righteous guides his friend's way rightly,
      but the way of the wicked will lead them astray.

27   A lazy man doesn't roast what he hunted;
      but when a man is diligent, his wealth is precious.

28   In the road of righteousness is life;
      no death is in its pathway.

13¹ A son who heeds his father's discipline is wise,
      but a scoffer doesn't listen to rebuke.

2   A [good] man enjoys good as a result of what he says,
      but the essence of the treacherous is violence.

3   He who guards his mouth preserves his life,
      but one who talks too much comes to ruin.

4   The lazy person wants but doesn't have;
      the diligent get their desires filled.

5   A righteous person hates lying,
      but the wicked is vile and disgraceful.

6   Righteousness protects him whose way is honest,
       but wickedness brings down the sinner.

7   There are those with nothing who pretend they are rich,
       also those with great wealth who pretend they are poor.

8   The rich man may have to ransom his life,
       but a poor man gets no threats.

9   The light of the righteous [shines] joyfully,
       but the lamp of the wicked will be extinguished.

10   Insolence produces only strife,
       but wisdom is found with those who take advice.

11   Wealth gotten by worthless means dwindles away,
       but he who amasses it by hard work will increase it.

12   Hope deferred makes the heart sick,
       but desire fulfilled is a tree of life.

13   He who despises a word will suffer for it,
       but he who respects a command will be rewarded.

14   The teaching of a wise man is a fountain of life,
       enabling one to avoid deadly traps.

15   Good common sense produces grace,
       but the way of the treacherous is rough.

16   Every cautious person acts with knowledge,
       but a fool parades his folly.

17   A wicked messenger falls into evil,
       but a faithful envoy brings healing.

18   Poverty and shame are for him who won't be taught,
       but he who heeds reproof will be honored.

19   Desire fulfilled is sweet to the soul,
       but turning away from evil is abhorrent to fools.

20   He who walks with the wise will become wise,
       but the companion of fools will suffer.

21   Evil pursues sinners,
       but prosperity will reward the righteous.

22   A good man leaves an inheritance to his grandchildren,
       but the wealth of a sinner is stored up for the righteous.

²³ The fields of the poor may yield much food,
  but some are swept away because of injustice.

²⁴ He who fails to use a stick hates his son,
  but he who loves him is careful to discipline him.

²⁵ The righteous person eats his fill,
  but the belly of the wicked is empty.

14 ¹ Every wise woman builds up her home,
  but a foolish one tears it down with her own hands.

² A person with upright conduct fears ADONAI,
  but a person who is devious scorns him.

³ From the mouth of a fool sprouts pride,
  but the lips of the wise protect them.

⁴ Where there are no oxen, the stalls are clean;
  but much is produced by the strength of an ox.

⁵ An honest witness will not lie,
  but a false witness lies with every breath.

⁶ A scoffer seeks wisdom in vain,
  but knowledge comes easily to someone with discernment.

⁷ Keep clear of a fool,
  for you won't hear a sensible word from him.

⁸ The wisdom of the cautious makes him know where he is going,
  but the folly of fools misleads them.

⁹ Guilt offerings make a mockery of fools;
  but among the upright there is good will.

¹⁰ The heart knows its own bitterness,
  and no stranger can share its joy.

¹¹ The house of the wicked will be destroyed,
  but the tent of the upright will flourish.

¹² There can be a way which seems right to a person,
  but at its end are the ways of death.

¹³ Even in laughter the heart can be sad,
  and joy may end in sorrow.

14 A backslider is filled up with his own ways,
   but a good person gets satisfaction from himself.

15 One who doesn't think believes every word,
   but the cautious understands his steps.

16 A wise person fears and turns away from evil,
   but a fool is reckless and overconfident.

17 He who is quick-tempered does stupid things,
   and one who does vile things is hated.

18 Thoughtless people inherit folly,
   but the cautious are crowned with knowledge.

19 The evil bow down before the good,
   and the wicked at the gates of the righteous.

20 The poor are disliked even by their peers,
   but the rich have many friends.

21 He who despises his fellow sins,
   but he who shows compassion to the humble is happy.

22 Won't those who plot evil go astray?
   But grace and truth are for those who plan good.

23 In all work there is profit,
   but mere talk produces only poverty.
24 The crown of the wise is their riches,
   but the folly of fools is just that — folly.

25 A truthful witness saves lives,
   but a liar misdirects [judgment].

26 In the fear of ADONAI is powerful security;
   for his children there will be a place of refuge.
27 The fear of ADONAI is a fountain of life
   enabling one to avoid deadly traps.

28 A king's glory lies in having many subjects;
   if the prince's people are few, it is his ruin.

29 Being slow to anger goes with great understanding,
   being quick-tempered makes folly still worse.

30 A tranquil mind gives health to the body,
   but envy rots the bones.

³¹ The oppressor of the poor insults his maker,
but he who is kind to the needy honors him.

³² The wicked are brought down by their wrongdoing,
but the righteous can be confident even at death.

³³ Wisdom is at rest in a person with discernment,
but in fools it has to call attention to itself.

³⁴ Righteousness makes a nation great,
but sin degrades any people.

³⁵ A king shows favor to a servant with good sense,
but his wrath strikes one who shames [him].

15 ¹ A gentle response deflects fury,
but a harsh word makes tempers rise.

² The tongue of the wise presents knowledge well,
but the mouth of a fool spews out folly.

³ The eyes of *Adonai* are everywhere,
watching the evil and the good.

⁴ A soothing tongue is a tree of life,
but when it twists things, it breaks the spirit.

⁵ A fool despises his father's discipline,
but he who heeds warnings is prudent.

⁶ The home of the righteous is a storehouse of treasure,
but the earnings of the wicked bring trouble.

⁷ The lips of the wise spread knowledge;
not so the hearts of fools.

⁸ *Adonai* detests the sacrifices of the wicked
but delights in the prayers of the upright.

⁹ *Adonai* detests the way of the wicked
but loves anyone who pursues righteousness.

¹⁰ Discipline is severe for one who leaves the way,
and whoever can't stand correction will die.

¹¹ Sh'ol and Abaddon lie open to *Adonai*;
so how much more people's hearts!

12   A scorner does not like being corrected;
      he won't go to the wise [for advice].

13   A glad heart makes a face happy,
      but heartache breaks the spirit.

14   The mind of a person with discernment seeks knowledge,
      but the mouth of a fool feeds on folly.

15   For the poor, every day is hard;
      but the good-hearted have a perpetual feast.

16   Better little with the fear of ADONAI
      than great wealth coupled with worry.

17   Better a vegetable dinner with love
      than a stall-fattened ox with hate.

18   Hot-tempered people stir up strife,
      but patient people quiet quarrels.

19   The lazy person's way seems overgrown by thorns,
      but the path of the upright is a level highway.

20   A wise son is a joy to his father,
      and only a fool despises his mother.

21   Folly appeals to one who lacks sense,
      but a person of discernment goes straight ahead.

22   Without deliberation, plans go wrong;
      but with many advisers, they succeed.

23   People take pleasure in anything they say;
      but a word at the right time, how good it is!

24   For the prudent, the path of life goes upward;
      thus he avoids Sh'ol below.

25   ADONAI will pull down the houses of the proud,
      but preserves intact the widow's boundaries.

26   ADONAI detests plans to do evil,
      but kind words are pure.

27   The greedy for gain brings trouble to his home,
      but he who hates bribes will live.

28   The mind of the righteous thinks before speaking,
      but the mouth of the wicked spews out evil stuff.

²⁹   ADONAI is far from the wicked,
        but he listens to the prayer of the righteous.

³⁰   A cheerful glance brings joy to the heart,
        and good news invigorates the bones.

³¹   He who heeds life-giving correction
        will be at home in the company of the wise.

³²   He who spurns discipline detests himself,
        but he who listens to correction grows in understanding.

³³   The discipline of wisdom is fear of ADONAI,
        so before being honored, a person must be humble.

16 ¹   A person is responsible to prepare his heart,
        but how the tongue speaks is from ADONAI.

²   All a man's ways are pure in his own view,
        but ADONAI weighs the spirit.

³   If you entrust all you do to ADONAI,
        your plans will achieve success.

⁴   ADONAI made everything for its purpose,
        even the wicked for the day of disaster.

⁵   ADONAI detests all those with proud hearts;
        be assured that they will not go unpunished.

⁶   Grace and truth atone for iniquity,
        and people turn from evil through fear of ADONAI.

⁷   When a man's ways please ADONAI,
        he makes even the man's enemies be at peace with him.

⁸   Better a little with righteousness
        than a huge income with injustice.

⁹   A person may plan his path,
        but ADONAI directs his steps.

¹⁰   Divine inspiration is on the lips of the king,
        so his mouth must be faithful when he judges.

¹¹   The balance and scales of justice have their origin in ADONAI;
        all the weights in the bag are his doing.

¹²   It is an abomination for a king to do evil,
        for the throne is made secure by righteousness.

13   The king should delight in righteous lips,
       and he should love someone who speaks what is right.

14   The king's anger is a herald of death,
       and one who is wise will appease it.

15   When the king's face brightens, it means life;
       his favor is like the clouds that bring spring rain.

16   How much better than gold it is to gain wisdom!
       Yes, rather than money, choose to gain understanding.

17   Avoiding evil is the highway of the upright;
       he who watches his step preserves his life.

18   Pride goes before destruction,
       and arrogance before failure.

19   Better to be humble among the poor
       than share the spoil with the proud.

20   He who has skill in a matter will succeed;
       he who trusts in ADONAI will be happy.

21   A wise-hearted person is said to have discernment,
       and sweetness of speech adds to learning.

22   Common sense is a fountain of life to one who has it,
       whereas fools are punished by their own folly.

23   The wise man's heart teaches his mouth,
       and to his lips it adds learning.

24   Pleasant words are like a honeycomb,
       sweet to the taste and healing for the body.

25   There can be a way which seems right to a person,
       but at its end are the ways of death.

26   A working man's appetite acts on his behalf,
       because his hunger presses him on.

27   A worthless person digs up evil [gossip] —
       it is like scorching fire on his lips.

28   A deceitful person stirs up strife,
       and a slanderer can separate even close friends.

29   A violent man lures his neighbor astray
       and leads him into evil ways.

30 One who winks knowingly is planning deceit;
    one who pinches his lips together has already done wrong.

31 White hair is a crown of honor
    obtained by righteous living.

32 He who controls his temper is better than a war hero,
    he who rules his spirit better than he who captures a city.

33 One can cast lots into one's lap,
    but the decision comes from ADONAI.

17 ¹ Better a dry piece of bread with calm
    than a house full of food but also full of strife.

2 An intelligent slave will rule a shameful son
    and share the inheritance with the brothers.

3 The crucible [tests] silver, and the furnace [tests] gold,
    but the one who tests hearts is ADONAI.

4 An evildoer heeds wicked lips;
    a liar listens to destructive talk.

5 He who mocks the poor insults his maker;
    he who rejoices at calamity will not go unpunished.

6 Grandchildren are the crown of the aged,
    while the glory of children is their ancestors.

7 Fine speech is unbecoming to a boor,
    and even less lying lips to a leader.

8 A bribe works like a charm, in the view of him who gives it —
    wherever it turns, it succeeds.

9 He who conceals an offense promotes love,
    but he who harps on it can separate even close friends.

10 A rebuke makes more impression on a person of understanding
    than a hundred blows on a fool.

11 An evil person seeks only rebellion,
    but a cruel messenger will be sent against him.

12 Rather meet a bear robbed of its cubs
    than encounter a fool in his folly.

13   Evil will not depart from the house
       of him who returns evil for good.

14   Starting a fight is like letting water through [a dike] —
       better stop the quarrel before it gets worse.

15   He who justifies the wicked and he who condemns the righteous —
       both alike are an abomination to *Adonai*.

16   Why would a fool wish to pay for wisdom
       when he has no desire to learn?

17   A friend shows his friendship at all times —
       it is for adversity that [such] a brother is born.

18   He who gives his hand to guarantee a loan
       for his neighbor lacks good sense.

19   Those who love quarreling love giving offense;
       those who make their gates tall are courting disaster.

20   A crooked-hearted person will find nothing good,
       and the perverse of speech will end in calamity.

21   He who fathers a fool does so to his sorrow,
       and the father of a boor has no joy.

22   A happy heart is good medicine,
       but low spirits sap one's strength.

23   From under a cloak a bad man takes a bribe
       to pervert the course of justice.

24   The discerning person focuses on wisdom there before him,
       but a fool's eyes wander to the ends of the earth.

25   A son who is a fool means anger for his father
       and bitterness for the mother who gave him birth.

26   To punish the innocent is not right,
       likewise to flog noble people for their uprightness.

27   A knowledgeable person controls his tongue;
       a discerning person controls his temper.

28   Even a fool, if he stays silent, is thought wise;
       he who keeps his mouth shut can pass for smart.

18 ¹   He who separates himself indulges his desires
and shows contempt for sound advice of any kind.

²   A fool takes no pleasure in trying to understand;
he only wants to express his own opinion.

³   When a wicked person comes, contempt comes too,
and with disdain, provocation.

⁴   The words of a man's mouth are deep water,
a gushing torrent, a fountain of wisdom.

⁵   It is not good to be partial to the guilty
and thus deprive the innocent of justice.

⁶   A fool's words get him into fights;
yes, his mouth calls out for a beating.

⁷   A fool's mouth is his ruin;
his words are a trap for him.

⁸   A slanderer's words are tasty morsels;
they slide right down into the belly.

⁹   Whoever is lazy in doing his work
is brother to the destroyer.

¹⁰   The name of ADONAI is a strong tower;
a righteous person runs to it and is raised high [above danger].

¹¹   The wealth of the rich is his fortified city,
like a high wall, in his own imagination.

¹²   Before being ruined, a person's heart is proud;
before being honored, a person must be humble.

¹³   To answer someone before hearing him out
is both stupid and embarrassing.

¹⁴   A person's spirit can sustain him when ill,
but a crushed spirit — who can bear it?

¹⁵   The mind of a person with discernment gets knowledge,
and the ear of the wise seeks knowledge.

¹⁶   A person's gift clears his way
and gives him access to the great.

¹⁷   The first to state his case seems right,
till the other one comes and cross-examines.

18 Casting lots puts an end to strife
    and separates powerful disputants.

19 It is harder to win an offended brother than a strong city;
    their fights are like the bars of a fortress.

20 A person's belly will be filled with the fruit of his mouth;
    with what his lips produce he will be filled.

21 The tongue has power over life and death;
    those who indulge it must eat its fruit.

22 He who finds a wife finds a great good;
    he has won the favor of ADONAI.

23 The poor man speaks beseechingly,
    the rich man's answer is blunt.

24 Some "friends" pretend to be friends,
    but a true friend sticks closer than a brother.

19 1 Better to be poor and live one's life uprightly
    than engage in crooked speech, for such a one is a fool.

2 To act without knowing how you function is not good;
   and if you rush ahead, you will miss your goal.

3 A person's own folly is what ruins his way,
   but he rages in his heart against ADONAI.

4 Wealth brings in many friends,
   but the poor man loses the one friend he has.

5 A false witness will not go unpunished;
   whoever breathes out lies will not escape.

6 Many ask favors of a generous person —
   to a giver of gifts, everyone is a friend.

7 A poor man's relatives all hate him;
   even more his friends stay away from him.
   He may pursue them with entreaties,
   but they aren't there to be found.

8 To acquire good sense is to love oneself;
   to treasure discernment is to prosper.

9   A false witness will not go unpunished;
         whoever breathes out lies will perish.

10   It isn't fitting for a fool to live in luxury,
         and even less for a slave to govern princes.

11   People with good sense are slow to anger,
         and it is their glory to overlook an offense.

12   A king's wrath is like the roaring of a lion,
         but his favor is like dew on the grass.

13   A son who is a fool is his father's ruin,
         and a nagging wife is like a leak that keeps dripping.

14   A house and wealth are inherited from ancestors,
         but a sensible wife is from ADONAI.

15   Laziness makes people fall asleep,
         and an idle person will go hungry.

16   He who keeps a *mitzvah* keeps himself safe,
         but he who doesn't care how he lives will die.

17   He who is kind to the poor is lending to ADONAI,
         and he will repay him for his good deed.

18   Discipline your child while there is hope,
         but don't get so angry that you kill him!

19   A violent-tempered person will be punished;
         if you try to save him from it, you make things worse.

20   Listen to advice, and accept discipline,
         so that in the end you will be wise.

21   One can devise many plans in one's mind,
         but ADONAI's plan will prevail.

22   A man's lust is his shame,
         and a poor man is better than a liar.

23   The fear of ADONAI leads to life;
         one who has it is satisfied and rests untouched by evil.

24   The lazy person buries his hand in the dish
         but doesn't even bother to bring it to his mouth.

25   If you strike a scorner,
          the simple will learn to act wisely;
      if you reprove the intelligent,
          he will understand what you mean.

26   One who mistreats his father and evicts his mother
          is a son who brings them shame and disgrace.

27   My son, if you stop heeding discipline,
          you will stray from the principles of knowledge.

28   A worthless witness mocks at justice,
          and the mouth of the wicked swallows wrongdoing.

29   Judgments are in store for scorners
          and blows for the backs of fools.

20 ¹   Wine is a mocker, strong liquor a rowdy;
          anyone led astray by it is unwise.

2   The dread of a king is like when a lion roars;
          he who makes him angry commits a life-threatening sin.

3   Avoiding quarrels brings a person honor;
          for any fool can explode in anger.

4   A lazy person won't plow in winter;
          so at harvest-time, when he looks, there is nothing.

5   The heart's real intentions are like deep water;
          but a person with discernment draws them out.

6   Most people announce that they show kindness,
          but who can find someone faithful [enough to do it]?

7   The righteous live a life of integrity;
          happy are their children after them.

8   The king seated on his judgment throne
          can winnow out all evil with his glance.

9   Who can say, "I have made my heart clean,
          I am cleansed from my sin"?

10   False weights and false measures —
          ADONAI detests them both.

11   The character of even a child is known by how he acts,
       by whether his deeds are pure and right.

12   The hearing ear and the seeing eye —
       ADONAI made them both.

13   If you love sleep, you will become poor;
       keep your eyes open, and you'll have plenty of food.

14   "Really bad stuff!" says the buyer [to the seller];
       then he goes off and brags [about his bargain].

15   A person may have gold and a wealth of pearls,
       but lips informed by knowledge are a precious jewel.

16   Seize his clothes, because he guaranteed a stranger's loan;
       take them as security for that unknown woman.

17   Food obtained by fraud may taste good,
       but later the mouth is full of gravel.

18   After consultation, plans succeed;
       so take wise advice when waging war.

19   A gossip goes around revealing secrets,
       so don't get involved with a talkative person.

20   Whoever curses his father or mother —
       his lamp will go out in total darkness.

21   Possessions acquired quickly at first
       will not be blessed in the end.

22   Don't say, "I'll pay back evil for evil";
       wait for ADONAI to save you.

23   ADONAI detests a double standard in weights,
       and false scales are not good.

24   A man's steps are ordered by ADONAI,
       so how can a person understand his own ways?

25   It is a snare to dedicate a gift to God rashly
       and reflect on the vows only afterwards.

26   A wise king winnows the wicked [from the righteous]
       and threshes them under the cartwheel.

27   The human spirit is a lamp of *Adonai*;
        it searches one's inmost being.

28   Grace and truth preserve a king;
        with grace he upholds his throne.

29   The pride of the young is their strength;
        the dignity of the old is gray hair.

30   Blows that wound purge away evil,
        yes, beatings [cleanse] one's inmost being.

21 ¹   The king's heart in *Adonai*'s hand is like streams of water —
        he directs it wherever he pleases.

2   All a person's ways are right in his own view,
        but *Adonai* weighs the heart.

3   To do what is right and just
        is more pleasing to *Adonai* than sacrifice.

4   Haughty looks, a proud heart —
        what the wicked plow is sin.

5   The plans of the diligent lead only to abundance;
        but all who rush in arrive only at want.

6   A fortune gained by a lying tongue
        is vapor dispersed [by] seekers of death.

7   The violence of the wicked will sweep them away,
        because they refuse to act justly.

8   A criminal's conduct is crooked,
        but the work of the pure is right.

9   It is better to live on a corner of the roof
        than to share the house with a nagging wife.

10   The wicked is set on evil;
        he doesn't pity even his neighbor.

11   When a scorner is punished, the simple become wiser;
        and when the wise is instructed, he takes hold of knowledge.

12   The Righteous One observes the house of the wicked;
        he overthrows the wicked to their ruin.

13   Whoever stops up his ears at the cry of the poor
          will himself cry, but not be answered.

14   A secret gift allays anger,
          and a bribe under the cloak the strongest fury.

15   Acting justly is a joy for the righteous
          but it terrifies evildoers.

16   The person who strays from the way of common sense
          will come to rest in the company of the dead.

17   Pleasure-lovers will suffer want;
          he who loves wine and oil won't get rich.

18   The wicked serve as a ransom for the righteous,
          and likewise the perfidious for the upright.

19   It is better to live in the desert
          than with a nagging, irritable wife.

20   In the home of the wise are fine treasures and oil,
          but a fool quickly devours it.

21   He who pursues righteousness and kindness
          finds life, prosperity and honor.

22   A wise man can go up into a city of warriors
          and undermine the strength in which it trusts.

23   Whoever guards his mouth and tongue
          keeps himself out of trouble.

24   "Scoffer" is what you call a proud, insolent person
          who acts with overweening conceit.

25   A lazy man's craving will kill him,
          because his hands refuse to work —
26   he covets greedily all day long;
          but a righteous person gives without holding back.

27   The sacrifice of the wicked is an abomination;
          how much more when he brings it with vile motives.

28   A lying witness is doomed,
          but one who heard [what was said] will testify successfully.

29 A wicked man puts on a bold face,
whereas the upright prepares his ways.

30 No wisdom, discernment or counsel
succeeds against ADONAI.

31 A horse may be prepared for the day of battle,
but victory comes from ADONAI.

22 1 Rather than wealth, choose a good reputation,
esteem over silver and gold.

2 Rich and poor have this in common —
ADONAI made them both.

3 The clever see trouble coming and hide;
the simple go on and pay the penalty.

4 The reward for humility is fear of ADONAI,
along with wealth, honor and life.

5 Thorns and snares beset the way of the stubborn;
he who values his life keeps his distance from them.

6 Train a child in the way he [should] go;
and, even when old, he will not swerve from it.

7 The rich rule the poor,
and the borrower is slave to the lender.

8 He who sows injustice reaps trouble,
and the rod of his angry outburst will fail.

9 He who is generous is blessed,
because he shares his food with the poor.

10 Throw the scoffer out, and quarreling goes too;
strife and insults cease.

11 He who loves the pure-hearted and is gracious in speech
will have the king as his friend.

12 The eyes of ADONAI protect [the man with] knowledge,
but he overturns the plans of a traitor.

13 A lazy man says, "There's a lion outside!
I'll be killed if I go out in the street!"

14   The mouth of an adulteress is a deep pit;
         the man with whom ADONAI is angry falls into it.

15   Doing wrong is firmly tied to the heart of a child,
         but the rod of discipline will drive it far away from him.

16   Both oppressing the poor to enrich oneself
         and giving to the rich yield only loss.

17   Pay attention, and listen to the words of the wise;
         apply your heart to my knowledge;
18   for it is pleasant to keep them deep within you;
         have all of them ready on your lips.
19   I want your trust to be in ADONAI;
         this is why I'm instructing you about them today.
20   I have written you worthwhile things
         full of good counsel and knowledge,
21   so you will know that these sayings are certainly true
         and bring back true sayings to him who sent you.

22   Don't exploit the helpless, because they are helpless,
         and don't crush the poor in court,
23   for ADONAI will plead their case for them
         and withhold life from those who defraud them.

24   Don't associate with an angry man;
         make no hot-tempered man your companion.
25   If you do, you may learn his ways
         and find yourself caught in a trap.

26   Don't be one of those who give pledges,
         guaranteeing loans made to others;
27   for if you don't have the wherewithal to pay,
         they will take your bed away from underneath you.

28   Don't move the ancient boundary stone
         set up by your ancestors.

29   Do you see a man skilled at his work?
         He will serve kings, not obscure people.

23 1   When you sit down to dine with a ruler,
         think carefully about who is before you.
2   If you have a big appetite,
         put a knife to your throat!
3   Don't be greedy for his delicacies,
         for they are deceptive food.

4   Don't exhaust yourself in pursuit of wealth;
      be smart enough to desist.
5   If you make your eyes rush at it,
      it's no longer there!
    For wealth will surely grow wings,
      like an eagle flying off to the sky.

6   Don't eat the food of a stingy man;
      don't be greedy for his delicacies.
7   For he is like someone who keeps accounts —
    "Eat! Drink!" he says to you,
      but he doesn't really mean it.
8   The little you eat you will vomit up,
      and your compliments will have been wasted.

9   Don't speak in the ears of a fool,
      for he will only despise the common sense in your words.

10   Don't move the ancient boundary stone
      or encroach on the land of the fatherless;
11   for their Redeemer is strong;
      he will take up their fight against you.

12   Apply your mind to discipline
      and your ears to words of knowledge.

13   Don't withhold discipline from a child —
      if you beat him with a stick, he won't die!
14   If you beat him with a stick,
      you will save him from Sh'ol.

15   My son, if your heart is wise,
      then my own heart too is glad;
16   my inmost being rejoices
      when your lips say what is right.

17   Don't envy sinners, but follow the example
      of those who always fear God;
18   for then you will have a future;
      what you hope for will not be cut off.

19   You, my son: listen, be wise,
      and set your mind on the right way.

20   Don't be one of those who guzzle wine
      or of those who eat meat to excess,
21   for both drunkard and glutton will become poor —
      drowsiness will clothe them with rags.

22   Listen to your father, who gave you life;
        and don't despise your mother when she gets old.

23   Buy the truth, don't sell it,
        also wisdom, discipline and discernment.

24   A righteous person's father will be filled with joy;
        yes, he whose son is wise will rejoice in him.
25   So let your father and mother be glad;
        let her who gave you birth rejoice.

26   My son, give me your heart;
        let your eyes observe my ways.

27   A prostitute is a deep ditch,
        and a forbidden woman like a narrow well.
28   She lies in wait to snatch her prey
        and adds to the number of faithless men.

29   Who has misery? Who has regret?
        Who fights and complains all the time?
    Who gets bruised for no good reason?
        Who has bloodshot eyes?
30   Those who spend their time over wine,
        those always trying out mixed drinks.
31   Don't gaze at the red wine
        as it gives its color to the cup.
    It may glide down smoothly now;
32   but in the end, it bites like a serpent —
        yes, it strikes like a poisonous snake.
33   Your eyes will see peculiar things,
        your mind will utter nonsense.
34   You will feel as if lying on the waves of the sea
        or sprawled on top of the mast —
35   "They hit me, but I didn't feel it!
        They beat me up, and I didn't even know it!
    When will I wake up? . . .
        I'll go get another drink."

24 ¹   Don't be envious of evil people,
        and don't desire to be with them.
2   For their minds are occupied with violence,
        and their lips speak of making trouble.

3   By wisdom a house is built,
        by understanding it is made secure,

4   and by knowledge its rooms are filled
      with all kinds of costly and pleasant possessions.

5   A wise man is strong;
      yes, a man of knowledge grows in strength.
6   For with clever strategy you wage your war,
      and victory comes from having many advisers.

7   Wisdom is too lofty for a fool;
      he keeps his mouth shut at the city gate.

8   He who plans to do evil
      people call a schemer.

9   The evil plans of the foolish are sin,
      and people detest a scorner.

10   If you slack off on a day of distress,
      your strength is small indeed.
11   Yes, rescue those being dragged off to death —
      won't you save those about to be killed?
12   If you say, "We knew nothing about it,"
      won't he who weighs hearts discern it?
    Yes, he who guards you will know it
      and repay each one as his deeds deserve.

13   My son, eat honey, for it is good;
      honeycomb drippings are sweet to your taste.
14   Know that wisdom is similar[ly sweet] to your soul;
      if you find it, then you will have a future,
      what you hope for will not be cut off.

15   Don't lurk like an outlaw near the home of the righteous,
      don't raid the place where he lives.
16   For though he falls seven times, he will get up again;
      it's the wicked who fail under stress.

17   Don't rejoice when your enemy falls;
      don't let your heart be glad when he stumbles.
18   For Adonai might see it, and it would displease him;
      he might withdraw his anger from your foe.

19   Don't get upset because of evildoers;
      don't be envious of the wicked.
20   For the evil person has no future —
      the lamp of the wicked will go out.

²¹ My son, don't get involved with revolutionaries,
    but fear *Adonai* and the king.
²² For disaster from them will suddenly appear,
    and who knows what ruin they both can cause?

²³ These also are sayings of the wise:

    Showing partiality in judgment is not good.
²⁴ He who tells the guilty, "You are innocent,"
    will be cursed by peoples, reviled by nations;
²⁵ but with those who condemn him, things will go well,
    and a good blessing will come upon them.

²⁶ Giving an honest answer
    is like giving a kiss.

²⁷ Prepare your outside work,
    and get things ready for yourself on the land;
    after that, build your house.

²⁸ Don't be a witness against your neighbor for no reason —
    would you use your lips to deceive?

²⁹ Don't say, "I'll do to him what he did to me,
    I'll pay him back what his deeds deserve."

³⁰ I passed by the field of the lazy man
    and the vineyard of the man lacking sense.
³¹ There it was, overgrown with thistles;
    the ground was covered with nettles,
    and its stone wall was broken down.
³² I looked, and I thought about it;
    I saw, and I learned this lesson:
³³ "I'll just lie here a bit, rest a little longer,
    just fold my hands for a little more sleep" —
³⁴ and poverty comes marching in on you,
    scarcity hits you like an invading soldier.

25 ¹ These also are proverbs of Shlomo; the men of Hizkiyah king of Y'hudah copied them out:

² God gets glory from concealing things;
    kings get glory from investigating things.
³ Like the sky for height or the earth for depth
    is the heart of kings — unfathomable.
⁴ Remove the impurities from the silver,
    and the smith has material to make a vessel.

5   Remove the wicked from the king's presence,
        and his throne will rest firmly on righteousness.

6   Don't put yourself forward in the king's presence;
        don't take a place among the great.

7   For it is better to be told, "Come up here,"
        than be degraded in the presence of a nobleman.

    What your eyes have seen,
8   don't rush to present in a dispute.
    For what will you do later on,
        if your neighbor puts you to shame?

9   Discuss your dispute with your neighbor,
        but don't reveal another person's secrets.

10   If you do, and he hears of it, he will disgrace you,
        and your bad reputation will stick.

11   Like apples of gold in settings of silver
        is a word appropriately spoken.

12   Like a gold earring, like a fine gold necklace
        is a wise reprover to a receptive ear.

13   Like the coldness of snow in the heat of the harvest
        is a faithful messenger to the one who sends him;
        he refreshes his master's spirit.

14   Like clouds and wind that bring no rain
        is he who boasts of gifts he never gives.

15   With patience a ruler may be won over,
        and a gentle tongue can break bones.

16   If you find honey, eat only what you need;
        for if you eat too much of it, you may throw it up;

17   so don't visit your neighbor too much,
        or he may get his fill of you and come to hate you.

18   Like a club, a sword or a sharp arrow
        is a person who gives false testimony against a neighbor.

19   Relying on an untrustworthy person in a time of trouble
        is like [relying on] a broken tooth or an unsteady leg.

20   Like removing clothes on a chilly day or like vinegar on soda
        is someone who sings songs to a heavy heart.

21   If someone who hates you is hungry, give him food to eat;
        and if he is thirsty, give him water to drink.

22   For you will heap fiery coals [of shame] on his head,
        and *Adonai* will reward you.

23 The north wind brings rain
    and a backbiting tongue, angry looks.

24 It is better to live on a corner of the roof
    than to share the house with a nagging wife.

25 Like cold water to a person faint from thirst
    is good news from a distant land.

26 Like a muddied spring or a polluted well
    is a righteous person who gives way before the wicked.

27 It isn't good to eat too much honey
    or to seek honor after honor.

28 Like a city breached, without walls,
    is a person who lacks self-control.

26 1 Like snow in summer or rain at harvest-time,
    so honor for a fool is out of place.

2 Like a fluttering sparrow or a flying swallow,
    an undeserved curse will come home to roost.

3 A whip for a horse, a bridle for a donkey,
    and a rod for the back of fools.

4 Don't answer a fool in terms of his folly,
    or you will be descending to his level;

5 but answer a fool as his folly deserves,
    so that he won't think he is wise.

6 Telling a message to a fool and sending him out
    is like cutting off one's feet and drinking violence.

7 The legs of the disabled hang limp and useless;
    likewise a proverb in the mouth of a fool.

8 Like one who ties his stone to the sling
    is he who gives honor to a fool.

9 Like a thorn branch in the hand of a drunk
    is a proverb in the mouth of a fool.

10 A master can make anything,
    but hiring a fool is like hiring some passer-by.

11 Just as a dog returns to his vomit,
    a fool repeats his folly.

12 Do you see someone who thinks himself wise?
    There is more hope for a fool than for him!

13 The lazy person says, "There's a lion in the streets!
    A lion is roaming loose out there!"

14   The door turns on its hinges,
        and the lazy man on his bed.

15   The lazy person buries his hand in the dish
        but is too tired to return it to his mouth.

16   A lazy man is wiser in his own view
        than seven who can answer with sense.

17   Like someone who grabs a dog by the ears
        is a passer-by who mixes in a fight not his own.

18   Like a madman shooting deadly arrows and firebrands
19   is one who deceives another, then says, "It was just a joke."

20   If there's no wood, the fire goes out;
        if nobody gossips, contention stops.

21   As coals are to embers and wood to fire
        is a quarrelsome person to kindling strife.

22   A slanderer's words are tasty morsels;
        they slide right down into the belly.

23   Like silver slag overlaid on a clay pot
        are lips that burn [with friendship] over a hating heart.

24   He who hates may hide it with his speech;
        but inside, he harbors deceit.

25   He may speak pleasantly, but don't trust him;
        for seven abominations are in his heart.

26   His hatred may be concealed by deceit,
        but his wickedness will be revealed in the assembly.

27   Whoever digs a pit will fall into it,
        and a stone will come back on the one who starts it rolling.

28   A lying tongue hates its victims,
        and a flattering mouth causes ruin.

27 ¹   Don't boast about tomorrow,
        for you don't know what the day may bring.

2   Let someone else praise you, not your own mouth,
        a stranger and not your own lips.

3   Stone is heavy and sand a dead weight,
        but a fool's provocation outweighs them both.

4   Fury is cruel and anger overwhelming,
        but who can stand up to jealousy?

5   Better open rebuke
         than hidden love.

6   Wounds from a friend are received as well-meant,
         but an enemy's kisses are insincere.

7   A person who is full loathes a honeycomb;
         but to the hungry, any bitter thing is sweet.

8   Like a bird that strays from its nest
         is a man who strays from his home.

9   Perfume and incense make the heart glad,
         [also] friendship sweet with advice from the heart.

10   Don't abandon a friend
         who is also a friend of your father.

     Don't enter your brother's house on the day of your calamity —
         better a neighbor nearby than a brother far away.

11   My son, become wise, and gladden my heart,
         so that I can answer my critics.

12   The clever see trouble coming and hide;
         the thoughtless go on and pay the penalty.

13   Seize his clothes because he guaranteed a stranger's loan;
         take them as security for that unknown woman.

14   Whoever greets his neighbor in a loud voice at dawn
         might just as well have cursed him.

15   A leak that keeps dripping on a rainy day
         and the nagging of a wife are the same —
16   whoever can restrain her can restrain the wind
         or keep perfume on his hand from making itself known.

17   Just as iron sharpens iron,
         a person sharpens the character of his friend.

18   Whoever tends the fig tree will eat its fruit,
         and he who is attentive to his master will be honored.

19   Just as water reflects the face,
         so one human heart reflects another.

20   Sh'ol and Abaddon are never satisfied,
          and human eyes are never satisfied.

21   The crucible [tests] silver, and the furnace [tests] gold,
          but a person [is tested] by [his reaction to] praise.

22   You can crush a fool in a mortar with a pestle,
        along with the grain being crushed;
          yet his foolishness will not leave him.

23   Take care to know the condition of your flocks,
          and pay attention to your herds.
24   For wealth doesn't last forever,
          neither does a crown through all generations.
25   When the hay has been mown, and the new grass appears,
          and the mountain greens have been gathered;
26   the lambs will provide your clothing,
          the goats will sell for enough to buy a field,
27   and there will be enough goat's milk
            to [buy] food for you and your household
            and maintenance for your servant-girls.

28 ¹   The wicked flee when no one pursues them;
          but the righteous, like lions, feel sure of themselves.

2   A land which transgresses [is punished by] having many rulers;
          but with a man of understanding and knowledge, stability is prolonged.

3   A poor man who oppresses the weak
          is like a downpour that sweeps away all the food.

4   Those who abandon *Torah* praise the wicked,
          but those who keep *Torah* fight them.

5   Evil people don't understand justice,
          but those who seek A DONAI understand everything.

6   Better to be poor and live an honest life
          than be crooked in one's ways, though rich.

7   A wise son observes *Torah*,
          but a friend of those lacking restraint shames his father.

8   He who increases his wealth by charging exorbitant interest
          amasses it for someone who will bestow it on the poor.

9
> If a person will not listen to *Torah*,
>> even his prayer is an abomination.

10
> Whoever causes the honest to pursue evil ways
> will himself fall into his own pit,
>> but the pure-hearted will inherit good.

11
> The rich man is wise in his own view,
>> but the poor who has discernment sees through him.

12
> When the just are triumphant, there is great rejoicing,
>> but when the wicked rise up, people hide.

13
> He who conceals his sins will not succeed;
>> he who confesses and abandons them will gain mercy.

14
> Happy the person who is never without fear,
>> but he who hardens his heart will fall into misfortune.

15
> Like a roaring lion or a bear prowling for food
>> is a wicked ruler over a poor people.

16
> A prince without discernment is a cruel oppressor,
>> but one who hates greed will prolong his life.

17
> Let a man weighed down with anyone's blood
>> flee to a pit; give him no support.

18
> Whoever lives blamelessly will be saved,
>> but he whose ways are crooked will fall in one [of those ways].

19
> He who farms his land will have plenty of food,
>> but he who follows futilities will have plenty of poverty.

20
> A trustworthy person will receive many blessings,
>> but one rushing to get rich will not go unpunished.

21
> To show partiality is not good,
>> though a person may do wrong for a crust of bread.

22
> He who is greedy rushes after riches,
>> not knowing that want will overtake him.

23
> He who rebukes another person
>> in the end gets more thanks than the flatterer.

24
> Whoever robs mother or father and says, "That's not a crime!"
>> is comrade to the destroyer.

25   A grasping disposition stirs up strife,
        but he who trusts in ADONAI will prosper.

26   He who trusts in himself is a fool,
        but he who lives by wisdom will escape.

27   He who gives to the poor will lack nothing,
        but he who hides his eyes will get curses in plenty.

28   When the wicked rise up, people hide;
        but when they perish, the righteous flourish.

29 1   He who remains stiffnecked after much rebuke
        will be suddenly and incurably broken.

2   When the righteous flourish, the people rejoice;
        but when the wicked are in power, the people groan.

3   Whoever loves wisdom brings joy to his father,
        but a patron of prostitutes wastes his wealth.

4   A king gives stability to a country by justice,
        but one who overtaxes it brings it to ruin.

5   A person who flatters his neighbor
        spreads a net for his own steps.

6   In an evil person's crime is a trap,
        but the righteous sing and rejoice.

7   The righteous understands the cause of the poor,
        but the wicked is unconcerned.

8   Scoffers can inflame a city,
        but the wise can calm the fury.

9   When a wise man argues with a foolish one,
        he meets anger and ridicule without relief.

10   Men of blood hate those who are pure
        and seek the life of the upright.

11   A fool gives vent to all his feelings,
        but the wise, thinking of afterwards, stills them.

12   If a ruler listens to lies,
        all his officials will be wicked.

13   The poor and the oppressor have this in common:
       ADONAI gives light to the eyes of both.

14   If a king steadfastly gives justice to the poor,
       his throne will be secure forever.

15   The rod and rebuke give wisdom,
       but a child left to himself brings shame on his mother.

16   When the wicked flourish, wrongdoing flourishes;
       but the righteous will witness their downfall.

17   Discipline your son, and he will give you rest;
       yes, he will be your delight.

18   Without a prophetic vision, the people throw off all restraint;
       but he who keeps *Torah* is happy.

19   A slave can't be disciplined with words;
       he may understand, but he won't respond.

20   Do you see someone too anxious to speak?
       There is more hope for a fool than for him.

21   A slave who is pampered from youth
       will in the end be ungrateful.

22   Angry people stir up strife;
       hot-tempered people commit many crimes.

23   The proud will be humbled,
       but the humble will be honored.

24   The accomplice of a thief hates himself;
       he hears himself put under oath but discloses nothing.

25   Fearing human beings is a snare;
       but he who trusts in ADONAI will be raised high [above danger].

26   Many seek the ruler's favor,
       but it is from ADONAI that each gets justice.

27   An unjust person is an abomination to the righteous,
       but he who lives uprightly is an abomination to the wicked.

30 ^{1} The words of Agur the son of Yakeh, the prophecy. The man says to Iti'el,
to Iti'el and Ukhal:

^{2} I am more boorish than anyone,
    I lack human discernment;
^{3} I have not learned enough wisdom
    to know the Holy One.

^{4} Who has gone up to heaven and come down?
Who has cupped the wind in the palms of his hands?
Who has wrapped up the waters in his cloak?
Who established all the ends of the earth?
What is his name, and what is his son's name?
Surely you know!

^{5} Every word of God's is pure;
    he shields those taking refuge in him.
^{6} Don't add anything to his words;
    or he will rebuke you, and you be found a liar.

^{7} [God,] I have asked two things of you;
    don't deny them to me as long as I live —
^{8} keep falsehood and futility far from me,
    and give me neither poverty nor wealth.
Yes, provide just the food I need today;
^{9} for if I have too much, I might deny you
    and say, "Who is ADONAI?"
And if I am poor, I might steal
    and thus profane the name of my God.

^{10} Never disparage a slave to his master,
    or he will curse you, and you will deserve it.

^{11} There is a type of people who curse their fathers
    and don't bless their mothers.
^{12} There is a type of people clean in their own view,
    but not cleansed from their filth.
^{13} There is a type of people — how haughty their look! —
    utterly supercilious!
^{14} There is a type of people whose teeth are like swords,
    yes, their fangs are knives;
they devour the poor from the earth,
    the needy from humankind.

^{15} The leech has two daughters;
    they cry, "Give! Give!"

Three things are never satisfied;
four never say, "Enough!" —
16   Sh'ol and a barren womb;
the earth, never satisfied with water;
and fire, which never says, "Enough!"

17 The eye that mocks his father
and scorns obeying his mother
will be pecked out by the ravens in the valley,
and the vultures will eat it.

18 Three things are too wonderful for me,
four beyond my knowledge —
19   the way of an eagle in the sky,
the way of a snake on a rock,
the way of a ship on the open sea,
and the way of a man with a girl.

20 This is how an unfaithful wife behaves:
she eats, wipes her mouth, and says, "I did nothing wrong."

21 Three things make the earth quake,
four things it can't bear —
22   a slave who becomes king,
a boor gorged with food,
23   a hated [wife] when her husband takes her [back],
and a slave-girl who inherits from her mistress.

24 Four things on the earth are small;
nevertheless, they are very wise —
25 the ants, a species not strong,
yet they store up their food in the summer;
26 the coneys, a species with little power,
yet they make their home in the rocks;
27 the locusts, who have no king,
yet they all march out in ranks;
28 and the spiders, which you can catch in your hand,
yet they are in the king's palace.

29 Three things are stately in their stride,
four of stately gait —
30   the lion, mightiest of beasts,
which turns aside for no one;
31   the greyhound, the billy-goat
and the king when his army is with him.

32   If you have been boorish, exalting yourself,
      or if you have been scheming,
         lay your hand on your mouth.
33   For as pressing milk produces butter
      and pressing the nose produces blood,
         so pressing out anger produces strife.

31 ¹ The words of King L'mu'el, the prophecy with which his mother disciplined him:

2   No, my son! No, son of my womb!
      No, son of my vows!
3   Don't give your strength to women
      or your ways to that which destroys kings.
4   It is not for kings, L'mu'el,
         not for kings to drink wine;
      it is not for rulers to ask,
         "Where can I find strong liquor?"
5   For they may drink, then forget what has been decreed,
         and pervert the justice due to the poor.
6   Give strong liquor to one who is perishing,
         wine to the deeply depressed;
7   let him drink, forget his poverty
         and cease to remember his troubles.

8   Speak up for those who can't speak for themselves,
         for the rights of all who need an advocate.
9   Speak up, judge righteously,
         defend the cause of the poor and the needy.

א   ¹⁰ Who can find a capable wife?
         Her value is far beyond that of pearls.
ב   ¹¹ Her husband trusts her from his heart,
         and she will prove a great asset to him.
ג   ¹² She works to bring him good, not harm,
         all the days of her life.

ד   ¹³ She procures a supply of wool and flax
         and works with willing hands.
ה   ¹⁴ She is like those merchant vessels,
         bringing her food from far away.
ו   ¹⁵ It's still dark when she rises to give food to her household
         and orders to the young women serving her.

ז   ¹⁶ She considers a field, then buys it,
         and from her earnings she plants a vineyard.

ח ¹⁷ She gathers her strength around her
and throws herself into her work.

ט ¹⁸ She sees that her business affairs go well;
her lamp stays lit at night.

י ¹⁹ She puts her hands to the staff with the flax;
her fingers hold the spinning rod.

כ ²⁰ She reaches out to embrace the poor
and opens her arms to the needy.

ל ²¹ When it snows, she has no fear for her household;
since all of them are doubly clothed.

מ ²² She makes her own quilts;
she is clothed in fine linen and purple.

נ ²³ Her husband is known at the city gates
when he sits with the leaders of the land.

ס ²⁴ She makes linen garments and sells them;
she supplies the merchants with sashes.

ע ²⁵ Clothed with strength and dignity,
she can laugh at the days to come.

פ ²⁶ When she opens her mouth, she speaks wisely;
on her tongue is loving instruction.

צ ²⁷ She watches how things go in her house,
not eating the bread of idleness.

ק ²⁸ Her children arise; they make her happy;
her husband too, as he praises her:

ר ²⁹ "Many women have done wonderful things,
but you surpass them all!"

ש ³⁰ Charm can lie, beauty can vanish,
but a woman who fears ADONAI should be praised.

ת ³¹ Give her a share in what she produces;
let her works speak her praises at the city gates.

Iyov
JOB

1 ¹ There was a man in the land of 'Utz whose name was Iyov. This man was blameless and upright; he feared God and shunned evil. ² Seven sons and three daughters were born to him. ³ He owned 7,000 sheep, 3,000 camels, 500 pairs of oxen and 500 female donkeys, as well as a great number of servants; so that he was the wealthiest man in the east.

⁴ It was the custom of his sons to give banquets, each on his set day in his own house; and they would invite their three sisters to eat and drink with them. ⁵ After a cycle of banquets, Iyov would send for them to come and be consecrated; then he would get up early in the morning and offer burnt offerings for each of them, because Iyov said, "My sons might have sinned and blasphemed God in their thoughts." This is what Iyov did every time.

⁶ It happened one day that the sons of God came to serve ADONAI, and among them came the Adversary [Hebrew: *Satan*]. ⁷ ADONAI asked the Adversary, "Where are you coming from?" The Adversary answered ADONAI, "From roaming through the earth, wandering here and there." ⁸ ADONAI asked the Adversary, "Did you notice my servant Iyov, that there's no one like him on earth, a blameless and upright man who fears God and shuns evil?" ⁹ The Adversary answered ADONAI, "Is it for nothing that Iyov fears God? ¹⁰ You've put a protective hedge around him, his house and everything he has. You've prospered his work, and his livestock are spread out all over the land. ¹¹ But if you reach out your hand and touch whatever he has, without doubt he'll curse you to your face!" ¹² ADONAI said to the Adversary, "Here! Everything he has is in your hands, except that you are not to lay a finger on his person." Then the Adversary went out from the presence of ADONAI.

¹³ One day when Iyov's sons and daughters were eating and drinking in their oldest brother's house, ¹⁴ a messenger came to him and said, "The oxen were plowing, with the donkeys grazing near them, ¹⁵ when a raiding party from Sh'va came and carried them off; they put the servants to the sword too, and I'm the only one who escaped to tell you."

¹⁶ While he was still speaking, another one came and said, "Fire from God fell from the sky and burned up the sheep and the servants; it completely destroyed them, and I'm the only one who escaped to tell you."

¹⁷ While he was still speaking, another one came and said, "The Kasdim, three bands of them, fell on the camels and carried them off; they put the servants to the sword too, and I'm the only one who escaped to tell you."

¹⁸ While he was still speaking, another one came and said, "Your sons and daughters were eating and drinking wine in their oldest brother's house, ¹⁹ when

suddenly a strong wind blew in from over the desert. It struck the four corners of the house, so that it fell on the young people; they are dead, and I'm the only one who escaped to tell you."

²⁰ Iyov got up, tore his coat, shaved his head, fell down on the ground and worshipped; ²¹ he said,

> "Naked I came from my mother's womb,
> and naked I will return there.
> ADONAI gave; ADONAI took;
> blessed be the name of ADONAI."

²² In all this Iyov neither committed a sin nor put blame on God.

2 ¹ Another day came when the sons of God came to serve ADONAI, and among them came the Adversary to serve ADONAI. ² ADONAI asked the Adversary, "Where are you coming from?" The Adversary answered ADONAI, "From roaming through the earth, wandering here and there." ³ ADONAI asked the Adversary, "Did you notice my servant Iyov, that there's no one like him on earth, a blameless and upright man who fears God and shuns evil, and that he still holds on to his integrity, even though you provoked me against him to destroy him for no reason?" ⁴ The Adversary answered ADONAI, "Skin for skin! A person will give up everything he has to save his life. ⁵ But if you reach out your hand and touch his flesh and bone, without doubt he'll curse you to your face!" ⁶ ADONAI said to the Adversary, "Here! He is in your hands, except that you are to spare his life."

⁷ Then the Adversary went out from the presence of ADONAI and struck Iyov down with horrible infected sores from the sole of his foot to the crown of his head. ⁸ He took a piece of a broken pot to scratch himself and sat down in the pile of ashes. ⁹ His wife asked him, "Why do you still hold on to your integrity? Curse God, and die!" ¹⁰ But he answered her, "You're talking like a low-class woman! Are we to receive the good at God's hands but reject the bad?" In all this Iyov did not say one sinful word.

¹¹ Now when Iyov's three friends heard of all the calamities that had overwhelmed him, they all came. Each came from his own home — Elifaz from Teiman, Bildad from Shuach and Tzofar from Na'amah. They had agreed to meet together in order to come and offer him sympathy and comfort. ¹² When they saw him from a distance, they couldn't even recognize him. They wept aloud, tore their coats and threw dust over their heads toward heaven. ¹³ Then they sat down with him on the ground. For seven days and seven nights, no one spoke a word to him; because they saw how much he was suffering. ¹⁴⁽³:¹⁾ At length, Iyov broke the silence and cursed the day of his [birth].

3 ¹⁽²⁾ Iyov said,

²⁽³⁾
> "Perish the day I was born
> and the night that said, 'A man is conceived.'

³⁽⁴⁾
> May that day be darkness,
> may God on high not seek it,
> may no light shine on it,

4(5)   may gloom dark as death defile it,
may clouds settle on it,
may it be terrified by its own blackness.

5(6)   "As for that night, may thick darkness seize it,
may it not be joined to the days of the year,
may it not be numbered among the months;

6(7)   may that night be desolate,
may no cry of joy be heard in it;

7(8)   may those who curse days curse it,
those who[se curses] could rouse Livyatan;

8(9)   may the stars of its twilight be dark,
may it look for light but get none,
may it never see the shimmer of dawn —

9(10)   because it didn't shut the doors of the womb I was in
and shield my eyes from trouble.

10(11)   "If I had been stillborn,
if I had died at birth,

11(12)   had there been no knees to receive me
or breasts for me to suck.

12(13)   Then I would be lying still and in peace,
I would have slept and been at rest,

13(14)   along with kings and their earthly advisers,
who rebuilt ruins for themselves,

14(15)   or with princes who had [plenty of] gold,
who filled their houses with silver.

15(16)   Or I could have been like a hidden, miscarried
child that never saw light.

16(17)   "There the wicked cease their raging,
there the weary are at rest,

17(18)   prisoners live at peace together
without hearing a taskmaster's yells.

18(19)   Great and small alike are there,
and the slave is free of his master.

19(20)   "So why must light be given to the miserable
and life to the bitter in spirit?

20(21)   They long for death, but it never comes;
they search for it more than for buried treasure;

21(22)   when at last they find the grave,
they are so happy they shout for joy.

22(23)   [Why give light] to a man who wanders blindly,
whom God shuts in on every side?

23(24)   "My sighing serves in place of my food,
and my groans pour out in a torrent;

24(25)   for the thing I feared has overwhelmed me,
        what I dreaded has happened to me.
25(26)   I have no peace, no quiet, no rest;
        and anguish keeps coming."

4 ¹ Then Elifaz the Teimani spoke up:

2   "If one tries to speak to you, will you mind?
        Yet who could keep from speaking?
3   You have given moral instruction to many,
        you have firmed up feeble hands,
4   your words have supported those who were stumbling,
        and you have strengthened the weak-kneed.

5   "But now it comes to you, and you are impatient;
        at the first touch, you are in shock.
6   Isn't your fear of God your assurance,
        and the integrity of your ways your hope?

7   "Think back: what innocent person has perished?
        Since when are the upright destroyed?
8   What I see is that those who plow sin
        and sow trouble reap just that.
9   At a breath from God, they perish;
        at a blast from his anger, they are consumed.
10   The lion may growl, the king lion may roar,
        but that old lion's teeth are broken;
11   so the lion succumbs from lack of prey,
        and the lion's cubs are scattered.

12   "For a word was stealthily brought to me,
        my ear caught only a whisper of it.
13   In passing thoughts flashing through visions at night,
        when sleep lies heavy on people,
14   a shiver of horror came over me;
        it made all my bones tremble.
15   Then a spirit passed in front of my face;
        the hair of my flesh stood on end.
16   It stood still,
        but I couldn't make out its appearance;
        yet the form stayed there before my eyes.
        Then I heard a subdued voice:
17   'Can a human be seen by God as righteous?
        Can a mortal be pure before his maker?
18   [God] doesn't trust his own servants,
        he finds fault even with his angels;
19   much more those living in houses of clay,
        whose foundation is in the dust.

20 They are crushed more easily than a worm;
shattered between morning and evening;
they perish forever, and no one takes notice.
21 Their cord within them is pulled up;
then they die, without ever gaining wisdom.'

5 1 "Call if you like, but will anyone answer?
To which of the holy ones will you turn?
2 For anger kills the fool,
and envy slays the silly.
3 I watch as a fool establishes roots,
but I curse his home with sudden [destruction] —
4 his children are far from help,
publicly humiliated, with no one to rescue;
5 the hungry eat up his harvest,
taking it even from among thorns,
while the thirsty are panting,
eager to swallow his wealth.
6 For misery does not come from the dust
or trouble spring from the ground.
7 No, people are born for trouble
as surely as sparks fly upward.

8 "If I were you, I would seek God;
I would make my plea to him.
9 For God does great deeds beyond investigation,
wonders beyond all reckoning.
10 He gives rain to the earth,
pours water down on the fields.
11 He raises the lowly on high
and lifts mourners to safety.
12 He frustrates the schemes of the cunning,
so that they achieve no success;
13 trapping the crafty in their own tricks
and foiling quickly the plans of the false.
14 They meet with darkness during the day,
groping at noon like at night.
15 But he saves the poor from the sword, their mouth,
and from the clutches of the strong;
16 so the poor can hope again;
and injustice shuts its mouth.

17 "How happy the person whom God corrects!
So don't despise *Shaddai*'s discipline.
18 For he wounds, but he bandages the sore;
his hands may strike, but they also heal.

19 He will rescue you from six disasters;
   yes, in seven no harm will touch you.
20 In famine, he will save you from death,
   and in war, from the power of the sword.
21 You will be shielded from the lash of the tongue,
   and you won't have to fear destruction when it comes —
22 you'll be able to laugh at destruction and famine.
   Also you won't have to fear wild animals,
23 for you will be in league with the stones in the field,
   and the wild animals will be at peace with you.
24 You will know that your tent is safe;
   you will look round your home and miss nothing.
25 You will know that your descendants are many,
   your offspring like grass [growing thick] in the fields.
26 You will come to your grave at a ripe old age,
   like a pile of grain that arrives in season.

27 "We've looked into this, and that's how it is;
   listen, and know that it's for your own good."

6 ¹ Iyov responded:

2 "I wish my frustration could be weighed,
   all my calamities laid on the scales!
3 They would outweigh the sands of the seas!
   No wonder, then, that my words come out stammered!
4 For the arrows of *Shaddai* find their mark in me,
   and my spirit is drinking in their poison;
   the terrors of God are arrayed against me.

5 "Does a wild donkey bray when it has grass?
   Does an ox low when it has fodder?
6 Can food without flavor be eaten without salt?
   Do egg whites have any taste?
7 I refuse to touch them;
   such food makes me sick.

8 "If only I could have my wish granted,
   and God would give me what I'm hoping for —
9 that God would decide to crush me,
   that he would let his hand loose and cut me off!
10 Then I would feel consoled;
   so that even in the face of unending pain,
   I would be able to rejoice;
   for I have not denied the words of the Holy One.

11 "Have I enough strength to go on waiting?
   What end can I expect, that I should be patient?

12   Is my strength the strength of stones?
     Is my flesh made of bronze?

13   Clearly, I have no help in myself;
     common sense has been driven from me.

14   "A friend should be kind to an unhappy man,
     even to one who abandons *Shaddai.*

15   But my brothers are as deceptive as *vadis,*
     as *vadi* streams that soon run dry;

16   they may turn dark with ice
     and be hidden by piled-up snow;

17   but as the weather warms up, they vanish;
     when it's hot, they disappear.

18   Their courses turn this way and that;
     they go up into the confusing waste and are lost.

19   The caravans from Tema look for them,
     the travelers from Sh'va hope to find them;

20   but they are disappointed, because they were confident;
     on arrival there, they are frustrated.

21   "For now, you have become like that —
     just seeing my calamity makes you afraid.

22   Did I say to you, 'Give me something,'
     or, 'From your wealth, offer a bribe on my behalf,'

23   or, 'Save me from the enemy's grip,'
     or, 'Redeem me from the clutches of oppressors'?

24   "Teach me, and I will be silent.
     Make me understand how I am at fault.

25   Honest words are forceful indeed,
     but what do your arguments prove?

26   Do you think [your own] words constitute argument,
     while the speech of a desperate man is merely wind?

27   I suppose you would even throw dice for an orphan
     or barter away your friend!

28   "So now, I beg you, look at me!
     Would I lie to your face?

29   Think it over, please; don't let wrong be done.
     Think it over again: my cause is just.

30   Am I saying something wrong?
     Can't I recognize trouble when I taste it?

7 1   "Human life on earth is like serving in the army;
     yes, we drudge through our days like a hired worker,

2   like a slave longing for shade,
     like a worker thinking only of his wages.

3   So I am assigned months of meaninglessness;
    troubled nights are my lot.
4   When I lie down, I ask,
    'When can I get up?'
    But the night is long, and I keep tossing
    to and fro until daybreak.
5   My flesh is clothed with worms and dirt,
    my skin forms scabs that ooze pus.
6   My days pass more swiftly than a weaver's shuttle
    and come to their end without hope.

7   "Remember that my life is but a breath;
    my eyes will never again see good times.
8   The eye that now sees me will see me no more;
    while your eyes are on me, I will be gone.
9   Like a cloud dissolving and disappearing,
    so he who descends to Sh'ol won't come back up.
10   He will not return again to his house,
    and his home will know him no more.

11   "Therefore I will not restrain my mouth
    but will speak in my anguish of spirit
    and complain in my bitterness of soul.
12   Am I the sea, or some sea monster,
    that you put a guard over me?
13   When I think that my bed will comfort me,
    that my couch will relieve my complaint,
14   then you terrify me with dreams
    and frighten me with visions.
15   I would rather be strangled;
    death would be better than these bones of mine.
16   I hate it! I won't live forever,
    so leave me alone, for my life means nothing.

17   "What are mere mortals, that you make so much of them?
    Why do you keep them on your mind?
18   Why examine them every morning
    and test them every moment?
19   Won't you ever take your eyes off of me,
    at least long enough for me to swallow my spit?

20   "Suppose I do sin — how do I harm you,
    you scrutinizer of humanity?
    Why have you made me your target,
    so that I am a burden to you?
21   Why don't you pardon my offense
    and take away my guilt?

For soon I will lie down in the dust;
you will seek me, but I will be gone."

8 ¹ Bildad the Shuchi spoke next:

2   "How long will you go on talking like this?
What you are saying is raging wind!
3   Does God distort judgment?
Does *Shaddai* pervert justice?
4   If your children sinned against him,
he left them to be victims of their own offense.

5   "If you will earnestly seek God
and plead for *Shaddai*'s favor,
6   if you are pure and upright;
then he will rouse himself for you
and fulfill your needs.
7   Then, although your beginnings were small,
your future will be very great indeed.

8   "Ask the older generation,
and consider what their ancestors found out;
9   for we who were born yesterday know nothing,
our days on earth are but a shadow.
10   They will teach you, they will tell you,
they will say what is in their hearts:
11   'Can papyrus grow except in a marsh?
Can swamp grass flourish without water?
12   While still green, before being cut down,
it dries up faster than any other plant.
13   Such are the paths of all who forget God;
the hope of a hypocrite will perish —
14   his confidence is mere gossamer,
his trust a spider's web.
15   He can lean on his house, but it won't stand;
he can hold on to it, but it won't last;
16   [for its destruction will come] like the lush growth
of a plant in the sun,
its shoots may spread out all over its garden,
17   but meanwhile its roots cause the stone house
to collapse, as it seizes hold of the rocks;
18   someone who tears it away from its place
denies he has ever seen it.
19   Yes, this is the "joy" of the way [of the godless],
and out of the dust will spring up others [like him].'

20   "Look, God will not reject a blameless man;
nor will he uphold wrongdoers.

21 He will yet fill your mouth with laughter
   and your lips with shouts of joy.
22 Those who hate you will be clothed with shame,
   and the tent of the wicked will cease to exist."

9 ¹ Then Iyov responded:

2 "Indeed, I know that this is so;
   but how can a human win a case against God?
3 Whoever might want to argue with him
   could not answer him one [question] in a thousand.
4 His heart is so wise, his strength so great —
   who can resist him and succeed?

5 "He moves the mountains, although they don't know it,
   when he overturns them in his anger.
6 He shakes the earth from its place;
   its supporting pillars tremble.
7 He commands the sun, and it fails to rise;
   he shuts up the stars under his seal.
8 He alone spreads out the sky
   and walks on the waves in the sea.
9 He made the Great Bear, Orion, the Pleiades
   and the hidden constellations of the south.
10 He does great, unsearchable things,
   wonders beyond counting.
11 He can go right by me, and I don't see him;
   he moves past without my being aware of him.
12 If he kills [people], who will ask why?
   Who will say to him, 'What are you doing?'
13 God will not withdraw his anger —
   even Rahav's supporters submit to him.

14 "How much less can I answer him
   and select my arguments against him!
15 Even if I were right, I wouldn't answer;
   I could only ask for mercy from my judge.
16 If I summoned him, and he answered me,
   I still can't believe he would listen to my plea.
17 He could break me with a storm;
   he could multiply my wounds for no reason,
18 to the point where I couldn't even breathe —
   with such bitterness he could fill me!
19 If it's a matter of force, look how mighty he is;
   if justice, who can summon him to court?
20 Even if I'm right, my own mouth will condemn me;
   if I'm innocent, it would pronounce me guilty.

21 "I am innocent. Don't I know myself?
  But I've had enough of this life of mine!
22 So I say it's all the same —
  he destroys innocent and wicked alike.
23 When disaster brings sudden death,
  he laughs at the plight of the innocent.
24 The earth has been given to the power of the wicked;
  he covers the faces of its judges —
  if it isn't he, then who is it?
25 My days pass on more swiftly than a runner;
  they flee without seeing anything good.
26 They skim by like skiffs built of reeds,
  like an eagle swooping down on its prey.

27 "If I say, 'I'll forget my complaining,
  I'll put off my sad face and be cheerful,'
28 then I'm still afraid of all my pain,
  and I know you will not hold me innocent.
29 I will be condemned,
  so why waste my efforts?
30 Even if I washed myself in melted snow
  and cleansed my hands with lye,
31 you would plunge me into the muddy pit,
  till my own clothes would detest me.

32 "For he is not merely human like me;
  there is no answer that I could give him
  if we were to come together in court.
33 There is no arbitrator between us
  who could lay his hand on us both.
34 If he would remove his rod from me
  and not let his terrors frighten me,
35 then I would speak without fear of him;
  for when I'm alone, I'm not afraid.

10 1 "I am just worn out.

  "By my life [I swear],
  I will never abandon my complaint;
  I will speak out in my soul's bitterness.
2 I will say to God, 'Don't condemn me!
  Tell me why you are contending with me.
3 Do you gain some advantage from oppressing,
  from spurning what your own hands made,
  from shining on the schemes of the wicked?
4 Do you have eyes of flesh?
  Do you see as humans see?

5   Are your days like the days of mortals?
      Are your years like human years,
6   that you have to seek my guilt
      and search out my sin?
7   You know that I won't be condemned,
      yet no one can rescue me from your power.
8   Your own hands shaped me, they made me;
      so why do you turn and destroy me?
9   Please remember that you made me, like clay;
      will you return me to dust?
10   Didn't you pour me out like milk,
      then let me thicken like cheese?
11   You clothed me with skin and flesh
      you knit me together with bones and sinews.
12   You granted me life and grace;
      your careful attention preserved my spirit.

13   "'Yet you hid these things in your heart;
      I know what your secret purpose was —
14   to watch until I would sin
      and then not absolve me of my guilt.
15   If I am wicked, woe to me! —
      but if righteous, I still don't dare raise my head,
      because I am so filled with shame,
      so soaked in my misery.
16   You rise up to hunt me like a lion,
      and you keep treating me in such peculiar ways.
17   You keep producing fresh witnesses against me,
      your anger against me keeps growing,
      your troops assail me, wave after wave.

18   "'Why did you bring me out of the womb?
      I wish I had died there where no eye could see me.
19   I would have been as if I had never existed,
      I would have been carried from womb to grave.
20   Aren't my days few? So stop!
      Leave me alone, so I can cheer up a little
21   before I go to the place of no return,
      to the land of darkness and death-dark gloom,
22   a land of gloom like darkness itself,
      of dense darkness and utter disorder,
      where even the light is dark.'"

11 ¹ Next Tzofar the Na'amati spoke up:

2   "Shouldn't this torrent of words be answered?
      Does talking a lot make a person right?

³ Is your babble supposed to put others to silence?
When you mock, is no one to make you ashamed?

⁴ "You claim that your teaching is pure;
you tell [God], 'I am clean in your sight.'

⁵ I wish that God would speak,
would open his mouth to answer you,

⁶ would tell you the secrets of wisdom,
which is worth twice as much as common sense.
Understand that God is demanding of you
less than your guilt deserves.

⁷ "Can you penetrate God's depths?
Can you find out *Shaddai*'s limits?

⁸ They're as high as heaven; what can you do?
They're deeper than Sh'ol; what can you know?

⁹ Their extent is longer than the earth
and broader than the sea.

¹⁰ If he passes through, puts in prison
and assembles [for judgment], who can prevent him?

¹¹ For he knows when people are worthless;
so if he sees iniquity, won't he look into it?

¹² "An empty man can gain understanding,
even if he was born like a wild donkey.

¹³ If you will set your heart right,
if you will spread out your hands toward him,

¹⁴ if you will put your iniquity at a distance
and not let unrighteousness remain in your tents,

¹⁵ then when you lift up your face, there will be no defect;
you will be firm and free from fear.

¹⁶ "For you will forget your misery;
you'll remember it like a flood that passed through long ago;

¹⁷ your life will be brighter than noon;
even its darkness will be like morning.

¹⁸ You will be confident, because there is hope;
you will look around you and lie down secure;

¹⁹ you will rest, and no one will make you afraid.
Many will seek your favor;

²⁰ but the eyes of the wicked will fail [to find comfort].
They will find no way to escape,
and their hope will turn to complete disappointment."

12 ¹ Iyov responded:

² "No doubt you are [the only] people [that matter];
and when you die, so will wisdom.

3   But I too have a brain, as much as you,
In no way am I inferior to you.
Besides, who doesn't know things like these?

4   "Anyone who calls on God,
and he answers him,
becomes a laughingstock to his friends —
they make fun of an innocent, blameless man.

5   Those at ease have contempt for misfortune,
for the blow that strikes somebody already staggering.

6   The tents of robbers prosper,
[the homes of] those who anger God are secure,
those who carry their gods in their hands.

7   "But ask the animals — they will teach you —
and the birds in the air — they will tell you;

8   or speak to the earth — it will teach you —
and the fish in the sea will inform you:

9   every one of them knows
that the hand of *Adonai* has done this!

10   In his hand is the life of every living thing
and the spirit of every human being.

11   Shouldn't the ear test words,
just as the palate tastes food?

12   Is wisdom [only] with aged men?
discernment [only] with long life?

13   "With God are wisdom and power;
he has [good] counsel and understanding.

14   When he breaks something down, it can't be rebuilt;
when he imprisons someone, he can't be released.

15   When he holds back water, there is drought;
when he sends it out, it overruns the land.

16   With him are strength and common sense;
both the misled and those who mislead are his.

17   He leads counselors away captive,
he makes fools of judges.

18   He removes authority from kings,
then binds them up [as prisoners].

19   He leads *cohanim* away captive
and overthrows those long in power.

20   Those who are trusted he deprives of speech,
and he removes the discernment of the aged.

21   He pours contempt on princes
and loosens the belt of the strong.

22   He discloses the deepest recesses of darkness
and brings light into shadows dark as death.

23 He makes nations great and destroys them;
   he enlarges nations, then leads them away.

24 He removes understanding from a country's leaders
   and makes them wander in trackless deserts.

25 They grope in unlit darkness;
   he makes them stagger like drunks.

13¹ "All this I have seen with my own eyes;
   with my own ears I have heard and understood it.

2 Whatever you know, I know too;
   I am not inferior to you.

3 However, it's *Shaddai* I want to speak with;
   I want to prove my case to God.

4 But you, what you do is whitewash with lies;
   you are all witch doctors!

5 I wish you would just stay silent;
   for you, that would be wisdom!

6 "Now listen to my reasoning,
   pay attention to how I present my dispute.

7 Is it for God's sake that you speak so wickedly?
   for him that you talk deceitfully?

8 Do you need to take his side
   and plead God's case for him?

9 If he examines you, will all go well?
   Can you deceive him, as one man deceives another?

10 If you are secretly flattering [him],
   he will surely rebuke you.

11 Doesn't God's majesty terrify you?
   Aren't you overcome with dread of him?

12 Your maxims are garbage-proverbs;
   your answers crumble like clay.

13 "So be quiet! Let me be! I'll do the talking,
   come on me what may!

14 Why am I taking my flesh in my teeth,
   taking my life in my hands?

15 Look, he will kill me — I don't expect more,
   but I will still defend my ways to his face.

16 And this is what will save me —
   that a hypocrite cannot appear before him.

17 "Listen closely, then, to my words;
   pay attention to what I am saying.

18 Here, now, I have prepared my case;
   I know I am in the right.

19 If anyone can contend with me,
   I will be quiet and die!

20   "Only grant two things to me, God;
        then I won't hide myself from your face —
21   take your hand away from me,
        and don't let fear of you frighten me.
22   Then, if you call, I will answer.
        Or let me speak, and you, answer me!
23   How many crimes and sins have I committed?
        Make me know my transgression and sin.
24   Why do you hide your face
        and think of me as your enemy?
25   Do you want to harass a wind-driven leaf?
        do you want to pursue a dry straw?
26   Is this why you draw up bitter charges against me
        and punish me for the faults of my youth?
27   You put my feet in the stocks,
        you watch me closely wherever I go,
        you trace out each footprint of mine —
28   though [my body] decays like something rotten
        or like a moth-eaten garment.

14 ¹   "A human being, born from a woman,
        lives a short, trouble-filled life.
2   He comes up like a flower and withers away,
        flees like a shadow, doesn't last.
3   You fix your eyes on a creature like this?
        You drag him to court with you?
4   Who can bring what is pure from something impure?
        No one!
5   Since his days are fixed in advance,
        the number of his months is known to you,
        and you have fixed the limits which he can't cross;
6   look away from him, and let him be;
        so that, like a hired worker,
        he can finish his day in peace.

7   "For a tree, there is hope
        that if cut down, it will sprout again,
        that its shoots will continue to grow.
8   Even if its roots grow old in the earth
        and its stump dies in the ground,
9   yet at the scent of water it will bud
        and put forth branches like a young plant.
10   But when a human being grows weak and dies,
        he expires; and then where is he?
11   Just as water in a lake disappears,
        as a river shrinks and dries up;
12   so a person lies down and doesn't arise —

until the sky no longer exists;
it will not awaken,
it won't be roused from its sleep.

13 "I wish you would hide me in Sh'ol,
conceal me until your anger has passed,
then fix a time and remember me!

14 If a man dies, will he live again?
I will wait all the days of my life
for my change to come.

15 You will call, and I will answer you;
you will long to see what you made again.

16 Whereas now you count each step of mine,
then you will not keep watch for my sin.

17 You will seal up my crime in a bag
and cover over my iniquity.

18 "Just as a mountain erodes and falls away,
its rock is removed from its place,

19 the water wears away its stones,
and the floods wash away its soil,
so you destroy a person's hope.

20 You overpower him, and he passes on;
you change his appearance and send him away.

21 His children earn honor, but he doesn't know it;
or they are brought low, but he doesn't notice.

22 He feels pain only for his own flesh;
he laments only for himself."

15 ¹ Then Elifaz the Teimani spoke:

2 "Should a wise man answer with hot-air arguments?
Should he fill up his belly with the hot east wind?

3 Should he reason with useless talk
or make speeches that do him no good?

4 "Why, you are abolishing fear of God
and hindering prayer to him!

5 Your iniquity is teaching you how to speak,
and deceit is your language of choice.

6 Your own mouth condemns you, not I;
your own lips testify against you.

7 "Were you the firstborn of the human race,
brought forth before the hills?

8 Do you listen in on God's secrets?
Do you limit wisdom to yourself?

9   What do you know that we don't know?
    What discernment do you have that we don't?
10 With us are gray-haired men, old men,
    men much older than your father.
11 Are the comfortings of God not enough for you,
    or a word that deals gently with you?
12 Why does your heart carry you away,
    and why do your eyes flash angrily,
13 so that you turn your spirit against God
    and let such words escape your mouth?

14 "What is a human being, that he could be innocent,
    someone born from a woman, that he could be righteous?
15 God doesn't trust even his holy ones;
    no, even the heavens are not innocent in his view.
16 How much less one loathesome and corrupt,
    a human being, who drinks iniquity like water.

17 "I will tell you — hear me out!
    I will recount what I have seen;
18 wise men have told it,
    and it wasn't hidden from their fathers either,
19 to whom alone the land was given —
    no foreigner passed among them.

20 "The wicked is in torment all his life,
    for all the years allotted to the tyrant.
21 Terrifying sounds are in his ears;
    in prosperity, robbers swoop down on him.
22 He despairs of returning from darkness —
    he is destined to meet the sword.
23 He wanders and looks for food, which isn't there.
    He knows the day of darkness is ready, at hand.
24 Distress and anguish overwhelm him,
    assaulting him like a king about to enter battle.

25 "He raises his hand against God
    and boldly defies Shaddai,
26 running against him with head held high
    and thickly ornamented shield.

27 "He lets his face grow gross and fat,
    and the rest of him bulges with blubber;
28 he lives in abandoned cities,
    in houses no one would inhabit,
    houses about to become ruins;
29 therefore he will not remain rich,

his wealth will not endure,
his produce will not bend
[the grain stalks] to the earth.

30 "He will not escape from darkness.
The flame will dry up his branches.
By a breath from the mouth of [God],
he will go away.

31 Let him not rely on futile methods,
thereby deceiving himself;
for what he will receive in exchange
will be only futility.

32 This will be accomplished in advance of its day.
His palm frond will not be fresh and green;

33 he will be like a vine that sheds its unripe grapes,
like an olive tree that drops its flowers.

34 "For the community of the ungodly is sterile;
fire consumes the tents of bribery.

35 They conceive trouble and give birth to evil;
their womb prepares deceit."

16 ¹ In response Iyov said:

2 "I have heard this stuff so often!
Such sorry comforters, all of you!

3 Is there no end to words of wind?
What provokes you to answer this way?

4 "If I were in your place,
I too could speak as you do —
I could string phrases together against you
and shake my head at you.

5 I could 'strengthen' you with my mouth,
with lip service I could 'ease your grief.'

6 If I speak, my own pain isn't eased;
and if I don't speak, it still doesn't leave.

7 "But now he has worn me out;
you have desolated this whole community of mine.

8 Besides, you have shriveled me up;
and this serves to witness against me.
My being so thin rises up against me
and testifies to my face.

9 He tears me apart in his anger;
he holds a grudge against me;
he gnashes on me with his teeth.

"My enemies look daggers at me.
10 Wide-mouthed, they gape at me;
with scorn, they slap my cheeks;
they gather themselves together against me.

11 "God delivers me to the perverse,
throws me into the hands of the wicked.
12 I was at peace, and he shook me apart.
Yes, he grabbed me by the neck and dashed me to pieces.
He set me up as his target —
13 his archers surrounded me.
He slashes my innards and shows no mercy,
he pours my gall on the ground.
14 He breaks in on me again and again,
attacking me like a warrior.

15 "I sewed sackcloth together to cover my skin
and laid my pride in the dust;
16 my face is red from crying,
and on my eyelids is a death-dark shadow.
17 Yet my hands are free from violence,
and my prayer is pure.

18 "Earth, don't cover my blood;
don't let my cry rest [without being answered].
19 Even now, my witness is in heaven;
my advocate is there on high.
20 With friends like these as intercessors,
my eyes pour out tears to God,
21 that he would arbitrate between a man and God,
just as one does for his fellow human being.
22 For I have but few years left
before I leave on the road of no return.

17 1 "My spirit is broken, my days are quenched,
I am marked for the grave.
2 Mockers are all around me;
my eye meets only their hostility.
3 Be my guarantor, yourself!
Who else will put up a pledge for me?
4 For you have shut their minds to common sense;
therefore you will not let them triumph.
5 Should people share with their friends
when their own children's eyes are so sad?

6 "He has made me a byword among the peoples,
a creature in whose face they spit.

7   I am nearly blind with grief,
    my limbs reduced to a shadow.
8   The upright are perplexed at this,
    the innocent aroused against the hypocrites.
9   Yet the righteous hold on to their way,
    and those with clean hands grow stronger and stronger.

10 "But as for you all, turn around! Come back! —
    yet I won't find a wise man among you.
11 My days are over, my plans cut off,
    which I had cherished so;
12 but they [try to] turn [my] night into day,
    [saying,] 'Light is near!' — in the face of darkness.

13 "If I hope for Sh'ol to be my house;
    if I spread my couch in the dark;
14 if I say to the pit, 'You are my father,'
    and to worms, 'You are my mother and sister,'
15 then where is my hope?
    And that hope of mine, who will see it?
16 Only those who go down with me
    to the bars of Sh'ol,
    when we rest together in the dust."

18 ¹ Bildad the Shuchi said,

2   "When will you put an end to words?
    Think about it — then we'll talk!
3   Why are we thought of as cattle,
    stupid in your view?
4   You can tear yourself to pieces in your anger,
    but the earth won't be abandoned just for your sake;
    not even a rock will be moved from its place.

5   "The light of the wicked will flicker and die,
    not a spark from his fire will shine,
6   the light in his tent is darkened,
    the lamp over him will be snuffed out.
7   His vigorous stride is shortened,
    his own plans make him trip and fall.
8   For his own feet plunge him into a net,
    he wanders into its meshes.
9   A trap grabs him by the heel,
    a snare catches hold of him.
10 A noose is hidden for him in the ground;
    pitfalls lie in his path.
11 Terrors overwhelm him on every side
    and scatter about his feet.

12   "Trouble is hungry for him,
         calamity ready for his fall;
13   disease eats away at his skin;
         the first stages of death devour him gradually.
14   What he relied on will be torn from his tent,
         and he will be marched before the king of terrors.

15   "What isn't his at all will live in his tent;
         sulfur will be scattered on his home.
16   His roots beneath him will dry up;
         above him, his branch will wither.
17   Memory of him will fade from the land,
         while abroad his name will be unknown.
18   He will be pushed from light into darkness
         and driven out of the world.

19   "Without son or grandson among his people,
         no one will remain in his dwellings.
20   Those who come after will be appalled at his fate,
         just as those there before were struck with horror.

21   "This is how things are in the homes of the wicked,
         and this is the place of those who don't know God."

19 ¹ Then Iyov answered:

2   "How long will you go on making me angry,
         crushing me with words?
3   You've insulted me ten times already;
         aren't you ashamed to treat me so badly?
4   Even if it's true that I made a mistake,
         my error stays with me.

5   "You may take a superior attitude toward me
         and cite my disgrace as proof against me;
6   but know that it's God who has put me in the wrong
         and closed his net around me.
7   If I cry, 'Violence!' no one hears me;
         I cry aloud, but there is no justice.

8   "He has fenced off my way, so that I can't pass;
         he has covered my paths with darkness.
9   He has stripped me of my glory
         and removed the crown from my head.
10   He tears every part of me down — I am gone;
         he uproots my hope like a tree.

11 "Inflamed with anger against me,
he counts me as one of his foes.

12 His troops advance together,
they make their way against me
and encamp around my tent.

13 "He has made my brothers keep their distance,
those who know me are wholly estranged from me,

14 my kinsfolk have failed me,
and my close friends have forgotten me.

15 Those living in my house consider me a stranger;
my slave-girls too — in their view I'm a foreigner.

16 I call my servant, and he doesn't answer,
even if I beg him for a favor!

17 "My wife can't stand my breath,
I am loathsome to my own family.

18 Even young children despise me —
if I stand up, they start jeering at me.

19 All my intimate friends abhor me,
and those I loved have turned against me.

20 My bones stick to my skin and flesh;
I have escaped by the skin of my teeth.

21 "Pity me, friends of mine, pity me!
For the hand of God has struck me!

22 Must you pursue me as God does,
never satisfied with my flesh?

23 I wish my words were written down,
that they were inscribed in a scroll,

24 that, engraved with iron and filled with lead,
they were cut into rock forever!

25 "But I know that my Redeemer lives,
that in the end he will rise on the dust;

26 so that after my skin has been thus destroyed,
then even without my flesh, I will see God.

27 I will see him for myself,
my eyes, not someone else's, will behold him.
My heart grows weak inside me!

28 "If you say, 'How will we persecute him?' —
the root of the matter is found in me.

29 You had best fear the sword,
for anger brings the punishment of the sword,
so that you will know there is judgment!"

20 [1] Tzofar the Na'amati replied,

[2] "My thoughts are pressing me to answer;
I feel such an urge to speak!

[3] I have heard reproof that outrages me,
but a spirit past my understanding gives me a reply.

[4] "Don't you know that ever since time began,
ever since humans were placed on earth,

[5] that the triumph of the wicked is always short-lived,
and the joy of the ungodly is gone in a moment?

[6] His pride may mount to the heavens,
his head may touch the clouds;

[7] but he will vanish completely, like his own dung —
those who used to see him will ask, 'Where is he?'

[8] Like a dream he flies off and is not found again;
like a vision in the night he is chased away.

[9] The eye which once saw him will see him no more,
his place will not behold him again.

[10] His children will have to pay back the poor;
his hands will restore their wealth.

[11] His bones may be filled with [the vigor of] his youth,
but it will join him lying in the dust.

[12] "Wickedness may taste sweet in his mouth,
he may savor and roll it around on his tongue,

[13] he may linger over it and not let it go
but keep it there in his mouth —

[14] yet in his stomach his food goes bad,
it works inside him like snake venom;

[15] the wealth he swallows he vomits back up;
God makes him disgorge it.

[16] He sucks the poison of asps,
the viper's fangs will kill him.

[17] He will not enjoy the rivers,
the streams flowing with honey and cream.

[18] He will have to give back what he toiled for;
he won't get to swallow it down —
to the degree that he acquired wealth,
he won't get to enjoy it.

[19] "For he crushed and abandoned the poor,
seizing houses he did not build,

[20] because his appetite would not let him rest,
in his greed he let nothing escape;

[21] nothing is left that he did not devour;
therefore his well-being will not last.

22 With all needs satisfied, he will be in distress;
the full force of misery will come over him.

23 "This is what will fill his belly! —
[God] will lay on him all his burning anger
and make it rain over him, into his insides.

24 If he flees from the weapon of iron,
the bow of bronze will pierce him through —

25 he pulls the arrow out of his back,
the shining tip comes out from his innards;
terrors come upon him.

26 "Total darkness is laid up for his treasures,
a fire fanned by no one will consume him,
and calamity awaits what is left in his tent.

27 The heavens will reveal his guilt,
and the earth will rise up against him.

28 The income of his household will be carried off;
his goods will flow away on the day of his wrath.

29 This is God's reward for the wicked,
the heritage God decrees for him."

21 ¹ Then Iyov responded:

2 "Listen carefully to my words;
let this be the comfort you give me.

3 Bear with me as I speak;
then, after I have spoken, you can go on mocking.

4 "As for me, is my complaint merely to other people?
Don't I have grounds for being short-tempered?

5 Look at me, and be appalled;
cover your mouth with your hand!

6 Whenever I recall it, I am in shock;
my whole body shudders.

7 "Why do the wicked go on living,
grow old and keep increasing their power?

8 They see their children settled with them,
their posterity assured.

9 Their houses are safe, with nothing to fear;
God's rod is not on them.

10 Their bulls are fertile without fail,
their cows get pregnant and don't miscarry.

11 They produce flocks of babies,
and their children dance around.

12 They sing with tambourines and lyres
and rejoice to the sound of the pipe.

13 They spend their days in prosperity
and go down to the grave in peace.

14 "Yet to God they said, 'Leave us alone!
We don't want to know about your ways.
15 What is *Shaddai*, that we should serve him?
What do we gain if we pray to him?'
16 Isn't their prosperity already theirs?
The plans of the wicked are far from me.

17 "How often is the lamp of the wicked put out?
How often does their calamity come upon them?
How often does [God] deal out pain in his anger,
18 to make them like straw in the wind,
like chaff carried off by a storm?
19 God lays up for their children
[the punishment for their] iniquity.
He should lay it on [the wicked] themselves,
so that they can feel it!
20 Let their own eyes see their own destruction
and themselves drink the wrath of *Shaddai*.
21 What joy can they have in their family after them,
given that their months are numbered?

22 "Can anyone teach God knowledge?
After all, he judges those who are on high.
23 One person dies in his full strength,
completely at ease and content;
24 his pails are full of milk,
and the marrow in his bones is moist.
25 Another dies with embittered heart,
never having tasted happiness.
26 They lie down alike in the dust,
and the worm covers them both.

27 "Look, I know what you are thinking
and your plans to do me wrong.
28 You ask, 'Where is the great man's house?
Where is the tent where the wicked once lived?'
29 Haven't you ever questioned travelers?
Don't you accept their testimony
30 that the evil man is saved on the day of disaster,
rescued on the day of wrath?
31 So who will confront him with his ways?
Who will repay him for what he has done?
32 For he is carried off to the grave,
people keep watch over his tomb,

33   the clods of the valley are sweet to him;
    so everyone follows his example,
    just as before him were countless others.

34   "Why offer me such meaningless comfort?
    Of your answers, only the perfidy remains."

22 ¹ Next Elifaz the Teimani replied:

2   "Can a human be of advantage to God?
    Can even the wisest benefit him?
3   Does *Shaddai* gain if you are righteous?
    Does he profit if you make your ways blameless?

4   "Is he rebuking you because you fear him?
    Is this why he enters into judgment with you?
5   Isn't it because your wickedness is great?
    Aren't your iniquities endless?

6   "For you kept your kinsmen's goods as collateral for no reason,
    you stripped the poorly clothed of what clothing they have,
7   you didn't give water to the weary to drink,
    you withheld food from the hungry.
8   As a wealthy man, an owner of land,
    and as a man of rank, who lives on it,
9   you sent widows away empty-handed
    and left the arms of orphans crushed.

10   "No wonder there are snares all around you,
    and sudden terror overwhelms you,
11   or darkness, so that you can't see,
    and a flood of water that covers you up!

12   "Isn't God in the heights of heaven,
    looking [down even] on the highest stars?
13   Yet you say, 'What does God know?
    Can he see through thick darkness to judge?
14   The clouds veil him off, so that he can't see;
    he just wanders around in heaven.'

15   "Are you going to keep to the old way,
    the one the wicked have trodden,
16   the ones snatched away before their time,
    whose foundations a flood swept away?
17   They said to God, 'Leave us alone!
    What can *Shaddai* do to us?'
18   Yet he himself had filled their homes with good things!
    (But the advice of the wicked is far away from me.)

19   The righteous saw this and rejoiced;
       the innocent laughed them to scorn —
20   'Indeed, our substance has not been not cut off,
       but the fire has consumed their wealth.'

21   "Learn to be at peace with [God];
       in this way good will come [back] to you.
22   Please! Receive instruction from his mouth,
       and take his words to heart.
23   If you return to *Shaddai*, you will be built up.
       If you drive wickedness far from your tents,
24   if you lay your treasure down in the dust
       and the gold of Ofir among the rocks in the *vadis*,
25   and let *Shaddai* be your treasure
       and your sparkling silver;
26   then *Shaddai* will be your delight,
       you will lift up your face to God;
27   you will entreat him, and he will hear you,
       and you will pay what you vowed;
28   what you decide to do will succeed,
       and light will shine on your path;
29   when someone is brought down, you will say, 'It was pride,
       because [God] saves the humble.'

30   "He delivers even the unclean;
       so if your hands are clean, you will be delivered."

23 ^{1} Then Iyov answered:

2   "Today too my complaint is bitter;
       my hand is weighed down because of my groaning.
3   I wish I knew where I could find him;
       then I would go to where he is.
4   I would state my case before him
       and fill my mouth with arguments.
5   I would know his answering words
       and grasp what he would tell me.
6   Would he browbeat me with his great power?
       No, he would pay attention to me.
7   There an upright person could reason with him;
       thus I might be forever acquitted by my judge.

8   "If I head east, he isn't there;
       if I head west, I don't detect him,
9   if I turn north, I don't spot him;
       in the south he is veiled, and I still don't see him.
10   Yet he knows the way I take;
       when he has tested me, I will come out like gold.

11 My feet have stayed in his footsteps;
I keep to his way without turning aside.
12 I don't withdraw from his lips' command;
I treasure his words more than my daily food.

13 "But he has no equal, so who can change him?
What he desires, he does.
14 He will accomplish what is decreed for me,
and he has many plans like this.
15 This is why I am terrified of him;
the more I think about it, the more afraid I am —
16 God has undermined my courage;
Shaddai frightens me.
17 Yet I am not cut off by the darkness;
he has protected me from the deepest gloom.

24 1 "Why are times not kept by *Shaddai*?
Why do those who know him not see his days?
2 There are those who move boundary markers;
they carry off flocks and pasture them;
3 they drive away the orphan's donkey;
as collateral, they seize the widow's ox.
4 They push the needy out of the way —
the poor of the land are forced into hiding;
5 like wild donkeys in the wilderness,
they have to go out and scavenge food,
[hoping that] the desert
will provide food for their children.
6 They must reap in fields that are not their own
and gather late grapes in the vineyards of the wicked.
7 They pass the night without clothing, naked,
uncovered in the cold,
8 wet with mountain rain,
and hugging the rock for lack of shelter.

9 "There are those who pluck orphans from the breast
and [those who] take [the clothes of] the poor in pledge,
10 so that they go about stripped, unclothed;
they go hungry, as they carry sheaves [of grain];
11 between these men's rows [of olives], they make oil;
treading their winepresses, they suffer thirst.
12 Men are groaning in the city,
the mortally wounded are crying for help,
yet God finds nothing amiss!

13 "There are those who rebel against the light —
they don't know its ways or stay in its paths.

14 The murderer rises with the light
to kill the poor and needy;
while at night he is like a thief.

15 The eye of the adulterer too waits for twilight;
he thinks, 'No eye will see me';
but [to be sure], he covers his face.

16 When it's dark, they break into houses;
in the daytime, they stay out of sight.
[None of them] know the light.

17 For to all of them deep darkness is like morning,
for the terrors of deep darkness are familiar to them.

18 "May they be scum on the surface of the water,
may their share of land be cursed,
may no one turn on the way of their vineyards,

19 may drought and heat steal away their snow water
and Sh'ol those who have sinned.

20 May the womb forget them,
may worms find them sweet,
may they no longer be remembered —
thus may iniquity be snapped like a stick.

21 They devour childless women
and give no help to widows.

22 "Yet God keeps pulling the mighty along —
they get up, even when not trusting their own lives.

23 However, even if God lets them rest in safety,
his eyes are on their ways.

24 They are exalted for a little while;
and then they are gone,
brought low, gathered in like all others,
shriveled up like ears of grain.

25 "And even if it isn't so now,
still no one can prove me a liar
and show that my words are worthless."

25 ¹ Bildad the Shuchi said,

2 "Dominion and fear belong to him;
he makes peace in his high places.

3 Can his armies be numbered?
On whom does his light not shine?

4 How then can humans be righteous with God?
How can those born of women be clean?

5 Why, before him even the moon lacks brightness,
and the stars themselves are not pure.

⁶   How much less a human, who is merely a maggot,
    a mortal, who is only a worm?!"

26 ¹ Then Iyov replied,

²   "What great help you bring to the powerless!
    what deliverance to the arm without strength!
³   Such wonderful advice for a man lacking wisdom!
    So much common sense you've expressed!
⁴   Who helped you to say these words?
    Whose spirit is it, coming forth from you?

⁵   "The ghosts of the dead tremble
    beneath the water, with its creatures.
⁶   Sh'ol is naked before him;
    Abaddon lies uncovered.
⁷   He stretches the north over chaos
    and suspends the earth on nothing.
⁸   He binds up the water in his thick clouds,
    yet no cloud is torn apart by it.
⁹   He shuts off the view of his throne
    by spreading his cloud across it.
¹⁰   He fixed a circle on the surface of the water,
    defining the boundary between light and dark.
¹¹   The pillars of heaven tremble,
    aghast at his rebuke.
¹²   He stirs up the sea with his power,
    and by his skill he strikes down Rahav.
¹³   With his Spirit he spreads the heavens;
    his hand pierces the fleeing serpent.
¹⁴   And these are but the fringes of his ways;
    how faint the echo we hear of him!
    But who is able to grasp the meaning
    of his thundering power?"

27 ¹ Iyov continued his speech:

²   "I swear by the living God,
    who is denying me justice,
    and by *Shaddai*,
    who deals with me so bitterly,
³   that as long as my life remains in me
    and God's breath is in my nostrils,
⁴   my lips will not speak unrighteousness,
    or my tongue utter deceit.
⁵   Far be it from me to say you are right;
    I will keep my integrity till the day I die.

⁶ I hold to my righteousness; I won't let it go;
my heart will not shame me as long as I live.

⁷ "May my enemy meet the doom of the wicked;
my foe the fate of the unrighteous.

⁸ For what hope does the godless have from his gain
when God takes away his life?

⁹ Will God hear his cry
when trouble comes upon him?

¹⁰ Will he take delight in *Shaddai*
and always call on God?

¹¹ "I am teaching you how God uses his power,
not hiding what *Shaddai* is doing.

¹² Look, you all can see for yourselves;
so why are you talking such empty nonsense?

¹³ "This is God's reward for the wicked man,
the heritage oppressors receive from *Shaddai*:

¹⁴ if his sons become many, they go to the sword;
and his children never have enough to eat.

¹⁵ Those of his who remain are buried by plague,
and their widows do not weep.

¹⁶ Even if he piles up silver like dust
and stores away clothing [in mounds] like clay —

¹⁷ he may collect it, but the just will wear it,
and the upright divide up the silver.

¹⁸ He builds his house weak as a spider's web,
as flimsy as a watchman's shack.

¹⁹ He may lie down rich, but his wealth yields nothing;
when he opens his eyes, it isn't there.

²⁰ Terrors overtake him like a flood;
at night a whirlwind steals him away.

²¹ The east wind carries him off, and he's gone;
it sweeps him far from his place.

²² Yes, it hurls itself at him, sparing nothing;
he does all he can to flee from its power.

²³ [People] clap their hands at him in derision
and hiss him out of his home.

28 ¹ "There are mines for silver
and places where gold is refined;

² iron is extracted from the earth,
and copper is smelted from ore.

³ Miners conquer the darkness
and dig as far in as they can,
to the ore in gloom and deep darkness.

4 There where no one lives, they break open a shaft;
the feet passing over are oblivious to them;
far from people, suspended in space,
they swing to and fro.

5 "While the earth is [peacefully] yielding bread,
underneath, it is being convulsed as if by fire;
6 its rocks have veins of sapphire,
and there are flecks of gold.
7 Birds of prey don't know that path,
no falcon's eye has seen it,
8 the proud beasts have never set foot on it,
no lion has ever passed over it.

9 "[The miner] attacks the flint,
overturns mountains at their roots,
10 and cuts out galleries in the rock,
all the while watching for something of value.
11 He dams up streams to keep them from flooding,
and brings what was hidden out into the light.

12 "But where can wisdom be found?
Where is the source of understanding?
13 No one knows its value,
and it can't be found in the land of the living.
14 The deep says, 'It isn't in me,'
and the sea says, 'It isn't with me.'
15 It can't be obtained with gold,
nor can silver be weighed out to buy it.
16 It can't be purchased with choice gold from Ofir,
or with precious onyx or sapphires.
17 Neither gold nor glass can be compared with it;
nor can it be exchanged for a bowl of fine gold,
18 let alone coral or crystal;
for indeed, the price of wisdom is above that of pearls.
19 It can't be compared with Ethiopian topaz,
and it can't be valued with pure gold.

20 "So where does wisdom come from?
Where is the source of understanding,
21 inasmuch as it is hidden from the eyes of all living
and kept secret from the birds flying around in the sky?
22 Destruction and Death say,
'We have heard a rumor about it with our ears.'

23 "God understands its way,
and he knows its place.

24	For he can see to the ends of the earth
	and view everything under heaven.
25	When he determined the force of the wind
	and parceled out water by measure,
26	when he made a law for the rain
	and cleared a path for the thunderbolts;
27	then he saw [wisdom] and declared it,
	yes, he set it up and searched it out.
28	And to human beings he said,
	'Look, fear of *Adonai* is wisdom!
	Shunning evil is understanding!'"

29 ¹ Iyov went on speaking:

2	"I wish I were as in the old days,
	back in the times when God watched over me;
3	when his lamp shone over my head,
	and I walked through the dark by its light;
4	as I was when I was young,
	and God's counsel graced my tent.
5	Then *Shaddai* was still with me,
	my children were around me;
6	my steps were awash in butter,
	and the rocks poured out for me streams of olive oil.
7	I would go out to the city gate
	and set up my seat in the open space;
8	when young men saw me they would hide themselves,
	while the aged arose and stood;
9	leaders refrained from speaking —
	they would lay their hands on their mouths;
10	the voices of nobles were silenced;
	their tongues stuck to their palates.
11	Any ear that heard me blessed me,
	any eye that saw me gave witness to me,
12	for I delivered the poor when they cried for assistance,
	the orphan too, who had no one to help him.
13	Those who had been about to die would bless me,
	and I made widows sing in their hearts for joy.
14	I clothed myself with righteousness, and it clothed itself with me;
	my justice was like a robe and a crown.
15	I was eyes for the blind,
	and I was feet for the lame.
16	I was a father to the needy,
	and I investigated the problems of those I didn't know.
17	I broke the jaws of the unrighteous
	and snatched the prey from his teeth.

18 "I said, 'I will die with my nest,
and I will live as long as a phoenix;
19 my root will spread till it reaches water,
and dew will stay all night on my branch;
20 my glory will always be fresh,
my bow always new in my hand.'

21 "People would listen to me;
they waited and were silent when I gave advice.
22 After I spoke, they didn't talk back;
my words were like drops [of dew] on them.
23 They waited for me as if for rain,
as if for spring rain, with their mouths open wide.
24 When I joked with them, they couldn't believe it;
and they never darkened the light on my face.
25 I chose their way [for them], sitting as chief;
I lived like a king in the army,
like one who comforts mourners.

30 1 "But now those younger than I
hold me in derision,
men whose fathers I wouldn't even
have put with the dogs that guarded my sheep.
2 What use to me was the strength in their hands?
All their vigor had left them.
3 Worn out by want and hunger,
they gnaw the dry ground in the gloom
of waste and desolation.
4 They pluck saltwort and bitter leaves;
these, with broom tree roots, are their food.
5 They are driven away from society,
with men shouting after them as after a thief,
6 to live in gullies and *vadis*,
in holes in the ground and caves in the rocks.
7 Among the bushes they howl like beasts
and huddle among the nettles,
8 irresponsible nobodies
driven from the land.

9 "Now I have become their song;
yes, I am a byword with them.
10 They loathe me, they stand aloof from me;
they don't hesitate to spit in my face!
11 For God has loosened my bowstring and humbled me;
they throw off restraint in my presence.

12   At my right the street urchins attack,
pushing me from place to place,
besieging me with their ways of destruction,
13   breaking up my path,
furthering my calamity —
even those who have no one to help them.
14   They move in as through a wide gap;
amid the ruin they roll on in waves.
15   Terrors tumble over me,
chasing my honor away like the wind;
my [hope of] salvation passes like a cloud.

16   "So now my life is ebbing away,
days of grief have seized me.
17   At night pain pierces me to the bone,
so that I never rest.
18   My clothes are disfigured by the force [of my disease];
they choke me like the collar of my coat.
19   [God] has thrown me into the mud;
I have become like dust and ashes.

20   "I call out to you [God], but you don't answer me;
I stand up to plead, but you just look at me.
21   You have turned cruelly against me;
with your powerful hand you keep persecuting me.
22   You snatch me up on the wind and make me ride it;
you toss me about in the tempest.
23   For I know that you will bring me to death,
the house assigned to everyone living.

24   "Surely [God] wouldn't strike at a ruin,
if in one's calamity one cried out to him for help.
25   Didn't I weep for those who were in trouble?
Didn't I grieve for the needy?
26   Yet when I hoped for good, what came was bad;
when I expected light, what came was darkness.
27   My insides are in turmoil; they can't find rest;
days of misery confront me.
28   I go about in sunless gloom,
I rise in the assembly and cry for help.
29   I have become a brother to jackals
and a companion of ostriches.
30   My skin is black and falling off me,
and my bones are burning with heat.
31   So my lyre is tuned for mourning,
my pipe to the voice of those who weep.

31 ¹ "I made a covenant with my eyes
not to let them lust after any girl.

² "What share does God give from above?
What is the heritage from *Shaddai* on high?

³ Isn't it calamity to the unrighteous?
disaster to those who do evil?

⁴ Doesn't he see my ways
and count all my steps?

⁵ "If I have gone along with falsehood,
if my feet have hurried to deceit;

⁶ then let me be weighed on an honest scale,
so that God will know my integrity.

⁷ "If my steps have wandered from the way,
if my heart has followed my eyes,
if the least dirt has stuck to my hands;

⁸ then let me sow and someone else eat,
let what grows from my fields be uprooted.

⁹ "If my heart has been enticed toward a woman,
and I have lain in wait at my neighbor's door;

¹⁰ then let my wife grind for another man,
and let others kneel on her.

¹¹ For that would be a heinous act,
a criminal offense,

¹² a fire that would burn to the depths of Abaddon,
uprooting all I produce.

¹³ "If I ever rejected my slave or slave-girl's cause,
when they brought legal action against me;

¹⁴ then what would I do if God stood up?
Were he to intervene, what answer could I give?

¹⁵ Didn't he who made me in the womb make them too?
Didn't the same one shape us both before our birth?

¹⁶ "If I held back anything needed by the poor
or made a widow's eye grow dim [with tears],

¹⁷ or ate my portion of food by myself,
without letting the orphan eat any of it —

¹⁸ No! From my youth he grew up
with me as if with a father,
and I have been her guide
from my mother's womb! —

¹⁹ or if I saw a traveler needing clothing,
someone in need who had no covering,

20   who didn't bless me from his heart
   for being warmed with the fleece from my sheep,
21   or if I lifted my hand against an orphan,
   knowing that no one would dare charge me in court;
22   then let my arm fall from its socket,
   and let my forearm be broken at the elbow!
23   For calamity from God has always terrified me;
   before his majesty I could never do a thing [like that].

24   "If I made gold my hope,
   if I said to fine gold, 'You are my security,'
25   if I took joy in my great wealth,
   in my having acquired so much;
26   or if, on seeing the shining sun
   or the full moon as it moved through the sky,
27   my heart was secretly seduced,
   so that I would wave them a kiss with my hand;
28   then this too would be a criminal offense,
   for I would have been lying to God on high.

29   "Did I rejoice at the destruction of him who hated me?
   Was I filled with glee when disaster overtook him?
30   No, I did not allow my mouth to sin
   by asking for his life with a curse.

31   "Was there anyone in my tent who didn't say,
   'No one can find a single person
   whom he has not filled with his meat'?
32   No stranger had to sleep in the street;
   I kept my house open to the traveler.

33   "If I concealed my sins, as most people do,
   by hiding my wrongdoing in my heart,
34   from fear of general gossip
   or dread of some family's contempt.
   keeping silent and not going outdoors —
35   I wish I had someone who would listen to me!
   Here is my signature; let *Shaddai* answer me!
   I wish I had the indictment my adversary has written!
36   I would carry it on my shoulder;
   I would bind it on me like a crown.
37   I would declare to him every one of my steps;
   I would approach him like a prince.

38   "If my land cried out against me,
   if its furrows wept together,
39   if I ate its produce without paying
   or made its owners despair;

40   then let thistles grow instead of wheat
         and noxious weeds instead of barley!

     "The words of Iyov are finished."

32 ¹ So these three men stopped trying to answer Iyov, because he remained convinced of his own righteousness.

² But then the anger of Elihu the son of Barakh'el the Buzi, from the family of Ram, blazed up against Iyov for thinking he was right and God wrong. ³ His anger also blazed up against his three friends, because they had found no answer to Iyov but condemned him anyway. ⁴ Elihu had waited to speak to Iyov because they were older than he; ⁵ however, when Elihu saw that these three had no answer, his anger flared up. ⁶ Elihu the son of Barakh'el the Buzi said:

     "I am young, and you are old,
         so I held back from telling you my opinion.
7   I said, 'Age should speak;
         an abundance of years should teach wisdom.'
8   But it is the spirit in a person, the breath from *Shaddai*,
         that gives him understanding —
9   it isn't [only] the great who are wise
         or the aged who know how to judge.
10   Therefore, I say, listen to me;
         I too will express my opinion.

11   "Here, I waited for your words,
         I listened to your reasoning,
         as you were searching for what to say.
12   I paid attention to you,
         but none of you convicted Iyov
         or refuted his arguments.
13   So don't say, 'We found the wise course —
         let God defeat him, not a human being.'
14   For he did not direct his words against me,
         and I won't answer him with your arguments.

15   "They are confused, they don't reply,
         words have failed them.
16   But must I wait just because they don't speak,
         just because they stand there, stuck for an answer?
17   No, I will now give my answer;
         I too will express my opinion.
18   For I am full of words;
         the spirit within me compels me.
19   Yes, my insides feel like new wine under pressure,
         like new wineskins ready to burst.

20 I must speak, to find relief;
and I will open my lips and answer.

21 I will show no favor to anyone,
and I will flatter no one;

22 I don't know how to flatter;
if I did, my maker would soon put an end to me.

33 1 "So, Iyov, please, hear my speech;
listen to all my words.

2 Look, I am opening my mouth;
the words are on the tip of my tongue.

3 I will say exactly what is on my mind;
what my lips know, they will speak sincerely.

4 It is the Spirit of God that made me,
the breath of *Shaddai* that gives me life.

5 So refute me, if you can;
organize your words, take your stand!

6 Look, before God I'm the same as you;
I too am fashioned from clay.

7 You don't need to be afraid of me;
my pressure on you will not be heavy.

8 "You spoke within my hearing,
and I heard what you said —

9 'I am clean, without transgression;
I am innocent, not guilty.

10 Yet [God] finds pretexts for accusing me;
he regards me as his enemy.

11 He puts my feet in the stocks
and watches wherever I go.'

12 "But in this, you are wrong; I will answer you:
God is greater than any mortal.

13 Why do you strive against him?
He will not defend his words —

14 God speaks once, even twice,
and still the hearer misses the point.

15 "In a dream, in a vision at night,
when slumber falls upon people,
as they sleep in their beds,

16 he opens people's ears
and seals the matter with a warning,

17 to turn a person away from his action
and protect a man from pride,

18 so that he will keep himself away from the pit
and from perishing by the sword.

19 "He is also warned by pain when in bed,
when all his bones are hurting;
20 so that he detests bread
as well as richer food.
21 His flesh wastes away, till one can't stand to look;
his bones protrude and become unsightly.
22 His soul comes close to the pit
and his life to those who bring death.

23 "If there is for him an angel,
a mediator, one among a thousand,
who can vouch for the man's uprightness;
24 then [God] is gracious to him and says,
'Redeem him from going down to the pit;
I have found a ransom.'
25 His flesh becomes fresher than that of a child,
he returns to the days of his youth.
26 He prays to God and is accepted by him,
so that he sees [God's] face with joy,
and [God] repays the man for his righteousness.
27 He declares before everyone, 'I sinned;
I perverted what was right,
and it gained me nothing.
28 [God] redeemed me from going into the pit,
and now my life sees light.'
29 God will accomplish all these things
twice, even three times, with a man,
30 to bring him back from the pit,
so that he can enjoy the light of the living.

31 "Pay attention, Iyov, listen to me;
keep quiet, and I will keep speaking.
32 If you have something to say, answer me;
speak, because I want to show that you are right.
33 If not, then listen to me;
keep quiet, and I will teach you wisdom."

34 ^{1} Elihu continued speaking:

2 "Hear my words, you sages!
Listen to me, you who know so much!
3 For the ear tests words,
just as the palate tastes food.
4 Let's choose for ourselves what is just;
let's decide among ourselves what is good.
5 For Iyov says, 'I am in the right,
but God is denying me justice.

6 Against justice, I am considered a liar;
  my wound is mortal, though I committed no crime.'

7 "Is there a man like Iyov,
  who drinks in scoffing like water,
8 who keeps company with evildoers
  and goes with wicked men,
9 since he thinks, 'It profits a person nothing
  to be in accord with God'?

10 "So listen to me, you men with sense!
  Far be it from God to do anything wicked!
11 For he pays people back for what they do
  and sees that each gets what his conduct deserves.
12 It is certain that God does nothing wicked;
  Shaddai will not pervert justice.
13 Did someone else put him in charge of the earth?
  Who else established the entire world?
14 If he were to take back man's heart to himself,
  if he gathered to himself his spirit and breath;
15 all flesh would instantly perish,
  everyone would return to dust.

16 "If you have any sense, [Iyov,] hear this;
  listen to what I am saying.
17-18 Should a hater of justice be in control?
  If you wouldn't tell a king, 'You're a scoundrel!'
  or nobles, 'You are wicked men!'
  then you shouldn't condemn the Just and Mighty One,
19 who is neither partial toward princes
  nor favors the rich over the poor,
  since they all are the work of his hands.
20 They may die in a moment, in the middle of the night —
  the people are shaken and pass away,
  the mighty are removed without human hands.
21 For he keeps watch on a person's ways;
  he sees his every step.
22 There is no darkness, no death-like gloom,
  where wrongdoers can hide;
23 for he doesn't give warning to people
  when they must appear before God in judgment.
24 He shatters the mighty without needing to investigate
  and sets up others in their place.
25 Therefore, aware of what they are doing,
  he overturns them by night, and they are crushed.
26 He strikes them as if they were common criminals
  in the open sight of others,

27 because they turned away from following him
and gave no thought to any of his ways,
28 thereby bringing before him the cries of the poor;
and he hears the cries of the oppressed.

29 "But if God is silent, who can accuse him;
if he hides his face, who can see him?
He may do this to nations and persons alike,
30 so that godless men will not become kings,
and the people will not be lured into traps.

31 "For has anyone said to God,
'I have been chastised without having offended;
32 teach me what I have failed to see;
and if I have done wrong, I will do it no more'?
33 Must his rewards meet your approval?
Well, you are the one who doesn't like them,
so you, not I, should pick the alternative;
come on, say what you think!
34 Intelligent people will tell me,
every wise man who hears me will say,
35 'Iyov is speaking without thinking;
his words lack discernment.'

36 "I wish Iyov would be kept on trial forever,
because he answers like wicked men.
37 For now to his sin he adds rebellion;
he [mockingly] claps his hands among us
and keeps adding to his words against God."

35 ¹ Elihu went on to say:

2 "Are you so convinced you are right,
that you say, 'I am more just than God'?
3 For you ask what advantage it is to you,
'How do I gain from not sinning?'

4 "Here is my answer to you,
to you and to your friends:
5 Look at the heavens and see;
observe the skies, high above you.
6 If you sin, how do you hurt him?
If your crimes are many, how do you affect him?
7 If you are righteous, what do you give him?
What benefit does he get from you?
8 Your wickedness can affect only others like you,
and your righteousness only other human beings.

9	People cry out from under many oppressions;
	they cry for help from under the fist of the mighty.
10	But no one asks, 'Where is God my maker,
	who causes glad songs to ring out at night,
11	who teaches us more than he teaches wild animals
	and makes us wiser than the birds in the air?'
12	They may cry out, but no one answers,
	because of evil men's pride.
13	For God will not listen to empty cries;
	Shaddai pays no attention to them.
14	All the more when you say that you don't see him!
	Just be patient; he's considering the matter.
15	But now, just because he doesn't get angry and punish,
	does it mean he doesn't know what arrogance is?
16	So Iyov is being futile when he opens his mouth;
	he is piling up words without knowledge."

36 ¹ Elihu added:

2	"Bear with me a little, and I will show you
	that there is more to say on God's behalf.
3	I may search far and wide for my arguments,
	but I will ascribe righteousness to God my maker.
4	For the fact is that my words are true;
	you have with you a man whose views are pure.
5	"Look, God is powerful and despises no one,
	powerful in his strength of understanding.
6	He does not preserve the lives of the wicked,
	but he gives justice to the poor.
7	He does not withdraw his eyes from the righteous;
	but when he sets kings on their throne forever,
	they may become proud;
8	if, then, they are bound in chains,
	held in oppressive cords,
9	he shows them the results of their doings,
	the crimes caused by their pride.
10	He sounds a warning in their ears
	and orders them to repent of their evil.
11	"If they pay attention and obey him,
	they spend their days in prosperity;
	their years pass pleasantly.
12	But if they don't pay attention,
	they perish by the sword
	and die without learning their lesson.
13	The godless in heart cherish their anger,
	not crying for help when he binds them.

14   Their soul perishes in their youth,
    and their life becomes depraved.

15   "God, with his affliction,
    delivers the afflicted;
    and he gets their attention
    by pressing on them.

16   Indeed [Iyov], he is drawing you
    away from distress
    to an untroubled open place,
    with rich food on your table.

17   But the judgment on the wicked
    applies fully to you,
    judgment and condemnation
    take hold [of them].

18   For beware of wrath
    when abundance entices you;
    don't let a big bribe
    turn you aside.

19   Will your great wealth help you?
    or all your efforts, no matter how strong?

20   Don't desire the night,
    when people suddenly die.

21   Be careful; turn away from wrongdoing;
    for because of this, you have been tested by affliction.

22   "Look, God is exalted in his strength;
    who is a teacher like him?

23   Who ever prescribed his course for him?
    Who ever said, 'What you are doing is wrong'?

24   Remember, rather, to magnify his work,
    of which many have sung.

25   Everyone has seen it,
    [but] humans see it [only] from a distance.

26   Look, God is great, beyond what we can know;
    the number of his years is uncountable.

27   "He makes the droplets of water,
    which condense into rain from his mist.

28   The clouds pour it down
    upon humankind in abundance.

29   Can anyone fathom the spreading of the clouds,
    or the crashes that come from his canopy?

30   See how he scatters his lightning over it
    and covers the roots of the sea.

31   By these things he judges the people
    and also gives food in plenty.

32 He gathers the lightning into his hands
and commands it to strike the target.

33 Its crashing announces its presence
and apprises the cattle of what is coming.

37¹ "At this, my own heart trembles
and leaps out of its place.

2 Just listen to the rumbling of his voice,
to the thunder that comes from his mouth!

3 He sends it out under all of heaven,
his lightning to the ends of the earth.

4 There follows a sound, a roar —
he is thundering with his majestic voice,
and he keeps releasing [the lightning]
even while his voice is being heard.

5 "God thunders wonderfully with his voice,
he does great things beyond our understanding.

6 He says to the snow, 'Fall on the earth!' —
likewise to the light rain, also to the downpour.

7 He brings all human activity to a stop,
so that everyone he has made can know it.

8 Then the animals go into their lairs
and hibernate in their dens.

9 "Out of its chamber comes the storm,
with cold out of the north.

10 By the breath of God, ice is given,
and the wide waters freeze over.

11 He weighs the clouds down with moisture,
and they flash forth his lightning.

12 He, by his plans, turns them around,
so they do what he commands them anywhere on earth;

13 he brings them forth on the earth
sometimes to punish, sometimes to express his grace.

14 "Listen to this, Iyov!
Stop, and consider God's wonders.

15 Do you know how God puts them in place,
how he causes lightning to flash from his cloud?

16 Do you know how he balances the clouds?
These are marvels of him who knows everything!

17 "You, sweltering in your clothing
as the earth lies still under a sultry south wind,

18 can you, with him, spread out the sky,
hard as a cast metal mirror?

19 Teach us what we should tell him,
for the darkness keeps us from organizing our case.

20 Is he to be told that I will speak?
Can a man speak at all when he is already swallowed up?

21 Now people don't see the light,
which is bright in the sky;
but then the wind blows
and clears [the clouds] away.

22 Out of the north comes a golden glow,
fearsome majesty surrounding God.

23 *Shaddai*, whom we cannot find,
whose power is immense,
in his great righteousness
does not pervert justice.

24 This is why people fear him;
he does not consider those
who think of themselves as wise."

38 ¹ Then *Adonai* answered Iyov out of the storm:

2 "Who is this, darkening my plans
with his ignorant words?

3 Stand up like a man, and brace yourself;
I will ask questions; and you, give the answers!

4 "Where were you when I founded the earth?
Tell me, if you know so much.

5 Do you know who determined its dimensions
or who stretched the measuring line across it?

6 On what were its bases sunk,
or who laid its cornerstone,

7 when the morning stars sang together,
and all the sons of God shouted for joy?

8 "Who shut up the sea behind closed doors
when it gushed forth from the womb,

9 when I made the clouds its blanket
and dense fog its swaddling cloth,

10 when I made the breakers its boundary
set its gates and bars,

11 and said, 'You may come this far, but no farther;
here your proud waves must stop'?

12 "Have you ever in your life called up the dawn
and made the morning know its place,

13 so that it could take hold of the edges of the earth
and shake the wicked out of it?
14 Then the earth is changed like clay under a seal,
until its colors are fixed like those of a garment.
15 But from the wicked the light is withheld,
and the arm raised [to strike] is broken.

16 "Have you gone down to the springs of the sea
or explored the limits of the deep?
17 Have the gates of death been revealed to you,
the gates of death-like darkness?
18 Have you surveyed the full extent of the earth?
Say so, if you know it all!

19 "Which way leads to where light has its home?
and darkness, where does it dwell?
20 If you knew, you could take each to its place
and set it on its homeward path.
21 You know, of course, because you were born then;
by now you must be very old!

22 "Have you gone into the storehouses for snow
or seen the storehouses for hail,
23 which I save for times of trouble,
for days of battle and war?

24 "By what path is light dispersed,
or the east wind poured out on the land?
25 Who cut a channel for the downpours,
or a way for the lightning and thunder,
26 causing it to rain where no one is,
in a desert without anyone there,
27 drenching the waste and desolate [ground],
till the tender grass sprouts?
28 Does the rain have a father?
Who is the father of dewdrops?
29 From whose womb does ice come?
Who gives birth to the frost of heaven,
30 when water becomes as hard as stone,
and the surface of the deep freezes solid?

31 "Can you tie up the cords of the Pleiades
or loosen the belt of Orion?
32 Can you lead out the constellations of the zodiac in their season
or guide the Great Bear and its cubs?
33 Do you know the laws of the sky?
Can you determine how they affect the earth?

34 "Can you raise your voice to the clouds
and make them cover you with a flood of rain?

35 Can you send lightning bolts on their way?
Will they say to you, 'Here we are'?

36 "Who put wisdom in people's inner parts?
Who gave understanding to the mind?

37 Who, by wisdom, can number the clouds?
Who can tilt the water-skins of heaven,

38 so that the dust becomes a mass [of mud],
and its clods stick together?

39 "Can you hunt prey for a lioness
or satisfy the appetite of the young lions,

40 when they crouch in their dens
or lie in ambush in their lairs?

41 Who provides food for the raven
when his young cry out to God
and wander about for lack of food?

39 1 "Do you know when mountain goats give birth?
Have you seen deer in labor?

2 Can you tell how many months they carry their young?
Do you know when they give birth,

3 when they crouch down and bring forth their young,
when they deliver their fawns?

4 Their young become strong, growing up in the open;
they leave and never return.

5 "Who lets the wild donkey roam freely?
Who sets the wild donkey loose from its shackles?

6 I made the 'Aravah its home,
the salty desert its place to live.

7 It scorns the noise of the city
and hears no driver's shouts.

8 It ranges over the hills for its pasture,
searching for anything green.

9 "Would a wild ox be willing to serve you?
Would it stay by your stall?

10 Could you tie a rope around its neck
and make it plow furrows for you?

11 Would you trust its great strength enough
to let it do your heavy work,

12 or rely on it to bring home your seed
and gather the grain from your threshing-floor?

13   "An ostrich's wings beat wildly,
        although its pinions lack plumage.
14   It leaves its eggs on the ground
        and lets them be warmed by the sand,
15   forgetting that a foot may crush them
        or a wild animal trample on them.
16   It treats its chicks heartlessly,
        as if they were not its own;
        even if her labor is in vain,
        it really doesn't care;
17   because God has deprived it of wisdom
        and given it no share in understanding.
18   When the time comes, it flaps its wings,
        scorning both horse and rider.

19   "Did you give the horse its strength?
        Did you clothe its neck with a mane?
20   Did you make him able to leap like a locust?
        Its majestic snorting is frightening!
21   It paws with force and exults with vigor,
        then charges into the battle;
22   mocking at fear, unafraid,
        it does not shy away from the sword.
23   The [rider's] quiver rattles over it,
        [his] gleaming spear and javelin.
24   Frenzied and eager, it devours the ground,
        scarcely believing the *shofar* has sounded.
25   At the sound of the *shofar* it whinnies;
        as from afar it scents the battle,
        the roar of the chiefs and the shouting.

26   "Is it your wisdom that sets the hawk soaring,
        spreading its wings toward the south?
27   Does the eagle fly up when you say so,
        to build its nest in the heights?
28   It lives and spends its nights on the cliffs;
        a rocky crag is its fortress.
29   From there it spots its prey,
        its eyes see it far off.
30   Its young ones suck up blood;
        wherever the slain are, there it is."

40 ¹ Continuing to address Iyov, A*donai* said:

2   "Does the critic still want to dispute *Shaddai*?
        Let him who wants to correct God give an answer!"

³ Then Iyov replied to ADONAI:

4 "I am too ashamed; I have nothing to say.
  I lay my hand over my mouth.
5 Yes, I spoke once, but I won't answer more;
  all right, twice, but I won't go on."

⁶ ADONAI answered Iyov out of the storm:

7 "Stand up like a man, and brace yourself;
  I will ask questions; and you, give the answers!

8 "Are you impugning my justice?
  Putting me in the wrong to prove yourself right?
9 Do you have an arm like God's?
  Can you thunder with a voice like his?
10 Come on, deck yourself with majesty and dignity,
  robe yourself in glory and splendor.
11 Let loose your furious anger,
  look at all who are proud, and humble them.
12 Look at all who are proud, and bring them down;
  tread down the wicked where they stand.
13 Bury them in the ground together,
  bind their faces in the hidden world.
14 If you do this, then I will confess to you
  that your own power can save you.

15 "Now consider Behemot, whom I made along with you.
  He eats grass like an ox.
16 What strength he has in his loins!
  What power in his stomach muscles!
17 He can make his tail as stiff as a cedar,
  the muscles in his thighs are like cables,
18 his bones are like bronze pipes,
  his limbs like iron bars.

19 "He ranks first among God's works.
  Only his maker can approach him with his sword.
20 The mountains produce food for him there,
  where all the wild animals play.
21 He lies down under the thorny lotus bushes
  and is hidden by the reeds in the swamp;
22 the lotus bushes cover him with their shade,
  and the willows by the stream surround him.
23 If the river overflows, it doesn't worry him;
  he is confident even if the Yarden rushes by his mouth.
24 Can anyone catch him by his eyes
  or pierce his nose with a hook?

25(41:1) "And Livyatan! Can you catch him with a fishhook
or hold his tongue down with a rope?

26(41:2) Can you put a ring in his nose
or pierce his jaw with a barb?

27(41:3) Will he entreat you at length?
Will he speak with you softly?

28(41:4) Will he agree with you
to be your slave forever?

29(41:5) Will you play with him as you would with a bird
or keep him on a string to amuse your little girls?

30(41:6) Will a group of fishermen turn him into a banquet?
Will they divide him among the merchants?

31(41:7) Can you fill his skin with darts
or his head with fish-spears?

32(41:8) If you lay your hand on him,
you won't forget the fight, and you'll never do it again!

41 ¹⁽⁹⁾ "Look, any hope [of capturing him] is futile—
one would fall prostrate at the very sight of him.

2(10) No one is fierce enough to rouse him,
so who can stand up to me?

3(11) Who has given me anything
and made me pay it back?
Everything belongs to me
under all of heaven.

4(12) "I have more to say about his limbs,
his strong talk, and his matchless strength.

5(13) Who can strip off his [scaly] garment?
Who can enter his jaws?

6(14) Who can pry open the doors of his face,
so close to his terrible teeth?

7(15) "His pride is his rows of scales,
tightly sealed together—

8(16) one is so close to the next
that no air can come between them;

9(17) they are stuck one to another,
interlocked and impervious.

10(18) "When he sneezes, light flashes out;
his eyes are like the shimmer of dawn.

11(19) From his mouth go fiery torches,
and sparks come flying out.

12(20) His nostrils belch steam
like a caldron boiling on the fire.

13(21) His breath sets coals ablaze;
flames pour from his mouth.

14(22)	"Strength resides in his neck,
	and dismay dances ahead of him [as he goes].
15(23)	The layers of his flesh stick together;
	they are firm on him, immovable.
16(24)	His heart is as hard as a stone,
	yes, hard as a lower millstone.
17(25)	When he rears himself up, the gods are afraid,
	beside themselves in despair.

18(26)	"If a sword touches him, it won't stick;
	neither will a spear, or a dart, or a lance.
19(27)	He regards iron as straw
	and bronze as rotten wood.
20(28)	An arrow can't make him flee;
	for him, slingstones are so much chaff.
21(29)	Clubs count as hay,
	and he laughs at a quivering javelin.
22(30)	His belly is as sharp as fragments of pottery,
	so he moves across the mud like a threshing-sledge.

23(31)	"He makes the depths seethe like a pot,
	he makes the sea [boil] like a perfume kettle.
24(32)	He leaves a shining wake behind him,
	making the deep seem to have white hair.

25(33)	"On earth there is nothing like him,
	a creature without fear.
26(34)	He looks straight at all high things.
	He is king over all proud beasts."

42 ¹ Then [at last,] Iyov gave *Adonai* this answer:

2   "I know that you can do everything,
       that no purpose of yours can be thwarted.

3   "[You asked,] 'Who is this, hiding counsel,
       without having knowledge?'
       Yes, I spoke, without understanding,
       of wonders far beyond me, which I didn't know.

4   "Please listen, and I will speak.
       [You said,] 'I will ask questions; and you, give me answers' —
5   I had heard about you with my ears,
       but now my eye sees you;
6   therefore I detest [myself]
       and repent in dust and ashes."

⁷ After *ADONAI* had spoken these words to Iyov, *ADONAI* said to Elifaz the Teimani, "My anger is blazing against you and your two friends, because, unlike my servant Iyov, you have not spoken rightly about me. ⁸ So now, get yourselves seven young bulls and seven rams, go to my servant Iyov, and offer up for yourselves a burnt offering. My servant Iyov will pray for you — because him I will accept — so that I won't punish you as your boorishness deserves; because you have not spoken rightly about me, as my servant Iyov has." ⁹ So Elifaz the Teimani, Bildad the Shuchi and Tzofar the Na'amati went and did what *ADONAI* had ordered them to do, and *ADONAI* accepted Iyov['s prayer].

¹⁰ When Iyov prayed for his friends, *ADONAI* restored his fortunes; *ADONAI* gave Iyov twice as much as he had had before. ¹¹ Then all his brothers and sisters came to him, also all who had known him before, and they ate a meal with him in his house. They consoled and comforted him for all the evils *ADONAI* had inflicted on him. Each one gave him a piece of silver and a gold ring. ¹² *ADONAI* blessed Iyov's later situation even more than his earlier one — he had 14,000 sheep, 6,000 camels, 1,000 pairs of oxen and 1,000 female donkeys.

¹³ He also had seven sons and three daughters. ¹⁴ The first he named Y'mimah; the second, K'tzi'ah; and the third, Keren-Hapukh. ¹⁵ Nowhere in the land could women be found as beautiful as Iyov's daughters; and their father gave them inheritances along with their brothers.

¹⁶ After this, Iyov lived 140 years, long enough to see his sons and grandsons, four generations. ¹⁷ Then, old and full of days, Iyov died.

*Shir-HaShirim**
SONG OF SOLOMON

1 ¹ The Ultimate Song, by Shlomo:

[She]   ² Let him smother me with kisses from his mouth,
for your love is better than wine.
    ³ Your anointing oils have a wonderful fragrance;
your name is like anointing oil poured out.
This is why young women love you —
    ⁴ "Take me with you. We will run after you."
The king has brought me into his rooms.

[Chorus]   We will be glad and rejoice for you.
We will praise your love more than wine.
How right it is for them to love you!

[She]   ⁵ I am dark tan but beautiful,
you daughters of Yerushalayim,
like the tents of Kedar,
like the curtains of Shlomo.
    ⁶ Don't stare at me because I'm dark;
it's the sun that tanned me.
My mother's sons were angry with me
and made me look after the vineyards.
But I haven't cared for my own vineyard.

    ⁷ Tell me, my love, where you pasture your flock,
where you have them rest at noon;
for why should I veil myself [like a whore]
beside the flocks of your friends?

[Chorus]   ⁸ If you do not know,
you most beautiful of women,
then follow the footprints of the flock
and let your kids graze by the shepherds' tents.

---

* *Shir-HaShirim* means "Song of Songs" or "The Ultimate Song."

[He]	9	My love, I compare you with my mare, pulling one of Pharaoh's chariots —
	10	your cheeks are lovely with ornaments, your neck with its strings of beads;
	11	we will make you ornaments of gold, studded with silver.
[She]	12	As the king reclines at table, my nard gives forth its perfume:
	13	to me the man I love is a sachet of myrrh lodged between my breasts;
	14	to me the man I love is a spray of henna flowers in the vineyards of 'Ein-Gedi.
[He]	15	Look at you, my love! How beautiful you are! Your eyes are doves —
[She]	16	— Look at you! So handsome, so pleasing, my darling! Our bed is the greenery;
	17	cedars are the beams of our houses, cypresses the rafters.
2	1	I am but a rose from the Sharon, just a lily in the valleys.
[He]	2	Like a lily among thorns is my darling among the other women.
[She]	3	Like an apple tree among the other trees in the forest is my darling among the other men. I love to sit in his shadow; his fruit is sweet to my taste.
	4	He brings me to the banquet hall; his banner over me is love.
	5	Sustain me with raisins, refresh me with apples, for I am sick with love.
	6	[I wish] his left arm [were] under my head, and his right arm around me.
	7	I warn you, daughters of Yerushalayim, by the gazelles and deer in the wilds, not to awaken or stir up love until it wants to arise!
	8	The voice of the man I love! Here he comes, bounding over the mountains, skipping over the hills!

9   My darling is like a gazelle or young stag.
There he is, standing outside our wall,
looking in through the windows,
peering in through the lattice.

10   My darling speaks; he is saying to me,
"Get up, my love! My beauty! Come away!

11   For you see that the winter has passed,
the rain is finished and gone,

12   the flowers are appearing in the countryside,
the time has come for [the birds] to sing,
and the cooing of doves can be heard in the land.

13   The fig trees are forming their unripe figs,
and the grapevines in bloom give out their perfume.
Get up, my love, my beauty!
Come away!"

[He]   14   My dove, hiding in holes in the rock,
in the secret recesses of the cliff,
let me see your face and hear your voice;
for your voice is sweet, and your face is lovely.

[She]   15   "Catch the foxes for us,
yes, the little foxes!
They are ruining the vineyards
when our vineyards are in bloom!"

16   My darling is mine, and I am his,
as he pastures his flock among the lilies.

17   Before the daytime breeze rises
and the shadows flee,
return, my love, like a stag or gazelle
on the hills of Beter.

3 1   Night after night on my bed
I looked for the man I love.
I looked for him, but I didn't find him.

2   "I will get up now and roam the city,
through the streets and the open places,
I will look for the man I love."
I looked for him, but I didn't find him.

3   The guards roaming the city found me.
"Have you seen the man I love?"

4   Scarcely had I left them,
when I found the man I love.
I took hold of him
and would not let him go
until I had brought him to my mother's house,
to the bedroom of the woman who conceived me.

⁵ I warn you, daughters of Yerushalayim,
by the gazelles and deer in the wilds,
not to awaken or stir up love
until it wants to arise!

⁶ Who is this, coming up from the desert
like a column of smoke,
perfumed with myrrh and frankincense,
chosen from the merchant's crushed spices?

⁷ It is Shlomo's litter,
escorted by sixty valiant men
chosen from Isra'el's finest;

⁸ all of them wield the sword
and are expert fighters;
each one has his sword ready at his side
to combat the terrors of night.

⁹ King Shlomo made himself a royal litter
of wood from the L'vanon.

¹⁰ He made its columns of silver,
its roof of gold, its seat of purple cloth;
its inside was lovingly inlaid
by the daughters of Yerushalayim.

¹¹ Daughters of Tziyon, come out,
and gaze upon King Shlomo,
wearing the crown with which his mother crowned him
on his wedding day, his day of joy!

[He] **4** ¹ How beautiful you are, my love!
How beautiful you are!
Your eyes are doves behind your veil.
Your hair is like a flock of goats
streaming down Mount Gil'ad.

² Your teeth are like a flock of shorn sheep
that have just come up from being washed;
each of them is matched,
and none of them is missing.

³ Your lips are like a scarlet thread,
and your mouth is lovely.
Your cheeks are like a pomegranate
split open behind your veil.

⁴ Your neck is like the tower of David,
built magnificently,
on which hang a thousand bucklers,
each one a brave warrior's shield.

⁵ Your two breasts are like two fawns,
twins of a gazelle grazing among lilies.

6 When the day's cool breeze comes up
and the shadows lengthen,
I will get myself to the mountain of myrrh
to the hill of frankincense.

7 Everything about you is beautiful, my love;
you are without a flaw.

8 Come with me from the L'vanon, my bride,
come with me from the L'vanon.
Come down from the heights of Amanah,
from the heights of S'nir and Hermon,
down from the lions' lairs
and the leopard-haunted hills.

9 My sister, my bride,
you have carried my heart away!
With just one glance, with one bead of your necklace
you have carried my heart away.

10 My sister, my bride,
how sweet is your love!
How much better your love than wine,
more fragrant your perfumes than any spice!

11 Your lips, my bride, drip honey;
honey and milk are under your tongue;
and the scent of your garments is like
the scent of the L'vanon.

12 My sister, my bride, is a garden locked up,
a pool covered over, a spring sealed shut.

13 You are an orchard that puts forth pomegranates
and other precious fruits, henna and nard —

14 nard, saffron and aromatic cane,
cinnamon and all kinds of frankincense trees,
myrrh, aloes, all the best spices.

15 You are a garden fountain,
a spring of running water,
flowing down from the L'vanon.

[She] 16 Awake, north wind! Come, south wind!
Blow on my garden to spread its fragrance.
Let my darling enter his garden
and eat its finest fruit.

[He] **5** 1 My sister, my bride, I have entered my garden;
I am gathering my myrrh and my spices;
I am eating my honeycomb along with my honey;
I am drinking my wine as well as my milk.

[Chorus]		Eat, friends, and drink,
		until you are drunk with love!
[She]	2	I am asleep, but my heart is awake.
		Listen! I hear my darling knocking!
[He]		Open for me, my sister, my love,
		my dove, my flawless one!
		For my head is wet with dew,
		my hair with the moisture of the night.
[She]	3	I've removed my coat; must I put it back on?
		I've washed my feet; must I dirty them again?
	4	The man I love put his hand through the hole by the door-latch,
		and my heart began pounding at the thought of him.
	5	I got up to open for the man I love.
		My hands were dripping with myrrh —
		pure myrrh ran off my fingers
		onto the handle of the bolt.
	6	I opened for my darling,
		but my darling had turned and gone.
		My heart had failed me when he spoke —
		I sought him, but I couldn't find him;
		I called him, but he didn't answer.
	7	The watchmen roaming the city found me;
		they beat me, they wounded me;
		they took away my cloak,
		those guardians of the walls!
	8	I charge you, daughters of Yerushalayim,
		that if you find the man I love,
		what are you to tell him?
		That I am sick with love.
[Chorus]	9	How does the man you love differ from any other,
		you most beautiful of women?
		How does the man you love differ from any other,
		that you should give us this charge?
[She]	10	The man I love is radiant and ruddy;
		he stands out among ten thousand.
	11	His head is like the finest gold;
		his locks are wavy and black as a raven.
	12	His eyes are like doves by running streams,
		bathed in milk and set just right.
	13	His cheeks are like beds of spices,

like banks of fragrant herbs.
His lips are like lilies
dripping with sweet myrrh.

14 His arms are rods of gold set with beryl,
his body polished ivory adorned with sapphires.

15 His legs are like pillars of marble
set on bases of pure gold.
His appearance is like the L'vanon,
as imposing as the cedars.

16 His words are sweetness itself;
he is altogether desirable.
This is my darling, and this is my friend,
daughters of Yerushalayim.

[Chorus] **6** 1 Where has your darling gone,
you most beautiful of women?
Which way did your darling turn,
so that we can help you find him?

[She] 2 My darling went down to his garden,
to the beds of spices,
to pasture his flock in the gardens
and to gather lilies.

3 I belong to the man I love, and he belongs to me;
he pastures his flock among the lilies.

[He] 4 You are as beautiful as Tirtzah, my love,
as lovely as Yerushalayim,
but formidable as an army
marching under banners.

5 Turn your eyes away from me,
because they overwhelm me!

Your hair is like a flock of goats
streaming down Gil'ad.

6 Your teeth are like a flock of sheep
that have just come up from being washed;
each of them is matched,
and none of them is missing.

7 Your cheeks are like a pomegranate
split open behind your veil.

8 There are sixty queens and eighty concubines,
as well as young women beyond number;

9 but my dove, my perfect one, is unique,
her mother's only child,
the darling of the one who bore her.

The daughters see her and call her happy;
the queens and concubines praise her.

10 "Who is this, shining forth like the dawn,
fair as the moon, bright as the sun" —
but formidable as an army
marching under banners?

[She] 11 I had gone down to the nut orchard
to see the fresh green plants in the valley,
to see if the vine had budded,
or if the pomegranate trees were in bloom.

12 Before I knew it, I found myself
in a chariot, and with me was a prince.

[Chorus] 7 1(6:13) Come back, come back, girl from Shulam!
Come back, come back to where we can see you!
Why are you looking at the girl from Shulam
as if she were dancing for two army camps?

[He] 2(1) How beautiful are your feet in sandals,
you daughter of princes!
The curves of your thighs are like a necklace
made by a skilled craftsman.

3(2) Your navel is like a round goblet
that never lacks spiced wine.
Your belly is a heap of wheat
encircled by lilies.

4(3) Your two breasts are like two fawns,
twins of a gazelle.

5(4) Your neck is like a tower of ivory,
your eyes like the pools in Heshbon
by the gate of Bat-Rabbim,
your nose like a tower in the L'vanon
overlooking Dammesek.

6(5) You hold your head like the Karmel,
and the hair on your head is like purple cloth —
the king is held captive in its tresses.

7(6) How beautiful you are, my love,
how charming, how delightful!

8(7) Your appearance is stately as a palm tree,
with its fruit clusters your breasts.

9(8) I said, "I will climb up into the palm tree,
I will take hold of its branches."
May your breasts be like clusters of grapes,
your breath as fragrant as apples,

10(9) and your mouth like the finest wine.

[She]   May the wine go straight to the man I love
and gently move the lips of those who are asleep.

11(10) I belong to my darling,
and his desire is for me.

12(11) Come, my darling, let's go out to the country
and spend the nights in the villages.

13(12) We'll get up early and go to the vineyards
to see if the vines have budded,
to see if their flowers have opened,
or if the pomegranate trees are in bloom.
There I will give you my love.

14(13) The mandrakes are sending out their fragrance,
all kinds of choice fruits are at our doors,
fruits both new and old, my darling,
which I have kept in store for you.

8 ¹   I wish you were my brother,
who nursed at my mother's breast;
then, if I met you outdoors, I could kiss you,
and no one would look down on me.

²   I would lead you and bring you to my mother's house,
and she would instruct me.
I would give you spiced wine to drink,
fresh juice from my pomegranates.

³   His left arm would be under my head
and his right arm around me.

⁴   I warn you, daughters of Yerushalayim,
not to awaken or stir up love
until it wants to arise!

[Chorus]   ⁵ Who is this, coming up from the desert,
leaning on her darling?

[He]   I awakened you under the apple tree.
It was there that your mother conceived you;
there she who bore you conceived you.

[She]   ⁶ Set me like a seal on your heart,
like a seal on your arm;
for love is as strong as death,
passion as cruel as Sh'ol;
its flashes are flashes of fire,
[as fierce as the] flame of *Yah*.

⁷   No amount of water can quench love,
torrents cannot drown it.

If someone gave all the wealth in his house for love,
he would gain only utter contempt.

[Chorus]　8　We have a little sister;
her breasts are still unformed.
What are we to do with our sister
when she is asked for in marriage?

9　If she is a wall,
we will build on her a palace of silver;
and if she is a door,
we will enclose her with panels of cedar.

[She]　10　I am a wall, and my breasts are like towers;
so in his view I am like one who brings peace.

11　Shlomo had a vineyard at Ba'al-Hamon,
and he gave the vineyard to caretakers;
each of them would pay for its fruit
a thousand pieces of silver.

12　My vineyard is mine; I tend it, myself.
You can have the thousand, Shlomo,
and the fruit-caretakers, two hundred!

[He]　13　You who live in the garden,
friends are listening for your voice.
Let me hear it! —

[She]　14　　　　　　　　— Flee, my darling!
Be like a gazelle or young stag
on the mountains of spices!

Rut

RUTH

1 ¹ Back in the days when the judges were judging, at a time when there was a famine in the land, a certain man from Beit-Lechem went to live in the territory of Mo'av — he, his wife and his two sons. ² The man's name was Elimelekh, his wife's name was Na'omi, and his two sons were named Machlon and Kilyon; they were Efratim from Beit-Lechem in Y'hudah. They arrived in the plain of Mo'av and settled there. ³ Elimelekh, Na'omi's husband, died; and she was left, she and her two sons. ⁴ They took wives for themselves from the women of Mo'av; the name of the one was 'Orpah; and the name of the other was Rut. They lived there for about ten years. ⁵ Then Machlon and Kilyon died, both of them; and the woman was left with neither her two sons nor her husband.

⁶ So she prepared to return with her daughters-in-law from the plain of Mo'av; for in the plain of Mo'av she had heard how ADONAI had paid attention to his people by giving them food. ⁷ She left the place where she was with her two daughters-in-law and took the road leading back to Y'hudah.

⁸ Na'omi said to her two daughters-in-law, "Each of you, go back to your mother's house. May ADONAI show grace to you, as you did to those who died and to me. ⁹ May ADONAI grant you security in the home of a new husband." Then she kissed them, but they began weeping aloud. ¹⁰ They said to her, "No; we want to return with you to your people." ¹¹ Na'omi said, "Go back, my daughters. Why do you want to go with me? Do I still have sons in my womb who could become your husbands? ¹² Go back, my daughters; go your way; for I'm too old to have a husband. Even if I were to say, 'I still have hope'; even if I had a husband tonight and bore sons; ¹³ would you wait for them until they grew up? Would you refuse to marry, just for them? No, my daughters. On your behalf I feel very bitter that the hand of ADONAI has gone out against me." ¹⁴ Again they wept aloud. Then 'Orpah kissed her mother-in-law good-bye. But Rut stuck with her. ¹⁵ She said, "Look, your sister-in-law has gone back to her people and to her god; go back, after your sister-in-law." ¹⁶ But Rut said,

> "Don't press me to leave you
> and stop following you;
> for wherever you go, I will go;
> and wherever you stay, I will stay.
> Your people will be my people
> and your God will be my God.
> ¹⁷ Where you die, I will die;
> and there I will be buried.
> May ADONAI bring terrible curses on me,

and worse ones as well,
if anything but death
separates you and me."

^{18} When Na'omi saw that she was determined to go with her, she said no more to her.
^{19} So the two of them went on until they came to Beit-Lechem. When they arrived in Beit-Lechem, the whole city was stirred with excitement over them. The women asked, "Can this be Na'omi?" ^{20} "Don't call me Na'omi [pleasant]," she answered them; "call me Marah [bitter], because *Shaddai* has made my life very bitter. ^{21} I went out full, and *Adonai* has brought me back empty. Why call me Na'omi? *Adonai* has testified against me, *Shaddai* has afflicted me." ^{22} This is how Na'omi returned, with Rut the woman from Mo'av, her daughter-in-law, accompanying her from the plain of Mo'av. They arrived in Beit-Lechem at the beginning of the barley harvest.

2 ^{1} Na'omi had a relative on her husband's side, a prominent and wealthy member of Elimelekh's clan, whose name was Bo'az. ^{2} Rut the woman from Mo'av said to Na'omi, "Let me go into the field and glean ears of grain behind anyone who will allow me to." She answered her, "Go, my daughter." ^{3} So she set out, arrived at the field and gleaned behind the reapers.

She happened to be in the part of the field that belonged to Bo'az from Elimelekh's clan, ^{4} when Bo'az arrived from Beit-Lechem. He said to the reapers, "*Adonai* be with you"; and they answered him, "*Adonai* bless you." ^{5} Then Bo'az asked his servant supervising the reapers, "Whose girl is this?" ^{6} The servant supervising the reapers answered, "She's a girl from Mo'av who returned with Na'omi from the plain of Mo'av. ^{7} She said, 'Please, let me glean and gather what falls from the sheaves behind the reapers.' So she went and has kept at it from morning until now, except for a little rest in the shelter."

^{8} Bo'az said to Rut, "Did you hear that, my daughter? Don't go to glean in another field, don't leave this place, but stick here with my working girls. ^{9} Keep your eyes on whichever field the reapers are working in, and follow the girls. I've ordered the young men not to bother you. Whenever you get thirsty, go and drink from the water jars the young men have filled."

^{10} She fell on her face, prostrating herself, and said to him, "Why are you showing me such favor? Why are you paying attention to me? After all, I'm only a foreigner." ^{11} Bo'az answered her, "I've heard the whole story, everything you've done for your mother-in-law since your husband died, including how you left your father and mother and the land you were born in to come to a people about whom you knew nothing beforehand. ^{12} May *Adonai* reward you for what you've done; may you be rewarded in full by *Adonai* the God of Isra'el, under whose wings you have come for refuge." ^{13} She said, "My lord, I hope I continue pleasing you. You have comforted and encouraged me, even though I'm not one of your servants."

^{14} When meal-time came, Bo'az said to her, "Come here, have something to eat, and dip your piece of bread in the [olive oil and] vinegar." She sat by the reapers, and they passed her some roasted grain. She ate till she was full, and she had some left over.

^{15} When she got up to glean, Bo'az ordered his young men, "Let her glean even among the sheaves themselves, without making her feel ashamed. ^{16} In fact, pull some ears of grain out from the sheaves on purpose. Leave them for her to glean, and don't rebuke her." ¹⁷ So she gleaned in the field until evening. When she beat out what she had gathered, it came to about a bushel of barley.

¹⁸ She picked it up and went back to the city. Her mother-in-law saw what she had gleaned, and Rut brought out and gave her what she had left over after eating her fill. ¹⁹ Her mother-in-law asked her, "Where did you glean today? Where were you working? Blessed be the one who took such good care of you!" She told her mother-in-law with whom she had been working; she said, "The name of the man with whom I was working today is Bo'az." ²⁰ Na'omi said to her daughter-in-law, "May he be blessed by ADONAI, who has never stopped showing grace, neither to the living nor to the dead." Na'omi also told her, "The man is closely related to us; he's one of our redeeming kinsmen." ²¹ Rut the woman from Mo'av said, "Moreover, he even said to me, 'Stay close to my young men until they've finished my harvest.'" ²² Na'omi said to Rut her daughter-in-law, "It's good, my daughter, for you to keep going out with his girls; so that you won't encounter hostility in some other field." ²³ So she stayed close to Bo'az's girls to glean, until the end of the barley and wheat harvests; and she lived with her mother-in-law.

3 ¹ Na'omi her mother-in-law said to her, "My daughter, I should be seeking security for you; so that things will go well with you. ² Now there's Bo'az our relative—you were with his girls. He's going to be winnowing barley tonight at the threshing-floor. ³ So bathe, anoint yourself, put on your good clothes, and go down to the threshing-floor; but don't reveal your presence to the man until he's finished eating and drinking. ⁴ Then, when he lies down, take note of where he's lying; later, go in, uncover his feet, and lie down. He will tell you what to do." ⁵ She responded, "I will do everything you tell me."

⁶ She went down to the threshing-floor and did everything as her mother-in-law had instructed her. ⁷ After Bo'az was through eating and drinking and was feeling good, he went to lie down at the end of the pile of grain. She stole in, uncovered his feet and lay down. ⁸ In the middle of the night the man was startled and turned over, and — there was a woman lying at his feet! ⁹ He asked, "Who are you?" and she answered, "I'm your handmaid Rut. Spread your robe over your handmaid, because you are a redeeming kinsman." ¹⁰ He said, "May ADONAI bless you, my daughter. Your latest kindness is even greater than your first, in that you didn't go after the young men, neither the rich ones nor the poor. ¹¹ And now, my daughter, don't be afraid. I will do for you everything you say, for all the city leaders among my people know that you are a woman of good character. ¹² Now, it is true that I am a redeeming kinsman; but there is a redeemer who is a closer relative than I am. ¹³ Stay tonight. If, in the morning, he will redeem you, fine!— let him redeem you. But if he doesn't want to redeem you, then, as ADONAI lives, I will redeem you. Now, lie down until morning."

¹⁴ She lay at his feet until morning; then, before [it was light enough that] people could recognize each other, she got up; because he said, "No one should know that the woman came to the threshing-floor." ¹⁵ He also said, "Bring the shawl you are wearing, and take hold of it." She held it while he put six measures of barley into it; then he went into the city.

¹⁶ When she came to her mother-in-law, she asked, "Who are you? My daughter?" She told her everything the man had done for her. ¹⁷ Then she added, "He gave me

these six measures of barley; because he said to me, "You shouldn't return to your mother-in-law with nothing." ¹⁸ Na'omi said, "My daughter, just stay where you are, until you learn how the matter comes out; for the man won't rest unless he resolves the matter today."

4 ¹ Meanwhile, Bo'az had gone up to the gate and had sat down there, when the redeemer of whom Bo'az had spoken passed by. "Such-and-such," he said, "come over, and sit down"; so he came over and sat down. ² He took ten of the city's leaders and said, "Sit down here"; and they sat down. ³ Then he said to the redeeming kinsman, "The parcel of land which used to belong to our relative Elimelekh is being offered for sale by Na'omi, who has returned from the plain of Mo'av. ⁴ I thought I should tell you about it and say, 'Buy it in the presence of the people sitting here and in the presence of the leaders of my people. If you want to redeem it, redeem it. But if it is not to be redeemed, then tell me, so that I can know, because there is no one else in line to redeem it, and I'm after you." He said, "I want to redeem it." ⁵ Then Bo'az said, "The same day you buy the field from Na'omi, you must also buy Rut the woman from Mo'av, the wife of the deceased [son], in order to raise up in the name of the deceased an heir for his property." ⁶ The redeemer said, "Then I can't redeem it for myself, because I might put my own inheritance at risk. You, take my right of redemption on yourself; because I can't redeem it."

⁷ In the past, this is what was done in Isra'el to validate all transactions involving redemption and exchange: a man took off his shoe and gave it to the other party; this was the form of attestation in Isra'el. ⁸ So the redeemer said to Bo'az, "Buy it for yourself," and took off his shoe. ⁹ Bo'az addressed the leaders and all the people: "You are witnesses today that I am purchasing from Na'omi all that belonged to Elimelekh and all that belonged to Kilyon and Machlon. ¹⁰ Also I am acquiring as my wife Rut the woman from Mo'av, the wife of Machlon, in order to raise up in the name of the deceased an heir for his property; so that the name of the deceased will not be cut off from his kinsmen and from the gate of his place. You are witnesses today." ¹¹ All the people at the gate and the leaders said, "We are witnesses. May ADONAI make the woman who has come into your house like Rachel and like Le'ah, who between them built up the house of Isra'el. Do worthy deeds in Efrat; become renowned in Beit-Lechem. ¹² May your house, because of the seed ADONAI will give you from this young woman, become like the house of Peretz, whom Tamar bore to Y'hudah."

¹³ So Bo'az took Rut, and she became his wife. He had sexual relations with her, ADONAI enabled her to conceive, and she gave birth to a son. ¹⁴ Then the women said to Na'omi, "Blessed be ADONAI, who today has provided you a redeemer! May his name be renowned in Isra'el. ¹⁵ May he restore your life and provide for your old age; for your daughter-in-law, who loves you and is better to you than seven sons, has given birth to him." ¹⁶ Na'omi took the child, laid it on her breast and became its nurse. ¹⁷ The women who were her neighbors gave it a name; they said, "A son has been born to Na'omi," and called it 'Oved. He was the father of Yishai the father of David.

¹⁸ Here is the genealogy of Peretz. Peretz was the father of Hetzron, ¹⁹ Hetzron was the father of Ram, Ram was the father of 'Amminadav, ²⁰ 'Amminadav was the father of Nachshon, Nachshon was the father of Salmon, ²¹ Salmon was the father of Bo'az, Bo'az was the father of 'Oved, ²² 'Oved was the father of Yishai, and Yishai was the father of David.

Eikhah

LAMENTATIONS

1 ¹ How lonely lies the city
that once thronged with people!
Once great among the nations,
now she is like a widow!
Once princess among provinces,
she has become a vassal.

² Bitterly she weeps at night,
tears running down her cheeks.
Not one of all her lovers
is there to comfort her.
Her friends have all betrayed her;
they have become her enemies.

³ Y'hudah has fled into exile
from oppression and endless slavery.
She lives among the nations,
but there she finds no rest.
Her pursuers have all overtaken her
in the midst of her distress.

⁴ The roads to Tziyon are mourning
because no one comes to the festivals.
Her gateways are all deserted,
her *cohanim* are groaning,
her unmarried girls are grieving —
how bitter it is for her!

⁵ Her foes have become the head,
her enemies relax,
for *Adonai* has made her suffer
because of her many sins.
Her young children have gone away
captive before the foe.

6   All splendor has departed
from the daughter of Tziyon.
Her princes have become like deer
unable to find pasture,
running on, exhausted,
fleeing from the hunter.

7   In the days of her affliction and anguish,
Yerushalayim remembers
all the treasures that were hers,
ever since ancient times.
Now her people fall into the power of the foe,
and she has no one to help her;
her enemies are gloating over her,
mocking her desolation.

8   Yerushalayim sinned grievously;
therefore she has become unclean.
All who honored her now despise her,
because they have seen her naked.
She herself also moans
and turns her face away.

9   Her filthiness was in her skirts;
she gave no thought to how it would end.
Hence her astounding downfall,
with no one to console her.
"Look, *Adonai*, how I suffer;
for the foe has triumphed!"

10   Enemies have reached out their hands
to seize all her treasures.
She has seen *Goyim* approach
and go inside her sanctuary,
those whom you forbade even
to enter your assembly.

11   All her people are groaning,
as they search for something to eat.
They barter their treasures for food
to keep themselves alive.
"Look, *Adonai*! See
how despised I am.

12   "May it not happen to you,
all you passers-by!

Just look, and see if there is any pain
like the pain inflicted on me,
which *Adonai* made me suffer
on the day of his blazing anger.

13 "From on high, he sent down fire
deep into my bones;
he spread a net to catch my feet;
he turned me back;
he left me desolate,
in misery all day long.

14 "My sins have been bound into a yoke,
knit together by his hand.
It weighs down on my neck,
and it saps my strength.
Adonai has put me into the power
of those I cannot withstand.

15 "All the strong men within my walls
Adonai has rejected.
He has set a specific time
for crushing my young men.
Adonai has trodden, like grapes in a winepress,
the virgin daughter of Y'hudah.

16 "Because of these things, I weep;
my eyes, my eyes stream with tears;
for anyone who could comfort me
and revive my courage is far away.
My children are in a state of shock,
because the enemy has prevailed."

17 Tziyon spreads out her hands,
but no one is there to console her.
Concerning Ya'akov, *Adonai* has ordered
those around him to be his foes;
Yerushalayim has become for them
an unclean, filthy thing.

18 "*Adonai* is in the right,
for I rebelled against his word.
Listen, please, all you peoples;
and see how I am in pain!
My young women and my young men
have gone into captivity.

19   "I called out to my lovers,
but they let me down.
My *cohanim* and leaders
perished in the city,
as they were seeking food
to keep themselves alive.

20   "See, ADONAI, how distressed I am!
Everything in me is churning!
My heart turns over inside me,
because I have been so rebellious.
Outside, the sword brings bereavement;
inside, it is like death.

21   "People have heard how I groan,
with no one to comfort me.
All my foes have heard of my trouble;
they are glad that you have done it.
Bring the day you have promised,
so that they will suffer like me!

22   "Let all their wickedness come before you.
Then do to them
as you have done to me
because of all my offenses.
For my groans are many,
and I am sick at heart."

2 ¹   How enveloped in darkness *Adonai*, in his anger,
has made the daughter of Tziyon!
He has thrown down from heaven to earth
the splendor of Isra'el,
forgotten his footstool [the sanctuary]
on the day of his anger.

2   Without pity *Adonai* swallowed up
all the dwellings of Ya'akov.
In his wrath he broke down the strongholds
of the daughter of Y'hudah,
brought them down to the ground,
thus profaning the kingdom and its rulers.

3   In his fierce anger he cut off
all the power of Isra'el,
withdrew his protecting right hand
at the approach of the enemy,
and blazed up in Ya'akov like a flaming fire
devouring everything around it.

4   He bent his bow like an enemy,
     with his right hand set like a foe.
     He killed all who were pleasant to see.
     In the tent of the daughter of Tziyon,
     he poured out his fury like fire.

5   *Adonai* became like an enemy;
     he swallowed up Isra'el,
     swallowed up all its palaces,
     and destroyed all its strongholds.
     For the daughter of Y'hudah
     he has multiplied mourning and moaning.

6   He wrecked his tabernacle as easily as a garden,
     destroyed his place of assembly.
     Adonai caused Isra'el to forget
     designated times and *Shabbat*s.
     In the heat of his anger
     he rejected both king and *cohen*.

7   *Adonai* rejected his altar,
     disowned his sanctuary,
     and gave her palace walls
     over to the power of the foe,
     who raised such shouts in the house of *Adonai*
     that it sounded like a festival day.

8   *Adonai* resolved to destroy
     the wall of the daughter of Tziyon.
     He measured it with his line and did not stay his hand
     until it was all in ruins.
     He brought grief to rampart and wall;
     together they lie dejected.

9   Her gates have sunk into the ground;
     he destroyed and broke their bars.
     Her king and rulers are among the *Goyim*,
     there is no more *Torah*,
     and her prophets do not receive
     visions from *Adonai*.

10   The leaders of the daughter of Tziyon
     sit on the ground in silence.
     They throw dust on their heads;
     they are wearing sackcloth.
     The unmarried women of Yerushalayim
     lower their heads to the ground.

11   My eyes are worn out from weeping,
      everything in me is churning;
      I am empty of emotion
      because of the wounds to my people,
      because children and infants are fainting away
      in the streets of the city.

12   They keep asking their mothers,
      "Where is something to eat or drink?"
      as they faint away
      in the streets of the city,
      gasping out their last breath
      in their mother's bosom.

13   What can be said to you, what can be compared with you,
      daughter of Yerushalayim?
      What example can I give to comfort you,
      virgin daughter of Tziyon?
      For your downfall is as vast as the sea;
      who can heal you?

14   The visions your prophets saw for you
      were futile, just a whitewash.
      They did not expose your guilt,
      so as to reverse your fortunes —
      no, the visions they saw for you
      were alluring, but futile.

15   All who pass your way
      clap their hands at you,
      hissing and shaking their heads
      at the daughter of Yerushalayim:
      "This city was called 'perfection in beauty'?
      'the joy of the whole earth'?"

16   All your adversaries
      open their mouths to jeer at you.
      They hiss, they grind their teeth;
      they say, "We have swallowed her up!
      This is the day we were waiting for,
      and now we have lived to see it!"

17   ADONAI has done what he planned,
      he has fulfilled his promise,
      which he decreed in ancient times.
      He has destroyed without pity,
      he has let the enemy gloat over you
      and filled your foes with pride.

18   Their hearts cried out to *Adonai*,
      "Wall of the daughter of Tziyon!
      Let your tears stream down
      like a torrent, day and night!
      Give yourself no respite,
      give your eyes no rest!

19   "Get up! Cry out in the night,
      at the beginning of every watch!
      Pour your heart out like water
      before the face of *Adonai*!
      Lift up your hands to him
      for the lives of your babies,
      who are fainting away from hunger
      at every streetcorner."

20   *ADONAI*, look and see
      who it is you have thus tormented!
      Should women eat the fruit of their wombs,
      the children they have held in their hands?
      Should *cohanim* and prophets be slaughtered
      in the sanctuary of *Adonai*?

21   Youths and old men are lying
      on the ground in the streets,
      my unmarried women and young men
      have fallen by the sword.
      You killed them on the day of your anger,
      you slaughtered them without pity.

22   You have summoned my terrors from every direction,
      as on a festival day.
      On the day of *ADONAI*'s anger,
      not one escaped; not one survived —
      the children I held in my arms and raised,
      my enemy has destroyed.

3 ¹   I am the man who has seen affliction
      under the rod of his fury.

2   He has led me and made me walk
      in darkness and not in light.

3   Against me alone he turns his hand
      again and again, all day.

4   He has worn away my skin and flesh,
      he has broken my bones.

5   He has besieged and surrounded me
      with bitterness and hardship.

6   He has made me live in darkness,
like those who are long dead.

7   He has walled me in, so I can't escape;
he has weighed me down with chains.

8   Even when I cry out, pleading for help,
he shuts out my prayer.

9   He has barred my way with blocks of stone,
he has made my paths crooked.

10   He lies in wait for me like a bear,
like a lion in hiding.

11   He has forced me aside and torn me to pieces,
leaving me stunned.

12   He has bent his bow and used me
as a target for his arrows.

13   He has pierced my vital organs
with shafts from his quiver.

14   I'm a laughingstock to all my people,
the butt of their taunts all day long.

15   He has filled me with bitterness,
sated me with wormwood.

16   He has broken my teeth with gravel
and pressed me down into ashes.

17   I have been so deprived of peace,
I have so forgotten what happiness is,

18   that I think, "My strength is gone,
and so is my hope in ADONAI."

19   Remember my utter misery,
the wormwood and the gall.

20   They are always on my mind;
this is why I am so depressed.

21   But in my mind I keep returning to something,
something that gives me hope —

22   that the grace of ADONAI is not exhausted,
that his compassion has not ended.

23   [On the contrary,] they are new every morning!
How great your faithfulness!

24   "ADONAI is all I have," I say;
"therefore I will put my hope in him.

25   ADONAI is good to those waiting for him,
to those who are seeking him out.

26 It is good to wait patiently
for the saving help of *Adonai*.

27 It is good for a man
to bear the yoke from his youth.

28 Let him sit alone in silence
when he has laid it on him.

29 Let him submit absolutely;
there may yet be hope.

30 Let him offer his cheek to the one who strikes it,
and receive his fill of insults.

31 For rejection by *Adonai*
does not last forever.

32 He may cause grief, but he will take pity,
in keeping with the greatness of his grace.

33 For he does not arbitrarily torment
or punish human beings.

34 When anyone tramples underfoot
any of the prisoners of the land;

35 when anyone deprives a person of justice,
in defiance of the Most High;

36 when someone is cheated of justice in court —
does *Adonai* not take note of such things?

37 Who can say something and have it happen
without *Adonai*'s commanding it?

38 Don't both bad things and good proceed
from the mouth of the Most High?

39 Why should anyone alive complain,
even a strong man, about the punishment for his sins?

40 Let us examine and test our ways
and return to *Adonai*.

41 Let us lift up our hearts and our hands
to God in heaven and say,

42 "We, for our part, have transgressed and rebelled;
you, for your part, have not forgiven.

43 "You have covered us with anger,
pursued and slaughtered us without pity.

44 You have covered yourself with a cloud so thick
that no prayer can pass through.

45 You have reduced us
to rubbish and filth among the peoples.

46   "All our adversaries
    open their mouths to jeer at us.
47   Panic and pitfall have come upon us,
    desolation and destruction.
48   My eyes stream with rivers of water
    over the destruction of the daughter of my people."

49   My eyes weep ceaselessly;
    there is no respite,
50   until ADONAI looks down
    and sees from heaven.
51   My eyes make me so upset
    at the fate of the women in my city.

52   Those who are my enemies for no reason
    hunted me down like a bird.
53   They forced me alive into a pit
    and threw stones on me.
54   Water rose above my head;
    I thought, "I am finished!"

55   I called on your name, ADONAI,
    from the bottom of the pit.
56   You heard my voice; don't close your ear
    at my sighs, at my cries.
57   You came near when I called to you;
    you said, "Don't be afraid."

58   Adonai, you defended my cause;
    you redeemed my life.
59   ADONAI, you see how I have been wronged;
    give judgment in my favor!
60   You have seen all their vindictiveness
    and all their plots against me.

61   You have heard their taunts, ADONAI,
    and all their plots against me,
62   the whispered murmurings of my foes
    against me all day long.
63   See how, whether they sit or stand,
    I am the butt of their taunts.

64   Repay them, ADONAI,
    as their deeds deserve.
65   Give them hardheartedness
    as your curse on them.

⁶⁶ Pursue them in anger!
Destroy them from under your heavens!

4 ¹ How the gold has lost its luster!
How the fine gold has changed!
How the stones of the sanctuary
lie scattered at every streetcorner!

² The precious sons of Tziyon,
as precious as fine gold —
to think they are now worth no more
than clay jars made by a potter!

³ Even jackals bare their breasts
in order to nurse their young,
but the daughters of my people have become as cruel
as ostriches in the desert.

⁴ The tongue of the baby at the breast
sticks to the roof of its mouth from thirst;
young children are begging for bread,
but no one is giving them any.

⁵ People who once ate only the best
lie dying in the streets;
those who were raised wearing purple
are clawing at piles of garbage.

⁶ For the offense of the daughter of my people
is greater than the sin of S'dom,
which was overthrown in an instant,
without a hand to help her.

⁷ Her princes were purer than snow;
they were whiter than milk,
their bodies more ruddy than pink pearls,
as beautiful as sapphires.

⁸ Now their faces are blacker than coal;
in the streets they go unrecognized.
Their skin has shriveled over their bones
and become as dry as a stick.

⁹ Those slain by the sword are better off
than those who are dying from hunger;
since these waste away as if pierced through,
for lack of food from the fields.

¹⁰ With their own hands compassionate women
have cooked their own children;
their children became their food
when the daughter of my people was destroyed.

¹¹ ADONAI has finished with his fury,
he has poured out his blazing wrath;
he kindled a fire in Tziyon
that consumed its very foundations.

¹² The kings of the earth could not believe,
neither could anyone living in the world,
that enemy or foe would ever enter
the gates of Yerushalayim.

¹³ It happened because of the sins of her prophets
and the offenses of her *cohanim*,
who, within her walls,
shed the blood of the righteous.

¹⁴ They wander in the streets like the blind;
they are so polluted with blood
that nobody is able
even to touch their clothing.

¹⁵ "Keep away! Unclean!" people shout at them,
"Keep away! Away! Don't touch us!"
They flee, to wander here and there;
but no nation allows them to stay.

¹⁶ ADONAI himself scattered them;
he will no longer look after them;
they had no respect for *cohanim*
and showed no kindness to the leaders.

¹⁷ As for us, our eyes are worn out
from looking in vain for help;
we kept on watching and watching
for a nation that couldn't save us.

¹⁸ They keep dogging our steps,
so that we can't go out in our streets.
Our end is near, our time is up;
yes, our end has come.

¹⁹ Those who pursued us were swifter
than eagles in the sky.

They chased us over the mountains
and waylaid us in the desert.

20 ADONAI's anointed, our life-breath,
was caught in their pits;
though of him we had said, "Under his protection,
we can live among the nations."

21 Rejoice, be glad, daughter of Edom,
who lives in the land of 'Utz.
To you too the cup will pass;
you will get drunk and strip yourself naked!

22 Your offenses, daughter of Tziyon, are atoned for;
he will keep you in exile no longer.
Your offenses, daughter of Edom, he will punish;
he will expose your sins.

5 1 Remember, ADONAI, what has happened to us;
look, and see our disgrace.
2 The land we possessed has been passed on to strangers,
our homes to foreigners.
3 We have become fatherless orphans,
our mothers now are widows.
4 We have to pay to drink our own water;
we have to buy our own wood.
5 The yoke is on our necks; we are persecuted;
we toil to exhaustion but are given no rest.
6 We made pacts with Egypt and Ashur
to get enough food.
7 Our ancestors sinned and no longer exist;
we bear the weight of their guilt.
8 We are ruled by slaves,
and there is no one to save us from their power.
9 We get our food at the peril of our lives
because of the sword in the desert.
10 Our skins are as black as a furnace
because of the searing blasts of famine.
11 They have raped the women of Tziyon,
virgins in the cities of Y'hudah.
12 Princes are hung up by their hands,
leaders receive no respect.
13 Young men are compelled to grind at the mill,
boys stagger under loads of wood.
14 The old men have deserted the city gate,
the young men have given up their music.

15 Joy has vanished from our hearts,
   our dancing has turned into mourning.
16 The crown has fallen from our heads.
   Woe to us! for we have sinned.
17 This is why our hearts are sick;
   this is why our eyes grow dim —
18 it's because of Mount Tziyon, so wasted
   that jackals have overrun it.
19 You, ADONAI, reign forever;
   your throne endures through all generations.
20 Why do you never remember us?
   Why abandon us for so long a time?
21 ADONAI, turn us back to you; and we will come back;
   renew our days, as they were in the past —
22 unless you have totally rejected us
   in a fury that knows no limits.

[ADONAI, turn us back to you; and we will come back;
renew our days, as they were in the past.]

Kohelet
ECCLESIASTES

1 ¹ The words of Kohelet the son of David, king in Yerushalayim:

²   Pointless! Pointless! — says Kohelet —
    Utterly meaningless! Nothing matters!
³   What does a person gain from all his labor
    at which he toils under the sun?

⁴   Generations come, generations go,
    but the earth remains forever.
⁵   The sun rises, the sun sets;
    then it speeds to its place and rises there.
⁶   The wind blows south,
    then it turns north;
    the wind blows all around
    and keeps returning to its rounds.
⁷   All the rivers flow to the sea,
    yet the sea is not full;
    to the place where the rivers flow,
    there they keep on flowing.

⁸   Everything is wearisome,
    more than one can express;
    the eye is not satisfied with seeing,
    the ear not filled up with hearing.
⁹   What has been is what will be,
    what has been done is what will be done,
    and there is nothing new
    under the sun.
¹⁰   Is there something of which it is said,
    "See, this is new"?
    It existed already in the ages before us.
¹¹   No one remembers the people of long ago;
    and those to come will not be remembered
    by those who come after them.

¹² I, Kohelet, have been king over Isra'el in Yerushalayim. ¹³ I wisely applied myself to seek out and investigate everything done under heaven. What a bothersome task God has given humanity to keep us occupied! ¹⁴ I have seen all the activities that are done under the sun, and it's all pointless, feeding on wind.

¹⁵   What is crooked can't be straightened;
     what is not there can't be counted.

¹⁶ I said to myself, "Look, I have acquired much wisdom, more than anyone ruling Yerushalayim before me." Yes, I experienced a great deal of wisdom and knowledge; ¹⁷ yet when I applied myself to understanding wisdom and knowledge, as well as stupidity and folly, I came to see that this too was merely feeding on wind.

¹⁸   For in much wisdom is much grief;
     the more knowledge, the more suffering.

2 ¹ I said to myself, "Come now, I will test myself with pleasure and enjoying good things"; but this too was pointless. ² Of laughter I said, "This is stupid," and of pleasure, "What's the use of it?"

³ I searched my mind for how to gratify my body with wine and, with my mind still guiding me with wisdom, how to pursue foolishness; my object was to find out what was the best thing for people to do during the short time they have under heaven to live. ⁴ I worked on a grand scale — I built myself palaces, planted myself vineyards, ⁵ and made myself gardens and parks; in them I planted all kinds of fruit trees. ⁶ I made myself pools from which to water the trees springing up in the forest. ⁷ I bought male and female slaves, and I had my home-born slaves as well. I also had growing herds of cattle and flocks of sheep, more than anyone before me in Yerushalayim. ⁸ I amassed silver and gold, the wealth of kings and provinces. I acquired male and female singers, things that provide sensual delight, and a good many concubines. ⁹ So I grew great, surpassing all who preceded me in Yerushalayim; my wisdom, too, stayed with me. ¹⁰ I denied my eyes nothing they wanted. I withheld no pleasure from myself; for I took pleasure in all my work, and this was my reward for all my work. ¹¹ Then I looked at all that my hands had accomplished and at the work I had toiled at; and I saw that it was all meaningless and feeding on wind, and that there was nothing to be gained under the sun.

¹² So I decided to look more carefully at wisdom, stupidity and foolishness; for what can the man who succeeds the king do, except what has already been done? ¹³ I saw that wisdom is more useful than foolishness, just as light is more useful than darkness.

¹⁴   The wise man has eyes in his head,
     but the fool walks in darkness.
     Yet the same fate awaits them all.

¹⁵ So I said to myself, "If the same thing happens to the fool as to me, then what did I gain by being wise?" and I thought to myself, "This too is pointless. ¹⁶ For the wise

man, like the fool, will not be long remembered, inasmuch as in the times to come, everything will long ago have been forgotten. The wise man, no less than the fool, must die." [17] So I came to hate life, because the activities done under the sun were loathesome to me, since everything is meaningless and feeding on wind. [18] I hated all the things for which I had worked under the sun, because I saw that I would have to leave them to the man who will come after me. [19] Who knows whether he will be a wise man or a fool? Yet he will have control over all the things I worked for and which demonstrated how wise I am under the sun. This too is pointless. [20] Thus I came to despair over all the things I had worked for under the sun. [21] Here is a man whose work is done with wisdom, knowledge and skill; yet he has to leave it to someone who has put no work into it. This is not only pointless, but a great evil. [22] For what does a person get from all his efforts and ambitions permeating the work he does under the sun? [23] His whole life is one of pain, and his work is full of stress; even at night his mind gets no rest. This too is pointless. [24] So there is nothing better for a man to do than eat, drink and and let himself enjoy the good that results from his work. I also realized that this is from God's hand. [25] For who will eat and who will enjoy except me? [26] For to the man who is good from [God's] viewpoint he gives wisdom, knowledge and joy; but to the sinner he gives the task of collecting and accumulating things to leave to him who is good from God's viewpoint. This too is pointless and feeding on wind.

3 [1] For everything there is a season,
a right time for every intention under heaven —
[2] a time to be born and a time to die,
a time to plant and a time to uproot,
[3] a time to kill and a time to heal,
a time to tear down and a time to build,
[4] a time to weep and a time to laugh,
a time to mourn and a time to dance,
[5] a time to throw stones and a time to gather stones,
a time to embrace and a time to refrain,
[6] a time to search and a time to give up,
a time to keep and a time to discard,
[7] a time to tear and a time to sew,
a time to keep silent and a time to speak,
[8] a time to love and a time to hate,
a time for war and a time for peace.

[9] What does the worker gain from his efforts? [10] I have seen the task God has given humanity to keep us occupied. [11] He has made everything suited to its time; also, he has given human beings an awareness of eternity; but in such a way that they can't fully comprehend, from beginning to end, the things God does. [12] I know that there is nothing better for them to do than to be happy and enjoy themselves as long as they live. [13] Still, the fact that everyone can eat and drink and enjoy the good that results from all his work, is a gift of God. [14] I know that

> whatever God does will last forever;
> there is nothing to add or subtract from it;
> and God has done it so that people will fear him.

¹⁵ That which was is here already;
> and that which will be has already been,
> but God seeks out what people chase after.

¹⁶ Another thing I observed under the sun:

> There, in the same place as justice, was wickedness;
> there, in the same place as righteousness, was wickedness.

¹⁷ I said to myself, "The righteous and the wicked God will judge, because there is a right time for every intention and for every action."

¹⁸ Concerning people, I said to myself, "God is testing them, so that they will see that by themselves they are just animals. ¹⁹ After all, the same things that happen to people happen to animals, the very same thing — just as the one dies, so does the other. Yes, their breath is the same; so that humans are no better than animals; since nothing matters, anyway. ²⁰ They all go to the same place; they all come from dust, and they all return to dust. ²¹ Who knows if the spirit of a human being goes upward and the spirit of an animal goes downward into the earth?" ²² So I concluded that there is nothing better for a person to do than take joy in his activities, that that is his allotted portion; for who can enable him to see what will happen after him?

4 ¹ But I turned away and thought about all the kinds of oppression being done under the sun.

> I saw the tears of the oppressed,
> and they had no one to comfort them.
> The power was on the side of their oppressors,
> and they had no one to comfort them.

² So I considered the dead happier, because they were already dead, than the living, who must still live their lives; ³ but happier than either of them is the one who has not yet been born, because he has not yet seen the evil things that are done under the sun.

⁴ Next I realized that all effort and achievement stem from one person's envy of another. This too is futility and feeding on wind.

⁵ Fools fold their arms together
> and eat their own flesh away.

⁶ Better an armload with tranquillity
> than both arms full of effort and feeding on wind.

⁷ Then I turned my attention to something else under the sun that is pointless: ⁸ the situation in which a solitary individual without a companion, with neither son nor

brother, keeps on working endlessly but never has enough wealth. "For whom" [he should ask], "am I working so hard and denying myself pleasure?" This too is truly pointless, a sorry business.

⁹ Two are better than one, in that their cooperative efforts yield this advantage: ¹⁰ if one of them falls, the other will help his partner up — woe to him who is alone when he falls and has no one to help him up. ¹¹ Again, if two people sleep together, they keep each other warm; but how can one person be warm by himself? ¹² Moreover, an attacker may defeat someone who is alone, but two can resist him; and a three-stranded cord is not easily broken.

¹³ Better a youth who is poor but wise
than a king who is old but foolish,
no longer willing to listen to advice.
¹⁴ True, he rose from prison to be king;
yet, while ruling, he became poor.

¹⁵ I observed that all who live and walk under the sun took the side of the youth mentioned first who would rule in place of the king, ¹⁶ and that no limit was set for the number of his subjects. Nevertheless, those who come afterwards will not regard him highly. This too is certainly pointless and feeding on wind.

¹⁷⁽⁵:¹⁾ Watch your step when you go to the house of God. Offering to listen is better than fools offering sacrifices, because they don't discern whether or not they are doing evil.

5 ¹⁽²⁾ Don't speak impulsively — don't be in a hurry
to give voice to your words before God.
For God is in heaven, and you are on earth;
so let your words be few.
²⁽³⁾ For nightmares come from worrying too much;
and a fool, when he speaks, chatters too much.

³⁽⁴⁾ If you make a vow to God, don't delay in discharging it. For God takes no pleasure in fools, so discharge your vow! ⁴⁽⁵⁾ Better not to make a vow than to make a vow and not discharge it. ⁵⁽⁶⁾ Don't let your words make you guilty, and don't tell the temple official that you made the vow by mistake. Why give God reason to be angry at what you say and destroy what you have accomplished? ⁶⁽⁷⁾ For [this is what happens when there are too] many dreams, aimless activities and words. Instead, just fear God!

⁷⁽⁸⁾ If you see the poor oppressed, rights violated and justice perverted in the province, don't be surprised; for a high official has one higher watching him, and there are others above them. ⁸⁽⁹⁾ But the greatest advantage to the country is when the king makes himself a servant to the land.

⁹⁽¹⁰⁾ The lover of money never has enough money;
the lover of luxury never has enough income.

This too is pointless.

10(11)   When the quantity of goods increases,
so does the number of parasites consuming them;
so the only advantage to the owner is
that he gets to watch them do it.

11(12)   The sleep of a working man is sweet,
whether he eats little or much;
but the overfullness of the rich
won't let them sleep at all.

12(13) Here is a gross evil which I have seen under the sun: the owner of wealth hoards it to his own hurt.

13(14)   Due to some misfortune,
the wealth turns to loss;
and then if he has fathered a son,
he has nothing to leave him.

14(15)   Just as he came from his mother's womb,
so he will go back naked as he came,
and for his efforts he will take nothing
that he can carry away in his hand.

15(16) This too is a gross evil, that in every respect as he came, so will he go; thus what profit does he have after toiling to earn the wind? 16(17) All his life he eats in darkness, in frustration, in sickness and in anger.

17(18) This is what I have seen to be good: that it is appropriate for a person to eat, drink and enjoy the good that results from all his work that he engages in under the sun for all the days of his life that God has given him, for this is his allotted portion. 18(19) Also, everyone to whom God has given riches and wealth, along with the power to enjoy it, so that he takes his allotted portion and finds pleasure in his work — this is a gift of God; 19(20) for he will not brood over the fact that his life is short, since God keeps him occupied with what will bring him joy.

6 ^{1} I have seen another evil under the sun, and it weighs heavily on people: ^{2} the case in which God gives someone riches, wealth and honor, so that he lacks nothing that he wants; but God does not give him the power to enjoy them, and some stranger gets to enjoy them — this is meaningless, evil, sick.

^{3} Suppose a man fathers a hundred children and lives many years, so that he has a long life, but he fails to enjoy himself; then, even if he were to [live indefinitely and therefore] never be buried, I say that it would be better to be born dead. ^{4} For the arrival of a stillborn baby is a futile thing, and its departure is in darkness; its name is [forgotten,] covered in darkness; ^{5} and although it has never seen or known the sun, it is more content than he is, ^{6} without enjoying himself, even if he were to live a thousand years twice over. Doesn't everyone go to the same place?

7   The purpose of all toil is to fill the mouth,
     yet the appetite is never satisfied.
8   What advantage has the wise over the fool,
     or the person with experience, if he is poor?
9   Better what the eyes can see
     than meandering desire.
     Yet this too is pointless
     and feeding on wind.

10   Whatever he is, he was named long ago,
     and it is known that he is merely human;
     moreover, he cannot defeat
     what is mightier than he [death].
11   There are many things that only add to futility,
     so how do humans benefit from them?
12   For who knows what is good for someone during life,
     during the days of his pointless life spent like a shadow?
     Who can tell what will happen under the sun
     after a person is gone?

7 1 A good name is better than perfumed oil,
     and the day of death better than the day of birth.
2   Better to go to a house of mourning
     than to go to a house of feasting,
     for all are destined to be mourned;
     the living should lay this to heart.
3   Grief is better than laughter,
     for sadness can improve a person.
4   The thoughts of the wise are in the house of mourning,
     but the thoughts of fools are in the house of pleasure.
5   It is better to hear the rebukes of the wise
     than to listen to the songs of fools.
6   For the laughter of fools is like the crackling of thorns
     burning under a pot; this too is pointless.
7   But oppression can make a wise man stupid;
     also a gift can destroy understanding.

8   The end of something is better than its beginning,
     so the patient are better than the proud.
9   Don't be quick to get angry,
     for [only] fools nurse anger.

10   Don't ask why the old days were better than now,
     because that is a foolish question.
11   Wisdom is good, along with possessions,
     an advantage to all who see the sun.
12   For wisdom is a shelter,

and money is a shelter,
but the advantage of knowledge is
that wisdom keeps the one who has it alive.

13 Consider the work of God:
who can make straight what he has made crooked?
14 When things are going well, enjoy yourself;
but when things are going badly, consider
that God made the one alongside the other,
so that people would learn nothing of their futures.
15 In my pointless life, I've seen everything —
from the righteous person perishing in his uprightness
to the wicked one who lives a long life
and keeps on doing wrong.
16 So don't be overly righteous or overly wise;
why should you disappoint yourself?
17 But don't be overly wicked, and don't be foolish;
why should you die before your time?
18 Don't grasp just one of these rules;
take hold of the other as well;
for he who is in fear of God
will live by both of them.
19 To a wise man wisdom is better protection
than ten rulers in a city.
20 For there isn't a righteous person on earth
who does [only] good and never sins.

21 Also, don't take seriously every word spoken,
such as when you hear your servant speaking badly of you;
22 because often, as you yourself know,
you have spoken badly of others.

23 All this I have put to the test of wisdom;
I said, "I will acquire wisdom";
but wisdom remained far away from me.
24 That which exists is far away
and deep, so deep, that it can't be discovered.

25 So I turned myself and my thoughts to know, search out and seek wisdom and the
reasons behind things, also to know how foolish it is to be wicked and how stupid to
act like a fool.

26 I found more bitter than death
the woman who is a trap,
whose heart is a snare
and whose hands are like prison chains.
The man who pleases God will escape from her,

but the sinner will be caught by her.

27 I have found this — says Kohelet —
adding one thing to another to reach a conclusion,

28 I searched a long time without finding it:
one man in a thousand I have found,
but a woman among all those I have not found.

29 This is the only thing I have found,
that God made human beings upright,
but they have devised many schemes.

8¹ Who can be compared with a wise person?
Who else knows what a thing means?
Wisdom lights up the face
and softens a grim appearance.

2 Keep the king's command
because of the oath before God.

3 Don't be quick to leave his presence,
and don't persist in doing what is wrong,
for he does whatever he pleases.

4 After all, his word is final;
who can challenge him, "Why are you doing that?"

5 Whoever obeys his command
will never come to harm,
and the wise person will know
the right time and judgment.

6 For to everything there is
a right time and a judgment,
since people are greatly troubled

7 by uncertainty over the future;
even when the event takes place,
who will tell them about it?

8 Just as no one has the power
to keep the wind from blowing,
so no one has power
over the day of death.
If one is drafted to fight a war,
one can't send a substitute;
likewise the wicked won't escape death
by their wickedness.

⁹ All this I have seen, as I applied my mind to everything done under the sun when one person tyrannizes another. ¹⁰ Thus I saw the wicked buried; they had even come from the Holy Place. But those who had acted uprightly were forgotten in the city. This too is a futile thing; ¹¹ because the punishment decreed for an evil act is not promptly carried out; therefore people who plan to do evil are strengthened in their intentions. ¹² For a sinner can do evil a hundred times and still live

a long life; although I know that in the end things will go well with those who fear God, because they fear him. ¹³ But things will not go well with the wicked; and, like a shadow, he will not prolong his days; because he doesn't fear God.

¹⁴ There is something frustrating that occurs on earth, namely, that there are righteous people to whom things happen as if they were doing wicked deeds; and, again, there are wicked people to whom things happen as if they were doing righteous deeds. I say that this too is pointless.

¹⁵ So I recommend enjoyment — a person can do nothing better under the sun than eat, drink and enjoy himself; this is what should accompany him as he does his work for as long as God gives him to live under the sun.

¹⁶ When I applied myself to gain wisdom and to observe how people occupy themselves on earth, that people's eyes don't see sleep either by day or by night, ¹⁷ then, on looking over all of God's work, I realized that it is impossible to grasp all the activity taking place under the sun; because even if a person works hard at searching it out, he won't grasp it; and even if a wise person thinks he knows it, he still won't be able to grasp it.

9 ¹ I applied myself to all of this, sifted through it and concluded that the righteous and the wise, along with their deeds, are in God's hands — a person cannot know whether these people and deeds will be rewarded with love or with hatred; all options are open. ² Anything can happen to anyone; the same thing can happen to the righteous as to the wicked, to the good and clean and to the unclean, to someone who offers a sacrifice and to someone who doesn't offer a sacrifice; it is the same for a good person as for a sinner, for someone who takes an oath rashly as for someone who fears to take an oath. ³ This is another evil among all those done under the sun, that the same events can occur to anyone. Truly, the human mind is full of evil; and as long as people live, folly is in their hearts; after which they go to be with the dead. ⁴ For as long as a person is linked with the living, there is hope — better to be a living dog than a dead lion! ⁵ For the living know that they will die, but the dead know nothing; there is no longer any reward for them, because all memory of them is lost. ⁶ What they loved, what they hated and what they envied all disappeared long ago, and they no longer have a share in anything done under the sun.

⁷   So go, eat your bread with joy,
       and drink your wine with a happy heart,
       for God has already accepted your deeds.
⁸   Let your clothing always be white,
       and never fail to perfume your head.

⁹ Enjoy life with the wife you have loved throughout your meaningless life that he has given you under the sun, all the days of your futility; for that is your allotted portion in life and in your labor that you work at under the sun. ¹⁰ Whatever task comes your way to do, do it with all your strength; because in Sh'ol, where you will go, there is neither working nor planning, neither knowledge nor wisdom.

¹¹ Yet another thing I observed under the sun is that races aren't won by the swift or battles by the strong, and that food doesn't go to the wise or wealth to the intelligent

or favor to the experts; rather, time and chance rule them all. ¹² For people don't know when their time will come any more than fish taken in the fatal net or birds caught in a snare; similarly, people are snared at an unfortunate time, when suddenly it falls on them.

¹³ Here is something else I have seen as wisdom under the sun, and it seemed important to me: ¹⁴ there was a small town with few people in it; and a great king came to attack it; he surrounded it and built massive siege-works against it. ¹⁵ Now there was found in it a man who was poor but wise, and by his wisdom he saved the city; yet afterwards, nobody remembered that poor man. ¹⁶ So, although I say that wisdom is better than strength, nevertheless the poor man's wisdom is despised; nobody pays attention to what he says.

17   A wise man speaking quietly is more worth heeding
        than the shouts of a ruler commanding fools.

18   Wisdom is better than weapons of war,
        but a person who makes a mistake can destroy much good.

10 ¹   Just as dead flies make perfumed oil stink,
        so a little folly outweighs wisdom and honor.

2   A wise man's heart leads him rightly,
        but a fool's heart leads him astray;

3   and when a fool travels, he has no good sense,
        thus showing everyone that he is a fool.

4   If a ruler gets angry at you, stay at your post,
        because calmness soothes great offenses.

5   Another evil I have seen under the sun,
        the kind of mistake rulers make, is that

6   fools are promoted to high positions,
        while the rich occupy humble places.

7   I have seen servants riding horses,
        while princes walk on foot like slaves.

8   He who digs a pit may fall into it;
        he who breaks through a wall may be bitten by a snake.

9   He who quarries stones may get hurt by them,
        he who chops wood puts himself in danger.

10   If the [hatchet's] iron [blade] is blunt,
        and [its user] doesn't sharpen it,
        he will have to exert more effort;
        but the expert has the advantage of his skill.

11   If a snake bites before it is charmed,
        the snake-charmer has no advantage.

12 The words spoken by the wise bring them favor,
but the lips of a fool swallow him up.
13 What he says starts with foolishness
and ends with wicked madness.
14 A fool keeps talking and talking,
yet no one knows what the future will bring —
can anyone tell a person
what will happen after he's gone?
15 The efforts of a fool wear him out;
he doesn't even know the way to town!

16 Woe to you, land, when your king is a child,
and your leaders start their parties in the morning!
17 Happy are you, land, when your king is well-born,
and your princes eat at the proper time,
in order to stay strong, not to get drunk!
18 When the owner is lazy, the roof sags;
when hands are idle, the house leaks.
19 Parties are made for having a good time,
wine adds cheer to life,
and money has an answer for everything.
20 Don't insult the king, not even in your thoughts;
and don't insult the wealthy, not even in your bedroom;
for a bird in the air might carry the news,
a creature with wings might repeat what you said.

11 ¹ Send your resources out over the seas;
eventually you will reap a return.
2 Divide your merchandise into seven or eight shares,
since you don't know what disasters may come on the earth.
3 If the clouds are full of rain,
they empty themselves on the earth.
Whether a tree falls toward the north or the south,
the place where the tree falls is where it stays.
4 He who keeps watching the wind will never sow;
he who keeps looking at the clouds will never reap.
5 Just as you don't know the way of the wind
or how bones grow in a pregnant woman's womb,
so you don't know the work of God,
the maker of everything.
6 In the morning, sow your seed;
and don't slack off until evening;
for you don't know which sowing will succeed,
this, or that, or if both will do well.
7 Then the light will be sweet,
and it will be a pleasure to see the sun.

8   For if a person lives many years,
let him take joy in them all;
yet remembering that there will be many days of darkness,
that all to come is futile.

9   Young person, if you spend your youth only having fun,
if you use your early years just to entertain yourself,
if you follow your heart as you live your life,
and let your eyes be your guide;
understand that for all these things
God will bring you to judgment.

10   Therefore, remove anger from your heart;
and keep from harming your body;
for neither adolescence nor youth
has any lasting value.

12 1   So remember your creator while you are young,
before the evil days come,
and the years approach when you will say,
"They no longer give me pleasure";

2   before the sun and the light grow dim,
also the moon and the stars;
before the clouds return after the rain;

3   on the day when the guards of the house are trembling,
and men of courage are bent over double;
when the women stop grinding grain,
because there are so few;
when the women at the windows
can no longer see out;

4   when the doors to the streets are kept shut;
when the noise from the grain-mill fades;
when a person is startled by the chirp of a bird,
yet their singing is hard to hear;

5   when they will be afraid to go up a hill,
and terrors will stalk the way,
even though the almond tree is in bloom;
when the locust can only drag itself along,
and the caper berry has no [aphrodisiac] effect —
because the person is headed for his eternal home,
and the mourners are already gathering
in the marketplace —

6   before the silver cord is snapped
the bowl of gold is cracked,
the pitcher is shattered at the spring,
the pulley is broken at the cistern,

7   the dust returns to earth, as it was,
and the spirit returns to God, who gave it!

⁸   Pointless! Meaningless! — says Kohelet,
        Nothing matters at all!

⁹ Not only was Kohelet wise, he also taught the people what he knew; also he weighed, researched and corrected many ethical sayings. ¹⁰ Kohelet worked to develop an attractive writing style, in which he expressed the truth straightforwardly. ¹¹ The sayings of the wise are as sharp as goads, and those given by leaders of assemblies are like well-fixed nails; [in this case,] they are presented by a single shepherd. ¹² In addition, my son, take heed: one can write many books — there's no end to it; and one can study so much that it wearies the flesh.

¹³ Here is the final conclusion, now that you have heard everything: fear God, and keep his *mitzvot*; this is what being human is all about. ¹⁴ For God will bring to judgment everything we do, including every secret, whether good or bad.

[Here is the final conclusion, now that you have heard everything: fear God, and keep his *mitzvot*; this is what being human is all about.]

Ester
ESTHER

1 ¹These events took place in the time of Achashverosh, the Achashverosh who ruled over 127 provinces from India to Ethiopia. ²It was in those days, when King Achashverosh sat on his royal throne in Shushan the capital, ³in the third year of his reign, that he gave a banquet for all his officials and courtiers. The army of Persia and Media, the nobles and the provincial officials were in attendance. ⁴He displayed the dazzling wealth of his kingdom and his great splendor for a long time, 180 days. ⁵At the end of that time, the king gave a seven-day banquet in the courtyard of the royal palace garden for all the people, both great and small, there in Shushan the capital. ⁶There were white cotton curtains and blue hangings fastened to silver rods, with cords of fine linen and purple; the columns were marble; the couches [for reclining at table] were of gold and silver on a mosaic flooring of malachite, marble, mother-of-pearl and onyx. ⁷Drinks were served in gold goblets, with each goblet different from the others. There was royal wine in abundance, as befits royal bounty. ⁸The drinking was not according to any fixed rule, for the king had ordered the stewards to serve each man what he wanted. ⁹Also Vashti the queen gave a banquet for the women in the royal house belonging to King Achashverosh.

¹⁰On the seventh day, when the king was in high spirits from the wine, he ordered Mehuman, Bizta, Harvona, Bigta, Avagta, Zetar and Karkas, the seven officers who attended him, ¹¹to bring Queen Vashti before the king with the royal crown, in order to show the people and the officials her beauty, for she was indeed a good-looking woman. ¹²But Queen Vashti refused to come at the order of the king, which he had sent through his officers. This enraged the king — his anger blazed inside him.

¹³As was the king's custom, he consulted sages well-versed in matters of law and justice. ¹⁴With him were Karshna, Shetar, Admata, Tarshish, Meres, Marsna and Memukhan, the seven vice-regents of Persia and Media, who were part of the king's inner circle and were the most important officials in the kingdom. ¹⁵[The king asked the sages,] "According to the law, what should we do to Queen Vashti, since she didn't obey the order of King Achashverosh conveyed by the officers?"

¹⁶Memukhan presented the king and vice-regents this answer: "Vashti the queen has wronged not only the king, but also all the officials and all the peoples in all the provinces of King Achashverosh; ¹⁷because this act of the queen's will become known to all the women, who will then start showing disrespect toward their own husbands; they will say, 'King Achashverosh ordered Vashti the queen to be brought before him, but she wouldn't come.' ¹⁸Moreover, the noble ladies of Persia and Media who hear of the queen's conduct will mention it to all the king's officials, which will bring about no end of disrespect and discord. ¹⁹If it pleases his majesty, let him issue

a royal decree — and let it be written as one of the laws of the Persians and Medes, which are irrevocable — that Vashti is never again to be admitted into the presence of King Achashverosh, and that the king give her royal position to someone better than she. ²⁰ When the edict made by the king is proclaimed throughout the length and breadth of the kingdom, then all wives will honor their husbands, whether great or small."

²¹ This advice pleased the king and the officials, so the king did what Memukhan had suggested — ²² he sent letters to all the royal provinces, to each province in its own script and to each people in their own language, that every man should be master in his own house and speak the language of his own people.

2 ¹ A while later, when King Achashverosh's anger had subsided, he remembered Vashti, what she had done and what had been decreed against her. ² The king's servants attending him said, "A search should be made for young, good-looking virgins. ³ The king should appoint officials in all the provinces of the kingdom to gather all the young, good-looking virgins to the house for the harem, in Shushan the capital. They should be put under the care of Hegai the king's officer in charge of the women, and he should give them the cosmetics they require. ⁴ Then, the girl who seems best to the king should become queen instead of Vashti." This proposal pleased the king, so he acted accordingly.

⁵ There was in Shushan the capital a man who was a Jew, whose name was Mordekhai the son of Ya'ir, the son of Shim'i, the son of Kish, a Binyamini. ⁶ He had been exiled from Yerushalayim with the captives exiled with Y'khanyah king of Y'hudah, whom N'vukhadnetzar king of Bavel had carried off. ⁷ He had raised Hadassah, that is, Ester, his uncle's daughter; because she had neither father nor mother. The girl was shapely and good-looking; after her father's and mother's death, Mordekhai had adopted her as his own daughter.

⁸ When the king's order and decree were proclaimed, and many girls assembled in Shushan the capital under the care of Hegai, Ester too was taken into the king's house and put under the care of Hegai, who was in charge of the women. ⁹ The girl pleased him and won his favor, so that he lost no time in giving her her cosmetics, her portions [of special food] and seven girls from the king's palace to attend her; he also promoted her and the girls attending her to the best place in the harem's quarters. ¹⁰ Ester did not disclose her people or family ties, because Mordekhai had instructed her not to tell anyone. ¹¹ Every day Mordekhai would walk around in front of the courtyard of the harem's house in order to know how Ester was doing and what was happening to her.

¹² Each girl had her turn to appear before King Achashverosh after she had undergone the full twelve-month preparation period prescribed for the women, consisting of a six-month treatment with oil of myrrh and six months with perfumes and other cosmetics for women. ¹³ Then, when the girl went to see the king, whatever she wanted would be given to her as she went from the harem's house to the king's palace. ¹⁴ She would go in the evening, and on the following day she would return to another part of the harem's house and be under the care of Sha'ashgaz the king's officer in charge of the concubines. She would not go to the king again unless he was especially pleased with her and had her summoned by name.

^{15} When the turn came for Ester the daughter of Avichayil, whom Mordekhai had adopted as his own daughter, to appear before the king, she didn't ask for anything other than what Hegai the king's officer in charge of the harem advised. Yet Ester was admired by all who saw her. ^{16} She was brought to King Achashverosh in his royal palace in the tenth month, Tevet, during the seventh year of his reign. ^{17} The king liked Ester more than any of his wives; none of the other virgins obtained such favor and approval from him. So he put the royal crown on her head and made her queen in place of Vashti.

^{18} The king then gave a great banquet in Ester's honor for all his officers and servants, decreed a holiday for the provinces and distributed gifts worthy of royal bounty.

^{19} When the girls would gather on other occasions, Mordekhai would sit at the King's Gate. ^{20} Ester had not yet revealed her family ties or her people, as Mordekhai had ordered her; for Ester continued obeying what Mordekhai told her to do, as she had when he was raising her. ^{21} On one of those occasions, when Mordekhai was sitting at the King's Gate, two of the king's officers, Bigtan and Teresh, from the group in charge of the private entryways, became angry and conspired to assassinate King Achashverosh. ^{22} But Mordekhai learned about it and told Ester the queen. Ester reported it to the king, crediting Mordekhai. ^{23} The matter was investigated, found to be true, and both were hanged on a stake. All this was recorded in the daily journal that was kept with the king.

3 ^{1} Some time later King Achashverosh began to single out Haman the son of Hamdata the Agagi for advancement; eventually he gave him precedence over all his fellow officers. ^{2} All the king's servants at the King's Gate would kneel and bow down before Haman, because the king had so ordered. But Mordekhai would neither kneel nor bow down to him. ^{3} The king's servants at the King's Gate asked Mordekhai, "Why don't you obey the king's order?" ^{4} But after they had confronted him a number of times without his paying attention to them, they told Haman, in order to find out whether Mordekhai's explanation that he was a Jew would suffice to justify his behavior. ^{5} Haman was furious when he saw that Mordekhai was not kneeling and bowing down to him. ^{6} However, on learning what people Mordekhai belonged to, it seemed to him a waste to lay hands on Mordekhai alone. Rather, he decided to destroy all of Mordekhai's people, the Jews, throughout the whole of Achashverosh's kingdom.

^{7} In the first month, the month of Nisan, in the twelfth year of Achashverosh, they began throwing *pur* (that is, they cast lots) before Haman every day and every month until the twelfth month, which is the month of Adar. ^{8} Then Haman said to Achashverosh, "There is a particular people scattered and dispersed among the peoples in all the provinces of your kingdom. Their laws are different from those of every other people; moreover, they don't observe the king's laws. It doesn't befit the king to tolerate them. ^{9} If it please the king, have a decree written for their destruction; and I will hand over 330 tons of silver to the officials in charge of the king's affairs to deposit in the royal treasury."

^{10} The king took his signet ring from his hand and gave it to Haman the son of Hamdata the Agagi, the enemy of the Jews. ^{11} The king said to Haman, "The money is given to you, and the people too, to do with as seems good to you."

^{12} The king's secretaries were summoned on the thirteenth day of the first month. They wrote down all Haman's orders to the king's army commanders and governors in all the provinces and to the officials of every people, to each province in its own script and to each people in their own language; everything was written in the name of King Achashverosh and sealed with the king's signet ring. ¹³ Letters were sent by courier to all the royal provinces "to destroy, kill and exterminate all Jews, from young to old, including small children and women, on a specific day, the thirteenth day of the twelfth month, the month of Adar, and to seize their goods as plunder." ¹⁴ A copy of the document to be issued as a decree in every province was to be publicly proclaimed to all the peoples, so that they would be ready for that day. ¹⁵ At the king's order the runners went out quickly, and the decree was issued in Shushan the capital. Then the king and Haman sat down for a drink together, but the city of Shushan was thrown into confusion.

4 ¹ When Mordekhai learned everything that had been done, he tore his clothes, put on sackcloth and ashes and went out through the city, lamenting and crying bitterly. ² He stopped before entering the King's Gate, since no one was allowed to go inside the King's Gate wearing sackcloth. ³ In every province reached by the king's order and decree, there was great mourning among the Jews, with fasting, weeping and wailing, as many lay down on sackcloth and ashes.

⁴ When the girls and officials attending Ester came and informed her of this, the queen became deeply distressed. She sent clothes for Mordekhai to wear instead of his sackcloth, but he wouldn't accept them. ⁵ So Ester summoned Hatakh, one of the king's officials attending her, and instructed him to go to Mordekhai and find out what this was all about and why. ⁶ Hatakh went out to Mordekhai in the open space in front of the King's Gate, ⁷ and Mordekhai told him everything that had happened to him and exactly how much silver Haman had promised to put in the royal treasury for the destruction of the Jews. ⁸ He also gave him a copy of the decree for their destruction issued in Shushan; so that he could show it to Ester, explain it to her, and then instruct her to approach the king, intercede with him and implore his favor on behalf of her people. ⁹ Hatakh returned and told Ester what Mordekhai had said.

¹⁰ Then Ester spoke to Hatakh and gave him this message for Mordekhai: ¹¹ "All the king's officials, as well as the people in the royal provinces, know that if anyone, man or woman, approaches the king in the inner courtyard without being summoned, there is just one law — he must be put to death — unless the king holds out the gold scepter for him to remain alive; and I haven't been summoned to the king for the past thirty days."

¹² Upon being told what Ester had said, Mordekhai ¹³ asked them to give Ester this answer: "Don't suppose that merely because you happen to be in the royal palace you will escape any more than the other Jews. ¹⁴ For if you fail to speak up now, relief and deliverance will come to the Jews from a different direction; but you and your father's family will perish. Who knows whether you didn't come into your royal position precisely for such a time as this."

¹⁵ Ester had them return this answer to Mordekhai: ¹⁶ "Go, assemble all the Jews to be found in Shushan, and have them fast for me, neither eating nor drinking for three days, night and day; also I and the girls attending me will fast the same way. Then I will go in to the king, which is against the law; and if I perish, I perish." ¹⁷ Then Mordekhai went his way and did everything Ester had ordered him to do.

5 ¹ On the third day, Ester put on her royal robes and stood in the inner courtyard of the king's palace, opposite the king's hall. The king was sitting on his royal throne in the king's hall, across from the entrance to the hall. ² When the king saw Ester the queen standing in the courtyard, she won his favor; so the king extended the gold scepter in his hand toward Ester. Ester approached and touched the tip of the scepter. ³ "What is it you want, Queen Ester?" the king asked her. "Whatever your request, up to half the kingdom, it will be given to you." ⁴ "If it is all right with the king," answered Ester, "let the king and Haman come today to the banquet I have prepared for him." ⁵ The king said, "Bring Haman quickly, so that what Ester has asked for can be done." ⁽⁶⁾ So the king and Haman came to the banquet Ester had prepared.

⁶⁽⁷⁾ At the banquet of wine the king again said to Ester, "Whatever your request, you will be granted it; whatever you want, up to half the kingdom, it will be done." ⁷⁽⁸⁾ Then Ester answered, "My request, what I want, is this: ⁸ if I have won the king's favor, if it pleases the king to grant my request and do what I want, let the king and Haman come to the banquet which I will prepare for them; and tomorrow I will do as the king has said."

⁹ That day Haman went out happy and in good spirits. But when Haman saw Mordekhai at the King's Gate, that he neither rose nor moved for him, Haman was infuriated with Mordekhai. ¹⁰ Nevertheless, Haman restrained himself and went home, where he summoned and brought his friends and Zeresh his wife. ¹¹ Haman boasted to them about his vast wealth, his many sons, and everything connected with how the king had promoted him and given him precedence over the other officials and servants of the king. ¹² "Indeed," Haman added, "Ester the queen let nobody into the banquet with the king that she had prepared except myself; and tomorrow, too, I am invited by her, together with the king. ¹³ Yet none of this does me any good at all, as long as I keep seeing Mordekhai the Jew remaining seated at the King's Gate." ¹⁴ At this Zeresh his wife and all his friends said to him, "Have a gallows seventy-five feet high constructed, and in the morning speak to the king about having Mordekhai hanged on it. Then go in, and enjoy yourself with the king at the banquet." Haman liked the idea, so he had a gallows made.

6 ¹ That night, the king couldn't sleep; so he ordered the records of the daily journal brought, and they were read to the king. ² It was found written that Mordekhai had told about Bigtana and Teresh, two of the king's officers from the group in charge of the private entryways, who had conspired to assassinate King Achashverosh. ³ The king asked, "What honor or distinction was conferred on Mordekhai for this?" The king's servants answered, "Nothing was done for him." ⁴ The king then asked, "Who's that in the courtyard?" For Haman had come into the outer courtyard of the king's palace to speak to the king about hanging Mordekhai on the gallows he had prepared for him. ⁵ The king's servants told him, "It's Haman standing there in the courtyard." The king said, "Have him come in." ⁶ So Haman came in. The king said to him, "What should be done for a man that the king wants to honor?" Haman thought to himself, "Whom would the king want to honor more than me?" ⁷ So Haman answered the king, "For a man the king wants to honor, ⁸ have royal robes brought which the king himself wears and the horse the king himself rides, with a royal crown on its head. ⁹ The robes and the horse should be handed over to one of the king's most respected officials, and they should put the robes on the man the king wants to honor and lead him on horseback through the streets of the city, proclaiming ahead of him, 'This is what is done for a man whom the king wants to honor.'" ¹⁰ The king said to Haman, "Hurry, and take the robes and the horse, as you said, and do this for Mordekhai the Jew, who sits at the King's Gate. Don't leave out anything you mentioned."

¹¹ So Haman took the robes and the horse, dressed Mordekhai and led him riding through the streets of the city, as he proclaimed ahead of him, "This is what is done for a man whom the king wants to honor." ¹² Then Mordekhai returned to the King's Gate; but Haman rushed home with his head covered in mourning.

¹³ After Haman had told Zeresh his wife and all his friends everything that had happened to him, his advisers and his wife Zeresh said to him, "If Mordekhai, before whom you have begun to fall, is a Jew, you will not get the better of him; on the contrary, your downfall before him is certain."

¹⁴ While they were still talking with him, the king's officials came, hurrying to bring Haman to the banquet Ester had prepared.

7 ¹ So the king and Haman went to Queen Ester's banquet; ² and the king again said to Ester at the wine banquet, "Whatever your request, Queen Ester, you will be granted it; whatever you want, up to half the kingdom, it will be done." ³ Ester the queen answered, "If I have won your favor, king, and if it pleases the king, then what I ask be given me is my own life and the lives of my people. ⁴ For we have been sold, I and my people, to be destroyed, killed, exterminated. If we had only been sold as men- and women-slaves, I would have remained quiet; since then [our] trouble would not have been worth the damage it would have caused the king [to alter the situation]." ⁵ King Achashverosh asked Ester the queen, "Who is he? Where is the man who dared to do such a thing?" ⁶ Ester said, "A ruthless enemy — it's this wicked Haman!" Haman stood aghast, terrified before the king and queen. ⁷ In a rage, the king got up from the wine banquet and went out to the palace garden. But Haman remained, pleading with Ester the queen to spare his life; for he could see that the king had decided to do him in. ⁸ Haman had just fallen on the couch where Ester was, when the king returned from the palace garden to the wine banquet. He shouted, "Is he even going to rape the queen here in the palace, before my very eyes?" The moment these words left the king's mouth, they covered Haman's face. ⁹ Harvonah, one of the king's attendants, said, "Look! The gallows seventy-five feet high that Haman made for Mordekhai, who spoke only good for the king, is standing at Haman's house." The king said, "Hang him on it." ¹⁰ So they hanged Haman on the gallows he had prepared for Mordekhai. Then the king's anger subsided.

8 ¹ That same day King Achashverosh gave the house of Haman, the enemy of the Jews, to Ester the queen. Also Mordekhai appeared before the king, for Ester had revealed his relationship to her. ² The king removed his signet ring, which he had taken back from Haman, and gave it to Mordekhai. Then Ester put Mordekhai in charge of Haman's house.

³ Again Ester spoke to the king; she fell at his feet and begged him with tears to put an end to the mischief Haman the Agagi had caused by the scheme he had worked out against the Jews. ⁴ The king extended the gold scepter toward Ester. So Ester got up and stood in front of the king. ⁵ She said, "If it pleases the king, if I have won his

favor, if the matter seem right to the king and if I have his approval, then let an order be written rescinding the letters devised by Haman the son of Hamdata the Agagi, which he wrote to destroy the Jews in all the royal provinces. ⁶For how can I bear to see the disaster that will overcome my people? How can I endure seeing the extermination of my kinsmen?" ⁷King Achashverosh said to Ester the queen and Mordekhai the Jew, "Listen! I gave Ester the house of Haman, and they hanged him on the gallows, because he threatened the lives of the Jews. ⁸You should issue a decree in the king's name for whatever you want concerning the Jews, and seal it with the king's signet ring; because a decree written in the king's name and sealed with the king's ring can't be rescinded by anyone."

⁹The king's secretaries were summoned at that time, on the twenty-third day of the third month, the month of Sivan; and a decree was written according to everything Mordekhai ordered concerning the Jews, to the army commanders, governors and officials of the provinces from India to Ethiopia, 127 provinces, to each province in its script and to each people in their language, also to the Jews in their script and language. ¹⁰They wrote in the name of King Achashverosh and sealed it with the king's signet ring; they sent the letters by couriers on horseback riding fast horses used in the king's service and bred from the royal stock. ¹¹The letters said that the king had granted the Jews in every city the right "to assemble and defend their lives by destroying, killing and exterminating any forces of any people or province that would attack them, their little ones or their women or would try to seize their goods as plunder ¹²on the designated day in any of the provinces of King Achashverosh, namely, the thirteenth day of the twelfth month, the month of Adar." ¹³A copy of the edict was to be issued as a decree in every province and proclaimed to all the peoples, and the Jews were to be ready on that day to take vengeance against their enemies. ¹⁴Couriers riding fast horses used in the king's service left quickly, pressed by the king's order; and the decree was issued in Shushan the capital.

¹⁵Meanwhile, Mordekhai left the king's presence arrayed in royal blue and white, wearing a large gold crown and a robe of fine linen and purple; and the city of Shushan shouted for joy. ¹⁶For the Jews, all was light, gladness, joy and honor. ¹⁷In every province and city where the king's order and decree arrived, the Jews had gladness and joy, a feast and a holiday. Many from the peoples of the land became Jews, because fear of the Jews had overcome them.

9 ¹The time approached for the king's order and decree to be carried out, the day when the enemies of the Jews hoped to overpower them. But, as it turned out, the opposite took place — the Jews overpowered those who hated them. Thus, on the thirteenth day of the twelfth month, the month of Adar, ²the Jews assembled in their cities throughout all the provinces of King Achashverosh to attack anyone who tried to do them harm; and no one was able to withstand them; because all the peoples were afraid of them. ³All the officials of the provinces, the army commanders, the governors and those occupied with the king's affairs helped the Jews; because they were afraid of Mordekhai. ⁴For Mordekhai had become a powerful person in the king's palace, and his fame had spread through all the provinces; Mordekhai continued to grow increasingly powerful.

⁵The Jews put all their enemies to the sword; there was great slaughter and destruction, as they did whatever they wanted to those who hated them; ⁶in Shushan

the capital, the Jews slaughtered 500 men. ^7-10 They put to death the ten sons of Haman the son of Hamdata, the enemy of the Jews — Parshandata, Dalfon, Aspata, Porata, Adalya, Aridata, Parmashta, Arisai, Aridai and Vaizata. But they did not touch the spoil.

^11 The same day, after the king had been told the number of those killed in Shushan the capital, ^12 he said to Ester the queen, "If the Jews have slaughtered 500 men in Shushan the capital and the ten sons of Haman, what have they done in the rest of the royal provinces! Now, whatever your request, you will be granted it; whatever more you want, it will be done." ^13 Ester replied, "If it pleases the king, let the Jews in Shushan act again tomorrow in accordance with today's decree; also have Haman's ten sons hanged on the gallows." ^14 The king ordered these things done — a decree was issued in Shushan, and they hanged Haman's ten sons. ^15 So the Jews in Shushan assembled also on the fourteenth day of the month of Adar and killed 300 men in Shushan, but they did not touch the spoil.

^16 The other Jews, those in the royal provinces, had assembled, defended their lives and won rest from their enemies, killing 75,000 of those who hated them, but without touching the spoil, ^17 on the thirteenth day of the month Adar. So on the fourteenth day of Adar they rested and made it a holiday for celebrating and rejoicing. ^18 However, the Jews of Shushan assembled on both the thirteenth and fourteenth days of Adar, so it was on the fifteenth that they rested and made it a holiday for celebrating and rejoicing. ^19 This is why the Jews of the villages, those who live in unwalled towns, make the fourteenth day of the month of Adar a day for celebrating and rejoicing, a holiday and a time for sending each other portions [of food].

^20 Mordekhai recorded these events and sent letters to all the Jews in all the provinces of King Achashverosh, both near and far, ^21 instructing them to observe the fourteenth day of the month of Adar and the fifteenth day, every year, ^22 [to commemorate] the days on which the Jews obtained rest from their enemies and the month which for them was turned from sorrow into gladness and from mourning into a holiday; they were to make them days of celebrating and rejoicing, sending portions [of food] to each other and giving gifts to the poor.

^23 So the Jews took it upon themselves to continue what they had already begun to do, and as Mordekhai had written to them; ^24 because Haman the son of Hamdata the Agagi, the enemy of the Jews, had plotted against the Jews to destroy them and had thrown *pur* (that is, "cast lots") to crush and destroy them; ^25 but when Ester came before the king, he ordered by letters that [Haman's] wicked scheme, which he had plotted against the Jews, should recoil on his own head, and that he and his sons should be hanged on the gallows. ^26 This is why these days have been called *Purim*, after the word *pur*. Thus, because of everything written in this letter, and what they had seen concerning this matter, and what had come upon them, ^27 the Jews resolved and took upon themselves, their descendants and all who might join them that without fail they would observe these two days in accordance with what was written in [this letter] and at the appointed time, every year; ^28 and that these days would be remembered and observed throughout every generation, every family, every province and every city; and that these days of *Purim* would never cease among the Jews or their memory be lost by their descendants.

^29 Then Ester the queen, the daughter of Avichayil, and Mordekhai the Jew, gave full written authority to confirm a second letter about *Purim*. ^30 He sent copies of it to all the Jews, to the 127 provinces of the kingdom of Achashverosh, ensuring their peace and security ³¹ and requiring the observance of these days of *Purim* at their designated times, as Mordekhai the Jew and Ester the queen had enjoined them, and as they had established for themselves and their descendants concerning the matters of fasting and lamenting. ³² At Ester's order these matters of *Purim* were confirmed and put in writing in the book.

10 ¹ King Achashverosh laid tribute on the land, the coasts and the islands. ² All the acts of his power and might, along with a full account of the high honor to which the king advanced Mordekhai, are written in the Annals of the Kings of Media and Persia. ³ For Mordekhai the Jew was second only to King Achashverosh; he was a great man among the Jews, popular with all his many countrymen. He sought the good of his people and interceded for the welfare of all their descendants.

all the Jews, to the 127 provinces of the kingdom of Achashverosh, ensuring their
peace and security, °° and requiring the observance of these days of Purim at their
designated times, as Mordechai the Jew and Ester the queen had enjoined them, and
as they had established for themselves and their descendants concerning the matters
of fasting and lamenting. °° At Ester's order these matters of Purim were confirmed
and put in writing in the book.

10¹ King Achashverosh laid tribute on the mainland coasts and the islands. ² All the
acts of his power and might, along with a full account of the high honor to which the
king advanced Mordechai, are written in the Annals of the Kings of Media and
Persia. ³ For Mordechai the Jew was second only to King Achashverosh; he was

Dani'el

DANIEL

1 ¹ In the third year of the reign of Y'hoyakim king of Y'hudah, N'vukhadnetzar
king of Bavel came to Yerushalayim and laid siege to it; ² and *Adonai* handed
Y'hoyakim king of Y'hudah over to him, along with some of the articles from the
house of God. He took them to the land of Shin'ar, to the house of his god and placed
the articles in the storehouse of his god.

³ The king ordered Ashp'naz, the eunuch serving as his chief officer, to bring
into the palace from the people of Isra'el some of royal or noble descent. ⁴ They were
to be boys without physical defect, handsome in appearance, versed in all kinds of
wisdom, quick to learn, discerning, and having the capacity to serve in the king's
palace; and he was to teach them the language and literature of the Kasdim. ⁵ The
king assigned them a daily portion of his own food and the wine he drank, and they
were to be cared for in this way for three years. At the end of this time they were to
become the king's attendants.

⁶ Among these, from the people of Y'hudah, were Dani'el, Hananyah,
Misha'el and 'Azaryah. ⁷ The chief officer gave them other names — to Dani'el he
gave the name Belt'shatzar; to Hananyah, Shadrakh; to Misha'el, Meishakh; and to
'Azaryah, 'Aved-N'go.

⁸ But Dani'el resolved that he would not defile himself with the king's food or
the wine he drank, so he asked the chief officer to be excused from defiling himself.
⁹ God caused the chief officer to be kind and sympathetic toward Dani'el; ¹⁰ however,
the chief officer said to Dani'el, "I'm afraid of my lord the king. After all, he has given
you an allowance of food and drink; so if he were to see you boys looking worse than
the others your age, you would be putting my own head in danger from the king."

¹¹ Then Dani'el said to the guard whom the chief officer had put in charge of
Dani'el, Hananyah, Misha'el and 'Azaryah, ¹² "Please! Try an experiment on your
servants — for ten days have them give us only vegetables to eat and water to drink.
¹³ Then see how we look, and compare us with how the boys who eat the king's food
look; and deal with your servants according to what you see." ¹⁴ He agreed to do
what they had asked and gave them a ten-day test. ¹⁵ At the end of ten days they
looked better and more robust than all the boys who were eating the king's food.
¹⁶ So the guard took away their food and the wine they were supposed to drink, and
gave them vegetables.

¹⁷ To these four boys God had given knowledge and skill in every aspect of learning and wisdom; moreover, Dani'el could understand all kinds of visions and dreams.
¹⁸ When the time the king had set for them to be presented came, the chief
officer presented them to N'vukhadnetzar; ¹⁹ and when the king spoke with them,

none was found among all of them to compare with Dani'el, Hananyah, Misha'el and 'Azaryah. So they entered the king's service; ²⁰ and in all matters requiring wisdom and understanding, whenever the king consulted them, he found them ten times better than all the magicians and exorcists in his entire kingdom. ²¹ So Dani'el remained there until the first year of King Koresh.

2 ¹ In the second year of the reign of N'vukhadnetzar, N'vukhadnetzar became so troubled by a series of dreams he had that he couldn't sleep. ² So the king ordered the magicians, exorcists, sorcerers and astrologers summoned to interpret the king's dreams to him. They came and stood in his presence. ³ The king said to them, "I had a dream which will keep troubling my spirit until I know what it means."

⁴ The astrologers spoke to the king in Aramaic: "May the king live forever! Tell your servants the dream, and we will interpret it." ⁵ The king answered the astrologers, "Here is what I have decided: if you don't tell me both the dream and its interpretation, you will be torn limb from limb and your houses reduced to rubble. ⁶ But if you do state the dream and its interpretation, I will give you presents, rewards and great honor. Just tell me the dream and its interpretation." ⁷ A second time they said, "Let his majesty tell his servants the dream, and we will interpret it." ⁸ The king replied, "I see you're only trying to gain time, because you see that I've decided ⁹ that if you don't tell me the dream, there is only one sentence passed on all of you. So you've conspired to mislead me with lies in the hope that time will change things. Now, just tell me the dream! That will convince me that you will also be able to give me its correct interpretation." ¹⁰ The astrologers answered the king, "Your majesty, nobody in the world can do this! Never has a king, no matter how great and powerful, asked such a thing of any magician or exorcist or astrologer. ¹¹ The king is asking a difficult thing; nobody but the gods could tell this to your majesty, and they don't live with mere mortals." ¹² At this the king flew into a rage and ordered all the sages of Bavel put to death. ¹³ When the decree was published that the sages were to be slain, they sought Dani'el and his companions in order to have them put to death.

¹⁴ Then, choosing his words carefully, Dani'el consulted Aryokh, captain of the royal guard, who had already gone out to kill the sages of Bavel. ¹⁵ He said to Aryokh, "Since you are the king's official, let me ask: why has the king issued such a harsh decree?" Aryokh explained the matter to Dani'el. ¹⁶ Then Dani'el went in and asked the king to give him time to tell the king the interpretation.

¹⁷ Dani'el went home and made the matter known to Hananyah, Misha'el and 'Azaryah, his companions; ¹⁸ so that they could ask the God of heaven for mercy concerning this secret, and thus save Dani'el and his companions from dying along with the other sages of Bavel. ¹⁹ Then the secret was revealed to Dani'el in a vision at night, and Dani'el blessed the God of heaven ²⁰ in these words:

> "Blessed be the name of God
> from eternity past to eternity future!
> For wisdom and power are his alone;
> ²¹ he brings the changes of seasons and times;
> he installs and deposes kings;

> he gives wisdom to the wise
> and knowledge to those with discernment.
> ²² He reveals deep and secret things;
> he knows what lies in the darkness;
> and light dwells with him.
> ²³ I thank and praise you, God of my ancestors,
> for giving me wisdom and power,
> and revealing to me what we wanted from you,
> for giving us the answer for the king."

²⁴ So Dani'el went to see Aryokh, whom the king had charged with destroying the sages of Bavel, and said to him, "Don't destroy the sages of Bavel! Bring me before the king, and I will give the king the interpretation." ²⁵ Quickly Aryokh brought Dani'el before the king and told him, "I have found one of the exiles of Y'hudah who will reveal the interpretation to his majesty." ²⁶ The king said to Dani'el (who had been renamed Belt'shatzar), "Can you tell me what I dreamt and what it means?" ²⁷ Dani'el answered the king, "No sage, exorcist, magician or astrologer can tell his majesty the secret he has asked about. ²⁸ But there is a God in heaven who unlocks mysteries, and he has revealed to King N'vukhadnetzar what will happen in the *acharit-hayamim.* Here are your dream and the visions you had in your head when you were in bed.

²⁹ "Your majesty, when you were in bed, you began thinking about what would take place in the future; and he who reveals secrets has revealed to you what will happen. ³⁰ Yet this secret has not been revealed to me because I am wiser than anyone living, but so that the meaning can be made known to your majesty, and then you can understand the thoughts of your own mind.

³¹ "Your majesty had a vision of a statue, very large and extremely bright; it stood in front of you and its appearance was terrifying. ³² The head of the statue was of fine gold, its chest and arms of silver, its trunk and thighs of bronze, ³³ its legs of iron, and its feet partly of iron and partly of clay. ³⁴ As you watched, a stone separated itself without any human hand, struck the statue on its feet made of iron and clay, and broke them in pieces. ³⁵ Then the iron, the clay, the bronze, the silver and the gold were all broken into pieces which became like the chaff on a threshing-floor in summer; the wind blew them away without leaving a trace. But the stone which had struck the statue grew into a huge mountain that filled the whole earth.

³⁶ "That is what you dreamt, and now we will give the king its interpretation. ³⁷ Your majesty, king of kings, to whom the God of heaven has given the kingdom, the power, the strength and the glory; ³⁸ so that wherever people, wild animals or birds in the air live, he has handed them over to you and enabled you to rule them all — you are the head of gold. ³⁹ But after you another kingdom will rise, inferior to you; then a third kingdom, of bronze, which will rule the whole world. ⁴⁰ The fourth kingdom will be as strong as iron. Iron can break anything into pieces, pulverize it and crush it. So just as iron can crush anything, this kingdom will break the other kingdoms into pieces and crush them. ⁴¹ Finally, you saw the feet and toes made partly of pottery clay and partly of iron; this will be a divided kingdom; yet it will have some of the firmness of iron, since you saw the iron mixed with clay from the ground. ⁴² Just as the toes of the feet were part iron and part clay, this kingdom will

be partly strong and partly brittle. ⁴³ You saw the iron mixed with clay; that means that they will cement their alliances by intermarriages; but they won't stick together any more than iron blends with clay.

⁴⁴ "In the days of those kings the God of heaven will establish a kingdom that will never be destroyed, and that kingdom will not pass into the hands of another people. It will break to pieces and consume all those kingdoms; but it, itself, will stand forever — ⁴⁵ like the stone you saw, which, without human hands, separated itself from the mountain and broke to pieces the iron, the bronze, the clay, the silver and the gold. The great God has revealed to the king what will come about in the future. The dream is true, and its interpretation is reliable."

⁴⁶ Then King N'vukhadnetzar fell on his face and worshipped Dani'el; he ordered that a grain offering and incense be offered to him. ⁴⁷ To Dani'el the king said, "Your God is indeed the God of gods, the Lord of kings and a revealer of secrets, since you have been able to reveal this secret." ⁴⁸ The king promoted Dani'el to a high rank, gave him many rich gifts and made him governor of the entire province of Bavel and head of all the sages of Bavel. ⁴⁹ At Dani'el's request, the king put Shadrakh, Meishakh and 'Aved-N'go in charge of the affairs of the province of Bavel, while Dani'el remained in attendance on the king.

3 ¹ N'vukhadnetzar the king had a gold statue made, ninety feet high and nine feet wide, which he set up on the plain of Dura, in the province of Bavel. ² Then N'vukhadnetzar the king summoned the viceroys, prefects, governors, judges, treasurers, counselors, sheriffs and all the provincial officials to assemble and come to the dedication of the statue which N'vukhadnetzar the king had set up. ³ The viceroys, prefects, governors, judges, treasurers, counselors, sheriffs and all the provincial officials assembled for the dedication of the statue which N'vukhadnetzar the king had set up. They stood in front of the statue that N'vukhadnetzar had set up; ⁴ and a herald proclaimed, "Peoples! Nations! Languages! You are ordered ⁵ that when you hear the sound of the horn, pipe, harp, zither, lute, bagpipe and the rest of the musical instruments, you are to fall down and worship the gold statue that N'vukhadnetzar the king has set up. ⁶ Whoever does not fall down and worship is to be thrown immediately into a blazing hot furnace." ⁷ Therefore, when all the peoples heard the sound of the horn, pipe, harp, zither, lute and the rest of the musical instruments, all the peoples, nations and languages fell down and worshipped the gold statue that N'vukhadnetzar the king had set up.

⁸ But then some Kasdim approached and began denouncing the Jews. ⁹ They said to N'vukhadnetzar the king, "May the king live forever! ¹⁰ Your majesty, you have ordered that everyone who hears sound of the horn, pipe, harp, zither, lute, bagpipe and the rest of the musical instruments is to fall down and worship the gold statue; ¹¹ and that whoever does not fall down and worship is to be thrown into a blazing hot furnace. ¹² There are some Jews whom you have put in charge of the affairs of the province of Bavel, Shadrakh, Meishakh and 'Aved-N'go; and these men, your majesty, have paid no attention to you. They do not serve your gods, and they do not worship the gold statue you set up."

¹³ In a raging fury N'vukhadnetzar ordered that Shadrakh, Meishakh and 'Aved-N'go be brought. When the men had been brought before the king, ¹⁴ N'vukhadnetzar said to them, "Shadrakh! Meishakh! 'Aved-N'go! Is it true that you neither serve my

gods nor worship the gold statue I set up? ¹⁵ All right, then. If you are prepared, when you hear the sound of the horn, pipe, harp, zither, lute, bagpipe and the rest of the musical instruments, to fall down and worship the gold statue, very well. But if you won't worship, you will immediately be thrown into a blazing hot furnace — and what god will save you from my power then?" ¹⁶ Shadrakh, Meishakh and 'Aved-N'go answered the king, "Your question doesn't require an answer from us. ¹⁷ Your majesty, if our God, whom we serve, is able to save us, he will save us from the blazing hot furnace and from your power. ¹⁸ But even if he doesn't, we want you to know, your majesty, that we will neither serve your gods nor worship the gold statue which you have set up."

¹⁹ N'vukhadnetzar became so utterly enraged that his face was distorted with anger against Shadrakh, Meishakh and 'Aved-N'go. He ordered the furnace made seven times hotter than usual. ²⁰ Then he ordered some of the strongest men in his army to tie up Shadrakh, Meishakh and 'Aved-N'go and throw them into the blazing hot furnace. ²¹ So these men were tied up in their cloaks, tunics, robes and other clothes, and thrown into the blazing hot furnace. ²² The king's order was so urgent and the furnace so overheated that the men carrying Shadrakh, Meishakh and 'Aved-N'go were burned to death by the flames. ²³ These three men, Shadrakh, Meishakh and 'Aved-N'go, fell, bound, into the blazing hot furnace.

²⁴ Suddenly N'vukhadnetzar sprang to his feet. Alarmed, he asked his advisers, "Didn't we throw three men, bound, into the flames?" They answered the king, "Yes, of course, your majesty." ²⁵ But he exclaimed, "Look! I see four men, not tied up, walking around there in the flames, unhurt; and the fourth looks like one of the gods!" ²⁶ N'vukhadnetzar approached the opening of the blazing hot furnace and said, "Shadrakh! Meishakh! 'Aved-N'go! You servants of El 'Elyon! Come out, and come here!" Shadrakh, Meishakh and 'Aved-N'go emerged from the flames. ²⁷ The viceroys, prefects, governors and royal advisers who were there saw that the fire had had no power on the bodies of these men — not even their hair was singed, their clothes looked the same, and they didn't smell of fire.

²⁸ N'vukhadnetzar said, "Blessed be the God of Shadrakh, Meishakh and 'Aved-N'go! He sent his angel to deliver his servants who trusted in him. They defied the royal order to the point of being willing to give up their bodies, in order not to serve or worship any god but their own God. ²⁹ Therefore I herewith decree that anyone, no matter from which people, nation or language, who says anything to insult the God of Shadrakh, Meishakh and 'Aved-N'go is to be torn limb from limb, and his house is to be reduced to rubble; because there is no other god who can save like this."

³⁰ Then the king gave Shadrakh, Meishakh and 'Aved-N'go higher rank in the province of Bavel.

³¹⁽⁴:¹⁾ [The following letter was sent out:]

"From: N'vukhadnetzar the king

"To: All the peoples, nations and languages living throughout the earth:

"Shalom rav! [Abundant peace!]

³²⁽⁴:²⁾ "I am pleased to recount the signs and wonders which the Most High God has done for me.

^{33(4:3)} "How great are his signs!
How powerful his wonders!
His kingdom lasts forever,
and he rules all generations.

4 ¹⁽⁴⁾ "I, N'vukhadnetzar, was contentedly living at home, enjoying the luxury of my palace; ²⁽⁵⁾ but as I lay on my bed, I had a dream which frightened me, followed by fantasies and visions in my head which frightened me even more. ³⁽⁶⁾ So I ordered all the sages of Bavel to present themselves to me, so that they could tell me the interpretation of the dream. ⁴⁽⁷⁾ When the magicians, exorcists, astrologers and diviners came, I told them the dream; but they couldn't interpret it for me. ⁵⁽⁸⁾ Finally, however, Dani'el (renamed Belt'shatzar, after the name of my god), in whom is the spirit of the holy gods, came before me; and I told him the dream: ⁶⁽⁹⁾ 'Belt'shatzar, chief of the magicians! Because I know that the spirit of the holy gods is in you, and no mystery is too difficult for you, tell me the meaning of the visions I saw in my dream. ⁷⁽¹⁰⁾ Here are the visions I had in my head as I lay on my bed: I looked, and there before me was a tree at the center of the earth; it was very tall. ⁸⁽¹¹⁾ The tree grew and became strong until its crown reached the sky, and it could be seen from anywhere on earth. ⁹⁽¹²⁾ Its foliage was beautiful and its fruit abundant; it produced enough food for everyone. The wild animals enjoyed its shade, the birds in the air lived in its branches, and it gave food to every living creature. ¹⁰⁽¹³⁾ I looked in the visions of my head as I lay on my bed, and there appeared a holy watcher coming down from heaven. ¹¹⁽¹⁴⁾ He cried out:

"'"Cut down the tree, cut off its branches,
strip off its leaves, scatter its fruit!
Let the wild animals flee from its shelter!
Let the birds abandon its branches!
¹²⁽¹⁵⁾ But leave the stump with its roots in the ground,
with a band of iron and bronze,
in the lush grass of the countryside;
let him be drenched with dew from the sky
and share the lot of animals in the pasture;
¹³⁽¹⁶⁾ let his heart and mind cease to be human
and become those of an animal;
and let seven seasons pass over him.

¹⁴⁽¹⁷⁾ "'"This order is issued by the watchers,
the sentence is announced by the holy ones,
so that all who live may know
that the Most High rules the human kingdom,
that he gives it to whomever he wishes
and can raise up over it the lowliest of mortals."

¹⁵⁽¹⁸⁾ "'This is the dream which I, King N'vukhadnetzar, saw. Now you, Belt'shatzar, tell me its interpretation. None of the sages of my kingdom

can tell me the interpretation, but you can do it, because the spirit of the holy gods is in you.'

$^{16(19)}$ "Dani'el, whose name was Belt'shatzar, was in shock awhile, frightened by his thoughts. The king said, 'Belt'shatzar, don't let the dream or the interpretation frighten you.' Belt'shatzar answered, 'My lord, if only the dream were about those who hate you, and the interpretation about your enemies! $^{17(20)}$ The tree you saw which grew and became strong until its crown reached the sky, and it could be seen throughout the whole earth, $^{18(21)}$ that had beautiful foliage and abundant fruit, enough to feed everyone, under which the wild animals lived, and on whose branches the birds in the air built their nests — $^{19(22)}$ it's you, your majesty! You have grown and become strong — your greatness has grown and reaches to heaven, and your rule extends to the end of the earth.

$^{20(23)}$ "'Now the king saw a holy watcher coming down from heaven, who said,

"'"Cut down the tree, and destroy it,
but leave the stump with its roots in the ground,
with a band of iron and bronze,
in the lush grass of the countryside;
let him be drenched with dew from the sky
and share the lot of the wild animals
until seven seasons pass over him."

$^{21(24)}$ "'This is the interpretation, your majesty; and it is the decree of the Most High that has come upon my lord the king:

$^{22(25)}$ "'You will be driven from human society
to live with the wild animals.
You will be made to eat grass like an ox
and be drenched with dew from the sky,
as seven seasons pass over you;
until you learn that the Most High
rules in the human kingdom
and gives it to whomever he pleases.

$^{23(26)}$ "'But since it was ordered to leave the stump of the tree with its roots, your kingdom will be kept for you until you have learned that Heaven rules everything. $^{24(27)}$ Therefore, your majesty, please take my advice: break with your sins by replacing them with acts of charity, and break with your crimes by showing mercy to the poor; this may extend the time of your prosperity.'

$^{25(28)}$ "All this happened to King N'vukhadnetzar. $^{26(29)}$ Twelve months later, as he was walking on the roof of the royal palace of Bavel, $^{27(30)}$ the king said, 'Bavel the great! I built it as a royal residence by my power and force to enhance the glory of my majesty!' ²⁸⁽³¹⁾ No sooner had the king spoken these words when a voice came down from heaven: 'King N'vukhadnetzar! These words are for you:

> "'The kingdom has left you.
> ²⁹⁽³²⁾ You will be driven from human society
> to live with the wild animals.
> You will be made to eat grass like an ox
> and be drenched with dew from the sky,
> as seven seasons pass over you,
> until you learn that the Most High
> rules in the human kingdom
> and gives it to whomever he pleases.'

³⁰⁽³³⁾ "Within the hour the word was fulfilled. N'vukhadnetzar was driven from human society, he ate grass like an ox, and his body was drenched with dew from the sky, until his hair had grown like eagles' feathers and his nails like birds' claws.

³¹⁽³⁴⁾ "When this period was over, I, N'vukhadnetzar, lifted my eyes toward heaven, and my understanding came back to me. I blessed the Most High, I praised and gave honor to him who lives forever.

> "'For his rulership is everlasting,
> his kingdom endures through all generations.
> ³²⁽³⁵⁾ All who live on earth are counted as nothing.
> He does what he wishes with the army of heaven
> and with those living on earth.
> No one can hold back his hand
> or ask him, "What are you doing?"'

³³⁽³⁶⁾ "It was at that moment that my understanding came back to me; and for the sake of the glory of my kingdom, my majesty and splendor also came back to me. My advisers and lords sought me out, I was re-established in my kingdom, and to my previous greatness even more was added. ³⁴⁽³⁷⁾ So now I, N'vukhadnetzar, praise, exalt and honor the King of heaven:

> "'For all his works are truth,
> and his ways are just;
> and he can humble those who walk in pride.'"

5 ¹ Belshatzar the king gave a great banquet for a thousand of his lords, and in the presence of the thousand he was drinking wine. ² While tasting the wine, Belshatzar ordered that the gold and silver vessels which his father N'vukhadnetzar had removed from the temple in Yerushalayim be brought; so that the king, his lords, his wives and his concubines could drink from them. ³ So they brought the gold vessels which had been removed from the sanctuary of the house of God in

Yerushalayim; and the king, his lords, his wives and his concubines drank from them. ⁴ They drank their wine and praised their gods made of gold, silver, bronze, iron, wood and stone.

⁵ Suddenly, the fingers of a human hand appeared and began writing on the plaster of the palace wall by the lampstand. When the king saw the palm of the hand that was writing, ⁶ the king's face took on a different look. As frightening thoughts rose up within him, his hip joints gave way and his knees started knocking together. ⁷ The king cried out to bring in the exorcists, astrologers and diviners. The king said to the sages of Bavel, "Whoever can read this inscription and tell me what it means will be dressed in royal purple, wear a gold chain around his neck and be one of the three men ruling the kingdom." ⁸ But although all the king's sages came in, none could read the inscription or tell the king what it meant. ⁹ Then King Belshatzar became terrified; his face turned pale, and his lords were thrown into confusion.

¹⁰ At this point the queen mother, because of what the king and his lords were saying, entered the banquet hall. The queen mother said, "May the king live forever! Don't be scared by your thoughts or let your face be so pale. ¹¹ There is a man in your kingdom in whom is the spirit of the holy gods. In the days of your father, he was found to have light, discernment and wisdom like the wisdom of the gods. King N'vukhadnetzar your father — the king, your father — made him chief of the magicians, exorcists, astrologers and diviners; ¹² because he was found to have an extraordinary spirit, knowledge, discernment, and the ability to interpret dreams, unlock mysteries and solve knotty problems. He is called Dani'el, but the king gave him the name Belt'shatzar. Now have Dani'el summoned, and he will tell you what this means."

¹³ Dani'el was brought into the king's presence. The king said to Dani'el, "Are you Dani'el, one of the exiles from Y'hudah whom the king my father brought out of Y'hudah? ¹⁴ I've heard about you that the spirit of the gods is in you, and that you have been found to have light, discernment and extraordinary wisdom. ¹⁵ Now the sages, the exorcists, were brought in to me so that they could read this inscription and tell me what it means, but they couldn't interpret it for me. ¹⁶ However, I've heard that you can give interpretations and solve knotty problems. Now if you can read the inscription and tell me what it means, you will be dressed in royal purple, wear a gold chain around your neck and be one of the three men ruling the kingdom."

¹⁷ Dani'el answered the king, "Keep your gifts, and give your rewards to someone else. However, I will read the inscription to the king and tell him what it means. ¹⁸ Your majesty, the Most High God gave N'vukhadnetzar your father the kingdom, as well as greatness, glory and majesty. ¹⁹ Because of the greatness he gave him, all the peoples, nations and languages trembled with fear before him. Anyone he wanted to, he put to death; anyone he wanted to, he kept alive; anyone he wanted to, he advanced; and anyone he wanted to, he humbled. ²⁰ But when he grew proud and his spirit became hard, he began treating people arrogantly, so he was deposed from his royal throne, and his glory was taken away from him. ²¹ He was driven from human society, his heart was made like that of an animal, he lived with the wild donkeys, he was fed with grass like an ox, and his body was drenched with dew from the sky; until he learned that the Most High God rules in the human kingdom and sets up over it whomever he pleases. ²² But, Belshatzar, you, his son, have not humbled your heart, even though you knew all this. ²³ Instead, you have exalted yourself against

the Lord of heaven by having them bring you the vessels from his house; and you and your lords, your wives and your concubines drank wine from them; then you offered praise to your gods of silver, gold, bronze, iron, wood and stone, which can't see, hear or know anything. Meanwhile, God, who holds your very breath in his hands, and to whom belongs everything you do, you have not glorified. ²⁴ This is why he sent the hand to write this inscription; ²⁵ and the inscription says, '*M'ne! M'ne! T'kel ufarsin.*' * ²⁶ This is what it means: '*M'ne!*' — God has counted up your kingdom and brought it to an end. ²⁷ '*T'kel*' — you are weighed on the balance-scale and come up short. ²⁸ '*P'res*' — your kingdom has been divided and given to the Medes and Persians."

²⁹ Then Belshatzar gave the order; and they clothed Dani'el in royal purple, put a gold chain around his neck and proclaimed of him that he was to be one of the three men ruling the kingdom.

³⁰ That very night Belshatzar, the king of the Kasdim, was killed.

6 ¹⁽⁵:³¹⁾ The kingdom passed to Daryavesh the Mede when he was about sixty-two years old. ²⁽¹⁾ Daryavesh decided to set over the kingdom 120 viceroys to rule throughout the entire kingdom, ³⁽²⁾ with three chiefs over them, of whom Dani'el was one, so that these viceroys could be responsible to them and so that the king's interests would be safeguarded. ⁴⁽³⁾ But because an extraordinary spirit was in this Dani'el, he so distinguished himself above the other chiefs and the viceroys that the king considered putting him in charge of the whole kingdom. ⁵⁽⁴⁾ The other chiefs and the viceroys tried to find a cause for complaint against Dani'el in regard to how he performed his governing duties, but they could find nothing to complain about, no fault; on the contrary, because he was so faithful, not a single instance of negligence or faulty administration could be found.

⁶⁽⁵⁾ Then these men said, "We're not going to find any cause for complaint against this Dani'el unless we can find something against him in regard to the law of his god." ⁷⁽⁶⁾ So these chiefs and viceroys descended on the king and said to him, "King Daryavesh, live forever! ⁸⁽⁷⁾ All the chiefs of the kingdom, along with the prefects, viceroys, advisers and governors, have met and agreed that the king should issue a decree putting in force the following law: 'Whoever makes a request of any god or man during the next thirty days, except of you, your majesty, is to be thrown into the lion pit.' ⁹⁽⁸⁾ Now, your majesty, issue this decree over your signature, so that it cannot be revoked, as required by the law of the Medes and Persians, which is itself irrevocable." ¹⁰⁽⁹⁾ So King Daryavesh signed the document, and the decree became law.

¹¹⁽¹⁰⁾ On learning that the document had been signed, Dani'el went home. The windows of his upstairs room were open in the direction of Yerushalayim; and there he kneeled down three times a day and prayed, giving thanks before his God, just as he had been doing before. ¹²⁽¹¹⁾ Then these men descended on Dani'el and found him making requests and pleading before his God. ¹³⁽¹²⁾ So they went to remind the king of his royal decree: "Didn't you sign a law prohibiting anyone from making requests of any god or man within thirty days, except yourself, your majesty, on pain of being

---

* *M'ne* — a *maneh* was a coin; Aramaic *mena* means "to count." *T'kel* is Aramaic for *shekel*, a unit of weight; Aramaic *tekilta* means "you are weighed." *P'res* (an Aramaic noun, plural *parsin*), is half a *maneh*; *p'ris* means "cut up, divided"; *Paras* is Persia. (The "f" in *ufarsin* is the Aramaic letter *peh*, sometimes pronounced "p" and sometimes, "f.")

thrown into the lion pit?" The king answered, "Yes, that is true, as required by the law of the Medes and Persians, which is itself irrevocable." ¹⁴⁽¹³⁾ They replied to the king, "That Dani'el, one of the exiles from Y'hudah, respects neither you, your majesty, nor the decree you signed; instead, he continues praying three times a day." ¹⁵⁽¹⁴⁾ When the king heard this report, he was very upset. He determined to save Dani'el and worked until sunset to find a way to rescue him. ¹⁶⁽¹⁵⁾ But these men descended on the king and said to him, "Remember, your majesty, that it is a law of the Medes and Persians that no decree or edict, once issued by the king, can be revoked."
¹⁷⁽¹⁶⁾ So the king gave the order, and they brought Dani'el and threw him into the lion pit. The king said to Dani'el, "Your God, whom you are always serving, will save you." ¹⁸⁽¹⁷⁾ A stone was brought to block the opening of the pit, and the king sealed it with his own signet and with the signet of his lords, so that nothing concerning Dani'el could be changed.

¹⁹⁽¹⁸⁾ Then the king returned to his palace. He spent the night fasting and refusing to be entertained, as sleep eluded him. ²⁰⁽¹⁹⁾ Early in the morning, the king got up and hurried to the lion pit. ²¹⁽²⁰⁾ On approaching the pit where Dani'el was, the king cried in a pained voice to Dani'el, "Dani'el, servant of the living God! Has your God, whom you are always serving, been able to save you from the lions?" ²²⁽²¹⁾ Then Dani'el answered the king, "May the king live forever! ²³⁽²²⁾ My God sent his angel to shut the lions' mouths, so they haven't hurt me. This is because before him I was found innocent; and also I have done no harm to you, your majesty." ²⁴⁽²³⁾ The king was overjoyed and ordered Dani'el taken up from the pit. So Dani'el was taken up from the pit, and he was found to be completely unharmed, because he had trusted in his God.

²⁵⁽²⁴⁾ Then the king gave an order, and they brought those men who had accused Dani'el, and they threw them into the lion pit — them, their children and their wives — and before they even reached the bottom of the pit, the lions had them in their control and broke all their bones to pieces.

²⁶⁽²⁵⁾ King Daryavesh wrote all the peoples, nations and languages living anywhere on earth:

"*Shalom rav!* [Abundant peace!]

²⁷⁽²⁶⁾ "I herewith issue a decree that everywhere in my kingdom, people are to tremble and be in awe of the God of Dani'el.

"For he is the living God;
he endures forever.
His kingdom will never be destroyed;
his rulership will last till the end.
²⁸⁽²⁷⁾ He saves, rescues, does signs and wonders
both in heaven and on earth.
He delivered Dani'el
from the power of the lions."

²⁹⁽²⁸⁾ So this Dani'el prospered during the reign of Daryavesh, and also during the reign of Koresh the Persian.

7 ^{1} In the first year of Belshatzar king of Bavel, Dani'el had a dream and visions in his head, as he was lying on his bed. He wrote the dream down, and this is his account: ^{2} "I had a vision at night; I saw there before me the four winds of the sky breaking out over the great sea, ^{3} and four huge animals came up out of the sea, each different from the others. ^{4} The first was like a lion, but it had eagle's wings. As I watched, its wings were plucked off, and it was lifted off the earth and made to stand on two feet like a man, and a human heart was given to it. ^{5} Then there was another animal, a second one, like a bear. It raised itself up on one side, and it had three ribs in its mouth between its teeth. It was told, 'Get up, and gorge yourself with flesh!' ^{6} After this, I looked; and there was another one, like a leopard with four bird's wings on its sides. The animal also had four heads, and it was given power to rule. ^{7} After this, I looked in the night visions; and there before me was a fourth animal, dreadful, horrible, extremely strong, and with great iron teeth. It devoured, crushed and stamped its feet on what was left. It was different from all the animals that had gone before it, and it had ten horns.

^{8} "While I was considering the horns, another horn sprang up among them, a little one, before which three of the first horns were plucked up by the roots. In this horn were eyes like human eyes and a mouth speaking arrogantly.

^{9} "As I watched, thrones were set in place;
   and the Ancient One took his seat.
   His clothing was white as snow,
    the hair on his head was like pure wool.
   His throne was fiery flames,
    with wheels of burning fire.
^{10} A stream of fire flowed from his presence;
   thousands and thousands ministered to him,
   millions and millions stood before him.
   Then the court was convened, and the books were opened.

^{11} "I kept watching. Then, because of the arrogant words which the horn was speaking, I watched as the animal was killed; its body was destroyed; and it was given over to be burned up completely. ^{12} As for the other animals, their rulership was taken away; but their lives were prolonged for a time and a season.

^{13} "I kept watching the night visions,
   when I saw, coming with the clouds of heaven,
   someone like a son of man.
   He approached the Ancient One
   and was led into his presence.
^{14} To him was given rulership,
   glory and a kingdom,
   so that all peoples, nations and languages
   should serve him.
   His rulership is an eternal rulership
   that will not pass away;
   and his kingdom is one
   that will never be destroyed.

¹⁵ "As for me, Dani'el, my spirit deep within me was troubled; the visions in my head frightened me. ¹⁶ I approached one of those standing by and asked him what all this really meant. He said that he would make me understand how to interpret these things. ¹⁷ 'These four huge animals are four kingdoms that will arise on earth. ¹⁸ But the holy ones of the Most High will receive the kingdom and possess the kingdom forever, yes, forever and ever.'

¹⁹ "Then I wanted to know what the fourth beast meant, the one that was different from all the others, so very terrifying, with iron teeth and bronze nails, which devoured, crushed and stamped its feet on what was left; ²⁰ and what the ten horns on its head meant; and the other horn which sprang up and before which three fell, the horn that had eyes and a mouth speaking arrogantly and seemed greater than the others. ²¹ I watched, and that horn made war with the holy ones and was winning, ²² until the Ancient One came, judgment was given in favor of the holy ones of the Most High, and the time came for the holy ones to take over the kingdom. ²³ This is what he said: 'The fourth animal will be a fourth kingdom on earth. It will be different from the other kingdoms; it will devour the whole earth, trample it down and crush it. ²⁴ As for the ten horns, out of this kingdom ten kings will arise; and yet another will arise after them. Now he will be different from the earlier ones, and he will put down three kings. ²⁵ He will speak words against the Most High and try to exhaust the holy ones of the Most High. He will attempt to alter the seasons and the law; and [the holy ones] will be handed over to him for a time, times and half a time. ²⁶ But when the court goes into session, he will be stripped of his rulership, which will be consumed and completely destroyed. ²⁷ Then the kingdom, the rulership and the greatness of the kingdoms under the whole heaven will be given to the holy people of the Most High. Their kingdom is an everlasting kingdom, and all rulers will serve and obey them.'"

²⁸ This is the end of the account. As for me, Dani'el, my thoughts frightened me so much that I turned pale; but I kept the matter to myself.

8 ¹ After that first vision, it was in the third year of the reign of King Belshatzar that another vision appeared to me, Dani'el. ² I looked into the vision; and as I looked, I found myself in Shushan the capital, in the province of 'Eilam. I looked into the vision, and I was by the Ulai canal. ³ I looked up; and as I watched, there in front of the stream stood a ram with two horns. The horns were long, but one was longer than the other, and the longer one came up later [than the other]. ⁴ I saw the ram pushing to the west, north and south; and no animals could stand up against it; nor was there anyone that could rescue from its power. So it did as it pleased and became very strong.

⁵ I was beginning to understand, when a male goat came from the west, passing over the whole earth without touching the ground. The goat had a prominent horn between its eyes. ⁶ It approached the ram with the two horns, which I had seen standing in front of the river, and charged it with savage force. ⁷ I watched as it advanced on the ram, filled with rage against it, and struck the ram, breaking its two horns. The ram was powerless to stand against it. It threw the ram to the ground and trampled it down, and there was no one that could rescue it from the goat's power. ⁸ The male goat then became extremely strong; but when it was strong, the big horn was broken; and in its place arose what appeared to be four horns in the directions of the four winds of heaven. ⁹ Out of one of them came a little horn which

grew extremely big in the directions of the south and east, and in the direction of the Glory. ¹⁰ It grew so great that it reached the army of heaven; it hurled some of the army and the stars to the ground and trampled on them. ¹¹ Yes, it even considered itself as great as the prince of the army; the regular burnt offering was taken away from him, and the place of his sanctuary was thrown down. ¹² Through sin, the army was put in its power, along with the regular burnt offering. It flung truth on the ground as it acted and prospered.

¹³ Then I heard a holy one speaking, and another holy one said to the speaker, "How long will the events of the vision last, this vision concerning the regular offering and the transgression which is so appalling, that allows the sanctuary and the army to be trampled underfoot?" ¹⁴ The first said to me, "Two thousand three hundred evenings and mornings, after which the sanctuary will be restored to its rightful state."

¹⁵ After I, Dani'el, had seen the vision and was trying to understand it, suddenly there stood in front of me someone who appeared to be a man. ¹⁶ I heard a human voice calling from between the banks of the Ulai, "Gavri'el, make this man understand the vision!" ¹⁷ He came up to where I was standing, and his approach so terrified me that I fell on my face. But he said to me, "Human being! Understand that the vision refers to the time of the end." ¹⁸ As he was speaking with me, I fell into a deep sleep, with my face toward the ground; but he touched me, set me on my feet, ¹⁹ and said, "I am going to explain to you what will happen at the end of the period of fury, because [the vision] has to do with the time at the end. ²⁰ You saw a ram with two horns which are the kings of Media and Persia. ²¹ The shaggy male goat is the king of Greece, and the prominent horn between its eyes is the first king. ²² As for the horn that broke and the four which rose up in its place, four kingdoms will arise out of this nation, but not with the power the first king had. ²³ In the latter part of their reign, when the evildoers have become as evil as possible, there will arise an arrogant king skilled in intrigue. ²⁴ His power will be great, but not with the power the first king had. He will be amazingly destructive, he will succeed in whatever he does, and he will destroy the mighty and the holy ones. ²⁵ He will succeed through craftiness and deceit, become swelled with pride, and destroy many people just when they feel the most secure. He will even challenge the prince of princes; but, without human intervention, he will be broken. ²⁶ The vision of the evenings and mornings which has been told is true; but you are to keep the vision secret, because it is about days in the distant future."

²⁷ I, Dani'el, grew weak and was ill for some days. Then I got up and took care of the king's affairs; but I was appalled at the vision and still couldn't understand it.

9 ¹ In the first year of Daryavesh the son of Achashverosh, a Mede by birth who was made king over the kingdom of the Kasdim — ² in the first year of his reign, I, Dani'el, was reading the Scriptures and thinking about the number of years which *Adonai* had told Yirmeyah the prophet would be the period of Yerushalayim's desolation, seventy years. ³ I turned to *Adonai*, God, to seek an answer, pleading with him in prayer, with fasting, sackcloth and ashes. ⁴ I prayed to *Adonai* my God and made this confession:

"Please, *Adonai*, great and fearsome God, who keeps his covenant and extends grace to those who love him and observe his *mitzvot*! ⁵ We have sinned, done wrong, acted wickedly, rebelled and turned away from your *mitzvot* and rulings. ⁶ We have not listened to your servants the prophets, who spoke in your name to our kings, our leaders, our ancestors and to all the people of the land.

⁷ "To you, *Adonai*, belongs righteousness; but to us today belongs shame — to us, the men of Y'hudah, the inhabitants of Yerushalayim and all Isra'el, including those nearby and those far away, throughout all the countries where you have driven them; because they broke faith with you. ⁸ Yes, ADONAI, shame falls on us, our kings, our leaders and our ancestors; because we sinned against you. ⁹ It is for *Adonai* our God to show compassion and forgiveness, because we rebelled against him. ¹⁰ We didn't listen to the voice of ADONAI our God, so that we could live by his laws, which he presented to us through his servants the prophets. ¹¹ Yes, all Isra'el flouted your *Torah* and turned away, unwilling to listen to your voice. Therefore the curse and oath written in the *Torah* of Moshe the servant of God was poured out on us, because we sinned against him. ¹² He carried out the threats he spoke against us and against our judges who judged us, by bringing upon us disaster so great that under all of heaven, nothing has been done like what has been done to Yerushalayim. ¹³ As written in the *Torah* of Moshe, this whole disaster came upon us. Yet we did not appease ADONAI our God by renouncing our wrongdoing and discerning your truth. ¹⁴ So ADONAI watched for the right moment to bring this disaster upon us, for ADONAI our God was just in everything he did, yet we didn't listen when he spoke.

¹⁵ "Now, *Adonai* our God, who brought your people out of the land of Egypt with a strong hand, thereby winning renown for yourself, as is the case today — we sinned, we acted wickedly. ¹⁶ *Adonai*, in keeping with all your justice, please allow your anger and fury to be turned away from your city Yerushalayim, your holy mountain; because it is due to our sins and the wrongdoings of our ancestors that Yerushalayim and your people have become objects of scorn among everyone around us. ¹⁷ Therefore, our God, listen to the prayer and pleadings of your servant; and cause your face to shine on your desolated sanctuary, for your own sake. ¹⁸ My God, turn your ear, and hear; open your eyes and see how desolated we are, as well as the city which bears your name. For we plead with you not because of our own righteousness, but because of your compassion. ¹⁹ *Adonai*, hear! *Adonai*, forgive! *Adonai*, pay attention, and don't delay action — for your own sake, my God, because your city and your people bear your name!"

²⁰ While I was speaking, praying, confessing my own sin and the sin of my people Isra'el, and pleading before ADONAI my God for the holy mountain of my God — ²¹ yes, while I was speaking in prayer, the man Gavri'el, whom I had seen in the vision at the beginning, swooped down on me in full flight at about the time of the evening sacrifice, ²² and explained things to me. He said, "I have come now, Dani'el, to enable you to understand this vision clearly. ²³ At the beginning of your prayers, an answer was given; and I have come to say what it is; because you are greatly loved. Therefore look into this answer, and understand the vision.

²⁴ "Seventy weeks have been decreed for your people and for your holy city for putting an end to the transgression, for making an end of sin, for forgiving iniquity, for bringing in everlasting justice, for setting the seal on vision and prophet, and for anointing the Especially Holy Place. ²⁵ Know, therefore, and discern that seven weeks [of years] will elapse between the issuing of the decree to restore and rebuild Yerushalayim until an anointed prince comes. It will remain built for sixty-two weeks [of years], with open spaces and moats; but these will be troubled times. ²⁶ Then, after the sixty-two weeks, *Mashiach* will be cut off and have nothing. The people of a prince yet to come will destroy the city and the sanctuary, but his end will come

with a flood, and desolations are decreed until the war is over. ²⁷ He will make a strong covenant with leaders for one week [of years]. For half of the week he will put a stop to the sacrifice and the grain offering. On the wing of detestable things the desolator will come and continue until the already decreed destruction is poured out on the desolator."

10 ¹ In the third year of Koresh king of Persia, a word was revealed to Dani'el, also called Belt'shatzar. The word was certain: a great war. He understood the word, having gained understanding in the vision.

² At that time I, Dani'el, had been mourning for three whole weeks. ³ I hadn't eaten any food that satisfied me — neither meat nor wine had entered my mouth, and I didn't anoint myself once, until three full weeks had passed.

⁴ On the twenty-fourth day of the first month, I was on the bank of the great river, the Tigris, ⁵ when I looked up, and there before me was a man dressed in linen wearing a belt made of fine Ufaz gold. ⁶ His body was like beryl, his face looked like lightning and his eyes like fiery torches; his arms and feet were the color of burnished bronze; and when he spoke, it sounded like the roar of a crowd. ⁷ Only I, Dani'el, saw the vision; the men who were with me did not see the vision; however, a great trembling fell over them; so that they rushed to hide themselves. ⁸ Thus I was left alone; and when I saw this great vision, there was no strength left in me — my face, normally pleasant-looking, became disfigured; and I had no strength.

⁹ I heard his voice speaking; and when I heard him speaking, I fell down in a faint, with my face to the ground. ¹⁰ Then a hand touched me and raised me, tottering, to my hands and knees. ¹¹ He said to me, "Dani'el, you are a greatly loved man. Now pay attention to the words I am saying to you, and stand upright; for it is to you that I have been sent now." After he had said this to me, I stood up, trembling. ¹² Then he said to me, "Don't be afraid, Dani'el; because since the first day that you determined to understand and to humble yourself before your God, your words have been heard; and I have come because of what you said. ¹³ The prince of the kingdom of Persia prevented me from coming for twenty-one days; but Mikha'el, one of the chief princes, came to assist me; so that I was no longer needed there with the kings of Persia. ¹⁴ So I have come to make you understand what will happen to your people in the *acharit-hayamim*; for there is still another vision which will relate to those days."

¹⁵ After he had said these things to me, I looked down at the ground and couldn't speak. ¹⁶ Then someone who looked like a human being touched my lips, after which I could open my mouth and speak; I said to the one standing in front of me, "My lord, it is because of the vision that I am seized with such anguish; I don't have any strength. ¹⁷ For how can this servant of my lord speak with my lord, when my strength and breath have failed me?" ¹⁸ Then, again someone who looked human touched me and revived me. ¹⁹ He said, "You man so greatly loved, don't be afraid. *Shalom* to you; and be strong, yes, truly strong." His speaking to me strengthened me, and I said, "My lord, keep speaking; because you've given me strength." ²⁰ Then he said, "Do you know why I came to you? Although now I must return to fight the prince of Persia; and when I leave, the prince of Greece will come; ²¹ nevertheless, I will tell you what is written in the Book of Truth. There is no one standing with me against them except Mikha'el your prince;

11 [1] however, I was already standing up to support and help Daryavesh the Mede in the first year of his reign. [2] What I am going to tell you now is true.

"Three kings will arise in Persia, followed by a fourth, who will be far wealthier than all of them; and when he has grown strong by means of his wealth, he will stir up everyone against the kingdom of Greece.

[3] "Then a powerful king will appear who will rule a vast kingdom and do whatever he pleases. [4] But once he appears, his kingdom will be broken up and divided to the four winds of heaven. It won't be inherited by his descendants, and it won't be ruled with the power he had, because his kingship will be uprooted and will pass to others than his own posterity.

[5] "The king in the south will be strong, and one of his princes will gain power over him and have dominion; his domain will be a great dominion. [6] After a number of years they will form an alliance. The daughter of the king of the south will approach the king of the north to make an agreement, but she won't retain her power; and he and his power won't last either. Rather, she will be surrendered, along with her attendants, her father and the one who supported her during those times. [7] But another branch from the same roots as hers will appear in her father's place. He will attack the army of the king of the north, enter his fortress and succeed in conquering them. [8] He will also carry off as booty to Egypt their gods, their cast metal images and their valuable gold and silver vessels. Then for some years, he will refrain from attacking the king of the north.

[9] "Afterwards, the king of the north will invade the kingdom of the king of the south, but he will retire to his own land. [10] His sons will rouse themselves to muster a large and powerful army, which will advance like a flood passing through. In another campaign, it will march on the enemy stronghold. [11] The king of the south, enraged, will set out to do battle with the king of the north, who, in turn, will muster a large army; but this army will be defeated by his enemy [12] and carried off. The conqueror will grow proud as he slaughters tens of thousands, yet he will not prevail. [13] Rather, the king of the north will again muster an army, larger than the first one, at the end of this period, after a number of years; it will be a large, well-supplied army. [14] Those will be times in which many will resist the king of the south; and the more violent ones among your own people will rebel in order to fulfill their vision; but they will fail.

[15] "Then the king of the north will come, set up siege-works and capture a fortified city; the forces of the south will be insufficient defense, even his elite troops will not be strong enough to resist. [16] The invader will do as he pleases; no one will be able to withstand him. So he will establish himself in the Land of Glory, and he will have the power to destroy it. [17] He will determinedly advance with the full force of his kingdom, but he will make an agreement with the king of the south and give him a daughter in marriage. His object will be to destroy him, but the agreement will not last or work out in his favor. [18] Next, he will put his attention on the coastlands and islands and capture many, but an army commander will put a stop to his outrages and cause his outrages to come back upon him. [19] After this, he will put his attention on the strongholds in his own land; but he will stumble, fall and not be seen again.

[20] "In his place will arise one who will send a tax collector through the Glorious Kingdom; but within a few days, he will be broken, though neither in anger nor in battle.

²¹ "There will arise in his place a despicable man not entitled to inherit the majesty of the kingdom, but he will come without warning and gain the kingdom by intrigue. ²² Large armies will be broken and swept away before him, as well as the prince of the covenant. ²³ Alliances will be made with him, but he will undermine them by deceit. Then, although he will have but a small following, he will emerge and become strong. ²⁴ Without warning, he will assail the most powerful men in each province and do things his predecessors never did, either recently or in the distant past; he will reward them with plunder, spoil and wealth while devising plots against their strongholds, but only for a time.

²⁵ "He will summon his power and courage against the king of the south with a great army, and the king of the south will fight back with a very large and powerful army; but he will not succeed, because of plots devised against him. ²⁶ Yes, those who shared his food will destroy him; his army will be swept away; and many will fall in the slaughter. ²⁷ These two kings, bent on mischief, will sit at the same table, speaking lies to each other; but none of this will succeed; because the appointed end will not have come yet. ²⁸ Then the king of the north will return to his own land with great wealth; with his heart set against the holy covenant, he will take action and then return home.

²⁹ "At the time designated, he will come back to the south. But this time, things will turn out differently than before; ³⁰ because ships from Kittim will come against him, so that his courage will fail him. Then, in retreat, he will take furious action against the holy covenant, again showing favor to those who abandon the holy covenant. ³¹ Armed forces will come at his order and profane the sanctuary and fortress. They will abolish the daily burnt offering and set up the abomination that causes desolation. ³² Those who act wickedly against the covenant he will corrupt with his blandishments, but the people who know their God will stand firm and prevail. ³³ Those among the people who have discernment will cause the rest of the people to understand what is happening; nevertheless, for a while they will fall victim to sword, fire, exile and pillage. ³⁴ When they stumble, they will receive a little help, although many who join them will be insincere. ³⁵ Even some of those with discernment will stumble, so that some of them will be refined, purified and cleansed for an end yet to come at the designated time.

³⁶ "The king will do as he pleases. He will exalt himself and consider himself greater than any god, and he will utter monstrous blasphemies against the God of gods. He will prosper only until the period of wrath is over, for what has been determined must take place. ³⁷ He will show no respect for the gods his ancestors worshipped, or for the god women worship — he won't show respect for any god, because he will consider himself greater than all of them. ³⁸ But instead, he will honor the god of strongholds; with gold, silver, precious stones and other costly things he will honor a god unknown to his ancestors. ³⁹ He will deal with the strongest fortresses with the help of a foreign god. He will confer honor on those he acknowledges, causing them to rule over many and distributing land as a reward.

⁴⁰ "When the time for the end comes, the king of the south will push at him; while the king of the north will attack him like a whirlwind, with chariots, cavalry and a large navy. He will invade countries, overrun them and move on. ⁴¹ He will also enter the Land of Glory, and many [countries] will come to grief, but these will be saved from his power — Edom, Mo'av and the people of 'Amon. ⁴² He will reach

out his hand to seize other countries too. The land of Egypt will not escape — ^{43} he will control the treasures of gold and silver, as well as everything else in Egypt of value. Put and Ethiopia will be subject to him. ^{44} However, news from the east and north will frighten him, so that he moves out in great fury to ruin and completely do away with many. ^{45} Finally, when he pitches the tents of his palace between the seas and the mountain of the holy Glory, he will come to his end, with no one to help him.

12 ^{1} "When that time comes, Mikha'el, the great prince who champions your people, will stand up; and there will be a time of distress unparalleled between the time they became a nation and that moment. At that time, your people will be delivered, everyone whose name is found written in the book. ^{2} Many of those sleeping in the dust of the earth will awaken, some to everlasting life and some to everlasting shame and abhorrence. ^{3} But those who can discern will shine like the brightness of heaven's dome, and those who turn many to righteousness like the stars forever and ever.

^{4} "But you, Dani'el, keep these words secret, and seal up the book until the time of the end. Many will rush here and there as knowledge increases."

^{5} Then I, Dani'el, looked; and I saw in front of me two others, one on this bank of the river and the other on its other bank. ^{6} One of them asked the man dressed in linen who was above the water of the river, "How long will these wonders last?" ^{7} The man dressed in linen who was above the water of the river raised his right and left hands toward heaven and swore by him who lives forever that it would be for a time, times and a half, and that it will be when the the power of the holy people is no longer being shattered that all these things will end.

^{8} I heard this, but I couldn't understand what it meant; so I asked, "Lord, what will be the outcome of all this?" ^{9} But he said, "Go your way, Dani'el; for these words are to remain secret and sealed until the time of the end. ^{10} Many will purify, cleanse and refine themselves; but the wicked will keep on acting wickedly, and none of the wicked will understand. But those with discernment will understand. ^{11} From the time the regular burnt offering is taken away and the abomination that causes desolation is set up, there will be 1,290 days. ^{12} How blessed will be anyone who waits and arrives at the 1,335 days. ^{13} But you, go your way until the end comes. Then you will rest and rise for your reward, at the end of days."

'Ezra
EZRA

1 ¹ In the first year of Koresh king of Persia, in order for the word of ADONAI prophesied by Yirmeyahu to be fulfilled, ADONAI stirred up the spirit of Koresh king of Persia to make a proclamation throughout his whole kingdom, which he also put in writing, as follows:

² "Here is what Koresh king of Persia says: ADONAI, the God of heaven, has given me all the kingdoms on earth; and he has charged me to build him a house in Yerushalayim, in Y'hudah. ³ Whoever there is among you of all his people, may his God be with him! He may go up to Yerushalayim, in Y'hudah, and build the house of ADONAI the God of Isra'el, the God who is in Yerushalayim. ⁴ Let every survivor, no matter where he lives, be helped by his neighbors with silver, gold, goods and animals, in addition to the voluntary offering for the house of God in Yerushalayim."

⁵ The heads of fathers' clans in Y'hudah and Binyamin, along with the *cohanim*, the *L'vi'im*, and indeed all whose spirit God had stirred, set out to go up and rebuild the house of ADONAI in Yerushalayim. ⁶ All their neighbors supported them by giving them articles of silver, gold, goods, animals, and valuables, besides all their voluntary offerings.

⁷ In addition, Koresh the king brought out the vessels from the house of ADONAI which N'vukhadnetzar had taken from Yerushalayim and put in the house of his god. ⁸ Koresh king of Persia had Mitr'dat the treasurer bring them out and make an inventory of them for Sheshbatzar the prince of Y'hudah. ⁹ The list was as follows:

Gold basins	30
Silver basins	1,000
Knives	29
¹⁰ Gold bowls	30
Silver bowls of a different kind	410
Other vessels	1,000

¹¹ In all there were 5,400 articles of gold and silver. Sheshbatzar took all of them along when the exiles were brought up from Bavel to Yerushalayim.

2 ¹ Here is a list of the people of the province who had been exiled, carried off to Bavel by N'vukhadnetzar king of Bavel, but who later returned from exile and went up to Yerushalayim and Y'hudah, each to his own city; ² they went with Z'rubavel, Yeshua, Nechemyah, S'rayah, Re'elyah, Mordekhai, Bilshan, Mispar, Bigvai, Rechum and Ba'anah.

The number of men from the people of Isra'el:

³	descendants of Par'osh	2,172
⁴	descendants of Sh'fatyah	372
⁵	descendants of Arach	775
⁶	descendants of Pachat-Mo'av,	
	from the descendants of Yeshua and Yo'av	2,812
⁷	descendants of 'Eilam	1,254
⁸	descendants of Zatu	945
⁹	descendants of Zakkai	760
¹⁰	descendants of Bani	642
¹¹	descendants of B'vai	623
¹²	descendants of 'Azgad	1,222
¹³	descendants of Adonikam	666
¹⁴	descendants of Bigvai	2,056
¹⁵	descendants of 'Adin	454
¹⁶	descendants of Ater, of Y'chizkiyah	98
¹⁷	descendants of Betzai	323
¹⁸	descendants of Yorah	112
¹⁹	descendants of Hashum	223
²⁰	descendants of Gibbar	95
²¹	descendants of Beit-Lechem	123
²²	people of N'tofah	56
²³	people of 'Anatot	128
²⁴	descendants of 'Azmavet	42
²⁵	descendants of Kiryat-'Arim, K'firah and Be'erot	743
²⁶	descendants of Ramah and Geva	621
²⁷	people of Mikhmas	122
²⁸	people of Beit-El and 'Ai	223
²⁹	descendants of N'vo	52
³⁰	descendants of Magbish	156
³¹	descendants of the other 'Eilam	1,254
³²	descendants of Harim	320
³³	descendants of Lod, Hadid and Ono	725
³⁴	descendants of Yericho	345
³⁵	descendants of S'na'ah	3,630

³⁶ The *cohanim*:

	descendants of Y'da'yah, of the house of Yeshua	973
³⁷	descendants of Immer	1,052
³⁸	descendants of Pash'chur	1,247
³⁹	descendants of Harim	1,017

⁴⁰ The *L'vi'im*:

	descendants of Yeshua and Kadmi'el,	
	of the descendants of Hodavyah	74

⁴¹ The singers:

    descendants of Asaf   128

⁴² The descendants of the gatekeepers:

    descendants of Shalum,
    descendants of Ater,
    descendants of Talmon,
    descendants of 'Akuv,
    descendants of Hatita, and
    descendants of Shovai —
    in all,   139

⁴³ The temple servants:

    descendants of Tzicha,
    descendants of Hasufa,
    descendants of Taba'ot,
⁴⁴   descendants of Keros,
    descendants of Sia'ha,
    descendants of Padon,
⁴⁵   descendants of L'vanah,
    descendants of Hagavah,
    descendants of 'Akuv,
⁴⁶   descendants of Hagav,
    descendants of Salmai,
    descendants of Hanan,
⁴⁷   descendants of Giddel,
    descendants of Gachar,
    descendants of Re'ayah,
⁴⁸   descendants of Retzin,
    descendants of N'koda,
    descendants of Gazam,
⁴⁹   descendants of 'Uza,
    descendants of Paseach,
    descendants of Besai,
⁵⁰   descendants of Asnah,
    descendants of Me'unim,
    descendants of N'fusim,
⁵¹   descendants of Bakbuk,
    descendants of Hakufa,
    descendants of Harhur,
⁵²   descendants of Batzlut,
    descendants of M'chida,
    descendants of Harsha,
⁵³   descendants of Barkos,
    descendants of Sisra,

descendants of Temach,
⁵⁴   descendants of N'tziach, and
descendants of Hatifa.

⁵⁵ The descendants of Shlomo's servants:

descendants of Sotai,
descendants of Hasoferet,
descendants of P'ruda,
⁵⁶   descendants of Ya'alah,
descendants of Darkon,
descendants of Giddel,
⁵⁷   descendants of Sh'fatyah,
descendants of Hatil,
descendants of Pokheret-Hatzvayim, and
descendants of Ami.

⁵⁸ All the temple servants and the
descendants of Shlomo's servants numbered   392

⁵⁹ The following went up from Tel-Melach, Tel-Harsha, K'ruv, Adan and Immer; but they could not state which fathers' clan they or their children belonged to, [so it was not clear] whether they were from Isra'el:

⁶⁰   descendants of D'layah,
descendants of Toviyah, and
descendants of N'koda   652

⁶¹ and of the descendants of the *cohanim*:

descendants of Havayah,
descendants of Hakotz, and
descendants of Barzillai, who took a wife from the
daughters of Barzillai the Gil'adi and was named after them.

⁶² These tried to locate their genealogical records, but they weren't found. Therefore they were considered defiled and were not allowed to serve as *cohanim*. ⁶³ The Tirshata told them not to eat any of the especially holy food until a *cohen* appeared who could consult the *urim* and *tumim*.

⁶⁴ The entire assembly numbered 42,360 — ⁶⁵ not including their male and female slaves, of whom there were 7,337. They also had 200 male and female singers.

⁶⁶ Their horses numbered 736; their mules, 245; ⁶⁷ their camels, 435; and their donkeys, 6,720.

⁶⁸ Some of the heads of fathers' clans, when they came to the house of *ADONAI* in Yerushalayim, made voluntary offerings for rebuilding the house of God on its site. ⁶⁹ According to their means they gave into the treasury for the work 61,000 gold *darkmonim* [about two-thirds of a ton], 5,000 *manim* of silver [just over three tons], and a hundred tunics for the *cohanim*.

^70^ So the *cohanim*, the *L'vi'im*, some of the people, the singers, the gatekeepers and the temple servants lived in their towns and all Isra'el in their towns.

3 ^1^ When the seventh month arrived, after the people of Isra'el had resettled in the towns, the people gathered with one accord in Yerushalayim. ^2^ Then Yeshua the son of Yotzadak with his fellow *cohanim*, and Z'rubavel the son of Sh'alti'el with his kinsmen, organized rebuilding the altar of the God of Isra'el; so that they could offer burnt offerings on it, as is written in the *Torah* of Moshe the man of God. ^3^ They set up the altar on its former bases. Despite feeling threatened by the peoples of the [surrounding] countries; they offered on it burnt offerings to ADONAI, the morning and evening burnt offerings.

^4^ They observed the festival of *Sukkot* as written, offering daily the number of burnt offerings prescribed for each day, ^5^ and afterwards the regular burnt offering, the offerings for *Rosh-Hodesh* and those for all the designated times set apart for ADONAI, as well as those of everyone who volunteered a voluntary offering to ADONAI. ^6^ From the first day of the seventh month, they began offering burnt offerings to ADONAI, even though the foundation of ADONAI's temple had not yet been laid. ^7^ They also gave money for the stone-workers and carpenters, as well as food, drink and olive oil for the people of Tzidon and Tzor bringing cedar logs from the L'vanon to the sea and on to Yafo, in accordance with the authorization granted by Koresh king of Persia.

^8^ In the second year after their arrival at the house of God in Yerushalayim, in the second month, Z'rubavel the son of Sh'alti'el, Yeshua the son of Yotzadak, the rest of their kinsmen the *cohanim* and *L'vi'im*, and all who had come out of exile to Yerushalayim began the project. They appointed the *L'vi'im* aged twenty and up to direct work in the house of ADONAI. ^9^ Yeshua and his sons and brothers, Kadmi'el and his sons, and Y'hudah's sons together directed the workers in the house of God; also the sons of Henadad, with their sons and their kinsmen the *L'vi'im*.

^10^ When the builders laid the foundation of the temple of ADONAI, the *cohanim* in their robes, with trumpets, and the *L'vi'im* the sons of Asaf, with cymbals, took their places to praise ADONAI, as David king of Isra'el had instructed. ^11^ They sang antiphonally, praising and giving "thanks to ADONAI, for he is good, for his grace continues forever" toward Isra'el. All the people raised a great shout of praise to ADONAI, because the foundation of the house of ADONAI had been laid. ^12^ But many of the *cohanim*, *L'vi'im* and heads of fathers' clans, the old men who had seen the first house standing on its foundation, wept out loud when they saw this house; while others shouted out loud for joy — ^13^ so that the people couldn't distinguish the noise of the joyful shouting from the noise of the people's weeping; for the people were shouting so loudly that the noise could be heard at a great distance.

4 ^1^ When the enemies of Y'hudah and Binyamin heard that the people from the exile were building a temple to ADONAI the God of Isra'el, ^2^ they approached Z'rubavel and the heads of fathers' clans and said to them, "Let us build along with you; for we seek your God, just as you do; and we have been sacrificing to him since the time of Esar-Hadon king of Ashur, who brought us here." ^3^ But Z'rubavel, Yeshua and the rest of the heads of fathers' clans in Isra'el answered them, "You and we have nothing in common that you should join us in building a house for our God. We will build by ourselves for ADONAI the God of Isra'el, as Koresh king of Persia ordered us to do."

[4] Then the people of the land began discouraging the people of Y'hudah, in order to make them afraid to build. [5] They also bribed officials to frustrate their plan throughout the lifetime of Koresh king of Persia and on into the reign of Daryavesh king of Persia. [6] During the reign of Achashverosh, at the beginning of his reign, they brought a charge in writing against the people living in Y'hudah and Yerushalayim. [7] Then, during the time of Artach'shashta, Bishlam, Mitr'dat, Tav'el and their other colleagues wrote Artach'shashta; the letter was written in Aramaic, using Aramaic script. [8] Rechum the district governor and Shimshai the secretary wrote a letter against Yerushalayim to Artach'shashta the king as follows:

[9] "From Rechum the district governor, Shimshai the secretary, their other colleagues, the judges, the officials, the Dina'im, the Afarsat'khim, the Tarp'lim, the Afarsim, the Ark'vim, the Bavlim, the Shushan'kayim, the Dehayim, the 'Elma'im, [10] the other nations whom the great and noble Asnapar deported and settled in Shomron, and the others who remain in the country beyond the [Euphrates] River."

[11] (This is the text of the letter they sent him.)

"To Artach'shashta the king from his servants the people beyond the River:

[12] "Let the king know that the Judeans who left you to come to us in Yerushalayim are building this rebellious and wicked city. They have finished the walls and are now digging the foundations. [13] So let the king know that if this city is rebuilt and the walls are finished, they will refuse to pay tribute, tax or toll; and this will reduce the royal revenue. [14] Now, because we eat the king's salt, and it is not right for us to see the king dishonored, we therefore are sending to inform the king, [15] so that a search can be made in the archives of your ancestors; in these archives you will find and ascertain that this city is indeed a rebellious city, the bane of kings and provinces, and that sedition has been fostered there since ancient times — which is why this city was destroyed. [16] We submit to the king that if this city is rebuilt and the walls are finished, you will soon lose possession of all territories beyond the River."

[17] The king sent this answer:

"To Rechum the district governor, Shimshai the secretary, their other colleagues living in Shomron, and the rest beyond the River:

"*Shalom!*

[18] "The letter you sent us has now been translated for me. [19] I ordered a search made, and it was found that this city has a long history of revolt against kings, that rebellion and sedition have been fostered there; [20] also that there have been powerful kings over Yerushalayim who ruled all the territory beyond the River; and tribute, taxes and tolls were paid to them.

[21] "So now, order that these men stop work and that this city not be rebuilt until I order it. [22] Take care not to neglect your duty; otherwise the harm may increase, to the damage of the king."

²³ When the text of King Artach'shashta's letter was read before Rechum, Shimshai the secretary and their colleagues, they hurried to Yerushalayim to the Judeans and stopped their work by force of arms. ²⁴ So the work on the house of God in Yerushalayim ceased; it remained at a standstill until the second year of the reign of Daryavesh king of Persia.

5 ¹ The prophets Hagai and Z'kharyah the son of 'Iddo prophesied to the Judeans in Yerushalayim and Y'hudah; they prophesied to them in the name of the God of Isra'el. ² Then Z'rubavel the son of Sh'alti'el and Yeshua the son of Yotzadak began rebuilding the house of God in Yerushalayim; with them were the prophets of God, helping them. ³ No sooner had they begun, when Tatnai the governor of the territory beyond the [Euphrates] River, Sh'tar-Boznai and their colleagues came and asked them, "Who gave you permission to rebuild this house and finish this wall? ⁴ What are the names of the men putting up this building?" ⁵ But the eye of their God was on the leaders of the Judeans, so they didn't stop them until the matter could come before Daryavesh and a reply in writing be received.

⁶ Here is the text of the letter which Tatnai the governor of the territory beyond the River, Sh'tar-Boznai and their fellow officials beyond the River sent to Daryavesh the king; ⁷ they sent him a letter in which it was written:

"To Daryavesh the king,

"Complete *shalom!*"

⁸ "Let the king know that we went to the province of Y'hudah, to the house of the great God. It is being rebuilt with large stones, and timber is being set in the walls. This work is being done energetically, and it is making good progress under the direction ⁹ of their leaders. We asked them, 'Who gave you permission to rebuild this house and finish this wall?' ¹⁰ We also asked them their names, so that we could write you the names of the men in charge of them.

¹¹ "They gave us this answer: 'We are the servants of the God of heaven and earth. We are rebuilding the house that was built many years ago, built and finished by a great king of Isra'el. ¹² But because our ancestors provoked the God of heaven, he handed them over to N'vukhadnetzar king of Bavel, the Kasdi; he destroyed this house and carried the people off to Bavel. ¹³ But in the first year of Koresh king of Bavel, Koresh the king gave authorization to rebuild this house of God. ¹⁴ Moreover, the gold and silver articles belonging to the house of God, which N'vukhadnetzar had removed from the temple in Yerushalayim and brought to the temple of Bavel, Koresh the king took out of the temple in Bavel; they were turned over to a man named Sheshbatzar, whom he had appointed governor. ¹⁵ He said to him, "Take these articles, go, put them in the temple in Yerushalayim, and let the house of God be rebuilt on its original site." ¹⁶ So this same Sheshbatzar came and laid the foundations of the house of God in Yerushalayim; it has been under construction ever since, and it isn't finished yet.

¹⁷ "'Now therefore, if it seems good to the king, let a search be made in the royal treasury there in Bavel to determine whether a decree was issued by Koresh the king to rebuild this house of God in Yerushalayim; and let the king send us his decision concerning this matter.'"

6 ¹ Daryavesh the king issued an order; and search was made in the archives building, where treasures were stored in Bavel; ² and there was found at Achm'ta, in the palace which is in the province of Media, a scroll on which was written the following:

"Memorandum:

³ "In the first year of Koresh the king, Koresh the king issued this decree: 'Concerning the house of God in Yerushalayim, let the house be rebuilt, the place where they offer sacrifices; and let its foundations be firmly laid. Its height is to be ninety feet and its breadth ninety feet, ⁴ with three rows of large stones and one row of new timber. The expenses are to be charged to the king's treasury. ⁵ Also let the gold and silver articles belonging to the house of God, which N'vukhadnetzar removed from the temple at Yerushalayim and brought to Bavel, be restored and returned to the temple in Yerushalayim, each item to its place; and you are to put them in the house of God.'

⁶ "Therefore, Tatnai governor of the territory beyond the River, Sh'tar-Boznai and your colleagues the officials beyond the River, stay away from there! ⁷ Let the work of this house of God alone. Let the governor of the Judeans and the leaders of the Judeans rebuild this house of God on its site.

⁸ "Moreover, I herewith issue this order concerning how you are to assist these leaders of the Judeans in rebuilding this house of God: the expenses of these men are to be defrayed promptly from the royal funds, from the taxes collected beyond the River, so that the work can continue. ⁹ Whatever they need — young bulls, rams and lambs — for burnt offerings to the God of heaven, wheat, salt, wine and olive oil, according to what the *cohanim* in Yerushalayim say, is to be given them daily without fail; ¹⁰ so that they can offer sacrifices with a fragrant aroma to the God of heaven and pray for the life of the king and his sons.

¹¹ "I also order that if anyone defies this order, a beam is to be pulled from his house; and he is to be lifted up and impaled on it. His house is to be reduced to rubble. ¹² May the God who has caused his name to be there overthrow any king or people that tries to defy it and destroy this house of God in Yerushalayim.

"I, Daryavesh, have issued this order. Let it be carried out to the letter."

¹³ Then Tatnai the governor of the territory beyond the [Euphrates] River, Sh'tar-Boznai and their colleagues obeyed strictly; because Daryavesh the king had given the order to do so.

¹⁴ The leaders of the Judeans made good progress with the rebuilding, thanks to the prophesying of Hagai the prophet and Z'kharyah the son of 'Iddo. They kept building until they were finished, in keeping with the command of the God of Isra'el and in accordance with the order of Koresh, Daryavesh and Artach'shashta king of Persia. ¹⁵ This house was finished on the third day of the month Adar, in the sixth year of the reign of Daryavesh the king. ¹⁶ The people of Isra'el, the *cohanim*, the *L'vi'im* and the other people from the exile joyfully dedicated this house of God. ¹⁷ At the dedication of this house of God they offered 100 young bulls, 200 rams, 400 lambs, and, as a sin offering for all Isra'el, twelve male goats, corresponding to the number of the tribes of Isra'el.

¹⁸ Then they installed the *cohanim* in their divisions and the *L'vi'im* in their orders for the service of God in Yerushalayim, as written in the book of Moshe.

¹⁹ The people from the exile kept *Pesach* on the fourteenth day of the first month. ²⁰ For the *cohanim* and *L'vi'im* had purified themselves together; all of them were pure. So they slaughtered the *Pesach* lambs for all the people from the exile and for their kinsmen the *cohanim* and for themselves. ²¹ The people of Isra'el who had returned from the exile and all those who had renounced the filthy practices of the nations living in the land in order to seek ADONAI the God of Isra'el, ate [the *Pesach* lamb] ²² and joyfully kept the feast of *matzah* for seven days; for ADONAI had filled them with joy by turning the heart of the king of Ashur toward them, so that he assisted them in the work of the house of God, the God of Isra'el.

7 ¹ After these events, during the reign of Artach'shashta king of Persia, 'Ezra the son of S'rayah, the son of 'Azaryah, the son of Hilkiyah, ² the son of Shalum, the son of Tzadok, the son of Achituv, ³ the son of Amaryah, the son of 'Azaryah, the son of M'rayot, ⁴ the son of Z'rachyah, the son of 'Uzi, the son of Buki, ⁵ the son of Avishua, the son of Pinchas, the son of Eli'ezer, the son of Aharon the *cohen hagadol* — ⁶ this 'Ezra went up from Bavel. He was a scribe, expert in the *Torah* of Moshe, which ADONAI the God of Isra'el had given; and the king granted him everything he asked for, since the hand of ADONAI his God was on him.

⁷ In the seventh year of Artach'shashta the king, some of the people of Isra'el, and some of the *cohanim*, *L'vi'im*, singers, gatekeepers and temple servants went up to Yerushalayim. ⁸ ['Ezra] arrived at Yerushalayim in the fifth month of the seventh year of the king. ⁹ He began going up to Yerushalayim from Bavel on the first day of the first month and arrived on the first day of the fifth month, since the good hand of his God was on him. ¹⁰ For 'Ezra had set his heart on studying and practicing the *Torah* of ADONAI and teaching Isra'el the laws and rulings.

¹¹ Here is the letter that King Artach'shashta gave 'Ezra the *cohen* and *Torah*-teacher, the student of matters relating to ADONAI's *mitzvot* and his laws for Isra'el:

¹² "From: Artach'shashta, king of kings

"To: 'Ezra the *cohen*, scribe of the law of the God of heaven, etc.:

"Herewith ¹³ I decree that everyone in my realm who belongs to the people of Isra'el, including their *cohanim* and *L'vi'im*, who, of his own free will, chooses to go with you to Yerushalayim, should go. ¹⁴ You are being sent by the king and his seven counselors to inquire how the law of your God, of which you have expert knowledge, is being applied in Y'hudah and Yerushalayim. ¹⁵ You are also to bring with you the silver and gold which the king and his counselors have voluntarily offered to the God of Isra'el, whose dwelling is in Yerushalayim; ¹⁶ together with all the silver and gold you receive throughout the province of Bavel and the voluntary offerings of the people and the *cohanim* that have been offered willingly for the house of their God in Yerushalayim.

¹⁷ "You are to spend this money carefully on young bulls, rams, and lambs, with their grain offerings and drink offerings; and offer them on the altar of the house of your God in Yerushalayim. ¹⁸ Whatever seems good to you and your kinsmen to do with the rest of the silver and gold, do it according to the will of your God.

¹⁹ "The articles given to you for the service of the house of your God, deliver to the God of Yerushalayim.

²⁰ "Whatever else may be needed for the house of your God that you have to supply, you may supply from the royal treasury.

²¹ "I, Artach'shashta the king, herewith order all the treasurers in the territory beyond the [Euphrates] River to do carefully anything 'Ezra the *cohen*, scribe of the law of the God of heaven, requires of you, ²² up to three-and-a-third tons of silver, 500 bushels of wheat, 500 gallons of wine, 500 gallons of olive oil and unlimited amounts of salt. ²³ Whatever is ordered by the God of heaven is to be performed exactly for the house of the God of heaven; for why should wrath come against the realm of the king and his sons? ²⁴ Moreover, we herewith proclaim to you that it will be illegal to impose tribute, taxes or tolls on any of the *cohanim*, *L'vi'im*, singers, gatekeepers, servants or laborers in this house of God.

²⁵ "And you, 'Ezra, making use of the wisdom you have from your God, are to appoint magistrates and judges to judge all the people in the territory beyond the River, that is, all who know the laws of your God; and you are to teach those who don't know them. ²⁶ Whoever refuses to obey the law of your God and the law of the king, let judgment be executed on him swiftly, whether it be death, banishment, confiscation of goods or imprisonment."

²⁷ Blessed be *Adonai*, the God of our ancestors, who has put such a thing as this in the heart of the king, to restore the beauty of the house of *Adonai* in Yerushalayim, ²⁸ and has extended mercy to me before the king and his counselors, and before all the king's most powerful officials.

So I took courage, since the hand of *Adonai* my God was on me, and I gathered together out of Isra'el key men to go up with me.

8 ¹ These are the heads of their fathers' clans, and this is the genealogy of those who went up with me from Bavel during the reign of Artach'shashta the king:

² of the descendants of Pinchas: Gershom;
of the descendants of Itamar: Dani'el;
of the descendants of David: Hatush;
³ of the descendants of Sh'khanyah:
of the descendants of Par'osh: Z'kharyah,
and with him 150 males officially registered;
⁴ of the descendants of Pachat-Mo'av: Ely'ho'einai the son of Z'rachyah,
and with him 200 males;
⁵ of the descendants of Sh'khanyah: the son of Yachazi'el,
and with him 300 males;
⁶ of the descendants of 'Adin: 'Eved the son of Yonatan,
and with him 50 males;
⁷ of the descendants of 'Eilam: Yesha'yah the son of 'Atalyah,
and with him 70 males;
⁸ of the descendants of Sh'fatyah: Z'vadyah the son of Mikha'el,
and with him 80 males;
⁹ of the descendants of Yo'av: 'Ovadyah the son of Yechi'el,
and with him 218 males;
¹⁰ of the descendants of Shlomit: the son of Yosifyah,
and with him 160 males;
¹¹ of the descendants of Bevai: Z'kharyah the son of Bevai,
and with him 28 males;
¹² of the descendants of 'Azgad: Yochanan the son of HaKatan,
and with him 110 males;
¹³ of the descendants of Adonikam: the younger ones, whose names were Elifelet, Ye'i'el and Sh'ma'yah,
and with them 60 males; and
¹⁴ of the descendants of Bigvai: 'Utai and Zakur,
and with them 70 males.

¹⁵ I assembled them by the river that runs to Ahava, and we camped there three days. I reviewed the people and the *cohanim* but found no *L'vi'im* there. ¹⁶ So I sent for Eli'ezer, Ari'el, Sh'ma'yah, Elnatan, Yariv, Elnatan, Natan, Z'kharyah and Meshulam, who were leaders, and also for Yoyariv and Elnatan, who were men of discernment. ¹⁷ I gave them instructions for Iddo, the leading man in a place called Kasifya, and told them what to say to Iddo and his brother, who were in charge of Kasifya, so that they would bring us men to minister in the house of our God. ¹⁸ Since the good hand of our God was on us, they brought us Ish-Sekhel from the descendants of Machli the son of Levi, the son of Isra'el; Sherevyah with eighteen of his sons and kinsmen; ¹⁹ Hashavyah, with Yesha'yah, from the descendants of M'rari, and twenty of his kinsmen and their sons; ²⁰ and from the temple servants, whom David and the princes had assigned to serve the *L'vi'im*, two hundred temple servants, all recorded by name.

²¹ Then, there at the Ahava River, I proclaimed a fast; so that we could humble ourselves before our God and ask a safe journey of him for ourselves, our little ones

and all our possessions. ²² For I would have been ashamed to ask the king for a detachment of soldiers and horsemen to protect us from enemies along the road, since we had said to the king, "The hand of our God is on all who seek him, for good; but his power and fury is against all who abandon him." ²³ So we fasted and asked our God for this, and he answered our prayer.

²⁴ Then I separated twelve of the chief *cohanim*, along with Sherevyah, Hashavyah and ten of their kinsmen. ²⁵ I weighed out to them the silver, the gold and the utensils for the house of our God contributed by the king, his counselors, his princes and all Isra'el present there. ²⁶ I weighed out and handed over to them twenty-one-and-a-half tons of silver, three-and-a-third tons of silver articles, three-and-a-third tons of gold, ²⁷ twenty gold bowls weighing twenty-one pounds, and two vessels of fine burnished bronze as precious as gold. ²⁸ Then I told them, "You are consecrated to ADONAI, the articles are holy, and the silver and gold are a voluntary offering for ADONAI the God of your ancestors. ²⁹ Guard them carefully, until you weigh them before the chief *cohanim* and *L'vi'im* and the leaders of the fathers' clans in Yerushalayim, in the rooms of the house of ADONAI." ³⁰ So the *cohanim* and *L'vi'im* received the consignment of silver and gold and the articles to bring to Yerushalayim, to the house of our God.

³¹ On the twelfth day of the first month, we left the Ahava River to go to Yerushalayim. The hand of our God was on us, and he protected us from enemies and surprise attacks along the road. ³² In time, we arrived at Yerushalayim, where we rested for three days. ³³ On the fourth day, the silver, gold and articles were weighed in the house of our God and handed over to M'remot the son of Uriyah the *cohen*; with him was El'azar the son of Pinchas; and with them were Yozavad the son of Yeshua and No'adyah the son of Binui, who were *L'vi'im*. ³⁴ The entire consignment was numbered and weighed, and at the same time the total weight was recorded.

³⁵ The exiles who had returned from captivity offered burnt offerings to the God of Isra'el — twelve young bulls for all Isra'el, ninety-six rams, seventy-seven lambs, and twelve male goats as a sin offering; all this was a burnt offering for ADONAI.

³⁶ They also delivered the king's orders to the king's viceroys and governors beyond the [Euphrates] River; and these gave their support to the people and to the house of God.

9 ¹ After these things had been done, the leaders approached me and said, "The people of Isra'el, the *cohanim* and the *L'vi'im* have not separated themselves from the peoples of the lands and their disgusting practices — the Kena'ani, Hitti, P'rizi, Y'vusi, 'Amoni, Mo'avi, Egyptians and Emori. ² They have taken some of the women from these nations as wives for themselves and their sons, so that the holy seed has assimilated to the peoples of the lands; moreover, the officials and leaders have been the main offenders in this treachery." ³ When I heard this, I tore my robe and tunic, pulled hair from my head and beard, and sat down in shock. ⁴ All who trembled at the words of the God of Isra'el assembled around me when confronted with the treachery of these exiles; and I sat there in shock until the evening offering.

⁵ At the evening offering, with my cloak and tunic torn, I got up from afflicting myself, fell on my knees, spread out my hands to ADONAI my God, ⁶ and said, "My God, I am ashamed. I blush to lift my face to you, my God! For our sins tower over

our heads; our guilt reaches up to heaven. ⁷ Since the times of our ancestors, we have been deeply guilty; and because of our sins, we, our kings and our *cohanim* have been handed over to the kings of the lands, to the sword, to exile, to pillage and to disgrace, as is the case today. ⁸ Now, for a brief moment, ADONAI our God has shown us the favor of allowing a remnant to escape and giving us a secure foothold in his holy place, in order for God to make things look brighter to us and revive us a little in our slavery. ⁹ For we are slaves. Yet our God has not abandoned us in our slavery, but has caused the kings of Persia to extend grace to us, reviving us, so that we can rebuild the house of our God, repair its ruins, and have a wall of defense in Y'hudah and Yerushalayim.

¹⁰"But now, our God, what are we to say after this? For we have abandoned your *mitzvot*, ¹¹ which you gave us through your servants the prophets when they said, 'The land which you are going to in order to take possession of it is a land defiled by the uncleanness of the peoples of the lands, because of their disgusting practices, which have filled it with their filth from one end to the other. ¹² Therefore, you are not to give your daughters to their sons or take their daughters for your sons; and you are not to promote their peace or prosperity ever. Only in this way will you grow strong, enjoy the good things of the land and leave it as a lasting inheritance to your children.' ¹³ Now, after all that has come upon us because of our evil deeds and our deep guilt — and even so, you, our God, have punished us less than our sins deserve and have given us a surviving remnant — ¹⁴ are we to break your *mitzvot* again by making marriages with the peoples who have these disgusting practices? Won't you become so angry with us that you would destroy us completely, so that there would be no surviving remnant and no one who escapes? ¹⁵ ADONAI, God of Isra'el! You are just; yet we have been left a surviving remnant that has escaped, as is the case today. Look, we are before you in our guilt; because of it, no one can stand in your presence."

10 ¹ While 'Ezra was praying and making confession, weeping and prostrated before the house of God, a huge crowd of Isra'el's men, women and children gathered around him; and the people were weeping bitterly. ² Sh'khanyah the son of Yechi'el, one of the descendants of 'Eilam, spoke up and said to 'Ezra, "We have acted treacherously toward our God by marrying foreign women from the peoples of the land. But in spite of this, there is still hope for Isra'el. ³ We should make a covenant with our God to send away all these wives, along with their children, in obedience to the advice of *Adonai* and of those who tremble at the *mitzvah* of our God; let us act in accordance with the *Torah*. ⁴ Stand up, and do your duty, for we are with you; take courage, and do it!"

⁵ 'Ezra stood up, and he made the chief *cohanim*, the *L'vi'im* and all Isra'el swear that they would act according to what had been said; and they took the oath. ⁶ 'Ezra then left his place in front of the house of God and went to the room of Y'hochanan the son of Elyashiv. After going there, he neither ate food nor drank water; because he was mourning over the treachery of the exiles.

⁷ A proclamation was issued throughout Y'hudah and Yerushalayim that all the exiles were to assemble in Yerushalayim; ⁸ and that whoever didn't come within three days, in answer to the summons from the officials and leaders, would forfeit all he owned and himself be banished from the community of the exiles.

⁹ All the men of Y'hudah and Binyamin assembled in Yerushalayim within the three days. It was the twentieth day of the ninth month. All the people sat in the open place in front of the house of God, trembling because of this matter and because of the heavy rain. ¹⁰ 'Ezra the *cohen* stood up and addressed them: "You have acted treacherously by marrying foreign women and have thus increased Isra'el's guilt. ¹¹ Now, therefore, make confession to ADONAI, the God of your ancestors; and do what will please him by separating yourselves from the peoples of the land and from the foreign women." ¹² In response, the whole assembly cried aloud, "Yes, our duty is to do as you have said. ¹³ But there are many people, and it's the rainy season — we can't stay out here in the open. Also, it isn't the work of a day or two; for there are many of us who have committed this crime. ¹⁴ Let our leaders represent the whole community; and let all those in our cities who have married foreign women appear at prearranged times, accompanied by the elders and judges of each city; until our God's fierce anger over this has been turned away from us." ¹⁵ Only Yonatan the son of 'Asah'el and Yachz'yah the son of Tikvah, supported by Meshulam and Shabtai the *Levi*, opposed this.

¹⁶ The exiles did as agreed. 'Ezra the *cohen* chose heads of fathers' clans by name, and they began their sessions to look into the matter on the first day of the tenth month. ¹⁷ They finished dealing with all the men who had married foreign women by the first day of the first month.

¹⁸ Among the *cohanim* were found these who had married foreign women: of the sons of Yeshua the son of Yotzadak and his brothers: Ma'aseiyah, Eli'ezer, Yariv and G'dalyah. ¹⁹ They promised that they would send their wives away; and since they were guilty, they offered a ram from the flock for their guilt. ²⁰ Of the sons of Immer: Hanani and Z'vadyah; ²¹ of the sons of Harim: Ma'aseiyah, Eliyah, Sh'ma'yah, Yechi'el and 'Uziyah; ²² of the sons of Pash'chur: Elyo'einai, Ma'aseiyah, Yishma'el, N'tan'el, Yozavad and El'asah.

²³ Of the *L'vi'im*: Yozavad, Shim'i, K'layah (also known as K'lita), P'tachyah, Y'hudah and Eli'ezer.

²⁴ Of the singers: Elyashiv.

Of the gatekeepers: Shalum, Telem and Uri.

²⁵ Of Isra'el: of the descendants of Par'osh: Ramyah, Yizziyah, Malkiyah, Miyamin, El'azar, Malkiyah and B'nayah; ²⁶ of the descendants of 'Eilam: Mattanyah, Z'kharyah, Yechi'el, 'Avdi, Yeremot and Eliyah; ²⁷ of the descendants of Zatu: Elyo'einai, Elyashiv, Mattanyah, Yeremot, Zavad and 'Aziza; ²⁸ of the descendants of B'vai: Y'hochanan, Hananyah, Zabai and 'Atlai; ²⁹ of the descendants of Bani: Meshulam, Malukh, 'Adayah, Yashuv, Sh'al and Ramot; ³⁰ of the descendants of Pachat-Mo'av: 'Adna, K'lal, B'nayah, Ma'aseiyah, Mattanyah, B'tzal'el, Binui and M'nasheh; ³¹ of the descendants of Harim: Eli'ezer, Yishiyah, Malkiyah, Sh'ma'yah, Shim'on, ³² Binyamin, Malukh, and Sh'maryah; ³³ of the descendants of Hashum: Matnai, Matatah, Zavad, Elifelet, Yeremai, M'nasheh and Shim'i; ³⁴ of the descendants of Bani: Ma'adai, 'Amram, U'el, ³⁵ B'nayah, Bedyah, K'luhu, ³⁶ Vanyah, M'remot, Elyashiv, ³⁷ Mattanyah, Matnai, Ya'asai, ³⁸ Bani, Binui, Shim'i, ³⁹ Shelemyah, Natan, 'Adayah, ⁴⁰ Makhnavdai, Shashai, Sharai, ⁴¹ 'Azar'el, Shelemyah, Sh'maryah, ⁴² Shalum, Amaryah and Yosef; and ⁴³ of the descendants of N'vo: Ye'i'el, Mattityah, Zavad, Z'vina, Yadai, Yo'el and B'nayah.

⁴⁴ All these had taken foreign wives, and some of them had wives by whom they had had children.

Nechemyah
NEHEMIAH

1 ¹ The words of Nechemyah the son of Hakhalyah:

It was in the month of Kislev, in the twentieth year, as I was in Shushan the capital, ² that Hanani, one of my kinsmen, came out of Y'hudah with some men; and I asked them about the remnant of Judeans who had escaped the exile, and about Yerushalayim. ³ They answered me, "The remnant of the exile left there in the province are in great distress and are held in contempt, the wall of Yerushalayim is in ruins, and its gates have been completely burned up."

⁴ On hearing this answer, I sat down and wept; I mourned for several days, fasting and praying before the God of heaven. ⁵ I said, "Please, *Adonai*! God of heaven! You great and fearsome God, who keeps his covenant and extends grace to those who love him and observe his *mitzvot*! ⁶ Let your ear now be attentive and your eyes be open, so that you will listen to the prayer of your servant, which I am praying before you these days, day and night, for the people of Isra'el your servants — even as I confess the sins of the people of Isra'el that we have committed against you. Yes, I and my father's house have sinned. ⁷ We have deeply offended you. We haven't observed the *mitzvot*, laws or rulings you ordered your servant Moshe. ⁸ Remember, please, the word you gave through your servant Moshe, 'If you break faith, I will scatter you among the peoples; ⁹ but if you return to me, observe my *mitzvot* and obey them, then, even if your scattered ones are in the most distant part of heaven, nevertheless, I will collect them from there and bring them to the place I have chosen for bearing my name.' ¹⁰ Now these are your servants, your people, whom you have redeemed by your great power and strong hand. ¹¹ *Adonai*, please, let your ear now be attentive to the prayer of your servant and to the prayer of your servants who take joy in fearing your name: please let your servant succeed today and win this man's compassion" — for I was the king's personal attendant.

2 ¹ In the month of Nisan in the twentieth year of Artach'shashta the king, it happened that I took the wine and brought it to the king. Prior to then I had never appeared sad in his presence. ² The king asked, "Why do you look so sad? You're not sick, so this must be some deep inner grief." At this, I became very fearful, ³ as I said to the king, "May the king live forever! Why shouldn't I look sad, when the city, the place where my ancestors' tombs are, lies in ruins; and its gates are completely burned up?" ⁴ The king asked me, "What is it that you want?" I prayed to the God of heaven, ⁵ then said to the king, "If it pleases the king, if your servant has won your favor, send me to Y'hudah, to the city of my ancestors' tombs, so that I can rebuild it." ⁶ With the queen sitting next to him, the king asked me, "How long is your trip going to take? When will you return?" So it pleased the king to send me, and I gave him a time.

⁷ I then said to the king, "If it pleases the king, have letters given to me for the governors of the territory beyond the [Euphrates] River, so that they will let me pass through until I reach Y'hudah; ⁸ and also a letter for Asaf the supervisor of the royal

forests, so that he will give me timber to make beams for the gates of the fortress belonging to the house, for the city wall and for the house I will be occupying." The king gave me these, according to the good hand of my God on me.

⁹ I went to the governors of the territory beyond the River and gave them the king's letters. The king had sent with me an escort of army captains and cavalry. ¹⁰ When Sanvalat the Horoni and Toviyah the servant, the 'Amoni, heard about this, they were very displeased that someone had come to promote the welfare of the people of Isra'el.

¹¹ So I reached Yerushalayim. After I had been there for three days, ¹² I got up during the night, I and a few men with me. I hadn't told anyone what my God had put in my heart to do for Yerushalayim; and I didn't take any animal with me except the animal on which I was riding. ¹³ I went out by night through the Valley Gate, to the Dragon's Well and the Dung Gate, and inspected the places where the walls of Yerushalayim were broken down and where its gates had been burned down. ¹⁴ Then I went on to the Fountain Gate and the King's Pool, but there was no room for the animal under me to pass. ¹⁵ So I went up the valley in the dark and went on inspecting the wall; then I turned back, entered through the Valley Gate and returned, ¹⁶ without the officials' knowing where I had gone or what I had done. Till then, I hadn't said anything about this to the Judeans, *cohanim*, nobles, officials or anyone who would be responsible for the work.

¹⁷ Afterwards, I said to them, "You see what a sad state we are in, how Yerushalayim lies in ruins, with it gates burned up. Come, let's rebuild the wall of Yerushalayim, so that we won't continue in disgrace." ¹⁸ I also told them of the gracious hand of my God that had been on me, also what the king had said to me. They said, "Let's start building at once," and energetically set out to do this good work.

¹⁹ When Sanvalat the Horoni, Toviyah the servant, the 'Amoni, and Geshem the Arab heard about it, they began mocking us and jeering, "What is this you are doing? Are you going to rebel against the king?" ²⁰ But I answered them: "The God of heaven will enable us to succeed. Therefore we his servants will set about rebuilding. But you have no share, right or history to commemorate in Yerushalayim."

3 ¹ Then Elyashiv the *cohen hagadol* set out with his fellow *cohanim*, and they rebuilt the Sheep Gate. They consecrated it and set up its doors; they consecrated it as far as the Tower of the Hundred and on to the Tower of Hanan'el. ² Next to him the men from Yericho built. Next to him Zakur the son of Imri built.

³ The sons of Hasna'ah rebuilt the Fish Gate; they installed its timber framework and set up its doors, along with its bolts and bars. ⁴ Next to them M'remot the son of Uriyah, the son of Hakotz, made repairs. Next to them Meshulam the son of Berekhyah, the son of Mesheizav'el, made repairs. Next to them Tzadok the son of Ba'ana made repairs. ⁵ Next to them the men from T'koa made repairs; but their nobles would not put their shoulders to the work of their Lord.

⁶ Yoyada the son of Paseach and Meshulam the son of B'sodyah made repairs to the Old City Gate; they installed its timber framework and set up its doors, along with its bolts and bars. ⁷ Next to them M'latyah the Giv'oni, Yadon the Meronoti and the men from Giv'on and Mitzpah made repairs; they worked for the people associated with the governor of the territory beyond the [Euphrates] River. ⁸ Next to them 'Uzi'el the son of Harhayah, goldsmiths, made repairs.

Next to him Hananyah, one of the perfume-makers, made repairs; they renovated Yerushalayim as far as the Broad Wall. [9] Next to them Refayah the son of Hur, leader of half the district of Yerushalayim, made repairs. [10] Next to him Y'dayah the son of Harumaf made repairs opposite his own house. Next to him Hatush the son of Hashavn'yah made repairs. [11] Malkiyah the son of Harim and Hashuv the son of Pachat-Mo'av made repairs on another section and on the Tower of the Ovens. [12] Next to him Shalum the son of HaLochesh, leader of half the district of Yerushalayim, he and his daughters, made repairs.

[13] Hanun and the people living in Zanoach repaired the Valley Gate; they rebuilt it and set up its doors, along with its bolts and bars; and they rebuilt 1,500 feet of the wall, as far as the Dung Gate.

[14] Malkiyah the son of Rechav, leader of the district of Beit-Hakerem, repaired the Dung Gate; he rebuilt it and set up its doors, along with its bolts and bars.

[15] Shalun the son of Kol-Hozeh, leader of the district of Mitzpah, repaired the Fountain Gate; he rebuilt it, covered it and set up its doors, along with its bolts and bars; he also rebuilt the wall of the Pool of Shelach, by the royal garden, as far as the stairs that go down from the City of David. [16] After him Nechemyah the son of Azbuk, leader of half the district of Beit-Tzur, made repairs from the place opposite the tombs of David as far as the artificial pool and the soldiers' barracks. [17] After him the *L'vi'im* made repairs: Rechum the son of Bani; next to him Hashavyah, leader of half the district of Ke'ilah, made repairs for his district. [18] After him their colleagues, Bavai the son of Henadad, leader of half the district of Ke'ilah, made repairs. [19] Next to him 'Ezer the son of Yeshua, leader of Mitzpah, made repairs on another section, opposite the ascent to the armory at the Angle. [20] After him Barukh the son of Zakkai worked diligently making repairs on another section, from the Angle to the door of the house of Elyashiv the *cohen hagadol*. [21] After him M'remot the son of Uriyah made repairs on another section, from the door of the house of Elyashiv to the end of the house of Elyashiv. [22] After him the *cohanim* from the plain made repairs. [23] After them Binyamin and Hashuv made repairs opposite their house. After them 'Azaryah the son of Ma'aseiyah, the son of 'Ananyah, made repairs next to his house. [24] After him Binui the son of Henadad repaired another section, from the house of 'Azaryah to the Angle and to the Corner. [25] Palal the son of Uzai made repairs opposite the Angle and the tower that projects out from the upper part of the royal palace near the Courtyard of the Guard.

After him P'dayah the son of Par'osh made repairs [26] (since the temple servants were living in the 'Ofel) as far as opposite the Water Gate to the east and the tower that projects out. [27] After him the men from T'koa repaired another section, opposite the great tower that projects out and on to the wall of the 'Ofel.

[28] Above the Horse Gate the *cohanim* made repairs, each one opposite his own house. [29] After them Tzadok the son of Immer made repairs opposite his house. After him Sh'ma'yah the son of Sh'khanyah, the keeper of the East Gate, made repairs. [30] After him Hananyah the son of Shelemyah and Hanun the sixth son of Tzalaf made repairs on another section. After him Meshulam the son of Berekhyah made repairs opposite his own room.

[31] After him Malkiyah, one of the goldsmiths, made repairs as far as the house of the temple servants and the merchants, opposite the Mustering Gate and on to the upper room at the corner. [32] Finally, between the upper room at the corner and the Sheep Gate the goldsmiths and merchants made repairs.

³³⁽⁴:¹⁾ But when Sanvalat heard that we were rebuilding the wall, he was furious. Greatly enraged, he ridiculed the Judeans; ³⁴⁽⁴:²⁾ before his kinsmen and the army of Shomron he said, "What are these pathetic Judeans doing? Are they going to rebuild anything they want? Are they going to sacrifice? Are they going to finish today? Are they going to recover useful stones from the piles of rubble, burned rubble at that?" ³⁵⁽⁴:³⁾ Toviyah the 'Amoni was with him, and he said, "Whatever they're building, why, if even a fox went up it, he'd knock their stone wall down!"

³⁶⁽⁴:⁴⁾ Our God, listen! We are being treated with contempt. Turn back their jeers on their own heads; give them over to be plundered in a land of exile. ³⁷⁽⁴:⁵⁾ Don't cover their guilt, don't let their sin be wiped out from before you; because they have insulted the builders to their face.

³⁸⁽⁴:⁶⁾ So we kept building the wall, which was soon joined together and completed to half its height all the way around; because the people worked with a will.

4 ¹⁽⁷⁾ But when Sanvalat, Toviyah, the Arabs, the 'Amonim and the Ashdodim heard that the repairs on the walls of Yerushalayim were going forward, and the breaks were being filled in, they became very angry. ²⁽⁸⁾ All of them together plotted to come and fight against Yerushalayim and thus throw us into confusion. ³⁽⁹⁾ However, we prayed to our God and, because of them, organized a watch against them day and night. ⁴⁽¹⁰⁾ Y'hudah was saying, "The strength of the people who carry loads away is starting to fail, and there is so much rubble that we can't build the wall." ⁵⁽¹¹⁾ Our enemies were saying, "They won't know or see anything, until we have already infiltrated them and begun killing them and stopping the work." ⁶⁽¹²⁾ And even the Judeans living near them came and must have said to us ten times, "From every place you must come back to us."

⁷⁽¹³⁾ So in the lower parts of the space behind the wall, I stationed men according to their families, with their swords, spears and bows. ⁸⁽¹⁴⁾ After inspecting them, I stood up and addressed the nobles, leaders and the rest of the people: "Don't be afraid of them! Remember *Adonai*, who is great and fearful; and fight for your brothers, sons, daughters, wives and homes." ⁹⁽¹⁵⁾ When our enemies heard that the plot was known to us, and God had foiled their plans, we all returned to the wall, everyone to his work. ¹⁰⁽¹⁶⁾ From then on, half of my men would do the work; and half of them held the spears, shields, bows and armor; while the leaders stood guard behind the entire house of Y'hudah, ¹¹⁽¹⁷⁾ as they continued building the wall. Those who carried loads held their loads with one hand and carried a weapon in the other. ¹²⁽¹⁸⁾ As for the construction-workers, each one had his sword sheathed at his side; that is how they built. The man to sound the alarm on the *shofar* stayed with me. ¹³⁽¹⁹⁾ I said to the nobles, the leaders and the rest of the people, "This is a great work, and it is spread out; we are separated on the wall, one far from another. ¹⁴⁽²⁰⁾ But wherever you are, when you hear the sound of the *shofar*, come to that place, to us. Our God will fight for us!"

¹⁵⁽²¹⁾ So we kept doing the work. Half of them held spears from daybreak until the stars appeared. ¹⁶⁽²²⁾ Also at that time I told the people, "Let everyone with a servant stay the night within Yerushalayim, so that at night they can be a guard for us, even as they work during the day." ¹⁷⁽²³⁾ I, my kinsmen, my servants and my bodyguards never took off our clothes, and everyone who went to get water took his weapon.

5 ¹ Then there arose a great outcry from the common people and their wives against their brothers the [wealthier] Judeans. ² Some of them said, "Counting our sons and daughters, there are a lot of us! Allow us to get grain for them, so that we can eat and stay alive." ³ There were also some who said, "We are mortgaging our fields, vineyards and homes in order to buy grain, because of the famine." ⁴ Yet others said, "We have borrowed money for the king's taxes against our fields and vineyards. ⁵ Now our flesh is no different from the flesh of our kinsmen, and our children are the same as their children; yet we are bringing our sons and daughters into bondage as slaves. Some of our daughters have gone into slavery already, and it's beyond our power to do anything about it, because other men have our fields and vineyards."

⁶ When I heard their outcry and the reasons for it, I became very angry. ⁷ I thought the matter over and then took issue with the nobles and rulers. I charged them, "You are lending against pledges, everyone to his brother"; and I summoned a great assembly to deal with them. ⁸ I said to them, "We, to the limit of our ability, have redeemed our brothers the Judeans who sold themselves to the pagans. Now you are selling your own brothers, and we will have to buy them back!" They stayed silent; they couldn't think of anything to say. ⁹ I also said, "What you are doing is not good! You should be living in fear of our God, so that our pagan enemies won't have grounds for deriding us. ¹⁰ Moreover, my brothers and my servants, I too have loaned them money and grain. Please, let's stop making it so burdensome to go into debt. ¹¹ Please! Today! Give them back their fields, vineyards, olive groves and homes; also the hundred pieces of silver and the grain, wine and olive oil you demand from them as interest."

¹² They answered, "We will give it back. We will require nothing from them. Yes, we will do it, just as you say." Then I called the *cohanim* and took an oath from them that they would do as they had promised. ¹³ Shaking out the fold in my garment, I said, "May God thus shake every man from his house and from his work who fails to live up to this promise — may he be shaken out like this and made empty." The whole assembly said, "*Amen!*" and praised *ADONAI*; and the people did as they had promised.

¹⁴ Besides that, from the time I was appointed their governor in the land of Y'hudah, from the twentieth year until the thirty-second year of Artach'shashta the king — that is, for twelve years — neither I nor my colleagues drew on the governor's living allowance. ¹⁵ The earlier governors, before me, had burdened the people, taxing them more than one-and-a-half pounds of silver *shekel*s for food and wine; and even their servants lorded it over the people. But I didn't, because I feared God. ¹⁶ Moreover, I put all my energy into working on this wall. We didn't buy any land, and all my servants were gathered there for the work.

¹⁷ There were 150 leaders and other Judeans who ate at my table, besides those who came to us from the surrounding nations. ¹⁸ Every day one ox, six choice sheep, and fowl were prepared for me, and every ten days a supply of all kinds of wine. Yet in spite of all this, I never claimed the governor's allowance, because the people were already bearing the heavy burden of their labor. ¹⁹ My God, remember favorably everything I have done for this people!

6 ¹ When it was reported to Sanvalat, Toviyah, Geshem the Arab and the rest of our enemies that I had rebuilt the wall and that not a single gap was left in it — although up to that time I hadn't yet set up the doors in the gateways — ² Sanvalat and Geshem sent me a message which said, "Come, let's meet together in one of the villages of the Ono Valley." But they were planning to do me harm; ³ so I sent them messengers with this message: "I'm too busy with important work to come down. Why should the work stop while I leave it to come down to you?" ⁴ They kept sending this sort of message to me — four times — and I answered them the same way.

⁵ The fifth time, with the same purpose, Sanvalat sent his servant to me with an open letter in his hand, ⁶ in which was written: "It is reported among the nations, and Geshem says it too, that you and the Judeans are planning a revolt, that this is why you are rebuilding the wall, and that you intend to be their king," and similar words; ⁷ "moreover, that you have also appointed prophets to proclaim about you in Yerushalayim, 'There is a king in Y'hudah!' A report along these lines is now going to be made to the king. Come now, therefore, and let's discuss this." ⁸ I sent him this answer; "Nothing like what you are saying is being done. You're making it all up in your head." ⁹ They were all just trying to scare us, thinking, "This will sap their strength and keep them from working." But now, [God,] increase my strength!

¹⁰ One day, when I went to the house of Sh'ma'yah the son of D'layah, the son of M'heitav'el, where he was confined, he said, "Let's meet together in the house of God, inside the temple, and let's shut the doors of the temple. For they are going to come and try to assassinate you; yes, they will come at night to kill you." ¹¹ I replied, "Should a man like me run away? Can a man like me go into the temple to save his life? I refuse to go in." ¹² Then I realized that God had not sent him, that he was making this prophecy against me, and that Toviyah and Sanvalat had bribed him to say it. ¹³ He had been hired to frighten me into following his suggestion and thus sin, so that they would have material for their unfavorable report about me and could taunt me with it. ¹⁴ My God, remember Toviyah and Sanvalat according to their deeds, also the prophet No'adyah and the other prophets trying to intimidate me.

¹⁵ So the wall was finished on the twenty-fifth day of the month Elul, in fifty-two days. ¹⁶ When all our enemies heard about it and the surrounding nations became afraid, our enemies' self-esteem fell severely; because they realized that this work had been accomplished by our God.

¹⁷ During this same period of time, the nobles of Y'hudah sent many letters to Toviyah, and Toviyah kept sending them replies. ¹⁸ For there were many in Y'hudah who had sworn allegiance to him, because he was the son-in-law of Sh'khanyah the son of Arach, and his son Y'hochanan had taken as his wife the daughter of Meshulam the son of Berekhyah. ¹⁹ They would even praise his good deeds in my presence, and they passed on my words to him. And Toviyah kept sending letters to intimidate me.

7 ¹ After the wall had been rebuilt, and I had set up its doors, and the gatekeepers, singers and *L'vi'im* had been appointed, ² I put my kinsman Hanani in charge of Yerushalayim, along with Hananyah the commander of the citadel. For he was a faithful man, and he feared God more than most. ³ I said to them, "The gates of Yerushalayim are not to be opened until the sun is hot; and while the gatekeepers are still on duty, have them shut the doors; and you, put up the bars. Appoint watchmen from among those living in Yerushalayim; assign each one his time to guard, and have each one serving near his own house."

⁴ The city was large and spacious, but there were few people in it, and the houses had not been rebuilt. ⁵ My God put it in my heart to assemble the nobles, the leaders and the people, so that they could be registered according to their genealogies.

I located the record of the genealogies of those who had come up at the beginning and found written in it:

⁶ "Here is a list of the people of the province who had been exiled, carried off to Bavel by N'vukhadnetzar king of Bavel, but who later returned from exile and went up to Yerushalayim and Y'hudah, each to his own city; ⁷ they went with Z'rubavel, Yeshua, Nechemyah, 'Azaryah, Ra'amyah, Nachmani, Mordekhai, Bilshan, Misperet, Bigvai, N'chum and Ba'anah.

"The number of men from the people of Isra'el:

8	descendants of Par'osh	2,172
9	descendants of Sh'fatyah	372
10	descendants of Arach	652
11	descendants of Pachat-Mo'av,	
	from the descendants of Yeshua and Yo'av	2,818
12	descendants of 'Eilam	1,254
13	descendants of Zatu	845
14	descendants of Zakkai	760
15	descendants of Binui	648
16	descendants of B'vai	628
17	descendants of 'Azgad	2,322
18	descendants of Adonikam	667
19	descendants of Bigvai	2,067
20	descendants of 'Adin	655
21	descendants of Ater, of Y'chizkiyah	98
22	descendants of Hashum	328
23	descendants of Betzai	324
24	descendants of Harif	112
25	descendants of Giv'on	95
26	people of Beit-Lechem and N'tofah	188
27	people of 'Anatot	128
28	people of Beit-'Azmavet	42
29	people of Kiryat-Ye'arim, K'firah and Be'erot	743
30	people of Ramah and Geva	621
31	people of Mikhmas	122
32	people of Beit-El and 'Ai	123
33	people from the other N'vo	52
34	people from the other 'Eilam	1,254
35	descendants of Harim	320
36	descendants of Yericho	345
37	descendants of Lod, Hadid and Ono	721
38	descendants of S'na'ah	3,930

³⁹ "The *cohanim*:

	descendants of Y'da'yah, of the house of Yeshua	973
40	descendants of Immer	1,052

| 41 | descendants of Pash'chur | 1,247 |
| 42 | descendants of Harim | 1,017 |

43 "The *L'vi'im*:

descendants of Yeshua, of Kadmi'el,
of the descendants of Hodvah 74

44 "The singers:

descendants of Asaf 148

45 "The gatekeepers:

descendants of Shalum,
descendants of Ater,
descendants of Talmon,
descendants of 'Akuv,
descendants of Hatita, and
descendants of Shovai 138

46 "The temple servants:

descendants of Tzicha,
descendants of Hasufa,
descendants of Taba'ot,

47   descendants of Keros,
descendants of Si'a,
descendants of Padon,

48   descendants of L'vanah,
descendants of Hagava,
descendants of Salmai,

49   descendants of Hanan,
descendants of Giddel,
descendants of Gachar,

50   descendants of Re'ayah,
descendants of Retzin,
descendants of N'koda,

51   descendants of Gazam,
descendants of 'Uza,
descendants of Paseach,

52   descendants of Besai,
descendants of Me'unim,
descendants of N'fish'sim,

53   descendants of Bakbuk,
descendants of Hakufa,
descendants of Harhur,

[54] descendants of Batzlit,
descendants of M'chida,
descendants of Harsha,
[55] descendants of Barkos,
descendants of Sisra,
descendants of Temach,
[56] descendants of N'tziach, and
descendants of Hatifa.

[57] "The descendants of Shlomo's servants:

descendants of Sotai,
descendants of Soferet,
descendants of P'rida,
[58] descendants of Ya'lah,
descendants of Darkon,
descendants of Giddel,
[59] descendants of Sh'fatyah,
descendants of Hatil,
descendants of Pokheret-Hatzvayim, and
descendants of Amon.

[60] "All the temple servants and the
descendants of Shlomo's servants numbered   392

[61] "The following went up from Tel-Melach, Tel-Harsha, K'ruv, Adon and Immer; but they could not state which fathers' clan they and their children belonged to, [so it was not clear] whether they were from Isra'el:

[62] descendants of D'layah,
descendants of Toviyah, and
descendants of N'koda   642

[63] and of the *cohanim*:

descendants of Havayah,
descendants of Hakotz, and
descendants of Barzillai, who took a wife from the
daughters of Barzillai the Gil'adi and was named after them.

[64] "These tried to locate their geneaolgical records, but they weren't found. Therefore they were considered defiled and were not allowed to serve as *cohanim*. [65] The *Tirshata* told them not to eat any of the especially holy food until a *cohen* appeared who could consult the *urim* and *tumim*.

[66] "The entire assembly numbered 42,360, [67] not including their male and female slaves, of whom there were 7,337. They also had 245 male and female singers. [68] Their horses numbered 736; their mules, 245; * [69] their camels, 435; and their donkeys, 6,720.

---

* Verse 68 is not included in some versions; it corresponds to 'Ezra 2:66.

^{70} "Some from among the heads of fathers' clans made contributions for the work. The *Tirshata* contributed to the treasury a thousand gold *darkmonim* [twenty-one pounds], fifty basins and 530 tunics for the *cohanim*. ^{71} Some of the heads of fathers' clans gave into the treasury for the work 20,000 gold *darkmonim* [420 pounds] and 2,200 silver *manim* [one-and-a-third tons]. ^{72} The rest of the people gave 20,000 gold *darkmonim*, 2,000 silver *manim* [about one-and-a-quarter tons] and sixty-seven tunics for the *cohanim*.

^{73} "So the *cohanim*, the *L'vi'im*, the gatekeepers, the singers, some of the people, the temple servants and all Isra'el lived in their towns."

$^{(8:1)}$ When the seventh month arrived, after the people of Isra'el had resettled in their towns,

8 ^{1} all the people gathered with one accord in the open space in front of the Water Gate and asked 'Ezra the *Torah*-teacher to bring the scroll of the *Torah* of Moshe, which ADONAI had commanded Isra'el. ^{2} 'Ezra the *cohen* brought the *Torah* before the assembly, which consisted of men, women and all children old enough to understand. It was the first day of the seventh month. ^{3} Facing the open space in front of the Water Gate, he read from it to the men, the women and the children who could understand from early morning until noon; and all the people listened attentively to the scroll of the *Torah*. ^{4} 'Ezra the *Torah*-teacher stood on a wood platform which they had made for the purpose; beside him on his right stood Mattityah, Shema, 'Anayah, Uriyah, Hilkiyah and Ma'aseiyah; while on his left were P'dayah, Misha'el, Malkiyah, Hashum, Hashbadanah, Z'kharyah and Meshulam. ^{5} 'Ezra opened the scroll where all the people could see him, because he was higher than all the people; when he opened it, all the people rose to their feet. ^{6} 'Ezra blessed ADONAI, the great God; and all the people answered, "*Amen! Amen!*" as they lifted up their hands, bowed their heads and fell prostrate before ADONAI with their faces to the ground. ^{7} The *L'vi'im* Yeshua, Bani, Sherevyah, Yamin, 'Akuv, Shabtai, Hodiyah, Ma'aseiyah, K'lita, 'Azaryah, Yozavad, Hanan and P'layah explained the *Torah* to the people, while the people remained in their places. ^{8} They read clearly from the scroll, in the *Torah* of God, translated it, and enabled them to understand the sense of what was being read.

^{9} Nechemyah the *Tirshata*, 'Ezra the *cohen* and *Torah*-teacher and the *L'vi'im* who taught the people said to all the people, "Today is consecrated to ADONAI your God; don't be mournful, don't weep." For all the people had been weeping when they heard the words of the *Torah*. ^{10} Then he said to them, "Go, eat rich food, drink sweet drinks, and send portions to those who can't provide for themselves; for today is consecrated to our Lord. Don't be sad, because the joy of ADONAI is your strength." ^{11} In this way the *L'vi'im* quieted the people, as they said, "Be quiet, for today is holy; don't be sad." ^{12} Then the people went off to eat, drink, send portions and celebrate; because they had understood the words that had been proclaimed to them.

^{13} On the second day, the heads of fathers' clans of all the people assembled with the *cohanim* and *L'vi'im* before 'Ezra the *Torah*-teacher to study the words of the *Torah*. ^{14} They found written in the *Torah* that ADONAI had ordered through Moshe that the people of Isra'el were to live in *sukkot* during the feast of the seventh month; ^{15} and that they were to announce and pass the word in all their cities and in Yerushalayim, "Go out to the mountains, and collect branches of olives, wild olives, myrtles, palms, and other leafy trees to make *sukkot*, as prescribed." ^{16} So the people went out, brought them and made *sukkot* for themselves, each one on the roof of his house, also in their courtyards, in the courtyards of the house of God, in the open space by the Water Gate and in the open space by the Efrayim Gate. ¹⁷ The entire community of those who had returned from the exile made *sukkot* and lived in the *sukkot*, for the people of Isra'el had not done this since the days of Yeshua the son of Nun. So there was very great joy. ¹⁸ Also they read every day, from the first day until the last day, in the scroll of the *Torah* of God. They kept the feast for seven days; then on the eighth day there was a solemn assembly, according to the rule.

9 ¹ On the twenty-fourth day of this month the people of Isra'el, wearing sackcloth and with dirt on them, assembled for a fast. ² Those descended from Isra'el separated themselves from all foreigners; then they stood up and confessed their own sins and the iniquities of their ancestors. ³ Standing where they were, they read in the scroll of the *Torah* of ADONAI their God for one-quarter of the day. For another quarter they confessed and prostrated themselves before ADONAI their God. ⁴ On the platform of the *L'vi'im* stood Yeshua, Bani, Kadmi'el, Sh'vanyah, Buni, Sherevyah, Bani and K'nani; they cried out loudly to ADONAI their God. ⁵ Then the *L'vi'im* Yeshua, Kadmi'el, Bani, Hashavn'yah, Sherevyah, Hodiyah, Sh'vanyah and P'tachyah said, "Stand up, and bless ADONAI your God from everlasting to everlasting; let them say:

> "'Blessed be your glorious name,
> exalted above all blessing and praise!

6
> "'You are ADONAI, you alone.
> You made heaven,
> the heaven of heavens, with all their array,
> the earth and all the things that are in it,
> the seas and all that is in them;
> and you preserve them all.
> The army of heaven worships you.

7
> "'You are ADONAI, the God who chose Avram,
> brought him out of Ur-Kasdim
> and gave him the name of Avraham.
8
> Finding that he was faithful to you,
> you made a covenant with him
> to give the land of the Kena'ani,
> the Hitti, Emori and P'rizi,
> the Y'vusi and the Girgashi,
> to give it to his descendants;
> and you have done what you promised,
> because you are just.

9
> "'You saw the distress of our ancestors in Egypt
> and heard their cry by the Sea of Suf.
10
> You performed signs and wonders against Pharaoh,
> against all his servants and the people of the land;

for you knew how arrogantly they treated them;
and you won yourself a name which is yours to this day.

11 You divided the sea ahead of them,
so that they could pass through the sea on dry land;
then you hurled their pursuers into the depths,
like a stone into turbulent waters.

12 "'In a column of cloud you led them by day,
and by night in a column of fire,
so that they would have light ahead of them
on the way that they were to go.

13 "'You descended on Mount Sinai
and spoke with them from heaven.
You gave them right rulings and true teachings,
good laws and *mitzvot*.

14 You revealed to them your holy *Shabbat*
and gave them *mitzvot*, laws and the *Torah*
through Moshe your servant.

15 "'For their hunger you gave them bread from heaven;
for their thirst you brought forth for them water from the rock.
You ordered them to enter and possess the land
you had sworn with your hand to give them.

16 "'But they and our ancestors were arrogant;
they stiffened their necks and ignored your *mitzvot*;

17 they refused to listen and paid no attention
to the wonders you had done among them.
No, they stiffened their necks, and in their rebellion
appointed a leader to return them to their slavery.
But because you are a God of forgiveness,
merciful, full of compassion,
slow to grow angry and full of grace,
you did not abandon them.

18 Even when they cast themselves a metal calf,
saying of it, "This is your god
that brought you up from Egypt,"
and committing other gross provocations;

19 still, you, in your great compassion,
did not abandon them in the desert.
The column of cloud did not leave them by day;
it kept leading them along the way.
By night the column of fire
kept showing them light and the path to take.

20 You also gave your good Spirit to teach them,
did not withhold *man* from their mouths
and provided them water to quench their thirst.

21 Yes, forty years you sustained them in the desert;
they lacked nothing —
their clothes did not wear out;
their feet did not swell up.

22 "'You gave them kingdoms and peoples;
you even gave them extra land,
so that they took possession of the land of Sichon,
also the land of the king of Heshbon
and the land of 'Og king of Bashan.
23 You made their children as numerous
as the countless stars in the sky.

"'Then you brought them into the land
about which you had said to their fathers
that they should go in and take possession of it.
24 So the children went in and possessed the land,
as you subdued ahead of them
the Kena'ani living in the land,
and handed them over to them,
along with their kings and the peoples of the land,
for them to do with as they wished.
25 They took fortified cities and fertile land,
possessed houses full of all kinds of good things,
dug-out cisterns, vineyards, olive groves,
fruit trees in plenty;
so they ate their fill and grew robust,
luxuriating in your great goodness.

26 "'Yet they disobeyed and rebelled against you,
throwing your *Torah* behind their backs.
They killed your prophets for warning them
that they should return to you
and committed other gross provocations.
27 So you handed them over to the power
of their adversaries, who oppressed them.
Yet in the time of their trouble,
when they cried out to you,
you heard from heaven, and in keeping
with your great compassion,
you gave them saviors to save them
from the power of their adversaries.
28 But as soon as they had gotten some relief,
they went back to do evil before you.
So you left them in the power of their enemies,
who came down hard on them.
Yet when they returned and cried out to you,

you heard from heaven many times
and saved them, according to your compassion.

29 You warned them, in order to bring them back
to your *Torah*; yet they were arrogant.
They paid no attention to your *mitzvot*,
but sinned against your rulings,
which, if a person does them,
he will have life through them.
However, they stubbornly turned their shoulders,
stiffened their necks and refused to hear.

30 Many years you extended them mercy
and warned them by your Spirit through your prophets;
yet they would not listen.
Therefore you handed them over
to the peoples of the lands.

31 Even so, in your great compassion,
you didn't completely destroy them;
nor did you abandon them,
for you are a compassionate and merciful God.

32 "'Now therefore, our God,
great, mighty, fearsome God,
who keeps both covenant and grace:
let not all this suffering seem little to you
that has come on us, our kings, our leaders,
our *cohanim*, our prophets, our ancestors,
and on all your people,
from the times of the kings of Ashur
until this very day.

33 There is no question that you are just
in all that has come upon us;
for you have treated us fairly.
It is we who have acted wickedly.

34 Our kings, our leaders, our *cohanim* and ancestors
did not keep your *Torah*,
pay attention to your *mitzvot*
or heed the warnings you gave them.

35 Even when they ruled their own kingdom,
even when you prospered them greatly,
in the great, rich land you gave them,
they did not serve you;
nor did they turn from their wicked deeds.

36 "'So here we are today, slaves.
Yes, in the land you gave our ancestors,
so that they could eat what it produces
and enjoy its good —

here we are in it, slaves!

37   Its rich yield now goes to the kings
you have set over us because of our sins;
they have power over our bodies,
they can do what they please to our livestock,
and we are in great distress!

10 ¹⁽⁹:³⁸⁾ "'In view of all this, we are making a binding covenant, putting it in writing and having it sealed by our leaders, our *L'vi'im* and our *cohanim*.'"

²⁽¹⁾ On the sealed document were the names of: Nechemyah the *Tirshata* the son of Hakhalyah, Tzedekyah, ³⁽²⁾ S'rayah, 'Azaryah, Yirmeyah, ⁴⁽³⁾ Pash'chur, Amaryah, Malkiyah, ⁵⁽⁴⁾ Hatush, Sh'vanyah, Malukh, ⁶⁽⁵⁾ Harim, M'remot, 'Ovadyah, ⁷⁽⁶⁾ Dani'el, Ginton, Barukh, ⁸⁽⁷⁾ Meshulam, Aviyah, Miyamin, ⁹⁽⁸⁾ Ma'azyah, Bilgai and Sh'ma'yah. These were the *cohanim*.

¹⁰⁽⁹⁾ The *L'vi'im* were: Yeshua the son of Azanyah, Binui a descendant of Henadad, Kadmi'el, ¹¹⁽¹⁰⁾ and their kinsmen Sh'vanyah, Hodiyah, K'lita, P'layah, Hanan, ¹²⁽¹¹⁾ Mikha, Rechov, Hashavyah, ¹³⁽¹²⁾ Zakur, Sherevyah, Sh'vanyah, ¹⁴⁽¹³⁾ Hodiyah, Bani and B'ninu.

¹⁵⁽¹⁴⁾ The leaders of the people: Par'osh, Pachat-Mo'av, 'Eilam, Zatu, Bani, ¹⁶⁽¹⁵⁾ Buni, 'Azgad, B'vai, ¹⁷⁽¹⁶⁾ Adoniyah, Bigvai, 'Adin, ¹⁸⁽¹⁷⁾ Ater, Hizkiyah, 'Azur, ¹⁹⁽¹⁸⁾ Hodiyah, Hashum, Betzai, ²⁰⁽¹⁹⁾ Harif, 'Anatot, Neivai, ²¹⁽²⁰⁾ Magpi'ash, Meshulam, Hezir, ²²⁽²¹⁾ Mesheizav'el, Tzadok, Yadua, ²³⁽²²⁾ P'latyah, Hanan, 'Anayah, ²⁴⁽²³⁾ Hoshea, Hananyah, Hashuv, ²⁵⁽²⁴⁾ HaLochesh, Pilcha, Shovek, ²⁶⁽²⁵⁾ Rechum, Hashavnah, Ma'aseiyah, ²⁷⁽²⁶⁾ Achiyah, Hanan, 'Anan, ²⁸⁽²⁷⁾ Malukh, Harim and Ba'anah.

²⁹⁽²⁸⁾ The rest of the people, the *cohanim*, the *L'vi'im*, the gatekeepers, the singers, the temple servants and all who had separated themselves from the peoples of the lands to the *Torah* of God, along with their wives, sons and daughters, everyone capable of knowing and understanding, ³⁰⁽²⁹⁾ joined their kinsmen and their leaders in swearing an oath, accompanied by a curse [in case of noncompliance], as follows:

"We will live by God's *Torah*, given by Moshe the servant of God, and will perform and obey all the *mitzvot*, rulings and laws of A*donai* our Lord.

³¹⁽³⁰⁾ "We will not give our daughters as wives to the peoples of the land or take their daughters as wives for our sons.

³²⁽³¹⁾ "If the peoples of the lands bring merchandise or food to sell on *Shabbat*, we will not buy from them on *Shabbat* or on a holy day.

"We will forego [planting and harvesting our fields] during the seventh year and collecting debts then.

³³⁽³²⁾ "We will impose on ourselves a yearly tax of one-third of a *shekel* [one-seventh of an ounce of silver] for the service of the house of our God, ³⁴⁽³³⁾ for the showbread, for the regular grain offering, for the regular burnt offering, for [the offerings] on *Shabbat*, on *Rosh-Hodesh*,

at the designated times and at other holy times, for the sin offerings to make atonement for Isra'el, and for all the work connected with the house of our God.

³⁵⁽³⁴⁾ "We, the *cohanim*, the *L'vi'im* and the people, will cast lots in connection with the wood offering, so that it will be brought to the house of our God according to our fathers' clans, at specified times, year by year, and then be burned on the altar of Aᴅᴏɴᴀɪ our God, as prescribed in the *Torah*.

³⁶⁽³⁵⁾ "Every year we will bring the firstfruits of our land and the firstfruits of all fruit from every kind of tree to the house of Aᴅᴏɴᴀɪ. ³⁷⁽³⁶⁾ "We will also bring the firstborn of our sons and of our livestock, as prescribed in the *Torah*, and the firstborn of our herds and flocks, to the house of our God, to the *cohanim* ministering in the house of our God.

³⁸⁽³⁷⁾ "We will bring the first of our dough, our contributions, the fruit of every kind of tree, wine and olive oil to the *cohanim* in the storerooms of the house of our God, along with the tenths from our land for the *L'vi'im*; since they, the *L'vi'im*, take the tenths in all the cities where we farm. ³⁹⁽³⁸⁾ The *cohen* the descendant of Aharon is to be with the *L'vi'im* when the *L'vi'im* take tenths. The *L'vi'im* will bring the tenth of the tenth to the house of our God, to the storerooms for supplies. ⁴⁰⁽³⁹⁾ For the people of Isra'el and the descendants of Levi are to bring the contribution of grain, wine and olive oil to the rooms where the equipment for the sanctuary, the ministering *cohanim*, the gatekeepers and the singers are. We will not abandon the house of our God."

11 ¹ The leaders of the people took up residence in Yerushalayim; while the rest of the people cast lots to bring one-tenth of them to live in Yerushalayim the holy city, with the other nine-tenths in the other cities. ² The people blessed all those who volunteered to live in Yerushalayim.

³ In the cities of Y'hudah, everyone lived on his own property — the people of Isra'el, the *cohanim*, the *L'vi'im*, the temple servants and the descendants of Shlomo's servants. But the leaders of the province lived in Yerushalayim. ⁴ Some of those living in Yerushalayim were from people of Y'hudah, and others were from people of Binyamin. Those from the people of Y'hudah were: 'Atayah the son of 'Uziyah, the son of Z'kharyah, the son of Amaryah, the son of Sh'fatyah, the son of Mahalal'el, from the descendants of Peretz; ⁵ and Ma'aseiyah the son of Barukh, the son of Kol-Hozeh, the son of Hazayah, the son of 'Adayah, the son of Yoyariv, the son of Z'kharyah, who belonged to the family of Shelah. ⁶ The total number of descendants of Peretz living in Yerushalayim was 468 courageous men.

⁷ These are the people of Binyamin: Salu the son of Meshulam, the son of Yo'ed, the son of P'dayah, the son of Kolayah, the son of Ma'aseiyah, the son of Iti'el, the son of Yesha'yah. ⁸ After him: Gabai, Salai; 928 in all. ⁹ Yo'el the son of Zikhri was their overseer, and Y'hudah the son of Hasnu'ah was second in charge of the city.

¹⁰ From the *cohanim*: Y'da'yah the son of Yoyariv, Yakhin, ¹¹ S'rayah the son of Hilkiyah, the son of Meshulam, the son of Tzadok, the son of M'rayot, the son of

Achituv, the supervisor of the house of God, ¹² and their kinsmen who did the work for the house; in all 822; and 'Adayah the son of Yerocham, the son of P'lalyah, the son of Amtzi, the son of Z'kharyah, the son of Pash'chur, the son of Malkiyah; ¹³ with his kinsmen, heads of fathers' clans, 242; and 'Amash'sai the son of 'Azar'el, the son of Achzai, the son of Meshillemot, the son of Immer; ¹⁴ with his kinsmen, courageous men, 128; their overseer was Zavdi'el the son of HaG'dolim.

¹⁵ From the *L'vi'im*: Sh'ma'yah the son of Hashuv, the son of 'Azrikam, the son of Hashavyah, the son of Buni, ¹⁶ and Shabtai and Yozavad, from the leaders of the *L'vi'im*, who were in charge of external affairs for the house of God; ¹⁷ and Matanyah the son of Mikha, the son of Zavdi, the son of Asaf, the leader who began the thanksgiving prayer; and Bakbukyah, the second among his kinsmen; and 'Avda the son of Shamua, the son of Galal, the son of Y'dutun. ¹⁸ All the *L'vi'im* in the holy city numbered 284.

¹⁹ The gatekeepers: 'Akuv, Talmon and their kinsmen, who kept watch at the gates, numbered 172.

²⁰ The rest of Isra'el, [the rest of] the *cohanim* and [the rest of] the *L'vi'im* were in all the cities of Y'hudah, each on his own property.

²¹ The temple servants lived in the 'Ofel; Tzicha and Gishpa were in charge of the temple servants.

²² The overseer of the *L'vi'im* in Yerushalayim was 'Uzi the son of Bani, the son of Hashavyah, the son of Matanyah, the son of Mikha, from the descendants of Asaf the singers; [he was] in charge of the work of the house of God. ²³ For they were subject to the king's orders; and there was a fixed schedule for the singers, assigning them their daily duties. ²⁴ P'tachyah the son of Mesheizav'el, from the descendants of Zerach the son of Y'hudah, was the king's deputy in all affairs concerning the people.

²⁵ As for the villages and their surrounding fields: some of the people of Y'hudah lived in Kiryat-Arba and its villages, in Divon and its villages, in Y'kabze'el and its villages, ²⁶ in Yeshua, in Moladah, in Beit-Pelet, ²⁷ in Hatzar-Shu'al and its villages, in Be'er-Sheva and its villages, ²⁸ in Ziklag, in M'khonah and its villages, ²⁹ in 'Ein-Rimmon, in Tzor'ah, in Yarmut, ³⁰ Zanoach, Adulam and their villages, in Lakhish and its surrounding fields, and in 'Azekah and its villages. Thus they occupied the territory from Be'er-Sheva as far as the Hinnom Valley.

³¹ The people of Binyamin lived from Geva onward, in Mikhmas and 'Ayah, in Beit-El and its villages, ³² and in 'Anatot, Nov, 'Ananyah, ³³ Hatzor, Ramah, Gittayim, ³⁴ Hadid, Tzvo'im, N'valat, ³⁵ Lud, Ono and Gei-Harashim.

³⁶ Of the *L'vi'im*, some divisions from Y'hudah settled in Binyamin.

12 ¹ These are the *cohanim* and *L'vi'im* who went up with Z'rubavel the son of Sh'alti'el, and Yeshua: S'rayah, Yirmeyah, 'Ezra, ² Amaryah, Malukh, Hatush, ³ Sh'khanyah, Rechum, M'remot, ⁴ 'Iddo, Gintoi, Achiyah, ⁵ Miyamin, Ma'adiyah, Bilgah, ⁶ Sh'ma'yah, Yoyariv, Y'da'yah, ⁷ Salu, 'Amok, Hilkiyah and Y'da'yah. These were the leaders of the *cohanim* and their kinsmen during the time of Yeshua.

⁸ The *L'vi'im*: Yeshua, Binui, Kadmi'el, Sherevyah, Y'hudah and Mattanyah, who was in charge of the songs of thanksgiving, he and his kinsmen, ⁹ with Bakbukyah and 'Uni, their kinsmen, singing antiphonally with them in the service.

¹⁰ Yeshua was the father of Yoyakim, Yoyakim was the father of Elyashiv, Elyashiv was the father of Yoyada, ¹¹ Yoyada was the father of Yonatan, and Yonatan was the father of Yadua.

[12] In the days of Yoyakim these were the *cohanim* who were heads of fathers' clans: of S'rayah, M'rayah; of Yirmeyah, Hananyah; [13] of 'Ezra, Meshulam; of Amaryah, Y'hochanan; [14] of M'likhu, Yonatan; of Sh'vanyah, Yosef; [15] of Harim, 'Adna; of M'rayot, Helkai; [16] of 'Iddo, Z'kharyah; of Ginton, Meshulam; [17] of Achiyah, Zikhri; of Minyamin, of Mo'adyah, Piltai; [18] of Bilgai, Shamua; of Sh'ma'yah, Y'honatan; [19] of Yoyariv, Matnai; of Y'da'yah, 'Uzi; [20] of Salai, Kallai; of 'Amok, 'Ever; [21] of Hilkiyah, Hashavyah; and of Y'da'yah, N'tan'el.

[22] As for the *L'vi'im*, the heads of fathers' clans in the days of Elyashiv, Yoyada, Yochanan and Yadua were recorded; also the *cohanim*, up to the reign of Daryavesh the Persian. [23] The descendants of Levi who were heads of fathers' clans were recorded in the annals until the days of Yochanan the [grand]son of Elyashiv. [24] The chiefs of the *L'vi'im* were Hashavyah, Sherevyah and Yeshua the son of Kadmi'el, with their kinsmen in an antiphonal choir, to praise and give thanks, in accordance with the order of David the man of God, choir opposite choir.

[25] Mattanyah, Bakbukyah, 'Ovadyah, Meshulam, Talmon and 'Akuv were the gatekeepers who guarded the supplies kept at the gates. [26] This was in the days of Yoyakim the son of Yeshua, the son of Yotzadak, and in the days of Nechemyah the governor and of 'Ezra the *cohen* and *Torah*-teacher.

[27] At the dedication of the wall of Yerushalayim, they sought out the *L'vi'im* from wherever they had settled to bring them to Yerushalayim and celebrate the dedication with hymns of thanksgiving and with songs accompanied by cymbals, lutes and lyres. [28] The trained singers assembled together from the area around Yerushalayim, the villages of the N'tofati, [29] Beit-Gilgal and the region of Geva and 'Azmavet; for the singers had built villages for themselves all around Yerushalayim.

[30] The *cohanim* and *L'vi'im* first purified themselves; then they purified the people, the gates and the wall; [31] and after that I brought the leaders of Y'hudah up onto the wall and appointed two large choirs to give thanks and to walk in procession. One went to the right on the wall toward the Dung Gate. [32] After them went Hosha'yah and half of the leaders of Y'hudah, [33] together with 'Azaryah, 'Ezra, Meshulam, [34] Y'hudah, Binyamin, Sh'ma'yah and Yirmeyah. [35] With them were some of the sons of the *cohanim* carrying trumpets, namely, Z'kharyah the son of Yonatan the son of Sh'ma'yah, the son of Mattanyah, the son of Mikhayah, the son of Zakur, the son of Asaf, [36] and his kinsmen, Sh'ma'yah, 'Azar'el, Milalai, Gilalai, Ma'ai, N'tan'el, Y'hudah and Hanani, who had the musical instruments of David the man of God. 'Ezra the *Torah*-teacher led them. [37] At the Fountain Gate they went straight ahead up the steps to the City of David, where the wall goes up, passed above the house of David, and went on to the Water Gate on the east.

[38] The other thanksgiving choir, consisting of half the people, walked on the wall to meet them, with myself following. They went above the Tower of the Furnaces to the Broad Wall, [39] above the Efrayim Gate, by the gate to the Old City, to the Fish Gate, the Tower of Hanan'el and the Tower of the Hundred, as far as the Sheep Gate, and halted at the Prison Gate.

[40] Thus stood the two choirs of those giving thanks in the house of God, with myself and half of the leaders with me. [41] The *cohanim* there included Elyakim, Ma'aseiyah, Minyamin, Mikhayah, Elyo'einai, Z'kharyah and Hananyah carrying trumpets; [42] also Ma'aseiyah, Sh'ma'yah, El'azar, 'Uzi, Y'hochanan, Malkiyah, 'Eilam and 'Ezer. The singers sang loudly, directed by Yizrachyah. [43] With joy they

offered great sacrifices that day, for God had made them celebrate with great joy. The women and children too rejoiced, so that the celebrating in Yerushalayim could be heard far off. ⁴⁴ At that time, men were appointed to be in charge of the storerooms for supplies, contributions, firstfruits and tenths, and to gather into them, from the fields belonging to the cities, the portions prescribed by the *Torah* for the *cohanim* and *L'vi'im*. For Y'hudah rejoiced over the *cohanim* and *L'vi'im* who took their position ⁴⁵ carrying out the duties of their God and the duties of purification, as also did the singers and gatekeepers, in accordance with the order of David and of Shlomo his son. ⁴⁶ For back in the days of David and Asaf, there had been leaders for those singing the songs of praise and thanksgiving to God. ⁴⁷ So in the days of Z'rubavel and in the days of Nechemyah, all Isra'el gave portions to the singers and gatekeepers as required daily. They set aside a portion for the *L'vi'im*, who, in turn set aside a portion for the descendants of Aharon.

13 ¹ It was also at that time, when they were reading in the scroll of Moshe, that it was found written that no 'Amoni or Mo'avi may ever enter the assembly of God, ² because they did not supply the people of Isra'el with food and water, but hired Bil'am against them to put a curse on them — although our God turned the curse into a blessing. ³ On hearing the *Torah*, they separated from Isra'el everyone of mixed ancestry.

⁴ Also, prior to this, Elyashiv the *cohen*, who had been put in charge of the storage rooms in the house of our God, and who was related by marriage to Toviyah, ⁵ had prepared for him a large room where formerly they had stored the grain offerings, frankincense, equipment and the tenths of grain, wine and olive oil ordered to be given to the *L'vi'im*, singers and gatekeepers, and the contributions for the *cohanim*. ⁶ During all this time I wasn't present in Yerushalayim; because in the thirty-second year of Artach'shashta king of Bavel, I went to see the king; then, after some time had passed, I asked permission from the king ⁷ and returned to Yerushalayim, where I found out about the terrible thing Elyashiv had done for Toviyah by preparing a room for him in the courtyards of the house of our God. ⁸ I was so furious that I threw all Toviyah's household goods out of the room. ⁹ Then, at my order, they cleansed the rooms; and I brought back the equipment of the house of God, the grain offerings and frankincense.

¹⁰ I also learned that the portions for the *L'vi'im* had not been given to them, so that the *L'vi'im* and singers who were supposed to be doing the work had deserted, each one to his own farm. ¹¹ I disputed with the leaders, demanding, "Why is the house of God abandoned?" I gathered the *L'vi'im* together and restored them to their stations; ¹² and then all Y'hudah brought the tenth of grain, wine and olive oil to the storerooms. ¹³ To supervise the storerooms I appointed Shelemyah the *cohen*, Tzadok the *Torah*-teacher and, from the *L'vi'im*, P'dayah; assisting them was Hanan the son of Zakur, the son of Mattanyah; for these were considered reliable. Their duty was to make the distribution to their kinsmen. ¹⁴ My God, remember me for this; don't wipe out my good deeds which I have done for the house of my God and for his service!

¹⁵ During this time I saw in Y'hudah some people who were treading winepresses on *Shabbat*, also bringing in heaps of grain and loading donkeys with it, likewise wine, grapes, figs and all kinds of loads; and they were bringing them into

Yerushalayim on the day of *Shabbat*. On the day when they were planning to sell the food, I warned them not to. ¹⁶ There were also living there people from Tzor who brought in fish and all kinds of goods, and sold them on *Shabbat* to the people in Y'hudah and even in Yerushalayim. ¹⁷ I disputed with the nobles of Y'hudah, demanding of them, "What is this terrible thing you are doing, profaning the day of *Shabbat*? ¹⁸ Didn't your ancestors do this, and didn't our God bring all this disaster on us and on this city? Yet you are bringing still more fury against Isra'el by profaning *Shabbat*!" ¹⁹ So when the gates of Yerushalayim began to grow dark before *Shabbat*, I ordered that the doors be shut; and I ordered that they not be reopened until after *Shabbat*. I put some of my servants in charge of the gates, to see to it that no loads be brought in on *Shabbat*. ²⁰ The merchants and sellers of all kinds of goods spent the night outside Yerushalayim once or twice, ²¹ until I warned them, "Why are you spending the night by the wall? Do it again, and I'll use force against you!" From then on they stopped coming on *Shabbat*. ²² Then I ordered the *L'vi'im* to purify themselves and come and guard the gates, in order to keep the day of *Shabbat* holy. My God, remember this too for me, and have mercy on me in keeping with the greatness of your grace!

²³ Also during this time I saw the Judeans who had married women from Ashdod, 'Amon and Mo'av; ²⁴ and their children, who spoke half in the language of Ashdod and couldn't speak in the language the Judeans spoke but only in the language of each people. ²⁵ I disputed with them and cursed them, and I beat some of them up and pulled out their hair. Then I made them swear by God, "You will not give your daughters as wives for their sons or take their daughters as wives for your sons or for yourselves. ²⁶ Wasn't it by doing these things that Shlomo king of Isra'el sinned? There was no king like him among many nations, and his God loved him, and God made him king over all Isra'el; nevertheless the foreign women caused even him to sin. ²⁷ Are we to give in to you and let you continue in this very great evil, breaking faith with our God by marrying foreign women?"

²⁸ One of the sons of Yoyada the son of Elyashiv, the *cohen hagadol*, had become son-in-law to Sanvalat the Horoni; so I drove him out of my presence. ²⁹ My God, remember them; because they have defiled the office of *cohen* and the covenant of the *cohanim* and *L'vi'im*.

³⁰ Thus I cleansed them of everything foreign, and I had the *cohanim* and *L'vi'im* resume their duties, each one in his appointed task. ³¹ I also made provision for the delivery of wood at stated times, and for the firstfruits. My God, remember me favorably.

Divrei-HaYamim Alef
1 CHRONICLES

1 ¹ Adam, Shet, Enosh, ² Keinan, Mahalal'el, Yered, ³ Hanokh, Metushelach, Lemekh, ⁴ Noach; Shem, Ham and Yefet.

⁵ The sons of Yefet: Gomer, Magog, Madai, Yavan, Tuval, Meshekh and Tiras. ⁶ The sons of Gomer: Ashkenaz, Difat and Togarmah. ⁷ The sons of Yavan: Elishah, Tarshishah, Kittim and Rodanim.

⁸ The sons of Ham: Kush, Mitzrayim, Put and Kena'an. ⁹ The sons of Kush: S'va, Havilah, Savta, Ra'ma and Savt'kha. The sons of Ra'ma: Sh'va and D'dan. ¹⁰ Kush fathered Nimrod, who was the first powerful ruler on earth. ¹¹ Mitzrayim fathered Ludim, 'Anamim, L'havim, Naftuchim, ¹² Patrusim, Kasluchim (from whom came the P'lishtim) and Kaftorim. ¹³ Kena'an was the father of Tzidon his firstborn, and also of Het, ¹⁴ the Y'vusi, the Emori, the Girgashi, ¹⁵ the Hivi, the 'Arki, the Sini, ¹⁶ the Arvadi, the Tz'mari and the Hamati.

¹⁷ The sons of Shem: 'Elam, Ashur, Arpakhshad, Lud, Aram, 'Utz, Hul, Geter and Meshekh. ¹⁸ Arpakhshad fathered Shelach, Shelach fathered 'Ever, ¹⁹ and to 'Ever were born two sons: the name of one was Peleg [division], because it was during his lifetime that the earth was divided; and his brother's name was Yoktan. ²⁰ Yoktan fathered Almodad, Shelef, Hatzar-Mavet, Yerach, ²¹ Hadoram, Uzal, Diklah, ²² 'Eival, Avima'el, Sh'va, ²³ Ofir, Havilah and Yovav; these were all sons of Yoktan.

²⁴ Shem, Arpakhshad, Shelach, ²⁵ 'Ever, Peleg, Re'u, ²⁶ S'rug, Nachor, Terach, ²⁷ Avram (also called Avraham).

²⁸ The sons of Avraham: Yitz'chak and Yishma'el. ²⁹ Here are their descendants: Yishma'el's firstborn N'vayot; then Kedar, Adbe'el, Mivsam, ³⁰ Mishma, Dumah, Masa, Hadad, Teima, ³¹ Y'tur, Nafish and Kedem. These are the sons of Yishma'el.

³² The sons of K'turah Avraham's concubine: she bore Zimran, Yokshan, Medan, Midyan, Yishbak and Shuach. The sons of Yokshan: Sh'va and D'dan. ³³ The sons of Midyan: 'Eifah, 'Efer, Hanokh, Avida and Elda'ah. These were all descendants of K'turah.

³⁴ Avraham fathered Yitz'chak. The sons of Yitz'chak: 'Esav and Isra'el. ³⁵ The sons of 'Esav: Elifaz, Re'u'el, Ye'ush, Ya'lam and Korach. ³⁶ The sons of Elifaz: Teman, Omar, Tzefi, Ga'tam, K'naz, Timna and 'Amalek. ³⁷ The sons of Re'u'el: Nachat, Zerach, Shamah and Mizah.

³⁸ The sons of Se'ir: Lotan, Shoval, Tziv'on, 'Anah, Dishon, Etzer and Dishan. ³⁹ The sons of Lotan: Hori and Homam; the sister of Lotan was Timna. ⁴⁰ The sons of Shoval: 'Alyan, Manachat, 'Eival, Sh'fi and Onam. The sons of Tziv'on: Ayah and 'Anah. ⁴¹ The son of 'Anah: Dishon. The sons of Dishon: Hamran,

Eshban, Yitran and K'ran. ⁴² The sons of Etzer: Bilhan, Za'avan and Ya'akan. The sons of Dishan: 'Utz and Aran.

⁴³ Following are the kings who ruled in the land of Edom before any king ruled over the people of Isra'el: Bela the son of B'or; the name of his city was Dinhavah. ⁴⁴ After Bela died, Yovav the son of Zerach from Botzrah took his place as king. ⁴⁵ After Yovav died, Husham from the land of the Temani took his place as king. ⁴⁶ After Husham died, Hadad the son of B'dad, who attacked Midyan on the plains of Mo'av, took his place as king; the name of his city was 'Avit. ⁴⁷ After Hadad died, Samlah from Masrekah took his place as king. ⁴⁸ After Samlah died, Sha'ul from Rechovot-by-the-River took his place as king. ⁴⁹ After Sha'ul died, Ba'al-Hanan the son of 'Akhbor took his place as king. ⁵⁰ After Ba'al-Hanan died, Hadad took his place as king; the name of his city was Pa'i; his wife's name was M'heitav'el the daughter of Matred the daughter of Mei-Zahav. ⁵¹ Then Hadad died.

The chieftains of Edom were: the chieftains of Timnah, 'Alvah, Y'tet, ⁵² Oholivamah, Elah, Pinon, ⁵³ Kenaz, Teman, Mivtzar, ⁵⁴ Magdi'el and 'Iram. These were the chieftains of Edom.

2 ¹ These are the sons of Isra'el: Re'uven, Shim'on, Levi, Y'hudah, Yissakhar, Z'vulun, ² Dan, Yosef, Binyamin, Naftali, Gad and Asher.

³ The sons of Y'hudah: 'Er, Onan and Shelah; the mother of these three was Bat-Shua the Kena'anit. 'Er, Y'hudah's firstborn, was wicked from ADONAI's perspective, so he killed him. ⁴ Tamar his daughter-in-law bore him Peretz and Zerach; thus Y'hudah had five sons altogether.

⁵ The sons of Peretz: Hetzron and Hamul. ⁶ The sons of Zerach: Zimri, Eitan, Heiman, Kalkol and Dara — five of them altogether. ⁷ The sons of Karmi: 'Akhar [troubler], who troubled Isra'el by violating the rule concerning things set aside to be destroyed. ⁸ The son of Eitan: 'Azaryah.

⁹ The sons born to Hetzron: Yerachme'el, Ram and K'luvai. ¹⁰ Ram fathered 'Amminadav; 'Amminadav fathered Nachshon prince of the descendants of Y'hudah; ¹¹ Nachshon fathered Salma; Salma fathered Bo'az; ¹² Bo'az fathered 'Oved; 'Oved fathered Yishai; ¹³ and Yishai fathered Eli'av his firstborn, Avinadav second, Shim'a third, ¹⁴ N'tan'el fourth, Radai fifth, ¹⁵ Otzem sixth, David seventh, ¹⁶ and their sisters Tz'ruyah and Avigayil. The sons of Tz'ruyah: Avshai, Yo'av and 'Asah'el, three of them. ¹⁷ Avigayil was the mother of 'Amasa; the father of 'Amasa was Yeter the Yishma'eli.

¹⁸ Kalev the son of Hetzron fathered sons with 'Azuvah his wife (and with Yeri'ot); these were her sons: Yesher, Shovav and Ardon. ¹⁹ After 'Azuvah died, Kalev married Efrat, who bore him Hur. ²⁰ Hur fathered Uri, and Uri fathered B'tzal'el. ²¹ Afterwards, Hetzron had sexual relations with the daughter of Machir the father of Gil'ad; he married her when he was sixty years old, and she bore him S'guv. ²² S'guv fathered Ya'ir, who had twenty-three cities in the land of Gil'ad. ²³ (But G'shur and Aram took Havot-Ya'ir away from them, along with K'nat and its villages — sixty cities.) All these were descendants of Machir the father of Gil'ad.

²⁴ After Hetzron died in Kalev-Efratah, Aviyah Hetzron's wife bore him Ash'chur the father of T'koa.

²⁵ The sons of Yerachme'el Hetzron's firstborn: Ram the firstborn, Bunah, Oren, Otzem and Achiyah. ²⁶ Yerachme'el had another wife, whose name was 'Atarah; she

was the mother of Onam. ²⁷ The sons of Ram the firstborn son of Yerachme'el: Ma'atz, Yamin and 'Eker. ²⁸ The sons of Onam: Shamai and Yada. The sons of Shamai: Nadav and Avishur. ²⁹ Avishur's wife was named Avichayil, and she bore him Achban and Molid. ³⁰ The sons of Nadav: Seled and Apayim. Seled died without having any children. ³¹ The son of Apayim: Yish'i. The son of Yish'i: Sheshan. The son of Sheshan: Achlai. ³² The sons of Yada the brother of Shamai: Yeter and Yonatan. Yeter died without having any children. ³³ The sons of Yonatan: Pelet and Zaza. These were the descendants of Yerachme'el.

³⁴ Sheshan had no sons, but daughters. Sheshan had a servant, an Egyptian, whose name was Yarcha; ³⁵ Sheshan gave his daughter in marriage to Yarcha his servant, and she bore him 'Atai. ³⁶ 'Atai fathered Natan, Natan fathered Zavad, ³⁷ Zavad fathered Eflal, Eflal fathered 'Oved, ³⁸ 'Oved fathered Yehu, Yehu fathered 'Azaryah, ³⁹ 'Azaryah fathered Heletz, Heletz fathered El'asah, ⁴⁰ El'asah fathered Sismai, Sismai fathered Shalum, ⁴¹ Shalum fathered Y'kamyah and Y'kamyah fathered Elishama.

⁴² The sons of Kalev the brother of Yerachme'el: Mesha his firstborn, who was the father of Zif; and the sons of Mareshah the father of Hevron. ⁴³ The sons of Hevron: Korach, Tapuach, Rekem and Shema. ⁴⁴ Shema fathered Racham the father of Yorke'am, and Rekem fathered Shamai. ⁴⁵ The son of Shamai was Ma'on, and Ma'on was the father of Beit-Tzur. ⁴⁶ 'Eifah, Kalev's concubine, bore Haran, Motza and Gazez; and Haran fathered Gazez. ⁴⁷ The sons of Yahdai: Regem, Yotam, Geshan, Pelet, 'Eifah and Sha'af. ⁴⁸ Ma'akhah, Kalev's concubine, bore Shever and Tirchanah. ⁴⁹ [The wife of] Sha'af the father of Madmanah bore Sh'va the father of Machbenah and the father of Giv'a. The daughter of Kalev was 'Akhsah. ⁵⁰ These were the descendants of Kalev.

The sons of Hur the firstborn of Efratah: Shoval the father of Kiryat-Ye'arim, ⁵¹ Salma the father of Beit-Lechem and Haref the father of Beit-Gader. ⁵² Shoval the father of Kiryat-Ye'arim had sons: HaRo'eh and half of the [inhabitants of] M'nuchot. ⁵³ The families of Kiryat-Ye'arim: the Yitri, the Puti, the Shumati and the Mishra'i; from them came the Tzor'ati and the Eshta'uli. ⁵⁴ The sons of Salma: Beit-Lechem, the N'tofati, 'Atrot-Beit-Yo'av, half of the Manachati, the Tzor'i, ⁵⁵ the families of scribes that lived in Ya'betz, the Tir'atim, the Shim'atim and the Sukhatim. These are the Kinim, who came from Hamat, father of the house of Rekhav.

3 ¹ These were the sons born to David in Hevron: the firstborn was Amnon, whose mother was Achino'am from Yizre'el; the second, Dani'el, whose mother was Avigayil from Karmel; ² the third, Avshalom, the son of Ma'akhah the daughter of Talmai king of G'shur; the fourth, Adoniyah the son of Haggit; ³ the fifth, Sh'fatyah, whose mother was Avital; and the sixth, Yitre'am, whose mother was his wife 'Eglah. ⁴ Six were born to David in Hevron. He ruled there seven years and six months; then he ruled in Yerushalayim thirty-three years.

⁵ These were born to him in Yerushalayim: Shim'a, Shovav, Natan, Shlomo, four whose mother was Bat-Shua the daughter of 'Ammi'el; ⁶ and nine others — Yivchar, Elishama, Elifelet, ⁷ Nogah, Nefeg, Yafia, ⁸ Elishama, Elyada and Elifelet. ⁹ All these were sons of David, apart from the sons of the concubines; Tamar was their sister.

¹⁰ Shlomo's son was Rechav'am, his son Aviyah, his son Asa, his son Y'hoshafat, ¹¹ his son Yoram, his son Achazyah, his son Yo'ash, ¹² his son Amatzyah, his son

'Azaryah, his son Yotam, ¹³ his son Achaz, his son Hizkiyahu, his son M'nasheh, ¹⁴ his son Amon and his son Yoshiyahu. ¹⁵ The sons of Yoshiyahu: Yochanan the firstborn, Y'hoyakim the second, Tzedekyah the third, and Shalum the fourth. ¹⁶ The sons of Y'hoyakim: Y'khonyah his son, and Tzedekyah his son. ¹⁷ The sons of Y'khonyah, also called Asir: Sh'alti'el his son; ¹⁸ also Malkiram, P'dayah, Shen'atzar, Y'kamyah, Hoshama and N'davyah. ¹⁹ The sons of P'dayah: Z'rubavel and Shim'i. The children of Z'rubavel: Meshulam, Hananyah and Shlomit their sister; ²⁰ also Hashuvah, Ohel, Berekhyah, Hasadyah and Yushav-Hesed — five. ²¹ The sons of Hananyah: P'latyah and Yesha'yah. His son was Refayah. His son was Arnan. His son was 'Ovadyah. And his son was Sh'khanyah. ²² The sons of Sh'khanyah: Sh'ma'yah and the sons of Sh'ma'yah — Hatush, Yig'al, Bariach, Ne'aryah and Shafat — six. ²³ The sons of Ne'aryah: Elyo'einai, Hizkiyah and 'Azrikam — three. ²⁴ The sons of Elyo'einai: Hodavyahu, Elyashiv, P'layah, 'Akuv, Yochanan, D'layah and 'Anani — seven.

4 ¹ The descendants of Y'hudah: Peretz, Hetzron, Karmi, Hur and Shoval. ² Re'ayah the son of Shoval fathered Yachat; Yachat fathered Achumai and Lahad. These are the families of the Tzor'ati. ³ These are [the sons] of the father of 'Eitam: Yizre'el, Yishma and Yidbash; their sister's name was Hatzlelponi. ⁴ P'nu'el fathered Geder, and 'Ezer fathered Hushah. These are the sons of Hur the firstborn of Efratah, the father of Beit-Lechem.

⁵ Ashur the father of T'koa had two wives, Hel'ah and Na'arah. ⁶ Na'arah bore him Achuzam, Hefer, Teimni and Achashtari; these were the sons of Na'arah. ⁷ The sons of Hel'ah were Tzeret, Tzochar and Etnan. ⁸ Kotz fathered 'Anuv, Tzovevah and the families of Acharchel the son of Harum. ⁹ Ya'betz was honored more than his brothers; his mother called him Ya'betz, she explained, "because I bore him in pain [Hebrew: 'otzev]." ¹⁰ Ya'betz called on the God of Isra'el: "Please bless me by enlarging my territory. May your hand be with me! Keep me from harm, so that it will not cause me pain [Hebrew: 'atzbi]." God granted his request.

¹¹ K'luv the brother of Shuchah fathered M'chir, who fathered Eshton. ¹² Eshton fathered Beit-Rafa, Paseach and T'chinah the father of 'Ir-Nachash. These are the men of Rekhah.

¹³ The sons of K'naz: 'Otni'el and S'rayah. The son of 'Otni'el: Hatat. ¹⁴ M'onotai fathered 'Ofrah, and S'rayah fathered Yo'av the father of Gei-Harashim; for they were craftsmen [Hebrew: harashim].

¹⁵ The sons of Kalev the son of Y'funeh: 'Iru, Elah and Na'am. The son of Elah: K'naz. ¹⁶ The sons of Yehallel'el: Zif, Zifah, Tirya and Asar'el. ¹⁷⁻¹⁸ The sons of 'Ezrah: Yeter, Mered, 'Efer and Yalon. These are the sons of Bityah the daughter of Pharaoh, whom Mered took as his wife: she conceived Miryam, Shamai and Yishbach the father of Esht'moa; while his Jewish wife bore Yered the father of G'dor, Hever the father of Sokho and Y'kuti'el the father of Zanoach.

¹⁹ The sons of the wife of Hodiyah the sister of Nacham were the father of Ke'ilah the Garmi and Esht'moa the Ma'akhati. ²⁰ The sons of Shimon: Amnon, Rinah, Ben-Hanan and Tilon. The sons of Yish'i: Zochet and Ben-Zochet.

²¹ The sons of Shelah the son of Y'hudah: 'Er the father of Lekha, La'adah the father of Mareshah and the clans of fine-linen-workers at Beit-Ashbea, ²² Yokim, the men of Kozeva, Saraf the ruler in Mo'av, and Yashuvi-Lechem (the records

are ancient). ²³ These were potters and inhabitants of N'ta'im and G'derah; they lived there, occupied with the king's work.

²⁴ The sons of Shim'on: N'mu'el, Yamin, Yariv, Zerach and Sha'ul. ²⁵ His son was Shalum, his son was Mivsam, and his son was Mishma. ²⁶ The descendants of Mishma: his son Hamu'el, his son Zakur, his son Shim'i. ²⁷ Shim'i had sixteen sons and six daughters, but his brothers did not have many children, so their clans did not increase like those of Y'hudah. ²⁸ They lived at Be'er-Sheva, Moladah, Hatzar-Shu'al, ²⁹ Bilhah, 'Etzem, Tolad, ³⁰ B'tu'el, Hormah, Ziklag, ³¹ Beit-Markavot, Hatzar-Susim, Beit-Bir'i and Sha'arayim. These were their cities until the reign of David. ³² Their villages were 'Eitam, 'Ayin, Rimmon, Tokhen and 'Ashan, five cities, ³³ along with all the villages surrounding these cities, as far as Ba'al. These are the places where they lived, and they have their official genealogy. ³⁴ Meshovav, Yamlekh, Yoshah the son of Amatzyah, ³⁵ Yo'el, Yehu the son of Yoshivyah the son of S'rayah the son of 'Asi'el, ³⁶ Elyo'einai, Ya'akovah, Y'shochayah, 'Asayah, 'Adi'el, Y'simi'el, B'nayah, ³⁷ Ziza the son of Shif'i the son of Alon the son of Y'da'yah the son of Shimri the son of Sh'ma'yah — ³⁸ these mentioned by name were princes in their clans, and their fathers' houses increased greatly. ³⁹ Seeking pasture for their flocks they went to the entrance of Geder, as far as the east side of the valley. ⁴⁰ They found rich, good pastures; and the land was spacious, quiet and peaceful. Those who had lived there previously belonged to Ham. ⁴¹ Those whose names are written above came during the time of Hizkiyahu king of Y'hudah; they attacked their tents and the Me'unim who were found there, destroyed them completely, and have lived there in place of them to this day; because there was pasture there for their flocks. ⁴² Some 500 of them who were descendants of Shim'on went to Mount Se'ir under the leadership of P'latyah, Ne'aryah, Refayah and Uzi'el the sons of Yish'i. ⁴³ They attacked the remnant of 'Amalek who had escaped and have lived there to this day.

5 ¹ The sons of Re'uven the firstborn of Isra'el — he was the firstborn, but because he defiled his father's bed, his birthright was given to the sons of Yosef the son of Isra'el, though not in such a way as for him to be regarded in the genealogy as the firstborn. ² For Y'hudah became greater than his brothers, inasmuch as the ruler came from him; nevertheless, the birthright went to Yosef. ³ So these are the sons of Re'uven the firstborn of Isra'el: Hanokh, Pallu, Hetzron and Karmi.

⁴ The descendants of Yo'el: his son Sh'ma'yah, his son Gog, his son Shim'i, ⁵ his son Mikhah, his son Re'ayah, his son Ba'al, ⁶ and his son Be'erah. Tilgat-Piln'eser king of Ashur carried him away captive; he was leader of the Re'uveni. ⁷ His brothers, by their clans, as listed in their genealogical records were: Ye'i'el the leader, Z'kharyah ⁸ and Bela the son of 'Azaz the son of Sh'ma the son of Yo'el. He lived in 'Aro'er, with territory extending to N'vo and Ba'al-M'on; ⁹ while to the east he occupied territory that extended to the beginning of the desert as one comes from the Euphrates River; because their cattle multiplied in the land of Gil'ad. ¹⁰ In the time of Sha'ul they went to war with the Hagri'im; after defeating them they occupied their tents throughout all the territory east of Gil'ad.

¹¹ The descendants of Gad lived across from them, in the territory from Bashan to Salkhah: ¹² Yo'el was the leader, Shafam second, then Yanai and Shafat in Bashan. ¹³ The houses of their fathers' brothers were: Mikha'el, Meshulam, Sheva, Yorai, Ya'kan, Zia and 'Ever — seven altogether. ¹⁴ These are the sons of Avichayil the son

of Huri the son of Yaroach the son of Gil'ad the son of Mikha'el the son of Yeshishai the son of Yachdo the son of Buz; ¹⁵ Achi the son of 'Avdi'el the son of Guni was leader of their fathers' house. ¹⁶ They lived in Gil'ad, in Bashan, in its towns and in all the pasture lands of the plain as far as their borders. ¹⁷ All these were listed in genealogies during the times of Yotam king of Y'hudah and Yarov'am king of Isra'el.

¹⁸ The descendants of Re'uven, the Gadi and the half-tribe of M'nasheh included 44,760 brave men who were available for warfare, able to take up shield and sword, shoot with the bow, or make use of other war skills. ¹⁹ These made war with the Hagri'im, Y'tur, Nafish and Nodav. ²⁰ They received help against them, so that the Hagri'im and all who were allied with them suffered defeat at their hands; because they cried out to God while they were fighting, and he did as they requested, because they put their trust in him. ²¹ From their livestock they carried off 50,000 camels, 250,000 sheep and 2,000 donkeys; they also took captive 100,000 persons. ²² Many were slaughtered, because the war was of God, and they lived in their territory until the captivity.

²³ The descendants of the half-tribe of M'nasheh lived and increased in the territory from Bashan to Ba'al-Hermon, S'nir and Mount Hermon. ²⁴ The leaders of their fathers' houses were: 'Efer, Yish'i, Eli'el, 'Azri'el, Yirmeyah, Hodavyah and Yachdi'el, strong, brave, famous men, leaders of their fathers' houses. ²⁵ But they broke faith with the God of their ancestors and prostituted themselves to the gods of the peoples of the land, whom God had destroyed ahead of them. ²⁶ So the God of Isra'el stirred up the spirit of Pul king of Ashur and the spirit of Tilgat-Piln'eser king of Ashur; and he carried them away as captives — the Re'uveni, the Gadi and the half-tribe of M'nasheh — and brought them to Halach, Havor, Hara and to the Gozan River, where they are to this day.

²⁷⁽⁶:¹⁾ The sons of Levi: Gershon, K'hat and M'rari. ²⁸⁽⁶:²⁾ The sons of K'hat: 'Amram, Yitz'har, Hevron and 'Uzi'el. ²⁹⁽⁶:³⁾ The children of 'Amram: Aharon, Moshe and Miryam. The sons of Aharon: Nadav, Avihu, El'azar and Itamar. ³⁰⁽⁶:⁴⁾ El'azar fathered Pinchas, Pinchas fathered Avishua, ³¹⁽⁶:⁵⁾ Avishua fathered Buki, Buki fathered 'Uzi, ³²⁽⁶:⁶⁾ 'Uzi fathered Z'rachyah, Z'rachyah fathered M'rayot, ³³⁽⁶:⁷⁾ M'rayot fathered Amaryah, Amaryah fathered Achituv, ³⁴⁽⁶:⁸⁾ Achituv fathered Tzadok, Tzadok fathered Achima'atz, ³⁵⁽⁶:⁹⁾ Achima'atz fathered 'Azaryah, 'Azaryah fathered Yochanan, ³⁶⁽⁶:¹⁰⁾ and Yochanan fathered 'Azaryah. He functioned as *cohen* in the house that Shlomo built in Yerushalayim. ³⁷⁽⁶:¹¹⁾ 'Azaryah fathered Amaryah, Amaryah fathered Achituv, ³⁸⁽⁶:¹²⁾ Achituv fathered Tzadok, Tzadok fathered Shalum, ³⁹⁽⁶:¹³⁾ Shalum fathered Hilkiyah, Hilkiyah fathered 'Azaryah, ⁴⁰⁽⁶:¹⁴⁾ 'Azaryah fathered S'rayah, S'rayah fathered Y'hotzadak, ⁴¹⁽⁶:¹⁵⁾ and Y'hotzadak went into captivity when ADONAI carried Y'hudah and Yerushalayim away at the hands of N'vukhadnetzar.

6 ¹⁽¹⁶⁾ The sons of Levi: Gershom, K'hat and M'rari. ²⁽¹⁷⁾ These are the names of the sons of Gershom: Livni and Shim'i. ³⁽¹⁸⁾ The sons of K'hat: 'Amram, Yitz'har, Hevron and 'Uzi'el. ⁴⁽¹⁹⁾ The sons of M'rari: Machli and Mushi.

These are the families of the *L'vi'im* according to father's clans: ⁵⁽²⁰⁾ [The descendants] of Gershom: his son Livni, his son Yachat, his son Zimah, ⁶⁽²¹⁾ his son Yo'ach, his son 'Iddo, his son Zerach, his son Ye'atrai.

⁷⁽²²⁾ The descendants of K'hat: his son 'Amminadav, his son Korach, his son Asir, ⁸⁽²³⁾ his son Elkanah, his son Evyasaf, his son Asir, ⁹⁽²⁴⁾ his son Tachat, his son

Uri'el, his son 'Uziyah and his son Sha'ul. ¹⁰⁽²⁵⁾ The sons of Elkanah: 'Amasai and Achimot. ¹¹⁽²⁶⁾ As for Elkanah, the sons of Elkanah: his son Tzofai, his son Nachat, ¹²⁽²⁷⁾ his son Eli'av, his son Yerocham and his son Elkanah. ¹³⁽²⁸⁾ The sons of Sh'mu'el: Vashni the firstborn, then Aviyah.

¹⁴⁽²⁹⁾ The descendants of M'rari: Machli, his son Livni, his son Shim'i, his son 'Uzah, ¹⁵⁽³⁰⁾ his son Shim'a, his son Hagiyah and his son 'Asayah. ¹⁶⁽³¹⁾ David appointed them to be in charge of the service of song in the house of ADONAI after the ark had found a permanent resting place. ¹⁷⁽³²⁾ They served as singers before the tabernacle of the tent of meeting, until Shlomo had built the house of ADONAI in Yerushalayim; and they carried out their tasks in a prescribed order.

¹⁸⁽³³⁾ Those who carried out these tasks and their descendants were — starting with descendants of the K'hati — Heman the singer, the son of Yo'el the son of Sh'mu'el, ¹⁹⁽³⁴⁾ the son of Elkanah, the son of Yerocham, the son of Eli'el, the son of Toach, ²⁰⁽³⁵⁾ the son of Tzuf, the son of Elkanah, the son of Machat, the son of 'Amasai, ²¹⁽³⁶⁾ the son of Elkanah, the son of Yo'el, the son of 'Azaryah, the son of Tz'fanyah, ²²⁽³⁷⁾ the son of Tachat, the son of Asir, the son of Evyasaf, the son of Korach, ²³⁽³⁸⁾ the son of Yitz'har, the son of K'hat, the son of Levi, the son of Isra'el.

²⁴⁽³⁹⁾ His brother Asaf, who stood on his right, was Asaf the son of Berekhyah, the son of Shim'a, ²⁵⁽⁴⁰⁾ the son of Mikha'el, the son of Ba'aseyah, the son of Malkiyah, ²⁶⁽⁴¹⁾ the son of Etni, the son of Zerach, the son of 'Adayah, ²⁷⁽⁴²⁾ the son of Eitan, the son of Zimah, the son of Shim'i, ²⁸⁽⁴³⁾ the son of Yachat, the son of Gershom, the son of Levi.

²⁹⁽⁴⁴⁾ On the left were their kinsmen the descendants of M'rari: Eitan the son of Kishi, the son of 'Avdi, the son of Malukh, ³⁰⁽⁴⁵⁾ the son of Hashavyah, the son of Amatzyah, the son of Hilkiyah, ³¹⁽⁴⁶⁾ the son of Amtzi, the son of Bani, the son of Shemer, ³²⁽⁴⁷⁾ the son of Machli, the son of Mushi, the son of M'rari, the son of Levi.

³³⁽⁴⁸⁾ Their kinsmen the *L'vi'im* were put in charge of all the service of the tabernacle of the house of God.

³⁴⁽⁴⁹⁾ But Aharon and his sons were the ones who offered on the altar of burnt offering and on the altar of incense for all the service of the Especially Holy Place and to make atonement for Isra'el, in keeping with all that Moshe the servant of God had ordered to be done. ³⁵⁽⁵⁰⁾ These are the descendants of Aharon: his son El'azar, his son Pinchas, his son Avishua, ³⁶⁽⁵¹⁾ his son Buki, his son 'Uzi, his son Z'rachyah, ³⁷⁽⁵²⁾ his son M'rayot, his son Amaryah, his son Achituv, ³⁸⁽⁵³⁾ his son Tzadok and his son Achima'atz.

³⁹⁽⁵⁴⁾ These were the settlements of the descendants of Aharon according to the territories assigned them: to the descendants of Aharon, of the clans of the K'hati — for the first lot fell to them — ⁴⁰⁽⁵⁵⁾ they gave Hevron in the land of Y'hudah with the open land surrounding it, ⁴¹⁽⁵⁶⁾ but the fields and the dependent villages of the city they gave to Kalev the son of Y'funeh. ⁴²⁽⁵⁷⁾ To the descendants of Aharon they gave the city of refuge Hevron, also Livnah with its surrounding open land, Yatir, Esht'moa with its surrounding open land, ⁴³⁽⁵⁸⁾ Hilen with its surrounding open land, D'vir with its surrounding open land, ⁴⁴⁽⁵⁹⁾ 'Ashan with its surrounding open land, Beit-Shemesh with its surrounding open land; ⁴⁵⁽⁶⁰⁾ and out of the tribe of Binyamin: Geva with its surrounding open land, 'Alemet with its surrounding open land and 'Anatot with its surrounding open land. All the cities for all their clans amounted to thirteen cities.

⁴⁶⁽⁶¹⁾ The rest of the descendants of K'hat were assigned by lot, clan by clan, ten cities from the half-tribe of M'nasheh. ⁴⁷⁽⁶²⁾ The descendants of Gershom were

assigned, clan by clan, thirteen cities from the tribes of Yissakhar, Asher, Naftali and M'nasheh in Bashan. ⁴⁸⁽⁶³⁾ To the descendants of M'rari were assigned by lot, clan by clan, twelve cities from the tribes of Re'uven, Gad and Z'vulun. ⁴⁹⁽⁶⁴⁾ So the people of Isra'el gave the *L'vi'im* these cities with the surrounding open land. ⁵⁰⁽⁶⁵⁾ From the tribes of the descendants of Y'hudah, Shim'on and Binyamin they assigned these cities mentioned by name.

⁵¹⁽⁶⁶⁾ Some of the clans of the descendants of K'hat were given cities in territory from the tribe of Efrayim. ⁵²⁽⁶⁷⁾ They gave them the city of refuge Sh'khem in the hills of Efrayim with the surrounding open land, also Gezer with the surrounding open land, ⁵³⁽⁶⁸⁾ Yokme'am with the surrounding open land, Beit-Horon with the surrounding open land, ⁵⁴⁽⁶⁹⁾ Ayalon with the surrounding open land, and Gat-Rimmon with the surrounding open land; ⁵⁵⁽⁷⁰⁾ and out of the half-tribe of M'nasheh: 'Aner with the surrounding open land and Bil'am with the surrounding open land, for the rest of the clans of the descendants of K'hat.

⁵⁶⁽⁷¹⁾ The descendants of Gershom were given, from the clans of the half-tribe of M'nasheh: Golan in Bashan with the surrounding open land and 'Ashtarot with the surrounding open land; ⁵⁷⁽⁷²⁾ and from the tribe of Yissakhar: Kedesh with the surrounding open land, Davrat with the surrounding open land, ⁵⁸⁽⁷³⁾ Ramot with the surrounding open land and 'Anem with the surrounding open land; ⁵⁹⁽⁷⁴⁾ and from the tribe of Asher: Mashal with the surrounding open land, 'Avdon with the surrounding open land, ⁶⁰⁽⁷⁵⁾ Hukok with the surrounding open land and Rechov with the surrounding open land; ⁶¹⁽⁷⁶⁾ and from the tribe of Naftali: Kedesh in the Galil with the surrounding open land, Hamon with the surrounding open land and Kiryatayim with the surrounding open land.

⁶²⁽⁷⁷⁾ To the rest [of the *L'vi'im*], the descendants of M'rari, were given, from the tribe of Z'vulun: Rimmono with the surrounding open land and Tavor with the surrounding open land; ⁶³⁽⁷⁸⁾ and beyond the Yarden at Yericho, on the east side of the Yarden, they were given, from the tribe of Re'uven: Betzer in the desert with the surrounding open land, Yahatz with the surrounding open land, ⁶⁴⁽⁷⁹⁾ K'demot with the surrounding open land and Mefa'at with the surrounding open land; ⁶⁵⁽⁸⁰⁾ and from the tribe of Gad: Ramot in Gil'ad with the surrounding open land, Machanayim with the surrounding open land, ⁶⁶⁽⁸¹⁾ Heshbon with the surrounding open land and Ya'zer with the surrounding open land.

7 ¹ The sons of Yissakhar were: Tola, Pu'ah, Yashuv and Shimron — four.

² The sons of Tola were: 'Uzi, Refayah, Yeri'el, Yachmai, Yivsam and Sh'mu'el. They were heads of their fathers' clans, descended from Tola; they were strong, brave men in their generations. In the time of David they numbered 22,600.

³ The son of 'Uzi was Yizrachyah, and the sons of Yizrachyah were: Mikha'el, 'Ovadyah, Yo'el and Yishiyah — five, all of them leaders. ⁴ With them, by their generations, in their fathers' clans, were army troops organized for war, 36,000 of them, because they had many women and children. ⁵ Their kinsmen among all the clans of Yissakhar, strong, brave men, numbered 87,000, listed in genealogical records.

⁶ [The sons of] Binyamin were: Bela, Bekher and Y'dia'el — three.

⁷ The sons of Bela were: Etzbon, 'Uzi, 'Uzi'el, Yerimot and 'Iri — five; they were leaders of fathers' clans, strong, brave men. They numbered 22,034, listed in genealogical records.

⁸ The sons of Bekher were: Z'mirah, Yo'ash, Eli'ezer, Elyo'enai, 'Omri, Yeremot, Aviyah, 'Anatot and 'Alemet; all these were sons of Bekher. ⁹ Listed in genealogical records by generations under leaders of fathers' clans, who were strong, brave men, were 20,200.

¹⁰ The son of Y'dia'el was Bilhan. The sons of Bilhan were: Ye'ush, Binyamin, Ehud, Kena'anah, Zeitan, Tarshish and Achishachar. ¹¹ All these were descendants of Y'dia'el, leaders of their fathers' clans, who were brave, strong men; they numbered 17,200, all fit to fight with the army.

¹² [More descendants of Binyamin:] Shupim, Hupim, the sons of 'Ir.

Hushim, the son of another [of Isra'el's sons, namely, Dan].

¹³ The sons of Naftali were: Yachtzi'el, Guni, Yetzer, Shalum, the sons of Bilhah.

¹⁴ The descendants of M'nasheh: his concubine the woman from Aram bore Makhir the father of Gil'ad; Asri'el [Gil'ad's son] was descended from her. ¹⁵ Makhir's wife was from the families of Hupim and Shupim, and his sister's name was Ma'akhah. M'nasheh's second son was Tz'lof'chad, and Tz'lof'chad had daughters. ¹⁶ Ma'akhah the wife of Makhir bore a son whom she named Peresh, the name of his brother was Sheresh, and his sons were Ulam and Rekem. ¹⁷ The son of Ulam was B'dan. These were the descendants of Gil'ad the son of Makhir the son of M'nasheh. ¹⁸ His sister Hammolekhet [the governor] bore Ish-Hod, Avi'ezer and Machlah. ¹⁹ The sons of Sh'mida were Achyan, Sh'khem, Lik'chi and Ani'am.

²⁰ The descendants of Efrayim were: Shutelach, his son Bered, his son Tachat, his son El'adah, his son Tachat, ²¹ his son Zavad and his son Shutelach; also 'Ezer and El'ad, whom the men of Gat born in the land killed when they came down to raid their cattle. ²² Efrayim their father mourned for a long time, and his kinsmen came to comfort him. ²³ Then he had sexual relations with his wife, and she conceived and bore a son whom he called B'ri'ah [in calamity], because his household had suffered a calamity. ²⁴ His daughter was She'erah, who built upper and lower Beit-Horon and Uzen-She'erah. ²⁵ Refach was his son, and Reshef, then his son Telach, his son Tachan ²⁶ his son La'dan, his son 'Ammihud, his son Elishama, ²⁷ his son Nun and his son Y'hoshua.

²⁸ Their possessions and settlements were Beit-El with its towns; Na'aran to the east; and to the west, Gezer with its towns; also Sh'khem with its towns, as far as 'Ayah and its towns; ²⁹ and, near the territory of the descendants of M'nasheh, Beit-Sh'an with its towns, Ta'nakh with its towns, Megiddo with its towns and Dor with its towns. In these places lived the descendants of Yosef the son of Isra'el.

³⁰ The children of Asher were: Yimnah, Yishvah, Yishvi, B'ri'ah and their sister Serach. ³¹ The sons of B'ri'ah were: Hever and Malki'el, who fathered Birzayit. ³² Hever fathered Yaflet, Shomer, Hotam and their sister Shua. ³³ The sons of Yaflet were: Pasakh, Bimhal and 'Ashvat; these were the sons of Yaflet. ³⁴ The sons of Shemer were: Achi, Rohgah, Hubah and Aram. ³⁵ The sons of his brother Helem were: Zofach, Yimnah, Shelesh and 'Amal. ³⁶ The sons of Zofach were: Suach, Harnefer, Shu'al, Beri, Yimrah, ³⁷ Betzer, Hod, Shama, Shilshah, Yitran and Be'era. ³⁸ The sons of Yeter were: Y'funeh, Pispah and Ara. ³⁹ The sons of 'Ula were: Arach, Hani'el and Ritzya. ⁴⁰ All these were descendants of Asher, leaders of their fathers' clans, elite, strong, brave men, the most important of the princes. Those fit for battle service, listed in genealogies, numbered 26,000 men.

8 ¹ Binyamin fathered Bela his firstborn son; his second, Ashbel; his third, Achrach; ² his fourth, Nochah; and his fifth, Rafa. ³ Bela had sons: Adar, Gera, Avihud, ⁴ Avishua, Na'aman, Achoach, ⁵ Gera, Sh'fufan and Huram. ⁶ These are the sons of Ehud, the heads of fathers' clans among the inhabitants of Geva (they were carried away captive to Manachat; ⁷ those who carried them off were Na'aman, Achiyah and Gera): he fathered 'Uzah and Achichud. ⁸ Shacharayim fathered children on the plains of Mo'av; after sending away his wives Hushim and Ba'ara, ⁹ it was through his wife Hodesh that he fathered: Yovav, Tzivya, Mesha, Malkam, ¹⁰ Ye'utz, Sokhya and Mirmah. These were his sons, heads of clans. ¹¹ Through Hushim he fathered Avituv and Elpa'al. ¹² The sons of Elpa'al: 'Ever, Mish'am, Shemed — he built Ono and Lod with its towns — ¹³ and B'ri'ah and Shema — they were heads of fathers' clans among the inhabitants of Ayalon, who drove away the people living in Gat.

¹⁴ Achyo, Shashak, Yeremot, ¹⁵ Z'vadyah, 'Arad, 'Eder, ¹⁶ Mikha'el, Yishpah and Yocha were the sons of B'ri'ah. ¹⁷ Z'vadyah, Meshulam, Hizki, Hever, ¹⁸ Yishm'rai, Yizli'ah and Yovav were the sons of Elpa'al. ¹⁹ Yakim, Zikhri, Zavdi, ²⁰ Eli'einai, Tziltai, Eli'el, ²¹ 'Adayah, B'rayah and Shimrat were the sons of Shim'i. ²² Yishpan, 'Eved, Eli'el, ²³ 'Avdon, Zikhri, Hanan, ²⁴ Hananyah, 'Eilam, 'Anatotyah, ²⁵ Yifdeyah and P'nu'el were the sons of Shashak. ²⁶ Shamsh'rai, Sh'charyah, 'Atalyah, ²⁷ Ya'areshyah, Eliyah and Zikhri were the sons of Yerocham. ²⁸ These were leaders of fathers' houses through all their generations, leading men who lived in Yerushalayim.

²⁹ In Giv'on lived the father of Giv'on, whose wife's name was Ma'akhah; ³⁰ and his firstborn son 'Avdon, Tzur, Kish, Ba'al, Nadav, ³¹ G'dor, Achyo and Zekher. ³² Miklot fathered Shim'ah. In contrast with some of their kinsmen, they and their families lived in Yerushalayim.

³³ Ner fathered Kish; Kish fathered Sha'ul; and Sha'ul fathered Y'honatan, Malkishua, Avinadav and Eshba'al. ³⁴ The son of Y'honatan was M'riv-Ba'al, and M'riv-Ba'al fathered Mikhah. ³⁵ The sons of Mikhah: Piton, Melekh, Ta'rea and Achaz. ³⁶ Achaz fathered Y'ho'adah; Y'ho'adah fathered 'Alemet, 'Azmavet and Zimri; Zimri fathered Motza; ³⁷ and Motza fathered Bin'a. His son was Rafah, his son was El'asah and his son was Atzel. ³⁸ Atzel had six sons, whose names were: 'Azrikam, Bokhru, Yishma'el, Sh'aryah, 'Ovadyah and Hanan; all these were sons of Atzel. ³⁹ The sons of his brother 'Eshek: Ulam his firstborn, Ye'ush the second and Elifelet the third. ⁴⁰ The sons of Ulam were strong, brave men, archers; they had many children and grandchildren, a hundred and fifty. All these were descendants of Binyamin.

9 ¹ So all Isra'el was listed by genealogies, and these were recorded in the book of the kings of Isra'el. Then Y'hudah was carried away captive to Bavel because of their unfaithfulness. ² The first people to return to their possessions in the cities were the Isra'elim, the *cohanim*, the *L'vi'im* and the temple servants. ³ In Yerushalayim lived some descendants of Y'hudah, some descendants of Binyamin and some descendants of Efrayim and of M'nasheh: ⁴ 'Utai the son of 'Ammihud, the son of 'Omri, the son of Imri, the son of Bani, from the descendants of Peretz the son of Y'hudah. ⁵ Of the Shiloni: 'Asayah the firstborn and his sons. ⁶ Of the descendants of Zerach: Ye'u'el and their kinsmen, 690. ⁷ Of the descendants of Binyamin: Salu the son of Meshulam the son of Hodavyah the son of Hasnu'ah, ⁸ Yivneyah the son of Yerocham, Elah the son of 'Uzi the son of Mikhri, Meshulam the son of Sh'fatyah the son of Re'u'el the son of Yivneyah, ⁹ and their kinsmen, according to their generations — altogether 956. All these men were leaders of fathers' clans.

¹⁰ Of the *cohanim*: Y'da'yah, Y'hoyariv, Yakhin, ¹¹ 'Azaryah the son of Hilkiyah the son of Meshulam the son of Tzadok the son of M'rayot the son of Achituv the ruler of the house of God, ¹² 'Adayah the son of Yerocham the son of Pash'chur the son of Malkiyah, Ma'asai the son of 'Adi'el the son of Yachzerah the son of Meshulam the son of Meshilmit the son of Immer, ¹³ and their kinsmen, leaders of their fathers' clans, 1,760 very competent men available for serving in the house of God.

¹⁴ Of the *L'vi'im*: Sh'ma'yah the son of Hashuv the son of 'Azrikam the son of Hashavyah, from the descendants of M'rari; ¹⁵ Bakbakar; Heresh; Galal; Matanyah the son of Mikha the son of Zikhri the son of Asaf; ¹⁶ 'Ovadyah the son of Sh'ma'yah the son of Galal the son of Y'dutun; and Berekhyah the son of Asa the son of Elkanah, who lived in the towns of the N'tofati.

¹⁷ The gatekeepers: Shalum, 'Akuv, Talmon, Achiman and their kinsmen; Shalum was the chief. ¹⁸ Previously they had guarded the king's gate to the east; they were gatekeepers for the camp of the descendants of Levi. ¹⁹ Shalum the son of Kore the son of Evyasaf the son of Korach and his kinsmen from his father's clan the Korchim were in charge of the work of the service, keepers of the gates of the tent. Their ancestors had been in charge of the camp of ADONAI, keepers of the entryway. ²⁰ Pinchas the son of El'azar had been ruler over them long before; ADONAI had been with him. ²¹ Z'kharyah the son of Meshelemyah guarded the entryway to the tent of meeting. ²² All these chosen to be gatekeepers numbered 212. Their genealogies were recorded in their towns; they had been appointed to their positions by David and Sh'mu'el the seer. ²³ They and their descendants supervised the gates of the house of ADONAI, that is, the house of the tent, by periods of duty. ²⁴ The gatekeepers served on the four sides, east, west, north and south. ²⁵ From time to time their kinsmen had to come in from their towns to help them for seven days.

²⁶ For the four chief gatekeepers were on permanent duty; they were the *L'vi'im* in charge of accommodations and supplies in the house of God. ²⁷ They spent their nights in the vicinity of the house of God, because they were in charge of it; they were responsible for opening it up each morning.

²⁸ Some of [the *L'vi'im*] were in charge of the articles used for the service; they had to keep records of them when bringing them in and out. ²⁹ Others were in charge of the equipment, the holy utensils, the fine flour, the wine, the olive oil, the frankincense and the spices. ³⁰ Some of the sons of the *cohanim* mixed together the ingredients for the perfumes. ³¹ Mattityah, one of the *L'vi'im*, who was the firstborn of Shalum the Korchi, was permanently in charge of baking operations. ³² Some of their kinsmen, from the descendants of the K'hati, were in charge of preparing the showbread every *Shabbat*. ³³ Also there were the singers, heads of fathers' clans among the *L'vi'im*. They lived in the accommodations and were free from other kinds of service, for they were employed in their own work day and night. ³⁴ These were heads of fathers' clans among the *L'vi'im*, according to their generations, and they were leaders; they lived in Yerushalayim.

³⁵ In Giv'on lived the father of Giv'on, Ye'i'el, whose his wife's name was Ma'akhah; ³⁶ and his firstborn son 'Avdon, Tzur, Kish, Ba'al, Ner, Nadav, ³⁷ G'dor, Achyo, Z'kharyah and Miklot. ³⁸ Miklot fathered Shim'am. In contrast with some of their kinsmen, they and their families lived in Yerushalayim.

³⁹ Ner fathered Kish; Kish fathered Sha'ul; and Sha'ul fathered Y'honatan, Malkishua, Avinadav and Eshba'al. ⁴⁰ The son of Y'honatan was M'riv-Ba'al, and M'riv-Ba'al fathered Mikhah. ⁴¹ The sons of Mikhah were: Piton, Melekh and Ta'rea. ⁴² Achaz fathered Ya'ra; Ya'ra fathered 'Alemet, 'Azmavet and Zimri; Zimri fathered Motza; ⁴³ and Motza fathered Bin'a. His son was Rafah, his son El'asah and his son Atzel. ⁴⁴ Atzel had six sons, whose names were: 'Azrikam, Bokhru, Yishma'el, Sh'aryah, 'Ovadyah and Hanan; all these were sons of Atzel.

10 ¹ Now the P'lishtim pressed their attack on Isra'el; and the men of Isra'el fled before the P'lishtim, leaving their dead on Mount Gilboa. ² The P'lishtim pursued Sha'ul; overtook him and his sons; and the P'lishtim killed Y'honatan, Avinadav and Malkishua, the sons of Sha'ul. ³ The fighting went hard against Sha'ul; then the archers overtook and wounded him, so that he was in agony. ⁴ Sha'ul said to his armor-bearer, "Draw your sword and run me through with it. Otherwise, these uncircumcised men will come and make sport of me." But his armor-bearer refused; he was too frightened. So Sha'ul took his sword and fell on it. ⁵ When his armor-bearer saw that Sha'ul was dead, he too fell on his own sword and died. ⁶ Thus Sha'ul, his three sons and all his household died together.

⁷ When all the men of Isra'el who were in the valley saw them fleeing and that Sha'ul and his sons were dead, they abandoned their cities and fled; then the P'lishtim came and lived in them.

⁸ The following day, when the P'lishtim came to strip the dead, they found Sha'ul and his sons lying dead on Mount Gilboa. ⁹ They stripped him, then took his head and his armor and sent them all over the territory of the P'lishtim to carry the news to their idols and to the people. ¹⁰ They put his armor in the temple of their gods and fastened his skull to the temple of Dagon. ¹¹ When everyone in Yavesh-Gil'ad heard all that the P'lishtim had done to Sha'ul, ¹² all their warriors set out, took away the body of Sha'ul and the bodies of his sons, brought them to Yavesh, buried their bones under the pistachio tree in Yavesh and fasted seven days.

¹³ So Sha'ul died for the transgression he committed against ADONAI, because of the word of ADONAI that he did not keep and because he sought the counsel of a spirit ¹⁴ instead of consulting ADONAI. Therefore ADONAI put him to death and turned the rulership over to David the son of Yishai.

11 ¹ Then all Isra'el gathered themselves to David in Hevron and said, "Here, we are your own flesh and bone. ² In the past, even when Sha'ul was king, it was you who led Isra'el's military campaigns; and ADONAI your God said to you, 'You will shepherd my people Isra'el, and you will be chief over my people Isra'el.'" ³ So all the leaders of Isra'el came to the king in Hevron; and David made a covenant with them in Hevron in the presence of ADONAI. Then they anointed David king over Isra'el, as ADONAI had said through Sh'mu'el.

⁴ David and all Isra'el went to Yerushalayim, also known as Y'vus; and the Y'vusi, the inhabitants of that region, were there. ⁵ The inhabitants of Y'vus taunted David by saying, "You won't get in here!" Nevertheless, David captured the stronghold of Tziyon, also known now as the City of David. ⁶ David said, "Whoever attacks the Y'vusi first will be commander-in-chief." Yo'av the son of Tz'ruyah attacked first and was made commander.

⁷ David lived in the stronghold; therefore they called it the City of David. ⁸ David built up the city around it, starting at the Millo [earth rampart] and going on around; while Yo'av repaired the rest of the city. ⁹ David grew greater and greater, because ADONAI-*Tzva'ot* was with him.

¹⁰ These are David's chief warriors, who, under his rulership, joined forces with him and with all Isra'el to make him king, as ADONAI had said concerning Isra'el; ¹¹ here is the list of David's warrior-heroes:

Yashov'am son of a Hakhmoni, the chief officer; he is the one who raised his spear against 300 men and killed them in a single encounter.

¹² After him was El'azar the son of Dodo the Achochi, one of the three warriors. ¹³ He was with David at Pas-Damim, where the P'lishtim had assembled for battle. There was a plot of ground full of barley; and when the people fled from the P'lishtim, ¹⁴ they stood in the middle of the plot and defended it, killing the P'lishtim; and ADONAI saved them with a great victory.

¹⁵ Three of the thirty leaders went down to the rock and came to David during harvest season at the cave of 'Adulam when the army of the P'lishtim had set up camp in the Refa'im Valley. ¹⁶ At that time David was in the fortress, and the garrison of the P'lishtim was in Beit-Lechem. ¹⁷ David had a craving and said, "I wish someone could give me water to drink from the well by the gate of Beit-Lechem!" ¹⁸ The three broke through the army of the P'lishtim, drew water from the well by the gate of Beit-Lechem, took it and brought it to David. But David would not drink it; instead, he poured it out to ADONAI ¹⁹ and said, "My God forbid that I should do such a thing! Am I to drink the blood of these men who went and put their lives in jeopardy? They risked their lives to bring it!" — and he would not consent to drink it. These are the things the three warrior-heroes did.

²⁰ Avishai the brother of Yo'av was chief of these three. He raised his spear against 300 men and killed them; thus he had a reputation even among the three. ²¹ Of the three in the second rank he had the most honor and was therefore made their leader; however, he did not achieve the status of the first three.

²² B'nayah the son of Y'hoyada, the son of a valiant man of Kavtze'el, was a man of many exploits. He struck down two lion-hearted men of Mo'av. One day when it was snowing, he went down into a pit and killed a lion. ²³ Here is how he killed an Egyptian, a man who was very tall, seven-and-a-half feet: the Egyptian had a spear in his hand the size of a weaver's beam; he went down to him with only a stick, seized the spear from the Egyptian's hand and killed him with his own spear. ²⁴ These are things that B'nayah the son of Y'hoyada did that earned him a name among the three warrior-heroes. ²⁵ He had more honor than the thirty, but he did not achieve the status of the first three. David put him in command of his personal guard.

²⁶ There were also these warrior-heroes:

'Asah'el the brother of Yo'av,
Elchanan the son of Dodo, from Beit-Lechem,
²⁷   Shammah the Harori,
Heletz the P'loni,
²⁸   'Ira son of 'Ikesh from T'koa,
Avi'ezer from 'Anatot,

29   Sibkhai the Hushati,
    'Ilai the Achochi,
30   Mahrai the N'tofati,
    Heled the son of Ba'anah the N'tofati,
31   Ittai the son of Rivai from Giv'ah, from the descendants of Binyamin,
    B'nayahu from Pir'aton,
32   Hurai from the *vadi*s of Ga'ash,
    Avi'el the 'Arvati,
33   'Azmavet the Bacharumi,
    Elyachba the Sha'alvoni,
34   the sons of Hashem the Gizoni,
    Y'honatan the son of Shageh the Harari,
35   Achi'am the son of Sakhar the Harari,
    Elifal the son of Ur,
36   Hefer the M'kherati,
    Achiyah the P'loni,
37   Hetzro the Karmeli,
    Na'arai the son of Ezbai,
38   Yo'el the brother of Natan,
    Mivchar the son of Hagri,
39   Tzelek the 'Amoni,
    Nachrai the Be'eroti, armor-bearer of Yo'av the son of Tz'ruyah,
40   'Ira the Yitri,
    Garev the Yitri,
41   Uriyah the Hitti,
    Zavad the son of Achlai,
42   'Adina the son of Shiza the Re'uveni, a leader among the Re'uveni,
    and thirty with him,
43   Hanan the son of Ma'akhah,
    Yoshafat the Mitni,
44   'Uziyah the 'Asht'rati
    Shama and Ye'i'el the sons of Hotam the 'Aro'eri,
45   Y'dia'el the son of Shimri,
    Yocha his brother, the Titzi,
46   Eli'el from Machavim,
    Yerivai and Yoshavyah the sons of Elna'am,
    Yitmah the Mo'avi,
47   Eli'el,
    'Oved,
    and Ya'asi'el from M'tzovayah.

12 ¹ Following are the men who joined David at Ziklag while he was still being kept away from Sha'ul the son of Kish; they were among the warriors who helped him fight his battles. ² They were archers who could use either hand to sling stones or shoot arrows from a bow; they were Sha'ul's kinsmen from Binyamin. ³ Their leader was Achi'ezer, then Yo'ash, the sons of Sh'ma'ah the Giv'ati, Y'zi'el, Pelet, the sons of 'Azmavet, B'rakhah, Yehu from 'Anatot, ⁴ Yishma'yah the Giv'oni, one of the strongest of the thirty and commander of the thirty, ⁵⁽⁴ᵇ⁾ Yirmeyah, Yachzi'el, Yochanan, Yozavad from G'derah, ⁶⁽⁵⁾ El'uzai, Yerimot, B'alyah, Sh'maryah, Sh'fatyah the Harufi, ⁷⁽⁶⁾ Elkanah, Yishiyahu, 'Azar'el, Yo'ezer, Yashov'am the Korchi, ⁸⁽⁷⁾ and Yo'elah and Z'vadyah the sons of Yerocham from G'dor.

⁹⁽⁸⁾ From the Gadi a number of strong, brave, trained fighting men defected to David at the fortress in the desert. They could handle shield and spear, they were as fierce as lions, and they were as fast as deer on the hills: ¹⁰⁽⁹⁾ 'Ezer was the leader, 'Ovadyah was second, Eli'av third, ¹¹⁽¹⁰⁾ Mishmanah fourth, Yirmeyah fifth, ¹²⁽¹¹⁾ 'Atai sixth, Eli'el seventh, ¹³⁽¹²⁾ Yochanan eighth, Elzavad ninth, ¹⁴⁽¹³⁾ Yirmeyah tenth, and Makhbanai eleventh. ¹⁵⁽¹⁴⁾ These descendants of Gad were army commanders; the least of them was worth a hundred, and the greatest worth a thousand. ¹⁶⁽¹⁵⁾ These are the men who crossed the Yarden during the first month, when it had overflowed all its banks, and drove out all those who lived in the valleys, both to the east and to the west.

¹⁷⁽¹⁶⁾ From the descendants of Binyamin and Y'hudah a number came to David at the fortress. ¹⁸⁽¹⁷⁾ When David went out to meet them, he said, "If you are coming to me in peace to help me, my heart will be bonded to yours. But if you are coming to betray me to my enemies, then, since I have done nothing wrong, may the God of our fathers see it and judge." ¹⁹⁽¹⁸⁾ Then the Spirit covered 'Amasai the chief commander, and he said:

"We are yours, David;
on your side, son of Yishai!
Peace, peace to you,
and peace to your helpers;
for your God helps you."

David welcomed them and made them senior officers.

²⁰⁽¹⁹⁾ From M'nasheh some defected to David when he was about to go with the P'lishtim to fight against Sha'ul; but they ended up not helping them; because the rulers of the P'lishtim, after consultation, sent David away, saying, "He will defect to his master Sha'ul at the cost of our heads." ²¹⁽²⁰⁾ As he was on his way to Ziklag, those who defected to him from M'nasheh included 'Adnach, Yozavad, Y'dia'el, Mikha'el, Yozavad, Elihu and Tziltai, commanders of thousands from M'nasheh. ²²⁽²¹⁾ They helped David against the raiding band, for they were all strong, brave men who were commanders in the army.

²³⁽²²⁾ Indeed, reinforcements to assist David reached him daily, until there was a great army, like the army of God. ²⁴⁽²³⁾ Following are the numbers of those who came armed for war to David in Hevron, in order to transfer to him the kingdom of Sha'ul, according to what ADONAI had said.

²⁵⁽²⁴⁾ The descendants of Y'hudah bearing shields and spears numbered 6,800, armed for war.

²⁶⁽²⁵⁾ Of the descendants of Shim'on, strong, brave men for war, there were 7,100.

²⁷⁽²⁶⁾ Of the descendants of Levi, there were 4,600. ²⁸⁽²⁷⁾ Y'hoyada was the leader of the house of Aharon, and with him were 3,700; ²⁹⁽²⁸⁾ also Tzadok, a young man, strong and brave, with twenty-two commanders from his father's family.

³⁰⁽²⁹⁾ Of the descendants of Binyamin the kinsmen of Sha'ul, there were 3,000; for up until then, the majority of them had remained loyal to the house of Sha'ul.

³¹⁽³⁰⁾ Of the descendants of Efrayim, there were 20,800 strong, brave men, well known in their fathers' families.

³²⁽³¹⁾ Of the half-tribe of M'nasheh, 18,000 were designated by name to come and make David king.

³³⁽³²⁾ Of the descendants of Yissakhar, men who understood the times and knew what Isra'el ought to do, there were 200 leaders, and all their kinsmen were under their command.

³⁴⁽³³⁾ Of Z'vulun, 50,000 men were fit for military service, experienced in war and able to use all kinds of weapons; they were brave, and none was doubleminded.

³⁵⁽³⁴⁾ Of Naftali, there were 1,000 officers, and with them 37,000 troops having shields and spears.

³⁶⁽³⁵⁾ Of Dan, 28,600 were experienced in war.

³⁷⁽³⁶⁾ Of Asher, 40,000 men were fit for military service and experienced in war.

³⁸⁽³⁷⁾ On the other side of the Yarden, from the Re'uveni, the Gadi and the half-tribe of M'nasheh, there were 120,000 with all kinds of weapons for battle.

³⁹⁽³⁸⁾ All these soldiers who were experienced in war came to Hevron whole-heartedly to make David king over all Isra'el, and all the rest from Isra'el were single-hearted in wanting to make David king. ⁴⁰⁽³⁹⁾ They remained there with David for three days, eating and drinking, for their kinsmen had prepared for them. ⁴¹⁽⁴⁰⁾ Moreover, those who were near them — and even those as far as Yissakhar, Z'vulun and Naftali — brought food on donkeys, camels, mules and oxen: baked goods, fig cakes, clusters of raisins, wine, oil, and oxen and sheep in abundance; for there was joy in Isra'el.

13 ¹ David consulted with the commanders of thousands and of hundreds — with every leader. ² Then David said to the entire assembly of Isra'el, "If it seems good to you, and if it is the will of ADONAI our God, let's send messengers to the rest of our kinsmen in the land of Isra'el, and also to the *cohanim* and *L'vi'im* in their cities with surrounding open land, asking them to join us; ³ and let's bring back the ark of our God to ourselves, since we didn't go after it when Sha'ul was king." ⁴ The whole assembly said they would do this, for in the view of all the people it seemed right.

⁵ So David summoned all Isra'el to come together, from Shichor in Egypt all the way to the entrance of Hamat, to bring the ark of God from Kiryat-Ye'arim. ⁶ David went up with all Isra'el to Ba'alah, that is, Kiryat-Ye'arim, which belonged to Y'hudah, to bring up from there the ark of God, ADONAI, who is enthroned above the *k'ruvim*, bearing the Name. ⁷ They set the ark of God on a new cart from the house of Avinadav, with 'Uza and Achyo, the sons of Avinadav, driving the cart. ⁸ David and all Isra'el celebrated in the presence of God with all their strength, with songs, lyres, lutes, tambourines, cymbals and trumpets.

⁹ When they arrived at Kidon's threshing-floor, the oxen stumbled; and 'Uza put out his hand to steady the ark. ¹⁰ But ADONAI's anger blazed up against 'Uza, and he struck him down, because he had put out his hand and touched the ark, so that he died there before God. ¹¹ It upset David that ADONAI had broken out against 'Uza; that place has been called Peretz-'Uza [breaking-out of 'Uza] ever since. ¹² That day, God frightened David; he asked, "How can I bring the ark of God to me?"

¹³ So David didn't bring the ark into the City of David; rather, David carried it aside into the house of 'Oved-'Edom the Gitti. ¹⁴ The ark of God stayed with the family of 'Oved-'Edom the Gitti in his house for three months; and *Adonai* blessed the household of 'Oved-'Edom and all he had.

14 ¹ Huram king of Tzor sent envoys to David with cedar logs, and with them stonemasons and carpenters, to build him a palace. ² David then knew that *Adonai* had set him up as king over Isra'el; because, for the sake of his people Isra'el, his royal power had been greatly increased.

³ David took more concubines and wives in Yerushalayim, and David became father of more sons and daughters. ⁴ Here are the names of the children born to him in Yerushalayim: Shamua, Shovav, Natan, Shlomo, ⁵ Yivchar, Elishua, Elpelet, ⁶ Nogah, Nefeg, Yafia, ⁷ Elishama, Be'elyada and Elifelet.

⁸ When the P'lishtim heard that David had been anointed king over all Isra'el, all the P'lishtim went up in search of David. On hearing of it, David went to attack them. ⁹ Now the P'lishtim came and made a raid in the Refa'im Valley. ¹⁰ David consulted God, asking, "Should I attack the P'lishtim? Will you hand them over to me?" *Adonai* answered David, "Attack; I will hand them over to you." ¹¹ So they went up to Ba'al-P'ratzim, and David defeated them there. David said, "God has broken through my enemies by my power like a river breaking through its banks." This is why they called the place Ba'al-P'ratzim [Lord of breaking through]. ¹² The P'lishtim had left their gods there, so David gave an order, and they were burned up completely.

¹³ The P'lishtim came up again and raided the valley. ¹⁴ David consulted God again, but God told him, "Don't attack them! Turn away from them, and engage them opposite the balsam trees. ¹⁵ When you hear the sound of marching in the tops of the balsam trees, move out, and attack; because God has gone out ahead of you to defeat the army of the P'lishtim." ¹⁶ David did as God had ordered him to do and pursued his attack on the army of the P'lishtim from Giv'on to Gezer.

¹⁷ So David's reputation spread to all countries, and *Adonai* brought the fear of him on all nations.

15 ¹ David erected buildings for himself in the City of David, prepared a place for the ark of God, and set up a tent for it. ² Then David said, "No one but the *L'vi'im* should carry the ark of God, because *Adonai* chose them to carry the ark of *Adonai* and to serve him forever."

³ David assembled all Isra'el in Yerushalayim to bring the ark of *Adonai* up to its place, which he had prepared for it. ⁴ David gathered together the descendants of Aharon and the *L'vi'im*: ⁵ from the descendants of K'hat: Uri'el the chief, and 120 of his kinsmen; ⁶ from the descendants of M'rari: 'Asayah the chief, and 220 of his kinsmen; ⁷ from the descendants of Gershom: Yo'el the chief, and 130 of his kinsmen; ⁸ from the descendants of Elitzafan: Sh'ma'yah the chief, and 200 of his kinsmen; ⁹ from the descendants of Hevron: Eli'el the chief, and eighty of his kinsmen; ¹⁰ and from the descendants of 'Uzi'el: 'Amminadav the chief, and 112 of his kinsmen.

¹¹ David called for Tzadok and Evyatar the *cohanim* and for the *L'vi'im* — Uri'el, 'Asayah, Yo'el, Sh'ma'yah, Eli'el and 'Amminadav — ¹² and said to them, "You are the clan leaders of the *L'vi'im*. Consecrate yourselves, both you and your kinsmen,

to bring the ark of ADONAI the God of Isra'el up to the place I have prepared for it. ¹³ It's because you weren't there the first time that ADONAI our God broke out against us. We didn't seek him out according to the rule." ¹⁴ So the *cohanim* and *L'vi'im* consecrated themselves to bring up the ark of ADONAI the God of Isra'el; ¹⁵ and the *L'vi'im* carried the ark of God on their shoulders with the poles on it, as Moshe had ordered, according to what ADONAI had said.

¹⁶ David spoke to the chief of the *L'vi'im* to appoint their kinsmen to be singers making use of musical instruments — lutes, lyres and cymbals — to play loudly and raise sounds of joy. ¹⁷ So the *L'vi'im* appointed Heman the son of Yo'el; of his kinsmen, Asaf the son of Berekhyahu; of the descendants of M'rari their kinsmen, Eitan the son of Kushayahu; ¹⁸ and with them their second-degree kinsmen Z'kharyahu, Ben, Ya'azi'el, Sh'miramot, Yechi'el, 'Uni, Eli'av, B'nayahu, Ma'aseiyahu, Mattityahu, Elif'lehu, Mikneyahu, with 'Oved-Edom and Ye'i'el the gatekeepers. ¹⁹ The singers Heman, Asaf and Eitan were appointed to sound the bronze cymbals. ²⁰ Z'kharyahu, 'Azi'el, Sh'miramot, Yechi'el, 'Uni, Eli'av, Ma'aseiyahu and B'nayahu were to play the lutes for *'alamot* [high-pitched music?]. ²¹ Mattityahu, Elif'lehu, Mikneyahu, 'Oved-Edom, Ye'i'el and 'Azazyahu were to play lyres to lead the *sh'minit* [low-pitched music?]. ²² K'nanyahu, chief of the *L'vi'im*, was in charge of the singing; he was put in charge of the singing because he was skillful at it. ²³ Berekhyahu and Elkanah were gatekeepers for the ark. ²⁴ Sh'vanyahu, Yoshafat, N'tan'el, 'Amasai, Z'kharyahu, B'nayahu and Eli'ezer the *cohanim* blew the trumpets in front of the ark of God. 'Oved-Edom and Yechiyah were gatekeepers for the ark.

²⁵ So David, the leaders of Isra'el and the commanders over thousands went to bring up the ark for the covenant of ADONAI out from the house of 'Oved-Edom with joy. ²⁶ Since God was helping the *L'vi'im* who were carrying the ark for the covenant of ADONAI, they sacrificed seven young bulls and seven rams. ²⁷ David, all the *L'vi'im* bearing the ark, the singers and K'nanyah the music leader for the singers were all wearing linen cloaks; and David was also wearing a linen ritual vest. ²⁸ So all Isra'el brought up the ark for the covenant of ADONAI with shouting; blowing on *shofar*s and trumpets; and cymbals sounding with lutes and lyres. ²⁹ As the ark for the covenant of ADONAI entered the City of David, Mikhal the daughter of Sha'ul, watching from the window, saw King David dancing and celebrating; and she was filled with contempt for him.

16 ¹ They brought the ark of God in and put it in the tent that David had set up for it; and they offered burnt offerings and peace offerings before God. ² When David had finished offering the burnt offering and peace offerings, he blessed the people in the name of ADONAI. ³ Then he distributed to everyone in Isra'el, to everyone there, both men and women, a loaf of bread, a portion of meat and a raisin cake.

⁴ He appointed certain *L'vi'im* to serve in front of the ark of ADONAI, to celebrate, and to thank and praise ADONAI the God of Isra'el: ⁵ Asaf, the leader; assisting him, Z'kharyah; then Ye'i'el, Sh'miramot, Yechi'el, Mattityahu, Eli'av, B'nayahu, 'Oved-Edom and Ye'i'el playing lutes and lyres, while Asaf played cymbals. ⁶ B'nayah and Yachzi'el the *cohanim* blew the trumpets continually before the ark for the covenant of God. ⁷ It was on that same day that David first ordered that thanks be given to ADONAI through Asaf and his kinsmen:

8   Give thanks to *Adonai*! Call on his name!
    Make his deeds known among the peoples.
9   Sing to him, sing praises to him!
    Talk about all his wonders.
10 Glory in his holy name;
    let those seeking *Adonai* have joyful hearts.
11 Seek *Adonai* and his strength;
    always seek his presence.
12 Remember the wonders he has done,
    his signs and his spoken judgments.

13 You descendants of Isra'el his servant,
    you offspring of Ya'akov, his chosen ones:
14 he is *Adonai* our God;
    his judgments are everywhere on earth.
15 Remember his covenant forever,
    the word he commanded to a thousand generations,
16 the covenant he made with Avraham;
    the oath he swore to Yitz'chak
17 and established as a law for Ya'akov,
    for Isra'el as an everlasting covenant:
18 "To you I will give the land of Kena'an
    as your allotted heritage."

19 When you were but few in number,
    and not only few, but aliens there too,
20 wandering from nation to nation,
    from this kingdom to that people,
21 he allowed no one to oppress them.
    Yes, for their sakes he rebuked even kings:
22 "Don't touch my anointed ones
    or do my prophets harm!"

23 Sing to *Adonai*, all the earth!
    Proclaim his victory day after day!
24 Declare his glory among the nations,
    his wonders among all peoples!

25 For *Adonai* is great, and greatly to be praised;
    he is to be feared more than all gods.
26 For all the gods of the peoples are nothing,
    but *Adonai* made the heavens.
27 In his presence are honor and majesty;
    in his place, strength and joy.

28 Give *Adonai* his due, you families from the peoples,
    give *Adonai* his due of glory and strength;

29   give ADONAI the glory due to his name;
bring an offering, and come into his presence.
Worship ADONAI in splendid, holy attire.

30   Tremble before him, all the earth!
The world is firmly established, immovable.

31   Let the heavens rejoice; let the earth be glad;
let them say among the nations, "ADONAI is king!"

32   Let the sea roar, and everything in it;
let the fields exult, and all that is in them.

33   Then the trees in the forest will sing before ADONAI,
because he has come to judge the earth.

34   Give thanks to ADONAI; for he is good,
for his grace continues forever.

35   Say: "Save us, God who can save us!
Gather and rescue us from the nations;
so that we can thank your holy name
and glory in praising you.

36   Blessed be ADONAI, the God of Isra'el,
from eternity past to eternity future!"

All the people said, "Amen!" and praised ADONAI.

³⁷ So, there before the ark for the covenant of ADONAI, David left Asaf and his kinsmen to perform the service regularly before the ark, as each day's work required; ³⁸ also 'Oved-Edom with their kinsmen, sixty-eight of them — 'Oved-Edom the son of Y'dutun and Hosah were gatekeepers.

³⁹ He left Tzadok the *cohen* with his kinsmen before the tabernacle of ADONAI at the high place in Giv'on ⁴⁰ to offer burnt offerings to ADONAI every morning and evening on the altar for burnt offerings, according to everything written in the *Torah* of ADONAI, which he gave to Isra'el. ⁴¹ With them were Heman and Y'dutun and the rest who were chosen and assigned by name to give thanks to ADONAI, because his grace continues forever. ⁴² With them were Heman and Y'dutun to play trumpets and cymbals, also instruments for the songs about God; while the sons of Y'dutun were assigned to the gate.

⁴³ Then the people all left for their homes, and David returned to bless his household.

17 ¹ After David had been living in his palace awhile, he said to Natan the prophet, "Here, I'm living in a cedar-wood palace; but the ark for the covenant of ADONAI is kept under a tent!" ² Natan said to David, "Go, do everything that is in your heart, for God is with you."

³ But that same night the word of God came to Natan: ⁴ "Go, and tell David my servant that this is what ADONAI says: 'You are not to build me a house to live in, ⁵ because from the day I brought up Isra'el until today, I never lived in a house; rather, I've gone from tent to tent and from one tabernacle to another. ⁶ Everywhere I traveled with all Isra'el, did I ever speak a word to any of the judges of Isra'el, whom I ordered to shepherd my people Isra'el, asking, "Why haven't you built me a cedar-wood house?"'

⁷ "Therefore say to my servant David that this is what ADONAI-*Tzva'ot* says: 'I took you from the sheep-yards, from following the sheep, to make you chief over my people Isra'el. ⁸ I have been with you wherever you went, I have destroyed all your enemies ahead of you; and I am making your reputation like the reputations of the greatest people on earth. ⁹ I will assign a place to my people Isra'el; I will plant them there, so that they can live in their own place without being disturbed any more. The wicked will no longer devastate them, as they did at the beginning, ¹⁰ and as they did from the time I ordered judges to be over my people Isra'el; instead, I will subdue all your enemies.

"'Moreover, I tell you that ADONAI will make you a house. ¹¹ When your days come to an end and you go to be with your ancestors, I will establish one of your descendants to succeed you, one of your own sons; and I will set up his rulership. ¹² He will build me a house, and I will establish his throne forever. ¹³ I will be a father for him, and he will be a son for me; I will not take my grace away from him, as I took it away from your predecessor. ¹⁴ Rather, I will maintain him in my house and in my kingdom forever; and his throne will be set up forever.'" ¹⁵ Natan told David all of these words and described this entire vision.

¹⁶ Then David went in, sat before ADONAI and said, "Who am I, ADONAI, God, and what is my family, that has caused you to bring me this far? ¹⁷ Yet in your view, God, even this was but a small thing; so you have said that your servant's dynasty will continue on into the distant future. You have regarded me, ADONAI, God, as a man of high rank. ¹⁸ What more can David say to you about the honor you are bestowing on your servant? For you know your servant intimately. ¹⁹ ADONAI, it is for your servant's sake and in accordance with your own heart that you have done all this greatness and revealed all these great things. ²⁰ ADONAI, there is no one like you, and there is no God besides you — everything we have heard confirms that. ²¹ Who can be compared with your people Isra'el? What other nation on earth did God set out to redeem and turn into a people for himself? You made yourself a reputation by doing great and terrifying things, as you drove out the nations from before your people, whom you redeemed from Egypt. ²² For you made your people Isra'el your people forever; and you, ADONAI, became their God. ²³ So now, ADONAI, let the word that you spoke concerning your servant and his house be confirmed forever; do what you have promised. ²⁴ May your name be confirmed and magnified forever; so that it will be said, 'ADONAI-*Tzva'ot* is the God of Isra'el and the God for Isra'el, and the dynasty of David your servant will be set up in your presence.' ²⁵ For you, my God, have disclosed to your servant that you will build him a house. This is why your servant has the courage to pray to you. ²⁶ Now, ADONAI, you are God; and you have made this wonderful promise to your servant; ²⁷ and now it has pleased you to bless the family of your servant and thereby cause it to continue forever in your presence. For you, ADONAI, have blessed, and it is blessed forever."

18 ¹ Some time afterwards, David attacked the P'lishtim and subdued them; David took Gat and its villages out of the hands of the P'lishtim. ² He also defeated Mo'av, so that the people of Mo'av became subjects of David and paid tribute.

³ David, on his way to establish his dominion as far as the Euphrates River, also defeated Hadar'ezer king of Tzovah near Hamat. ⁴ David captured 1,000 chariots, 7,000 horsemen and 20,000 foot soldiers. He reserved enough horses for 100 chariots

and disabled the rest. ⁵ When the people of Aram from Dammesek came to the aid of Hadar'ezer king of Tzovah, David killed 22,000 men of Aram. ⁶ Then David put [garrisons] among the people of Aram in Dammesek; Aram became subject to David and paid tribute. ADONAI gave victory to David wherever he went.

⁷ David took the gold shields which Hadar'ezer's servants were wearing and brought them to Yerushalayim. ⁸ From Tivchat and Kun, cities of Hadar'ezer, King David took a great quantity of bronze, which Shlomo used to make the bronze "Sea," the columns and various bronze articles.

⁹ When To'u king of Hamat heard that David had defeated the entire army of Hadar'ezer king of Tzovah, ¹⁰ he sent Hadoram his son to King David to greet and congratulate him on fighting and defeating Hadar'ezer — for Hadar'ezer had been at war with To'u — and [he sent] all kinds of articles made of silver, gold and bronze, ¹¹ which King David dedicated to ADONAI, along with the silver and gold that he had carried off from all the nations — from Edom, Mo'av, the people of 'Amon, the P'lishtim and 'Amalek. ¹² Moreover, Avishai the son of Tz'ruyah killed 18,000 men from Edom in the Salt Valley. ¹³ David stationed garrisons in Edom, and all the people of Edom became subject to him. ADONAI gave victory to David wherever he went.

¹⁴ David ruled over all Isra'el; he administered law and justice for all his people. ¹⁵ Yo'av the son of Tz'ruyah was commander of the army, Y'hoshafat the son of Achilud was chief adviser, ¹⁶ Tzadok the son of Achituv and Avimelekh the son of Evyatar were *cohanim*, Shavsha was secretary, ¹⁷ B'nayahu the son of Y'hoyada was in charge of the K'reti and P'leti [serving as the king's bodyguards], and David's sons were the king's chief personal advisers.

19 ¹ Some time later, when Nachash the king of the people of 'Amon died, his son became king in his place. ² David said, "I will be kind to Hanun the son of Nachash, because his father showed grace to me." So David sent messengers to comfort him about his father.

David's servants entered the territory of the people of 'Amon to go to Hanun and comfort him; ³ but the leaders of the people of 'Amon said to Hanun, "Do you really think David is honoring your father by sending people to comfort you? Haven't his servants come to you in order to look the city over, overthrow it and reconnoiter the land?" ⁴ So Hanun took David's servants, shaved them, cut off their clothes halfway up, at their hips, and then sent them away. ⁵ Some people reported to David how the men had been treated. He sent a delegation to meet them, because the men had been deeply humiliated. The king said, "Stay in Yericho until your beards have grown back, and then return."

⁶ Aware that they had made themselves utterly abhorrent to David, Hanun and the people of 'Amon sent thirty-three tons of silver to hire chariots and horsemen from Aram-Naharayim, Aram-Ma'akhah and Tzovah. ⁷ They hired 32,000 chariots, as well as the king of Ma'akhah with his people, who came and pitched their camp in front of Meidva. Then the people of 'Amon assembled themselves from their cities and went out to fight. ⁸ When David heard of it, he sent Yo'av with his entire army of trained soldiers.

⁹ The army of 'Amon came out and went into battle formation at the city gate, while the kings who had come were alone in the countryside. ¹⁰ When Yo'av saw that he would be fighting on two fronts, ahead and behind, he chose the best troops of

Isra'el to deploy against Aram; ¹¹ while the rest of the army he put under the command of Avishai his brother to deploy against the army of 'Amon. ¹² He said, "If Aram is too strong for me, you help me; but if the army of 'Amon is too strong for you, then I will help you. ¹³ Take courage, and let's be strong for the sake of our people and the cities of our God. May *Adonai* do what seems good to him."

¹⁴ So Yo'av and the people with him went to engage Aram in battle, and they fled before him. ¹⁵ When the people of 'Amon saw that Aram had fled, they likewise fled before Avishai his brother and retreated into the city. Then Yo'av went to Yerushalayim.

¹⁶ When Aram saw that Isra'el had gotten the better of them, they sent messengers and brought out the people of Aram who lived beyond the [Euphrates] River, with Shofakh the commander of Hadar'ezer's army at their head. ¹⁷ It was reported to David; so he gathered all Isra'el together and crossed the Yarden to engage them. David deployed his forces for battle against Aram; and after he had done so, fought them. ¹⁸ But Aram fled before Isra'el; David killed 7,000 chariot-drivers and 40,000 foot soldiers from Aram; and he killed Shofakh the commander of the army. ¹⁹ When all Hadar'ezer's servants saw that they had been defeated by Isra'el, they made peace with David and became his subjects; and Aram would no longer help the people of 'Amon.

20 ¹ In the spring, at the time when kings go out to war, Yo'av led the army out in force and laid waste to the country of the people of 'Amon; then he came and laid siege to Rabbah. But David stayed in Yerushalayim, while Yo'av attacked Rabbah and destroyed it. ² David took the crown off Malkam's head and found it to weigh sixty-six pounds, with its gold and precious stones; and it was placed on David's head. He carried off great quantities of spoil from the city. ³ In addition, he brought out the people who were in it and set them to work with saws, iron harrows and axes. This is what he did to all the cities of the people of 'Amon. Then David and all the people returned to Yerushalayim.

⁴ A while after this there was war at Gezer with the P'lishtim. Sibkhai the Hushati killed Sipai, one of the giants, and they were defeated. ⁵ There was more war with the P'lishtim; and Elchanan the son of Ya'ir killed Lachmi the brother of Golyat the Gitti, who had a spear with a shaft like a weaver's beam. ⁶ There was again war at Gat, where there was a very tall man whose fingers and toes numbered twenty-four, six [fingers on each hand] and six [toes on each foot]; and he too was a son of the giant. ⁷ When he mocked Isra'el, Y'honatan the son of Shim'a David's brother killed him. ⁸ These were sons of the giant in Gat; they fell at the hands of David and his servants.

21 ¹ The Adversary [Hebrew: *Satan*] now rose up against Isra'el and incited David to take a census of Isra'el. ² David said to Yo'av and the leaders of the people, "Go, take a census of Isra'el from Be'er-Sheva to Dan; then report to me, so that I can know how many of them there are." ³ Yo'av said, "May *Adonai* make his people a hundred times as many as they are now! But, my lord the king, aren't they all my lord's servants in any case? Why does my lord the king require this? Why should he bring guilt upon Isra'el?" ⁴ Nevertheless, the king's word prevailed against Yo'av. So Yo'av left and went through all Isra'el, after which he came to Yerushalayim.

⁵ Yo'av reported the results of the census to David: in Isra'el were 1,100,000 men who could handle a sword, while Y'hudah had 470,000 men who could handle a sword. ⁶ But he didn't count Levi and Binyamin among them, because the king's order was hateful to Yo'av.

⁷ God was displeased with this and therefore punished Isra'el. ⁸ David said to God, "I have greatly sinned by doing this. But now, please! Put aside your servant's sin, for I have done a very foolish thing." ⁹ ADONAI spoke to Gad, David's seer: ¹⁰ "Go and tell David that ADONAI says, 'I am offering you a choice of three punishments: choose one of them, and I will execute it against you.'" ¹¹ Gad came to David and said to him, "Take your choice: ¹² three years of famine; or three months of being swept away by your enemies, while your enemies' sword overwhelms you; or three days of ADONAI's sword — plague in the land, with the angel of ADONAI destroying everywhere in Isra'el's territory. Now think about what answer I should give to the one who sent me."

¹³ David said to Gad, "This is very hard for me. Let me fall into the hand of ADONAI, because his mercies are very great, rather than have me fall into the hand of man." ¹⁴ So ADONAI sent a plague on Isra'el; 70,000 of the people of Isra'el died.

¹⁵ God also sent an angel to destroy Yerushalayim, but when he was about to carry out the destruction, ADONAI saw it and changed his mind about causing such distress; so he said to the destroying angel, "Enough! Now withdraw your hand." The angel of ADONAI was standing at the threshing-floor of Ornan the Y'vusi. ¹⁶ David raised his eyes and saw the angel of ADONAI standing between the earth and the sky, and in his hand was a drawn sword stretched out over Yerushalayim. Then David and the leaders, wearing sackcloth, fell on their faces. ¹⁷ David said to God, "Wasn't it I who ordered the census of the people? Yes, I am the one who has sinned and done something very wicked. But these sheep, what have they done? Please! Let your hand be against me and my father's family, but not against your people, striking them with this plague!"

¹⁸ Then the angel of ADONAI ordered Gad to tell David to go and set up an altar to ADONAI on the threshing-floor of Ornan the Y'vusi. ¹⁹ David went up at Gad's word, spoken in ADONAI's name. ²⁰ Ornan turned back and saw the angel, and his four sons who were with him hid themselves. As Ornan was threshing wheat, ²¹ David approached Ornan. When Ornan looked and saw David, he went out from the threshing-floor and prostrated himself before David with his face to the ground. ²² Then David said to Ornan, "Let me have the parcel with this threshing-floor, so that I can build on it an altar to ADONAI — I will pay you its full value — so that the plague will be lifted from the people." ²³ Ornan said to David, "Take it for yourself, and let my lord the king do what seems good to him. I'm giving you the oxen for the burnt offerings, the threshing-sledges for firewood and the wheat for the grain offering — I'm giving it all." ²⁴ But King David said to Ornan, "No; I insist on buying it from you at the full price. I refuse to take what is yours for ADONAI or offer a burnt offering that costs me nothing." ²⁵ So David bought the place from Ornan for 600 *shekel*s of gold by weight [fifteen pounds]. ²⁶ Then David built an altar to ADONAI there and offered burnt offerings and peace offerings. He called on ADONAI, who answered him from heaven by fire on the altar for burnt offerings. ²⁷ ADONAI gave an order to the angel, and he put his sword back in its sheath. ²⁸ When David saw that ADONAI had answered him

at the threshing-floor of Ornan the Y'vusi, he sacrificed there. ²⁹ For at that time the tabernacle of ADONAI, which Moshe had made in the desert, together with the altar for burnt offerings, were in the high place at Giv'on. ³⁰ But David could not go into its presence to consult God, because the sword of the angel of ADONAI had struck him with terror.

22 ¹ Then David said, "This is the house of ADONAI, God; and this is the altar Isra'el is to use for burnt offerings." ² David ordered that the foreigners in the land of Isra'el should be assembled, and he appointed stone-workers to shape stones for building the house of God. ³ David prepared a large store of iron from which to make nails and clamps for the gateway doors and, a quantity of bronze too great to weigh, ⁴ and cedar logs beyond numbering — because the Tzidonim and the people from Tzor brought cedar logs in abundance to David.

⁵ David said, "Shlomo my son is young and inexperienced, while the house to be built for ADONAI must be so magnificent and splendid that its fame and glory will be known in every country; so I will make preparations for him." Therefore David made extensive preparations before his death. ⁶ Then he summoned Shlomo his son and charged him to build a house for ADONAI, the God of Isra'el. ⁷ "My son," said David to Shlomo, "my heart was set on building a house for the name of ADONAI my God. ⁸ But a message from ADONAI came to me, 'You have shed much blood and fought great wars. You are not to build a house for my name, because you have shed so much blood on the earth in my sight. ⁹ But you will have a son who will be a man of rest. I will give him rest from all his enemies that surround him; for his name is to be Shlomo, and during his reign I will give peace [Hebrew: *shalom*] and quiet to Isra'el. ¹⁰ It is he who will build a house for my name. He will be my son and I will be his father, and I will establish the throne of his kingdom over Isra'el forever.'

¹¹ "Now, my son, may ADONAI be with you and give you success as you build the house of ADONAI your God, in keeping with what he said about you. ¹² May ADONAI give you common sense and understanding, and may he give you his orders concerning Isra'el, so that you will observe the *Torah* of ADONAI your God. ¹³ Then you will succeed, if you take care to obey the laws and rulings that ADONAI ordered Moshe concerning Isra'el. Be strong, be bold; don't be afraid or become discouraged!

¹⁴ "Now look: despite my difficulties, I have prepared for the house of ADONAI 3,300 tons of gold, 33,000 tons of silver, and so much bronze and iron that it can't be weighed. I've also prepared timber and stone, and you can add to it. ¹⁵ Moreover, you have plenty of workers — quarrymen, stone-workers, lumbermen, and all kinds of skilled craftsmen to do whatever has to be done with ¹⁶ the gold, silver, bronze and iron—they're beyond number. So get up, and get to work! And may ADONAI be with you."

¹⁷ David also ordered all the leaders of Isra'el to help Shlomo his son: ¹⁸ "Isn't ADONAI your God with you? Hasn't he given you rest on every side? For he has put the inhabitants of the land under my power — the land has been subdued before ADONAI and his people. ¹⁹ Now set your heart and being on seeking ADONAI your God. Get up, and build the sanctuary for ADONAI, God. Then you can bring the ark for the covenant of ADONAI and the holy articles of God into the house that will be built for the name of ADONAI."

23 ¹ David had now grown old; he had lived many years; so he made Shlomo his son king over Isra'el.

² Then he assembled all the leaders of Isra'el, with the *cohanim* and *L'vi'im*. ³ A census of *L'vi'im* thirty years old and over was taken, and their number came to 38,000. ⁴ Of these, 24,000 were to oversee the work on the house of ADONAI, while 6,000 were officials and judges, ⁵ 4,000 were gatekeepers, and 4,000 sang praise to ADONAI "with the instruments I made for the purpose of singing praise."

⁶ David organized them into divisions named after the sons of Levi — Gershon, K'hat and M'rari.

⁷ For the Gershuni: La'dan and Shim'i. ⁸ The sons of La'dan: Yechi'el the chief, Zetam and Yo'el — three. ⁹ The sons of Shim'i: Shlomit, Hazi'el and Haran — three. These were the heads of the clans of La'dan. ¹⁰ The sons of Shim'i: Yachat, Zina Ye'ush and B'ri'ah. These four were the sons of Shim'i. ¹¹ Yachat was the chief and Zizah the second, then Ye'ush and B'ri'ah, who did not have many descendants and were therefore counted as one clan.

¹² The sons of K'hat: 'Amram, Yitz'har, Hevron and 'Uzi'el — four. ¹³ The sons of 'Amram: Aharon and Moshe. Aharon was set apart to be consecrated as especially holy, he and his sons forever; so that they might bring offerings before ADONAI, perform the service for him and bless in his name forever. ¹⁴ But as for Moshe the man of God, his sons are included with the tribe of Levi. ¹⁵ The sons of Moshe: Gershom and Eli'ezer. ¹⁶ The sons of Gershom: Sh'vu'el the chief. ¹⁷ The sons of Eli'ezer were: Rechavyah the chief. Eli'ezer had no other sons, but the sons of Rechavyah were very numerous.

¹⁸ The sons of Yitz'har: Shlomit the chief. ¹⁹ The sons of Hevron: Yeriyahu the chief, Amaryah the second, Yachzi'el the third and Y'kam'am the fourth. ²⁰ The sons of 'Uzi'el: Mikhah the chief and Yishiyah the second.

²¹ The sons of M'rari: Machli and Mushi. The sons of Machli: El'azar and Kish. ²² El'azar died without having sons, but daughters only; their cousins, the sons of Kish, married them. ²³ Mushi had three sons — Machli, 'Eder and Yeremot.

²⁴ These were the descendants of Levi, according to their clans, the heads of clans according to their listing in the register, who did the work for the service of the house of ADONAI, those twenty years old and over. ²⁵ For David said, "ADONAI the God of Isra'el has given rest to his people, and he lives in Yerushalayim forever. ²⁶ The *L'vi'im* will no longer have to carry the tabernacle and all the equipment that goes with it for its service." ²⁷ For, according to David's last instructions, the descendants of Levi twenty years old and over were to be counted. ²⁸ Their role was to assist the descendants of Aharon with the service of the house of ADONAI in the courtyards and rooms, and with purification of all the holy articles — in other words, with the work needed to minister in the house of God. ²⁹ They were to assist with the showbread and the finely ground flour needed for grain offerings, no matter whether of *matzah*, pan-baked bread or mixed with oil, and no matter what shape or size. ³⁰ They were to stand every morning to sing thanks and praises to ADONAI, and likewise every evening. ³¹ They were to be present regularly before ADONAI whenever burnt offerings were offered to ADONAI on *Shabbat*, at *Rosh-Hodesh*, and at the other designated times, in the numbers required by the rules for sacrifices. ³² Finally, for the service in the house of ADONAI they were to perform their duties in relation to the tent of meeting, the Holy Place and their kinsmen the descendants of Aharon.

24 [1] The divisions of the descendants of Aharon were as follows:

The sons of Aharon: Nadav, Avihu, El'azar and Itamar. [2] But Nadav and Avihu died before their father and had no children; therefore El'azar and Itamar functioned as the *cohanim.* [3] David, together with Tzadok from the descendants of El'azar, and Achimelekh from the descendants of Itamar, arranged them in divisions for service. [4] There were more men who were chiefs found among the descendants of El'azar than among the descendants of Itamar; therefore there were sixteen divisions of the descendants of El'azar, headed by clan leaders, and eight divisions of the descendants of Itamar, according to their clans. [5] They were assigned [periods of service] by lot, the one group equally with the other, since both the descendants of El'azar and the descendants of Itamar had officers of the sanctuary and officers of God. [6] Sh'ma'yah the son of N'tan'el the secretary, one of the *L'vi'im,* recorded them in the presence of the king, the officers, Tzadok the *cohen,* Achimelekh the son of Evyatar, and the clan leaders of the *cohanim* and of the *L'vi'im* — with two clan divisions taken from El'azar for each one from Itamar.

[7]   The first lot drawn was for Y'hoyariv,
            the second for Y'da'yah,
[8]   the third for Harim,
            the fourth for S'orim,
[9]   the fifth for Malkiyah,
            the sixth for Miyamin,
[10]   the seventh for Hakotz,
            the eighth for Aviyah,
[11]   the ninth for Yeshua,
            the tenth for Sh'khanyahu,
[12]   the eleventh for Elyashiv,
            the twelfth for Yakim,
[13]   the thirteenth for Hupah,
            the fourteenth for Yeshev'av,
[14]   the fifteenth for Bilgah,
            the sixteenth for Immer,
[15]   the seventeenth for Hezir,
            the eighteenth for HaPitzetz,
[16]   the nineteenth for P'tachyah,
            the twentieth for Yechezk'el,
[17]   the twenty-first for Yakhin,
            the twenty-second for Gamul,
[18]   the twenty-third for D'layahu, and
            the twenty-fourth for Ma'azyahu.

[19] These are the divisions and the sequence in which they served in the house of ADONAI, in accordance with the rule they were given through Aharon their ancestor, as ADONAI the God of Isra'el had ordered him.
    [20] The rest of the descendants of Levi: of the descendants of 'Amram, Shuva'el; of the descendants of Shuva'el, Yechd'yah. [21] Of Rechavyahu: of the descendants of Rechavyahu, Yishiyah the chief. [22] Of the Yitz'hari, Shlomot; of the descendants of

Shlomot, Yachat. ²³ Of the sons [of Hevron]: Yeriyahu, Amaryahu second, Yachzi'el third and Y'kam'am fourth. ²⁴ The descendants of 'Uzi'el: Mikhah; of the descendants of Mikhah, Shamir. ²⁵ The brother of Mikhah: Yishiyah; of the descendants of Yishiyah, Z'kharyahu.

²⁶ The sons of M'rari: Machli and Mushi. The descendants of his son Ya'aziyahu, ²⁷ that is, the descendants of M'rari through his descendant Ya'aziyahu: Shoham, Zakur and 'Ivri. ²⁸ Of Machli: El'azar, who had no sons. ²⁹ Of Kish: the descendants of Kish, Yerachme'el. ³⁰ And the sons of Mushi: Machli, 'Eder and Yerimot.

These were the descendants of the *L'vi'im* according to their clans. ³¹ These likewise cast lots, as had their kinsmen the descendants of Aharon, in the presence of David the king, Tzadok, Achimelekh, and the clan leaders of the *cohanim* and of the *L'vi'im*; with the senior and junior clans casting lots equally.

25 ¹ For the service, David and the army commanders selected some of the descendants of Asaf, of Heman and of Y'dutun to prophesy with lyres, lutes and cymbals. The list of those doing this work, according to the type of work performed was:

² Of the descendants of Asaf: Zakur, Yosef, N'tanyah and Asar'elah; the sons of Asaf were with Asaf, who prophesied according to the direction of the king. ³ Of Y'dutun, the descendants of Y'dutun: G'dalyahu, Tzeri, Yesha'yahu, Hashavyahu, Mattityahu — six, with their father Y'dutun, who, accompanied by the lyre, prophesied thanks and praise to Adonai. ⁴ Of Heman, the sons of Heman: Bukiyahu, Mattanyahu, 'Uzi'el, Sh'vu'el, Yerimot, Hananyah, Hanani, Eli'atah, Gidalti, Romamti-'ezer, Yoshb'kashah, Maloti, Hotir and Machzi'ot; ⁵ all these sons of Heman, the king's seer in matters pertaining to God, were there to exalt [God]. God gave Heman fourteen sons and three daughters. ⁶ They were all with their fathers Asaf, Y'dutun and Heman to sing with cymbals, lutes and lyres in the house of Adonai, serving in the house of God under the direction of the king. ⁷ Their number, together with their kinsmen who had been instructed in singing to Adonai, was 288, all well trained. ⁸ Whether great or small, teacher or *talmid*, they cast lots for their term of duty.

⁹ The first lot for Asaf fell to Yosef;
the second to G'dalyah; he, his brothers and his sons numbered twelve;
¹⁰ the third to Zakur, his sons and brothers, twelve;
¹¹ the fourth to Izri, his sons and brothers, twelve;
¹² the fifth to N'tanyahu, his sons and brothers, twelve;
¹³ the sixth to Bukiyahu, his sons and brothers, twelve;
¹⁴ the seventh to Y'sar'elah, his sons and brothers, twelve;
¹⁵ the eighth to Yesha'yahu, his sons and brothers, twelve;
¹⁶ the ninth to Mattanyahu, his sons and brothers, twelve;
¹⁷ the tenth to Shim'i, his sons and brothers, twelve;
¹⁸ the eleventh to 'Azar'el, his sons and brothers, twelve;
¹⁹ the twelfth to Hashavyah, his sons and brothers, twelve;
²⁰ the thirteenth to Shuva'el, his sons and brothers, twelve;
²¹ the fourteenth to Mattityahu, his sons and brothers, twelve;
²² the fifteenth to Yeremot, his sons and brothers, twelve;
²³ the sixteenth to Hananyahu, his sons and brothers, twelve;
²⁴ the seventeenth to Yoshb'kashah, his sons and brothers, twelve;

25 the eighteenth to Hanani, his sons and brothers, twelve;

26 the nineteenth to Maloti, his sons and brothers, twelve;

27 the twentieth to Eli'atah, his sons and brothers, twelve;

28 the twenty-first to Hotir, his sons and brothers, twelve;

29 the twenty-second to Gidalti, his sons and brothers, twelve;

30 the twenty-third to Machzi'ot, his sons and brothers, twelve; and

31 the twenty-fourth to Romamti-'ezer, his sons and brothers, twelve.

26 ¹ The divisions of the gatekeepers:

Of the Korchim: Meshelemyahu the son of Kore, of the descendants of Asaf. ² Meshelemyahu had sons: Z'kharyahu the firstborn, Y'dia'el the second, Z'vadyahu the third, Yatni'el the fourth, ³ 'Eilam the fifth, Y'hochanan the sixth and Ely'ho'einai the seventh.

⁴ 'Oved-Edom had sons: Sh'ma'yah the firstborn, Y'hozavad the second son, Yo'ach the third, Sakhar the fourth, N'tan'el the fifth, ⁵ 'Ammi'el the sixth, Yissakhar the seventh, and Pe'ultai the eighth; for God blessed him. ⁶ To his son Sh'ma'yah were born sons who ruled over their father's clan, because they were strong, brave men. ⁷ The sons of Sh'ma'yah: 'Otni, Refa'el and his brothers 'Oved and Elzavad, valiant men; also Elihu and S'makhyahu. ⁸ These were all from the sons of 'Oved-Edom, they and their sons and brothers, men of ability and strength for service, sixty-two from 'Oved-Edom.

⁹ Meshelemyahu had sons and brothers, valiant men, eighteen. ¹⁰ Hosah, from the descendants of M'rari, had sons: Shimri the chief, for although he was not the firstborn, nevertheless his father made him the chief; ¹¹ Hilkiyahu the second, T'valyahu the third and Z'kharyahu the fourth; all the sons and brothers of Hosah were thirteen.

¹² These divisions of the gatekeepers, under their chief men, had duties, just as their kinsmen did, serving in the house of ADONAI. ¹³ Great or small, they cast lots according to their clans for every gate. ¹⁴ The lot for the east gate fell to Shelemyahu. Then they cast lots for his son Z'kharyahu, a sensible adviser, and he was allotted the north gate. ¹⁵ 'Oved-Edom was allotted the south gate and his sons the storehouse. ¹⁶ Shupim and Hosah were allotted the west gate and the Shallekhet Gate at the highway that goes up, with corresponding guards. ¹⁷ For the east there were six L'vi'im, for the north four a day, for the south four a day, for the Storehouse two and two, ¹⁸ while for the courtyard to the west there were four at the highway and two at the courtyard itself. ¹⁹ These were the divisions of the gatekeepers, consisting of descendants of the Korchim and descendants of M'rari.

²⁰ Of the L'vi'im, Achiyah was responsible for the stores in the house of God and the stores of holy articles. ²¹ The sons of La'dan, the descendants of the Gershuni belonging to La'dan, the heads of clans belonging to La'dan the Gershuni: Yechi'eli; ²² and the sons of Yechi'eli: Zetam and Yo'el his brother, over the stores in the house of ADONAI. ²³ Of the 'Amrami, of the Yitz'hari, of the Hevroni, of the 'Uzi'eli, ²⁴ Sh'vu'el the descendant of Gershom, the son of Moshe, was in charge of the stores.

²⁵ His kinsmen: from Eli'ezer: Rechavyahu his son, Yesha'yahu his son, Yoram his son, Zikhri his son and Shlomit his son. ²⁶ This Shlomit and his kinsmen were in charge of all the stores of the dedicated things that David the king, the clan heads,

the captains over thousands and hundreds and the commanders of the army had dedicated. ²⁷ From the spoil won in wars they had dedicated these things to repair the house of ADONAI. ²⁸ Also included was all that Sh'mu'el the seer, Sha'ul the son of Kish, Avner the son of Ner and Yo'av the son of Tz'ruyah had dedicated. In short, if anyone had dedicated anything, Shlomit and his brothers were in charge of it.

²⁹ Of the Yitz'hari: K'nanyahu and his sons were assigned to be over Isra'el in regard to outside business as officers and judges. ³⁰ Of the Hevroni: Hashavyah and his kinsmen, 1,700 valiant men, had the oversight of Isra'el west of the Yarden in regard to all the business of ADONAI and the service of the king. ³¹ Yeriyah was chief of the Hevroni according to their generations by clans. In the fortieth year of David's reign the Hevroni were sought out, and there were found among them strong, brave men at Ya'zer in Gil'ad. ³² King David appointed 2,700 of his kinsmen, valiant men and clan leaders, as overseers over the Re'uveni, the Gadi and the half-tribe of the M'nashi for every matter pertaining to God and for the affairs of the king.

27 ¹ The people of Isra'el, registered according to their clan leaders, were drafted for army duty under captains of thousands and of hundreds, and officers serving the king, in divisions of 24,000 each, for month-long terms of duty covering all the months of the year.

² Over the first division, for the first month, was Yashov'am the son of Zavdi'el; there were 24,000 in his division. ³ He was from the descendants of Peretz and was in charge of all the army captains during the first month.

⁴ Over the division for the second month was Dodai the Achochi; Miklot was the chief officer of his division; there were 24,000 in his division.

⁵ The third army commander, for the third month, was B'nayah the son of Y'hoyada the chief *cohen*; there were 24,000 in his division. ⁶ This is the same B'nayah who was one of the thirty heroes and was over the thirty; his son 'Ammizavad was in his division.

⁷ The fourth commander, for the fourth month, was 'Asah'el the brother of Yo'av, with Z'vadyah his son after him; there were 24,000 in his division.

⁸ The fifth commander, for the fifth month, was Shamhut from Yizrach; there were 24,000 in his division.

⁹ The sixth commander, for the sixth month, was 'Ira the son of 'Ikesh from T'koa; there were 24,000 in his division.

¹⁰ The seventh commander, for the seventh month, was Heletz the P'loni, from the descendants of Efrayim; there were 24,000 in his division.

¹¹ The eighth commander, for the eighth month, was Sibkhai the Hushati, from the Zarchi; there were 24,000 in his division.

¹² The ninth commander, for the ninth month, was Avi'ezer from 'Anatot, from the Ben-Y'mini; there were 24,000 in his division.

¹³ The tenth commander, for the tenth month, was Mahrai, the N'tofati, from the Zarchi; there were 24,000 in his division.

¹⁴ The eleventh commander, for the eleventh month, was B'nayah from Pir'aton, from the descendants of Efrayim; there were 24,000 in his division.

¹⁵ The twelfth commander, for the twelfth month, was Heldai the N'tofati, from 'Otni'el; there were 24,000 in his division.

^{16} Over the the tribes of Isra'el:

leader of the Re'uveni: Eli'ezer the son of Zikhri;
of the Shim'oni: Sh'fatyah the son of Ma'akhah;
^{17} of Levi: Hashavyah the son of K'mu'el;
of Aharon: Tzadok;
^{18} of Y'hudah: Elihu, one of David's brothers;
of Yissakhar: 'Omri the son of Mikha'el;
^{19} of Z'vulun: Yishma'yahu the son of 'Ovadyah;
of Naftali: Yerimot the son of 'Azri'el;
^{20} of the descendants of Efrayim: Hoshea the son of 'Azazyahu;
of the half-tribe of M'nasheh: Yo'el the son of P'dayah;
^{21} of the half-tribe of M'nasheh in Gil'ad: Yiddo the son of Z'kharyahu;
of Binyamin: Ya'asi'el the son of Avner;
^{22} of Dan: 'Azar'el the son of Yerocham.

These were the commanders of the tribes of Isra'el.

^{23} But David did not include in the registration those twenty years old or less, because ADONAI had said he would increase Isra'el's numbers like the stars in the sky. ^{24} Yo'av the son of Tz'ruyah began a census of these, but he did not finish, and wrath came upon Isra'el because of this; moreover the number was not entered into the Annals of King David.

^{25} In charge of the king's supplies was 'Azmavet the son of 'Adi'el. In charge of the supplies in the countryside, the cities, the villages and the fortresses was Y'honatan the son of 'Uziyahu. ^{26} In charge of farmers working the land was 'Ezri the son of K'luv. ^{27} In charge of the vineyards was Shim'i the Ramati, while Zavdi the Shifmi was responsible for the produce from the vineyards for the wine-cellars. ^{28} In charge of the olive and sycamore-fig trees in the Sh'felah was Ba'al-Hanan from G'derah, while Yo'ash was put over the storehouses for olive oil. ^{29} In charge of the herds of livestock feeding in the Sharon was Shirtai from the Sharon, while Shafat the son of Adlai was put over herds in the valleys. ^{30} Ovil the Yishma'eli was put over the camels, Yechd'yahu the Meronoti over the donkeys ^{31} and Yaziz the Hagri over the flocks [of sheep and goats]. All of these were responsible for King David's property.

^{32} Y'honatan David's uncle was an adviser, a man of understanding and a secretary. Yechi'el the son of Hachmoni took care of the king's sons. ^{33} Achitofel was an adviser to the king. Hushai the Archi was the king's confidant; ^{34} and after Achitofel were Y'hoyada the son of B'nayah and Evyatar. Yo'av was commander of the king's army.

28 ^{1} David assembled in Yerushalayim all the leaders of Isra'el — the leaders of the tribes, the commanders of the divisions serving the king, the captains of thousands and of hundreds, and the supervisors over the property and livestock of the king, along with his sons, the officials, the warrior-heroes, and anyone else who was a leader. ^{2} Then David the king rose to his feet and said: "My kinsmen and my people! Listen to me! I set my heart on building a house where the ark for the covenant of ADONAI could remain at rest. It would have been God's footstool, and I prepared to build it. ³ But God said to me, 'You are not to build a house for my name, because you are a man of war, you have shed blood.' ⁴ However, ADONAI the God of Isra'el chose me out of my father's whole family to be king over Isra'el forever; for he chose Y'hudah to be the leader; and in the house of Y'hudah, in the house of my father, and among the sons of my father, it was his pleasure to make me king over all Isra'el; ⁵ and of all my sons — for ADONAI has given me many sons — he has chosen Shlomo my son to sit on the throne of the kingdom of ADONAI over Isra'el.

⁶ "Moreover, he said to me, 'Shlomo your son will build my house and court-yards, for I have chosen him to be a son to me, and I will be a father to him. ⁷ I will establish his kingdom forever, if he uses his strength to obey my *mitzvot* and abide by my rulings, as [he is doing] currently.' ⁸ Now therefore, in the sight of all Isra'el, the community of ADONAI, and in the hearing of our God, observe and seek out all the *mitzvot* of ADONAI your God, so that you may continue to possess this good land and leave it as an inheritance to your descendants after you forever.

⁹ "As for you, Shlomo my son, know the God of your father. Serve him whole-heartedly and with desire in your being; for ADONAI searches all hearts and under-stands all the inclinations of people's thoughts. If you seek him, he will let himself be found by you; but if you abandon him, he will reject you forever. ¹⁰ See now that ADONAI has chosen you to build a house for the sanctuary; so be strong, and do it!"

¹¹ Then David gave Shlomo his son the designs for the hall [of the temple], its buildings, its supply areas, its upper rooms, its inside rooms, and the place for the ark-cover; ¹² also the designs for everything he had been given by the Spirit — for the courtyards of the house of ADONAI, for all the rooms surrounding it, for the storehouses in the house of God, for the storehouses for the holy articles, ¹³ and for the areas set aside for the *cohanim* and the *L'vi'im*; [arrangements] for the work involved in the service of the house of ADONAI and for all the articles needed for the service of the house of ADONAI; ¹⁴ [lists] of the weights of gold needed for the gold items to be used for various purposes, and the weights of silver needed for the silver items to be used for various purposes — ¹⁵ the weight of the gold needed for the gold *menorah*s, the weight needed for each *menorah* and for its lamps; and for the *menorah*s of silver, the weight of silver needed for each *menorah* and for its lamps, according to the way each *menorah* was to be used; ¹⁶ also the gold by weight for the tables for the showbread, for each table; and silver for the tables made of silver; ¹⁷ the gold for the pure gold forks, basins and jars, and for the gold bowls by weight for each bowl; also for the silver bowls by weight for each bowl; ¹⁸ and for the incense altar, refined gold by weight; and gold for the design of the chariot and the *k'ruvim* with their wings spread out to cover the ark for the covenant of ADONAI. ¹⁹ "All this is in writing, as ADONAI, with his hand on me, has given me good sense in working out these detailed plans."

²⁰ Then David said to Shlomo his son, "Be strong, be bold, and do it! Don't be afraid or become discouraged! For ADONAI, God, my God, is with you. He will not fail you or abandon you until all the work for the service in the house of ADONAI has been finished. ²¹ See, there are the divisions of the *cohanim* and *L'vi'im* for all the service in the house of God. For every kind of work, you will have with you every man who is willing and skilled, for every kind of service. Also the captains and all the people will be completely at your disposal."

29 ¹ To the whole community, David the king said, "Shlomo my son is the only one God has chosen. But he is still young and inexperienced, whereas the work to be done is great; because the palace is not for anyone human, but for ADONAI, God. ² Now I have used all my strength to prepare for the house of my God the gold needed for the articles of gold, the silver for the articles of silver, the bronze for the articles of bronze, the iron for the articles of iron, the wood for the articles of wood, onyx stones, gemstones to be set, brilliant stones of various colors, all kinds of precious stones, as well as marble in abundance. ³ In addition, because my desire is set on the house of my God, since I have my own supply of gold and silver, I herewith give it to the house of my God — over and above everything I have prepared for the holy house — ⁴ ninety-nine tons of gold from the gold of Ofir and 231 tons of refined silver to be used for overlaying the walls of the houses. ⁵ The gold is for whatever is to be made of gold, and the silver is for whatever is to be made of silver; and they may be used for anything to be made by craftsmen. Therefore, who offers willingly to consecrate himself today to ADONAI?"

⁶ Then the clan leaders, the leaders of the tribes of Isra'el, the captains of thousands and of hundreds, along with the supervisors over the king's work offered willingly. ⁷ They gave for the service of the house of God 165 tons of gold, 330 tons of silver, 594 tons of bronze and 3,300 tons of iron. ⁸ Those who had precious stones gave them to the storehouse of the house of ADONAI, supervised by Yechi'el the Gershuni.

⁹ The people were filled with joy, because they had given willingly — wholeheartedly they had given willingly to ADONAI; and David the king too was completely filled with joy, ¹⁰ as he blessed ADONAI before the entire community: "Blessed be you, ADONAI, the God of Isra'el our father, forever and ever. ¹¹ Yours, ADONAI, is the greatness, the power, the glory, the victory and the majesty; for everything in heaven and on earth is yours. The kingdom is yours, ADONAI; and you are exalted as head over all. ¹² Riches and honor come from you, you rule everything, in your hand is power and strength, you have the capacity to make great and to give strength to all. ¹³ Therefore, our God, we thank you and praise your glorious name.

¹⁴ "But who am I, and what is my people, that we should be able to give so willingly in this way? For all things come from you, so that we have given you what is already yours. ¹⁵ For in your presence we are temporary residents, just passing through, as all our ancestors were — our days on earth are like a shadow, without hope. ¹⁶ ADONAI our God, all these supplies that we have prepared in order to build you a house for your holy name come from your own hand, all of it is already yours. ¹⁷ I know also, my God, that you test the heart and take pleasure in integrity. As for myself, I have given all these things willingly, in the integrity of my heart; and now, with joy, I have seen your people who are present here give willingly to you. ¹⁸ ADONAI, God of Avraham, Yitz'chak and Isra'el our ancestors, guard forever the inclinations of the thoughts in the hearts of your people; direct their hearts to you; ¹⁹ and give to Shlomo my son wholeheartedness to obey your *mitzvot*, instructions and rules, to do all these things, and to build the palace for which I have made provision."

²⁰ Then David said to all the community, "Now bless ADONAI your God." All the community blessed ADONAI, the God of their ancestors, bowing their heads and prostrating themselves before ADONAI and before the king. ²¹ On the following day they presented sacrifices to ADONAI and offered burnt offerings to ADONAI — a thousand bulls, a thousand rams and a thousand lambs, with their drink offerings — and

sacrifices in abundance for all Isra'el. ²² They ate and drank before ADONAI that day with great joy.

Then, for the second time, they made Shlomo the son of David king, anointing him before ADONAI to be king, and Tzadok to be *cohen*. ²³ Shlomo sat on the throne of ADONAI as king in place of David his father and prospered, and all Isra'el obeyed him. ²⁴ All the leaders, the warrior-heroes and likewise the sons of King David submitted themselves to Shlomo the king. ²⁵ ADONAI gave Shlomo exceedingly great power, in full view of all Isra'el, and bestowed on him royal majesty such as had not been seen on any king before him in Isra'el.

²⁶ Now David the son of Yishai ruled over all Isra'el. ²⁷ The duration of his reign over Isra'el was forty years; he reigned seven years in Hevron, and he reigned thirty-three years in Yerushalayim. ²⁸ Then he died, at a ripe old age, full of years, riches and honor; and Shlomo his son reigned in his place. ²⁹ The activities of David the king, from first to last, are written in the records of Sh'mu'el the seer, Natan the prophet and Gad the seer, ³⁰ with all his reign and his power, and the events that he, Isra'el and the kingdoms of other countries experienced.

Divrei-HaYamim Bet
2 CHRONICLES

1 ¹ Shlomo the son of David grew stronger in his rulership; ADONAI his God was with him, making him greater and greater.

² Shlomo spoke to all Isra'el — to the captains of thousands and of hundreds, to the judges and to every leader in all Isra'el, the heads of clans. ³ Shlomo and the whole community with him went to the high place at Giv'on, because in that place was God's tent of meeting, which Moshe the servant of ADONAI had made in the desert. ⁴ But the ark of God David had brought up from Kiryat-Ye'arim to the place he had prepared for it — he had set up a tent for it in Yerushalayim. ⁵ The bronze altar crafted by B'tzal'el the son of Uri, the son of Hur, had been placed before the tabernacle of ADONAI; and there Shlomo and the community consulted him. ⁶ On the bronze altar at the tent of meeting Shlomo offered a thousand burnt offerings before ADONAI.

⁷ That night God appeared to Shlomo and said to him, "Tell me what I should give you." ⁸ Shlomo said to God, "You showed much grace to your servant David my father and have made me king in his place. ⁹ Now, ADONAI, God, you have been faithful to your promise to David my father; for you have made me king over a people as numerous as the grains of dust on the earth. ¹⁰ So now, give me wisdom and knowledge; so that I will be able to lead this people. For who is equal to judging this great people of yours?"

¹¹ God said to Shlomo, "Because you set your heart on this — because, instead of asking for riches, wealth, honor, the death of those who hate you, or long life, you asked for wisdom and knowledge for yourself, so that you would be able to judge my people, over whom I made you king — ¹² not only are wisdom and knowledge being given to you, but I will also give you riches, wealth and honor such as no king before you has ever had; and no king after you will have as much." ¹³ So Shlomo came away from the high place at Giv'on, from in front of the tent of meeting, to Yerushalayim; and he ruled over Isra'el.

¹⁴ Shlomo amassed chariots and horsemen; he had 1,400 chariots and 12,000 horsemen; he placed them in the chariot cities and with the king in Yerushalayim. ¹⁵ The king made silver and gold in Yerushalayim as common as stones, and he made cedars as abundant as sycamore-fig trees in the Sh'felah. ¹⁶ Shlomo's horses had been brought from Egypt and from Keve, with the king's agents having bought them from the dealers in Keve at the going price. ¹⁷ A chariot brought from Egypt cost fifteen pounds of silver *shekels* and a horse three-and-three-quarters pounds [of *shekels*]; all the kings of the Hittim and the kings of Aram purchased them at these prices through Shlomo's agents.

¹⁸⁽²:¹⁾ Shlomo then decided to build a house for the name of ADONAI and a royal palace for himself.

2 ¹⁽²⁾ Shlomo enlisted 70,000 men who carried loads, another 80,000 men who were stonecutters in the hills and 3,600 supervising them. ²⁽³⁾ Then Shlomo sent this message to Huram the king of Tzor: "[Deal with me] as you dealt with David my father when you sent him cedar logs, so that he could build himself a palace to live in. ³⁽⁴⁾ Here, I am about to build a house for the name of ADONAI my God, to dedicate it to him, and to burn before him incense made of sweet spices; the house will also be for the continuing showbread and for the burnt offerings presented every morning and evening, on the *shabbat*s, at every *Rosh-Hodesh*, and at the designated times of ADONAI our God. This is a perpetual regulation for Isra'el. ⁴⁽⁵⁾ The house I will build will be great, because our God is greater than all gods. ⁵⁽⁶⁾ But who is equal to building him a house? Why, heaven itself, even the heaven of heavens, cannot contain him; so who am I to build him a house, except to offer sacrifices before him?

⁶⁽⁷⁾ "Now, therefore, send me a man skilled at working with gold, silver, bronze and iron; dealing with purple, crimson, and blue dyed materials; and capable of doing all kinds of engraving. He will be with the skilled craftsmen I have with me in Y'hudah and Yerushalayim, whom David my father provided. ⁷⁽⁸⁾ Also send me cedar, cypress and sandalwood logs from the L'vanon; for I know that your servants are skilled in cutting timber in the L'vanon. I will have my servants work together with your servants ⁸⁽⁹⁾ to prepare me an abundant supply of timber, for the house I am about to build must be magnificent and wonderful. ⁹⁽¹⁰⁾ I will give your servants, the woodcutters who cut the timber, 100,000 bushels of cracked wheat, 100,000 bushels of barley, 100,000 gallons of wine, and 100,000 gallons of olive oil."

¹⁰⁽¹¹⁾ Huram the king of Tzor wrote this answer and sent it to Shlomo: "Because the Lord loves his people, he has made you king over them." ¹¹⁽¹²⁾ Huram continued, "Blessed be ADONAI, the God of Isra'el, who made heaven and earth, who has given David the king a wise, knowledgeable son with common sense to build a house for ADONAI and a royal palace for himself. ¹²⁽¹³⁾ Now I am sending a man of skill and

understanding, my master craftsman Huram, ^{13(14)} the son of a woman who was one of the daughters of Dan, while his father was a man from Tzor. He is skilled in working gold, silver, bronze, iron, stone, and timber, as well as purple and blue dyed materials, fine linen and crimson material; he can do any kind of engraving; and he can make all the equipment necessary to accomplish any task assigned to him, with the help of your craftsmen and those of my lord David your father. ^{14(15)} Therefore let my lord send his servants the wheat, barley, oil and wine he has spoken of; ^{15(16)} and we will cut wood from the L'vanon, as much as you need; we will float it to you as rafts by sea to Yafo, and you will take it up to Yerushalayim."

^{16(17)} Shlomo took a census of all the foreigners in the land of Isra'el, following the pattern of the census of David his father; they were found to number 153,600. ^{17(18)} He appointed 70,000 of them to carry loads, 80,000 to be stonecutters in the hills and 3,600 as supervisors to assign the people their work.

3 ^1 Then Shlomo began to build the house of ADONAI in Yerushalayim on Mount Moriyah, where ADONAI had appeared to David his father. Provision had been made for this at the place David had chosen, the threshing-floor of Ornan the Y'vusi. ^2 He began building in the fourth year of his reign, on the second day of the second month.

^3 These are the foundations Shlomo laid for building the house of God: the length in old-standard cubits was sixty cubits [105 feet] and the width twenty cubits [thirty-five feet]. ^4 The length of the hall fronting the house was the same as the house's width, thirty-five feet and the height 210 [feet]; and he overlaid it with pure gold.

^5 The larger house he covered with cypress-wood, which he overlaid with fine gold and embossed with palm trees and chains. ^6 He also decorated the building with precious stones and gold from Parvayim, ^7 overlaying the house and its beams, thresholds, walls and doors with gold and carving k'ruvim on the walls.

^8 Then he made the Especially Holy Place; its length matched the width of the house, thirty-five feet, and its width was thirty-five feet. He overlaid it with twenty tons of fine gold. ^9 The weight of the nails was one-and-a-quarter pounds of gold, and he overlaid the upper rooms with gold.

^10 Inside the Especially Holy Place he made two k'ruvim of cast metal, and they overlaid them with gold. ^11 The wings of the k'ruvim were thirty-five feet long — the wing of the one keruv was eight-and-three-quarters feet long and touched the wall of the house; the other wing was also eight-and-three-quarters feet long, so that it touched the wing of the other keruv. ^12 The wing of the other keruv was eight-and-three-quarters feet long, touching the wall of the house; and the other wing was also eight-and-three-quarters feet long, touching the wing of the first keruv. ^13 The wings of these k'ruvim spread out over thirty-five feet. They stood on their feet with their faces turned inward.

^14 He made the curtain of blue, purple and crimson material and of fine linen, with a design of k'ruvim worked into it.

^15 In front of the house he made two columns sixty-one-and-a-quarter feet high, with a capital of eight-and-three-quarters feet on top of each. ^16 He made chains in the sanctuary and added them to the tops of the columns, and he made a hundred pomegranates and attached them to the chains. ^17 He erected the columns in front of the temple, one on the right and the other on the left; the one on the right he called Yakhin, and the one on the left he called Bo'az.

4 ¹ He made an altar of bronze thirty-five feet long, thirty-five feet wide and seventeen-and-a-half feet high. ² He made the cast metal "Sea" circular, seventeen-and-a-half feet from rim to rim, eight-and-three quarters feet high and fifty-two-and-a-half feet in circumference. ³ Below the rim a ring of ox-like figures encircled it, ten for every twenty-one inches all the way around the Sea. The oxen were in two rows; they were cast when the Sea was cast. ⁴ It rested on twelve oxen, three looking north, three looking west, three looking south and three looking east, all with their hindquarters toward the center. The Sea was set on top of them. ⁵ It was a handbreadth thick, its rim was made like the rim of a cup, like the flower of a lily; and its capacity was 16,500 gallons. ⁶ He also made ten basins for washing and put five on the right and five on the left. Items needed for the burnt offerings would be cleansed in these, but the Sea was for the *cohanim* to wash in.

⁷ He made the ten *menorah*s of gold in accordance with their specifications and set them in the temple, five on the right and five on the left. ⁸ He also made ten tables and put them in the temple, five on the right and five on the left. And he made a hundred basins of gold.

⁹ He made the courtyard for the *cohanim* and the great courtyard, also the doors to the courtyard, which he overlaid with bronze.

¹⁰ The Sea he placed on the right side [of the house], toward the southeast.

¹¹ Huram made the ash pots, shovels and sprinkling basins. With that, Huram completed the work he had been doing for King Shlomo in the house of God — ¹² the two columns, the two moldings, the two capitals on top of the columns, the two nettings covering the two moldings of the capitals atop the columns, ¹³ and the 400 pomegranates for the two nettings, two rows of pomegranates for each netting, to cover the two moldings of the capitals atop the columns. ¹⁴ He also made the trolleys, the basins on the trolleys, ¹⁵ the one Sea, the twelve oxen under it, ¹⁶ the ash pots, the shovels, the forks and all the other equipment for it. All these articles that Huram the master craftsman made for King Shlomo in the house of ADONAI were of brilliant bronze. ¹⁷ The king cast them in the plain of the Yarden, in the clay ground between Sukkot and Tz'redah. ¹⁸ Shlomo made so many of these objects that the total weight of the bronze could not be determined.

¹⁹ Shlomo made all the objects that were inside the house of God: the gold altar; the table on which the showbread was displayed; ²⁰ the *menorah*s with their lamps to burn in front of the sanctuary as specified, of pure gold; ²¹ the flowers, lamps and tongs of gold, solid gold; ²² and the snuffers, bowls, cups and fire pans of pure gold. As for the entryway to the house, the inner doors for the Especially Holy Place and the doors of the house (that is, of the temple) were of gold.

5 ¹ Thus all the work that Shlomo did for the house of ADONAI was finished. Then Shlomo brought in the gifts which David his father had consecrated — the silver, the gold and all the utensils — and put them in the treasuries of the house of God.

² Shlomo assembled all the leaders of Isra'el and all the heads of the tribes and the chiefs of the paternal clans of the people of Isra'el, to Yerushalayim, to bring the ark for the covenant of ADONAI out of the City of David, also known as Tziyon. ³ All the people of Isra'el assembled before the king at the festival in the seventh month. ⁴ All the leaders of Isra'el came. The *L'vi'im* took the ark ⁵ and brought up the ark,

the tent of meeting and all the holy utensils that were in the tent; these are what the *cohanim* and *L'vi'im* brought up. ⁶ King Shlomo and the whole community of Isra'el who had assembled in his presence were in front of the ark, sacrificing sheep and oxen in numbers beyond counting or recording. ⁷ The *cohanim* brought the ark for the covenant of A*DONAI* in to its place inside the sanctuary of the house, to the Especially Holy Place, under the wings of the *k'ruvim*. ⁸ For the *k'ruvim* spread out their wings over the place for the ark, covering the ark and its poles from above. ⁹ The poles were so long that their ends could be seen [extending] from the ark into the sanctuary, but they could not be seen from outside; they are there to this day. ¹⁰ There was nothing in the ark except the two tablets Moshe put there at Horev, when A*DONAI* made the covenant with the people of Isra'el at the time of their leaving Egypt.

¹¹ When the *cohanim* came out of the Holy Place (for all the *cohanim* who were present had consecrated themselves; they didn't keep to their divisions; ¹² also the *L'vi'im* who were the singers, all of them — Asaf, Heman, Y'dutun and their sons and relatives — dressed in fine linen, with cymbals, lutes and lyres, stood on the east side of the altar; and with them 120 *cohanim* sounding trumpets), ¹³ then, when the trumpeters and singers were playing in concord, to be heard harmoniously praising and thanking A*DONAI*, and they lifted their voices together with the trumpets, cymbals and other musical instruments to praise A*DONAI*: "for he is good, for his grace continues forever" — then, the house, the house of A*DONAI*, was filled with a cloud; ¹⁴ so that because of the cloud, the *cohanim* could not stand up to perform their service; for the glory of A*DONAI* filled the house of God.

6 ¹ Shlomo said, "A*DONAI* said he would live in thick darkness. ² But I have built you a magnificent house, a place where you can live forever."

³ Then the king turned around and blessed the whole community of Isra'el. The whole community of Isra'el stood ⁴ as he said, "Blessed be A*DONAI*, the God of Isra'el, who spoke to my father David with his mouth and fulfilled his promise with his hand. He said, ⁵ 'Since the day I brought my people out of Egypt, I chose no city from any of the tribes of Isra'el to build a house, so that my name might be there; nor did I choose anyone to be the leader of my people Isra'el. ⁶ But now I have chosen Yerushalayim, so that my name can be there; and I have chosen David to be over my people Isra'el.' ⁷ It was in the heart of David my father to build a house for the name of A*DONAI* the God of Isra'el; ⁸ but A*DONAI* said to David my father, 'Although it was in your heart to build a house for my name, and you did well that it was in your heart, ⁹ nevertheless you will not build the house. Rather, you will father a son, and it will be he who will build the house for my name.' ¹⁰ Now A*DONAI* has fulfilled this spoken word of his; for I have succeeded my father and sit on the throne of Isra'el, as A*DONAI* promised; and I have built the house for the name of A*DONAI* the God of Isra'el. ¹¹ And there I have placed the ark containing the covenant of A*DONAI*, which he made with the people of Isra'el."

¹² Then he stood before the altar of A*DONAI* in the presence of the whole community of Isra'el, spread out his hands — ¹³ for Shlomo had made a bronze platform eight-and-three quarters feet long, eight-and-three-quarters feet wide and five-and-a-quarter feet high and had set it up in the middle of the courtyard. He stood on it, then got down on his knees before the whole community, spread out his hands toward heaven,

¹⁴ and said, "*ADONAI*, God of Isra'el, there is no God like you in heaven or on earth. You keep covenant with your servants and show them grace, provided they live in your presence with all their heart. ¹⁵ You have kept your promise to your servant David, my father; you spoke with your mouth and fulfilled it with your hand; so it is today. ¹⁶ Now therefore, *ADONAI*, God of Isra'el, keep what you promised to your servant David, my father, when you said, 'You will never lack a man in my presence to sit on the throne of Isra'el, if only your children are careful about what they do, so that they live by my *Torah*, just as you have lived in my presence.' ¹⁷ Now therefore, *ADONAI*, God of Isra'el, please let your word, which you spoke to your servant David, my father, be confirmed.

¹⁸ "But can God actually live with human beings on the earth? Why, heaven itself, even the heaven of heavens, cannot contain you; so how much less this house I have built? ¹⁹ Even so, *ADONAI* my God, pay attention to your servant's prayer and plea, listen to the cry and prayer that your servant is praying before you, ²⁰ that your eyes will be open toward this house day and night — toward the place where you said you would put your name — to listen to the prayer your servant will pray toward this place. ²¹ Yes, listen to the pleas of your servant, and also those of your people Isra'el when they pray toward this place. Hear from where you live, from heaven; and when you hear, forgive!

²² "If a person sins against a fellow member of the community, and he is made to swear under oath, and he comes and swears before your altar in this house; ²³ then hear from heaven, act and judge your servants, paying back the wicked, so that his way of life devolves on his own head, and vindicating the one who is right, giving him what his righteousness deserves.

²⁴ "If your people Isra'el sin against you and in consequence are defeated by an enemy; then if they turn back to you, acknowledge your name, and pray and make their plea to you in this house, ²⁵ hear from heaven, forgive the sin of your people Isra'el, and bring them back to the land you gave to them and their ancestors.

²⁶ "When they sin against you, and in consequence the sky is shut, so that there is no rain; then if they pray toward this place, acknowledge your name and turn from their sin when you have brought them low; ²⁷ hear in heaven, forgive the sin of your servants and of your people Isra'el — since you keep teaching them the good way by which they should live — and send down rain on your land, which you have given your people as their inheritance.

²⁸ "If there is famine in the land, or blight, windstorm, mildew, locusts or shearer-worms; or if their enemies besiege them in any of their cities — no matter what kind of plague or sickness it is; ²⁹ then, regardless of what prayer or plea anyone among all your people Isra'el makes — for each individual will know his own plague and his own pain — and the person spreads out his hands toward this house; ³⁰ then hear from heaven where you live, and forgive; also, since you know what is in each one's heart, give each person what his conduct deserves (because you, and only you, know human hearts), ³¹ so that they will fear you and therefore live according to your ways throughout the time they live in the land you gave our ancestors.

³² "Also the foreigner who does not belong to your people Isra'el — when he comes from a distant country because of your great reputation, your mighty hand and your outstretched arm, when they come and pray toward this house; ³³ then hear from heaven, from where you live; and act in accordance with everything about

which the foreigner is calling to you; so that all the peoples of the earth will know your name and fear you, as does your people Isra'el, and so that they will know that this house which I have built bears your name. ³⁴ "If your people go out to fight their enemies, no matter by which way you send them, and they pray to you toward the city you chose and the house I built for your name; ³⁵ then, from heaven, hear their prayer and plea, and uphold their cause.

³⁶ "If they sin against you — for there is no one who doesn't sin — and you are angry with them and hand them over to the enemy, so that they carry them off captive to a land far away or nearby; ³⁷ then, if they come to their senses in the land where they have been carried away captive, turn back and make their plea to you in the land where they are being held captive, saying, 'We sinned, we acted wrongly, we behaved wickedly,' ³⁸ if, in the land where they were brought and are being held captive, they return to you with all their heart and being and pray to you toward their own land, which you gave to their ancestors, toward the city you chose and toward the house I have built for your name; ³⁹ then, from heaven, from where you live, hear their prayer and pleas, uphold their cause, and forgive your people who have sinned against you.

⁴⁰ "Now, my God, please, let your eyes be open, and let your ears pay attention to the prayer being made in this place.

⁴¹   "Now go up, ADONAI, God, to your place of rest,
      you and the ark through which you give strength.

      "May your *cohanim*, ADONAI, God, be clothed with salvation;
      may those loyal to you take joy in good.

⁴²   "ADONAI, God, don't turn away the face of your anointed one;
      remember the mercies of your servant David."

7 ¹ When Shlomo had finished praying, fire came down from heaven and consumed the burnt offering and the sacrifices; and the glory of ADONAI filled the house, ² so that the *cohanim* could not enter the house of ADONAI; because the glory of ADONAI filled ADONAI's house. ³ All the people of Isra'el saw when the fire came down, and the glory of ADONAI was on the house; they bowed down with their faces to the ground on the flooring; prostrating themselves, they gave thanks to ADONAI, "for he is good, for his grace continues forever."

⁴ Then the king and all the people offered sacrifices before ADONAI. ⁵ King Shlomo offered a sacrifice of 22,000 oxen and 120,000 sheep. Thus the king and all the people dedicated the house of God. ⁶ The *cohanim* stood at their appointed stations, while the *L'vi'im* used the instruments that David the king had provided for making music to ADONAI in order to "give thanks to ADONAI, for his grace continues forever," by means of the praises David had composed. Opposite them the *cohanim* sounded trumpets; and all Isra'el stood up. ⁷ Shlomo also consecrated the center of the court-yard in front of the house of ADONAI; because he had to offer the burnt offerings and the fat of the peace offerings there. For the bronze altar which Shlomo had made could not receive the burnt offering, the grain offering and the fat. ⁸ So Shlomo celebrated the festival at that time for seven days, together with all Isra'el, an enormous gathering;

[they had come all the way] from the entrance of Hamat to the *Vadi* [of Egypt]. ⁹ On the eighth day they held a solemn assembly, having observed the dedication of the altar for seven days and the festival for seven days. ¹⁰ Then, on the twenty-third day of the seventh month, he sent the people away to their tents full of joy and glad of heart for all the goodness ADONAI had shown to David, to Shlomo and to Isra'el his people.

¹¹ Thus Shlomo finished the house of ADONAI and the royal palace. Everything that Shlomo had set his heart on making in the house of ADONAI and in his own palace he accomplished successfully.

¹² ADONAI appeared to Shlomo by night and said to him, "I have heard your prayer and have chosen this place for myself as a house of sacrifice. ¹³ If I shut up the sky, so that there is no rain; or if I order locusts to devour the land; or if I send an epidemic of sickness among my people; ¹⁴ then, if my people, who bear my name, will humble themselves, pray, seek my face and turn from their evil ways, I will hear from heaven, forgive their sin and heal their land. ¹⁵ Now my eyes will be open and my ears will pay attention to the prayer made in this place. ¹⁶ For now I have chosen and consecrated this house, so that my name can be there forever; my eyes and heart will always be there. ¹⁷ As for you, if you will live in my presence, as did David your father, doing everything I have ordered you to do, and keeping my laws and rulings; ¹⁸ then I will establish the throne of your rulership, as I covenanted with David your father when I said, 'You will never lack a man to be ruler in Isra'el.' ¹⁹ But if you turn away and abandon my regulations and *mitzvot* which I have set before you, and go and serve other gods, worshipping them; ²⁰ then I will pull them up by the roots out of the land I have given them. This house, which I consecrated for my name, I will eject from my sight; and I will make it an example to avoid and an object of scorn among all peoples. ²¹ This house, now so exalted — everyone passing by will be shocked at the sight of it and will ask, 'Why has ADONAI done this to this land and to this house?' ²² But the answer will be, 'It's because they abandoned ADONAI the God of their ancestors, who brought them out of the land of Egypt, and took hold of other gods, worshipping and serving them; this is why [ADONAI] brought all these calamities on them.'"

8 ¹ At the end of twenty years, during which time Shlomo had built the house of ADONAI and his own palace, ² Shlomo built up the cities which Huram had given to Shlomo and had the people of Isra'el live there.

³ Then Shlomo attacked Hamat-Tzovah and defeated it. ⁴ He built Tadmor in the desert and all the cities for storing supplies that he built in Hamat. ⁵ He also built Upper Beit-Horon and Lower Beit-Horon, fortified cities with walls, gates and bars; ⁶ Ba'alat; and all the cities that Shlomo had for storing supplies, all the cities for his chariots, the cities for his horsemen, and all the other buildings Shlomo wanted to build in Yerushalayim, in the L'vanon and throughout the land he ruled.

⁷ As for all the people still left from the Hitti, Emori, P'rizi, Hivi, and Y'vusi, who were not part of Isra'el, ⁸ from their descendants remaining after them in the land, whom the people of Isra'el did not exterminate — from them Shlomo levied [his forced laborers], as it is to this day. ⁹ But Shlomo did not raise any of his slaves from the people of Isra'el; rather, these were the soldiers, his chief commanders, and the officials in charge of his chariots and horsemen. ¹⁰ King Shlomo had 250 chief officers in charge of the people.

¹¹ Shlomo brought up Pharaoh's daughter from the City of David to the house he had built for her; because he said, "No wife of mine is going to live in the house of David king of Isra'el, since the [buildings] where the ark of ADONAI has been are holy." ¹² Then Shlomo offered burnt offerings to ADONAI on the altar of ADONAI that he had built in front of the vestibule, ¹³ as each day required, offering according to the *mitzvah* of Moshe on *Shabbat*s, at *Rosh-Hodesh* and at the designated times three times a year — the festivals of *Matzah*, *Shavu'ot* and *Sukkot*. ¹⁴ As David his father had ordered, he appointed the divisions of the *cohanim* for their service and the *L'vi'im* to their tasks — to praise and to perform their service in the presence of the *cohanim* according to each day's requirements. He also appointed the gatekeepers by their divisions to be at every gate, for David the man of God had so ordered. ¹⁵ They did not deviate from the king's order to the *cohanim* and *L'vi'im* in any matter or in regard to the supplies. ¹⁶ All the work of Shlomo was organized in this way from the day ground was broken for the house of ADONAI until everything had been accomplished, and the house of ADONAI had been completed.

¹⁷ Shlomo went to 'Etzyon-Gever and Elot on the shore of the sea in the land of Edom. ¹⁸ Huram sent some of his servants with ships, and others that were experienced sailors who understood the sea; they went with Shlomo's servants to Ofir and took from there fifteen tons of gold, which they brought back to King Shlomo.

9 ¹ When the queen of Sh'va heard what was being said about Shlomo, she came to test him with difficult questions in Yerushalayim, accompanied by a very great retinue, including camels bearing spices and gold in abundance, and precious stones. When she appeared before Shlomo, she spoke with him about everything on her heart; ² and Shlomo answered all her questions; nothing was hidden from the king that he could not explain to her. ³ After the queen of Sh'va had seen Shlomo's wisdom, the palace he had built, ⁴ the food at his table, the manner of seating his officials, the manner in which his staff served him and how they were dressed, his personal servants and how they were dressed, and his manner of going up to the house of ADONAI, it left her breathless. ⁵ She said to the king, "What I heard in my own country about your deeds and your wisdom is true, ⁶ but I couldn't believe the report until I came and saw for myself. Actually, they didn't tell me even half of how great your wisdom is. In reality, you surpass the reports I heard. ⁷ How happy your people must be, how happy these servants of yours who are always here attending you and get to hear your wisdom! ⁸ Blessed be ADONAI your God, who took pleasure in you to put you on his throne, so that you could be king for ADONAI your God. Because of your God's love for Isra'el, to establish them forever, he has made you king over them, to administer law and judgment." ⁹ Then she gave the king four tons of gold, spices in great abundance, and precious stones; there had never been spices like those the queen of Sh'va gave to King Shlomo.

¹⁰ Huram's servants and Shlomo's servants, who had brought the gold from Ofir, now brought sandalwood and precious stones. ¹¹ The king used the sandalwood to make walkways for the house of ADONAI and for the royal palace, also lyres and lutes for the singers. None like these had been seen before in the land of Y'hudah. ¹² King Shlomo gave the queen of Sh'va everything she wanted, whatever she asked, more than what she had brought to the king. After this, she returned and went back to her own country, she and her servants.

^{13} The weight of the gold Shlomo received annually came to twenty-two tons, ^{14} besides that which came from customs duties and sales taxes; also all the Arab kings and regional governors brought gold and silver to Shlomo. ^{15} King Shlomo made 200 large shields of hammered gold; fifteen pounds of hammered gold went into one shield. ^{16} He made 300 more shields of hammered gold, with seven-and-a-half pounds going into one shield; the king put these in the House of the L'vanon Forest.

^{17} The king also made a great throne of ivory and overlaid it with pure gold. ^{18} The throne had six steps and a gold footstool; these were fastened to the throne. There were arms on either side of the seat, two lions standing beside the arms, ^{19} and twelve more lions standing on each side of the six steps. Nothing like it had ever been made in any kingdom.

^{20} All King Shlomo's drinking vessels were of gold; and all the utensils in the House of the L'vanon Forest were of pure gold; for in Shlomo's time, silver was regarded as having little value. ^{21} The king had ships that could go to Tarshish with Huram's servants; once every three years the "Tarshish" ships came in, bringing gold, silver, ivory, apes and peacocks.

^{22} So King Shlomo surpassed all the kings on earth in both wealth and wisdom. ^{23} All the kings on earth sought to have an audience with Shlomo, in order to hear his wisdom, which God had put in his heart. ^{24} Each one brought his present — articles of silver, articles of gold, clothing, armor, spices, horses and mules; and this continued year after year.

^{25} Shlomo also had 4,000 stalls of horses for his chariots and his 12,000 horsemen; he assigned them to the chariot cities and to the king in Yerushalayim. ^{26} He ruled over all the kingdoms from the [Euphrates] River through the land of the P'lishtim to the border of Egypt. ^{27} The king made silver in Yerushalayim as common as stones, and he made cedars as abundant as sycamore-fig trees are in the Sh'felah. ^{28} They brought horses for Shlomo from Egypt and from all countries.

^{29} Other activities of Shlomo, from beginning to end, are written in the records of Natan the prophet, in the prophecy of Achiyah of Shiloh and in the visions of Ye'do the seer concerning Yarov'am the son of N'vat. ^{30} Shlomo reigned in Yerushalayim over all Isra'el for forty years. ^{31} Then Shlomo slept with his ancestors and was buried in the City of David his father, and Rechav'am his son became king in his place.

10 ^{1} Rechav'am went to Sh'khem, where all Isra'el had come in order to proclaim him king. ^{2} When Yarov'am the son of N'vat heard of it, he returned from Egypt, where he had fled from Shlomo. ^{3} They sent and summoned him, so Yarov'am and all Isra'el came and said to Rechav'am, ^{4} "Your father laid a harsh yoke on us. But if you will lighten the harsh service we had to render your father and ease his heavy yoke that he put on us, we will serve you." ^{5} He said to them, "Come back to me after three days." So the people left.

^{6} King Rechav'am consulted the older men who had been in attendance on Shlomo his father during his lifetime and asked, "What advice would you give me as to how to answer these people?" ^{7} They said to him, "If you will treat these people kindly, pleasing them and giving them favorable consideration, they will be your servants forever." ^{8} But he didn't take the advice the older men gave him; instead he consulted the young men he had grown up with, who were now his attendants. ⁹ He said to them, "What advice would you give me, so that we can give an answer to these people who said to me, 'Lighten the yoke that your father laid on us'?" ¹⁰ The young men he had grown up with said to him, "The people who said to you, 'Your father made our yoke heavy, but you, make it lighter for us' — here's the answer you should give them: 'My little finger is thicker than my father's waist! ¹¹ Yes, my father burdened you with a heavy yoke, but I will make it heavier! My father controlled you with whips, but I [will control you] with scorpions!'"

¹² So Yarov'am and all the people came to Rechav'am the third day, as the king had requested by saying, "Come to me again the third day"; ¹³ and the king answered them harshly. Abandoning the advice of the older men, King Rechav'am ¹⁴ addressed them according to the advice of the young men and said, "I will make your yoke heavy, and I will add to it! My father controlled you with whips, but I will control you with scorpions!" ¹⁵ So the king didn't listen to the people; and that was something God brought about, so that Adonai could fulfill his word, which he had spoken through Achiyah from Shiloh to Yarov'am the son of N'vat.

¹⁶ When all Isra'el [saw] that the king wasn't listening to them, the people answered the king,

> "Do we have any share in David?
> We have no heritage in the son of Yishai!
> Everyone to your tents, Isra'el!
> Care for your own house, David!"

So all Isra'el left for their tents.

¹⁷ But as for the people of Isra'el living in the cities of Y'hudah, Rechav'am ruled over them. ¹⁸ King Rechav'am then sent Hadoram, who was in charge of forced labor; but the people of Isra'el stoned him to death. King Rechav'am managed to mount his chariot and flee to Yerushalayim. ¹⁹ Isra'el has been in rebellion against the dynasty of David to this day.

11 ¹ When Rechav'am arrived in Yerushalayim, he assembled the house of Y'hudah and Binyamin, 180,000 select soldiers, to fight Isra'el and bring the rulership back to Rechav'am. ² But this word of Adonai came to Sh'ma'yah the man of God: ³ "Speak to Rechav'am the son of Shlomo, king of Y'hudah, and to all Isra'el in Y'hudah and Binyamin; tell them ⁴ that this is what Adonai says: 'You are not to go up and fight your brothers! Every man is to go back home, because this is my doing.'" They paid attention to the words of Adonai and turned back from attacking Yarov'am.

⁵ Rechav'am lived in Yerushalayim and built cities for defense in Y'hudah — ⁶ he built Beit-Lechem, 'Eitam, T'koa, ⁷ Beit-Tzur, Sokho, 'Adulam, ⁸ Gat, Mareshah, Zif, ⁹ Adorayim, Lakhish, 'Azekah, ¹⁰ Tzor'ah, Ayalon and Hevron; these are fortified cities in Y'hudah and Binyamin. ¹¹ He fortified the strongholds, appointed captains in charge of them and supplied them with food, olive oil and wine. ¹² In every city he put shields and spears, making them very strong. Y'hudah and Binyamin stuck with him.

¹³ The *cohanim* and *L'vi'im* from wherever they lived throughout all Isra'el made themselves available to Rechav'am. ¹⁴ The *L'vi'im* left their pasture lands and property and came to Y'hudah and Yerushalayim; since Yarov'am and his sons had

thrown them out, not allowing them to function as *cohanim* for A<small>DONAI</small>, ¹⁵ and had appointed for himself *cohanim* for the high places and for the images of goat-demons and calves that he had made. ¹⁶ Those from all the tribes of Isra'el who had set their hearts on seeking A<small>DONAI</small>, the God of Isra'el, followed them to Yerushalayim to sacrifice to A<small>DONAI</small>, the God of their fathers. ¹⁷ For three years they strengthened the kingdom of Y'hudah and made Rechav'am the son of Shlomo strong, because for three years they followed the way of life of David and Shlomo.

¹⁸ Rechav'am married Machalat the daughter of Yerimot the son of David and Avichayil the daughter of Eli'av the son of Yishai; ¹⁹ and she became the mother of his sons Ye'ush, Sh'maryah and Zaham. ²⁰ After her, he married Ma'akhah the daughter of Avshalom; she became the mother of Aviyah, 'Atai, Ziza and Shlomit. ²¹ Rechav'am loved Ma'akhah more than all his other wives and concubines — for he had eighteen wives and sixty concubines and was the father of twenty-eight sons and sixty daughters. ²² Rechav'am appointed Aviyah the son of Ma'akhah chief, the leader of his brothers, because he intended to make him king. ²³ He was wise in his treatment of his sons, sending all of them throughout the territory of Y'hudah and Binyamin, to every fortified city, providing them with plenty of supplies and seeking for them many wives.

12 ¹ But in time, after Rechav'am had consolidated his rulership and had become strong, he, and with him all Isra'el, abandoned the *Torah* of A<small>DONAI</small>. ² In the fifth year of King Rechav'am, Shishak king of Egypt attacked Yerushalayim, because they had acted faithlessly toward A<small>DONAI</small>. ³ He came out of Egypt with 1,200 chariots, 60,000 horsemen and a numberless army including Luvim, Suki'im and Ethiopians. ⁴ He captured the fortified cities of Y'hudah, then went to Yerushalayim.

⁵ Now Sh'ma'yah the prophet came to Rechav'am and the leaders of Y'hudah who had gathered in Yerushalayim because of Shishak and said to them, "Here is what A<small>DONAI</small> says: 'Because you have abandoned me, I have abandoned you to the hands of Shishak.'" ⁶ In response, the leaders of Isra'el and the king humbled themselves; they said, "A<small>DONAI</small> is right." ⁷ When A<small>DONAI</small> saw that they had humbled themselves, this word of A<small>DONAI</small> came to Sh'ma'yah: "Because they have humbled themselves, I will not destroy them but will grant them a measure of deliverance. My wrath will not be poured out on Yerushalayim through Shishak. ⁸ However, they will become his slaves, so that they will come to appreciate the difference between serving me and serving earthly kingdoms."

⁹ So Shishak king of Egypt attacked Yerushalayim. He took the treasures in the house of A<small>DONAI</small> and the treasures in the royal palace — he took everything, including the gold shields Shlomo had made. ¹⁰ To replace them, King Rechav'am made shields of bronze, which he entrusted to the commanders of the contingent guarding the gate to the royal palace. ¹¹ Whenever the king went to the house of A<small>DONAI</small>, the guard would come and get the shields; later they would return them to the guardroom.

¹² After he humbled himself, the anger of A<small>DONAI</small> turned away from him, so that he did not altogether destroy him; moreover, some good things were found in Y'hudah. ¹³ So King Rechav'am consolidated his rule in Yerushalayim.

Rechav'am was forty-one years old when he began his reign; and he ruled seventeen years in Yerushalayim, the city A<small>DONAI</small> had chosen from all the tribes of Isra'el to bear his name; his mother's name was Na'amah the 'Amonit. ¹⁴ He did what was evil, because he had not set his heart on seeking A<small>DONAI</small>. ¹⁵ The activities of

Rechav'am from beginning to end are written in the genealogically organized histories of Sh'ma'yah the prophet and 'Iddo the seer. But there were continual wars between Rechav'am and Yarov'am. ¹⁶ Rechav'am slept with his ancestors and was buried in the City of David. Then Aviyah his son became king in his place.

13 ¹ It was in the eighteenth year of King Yarov'am that Aviyah began his reign over Y'hudah. ² He ruled three years in Yerushalayim; his mother's name was Mikhayahu the daughter of Uri'el from Giv'ah.

There was war between Aviyah and Yarov'am. ³ Aviyah joined the battle with an army of valiant soldiers, 400,000 select troops; while Yarov'am took the field against him with 800,000 select troops who were valiant, strong men.

⁴ Aviyah, standing on Mount Z'marayim, in the hills of Efrayim, cried, "Yarov'am and all Isra'el! Listen to me! ⁵ Don't you know that ADONAI, the God of Isra'el, gave rulership over Isra'el to David forever, to him and his descendants, by a covenant of salt [which is unbreakable]? ⁶ Yet Yarov'am the son of N'vat, servant to Shlomo the son of David, rose in rebellion against his lord. ⁷ There rallied around him worthless brutes who were too strong for Rechav'am the son of Shlomo to withstand when he was young and inexperienced. ⁸ Now you expect to withstand the kingdom of ADONAI in the hands of the descendants of David. Yes, there are a great number of you, and you have with you the gold calves that Yarov'am made as gods for you. ⁹ Yes, you drove out the *cohanim* of ADONAI, the descendants of Aharon, and the *L'vi'im*; and you made yourselves priests as do the peoples in other countries, so that anyone who comes to consecrate himself with a young bull and seven rams can become a priest of those non-gods.

¹⁰ "But we are different. ADONAI is our God, and we have not abandoned him. We have *cohanim* performing the service for ADONAI, descendants of Aharon. With the *L'vi'im* doing their work, ¹¹ they burn to ADONAI every morning and evening burnt offerings and sweet incense; they arrange the showbread on the pure table, and they prepare the gold *menorah* with its lamps to burn every evening. For we observe the order of ADONAI our God. But you have abandoned him.

¹² "So look here! God is with us, leading us and his *cohanim* with the battle trumpets to sound an alarm against you. People of Isra'el! Don't fight against ADONAI, the God of your ancestors; because you will not succeed."

¹³ But Yarov'am prepared to ambush them from behind, so that the main body was ahead of Y'hudah, while the ambush was behind them. ¹⁴ Thus when Y'hudah looked back, the battle had to be fought in front of them and behind them.

They cried to ADONAI, and the *cohanim* sounded the trumpets. ¹⁵ Then the men of Y'hudah gave forth a shout, and as the men of Y'hudah shouted, God struck Yarov'am and all Isra'el before Aviyah and Y'hudah. ¹⁶ The people of Isra'el fled before Y'hudah, and God handed them over to them. ¹⁷ Aviyah and his army inflicted a great slaughter on them — 500,000 of Isra'el's select soldiers fell dead. ¹⁸ Thus the people of Isra'el were subdued that time, and the people of Y'hudah won the victory, because they relied on ADONAI the God of their ancestors. ¹⁹ Aviyah pursued Yarov'am, taking from him the towns of Beit-El with its villages, Y'shanah with its villages and 'Efrayin with its villages. ²⁰ Yarov'am did not recover his strength during the time of Aviyahu. Finally ADONAI struck him, and he died. ²¹ But Aviyahu grew strong; he married fourteen wives and became the father of twenty-two sons and sixteen daughters.

²² Other activities of Aviyah, together with his ways of doing things and his sayings, are recorded in the commentary of the prophet 'Iddo. ²³⁽¹⁴:¹⁾ Aviyah slept with his ancestors, and they buried him in the City of David. Then Asa his son became king in his place; during his time the land was quiet for ten years.

14 ¹⁽²⁾ Asa did what was good and right from the perspective of ADONAI his God; ²⁽³⁾ for he removed the foreign altars and the high places, smashing the standing-stones and chopping down the sacred poles. ³⁽⁴⁾ He ordered Y'hudah to seek ADONAI, the God of their ancestors, and to obey the *Torah* and the *mitzvah*. ⁴⁽⁵⁾ He removed the high places and pillars for sun-worship from all the cities of Y'hudah, and under him the kingdom was quiet.

⁵⁽⁶⁾ Because the land was quiet, and he had no war during those years, since ADONAI had given him rest, he built fortified cities in Y'hudah. ⁶⁽⁷⁾ "Let's build these cities," he said to Y'hudah; "we'll surround them with walls, towers, gates and bars. The land is there for us to use, because we have sought ADONAI our God; we have sought him, and he has given us peace on every side." So they built and prospered.

⁷⁽⁸⁾ Asa had an army of 300,000 men from Y'hudah, equipped with shields and spears, and another 280,000 from Binyamin, with shields and bows; all were brave, strong men. ⁸⁽⁹⁾ Zerach the Ethiopian came out to attack them with an army of one million and three hundred chariots. When he arrived at Mareshah, ⁹⁽¹⁰⁾ Asa went out to fight him, and the forces were arranged for battle in the Tz'fat Valley at Mareshah.

¹⁰⁽¹¹⁾ Asa cried out to ADONAI his God, "ADONAI, there is no one besides yourself, strong or weak, who can help. Help us, ADONAI our God, because we are relying on you, and we are coming against this vast throng in your name. You are ADONAI our God; don't let human beings stop you!" ¹¹⁽¹²⁾ So ADONAI struck the Ethiopians before Asa and Y'hudah, and the Ethiopians fled. ¹²⁽¹³⁾ Asa and the army with him pursued them to G'rar, and the Ethiopians were defeated beyond recovery; they were shattered before ADONAI and his army, who carried off much spoil. ¹³⁽¹⁴⁾ Then they attacked all the cities in the vicinity of G'rar, for a panic from ADONAI had overcome them. They plundered all the cities, for they were full of spoil. ¹⁴⁽¹⁵⁾ They also attacked the tents of those tending the livestock and carried off sheep and camels in abundance. Then they returned to Yerushalayim.

15 ¹ The Spirit of God came on 'Azaryah the son of 'Oded; ² he went out to meet Asa and said to him, "Listen to me, Asa, and all Y'hudah and Binyamin! ADONAI is with you, as long as you are with him; if you seek him, you will find him; but if you abandon him, he will abandon you! ³ For a long time Isra'el was without the true God, without a *cohen* who could teach, and without *Torah*. ⁴ But when, in their distress, they turned to ADONAI the God of Isra'el and sought him, they found him. ⁵ In those times people going about their business were insecure, and great disturbances afflicted all the inhabitants of the lands; ⁶ so that they were shattered to pieces, nation against nation and city against city, as God troubled them with every kind of distress. ⁷ But you, be strong, and don't slack off; for your work will be rewarded."

⁸ When Asa heard these words prophesied by 'Oded the prophet, it gave him courage to throw the disgusting things out of the whole land of Y'hudah and Binyamin and out of the cities he had captured in the hills of Efrayim; he also renewed the altar of ADONAI which was in front of the vestibule of ADONAI. ⁹ Then he gathered all Y'hudah

and Binyamin, along with those from Efrayim, M'nasheh and Shim'on who were staying with him (for they had defected to him in large numbers upon seeing that ADONAI his God was with him). [10] They assembled together at Yerushalayim in the third month of the fifteenth year of Asa's reign. [11] That day they sacrificed to ADONAI 700 oxen and 7,000 sheep from the spoil they had brought; [12] and they entered into a covenant to seek ADONAI, the God of their ancestors, with all their heart and with all their being; [13] [they also agreed] that whoever refused to seek ADONAI the God of Isra'el should be put to death, whether small or great, man or woman. [14] They swore this to ADONAI in a loud voice, with shouting and blowing of trumpets and *shofars*. [15] All Y'hudah was full of joy at this oath; for they had sworn with all their heart and had sought him with all their will; and they found him, and ADONAI gave them rest all around.

[16] Asa the king also deposed Ma'akhah his [grand]mother from her position as queen mother, because she had made a disgusting image for an *asherah*. Asa cut down this image of hers, chopped it into tiny pieces and burned it in *Vadi* Kidron. [17] But the high places were not removed from Isra'el. Nevertheless, Asa was wholehearted throughout his life. [18] He brought into the house of God all the articles his father had consecrated, also the things he himself had consecrated — silver, gold and utensils. [19] There was no more war through the thirty-fifth year of Asa's reign.

16 [1] In the thirty-sixth year of Asa's reign, Ba'asha king of Isra'el attacked Y'hudah, and he fortified Ramah to prevent anyone's leaving or entering the territory of Asa king of Y'hudah. [2] Then Asa removed silver and gold from the treasures of the house of ADONAI and the royal palace; and sent this message to Ben-Hadad king of Aram, who lived in Dammesek: [3] "There is a covenant between me and you, as there was between my father and your father. Here, I am sending you silver and gold; go, and break your covenant with Ba'asha king of Isra'el, so that he will leave me alone." [4] Ben-Hadad did as King Asa had asked — he sent the commanders of his armies against the cities of Isra'el, attacking 'Iyon, Dan, Avel-Mayim and all the storage-cities of Naftali. [5] As soon as Ba'asha heard of it, he stopped building Ramah and abandoned his work. [6] Asa the king took all Y'hudah and carried off the stones and timber which Ba'asha had used to fortify Ramah. With them he fortified Geva and Mitzpah.

[7] It was around then that Hanani the seer came to Asa king of Y'hudah and said to him, "Because you relied on the king of Aram and didn't rely on ADONAI your God, the king of Aram's army has escaped from your power. [8] The army of the Ethiopians and Luvim was huge, wasn't it? How many chariots and horsemen did they have? Yet because you relied on ADONAI, he handed them over to you. [9] For the eyes of ADONAI move here and there throughout the whole earth, to show himself strong on behalf of those who are wholehearted toward him. You acted foolishly in this regard; for from now on, you will have war." [10] But Asa became angry at the seer; in fact, because of his rage at him over this matter he threw him in prison. Moreover, at the same time, he mistreated some of the people.

[11] The activities of Asa from beginning to end are recorded in the Annals of the Kings of Y'hudah and Isra'el. [12] In the thirty-ninth year of his reign, Asa suffered from a disease in his legs. It was a very serious disease, yet even with this disease he did not seek out ADONAI but turned to the physicians. [13] Asa slept with his ancestors, dying in the forty-first year

of his reign. ¹⁴ They buried him in his own burial cave, which he had ordered cut for himself in the City of David. They laid him in a bed filled with sweet spices of various kinds, expertly compounded; and a very great fire was kindled in his honor.

17 ¹ Then Y'hoshafat his son became king in his place. He strengthened his position against Isra'el ² by placing forces in all the fortified cities of Y'hudah, and by garrisoning troops in the territory of Y'hudah and in the cities of Efrayim that Asa his father had captured. ³ ADONAI was with Y'hoshafat, because he lived according to the first ways of his ancestor David, not seeking the *ba'alim*, ⁴ but seeking the God of his father and living by his *mitzvot*, not by what Isra'el did. ⁵ Therefore ADONAI consolidated his rulership; all Y'hudah brought presents to Y'hoshafat, so that he had wealth and honor in abundance. ⁶ In his heart he highly regarded ADONAI's ways; moreover, he removed the high places and sacred poles from Y'hudah.

⁷ In the third year of his reign he sent his leading men Ben-Chayil, 'Ovadyah, Z'kharyah, N'tan'el and Mikhayahu to teach in the cities of Y'hudah; ⁸ with them were the *L'vi'im* Sh'ma'yahu, N'tanyahu, Z'vadyahu, 'Asah'el, Sh'miramot, Y'honatan, Adoniyahu, Tuviyahu and Tov-Adoniyah, the *L'vi'im*; and with them Elishama and Y'horam the *cohanim*. ⁹ They taught in Y'hudah, having a scroll of the *Torah* of ADONAI with them; they circulated through all the cities of Y'hudah, teaching among the people.

¹⁰ A panic from ADONAI seized all the kingdoms in the lands surrounding Y'hudah, so that they did not make war against Y'hoshafat. ¹¹ Some of the P'lishtim brought Y'hoshafat gifts and silver as tribute; the Arabs too brought him flocks — 7,700 rams and 7,700 male goats.

¹² So Y'hoshafat grew increasingly powerful. In Y'hudah he built fortresses and storage cities. ¹³ He had many projects in the cities of Y'hudah; and in Yerushalayim he had warriors, strong brave men. ¹⁴ Here is a listing of them by clans: from Y'hudah, the captains of thousands: 'Adnah the leader, and with him 300,000 strong, brave men; ¹⁵ next to him Y'hochanan the leader, and with him 280,000; ¹⁶ next to him 'Amasyah the son of Zikhri, who volunteered to serve ADONAI, and with him 200,000 strong, brave men. ¹⁷ From Binyamin: Elyada, a strong, brave man, and with him 200,000 equipped with bows and shields; ¹⁸ next to him Y'hozavad, and with him 180,000 prepared for war. ¹⁹ These served the king, in addition to those the king assigned to the fortified cities throughout all Y'hudah.

18 ¹ Y'hoshafat had wealth and honor in abundance, and by marriage he allied himself with Ach'av. ² After some years he went down to Ach'av in Shomron. Ach'av slaughtered sheep and oxen in abundance for him and the people with him, and persuaded him to go up with him to Ramot-Gil'ad. ³ Ach'av king of Isra'el said to Y'hoshafat king of Y'hudah, "Will you go with me to Ramot-Gil'ad?" He answered him, "I'm with you all the way; think of my troops as yours; we will join you in this war." ⁴ But Y'hoshafat said to the king of Isra'el, "First, we should seek the word of ADONAI."

⁵ So the king of Isra'el assembled the prophets, 400 men. "Should we attack Ramot-Gil'ad?" he asked them, "Or should I hold off?" They said, "Attack. God will hand it over to the king." ⁶ But Y'hoshafat said, "Besides these, isn't there a prophet of ADONAI here that we can consult?" ⁷ The king of Isra'el said to Y'hoshafat, "Yes, there is still one man through whom we can consult ADONAI; but I hate him,

because he never prophesies anything good for me, only bad! It's Mikhay'hu the son of Yimlah." Y'hoshafat replied, "The king shouldn't say such a thing."

⁸ Then the king called an officer and said, "Quickly! Bring Mikhay'hu the son of Yimlah." ⁹ Now the king of Isra'el and Y'hoshafat the king of Y'hudah were each sitting on his throne, dressed in their royal robes; they were sitting in a threshing-floor at the entrance to the gate of Shomron; and all the prophets were there, prophesying in their presence. ¹⁰ Tzidkiyah the son of Kena'anah had made himself some horns out of iron and said, "This is what ADONAI says: 'With these you will gore Aram until they are destroyed.'" ¹¹ All the prophets prophesied the same thing: "Go up and attack Ramot-Gil'ad. You will succeed, because ADONAI will hand it over to the king."

¹² The messenger who had gone to call Mikhay'hu said to him, "Here, now, the prophets are unanimously predicting success for the king. Please let your word be like one of theirs — say something good." ¹³ But Mikhay'hu answered, "As ADONAI lives, whatever my God says is what I will say."

¹⁴ When he reached the king, the king asked him, "Mikhay'hu, should we go up and attack Ramot-Gil'ad, or should we hold off?" He answered, "Go up, you will succeed, they will be handed over to you." ¹⁵ The king said to him, "How many times do I have to warn you to tell me nothing but the truth in the name of ADONAI?" ¹⁶ Then he said, "I saw all Isra'el scattered over the hills like sheep without a shepherd; and ADONAI said, 'These men have no leader; let everyone go home in peace.'" ¹⁷ The king of Isra'el said to Y'hoshafat, "Didn't I tell you that he wouldn't prophesy good things about me, but bad?"

¹⁸ Mikhay'hu continued: "Therefore, hear the word of ADONAI. I saw ADONAI sitting on his throne with the whole army of heaven standing on his right and on his left. ¹⁹ ADONAI asked, 'Who will entice Ach'av king of Isra'el to go up to his death at Ramot-Gil'ad?' One of them said, 'Do it this way,' and another, 'Do it that way.' ²⁰ Then a spirit stepped up, stood in front of ADONAI and said, 'I will entice him.' ADONAI asked, 'How?' ²¹ He answered, 'I will go and be a deceiving spirit in the mouths of all his prophets.' ADONAI said, 'You will succeed in enticing him. Go, and do it.' ²² So now ADONAI has put a deceiving spirit in the mouths of these prophets of yours; meanwhile, ADONAI has ordained disaster for you."

²³ Then Tzidkiyah the son of Kena'anah came up, slapped Mikhay'hu in the face and said, "And how did the Spirit of ADONAI leave me to speak to you?" ²⁴ Mikhay'hu said, "You'll find out the day you go into an inside room, trying to hide."

²⁵ The king of Isra'el said, "Seize Mikhay'hu, and take him back to Amon the governor of the city and Yo'ash the king's son. ²⁶ Say, 'The king says to put this man in prison; and feed him only bread and water, and not much of that, until I come back in peace.'" ²⁷ Mikhay'hu said, "If you return in peace at all, ADONAI has not spoken through me!" Then he added, "Did you hear me, you peoples, all of you?"

²⁸ So the king of Isra'el and Y'hoshafat the king of Y'hudah went up to Ramot-Gil'ad. ²⁹ The king of Isra'el said to Y'hoshafat, "I will disguise myself and go into battle; but you, put on your robes." So the king of Isra'el disguised himself and went into battle. ³⁰ Now the king of Aram had ordered his chariot commanders, "Don't attack anyone of either high or low rank, only the king of Isra'el." ³¹ So when the chariot commanders saw Y'hoshafat they said, "This is the king of Isra'el," and turned to attack him. But Y'hoshafat called out, and ADONAI came

to his aid — God moved them to leave him alone, ³² so that when the chariot commanders saw that he wasn't the king of Isra'el, they stopped pursuing him. ³³ However, one soldier shot an arrow at random and struck the king of Isra'el between his lower armor and the breastplate. The king said to his chariot-driver, "Turn the reins and take me out of the fighting; I'm collapsing from my wounds." ³⁴ But the fighting grew fiercer that day; and although the king of Isra'el propped himself upright in his chariot facing Aram until evening, around sunset he died.

19 ¹ Then Y'hoshafat the king of Y'hudah returned home to Yerushalayim in peace. ² Yehu the son of Hanani the seer went out to meet him and said to King Y'hoshafat, "Should you help the wicked and befriend those who hate ADONAI? Because of this, ADONAI's anger is upon you. ³ Still, there is some good in you, in that you have removed the sacred poles from the land and have set your heart on seeking God."

⁴ So Y'hoshafat lived in Yerushalayim and again circulated among the people from Be'er-Sheva to the hills of Efrayim, bringing them back to ADONAI, the God of their ancestors.

⁵ He appointed judges throughout the land in all the fortified cities of Y'hudah, city by city, ⁶ and instructed the judges, "Think about what you are doing: you are not dispensing justice by merely human standards but on behalf of ADONAI; he is with you when you deliver a verdict. ⁷ Therefore, let the fear of ADONAI be upon you; be careful what you do; for ADONAI our God does not allow dishonesty, partiality or bribe-taking."

⁸ In Yerushalayim Y'hoshafat appointed some of the *L'vi'im*, *cohanim* and clan heads of Isra'el to judge in matters concerning ADONAI and in civil cases. After they had returned to Yerushalayim, ⁹ he charged them, "Here is what you are to do faithfully and wholeheartedly, in fear of ADONAI: ¹⁰ when an issue comes before you from your brothers who live in their cities, whether it's a case involving bloodshed or a question as to which teaching, *mitzvah*, law or ruling applies, you must warn them; so that they won't incur guilt toward ADONAI and thereby bring anger on both you and your kinsmen. Do this, and you won't incur guilt. ¹¹ Amaryahu the chief *cohen* is over you in all matters concerning ADONAI, and Z'vadyahu the son of Yishma'el, chief of the house of Y'hudah, in all the king's matters. The officers of the *L'vi'im* are at your service. Be strong, and act, and may ADONAI be with the good."

20 ¹ Some time later, the people of Mo'av and the people of 'Amon with other 'Amonim came up to fight Y'hoshafat. ² Y'hoshafat was told, "A huge army from beyond the [Dead] Sea, from Aram, is on its way to fight you; right now they are in Hatzatzon-Tamar" (that is, 'Ein-Gedi). ³ Y'hoshafat was frightened, so he determined to seek ADONAI. He proclaimed a fast throughout all Y'hudah, ⁴ and Y'hudah assembled to seek help from ADONAI; they came from all the cities of Y'hudah to seek ADONAI.

⁵ Standing in front of the new courtyard in the house of ADONAI, among those assembled from Y'hudah and Yerushalayim, ⁶ he said: "ADONAI, God of our ancestors, you alone are God in heaven. You rule all the kingdoms of the nations. In your hand are power and strength, so that no one can withstand you. ⁷ You, our God, drove out those living in the land ahead of your people Isra'el and gave it forever to the descendants of Avraham your friend. ⁸ They lived in it, built you a sanctuary in it

for your name, and said, ⁹ 'If calamity strikes us, such as war, judgment, disease or famine, we will stand before this house — that is, before you, since your name is in this house — and cry to you in our distress; and you will hear us and rescue us.'

¹⁰ "So now, see: the people of 'Amon, Mo'av and Mount Se'ir, whom you would not let Isra'el invade when they came out of the land of Egypt, so that they turned away from them and did not destroy them, ¹¹ are now repaying us [evil]; they have come to throw us out of your possession, which you gave us as an inheritance. ¹² Our God! Won't you execute judgment against them? For we haven't strength enough to defeat this huge horde coming against us, and we don't know what to do, but our eyes are on you."

¹³ All Y'hudah stood before ADONAI with their little ones, their wives and their children. ¹⁴ Then, in the middle of the assembly, the Spirit of ADONAI came upon Yachzi'el the son of Z'kharyahu, the son of B'nayah, the son of Ye'i'el, the son of Matanyah the Levi, from the descendants of Asaf. ¹⁵ He said, "Listen, all Y'hudah, you who live in Yerushalayim and King Y'hoshafat: here is what ADONAI is saying to you: 'Don't be afraid or distressed by this great horde; for the battle is not yours, but God's. ¹⁶ Tomorrow, go down against them. They will be coming up by the ascent of Tzitz, and you will find them at the end of the vadi, before the Yeru'el Desert. ¹⁷ You won't even need to fight this battle! Just take your positions, Y'hudah and Yerushalayim, stand still, and watch how ADONAI will deliver you! Don't be afraid or distressed; tomorrow, go out against them; for ADONAI is with you.'"

¹⁸ Y'hoshafat bowed his head with his face to the ground; while all Y'hudah and the inhabitants of Yerushalayim fell down before ADONAI, worshipping ADONAI; ¹⁹ and the L'vi'im from the descendants of the K'hati and the descendants of the Korchi, stood up and praised ADONAI the God of Isra'el at the top of their voices.

²⁰ The next morning, they rose early and went out into the T'koa Desert. As they left, Y'hoshafat stood and said, "Listen to me, Y'hudah and you inhabitants of Yerushalayim!

"Trust in ADONAI your God,
and you will be safe.
Trust in his prophets,
and you will succeed."

²¹ After consulting with the people, he appointed those who would sing to ADONAI and praise the splendor of his holiness as they went out ahead of the army, saying, "Give thanks to ADONAI, for his grace continues forever." ²² Then, during the time when they were singing and praising, ADONAI brought a surprise attack against the people of 'Amon, Mo'av and Mount Se'ir who had come to fight Y'hudah; and they were defeated. ²³ What happened was that the people of 'Amon and Mo'av began attacking those people who lived by Mount Se'ir, to kill and destroy them completely; and when they had finished off the people from Se'ir, they set to work slaughtering one another. ²⁴ So when Y'hudah reached the watchtower overlooking the desert, they looked toward the horde; and there in front of them were corpses fallen to the ground; none had escaped. ²⁵ Y'hoshafat and his army came to take the spoil from them and found among them personal property in abundance and corpses with precious jewels, which they stripped off for themselves until they couldn't carry

any more. They took three days just to collect the spoil, there was so much. ²⁶ On the fourth day, they assembled in the Valley of B'rakhah [blessing], where they blessed ADONAI; hence that place is called the Valley of B'rakhah to this day.

²⁷ Then they returned, everyone from Y'hudah and Yerushalayim, with Y'hoshafat leading them joyfully back to Yerushalayim; for ADONAI had caused them to rejoice over their enemies. ²⁸ They came to Yerushalayim with lyres, lutes and trumpets and went to the house of ADONAI. ²⁹ A panic from God was on all the kingdoms of the countries when they heard that ADONAI had fought against the enemies of Isra'el. ³⁰ So Y'hoshafat's rule was a quiet one, because his God gave him rest all around.

³¹ Y'hoshafat ruled over Y'hudah; he was thirty-five years old when he began his reign, and he ruled twenty-five years in Yerushalayim. His mother's name was 'Azuvah the daughter of Shilchi. ³² He lived in the manner of Asa his father and did not turn away from it, doing what was right from ADONAI's perspective; ³³ although the high places were not taken away, and the people had not yet set their hearts toward the God of their ancestors. ³⁴ Other activities of Y'hoshafat, from beginning to end, are written in the records of Yehu the son of Hanani, which have been inserted in the Annals of the Kings of Isra'el.

³⁵ It was after this that Y'hoshafat joined up with Achazyah king of Isra'el, who was acting very wickedly. ³⁶ He joined together with him to build large ships capable of going to Tarshish; they made the ships in 'Etzyon-Gever. ³⁷ Then Eli'ezer the son of Dodavahu from Mareshah prophesied against Y'hoshafat: "Because you joined yourself with Achazyah, ADONAI is wrecking your project." And the ships were wrecked, so that they couldn't go to Tarshish.

21 ¹ Y'hoshafat slept with his ancestors and was buried with his ancestors in the City of David, and Y'horam his son became king in his place. ² He had brothers who were sons of Y'hoshafat — 'Azaryah, Yechi'el, Z'kharyahu, 'Azaryahu, Mikha'el and Sh'fatyahu; all these were sons of Y'hoshafat king of Isra'el. ³ Their father had given them lavish gifts of silver, gold and other items of value, as well as fortified cities in Y'hudah; but he had given the kingdom to Y'horam, because he was the firstborn. ⁴ But when Y'horam had taken control of his father's kingdom and consolidated his rule, he put to the sword all his brothers and a number of the leading men in Isra'el.

⁵ He was thirty-two years old when he began his reign, and he ruled eight years in Yerushalayim. ⁶ He lived after the example of the kings of Isra'el, as did the house of Ach'av; because he had married Ach'av's daughter; he did what was evil from ADONAI's perspective. ⁷ However, ADONAI was unwilling to destroy the house of David, because of the covenant he had made with David; inasmuch as he had promised to give him and his children a lamp that would burn forever.

⁸ During his time Edom revolted against Y'hudah and set up its own king. ⁹ Then Y'horam crossed with his commanders and all his chariots. Under cover of night, he and his chariot commanders attacked and defeated Edom, who had surrounded him. ¹⁰ Nevertheless, since that day Edom has remained free of Y'hudah's domination. Livnah revolted against him at the same time, because he had abandoned ADONAI the God of his ancestors. ¹¹ Moreover, he built high places in the hills of Y'hudah, caused the people living in Yerushalayim to prostitute themselves and drew Y'hudah away.

¹² A letter came to him from Eliyahu the prophet which said, "Here is what ADONAI, the God of David your ancestor, says: 'You have not lived by the examples of Y'hoshafat your father or Asa king of Y'hudah. ¹³ Instead you have lived by the example of the kings of Isra'el and have caused Y'hudah and the people living in Yerushalayim to prostitute themselves, just as the house of Ach'av caused [Isra'el] to prostitute themselves. Moreover, you killed your brothers from your father's house, men better than you. ¹⁴ Because of all this, ADONAI is going to strike your people with a terrible disease, also your children, your wives and everything you have. ¹⁵ You will be very ill from a disease in your intestines, until your intestines protrude, because of the effects of this disease, day after day.'"

¹⁶ Then ADONAI aroused against Y'horam the spirit of the P'lishtim and of the Arabs near the Ethiopians; ¹⁷ and they came up to attack Y'hudah. They broke in and carried off all the personal property they could find in the royal palace, as well as his children and his wives; so that no son was left to him except Y'ho'achaz his youngest son.

¹⁸ After all this, ADONAI struck him in his intestines with an incurable disease. ¹⁹ In time, after two years, his intestines protruded because of his disease, and he suffered a most painful death. His people kindled no fire for him, as had been done for his ancestors. ²⁰ He was thirty-two years old when he began his reign, he ruled in Yerushalayim for eight years, and he left without joy. They buried him in the City of David, but not in the tombs of the kings.

22 ¹ The people living in Yerushalayim made Achazyah his youngest son king in place of him, since the raiding party that had invaded the camp with the Arabs had killed all the older ones. So Achazyah the son of Y'horam king of Y'hudah reigned. ² Achazyah was forty-two years old when he began his reign, and he ruled for one year in Yerushalayim. His mother's name was 'Atalyahu the daughter of 'Omri. ³ He too lived after the example of the house of Ach'av, because his mother was his counselor in acting wickedly. ⁴ So he did what was evil from ADONAI's perspective, as had the house of Ach'av; because, to his destruction, they were his counselors after his father died; ⁵ and he lived his life by their advice.

With Y'horam the son of Ach'av, king of Isra'el, he went to war against Haza'el king of Aram at Ramot-Gil'ad, where the Aramim wounded Y'horam. ⁶ He returned to Yizre'el to be healed of the wounds which they had inflicted on him at Ramah while fighting Haza'el king of Aram. Achazyah the son of Y'horam, king of Y'hudah, went down to visit Y'horam the son of Ach'av in Yizre'el, because he was not feeling well. ⁷ Through Achazyah's visit to Y'horam, God brought about his downfall. After he arrived, he accompanied Y'horam against Yehu the son of Nimshi, whom ADONAI had anointed to cut off the house of Ach'av. ⁸ But it happened that when Yehu was executing judgment on the house of Ach'av, he found the leading men of Y'hudah and Achazyah's nephews in attendance on Achazyah and killed them. ⁹ Then he went searching for Achazyah; they caught him where he had been hiding in Shomron, brought him to Yehu and killed him. But [his subjects] buried him, because they said, "He was the [grand]son of Y'hoshafat, who sought ADONAI with all his heart."

At this point there was no one in the house of Achazyah strong enough to rule the kingdom. ¹⁰ When 'Atalyah the mother of Achazyah saw that her son was dead, she set about destroying the entire royal family of the house of Y'hudah. ¹¹ But Y'hoshav'at the daughter of the king took Yo'ash the son of Achazyah, stole him away from among the princes who were being slaughtered, and sequestered him and his nurse in a bedroom. Thus Y'hoshav'at the daughter of King Y'horam, wife of Y'hoyada the *cohen* and sister of Achazyah, hid him from 'Atalyah, so that he was not killed. ^{12} He remained hidden with them in the house of God for six years; during this time 'Atalyah ruled the land.

23 ^{1} In the seventh year Y'hoyada took courage and formed a conspiracy with certain captains of hundred-man platoons — 'Azaryah the son of Yerocham, Yishma'el the son of Y'hochanan, 'Azaryah the son of 'Oved, Ma'aseiyahu the son of 'Adayahu and Elishafat the son of Zikhri. ^{2} They canvassed Y'hudah and gathered the *L'vi'im* from all the cities of Y'hudah, together with the clan heads of Isra'el, and came to Yerushalayim. ^{3} The whole assembly made an agreement with the king in the house of God. [Y'hoyada] addressed them: "Here! The king's son will reign, as A$_{DONAI}$ said in regard to the descendants of David! ^{4} Here is what you are to do: of you *cohanim* and *L'vi'im* who come on duty on *Shabbat*, a third are to guard the gates, ^{5} a third the royal palace and a third the Gate of the Foundation; while all the people are to remain in the courtyards of the house of A$_{DONAI}$. ^{6} No one is to enter the house of A$_{DONAI}$ except the *cohanim* and those *L'vi'im* who are actually performing the service. These may enter, because they are holy; but all the people are to observe A$_{DONAI}$'s order. ^{7} The *L'vi'im* are to surround the king, each man with his weapons in his hand. Anyone who enters the house is to be killed. Stay with the king whenever he enters or leaves."

^{8} The *L'vi'im* and all Y'hudah did exactly as Y'hoyada the *cohen* ordered. Each took his men, those coming on duty on *Shabbat* and those going off duty on *Shabbat* (for Y'hoyada the *cohen* did not dismiss the divisions). ^{9} Y'hoyada the *cohen* issued to the captains of hundreds the spears and the large and small shields that had been King David's and were kept in the house of God. ^{10} He then positioned all the people, each man with his weapon in his hand, from the right side of the house to the left side of the house, alongside the altar, alongside [the exterior of] the house and around the king. ^{11} Then they brought out the king's son, crowned him, gave him [a copy of] the testimony and thus made him king. Y'hoyada and his sons anointed him, and they shouted, "Long live the king!"

^{12} When 'Atalyah heard the sound of the people running and praising the king, she entered the house of A$_{DONAI}$ where the people were, ^{13} looked and saw the king standing there on his platform at the entrance, with the leaders and trumpeters next to the king. All the people of the land were celebrating and blowing the trumpets; while the singers with their musical instruments were leading songs of praise. At this, 'Atalyah tore her clothes and cried, "Treason! Treason!" ^{14} Y'hoyada the *cohen* brought out the captains of hundreds who were in charge of the army and said to them, "Escort her out past the ranks [of guards]; but anyone who follows her, let him be put to the sword." For the *cohen* had said, "Do not put her to death in the house of A$_{DONAI}$." ^{15} So they took her by force and led her by the horses' entry to the king's palace, and there they put her to death.

^{16} Y'hoyada made a covenant between himself, all the people and the king, that they would be A$_{DONAI}$'s people. ^{17} Then all the people went to the house of Ba'al and broke it down; they smashed his altars and images and killed Mattan the priest of Ba'al in front of the altars.

[18] Y'hoyada appointed officers for the house of ADONAI under the supervision of the cohanim and L'vi'im, whom David had assigned turns of duty in the house of ADONAI, to offer the burnt offerings of ADONAI, as written in the Torah of Moshe, with rejoicing and singing in keeping with David's orders. [19] He stationed guards at the gates of the house of ADONAI, so that no one who was unclean in any respect could enter. [20] He took the captains of hundreds, the men of rank, the rulers of the people and all the people of the land; and they brought the king down from the house of ADONAI, going through the Upper Gate to the royal palace, and seated the king on the royal throne. [21] All the people of the land celebrated, and at last the city was quiet. That is how they killed 'Atalyah with the sword.

24 [1] Yo'ash was seven years old when he began his reign, and he reigned forty years in Yerushalayim. His mother's name was Tzivyah, from Be'er-Sheva. [2] Yo'ash did what was right from ADONAI's perspective throughout the lifetime of Y'hoyada the cohen. [3] Y'hoyada chose two wives for him, and he became the father of sons and daughters.

[4] Some time later, Yo'ash decided to restore the house of ADONAI. [5] He gathered the cohanim and L'vi'im and said to them, "Go out to the cities of Y'hudah, and collect money each year from all Isra'el to repair the house of your God. See that you do this promptly." But when the L'vi'im procrastinated, [6] the king summoned Y'hoyada the chief and said to him, "Why haven't you demanded that the L'vi'im bring in from Y'hudah and Yerushalayim the tax prescribed by Moshe the servant of ADONAI and by the community of Isra'el, for the tent of the testimony?" [7] For the sons of that wicked 'Atalyahu had broken up the house of God, and they had given all the consecrated things belonging to the house of ADONAI to the ba'alim.

[8] Then, at the king's order, they made a box and placed it outside the entrance to the house of ADONAI. [9] They proclaimed throughout Y'hudah and Yerushalayim that the tax Moshe the servant of God had imposed on Isra'el in the desert should be brought in for ADONAI. [10] All the leaders and all the people were glad to bring in their contributions and put them in the box, until it was full. [11] When the box was brought to the king's officials by the L'vi'im, and when they saw how much money there was, the king's secretary and the chief cohen's official came and emptied the box; then they took it and returned it to its place. They did this daily, and they collected money in abundance.

[12] The king and Y'hoyada gave it to those in charge of taking care of the house of ADONAI. They, in turn, hired stone-workers and carpenters to restore the house of ADONAI, also iron- and bronze-workers to repair the house of ADONAI. [13] The workers got on with their tasks, so that the restoration progressed well, until they had returned the house of God to its earlier condition and strengthened it. [14] When they had finished, they brought the rest of the money to the king and Y'hoyada, and it was used to make equipment for the house of ADONAI — articles for ministry, buckets, fire pans, and utensils of gold and silver. So they offered burnt offerings in the house of ADONAI regularly throughout the time of Y'hoyada.

[15] But Y'hoyada grew old; and when he was full of days, he died. He was 130 years old when he died. [16] They buried him in the City of David among the kings, because he had served Isra'el, God and his house well.

¹⁷ After Y'hoyada died, the leaders of Y'hudah came and prostrated themselves before the king. Then the king listened to them; ¹⁸ and they abandoned the house of ADONAI the God of their ancestors and served the sacred poles and the idols. In consequence of their guilt, [God's] anger fell on Y'hudah and Yerushalayim. ¹⁹ In spite of this, he sent them prophets to bring them back to ADONAI; they warned them, but they wouldn't pay attention. ²⁰ The Spirit of God covered Z'kharyah the son of Y'hoyada the *cohen*; he stood above the people and addressed them: "Thus says God: 'Why are you transgressing the *mitzvot* of ADONAI and courting disaster? Because you have abandoned ADONAI, he has abandoned you.'" ²¹ But they conspired against him and stoned him to death at the order of the king in the courtyard of the house of ADONAI. ²² Thus Yo'ash the king did not remember the kindness which Y'hoyada, [Z'kharyah's] father, had done for him, but put his son to death. As he was dying he said, "May ADONAI see this and take vengeance!"

²³ The following spring, the army of Aram came up against him. They attacked Y'hudah and Yerushalayim, slaughtered all the people's leaders and sent all their spoil to the king of Dammesek. ²⁴ Although the army of Aram attacked with only a small company of men, ADONAI handed over a very great army to them, because they had abandoned ADONAI the God of their ancestors. Thus they executed judgment against Yo'ash.

²⁵ After they had left him — and they left him seriously wounded — his own servants conspired against him because he had shed the blood of the sons of Y'hoyada the *cohen*; and they killed him in his own bed. After he died, they buried him in the City of David, but they didn't bury him in the tombs of the kings. ²⁶ Those who conspired against him were Zavad the son of Shim'at the 'Amonit and Y'hozavad the son of Shimrit the Mo'avit.

²⁷ As for his sons, the heavy tribute imposed on him, and the rebuilding of the house of God, they are recorded in the commentary of the Annals of the Kings. Then Amatzyahu his son took his place as king.

25 ¹ Amatzyahu was twenty-five years old when he began his reign, and he ruled for twenty-nine years in Yerushalayim. His mother's name was Y'ho'adan, from Yerushalayim. ² He did what was right from ADONAI's perspective, but not wholeheartedly.

³ As soon as he had the kingdom firmly in his control, he put to death the servants of his who had assassinated the king his father. ⁴ But he did not put their children to death; rather, he acted according to what is written in the *Torah*, in the scroll of Moshe, as ADONAI ordered when he said, "Fathers are not to die for the children, nor are the children to die for the fathers; every person will die for his own sin."

⁵ Amatzyahu assembled Y'hudah together and put them in order by clans under captains of thousands and captains of hundreds — all Y'hudah and Binyamin. He registered everyone twenty years old and older, and found that there were 300,000 select troops able to go to war, capable of using spears and shields. ⁶ He also hired 100,000 strong, brave men from Isra'el for three-and-a-third tons of silver. ⁷ But a man of God came to him and said, "King, don't let the army of Isra'el go with you; because ADONAI is not with Isra'el or with any of the people of Efrayim. ⁸ And if you do go, then no matter how fiercely you fight, God will cause you to fail before the enemy. For God has the power to help and to cause failure." ⁹ Amatzyahu said to the man of God, "But what do we do about the three-and-a-third tons [of silver] I paid

for Isra'el's army?" The man of God answered, "*ADONAI* can give you far more than that!" ¹⁰ Then Amatzyahu separated out the battalion that had come to him from Efrayim and told them to go back home — which made their anger burn hotly against Y'hudah, and they returned home enraged.

¹¹ Amatzyahu took courage, led his people out and went to the Salt Valley, where he killed 10,000 of the people of Se'ir. ¹² The people of Y'hudah took another 10,000 away alive, brought them to the top of the Rock and threw them off the top of the Rock, so that they were all dashed to pieces.

¹³ Meanwhile, the men in the army that Amatzyahu had sent back and hadn't allowed to join him in battle fell on the cities of Y'hudah, all the way from Shomron to Beit-Horon, killed 3,000 of them and took much spoil.

¹⁴ After Amatzyahu returned from the slaughter of the people from Edom, he brought the gods of the people of Se'ir and set them up as his own gods, prostrating himself before them and offering incense to them. ¹⁵ As a result, the anger of *ADONAI* blazed up against Amatzyah, and he sent him a prophet, who said to him, "Why have you sought out the gods of those people, when they couldn't even rescue their own people from you?" ¹⁶ But as [the prophet] was speaking to him, he interrupted him: "Were you made an adviser to the king? You had better stop before you get yourself killed!" So the prophet stopped, but he added, "I know that God is planning to destroy you for having done this and for refusing to listen to my advice."

¹⁷ Then, after taking counsel, Amatzyah king of Y'hudah sent a challenge to Yo'ash the son of Y'ho'achaz, the son of Yehu, king of Isra'el: "Come on, let's have it out face-to-face." ¹⁸ Yo'ash the king of Isra'el sent this reply to Amatzyah king of Y'hudah: "Once, in the L'vanon, the thistle sent a message to the cedar: 'Give your daughter to my son in marriage.' But a wild animal passed by the thistle and squashed it. ¹⁹ You say you defeated Edom, which is true; so you're excited and itching for more glory. But now, stay home! Why provoke calamity, to your own ruin, yours and Y'hudah's too?" ²⁰ But Amatzyah wouldn't listen. And this was from God, so that he could hand them over [to their enemies], because they had sought the gods of Edom. ²¹ So Yo'ash king of Isra'el went up; and he and Amatzyah king of Y'hudah had it out face-to-face at Beit-Shemesh, which belongs to Y'hudah. ²² Y'hudah was defeated by Isra'el, and every man fled to his tent. ²³ Yo'ash king of Isra'el took Amatzyah king of Y'hudah, the son of Yo'ash the son of Y'ho'achaz, prisoner at Beit-Shemesh. Then he brought him to Yerushalayim and demolished the wall of Yerushalayim between the Gate of Efrayim and the Corner Gate, a section 600 feet long. ²⁴ [He took] all the gold and silver, all the articles he could find in the house of God, with 'Oved-Edom, and the treasures of the royal palace, together with hostages; then he returned to Shomron.

²⁵ Amatzyahu the son of Yo'ash, king of Y'hudah, lived another fifteen years after the death of Yo'ash son of Y'ho'achaz king of Isra'el. ²⁶ Other activities of Amatzyah, from beginning to end, are recorded in the Annals of the Kings of Y'hudah and Isra'el.

²⁷ From the time that Amatzyahu turned away from following *ADONAI*, they formed a conspiracy against him in Yerushalayim. So he fled to Lakhish; but they followed him to Lakhish and killed him there. ²⁸ They brought his body back on horses and buried him with his ancestors in the City of Y'hudah.

26 ¹ Meanwhile, all the people of Y'hudah had taken 'Uziyahu at the age of sixteen and made him king in place of his father Amatzyahu. ² He recovered Eilot for Y'hudah and rebuilt it; it was after this that the king [Amatzyahu] slept with his ancestors.

³ 'Uziyahu was sixteen years old when he began his reign, and he ruled for fifty-two years in Yerushalayim. His mother's name was Y'kholyahu, from Yerushalayim. ⁴ He did what was right from ADONAI's perspective, following the example of everything his father Amatzyahu had done. ⁵ He consulted God during the lifetime of Z'kharyahu, who understood visions of God; and as long as he consulted ADONAI, God gave him success.

⁶ He went out to fight the P'lishtim, breaking down the walls of Gat, Yavneh and Ashdod; and he built cities in the area of Ashdod and among the P'lishtim. ⁷ God helped him against the P'lishtim, against the Arabs living in Gur-Ba'al, and against the Me'unim. ⁸ The 'Amonim brought tribute to 'Uziyahu, and his fame spread abroad as far as the Egyptian frontier, since he kept growing stronger.

⁹ 'Uziyahu built towers in Yerushalayim at the Corner Gate, at the Valley Gate and at the Angle, and fortified them. ¹⁰ He built towers in the desert and dug many cisterns, because he had much livestock, likewise in the Sh'felah and the coastal plain. He had farmers and vineyard-workers in the hills and in the fertile lands, because he loved the soil.

¹¹ 'Uziyahu had a standing army of fit soldiers divided into units according to the census taken by the secretary Ye'i'el and the officer Ma'aseiyah, under the direction of Hananyah, one of the king's officials. ¹² The total number of clan heads over these strong, brave men was 2,600. ¹³ They directed a trained army of 307,500 fighting men, a strong force supporting the king in war against the enemy. ¹⁴ 'Uziyahu equipped them, the whole army, with shields, spears, helmets, armor, bows and slingstones.

¹⁵ In Yerushalayim he built devices designed by experts for the towers and angles, from which to shoot arrows and lob large stones. His fame spread far and wide, for he was miraculously helped, until he became strong.

¹⁶ But when he was strong, he became arrogant, which caused him to become corrupt, so that he sinned against ADONAI his God by going into the temple of ADONAI to burn incense on the incense altar. ¹⁷ 'Azaryahu the *cohen* went in after him, and with him were eighty of ADONAI's *cohanim*, brave men. ¹⁸ They stood up to 'Uziyahu the king; they told him, "It isn't your job, 'Uziyahu, to burn incense to ADONAI! The job of burning incense belongs to the *cohanim*, the descendants of Aharon, who have been consecrated. Get out of the sanctuary! You have trespassed, and ADONAI, God, will not honor you for this." ¹⁹ This made 'Uziyahu angry as he stood there with a censer in his hand ready to burn incense; and in his anger at the *cohanim*, *tzara'at* broke out on his forehead right in front of the *cohanim* in the house of ADONAI beside the altar for incense. ²⁰ 'Azaryahu the chief *cohen* and all the *cohanim* stared at him — there he was, with *tzara'at* on his forehead! Quickly they threw him out of there; and indeed, he himself hurried to get out, because ADONAI had struck him. ²¹ 'Uziyahu the king had *tzara'at* until his dying day; he lived in a separate house because he had *tzara'at*, and was not allowed into the house of ADONAI. Meanwhile, Yotam the king's son ran the king's household and was regent over the people of the land.

²² Other activities of 'Uziyahu, from beginning to end, were recorded by Yesha'yahu the prophet, the son of Amotz. ²³ So 'Uziyahu slept with his ancestors,

and they buried him with his ancestors in the graveyard belonging to the kings, because they said, "He had *tzara'at.*" Then Yotam his son took his place as king.

27 ¹ Yotam was twenty-five years old when he began his reign, and he ruled for sixteen years in Yerushalayim. His mother's name was Yerushah the daughter of Tzadok. ² He did what was right from ADONAI's perspective, following the example of everything his father 'Uziyahu had done, except that he did not enter the temple of ADONAI. Nevertheless, the people acted corruptly.

³ He built the Upper Gate of the house of ADONAI and added considerably to the wall of the 'Ofel. ⁴ He built cities in the hills of Y'hudah, and in the wooded areas he built forts and towers.

⁵ He fought with the king of the people of 'Amon and defeated them. That year the people of 'Amon paid him tribute of three-and-a-third tons of silver, 50,000 bushels of wheat and 50,000 [bushels] of barley. The people of 'Amon paid him the same amount the second and third years also. ⁶ Thus Yotam became strong, because he prepared his ways [of doing things] before ADONAI his God.

⁷ Other activities of Yotam, all his wars and his ways [of doing things] are recorded in the Annals of the Kings of Isra'el and Y'hudah. ⁸ He was twenty-five years old when he began his reign, and he ruled for sixteen years in Yerushalayim. ⁹ Yotam slept with his ancestors and they buried him in the City of David. Then Achaz his son took his place as king.

28 ¹ Achaz was twenty years old when he began his reign, and he ruled sixteen years in Yerushalayim. But he did not do what was right from the perspective of ADONAI, as David his ancestor had done. ² Rather, he lived in the manner of the kings of Isra'el and made cast metal images for the *ba'alim.* ³ Moreover, he made offerings in the Ben-Hinnom Valley and even burned up his own children as sacrifices, in keeping with the horrible practices of the pagans, whom ADONAI had thrown out ahead of the people of Isra'el. ⁴ He also sacrificed and offered on the high places, on the hills and under any green tree.

⁵ Because of this, ADONAI his God handed him over to the king of Aram; they attacked him and carried off from his people a great number of captives, bringing them to Dammesek.

In addition, he was handed over to the king of Isra'el, who inflicted on him a great massacre. ⁶ For Pekach the son of Remalyah killed in Y'hudah 120,000 men in one day, all of them brave men, because they had abandoned ADONAI, the God of their ancestors. ⁷ And Zikhri, a champion from Efrayim, killed Ma'aseiyah the king's son, 'Azrikam the administrator of the household and Elkanah, who was second only to the king. ⁸ The people of Isra'el took captive from their kinsmen 200,000 wives, sons and daughters; they also captured from them much spoil, which they brought to Shomron.

⁹ But a prophet of ADONAI named 'Oded was there; he went out to meet the army coming to Shomron and said to them, "Look, it's because ADONAI the God of your fathers was angry with Y'hudah that he has handed them over to you, and you have slaughtered them in a fury that has reached up to heaven. ¹⁰ Now you intend to force the people from Y'hudah and Yerushalayim into subjection as your slaves; but haven't you guilty deeds of your own that you committed against ADONAI your God?

¹¹ Therefore listen to me now; and send the captives back, the people you have taken captive from your kinsmen; because the fierce anger of ADONAI is on you."

¹² At this, some of the leaders of the people of Efrayim — 'Azaryahu the son of Y'hochanan, Berekhyahu the son of Meshilemot, Y'chizkiyah the son of Shalum and 'Amasa the son of Hadlai — protested against those who were returning from the war, ¹³ saying to them, "Don't bring the captives here, because you intend to do something that will bring guilt on us against ADONAI. It will only add to our sins and guilt, for our guilt is great, and there is fierce anger against Isra'el."

¹⁴ So the armed soldiers left the captives and the spoil there with the leaders and the whole community; ¹⁵ while the men named above took charge of the captives and from the spoil clothed those among them who were inadequately clothed, giving them garments and shoes, providing them food and drink and anointing them with oil. After placing all the weak among them on donkeys, they brought them to Yericho, the City of Date-Palms, to their kinsmen; only then did they return to Shomron.

¹⁶ It was at that time that King Achaz sent to the kings of Ashur to help him. ¹⁷ For again the people from Edom had come, attacking Y'hudah and carrying off captives. ¹⁸ The P'lishtim too had invaded the cities in the Sh'felah and in the Negev of Y'hudah; they had captured Beit-Shemesh, Ayalon, G'derot, Sokho with its villages, Timnah with its villages and Gimzo with its villages; and they settled there. ¹⁹ For ADONAI brought Y'hudah low because of Achaz king of Isra'el, since he had caused disturbances in Y'hudah and acted very treacherously against ADONAI.

²⁰ Tilgat-Piln'eser king of Ashur attacked and besieged Achaz instead of strengthening him — ²¹ even though Achaz had stripped the house of ADONAI and the palaces of the king and princes and had given the plunder to the king of Ashur, it didn't help him at all.

²² During his time of distress this same King Achaz added to his treachery against ADONAI ²³ by sacrificing to the gods of Dammesek, who had attacked him, reasoning, "The gods of the kings of Aram helped them, so I will sacrifice to them, and then they'll help me." But they became the ruin of him and of all Isra'el. ²⁴ Achaz collected the equipment from the house of God, broke to pieces the equipment from the house of God and sealed the doors of the house of ADONAI; then he made himself altars in every corner of Yerushalayim. ²⁵ In every city of Y'hudah he made high places for offering to other gods, thus provoking ADONAI the God of his ancestors.

²⁶ Other activities of Achaz and his ways [of doing things], from beginning to end, are recorded in the Annals of the Kings of Y'hudah and Isra'el. ²⁷ Achaz slept with his ancestors, and they buried him in the city, in Yerushalayim; because they did not bring him to the tombs of the kings of Isra'el. Then Hizkiyahu his son took his place as king.

29 ¹ Hizkiyahu was twenty-five years old when he began his reign, and he ruled for twenty-nine years in Yerushalayim. His mother's name was Aviyah the daughter of Z'kharyah. ² He did what was right from ADONAI's perspective, following the example of everything David his ancestor had done.

³ In the first month of the first year of his reign, he reopened the doors of the house of ADONAI and repaired them. ⁴ Then he brought in the cohanim and L'vi'im, assembled them in the open space to the east, ⁵ and said to them, "Listen to me, L'vi'im: consecrate yourselves now, consecrate the house of ADONAI the God of your

ancestors, and remove the filth from the Holy Place. [6] For our ancestors acted treacherously, they did what is evil from the perspective of ADONAI our God, they abandoned him, they turned their faces away from where ADONAI lives and turned their backs on him. [7] They sealed the doors of the vestibule, put out the lamps and stopped burning incense and offering burnt offerings in the Holy Place to the God of Isra'el.

[8] "Because of this, ADONAI's anger has settled on Y'hudah and Yerushalayim; and he has made them an object of horror, astonishment and mocking — as you can see with your own eyes. [9] Here, our ancestors have fallen by the sword; and on this account our sons, daughters and wives have gone into captivity.

[10] "Now it is in my heart to make a covenant with ADONAI the God of Isra'el, so that his furious anger will turn away from us. [11] My sons, now is not a time for being negligent; for you are the ones ADONAI chose to stand before him and serve him as his ministers, offering him incense."

[12] Then the L'vi'im set about the task — Machat the son of 'Amasai and Yo'el the son of 'Azaryahu from the descendants of the K'hati; of the sons of M'rari, Kish the son of 'Avdi and 'Azaryahu the son of Yehallel'el; of the Gershuni, Yo'ach the son of Zimah and 'Eden the son of Yo'ach; [13] of the descendants of Elitzafan, Shimri and Ye'i'el; of the descendants of Asaf, Z'kharyahu and Matanyahu; [14] of the descendants of Heman, Yechi'el and Shim'i; and of the descendants of Y'dutun, Sh'ma'yah and 'Uzi'el.

[15] They gathered their kinsmen, consecrated themselves and, in keeping with the king's order and ADONAI's words, went in to cleanse the house of ADONAI. [16] The cohanim went in to cleanse the inner part of the house of ADONAI; all the unclean things they found in the sanctuary of ADONAI they brought out into the courtyard of the house of ADONAI, where the L'vi'im took and carried them out to Vadi Kidron. [17] They began consecrating on the first day of the first month, and on the eighth day of the month they reached the vestibule of ADONAI. Then they consecrated the house of ADONAI in eight more days; so that on the sixteenth day of the first month, they had finished. [18] Then they went to Hizkiyahu the king in [the palace] and said, "We have cleansed all the house of ADONAI, including the altar for burnt offerings, with all its equipment, and the table for the showbread, with all its equipment. [19] Moreover, we have reconditioned and consecrated all the articles that King Achaz threw out during his reign, when he was sinning; and they are there, in front of the altar of ADONAI."

[20] Next morning, Hizkiyahu the king got up early, gathered the leading men of the city and went up to the house of ADONAI. [21] They brought seven bulls, seven rams, seven lambs and seven male goats as a sin offering for the kingdom, for the sanctuary and for Y'hudah; and he ordered the cohanim to offer them on the altar of ADONAI. [22] After slaughtering the bulls, the cohanim took the blood and splashed it against the altar. Next, they slaughtered the rams and splashed the blood against the altar and also slaughtered the lambs and splashed the blood against the altar. [23] After bringing the male goats for the sin offering close to the king and the assembly and laying their hands on them, [24] the cohanim slaughtered them and made a sin offering with their blood on the altar to make atonement for all Isra'el; for the king had ordered that the burnt offering and the sin offering should be for all Isra'el.

[25] He stationed the L'vi'im in the house of ADONAI with cymbals, lyres and lutes, in keeping with the order of David, Gad the king's seer and Natan the prophet; for the mitzvah had come from ADONAI through his prophets. [26] The L'vi'im stood with

the instruments of David and the *cohanim* with the trumpets. ²⁷ Hizkiyahu ordered that the burnt offering should be offered on the altar. The moment the burnt offering began, the song of Adonai also began, accompanied by the trumpets and the instruments of David king of Isra'el. ²⁸ The whole assembly prostrated themselves, the singers sang, and the trumpeters sounded; all this continued until the burnt offering was finished.

²⁹ When the offering was over, the king and everyone present with him bowed down and prostrated themselves. ³⁰ Then Hizkiyahu the king and the leaders ordered the *L'vi'im* to sing praises to Adonai, using the words of David and of Asaf the seer. They sang praises until they were filled with joy, and they bowed their heads and prostrated themselves.

³¹ Hizkiyahu responded by saying, "Now that you have consecrated yourselves to Adonai, come close, and bring sacrifices and thank offerings into the house of Adonai." So the community brought in sacrifices and thank offerings, and as many as were willing volunteered burnt offerings. ³² In all, the burnt offerings brought by the congregation totaled 70 bulls, 100 rams and 200 lambs; all these were for a burnt offering to Adonai. ³³ The consecrated gifts amounted to 600 oxen and 3,000 sheep. ³⁴ Only there weren't enough *cohanim* to skin and butcher all the burnt offerings, so their colleagues the *L'vi'im* assisted them until the work was finished and the *cohanim* had consecrated themselves (for the *L'vi'im* had been more diligent to consecrate themselves than the *cohanim*). ³⁵ Besides the abundance of burnt offerings, there was the fat of the peace offerings and drink offerings for each burnt offering.

Thus the service of the house of Adonai was restored. ³⁶ Hizkiyahu and all the people rejoiced over what God had prepared for the people, since it had all happened so suddenly.

30 ¹ Then Hizkiyahu sent to all Isra'el and Y'hudah, and wrote letters also to Efrayim and M'nasheh, summoning them to the house of Adonai in Yerushalayim, to keep the *Pesach* to Adonai the God of Isra'el. ² For the king, his officials and the entire Yerushalayim community had agreed to keep the *Pesach* in the second month. ³ They had not been able to observe it at the proper time because the *cohanim* had not consecrated themselves in sufficient number; also the people had not assembled in Yerushalayim. ⁴ The idea had seemed right to the king and to the whole community; ⁵ so they issued a decree that it should be proclaimed throughout all Isra'el, from Be'er-Sheva to Dan, that they should come to keep the *Pesach* to Adonai the God of Isra'el at Yerushalayim; for only a few had been observing it as prescribed.

⁶ So runners went with the letters from the king and his officers throughout all Isra'el and Y'hudah. They conveyed the king's order: "People of Isra'el! Turn back to Adonai, the God of Avraham, Yitz'chak and Ya'akov! Then he will return to those of you who remain, who escaped capture by the kings of Ashur. ⁷ Don't be like your ancestors, or like your kinsmen who sinned against Adonai the God of their ancestors, with the result that he allowed them to become an object of horror, as you see. ⁸ Don't be stiffnecked now, as your ancestors were. Instead, yield yourselves to Adonai; enter his sanctuary, which he has made holy forever; and serve Adonai your God; so that his fierce anger will turn away from you. ⁹ For if you turn back to Adonai, your kinsmen and children will find that those who took them captive will have compassion on them, and they will come back to this land. Adonai your God is compassionate and merciful; he will not turn his face away from you if you return to him."

¹⁰ So the runners passed from city to city through the territory of Efrayim and M'nasheh, as far as Z'vulun; but the people laughed at them and made fun of them. ¹¹ Nevertheless, some from Asher, M'nasheh and Z'vulun were humble enough to come to Yerushalayim. ¹² Also in Y'hudah the hand of God was at work, uniting their hearts to do what the king and the leaders had ordered in accordance with the word of ADONAI.

¹³ Thus, many people assembled in Yerushalayim to keep the festival of *Matzot* in the second month, a huge crowd. ¹⁴ First they set about removing the altars that were in Yerushalayim, and they also removed all the altars for incense and threw them in *Vadi* Kidron. ¹⁵ Then they slaughtered the *Pesach* lamb on the fourteenth day of the second month. Ashamed of themselves, the *cohanim* and *L'vi'im* had consecrated themselves and brought burnt offerings into the house of ADONAI. ¹⁶ Now they stood at their stations, as prescribed in the *Torah* of Moshe the man of God; the *cohanim* splashed the blood given to them by the *L'vi'im*. ¹⁷ For there were many in the assembly who had not consecrated themselves; therefore the *L'vi'im* were responsible for slaughtering the *Pesach* lambs and consecrating them to ADONAI on behalf of everyone who was not clean. ¹⁸ For a large number of the people, especially from Efrayim, M'nasheh, Yissakhar and Z'vulun, had not cleansed themselves but ate the *Pesach* lamb anyway, despite what is written. For Hizkiyahu had prayed for them, "May ADONAI, who is good, pardon ¹⁹ everyone who sets his heart on seeking God, ADONAI, the God of his ancestors, even if he hasn't undergone the purification prescribed in connection with holy things." ²⁰ ADONAI heard Hizkiyahu and healed the people.

²¹ The people of Isra'el there in Yerushalayim observed the festival of *Matzot* for seven days with great joy; while every day the *L'vi'im* and *cohanim* praised ADONAI, singing to ADONAI with the accompaniment of loud instruments. ²² Hizkiyahu spoke encouragingly to all the *L'vi'im* who were well skilled in the service of ADONAI. Thus they ate throughout the festival for the seven days, offering sacrifices of peace offerings and giving thanks to ADONAI, the God of their ancestors.

²³ Then the whole assembly decided to celebrate for yet another seven days, and they observed those seven days too with joy. ²⁴ For Hizkiyahu king of Y'hudah gave the assembly a thousand bulls and seven thousand sheep for offerings, while the leaders gave the assembly a thousand bulls and ten thousand sheep; and great numbers of *cohanim* consecrated themselves. ²⁵ All the people who had assembled from Y'hudah rejoiced, as did the *cohanim* and *L'vi'im*, those assembled from Isra'el, and the foreigners who had come from the territory of Isra'el or who lived in Y'hudah. ²⁶ So there was great joy in Yerushalayim; for since the time of Shlomo the son of David, king of Isra'el, there had been nothing like it in Yerushalayim. ²⁷ Then the *cohanim*, who were *L'vi'im*, stood up and blessed the people; [ADONAI] heard their voice, and their prayer came up to the holy place where he lives, heaven.

31 ¹ After all this was over, all Isra'el who were there went out to the cities of Y'hudah and smashed the standing-stones, chopped down the sacred poles, and broke down the high places and altars throughout Y'hudah, Binyamin, Efrayim and M'nasheh, until they had destroyed them all. Then all the people of Isra'el returned to their own cities, each to his own possession.

² Hizkiyahu re-established the divisions of the *cohanim* and *L'vi'im* in accordance with the way the divisions had been before, with each man assigned his task, both

the *cohanim* and the *L'vi'im*, for burnt offerings and for peace offerings, to serve, to give thanks and to praise at the gates of ADONAI's camp. ³ He determined a portion of the king's property to be given for the burnt offerings, that is, for the morning and evening burnt offerings and for burnt offerings on *Shabbats, Rosh-Hodesh* and the designated times, as prescribed by the *Torah* of ADONAI. ⁴ He also ordered the people living in Yerushalayim to contribute the portion meant for the *cohanim* and *L'vi'im*, so that they would be submitting themselves to the *Torah* of ADONAI. ⁵ As soon as the order was issued, the people of Isra'el gave in abundance from the firstfruits of the grain, wine, olive oil, honey and other agricultural produce; they brought the required tenth and more. ⁶ The people of Isra'el and Y'hudah living in the cities of Y'hudah also brought the required tenth of oxen and sheep and the required tenth of consecrated gifts that had been dedicated to ADONAI their God, and piled them in heaps. ⁷ They began accumulating these heaps in the third month and completed them in the seventh month. ⁸ When Hizkiyahu and the leaders came and saw the heaps, they blessed ADONAI and his people Isra'el. ⁹ When Hizkiyahu asked the *cohanim* and *L'vi'im* about the heaps, ¹⁰ 'Azaryahu the chief *cohen*, from the house of Tzadok, answered him, "Ever since the people began bringing offerings into the house of ADONAI, we have had enough to eat and plenty left over; for ADONAI has blessed his people, and what is left over is this massive supply."

¹¹ Then Hizkiyahu ordered storerooms prepared in the house of ADONAI. After preparing them, ¹² they faithfully brought in the offerings, the required tenths and the consecrated things. Konanyahu the *Levi* was put in charge of them, with Shim'i his brother as his assistant. ¹³ Hizkiyahu the king and 'Azaryahu the ruler of the house of God appointed Yechi'el, 'Azazyahu, Nachat, 'Asah'el, Yerimot, Yozavad, Eli'el, Yismachyah, Machat and B'nayahu as supervisors to serve under Konanyah and Shim'i his brother. ¹⁴ Kore the son of Yimnah the *Levi*, gatekeeper at the East Gate, was responsible for the voluntary offerings to God; he had to distribute the offerings made to ADONAI and the especially holy gifts. ¹⁵ Under him were 'Eden, Minyamin, Yeshua, Sh'ma'yahu, Amaryahu and Sh'khanyahu, in the cities of the *cohanim*, faithfully making the distributions to their kinsmen by divisions, to great and small alike. ¹⁶ Every male three years and older entitled to enter the house of ADONAI was given his daily share for performing his duties according to his division, regardless of how he was recorded in the genealogies. ¹⁷ Likewise, those recorded in the genealogies of the *cohanim* by clans received shares, as did the *L'vi'im* twenty years and older who were performing their duties in their assigned divisions. ¹⁸ When shares were assigned, all their little ones, wives, sons and daughters were also recorded in the genealogies, throughout the entire community; for in their faithfulness to this task they consecrated themselves. ¹⁹ Finally, shares were assigned to the descendants of Aharon, the *cohanim*, who lived in the pasture-lands surrounding their cities — in each city they were mentioned by name. Thus portions were distributed to all the males among the *cohanim* and to all whose genealogies showed that they belonged to the *L'vi'im*.

²⁰ This is what Hizkiyahu did throughout all Y'hudah. He accomplished things that were good, right and faithful before ADONAI his God. ²¹ Every project that he undertook in order to seek his God, whether in the service of the house of God or in connection with the *Torah* and the *mitzvot*, he did with all his heart; and so he succeeded.

32 ^{1} After these events and this faithfulness of [Hizkiyahu's], Sancheriv king of Ashur came, invaded Y'hudah and besieged the fortified cities, thinking that he would break in [and capture] them. ^{2} When Hizkiyahu saw that Sancheriv had come and intended to attack Yerushalayim, ^{3} he consulted his leading men and military advisers about sealing off the water in the springs outside the city. After gaining their support, ^{4} a large crowd was gathered to block all the springs and the stream flowing through the countryside. They reasoned, "Why should the kings of Ashur come and find an ample supply of water?" ^{5} Then, taking courage, he rebuilt all the broken sections of the wall, raised towers on it, built another wall outside that, strengthened the Millo in the City of David, and made a large quantity of spears and shields. ^{6} He appointed military commanders over the people, then gathered them before him in the open space at the city gate and spoke these words of encouragement to them: ^{7} "Be strong! Take courage! Don't be afraid or distressed on account of the king of Ashur or all the horde he brings with him. For the One with us is greater than the one with him — ^{8} he has human strength, but we have ADONAI our God to help us and fight our battles!" The people took heart at the words of Hizkiyahu king of Y'hudah.

^{9} After this, while Sancheriv and all his army were besieging Lakhish, he sent his envoys to Yerushalayim, to Hizkiyahu king of Y'hudah and to all Y'hudah who were there in Yerushalayim, with this message: ^{10} "This is what Sancheriv king of Ashur says: 'What gives you the confidence that you can endure a siege against Yerushalayim? ^{11} Hasn't Hizkiyahu deluded you? Isn't he condemning you to death by starvation and thirst when he says, "ADONAI our God will save us from the king of Ashur"? ^{12} Isn't this the same Hizkiyahu who removed [your God's] high places and altars and ordered Y'hudah and Yerushalayim to worship before one altar and offer sacrifices only on it? ^{13} Don't you realize what I and my ancestors have done to all the peoples of the other countries? Were the gods of these nations able to do a thing to rescue their country from me? ^{14} Who of all the gods of those nations that my ancestors completely destroyed was able to rescue his people from me? How then will your God rescue you from me? ^{15} Don't let Hizkiyahu mislead you or delude you this way, don't believe him. For no god of any nation or kingdom has ever been able to rescue his people from me or my ancestors; how much less will your God rescue you from me!'"

^{16} His envoys kept on speaking against ADONAI, God; and against his servant Hizkiyahu. ^{17} He also wrote a letter insulting ADONAI the God of Isra'el and speaking against him; it said, "Just as the gods of the nations of the other countries could not rescue their people from me, likewise Hizkiyahu's God will not rescue his people from me."

^{18} They were shouting loudly in the language of the Judeans to the people of Yerushalayim who were on the wall in order to terrify them and make them fearful, so that they could capture the city. ^{19} They spoke about the God of Yerushalayim in the same way as about the gods of the other peoples of the earth, which are merely human artifacts. ^{20} Because of this, Hizkiyahu the king and Yesha'yahu the prophet, the son of Amotz, prayed and cried out to heaven. ^{21} Then ADONAI sent an angel, who cut down the valiant warriors, the leaders and the officers in the king of Ashur's camp, so that he had to return shamefaced to his own country. When he entered the house of his god, his own sons, whom he himself had fathered, put him to death with the sword there.

²² In this way ADONAI rescued Hizkiyahu and those living in Yerushalayim from Sancheriv the king of Ashur and from everyone, caring for them in every respect. ²³ Many people brought gifts to ADONAI in Yerushalayim and items of value to Hizkiyahu king of Y'hudah, so that from then on he was regarded highly by all the nations.

²⁴ Around this time, Hizkiyahu became ill to the point of death. But he prayed to ADONAI, who answered him, even giving him a sign. ²⁵ However, Hizkiyahu did not respond commensurately with the benefit done for him, because he had grown proud; thus he brought anger on himself and on Y'hudah and Yerushalayim as well. ²⁶ But Hizkiyahu then humbled himself for his pride, both he and the people living in Yerushalayim, so that ADONAI's anger did not strike them during Hizkiyahu's lifetime.

²⁷ Hizkiyahu had vast riches and great honor. He provided himself with storage places for silver, gold, precious stones, spices, shields and all kinds of valuable articles; ²⁸ also storehouses for the harvest of grain, wine and olive oil; and stalls for all kinds of livestock and pens for the flocks. ²⁹ He provided cities for himself and purchased flocks and herds in abundance, for God had made him extremely wealthy.

³⁰ It was this same Hizkiyahu who blocked the upper outlet of the Gichon Spring and diverted the water straight down on the west side of the City of David.

Hizkiyahu succeeded in all that he did. ³¹ However, in the matter of the ambassadors from the princes of Bavel, who sent to him to learn of the marvel that had taken place in the land, God left him by himself, in order to test him, so that he might know everything that was in his heart.

³² Other activities of Hizkiyahu and his good deeds are recorded in the vision of Yesha'yahu the prophet, the son of Amotz, and in the Annals of the Kings of Y'hudah and Isra'el. ³³ Then Hizkiyahu slept with his ancestors, and they buried him by the path leading up to the tombs of the descendants of David. All Y'hudah and the people living in Yerushalayim honored him when he died, after which M'nasheh his son took his place as king.

33 ¹ M'nasheh was twelve years old when he began his reign, and he ruled for fifty-five years in Yerushalayim. ² He did what was evil from ADONAI's perspective, following the disgusting practices of the nations whom ADONAI had expelled ahead of the people of Isra'el. ³ For he rebuilt the high places which Hizkiyahu his father had smashed; he erected altars for the *ba'alim*, made sacred poles and worshipped all the army of heaven and served them. ⁴ He erected altars in the house of ADONAI, concerning which ADONAI had said, "My name will be in Yerushalayim forever." ⁵ He erected altars for all the army of heaven in the two courtyards of the house of ADONAI. ⁶ He made his children pass through the fire [as a sacrifice] in the Ben-Hinnom Valley. He practiced soothsaying, divination and sorcery; and he appointed mediums and persons who used spirit guides. He did much that was evil from ADONAI's perspective, thus provoking him to anger. ⁷ He set the carved image of the idol he had made in the house of God, concerning which God had told David and Shlomo his son, "In this house and in Yerushalayim, which I have chosen out of all the tribes of Isra'el, I will put my name forever. ⁸ Also I will not remove the feet of Isra'el from the land I assigned your ancestors, if only they will take heed to obey every order I have given them, that is, all the *Torah*, laws and rulings that came through Moshe." ⁹ M'nasheh caused Y'hudah and the people of Yerushalayim to go astray, so that they did even worse things than the nations whom ADONAI destroyed ahead of the people of Isra'el.

¹⁰ *ADONAI* spoke to M'nasheh and to his people, but they paid no attention. ¹¹ Therefore *ADONAI* brought against them the commanders of the king of Ashur's army. They took M'nasheh captive with hooks, bound him in chains and carried him off to Bavel. ¹² Then, when he was in distress, he began to appease the anger of *ADONAI*, abjectly humbling himself before the God of his ancestors. ¹³ He prayed to him; and God was moved by his plea, paid attention to his entreaty and brought him back to Yerushalayim, to his kingly office. Then M'nasheh understood that *ADONAI* really is God.

¹⁴ After this he built an outer wall for the City of David on the west side of Gichon, in the valley, extending as far as the entrance at the Fish Gate; it encompassed the 'Ofel, and he built it very high. He stationed army commanders in all the fortified cities of Y'hudah. ¹⁵ He removed the foreign gods and the idol from the house of *ADONAI* and all the altars he had built on the hill of the house of *ADONAI* and in Yerushalayim, and threw them out of the city. ¹⁶ He repaired the altar of *ADONAI* and offered on it sacrifices as peace offerings and for thanksgiving; and he ordered Y'hudah to serve *ADONAI* the God of Isra'el. ¹⁷ However, the people continued sacrificing on the high places, although only to *ADONAI* their God.

¹⁸ Other activities of M'nasheh, his prayer to his God and the words of the seers who spoke to him in the name of *ADONAI* the God of Isra'el are recorded in the Annals of the Kings of Isra'el. ¹⁹ Also his prayer and how God was moved by his plea, all his sin and disloyalty, and the locations where he built high places and set up the sacred poles and carved images before he humbled himself are written in the History of the Seers.

²⁰ Then M'nasheh slept with his ancestors and was buried at his own house, and Amon his son took his place as king.

²¹ Amon was twenty-two years old when he began his reign, and he ruled for two years in Yerushalayim. ²² He did what was evil from *ADONAI*'s perspective, as had M'nasheh his father. Amon sacrificed to all the carved images that M'nasheh his father had made, and served them. ²³ He did not humble himself before *ADONAI*, as M'nasheh his father had done; rather, this Amon kept adding to his guilt.

²⁴ His servants conspired against him and put the king to death in his own palace. ²⁵ But the people of the land put to death all those who had been part of the conspiracy against King Amon. Then the people of the land made Yoshiyahu his son king in place of him.

34 ¹ Yoshiyahu was eight years old when he began his reign, and he ruled for thirty-one years in Yerushalayim. ² He did what was right from *ADONAI*'s perspective, living entirely in the manner of David his ancestor and turning away neither to the right nor to the left.

³ For in the eighth year of his reign, when he was still young, he began seeking after the God of David his father; and in the twelfth year, he began cleansing Y'hudah and Yerushalayim from the high places, the sacred poles, and the carved and cast metal images. ⁴ In his presence they broke down the altars of the *ba'alim*, and he chopped down the pillars for sun-worship mounted above them. He smashed the sacred poles and the carved and cast metal images, grinding them to dust, which he threw on the graves of those who had sacrificed to them. ⁵ He burned the bones of the priests on their altars, thus cleansing Y'hudah and Yerushalayim. ⁶ He did likewise in the cities of M'nasheh, Efrayim, Shim'on and even as far as Naftali, in their

surrounding ruins. ⁷ He broke down the altars, beat the sacred poles and carved images to powder and chopped down the pillars for sun-worship throughout all the land of Isra'el. Then he returned to Yerushalayim.

⁸ In the eighteenth year of his reign, after he had cleansed the land and the house, he sent Shafan the son of Atzalyahu, Ma'aseiyah the governor of the city and Yo'ach the son of Yo'achaz the recorder to repair the house of ADONAI his God. ⁹ They went to Hilkiyahu the *cohen hagadol* and handed over to him the money that had been brought into the house of God, which the *L'vi'im* who guarded the doors had collected from M'nasheh, Efrayim, the rest of Isra'el and all Y'hudah and Binyamin. Then they returned to Yerushalayim. ¹⁰ They gave it to the supervisors of the work being done in the house of ADONAI; and those doing the work in the house of ADONAI used it to repair and restore the house — ¹¹ that is, they gave it to the carpenters and construction-workers to purchase worked stone, timber for the crossbeams and roof beams for the houses which the kings of Y'hudah had destroyed. ¹² The men did the work faithfully. Their supervisors were Yachat and 'Ovadyahu, *L'vi'im* from the descendants of M'rari, also Z'kharyah and Meshulam from the descendants of the K'hatim to give direction; and other *L'vi'im*, all of whom could accompany singing with musical instruments. ¹³ They supervised those carrying the loads and everyone doing any kind of work; and there were also *L'vi'im* who were secretaries, officials and gatekeepers.

¹⁴ While bringing out the money that had been brought into the house of ADONAI, Hilkiyahu the *cohen* found the scroll of the *Torah* of ADONAI given by Moshe. ¹⁵ Hilkiyahu said to Shafan the secretary, "I have found the scroll of the *Torah* in the house of ADONAI." Hilkiyahu gave the scroll to Shafan. ¹⁶ Shafan the secretary brought the scroll to the king.

Turning to the king, he gave him this report: "Your servants are doing everything you ordered them to do. ¹⁷ They have poured out the money found in the house of ADONAI and handed it over to the supervisors and workers." ¹⁸ Then Shafan the secretary told the king, "Hilkiyahu the *cohen hagadol* gave me a scroll." Shafan read it aloud before the king. ¹⁹ After the king had heard what was written in the *Torah*, he tore his clothes. ²⁰ Then the king issued this order to Hilkiyahu, Achikam the son of Shafan, 'Avdon the son of Mikhah, Shafan the secretary and 'Asayah the king's servant: ²¹ "Go, and consult ADONAI for me and for the people left in Isra'el and Y'hudah in regard to what is written in this scroll which has been found. For ADONAI must be furious at us, since our ancestors did not observe the word of ADONAI and do everything written in this scroll." ²² So Hilkiyahu and those the king had ordered went to Huldah the prophet, the wife of Shalum the son of Tok'hat, the son of Hasrat, keeper of the wardrobe — she lived in the Second Quarter of Yerushalayim — and spoke with her about this. ²³ She told them, "ADONAI the God of Isra'el says to tell the man who sent you to me ²⁴ that ADONAI says this: 'I am going to bring calamity on this place and on its inhabitants, all the curses written in the scroll they read to the king of Y'hudah; ²⁵ because they have abandoned me and offered to other gods, in order to provoke me with everything they do. Therefore my anger is poured out on this place and will not be quenched.'

²⁶ "But you are to tell the king of Y'hudah, who sent you to consult ADONAI, that ADONAI the God of Isra'el also says this: 'In regard to the words you have heard, ²⁷ because your heart was tender, and you humbled yourself before God when

you heard his words against this place and its inhabitants — you humbled yourself before me, tore your clothes and cried before me — I have also heard you,' says
ADONAI. ²⁸ 'Here, I will gather you to your ancestors; you will go to your grave in
peace; and your eyes will not see all the calamity I am going to bring on this place
and its inhabitants.'" So they brought back word to the king.

²⁹ Then the king summoned and assembled all the leaders of Y'hudah and
Yerushalayim. ³⁰ The king went up to the house of ADONAI with all the men of Y'hudah,
those living in Yerushalayim, the *cohanim*, the *L'vi'im* and all the people, both great
and small; and he read in their hearing everything written in the scroll of the covenant that had been found in the house of ADONAI. ³¹ The king stood in his place and
made a covenant in the presence of ADONAI to live following ADONAI, observing his
mitzvot, instructions and laws wholeheartedly and with all his being, so as to perform
the words of the covenant written in this scroll. ³² Then, after he had all the people in
Yerushalayim and Binyamin stand in affirmation of it, the inhabitants of Yerushalayim
acted in accordance with the covenant of God, the God of their ancestors.

³³ Yoshiyahu removed all the abominable idols from all the territories belonging
to the people of Isra'el, and he made everyone in Isra'el serve ADONAI their God. Throughout his lifetime, they did not stop following ADONAI, the God of their ancestors.

35 ¹ Yoshiyahu kept *Pesach* to ADONAI in Yerushalayim. They slaughtered the *Pesach*
lamb on the fourteenth day of the first month. ² He assigned the *cohanim* to their
posts and encouraged them to perform the service of the house of ADONAI. ³ To the
L'vi'im who were teaching all Isra'el and were holy for ADONAI he said, "Put the holy
ark in the house which Shlomo the son of David, king of Isra'el, built; after this,
you will not have to carry it again. Now serve ADONAI your God and his people
Isra'el. ⁴ Organize yourselves by clans and duty divisions according to the arrangement written down by David king of Isra'el and Shlomo his son. ⁵ Stand in the Holy
Place according to the divisions of the clans of your kinsmen the ordinary people,
with part of a clan of *L'vi'im* serving each clan [of Isra'el]. ⁶ Then slaughter the
Pesach lamb, consecrate yourselves, prepare what your kinsmen need, and act
according to the word of ADONAI given through Moshe."

⁷ Yoshiyahu gave the ordinary people, to all who were present, 30,000 lambs
and kids from the flock, all of them for *Pesach* offerings, and 3,000 bulls. These
were from the king's personal property. ⁸ Also his leading men voluntarily gave to
the people and to the *cohanim* and *L'vi'im*. Hilkiyah, Z'kharyahu and Yechi'el, the
rulers of the house of God, gave the *cohanim* 2,600 [lambs and kids] and 300 oxen
for *Pesach* offerings. ⁹ Konanyah, his brothers Sh'ma'yah and N'tan'el, and
Hashavyah, Ye'i'el and Yozavad, the head *L'vi'im*, gave the *L'vi'im* 5,000 [lambs
and kids] and 500 oxen for *Pesach* offerings.

¹⁰ So the service was prepared; the *cohanim* stood at their posts; and the *L'vi'im*
worked in their divisions, in keeping with the king's order. ¹¹ They slaughtered the
Pesach lamb; the *cohanim* splashed [the blood, which they received from the *L'vi'im*],
and the *L'vi'im* skinned and butchered them. ¹² They removed the portions to be burned,
in order to give them to the divisions of the clans of the ordinary people to present to
ADONAI, as written in the scroll of Moshe. They did the same with the oxen. ¹³ They
roasted the *Pesach* lamb over fire, according to the rule; while they boiled the holy
offerings in pots, kettles and pans and carried them quickly to all the ordinary people.

^{14} Afterwards, they prepared food for themselves and for the *cohanim*; because the *cohanim*, the descendants of Aharon, were busy till nightfall offering the fat and the portions to be burned up; this is why the *L'vi'im* prepared food both for themselves and for the *cohanim* the descendants of Aharon.

^{15} The singers the sons of Asaf were at their posts, as ordered by David — Asaf, Heman and Y'dutun the king's seer. The gatekeepers were at every gate, and they did not need to leave their posts, because their brothers the *L'vi'im* prepared [food] for them.

^{16} Thus all the service of A$_{DONAI}$ was prepared the same day for observing *Pesach* and offering burnt offerings on the altar of A$_{DONAI}$, in accordance with the order of King Yoshiyahu. ^{17} The people of Isra'el who were present observed the *Pesach* at that time and the festival of *Matzot* for seven days. ^{18} No *Pesach* like that had been kept in Isra'el since the days of Sh'mu'el the prophet, and none of the kings of Isra'el observe a *Pesach* such as Yoshiyahu observed, with the *cohanim*, *L'vi'im*, all Y'hudah, those of Isra'el who were present, and the inhabitants of Yerushalayim. ^{19} This *Pesach* was observed in the eighteenth year of Yoshiyahu.

^{20} After all this, and after Yoshiyahu had restored the house, N'kho king of Egypt went up to attack Kark'mish by the Euphrates River. King Yoshiyahu went out to oppose him; ^{21} but N'kho sent envoys to him with this message: "Do I have a conflict with you, king of Y'hudah? No, I am not coming today to attack you, but to attack the dynasty with whom I am at war. God has ordered to speed me along; so don't meddle with God, who is with me; so that he won't destroy you." ^{22} Nevertheless, Yoshiyahu was determined to go after him. He disguised himself in order to fight against him and wouldn't listen to what N'kho said, which was from the mouth of God. Then he went to fight in the Megiddo Valley. ^{23} There archers shot King Yoshiyahu. The king said to his servants, "Take me away, because I'm badly wounded." ^{24} So his servants took him out of the chariot, transferred him to his second chariot and brought him to Yerushalayim. But he died, and he was buried in the tombs of his ancestors. All Y'hudah and Yerushalayim mourned Yoshiyahu. ^{25} Yirmeyahu composed a lament for Yoshiyahu; and all the men and women singers have sung of Yoshiyahu in their laments till this day. They made singing them a law in Isra'el, and they are recorded in the Laments.

^{26} Other activities of Yoshiyahu and all his good deeds in keeping with what is written in the *Torah* of A$_{DONAI}$, ^{27} also his accomplishments from beginning to end, are recorded in the Annals of the Kings of Isra'el and Y'hudah.

36 ^{1} Then the people of the land took Y'ho'achaz the son of Yoshiyahu and made him king in his father's place, in Yerushalayim.

^{2} Y'ho'achaz was twenty-three years old when he began his reign, and he ruled for three months in Yerushalayim. ^{3} But the king of Egypt deposed him in Yerushalayim and imposed a penalty on the land of three-and-a-third tons of silver and sixty-six pounds of gold. ^{4} Then the king of Egypt made Elyakim his brother king over Y'hudah and Yerushalayim, changing his name to Y'hoyakim; N'kho took Yo'achaz his brother and carried him off to Egypt.

^{5} Y'hoyakim was twenty-five years old when he began his reign, and he ruled for eleven years in Yerushalayim. He did what was evil from the perspective of A$_{DONAI}$ his God. ^{6} N'vukhadnetzar king of Bavel attacked him and bound him in chains to carry him off to Bavel. ⁷ N'vukhadnetzar also carried the articles in the house of ADONAI away to Bavel and put them in his temple in Bavel. ⁸ Other activities of Y'hoyakim, including all the abominations he did publicly and those discovered later, are recorded in the Annals of the Kings of Isra'el and Y'hudah. Then Y'hoyakhin his son took his place as king.

⁹ Y'hoyakhin was eight years old when he began his reign, and he ruled in Yerushalayim for three months and ten days. He did what was evil from ADONAI's perspective. ¹⁰ In the spring, King N'vukhadnetzar sent and had him brought to Bavel together with the valuable articles from the house of ADONAI, and made Tzedekyah his brother king over Y'hudah and Yerushalayim.

¹¹ Tzedekyah was twenty-one years old when he began his reign, and he ruled for eleven years in Yerushalayim. ¹² He did what was evil from the perspective of ADONAI his God. He did not humble himself before Yirmeyahu the prophet speaking on behalf of ADONAI.

¹³ He also rebelled against King N'vukhadnetzar, who had made him swear loyalty to him by God; instead, he became stiffnecked and hardhearted, refusing to turn to ADONAI the God of Isra'el. ¹⁴ In addition, the chief *cohanim* and the people grew increasingly unfaithful, following all the abominable practices of the other nations; and they polluted the house of ADONAI, which he had consecrated in Yerushalayim. ¹⁵ Time after time, and frequently, ADONAI, the God of their ancestors, sent word to them through his messengers; because he had compassion on his people and on the place where he lived. ¹⁶ But they ridiculed God's messengers, treating his words with contempt and scoffing at his prophets, until the anger of ADONAI rose up against his people to the extent that there was no longer any remedy.

¹⁷ Therefore he brought upon them the king of the Kasdim, who put their young men to the sword in the house of their sanctuary. They had no compassion on either young men or young women, old men or gray-haired; God handed all of them over to him. ¹⁸ All the articles in the house of God, great and small; the supplies in the house of ADONAI; and the supplies of the king and his leading men — all these he brought to Bavel. ¹⁹ Then they burned down the house of God, broke down the wall of Yerushalayim, put to flames all its palaces and destroyed everything in it of worth. ²⁰ Those who had escaped the sword he carried off to Bavel, and they became slaves to him and his sons until the reign of the kingdom of Persia. ²¹ Thus was fulfilled the word of ADONAI spoken by Yirmeyahu, "until the land has been paid her *Shabbat*s" — for as long as it lay desolate, it kept *Shabbat*, until seventy years had passed.

²² Now in the first year of Koresh king of Persia, so that the word of ADONAI spoken by Yirmeyahu might be fulfilled, ADONAI activated the spirit of Koresh king of Persia to proclaim throughout his entire kingdom, and put in writing as well: ²³ "Here is what Koresh king of Persia says: ADONAI, the God of heaven, has given me all the kingdoms on earth, and he has charged me to build him a house in Yerushalayim, in Y'hudah. Whoever there is among you of all his people, may ADONAI his God be with him! He may go up ...."

The Good News of Yeshua the Messiah, as Reported by

Mattityahu

MATTHEW

1 ¹ This is the genealogy of Yeshua the Messiah, son of David, son of Avraham:

² Avraham was the father of Yitz'chak,
Yitz'chak was the father of Ya'akov,
Ya'akov was the father of Y'hudah and his brothers,
³ Y'hudah was the father of Peretz and Zerach (their mother was Tamar),
Peretz was the father of Hetzron,
Hetzron was the father of Ram,
⁴ Ram was the father of 'Amminadav,
'Amminadav was the father of Nachshon,
Nachshon was the father of Salmon,
⁵ Salmon was the father of Bo'az (his mother was Rachav),
Bo'az was the father of 'Oved (his mother was Rut),
'Oved was the father of Yishai,
⁶ Yishai was the father of David the king.

David was the father of Shlomo (his mother was the wife of Uriyah),
⁷ Shlomo was the father of Rechav'am,
Rechav'am was the father of Aviyah,
Aviyah was the father of Asa,
⁸ Asa was the father of Y'hoshafat,
Y'hoshafat was the father of Yoram,
Yoram was the father of 'Uziyahu,
⁹ 'Uziyahu was the father of Yotam,
Yotam was the father of Achaz,
Achaz was the father of Hizkiyahu,
¹⁰ Hizkiyahu was the father of M'nasheh,
M'nasheh was the father of Amon,
Amon was the father of Yoshiyahu,
¹¹ Yoshiyahu was the father of Y'khanyahu and his brothers
at the time of the Exile to Bavel.

¹² After the Babylonian Exile, Y'khanyahu was the father of Sh'altiel,
Sh'altiel was the father of Z'rubavel,
¹³ Z'rubavel was the father of Avihud,
Avihud was the father of Elyakim,
Elyakim was the father of 'Azur,

14   'Azur was the father of Tzadok,
      Tzadok was the father of Yakhin,
      Yakhin was the father of El'ichud,

15   El'ichud was the father of El'azar,
      El'azar was the father of Mattan,
      Mattan was the father of Ya'akov,

16   Ya'akov was the father of Yosef the husband of Miryam,
        from whom was born the Yeshua who was called the Messiah.

17   Thus there were fourteen generations from Avraham to David,
      fourteen generations from David to the Babylonian Exile,
      and fourteen generations from the Babylonian Exile to the Messiah.

[18] Here is how the birth of Yeshua the Messiah took place. When his mother Miryam was engaged to Yosef, before they were married, she was found to be pregnant from the *Ruach HaKodesh*. [19] Her husband-to-be, Yosef, was a man who did what was right; so he made plans to break the engagement quietly, rather than put her to public shame. [20] But while he was thinking about this, an angel of ADONAI appeared to him in a dream and said, "Yosef, son of David, do not be afraid to take Miryam home with you as your wife; for what has been conceived in her is from the *Ruach HaKodesh*. [21] She will give birth to a son, and you are to name him Yeshua, [which means 'ADONAI saves,'] because he will save his people from their sins."

[22] All this happened in order to fulfill what ADONAI had said through the prophet,

23   **"The virgin will conceive and bear a son,**
      and they will call him 'Immanu El.'"[a]

(The name means, "God is with us.")

[24] When Yosef awoke he did what the angel of ADONAI had told him to do — he took Miryam home to be his wife, [25] but he did not have sexual relations with her until she had given birth to a son, and he named him Yeshua.

2 [1] After Yeshua was born in Beit-Lechem in the land of Y'hudah during the time when Herod was king, Magi from the east came to Yerushalayim [2] and asked, "Where is the new-born King of the Jews? For we saw his star in the east and have come to worship him." [3] When King Herod heard of this he became very agitated, and so did everyone else in Yerushalayim. [4] He called together all the head *cohanim* and *Torah*-teachers of the people and asked them, "Where will the Messiah be born?" [5] "In Beit-Lechem of Y'hudah," they replied, "because the prophet wrote,

6   **'And you, Beit-Lechem in the land of Y'hudah,**
      are by no means the least among the rulers of Y'hudah;
      for from you will come a Ruler
      who will shepherd my people Isra'el.'"[b]

---

[a] Isaiah 7:14   [b] Micah 5:1(2)

⁷ Herod summoned the Magi to meet with him privately and asked them exactly when the star had appeared. ⁸ Then he sent them to Beit-Lechem with these instructions: "Search carefully for the child; and when you find him, let me know, so that I too may go and worship him."

⁹ After they had listened to the king, they went away; and the star which they had seen in the east went in front of them until it came and stopped over the place where the child was. ¹⁰ When they saw the star, they were overjoyed. ¹¹ Upon entering the house, they saw the child with his mother Miryam; and they prostrated themselves and worshipped him. Then they opened their bags and presented him gifts of gold, frankincense and myrrh. ¹² But they had been warned in a dream not to return to Herod, so they took another route back to their own country.

¹³ After they had gone, an angel of ADONAI appeared to Yosef in a dream and said, "Get up, take the child and his mother, and escape to Egypt, and stay there until I tell you to leave. For Herod is going to look for the child in order to kill him." ¹⁴ So he got up, took the child and his mother, and left during the night for Egypt, ¹⁵ where he stayed until Herod died. This happened in order to fulfill what ADONAI had said through the prophet,

"Out of Egypt I called my son."[c]

¹⁶ Meanwhile, when Herod realized that the Magi had tricked him, he was furious and gave orders to kill all the boys in and around Beit-Lechem who were two years old or less, calculating from the time the Magi had told him. ¹⁷ In this way were fulfilled the words spoken through the prophet Yirmeyahu,

¹⁸ **"A voice was heard in Ramah,**
sobbing and lamenting loudly.
It was Rachel sobbing for her children
and refusing to be comforted,
because they are no longer alive."[d]

¹⁹ After Herod's death, an angel of ADONAI appeared in a dream to Yosef in Egypt ²⁰ and said, "Get up, take the child and his mother, and go to *Eretz-Yisra'el*, for those who wanted to kill the child are dead." ²¹ So he got up, took the child and his mother, and went back to *Eretz-Yisra'el*. ²² However, when he heard that Archelaus had succeeded his father Herod as king of Y'hudah, he was afraid to go there. Warned in a dream, he withdrew to the Galil ²³ and settled in a town called Natzeret, so that what had been spoken by the prophets might be fulfilled, that he will be called a *Natzrati*.

3 ¹ It was during those days that Yochanan the Immerser arrived in the desert of Y'hudah and began proclaiming the message, ² "Turn from your sins to God, for the Kingdom of Heaven is near!" ³ This is the man Yesha'yahu was talking about when he said,

"The voice of someone crying out:
'In the desert prepare the way of ADONAI!
Make straight paths for him!'"[e]

---

[c] Hosea 11:1   [d] Jeremiah 31:14(15)   [e] Isaiah 40:3

⁴ Yochanan wore clothes of camel's hair with a leather belt around his waist, and his food was locusts and wild honey. ⁵ People went out to him from Yerushalayim, from all Y'hudah, and from the whole region around the Yarden. ⁶ Confessing their sins, they were immersed by him in the Yarden River.

⁷ But when Yochanan saw many of the *P'rushim* and *Tz'dukim* coming to be immersed by him, he said to them, "You snakes! Who warned you to escape the coming punishment? ⁸ If you have really turned from your sins to God, produce fruit that will prove it! ⁹ And don't suppose you can comfort yourselves by saying, 'Avraham is our father'! For I tell you that God can raise up for Avraham sons from these stones! ¹⁰ Already the axe is at the root of the trees, ready to strike; every tree that doesn't produce good fruit will be chopped down and thrown in the fire! ¹¹ It's true that I am immersing you in water so that you might turn from sin to God; but the one coming after me is more powerful than I — I'm not worthy even to carry his sandals — and he will immerse you in the *Ruach HaKodesh* and in fire. ¹² He has with him his winnowing fork; and he will clear out his threshing floor, gathering his wheat into the barn but burning up the straw with unquenchable fire!"

¹³ Then Yeshua came from the Galil to the Yarden to be immersed by Yochanan. ¹⁴ But Yochanan tried to stop him. "You are coming to me? I ought to be immersed by you!" ¹⁵ However, Yeshua answered him, "Let it be this way now, because we should do everything righteousness requires." Then Yochanan let him. ¹⁶ As soon as Yeshua had been immersed, he came up out of the water. At that moment heaven was opened, he saw the Spirit of God coming down upon him like a dove, ¹⁷ and a voice from heaven said, "This is my Son, whom I love; I am well pleased with him."

4 ¹ Then the Spirit led Yeshua up into the wilderness to be tempted by the Adversary. ² After Yeshua had fasted forty days and nights, he was hungry. ³ The Tempter came and said to him, "If you are the Son of God, order these stones to become bread." ⁴ But he answered, "The *Tanakh* says,

> **'Man does not live on bread alone,**
> **but on every word that comes from the mouth of ADONAI'"***ⁱ*

⁵ Then the Adversary took him to the holy city and set him on the highest point of the Temple. ⁶ "If you are the Son of God," he said, "jump! For the *Tanakh* says,

> **'He will order his angels to be responsible for you. . . .**
> **They will support you with their hands,**
> **so that you will not hurt your feet on the stones.'"***ᵍ*

⁷ Yeshua replied to him, "But it also says, **'Do not put ADONAI your God to the test.'"***ʰ*

⁸ Once more, the Adversary took him up to the summit of a very high mountain, showed him all the kingdoms of the world in all their glory, ⁹ and said to him, "All this I will give you if you will bow down and worship me." ¹⁰ "Away with you, Satan!" Yeshua told him, "For the *Tanakh* says,

---

ⁱ Deuteronomy 8:3   *ᵍ* Psalm 91:11–12   *ʰ* Deuteronomy 6:16

'Worship *Adonai* your God, and serve only him.'"[i]

[11] Then the Adversary let him alone, and angels came and took care of him.

[12] When Yeshua heard that Yochanan had been put in prison, he returned to the Galil; [13] but he left Natzeret and came to live in K'far-Nachum, a lake shore town near the boundary between Z'vulun and Naftali. [14] This happened in order to fulfill what Yesha'yahu the prophet had said,

[15]   "Land of Z'vulun and land of Naftali,
         toward the lake, beyond the Yarden, Galil-of-the-*Goyim* —
[16]   the people living in darkness
         have seen a great light;
         upon those living in the region, in the shadow of death,
         light has dawned."[j]

[17] From that time on, Yeshua began proclaiming, "Turn from your sins to God, for the Kingdom of Heaven is near!"

[18] As Yeshua walked by Lake Kinneret, he saw two brothers who were fishermen — Shim'on, known as Kefa, and his brother Andrew — throwing their net into the lake. [19] Yeshua said to them, "Come after me, and I will make you fishers for men!" [20] At once they left their nets and went with him.

[21] Going on from there, he saw two other brothers — Ya'akov Ben-Zavdai and Yochanan his brother — in the boat with their father Zavdai, repairing their nets; and he called them. [22] At once they left the boat and their father and went with Yeshua.

[23] Yeshua went all over the Galil teaching in their synagogues, proclaiming the Good News of the Kingdom, and healing people from every kind of disease and sickness. [24] Word of him spread throughout all Syria, and people brought to him all who were ill, suffering from various diseases and pains, and those held in the power of demons, and epileptics and paralytics; and he healed them. [25] Huge crowds followed him from the Galil, the Ten Towns, Yerushalayim, Y'hudah, and 'Ever-HaYarden.

5 [1] Seeing the crowds, Yeshua walked up the hill. After he sat down, his *talmidim* came to him, [2] and he began to speak. This is what he taught them:

[3]   "How blessed are the poor in spirit!
         for the Kingdom of Heaven is theirs.

[4]   "How blessed are those who mourn!
         for they will be comforted.

[5]   "How blessed are **the meek!**
         for they **will inherit the Land!**[k]

[6]   "How blessed are those who hunger and thirst for righteousness!
         for they will be filled.

---

[i] Deuteronomy 6:13–14   [j] Isaiah 8:23(9:1)–9:1(2)   [k] Psalm 37:11

7   "How blessed are those who show mercy!
          for they will be shown mercy.

8   "How blessed are the pure in heart!
          for they will see God.

9   "How blessed are those who make peace!
          for they will be called sons of God.

10   "How blessed are those who are persecuted
          because they pursue righteousness!
          for the Kingdom of Heaven is theirs.

[11] "How blessed you are when people insult you and persecute you and tell all kinds of vicious lies about you because you follow me! [12] Rejoice, be glad, because your reward in heaven is great — they persecuted the prophets before you in the same way.

[13] "You are salt for the Land. But if salt becomes tasteless, how can it be made salty again? It is no longer good for anything except being thrown out for people to trample on.

[14] "You are light for the world. A town built on a hill cannot be hidden. [15] Likewise, when people light a lamp, they don't cover it with a bowl but put it on a lampstand, so that it shines for everyone in the house. [16] In the same way, let your light shine before people, so that they may see the good things you do and praise your Father in heaven.

[17] "Don't think that I have come to abolish the *Torah* or the Prophets. I have come not to abolish but to complete. [18] Yes indeed! I tell you that until heaven and earth pass away, not so much as a *yud* or a stroke will pass from the *Torah* — not until everything that must happen has happened. [19] So whoever disobeys the least of these *mitzvot* and teaches others to do so will be called the least in the Kingdom of Heaven. But whoever obeys them and so teaches will be called great in the Kingdom of Heaven. [20] For I tell you that unless your righteousness is far greater than that of the *Torah*-teachers and *P'rushim*, you will certainly not enter the Kingdom of Heaven!

[21] "You have heard that our fathers were told, **'Do not murder,'**[i] and that anyone who commits murder will be subject to judgment. [22] But I tell you that anyone who nurses anger against his brother will be subject to judgment; that whoever calls his brother, 'You good-for-nothing!' will be brought before the *Sanhedrin*; that whoever says, 'Fool!' incurs the penalty of burning in the fire of Gei-Hinnom! [23] So if you are offering your gift at the Temple altar and you remember there that your brother has something against you, [24] leave your gift where it is by the altar, and go, make peace with your brother. Then come back and offer your gift. [25] If someone sues you, come to terms with him quickly, while you and he are on the way to court; or he may hand you over to the judge, and the judge to the officer of the court, and you may be thrown in jail! [26] Yes indeed! I tell you, you will certainly not get out until you have paid the last penny.

---

[i] Exodus 20:13, Deuteronomy 5:17

1228

27 “You have heard that our fathers were told, **‘Do not commit adultery.’**[m]
28 But I tell you that a man who even looks at a woman with the purpose of lusting
after her has already committed adultery with her in his heart. 29 If your right eye
makes you sin, gouge it out and throw it away! Better that you should lose one part
of you than have your whole body thrown into Gei-Hinnom. 30 And if your right
hand makes you sin, cut it off and throw it away! Better that you should lose one part
of you than have your whole body thrown into Gei-Hinnom.

31 “It was said, **‘Whoever divorces his wife must give her a *get*.’**[n] 32 But I tell
you that anyone who divorces his wife, except on the ground of fornication, makes
her an adulteress; and that anyone who marries a divorcee commits adultery.

33 “Again, you have heard that our fathers were told, **‘Do not break your
oath,’** and **‘Keep your vows to *Adonai*.’**[o] 34 But I tell you not to swear at all —
not ‘by **heaven**,’ because it **is** God’s **throne**; 35 not ‘by **the earth**,’ because it **is** his
footstool;[p] and not ‘by Yerushalayim,’ because it is **the city of the Great King.**[q] 36 And
don’t swear by your head, because you can’t make a single hair white or black. 37 Just
let your ‘Yes’ be a simple ‘Yes,’ and your ‘No’ a simple ‘No’; anything more than
this has its origin in evil.

38 “You have heard that our fathers were told, **‘Eye for eye and tooth for
tooth.’**[r] 39 But I tell you not to stand up against someone who does you wrong. On the
contrary, if someone hits you on the right cheek, let him hit you on the left cheek
too! 40 If someone wants to sue you for your shirt, let him have your coat as
well! 41 And if a soldier forces you to carry his pack for one mile, carry it for two!
42 When someone asks you for something, give it to him; when someone wants
to borrow something from you, lend it to him.

43 “You have heard that our fathers were told, ‘**Love your neighbor**[s] — and
hate your enemy.’ 44 But I tell you, love your enemies! Pray for those who persecute
you! 45 Then you will become children of your Father in heaven. For he makes
his sun shine on good and bad people alike, and he sends rain to the righteous
and the unrighteous alike. 46 What reward do you get if you love only those who
love you? Why, even tax-collectors do that! 47 And if you are friendly only to
your friends, are you doing anything out of the ordinary? Even the *Goyim* do that!
48 Therefore, be perfect, just as your Father in heaven is perfect.

6 1 “Be careful not to parade your acts of *tzedakah* in front of people in order to be seen
by them! If you do, you have no reward from your Father in heaven. 2 So, when you do
tzedakah, don’t announce it with trumpets to win people’s praise, like the hypocrites
in the synagogues and on the streets. Yes! I tell you, they have their reward
already! 3 But you, when you do *tzedakah*, don’t even let your left hand know
what your right hand is doing. 4 Then your *tzedakah* will be in secret; and your
Father, who sees what you do in secret, will reward you.

5 “When you pray, don’t be like the hypocrites, who love to pray standing in the
synagogues and on street corners, so that people can see them. Yes! I tell you, they
have their reward already! 6 But you, when you pray, go into your room, close the

[m] Exodus 20:13(14); Deuteronomy 5:17(18)
[n] Deuteronomy 24:1
[o] Leviticus 19:12; Numbers 30:3(2); Deuteronomy 23:22(21)
[p] Isaiah 66:1
[q] Psalm 48:3(2)
[r] Exodus 21:24; Leviticus 24:20; Deuteronomy 19:21
[s] Leviticus 19:18

door, and pray to your Father in secret. Your Father, who sees what is done in secret, will reward you.

⁷ "And when you pray, don't babble on and on like the pagans, who think God will hear them better if they talk a lot. ⁸ Don't be like them, because your Father knows what you need before you ask him. ⁹ You, therefore, pray like this:

'Our Father in heaven!
     May your Name be kept holy.
¹⁰   May your Kingdom come,
       your will be done on earth as in heaven.
¹¹   Give us the food we need today.
¹²   Forgive us what we have done wrong,
       as we too have forgiven those who have wronged us.
¹³   And do not lead us into hard testing,
       but keep us safe from the Evil One.
    *For kingship, power and glory are yours forever.
    Amen.'

¹⁴ For if you forgive others their offenses, your heavenly Father will also forgive you; ¹⁵ but if you do not forgive others their offenses, your heavenly Father will not forgive yours.

¹⁶ "Now when you fast, don't go around looking miserable, like the hypocrites. They make sour faces so that people will know they are fasting. Yes! I tell you, they have their reward already! ¹⁷ But you, when you fast, wash your face and groom yourself, ¹⁸ so that no one will know you are fasting — except your Father, who is with you in secret. Your Father, who sees what is done in secret, will reward you.

¹⁹ "Do not store up for yourselves wealth here on earth, where moths and rust destroy, and burglars break in and steal. ²⁰ Instead, store up for yourselves wealth in heaven, where neither moth nor rust destroys, and burglars do not break in or steal. ²¹ For where your wealth is, there your heart will be also. ²² 'The eye is the lamp of the body.' So if you have a 'good eye' [that is, if you are generous] your whole body will be full of light; ²³ but if you have an 'evil eye' [if you are stingy] your whole body will be full of darkness. If, then, the light in you is darkness, how great is that darkness! ²⁴ No one can be slave to two masters; for he will either hate the first and love the second, or scorn the second and be loyal to the first. You can't be a slave to both God and money.

²⁵ "Therefore, I tell you, don't worry about your life — what you will eat or drink; or about your body — what you will wear. Isn't life more than food and the body more than clothing? ²⁶ Look at the birds flying about! They neither plant nor harvest, nor do they gather food into barns; yet your heavenly Father feeds them. Aren't you worth more than they are? ²⁷ Can any of you by worrying add a single hour to his life?

²⁸ "And why be anxious about clothing? Think about the fields of wild irises, and how they grow. They neither work nor spin thread, ²⁹ yet I tell you that not even

---

* The latter half of verse 13 is not found in the oldest manuscripts.

Shlomo in all his glory was clothed as beautifully as one of these. ³⁰ If this is how God clothes grass in the field — which is here today and gone tomorrow, thrown in an oven — won't he much more clothe you? What little trust you have!

³¹ "So don't be anxious, asking, 'What will we eat?,' 'What will we drink?' or 'How will we be clothed?' ³² For it is the pagans who set their hearts on all these things. Your heavenly Father knows you need them all. ³³ But seek first his Kingdom and his righteousness, and all these things will be given to you as well. ³⁴ Don't worry about tomorrow — tomorrow will worry about itself! Today has enough *tsuris* already!

7 ¹ "Don't judge, so that you won't be judged. ² For the way you judge others is how you will be judged — the measure with which you measure out will be used to measure to you. ³ Why do you see the splinter in your brother's eye but not notice the log in your own eye? ⁴ How can you say to your brother, 'Let me take the splinter out of your eye,' when you have the log in your own eye? ⁵ You hypocrite! First, take the log out of your own eye; then you will see clearly, so that you can remove the splinter from your brother's eye!

⁶ "Don't give to dogs what is holy, and don't throw your pearls to the pigs. If you do, they may trample them under their feet, then turn and attack you.

⁷ "Keep asking, and it will be given to you; keep seeking, and you will find; keep knocking, and the door will be opened to you. ⁸ For everyone who keeps asking receives; he who keeps seeking finds; and to him who keeps knocking, the door will be opened. ⁹ Is there anyone here who, if his son asks him for a loaf of bread, will give him a stone? ¹⁰ or if he asks for a fish, will give him a snake? ¹¹ So if you, even though you are bad, know how to give your children gifts that are good, how much more will your Father in heaven keep giving good things to those who keep asking him!

¹² "Always treat others as you would like them to treat you; that sums up the teaching of the *Torah* and the Prophets.

¹³ "Go in through the narrow gate; for the gate that leads to destruction is wide and the road broad, and many travel it; ¹⁴ but it is a narrow gate and a hard road that leads to life, and only a few find it.

¹⁵ "Beware of the false prophets! They come to you wearing sheep's clothing, but underneath they are hungry wolves! ¹⁶ You will recognize them by their fruit. Can people pick grapes from thorn bushes, or figs from thistles? ¹⁷ Likewise, every healthy tree produces good fruit, but a poor tree produces bad fruit. ¹⁸ A healthy tree cannot bear bad fruit, or a poor tree good fruit. ¹⁹ Any tree that does not produce good fruit is cut down and thrown in the fire! ²⁰ So you will recognize them by their fruit.

²¹ "Not everyone who says to me, 'Lord, Lord!' will enter the Kingdom of Heaven, only those who do what my Father in heaven wants. ²² On that Day, many will say to me, 'Lord, Lord! Didn't we prophesy in your name? Didn't we expel demons in your name? Didn't we perform many miracles in your name?' ²³ Then I will tell them to their faces, 'I never knew you! **Get away from me, you workers of lawlessness!**'ᵗ

ᵗ Psalm 6:9(8)

²⁴ "So, everyone who hears these words of mine and acts on them will be like a sensible man who built his house on bedrock. ²⁵ The rain fell, the rivers flooded, the winds blew and beat against that house, but it didn't collapse, because its foundation was on rock. ²⁶ But everyone who hears these words of mine and does not act on them will be like a stupid man who built his house on sand. ²⁷ The rain fell, the rivers flooded, the wind blew and beat against that house, and it collapsed — and its collapse was horrendous!"

²⁸ When Yeshua had finished saying these things, the crowds were amazed at the way he taught, ²⁹ for he was not instructing them like their *Torah*-teachers but as one who had authority himself.

8 ¹ After Yeshua had come down from the hill, large crowds followed him. ² Then a man afflicted with *tzara'at* came, kneeled down in front of him and said, "Sir, if you are willing, you can make me clean." ³ Yeshua reached out his hand, touched him and said, "I am willing! Be cleansed!" And at once he was cleansed from his *tzara'at*. ⁴ Then Yeshua said to him, "See that you tell no one; but as a testimony to the people, go and let the *cohen* examine you, and offer the sacrifice that Moshe commanded."

⁵ As Yeshua entered K'far-Nachum, a Roman army officer came up and pleaded for help. ⁶ "Sir, my orderly is lying at home paralyzed and suffering terribly!" ⁷ Yeshua said, "I will go and heal him." ⁸ But the officer answered, "Sir, I am unfit to have you come into my home. Rather, if you will only give the command, my orderly will recover. ⁹ For I too am a man under authority. I have soldiers under me, and I say to this one, 'Go!' and he goes; to another, 'Come!' and he comes; to my slave, 'Do this!' and he does it." ¹⁰ On hearing this Yeshua was amazed and said to the people following him, "Yes! I tell you, I have not found anyone in Isra'el with such trust! ¹¹ Moreover, I tell you that many will come from the east and from the west to take their places at the feast in the Kingdom of Heaven with Avraham, Yitz'chak and Ya'akov. ¹² But those born for the Kingdom will be thrown outside in the dark, where people will wail and grind their teeth!" ¹³ Then Yeshua said to the officer, "Go; let it be for you as you have trusted." And his orderly was healed at that very moment.

¹⁴ Yeshua went to Kefa's home and there saw Kefa's mother-in-law sick in bed with a fever. ¹⁵ He touched her hand, the fever left her, and she got up and began helping him.

¹⁶ When evening came, many people held in the power of demons were brought to him. He expelled the spirits with a word and healed all who were ill. ¹⁷ This was done to fulfill what had been spoken through the prophet Yesha'yahu,

> **"He himself took our weaknesses**
> **and bore our diseases"**ᵘ

¹⁸ When Yeshua saw the crowd around him, he gave orders to cross to the other side of the lake. ¹⁹ A *Torah*-teacher approached and said to him, "Rabbi, I will follow you wherever you go." ²⁰ Yeshua said to him, "The foxes have holes, and the birds

---

ᵘ Isaiah 53:4

flying about have nests, but the Son of Man has no home of his own." ²¹ Another of the *talmidim* said to him, "Sir, first let me go and bury my father." ²² But Yeshua replied, "Follow me, and let the dead bury their own dead."

²³ He boarded the boat, and his *talmidim* followed. ²⁴ Then, without warning, a furious storm arose on the lake, so that waves were sweeping over the boat. But Yeshua was sleeping. ²⁵ So they came and roused him, saying, "Sir! Help! We're about to die!" ²⁶ He said to them, "Why are you afraid? So little trust you have!" Then he got up and rebuked the winds and the waves, and there was a dead calm. ²⁷ The men were astounded. They asked, "What kind of man is this, that even the winds and sea obey him?"

²⁸ When Yeshua arrived at the other side of the lake, in the Gadarenes' territory, there came out of the burial caves two men controlled by demons, so violent that no one dared travel on that road. ²⁹ They screamed, "What do you want with us, Son of God? Have you come here to torture us before the appointed time?" ³⁰ Now some distance from them a large herd of pigs was feeding. ³¹ The demons begged him, "If you are going to drive us out, send us into the herd of pigs." ³² "All right, go!" he told them. So they came out and went into the pigs, whereupon the entire herd rushed down the hillside into the lake and drowned. ³³ The swineherds fled, went off to the town and told the whole story, including what had happened to the demonized men. ³⁴ At this, the whole town came out to meet Yeshua. When they saw him, they begged him to leave their district.

9 ¹ So he stepped into a boat, crossed the lake again and came to his own town. ² Some people brought him a paralyzed man lying on a mattress. When Yeshua saw their trust, he said to the paralyzed man, "Courage, son! Your sins are forgiven." ³ On seeing this, some of the *Torah*-teachers said among themselves, "This man is blaspheming!" ⁴ Yeshua, knowing what they were thinking, said, "Why are you entertaining evil thoughts in your hearts? ⁵ Tell me, which is easier to say — 'Your sins are forgiven' or 'Get up and walk'? ⁶ But look! I will prove to you that the Son of Man has authority on earth to forgive sins." He then said to the paralyzed man, "Get up, pick up your mattress, and go home!" ⁷ And the man got up and went home. ⁸ When the crowds saw this, they were awestruck and said a *b'rakhah* to God the Giver of such authority to human beings.

⁹ As Yeshua passed on from there he spotted a tax-collector named Mattityahu sitting in his collection booth. He said to him, "Follow me!" and he got up and followed him.

¹⁰ While Yeshua was in the house eating, many tax-collectors and sinners came and joined him and his *talmidim* at the meal. ¹¹ When the *P'rushim* saw this, they said to his *talmidim*, "Why does your rabbi eat with tax-collectors and sinners?" ¹² But Yeshua heard the question and answered, "The ones who need a doctor aren't the healthy but the sick. ¹³ As for you, go and learn what this means: **'I want compassion rather than animal-sacrifices.'**ᵛ For I didn't come to call the 'righteous,' but sinners!"

¹⁴ Next, Yochanan's *talmidim* came to him and asked, "Why is it that we and the *P'rushim* fast frequently, but your *talmidim* don't fast at all?" ¹⁵ Yeshua said to them, "Can wedding guests mourn while the bridegroom is still with them? But the time will come when the bridegroom is taken away from them; then they will fast.

ᵛ Hosea 6:6

^{16} No one patches an old coat with a piece of unshrunk cloth, because the patch tears away from the coat and leaves a worse hole. ^{17} Nor do people put new wine in old wineskins; if they do, the skins burst, the wine spills and the wineskins are ruined. No, they pour new wine into freshly prepared wineskins, and in this way both are preserved."

^{18} While he was talking, an official came in, kneeled down in front of him and said, "My daughter has just died. But if you come and lay your hand on her, she will live." ^{19} Yeshua, with his *talmidim*, got up and followed him.

^{20} A woman who had had a hemorrhage for twelve years approached him from behind and touched the *tzitzit* on his robe. ^{21} For she said to herself, "If I can only touch his robe, I will be healed." ^{22} Yeshua turned, saw her and said, "Courage, daughter! Your trust has healed you." And she was instantly healed.

^{23} When Yeshua arrived at the official's house and saw the flute-players, and the crowd in an uproar, ^{24} he said, "Everybody out! The girl isn't dead, she's only sleeping!" And they jeered at him. ^{25} But after the people had been put outside, he entered and took hold of the girl's hand, and she got up. ^{26} News of this spread through all that region.

^{27} As Yeshua went on from there, two blind men began following him, shouting, "Son of David! Take pity on us!" ^{28} When he entered the house, the blind men came up, and Yeshua said to them, "Do you believe that I have the power to do this?" They replied, "Yes, sir." ^{29} Then he touched their eyes and said, "Let it happen to you according to your trust"; ^{30} and their sight was restored. Yeshua warned them severely, "See that no one knows about it." ^{31} But instead, they went away and talked about him throughout that district.

^{32} As they were going, a man controlled by a demon and unable to speak was brought to Yeshua. ^{33} After the demon was expelled the man who had been mute spoke, and the crowds were amazed. "Nothing like this has ever been seen in Isra'el," they said. ^{34} But the *P'rushim* said, "It is through the ruler of the demons that he expels demons."

^{35} Yeshua went about all the towns and villages, teaching in their synagogues, proclaiming the Good News of the Kingdom, and healing every kind of disease and weakness. ^{36} When he saw the crowds, he had compassion on them because they were harried and helpless, like sheep without a shepherd. ^{37} Then he said to his *talmidim*, "The harvest is rich, but the workers are few. ^{38} Pray that the Lord of the harvest will send out workers to gather in his harvest."

10 ^{1} Yeshua called his twelve *talmidim* and gave them authority to drive out unclean spirits and to heal every kind of disease and weakness. ^{2} These are the names of the twelve emissaries:

> First, Shim'on, called Kefa, and Andrew his brother,
> Ya'akov Ben-Zavdai and Yochanan his brother,
> ^{3} Philip and Bar-Talmai,
> T'oma and Mattityahu the tax-collector,
> Ya'akov Bar-Halfai and Taddai,
> ^{4} Shim'on the Zealot, and Y'hudah from K'riot, who betrayed him.

^{5} These twelve Yeshua sent out with the following instructions: "Don't go into the territory of the *Goyim*, and don't enter any town in Shomron, ^{6} but go rather to the lost sheep of the house of Isra'el. ⁷ As you go, proclaim, 'The Kingdom of Heaven is near,' ⁸ heal the sick, raise the dead, cleanse those afflicted with *tzara'at*, expel demons. You have received without paying, so give without asking payment. ⁹ Don't take money in your belts, no gold, no silver, no copper; ¹⁰ and for the trip don't take a pack, an extra shirt, shoes or a walking stick — a worker should be given what he needs.

¹¹ "When you come to a town or village, look for someone trustworthy and stay with him until you leave. ¹² When you enter someone's household, say, '*Shalom aleikhem!*' ¹³ If the home deserves it, let your *shalom* rest on it; if not, let your *shalom* return to you. ¹⁴ But if the people of a house or town will not welcome you or listen to you, leave it and shake its dust from your feet! ¹⁵ Yes, I tell you, it will be more tolerable on the Day of Judgment for the people of S'dom and 'Amora than for that town!

¹⁶ "Pay attention! I am sending you out like sheep among wolves, so be as prudent as snakes and as harmless as doves. ¹⁷ Be on guard, for there will be people who will hand you over to the local *Sanhedrin*s and flog you in their synagogues. ¹⁸ On my account you will be brought before governors and kings as a testimony to them and to the *Goyim*. ¹⁹ But when they bring you to trial, do not worry about what to say or how to say it; when the time comes, you will be given what you should say. ²⁰ For it will not be just you speaking, but the Spirit of your heavenly Father speaking through you.

²¹ "A brother will betray his brother to death, and a father his child; children will turn against their parents and have them put to death. ²² Everyone will hate you because of me, but whoever holds out till the end will be preserved from harm. ²³ When you are persecuted in one town, run away to another. Yes indeed; I tell you, you will not finish going through the towns of Isra'el before the Son of Man comes.

²⁴ "A *talmid* is not greater than his rabbi, a slave is not greater than his master. ²⁵ It is enough for a *talmid* that he become like his rabbi, and a slave like his master. Now if people have called the head of the house Ba'al-Zibbul, how much more will they malign the members of his household! ²⁶ So do not fear them; for there is nothing covered that will not be uncovered, or hidden that will not be known. ²⁷ What I tell you in the dark, speak in the light; what is whispered in your ear, proclaim on the housetops.

²⁸ "Do not fear those who kill the body but are powerless to kill the soul. Rather, fear him who can destroy both soul and body in Gei-Hinnom. ²⁹ Aren't sparrows sold for next to nothing, two for an assarion? Yet not one of them will fall to the ground without your Father's consent. ³⁰ As for you, every hair on your head has been counted. ³¹ So do not be afraid, you are worth more than many sparrows.

³² "Whoever acknowledges me in the presence of others I will also acknowledge in the presence of my Father in heaven. ³³ But whoever disowns me before others I will disown before my Father in heaven.

³⁴ "Don't suppose that I have come to bring peace to the Land. It is not peace I have come to bring, but a sword! ³⁵ For I have come to set

³⁶   **a man against his father,**
            a daughter against her mother,
            a daughter-in-law against her mother-in-law,
            so that **a man's enemies will be the members of his own household.**ʷ

ʷ Micah 7:6

³⁷ Whoever loves his father or mother more than he loves me is not worthy of me; anyone who loves his son or daughter more than he loves me is not worthy of me. ³⁸ And anyone who does not take up his execution-stake and follow me is not worthy of me. ³⁹ Whoever finds his own life will lose it, but the person who loses his life for my sake will find it.

⁴⁰ "Whoever receives you is receiving me, and whoever receives me is receiving the One who sent me. ⁴¹ Anyone who receives a prophet because he is a prophet will receive the reward a prophet gets, and anyone who receives a *tzaddik* because he is a *tzaddik* will receive the reward a *tzaddik* gets. ⁴² Indeed, if someone gives just a cup of cold water to one of these little ones because he is my *talmid* — yes! — I tell you, he will certainly not lose his reward!"

11 ¹ After Yeshua had finished instructing the twelve *talmidim*, he went on from there to teach and preach in the towns nearby.

² Meanwhile, Yochanan the Immerser, who had been put in prison, heard what the Messiah had been doing; so he sent a message to him through his *talmidim*, ³ asking, "Are you the one who is to come, or should we look for someone else?" ⁴ Yeshua answered, "Go and tell Yochanan what you are hearing and seeing — ⁵ **the blind are seeing again, the lame are** walking, people with *tzara'at* are being cleansed, **the deaf are hearing,**ˣ the dead are being raised,ʸ **the Good News is being told to the poor**ᶻ — ⁶ and how blessed is anyone not offended by me!"

⁷ As they were leaving, Yeshua began speaking about Yochanan to the crowds: "What did you go out to the desert to see? Reeds swaying in the breeze? ⁸ No? then what did you go out to see? Someone who was well dressed? Well-dressed people live in kings' palaces. ⁹ *Nu*, so why did you go out? To see a prophet! Yes! and I tell you he's much more than a prophet. ¹⁰ This is the one about whom the *Tanakh* says,

> **'See, I am sending out my messenger ahead of you;**
> **he will prepare your way before you.'**ᵃ

¹¹ Yes! I tell you that among those born of women there has not arisen anyone greater than Yochanan the Immerser! Yet the one who is least in the Kingdom of Heaven is greater than he! ¹² From the time of Yochanan the Immerser until now, the Kingdom of Heaven has been suffering violence; yes, violent ones are trying to snatch it away. ¹³ For all the prophets and the *Torah* prophesied until Yochanan. ¹⁴ Indeed, if you are willing to accept it, he is Eliyahu, whose coming was predicted. ¹⁵ If you have ears, then hear!

¹⁶ "Oh, what can I compare this generation with? They're like children sitting in the marketplaces, calling out to each other,

¹⁷
> 'We made happy music,
>   but you wouldn't dance!
> We made sad music,
>   but you wouldn't cry!'

¹⁸ For Yochanan came, fasting, not drinking — so they say, 'He has a demon.' ¹⁹ The Son of Man came, eating freely and drinking wine — so they say, 'Aha! A glutton

---

ˣ Isaiah 35:5–6   ʸ Isaiah 26:19   ᶻIsaiah 61:1   ᵃMalachi 3:1

and a drunkard! A friend of tax-collectors and sinners!' Well, the proof of wisdom is in the actions it produces."

²⁰ Then Yeshua began to denounce the towns in which he had done most of his miracles, because the people had not turned from their sins to God. ²¹ "Woe to you, Korazin! Woe to you, Beit-Tzaidah! Why, if the miracles done in you had been done in Tzor and Tzidon, they would long ago have put on sackcloth and ashes as evidence that they had changed their ways. ²² But I tell you it will be more bearable for Tzor and Tzidon than for you on the Day of Judgment! ²³ And you, K'far-Nachum, will you be **exalted to heaven? No, you will be brought down to Sh'ol!**ᵇ For if the miracles done in you had been done in S'dom, it would still be in existence today. ²⁴ But I tell you that on the Day of Judgment it will be more bearable for the land of S'dom than for you!"

²⁵ It was at that time that Yeshua said, "I thank you, Father, Lord of heaven and earth, that you concealed these things from the sophisticated and educated and revealed them to ordinary folks. ²⁶ Yes, Father, I thank you that it pleased you to do this.

²⁷ "My Father has handed over everything to me. Indeed, no one fully knows the Son except the Father, and no one fully knows the Father except the Son and those to whom the Son wishes to reveal him.

²⁸ "Come to me, all of you who are struggling and burdened, and I will give you rest. ²⁹ Take my yoke upon you and learn from me, because I am gentle and humble in heart, **and you will find rest for your souls.**ᶜ ³⁰ For my yoke is easy, and my burden is light."

12 ¹ One *Shabbat* during that time, Yeshua was walking through some wheat fields. His *talmidim* were hungry, so they began picking heads of grain and eating them. ² On seeing this, the *P'rushim* said to him, "Look! Your *talmidim* are violating *Shabbat!*" ³ But he said to them, "Haven't you ever read what David did when he and those with him were hungry? ⁴ He entered the House of God and ate the Bread of the Presence!" — which was prohibited, both to him and to his companions; it is permitted only to the *cohanim*. ⁵ "Or haven't you read in the *Torah* that on *Shabbat* the *cohanim* profane *Shabbat* and yet are blameless? ⁶ I tell you, there is in this place something greater than the Temple! ⁷ If you knew what **'I want compassion rather than animal-sacrifice'**ᵈ meant, you would not condemn the innocent. ⁸ For the Son of Man is Lord of *Shabbat!*"

⁹ Going on from that place, he went into their synagogue. ¹⁰ A man there had a shriveled hand. Looking for a reason to accuse him of something, they asked him, "Is healing permitted on *Shabbat?*" ¹¹ But he answered, "If you have a sheep that falls in a pit on *Shabbat*, which of you won't take hold of it and lift it out? ¹² How much more valuable is a man than a sheep! Therefore, what is permitted on *Shabbat* is to do good." ¹³ Then to the man he said, "Hold out your hand." As he held it out, it became restored, as sound as the other one. ¹⁴ But the *P'rushim* went out and began plotting how they might do away with Yeshua. ¹⁵ Aware of this, he left that area.

Many people followed him; and he healed them all ¹⁶ but warned them not to make him known. ¹⁷ This was to fulfill what had been spoken through Yesha'yahu the prophet,

---

ᵇ Isaiah 14:13, 15   ᶜ Jeremiah 6:16   ᵈ Hosea 6:6

18	**"Here is my servant, whom I have chosen,** **my beloved, with whom I am well pleased;** **I will put my Spirit on him,** **and he will announce justice to the Gentiles.**
19	**He will not fight or shout,** **no one will hear his voice in the streets;**
20	**he will not snap off a broken reed** **or snuff out a smoldering wick** **until he has brought justice through to victory.**
21	**In him the Gentiles will put their hope."**^e

²² Then some people brought him a man controlled by demons who was blind and mute; and Yeshua healed him, so that he could both speak and see. ²³ The crowds were astounded and asked, "This couldn't be the Son of David, could it?" ²⁴ But when the *P'rushim* heard of it, they said, "It is only by Ba'al-Zibbul" — the ruler of the demons — "that this man drives out demons."

²⁵ However, knowing what they were thinking, Yeshua said to them, "Every kingdom divided against itself will be ruined, and every city or household divided against itself will not survive. ²⁶ If Satan drives out Satan, he is divided against himself; so how can his kingdom survive? ²⁷ Besides, if I drive out demons by Ba'al-Zibbul, by whom do your people drive them out? So, they will be your judges! ²⁸ But if I drive out demons by the Spirit of God, then the Kingdom of God has come upon you!

²⁹ "Or again, how can someone break into a strong man's house and make off with his possessions unless he first ties up the strong man? After that he can ransack his house. ³⁰ "Those who are not with me are against me, and those who do not gather with me are scattering. ³¹ Because of this, I tell you that people will be forgiven any sin and blasphemy, but blaspheming the *Ruach HaKodesh* will not be forgiven. ³² One can say something against the Son of Man and be forgiven; but whoever keeps on speaking against the *Ruach HaKodesh* will never be forgiven, neither in the *'olam hazeh* nor in the *'olam haba*.

³³ "If you make a tree good, its fruit will be good; and if you make a tree bad, its fruit will be bad; for a tree is known by its fruit. ³⁴ You snakes! How can you who are evil say anything good? For the mouth speaks what overflows from the heart. ³⁵ The good person brings forth good things from his store of good, and the evil person brings forth evil things from his store of evil. ³⁶ Moreover, I tell you this: on the Day of Judgment people will have to give account for every careless word they have spoken; ³⁷ for by your own words you will be acquitted, and by your own words you will be condemned."

³⁸ At this some of the *Torah*-teachers said, "Rabbi, we want to see a miraculous sign from you." ³⁹ He replied, "A wicked and adulterous generation asks for a sign? No! None will be given to it but the sign of the prophet Yonah. ⁴⁰ For just as Yonah **was three days and three nights in the belly of the sea-monster,**^f so will the Son of Man be three days and three nights in the depths of the earth. ⁴¹ The people of Ninveh will stand up at the Judgment with this generation and condemn it, for they turned from their sins to God when Yonah preached, but what is here now is greater than

---

^e Isaiah 42:1–4   ^f Jonah 2:1(1:17)

Yonah. ⁴² The Queen of the South will stand up at the Judgment with this generation and condemn it, for she came from the ends of the earth to hear the wisdom of Shlomo, but what is here now is greater than Shlomo.

⁴³ "When an unclean spirit comes out of a person, it travels through dry country seeking rest and does not find it. ⁴⁴ Then it says to itself, 'I will return to the house I left.' When it arrives, it finds the house standing empty, swept clean and put in order. ⁴⁵ Then it goes and takes with it seven other spirits more evil than itself, and they come and live there — so that in the end, the person is worse off than he was before. This is how it will be for this wicked generation."

⁴⁶ He was still speaking to the crowd when his mother and brothers appeared outside, asking to talk with him. ⁴⁷* ⁴⁸ But to the one who had informed him he replied, "Who is my mother? Who are my brothers?" ⁴⁹ Pointing to his *talmidim*, he said, "Look! Here are my mother and my brothers! ⁵⁰ Whoever does what my Father in heaven wants, that person is my brother and sister and mother."

13 ¹ That same day, Yeshua went out of the house and sat down by the lake; ² but such a large crowd gathered around him that he got into a boat and sat there while the crowd stood on the shore. ³ He told them many things in parables:

"A farmer went out to sow his seed. ⁴ As he sowed, some seed fell alongside the path; and the birds came and ate it up. ⁵ Other seed fell on rocky patches where there was not much soil. It sprouted quickly because the soil was shallow; ⁶ but when the sun had risen, the young plants were scorched; and since their roots were not deep, they dried up. ⁷ Other seed fell among thorns, which grew up and choked the plants. ⁸ But others fell into rich soil and produced grain, a hundred or sixty or thirty times as much as had been sown. ⁹ Those who have ears, let them hear!"

¹⁰ Then the *talmidim* came and asked Yeshua, "Why are you speaking to them in parables?" ¹¹ He answered, "Because it has been given to you to know the secrets of the Kingdom of Heaven, but it has not been given to them. ¹² For anyone who has something will be given more, so that he will have plenty; but from anyone who has nothing, even what he does have will be taken away. ¹³ Here is why I speak to them in parables: they look without seeing and listen without hearing or understanding. ¹⁴ That is, in them is fulfilled the prophecy of Yesha'yahu which says,

> **'You will keep on hearing but never understand,**
> **and keep on seeing but never perceive,**
> ¹⁵ **because the heart of this people has become dull —**
> **with their ears they barely hear,**
> **and their eyes they have closed,**
> **so as not to see with their eyes,**
> **hear with their ears,**
> **understand with their heart,**
> **and do *t'shuvah*,**
> **so that I could heal them.'ᵍ**

ᵍ Isaiah 6:9–10

* Some manuscripts include verse 47: Someone told him, "Your mother and brothers are standing outside, asking to talk with you."

¹⁶ But you, how blessed are your eyes, because they see, and your ears, because they hear! ¹⁷ Yes indeed! I tell you that many a prophet and many a *tzaddik* longed to see the things you are seeing but did not see them, and to hear the things you are hearing but did not hear them.

¹⁸ "So listen to what the parable of the sower means. ¹⁹ Whoever hears the message about the Kingdom, but doesn't understand it, is like the seed sown along the path — the Evil One comes and seizes what was sown in his heart. ²⁰ The seed sown on rocky ground is like a person who hears the message and accepts it with joy at once, ²¹ but has no root in himself. So he stays on for a while; but as soon as some trouble or persecution arises on account of the message, he immediately falls away. ²² Now the seed sown among thorns stands for someone who hears the message, but it is choked by the worries of the world and the deceitful glamor of wealth, so that it produces nothing. ²³ However, what was sown on rich soil is the one who hears the message and understands it; such a person will surely bear fruit, a hundred or sixty or thirty times what was sown."

²⁴ Yeshua put before them another parable. "The Kingdom of Heaven is like a man who sowed good seed in his field; ²⁵ but while people were sleeping, his enemy came and sowed weeds among the wheat, then went away. ²⁶ When the wheat sprouted and formed heads of grain, the weeds also appeared. ²⁷ The owner's servants came to him and said, 'Sir didn't you sow good seed in your field? Where have the weeds come from?' ²⁸ He answered, 'An enemy has done this.' The servants asked him, 'Then do you want us to go and pull them up?' ²⁹ But he said, 'No, because if you pull up the weeds, you might uproot some of the wheat at the same time. ³⁰ Let them both grow together until the harvest; and at harvest-time I will tell the reapers to collect the weeds first and tie them in bundles to be burned, but to gather the wheat into my barn.'"

³¹ Yeshua put before them another parable. "The Kingdom of Heaven is like a mustard seed which a man takes and sows in his field. ³² It is the smallest of all seeds, but when it grows up it is larger than any garden plant and becomes a tree, so that the birds flying about come and nest in its branches."

³³ And he told them yet another parable. "The Kingdom of Heaven is like yeast that a woman took and mixed with a bushel of flour, then waited until the whole batch of dough rose."

³⁴ All these things Yeshua said to the crowds in parables; indeed, he said nothing to them without using a parable. ³⁵ This was to fulfill what had been spoken through the prophet,

> **"I will open my mouth in parables,**
> **I will say what has been hidden since the creation of the universe."**ʰ

³⁶ Then he left the crowds and went into the house. His *talmidim* approached him and said, "Explain to us the parable of the weeds in the field." ³⁷ He answered, "The one who sows the good seed is the Son of Man; ³⁸ the field is the world. As for the good seed, these are the people who belong to the Kingdom; and the weeds are the people who belong to the Evil One. ³⁹ The enemy who sows them is the Adversary,

---

ʰ Psalm 78:2

the harvest is the end of the age, and the harvesters are angels. ⁴⁰ Just as the weeds are collected and burned up in the fire, so will it be at the end of the age. ⁴¹ The Son of Man will send forth his angels, and they will collect out of his Kingdom all the things that cause people to sin and all the people who are far from *Torah*; ⁴² and they will throw them into the fiery furnace, where people will wail and grind their teeth. ⁴³ Then the righteous will shine forth like the sun in the Kingdom of their Father. Whoever has ears, let him hear!

⁴⁴ "The Kingdom of Heaven is like a treasure hidden in a field. A man found it, hid it again, then in great joy went and sold everything he owned, and bought that field.

⁴⁵ "Again, the Kingdom of Heaven is like a merchant on the lookout for fine pearls. ⁴⁶ On finding one very valuable pearl he went away, sold everything he owned and bought it.

⁴⁷ "Once more, the Kingdom of Heaven is like a net thrown into the lake, that caught all kinds of fish. ⁴⁸ When it was full, the fishermen brought the net up onto the shore, sat down and collected the good fish in baskets, but threw the bad fish away. ⁴⁹ So it will be at the close of the age — the angels will go forth and separate the evil people from among the righteous ⁵⁰ and throw them into the fiery furnace, where they will wail and grind their teeth.

⁵¹ "Have you understood all these things?" "Yes," they answered. ⁵² He said to them, "So then, every *Torah*-teacher who has been made into a *talmid* for the Kingdom of Heaven is like the owner of a home who brings out of his storage room both new things and old."

⁵³ When Yeshua had finished these parables, he left ⁵⁴ and went to his home town. There he taught them in their synagogue in a way that astounded them, so that they asked, "Where do this man's wisdom and miracles come from? ⁵⁵ Isn't he the carpenter's son? Isn't his mother called Miryam? and his brothers Ya'akov, Yosef, Shim'on and Y'hudah? ⁵⁶ And his sisters, aren't they all with us? So where does he get all this?" ⁵⁷ And they took offense at him. But Yeshua said to them, "The only place people don't respect a prophet is in his home town and in his own house." ⁵⁸ And he did few miracles there because of their lack of trust.

14 ¹ Around that time, Herod, the regional governor, heard of the fame of Yeshua ² and said to his attendants, "This must be Yochanan the Immerser. He has been raised from the dead; that is why these miraculous powers are at work in him."

³ For Herod had arrested Yochanan, put him in chains and thrown him in prison because of Herodias, the wife of his brother Philip; ⁴ since Yochanan had told Herod, "It violates the *Torah* for you to have her as your wife." ⁵ Herod had wanted to put Yochanan to death; but he was afraid of the people, in whose eyes Yochanan was a prophet. ⁶ However, at Herod's birthday celebration, Herodias' daughter danced before the company and pleased Herod so much ⁷ that he promised with an oath to give her whatever she asked. ⁸ Prompted by her mother, she said, "Give me here on a platter the head of Yochanan the Immerser." ⁹ The king became deeply upset; but out of regard for the oaths he had sworn before his dinner guests, he ordered that her wish be granted, ¹⁰ and sent and had Yochanan beheaded in prison. ¹¹ The head was brought on a platter to the girl, and she gave it to her mother. ¹² Yochanan's *talmidim* came, took the body and buried it; then they went and told Yeshua.

¹³ On hearing about this, Yeshua left in a boat to be by himself in the wilderness. But the people learned of it and followed him from the towns by land. ¹⁴ So when he came ashore, he saw a huge crowd; and, filled with compassion for them, he healed those of them who were sick.

¹⁵ As evening approached, the *talmidim* came to him and said, "This is a remote place and it's getting late. Send the crowds away, so that they can go and buy food for themselves in the villages." ¹⁶ But Yeshua replied, "They don't need to go away. Give them something to eat, yourselves!" ¹⁷ "All we have with us," they said, "is five loaves of bread and two fish." ¹⁸ He said, "Bring them here to me." ¹⁹ After instructing the crowds to sit down on the grass, he took the five loaves and the two fish and, looking up toward heaven, made a *b'rakhah*. Then he broke the loaves and gave them to the *talmidim*, who gave them to the crowds. ²⁰ They all ate as much as they wanted, and they took up twelve baskets full of the pieces left over. ²¹ Those eating numbered about five thousand men, plus women and children.

²² Immediately he had the *talmidim* get in the boat and go on ahead of him to the other side, while he sent the crowds away. ²³ After he had sent the crowds away, he went up into the hills by himself to pray. Night came on, and he was there alone. ²⁴ But by this time, the boat was several miles from shore, battling a rough sea and a headwind. ²⁵ Around four o'clock in the morning, he came toward them, walking on the lake! ²⁶ When the *talmidim* saw him walking on the lake, they were terrified. "It's a ghost!" they said and screamed with fear. ²⁷ But at once Yeshua spoke to them. "Courage," he said, "it is I. Stop being afraid." ²⁸ Then Kefa called to him, "Lord, if it is really you, tell me to come to you on the water." ²⁹ "Come!" he said. So Kefa got out of the boat and walked on the water toward Yeshua. ³⁰ But when he saw the wind, he became afraid; and as he began to sink, he yelled, "Lord! Save me!" ³¹ Yeshua immediately stretched out his hand, took hold of him, and said to him, "Such little trust! Why did you doubt?" ³² As they went up into the boat, the wind ceased. ³³ The men in the boat fell down before him and exclaimed, "You really are God's son!"

³⁴ Having made the crossing, they landed at Ginosar. ³⁵ When the people of the place recognized him, they sent word throughout the neighborhood and brought him everyone who was ill. ³⁶ They begged him that the sick people might only touch the *tzitzit* on his robe, and all who touched it were completely healed.

15 ¹ Then some *P'rushim* and *Torah*-teachers from Yerushalayim came to Yeshua and asked him, ² "Why is it that your *talmidim* break the Tradition of the Elders? They don't do *n'tilat-yadayim* before they eat!" ³ He answered, "Indeed, why do you break the command of God by your tradition? ⁴ For God said, **'Honor your father and mother,'***ⁱ* and **'Anyone who curses his father or mother must be put to death.'***ʲ* ⁵ But you say, 'If anyone says to his father or mother, "I have promised to give to God what I might have used to help you," ⁶ then he is rid of his duty to honor his father or mother.' Thus by your tradition you make null and void the word of God! ⁷ You hypocrites! Yesha'yahu was right when he prophesied about you,

⁸   **'These people honor me with their lips,**
         but their hearts are far away from me.

ⁱ Exodus 20:12; Deuteronomy 5:16   *ʲ* Exodus 21:17; Leviticus 20:9

9   **Their worship of me is useless,**
        because they teach man-made rules as if they were doctrines.'"[k]

¹⁰ Then he called the crowd to him and said, "Listen and understand this! ¹¹ What makes a person unclean is not what goes into his mouth; rather, what comes out of his mouth, that is what makes him unclean!"

¹² The *talmidim* came to him and said, "Do you know that the *P'rushim* were offended by what you said?" ¹³ He replied, "Every plant that my Father in heaven has not planted will be pulled up by the roots. ¹⁴ Let them be. They are blind guides. When a blind man guides another blind man, both will fall in a pit."

¹⁵ Kefa said to him, "Explain the parable to us." ¹⁶ So he said, "Don't you understand even now? ¹⁷ Don't you see that anything that enters the mouth goes into the stomach and passes out into the latrine? ¹⁸ But what comes out of your mouth is actually coming from your heart, and that is what makes a person unclean. ¹⁹ For out of the heart come forth wicked thoughts, murder, adultery and other kinds of sexual immorality, theft, lies, slanders. . . . ²⁰ These are what really make a person unclean, but eating without doing *n'tilat-yadayim* does not make a person unclean."

²¹ Yeshua left that place and went off to the region of Tzor and Tzidon. ²² A woman from Kena'an who was living there came to him, pleading, "Sir, have pity on me. Son of David! My daughter is cruelly held under the power of demons!" ²³ But Yeshua did not say a word to her. Then his *talmidim* came to him and urged him, "Send her away, because she is following us and keeps pestering us with her crying." ²⁴ He said, "I was sent only to the lost sheep of the house of Isra'el." ²⁵ But she came, fell at his feet and said, "Sir, help me!" ²⁶ He answered, "It is not right to take the children's food and toss it to their pet dogs." ²⁷ She said, "That is true, sir, but even the dogs eat the leftovers that fall from their master's table." ²⁸ Then Yeshua answered her, "Lady, you are a person of great trust. Let your desire be granted." And her daughter was healed at that very moment.

²⁹ Yeshua left there and went along the shore of Lake Kinneret. He climbed a hill and sat down; ³⁰ and large crowds came to him, bringing with them the lame, the blind, the crippled, the mute and many others. They laid them at his feet, and he healed them. ³¹ The people were amazed as they saw mute people speaking, crippled people cured, lame people walking and blind people seeing; and they said a *b'rakhah* to the God of Isra'el.

³² Yeshua called his *talmidim* to him and said, "I feel sorry for these people, because they have been with me three days, and now they have nothing to eat. I don't want to send them away hungry, because they might collapse on the way home." ³³ The *talmidim* said to him, "Where will we find enough loaves of bread in this remote place to satisfy so big a crowd?" ³⁴ Yeshua asked them, "How many loaves do you have?" They said, "Seven, and a few fish." ³⁵ After telling the crowd to sit down on the ground, ³⁶ he took the seven loaves and the fish, made a *b'rakhah*, broke the loaves and gave them to the *talmidim*, who gave them to the people. ³⁷ Everyone ate his fill, and they took seven large baskets full of the leftover pieces. ³⁸ Those eating numbered four thousand men, plus women and children. ³⁹ After sending the crowd away, he got in the boat and went off to the region of Magadan.

---

[k] Isaiah 29:13

16 ^{1} Then some *P'rushim* and *Tz'dukim* came to trap Yeshua by asking him to show them a miraculous sign from Heaven. ^{2} But his response was, "When it is evening, you say, 'Fair weather ahead,' because the sky is red; ^{3} and in the morning you say, 'Storm today!' because the sky is red and overcast. You know how to read the appearance of the sky, but you can't read the signs of the times! ^{4} A wicked and adulterous generation is asking for a sign? It will certainly not be given a sign — except the sign of Yonah!" With that he left them and went off.

^{5} The *talmidim*, in crossing to the other side of the lake, had forgotten to bring any bread. ^{6} So when Yeshua said to them, "Watch out! Guard yourselves against the *hametz* of the *P'rushim* and *Tz'dukim*," ^{7} they thought he said it because they hadn't brought bread. ^{8} But Yeshua, aware of this, said, "Such little trust you have! Why are you talking with each other about not having bread? ^{9} Don't you understand yet? Don't you remember the five loaves of the five thousand and how many baskets you filled? ^{10} Or the seven loaves of the four thousand and how many baskets you filled? ^{11} How can you possibly think I was talking to you about bread? Guard yourselves from the *hametz* of the *P'rushim* and *Tz'dukim*!" ^{12} Then they understood — they were to guard themselves not from yeast for bread but from the teaching of the *P'rushim* and *Tz'dukim*.

^{13} When Yeshua came into the territory around Caesarea Philippi, he asked his *talmidim*, "Who are people saying the Son of Man is?" ^{14} They said, "Well, some say Yochanan the Immerser, others Eliyahu, still others Yirmeyahu or one of the prophets." ^{15} "But you," he said to them, "who do you say I am?" ^{16} Shim'on Kefa answered, "You are the *Mashiach*, the Son of the living God." ^{17} "Shim'on Bar-Yochanan," Yeshua said to him, "how blessed you are! For no human being revealed this to you, no, it was my Father in heaven. ^{18} I also tell you this: you are Kefa," [which means 'Rock,'] "and on this rock I will build my Community, and the gates of Sh'ol will not overcome it. ^{19} I will give you the keys of the Kingdom of Heaven. Whatever you prohibit on earth will be prohibited in heaven, and whatever you permit on earth will be permitted in heaven." ^{20} Then he warned the *talmidim* not to tell anyone that he was the Messiah.

^{21} From that time on, Yeshua began making it clear to his *talmidim* that he had to go to Yerushalayim and endure much suffering at the hands of the elders, the head *cohanim* and the *Torah*-teachers; and that he had to be put to death; but that on the third day, he had to be raised to life. ^{22} Kefa took him aside and began rebuking him, "Heaven be merciful, Lord! By no means will this happen to you!" ^{23} But Yeshua turned his back on Kefa, saying, "Get behind me, Satan! You are an obstacle in my path, because your thinking is from a human perspective, not from God's perspective!"

^{24} Then Yeshua told his *talmidim*, "If anyone wants to come after me, let him say 'No' to himself, take up his execution-stake, and keep following me. ^{25} For whoever wants to save his own life will destroy it, but whoever destroys his life for my sake will find it. ^{26} What good will it do someone if he gains the whole world but forfeits his life? Or, what can a person give in exchange for his life? ^{27} For the Son of Man will come in his Father's glory, with his angels; and then he will repay everyone according to his conduct. ^{28} Yes! I tell you that there are some people standing here who will not experience death until they see the Son of Man coming in his Kingdom!"

17 ¹ Six days later, Yeshua took Kefa, Ya'akov and his brother Yochanan and led them up a high mountain privately. ² As they watched, he began to change form — his face shone like the sun, and his clothing became as white as light. ³ Then they looked and saw Moshe and Eliyahu speaking with him. ⁴ Kefa said to Yeshua, "It's good that we're here, Lord. I'll put up three shelters if you want — one for you, one for Moshe and one for Eliyahu." ⁵ While he was still speaking, a bright cloud enveloped them; and a voice from the cloud said, "This is my Son, whom I love, with whom I am well pleased. Listen to him!" ⁶ When the *talmidim* heard this, they were so frightened that they fell face down on the ground. ⁷ But Yeshua came and touched them. "Get up!" he said, "Don't be afraid." ⁸ So they opened their eyes, looked up and saw only Yeshua by himself.

⁹ As they came down the mountain, Yeshua ordered them, "Don't tell anyone what you have seen until the Son of Man has been raised from the dead." ¹⁰ The *talmidim* asked him, "Then why do the *Torah*-teachers say that Eliyahu must come first?" ¹¹ He answered, "On the one hand, Eliyahu is coming and will restore all things; ¹² on the other hand, I tell you that Eliyahu has come already, and people did not recognize him but did whatever they pleased to him. In the same way, the Son of Man too is about to suffer at their hands." ¹³ Then the *talmidim* understood that he was talking to them about Yochanan the Immerser.

¹⁴ As they came up to the crowd, a man approached Yeshua, kneeled down in front of him, ¹⁵ and said, "Sir, have mercy on my son, because he is an epileptic and has such terrible fits that he often falls into the fire or into the water. ¹⁶ I brought him to your *talmidim*, but they couldn't heal him." ¹⁷ Yeshua answered, "Perverted people, without any trust! How long will I be with you? How long must I put up with you? Bring him here to me!" ¹⁸ Yeshua rebuked the demon, and it came out of the boy, so that from that moment he was healed.

¹⁹ Then the *talmidim* went to him privately and said, "Why couldn't we drive it out?" ²⁰ He said to them, "Because you have such little trust! Yes! I tell you that if you have trust as tiny as a mustard seed, you will be able to say to this mountain, 'Move from here to there!' and it will move; indeed, nothing will be impossible for you!" ²¹*

²² As they were going about together in the Galil, Yeshua said to them, "The Son of Man is about to be betrayed into the hands of people ²³ who will put him to death, and on the third day he will be raised." And they were filled with sadness.

²⁴ When they came to K'far-Nachum, the collectors of the half-*shekel* came to Kefa and said, "Doesn't your rabbi pay the Temple tax?" ²⁵ "Of course he does," said Kefa. When he arrived home, Yeshua spoke first. "Shim'on, what's your opinion? The kings of the earth — from whom do they collect duties and taxes? From their sons or from others?" ²⁶ "From others," he answered. "Then," said Yeshua, "The sons are exempt. ²⁷ But to avoid offending them — go to the lake, throw out a line, and take the first fish you catch. Open its mouth, and you will find a *shekel*. Take it and give it to them for me and for you."

18 ¹ At that moment the *talmidim* came to Yeshua and asked, "Who is the greatest in the Kingdom of Heaven?" ² He called a child to him, stood him among them, ³ and said, "Yes! I tell you that unless you change and become like little children, you

---

*Some manuscripts include verse 21: But this kind does not go out except through prayer and fasting."

won't even enter the Kingdom of Heaven! ⁴ So the greatest in the Kingdom is whoever makes himself as humble as this child. ⁵ Whoever welcomes one such child in my name welcomes me; ⁶ and whoever ensnares one of these little ones who trust me, it would be better for him to have a millstone hung around his neck and be drowned in the open sea! ⁷ Woe to the world because of snares! For there must be snares, but woe to the person who sets the snare!

⁸ "So if your hand or foot becomes a snare for you, cut it off and throw it away! Better that you should be maimed or crippled and obtain eternal life than keep both hands or both feet and be thrown into everlasting fire! ⁹ And if your eye is a snare for you, gouge it out and fling it away! Better that you should be one-eyed and obtain eternal life than keep both eyes and be thrown into the fire of Gei-Hinnom. ¹⁰ See that you never despise one of these little ones, for I tell you that their angels in heaven are continually seeing the face of my Father in heaven. ¹¹*

¹² "What's your opinion? What will somebody do who has a hundred sheep, and one of them wanders away? Won't he leave the ninety-nine on the hillsides and go off to find the stray? ¹³ And if he happens to find it? Yes! I tell you he is happier over it than over the ninety-nine that never strayed! ¹⁴ Thus your Father in heaven does not want even one of these little ones to be lost.

¹⁵ "Moreover, if your brother commits a sin against you, go and show him his fault — but privately, just between the two of you. If he listens to you, you have won back your brother. ¹⁶ If he doesn't listen, take one or two others with you so that **every accusation can be supported by the testimony of two or three witnesses.**¹ ¹⁷ If he refuses to hear them, tell the congregation; and if he refuses to listen even to the congregation, treat him as you would a pagan or a tax-collector. ¹⁸ Yes! I tell you people that whatever you prohibit on earth will be prohibited in heaven, and whatever you permit on earth will be permitted in heaven. ¹⁹ To repeat, I tell you that if two of you here on earth agree about anything people ask, it will be for them from my Father in heaven. ²⁰ For wherever two or three are assembled in my name, I am there with them."

²¹ Then Kefa came up and said to him, "Rabbi, how often can my brother sin against me and I have to forgive him? As many as seven times?" ²² "No, not seven times," answered Yeshua, "but seventy times seven! ²³ Because of this, the Kingdom of Heaven may be compared with a king who decided to settle accounts with his deputies. ²⁴ Right away they brought forward a man who owed him many millions; ²⁵ and since he couldn't pay, his master ordered that he, his wife, his children and all his possessions be sold to pay the debt. ²⁶ But the servant fell down before him. 'Be patient with me,' he begged, 'and I will pay back everything.' ²⁷ So out of pity for him, the master let him go and forgave the debt.

²⁸ "But as that servant was leaving, he came upon one of his fellow servants who owed him some tiny sum. He grabbed him and began to choke him, crying, 'Pay back what you owe me!' ²⁹ His fellow servant fell before him and begged, 'Be patient with me, and I will pay you back.' ³⁰ But he refused; instead, he had him thrown in jail until he should repay the debt. ³¹ When the other servants saw what had happened, they were extremely distressed; and they went and told their master everything that had taken place. ³² Then the master summoned his servant and said, 'You wicked servant! I forgave you all that debt just because you begged me to do it.

---

*Some manuscripts include verse 11: For the Son of Man came to save the lost. ¹ Deuteronomy 19:15

33 Shouldn't you have had pity on your fellow servant, just as I had pity on you?'
34 And in anger his master turned him over to the jailers for punishment until he paid
back everything he owed. 35 This is how my heavenly Father will treat you, unless
you each forgive your brother from your hearts."

19 1 When Yeshua had finished talking about these things, he left the Galil and
traveled down the east side of the Yarden River until he passed the border of Y'hudah.
2 Great crowds followed him, and he healed them there.

3 Some *P'rushim* came and tried to trap him by asking, "Is it permitted for a man
to divorce his wife on any ground whatever?" 4 He replied, "Haven't you read that at
the beginning the Creator **made them male and female**,[m] 5 and that he said, **'For
this reason a man should leave his father and mother and be united with his
wife, and the two are to become one flesh'**?[n] 6 Thus they are no longer two, but one.
So then, no one should split apart what God has joined together."

7 They said to him, "Then why did Moshe give the commandment that a man
should **hand his wife a *get*** and divorce her?"[o] 8 He answered, "Moshe allowed you
to divorce your wives because your hearts are so hardened. But this is not how it was
at the beginning. 9 Now what I say to you is that whoever divorces his wife, except
on the ground of sexual immorality, and marries another woman commits adultery!"

10 The *talmidim* said to him, "If that is how things are between husband and
wife, it would be better not to marry!" 11 He said to them, "Not everyone grasps this
teaching, only those for whom it is meant. 12 For there are different reasons why men
do not marry — some because they were born without the desire, some because they
have been castrated, and some because they have renounced marriage for the sake of
the Kingdom of Heaven. Whoever can grasp this, let him do so."

13 Then children were brought to him so that he might lay his hands on them and
pray for them, but the *talmidim* rebuked the people bringing them. 14 However, Yeshua
said, "Let the children come to me, don't stop them, for the Kingdom of Heaven
belongs to such as these." 15 Then, after laying his hands on them, he went on his way.

16 A man approached Yeshua and said, "Rabbi, what good thing should I do in
order to have eternal life?" He said to him, 17 "Why are you asking me about good?
There is One who is good! But if you want to obtain eternal life, observe the *mitzvot*."
18 The man asked him, "Which ones?" and Yeshua said, "**Don't murder, don't commit
adultery, don't steal, don't give false testimony**[p] 19 **honor father and mother**[q] and
love your neighbor as yourself."[r] 20 The young man said to him, "I have kept all
these; where do I still fall short?" 21 Yeshua said to him, "If you are serious about
reaching the goal, go and sell your possessions, give to the poor, and you will have
riches in heaven. Then come, follow me!" 22 But when the young man heard this, he
went away sad, because he was wealthy.

23 Then Yeshua said to his *talmidim*, "Yes. I tell you that it will be very hard for
a rich man to enter the Kingdom of Heaven. 24 Furthermore, I tell you that it is easier
for a camel to pass through a needle's eye than for a rich man to enter the Kingdom
of God." 25 When the *talmidim* heard this they were utterly amazed. "Then who,"

---

[m] Genesis 1:27, 5:2 [n] Genesis 2:24 [o] Deuteronomy 24:1, 3
[p] Exodus 20:13(13–16); Deuteronomy 5:17(17–20) [q] Exodus 20:12; Deuteronomy 5:16
[r] Leviticus 19:18

they asked, "can be saved?" ²⁶ Yeshua looked at them and said, "Humanly, this is impossible; but with God everything is possible." ²⁷ Kefa replied, "Look, we have left everything and followed you. So what will we have?" ²⁸ Yeshua said to them, "Yes. I tell you that in the regenerated world, when the Son of Man sits on his glorious throne, you who have followed me will also sit on twelve thrones and judge the twelve tribes of Isra'el. ²⁹ Everyone who has left houses, brothers, sisters, father, mother, children or fields for my sake will receive a hundred times more, and he will obtain eternal life. ³⁰ But many who are first will be last, and many who are last will be first.

20 ¹ "The Kingdom of Heaven is like a farmer who went out at daybreak to hire workers for his vineyard. ² After agreeing with the workers on a wage of one denarius, [the standard daily wage,] he sent them off to his vineyard. ³ Then, on going out at about nine in the morning, he saw more men standing around in the market-square doing nothing, ⁴ and said to them, 'You go to the vineyard too — I'll pay you a fair wage.' So they went. ⁵ At noon, and again around three in the afternoon, he did the same thing. ⁶ About an hour before sundown, he went out, found still others standing around, and asked them, 'Why have you been standing here all day, doing nothing?' ⁷ They said to him, 'Because no one hired us.' 'You too,' he told them, 'go to the vineyard.'

⁸ "When evening came, the owner of the vineyard said to his foreman, 'Call the workers and pay them their wages, starting with the last ones hired and ending with the first.' ⁹ The workers who came an hour before sunset each received a denarius, ¹⁰ so the workers who came first expected they would get more, but each of them also received just a denarius. ¹¹ On receiving their wages, they began grumbling to the farmer, ¹² 'These latecomers have worked only one hour, while we have borne the brunt of the day's work in the hot sun, yet you have put them on an equal footing with us!' ¹³ But he answered one of them, 'Look, friend, I'm not being unfair with you. Didn't you agree to work today for a denarius? ¹⁴ Now take your pay and go! I choose to give the last worker as much as I'm giving you. ¹⁵ Haven't I the right to do what I want with what belongs to me? Or do you begrudge my generosity?' ¹⁶ Thus the last ones will be first and the first last."

¹⁷ As Yeshua was going up to Yerushalayim, he took the twelve *talmidim* aside by themselves and said to them, as they went on their way, ¹⁸ "We are now going up to Yerushalayim, where the Son of Man will be handed over to the head *cohanim* and *Torah*-teachers. They will sentence him to death ¹⁹ and turn him over to the *Goyim*, who will jeer at him, beat him and execute him on a stake as a criminal. But on the third day, he will be raised."

²⁰ Then Zavdai's sons came to Yeshua with their mother. She bowed down, begging a favor from him. ²¹ He said to her, "What do you want?" She replied, "Promise that when you become king, these two sons of mine may sit, one on your right and the other on your left." ²² But Yeshua answered, "You people don't know what you are asking. Can you drink the cup that I am about to drink?" They said to him, "We can." ²³ He said to them, "Yes, you will drink my cup. But to sit on my right and on my left is not mine to give, it is for those for whom my Father has prepared it."

²⁴ Now when the other ten heard about this, they were outraged at the two brothers. ²⁵ But Yeshua called them and said, "You know that among the *Goyim*, those who are supposed to rule them become tyrants, and their superiors become dictators. ²⁶ Among you, it must not be like that. On the contrary, whoever among you wants to be a

leader must become your servant, ²⁷ and whoever wants to be first must be your slave! ²⁸ For the Son of Man did not come to be served, but to serve — and to give his life as a ransom for many."

²⁹ As they were leaving Yericho, a large crowd followed Yeshua. ³⁰ Two blind men sitting by the side of the road heard that he was passing by and shouted, "Son of David! Have pity on us!" ³¹ The crowd scolded them and told them to be quiet, but they shouted all the louder, "Lord! Son of David! Have pity on us!" ³² Yeshua stopped, called them and said, "What do you want me to do for you?" ³³ They said to him, "Lord, open our eyes." ³⁴ Filled with tenderness, Yeshua touched their eyes; and instantly they received their sight and followed him.

21 ¹ As they were approaching Yerushalayim, they came to Beit-Pagei on the Mount of Olives. Yeshua sent two *talmidim* ² with these instructions: "Go into the village ahead of you, and you will immediately find a donkey tethered there with its colt. Untie them and bring them to me. ³ If anyone says anything to you, tell him, 'The Lord needs them'; and he will let them go at once." ⁴ This happened in order to fulfill what had been spoken through the prophet,

⁵   **"Say to the daughter of Tziyon,**
     'Look! Your King is coming to you,
     riding humbly on a donkey,
     and on a colt, the offspring of a beast of burden!'*ˢ

⁶ So the *talmidim* went and did as Yeshua had directed them. ⁷ They brought the donkey and the colt and put their robes on them, and Yeshua sat on them. ⁸ Crowds of people carpeted the road with their clothing, while others cut branches from trees and spread them on the road. ⁹ The crowds ahead of him and behind shouted,

"Please! Deliver us!"*

to the Son of David;

"Blessed is he who comes in the name of *Adonai*!"ᵗ

"You in the highest heaven! **Please! Deliver us!"***

¹⁰ When he entered Yerushalayim, the whole city was stirred. "Who is this?" they asked. ¹¹ And the crowds answered, "This is Yeshua, the prophet from Natzeret in the Galil."

¹² Yeshua entered the Temple grounds and drove out those who were doing business there, both the merchants and their customers. He upset the desks of the money-changers and knocked over the benches of those who were selling pigeons. ¹³ He said to them, "It has been written, **'My house will be called a house of prayer.'**ᵘ But you are making it into a **den of robbers!"**ᵛ

ˢ Zechariah 9:9   ᵗ Psalm 118:25–26   ᵘ Isaiah 56:7
ᵛ Jeremiah 7:11

* Greek *Ôsanna* (English "Hosanna") transliterates Hebrew *Hosha na*, which means "Please! Save [us]!"

¹⁴ Blind and lame people came up to him in the Temple, and he healed them.
¹⁵ But when the head *cohanim* and *Torah*-teachers saw the wonderful things he was
doing, and the children crying out in the Temple, "**Please deliver us!**"* to the Son of
David, they were furious. ¹⁶ They said to him, "Do you hear what they're saying?"
Yeshua replied, "Of course! Haven't you ever read,

> **'From the mouths of children and infants
> you have prepared praise for yourself'?**"ˣ

¹⁷ With that, he left them and went outside the city to Beit-Anyah, where he spent
the night.

¹⁸ The next morning, on his way back to the city, he felt hungry. ¹⁹ Spotting
a fig tree by the road, he went up to it but found nothing on it except leaves. So
he said to it, "May you never again bear fruit!" and immediately the fig tree
dried up. ²⁰ The *talmidim* saw this and were amazed. "How did the fig tree dry up so
quickly?" they asked. ²¹ Yeshua answered them, "Yes! I tell you, if you have
trust and don't doubt, you will not only do what was done to this fig tree; but even if
you say to this mountain, 'Go and throw yourself into the sea!' it will be done. ²² In
other words, you will receive everything you ask for in prayer, no matter what it is,
provided you have trust."

²³ He went into the Temple area; and as he was teaching, the head *cohanim* and
the elders of the people approached him and demanded, "What *s'mikhah* do you
have that authorizes you to do these things? And who gave you this *s'mikhah*?"
²⁴ Yeshua answered, "I too will ask you a question. If you answer it, then I will tell
you by what *s'mikhah* I do these things. ²⁵ The immersion of Yochanan — where did
it come from? From Heaven or from a human source?" They discussed it among
themselves: "If we say, 'From Heaven,' he will say, 'Then why didn't you believe
him?' ²⁶ But if we say, 'From a human source,' we are afraid of the people, for they
all regard Yochanan as a prophet." ²⁷ So they answered Yeshua, "We don't know."
And he replied, "Then I won't tell you by what *s'mikhah* I do these things.

²⁸ "But give me your opinion: a man had two sons. He went to the first and said,
'Son, go and work today in the vineyard.' ²⁹ He answered, 'I don't want to'; but later he
changed his mind and went. ³⁰ The father went to his other son and said the same thing.
This one answered, 'I will, sir'; but he didn't go. ³¹ Which of the two did what his
father wanted?" "The first," they replied. "That's right!" Yeshua said to them. "I tell
you that the tax-collectors and prostitutes are going into the Kingdom of God ahead
of you! ³² For Yochanan came to you showing the path to righteousness, and you wouldn't
trust him. The tax-collectors and prostitutes trusted him; but you, even after you saw
this, didn't change your minds later and trust him.

³³ "Now listen to another parable. There was a farmer who planted a vineyard. He
put a wall around it, dug a pit for the winepress and built a tower; then he rented it to
tenants and left. ³⁴ When harvest-time came, he sent his servants to the tenants to collect
his share of the crop. ³⁵ But the tenants seized his servants — this one they beat up, that
one they killed, another they stoned. ³⁶ So he sent some other servants, more than the

---

ˣ Psalm 8:3(2)
* See note, p. 1249.

first group, and they did the same to them. ³⁷ Finally, he sent them his son, saying, 'My son they will respect.' ³⁸ But when the tenants saw the son, they said to each other, 'This is the heir. Come, let's kill him and take his inheritance!' ³⁹ So they grabbed him, threw him out of the vineyard and killed him. ⁴⁰ Now when the owner of the vineyard comes, what will he do to those tenants?" ⁴¹ They answered him, "He will viciously destroy those vicious men and rent out the vineyard to other tenants who will give him his share of the crop when it's due." ⁴² Yeshua said to them, "Haven't you ever read in the *Tanakh*,

'The very rock which the builders rejected
has become the cornerstone!
This has come from Adonai,
and in our eyes it is amazing'?ʸ

⁴³ Therefore, I tell you that the Kingdom of God will be taken away from you and given to the kind of people that will produce its fruit!" ⁴⁴*

⁴⁵ As the head *cohanim* and the *P'rushim* listened to his stories, they saw that he was speaking about them. ⁴⁶ But when they set about to arrest him, they were afraid of the crowds; because the crowds considered him a prophet.

22 ¹ Yeshua again used parables in speaking to them: ² "The Kingdom of Heaven is like a king who prepared a wedding feast for his son, ³ but when he sent his slaves to summon the invited guests to the wedding, they refused to come. ⁴ So he sent some more slaves, instructing them to tell the guests, 'Look, I've prepared my banquet, I've slaughtered my bulls and my fattened cattle, and everything is ready. Come to the wedding!' ⁵ But they weren't interested and went off, one to his farm, another to his business; ⁶ and the rest grabbed his slaves, mistreated them and killed them. ⁷ The king was furious and sent his soldiers, who killed those murderers and burned down their city.

⁸ "Then he said to his slaves, 'Well, the wedding feast is ready; but the ones who were invited didn't deserve it. ⁹ So go out to the street-corners and invite to the banquet as many as you find.' ¹⁰ The slaves went out into the streets, gathered all the people they could find, the bad along with the good; and the wedding hall was filled with guests.

¹¹ "Now when the king came in to look at the guests, he saw there a man who wasn't dressed for a wedding; so he asked him, ¹² 'Friend, how did you get in here without wedding clothes?' The man was speechless. ¹³ Then the king said to the servants, 'Bind him hand and foot, and throw him outside in the dark!' In that place people will wail and grind their teeth, ¹⁴ for many are invited, but few are chosen."

¹⁵ Then the *P'rushim* went away and put together a plan to trap Yeshua with his own words. ¹⁶ They sent him some of their *talmidim* and some members of Herod's party. They said, "Rabbi, we know that you tell the truth and really teach what God's way is. You aren't concerned with what other people think about you, since you pay no attention to a person's status. ¹⁷ So tell us your opinion: does *Torah* permit

---

ʸ Psalm 118:22–23
* Some manuscripts include verse 44: Whoever falls on this stone will be broken in pieces; but if it falls on him, he will be crushed to powder!"

paying taxes to the Roman Emperor or not?" ¹⁸ Yeshua, however, knowing their malicious intent, said, "You hypocrites! Why are you trying to trap me? ¹⁹ Show me the coin used to pay the tax!" They brought him a denarius; ²⁰ and he asked them, "Whose name and picture are these?" ²¹ "The Emperor's," they replied. Yeshua said to them, *"Nu*, give the Emperor what belongs to the Emperor. And give to God what belongs to God!" ²² On hearing this, they were amazed; and they left him and went away.

²³ That same day, some *Tz'dukim* came to him. They are the ones who say there is no such thing as resurrection, so they put to him a *sh'eilah*: ²⁴ "Rabbi, Moshe said, **'If a man dies childless, his brother must marry his widow and have children to preserve the man's family line.'**ᶻ ²⁵ There were seven brothers. The first one married and then died; and since he had no children, he left his widow to his brother. ²⁶ The same thing happened to the second brother, and the third, and finally to all seven. ²⁷ After them all, the woman died. ²⁸ Now in the Resurrection — of the seven, whose wife will she be? For they all married her."

²⁹ Yeshua answered them, "The reason you go astray is that you are ignorant both of the *Tanakh* and of the power of God. ³⁰ For in the Resurrection, neither men nor women will marry; rather, they will be like angels in heaven. ³¹ And as for whether the dead are resurrected, haven't you read what God said to you, ³² **'I am the God of Avraham, the God of Yitz'chak and the God of Ya'akov'?**ᵃ He is God not of the dead but of the living!"

³³ When the crowds heard how he taught, they were astounded; ³⁴ but when the *P'rushim* learned that he had silenced the *Tz'dukim*, they got together, ³⁵ and one of them who was a *Torah* expert asked a *sh'eilah* to trap him: ³⁶ "Rabbi, which of the *mitzvot* in the *Torah* is the most important?" ³⁷ He told him, **"'You are to love ADONAI your God with all your heart and with all your soul and with all your strength.'**ᵇ ³⁸ This is the greatest and most important *mitzvah*. ³⁹ And a second is similar to it, **'You are to love your neighbor as yourself.'**ᶜ ⁴⁰ All of the *Torah* and the Prophets are dependent on these two *mitzvot*."

⁴¹ Then, turning to the assembled *P'rushim*, Yeshua put a *sh'eilah* to them: ⁴² "Tell me your view concerning the Messiah: whose son is he?" They said to him, "David's." ⁴³ "Then how is it," he asked them, "that David, inspired by the Spirit, calls him 'Lord,' when he says,

⁴⁴ **'ADONAI said to my Lord,**
 "Sit here at my right hand
 until I put your enemies under your feet"'?ᵈ

⁴⁵ If David thus calls him 'Lord,' how is he his son?" ⁴⁶ No one could think of anything to say in reply; and from that day on, no one dared put to him another *sh'eilah*.

23 ¹ Then Yeshua addressed the crowds and his *talmidim*: ² "The *Torah*-teachers and the *P'rushim*," he said, "sit in the seat of Moshe. ³ So whatever they tell you, take care

---

ᶻ Deuteronomy 25:5–6   ᵃ Exodus 3:6   ᵇ Deuteronomy 6:5
ᶜ Leviticus 19:18   ᵈ Psalm 110:1

to do it. But don't do what they do, because they talk but don't act! ⁴ They tie heavy loads onto people's shoulders but won't lift a finger to help carry them. ⁵ Everything they do is done to be seen by others; for they make their *t'fillin* broad and their *tzitziyot* long, ⁶ they love the place of honor at banquets and the best seats in the synagogues, ⁷ and they love being greeted deferentially in the marketplaces and being called 'Rabbi.'

⁸ "But you are not to let yourselves be called 'Rabbi'; because you have one Rabbi, and you are all each other's brothers. ⁹ And do not call anyone on earth 'Father,' because you have one Father, and he is in heaven. ¹⁰ Nor are you to let yourselves be called 'leaders,' because you have one Leader, and he is the Messiah! ¹¹ The greatest among you must be your servant, ¹² for whoever promotes himself will be humbled, and whoever humbles himself will be promoted.

¹³ "But woe to you hypocritical *Torah*-teachers and *P'rushim*! For you are shutting the Kingdom of Heaven in people's faces, neither entering yourselves nor allowing those who wish to enter to do so. ¹⁴ *

¹⁵ "Woe to you hypocritical *Torah*-teachers and *P'rushim*! You go about over land and sea to make one proselyte; and when you succeed, you make him twice as fit for Gei-Hinnom as you are!

¹⁶ "Woe to you, you blind guides! You say, 'If someone swears by the Temple, he is not bound by his oath; but if he swears by the gold in the Temple, he is bound.' ¹⁷ You blind fools! Which is more important? the gold? or the Temple which makes the gold holy? ¹⁸ And you say, 'If someone swears by the altar, he is not bound by his oath; but if he swears by the offering on the altar, he is bound.' ¹⁹ Blind men! Which is more important? the sacrifice? or the altar which makes the sacrifice holy? ²⁰ So someone who swears by the altar swears by it and everything on it. ²¹ And someone who swears by the Temple swears by it and the One who lives in it. ²² And someone who swears by heaven swears by God's throne and the One who sits on it.

²³ "Woe to you hypocritical *Torah*-teachers and *P'rushim*! You pay your tithes of mint, dill and cumin; but you have neglected the weightier matters of the *Torah* — justice, mercy, trust. These are the things you should have attended to — without neglecting the others! ²⁴ Blind guides! — straining out a gnat, meanwhile swallowing a camel!

²⁵ "Woe to you hypocritical *Torah*-teachers and *P'rushim*! You clean the outside of the cup and the dish, but inside they are full of robbery and self-indulgence. ²⁶ Blind *Parush*! First clean the inside of the cup, so that the outside may be clean too.

²⁷ "Woe to you hypocritical *Torah*-teachers and *P'rushim*! You are like whitewashed tombs, which look fine on the outside but inside are full of dead people's bones and all kinds of rottenness. ²⁸ Likewise, you appear to people from the outside to be good and honest, but inwardly you are full of hypocrisy and far from *Torah*.

²⁹ "Woe to you hypocritical *Torah*-teachers and *P'rushim*! You build tombs for the prophets and decorate the graves of the *tzaddikim*, ³⁰ and you say, 'Had we lived

---

*Some manuscripts include verse 14: Woe to you hypocritical *Torah*-teachers and *P'rushim*! For you swallow up widow's houses while making a show of *davvening* at great length. Because of this your punishment will be all the worse!

when our fathers did, we would never have taken part in killing the prophets.' ³¹ In this you testify against yourselves that you are worthy descendants of those who murdered the prophets. ³² Go ahead then, finish what your fathers started!

³³ "You snakes! Sons of snakes! How can you escape being condemned to Gei-Hinnom? ³⁴ Therefore I am sending you prophets and sages and *Torah*-teachers — some of them you will kill, indeed, you will have them executed on stakes as criminals; some you will flog in your synagogues and pursue from town to town. ³⁵ And so, on you will fall the guilt for all the innocent blood that has ever been shed on earth, from the blood of innocent Hevel to the blood of Z'kharyah Ben-Berekhyah, whom you murdered between the Temple and the altar. ³⁶ Yes! I tell you that all this will fall on this generation!

³⁷ "Yerushalayim! Yerushalayim! You kill the prophets! You stone those who are sent to you! How often I wanted to gather your children, just as a hen gathers her chickens under her wings, but you refused! ³⁸ Look! **God is abandoning your house to you, leaving it desolate.**ᵉ ³⁹ For I tell you, from now on, you will not see me again until you say, **'Blessed is he who comes in the name of *Adonai*.'**ᶠ

24 ¹ As Yeshua left the Temple and was going away, his *talmidim* came and called his attention to its buildings. ² But he answered them, "You see all these? Yes! I tell you, they will be totally destroyed — not a single stone will be left standing!"

³ When he was sitting on the Mount of Olives, the *talmidim* came to him privately. "Tell us," they said, "when will these things happen? And what will be the sign that you are coming, and that the *'olam hazeh* is ending?"

⁴ Yeshua replied: "Watch out! Don't let anyone fool you! ⁵ For many will come in my name, saying, 'I am the Messiah!' and they will lead many astray. ⁶ You will hear the noise of wars nearby and the news of wars far off; see to it that you don't become frightened. Such things must happen, but the end is yet to come. ⁷ For peoples will fight each other, nations will fight each other, and there will be famines and earthquakes in various parts of the world; ⁸ all this is but the beginning of the 'birth-pains.' ⁹ At that time you will be arrested and handed over to be punished and put to death, and all peoples will hate you because of me. ¹⁰ At that time many will be trapped into betraying and hating each other, ¹¹ many false prophets will appear and fool many people; ¹² and many people's love will grow cold because of increased distance from *Torah*. ¹³ But whoever holds out till the end will be delivered. ¹⁴ And this Good News about the Kingdom will be announced throughout the whole world as a witness to all the *Goyim*. It is then that the end will come.

¹⁵ "So when you see **the abomination that causes desolation** spoken about through the prophet Dani'el standing in the Holy Place"ᵍ (let the reader understand the allusion), ¹⁶ "that will be the time for those in Y'hudah to escape to the hills. ¹⁷ If someone is on the roof, he must not go down to gather his belongings from his house; ¹⁸ if someone is in the field, he must not turn back to get his coat. ¹⁹ What a terrible time it will be for pregnant women and nursing mothers! ²⁰ Pray that you will not have to escape in winter or on *Shabbat*. ²¹ **For there will be trouble then worse than there has ever been from the beginning of the world until now, and there will be nothing like it again!**ʰ ²² Indeed, if the length of this

---

ᵉ Jeremiah 22:5   ᶠ Psalm 118:26   ᵍ Daniel 9:27, 11:31, 12:11   ʰ Joel 2:2, Daniel 12:1

time had not been limited, no one would survive; but for the sake of those who have been chosen, its length will be limited.

²³ "At that time, if someone says to you, 'Look! Here's the Messiah!' or, 'There he is!' don't believe him. ²⁴ For there will appear false Messiahs and false prophets performing great miracles — amazing things! — so as to fool even the chosen, if possible. ²⁵ There! I have told you in advance! ²⁶ So if people say to you, 'Listen! He's out in the desert!' don't go; or, 'Look! He's hidden away in a secret room!' don't believe it. ²⁷ For when the Son of Man does come, it will be like lightning that flashes out of the east and fills the sky to the western horizon. ²⁸ Wherever there's a dead body, that's where you find the vultures.

²⁹ "But immediately following the trouble of those times,

> **the sun will grow dark,**
> **the moon will stop shining,**ⁱ
> **the stars will fall from the sky,**
> **and the powers in heaven will be shaken.**ʲ

³⁰ "Then the sign of the Son of Man will appear in the sky, **all the tribes of the Land will mourn,**ᵏ and they will see **the Son of Man coming on the clouds of heaven** with tremendous power and glory.ˡ ³¹ He will send out his angels **with a great *shofar*;**ᵐ and they will gather together his chosen people from the four winds, from one end of heaven to the other.

³² "Now let the fig tree teach you its lesson: when its branches begin to sprout and leaves appear, you know that summer is approaching. ³³ In the same way, when you see all these things, you are to know that the time is near, right at the door. ³⁴ Yes! I tell you that this people will certainly not pass away before all these things happen. ³⁵ Heaven and earth will pass away, but my words will never pass away.

³⁶ "But when that day and hour will come, no one knows — not the angels in heaven, not the Son, only the Father. ³⁷ For the Son of Man's coming will be just as it was in the days of Noach. ³⁸ Back then, before the Flood, people went on eating and drinking, taking wives and becoming wives, right up till the day Noach entered the ark; ³⁹ and they didn't know what was happening until the Flood came and swept them all away. It will be just like that when the Son of Man comes. ⁴⁰ Then there will be two men in a field — one will be taken and the other left behind. ⁴¹ There will be two women grinding flour at the mill — one will be taken and the other left behind. ⁴² So stay alert, because you don't know on what day your Lord will come. ⁴³ But you do know this: had the owner of the house known when the thief was coming, he would have stayed awake and not allowed his house to be broken into. ⁴⁴ Therefore you too must always be ready, for the Son of Man will come when you are not expecting him.

⁴⁵ "Who is the faithful and sensible servant whose master puts him in charge of the household staff, to give them their food at the proper time? ⁴⁶ It will go well with that servant if he is found doing his job when his master comes. ⁴⁷ Yes, I tell you that he will put him in charge of all he owns. ⁴⁸ But if that servant is wicked and says to himself, 'My master is taking his time'; ⁴⁹ and he

---

ⁱ Isaiah 13:10; Ezekiel 32:7; Joel 2:10; 3:4(2:31); 4:15(3:15)   ʲ Isaiah 34:4; Haggai 2:6, 21
ᵏ Zechariah 12:10–14   ˡ Daniel 7:13–14   ᵐ Isaiah 27:13

starts beating up his fellow servants and spends his time eating and drinking with drunkards; ⁵⁰ then his master will come on a day the servant does not expect, at a time he doesn't know; ⁵¹ and he will cut him in two and put him with the hypocrites, where people will wail and grind their teeth!

25 ¹ "The Kingdom of Heaven at that time will be like ten bridesmaids who took their lamps and went out to meet the groom. ² Five of them were foolish and five were sensible. ³ The foolish ones took lamps with them but no oil, ⁴ whereas the others took flasks of oil with their lamps. ⁵ Now the bridegroom was late, so they all went to sleep. ⁶ It was the middle of the night when the cry rang out, 'The bridegroom is here! Go out to meet him!' ⁷ The girls all woke up and prepared their lamps for lighting. ⁸ The foolish ones said to the sensible ones, 'Give us some of your oil, because our lamps are going out.' ⁹ 'No,' they replied, 'there may not be enough for both you and us. Go to the oil dealers and buy some for yourselves.' ¹⁰ But as they were going off to buy, the bridegroom came. Those who were ready went with him to the wedding feast, and the door was shut. ¹¹ Later, the other bridesmaids came. 'Sir! Sir!' they cried, 'Let us in!' ¹² But he answered, 'Indeed! I tell you, I don't know you!' ¹³ So stay alert, because you know neither the day nor the hour.

¹⁴ "For it will be like a man about to leave home for awhile, who entrusted his possessions to his servants. ¹⁵ To one he gave five talents [equivalent to a hundred years' wages]; to another, two talents; and to another, one talent — to each according to his ability. Then he left. ¹⁶ The one who had received five talents immediately went out, invested it and earned another five. ¹⁷ Similarly, the one given two earned another two. ¹⁸ But the one given one talent went off, dug a hole in the ground and hid his master's money.

¹⁹ "After a long time, the master of those servants returned to settle accounts with them. ²⁰ The one who had received five talents came forward bringing the other five and said, 'Sir, you gave me five talents; here, I have made five more.' ²¹ His master said to him, 'Excellent! You are a good and trustworthy servant. You have been faithful with a small amount, so I will put you in charge of a large amount. Come and join in your master's happiness!' ²² Also the one who had received two came forward and said, 'Sir, you gave me two talents; here, I have made two more.' ²³ His master said to him, 'Excellent! you are a good and trustworthy servant. You have been faithful with a small amount, so I will put you in charge of a large amount. Come and join in your master's happiness!'

²⁴ "Now the one who had received one talent came forward and said, 'I knew you were a hard man. You harvest where you didn't plant and gather where you didn't sow seed. ²⁵ I was afraid, so I went and hid your talent in the ground. Here! Take what belongs to you!' ²⁶ 'You wicked, lazy servant!' said his master, 'So you knew, did you, that I harvest where I haven't planted? and that I gather where I didn't sow seed? ²⁷ Then you should have deposited my money with the bankers, so that when I returned, I would at least have gotten back interest with my capital! ²⁸ Take the talent from him and give it to the one who has ten. ²⁹ For everyone who has something will be given more, so that he will have more than enough; but from anyone who has nothing, even what he does have will be taken away. ³⁰ As for this worthless servant, throw him out in the dark, where people will wail and grind their teeth!'

[31] "When the Son of Man comes in his glory, accompanied by all the angels, he will sit on his glorious throne. [32] All the nations will be assembled before him, and he will separate people one from another as a shepherd separates sheep from goats. [33] The 'sheep' he will place at his right hand and the 'goats' at his left.

[34] "Then the King will say to those on his right, 'Come, you whom my Father has blessed, take your inheritance, the Kingdom prepared for you from the founding of the world. [35] For I was hungry and you gave me food, I was thirsty and you gave me something to drink, I was a stranger and you made me your guest, [36] I needed clothes and you provided them, I was sick and you took care of me, I was in prison and you visited me.' [37] Then the people who have done what God wants will reply, 'Lord, when did we see you hungry and feed you, or thirsty and give you something to drink? [38] When did we see you a stranger and make you our guest, or needing clothes and provide them? [39] When did we see you sick or in prison, and visit you?' [40] The King will say to them, 'Yes! I tell you that whenever you did these things for one of the least important of these brothers of mine, you did them for me!'

[41] "Then he will also speak to those on his left, saying, 'Get away from me, you who are cursed! Go off into the fire prepared for the Adversary and his angels! [42] For I was hungry and you gave me no food, thirsty and you gave me nothing to drink, [43] a stranger and you did not welcome me, needing clothes and you did not give them to me, sick and in prison and you did not visit me.' [44] Then they too will reply, 'Lord, when did we see you hungry, thirsty, a stranger, needing clothes, sick or in prison, and not take care of you?' [45] And he will answer them, 'Yes! I tell you that whenever you refused to do it for the least important of these people, you refused to do it for me!' [46] They will go off to eternal punishment, but those who have done what God wants will go to eternal life."

26 [1] When Yeshua had finished speaking, he said to his *talmidim*, [2] "As you know, *Pesach* is two days away, and the Son of Man will be handed over to be nailed to the execution-stake."

[3] Then the head *cohanim* and the elders of the people gathered in the palace of Kayafa the *cohen hagadol*. [4] They made plans to arrest Yeshua surreptitiously and have him put to death; [5] but they said, "Not during the festival, or the people will riot."

[6] Yeshua was in Beit-Anyah, at the home of Shim'on, the man who had had *tzara'at*. [7] A woman who had an alabaster jar filled with very expensive perfume approached Yeshua while he was eating and began pouring it on his head. [8] When the *talmidim* saw it, they became very angry. "Why this waste?" they asked. [9] "This could have been sold for a lot of money and given to the poor." [10] But Yeshua, aware of what was going on, said to them, "Why are you bothering this woman? She has done a beautiful thing for me. [11] The poor you will always have with you, but you will not always have me. [12] She poured this perfume on me to prepare my body for burial. [13] Yes! I tell you that throughout the whole world, wherever this Good News is proclaimed, what she has done will be told in her memory."

[14] Then one of the Twelve, the one called Y'hudah from K'riot, went to the head *cohanim* [15] and said, "What are you willing to give me if I turn Yeshua over to you?" **They counted out thirty silver coins and gave them** to Y'hudah.[n] [16] From then on he looked for a good opportunity to betray him.

---

[n] Zechariah 11:12

1257

¹⁷ On the first day for *matzah*, the *talmidim* came to Yeshua and asked, "Where do you want us to prepare your *Seder*?" ¹⁸ "Go into the city, to so-and-so," he replied, "and tell him that the Rabbi says, 'My time is near, my *talmidim* and I are celebrating *Pesach* at your house.'" ¹⁹ The *talmidim* did as Yeshua directed and prepared the *Seder*.

²⁰ When evening came, Yeshua reclined with the twelve *talmidim*; ²¹ and as they were eating, he said, "Yes, I tell you that one of you is going to betray me." ²² They became terribly upset and began asking him, one after the other, "Lord, you don't mean me, do you?" ²³ He answered, "The one who dips his *matzah* in the dish with me is the one who will betray me. ²⁴ The Son of Man will die just as the *Tanakh* says he will; but woe to that man by whom the Son of Man is betrayed! It would have been better for him had he never been born!" ²⁵ Y'hudah, the one who was betraying him, then asked, "Surely, Rabbi, you don't mean me?" He answered, "The words are yours."

²⁶ While they were eating, Yeshua took a piece of *matzah*, made the *b'rakhah*, broke it, gave it to the *talmidim* and said, "Take! Eat! This is my body!" ²⁷ Also he took a cup of wine, made the *b'rakhah*, and gave it to them, saying, "All of you, drink from it! ²⁸ For this is my blood, which ratifies the New Covenant, my blood shed on behalf of many, so that they may have their sins forgiven. ²⁹ I tell you, I will not drink this 'fruit of the vine' again until the day I drink new wine with you in my Father's Kingdom."

³⁰ After singing the *Hallel*, they went out to the Mount of Olives. ³¹ Yeshua then said to them, "Tonight you will all lose faith in me, as the *Tanakh* says, **'I will strike the shepherd dead, and the sheep of the flock will be scattered.'**ᵒ ³² But after I have been raised, I will go ahead of you into the Galil." ³³ "I will never lose faith in you," Kefa answered, "even if everyone else does." ³⁴ Yeshua said to him, "Yes! I tell you that tonight before the rooster crows, you will disown me three times!" ³⁵ "Even if I must die with you," Kefa replied, "I will never disown you!" And all the *talmidim* said the same thing.

³⁶ Then Yeshua went with his *talmidim* to a place called Gat-Sh'manim and said to them, "Sit here while I go over there and pray." ³⁷ He took with him Kefa and Zavdai's two sons. Grief and anguish came over him, ³⁸ and he said to them, "My heart is so filled with sadness that I could die! Remain here and stay awake with me." ³⁹ Going on a little farther, he fell on his face, praying, "My Father, if possible, let this cup pass from me! Yet — not what I want, but what you want!" ⁴⁰ He returned to the *talmidim* and found them sleeping. He said to Kefa, "Were you so weak that you couldn't stay awake with me for even an hour? ⁴¹ Stay awake, and pray that you will not be put to the test — the spirit indeed is eager, but human nature is weak."

⁴² A second time he went off and prayed. "My Father, if this cup cannot pass away unless I drink it, let what you want be done." ⁴³ Again he returned and found them sleeping, their eyes were so heavy.

⁴⁴ Leaving them again, he went off and prayed a third time, saying the same words. ⁴⁵ Then he came to the *talmidim* and said, "For now, go on sleeping, take your rest. . . . Look! The time has come for the Son of Man to be betrayed into the hands of sinners. ⁴⁶ Get up! Let's go! Here comes my betrayer!"

ᵒ Zechariah 13:7

⁴⁷ While Yeshua was still speaking, Y'hudah (one of the Twelve!) came, and with him a large crowd carrying swords and clubs, from the head *cohanim* and elders of the people. ⁴⁸ The betrayer had arranged to give them a signal: "The man I kiss is the one you want — grab him!" ⁴⁹ He went straight up to Yeshua, said, "*Shalom*, Rabbi!" and kissed him. ⁵⁰ Yeshua said to him, "Friend, do what you came to do." Then they moved forward, laid hold of Yeshua and arrested him.

⁵¹ At that, one of the men with Yeshua reached for his sword, drew it out and struck at the servant of the *cohen hagadol*, cutting off his ear. ⁵² Yeshua said to him, "Put your sword back where it belongs, for everyone who uses the sword will die by the sword. ⁵³ Don't you know that I can ask my Father, and he will instantly provide more than a dozen armies of angels to help me? ⁵⁴ But if I did that, how could the passages in the *Tanakh* be fulfilled that say it has to happen this way?"

⁵⁵ Then Yeshua addressed the crowd: "So you came out to take me with swords and clubs, the way you would the leader of a rebellion? Every day I sat in the Temple court, teaching; and you didn't seize me then. ⁵⁶ But all this has happened so that what the prophets wrote may be fulfilled." Then the *talmidim* all deserted him and ran away.

⁵⁷ Those who had seized Yeshua led him off to Kayafa the *cohen hagadol*, where the *Torah*-teachers and elders were assembled. ⁵⁸ Kefa followed him at a distance as far as the courtyard of the *cohen hagadol*; then he went inside and sat down with the guards to see what the outcome would be.

⁵⁹ The head *cohanim* and the whole *Sanhedrin* looked for some false evidence against Yeshua, so that they might put him to death. ⁶⁰ But they didn't find any, even though many liars came forward to give testimony. At last, however, two people came forward and said, ⁶¹ "This man said, 'I can tear down God's Temple and build it again in three days.'" ⁶² The *cohen hagadol* stood up and said, "Have you nothing to say to the accusation these men are making?" ⁶³ Yeshua remained silent. The *cohen hagadol* said to him, "I put you under oath! By the living God, tell us if you are the *Mashiach*, the Son of God!" ⁶⁴ Yeshua said to him, "The words are your own. But I tell you that one day you will see **the Son of Man sitting at the right hand of** *HaG'vurah* and **coming on the clouds of heaven.**"ᵖ ⁶⁵ At this, the *cohen hagadol* tore his robes. "Blasphemy!" he said. "Why do we still need witnesses? You heard him blaspheme! ⁶⁶ What is your verdict?" "Guilty," they answered. "He deserves death!" ⁶⁷ Then they spit in his face and pounded him with their fists; and those who were beating him ⁶⁸ said, "Now, you 'Messiah,' 'prophesy' to us: who hit you that time?"

⁶⁹ Kefa was sitting outside in the courtyard when a servant girl came up to him. "You too were with Yeshua from the Galil," she said. ⁷⁰ But he denied it in front of everyone — "I don't know what you're talking about!" ⁷¹ He went out onto the porch, and another girl saw him and said to the people there, "This man was with Yeshua of Natzeret." ⁷² Again he denied it, swearing, "I don't know the man!" ⁷³ After a little while, the bystanders approached Kefa and said, "You must be one of them — your accent gives you away." ⁷⁴ This time he began to invoke a curse on himself as he swore, "I do not know the man!" — and immediately a rooster crowed. ⁷⁵ Kefa remembered what Yeshua had said, "Before the rooster crows, you will disown me three times"; and he went outside and cried bitterly.

ᵖ Daniel 7:13; Psalm 110:1

27 ¹ Early in the morning, all the head *cohanim* and elders met to plan how to bring about Yeshua's death. ² Then they put him in chains, led him away and handed him over to Pilate the governor.

³ When Y'hudah, who had betrayed him, saw that Yeshua had been condemned, he was seized with remorse and returned the thirty silver coins to the head *cohanim* and elders, ⁴ saying, "I sinned in betraying an innocent man to death." "What is that to us?" they answered. "That's your problem." ⁵ Hurling the pieces of silver into the sanctuary, he left; then he went off and hanged himself.

⁶ The head *cohanim* took the silver coins and said, "It is prohibited to put this into the Temple treasury, because it is blood money." ⁷ So they decided to use it to buy the potter's field as a cemetery for foreigners. ⁸ This is how it came to be called the Field of Blood, a name it still bears. ⁹ Then what Yirmeyahu the prophet spoke was fulfilled, **"And they took the thirty silver coins, which was the price the people of Isra'el had agreed to pay for him, ¹⁰ and used them to buy the potter's field, just as the Lord directed me."**ᵍ

¹¹ Meanwhile, Yeshua was brought before the governor, and the governor put this question to him: "Are you the King of the Jews?" Yeshua answered, "The words are yours." ¹² But when he was accused by the head *cohanim* and elders, he gave no answer. ¹³ Then Pilate said to him, "Don't you hear all these charges they are making against you?" ¹⁴ But to the governor's great amazement, he did not say a single word in reply to the accusations.

¹⁵ It was the governor's custom during a festival to set free one prisoner, whomever the crowd asked for. ¹⁶ There was at that time a notorious prisoner being held, named Yeshua Bar-Abba. ¹⁷ So when a crowd had gathered, Pilate said to them, "Whom do you want me to set free for you? Bar-Abba? or Yeshua, called 'the Messiah'?" ¹⁸ For he understood that it was out of jealousy that they had handed him over. ¹⁹ While he was sitting in court, his wife sent him a message, "Leave that innocent man alone. Today in a dream I suffered terribly because of him." ²⁰ But the head *cohanim* persuaded the crowd to ask for Bar-Abba's release and to have Yeshua executed on the stake. ²¹ "Which of the two do you want me to set free for you?" asked the governor. "Bar-Abba!" they answered. ²² Pilate said to them, "Then what should I do with Yeshua, called 'the Messiah'?" They all said, "Put him to death on the stake! Put him to death on the stake!" ²³ When he asked, "Why? What crime has he committed?" they shouted all the louder, "Put him to death on the stake!" ²⁴ When Pilate saw that he was accomplishing nothing, but rather that a riot was starting, he took water, washed his hands in front of the crowd, and said, "My hands are clean of this man's blood; it's your responsibility." ²⁵ All the people answered, "His blood is on us and on our children!" ²⁶ Then he released to them Bar-Abba; but Yeshua, after having him whipped, he handed over to be executed on a stake.

²⁷ The governor's soldiers took Yeshua into the headquarters building, and the whole battalion gathered around him. ²⁸ They stripped off his clothes and put on him a scarlet robe, ²⁹ wove thorn-branches into a crown and put it on his head, and put a stick in his right hand. Then they kneeled down in front of him and made fun of him: "Hail to the King of the Jews!" ³⁰ They spit on him and

---

ᵍ Zechariah 11:12–13, where Hebrew *yotzer* means "treasury"; here it means "potter" (see v. 7).

used the stick to beat him about the head. [31] When they had finished ridiculing him, they took off the robe, put his own clothes back on him and led him away to be nailed to the execution-stake.

[32] As they were leaving, they met a man from Cyrene named Shim'on; and they forced him to carry Yeshua's execution-stake. [33] When they arrived at a place called Gulgolta (which means "place of a skull"), [34] they gave him wine mixed with bitter gall to drink; but after tasting it, he would not drink it. [35] After they had nailed him to the stake, they divided his clothes among them by throwing dice. [36] Then they sat down to keep watch over him there. [37] Above his head they placed the written notice stating the charge against him,

THIS IS YESHUA
THE KING OF THE JEWS

[38] Then two robbers were placed on execution-stakes with him, one on the right and one on the left. [39] People passing by hurled insults at him, **shaking their heads**[r] [40] and saying, "So you can destroy the Temple, can you, and rebuild it in three days? Save yourself, if you are the Son of God, and come down from the stake!" [41] Likewise, the head *cohanim* jeered at him, along with the *Torah*-teachers and elders, [42] "He saved others, but he can't save himself!" "So he's King of Isra'el, is he? Let him come down now from the stake! Then we'll believe him!" [43] **"He trusted God? So, let him rescue him if he wants him!**[s] After all, he did say, 'I'm the Son of God'!" [44] Even the robbers nailed up with him insulted him in the same way.

[45] From noon until three o'clock in the afternoon, all the Land was covered with darkness. [46] At about three, Yeshua uttered a loud cry, *"Eli! Eli! L'mah sh'vaktani? (My God! My God! Why have you deserted me?)"*[t] [47] On hearing this, some of the bystanders said, "He's calling for Eliyahu." [48] Immediately one of them ran and took a sponge, soaked it in **vinegar**, put it on a stick and gave it to him **to drink.**[u] [49] The rest said, "Wait! Let's see if Eliyahu comes and rescues him." [50] But Yeshua, again crying out in a loud voice, yielded up his spirit.

[51] At that moment the *parokhet* in the Temple was ripped in two from top to bottom; and there was an earthquake, with rocks splitting apart. [52] Also the graves were opened, and the bodies of many holy people who had died were raised to life; [53] and after Yeshua rose, they came out of the graves and went into the holy city, where many people saw them. [54] When the Roman officer and those with him who were keeping watch over Yeshua saw the earthquake and what was happening, they were awestruck and said, "He really was a son of God."

[55] There were many women there, looking on from a distance; they had followed Yeshua from the Galil, helping him. [56] Among them were Miryam from Magdala, Miryam the mother of Ya'akov and Yosef, and the mother of Zavdai's sons.

[57] Towards evening, there came a wealthy man from Ramatayim named Yosef, who was himself a *talmid* of Yeshua. [58] He approached Pilate and asked for Yeshua's body, and Pilate ordered it to be given to him. [59] Yosef took the body, wrapped it in a clean linen sheet, [60] and laid it in his own tomb, which he had recently had cut out of the rock. After rolling a large stone in front of the entrance to

---

[r] Psalm 22:8(7)   [s] Psalm 22:9(8)   [t] Psalm 22:2(1)   [u] Psalm 69:22(21)

the tomb, he went away. [61] Miryam of Magdala and the other Miryam stayed there, sitting opposite the grave.

[62] Next day, after the preparation, the head *cohanim* and the *P'rushim* went together to Pilate [63] and said, "Sir, we remember that that deceiver said while he was still alive, 'After three days I will be raised.' [64] Therefore, order that the grave be made secure till the third day; otherwise the *talmidim* may come, steal him away and say to the people, 'He was raised from the dead'; and the last deception will be worse than the first." [65] Pilate said to them, "You may have your guard. Go and make the grave as secure as you know how." [66] So they went and made the grave secure by sealing the stone and putting the guard on watch.

28 [1] After *Shabbat*, as the next day was dawning, Miryam of Magdala and the other Miryam went to see the grave. [2] Suddenly there was a violent earthquake, for an angel of *Adonai* came down from heaven, rolled away the stone and sat on it. [3] His appearance was like lightning, and his clothes were as white as snow. [4] The guards were so terrified at him that they trembled and became like dead men. [5] But the angel said to the women, "Don't be afraid. I know you are looking for Yeshua, who was executed on the stake. [6] He is not here, because he has been raised — just as he said! Come and look at the place where he lay. [7] Then go quickly and tell the *talmidim*, 'He has been raised from the dead, and now he is going to the Galil ahead of you. You will see him there.' Now I have told you."

[8] So they left the tomb quickly, frightened yet filled with joy; and they ran to give the news to his *talmidim*. [9] Suddenly Yeshua met them and said, "Shalom!" They came up and took hold of his feet as they fell down in front of him. [10] Then Yeshua said to them, "Don't be afraid! Go and tell my brothers to go to the Galil, and they will see me there."

[11] As they were going, some of the guards went into the city and reported to the head *cohanim* everything that had happened. [12] Then they met with the elders; and after discussing the matter, they gave the soldiers a sizeable sum of money [13] and said to them, "Tell people, 'His *talmidim* came during the night and stole his body while we were sleeping.' [14] If the governor hears of it, we will put things right with him and keep you from getting in trouble." [15] The soldiers took the money and did as they were told, and this story has been spread about by Judeans till this very day.

[16] So the eleven *talmidim* went to the hill in the Galil where Yeshua had told them to go. [17] When they saw him, they prostrated themselves before him; but some hesitated. [18] Yeshua came and talked with them. He said, "All authority in heaven and on earth has been given to me. [19] Therefore, go and make people from all nations into *talmidim*, immersing them into the reality of the Father, the Son and the *Ruach HaKodesh*, [20] and teaching them to obey everything that I have commanded you. And remember! I will be with you always, yes, even until the end of the age."

The Good News of Yeshua the Messiah,
as Reported by

MARK

1 ¹ The beginning of the Good News of Yeshua the Messiah, the Son of God: ² It is written in the prophet Yesha'yahu,

> **"See, I am sending my messenger ahead of you;**
> **he will prepare the way before** you."*ᵃ*

³
> **"The voice of someone crying out:**
> **'In the desert prepare the way for** ADONAI!
> **Make straight paths for** him!'"*ᵇ*

⁴ So it was that Yochanan the Immerser appeared in the desert, proclaiming an immersion involving turning to God from sin in order to be forgiven. ⁵ People went out to him from all over Y'hudah, as did all the inhabitants of Yerushalayim. Confessing their sins, they were immersed by him in the Yarden River. ⁶ Yochanan wore clothes of camel's hair, with a leather belt around his waist; he ate locusts and wild honey. ⁷ He proclaimed: "After me is coming someone who is more powerful than I — I'm not worthy even to bend down and untie his sandals. ⁸ I have immersed you in water, but he will immerse you in the *Ruach HaKodesh.*"

⁹ Shortly thereafter, Yeshua came from Natzeret in the Galil and was immersed in the Yarden by Yochanan. ¹⁰ Immediately upon coming up out of the water, he saw heaven torn open and the Spirit descending upon him like a dove; ¹¹ then a voice came from heaven, "You are my Son, whom I love; I am well pleased with you."

¹² Immediately the Spirit drove him out into the wilderness, ¹³ and he was in the wilderness forty days being tempted by the Adversary. He was with the wild animals, and the angels took care of him.

¹⁴ After Yochanan had been arrested, Yeshua came into the Galil proclaiming the Good News from God:

¹⁵
> "The time has come,
> God's Kingdom is near!
> Turn to God from your sins
> and believe the Good News!"

¹⁶ As he walked beside Lake Kinneret, he saw Shim'on and Andrew, Shim'on's brother, casting a net into the lake; for they were fishermen. ¹⁷ Yeshua said to them, "Come, follow me, and I will make you into fishers for men!" ¹⁸ At once they left their nets and followed him.

ᵃ Malachi 3:1   *ᵇ* Isaiah 40:3

^{19} Going on a little farther, he saw Ya'akov Ben-Zavdai and Yochanan, his brother, in their boat, repairing their nets. ^{20} Immediately he called them, and they left their father Zavdai in the boat with the hired men and went after Yeshua.

^{21} They entered K'far-Nachum, and on *Shabbat* Yeshua went into the synagogue and began teaching. ^{22} They were amazed at the way he taught, for he did not instruct them like the *Torah*-teachers but as one who had authority himself.

^{23} In their synagogue just then was a man with an unclean spirit in him, who shouted, ^{24} "What do you want with us, Yeshua from Natzeret? Have you come to destroy us? I know who you are — the Holy One of God!" ^{25} But Yeshua rebuked the unclean spirit, "Be quiet and come out of him!" ^{26} Throwing the man into a convulsion, it gave a loud shriek and came out of him. ^{27} They were all so astounded that they began asking each other, "What is this? A new teaching, one with authority behind it! He gives orders even to the unclean spirits, and they obey him!" ^{28} And the news about him spread quickly through the whole region of the Galil.

^{29} They left the synagogue and went with Ya'akov and Yochanan to the home of Shim'on and Andrew. ^{30} Shim'on's mother-in-law was lying sick with a fever, and they told Yeshua about her. ^{31} He came, took her by the hand and lifted her onto her feet. The fever left her, and she began helping them.

^{32} That evening after sundown, they brought to Yeshua all who were ill or held in the power of demons, ^{33} and the whole town came crowding around the door. ^{34} He healed many who were ill with various diseases and expelled many demons, but he did not allow the demons to speak, because they knew who he was.

^{35} Very early in the morning, while it was still dark, Yeshua got up, left, went away to a lonely spot and stayed there praying. ^{36} But Shim'on and those with him went after him; ^{37} and when they found him, they said, "Everybody is looking for you." ^{38} He answered, "Let's go somewhere else — to the other villages around here. I have to proclaim the message there too — in fact this is why I came out." ^{39} So he traveled all through the Galil, preaching in their synagogues and expelling demons.

^{40} A man afflicted with *tzara'at* came to Yeshua and begged him on his knees, "If you are willing, you can make me clean." ^{41} Moved with pity, Yeshua reached out his hand, touched him and said to him, "I am willing! Be cleansed!" ^{42} Instantly the *tzara'at* left him, and he was cleansed. ^{43} Yeshua sent him away with this stern warning: ^{44} "See to it that you tell no one; instead, as a testimony to the people, go and let the *cohen* examine you, and offer for your cleansing what Moshe commanded." ^{45} But he went out and began spreading the news, talking freely about it; so that Yeshua could no longer enter a town openly but stayed out in the country, where people continued coming to him from all around.

2 ^{1} After a while, Yeshua returned to K'far-Nachum. The word spread that he was back, ^{2} and so many people gathered around the house that there was no longer any room, not even in front of the door. While he was preaching the message to them, ^{3} four men came to him carrying a paralyzed man. ^{4} They could not get near Yeshua because of the crowd, so they stripped the roof over the place where he was, made an opening, and lowered the stretcher with the paralytic lying on it. ^{5} Seeing their trust, Yeshua said to the paralyzed man, "Son, your sins are forgiven." ^{6} Some *Torah*-teachers sitting there thought to themselves, ^{7} "How can this fellow say such a thing? He is blaspheming! Who can forgive sins except God?" ^{8} But immediately Yeshua, perceiving in his spirit what they were thinking, said to them, "Why are you thinking these things? ⁹Which is easier to say to the paralyzed man? 'Your sins are forgiven'? or 'Get up, pick up your stretcher and walk'? ¹⁰But look! I will prove to you that the Son of Man has authority on earth to forgive sins." He then said to the paralytic, ¹¹"I say to you: get up, pick up your stretcher and go home!" ¹²In front of everyone the man got up, picked up his stretcher at once and left. They were all utterly amazed and praised God, saying, "We have never seen anything like this!"

¹³Yeshua went out again by the lake. All the crowd came to him, and he began teaching them. ¹⁴As he passed on from there, he saw Levi Ben-Halfai sitting in his tax-collection booth and said to him, "Follow me!" And he got up and followed him.

¹⁵As Yeshua was in Levi's house eating, many tax-collectors and sinners were sitting with Yeshua and his *talmidim*, for there were many of them among his followers. ¹⁶When the *Torah*-teachers and the *P'rushim* saw that he was eating with sinners and tax-collectors, they said to his *talmidim*, "Why does he eat with tax-collectors and sinners?" ¹⁷But, hearing the question, Yeshua answered them, "The ones who need a doctor aren't the healthy but the sick. I didn't come to call the 'righteous' but sinners!"

¹⁸Also Yochanan's *talmidim* and the *P'rushim* were fasting; and they came and asked Yeshua, "Why is it that Yochanan's *talmidim* and the *talmidim* of the *P'rushim* fast, but your *talmidim* don't fast?" ¹⁹Yeshua answered them, "Can wedding guests fast while the bridegroom is still with them? As long as they have the bridegroom with them, fasting is out of the question. ²⁰But the time will come when the bridegroom is taken away from them; and when that day comes, they will fast. ²¹No one sews a piece of unshrunk cloth on an old coat; if he does, the new patch tears away from the old cloth and leaves a worse hole. ²²And no one puts new wine in old wineskins; if he does, the wine will burst the skins, and both the wine and the skins will be ruined. Rather, new wine is for freshly prepared wineskins."

²³One *Shabbat* Yeshua was passing through some wheat fields; and as they went along, his *talmidim* began picking heads of grain. ²⁴The *P'rushim* said to him, "Look! Why are they violating *Shabbat*?" ²⁵He said to them, "Haven't you ever read what David did when he and those with him were hungry and needed food? ²⁶He entered the House of God when Evyatar was *cohen gadol* and ate the Bread of the Presence," — which is forbidden for anyone to eat but the *cohanim* — "and even gave some to his companions." ²⁷Then he said to them, "*Shabbat* was made for mankind, not mankind for *Shabbat*; ²⁸So the Son of Man is Lord even of *Shabbat*."

3 ¹Yeshua went again into a synagogue, and a man with a shriveled hand was there. ²Looking for a reason to accuse him of something, people watched him carefully to see if he would heal him on *Shabbat*. ³He said to the man with the shriveled hand, "Come up where we can see you!" ⁴Then to them he said, "What is permitted on *Shabbat*? Doing good or doing evil? Saving life or killing?" But they said nothing. ⁵Then, looking them over and feeling both anger with them and sympathy for them at the stoniness of their hearts, he said to the man, "Hold out your hand." As he held it out, it became restored. ⁶The *P'rushim* went out and immediately began plotting with some members of Herod's party how to do away with him.

⁷Yeshua went off with his *talmidim* to the lake, and great numbers followed him from the Galil. ⁸When they heard what he was doing, great numbers also followed

him from Y'hudah, Yerushalayim, Idumea, the territory beyond the Yarden, and the Tzor-Tzidon area. ⁹ He told his *talmidim* to have a boat ready for him, so that he could escape the crush of the crowd if necessary, ¹⁰ for he had healed many people, and all the sick kept pressing forward to touch him. ¹¹ Whenever the unclean spirits saw him, they would fall down in front of him and scream, "You are the Son of God!" ¹² But he warned them strictly not to make him known.

¹³ Then he went up into the hill country and summoned to himself those he wanted, and they came to him. ¹⁴ He appointed twelve to be with him, to be sent out to preach ¹⁵ and to have authority to expel demons:

¹⁶ Shim'on, to whom he gave another name, "Kefa";

¹⁷ Ya'akov Ben-Zavdai and Yochanan, Ya'akov's brother — to them he gave the name "B'nei-Regesh" (that is, "Thunderers");

¹⁸ Andrew, Philip, Bar-Talmai, Mattityahu, T'oma, Ya'akov Ben-Halfai, Taddai, Shim'on the Zealot,

¹⁹ and Y'hudah from K'riot, the one who betrayed him.

Then he entered a house; ²⁰ and once more, such a crowd came together that they couldn't even eat. ²¹ When his family heard about this, they set out to take charge of him; for they said, "He's out of his mind!"

²² The *Torah*-teachers who came down from Yerushalayim said, "He has Ba'al-Zibbul in him," and "It is by the ruler of the demons that he expels the demons." ²³ But he called them and spoke to them in parables: "How can Satan expel Satan? ²⁴ If a kingdom is divided against itself, that kingdom can't survive; ²⁵ and if a household is divided against itself, that household can't survive. ²⁶ So if Satan has rebelled against himself and is divided, he can't survive either; and that's the end of him. ²⁷ Furthermore, no one can break into a strong man's house and make off with his possessions unless he first ties up the strong man. After that, he can ransack his house. ²⁸ Yes! I tell you that people will be forgiven all sins and whatever blasphemies they utter; ²⁹ however, someone who blasphemes against the *Ruach HaKodesh* never has forgiveness but is guilty of an eternal sin." ³⁰ For they had been saying, "He has an unclean spirit in him."

³¹ Then his mother and brothers arrived. Standing outside, they sent a message asking for him. ³² A crowd was sitting around him; and they said to him, "Your mother and your brothers are outside, asking for you." ³³ He replied, "Who are my mother and my brothers?" ³⁴ Looking at those seated in a circle around him, he said, "See! Here are my mother and my brothers! ³⁵ Whoever does what God wants is my brother, sister and mother!"

4 ¹ Again Yeshua began to teach by the lake, but the crowd that gathered around him was so large that he got into a boat on the lake and sat there, while the crowd remained on shore at the water's edge. ² He taught them many things in parables. In the course of his teaching, he said to them: ³ "Listen! A farmer went out to sow his seed. ⁴ As he sowed, some seed fell alongside the path; and the birds came and ate it up. ⁵ Other seed fell on rocky patches where there was not much soil. It sprouted quickly because the soil was shallow; ⁶ but when the sun rose, the young plants were scorched; and since their roots were not deep, they dried up. ⁷ Other seed fell among thorns, which grew up and choked it; so that it yielded no grain. ⁸ But other seed fell into rich soil and produced grain; it sprouted, and grew, and yielded a crop — thirty, sixty, even a hundred times what was sown." [9] And he concluded, "Whoever has ears to hear with, let him hear!"

[10] When Yeshua was alone, the people around him with the Twelve asked him about the parables. [11] He answered them, "To you the secret of the Kingdom of God has been given; but to those outside, everything is in parables, [12] so that

> **they may be always looking but never seeing;**
> **always listening but never understanding.**
> **Otherwise, they might turn and be forgiven!"[c]**

[13] Then Yeshua said to them, "Don't you understand this parable? How will you be able to understand any parable? [14] The sower sows the message. [15] Those alongside the path where the message is sown are people who no sooner hear it than the Adversary comes and takes away the message sown in them. [16] Likewise, those receiving seed on rocky patches are people who hear the message and joyfully accept it at once; [17] but they have no root in themselves. So they hold out for a while, but as soon as some trouble or persecution arises on account of the message, they immediately fall away. [18] Others are those sown among thorns — they hear the message; [19] but the worries of the world, the deceitful glamor of wealth and all the other kinds of desires push in and choke the message; so that it produces nothing. [20] But those sown on rich soil hear the message, accept it and bear fruit — thirty, sixty or a hundredfold."

[21] He said to them, "A lamp isn't brought in to be put under a bowl or under the bed, is it? Wouldn't you put it on a lampstand? [22] Indeed, nothing is hidden, except to be disclosed; and nothing is covered up, except to come out into the open. [23] Those who have ears to hear with, let them hear!"

[24] He also said to them, "Pay attention to what you are hearing! The measure with which you measure out will be used to measure to you — and more besides! [25] For anyone who has something will be given more; but from anyone who has nothing, even what he does have will be taken away."

[26] And he said, "The Kingdom of God is like a man who scatters seed on the ground. [27] Nights he sleeps, days he's awake; and meanwhile the seeds sprout and grow — how, he doesn't know. [28] By itself the soil produces a crop — first the stalk, then the head, and finally the full grain in the head. [29] But as soon as the crop is ready, the man comes with his sickle, because it's harvest-time."

[30] Yeshua also said, "With what can we compare the Kingdom of God? What illustration should we use to describe it? [31] It is like a mustard seed, which, when planted, is the smallest of all the seeds in the field; [32] but after it has been planted, it grows and becomes the largest of all the plants, with such big branches that the birds flying about can build nests in its shade."

[33] With many parables like these he spoke the message to them, to the extent that they were capable of hearing it. [34] He did not say a thing to them without using a parable; when he was alone with his own *talmidim* he explained everything to them.

[35] That day, when evening had come, Yeshua said to them, "Let's cross to the other side of the lake." [36] So, leaving the crowd behind, they took him just as he was,

---

[c] Isaiah 6:9–10

in the boat; and there were other boats with him. ³⁷ A furious windstorm arose, and the waves broke over the boat, so that it was close to being swamped. ³⁸ But he was in the stern on a cushion, asleep. They woke him and said to him, "Rabbi, doesn't it matter to you that we're about to be killed?" ³⁹ He awoke, rebuked the wind and said to the waves, "Quiet! Be still!" The wind subsided, and there was a dead calm. ⁴⁰ He said to them, "Why are you afraid? Have you no trust even now?" ⁴¹ But they were terrified and asked each other, "Who can this be, that even the wind and the waves obey him?"

5 ¹ Yeshua and his *talmidim* arrived at the other side of the lake, in the Gerasenes' territory. ² As soon as he disembarked, a man with an unclean spirit came out of the burial caves to meet him. ³ He lived in the burial caves; and no one could keep him tied up, not even with a chain. ⁴ He had often been chained hand and foot, but he would snap the chains and break the irons off his feet, and no one was strong enough to control him. ⁵ Night and day he wandered among the graves and through the hills, howling and gashing himself with stones.

⁶ Seeing Yeshua from a distance, he ran and fell on his knees in front of him ⁷ and screamed at the top of his voice, "What do you want with me, Yeshua, Son of God *Ha'Elyon*? I implore you in God's name! Don't torture me!" ⁸ For Yeshua had already begun saying to him, "Unclean spirit, come out of this man!" ⁹ Yeshua asked him, "What's your name?" "My name is Legion," he answered, "there are so many of us"; ¹⁰ and he kept begging Yeshua not to send them out of that region.

¹¹ Now there was a large herd of pigs feeding near the hill, ¹² and the unclean spirits begged him, "Send us to the pigs, so we can go into them." ¹³ Yeshua gave them permission. They came out and entered the pigs; and the herd, numbering around two thousand, rushed down the hillside into the lake and were drowned. ¹⁴ The swineherds fled and told it in the town and in the surrounding country, and the people went to see what had happened. ¹⁵ They came to Yeshua and saw the man who had had the legion of demons, sitting there, dressed and in his right mind; and they were frightened. ¹⁶ Those who had seen it told what had happened to the man controlled by demons and to the pigs; ¹⁷ and the people began begging Yeshua to leave their district.

¹⁸ As he was getting into the boat, the man who had been demonized begged him to be allowed to go with him. ¹⁹ But Yeshua would not permit it. Instead, he said to him, "Go home to your people, and tell them how much Adonai in his mercy has done for you." ²⁰ He went off and began proclaiming in the Ten Towns how much Yeshua had done for him, and everyone was amazed.

²¹ Yeshua crossed in the boat to the other side of the lake, and a great crowd gathered around him. ²² There came to him a synagogue official, Ya'ir by name, who fell at his feet ²³ and pleaded desperately with him, "My little daughter is at the point of death. Please! Come and lay your hands on her, so that she will get well and live!" ²⁴ He went with him; and a large crowd followed, pressing all around him. ²⁵ Among them was a woman who had had a hemorrhage for twelve years ²⁶ and had suffered a great deal under many physicians. She had spent her life savings; yet instead of improving, she had grown worse. ²⁷ She had heard about Yeshua, so she came up behind him in the crowd and touched his robe; ²⁸ for she said, "If I touch even his clothes, I will be healed." ²⁹ Instantly the hemorrhaging stopped, and she

felt in her body that she had been healed from the disease. ³⁰ At the same time, Yeshua, aware that power had gone out from him, turned around in the crowd and asked, "Who touched my clothes?" ³¹ His *talmidim* responded, "You see the people pressing in on you; and still you ask, 'Who touched me?'" ³² But he kept looking around to see who had done it. ³³ The woman, frightened and trembling, because she knew what had happened to her, came and fell down in front of him and told him the whole truth. ³⁴ "Daughter," he said to her, "your trust has healed you. Go in peace, and be healed of your disease."

³⁵ While he was still speaking, people from the synagogue official's house came, saying, "Your daughter has died. Why bother the rabbi any longer?" ³⁶ Ignoring what they had said, Yeshua told the synagogue official, "Don't be afraid, just keep trusting." ³⁷ He let no one follow him except Kefa, Ya'akov and Yochanan, Ya'akov's brother. ³⁸ When they came to the synagogue official's house, he found a great commotion, with people weeping and wailing loudly. ³⁹ On entering, he said to them, "Why all this commotion and weeping? The child isn't dead, she's just asleep!" ⁴⁰ And they jeered at him. But he put them all outside, took the child's father and mother and those with him, and went in where the child was. ⁴¹ Taking her by the hand, he said to her, *"Talita, kumi!"* (which means, "Little girl, I say to you, get up!"). ⁴² At once the girl got up and began walking around; she was twelve years old. Everybody was utterly amazed. ⁴³ He gave them strict orders to say nothing about this to anyone, and told them to give her something to eat.

6 ¹ Then Yeshua left and went to his home town, and his *talmidim* followed him. ² On *Shabbat* he started to teach in the synagogue, and many who heard him were astounded. They asked, "Where did this man get all this? What is this wisdom he has been given? What are these miracles worked through him? ³ Isn't he just the carpenter? the son of Miryam? the brother of Ya'akov and Yosi and Y'hudah and Shim'on? Aren't his sisters here with us?" And they took offense at him. ⁴ But Yeshua said to them. "The only place people don't respect a prophet is in his home town, among his own relatives, and in his own house." ⁵ So he could do no miracles there, other than lay his hands on a few sick people and heal them. ⁶ He was amazed at their lack of trust.

Then he went through the surrounding towns and villages, teaching.

⁷ Yeshua summoned the Twelve and started sending them out in pairs, giving them authority over the unclean spirits. ⁸ He instructed them, "Take nothing for your trip except a walking stick — no bread, no pack, no money in your belt. ⁹ Wear shoes but not an extra shirt. ¹⁰ Whenever you enter a house, stay there until you leave the place; ¹¹ and if the people of some place will not welcome you, and they refuse to hear you, then, as you leave, shake the dust off your feet as a warning to them."

¹² So they set out and preached that people should turn from sin to God, ¹³ they expelled many demons, and they anointed many sick people with oil and healed them.

¹⁴ Meanwhile, King Herod heard about this, for Yeshua's reputation had spread. Some were saying, "Yochanan the Immerser has been raised from the dead; that is why these miraculous powers are at work in him." ¹⁵ Others said, "It is Eliyahu!" and still others, "He is a prophet, like one of the old prophets." ¹⁶ But when Herod heard about it, he said, "Yochanan, whom I had beheaded, has been raised."

[17] For Herod had sent and had Yochanan arrested and chained in prison because of Herodias, the wife of his brother Philip. Herod had married her, [18] but Yochanan had told him, "It violates the *Torah* for you to marry your brother's wife." [19] So Herodias had a grudge against him and wanted him put to death. But this she could not accomplish, [20] because Herod stood in awe of Yochanan and protected him, for he knew that he was a *tzaddik*, a holy man. Whenever he heard him, he became deeply disturbed; yet he liked to listen to him.

[21] Finally, the opportunity came. Herod gave a banquet on his birthday for his nobles and officers and the leading men of the Galil. [22] The daughter of Herodias came in and danced, and she pleased Herod and his guests. The king said to the girl, "Ask me for whatever you want; I will give it to you"; [23] and he made a vow to her, "Whatever you ask me, I will give you, up to half my kingdom." [24] So she went out and said to her mother, "What should I ask for?" She said, "The head of Yochanan the Immerser." [25] At once the daughter hurried back to the king and announced her request: "I want you to give me right now on a platter the head of Yochanan the Immerser." [26] Herod was appalled; but out of regard for the oaths he had sworn before his dinner guests, he did not want to break his word to her. [27] So the king immediately sent a soldier from his personal guard with orders to bring Yochanan's head. The soldier went and beheaded Yochanan in the prison, [28] brought his head on a platter, and gave it to the girl; and the girl gave it to her mother. [29] When Yochanan's *talmidim* heard of it, they came and took the body and laid it in a grave.

[30] Those who had been sent out rejoined Yeshua and reported to him all they had done and taught. [31] There were so many people coming and going that they couldn't even take time to eat, so he said to them, "Come with me by yourselves to a place where we can be alone, and you can get some rest." [32] They went off by themselves to an isolated spot; [33] but many people, seeing them leave and recognizing them, ran ahead on foot from all the towns and got there first. [34] When Yeshua came ashore, he saw a huge crowd. Filled with compassion for them, because they were like sheep without a shepherd, he began teaching them many things.

[35] By this time, the hour was late. The *talmidim* came to him and said, "This is a remote place, and it's getting late. [36] Send the people away, so that they can go and buy food for themselves in the farms and towns around here." [37] But he answered them, "Give them something to eat, yourselves!" They replied, "We are to go and spend thousands on bread, and give it to them to eat?" [38] He asked them, "How many loaves do you have? Go and check." When they had found out, they said, "Five. And two fish." [39] Then he ordered all the people to sit down in groups on the green grass. [40] They sat down in groups of fifty or a hundred. [41] Then he took the five loaves and the two fish, and, looking up toward heaven, made a *b'rakhah*. Next he broke up the loaves and began giving them to the *talmidim* to distribute. He also divided up the two fish among them all. [42] They all ate as much as they wanted, [43] and they took up twelve baskets full of the broken pieces and fish. [44] Those who ate the loaves numbered five thousand men.

[45] Immediately Yeshua had his *talmidim* get in the boat and go on ahead of him toward the other side of the lake, toward Beit-Tzaidah, while he sent the crowds away. [46] After he had left them, he went into the hills to pray. [47] When night came, the boat was out on the lake, and he was by himself on land. [48] He saw that they were having difficulty rowing, because the wind was against them; so at around four o'clock

in the morning he came toward them, walking on the lake! He meant to come alongside them; ^{49} but when they saw him walking on the lake, they thought it was a ghost and let out a shriek; ^{50} for they had all seen him and were terrified. However, he spoke to them. "Courage," he said, "it is I. Stop being afraid!" ^{51} He got into the boat with them, and the wind ceased. They were completely astounded, ^{52} for they did not understand about the loaves; on the contrary, their hearts had been made stonelike.

^{53} After they had made the crossing, they landed at Ginosar and anchored. ^{54} As soon as they got out of the boat, the people recognized him ^{55} and began running around throughout that whole region and bringing sick people on their stretchers to any place where they heard he was. ^{56} Wherever he went, in towns, cities or country, they laid the sick in the marketplaces. They begged him to let them touch even the *tzitzit* on his robe, and all who touched it were healed.

7 ^{1} The *P'rushim* and some of the *Torah*-teachers who had come from Yerushalayim gathered together with Yeshua ^{2} and saw that some of his *talmidim* ate with ritually unclean hands, that is, without doing *n'tilat-yadayim*. ^{3} (For the *P'rushim*, and indeed all the Judeans, holding fast to the Tradition of the Elders, do not eat unless they have given their hands a ceremonial washing. ^{4} Also, when they come from the marketplace they do not eat unless they have rinsed their hands up to the wrist; and they adhere to many other traditions, such as washing cups, pots and bronze vessels.)

^{5} The *P'rushim* and the *Torah*-teachers asked him, "Why don't your *talmidim* live in accordance with the Tradition of the Elders, but instead eat with ritually unclean hands?" ^{6} Yeshua answered them, "Yesha'yahu was right when he prophesied about you hypocrites — as it is written,

> **'These people honor me with their lips,**
> **but their hearts are far away from me.**
> ^{7} **Their worship of me is useless,**
> **because they teach man-made rules as if they were doctrines.'**^{d}

^{8} "You depart from God's command and hold onto human tradition. ^{9} Indeed," he said to them, "you have made a fine art of departing from God's command in order to keep your tradition! ^{10} For Moshe said, '**Honor your father and your mother,**'^{e} and '**Anyone who curses his father or mother must be put to death.**'^{f} ^{11} But you say, 'If someone says to his father or mother, "I have promised as a *korban*" ' " (that is, as a gift to God) " ' "what I might have used to help you," ' ^{12} then you no longer let him do anything for his father or mother. ^{13} Thus, with your tradition which you had handed down to you, you nullify the Word of God! And you do other things like this."

^{14} Then Yeshua called the people to him again and said, "Listen to me, all of you, and understand this! ^{15} There is nothing outside a person which, by going into him, can make him unclean. Rather, it is the things that come out of a person which make a person unclean!" ^{16}*

^{17} When he had left the people and entered the house, his *talmidim* asked him about the parable. ^{18} He replied to them, "So you too are without understanding?

---

^{d} Isaiah 29:13 ^{e} Exodus 20:12; Deuteronomy 5:16 ^{f} Exodus 21:17; Leviticus 20:9
*Some manuscripts include verse 7:16: "Anyone who has ears that can hear, let him hear!"

Don't you see that nothing going into a person from outside can make him unclean? [19] For it doesn't go into his heart but into his stomach, and it passes out into the latrine." (Thus he declared all foods ritually clean.) [20] "It is what comes out of a person," he went on, "that makes him unclean. [21] For from within, out of a person's heart, come forth wicked thoughts, sexual immorality, theft, murder, adultery, [22] greed, malice, deceit, indecency, envy, slander, arrogance, foolishness.... [23] All these wicked things come from within, and they make a person unclean."

[24] Next, Yeshua left that district and went off to the vicinity of Tzor and Tzidon. There he found a house to stay in and wanted to remain unrecognized, but keeping hidden proved impossible. [25] Instead, a woman whose little daughter had an unclean spirit in her came to him and fell down at his feet. [26] The woman was a Greek, by birth a Syro-phoenician, and she begged him to drive the demon out of her daughter. [27] He said, "Let the children be fed first, for it is not right to take the children's food and toss it to their pet dogs." [28] She answered him, "That is true, sir; but even the dogs under the table eat the children's leftovers." [29] Then he said to her, "For such an answer you may go on home; the demon has left your daughter." [30] She went back home and found the child lying on the couch, the demon gone.

[31] Then he left the district of Tzor and went through Tzidon to Lake Kinneret and on to the region of the Ten Towns. [32] They brought him a man who was deaf and had a speech impediment and asked Yeshua to lay his hand on him. [33] Taking him off alone, away from the crowd, Yeshua put his fingers into the man's ears, spat, and touched his tongue; [34] then, looking up to heaven, he gave a deep groan and said to him, "*Hippatach!*" (that is, "Be opened!"). [35] His ears were opened, his tongue was freed, and he began speaking clearly. [36] Yeshua ordered the people to tell no one; but the more he insisted, the more zealously they spread the news. [37] People were overcome with amazement. "Everything he does, he does well!" they said. "He even makes the deaf hear and the dumb speak!"

8 [1] It was during that time that another large crowd gathered, and they had nothing to eat. Yeshua called his *talmidim* to him and said to them, [2] "I feel sorry for these people, because they have been with me three days, and now they have nothing to eat. [3] If I send them off to their homes hungry, they will collapse on the way; some of them have come a long distance." [4] His *talmidim* said to him, "How can anyone find enough bread to satisfy these people in a remote place like this?" [5] "How many loaves do you have?" he asked them. They answered, "Seven." [6] He then told the crowd to sit down on the ground, took the seven loaves, made a *b'rakhah*, broke the loaves and gave them to his *talmidim* to serve to the people. [7] They also had a few fish; making a *b'rakhah* over them he also ordered these to be served. [8] The people ate their fill; and the *talmidim* took up the leftover pieces, seven large basketsful. [9] About four thousand were there. [10] After sending them away, Yeshua got into the boat with his *talmidim* and went off to the district of Dalmanuta.

[11] The *P'rushim* came and began arguing with him; they wanted him to give them a sign from Heaven, because they were out to trap him. [12] With a sigh that came straight from his heart, he said, "Why does this generation want a sign? Yes! I tell you, no sign will be given to this generation!" [13] With that, he left them, got into the boat again and went off to the other side of the lake.

^{14} Now the *talmidim* had forgotten to bring bread and had with them in the boat only one loaf. ^{15} So when Yeshua said to them, "Watch out! Guard yourselves from the *hametz* of the *P'rushim* and the *hametz* of Herod," ^{16} they thought he had said it because they had no bread. ^{17} But, aware of this, he said, "Why are you talking with each other about having no bread? Don't you see or understand yet? Have your hearts been made like stone? ^{18} You have eyes — don't you see? You have ears — don't you hear? And don't you remember? ^{19} When I broke the five loaves for the five thousand, how many baskets full of broken pieces did you collect?" "Twelve," they answered him. ^{20} "And when I broke the seven loaves for the four thousand, how many baskets full of broken pieces did you collect?" "Seven," they answered. ^{21} He said to them, "And you still don't understand?"

^{22} They came to Beit-Tzaidah. Some people brought him a blind man and begged Yeshua to touch him. ^{23} Taking the blind man's hand, he led him outside the town. He spit in his eyes, put his hands on him and asked him, "Do you see anything?" ^{24} He looked up and said, "I see people, but they look like walking trees." ^{25} Then he put his hands on the blind man's eyes again. He peered intently, and his eyesight was restored, so that he could see everything distinctly. ^{26} Yeshua sent him home with the words, "Don't go into town."

^{27} Yeshua and his *talmidim* went on to the towns of Caesarea Philippi. On the way, he asked his *talmidim*, "Who are people saying I am?" ^{28} "Some say you are Yochanan the Immerser," they told him, "others say Eliyahu, and still others, one of the prophets." ^{29} "But you," he asked, "who do you say I am?" Kefa answered, "You are the *Mashiach*." ^{30} Then Yeshua warned them not to tell anyone about him. ^{31} He began teaching them that the Son of Man had to endure much suffering and be rejected by the elders, the head *cohanim* and the *Torah*-teachers; and that he had to be put to death; but that after three days, he had to rise again. ^{32} He spoke very plainly about it. Kefa took him aside and began rebuking him. ^{33} But, turning around and looking at his *talmidim*, he rebuked Kefa. "Get behind me, Satan!" he said, "For your thinking is from a human perspective, not from God's perspective!"

^{34} Then Yeshua called the crowd and his *talmidim* to him and told them, "If anyone wants to come after me, let him say 'No' to himself, take up his execution-stake, and keep following me. ^{35} For whoever wants to save his own life will destroy it, but whoever destroys his life for my sake and for the sake of the Good News will save it. ^{36} Indeed, what will it benefit a person if he gains the whole world but forfeits his life? ^{37} What could a person give in exchange for his life? ^{38} For if someone is ashamed of me and of what I say in this adulterous and sinful generation, the Son of Man also will be ashamed of him when he comes in his Father's glory with the holy angels. **9** ^{1} Yes!" he went on, "I tell you that there are some people standing here who will not experience death until they see the Kingdom of God come in a powerful way!"

^{2} Six days later, Yeshua took Kefa, Ya'akov and Yochanan and led them up a high mountain privately. As they watched, he began to change form, ^{3} and his clothes became dazzlingly white, whiter than anyone in the world could possibly bleach them. ^{4} Then they saw Eliyahu and Moshe speaking with Yeshua. ^{5} Kefa said to Yeshua, "It's good that we're here, Rabbi! Let's put up three shelters — one for you, one for Moshe and one for Eliyahu." ^{6} (He didn't know what to say, they were so frightened.) ^{7} Then a cloud enveloped them; and a voice came out of the cloud, "This is my

Son, whom I love. Listen to him!" ⁸ Suddenly, when they looked around, they no longer saw anyone with them except Yeshua.

⁹ As they came down the mountain, he warned them not to tell anyone what they had seen until after the Son of Man had risen from the dead. ¹⁰ So they kept the matter to themselves; but they continued asking each other, "What is this 'rising from the dead'?" ¹¹ They also asked him, "Why do the *Torah*-teachers say that Eliyahu has to come first?" ¹² "Eliyahu will indeed come first," he answered, "and he will restore everything. Nevertheless, why is it written in the *Tanakh* that the Son of Man must suffer much and be rejected? ¹³ There's more to it: I tell you that Eliyahu has come, and they did whatever they pleased to him, just as the *Tanakh* says about him."

¹⁴ When they got back to the *talmidim*, they saw a large crowd around them and some *Torah*-teachers arguing with them. ¹⁵ As soon as the crowd saw him, they were surprised and ran out to greet him. ¹⁶ He asked them, "What's the discussion about?" ¹⁷ One of the crowd gave him the answer: "Rabbi, I brought my son to you because he has an evil spirit in him that makes him unable to talk. ¹⁸ Whenever it seizes him, it throws him to the ground — he foams at the mouth, grinds his teeth and becomes stiff all over. I asked your *talmidim* to drive the spirit out, but they couldn't do it." ¹⁹ "People without any trust!" he responded. "How long will I be with you? How long must I put up with you? Bring him to me!" ²⁰ They brought the boy to him; and as soon as the spirit saw him, it threw the boy into a convulsion. ²¹ Yeshua asked the boy's father, "How long has this been happening to him?" "Ever since childhood," he said; ²² "and it often tries to kill him by throwing him into the fire or into the water. But if you can do anything, have pity on us and help us!" ²³ Yeshua said to him, "What do you mean, 'if you can'? Everything is possible to someone who has trust!" ²⁴ Instantly the father of the child exclaimed, "I do trust — help my lack of trust!" ²⁵ When Yeshua saw that the crowd was closing in on them, he rebuked the unclean spirit, saying to it, "You deaf and dumb spirit! I command you: come out of him, and never go back into him again!" ²⁶ Shrieking and throwing the boy into a violent fit, it came out. The boy lay there like a corpse, so that most of the people said he was dead. ²⁷ But Yeshua took him by the hand and raised him to his feet, and he stood up.

²⁸ After Yeshua had gone indoors, his *talmidim* asked him privately, "Why couldn't we drive it out?" ²⁹ He said to them "This is the kind of spirit that can be driven out only by prayer."

³⁰ After leaving that place, they went on through the Galil. Yeshua didn't want anyone to know, ³¹ because he was teaching his *talmidim*. He told them, "The Son of Man will be betrayed into the hands of men who will put him to death; but after he has been killed, three days later he will rise." ³² But they didn't understand what he meant, and they were afraid to ask him.

³³ They arrived at K'far-Nachum. When Yeshua was inside the house, he asked them, "What were you discussing as we were traveling?" ³⁴ But they kept quiet; because on the way, they had been arguing with each other about who was the greatest. ³⁵ He sat down, summoned the Twelve and said to them, "If anyone wants to be first, he must make himself last of all and servant of all." ³⁶ He took a child and stood him among them. Then he put his arms around him and said to them, ³⁷ "Whoever welcomes one such child in my name welcomes me, and whoever welcomes me welcomes not me but the One who sent me."

³⁸ Yochanan said to him, "Rabbi, we saw a man expelling demons in your name; and because he wasn't one of us, we told him to stop." ³⁹ But Yeshua said, "Don't stop him, because no one who works a miracle in my name will soon after be able to say something bad about me. ⁴⁰ For whoever is not against us is for us. ⁴¹ Indeed, whoever gives you even a cup of water to drink because you come in the name of the Messiah — yes! I tell you that he will certainly not lose his reward.

⁴² "Whoever ensnares one of these little ones who trust me — it would be better for him to have a millstone hung around his neck and be thrown in the sea. ⁴³ If your hand makes you sin, cut it off! Better that you should be maimed but obtain eternal life, rather than keep both hands and go to Gei-Hinnom, to unquenchable fire! ⁴⁴* ⁴⁵ And if your foot makes you sin, cut it off! Better that you should be lame but obtain eternal life, rather than keep both feet and be thrown into Gei-Hinnom! ⁴⁶* ⁴⁷ And if your eye makes you sin, pluck it out! Better that you should be one-eyed but enter the Kingdom of God, rather than keep both eyes and be thrown into Gei-Hinnom,

⁴⁸   **where their worm does not die,
and the fire is not quenched.**ᵍ

⁴⁹ Indeed, everyone is going to be salted with fire. ⁵⁰ Salt is excellent, but if it loses its saltiness, how will you season it? So have salt in yourselves — that is, be at peace with each other."

10 ¹ Then Yeshua left that place and went into the regions of Y'hudah and the territory beyond the Yarden. Again crowds gathered around him; and again, as usual, he taught them. ² Some *P'rushim* came up and tried to trap him by asking him, "Does the *Torah* permit a man to divorce his wife?" ³ He replied, "What did Moshe command you?" ⁴ They said, "Moshe allowed a man to **hand his wife a** *get* and divorce her."ʰ ⁵ But Yeshua said to them, "He wrote this commandment for you because of your hardheartedness. ⁶ However, at the beginning of creation, God **made them male and female.**ⁱ ⁷ **For this reason, a man should leave his father and mother and be united with his wife,** ⁸ **and the two are to become one flesh.**ʲ Thus they are no longer two, but one. ⁹ So then, no one should break apart what God has joined together." ¹⁰ When they were indoors once more, the *talmidim* asked him about this. ¹¹ He said to them, "Whoever divorces his wife and marries another woman commits adultery against his wife; ¹² and if a wife divorces her husband and marries another man, she too commits adultery."

¹³ People were bringing children to him so that he might touch them, but the *talmidim* rebuked those people. ¹⁴ However, when Yeshua saw it, he became indignant and said to them, "Let the children come to me, don't stop them, for the Kingdom of God belongs to such as these. ¹⁵ Yes! I tell you, whoever does not receive the Kingdom of God like a child will not enter it!" ¹⁶ And he took them in his arms, laid his hands on them, and made a *b'rakhah* over them.

¹⁷ As he was starting on his way, a man ran up, kneeled down in front of him and asked, "Good rabbi, what should I do to obtain eternal life?" ¹⁸ Yeshua said to him,

---

ᵍ Isaiah 66:24   ʰ Deuteronomy 24:1, 3   ⁱ Genesis 1:27, 5:2   ʲ Genesis 2:24
*Some manuscripts include identical verses 9:44, 46: **where their worm does not die, and the fire is not quenched.** (Isaiah 66:24)

"Why are you calling me good? No one is good except God! [19] You know the *mitzvot* — **'Don't murder, don't commit adultery, don't steal, don't give false testimony,** don't defraud, **honor your father and mother,**....'"[k] [20] "Rabbi," he said, "I have kept all these since I was a boy." [21] Yeshua, looking at him, felt love for him and said to him, "You're missing one thing. Go, sell whatever you own, give to the poor, and you will have riches in heaven. Then come, follow me!" [22] Shocked by this word, he went away sad; because he was a wealthy man.

[23] Yeshua looked around and said to his *talmidim,* "How hard it is going to be for people with wealth to enter the Kingdom of God!" [24] The *talmidim* were astounded at these words; but Yeshua said to them again, "My friends, how hard it is to enter the Kingdom of God! [25] It's easier for a camel to pass through a needle's eye than for a rich man to enter the Kingdom of God." [26] They were utterly amazed and said to him, "Then who can be saved?" [27] Yeshua looked at them and said, "Humanly, it is impossible, but not with God; with God, everything is possible." [28] Kefa began saying to him, "Look, we have left everything and followed you." [29] Yeshua said, "Yes! I tell you that there is no one who has left house, brothers, sisters, mother, father, children or fields, for my sake and for the sake of the Good News, [30] who will not receive a hundred times over, now, in the *'olam hazeh,* homes, brothers, sisters, mothers, children and lands — with persecutions! — and in the *'olam haba,* eternal life. [31] But many who are first will be last, and many who are last will be first!"

[32] They were on the road going up to Yerushalayim. Yeshua was walking ahead of them, and they were amazed — and those following were afraid. So again taking the Twelve along with him, he began telling them what was about to happen to him. [33] "We are now going up to Yerushalayim, where the Son of Man will be handed over to the head *cohanim* and the *Torah*-teachers. They will sentence him to death and turn him over to the *Goyim,* [34] who will **jeer at him, spit on him, beat him** and kill him; but **after three days, he will rise.**"[l]

[35] Ya'akov and Yochanan, the sons of Zavdai, came up to him and said, "Rabbi, we would like you to do us a favor." [36] He said to them, "What do you want me to do for you?" [37] They replied, "When you are in your glory, let us sit with you, one on your right and the other on your left." [38] But Yeshua answered, "You don't know what you're asking! Can you drink the cup that I am drinking? or be immersed with the immersion that I must undergo?" [39] They said to him, "We can." Yeshua replied, "The cup that I am drinking, you will drink; and the immersion I am being immersed with, you will undergo. [40] But to sit on my right and on my left is not mine to give. Rather, it is for those for whom it has been prepared."

[41] When the other ten heard about this, they became outraged at Ya'akov and Yochanan. [42] But Yeshua called them to him and said to them, "You know that among the *Goyim,* those who are supposed to rule them become tyrants, and their superiors become dictators. [43] But among you, it must not be like that! On the contrary, whoever among you wants to be a leader must be your servant; [44] and whoever wants to be first among you must become everyone's slave! [45] For the Son of Man did not come to be served, but to serve — and to give his life as a ransom for many."

---

[k] Exodus 20:12–13(16); Deuteronomy 5:16–17(20)   [l] Isaiah 50:6, Hosea 6:2

⁴⁶ They came to Yericho; and as Yeshua was leaving Yericho with his *talmidim* and a great crowd, a blind beggar, Bar-Timai (son of Timai), was sitting by the side of the road. ⁴⁷ When he heard that it was Yeshua from Natzeret, he started shouting, "Yeshua! Son of David! Have pity on me!" ⁴⁸ Many people scolded him and told him to be quiet, but he shouted all the louder, "Son of David! Have pity on me!" ⁴⁹ Yeshua stopped and said, "Call him over!" They called to the blind man, "Courage! Get up! He's calling for you!" ⁵⁰ Throwing down his blanket, he jumped up and came over to Yeshua. ⁵¹ "What do you want me to do for you?" asked Yeshua. The blind man said to him, "Rabbi, let me be able to see again." ⁵² Yeshua said to him, "Go! Your trust has healed you." Instantly he received his sight and followed him on the road.

11 ¹ As they were approaching Yerushalayim, near Beit-Pagei and Beit-Anyah, by the Mount of Olives, Yeshua sent two of his *talmidim* ² with these instructions: "Go into the village ahead of you; and as soon as you enter it, you will find a colt tied there that has never been ridden. Untie it, and bring it here. ³ If anyone asks you, 'Why are you doing this?' tell him, 'The Lord needs it,' and he will send it here right away."

⁴ They went off and found a colt in the street tied in a doorway, and they untied it. ⁵ The bystanders said to them, "What are you doing, untying that colt?" ⁶ They gave the answer Yeshua had told them to give, and they let them continue. ⁷ They brought the colt to Yeshua and threw their robes on it, and he sat on it.

⁸ Many people carpeted the road with their clothing, while others spread out green branches which they had cut in the fields. ⁹ Those who were ahead and those behind shouted,

> **"Please! Deliver us!"** *ᵐ* *

> **"Blessed is he who comes in the name of A**DONAI**!"** *ⁿ*

¹⁰   "Blessed is the coming Kingdom of our father David!"

and,

> **"You in the highest heaven! Please! Deliver us!"** *ᵒ* *

¹¹ Yeshua entered Yerushalayim, went into the Temple courts and took a good look at everything; but since it was now late, he went out with the Twelve to Beit-Anyah.

¹² The next day, as they came back from Beit-Anyah, he felt hungry. ¹³ Spotting in the distance a fig tree in leaf, he went to see if he could find anything on it. When he came up to it, he found nothing but leaves; for it wasn't fig season. ¹⁴ He said to it, "May no one ever eat fruit from you again!" And his *talmidim* heard what he said.

¹⁵ On reaching Yerushalayim, he entered the Temple courts and began driving out those who were carrying on business there, both the merchants and their customers. He also knocked over the desks of the money-changers, upset the benches of the pigeon-dealers, ¹⁶ and refused to let anyone carry merchandise through the Temple courts. ¹⁷ Then, as he taught them, he said, "Isn't it written in the *Tanakh*, '**My house**

ᵐ Psalm 118:25   ⁿ Psalm 118:26   ᵒ Psalm 118:25
*See note, p. 1249.

will be called a house of prayer for all the *Goyim*.'[p] But you have made it into a
den of robbers!"[q] 18 The head *cohanim* and the *Torah*-teachers heard what he said
and tried to find a way to do away with him; they were afraid of him, because the
crowds were utterly taken by his teaching. 19 When evening came, they left the city.
20 In the morning, as the *talmidim* passed by, they saw the fig tree withered all
the way to its roots. 21 Kefa remembered and said to Yeshua, "Rabbi! Look! The fig
tree that you cursed has dried up!" 22 He responded, "Have the kind of trust that
comes from God! 23 Yes! I tell you that whoever does not doubt in his heart but trusts
that what he says will happen can say to this mountain, 'Go and throw yourself into
the sea!' and it will be done for him. 24 Therefore, I tell you, whatever you ask for in
prayer, trust that you are receiving it, and it will be yours. 25 And when you stand
praying, if you have anything against anyone, forgive him; so that your Father in
heaven may also forgive your offenses." 26 *
27 They went back into Yerushalayim; and as he was walking in the Temple
courts, there came to him the head *cohanim*, the *Torah*-teachers and the elders; 28 and
they said to him, "What *s'mikhah* do you have that authorizes you to do these things?
Who gave you this *s'mikhah* authorizing you to do them?" 29 Yeshua said to them, "I
will ask you just one question: answer me, and I will tell you by what *s'mikhah* I do
these things. 30 The immersion of Yochanan — was it from Heaven or from a human
source? Answer me." 31 They discussed it among themselves: "If we say, 'From
Heaven,' he will say, 'Then why didn't you believe him?' 32 But if we say, 'From a
human source, . . .' " — they were afraid of the people, for they all regarded Yochanan
as a genuine prophet. 33 So they answered Yeshua, "We don't know." "Then," he
replied, "I won't tell you by what *s'mikhah* I do these things."

12 1 Yeshua began speaking to them in parables. "A man planted a vineyard. He put
a wall around it, dug a pit for the wine press and built a tower; then he rented it
to tenant-farmers and left. 2 When harvest-time came, he sent a servant to the
tenants to collect his share of the crop from the vineyard. 3 But they took him,
beat him up and sent him away empty-handed. 4 So he sent another servant; this
one they punched in the head and insulted. 5 He sent another one, and him they
killed; and so with many others — some they beat up, others they killed. 6 He
had still one person left, a son whom he loved; in the end, he sent him to them,
saying, 'My son they will respect.' 7 But the tenants said to each other, 'This is
the heir. Come, let's kill him, and the inheritance will be ours!' 8 So they seized
him, killed him and threw him out of the vineyard. 9 What will the owner of the
vineyard do? He will come, destroy those tenants and give the vineyard to others!
10 Haven't you read the passage in the *Tanakh* that says,

'The very rock which the builders rejected
has become the cornerstone!
11 **This has come from *Adonai*,**
and in our eyes it is amazing'?"[r]

[p] Isaiah 56:7 [q] Jeremiah 7:11 [r] Psalm 118:22–23
* Some manuscripts include verse 11:26: But if you do not forgive, your Father in heaven will not forgive your offenses."

[12] They set about to arrest him, for they recognized that he had told the parable with reference to themselves. But they were afraid of the crowd, so they left him and went away.

[13] Next they sent some *P'rushim* and some members of Herod's party to him in order to trap him with a *sh'eilah*. [14] They came and said to him, "Rabbi, we know that you tell the truth and are not concerned with what people think about you, since you pay no attention to a person's status but really teach what God's way is. Does *Torah* say that taxes are to be paid to the Roman Emperor, or not?" [15] But he, knowing their hypocrisy, said to them, "Why are you trying to trap me? Bring me a denarius so I can look at it." [16] They brought one; and he asked them, "Whose name and picture are these?" "The Emperor's," they replied. [17] Yeshua said, "Give the Emperor what belongs to the Emperor. And give to God what belongs to God!" And they were amazed at him.

[18] Then some *Tz'dukim* came to him. They are the ones who say there is no such thing as resurrection, so they put to him a *sh'eilah*: [19] "Rabbi, Moshe wrote for us that **if a man's brother dies and leaves a wife but no child, his brother must take the wife and have children to preserve the man's family line.**[s] [20] There were seven brothers. The first one took a wife, and when he died, he left no children. [21] Then the second one took her and died without leaving children, and the third likewise, [22] and none of the seven left children. Last of all, the woman also died. [23] In the Resurrection, whose wife will she be? For all seven had her as wife."

[24] Yeshua said to them, "Isn't this the reason that you go astray? because you are ignorant both of the *Tanakh* and of the power of God? [25] For when people rise from the dead, neither men nor women marry — they are like angels in heaven. [26] And as for the dead being raised, haven't you read in the book of Moshe, in the passage about the bush, how God said to him, '**I am the God of Avraham, the God of Yitz'chak and the God of Ya'akov**'?[t27] He is God not of the dead, but of the living! You are going far astray!"

[28] One of the *Torah*-teachers came up and heard them engaged in this discussion. Seeing that Yeshua answered them well, he asked him, "Which is the most important *mitzvah* of them all?" [29] Yeshua answered, "The most important is,

> '**Sh'ma Yisra'el, ADONAI Eloheinu, ADONAI echad** [Hear, O Isra'el, the LORD our God, the LORD is one], [30] **and you are to love ADONAI your God with all your heart, with all your soul,** with all your understanding **and with all your strength.**'[u]

[31] The second is this:

> '**You are to love your neighbor as yourself.**'[v]

There is no other *mitzvah* greater than these." [32] The *Torah*-teacher said to him, "Well said, Rabbi; you speak the truth when you say that he is one, and that there is no other besides him; [33] and that loving him with all one's heart, understanding and strength, and loving one's neighbor as oneself, mean more than all the burnt offerings

---

[s] Deuteronomy 25:5–6   [t] Exodus 3:6   [u] Deuteronomy 6:4–5   [v] Leviticus 19:18

and sacrifices." ³⁴ When Yeshua saw that he responded sensibly, he said to him, "You are not far from the Kingdom of God." And after that, no one dared put to him another *sh'eilah*.

³⁵ As Yeshua was teaching in the Temple, he asked, "How is it that the *Torah*-teachers say the Messiah is the Son of David? ³⁶ David himself, inspired by the *Ruach HaKodesh*, said,

> '*Adonai* said to my Lord,
> **"Sit here at my right hand**
> **until I put your enemies under your feet."** ʷ

³⁷ David himself calls him 'Lord'; so how is he his son?"

The great crowd listened eagerly to him. ³⁸ As he taught them, he said, "Watch out for the kind of *Torah*-teachers who like to walk around in robes and be greeted deferentially in the marketplaces, ³⁹ who like to have the best seats in the synagogues and take the places of honor at banquets, ⁴⁰ who like to swallow up widows' houses while making a show of *davvening* at great length. Their punishment will be all the worse!"

⁴¹ Then Yeshua sat down opposite the Temple treasury and watched the crowd as they put money into the offering-boxes. Many rich people put in large sums, ⁴² but a poor widow came and put in two small coins. ⁴³ He called his *talmidim* to him and said to them, "Yes! I tell you, this poor widow has put more in the offering-box than all the others making donations. ⁴⁴ For all of them, out of their wealth, have contributed money they can easily spare; but she, out of her poverty, has given everything she had to live on."

13 ¹ As Yeshua came out of the Temple, one of the *talmidim* said to him, "Look, Rabbi! What huge stones! What magnificent buildings!" ² "You see all these great buildings?" Yeshua said to him, "They will be totally destroyed — not a single stone will be left standing!"

³ As he was sitting on the Mount of Olives opposite the Temple, Kefa, Ya'akov, Yochanan and Andrew asked him privately, ⁴ "Tell us, when will these things happen? And what sign will show when all these things are about to be accomplished?"

⁵ Yeshua began speaking to them: "Watch out! Don't let anyone fool you! ⁶ Many will come in my name, saying, 'I am he!' and they will fool many people. ⁷ When you hear the noise of wars nearby and the news of wars far off, don't become frightened. Such things must happen, but the end is yet to come. ⁸ For peoples will fight each other, and nations will fight each other, there will be earthquakes in various places, there will be famines; this is but the beginning of the 'birth pains.'

⁹ "But you, watch yourselves! They will hand you over to the local *Sanhedrin*s, you will be beaten up in synagogues, and on my account you will stand before governors and kings as witnesses to them. ¹⁰ Indeed, the Good News has to be proclaimed first to all the *Goyim*. ¹¹ Now when they arrest you and bring you to trial, don't worry beforehand about what to say. Rather, say whatever is given you when the time comes; for it will not be just you speaking, but the *Ruach HaKodesh*. ¹² Brother will betray brother to death, and a father his child; children will turn against

---

ʷ Psalm 110:1

their parents and have them put to death; ¹³ and everyone will hate you because of me. But whoever holds out till the end will be delivered.

¹⁴ "Now when you see **the abomination that causes devastation**ˣ standing where it ought not to be" (let the reader understand the allusion), "that will be the time for those in Y'hudah to escape to the hills. ¹⁵ If someone is on the roof, he must not go down and enter his house to take any of his belongings; ¹⁶ if someone is in the field, he must not turn back to get his coat. ¹⁷ What a terrible time it will be for pregnant women and nursing mothers! ¹⁸ Pray that it may not happen in winter. ¹⁹ For there will be **worse trouble** at that time **than there has ever been from the very beginning,** when God created the universe, **until now; and there will be nothing like it again.**ʸ ²⁰ Indeed, if God had not limited the duration of the trouble, no one would survive; but for the sake of the elect, those whom he has chosen, he has limited it.

²¹ "At that time, if anyone says to you, 'Look! Here's the Messiah!' or, 'See, there he is!' — don't believe him! ²² There will appear false Messiahs and false prophets performing signs and wonders for the purpose, if possible, of misleading the chosen. ²³ But you, watch out! I have told you everything in advance! ²⁴ In those days, after that trouble,

> **the sun will grow dark,**
> **the moon will stop shining,**
> ²⁵ **the stars will fall from the sky,**
> **and the powers in heaven will be shaken.**ᶻ

²⁶ Then they will see **the Son of Man coming in clouds** with tremendous power and glory.ᵃ ²⁷ He will send out his angels and gather together his chosen people from the four winds, from the ends of the earth to the ends of heaven.

²⁸ "Now let the fig tree teach you its lesson: when its branches begin to sprout and leaves appear, you know that summer is approaching. ²⁹ In the same way, when you see all these things happening, you are to know that the time is near, right at the door. ³⁰ Yes! I tell you that this people will certainly not pass away before all these things happen. ³¹ Heaven and earth will pass away, but my words will certainly not pass away. ³² However, when that day and hour will come, no one knows — not the angels in heaven, not the Son, just the Father. ³³ Stay alert! Be on your guard! For you do not know when the time will come.

³⁴ "It's like a man who travels away from home, puts his servants in charge, each with his own task, and tells the doorkeeper to stay alert. ³⁵ So stay alert! for you don't know when the owner of the house will come, ³⁶ whether it will be evening, midnight, cockcrow or morning — you don't want him to come suddenly and find you sleeping! ³⁷ And what I say to you, I say to everyone: stay alert!"

14 ¹ It was now two days before *Pesach* (that is, the festival of *Matzah*), and the head *cohanim* and the *Torah*-teachers were trying to find some way to arrest Yeshua surreptitiously and have him put to death; ² for they said, "Not during the festival, or the people will riot."

ˣ Daniel 9:27; 11:31; 12:11   ʸ Joel 2:2; Daniel 12:1   ᶻ Isaiah 13:10; 34:4; Ezekiel 32:7;
Joel 2:10; 3:4 (2:31); 4:15(3:15); Haggai 2:6, 21   ᵃ Daniel 7:13–14

[3] While he was in Beit-Anyah in the home of Shim'on (a man who had had *tzara'at*), and as he was eating, a woman came with an alabaster jar of perfume, pure oil of nard, very costly. She broke the jar and poured the perfume over Yeshua's head. [4] But some there angrily said to themselves, "Why this waste of perfume? [5] It could have been sold for a year's wages and given to the poor!" And they scolded her. [6] But he said, "Let her be. Why are you bothering her? She has done a beautiful thing for me. [7] For you will always have the poor with you; and whenever you want to, you can help them. But you will not always have me. [8] What she could do, she did do — in advance she poured perfume on my body to prepare it for burial. [9] Yes! I tell you that wherever in the whole world this Good News is proclaimed, what she has done will be told in her memory."

[10] Then Y'hudah from K'riot, who was one of the Twelve, went to the head *cohanim* in order to betray Yeshua to them. [11] They were pleased to hear this and promised to give him money. And he began looking for a good opportunity to betray Yeshua.

[12] On the first day for *matzah*, when they slaughtered the lamb for *Pesach*, Yeshua's *talmidim* asked him, "Where do you want us to go and prepare your *Seder*?" [13] He sent two of his *talmidim* with these instructions: "Go into the city, and a man carrying a jar of water will meet you. Follow him; [14] and whichever house he enters, tell him that the Rabbi says, 'Where is the guest room for me, where I am to eat the *Pesach* meal with my *talmidim*?' [15] He will show you a large room upstairs, furnished and ready. Make the preparations there." [16] The *talmidim* went off, came to the city and found things just as he had told them they would be; and they prepared the *Seder*.

[17] When evening came, Yeshua arrived with the Twelve. [18] As they were reclining and eating, Yeshua said, "Yes! I tell you that one of you is going to betray me." [19] They became upset and began asking him, one after the other, "You don't mean me, do you?" [20] "It's one of the Twelve," he said to them, "someone dipping *matzah* in the dish with me. [21] For the Son of Man will die, just as the *Tanakh* says he will; but woe to that man by whom the Son of Man is betrayed! It would have been better for him had he never been born!"

[22] While they were eating, Yeshua took a piece of *matzah*, made the *b'rakhah*, broke it, gave it to them and said, "Take it! This is my body." [23] Also he took a cup of wine, made the *b'rakhah*, and gave it to them; and they all drank. [24] He said to them, "This is my blood, which ratifies the New Covenant, my blood shed on behalf of many people. [25] Yes! I tell you, I will not drink this 'fruit of the vine' again until the day I drink new wine in the Kingdom of God."

[26] After singing the *Hallel*, they went out to the Mount of Olives. [27] Yeshua said to them, "You will all lose faith in me, for the *Tanakh* says,

**'I will strike the shepherd dead,
and the sheep will be scattered.'**[b]

[28] But after I have been raised, I will go ahead of you into the Galil." [29] Kefa said to him, "Even if everyone else loses faith in you, I won't." [30] Yeshua replied, "Yes! I tell you that this very night, before the rooster crows twice, you will disown me three

---

[b] Zechariah 13:7

times!" [31] But Kefa kept insisting, "Even if I must die with you, I will never disown you!" And they all said the same thing.

[32] They went to a place called Gat Sh'manim; and Yeshua said to his *talmidim*, "Sit here while I pray." [33] He took with him Kefa, Ya'akov and Yochanan. Great distress and anguish came over him; [34] and he said to them, "My heart is so filled with sadness that I could die! Remain here and stay awake." [35] Going on a little farther, he fell on the ground and prayed that if possible, the hour might pass from him; [36] "*Abba!*" (that is, "Dear Father!") "All things are possible for you. Take this cup away from me! Still, not what I want, but what you want." [37] He came and found them sleeping; and he said to Kefa, "Shim'on, are you asleep? Couldn't you stay awake one hour? [38] Stay awake, and pray that you will not be put to the test — the spirit indeed is eager, but human nature is weak."

[39] Again he went away and prayed, saying the same words; [40] and again he came and found them sleeping, their eyes were so very heavy; and they didn't know what to answer him.

[41] The third time, he came and said to them, "For now, go on sleeping, take your rest. . . .There, that's enough! The time has come! Look! The Son of Man is being betrayed into the hands of sinners! [42] Get up! Let's go! Here comes my betrayer!"

[43] While Yeshua was still speaking, Y'hudah (one of the Twelve!) came, and with him a crowd carrying swords and clubs, from the head *cohanim*, the *Torah*-teachers and the elders. [44] The betrayer had arranged to give them a signal: "The man I kiss is the one you want. Grab him, and take him away under guard." [45] As he arrived, he went right up to Yeshua, said, "Rabbi!" and kissed him. [46] Then they laid hold of Yeshua and arrested him; [47] but one of the people standing nearby drew his sword and struck at the servant of the *cohen hagadol*, cutting off his ear.

[48] Yeshua addressed them: "So you came out to take me with swords and clubs, the way you would the leader of a rebellion? [49] Every day I was with you in the Temple court, teaching, and you didn't seize me then! But let the *Tanakh* be fulfilled." [50] And they all deserted him and ran away. [51] There was one young man who did try to follow him; but he was wearing only a nightshirt; and when they tried to seize him, [52] he slipped out of the nightshirt and ran away naked.

[53] They led Yeshua to the *cohen hagadol*, with whom all the head *cohanim*, elders and *Torah*-teachers were assembling. [54] Kefa followed him at a distance right into the courtyard of the *cohen hagadol*, where he sat down with the guards and warmed himself by the fire.

[55] The head *cohanim* and the whole *Sanhedrin* tried to find evidence against Yeshua, so that they might have him put to death, but they couldn't find any. [56] For many people gave false evidence against him, but their testimonies didn't agree. [57] Some stood up and gave this false testimony: [58] "We heard him say, 'I will destroy this Temple made with hands; and in three days I will build another one, not made with hands.'" [59] Even so, their testimonies didn't agree.

[60] The *cohen hagadol* stood up in the front and asked Yeshua, "Have you nothing to say to the accusations these men are making?" [61] But he remained silent and made no reply. Again the *cohen hagadol* questioned him: "Are you the *Mashiach*, *Ben-HaM'vorakh?*" [62] "I AM," answered Yeshua. "Moreover, you will see **the Son of Man sitting at the right hand of** *HaG'vurah* and **coming on the clouds**

of heaven."[c] [63] At this, the *cohen hagadol* tore his clothes and said, "Why do we still need witnesses? [64] You heard him blaspheme! What is your decision?" And they all declared him guilty and subject to the death penalty.

[65] Then some began spitting at him; and after blindfolding him, they started pounding him with their fists and saying to him, "Let's see you prophesy!" And as the guards took him, they beat him too.

[66] Meanwhile, Kefa was still in the courtyard below. One of the serving-girls of the *cohen hagadol* [67] saw Kefa warming himself, took a look at him, and said, "You were with the man from Natzeret, Yeshua!" [68] But he denied it, saying, "I haven't the faintest idea what you're talking about!" He went outside into the entryway, and a rooster crowed. [69] The girl saw him there and started telling the bystanders, "This fellow is one of them." [70] Again he denied it. A little later, the bystanders themselves said to Kefa, "You must be one of them, because you're from the Galil." [71] At this he began to invoke a curse on himself as he swore, "I do not know this man you are telling me about!" — [72] and immediately the rooster crowed a second time. Then Kefa remembered what Yeshua had said to him, "Before the rooster crows twice, you will disown me three times." And throwing himself down, he burst into tears.

15 [1] As soon as it was morning, the head *cohanim* held a council meeting with the elders, the *Torah*-teachers and the whole *Sanhedrin*. Then they put Yeshua in chains, led him away and handed him over to Pilate. [2] Pilate put this question to him: "Are you the King of the Jews?" He answered him, "The words are yours." [3] The head *cohanim* too made accusations against him, [4] and Pilate again inquired of him, "Aren't you going to answer? Look how many charges they are making against you!" [5] But Yeshua made no further response, to Pilate's amazement.

[6] Now during a festival, Pilate used to set free one prisoner, whomever the crowd requested. [7] There was in prison among the rebels who had committed murder during the insurrection a man called Bar-Abba. [8] When the crowd came up and began asking Pilate to do for them what he usually did, [9] he asked them, "Do you want me to set free for you the 'King of the Jews'?" [10] For it was evident to him that it was out of jealousy that the head *cohanim* had handed him over. [11] But the head *cohanim* stirred up the crowd to have him release Bar-Abba for them instead. [12] Pilate again said to them, "Then what should I do with the man you call the King of the Jews?" [13] They shouted back, "Put him to death on the stake!" [14] He asked, "Why? What crime has he committed?" But they only shouted louder, "Put him to death on the stake!" [15] So Pilate, wishing to satisfy the mob, set Bar-Abba free for them; but he had Yeshua whipped and then handed him over to be executed on the stake.

[16] The soldiers led him away inside the palace (that is, the headquarters building) and called together the whole battalion. [17] They dressed him in purple and wove thorn branches into a crown, which they put on him. [18] Then they began to salute him, "Hail to the King of the Jews!" [19] They hit him on the head with a stick, spat on him and kneeled in mock worship of him. [20] When they had finished ridiculing him, they took off the purple robe, put his own clothes back on him and led him away to be nailed to the execution-stake.

---

[c] Daniel 7:13; Psalm 110:1

²¹ A certain man from Cyrene, Shim'on, the father of Alexander and Rufus, was passing by on his way in from the country; and they forced him to carry the stake. ²² They brought Yeshua to a place called Gulgolta (which means "place of a skull"), ²³ and they gave him wine spiced with myrrh, but he didn't take it. ²⁴ Then they nailed him to the execution-stake; and they divided his clothes among themselves, throwing dice to determine what each man should get. ²⁵ It was nine in the morning when they nailed him to the stake. ²⁶ Over his head, the written notice of the charge against him read,

THE KING OF THE JEWS

²⁷ On execution-stakes with him they placed two robbers, one on his right and one on his left. ²⁸ * ²⁹ People passing by hurled insults at him, shaking their heads and saying, "Aha! So you can destroy the Temple, can you, and rebuild it in three days? ³⁰ Save yourself and come down from the stake!" ³¹ Likewise, the head *cohanim* and the *Torah*-teachers made fun of him, saying to each other, "He saved others, but he can't save himself!" ³² and, "So he's the Messiah, is he? The King of Isra'el? Let him come down now from the stake! If we see that, then we'll believe him!" Even the men nailed up with him insulted him.

³³ At noon, darkness covered the whole Land until three o'clock in the afternoon. ³⁴ At three, he uttered a loud cry, **"*Elohi! Elohi! L'mah sh'vaktani?*"** (which means, **"My God! My God! Why have you deserted me?"**)*ᵈ* ³⁵ On hearing this, some of the bystanders said, "Look! He's calling for Eliyahu!" ³⁶ One ran and soaked a sponge in **vinegar**, put it on a stick and **gave** it to him **to drink**.*ᵉ* "Wait!" he said, "Let's see if Eliyahu will come and take him down." ³⁷ But Yeshua let out a loud cry and gave up his spirit. ³⁸ And the *parokhet* in the Temple was torn in two from top to bottom. ³⁹ When the Roman officer who stood facing him saw the way he gave up his spirit, he said, "This man really was a son of God!"

⁴⁰ There were women looking on from a distance; among them were Miryam from Magdala, Miryam the mother of the younger Ya'akov and of Yosi, and Shlomit. ⁴¹ These women had followed him and helped him when he was in the Galil. And many other women were there who had come up with him to Yerushalayim.

⁴² Since it was Preparation Day (that is, the day before a *Shabbat*), as evening approached, ⁴³ Yosef of Ramatayim, a prominent member of the *Sanhedrin* who himself was also looking forward to the Kingdom of God, went boldly to Pilate and asked for Yeshua's body. ⁴⁴ Pilate was surprised to hear that he was already dead, so he summoned the officer and asked him if he had been dead awhile. ⁴⁵ After he had gotten confirmation from the officer that Yeshua was dead, he granted Yosef the corpse. ⁴⁶ Yosef purchased a linen sheet; and after taking Yeshua down, he wrapped him in the linen sheet, laid him in a tomb which had been cut out of the rock, and rolled a stone against the entrance to the tomb. ⁴⁷ Miryam of Magdala and Miryam the mother of Yosi saw where he had been laid.

ᵈ Psalm 22:2(1)   *ᵉ* Psalm 69:22(21)

* Some manuscripts include verse 15:28: And the passage from the Tanakh was fulfilled which says, **"He was counted with transgressors."** (Isaiah 53:12)

16 [1] When *Shabbat* was over, Miryam of Magdala, Miryam the mother of Ya'akov, and Shlomit bought spices in order to go and anoint Yeshua. [2] Very early the next day, just after sunrise, they went to the tomb. [3] They were asking each other, "Who will roll away the stone from the entrance to the tomb for us?" [4] Then they looked up and saw that the stone, even though it was huge, had been rolled back already. [5] On entering the tomb, they saw a young man dressed in a white robe sitting on the right; and they were dumbfounded. [6] But he said, "Don't be so surprised! You're looking for Yeshua from Natzeret, who was executed on the stake. He has risen, he's not here! Look at the place where they laid him. [7] But go and tell his *talmidim*, especially Kefa, that he is going to the Galil ahead of you. You will see him there, just as he told you." [8] Trembling but ecstatic they went out and fled from the tomb, and they said nothing to anyone, because they were afraid.

*[9] When Yeshua rose early on Sunday, he appeared first to Miryam of Magdala, from whom he had expelled seven demons. [10] She went and told those who had been with him, as they were crying and mourning. [11] But when they heard that he was alive and that she had seen him, they wouldn't believe it.

[12] After that, Yeshua appeared in another form to two of them as they were walking into the country. [13] They went and told the others, but they didn't believe them either.

[14] Later, Yeshua appeared to the Eleven as they were eating, and he reproached them for their lack of trust and their spiritual insensitivity in not having believed those who had seen him after he had risen. [15] Then he said to them, "As you go throughout the world, proclaim the Good News to all creation. [16] Whoever trusts and is immersed will be saved; whoever does not trust will be condemned. [17] And these signs will accompany those who do trust: in my name they will drive out demons, speak with new tongues, [18] not be injured if they handle snakes or drink poison, and heal the sick by laying hands on them."

[19] So then, after he had spoken to them, the Lord Yeshua was taken up into heaven and **sat at the right hand of God**.*[20] And they went out and proclaimed everywhere, the Lord working with them and confirming the message by the accompanying signs.

---

[f] Psalm 110:1
*Verses 9–20 are found in many ancient Greek manuscripts but not in the two oldest ones.

The Good News of Yeshua the Messiah,
as Reported by

LUKE

1 ¹Dear Theophilos:

Concerning the matters that have taken place among us, many people have undertaken to draw up accounts ²based on what was handed down to us by those who from the start were eyewitnesses and proclaimers of the message. ³Therefore, Your Excellency, since I have carefully investigated all these things from the beginning, it seemed good to me that I too should write you an accurate and ordered narrative, ⁴so that you might know how well-founded are the things about which you have been taught.

⁵In the days of Herod, King of Y'hudah, there was a *cohen* named Z'kharyah who belonged to the Aviyah division. His wife was a descendant of Aharon, and her name was Elisheva. ⁶Both of them were righteous before God, observing all the *mitzvot* and ordinances of ADONAI blamelessly. ⁷But they had no children, because Elisheva was barren; and they were both well along in years.

⁸One time, when Z'kharyah was fulfilling his duties as *cohen* during his division's period of service before God, ⁹he was chosen by lot (according to the custom among the *cohanim*) to enter the Temple and burn incense. ¹⁰All the people were outside, praying, at the time of the incense burning, ¹¹when there appeared to him an angel of ADONAI standing to the right of the incense altar. ¹²Z'kharyah was startled and terrified at the sight. ¹³But the angel said to him, "Don't be afraid, Z'kharyah; because your prayer has been heard. Your wife Elisheva will bear you a son, and you are to name him Yochanan. ¹⁴He will be a joy and a delight to you, and many people will rejoice when he is born, ¹⁵for he will be great in the sight of ADONAI. He is never to drink wine or other liquor, and he will be filled with the *Ruach HaKodesh* even from his mother's womb. ¹⁶He will turn many of the people of Isra'el to ADONAI their God. ¹⁷He will go out ahead of ADONAI in the spirit and power of **Eliyahu** to **turn the hearts of fathers to their children**[a] and the disobedient to the wisdom of the righteous, to make ready for ADONAI a people prepared."

¹⁸Z'kharyah said to the angel, "How can I be sure of this? For I am an old man; my wife too is well on in years." ¹⁹"I am Gavri'el," the angel answered him, "and I stand in the presence of God. I was sent to speak to you, to give you this good news. ²⁰Now, because you didn't believe what I said, which will be fulfilled when the time comes, you will be silent, unable to speak until the day these things take place."

²¹Meanwhile, the people were waiting for Z'kharyah; they were surprised at his taking so long in the Temple. ²²But when he came out unable to talk to them, they realized that he had seen a vision in the Temple; speechless, he communicated to them with signs.

---

[a] Malachi 3:23–24(4:5–6)

²³ When the period of his Temple service was over, he returned home. ²⁴ Following this, Elisheva his wife conceived, and she remained five months in seclusion, saying, ²⁵ "*Adonai* has done this for me; he has shown me favor at this time, so as to remove my public disgrace."

²⁶ In the sixth month, the angel Gavri'el was sent by God to a city in the Galil called Natzeret, ²⁷ to a virgin engaged to a man named Yosef, of the house of David; the virgin's name was Miryam. ²⁸ Approaching her, the angel said, "*Shalom*, favored lady! *Adonai* is with you!" ²⁹ She was deeply troubled by his words and wondered what kind of greeting this might be. ³⁰ The angel said to her, "Don't be afraid, Miryam, for you have found favor with God. ³¹ Look! You will become pregnant, you will give birth to a son, and you are to name him Yeshua. ³² He will be great, he will be called Son of *Ha'Elyon*. *Adonai*, God, will give him the throne of his forefather David; ³³ and he will rule the House of Ya'akov forever — there will be no end to his Kingdom." ³⁴ "How can this be," asked Miryam of the angel, "since I am a virgin?" ³⁵ The angel answered her,

> "The *Ruach HaKodesh* will come over you,
> the power of *Ha'Elyon* will cover you.
> Therefore the holy child born to you
> will be called the Son of God.

³⁶ "You have a relative, Elisheva, who is an old woman; and everyone says she is barren. But she has conceived a son and is six months pregnant! ³⁷ For with God, nothing is impossible." ³⁸ Miryam said, "I am the servant of *Adonai*; may it happen to me as you have said." Then the angel left her.

³⁹ Without delay, Miryam set out and hurried to the town in the hill country of Y'hudah ⁴⁰ where Z'kharyah lived, entered his house and greeted Elisheva. ⁴¹ When Elisheva heard Miryam's greeting, the baby in her womb stirred. Elisheva was filled with the *Ruach HaKodesh* ⁴² and spoke up in a loud voice,

> "How blessed are you among women!
> And how blessed is the child in your womb!

⁴³ "But who am I, that the mother of my Lord should come to me? ⁴⁴ For as soon as the sound of your greeting reached my ears, the baby in my womb leaped for joy! ⁴⁵ Indeed you are blessed, because you have trusted that the promise *Adonai* has made to you will be fulfilled."

⁴⁶ Then Miryam said,

> **"My soul magnifies *Adonai*;**
> ⁴⁷ **and my spirit rejoices in God, my Savior,**
> ⁴⁸ who **has taken notice of** his **servant-girl**
> **in her humble position.**ᵇ
> For — imagine it! — from now on, all generations will call me blessed!
> ⁴⁹ "The Mighty One has done great things for me!

ᵇ 1 Samuel 1:11; 2:1

Indeed, **his name is holy**; [50] and in every generation
he has **mercy on those who fear him**.[c]

[51]   "He has performed mighty deeds with his arm,
            routed the secretly proud,
[52]   brought down rulers from their thrones,
            raised up the humble,
[53]   filled the hungry with good things,
            but sent the rich away empty.

[54]   "He has taken the part of his servant Isra'el,
            mindful of the mercy
[55]   which he promised to our fathers,
            to Avraham and his seed forever."

[56] Miryam stayed with Elisheva for about three months and then returned home.

[57] The time arrived for Elisheva to have her baby, and she gave birth to a
son. [58] Her neighbors and relatives heard how good ADONAI had been to her, and
they rejoiced with her.

[59] On the eighth day, they came to do the child's *b'rit-milah*. They were about to
name him Z'kharyah, after his father, [60] when his mother spoke up and said, "No, he
is to be called Yochanan." [61] They said to her, "None of your relatives has that name,"
[62] and they made signs to his father to find out what he wanted him called. [63] He
motioned for a writing tablet, and to everyone's surprise he wrote, "His name is
Yochanan." [64] At that moment, his power of speech returned, and his first words were
a *b'rakhah* to God. [65] All their neighbors were awestruck; and throughout the hill
country of Y'hudah, people talked about all these things. [66] Everyone who heard of
them said to himself, "What is this child going to be?" For clearly the hand of ADONAI
was with him.

[67] His father Z'kharyah was filled with the *Ruach HaKodesh* and spoke this
prophecy:

[68]   "**Praised be ADONAI, the God of Isra'el**,[d]
            because he has visited and made a ransom to liberate his people
[69]   by raising up for us a mighty Deliverer
            who is a descendant of his servant David.
[70]   It is just as he has spoken
            through the mouth of the prophets from the very beginning —
[71]   that we should be delivered from our enemies
            and from the power of all who hate us.

[72]   "This has happened so that he might show
            the mercy promised to our fathers —
        that he would remember his holy covenant,
[73]   the oath he swore before *Avraham avinu*

---

[c] Psalms 103:17; 111:9   [d] Psalms 41:14(13); 72:18; 106:48

74   to grant us that we, freed from our enemies,
        would serve him without fear,
75   in holiness and righteousness
        before him all our days.

76   You, child, will be called a prophet of *Ha'Elyon*;
        you will **go before the Lord to prepare his way**ᵉ
77   by spreading the knowledge among his people
        that deliverance comes by having sins forgiven
78   through our God's most tender mercy,
        which causes the Sunrise to visit us from Heaven,
79   to **shine on those in darkness, living in the shadow of death,**ᶠ
        and to guide our feet into the paths of peace."

⁸⁰ The child grew and became strong in spirit, and he lived in the wilderness until the time came for him to appear in public to Isra'el.

2 ¹ Around this time, Emperor Augustus issued an order for a census to be taken throughout the Empire. ² This registration, the first of its kind, took place when Quirinius was governing in Syria. ³ Everyone went to be registered, each to his own town. ⁴ So Yosef, because he was a descendant of David, went up from the town of Natzeret in the Galil to the town of David, called Beit-Lechem, in Y'hudah, ⁵ to be registered, with Miryam, to whom he was engaged, and who was pregnant. ⁶ While they were there, the time came for her to give birth; ⁷ and she gave birth to her first child, a son. She wrapped him in cloth and laid him down in a feeding trough, because there was no space for them in the living-quarters.

⁸ In the countryside nearby were some shepherds spending the night in the fields, guarding their flocks, ⁹ when an angel of *Adonai* appeared to them, and the *Sh'khinah* of *Adonai* shone around them. They were terrified; ¹⁰ but the angel said to them, "Don't be afraid, because I am here announcing to you Good News that will bring great joy to all the people. ¹¹ This very day, in the town of David, there was born for you a Deliverer who is the Messiah, the Lord. ¹² Here is how you will know: you will find a baby wrapped in cloth and lying in a feeding trough." ¹³ Suddenly, along with the angel was a vast army from heaven praising God:

14   "In the highest heaven, glory to God!
    And on earth, peace among people of good will!"

¹⁵ No sooner had the angels left them and gone back into heaven than the shepherds said to one another, "Let's go over to Beit-Lechem and see this thing that has happened, that *Adonai* has told us about." ¹⁶ Hurrying off, they came and found Miryam and Yosef, and the baby lying in the feeding trough. ¹⁷ Upon seeing this, they made known what they had been told about this child; ¹⁸ and all who heard were amazed by what the shepherds said to them. ¹⁹ Miryam treasured all these

---

ᵉ Malachi 3:1; Isaiah 40:3   ᶠ Isaiah 9:1(2)

things and kept mulling them over in her heart. [20]Meanwhile, the shepherds returned, glorifying and praising God for everything they had heard and seen; it had been just as they had been told.

[21] On the eighth day, when it was time for his *b'rit-milah*, he was given the name Yeshua, which is what the angel had called him before his conception.

[22] When the time came for their purification according to the *Torah* of Moshe, they took him up to Yerushalayim to present him to ADONAI [23] (as it is written in the *Torah* of ADONAI, "**Every firstborn male is to be consecrated to** ADONAI"[g]) [24] and also to offer a sacrifice of **a pair of doves or two young pigeons,**[h] as required by the *Torah* of ADONAI.

[25] There was in Yerushalayim a man named Shim'on. This man was a *tzaddik*, he was devout, he waited eagerly for God to comfort Isra'el, and the *Ruach HaKodesh* was upon him. [26] It had been revealed to him by the *Ruach HaKodesh* that he would not die before he had seen the Messiah of ADONAI. [27] Prompted by the Spirit, he went into the Temple courts; and when the parents brought in the child Yeshua to do for him what the *Torah* required, [28] Shim'on took him in his arms, made a *b'rakhah* to God, and said,

[29]   "Now, ADONAI, according to your word,
        your servant is at peace as you let him go;
[30]   for I have seen with my own eyes your *yeshu'ah*,
[31]   which you prepared in the presence of all peoples —
[32]   a light that will bring revelation to the *Goyim*
        and glory to your people Isra'el."

[33] Yeshua's father and mother were marvelling at the things Shim'on was saying about him. [34] Shim'on blessed them and said to the child's mother, Miryam,

    "This child will cause many in Isra'el to fall and to rise,
        he will become a sign whom people will speak against;
[35]   moreover, a sword will pierce your own heart too.
    All this will happen in order to reveal many people's inmost thoughts."

[36] There was also a prophet named Hannah Bat-P'nu'el, of the tribe of Asher. She was a very old woman — she had lived with her husband seven years after her marriage [37] and had remained a widow ever since; now she was eighty-four. She never left the Temple grounds but worshipped there night and day, fasting and praying. [38] She came by at that moment and began thanking God and speaking about the child to everyone who was waiting for Yerushalayim to be liberated.

[39] When Yosef and Miryam had finished doing everything required by the *Torah* of ADONAI, they returned to the Galil, to their town Natzeret.

[40] The child grew and became strong and filled with wisdom — God's favor was upon him.

[41] Every year Yeshua's parents went to Yerushalayim for the festival of *Pesach*. [42] When he was twelve years old, they went up for the festival, as custom required.

---

[g] Exodus 13:2, 12, 15   [h] Leviticus 12:8

^{43} But after the festival was over, when his parents returned, Yeshua remained in Yerushalayim. They didn't realize this; ^{44} supposing that he was somewhere in the caravan, they spent a whole day on the road before they began searching for him among their relatives and friends. ^{45} Failing to find him, they returned to Yerushalayim to look for him. ^{46} On the third day they found him — he was sitting in the Temple court among the rabbis, not only listening to them but questioning what they said; ^{47} and everyone who heard him was astonished at his insight and his responses. ^{48} When his parents saw him, they were shocked; and his mother said to him, "Son! Why have you done this to us? Your father and I have been terribly worried looking for you!" ^{49} He said to them, "Why did you have to look for me? Didn't you know that I had to be concerning myself with my Father's affairs?" ^{50} But they didn't understand what he meant.

^{51} So he went with them to Natzeret and was obedient to them. But his mother stored up all these things in her heart.

^{52} And Yeshua grew both in wisdom and in stature, gaining favor both with other people and with God.

3 ^{1} In the fifteenth year of Emperor Tiberius' rule; when Pontius Pilate was governor of Y'hudah, Herod ruler of the Galil, his brother Philip ruler of Iturea and Trachonitis, and Lysanias ruler of Abilene, ^{2} with 'Anan and Kayafa being the *cohanim g'dolim*; the word of God came to Yochanan Ben-Z'kharyah in the desert. ^{3} He went all through the Yarden region proclaiming an immersion involving turning to God from sin in order to be forgiven. ^{4} It was just as had been written in the book of the sayings of the prophet Yesha'yahu,

> **The voice of someone crying out:**
>   **'In the desert prepare the way for A*DONAI*!**
>   **Make straight paths for** him!
> ^{5} **Every valley must be filled in,**
>   **every mountain and hill leveled off;**
>   **the winding roads must be straightened**
>   **and the rough ways made smooth.**
> ^{6} **Then all humanity will see God's deliverance.'"**^{i}

^{7} Therefore, Yochanan said to the crowds who came out to be immersed by him, "You snakes! Who warned you to escape the coming punishment? ^{8} If you have really turned from your sins, produce fruit that will prove it! And don't start saying to yourselves, 'Avraham is our father'! For I tell you that God can raise up for Avraham sons from these stones! ^{9} Already the axe is at the root of the trees, ready to strike; every tree that doesn't produce good fruit will be chopped down and thrown in the fire!"

^{10} The crowds asked Yochanan, "So then, what should we do?" ^{11} He answered, "Whoever has two coats should share with somebody who has none, and whoever has food should do the same." ^{12} Tax-collectors also came to be immersed; and they asked him, "Rabbi, what should we do?" ^{13} "Collect no more than the government assesses," he told them. ^{14} Some soldiers asked him, "What about us? What should

---

^{i} Isaiah 40:3–5

we do?" To them he said, "Don't intimidate anyone, don't accuse people falsely, and be satisfied with your pay."

¹⁵ The people were in a state of great expectancy, and everyone was wondering whether perhaps Yochanan himself might be the Messiah; ¹⁶ so Yochanan answered them all, "I am immersing you in water, but he who is coming is more powerful than I — I'm not worthy to untie his sandals! He will immerse you in the *Ruach HaKodesh* and in fire. ¹⁷ He has with him his winnowing fork to clear out his threshing floor and gather his wheat into his barn, but he will burn up the straw with unquenchable fire!" ¹⁸ And with many other warnings besides these he announced the Good News to the people.

¹⁹ But Yochanan also denounced Herod the regional governor for taking as his own wife Herodias, the wife of his brother, and for all the other wicked things Herod had done; ²⁰ whereupon Herod added this to the rest: he locked up Yochanan in prison.

²¹ While all the people were being immersed, Yeshua too was immersed. As he was praying, heaven was opened; ²² the *Ruach HaKodesh* came down on him in physical form like a dove; and a voice came from heaven, "You are my Son, whom I love; I am well pleased with you."

²³ Yeshua was about thirty years old when he began his public ministry. It was supposed that he was a son of Yosef who was of Eli,
²⁴ of Mattat, of Levi, of Malki, of Yannai, of Yosef,
²⁵ of Mattityahu, of Amotz, of Nachum, of Hesli, of Naggai,
²⁶ of Machat, of Mattityahu, of Shim'i, of Yosef, of Yodah,
²⁷ of Yochanan, of Reisha, of Z'rubavel, of Sh'altiel, of Neri,
²⁸ of Malki, of Addi, of Kosam, of Elmadan, of Er,
²⁹ of Yeshua, of Eli'ezer, of Yoram, of Mattat, of Levi,
³⁰ of Shim'on, of Y'hudah, of Yosef, of Yonam, of Elyakim,
³¹ of Mal'ah, of Manah, of Mattatah, of Natan, of David,
³² of Yishai, of 'Oved, of Bo'az, of Salmon, of Nachshon,
³³ of Amminadav, of Admin, of Arni, of Hetzron, of Peretz, of Y'hudah,
³⁴ of Ya'akov, of Yitz'chak, of Avraham, of Terach, of Nachor,
³⁵ of S'rug, of Re'u, of Peleg, of 'Ever, of Shelah,
³⁶ of Keinan, of Arpakhshad, of Shem, of Noach, of Lemekh,
³⁷ of Metushelach, of Hanokh, of Yered, of Mahalal'el, of Keinan,
³⁸ of Enosh, of Shet, of Adam, of God.

4 ¹ Then Yeshua, filled with the *Ruach HaKodesh*, returned from the Yarden and was led by the Spirit in the wilderness ² for forty days of testing by the Adversary. During that time he ate nothing, and afterwards he was hungry. ³ The Adversary said to him, "If you are the Son of God, order this stone to become bread." ⁴ Yeshua answered him, "The *Tanakh* says, **'Man does not live on bread alone.'**"ʲ

⁵ The Adversary took him up, showed him in an instant all the kingdoms of the world, ⁶ and said to him, "I will give you all this power and glory. It has been handed over to me, and I can give it to whomever I choose. ⁷ So if you will worship me, it will all be yours." ⁸ Yeshua answered him, "The *Tanakh* says, **'Worship ADONAI your God and serve him** only.'"ᵏ

ʲ Deuteronomy 8:3   ᵏ Deuteronomy 6:13–14

⁹ Then he took him to Yerushalayim, set him on the highest point of the Temple and said to him, "If you are the Son of God, jump from here! ¹⁰ For the *Tanakh* says,

> '**He will order his angels**
> **to be responsible for you and to protect you.**
> ¹¹ **They will support you with their hands,**
> **so that you will not hurt your feet on the stones.**'"ˡ

¹² Yeshua answered him, "It also says, '**Do not put** Aᴅᴏɴᴀɪ **your God to the test.**'"ᵐ ¹³ When the Adversary had ended all his testings, he let him alone until an opportune time.

¹⁴ Yeshua returned to the Galil in the power of the Spirit, and reports about him spread throughout the countryside. ¹⁵ He taught in their synagogues, and everyone respected him.

¹⁶ Now when he went to Natzeret, where he had been brought up, on *Shabbat* he went to the synagogue as usual. He stood up to read, ¹⁷ and he was given the scroll of the prophet Yesha'yahu. Unrolling the scroll, he found the place where it was written,

> ¹⁸ **"The Spirit of** Aᴅᴏɴᴀɪ **is upon me**
> **because he has anointed me**
> **to announce Good News to the poor;**
> **he has sent me to proclaim freedom for the imprisoned**
> **and renewed sight for the blind,**
> **to release those who have been crushed,**
> ¹⁹ **to proclaim a year of the favor of** Aᴅᴏɴᴀɪ**."**ⁿ

²⁰ After closing the scroll and returning it to the *shammash*, he sat down; and the eyes of everyone in the synagogue were fixed on him. ²¹ He started to speak to them: "Today, as you heard it read, this passage of the *Tanakh* was fulfilled!" ²² Everyone was speaking well of him and marvelling that such appealing words were coming from his mouth. They were even asking, "Can this be Yosef's son?"

²³ Then Yeshua said to them, "No doubt you will quote to me this proverb — "'Doctor, cure yourself!' We've heard about all the things that have been going on over in K'far-Nachum; now do them here in your home town!' ²⁴ Yes!" he said, "I tell you that no prophet is accepted in his home town. ²⁵ It's true, I'm telling you — when Eliyahu was in Isra'el, and the sky was sealed off for three-and-a-half years, so that all the Land suffered a severe famine, there were many widows; ²⁶ but Eliyahu was sent to none of them, only to a widow in Tzarfat in the land of Tzidon. ²⁷ Also there were many people with *tzara'at* in Isra'el during the time of the prophet Elisha; but not one of them was healed, only Na'aman the Syrian."

²⁸ On hearing this, everyone in the synagogue was filled with fury. ²⁹ They rose up, drove him out of town and dragged him to the edge of the cliff on which their town was built, intending to throw him off. ³⁰ But he walked right through the middle of the crowd and went away.

ˡ Psalm 91:11–12   ᵐ Deuteronomy 6:16   ⁿ Isaiah 61:1–2; 58:6

[31] He went down to K'far-Nachum, a town in the Galil, and made a practice of teaching them on *Shabbat*. [32] They were amazed at the way he taught, because his word carried the ring of authority.

[33] In the synagogue there was a man who had an unclean demonic spirit, who shouted in a loud voice, [34] "Yaah! What do you want with us, Yeshua from Natzeret? Have you come to destroy us? I know who you are — the Holy One of God!" [35] But Yeshua rebuked it: "Be quiet, and come out of him!" The demonic spirit threw the man down in the middle of the crowd and came out of him, having done him no harm. [36] They were all astounded and said to one another, "What kind of teaching is this? Why, he gives orders with power and authority to the unclean spirits, and they come out!" [37] And reports about him went out through the whole surrounding district.

[38] Leaving the synagogue, he went to Shim'on's house. Shim'on's mother-in-law was suffering from a high fever, and they asked him to do something for her. [39] So, standing over her, he rebuked the fever; and it left her. She immediately got up and began helping them.

[40] After sunset, all those who had people sick with various diseases brought them to Yeshua, and he put his hands on each one of them and healed them; [41] also demons came out of many, crying, "You are the Son of God!" But, rebuking them, he did not permit them to say that they knew he was the Messiah.

[42] When day had come, he left and went away to a lonely spot. The people looked for him, came to him and would have kept him from leaving them. [43] But he said to them, "I must announce the Good News of the Kingdom of God to the other towns too — this is why I was sent." [44] He also spent time preaching in the synagogues of Y'hudah.

5 [1] One day, as Yeshua was standing on the shore of Lake Kinneret, with the people pressing in around him in order to hear the word of God, [2] he noticed two boats pulled up on the beach, left there by the fishermen, who were cleaning their nets. [3] He got into one of the boats, the one belonging to Shim'on, and asked him to put out a little way from shore. Then he sat down and taught the people from the boat.

[4] When he had finished speaking, he said to Shim'on, "Put out into deep water, and let down your nets for a catch." [5] Shim'on answered, "We've worked hard all night long, Rabbi, and haven't caught a thing! But if you say so, I'll let down the nets." [6] They did this and took in so many fish that their nets began to tear. [7] So they motioned to their partners in the other boat to come and help them; and they came and filled both boats to the point of sinking. [8] When he saw this, Shim'on Kefa fell at Yeshua's knees and said, "Get away from me, sir, because I'm a sinner!" [9] For astonishment had seized him and everyone with him at the catch of fish they had taken, [10] and likewise both Ya'akov and Yochanan, Shim'on's partners. "Don't be frightened," Yeshua said to Shim'on, "from now on you will be catching men — alive!" [11] And as soon as they had beached their boats, they left everything behind and followed him.

[12] Once, when Yeshua was in one of the towns, there came a man completely covered with *tzara'at*. On seeing Yeshua, he fell on his face and begged him, "Sir, if you are willing, you can make me clean." [13] Yeshua reached out his hand and touched him, saying, "I am willing! Be cleansed!" Immediately the *tzara'at* left him. [14] Then Yeshua warned him not to tell anyone. "Instead, as a testimony to the people, go straight to the *cohen* and make an offering for your cleansing, as Moshe commanded."

¹⁵ But the news about Yeshua kept spreading all the more, so that huge crowds would gather to listen and be healed of their sicknesses. ¹⁶ However, he made a practice of withdrawing to remote places in order to pray.

¹⁷ One day when Yeshua was teaching, there were *P'rushim* and *Torah*-teachers present who had come from various villages in the Galil and Y'hudah, also from Yerushalayim; and the power of ADONAI was with him to heal the sick. ¹⁸ Some men came carrying a paralyzed man lying on a bed. They wanted to bring him inside and lay him in front of Yeshua, ¹⁹ but they couldn't find a way to get him in because of the crowd. So they went up onto the roof and lowered him on his mattress through the tiles into the middle of the gathering, right in front of Yeshua. ²⁰ When Yeshua saw their trust, he said, "Friend, your sins are forgiven you." ²¹ The *Torah*-teachers and the *P'rushim* began thinking, "Who is this fellow that speaks such blasphemies? Who can forgive sin except God?" ²² But Yeshua, knowing what they were thinking, answered, "Why are you turning over such thoughts in your hearts? ²³ Which is easier to say? 'Your sins are forgiven you'? or 'Get up and walk'? ²⁴ But look! I will prove to you that the Son of Man has authority on earth to forgive sins." He then said to the paralytic, "I say to you: get up, pick up your mattress and go home!" ²⁵ Immediately, in front of everyone, he stood up, picked up what he had been lying on, and went home praising God. ²⁶ Amazement seized them all, and they made a *b'rakhah* to God; they were awestruck, saying, "We have seen extraordinary things today."

²⁷ Later Yeshua went out and saw a tax-collector named Levi sitting in his tax-collection booth; and he said to him, "Follow me!" ²⁸ He got up, left everything and followed him.

²⁹ Levi gave a banquet at his house in Yeshua's honor, and there was a large group of tax-collectors and others at the table with them. ³⁰ The *P'rushim* and their *Torah*-teachers protested indignantly against his *talmidim*, saying, "Why do you eat and drink with tax-collectors and sinners?" ³¹ It was Yeshua who answered them: "The ones who need a doctor aren't the healthy but the sick. ³² I have not come to call the 'righteous,' but rather to call sinners to turn to God from their sins."

³³ Next they said to him, "Yochanan's *talmidim* are always fasting and *davvening*, and likewise the *talmidim* of the *P'rushim*; but yours go on eating and drinking." ³⁴ Yeshua said to them, "Can you make wedding guests fast while the bridegroom is still with them? ³⁵ The time will come when the bridegroom will be taken away from them; and when that time comes, they will fast." ³⁶ Then he gave them an illustration: "No one tears a piece from a new coat and puts it on an old one; if he does, not only will the new one continue to rip, but the piece from the new will not match the old. ³⁷ Also, no one puts new wine into old wineskins; if he does, the new wine will burst the skins and be spilled, and the skins too will be ruined. ³⁸ On the contrary, new wine must be put into freshly prepared wineskins. ³⁹ Besides that, after drinking old wine, people don't want new; because they say, 'The old is good enough.'"

6 ¹ One *Shabbat*, while Yeshua was passing through some wheat fields, his *talmidim* began plucking the heads of grain, rubbing them between their hands and eating the seeds. ² Some of the *P'rushim* said, "Why are you violating *Shabbat*?" ³ Yeshua answered them, "Haven't you ever read what David did when he and his companions were hungry? ⁴ He entered the House of God and took and ate the Bread of the

Presence" — which no one is permitted to eat but the *cohanim*. [5] "The Son of Man," he concluded, "is Lord of *Shabbat*."

[6] On another *Shabbat*, when Yeshua had gone into the synagogue and was teaching, a man was there who had a shriveled hand. [7] The *Torah*-teachers and *P'rushim* watched Yeshua carefully to see if he would heal on *Shabbat*, so that they could accuse him of something. [8] But he knew what they were thinking and said to the man with the shriveled hand, "Come up and stand where we can see you!" He got up and stood there. [9] Then Yeshua said to them, "I ask you now: what is permitted on *Shabbat*? Doing good or doing evil? Saving life or destroying it?" [10] Then, after looking around at all of them, he said to the man, "Hold out your hand." As he held it out, his hand was restored. [11] But the others were filled with fury and began discussing with each other what they could do to Yeshua.

[12] It was around that time that Yeshua went out to the hill country to pray, and all night he continued in prayer to God. [13] When day came, he called his *talmidim* and chose from among them twelve to be known as emissaries:

[14] Shim'on, whom he named Kefa; Andrew, his brother; Ya'akov; Yochanan; Philip; Bar-Talmai;

[15] Mattityahu; T'oma; Ya'akov Ben-Halfai;

[16] Shim'on, the one called the Zealot; Y'hudah Ben-Ya'akov; and Y'hudah from K'riot, who turned traitor.

[17] Then he came down with them and stood on a level place. A large crowd of his *talmidim* was there with great numbers of people from all Y'hudah, Yerushalayim and the coast around Tzor and Tzidon; they had come to hear him and be healed of their diseases. [18] Those who were troubled with unclean spirits were being healed; [19] and the whole crowd was trying to touch him, because power kept going out from him, healing everyone. [20] He looked at his *talmidim* and said:

"How blessed are you poor!
for the Kingdom of God is yours.

[21]   "How blessed are you who are hungry!
for you will be filled.

"How blessed are you who are crying now!
for you will laugh.

[22] "How blessed you are whenever people hate you and ostracize you and insult you and denounce you as a criminal on account of the Son of Man. [23] Be glad when that happens; yes, dance for joy! because in heaven your reward is great. For that is just how their fathers treated the prophets.

[24]   "But woe to you who are rich,
for you have already had all the comfort you will get!

[25]   "Woe to you who are full now,
for you will go hungry!

"Woe to you who are laughing now,
for you will mourn and cry!

²⁶ "Woe to you when people speak well of you, for that is just how their fathers treated the false prophets!

²⁷ Nevertheless, to you who are listening, what I say is this:

"Love your enemies!
Do good to those who hate you,
²⁸ bless those who curse you,
pray for those who mistreat you.

²⁹ "If someone hits you on one cheek,
offer the other too;
if someone takes your coat,
let him have your shirt as well.

³⁰ "If someone asks you for something,
give it to him;
if someone takes what belongs to you,
don't demand it back.

³¹ "Treat other people as you would like them to treat you. ³² What credit is it to you if you love only those who love you? Why, even sinners love those who love them. ³³ What credit is it to you if you do good only to those who do good to you? Even sinners do that. ³⁴ What credit is it to you if you lend only to those who you expect will pay you back? Even sinners lend to each other, expecting to be repaid in full. ³⁵ But love your enemies, do good, and lend expecting nothing back! Your reward will be great, and you will be children of *Ha'Elyon*; for he is kind to the ungrateful and the wicked. ³⁶ Show compassion, just as your Father shows compassion.

³⁷ "Don't judge,
and you won't be judged.
Don't condemn,
and you won't be condemned.

"Forgive,
and you will be forgiven.
³⁸ Give,
and you will receive gifts —

the full measure, compacted, shaken together and overflowing, will be put right in your lap. For the measure with which you measure out will be used to measure back to you!"

³⁹ He also told them a parable: "Can one blind man lead another blind man? Won't they both fall into a pit? ⁴⁰ A *talmid* is not above his rabbi; but each one, when he is fully trained, will be like his rabbi. ⁴¹ So why do you see the splinter in your

brother's eye, but not notice the log in your own eye? ⁴²How can you say to your brother, 'Brother, let me remove the splinter from your eye,' when you yourself don't see the log in your own eye? You hypocrite! First take the log out of your own eye; then you will see clearly, so that you can remove the splinter from your brother's eye!

⁴³"For no good tree produces bad fruit, nor does a bad tree produce good fruit. ⁴⁴Each tree is recognized by its own fruit — figs aren't picked from thorn bushes, nor grapes from a briar patch. ⁴⁵The good person produces good things from the store of good in his heart, while the evil person produces evil things from the store of evil in his heart. For his mouth speaks what overflows from his heart.

⁴⁶"Why do you call me, 'Lord! Lord!' but not do what I say? ⁴⁷Everyone who comes to me, hears my words and acts on them — I will show you what he is like: ⁴⁸he is like someone building a house who dug deep and laid the foundation on bedrock. When a flood came, the torrent beat against that house but couldn't shake it, because it was constructed well. ⁴⁹And whoever hears my words but doesn't act on them is like someone who built his house on the ground without any foundation. As soon as the river struck it, it collapsed and that house became a horrendous wreck!"

7 ¹When Yeshua had finished speaking to the people, he went back to K'far-Nachum. ²A Roman army officer there had a servant he regarded highly, who was sick to the point of death. ³Hearing about Yeshua, the officer sent some Jewish elders to him with the request that he come and heal his servant. ⁴They came to Yeshua and pleaded earnestly with him, "He really deserves to have you do this, ⁵for he loves our people — in fact, he built the synagogue for us!" ⁶So Yeshua went with them. He had not gone far from the house, when the officer sent friends who said to him, "Sir, don't trouble yourself. I'm not worthy to have you come under my roof — ⁷this is why I didn't presume to approach you myself. Instead, just give a command and let my servant recover. ⁸For I too am a man set under authority. I have soldiers under me; and I say to this one, 'Go!' and he goes; and to another, 'Come!' and he comes; and to my slave, 'Do this!' and he does it." ⁹Yeshua was astonished at him when he heard this; and he turned and said to the crowd following him, "I tell you, not even in Isra'el have I found such trust!" ¹⁰When the messengers got back to the officer's house, they found the servant in good health.

¹¹The next day Yeshua, accompanied by his *talmidim* and a large crowd, went to a town called Na'im. ¹²As he approached the town gate, a dead man was being carried out for burial. His mother was a widow, this had been her only son, and a sizeable crowd from the town was with her. ¹³When the Lord saw her, he felt compassion for her and said to her, "Don't cry." ¹⁴Then he came close and touched the coffin, and the pallbearers halted. He said, "Young man, I say to you: get up!" ¹⁵The dead man sat up and began to speak, and Yeshua **gave him to his mother.**ᵒ ¹⁶They were all filled with awe and gave glory to God, saying, "A great prophet has appeared among us," and, "God has come to help his people." ¹⁷This report about him spread throughout all Y'hudah and the surrounding countryside.

¹⁸Yochanan's *talmidim* informed him of all these things. Then Yochanan called two of his *talmidim* ¹⁹and sent them to the Lord to ask, "Are you the one who is to come? Or should we look for someone else?" ²⁰When the men came to him, they said,

---

ᵒ 1 Kings 17:23

"Yochanan the Immerser has sent us to you to ask, 'Are you the one who is to come?
Or should we keep looking — for someone else?'" [21] Right then he was healing many
people of diseases, pains and evil spirits, and giving sight to many who were blind. [22] So
he answered them by saying, "Go, tell Yochanan what you have been seeing and hearing: **the blind are seeing again, the lame are** walking, people with *tzara'at* are being
cleansed, **the deaf are hearing**, the dead are being raised, **the Good News is being
told to the poor**[p] — [23] and how blessed is anyone not offended by me!"

[24] When the messengers from Yochanan had gone, Yeshua began speaking to the
crowds about Yochanan: "What did you go out into the desert to see? Reeds swaying
in the breeze? [25] No? Then what did you go out to see? Someone who was well
dressed? But people who dress beautifully and live in luxury are found in kings'
palaces. [26] *Nu*, so what did you go out to see? A prophet! Yes, and I tell you he's
much more than a prophet. [27] This is the one about whom the *Tanakh* says,

> '**See, I am sending out my messenger** ahead of you;
> **he will prepare your way before you.**'[q]

[28] I tell you that among those born of women there has not arisen anyone greater than
Yochanan the Immerser! Yet the one who is least in the Kingdom of Heaven is greater
than he!"

[29] All the people who heard him, even the tax-collectors, by undergoing
Yochanan's immersion acknowledged that God was right; [30] but the *P'rushim* and
the *Torah*-teachers, by not letting themselves be immersed by him, nullified for themselves God's plan.

[31] "Therefore," said the Lord, "how can I describe the people of this generation?
What are they like? [32] They are like children sitting in the marketplaces, calling to
one another,

> 'We made happy music, but you wouldn't dance!
> We made sad music, but you wouldn't cry!'

[33] For Yochanan has come not eating bread and not drinking wine; and you say, 'He
has a demon!' [34] The Son of Man has come eating and drinking; and you say, 'Aha!
A glutton and a drunkard! A friend of tax-collectors and sinners!' [35] Well, the proof of
wisdom is in all the kinds of people it produces."

[36] One of the *P'rushim* invited Yeshua to eat with him, and he went into the
home of the *Parush* and took his place at the table. [37] A woman who lived in that
town, a sinner, who was aware that he was eating in the home of the *Parush*, brought
an alabaster box of very expensive perfume, [38] stood behind Yeshua at his feet and
wept until her tears began to wet his feet. Then she wiped his feet with her own hair,
kissed his feet and poured the perfume on them.

[39] When the *Parush* who had invited him saw what was going on, he said to
himself, "If this man were really a prophet, he would have known who is touching
him and what sort of woman she is, that she is a sinner." [40] Yeshua answered, "Shim'on,
I have something to say to you." "Say it, Rabbi," he replied. [41] "A certain creditor

---

[p] Isaiah 35:5–6; 26:19; 61:1 [q] Malachi 3:1

had two debtors; the one owed ten times as much as the other. [42] When they were unable to pay him back, he canceled both their debts. Now which of them will love him more?" [43] Shim'on answered, "I suppose the one for whom he canceled the larger debt." "Your judgment is right," Yeshua said to him.

[44] Then, turning to the woman, he said to Shim'on, "Do you see this woman? I came into your house — you didn't give me water for my feet, but this woman has washed my feet with her tears and dried them with her hair! [45] You didn't give me a kiss; but from the time I arrived, this woman has not stopped kissing my feet! [46] You didn't put oil on my head, but this woman poured perfume on my feet! [47] Because of this, I tell you that her sins — which are many! — have been forgiven, because she loved much. But someone who has been forgiven only a little loves only a little." [48] Then he said to her, "Your sins have been forgiven." [49] At this, those eating with him began saying among themselves, "Who is this fellow that presumes to forgive sins?" [50] But he said to the woman, "Your trust has saved you; go in peace."

8 [1] After this, Yeshua traveled about from town to town and village to village, proclaiming the Good News of the Kingdom of God. With him were the Twelve, [2] and a number of women who had been healed from evil spirits and illnesses — Miryam (called Magdalit), from whom seven demons had gone out; [3] Yochanah the wife of Herod's finance minister Kuza; Shoshanah; and many other women who drew on their own wealth to help him.

[4] After a large crowd had gathered from the people who kept coming to him from town after town, Yeshua told this parable: [5] "A farmer went out to sow his seed. As he sowed, some fell along the path and was stepped on, and the birds flying around ate it up. [6] Some fell on rock; and after it sprouted, it dried up from lack of moisture. [7] Some fell in the midst of thorns, and the thorns grew up with it and choked it. [8] But some fell into rich soil, and grew, and produced a hundred times as much as had been sown." After saying this, he called out, "Whoever has ears to hear with, let him hear!"

[9] His *talmidim* asked him what this parable might mean, [10] and he said, "To you it has been given to know the secrets of the Kingdom of God; but the rest are taught in parables, so that they may **look but not see, and listen but not understand.**[r]

[11] "The parable is this: the seed is God's message. [12] The ones along the path are those who hear, but then the Adversary comes and takes the message out of their hearts, in order to keep them from being saved by trusting it. [13] The ones on rock are those who, when they hear the word, accept it with joy; but these have no root — they go on trusting for awhile; but when a time of testing comes, they apostatize. [14] As for what fell in the midst of thorns these are the ones who hear; but as they go along, worries and wealth and life's gratifications crowd in and choke them, so that their fruit never matures. [15] But what fell in rich soil — these are the ones who, when they hear the message, hold onto it with a good, receptive heart; and by persevering, they bring forth a harvest.

[16] "No one who has lit a lamp covers it with a bowl or puts it under a bed; no, he puts it on a stand; so that those coming in may see the light. [17] For nothing is hidden

---

[r] Isaiah 6:9

that will not be disclosed, nothing is covered up that will not be known and come out into the open. [18] Pay attention, then, to how you hear! For anyone who has something will be given more; but from anyone who has nothing, even what he seems to have will be taken away."

[19] Then Yeshua's mother and brothers came to see him, but they couldn't get near him because of the crowd. [20] It was reported to him, "Your mother and your brothers are standing outside and want to see you." [21] But he gave them this answer: "My mother and brothers are those who hear God's message and act on it!"

[22] One day Yeshua got into a boat with his *talmidim* and said to them, "Let's cross to the other side of the lake." [23] So they set out; and as they were sailing, he fell asleep. A windstorm came down on the lake, so that the boat began to fill up with water, putting them in great danger. [24] They went and woke him, saying, "Rabbi! Rabbi! We're about to die!" He woke up, rebuked the wind and the rough water; and they calmed down, so that it was still. [25] Then he said to the *talmidim*, "Where is your trust?" Awestruck, they marveled, asking one another, "Who can this be, that he commands even the wind and the water, and they obey him?"

[26] They sailed on and landed in the region of the Gerasenes, which is opposite the Galil. [27] As Yeshua stepped ashore, a man from the town who had demons came to meet him. For a long time he had not worn clothes; and he lived, not in a house, but in the burial caves. [28] Catching sight of Yeshua, he screamed, fell down in front of him and yelled, "Yeshua! Son of God *Ha'Elyon*! What do you want with me? I beg you, don't torture me!" [29] For Yeshua had ordered the unclean spirit to come out of the man. It had often taken hold of him — he had been kept under guard, chained hand and foot, but had broken the bonds and been driven by the demon into the desert. [30] Yeshua asked him, "What is your name?" "Legion," he said, because many demons had entered him. [31] They begged Yeshua not to order them to go off into the Bottomless Pit.

[32] Now there was a herd of many pigs, feeding on the hill; and the demons begged him to let them go into these. So he gave them permission. [33] The demons came out of the man and entered the pigs, whereupon the herd rushed down the hillside into the lake and were drowned.

[34] When the swineherds saw what had happened, they fled and told it in the town and in the country; [35] and the people came out to see for themselves. They came to Yeshua and found the man out of whom the demons had gone, sitting — dressed and in his right mind — at the feet of Yeshua; and they were frightened. [36] Those who had seen it told how the formerly demonized man had been delivered.

[37] Then all the people of the Gerasene district asked him to leave them, for they had been seized with great fear. So he boarded the boat and returned. [38] The man from whom the demons had gone out begged that he might go with him; but Yeshua sent him away, saying, [39] "Go back to your home and tell how much God has done for you." He went away proclaiming throughout the whole town how much Yeshua had done for him.

[40] When Yeshua got back, the crowd welcomed him; for they were all expecting him. [41] Then there came a man named Ya'ir who was president of the synagogue. Falling at Yeshua's feet, he pleaded with him to come to his house; [42] for he had an only daughter, about twelve years old; and she was dying.

As he went, with the crowds on every side virtually choking him, [43] a woman who had had a hemorrhage for twelve years, and could not be healed by anyone,

⁴⁴ came up behind him and touched the *tzitzit* on his robe; instantly her hemorrhaging stopped. ⁴⁵ Yeshua asked, "Who touched me?" When they all denied doing it, Kefa said, "Rabbi! The crowds are hemming you in and jostling you!" ⁴⁶ But Yeshua said, "Someone did touch me, because I felt power go out of me." ⁴⁷ Seeing she could not escape notice, the woman, quaking with fear, threw herself down before him and confessed in front of everyone why she had touched him and how she had been instantly healed. ⁴⁸ He said to her, "My daughter, your trust has saved you; go in peace."

⁴⁹ While Yeshua was still speaking, a man came from the synagogue president's house. "Your daughter has died," he said. "Don't bother the rabbi any more." ⁵⁰ But on hearing this, Yeshua answered him, "Don't be afraid! Just go on trusting, and she will be made well." ⁵¹ When he arrived at the house, he didn't allow anyone to go in with him except Kefa, Yochanan, Ya'akov and the child's father and mother ⁵² All the people were wailing and mourning for her; but he said, "Don't weep; she hasn't died, she's sleeping." ⁵³ They jeered at him, since they knew she had died. ⁵⁴ But he took her by the hand, called out, "Little girl, get up!" ⁵⁵ and her spirit returned. She stood up at once, and he directed that something be given her to eat. ⁵⁶ Her parents were astounded, but he instructed them to tell no one what had happened.

9 ¹ Calling together the Twelve, Yeshua gave them power and authority to expel all the demons and to cure diseases; ² and he sent them out to proclaim the Kingdom of God and to heal. ³ He said to them, "Take nothing for your trip — neither a walking stick nor a pack, neither bread nor money; and don't have two shirts. ⁴ Whatever house you enter, stay there and go out from there. ⁵ Wherever they don't welcome you, shake the dust from your feet when you leave that town as a warning to them." ⁶ They set out and went through village after village, healing and announcing the Good News everywhere.

⁷ Herod the governor heard about all that was going on and was perplexed, because it was said by some that Yochanan had been raised from the dead, ⁸ by others that Eliyahu had appeared, and by others that one of the prophets of long ago had come back to life. ⁹ Herod said, "I had Yochanan beheaded, so who is this about whom I keep hearing such things?" And he began trying to see him.

¹⁰ On their return, the emissaries detailed to Yeshua what they had done. Then, taking them with him, he withdrew by himself to a town called Beit-Tzaidah. ¹¹ But the crowds found out and followed him. Welcoming them, he went on to speak to them about the Kingdom of God and to heal those who needed to be healed.

¹² The day began to draw to a close. The Twelve came to him and said, "Send the crowd away, so that they can go and get lodging and food in the towns and farms around here, because where we are is a remote place." ¹³ But he said to them, "Give them something to eat, yourselves!" They said, "We have no more than five loaves of bread and two fish — unless we ourselves are supposed to go and buy food for all these people!" ¹⁴ (For there were about five thousand men.) He said to his *talmidim*, "Make them sit down in groups of about fifty each." ¹⁵ They did what he told them and had them all sit down. ¹⁶ Then he took the five loaves and the two fish and, looking up toward heaven, made a *b'rakhah*, broke the loaves and began giving them to the *talmidim* to distribute to the crowd. ¹⁷ Everyone ate as much as he wanted; and they took up what was left over, twelve baskets full of broken pieces.

¹⁸ Once when Yeshua was praying in private, his *talmidim* were with him; and he asked them, "Who are the crowds saying I am?" ¹⁹ They answered, "Yochanan the

Immerser; but others say Eliyahu, and others that some prophet of long ago has risen." ²⁰ "But you," he said to them, "who do you say I am?" Kefa answered, "The *Mashiach* of God!" ²¹ However, he, warning them, ordered them to tell this to no one, ²² adding, "The Son of Man has to endure much suffering and be rejected by the elders, the head *cohanim* and the *Torah*-teachers; and he has to be put to death; but on the third day, he has to be raised to life."

²³ Then to everyone he said, "If anyone wants to come after me, let him say 'No' to himself, take up his execution-stake daily and keep following me. ²⁴ For whoever tries to save his own life will destroy it, but whoever destroys his life on my account will save it. ²⁵ What will it benefit a person if he gains the whole world but destroys or forfeits his own life? ²⁶ For if someone is ashamed of me and of what I say, the Son of Man will be ashamed of him when he comes in his glory and that of the Father and of the holy angels. ²⁷ I tell you the truth, there are some people standing here who will not experience death until they see the Kingdom of God."

²⁸ About a week after Yeshua said these things, he took Kefa, Yochanan and Ya'akov with him and went up to the hill country to pray. ²⁹ As he was praying, the appearance of his face changed; and his clothing became gleaming white. ³⁰ Suddenly there were two men talking with him — Moshe and Eliyahu! ³¹ They appeared in glorious splendor and spoke of his exodus, which he was soon to accomplish in Yerushalayim. ³² Kefa and those with him had been sound asleep; but on becoming fully awake, they saw his glory and the two men standing with him. ³³ As the men were leaving Yeshua, Kefa said to him, not knowing what he was saying, "It's good that we're here, Rabbi! Let's put up three shelters — one for you, one for Moshe and one for Eliyahu." ³⁴ As he spoke, a cloud came and enveloped them. They were frightened as they entered the cloud; ³⁵ and a voice came out of the cloud, saying, "This is my Son, whom I have chosen. Listen to him!" ³⁶ When the voice spoke, Yeshua was alone once more. They kept quiet — at that time they told no one anything of what they had seen.

³⁷ The next day, as they were coming down out of the hill country, a large crowd met him. ³⁸ Suddenly a man in the crowd shouted, "Rabbi! Look at my son, I beg you, because he's my only child! ³⁹ What happens is this: a spirit seizes him, and suddenly it lets out a shriek and throws him into convulsions with foaming at the mouth; and only with difficulty will it leave him. It's destroying him! ⁴⁰ I asked your *talmidim* to drive the spirit out, but they couldn't." ⁴¹ "Perverted people, without any trust!" Yeshua answered, "How long do I have to be with you and put up with you? Bring your son here." ⁴² Even as the boy was coming, the demon dashed him to the ground and threw him into a fit. But Yeshua rebuked the unclean spirit, healed the boy and gave him back to his father. ⁴³ All were struck with amazement at the greatness of God. While they were all marvelling at everything Yeshua was doing, he said to his *talmidim*, ⁴⁴ "Listen very carefully to what I'm going to say. The Son of Man is about to be betrayed into the hands of men." ⁴⁵ But they didn't understand what he meant by this. It had been concealed from them so that they would not grasp its meaning, and they were afraid to ask him about it.

⁴⁶ An argument arose among the *talmidim* as to which of them might be the greatest. ⁴⁷ But Yeshua, knowing the thoughts of their hearts, took a child, stood him beside himself, ⁴⁸ and said to them, "Whoever welcomes this child in my name welcomes me, and whoever welcomes me welcomes the One who sent me. In other

words, the one who is least among you all — this is the one who is great." ⁴⁹ Yochanan responded, "Rabbi, we saw someone expelling demons in your name; and we stopped him because he doesn't follow you along with us." ⁵⁰ Yeshua said to him, "Don't stop such people, because whoever isn't against you is for you."

⁵¹ As the time approached for him to be taken up into heaven, he made his decision to set out for Yerushalayim. ⁵² He sent messengers ahead of him, who went and entered a village in Shomron to make preparations for him. ⁵³ However, the people there would not let him stay, because his destination was Yerushalayim. ⁵⁴ When the *talmidim* Ya'akov and Yochanan saw this, they said, "Sir, do you want us to call down **fire from heaven to destroy** them?"ˢ ⁵⁵ But he turned and rebuked them.* ⁵⁶ And they went on to another village.

⁵⁷ As they were traveling on the road, a man said to him, "I will follow you wherever you go." ⁵⁸ Yeshua answered him, "The foxes have holes, and the birds flying about have nests, but the Son of Man has no home of his own." ⁵⁹ To another he said, "Follow me!" but the man replied, "Sir, first let me go away and bury my father." ⁶⁰ Yeshua said, "Let the dead bury their own dead; you, go and proclaim the Kingdom of God!" ⁶¹ Yet another said, "I will follow you, sir, but first let me say good-by to the people at home." ⁶² To him Yeshua said, "No one who puts his hand to the plow and keeps looking back is fit to serve in the Kingdom of God."

10 ¹ After this, the Lord appointed seventy other *talmidim* and sent them on ahead in pairs to every town and place where he himself was about to go. ² He said to them, "To be sure, there is a large harvest. But there are few workers. Therefore, plead with the Lord of the Harvest that he speed workers out to gather in his harvest. ³ Get going now, but pay attention! I am sending you out like lambs among wolves. ⁴ Don't carry a money-belt or a pack, and don't stop to *shmoose* with people on the road.

⁵ "Whenever you enter a house, first say, 'Shalom!' to the household. ⁶ If a seeker of *shalom* is there, your 'Shalom!' will find its rest with him; and if there isn't, it will return to you. ⁷ Stay in that same house, eating and drinking what they offer, for a worker deserves his wages — don't move about from house to house.

⁸ "Whenever you come into a town where they make you welcome, eat what is put in front of you. ⁹ Heal the sick there, and tell them, 'The Kingdom of God is near you.' ¹⁰ But whenever you enter a town and they don't make you welcome, go out into its streets and say, ¹¹ 'Even the dust of your town that sticks to our feet we wipe off as a sign against you! But understand this: the Kingdom of God is near!' ¹² I tell you, it will be more tolerable on the Day of Judgment for S'dom than for that town.

¹³ "Woe to you, Korazin! Woe to you, Beit-Tzaidah! For if the miracles done in you had been done in Tzor and Tzidon, they would long ago have put on sackcloth and ashes as evidence that they had changed their ways. ¹⁴ But at the Judgment it will be more bearable for Tzor and Tzidon than for you!

¹⁵ "And you, K'far-Nachum, will you be **exalted to heaven**? **No, you will be brought down to Sh'ol!**ᵗ

ˢ 2 Kings 1:9–16   ᵗ Isaiah 14:13, 15
* Some manuscripts have verses 9:55b–56a: . . . and he said, "You don't know what Spirit you are of;
⁵⁶ for the Son of Man did not come to destroy people's lives, but to save."

[16] "Whoever listens to you listens to me, also whoever rejects you rejects me, and whoever rejects me rejects the One who sent me."

[17] The seventy came back jubilant. "Lord," they said, "with your power, even the demons submit to us!" [18] Yeshua said to them, "I saw Satan fall like lightning from heaven. [19] Remember, I have given you authority; so you can trample down snakes and scorpions, indeed, all the Enemy's forces; and you will remain completely unharmed. [20] Nevertheless, don't be glad that the spirits submit to you; be glad that your names have been recorded in heaven."

[21] At that moment he was filled with joy by the *Ruach HaKodesh* and said, "Father, Lord of heaven and earth, I thank you because you concealed these things from the sophisticated and educated, yet revealed them to ordinary people. Yes, Father, I thank you that it pleased you to do this.

[22] "My Father has handed over everything to me. Indeed, no one fully knows who the Son is except the Father, and who the Father is except the Son and those to whom the Son wishes to reveal him." [23] Then, turning to the *talmidim*, he said, privately, "How blessed are the eyes that see what you are seeing! [24] Indeed, I tell you that many prophets and kings wanted to see the things you are seeing but did not see them, and to hear the things you are hearing but did not hear them."

[25] An expert in *Torah* stood up to try and trap him by asking, "Rabbi, what should I do to obtain eternal life?" [26] But Yeshua said to him, "What is written in the *Torah*? How do you read it?" [27] He answered, "**You are to love ADONAI your God with all your heart, with all your soul, with all your strength** and with all your understanding; and **your neighbor as yourself**."[u] [28] "That's the right answer," Yeshua said. "Do this, and you will have life."

[29] But he, wanting to justify himself, said to Yeshua, "And who is my '**neighbor**'?" [30] Taking up the question, Yeshua said: "A man was going down from Yerushalayim to Yericho when he was attacked by robbers. They stripped him naked and beat him up, then went off, leaving him half dead. [31] By coincidence, a *cohen* was going down on that road; but when he saw him, he passed by on the other side. [32] Likewise a *Levi* who reached the place and saw him also passed by on the other side.

[33] "But a man from Shomron who was traveling came upon him; and when he saw him, he was moved with compassion. [34] So he went up to him, put oil and wine on his wounds and bandaged them. Then he set him on his own donkey, brought him to an inn and took care of him. [35] The next day, he took out two days' wages, gave them to the innkeeper and said, 'Look after him; and if you spend more than this, I'll pay you back when I return.' [36] Of these three, which one seems to you to have become the '**neighbor**' of the man who fell among robbers?" [37] He answered, "The one who showed mercy toward him." Yeshua said to him, "You go and do as he did."

[38] On their way Yeshua and his *talmidim* came to a village where a woman named Marta welcomed him into her home. [39] She had a sister called Miryam who also sat at the Lord's feet and heard what he had to say. [40] But Marta was busy with all the work to be done; so, going up to him, she said, "Sir, don't you care that my sister has been leaving me to do all the work by myself?" [41] However, the Lord answered her, "Marta, Marta, you are fretting and worrying about so many things!

---

[u] Deuteronomy 6:5; Leviticus 19:18

⁴² But there is only one thing that is essential. Miryam has chosen the right thing, and it won't be taken away from her."

11 ¹ One time Yeshua was in a certain place praying. As he finished, one of the *talmidim* said to him, "Sir, teach us to pray, just as Yochanan taught his *talmidim*." ² He said to them, "When you pray, say:

'Father,

    May your name be kept holy.

    May your Kingdom come.

³   Give us each day the food we need.

⁴   Forgive us our sins, for we too forgive everyone who has wronged us.

    And do not lead us to hard testing.'"

⁵ He also said to them, "Suppose one of you has a friend; and you go to him in the middle of the night and say to him, 'Friend, lend me three loaves of bread, ⁶ because a friend of mine who has been travelling has just arrived at my house, and I have nothing for him to eat.' ⁷ Now the one inside may answer, 'Don't bother me! The door is already shut, my children are with me in bed — I can't get up to give you anything!' ⁸ But I tell you, even if he won't get up because the man is his friend, yet because of the man's *hutzpah* he will get up and give him as much as he needs.

⁹ "Moreover, I myself say to you: keep asking, and it will be given to you; keep seeking, and you will find; keep knocking, and the door will be opened to you. ¹⁰ For everyone who goes on asking receives; and he who goes on seeking finds; and to him who continues knocking, the door will be opened.

¹¹ "Is there any father here who, if his son asked him for a fish, would instead of a fish give him a snake? ¹² or if he asked for an egg would give him a scorpion? ¹³ So if you, even though you are bad, know how to give your children gifts that are good, how much more will the Father keep giving the *Ruach HaKodesh* from heaven to those who keep asking him!"

¹⁴ He was expelling a demon that was mute. When the demon had gone out, the man who had been mute spoke; and the people were astounded. ¹⁵ But some of them said, "It is by Ba'al-Zibbul" — the ruler of the demons — "that he expels the demons." ¹⁶ And others, trying to trap him, demanded from him a sign from Heaven. ¹⁷ But he, knowing what they were thinking, said to them, "Every kingdom divided against itself will be ruined, with one house collapsing on another. ¹⁸ So if the Adversary too is divided against himself, how can his kingdom survive? I'm asking because you claim it is by Ba'al-Zibbul that I drive out the demons. ¹⁹ If I drive out demons by Ba'al-Zibbul, by whom do your people drive them out? So, they will be your judges! ²⁰ But if I drive out demons by the **finger of God**,^v then the Kingdom of God has come upon you!

²¹ "When a strong man who is fully equipped for battle guards his own house, his possessions are secure. ²² But when someone stronger attacks and defeats him, he carries off all the armor and weaponry on which the man was depending, and divides

^v Exodus 8:15(19), 31:18

up the spoils. [23] Those who are not with me are against me, and those who do not gather with me are scattering.

[24] "When an unclean spirit comes out of a person, it travels through dry country seeking rest. On finding none, it says, 'I will return to the house I left.' [25] When it arrives, it finds the house swept clean and put in order. [26] Then it goes and takes seven other spirits more evil than itself, and they come and live there — so that in the end the person is worse off than he was before."

[27] As Yeshua was saying these things, a woman in the crowd raised her voice to call out, "How blessed is the mother that gave birth to you and nursed you from her breast!" [28] But he said, "Far more blessed are those who hear the word of God and obey it!"

[29] As the people crowded around him, Yeshua went on to say, "This generation is a wicked generation! It asks for a sign, but no sign will be given to it — except the sign of Yonah. [30] For just as Yonah became a sign to the people of Ninveh, so will the Son of Man be for this generation. [31] The Queen of the South will appear at the Judgment with the people of this generation and condemn them; for she came from the ends of the earth to hear the wisdom of Shlomo, and what is here now is greater than Shlomo. [32] The people of Ninveh will stand up at the Judgment with this generation and condemn it, for they turned to God from their sins when Yonah preached, and what is here now is greater than Yonah.

[33] "No one who has kindled a lamp hides it or places it under a bowl; rather, he puts it on a stand, so that those coming in may see its light. [34] The lamp of your body is the eye. When you have a 'good eye,' [that is, when you are generous,] your whole body is full of light; but when you have an 'evil eye,' [when you are stingy,] your body is full of darkness. [35] So take care that the light in you is not darkness! [36] If, then, your whole body is filled with light, with no part dark, it will be wholly lighted, as when a brightly lit lamp shines on you."

[37] As Yeshua spoke, a *Parush* asked him to eat dinner with him; so he went in and took his place at the table; [38] and the *Parush* was surprised that he didn't begin by doing *n'tilat yadayim* before the meal. [39] However, the Lord said to him, "Now then, you *P'rushim*, you clean the outside of the cup and plate; but inside, you are full of robbery and wickedness. [40] Fools! Didn't the One who made the outside make the inside too? [41] Rather, give as alms what is inside, and then everything will be clean for you!

[42] "But woe to you *P'rushim*! You pay your tithes of mint and rue and every garden herb, but you ignore justice and the love of God. You have an obligation to do these things — but without disregarding the others!

[43] "Woe to you *P'rushim*, because you love the best seat in the synagogue and being greeted deferentially in the marketplaces!

[44] "Woe to you, because you are like unmarked graves, which people walk over without knowing it."

[45] One of the experts in *Torah* answered him, "Rabbi, by saying these things you are insulting us also." [46] Yeshua said, "Woe to you *Torah* experts too! You load people down with burdens they can hardly bear, and you won't lift a finger to help them!

[47] "Woe to you! You build tombs in memory of the prophets, but your fathers murdered them! [48] Thus you testify that you completely approve of what your fathers did — they did the killing, you do the building! [49] Therefore the Wisdom of God said, 'I will send them prophets and emissaries; they will kill some and persecute others';

⁵⁰ so that on this generation will fall the responsibility for all the prophets' blood that has been shed since the world was established, ⁵¹ from the blood of Hevel to the blood of Z'kharyah, who was killed between the altar and the Holy Place. Yes, I tell you, the responsibility for it will fall on this generation!

⁵² "Woe to you *Torah* experts! For you have taken away the key of knowledge! Not only did you yourselves not go in, you also have stopped those who were trying to enter!"

⁵³ As Yeshua left that place, the *Torah*-teachers and the *P'rushim* began to oppose him bitterly and to provoke him to express his views on all sorts of subjects, ⁵⁴ laying traps to catch him in something he might say.

12 ¹ Meanwhile, as a crowd in the tens of thousands gathered so closely as to trample each other down, Yeshua began to say to his *talmidim* first, "Guard yourselves from the *hametz* of the *P'rushim*, by which I mean their hypocrisy. ² There is nothing covered up that will not be uncovered, or hidden that will not become known. ³ What you have spoken in the dark will be heard in the light, and what you have whispered behind closed doors will be proclaimed on the housetops.

⁴ "My friends, I tell you: don't fear those who kill the body but then have nothing more they can do. ⁵ I will show you whom to fear: fear him who after killing you has authority to throw you into Gei-Hinnom! Yes, I tell you, this is the one to fear! ⁶ Aren't sparrows sold for next to nothing, five for two assarions? And not one of them has been forgotten by God. ⁷ Why, every hair on your head has been counted! Don't be afraid, you are worth more than many sparrows.

⁸ "Moreover, I tell you, whoever acknowledges me in the presence of others, the Son of Man will also acknowledge in the presence of God's angels. ⁹ But whoever disowns me before others will be disowned before God's angels. ¹⁰ Also, everyone who says something against the Son of Man will have it forgiven him; but whoever has blasphemed the *Ruach HaKodesh* will not be forgiven.

¹¹ "When they bring you before the synagogues and the ruling powers and the authorities, don't worry about how you will defend yourself or what you will say; ¹² because when the time comes, the *Ruach HaKodesh* will teach you what you need to say."

¹³ Someone in the crowd said to him, "Rabbi, tell my brother to share with me the property we inherited." ¹⁴ But Yeshua answered him, "My friend, who appointed me judge or arbitrator over you?" ¹⁵ Then to the people he said, "Be careful to guard against all forms of greed, because even if someone is rich, his life does not consist in what he owns." ¹⁶ And he gave them this illustration: "There was a man whose land was very productive. ¹⁷ He debated with himself, 'What should I do? I haven't enough room for all my crops.' ¹⁸ Then he said, 'This is what I will do: I'll tear down my barns and build bigger ones, and I'll store all my wheat and other goods there. ¹⁹ Then I'll say to myself, "You're a lucky man! You have a big supply of goods laid up that will last many years. Start taking it easy! Eat! Drink! Enjoy yourself!"' ²⁰ But God said to him, 'You fool! This very night you will die! And the things you prepared — whose will they be?' ²¹ That's how it is with anyone who stores up wealth for himself without being rich toward God."

²² To his *talmidim* Yeshua said, "Because of this I tell you, don't worry about your life — what you will eat or drink; or about your body — what you will wear.

²³ For life is more than food, and the body is more than clothing. ²⁴ Think about the ravens! They neither plant nor harvest, they have neither storerooms nor barns, yet God feeds them. You are worth much more than the birds! ²⁵ Can any of you by worrying add an hour to his life? ²⁶ If you can't do a little thing like that, why worry about the rest? ²⁷ Think about the wild irises, and how they grow. They neither work nor spin thread; yet, I tell you, not even Shlomo in all his glory was clothed as beautifully as one of these. ²⁸ If this is how God clothes grass, which is alive in the field today and thrown in the oven tomorrow, how much more will he clothe you! What little trust you have!

²⁹ "In other words, don't strive after what you will eat and what you will drink — don't be anxious. ³⁰ For all the pagan nations in the world set their hearts on these things. Your Father knows that you need them too. ³¹ Rather, seek his Kingdom; and these things will be given to you as well. ³² Have no fear, little flock, for your Father has resolved to give you the Kingdom! ³³ Sell what you own and do *tzedakah* — make for yourselves purses that don't wear out, riches in heaven that never fail, where no burglar comes near, where no moth destroys. ³⁴ For where your wealth is, there your heart will be also.

³⁵ "Be dressed for action and have your lamps lit, ³⁶ like people waiting for their master's return after a wedding feast; so that when he comes and knocks, they will open the door for him without delay. ³⁷ Happy the slaves whom the master finds alert when he comes! Yes! I tell you he will put on his work clothes, seat them at the table, and come serve them himself! ³⁸ Whether it is late at night or early in the morning, if this is how he finds them, those slaves are happy.

³⁹ "But notice this: no house-owner would let his house be broken into if he knew when the thief was coming. ⁴⁰ You too, be ready! For the Son of Man will come when you are not expecting him."

⁴¹ Kefa said, "Sir, are you telling this parable for our benefit only or for everyone's?" ⁴² The Lord replied, "*Nu*, who is the faithful and sensible manager whose master puts him in charge of the household staff to give them their share of food at the proper time? ⁴³ It will go well with that servant if he is found doing his job when his master comes. ⁴⁴ Yes, I tell you he will put him in charge of all he owns. ⁴⁵ But if that servant says to himself, 'My master is taking his time coming,' and starts bullying the men- and women-servants, and eating and drinking, getting drunk, ⁴⁶ then his master will come on a day when the servant isn't expecting him, at a time he doesn't know in advance; his master will cut him in two and put him with the disloyal. ⁴⁷ Now the servant who knew what his master wanted but didn't prepare or act according to his will, will be whipped with many lashes; ⁴⁸ however, the one who did what deserves a beating, but didn't know, will receive few lashes. From him who has been given much, much will be demanded — from someone to whom people entrust much, they ask still more.

⁴⁹ "I have come to set fire to the earth! And how I wish it were already kindled! ⁵⁰ I have an immersion to undergo — how pressured I feel till it's over! ⁵¹ Do you think that I have come to bring peace in the Land? Not peace, I tell you, but division! ⁵² For from now on, a household of five will be divided, three against two, two against three.

⁵³   Father will be divided against son
       and **son against father**,

mother against daughter
and **daughter against mother**,
mother-in-law against her daughter-in-law
and **daughter-in-law against mother-in-law**."ʷ

⁵⁴ Then to the crowds Yeshua said, "When you see a cloud-bank rising in the west, at once you say that a rainstorm is coming; ⁵⁵ and when the wind is from the south, you say there will be a heat wave, and there is. ⁵⁶ Hypocrites! You know how to interpret the appearance of the earth and the sky — how is it that you don't know how to interpret this present time? ⁵⁷ Why don't you decide for yourselves what is the right course to follow? ⁵⁸ If someone brings a lawsuit against you, take pains to settle with him first; otherwise he will take the matter to court, and the judge will turn you over to the bailiff, and the bailiff will throw you in jail. ⁵⁹ I tell you, you won't get out of there till you have paid the last penny!"

13 ¹ Just then, some people came to tell Yeshua about the men from the Galil whom Pilate had slaughtered even while they were slaughtering animals for sacrifice. ² His answer to them was, "Do you think that just because they died so horribly, these folks from the Galil were worse sinners than all the others from the Galil? ³ No, I tell you. Rather, unless you turn to God from your sins, you will all die as they did! ⁴ "Or what about those eighteen people who died when the tower at Shiloach fell on them? Do you think they were worse offenders than all the other people living in Yerushalayim? ⁵ No, I tell you. Rather, unless you turn from your sins, you will all die similarly."

⁶ Then Yeshua gave this illustration: "A man had a fig tree planted in his vineyard, and he came looking for fruit but didn't find any. ⁷ So he said to the man who took care of the vineyard, 'Here, I've come looking for fruit on this fig tree for three years now without finding any. Cut it down — why let it go on using up the soil?' ⁸ But he answered, 'Sir, leave it alone one more year. I'll dig around it and put manure on it. ⁹ If it bears fruit next year, well and good; if not, you will have it cut down then.'"

¹⁰ Yeshua was teaching in one of the synagogues on *Shabbat*. ¹¹ A woman came up who had a spirit which had crippled her for eighteen years; she was bent double and unable to stand erect at all. ¹² On seeing her, Yeshua called her and said to her, "Lady, you have been set free from your weakness!" ¹³ He put his hands on her, and at once she stood upright and began to glorify God.

¹⁴ But the president of the synagogue, indignant that Yeshua had healed on *Shabbat*, spoke up and said to the congregation, "There are six days in the week for working; so come during those days to be healed, not on *Shabbat*!" ¹⁵ However, the Lord answered him, "You hypocrites! Each one of you on *Shabbat* — don't you unloose your ox or your donkey from the stall and lead him off to drink? ¹⁶ This woman is a daughter of Avraham, and the Adversary kept her tied up for eighteen years! Shouldn't she be freed from this bondage on *Shabbat*?" ¹⁷ By these words, Yeshua put to shame the people who opposed him; but the rest of the crowd were happy about all the wonderful things that were taking place through him.

ʷ Micah 7:6

¹⁸ So he went on to say, "What is the Kingdom of God like? With what will we compare it? ¹⁹ It is like a mustard seed that a man took and planted in his own garden, and it grew and became a tree, and the birds flying about nested in its branches."

²⁰ Again he said, "With what will I compare the Kingdom of God? ²¹ It is like yeast that a woman took and mixed with a bushel of flour, then waited until the whole batch of dough rose."

²² Yeshua continued traveling through town after town and village after village, teaching and making his way toward Yerushalayim. ²³ Someone asked him, "Are only a few people being saved?" ²⁴ He answered, "Struggle to get in through the narrow door, because — I'm telling you! — many will be demanding to get in and won't be able to, ²⁵ once the owner of the house has gotten up and shut the door. You will stand outside, knocking at the door and saying, 'Lord! Open up for us!' But he will answer, 'I don't know you or where you come from!' ²⁶ Then you will say, 'We ate and drank with you! you taught in our streets!' ²⁷ and he will tell you, 'I don't know where you're from. Get away from me, all you workers of wickedness!' ²⁸ You will cry and grind your teeth when you see Avraham, Yitz'chak, Ya'akov and all the prophets inside the Kingdom of God, but yourselves thrown outside. ²⁹ Moreover, people will come from the east, the west, the north and the south to sit at table in the Kingdom of God. ³⁰ And notice that some who are last will be first, and some who are first will be last."

³¹ Just at that moment, some *P'rushim* came up and said to Yeshua, "Get out and go away from here, because Herod wants to kill you!" ³² He said to them, "Go, tell that fox, 'Pay attention: today and tomorrow I am driving out demons and healing people, and on the third day I reach my goal.' ³³ Nevertheless, I must keep travelling today, tomorrow and the next day; because it is unthinkable that a prophet should die anywhere but in Yerushalayim.

³⁴ "Yerushalayim! Yerushalayim! You kill the prophets! You stone those who are sent to you! How often I wanted to gather your children, just as a hen gathers her chickens under her wings, but you refused! ³⁵ Look! God is abandoning your house to you! I tell you, you will not see me again until you say, **'Blessed is he who comes in the name of *Adonai*!'**ˣ

14 ¹ One *Shabbat* Yeshua went to eat in the home of one of the leading *P'rushim*, and they were watching him closely. ² In front of him was a man whose body was swollen with fluid. ³ Yeshua spoke up and asked the *Torah* experts and *P'rushim*, "Does the *Torah* allow healing on *Shabbat* or not?" ⁴ But they said nothing. So, taking hold of him, he healed him and sent him away. ⁵ To them he said, "Which of you, if a son or an ox falls into a well, will hesitate to haul him out on *Shabbat*?" ⁶ And to these things they could give no answer.

⁷ When Yeshua noticed how the guests were choosing for themselves the best seats at the table, he told them this parable: ⁸ "When you are invited by someone to a wedding feast, don't sit down in the best seat; because if there is someone more important than you who has been invited, ⁹ the person who invited both of you might come and say to you, 'Give this man your place.' Then you will be humiliated as you go to take the least important place. ¹⁰ Instead, when you are invited, go and sit in the least important place; so that when the one who invited you comes, he will say to

---

ˣ Psalm 118:26

you, 'Go on up to a better seat.' Then you will be honored in front of everyone sitting with you. ¹¹ Because everyone who exalts himself will be humbled, but everyone who humbles himself will be exalted."

¹² Yeshua also said to the one who had invited him, "When you give a lunch or a dinner, don't invite your friends, brothers, relatives or rich neighbors; for they may well invite you in return, and that will be your repayment. ¹³ Instead, when you have a party, invite poor people, disfigured people, the crippled, the blind! ¹⁴ How blessed you will be that they have nothing with which to repay you! For you will be repaid at the resurrection of the righteous."

¹⁵ On hearing this, one of the people at the table with Yeshua said to him, "How blessed are those who eat bread in the Kingdom of God!" ¹⁶ But he replied, "Once a man gave a banquet and invited many people. ¹⁷ When the time came for the banquet, he sent his slave to tell those who had been invited, 'Come! Everything is ready!' ¹⁸ But they responded with a chorus of excuses. The first said to him, 'I've just bought a field, and I have to go out and see it. Please accept my apologies.' ¹⁹ Another said, 'I've just bought five yoke of oxen, and I'm on my way to test them out. Please accept my apologies.' ²⁰ Still another said, 'I have just gotten married, so I can't come.' ²¹ The slave came and reported these things to his master.

"Then the owner of the house, in a rage, told his slave, 'Quick, go out into the streets and alleys of the city; and bring in the poor, the disfigured, the blind and the crippled!' ²² The slave said, 'Sir, what you ordered has been done, and there is still room.' ²³ The master said to the slave, 'Go out to the country roads and boundary walls, and insistently persuade people to come in, so that my house will be full. ²⁴ I tell you, not one of those who were invited will get a taste of my banquet!'"

²⁵ Large crowds were traveling along with Yeshua. Turning, he said to them, ²⁶ "If anyone comes to me and does not hate his father, his mother, his wife, his children, his brothers and his sisters, yes, and his own life besides, he cannot be my *talmid.* ²⁷ Whoever does not carry his own execution-stake and come after me cannot be my *talmid.*

²⁸ "Suppose one of you wants to build a tower. Don't you sit down and estimate the cost, to see if you have enough capital to complete it? ²⁹ If you don't, then when you have laid the foundation but can't finish, all the onlookers start making fun of you ³⁰ and say, 'This is the man who began to build, but couldn't finish!'

³¹ "Or again, suppose one king is going out to wage war with another king. Doesn't he first sit down and consider whether he, with his ten thousand troops, has enough strength to meet the other one, who is coming against him with twenty thousand? ³² If he hasn't, then while the other is still far away, he sends a delegation to inquire about terms for peace.

³³ "So every one of you who doesn't renounce all that he has cannot be my *talmid.* ³⁴ Salt is excellent. But if even the salt becomes tasteless, what can be used to season it? ³⁵ It is fit for neither soil nor manure — people throw it out. Those who have ears that can hear, let them hear!"

15 ¹ The tax-collectors and sinners kept gathering around to hear Yeshua, ² and the *P'rushim* and *Torah*-teachers kept grumbling. "This fellow," they said, "welcomes sinners — he even eats with them!" ³ So he told them this parable: ⁴ "If one of you has a hundred sheep and loses one of them, doesn't he leave the other ninety-nine in the desert and go after the lost one until he finds it? ⁵ When he does find it, he joyfully hoists it onto his shoulders; ⁶ and when he gets home, he calls his friends and neighbors together and says, 'Come, celebrate with me, because I have found my lost sheep!' ⁷ I tell you that in the same way, there will be more joy in heaven over one sinner who turns to God from his sins than over ninety-nine righteous people who have no need to repent.

⁸ "Another example: what woman, if she has ten drachmas and loses one of these valuable coins, won't light a lamp, sweep the house and search all over until she finds it? ⁹ And when she does find it, she calls her friends and neighbors together and says, 'Come, celebrate with me, because I have found the drachma I lost.' ¹⁰ In the same way, I tell you, there is joy among God's angels when one sinner repents."

¹¹ Again Yeshua said, "A man had two sons. ¹² The younger of them said to his father, 'Father, give me the share of the estate that will be mine.' So the father divided the property between them. ¹³ As soon as he could convert his share into cash, the younger son left home and went off to a distant country, where he squandered his money in reckless living. ¹⁴ But after he had spent it all, a severe famine arose throughout that country, and he began to feel the pinch.

¹⁵ "So he went and attached himself to one of the citizens of that country, who sent him into his fields to feed pigs. ¹⁶ He longed to fill his stomach with the carob pods the pigs were eating, but no one gave him any.

¹⁷ "At last he came to his senses and said, 'Any number of my father's hired workers have food to spare; and here I am, starving to death! ¹⁸ I'm going to get up and go back to my father and say to him, "Father, I have sinned against Heaven and against you; ¹⁹ I am no longer worthy to be called your son; treat me like one of your hired workers." ' ²⁰ So he got up and started back to his father.

"But while he was still a long way off, his father saw him and was moved with pity. He ran and threw his arms around him and kissed him warmly. ²¹ His son said to him, 'Father, I have sinned against Heaven and against you; I am no longer worthy to be called your son —' ²² but his father said to his slaves, 'Quick, bring out a robe, the best one, and put it on him; and put a ring on his finger and shoes on his feet; ²³ and bring the calf that has been fattened up, and kill it. Let's eat and have a celebration! ²⁴ For this son of mine was dead, but now he's alive again! He was lost, but now he has been found!' And they began celebrating.

²⁵ "Now his older son was in the field. As he came close to the house, he heard music and dancing. ²⁶ So he called one of the servants and asked, 'What's going on?' ²⁷ The servant told him, 'Your brother has come back, and your father has slaughtered the calf that was fattened up, because he has gotten him back safe and sound.' ²⁸ But the older son became angry and refused to go inside.

"So his father came out and pleaded with him. ²⁹ 'Look,' the son answered, 'I have worked for you all these years, and I have never disobeyed your orders. But you have never even given me a young goat, so that I could celebrate with my friends. ³⁰ Yet this son of yours comes, who squandered your property with prostitutes, and for him you slaughter the fattened calf!' ³¹ 'Son, you are always with me,' said the father, 'and everything I have is yours. ³² We had to celebrate and rejoice, because this brother of yours was dead but has come back to life — he was lost but has been found.'"

16 [1] Speaking to the *talmidim*, Yeshua said: "There was a wealthy man who employed a general manager. Charges were brought to him that his manager was squandering his resources. [2] So he summoned him and asked him, 'What is this I hear about you? Turn in your accounts, for you can no longer be manager.'

[3] "'What am I to do?' said the manager to himself. 'My boss is firing me, I'm not strong enough to dig ditches, and I'm ashamed to go begging. [4] Aha! I know what I'll do — something that will make people welcome me into their homes after I've lost my job here!'

[5] "So, after making appointments with each of his employer's debtors, he said to the first, 'How much do you owe my boss?' [6] 'Eight hundred gallons of olive oil,' he replied. 'Take your note back,' he told him. 'Now, quickly! Sit down and write one for four hundred!' [7] To the next he said, 'And you, how much do you owe?' 'A thousand bushels of wheat,' he replied. 'Take your note back and write one for eight hundred.'

[8] "And the employer of this dishonest manager applauded him for acting so shrewdly! For the worldly have more *sekhel* than those who have received the light — in dealing with their own kind of people!

[9] "Now what I say to you is this: use worldly wealth to make friends for yourselves, so that when it gives out, you may be welcomed into the eternal home. [10] Someone who is trustworthy in a small matter is also trustworthy in large ones, and someone who is dishonest in a small matter is also dishonest in large ones. [11] So if you haven't been trustworthy in handling worldly wealth, who is going to trust you with the real thing? [12] And if you haven't been trustworthy with what belongs to someone else, who will give you what ought to belong to you? [13] No servant can be slave to two masters, for he will either hate the first and love the second, or scorn the second and be loyal to the first. You can't be a slave to both God and money."

[14] The *P'rushim* heard all this, and since they were money-lovers, they ridiculed him. [15] He said to them, "You people make yourselves look righteous to others, but God knows your hearts; what people regard highly is an abomination before God! [16] Up to the time of Yochanan there were the *Torah* and the Prophets. Since then the Good News of the Kingdom of God has been proclaimed, and everyone is pushing to get in. [17] But it is easier for heaven and earth to pass away than for one stroke of a letter in the *Torah* to become void. [18] Every man who divorces his wife and marries another woman commits adultery, and a man who marries a woman divorced by her husband commits adultery.

[19] "Once there was a rich man who used to dress in the most expensive clothing and spent his days in magnificent luxury. [20] At his gate had been laid a beggar named El'azar who was covered with sores. [21] He would have been glad to eat the scraps that fell from the rich man's table; but instead, even the dogs would come and lick his sores. [22] In time the beggar died and was carried away by the angels to Avraham's side; the rich man also died and was buried.

[23] "In Sh'ol, where he was in torment, the rich man looked up and saw Avraham far away with El'azar at his side. [24] He called out, 'Father Avraham, take pity on me, and send El'azar just to dip the tip of his finger in water to cool my tongue, because I'm in agony in this fire!' [25] However, Avraham said, 'Son, remember that when you were alive, you got the good things while he got the bad; but now he gets his consolation here, while you are the one in agony. [26] Yet that isn't all: between you and us a

deep rift has been established, so that those who would like to pass from here to you cannot, nor can anyone cross over from there to us.'

²⁷ "He answered, 'Then, father, I beg you to send him to my father's house, ²⁸ where I have five brothers, to warn them; so that they may be spared having to come to this place of torment too.' ²⁹ But Avraham said, 'They have Moshe and the Prophets; they should listen to them.' ³⁰ However, he said, 'No, father Avraham, they need more. If someone from the dead goes to them, they'll repent!' ³¹ But he replied, 'If they won't listen to Moshe and the Prophets, they won't be convinced even if someone rises from the dead!'"

17 ¹ Yeshua said to his *talmidim*, "It is impossible that snares will not be set. But woe to the person who sets them! ² It would be to his advantage that he have a millstone hung around his neck and he be thrown into the sea, rather than that he ensnare one of these little ones. ³ Watch yourselves! If your brother sins, rebuke him; and if he repents, forgive him. ⁴ Also, if seven times in one day he sins against you, and seven times he comes to you and says, 'I repent,' you are to forgive him." ⁵ The emissaries said to the Lord, "Increase our trust." ⁶ The Lord replied, "If you had trust as tiny as a mustard seed, you could say to this fig tree, 'Be uprooted and replanted in the sea!' and it would obey you. ⁷ If one of you has a slave tending the sheep or plowing, when he comes back from the field, will you say to him, 'Come along now, sit down and eat'? ⁸ No, you'll say, 'Get my supper ready, dress for work, and serve me until I have finished eating and drinking; after that, you may eat and drink.' ⁹ Does he thank the slave because he did what he was told to do? No! ¹⁰ It's the same with you — when you have done everything you were told to do, you should be saying, 'We're just ordinary slaves, we have only done our duty.'"

¹¹ On his way to Yerushalayim, Yeshua passed along the border country between Shomron and the Galil. ¹² As he entered one of the villages, ten men afflicted with *tzara'at* met him. They stood at a distance ¹³ and called out, "Yeshua! Rabbi! Have pity on us!" ¹⁴ On seeing them, he said, "Go and let the *cohanim* examine you!" And as they went, they were cleansed. ¹⁵ One of them, as soon as he noticed that he had been healed, returned shouting praises to God, ¹⁶ and fell on his face at Yeshua's feet to thank him. Now he was from Shomron. ¹⁷ Yeshua said, "Weren't ten cleansed? Where are the other nine? ¹⁸ Was no one found coming back to give glory to God except this foreigner?" ¹⁹ And to the man from Shomron he said, "Get up, you may go; your trust has saved you."

²⁰ The *P'rushim* asked Yeshua when the Kingdom of God would come. "The Kingdom of God," he answered, "does not come with visible signs; ²¹ nor will people be able to say, 'Look! Here it is!' or, 'Over there!' Because, you see, the Kingdom of God is among you." ²² Then he said to his *talmidim*, "The time is coming when you will long to see even one of the days of the Son of Man, but you will not see it. ²³ People will say to you, 'Look! Right here!' or, 'See! Over there!' Don't run off, don't follow them, ²⁴ because the Son of Man in his day will be like lightning that flashes and lights up the sky from one horizon to the other. ²⁵ But first he must endure horrible suffering and be rejected by this generation.

²⁶ "Also, at the time of the Son of Man, it will be just as it was at the time of Noach. ²⁷ People ate and drank, and men and women married, right up until the day Noach entered the ark; then the flood came and destroyed them all. ²⁸ Likewise, as it

was in the time of Lot — people ate and drank, bought and sold, planted and built; ²⁹ but the day Lot left S'dom, fire and sulfur rained down from heaven and destroyed them all. ³⁰ That is how it will be on the day the Son of Man is revealed. ³¹ On that day, if someone is on the roof with his belongings in his house, he must not go down to take them away. Similarly, if someone is in the field, he must not turn back — ³² remember Lot's wife! ³³ Whoever aims at preserving his own life will lose it, but whoever loses his life will stay alive. ³⁴ I tell you, on that night there will be two people in one bed — one will be taken and the other left behind. ³⁵ There will be two women grinding grain together — one will be taken and the other left behind." ³⁶ *

³⁷ They asked him, "Where, Lord?" He answered, "Wherever there's a dead body, that's where the vultures gather."

18 ¹ Then Yeshua told his *talmidim* a parable, in order to impress on them that they must always keep praying and not lose heart. ² "In a certain town, there was a judge who neither feared God nor respected other people. ³ There was also in that town a widow who kept coming to him and saying, 'Give me a judgment against the man who is trying to ruin me.' ⁴ For a long time he refused; but after awhile, he said to himself, 'I don't fear God, and I don't respect other people; ⁵ but because this widow is such a *nudnik*, I will see to it that she gets justice — otherwise, she'll keep coming and pestering me till she wears me out!'

⁶ Then the Lord commented, "Notice what this corrupt judge says. ⁷ Now won't God grant justice to his chosen people who cry out to him day and night? Is he delaying long over them? ⁸ I tell you that he will judge in their favor, and quickly! But when the Son of Man comes, will he find this trust on the earth at all?"

⁹ Also, to some who were relying on their own righteousness and looking down on everyone else, he told this parable: ¹⁰ "Two men went up to the Temple to pray, one a *Parush* and the other a tax-collector. ¹¹ The *Parush* stood and prayed to himself, 'O God! I thank you that I am not like the rest of humanity — greedy, dishonest, immoral, or like this tax-collector! ¹² I fast twice a week, I pay tithes on my entire income, . . .' ¹³ But the tax-collector, standing far off, would not even raise his eyes toward heaven, but beat his breast and said, 'God! Have mercy on me, sinner that I am!' ¹⁴ I tell you, this man went down to his home right with God rather than the other. For everyone who exalts himself will be humbled, but everyone who humbles himself will be exalted."

¹⁵ People brought him babies to touch; but when the *talmidim* saw the people doing this, they rebuked them. ¹⁶ However, Yeshua called the children to him and said, "Let the children come to me, and stop hindering them, because the Kingdom of God belongs to such as these. ¹⁷ Yes! I tell you that whoever does not receive the Kingdom of God like a little child will not enter it at all!"

¹⁸ One of the leaders asked him, "Good rabbi, what should I do to obtain eternal life?" ¹⁹ Yeshua said to him, "Why are you calling me good? No one is good but God! ²⁰ You know the *mitzvot* — **'Don't commit adultery, don't murder, don't steal, don't give false testimony, honor your father and mother, . . .'**ʸ ²¹ He replied, "I have kept all these since I was a boy." ²² On hearing this Yeshua said to him, "There

---

ʸ Exodus 20:12–13(16); Deuteronomy 5:16–17(20)

* Some manuscripts have verse 36: Two men will be in a field — one will be taken and the other left behind."

is one thing you still lack. Sell whatever you have, distribute the proceeds to the poor, and you will have riches in heaven. Then come, follow me!" ²³ But when the man heard this, he became very sad, because he was very rich.

²⁴ Yeshua looked at him and said, "How hard it is for people with wealth to enter the Kingdom of God! ²⁵ It's easier for a camel to pass through a needle's eye than for a rich man to enter the Kingdom of God!" ²⁶ Those who heard this asked, "Then who can be saved?" ²⁷ He said, "What is impossible humanly is possible with God."

²⁸ Kefa said, "Look, we have left our homes and followed you." ²⁹ Yeshua answered them, "Yes! I tell you that everyone who has left house, wife, brothers, parents or children, for the sake of the kingdom of God, ³⁰ will receive many times as much in the *'olam hazeh*, and in the *'olam haba* eternal life."

³¹ Then, taking the Twelve, Yeshua said to them, "We are now going up to Yerushalayim, where everything written through the prophets about the Son of Man will come true. ³² For he will be handed over to the *Goyim* and be ridiculed, insulted and spat upon. ³³ Then, after they have beaten him, they will kill him. But on the third day he will rise." ³⁴ However, they understood none of this; its meaning had been hidden from them, and they had no idea what he was talking about.

³⁵ As Yeshua approached Yericho, a blind man was sitting by the road, begging. ³⁶ When he heard the crowd going past, he asked what it was all about; ³⁷ and they told him, "Yeshua from Natzeret is passing by." ³⁸ He called out, "Yeshua! Son of David! Have pity on me!" ³⁹ Those in front scolded him in order to get him to shut up, but he shouted all the louder, "Son of David! Have pity on me!" ⁴⁰ Yeshua stopped and ordered the man to be brought to him. When he had come, Yeshua asked him, ⁴¹ "What do you want me to do for you?" The blind man said, "Lord, let me be able to see." ⁴² Yeshua said to him, "See again! your trust has healed you!" ⁴³ Instantly he received his sight and began following him, glorifying God; and when all the people saw it, they too praised God.

19 ¹ Yeshua entered Yericho and was passing through, ² when a man named Zakkai appeared who was a chief tax-collector and a wealthy man. ³ He was trying to see who Yeshua was; but, being short, he couldn't, because of the crowd. ⁴ So he ran on ahead and climbed a fig tree in order to see him, for Yeshua was about to pass that way. ⁵ When he came to the place, he looked up and said to him, "Zakkai! Hurry! Come down, because I have to stay at your house today!" ⁶ He climbed down as fast as he could and welcomed Yeshua joyfully. ⁷ Everyone who saw it began muttering, "He has gone to be the house-guest of a sinner." ⁸ But Zakkai stood there and said to the Lord, "Here, Lord, I am giving half of all I own to the poor; and if I have cheated anyone, I will pay him back four times as much." ⁹ Yeshua said to him, "Today salvation has come to this house, inasmuch as this man too is a son of Avraham. ¹⁰ For the Son of Man came to seek and save what was lost."

¹¹ While they were listening to this, Yeshua went on to tell a parable, because he was near Yerushalayim, and the people supposed that the Kingdom of God was about to appear at any moment. ¹² Therefore he said, "A nobleman went to a country far away to have himself crowned king and then return. ¹³ Calling ten of his servants, he gave them ten *manim* [a *maneh* is about three months' wages] and said to them, 'Do business with this while I'm away.' ¹⁴ But his countrymen hated him, and they sent a delegation after him to say, 'We don't want this man to rule over us.'

¹⁵ "However, he returned, having been made king, and sent for the servants to whom he had given the money, to find out what each one had earned in his business dealings. ¹⁶ The first one came in and said, 'Sir, your *maneh* has earned ten more *manim.*' ¹⁷ 'Excellent!' he said to him. 'You are a good servant. Because you have been trustworthy in a small matter, I am putting you in charge of ten towns.' ¹⁸ The second one came and said, 'Sir, your *maneh* has earned five more *manim;* ¹⁹ and to this one he said, 'You be in charge of five towns.'

²⁰ "Then another one came and said, 'Sir, here is your *maneh.* I kept it hidden in a piece of cloth, ²¹ because I was afraid of you — you take out what you didn't put in, and you harvest what you didn't plant.' ²² To him the master said, 'You wicked servant! I will judge you by your own words! So you knew, did you, that I was a severe man, taking out what I didn't put in and harvesting what I didn't plant? ²³ Then why didn't you put my money in the bank? Then, when I returned, I would have gotten it back with interest!' ²⁴ To those standing by, he said, 'Take the *maneh* from him and give it to the one with ten *manim.*' ²⁵ They said to him, 'Sir, he already has ten *manim!*' ²⁶ But the master answered, 'I tell you, everyone who has something will be given more; but from anyone who has nothing, even what he does have will be taken away. ²⁷ However, as for these enemies of mine who did not want me to be their king, bring them here and execute them in my presence!'"

²⁸ After saying this, Yeshua went on and began the ascent to Yerushalayim. ²⁹ As he approached Beit-Pagei and Beit-Anyah, by the Mount of Olives, he sent two *talmidim,* ³⁰ instructing them, "Go into the village ahead; on entering it, you will find a colt tied up that has never been ridden. Untie it and bring it here. ³¹ If anyone asks why you are untying it, tell him, 'The Lord needs it.'" ³² Those who were sent went off and found it just as he had told them. ³³ As they were untying the colt, its owners said to them, "Why are you untying the colt?" ³⁴ and they said, "Because the Lord needs it." ³⁵ They brought it to Yeshua; and, throwing their robes on the colt, they put Yeshua on it. ³⁶ As he went along, people carpeted the road with their clothing; ³⁷ and as he came near Yerushalayim, where the road descends from the Mount of Olives, the entire band of *talmidim* began to sing and praise God at the top of their voices for all the powerful works they had seen:

³⁸   **"Blessed is** the King **who is coming in the name of** *ADONAI***!"**ᶻ

     "Shalom in heaven!"

and

     "Glory in the highest places!"

³⁹ Some of the *P'rushim* in the crowd said to him, "Rabbi! Reprimand your *talmidim!*" ⁴⁰ But he answered them, "I tell you that if they keep quiet, the stones will shout!"

⁴¹ When Yeshua had come closer and could see the city, he wept over it, ⁴² saying, "If you only knew today what is needed for *shalom*! But for now it is hidden from

---

ᶻ Psalm 118:26

your sight. ⁴³ For the days are coming upon you when your enemies will set up a barricade around you, encircle you, hem you in on every side, ⁴⁴ and dash you to the ground, you and your children within your walls, leaving not one stone standing on another — and all because you did not recognize your opportunity when God offered it!"

⁴⁵ Then Yeshua entered the Temple grounds and began driving out those doing business there, ⁴⁶ saying to them, "The *Tanakh* says, **'My House is to be a house of prayer,'** *ᵃ* but you have made it into a **den of robbers!"** *ᵇ*

⁴⁷ Every day he taught at the Temple. The head *cohanim*, the *Torah*-teachers and the leaders of the people tried to find a way of putting an end to him; ⁴⁸ but they couldn't find any way of doing it, because all the people were hanging onto his every word.

20 ¹ One day, as Yeshua was teaching the people at the Temple, making known the Good News, the head *cohanim* and the *Torah*-teachers, along with the elders, came up to him ² and said, "Tell us, what *s'mikhah* do you have that authorizes you to do these things? Who gave you this *s'mikhah*?" ³ He answered, "I too will ask you a question. Tell me, ⁴ the immersion of Yochanan — was it from Heaven or from a human source?" ⁵ They discussed it among themselves, saying, "If we say, 'From Heaven,' he will say, 'Then why didn't you believe him?' ⁶ But if we say, 'From a human source,' all the people will stone us, because they're convinced that Yochanan was a prophet." ⁷ So they answered, "We don't know where it came from." ⁸ Yeshua said to them, "Then I won't tell you by what *s'mikhah* I do these things."

⁹ Next Yeshua told the people this parable: "A man planted a vineyard, rented it to tenant-farmers and went away for a long time. ¹⁰ When the time came, he sent a servant to the tenants to receive his share of the crop from the vineyard; but the tenants beat him up and sent him away empty-handed. ¹¹ He sent another servant; they beat him too, insulted him and sent him away empty-handed. ¹² He sent yet a third; this one they wounded and threw out.

¹³ "Then the owner of the vineyard said, 'What am I to do? I will send my son, whom I love; maybe they will respect him.' ¹⁴ But when the tenants saw him, they discussed it among themselves and said, 'This is the heir; let's kill him, so that the inheritance will be ours!' ¹⁵ And they threw him out of the vineyard and killed him.

"Now what will the owner of the vineyard do to them? ¹⁶ He will come and put an end to those tenants and give the vineyard to others!" When the people heard this, they said, "Heaven forbid!" ¹⁷ But Yeshua looked searchingly at them and said, "Then what is this which is written in the *Tanakh*,

> **'The very rock which the builders rejected**
> **has become the cornerstone'?** *ᶜ*

¹⁸ Whoever falls on that stone will be broken in pieces; but if it falls on him, he will be crushed to powder!"

¹⁹ The *Torah*-teachers and the head *cohanim* would have seized him at that very moment, because they knew that he had aimed this parable at them, but they were afraid of the people.

ᵃ Isaiah 56:7   *ᵇ* Jeremiah 7:11   *ᶜ* Psalm 118:22

²⁰ So they kept a close watch on the situation. They sent spies who hypocritically represented themselves as righteous, so that they might seize hold of something Yeshua said, as an excuse to hand him over to the jurisdiction and authority of the governor. ²¹ They put to him this *sh'eilah*: "Rabbi, we know that you speak and teach straightforwardly, showing no partiality but really teaching what God's way is. ²² Does *Torah* permit us to pay taxes to the Roman Emperor or not?" ²³ But he, spotting their craftiness, said to them, ²⁴ "Show me a denarius! Whose name and picture does it have?" "The Emperor's," they replied. ²⁵ "Then," he said to them, "give the Emperor what belongs to the Emperor. And give God what belongs to God!" ²⁶ They were unable to trap him by anything he said publicly; indeed, amazed at his answer, they fell silent.

²⁷ Some *Tz'dukim*, who say there is no resurrection, came to Yeshua ²⁸ and put to him a *sh'eilah*: "Rabbi, Moshe wrote for us that **if a man dies leaving a wife but no children, his brother must take the wife and have children to preserve the man's family line.**ᵈ ²⁹ Now there were seven brothers. The first took a wife and died child-less, ³⁰ then the second ³¹ and third took her, and likewise all seven, but they all died without leaving children. ³² Lastly, the woman also died. ³³ In the Resurrection, which one's wife will she be? For all seven were married to her."

³⁴ Yeshua said to them, "In this age, men and women marry; ³⁵ but those judged worthy of the age to come, and of resurrection from the dead, do not get married, ³⁶ because they can no longer die. Being children of the Resurrection, they are like angels; indeed, they are children of God.

³⁷ "But even Moshe showed that the dead are raised; for in the passage about the bush, he calls ADONAI **'the God of Avraham, the God of Yitz'chak and the God of Ya'akov.'**ᵉ ³⁸ Now he is not God of the dead, but of the living — to him all are alive."

³⁹ Some of the *Torah*-teachers answered, "Well spoken, Rabbi." ⁴⁰ For they no longer dared put to him a *sh'eilah*. ⁴¹ But he said to them, "How is it that people say the Messiah is David's son? ⁴² For David himself says in the book of Psalms,

⁴³   **'ADONAI said to my Lord,**
       "Sit at my right hand
       until I make your enemies your footstool."'ᶠ

⁴⁴ David thus calls him 'Lord.' So how can he be David's son?"

⁴⁵ Within the hearing of all the people, Yeshua said to his *talmidim*, ⁴⁶ "Watch out for the kind of *Torah*-teachers that like to walk around in robes and be greeted defer-entially in the marketplaces, the kind that like to have the best seats in the synagogues and the places of honor at banquets, ⁴⁷ the kind that swallow up widows' houses while making a show of *davvening* at great length. Their punishment will be all the worse!"

21 ¹ Then Yeshua looked up, and as he watched the rich placing their gifts into the Temple offering-boxes, ² he also saw a poor widow put in two small coins. ³ He said, "I tell you the truth, this poor widow has put in more than all the others. ⁴ For they, out of their wealth, have contributed money they could easily spare; but she, out of her poverty, has given all she had to live on."

ᵈ Deuteronomy 25:5   ᵉ Exodus 3:6   ᶠ Psalm 110:1

⁵ As some people were remarking about the Temple, how beautiful its stone-work and memorial decorations were, he said, ⁶ "The time is coming when what you see here will be totally destroyed — not a single stone will be left standing!" ⁷ They asked him, "Rabbi, if this is so, when will these events take place? And what sign will show that they are about to happen?" ⁸ He answered, "Watch out! Don't be fooled! For many will come in my name, saying, 'I am he!' and, 'The time has come!' Don't go after them. ⁹ And when you hear of wars and revolutions, don't panic. For these things must happen first, but the end will not follow immediately."

¹⁰ Then he told them, "Peoples will fight each other, nations will fight each other, ¹¹ there will be great earthquakes, there will be epidemics and famines in various places, and there will be fearful sights and great signs from Heaven. ¹² But before all this, they will arrest you and persecute you, handing you over to the synagogues and prisons; and you will be brought before kings and governors. This will all be on account of me, ¹³ but it will prove an opportunity for you to bear witness. ¹⁴ So make up your minds not to worry, rehearsing your defense beforehand; ¹⁵ for I myself will give you an eloquence and a wisdom that no adversary will be able to resist or refute. ¹⁶ You will be betrayed even by parents, brothers, relatives and friends; some of you they will have put to death; ¹⁷ and every-one will hate you because of me. ¹⁸ But not a hair of your head will be lost. ¹⁹ By standing firm you will save your lives.

²⁰ "However, when you see Yerushalayim surrounded by armies, then you are to understand that she is about to be destroyed. ²¹ Those in Y'hudah must escape to the hills, those inside the city must get out, and those in the country must not enter it. ²² For these are the days of vengeance, when everything that has been written in the *Tanakh* will come true. ²³ What a terrible time it will be for pregnant women and nursing mothers! For there will be great distress in the Land and judgment on the people. ²⁴ Some will fall by the edge of the sword, others will be carried into all the countries of the *Goyim*, and Yerushalayim will be trampled down by the *Goyim* until the age of the *Goyim* has run its course.

²⁵ "There will appear signs in the sun, moon and stars; and on earth, nations will be in anxiety and bewilderment at the sound and surge of the sea, ²⁶ as people faint with fear at the prospect of what is overtaking the world; for **the powers in heaven will be shaken.**ᵍ ²⁷ And then they will see **the Son of Man coming in a cloud** with tremendous power and glory.ʰ ²⁸ When these things start to happen, stand up and hold your heads high; because you are about to be liberated!"

²⁹ Then he told them a parable: "Look at the fig tree, indeed all the trees. ³⁰ As soon as they sprout leaves, you can see for yourselves that summer is near. ³¹ In the same way, when you see these things taking place, you are to know that the Kingdom of God is near! ³² Yes! I tell you that this people will certainly not pass away before it has all happened. ³³ Heaven and earth will pass away, but my words will certainly not pass away.

³⁴ "But keep watch on yourselves, or your hearts will become dulled by carousing, drunkenness and the worries of everyday living, and that Day will be sprung upon you suddenly like a trap! ³⁵ For it will close in on everyone, no matter where they live, throughout the whole world. ³⁶ Stay alert, always praying that you

---

ᵍ Haggai 2:6, 21   ʰ Daniel 7:13–14

will have the strength to escape all the things that will happen and to stand in the presence of the Son of Man."

³⁷ Yeshua spent his days at the Temple, teaching; while at night he went out and stayed on the hill called the Mount of Olives. ³⁸ All the people would rise with the dawn to come and hear him at the Temple courts.

22 ¹ But the festival of *Matzah*, known as *Pesach*, was approaching; ² and the head *cohanim* and the *Torah*-teachers began trying to find some way to get rid of Yeshua, because they were afraid of the people.

³ At this point the Adversary went into Y'hudah from K'riot, who was one of the Twelve. ⁴ He approached the head *cohanim* and the Temple guard and discussed with them how he might turn Yeshua over to them. ⁵ They were pleased and offered to pay him money. ⁶ He agreed and began looking for a good opportunity to betray Yeshua without the people's knowledge.

⁷ Then came the day of *matzah*, on which the Passover lamb had to be killed. ⁸ Yeshua sent Kefa and Yochanan, instructing them, "Go and prepare our *Seder*, so we can eat." ⁹ They asked him, "Where do you want us to prepare it?" ¹⁰ He told them, "As you're going into the city, a man carrying a jar of water will meet you. Follow him into the house he enters, ¹¹ and say to its owner, 'The Rabbi says to you, "Where is the guest room, where I am to eat the *Pesach* meal with my *talmidim*?" ' ¹² He will show you a large room upstairs already furnished; make the preparations there." ¹³ They went and found things just as Yeshua had told them they would be, and they prepared for the *Seder*.

¹⁴ When the time came, Yeshua and the emissaries reclined at the table, ¹⁵ and he said to them, "I have really wanted so much to celebrate this *Seder* with you before I die! ¹⁶ For I tell you, it is certain that I will not celebrate it again until it is given its full meaning in the Kingdom of God."

¹⁷ Then, taking a cup of wine, he made the *b'rakhah* and said, "Take this and share it among yourselves. ¹⁸ For I tell you that from now on, I will not drink the 'fruit of the vine' until the Kingdom of God comes." ¹⁹ Also, taking a piece of *matzah*, he made the *b'rakhah*, broke it, gave it to them and said, "This is my body, which is being given for you; do this in memory of me." ²⁰ He did the same with the cup after the meal, saying, "This cup is the New Covenant, ratified by my blood, which is being poured out for you.

²¹ "But look! The person who is betraying me is here at the table with me! ²² The Son of Man is going to his death according to God's plan, but woe to that man by whom he is being betrayed!" ²³ They began asking each other which of them could be about to do such a thing.

²⁴ An argument arose among them as to which of them should be considered the greatest. ²⁵ But Yeshua said to them, "The kings of the *Goyim* lord it over them; and those in authority over them are given the title, 'Benefactor.' ²⁶ But not so with you! On the contrary, let the greater among you become like the younger, and one who rules like one who serves. ²⁷ For who is greater? The one reclining at the table? or the one who serves? It's the one reclining at the table, isn't it? But I myself am among you like one who serves.

²⁸ "You are the ones who have stayed with me throughout my trials. ²⁹ Just as my Father gave me the right to rule, so I give you an appointment, ³⁰ namely, to eat

and drink at my table in my Kingdom and to sit on thrones judging the twelve tribes of Isra'el.

[31] "Shim'on, Shim'on, listen! The Adversary demanded to have you people for himself, to sift you like wheat! [32] But I prayed for you, Shim'on, that your trust might not fail. And you, once you have turned back in repentance, strengthen your brothers!" [33] Shim'on said to him, "Lord, I am prepared to go with you both to prison and to death!" [34] Yeshua replied, "I tell you, Kefa, the rooster will not crow today until you have denied three times that you know me."

[35] He said to them, "When I sent you out without wallet, pack or shoes, were you ever short of anything?" "Not a thing," they answered. [36] "But now," he said, if you have a wallet or a pack, take it; and if you don't have a sword, sell your robe to buy one. [37] For I tell you this: the passage from the *Tanakh* that says, **'He was counted with transgressors,'**[i] has to be fulfilled in me; since what is happening to me has a purpose." [38] They said, "Look, Lord, there are two swords right here!" "Enough!" he replied.

[39] On leaving, Yeshua went as usual to the Mount of Olives; and the *talmidim* followed him. [40] When he arrived, he said to them, "Pray that you won't be put to the test." [41] He went about a stone's throw away from them, kneeled down and prayed, [42] "Father, if you are willing, take this cup away from me; still, let not my will but yours be done." [43] There appeared to him an angel from heaven giving him strength, [44] and in great anguish he prayed more intensely, so that his sweat became like drops of blood falling to the ground. [45] On rising from prayer and coming to the *talmidim*, he found them sleeping because of their grief. [46] He said to them, "Why are you sleeping? Get up and pray that you won't be put to the test!"

[47] While he was still speaking, a crowd of people arrived, with the man called Y'hudah (one of the Twelve!) leading them. He came up to Yeshua to kiss him, [48] but Yeshua said to him, "Y'hudah, are you betraying the Son of Man with a kiss?" [49] When his followers saw what was going to happen, they said, "Lord, should we use our swords?" [50] One of them struck at the slave of the *cohen hagadol* and cut off his right ear. [51] But Yeshua answered, "Just let me do this," and, touching the man's ear, he healed him.

[52] Then Yeshua said to the head *cohanim*, the officers of the Temple guard and the elders who had come to seize him, "So you came out just as you would to the leader of a rebellion, with swords and clubs? [53] Every day I was there with you in the Temple court, yet you didn't arrest me. But this is your hour — the hour when darkness rules."

[54] Having seized him, they led him away and brought him into the house of the *cohen hagadol*. Kefa followed at a distance; [55] but when they had lit a fire in the middle of the courtyard and sat down together, Kefa joined them. [56] One of the servant girls saw him sitting in the light of the fire, stared at him and said, "This man also was with him." [57] But he denied it: "Lady, I don't even know him." [58] A little later, someone else saw him and said, "You're one of them too"; but Kefa said, "Man, I am not!" [59] About an hour later, another man asserted emphatically, "There can be no doubt that this fellow was with him, because he too is from the Galil!" [60] But Kefa said, "Man, I don't know what you're talking about!" And instantly, while he was still speaking, a rooster crowed. [61] The Lord turned and looked straight

---

[i] Isaiah 53:12

at Kefa; and Kefa remembered what the Lord had said, "Before the rooster crows today, you will deny me three times." ^{62} And he went outside and cried bitterly.

^{63} Meanwhile, the men who were holding Yeshua made fun of him. They beat him, ^{64} blindfolded him, and kept asking him, "Now, 'prophesy'! Who hit you that time?" ^{65} And they said many other insulting things to him.

^{66} At daybreak, the people's council of elders, including both head *cohanim* and *Torah*-teachers, met and led him off to their *Sanhedrin*, ^{67} where they said, "If you are the *Mashiach*, tell us." He answered, "If I tell you, you won't believe me; ^{68} and if I ask you, you won't answer. ^{69} But from now on, the Son of Man will be **sitting at the right hand of** *HaG'vurah*,"^{j} ^{70} They all said, "Does this mean, then, that you are the Son of God?" And he answered them, "You say I am." ^{71} They said, "Why do we need additional testimony? We have heard it ourselves from his own mouth!"

23 ^{1} With that, the whole *Sanhedrin* got up and brought Yeshua before Pilate, ^{2} where they started accusing him. "We found this man subverting our nation, forbidding us to pay taxes to the Emperor and claiming that he himself is the Messiah — a king!" ^{3} Pilate asked him, "Are you the king of the Jews?" And he answered him, "The words are yours." ^{4} Pilate said to the head *cohanim* and the crowds, "I find no ground for a charge against this man." ^{5} But they persisted. "He is inciting the people with his teaching throughout all Y'hudah — he started in the Galil, and now he's here!" ^{6} On hearing this, Pilate asked if the man was from the Galil; ^{7} and when he learned that he was under Herod's jurisdiction, he sent him over to Herod, who at that time happened to be in Yerushalayim too.

^{8} Herod was delighted to see Yeshua, because he had heard about him and for a long time had been wanting to meet him; indeed, he hoped to see him perform some miracle. ^{9} He questioned him at great length, but Yeshua made no reply. ^{10} However, the head *cohanim* and the *Torah*-teachers stood there, vehemently pressing their case against him. ^{11} Herod and his soldiers treated Yeshua with contempt and made fun of him. Then, dressing him in an elegant robe, they sent him back to Pilate. ^{12} That day Herod and Pilate became friends with each other; previously they had been enemies.

^{13} Pilate summoned the head *cohanim*, the leaders and the people, ^{14} and said to them, "You brought this man before me on a charge of subverting the people. I examined him in your presence and did not find the man guilty of the crime you are accusing him of. ^{15} And neither did Herod, because he sent him back to us. Clearly, he has not done anything that merits the death penalty. ^{16} Therefore, what I will do is have him flogged and release him." ^{17*} ^{18} But with one voice they shouted, "Away with this man! Give us Bar-Abba!" ^{19} (He was a man who had been thrown in prison for causing a riot in the city and for murder.) ^{20} Pilate appealed to them again, because he wanted to release Yeshua. ^{21} But they yelled, "Put him to death on the stake! Put him to death on the stake!" ^{22} A third time he asked them, "But what has this man done wrong? I haven't found any reason to put him to death. So I'm going to have him flogged and set free." ^{23} But they went on yelling insistently, demanding that he be executed on the stake; and their shouting prevailed. ^{24} Pilate decided to grant their demand; ^{25} he released the

---

^{j} Psalm 110:1
* Some manuscripts have verse 17: For he was required to release one man to them at the festival.

man who had been thrown in prison for insurrection and murder, the one they had asked for; and Yeshua he surrendered to their will.

²⁶ As the Roman soldiers led Yeshua away, they grabbed hold of a man from Cyrene named Shim'on, who was on his way in from the country. They put the execution-stake on his back and made him carry it behind Yeshua. ²⁷ Large numbers of people followed, including women crying and wailing over him. ²⁸ Yeshua turned to them and said, "Daughters of Yerushalayim, don't cry for me; cry for yourselves and your children! ²⁹ For the time is coming when people will say, 'The childless women are the lucky ones — those whose wombs have never borne a child, whose breasts have never nursed a baby! ³⁰ Then

> They will begin to **say to the mountains, 'Fall on us!'**
> and to the hills, 'Cover us!'**ᵏ

³¹ For if they do these things when the wood is green, what is going to happen when it's dry?"

³² Two other men, both criminals, were led out to be executed with him. ³³ When they came to the place called The Skull, they nailed him to a stake; and they nailed the criminals to stakes, one on the right and one on the left. ³⁴ Yeshua said, "Father, forgive them; they don't understand what they are doing."

> **They divided up his clothes by throwing dice.**ˡ ³⁵ The people stood **watching**, and the rulers **sneered at** him.ᵐ "He saved others," they said, "so if he really is the Messiah, the one chosen by God, let him save himself!" ³⁶ The soldiers too ridiculed him; they came up, offered him **vinegar**ⁿ ³⁷ and said, "If you are the king of the Jews, save yourself!" ³⁸ And there was a notice over him which read,

> THIS IS
> THE KING OF THE JEWS

³⁹ One of the criminals hanging there hurled insults at him. "Aren't you the Messiah? Save yourself and us!" ⁴⁰ But the other one spoke up and rebuked the first, saying, "Have you no fear of God? You're getting the same punishment as he is. ⁴¹ Ours is only fair; we're getting what we deserve for what we did. But this man did nothing wrong." ⁴² Then he said, "Yeshua, remember me when you come as King." ⁴³ Yeshua said to him, "Yes! I promise that you will be with me today in Gan-'Eden."

⁴⁴ It was now about noon, and darkness covered the whole Land until three o'clock in the afternoon; ⁴⁵ the sun did not shine. Also the *parokhet* in the Temple was split down the middle. ⁴⁶ Crying out with a loud voice, Yeshua said, "Father! **Into your hands I commit my spirit.**ᵒ With these words he gave up his spirit.

⁴⁷ When the Roman officer saw what had happened, he began to praise God and said, "Surely this man was innocent!" ⁴⁸ And when all the crowds that had gathered to watch the spectacle saw the things that had occurred, they returned home beating their breasts. ⁴⁹ All his friends, including the women who had accompanied him from the Galil, had been standing at a distance; they saw it all.

ᵏ Hosea 10:8 ˡ Psalm 22:19(18) ᵐ Psalm 22:8(7)
ⁿ Psalm 69:22(21) ᵒ Psalm 31:6(5)

^{50} There was a man named Yosef, a member of the *Sanhedrin*. He was a good man, a *tzaddik*; ^{51} and he had not been in agreement with either the *Sanhedrin*'s motivation or their action. He came from the town of Ramatayim, a town of the Judeans; and he looked forward to the Kingdom of God. ^{52} This man approached Pilate and asked for Yeshua's body. ^{53} He took it down, wrapped it in a linen sheet, and placed it in a tomb cut into the rock, that had never been used.

^{54} It was Preparation Day, and a *Shabbat* was about to begin. ^{55} The women who had come with Yeshua from the Galil followed; they saw the tomb and how his body was placed in it. ^{56} Then they went back home to prepare spices and ointments.

On *Shabbat* the women rested, in obedience to the commandment;

24 ^{1} but the next day, while it was still very early, they took the spices they had prepared, went to the tomb, ^{2} and found the stone rolled away from the tomb! ^{3} On entering, they discovered that the body of the Lord Yeshua was gone! ^{4} They were standing there, not knowing what to think about it, when suddenly two men in dazzlingly bright clothing stood next to them. ^{5} Terror-stricken, they bowed down with their faces to the ground. The two men said to them, "Why are you looking for the living among the dead? ^{6} He is not here; he has been raised. Remember how he told you while he was still in the Galil, ^{7} 'The Son of Man must be delivered into the hands of sinful men and be executed on a stake as a criminal, but on the third day be raised again'?" ^{8} Then they remembered his words; ^{9} and, returning from the tomb, they told everything to the Eleven and to all the rest. ^{10} The women who told the emissaries these things were Miryam of Magdala, Yochanah, Miryam the mother of Ya'akov, and the others in their circle.

^{11} But the emissaries didn't believe them; in fact, they thought that what they said was utter nonsense! ^{12} However, Kefa got up and ran to the tomb. Stooping down, he saw only the burial cloths and went home wondering what had happened.

^{13} That same day, two of them were going toward a village about seven miles from Yerushalayim called Amma'us, ^{14} and they were talking with each other about all the things that had happened. ^{15} As they talked and discussed, Yeshua himself came up and walked along with them, ^{16} but something kept them from recognizing him. ^{17} He asked them, "What are you talking about with each other as you walk along?" They stopped short, their faces downcast; ^{18} and one of them, named Cleopas, answered him, "Are you the only person staying in Yerushalayim that doesn't know the things that have been going on there the last few days?" ^{19} "What things?" he asked them. They said to him, "The things about Yeshua from Natzeret. He was a prophet and proved it by the things he did and said before God and all the people. ^{20} Our head *cohanim* and our leaders handed him over, so that he could be sentenced to death and executed on a stake as a criminal. ^{21} And we had hoped that he would be the one to liberate Isra'el! Besides all that, today is the third day since these things happened; ^{22} and this morning, some of the women astounded us. They were at the tomb early ^{23} and couldn't find his body, so they came back; but they also reported that they had seen a vision of angels who say he's alive! ^{24} Some of our friends went to the tomb and found it exactly as the women had said, but they didn't see him."

^{25} He said to them, "Foolish people! So unwilling to put your trust in everything the prophets spoke! ^{26} Didn't the Messiah have to die like this before entering his glory?"

²⁷ Then, starting with Moshe and all the prophets, he explained to them the things that can be found throughout the *Tanakh* concerning himself.

²⁸ They approached the village where they were going. He made as if he were going on farther; ²⁹ but they held him back, saying, "Stay with us, for it's almost evening, and it's getting dark." So he went in to stay with them. ³⁰ As he was reclining with them at the table, he took the *matzah*, made the *b'rakhah*, broke it and handed it to them. ³¹ Then their eyes were opened, and they recognized him. But he became invisible to them. ³² They said to each other, "Didn't our hearts burn inside us as he spoke to us on the road, opening up the *Tanakh* to us?"

³³ They got up at once, returned to Yerushalayim and found the Eleven gathered together with their friends, ³⁴ saying, "It's true! The Lord has risen! Shim'on saw him!" ³⁵ Then the two told what had happened on the road and how he had become known to them in the breaking of the *matzah*.

³⁶ They were still talking about it when — there he was, standing among them! ³⁷ Startled and terrified, they thought they were seeing a ghost. ³⁸ But he said to them, "Why are you so upset? Why are these doubts welling up inside you? ³⁹ Look at my hands and my feet — it is I, myself! Touch me and see — a ghost doesn't have flesh and bones, as you can see I do." ⁴⁰ As he said this, he showed them his hands and feet. ⁴¹ While they were still unable to believe it for joy and stood there dumbfounded, he said to them, "Have you something here to eat?" ⁴² They gave him a piece of broiled fish, ⁴³ which he took and ate in their presence.

⁴⁴ Yeshua said to them, "This is what I meant when I was still with you and told you that everything written about me in the *Torah* of Moshe, the Prophets and the Psalms had to be fulfilled." ⁴⁵ Then he opened their minds, so that they could understand the *Tanakh*, ⁴⁶ telling them, "Here is what it says: the Messiah is to suffer and to rise from the dead on the third day; ⁴⁷ and in his name repentance leading to forgiveness of sins is to be proclaimed to people from all nations, starting with Yerushalayim. ⁴⁸ You are witnesses of these things. ⁴⁹ Now I am sending forth upon you what my Father promised, so stay here in the city until you have been equipped with power from above."

⁵⁰ He led them out toward Beit-Anyah; then, raising his hands, he said a *b'rakhah* over them; ⁵¹ and as he was blessing them, he withdrew from them and was carried up into heaven. ⁵² They bowed in worship to him, then returned to Yerushalayim, overflowing with joy. ⁵³ And they spent all their time in the Temple courts, praising God.

The Good News of Yeshua the Messiah, as Reported by

Yochanan

JOHN

1 ¹   In the beginning was the Word,
        and the Word was with God,

      and the Word was God.
²   He was with God in the beginning.

³   All things came to be through him,
        and without him nothing made had being.

⁴   In him was life,
        and the life was the light of mankind.

⁵   The light shines in the darkness,
        and the darkness has not suppressed it.

⁶ There was a man sent from God whose name was Yochanan. ⁷ He came to be a testimony, to bear witness concerning the light; so that through him, everyone might put his trust in God and be faithful to him. ⁸ He himself was not that light; no, he came to bear witness concerning the light.

⁹   This was the true light,
        which gives light to everyone entering the world.

¹⁰   He was in the world — the world came to be through him —
        yet the world did not know him.

¹¹   He came to his own homeland,
        yet his own people did not receive him.

¹² But to as many as did receive him, to those who put their trust in his person and power, he gave the right to become children of God, ¹³ not because of bloodline, physical impulse or human intention, but because of God.

¹⁴   The Word became a human being and lived with us,
        and we saw his *Sh'khinah*,

the *Sh'khinah* of the Father's only Son,
full of grace and truth.

[15] Yochanan witnessed concerning him when he cried out, "This is the man I was talking about when I said, 'The one coming after me has come to rank ahead of me, because he existed before me.'"

[16]   We have all received from his fullness,
yes, grace upon grace.

[17]   For the *Torah* was given through Moshe;
grace and truth came through Yeshua the Messiah.

[18] No one has ever seen God; but the only and unique Son, who is identical with God and is at the Father's side — he has made him known.
[19] Here is Yochanan's testimony: when the Judeans sent *cohanim* and *L'vi'im* from Yerushalayim to ask him, "Who are you?" [20] he was very straightforward and stated clearly, "I am not the Messiah." [21] "Then who are you?" they asked him. "Are you Eliyahu?" "No, I am not," he said. "Are you 'the prophet,' the one we're expecting?" "No," he replied. [22] So they said to him, "Who are you? — so that we can give an answer to the people who sent us. What do you have to say about yourself?" [23] He answered in the words of Yesha'yahu the prophet, "I am

The voice of someone crying out:
'In the desert make the way of ADONAI **straight!'"**[a]

[24] Some of those who had been sent were *P'rushim*. [25] They asked him, "If you are neither the Messiah nor Eliyahu nor 'the prophet,' then why are you immersing people?" [26] To them Yochanan replied, "I am immersing people in water, but among you is standing someone whom you don't know. [27] He is the one coming after me — I'm not good enough even to untie his sandal!" [28] All this took place in Beit-Anyah, east of the Yarden, where Yochanan was immersing.
[29] The next day, Yochanan saw Yeshua coming toward him and said, "Look! God's lamb! The one who is taking away the sin of the world! [30] This is the man I was talking about when I said, 'After me is coming someone who has come to rank above me, because he existed before me.' [31] I myself did not know who he was, but the reason I came immersing with water was so that he might be made known to Isra'el." [32] Then Yochanan gave this testimony: "I saw the Spirit coming down from heaven like a dove, and remaining on him. [33] I myself did not know who he was, but the one who sent me to immerse in water said to me, 'The one on whom you see the Spirit descending and remaining, this is the one who immerses in the *Ruach HaKodesh*.' [34] And I have seen and borne witness that this is the Son of God."
[35] The next day, Yochanan was again standing with two of his *talmidim*. [36] On seeing Yeshua walking by, he said, "Look! God's lamb!" [37] His two *talmidim* heard him speaking, and they followed Yeshua. [38] Yeshua turned and saw them following him, and he asked them, "What are you looking for?" They said to him, "Rabbi!"

---

[a] Isaiah 40:3

(which means "Teacher!") "Where are you staying?" ³⁹ He said to them, "Come and see." So they went and saw where he was staying, and remained with him the rest of the day—it was about four o'clock in the afternoon. ⁴⁰ One of the two who had heard Yochanan and had followed Yeshua was Andrew the brother of Shim'on Kefa.

⁴¹ The first thing he did was to find his brother Shim'on and tell him, "We've found the *Mashiach*!" (The word means "one who has been anointed.") ⁴² He took him to Yeshua. Looking at him, Yeshua said, "You are Shim'on Bar-Yochanan; you will be known as Kefa." (The name means "rock.")

⁴³ The next day, having decided to leave for the Galil, Yeshua found Philip and said, "Follow me!" ⁴⁴ Philip was from Beit-Tzaidah, the town where Andrew and Kefa lived. ⁴⁵ Philip found Natan'el and told him, "We've found the one that Moshe wrote about in the *Torah*, also the Prophets—it's Yeshua Ben-Yosef from Natzeret!" ⁴⁶ Natan'el answered him, "Natzeret? Can anything good come from there?" "Come and see," Philip said to him. ⁴⁷ Yeshua saw Natan'el coming toward him and remarked about him, "Here's a true son of Isra'el—nothing false in him!" ⁴⁸ Natan'el said to him, "How do you know me?" Yeshua answered him, "Before Philip called you, when you were under the fig tree, I saw you." ⁴⁹ Natan'el said, "Rabbi, you are the Son of God! You are the King of Isra'el!" ⁵⁰ Yeshua answered him, "you believe all this just because I told you I saw you under the fig tree? You will see greater things than that!" ⁵¹ Then he said to him, "Yes indeed! I tell you that you will see **heaven** opened and **the angels of God going up and coming down**ᵇ on the Son of Man!"

2 ¹ On Tuesday* there was a wedding at Kanah in the Galil; and the mother of Yeshua was there. ² Yeshua too was invited to the wedding, along with his *talmidim*. ³ The wine ran out, and Yeshua's mother said to him, "They have no more wine." ⁴ Yeshua replied, "Mother, why should that concern me? — or you? My time hasn't come yet." ⁵ His mother said to the servants, "Do whatever he tells you." ⁶ Now six stone water-jars were standing there for the Jewish ceremonial washings, each with a capacity of twenty or thirty gallons. ⁷ Yeshua told them, "Fill the jars with water," and they filled them to the brim. ⁸ He said, "Now draw some out, and take it to the man in charge of the banquet"; and they took it. ⁹ The man in charge tasted the water; it had now turned into wine! He did not know where it had come from, but the servants who had drawn the water knew. So he called the bridegroom ¹⁰ and said to him, "Everyone else serves the good wine first and the poorer wine after people have drunk freely. But you have kept the good wine until now!" ¹¹ This, the first of Yeshua's miraculous signs, he did at Kanah in the Galil; he manifested his glory, and his *talmidim* came to trust in him. ¹² Afterwards, he, his mother and brothers, and his *talmidim* went down to K'far-Nachum and stayed there a few days.

¹³ It was almost time for the festival of *Pesach* in Y'hudah, so Yeshua went up to Yerushalayim. ¹⁴ In the Temple grounds he found those who were selling cattle, sheep and pigeons, and others who were sitting at tables exchanging money. ¹⁵ He made a whip from cords and drove them all out of the Temple grounds, the sheep and cattle

---

* Greek: the third day, equivalent to Hebrew *yom shlishi*
ᵇ Genesis 28:12

as well. He knocked over the money-changers' tables, scattering their coins; [16] and to the pigeon-sellers he said, "Get these things out of here! How dare you turn my Father's house into a market?" [17] (His *talmidim* later recalled that the *Tanakh* says, **"Zeal for your house will devour me."** [c]) [18] So the Judeans confronted him by asking him, "What miraculous sign can you show us to prove you have the right to do all this?" [19] Yeshua answered them, "Destroy this temple, and in three days I will raise it up again." [20] The Judeans said, "It took 46 years to build this Temple, and you're going to raise it in three days?" [21] But the "temple" he had spoken of was his body. [22] Therefore, when he was raised from the dead, his *talmidim* remembered that he had said this, and they trusted in the *Tanakh* and in what Yeshua had said.

[23] Now while Yeshua was in Yerushalayim at the *Pesach* festival, there were many people who "believed in his name" when they saw the miracles he performed. [24] But he did not commit himself to them, for he knew what people are like — [25] that is, he didn't need anyone to inform him about a person, because he knew what was in the person's heart.

3 [1] There was a man among the *P'rushim*, named Nakdimon, who was a ruler of the Judeans. [2] This man came to Yeshua by night and said to him, "Rabbi, we know it is from God that you have come as a teacher; for no one can do these miracles you perform unless God is with him." [3] "Yes, indeed," Yeshua answered him, "I tell you that unless a person is born again from above, he cannot see the Kingdom of God."

[4] Nakdimon said to him, "How can a grown man be 'born'? Can he go back into his mother's womb and be born a second time?" [5] Yeshua answered, "Yes, indeed, I tell you that unless a person is born from water and the Spirit, he cannot enter the Kingdom of God. [6] What is born from the flesh is flesh, and what is born from the Spirit is spirit. [7] Stop being amazed at my telling you that you must be born again from above! [8] The wind blows where it wants to, and you hear its sound, but you don't know where it comes from or where it's going. That's how it is with everyone who has been born from the Spirit."

[9] Nakdimon replied, "How can this happen?" [10] Yeshua answered him, "You hold the office of teacher in Isra'el, and you don't know this? [11] Yes, indeed! I tell you that what we speak about, we know; and what we give evidence of, we have seen; but you people don't accept our evidence! [12] If you people don't believe me when I tell you about the things of the world, how will you believe me when I tell you about the things of heaven? [13] No one has gone up into heaven; there is only the one who has come down from heaven, the Son of Man. [14] Just as Moshe lifted up the serpent in the desert, so must the Son of Man be lifted up; [15] so that everyone who trusts in him may have eternal life.

[16] "For God so loved the world that he gave his only and unique Son, so that everyone who trusts in him may have eternal life, instead of being utterly destroyed. [17] For God did not send the Son into the world to judge the world, but rather so that through him, the world might be saved. [18] Those who trust in him are not judged; those who do not trust have been judged already, in that they have not trusted in the one who is God's only and unique Son.

---

[c] Psalm 69:10(9)

[19] "Now this is the judgment: the light has come into the world, but people loved the darkness rather than the light. Why? Because their actions were wicked. [20] For everyone who does evil things hates the light and avoids it, so that his actions won't be exposed. [21] But everyone who does what is true comes to the light, so that all may see that his actions are accomplished through God."

[22] After this, Yeshua and his *talmidim* went out into the countryside of Y'hudah, where he stayed awhile with them and immersed people. [23] Yochanan too was immersing at Einayim, near Shalem, because there was plenty of water there; and people kept coming to be immersed. [24] (This was before Yochanan's imprisonment.)

[25] A discussion arose between some of Yochanan's *talmidim* and a Judean about ceremonial washing; [26] and they came to Yochanan and said to him, "Rabbi, you know the man who was with you on the other side of the Yarden, the one you spoke about? Well, here he is, immersing; and everyone is going to him!" [27] Yochanan answered, "No one can receive anything unless it has been given to him from Heaven. [28] You yourselves can confirm that I did not say I was the Messiah, but that I have been sent ahead of him. [29] The bridegroom is the one who has the bride; but the bridegroom's friend, who stands and listens to him, is overjoyed at the sound of the bridegroom's voice. So this joy of mine is now complete. [30] He must become more important, while I become less important.

[31] "He who comes from above is above all. He who is from the earth is from the earth and talks from an earthly point of view; he who comes from heaven is above all. [32] He testifies about what he has actually seen and heard, yet no one accepts what he says! [33] Whoever does accept what he says puts his seal on the fact that God is true, [34] because the one whom God sent speaks God's words. For God does not give him the Spirit in limited degree — [35] the Father loves the Son and has put everything in his hands. [36] Whoever trusts in the Son has eternal life. But whoever disobeys the Son will not see that life but remains subject to God's wrath."

4 [1] When Yeshua learned that the *P'rushim* had heard he was making and immersing more *talmidim* than Yochanan [2] (although it was not Yeshua himself who immersed but his *talmidim*), [3] Yeshua left Y'hudah and set out again for the Galil. [4] This meant that he had to pass through Shomron.

[5] He came to a town in Shomron called Sh'khem, near the field Ya'akov had given to his son Yosef. [6] Ya'akov's Well was there; so Yeshua, exhausted from his travel, sat down by the well; it was about noon. [7] A woman from Shomron came to draw some water; and Yeshua said to her, "Give me a drink of water." [8] (His *talmidim* had gone into town to buy food.) [9] The woman from Shomron said to him, "How is it that you, a Jew, ask for water from me, a woman of Shomron?" (For Jews don't associate with people from Shomron.) [10] Yeshua answered her, "If you knew God's gift, that is, who it is saying to you, 'Give me a drink of water,' then you would have asked him; and he would have given you living water."

[11] She said to him, "Sir, you don't have a bucket, and the well is deep; so where do you get this 'living water'? [12] You aren't greater than our father Ya'akov, are you? He gave us this well and drank from it, and so did his sons and his cattle." [13] Yeshua answered, "Everyone who drinks this water will get thirsty again, [14] but whoever drinks the water I will give him will never be thirsty again! On the contrary, the water I give him will become a spring of water inside him, welling up into eternal life!"

[15] "Sir, give me this water," the woman said to him, "so that I won't have to be thirsty and keep coming here to draw water." [16] He said to her, "Go, call your husband, and come back." [17] She answered, "I don't have a husband." Yeshua said to her, "You're right, you don't have a husband! [18] You've had five husbands in the past, and you're not married to the man you're living with now! You've spoken the truth!"

[19] "Sir, I can see that you are a prophet," the woman replied. [20] "Our fathers worshipped on this mountain, but you people say that the place where one has to worship is in Yerushalayim." [21] Yeshua said, "Lady, believe me, the time is coming when you will worship the Father neither on this mountain nor in Yerushalayim. [22] You people don't know what you are worshipping; we worship what we do know, because salvation comes from the Jews. [23] But the time is coming — indeed, it's here now — when the true worshippers will worship the Father spiritually and truly, for these are the kind of people the Father wants worshipping him. [24] God is spirit; and worshippers must worship him spiritually and truly."

[25] The woman replied, "I know that *Mashiach* is coming" (that is, "the one who has been anointed"). "When he comes, he will tell us everything." [26] Yeshua said to her, "I, the person speaking to you, am he."

[27] Just then, his *talmidim* arrived. They were amazed that he was talking with a woman; but none of them said, "What do you want?" or, "Why are you talking with her?" [28] So the woman left her water-jar, went back to the town and said to the people there, [29] "Come, see a man who told me everything I've ever done. Could it be that this is the Messiah?" [30] They left the town and began coming toward him.

[31] Meanwhile, the *talmidim* were urging Yeshua, "Rabbi, eat something." [32] But he answered, "I have food to eat that you don't know about." [33] At this, the *talmidim* asked one another, "Could someone have brought him food?" [34] Yeshua said to them, "My food is to do what the one who sent me wants and to bring his work to completion. [35] Don't you have a saying, 'Four more months and then the harvest'? Well, what I say to you is: open your eyes and look at the fields! They're already ripe for harvest! [36] The one who reaps receives his wages and gathers fruit for eternal life, so that the reaper and the sower may be glad together — [37] for in this matter, the proverb, 'One sows and another reaps,' holds true. [38] I sent you to reap what you haven't worked for. Others have done the hard labor, and you have benefited from their work."

[39] Many people from that town in Shomron put their trust in him because of the woman's testimony, "He told me all the things I did." [40] So when these people from Shomron came to him, they asked him to stay with them. He stayed two days, [41] and many more came to trust because of what he said. [42] They said to the woman, "We no longer trust because of what you said, because we have heard for ourselves. We know indeed that this man really is the Savior of the world."

[43] After the two days, he went on from there toward the Galil. [44] Now Yeshua himself said, "A prophet is not respected in his own country." [45] But when he arrived in the Galil, the people there welcomed him, because they had seen all he had done at the festival in Yerushalayim; since they had been there too.

[46] He went again to Kanah in the Galil, where he had turned the water into wine. An officer in the royal service was there; his son was ill in K'far-Nachum. [47] This man, on hearing that Yeshua had come from Y'hudah to the Galil, went and asked him to come down and heal his son, for he was at the point of death. [48] Yeshua answered, "Unless you people see signs and miracles, you simply will not trust!"

⁴⁹ The officer said to him, "Sir, come down before my child dies." ⁵⁰ Yeshua replied, "You may go, your son is alive." The man believed what Yeshua said and left. ⁵¹ As he was going down, his servants met him with the news that his son was alive ⁵² So he asked them at what time he had gotten better; and they said, "The fever left him yesterday at one o'clock in the afternoon." ⁵³ The father knew that that was the very hour when Yeshua had told him, "Your son is alive"; and he and all his household trusted. ⁵⁴ This was a second sign that Yeshua did; he did it after he had come from Y'hudah into the Galil.

5 ¹ After this, there was a Judean festival; and Yeshua went up to Yerushalayim. ² In Yerushalayim, by the Sheep Gate, is a pool called in Aramaic, Beit-Zata, ³ in which lay a crowd of invalids — blind, lame, crippled. ⁴* ⁵ One man was there who had been ill for thirty-eight years. ⁶ Yeshua, seeing this man and knowing that he had been there a long time, said to him, "Do you want to be healed?" ⁷ The sick man answered, "I have no one to put me in the pool when the water is disturbed; and while I'm trying to get there, someone goes in ahead of me." ⁸ Yeshua said to him, "Get up, pick up your mat and walk!" ⁹ Immediately the man was healed, and he picked up his mat and walked.

Now that day was *Shabbat*, ¹⁰ so the Judeans said to the man who had been healed, "It's *Shabbat*! It's against *Torah* for you to carry your mat!" ¹¹ But he answered them, "The man who healed me — he's the one who told me, 'Pick up your mat and walk.'" ¹² They asked him, "Who is the man who told you to pick it up and walk?" ¹³ But the man who had been healed didn't know who it was, because Yeshua had slipped away into the crowd.

¹⁴ Afterwards Yeshua found him in the Temple court and said to him, "See, you are well! Now stop sinning, or something worse may happen to you!" ¹⁵ The man went off and told the Judeans it was Yeshua who had healed him; ¹⁶ and on account of this, the Judeans began harassing Yeshua because he did these things on *Shabbat*.

¹⁷ But he answered them, "My Father has been working until now, and I too am working." ¹⁸ This answer made the Judeans all the more intent on killing him — not only was he breaking *Shabbat*; but also, by saying that God was his own Father, he was claiming equality with God. ¹⁹ Therefore, Yeshua said this to them: "Yes, indeed! I tell you that the Son cannot do anything on his own, but only what he sees the Father doing; whatever the Father does, the Son does too. ²⁰ For the Father loves the Son and shows him everything he does; and he will show him even greater things than these, so that you will be amazed. ²¹ Just as the Father raises the dead and makes them alive, so too the Son makes alive anyone he wants. ²² The Father does not judge anyone but has entrusted all judgment to the Son, ²³ so that all may honor the Son as they honor the Father. Whoever fails to honor the Son is not honoring the Father who sent him. ²⁴ Yes, indeed! I tell you that whoever hears what I am saying and trusts the One who sent me has eternal life — that is, he will not come up for judgment but has already crossed over from death to life! ²⁵ Yes, indeed! I tell you that there is coming a time — in fact, it's already here — when the dead will hear the voice of the Son of God, and those who listen will come to life. ²⁶ For just as the Father has life in

* Some manuscripts have verses 3b–4: . . . , waiting for the water to move; ⁴ for at certain times an angel of A*DONAI* went down into the pool and disturbed the water, and whoever stepped into the water first after it was disturbed was healed of whatever disease he had.

himself, so he has given the Son life to have in himself. ²⁷ Also he has given him authority to execute judgment, because he is the Son of Man. ²⁸ Don't be surprised at this; because the time is coming when all who are in the grave will hear his voice ²⁹ and come out — those who have done good to a resurrection of life, and those who have done evil to a resurrection of judgment. ³⁰ I can't do a thing on my own. As I hear, I judge; and my judgment is right; because I don't seek my own desire, but the desire of the one who sent me.

³¹ "If I testify on my own behalf, my testimony is not valid. ³² But there is someone else testifying on my behalf, and I know that the testimony he is making is valid — ³³ you have sent to Yochanan, and he has testified to the truth. ³⁴ Not that I collect human testimony; rather, I say these things so that you might be saved. ³⁵ He was a lamp burning and shining, and for a little while you were willing to bask in his light.

³⁶ "But I have a testimony that is greater than Yochanan's. For the things the Father has given me to do, the very things I am doing now, testify on my behalf that the Father has sent me.

³⁷ "In addition, the Father who sent me has himself testified on my behalf. But you have never heard his voice or seen his shape; ³⁸ moreover, his word does not stay in you, because you don't trust the one he sent. ³⁹ You keep examining the *Tanakh* because you think that in it you have eternal life. Those very Scriptures bear witness to me, ⁴⁰ but you won't come to me in order to have life!

⁴¹ "I don't collect praise from men, ⁴² but I do know you people — I know that you have no love for God in you! ⁴³ I have come in my Father's name, and you don't accept me; if someone else comes in his own name, him you will accept. ⁴⁴ How can you trust? You're busy collecting praise from each other, instead of seeking praise from God only.

⁴⁵ "But don't think that it is I who will be your accuser before the Father. Do you know who will accuse you? Moshe, the very one you have counted on! ⁴⁶ For if you really believed Moshe, you would believe me; because it was about me that he wrote. ⁴⁷ But if you don't believe what he wrote, how are you going to believe what I say?"

6 ¹ Some time later, Yeshua went over to the far side of Lake Kinneret (that is, Lake Tiberias), ² and a large crowd followed him, because they had seen the miracles he had performed on the sick. ³ Yeshua went up into the hills and sat down there with his *talmidim*. ⁴ Now the Judean festival of *Pesach* was coming up; ⁵ so when Yeshua looked up and saw that a large crowd was approaching, he said to Philip, "Where will we be able to buy bread, so that these people can eat?" ⁶ (Now Yeshua said this to test Philip, for Yeshua himself knew what he was about to do.) ⁷ Philip answered, "Half a year's wages wouldn't buy enough bread for them — each one would get only a bite!" ⁸ One of the *talmidim*, Andrew the brother of Shim'on Kefa, said to him, ⁹ "There's a young fellow here who has five loaves of barley bread and two fish. But how far will they go among so many?"

¹⁰ Yeshua said, "Have the people sit down." There was a lot of grass there, so they sat down. The number of men was about five thousand. ¹¹ Then Yeshua took the loaves of bread, and, after making a *b'rakhah*, gave to all who were sitting there, and likewise with the fish, as much as they wanted. ¹² After they had eaten their fill, he told his *talmidim*, "Gather the leftover pieces, so that nothing gets wasted." ¹³ They gathered them and filled twelve baskets with the pieces from the five barley loaves left by those who had eaten.

¹⁴ When the people saw the miracle he had performed, they said, "This has to be 'the prophet' who is supposed to come into the world." ¹⁵ Yeshua knew that they were on the point of coming and seizing him, in order to make him king; so he went back to the hills again. This time he went by himself.

¹⁶ When evening came, his *talmidim* went down to the lake, ¹⁷ got into a boat and set out across the lake toward K'far-Nachum. By now it was dark, Yeshua had not yet joined them, ¹⁸ and the sea was getting rough, because a strong wind was blowing. ¹⁹ They had rowed three or four miles when they saw Yeshua approaching the boat, walking on the lake! They were terrified; ²⁰ but he said to them, "Stop being afraid, it is I." ²¹ Then they were willing to take him into the boat, and instantly the boat reached the land they were heading for.

²² The next day, the crowd which had stayed on the other side of the lake noticed that there had been only one boat there, and that Yeshua had not entered the boat with his *talmidim*, but that the *talmidim* had been alone when they sailed off. ²³ Then other boats, from Tiberias, came ashore near the place where they had eaten the bread after the Lord had made the *b'rakhah*. ²⁴ Accordingly, when the crowd saw that neither Yeshua nor his *talmidim* were there, they themselves boarded the boats and made for K'far-Nachum in search of Yeshua.

²⁵ When they found him on the other side of the lake, they asked him, "Rabbi, when did you get here?" ²⁶ Yeshua answered, "Yes, indeed! I tell you, you're not looking for me because you saw miraculous signs, but because you ate the bread and had all you wanted! ²⁷ Don't work for the food which passes away but for the food that stays on into eternal life, which the Son of Man will give you. For this is the one on whom God the Father has put his seal."

²⁸ So they said to him, "What should we do in order to perform the works of God?" ²⁹ Yeshua answered, "Here's what the work of God is: to trust in the one he sent!"

³⁰ They said to him, "*Nu*, what miracle will you do for us, so that we may see it and trust you? What work can you perform? ³¹ Our fathers ate *man* in the desert — as it says in the *Tanakh*, '**He gave them bread from heaven** to eat.'*ᵈ* ³² Yeshua said to them, "Yes, indeed! I tell you it wasn't Moshe who gave you the bread from heaven. But my Father is giving you the genuine bread from heaven; ³³ for God's bread is the one who comes down out of heaven and gives life to the world."

³⁴ They said to him, "Sir, give us this bread from now on." ³⁵ Yeshua answered, "I am the bread which is life! Whoever comes to me will never go hungry, and whoever trusts in me will never be thirsty. ³⁶ I told you that you have seen but still don't trust. ³⁷ Everyone the Father gives me will come to me, and whoever comes to me I will certainly not turn away. ³⁸ For I have come down from heaven to do not my own will but the will of the One who sent me. ³⁹ And this is the will of the One who sent me: that I should not lose any of all those he has given me but should raise them up on the Last Day. ⁴⁰ Yes, this is the will of my Father: that all who see the Son and trust in him should have eternal life, and that I should raise them up on the Last Day."

⁴¹ At this the Judeans began grumbling about him because he said, "I am the bread which has come down from heaven." ⁴² They said, "Isn't this Yeshua Ben-Yosef? We know his father and mother! How can he now say, 'I have come down from heaven'?" ⁴³ Yeshua answered them, "Stop grumbling to each other! ⁴⁴ No one can come to me

---

ᵈ Psalm 78:24; Nehemiah 9:15

unless the Father — the One who sent me — draws him. And I will raise him up on the Last Day. [45] It is written in the Prophets, **'They will all be taught by ADONAI.'**[e] Everyone who listens to the Father and learns from him comes to me. [46] Not that anyone has seen the Father except the one who is from God — he has seen the Father. [47] Yes, indeed! I tell you, whoever trusts has eternal life: [48] I am the bread which is life. [49] Your fathers ate the *man* in the desert; they died. [50] But the bread that comes down from heaven is such that a person may eat it and not die. [51] I am the living bread that has come down from heaven; if anyone eats this bread, he will live forever. Furthermore, the bread that I will give is my own flesh; and I will give it for the life of the world."

[52] At this, the Judeans disputed with one another, saying, "How can this man give us his flesh to eat?" [53] Then Yeshua said to them, "Yes, indeed! I tell you that unless you eat the flesh of the Son of Man and drink his blood, you do not have life in yourselves. [54] Whoever eats my flesh and drinks my blood has eternal life — that is, I will raise him up on the Last Day. [55] For my flesh is true food, and my blood is true drink. [56] Whoever eats my flesh and drinks my blood lives in me, and I live in him. [57] Just as the living Father sent me, and I live through the Father, so also whoever eats me will live through me. [58] So this is the bread that has come down from heaven — it is not like the bread the fathers ate; they're dead, but whoever eats this bread will live forever!" [59] He said these things as he was teaching in a synagogue in K'far-Nachum.

[60] On hearing it, many of his *talmidim* said, "This is a hard word — who can bear to listen to it?" [61] But Yeshua, aware that his *talmidim* were grumbling about this, said to them, "This is a trap for you? [62] Suppose you were to see the Son of Man going back up to where he was before? [63] It is the Spirit who gives life, the flesh is no help. The words I have spoken to you are Spirit and life, [64] yet some among you do not trust." (For Yeshua knew from the outset which ones would not trust him, also which one would betray him.) [65] "This," he said, "is why I told you that no one can come to me unless the Father has made it possible for him."

[66] From this time on, many of his *talmidim* turned back and no longer traveled around with him. [67] So Yeshua said to the Twelve, "Don't you want to leave too?" [68] Shim'on Kefa answered him, "Lord, to whom would we go? You have the word of eternal life. [69] We have trusted, and we know that you are the Holy One of God." [70] Yeshua answered them, "Didn't I choose you, the Twelve? Yet one of you is an adversary." [71] (He was speaking of Y'hudah Ben-Shim'on, from K'riot; for this man — one of the Twelve! — was soon to betray him.)

7 [1] After this, Yeshua traveled around in the Galil, intentionally avoiding Y'hudah because the Judeans were out to kill him. [2] But the festival of *Sukkot* in Y'hudah was near; [3] so his brothers said to him, "Leave here and go into Y'hudah, so that your *talmidim* can see the miracles you do; [4] for no one who wants to become known acts in secret. If you're doing these things, show yourself to the world!" [5] (His brothers spoke this way because they had not put their trust in him.) [6] Yeshua said to them, "My time has not yet come; but for you, any time is right. [7] The world can't hate you, but it does hate me, because I keep telling it how wicked its ways are. [8] You, go on up

---

[e] Isaiah 54:13

to the festival; as for me, I am not going up to this festival now, because the right time for me has not yet come." [9] Having said this, he stayed on in the Galil.

[10] But after his brothers had gone up to the festival, he too went up, not publicly but in secret. [11] At the festival, the Judeans were looking for him. "Where is he?" they asked. [12] And among the crowds there was much whispering about him. Some said, "He's a good man"; but others said, "No, he is deceiving the masses." [13] However, no one spoke about him openly, for fear of the Judeans.

[14] Not until the festival was half over did Yeshua go up to the Temple courts and begin to teach. [15] The Judeans were surprised: "How does this man know so much without having studied?" they asked. [16] So Yeshua gave them an answer: "My teaching is not my own, it comes from the One who sent me. [17] If anyone wants to do his will, he will know whether my teaching is from God or I speak on my own. [18] A person who speaks on his own is trying to win praise for himself; but a person who tries to win praise for the one who sent him is honest, there is nothing false about him. [19] Didn't Moshe give you the *Torah*? Yet not one of you obeys the *Torah*! Why are you out to kill me?" [20] "You have a demon!" the crowd answered. "Who's out to kill you?" [21] Yeshua answered them, "I did one thing; and because of this, all of you are amazed. [22] Moshe gave you *b'rit-milah* — not that it came from Moshe but from the Patriarchs — and you do a boy's *b'rit-milah* on *Shabbat*. [23] If a boy is circumcised on *Shabbat* so that the *Torah* of Moshe will not be broken, why are you angry with me because I made a man's whole body well on *Shabbat*? [24] Stop judging by surface appearances, and judge the right way!"

[25] Some of the Yerushalayim people said, "Isn't this the man they're out to kill? [26] Yet here he is, speaking openly; and they don't say anything to him. It couldn't be, could it, that the authorities have actually concluded he's the Messiah? [27] Surely not — we know where this man comes from; but when the Messiah comes, no one will know where he comes from." [28] Whereupon Yeshua, continuing to teach in the Temple courts, cried out, "Indeed you do know me! And you know where I'm from! And I have not come on my own! The One who sent me is real. But him you don't know! [29] I do know him, because I am with him, and he sent me!"

[30] At this, they tried to arrest him; but no one laid a hand on him; because his time had not yet come. [31] However, many in the crowd put their trust in him and said, "When the Messiah comes, will he do more miracles than this man has done?"

[32] The *P'rushim* heard the crowd whispering these things about Yeshua; so the head *cohanim* and the *P'rushim* sent some of the Temple guards to arrest him. [33] Yeshua said, "I will be with you only a little while longer; then I will go away to the One who sent me. [34] You will look for me and not find me; indeed, where I am, you cannot come." [35] The Judeans said to themselves, "Where is this man about to go, that we won't find him? Does he intend to go to the Greek Diaspora and teach the Greek-speaking Jews? [36] And when he says, 'You will look for me and not find me; indeed, where I am, you cannot come' — what does he mean?"

[37] Now on the last day of the festival, *Hoshana Rabbah*, Yeshua stood and cried out, "If anyone is thirsty, let him keep coming to me and drinking! [38] Whoever puts his trust in me, as the Scripture says, rivers of living water will flow from his inmost being!" [39] (Now he said this about the Spirit, whom those who trusted in him were to receive later — the Spirit had not yet been given, because Yeshua had not yet been glorified.)

⁴⁰ On hearing his words, some people in the crowd said, "Surely this man is 'the prophet'"; ⁴¹ others said, "This is the Messiah." But others said, "How can the Messiah come from the Galil? ⁴² Doesn't the *Tanakh* say that the Messiah is from **the seed of David**ᶠ and comes **from Beit-Lechem,**ᵍ the village where David lived?" ⁴³ So the people were divided because of him. ⁴⁴ Some wanted to arrest him, but no one laid a hand on him.

⁴⁵ The guards came back to the head *cohanim* and the *P'rushim*, who asked them, "Why didn't you bring him in?" ⁴⁶ The guards replied, "No one ever spoke the way this man speaks!" ⁴⁷ "You mean you've been taken in as well?" the *P'rushim* retorted. ⁴⁸ "Has any of the authorities trusted him? Or any of the *P'rushim*? No! ⁴⁹ True, these *'am-ha'aretz* do, but they know nothing about the *Torah*, they are under a curse!"

⁵⁰ Nakdimon, the man who had gone to Yeshua before and was one of them, said to them, ⁵¹ "Our *Torah* doesn't condemn a man — does it? — until after hearing from him and finding out what he's doing." ⁵² They replied, "You aren't from the Galil too, are you? Study the *Tanakh*, and see for yourself that no prophet comes from the Galil!" *⁵³ Then they all left, each one to his own home.

8 ¹ But Yeshua went to the Mount of Olives. ² At daybreak, he appeared again in the Temple Court, where all the people gathered around him, and he sat down to teach them. ³ The *Torah*-teachers and the *P'rushim* brought in a woman who had been caught committing adultery and made her stand in the center of the group. ⁴ Then they said to him, "Rabbi, this woman was caught in the very act of committing adultery. ⁵ Now in our *Torah*, Moshe commanded that such a woman be stoned to death. What do you say about it?" ⁶ They said this to trap him, so that they might have ground for bringing charges against him; but Yeshua bent down and began writing in the dust with his finger. ⁷ When they kept questioning him, he straightened up and said to them, "The one of you who is without sin, let him be the first to throw a stone at her." ⁸ Then he bent down and wrote in the dust again. ⁹ On hearing this, they began to leave, one by one, the older ones first, until he was left alone, with the woman still there. ¹⁰ Standing up, Yeshua said to her, "Where are they? Has no one condemned you?" ¹¹ She said, "No one, sir." Yeshua said, "Neither do I condemn you. Now go, and don't sin any more."

¹² Yeshua spoke to them again: "I am the light of the world; whoever follows me will never walk in darkness but will have the light which gives life." ¹³ So the *P'rushim* said to him, "Now you're testifying on your own behalf; your testimony is not valid." ¹⁴ Yeshua answered them, "Even if I do testify on my own behalf, my testimony is indeed valid; because I know where I came from and where I'm going; but you do not know where I came from or where I'm going. ¹⁵ You judge by merely human standards. As for me, I pass judgment on no one; ¹⁶ but if I were indeed to pass judgment, my judgment would be valid; because it is not I alone who judge, but I and the One who sent me. ¹⁷ And even in your *Torah* it is written that the testimony of two people is valid. ¹⁸ I myself testify on my own behalf, and so does the Father who sent me."

ᶠ 2 Samuel 7:12   ᵍ Micah 5:1(2)
* Most scholars believe that 7:53–8:11 is not from the pen of Yochanan. Many are of the opinion that it is a true story about Yeshua written by another of his *talmidim*.

[19] They said to him, "Where is this 'father' of yours?" Yeshua answered, "You know neither me nor my Father; if you knew me, you would know my Father too." [20] He said these things when he was teaching in the Temple treasury room; yet no one arrested him, because his time had not yet come.

[21] Again he told them, "I am going away, and you will look for me, but you will die in your sin — where I am going, you cannot come." [22] The Judeans said, "Is he going to commit suicide? Is that what he means when he says, 'Where I am going, you cannot come'?" [23] Yeshua said to them, "You are from below, I am from above; you are of this world, I am not of this world. [24] This is why I said to you that you will die in your sins; for if you do not trust that I AM [who I say I am], you will die in your sins."

[25] At this, they said to him, "You? Who are you?" Yeshua answered, "Just what I've been telling you from the start. [26] There are many things I could say about you, and many judgments I could make. However, the One who sent me is true; so I say in the world only what I have heard from him." [27] They did not understand that he was talking to them about the Father. [28] So Yeshua said, "When you lift up the Son of Man, then you will know that I AM [who I say I am], and that of myself I do nothing, but say only what the Father has taught me. [29] Also, the One who sent me is still with me; he did not leave me to myself, because I always do what pleases him."

[30] Many people who heard him say these things trusted in him. [31] So Yeshua said to the Judeans who had trusted him, "If you obey what I say, then you are really my *talmidim*, [32] you will know the truth, and the truth will set you free." [33] They answered, "We are the seed of Avraham and have never been slaves to anyone; so what do you mean by saying, 'You will be set free'?" [34] Yeshua answered them, "Yes, indeed! I tell you that everyone who practices sin is a slave of sin. [35] Now a slave does not remain with a family forever, but a son does remain with it forever. [36] So if the Son frees you, you will really be free! [37] I know you are the seed of Avraham. Yet you are out to kill me, because what I am saying makes no headway in you. [38] I say what my Father has shown me; you do what your father has told you!"

[39] They answered him, "Our father is Avraham." Yeshua replied, "If you are children of Avraham, then do the things Avraham did! [40] As it is, you are out to kill me, a man who has told you the truth which I heard from God. Avraham did nothing like that! [41] You are doing the things your father does." "We're not illegitimate children!" they said to him. "We have only one Father — God!" [42] Yeshua replied to them, "If God were your Father, you would love me; because I came out from God; and now I have arrived here. I did not come on my own; he sent me. [43] Why don't you understand what I'm saying? Because you can't bear to listen to my message. [44] You belong to your father, Satan, and you want to carry out your father's desires. From the start he was a murderer, and he has never stood by the truth, because there is no truth in him. When he tells a lie, he is speaking in character; because he is a liar — indeed, the inventor of the lie! [45] But as for me, because I tell the truth you don't believe me. [46] Which one of you can show me where I'm wrong? If I'm telling the truth, why don't you believe me? [47] Whoever belongs to God listens to what God says; the reason you don't listen is that you don't belong to God."

[48] The Judeans answered him, "Aren't we right in saying you are from Shomron and have a demon?" [49] Yeshua replied, "Me? I have no demon. I am honoring my Father. But you dishonor me. [50] I am not seeking praise for myself. There is One who

is seeking it, and he is the judge. [51] Yes, indeed! I tell you that whoever obeys my teaching will never see death."

[52] The Judeans said to him, "Now we know for sure that you have a demon! Avraham died, and so did the prophets; yet you say, 'Whoever obeys my teaching will never taste death.' [53] *Avraham avinu* died; you aren't greater than he, are you? And the prophets also died. Who do you think you are?" [54] Yeshua answered, "If I praise myself, my praise counts for nothing. The One who is praising me is my Father, the very one about whom you keep saying, 'He is our God.' [55] Now you have not known him, but I do know him; indeed, if I were to say that I don't know him, I would be a liar like you! But I do know him, and I obey his word. [56] Avraham, your father, was glad that he would see my day; then he saw it and was overjoyed."

[57] "Why, you're not yet fifty years old," the Judeans replied, "and you have seen Avraham?" [58] Yeshua said to them, "Yes, indeed! Before Avraham came into being, I AM!" [59] At this, they picked up stones to throw at him; but Yeshua was hidden and left the Temple grounds.

9 [1] As Yeshua passed along, he saw a man blind from birth. [2] His *talmidim* asked him, "Rabbi, who sinned — this man or his parents — to cause him to be born blind?" [3] Yeshua answered, "His blindness is due neither to his sin nor to that of his parents; it happened so that God's power might be seen at work in him. [4] As long as it is day, we must keep doing the work of the One who sent me; the night is coming, when no one can work. [5] While I am in the world, I am the light of the world."

[6] Having said this, he spit on the ground, made some mud with the saliva, put the mud on the man's eyes, [7] and said to him, "Go, wash off in the Pool of Shiloach!" (The name means "sent.") So he went and washed and came away seeing.

[8] His neighbors and those who previously had seen him begging said, "Isn't this the man who used to sit and beg?" [9] Some said, "Yes, he's the one"; while others said, "No, but he looks like him." However, he himself said, "I'm the one." [10] "How were your eyes opened?" they asked him. [11] He answered, "The man called Yeshua made mud, put it on my eyes, and told me, 'Go to Shiloach and wash!' So I went; and as soon as I had washed, I could see." [12] They said to him, "Where is he?" and he replied, "I don't know."

[13] They took the man who had been blind to the *P'rushim*. [14] Now the day on which Yeshua had made the mud and opened his eyes was *Shabbat*. [15] So the *P'rushim* asked him again how he had become able to see; and he told them, "He put mud on my eyes, then I washed, and now I can see." [16] At this, some of the *P'rushim* said, "This man is not from God, because he doesn't keep *Shabbat*." But others said, "How could a man who is a sinner do miracles like these?" And there was a split among them. [17] So once more they spoke to the blind man: "Since you're the one whose eyes he opened, what do you say about him?" He replied: "He is a prophet."

[18] The Judeans, however, were unwilling to believe that he had formerly been blind, but now could see, until they had summoned the man's parents. [19] They asked them, "Is this your son, who you say was born blind? How is it that now he can see?" [20] His parents answered, "We know that this is our son and that he was born blind; [21] but how it is that he can see now, we don't know; nor do we know who opened his eyes. Ask him — he's old enough, he can speak for himself!" [22] The parents said this because they were afraid of the Judeans, for the Judeans had already agreed that

anyone who acknowledged Yeshua as the Messiah would be banned from the synagogue. ²³ This is why his parents said, "He's old enough, ask him."

²⁴ So a second time they called the man who had been blind; and they said to him, "Swear to God that you will tell the truth! We know that this man is a sinner." ²⁵ He answered, "Whether he's a sinner or not I don't know. One thing I do know: I was blind, now I see." ²⁶ So they said to him, "What did he do to you? How did he open your eyes?" ²⁷ "I already told you," he answered, "and you didn't listen. Why do you want to hear it again? Maybe you too want to become his *talmidim*?" ²⁸ Then they railed at him. "You may be his *talmid*," they said, "but we are *talmidim* of Moshe! ²⁹ We know that God has spoken to Moshe, but as for this fellow — we don't know where he's from!" ³⁰ "What a strange thing," the man answered, "that you don't know where he's from — considering that he opened my eyes! ³¹ We know that God doesn't listen to sinners; but if anyone fears God and does his will, God does listen to him. ³² In all history no one has ever heard of someone's opening the eyes of a man born blind. ³³ If this man were not from God, he couldn't do a thing!" ³⁴ "Why, you *mamzer*!" they retorted, "Are you lecturing us?" And they threw him out.

³⁵ Yeshua heard that they had thrown the man out. He found him and said, "Do you trust in the Son of Man?" ³⁶ "Sir," he answered, "tell me who he is, so that I can trust in him." ³⁷ Yeshua said to him, "You have seen him. In fact, he's the one speaking with you now." ³⁸ "Lord, I trust!" he said, and he kneeled down in front of him.

³⁹ Yeshua said, "It is to judge that I came into this world, so that those who do not see might see, and those who do see might become blind." ⁴⁰ Some of the *P'rushim* nearby heard this and said to him, "So we're blind too, are we?" ⁴¹ Yeshua answered them, "If you were blind, you would not be guilty of sin. But since you still say, 'We see,' your guilt remains.

10 ¹ "Yes, indeed! I tell you, the person who doesn't enter the sheep-pen through the door, but climbs in some other way, is a thief and a robber. ² But the one who goes in through the gate is the sheep's own shepherd. ³ This is the one the gate-keeper admits, and the sheep hear his voice. He calls his own sheep, each one by name, and leads them out. ⁴ After taking out all that are his own, he goes on ahead of them; and the sheep follow him because they recognize his voice. ⁵ They never follow a stranger but will run away from him, because strangers' voices are unfamiliar to them."

⁶ Yeshua used this indirect manner of speaking with them, but they didn't understand what he was talking to them about. ⁷ So Yeshua said to them again, "Yes, indeed! I tell you that I am the gate for the sheep. ⁸ All those who have come before me have been thieves and robbers, but the sheep didn't listen to them. ⁹ I am the gate; if someone enters through me, he will be safe and will go in and out and find pasture. ¹⁰ The thief comes only in order to steal, kill and destroy; I have come so that they may have life, life in its fullest measure.

¹¹ "I am the good shepherd. The good shepherd lays down his life for the sheep. ¹² The hired hand, since he isn't a shepherd and the sheep aren't his own, sees the wolf coming, abandons the sheep and runs away. Then the wolf drags them off and scatters them. ¹³ The hired worker behaves like this because that's all he is, a hired worker; so it doesn't matter to him what happens to the sheep. ¹⁴ I am the good shepherd; I know my own, and my own know me — ¹⁵ just as the Father knows me, and I know the Father — and I lay down my life on behalf of the sheep.

¹⁶ Also I have other sheep which are not from this pen; I need to bring them, and they will hear my voice; and there will be one flock, one shepherd.

¹⁷ "This is why the Father loves me: because I lay down my life — in order to take it up again! ¹⁸ No one takes it away from me; on the contrary, I lay it down of my own free will. I have the power to lay it down, and I have the power to take it up again. This is what my Father commanded me to do."

¹⁹ Again there was a split among the Judeans because of what he said. ²⁰ Many of them said, "He has a demon!" and "He's *meshugga*! Why do you listen to him?" ²¹ Others said, "These are not the deeds of a man who is demonized — how can a demon open blind people's eyes?"

²² Then came *Hanukkah* in Yerushalayim. It was winter, ²³ and Yeshua was walking around inside the Temple area, in Shlomo's Colonnade. ²⁴ So the Judeans surrounded him and said to him, "How much longer are you going to keep us in suspense? If you are the Messiah, tell us publicly!" ²⁵ Yeshua answered them, "I have already told you, and you don't trust me. The works I do in my Father's name testify on my behalf, ²⁶ but the reason you don't trust is that you are not included among my sheep. ²⁷ My sheep listen to my voice, I recognize them, they follow me, ²⁸ and I give them eternal life. They will absolutely never be destroyed, and no one will snatch them from my hands. ²⁹ My Father, who gave them to me, is greater than all; and no one can snatch them from the Father's hands. ³⁰ I and the Father are one."

³¹ Once again the Judeans picked up rocks in order to stone him. ³² Yeshua answered them, "You have seen me do many good deeds that reflect the Father's power; for which one of these deeds are you stoning me?" ³³ The Judeans replied, "We are not stoning you for any good deed, but for blasphemy — because you, who are only a man, are making yourself out to be God [Hebrew: *Elohim*]." ³⁴ Yeshua answered them, "Isn't it written in your *Torah*, **'I have said, "You people are Elohim' "**?*ʰ* ³⁵ If he called '*elohim*' the people to whom the word of *Elohim* was addressed (and the *Tanakh* cannot be broken), ³⁶ then are you telling the one whom the Father set apart as holy and sent into the world, 'You are committing blasphemy,' just because I said, 'I am a son of *Elohim*'?

³⁷ "If I am not doing deeds that reflect my Father's power, don't trust me. ³⁸ But if I am, then, even if you don't trust me, trust the deeds; so that you may understand once and for all that the Father is united with me, and I am united with the Father." ³⁹ One more time they tried to arrest him, but he slipped out of their hands.

⁴⁰ He went off again beyond the Yarden, where Yochanan had been immersing at first, and stayed there. ⁴¹ Many people came to him and said, "Yochanan performed no miracles, but everything Yochanan said about this man was true." ⁴² And many people there put their trust in him.

11 ¹ There was a man who had fallen sick. His name was El'azar, and he came from Beit-Anyah, the village where Miryam and her sister Marta lived. ² (This Miryam, whose brother El'azar had become sick, is the one who poured perfume on the Lord and wiped his feet with her hair.) ³ So the sisters sent a message to Yeshua, "Lord, the man you love is sick." ⁴ On hearing it, he said, "This sickness will not end in death. No, it is for God's glory, so that the Son of God may receive glory through it."

ʰ Psalm 82:6

⁵ Yeshua loved Marta and her sister and El'azar; ⁶ so when he heard he was sick, first he stayed where he was two more days; ⁷ then, after this, he said to the *talmidim*, "Let's go back to Y'hudah." ⁸ The *talmidim* replied, "Rabbi! Just a short while ago the Judeans were out to stone you — and you want to go back there?" ⁹ Yeshua answered, "Aren't there twelve hours of daylight? If a person walks during daylight, he doesn't stumble; because he sees the light of this world. ¹⁰ But if a person walks at night, he does stumble; because he has no light with him."

¹¹ Yeshua said these things, and afterwards he said to the *talmidim*, "Our friend El'azar has gone to sleep; but I am going in order to wake him up." ¹² The *talmidim* said to him, "Lord, if he has gone to sleep, he will get better." ¹³ Now Yeshua had used the phrase to speak about El'azar's death, but they thought he had been talking literally about sleep. ¹⁴ So Yeshua told them in plain language, "El'azar has died. ¹⁵ And for your sakes, I am glad that I wasn't there, so that you may come to trust. But let's go to him." ¹⁶ Then T'oma (the name means "twin") said to his fellow *talmidim*, "Yes, we should go, so that we can die with him!"

¹⁷ On arrival, Yeshua found that El'azar had already been in the tomb for four days. ¹⁸ Now Beit-Anyah was about two miles from Yerushalayim, ¹⁹ and many of the Judeans had come to Marta and Miryam in order to comfort them at the loss of their brother. ²⁰ So when Marta heard that Yeshua was coming, she went out to meet him; but Miryam continued sitting *shiv'ah* in the house.

²¹ Marta said to Yeshua, "Lord, if you had been here, my brother would not have died. ²² Even now I know that whatever you ask of God, God will give you." ²³ Yeshua said to her, "Your brother will rise again." ²⁴ Marta said, "I know that he will rise again at the Resurrection on the Last Day." ²⁵ Yeshua said to her, "I AM the Resurrection and the Life! Whoever puts his trust in me will live, even if he dies; ²⁶ and everyone living and trusting in me will never die. Do you believe this?" ²⁷ She said to him, "Yes, Lord, I believe that you are the Messiah, the Son of God, the one coming into the world."

²⁸ After saying this, she went off and secretly called Miryam, her sister: "The Rabbi is here and is calling for you." ²⁹ When she heard this, she jumped up and went to him. ³⁰ Yeshua had not yet come into the village but was still where Marta had met him; ³¹ so when the Judeans who had been with Miryam in the house comforting her saw her get up quickly and go out, they followed her, thinking she was going to the tomb to mourn there.

³² When Miryam came to where Yeshua was and saw him, she fell at his feet and said to him, "Lord, if you had been here, my brother would not have died." ³³ When Yeshua saw her crying, and also the Judeans who came with her crying, he was deeply moved and also troubled. ³⁴ He said, "Where have you buried him?" They said, "Lord, come and see." ³⁵ Yeshua cried; ³⁶ so the Judeans there said, "See how he loved him!" ³⁷ But some of them said, "He opened the blind man's eyes. Couldn't he have kept this one from dying?"

³⁸ Yeshua, again deeply moved, came to the tomb. It was a cave, and a stone was lying in front of the entrance. ³⁹ Yeshua said, "Take the stone away!" Marta, the sister of the dead man, said to Yeshua, "By now his body must smell, for it has been four days since he died!" ⁴⁰ Yeshua said to her, "Didn't I tell you that if you keep trusting, you will see the glory of God?" ⁴¹ So they removed the stone. Yeshua looked upward and said, "Father, I thank you that you have heard me. ⁴² I myself know that you

always hear me, but I say this because of the crowd standing around, so that they may believe that you have sent me." ⁴³ Having said this, he shouted, "El'azar! Come out!" ⁴⁴ The man who had been dead came out, his hands and feet wrapped in strips of linen and his face covered with a cloth. Yeshua said to them, "Unwrap him, and let him go!" ⁴⁵ At this, many of the Judeans who had come to visit Miryam, and had seen what Yeshua had done, trusted in him.

⁴⁶ But some of them went off to the *P'rushim* and told them what he had done. ⁴⁷ So the head *cohanim* and the *P'rushim* called a meeting of the *Sanhedrin* and said, "What are we going to do? — for this man is performing many miracles. ⁴⁸ If we let him keep going on this way, everyone will trust in him, and the Romans will come and destroy both the Temple and the nation." ⁴⁹ But one of them, Kayafa, who was *cohen gadol* that year, said to them, "You people don't know anything! ⁵⁰ You don't see that it's better for you if one man dies on behalf of the people, so that the whole nation won't be destroyed." ⁵¹ Now he didn't speak this way on his own initiative; rather, since he was *cohen gadol* that year, he was prophesying that Yeshua was about to die on behalf of the nation, ⁵² and not for the nation alone, but so that he might gather into one the scattered children of God.

⁵³ From that day on, they made plans to have him put to death. ⁵⁴ Therefore Yeshua no longer walked around openly among the Judeans but went away from there into the region near the desert, to a town called Efrayim, and stayed there with his *talmidim*.

⁵⁵ The Judean festival of *Pesach* was near, and many people went up from the country to Yerushalayim to perform the purification ceremony prior to *Pesach*. ⁵⁶ They were looking for Yeshua, and as they stood in the Temple courts they said to each other, "What do you think? that he simply won't come to the festival?" ⁵⁷ Moreover, the head *cohanim* and the *P'rushim* had given orders that anyone knowing Yeshua's whereabouts should inform them, so that they could have him arrested.

12 ¹ Six days before *Pesach*, Yeshua came to Beit-Anyah, where El'azar lived, the man Yeshua had raised from the dead; ² so they gave a dinner there in his honor. Marta served the meal, and El'azar was among those at the table with him. ³ Miryam took a whole pint of pure oil of spikenard, which is very expensive, poured it on Yeshua's feet and wiped his feet with her hair, so that the house was filled with the fragrance of the perfume. ⁴ But one of the *talmidim*, Y'hudah from K'riot, the one who was about to betray him, said, ⁵ "This perfume is worth a year's wages! Why wasn't it sold and the money given to the poor?" ⁶ Now he said this not out of concern for the poor, but because he was a thief — he was in charge of the common purse and used to steal from it. ⁷ Yeshua said, "Leave her alone! She kept this for the day of my burial. ⁸ You always have the poor among you, but you will not always have me."

⁹ A large crowd of Judeans learned that he was there; and they came not only because of Yeshua, but also so that they could see El'azar, whom he had raised from the dead. ¹⁰ The head *cohanim* then decided to do away with El'azar too, ¹¹ since it was because of him that large numbers of the Judeans were leaving their leaders and putting their trust in Yeshua.

¹² The next day, the large crowd that had come for the festival heard that Yeshua was on his way into Yerushalayim. ¹³ They took palm branches and went out to meet him, shouting,

"Deliver us!"[i]

"Blessed is he who comes in the name of ADONAI,[j] the King of Isra'el!"

[14] After finding a donkey colt, Yeshua mounted it, just as the *Tanakh* says —

[15]   **"Daughter of Tziyon, don't be afraid!**
     Look! your King is coming,
     sitting on a donkey's colt."[k]

[16] His *talmidim* did not understand this at first; but after Yeshua had been glorified, then they remembered that the *Tanakh* said this about him, and that they had done this for him. [17] The group that had been with him when he called El'azar out of the tomb and raised him from the dead had been telling about it. [18] It was because of this too that the crowd came out to meet him — they had heard that he had performed this miracle. [19] The *P'rushim* said to each other, "Look, you're getting nowhere! Why, the whole world has gone after him!"

[20] Among those who went up to worship at the festival were some Greek-speaking Jews. [21] They approached Philip, the one from Beit-Tzaidah in the Galil, with a request. "Sir," they said, "we would like to see Yeshua." [22] Philip came and told Andrew; then Andrew and Philip went and told Yeshua. [23] Yeshua gave them this answer: "The time has come for the Son of Man to be glorified. [24] Yes, indeed! I tell you that unless a grain of wheat that falls to the ground dies, it stays just a grain; but if it dies, it produces a big harvest. [25] He who loves his life loses it, but he who hates his life in this world will keep it safe right on into eternal life! [26] If someone is serving me, let him follow me; wherever I am, my servant will be there too. My Father will honor anyone who serves me.

[27] "Now I am in turmoil. What can I say — 'Father, save me from this hour'? No, it was for this very reason that I have come to this hour. I will say this: [28] 'Father, glorify your name!'" At this a *bat-kol* came out of heaven, "I have glorified it before, and I will glorify it again!" [29] The crowd standing there and hearing it said that it had thundered; others said, "An angel spoke to him." [30] Yeshua answered, "This *bat-kol* did not come for my sake but for yours. [31] Now is the time for this world to be judged, now the ruler of this world will be expelled. [32] As for me, when I am lifted up from the earth, I will draw everyone to myself." [33] He said this to indicate what kind of death he would die.

[34] The crowd answered, "We have learned from the *Torah* that the Messiah remains forever. How is it that you say the Son of Man has to be 'lifted up'? Who is this 'Son of Man'?" [35] Yeshua said to them, "The light will be with you only a little while longer. Walk while you have the light, or the dark will overtake you; he who walks in the dark doesn't know where he's going. [36] While you have the light, put your trust in the light, so that you may become people of light." Yeshua said these things, then went off and kept himself hidden from them.

[37] Even though he had performed so many miracles in their presence, they still did not put their trust in him, [38] in order that what Yesha'yahu the prophet had said might be fulfilled,

---

[i] Psalm 118:25   [j] Psalm 118:26   [k] Zechariah 9:9

> "*ADONAI*, who has believed our report?
> To whom has the arm of *ADONAI* been revealed?"[l]

³⁹ The reason they could not believe was — as Yesha'yahu said elsewhere —

⁴⁰　　**"He has blinded their eyes**
　　and hardened their hearts,
　　so that they do not see with their eyes,
　　understand with their hearts,
　　and do *t'shuvah*,
　　so that I could heal them."[m]

⁴¹ (Yesha'yahu said these things because he saw the *Sh'khinah* of Yeshua and spoke about him.) ⁴² Nevertheless, many of the leaders did trust in him; but because of the *P'rushim* they did not say so openly, out of fear of being banned from the synagogue; ⁴³ for they loved praise from other people more than praise from God.

⁴⁴ Yeshua declared publicly, "Those who put their trust in me are trusting not merely in me, but in the One who sent me. ⁴⁵ Also those who see me see the One who sent me. ⁴⁶ I have come as a light into the world, so that everyone who trusts in me might not remain in the dark. ⁴⁷ If anyone hears what I am saying and does not observe it, I don't judge him; for I did not come to judge the world, but to save the world. ⁴⁸ Those who reject me and don't accept what I say have a judge — the word which I have spoken will judge them on the Last Day. ⁴⁹ For I have not spoken on my own initiative, but the Father who sent me has given me a command, namely, what to say and how to say it. ⁵⁰ And I know that his command is eternal life. So what I say is simply what the Father has told me to say."

13 ¹ It was just before the festival of *Pesach*, and Yeshua knew that the time had come for him to pass from this world to the Father. Having loved his own people in the world, he loved them to the end. ² They were at supper, and the Adversary had already put the desire to betray him into the heart of Y'hudah Ben-Shim'on from K'riot. ³ Yeshua was aware that the Father had put everything in his power, and that he had come from God and was returning to God. ⁴ So he rose from the table, removed his outer garments and wrapped a towel around his waist. ⁵ Then he poured some water into a basin and began to wash the feet of the *talmidim* and wipe them off with the towel wrapped around him.

⁶ He came to Shim'on Kefa, who said to him, "Lord! You are washing my feet?" ⁷ Yeshua answered him, "You don't understand yet what I am doing, but in time you will understand." ⁸ "No!" said Kefa, "You will never wash my feet!" Yeshua answered him, "If I don't wash you, you have no share with me." ⁹ "Lord," Shim'on Kefa replied, "not only my feet, but my hands and head too!" ¹⁰ Yeshua said to him, "A man who has had a bath doesn't need to wash, except his feet — his body is already clean. And you people are clean, but not all of you." ¹¹ (He knew who was betraying him; this is why he said, "Not all of you are clean.")

---

[l] Isaiah 53:1　　[m] Isaiah 6:10

¹² After he had washed their feet, taken back his clothes and returned to the table, he said to them, "Do you understand what I have done to you? ¹³ You call me 'Rabbi' and 'Lord,' and you are right, because I am. ¹⁴ Now if I, the Lord and Rabbi, have washed your feet, you also should wash each other's feet. ¹⁵ For I have set you an example, so that you may do as I have done to you. ¹⁶ Yes, indeed! I tell you, a slave is not greater than his master, nor is an emissary greater than the one who sent him. ¹⁷ If you know these things, you will be blessed if you do them.

¹⁸ "I'm not talking to all of you — I know which ones I have chosen. But the words of the *Tanakh* must be fulfilled that say, **'The one eating my bread has turned against me.'**ⁿ ¹⁹ I'm telling you now, before it happens; so that when it does happen, you may believe that I AM [who I say I am]. ²⁰ Yes, indeed! I tell you that a person who receives someone I send receives me, and that anyone who receives me receives the One who sent me."

²¹ After saying this, Yeshua, in deep anguish of spirit, declared, "Yes, indeed! I tell you that one of you will betray me." ²² The *talmidim* stared at one another, totally mystified — whom could he mean? ²³ One of his *talmidim*, the one Yeshua particularly loved, was reclining close beside him. ²⁴ So Shim'on Kefa motioned to him and said, "Ask which one he's talking about." ²⁵ Leaning against Yeshua's chest, he asked Yeshua, "Lord, who is it?" ²⁶ Yeshua answered, "It's the one to whom I give this piece of *matzah* after I dip it in the dish." So he dipped the piece of *matzah* and gave it to Y'hudah Ben-Shim'on from K'riot. ²⁷ As soon as Y'hudah took the piece of *matzah*, the Adversary went into him. "What you are doing, do quickly!" Yeshua said to him. ²⁸ But no one at the table understood why he had said this to him. ²⁹ Some thought that since Y'hudah was in charge of the common purse, Yeshua was telling him, "Buy what we need for the festival," or telling him to give something to the poor. ³⁰ As soon as he had taken the piece of *matzah*, Y'hudah went out, and it was night.

³¹ After Y'hudah had left, Yeshua said, "Now the Son of Man has been glorified, and God has been glorified in him. ³² If the Son has glorified God, God will himself glorify the Son, and will do so without delay. ³³ Little children, I will be with you only a little longer. You will look for me; and, as I said to the Judeans, 'Where I am going, you cannot come,' now I say it to you as well.

³⁴ "I am giving you a new command: that you keep on loving each other. In the same way that I have loved you, you are also to keep on loving each other. ³⁵ Everyone will know that you are my *talmidim* by the fact that you have love for each other."

³⁶ Shim'on Kefa said to him, "Lord, where are you going?" Yeshua answered, "Where I am going, you cannot follow me now; but you will follow later." ³⁷ "Lord," Kefa said to him, "why can't I follow you now? I will lay down my life for you!" ³⁸ Yeshua answered, "You will lay down your life for me? Yes, indeed! I tell you, before the rooster crows you will disown me three times.

14 ¹ "Don't let yourselves be disturbed. Trust in God and trust in me. ² In my Father's house are many places to live. If there weren't, I would have told you; because I am going there to prepare a place for you. ³ Since I am going and preparing a place for you, I will return to take you with me; so that where I am, you may be also. ⁴ Furthermore, you know where I'm going; and you know the way there."

ⁿ Psalm 41:10(9)

[5] T'oma said to him, "Lord, we don't know where you're going; so how can we know the way?" [6] Yeshua said, "I AM the Way — and the Truth and the Life; no one comes to the Father except through me. [7] Because you have known me, you will also know my Father; from now on, you do know him — in fact, you have seen him."

[8] Philip said to him, "Lord, show us the Father, and it will be enough for us." [9] Yeshua replied to him, "Have I been with you so long without your knowing me, Philip? Whoever has seen me has seen the Father; so how can you say, 'Show us the Father'? [10] Don't you believe that I am united with the Father, and the Father united with me? What I am telling you, I am not saying on my own initiative; the Father living in me is doing his own works. [11] Trust me, that I am united with the Father, and the Father united with me. But if you can't, then trust because of the works themselves. [12] Yes, indeed! I tell you that whoever trusts in me will also do the works I do! Indeed, he will do greater ones, because I am going to the Father. [13] In fact, whatever you ask for in my name, I will do; so that the Father may be glorified in the Son. [14] If you ask me for something in my name, I will do it.

[15] "If you love me, you will keep my commands; [16] and I will ask the Father, and he will give you another comforting Counselor like me, the Spirit of Truth, to be with you forever. [17] The world cannot receive him, because it neither sees nor knows him. You know him, because he is staying with you and will be united with you. [18] I will not leave you orphans — I am coming to you. [19] In just a little while, the world will no longer see me; but you will see me. Because I live, you too will live. [20] When that day comes, you will know that I am united with my Father, and you with me, and I with you. [21] Whoever has my commands and keeps them is the one who loves me, and the one who loves me will be loved by my Father, and I will love him and reveal myself to him."

[22] Y'hudah (not the one from K'riot) said to him, "What has happened, Lord, that you are about to reveal yourself to us and not to the world?" [23] Yeshua answered him, "If someone loves me, he will keep my word; and my Father will love him, and we will come to him and make our home with him. [24] Someone who doesn't love me doesn't keep my words — and the word you are hearing is not my own but that of the Father who sent me.

[25] "I have told you these things while I am still with you. [26] But the Counselor, the *Ruach HaKodesh*, whom the Father will send in my name, will teach you everything; that is, he will remind you of everything I have said to you.

[27] "What I am leaving with you is *shalom* — I am giving you my *shalom*. I don't give the way the world gives. Don't let yourselves be upset or frightened. [28] You heard me tell you, 'I am leaving, and I will come back to you.' If you loved me, you would have been glad that I am going to the Father; because the Father is greater than I.

[29] "Also, I have said it to you now, before it happens; so that when it does happen, you will trust. [30] I won't be talking with you much longer, because the ruler of this world is coming. He has no claim on me; [31] rather, this is happening so that the world may know that I love the Father, and that I do as the Father has commanded me.

"Get up! Let's get going!

15 [1] "I am the real vine, and my Father is the gardener. [2] Every branch which is part of me but fails to bear fruit, he cuts off; and every branch that does bear fruit, he prunes, so that it may bear more fruit. [3] Right now, because of the word which I have spoken to you, you are pruned. [4] Stay united with me, as I will with you — for just as the branch can't put forth fruit by itself apart from the vine, so you can't bear fruit apart from me.

[5] "I am the vine and you are the branches. Those who stay united with me, and I with them, are the ones who bear much fruit; because apart from me you can't do a thing. [6] Unless a person remains united with me, he is thrown away like a branch and dries up. Such branches are gathered and thrown into the fire, where they are burned up.

[7] "If you remain united with me, and my words with you, then ask whatever you want, and it will happen for you. [8] This is how my Father is glorified — in your bearing much fruit; this is how you will prove to be my *talmidim*.

[9] "Just as my Father has loved me, I too have loved you; so stay in my love. [10] If you keep my commands, you will stay in my love — just as I have kept my Father's commands and stay in his love. [11] I have said this to you so that my joy may be in you, and your joy be complete.

[12] "This is my command: that you keep on loving each other just as I have loved you. [13] No one has greater love than a person who lays down his life for his friends. [14] You are my friends, if you do what I command you. [15] I no longer call you slaves, because a slave doesn't know what his master is about; but I have called you friends, because everything I have heard from my Father I have made known to you. [16] You did not choose me, I chose you; and I have commissioned you to go and bear fruit, fruit that will last; so that whatever you ask from the Father in my name he may give you. [17] This is what I command you: keep loving each other!

[18] "If the world hates you, understand that it hated me first. [19] If you belonged to the world, the world would have loved its own. But because you do not belong to the world — on the contrary, I have picked you out of the world — therefore the world hates you. [20] Remember what I told you, 'A slave is not greater than his master.' If they persecuted me, they will persecute you too; if they kept my word, they will keep yours too. [21] But they will do all this to you on my account, because they don't know the One who sent me.

[22] "If I had not come and spoken to them, they wouldn't be guilty of sin; but now, they have no excuse for their sin. [23] Whoever hates me hates my Father also. [24] If I had not done in their presence works which no one else ever did, they would not be guilty of sin; but now, they have seen them and have hated both me and my Father. [25] But this has happened in order to fulfill the words in their *Torah* which read, **'They hated me for no reason at all.'**[o]

[26] "When the Counselor comes, whom I will send you from the Father — the Spirit of Truth, who keeps going out from the Father — he will testify on my behalf. [27] And you testify too, because you have been with me from the outset.

16 [1] "I have told you these things so that you won't be caught by surprise. [2] They will ban you from the synagogue; in fact, the time will come when anyone who kills you will think he is serving God! [3] They will do these things because they have

---

[o] Psalms 35:19; 69:5(4)

understood neither the Father nor me. ⁴But I have told you this, so that when the time comes for it to happen, you will remember that I told you. I didn't tell you this at first, because I was with you. ⁵But now I am going to the One who sent me.

"Not one of you is asking me, 'Where are you going?' ⁶Instead, because I have said these things to you, you are overcome with grief. ⁷But I tell you the truth, it is to your advantage that I go away; for if I don't go away, the comforting Counselor will not come to you. However, if I do go, I will send him to you.

⁸"When he comes, he will show that the world is wrong about sin, about righteousness and about judgment — ⁹about sin, in that people don't put their trust in me; ¹⁰about righteousness, in that I am going to the Father and you will no longer see me; ¹¹about judgment, in that the ruler of this world has been judged.

¹²"I still have many things to tell you, but you can't bear them now. ¹³However, when the Spirit of Truth comes, he will guide you into all the truth; for he will not speak on his own initiative but will say only what he hears. He will also announce to you the events of the future. ¹⁴He will glorify me, because he will receive from what is mine and announce it to you. ¹⁵Everything the Father has is mine; this is why I said that he receives from what is mine and will announce it to you.

¹⁶"In a little while, you will see me no more; then, a little while later, you will see me." ¹⁷At this, some of the *talmidim* said to one another, "What is this that he's telling us, 'In a little while, you won't see me; then, a little while later, you will see me'? and, 'I am going to the Father'?" ¹⁸They went on saying, "What is this 'little while'? We don't understand what he's talking about."

¹⁹Yeshua knew that they wanted to ask him, so he said to them, "Are you asking each other what I meant by saying, 'In a little while, you won't see me; and then, a little while later, you will see me'? ²⁰Yes, it's true. I tell you that you will sob and mourn, and the world will rejoice; you will grieve, but your grief will turn to joy. ²¹When a woman is giving birth, she is in pain; because her time has come. But when the baby is born, she forgets her suffering out of joy that a child has come into the world. ²²So you do indeed feel grief now, but I am going to see you again. Then your hearts will be full of joy, and no one will take your joy away from you.

²³"When that day comes, you won't ask anything of me! Yes, indeed! I tell you that whatever you ask from the Father, he will give you in my name. ²⁴Till now you haven't asked for anything in my name. Keep asking, and you will receive, so that your joy may be complete.

²⁵"I have said these things to you with the help of illustrations; however, a time is coming when I will no longer speak indirectly but will talk about the Father in plain language. ²⁶When that day comes, you will ask in my name. I am not telling you that I will pray to the Father on your behalf, ²⁷for the Father himself loves you, because you have loved me and have believed that I came from God.

²⁸"I came from the Father and have come into the world; again, I am leaving the world and returning to the Father."

²⁹The *talmidim* said to him, "Look, you're talking plainly right now, you're not speaking indirectly at all. ³⁰Now we know that you know everything, and that you don't need to have people put their questions into words. This makes us believe that you came from God."

³¹Yeshua answered, "Now you do believe. ³²But a time is coming — indeed it has come already — when you will be scattered, each one looking out for himself;

and you will leave me all alone. Yet I am not alone; because the Father is with me. ³³ "I have said these things to you so that, united with me, you may have *shalom*. In the world, you have *tsuris*. But be brave! I have conquered the world!"

17 ¹ After Yeshua had said these things, he looked up toward heaven and said, "Father, the time has come. Glorify your Son, so that the Son may glorify you — ² just as you gave him authority over all mankind, so that he might give eternal life to all those whom you have given him. ³ And eternal life is this: to know you, the one true God, and him whom you sent, Yeshua the Messiah.

⁴ "I glorified you on earth by finishing the work you gave me to do. ⁵ Now, Father, glorify me alongside yourself. Give me the same glory I had with you before the world existed.

⁶ "I made your name known to the people you gave me out of the world. They were yours, you gave them to me, and they have kept your word. ⁷ Now they know that everything you have given me is from you, ⁸ because the words you gave me I have given to them, and they have received them. They have really come to know that I came from you, and they have come to trust that you sent me.

⁹ "I am praying for them. I am not praying for the world, but for those you have given to me, because they are yours. ¹⁰ Indeed, all I have is yours, and all you have is mine, and in them I have been glorified. ¹¹ Now I am no longer in the world. They are in the world, but I am coming to you. Holy Father, guard them by the power of your name, which you have given to me, so that they may be one, just as we are. ¹² When I was with them, I guarded them by the power of your name, which you have given to me; yes, I kept watch over them; and not one of them was destroyed (except the one meant for destruction, so that the *Tanakh* might be fulfilled). ¹³ But now, I am coming to you; and I say these things while I am still in the world so that they may have my joy made complete in themselves.

¹⁴ "I have given them your word, and the world hated them, because they do not belong to the world — just as I myself do not belong to the world. ¹⁵ I don't ask you to take them out of the world, but to protect them from the Evil One. ¹⁶ They do not belong to the world, just as I do not belong to the world. ¹⁷ Set them apart for holiness by means of the truth — your word is truth. ¹⁸ Just as you sent me into the world, I have sent them into the world. ¹⁹ On their behalf I am setting myself apart for holiness, so that they too may be set apart for holiness by means of the truth.

²⁰ "I pray not only for these, but also for those who will trust in me because of their word, ²¹ that they may all be one. Just as you, Father, are united with me and I with you, I pray that they may be united with us, so that the world may believe that you sent me. ²² The glory which you have given to me, I have given to them; so that they may be one, just as we are one — ²³ I united with them and you with me, so that they may be completely one, and the world thus realize that you sent me, and that you have loved them just as you have loved me.

²⁴ "Father, I want those you have given me to be with me where I am; so that they may see my glory, which you have given me because you loved me before the creation of the world. ²⁵ Righteous Father, the world has not known you, but I have known you, and these people have known that you sent me. ²⁶ I made your name known to them, and I will continue to make it known; so that the love with which you have loved me may be in them, and I myself may be united with them."

18 ¹ After Yeshua had said all this, he went out with his *talmidim* across the stream that flows in winter through the *Vadi* Kidron, to a spot where there was a grove of trees; and he and his *talmidim* went into it. ² Now Y'hudah, who was betraying him, also knew the place; because Yeshua had often met there with his *talmidim*. ³ So Y'hudah went there, taking with him a detachment of Roman soldiers and some Temple guards provided by the head *cohanim* and the *P'rushim*; they carried weapons, lanterns and torches. ⁴ Yeshua, who knew everything that was going to happen to him, went out and asked them, "Whom do you want?" ⁵ "Yeshua from Natzeret," they answered. He said to them, "I AM." Also standing with them was Y'hudah, the one who was betraying him. ⁶ When he said, "I AM," they went backward from him and fell to the ground. ⁷ So he inquired of them once more, "Whom do you want?" and they said, "Yeshua from Natzeret." ⁸ "I told you, 'I AM,'" answered Yeshua, "so if I'm the one you want, let these others go." ⁹ This happened so that what he had said might be fulfilled, "I have not lost one of those you gave me."

¹⁰ Then Shim'on Kefa, who had a sword, drew it and struck the slave of the *cohen hagadol*, cutting off his right ear; the slave's name was Melekh. ¹¹ Yeshua said to Kefa, "Put your sword back in its scabbard! This is the cup the Father has given me; am I not to drink it?"

¹² So the detachment of Roman soldiers and their captain, together with the Temple Guard of the Judeans, arrested Yeshua, tied him up, ¹³ and took him first to 'Anan, the father-in-law of Kayafa, who was *cohen gadol* that fateful year. ¹⁴ (It was Kayafa who had advised the Judeans that it would be good for one man to die on behalf of the people.) ¹⁵ Shim'on Kefa and another *talmid* followed Yeshua. The second *talmid* was known to the *cohen hagadol*, and he went with Yeshua into the courtyard of the *cohen hagadol*; ¹⁶ but Kefa stood outside by the gate. So the other *talmid*, the one known to the *cohen hagadol*, went back out and spoke to the woman on duty at the gate, then brought Kefa inside. ¹⁷ The woman at the gate said to Kefa, "Aren't you another of that man's *talmidim*?" He said, "No, I'm not." ¹⁸ Now the slaves and guards had lit a fire because it was cold, and they were standing around it warming themselves; Kefa joined them and stood warming himself too.

¹⁹ The *cohen hagadol* questioned Yeshua about his *talmidim* and about what he taught. ²⁰ Yeshua answered, "I have spoken quite openly to everyone; I have always taught in a synagogue or in the Temple where all Jews meet together, and I have said nothing in secret; ²¹ so why are you questioning me? Question the ones who heard what I said to them; look, they know what I said." ²² At these words, one of the guards standing by slapped Yeshua in the face and said, "This is how you talk to the *cohen hagadol*?" ²³ Yeshua answered him, "If I said something wrong, state publicly what was wrong; but if I was right, why are you hitting me?" ²⁴ So 'Anan sent him, still tied up, to Kayafa the *cohen hagadol*.

²⁵ Meanwhile, Shim'on Kefa was standing and warming himself. They said to him, "Aren't you also one of his *talmidim*?" He denied it, saying, "No, I am not." ²⁶ One of the slaves of the *cohen hagadol*, a relative of the man whose ear Kefa had cut off, said, "Didn't I see you with him in the grove of trees?" ²⁷ So again Kefa denied it, and instantly a rooster crowed.

²⁸ They led Yeshua from Kayafa to the governor's headquarters. By now it was early morning. They did not enter the headquarters building because they didn't want to become ritually defiled and thus unable to eat the *Pesach* meal. ²⁹ So Pilate went

outside to them and said, "What charge are you bringing against this man?" ³⁰ They answered, "If he hadn't done something wrong, we wouldn't have brought him to you." ³¹ Pilate said to them, "You take him and judge him according to your own law." The Judeans replied, "We don't have the legal power to put anyone to death." ³² This was so that what Yeshua had said, about how he was going to die, might be fulfilled.

³³ So Pilate went back into the headquarters, called Yeshua and said to him, "Are you the king of the Jews?" ³⁴ Yeshua answered, "Are you asking this on your own, or have other people told you about me?" ³⁵ Pilate replied, "Am I a Jew? Your own nation and head *cohanim* have handed you over to me; what have you done?" ³⁶ Yeshua answered, "My kingship does not derive its authority from this world's order of things. If it did, my men would have fought to keep me from being arrested by the Judeans. But my kingship does not come from here." ³⁷ "So then," Pilate said to him, "You are a king, after all." Yeshua answered, "You say I am a king. The reason I have been born, the reason I have come into the world, is to bear witness to the truth. Every one who belongs to the truth listens to me." ³⁸ Pilate asked him, "What is truth?"

Having said this, Pilate went outside again to the Judeans and told them, "I don't find any case against him. ³⁹ However, you have a custom that at Passover I set one prisoner free. Do you want me to set free for you the 'king of the Jews'?" ⁴⁰ But they yelled back, "No, not this man but Bar-Abba!" (Bar-Abba was a revolutionary.)

19 ¹ Pilate then took Yeshua and had him flogged. ² The soldiers twisted thorn-branches into a crown and placed it on his head, put a purple robe on him, ³ and went up to him, saying over and over, "Hail, 'king of the Jews'!" and hitting him in the face.

⁴ Pilate went outside once more and said to the crowd, "Look, I'm bringing him out to you to get you to understand that I find no case against him." ⁵ So Yeshua came out, wearing the thorn-branch crown and the purple robe. Pilate said to them, "Look at the man!" ⁶ When the head *cohanim* and the Temple guards saw him they shouted, "Put him to death on the stake! Put him to death on the stake!" Pilate said to them, "You take him out yourselves and put him to death on the stake, because I don't find any case against him." ⁷ The Judeans answered him, "We have a law; according to that law, he ought to be put to death, because he made himself out to be the Son of God." ⁸ On hearing this, Pilate became even more frightened.

⁹ He went back into the headquarters and asked Yeshua, "Where are you from?" But Yeshua didn't answer. ¹⁰ So Pilate said to him, "You refuse to speak to me? Don't you understand that it is in my power either to set you free or to have you executed on the stake?" ¹¹ Yeshua answered, "You would have no power over me if it hadn't been given to you from above; this is why the one who handed me over to you is guilty of a greater sin." ¹² On hearing this, Pilate tried to find a way to set him free; but the Judeans shouted, "If you set this man free, it means you're not a 'Friend of the Emperor'! Everyone who claims to be a king is opposing the Emperor!" ¹³ When Pilate heard what they were saying, he brought Yeshua outside and sat down on the judge's seat in the place called The Pavement (in Aramaic, *Gabta*); ¹⁴ it was about noon on Preparation Day for *Pesach*. He said to the Judeans, "Here's your king!" ¹⁵ They shouted, "Take him away! Take him away! Put him to death on the stake!" Pilate said to them, "You want me to execute your king on a stake?" The head *cohanim* answered, "We have no king but the Emperor." ¹⁶ Then Pilate handed Yeshua over to them to have him put to death on the stake.

So they took charge of Yeshua. [17] Carrying the stake himself he went out to the place called Skull (in Aramaic, *Gulgolta*). [18] There they nailed him to the stake along with two others, one on either side, with Yeshua in the middle. [19] Pilate also had a notice written and posted on the stake; it read,

YESHUA FROM NATZERET
THE KING OF THE JEWS

[20] Many of the Judeans read this notice, because the place where Yeshua was put on the stake was close to the city; and it had been written in Hebrew, in Latin and in Greek. [21] The Judeans' head *cohanim* therefore said to Pilate, "Don't write, 'The King of the Jews,' but 'He said, "I am King of the Jews."'" [22] Pilate answered, "What I have written, I have written."

[23] When the soldiers had nailed Yeshua to the stake, they took his clothes and divided them into four shares, a share for each soldier, with the under-robe left over. Now the under-robe was seamless, woven in one piece from top to bottom; [24] so they said to one another, "We shouldn't tear it in pieces; let's draw for it." This happened in order to fulfill the words from the *Tanakh*,

"They divided my clothes among themselves
and gambled for my robe."[*p*]

This is why the soldiers did these things.

[25] Nearby Yeshua's execution stake stood his mother, his mother's sister Miryam the wife of K'lofah, and Miryam from Magdala. [26] When Yeshua saw his mother and the *talmid* whom he loved standing there, he said to his mother, "Mother, this is your son." [27] Then he said to the *talmid*, "This is your mother." And from that time on, the *talmid* took her into his own home.

[28] After this, knowing that all things had accomplished their purpose, Yeshua, in order to fulfill the words of the *Tanakh*, said, "I'm thirsty." [29] A jar full of cheap sour wine was there; so they soaked a sponge in the wine, coated it with oregano leaves and held it up to his mouth. [30] After Yeshua had taken the wine, he said, "It is accomplished!" And, letting his head droop, he delivered up his spirit.

[31] It was Preparation Day, and the Judeans did not want the bodies to remain on the stake on *Shabbat*, since it was an especially important *Shabbat*. So they asked Pilate to have the legs broken and the bodies removed. [32] The soldiers came and broke the legs of the first man who had been put on a stake beside Yeshua, then the legs of the other one; [33] but when they got to Yeshua and saw that he was already dead, they didn't break his legs. [34] However, one of the soldiers stabbed his side with a spear, and at once blood and water flowed out. [35] The man who saw it has testified about it, and his testimony is true. And he knows that he tells the truth, so you too can trust. [36] For these things happened in order to fulfill this passage of the *Tanakh*:

"Not one of his bones will be broken."[*q*]

[*p*] Psalm 22:19(18)   [*q*] Psalm 34:21(20); Exodus 12:46; Numbers 9:12

³⁷ And again, another passage says,

"They will look at him whom they have pierced."^r

³⁸ After this, Yosef of Ramatayim, who was a *talmid* of Yeshua, but a secret one out of fear of the Judeans, asked Pilate if he could have Yeshua's body. Pilate gave his consent, so Yosef came and took the body away. ³⁹ Also Nakdimon, who at first had gone to see Yeshua by night, came with some seventy pounds of spices — a mixture of myrrh and aloes. ⁴⁰ They took Yeshua's body and wrapped it up in linen sheets with the spices, in keeping with Judean burial practice. ⁴¹ In the vicinity of where he had been executed was a garden, and in the garden was a new tomb in which no one had ever been buried. ⁴² So, because it was Preparation Day for the Judeans, and because the tomb was close by, that is where they buried Yeshua.

20 ¹ Early on the first day of the week, while it was still dark, Miryam from Magdala went to the tomb and saw that the stone had been removed from the tomb. ² So she came running to Shim'on Kefa and the other *talmid*, the one Yeshua loved, and said to them, "They've taken the Lord out of the tomb, and we don't know where they've put him!"

³ Then Kefa and the other *talmid* started for the tomb. ⁴ They both ran, but the other *talmid* outran Kefa and reached the tomb first. ⁵ Stooping down, he saw the linen burial-sheets lying there but did not go in. ⁶ Then, following him, Shim'on Kefa arrived, entered the tomb and saw the burial-sheets lying there, ⁷ also the cloth that had been around his head, lying not with the sheets but in a separate place and still folded up. ⁸ Then the other *talmid*, who had arrived at the tomb first, also went in; he saw, and he trusted. ⁹ (They had not yet come to understand that the *Tanakh* teaches that the Messiah has to rise from the dead.)

¹⁰ So the *talmidim* returned home, ¹¹ but Miryam stood outside crying. As she cried, she bent down, peered into the tomb, ¹² and saw two angels in white sitting where the body of Yeshua had been, one at the head and one at the feet. ¹³ "Why are you crying?" they asked her. "They took my Lord," she said to them, "and I don't know where they have put him."

¹⁴ As she said this, she turned around and saw Yeshua standing there, but she didn't know it was he. ¹⁵ Yeshua said to her, "Lady, why are you crying? Whom are you looking for?" Thinking he was the gardener, she said to him, "Sir, if you're the one who carried him away, just tell me where you put him; and I'll go and get him myself." ¹⁶ Yeshua said to her, "Miryam!" Turning, she cried out to him in Hebrew, "*Rabbani!*" (that is, "Teacher!") ¹⁷ "Stop holding onto me," Yeshua said to her, "because I haven't yet gone back to the Father. But go to my brothers, and tell them that I am going back to my Father and your Father, to my God and your God." ¹⁸ Miryam of Magdala went to the *talmidim* with the news that she had seen the Lord and that he had told her this.

¹⁹ In the evening that same day, the first day of the week, when the *talmidim* were gathered together behind locked doors out of fear of the Judeans, Yeshua came, stood in the middle and said, "*Shalom aleikhem!*" ²⁰ Having greeted them, he showed

---

^r Zechariah 12:10

them his hands and his side. The *talmidim* were overjoyed to see the Lord. ²¹ "*Shalom aleikhem!*" Yeshua repeated. "Just as the Father sent me, I myself am also sending you." ²² Having said this, he breathed on them and said to them, "Receive the *Ruach HaKodesh!* ²³ If you forgive someone's sins, their sins are forgiven; if you hold them, they are held."

²⁴ Now T'oma (the name means "twin"), one of the Twelve, was not with them when Yeshua came. ²⁵ When the other *talmidim* told him, "We have seen the Lord," he replied, "Unless I see the nail marks in his hands, put my finger into the place where the nails were and put my hand into his side, I refuse to believe it."

²⁶ A week later his *talmidim* were once more in the room, and this time T'oma was with them. Although the doors were locked, Yeshua came, stood among them and said, "*Shalom aleikhem!*" ²⁷ Then he said to T'oma, "Put your finger here, look at my hands, take your hand and put it into my side. Don't be lacking in trust, but have trust!" ²⁸ T'oma answered him, "My Lord and my God!" ²⁹ Yeshua said to him, "Have you trusted because you have seen me? How blessed are those who do not see, but trust anyway!"

³⁰ In the presence of the *talmidim* Yeshua performed many other miracles which have not been recorded in this book. ³¹ But these which have been recorded are here so that you may trust that Yeshua is the Messiah, the Son of God, and that by this trust you may have life because of who he is.

21 ¹ After this, Yeshua appeared again to the *talmidim* at Lake Tiberias. Here is how it happened: ² Shim'on Kefa and T'oma (his name means "twin") were together with Natan'el from Kanah in the Galil, the sons of Zavdai, and two other *talmidim*. ³ Shim'on Kefa said, "I'm going fishing." They said to him, "We're coming with you." They went and got into the boat, but that night they didn't catch anything. ⁴ However, just as day was breaking, Yeshua stood on shore, but the *talmidim* didn't know it was he. ⁵ He said to them, "You don't have any fish, do you?" "No," they answered him. ⁶ He said to them, "Throw in your net to starboard and you will catch some." So they threw in their net, and there were so many fish in it that they couldn't haul it aboard. ⁷ The *talmid* Yeshua loved said to Kefa, "It's the Lord!" On hearing it was the Lord, Shim'on Kefa threw on his coat, because he was stripped for work, and plunged into the lake; ⁸ but the other *talmidim* followed in the boat, dragging the net full of fish; for they weren't far from shore, only about a hundred yards. ⁹ When they stepped ashore, they saw a fire of burning coals with a fish on it, and some bread. ¹⁰ Yeshua said to them, "Bring some of the fish you have just caught." ¹¹ Shim'on Kefa went up and dragged the net ashore. It was full of fish, 153 of them; but even with so many, the net wasn't torn. ¹² Yeshua said to them, "Come and have breakfast." None of the *talmidim* dared to ask him, "Who are you?" They knew it was the Lord. ¹³ Yeshua came, took the bread and gave it to them, and did the same with the fish. ¹⁴ This was now the third time Yeshua had appeared to the *talmidim* after being raised from the dead.

¹⁵ After breakfast, Yeshua said to Shim'on Kefa, "Shim'on Bar-Yochanan, do you love me more than these?" He replied, "Yes, Lord, you know I'm your friend." He said to him, "Feed my lambs." ¹⁶ A second time he said to him, "Shim'on Bar-Yochanan, do you love me?" He replied, "Yes, Lord, you know I'm your friend." He said to him, "Shepherd my sheep." ¹⁷ The third time he said to him, "Shim'on Bar-

Yochanan, are you my friend?" Shim'on was hurt that he questioned him a third time: "Are you my friend?" So he replied, "Lord, you know everything! You know I'm your friend!" Yeshua said to him, "Feed my sheep! ^{18} Yes, indeed! I tell you, when you were younger, you put on your clothes and went where you wanted. But when you grow old, you will stretch out your hands, and someone else will dress you and carry you where you do not want to go." ^{19} He said this to indicate the kind of death by which Kefa would bring glory to God. Then Yeshua said to him, "Follow me!"

^{20} Kefa turned and saw the *talmid* Yeshua especially loved following behind, the one who had leaned against him at the supper and had asked, "Who is the one who is betraying you?" ^{21} On seeing him, Kefa said to Yeshua, "Lord, what about him?" ^{22} Yeshua said to him, "If I want him to stay on until I come, what is it to you? You, follow me!" ^{23} Therefore the word spread among the brothers that that *talmid* would not die. However, Yeshua didn't say he wouldn't die, but simply, "If I want him to stay on until I come, what is it to you?"

^{24} This one is the *talmid* who is testifying about these things and who has recorded them.

And we know that his testimony is true.

^{25} But there are also many other things Yeshua did; and if they were all to be recorded, I don't think the whole world could contain the books that would have to be written!

The

ACTS

of the Emissaries of Yeshua the Messiah

1 ¹ Dear Theophilos:
In the first book, I wrote about everything Yeshua set out to do and teach, ² until the day when, after giving instructions through the *Ruach HaKodesh* to the emissaries whom he had chosen, he was taken up into heaven.

³ After his death he showed himself to them and gave many convincing proofs that he was alive. During a period of forty days they saw him, and he spoke with them about the Kingdom of God.

⁴ At one of these gatherings, he instructed them not to leave Yerushalayim but to "wait for what the Father promised, which you heard about from me. ⁵ For Yochanan used to immerse people in water; but in a few days, you will be immersed in the *Ruach HaKodesh!*"

⁶ When they were together, they asked him, "Lord, are you at this time going to restore self-rule to Isra'el?" ⁷ He answered, "You don't need to know the dates or the times; the Father has kept these under his own authority. ⁸ But you will receive power when the *Ruach HaKodesh* comes upon you; you will be my witnesses both in Yerushalayim and in all Y'hudah and Shomron, indeed to the ends of the earth!"

⁹ After saying this, he was taken up before their eyes; and a cloud hid him from their sight. ¹⁰ As they were staring into the sky after him, suddenly they saw two men dressed in white standing next to them. ¹¹ The men said, "You Galileans! Why are you standing, staring into space? This Yeshua, who has been taken away from you into heaven, will come back to you in just the same way as you saw him go into heaven."

¹² Then they returned the *Shabbat*-walk distance from the Mount of Olives to Yerushalayim. ¹³ After entering the city, they went to the upstairs room where they were staying. The names of the emissaries were Kefa, Ya'akov, Yochanan, Andrew, Philip, T'oma, Bar-Talmai, Mattityahu, Ya'akov Ben-Halfai, Shim'on "the Zealot," and Y'hudah Ben-Ya'akov. ¹⁴ These all devoted themselves single-mindedly to prayer, along with some women, including Miryam (Yeshua's mother), and his brothers.

¹⁵ During this period, when the group of believers numbered about 120, Kefa stood up and addressed his fellow-believers: ¹⁶ "Brothers, the *Ruach HaKodesh* spoke in advance through David about Y'hudah, and these words of the *Tanakh* had to be fulfilled. He was guide for those who arrested Yeshua — ¹⁷ he was one of us and had been assigned a part in our work." ¹⁸ (With the money Y'hudah received for his evil deed, he bought a field; and there he fell to his death. His body swelled up and burst open, and all his insides spilled out. ¹⁹ This became known to everyone in Yerushalayim, so they called that field Hakal-D'ma — which in their language means "Field of Blood"). ²⁰ "Now," said Kefa, "it is written in the book of Psalms,

> **'Let his estate become desolate,**
> **let there be no one to live in it';**ᵃ

and

> **'Let someone else take his place as a supervisor.'**ᵇ

²¹ Therefore, one of the men who have been with us continuously throughout the time the Lord Yeshua traveled around among us, ²² from the time Yochanan was immersing people until the day Yeshua was taken up from us — one of these must become a witness with us to his resurrection."

²³ They nominated two men — Yosef Bar-Sabba, surnamed Justus, and Mattityahu. ²⁴ Then they prayed, "Lord, you know everyone's heart. Show us which of these two you have chosen ²⁵ to take over the work and the office of emissary that Y'hudah abandoned to go where he belongs." ²⁶ Then they drew lots to decide between the two, and the lot fell to Mattityahu. So he was added to the eleven emissaries.

2 ¹ The festival of *Shavu'ot* arrived, and the believers all gathered together in one place. ² Suddenly there came a sound from the sky like the roar of a violent wind, and it filled the whole house where they were sitting. ³ Then they saw what looked like tongues of fire, which separated and came to rest on each one of them. ⁴ They were all filled with the *Ruach HaKodesh* and began to talk in different languages, as the Spirit enabled them to speak.

⁵ Now there were staying in Yerushalayim religious Jews from every nation under heaven. ⁶ When they heard this sound, a crowd gathered; they were confused, because each one heard the believers speaking in his own language. ⁷ Totally amazed, they asked, "How is this possible? Aren't all these people who are speaking from the Galil? ⁸ How is it that we hear them speaking in our native languages? ⁹ We are Parthians, Medes, Elamites; residents of Mesopotamia, Y'hudah, Cappadocia, Pontus, Asia, ¹⁰ Phrygia, Pamphylia, Egypt, the parts of Libya near Cyrene; visitors from Rome; ¹¹ Jews by birth and proselytes; Jews from Crete and from Arabia. . . ! How is it that we hear them speaking in our own languages about the great things God has done?" ¹² Amazed and confused, they all went on asking each other, "What can this mean?" ¹³ But others made fun of them and said, "They've just had too much wine!"

¹⁴ Then Kefa stood up with the Eleven and raised his voice to address them: "You Judeans, and all of you staying here in Yerushalayim! Let me tell you what this means! Listen carefully to me!

¹⁵ "These people aren't drunk, as you suppose — it's only nine in the morning. ¹⁶ No, this is what was spoken about through the prophet Yo'el:

¹⁷
> **'ADONAI says:**
> **"In the Last Days,**
> **I will pour out from my Spirit upon everyone.**
> **Your sons and daughters will prophesy,**
> **your young men will see visions,**

ᵃ Psalm 69:26(25) ᵇ Psalm 109:8

18   **Even on my slaves, both men and women,**
    will I pour out from my Spirit in those days;
    and they will prophesy.

19   **I will perform miracles in the sky above**
    and signs on the earth below —
    blood, fire and thick smoke.

20   **The sun will become dark**
    and the moon blood
    before the great and fearful Day of ADONAI comes.

21   **And then, whoever calls on the name of ADONAI will be saved.'"**[c]

22 "Men of Isra'el! Listen to this! Yeshua from Natzeret was a man demonstrated to you to have been from God by the powerful works, miracles and signs that God performed through him in your presence. You yourselves know this. 23 This man was arrested in accordance with God's predetermined plan and foreknowledge; and, through the agency of persons not bound by the *Torah*, you nailed him up on a stake and killed him!

24 "But God has raised him up and freed him from the suffering of death; it was impossible that death could keep its hold on him. 25 For David says this about him:

    'I saw ADONAI always before me,
    for he is at my right hand,
    so that I will not be shaken.

26   **For this reason, my heart was glad;**
    and my tongue rejoiced;
    and now my body too will live on in the certain hope

27   **that you will not abandon me to Sh'ol**
    or let your Holy One see decay.

28   **You have made known to me the ways of life;**
    you will fill me with joy by your presence.'[d]

29 "Brothers, I know I can say to you frankly that the patriarch David died and was buried — his tomb is with us to this day. 30 Therefore, since he was a prophet and knew that God had sworn an oath to him that one of his descendants would sit on his throne, 31 he was speaking in advance about the resurrection of the Messiah, that it was he who was not abandoned in Sh'ol and whose flesh did not see decay. 32 God raised up this Yeshua! And we are all witnesses of it!

33 "Moreover, he has been exalted to **the right hand of God**; has received from the Father what he promised, namely, the *Ruach HaKodesh*; and has poured out this gift, which you are both seeing and hearing. 34 For David did not ascend into heaven. But he says,

35   **'ADONAI said to my Lord,**
    "Sit at my right hand
    until I make your enemies a footstool for your feet."'[e]

---

[c] Joel 3:1–5(2:28–32)   [d] Psalm 16:8–11   [e] Psalm 110:1

³⁶ Therefore, let the whole house of Isra'el know beyond doubt that God has made him both Lord and Messiah — this Yeshua, whom you executed on a stake!"

³⁷ On hearing this, they were stung in their hearts; and they said to Kefa and the other emissaries, "Brothers, what should we do?" ³⁸ Kefa answered them, "Turn from sin, return to God, and each of you be immersed on the authority of Yeshua the Messiah into forgiveness of your sins, and you will receive the gift of the *Ruach HaKodesh!* ³⁹ For the promise is for you, for your children, and for those far away — as many as ADONAI our God may call!"

⁴⁰ He pressed his case with many other arguments and kept pleading with them, "Save yourselves from this perverse generation!"

⁴¹ So those who accepted what he said were immersed, and there were added to the group that day about three thousand people.

⁴² They continued faithfully in the teaching of the emissaries, in fellowship, in breaking bread and in the prayers. ⁴³ Everyone was filled with awe, and many miracles and signs took place through the emissaries. ⁴⁴ All those trusting in Yeshua stayed together and had everything in common; ⁴⁵ in fact, they sold their property and possessions and distributed the proceeds to all who were in need. ⁴⁶ Continuing faithfully and with singleness of purpose to meet in the Temple courts daily, and breaking bread in their several homes, they shared their food in joy and simplicity of heart, ⁴⁷ praising God and having the respect of all the people. And day after day the Lord kept adding to them those who were being saved.

3 ¹ One afternoon at three o'clock, the hour of *minchah* prayers, as Kefa and Yochanan were going up to the Temple, ² a man crippled since birth was being carried in. Every day people used to put him at the Beautiful Gate of the Temple, so that he could beg from those going into the Temple court. ³ When he saw Kefa and Yochanan about to enter, he asked them for some money. ⁴ But they stared straight at him; and Kefa said, "Look at us!" ⁵ The crippled man fixed his attention on them, expecting to receive something from them. ⁶ Kefa said, "I don't have silver, and I don't have gold, but what I do have I give to you: in the name of the Messiah, Yeshua of Natzeret, walk!" ⁷ And taking hold of him by his right hand, Kefa pulled him up. Instantly his feet and ankles became strong; ⁸ so that he sprang up, stood a moment, and began walking. Then he entered the Temple court with them, walking and leaping and praising God! ⁹ Everyone saw him walking and praising God. ¹⁰ They recognized him as the same man who had formerly sat begging at the Beautiful Gate of the Temple, and they were utterly amazed and confounded at what had happened to him. ¹¹ While he clung to Kefa and Yochanan, all the people came running in astonishment toward them in Shlomo's Colonnade.

¹² Seeing this, Kefa addressed the people: "Men of Isra'el! Why are you amazed at this? Or why do you stare at us as if we had made this man walk through some power or godliness of our own? ¹³ **The God of Avraham, Yitz'chak and Ya'akov, the God of our fathers,**ʲ has glorified his servant Yeshua — the same Yeshua you handed over and disowned before Pilate, even after he had decided to release him. ¹⁴ You denied the holy and innocent one, and instead asked for the reprieve of a murderer! ¹⁵ You killed the author of life!

ʲ Exodus 3:6, 15

"But God has raised him from the dead! Of this we are witnesses. ¹⁶ And it is through putting trust in his name that his name has given strength to this man whom you see and know. Yes, it is the trust that comes through Yeshua which has given him this perfect healing in the presence of you all.

¹⁷ "Now, brothers, I know that you did not understand the significance of what you were doing; neither did your leaders. ¹⁸ But this is how God fulfilled what he had announced in advance, when he spoke through all the prophets, namely, that his Messiah was to die.

¹⁹ "Therefore, repent and turn to God, so that your sins may be erased; ²⁰ so that times of refreshing may come from the Lord's presence; and he may send the Messiah appointed in advance for you, that is, Yeshua. ²¹ He has to remain in heaven until the time comes for restoring everything, as God said long ago, when he spoke through the holy prophets. ²² For Moshe himself said, **'A***DONAI* **will raise up for you a prophet like me from among your brothers. You are to listen to everything he tells you.** ²³ **Everyone who fails to listen to that prophet will be removed from the people and destroyed.'**ᵍ ²⁴ Indeed, all the prophets announced these days, starting with Sh'mu'el and continuing through all who followed.

²⁵ "You are the sons of the prophets; and you are included in the covenant which God made with our fathers when he said to Avraham, **'By your seed will all the families of the earth be blessed.'**ʰ ²⁶ So it is to you first that God has sent his servant whom he has raised up, so that he might bless you by turning each one of you from your evil ways."

4 ¹ Kefa and Yochanan were still speaking to the people when the *cohanim*, the captain in charge of the Temple police, and the *Tz'dukim* came upon them, ² very annoyed that they were teaching the people the doctrine of resurrection from the dead and offering Yeshua as proof. ³ The Temple police arrested them; and since it was already evening, they put them in custody overnight. ⁴ However, many of those who heard the message trusted; the number of men alone was about five thousand.

⁵ The next day, the people's rulers, elders and *Torah*-teachers assembled in Yerushalayim, ⁶ along with 'Anan the *cohen hagadol*, Kayafa, Yochanan, Alexander and the other men from the family of the *cohen hagadol*. ⁷ They had the emissaries stand before them and asked, "By what power or in what name did you do this?"

⁸ Then Kefa, filled with the *Ruach HaKodesh*, said to them, "Rulers and elders of the people! ⁹ If we are being examined today about a good deed done for a disabled person, if you want to know how he was restored to health, ¹⁰ then let it be known to you and to all the people of Isra'el that it is in the name of the Messiah, Yeshua from Natzeret, whom you had executed on a stake as a criminal but whom God has raised from the dead, that this man stands before you perfectly healed. ¹¹ "This Yeshua is the **stone rejected by** you **builders** which **has become the cornerstone**.ⁱ ¹² There is salvation in no one else! For there is no other name under heaven given to mankind by whom we must be saved!"

¹³ When they saw how bold Kefa and Yochanan were, even though they were untrained *'am-ha'aretz*, they were amazed; also they recognized them as having been with Yeshua. ¹⁴ Moreover, since they could see the man who had been healed

---

ᵍ Deuteronomy 18:15–16 ʰ Genesis 22:18; 26:4 ⁱ Psalm 118:22

standing right there beside them, there was nothing they could say to discredit the healing. ¹⁵ So they told them to step away from the *Sanhedrin* while they discussed the matter privately. ¹⁶ "What can we do with these men?" they asked each other. "Why, anyone in Yerushalayim can see that a remarkable miracle has come about through them — we can't possibly deny that. ¹⁷ But to prevent it from spreading any further among the people, let's warn them not to speak any more to anyone in this name."

¹⁸ So they called them in again and ordered them under no circumstances to speak or teach in the name of Yeshua. ¹⁹ But Kefa and Yochanan answered, "You must judge whether it is right in the sight of God to listen to you rather than God. ²⁰ As for us, we can't help talking about what we have actually seen and heard." ²¹ They threatened them some more but finally let them go — they couldn't punish them because of the people, for everyone was praising God over what had happened, ²² since the man who had been miraculously healed was more than forty years old.

²³ Upon being released, they went back to their friends and reported what the head *cohanim* and elders had said to them. ²⁴ When they heard it, they raised their voices to God with singleness of heart. "Master," they prayed, "You **made heaven, earth, the sea and everything in them.**ʲ ²⁵ By the *Ruach HaKodesh*, through the mouth of our father David, your servant, you said,

> **'Why did the nations rage**
> **and the peoples devise useless plans?**
> ²⁶ **The kings of the earth took their stand;**
> **and the rulers assembled together**
> **against** *ADONAI*
> **and against his Messiah.'ᵏ**

²⁷ "This has come true in this city, since Herod and Pontius Pilate, with *Goyim* and the peoples of Isra'el, all assembled against your holy servant Yeshua, whom you made Messiah, ²⁸ to do what your power and plan had already determined beforehand should happen.

²⁹ "So now, Lord, take note of their threats; and enable your slaves to speak your message with boldness! ³⁰ Stretch out your hand to heal and to do signs and miracles through the name of your holy servant Yeshua!"

³¹ While they were still praying, the place where they were gathered was shaken. They were all filled with the *Ruach HaKodesh*, and they spoke God's message with boldness.

³² All the many believers were one in heart and soul, and no one claimed any of his possessions for himself, but everyone shared everything he had. ³³ With great power the emissaries continued testifying to the resurrection of the Lord Yeshua, and they were all held in high regard. ³⁴ No one among them was poor, since those who owned lands or houses sold them and turned over the proceeds ³⁵ to the emissaries to distribute to each according to his need. ³⁶ Thus Yosef, whom the emissaries called Bar-Nabba (which means "the Exhorter"), a *Levi* and a native of Cyprus, ³⁷ sold a field which belonged to him and brought the money to the emissaries.

ʲ Psalm 146:6   ᵏ Psalm 2:1–2

5 [1] But there was a man named Hananyah who, with his wife Shappirah, sold some property [2] and, with his wife's knowledge, withheld some of the proceeds for himself; although he did bring the rest to the emissaries. [3] Then Kefa said, "Why has the Adversary so filled your heart that you lie to the *Ruach HaKodesh* and keep back some of the money you received for the land? [4] Before you sold it, the property was yours; and after you sold it, the money was yours to use as you pleased. So what made you decide to do such a thing? You have lied not to human beings but to God!"

[5] On hearing these words, Hananyah fell down dead; and everyone who heard about it was terrified. [6] The young men got up, wrapped his body in a shroud, carried him out and buried him.

[7] Some three hours later, his wife came in, unaware of what had happened. [8] Kefa challenged her: "Tell me, is it true that you sold the land for such-and-such a price?" "Yes," she answered, "that is what we were paid for it." [9] But Kefa came back at her, "Then why did you people plot to test the Spirit of the Lord? Listen! The men who buried your husband are at the door. They will carry you out too!" [10] Instantly she collapsed at his feet and died. The young men entered, found her there dead, carried her out and buried her beside her husband. [11] As a result of this, great fear came over the whole Messianic community, and indeed over everyone who heard about it.

[12] Meanwhile, through the emissaries many signs and miracles continued to be done among the people. United in mind and purpose, the believers met in Shlomo's Colonnade; [13] and no one else dared to join them. Nevertheless, the people continued to regard them highly; [14] and throngs of believers were added to the Lord, both men and women. [15] They went so far as to bring the sick into the streets and lay them on mattresses and stretchers, so that at least Kefa's shadow might fall on them as he passed by. [16] Crowds also gathered from the towns around Yerushalayim, bringing the sick and those afflicted with unclean spirits; and every one of them was healed.

[17] But the *cohen hagadol* and his associates, who were members of the party of the *Tz'dukim*, were filled with jealousy. [18] They arrested the emissaries and put them in the public jail. [19] But during the night, an angel of *Adonai* opened the doors of the prison, led them out and said, [20] "Go, stand in the Temple court and keep telling the people all about this new life!" [21] After hearing that, they entered the Temple area about dawn and began to teach.

Now the *cohen hagadol* and his associates came and called a meeting of the *Sanhedrin* (that is, of Isra'el's whole assembly of elders) and sent to the jail to have them brought. [22] But the officers who went did not find them in the prison. So they returned and reported, [23] "We found the jail securely locked and the guards standing at the doors; but when we opened it, we found no one inside!" [24] When the captain of the Temple police and the head *cohanim* heard these things, they were puzzled and wondered what would happen next.

[25] Then someone came and reported to them, "Listen! The men you ordered put in prison are standing in the Temple court, teaching the people!" [26] The captain and his officers went and brought them, but not with force; because they were afraid of being stoned by the people. [27] They conducted them to the *Sanhedrin*, where the *cohen hagadol* demanded of them, [28] "We gave you strict orders not to teach in this name! Look here! you have filled Yerushalayim with your teaching; moreover, you are determined to make us responsible for this man's death!"

²⁹ Kefa and the other emissaries answered, "We must obey God, not men. ³⁰ **The God of our fathers**[l] raised up Yeshua, whereas you men killed him by having him **hanged on a stake.**[m] ³¹ God has exalted this man **at his right hand**[n] as Ruler and Savior, in order to enable Isra'el to do *t'shuvah* and have her sins forgiven. ³² We are witnesses to these things; so is the *Ruach HaKodesh*, whom God has given to those who obey him."

³³ On hearing this, the members of the *Sanhedrin* were infuriated and wanted to put the emissaries to death. ³⁴ But one of the members of the *Sanhedrin* rose to his feet, a *Parush* named Gamli'el, a teacher of the *Torah* highly respected by all the people. He ordered the men put outside for a little while ³⁵ and then addressed the court: "Men of Isra'el, take care what you do to these people. ³⁶ Some time ago, there was a rebellion under Todah, who claimed to be somebody special; and a number of men, maybe four hundred, rallied behind him. But upon his being put to death, his whole following was broken up and came to nothing. ³⁷ After this, Y'hudah HaG'lili led another uprising, back at the time of the enrollment for the Roman tax; and he got some people to defect to him. But he was killed, and all his followers were scattered. ³⁸ So in the present case, my advice to you is not to interfere with these people, but to leave them alone. For if this idea or this movement has a human origin, it will collapse. ³⁹ But if it is from God, you will not be able to stop them; you might even find yourselves fighting God!"

They heeded his advice. ⁴⁰ After summoning the emissaries and flogging them, they commanded them not to speak in the name of Yeshua, and let them go. ⁴¹ The emissaries left the *Sanhedrin* overjoyed at having been considered worthy of suffering disgrace on account of him. ⁴² And not for a single day, either in the Temple court or in private homes, did they stop teaching and proclaiming the Good News that Yeshua is the Messiah.

6 ¹ Around this time, when the number of *talmidim* was growing, the Greek-speaking Jews began complaining against those who spoke Hebrew that their widows were being overlooked in the daily distribution. ² So the Twelve called a general meeting of the *talmidim* and said, "It isn't appropriate that we should neglect the Word of God in order to serve tables. ³ Brothers, choose seven men from among yourselves who are known to be full of the Spirit and wisdom. We will appoint them to be in charge of this important matter, ⁴ but we ourselves will give our full attention to praying and to serving the Word."

⁵ What they said was agreeable to the whole gathering. They chose Stephen, a man full of faith and the *Ruach HaKodesh*, Philip, Prochoros, Nikanor, Timon, Parmenas and Nicholas, who was a proselyte from Antioch. ⁶ They presented these men to the emissaries, who prayed and laid their hands on them.

⁷ So the word of God continued to spread. The number of *talmidim* in Yerushalayim increased rapidly, and a large crowd of *cohanim* were becoming obedient to the faith.

⁸ Now Stephen, full of grace and power, performed great miracles and signs among the people. ⁹ But opposition arose from members of the Synagogue of the Freed Slaves (as it was called), composed of Cyrenians, Alexandrians and people

---

[l] Exodus 3:15   [m] Deuteronomy 21:22–23   [n] Psalm 110:1

from Cilicia and the province of Asia. They argued with Stephen, 10 but they could
not stand up against his wisdom or the Spirit by which he spoke.
11 So they secretly persuaded some men to allege, "We heard him speak
blasphemously against Moshe and against God." 12 They stirred up the people, as
well as the elders and the *Torah*-teachers; so they came and arrested him and led him
before the *Sanhedrin*. 13 There they set up false witnesses who said, "This man never
stops speaking against this holy place and against the *Torah*; 14 for we have heard
him say that Yeshua from Natzeret will destroy this place and will change the
customs Moshe handed down to us."
15 Everyone sitting in the *Sanhedrin* stared at Stephen and saw that his face
looked like the face of an angel.

7 1 The *cohen hagadol* asked, "Are these accusations true?" 2 and Stephen said:
"Brothers and fathers, listen to me! The God of glory appeared to Avraham
avinu in Mesopotamia before he lived in Haran 3 **and said to him, 'Leave your land
and your family, and go into the land that I will show you.'**[o] 4 So he left the land of
the Kasdim and lived in Haran. After his father died, God made him move to this
land where you are living now. 5 He gave him no inheritance in it, **not even space for
one foot**;[p] yet he promised to **give it to him as a possession and to his descendants
after him**,[q] even though at the time he was childless. 6 What God said to him was,
**'Your descendants will be aliens in a foreign land, where they will be in slavery
and oppressed for four hundred years**. 7 But I will judge the nation that enslaves
them,' God said, **'and afterwards they will leave and worship me in this place.'**[r]
8 And he gave him *b'rit-milah*. So he became the father of Yitz'chak and did his
b'rit-milah on the eighth day, and Yitz'chak became the father of Ya'akov, and Ya'akov
became the father of the Twelve Patriarchs.
9 "Now the Patriarchs **grew jealous of Yosef and sold** him into slavery **in Egypt**.
But *Adonai* was with him;[s] 10 he rescued him from all his troubles and **gave him
favor and wisdom before Pharaoh, king of Egypt, who appointed him chief
administrator over Egypt and over all his household.**[t] 11 **Now there came a famine** that caused much suffering **throughout Egypt and Kena'an**[u] 12 But when Ya'akov
heard that there was grain in Egypt, he sent our fathers there the first time. 13 The
second time, Yosef **revealed his identity to his brothers**,[v] and Yosef's family became
known to Pharaoh. 14 Yosef then sent for his father Ya'akov and all his relatives,
seventy-five people. 15 And Ya'akov went down to Egypt; there he died, as did our other
ancestors. 16 Their bodies were removed to Sh'khem and buried in the tomb Avraham
had bought from the family of Hamor in Sh'khem for a certain sum of money.
17 "As the time drew near for the fulfillment of the promise God had made to
Avraham, the number of our people in Egypt **increased greatly**, 18 until **there arose
another king over Egypt who had no knowledge of Yosef**.[w] 19 With cruel cunning
this man forced our fathers to put their newborn babies outside their homes, so that
they would not survive.

---

[o] Genesis 12:1 [p] Deuteronomy 2:5
[q] Genesis 12:7; 13:15; 15:4, 7, 18–21; 17:8; 24:7; 48:4
[r] Genesis 15:13–14, 16 [s] Genesis 37:11, 28; 39:1–3, 21, 23 [t] Genesis 41:37–44
[u] Genesis 41:54; 42:5 [v] Genesis 45:1 [w] Exodus 1:7–8

[20] "It was then that Moshe was born, and he was beautiful in God's sight. For three months he was reared in his father's house; [21] and when he was put out of his home, Pharaoh's daughter took him and brought him up as her own son. [22] So Moshe was trained in all the wisdom of the Egyptians and became both a powerful speaker and a man of action.

[23] "But when he was forty years old, the thought came to him to visit his brothers, the people of Isra'el. [24] On seeing one of them being mistreated, he went to his defense and took revenge by striking down the Egyptian. [25] He supposed his brothers would understand that God was using him to rescue them, but they didn't understand. [26] When he appeared the next day, as they were fighting, and tried to make peace between them by saying, 'Men, you are brothers! Why do you want to hurt each other?' [27] the one who was mistreating his fellow pushed Moshe away and said, **'Who made you a ruler and judge over us?** [28] **Do you want to kill me, the way you killed that Egyptian yesterday?'**[x] [29] On hearing this, Moshe fled the country and became an exile in the land of Midyan, where he had two sons.

[30] "After forty more years, an angel **appeared to him in the desert** near Mount Sinai **in the flames of a burning thorn bush.** [31] When Moshe saw this, he was amazed at the sight; and as he approached to get a better look, there came the voice of ADONAI, [32] **'I am the God of your fathers, the God of Avraham, Yitz'chak and Ya'akov.' But Moshe trembled with fear and didn't dare to look.** [33] ADONAI said to him, **'Take off your sandals, because the place where you are standing is holy ground.** [34] **I have clearly seen how My people are being oppressed in Egypt, I have heard their cry, and I have come down to rescue them, and now I will send you to Egypt.'**[y]

[35] "This Moshe, whom they rejected, saying, **'Who made you a ruler and judge?'** is the very one whom God sent as both ruler and ransomer by means of the angel that appeared to him in the thorn bush. [36] This man led them out, performing miracles and signs in Egypt, at the Red Sea and in the wilderness for forty years. [37] This is the Moshe who said to the people of Isra'el, **'God will raise up a prophet like me from among your brothers'**[z] [38] This is the man who was in the assembly in the wilderness, accompanied by the angel that had spoken to him at Mount Sinai and by our fathers, the man who was given living words to pass on to us.

[39] "But our fathers did not want to obey him. On the contrary, they rejected him and in their hearts turned to Egypt, [40] saying to Aharon, **'Make us some gods to lead us; because this Moshe, who led us out of Egypt — we don't know what has become of him.'**[a] [41] That was when they made an idol in the shape of a calf and offered a sacrifice to it and held a celebration in honor of what they had made with their own hands. [42] So God turned away from them and gave them over to **worship the stars**[b] — as has been written in the book of the prophets,

> **'People of Isra'el, it was not to me**
> **that you offered slaughtered animals**
> **and sacrifices for forty years in the wilderness!**
[43] **No, you carried the tent of Molekh**

---

[x] Exodus 2:14 [y] Exodus 3:1–2 [z] Deuteronomy 18:15
[a] Exodus 32:1, 23 [b] Jeremiah 19:13

and the star of your god Reifan,
the idols you made so that you could worship them.
Therefore, I will send you into exile beyond Bavel.'^{c}

^{44} "Our fathers had the Tent of Witness in the wilderness. It had been made just as God, who spoke to Moshe, had ordered it made, according to the pattern Moshe had seen. ^{45} Later on, our fathers who had received it brought it in with Y'hoshua when they took the Land away from the nations that God drove out before them.

"So it was until the days of David. ^{46} He enjoyed God's favor and asked if he might provide a dwelling place for the God of Ya'akov ^{47} and Shlomo did build him a house. ^{48} But *Ha'Elyon* does not live in places made by hand! As the prophet says,

^{49} **'Heaven is my throne,' says** A*DONAI,*
          'and the earth is my footstool.
       What kind of house could you build for me?
       What kind of place could you devise for my rest?
^{50} **Didn't I myself make all these things?'**^{d}

^{51} "**Stiffnecked people,**^{e} with **uncircumcised hearts and ears!**^{f} You continually **oppose the** *Ruach HaKodesh!*^{g} You do the same things your fathers did! ^{52} Which of the prophets did your fathers not persecute? They killed those who told in advance about the coming of the *Tzaddik,* and now you have become his betrayers and murderers! — ^{53} you! — who receive the *Torah* as having been delivered by angels — but do not keep it!"

^{54} On hearing these things, they were cut to their hearts and ground their teeth at him. ^{55} But he, full of the *Ruach HaKodesh,* looked up to heaven and saw God's *Sh'khinah,* with Yeshua standing **at the right hand of God**. ^{56} "Look!" he exclaimed, "I see heaven opened and the Son of Man standing **at the right hand of God!"**^{h}

^{57} At this, they began yelling at the top of their voices, so that they wouldn't have to hear him; and with one accord, they rushed at him, ^{58} threw him outside the city and began stoning him. And the witnesses laid down their coats at the feet of a young man named Sha'ul.

^{59} As they were stoning him, Stephen called out to God, "Lord Yeshua! Receive my spirit!" ^{60} Then he kneeled down and shouted out, "Lord! Don't hold this sin against them!" With that, he died;

8 ^{1} and Sha'ul gave his approval to his murder.

Starting with that day, there arose intense persecution against the Messianic Community in Yerushalayim; all but the emissaries were scattered throughout the regions of Y'hudah and Shomron. ^{2} Some godly men buried Stephen and mourned him deeply. ^{3} But Sha'ul set out to destroy the Messianic Community — entering house after house, he dragged off both men and women and handed them over to be put in prison. ^{4} However, those who were scattered announced the Good News of the Word wherever they went.

---

^{c} Amos 5:25–27 ^{d} Isaiah 66:1–2 ^{e} Exodus 32:9; 33:3, 5
^{f} Leviticus 26:41; Jeremiah 6:10; 9:25(26) ^{g} Isaiah 63:10 ^{h} Psalm 110:1

⁵ Now Philip went down to a city in Shomron and was proclaiming the Messiah to them; ⁶ and the crowds were paying close attention to what Philip said, as they heard and saw the miraculous signs he was doing. ⁷ For many people were having unclean spirits driven out of them, shrieking; also many paralytics and crippled persons were being healed; ⁸ so that there was great joy in that city.

⁹ But there was a man named Shim'on in the city who for some time had been practicing magic and astonishing the nation of Shomron, claiming to be somebody great. ¹⁰ Everyone gave heed to him, from the lowest to the highest, saying, "This man is the power of God called 'The Great Power'." ¹¹ They followed him because for a considerable time he had amazed them with his magic.

¹² But when they came to believe Philip, as he announced the Good News concerning the Kingdom of God and the name of Yeshua the Messiah, they were immersed, both men and women. ¹³ Moreover, Shim'on himself came to believe; and after being immersed, he attached himself closely to Philip; and he was amazed as he saw the miraculous signs and great works of power that kept taking place.

¹⁴ When the emissaries in Yerushalayim heard that Shomron had received the Word of God, they sent them Kefa and Yochanan, ¹⁵ who came down and prayed for them, that they might receive the *Ruach HaKodesh*. ¹⁶ For until then he had not come upon any of them; they had only been immersed into the name of the Lord Yeshua. ¹⁷ Then, as Kefa and Yochanan placed their hands on them, they received the *Ruach HaKodesh*.

¹⁸ Shim'on saw that the Spirit was given when the emissaries placed their hands on them, and he offered them money. ¹⁹ "Give this power to me, too," he said, "so that whoever I place my hands on will receive the *Ruach HaKodesh*." ²⁰ But Kefa said to him, "Your silver go to ruin — and you with it, for thinking the free gift of God can be bought! ²¹ You have no part at all in this matter; because in the eyes of God, your heart is crooked. ²² So repent of this wickedness of yours, and pray to the Lord. Perhaps you will yet be forgiven for holding such a thought in your heart. ²³ For I see that you are extremely bitter and completely under the control of sin!" ²⁴ Shim'on answered, "Pray to the Lord for me, so that none of the things you have spoken about will happen to me."

²⁵ Then, after giving a thorough witness and speaking the Word of the Lord, Kefa and Yochanan started back to Yerushalayim, announcing the Good News to many villages in Shomron.

²⁶ An angel of ADONAI said to Philip, "Get up, and go southward on the road that goes down from Yerushalayim to 'Azah, the desert road." ²⁷ So he got up and went. On his way, he caught sight of an Ethiopian, a eunuch who was minister in charge of all the treasure of the Kandake, or queen, of Ethiopia. He had been to Yerushalayim to worship; ²⁸ and now, as he was returning home, he was sitting in his chariot, reading the prophet Yesha'yahu. ²⁹ The Spirit said to Philip, "Go over to this chariot, and stay close to it." ³⁰ As Philip ran up, he heard the Ethiopian reading from Yesha'yahu the prophet. "Do you understand what you're reading?" he asked. ³¹ "How can I," he said, "unless someone explains it to me?" And he invited Philip to climb up and sit with him.

³² Now the portion of the *Tanakh* that he was reading was this:

> **"He was like a sheep led to be slaughtered;**
> **like a lamb silent before the shearer, he does not open his mouth.**

³³ **He was humiliated and denied justice.**
Who will tell about his descendants,
since his life has been taken from the earth?"[i]

³⁴ The eunuch said to Philip, "Here's my question to you — is the prophet talking about himself or someone else?" ³⁵ Then Philip started to speak — beginning with that passage, he went on to tell him the Good News about Yeshua.

³⁶ As they were going down the road, they came to some water; and the eunuch said, "Look! Here's some water! Is there any reason why I shouldn't be immersed?" ³⁷ * ³⁸ He ordered the chariot to stop; then both Philip and the eunuch went down into the water, and Philip immersed him. ³⁹ When they came up out of the water, the Spirit of the Lord snatched Philip away. The eunuch saw no more of him, because he continued on his way — full of joy. ⁴⁰ But Philip showed up at Ashdod and continued proclaiming the Good News as he went through all the towns until he came to Caesarea.

9 ¹ Meanwhile, Sha'ul, still breathing murderous threats against the Lord's *talmidim*, went to the *cohen hagadol* ² and asked him for letters to the synagogues in Dammesek, authorizing him to arrest any people he might find, whether men or women, who belonged to "the Way," and bring them back to Yerushalayim.

³ He was on the road and nearing Dammesek, when suddenly a light from heaven flashed all around him. ⁴ Falling to the ground, he heard a voice saying to him, "Sha'ul! Sha'ul! Why do you keep persecuting me?" ⁵ "Sir, who are you?" he asked. "I am Yeshua, and you are persecuting me. ⁶ But get up, and go into the city, and you will be told what you have to do."

⁷ The men traveling with him stood speechless, hearing the voice but seeing no one. ⁸ They helped Sha'ul get up off the ground; but when he opened his eyes, he could see nothing. So, leading him by the hand, they brought him into Dammesek. ⁹ For three days he remained unable to see, and he neither ate nor drank.

¹⁰ There was a *talmid* in Dammesek, Hananyah by name; and in a vision the Lord said to him, "Hananyah!" He said, "Here I am, Lord." ¹¹ The Lord said to him, "Get up and go to Straight Street, to Y'hudah's house; and ask for a man from Tarsus named Sha'ul; for he is praying, ¹² and in a vision he has seen a man named Hananyah coming in and placing his hands on him to restore his sight." ¹³ But Hananyah answered, "Lord, many have told me about this man, how much harm he has done to your people in Yerushalayim; ¹⁴ and here he has a warrant from the head *cohanim* to arrest everyone who calls on your name." ¹⁵ But the Lord said to him, "Go, because this man is my chosen instrument to carry my name to the *Goyim*, even to their kings, and to the sons of Isra'el as well. ¹⁶ For I myself will show him how much he will have to suffer on account of my name."

¹⁷ So Hananyah left and went into the house. Placing his hands on him, he said, "Brother Sha'ul, the Lord — Yeshua, the one who appeared to you on the road as you were coming here — has sent me so that you may see again and be filled with

---

[i] Isaiah 53:7–8

* Some manuscripts include verse 37: And Philip said, "If you believe with all your heart, you may." He answered, "I believe that Yeshua the Messiah is the Son of God."

the *Ruach HaKodesh.*" [18] In that moment, something like scales fell away from Sha'ul's eyes; and he could see again. He got up and was immersed; [19] then he ate some food and regained his strength.

Sha'ul spent some days with the *talmidim* in Dammesek, [20] and immediately he began proclaiming in the synagogues that Yeshua is the Son of God. [21] All who heard him were amazed. They asked, "Isn't he the man who in Yerushalayim was trying to destroy the people who call on this name? In fact, isn't that why he came here, to arrest them and bring them back to the head *cohanim?*" [22] But Sha'ul was being filled with more and more power and was creating an uproar among the Jews living in Dammesek with his proofs that Yeshua is the Messiah.

[23] Quite some time later, the non-believing Jews gathered together and made plans to kill him; [24] but their plot became known to Sha'ul. They were watching the gates day and night in order to do away with him; [25] but under cover of night, his *talmidim* took him and let him down over the city wall, lowering him in a large basket.

[26] On reaching Yerushalayim, he tried to join the *talmidim*; but they were all afraid of him — they didn't believe he was a *talmid.* [27] However, Bar-Nabba got hold of him and took him to the emissaries. He told them how Sha'ul had seen the Lord while traveling, that the Lord had spoken to him, and how in Dammesek Sha'ul had spoken out boldly in the name of Yeshua. [28] So he remained with them and went all over Yerushalayim continuing to speak out boldly in the name of the Lord. [29] He talked and debated with the Greek-speaking Jews, but they began making attempts to kill him. [30] When the brothers learned of it, they brought him down to Caesarea and sent him away to Tarsus.

[31] Then the Messianic community throughout Y'hudah, the Galil and Shomron enjoyed peace and was built up. They lived in the fear of the Lord, with the counsel of the *Ruach HaKodesh*; and their numbers kept multiplying.

[32] As Kefa traveled around the countryside, he came down to the believers in Lud. [33] There he found a man named Aeneas who had lain bedridden for eight years, because he was paralyzed. [34] Kefa said to him, "Aeneas! Yeshua the Messiah is healing you! Get up, and make your bed!" [35] Everyone living in Lud and the Sharon saw him, and they turned to the Lord.

Now in Yafo there was a *talmidah* named Tavita [36] (which means "gazelle"); she was always doing *tzedakah* and other good deeds. [37] It happened that just at that time, she took sick and died. After washing her, they laid her in a room upstairs. [38] Lud is near Yafo, and the *talmidim* had heard that Kefa was there, so they sent two men to him and urged him, "Please come to us without delay." [39] Kefa got up and went with them.

When he arrived, they led him into the upstairs room. All the widows stood by him, sobbing and showing all the dresses and coats Tavita had made them while she was still with them. [40] But Kefa put them all outside, kneeled down and prayed. Then, turning to the body, he said, "Tavita! Get up!" She opened her eyes; and on seeing Kefa, she sat up. [41] He offered her his hand and helped her to her feet; then, calling the believers and the widows, he presented her to them alive. [42] This became known all over Yafo, and many people put their trust in the Lord. [43] Kefa stayed on in Yafo for some time with a man named Shim'on, a leather-tanner.

10 ¹ There was a man in Caesarea named Cornelius, a Roman army officer in what was called the Italian Regiment. ² He was a devout man, a "God-fearer," as was his whole household; he gave generously to help the Jewish poor and prayed regularly to God. ³ One afternoon around three o'clock he saw clearly in a vision an angel of God coming in and saying to him, "Cornelius!" ⁴ Cornelius stared at the angel, terrified. "What is it, sir?" he asked. "Your prayers," replied the angel, "and your acts of charity have gone up into God's presence, so that he has you on his mind. ⁵ Now send some men to Yafo to bring back a man named Shim'on, also called Kefa. ⁶ He's staying with Shim'on the leather-tanner, who has a house by the sea." ⁷ As the angel that had spoken to him went away, Cornelius called two of his household slaves and one of his military aides, who was a godly man; ⁸ he explained everything to them and sent them to Yafo.

⁹ The next day about noon, while they were still on their way and approaching the city, Kefa went up onto the roof of the house to pray. ¹⁰ He began to feel hungry and wanted something to eat; but while they were preparing the meal, he fell into a trance ¹¹ in which he saw heaven opened, and something that looked like a large sheet being lowered to the ground by its four corners. ¹² In it were all kinds of four-footed animals, crawling creatures and wild birds. ¹³ Then a voice came to him, "Get up, Kefa, slaughter and eat!" ¹⁴ But Kefa said, "No, sir! Absolutely not! I have never eaten food that was unclean or *treif*." ¹⁵ The voice spoke to him a second time: "Stop treating as unclean what God has made clean." ¹⁶ This happened three times, and then the sheet was immediately taken back up into heaven.

¹⁷ Kefa was still puzzling over the meaning of the vision he had seen, when the men Cornelius had sent, having inquired for Shim'on's house, stood at the gate ¹⁸ and called out to ask if the Shim'on known as Kefa was staying there. ¹⁹ While Kefa's mind was still on the vision, the Spirit said, "Three men are looking for you. ²⁰ Get up, go downstairs, and have no misgivings about going with them, because I myself have sent them."

²¹ So Kefa went down and said to the men, "You were looking for me? Here I am. What brings you here?" ²² They answered, "Cornelius. He's a Roman army officer, an upright man and a God-fearer, a man highly regarded by the whole Jewish nation; and he was told by a holy angel to have you come to his house and listen to what you have to say." ²³ So Kefa invited them to be his guests.

The next day, he got up and went with them, accompanied by some of the brothers from Yafo; ²⁴ and he arrived at Caesarea the day after that. Cornelius was expecting them — he had already called together his relatives and close friends. ²⁵ As Kefa entered the house, Cornelius met him and fell prostrate at his feet. ²⁶ But Kefa pulled him to his feet and said, "Stand up! I myself am just a man."

²⁷ As he talked with him, Kefa went inside and found many people gathered. ²⁸ He said to them, "You are well aware that for a man who is a Jew to have close association with someone who belongs to another people, or to come and visit him, is something that just isn't done. But God has shown me not to call any person common or unclean; ²⁹ so when I was summoned, I came without raising any questions. Tell me, then, why did you send for me?"

³⁰ Cornelius answered, "Three days ago around this time, I was at *minchah* prayers in my house, when suddenly a man in shining clothes stood in front of me ³¹ and said, 'God has heard your prayer and remembered your acts of charity. ³² Now send to

Yafo and ask for Shim'on, known as Kefa; he is staying in the house of Shim'on, a leather-tanner, by the sea.' ³³ So I sent for you immediately, and you have been kind enough to come. Now all of us are here in the presence of God to hear everything the Lord has ordered you to say."

³⁴ Then Kefa addressed them: "I now understand that God does not play favorites, ³⁵ but that whoever fears him and does what is right is acceptable to him, no matter what people he belongs to.

³⁶ "Here is the message that he sent to the sons of Isra'el announcing *shalom* through Yeshua the Messiah, who is Lord of everything. ³⁷ You know what has been going on throughout Y'hudah, starting from the Galil after the immersion that Yochanan proclaimed; ³⁸ how God anointed Yeshua from Natzeret with the *Ruach HaKodesh* and with power; how Yeshua went about doing good and healing all the people oppressed by the Adversary, because God was with him.

³⁹ "As for us, we are witnesses of everything he did, both in the Judean countryside and in Yerushalayim. They did away with him by **hanging him on a stake;**[j] ⁴⁰ but God raised him up on the third day and let him be seen, ⁴¹ not by all the people, but by witnesses God had previously chosen, that is, by us, who ate and drank with him after he had risen again from the dead.

⁴² "Then he commanded us to proclaim and attest to the Jewish people that this man has been appointed by God to judge the living and the dead. ⁴³ All the prophets bear witness to him, that everyone who puts his trust in him receives forgiveness of sins through his name."

⁴⁴ Kefa was still saying these things when the *Ruach HaKodesh* fell on all who were hearing the message. ⁴⁵ All the believers from the Circumcision faction who had accompanied Kefa were amazed that the gift of the *Ruach HaKodesh* was also being poured out ⁴⁶ on the *Goyim*, for they heard them speaking in tongues and praising God. Kefa's response was, ⁴⁷ "Is anyone prepared to prohibit these people from being immersed in water? After all, they have received the *Ruach HaKodesh*, just as we did." ⁴⁸ And he ordered that they be immersed in the name of Yeshua the Messiah. Then they asked Kefa to stay on with them for a few days.

11 ¹ The emissaries and the brothers throughout Y'hudah heard that the *Goyim* had received the word of God; ² but when Kefa went up to Yerushalayim, the members of the Circumcision faction criticized him, ³ saying, "You went into the homes of uncircumcised men and even ate with them!"

⁴ In reply, Kefa began explaining in detail what had actually happened: ⁵ "I was in the city of Yafo, praying; and in a trance I had a vision. I saw something like a large sheet being lowered by its four corners from heaven, and it came down to me. ⁶ I looked inside and saw four-footed animals, beasts of prey, crawling creatures and wild birds. ⁷ Then I heard a voice telling me, 'Get up, Kefa, slaughter and eat!' ⁸ I said, 'No, sir! Absolutely not! Nothing unclean or *treif* has ever entered my mouth!' ⁹ But the voice spoke again from heaven: 'Stop treating as unclean what God has made clean.' ¹⁰ This happened three times, and then everything was pulled back up into heaven.

¹¹ "At that very moment, three men who had been sent to me from Caesarea arrived at the house where I was staying; ¹² and the Spirit told me to have no misgivings

---

[j] Deuteronomy 21:23

about going back with them. These six brothers also came with me, and we went into the man's house. ¹³ He told us how he had seen the angel standing in his house and saying, 'Send to Yafo and bring back Shim'on, known as Kefa. ¹⁴ He has a message for you which will enable you and your whole household to be saved.'

¹⁵ "But I had hardly begun speaking when the *Ruach HaKodesh* fell on them, just as on us at the beginning! ¹⁶ And I remembered that the Lord had said, 'Yochanan used to immerse people in water, but you will be immersed in the *Ruach HaKodesh*.' ¹⁷ Therefore, if God gave them the same gift as he gave us after we had come to put our trust in the Lord Yeshua the Messiah, who was I to stand in God's way?"

¹⁸ On hearing these things, they stopped objecting and began to praise God, saying, "This means that God has enabled the *Goyim* as well to do *t'shuvah* and have life!"

¹⁹ Now those who had been scattered because of the persecution which had arisen over Stephen went as far as Phoenicia, Cyprus and Antioch; they spoke God's word, but only to Jews. ²⁰ However, some of these, men from Cyprus and Cyrene, when they arrived at Antioch, began speaking to the Greeks too, proclaiming the Good News of the Lord Yeshua. ²¹ The hand of the Lord was with them, and a great number of people trusted and turned to the Lord.

²² News of this reached the ears of the Messianic community in Yerushalayim, and they sent Bar-Nabba to Antioch. ²³ On arriving and seeing for himself the grace of God at work, he was glad; and he encouraged them all to remain true to the Lord with their whole hearts; ²⁴ for he was a good man, full of the *Ruach HaKodesh* and trust.

²⁵ Then Bar-Nabba went off to Tarsus to look for Sha'ul. ²⁶ and when he found him, he brought him to Antioch. They met with the congregation there for a whole year and taught a sizeable crowd. Also it was in Antioch that the *talmidim* for the first time were called "Messianic."

²⁷ During this time, some prophets came down from Yerushalayim to Antioch; ²⁸ and one of them named Agav stood up and through the Spirit predicted that there was going to be a severe famine throughout the Roman Empire. (It took place while Claudius was Emperor.) ²⁹ So the *talmidim* decided to provide relief to the brothers living in Y'hudah, each according to his means; ³⁰ and they did it, sending their contribution to the elders in the care of Bar-Nabba and Sha'ul.

12 ¹ It was around this time that King Herod began arresting and persecuting certain members of the Messianic community; ² and he had Ya'akov, Yochanan's brother, put to death by the sword. ³ When Herod saw how much this pleased the Judeans, he went on to arrest Kefa as well. It was during the Days of *Matzah*, ⁴ so when Herod seized him, he threw him in prison, handing him over to be guarded by four squads of four soldiers each, with the intention of bringing him to public trial after *Pesach*. ⁵ So Kefa was being held under watch in prison, but intense prayer was being made to God on his behalf by the Messianic community.

⁶ The night before Herod was going to bring him to trial, Kefa was sleeping between two soldiers. He was bound with two chains; and guards were at the door, keeping watch over the prison. ⁷ Suddenly an angel of *ADONAI* stood there, and a light shone in the cell. He tapped Kefa's side and woke him. "Hurry! Get up!" he said; and the chains fell off his hands. ⁸ The angel said to him, "Put on your clothes and

sandals," and he did. "Throw on your robe," he said, "and follow me!" ⁹ Going out, Kefa followed him but did not realize that what was happening through the angel was real — he thought he was seeing a vision. ¹⁰ Having passed a first guard and a second, they arrived at the iron gate leading to the city. This opened to them by itself, and they made their exit. They went down the length of one street, and suddenly the angel left him. ¹¹ Then Kefa came to himself and said, "Now I know for sure that the Lord sent his angel to rescue me from Herod's power and from everything the Judean people were hoping for."

¹² Realizing what had happened, he went to the house of Miryam the mother of Yochanan (surnamed Mark), where many people had gathered to pray. ¹³ He knocked at the outside door, and a servant named Rhoda came to answer. ¹⁴ She recognized Kefa's voice and was so happy that she ran back in without opening the door, and announced that Kefa was standing outside. ¹⁵ "You're out of your mind!" they said to her. But she insisted it was true. So they said, "It is his angel." ¹⁶ Meanwhile, Kefa kept knocking; and when they opened the door and saw him, they were amazed. ¹⁷ Motioning to them with his hand to be quiet, he told them how the Lord had brought him out of the prison and said, "Tell all this to Ya'akov and the brothers." Then he left and went elsewhere.

¹⁸ When daylight came, there was no small commotion among the soldiers over what had become of Kefa. ¹⁹ Herod had a thorough search made for him, but they failed to find him, so he cross-examined the guards and ordered them put to death. Then Herod went down from Y'hudah to Caesarea and spent some time there.

²⁰ Now Herod was very angry with the people of Tzor and Tzidon, so they joined together and sought an audience with him. After securing the support of Blastus, the king's chief personal servant, they asked for peace; because they depended on the king's lands for their food supply. ²¹ A day was set, and Herod in his royal robes sat on the throne and made a speech to them. ²² The mob cried out, "This is the voice of a god, not a man!" ²³ At once, because Herod did not give the glory to God, an angel of ADONAI struck him down. He was eaten away by worms and died.

²⁴ But the word of the Lord went on growing and being multiplied.

²⁵ Bar-Nabba and Sha'ul, having completed their errand, returned from Yerushalayim, bringing with them Yochanan, surnamed Mark.

13 ¹ In the Antioch congregation were prophets and teachers — Bar-Nabba, Shim'on (known as "the Black"), Lucius (from Cyrene), Menachem (who had been brought up with Herod the governor) and Sha'ul. ² One time when they were worshipping the Lord and fasting, the *Ruach HaKodesh* said to them, "Set aside for me Bar-Nabba and Sha'ul for the work to which I have called them." ³ After fasting and praying, they placed their hands on them and sent them off.

⁴ So these two, after they had been sent out by the *Ruach HaKodesh*, went down to Seleucia and from there sailed to Cyprus. ⁵ After landing in Salamis, they began proclaiming the word of God in the synagogues, with Yochanan (Mark) as an assistant; ⁶ and thus they made their way throughout the whole island.

They ended up in Paphos, where they found a Jewish sorcerer and pseudo-prophet named Bar-Yeshua. ⁷ He had attached himself to the governor, Sergius Paulus, who was an intelligent man. Now the governor had called for Bar-Nabba and Sha'ul and was anxious to hear the message about God; ⁸ but the sorcerer Elymas (for that is how his name is translated) opposed them, doing his best to turn the governor away from the faith. ⁹ Then Sha'ul, also known as Paul, filled with the *Ruach HaKodesh*, stared straight at him and said, ¹⁰ "You son of Satan, full of fraud and evil! You enemy of everything good! Won't you ever stop **making crooked the straight paths of the Lord?**ᵏ ¹¹ So now, look! The hand of the Lord is upon you; and for a while you will be blind, unable to see the sun." Immediately mist and darkness came over Elymas; and he groped about, trying to find someone to lead him by the hand. ¹² Then, on seeing what had happened, the governor trusted, astounded by the teaching about the Lord.

¹³ Having set sail from Paphos, Sha'ul and his companions arrived at Perga in Pamphylia. There Yochanan left them and returned to Yerushalayim, ¹⁴ but the others went on from Perga to Pisidian Antioch, and on *Shabbat* they went into the synagogue and sat down. ¹⁵ After the reading from the *Torah* and from the Prophets, the synagogue leaders sent them a message, "Brothers, if any of you has a word of exhortation for the people, speak!" ¹⁶ So Sha'ul stood, motioned with his hand, and said:

"Men of Isra'el and God-fearers, listen! ¹⁷ The God of this people Isra'el chose our fathers. He made the people great during the time when they were living as aliens in Egypt and **with a stretched-out arm he led them out of that land.**ˡ ¹⁸ For some **forty years**ᵐ he took care of them in the desert, ¹⁹ and after he had destroyed **seven nations**ⁿ in the land of Kena'an he gave their land to his people as an inheritance. ²⁰ All this took about 450 years. After that, **he gave them judges,**ᵒ down to the prophet Sh'mu'el. ²¹ Then they asked for a king, and God gave them Sha'ul Ben-Kish, a man from the tribe of Binyamin. After forty years, ²² God removed him and raised up David as king for them, making his approval known with these words, '**I found David** Ben-Yishai to be **a man after my own heart**; he will do everything I want.'ᵖ

²³ "In keeping with his promise, God has brought to Isra'el from this man's descendants a deliverer, Yeshua. ²⁴ Now before the coming of Yeshua, Yochanan proclaimed to all the people of Isra'el an immersion in connection with turning to God from sin. ²⁵ But as Yochanan was ending his work, he said, 'Who do you suppose I am? Well — I'm not! But after me is coming someone, the sandals of whose feet I am unworthy to untie.'

²⁶ "Brothers! — sons of Avraham and those among you who are 'God-fearers'! It is to us that the message of this deliverance has been sent! ²⁷ For the people living in Yerushalayim and their leaders did not recognize who Yeshua was or understand the message of the Prophets read every *Shabbat*, so they fulfilled that message by condemning him. ²⁸ They could not find any legitimate ground for a death sentence; nevertheless they asked Pilate to have him executed; ²⁹ and when they had carried out all the things written about him, he was taken down from the **stake**ᵍ and placed in a tomb.

³⁰ "But God raised him from the dead! ³¹ He appeared for many days to those who had come up with him from the Galil to Yerushalayim; and they are now his witnesses to the people.

³² "As for us, we are bringing you the Good News that what God promised to the fathers, ³³ he has fulfilled for us the children in raising up Yeshua, as indeed it is

---

ᵏ Proverbs 10:9   ˡ Exodus 6:6; 12:51   ᵐ Exodus 16:35; Numbers 14:34   ⁿ Deuteronomy 7:1
ᵒ Judges 2:16   ᵖ Psalm 89:21(20); 1 Samuel 13:14   ᵍ Deuteronomy 21:23

written in the second Psalm,

**'You are my Son;
today I have become your Father.'**[r]

³⁴ And as for his raising him up from the dead, to return to decay no more, he said,

'I will give the holy and trustworthy things of David to you.'[s]

³⁵ This is explained elsewhere:

'You will not let your Holy One see decay.'[t]

³⁶ For David did indeed serve God's purposes in his own generation; but after that, he died, was buried with his fathers and did **see decay**. ³⁷ However, the one God raised up did not **see decay**.

³⁸ "Therefore, brothers, let it be known to you that through this man is proclaimed forgiveness of sins! ³⁹ That is, God clears everyone who puts his trust in this man, even in regard to all the things concerning which you could not be cleared by the *Torah* of Moshe.

⁴⁰ "Watch out, then, so that this word found in the Prophets may not happen to you:

⁴¹   **'You mockers! Look, and marvel, and die!
For in your own time, I am doing a work
that you simply will not believe,
even if someone explains it to you!' "**[u]

⁴² As they left, the people invited Sha'ul and Bar-Nabba to tell them more about these matters the following *Shabbat*. ⁴³ When the synagogue meeting broke up, many of the born Jews and devout proselytes followed Sha'ul and Bar-Nabba, who spoke with them and urged them to keep holding fast to the love and kindness of God.

⁴⁴ The next *Shabbat*, nearly the whole city gathered together to hear the message about the Lord; ⁴⁵ but when the Jews who had not believed saw the crowds, they were filled with jealousy and spoke up against what Sha'ul was saying and insulted him. ⁴⁶ However, Sha'ul and Bar-Nabba answered boldly: "It was necessary that God's word be spoken first to you. But since you are rejecting it and are judging yourselves unworthy of eternal life — why, we're turning to the *Goyim*! ⁴⁷ For that is what *Adonai* has ordered us to do:

**'I have set you as a light for the *Goyim*,
to be for deliverance to the ends of the earth.' "**[v]

⁴⁸ The Gentiles were very happy to hear this. They honored the message about the Lord, and as many as had been appointed to eternal life came to trust. ⁴⁹ And the message about the Lord was carried throughout the whole region.

---

[r] Psalm 2:7   [s] Isaiah 55:3   [t] Psalm 16:10
[u] Habakkuk 1:5   [v] Isaiah 49:6

^{50} But the unbelieving Jews stirred up the women 'God-fearers' of high social standing and the leading men of the city, and they organized persecution against Sha'ul and Bar-Nabba and expelled them from their district. ^{51} However, Sha'ul and Bar-Nabba shook off the dust of their feet against them and went on to Iconium; ^{52} and the *talmidim* were filled with joy and with the *Ruach HaKodesh*.

14 ^{1} In Iconium the same thing happened — they went into the synagogue and spoke in such a way that a large number of both Jews and Greeks came to trust. ^{2} But the Jews who would not be persuaded stirred up the Gentiles and poisoned their minds against the brothers. ^{3} Therefore, Sha'ul and Bar-Nabba remained for a long time, speaking boldly about the Lord, who bore witness to the message about his love and kindness by enabling them to perform signs and miracles. ^{4} However, the people of the city were divided — some sided with the unbelieving Jews, others with the emissaries.

^{5} Eventually the unbelievers, both Jews and Gentiles, together with their leaders, made a move to mistreat the emissaries, even to stone them; ^{6} but they learned of it and escaped to Lystra and Derbe, towns in Lycaonia, and to the surrounding country, ^{7} where they continued proclaiming the Good News.

^{8} There was a man living in Lystra who could not use his feet — crippled from birth, he had never walked. ^{9} This man listened to Sha'ul speaking. Sha'ul, looking at him intently and seeing that he had faith to be healed, ^{10} said with a loud voice, "Stand up on your feet!" He jumped up and began to walk. ^{11} When the crowds saw what Sha'ul had done, they began to shout in the Lycaonian language, "The gods have come down to us in the form of men!" ^{12} They began calling Bar-Nabba "Zeus" and Sha'ul "Hermes," since he did most of the talking; ^{13} and the priest of Zeus, whose temple was just outside the city, brought bulls and wreaths to the city gates, intending to offer a sacrifice to them with the people.

^{14} When the emissaries Bar-Nabba and Sha'ul heard of it, they tore their clothes and ran into the crowd, shouting, ^{15} "Men! Why are you doing this? We're just men, human like you! We are announcing Good News to you — turn from these worthless things to the living **God who made heaven and earth and the sea and everything in them!**^{w} ^{16} In times past, he allowed all peoples to walk in their own ways; ^{17} yet he did not leave himself without evidence of his nature; because he does good things, giving you rain from heaven and crops in their seasons, filling you with food and your hearts with happiness!" ^{18} Even saying this barely kept the crowds from sacrificing to them.

^{19} Then some unbelieving Jews came from Antioch and Iconium. They won over the crowds, stoned Sha'ul and dragged him outside the city, thinking he was dead. ^{20} But as the *talmidim* gathered around him, he got up and went back into the town. The next day, he left with Bar-Nabba for Derbe.

^{21} After proclaiming the Good News in that city and making many people into *talmidim*, they returned to Lystra, Iconium and Antioch, ^{22} strengthening the *talmidim*, encouraging them to remain true to the faith, and reminding them that it is through many hardships that we must enter the Kingdom of God. ^{23} After appointing elders for them in every congregation, Sha'ul and Bar-Nabba, with prayer and fasting, committed them to the Lord in whom they had put their trust.

---

^{w} Psalm 146:6

²⁴ Passing through Pisidia, they came to Pamphylia. ²⁵ After speaking the message in Perga, they came down to Attalia; and from there, they sailed back to Antioch, ²⁶ the place where they had been handed over to the care of God for the work which they had now completed.

²⁷ When they arrived, they gathered the Messianic community together and reported what God had done through them, that he had opened a door of faith to the Gentiles. ²⁸ And they stayed for some time there with the *talmidim*.

15 ¹ But some men came down from Y'hudah to Antioch and began teaching the brothers, "You can't be saved unless you undergo *b'rit-milah* in the manner prescribed by Moshe." ² This brought them into no small measure of discord and dispute with Sha'ul and Bar-Nabba. So the congregation assigned Sha'ul, Bar-Nabba and some of themselves to go and put this *sh'eilah* before the emissaries and the elders up in Yerushalayim.

³ After being sent off by the congregation, they made their way through Phoenicia and Shomron, recounting in detail how the Gentiles had turned to God; and this news brought great joy to all the brothers.

⁴ On arrival in Yerushalayim, they were welcomed by the Messianic community, including the emissaries and the elders; and they reported what God had done through them. ⁵ But some of those who had come to trust were from the party of the *P'rushim*; and they stood up and said, "It is necessary to circumcise them and direct them to observe the *Torah* of Moshe."

⁶ The emissaries and the elders met to look into this matter. ⁷ After lengthy debate, Kefa got up and said to them, "Brothers, you yourselves know that a good while back, God chose me from among you to be the one by whose mouth the *Goyim* should hear the message of the Good News and come to trust. ⁸ And God, who knows the heart, bore them witness by giving the *Ruach HaKodesh* to them, just as he did to us; ⁹ that is, he made no distinction between us and them, but cleansed their heart by trust. ¹⁰ So why are you putting God to the test now by placing a yoke on the neck of the *talmidim* which neither our fathers nor we have had the strength to bear? ¹¹ No, it is through the love and kindness of the Lord Yeshua that we trust and are delivered—and it's the same with them."

¹² Then the whole assembly kept still as they listened to Bar-Nabba and Sha'ul tell what signs and miracles God had done through them among the Gentiles. ¹³ Ya'akov broke the silence to reply. "Brothers," he said, "hear what I have to say. ¹⁴ Shim'on has told in detail what God did when he first began to show his concern for taking from among the *Goyim* a people to bear his name. ¹⁵ And the words of the Prophets are in complete harmony with this for it is written,

¹⁶   **"'After this, I will return;**
       and I will rebuild the fallen tent of David.
       I will rebuild its ruins,
       I will restore it,
¹⁷   **so that the rest of mankind may seek the Lord,**
       that is, all the *Goyim* who have been called by my name,"
¹⁸   **says *ADONAI*, who is doing these things.'**ˣ

ˣ Amos 9:11–12

All this has been known for ages.

[19] "Therefore, my opinion is that we should not put obstacles in the way of the *Goyim* who are turning to God. [20] Instead, we should write them a letter telling them to abstain from things polluted by idols, from fornication, from what is strangled and from blood. [21] For from the earliest times, Moshe has had in every city those who proclaim him, with his words being read in the synagogues every *Shabbat*."

[22] Then the emissaries and the elders, together with the whole Messianic community, decided to select men from among themselves to send to Antioch with Sha'ul and Bar-Nabba. They sent Y'hudah, called Bar-Sabba, and Sila, both leading men among the brothers, [23] with the following letter:

From: The emissaries and the elders, your brothers
To: The brothers from among the Gentiles throughout Antioch, Syria and Cilicia:

Greetings!

[24]   We have heard that some people went out from among us without our authorization, and that they have upset you with their talk, unsettling your minds. [25] So we have decided unanimously to select men and send them to you with our dear friends Bar-Nabba and Sha'ul, [26] who have dedicated their lives to upholding the name of our Lord, Yeshua the Messiah. [27] So we have sent Y'hudah and Sila, and they will confirm in person what we are writing.

[28]   For it seemed good to the *Ruach HaKodesh* and to us not to lay any heavier burden on you than the following requirements: [29] to abstain from what has been sacrificed to idols, from blood, from things strangled, and from fornication. If you keep yourselves from these, you will be doing the right thing.

Shalom!

[30] The messengers were sent off and went to Antioch, where they gathered the group together and delivered the letter. [31] After reading it, the people were delighted by its encouragement. [32] Y'hudah and Sila, who were also prophets, said much to encourage and strengthen the brothers. [33] After they had spent some time there, they were sent off with a greeting of "*Shalom*!" from the brothers to those who had sent them. [34]* [35] But Sha'ul and Bar-Nabba stayed in Antioch, where they and many others taught and proclaimed the Good News of the message about the Lord.

[36] After some time, Sha'ul said to Bar-Nabba, "Let's go back and visit the brothers in all the towns where we proclaimed the message about the Lord, and see how they're doing." [37] Now Bar-Nabba wanted to take with them Yochanan, the one called Mark. [38] But Sha'ul thought it would be unwise to take this man with them, since he had gone off and left them in Pamphylia to do the work by themselves. [39] There was such sharp disagreement over this that they separated from each other, with Bar-Nabba taking Mark and sailing off to Cyprus.

---

* Some manuscripts include verse 34: But it seemed good to Sila to stay there.

^{40} However, Sha'ul chose Sila and left, after the brothers had committed him to the love and kindness of the Lord. ^{41} He went through Syria and Cilicia, strengthening the congregations.

16 ^{1} Sha'ul came down to Derbe and went on to Lystra, where there lived a *talmid* named Timothy. He was the son of a Jewish woman who had come to trust, and a Greek father. ^{2} All the brothers in Lystra and Iconium spoke well of Timothy. ^{3} Sha'ul wanted Timothy to accompany him; so he took him and did a *b'rit-milah*, because of the Jews living in those areas; for they all knew that his father had been a Greek.

^{4} As they went on through the towns, they delivered to the people the decisions reached by the emissaries and the elders in Yerushalayim for them to observe. ^{5} Accordingly, the congregations were strengthened in the faith and increased in number day by day.

^{6} They traveled through the region of Phrygia and Galatia, because they had been prevented by the *Ruach HaKodesh* from speaking the message in the province of Asia. ^{7} When they came to the frontier of Mysia, they tried to go into Bithynia; but the Spirit of Yeshua would not let them. ^{8} So, after passing by Mysia, they came down to Troas.

^{9} There a vision appeared to Sha'ul at night. A man from Macedonia was standing and begging him, "Come over to Macedonia and help us!" ^{10} As soon as he had seen the vision, we lost no time getting ready to leave for Macedonia; for we concluded that God had called us to proclaim the Good News to them.

^{11} Sailing from Troas, we made a straight run to Samothrace; the next day we went to Neapolis; ^{12} and from there, we went on to Philippi, a Roman colony and the leading city of that part of Macedonia. We spent a few days in this city; ^{13} then on *Shabbat*, we went outside the gate to the riverside, where we understood a *minyan* met. We sat down and began speaking to the women who had gathered there. ^{14} One of those listening was a woman from the city of Thyatira named Lydia, a dealer in fine purple cloth. She was already a "God-fearer," and the Lord opened up her heart to respond to what Sha'ul was saying. ^{15} After she and the members of her household had been immersed, she gave us this invitation: "If you consider me to be faithful to the Lord, come and stay in my house." And she insisted till we went.

^{16} Once, when we were going to the place where the *minyan* gathered, we were met by a slave girl who had in her a snake-spirit that enabled her to predict the future. She earned a lot of money for her owners by telling fortunes. ^{17} This girl followed behind Sha'ul and the rest of us and kept screaming, "These men are servants of God *Ha'Elyon*! They're telling you how to be saved!" ^{18} She kept this up day after day, until Sha'ul, greatly disturbed, turned and said to the spirit, "In the name of Yeshua the Messiah, I order you to come out of her!" And the spirit did come out, at that very moment.

^{19} But when her owners saw that what had come out was any further prospect of profit for them, they seized Sha'ul and Sila and dragged them to the market square to face the authorities. ^{20} Bringing them to the judges, they said, "These men are causing a lot of trouble in our city, since they are Jews. ^{21} What they are doing is advocating customs that are against the law for us to accept or practice, since we are Romans." ^{22} The mob joined in the attack against them, and the judges tore their clothes off them and ordered that they be flogged. ^{23} After giving them a severe beating, they threw them in prison, charging the jailer to guard them securely. ²⁴Upon receiving such an order, he threw them into the inner cell and clamped their feet securely between heavy blocks of wood.

²⁵Around midnight, Sha'ul and Sila were praying and singing hymns to God, while the other prisoners listened attentively. ²⁶Suddenly there was a violent earthquake which shook the prison to its foundations. All the doors flew open and everyone's chains came loose. ²⁷The jailer awoke, and when he saw the doors open he drew his sword and was about to kill himself, for he assumed that the prisoners had escaped. ²⁸But Sha'ul shouted, "Don't harm yourself! We're all here!"

²⁹Calling for lights, the jailer ran in, began to tremble and fell down in front of Sha'ul and Sila. ³⁰Then, leading them outside, he said, "Men, what must I do to be saved?" ³¹They said, "Trust in the Lord Yeshua, and you will be saved — you and your household!" ³²Whereupon they told him and everyone in his household the message about the Lord.

³³Then, even at that late hour of the night, the jailer took them and washed off their wounds; and without delay, he and all his people were immersed. ³⁴After that, he brought them up to his house and set food in front of them; and he and his entire household celebrated their having come to trust in God.

³⁵The next morning, the judges sent police officers with the order, "Release those men." ³⁶The jailer told Sha'ul, "The judges have sent word to release both of you. So come out, and go on your way in peace." ³⁷But Sha'ul said to the officers, "After flogging us in public when we hadn't been convicted of any crime and are Roman citizens, they threw us in prison. Now they want to get rid of us secretly? Oh, no! Let them come and escort us out themselves!"

³⁸The officers reported these words to the judges, who became frightened when they heard that Sha'ul and Sila were Roman citizens. ³⁹They came and apologized to them; then, after escorting them out, requested them to leave the city. ⁴⁰From the prison they went to Lydia's house, and after seeing and encouraging the brothers they departed.

17 ¹After passing through Amphipolis and Apollonia, Sha'ul and Sila came to Thessalonica, where there was a synagogue. ²According to his usual practice, Sha'ul went in; and on three *Shabbat*s he gave them *drash*es from the *Tanakh*, ³explaining and proving that the Messiah had to suffer and rise again from the dead, and that "this Yeshua whom I am proclaiming to you is the Messiah." ⁴Some of the Jews were persuaded and threw in their lot with Sha'ul and Sila, as did a great many of the Greek men who were "God-fearers," and not a few of the leading women.

⁵But the unbelieving Jews grew jealous; so they got together some vicious men from the riffraff hanging around in the market square, collected a crowd and started a riot in the city. They attacked Jason's house, hoping to bring Sha'ul and Sila out to the mob. ⁶But when they didn't find them, they dragged Jason and some other brothers before the city authorities and shouted, "These men who have turned the whole world upside down have come here too! ⁷And Jason has let them stay in his home! All of them are defying the decrees of the Emperor; because they assert that there is another king, Yeshua!" ⁸Their words threw the crowd and the authorities into a turmoil, ⁹so that only after Jason and the others had posted bond did they let them go. ¹⁰But as soon as night fell, the brothers sent Sha'ul and Sila off to Berea.

As soon as they arrived, they went to the synagogue. [11] Now the people here were of nobler character than the ones in Thessalonica; they eagerly welcomed the message, checking the *Tanakh* every day to see if the things Sha'ul was saying were true. [12] Many of them came to trust, as did a number of prominent Greek women and not a few Greek men.

[13] But when the unbelieving Jews of Thessalonica learned that the word of God had been proclaimed by Sha'ul in Berea as well, they went there too to make trouble and agitate the crowds. [14] The brothers sent Sha'ul away at once to go down to the seacoast, while Sila and Timothy stayed behind. [15] Sha'ul's escort went with him as far as Athens, then left with instructions for Sila and Timothy to come as quickly as they could.

[16] While Sha'ul was waiting for them in Athens, his spirit within him was disturbed at the sight of the city full of idols. [17] So he began holding discussions in the synagogue with the Jews and the "God-fearers," and in the market square every day with the people who happened to be there.

[18] Also a group of Epicurean and Stoic philosophers started meeting with him. Some asked, "What is this babbler trying to say?" Others, because he proclaimed the Good News about Yeshua and the resurrection, said, "He sounds like a propagandist for foreign gods." [19] They took and brought him before the High Council, saying, "May we know what this new teaching is that you are presenting? [20] Some of the things we are hearing from you strike us as strange, and we would like to know what they mean." [21] (All the Athenians and the foreigners living there used to spend their spare time talking or hearing about the latest intellectual fads.)

[22] Sha'ul stood up in the Council meeting and said, "Men of Athens: I see how very religious you are in every way! [23] For as I was walking around, looking at your shrines, I even found an altar which had been inscribed, 'To An Unknown God.' So, the one whom you are already worshipping in ignorance — this is the one I proclaim to you.

[24] "The God who made the universe and everything in it, and who is Lord of heaven and earth, does not live in man-made temples; [25] nor is he served by human hands, as if he lacked something; since it is he himself who gives life and breath and everything to everyone.

[26] "From one man he made every nation living on the entire surface of the earth, and he fixed the limits of their territories and the periods when they would flourish. [27] God did this so that people would look for him and perhaps reach out and find him although in fact, he is not far from each one of us, [28] 'for in him we live and move and exist.' Indeed, as some of the poets among you have said, 'We are actually his children.' [29] So, since we are children of God, we shouldn't suppose that God's essence resembles gold, silver or stone shaped by human technique and imagination.

[30] "In the past, God overlooked such ignorance; but now he is commanding all people everywhere to turn to him from their sins. [31] For he has set a Day when he will judge the inhabited world, and do it justly, by means of a man whom he has designated. And he has given public proof of it by resurrecting this man from the dead."

[32] At the mention of a resurrection of dead people, some began to scoff; while others said, "We want to hear you again on this subject." [33] So Sha'ul left the meeting. [34] But some men stayed with him and came to trust, including the High Council member Dionysius; there was also a woman named Damaris; and others came to trust along with them.

18 ¹ After this, Sha'ul left Athens and went to Corinth, ² where he met a Jewish man named Aquila, originally from Pontus but having recently come with his wife Priscilla from Italy, because Claudius had issued a decree expelling all the Jews from Rome. Sha'ul went to see them; ³ and because he had the same trade as they, making tents, he stayed on with them; and they worked together.

⁴ Sha'ul also began carrying on discussions every *Shabbat* in the synagogue, where he tried to convince both Jews and Greeks. ⁵ But after Sila and Timothy arrived from Macedonia, Sha'ul felt pressed by the urgency of the message and testified in depth to the Jews that Yeshua is the Messiah. ⁶ However when they set themselves against him and began hurling insults, he shook out his clothes and said to them, "Your blood be on your own heads! For my part, I am clean; from now on, I will go to the *Goyim!*"

⁷ So he left them and went into the home of a "God-fearer" named Titius Justus, whose house was right next door to the synagogue. ⁸ Crispus, the president of the synagogue, came to trust in the Lord, along with his whole household; also many of the Corinthians who heard trusted and were immersed.

⁹ One night, in a vision, the Lord said to Sha'ul, "Don't be afraid, but speak right up, and don't stop, ¹⁰ because I am with you. No one will succeed in harming you, for I have many people in this city." ¹¹ So Sha'ul stayed there for a year and a half, teaching them the word of God.

¹² But when Gallio became the Roman governor of Achaia, the unbelieving Jews made a concerted attack on Sha'ul and took him to court, ¹³ saying, "This man is trying to persuade people to worship God in ways that violate the *Torah*." ¹⁴ Sha'ul was just about to open his mouth, when Gallio said to the Jews, "Listen, you Jews, if this were a case of inflicted injury or a serious crime, I could reasonably be expected to hear you out patiently. ¹⁵ But since it involves questions about words and names and your own law, then you must deal with it yourselves. I flatly refuse to judge such matters." ¹⁶ And he had them ejected from the court. ¹⁷ They all grabbed Sosthenes, the president of the synagogue, and gave him a beating in full view of the bench; but Gallio showed no concern whatever.

¹⁸ Sha'ul remained for some time, then said good-bye to the brothers and sailed off to Syria, after having his hair cut short in Cenchrea, because he had taken a vow; with him were Priscilla and Aquila.

¹⁹ They came to Ephesus, and he left them there; but he himself went into the synagogue and held dialogue with the Jews. ²⁰ When they asked him to stay with them longer, he declined; ²¹ however, in his farewell he said, "God willing, I will come back to you." Then he set sail from Ephesus.

²² After landing at Caesarea, he went up to Yerushalayim and greeted the Messianic community. Then he came down to Antioch, ²³ spent some time there, and afterwards set out and passed systematically through the region of Galatia and Phrygia, strengthening all the *talmidim*.

²⁴ Meanwhile, a Jewish man named Apollos, a native of Alexandria, came to Ephesus. He was an eloquent speaker with a thorough knowledge of the *Tanakh*. ²⁵ This man had been informed about the Way of the Lord, and with great spiritual fervor he spoke and taught accurately the facts about Yeshua, but he knew only the immersion of Yochanan. ²⁶ He began to speak out boldly in the synagogue; but when Priscilla and Aquila heard him, they took him aside and explained to him the Way of

God in fuller detail. ²⁷ When he made plans to cross over into Achaia, the brothers encouraged him and wrote the *talmidim* there to welcome him. On arrival, he greatly helped those who through grace had come to trust; ²⁸ for he powerfully and conclusively refuted the unbelieving Jews in public, demonstrating by the *Tanakh* that Yeshua is the Messiah.

19 ¹ While Apollos was in Corinth, Sha'ul completed his travels through the inland country and arrived at Ephesus, where he found a few *talmidim*. ² He asked them, "Did you receive the *Ruach HaKodesh* when you came to trust?" "No," they said to him, "we have never even heard that there is such a thing as the *Ruach HaKodesh*." ³ "In that case," he said, "into what were you immersed?" "The immersion of Yochanan," they answered. ⁴ Sha'ul said, "Yochanan practiced an immersion in connection with turning from sin to God; but he told the people to put their trust in the one who would come after him, that is, in Yeshua." ⁵ On hearing this, they were immersed into the name of the Lord Yeshua; ⁶ and when Sha'ul placed his hands on them, the *Ruach HaKodesh* came upon them; so that they began speaking in tongues and prophesying. ⁷ In all, there were about twelve of these men.

⁸ Sha'ul went into the synagogue; and for three months he spoke out boldly, engaging in dialogue and trying to persuade people about the Kingdom of God. ⁹ But some began hardening themselves and refusing to listen; and when these started defaming the Way before the whole synagogue, Sha'ul withdrew, took the *talmidim* with him, and commenced holding daily dialogues in Tyrannus's *yeshivah*. ¹⁰ This went on for two years; so that everyone, both Jews and Greeks, living in the province of Asia heard the message about the Lord.

¹¹ God did extraordinary miracles through Sha'ul. ¹² For instance, handkerchiefs and aprons that had touched him were brought to sick people; they would recover from their ailments; and the evil spirits would leave them.

¹³ Then some of the Jewish exorcists who traveled from place to place tried to make use of the name of the Lord Yeshua in connection with people who had evil spirits. They would say, "I exorcise you by the Yeshua that Sha'ul is proclaiming!" ¹⁴ One time, seven sons of a Jewish *cohen gadol* named Skeva were doing this; ¹⁵ and the evil spirit answered them. It said, "Yeshua I know. And Sha'ul I recognize. But you? Who are you?" ¹⁶ Then the man with the evil spirit fell upon them, overpowered them and gave them such a beating that they ran from the house, naked and bleeding.

¹⁷ When all this became known to the residents of Ephesus, fear fell on all of them, Jews and Greeks alike; and the name of the Lord Yeshua came to be held in high regard. ¹⁸ Many of those who had earlier made professions of faith now came and admitted publicly their evil deeds; ¹⁹ and a considerable number of those who had engaged in occult practices threw their scrolls in a pile and burned them in public. When they calculated the value of the scrolls, it came to fifty thousand *drachma*s. ²⁰ Thus the message about the Lord continued in a powerful way to grow in influence.

²¹ Some time later, Sha'ul decided by the Spirit to pass through Macedonia and Achaia and then go to Yerushalayim. "After I have been there," he said, "I must visit Rome." ²² So he dispatched two of his helpers, Timothy and Erastus, to Macedonia; but he himself remained in the province of Asia for awhile.

²³ It was at this time that a major furor arose concerning the Way. ²⁴ There was a silversmith named Demetrius who manufactured from silver, objects connected with

the worship of the goddess Artemis; and he provided no small amount of work for the craftsmen. ²⁵ He called a meeting of them and of those engaged in similar trades, and said, "Men, you understand that this line of business provides us our living. ²⁶ And you can see and hear for yourselves that not only here in Ephesus, but in practically the whole province of Asia, this Sha'ul has convinced and turned away a considerable crowd by saying that man-made gods aren't gods at all. ²⁷ Now the danger is not only that the reputation of our trade will suffer, but that the temple of the great goddess Artemis will come to be taken lightly. It could end up with the goddess herself, who is worshipped throughout the province of Asia and indeed throughout the whole world, being ignominiously brought down from her divine majesty!"

²⁸ Hearing this, they were filled with rage and began bellowing, "Great is Artemis of the Ephesians!" ²⁹ Soon the whole city was in an uproar. As one man, the mob rushed into the theater, dragging along Gaius and Aristarchus, Sha'ul's traveling companions from Macedonia. ³⁰ Sha'ul himself wanted to appear before the crowd, but the *talmidim* wouldn't let him. ³¹ Even some of the officials of the province, friends of his, sent a message begging him not to risk entering the theater. ³² Meanwhile, some were shouting one thing and others something else, because the assembly was in complete confusion, and the great majority didn't even know why they were there. ³³ Some of the crowd explained the situation to Alexander, whom the Jews had pushed to the front. So Alexander motioned for silence, hoping to make a defense speech to the people. ³⁴ But as soon as they recognized that he was a Jew, they began bellowing in unison, "Great is Artemis of the Ephesians!" and they kept it up for about two hours.

³⁵ At last, the city clerk was able to quiet the crowd. "Men of Ephesus!" he said, "Is there anyone who doesn't know that the city of Ephesus is the guardian of the temple of the great Artemis, and of the sacred stone which fell from the sky? ³⁶ Since this is beyond dispute, you had better calm down and not do anything rash. ³⁷ For you have brought these men here who have neither robbed the temple nor insulted your goddess. ³⁸ So if Demetrius and his fellow craftsmen have a complaint against anyone, the courts are open and the judges are there — let them bring charges and counter-charges. ³⁹ But if there is something more you want, it will have to be settled in a lawful assembly. ⁴⁰ For we are in danger of being accused of rioting on account of what has happened today. There is no justification for it; and if we are asked, we will be unable to give any reasonable explanation for this disorderly gathering." ⁴¹ And with these words, he dismissed the assembly.

20 ¹ After the furor died down, Sha'ul sent for the *talmidim* and encouraged them, then took his leave and set out on his way to Macedonia. ² He went through that area, and, after saying much to encourage them, passed on to Greece, ³ where he spent three months. As he was preparing to set sail for Syria, he discovered a plot against him by the unbelieving Jews; so he changed his mind and decided to return by way of Macedonia. ⁴ Sopater from Berea, the son of Pyrrhus, accompanied him; as did Aristarchus and Secundus from Thessalonica, Gaius from Derbe, Timothy, and Tychicus and Trophimus from the province of Asia. ⁵ These men went on and waited for us in Troas, ⁶ while we sailed from Philippi after the Days of *Matzah*. Five days later, we met them in Troas, where we spent a week.

[7] On *Motza'ei-Shabbat*, when we were gathered to break bread, Sha'ul addressed them. Since he was going to leave the next day, he kept talking until midnight. [8] Now there were many oil lamps burning in the upstairs room where we were meeting, [9] and there was a young fellow named Eutychus sitting on the window-sill. As Sha'ul's *drash* went on and on, Eutychus grew sleepier and sleepier; until finally he went sound asleep and fell from the third story to the ground. When they picked him up, he was dead. [10] But Sha'ul went down, threw himself onto him, put his arms around him and said, "Don't be upset, he's alive!" [11] Then he went back upstairs, broke the bread and ate. He continued talking with them till daylight, then left. [12] So, greatly relieved, they brought the boy home alive.

[13] We went on ahead to the ship and set sail for Assos, where we were planning to take Sha'ul aboard — he had arranged this because he wanted to go there by land. [14] After he met us at Assos, we took him aboard and went on to Mitylene. [15] The next day, we sailed from there and arrived off Chios; the following day, we crossed over to Samos; and the day after that, we reached Miletus. [16] For Sha'ul had decided to bypass Ephesus on his voyage, in order to avoid losing time in the province of Asia, because he was hurrying to get to Yerushalayim, if possible in time to celebrate *Shavu'ot*.

[17] But he did send from Miletus to Ephesus, summoning the elders of the Messianic community. [18] When they arrived, he said to them, "You yourselves know how, from the first day I set foot in the province of Asia, I was with you the whole time, [19] serving the Lord with much humility and with tears, in spite of the tests I had to undergo because of the plots of the unbelieving Jews. [20] You know that I held back nothing that could be helpful to you, and that I taught you both in public and from house to house, [21] declaring with utmost seriousness the same message to Jews and Greeks alike: turn from sin to God; and put your trust in our Lord, Yeshua the Messiah.

[22] "And now, compelled by the Spirit, I am going to Yerushalayim. I don't know what will happen to me there, [23] other than that in every city the *Ruach HaKodesh* keeps warning me that imprisonment and persecution await me. [24] But I consider my own life of no importance to me whatsoever, as long as I can finish the course ahead of me, the task I received from the Lord Yeshua — to declare in depth the Good News of God's love and kindness.

[25] "Now, listen! I know that none of you people among whom I have gone about proclaiming the Kingdom will ever see me again. [26] Therefore, I testify on this day that I am innocent of the blood of all. [27] For I did not shrink from proclaiming to you the whole plan of God.

[28] "Watch out for yourselves, and for all the flock in which the *Ruach HaKodesh* has placed you as leaders, to shepherd God's Messianic community, which he won for himself at the cost of his own Son's blood. [29] I know that after I leave, savage wolves will come in among you; and they won't spare the flock. [30] Even from among your own number, men will arise and teach perversions of the truth, in order to drag away the *talmidim* after themselves. [31] So stay alert! Remember that for three years, night and day, with tears in my eyes, I never stopped warning you!

[32] "And now I entrust you to the care of the Lord and to the message of his love and kindness, for it can build you up and give you an inheritance among all those who have been set apart for God.

³³ "I have not wanted for myself anyone's silver or gold or clothing. ³⁴ You yourselves know that these hands of mine have provided not only for my own needs, but for the needs of my co-workers as well. ³⁵ In everything I have given you an example of how, by working hard like this, you must help the weak, remembering the words of the Lord Yeshua himself, 'There is more happiness in giving than in receiving.'"

³⁶ When he had finished speaking, Sha'ul kneeled down with them all and prayed. ³⁷ They were all in tears as they threw their arms around his neck and kissed him farewell. ³⁸ What saddened them the most was his remark that they would never see him again. Then they accompanied him to the ship.

21 ¹ After we had torn ourselves away from the Ephesian elders, we set sail and made a straight run to Cos. The next day we went to Rhodes, and from there to Patara. ² On finding a ship that was crossing over to Phoenicia, we embarked and set sail. ³ After sighting Cyprus, we passed it on the left, sailed to Syria and landed at Tzor, because that was where the ship was unloading its cargo. ⁴ Having searched out the *talmidim* there, we remained for a week. Guided by the Spirit, they told Sha'ul not to go up to Yerushalayim; ⁵ but when the week was over, we left to continue our journey. All of them, with their wives and children, accompanied us until we were outside the town. Kneeling on the beach and praying, ⁶ we said good-bye to each other. Then we boarded the ship, and they returned home.

⁷ When the voyage from Tzor was over, we arrived at Ptolemais. There we greeted the brothers and stayed with them overnight. ⁸ The following day, we left and came to Caesarea, where we went to the home of Philip the proclaimer of the Good News, one of the Seven, and stayed with him. ⁹ He had four unmarried daughters with the gift of prophecy.

¹⁰ While we were staying there, a prophet named Agav came down from Y'hudah ¹¹ to visit us. He took Sha'ul's belt, tied up his own hands and feet and said, "Here is what the *Ruach HaKodesh* says: the man who owns this belt — the Judeans in Yerushalayim will tie him up just like this and hand him over to the *Goyim*." ¹² When we heard this, both we and the people there begged him not to go up to Yerushalayim; ¹³ but Sha'ul answered, "What are you doing, crying and trying to weaken my resolve? I am prepared not only to be tied up, but even to die in Yerushalayim for the name of the Lord Yeshua." ¹⁴ And when he would not be convinced, we said, "May the Lord's will be done," and kept quiet.

¹⁵ So at the end of our stay, we packed and went up to Yerushalayim; ¹⁶ and with us went some of the *talmidim* from Caesarea. They brought us to the home of the man with whom we were to stay, Mnason from Cyprus, who had been a *talmid* since the early days.

¹⁷ In Yerushalayim, the brothers received us warmly. ¹⁸ The next day Sha'ul and the rest of us went in to Ya'akov, and all the elders were present. ¹⁹ After greeting them, Sha'ul described in detail each of the things God had done among the Gentiles through his efforts.

²⁰ On hearing it, they praised God; but they also said to him, "You see, brother, how many tens of thousands of believers there are among the Judeans, and they are all zealots for the *Torah*. ²¹ Now what they have been told about you is that you are teaching all the Jews living among the *Goyim* to apostatize from Moshe, telling them not to have a *b'rit-milah* for their sons and not to follow the traditions.

²² "What, then, is to be done? They will certainly hear that you have come. ²³ So do what we tell you. We have four men who are under a vow. ²⁴ Take them with you, be purified with them, and pay the expenses connected with having their heads shaved. Then everyone will know that there is nothing to these rumors which they have heard about you; but that, on the contrary, you yourself stay in line and keep the *Torah*.

²⁵ "However, in regard to the *Goyim* who have come to trust in Yeshua, we all joined in writing them a letter with our decision that they should abstain from what had been sacrificed to idols, from blood, from what is strangled and from fornication."

²⁶ The next day Sha'ul took the men, purified himself along with them and entered the Temple to give notice of when the period of purification would be finished and the offering would have to be made for each of them. ²⁷ The seven days were almost up when some unbelieving Jews from the province of Asia saw him in the Temple, stirred up all the crowd and grabbed him. ²⁸ "Men of Isra'el, help!" they shouted. "This is the man who goes everywhere teaching everyone things against the people, against the *Torah* and against this place! And now he has even brought some *Goyim* into the Temple and defiled this holy place!" ²⁹ (They had previously seen Trophimus from Ephesus in the city with him and assumed that Sha'ul had brought him into the Temple.)

³⁰ The whole city was aroused, and people came running from all over. They seized Sha'ul and dragged him out of the Temple, and at once the gates were shut. ³¹ But while they were attempting to kill him, word reached the commander of the Roman battalion that all Yerushalayim was in turmoil. ³² Immediately he took officers and soldiers and charged down upon them. As soon as they saw the commander, they quit beating Sha'ul.

³³ Then the commander came up, arrested him and ordered him to be tied up with two chains. He asked who he was and what he had done. ³⁴ Everyone in the crowd shouted something different; so, since he couldn't find out what had happened because of the uproar, he ordered him brought to the barracks. ³⁵ When Sha'ul got to the steps, he actually had to be carried by the soldiers, because the mob was so wild — ³⁶ the crowd kept following and screaming, "Kill him!"

³⁷ As Sha'ul was about to be brought into the barracks, he said to the commander, "Is it all right if I say something to you?" The commander said, "You know Greek! ³⁸ Say, aren't you that Egyptian who tried to start a revolution a while back, and led four thousand armed terrorists out into the desert?" ³⁹ Sha'ul said, "I am a Jew from Tarsus in Cilicia, a citizen of an important city; and I ask your permission to let me speak to the people."

⁴⁰ Having received permission, Sha'ul stood on the steps and motioned with his hand to the people. When they finally became still, he addressed them in Hebrew:

22 ¹ "Brothers and fathers! Listen to me as I make my defense before you now!" ² When they heard him speaking to them in Hebrew, they settled down more; so he continued: ³ "I am a Jew, born in Tarsus of Cilicia, but brought up in this city and trained at the feet of Gamli'el in every detail of the *Torah* of our forefathers. I was a zealot for God, as all of you are today. ⁴ I persecuted to death the followers of this Way, arresting both men and women and throwing them in prison. ⁵ The *cohen hagadol* and the whole *Sanhedrin* can also testify to this. Indeed, after receiving letters from them to their colleagues in Dammesek, I was on my way there in order to arrest the ones in that city too and bring them back to Yerushalayim for punishment.

⁶ "As I was traveling and approaching Dammesek, around noon, suddenly a brilliant light from heaven flashed all around me! ⁷ I fell to the ground and heard a voice saying to me, 'Sha'ul! Sha'ul! Why do you keep persecuting me?' ⁸ I answered, 'Sir, who are you?' 'I am Yeshua from Natzeret,' he said to me, 'and you are persecuting me!' ⁹ Those who were with me did see the light, but they didn't hear the voice of the one who was speaking to me. ¹⁰ I said 'What should I do, Lord?' And the Lord said to me, 'Get up, and go into Dammesek, and there you will be told about everything that has been laid out for you to do.' ¹¹ I had been blinded by the brightness of the light, so my companions led me by the hand into Dammesek.

¹² "A man named Hananyah, an observant follower of the *Torah* who was highly regarded by the entire Jewish community there, ¹³ came to me, stood by me and said, 'Brother Sha'ul, see again!' And at that very moment, I recovered my sight and saw him. ¹⁴ He said, 'The **God of our fathers**ʸ determined in advance that you should know his will, see the *Tzaddik* and hear his voice; ¹⁵ because you will be a witness for him to everyone of what you have seen and heard. ¹⁶ So now, what are you waiting for? Get up, immerse yourself and have your sins washed away as you call on his name.'

¹⁷ "After I had returned to Yerushalayim, it happened that as I was praying in the Temple, I went into a trance, ¹⁸ and I saw Yeshua. 'Hurry!' he said to me, 'Get out of Yerushalayim immediately, because they will not accept what you have to say about me.' ¹⁹ I said, 'Lord, they know themselves that in every synagogue I used to imprison and flog those who trusted in you; ²⁰ also that when the blood of your witness Stephen was being shed, I was standing there too, in full agreement; I was even looking after the clothes of the ones who were killing him!' ²¹ But he said, 'Get going! For I am going to send you far away — to the *Goyim!*'"

²² They had been listening to him up to this point; but now they shouted at the top of their lungs, "Rid the earth of such a man! He's not fit to live!" ²³ They were screaming, waving their clothes and throwing dust into the air; ²⁴ so the commander ordered him brought into the barracks and directed that he be interrogated and whipped, in order to find out why they were yelling at him like this.

²⁵ But as they were stretching him out with thongs to be flogged, Sha'ul said to the captain standing by, "Is it legal for you to whip a man who is a Roman citizen and hasn't even had a trial?" ²⁶ When the captain heard that, he went and reported it to the commander, "Do you realize what you're doing? This man is a Roman citizen!" ²⁷ The commander came and said to Sha'ul, "Tell me, are you a Roman citizen?" "Yes," he said. ²⁸ The commander replied, "I bought this citizenship for a sizeable sum of money." "But I was born to it," Sha'ul said. ²⁹ At once the men who had been about to interrogate him drew back from him; and the commander was afraid too, because he realized that he had put this man who was a Roman citizen in chains.

³⁰ However, the next day, since he wanted to know the specific charge the Judeans were bringing against him, he released him and ordered the head *cohanim* and the whole *Sanhedrin* to meet. Then he brought Sha'ul down and put him in front of them.

ʸExodus 3:15

23 ¹ Sha'ul looked straight at them and said, "Brothers, I have been discharging my obligations to God with a perfectly clear conscience, right up until today." ² But the *cohen hagadol*, Hananyah, ordered those standing near him to strike him on the mouth. ³ Then Sha'ul said to him, "God will strike you, you whitewashed wall! Will you sit there judging me according to the *Torah*, yet in violation of the *Torah* order me to be struck?" ⁴ The men nearby said, "This is the *cohen hagadol* of God that you're insulting!" ⁵ Sha'ul said, "I didn't know, brothers, that he was the *cohen hagadol*; for it says in the *Torah*, '**You are not to speak disparagingly of a ruler of your people.**'"

⁶ But knowing that one part of the *Sanhedrin* consisted of *Tz'dukim* and the other of *P'rushim*, Sha'ul shouted, "Brothers, I myself am a *Parush* and the son of *P'rushim*; and it is concerning the hope of the resurrection of the dead that I am being tried!" ⁷ When he said this, an argument arose between the *P'rushim* and the *Tz'dukim*, and the crowd was divided. ⁸ For the *Tz'dukim* deny the resurrection and the existence of angels and spirits; whereas the *P'rushim* acknowledge both. ⁹ So there was a great uproar, with some of the *Torah*-teachers who were on the side of the *P'rushim* standing up and joining in — "We don't find anything wrong with this man; and if a spirit or an angel spoke to him, what of it?" ¹⁰ The dispute became so violent that the commander, fearing that Sha'ul would be torn apart by them, ordered the soldiers to go down, take him by force and bring him back into the barracks.

¹¹ The following night, the Lord stood by him and said, "Take courage! For just as you have borne a faithful witness to me in Yerushalayim, so now you must bear witness in Rome."

¹² The next day, some of the Judeans formed a conspiracy. They took an oath, saying they would neither eat nor drink until they had killed Sha'ul; ¹³ more than forty were involved in this plot. ¹⁴ They went to the head *cohanim* and the elders and said, "We have bound ourselves by an oath to taste no food until we have killed Sha'ul. ¹⁵ What you are to do is make it appear to the commander that you and the *Sanhedrin* want to get more accurate information about Sha'ul's case, so that he will bring him down to you; while we, for our part, are prepared to kill him before he ever gets here."

¹⁶ But the son of Sha'ul's sister got wind of the planned ambush, and he went into the barracks and told Sha'ul. ¹⁷ Sha'ul called one of the officers and said, "Take this man up to the commander; he has something to tell him." ¹⁸ So he took him and brought him to the commander and said, "The prisoner Sha'ul called me and asked me to bring this young man to you, because he has something to tell you." ¹⁹ The commander took him by the hand, led him aside privately and asked, "What is it you have to tell me?" ²⁰ He said, "The Judeans have agreed to ask you tomorrow to bring Sha'ul down to the *Sanhedrin* on the pretext that they want to investigate his case more thoroughly. ²¹ But don't let yourself be talked into it, because more than forty men are lying in wait for him. They have taken an oath neither to eat nor to drink until they kill him; and they are ready now, only waiting for you to give your consent to their request."

²² The commander let the young man go, cautioning him, "Don't tell anyone that you have reported this to me." ²³ Then he summoned two of the captains and said, "Get two hundred infantry soldiers ready to leave for Caesarea at nine o'clock tonight, and seventy mounted cavalry and two hundred spearmen; ²⁴ also provide

---

^z Exodus 22:27(28)

replacements for Sha'ul's horse when it gets tired; and bring him through safely to Felix the governor." ²⁵ And the commander wrote the following letter:

²⁶ From: Claudius Lysias
To: His Excellency, Governor Felix:

Greetings!

²⁷ This man was seized by the Judeans and was about to be killed by them, when I came on the scene with my troops and rescued him. After learning that he was a Roman citizen, ²⁸ I wanted to understand exactly what they were charging him with; so I brought him down to their "*Sanhedrin*."

²⁹ I found that he was charged in connection with questions of their "*Torah*" but that there was no charge deserving death or prison.

³⁰ But when I was informed of a plot against the man, I immediately sent him to you and also ordered his accusers to state their case against him before you.

³¹ So the soldiers, following their orders, took Sha'ul during the night and brought him to Antipatris, ³² then returned to the barracks after leaving the cavalry to go on with him. ³³ The cavalry took him to Caesarea, delivered the letter to the governor, and handed Sha'ul over to him. ³⁴ The governor read the letter and asked what province he was from. On learning he was from Cilicia, ³⁵ he said, "I will give you a full hearing after your accusers have also arrived," and ordered him to be kept under guard in Herod's headquarters.

24 ¹ After five days, the *cohen hagadol* Hananyah came down with some elders and a lawyer named Tertullus, and they presented their case against Sha'ul to the governor. ² Sha'ul was called, and Tertullus began to make the charges: "Felix, your Excellency, it is because of you that we enjoy unbroken peace, and it is your foresight that has brought to this nation ³ so many reforms in so many areas. It is with the utmost gratitude that we receive this. ⁴ But, in order not to take up too much of your time, I beg your indulgence to give us a brief hearing.

⁵ "We have found this man a pest. He is an agitator among all the Jews throughout the world and a ringleader of the sect of the *Natzratim*. ⁶ He even tried to profane the Temple, but we arrested him. ⁷ * ⁸ By questioning this man yourself, you will be able to learn all about the things of which we are accusing him." ⁹ The Judeans also joined in the accusation and alleged that these were the facts.

¹⁰ When the governor motioned for Sha'ul to speak, he replied, "I know that you have been judge over this nation for a number of years, so I am glad to make my defense. ¹¹ As you can verify for yourself, it has not been more than twelve days

---

* Some manuscripts include verses 6b–8a: We wanted to try him under our own law, ⁷ but Lysias the commander intervened. He took him out of our hands by force ⁸ and ordered his accuser to appear before you.

since I went up to worship in Yerushalayim; [12] and neither in the Temple nor in the synagogues nor anywhere else in the city did they find me either arguing with anyone or collecting a crowd. [13] Nor can they give any proof of the things of which they are accusing me.

[14] "But this I do admit to you: I worship the **God of our fathers**[a] in accordance with the Way (which they call a sect). I continue to believe everything that accords with the *Torah* and everything written in the Prophets. [15] And I continue to have a hope in God — which they too accept — that there will be a resurrection of both the righteous and the unrighteous. [16] Indeed, it is because of this that I make a point of always having a clear conscience in the sight of both God and man.

[17] "After an absence of several years, I came to Yerushalayim to bring a charitable gift to my nation and to offer sacrifices. [18] It was in connection with the latter that they found me in the Temple. I had been ceremonially purified, I was not with a crowd, and I was not causing a disturbance. [19] But some Jews from the province of Asia — they ought to be here before you to make a charge if they have anything against me! [20] Or else, let these men themselves say what crime they found me guilty of when I stood in front of the *Sanhedrin*, [21] other than this one thing which I shouted out when I was standing among them: 'I am on trial before you today because I believe in the resurrection of the dead!'"

[22] But Felix, who had rather detailed knowledge of things connected with the Way, put them off, saying, "When Lysias the commander comes down, I will decide your case." [23] He ordered the captain to keep Sha'ul in custody, but to let him have considerable liberty and not prevent any of his friends from taking care of his needs.

[24] After some days, Felix came with his wife Drusilla, who was Jewish. He sent for Sha'ul and listened to him as he spoke about trusting in the Messiah Yeshua. [25] But when Sha'ul began to discuss righteousness, self-control and the coming Judgment, Felix became frightened and said, "For the time being, go away! I will send for you when I get a chance." [26] At the same time, he hoped that Sha'ul would offer him a bribe; so he sent for him rather often and kept talking with him.

[27] After two years, Felix was succeeded by Porcius Festus; but because Felix wanted to grant the Judeans a favor, he left Sha'ul still a prisoner.

25 [1] Three days after Festus had entered the province, he went up from Caesarea to Yerushalayim. [2] There the head *cohanim* and the Judean leaders informed him of the case against Sha'ul, and they asked him [3] to do them the favor of having the man sent to Yerushalayim. (They had plotted to have him ambushed and killed *en route*.) [4] Festus replied that Sha'ul was being kept under guard in Caesarea, and that he was about to go there shortly himself. [5] "So," he said, "let competent men among you come down with me and press charges against the man, if he has done something wrong."

[6] After staying with them at most eight or ten days, Festus went down to Caesarea; and on the following day, he took his seat in court and ordered Sha'ul to be brought in. [7] When he arrived, the Judeans who had come down from Yerushalayim stood around him, bringing many serious charges against him which they could not prove. [8] In reply, Sha'ul said, "I have committed no offense — not against the *Torah* to which the Jews hold, not against the Temple, and not against the Emperor."

---

[a] Exodus 3:15

⁹ But Festus, wanting to do the Judeans a favor, asked Sha'ul, "Would you be willing to go up to Yerushalayim and be tried before me there on these charges?" ¹⁰ Sha'ul replied, "I am standing right now in the court of the Emperor, and this is where I should be tried. I have done no wrong to the Judeans, as you very well know. ¹¹ If I am a wrongdoer, if I have done something for which I deserve to die, then I am ready to die. But if there is nothing to these charges which they are bringing against me, no one can give me to them just to grant a favor! I appeal to the Emperor!" ¹² Then Festus, after talking with his advisers, answered, "You have appealed to the Emperor; you will go to the Emperor!"

¹³ After some days, King Agrippa and Bernice arrived at Caesarea to pay their respects to Festus. ¹⁴ Since they were staying on there for some time, Festus had the opportunity to acquaint the king with Sha'ul's situation. "There is a man here," he said, "who was left behind in custody by Felix. ¹⁵ When I was in Yerushalayim, the head *cohanim* and the elders of the Judeans informed me about him and asked me to pronounce judgment against him. ¹⁶ My answer to them was that it is not the custom with Romans to give up an accused man just to grant a favor, before he has met his accusers face to face and had the opportunity to defend himself against the charge. ¹⁷ So when they arrived here with me, I did not delay, but took my seat in court the next day and ordered the man brought in.

¹⁸ "When the accusers stood up, instead of charging him with some serious crime as I had expected, ¹⁹ they disputed with him about certain points of their own religion, and particularly about somebody called Yeshua, who had died, but who Sha'ul claimed was alive. ²⁰ Being at a loss as to how to investigate such questions, I asked him if he would be willing to go to Yerushalayim and be tried on these matters there. ²¹ But since Sha'ul appealed to be kept in custody and have his case decided by His Imperial Majesty, I ordered him held until I could send him to the Emperor."

²² Agrippa said to Festus, "I myself have been wanting to hear the man." "Tomorrow," he replied, "you will hear him."

²³ So the next day, Agrippa and Bernice came with much pageantry; they entered the audience room accompanied by military commanders and the prominent men of the city. Then, at the command of Festus, Sha'ul was brought in. ²⁴ Festus said, "King Agrippa and all of you here with us, do you see this man? The whole Judean community has complained to me about him both in Yerushalayim and here, crying that he shouldn't be allowed to remain alive. ²⁵ But I discovered that he had done nothing that deserves a death sentence. Now when he himself appealed to the Emperor, I decided to send him. ²⁶ However, I have nothing specific to write to His Majesty about him. This is why I have brought him before all of you, and especially before you, King Agrippa — so that after we have examined him, I might have something to write. ²⁷ It seems irrational to me to send a prisoner without also indicating what the charges against him are."

26 ¹ Agrippa said to Sha'ul, "You have permission to speak on your own behalf." Then Sha'ul motioned with his hand and began his defense:

² "King Agrippa, I consider myself fortunate that it is before you today that I am defending against all the charges made against me by Jews, ³ because you are so well informed about all the Jewish customs and controversies. Therefore, I beg you to listen to me patiently.

⁴"So then! All Jews know how I lived my life from my youth on, both in my own country and in Yerushalayim. ⁵They have known me for a long time; and if they are willing, they can testify that I have followed the strictest party in our religion — that is, I have lived as a *Parush*. ⁶How ironic it is that I stand on trial here because of my hope in the promise made to our fathers! ⁷It is the fulfillment of this very promise that our twelve tribes hope to attain, as they resolutely carry on their acts of worship night and day; yet it is in connection with this hope, your Majesty, that I am being accused by Jews! ⁸Why do you people consider it incredible that God raises the dead?

⁹"I used to think it was my duty to do all I could to combat the name of Yeshua from Natzeret; ¹⁰and in Yerushalayim I did so. After receiving authority from the head *cohanim*, I myself threw many of God's people in prison; when they were put to death, I cast my vote against them. ¹¹Often I went from one synagogue to another, punishing them and trying to make them blaspheme; and in my wild fury against them, I even went so far as to persecute them in cities outside the country.

¹²"On one such occasion, I was traveling to Dammesek with the full authority and power of the head *cohanim*. ¹³I was on the road, and it was noon, your Majesty, when I saw a light from heaven, brighter than the sun, shining around me and my traveling companions. ¹⁴We all fell to the ground; and then I heard a voice saying to me, in Hebrew, 'Sha'ul! Sha'ul! Why do you keep persecuting me? It's hard on you to be kicking against the ox-goads!' ¹⁵I said, 'Who are you, sir?' and the Lord answered, 'I am Yeshua, and you are persecuting me! ¹⁶But get up, and stand on your feet! I have appeared to you to appoint you to serve and bear witness to what you have already seen of me, and to what you will see when I appear to you in the future. ¹⁷I will deliver you from the People and from the *Goyim*. I am sending you ¹⁸to open their eyes; so that they will turn from darkness to light, from the power of the Adversary to God, and thus receive forgiveness of sins and a place among those who have been separated for holiness by putting their trust in me.'

¹⁹"So, King Agrippa, I did not disobey the vision from heaven! ²⁰On the contrary, I announced first in Dammesek, then in Yerushalayim and throughout Y'hudah, and also to the *Goyim*, that they should turn from their sins to God and then do deeds consistent with that repentance. ²¹It was because of these things that Jews seized me in the Temple and tried to kill me. ²²However, I have had God's help; so to this day, I stand testifying to both small and great, saying nothing but what both the prophets and Moshe said would happen — ²³that the Messiah would die, and that he, as the first to rise from the dead, would proclaim light to both the People and the *Goyim*."

²⁴But just as he reached this point in his defense, Festus shouted at the top of his voice, "Sha'ul, you're out of your mind! So much learning is driving you crazy!"

²⁵But Sha'ul said, "No, I am not 'crazy,' Festus, your Excellency; on the contrary, I am speaking words of truth and sanity. ²⁶For the king understands these matters, so to him I express myself freely, because I am sure that none of these things have been hidden from him. After all, they didn't happen in some back alley. ²⁷King Agrippa, do you believe the prophets? I know you believe!"

²⁸Agrippa said to Sha'ul, "In this short time, you're trying to convince me to become Messianic?" ²⁹Sha'ul replied, "Whether it takes a short time or a long time, I wish to God that not only you, but also everyone hearing me today, might become just like me except for these chains!"

^{30} Then the king got up, and with him the governor and Bernice and the others sitting with them. ^{31} After they had left, they said to one another, "This man is doing nothing that deserves either death or prison." ^{32} And Agrippa said to Festus, "If he hadn't appealed to the Emperor, he could have been released."

27 ^{1} Once it had been decided that we should set sail for Italy, they handed Sha'ul and some other prisoners over to an officer of the Emperor's Regiment named Julius. ^{2} We embarked in a ship from Adramyttium which was about to sail to the ports along the coast of the province of Asia, and put out to sea, accompanied by Aristarchus, a Macedonian from Thessalonica. ^{3} The next day, we landed at Tzidon; and Julius considerately allowed Sha'ul to go visit his friends and receive what he needed. ^{4} Putting to sea from there, we sailed close to the sheltered side of Cyprus because the winds were against us, ^{5} then across the open sea along the coasts of Cilicia and Pamphylia; and so we reached Myra in Lycia.

^{6} There the Roman officer found an Alexandrian vessel sailing to Italy and put us aboard. ^{7} For a number of days we made little headway, and we arrived off Cnidus only with difficulty. The wind would not let us continue any farther along the direct route; so we ran down along the sheltered side of Crete from Cape Salmone; ^{8} and, continuing to struggle on, hugging the coast, we reached a place called Pleasant Harbor, near the town of Lasea.

^{9} Since much time had been lost, and continuing the voyage was risky, because it was already past *Yom-Kippur*, Sha'ul advised them, ^{10} "Men, I can see that our voyage is going to be a catastrophe, not only with huge losses to the cargo and the ship but with loss of our lives as well." ^{11} However, the officer paid more attention to the pilot and the ship's owner than to what Sha'ul said. ^{12} Moreover, since the harbor was not well suited to sitting out the winter, the majority reached the decision to sail on from there in the hope of reaching Phoenix, another harbor in Crete, and wintering there, where it is protected from the southwest and northwest winds.

^{13} When a gentle southerly breeze began to blow, they thought that they had their goal within grasp; so they raised the anchor and started coasting by Crete close to shore. ^{14} But before long there struck us from land a full gale from the northeast, the kind they call an Evrakilon. ^{15} The ship was caught up and unable to face the wind, so we gave way to it and were driven along.

^{16} As we passed into the lee of a small island called Cauda, we managed with strenuous effort to get control of the lifeboat. ^{17} They hoisted it aboard, then fastened cables tightly around the ship itself to reinforce it. Fearing they might run aground on the Syrtis sandbars, they lowered the topsails and thus continued drifting. ^{18} But because we were fighting such heavy weather, the next day they began to jettison non-essentials; ^{19} and the third day, they threw the ship's sailing equipment overboard with their own hands. ^{20} For many days neither the sun nor the stars appeared, while the storm continued to rage, until gradually all hope of survival vanished.

^{21} It was then, when they had gone a long time without eating, that Sha'ul stood up in front of them and said, "You should have listened to me and not set out from Crete; if you had, you would have escaped this disastrous loss. ^{22} But now, my advice to you is to take heart; because not one of you will lose his life — only the ship will be lost. ^{23} For this very night, there stood next to me an angel of the God to whom I belong and whom I serve. ^{24} He said, 'Don't be afraid, Sha'ul! You have to stand before the Emperor. Look! God has granted you all those who are sailing with you.' ²⁵ So, men, take heart! For I trust God and believe that what I have been told will come true. ²⁶ Nevertheless, we have to run aground on some island."

²⁷ It was the fourteenth night, and we were still being driven about in the Adriatic Sea, when around midnight the sailors sensed that we were nearing land. ²⁸ So they dropped a plumbline and found the water one hundred and twenty feet deep. A little farther on, they took another sounding and found it ninety feet. ²⁹ Fearing we might run on the rocks, they let out four anchors from the stern and prayed for daylight to come.

³⁰ At this point, the crew made an attempt to abandon ship — they lowered the lifeboat into the sea, pretending that they were about to let out some anchors from the bow. ³¹ Sha'ul said to the officer and the soldiers, "Unless these men remain aboard the ship, you yourselves cannot be saved." ³² Then the soldiers cut the ropes holding the lifeboat and let it go.

³³ Just before daybreak, Sha'ul urged them all to eat, saying, "Today is the fourteenth day you have been in suspense, going hungry, eating nothing. ³⁴ Therefore I advise you to take some food; you need it for your own survival. For not one of you will lose so much as a hair from his head." ³⁵ When he had said this, he took bread, said the *b'rakhah* to God in front of everyone, broke it and began to eat. ³⁶ With courage restored, they all ate some food themselves. ³⁷ Altogether there were 276 of us on board the ship. ³⁸ After they had eaten all they wanted, they lightened the ship by dumping the grain into the sea.

³⁹ When day broke, they didn't recognize the land; but they noticed a bay with a sand beach, where they decided to run the ship aground if they could. ⁴⁰ So they cut away the anchors and left them in the sea; at the same time, they loosened the ropes that held the rudders out of the water. Then they hoisted the foresail to the wind and headed for the beach. ⁴¹ But they encountered a place where two currents meet, and ran the vessel aground on the sandbar there. The bow stuck and would not move, while the pounding of the surf began to break up the stern.

⁴² At this point the soldiers' thought was to kill the prisoners, so that none of them would swim off and escape. ⁴³ But the officer, wanting to save Sha'ul, kept them from carrying out their plan. He ordered those who could swim to throw themselves overboard first and head for shore, ⁴⁴ and the rest to use planks or whatever they could find from the ship. Thus it was that everyone reached land safely.

28 ¹ After our escape, we learned that the island was called Malta. ² Its people showed extraordinary kindness — it was cold and it had started to rain, so they lit a bonfire and welcomed us all. ³ Sha'ul had gathered a bundle of sticks and was adding them to the fire, when a poisonous snake, driven out by the heat, fastened itself to his hand. ⁴ The islanders saw the creature hanging from Sha'ul's hand and said to one another, "This man must be a murderer. Even though he escaped the sea, justice has not allowed him to live." ⁵ But he shook the snake off into the fire and suffered no harm. ⁶ They waited, expecting him to swell up or suddenly fall down dead; but after waiting a long time and seeing that nothing amiss was happening to him, they reversed their opinion and said he was a god.

⁷ Nearby were lands belonging to the governor of the island, whose name was Publius. He received us in a friendly manner and put us up for three days. ⁸ Now it so happened that Publius' father was lying in bed, sick with fever attacks and dysentery.

Sha'ul went in to him, prayed, placed his hands on him and healed him. ⁹ After this happened, the rest of those on the island who had ailments came and were healed. ¹⁰ They heaped honors on us; and when the time came for us to sail, they provided the supplies we needed.

¹¹ After three months, we sailed away on a ship from Alexandria called "Twin Gods," which had passed the winter at the island. ¹² We landed at Syracuse and stayed three days. ¹³ From there, we arrived at Rhegium by tacking; but after one day, a south wind sprang up; so we made it to Puteoli the second day. ¹⁴ There we found brothers who invited us to spend a week with them. And so we went on toward Rome.

¹⁵ The brothers there had heard about us and came as far as Appian Market and Three Inns to meet us. When Sha'ul saw them, he thanked God and took courage. ¹⁶ And when we arrived at Rome, the officer allowed Sha'ul to stay by himself, though guarded by a soldier.

¹⁷ After three days Sha'ul called a meeting of the local Jewish leaders. When they had gathered, he said to them: "Brothers, although I have done nothing against either our people or the traditions of our fathers, I was made a prisoner in Yerushalayim and handed over to the Romans. ¹⁸ They examined me and were ready to release me, because I had done nothing to justify a death sentence. ¹⁹ But when the Judeans objected, I was forced to appeal to the Emperor — not that I had any charge to make against my own people. ²⁰ This is why I have asked to see you and speak with you, for it is because of the hope of Isra'el that I have this chain around me."

²¹ They said to him, "We have not received any letters about you from Y'hudah, and none of the brothers who have come from there has reported or said anything bad about you. ²² But we do think it would be appropriate to hear your views from you, yourself; for all we know about this sect is that people everywhere speak against it."

²³ So they arranged a day with him and came to his quarters in large numbers. From morning until evening he explained the matter to them, giving a thorough witness about the Kingdom of God and making use of both the *Torah* of Moshe and the Prophets to persuade them about Yeshua. ²⁴ Some were convinced by what he said, ²⁵ while others refused to believe.

So they left, disagreeing among themselves, after Sha'ul had made one final statement: "The *Ruach HaKodesh* spoke well in saying to your fathers through Yesha'yahu the prophet,

²⁶   'Go to this people and say,
       "You will keep on hearing but never understand,
       and you will keep on seeing but never perceive,
²⁷   because the heart of this people has grown thick —
       with their ears they barely hear,
       and their eyes they have closed,
       for fear that they should see with their eyes,
       hear with their ears,
       understand with their heart,
       and do *t'shuvah*,
       so that I could heal them.'"ᵇ

ᵇ Isaiah 6:9–10

²⁸ Therefore, let it be known to you that this salvation of God has been sent to the *Goyim*, and they will listen!" ²⁹ *

³⁰ Sha'ul remained two whole years in a place he rented for himself; and he continued receiving all who came to see him, ³¹ openly and without hindrance proclaiming the Kingdom of God and teaching about the Lord Yeshua the Messiah.

---

* Some manuscripts include verse 29: After he had said this, the Jews left, arguing vehemently among themselves.

The Letter from Yeshua's Emissary Sha'ul (Paul)
to the Messianic Community in Rome

ROMANS

1 ¹ From: Sha'ul, a slave of the Messiah Yeshua, an emissary because I was called and set apart for the Good News of God.

² God promised this Good News in advance through his prophets in the *Tanakh*. ³ It concerns his Son — he is descended from David physically; ⁴ he was powerfully demonstrated to be Son of God spiritually, set apart by his having been resurrected from the dead; he is Yeshua the Messiah, our Lord. ⁵ Through him we received grace and were given the work of being an emissary on his behalf promoting trust-grounded obedience among all the Gentiles, ⁶ including you, who have been called by Yeshua the Messiah.

⁷ To: All those in Rome whom God loves, who have been called, who have been set apart for him:

Grace to you and *shalom* from God our Father and the Lord Yeshua the Messiah.

⁸ First, I thank my God through Yeshua the Messiah for all of you, because the report of your trust is spreading throughout the whole world. ⁹ For God, whom I serve in my spirit by spreading the Good News about his Son, is my witness that I regularly remember you ¹⁰ in my prayers; and I always pray that somehow, now or in the future, I might, by God's will, succeed in coming to visit you. ¹¹ For I long to see you, so that I might share with you some spiritual gift that can make you stronger — ¹² or, to put it another way, so that by my being with you, we might, through the faith we share, encourage one another. ¹³ Brothers, I want you to know that although I have been prevented from visiting you until now, I have often planned to do so, in order that I might have some fruit among you, just as I have among the other Gentiles. ¹⁴ I owe a debt to both civilized Greeks and uncivilized people, to both the educated and the ignorant; ¹⁵ therefore I am eager to proclaim the Good News also to you who live in Rome.

¹⁶ For I am not ashamed of the Good News, since it is God's powerful means of bringing salvation to everyone who keeps on trusting, to the Jew especially, but equally to the Gentile. ¹⁷ For in it is revealed how God makes people righteous in his sight; and from beginning to end it is through trust — as the *Tanakh* puts it, **"But the person who is righteous will live his life by trust."**[a]

¹⁸ What is revealed is God's anger from heaven against all the godlessness and wickedness of people who in their wickedness keep suppressing the truth; ¹⁹ because what is known about God is plain to them, since God has made it plain to them. ²⁰ For ever since the creation of the universe his invisible qualities — both his eternal power and his divine nature — have been clearly seen, because they can be understood from what he has made. Therefore, they have no excuse; ²¹ because, although they

---

[a] Habakkuk 2:4

1402

know who God is, they do not glorify him as God or thank him. On the contrary, they have become futile in their thinking; and their undiscerning hearts have become darkened. ²² Claiming to be wise, they have become fools! ²³ In fact, they have exchanged the glory of the immortal God for mere images, like a mortal human being, or like birds, animals or reptiles!

²⁴ This is why God has given them up to the vileness of their hearts' lusts, to the shameful misuse of each other's bodies. ²⁵ They have exchanged the truth of God for falsehood, by worshipping and serving created things, rather than the Creator — praised be he for ever. *Amen.* ²⁶ This is why God has given them up to degrading passions; so that their women exchange natural sexual relations for unnatural; ²⁷ and likewise the men, giving up natural relations with the opposite sex, burn with passion for one another, men committing shameful acts with other men and receiving in their own persons the penalty appropriate to their perversion. ²⁸ In other words, since they have not considered God worth knowing, God has given them up to worthless ways of thinking; so that they do improper things. ²⁹ They are filled with every kind of wickedness, evil, greed and vice; stuffed with jealousy, murder, quarrelling, dishonesty and ill-will; they are gossips, ³⁰ slanderers, haters of God; they are insolent, arrogant and boastful; they plan evil schemes; they disobey their parents; ³¹ they are brainless, faithless, heartless and ruthless. ³² They know well enough God's righteous decree that people who do such things deserve to die; yet not only do they keep doing them, but they applaud others who do the same.

2 ¹ Therefore you have no excuse, whoever you are, passing judgment; for when you judge someone else, you are passing judgment against yourself; since you who are judging do the same things he does. ² We know that God's judgment lands impartially on those who do such things; ³ do you think that you, a mere man passing judgment on others who do such things, yet doing them yourself, will escape the judgment of God? ⁴ Or perhaps you despise the riches of his kindness, forbearance and patience; because you don't realize that God's kindness is intended to lead you to turn from your sins. ⁵ But by your stubbornness, by your unrepentant heart, you are storing up anger for yourself on the Day of Anger, when God's righteous judgment will be revealed; ⁶ for he **will pay back each one according to his deeds.**[b] ⁷ To those who seek glory, honor and immortality by perseverance in doing good, he will pay back eternal life. ⁸ But to those who are self-seeking, who disobey the truth and obey evil, he will pay back wrath and anger.

⁹ Yes, he will pay back misery and anguish to every human being who does evil, to the Jew first, then to the Gentile; ¹⁰ but glory and honor and *shalom* to everyone who keeps doing what is good, to the Jew first, then to the Gentile. ¹¹ For God does not show favoritism. ¹² All who have sinned outside the framework of *Torah* will die outside the framework of *Torah*; and all who have sinned within the framework of *Torah* will be judged by *Torah*. ¹³ For it is not merely the hearers of *Torah* whom God considers righteous; rather, it is the doers of what *Torah* says who will be made righteous in God's sight. ¹⁴ For whenever Gentiles, who have no *Torah*, do naturally what the *Torah* requires, then these, even though they don't have *Torah*, for

[b] Psalm 62:13(12), Proverbs 24:12

themselves are *Torah*! [15] For their lives show that the conduct the *Torah* dictates is **written in their hearts.**[c] Their consciences also bear witness to this, for their conflicting thoughts sometimes accuse them and sometimes defend them [16] on a day when God passes judgment on people's inmost secrets. (According to the Good News as I proclaim it, he does this through the Messiah Yeshua.)

[17] But if you call yourself a Jew and rest on *Torah* and boast about God [18] and know his will and give your approval to what is right, because you have been instructed from the *Torah*; [19] and if you have persuaded yourself that you are a guide to the blind, a light in the darkness, [20] an instructor for the spiritually unaware and a teacher of children, since in the *Torah* you have the embodiment of knowledge and truth; [21] then, you who teach others, don't you teach yourself? Preaching, **"Thou shalt not steal,"**[d] do you steal? [22] Saying, **"Thou shalt not commit adultery,"**[e] do you commit adultery? Detesting idols, do you commit idolatrous acts? [23] You who take such pride in *Torah*, do you, by disobeying the *Torah*, dishonor God? — [24] as it says in the *Tanakh*, **"For it is because of you that God's name is blasphemed by the Goyim."**[f] [25] For circumcision is indeed of value if you do what *Torah* says. But if you are a transgressor of *Torah*, your circumcision has become uncircumcision! [26] Therefore, if an uncircumcised man keeps the righteous requirements of the *Torah*, won't his uncircumcision be counted as circumcision? [27] Indeed, the man who is physically uncircumcised but obeys the *Torah* will stand as a judgment on you who have had a *b'rit-milah* and have *Torah* written out but violate it! [28] For the real Jew is not merely Jewish outwardly: true circumcision is not only external and physical. [29] On the contrary, the real Jew is one inwardly; and true circumcision is of the heart, spiritual not literal; so that his praise comes not from other people but from God.

3 [1] Then what advantage has the Jew? What is the value of being circumcised? [2] Much in every way! In the first place, the Jews were entrusted with the very words of God. [3] If some of them were unfaithful, so what? Does their faithlessness cancel God's faithfulness? [4] Heaven forbid! God would be true even if everyone were a liar! — as the *Tanakh* says,

> **"so that you, God, may be proved right in your words**
> **and win the verdict when you are put on trial."**[g]

[5] Now if our unrighteousness highlights God's righteousness, what should we say? That God is unrighteous to inflict his anger on us? (I am speaking here the way people commonly do.) [6] Heaven forbid! Else, how could God judge the world? [7] "But," you say, "if, through my lie, God's truth is enhanced and brings him greater glory, why am I still judged merely for being a sinner?" [8] Indeed! Why not say (as some people slander us by claiming we do say), "Let us do evil, so that good may come of it"? Against them the judgment is a just one!

[9] So are we Jews better off? Not entirely; for I have already made the charge that all people, Jews and Gentiles alike, are controlled by sin. [10] As the *Tanakh* puts it,

---

[c] Jeremiah 31:32(33)   [d] Exodus 20:13(15), Deuteronomy 5:17(19)   [e] Exodus 20:13(14),
Deuteronomy 5:17(18)   [f] Isaiah 52:5, Ezekiel 36:20   [g] Psalm 51:6 (4)

"There is no one righteous, not even one!
No one understands,
11   no one seeks God,
12   all have turned away
and at the same time become useless;
there is no one who shows kindness, not a single one!"[h]

13   "Their throats are open graves,
they use their tongues to deceive.[i]
Vipers' venom is under their lips.[j]
14   Their mouths are full of curses and bitterness.[k]

15   "Their feet rush to shed blood,
16   in their ways are ruin and misery,
17   and the way of *shalom* they do not know.[l]

18   "There is no fear of God before their eyes."[m]

[19] Moreover, we know that whatever the *Torah* says, it says to those living within the framework of the *Torah*, in order that every mouth may be stopped and the whole world be shown to deserve God's adverse judgment. [20] **For in his sight no one alive will be considered righteous**[n] on the ground of legalistic observance of *Torah* commands, because what *Torah* really does is show people how sinful they are.

[21] But now, quite apart from *Torah*, God's way of making people righteous in his sight has been made clear — although the *Torah* and the Prophets give their witness to it as well — [22] and it is a righteousness that comes from God, through the faithfulness of Yeshua the Messiah, to all who continue trusting. For it makes no difference whether one is a Jew or a Gentile, [23] since all have sinned and come short of earning God's praise. [24] By God's grace, without earning it, all are granted the status of being considered righteous before him, through the act redeeming us from our enslavement to sin that was accomplished by the Messiah Yeshua. [25] God put Yeshua forward as the *kapparah* for sin through his faithfulness in respect to his bloody sacrificial death. This vindicated God's righteousness; because, in his forbearance, he had passed over [with neither punishment nor remission] the sins people had committed in the past; [26] and it vindicates his righteousness in the present age by showing that he is righteous himself and is also the one who makes people righteous on the ground of Yeshua's faithfulness.

[27] So what room is left for boasting? None at all! What kind of *Torah* excludes it? One that has to do with legalistic observance of rules? No, rather, a *Torah* that has to do with trusting. [28] Therefore, we hold the view that a person comes to be considered righteous by God on the ground of trusting, which has nothing to do with legalistic observance of *Torah* commands.

[29] Or is God the God of the Jews only? Isn't he also the God of the Gentiles? Yes, he is indeed the God of the Gentiles; [30] because, as you will admit, **God is one.**[o]

---

[h] Psalm 14:1–3, 53:2–4(1–3)   [i] Psalm 5:10(9)   [j] Psalm 140:4(3)   [k] Psalm 10:7
[l] Isaiah 59:7–8, Proverbs 1:16   [m] Psalm 36:2(1)   [n] Psalm 143:2   [o] Deuteronomy 6:4

Therefore, he will consider righteous the circumcised on the ground of trusting and the uncircumcised through that same trusting. 31 Does it follow that we abolish *Torah* by this trusting? Heaven forbid! On the contrary, we confirm *Torah*.

4 1 Then what should we say Avraham, our forefather, obtained by his own efforts? 2 For if Avraham came to be considered righteous by God because of legalistic observances, then he has something to boast about. But this is not how it is before God! 3 For what does the *Tanakh* say? **"Avraham put his trust in God, and it was credited to his account as righteousness."**[p] 4 Now the account of someone who is working is credited not on the ground of grace but on the ground of what is owed him. 5 However, in the case of one who is not working but rather is trusting in him who makes ungodly people righteous, his trust is credited to him as righteousness.

6 In the same way, the blessing which David pronounces is on those whom God credits with righteousness apart from legalistic observances:

7 **"Blessed are those whose transgressions are forgiven,**
whose sins are covered over;
8 **Blessed is the man whose sin *Adonai***
will not reckon against his account."[q]

9 Now is this blessing for the circumcised only? Or is it also for the uncircumcised? For we say that Avraham's **trust was credited to his account as righteousness**; 10 but what state was he in when it was so credited — circumcision or uncircumcision? Not in circumcision, but in uncircumcision! 11 In fact, he received circumcision as a sign, as a seal of the righteousness he had been credited with on the ground of the trust he had while he was still uncircumcised. This happened so that he could be the father of every uncircumcised person who trusts and thus has righteousness credited to him, 12 and at the same time be the father of every circumcised person who not only has had a *b'rit-milah*, but also follows in the footsteps of the trust which *Avraham avinu* had when he was still uncircumcised.

13 For the promise to Avraham and his **seed**[r] that he would inherit the world did not come through legalism but through the righteousness that trust produces. 14 For if the heirs are produced by legalism, then trust is pointless and the promise worthless. 15 For what law brings is punishment. But where there is no law, there is also no violation.

16 The reason the promise is based on trusting is so that it may come as God's free gift, a promise that can be relied on by all the **seed**, not only those who live within the framework of the *Torah*, but also those with the kind of trust Avraham had — *Avraham avinu* for all of us. 17 This accords with the *Tanakh*, where it says, **"I have appointed you to be a father to many nations."**[s] Avraham is our father in God's sight because he trusted God as the one who gives life to the dead and calls nonexistent things into existence. 18 For he was past hope, yet in hope he trusted that he would indeed become **a father to many nations**, in keeping with what he had been told, **"So many will your seed be."**[t] 19 His trust did not waver when he considered his own body — which was as good as dead, since he was about a hundred years old — or when he considered that Sarah's womb was dead too. 20 He did not by lack of trust

---

[p] Genesis 15:6 [q] Psalm 32:1–2 [r] Genesis 15:3, 5 [s] Genesis 17:5 [t] Genesis 15:5

decide against God's promises. On the contrary, by trust he was given power as he gave glory to God, ^{21} for he was fully convinced that what God had promised he could also accomplish. ^{22} This is why it **was credited to his account as righteousness."**

^{23} But the words, **"it was credited to his account . . . ,"** were not written for him only. ^{24} They were written also for us, who will certainly have our account credited too, because we have trusted in him who raised Yeshua our Lord from the dead — ^{25} Yeshua, who was delivered over to death because of our offenses and raised to life in order to make us righteous.

5 ^{1} So, since we have come to be considered righteous by God because of our trust, let us continue to have *shalom* with God through our Lord, Yeshua the Messiah. ^{2} Also through him and on the ground of our trust, we have gained access to this grace in which we stand; so let us boast about the hope of experiencing God's glory. ^{3} But not only that, let us also boast in our troubles; because we know that trouble produces endurance, ^{4} endurance produces character, and character produces hope; ^{5} and this hope does not let us down, because God's love for us has already been poured out in our hearts through the *Ruach HaKodesh* who has been given to us.

^{6} For while we were still helpless, at the right time, the Messiah died on behalf of ungodly people. ^{7} Now it is a rare event when someone gives up his life even for the sake of somebody righteous, although possibly for a truly good person one might have the courage to die. ^{8} But God demonstrates his own love for us in that the Messiah died on our behalf while we were still sinners. ^{9} Therefore, since we have now come to be considered righteous by means of his bloody sacrificial death, how much more will we be delivered through him from the anger of God's judgment! ^{10} For if we were reconciled with God through his Son's death when we were enemies, how much more will we be delivered by his life, now that we are reconciled! ^{11} And not only will we be delivered in the future, but we are boasting about God right now, because he has acted through our Lord Yeshua the Messiah, through whom we have already received that reconciliation.

^{12} Here is how it works: it was through one individual that sin entered the world, and through sin, death; and in this way death passed through to the whole human race, inasmuch as everyone sinned. ^{13} Sin was indeed present in the world before *Torah* was given, but sin is not counted as such when there is no *Torah*. ^{14} Nevertheless death ruled from Adam until Moshe, even over those whose sinning was not exactly like Adam's violation of a direct command. In this, Adam prefigured the one who was to come.

^{15} But the free gift is not like the offense. For if, because of one man's offense, many died, then how much more has God's grace, that is, the gracious gift of one man, Yeshua the Messiah, overflowed to many! ^{16} No, the free gift is not like what resulted from one man's sinning; for from one sinner came judgment that brought condemnation; but the free gift came after many offenses and brought acquittal. ^{17} For if, because of the offense of one man, death ruled through that one man; how much more will those receiving the overflowing grace, that is, the gift of being considered righteous, rule in life through the one man Yeshua the Messiah!

^{18} In other words, just as it was through one offense that all people came under condemnation, so also it is through one righteous act that all people come to be

---

" Genesis 15:6

considered righteous. ^{19} For just as through the disobedience of the one man, many were made sinners, so also through the obedience of the other man, many will be made righteous. ^{20} And the *Torah* came into the picture so that the offense would proliferate; but where sin proliferated, grace proliferated even more. ^{21} All this happened so that just as sin ruled by means of death, so also grace might rule through causing people to be considered righteous, so that they might have eternal life, through Yeshua the Messiah, our Lord.

6 ^{1} So then, are we to say, "Let's keep on sinning, so that there can be more grace"? ^{2} Heaven forbid! How can we, who have died to sin, still live in it? ^{3} Don't you know that those of us who have been immersed into the Messiah Yeshua have been immersed into his death? ^{4} Through immersion into his death we were buried with him; so that just as, through the glory of the Father, the Messiah was raised from the dead, likewise we too might live a new life. ^{5} For if we have been united with him in a death like his, we will also be united with him in a resurrection like his. ^{6} We know that our old self was put to death on the execution-stake with him, so that the entire body of our sinful propensities might be destroyed, and we might no longer be enslaved to sin. ^{7} For someone who has died has been cleared from sin. ^{8} Now since we died with the Messiah, we trust that we will also live with him. ^{9} We know that the Messiah has been raised from the dead, never to die again; death has no authority over him. ^{10} For his death was a unique event that need not be repeated; but his life, he keeps on living for God. ^{11} In the same way, consider yourselves to be dead to sin but alive for God, by your union with the Messiah Yeshua.

^{12} Therefore, do not let sin rule in your mortal bodies, so that it makes you obey its desires; ^{13} and do not offer any part of yourselves to sin as an instrument for wickedness. On the contrary, offer yourselves to God as people alive from the dead, and your various parts to God as instruments for righteousness. ^{14} For sin will not have authority over you; because you are not under legalism but under grace.

^{15} Therefore, what conclusion should we reach? "Let's go on sinning, because we're not under legalism but under grace"? Heaven forbid! ^{16} Don't you know that if you present yourselves to someone as obedient slaves, then, of the one whom you are obeying, you are slaves — whether of sin, which leads to death, or of obedience, which leads to being made righteous? ^{17} By God's grace, you, who were once slaves to sin, obeyed from your heart the pattern of teaching to which you were exposed; ^{18} and after you had been set free from sin, you became enslaved to righteousness. ^{19} (I am using popular language because your human nature is so weak.) For just as you used to offer your various parts as slaves to impurity and lawlessness, which led to more lawlessness; so now offer your various parts as slaves to righteousness, which leads to being made holy, set apart for God. ^{20} For when you were slaves of sin, you were free in relationship to righteousness; ^{21} but what benefit did you derive from the things of which you are now ashamed? The end result of those things was death. ^{22} However, now, freed from sin and enslaved to God, you do get the benefit — it consists in being made holy, set apart for God, and its end result is eternal life. ^{23} For what one earns from sin is death; but eternal life is what one receives as a free gift from God, in union with the Messiah Yeshua, our Lord.

7 [1] Surely you know, brothers — for I am speaking to those who understand *Torah* — that the *Torah* has authority over a person only so long as he lives? [2] For example, a married woman is bound by *Torah* to her husband while he is alive; but if the husband dies, she is released from the part of the *Torah* that deals with husbands. [3] Therefore, while the husband is alive, she will be called an adulteress if she marries another man; but if the husband dies, she is free from that part of the *Torah*; so that if she marries another man, she is not an adulteress.

[4] Thus, my brothers, you have been made dead with regard to the *Torah* through the Messiah's body, so that you may belong to someone else, namely, the one who has been raised from the dead, in order for us to bear fruit for God. [5] For when we were living according to our old nature, the passions connected with sins worked through the *Torah* in our various parts, with the result that we bore fruit for death. [6] But now we have been released from this aspect of the *Torah*, because we have died to that which had us in its clutches, so that we are serving in the new way provided by the Spirit and not in the old way of outwardly following the letter of the law.

[7] Therefore, what are we to say? That the *Torah* is sinful? Heaven forbid! Rather, the function of the *Torah* was that without it, I would not have known what sin is. For example, I would not have become conscious of what greed is if the *Torah* had not said, **"Thou shalt not covet."**[v] [8] But sin, seizing the opportunity afforded by the commandment, worked in me all kinds of evil desires — for apart from *Torah*, sin is dead. [9] I was once alive outside the framework of *Torah*. But when the commandment really encountered me, sin sprang to life, [10] and I died. The commandment that was intended to bring me life was found to be bringing me death! [11] For sin, seizing the opportunity afforded by the commandment, deceived me; and through the commandment, sin killed me. [12] So the *Torah* is holy; that is, the commandment is holy, just and good.

[13] Then did something good become for me the source of death? Heaven forbid! Rather, it was sin working death in me through something good, so that sin might be clearly exposed as sin, so that sin through the commandment might come to be experienced as sinful beyond measure. [14] For we know that the *Torah* is of the Spirit; but as for me, I am bound to the old nature, sold to sin as a slave. [15] I don't understand my own behavior — I don't do what I want to do; instead, I do the very thing I hate! [16] Now if I am doing what I don't want to do, I am agreeing that the *Torah* is good. [17] But now it is no longer "the real me" doing it, but the sin housed inside me. [18] For I know that there is nothing good housed inside me — that is, inside my old nature. I can want what is good, but I can't do it! [19] For I don't do the good I want; instead, the evil that I don't want is what I do! [20] But if I am doing what "the real me" doesn't want, it is no longer "the real me" doing it but the sin housed inside me. [21] So I find it to be the rule, a kind of perverse *"torah,"* that although I want to do what is good, evil is right there with me! [22] For in my inner self I completely agree with God's *Torah*; [23] but in my various parts, I see a different *"torah,"* one that battles with the *Torah* in my mind and makes me a prisoner of sin's *"torah,"* which is operating in my various parts. [24] What a miserable creature I am! Who will rescue me from this body bound for death? [25] Thanks be to God [, he will]! — through Yeshua the Messiah, our Lord!

---

[v] Exodus 20:14(17), Deuteronomy 5:18(21)

To sum up: with my mind, I am a slave of God's *Torah*; but with my old nature, I am a slave of sin's "*Torah.*"

8 ¹ Therefore, there is no longer any condemnation awaiting those who are in union with the Messiah Yeshua. ² Why? Because the *Torah* of the Spirit, which produces this life in union with Messiah Yeshua, has set me free from the "*Torah*" of sin and death. ³ For what the *Torah* could not do by itself, because it lacked the power to make the old nature cooperate, God did by sending his own Son as a human being with a nature like our own sinful one [but without sin]. God did this in order to deal with sin, and in so doing he executed the punishment against sin in human nature, ⁴ so that the just requirement of the *Torah* might be fulfilled in us who do not run our lives according to what our old nature wants but according to what the Spirit wants. ⁵ For those who identify with their old nature set their minds on the things of the old nature, but those who identify with the Spirit set their minds on the things of the Spirit. ⁶ Having one's mind controlled by the old nature is death, but having one's mind controlled by the Spirit is life and *shalom*. ⁷ For the mind controlled by the old nature is hostile to God, because it does not submit itself to God's *Torah* — indeed, it cannot. ⁸ Thus, those who identify with their old nature cannot please God.

⁹ But you, you do not identify with your old nature but with the Spirit — provided the Spirit of God is living inside you, for anyone who doesn't have the Spirit of the Messiah doesn't belong to him. ¹⁰ However, if the Messiah is in you, then, on the one hand, the body is dead because of sin; but, on the other hand, the Spirit is giving life because God considers you righteous. ¹¹ And if the Spirit of the One who raised Yeshua from the dead is living in you, then the One who raised the Messiah Yeshua from the dead will also give life to your mortal bodies through his Spirit living in you.

¹² So then, brothers, we don't owe a thing to our old nature that would require us to live according to our old nature. ¹³ For if you live according to your old nature, you will certainly die; but if, by the Spirit, you keep putting to death the practices of the body, you will live.

¹⁴ All who are led by God's Spirit are God's sons. ¹⁵ For you did not receive a spirit of slavery to bring you back again into fear; on the contrary, you received the Spirit, who makes us sons and by whose power we cry out, "*Abba!*" (that is, "Dear Father!"). ¹⁶ The Spirit himself bears witness with our own spirits that we are children of God; ¹⁷ and if we are children, then we are also heirs, heirs of God and joint-heirs with the Messiah — provided we are suffering with him in order also to be glorified with him.

¹⁸ I don't think the sufferings we are going through now are even worth comparing with the glory that will be revealed to us in the future. ¹⁹ The creation waits eagerly for the sons of God to be revealed; ²⁰ for the creation was made subject to frustration — not willingly, but because of the one who subjected it. But it was given a reliable hope ²¹ that it too would be set free from its bondage to decay and would enjoy the freedom accompanying the glory that God's children will have. ²² We know that until now, the whole creation has been groaning as with the pains of childbirth; ²³ and not only it, but we ourselves, who have the firstfruits of the Spirit, groan inwardly as we continue waiting eagerly to be made sons — that is, to have our whole bodies redeemed and set free. ²⁴ It was in this hope that we were saved. But if we see what we hope for, it isn't

hope — after all, who hopes for what he already sees? ²⁵ But if we continue hoping for something we don't see, then we still wait eagerly for it, with perseverance.

²⁶ Similarly, the Spirit helps us in our weakness; for we don't know how to pray the way we should. But the Spirit himself pleads on our behalf with groanings too deep for words; ²⁷ and the one who searches hearts knows exactly what the Spirit is thinking, because his pleadings for God's people accord with God's will. ²⁸ Furthermore, we know that God causes everything to work together for the good of those who love God and are called in accordance with his purpose; ²⁹ because those whom he knew in advance, he also determined in advance would be conformed to the pattern of his Son, so that he might be the firstborn among many brothers; ³⁰ and those whom he thus determined in advance, he also called; and those whom he called, he also caused to be considered righteous; and those whom he caused to be considered righteous he also glorified!

³¹ What, then, are we to say to these things? If God is for us, who can be against us? ³² He who did not spare even his own Son, but gave him up on behalf of us all — is it possible that, having given us his Son, he would not give us everything else too? ³³ So who will bring a charge against God's chosen people? Certainly not God — he is the one who causes them to be considered righteous! ³⁴ Who punishes them? Certainly not the Messiah Yeshua, who died and — more than that — has been raised, is at the right hand of God and is actually pleading on our behalf! ³⁵ Who will separate us from the love of the Messiah? Trouble? Hardship? Persecution? Hunger? Poverty? Danger? War? ³⁶ As the *Tanakh* puts it,

> **"For your sake we are being put to death all day long,**
> **we are considered sheep to be slaughtered."**[w]

³⁷ No, in all these things we are superconquerors, through the one who has loved us. ³⁸ For I am convinced that neither death nor life, neither angels nor other heavenly rulers, neither what exists nor what is coming, ³⁹ neither powers above nor powers below, nor any other created thing will be able to separate us from the love of God which comes to us through the Messiah Yeshua, our Lord.

9 ¹ I am speaking the truth — as one who belongs to the Messiah, I do not lie; and also bearing witness is my conscience, governed by the *Ruach HaKodesh*: ² my grief is so great, the pain in my heart so constant, ³ that I could wish myself actually under God's curse and separated from the Messiah, if it would help my brothers, my own flesh and blood, ⁴ the people of Isra'el! They were made God's children, the *Sh'khinah* has been with them, the covenants are theirs, likewise the giving of the *Torah*, the Temple service and the promises; ⁵ the Patriarchs are theirs; and from them, as far as his physical descent is concerned, came the Messiah, who is over all. Praised be *ADONAI* for ever! *Amen.*

⁶ But the present condition of Isra'el does not mean that the Word of God has failed. For not everyone from Isra'el is truly part of Isra'el; ⁷ indeed, not all the descendants are **seed of Avraham;**[x] rather, **"What is to be called your 'seed' will be in Yitz'chak."**[y] ⁸ In other words, it is not the physical children who are children of God, but the children the promise refers to who are considered **seed.** ⁹ For this is what the

---

[w] Psalm 44:23(22)   [x] 2 Chronicles 20:7, Psalm 105:6   [y] Genesis 21:12

promise said: "At the time set, I will come; and Sarah will have a son."[z] [10] And even more to the point is the case of Rivkah; for both her children were conceived in a single act with Yitz'chak, our father; [11] and before they were born, before they had done anything at all, either good or bad (so that God's plan might remain a matter of his sovereign choice, not dependent on what they did, but on God, who does the calling), [12] it was said to her, "The older will serve the younger."[a] [13] This accords with where it is written, "Ya'akov I loved, but Esav I hated."[b]

[14] So are we to say, "It is unjust for God to do this"? Heaven forbid! [15] For to Moshe he says, "I will have mercy on whom I have mercy, and I will pity whom I pity."[c] [16] Thus it doesn't depend on human desires or efforts, but on God, who has mercy. [17] For the *Tanakh* says to Pharaoh, "It is for this very reason that I raised you up, so that in connection with you I might demonstrate my power, so that my name might be known throughout the world."[d] [18] So then, he has mercy on whom he wants, and he hardens whom he wants.

[19] But you will say to me, "Then why does he still find fault with us? After all, who resists his will?" [20] Who are you, a mere human being, to talk back to God? Will what is formed say to him who formed it, "Why did you make me this way?"[e] [21] Or has the potter no right to make from a given lump of clay this pot for honorable use and that one for dishonorable? [22] Now what if God, even though he was quite willing to demonstrate his anger and make known his power, patiently put up with people who deserved punishment and were ripe for destruction? [23] What if he did this in order to make known the riches of his glory to those who are the objects of his mercy, whom he prepared in advance for glory — [24] that is, to us, whom he called not only from among the Jews but also from among the Gentiles? [25] As indeed he says in Hoshea,

> "Those who were not my people I will call my people;
> her who was not loved I will call loved;
> [26] and in the very place where they were told,
> 'You are not my people,'
> there they will be called sons of the living God!"[f]

[27] But Yesha'yahu, referring to Isra'el, cries out,

> "Even if the number of people in Isra'el is as large
> as the number of grains of sand by the sea,
> only a remnant will be saved.
> [28] For *Adonai* will fulfill his word on the earth
> with certainty and without delay."[g]

[29] Also, as Yesha'yahu said earlier,

> "If *Adonai-Tzva'ot* had not left us a seed,
> we would have become like S'dom,
> we would have resembled 'Amora."[h]

---

[z] Genesis 18:14
[c] Exodus 33:19
[f] Hosea 2:25 (23), 2:1(1:10)

[a] Genesis 25:23
[d] Exodus 9:16
[g] Isaiah 10:22–23

[b] Malachi 1:2–3
[e] Isaiah 29:16, 45:9
[h] Isaiah 1:9

³⁰ So, what are we to say? This: that Gentiles, even though they were not striving for righteousness, have obtained righteousness; but it is a righteousness grounded in trusting! ³¹ However, Isra'el, even though they kept pursuing a *Torah* that offers righteousness, did not reach what the *Torah* offers. ³² Why? Because they did not pursue righteousness as being grounded in trusting but as if it were grounded in doing legalistic works. They stumbled over the **stone that makes people stumble.**ⁱ ³³ As the *Tanakh* puts it,

> **"Look, I am laying in Tziyon**
> **a stone that will make people stumble,**
> **a rock that will trip them up.**
> **But he who rests his trust on** it
> **will not be humiliated."**ʲ

10 ¹ Brothers, my heart's deepest desire and my prayer to God for Isra'el is for their salvation; ² for I can testify to their zeal for God. But it is not based on correct understanding; ³ for, since they are unaware of God's way of making people righteous and instead seek to set up their own, they have not submitted themselves to God's way of making people righteous. ⁴ For the goal at which the *Torah* aims is the Messiah, who offers righteousness to everyone who trusts. ⁵ For Moshe writes about the righteousness grounded in the *Torah* that **the person who does these things will attain life through them.**ᵏ ⁶ Moreover, the righteousness grounded in trusting says:

> **"Do not say in your heart, 'Who will ascend to heaven?'"** —

that is, to bring the Messiah down — ⁷ or,

> **"'Who will** descend into Sh'ol?'"** —

that is, to bring the Messiah up from the dead. ⁸ What, then, does it say?

> **"The word is near you, in your mouth and in your heart."**ˡ —

that is, the word about trust which we proclaim, namely, ⁹ that if you acknowledge publicly with your mouth that Yeshua is Lord and trust in your heart that God raised him from the dead, you will be delivered. ¹⁰ For with the heart one goes on trusting and thus continues toward righteousness, while with the mouth one keeps on making public acknowledgement and thus continues toward deliverance. ¹¹ For the passage quoted says that *everyone* who **rests his trust on** him **will not be humiliated.**ᵐ ¹² That means that there is no difference between Jew and Gentile — ADONAI *is* the same for everyone, rich toward everyone who calls on him, ¹³ since *everyone* **who calls on the name of** ADONAI **will be delivered.**ⁿ

¹⁴ But how can they call on someone if they haven't trusted in him? And how can they trust in someone if they haven't heard about him? And how can they hear

---

ⁱ Isaiah 8:14
ˡ Deuteronomy 30:11–14
ʲ Isaiah 28:16
ᵐ Isaiah 28:16
ᵏ Leviticus 18:5
ⁿ Joel 3:5(2:32)

about someone if no one is proclaiming him? [15] And how can people proclaim him unless God sends them? — as the *Tanakh* puts it, **"How beautiful are the feet of those announcing good news about good things!"**[o]

[16] The problem is that they haven't all paid attention to the Good News and obeyed it. For Yesha'yahu says,

> **"A***DONAI***, who has trusted what he has heard from us?"**[p]

[17] So trust comes from what is heard, and what is heard comes through a word proclaimed about the Messiah.

[18] "But, I say, isn't it rather that they didn't hear?" No, they did hear —

> **"Their voice has gone out throughout the whole world**
> **and their words to the ends of the earth."**[q]

[19] "But, I say, isn't it rather that Isra'el didn't understand?"

> **"I will provoke you to jealousy over a non-nation,**
> **over a nation void of understanding I will make you angry."**[r]

[20] Moreover, Yesha'yahu boldly says,

> **"I was found by those who were not looking for me,**
> **I became known to those who did not ask for me"**;[s]

[21] but to Isra'el he says,

> **"All day long I held out my hands**
> **to a people who kept disobeying and contradicting."**[t]

11 [1] "In that case, I say, isn't it that God has repudiated his people?" Heaven forbid! For I myself am a son of Isra'el, from the **seed of Avraham,**[u] of the tribe of Binyamin. [2] **God has not repudiated his people,**[v] whom he chose in advance. Or don't you know what the *Tanakh* says about Eliyahu? He pleads with God against Isra'el, [3] **"A***DONAI***, they have killed your prophets and torn down your altars, and I'm the only one left, and now they want to kill me too!"**[w] [4] But what is God's answer to him? **"I have kept for myself seven thousand men who have not knelt down to Ba'al."**[x] [5] It's the same way in the present age: there is a remnant, chosen by grace. [6] (Now if it is by grace, it is accordingly not based on legalistic works; if it were otherwise, grace would no longer be grace.) [7] What follows is that Isra'el has not attained the goal for which she is striving. The ones chosen have obtained it, but the rest have been made stonelike, [8] just as the *Tanakh* says,

[o] Isaiah 52:7   [p] Isaiah 53:1   [q] Psalm 19:5(4)   [r] Deuteronomy 32:21
[s] Isaiah 65:1   [t] Isaiah 65:2   [u] 2 Chronicles 20:7, Psalm 105:6
[v] 1 Samuel 12:22, Psalm 94:14   [w] 1 Kings 19:10, 14   [x] 1 Kings 19:18

1414

"God has given them a spirit of dullness —
eyes that do not see
and ears that do not hear,
right down to the present day."[y]

[9] And David says,

"Let their dining table become for them
    a snare and a trap, a pitfall and a punishment.
[10] Let their eyes be darkened, so that they can't see,
    with their backs bent continually."[z]

[11] "In that case, I say, isn't it that they have stumbled with the result that they have permanently fallen away?" Heaven forbid! Quite the contrary, it is by means of their stumbling that the deliverance has come to the Gentiles, in order to **provoke them to jealousy**.[a] [12] Moreover, if their stumbling is bringing riches to the world — that is, if Isra'el's being placed temporarily in a condition less favored than that of the Gentiles is bringing riches to the latter — how much greater riches will Isra'el in its fullness bring them!

[13] However, to those of you who are Gentiles I say this: since I myself am an emissary sent to the Gentiles, I make known the importance of my work [14] in the hope that somehow I may **provoke** some of my own people **to jealousy** and save some of them! [15] For if their casting Yeshua aside means reconciliation for the world, what will their accepting him mean? It will be life from the dead!

[16] Now if the *hallah* offered as firstfruits is holy, so is the whole loaf. And if the root is holy, so are the branches. [17] But if some of the branches were broken off, and you — a wild olive — were grafted in among them and have become equal sharers in the rich root of the olive tree, [18] then don't boast as if you were better than the branches! However, if you do boast, remember that you are not supporting the root, the root is supporting you. [19] So you will say, "Branches were broken off so that I might be grafted in." [20] True, but so what? They were broken off because of their lack of trust. However, you keep your place only because of your trust. So don't be arrogant; on the contrary, be terrified! [21] For if God did not spare the natural branches, he certainly won't spare you! [22] So take a good look at God's kindness and his severity: on the one hand, severity toward those who fell off; but, on the other hand, God's kindness toward you — provided you maintain yourself in that kindness! Otherwise, you too will be cut off! [23] Moreover, the others, if they do not persist in their lack of trust, will be grafted in; because God is able to graft them back in. [24] For if you were cut out of what is by nature a wild olive tree and grafted, contrary to nature, into a cultivated olive tree, how much more will these natural branches be grafted back into their own olive tree!

[25] For, brothers, I want you to understand this truth which God formerly concealed but has now revealed, so that you won't imagine you know more than you actually do. It is that stoniness, to a degree, has come upon Isra'el, until the Gentile world enters in its fullness; [26] and that it is in this way that all Isra'el will be saved. As the *Tanakh* says,

---

[y] Deuteronomy 29:3(4), Isaiah 29:10   [z] Psalm 69:23–24(22–23)   [a] Deuteronomy 32:21

> **"Out of Tziyon will come the Redeemer;**
> **he will turn away ungodliness from Ya'akov**
> 27 **and this will be my covenant with them, . . .**
> **when I take away their sins."**[b]

²⁸ With respect to the Good News they are hated for your sake. But with respect to being chosen they are loved for the Patriarchs' sake, ²⁹ for God's free gifts and his calling are irrevocable. ³⁰ Just as you yourselves were disobedient to God before but have received mercy now because of Isra'el's disobedience; ³¹ so also Isra'el has been disobedient now, so that by your showing them the same mercy that God has shown you, they too may now receive God's mercy. ³² For God has shut up all mankind together in disobedience, in order that he might show mercy to all.

33   O the depth of the riches
            and the wisdom and knowledge of God!
        How inscrutable are his judgments!
            How unsearchable are his ways!

34   For, **'Who has known the mind of A**DONAI**?**
            Who has been his counselor?'[c]
35   Or, **'Who has given him anything**
            and made him pay it back?'[d]

36   For from him and through him
            and to him are all things.
        To him be the glory forever!
            Amen.

12 ¹ I exhort you, therefore, brothers, in view of God's mercies, to offer yourselves as a sacrifice, living and set apart for God. This will please him; it is the logical "Temple worship" for you. ² In other words, do not let yourselves be conformed to the standards of the *'olam hazeh.* Instead, keep letting yourselves be transformed by the renewing of your minds; so that you will know what God wants and will agree that what he wants is good, satisfying and able to succeed. ³ For I am telling every single one of you, through the grace that has been given to me, not to have exaggerated ideas about your own importance. Instead, develop a sober estimate of yourself based on the standard which God has given to each of you, namely, trust. ⁴ For just as there are many parts that compose one body, but the parts don't all have the same function; ⁵ so there are many of us, and in union with the Messiah we comprise one body, with each of us belonging to the others. ⁶ But we have gifts that differ and which are meant to be used according to the grace that has been given to us. If your gift is prophecy, use it to the extent of your trust; ⁷ if it is serving, use it to serve; if you are a teacher, use your gift in teaching; ⁸ if you are a counselor, use your gift to comfort and exhort; if you are someone who gives, do it simply and generously; if you are in a position of leadership, lead with diligence and zeal; if you are one who does acts of mercy, do them cheerfully.

---

b Isaiah 59:20–21, 27:9   *c* Isaiah 40:13   *d* Job 41:3(11)

⁹ Don't let love be a mere outward show. Recoil from what is evil, and cling to what is good. ¹⁰ Love each other devotedly and with brotherly love; and set examples for each other in showing respect. ¹¹ Don't be lazy when hard work is needed, but serve the Lord with spiritual fervor. ¹² Rejoice in your hope, be patient in your troubles, and continue steadfastly in prayer. ¹³ Share what you have with God's people, and practice hospitality.

¹⁴ Bless those who persecute you — bless them, don't curse them! ¹⁵ Rejoice with those who rejoice, and weep with those who weep. ¹⁶ Be sensitive to each other's needs — don't think yourselves better than others, but make humble people your friends. Don't be conceited. ¹⁷ Repay no one evil for evil, but try to do what everyone regards as good. ¹⁸ If possible, and to the extent that it depends on you, live in peace with all people. ¹⁹ Never seek revenge, my friends; instead, leave that to God's anger; for in the *Tanakh* it is written,

> "*ADONAI* says, 'Vengeance is my responsibility; I will repay.'"ᵉ

²⁰ On the contrary,

> "If your enemy is hungry, feed him;
> if he is thirsty, give him something to drink.
> For by doing this, you will heap
> fiery coals [of shame] on his head."ᶠ

²¹ Do not be conquered by evil, but conquer evil with good.

13 ¹ Everyone is to obey the governing authorities. For there is no authority that is not from God, and the existing authorities have been placed where they are by God. ² Therefore, whoever resists the authorities is resisting what God has instituted; and those who resist will bring judgment on themselves. ³ For rulers are no terror to good conduct, but to bad. Would you like to be unafraid of the person in authority? Then simply do what is good, and you will win his approval; ⁴ for he is God's servant, there for your benefit. But if you do what is wrong, be afraid! Because it is not for nothing that he holds the power of the sword; for he is God's servant, there as an avenger to punish wrongdoers. ⁵ Another reason to obey, besides fear of punishment, is for the sake of conscience. ⁶ This is also why you pay taxes; for the authorities are God's public officials, constantly attending to these duties. ⁷ Pay everyone what he is owed: if you owe the tax-collector, pay your taxes; if you owe the revenue-collector, pay revenue; if you owe someone respect, pay him respect; if you owe someone honor, pay him honor. ⁸ Don't owe anyone anything — except to love one another; for whoever loves his fellow human being has fulfilled *Torah*. ⁹ For the commandments, **"Don't commit adultery," "Don't murder," "Don't steal," "Don't covet,"**ᵍ and any others are summed up in this one rule: **"Love your neighbor as yourself."**ʰ ¹⁰ Love does not do harm to a neighbor; therefore love is the fullness of *Torah*.

ᵉ Deuteronomy 32:41
ᵍ Exodus 20:13–14(17), Deuteronomy 5:17–18(21)

ᶠ Proverbs 25:21–22
ʰ Leviticus 19:18

¹¹ Besides all this, you know at what point of history we stand; so it is high time for you to rouse yourselves from sleep; for the final deliverance is nearer than when we first came to trust. ¹² The night is almost over, the day is almost here. So let us put aside the deeds of darkness and arm ourselves with the weapons of light. ¹³ Let us live properly, as people do in the daytime — not partying and getting drunk, not engaging in sexual immorality and other excesses, not quarrelling and being jealous. ¹⁴ Instead, clothe yourselves with the Lord Yeshua the Messiah; and don't waste your time thinking about how to provide for the sinful desires of your old nature.

14 ¹ Now as for a person whose trust is weak, welcome him — but not to get into arguments over opinions. ² One person has the trust that will allow him to eat anything, while another whose trust is weak eats only vegetables. ³ The one who eats anything must not look down on the one who abstains; and the abstainer must not pass judgment on the one who eats anything, because God has accepted him — ⁴ who are you to pass judgment on someone else's servant? It is before his own master that he will stand or fall; and the fact is that he will stand, because the Lord is able to make him stand.

⁵ One person considers some days more holy than others, while someone else regards them as being all alike. What is important is for each to be fully convinced in his own mind. ⁶ He who observes a day as special does so to honor the Lord. Also he who eats anything, eats to honor the Lord, since he gives thanks to God; likewise the abstainer abstains to honor the Lord, and he too gives thanks to God. ⁷ For none of us lives only in relation to himself, and none of us dies only in relation to himself; ⁸ for if we live, we live in relation to the Lord; and if we die, we die in relation to the Lord. So whether we live or die, we belong to the Lord — ⁹ indeed, it was for this very reason that the Messiah died and came back to life, so that he might be Lord of both the dead and the living. ¹⁰ You then, why do you pass judgment on your brother? Or why do you look down on your brother? For all of us will stand before God's judgment seat; ¹¹ since it is written in the *Tanakh*,

> **"As I live, says Adonai, every knee will bend before me,**
> **and every tongue will publicly acknowledge God."**[i]

¹² So then, every one of us will have to give an account of himself to God.

¹³ Therefore, let's stop passing judgment on each other! Instead, make this one judgment — not to put a stumbling block or a snare in a brother's way. ¹⁴ I know — that is, I have been persuaded by the Lord Yeshua the Messiah — that nothing is unclean in itself. But if a person considers something unclean, then for him it is unclean; ¹⁵ and if your brother is being upset by the food you eat, your life is no longer one of love. Do not, by your eating habits, destroy someone for whom the Messiah died! ¹⁶ Do not let what you know to be good, be spoken of as bad; ¹⁷ for the Kingdom of God is not eating and drinking, but righteousness, *shalom* and joy in the *Ruach HaKodesh*. ¹⁸ Anyone who serves the Messiah in this fashion both pleases God and wins the approval of other people.

---

[i] Isaiah 45:23

[19] So then, let us pursue the things that make for *shalom* and mutual upbuilding. [20] Don't tear down God's work for the sake of food. True enough, all things are clean; but it is wrong for anybody by his eating to cause someone to fall away. [21] What is good is not to eat meat or drink wine or do anything that causes your brother to stumble. [22] The belief you hold about such things, keep between yourself and God. Happy the person who is free of self-condemnation when he approves of something! [23] But the doubter comes under condemnation if he eats, because his action is not based on trust. And anything not based on trust is a sin.

15 [1] So we who are strong have a duty to bear the weaknesses of those who are not strong, rather than please ourselves. [2] Each of us should please his neighbor and act for his good, thus building him up. [3] For even the Messiah did not please himself; rather, as the *Tanakh* says, **'The insults of those insulting you fell on me.'**[j] [4] For everything written in the past was written to teach us, so that with the encouragement of the *Tanakh* we might patiently hold on to our hope. [5] And may God, the source of encouragement and patience, give you the same attitude among yourselves as the Messiah Yeshua had, [6] so that with one accord and with one voice you may glorify the God and Father of our Lord Yeshua the Messiah.

[7] So welcome each other, just as the Messiah has welcomed you into God's glory. [8] For I say that the Messiah became a servant of the Jewish people in order to show God's truthfulness by making good his promises to the Patriarchs, [9] and in order to show his mercy by causing the Gentiles to glorify God — as it is written in the *Tanakh*,

> **"Because of this I will acknowledge you among the Gentiles**
> **and sing praise to your name."**[k]

[10] And again it says,

> **"Gentiles, rejoice with his people."**[l]

[11] And again,

> **"Praise ADONAI, all Gentiles!**
> **Let all peoples praise him!"**[m]

[12] And again, Yesha'yahu says,

> **"The root of Yishai will come,**
> **he who arises to rule Gentiles;**
> **Gentiles will put their hope in him."**[n]

[13] May God, the source of hope, fill you completely with joy and *shalom* as you continue trusting, so that by the power of the *Ruach HaKodesh* you may overflow with hope.

---

[j] Psalm 69:10(9)   [k] 2 Samuel 22:50, Psalm 18:50(49)   [l] Deuteronomy 32:43
[m] Psalm 117:1   [n] Isaiah 11:10

¹⁴Now I myself am convinced, my brothers, that you are full of goodness, filled with knowledge and well able to counsel each other. ¹⁵But on some points I have written you quite boldly by way of reminding you about them, because of the grace God has given me ¹⁶to be a servant of the Messiah Yeshua for the Gentiles, with the priestly duty of presenting the Good News of God, so that the Gentiles may be an acceptable offering, made holy by the *Ruach HaKodesh.*

¹⁷In union with the Messiah Yeshua, then, I have reason to be proud of my service to God; ¹⁸for I will not dare speak of anything except what the Messiah has accomplished through me to bring the Gentiles to obedience by my words and deeds, ¹⁹through the power of signs and miracles, through the power of the Spirit of God. So from Yerushalayim all the way to Illyricum I have fully proclaimed the Good News of the Messiah. ²⁰I have always made it my ambition to proclaim the Good News where the Messiah was not yet known, so that I would not be building on someone else's foundation, ²¹but rather, as the *Tanakh* puts it,

**"Those who have not been told about him will see,
and those who have not heard will understand."**ᵒ

²²This is also why I have so often been prevented from visiting you. ²³But now, since there is no longer a place in these regions that needs me, and since I have wanted for many years to come to you, ²⁴I hope to see you as I pass through on my way to Spain, and to have you help me travel there after I have enjoyed your company awhile.

²⁵But now I am going to Yerushalayim with aid for God's people there. ²⁶For Macedonia and Achaia thought it would be good to make some contribution to the poor among God's people in Yerushalayim. ²⁷They were pleased to do it, but the fact is that they owe it to them. For if the Gentiles have shared with the Jews in spiritual matters, then the Gentiles clearly have a duty to help the Jews in material matters. ²⁸So when I have finished this task and made certain that they have received this fruit, I will leave for Spain and visit you on my way there; ²⁹and I know that when I come to you, it will be with the full measure of the Messiah's blessings. ³⁰And now I urge you, brothers, by our Lord Yeshua the Messiah and by the love of the Spirit, to join me in my struggle by praying to God on my behalf ³¹that I will be rescued from the unbelievers in Y'hudah, and that my service for Yerushalayim will be acceptable to God's people there. ³²Then, if it is God's will, I will come to you with joy and have a time of rest among you. ³³Now may the God of *shalom* be with you all. *Amen.*

16 ¹I am introducing to you our sister Phoebe, *shammash* of the congregation at Cenchrea, ²so that you may welcome her in the Lord, as God's people should, and give her whatever assistance she may need from you; for she has been a big help to many people — including myself.

³Give my greetings to Priscilla and Aquila, my fellow workers for the Messiah Yeshua. ⁴They risked their necks to save my life; not only I thank them, but also all the Messianic communities among the Gentiles. ⁵And give my greetings to the congregation that meets in their house.

ᵒIsaiah 52:15

Give my greetings to my dear friend Epaenetus, who was the first person in the province of Asia to put his trust in the Messiah.

⁶ Give my greetings to Miryam, who has worked very hard for you.

⁷ Greetings to Andronicus and Junia, relatives of mine who were in prison with me. They are well known among the emissaries; also they came to trust in the Messiah before I did.

⁸ Greetings to Ampliatus, my dear friend in the Lord.

⁹ Greetings to Urbanus, our fellow worker for the Messiah, and to my dear friend Stachys.

¹⁰ Greetings to Appeles, whose trust in the Messiah has been tested and proved. Greet those in the household of Aristobulus.

¹¹ Greet my relative, Herodion.

¹² Greet Tryphaena and Tryphosa, women who are working hard for the Lord.

Greet my dear friend Persis, another woman who has done a lot of hard work for the Lord.

¹³ Greet Rufus, chosen by the Lord, and his mother, who has been a mother to me too.

¹⁴ Greet Asyncritus, Phlegon, Hermes, Patrobas, Hermas and the brothers who are with them.

¹⁵ Greet Philologus, Julia, Nereus and his sister, and Olympas, and all of God's people who are with them.

¹⁶ Greet one another with a holy kiss. All the Messiah's congregations send their greetings to you.

¹⁷ I urge you, brothers, to watch out for those who cause divisions and put snares alongside the teaching in which you have been trained — keep away from them. ¹⁸ For men like these are not serving our Lord the Messiah but their own belly; by smooth talk and flattery they deceive the innocent. ¹⁹ For everyone has heard about your obedience; therefore I rejoice over you. However, I want you to be wise concerning good, but innocent concerning evil. ²⁰ And God, the source of *shalom*, will soon crush the Adversary under your feet.

The grace of our Lord Yeshua be with you.

²¹ Timothy, my fellow-worker, sends greetings to you; so do Lucius, Jason and Sosipater, my relatives.

²² I, Tertius, the one writing down this letter, greet you in the Lord.

²³ My host Gaius, in whose home the whole congregation meets, greets you. Erastus the city treasurer and brother Quartus greet you. ²⁴*

25   Now to God, who can strengthen you, according to my Good News,
        in harmony with the revelation of the secret truth
        which is the proclamation of Yeshua the Messiah,
        kept hidden in silence for ages and ages,

26   but manifested now through prophetic writings,
        in keeping with the command of God the Eternal,
        and communicated to all the Gentiles

---

* Some manuscripts have verse 24: The grace of our Lord Yeshua the Messiah be with you all. *Amen.*

to promote in them trust-grounded obedience —
²⁷ to the only wise God, through Yeshua the Messiah,
be the glory forever and ever!

Amen.

The First Letter from Yeshua's Emissary Sha'ul (Paul)
to the Messianic Community in Corinth

1 CORINTHIANS

1 ¹ From: Sha'ul, called by God's will to be an emissary of the Messiah Yeshua; and from brother Sosthenes

² To: God's Messianic community in Corinth, consisting of those who have been set apart by Yeshua the Messiah and called to be God's holy people — along with everyone everywhere who calls on the name of our Lord Yeshua the Messiah, their Lord as well as ours:

³ Grace to you and *shalom* from God our Father and the Lord Yeshua the Messiah.

⁴ I thank my God always for you because of God's love and kindness given to you through the Messiah Yeshua, ⁵ in that you have been enriched by him in so many ways, particularly in power of speech and depth of knowledge. ⁶ Indeed, the testimony about the Messiah has become firmly established in you; ⁷ so that you are not lacking any spiritual gift and are eagerly awaiting the revealing of our Lord Yeshua the Messiah. ⁸ He will enable you to hold out until the end and thus be blameless on the Day of our Lord Yeshua the Messiah — ⁹ God is trustworthy: it was he who called you into fellowship with his Son, Yeshua the Messiah, our Lord.

¹⁰ Nevertheless, brothers, I call on you in the name of our Lord Yeshua the Messiah to agree, all of you, in what you say, and not to let yourselves remain split into factions but be restored to having a common mind and a common purpose. ¹¹ For some of Chloe's people have made it known to me, my brothers, that there are quarrels among you. ¹² I say this because one of you says, "I follow Sha'ul"; another says, "I follow Apollos"; another, "I follow Kefa"; while still another says, "I follow the Messiah!" ¹³ Has the Messiah been split in pieces? Was it Sha'ul who was put to death on a stake for you? Were you immersed into the name of Sha'ul? ¹⁴ I thank God that I didn't immerse any of you except Crispus and Gaius — ¹⁵ otherwise someone might say that you were indeed immersed into my name. ¹⁶ (Oh yes, I did also immerse Stephanas and his household; beyond that, I can't remember whether I immersed anyone else.)

¹⁷ For the Messiah did not send me to immerse but to proclaim the Good News — and to do it without relying on "wisdom" that consists of mere rhetoric, so as not to rob the Messiah's execution-stake of its power. ¹⁸ For the message about the execution-stake is nonsense to those in the process of being destroyed, but to us in the process of being saved it is the power of God. ¹⁹ Indeed, the *Tanakh* says,

> **"I will destroy the wisdom of the wise**
> **and frustrate the intelligence of the intelligent."**[a]

---

[a] Isaiah 29:14

1423

²⁰ Where does that leave the philosopher, the *Torah*-teacher, or any of today's think-ers? Hasn't God made this world's wisdom look pretty foolish? ²¹ For God's wisdom ordained that the world, using its own wisdom, would not come to know him. There-fore God decided to use the "nonsense" of what we proclaim as his means of saving those who come to trust in it. ²² Precisely because Jews ask for signs and Greeks try to find wisdom, ²³ we go on proclaiming a Messiah executed on a stake as a criminal! To Jews this is an obstacle, and to Greeks it is nonsense; ²⁴ but to those who are called, both Jews and Greeks, this same Messiah is God's power and God's wisdom! ²⁵ For God's "nonsense" is wiser than humanity's "wisdom."

And God's "weakness" is stronger than humanity's "strength." ²⁶ Just look at yourselves, brothers — look at those whom God has called! Not many of you are wise by the world's standards, not many wield power or boast noble birth. ²⁷ But God chose what the world considers nonsense in order to shame the wise; God chose what the world considers weak in order to shame the strong; ²⁸ and God chose what the world looks down on as common or regards as nothing in order to bring to nothing what the world considers important; ²⁹ so that no one should boast before God. ³⁰ It is his doing that you are united with the Messiah Yeshua. He has become wisdom for us from God, and righteousness and holiness and redemption as well! ³¹ Therefore — as the *Tanakh* says — **"Let anyone who wants to boast, boast about ADONAI."**[b]

2 ¹ As for me, brothers, when I arrived among you, it was not with surpassing eloquence or wisdom that I came announcing to you the previously concealed truth about God; ² for I had decided that while I was with you I would forget everything except Yeshua the Messiah, and even him only as someone who had been executed on a stake as a criminal. ³ Also I myself was with you as somebody weak, nervous and shaking all over from fear; ⁴ and neither the delivery nor the content of my message relied on compelling words of "wisdom" but on a demonstration of the power of the Spirit, ⁵ so that your trust might not rest on human wisdom but on God's power.

⁶ Yet there is a wisdom that we are speaking to those who are mature enough for it. But it is not the wisdom of this world or of this world's leaders, who are in the process of passing away. ⁷ On the contrary, we are communicating a secret wisdom from God which has been hidden until now but which, before history began, God had decreed would bring us glory. ⁸ Not one of this world's leaders has understood it; because if they had, they would not have executed the Lord from whom this glory flows. ⁹ But, as the *Tanakh* says,

> **"No eye has seen, no ear has heard**
> **and no one's heart has imagined**
> **all the things that God has prepared**
> **for those who love him."**[c]

¹⁰ It is to us, however, that God has revealed these things. How? Through the Spirit. For the Spirit probes all things, even the profoundest depths of God. ¹¹ For who knows the inner workings of a person except the person's own spirit inside him? So too no one knows the inner workings of God except God's Spirit. ¹² Now we have

---

[b] Jeremiah 9:23(24)   [c] Isaiah 64:3(4), 52:15

not received the spirit of the world but the Spirit of God, so that we might understand the things God has so freely given us. ¹³ These are the things we are talking about when we avoid the manner of speaking that human wisdom would dictate and instead use a manner of speaking taught by the Spirit, by which we explain things of the Spirit to people who have the Spirit. ¹⁴ Now the natural man does not receive the things from the Spirit of God — to him they are nonsense! Moreover, he is unable to grasp them, because they are evaluated through the Spirit. ¹⁵ But the person who has the Spirit can evaluate everything, while no one is in a position to evaluate him.

¹⁶   **For who has known the mind of ADONAI?**
       Who will counsel him?[d]

But we have the mind of the Messiah!

3 ¹ As for me, brothers, I couldn't talk to you as spiritual people but as worldly people, as babies, so far as experience with the Messiah is concerned. ² I gave you milk, not solid food, because you were not yet ready for it. But you aren't ready for it now either! ³ For you are still worldly! Isn't it obvious from all the jealousy and quarrelling among you that you are worldly and living by merely human standards? ⁴ For when one says, "I follow Sha'ul" and another, "I follow Apollos," aren't you being merely human? ⁵ After all, what is Apollos? What is Sha'ul? Only servants through whom you came to trust. Indeed, it was the Lord who brought you to trust through one of us or through another. ⁶ I planted the seed, and Apollos watered it, but it was God who made it grow. ⁷ So neither the planter nor the waterer is anything, only God who makes things grow — ⁸ planter and waterer are the same.

However, each will be rewarded according to his work. ⁹ For we are God's co-workers; you are God's field, God's building. ¹⁰ Using the grace God gave me, I laid a foundation, like a skilled master-builder; and another man is building on it. But let each one be careful how he builds. ¹¹ For no one can lay any foundation other than the one already laid, which is Yeshua the Messiah. ¹² Some will use gold, silver or precious stones in building on this foundation; while others will use wood, grass or straw. ¹³ But each one's work will be shown for what it is; the Day will disclose it, because it will be revealed by fire — the fire will test the quality of each one's work. ¹⁴ If the work someone has built on the foundation survives, he will receive a reward; ¹⁵ if it is burned up, he will have to bear the loss: he will still escape with his life, but it will be like escaping through a fire.

¹⁶ Don't you know that you people are God's temple and that God's Spirit lives in you? ¹⁷ So if anyone destroys God's temple, God will destroy him. For God's temple is holy, and you yourselves are that temple.

¹⁸ Let no one fool himself. If someone among you thinks he is wise (by this world's standards), let him become "foolish," so that he may become really wise. ¹⁹ For the wisdom of this world is nonsense, as far as God is concerned; inasmuch as the *Tanakh* says, **"He traps the wise in their own cleverness,"**[e] ²⁰ and again, **"ADONAI knows that the thoughts of the wise are worthless."**[f] ²¹ So let no one boast about

---

[d] Isaiah 40:13   [e] Job 5:13   [f] Psalm 94:11

human beings, for all things are yours — ²² whether Sha'ul or Apollos or Kefa or the world or life or death or the present or the future: they all belong to you, ²³ and you belong to the Messiah, and the Messiah belongs to God.

4 ¹ So, you should regard us as the Messiah's servants, as trustees of God's secret truths. ² Now the one thing that is asked of a trustee is that he be found trustworthy. ³ And it matters very little to me how I am evaluated by you or by any human court; in fact, I don't even evaluate myself. ⁴ I am not aware of anything against me, but this does not make me innocent. The one who is evaluating me is the Lord. ⁵ So don't pronounce judgment prematurely, before the Lord comes; for he will bring to light what is now hidden in darkness; he will expose the motives of people's hearts; and then each will receive from God whatever praise he deserves.

⁶ Now in what I have said here, brothers, I have used myself and Apollos as examples to teach you not to go beyond what the *Tanakh* says, proudly taking the side of one leader against another. ⁷ After all, what makes you so special? What do you have that you didn't receive as a gift? And if in fact it was a gift, why do you boast as if it weren't? ⁸ You are glutted already? You are rich already? You have become kings, even though we are not? Well, I wish you really were kings, so that we might share the kingship with you! ⁹ For I think God has been placing us emissaries on display at the tail of the parade, like men condemned to die in the public arena: we have become a spectacle before the whole universe, angels as well as men. ¹⁰ For the Messiah's sake we are fools, but united with the Messiah you are wise! We are weak, but you are strong; you are honored, but we are dishonored. ¹¹ Till this very moment we go hungry and thirsty, we are dressed in rags, we are treated roughly, we wander from place to place, ¹² we exhaust ourselves working with our own hands for our living. When we are cursed, we keep on blessing; when we are persecuted, we go on putting up with it; ¹³ when we are slandered, we continue making our appeal. We are the world's garbage, the scum of the earth — yes, to this moment!

¹⁴ I am not writing you this to make you feel ashamed, but, as my dear children, to confront you and get you to change. ¹⁵ For even if you have ten thousand trainers in connection with the Messiah, you do not have many fathers; for in connection with the Messiah Yeshua it was I who became your father by means of the Good News. ¹⁶ Therefore I urge you to imitate me. ¹⁷ This is why I have sent you Timothy, my beloved and trustworthy child in the Lord. He will remind you of the way of life I follow in union with the Messiah Yeshua and teach everywhere in every congregation.

¹⁸ When I didn't come to visit you, some of you became arrogant. ¹⁹ But I am coming to you soon, if the Lord wills; and I will take cognizance not of the talk of these arrogant people but of their power. ²⁰ For the Kingdom of God is not a matter of words but of power. ²¹ Which do you prefer — should I come to you with a stick? or with love in a spirit of gentleness?

5 ¹ It is actually being reported that there is sexual sin among you, and it is sexual sin of a kind that is condemned even by pagans — a man is living with his stepmother! ² And you stay proud? Shouldn't you rather have felt some sadness that would have led you to remove from your company the man who has done this thing? ³ For I myself, even though I am absent physically, am with you spiritually; and I have already judged the man who has done this as if I were present. ⁴ In the name of the

Lord Yeshua, when you are assembled, with me present spiritually and the power of our Lord Yeshua among us, ⁵ hand over such a person to the Adversary for his old nature to be destroyed, so that his spirit may be saved in the Day of the Lord.

⁶ Your boasting is not good. Don't you know the saying, "It takes only a little *hametz* to leaven a whole batch of dough?" ⁷ Get rid of the old *hametz*, so that you can be a new batch of dough, because in reality you are unleavened. For our *Pesach* lamb, the Messiah, has been sacrificed. ⁸ So let us celebrate the *Seder* not with leftover *hametz*, the *hametz* of wickedness and evil, but with the *matzah* of purity and truth.

⁹ In my earlier letter I wrote you not to associate with people who engage in sexual immorality. ¹⁰ I didn't mean the sexually immoral people outside your community, or the greedy, or the thieves or the idol-worshippers — for then you would have to leave the world altogether! ¹¹ No, what I wrote you was not to associate with anyone who is supposedly a brother but who also engages in sexual immorality, is greedy, worships idols, is abusive, gets drunk or steals. With such a person you shouldn't even eat! ¹² For what business is it of mine to judge outsiders? Isn't it those who are part of the community that you should be judging? ¹³ God will judge those who are outside. Just **expel the evildoer from among yourselves.**[g]

6 ¹ How dare one of you with a complaint against another go to court before pagan judges and not before God's people? ² Don't you know that God's people are going to judge the universe? If you are going to judge the universe, are you incompetent to judge these minor matters? ³ Don't you know that we will judge angels, not to mention affairs of everyday life? ⁴ So if you require judgments about matters of everyday life, why do you put them in front of men who have no standing in the Messianic Community? ⁵ I say, shame on you! Can it be that there isn't one person among you wise enough to be able to settle a dispute between brothers? ⁶ Instead, a brother brings a lawsuit against another brother, and that before unbelievers!

⁷ Actually, if you are bringing lawsuits against each other, it is already a defeat for you. Why not rather be wronged? Why not rather be cheated? ⁸ Instead, you yourselves wrong and cheat; and you do it to your own brothers! ⁹ Don't you know that unrighteous people will have no share in the Kingdom of God? Don't delude yourselves — people who engage in sex before marriage, who worship idols, who engage in sex after marriage with someone other than their spouse, who engage in active or passive homosexuality, ¹⁰ who steal, who are greedy, who get drunk, who assail people with contemptuous language, who rob — none of them will share in the Kingdom of God. ¹¹ Some of you used to do these things. But you have cleansed yourselves, you have been set apart for God, you have come to be counted righteous through the power of the Lord Yeshua the Messiah and the Spirit of our God.

¹² You say, "For me, everything is permitted"? Maybe, but not everything is helpful. "For me, everything is permitted"? Maybe, but as far as I am concerned, I am not going to let anything gain control over me. ¹³ "Food is meant for the stomach and the stomach for food"? Maybe, but God will put an end to both of them. Anyhow, the body is not meant for sexual immorality but for the Lord, and the Lord is for the body. ¹⁴ God raised up the Lord, and he will raise us up too by his power.

---

[g] Deuteronomy 13:6(5); 17:7,12; 19:19; 21:21; 22:21, 24; 24:7

¹⁵ Don't you know that your bodies are parts of the Messiah? So, am I to take parts of the Messiah and make them parts of a prostitute? Heaven forbid! ¹⁶ Don't you know that a man who joins himself to a prostitute becomes physically one with her? For the *Tanakh* says, **"The two will become one flesh";**[h] ¹⁷ but the person who is joined to the Lord is one spirit. ¹⁸ Run from sexual immorality! Every other sin a person commits is outside the body, but the fornicator sins against his own body. ¹⁹ Or don't you know that your body is a temple for the *Ruach HaKodesh* who lives inside you, whom you received from God? The fact is, you don't belong to yourselves; ²⁰ for you were bought at a price. So use your bodies to glorify God.

7 ¹ Now to deal with the questions you wrote about: "Is it good for a man to keep away from women?" ² Well, because of the danger of sexual immorality, let each man have his own wife and each woman her own husband. ³ The husband should give his wife what she is entitled to in the marriage relationship, and the wife should do the same for her husband. ⁴ The wife is not in charge of her own body, but her husband is; likewise, the husband is not in charge of his own body, but his wife is. ⁵ Do not deprive each other, except for a limited time, by mutual agreement, and then only so as to have extra time for prayer; but afterwards, come together again. Otherwise, because of your lack of self-control, you may succumb to the Adversary's temptation. ⁶ I am giving you this as a suggestion, not as a command. ⁷ Actually, I wish everyone were like me; but each has his own gift from God, one this, another that.

⁸ Now to the single people and the widows I say that it is fine if they remain unmarried like me; ⁹ but if they can't exercise self-control, they should get married; because it is better to get married than to keep burning with sexual desire.

¹⁰ To those who are married I have a command, and it is not from me but from the Lord: a woman is not to separate herself from her husband. ¹¹ But if she does separate herself, she is to remain single or be reconciled with her husband. Also, a husband is not to leave his wife.

¹² To the rest I say — I, not the Lord: if any brother has a wife who is not a believer, and she is satisfied to go on living with him, he should not leave her. ¹³ Also, if any woman has an unbelieving husband who is satisfied to go on living with her, she is not to leave him. ¹⁴ For the unbelieving husband has been set aside for God by the wife, and the unbelieving wife has been set aside for God by the brother — otherwise your children would be "unclean," but as it is, they are set aside for God. ¹⁵ But if the unbelieving spouse separates himself, let him be separated. In circumstances like these, the brother or sister is not enslaved — God has called you to a life of peace. ¹⁶ For how do you know, wife, whether you will save your husband? Or how do you know, husband, whether you will save your wife?

¹⁷ Only let each person live the life the Lord has assigned him and live it in the condition he was in when God called him. This is the rule I lay down in all the congregations. ¹⁸ Was someone already circumcised when he was called? Then he should not try to remove the marks of his circumcision. Was someone uncircumcised when he was called? He shouldn't undergo *b'rit-milah*. ¹⁹ Being circumcised means nothing, and being uncircumcised means nothing; what does mean something is

---

[h] Genesis 2:24

keeping God's commandments. ²⁰ Each person should remain in the condition he was in when he was called.

²¹ Were you a slave when you were called? Well, don't let it bother you; although if you can gain your freedom, take advantage of the opportunity. ²² For a person who was a slave when he was called is the Lord's freedman; likewise, someone who was a free man when he was called is a slave of the Messiah. ²³ You were bought at a price, so do not become slaves of other human beings. ²⁴ Brothers, let each one remain with God in the condition in which he was called.

²⁵ Now the question about the unmarried: I do not have a command from the Lord, but I offer an opinion as one who by the Lord's mercy is worthy to be trusted. ²⁶ I suppose that in a time of stress like the present it is good for a person to stay as he is. ²⁷ That means that if a man has a wife, he should not seek to be free of her; and if he is unmarried, he should not look for a wife. ²⁸ But if you marry you do not sin, and if a girl marries she does not sin. It is just that those who get married will have the normal problems of married life, and I would rather spare you. ²⁹ What I am saying, brothers, is that there is not much time left: from now on a man with a wife should live as if he had none — ³⁰ and those who are sad should live as if they weren't, those who are happy as if they weren't, ³¹ and those who deal in worldly affairs as if not engrossed in them — because the present scheme of things in this world won't last much longer. ³² What I want is for you to be free of concern. An unmarried man concerns himself with the Lord's affairs, ³³ with how to please the Lord; but the married man concerns himself with the world's affairs, with how to please his wife; ³⁴ and he finds himself split. Likewise the woman who is no longer married or the girl who has never been married concerns herself with the Lord's affairs, with how to be holy both physically and spiritually; but the married woman concerns herself with the world's affairs, with how to please her husband. ³⁵ I am telling you this for your own benefit, not to put restrictions on you — I am simply concerned that you live in a proper manner and serve the Lord with undivided devotion.

³⁶ Now if a man thinks he is behaving dishonorably by treating his fiancée this way, and if there is strong sexual desire, so that marriage is what ought to happen; then let him do what he wants — he is not sinning: let them get married. ³⁷ But if a man has firmly made up his mind, being under no compulsion but having complete control over his will, if he has decided within himself to keep his fiancée a virgin, he will be doing well. ³⁸ So the man who marries his fiancée will do well, and the man who doesn't marry will do better.

³⁹ A wife is bound to her husband as long as he lives, but if the husband dies she is free to marry anyone she wishes, provided he is a believer in the Lord. ⁴⁰ However, in my opinion, she will be happier if she remains unmarried, and in saying this I think I have God's Spirit.

8 ¹ Now about food sacrificed to idols: we know that, as you say, "We all have knowledge." Yes, that is so, but "knowledge" puffs a person up with pride; whereas love builds up. ² The person who thinks he "knows" something doesn't yet know in the way he ought to know. ³ However, if someone loves God, God knows him.

⁴ So, as for eating food sacrificed to idols, we "know" that, as you say, "An idol has no real existence in the world, and there is only one God." ⁵ For even if there are so-called "gods," either in heaven or on earth — as in fact there are "gods" and

"lords" galore — ⁶yet for us there is one God, the Father, from whom all things come and for whom we exist; and one Lord, Yeshua the Messiah, through whom were created all things and through whom we have our being.

⁷But not everyone has this knowledge. Moreover, some people are still so accustomed to idols that when they eat food which has been sacrificed to them, they think of it as really affected by the idol; and their consciences, being weak, are thus defiled. ⁸Now food will not improve our relationship with God — we will be neither poorer if we abstain nor richer if we eat. ⁹However watch out that your mastery of the situation does not become a stumbling block to the weak. ¹⁰You have this "knowledge"; but suppose someone with a weak conscience sees you sitting, eating a meal in the temple of an idol. Won't he be built up wrongly to eat this food which has been sacrificed to idols? ¹¹Thus by your "knowledge" this weak person is destroyed, this brother for whom the Messiah died; ¹²and so, when you sin against the brothers by wounding their conscience when it is weak, you are sinning against the Messiah!

¹³To sum up, if food will be a snare for my brother, I will never eat meat again, lest I cause my brother to sin.

9 ¹Am I not a free man? Am I not an emissary of the Messiah? Haven't I seen Yeshua our Lord? And aren't you yourselves the result of my work for the Lord? ²Even if to others I am not an emissary, at least I am to you; for you are living proof that I am the Lord's emissary. ³That is my defense when people put me under examination.

⁴Don't we have the right to be given food and drink? ⁵Don't we have the right to take along with us a believing wife, as do the other emissaries, also the Lord's brothers and Kefa? ⁶Or are Bar-Nabba and I the only ones required to go on working for our living? ⁷Did you ever hear of a soldier paying his own expenses? or of a farmer planting a vineyard without eating its grapes? Who shepherds a flock without drinking some of the milk? ⁸What I am saying is not based merely on human authority, because the *Torah* says the same thing — ⁹for in the *Torah* of Moshe it is written, **"You are not to put a muzzle on an ox when it is treading out the grain."***ⁱ* If God is concerned about cattle, ¹⁰all the more does he say this for our sakes. Yes, it was written for us, meaning that he who plows and he who threshes should work expecting to get a share of the crop. ¹¹If we have sown spiritual seed among you, is it too much if we reap a material harvest from you? ¹²If others are sharing in this right to be supported by you, don't we have a greater claim to it?

But we don't make use of this right. Rather, we put up with all kinds of things so as not to impede in any way the Good News about the Messiah. ¹³Don't you know that those who work in the Temple get their food from the Temple, and those who serve at the altar get a share of the sacrifices offered there? ¹⁴In the same way, the Lord directed that those who proclaim the Good News should get their living from the Good News.

¹⁵But I have not made use of any of these rights. Nor am I writing now to secure them for myself, for I would rather die than be deprived of my ground for boasting! ¹⁶For I can't boast merely because I proclaim the Good News — this I do from inner compulsion: woe is me if I don't proclaim the Good News! ¹⁷For if I do this willingly, I have a reward; but if I do it unwillingly, I still do it, simply because I've

---

*ⁱ*Deuteronomy 25:4

been entrusted with a job. [18] So then, what is my reward? Just this: that in proclaiming the Good News I can make it available free of charge, without making use of the rights to which it entitles me.

[19] For although I am a free man, not bound to do anyone's bidding, I have made myself a slave to all in order to win as many people as possible. [20] That is, with Jews, what I did was put myself in the position of a Jew, in order to win Jews. With people in subjection to a legalistic perversion of the *Torah*, I put myself in the position of someone under such legalism, in order to win those under this legalism, even though I myself am not in subjection to a legalistic perversion of the *Torah*. [21] With those who live outside the framework of *Torah*, I put myself in the position of someone outside the *Torah* in order to win those outside the *Torah* — although I myself am not outside the framework of God's *Torah* but within the framework of *Torah* as upheld by the Messiah. [22] With the "weak" I became "weak," in order to win the "weak." With all kinds of people I have become all kinds of things, so that in all kinds of circumstances I might save at least some of them.

[23] But I do it all because of the rewards promised by the Good News, so that I may share in them along with the others who come to trust. [24] Don't you know that in a race all the runners compete, but only one wins the prize? So then, run to win! [25] Now every athlete in training submits himself to strict discipline, and he does it just to win a laurel wreath that will soon wither away. But we do it to win a crown that will last forever. [26] Accordingly, I don't run aimlessly but straight for the finish line; I don't shadow-box but try to make every punch count. [27] I treat my body hard and make it my slave so that, after proclaiming the Good News to others, I myself will not be disqualified.

10 [1] For, brothers, I don't want you to miss the significance of what happened to our fathers. All of them were guided by the pillar of cloud, and they all passed through the sea, [2] and in connection with the cloud and with the sea they all immersed themselves into Moshe, [3] also they all ate the same food from the Spirit, [4] and they all drank the same drink from the Spirit — for they drank from a Spirit-sent Rock which followed them, and that Rock was the Messiah. [5] Yet with the majority of them God was not pleased, so their bodies were strewn across the desert.

[6] Now these things took place as prefigurative historical events, warning us not to set our hearts on evil things as they did. [7] Don't be idolaters, as some of them were — as the *Tanakh* puts it, **"The people sat down to eat and drink, then got up to indulge in revelry."**[j] [8] And let us not engage in sexual immorality, as some of them did, with the consequence that 23,000 died in a single day. [9] And let us not put the Messiah to the test, as some of them did, and were destroyed by snakes. [10] And don't grumble, as some of them did, and were destroyed by the Destroying Angel.

[11] These things happened to them as prefigurative historical events, and they were written down as a warning to us who are living in the *acharit-hayamim*. [12] Therefore, let anyone who thinks he is standing up be careful not to fall! [13] No temptation has seized you beyond what people normally experience, and God can be trusted not to allow you to be tempted beyond what you can bear. On the contrary, along with the temptation he will also provide the way out, so that you will be able to endure.

---

[j] Exodus 32:6

¹⁴ Therefore, my dear friends, run from idolatry! ¹⁵ I speak to you as sensible people; judge for yourselves what I am saying. ¹⁶ The "cup of blessing" over which we make the *b'rakhah* — isn't it a sharing in the bloody sacrificial death of the Messiah? The bread we break, isn't it a sharing in the body of the Messiah? ¹⁷ Because there is one loaf of bread, we who are many constitute one body, since we all partake of the one loaf of bread. ¹⁸ Look at physical Isra'el: don't those who eat the sacrifices participate in the altar? ¹⁹ So, what am I saying? That food sacrificed to idols has any significance in itself? or that an idol has significance in itself? ²⁰ No, what I am saying is that the things which pagans sacrifice, they sacrifice not to God but to demons; and I don't want you to become sharers of the demons! ²¹ You can't drink both a cup of the Lord and a cup of demons, you can't partake in both a meal of the Lord and a meal of demons. ²² Or are we trying to make the Lord jealous? We aren't stronger than he is, are we?

²³ "Everything is permitted," you say? Maybe, but not everything is helpful. "Everything is permitted?" Maybe, but not everything is edifying. ²⁴ No one should be looking out for his own interests, but for those of his fellow. ²⁵ Eat whatever is sold in the meat market without raising questions of conscience, ²⁶ for **the earth and everything in it belong to the Lord.**ᵏ ²⁷ If some unbeliever invites you to a meal, and you want to go, eat whatever is put in front of you without raising questions of conscience. ²⁸ But if someone says to you, "This meat was offered as a sacrifice," then don't eat it, out of consideration for the person who pointed it out and also for conscience's sake — ²⁹ however, I don't mean your conscience but that of the other person. You say, "Why should my freedom be determined by someone else's conscience? ³⁰ If I participate with thankfulness, why am I criticized over something for which I myself bless God?" ³¹ Well, whatever you do, whether it's eating or drinking or anything else, do it all so as to bring glory to God. ³² Do not be an obstacle to anyone — not to Jews, not to Gentiles, and not to God's Messianic Community. ³³ Just as I try to please everyone in everything I do, not looking out for my own interests but for those of the many, so that they may be saved;

11 ¹ try to imitate me, even as I myself try to imitate the Messiah.

² Now I praise you because you have remembered everything I told you and observe the traditions just the way I passed them on to you. ³ But I want you to understand that the head of every man is the Messiah, and the head of a wife is her husband, and the head of the Messiah is God. ⁴ Every man who prays or prophesies wearing something down over his head brings shame to his head, ⁵ but every woman who prays or prophesies with her head unveiled brings shame to her head — there is no difference between her and a woman who has had her head shaved. ⁶ For if a woman is not veiled, let her also have her hair cut short; but if it is shameful for a woman to wear her hair cut short or to have her head shaved, then let her be veiled. ⁷ For a man indeed should not have his head veiled, because he is the image and glory of God, and the woman is the glory of man. ⁸ For man was not made from woman, but woman from man; ⁹ and indeed man was not created for the sake of the woman but woman for the sake of the man. ¹⁰ The reason a woman should show by veiling her head that she is under authority has to do with the angels. ¹¹ Nevertheless,

---

ᵏ Psalm 24:1, 50:12, 89:12(11)

in union with the Lord neither is woman independent of man nor is man independent of woman; ¹²for as the woman was made from the man, so also the man is now born through the woman. But everything is from God. ¹³Decide for yourselves: is it appropriate for a woman to pray to God when she is unveiled? ¹⁴Doesn't the nature of things itself teach you that a man who wears his hair long degrades himself? ¹⁵But a woman who wears her hair long enhances her appearance, because her hair has been given to her as a covering. ¹⁶However, if anyone wants to argue about it, the fact remains that we have no such custom, nor do the Messianic communities of God.

¹⁷But in giving you this next instruction I do not praise you, because when you meet together it does more harm than good! ¹⁸For, in the first place, I hear that when you gather together as a congregation you divide up into cliques; and to a degree I believe it ¹⁹(granted that there must be some divisions among you in order to show who are the ones in the right). ²⁰Thus, when you gather together, it is not to eat a meal of the Lord; ²¹because as you eat your meal, each one goes ahead on his own; so that one stays hungry while another is already drunk! ²²Don't you have homes to eat and drink in? Or are you trying to show your contempt for God's Messianic community and embarrass those who are poor? What am I supposed to say to you? Am I supposed to praise you? Well, for this I don't praise you!

²³For what I received from the Lord is just what I passed on to you — that the Lord Yeshua, on the night he was betrayed, took bread; ²⁴and after he had made the *b'rakhah* he broke it and said, "This is my body, which is for you. Do this as a memorial to me"; ²⁵likewise also the cup after the meal, saying, "This cup is the New Covenant effected by my blood; do this, as often as you drink it, as a memorial to me." ²⁶For as often as you eat this bread and drink the cup, you proclaim the death of the Lord, until he comes.

²⁷Therefore, whoever eats the Lord's bread or drinks the Lord's cup in an unworthy manner will be guilty of desecrating the body and blood of the Lord! ²⁸So let a person examine himself first, and then he may eat of the bread and drink from the cup; ²⁹for a person who eats and drinks without recognizing the body eats and drinks judgment upon himself. ³⁰This is why many among you are weak and sick, and some have died! ³¹If we would examine ourselves, we would not come under judgment. ³²But when we are judged by the Lord, we are being disciplined, so that we will not be condemned along with the world.

³³So then, my brothers, when you gather together to eat, wait for one another. ³⁴If someone is hungry, he should eat at home, so that when you meet together it will not result in judgment.

As for the other matters, I will instruct you about them when I come.

12 ¹But, brothers, I do not want you to go on being ignorant about the things of the Spirit. ²You know that when you were pagans, no matter how you felt you were being led, you were being led astray to idols, which can't speak at all. ³Therefore, I want to make it clear to you that no one speaking by the Spirit of God ever says, "Yeshua is cursed!" and no one can say, "Yeshua is Lord," except by the *Ruach HaKodesh*.

⁴Now there are different kinds of gifts, but the same Spirit gives them. ⁵Also there are different ways of serving, but it is the same Lord being served. ⁶And there are different modes of working, but it is the same God working them all in everyone. ⁷Moreover, to each person is given the particular manifestation of the Spirit that will

be for the common good. ⁸ To one, through the Spirit, is given a word of wisdom; to another, a word of knowledge, in accordance with the same Spirit; ⁹ to another, faith, by the same Spirit; and to another, gifts of healing, by the one Spirit; ¹⁰ to another, the working of miracles; to another, prophecy; to another, the ability to judge between spirits; to another, the ability to speak in different kinds of tongues; and to yet another, the ability to interpret tongues. ¹¹ One and the same Spirit is at work in all these things, distributing to each person as he chooses. ¹² For just as the body is one but has many parts; and all the parts of the body, though many, constitute one body; so it is with the Messiah. ¹³ For it was by one Spirit that we were all immersed into one body, whether Jews or Gentiles, slaves or free; and we were all given the one Spirit to drink.

¹⁴ For indeed the body is not one part but many. ¹⁵ If the foot says, "I'm not a hand, so I'm not part of the body," that doesn't make it stop being part of the body. ¹⁶ And if the ear says, "I'm not an eye, so I'm not part of the body," that doesn't make it stop being part of the body. ¹⁷ If the whole body were an eye, how could it hear? If it were all hearing, how could it smell? ¹⁸ But as it is, God arranged each of the parts in the body exactly as he wanted them. ¹⁹ Now if they were all just one part, where would the body be? ²⁰ But as it is, there are indeed many parts, yet just one body. ²¹ So the eye cannot say to the hand, "I don't need you"; or the head to the feet, "I don't need you." ²² On the contrary, the parts of the body that seem to be less important turn out to be all the more necessary; ²³ and upon body parts which we consider less dignified we bestow greater dignity; and the parts that aren't attractive are the ones we make as attractive as we can, ²⁴ while our attractive parts have no need for such treatment. Indeed, God has put the body together in such a way that he gives greater dignity to the parts that lack it, ²⁵ so that there will be no disagreements within the body, but rather all the parts will be equally concerned for all the others. ²⁶ Thus if one part suffers, all the parts suffer with it; and if one part is honored, all the parts share its happiness.

²⁷ Now you together constitute the body of the Messiah, and individually you are parts of it. ²⁸ And God has placed in the Messianic Community first, emissaries; second, prophets; third, teachers; then those who work miracles; then those with gifts of healing; those with ability to help; those skilled in administration; and those who speak in various tongues. ²⁹ Not all are emissaries, are they? Not all are prophets, are they? or teachers? or miracle-workers? ³⁰ Not all have gifts of healing, not all speak in tongues, not all interpret, do they? ³¹ Eagerly seek the better gifts.

But now I will show you the best way of all.

13 ¹   I may speak in the tongues of men, even angels;
        but if I lack love, I have become merely
        blaring brass or a cymbal clanging.

²   I may have the gift of prophecy,
        I may fathom all mysteries, know all things,
        have all faith — enough to move mountains;
        but if I lack love, I am nothing.

³   I may give away everything that I own,
        I may even hand over my body to be burned;
        but if I lack love, I gain nothing.

⁴ Love is patient and kind, not jealous, not boastful,
⁵ not proud, rude or selfish, not easily angered,
and it keeps no record of wrongs.
⁶ Love does not gloat over other people's sins
but takes its delight in the truth.
⁷ Love always bears up, always trusts,
always hopes, always endures.

⁸ Love never ends; but prophecies will pass,
tongues will cease, knowledge will pass.
⁹ For our knowledge is partial, and our prophecy partial;
¹⁰ but when the perfect comes, the partial will pass.

¹¹ When I was a child, I spoke like a child,
thought like a child, argued like a child;
now that I have become a man,
I have finished with childish ways.

¹² For now we see obscurely in a mirror,
but then it will be face to face.
Now I know partly; then I will know fully,
just as God has fully known me.

¹³ But for now, three things last —
trust, hope, love;
and the greatest of these is love.

14 ¹ Pursue love!

However, keep on eagerly seeking the things of the Spirit; and especially seek to be able to prophesy. ² For someone speaking in a tongue is not speaking to people but to God, because no one can understand, since he is uttering mysteries in the power of the Spirit. ³ But someone prophesying is speaking to people, edifying, encouraging and comforting them. ⁴ A person speaking in a tongue does edify himself, but a person prophesying edifies the congregation. ⁵ I wish you would all speak in tongues, but even more I wish you would all prophesy. The person who prophesies is greater than the person who speaks in tongues, unless someone gives an interpretation, so that the congregation can be edified.

⁶ Brothers, suppose I come to you now speaking in tongues. How can I be of benefit to you unless I bring you some revelation or knowledge or prophecy or teaching? ⁷ Even with lifeless musical instruments, such as a flute or a harp, how will anyone recognize the melody if one note can't be distinguished from another? ⁸ And if the bugle gives an unclear sound, who will get ready for battle? ⁹ It's the same with you: how will anyone know what you are saying unless you use your tongue to produce intelligible speech? You will be talking to the air! ¹⁰ There are undoubtedly all kinds of sounds in the world, and none is altogether meaningless; ¹¹ but if I don't know what a person's sounds mean, I will be a foreigner to the speaker and the speaker will be a foreigner to me. ¹² Likewise with you:

since you eagerly seek the things of the Spirit, seek especially what will help in edifying the congregation.

[13] Therefore someone who speaks in a tongue should pray for the power to interpret. [14] For if I pray in a tongue, my spirit does pray, but my mind is unproductive. [15] So, what about it? I will pray with my spirit, but I will also pray with my mind; I will sing with my spirit, but I will also sing with my mind. [16] Otherwise, if you are giving thanks with your spirit, how will someone who has not yet received much instruction be able to say, "Amen," when you have finished giving thanks, since he doesn't know what you are saying? [17] For undoubtedly you are giving thanks very nicely, but the other person is not being edified. [18] I thank God that I speak in tongues more than all of you, [19] but in a congregation meeting I would rather say five words with my mind in order to instruct others than ten thousand words in a tongue!

[20] Brothers, don't be children in your thinking. In evil, be like infants; but in your thinking, be grown-up. [21] In the *Torah* it is written,

> **"By other tongues,**
> **by the lips of foreigners**
> **I will speak to this people.**
> **But even then they will not listen to me,"**
> says ADONAI.[1]

[22] Thus tongues are a sign not for believers but for unbelievers, while prophecy is not for unbelievers but for believers. [23] So if the whole congregation comes together with everybody speaking in tongues, and uninstructed people or unbelievers come in, won't they say you're crazy? [24] But if you all prophesy, and some unbeliever or uninstructed person enters, he is convicted of sin by all, he is brought under judgment by all, [25] and the secrets of his heart are laid bare; so he falls on his face and worships God, saying, "God is really here among you!"

[26] What is our conclusion, brothers? Whenever you come together, let everyone be ready with a psalm or a teaching or a revelation, or ready to use his gift of tongues or give an interpretation; but let everything be for edification. [27] If the gift of tongues is exercised, let it be by two or at most three, and each in turn; and let someone interpret. [28] And if there is no one present who can interpret, let the people who speak in tongues keep silent when the congregation meets — they can speak to themselves and to God. [29] Let two or three prophets speak, while the others weigh what is said. [30] And if something is revealed to a prophet who is sitting down, let the first one be silent. [31] For you can all prophesy one by one, with the result that all will learn something and all will be encouraged. [32] Also, the prophets' spirits are under the prophets' control; [33] for God is not a God of unruliness but of *shalom*.

As in all the congregations of God's people, [34] let the wives remain silent when the congregation meets; they are certainly not permitted to speak out. Rather, let them remain subordinate, as also the *Torah* says; [35] and if there is something they want to know, let them ask their own husbands at home; for it is shameful for a woman to speak out in a congregational meeting.

_____

[1] Isaiah 28:11–12

³⁶ Did the word of God originate with you? Or are you the only people it has reached? ³⁷ If anyone thinks he is a prophet or is endowed with the Spirit, let him acknowledge that what I am writing you is a command of the Lord. ³⁸ But if someone doesn't recognize this, then let him remain unrecognized.

³⁹ So, my brothers, eagerly seek to prophesy; and do not forbid speaking in tongues; ⁴⁰ but let all things be done in a proper and orderly way.

15 ¹ Now, brothers, I must remind you of the Good News which I proclaimed to you, and which you received, and on which you have taken your stand, ² and by which you are being saved — provided you keep holding fast to the message I proclaimed to you. For if you don't, your trust will have been in vain. ³ For among the first things I passed on to you was what I also received, namely this: the Messiah died for our sins, in accordance with what the *Tanakh* says; ⁴ and he was buried; and he was raised on the third day, in accordance with what the *Tanakh* says; ⁵ and he was seen by Kefa, then by the Twelve; ⁶ and afterwards he was seen by more than five hundred brothers at one time, the majority of whom are still alive, though some have died. ⁷ Later he was seen by Ya'akov, then by all the emissaries; ⁸ and last of all he was seen by me, even though I was born at the wrong time. ⁹ For I am the least of all the emissaries, unfit to be called an emissary, because I persecuted the Messianic Community of God. ¹⁰ But by God's grace I am what I am, and his grace towards me was not in vain; on the contrary, I have worked harder than all of them, although it was not I but the grace of God with me. ¹¹ Anyhow, whether I or they, this is what we proclaim, and this is what you believed.

¹² But if it has been proclaimed that the Messiah has been raised from the dead, how is it that some of you are saying there is no such thing as a resurrection of the dead? ¹³ If there is no resurrection of the dead, then the Messiah has not been raised; ¹⁴ and if the Messiah has not been raised, then what we have proclaimed is in vain; also your trust is in vain; ¹⁵ furthermore, we are shown up as false witnesses for God in having testified that God raised up the Messiah, whom he did not raise if it is true that the dead are not raised. ¹⁶ For if the dead are not raised, then the Messiah has not been raised either; ¹⁷ and if the Messiah has not been raised, your trust is useless, and you are still in your sins. ¹⁸ Also, if this is the case, those who died in union with the Messiah are lost. ¹⁹ If it is only for this life that we have put our hope in the Messiah, we are more pitiable than anyone.

²⁰ But the fact is that the Messiah *has* been raised from the dead, the firstfruits of those who have died. ²¹ For since death came through a man, also the resurrection of the dead has come through a man. ²² For just as in connection with Adam all die, so in connection with the Messiah all will be made alive. ²³ But each in his own order: the Messiah is the firstfruits; then those who belong to the Messiah, at the time of his coming; ²⁴ then the culmination, when he hands over the Kingdom to God the Father, after having put an end to every rulership, yes, to every authority and power. ²⁵ For he has to rule until he puts all his enemies under his feet. ²⁶ The last enemy to be done away with will be death, ²⁷ for **"He put everything in subjection under his feet."**ᵐ But when it says that **"everything"** has been subjected, obviously the word does not include God, who is himself the one subjecting everything to the Messiah.

ᵐ Psalm 8:7(6)

²⁸ Now when everything has been subjected to the Son, then he will subject himself to God, who subjected everything to him; so that God may be everything in everyone.

²⁹ Were it otherwise, what would the people accomplish who are immersed on behalf of the dead? If the dead are not actually raised, why are people immersed for them? ³⁰ For that matter, we ourselves — why do we keep facing danger hour by hour? ³¹ Brothers, by the right to be proud which the Messiah Yeshua our Lord gives me, I solemnly tell you that I die every day. ³² If my fighting with "wild beasts" in Ephesus was done merely on a human basis, what do I gain by it? If dead people are not raised, we might as well live by the saying, **"Let's eat and drink, for tomorrow we die!"**ⁿ ³³ Don't be fooled. "Bad company ruins good character." ³⁴ Come to your senses! Live righteously and stop sinning! There are some people who lack knowledge of God — I say this to your shame.

³⁵ But someone will ask, "In what manner are the dead raised? What sort of body do they have?" ³⁶ Stupid! When you sow a seed, it doesn't come alive unless it first dies. ³⁷ Also, what you sow is not the body that will be, but a bare seed of, say, wheat or something else; ³⁸ but God gives it the body he intended for it; and to each kind of seed he gives its own body. ³⁹ Not all living matter is the same living matter; on the contrary, there is one kind for human beings, another kind of living matter for animals, another for birds and another for fish. ⁴⁰ Further, there are heavenly bodies and earthly bodies; but the beauty of heavenly bodies is one thing, while the beauty of earthly bodies is something else. ⁴¹ The sun has one kind of beauty, the moon another, the stars yet another; indeed, each star has its own individual kind of beauty.

⁴² So it is with the resurrection of the dead. When the body is "sown," it decays; when it is raised, it cannot decay. ⁴³ When sown, it is without dignity; when raised, it will be beautiful. When sown, it is weak; when raised, it will be strong. ⁴⁴ When sown, it is an ordinary human body; when raised, it will be a body controlled by the Spirit. If there is an ordinary human body, there is also a body controlled by the Spirit. ⁴⁵ In fact, the *Tanakh* says so: Adam, the first man, **became a living human being;**ᵒ but the last "Adam" has become a life-giving Spirit. ⁴⁶ Note, however, that the body from the Spirit did not come first, but the ordinary human one; the one from the Spirit comes afterwards. ⁴⁷ The first man is from the earth, made of dust; the second man is from heaven. ⁴⁸ People born of dust are like the man of dust, and people born from heaven are like the man from heaven; ⁴⁹ and just as we have borne the image of the man of dust, so also we will bear the image of the man from heaven.

⁵⁰ Let me say this, brothers: flesh and blood cannot share in the Kingdom of God, nor can something that decays share in what does not decay. ⁵¹ Look, I will tell you a secret — not all of us will die! But we will all be changed! ⁵² It will take but a moment, the blink of an eye, at the final *shofar*. For the *shofar* will sound, and the dead will be raised to live forever, and we too will be changed. ⁵³ For this material which can decay must be clothed with imperishability, this which is mortal must be clothed with immortality. ⁵⁴ When what decays puts on imperishability and what is mortal puts on immortality, then this passage in the *Tanakh* will be fulfilled:

ⁿ Isaiah 22:13, 56:12   ᵒ Genesis 2:7

"Death is swallowed up in victory.[p]

55   **"Death, where is your victory?**
    Death, where is your sting?"[q]

[56] The sting of death is sin; and sin draws its power from the *Torah*; [57] but thanks be to God, who gives us the victory through our Lord Yeshua the Messiah!

[58] So, my dear brothers, stand firm and immovable, always doing the Lord's work as vigorously as you can, knowing that united with the Lord your efforts are not in vain.

16 [1] Now, in regard to the collection being made for God's people: you are to do the same as I directed the congregations in Galatia to do. [2] Every week, on *Motza'ei-Shabbat*, each of you should set some money aside, according to his resources, and save it up; so that when I come I won't have to do fundraising. [3] And when I arrive, I will give letters of introduction to the people you have approved, and I will send them to carry your gift to Yerushalayim. [4] If it seems appropriate that I go too, they will go along with me.

[5] I will visit you after I have gone through Macedonia, for I am intending to pass through Macedonia, [6] and I may stay with you or even spend the winter, so that you may help me continue my travels wherever I may go. [7] For I don't want to see you now, when I am only passing through; because I am hoping to spend some time with you, if the Lord allows it. [8] But I will remain in Ephesus until *Shavu'ot*, [9] because a great and important door has opened for my work, and there are many people opposing me.

[10] If Timothy comes, see that he has nothing to be afraid of while he is with you; for he is doing the Lord's work, just as I am. [11] So let no one treat him with disrespect. Help him on his way in peace, so that he will return to me, for the brothers and I are expecting him.

[12] As for brother Apollos, I strongly urged him to go and visit you along with the other brothers; and although it was not at all his desire to come at this time, he will come when he has the opportunity.

[13] Stay alert, stand firm in the faith, behave like a *mentsh*, grow strong. [14] Let everything you do be done in love.

[15] Now, brothers, you know that the household of Stephanas were the first people in Achaia to put their trust in the Messiah, and they have devoted themselves to serving God's people. [16] I urge you to submit yourselves to people like these and to everyone who works and toils with them. [17] I am glad that Stephanas and Fortunatus and Achaicus are here, because they have helped make up for your not being here. [18] They have refreshed my spirit, just as they have yours. I want you to show appreciation for people like these.

[19] The congregations in the province of Asia send greetings to you. Aquila and Priscilla greet you in union with the Lord, as does the congregation that meets in their house. [20] All the brothers send you their greetings. Greet one another with a holy kiss.

---

[p] Isaiah 25:8   [q] Hosea 13:14

21 *Now, I Sha'ul, greet you in my own handwriting.*

22 *If anyone does not love the Lord, a curse on him! Marana, ta!*
[Our Lord, come!]

23 *May the grace of the Lord Yeshua be with you.*

24 *My love is with you all, in union with the Messiah Yeshua.*

The Second Letter from Yeshua's Emissary Sha'ul (Paul) to the Messianic Community in Corinth

2 CORINTHIANS

1 ¹ From: Sha'ul, by God's will an emissary of the Messiah Yeshua, and brother Timothy

To: God's Messianic community in Corinth, along with all God's people throughout Achaia:

² Grace to you and *shalom* from God our Father and the Lord Yeshua the Messiah.

³ Praised be God, Father of our Lord Yeshua the Messiah, compassionate Father, God of all encouragement and comfort; ⁴ who encourages us in all our trials, so that we can encourage others in whatever trials they may be undergoing with the encouragement we ourselves have received from God.

⁵ For just as the Messiah's sufferings overflow into us, so through the Messiah our encouragement also overflows. ⁶ So if we undergo trials, it is for your encouragement and deliverance; and if we are encouraged, that should encourage you when you have to endure sufferings like those we are experiencing. ⁷ Moreover, our hope for you remains staunch, because we know that as you share in the sufferings, you will also share in the encouragement.

⁸ For, brothers, we want you to know about the trials we have undergone in the province of Asia. The burden laid on us was so far beyond what we could bear that we even despaired of living through it. ⁹ In our hearts we felt we were under sentence of death. However, this was to get us to rely not on ourselves but on God, who raises the dead! ¹⁰ He rescued us from such deadly peril, and he will rescue us again! The one in whom we have placed our hope will indeed continue to rescue us. ¹¹ And you must add your help by praying for us; for the more people there are praying, the more people there will be to give thanks when their prayer for us is answered.

¹² For we take pride in this: that our conscience assures us that in our dealings with the world, and especially with you, we have conducted ourselves with frankness and godly pureness of motive — not by worldly wisdom but by God-given grace. ¹³ There are no hidden meanings in our letters other than what you can read and understand; and my hope is that you will understand fully, ¹⁴ as indeed you have already understood us in part; so that on the Day of our Lord Yeshua you can be as proud of us as we are of you.

¹⁵ So sure was I of this that I had planned to come and see you, so that you might have the benefit of a second visit. ¹⁶ I wanted to visit you on my way to Macedonia, visit you again on my way back from Macedonia, and then have you send me on my way to Y'hudah.

¹⁷ Did I make these plans lightly? Or do I make plans the way a worldly man does, ready to say, "Yes, yes," and "No, no," in the same breath? ¹⁸ As surely as God is trustworthy, we don't say "Yes" when we mean "No." ¹⁹ For the Son of God, the Messiah Yeshua, who was proclaimed among you through us — that is, through me and Sila and Timothy — was not a yes-and-no man; on the contrary, with him it is

always "Yes!" ^{20}For however many promises God has made, they all find their "Yes" in connection with him; that is why it is through him that we say the "*Amen*" when we give glory to God. ^{21}Moreover, it is God who sets both us and you in firm union with the Messiah; he has anointed us, ^{22}put his seal on us, and given us his Spirit in our hearts as a guarantee for the future.

^{23}I call God to witness — he knows what my life is like — that the reason I held back from coming to Corinth was out of consideration for you! ^{24}We are not trying to dictate how you must live out your trust in the Messiah, for in your trust you are standing firm. Rather, we are working with you for your own happiness.

2 ^{1}So I made up my mind that I would not pay you another painful visit. ^{2}For if I cause you pain, who is left to make me happy except the people I have pained? ^{3}Indeed, this is why I wrote as I did — so that when I came, I would not have to be pained by those who ought to be making me happy; for I had enough confidence in all of you to believe that unless I could be happy, none of you could be happy either. ^{4}I wrote to you with a greatly distressed and anguished heart, and with many tears, not in order to cause you pain, but to get you to realize how very much I love you.

^{5}Now if someone has been a cause of pain, it is not I whom he has pained, but, in some measure — I don't want to overstate it — all of you. ^{6}For such a person the punishment already imposed on him by the majority is sufficient, ^{7}so that now you should do the opposite — forgive him, encourage him, comfort him. Otherwise such a person might be swallowed up in overwhelming depression. ^{8}So I urge you to show that you really do love him. ^{9}The reason I wrote you was to see if you would pass the test, to see if you would fully obey me. ^{10}Anyone you forgive, I forgive too. For indeed, whatever I have forgiven, if there has been anything to forgive, has been for your sake in the presence of the Messiah ^{11}so that we will not be taken advantage of by the Adversary — for we are quite aware of his schemes!

^{12}Now when I went to Troas to proclaim the Good News of the Messiah, since a door had been opened for me by the Lord, ^{13}I could not rest, because I failed to find my brother Titus. So I left the people there and went on to Macedonia.

^{14}But thanks be to God, who in the Messiah constantly leads us in a triumphal procession and through us spreads everywhere the fragrance of what it means to know him! ^{15}For to God we are the aroma of the Messiah, both among those being saved and among those being lost; ^{16}to the latter, we are the smell of death leading only to more death; but to the former, we are the sweet smell of life leading to more life. Who is equal to such a task? ^{17}For we are not like a lot of folks who go about huckstering God's message for a fee; on the contrary, we speak out of a sincere heart, as people sent by God, standing in God's presence, living in union with the Messiah.

3 ^{1}Are we starting to recommend ourselves again? Or do we, like some, need letters of recommendation either to you or from you? ^{2}You yourselves are our letter of recommendation, written on our hearts, known and read by everyone. ^{3}You make it clear that you are a letter from the Messiah placed in our care, written not with ink but by the Spirit of the living God, not on stone tablets but on human hearts.

^{4}Such is the confidence we have through the Messiah toward God. ^{5}It is not that we are competent in ourselves to count anything as having come from us; on the contrary, our competence is from God. ^{6}He has even made us competent to be workers serving a New Covenant, the essence of which is not a written text but the Spirit. For the written text brings death, but the Spirit gives life.

⁷ Now if that which worked death, by means of a written text engraved on stone tablets, came with glory — such glory that the people of Isra'el could not stand to look at Moshe's face because of its brightness, even though that brightness was already fading away — ⁸ won't the working of the Spirit be accompanied by even greater glory? ⁹ For if there was glory in what worked to declare people guilty, how much more must the glory abound in what works to declare people innocent! ¹⁰ In fact, by comparison with this greater glory, what was made glorious before has no glory now. ¹¹ For if there was glory in what faded away, how much more glory must there be in what lasts.

¹² Therefore, with a hope like this, we are very open — ¹³ unlike Moshe, who put a veil over his face, so that the people of Isra'el would not see the fading brightness come to an end.

¹⁴ What is more, their minds were made stonelike; for to this day the same veil remains over them when they read the Old Covenant; it has not been unveiled, because only by the Messiah is the veil taken away. ¹⁵ Yes, till today, whenever Moshe is read, a veil lies over their heart. ¹⁶ **"But,"** says the *Torah*, **"whenever someone turns to** A*DONAI*, **the veil is taken away."**[a] ¹⁷ Now, "A*DONAI*" in this text means the Spirit. And where the Spirit of A*DONAI* is, there is freedom. ¹⁸ So all of us, with faces unveiled, see as in a mirror the glory of the Lord; and we are being changed into his very image, from one degree of glory to the next, by A*DONAI* the Spirit.

4 ¹ God has shown us such mercy that we do not lose courage as we do the work he has given us. ² Indeed, we refuse to make use of shameful underhanded methods, employing deception or distorting God's message. On the contrary, by making very clear what the truth is, we commend ourselves to everyone's conscience in the sight of God. ³ So if indeed our Good News is veiled, it is veiled only to those in the process of being lost. ⁴ They do not come to trust because the god of the *'olam hazeh* has blinded their minds, in order to prevent them from seeing the light shining from the Good News about the glory of the Messiah, who is the image of God. ⁵ For what we are proclaiming is not ourselves, but the Messiah Yeshua as Lord, with ourselves as slaves for you because of Yeshua. ⁶ For it is the God who once said, "Let light shine out of darkness," who has made his light shine in our hearts, the light of the knowledge of God's glory shining in the face of the Messiah Yeshua.

⁷ But we have this treasure in clay jars, so that it will be evident that such overwhelming power comes from God and not from us. ⁸ We have all kinds of troubles, but we are not crushed; we are perplexed, yet not in despair; ⁹ persecuted, yet not abandoned; knocked down, yet not destroyed. ¹⁰ We always carry in our bodies the dying of Yeshua, so that the life of Yeshua may be manifested in our bodies too. ¹¹ For we who are alive are always being handed over to death for Yeshua's sake, so that Yeshua's life also might be manifested in our mortal bodies. ¹² Thus death is at work in us but life in you.

¹³ The *Tanakh* says, **"I trusted, therefore I spoke."**[b] Since we have that same Spirit who enables us to trust, we also trust and therefore speak; ¹⁴ because we know

---

[a] Exodus 34:34   [b] Psalm 116:10

that he who raised the Lord Yeshua will also raise us with Yeshua and bring us along with you into his presence. ^{15} All this is for your sakes, so that as grace flows out to more and more people, it may cause thanksgiving to overflow and bring glory to God.

^{16} This is why we do not lose courage. Though our outer self is heading for decay, our inner self is being renewed daily. ^{17} For our light and transient troubles are achieving for us an everlasting glory whose weight is beyond description. ^{18} We concentrate not on what is seen but on what is not seen, since things seen are temporary, but things not seen are eternal.

5 ^{1} We know that when the tent which houses us here on earth is torn down, we have a permanent building from God, a building not made by human hands, to house us in heaven. ^{2} For in this tent, our earthly body, we groan with desire to have around us the home from heaven that will be ours. ^{3} With this around us we will not be found naked. ^{4} Yes, while we are in this body, we groan with the sense of being oppressed: it is not so much that we want to take something off, but rather to put something on over it; so that what must die may be swallowed up by the Life. ^{5} Moreover, it is God who has prepared us for this very thing, and as a pledge he has given us his Spirit.

^{6} So we are always confident — we know that so long as we are at home in the body, we are away from our home with the Lord; ^{7} for we live by trust, not by what we see. ^{8} We are confident, then, and would much prefer to leave our home in the body and come to our home with the Lord.

^{9} Therefore, whether at home or away from home, we try our utmost to please him; ^{10} for we must all appear before the Messiah's court of judgment, where everyone will receive the good or bad consequences of what he did while he was in the body.

^{11} So it is with the fear of the Lord before us that we try to persuade people. Moreover, God knows us as we really are; and I hope that in your consciences you too know us as we really are. ^{12} We are not recommending ourselves to you again but giving you a reason to be proud of us, so that you will be able to answer those who boast about a person's appearance rather than his inner qualities. ^{13} If we are insane, it is for God's sake; and if we are sane, it is for your sake. ^{14} For the Messiah's love has hold of us, because we are convinced that one man died on behalf of all mankind (which implies that all mankind was already dead), ^{15} and that he died on behalf of all in order that those who live should not live any longer for themselves but for the one who on their behalf died and was raised. ^{16} So from now on, we do not look at anyone from a worldly viewpoint. Even if we once regarded the Messiah from a worldly viewpoint, we do so no longer. ^{17} Therefore, if anyone is united with the Messiah, he is a new creation — the old has passed; look, what has come is fresh and new! ^{18} And it is all from God, who through the Messiah has reconciled us to himself and has given us the work of that reconciliation, ^{19} which is that God in the Messiah was reconciling mankind to himself, not counting their sins against them, and entrusting to us the message of reconciliation. ^{20} Therefore we are ambassadors of the Messiah; in effect, God is making his appeal through us. What we do is appeal on behalf of the Messiah, "Be reconciled to God! ^{21} God made this sinless man be a sin offering on our behalf, so that in union with him we might fully share in God's righteousness."

6 ^{1} As God's fellow-workers we also urge you not to receive his grace and then do nothing with it. ^{2} For he says,

> **"At the acceptable time I heard you;**
> **in the day of salvation I helped you."ᶜ**

³ We try not to put obstacles in anyone's path, so that no one can find fault with the work we do. ⁴ On the contrary, we try to commend ourselves in every way as workers for God by continually enduring troubles, hardships, calamities, ⁵ beatings, imprisonments, riots, overwork, lack of sleep and food. ⁶ We commend ourselves by our purity, knowledge, patience and kindness; by the *Ruach HaKodesh;* by genuineness of love ⁷ and truthfulness of speech; and by God's power. We commend ourselves through our use of righteous weapons, whether for pressing our cause or defending it; ⁸ through being honored and dishonored, praised and blamed, considered deceptive and sincere, ⁹ unknown and famous. And we commend ourselves as God's workers headed for death, yet look! we're alive! as punished, yet not killed; ¹⁰ as having reason to be sad, yet always filled with joy; as poor, yet making many people rich; as having nothing, yet having everything!

¹¹ Dear friends in Corinth! We have spoken frankly to you, we have opened our hearts wide. ¹² Any constraint you feel has not been imposed by us, but by your own inner selves. ¹³ So, just to be "fair" (I am using the language of children), open wide your hearts too.

¹⁴ Do not yoke yourselves together in a team with unbelievers. For how can righteousness and lawlessness be partners? What fellowship does light have with darkness? ¹⁵ What harmony can there be between the Messiah and B'liya'al? What does a believer have in common with an unbeliever? ¹⁶ What agreement can there be between the temple of God and idols? For we are the temple of the living God — as God said,

> **"I will house myself in them, . . .**
> **and I will walk among you.**
> **I will be their God,**
> **and they will be my people."ᵈ**

¹⁷ Therefore *ADONAI* says,

> **"'Go out from their midst;**
> **separate yourselves;**
> **don't even touch what is unclean.ᵉ**
> **Then I myself will receive you.ᶠ**
> ¹⁸ **In fact, I will be your Father,**
> **and you will be my sons** and daughters.'**

says *ADONAI-Tzva'ot*."ᵍ

7 ¹ Therefore, my dear friends, since we have these promises, let us purify ourselves from everything that can defile either body or spirit, and strive to be completely holy, out of reverence for God.

ᶜ Isaiah 49:8   ᵈ Leviticus 26:12; Exodus 6:7; Jeremiah 31:32(33), 32:38; Ezekiel 37:27
ᵉ Isaiah 52:11   ᶠ Ezekiel 20:34, 41   ᵍ 2 Samuel 7:14, Isaiah 43:6

² Make room for us in your hearts — we haven't wronged anyone, we haven't corrupted anyone, we haven't exploited anyone. ³ I am not saying this to put blame on you, for I have already said that you have a place in our hearts, whether we live together or die together; ⁴ that I am very confident in you; that I am very proud of you; that you have filled me with encouragement; and that in spite of all our troubles, I am overflowing with joy.

⁵ For indeed when we came into Macedonia, our bodies had no rest. On the contrary, we faced all kinds of troubles — altercations without, apprehensions within. ⁶ But God, who encourages the downhearted, encouraged us with the arrival of Titus! ⁷ However, it was not only his arrival which encouraged us, but also how encouraged he was about you, as he told us how you long to see me, how distressed you are over my situation, how zealous you are in my defense — this news made me even happier!

⁸ If I caused you pain by my letter, I do not regret it. Even if I did regret it before — for I do see that that letter did distress you, though only for a short time — ⁹ now I rejoice not because you were pained, but because the pain led you to turn back to God. For you handled the pain in God's way, so that you were not harmed by us at all. ¹⁰ Pain handled in God's way produces a turning from sin to God which leads to salvation, and there is nothing to regret in that! But pain handled in the world's way produces only death. ¹¹ For just look at what handling the pain God's way produced in you! What earnest diligence, what eagerness to clear yourselves, what indignation, what fear, what longing, what zeal, what readiness to put things right! In everything you have proved yourselves blameless in the matter. ¹² So even though I wrote to you, it was not for the sake of either the one who did the wrong or the one wronged, but so that before God you could see for yourselves how deep is your devotion to us. ¹³ This is the reason we have been encouraged.

Besides our own encouragement, we had the even greater joy of seeing how happy Titus was, because all of you set his mind at rest. ¹⁴ For I had boasted somewhat about you to him, and now I have not been made to look foolish. On the contrary, just as everything we have said to you is true, so too our boasting in front of Titus has proved true. ¹⁵ And his affection for you is all the greater as he remembers how ready you were to obey and how you received him with reverence and respect. ¹⁶ I am glad that I can have such complete confidence in you.

8 ¹ Now, brothers, we must tell you about the grace God has given the congregations in Macedonia. ² Despite severe trials, and even though they are desperately poor, their joy has overflowed in a wealth of generosity. ³ I tell you they have not merely given according to their means, but of their own free will they have given beyond their means. ⁴ They begged and pleaded with us for the privilege of sharing in this service for God's people. ⁵ Also, they didn't do this in the way we had expected, but first they gave themselves to the Lord, which means, by God's will, to us.

⁶ All this has led us to urge Titus to bring this same gracious gift to completion among you, since he has already made a beginning of it. ⁷ Just as you excel in everything — in faith, in speech, in knowledge, in diligence of every kind, and in your love for us — see that you excel in this gift too. ⁸ I am not issuing an order; rather, I am testing the genuineness of your love against the diligence of others. ⁹ For you know how generous our Lord Yeshua the Messiah was — for your sakes he impoverished himself, even though he was rich, so that he might make you rich by means

of his poverty. ¹⁰ As I say, in regard to this matter I am only giving an opinion. A year ago you were not only the first to take action but the first to want to do so. Now it would be to your advantage ¹¹ to finish what you started, so that your eagerness in wanting to commence the project may be matched by your eagerness to complete it, as you contribute from what you have. ¹² For if the eagerness to give is there, the acceptability of the gift will be measured by what you have, not by what you don't have. ¹³ It is not that relief for others should cause trouble for you, but that there should be a kind of reciprocity: ¹⁴ at present your abundance can help those in need; so that when you are in need, their abundance can help you — thus there is reciprocity. ¹⁵ It is as the *Tanakh* says,

> **"He who gathered much had nothing extra,**
> **and he who gathered little had nothing lacking."**[h]

¹⁶ Now I thank God for making Titus as devoted to you as we are; ¹⁷ for he not only responded to our urging, but, being so devoted, he is coming to you on his own initiative. ¹⁸ And with him we are sending the brother whose work for the Good News is praised in all the congregations; ¹⁹ not only that, he has also been appointed by the congregations to travel with us, so that the way we administer this charitable work will bring honor to the Lord and show our eagerness to help. ²⁰ Our aim in this is to show that our conduct in dealing with these substantial sums is above reproach; ²¹ for **we take pains to do what is right** not only **in the sight of God** but **also** in the sight of **other people.**[i] ²² With these two we are sending another brother of ours, one whose diligence we have tested many times in many ways, but who is now all the more diligent because of his great confidence in you. ²³ As for Titus, he is my partner who works with me on your behalf; and the other brothers with him are emissaries of the congregations and bring honor to the Messiah. ²⁴ So the love you show these men will justify our pride in you to them, and through them to the congregations that sent them.

9 ¹ There is really no need for me to write you about this offering for God's people — ² I know how eager you are, and I boast about you to the Macedonians. I tell them, "Achaia has been ready since last year," and it was your zeal that stirred up most of them. ³ But now I am sending the brothers so that our boast about you in this regard will not prove hollow, so that you will be ready, as I said you would be. ⁴ For if some Macedonians were to come with me and find you unprepared, we would be humiliated at having been so confident — to say nothing of how you would feel. ⁵ So I thought it necessary to urge these brothers to go on to you ahead of me and prepare your promised gift in plenty of time; this way it will be ready when I come and will be a genuine gift, not something extracted by pressure.

⁶ Here's the point: he who plants sparingly also harvests sparingly. ⁷ Each should give according to what he has decided in his heart, not grudgingly or under compulsion, for **God loves a cheerful giver.**[j] ⁸ Moreover, God has the power to provide you with every gracious gift in abundance, so that always in every way you will have all you need yourselves and be able to provide abundantly for every good cause — ⁹ as the *Tanakh* says,

---

[h] Exodus 16:18   [i] Proverbs 3:4 (Septuagint)   [j] Proverbs 22:8 (Septuagint)

> "He gave generously to the poor;
> his *tzedakah* lasts forever."[k]

[10] He who provides both seed for the planter and bread for food will supply and multiply your seed and increase the harvest of your *tzedakah*. [11] You will be enriched in every way, so that you can be generous in everything. And through us your generosity will cause people to thank God, [12] because rendering this holy service not only provides for the needs of God's people, but it also overflows in the many thanks people will be giving to God. [13] In offering this service you prove to these people that you glorify God by actually doing what your acknowledgement of the Good News of the Messiah requires, namely, sharing generously with them and with everyone. [14] And in their prayers for you they will feel a strong affection for you because of how gracious God has been to you. [15] Thanks be to God for his indescribable gift!

10 [1] Now it is I myself, Sha'ul, making an appeal to you with the meekness and forbearance that come from the Messiah, I who am considered timid when face-to-face with you but intimidating from a distance. [2] But I beg you not to force me to be intimidating when I am with you, as I expect to be toward some who regard us as living in a worldly way. [3] For although we do live in the world, we do not wage war in a worldly way; [4] because the weapons we use to wage war are not worldly. On the contrary, they have God's power for demolishing strongholds. We demolish arguments [5] and every arrogance that raises itself up against the knowledge of God; we take every thought captive and make it obey the Messiah. [6] And when you have become completely obedient, then we will be ready to punish every act of disobedience.

[7] You are looking at the surface of things. If anyone is convinced that he belongs to the Messiah, he should remind himself that we belong to the Messiah as much as he does. [8] For even if I boast a little too much about the authority the Lord has given us — authority to build you up, not tear you down — I am not ashamed. [9] My object is not to seem as if I were trying to frighten you with these letters. [10] Someone says, "His letters are weighty and powerful, but when he appears in person he is weak, and as a speaker he is nothing." [11] Such a person should realize that what we say in our letters when absent, we will do when present.

[12] We don't dare class or compare ourselves with some of the people who advertise themselves. In measuring themselves against each other and comparing themselves with each other, they are simply stupid. [13] We will not boast about what lies outside the area of work which God has given us; rather, we will boast within our assigned area, and that area does reach as far as you. [14] We are not overextending our boasting as if we had not reached as far as you; for we did come all the way to you with the Good News of the Messiah. [15] We do not boast about the area in which others labor; but our hope is that as your trust grows, we will be magnified in your midst in relation to our own area of work, so that we can go on to do even more, [16] namely, to proclaim the Good News in regions beyond you. Our hope is not to boast about the work already done by someone else.

---

[k] Psalm 112:9

¹⁷ So, **let anyone who wants to boast, boast about** *ADONAI*;[*][18] because it is not the one who recommends himself who is worthy of approval, but the one whom the Lord recommends.

11 ¹ I would like you to bear with me in a little foolishness — please do bear with me! ² For I am jealous for you with God's kind of jealousy; since I promised to present you as a pure virgin in marriage to your one husband, the Messiah; ³ and I fear that somehow your minds may be seduced away from simple and pure devotion to the Messiah, just as Havah was deceived by the serpent and his craftiness. ⁴ For if someone comes and tells you about some other Yeshua than the one we told you about, or if you receive a spirit different from the one you received or accept some so-called "good news" different from the Good News you already accepted, you bear with him well enough! ⁵ For I don't consider myself in any way inferior to these "super-emissaries." ⁶ I may not be a skilled speaker, but I do have the knowledge; anyhow, we have made this clear to you in every way and in every circumstance.

⁷ Or did I sin in humbling myself so that you could be exalted, in proclaiming God's Good News to you free of charge? ⁸ I robbed other congregations by accepting support from them in order to serve you. ⁹ And when I was with you and had needs, I did not burden anyone: my needs were met by the brothers who came from Macedonia. In nothing have I been a burden to you, nor will I be. ¹⁰ The truthfulness of the Messiah is in me, so that this boast concerning me is not going to be silenced anywhere in Achaia. ¹¹ Why won't I ever accept your support? Is it that I don't love you? God knows I do! ¹² No, I do it — and will go on doing it — in order to cut the ground from under those who want an excuse to boast that they work the same way we do. ¹³ The fact is that such men are pseudo-emissaries: they tell lies about their work and masquerade as emissaries of the Messiah. ¹⁴ There is nothing surprising in that, for the Adversary himself masquerades as an angel of light; ¹⁵ so it's no great thing if his workers masquerade as servants of righteousness. They will meet the end their deeds deserve.

¹⁶ I repeat: don't let anyone think I am a fool. But even if you do, at least receive me as a fool; so that I too may do a little boasting! ¹⁷ What I am saying is not in accordance with the Lord; rather, this conceited boasting is spoken as a fool would speak. ¹⁸ Since many people boast in a worldly way, I too will boast this way. ¹⁹ For since you yourselves are so wise, you gladly put up with fools! ²⁰ You put up with it if someone makes slaves of you, exploits you, takes you in, puffs himself up, slaps you in the face. ²¹ To my shame, I must admit that we have been too "weak" to do such things!

But if anyone dares to boast about something — I'm talking like a fool! — I am just as daring. ²² Are they Hebrew-speakers? So am I. Are they of the people of Isra'el? So am I. Are they descendants of Avraham? So am I. ²³ Are they servants of the Messiah? (I'm talking like a madman!) I'm a better one! I've worked much harder, been imprisoned more often, suffered more beatings, been near death over and over. ²⁴ Five times I received "forty lashes less one" from the Jews. ²⁵ Three times I was beaten with rods. Once I was stoned. Three times I was shipwrecked. I spent a night and a day in the open sea. ²⁶ In my many travels I have been exposed to danger

---

[*] Jeremiah 9:23(24)

from rivers, danger from robbers, danger from my own people, danger from Gentiles, danger in the city, danger in the desert, danger at sea, danger from false brothers. ²⁷ I have toiled and endured hardship, often not had enough sleep, been hungry and thirsty, frequently gone without food, been cold and naked. ²⁸ And besides these external matters, there is the daily pressure of my anxious concern for all the congregations. ²⁹ Who is weak without my sharing his weakness? Who falls into sin without my burning inside?

³⁰ If I must boast, I will boast about things that show how weak I am. ³¹ God the Father of the Lord Yeshua — blessed be he forever — knows that I am not lying! ³² When I was in Dalmanuta, the governor under King Aretas had the city of Dalmanuta guarded in order to arrest me; ³³ but I was lowered in a basket through an opening in the wall and escaped his clutches.

12 ¹ I have to boast. There is nothing to be gained by it, but I will go on to visions and revelations of the Lord. ² I know a man in union with the Messiah who fourteen years ago was snatched up to the third heaven; whether he was in the body or outside the body I don't know, God knows. ³ And I know that such a man — whether in the body or apart from the body I don't know, God knows — ⁴ was snatched into Gan-'Eden and heard things that cannot be put into words, things unlawful for a human being to utter. ⁵ About such a man I will boast; but about myself I will not boast, except in regard to my weaknesses. ⁶ If I did want to boast, I would not be foolish; because I would be speaking the truth. But, because of the extraordinary greatness of the revelations, I refrain, so that no one will think more of me than what my words or deeds may warrant. ⁷ Therefore, to keep me from becoming overly proud, I was given a thorn in my flesh, a messenger from the Adversary to pound away at me, so that I wouldn't grow conceited. ⁸ Three times I begged the Lord to take this thing away from me; ⁹ but he told me, "My grace is enough for you, for my power is brought to perfection in weakness." Therefore, I am very happy to boast about my weaknesses, in order that the Messiah's power will rest upon me. ¹⁰ Yes, I am well pleased with weaknesses, insults, hardships, persecutions and difficulties endured on behalf of the Messiah; for it is when I am weak that I am strong.

¹¹ I have behaved like a fool, but you forced me to do it — you who should have been commending me. For I am in no way inferior to the "super-emissaries," even if I am nothing. ¹² The things that prove I am an emissary — signs, wonders and miracles — were done in your presence, despite what I had to endure. ¹³ Is there any way in which you have been behind any of the other congregations, other than in my not having been a burden to you? For this unfairness, please forgive me!

¹⁴ Look, I am ready this third time to come and visit you; and I will not be a burden to you; for it is not what you own that I want, but you! Children are not supposed to save up for their parents, but parents for their children. ¹⁵ And as for me, I will most gladly spend everything I have and be spent myself too for your sakes. If I love you more, am I to be loved less?

¹⁶ Let it be granted, then, that I was not a burden to you; but, crafty fellow that I am, I took you with trickery! ¹⁷ Was it perhaps through someone I sent you ¹⁸ that I took advantage of you? I urged Titus to go and sent the brother with him; Titus didn't take advantage of you, did he? Didn't we live by the same Spirit and show you the same path?

¹⁹ Perhaps you think that all this time we have been defending ourselves before you. No, we have been speaking in the sight of God, as those united with the Messiah should; and, my dear friends, it is all for your upbuilding. ²⁰ For I am afraid of coming and finding you not the way I want you to be, and also of not being found the way you want me to be. I am afraid of finding quarreling and jealousy, anger and rivalry, slander and gossip, arrogance and disorder. ²¹ I am afraid that when I come again, my God may humiliate me in your presence, and that I will be grieved over many of those who sinned in the past and have not repented of the impurity, fornication and debauchery that they have engaged in.

13 ¹ This will be the third time that I have come to visit you. **Any charge must be established by the testimony of two or three witnesses.**^*m* ² To those who sinned in the past and to the rest I say beforehand while absent the same thing I said when I was with you the second time: if I come again I will not spare you — ³ since you are looking for proof of the Messiah speaking in me. He is not weak in dealing with you, but he is powerful among you. ⁴ For although he was executed on a stake in weakness, now he lives by God's power. And we too are weak in union with him, but in dealing with you we will live with him by God's power.

⁵ Examine yourselves to see whether you are living the life of trust. Test yourselves. Don't you realize that Yeshua the Messiah is in you? — unless you fail to pass the test. ⁶ But I hope you will realize that we are not failures. ⁷ And we pray to God that you will do nothing wrong. We are not concerned with our appearing successful, but with your doing what is right, even if we appear to be failures. ⁸ For we cannot act against the truth, only for it. ⁹ So we rejoice whenever we are weak and you are strong; indeed, what we pray for is that you become perfect. ¹⁰ I write these things while away from you, so that when I am with you I will not have to use my authority to deal sharply with you, for the Lord gave it to me for building up and not for tearing down.

¹¹ And now, brothers, *shalom!* Put yourselves in order, pay attention to my advice, be of one mind, live in *shalom* — and the God of love and *shalom* will be with you.

¹² Greet one another with a holy kiss.

¹³ All God's people send greetings to you.

¹⁴ The grace of the Lord Yeshua the Messiah,
the love of God
and the fellowship of the *Ruach HaKodesh*
be with you all.

---

^*m* Deuteronomy 19:15

The Letter from Yeshua's Emissary Sha'ul (Paul) to the Messianic Community in Galatia

GALATIANS

1 ¹ From: Sha'ul, an emissary — I received my commission not from human beings or through human mediation but through Yeshua the Messiah and God the Father, who raised him from the dead — also from all the brothers with me

² To: The Messianic communities in Galatia:

³ Grace and *shalom* to you from God our Father and from the Lord Yeshua the Messiah, ⁴ who gave himself for our sins, so that he might deliver us from the present evil world-system, in obedience to the will of God, our Father. ⁵ To him be the glory forever and ever! *Amen.*

⁶ I am astounded that you are so quick to remove yourselves from me, the one who called you by the Messiah's grace, and turn to some other supposedly "Good News," ⁷ which is not good news at all! What is really happening is that certain people are pestering you and trying to pervert the genuine Good News of the Messiah. ⁸ But even if we — or, for that matter, an angel from heaven! — were to announce to you some so-called "Good News" contrary to the Good News we did announce to you, let him be under a curse forever! ⁹ We said it before, and I say it again: if anyone announces "Good News" contrary to what you received, let him be under a curse forever!

¹⁰ Now does that sound as if I were trying to win human approval? No! I want God's approval! Or that I'm trying to cater to people? If I were still doing that, I would not be a servant of the Messiah.

¹¹ Furthermore, let me make clear to you, brothers, that the Good News as I proclaim it is not a human product; ¹² because neither did I receive it from someone else nor was I taught it — it came through a direct revelation from Yeshua the Messiah. ¹³ For you have heard about my former way of life in [traditional] Judaism — how I did my best to persecute God's Messianic Community and destroy it; ¹⁴ and how, since I was more of a zealot for the traditions handed down by my forefathers than most Jews my age, I advanced in [traditional] Judaism more rapidly than they did.

¹⁵ But when God, who picked me out before I was born and called me by his grace, chose ¹⁶ to reveal his Son to me, so that I might announce him to the Gentiles, I did not consult anyone; ¹⁷ and I did not go up to Yerushalayim to see those who were emissaries before me. Instead, I immediately went off to Arabia and afterwards returned to Dammesek. ¹⁸ Not until three years later did I go up to Yerushalayim to make Kefa's acquaintance, and I stayed with him for two weeks, ¹⁹ but I did not see any of the other emissaries except Ya'akov the Lord's brother. ²⁰ (Concerning these matters I am writing you about, I declare before God that I am not lying!) ²¹ Next I went to Syria and Cilicia; ²² but in Y'hudah, the Messianic congregations didn't even know what I looked like — ²³ they were only hearing the report, "The one who used to persecute us now preaches the Good News of the faith he was formerly out to destroy"; ²⁴ and they praised God for me.

2 [1] Then after fourteen years I again went up to Yerushalayim, this time with Bar-Nabba; and I took with me Titus. [2] I went up in obedience to a revelation, and I explained to them the Good News as I proclaim it among the Gentiles — but privately, to the acknowledged leaders. I did this out of concern that my current or previous work might have been in vain.

[3] But they didn't force my Gentile companion Titus to undergo *b'rit-milah*. [4] Indeed, the question came up only because some men who pretended to be brothers had been sneaked in — they came in surreptitiously to spy out the freedom we have in the Messiah Yeshua, so that they might enslave us. [5] Not even for a minute did we give in to them, so that the truth of the Good News might be preserved for you.

[6] Moreover, those who were the acknowledged leaders — what they were makes no difference to me; God does not judge by outward appearances — these leaders added nothing to me. [7] On the contrary, they saw that I had been entrusted with the Good News for the Uncircumcised, just as Kefa had been for the Circumcised; [8] since the One working in Kefa to make him an emissary to the Circumcised had worked in me to make me an emissary to the Gentiles. [9] So, having perceived what grace had been given to me, Ya'akov, Kefa and Yochanan, the acknowledged pillars of the community, extended to me and Bar-Nabba the right hand of fellowship; so that we might go to the Gentiles, and they to the Circumcised. [10] Their only request was that we should remember the poor — which very thing I have spared no pains to do.

[11] Furthermore, when Kefa came to Antioch, I opposed him publicly, because he was clearly in the wrong. [12] For prior to the arrival of certain people from [the community headed by] Ya'akov, he had been eating with the Gentile believers; but when they came, he withdrew and separated himself, because he was afraid of the faction who favored circumcising Gentile believers. [13] And the other Jewish believers became hypocrites along with him, so that even Bar-Nabba was led astray by their hypocrisy. [14] But when I saw that they were not walking a straight path, keeping in line with the truth of the Good News, I said to Kefa, right in front of everyone, "If you, who are a Jew, live like a *Goy* and not like a Jew, why are you forcing the *Goyim* to live like Jews? [15] We are Jews by birth, not so-called '*Goyishe* sinners'; [16] even so, we have come to realize that a person is not declared righteous by God on the ground of his legalistic observance of *Torah* commands, but through the Messiah Yeshua's trusting faithfulness. Therefore, we too have put our trust in Messiah Yeshua and become faithful to him, in order that we might be declared righteous on the ground of the Messiah's trusting faithfulness and not on the ground of our legalistic observance of *Torah* commands. For on the ground of legalistic observance of *Torah* commands, **no one will be declared righteous.**[a]

[17] But if, in seeking to be declared righteous by God through our union with the Messiah, we ourselves are indeed found to be sinners, then is the Messiah an aider and abettor of sin? Heaven forbid! [18] Indeed, if I build up again the legalistic bondage which I destroyed, I really do make myself a transgressor. [19] For it was through letting the *Torah* speak for itself that I died to its traditional legalistic misinterpretation, so that I might live in direct relationship with God. [20] When the Messiah was executed on the stake as a criminal, I was too; so that my proud ego no longer lives. But the Messiah lives in me, and the life I now live in my body I live by the same

---

[a] Psalm 143:2

trusting faithfulness that the Son of God had, who loved me and gave himself up for me. ²¹ I do not reject God's gracious gift; for if the way in which one attains righteousness is through legalism, then the Messiah's death was pointless.

3 ¹ You stupid Galatians! Who has put you under a spell? Before your very eyes Yeshua the Messiah was clearly portrayed as having been put to death as a criminal! ² I want to know from you just this one thing: did you receive the Spirit by legalistic observance of *Torah* commands or by trusting in what you heard and being faithful to it? ³ Are you that stupid? Having begun with the Spirit's power, do you think you can reach the goal under your own power? ⁴ Have you suffered so much for nothing? If that's the way you think, your suffering certainly will have been for nothing! ⁵ What about God, who supplies you with the Spirit and works miracles among you — does he do it because of your legalistic observance of *Torah* commands or because you trust in what you heard and are faithful to it?

⁶ It was the same with Avraham: **"He trusted in God and was faithful to him, and that was credited to his account as righteousness."**ᵇ ⁷ Be assured, then, that it is those who live by trusting and being faithful who are really children of Avraham. ⁸ Also the *Tanakh*, foreseeing that God would consider the Gentiles righteous when they live by trusting and being faithful, told the Good News to Avraham in advance by saying, **"In connection with you, all the *Goyim* will be blessed."**ᶜ ⁹ So then, those who rely on trusting and being faithful are blessed along with Avraham, who trusted and was faithful.

¹⁰ For everyone who depends on legalistic observance of *Torah* commands lives under a curse, since it is written, **"Cursed is everyone who does not keep on doing everything written in the Scroll of the *Torah*."**ᵈ ¹¹ Now it is evident that no one comes to be declared righteous by God through legalism, since **"The person who is righteous will attain life by trusting and being faithful."**ᵉ ¹² Furthermore, legalism is not based on trusting and being faithful, but on [a misuse of] the text that says, **"Anyone who does these things will attain life through them."**ᶠ ¹³ The Messiah redeemed us from the curse pronounced in the *Torah* by becoming cursed on our behalf; for the *Tanakh* says, **"Everyone who hangs from a stake comes under a curse."**ᵍ ¹⁴ Yeshua the Messiah did this so that in union with him the Gentiles might receive the blessing announced to Avraham, so that through trusting and being faithful, we might receive what was promised, namely, the Spirit.

¹⁵ Brothers, let me make an analogy from everyday life: when someone swears an oath, no one else can set it aside or add to it. ¹⁶ Now the promises were made to Avraham and to his seed. It doesn't say, "and to seeds," as if to many; on the contrary, it speaks of one — **"and to your seed"**ʰ — and this "one" is the Messiah. ¹⁷ Here is what I am saying: the legal part of the *Torah*, which came into being 430 years later, does not nullify an oath sworn by God, so as to abolish the promise. ¹⁸ For if the inheritance comes from the legal part of the *Torah*, it no longer comes from a promise. But God gave it to Avraham through a promise.

¹⁹ So then, why the legal part of the *Torah*? It was added in order to create transgressions, until the coming of the **seed** about whom the promise had been made.

ᵇ Genesis 15:6   ᶜ Genesis 12:3   ᵈ Deuteronomy 27:26   ᵉ Habakkuk 2:4
ᶠ Leviticus 18:5   ᵍ Deuteronomy 21:22–23   ʰ Genesis 12:7; 13:15; 17:7; 24:7

Moreover, it was handed down through angels and a mediator. ²⁰ Now a mediator implies more than one, but God is one.

²¹ Does this mean that the legal part of the *Torah* stands in opposition to God's promises? Heaven forbid! For if the legal part of the *Torah* which God gave had had in itself the power to give life, then righteousness really would have come by legalistically following such a *Torah*. ²² But instead, the *Tanakh* shuts up everything under sin; so that what had been promised might be given, on the basis of Yeshua the Messiah's trusting faithfulness, to those who continue to be trustingly faithful.

²³ Now before the time for this trusting faithfulness came, we were imprisoned in subjection to the system which results from perverting the *Torah* into legalism, kept under guard until this yet-to-come trusting faithfulness would be revealed. ²⁴ Accordingly, the *Torah* functioned as a custodian until the Messiah came, so that we might be declared righteous on the ground of trusting and being faithful. ²⁵ But now that the time for this trusting faithfulness has come, we are no longer under a custodian.

²⁶ For in union with the Messiah, you are all children of God through this trusting faithfulness; ²⁷ because as many of you as were immersed into the Messiah have clothed yourselves with the Messiah, in whom ²⁸ there is neither Jew nor Gentile, neither slave nor freeman, neither male nor female; for in union with the Messiah Yeshua, you are all one. ²⁹ Also, if you belong to the Messiah, you are seed of Avraham and heirs according to the promise.

4 ¹ What I am saying is that as long as the heir is a minor he is no different from a slave, even though he is the legal owner of the estate; ² rather, he is subject to guardians and caretakers until the time previously set by his father. ³ So it is with us — when we were "children" we were slaves to the elemental spirits of the universe; ⁴ but when the appointed time arrived, God sent forth his Son. He was born from a woman, born into a culture in which legalistic perversion of the *Torah* was the norm, ⁵ so that he might redeem those in subjection to this legalism and thus enable us to be made God's sons. ⁶ Now because you are sons, God has sent forth into our hearts the Spirit of his Son, the Spirit who cries out, "Abba!" (that is, "Dear Father!"). ⁷ So through God you are no longer a slave but a son, and if you are a son you are also an heir.

⁸ In the past, when you did not know God, you served as slaves beings which in reality are non-gods. ⁹ But now you do know God, and, more than that, you are known by God. So how is it that you turn back again to those weak and miserable elemental spirits? Do you want to enslave yourselves to them once more? ¹⁰ You observe special days, months, seasons and years! ¹¹ I fear for you that my work among you has been wasted!

¹² Brothers, I beg of you: put yourselves in my place — after all, I put myself in your place. It isn't that you have done me any wrong — ¹³ you know that it was because I was ill that I proclaimed the Good News to you at first; ¹⁴ and even though my physical condition must have tempted you to treat me with scorn, you did not display any sign of disdain or disgust. No, you welcomed me as if I had been an angel of God, as if I had been the Messiah Yeshua himself! ¹⁵ So what has become of the joy you felt? For I bear you witness that had it been possible, you would have gouged out your eyes and given them to me. ¹⁶ Have I now become your enemy because I tell you the truth? ¹⁷ True, these teachers are zealous for you, but their motives are not good. They want to separate you from us so that you will become

zealous for them. [18] To be zealous is good, provided always that the cause is good. Indeed, whether I am present with you or not, [19] my dear children, I am suffering the pains of giving birth to you all over again — and this will go on until the Messiah takes shape in you. [20] I wish I could be present with you now and change my tone of voice. I don't know what to do with you.

[21] Tell me, you who want to be in subjection to the system that results from perverting the *Torah* into legalism, don't you hear what the *Torah* itself says? [22] It says that Avraham had two sons, one by the slave woman and one by the free woman. [23] The one by the slave woman was born according to the limited capabilities of human beings, but the one by the free woman was born through the miracle-working power of God fulfilling his promise. [24] Now, to make a *midrash* on these things: the two women are two covenants. One is from Mount Sinai and bears children for slavery — this is Hagar. [25] Hagar is Mount Sinai in Arabia; she corresponds to the present Yerushalayim, for she serves as a slave along with her children. [26] But the Yerushalayim above is free, and she is our mother; [27] for the *Tanakh* says,

> **"Rejoice, you barren woman who does not bear children!**
> **Break forth and shout, you who are not in labor!**
> **For the deserted wife will have more children**
> **than the one whose husband is with her!"**[i]

[28] You, brothers, like Yitz'chak, are children referred to in a promise of God. [29] But just as then the one born according to limited human capability persecuted the one born through the Spirit's supernatural power, so it is now. [30] Nevertheless, what does the *Tanakh* say? **"Get rid of the slave woman and her son, for by no means will the son of the slave woman inherit along with the son of the free woman!"**[j] [31] So, brothers, we are children not of the slave woman, but of the free woman.

5 [1] What the Messiah has freed us for is freedom! Therefore, stand firm, and don't let yourselves be tied up again to a yoke of slavery. [2] Mark my words — I, Sha'ul, tell you that if you undergo *b'rit-milah* the Messiah will be of no advantage to you at all! [3] Again, I warn you: any man who undergoes *b'rit-milah* is obligated to observe the entire *Torah*! [4] You who are trying to be declared righteous by God through legalism have severed yourselves from the Messiah! You have fallen away from God's grace! [5] For it is by the power of the Spirit, who works in us because we trust and are faithful, that we confidently expect our hope of attaining righteousness to be fulfilled. [6] When we are united with the Messiah Yeshua, neither being circumcised nor being uncircumcised matters; what matters is trusting faithfulness expressing itself through love.

[7] You were running the race well; who has stopped you from following the truth? [8] Whatever means of persuasion he used was not from the One who calls you. [9] "It takes only a little *hametz* to leaven the whole batch of dough." [10] I am confident that since you are united with the Lord, you will take no other view; and I am confident that the one who has been disturbing you, whoever he may be, will have to bear his punishment.

---

[i] Isaiah 54:1   [j] Genesis 21:10

[11] And as for me, brothers, if I am still preaching that circumcision is necessary, why am I still being persecuted? If that were the case, my preaching about the execution-stake would cause no offense whatever. [12] I wish the people who are bothering you would go the whole way and castrate themselves!

[13] For, brothers, you were called to be free. Only do not let that freedom become an excuse for allowing your old nature to have its way. Instead, serve one another in love. [14] For the whole of the *Torah* is summed up in this one sentence: **"Love your neighbor as yourself"**;[k] [15] but if you go on snapping at each other and tearing each other to pieces, watch out, or you will be destroyed by each other!

[16] What I am saying is this: run your lives by the Spirit. Then you will not do what your old nature wants. [17] For the old nature wants what is contrary to the Spirit, and the Spirit wants what is contrary to the old nature. These oppose each other, so that you find yourselves unable to carry out your good intentions. [18] But if you are led by the Spirit, then you are not in subjection to the system that results from perverting the *Torah* into legalism.

[19] And it is perfectly evident what the old nature does. It expresses itself in sexual immorality, impurity and indecency; [20] involvement with the occult and with drugs; in feuding, fighting, becoming jealous and getting angry; in selfish ambition, factionalism, intrigue [21] and envy; in drunkenness, orgies and things like these. I warn you now as I have warned you before: those who do such things will have no share in the Kingdom of God!

[22] But the fruit of the Spirit is love, joy, peace, patience, kindness, goodness, faithfulness, [23] humility, self control. Nothing in the *Torah* stands against such things.

[24] Moreover, those who belong to the Messiah Yeshua have put their old nature to death on the stake, along with its passions and desires. [25] Since it is through the Spirit that we have Life, let it also be through the Spirit that we order our lives day by day.

[26] Let us not become conceited, provoking and envying each other.

6 [1] Brothers, suppose someone is caught doing something wrong. You who have the Spirit should set him right, but in a spirit of humility, keeping an eye on yourselves so that you won't be tempted too. [2] Bear one another's burdens — in this way you will be fulfilling the *Torah's* true meaning, which the Messiah upholds. [3] For if anyone thinks he is something when he is really nothing, he is fooling himself. [4] So let each of you scrutinize his own actions. Then if you do find something to boast about, at least the boasting will be based on what you have actually done and not merely on a judgment that you are better than someone else; [5] for each person will carry his own load. [6] But whoever is being instructed in the Word should share all the good things he has with his instructor. [7] Don't delude yourselves: no one makes a fool of God! A person reaps what he sows. [8] Those who keep sowing in the field of their old nature, in order to meet its demands, will eventually reap ruin; but those who keep sowing in the field of the Spirit will reap from the Spirit everlasting life. [9] So let us not grow weary of doing what is good; for if we don't give up, we will in due time reap the harvest. [10] Therefore, as the opportunity arises, let us do what is good to everyone, and especially to the family of those who are trustingly faithful.

---

[k] Leviticus 19:18

¹¹ Look at the large letters I use as I close in my own handwriting.

¹² It is those who want to look good outwardly who are trying to get you to be circumcised. The only reason they are doing it is to escape persecution for preaching about the Messiah's execution-stake. ¹³ For even those who are getting circumcised don't observe the Torah. On the contrary, they want you to get circumcised so that they can boast of having gained your adherence. ¹⁴ But as for me, Heaven forbid that I should boast about anything except the execution-stake of our Lord Yeshua the Messiah! Through him, as far as I am concerned, the world has been put to death on the stake; and through him, as far as the world is concerned, I have been put to death on the stake.

¹⁵ For neither being circumcised nor being uncircumcised matters; what matters is being a new creation. ¹⁶ And as many as order their lives by this rule, shalom upon them and mercy, and upon the Isra'el of God!

¹⁷ From now on, I don't want anyone to give me any more tsuris, because I have scars on my body to prove that I belong to Yeshua!

¹⁸ The grace of our Lord Yeshua the Messiah be with your spirit, brothers. Amen.

The Letter from Yeshua's Emissary Sha'ul (Paul) to the Messianic Community in Ephesus

EPHESIANS

1 [1] From: Sha'ul, by God's will an emissary of the Messiah Yeshua

To: God's people living in Ephesus, that is, those who are trusting in the Messiah Yeshua:

[2] Grace to you and *shalom* from God our Father and the Lord Yeshua the Messiah.

[3] Praised be *ADONAI*, Father of our Lord Yeshua the Messiah, who in the Messiah has blessed us with every spiritual blessing in heaven. [4] In the Messiah he chose us in love before the creation of the universe to be holy and without defect in his presence — [5] He determined in advance that through Yeshua the Messiah we would be his sons — in keeping with his pleasure and purpose — [6] so that we would bring him praise commensurate with the glory of the grace he gave us through the Beloved One.

[7] In union with him, through the shedding of his blood, we are set free — our sins are forgiven; this accords with the wealth of the grace [8] he has lavished on us. In all his wisdom and insight [9] he has made known to us his secret plan, which by his own will he designed beforehand in connection with the Messiah [10] and will put into effect when the time is ripe — his plan to place everything in heaven and on earth under the Messiah's headship.

[11] Also in union with him we were given an inheritance, we who were picked in advance according to the purpose of the One who effects everything in keeping with the decision of his will, [12] so that we who earlier had put our hope in the Messiah would bring him praise commensurate with his glory.

[13] Furthermore, you who heard the message of the truth, the Good News offering you deliverance, and put your trust in the Messiah were sealed by him with the promised *Ruach HaKodesh*, [14] who guarantees our inheritance until we come into possession of it and thus bring him praise commensurate with his glory.

[15] For this reason, ever since I heard about your trust in the Lord Yeshua and your love for all God's people, [16] I have not stopped giving thanks for you. In my prayers I keep asking [17] the God of our Lord Yeshua the Messiah, the glorious Father, to give you a spirit of wisdom and revelation, so that you will have full knowledge of him. [18] I pray that he will give light to the eyes of your hearts, so that you will understand the hope to which he has called you, what rich glories there are in the inheritance he has promised his people, [19] and how surpassingly great is his power working in us who trust him. It works with the same mighty strength he used [20] when he worked in the Messiah to raise him from the dead and seat him at his right hand in heaven, [21] far above every ruler, authority, power, dominion or any other name that can be named either in the *'olam hazeh* or in the *'olam haba*. [22] Also, he has **put all things under his feet**[a]

---

[a] Psalm 8:7(6)

and made him head over everything for the Messianic Community, ^{23} which is his body, the full expression of him who fills all creation.

2 ^{1} You used to be dead because of your sins and acts of disobedience. ^{2} You walked in the ways of the *'olam hazeh* and obeyed the Ruler of the Powers of the Air, who is still at work among the disobedient. ^{3} Indeed, we all once lived this way — we followed the passions of our old nature and obeyed the wishes of our old nature and our own thoughts. In our natural condition we were headed for God's wrath, just like everyone else.

^{4} But God is so rich in mercy and loves us with such intense love ^{5} that, even when we were dead because of our acts of disobedience, he brought us to life along with the Messiah — it is by grace that you have been delivered. ^{6} That is, God raised us up with the Messiah Yeshua and seated us with him in heaven, ^{7} in order to exhibit in the ages to come how infinitely rich is his grace, how great is his kindness toward us who are united with the Messiah Yeshua. ^{8} For you have been delivered by grace through trusting, and even this is not your accomplishment but God's gift. ^{9} You were not delivered by your own actions; therefore no one should boast. ^{10} For we are of God's making, created in union with the Messiah Yeshua for a life of good actions already prepared by God for us to do.

^{11} Therefore, remember your former state: you Gentiles by birth — called the Uncircumcised by those who, merely because of an operation on their flesh, are called the Circumcised — ^{12} at that time had no Messiah. You were estranged from the national life of Isra'el. You were foreigners to the covenants embodying God's promise. You were in this world without hope and without God.

^{13} But now, you who were once far off have been brought near through the shedding of the Messiah's blood. ^{14} For he himself is our *shalom* — he has made us both one and has broken down the *m'chitzah* which divided us ^{15} by destroying in his own body the enmity occasioned by the *Torah*, with its commands set forth in the form of ordinances. He did this in order to create in union with himself from the two groups a single new humanity and thus make *shalom*, ^{16} and in order to reconcile to God both in a single body by being executed on a stake as a criminal and thus in himself killing that enmity.

^{17} Also, when he came, **he announced as Good News *shalom* to** you **far off and *shalom* to those nearby**,^{b} ^{18} news that through him we both have access in one Spirit to the Father.

^{19} So then, you are no longer foreigners and strangers. On the contrary, you are fellow-citizens with God's people and members of God's family. ^{20} You have been built on the foundation of the emissaries and the prophets, with the cornerstone being Yeshua the Messiah himself. ^{21} In union with him the whole building is held together, and it is growing into a holy temple in union with the Lord. ^{22} Yes, in union with him, you yourselves are being built together into a spiritual dwelling-place for God!

3 ^{1} It is a consequence of this that I, Sha'ul, am a prisoner of the Messiah Yeshua on behalf of you Gentiles. ^{2} I assume that you have heard of the work God in his grace has given me to do for your benefit, ^{3} and that it was by a revelation that this secret plan was made known to me. I have already written about it briefly, ^{4} and if you read

---

^{b} Isaiah 57:19

what I have written, you will grasp how I understand this secret plan concerning the Messiah. ⁵ In past generations it was not made known to mankind, as the Spirit is now revealing it to his emissaries and prophets, ⁶ that in union with the Messiah and through the Good News the Gentiles were to be joint heirs, a joint body and joint sharers with the Jews in what God has promised. ⁷ I became a servant of this Good News by God's gracious gift, which he gave me through the operation of his power. ⁸ To me, the least important of all God's holy people, was given this privilege of announcing to the Gentiles the Good News of the Messiah's unfathomable riches, ⁹ and of letting everyone see how this secret plan is going to work out. This plan, kept hidden for ages by God, the Creator of everything, ¹⁰ is for the rulers and authorities in heaven to learn, through the existence of the Messianic Community, how many-sided God's wisdom is. ¹¹ This accords with God's age-old purpose, accomplished in the Messiah Yeshua, our Lord. ¹² In union with him, through his faithfulness, we have boldness and confidence when we approach God. ¹³ So I ask you not to be discouraged by the troubles I endure on your behalf — it is all for your glory.

¹⁴ For this reason, I fall on my knees before the Father, ¹⁵ from whom every family in heaven and on earth receives its character. ¹⁶ I pray that from the treasures of his glory he will empower you with inner strength by his Spirit, ¹⁷ so that the Messiah may live in your hearts through your trusting. Also I pray that you will be rooted and founded in love, ¹⁸ so that you, with all God's people, will be given strength to grasp the breadth, length, height and depth of the Messiah's love, ¹⁹ yes, to know it, even though it is beyond all knowing, so that you will be filled with all the fullness of God.

²⁰ Now to him who by his power working in us is able to do far beyond anything we can ask or imagine, ²¹ to him be glory in the Messianic Community and in the Messiah Yeshua from generation to generation forever. *Amen.*

4 ¹ Therefore I, the prisoner united with the Lord, beg you to lead a life worthy of the calling to which you have been called.

² Always be humble, gentle and patient, bearing with one another in love, ³ and making every effort to preserve the unity the Spirit gives through the binding power of *shalom.* ⁴ There is one body and one Spirit, just as when you were called you were called to one hope. ⁵ And there is one Lord, one trust, one immersion, ⁶ and one God, the Father of all, who rules over all, works through all and is in all.

⁷ Each one of us, however, has been given grace to be measured by the Messiah's bounty. ⁸ This is why it says,

> **"After** he **went up into the heights,**
> he **led captivity captive**
> **and** he gave **gifts to mankind."**ᶜ

⁹ Now this phrase, **"he went up,"** what can it mean if not that he first went down into the lower parts, that is, the earth? ¹⁰ The one who went down is himself the one who also **went up**, far above all of heaven, in order to fill all things. ¹¹ Furthermore, **he gave** some people as emissaries, some as prophets, some as proclaimers of the Good

ᶜ Psalm 68:19(18)

News, and some as shepherds and teachers. ^{12}Their task is to equip God's people for the work of service that builds the body of the Messiah, ^{13} until we all arrive at the unity implied by trusting and knowing the Son of God, at full manhood, at the standard of maturity set by the Messiah's perfection.

^{14}We will then no longer be infants tossed about by the waves and blown along by every wind of teaching, at the mercy of people clever in devising ways to deceive. ^{15}Instead, speaking the truth in love, we will in every respect grow up into him who is the head, the Messiah. ^{16}Under his control, the whole body is being fitted and held together by the support of every joint, with each part working to fulfill its function; this is how the body grows and builds itself up in love.

^{17}Therefore I say this — indeed, in union with the Lord I insist on it: do not live any longer as the pagans live, with their sterile ways of thinking. ^{18}Their intelligence has been shrouded in darkness, and they are estranged from the life of God, because of the ignorance in them, which in turn comes from resisting God's will. ^{19}They have lost all feeling, so they have abandoned themselves to sensuality, practicing any kind of impurity and always greedy for more. ^{20}But this is not the lesson you learned from the Messiah! ^{21}If you really listened to him and were instructed about him, then you learned that since what is in Yeshua is truth, ^{22}then, so far as your former way of life is concerned, you must strip off your old nature, because your old nature is thoroughly rotted by its deceptive desires; ^{23}and you must let your spirits and minds keep being renewed, ^{24}and clothe yourselves with the new nature created to be godly, which expresses itself in the righteousness and holiness that flow from the truth.

^{25}Therefore, stripping off falsehood, **let everyone speak truth with his neighbor,**^{d} because we are intimately related to each other as parts of a body. ^{26}**Be angry, but don't sin**^{e} — don't let the sun go down before you have dealt with the cause of your anger; ^{27}otherwise you leave room for the Adversary.

^{28}The thief must stop stealing; instead, he should make an honest living by his own efforts. This way he will be able to share with those in need.

^{29}Let no harmful language come from your mouth, only good words that are helpful in meeting the need, words that will benefit those who hear them. ^{30}Don't cause grief to God's *Ruach HaKodesh*, for he has stamped you as his property until the day of final redemption. ^{31}Get rid of all bitterness, rage, anger, violent assertiveness and slander, along with all spitefulness. ^{32}Instead, be kind to each other, tenderhearted; and forgive each other, just as in the Messiah God has also forgiven you.

5 ^{1} So imitate God, as his dear children; ^{2} and live a life of love, just as also the Messiah loved us, indeed, on our behalf gave himself up as an offering, as a slaughtered sacrifice to God with a pleasing fragrance. ^{3} Among you there should not even be mentioned sexual immorality, or any kind of impurity, or greed; these are utterly inappropriate for God's holy people. ^{4} Also out of place are obscenity and stupid talk or coarse language; instead, you should be giving thanks. ^{5} For of this you can be sure: every sexually immoral, impure or greedy person — that is, every idol-worshipper — has no share in the Kingdom of the Messiah and of God. ^{6} Let no one deceive you with empty talk; for it is because of these things that God's judgment is coming on those who disobey him. ^{7} So don't become partners with them!

---

^{d} Zechariah 8:16 ^{e} Psalm 4:5(4)

⁸ For you used to be darkness; but now, united with the Lord, you are light. Live like children of light, ⁹ for the fruit of the light is in every kind of goodness, rightness and truth — ¹⁰ try to determine what will please the Lord. ¹¹ Have nothing to do with the deeds produced by darkness, but instead expose them, ¹² for it is shameful even to speak of the things these people do in secret. ¹³ But everything exposed to the light is revealed clearly for what it is, ¹⁴ since anything revealed is a light. This is why it says,

> "Get up, sleeper! Arise from the dead,
> and the Messiah will shine on you!"

¹⁵ Therefore, pay careful attention to how you conduct your life — live wisely, not unwisely. ¹⁶ Use your time well, for these are evil days. ¹⁷ So don't be foolish, but try to understand what the will of the Lord is.

¹⁸ Don't get drunk with wine, because it makes you lose control. Instead, keep on being filled with the Spirit — ¹⁹ sing psalms, hymns and spiritual songs to each other; sing to the Lord and make music in your heart to him; ²⁰ always give thanks for everything to God the Father in the name of our Lord Yeshua the Messiah.

²¹ Submit to one another in fear of the Messiah. ²² Wives should submit to their husbands as they do to the Lord; ²³ because the husband is head of the wife, just as the Messiah, as head of the Messianic Community, is himself the one who keeps the body safe. ²⁴ Just as the Messianic Community submits to the Messiah, so also wives should submit to their husbands in everything.

²⁵ As for husbands, love your wives, just as the Messiah loved the Messianic Community, indeed, gave himself up on its behalf, ²⁶ in order to set it apart for God, making it clean through immersion in the *mikveh*, so to speak, ²⁷ in order to present the Messianic Community to himself as a bride to be proud of, without a spot, wrinkle or any such thing, but holy and without defect. ²⁸ This is how husbands ought to love their wives — like their own bodies; for the man who loves his wife is loving himself. ²⁹ Why, no one ever hated his own flesh! On the contrary, he feeds it well and takes care of it, just as the Messiah does the Messianic Community, ³⁰ because we are parts of his Body. ³¹ **"Therefore a man will leave his father and mother and remain with his wife, and the two will become one."**[f] ³² There is profound truth hidden here, which I say concerns the Messiah and the Messianic Community. ³³ However, the text also applies to each of you individually: let each man love his wife as he does himself, and see that the wife respects her husband.

6 ¹ Children, what you should do in union with the Lord is obey your parents, for this is right. ² **"Honor your father and mother"** — this is the first commandment that embodies a promise — ³ **"so that it may go well with you, and you may live long in the Land."**[g]

⁴ Fathers, don't irritate your children and make them resentful; instead, raise them with the Lord's kind of discipline and guidance.

⁵ Slaves, obey your human masters with the same fear, trembling and single-heartedness with which you obey the Messiah. ⁶ Don't obey just to win their favor,

---

[f] Genesis 2:24   [g] Exodus 20:12; Deuteronomy 5:16

serving only when they are watching you; but serve as slaves of the Messiah, doing what God wants with all your heart. ⁷ Work willingly as slaves, as people do who are serving not merely human beings but the Lord. ⁸ Remember that whoever does good work, whether he be a slave or a free man, will be rewarded by the Lord.

⁹ And masters, treat your slaves the same way. Don't threaten them. Remember that in heaven both you and they have the same Master, and he has no favorites.

¹⁰ Finally, grow powerful in union with the Lord, in union with his mighty strength! ¹¹ Use all the armor and weaponry that God provides, so that you will be able to stand against the deceptive tactics of the Adversary. ¹² For we are not struggling against human beings, but against the rulers, authorities and cosmic powers governing this darkness, against the spiritual forces of evil in the heavenly realm. ¹³ So take up every piece of war equipment God provides; so that when the evil day comes, you will be able to resist; and when the battle is won, you will still be standing. ¹⁴ Therefore, stand! Have the belt of **truth buckled around** your **waist,**ʰ **put on righteousness for a breastplate,**ⁱ ¹⁵ and wear on your **feet the readiness that comes from the Good News of** shalom.ʲ ¹⁶ Always carry the shield of trust, with which you will be able to extinguish all the flaming arrows of the Evil One. ¹⁷ And take **the helmet of deliverance;**ᵏ along with the sword given by the Spirit, that is, the Word of God; ¹⁸ as you pray at all times, with all kinds of prayers and requests, in the Spirit, vigilantly and persistently, for all God's people.

¹⁹ And pray for me, too, that whenever I open my mouth, the words will be given to me to be bold in making known the secret of the Good News, ²⁰ for which I am an ambassador in chains. Pray that I may speak boldly, the way I should.

²¹ Now, so that you may also be informed about how I am and what I am doing, Tychicus, the dear brother and a faithful worker for the Lord, will tell you everything. ²² This is the very reason I have sent him to you, so that you may know how we are getting along and so that he may comfort and encourage you.

²³ *Shalom* to the brothers. May God the Father and the Lord Yeshua the Messiah give you love and trust. ²⁴ Grace be to all who love our Lord Yeshua the Messiah with undying love.

ʰ Isaiah 11:5   ⁱ Isaiah 59:17   ʲ Isaiah 52:7   ᵏ Isaiah 59:17

The Letter from Yeshua's Emissary Sha'ul (Paul) to the Messianic Community in Philippi

PHILIPPIANS

1 ¹ From: Sha'ul and Timothy, slaves of the Messiah Yeshua

To: All God's people united with the Messiah Yeshua and living in Philippi, along with the congregation leaders and *shammashim*:

² Grace to you and *shalom* from God our Father and the Lord Yeshua the Messiah.

³ I thank my God every time I think of you. ⁴ Whenever I pray for all of you I always pray with joy, ⁵ because you have shared in proclaiming the Good News from the very first day until now. ⁶ And I am sure of this: that the One who began a good work among you will keep it growing until it is completed on the Day of the Messiah Yeshua. ⁷ It is right for me to think this way about you all, because I have you on my heart; for whether I am in chains or defending and establishing the Good News, you are all sharing with me in this privileged work. ⁸ God can testify how I long for all of you with the deep affection of the Messiah Yeshua.

⁹ And this is my prayer: that your love may more and more overflow in fullness of knowledge and depth of discernment, ¹⁰ so that you will be able to determine what is best and thus be pure and without blame for the Day of the Messiah, ¹¹ filled with the fruit of righteousness that comes through Yeshua the Messiah — to the glory and praise of God.

¹² Now, brothers, I want you to know that what has happened to me has helped in advancing the Good News. ¹³ It has become clear to the whole palace and to everyone else that it is because of the Messiah that I am in chains. ¹⁴ Also, my being in prison has given most of the brothers in the Lord confidence, so that they have become much more bold in speaking the word of God fearlessly. ¹⁵ True, some are proclaiming the Messiah out of jealousy and rivalry, but others are doing it in goodwill. ¹⁶ The latter act from love, aware that I am put where I am for defending the Good News; ¹⁷ while the former announce the Messiah out of selfish ambition, with impure motives, supposing they can stir up trouble for me in prison. ¹⁸ But so what? All that matters is that in every way, whether honestly or in pretense, the Messiah is being proclaimed; and in that I rejoice.

Yes, and I will continue to rejoice, ¹⁹ for I know that **this will work out for my deliverance**,*ᵃ* because of your prayers and the support I get from the Spirit of Yeshua the Messiah. ²⁰ It all accords with my earnest expectation and hope that I will have nothing to be ashamed of; but rather, now, as always, the Messiah will be honored by my body, whether it is alive or dead. ²¹ For to me, life is the Messiah, and death is gain. ²² But if by living on in the body I can do fruitful work, then I don't know which to choose. ²³ I am caught in a dilemma: my desire is to go off and be with the Messiah — that is better by far — ²⁴ but because of you, the greater need is to stay on in the body.

ᵃ Job 13:16

²⁵ Yes, I am convinced of this; so I know I will stay on with you in order to help you progress in the faith and have joy in it. ²⁶ Then, through my being with you again, you will have even greater reason for boasting about the Messiah Yeshua.

²⁷ Only conduct your lives in a way worthy of the Good News of the Messiah; so that whether I come and see you or I hear about you from a distance, you stand firm, united in spirit, fighting with one accord for the faith of the Good News, ²⁸ not frightened by anything the opposition does. This will be for them an indication that they are headed for destruction and you for deliverance. And this is from God; ²⁹ because for the Messiah's sake it has been granted to you not only to trust in him but also to suffer on his behalf, ³⁰ to fight the same battles you once saw me fight and now hear that I am still fighting.

2 ¹ Therefore, if you have any encouragement for me from your being in union with the Messiah, any comfort flowing from love, any fellowship with me in the Spirit, or any compassion and sympathy, ² then complete my joy by having a common purpose and a common love, by being one in heart and mind. ³ Do nothing out of rivalry or vanity; but, in humility, regard each other as better than yourselves — ⁴ look out for each other's interests and not just for your own.

⁵ Let your attitude toward one another be governed by your being in union with the Messiah Yeshua:

⁶   Though he was in the form of God,
      he did not regard equality with God
      something to be possessed by force.
⁷   On the contrary, he emptied himself,
      in that he took the form of a slave
      by becoming like human beings are.

    And when he appeared as a human being,
⁸   he humbled himself still more
      by becoming obedient even to death —
      death on a stake as a criminal!
⁹   Therefore God raised him to the highest place
      and gave him the name above every name;

¹⁰   that in honor of the name given Yeshua,
      every knee will bow —
      in heaven, on earth and under the earth —
¹¹   **and every tongue will acknowledge**ᵇ
      that Yeshua the Messiah is *ADONAI* —
      to the glory of God the Father.

¹² So, my dear friends, just as you have always obeyed when I was with you, it is even more important that you obey now when I am away from you: keep working out your deliverance **with fear and trembling,**ᶜ ¹³ for God is the one working among you both

---

ᵇ Isaiah 45:23   ᶜ Psalm 2:11

the willing and the working for what pleases him. ¹⁴ Do everything without *kvetching* or arguing, ¹⁵ so that you may be blameless and pure children of God, without defect in the midst of **a twisted and perverted generation,**ᵈ among whom you shine like stars in the sky, ¹⁶ as you hold on to the Word of Life. If you do this, I will be able to boast, when the Day of the Messiah comes, that I did not run or toil for nothing. ¹⁷ Indeed, even if my lifeblood is poured out as a drink offering over the sacrifice and service of your faith, I will still be glad and rejoice with you all. ¹⁸ Likewise, you too should be glad and rejoice with me.

¹⁹ But I hope in the Lord Yeshua to send Timothy to you shortly, so that I too may be cheered by knowing how you are doing. ²⁰ I have no one who compares with him, who will care so sincerely for your welfare — ²¹ people all put their own interests ahead of the Messiah Yeshua's. ²² But you know his character, that like a child with his father he slaved with me to advance the Good News. ²³ So I hope to send him just as soon as I see how things will go with me, ²⁴ and I am confident in the Lord that before long I myself will come too.

²⁵ Also I considered it necessary to send you Epaphroditus, my brother, fellow-worker and fellow-soldier, the emissary whom you sent to take care of my needs; ²⁶ since he has been longing for you all and has been distressed because you heard he was ill. ²⁷ Indeed he was ill, close to death; but God had mercy on him — and not only on him, but also on me — otherwise I would have had sorrow piled on sorrow. ²⁸ Therefore, I am all the more eager to send him, so that you may rejoice when you see him again; and I, for my part, may be less sad. ²⁹ So give him a joyful welcome in the Lord; honor such people. ³⁰ For he risked his life and nearly died working for the Messiah, in order to give me the help you were not in a position to give.

3 ¹ In conclusion, my brothers: rejoice in union with the Lord.

It is no trouble for me to repeat what I have written you before, and for you it will be a safeguard: ² beware of the dogs, those evildoers, the Mutilated! ³ For it is we who are the Circumcised, we who worship by the Spirit of God and make our boast in the Messiah Yeshua! We do not put confidence in human qualifications, ⁴ even though I certainly have grounds for putting confidence in such things. If anyone else thinks he has grounds for putting confidence in human qualifications, I have better grounds:

⁵ · *b'rit-milah* on the eighth day,
· by birth belonging to the people of Isra'el,
· from the tribe of Binyamin,
· a Hebrew-speaker, with Hebrew-speaking parents,
· in regard to the *Torah,* a *Parush,*
⁶ · in regard to zeal, a persecutor of the Messianic Community,
· in regard to the righteousness demanded by legalism, blameless.

⁷ But the things that used to be advantages for me, I have, because of the Messiah, come to consider a disadvantage. ⁸ Not only that, but I consider everything a disadvantage in comparison with the supreme value of knowing the Messiah Yeshua as my Lord. It was because of him that I gave up everything and regard it all as garbage,

---

ᵈ Deuteronomy 32:5

in order to gain the Messiah ⁹ and be found in union with him, not having any righteousness of my own based on legalism, but having that righteousness which comes through the Messiah's faithfulness, the righteousness from God based on trust. ¹⁰ Yes, I gave it all up in order to know him, that is, to know the power of his resurrection and the fellowship of his sufferings as I am being conformed to his death, ¹¹ so that somehow I might arrive at being resurrected from the dead. ¹² It is not that I have already obtained it or already reached the goal — no, I keep pursuing it in the hope of taking hold of that for which the Messiah Yeshua took hold of me. ¹³ Brothers, I, for my part, do not think of myself as having yet gotten hold of it; but one thing I do: forgetting what is behind me and straining forward toward what lies ahead, ¹⁴ I keep pursuing the goal in order to win the prize offered by God's upward calling in the Messiah Yeshua. ¹⁵ Therefore, as many of us as are mature, let us keep paying attention to this; and if you are differently minded about anything, God will also reveal this to you. ¹⁶ Only let our conduct fit the level we have already reached.

¹⁷ Brothers, join in imitating me, and pay attention to those who live according to the pattern we have set for you. ¹⁸ For many — I have told you about them often before, and even now I say it with tears — live as enemies of the Messiah's execution-stake. ¹⁹ They are headed for destruction! Their god is the belly; they are proud of what they ought to be ashamed of, since they are concerned about the things of the world. ²⁰ But we are citizens of heaven, and it is from there that we expect a Deliverer, the Lord Yeshua the Messiah. ²¹ He will change the bodies we have in this humble state and make them like his glorious body, using the power which enables him to bring everything under his control.

4 ¹ So, my brothers, whom I love and long for, my joy and my crown, my dear friends, keep standing firm in union with the Lord.

² I beg Evodia and I beg Syntyche to agree with each other in union with the Lord. ³ I also request you, loyal Syzygus, to help these women; for they have worked hard proclaiming the Good News with me, along with Clement and the rest of my fellow-workers whose names are in the Book of Life.

⁴ Rejoice in union with the Lord always! I will say it again: rejoice! ⁵ Let everyone see how reasonable and gentle you are. The Lord is near! ⁶ Don't worry about anything; on the contrary, make your requests known to God by prayer and petition, with thanksgiving. ⁷ Then God's *shalom*, passing all understanding, will keep your hearts and minds safe in union with the Messiah Yeshua. ⁸ In conclusion, brothers, focus your thoughts on what is true, noble, righteous, pure, lovable or admirable, on some virtue or on something praiseworthy. ⁹ Keep doing what you have learned and received from me, what you have heard and seen me doing; then the God who gives *shalom* will be with you.

¹⁰ In union with the Lord I greatly rejoice that now, after this long time, you have let your concern for me express itself again. Of course, you were concerned for me all along, but you had no opportunity to express it. ¹¹ Not that I am saying this to call attention to any need of mine; since, as far as I am concerned, I have learned to be content regardless of circumstances. ¹² I know what it is to be in want, and I know what it is to have more than enough — in everything and in every way I have learned the secret of being full and being hungry, of having abundance and being in need. ¹³ I can do all things through him who gives me power.

[14] Nevertheless, it was good of you to share in my trouble. [15] And you Philippians yourselves know that in the early days of my work spreading the Good News, when I left Macedonia, not a single congregation shared with me in the matter of giving and receiving — only you. [16] Indeed, in Thessalonica when I needed it, you sent me aid twice. [17] I am not seeking the gift; rather, I am looking for what will increase the credit balance of your account. [18] I have been more than paid in full: I have been filled, since I have received from Epaphroditus the gifts you sent — they are **a fragrant aroma,**[e] an acceptable sacrifice, one that pleases God well. [19] Moreover, my God will fill every need of yours according to his glorious wealth, in union with the Messiah Yeshua. [20] And to God our Father be the glory forever and ever. *Amen.*

[21] Greet each of God's people in the Messiah Yeshua. The brothers with me send their greetings to you. [22] All God's people send greetings, but especially those in the Emperor's household.

[23] The grace of the Lord Yeshua the Messiah be with your spirit.

---

[e] Genesis 8:21; Exodus 29:18

The Letter from Yeshua's Emissary Sha'ul (Paul)
to the Messianic Community in Colosse

COLOSSIANS

1 ¹ From: Sha'ul, by God's will an emissary of the Messiah Yeshua, and brother Timothy

² To: God's people in Colosse, faithful brothers in the Messiah:

Grace to you and *shalom* from God our Father.

³ Whenever we pray, we always give thanks for you to God, the Father of our Lord Yeshua the Messiah. ⁴ For we have heard of your trust in the Messiah Yeshua and of the love you have for all God's people. ⁵ Both spring from the confident hope that you will receive what is stored up for you in heaven. You heard of this earlier in the message about the truth. This Good News ⁶ has made its presence felt among you, just as it is also **being fruitful and multiplying**ᵃ throughout the world in the same way as it has among you since the day you heard and understood the grace of God as it really is. ⁷ You learned it from Epaphras, our dear fellow-slave and a faithful worker for the Messiah on your behalf; ⁸ and he has told us about the love which the Spirit has given you.

⁹ Therefore, from the day we heard of it, we have not stopped praying for you, asking God to fill you with the knowledge of his will in all the wisdom and understanding which the Spirit gives; ¹⁰ so that you may live lives worthy of the Lord and entirely pleasing to him, **being fruitful** in every good work **and multiply**ing in the full knowledge of God. ¹¹ We pray that you will be continually strengthened with all the power that comes from his glorious might; so that you will be able to persevere and be patient in any situation, joyfully ¹² giving thanks to the Father for having made you fit to share in the inheritance of his people in the light. ¹³ He has rescued us from the domain of darkness and transferred us into the Kingdom of his dear Son.

¹⁴ It is through his Son that we have redemption — that is, our sins have been forgiven. ¹⁵ He is the visible image of the invisible God. He is supreme over all creation, ¹⁶ because in connection with him were created all things — in heaven and on earth, visible and invisible, whether thrones, lordships, rulers or authorities — they have all been created through him and for him. ¹⁷ He existed before all things, and he holds everything together.

¹⁸ Also he is head of the Body, the Messianic Community — he is the beginning, the firstborn from the dead, so that he might hold first place in everything. ¹⁹ For it pleased God to have his full being live in his Son ²⁰ and through his Son to reconcile to himself all things, whether on earth or in heaven, making peace through him, through having his Son shed his blood by being executed on a stake.

²¹ In other words, you, who at one time were separated from God and had a hostile attitude towards him because of your wicked deeds, ²² he has now reconciled

---

ᵃ Genesis 1:28

1470

in the Son's physical body through his death; in order to present you holy and without defect or reproach before himself — ²³ provided, of course, that you continue in your trusting, grounded and steady, and don't let yourselves be moved away from the hope offered in the Good News you heard.

This is the Good News that has been proclaimed in all creation under heaven; and I, Sha'ul, have become a servant of it. ²⁴ I rejoice in my present sufferings on your behalf! Yes, I am completing in my own flesh what has been lacking of the Messiah's afflictions, on behalf of his Body, the Messianic Community. ²⁵ I became a servant of the Good News because God gave me this work to do for your benefit. The work is to make fully known the message from God, ²⁶ the secret hidden for generations, for ages, but now made clear to the people he has set apart for himself. ²⁷ To them God wanted to make known how great among the Gentiles is the glorious richness of this secret. And the secret is this: the Messiah is united with you people! In that rests your hope of glory! ²⁸ We, for our part, proclaim him; we warn, confront and teach everyone in all wisdom; so that we may present everyone as having reached the goal, united with the Messiah. ²⁹ It is for this that I toil, striving with all the energy that he stirs up in me so mightily.

2 ¹ For I want you to know how hard I work for you, for those in Laodicea, and for the rest of those who have not met me personally. ² My purpose is that they may be encouraged, that they may be joined together in love, and that they may have all the riches derived from being assured of understanding and fully knowing God's secret truth, which is — the Messiah! ³ It is in him that all the treasures of wisdom and knowledge are hidden.

⁴ I say this so that no one will fool you with plausible but specious arguments. ⁵ For although I am away from you physically, I am with you in spirit, rejoicing as I see the disciplined and resolute firmness of your trust in the Messiah. ⁶ Therefore, just as you received the Messiah Yeshua as Lord, keep living your life united with him. ⁷ Remain deeply rooted in him; continue being built up in him and confirmed in your trust, the way you were taught, so that you overflow in thanksgiving.

⁸ Watch out, so that no one will take you captive by means of philosophy and empty deceit, following human tradition which accords with the elemental spirits of the world but does not accord with the Messiah. ⁹ For in him, bodily, lives the fullness of all that God is. ¹⁰ And it is in union with him that you have been made full — he is the head of every rule and authority.

¹¹ Also it was in union with him that you were circumcised with a circumcision not done by human hands, but accomplished by stripping away the old nature's control over the body. In this circumcision done by the Messiah, ¹² you were buried along with him by being immersed; and in union with him, you were also raised up along with him by God's faithfulness that worked when he raised Yeshua from the dead. ¹³ You were dead because of your sins, that is, because of your "foreskin," your old nature. But God made you alive along with the Messiah by forgiving you all your sins. ¹⁴ He wiped away the bill of charges against us. Because of the regulations, it stood as a testimony against us; but he removed it by nailing it to the execution-stake. ¹⁵ Stripping the rulers and authorities of their power, he made a public spectacle of them, triumphing over them by means of the stake.

16 So don't let anyone pass judgment on you in connection with eating and drinking, or in regard to a Jewish festival or *Rosh-Hodesh* or *Shabbat.* 17 These are a shadow of things that are coming, but the body is of the Messiah.

18 Don't let anyone deny you the prize by insisting that you engage in self-mortification or angel-worship. Such people are always going on about some vision they have had, and they vainly puff themselves up by their worldly outlook. 19 They fail to hold to the Head, from whom the whole Body, receiving supply and being held together by its joints and ligaments, grows as God makes it grow. 20 If, along with the Messiah, you died to the elemental spirits of the world, then why, as if you still belonged to the world, are you letting yourselves be bothered by its rules? — 21 "Don't touch this!" "Don't eat that!" "Don't handle the other!" 22 Such prohibitions are concerned with things meant to perish by being used [not by being avoided!], and they are based on **man-made rules and teachings.**[b] 23 They do indeed have the outward appearance of wisdom, with their self-imposed religious observances, false humility and asceticism; but they have no value at all in restraining people from indulging their old nature.

3 1 So if you were raised along with the Messiah, then seek the things above, where the Messiah is **sitting at the right hand of God.**[c] 2 Focus your minds on the things above, not on things here on earth. 3 For you have died, and your life is hidden with the Messiah in God. 4 When the Messiah, who is our life, appears, then you too will appear with him in glory!

5 Therefore, put to death the earthly parts of your nature — sexual immorality, impurity, lust, evil desires and greed (which is a form of idolatry); 6 for it is because of these things that God's anger is coming on those who disobey him. 7 True enough, you used to practice these things in the life you once lived; 8 but now, put them all away — anger, exasperation, meanness, slander and obscene talk. 9 Never lie to one another; because you have stripped away the old self, with its ways, 10 and have put on the new self, which is continually being renewed in fuller and fuller knowledge, closer and closer to the image of its Creator. 11 The new self allows no room for discriminating between Gentile and Jew, circumcised and uncircumcised, foreigner, savage, slave, free man; on the contrary, in all, the Messiah is everything.

12 Therefore, as God's chosen people, holy and dearly loved, clothe yourselves with feelings of compassion and with kindness, humility, gentleness and patience. 13 Bear with one another; if anyone has a complaint against someone else, forgive him. Indeed, just as the Lord has forgiven you, so you must forgive.

14 Above all these, clothe yourselves with love, which binds everything together perfectly; 15 and let the *shalom* which comes from the Messiah be your heart's decision-maker, for this is why you were called to be part of a single Body.

And be thankful — 16 let the Word of the Messiah, in all its richness, live in you, as you teach and counsel each other in all wisdom, and as you sing psalms, hymns and spiritual songs with gratitude to God in your hearts. 17 That is, everything you do or say, do in the name of the Lord Yeshua, giving thanks through him to God the Father.

18 Wives, subject yourselves to your husbands, as is appropriate in the Lord. 19 Husbands, love your wives and don't treat them harshly.

[b] Isaiah 29:13   [c] Psalm 110:1

^{20} Children, obey your parents in everything; for this pleases the Lord.

^{21} Fathers, don't irritate your children and make them resentful, or they will become discouraged.

^{22} Slaves, obey your human masters in everything, not serving only when they are watching you, to win their favor, but single-heartedly, fearing the Lord. ^{23} Whatever work you do, put yourself into it, as those who are serving not merely other people, but the Lord. ^{24} Remember that as your reward, you will receive the inheritance from the Lord. You are slaving for the Lord, for the Messiah. ^{25} Don't worry — whoever is doing wrong will be paid in kind for his wrong, and there is no favoritism shown.

4 ^{1} Masters, treat your slaves justly and fairly. Remember that you too have a Master in heaven.

^{2} Keep persisting in prayer, staying alert in it and being thankful. ^{3} Include prayer for us, too, that God may open a door for us to proclaim the message about the secret of the Messiah — for that is why I am in prison. ^{4} And pray that I may speak, as I should, in a way that makes the message clear.

^{5} Behave wisely toward outsiders, making full use of every opportunity — ^{6} let your conversation always be gracious and interesting, so that you will know how to respond to any particular individual.

^{7} Our dear brother Tychicus, who is a faithful worker and fellow-slave in the Lord, will give you all the news about me. ^{8} I have sent him to you for this very reason — so that you might know how we are, and so that he might encourage you. ^{9} I have sent him with Onesimus, the dear and faithful brother, who is one of you; they will tell you everything that has happened here.

^{10} Aristarchus, my fellow prisoner, sends greetings, as does Mark, Bar-Nabba's cousin, concerning whom you have received instructions — if he comes to you, welcome him. ^{11} Yeshua, the one called Justus, also sends greetings. These three are among the Circumcised; and among my fellow workers for the Kingdom of God, only they have turned out to be a comfort to me.

^{12} Epaphras sends greetings; he is one of you, a slave of the Messiah Yeshua who always agonizes in his prayer on your behalf, praying that you may stand firm, mature and fully confident, as you devote yourselves completely to God's will. ^{13} For I can testify to him that he works hard for you and for those in Laodicea and Hierapolis.

^{14} Our dear friend Luke, the doctor, and Demas send you greetings.

^{15} Give my greetings to the brothers in Laodicea, also to Nympha and the congregation that meets in her home. ^{16} After this letter has been read to you, have it read also in the congregation of the Laodiceans; and you, in turn, are to read the letter that will come from Laodicea. ^{17} And tell Archippus, "See that you complete the task you were given in the Lord."

^{18} *This greeting I, Sha'ul, write with my own hand.*

Remember my imprisonment!

Grace be with you!

The First Letter from Yeshua's Emissary Sha'ul (Paul)
to the Messianic Community in Thessalonica

1 THESSALONIANS

1 ¹ From: Sha'ul, Sila and Timothy

To: The Messianic Community of the Thessalonians, united with God the Father and the Lord Yeshua the Messiah:

Grace to you and *shalom*.

² We always thank God for all of you, regularly mentioning you in our prayers, ³ calling to mind before God our Father what our Lord Yeshua the Messiah has brought about in you — how your trust produces action, your love hard work, and your hope perseverance. ⁴ We know, brothers, that God has loved and chosen you; ⁵ that the Good News we brought did not become for you a matter only of words, but also one of power, the *Ruach HaKodesh* and total conviction — just as you know how we lived for your sakes when we were with you. ⁶ You, indeed, became imitators of us and of the Lord; so that even though you were going through severe troubles, you received the Word with joy from the *Ruach HaKodesh*.

⁷ Thus you became a pattern for all the believers in Macedonia and Achaia; ⁸ for the Lord's message sounded forth from you not only in Macedonia and Achaia, but everywhere your trust toward God became known. The result is that we don't need to say anything; ⁹ since they themselves keep telling us about the welcome we received from you and how you turned to God from idols, to serve the true God, the one who is alive, ¹⁰ and to wait for his Son Yeshua, whom he raised from the dead, to appear from heaven and rescue us from the impending fury of God's judgment.

2 ¹ You yourselves know, brothers, that our visit to you was not fruitless. ² On the contrary, although we had already suffered and been outraged in Philippi, as you know, we had the courage, united with our God, to tell you the Good News even under great pressure. ³ For the appeal we make does not flow from error or from impure motives, neither do we try to trick people. ⁴ Instead, since God has tested us and found us fit to be entrusted with Good News, this is how we speak: not to win favor with people but with God, who tests our hearts. ⁵ For, as you know, never did we employ flattering talk, nor did we put on a false front to mask greed — God is witness. ⁶ Nor did we seek human praise — either from you or from others. ⁷ As emissaries of the Messiah, we could have made our weight felt; but instead, we were gentle when we were with you, like a mother feeding and caring for her children. ⁸ We were so devoted to you that we were glad to share with you not only God's Good News but also our own lives, because you had become very dear to us. ⁹ For you remember, brothers, our toil and hardship, how we worked night and day not to put a burden on any of you while we were proclaiming God's Good News to you. ¹⁰ You are witnesses, and so is God, of how holy, righteous and blameless our behavior was in the sight of you believers; ¹¹ for you know that we treated each one of you the way a father treats his children — ¹²we encouraged you and comforted you and appealed to you to lead lives worthy of God, who calls you into his Kingdom and glory.

¹³Another reason we regularly thank God is that when you heard the Word of God from us, you received it not merely as a human word, but as it truly is, God's Word, which is at work in you believers. ¹⁴For, brothers, you came to be imitators of God's congregations in Y'hudah that are united with the Messiah Yeshua — you suffered the same things from your countrymen as they did from the Judeans who ¹⁵both killed the Lord Yeshua and the prophets, and chased us out too. They are displeasing God and opposing all mankind ¹⁶by trying to keep us from speaking to the Gentiles, so that they may be delivered. Their object seems to be always to make their sins as bad as possible! But God's fury will catch up with them in the end.

¹⁷And as for us, brothers, when we were deprived of your company for a short time — in person, but not in thought — we missed you and tried hard to come and see you. ¹⁸We wanted so much to come to you — I, Sha'ul, tried more than once — but the Adversary stopped us. ¹⁹For when our Lord Yeshua returns, what will be our hope, our joy, our crown to boast about? Won't it be you? ²⁰Yes, you are our glory and our joy!

3 ¹So when we could no longer stand it, we agreed to be left in Athens alone ²and sent Timothy, our brother and God's fellow worker for the Good News of the Messiah, to make you solid and encourage you in your trust; ³so that none of you would let these persecutions unsettle him. For you yourselves know that these are bound to come to us; ⁴even when we were with you, we kept telling you in advance that we were about to be persecuted; and indeed it has happened, as you know. ⁵That is the reason why, after I could stand it no longer, I sent to find out about your trust. I was afraid that somehow the Tempter had tempted you, and our hard work had been wasted.

⁶But now Timothy has come to us from you, bringing good news about your trust and love, and telling us that you remember us well and are always longing to see us, just as we long to see you. ⁷Because of this, brothers, in spite of all our trouble and distress, we were comforted over you — because of your trust; ⁸so that now we are alive; since you continue to stand fast, united with the Lord.

⁹Indeed, how can we thank God enough for you or express to our God all the joy we feel because of you? ¹⁰Night and day we pray as hard as we can that we will be able to see you face to face and supply whatever shortcomings there may be in your trust. ¹¹May God our Father and our Lord Yeshua direct our way to you.

¹²And as for you, may the Lord make you increase and overflow in love toward each other, indeed, toward everyone, just as we do toward you; ¹³so that he may give you the inner strength to be blameless, by reason of your holiness, when you stand before God our Father at the coming of our Lord Yeshua with all his angels.

4 ¹Therefore, brothers, just as you learned from us how you had to live in order to please God, and just as you are living this way now, we ask you — indeed, united with the Lord Yeshua, we urge you — to keep doing so more and more. ²For you know what instructions we gave you on the authority of the Lord Yeshua. ³What God wants is that you be holy, that you keep away from sexual immorality, ⁴that each of you know how to manage his sexual impulses in a holy and honorable manner,

⁵ without giving in to lustful desires, like the pagans who don't know God. ⁶ No one should wrong his brother in this matter or take advantage of him, because the Lord punishes all who do such things — as we have explained to you before at length. ⁷ For God did not call us to live an unclean life but a holy one. ⁸ Therefore, whoever rejects this teaching is rejecting not a man but God, indeed, the One who gives you the *Ruach HaKodesh*, which is his.

⁹ Concerning love for the brothers we do not need to write you, for you yourselves have been taught by God to love each other; ¹⁰ and you do love all the brothers throughout Macedonia. But we urge you, brothers, to do it even more.

¹¹ Also, make it your ambition to live quietly, to mind your own business and to earn your living by your own efforts — just as we told you. ¹² Then your daily life will gain the respect of outsiders, and you will not be dependent on anyone.

¹³ Now, brothers, we want you to know the truth about those who have died; otherwise, you might become sad the way other people ¹⁴ do who have nothing to hope for. For since we believe that Yeshua died and rose again, we also believe that in the same way God, through Yeshua, will take with him those who have died. ¹⁵ When we say this, we base it on the Lord's own word: we who remain alive when the Lord comes will certainly not take precedence over those who have died. ¹⁶ For the Lord himself will come down from heaven with a rousing cry, with a call from one of the ruling angels, and with God's *shofar*; those who died united with the Messiah will be the first to rise; ¹⁷ then we who are left still alive will be caught up with them in the clouds to meet the Lord in the air; and thus we will always be with the Lord. ¹⁸ So encourage each other with these words.

5 ¹ But you have no need to have anything written to you, brothers, about the times and dates when this will happen; ² because you yourselves well know that the Day of the Lord will come like a thief in the night. ³ When people are saying, "Everything is so peaceful and secure," then destruction will suddenly come upon them, the way labor pains come upon a pregnant woman, and there is no way they will escape.

⁴ But you, brothers, are not in the dark, so that the Day should take you by surprise like a thief; ⁵ for you are all people who belong to the light, who belong to the day. We don't belong to the night or to darkness, ⁶ so let's not be asleep, like the rest are; on the contrary, let us stay alert and sober. ⁷ People who sleep, sleep at night; and people who get drunk, get drunk at night. ⁸ But since we belong to the day, let us stay sober, **putting on** trust and love **as a breastplate and the hope of being delivered as a helmet**.ᵃ ⁹ For God has not intended that we should experience his fury, but that we should gain deliverance through our Lord Yeshua the Messiah, ¹⁰ who died on our behalf so that whether we are alive or dead, we may live along with him. ¹¹ Therefore, encourage each other, and build each other up — just as you are doing.

¹² We ask you, brothers, to respect those who are working hard among you, those who are guiding you in the Lord and confronting you in order to help you change. ¹³ Treat them with the highest regard and love because of the work they are doing. Live at peace among yourselves; ¹⁴ but we urge you, brothers, to confront

---

ᵃ Isaiah 59:17

those who are lazy, your aim being to help them change, to encourage the timid, to assist the weak, and to be patient with everyone.

15 See that no one repays evil for evil; on the contrary, always try to do good to each other, indeed, to everyone.

16 Always be joyful. 17 Pray regularly. 18 In everything give thanks, for this is what God wants from you who are united with the Messiah Yeshua.

19 Don't quench the Spirit, 20 don't despise inspired messages. 21 But do test everything — hold onto what is good, 22 but keep away from every form of evil.

23 May the God of *shalom* make you completely holy — may your entire spirit, soul and body be kept blameless for the coming of our Lord Yeshua the Messiah. 24 The one calling you is faithful, and he will do it.

25 Brothers, keep praying for us.

26 Greet all the brothers with a holy kiss.

27 I charge you in the Lord to have this letter read to all the brothers.

28 The grace of our Lord Yeshua the Messiah be with you.

2 THESSALONIANS

1 [1] From: Sha'ul, Sila and Timothy

To: The Messianic Community of the Thessalonians, united with God our Father and the Lord Yeshua the Messiah:

[2] Grace to you and *shalom* from God the Father and the Lord Yeshua the Messiah.

[3] We have to keep thanking God for you always, brothers, as is appropriate; because your trust continues to grow greater, and the love you each have for one another continues to increase. [4] Therefore, we boast about you in the congregations of God because of your perseverance and trust in all the persecutions and troubles you are going through. [5] This is clear evidence that God's judgment is just; and as a result, you will be counted worthy of the Kingdom of God for which you are suffering. [6] For it is justice for God to pay back trouble to those who are troubling you, [7] and to give rest along with us to you who are being troubled, when the Lord Yeshua is revealed from heaven with his mighty angels [8] **in a fiery flame. Then he will punish those who don't know God,**[a] that is, those who don't listen to the Good News of our Lord Yeshua and obey it. [9] They will suffer the just penalty of eternal destruction, **far away from the face of the Lord and the glory of his might.**[b] [10] On that Day, when he comes to be glorified by his holy people and admired by all who have trusted, you will be among them, because you trusted our witness to you.

[11] With this in view, we always pray for you that our God may make you worthy of his calling and may fulfill by his power every good purpose of yours and every action stemming from your trust. [12] In this way, the name of our Lord Yeshua will be glorified in you, and you in him, in accordance with the grace of our God and the Lord Yeshua the Messiah.

2 [1] But in connection with the coming of our Lord Yeshua the Messiah and our gathering together to meet him, we ask you, brothers, [2] not to be easily shaken in your thinking or anxious because of a spirit or a spoken message or a letter supposedly from us claiming that the Day of the Lord has already come. [3] Don't let anyone deceive you in any way.

For the Day will not come until after the Apostasy has come and the man who separates himself from *Torah* has been revealed, the one destined for doom. [4] He will oppose himself to **everything** that people call a **god** or make an object of worship; **he will put himself above** them all, so that he will sit in the Temple **of God** and proclaim that he himself is **God.**[c]

[5] Don't you remember that when I was still with you, I used to tell you these things? [6] And now you know what is restraining, so that he may be revealed in his

---

[a] Isaiah 66:15; Jeremiah 10:25; Psalm 79:6   [b] Isaiah 2:10, 19, 21   [c] Ezekiel 28:2

own time. ⁷For already this separating from *Torah* is at work secretly, but it will be secretly only until he who is restraining is out of the way. ⁸Then the one who embodies separation from *Torah* will be revealed, the one whom the Lord Yeshua **will slay with the breath of his mouth**ᵈ and destroy by the glory of his coming.

⁹When this man who avoids *Torah* comes, the Adversary will give him the power to work all kinds of false miracles, signs and wonders. ¹⁰He will enable him to deceive, in all kinds of wicked ways, those who are headed for destruction because they would not receive the love of the truth that could have saved them. ¹¹This is why God is causing them to go astray, so that they will believe the Lie. ¹²The result will be that all who have not believed the truth, but have taken their pleasure in wickedness, will be condemned.

¹³But we have to keep thanking God for you always, brothers whom the Lord loves, because God chose you as firstfruits for deliverance by giving you the holiness that has its origin in the Spirit and the faithfulness that has its origin in the truth. ¹⁴He called you to this through our Good News, so that you could have the glory of our Lord Yeshua the Messiah.

¹⁵Therefore, brothers, stand firm; and hold to the traditions you were taught by us, whether we spoke them or wrote them in a letter. ¹⁶And may our Lord Yeshua the Messiah himself and God our Father, who has loved us and by his grace given us eternal comfort and a good hope, ¹⁷comfort your hearts and strengthen you in every good word and deed.

3 ¹Finally, brothers, pray for us that the Lord's message may spread rapidly and receive honor, just as it did with you; ²and that we may be rescued from wicked and evil people, for not everyone has trust. ³But the Lord is worthy of trust; he will make you firm and guard you from the Evil One. ⁴Yes, united with the Lord we are confident about you, that you are doing the things we are telling you to do, and that you will keep on doing them. ⁵May the Lord direct your hearts into God's love and the perseverance which the Messiah gives.

⁶Now, in the name of the Lord Yeshua the Messiah we command you, brothers, to stay away from any brother who is leading a life of idleness, a life not in keeping with the tradition you received from us. ⁷For you yourselves know how you must imitate us, that we were not idle when we were among you. ⁸We did not accept anyone's food without paying; on the contrary, we labored and toiled, day and night, working so as not to be a burden to any of you. ⁹It was not that we hadn't the right to be supported, but so that we could make ourselves an example to imitate. ¹⁰For even when we were with you, we gave you this command: if someone won't work, he shouldn't eat! ¹¹We hear that some of you are leading a life of idleness — not busy working, just busybodies! ¹²We command such people — and in union with the Lord Yeshua the Messiah we urge them — to settle down, get to work, and earn their own living. ¹³And you brothers who are doing what is good, don't slack off! ¹⁴Furthermore, if anyone does not obey what we are saying in this letter, take note of him and have nothing to do with him, so that he will be ashamed. ¹⁵But don't consider him an enemy; on the contrary, confront him as a brother and try to help him change.

ᵈIsaiah 11:4; Job 4:9

¹⁶ Now may the Lord of *shalom* himself give you *shalom* always in all ways. The Lord be with all of you.

¹⁷ *The greeting in my own handwriting: From Sha'ul. This is the mark of genuineness in every letter, this is what my handwriting looks like.*

¹⁸ *The grace of our Lord Yeshua the Messiah be with you all.*

1 TIMOTHY

1 ¹ From: Sha'ul, an emissary of the Messiah Yeshua by command of God our deliverer and the Messiah Yeshua our hope,

² To: Timothy, a true son because of your trust:

Grace, mercy and *shalom* from God the Father and the Messiah Yeshua our Lord.

³ As I counseled you when I was leaving for Macedonia, stay on in Ephesus, so that you may order certain people who are teaching a different doctrine to stop. ⁴ Have them stop devoting their attention to myths and never-ending genealogies; these divert people to speculating instead of doing God's work, which requires trust. ⁵ The purpose of this order is to promote love from a clean heart, from a good conscience and from sincere trust. ⁶ Some, by aiming amiss, have wandered off into fruitless discussion. ⁷ They want to be teachers of *Torah*, but they understand neither their own words nor the matters about which they make such emphatic pronouncements. ⁸ We know that the *Torah* is good, provided one uses it in the way the *Torah* itself intends. ⁹ We are aware that *Torah* is not for a person who is righteous, but for those who are heedless of *Torah* and rebellious, ungodly and sinful, wicked and worldly, for people who kill their fathers and mothers, for murderers, ¹⁰ the sexually immoral — both heterosexual and homosexual — slave dealers, liars, perjurers, and anyone who acts contrary to the sound teaching ¹¹ that accords with the Good News of the glorious and blessed God.

This Good News was entrusted to me; ¹² and I thank the one who has given me strength, the Messiah Yeshua, our Lord, that he considered me trustworthy enough to put me in his service, ¹³ even though I used to be a man who blasphemed and persecuted and was arrogant! But I received mercy because I had acted in unbelief, not understanding what I was doing. ¹⁴ Our Lord's grace overflowed to me with trust and love that come through the Messiah Yeshua. ¹⁵ So here is a statement you can trust, one that fully deserves to be accepted: the Messiah came into the world to save sinners, and I'm the number one sinner! ¹⁶ But this is precisely why I received mercy — so that in me, as the number one sinner, Yeshua the Messiah might demonstrate how very patient he is, as an example to those who would later come to trust in him and thereby have eternal life. ¹⁷ So to the King — eternal, imperishable and invisible, the only God there is — let there be honor and glory for ever and ever! *Amen.*

¹⁸ This charge, son Timothy, I put to you, in keeping with the prophecies already made about you, so that by these prophecies you may fight the good fight, ¹⁹ armed with trust and a good conscience. By rejecting conscience, some have made shipwreck of their trust; ²⁰ among them are Hymenaeus and Alexander. I have turned them over to the Adversary, so that they will learn not to insult God.

2 ¹ First of all, then, I counsel that petitions, prayers, intercessions and thanksgivings be made for all human beings, ² including kings and all in positions of prominence; so that we may lead quiet and peaceful lives, being godly and upright in everything. ³ This is what God, our Deliverer, regards as good; this is what meets his approval.

⁴ He wants all humanity to be delivered and come to full knowledge of the truth. ⁵ For **God is one**;ᵃ and there is but one Mediator between God and humanity, Yeshua the Messiah, himself human, ⁶ who gave himself as a ransom on behalf of all, thus providing testimony to God's purpose at just the right time. ⁷ This is why I myself was appointed a proclaimer, even an emissary — I am telling the truth, not lying! — a trustworthy and truthful teacher of the *Goyim*.

⁸ Therefore, it is my wish that when the men pray, no matter where, they should lift up hands that are holy — they should not become angry or get into arguments.

⁹ Likewise, the women, when they pray, should be dressed modestly and sensibly in respectable attire, not with elaborate hairstyles and gold jewelry, or pearls, or expensive clothes. ¹⁰ Rather, they should adorn themselves with what is appropriate for women who claim to be worshipping God, namely, good deeds.

¹¹ Let a woman learn in peace, fully submitted; ¹² but I do not permit a woman to teach a man or exercise authority over him; rather, she is to remain at peace. ¹³ For Adam was formed first, then Havah. ¹⁴ Also it was not Adam who was deceived, but the woman who, on being deceived, became involved in the transgression. ¹⁵ Nevertheless, the woman will be delivered through childbearing, provided that she continues trusting, loving and living a holy life with modesty.

3 ¹ Here is a statement you can trust: anyone aspiring to be a congregation leader is seeking worthwhile work. ² A congregation leader must be above reproach, he must be faithful to his wife, temperate, self-controlled, orderly, hospitable and able to teach. ³ He must not drink excessively or get into fights; rather, he must be kind and gentle. He must not be a lover of money. ⁴ He must manage his own household well, having children who obey him with all proper respect; ⁵ for if a man can't manage his own household, how will he be able to care for God's Messianic Community? ⁶ He must not be a new believer, because he might become puffed up with pride and thus fall under the same judgment as did the Adversary. ⁷ Furthermore, he must be well regarded by outsiders, so that he won't fall into disgrace and into the Adversary's trap.

⁸ Likewise, the *shammashim* must be of good character, people whose word can be trusted. They must not give themselves to excessive drinking or be greedy for dishonest gain. ⁹ They must possess the formerly hidden truth of the faith with a clean conscience. ¹⁰ And first, let them be tested; then, if they prove themselves blameless, let them be appointed *shammashim*. ¹¹ Similarly, the wives must be of good character, not gossips, but temperate, faithful in everything. ¹² Let the *shammashim* each be faithful to his wife, managing his children and household well. ¹³ For those who serve well as *shammashim* gain good standing for themselves and much boldness in the trust that comes through Yeshua the Messiah.

¹⁴ I hope to visit you soon; but I am writing these things ¹⁵ so that if I am delayed, you may know how one should behave in the household of God, which is the

---

ᵃ Deuteronomy 6:4

Messianic Community of the living God, the pillar and support of the truth. ¹⁶Great beyond all question is the formerly hidden truth underlying our faith:

> He was manifested physically
> > and proved righteous spiritually,
> > seen by angels
> > and proclaimed among the nations,
> > trusted throughout the world
> > and raised up in glory to heaven.

4 ¹The Spirit expressly states that in the *acharit-hayamim* some people will apostatize from the faith by paying attention to deceiving spirits and things taught by demons. ²Such teachings come from the hypocrisy of liars whose own consciences have been burned, as if with a red-hot branding iron. ³They forbid marriage and require abstinence from foods which God created to be eaten with thanksgiving by those who have come to trust and to know the truth. ⁴For everything created by God is good, and nothing received with thanksgiving needs to be rejected, ⁵because the word of God and prayer make it holy.

⁶If you present all this to the brothers, you will be serving the Messiah Yeshua well; it will show that you have digested the words of the faith and of the good teaching which you have followed. ⁷But refuse godless *bubbe-meises*, and exercise yourself in godliness. ⁸For although physical exercise does have some value, godliness is valuable for everything, since it holds promise both for the present life and for the life to come. ⁹Here is a statement you can trust, one that fully deserves to be accepted ¹⁰(indeed, it is for this that we toil and strive): we have our hope set on a living God who is the deliverer of all humanity, especially of those who trust.

¹¹Command these things and teach them. ¹²Don't let anyone look down on you because of your youth; on the contrary, set the believers an example in your speech, behavior, love, trust and purity. ¹³Until I come, pay attention to the public reading of the Scriptures. ¹⁴Do not neglect your gift, which you were given through a prophecy when the body of elders gave you *s'mikhah*. ¹⁵Be diligent about this work, throw yourself into it, so that your progress may be clear to everyone. ¹⁶Pay attention to yourself and to the teaching, continue in it, for by so doing you will deliver both yourself and those who hear you.

5 ¹Do not rebuke an older man sharply, but appeal to him as you would to a father; treat younger men like brothers, ²older women like mothers and younger women like sisters, with absolute purity.

³Show respect to widows who are really in need. ⁴But if a widow has children or grandchildren, first let them learn to do their religious duty to their own family and thus repay some of the debt they owe their forebears, for this is what is acceptable in the sight of God. ⁵Now the widow who is really in need, the one who has been left all alone, has set her hope on God and continues in petitions and prayers night and day. ⁶But the one who is self-indulgent is already dead, even though she lives. ⁷And instruct them about this, so that they will not be open to blame. ⁸Moreover, anyone who does not provide for his own people, especially for his family, has disowned the faith and is worse than an unbeliever.

⁹ Let a widow be enrolled on the list of widows only if she is more than sixty years old, was faithful to her husband, ¹⁰ and is known for her good deeds — as one who has reared her children well, showed hospitality, washed the feet of God's people, helped those in trouble, and engaged in all kinds of good work.

¹¹ But refuse to enroll younger widows, for when they begin to feel natural passions that alienate them from the Messiah, they want to get married. ¹² This brings them under condemnation for having set aside the trust they had at first. ¹³ Besides that, they learn to be idle, going around from house to house; and not only idle, but gossips and busybodies, saying things they shouldn't. ¹⁴ Therefore, I would rather the young widows get married, have children and take charge of their homes, so as to give the opposition no occasion for slandering us. ¹⁵ For already some have turned astray to follow the Adversary.

¹⁶ If any believing woman has relatives who are widows, she should provide relief for them — the congregation shouldn't be burdened, so that it may help the widows who are really in need.

¹⁷ The leaders who lead well should be considered worthy of double honor, especially those working hard at communicating the Word and at teaching. ¹⁸ For the *Tanakh* says, **"You are not to muzzle an ox when it is treading out the grain,"**[b] in other words, "The worker deserves his wages." ¹⁹ Never listen to any accusation against a leader unless it is supported **by two or three witnesses.**[c] ²⁰ Rebuke before the whole assembly those leaders who continue sinning, as a warning to the others. ²¹ Before God, the Messiah Yeshua and the chosen angels, I solemnly charge you to observe these instructions, not pre-judging and not doing anything out of favoritism. ²² Do not be hasty in granting *s'mikhah* to anyone, and do not share in other people's sins — keep yourself pure.

²³ Stop drinking water; instead, use a little wine for the sake of your digestion and because of your frequent illnesses.

²⁴ The sins of some people are obvious and go ahead of them to judgment, but the sins of others follow afterwards. ²⁵ Likewise, good deeds are obvious; and even when they are not, they can't stay hidden.

6 ¹ Those who are under the yoke of slavery should regard their masters as worthy of full respect, so that the name of God and the teaching will not be brought into disrepute. ² And those who have believing masters are not to show them less respect on the ground that they are brothers; on the contrary, they should serve all the more diligently, since those benefiting from their service are believers whom they love.

Teach and exhort people about these things. ³ If anyone teaches differently and does not agree to the sound precepts of our Lord Yeshua the Messiah and to the doctrine that is in keeping with godliness, ⁴ he is swollen with conceit and understands nothing. Instead, he has a morbid desire for controversies and word-battles, out of which come jealousy, dissension, insults, evil suspicions, ⁵ and constant wrangling among people whose minds no longer function properly and who have been deprived of the truth, so that they imagine that religion is a road to riches. ⁶ Now true religion does bring great riches, but only to those who are content with what they have. ⁷ For we have brought nothing into the world; and we can take nothing out of it;

---

[b] Deuteronomy 25:4   [c] Deuteronomy 17:6; 19:15

^{8} so if we have food and clothing, we will be satisfied with these. ^{9} Furthermore, those whose goal is to be rich fall into temptation; they get trapped in many foolish and hurtful ambitions which plunge them into ruin and destruction. ^{10} For the love of money is a root of all the evils; because of this craving, some people have wandered away from the faith and pierced themselves to the heart with many pains.

^{11} But you, as a man of God, flee from these things; and pursue righteousness, godliness, faithfulness, love, steadfastness, gentleness. ^{12} Fight the good fight of the faith, take hold of the eternal life to which you were called when you testified so well to your faith before many witnesses. ^{13} I charge you before God, who gives life to all things, and before the Messiah Yeshua, who in his witness to Pontius Pilate gave the same good testimony, ^{14} to obey your commission spotlessly and irreproachably until our Lord Yeshua the Messiah appears. ^{15} His appearing will be brought about in its own time by the blessed and sole Sovereign, who is King of kings and Lord of lords, ^{16} who alone is immortal, who dwells in unapproachable light that no human being has ever seen or can see — to him be honor and eternal power. *Amen.*

^{17} As for those who do have riches in this present world, charge them not to be proud and not to let their hopes rest on the uncertainties of riches but to rest their hopes on God, who richly provides us with all things for our enjoyment. ^{18} Charge them to do good, to be rich in good deeds, to be generous and ready to share. ^{19} In this way they will treasure up for themselves a good foundation for the future, so that they may lay hold of the real life.

^{20} Oh, Timothy! Keep safe what has been entrusted to you. Turn away from the ungodly babblings and the argumentative opposition of what is falsely called "knowledge." ^{21} For many who promise this "knowledge" have missed the mark, as far as the faith is concerned. Grace be with you.

The Second Letter from Yeshua's Emissary Sha'ul (Paul)
to Timothy

2 TIMOTHY

1 ¹From: Sha'ul, an emissary of the Messiah Yeshua by God's will, which holds forth a promise of life through being united with Messiah Yeshua ²To: Timothy, my dear son:

Grace, mercy and *shalom* from God the Father and the Messiah Yeshua, our Lord. ³I give thanks to God, whom, like my forbears, I worship with a clean conscience, as I regularly remember you in my prayers night and day. ⁴I am reminded of your tears, and I long to see you, so that I might be filled with joy. ⁵I recall your sincere trust, the same trust that your grandmother Lois and your mother Eunice had first; and I am convinced that you too now have this trust.

⁶For this reason, I am reminding you to fan the flame of God's gift, which you received through *s'mikhah* from me. ⁷For God gave us a Spirit who produces not timidity, but power, love and self-discipline. ⁸So don't be ashamed of bearing testimony to our Lord or to me, his prisoner. On the contrary, accept your share in suffering disgrace for the sake of the Good News. God will give you the strength for it, ⁹since he delivered us and called us to a life of holiness as his people. It was not because of our deeds, but because of his own purpose and the grace which he gave to us who are united with the Messiah Yeshua. He did this before the beginning of time, ¹⁰but made it public only now through the appearing of our Deliverer, the Messiah Yeshua, who abolished death and, through the Good News, revealed life and immortality.

¹¹It was for this Good News that I was appointed a proclaimer, emissary and teacher of the *Goyim*; ¹²and this is why I suffer as I do. But I am not ashamed, because I know him in whom I have put my trust, and I am persuaded that he can keep safe until that Day what he has entrusted to me. ¹³Follow the pattern of the sound teachings you have heard from me, with trust and the love which is yours in the Messiah Yeshua. ¹⁴Keep safe the great treasure that has been entrusted to you, with the help of the *Ruach HaKodesh*, who lives in us.

¹⁵You know that everyone in the province of Asia turned away from me, including Phygelus and Ermogenes. ¹⁶May the Lord show mercy to the household of Onesiphorus, because he was often a comfort to me and was not ashamed of my being in prison. ¹⁷On the contrary, when he came to Rome, he diligently searched for me and found me. ¹⁸May the Lord grant it to him to find mercy from *Adonai* on that Day. And you know very well how much he helped me in Ephesus.

2 ¹So then, you, my son, be empowered by the grace that comes from the Messiah Yeshua. ²And the things you heard from me, which were supported by many witnesses, these things commit to faithful people, such as will be competent to teach others also. ³Accept your share in suffering disgrace as a good soldier of the Messiah Yeshua. ⁴No soldier on duty gets involved with civilian affairs, since he has to please his commanding officer. ⁵ Also an athlete can't win a contest unless he competes according to the rules. ⁶ The farmer who has done the hard work should be the first to receive a share of the harvest. ⁷ Think about what I am saying, for the Lord will enable you to understand everything.

⁸ Remember Yeshua the Messiah, who was raised from the dead, who was a descendant of David. This is the Good News I proclaim, ⁹ and for which I am suffering to the point of being bound in chains — but the Word of God is not bound in chains! ¹⁰ Why do I persevere through it all? For the sake of those who have been chosen, so that they too may obtain the deliverance that comes through the Messiah Yeshua, with eternal glory. ¹¹ Here is a statement you can trust:

> If we have died with him,
> we will also live with him.
>
> ¹² If we persevere,
> we will also rule with him
>
> If we disown him,
> he will also disown us.
>
> ¹³ If we are faithless,
> he remains faithful,
> for he cannot disown himself.

¹⁴ Keep reminding people of this, and charge them solemnly before the Lord not to engage in word-battles. They accomplish nothing useful and are a catastrophe for the hearers! ¹⁵ Do all you can to present yourself to God as someone worthy of his approval, as a worker with no need to be ashamed, because he deals straightforwardly with the Word of the Truth. ¹⁶ But keep away from godless babbling, for those who engage in it will only become more ungodly, ¹⁷ and their teaching will eat away at people like gangrene. Hymenaeus and Philetus are among these; ¹⁸ they have missed the mark, as far as the truth is concerned, by saying that our resurrection has already taken place; and they are overturning some people's faith. ¹⁹ Nevertheless, God's firm foundation stands, stamped with these words:

"The Lord knows his own,"ᵃ

and,

**"Let everyone who claims he belongs to the Lord
stand apart from wrongdoing."**ᵇ

²⁰ In a large house there are dishes and pots not only of gold and silver, but also of wood and clay. That is, some are meant for honorable use and some for dishonorable. ²¹ If a person keeps himself free of defilement by the latter, he will be a vessel set aside for honorable use by the master of the house and ready for every kind of good work. ²² So, flee the passions of youth; and, along with those who call on the Lord

---

ᵃ Numbers 16:5; Nahum 1:7   ᵇ Numbers 16:26

from a pure heart, pursue righteousness, faithfulness, love and peace. ²³ But stay away from stupid and ignorant controversies — you know that they lead to fights, ²⁴ and a slave of the Lord shouldn't fight. On the contrary, he should be kind to everyone, a good teacher, and not resentful when mistreated. ²⁵ Also he should be gentle as he corrects his opponents. For God may perhaps grant them the opportunity to turn from their sins, acquire full knowledge of the truth, ²⁶ come to their senses and escape the trap of the Adversary, after having been captured alive by him to do his will.

3 ¹ Moreover, understand this: in the *acharit-hayamim* will come trying times. ² People will be self-loving, money-loving, proud, arrogant, insulting, disobedient to parents, ungrateful, unholy, ³ heartless, unappeasable, slanderous, uncontrolled, brutal, hateful of good, ⁴ traitorous, headstrong, swollen with conceit, loving pleasure rather than God, ⁵ as they retain the outer form of religion but deny its power.

Stay away from these people! ⁶ For some of them worm their way into homes and get control of weak-willed women who are heaped with sins and swayed by various impulses, ⁷ who are always learning but never able to come to full knowledge of the truth. ⁸ In the same way as Jannes and Jambres opposed Moshe, so also these people oppose the truth. They are people with corrupted minds, whose trust cannot pass the test. ⁹ However, they won't get very far; because everyone will see how stupid they are, just as happened with those two.

¹⁰ But you, you have closely followed my teaching, conduct, purpose in life, trust, steadfastness, love and perseverance — ¹¹ as well as the persecutions and sufferings that came my way in Antioch, Iconium and Lystra. What persecutions I endured! Yet the Lord rescued me from all of them. ¹² And indeed, all who want to live a godly life united with the Messiah Yeshua will be persecuted, ¹³ while evil people and impostors will go from bad to worse, deceiving others and being deceived themselves.

¹⁴ But you, continue in what you have learned and have become convinced of, recalling the people from whom you learned it; ¹⁵ and recalling too how from childhood you have known the Holy Scriptures, which can give you the wisdom that leads to deliverance through trusting in Yeshua the Messiah. ¹⁶ All Scripture is God-breathed and is valuable for teaching the truth, convicting of sin, correcting faults and training in right living; ¹⁷ thus anyone who belongs to God may be fully equipped for every good work.

4 ¹ I solemnly charge you before God and the Messiah Yeshua, who will judge the living and the dead when he appears and establishes his Kingdom: ² proclaim the Word! Be on hand with it whether the time seems right or not. Convict, censure and exhort with unfailing patience and with teaching.

³ For the time is coming when people will not have patience for sound teaching, but will cater to their passions and gather around themselves teachers who say whatever their ears itch to hear. ⁴ Yes, they will stop listening to the truth, but will turn aside to follow myths.

⁵ But you, remain steady in every situation, endure suffering, do the work that a proclaimer of the Good News should, and do everything your service to God requires.

⁶ For as for me, I am already being poured out on the altar; yes, the time for my departure has arrived. ⁷ I have fought the good fight, I have finished the race, I have

kept the faith. ⁸ All that awaits me now is the crown of righteousness which the Lord, "the Righteous Judge," will award to me on that Day — and not only to me, but also to all who have longed for him to appear.

⁹ Do your best to come to me soon. ¹⁰ For Demas, because he has fallen in love with this present world, has deserted me and gone off to Thessalonica; Crescens has gone to Galatia; Titus has gone to Dalmatia — ¹¹ only Luke is with me. Take Mark, and bring him with you, because he is a very useful helper in my work. ¹² But Tychicus I have sent to Ephesus. ¹³ When you come, bring the coat which I left with Carpus in Troas, also the scrolls and especially the parchments. ¹⁴ Alexander the metalworker did me a great deal of harm; the Lord will **render to him according to his works;**ᶜ ¹⁵ and you should guard against him, because he bitterly opposed everything we said.

¹⁶ The first time I had to present my defense, no one stood by me; everyone deserted me — may it not be counted against them. ¹⁷ But the Lord stood by me and gave me power to proclaim the full message for all the *Goyim* to hear, and I was **rescued from the lion's mouth.**ᵈ ¹⁸ The Lord will rescue me from every evil attack and bring me safely into his heavenly Kingdom. To him be the glory forever and ever. *Amen.*

¹⁹ Greet Priscilla and Aquila and the household of Onesiphorus. ²⁰ Erastus has remained in Corinth, and Trophimus I left ill at Miletus. ²¹ Do your best to come before winter. Eubulus sends greetings to you, as do Pudens, Linus, Claudia and all the brothers.

²² The Lord be with your spirit. Grace be with you.

ᶜ 2 Samuel 3:39; Psalms 28:4; 62:13(12); Proverbs 24:12
ᵈ Psalm 22:22(21); Daniel 6:21(20), 23(22)

TITUS

1 ¹ From: Sha'ul, God's slave and an emissary of Yeshua the Messiah, sent to promote among God's chosen people the trust and knowledge of truth which lead to godliness ² and which are based on the certain hope of eternal life. God, who does not lie, promised that life before the beginning of time ³ but made public this word of his in its own season through a proclamation with which I have been entrusted by order of God, our Deliverer.

⁴ To: Titus, a true son in the faith we share:

Grace and *shalom* from God the Father and from the Messiah Yeshua, our Deliverer. ⁵ The reason I left you in Crete was so that you might attend to the matters still not in order and appoint congregation leaders in each city — those were my instructions. ⁶ A leader must be blameless, husband to one wife, with believing children who do not have a reputation for being wild or rebellious. ⁷ For an overseer, as someone entrusted with God's affairs, must be blameless — he must not be self-willed or quick-tempered, he must not drink excessively, get into fights or be greedy for dishonest gain. ⁸ On the contrary, he must be hospitable, devoted to good, sober-mindedness, uprightness, holiness and self-control. ⁹ He must hold firmly to the trustworthy Message that agrees with the doctrine; so that by his sound teaching he will be able to exhort and encourage, and also to refute those who speak against it.

¹⁰ For there are many, especially from the Circumcision faction, who are rebellious, who delude people's minds with their worthless and misleading talk. ¹¹ They must be silenced; because they are upsetting entire households by teaching what they have no business teaching, and doing it for the sake of dishonest gain. ¹² Even one of the Cretans' own prophets has said, "Cretans are always liars, evil brutes, lazy gluttons" — ¹³ and it's true! For this reason, you must be severe when you rebuke those who have followed this false teaching, so that they will come to be sound in their trust ¹⁴ and no longer pay attention to Judaistic myths or to the commands of people who reject the truth.

¹⁵ To all who are themselves pure, everything is pure. But to those who are defiled and without trust, nothing is pure — even their minds and consciences have been defiled. ¹⁶ They claim to know God, but with their actions they deny him. They are detestable and disobedient; they have proved themselves unfit to do anything good.

2 ¹ But you, explain what kind of behavior goes along with sound teaching. ² Tell the older men to be serious, sensible, self-controlled and sound in their trust, love and perseverance.

³ Likewise, tell the older women to behave the way people leading a holy life should. They shouldn't be slanderers or slaves to excessive drinking. They should teach what is good, ⁴ thus training the younger women to love their husbands and

children, [5] to be self-controlled and pure, to take good care of their homes and submit to their husbands. In this way, God's message will not be brought into disgrace.

[6] Similarly, urge the young men to be self-controlled, [7] and in everything set them an example yourself by doing what is good. When you are teaching, have integrity and be serious; [8] let everything you say be so wholesome that an opponent will be put to shame because he will have nothing bad to say about us.

[9] Tell slaves to submit to their masters in everything, to give satisfaction without talking back [10] or pilfering. On the contrary, they should demonstrate complete faithfulness always, so that in every way they will make the teaching about God our Deliverer more attractive.

[11] For God's grace, which brings deliverance, has appeared to all people. [12] It teaches us to renounce godlessness and worldly pleasures, and to live self-controlled, upright and godly lives now, in this age; [13] while continuing to expect the blessed fulfillment of our certain hope, which is the appearing of the *Sh'khinah* of our great God and the appearing of our Deliverer, Yeshua the Messiah. [14] He gave himself up on our behalf in order to free us from all violation of *Torah* and purify for himself a people who would be his own, eager to do good.

[15] These are the things you should say. Encourage and rebuke with full authority; don't let anyone look down on you.

3 [1] Remind people to submit to the government and its officials, to obey them, to be ready to do any honorable kind of work, [2] to slander no one, to avoid quarrelling, to be friendly, and to behave gently towards everyone.

[3] For at one time, we too were foolish and disobedient, deceived and enslaved by a variety of passions and pleasures. We spent our lives in evil and envy; people hated us, and we hated each other. [4] But when the kindness and love for mankind of God our Deliverer was revealed, [5] he delivered us. It was not on the ground of any righteous deeds we had done, but on the ground of his own mercy. He did it by means of the *mikveh* of rebirth and the renewal brought about by the *Ruach HaKodesh*, [6] whom he poured out on us generously through Yeshua the Messiah, our Deliverer. [7] He did it so that by his grace we might come to be considered righteous by God and become heirs, with the certain hope of eternal life. [8] You can trust what I have just said, and I want you to speak with confidence about these things, so that those who have put their trust in God may apply themselves to doing good deeds. These are both good in themselves and valuable to the community.

[9] But avoid stupid controversies, genealogies, quarrels and fights about the *Torah*; because they are worthless and futile. [10] Warn a divisive person once, then a second time; and after that, have nothing more to do with him. [11] You may be sure that such a person has been perverted and is sinning: he stands self-condemned.

[12] When I send Artemas or Tychicus to you, do your best to come to me in Nicopolis, for I have decided to spend the winter there. [13] Do your best to help Zenas the *Torah* expert and Apollos with their arrangements for travelling, so that they will lack nothing. [14] And have our people learn to apply themselves to doing good deeds that meet genuine needs, so that they will not be unproductive.

[15] All who are with me send you greetings. Give our greetings to our friends in the faith.

Grace be with you all.

The Letter from Yeshua's Emissary Sha'ul (Paul) to Philemon

PHILEMON

[1] From: Sha'ul, a prisoner for the sake of the Messiah Yeshua, and brother Timothy
To: Our dear fellow-worker Philemon, [2] along with sister Apphia, our fellow-soldier Archippus and the congregation that gathers in your home:

[3] Grace and *shalom* to you from God our Father and the Lord Yeshua the Messiah.

[4] I thank my God every time I mention you in my prayers, Philemon, [5] for I am hearing about your love and commitment to the Lord Yeshua and to all God's people. [6] I pray that the fellowship based on your commitment will produce full understanding of every good thing that is ours in union with the Messiah. [7] For your love has given me much joy and encouragement. Brother, you have refreshed the hearts of God's people.

[8] Therefore, I would not hesitate, in union with the Messiah, to direct you to do the thing you ought to do. [9] But since I, Sha'ul, am the kind of person I am, an old man and now for the Messiah Yeshua's sake a prisoner besides, I prefer to appeal to you on the basis of love. [10] My request to you concerns my son, of whom I became the father while here in prison, Onesimus. [11] His name means "useful," and although he was once useless to you, he has now become most useful — not only to you but also to me; [12] so that in returning him to you I am sending a part of my very heart. [13] I would dearly have loved to keep him with me, in order for him to serve me in your place while I am in prison because of the Good News. [14] But I didn't want to do anything without your consent, so that the good you do for me may be voluntary and not forced.

[15] Perhaps the reason he was separated from you for a brief period was so that you could have him back forever, [16] no longer as a slave but as more than a slave, as a dear brother. And that he is, especially to me. But how much dearer he must be to you, both humanly and in union with the Lord!

[17] So if you are in fellowship with me, receive him as you would me. [18] And if he has wronged you in any way or owes you anything, charge it to me.

[19] *I, Sha'ul, write with my own hand. I will repay it.* (I won't mention, of course, that you owe me your very life.) [20] Yes, brother, please do me this favor in the Lord; refresh my heart in the Messiah.

[21] Trusting that you will respond positively, I write knowing that you will indeed do more than I am asking.

[22] One more thing: please get a room ready for me. For I hope that through the prayers of you all God will give me a chance to visit you.

[23] Epaphras, my fellow-prisoner for the sake of the Messiah Yeshua, sends greetings to you, [24] as do Mark, Aristarchus, Demas and Luke, my fellow-workers.

[25] The grace of the Lord Yeshua the Messiah be with your spirit.

To a Group of
Messianic Jews
HEBREWS

1 [1] In days gone by, God spoke in many and varied ways to the Fathers through the prophets. [2] But now, in the *acharit-hayamim*, he has spoken to us through his Son, to whom he has given ownership of everything and through whom he created the universe. [3] This Son is the radiance of the *Sh'khinah*, the very expression of God's essence, upholding all that exists by his powerful word; and after he had, through himself, made purification for sins, he **sat down at the right hand of** *HaG'dulah BaM'romim.*[a]

[4] So he has become much better than angels, and the name God has given him is superior to theirs. [5] For to which of the angels did God ever say,

> **"You are my Son;**
> **today I have become your Father"?**[b]

Also, God never said of any angel,

> **"I will be his Father,**
> **and he will be my Son."**[c]

[6] And again, when God brings his Firstborn into the world, he says,

> **"Let all God's angels worship him."**[d]

[7] Indeed, when speaking of angels, he says,

> **". . . who makes his angels winds**
> **and his servants fiery flames";**[e]

[8] but to the Son, he says,

> **"Your throne, O God, will last forever and ever;**
> **you rule your Kingdom with a scepter of equity;**
> [9] **you have loved righteousness and hated wickedness.**

---

[a] Psalm 110:1   [b] Psalm 2:7   [c] 2 Samuel 7:14; 1 Chronicles 17:13
[d] Psalm 97:7   [e] Psalm 104:4

> **Therefore, O God, your God has anointed you**
> **with the oil of joy in preference to your companions";**[f]

¹⁰ and,

> **"In the beginning, ADONAI, you laid the foundations of the earth;**
> **heaven is the work of your hands.**
> ¹¹ **They will vanish, but you will remain;**
> **like clothing, they will all grow old;**
> ¹² **and you will fold them up like a coat.**
> **Yes, they will be changed like clothing,**
> **but you remain the same,**
> **your years will never end."**[g]

¹³ Moreover, to which of the angels has he ever said,

> **"Sit at my right hand**
> **until I make your enemies a footstool for your feet"?**[h]

¹⁴ Aren't they all merely spirits who serve, sent out to help those whom God will deliver?

2 ¹ Therefore, we must pay much more careful heed to the things we have heard, so that we will not drift away. ² For if the word God spoke through angels became binding, so that every violation and act of disobedience received its just deserts in full measure, ³ then how will we escape if we ignore such a great deliverance? This deliverance, which was first declared by the Lord, was confirmed to us by those who heard him; ⁴ while God also bore witness to it with various signs, wonders and miracles, and with gifts of the *Ruach HaKodesh* which he distributed as he chose.

⁵ For it was not to angels that God subjected the *'olam haba* — which is what we are talking about. ⁶ And there is a place where someone has given this solemn testimony:

> **"What is mere man, that you concern yourself with him?**
> **or the son of man, that you watch over him with such care?**
> ⁷ **You made him a little lower than the angels,**
> **you crowned him with glory and honor,**
> ⁸ **you put everything in subjection under his feet."**[i]

In subjecting **everything** to him, he left nothing unsubjected to him. However, at present, we don't see **everything** subjected to him — at least, not yet. ⁹ But we do see Yeshua — who indeed **was made** for a little while **lower than the angels** — now **crowned with glory and honor** because he suffered death, so that by God's grace he might taste death for all humanity. ¹⁰ For in bringing many sons to glory, it was only fitting that God, the Creator and Preserver of everything, should bring the Initiator of their deliverance to the goal through sufferings. ¹¹ For both Yeshua, who sets people

---

[f] Psalm 45:7–8(6–7) [g] Psalm 102:26–28(25–27) [h] Psalm 110:1 [i] Psalm 8:5–7(4–6)

apart for God, and the ones being set apart have a common origin — this is why he is not ashamed to call them **brothers** [12] when he says,

> **"I will proclaim your name to my brothers;**
> **in the midst of the congregation I will sing your praise."[j]**

[13] Also,

> **"I will put my trust in him, . . ."[k]**

and then it goes on,

> **"Here I am, along with the children God has given me."[l]**

[14] Therefore, since the children share a common physical nature as human beings, he became like them and shared that same human nature; so that by his death he might render ineffective the one who had power over death (that is, the Adversary) [15] and thus set free those who had been in bondage all their lives because of their fear of death.

[16] Indeed, it is obvious that he does not take hold of angels to help them; on the contrary,

> **"He takes hold of the seed of Avraham."[m]**

[17] This is why he had to become like his brothers in every respect — so that he might become a merciful and faithful *cohen gadol* in the service of God, making a *kapparah* for the sins of the people. [18] For since he himself suffered death when he was put to the test, he is able to help those who are being tested now.

3 [1] Therefore, brothers whom God has set apart, who share in the call from heaven, think carefully about Yeshua, whom we acknowledge publicly as God's emissary and as *cohen gadol*. [2] He was **faithful** to God, who appointed him; just as

> **"Moshe was faithful in all God's house."[n]**

[3] But Yeshua deserves more honor than Moshe, just as the builder of the **house** deserves more honor than the **house**. [4] For every **house** is built by someone, but the one who built everything is God. [5] Also, **Moshe was faithful *in* all God's house**, as a **servant** giving witness to things God would divulge later. [6] But the Messiah, as Son, **was faithful *over* God's house**. And we are that **house** of his, provided we hold firmly to the courage and confidence inspired by what we hope for.

[7] Therefore, as the *Ruach HaKodesh* says,

> **"Today, if you hear God's voice,**
> [8]   **don't harden your hearts, as you did in the Bitter Quarrel**

---

[j] Psalm 22:23(22)   [k] Isaiah 8:17   [l] Isaiah 8:18 (Septuagint)
[m] Isaiah 41:8–9   [n] Numbers 12:7

⁹   on that day in the Wilderness when you put God to the test.
    Yes, your fathers put me to the test;
    they challenged me, and they saw my work for forty years!
¹⁰   Therefore, I was disgusted with that generation —
    I said, 'Their hearts are always going astray,
    they have not understood how I do things';
¹¹   in my anger, I swore
    that they would not enter my rest."*o*

¹² Watch out, brothers, so that there will not be in any one of you an evil heart lacking trust, which could lead you to apostatize from the living God! ¹³ Instead, keep exhorting each other every day, as long as it is called **Today**, so that none of you will become **harden**ed by the deceit of sin. ¹⁴ For we have become sharers in the Messiah, provided, however, that we hold firmly to the conviction we began with, right through until the goal is reached.

¹⁵ Now where it says,

> "**Today, if you hear God's voice,**
> **don't harden your hearts, as you did in the Bitter Quarrel,**"*p*

¹⁶ who were the people who, after they **heard, quarrel**ed so **bitter**ly? All those whom Moshe brought out of Egypt. ¹⁷ And with whom was God **disgusted for forty years**? Those who sinned — yes, they fell dead in the **Wilderness**! ¹⁸ And to whom was it that he **swore that they would not enter** his **rest**? Those who were disobedient. ¹⁹ So we see that they were unable to **enter** because of lack of trust.

4 ¹ Therefore, let us be terrified of the possibility that, even though the promise of **enter**ing his **rest** remains, any one of you might be judged to have fallen short of it; ² for Good News has also been proclaimed to us, just as it was to them. But the message they **heard** didn't do them any good, because those who heard it did not combine it with trust. ³ For it is we who have trusted who **enter** the **rest**.

It is just as he said,

> "**And in my anger, I swore**
> **that they would not enter my rest.**"*q*

He swore this even though his **works** have been in existence since the founding of the universe. ⁴ For there is a place where it is said, concerning the seventh day,

> "**And God rested on the seventh day from all his works.**"*r*

⁵ And once more, our present text says,

> "**They will not enter my rest.**"*s*

---

o Psalm 95:7–11   *p* Psalm 95:7–8   *q* Psalm 95:11
r Genesis 2:2   *s* Psalm 95:11

⁶ Therefore, since it still remains for some to **enter** it, and those who received the Good News earlier did **not enter,** ⁷ he again fixes a certain day, "**Today,**" saying through David, so long afterwards, in the text already given,

"Today, if you hear God's voice, don't harden your hearts."ᵗ

⁸ For if Y'hoshua had given them rest, God would not have spoken later of another "day."

⁹ So there remains a *Shabbat*-keeping for God's people. ¹⁰ For the one who has **enter**ed God's **rest** has also **rested from his** own **works,** as God did from his. ¹¹ Therefore, let us do our best to **enter** that **rest**; so that no one will fall short because of the same kind of disobedience.

¹² See, the Word of God is alive! It is at work and is sharper than any double-edged sword — it cuts right through to where soul meets spirit and joints meet marrow, and it is quick to judge the inner reflections and attitudes of the heart. ¹³ Before God, nothing created is hidden, but all things are naked and open to the eyes of him to whom we must render an account.

¹⁴ Therefore, since we have a great *cohen gadol* who has passed through to the highest heaven, Yeshua, the Son of God, let us hold firmly to what we acknowledge as true. ¹⁵ For we do not have a *cohen gadol* unable to empathize with our weaknesses; since in every respect he was tempted just as we are, the only difference being that he did not sin. ¹⁶ Therefore, let us confidently approach the throne from which God gives grace, so that we may receive mercy and find grace in our time of need.

5 ¹ For every *cohen gadol* taken from among men is appointed to act on people's behalf with regard to things concerning God, to offer gifts and sacrifices for sins. ² He can deal gently with the ignorant and with those who go astray, since he too is subject to weakness. ³ Also, because of this weakness, he has to offer sacrifices for his own sins, as well as those of the people. ⁴ And no one takes this honor upon himself, rather, he is called by God, just as Aharon was.

⁵ So neither did the Messiah glorify himself to become *cohen gadol*; rather, it was the One who said to him,

> **"You are my Son;**
> **today I have become your Father."**ᵘ

⁶ Also, as he says in another place,

> **"You are a *cohen* forever,**
> **to be compared with Malki-Tzedek."**ᵛ

⁷ During Yeshua's life on earth, he offered up prayers and petitions, crying aloud and shedding tears, to the One who had the power to deliver him from death; and he was heard because of his godliness. ⁸ Even though he was the Son, he learned obedience through his sufferings. ⁹ And after he had been brought to the goal, he became the

---

ᵗ Psalm 95:7–8   ᵘ Psalm 2:7   ᵛ Psalm 110:4

source of eternal deliverance to all who obey him, ¹⁰ since he had been proclaimed by God as a *cohen gadol* **to be compared with Malki-Tzedek**.

¹¹ We have much to say about this subject, but it is hard to explain, because you have become sluggish in understanding. ¹² For although by this time you ought to be teachers, you need someone to teach you the very first principles of God's Word all over again! You need milk, not solid food! ¹³ Anyone who has to drink milk is still a baby, without experience in applying the Word about righteousness. ¹⁴ But solid food is for the mature, for those whose faculties have been trained by continuous exercise to distinguish good from evil.

6 ¹ Therefore, leaving behind the initial lessons about the Messiah, let us go on to maturity, not laying again the foundation of turning from works that lead to death, trusting God, ² and instruction about washings, *s'mikhah*, the resurrection of the dead and eternal punishment. ³ And, God willing, this is what we will do.

⁴ For when people have once been enlightened, tasted the heavenly gift, become sharers in the *Ruach HaKodesh*, ⁵ and tasted the goodness of God's Word and the powers of the *'olam haba* — ⁶ and then have fallen away — it is impossible to renew them so that they turn from their sin, as long as for themselves they keep executing the Son of God on the stake all over again and keep holding him up to public contempt. ⁷ For the land that soaks up frequent rains and then brings forth a crop useful to its owners receives a blessing from God; ⁸ but **if it keeps producing thorns and thistles**, it fails the test and is close to being **cursed**;ʷ in the end, it will be burned.

⁹ Now even though we speak this way, dear friends, we are confident that you have the better things that come with being delivered. ¹⁰ For God is not so unfair as to forget your work and the love you showed for him in your past service to his people — and in your present service too. ¹¹ However, we want each one of you to keep showing the same diligence right up to the end, when your hope will be realized; ¹² so that you will not become sluggish, but will be imitators of those who by their trust and patience are receiving what has been promised.

¹³ For when God made his promise to Avraham, he swore an oath to do what he had promised; and since there was no one greater than himself for him to swear by, **he swore by himself**ˣ ¹⁴ and said,

> **"I will certainly bless you,**
> **and I will certainly give you many descendants";**ʸ

¹⁵ and so, after waiting patiently, Avraham saw the promise fulfilled. ¹⁶ Now people swear oaths by someone greater than themselves, and confirmation by an oath puts an end to all dispute. ¹⁷ Therefore, when God wanted to demonstrate still more convincingly the unchangeable character of his intentions to those who were to receive what he had promised, he added an oath to the promise; ¹⁸ so that through two unchangeable things, in neither of which God could lie, we, who have fled to take a firm hold on the hope set before us, would be strongly encouraged. ¹⁹ We have this hope as a sure and safe anchor for ourselves, a hope that goes right on through to what is inside the *parokhet*, ²⁰ where a forerunner has entered on our

---

ʷ Genesis 3:17–18   ˣ Genesis 22:16   ʸ Genesis 22:17

behalf, namely, Yeshua, who has become **a *cohen gadol* forever, to be compared with Malki-Tzedek.**[z]

7 ¹ This **Malki-Tzedek, king of Shalem, a *cohen* of God *Ha'Elyon*, met Avraham on his way back from the slaughter of the kings and blessed him;** ² also Avraham **gave him a tenth of everything.**[a]

Now first of all, by translation of his name, he is "king of righteousness"; and then he is also **king of Shalem**, which means "king of peace."

³ There is no record of his father, mother, ancestry, birth or death; rather, like the Son of God, he continues as a *cohen* for all time.

⁴ Just think how great he was! Even the Patriarch Avraham **gave him a tenth** of the choicest spoils. ⁵ Now the descendants of Levi who became *cohanim* have a commandment in the *Torah* to take a tenth of the income of the people, that is, from their own brothers, despite the fact that they too are descended from Avraham. ⁶ But Malki-Tzedek, even though he was not descended from Levi, took a tenth from Avraham.

Also, he blessed Avraham, the man who received God's promises; ⁷ and it is beyond all dispute that the one who blesses has higher status than the one who receives the blessing.

⁸ Moreover, in the case of the *cohanim*, the tenth is received by men who die; while in the case of Malki-Tzedek, it is received by someone who is testified to be still alive.

⁹ One might go even further and say that Levi, who himself receives tenths, paid a tenth through Avraham; ¹⁰ inasmuch as he was still in his ancestor Avraham's body when Malki-Tzedek met him.

¹¹ Therefore, if it had been possible to reach the goal through the system of *cohanim* derived from Levi (since in connection with it, the people were given the *Torah*), what need would there have been for another, different kind of *cohen*, the one spoken of as **to be compared with Malki-Tzedek** and not to be compared with Aharon? ¹² For if the system of *cohanim* is transformed, there must of necessity occur a transformation of *Torah*. ¹³ The one about whom these things are said belongs to another tribe, from which no one has ever served at the altar; ¹⁴ for everyone knows that our Lord arose out of Y'hudah, and that Moshe said nothing about this tribe when he spoke about *cohanim*.

¹⁵ It becomes even clearer if a "different kind of *cohen*," one like Malki-Tzedek, arises, ¹⁶ one who became a *cohen* not by virtue of a rule in the *Torah* concerning physical descent, but by virtue of the power of an indestructible life. ¹⁷ For it is stated,

> **"You are a *cohen* FOREVER,
> to be compared with Malki-Tzedek."**[b]

¹⁸ Thus, on the one hand, the earlier rule is set aside because of its weakness and inefficacy ¹⁹ (for the *Torah* did not bring anything to the goal); and, on the other hand, a hope of something better is introduced, through which we are drawing near to God.

---

[z] Psalm 110:4   [a] Genesis 14:17–20   [b] Psalm 110:4

²⁰ What is more, God swore an oath. For no oath was sworn in connection with those who become *cohanim* now; ²¹ but Yeshua became a *cohen* by the oath which God swore when he said to him,

> "*Adonai* has sworn and will not change his mind,
> 'You are a *cohen* forever.'"ᶜ

²² Also this shows how much better is the covenant of which Yeshua has become guarantor.

²³ Moreover, the present *cohanim* are many in number, because they are prevented by death from continuing in office. ²⁴ But because he lives forever, his position as *cohen* does not pass on to someone else; ²⁵ and consequently, he is totally able to deliver those who approach God through him; since he is alive forever and thus forever able to intercede on their behalf.

²⁶ This is the kind of *cohen gadol* that meets our need — holy, without evil, without stain, set apart from sinners and raised higher than the heavens; ²⁷ one who does not have the daily necessity, like the other *cohanim g'dolim*, of offering up sacrifices first for their own sins and only then for those of the people; because he offered one sacrifice, once and for all, by offering up himself. ²⁸ For the *Torah* appoints as *cohanim g'dolim* men who have weakness; but the text which speaks about the swearing of the oath, a text written later than the *Torah*, appoints a Son who has been brought to the goal forever.

8 ¹ Here is the whole point of what we have been saying: we do have just such a *cohen gadol* as has been described. And he does **sit at the right hand of** *HaG'dulah* in heaven.ᵈ ² There he serves in the Holy Place, that is, in the true Tent of Meeting, the one erected not by human beings but by *Adonai*.

³ For every *cohen gadol* is appointed to offer both gifts and sacrifices; so this *cohen gadol* too has to have something he can offer. ⁴ Now if he were on earth, he wouldn't be a *cohen* at all, since there already are *cohanim* offering the gifts required by the *Torah*. ⁵ But what they are serving is only a copy and shadow of the heavenly original; for when Moshe was about to erect the Tent, God warned him, **"See to it that you make everything according to the pattern you were shown on the mountain."**ᵉ

⁶ But now the work Yeshua has been given to do is far superior to theirs, just as the covenant he mediates is better. For this covenant has been given as *Torah* on the basis of better promises. ⁷ Indeed, if the first covenant had not given ground for faultfinding, there would have been no need for a second one. ⁸ For God does find fault with the people when he says,

> "'See! The days are coming,' says *Adonai*,
> 'when I will establish
> **over the house of Isra'el and over the house of Y'hudah**
> **a new covenant.**

ᶜ Psalm 110:4   ᵈ Psalm 110:1   ᵉ Exodus 25:40

9   **"'It will not be like the covenant**
    which I made with their fathers
    on the day when I took them by their hand
    and led them forth out of the land of Egypt;
    because they, for their part,
    did not remain faithful to my covenant;
    so I, for my part,
    stopped concerning myself with them,'
    says *ADONAI.*

10   **"'For this is the covenant which I will make**
    with the house of Isra'el after those days,'
    says *ADONAI*:

        'I will put my *Torah* in their minds
        and write it on their hearts;
        I will be their God,
        and they will be my people.

11   **"'None of them will teach his fellow-citizen**
    or his brother, saying, "Know *ADONAI*!"
    For all will know me,
    from the least of them to the greatest,
12   **because I will be merciful toward their wickednesses**
    and remember their sins no more.'"*ᶠ*

¹³ By using the term, **"new,"** he has made the first covenant "old"; and something being made old, something in the process of aging, is on its way to vanishing altogether.

9 ¹ Now the first covenant had both regulations for worship and a Holy Place here on earth. ² A tent was set up, the outer one, which was called the Holy Place; in it were the *menorah*, the table and the Bread of the Presence. ³ Behind the second *parokhet* was a tent called the Holiest Place, ⁴ which had the golden altar for burning incense and the Ark of the Covenant, entirely covered with gold. In the Ark were the gold jar containing the *man*, Aharon's rod that sprouted and the stone Tablets of the Covenant; ⁵ and above it were the *k'ruvim* representing the *Sh'khinah*, casting their shadow on the lid of the Ark — but now is not the time to discuss these things in detail.

⁶ With things so arranged, the *cohanim* go into the outer tent all the time to discharge their duties; ⁷ but only the *cohen hagadol* enters the inner one; and he goes in only once a year, and he must always bring blood, which he offers both for himself and for the sins committed in ignorance by the people. ⁸ By this arrangement, the *Ruach HaKodesh* showed that so long as the first Tent had standing, the way into the Holiest Place was still closed. ⁹ This symbolizes the present age and indicates that the conscience of the person performing the service cannot be brought to the goal by

---

ᶠ Jeremiah 31:30–33(31–34)

the gifts and sacrifices he offers. ¹⁰ For they involve only food and drink and various ceremonial washings — regulations concerning the outward life, imposed until the time for God to reshape the whole structure.

¹¹ But when the Messiah appeared as *cohen gadol* of the good things that are happening already, then, through the greater and more perfect Tent which is not man-made (that is, it is not of this created world), ¹² he entered the Holiest Place once and for all.

And he entered not by means of the blood of goats and calves, but by means of his own blood, thus setting people free forever. ¹³ For if sprinkling ceremonially unclean persons with the blood of goats and bulls and the ashes of a heifer restores their outward purity; ¹⁴ then how much more the blood of the Messiah, who, through the eternal Spirit, offered himself to God as a sacrifice without blemish, will purify our conscience from works that lead to death, so that we can serve the living God!

¹⁵ It is because of this death that he is mediator of a **new covenant** [or **will**].*ᵍ* Because a death has occurred which sets people free from the transgressions committed under the first covenant, those who have been called may receive the promised eternal inheritance. ¹⁶ For where there is a will, there must necessarily be produced evidence of its maker's death, ¹⁷ since a will goes into effect only upon death; it never has force while its maker is still alive.

¹⁸ This is why the first covenant too was inaugurated with blood. ¹⁹ After Moshe had proclaimed every command of the *Torah* to all the people, he took the blood of the calves with some water and used scarlet wool and hyssop to sprinkle both the scroll itself and all the people; ²⁰ and he said, **"This is the blood of the covenant which God has ordained for you."**ʰ ²¹ Likewise, he sprinkled with the blood both the Tent and all the things used in its ceremonies. ²² In fact, according to the *Torah*, almost everything is purified with blood; indeed, without the shedding of blood there is no forgiveness of sins.

²³ Now this is how the copies of the heavenly things had to be purified, but the heavenly things themselves require better sacrifices than these. ²⁴ For the Messiah has entered a Holiest Place which is not man-made and merely a copy of the true one, but into heaven itself, in order to appear now on our behalf in the very presence of God.

²⁵ Further, he did not enter heaven to offer himself over and over again, like the *cohen hagadol* who enters the Holiest Place year after year with blood that is not his own; ²⁶ for then he would have had to suffer death many times — from the founding of the universe on. But as it is, he has appeared once at the end of the ages in order to do away with sin through the sacrifice of himself. ²⁷ Just as human beings have to die once, but after this comes judgment, ²⁸ so also the Messiah, having been offered once to **bear the sins of many**,ⁱ will appear a second time, not to deal with sin, but to deliver those who are eagerly waiting for him.

10 ¹ For the *Torah* has in it a shadow of the good things to come, but not the actual manifestation of the originals. Therefore, it can never, by means of the same sacrifices repeated endlessly year after year, bring to the goal those who approach the Holy Place to offer them. ² Otherwise, wouldn't the offering of those sacrifices have ceased? For if the people performing the service had been cleansed once and

---

ᵍ Jeremiah 31:30(31)   ʰ Exodus 24:8   ⁱ Isaiah 53:12

for all, they would no longer have sins on their conscience. ³ No, it is quite the contrary — in these sacrifices is a reminder of sins, year after year. ⁴ For it is impossible that the blood of bulls and goats should take away sins.

⁵ This is why, on coming into the world, he says,

> **"It has not been your will**
> **to have an animal sacrifice and a meal offering;**
> **rather, you have prepared for me a body.**
> ⁶ **No, you have not been pleased**
> **with burnt offerings and sin offerings.**
> ⁷ **Then I said, 'Look!**
> **In the scroll of the book**
> **it is written about me.**
> **I have come to do your will.'"**ʲ

⁸ In saying first, "**You** neither **willed** nor were **pleased with animal sacrifices, meal offerings, burnt offerings and sin offerings,**" things which are offered in accordance with the *Torah*; ⁹ and then, "**Look, I have come to do your will**"; he takes away the first system in order to set up the second. ¹⁰ It is in connection with this **will** that we have been separated for God and made holy, once and for all, through the **offering** of Yeshua the Messiah's **body.**

¹¹ Now every *cohen* stands every day doing his service, offering over and over the same sacrifices, which can never take away sins. ¹² But this one, after he had offered for all time a single sacrifice for sins, **sat down at the right hand of** God, ¹³ from then on to wait **until** his **enemies** be made **a footstool for** his **feet.**ᵏ ¹⁴ For by a single offering he has brought to the goal for all time those who are being set apart for God and made holy.

¹⁵ And the *Ruach HaKodesh* too bears witness to us; for after saying,

> ¹⁶ **" 'This is the covenant which I will make**
> **with them after those days,' says** Aᴅᴏɴᴀɪ:
> **'I will put my *Torah* on their hearts,**
> **and write it on their minds . . . ,' "**ˡ

¹⁷ he then adds,

> **" 'And their sins and their wickednesses**
> **I will remember no more.' "**ᵐ

¹⁸ Now where there is forgiveness for these, an offering for sins is no longer needed.
¹⁹ So, brothers, we have confidence to use the way into the Holiest Place opened by the blood of Yeshua. ²⁰ He inaugurated it for us as a new and living way through the *parokhet*, by means of his flesh. ²¹ We also have a great *cohen* over God's household. ²² Therefore, let us approach the Holiest Place with a sincere heart, in the full assurance that comes from trusting — with our hearts **sprinkled clean**

ʲ Psalm 40:7–9(6–8)   ᵏ Psalm 110:1   ˡ Jeremiah 31:32(33)   ᵐ Jeremiah 31:33(34) from a bad conscience and our bodies washed with **pure water**.*[n]* ^{23} Let us continue holding fast to the hope we acknowledge, without wavering; for the One who made the promise is trustworthy. ^{24} And let us keep paying attention to one another, in order to spur each other on to love and good deeds, ^{25} not neglecting our own congregational meetings, as some have made a practice of doing, but, rather, encouraging each other.

And let us do this all the more as you see the Day approaching. ^{26} For if we deliberately continue to sin after receiving the knowledge of the truth, there no longer remains a sacrifice for sins, ^{27} but only the terrifying prospect of Judgment, of **raging fire that will consume the enemies**.*[o]*

^{28} Someone who disregards the *Torah* of Moshe is **put to death** without mercy **on the word of two or three witnesses**.*[p]* ^{29} Think how much worse will be the punishment deserved by someone who has trampled underfoot the Son of God; who has treated as something common the **blood of the covenant**[q] which made him holy; and who has insulted the Spirit, giver of God's grace!

^{30} For the One we know is the One who said,

> **"Vengeance is my responsibility;**
> **I will repay,"**

and then said,

> **"ADONAI will judge his people."**[r]

^{31} It is a terrifying thing to fall into the hands of the living God!

^{32} But remember the earlier days, when, after you had received the light, you endured a hard struggle with sufferings. ^{33} Sometimes you were publicly disgraced and persecuted, while at other times you stood loyally by those who were treated this way. ^{34} For you shared the sufferings of those who had been put in prison. Also when your possessions were seized, you accepted it gladly; since you knew that what you possessed was better and would last forever.

^{35} So don't throw away that courage of yours, which carries with it such a great reward. ^{36} For you need to hold out; so that, by having done what God wills, you may receive what he has promised. ^{37} For

> **"There is so, so little time!**
> **The One coming will indeed come,**
> **he will not delay.**
> ^{38} **But the person who is righteous**
> **will live his life by trusting,**
> **and if he shrinks back,**
> **I will not be pleased with him."**[s]

^{39} However, we are not the kind who **shrink back** and are destroyed; on the contrary, we keep **trusting** and thus preserve our lives!

---

[n] Ezekiel 36:25   *[o]* Isaiah 26:11   *[p]* Deuteronomy 17:6; 19:15
[q] Exodus 24:8   *[r]* Deuteronomy 32:35–36   *[s]* Habakkuk 2:3-4

11 [1] **Trusting**[t] is being confident of what we hope for, convinced about things we do not see. [2] It was for this that Scripture attested the merit of the people of old.

[3] By **trusting**, we understand that the universe was created through a spoken word of God, so that what is seen did not come into being out of existing phenomena.

[4] By **trusting**, Hevel offered a greater sacrifice than Kayin; because of this, he was attested as righteous, with God giving him this testimony on the ground of his gifts. Through having **trusted**, he still continues to speak, even though he is dead.

[5] By **trusting**, Hanokh was taken away from this life without seeing death — **"He was not to be found, because God took him away"** — for he has been attested as having been, prior to being taken away, **well pleasing to God.**[u] [6] And without **trusting**, it is impossible to be **well pleasing to God**, because whoever approaches him must **trust** that he does exist and that he becomes a Rewarder to those who seek him out.

[7] By **trusting**, Noach, after receiving divine warning about things as yet unseen, was filled with holy fear and built an ark to save his household. Through this **trusting**, he put the world under condemnation and received the righteousness that comes from **trusting**.

[8] By **trusting**, Avraham obeyed, after being called to **go out**[v] to a place which God would give him as a possession; indeed, he **went out** without knowing where he was going. [9] By **trusting**, he lived as a temporary resident in the Land of the promise, as if it were not his, staying in tents with Yitz'chak and Ya'akov, who were to receive what was promised along with him. [10] For he was looking forward to the city with permanent foundations, of which the architect and builder is God.

[11] By **trusting**, he received potency to father a child, even when he was past the age for it, as was Sarah herself; because he regarded the One who had made the promise as **trust**worthy. [12] Therefore this one man, who was virtually dead, fathered descendants

> as numerous as the stars in the sky,
> and as countless as the grains of the sand on the seashore.[w]

[13] All these people kept on **trusting** until they died, without receiving what had been promised. They had only seen it and welcomed it from a distance, while acknowledging that they were **aliens and temporary residents on the earth.**[x] [14] For people who speak this way make it clear that they are looking for a fatherland. [15] Now if they were to keep recalling the one they left, they would have an opportunity to return; [16] but as it is, they aspire to a better fatherland, a heavenly one. This is why God is not ashamed to be called *their* God, for he has prepared for them a city.

[17] By **trusting**, Avraham, when he was put to the test, offered up Yitz'chak as a sacrifice. Yes, he offered up his only son, he who had received the promises, [18] to whom it had been said, **"What is called your 'seed' will be in Yitz'chak."**[y] [19] For he had concluded that God could even raise people from the dead! And, figuratively speaking, he did so receive him.

---

[t] Habakkuk 2:4   [u] Genesis 5:24   [v] Genesis 12:1   [w] Genesis 15:5–6; 22:17; 32:13(12);
Exodus 32:13; Deuteronomy 1:10; 10:22   [x] 1 Chronicles 29:15   [y] Genesis 21:12

²⁰ By **trusting,** Yitz'chak, in his blessings over Ya'akov and Esav, made reference to events yet to come.

²¹ By **trusting,** Ya'akov, when he was dying, blessed each of Yosef's sons, **leaning on his walking-stick as he bowed in prayer.**ᶻ

²² By **trusting,** Yosef, near the end of his life, remembered about the Exodus of the people of Isra'el and gave instructions about what to do with his bones.

²³ By **trusting,** the parents of Moshe **hid him for three months** after he was born, **because they saw that he was a beautiful child,**ᵃ and they weren't afraid of the king's decree.

²⁴ By **trusting,** Moshe, **after he had grown up,**ᵇ refused to be called the son of Pharaoh's daughter. ²⁵ He chose being mistreated along with God's people rather than enjoying the passing pleasures of sin. ²⁶ He had come to regard abuse suffered on behalf of the Messiah as greater riches than the treasures of Egypt, for he kept his eyes fixed on the reward.

²⁷ By **trusting,** he left Egypt, not fearing the king's anger; he persevered as one who sees the unseen.

²⁸ By **trusting,** he obeyed the requirements for the *Pesach,* including the smearing of the blood, so that the Destroyer of the firstborn would not touch the firstborn of Isra'el.

²⁹ By **trusting,** they walked through the Red Sea as through dry land; when the Egyptians tried to do it, the sea swallowed them up.

³⁰ By **trusting,** the walls of Yericho fell down — after the people had marched around them for seven days.

³¹ By **trusting,** Rachav the prostitute welcomed the spies and therefore did not die along with those who were disobedient.

³² What more should I say? There isn't time to tell about Gid'on, Barak, Shimshon, Yiftach, David, Sh'mu'el and the prophets; ³³ who, through **trusting,** conquered kingdoms, worked righteousness, received what was promised, **shut the mouths of lions,**ᶜ ³⁴ quenched the power of fire, escaped the edge of the sword, had their weakness turned to strength, grew mighty in battle and routed foreign armies. ³⁵ Women received back their dead resurrected; other people were stretched on the rack and beaten to death, refusing to be ransomed, so that they would gain a better resurrection. ³⁶ Others underwent the trials of being mocked and whipped, then chained and imprisoned. ³⁷ They were stoned, sawed in two, murdered by the sword; they went about clothed in sheepskins and goatskins, destitute, persecuted, mistreated, ³⁸ wandering about in deserts and mountains, living in caves and holes in the ground! The world was not worthy of them!

³⁹ All of these had their merit attested because of their **trusting.** Nevertheless, they did not receive what had been promised, ⁴⁰ because God had planned something better that would involve us, so that only with us would they be brought to the goal.

12 ¹ So then, since we are surrounded by such a great cloud of witnesses, let us, too, put aside every impediment — that is, the sin which easily hampers our forward movement — and keep running with endurance in the contest set before us, ² looking away to the Initiator and Completer of that **trusting,**ᵈ Yeshua — who, in exchange

---

ᶻ Genesis 47:31 (Septuagint)   ᵃ Exodus 2:2   ᵇ Exodus 2:11
ᶜ Daniel 6:23(22)   ᵈ Habakkuk 2:4

for obtaining the joy set before him, endured execution on a stake as a criminal, scorning the shame, and has sat down **at the right hand of** the throne of God.ᵉ ³ Yes, think about him who endured such hostility against himself from sinners, so that you won't grow tired or **become despondent**. ⁴ You have not yet resisted to the point of shedding blood in the contest against sin.

⁵ Also you have forgotten the counsel which speaks with you as sons:

> **"My son, don't despise the discipline of** ADONAI
> **or become despondent when he corrects you.**
> ⁶ **For** ADONAI **disciplines those he loves**
> **and whips everyone he accepts as a son."**ᶠ

⁷ Regard your endurance as **discipline**; God is dealing with you as **sons**. For what son goes undisciplined by his father? ⁸ All legitimate sons undergo **discipline**; so if you don't, you're a *mamzer* and not a son!

⁹ Furthermore, we had physical fathers who disciplined us, and we respected them; how much more should we submit to our spiritual Father and live! ¹⁰ For they disciplined us only for a short time and only as best they could; but he disciplines us in a way that provides genuine benefit to us and enables us to share in his holiness. ¹¹ Now, all **discipline**, while it is happening, does indeed seem painful, not enjoyable; but for those who have been trained by it, it later produces its peaceful fruit, which is righteousness. ¹² So,

> **strengthen your drooping arms,**
> **and steady your tottering knees;**ᵍ

¹³ and

> **make a level path for your feet;**ʰ

so that what has been injured will not get wrenched out of joint but rather will be healed.

¹⁴ Keep pursuing *shalom* with everyone and the holiness without which no one will see the Lord. ¹⁵ See to it that no one misses out on God's grace, that no **root of bitterness**ⁱ springing up causes trouble and thus contaminates many, ¹⁶ and that no one is sexually immoral, or godless like Esav, who in exchange for a single meal gave up his rights as the firstborn. ¹⁷ For you know that afterwards, when he wanted to obtain his father's blessing, he was rejected; indeed, even though he sought it with tears, his change of heart was to no avail.

¹⁸ For you have not come to a tangible mountain, to an ignited fire, to darkness, to murk, to a whirlwind, ¹⁹ to the sound of a *shofar*, and to a voice whose words made the hearers beg that no further message be given to them — ²⁰ for they couldn't bear what was being commanded them, **"If even an animal touches the mountain, it is to be stoned to death";**ʲ ²¹ and so terrifying was the sight that Moshe said, **"I am quaking with dread."**ᵏ

ᵉ Psalm 110:1   ᶠ Proverbs 3:11–12   ᵍ Isaiah 35:3
ʰ Proverbs 4:26   ⁱ Deuteronomy 29:17(18)   ʲ Exodus 19:12–13
ᵏ Deuteronomy 9:19

²² On the contrary, you have come to Mount Tziyon, that is, the city of the living God, heavenly Yerushalayim; to myriads of angels in festive assembly; ²³ to a community of the firstborn whose names have been recorded in heaven; to a Judge who is God of everyone; to spirits of righteous people who have been brought to the goal; ²⁴ to the mediator of a new covenant, Yeshua; and to the sprinkled blood that speaks better things than that of Hevel.

²⁵ See that you don't reject the One speaking! For if those did not escape who rejected him when he gave divine warning on earth, think how much less we will escape if we turn away from him when he warns from heaven. ²⁶ Even then, his voice shook the earth; but now, he has made this promise:

> **"One more time I will shake**
> **not only the earth, but heaven too!"**[l]

²⁷ And this phrase, "**one more time**," makes clear that the things shaken are removed, since they are created things, so that the things not shaken may remain. ²⁸ Therefore, since we have received an un**shake**able Kingdom, let us have grace, through which we may offer service that will please God, with reverence and fear. ²⁹ For indeed,

> "Our **God is a consuming fire!**"[m]

13 ¹ Let brotherly friendship continue; ² but don't forget to be friendly to outsiders; for in so doing, some people, without knowing it, have entertained angels. ³ Remember those in prison and being mistreated, as if you were in prison with them and undergoing their torture yourselves.

⁴ Marriage is honorable in every respect; and, in particular, sex within marriage is pure. But God will indeed punish fornicators and adulterers.

⁵ Keep your lives free from the love of money; and be satisfied with what you have; for God himself has said, **"I will never fail you or abandon you."**[n] ⁶ Therefore, we say with confidence,

> "**ADONAI** is my helper; I will not be afraid —
> what can a human being do to me?"[o]

⁷ Remember your leaders, those who spoke God's message to you. Reflect on the results of their way of life, and imitate their trust — ⁸ Yeshua the Messiah is the same yesterday, today and forever.

⁹ Do not be carried away by various strange teachings; for what is good is for the heart to be strengthened by grace, not by foods. People who have made these the focus of their lives have not benefited thereby.

¹⁰ We have an altar from which those who serve in the Tent are not permitted to eat. ¹¹ For the *cohen hagadol* brings the blood of animals into the Holiest Place as a sin offering, but their bodies are **burned outside the camp**.[p] ¹² So too Yeshua suffered death outside the gate, in order to make the people holy through his own blood.

---

[l] Haggai 2:6, 21   [m] Deuteronomy 4:24; 9:3; Isaiah 33:14   [n] Deuteronomy 31:6
[o] Psalm 118:6   [p] Leviticus 16:27

[13] Therefore, let us go out to him who is **outside the camp** and share his disgrace. [14] For we have no permanent city here; on the contrary, we seek the one to come. [15] Through him, therefore, **let us offer God a sacrifice of praise** continually.[q] For this is the natural product of lips that acknowledge his name.

[16] But don't forget doing good and sharing with others, for with such **sacrifices** God is well pleased.

[17] Obey your leaders and submit to them, for they keep watch over your lives, as people who will have to render an account. So make it a task of joy for them, not one of groaning; for that is of no advantage to you.

[18] Keep praying for us, for we are certain that we have a clear conscience and want to conduct ourselves properly in everything we do. [19] And all the more I beg you to do this, so that I may be restored to you that much sooner.

[20] The God of *shalom* brought up from the dead the great Shepherd of the sheep, our Lord Yeshua, by the blood of an eternal covenant. [21] May God equip you with every good thing you need to do his will; and may he do in us whatever pleases him, through Yeshua the Messiah. To him be the glory forever and ever. *Amen.*

[22] Now I urge you, brothers, to bear with my message of exhortation; for I have written you only briefly.

[23] Know that our brother Timothy has been released. If he comes soon enough, I will bring him with me when I come to see you.

[24] Greet all your leaders and all God's people. The people from Italy send greetings to you.

[25] Grace be with you all.

---

[q] Leviticus 7:12; 22:29; Psalms 50:14, 23; 107:22; 116:17; 2 Chronicles 29:31

The Letter from

Ya'akov

JAMES

1 [1] From: Ya'akov, a slave of God and of the Lord Yeshua the Messiah
To: The Twelve Tribes in the Diaspora:
Shalom!
[2] Regard it all as joy, my brothers, when you face various kinds of temptations; [3] for you know that the testing of your trust produces perseverance. [4] But let perseverance do its complete work; so that you may be complete and whole, lacking in nothing. [5] Now if any of you lacks wisdom, let him ask God, who gives to all generously and without reproach; and it will be given to him. [6] But let him ask in trust, doubting nothing; for the doubter is like a wave in the sea being tossed and driven by the wind. [7] Indeed that person should not think that he will receive anything from the Lord, [8] because he is double-minded, unstable in all his ways.

[9] Let the brother in humble circumstances boast about his high position. [10] But let the rich brother boast about his being humbled; since, like a wildflower, he will pass away. [11] For just as the sun rises with the *sharav* and dries up the plant, so that its flower falls off and its beauty is destroyed, so too the rich person going about his business will wither away.

[12] How blessed is the man who perseveres through temptation! For after he has passed the test, he will receive as his crown the Life which God has promised to those who love him. [13] No one being tempted should say, "I am being tempted by God." For God cannot be tempted by evil, and God himself tempts no one. [14] Rather, each person is being tempted whenever he is being dragged off and enticed by the bait of his own desire. [15] Then, having conceived, the desire gives birth to sin; and when sin is fully grown, it gives birth to death. [16] Don't delude yourselves, my dear brothers.

[17] Every good act of giving and every perfect gift is from above, coming down from the Father who made the heavenly lights; with him there is neither variation nor darkness caused by turning. [18] Having made his decision, he gave birth to us through a Word that can be relied upon, in order that we should be a kind of firstfruits of all that he created. [19] Therefore, my dear brothers, let every person be quick to listen but slow to speak, slow to get angry; [20] for a person's anger does not accomplish God's righteousness!

[21] So rid yourselves of all vulgarity and obvious evil, and receive meekly the Word implanted in you that can save your lives. [22] Don't deceive yourselves by only hearing what the Word says, but do it! [23] For whoever hears the Word but doesn't do what it says is like someone who looks at his face in a mirror, [24] who looks at himself, goes away and immediately forgets what he looks like. [25] But if a person looks closely

into the perfect *Torah*, which gives freedom, and continues, becoming not a forgetful hearer but a doer of the work it requires, then he will be blessed in what he does. ²⁶ Anyone who thinks he is religiously observant but does not control his tongue is deceiving himself, and his observance counts for nothing. ²⁷ The religious observance that God the Father considers pure and faultless is this: to care for orphans and widows in their distress and to keep oneself from being contaminated by the world.

2 ¹ My brothers, practice the faith of our Lord Yeshua, the glorious Messiah, without showing favoritism. ² Suppose a man comes into your synagogue wearing gold rings and fancy clothes, and also a poor man comes in dressed in rags. ³ If you show more respect to the man wearing the fancy clothes and say to him, "Have this good seat here," while to the poor man you say, "You, stand over there," or, "Sit down on the floor by my feet," ⁴ then aren't you creating distinctions among yourselves, and haven't you made yourselves into judges with evil motives?

⁵ Listen, my dear brothers, hasn't God chosen the poor of the world to be rich in faith and to receive the Kingdom which he promised to those who love him? ⁶ But you despise the poor! Aren't the rich the ones who oppress you and drag you into court? ⁷ Aren't they the ones who insult the good name of Him to whom you belong? ⁸ If you truly attain the goal of Kingdom *Torah*, in conformity with the passage that says, **"Love your neighbor as yourself,"**[a] you are doing well. ⁹ But if you show favoritism, your actions constitute sin, since you are convicted under the *Torah* as transgressors.

¹⁰ For a person who keeps the whole *Torah*, yet stumbles at one point, has become guilty of breaking them all. ¹¹ For the One who said, **"Don't commit adultery,"**[b] also said, **"Don't murder."**[c] Now, if you don't commit adultery but do murder, you have become a transgressor of the *Torah*.

¹² Keep speaking and acting like people who will be judged by a *Torah* which gives freedom. ¹³ For judgment will be without mercy toward one who doesn't show mercy; but mercy wins out over judgment.

¹⁴ What good is it, my brothers, if someone claims to have faith but has no actions to prove it? Is such "faith" able to save him? ¹⁵ Suppose a brother or sister is without clothes and daily food, ¹⁶ and someone says to him, "*Shalom!* Keep warm and eat hearty!" without giving him what he needs, what good does it do? ¹⁷ Thus, faith by itself, unaccompanied by actions, is dead.

¹⁸ But someone will say that you have faith and I have actions. Show me this faith of yours without the actions, and I will show you my faith by my actions! ¹⁹ You believe that **"God is one"**?[d] Good for you! The demons believe it too — the thought makes them shudder with fear!

²⁰ But, foolish fellow, do you want to be shown that such "faith" apart from actions is barren? ²¹ Wasn't *Avraham avinu* declared righteous because of actions when he offered up his son Yitz'chak on the altar? ²² You see that his faith worked with his actions; by the actions the faith was made complete; ²³ and the passage of the *Tanakh* was fulfilled which says, **"Avraham had faith in God, and it was credited to his account as righteousness."**[e] He was even called **God's friend.**[f]

---

[a] Leviticus 19:18   [b] Exodus 20:13(14); Deuteronomy 5:17(18)   [c] Exodus 20:13; Deuteronomy 5:17
[d] Deuteronomy 6:4   [e] Genesis 15:6   [f] Isaiah 41:8; 2 Chronicles 20:7

²⁴ You see that a person is declared righteous because of actions and not because of faith alone.

²⁵ Likewise, wasn't Rachav the prostitute also declared righteous because of actions when she welcomed the messengers and sent them out by another route? ²⁶ Indeed, just as the body without a spirit is dead, so too faith without actions is dead.

3 ¹ Not many of you should become teachers, my brothers, since you know that we will be judged more severely. ² For we all stumble in many ways; if someone does not stumble in what he says, he is a mature man who can bridle his whole body. ³ If we put a bit into a horse's mouth to make it obey us, we control its whole body as well. ⁴ And think of a ship — although it is huge and is driven by strong winds, yet the pilot can steer it wherever he wants with just a small rudder. ⁵ So too the tongue is a tiny part of the body, yet it boasts great things. See how a little fire sets a whole forest ablaze! ⁶ Yes, the tongue is a fire, a world of wickedness. The tongue is so placed in our body that it defiles every part of it, setting ablaze the whole of our life; and it is set on fire by Gei-Hinnom itself. ⁷ For people have tamed and continue to tame all kinds of animals, birds, reptiles and sea creatures; ⁸ but the tongue no one can tame — it is an unstable and evil thing, full of death-dealing poison! ⁹ With it we bless *Adonai*, the Father; and with it we curse people, who were made **in the image of God**.*ᵍ* ¹⁰ Out of the same mouth come blessing and cursing! Brothers, it isn't right for things to be this way. ¹¹ A spring doesn't send both fresh and bitter water from the same opening, does it? ¹² Can a fig tree yield olives, my brothers? or a grapevine, figs? Neither does salt water produce fresh.

¹³ Who among you is wise and understanding? Let him demonstrate it by his good way of life, by actions done in the humility that grows out of wisdom. ¹⁴ But if you harbor in your hearts bitter jealousy and selfish ambition, don't boast and attack the truth with lies! ¹⁵ This wisdom is not the kind that comes down from above; on the contrary, it is worldly, unspiritual, demonic. ¹⁶ For where there are jealousy and selfish ambition, there will be disharmony and every foul practice. ¹⁷ But the wisdom from above is, first of all, pure, then peaceful, kind, open to reason, full of mercy and good fruits, without partiality and without hypocrisy. ¹⁸ And peacemakers who sow seed in peace raise a harvest of righteousness.

4 ¹ What is causing all the quarrels and fights among you? Isn't it your desires battling inside you? ² You desire things and don't have them. You kill, and you are jealous, and you still can't get them. So you fight and quarrel. The reason you don't have is that you don't pray! ³ Or you pray and don't receive, because you pray with the wrong motive, that of wanting to indulge your own desires.

⁴ You unfaithful wives! Don't you know that loving the world is hating God? Whoever chooses to be the world's friend makes himself God's enemy! ⁵ Or do you suppose the Scripture speaks in vain when it says that there is a spirit in us which longs to envy? ⁶ But the grace he gives is greater, which is why it says,

> **"God opposes the arrogant,**
> **but to the humble he gives grace."***ʰ*

ᵍ Genesis 1:26–27   *ʰ* Proverbs 3:34

⁷ Therefore, submit to God. Moreover, take a stand against the Adversary, and he will flee from you. ⁸ Come close to God, and he will come close to you. Clean your hands, sinners; and purify your hearts, you double-minded people! ⁹ Wail, mourn, sob! Let your laughter be turned into mourning and your joy into gloom! ¹⁰ Humble yourselves before the Lord, and he will lift you up.

¹¹ Brothers, stop speaking against each other! Whoever speaks against a brother or judges a brother is speaking against *Torah* and judging *Torah*. And if you judge *Torah*, you are not a doer of what *Torah* says, but a judge. ¹² There is but one Giver of *Torah*; he is also the Judge, with the power to deliver and to destroy. Who do you think you are, judging your fellow human being?

¹³ Now listen, you who say, "Today or tomorrow we will go to such-and-such a city, stay there a year trading and make a profit"! ¹⁴ You don't even know if you will be alive tomorrow! For all you are is a mist that appears for a little while and then disappears. ¹⁵ Instead, you ought to say, "If ADONAI wants it to happen, we will live" to do this or that. ¹⁶ But as it is, in your arrogance you boast. All such boasting is evil. ¹⁷ So then, anyone who knows the right thing to do and fails to do it is committing a sin.

5 ¹ Next, a word for the rich: weep and wail over the hardships coming upon you! ² Your riches have rotted, and your clothes have become moth-eaten; ³ your gold and silver have corroded, and their corrosion will be evidence against you and will eat up your flesh like fire! This is the *acharit-hayamim*, and you have been storing up wealth! ⁴ Listen! The wages you have fraudulently withheld from the workers who mowed your fields are calling out against you, and the outcries of those who harvested have reached the ears of ADONAI-*Tzva'ot*. ⁵ You have led a life of luxury and self-indulgence here on earth — in a time of slaughter, you have gone on eating to your heart's content. ⁶ You have condemned, you have murdered the innocent; they have not withstood you.

⁷ So, brothers, be patient until the Lord returns. See how the farmer waits for the precious "fruit of the earth" — he is patient over it until it receives **the fall and spring rains**.*ⁱ* ⁸ You too, be patient; keep up your courage; for the Lord's return is near. ⁹ Don't grumble against one another, brothers, so that you won't come under condemnation — look! the Judge is standing at the door! ¹⁰ As an example of suffering mistreatment and being patient, brothers, take the prophets who spoke in the name of ADONAI. ¹¹ Look, we regard those who persevered as blessed. You have heard of the perseverance of Iyov, and you know what the purpose of ADONAI was, that ADONAI **is very compassionate and merciful**.*ʲ*

¹² Above all, brothers, stop swearing oaths — not "By heaven," not "By the earth," and not by any other formula; rather, let your "Yes" be simply "Yes" and your "No" simply "No," so that you won't fall under condemnation.

¹³ Is someone among you in trouble? He should pray. Is someone feeling good? He should sing songs of praise.

¹⁴ Is someone among you ill? He should call for the elders of the congregation. They will pray for him and rub olive oil on him in the name of the Lord. ¹⁵ The prayer offered with trust will heal the one who is ill — the Lord will restore his health; and if he has committed sins, he will be forgiven. ¹⁶ Therefore, openly acknowledge your

---

*ⁱ*Deuteronomy 11:14; Jeremiah 5:24; Joel 2:23   *ʲ*Exodus 34:6; Psalms 103:8; 111:4

sins to one another, and pray for each other, so that you may be healed. The prayer of a righteous person is powerful and effective. ¹⁷Eliyahu was only a human being like us; yet he prayed fervently that it might not rain, and no rain fell on the Land for three years and six months. ¹⁸Then he prayed again, and heaven gave rain, and the Land produced its crops.

¹⁹My brothers, if one of you wanders from the truth, and someone causes him to return, ²⁰you should know that whoever turns a sinner from his wandering path will save him from death and **cover many sins.**^k

ᵏProverbs 10:12

The First Letter from Yeshua's Emissary Kefa

1 Kefa

1 PETER

1 ¹ From: Kefa, an emissary of Yeshua the Messiah

To: God's chosen people, living as aliens in the Diaspora — in Pontus, Galatia, Cappadocia, the province of Asia, and Bythinia — ² chosen according to the fore-knowledge of God the Father and set apart by the Spirit for obeying Yeshua the Messiah and for sprinkling with his blood:

Grace and *shalom* be yours in full measure.

³ Praised be God, Father of our Lord Yeshua the Messiah, who, in keeping with his great mercy, has caused us, through the resurrection of Yeshua the Messiah from the dead, to be born again to a living hope, ⁴ to an inheritance that cannot decay, spoil or fade, kept safe for you in heaven. ⁵ Meanwhile, through trusting, you are being protected by God's power for a deliverance ready to be revealed at the Last Time. ⁶ Rejoice in this, even though for a little while you may have to experience grief in various trials. ⁷ Even gold is tested for genuineness by fire. The purpose of these trials is so that your trust's genuineness, which is far more valuable than perishable gold, will be judged worthy of praise, glory and honor at the revealing of Yeshua the Messiah.

⁸ Without having seen him, you love him. Without seeing him now, but trusting in him, you continue to be full of joy that is glorious beyond words. ⁹ And you are receiving what your trust is aiming at, namely, your deliverance.

¹⁰ The prophets, who prophesied about this gift of deliverance that was meant for you, pondered and inquired diligently about it. ¹¹ They were trying to find out the time and circumstances to which the Spirit of the Messiah in them was referring in predicting the Messiah's sufferings and the glorious things to follow. ¹² It was revealed to them that their service when they spoke about these things was not for their own benefit, but for yours. And these same things have now been proclaimed to you by those who communicated the Good News to you through the *Ruach HaKodesh* sent from heaven. Even angels long to look into these things!

¹³ Therefore, get your minds ready for work, keep yourselves under control, and fix your hopes fully on the gift you will receive when Yeshua the Messiah is revealed. ¹⁴ As people who obey God, do not let yourselves be shaped by the evil desires you used to have when you were still ignorant. ¹⁵ On the contrary, following the Holy One who called you, become holy yourselves in your entire way of life; ¹⁶ since the *Tanakh* says,

"You are to be holy because I am holy."[a]

---

[a] Leviticus 11:44, 45; 19:2; 20:7

^{17} Also, if you are addressing as Father the one who judges impartially according to each person's actions, you should live out your temporary stay on earth in fear. ^{18} You should be aware that the ransom paid to free you from the worthless way of life which your fathers passed on to you did not consist of anything perishable like silver or gold; ^{19} on the contrary, it was the costly bloody sacrificial death of the Messiah, as of a lamb without defect or spot. ^{20} God knew him before the founding of the universe, but revealed him in the *acharit-hayamim* for your sakes. ^{21} Through him you trust in God, who raised him from the dead and gave him glory; so that your trust and hope are in God.

^{22} Now that you have purified yourselves by obeying the truth, so that you have a sincere love for your brothers, love each other deeply, with all your heart. ^{23} You have been born again not from some seed that will decay, but from one that cannot decay, through the living **Word of** God that **lasts forever**. ^{24} For

> **all humanity is like grass,**
> **all its glory is like a wildflower —**
> **the grass withers, and the flower falls off;**
> ^{25} **but the Word of** A*DONAI* **lasts forever.**^{b}

Moreover, this **Word** is the Good News which has been proclaimed to you.

2 ^{1} Therefore, rid yourselves of all malice, of all deceit, hypocrisy and envy, and of all the ways there are of speaking against people; ^{2} and be like newborn babies, thirsty for the pure milk of the **Word**; so that by it, you may grow up into deliverance. ^{3} For you have **tasted that** A*DONAI* **is good.**^{c}

^{4} As you come to him, the living **stone**, rejected by people but **chosen** by God and **precious** to him, ^{5} you yourselves, as living **stone**s, are being built into a spiritual house to be *cohanim* set apart for God to offer spiritual sacrifices acceptable to him through Yeshua the Messiah. ^{6} This is why the *Tanakh* says,

> **"Look! I am laying in Tziyon a stone,**
> **a chosen and precious cornerstone;**
> **and whoever rests his trust on it**
> **will certainly not be humiliated."**^{d}

^{7} Now to you who keep **trust**ing, he is **precious**. But to those who are not **trust**ing,

> **"The very stone that the builders rejected**
> **has become the cornerstone";**^{e}

^{8} also he is

> **a stone that will make people stumble,**
> **a rock over which they will trip.**^{f}

---

^{b} Isaiah 40:6–8 ^{c} Psalm 34:9(8) ^{d} Isaiah 28:16
^{e} Psalm 118:22 ^{f} Isaiah 8:14

They are **stumbl**ing at the Word, disobeying it — as had been planned. [9] But you are **a chosen people,**[g] **the King's** *cohanim,*[h] **a holy nation,**[i] **a people for God to possess!**[j] Why? In order for you to declare the praises of the One who called you out of darkness into his wonderful light. [10] Once you were **not a people**, but now you are **God's people**; before, you **had not received mercy**, but now you **have received mercy**.[k]

[11] Dear friends, I urge you as **aliens and temporary residents**[l] not to give in to the desires of your old nature, which keep warring against you; [12] but to live such good lives among the pagans that even though they now speak against you as evildoers, they will, as a result of seeing your good actions, give glory to God on the Day of his coming. [13] For the sake of the Lord, submit yourselves to every human authority — whether to the emperor as being supreme, [14] or to governors as being sent by him to punish wrongdoers and praise those who do what is good. [15] For it is God's will that your doing good should silence the ignorant talk of foolish people. [16] Submit as people who are free, but not letting your freedom serve as an excuse for evil; rather, submit as God's slaves. [17] Be respectful to all — keep loving the brotherhood, fearing God and honoring the emperor.

[18] Household servants, submit yourselves to your masters, showing them full respect — and not only those who are kind and considerate, but also those who are harsh. [19] For it is a grace when someone, because he is mindful of God, bears up under the pain of undeserved punishment. [20] For what credit is there in bearing up under a beating you deserve for doing something wrong? But if you bear up under punishment, even though you have done what is right, God looks on it with favor. [21] Indeed, this is what you were called to; because the Messiah too suffered, on your behalf, leaving an example so that you should follow in his steps.

[22]   **"He committed no sin,**
         nor was any deceit found on his lips."[m]

[23] When he was insulted, he didn't retaliate with insults; when he suffered, he didn't threaten, but handed them over to him who judges justly. [24] **He** himself **bore our sins**[n] in his body on the **stake,**[o] so that we might die to sins and live for righteousness — **by his wounds you were healed**.[p] [25] For you used to be **like sheep gone astray**, but now **you have turned to**[q] the Shepherd, who watches over you.

3 [1] In the same way, wives, submit to your husbands; so that even if some of them do not believe the Word, they will be won over by your conduct, without your saying anything, [2] as they see your respectful and pure behavior. [3] Your beauty should not consist in externals such as fancy hairstyles, gold jewelry or what you wear; [4] rather, let it be the inner character of your heart, with the imperishable quality of a gentle and quiet spirit. In God's sight this is of great value. [5] This is how the holy women of the past who put their hope in God used to adorn themselves and submit to their husbands, [6] the way Sarah obeyed

---

[g] Isaiah 43:20; Deuteronomy 7:6; 10:15
[j] Isaiah 43:21; Exodus 19:5
Psalm 39:13(12); 1 Chronicles 29:15
[o] Deuteronomy 21:22–23

[h] Exodus 19:6; Isaiah 61:6
[k] Hosea 2:25(23)
[m] Isaiah 53:9
[p] Isaiah 53:5

[i] Exodus 19:6
[l] Genesis 23:4; 47:4;
[n] Isaiah 53:4,12
[q] Isaiah 53:6

Avraham, honoring him as her lord. You are her daughters if you do what is right and do not succumb to fear.

⁷ You husbands, likewise, conduct your married lives with understanding. Although your wife may be weaker physically, you should respect her as a fellow-heir of the gift of Life. If you don't, your prayers will be blocked.

⁸ Finally, all of you, be one in mind and feeling; love as brothers; and be compassionate and humble-minded, ⁹ not repaying evil with evil or insult with insult, but, on the contrary, with blessing. For it is to this that you have been called, so that you may receive a blessing. ¹⁰ For

"Whoever wants to love life and see good days
   must keep his tongue from evil and his lips from speaking deceit,
¹¹   turn from evil and do good,
   seek peace and chase after it.
¹² For ADONAI keeps his eyes on the righteous,
   and his ears are open to their prayers;
   but the face of ADONAI is against
   those who do evil things."ʳ

¹³ For who will hurt you if you become zealots for what is good? ¹⁴ But even if you do suffer for being righteous, you are blessed! Moreover, **don't fear what they fear or be disturbed**, ¹⁵ but **treat** the Messiah **as holy, as Lord** in your hearts;ˢ while remaining always ready to give a reasoned answer to anyone who asks you to explain the hope you have in you — yet with humility and fear, ¹⁶ keeping your conscience clear, so that when you are spoken against, those who abuse the good behavior flowing from your union with the Messiah may be put to shame. ¹⁷ For if God has in fact willed that you should suffer, it is better that you suffer for doing what is good than for doing what is evil.

¹⁸ For the Messiah himself died for sins, once and for all, a righteous person on behalf of unrighteous people, so that he might bring you to God. He was put to death in the flesh but brought to life by the Spirit; ¹⁹ and in this form he went and made a proclamation to the imprisoned spirits, ²⁰ to those who were disobedient long ago, in the days of Noach, when God waited patiently during the building of the ark, in which a few people — to be specific, eight — were delivered by means of water. ²¹ This also prefigures what delivers us now, the water of immersion, which is not the removal of dirt from the body, but one's pledge to keep a good conscience toward God, through the resurrection of Yeshua the Messiah. ²² He has gone into heaven and is **at the right hand of God**,ᵗ with angels, authorities and powers subject to him.

4 ¹ Therefore, since the Messiah suffered physically, you too are to arm yourselves with the same attitude. For whoever has suffered physically is finished with sin, ² with the result that he lives the rest of his earthly life no longer controlled by human desires, but by God's will. ³ For you have spent enough time already living the way the pagans want you to live — in debauchery, lust, drunkenness, orgies, wild parties and forbidden idol-worship. ⁴ They think it strange that you don't plunge with them

---

ʳ Psalm 34:13-17(12-16)   ˢ Isaiah 8:12-13   ᵗ Psalm 110:1

into the same flood of dissoluteness, and so they heap insults on you. ⁵ But they will have to give an account to him who stands ready to judge the living and the dead. ⁶ This is why he was proclaimed to those who have died; it was so that, although physically they would receive the judgment common to all humanity, they might live by the Spirit in the way that God has provided.

⁷ The accomplishing of the goal of all things is close at hand. Therefore, keep alert and self-controlled, so that you can pray. ⁸ More than anything, keep loving each other actively; because **love covers many sins**." ⁹ Welcome one another into your homes without grumbling. ¹⁰ As each one has received some spiritual gift, he should use it to serve others, like good managers of God's many-sided grace — ¹¹ if someone speaks, let him speak God's words; if someone serves, let him do so out of strength that God supplies; so that in everything God may be glorified through Yeshua the Messiah — to him be glory and power forever and ever. *Amen.*

¹² Dear friends, don't regard as strange the fiery ordeal occurring among you to test you, as if something extraordinary were happening to you. ¹³ Rather, to the extent that you share the fellowship of the Messiah's sufferings, rejoice; so that you will rejoice even more when his *Sh'khinah* is revealed. ¹⁴ If you are being insulted because you bear the name of the Messiah, how blessed you are! For the Spirit of the *Sh'khinah*, that is, the Spirit of God, is resting on you! ¹⁵ Let none of you suffer for being a murderer or a thief or an evildoer or a meddler in other people's affairs. ¹⁶ But if anyone suffers for being Messianic, let him not be ashamed; but let him bring glory to God by the way he bears this name. ¹⁷ For the time has come for the judgment to begin. It begins with the household of God; and if it starts with us, what will the outcome be for those who are disobeying God's Good News? —

¹⁸   **"If the righteous is barely delivered,**
       where will the ungodly and sinful end up?"ᵛ

¹⁹ So let those who are suffering according to God's will entrust themselves to a faithful Creator by continuing to do what is good.

5 ¹ Therefore, I urge the congregation leaders among you, as a fellow-leader and witness to the Messiah's sufferings, as well as a sharer in the glory to be revealed: ² shepherd the flock of God that is in your care, exercising oversight not out of constraint, but willingly, as God wants; and not out of a desire for dishonest gain, but with enthusiasm; ³ also not as *machers* domineering over those in your care, but as people who become examples to the flock. ⁴ Then, when the Chief Shepherd appears, you will receive glory as your unfading crown.

⁵ Likewise, you who are less experienced, submit to leaders. Further, all of you should clothe yourselves in humility toward one another, because

     God opposes the arrogant,
     but to the humble he gives grace.ʷ

ᵘ Proverbs 10:12   ᵛ Proverbs 11:31   ʷ Proverbs 3:34

⁶ Therefore, humble yourselves under the mighty hand of God, so that at the right time he may lift you up. ⁷ Throw all your anxieties upon him, because he cares about you.

⁸ Stay sober, stay alert! Your enemy, the Adversary, stalks about like a roaring lion looking for someone to devour. ⁹ Stand against him, firm in your trust, knowing that your brothers throughout the world are going through the same kinds of suffering. ¹⁰ You will have to suffer only a little while; after that, God, who is full of grace, the one who called you to his eternal glory in union with the Messiah, will himself restore, establish and strengthen you and make you firm. ¹¹ To him be the power forever and ever. *Amen.*

¹² Through Sila, whom I regard as a faithful brother, I have written you briefly, encouraging you and giving my witness that this is God's true grace. Stand firm in it!

¹³ Your sister congregation in Bavel, chosen along with you, sends greetings to you, as does my son Mark. ¹⁴ Greet each other with a kiss of love.

"*Shalom aleikhem!*" to all who belong to the Messiah.

The Second Letter from Yeshua's Emissary Kefa

2 Kefa
2 PETER

1 ¹ From: Shim'on Kefa, a slave and emissary of Yeshua the Messiah

To: Those who, through the righteousness of our God and of our Deliverer Yeshua the Messiah, have been given the same kind of trust as ours:

² May grace and *shalom* be yours in full measure, as you come to a full knowledge of God and Yeshua our Lord.

³ God's power has given us everything we need for life and godliness, through our knowing the One who called us to his own glory and goodness. ⁴ By these he has given us valuable and superlatively great promises, so that through them you might come to share in God's nature and escape the corruption which evil desires have brought into the world.

⁵ For this very reason, try your hardest to furnish your faith with goodness, goodness with knowledge, ⁶ knowledge with self-control, self-control with perseverance, perseverance with godliness, ⁷ godliness with brotherly affection, and brotherly affection with love. ⁸ For if you have these qualities in abundance, they keep you from being barren and unfruitful in the knowledge of our Lord Yeshua the Messiah. ⁹ Indeed, whoever lacks them is blind, so shortsighted that he forgets that his past sins have been washed away. ¹⁰ Therefore, brothers, try even harder to make your being called and chosen a certainty. For if you keep doing this, you will never stumble. ¹¹ Thus you will be generously supplied with everything you need to enter the eternal Kingdom of our Lord and Deliverer, Yeshua the Messiah.

¹² For this reason, I will always remind you about these things, even though you know them and are firmly established in the truth you already have. ¹³ And I consider it right to keep stirring you up with reminders, as long as I am in the tent of this body. ¹⁴ I know that I will soon lay aside this tent of mine, as our Lord Yeshua the Messiah has made clear to me. ¹⁵ And I will do my best to see that after my exodus, you will be able to remember these things at all times.

¹⁶ For when we made known to you the power and the coming of our Lord Yeshua the Messiah, we did not rely on cunningly contrived myths. On the contrary, we saw his majesty with our own eyes. ¹⁷ For we were there when he received honor and glory from God the Father; and the voice came to him from the grandeur of the *Sh'khinah*, saying, "This is my son, whom I love; I am well pleased with him!" ¹⁸ We heard this voice come out of heaven when we were with him on the holy mountain.

¹⁹ Yes, we have the prophetic Word made very certain. You will do well to pay attention to it as to a light shining in a dark, murky place, until the Day dawns and the Morning Star rises in your hearts. ²⁰ First of all, understand this: no prophecy of

Scripture is to be interpreted by an individual on his own; ²¹ for never has a prophecy come as a result of human willing — on the contrary, people moved by the *Ruach HaKodesh* spoke a message from God.

2 ¹ But among the people there were also false prophets, just as there will be false teachers among you. Under false pretenses they will introduce destructive heresies, even denying the Master who bought them, and thus bring on themselves swift destruction. ² Many will follow their debaucheries; and because of them, the true Way will be maligned. ³ In their greed they will exploit you with fabricated stories.

Their punishment, decreed long ago, is not idle; their destruction is not asleep! ⁴ For God did not spare the angels who sinned; on the contrary, he put them in gloomy dungeons lower than Sh'ol to be held for judgment. ⁵ And he did not spare the ancient world; on the contrary, he preserved Noach, a herald of righteousness, with seven others, and brought the Flood upon a world of ungodly people. ⁶ And he condemned the cities of S'dom and 'Amora, reducing them to ashes and ruin, as a warning to those in the future who would live ungodly lives; ⁷ but he rescued Lot, a righteous man who was distressed by the debauchery of those unprincipled people; ⁸ for the wicked deeds which that righteous man saw and heard, as he lived among them, tormented his righteous heart day after day. ⁹ So the Lord knows how to rescue the godly from trials and how to hold the wicked until the Day of Judgment while continuing to punish them, ¹⁰ especially those who follow their old natures in lust for filth and who despise authority.

Presumptuous and self-willed, these false teachers do not tremble at insulting angelic beings; ¹¹ whereas angels, though stronger and more powerful, do not bring before the Lord an insulting charge against them. ¹² But these people, acting without thinking, like animals without reason, born to be captured and destroyed, insult things about which they have no knowledge. When they are destroyed, their destruction will be total — ¹³ they will be paid back harm as wages for the harm they are doing.

Their idea of pleasure is carousing in broad daylight; they are spots and defects reveling in their deceptions as they share meals with you — ¹⁴ for they have eyes always on the lookout for a woman who will commit adultery, eyes that never stop sinning; and they have a heart that has exercised itself in greed; so that they seduce unstable people. What a cursed brood!

¹⁵ These people have left the straight way and wandered off to follow the way of Bil'am Ben-B'or, who loved the wages of doing harm ¹⁶ but was rebuked for his sin — a dumb beast of burden spoke out with a human voice and restrained the prophet's insanity! ¹⁷ Waterless springs they are, mists driven by a gust of wind; for them has been reserved the blackest darkness. ¹⁸ Mouthing grandiosities of nothingness, they play on the desires of the old nature, in order to seduce with debaucheries people who have just begun to escape from those whose way of life is wrong.

¹⁹ They promise them freedom, but they themselves are slaves of corruption; for a person is slave to whatever has defeated him. ²⁰ Indeed, if they have once escaped the pollutions of the world through knowing our Lord and Deliverer, Yeshua the Messiah, and then have again become entangled and defeated by them, their latter condition has become worse than their former. ²¹ It would have been better for them not to have known the Way of righteousness than, fully knowing, to turn from the holy command delivered to them. ²² What has happened to them

accords with the true proverb, "**A dog returns to its own vomit**."*a* Yes, "The pig washed itself, only to wallow in the mud!"

3 ¹ Dear friends, I am writing you now this second letter; and in both letters I am trying to arouse you to wholesome thinking by means of reminders; ² so that you will keep in mind the predictions of the holy prophets and the command given by the Lord and Deliverer through your emissaries.

³ First, understand this: during the Last Days, scoffers will come, following their own desires ⁴ and asking, "Where is this promised 'coming' of his? For our fathers have died, and everything goes on just as it has since the beginning of creation." ⁵ But, wanting so much to be right about this, they overlook the fact that it was by God's Word that long ago there were heavens, and there was land which arose out of water and existed between the waters, ⁶ and that by means of these things the world of that time was flooded with water and destroyed. ⁷ It is by that same Word that the present heavens and earth, having been preserved, are being kept for fire until the Day of Judgment, when ungodly people will be destroyed.

⁸ Moreover, dear friends, do not ignore this: with the Lord, one day is like a thousand years and **a thousand years like** one **day**ᵇ ⁹ The Lord is not slow in keeping his promise, as some people think of slowness; on the contrary, he is patient with you; for it is not his purpose that anyone should be destroyed, but that everyone should turn from his sins. ¹⁰ However, the Day of the Lord will come "like a thief." On that Day the heavens will disappear with a roar, the elements will melt and disintegrate, and the earth and everything in it will be burned up.

¹¹ Since everything is going to be destroyed like this, what kind of people should you be? You should lead holy and godly lives, ¹² as you wait for the Day of God and work to hasten its coming. That Day will bring on the destruction of the heavens by fire, and the elements will melt from the heat; ¹³ but we, following along with his promise, wait for **new heavens and a new earth**,ᶜ in which righteousness will be at home. ¹⁴ Therefore, dear friends, as you look for these things, do everything you can to be found by him without spot or defect and at peace. ¹⁵ And think of our Lord's patience as deliverance, just as our dear brother Sha'ul also wrote you, following the wisdom God gave him. ¹⁶ Indeed, he speaks about these things in all his letters. They contain some things that are hard to understand, things which the uninstructed and unstable distort, to their own destruction, as they do the other Scriptures.

¹⁷ But you, dear friends, since you know this in advance, guard yourselves; so that you will not be led away by the errors of the wicked and fall from your own secure position. ¹⁸ And keep growing in grace and knowledge of our Lord and Deliverer, Yeshua the Messiah. To him be the glory, both now and forever! *Amen.*

---

a Proverbs 26:11   *b* Psalm 90:4   *c* Isaiah 65:17; 66:22

The First Letter from Yeshua's Emissary Yochanan

1 Yochanan

1 JOHN

1 ¹ The Word, which gives life!
He existed from the beginning.
We have heard him,
we have seen him with our eyes,
we have contemplated him,
we have touched him with our hands!

² The life appeared,
and we have seen it.
We are testifying to it
and announcing it to you —
eternal life!

He was with the Father,
and he appeared to us.

³ What we have seen and heard,
we are proclaiming to you;
so that you too
may have fellowship with us.
Our fellowship is with the Father
and with his Son, Yeshua the Messiah.

⁴ We are writing these things
so that our joy may be complete.

⁵ And this is the message which we have heard from him and proclaim to you: God is light, and there is no darkness in him — none!

⁶ If we claim to have fellowship with him while we are walking in the darkness, we are lying and not living out the truth. ⁷ But if we are walking in the light, as he is in the light, then we have fellowship with each other, and the blood of his Son Yeshua purifies us from all sin.

⁸ If we claim not to have sin, we are deceiving ourselves, and the truth is not in us. ⁹ If we acknowledge our sins, then, since he is trustworthy and just, he will forgive them and purify us from all wrongdoing.

¹⁰ If we claim we have not been sinning, we are making him out to be a liar, and his Word is not in us.

2 ¹ My children, I am writing you these things so that you won't sin. But if anyone does sin, we have Yeshua the Messiah, the *Tzaddik*, who pleads our cause with the Father. ² Also, he is the *kapparah* for our sins — and not only for ours, but also for those of the whole world.

³ The way we can be sure we know him is if we are obeying his commands. ⁴ Anyone who says, "I know him," but isn't obeying his commands is a liar — the truth is not in him. ⁵ But if someone keeps doing what he says, then truly love for God has been brought to its goal in him. This is how we are sure that we are united with him. ⁶ A person who claims to be continuing in union with him ought to conduct his life the way he did.

⁷ Dear friends, I am not writing you a new command. On the contrary, it is an old command, which you have had from the beginning; the old command is the message which you have heard before. ⁸ Yet I am writing you a new command, and its reality is seen both in him and in you, because the darkness is passing away and the true light is already shining. ⁹ Anyone who claims to be in this light while hating his brother is still in the dark. ¹⁰ The person who keeps loving his brother remains in the light, and there is nothing in him that could make him trip. ¹¹ But the person who hates his brother is in the dark — yes, he is walking in the dark, and he doesn't know where he is going, because the darkness has blinded his eyes.

¹²   You children, I am writing you
        because your sins have been forgiven for his sake.
¹³   You fathers, I am writing you
        because you have known him who has existed from the beginning.
    You young people, I am writing you
        because you have overcome the Evil One.
¹⁴   You children, I have written you
        because you have known the Father.
    You fathers, I have written you
        because you have known him who has existed from the beginning.
    You young people, I have written you
        because you are strong —
        the Word of God remains in you,
        and you have overcome the Evil One.

¹⁵ Do not love the world or the things of the world. If someone loves the world, then love for the Father is not in him; ¹⁶ because all the things of the world — the desires of the old nature, the desires of the eyes, and the pretensions of life — are not from the Father but from the world. ¹⁷ And the world is passing away, along with its desires. But whoever does God's will remains forever.

¹⁸ Children, this is the Last Hour. You have heard that an Anti-Messiah is coming; and in fact, many anti-Messiahs have arisen now — which is how we know that this is the Last Hour. ¹⁹ They went out from us, but they weren't part of us; for had they been part of us, they would have remained with us.

²⁰ But you have received the Messiah's anointing from *HaKadosh*, and you know all this. ²¹ It is not because you don't know the truth that I have written to you, but because you do know it, and because no lie has its origin in the truth. ²² Who is a liar

at all, if not the person who denies that Yeshua is the Messiah? Such a person is an anti-Messiah — he is denying the Father and the Son. ²³ Everyone who denies the Son is also without the Father, but the person who acknowledges the Son has the Father as well. ²⁴ Let what you heard from the beginning remain in you. If what you heard from the beginning remains in you, you will also remain in union with both the Son and the Father. ²⁵ And this is what he has promised us: eternal life.

²⁶ I have written you these things about the people who are trying to deceive you. ²⁷ As for you, the Messianic anointing you received from the Father remains in you, so that you have no need for anyone to teach you. On the contrary, as his Messianic anointing continues to teach you about all things, and is true, not a counterfeit, so, just as he taught you, remain united with him.

²⁸ And now, children, remain united with him; so that when he appears, we may have confidence and not shrink back from him in shame at his coming. ²⁹ If you know that he is righteous, you should also know that he is the Father of everyone who does what is right.

3 ¹ See what love the Father has lavished on us in letting us be called God's children! For that is what we are. The reason the world does not know us is that it has not known him. ² Dear friends, we are God's children now; and it has not yet been made clear what we will become. We do know that when he appears, we will be like him; because we will see him as he really is.

³ And everyone who has this hope in him continues purifying himself, since God is pure. ⁴ Everyone who keeps sinning is violating *Torah* — indeed, sin is violation of *Torah*. ⁵ You know that he appeared in order to take away sins, and that there is no sin in him. ⁶ So no one who remains united with him continues sinning; everyone who does continue sinning has neither seen him nor known him.

⁷ Children, don't let anyone deceive you — it is the person that keeps on doing what is right who is righteous, just as God is righteous. ⁸ The person who keeps on sinning is from the Adversary, because from the very beginning the Adversary has kept on sinning. It was for this very reason that the Son of God appeared, to destroy these doings of the Adversary. ⁹ No one who has God as his Father keeps on sinning, because the seed planted by God remains in him. That is, he cannot continue sinning, because he has God as his Father. ¹⁰ Here is how one can distinguish clearly between God's children and those of the Adversary: everyone who does not continue doing what is right is not from God.

Likewise, anyone who fails to keep loving his brother is not from God. ¹¹ For this is the message which you have heard from the beginning: that we should love each other ¹² and not be like Kayin, who was from the Evil One and murdered his own brother. Why did he murder him? Because his own actions were evil, and his brother's were righteous. ¹³ Don't be amazed, brothers, if the world hates you. ¹⁴ We, for our part, know that we have passed from death to life because we keep loving the brothers. The person who fails to keep on loving is still under the power of death. ¹⁵ Everyone who hates his brother is a murderer, and you know that no murderer has eternal life in him.

¹⁶ The way that we have come to know love is through his having laid down his life for us. And we ought to lay down our lives for the brothers! ¹⁷ If someone has worldly possessions and sees his brother in need, yet closes his heart against him,

how can he be loving God? ^{18} Children, let us love not with words and talk, but with actions and in reality!

^{19} Here is how we will know that we are from the truth and will set our hearts at rest in his presence: ^{20} if our hearts know something against us, God is greater than our hearts, and he knows everything. ^{21} Dear friends, if our hearts know nothing against us, we have confidence in approaching God; ^{22} then, whatever we ask for, we receive from him; because we are obeying his commands and doing the things that please him.

^{23} This is his command: that we are to trust in the person and power of his Son Yeshua the Messiah and to keep loving one another, just as he commanded us. ^{24} Those who obey his commands remain united with him and he with them.

Here is how we know that he remains united with us: by the Spirit whom he gave us.

4 ^{1} Dear friends, don't trust every spirit. On the contrary, test the spirits to see whether they are from God; because many false prophets have gone out into the world. ^{2} Here is how you recognize the Spirit of God: every spirit which acknowledges that Yeshua the Messiah came as a human being is from God, ^{3} and every spirit which does not acknowledge Yeshua is not from God — in fact, this is the spirit of the Anti-Messiah. You have heard that he is coming. Well, he's here now, in the world already!

^{4} You, children, are from God and have overcome the false prophets, because he who is in you is greater than he who is in the world. ^{5} They are from the world; therefore, they speak from the world's viewpoint; and the world listens to them. ^{6} We are from God. Whoever knows God listens to us; whoever is not from God doesn't listen to us. This is how we distinguish the Spirit of truth from the spirit of error.

^{7} Beloved friends, let us love one another; because love is from God; and everyone who loves has God as his Father and knows God. ^{8} Those who do not love, do not know God; because God is love. ^{9} Here is how God showed his love among us: God sent his only Son into the world, so that through him we might have life. ^{10} Here is what love is: not that we have loved God, but that he loved us and sent his Son to be the *kapparah* for our sins.

^{11} Beloved friends, if this is how God loved us, we likewise ought to love one another. ^{12} No one has ever seen God; if we love one another, God remains united with us, and our love for him has been brought to its goal in us. ^{13} Here is how we know that we remain united with him and he with us: he has given to us from his own Spirit. ^{14} Moreover, we have seen and we testify that the Father has sent his Son as Deliverer of the world. ^{15} If someone acknowledges that Yeshua is the Son of God, God remains united with him, and he with God. ^{16} Also we have come to know and trust the love that God has for us. God is love; and those who remain in this love remain united with God, and God remains united with them.

^{17} Here is how love has been brought to maturity with us: as the Messiah is, so are we in the world. This gives us confidence for the Day of Judgment. ^{18} There is no fear in love. On the contrary, love that has achieved its goal gets rid of fear, because fear has to do with punishment; the person who keeps fearing has not been brought to maturity in regard to love.

^{19} We ourselves love now because he loved us first. ^{20} If anyone says, "I love God," and hates his brother, he is a liar. For if a person does not love his brother, whom he has seen, then he cannot love God, whom he has not seen. ²¹ Yes, this is the command we have from him: whoever loves God must love his brother too.

5 ¹ Everyone who believes that Yeshua is the Messiah has God as his father, and everyone who loves a father loves his offspring too. ² Here is how we know that we love God's children: when we love God, we also do what he commands. ³ For loving God means obeying his commands. Moreover, his commands are not burdensome, ⁴ because everything which has God as its Father overcomes the world. And this is what victoriously overcomes the world: our trust. ⁵ Who does overcome the world if not the person who believes that Yeshua is the Son of God?

⁶ He is the one who came by means of water and blood, Yeshua the Messiah — not with water only, but with the water and the blood. And the Spirit bears witness, because the Spirit is the truth. ⁷ There are three witnesses — ⁸ the Spirit, the water and the blood — and these three are in agreement. ⁹ If we accept human witness, God's witness is stronger, because it is the witness which God has given about his Son. ¹⁰ Those who keep trusting in the Son of God have this witness in them. Those who do not keep trusting God have made him out to be a liar, because they have not trusted in the witness which God has given about his Son. ¹¹ And this is the witness: God has given us eternal life, and this life is in his Son. ¹² Those who have the Son have the life; those who do not have the Son of God do not have the life. ¹³ I have written you these things so that you may know that you have eternal life — you who keep trusting in the person and power of the Son of God.

¹⁴ This is the confidence we have in his presence: if we ask anything that accords with his will, he hears us. ¹⁵ And if we know that he hears us — whatever we ask — then we know that we have what we have asked from him.

¹⁶ If anyone sees his brother committing a sin that does not lead to death, he will ask; and God will give him life for those whose sinning does not lead to death. There is sin that does lead to death; I am not saying he should pray about that. ¹⁷ All wrongdoing is sin, but there is sin that does not lead to death.

¹⁸ We know that everyone who has God as his Father does not go on sinning; on the contrary, the Son born of God protects him, and the Evil One does not touch him.

¹⁹ We know that we are from God, and that the whole world lies in the power of the Evil One.

²⁰ And we know that the Son of God has come and has given us discernment, so that we may know who is genuine; moreover, we are united with the One who is genuine, united with his Son Yeshua the Messiah. He is the genuine God and eternal life.

²¹ Children, guard yourselves against false gods!

The Second Letter from Yeshua's Emissary Yochanan

2 Yochanan
2 JOHN

[1] From: The Elder

To: The chosen lady and her children, whom I love in truth — and not only I but also all who have come to know the truth — [2] because of the Truth which remains united with us and will be with us forever:

[3] Grace, mercy and *shalom* will be with us from God the Father and from Yeshua the Messiah, the Son of the Father, in truth and love.

[4] I was very happy when I found some of your children living in truth, just as the Father commanded us. [5] And now, dear lady, I am requesting that we love one another — not as if this were a new command I am writing you, for it is the one which we have had from the beginning. [6] Moreover, love is this: that we should live according to his commands. This is the command, as you people have heard from the beginning; live by it!

[7] For many deceivers have gone out into the world, people who do not acknowledge Yeshua the Messiah's coming as a human being. Such a person is a deceiver and an anti-Messiah. [8] Watch yourselves, so that you won't lose what you have worked for, but will receive your full reward. [9] Everyone who goes ahead and does not remain true to what the Messiah has taught does not have God. Those who remain true to his teaching have both the Father and the Son. [10] If someone comes to you and does not bring this teaching, don't welcome him into your home. Don't even say, "*Shalom!*" to him; [11] for the person who says, "*Shalom!*" to him shares in his evil deeds.

[12] Although I have much to write you people, I would rather not use paper and ink. Instead, I hope to come and see you and to talk with you face to face, so that our joy may be complete.

[13] The children of your chosen sister send you their greetings.

3 Yochanan
3 JOHN

¹ From: The Elder

To: Dear Gaius, whom I love in truth:

² Dear friend, I am praying that everything prosper with you and that you be in good health, as I know you are prospering spiritually. ³ For I was so happy when some brothers came and testified how faithful you are to the truth, as you continue living in the truth. ⁴ Nothing gives me greater joy than hearing that my children are living in the truth.

⁵ Dear friend, you are faithful in all the work you are doing for the brothers, even when they are strangers to you. ⁶ They have testified to your love in front of the congregation. You will be doing well if you send them on their way in a manner worthy of God, ⁷ since it was for the sake of *HaShem* that they went out without accepting anything from the *Goyim*. ⁸ It is we, therefore, who should support such people; so that we may share in their work for the truth.

⁹ I wrote something to the congregation; but Diotrephes, who likes to be the *macher* among them, doesn't recognize our authority. ¹⁰ So if I come, I will bring up everything he is doing, including his spiteful and groundless gossip about us. And as if that weren't enough for him, he refuses to recognize the brothers' authority either; moreover, he stops those who want to do so and tries to drive them out of the congregation!

¹¹ Dear friend, don't imitate the bad, but the good. Those who do what is good are from God; those who do what is bad are not from God.

¹² Everyone speaks well of Demetrius, and so does the truth itself. We vouch for him, and you know that our testimony is true.

¹³ I have much to write you, but I don't want to write with pen and ink; ¹⁴ however, I am hoping to see you very soon, and we will speak face to face.

Shalom to you. Your friends send you their greetings. Greet each of our friends by name.

The Letter from
Y'hudah
JUDE

¹ From: Y'hudah, a slave of Yeshua the Messiah and a brother of Ya'akov
To: Those who have been called, who are loved by God the Father and kept for
Yeshua the Messiah:

² May mercy, love and *shalom* be yours in full measure.

³ Dear friends, I was busily at work writing to you about the salvation we share,
when I found it necessary to write, urging you to keep contending earnestly for the
faith which was once and for all passed on to God's people. ⁴ For certain individuals,
the ones written about long ago as being meant for this condemnation, have wormed
their way in — ungodly people who pervert God's grace into a license for debauchery
and disown our only Master and Lord, Yeshua the Messiah.

⁵ Since you already know all this, my purpose is only to remind you that ADONAI,
who once delivered the people from Egypt, later destroyed those who did not trust.
⁶ And the angels that did not keep within their original authority, but abandoned their
proper sphere, he has kept in darkness, bound with everlasting chains for the
Judgment of the Great Day. ⁷ And S'dom, 'Amora and the surrounding cities,
following a pattern like theirs, committing sexual sins and perversions, lie exposed
as a warning of the everlasting fire awaiting those who must undergo punishment.

⁸ Likewise, these people, with their visions, defile their own flesh, despise
godly authority and insult angelic beings. ⁹ When Mikha'el, one of the ruling
angels, took issue with the Adversary, arguing over the body of Moshe, he did
not dare bring against him an insulting charge, but said, "May ADONAI rebuke
you." ¹⁰ However, these people insult anything they don't understand; and what
they do understand naturally, without thinking, like animals — by these things
they are destroyed!

¹¹ Woe to them, in that they have walked the road of Kayin, they have given
themselves over for money to the error of Bil'am, they have been destroyed in the
rebellion of Korach. ¹² These men are filthy spots at your festive gatherings meant to
foster love; they share your meals without a qualm, while caring only for themselves.
They are waterless clouds carried along by the winds; trees without fruit even in
autumn, and doubly dead because they have been uprooted; ¹³ savage sea-waves
heaving forth their shameful deeds like foam; wandering stars for whom the blackest
darkness has been reserved forever.

¹⁴ Moreover, Hanokh, in the seventh generation starting with Adam, also
prophesied about these men, saying, "Look! ADONAI came with his myriads of holy
ones ¹⁵ to execute judgment against everyone, that is, to convict all the godless for

their godless deeds which they have done in such a godless way, and for all the harsh words these godless sinners have spoken against him."

16 These people are grumblers and complainers, they follow their evil passions, their mouths speak grandiosities, and they flatter others to gain advantage.

17 But you, dear friends, keep in mind the words spoken in advance by the emissaries of our Lord Yeshua the Messiah. 18 They told you, "During the *acharit-hayamim* there will be scoffers following their own godless passions." 19 These are the people who cause divisions. They are controlled by their impulses, because they don't have the Spirit.

20 But you, dear friends, build yourselves up in your most holy faith, and pray in union with the *Ruach HaKodesh*. 21 Thus keep yourselves in God's love, as you wait for our Lord Yeshua the Messiah to give you the mercy that leads to eternal life.

22 Rebuke some who are disputing; 23 save others, snatching them out of the fire; and to yet others, show mercy, but with fear, hating even the clothes stained by their vices.

24 Now,

> to the one who can keep you from falling
>   and set you without defect and full of joy
>   in the presence of his *Sh'khinah* —

25 to God alone, our Deliverer,
>   through Yeshua the Messiah, our Lord —
> be glory, majesty, power and authority
>   before all time, now and forever.

Amen.

The
REVELATION
of Yeshua the Messiah to Yochanan (John)

1 [1] This is the revelation which God gave to Yeshua the Messiah, so that he could show his servants what must happen very soon. He communicated it by sending his angel to his servant Yochanan, [2] who bore witness to the Word of God and to the testimony of Yeshua the Messiah, as much as he saw. [3] Blessed are the reader and hearers of the words of this prophecy, provided they obey the things written in it! For the time is near!

[4] From: Yochanan

To: The seven Messianic communities in the province of Asia:

Grace and *shalom* to you from the One who is, who was and who is coming; from the sevenfold Spirit before his throne; [5] and from Yeshua the Messiah, the faithful witness, the firstborn from the dead and the ruler of the earth's kings.

To him, the one who loves us, who has freed us from our sins at the cost of his blood, [6] who has caused us to be a kingdom, that is, *cohanim* for God, his Father — to him be the glory and the rulership forever and ever. *Amen.*

[7]   **Look! He is coming with the clouds!**[a]
    Every eye will see him,
    including those who **pierced him**;
    and **all the tribes of the Land will mourn him.**[b]

Yes! *Amen!*

[8]   "I am the 'A' and the 'Z,'" says *ADONAI*,
    God of heaven's armies,
    the One who is, who was and who is coming.

[9] I, Yochanan, am a brother of yours and a fellow-sharer in the suffering, kingship and perseverance that come from being united with Yeshua. I had been exiled to the island called Patmos for having proclaimed the message of God and borne witness to Yeshua. [10] I came to be, in the Spirit, on the Day of the Lord; and I heard behind me a loud voice, like a trumpet, [11] saying, "Write down what you see on a scroll, and send it to the seven Messianic communities — Ephesus, Smyrna, Pergamum, Thyatira, Sardis, Philadelphia and Laodicea!" [12] I turned around to see who was speaking to me; and when I had turned, I saw seven gold *menorah*s; [13] and among the *menorah*s was someone **like a Son of Man, wearing a robe down to his feet** and **a gold band around** his chest.[c] [14] His head and hair were as white as

---

[a] Daniel 7:13   [b] Zechariah 12:10–14   [c] Daniel 7:13; 10:5

snow-white wool, **his eyes like a fiery flame**, ¹⁵ **his feet like burnished brass** refined in a furnace, and **his voice like the sound of rushing waters.**[d] ¹⁶ In his right hand he held seven stars, out of his mouth went a sharp double-edged sword, and his face was like the sun shining in full strength.

¹⁷ When I saw him, I fell down at his feet like a dead man. He placed his right hand upon me and said, "Don't be afraid! I am the First and the Last, ¹⁸ the Living One. I was dead, but look! — I am alive forever and ever! And I hold the keys to Death and Sh'ol. ¹⁹ So write down what you see, both what is now, and what will happen afterwards. ²⁰ Here is the secret meaning of the seven stars you saw in my right hand, and of the seven gold *menorah*s: the seven stars are the angels of the seven Messianic communities, and the seven *menorah*s are the seven Messianic communities.

2 ¹ "To the angel of the Messianic Community in Ephesus, write: 'Here is the message from the one who holds the seven stars in his right hand and walks among the seven gold *menorah*s: ² "I know what you have been doing, how hard you have worked, how you have persevered, and how you can't stand wicked people; so you tested those who call themselves emissaries but aren't — and you found them to be liars. ³ You are persevering, and you have suffered for my sake without growing weary. ⁴ But I have this against you: you have lost the love you had at first. ⁵ Therefore, remember where you were before you fell, turn from this sin, and do what you used to do before. Otherwise, I will come to you and remove your *menorah* from its place — if you don't turn from your sin! ⁶ But you have this in your favor: you hate what the Nicolaitans do — I hate it too. ⁷ Those who have ears, let them hear what the Spirit is saying to the Messianic communities. To him winning the victory I will give the right to eat from the Tree of Life which is in God's Gan-'Eden.'"

⁸ "To the angel of the Messianic Community in Smyrna, write: 'Here is the message from the First and the Last, who died and came alive again: ⁹ "I know how you are suffering and how poor you are (though in fact you are rich!), and I know the insults of those who call themselves Jews but aren't — on the contrary, they are a synagogue of the Adversary. ¹⁰ Don't be afraid of what you are about to suffer. Look, the Adversary is going to have some of you thrown in prison, in order to put you to the test; and you will face an ordeal for ten days. Remain faithful, even to the point of death; and I will give you life as your crown. ¹¹ Those who have ears, let them hear what the Spirit is saying to the Messianic communities. He who wins the victory will not be hurt at all by the second death.'"

¹² "To the angel of the Messianic Community in Pergamum, write: 'Here is the message from the one who has the sharp double-edged sword: ¹³ "I know where you are living, there where the Adversary's throne is. Yet you are holding onto my name. You did not deny trusting me even at the time when my faithful witness Antipas was put to death in your town, there where the Adversary lives. ¹⁴ Nevertheless, I have a few things against you: you have some people who hold to the teaching of Bil'am, who taught Balak to set a trap for the people of Isra'el, so that they would eat food that had been sacrificed to idols and commit sexual sin. ¹⁵ Likewise, you too have

---

[d] Daniel 10:6; Ezekiel 1:24; 43:2

people who hold to the teaching of the Nicolaitans. ¹⁶Therefore, turn from these sins. Otherwise, I will come to you very soon and make war against them with the sword of my mouth. ¹⁷Those who have ears, let them hear what the Spirit is saying to the Messianic communities. To him winning the victory I will give some of the hidden *man*. I will also give him a white stone, on which is written a new name that nobody knows except the one receiving it.'"

¹⁸"To the angel of the Messianic Community in Thyatira, write: 'Here is the message from the Son of God, whose eyes are like a fiery flame and whose feet are like burnished brass: ¹⁹I know what you are doing, your love, trust, service and perseverance. And I know that you are doing more now than before. ²⁰But I have this against you: you continue to tolerate that Izevel woman, the one who claims to be a prophet, but is teaching and deceiving my servants to commit sexual sin and eat food that has been sacrificed to idols. ²¹I gave her time to turn from her sin, but she doesn't want to repent of her immorality. ²²So I am throwing her into a sickbed; and those who commit adultery with her I am throwing into great trouble, unless they turn from the sins connected with what she does; ²³and I will strike her children dead! Then all the Messianic communities will know that I am the one who searches minds and hearts, and that I will give to each of you what your deeds deserve. ²⁴But to the rest of you in Thyatira, to those who do not hold this teaching, who have not learned what some people call the 'deep things' of the Adversary, I say this: I am not loading you up with another burden; ²⁵only hold fast to what you have until I come. ²⁶To him who wins the victory and does what I want until the goal is reached,

    I will give him authority over the **nations;**
²⁷   he **will** rule **them with a staff of iron**
    and dash them to pieces like pottery,ᵉ

²⁸just as I have received authority from my Father. I will also give him the morning star. ²⁹Those who have ears, let them hear what the Spirit is saying to the Messianic communities.'"

3 ¹"To the angel of the Messianic Community in Sardis, write: 'Here is the message from the one who has the sevenfold Spirit of God and the seven stars: "I know what you are doing — you have a reputation for being alive, but in fact you are dead! ²Wake up, and strengthen what remains, before it dies too! For I have found what you are doing incomplete in the sight of my God. ³So remember what you received and heard, and obey it, and turn from your sin! For if you don't wake up, I will come like a thief; and you don't know at what moment I will come upon you. ⁴Nevertheless, you do have a few people in Sardis who have not soiled their clothes; and they will walk with me, clothed in white, because they are worthy. ⁵He who wins the victory will, like them, be dressed in white clothing; and I will not blot his name out of the Book of Life; in fact, I will acknowledge him individually before my Father and before his angels. ⁶Those who have ears, let them hear what the Spirit is saying to the Messianic communities.'"

ᵉ Psalm 2:8–9

⁷ "To the angel of the Messianic Community in Philadelphia, write: 'Here is the message of *HaKadosh*, the True One, the one who has **the key of David, who, if he opens something, no one else can shut it, and if he closes something, no one else can open it**.ᶠ ⁸ "I know what you are doing. Look, I have put in front of you an open door, and no one can shut it. I know that you have but little power, yet you have obeyed my message and have not disowned me. ⁹ Here, I will give you some from the synagogue of the Adversary, those who call themselves Jews but aren't — on the contrary, they are lying — see, I will cause them to come and prostrate themselves at your feet, and they will know that I have loved you. ¹⁰ Because you did obey my message about persevering, I will keep you from the time of trial coming upon the whole world to put the people living on earth to the test. ¹¹ I am coming soon; hold on to what you have, so that no one will take away your crown. ¹² I will make him who wins the victory a pillar in the Temple of my God, and he will never leave it. Also I will write on him the name of my God and the name of my God's city, the new Yerushalayim coming down out of heaven from my God, and my own new name. ¹³ Those who have ears, let them hear what the Spirit is saying to the Messianic communities.'"

¹⁴ "To the angel of the Messianic Community in Laodicea, write: 'Here is the message from the *Amen*, the faithful and true witness, the Ruler of God's creation: ¹⁵ "I know what you are doing: you are neither cold nor hot. How I wish you were either one or the other! ¹⁶ So, because you are lukewarm, neither cold nor hot, I will vomit you out of my mouth! ¹⁷ For you keep saying, '**I am rich, I have gotten rich**,ᵍ I don't need a thing!' You don't know that you are the one who is wretched, pitiable, poor, blind and naked! ¹⁸ My advice to you is to buy from me gold refined by fire, so that you may be rich; and white clothing, so that you may be dressed and not have to be ashamed of your nakedness; and eyesalve to rub on your eyes, so that you may see. ¹⁹ As for me, I rebuke and discipline everyone I love; so exert yourselves, and turn from your sins! ²⁰ Here, I'm standing at the door, knocking. If someone hears my voice and opens the door, I will come in to him and eat with him, and he will eat with me. ²¹ I will let him who wins the victory sit with me on my throne, just as I myself also won the victory and sat down with my Father on his throne. ²² Those who have ears, let them hear what the Spirit is saying to the Messianic communities."'"

4 ¹ After these things, I looked; and there before me was a door standing open in heaven; and the voice like a trumpet which I had heard speaking with me before said, "Come up here, and I will show you what must happen after these things." ² Instantly I was in the Spirit, and there before me in heaven stood a throne, and on the throne Someone was sitting. ³ The One sitting there gleamed like diamonds and rubies, and a rainbow shining like emerald encircled the throne.

⁴ Surrounding the throne were twenty-four other thrones, and on the thrones sat twenty-four elders dressed in white clothing and wearing gold crowns on their heads. ⁵ From the throne came forth lightnings, voices and thunderings; and before the throne were seven flaming torches, which are the sevenfold Spirit of God. ⁶ In front of the throne was what looked like a sea of glass, clear as crystal.

ᶠ Isaiah 22:22   ᵍ Hosea 12:9(8)

In the center, around the throne, were four living beings covered with eyes in front and behind. ⁷ **The first** living being was like **a lion, the second** living being was like **an ox, the third** living being had **a face** that looked **human, and the fourth** living being was like a flying **eagle.**ʰ ⁸ **Each** of the four living beings **had six wings**ⁱ and was covered with eyes inside and out; and day and night they never stop saying,

> **"Holy, holy, holy is** Aᴅᴏɴᴀɪ**, God of heaven's armies**ʲ
> the One who was, who is and who is coming!"

⁹ And whenever the living beings give glory, honor and thanks to the One sitting on the throne, to the One who lives forever and ever, ¹⁰ the twenty-four elders fall down before the One sitting on the throne, who lives forever and ever, and worship him. They throw their crowns in front of the throne and say,

¹¹
> "You are worthy, Aᴅᴏɴᴀɪ *Eloheinu,*
> to have glory, honor and power,
> because you created all things —
> yes, because of your will they were created
> and came into being!"

5 ¹ Next I saw in the right hand of the One sitting on the throne a scroll with writing on both sides and sealed with seven seals; ² and I saw a mighty angel proclaiming in a loud voice, "Who is worthy to open the scroll and break its seals?" ³ But no one in heaven, on earth or under the earth was able to open the scroll or look inside it. ⁴ I cried and cried, because no one was found worthy to open the scroll or look inside it. ⁵ One of the elders said to me, "Don't cry. Look, the Lion of the tribe of Y'hudah, the Root of David, has won the right to open the scroll and its seven seals."

⁶ Then I saw standing there with the throne and the four living beings, in the circle of the elders, a Lamb that appeared to have been slaughtered. He had seven horns and seven eyes, which are the sevenfold Spirit of God sent out into all the earth. ⁷ He came and took the scroll out of the right hand of the One sitting on the throne. ⁸ When he took the scroll, the four living beings and the twenty-four elders fell down in front of the Lamb. Each one held a harp and gold bowls filled with pieces of incense, which are the prayers of God's people; ⁹ and they sang a new song,

> "You are worthy to take the scroll and break its seals;
>> because you were slaughtered;
> at the cost of blood you ransomed for God
>> persons from every tribe, language, people and nation.
¹⁰
> You made them into a kingdom for God to rule,
>> *cohanim* to serve him;
> and they will rule over the earth."

ʰ Ezekiel 1:5–10   ⁱ Isaiah 6:2   ʲ Isaiah 6:3; Amos 3:13; 4:13

¹¹ Then I looked, and I heard the sound of a vast number of angels — thousands and thousands, millions and millions! They were all around the throne, the living beings and the elders; ¹² and they shouted out,

> "Worthy is the slaughtered Lamb to receive
> power, riches, wisdom, strength,
> honor, glory and praise!"

¹³ And I heard every creature in heaven, on earth, under the earth and on the sea — yes, everything in them — saying,

> "To the One sitting on the throne
> and to the Lamb
> belong praise, honor, glory and power
> forever and ever!"

¹⁴ The four living beings said, "*Amen!*" and the elders fell down and worshipped.

6 ¹ Next I watched as the Lamb broke the first of the seven seals, and I heard one of the four living beings say in a thundering voice, "Go!" ² I looked, and there in front of me was a white horse; its rider had a bow and was given a crown; and he rode off as a conqueror to conquer.

³ When he broke the second seal, I heard the second living being say, "Go!" ⁴ Another horse went out, a red one; and its rider was given the power to take peace away from the earth and make people slaughter each other. He was given a great sword.

⁵ When he broke the third seal, I heard the third living being say, "Go!" I looked, and there in front of me was a black horse, and its rider held in his hand a pair of scales. ⁶ Then I heard what sounded like a voice from among the four living beings say, "Two pounds of wheat for a day's wages! Six pounds of barley for the same price! But don't damage the oil or the wine!"

⁷ When he broke the fourth seal, I heard the voice of the fourth living being say, "Go!" ⁸ I looked, and there in front of me was a pallid, sickly-looking horse. Its rider's name was Death, and Sh'ol followed behind him. They were given authority to kill one-quarter of the world by war, by famine, by plagues and with the wild animals of the earth.

⁹ When the Lamb broke the fifth seal, I saw underneath the altar the souls of those who had been put to death for proclaiming the Word of God, that is, for bearing witness. ¹⁰ They cried out in a loud voice, "Sovereign Ruler, *HaKadosh*, the True One, how long will it be before you judge the people living on earth and avenge our blood?" ¹¹ Each of them was given a white robe; and they were told to wait a little longer, until the full number of their fellow-servants should be reached, of their brothers who would be killed, just as they had been.

¹² Then I watched as he broke the sixth seal, and there was a great earthquake, the sun turned black as sackcloth worn in mourning, and the full moon became blood-red. ¹³ The stars fell from heaven to earth just as a fig tree drops its figs when shaken by a strong wind. ¹⁴ The sky receded like a scroll being rolled up, and every mountain and island was moved from its place. ¹⁵ Then the earth's kings, the rulers, the generals, the rich and the mighty — indeed, everyone, slave and free — hid himself

in caves and among the rocks in the mountains, ¹⁶ **and said to the mountains and rocks, "Fall on us, and hide us**ᵏ from the face of the One sitting on the throne and from the fury of the Lamb! ¹⁷ For the Great Day of their fury has come, and who can stand?"

7 ¹ After this, I saw four angels standing at the four corners of the earth, holding back the four winds of the earth, so that no wind would blow on the land, on the sea or on any tree. ² I saw another angel coming up from the east with a seal from the living God, and he shouted to the four angels who had been given power to harm the land and the sea, ³ "Do not harm the land or the sea or the trees until we have sealed the servants of our God on their foreheads!" ⁴ I heard how many were sealed — 144,000 from every tribe of the people of Isra'el:

5	From the tribe of Y'hudah	12,000 were sealed,
	from the tribe of Re'uven	12,000,
	from the tribe of Gad	12,000,
6	from the tribe of Asher	12,000,
	from the tribe of Naftali	12,000,
	from the tribe of M'nasheh	12,000,
7	from the tribe of Shim'on	12,000,
	from the tribe of Levi	12,000,
	from the tribe of Yissakhar	12,000,
8	from the tribe of Z'vulun	12,000,
	from the tribe of Yosef	12,000,
	from the tribe of Binyamin	12,000.

⁹ After this, I looked; and there before me was a huge crowd, too large for anyone to count, from every nation, tribe, people and language. They were standing in front of the throne and in front of the Lamb, dressed in white robes and holding palm branches in their hands; ¹⁰ and they shouted,

> "Victory to our God,
> who sits on the throne,
> and to the Lamb!"

¹¹ All the angels stood around the throne, the elders and the four living beings; they fell face down before the throne and worshipped God, saying,

12   *"Amen!*

> "Praise and glory, wisdom and thanks,
> honor and power and strength
> belong to our God forever and ever!

> *"Amen!"*

ᵏ Hosea 10:8

¹³ One of the elders asked me, "These people dressed in white robes — who are they, and where are they from?" ¹⁴ "Sir," I answered, "you know." Then he told me, "These are the people who have come out of the Great Persecution. They have washed their robes and made them white with the blood of the Lamb. ¹⁵ That is why they are before God's throne.

"Day and night they serve him in his Temple;
and the One who sits on the throne
will put his *Sh'khinah* upon them.

16 **"They will never again be hungry,**
they will never again be thirsty,
the sun will not beat down on them,
nor will any burning heat.ˡ

17 "For the Lamb at the center of the throne
will shepherd them, will lead them
to springs of living water,ᵐ
and God will wipe every tear from their eyes."ⁿ

8 ¹ When the Lamb broke the seventh seal, there was silence in heaven for what seemed like half an hour. ² Then I saw the seven angels who stand before God, and they were given seven *shofars*. ³ Another angel came and stood at the altar with a gold incense-bowl, and he was given a large quantity of incense to add to the prayers of all God's people ⁴ on the gold altar in front of the throne. The smoke of the incense went up with the prayers of God's people from the hand of the angel before God. ⁵ Then the angel took the incense-bowl, filled it with fire from the altar and threw it down onto the earth; and there followed peals of thunder, voices, flashes of lightning and an earthquake.

⁶ Now the seven angels with the seven *shofars* prepared to sound them.

⁷ The first one sounded his *shofar*; and there came hail and fire mingled with blood, and it was thrown down upon the earth. A third of the earth was burned up, a third of the trees were burned up, and all green grass was burned up.

⁸ The second angel sounded his *shofar*, and what looked like an enormous blazing mountain was hurled into the sea. A third of the sea turned to blood, ⁹ a third of the living creatures in the sea died, and a third of the ships were destroyed.

¹⁰ The third angel sounded his *shofar*; and a great star, blazing like a torch, fell from the sky onto a third of the rivers and onto the springs of water. ¹¹ The name of the star was "Bitterness," and a third of the water became bitter, and many people died from the water that had been turned bitter.

¹² The fourth angel sounded his *shofar*; and a third of the sun was struck, also a third of the moon and a third of the stars; so that a third of them were darkened, the day had a third less light, and the night likewise.

¹³ Then I looked, and I heard a lone eagle give a loud cry, as it flew in mid-heaven, "Woe! Woe! Woe to the people living on earth, because of the remaining blasts from the three angels who have yet to sound their *shofars*!"

ˡ Isaiah 49:10   ᵐ Isaiah 49:10; Jeremiah 2:13; Ezekiel 34:23; Psalm 23:1–2   ⁿ Isaiah 25:8

9 ^{1} The fifth angel sounded his *shofar*; and I saw a star that had fallen out of heaven onto the earth, and he was given the key to the shaft leading down to the Abyss. ^{2} He opened the shaft of the Abyss, and there went up smoke from the shaft like the smoke of a huge furnace; the sun was darkened, and the sky too, by the smoke from the shaft. ^{3} Then out of the smoke onto the earth came locusts, and they were given power like the power scorpions have on earth. ^{4} They were instructed not to harm the grass on the earth, any green plant or any tree, but only the people who did not have the seal of God on their foreheads. ^{5} The locusts were not allowed to kill them, only to inflict pain on them for five months; and the pain they caused was like the pain of a scorpion sting. ^{6} In those days people will seek death but will not find it; they will long to die, but death will elude them.

^{7} Now these locusts looked like horses outfitted for battle. On their heads were what looked like crowns of gold, and their faces were like human faces. ^{8} They had hair like women's hair, and their teeth were like those of lions. ^{9} Their chests were like iron breastplates, and the sound their wings made was like the roar of many horses and chariots rushing into battle. ^{10} They had tails like those of scorpions, with stings; and in their tails was their power to hurt people for five months. ^{11} They had as king over them the angel of the Abyss, whose name in Hebrew is "*Abaddon*" and in our language, "Destroyer."

^{12} The first woe has passed, but there are still two woes to come.

^{13} The sixth angel sounded his *shofar*, and I heard a voice from the four horns of the gold altar before God, ^{14} saying to the sixth angel, the one with the *shofar*, "Release the four angels that are bound at the great river Euphrates!" ^{15} And they were released. These four angels had been kept ready for this moment, for this day and month and year, to kill a third of mankind; ^{16} and the number of cavalry soldiers was two hundred million! — I heard the number.

^{17} Here is how the horses looked in the vision: the riders had breastplates that were fire-red, iris-blue and sulfur-yellow; the horses' heads were like lions' heads; and from their mouths issued fire, smoke and sulfur. ^{18} It was these three plagues that killed a third of mankind — the fire, smoke and sulfur issuing from the horses' mouths. ^{19} For the power of the horses was in their mouths — and also in their tails, for their tails were like snakes with heads, and with them they could cause injury.

^{20} The rest of mankind, those who were not killed by these plagues, even then did not turn from what they had made with their own hands — they did not stop worshipping demons and **idols made of gold, silver, bronze, stone and wood, which cannot see or hear or walk**.^{o} ^{21} Nor did they turn from their murdering, their involvement with the occult and with drugs, their sexual immorality or their stealing.

10 ^{1} Next I saw another mighty angel coming down from heaven. He was dressed in a cloud, with a rainbow over his head; his face was like the sun, his legs like columns of fire; ^{2} and he had a little scroll lying open in his hand. He planted his right foot on the sea and his left foot on the land, ^{3} and shouted in a voice as loud as the roar of a lion; and when he shouted, seven thunderclaps sounded with voices that spoke. ^{4} When the seven thunders spoke, I was about to write; but I heard a voice from heaven say,

---

^{o} Psalms 115:4–7; 135:15–17; Daniel 5:23

"Seal up the things the seven thunders said,
do not write them down!"

5 Then the angel I saw standing on the sea and on the land **lifted his right hand
toward heaven** 6 and swore by the One who lives forever and ever,[p] **who created
heaven and what is in it, earth and what is in it, and the sea and what is in it**:[q]
"There will be no more delay; 7 on the contrary, in the days of the sound from the
seventh angel when he sounds his *shofar*, the hidden plan of God will be brought to
completion, the Good News as he proclaimed it to his servants the prophets."
8 Next the voice which I had heard from heaven spoke to me again and said,
"Go, take the scroll lying open in the hand of the angel standing on the sea and on the
land!" 9 So I went over to the angel and asked him to give me the little scroll; and he
said to me, "Take it and eat it. It will turn your stomach bitter, but in your mouth it
will be sweet as honey." 10 I took the little scroll from the angel's hand and ate it; and
in my mouth it was sweet as honey; but after I had swallowed it, my stomach turned
bitter. 11 Then I was told, "You must prophesy again about many peoples, nations,
languages and kings."

11 1 I was given a measuring rod like a stick and told, "Get up, and measure the Temple
of God and the altar, and count how many people are worshipping there! 2 But the
court outside the Temple, leave that out; don't measure it; because it has been given
to the *Goyim*, and they will trample over the holy city for forty-two months.
3 "Also I will give power to my two witnesses; and they will prophesy for 1,260
days, dressed in sackcloth." 4 These are the two olive trees and the two *menorah*s
standing before the Lord of the earth. 5 If anyone tries to do them harm, fire
comes out of their mouth and consumes their enemies — yes, if anyone tries to
harm them, that is how he must die. 6 They have the authority to shut up the sky,
so that no rain falls during the period of their prophesying; also they have the
authority to turn the waters into blood and to strike the earth with every kind of
plague as often as they want.
7 When they finish their witnessing, the beast coming up out of the Abyss will
fight against them, overcome them and kill them; 8 and their dead bodies will lie in
the main street of the great city whose name, to reflect its spiritual condition, is
"S'dom" and "Egypt" — the city where their Lord was executed on a stake. 9 Some
from the nations, tribes, languages and peoples see their bodies for three-and-a-half
days and do not permit the corpses to be placed in a tomb. 10 The people living in the
Land rejoice over them, they celebrate and send each other gifts, because these two
prophets tormented them so.
11 But after the three-and-a-half days a breath of life from God entered them,
they stood up on their feet, and great fear fell on those who saw them. 12 Then the two
heard a loud voice from heaven saying to them, "Come up here!" And they went up into
heaven in a cloud, while their enemies watched them. 13 In that hour there was a great
earthquake, and a tenth of the city collapsed. Seven thousand people were killed in the
earthquake, and the rest were awestruck and gave glory to the God of heaven.
14 The second woe has passed; see, the third woe is coming quickly.

---

[p] Deuteronomy 32:40; Daniel 12:7 [q] Nehemiah 9:6; see also Exodus 20:11; Psalm 146:6

^{15} The seventh angel sounded his *shofar*; and there were loud voices in heaven, saying,

> "The kingdom of the world
> has become the Kingdom
> of our Lord and his Messiah,
> and he will rule forever and ever!"

^{16} The twenty-four elders sitting on their thrones in God's presence fell on their faces and worshipped God, ^{17} saying,

> "We thank you, ADONAI,
> **God of heaven's armies,**^{r}
> the One who is and was,
> that you have taken your power
> and have begun to rule.

^{18}
> **"The *Goyim* raged.**^{s}
> But now your rage has come,
> the time for the dead to be judged,
> the time for rewarding your servants the prophets
> and your holy people,
> those who stand in awe of your name,
> both small and great.
> It is also the time for destroying
> those who destroy the earth."

^{19} Then the Temple of God in heaven was opened, and the Ark of the Covenant was seen in his Temple; and there were flashes of lightning, voices, peals of thunder, an earthquake and violent hail.

12 ^{1} Now a great sign was seen in heaven — a woman clothed with the sun, under her feet the moon, and on her head a crown of twelve stars. ^{2} She was pregnant and about to give birth, and she screamed in the agony of labor.

^{3} Another sign was seen in heaven: there was a great red dragon with seven heads and ten horns, and on its heads were seven royal crowns. ^{4} Its tail swept a third of the stars out of heaven and threw them down to the earth. It stood in front of the woman about to give birth, so that it might devour the child the moment it was born.

^{5} She gave birth to a son, a male child, the one who **will rule all the nations with a staff of iron.**^{t} But her child was snatched up to God and his throne; ^{6} and she fled into the desert, where she has a place prepared by God so that she can be taken care of for 1,260 days.

^{7} Next there was a battle in heaven — Mikha'el and his angels fought against the dragon, and the dragon and his angels fought back. ^{8} But it was not strong enough to

---

^{r} Amos 3:13; 4:13 ^{s} Psalm 2:1 ^{t} Psalm 2:9

win, so that there was no longer any place for them in heaven. ⁹The great dragon was thrown out, that ancient serpent, also known as the Devil and Satan [the Adversary], the deceiver of the whole world. He was hurled down to the earth, and his angels were hurled down with him.

¹⁰Then I heard a loud voice in heaven saying,

> "Now have come God's victory, power and kingship,
> and the authority of his Messiah;
> because the Accuser of our brothers,
> who accuses them day and night before God,
> has been thrown out!

¹¹
> "They defeated him because of the Lamb's blood
> and because of the message of their witness.
> Even when facing death
> they did not cling to life.

¹²
> "Therefore, rejoice, heaven and you who live there!
> But woe to you, land and sea,
> for the Adversary has come down to you,
> and he is very angry, because he knows that his time is short!"

¹³When the dragon saw that he had been hurled down to the earth, he went in pursuit of the woman who had given birth to the male child. ¹⁴But the woman was given the two wings of the great eagle, so that she could fly to her place in the desert, where she is taken care of for **a season and two seasons and half a season**,ᵃ away from the serpent's presence. ¹⁵The serpent spewed water like a river out of its mouth after the woman, in order to sweep her away in the flood; ¹⁶but the land came to her rescue — it opened its mouth and swallowed up the river which the dragon had spewed out of its mouth. ¹⁷The dragon was infuriated over the woman and went off to fight the rest of her children, those who obey God's commands and bear witness to Yeshua.

¹⁸Then the dragon stood on the seashore;

13 ¹and I saw a beast come up out of the sea, with ten horns and seven heads. On its horns were ten royal crowns and on its heads blasphemous names. ²The beast which I saw was like a leopard, but with feet like those of a bear and a mouth like the mouth of a lion. To it the dragon gave its power, its throne and great authority. ³One of the heads of the beast appeared to have received a fatal wound, but its fatal wound was healed, and the whole earth followed after the beast in amazement. ⁴They worshipped the dragon, because he had given his authority to the beast; and they worshipped the beast, saying,

> "Who is like the beast?
> Who can fight against it?"

ᵃ Daniel 7:25; 12:7

⁵ It was given a mouth speaking arrogant blasphemies; and it was given authority to act for forty-two months. ⁶ So it opened its mouth in blasphemies against God to insult his name and his *Sh'khinah*, and those living in heaven; ⁷ it was allowed to make war on God's holy people and to defeat them; and it was given authority over every tribe, people, language and nation. ⁸ Everyone living on earth will worship it except those whose names are written in the Book of Life belonging to the Lamb slaughtered before the world was founded. ⁹ Those who have ears, let them hear!

10   **"If anyone is meant for captivity,**
       into captivity he goes!
       If anyone is to be killed with the sword,
       with the sword he is to be killed!"ᵛ

This is when God's holy people must persevere and trust!

¹¹ Then I saw another beast coming up out of the earth. It had two horns like those of a lamb, but it spoke like a dragon. ¹² It exercises all the authority of the first beast in its presence; and it makes the earth and its inhabitants worship the first beast, the one whose fatal wound had been healed. ¹³ It performs great miracles, even causing fire to come down from heaven onto the earth as people watch. ¹⁴ It deceives the people living on earth by the miracles it is allowed to perform in the presence of the beast, and it tells them to make an image honoring the beast that was struck by the sword but came alive again. ¹⁵ It was allowed to put breath into the image of the beast, so that the image of the beast could even speak; and it was allowed to cause anyone who would not worship the image of the beast to be put to death. ¹⁶ Also it forces everyone — great and small, rich and poor, free and slave — to receive a mark on his right hand or on his forehead ¹⁷ preventing anyone from buying or selling unless he has the mark, that is, the name of the beast or the number of its name. ¹⁸ This is where wisdom is needed; those who understand should count the number of the beast, for it is the number of a person, and its number is 666.

14 ¹ Then I looked, and there was the Lamb standing on Mount Tziyon; and with him were 144,000 who had his name and his Father's name written on their foreheads. ² I heard a sound from heaven like the sound of rushing waters and like the sound of pealing thunder; the sound I heard was also like that of harpists playing on their harps. ³ They were singing a new song before the throne and before the four living beings and the elders, and no one could learn the song except the 144,000 who have been ransomed from the world. ⁴ These are the ones who have not defiled themselves with women, for they are virgins; they follow the Lamb wherever he goes; they have been ransomed from among humanity as firstfruits for God and the Lamb; ⁵ on their lips no lie was found — they are without defect.

⁶ Next I saw another angel flying in mid-heaven with everlasting Good News to proclaim to those living on the earth — to every nation, tribe, language and people. ⁷ In a loud voice he said,

---

ᵛ Jeremiah 15:2, 43:11

"Fear God, give him glory,
for the hour has come when he will pass judgment!
Worship the One who made heaven and earth,
the sea and the springs of water!"

⁸ Another angel, a second one, followed, saying,

"She has fallen! She has fallen!
Bavel the Great!"[w]
She made all the nations drink the wine
of God's fury caused by her whoring!"

⁹ Another angel, a third one, followed them and said in a loud voice, "If anyone worships the beast and its image and receives the mark on his forehead or on his hand, ¹⁰ he will indeed drink the wine of God's fury poured undiluted into the cup of his rage. He will be tormented by fire and sulfur before the holy angels and before the Lamb, ¹¹ and the smoke from their tormenting goes up forever and ever. They have no rest, day or night, those who worship the beast and its image and those who receive the mark of its name." ¹² This is when perseverance is needed on the part of God's people, those who observe his commands and exercise Yeshua's faithfulness.

¹³ Next I heard a voice from heaven saying, "Write: 'How blessed are the dead who die united with the Lord, from now on!' 'Yes,' says the Spirit, 'now they may rest from their efforts, for the things they have accomplished follow along with them.'"

¹⁴ Then I looked, and there before me was a white cloud. Sitting on the cloud was someone **like a Son of Man**[x] with a gold crown on his head and a sharp sickle in his hand. ¹⁵ Another angel came out of the Temple and shouted to the one sitting on the cloud, "Start using your sickle to reap, because the time to reap has come — the earth's harvest is ripe!" ¹⁶ The one sitting on the cloud swung his sickle over the earth, and the earth was harvested.

¹⁷ Another angel came out of the Temple in heaven, and he too had a sharp sickle. ¹⁸ Then out from the altar went yet another angel, who was in charge of the fire; and he called in a loud voice to the one with the sharp sickle, "Use your sharp sickle, and gather the clusters of grapes from the earth's vine, because they are ripe!" ¹⁹ The angel swung his sickle down onto the earth, gathered the earth's grapes and threw them into the great winepress of God's fury. ²⁰ The winepress was trodden outside the city, and blood flowed from the winepress as high as the horses' bridles for two hundred miles!

15 ¹ Then I saw another sign in heaven, a great and wonderful one — seven angels with the seven plagues that are the final ones; because with them, God's fury is finished. ² I saw what looked like a sea of glass mixed with fire. Those defeating the beast, its image and the number of its name were standing by the sea of glass, holding harps which God had given them. ³ They were singing the song of Moshe, the servant of God, and the song of the Lamb:

ʷ Isaiah 21:9   ˣ Daniel 7:13

"Great and wonderful are the things you have done,
    *A*DONAI, **God of heaven's armies!**[y]
Just and true are your ways,
    king of the nations!
4   *A*DONAI, who will not fear and glorify your name?
    because you alone are holy.
All nations will come and worship before you,
    for your righteous deeds have been revealed."

⁵ After this I looked, and the sanctuary (that is, the Tent of Witness in heaven) was opened, ⁶ and out of the sanctuary came the seven angels with the seven plagues. They were dressed in clean bright linen and had gold belts around their chests. ⁷ One of the four living beings gave to the seven angels seven gold bowls filled with the fury of God, who lives forever and ever. ⁸ Then the sanctuary was filled with smoke from God's *Sh'khinah*, that is, from his power; and no one could enter the sanctuary until the seven plagues of the seven angels had accomplished their purpose.

16 ¹ I heard a loud voice from the sanctuary say to the seven angels, "Go, and pour out on the earth the seven bowls of God's fury!"

² So the first one went and poured his bowl onto the earth, and disgusting and painful sores appeared on all the people who had the mark of the beast and worshipped its image.

³ The second one poured out his bowl into the sea, and it became like the blood of a dead person, and every living thing in the sea died.

⁴ The third one poured out his bowl into the rivers and springs of water, and they turned to blood. ⁵ Then I heard the angel of the waters say,

"O *HaKadosh*, the One who is and was,
    you are just in these judgments of yours.
6   They poured out the blood of your people and your prophets,
    so you have made them drink blood. They deserve it!"

⁷ Then I heard the altar say,

"Yes, *A*DONAI, **God of heaven's armies,**[z]
    your judgments are true and just!"

⁸ The fourth one poured out his bowl on the sun, and it was permitted to burn people with fire. ⁹ People were burned by the intense heat; yet they cursed the name of God, who had the authority over these plagues, instead of turning from their sins to give him glory.

¹⁰ The fifth one poured out his bowl on the throne of the beast, and its kingdom grew dark. People gnawed on their tongues from the pain, ¹¹ yet they cursed the God of heaven because of their pains and sores, and did not turn from their sinful deeds.

---

[y] Amos 3:13, 4:13   [z] Amos 3:13; 4:13

¹² The sixth one poured out his bowl on the great river Euphrates, and its water dried up, in order to prepare the way for the kings from the east. ¹³ And I saw three unclean spirits that looked like frogs; they came from the mouth of the dragon, from the mouth of the beast and from the mouth of the false prophet. ¹⁴ They are miracle-working demonic spirits which go out to the kings of the whole inhabited world to assemble them for the War of the Great Day of ADONAI-Tzva'ot. ¹⁵ ("Look! I am coming like a thief! How blessed are those who stay alert and keep their clothes clean, so that they won't be walking naked and be publicly put to shame!") ¹⁶ And they gathered the kings to the place which in Hebrew is called Har Megiddo.

¹⁷ The seventh one poured out his bowl on the air, and a loud voice came out of the Temple from the throne, saying, "It is done!" ¹⁸ There were flashes of lightning, voices and peals of thunder; and there was a massive earthquake, such as has never occurred since mankind has been on earth, so violent was the earthquake. ¹⁹ The great city was split into three parts, the cities of the nations fell, and God remembered Bavel the Great and made her drink the wine from the cup of his raging fury. ²⁰ Every island fled, and no mountains were to be found. ²¹ And huge seventy-pound hailstones fell on people from the sky. But the people cursed God for the plague of hail, that it was such a terrible plague.

17 ¹ Then came one of the angels with the seven bowls; and he said to me, "Come, I will show you the judgment of the great whore who is sitting by many waters. ² The kings of the earth went whoring with her, and the people living on earth have become drunk from the wine of her whoring." ³ He carried me off in the Spirit to a desert, and I saw a woman sitting on a scarlet beast filled with blasphemous names and having seven heads and ten horns. ⁴ The woman was dressed in purple and scarlet and glittered with gold, precious stones and pearls. In her hand was a gold cup filled with the obscene and filthy things produced by her whoring. ⁵ On her forehead was written a name with a hidden meaning,

BAVEL THE GREAT
MOTHER OF WHORES AND OF
THE EARTH'S OBSCENITIES

⁶ I saw the woman drunk from the blood of God's people, that is, from the blood of the people who testify about Yeshua.

On seeing her, I was altogether astounded. ⁷ Then the angel said to me, "Why are you astounded? I will tell you the hidden meaning of the woman and of the beast with seven heads and ten horns that was carrying her. ⁸ The beast you saw once was, now is not, and will come up from the Abyss; but it is on its way to destruction. The people living on earth whose names have not been written in the Book of Life since the founding of the world will be astounded to see the beast that once was, now is not, but is to appear. ⁹ This calls for a mind with wisdom: the seven heads are seven hills on which the woman is sitting; also they are seven kings — ¹⁰ five have fallen, one is living now and the other is yet to come; and when he does come, he must remain only a little while. ¹¹ The beast which once was and now is not is an eighth king; it comes from the seven and is on its way to destruction. ¹² The ten horns you saw are ten kings who have not yet begun to rule, but they receive power as kings for one hour, along with the beast. ^{13} They have one mind, and they hand over their power and authority to the beast. ^{14} They will go to war against the Lamb, but the Lamb will defeat them, because he is Lord of lords and King of kings, and those who are called, chosen and faithful will overcome along with him."

^{15} Then he said to me, "The waters that you saw, where the whore is sitting, are peoples, crowds, nations and languages. ^{16} As for the ten horns that you saw and the beast, they will hate the whore, bring her to ruin, leave her naked, eat her flesh and consume her with fire. ^{17} For God put it in their hearts to do what will fulfill his purpose, that is, to be of one mind and give their kingdom to the beast until God's words have accomplished their intent. ^{18} And the woman you saw is the great city that rules over the kings of the earth."

18 ^{1} After these things, I saw another angel coming down from heaven. He had great authority, the earth was lit up by his splendor. ^{2} He cried out in a strong voice,

> "She has fallen! She has fallen!
> **Bavel the Great!**^{a}
> She has become a home for demons,
> a prison for every unclean spirit,
> a prison for every unclean, hated bird.

3
> "For all the nations have drunk of the wine
> of God's fury caused by her whoring —
> yes, the kings of the earth went whoring with her,
> and from her unrestrained love of luxury
> the world's businessmen have grown rich."

^{4} Then I heard another voice out of heaven say:

> "My people, come out of her!
> so that you will not share in her sins,
> so that you will not be infected by her plagues,
5
> for her sins are a sticky mass piled up to heaven,
> and God has remembered her crimes.

6
> "Render to her as she rendered to others!
> Pay her back double for what she has done!
> Use the cup in which she has brewed
> to brew her a double-sized drink!

7
> "Give her as much torment and sorrow
> as the glory and luxury she gave herself!
> For in her heart she says, 'I sit a queen —
> I am not a widow, I will never see sorrow.'

---

^{a} Isaiah 21:9

8 "Therefore, her plagues will come in a single day —
 death, sorrow and famine;
 and she will be burned with fire,
 because ADONAI, God, her Judge, is mighty"

9 The kings of the earth who went whoring with her and shared her luxury will sob and wail over her when they see the smoke as she burns. 10 Standing at a distance, for fear of her torment, they will say,

 "Oh no! The great city!
 Bavel, the mighty city!
 In a single hour
 your judgment has come!"

11 The world's businessmen weep and mourn over her, because no one is buying their merchandise any more — 12 stocks of gold and silver, gems and pearls, fine linen and purple, silk and scarlet, all rare woods, all ivory goods, all kinds of things made of scented wood, brass, iron and marble; 13 cinnamon, cardamom, incense, myrrh, frankincense, wine, oil, flour, grain, cattle, sheep, horses, chariots — and bodies — and people's souls.

14 The fruits you lusted for with all your heart have gone!
 All the luxury and flashiness have been destroyed, never to return!

15 The sellers of these things, who got rich from her, will stand at a distance, for fear of her torment, weeping and mourning, 16 and saying,

 "Oh no! The great city used to wear fine linen, purple and scarlet!
 She glittered with gold, precious stones and pearls!
17 Such great wealth —
 in a single hour, ruined!"

All the ship masters, passengers, sailors and everyone making his living from the sea stood at a distance 18 and cried out when they saw the smoke as she burned, "What city was like the great city?" 19 And they threw dust on their heads as they wept and mourned, saying,

 "Oh no! The great city!
 The abundance of her wealth
 made all the ship owners rich!
 In a single hour she is ruined!"

20 Rejoice over her, heaven!
 Rejoice, people of God,
 emissaries and prophets!
 For in judging her, God has vindicated you.

²¹ Then a mighty angel picked up a boulder the size of a great millstone, and hurled it into the sea, saying,

> "With violence like this
> will the great city Bavel
> be hurled down,
> never to be found again!

22
> "The sound of harpists and musicians,
> flute-players and trumpeters
>   will never again be heard in you.
> No worker of any trade
>   will ever again be found in you,
> the sound of a mill
>   will never again be heard in you,

23
> the light of a lamp
>   will never again shine in you,
> the voice of bridegroom and bride
>   will never again be heard in you.

> "For your businessmen were the most powerful on earth,
> all the nations were deceived by your magic spell.

24
> "In her was found the blood of prophets and of God's people,
> indeed, of all who have ever been slaughtered on earth!"

19 ¹ After these things, I heard what sounded like the roar of a huge crowd in heaven, shouting,

> "*Halleluyah*!
> The victory, the glory, the power of our God!

2
> For his judgments are true and just.
> He has judged the great whore
> who corrupted the earth with her whoring.
> He has taken vengeance on her
> who has the blood of his servants on her hands."

³ And a second time they said,

> "*Halleluyah*!
> Her smoke goes up forever and ever!"

⁴ The twenty-four elders and the four living beings fell down and worshipped God, sitting on the throne, and said,

> "*Amen*!
> *Halleluyah*!"

⁵ A voice went out from the throne, saying,

> "Praise our God, all you his servants,
> you who fear him, small and great!"

⁶ Then I heard what sounded like the roar of a huge crowd, like the sound of rushing waters, like loud peals of thunder, saying,

> "*Halleluyah*!
> **ADONAI, God of heaven's armies,**[b]
> has begun his reign!

⁷
> "Let us rejoice and be glad!
> Let us give him the glory!
> For the time has come for the
> wedding of the Lamb,
> and his Bride has prepared herself —

⁸
> fine linen, bright and clean
> has been given her to wear."

("Fine linen" means the righteous deeds of God's people.)

⁹ The angel said to me, "Write: 'How blessed are those who have been invited to the wedding feast of the Lamb!'" Then he added, "These are God's very words." ¹⁰ I fell at his feet to worship him; but he said, "Don't do that! I'm only a fellow-servant with you and your brothers who have the testimony of Yeshua. Worship God! For the testimony of Yeshua is the Spirit of prophecy."

¹¹ Next I saw heaven opened, and there before me was a white horse. Sitting on it was the one called Faithful and True, and it is in righteousness that he passes judgment and goes to battle. ¹² His eyes were like a fiery flame, and on his head were many royal crowns. And he had a name written which no one knew but himself. ¹³ He was wearing a robe that had been soaked in blood, and the name by which he is called is, "THE WORD OF GOD." ¹⁴ The armies of heaven, clothed in fine linen, white and pure, were following him on white horses. ¹⁵ And out of his mouth comes a sharp sword with which to strike down nations — **"He will rule them with a staff of iron."**[c] It is he who treads the winepress from which flows the wine of the furious rage of *ADONAI*, God of heaven's armies. ¹⁶ And on his robe and on his thigh he has a name written:

KING OF KINGS
AND
LORD OF LORDS.

¹⁷ Then I saw an angel standing in the sun, and he cried out in a loud voice to all the birds that fly about in mid-heaven, "Come, gather together for the great feast God is giving, ¹⁸ to eat the flesh of kings, the flesh of generals, the flesh of important men, the flesh of horses and their riders and the flesh of all kinds of people, free and slave, small and great!" ¹⁹ I saw the beast and the kings of the earth and their armies

---

[b] Amos 3:13; 4:13   [c] Psalm 2:9

gathered together to do battle with the rider of the horse and his army. ²⁰ But the beast was taken captive, and with it the false prophet who, in its presence, had done the miracles which he had used to deceive those who had received the mark of the beast and those who had worshipped his image. The beast and the false prophet were both thrown alive into the lake of fire that burns with sulfur. ²¹ The rest were killed with the sword that goes out of the mouth of the rider on the horse, and all the birds gorged themselves on their flesh.

20 ¹ Next I saw an angel coming down from heaven, who had the key to the Abyss and a great chain in his hand. ² He seized the dragon, that ancient serpent, who is the Devil and Satan [the Adversary], and chained him up for a thousand years. ³ He threw him into the Abyss, locked it and sealed it over him; so that he could not deceive the nations any more until the thousand years were over. After that, he has to be set free for a little while.

⁴ Then I saw thrones, and those seated on them received authority to judge. And I saw the souls of those who had been beheaded for testifying about Yeshua and proclaiming the Word of God, also those who had not worshipped the beast or its image and had not received the mark on their foreheads and on their hands. They came to life and ruled with the Messiah for a thousand years. ⁵ (The rest of the dead did not come to life until the thousand years were over.) This is the first resurrection. ⁶ Blessed and holy is anyone who has a part in the first resurrection; over him the second death has no power. On the contrary, they will be *cohanim* of God and of the Messiah, and they will rule with him for the thousand years.

⁷ When the thousand years are over, the Adversary will be set free from his prison ⁸ and will go out to deceive the nations in the four quarters of the earth, **Gog and Magog,**^{d} to gather them for the battle. Their number is countless as the sand on the seashore; ⁹ and they came up over the breadth of the Land and surrounded the camp of God's people and the city he loves. But fire came down from heaven and consumed them. ¹⁰ The Adversary who had deceived them was hurled into the lake of fire and sulfur, where the beast and the false prophet were; and they will be tormented day and night forever and ever.

¹¹ Next I saw a great white throne and the One sitting on it. Earth and heaven fled from his presence, and no place was found for them. ¹² And I saw the dead, both great and small, standing in front of the throne. Books were opened; and another book was opened, the Book of Life; and the dead were judged from what was written in the books, according to what they had done. ¹³ The sea gave up the dead in it; and Death and Sh'ol gave up the dead in them; and they were judged, each according to what he had done. ¹⁴ Then Death and Sh'ol were hurled into the lake of fire. This is the second death — the lake of fire. ¹⁵ Anyone whose name was not found written in the Book of Life was hurled into the lake of fire.

21 ¹ Then I saw **a new heaven and a new earth,**^{e} for the old heaven and the old earth had passed away, and the sea was no longer there. ² Also I saw the holy city, New Yerushalayim, coming down out of heaven from God, prepared like a bride beautifully dressed for her husband. ³ I heard a loud voice from the throne say, "See!

---

^{d} Ezekiel 38:2 ^{e} Isaiah 65:17, 66:22

God's *Sh'khinah* is with mankind, **and he will live with them. They will be his people, and he himself, God-with-them, will be their God.**ᶠ ⁴ He will wipe away every tear from their eyes. There will no longer be any death; and there will no longer be any mourning, crying or pain; because the old order has passed away."

⁵ Then the One sitting on the throne said, "Look! I am making everything new!" Also he said, "Write, 'These words are true and trustworthy!'" ⁶ And he said to me, "It is done! I am the 'A' and the 'Z,' the Beginning and the End. To anyone who is thirsty I myself will give water free of charge from the Fountain of Life. ⁷ He who wins the victory will receive these things, and I will be his God, and he will be my son. ⁸ But as for the cowardly, the untrustworthy, the vile, the murderers, the sexually immoral, those involved with the occult and with drugs, idol-worshippers, and all liars — their destiny is the lake burning with fire and sulfur, the second death."

⁹ One of the seven angels having the seven bowls full of the seven last plagues approached me and said, "Come! I will show you the Bride, the Wife of the Lamb." ¹⁰ He carried me off in the Spirit to the top of a great, high mountain and showed me the holy city, Yerushalayim, coming down out of heaven from God. ¹¹ It had the *Sh'khinah* of God, so that its brilliance was like that of a priceless jewel, like a crystal-clear diamond. ¹² It had a great, high wall with twelve gates; at the gates were twelve angels; and inscribed on the gates were the names of the twelve tribes of Isra'el. ¹³ There were three gates to the east, three gates to the north, three gates to the south and three gates to the west. ¹⁴ The wall of the city was built on twelve foundation-stones, and on these were the twelve names of the twelve emissaries of the Lamb.

¹⁵ The angel speaking with me had a gold measuring-rod with which to measure the city, its gates and its wall. ¹⁶ The city is laid out in a square, its length equal to its width. With his rod he measured the city at 1,500 miles, with length, width and height the same. ¹⁷ He measured its wall at 216 feet by human standards of measurement, which the angel was using. ¹⁸ The wall was made of diamond and the city of pure gold resembling pure glass. ¹⁹ The foundations of the city wall were decorated with all kinds of precious stones — the first foundation stone was diamond, the second sapphire, the third chalcedony, the fourth emerald, ²⁰ the fifth sardonyx, the sixth carnelian, the seventh chrysolite, the eighth beryl, the ninth topaz, the tenth chrysoprase, the eleventh turquoise and the twelfth amethyst. ²¹ The twelve gates were twelve pearls, with each gate made of a single pearl. The city's main street was pure gold, transparent as glass.

²² I saw no Temple in the city, for ADONAI, God of heaven's armies, is its Temple, as is the Lamb. ²³ The city has no need for the sun or the moon to shine on it, because God's *Sh'khinah* gives it light, and its lamp is the Lamb. ²⁴ The nations will walk by its light, and the kings of the earth will bring their splendor into it. ²⁵ Its gates will never close, they stay open all day because night will not exist there, ²⁶ and the honor and splendor of the nations will be brought into it. ²⁷ Nothing impure may enter it, nor anyone who does shameful things or lies; the only ones who may enter are those whose names are written in the Lamb's Book of Life.

22 ¹ Next the angel showed me the river of the water of life, sparkling like crystal, flowing from the throne of God and of the Lamb. ² Between the main street and the

---

ᶠ Leviticus 26:11–12; Isaiah 7:14; 8:8,10; Jeremiah 31:33(34); Ezekiel 37:27; 2 Chronicles 6:18

river was the Tree of Life producing twelve kinds of fruit, a different kind every month; and the leaves of the tree were for healing the nations — [3] no longer will there be any curses. The throne of God and of the Lamb will be in the city, and his servants will worship him; [4] they will see his face, and his name will be on their foreheads. [5] Night will no longer exist, so they will need neither the light of a lamp nor the light of the sun, because ADONAI, God, will shine upon them. And they will reign as kings forever and ever.

[6] Then he said to me, "These words are true and trustworthy: ADONAI, God of the spirits of the prophets, sent his angel to show his servants the things that must happen soon."

[7] "Look! I am coming very soon. Blessed is the person who obeys the words of the prophecy written in this book!"

[8] Then I, Yochanan, the one hearing and seeing these things, when I heard and saw them, I fell down to worship at the feet of the angel showing them to me. [9] But he said to me, "Don't do that! I am only a fellow-servant with you and your brothers, the prophets and the people who obey the words in this book. Worship God!"

[10] Then he said to me, "Don't **seal up the words of the prophecy in this book,**[g] because the time of their fulfillment is near.

[11]   "Whoever keeps acting wickedly, let him go on acting wickedly;
whoever is filthy, let him go on being made filthy.

"Also, whoever is righteous, let him go on doing what is righteous;
and whoever is holy, let him go on being made holy."

[12] "Pay attention!" [says Yeshua,] "I am coming soon, and my rewards are with me to give to each person according to what he has done. [13] I am the 'A' and the 'Z,' the First and the Last, the Beginning and the End."

[14] How blessed are those who wash their robes, so that they have the right to eat from the Tree of Life and go through the gates into the city! [15] Outside are the homosexuals, those involved with the occult and with drugs, the sexually immoral, murderers, idol-worshippers, and everyone who loves and practices falsehood. [16] "I, Yeshua, have sent my angel to give you this testimony for the Messianic communities. I am the Root and Offspring of David, the bright Morning Star. [17] The Spirit and the Bride say, 'Come!' Let anyone who hears say, 'Come!' And let anyone who is thirsty come — let anyone who wishes, take the water of life free of charge."

[18] I warn everyone hearing the words of the prophecy in this book that if anyone adds to them, God will add to him the plagues written in this book. [19] And if anyone takes anything away from the words in the book of this prophecy, God will take away his share in the Tree of Life and the holy city, as described in this book.

[20] "The one who is testifying to these things says, 'Yes, I am coming soon!'"
Amen! Come, Lord Yeshua!

[21] May the grace of the Lord Yeshua be with all!

[g] Daniel 12:4

Pronouncing Explanatory Glossary

Format. Names of persons and places are printed in ordinary type, other terms in *italics*. All terms are Hebrew except where [A] indicates Aramaic, [Y] Yiddish, and [O] some other language. Usual English renderings are shown in parentheses, unless the usual ones are the same as the *CJB* ones or differ only by reason of apostrophes. The definition or explanation, if there is one, follows a dash. In the case of *B'rit Hadashah* names and terms, there is given at the end of each entry the book, chapter and verse of the *B'rit Hadashah* where the name or term first appears (see abbreviations below); a "+" means it appears in at least one subsequent verse; "f." or "ff." means it appears again only in the verse or verses immediately following. *Tanakh* names and terms are generally not explained, although translations are given where needed.

Pronunciation. Vowels are pronounced as boldfaced in the following words: f**a**ther, **ai**sle, b**e**d, n**ee**d, n**ei**gh, wh**e**y, mar**i**ne (accented on last syllable) or **i**nvest (not accented), **o**bey, r**u**le. As for consonants, "*ch*" is pronounced as in Johann Sebastian Ba**ch**, and so is "*kh*"; "*g*" is always hard (**g**ive); other consonants are more or less as in English. The guttural stop *alef* is represented by an apostrophe (') before a vowel, except at the beginning of a word (example: Natan'el is pronounced Na‧tan‧**'el** and not Na‧ta‧**nel**). The stronger guttural stop *'ayin* (closer to the hard "g" sound) is represented by a reverse apostrophe (‘) before or after a vowel.

Dots separate syllables unless hyphens or apostrophes do the job already. Accented syllables are printed in **boldface**. Except where an asterisk (*) follows the word, the pronunciation shown for Hebrew and Aramaic is that used in Israel, where at least 90% of all words are accented on the last syllable; many of the exceptions, in which the next-to-last syllable is accented, end with "ch," with a vowel followed by "a," or with "e" in the last syllable. Ashkenazic (German and eastern European) pronunciations common in English-speaking countries often shift "a" sounds towards "o," turn some "*t*'s" into "*s*'s," and accent the next-to-last syllable where the Israelis accent the last, *e.g.*, **Shab‧**bos instead of Shab‧**bat**.

Section XVI of the Introduction tells more about how to pronounce Hebrew. An asterisk (*) means: See "Accentuation" paragraph on p. liii.

References to Books of the Bible. Books of the *Tanakh* are not abbreviated in the Glossary. The books of the *B'rit Hadashah* are abbreviated as follows:

Ac	Acts	MJ	Messianic Jews (Hebrews)	1Ti	1 Timothy
1C	1 Corinthians	Mk	Mark	2Ti	2 Timothy
2C	2 Corinthians	Mt	Mattityahu (Matthew)	Ti	Titus
Co	Colossians	Pm	Philemon	1Y	1 Yochanan (1 John)
Ep	Ephesians	Pp	Philippians	2Y	2 Yochanan (2 John)
Ga	Galatians	Ro	Romans	3Y	3 Yochanan (3 John)
1K	1 Kefa (1 Peter)	Rv	Revelation	Ya	Ya‘akov (James)
2K	2 Kefa (2 Peter)	1Th	1 Thessalonians	Yd	Y'hudah (Jude)
Lk	Luke	2Th	2 Thessalonians	Yn	Yochanan (John)

A·bad·**don**—The king and/or angel of the Bottomless Pit (Abyss). From the Hebrew root a-b-d, "lose, destroy." The Greek translation of the name is *Apollyon*, which means "Destroyer." Rv 9:11.

Ab·ba [A]—An affectionate way to say "father," hence, "Dear father," "Dad." or even "Daddy." Though originally Aramaic the word was incorporated into ancient Hebrew. Israeli children call their fathers, "Abba" Mk 14:36+.

A·char·**chel** (Aharhel)

A·*cha·rei Mot*—Parashah 29; Leviticus 16:1–18:30

a·cha·rit-ha·ya·mim—Literally, "the end of the days." The End Times or "latter days," when the *'olam hazeh* is coming to a close and the *'olam haba* is about to begin. 1C 10:11+.

A·chas·**bai** (Ahasbai)

A·chash·**ta**·ri (Haahashtari)

A·chash·ve·**rosh** (Ahasuerus)

Ach·**'av** (Ahab)

A·**chaz** (Ahaz)—King of Y'hudah, father of Hezekiah; in Messianic genealogy. Mt. 1:9.

A·chaz·**yah**, -**ya**·hu (Ahaziah)

Ach·**ban** (Ahban)

A·**cher** (Aher)

A·**chi** (Ahi)

Ach·i·**'am** (Ahiam)

Ach·i·**chud** (Ahihud)

Ach·i·**'e**·zer (Ahiezer)

Ach·i·**hud** (Ahihud)

Ach·i·**kam** (Ahikam)

Ach·i·**lud** (Ahilud)

Ach·i·ma·**'atz** (Ahimaaz)

Ach·i·**man** (Ahiman)

Ach·i·**me**·lekh (Ahimelech)

Ach·i·**mot** (Ahimoth)

Ach·i·na·**dav** (Ahinadab)

Ach·i·no·**'am** (Ahinoam)

Ach·i·**ra** (Ahira)

Ach·i·**ram** (Ahiram)

Ach·i·ra·**mi** (Ahiramite)

Ach·i·sa·**makh** (Ahisamach)

Ach·i·**sha**·char (Ahishahar)

Ach·i·**shar** (Ahishar)

Ach·i·**to**·fel (Ahithophel)

Ach·i·**tuv** (Ahitub)

Ach·i·**yah** (Ahiah, Ahijah)

Ach·**lai** (Ahlai)

Ach·**lav** (Ahlab)

Ach·m'·**ta** (Achmetha)

A·**cho**·ach (Ahoah)

A·cho·**chi** (Ahohite)

Ach·**rach** (Aharah)

A·chu·**mai** (Ahumai)

A·chu·**zam** (Ahuzam)

A·chu·**zat** (Ahuzat)

Ach·**yan** (Ahian)

Ach·**yo** (Ahio)

Ach·**zai** (Ahazai)

'Ad·'a·**dah**

'A·**dah**

A·dal·**ya** (Adalia)

A·**dam**—the first man; the word means "man" or "human" generically; from Hebrew root *a-d-m*, "red" from which also comes the word *a-da-mah* "earth" Lk 3:38+.

A·da·mi-**Ne**·kev (Adaminekeb)

A·**dan**

A·**dar**—12th month of the biblical year, 6th month of the modern Jewish year (in February–March)

'A·da·**yah**, -**ya**·hu (Adaiah)

Ad·be·**'el**

Ad·**di**—in Messianic genealogy. Lk 3:28.

'A·di·**'el**

'A·**din**

'A·di·**na**

'A·di·**no**

'A·di·**ta**·yim (Adithaim)

Ad·**lai**

Ad·**mah**

Ad·ma·**ta** (Admatha)

Ad·**min**—in Messianic genealogy. Lk 3:33.

'Ad·**na**

'Ad·**nach** (Adnah)

'Ad·**nah**

A·**don**

A·do·nai—literally, "my Lord," a word the Hebrew Bible uses to refer to God. When in large and small capital letters in the *CJB* (A·DO·NAI), it represents the tetragrammaton, the Hebrew name of God consisting of the four letters, *Yud-Heh-Vav-Heh*, sometimes rendered in English as Jehovah or Yahweh, but usually as LORD, sometimes as GOD. Mt 1:20+.

A·DO·NAI *E·lo·hei-Tzva·'ot* (LORD God of Hosts)

A·DO·NAI *E·lo·hei·nu*—LORD our God (see *elohim*). Mk 12:29.

A·DO·NAI (the LORD our God)

A·do·nai E·LO·HIM (the Lord GOD)

A·do·nai E·LO·HIM Elohei-Tzva'ot (the Lord GOD, God of Hosts)

A·do·nai E·LO·HIM-Tzva·'ot (the Lord GOD of Hosts)

A·DO·NAI Nis·si—the LORD my Banner/Miracle

A·DO·NAI-Sha·lom—the LORD of Peace

A·DO·NAI Sha·mah—the LORD is there

A·DO·NAI Tzid·ke·nu (the LORD our Righteousness)

A·DO·NAI-Tzva·'ot (the Lord of Sabaoth)—LORD of (heaven's) armies, LORD of Hosts. Ro 9:29+.

A·DO·NAI Yir·'eh—the LORD will see [to it]

A·do·ni-Be·zek

A·do·ni·kam

A·do·ni·ram

A·do·ni-Tze·dek (Adoni·zedek)

A·do·ni·yah, -ya·hu (Adonijah)

A·do·ram

A·do·ra·yim (Adoraim)

Ad·ra·me·lekh (Adrammelech)

Ad·ri·'el

A·du·lam (Adullam)

'A·du·lam (Adullam)

'A·du·la·mi (Adullamite)

A·far·sat'·khim (Apharesattechites)

A·far·sim (Apharesites)

A·fek (Aphek)

A·fe·kah (Aphekah)

A·fi·ach (Aphiah)

A·fik (Aphik)

A·gag

A·ga·gi (Agagite)

A·gav (Agabus)—a New Testament prophet. Ac 11:28; 21:10.

A·ge (Agee)

A·gur

A·ha·ron (Aaron)—Moshe's brother; traditionally the first *cohen gadol*. Lk 1:5+.

A·ha·va

'Ai

'A·kan

'A·khan (Achan)

'A·khar (Achar)

'Akh·bor (Achbor)

A·khish (Achish)

A·khor (Achor)

'Akh·sah (Achsah)

Akh·shaf (Achshaph)

Akh·ziv (Achzib)

Ak·kad (Accad)

'Ak·ko (Accho)

'Ak·rab·bim

'A·kuv (Akkub)

A·la·me·lekh (Alammelech)

'a·la·mot (alamoth)—high-pitched musical instruments

A·lef (Aleph)—1st letter of Hebrew alphabet

'A·le·met (Alemeth)

Al·mo·dad

'Al·mon

Al·mon-Div·la·ta·yim (Almon Diblataim)

A·lon (Allon)

A·lon-Ba·khut (AllonBachuth)

A·lot (Aloth)

A·lush

'Al·vah

'Al·van

'Al·yan (Alian)

'Am·'ad

a·mah—cubit

'A·mal

'A·ma·lek

'A·ma·le·ki, -kim (Amalakite, -s)

A·mam

A·ma·**nah** (Amana)
A·mar·**yah** (Amariah)
A·mar·**ya**·hu (Amariah)
'A·ma·**sa**
'A·ma·**sai**
'A·mash'·**sai** (Amashai)
'A·mas·**yah** (Amasiah)
A·matz·**yah**, -**ya**·hu (Amaziah)
A·***men***—"It is true," "So be it," "May it become true." Spoken after a prayer or statement to indicate agreement. (1) Most translators take Yeshua's "*Amen*" as referring forward to what he was about to say: "Truly, I say to you, . . ." But there is no other instance of "*Amen*" pointing forward in early Jewish literature, and the context does not require it. Yeshua uses "*Amen*" to refer back, either seriously or ironically, to what he or someone else has said, or to what has just happened. Mt 5:18+. (2) Occasionally the term indicates to the congregation to say "*Amen*" at the end of a prayer. Mt 6:13+.
'*am·ha·'a·retz*—literally, "people of the Land" , that is, ordinary, unlearned people; used pejoratively in the first century: "boors." May be used as a singular noun to describe an individual: "He's just an *am-ha'aretz*." Yn 7:49; Ac 4:13.
A·**mi** (Ammi)
A·mi·**tai** (Amittai)
Am·**ma**·'us (Emmaus)—town of uncertain location about seven miles from Jerusalem. Lk 24:13.
'Am·**mi**
'Am·mi·**'el**
'Am·mi·**hud**
'Am·mi·na·**dav** (Amminadab)—in Messianic genealogy. Mt 1:4; Lk 3:33.
'Am·mi·shad·**dai**
'Am·mi·za·**vad** (Ammizabad)
Am·**non**
'A·**mok**
A·**mon**—in Messianic genealogy. Mt 1:10.

'A·**mon** (Ammon)
'A·mo·**ni**, -**nim** (Ammonite, -s)
'A·mo·**nit** (Ammonite woman)
'A·mo·**ra** (Gomorrah, Gomorrha)— wicked city near the Dead Sea destroyed by God in the days of Avraham and Lot (Genesis 19), therefore a symbol of unrepentance. Mt 10:15+.
'A·**mos**
A·**motz** (Amos)—in Messianic genealogy, Lk 3:25.
Am·ra·**fel** (Amraphel)
'Am·**ram**
'Am·ra·**mi** (Amramite)
Am·**tzi** (Amzi)
A·na·cha·**rat** (Anaharath)
'A·**nah**
'A·**nak**
'A·na·**kim** (Anakims)
'A·na·**me**·lekh (Anammelech)
'A·na·**mim**
'A·**nan** (Annas)—*cohen gadol* when Yochanan and Yeshua were young, later a behind-the-scenes power. Lk 3:2+.
'A·**nani**
'A·nan·**yah** (Ananiah)
'A·**nat** (Anath)
'A·na·**tot** (Anathoth)
'A·na·tot·**yah** (Anthothijah)
'A·**nav** (Anab)
'A·na·**yah** (Anaiah)
'A·**nem**
'A·**ner**
A·ni·**'am**
'A·**nim**
'A·**nuv** (Anub)
'An·tot·**yah** (Antothijah)
A·**pa**·yim (Appaim)
'Ar
A·**ra**
A·**rach** (Arah)
'A·**rad**
A·**ram**—Syria
A·**ram**-Ma·'a·**khah** (Aram-maacah, Syria-maachah)

A·**ram**-Na·ha·**ra**·yim (Aram-naharaim)—
   Mesopotamia

A·**ram**-Tzo·**vah** (Aram-zobah)—Syrians
   of Zoba

A·ra·**mi** (Aramite)—Syrian, Syrians

A·ra·**mim**—Syrians

A·**ran**

A·ra·**rat**

A·ra·**ri** (Ararite)

A·**rav** (Arab)

'A·ra·**vah**—desert plain south of the
   Dead Sea

A·rav·**nah** (Araunah)

Ar·**ba**

Ar·**bi** (Arbite)

Ar·**chi** (Archite)

Ard

Ar·**di** (Ardite)

Ar·**don**

Ar·'e·**li** (Arelites)

Ar·**gov** (Argob)

A·ri·**dai**

A·ri·da·**ta** (Aridatha)

A·ri·**'el**

a·ri·'el—lion of God, fireplace on God's
   altar

A·ri·**sai**

Ar·**ki** (Arkite)

'Ar·**ki** (Arkite)

Ark'·**vim** (Archevites)

Ar·mo·**ni**

Ar·**nan**

Ar·**ni**—in Messianic genealogy. Some
   versions have Ram (Aram). Lk 3:33.

Ar·**non**

A·**rod**

A·ro·**di**

'A·ro·**'er**

'A·ro·**'e·ri** (Aroerite)

Ar·**pad**

Ar·pakh·**shad** (Arphaxad)—in Messianic
   genealogy. Lk 3:36.

A·rtach'·**shash·ta** (Artaeres)

Ar·**tza** (Arza)

A·ru·**bot** (Aruboth)

A·ru·**mah**

Ar·**vad**

Ar·va·**di** (Arvadite)

'Ar·va·**ti** (Arbathite)

Ar·**yeh** (Arieh)

Ar·**yokh** (Arioch)

A·**sa**—Judean king; in Messianic genealogy. Mt 1:7.

A·**saf** (Asaph)

'A·sah·**'el**

A·sar·**'el** (Asareel)

A·sar·**'e·lah**

'A·sa·**yah** (Asahiah)

'A·**shan**

Ash·**bel**

Ash·be·**li** (Ashbelite)

Ash·**dod** (Azotus)—one of the five
   Philistine cities, located on Mediterranean coast of Israel, 20 miles south
   of modern Tel Aviv. Ac 8:40.

Ash·do·**dim** (Ashdodites)

A·**sher** (Aser)—one of the twelve tribes
   of Israel. Lk 2:36; Rv 7:6.

a·she·rah, -rim (Astarte, idol; -s)—
   carved image of a pagan goddess

A·she·**ri** (Asherites)

A·shi·**ma**

Ash'·**chur** (Ashur)

Ash·ke·**lon**

Ash·ke·**naz**

Ash·**nah**

Ash·p'·**naz** (Ashpenaz)

'**ash·ta·rot** (Ashtoreth)—images of
   Phoenician goddess

'Ash·**to·ret** (Ashtoreth)—Phoenician
   goddess, place-name

'Ash·t'·ra·**ti** (Ashterathite)

A·**shur** (Asshur)—Assyria

A·shu·**ri**, -**rim** (Ashurite, -s)—Assyrian, -s

'Ash·**vat** (Asvath)

'A·si·**'el**

A·**sir** (Assir)

As·**nah**

As·na·**par** (Asnapper)

As·pa·**ta** (Aspatha)

As·ri·**'el**

As·ri·**'e·li** (Asrielites)

'As·**vat** (Ashvat)

A·**tad**

'A·tai (Attai)
'A·takh (Athach)
'A·tal·yah, -ya·hu (Athaliah)
'A·ta·rah
A·ta·rim (Atharim)
'A·ta·rot (Ataroth)
'A·ta·yah (Athaiah)
A·ter
'At·lai (Athlai)
'At·rot-A·dar (Ataroth-addar)
'At·rot-Beit-Yo·'av (Ataroth the house of Jacob)
'At·rot-Sho·fan (Ataroth Shophan)
A·tzal·ya·hu (Azaliah)
'Atz·bi (Azbi)
A·tzal (Azal)
A·tzel (Azal)
'A·tzem (Azem)
'atz·bi—my pain
'Atz·mon (Azmon)
'A·va
A·vag·ta (Abagtha)
'A·va·rim (Abarim)
'Av·da (Abda)
'Av·de·'el (Abdeel)
'Av·di (Abdi)
'Av·di·'el (Abdiel)
'Av·don (Abdon)
'Aved-N'·go (Abed-nego)
A·vel (Abel)
A·vel-Ha-Shee·tim (Abel-shittim)
A·vel-K'·ra·mim (Abel-keramim)
A·vel-M'·cho·lah (Abel-meholah)
A·vel-Mitz·ra·yim (Abel-mizraim)
A·ven
A·vi (Abi)
A·vi-'Ad (Eternal Father)
A·vi-'Al·von (Abi-Albon)
A·vi·'a·saf (Abiasaph, Ebiasaph)
A·vi·cha·yil (Abihail)
A·vi·da (Abidah)
A·vi·dan (Abidan)
A·vi·'el (Abiel)
A·vi·'e·zer (Abiezer)
A·vi·'ez·ri (Abiezrite)
A·vi·gal (Abigail)
A·vi·ga·yil (Abigail)

A·vi·hu (Abihu)
Av·i·hud (Abihud, Abiud)—in Messianic genealogy. Mt 1:13.
'A·vim (Avvites)
A·vi·ma·'el (Abimael)
A·vi·me·lekh (Abimelech)
A·vi·na·dav (Abinadab)
A·vi·ner (Abner)
A·vi·no·'am (Abinoam)
a·vi·nu—our father. Lk 1:73+.
A·vi·ram (Abiram)
A·vi·shag (Abishag)
A·vi·shai (Abishai)
A·vi·sha·lom (Abishalom)
A·vi·shu·a (Abishua)
A·vi·shur (Abishur)
'A·vit (Avith)
A·vi·tal (Abital)
A·vi·tuv (Abitub)
A·viv (Abib)—1st month of the biblical year, corresponding to the modern Jewish month of Nisan (see glossary entry there).
A·vi·yah, -ya·hu (Abijah, Abia)—(1) king of Y'hudah and ancestor of King David; in Messianic genealogy. Mt. 1:7. (2) one of the twenty-four divisions of the Levitical priesthood. Lk 1:5.
A·vi·yam (Abijam)
Av·ner (Abner)
Av·ra·ham (Abraham)—First of the three Patriarchs of the Jewish people. Mt 1:1+.
Av·ra·ham a·vi·nu—Abraham, our father. Lk 1:73+.
Av·ram (Abram)
Av·ro·nah (Ebronah)
Av·shai (Abishai)
Av·sha·lom (Absalom)
A·vi·sha·lom (Abishalom)
A·yah (Aiah, Aija)
'A·yah (Aiah, Aija)
A·ya·lon (Aijalon)
'A·yat (Aiath)
'A·yin (Ayin)—16th letter of Hebrew alphabet

1561

'A·zah (Gaza)—Philip took "the road that goes down from Yerushalayim to 'Azah, the desert road.'" 'Azah, some 40 miles south of modern Tel Aviv, was the southernmost of the five Philistine cities. A modern " 'Azah Road" heads from downtown Yerushalayim towards Gaza and the Negev desert for a mile or so before it gets another name. Ac 8:26.

'A·zan (Azzan)

A·zan·**yah** (Azaniah)

'A·zar·'el (Azareel)

'A·zar·yah, -**ya·**hu (Azariah)

'A·zaz

'Az·'a·zel — a scapegoat, goat demon

'A·zaz·ya·hu (Azaziah)

Az·**buk**

'A·ze·kah

'Az·gad

'A·zi·'el

'A·zi·za

'Az·ma·vet (Azmaveth)

Az·**not**-Ta·**vor** (Aznoth-tabor)

'Az·ri·'el

'Az·ri·kam

'A·zur (Azor)—in Messianic genealogy. Mt 1:13.

'A·zu·vah (Azubah) — Abandoned

Az·za·**ti** (Gazathites)

Ba·'al (Baal)—the chief male god of the Phoenicians and Canaanites. The word means "lord," "master," and by extension, "husband." Ro 11:4.

Ba·'al-**B'rit** (Baal-berith)

Ba·'al-Cha-**nan** (Baal-hanan)

Ba·'al-**Gad**

Ba·'al-Ha-**mon**

Ba·'al-Ha-**nan**

Ba·'al-Ha-**tzor** (Baal-hazor)

Ba·'al-Her·**mon**

Ba·'al-M·**'on** (Baal-meon)

Ba·'al-P.**'or** (Baal-peor)

Ba·'al-P'rat·**zim** (Baal-perazim)

Ba·'al-Sha·li·**shah** (Baal-shalisha)

Ba·'al-Ta·**mar**

Ba·'al-Tz'·**fon** (Baal-zephon)

Ba·'al-Zib·**bul** (Beelzevul) or **Ba·**'al-**Z'vuv** (Beelzebub, Baal-zebub); the manuscripts differ—derogatory names for the Adversary (Satan; see Mt 4:1). The latter is the name of a Philistine god (2 Kings 1:2) and means "lord of the flies." The former means "lord of heaven, lord of a high abode," hence "prince"; but it also suggests a word play on zevel, "rubbish, excrement." Mt 10:25+.

Ba·'a·**lah**

Ba·'a·**lat** (Baalath)

Ba·'a·**lat**-Be·**'er** (Baalath-beer)

Ba·'a·**lei**-Y'hu·**dah** (Baale-judah)

Ba·'a·*li* (Baali)—my lord, my husband

ba·'a·*lim* (Baalim)—pagan gods

Ba·'a·**lis**

Ba·'a·**na**

Ba·'a·**nah**

Ba·'a·**ra**

Ba·'a·se·**yah** (Baaseiah)

Ba·'a·**sha**

Ba·cha·ru·**mi** (Bacharumite)

Ba·chu·**rim** (Bahurim)

Ba·**kha** (Baca)

Bak·ba·**kar**

Bak·**buk**

Bak·buk·**yah** (Bakbukiah)

Bakh·**ri** (Bachrites)

Bal·'a·**dan**

Ba·lah

Ba·**lak** (Balac)—king of Moab who hired Bil'am to curse Israel (Numbers 22–24). Rv 2:14.

Ba·lak—Parashah 40; Numbers 22:2–25:9

Bal·**'i** (Belaites)

B·'al·**yah** (Bealiah)

Ba·**mah**

Ba·**mot** (Bamoth)

Ba·**mot**-Ba·**'al** (Bamoth-baal)

Ba·**ni**

bar [A]—son. "Bar-" before a name means "son of" or "descendant of," by extension it can also mean "having the properties of." Compare *ben*. Mt 10:3+.

Bar-**Ab**-ba (Barabbas) [A]—criminal released by Pontius Pilate instead of Yeshua the Messiah. The Aramaic name means "son of father." Mt 27:16+.

Ba-**rak**—D'vorah's general who defeated the Canaanite general, Sisera (Judges 4–5). MJ 11:32.

Ba-rakh-**'el** (Barachel)

Bar-chu-**mi** (Barhumite)

Ba-**ri**-ach (Bariah)

Bar-**kos**

Bar-**Nab**-ba (Barnabas) [A]—*talmid* who worked with Sha'ul of Tarsus. In the New Testament the name is said to mean "the Exhorter"; it may be related to the Hebrew word *navi*, "prophet." Ac 4:36+.

Ba-**rukh** (Baruch)

Bar-**Sab**-ba (Barsabbas; the name may possibly be Bar-S*habbat*, "son of *Shabbat*") [A]—surname of two figures. (1) One of the two candidates to replace Y'hudah from K'riot as an emissary of Yeshua. Ac 1:23. (2) Disciple sent with Sila to Antioch bearing a letter from the emissaries. Ac 15:22.

Bar-Tal-**mai** (Bartholomew) [A]—one of the twelve emissaries. The name may mean "son of *ptolemy*," that is, son of an Egyptian ruler. Mt 10:3+.

Bar-Ti-**mai** (Bartimaeus) [A]—blind beggar whom Yeshua healed (see Timai). Mk 10:46.

Bar-Ye-**shu**-a (Barjesus) [A]—false prophet also called Elymas. Ac 13:6.

Bar-Yo-cha-**nan** (Barjona, son of John) [A]—Shim'on Kefa (Peter) is identified as Shim'on, son of Yochanan. Mt 16:17; Yn 21:15–17.

Bar-zil-**lai**

Ba'-sha (Baasha)

Ba-**shan**

Bas-**mat** (Basmath)

bat—daughter. "*Bat-*" before a name means "daughter of." Lk 2:36.

Bat-Gal-**lim** (daughter of Gallim)

bat-kol—voice from heaven; literally, "daughter of a voice." Mt 3:17; Yn 12:28.

Bat-Rab-**bim** (Bath-rabbim)

Bat-**She**-va (Bath-sheba)

Bat-**Shu**-a (Bath-shua)

Batz-**lit** (Bazlith)

Batz-**lut** (Bazluth)

Ba-**vai**

Ba-**vel** (Babel, Babylon)

Bav-**lim** (Babylonians)

B'-chuk-ko-*tai*—Parashah 33; Leviticus 26:3–27:34

B'-**dad**

B'-**dan**

Be-'a-**lot** (Bealoth)

Bed-**yah** (Bedeiah)

Be-'el-ya-**da** (Beeliada)

Be-**'er**

Be-'e-**ra**

Be-'e-**rah**

Be-'er-E-**lim**

Be-'e-**ri**

Be-'er-La-**chai**-Ro-**'i** (Beer-lahai-roi)

Be-'e-**rot** (Beeroth)

Be-'e-ro-**ti**, -ro-**tim** (Beerothite, -s)

Be-'er-**She**-va (Beer-sheba)

Be-he-**mot** (Behemoth)

Beit-'**A**-nat (Beth-anath)

Beit-'**A**-not (Beth-anoth)

Beit-An-**yah** (Bethany)—the name means "house of poverty." (1) Village east of Yerushalayim, on the Mount of Olives. Mt 21:17+. (2) Village on east bank of Yarden River. Yn 1:28.

Beit-'**A**-ra-**vah** (Beth-arabah)

Beit-Ar-**bel** (Beth-arbel)

Beit-Ash-**be**-a (house of Ashbea)

Beit-**A**-ven (Beth-aven)

Beit-'**Az**-ma-vet (Beth-azmaveth)

Beit-Ba-'al-M-**'on** (Beth-baal-meon)

Beit-Ba-**rah** (Beth-barah)

Beit-Bir-**'i** (Beth-birei)

Beit-Da-**gon** (Beth-dagon)

Beit-Dib-la-**ta**-yim (Beth-diblathaim)

Beit-'**E**-den (house of Eden)

Beit-**El** (Beth-el)

Beit-'**E**-mek (Beth-emek)

Beit-Ga·**der** (Beth-gader)
Beit-Ga·**mul** (Beth-gamul)
Beit-Gil·**gal**
Beit-Ha·**'E**·tzel
Beit-Ha·**Gan**
Beit-Ha·Ke·rem (Beth-haccerem)
Beit-Ha·**ram**
Beit-Ha·**ran** (Beth-haran)
Beit-Ha·Ye·shi·**mot** (Beth-jeshimoth)
Beit-Hog·**lah** (Beth-hoglah)
Beit-Ho·**ron** (Beth-horon)
Beit-**Kar**
Beit-Lach·**mi** (Bethlehemite)
Beit-**Le**·chem (Bethlehem)—birthplace
    of Yeshua and of King David; liter-
    ally, "house of bread." Mt 2:1+.
Beit-L'·va·**'ot** (Beth-lebaoth)
Beit-Ma·**'a**·**khah** (Beth-maachah)
Beit-Mar·ka·**vot** (Beth-marcaboth)
Beit-Mil·**lo** (house of Millo)
Beit-M·**'on** (Beth-meon)
Beit-Nim·**rah** (Beth-nimrah)
Beit-Pa·**gei** (Bethphage)—village east of
    Jerusalem, on the Mount of Olives,
    near Beit-Anyah. Mt 21:1+.
Beit-Pa·**tzetz** (Beth-pazzez)
Beit-Pe·let (Beth-palet)
Beit-P·**'or** (Beth-peor)
Beit-Ra·**fa** (Beth-rapha)
Beit-Re·**chov** (Beth-rehob)
Beit-Sh·**'an** (Beth-shean)
Beit-Shee·**tah** (Beth-shittah)
Beit-**She**·mesh (Beth-shemesh)
Beit-Shim·**shi** (Beth-shemite)
Beit-Ta·**pu**·ach (Beth-tappuah)
Beit-Tzai·**dah** (Bethsaida)—literally,
    "house of nets." Native town of An-
    drew, Kefa and Philip on the west side
    of Lake Kinneret. Mt 11:21+.
Beit-**Tzur** (Beth-zur)
Beit-Ye·shi·**mot** (Beth-jeshimot)
Beit-**Za**·ta (Bethzatha); some manuscripts
    have Beit-Hisda (Bethesda) [A]—
    location of pool where Yeshua healed
    a man ill for 38 years. Beit-Zata may
    mean "house of olives"; Beit-Hisda
    means "house of mercy." Yn 5:2.

Be·kher (Becher)
Bel
Be·la
Bel·sha·**tzar** (Belshazzar)
Bel·t'·sha·**tzar** (Belteshazzar)
ben—son. "Ben-" before a name means
    "son of" or "descendant of"; by exten-
    sion it can also mean "having the prop-
    erties of." Compare *bar*. Mt 4:21+.
Ben-'Am·**mi**
Ben-Cha·**yil** (Ben-hail)
Ben-Ha·**dad**
Ben·Ha M'vo·rakh—Son of the Blessed,
    i.e., Son of God. Mk 14:61.
Ben-Ha·**nan**
Ben-Hin·**nom** (son of Hinnom)
Ben-O·**ni** (Benoni)
Ben-Y'·mi·**ni** (Benjamite)
Ben-**Zo**·chet (Ben-zoheth)
Be·**'on**
Be·**ra**
Be·red
Be·rekh·**yah**, -ya·hu (Berachiah, Barachiah,
    Barachias)—ancestor of the prophet
    Z'kharyah. Mt 23:35.
Be·**ri**
Be·**rim** (Beriites)
Be·ro·**tah** (Berothah)
Be·ro·**tai** (Berothai)
Be·**sai**
B'esh·t'·**rah** (Beeshterah)
Bet (Beth)—2nd letter of the Hebrew
    alphabet
Be·ten
Be·ter (Bether)
Be·**tzai** (Bezai)
Be·tzer (Bezer)
Bid·**kar**
Be·'u·**lah**—Married
Be·zek
B'·ha·'alot ·kha—Parashah 36; Numbers
    8:1–12:16
B'·har—Parashah 32; Leviticus 25:1–26:2
Bid·**kar**
Big·**ta** (Bigtha)
Big·**tan** (Bigthan)
Big·**ta**·na (Bigthana)

Big·vai
Bik·'at-A·ven (plain of Aven)
Bi·khri (Bichri)
Bil·'am Ben-B·'or (Balaam son of Beor (Bosor))—Midianite prophet hired by King Balak of Moab to curse Israel. Although he obeyed God and not Balak in blessing Israel, he led Israel astray into idol worship, including both sexual sin and eating sacrifices offered to idols (Numbers 22–25, 31; Psalm 106). 2 Kefa 2:15+.
Bil·dad
Bil·gah
Bil·gai
Bil·hah
Bil·han
Bil·shan
Bim·hal
Bin·'a (Binea)
Bi·nu·i (Binnui)
Bin·ya·min (Benjamin)—one of the twelve tribes of Israel. The name means "son of (the) right (hand)." Ac 13:21+.
Bin·ya·mi·ni (Benjamite)
Bir·sha
Bir·za·yit (Birzaith)
Bish·lam
Bit·ron (Bithron)
Bit·yah (Bithiah)
Biz·ta (Biztha)
Biz·yot-Yah (Bizjothjah)
B'·kho·rat (Bechorath)
B'li·ya·'al (Belial)—another name for Satan, the Adversary. The Hebrew means "without profit, worthless." 2C 6:15.
B'·mid·bar—Parashah 34; Numbers 1:1–4:20
B'·na·yah, -ya·hu (Benaiah)
B'·nei-Brak (Bene-berak)
B'nei-Re·gesh—Greek *Boanergês* transliterates either this phrase, which means "sons of rage, sons of tumult," or Hebrew B'nei-Ro·gez, "sons of anger." Both fit the translation supplied by the text itself, "Thunderers." Yeshua gave this name to Zavdai's sons,

probably because of their fiery zeal (Mk 9:38; Lk 9:54). Mk 3:17.
B'·nei-Ya·'a·kan (Bene-jaakan)
B'·ni·nu (Beninu)
Bo—Parashah 15; Exodus 10:1–13:16
Bo·'az (Boaz, Boöz)—the great-grandfather of King David, in Messianic genealogy. Mt 1:5; Lk 3:32.
Bo·khim (Bochim)
Bokh·ru (Bocheru)
B·'or (Beor)—see Bil'am ben-B'or
Bo·tzetz (Bozez)
Botz·kat (Bozkath)
Botz·rah (Bozrah)
Boz·kat
b'ra·khah, -khot—blessing(s), benediction(s). The word comes from *berekh* ("knee") and shows the connection between worship and kneeling. To "make a *B'rakhah*" is to say a blessing, to bless. Mt 9:8+.
B'ra·khah (Berachah)
B'ra·yah (Beraiah)
B'·re·sheet—Parashah 1; Genesis 1:1–6:8
B'ri·'ah (Beriah)
B'ri·'i (Beriites)
b'rit—covenant, contract. The major biblical covenants are those God made through Noach (Genesis 9), Avraham (Genesis 17), Moshe (Exodus 19–24), David (2 Samuel 7) and Yeshua (Jeremiah 31; Mt 26:28+). The first is with all mankind, the next three relate primarily to the Jewish people, and the last, though made with the Jewish people, brings all mankind into relationship with all the covenants.
B'rit Ha·da·shah—New Covenant, New Testament. The term is used in the Introduction but not in the text of the *Complete Jewish Bible*. (However, the New Covenant is mentioned at Mt 26:28; Mk 14:24; Lk 22:20; 1C 11:25; Ga 4:24; and throughout MJ 7:22–10:31; as well as in the *Tanakh* at Jeremiah 31:30–33(31–34)).

b'rit-mi·lah—literally, "covenant of circumcision" (see Genesis 17). The term can mean either the act or the ceremony of covenantal circumcision, which is normally performed on the eighth day of a male Jew's life and required of any male Gentile who converts to Judaism. Lk 1:59+.

B'ro·**dakh**-Bal·'a·**dan** (Berodach-baladan)

B'·shal·lach—Parashah 16; Exodus 13:17–17:16

B'·sod·**yah** (Besodeiah)

B'·to·**nim** (Betonim)

B'·tu·**'el** (Bethuel)

B'·**tul** (Bethul)

B'·tzal·**'el** (Bezalel)

bub·be·mei·ses [Y]—"old wives' tales"; literally, "grandmothers' stories." 1Ti 4:7.

Bu·**ki** (Bukki)

Bu·ki·**ya**·hu (Bukkiah)

Bul

Bu·**nah**

Bu·**ni** (Bunni)

Buz

Bu·**zi** (Buzite)

B'·**vai** (Bebai)

co·hen, pl. *co·ha·nim*—priest (in the temple or tabernacle). Mt 2:4+.

co·hen ga·dol, pl. *co·ha·nim g'do·lim*—high priest. *Co·hen ha·ga·dol* means "the high priest." Mt 26:3+.

Da·**be**·shet (Dabbeset)

Da·**gon**

Da·let (Daleth)—4th letter of Hebrew alphabet

Dal·**fon** (Dalphon)

Dal·ma·**nu**·ta (Dalmanutha)—place of uncertain location along west shore of Lake Kinneret; perhaps identical with or near Magdala. Mk 8:10.

Dam·**me**·sek (Damascus)—ancient city, now capital of modem Syria. Ac 9:2+.

Dan

Da·**nah** (Dannah)

Da·ni·**'el**—*Tanakh* prophet. Mt 24:15.

Dan-**Ya**'an (Dan-jaan)

Da·**ra**

Dar·**da**

Dar·**kon**

Dar·**ya**·vesh (Darius)

Da·**tan** (Dathan)

Da·**vid**—king of Israel and ancestor of Yeshua the Messiah. Mt 1:1+.

Dav·**rat** (Dabareh)

dav·ven·ing [Y]—praying. Mt 23:14+.

D'·**dan** (Dedan)

D'·da·**nim** (Dedanim)

De·ha·**yim** (Dehavites)

De·**ker** (Dekar)

de·na·ri·us [O]—a Roman coin, the standard daily wage for a common laborer. Mt 20:2+.

De·**'u**·**'el**

Di·a·spo·ra, the [O]—the Dispersion, i.e., the scattering of the Jewish people in exile (Hebrew *galut*) to the far corners of the earth which began during the reign of the Judean kings but was hastened by the Assyrian conquest (732 B.C.E.), the Babylonian conquest (586 B.C.E.), the destruction of the Temple (70 C.E.) and the Bar-Kokhva Rebellion (132–135 C.E.). It continues to this day, but reversal started in the 19th century as Jews began returning to *Eretz-Yisra'el*. Today 4.5 million Jews live in Israel and between 9 and 13 million in the Diaspora. Ya 1:1+.

Di·**bon**

Dib·**ri**

Di·**fat** (Diphath)

Dik·**lah** (Diklah)

Dil·**'an** (Dilean)

Dim·**nah**

Di·**mon**

Di·mo·**nah**

Di·**nah**

Din·ha·**vah** (Dinhabah)

Di·**shan**

Di·**shon**

Div·**lah** (Diblat)

Div·la·**yim** (Diblaim)

Di·**von** (Dibon)

Di·von-Gad (Dibon-gad)
Di·za·hav (Dizahab)
D'·la·yah, -ya·hu (Delaiah)
D'·li·lah (Delilah)
Do·dai
Do·da·nim
Do·da·va·hu (Dodavah)
Do·do
Dof·kah (Dophkah)
Do·'eg
Dor
Do·tan (Dothan)
Dov·rat (Daberath)
drash, pl. dra·shot—homily, sermon, teaching, Bible study. Ac 17:2.
Du·mah
Du·ra
D'·va·rim—Parashah 44; Deuteronomy 1:1–3:22
D'·vir (Debir)
D'·vo·rah (Deborah)
e·chad—one, unity
E·chi (Ehi)
'Ed
'E·den
'E·der
E·dom
E·do·mi (Edomite, -s)
Ed·re·'i
Ee·ma [A]—Mommy
'E·fai (Ephai)
'E·fer (Epher)
E·fes-Da·mim (Ephes-dammim)
Ef·lal (Ephlal)
E·fod (Ephod)
Ef·rat (Ephrath)
Ef·ra·tah (Ephrathah)
Ef·ra·ti, -tim (Ephrathite, -s)
E·fra·yim (Ephraim)—one of the two sons of Yosef the son of the Patriarch Ya'akov, hence a half-tribe (see M'nasheh); in the New Testament Efrayim is mentioned only as a town northeast of Yerushalayim. Yn 11:54.
'Ef·ra·yin (Ephrain)
'Ef·ron (Ephron)
'Eg·lah

'Eg·lat-Shli·shi·yah
Eg·la·yim (Eglaim)
'Eg·lon
E·hud
'Ei·fah (Ephah)
'ei·fah (ephah)—bushel dry-measure
'Ei·lam (Elam)
Eil-Pa'·ran (El-paran)
Ei·lat (Elat)
Ei·lim (Elim)
Ei·lon (Elon)
Ei·lon-Beit-Ha·nan (Elon-beth-hanan)
Ei·lot (Elot)
Ei·mim (Emim)
Ei·na·yim (Aenon, Ainon, Enon)—place "near Shalem" where Yochanan immersed; the name means "springs." It may be near Beit-Sh'an in the north, near Sh'khem in Samaria, or northeast of Yerushalayim. Yn 3:23.
'Ein-Dor (En-dor)
'Ein-'Eg·la·yim (En-eglaim)
'Ein-Ga·nim (En-gannim)
'Ein-Ge·di (En-gedi)
'Ein-Ha·dah (En-haddah)
'Ein-Ha-Ko·rei (En-hakkore)
'Ein-Ha·rod (well of Harod)
'Ein-Ha·tzor (En-hazor)
'Ein-Mish·pat (En-mishpat)
'Ein-Rim·mon (En-rimmon)
'Ein-Ro·gel (Em-rogel)
'Ein-She·mesh (En-shemesh)
'Ein-Ta·pu·ach (En-tappuah)
Ei·tam (Etam)
'Ei·tam (Etam)
Ei·tan (Etan)
'Ei·val (Ebal)
'E·ker
'E·kev—Parashah 46; Deuteronomy 7:12–11:25
'E·kron
'E·kro·nim (Ekronites)
El-Beit-El (El Beth-el)
El-B'rit (god Berith)
El-E·lo·hei-Yis·ra·'el
El 'El·yon—God Most High
El Gib·bor—Mighty God

El Ro·'i—you, God, see me
El Shad·dai—God Almighty
El-To·lad
E·la (Elah)
El·'ad (Elead)
El·'a·dah (Eladah)
E·lah
El·'a·leh (Elealeh)
'E·lam
El·'a·sah (Eleasah)
E·la·sar (Ellasar)
El·'a·zar (Eleazar, Lazarus)—(1) Ancestor of Yeshua. Mt 1:15. (2) Beggar outside rich man's home in story told by Yeshua. Lk 16:20ff. (3) Brother of Marta and Miryam #6; Yeshua raised him from the dead. Yn 11:1ff.
El·cha·nan (Elhanan)
El·da·'ah
El·dad
E·lef (Eleph)
E·li (Heli)—in Messianic genealogy; father or grandfather of Yosef #3, or father of Miryam #2, depending on interpretation. Lk 3:23.
E·li! E·li! L'mah sh'vak·ta·ni? [A]— "which means, 'My God! My God! Why have you deserted me?' " Mt 27:46.
E·li·'am
E·li·'av (Eliab)
E·li·cho·ref (Elihoreph)
El·'i·chud (Eliud)—in Messianic genealogy. Mt 1:14–15.
E·li·dad
E·li·'ei·nai (Elienai)
E·li·'el
Eli·'e·zer—in Messianic genealogy. Lk 3:29.
E·li·fal (Eliphal)
E·li·faz (Eliphaz)
E·li·fe·let (Eliphalet)
E·li·f'le·hu (Elipheleh)
E·li·hu
E·li·ka
E·li·me·lekh (Elimelech)
E·li·sha (Eliseus)—*Tanakh* prophet and miracle-worker, Eliyahu's disciple. Lk 4:27.

E·li·sha·fat (Elishaphat)
E·li·shah
E·li·sha·ma
E·li·she·va (Elisabeth, Elizabeth, Elisheba)—mother of Yochanan the Immerser. Lk 1:5+.
E·li·shu·a
E·li·tza·fan (Elizaphan)
E·li·tzur (Elizur)
E·li·yah, -ya·hu (Elijah, Elias)—*Tanakh* prophet and miracle-worker who did not die but was taken up into heaven. Malachi 3:23 (4:5) says he will herald "the great and terrible day of *ADONAI*." Therefore Jewish tradition regards him as the forerunner of the Messiah. Mt 11:14+.
E·li·'a·tah (Eliathah)
El·ka·nah
El·ko·shi (Elkoshite)
El·ma·dan (Elmadam, Elmodam)—in Messianic genealogy. Lk 3:28.
'El·ma·'im (Elamites)
El·na·'am
El·na·tan (Elnathan)
E·lo·hi! E·lo·hi! L'mah sh'vak·ta·ni? [A]—"which means, 'My God! My God! Why have you deserted me?' " Mk 15:34.
E·lo·hei·nu—our God
E·lo·him—God; *e·lo·him* means "gods" and "judges." Yeshua uses all three meanings in his word-play at Yn 10:33–36.
E·lon
E·lo·ni (Elonite)
E·lot
El·pa·'al
El·pe·let (Elpalet)
El·t'ke (Eltekeh)
El·t'keh (Eltekeh)
El·t'kon (Eltekon)
El·tza·fan (Elzaphan)
E·lul
El·'u·zai
El·yach·ba (Eliahba)
El·ya·da (Eliada)

El·ya·**kim** (Eliakim)—two persons in Messianic genealogy. The name means "God will raise up." Mt 1:13; Lk 3:30.

El·ya·**saf** (Eliasaph)

El·ya·**shiv** (Eliashib)

El·y'ho·'ei·**nai** (Elihoenai)

El·yo·'ei·**nai** (Elioenai)

El·yo·'e·**nai** (Elioenai)

'*El·yon*—Most High

El·za·**vad** (Elzabad)

'E·mek-K'·**tzitz** (Emek-keziz)

E·**mim**

E·*mor*—Parashah 31; Leviticus 21:1– 24:23

E·mo·**ri**, -**rim** (Amorite, -s)

'E·**nam**

'E·**nan**

E·**nosh** (Enos)—grandson of Adam, in Messianic genealogy. Lk 3:38.

'Er (Er)—in Messianic genealogy. Lk 3:28.

'E·**ran**

'E·ra·**ni** (Eranite)

E·**rekh** (Erech)

E·*retz-Yis·ra·'el*—the Land of Israel. In the New Testament this territory is called *Eretz-Yisra'el*, Isra'el, Kena'an (see glossary entries), and, most often, simply "the Land." See Introduction, page xliii. Mt 2:20–21.

'E·**ri** (Erite)

E·**sar**-Ha·**don** (Esarhaddon)

E·**sav** (Esau)—brother of *Ya'akov avinu.* Ro 9:13+.

Esh·**'an** (Eshean)

Esh·ba·**'al**

Esh·**ban**

'E·shek

Esh·**kol** (Eshcol)

Esh·ta·**'ol**

Esh·ta·'u·**li** (Eshtaulite)

Esh·t'·**mo·a**

Esh·t'·**moh**

Esh·**ton**

Es·**ter** (Esther)

E·**tam** (Etham)

E·ta·**nim** (Ethanim)

Et·ba·**'al** (Ethbaal)

'E·**ter** (Ether)

'**Et**-Ka·**tzin** (Ethkazin)

Et·**nan** (Ethnan)

Et·**ni** (Ethni)

Etz·**bon** (Ezbon)

'E·**tzem** (Ezem)

E·**tzer** (Ezar)

'Etz·**ni** (Eznite)

'Etz·**yon**-Gever (Ezion-geber)

'E·**ved** (Ebed)

'E·**ved**-Me·lekh (Ebed-melech)

E·ven-'E·**zer** (Eben-ezer)

E·**ver** (Eber, Heber)—ancestor of Avraham, in Messianic genealogy. Lk 3:35.

'**E**·ver-Ha·Yar·**den**—a part of *Eretz-Yisra'el* on the east bank of the Jordan river in what is now the country of Jordan. Mt 4:25.

E·**vetz** (Ebez)

E·**vi**

'Ev·**ron** (Ebron)

Ev·ya·**saf** (Ebiasaph)

Ev·ya·**tar** (Abiathar)—*cohen gadol* at the time of King David. Mk 2:26.

E·**veel**-M'ro·dakh (Evil-merodach)

Ez·**bai**

'**E**·zer

'**Ez**·ra*

Ez·ra·**chi** (Ezrahite)

'Ez·**rah** (Ezrah)

'Ez·**ri**

Ga·**bai** (Gabbai)

Gab·ta [A]—"the place called the Pavement." Yn 19:13.

Ga·**cham** (Gaham)

Ga·**char** (Gahar)

Gad—one of the twelve tribes of Israel. Rv 7:5.

Ga·**di** (Gadite, -s)

Ga·di·**'el** (Gaddiel)

Ga·'al

Ga·'ash

Ga'·**tam**

Gal-'Ed (Galeed)

Ga·lal

Ga·lil, the (Galilee)—the Galil is the portion of *Eretz-Yisra'el* west of Lake Kinneret and north of the Yizre'el (Jezreel) Valley. Mt 2:22+.

Ga·lil-of-the-*Go·yim* (Galilee of the nations)—the portion of *Eretz-Yisra'el* east of the Galil and of Lake Kinneret in what is now the country of Jordan. Its name describes the fact that it was inhabited largely by non-Jews. Mt 4:15.

Gal·lim

Ga·ma·dim (Gammadim)

Gam·li·'el (Gamaliel)—a major figure in non-Messianic Judaism, the first to be given the title *Rabban* ("our great one"). Of him the *Mishna* says, "When *Rabban* Gamli'el the Elder died, the glory of the *Torah* ceased, and purity and modesty died." (*Sotah* 9:15) He was Sha'ul's teacher, and he warned the *Sanhedrin not* to act rashly against the Messianic Jews. Ac 5:34–39; 22:3.

Ga·mul

Gan-'E·den (Paradise)—literally, "Garden of Eden"; in Judaism the term also refers to Paradise. Lk 23:43.

Ga·rev (Gareb)

Gar·mi (Garmite)

Gat (Gath)

Gat-He·fer (Gath-hepher)

Gat-Rim·mon (Gath-rimmon)

Gat-Sh'ma·nim (Gethsemane)—garden where Yeshua prayed and was apprehended by the Temple police. The term is odd, meaning, literally, "winepress of oils." Since it is located on the flank of the Mount of Olives, it is presumed that the garden was an olive orchard with an olive-oil press. Mt 26:36+.

Gav·ri·'el (Gabriel)—Angel sent in the *Tanakh* to Dani'el and in the New Testament to Z'kharyah #2 and Miryam #2. Lk 1:19, 26.

Ga·zam (Gazzam)

Ga·zez

G'dal·yah, -ya·hu (Gedaliah)

G'de·rah (Gederah)

G'de·rot (Gederoth)

G'de·ro·ta·yim (Gederothaim)

G'·dor (Gedor)

Ge·der

Gei·cha·zi (Gehazi)

Gei-Ha·ra·shim (Ge-harashim)

Gei-Hin·nom (Gehenna)—literally, "valley of Hinnom"; called the Valley of the son of Hinnom in the *Tanakh.* Located south of (the Old City of) Yerushalayim; where the city's rubbish was burned; hence, metaphorically, because of the fires, hell. Mt 5:22+.

Ge·ra

ge·rah—one-twentieth of a *shekel* , one-fiftieth of an ounce

Ger·shom

Ger·shon

Ger·shu·ni (Gershonite)

Ge·shan (Gesham)

Ge·shem

get—rabbinic term for a "writing of divorcement," as spoken of in Deuteronomy 24:1–4. Mt 5:31+.

Ge·ter (Gether)

Ge·'u·'el (Geuel)

Ge·va (Geba)

Ge·ver (Geber)

Ge·vim (Gebim)

Ge·zer (Gezer)

Gi·ach (Giah)

Gib·bar

Gib'·ton (Gibbethon)

Gi·chon (Gihon)

Gi·dal·ti (Giddalti)

Gid·del

Gid·'om

Gid·'on (Gideon, Gedeon)—a judge of Israel (Judges 6–8). MJ 11:32.

Gid·'on·i (Gideoni)

Gil·'ad (Gilead)

Gil·'a·di (Gileadite)

Gi·la·lai

Gil·**bo**·a
Gil·**gal**
Gi·**loh**
Gi·lo·ni (Gilonite)
Gi·mel—3rd letter of Hebrew alphabet
Gim·**zo**
Gi·**nat** (Ginath)
Gi·no·**sar** (Gennesaret)—town on north-
　　west coast of Lake Kinneret. Mt
　　14:34+.
Gin·**to**·i (Ginnetho)
Gin·**ton** (Ginnethon)
Gir·ga·**shi** (Girgashite, -s)
Gish·**pa** (Gispa)
Git·**ta**·yim (Gittaim)
Git·**ti**, -**tim** (Gittite, -s)
git·tit (gittith)—a musical instrument
Giv·**'a** (Gibea)
Giv·**'ah** (Gibeah)
Giv·**'at**-Bin·ya·**min** (Gibeah of Ben-
　　jamin)
Giv·**'at**-Ha-'A·ra·**lot**—the hill of fore-
　　skins
Giv·**'a**·**ti** (Gibeathite)
Giv·**'at**-Mo·**reh** (the hill of Moreh)
Giv·**'at**-Sha·**'ul** (Gibeah of Saul)
Giv·**li** (Giblite)
Giv·**'on** (Gibeon)
Giv·**'o**·**ni**, -**nim** (Gibeonite, -s)
Gi·zo·**ni** (Gizonite)
Giz·**ri** (Gezrite)
G'li·**lot** (Geliloth)
G'mal·**li** (Gemalli)
G'mar·**yah**, -**ya**·hu (Gemariah)
G'nu·**vat** (Genubath)
Go·**'ah** (Goath)
Gog—prince from the land of Magog,
　　leads final battle against God (Ezekiel
　　38–39). Rv 20:8.
go·fer wood (gopher wood)
Go·**lan**
Gol·**yat** (Goliath)
Go·mer
Go·shen
Gov
Goy, pl. *Go·yim*—corresponding to the
　　Greek word *ethnos* in the New

Testament, variously rendered "Gentile," "nation," "pagan," "non-Jew,"
and "*Goy*"; other versions sometimes
translate it "heathen." As used among
English-speaking Jews *Goyim* means
"Non-Jews," i.e., those outside "our
group"; as with all words employed
in this way, it can have a positive, a
neutral or a negative connotation,
depending on the speaker and the
situation. In the *CJB*, to avoid sug-
gesting exclusivist overtones when
the text does not intend them, the
word is used rather rarely and then
only when God is speaking or when
a Jew is addressing other Jews. Mt
5:47+.
Goy·i·she [Y]—Gentile (adjective). Ga
2:15.
Go·**zan**
G'·**rar** (Gerar)
G'·**shur** (Geshur)
G'shu·**ri** (Geshurite)
Gud·**god** (Gudgodah)
Gul·**gol**·ta (Golgotha, Calvary) [A]—
"which means 'place of a skull,'" the
place where Yeshua was executed on
a stake. Archeologists are in general
agreement that the traditional site of
Gulgolta, in the Church of the Holy
Sepulchre within the Old City of
Yerushalayim, is the correct one. Mt
27:33+.
Gu·**ni**
Gur
Gur-**Ba**·'al
G'val (Gebal)
Ha·'a·zi·nu—Parashah 53; Deuteronomy
　　32:1–52
Hach·mo·**ni**
Ha·**dad**
Ha·dad·**'e**·zer
Ha·dad-Rim·**mon**
Ha·**dar**
Ha·dar·**'e**·zer
Ha·**das**·sah*
Ha·da·**tah** (Hadattah)

Ha·did

Had·lai

Ha·do·ram

Had·rakh (Hadrach)

Ha·'El·yon—"the Most High," "the Highest," i.e., God. Mk 5:7+.

Ha·fa·ra·yim (Hapharaim)

Haf·ta·rah—synagogue reading from the Prophets

Ha·gar (Agar)—Sarah's handmaiden (Genesis 16; 21). Ga 4:24f.

Ha·gav (Hagab)

Ha·ga·va (Hagaba)

Ha·ga·vah (Hagabah)

Ha-G'do·lim (Haggedolim)

Ha·G'du·lah—"the Greatness," "the Majesty," *i.e., Y-H-V-H*. MJ 8:1.

Ha·G'du·lah Ba·M'ro·mim—"the Greatness on High," a euphemism for *Y-H-V-H*. MJ 1:3.

Hag·gi

Hag·git (Haggith)

Ha·gi·yah (Haggiah)

Hag·ri (Haggeri)

Hag·ri·'im (Hagrites)

Hag·rim (Haggarenes)

Ha·G'vu·rah—"the Power," a euphemism for *Y-H-V-H*. Mt 26:64.

Ha·kal·D'ma (Akeldama, Aceldama) [A]—"which in their language means 'Field of Blood'." Ac 1:19.

Ha·Ka·tan (Hakkatan)

Ha·khal·yah (Hachaliah)

Ha·khi·lah (Hachilah)

Hakh·mo·ni (Hachmoni)

Ha·Ka·dosh—"the Holy One," a euphemism for *Y-H-V-H*. 1Yn 2:20.

Ha·kotz (Hakkoz, Koz)

Ha·ku·fa (Hakupha)

Ha·lach (Halah)

Hal·chul (Halhul)

Hal·fai (Alphaeus, Alpheus)—father of Ya'akov Ben-Halfai, who was one of Yeshua's twelve *talmidim*. Mt 10:3+.

Ha·li

Hal·lah—loaf or cake. The modern popular meaning is the special bread

eaten on *Shabbat*. But in Romans 11:16 it refers to the share of the dough set aside for the *cohanim* in accordance with Numbers 15:20 (where the word appears) and *Mishna* tractate *Hallah*.

Hal·lel—literally, "praise." The "Egyptian" *Hallel* consists of Psalms 113–118; the "Great" *Hallel* is Psalm 136. Both are recited as part of the *Seder* service. Mt 26:30+.

Hal·le·lu·yah! (Hallelujah!)—a command in the plural, "Praise *Yah!*" (*Yah* is a name of God; see Psalm 68:5 (4)). Sometimes rendered: "Praise the LORD!" Rv 19:1ff.

Ha-Lo·chesh (Hallohesh)

Ham

Ha·man

Ha·mat (Hamath)

Ha·mat-Tzo·vah (Hammath-zobah)

Ha·ma·ti (Hamathite)

Ham·da·ta (Hammedatha)

Ha·metz—leavened dough, either cooked or not. The term is also used loosely to refer to the yeast or other leavening agent itself. Mt 16:6+.

Ha·Mitz·pah (Mizpah)

Ham·mot-Dor (Hammoth-dor)

Ha·mon (Hammon)

Ha·mor (Hamor, Emmor)—Owner of a field in Sh'khem. Ac 7:16.

Ham·ran

Ha·mu·'el

Ha·mul

Ha·mu·li (Hamulite)

Ha·mu·tal

Ha·M'vo·rakh—"the Blessed One," a euphemism for *Yud-Heh-Vav-Heh*. Mk 14:61.

Ha·nam·'el (Hanameel)

Ha·nan

Ha·na·ni

Ha·nan·yah, -ya·hu (Ananias, Hananiah)— (1) Believer who lied to the Holy Spirit. Ac 5:1+. (2) Messianic Jew in Damascus who prayed for Sha'ul to receive his sight. Ac 9:10+. (3) *Cohen gadol* at the time of Sha'ul's trial. Ac 23:2+.

Ha·na·ton (Hannathon)

Ha·ni·'el (Hanniel)

Han·nah

Han·nah Bat-P'nu·'el (Anna the daughter of Phanuel)—aged prophet who spoke about Yeshua. Lk 2:36.

Han·nes (Hanes)

Ha·nokh (Enoch)—seventh in descent from Adam in Messianic genealogy. According to Genesis 5:24 he did not die, at least not in the usual way, but "walked with God, and he was not, for God took him." Lk 3:37+

Ha·no·khi (Hanochite)

Ha·nuk·kah—the Feast of Dedication, honoring Temple rededication by the Maccabees (164 B.C.E.) after its profanation under Seleucid king Antiochus IV. Yn 10:22 is the first recorded mention of this Jewish holiday.

Ha·nun

Ha·Pi·tzetz (Happizzez)

Ha·ra

Ha·ra·dah

Ha·ran (Haran, Charran)—city in the Fertile Crescent (near the border between modern Syria and Turkey) where *Avraham avinu* stopped for many years before continuing on to Kena'an. Ac 7:2ff.

Ha·ra·ri (Hararite)

ha·ra·shim—craftsmen

Har·chas (Harhas)

Ha·ref (Hareph)

Har·ha·yah (Harhaiah)

Har·hur

Ha·rif (Hariph)

Ha·rim

Har-Me·gid·do (Armageddon)—the "hill of Megiddo," an ancient town with more than twenty archeological layers covering the period from nearly 6000 years ago until the fourth century

B.C.E. It was chosen again and again as the site for a city because of its strategic location guarding a pass on the *Via Maris* (the "Way of the Sea") joining Egypt and Assyria and overlooking the Valley of Yizre'el (Jezreel, Esdraelon), apparently the site of the final eschatological battle. However, Greek *armageddon* could be rendering Har Migdo ("hill of his glory"), in which case it refers to Mount Tziyon in Yerushalayim. Rv 16:16.

Har·mo·nah

Har·ne·fer (Harnepher)

Ha·ro·di (Harodite)

Ha·ro·'eh (Haroeh)

Ha·ro·ri (Harorite)

Ha·ro·shet-Ha-Go·yim

Har·sha

Ha·ru·fi (Haruphite)

Ha·rum

Ha·ru·maf (Harumaph)

Ha·rutz (Haruz)

Har·vo·na (Harbonah)

Har·vo·nah (Harbonah)

Ha·sad·yah (Hasadiah)

Ha·shav·nah (Hashabnah)

Ha·shav·n'·yah (Hashabniah)

Ha·shav·yah, -ya·hu (Hashabiah)

Hash·ba·da·nah (Hashbadana)

Ha·shem

Ha·Shem—"the Name," i.e., *Y-H-V-H,* hence a euphemism for God. 3Y 7.

Ha·Shmo·nah

Ha·shum

Ha·shuv (Hashub)

Ha·shu·vah (Hashubah)

Ha·sna·'ah (Hassenaah)

Ha·snu·'ah (Hassenuah)

Ha·so·fe·ret (Hassophereth)

Has·rat (Hasrah)

Ha·su·fa (Hasupha)

Ha·takh (Hathach)

Ha·tat (Hathath)

Ha·ti·fa (Hatipha)

Ha·til (Hattil)

Ha·ti·**ta**
Ha·**tush** (Hattush)
Ha·tza·**'el** (Hazael)
Ha·**tzar**-A·**dar** (Hazar-addar)
Ha·**tzar**-'Ei·**nan** (Hazar-enan)
Ha·**tzar**-'Ei·**non** (Hazar-enon)
Ha·**tzar**-'E·**nan** (Hazar-enan)
Ha·**tzar**-Ga·**dah** (Hazar-gaddah)
Ha·**tzar**-Ma·vet (Hazar-maveth)
Ha·**tzar**-Shu·**'al** (Hazar-shual)
Ha·**tzar**-Su·**sah** (Hazar-susah)
Ha·**tzar**-Su·**sim** (Hazar-susim)
Ha·tza·**tzon**-Ta·**mar** (Hazazon-tamar)
Ha·**tzer**-Ha·ti·**khon** (Hazar-hatticon)
Ha·tze·**rot** (Hazeroth)
Hatz·lel·**po**·ni (Hazelelponi)
Ha·**tzor** (Hazor)
Ha·**vah** (Eve)—the first woman. 2C 11:3;
   1Ti 2:13.
Ha·va·tzin·**yah** (Habaziniah)
Ha·va·**yah** (Habaiah)
Ha·vi·**lah**
Ha·**vor** (Habor)
Ha·**vot**-Ya·**'ir** (Havoth-jair)
Hav·**ran** (Hauran)
Hay·yei-Sa·rah—Parashah 5; Genesis
   23:1–25:18
Ha·za·**'el**
Ha·za·**yah** (Hazaiah)
Ha·zi·**'el**
Ha·**zo**
He·fer (Hepher)
Hef·**ri** (Hepherite)
Hef·tzi·**Vah** (Hepzibah)—My delight
   is in her.
He·**gai**
Heh—5th letter of Hebrew alphabet
Hei·**lam** (Helam)
Hei·**man** (Heman)
Hel·**'ah**
Hel·**bah**
Hel·**bon**
Hel·**dai**
He·led
He·lef (Heleph)
He·lek
He·lem

He·letz (Helez)
He·lev (Heleb)
Hel·**kai**
Hel·**kat** (Helkath)
Hel·**kat**-Ha·tzu·**rim** (Helkath-hazzurim)
Hel·**ki** (Helekites)
He·**lon**
He·**mam**
He·**man**
Hem·**dan**
He·**na**
He·na·**dad**
He·res
He·resh
Her·**mon**
He·sed
Hesh·**bon**
Hesh·**mon**
Hes·**li** (Esli)—in Messianic genealogy.
   Lk 3:25.
Het (Heth, Kheth)—8th letter of Hebrew
   alphabet
Het·**lon** (Hethlon)
Hetz·**rai** (Hezrai)
Hetz·**ro** (Hezro)
Hetz·**ron** (Hezron, Esrom)—ancestor of
   Avraham, in genealogy of Yeshua. Mt
   1:3; Lk 3:33.
Hetz·ro·**ni** (Hezronite)
He·**vel** (Abel)—Adam and Eve's second
   son, killed by Kayin (Genesis 4). Mt
   23:35+.
He·**ver** (Heber)
Hev·**ri** (Heberite)
Hev·**ron** (Hebron)
Hev·ro·**ni** (Hebronite)
He·**zir**
Hez·**yon** (Hezion)
Hid·**dai**
Hig·ga·yon—a musical notation
Hi·**'el**
Hi·**len**
Hil·ki·**yah**, -**ya**·hu (Hilkiah)
Hil·**lel**
Hin·**nom**
Hip·pa·tach! (Ephphatha!)—"Be opened!"
   Mk 7:34.

Hi·rah
Hi·ram
Hit·ti, **-tim** (Hittite, -s)
Hiv·vi (Hivite, -s)
Hiz·ki (Hezeki)
Hiz·ki·yah, **-ya·hu** (Hezekiah, Ezekias)—
king of Judah, in Messianic genealogy.
Mt 1:9–10.
Hod
Ho·dav·yah, **-ya·hu** (Hodaviah)
Ho·di·yah (Hodiah)
Hod·vah (Hodevah)
Hof·ni (Hophni)
Hog·lah
Ho·ham
Ho·lon
Ho·mam
Hor-Ha-Gid·gad
Ho·ram
Ho·rem
Ho·resh
Ho·rev (Horeb)
Ho·ri
Ho·rim (Horites)
Hor·mah
Ho·ro·na·yim (Horonaim)
Ho·ro·ni (Horonite)
Ho·sah
Ho·sha·ma
Ho·sha·na Rab·bah—literally, the "great
hosanna," the "great save-us-please."
It refers to the last day, "the great
day," of the week-long *Sukkot* festi-
val, when, in Temple times, water was
brought from the Pool of Shiloach for
a brilliant ceremony. The day is still
noted in modern Judaism. Yn 7:37.
Ho·sha'·yah (Hoshaiah)
Ho·she·a (Hosea, Osee)—one of the twelve
"minor prophets" in the *Tanakh*. Ro 9:25.
Ho·tam (Hotham)
Ho·tir (Hothir)
Ho·vah (Hobah)
Ho·va·lim—bound together
Ho·vav (Hobab)
Hu·bah (Jehubbah)
Hu·fam (Hupham)

Hu·fa·mi (Huphamite)
Huk·kat—Parashah 39; Numbers 19:1–22:1
Hu·kok
Hul
Hul·dah
Hum·tah
hu·pah—wedding canopy
Hu·pim (Huppim)
Hur
Hu·rai
Hu·ram
Hu·ri
Hu·shah
Hu·shai
Hu·sham
Hu·sha·ti (Hushathite)
Hu·shim
hutz·pah—boldness, audacity, insolence,
nerve, gall, or a combination thereof,
weighted according to the situational
need. Lk 11:8.
Ib·tzan (Ibzan)
'Id·do
I·'e·zer
I·'ez·ri (Iezerites)
'I·kesh (Ikkesh)
I-Kha·vod (Ichabod)
'I·lai
'Im·ma·nu El (Immanuel, Emmanuel)—
Name to be given to the child of the
'almah (young woman, virgin) in
Isaiah 7:14 and applied by Mattityahu
to Yeshua. The name means "God
with us" or "God is with us." Mt 1:23.
Im·mer
Im·ri
'Ir
'Ir-Ha·me·lach—city of salt
'Ir-Na·chash (Ir-nahash)
'Ir-She·mesh (Ir-shemesh)
'I·ra
'I·rad
'I·ram
'I·ri
'I·ru
ish—man
i·shah—woman

Ish-**Bo**·shet (Ish-boshet)
Ish-**Hod**
I·shi—my husband, my man
Ish-**Se**·khel
Is·ra·**'el**—(1) The descendants of the
Patriarch Ya'akov, who is himself called
Isra'el (Genesis 32:29(28), i.e., the
Jewish people. Mt 2:6+. (2) The Land
of Isra'el. Mt 2:20–21; 10:23; Lk 4:25,
27. (3) Those within Isra'el who remain
faithful to God. Ro 9:6, and perhaps
implied at 1C 10:18 and/or Ga 6:16.
(4) All Jewish and Gentile believers in
God and his Messiah Yeshua. Perhaps
implied at Ga 6:16 and/or Ep 2:12–13.
I·ta·**mar** (Ithamar)
I·ti·**'el** (Ithiel)
It·**tai**
'I·vah
'Iv·ri (Ibri)
'I·yei-Ha'A·va·**rim** (Iyeabarim)
'I·yim
'I·yon (Ijon)
I·**yov** (Job)—the world's best-known
sufferer, who learned from his suf-
ferings. Ya 5:11.
I·**ze**·vel (Jezebel)—wife of King Ahab of
Israel, encouraged idolatry. Rv 2:20.
Iz·**ri**
Ka·**bon** (Cabbon)
Ka·**desh**
Ka·**desh**-Bar·**ne**·a
Kad·mi·**'el**
Kad·mo·**ni** (Kadmonite)
Kaf (Kaph)—11th letter of Hebrew
alphabet
Kaf·**tor** (Caphtor)
Kaf·to·**rim** (Caphthorim)
Ka·**lev** (Caleb)
Ka·**lev**-Ef·**ra**·tah (Caleb Ephratah)
Kal·**kol** (Calcol)
Kal·**lai** (Kallai)
Kal·**neh** (Calneh)
Ka·**mon** (Camon)
Ka·**nah** (Cana)—town in the Galil where
Yeshua did two miracles. Home of
Yeshua's *talmid* Natan'el. Possibly

identical with the Arab town of Kana-
el-Jelil ("Jelil" is the Arabic form of
"Galil"), about five miles north of
Tzippori (Sepphoris), near Natzeret.
Yn 2:1+.
Ka·**neh** (Canneh)
kap·pa·rah—atonement, expiation, propi-
tiation; more loosely: forgiveness,
pardon. Ro 3:23; MJ 2:17; 1Y 2:2; 4:10.
Ka·**re**·ach (Kareah, Careah)
Ka·**ri** (Carite)
Kar·**ka** (Karkaa)
Kar·**kas** (Carcas)
Kar·**k'**·**mish** (Carchemish)
Kar·**kor**
Kar·**mel** (Carmel)
Kar·me·**li** (Carmelite)
Kar·**mi** (Carmi, Carmite)
Kar·**shna** (Carshena)
Kar·**tah**
Kar·**tan**
Kas·**di**, -**dim** (Chaldean, -s)
Ka·sif·**ya** (Casiphia)
Kas·lu·**chim** (Casluhim)
kav la-kav—line by line
Kav·tze·**'el** (Kabzeel)
Ka·**vul** (Cabul)
Ka·ya·**fa** (Caiaphas)—*cohen gadol* at the
time of Yeshua. Mt 26:3+.
Ka·**yin** (Cain)—Adam and Eve's first
son, who killed Hevel (Genesis 4).
MJ 11:4+.
K'·**dar** (Kedar)
K'de·**mot** (Kedemoth)
K'dor·la·**'o**·mer (Chedorlaomer)
K'·do·shim—Parashah 30; Leviticus
19:1–20:27
Ke·**dar** (Kedar)
Ke·dem
Ke·desh
Ked·**mah** (Kedemah)
Ke·**fa** (Cephas, Peter)—name given by
Yeshua to Shim'on Bar-Yochanan; it
means "rock" in Aramaic, as does the
Greek equivalent, *petros*. Mt 4:18+.
Kei·**dar** (Kedar)
Ke·**'i**·**lah** (Keilah)

Kei·nan (Cainan)—great-grandson of Adam; in Messianic genealogy. Lk 3:37.

Kei·ni (Kenite, -s)
Ke·lach (Calah)
Ke·na·'an (Canaan, Chanaan)—ancient name for the Land of Israel used at Mt 15:22 to identify the origin of the Gentile woman who approached Yeshua in the region of Tzor and Tzidon, and twice in an historical setting (Ac 7:11; 13:19); in the latter Sha'ul points out that God gave Kena'an to the people of Israel as an inheritance. See more at *Eretz-Yisra'el.*

Ke·na·'a·nah (Chenaanah)
Ke·na·'a·ni, -nim (Canaanite, -s)
Ke·na·'a·nit (Canaanite woman)
Ke·nan
Ke·naz
Ke·ni (Kenite)
Ke·ren-Ha·pukh (Keren-happuch)
Ke·ros
ke·ruv (cherub)—see glossary entry at the plural, *k'ru·vim.*
Ke·sed (Chesed)
Ke·ve
Ke·veh (Kue)
K'far-Ha·'a·mo·nah (Cephar-ammonah)
K'far-Na·chum (Capernaum)—town on northwest shore of Lake Kinneret where Yeshua did much of his ministry. The name means "village of Nahum." Mt 4:13+.

K'fi·rah (Chephirah)
K'·hat (Kohath)
K'·ha·ti, -tim (Kohathite, -s)
K'·he·lah (Kehelathah)
Khim·ham (Chimham)
Ki·don (Chidon)
Kid·ron (Cedron)—valley east of the Old City of Yerushalayim, separating it from the Mount of Olives. Yn 18:1.
Kil·'av (Chileab)
Kil·mad (Chilmad)
Kil·yon (Chilion)

Kim·ham (Chimham)
Ki·nah
Ki·nim (Kenites)
Kin·ne·ret, Lake—modern Israel's name for the Sea of Galilee. The name or a variant is found seven times in the *Tanakh,* first at Numbers 34:11, where it is rendered in most English versions as "Chinnereth." Mt 4:18+.

Kin·n'·rot (Chinneroth)
Kir
Kir-Ha·re·set (Kir-hareseth)
Kir-He·res
Kir·yat-Ar·ba (Kirjath-arba)
Kir·yat-'A·rim (Kirjath-arim)
Kir·ya·ta·yim (Kirjathaim)
Kir·yat-Ba·'al (Kirjath-baal)
Kir·yat-Hu·tzot (Kirjath-huzoth)
Kir·yat-San·na (Kirjath-sannah)
Kir·yat-Se·fer (Kirjath-sepher)
Kir·yat-Ye·'a·rim (Kirjath-jearim)
Kish—father of Israel's first king, Sha'ul. Ac 13:21.
Ki·shi
Ki·shon
Kish·yon (Kishion)
Kis·lev (Chisleu)
Kis·lon (Chislon)
Kis·lot-Ta·vor (Chisloth-tabor)
Ki Ta·vo—Parashah 50; Deuteronomy 26:1–29:8
Ki Te·tze—Parashah 49; Deuteronomy 21:10–25:19
Ki Tis·sa—Parashah 21; Exodus 30:11–34:35
Kit·lish (Kithlish)
Kit·ron
Kit·ti·'im (Kittim)
Kit·tim
Kiv·rot-Ha-Ta·'a·vah (Kibroth-hattaavah)
Kiv·tza·yim (Kibzaim)
Ki·yun (Chiun)
K'·lal (Chelal)
K'li·ta (Kelita)
K'lo·fah (Clopas, Cleopas, Cleophas)—Yeshua's uncle-by-marriage Yn 19:25.
K'·luv (Chelub)

K'lu·**vai** (Chelubai)
K'·**mosh** (Chemosh)
K'mu·**'el** (Kemuel)
K'na·**ni** (Chenani)
K'nan·**yah**, -**ya**·hu (Chenaniah)
K'·**nat** (Kenath)
K'·**naz** (Kenaz)
K'ni·**zi** (Kenizzite)
Ko·a
Kol-Ho·**zeh** (Colhozeh)
Ko·la·**yah** (Kolaiah)
Ko·nan·**yah**, -**ya**·hu (Cononiah)
Ko·ni·**ya**·hu (Coniah)
Ko·rach (Korah, Core)—Levite who led rebellion against Moshe in the desert; God punished Korach by having the earth swallow him alive (Numbers 16; 26). Yd 11.
Ko·rach—Parashah 38; Numbers 16:1–18:32
Kor-'A·**shan** (Corashan)
Ko·ra·**zin** (Chorazin)—city on the shore of Lake Kinneret two miles north of K'far-Nachum. Mt 11:21+.
kor·ban (corban)—sacrifice, i.e., an animal sacrifice, but Mark explains the term as meaning "a gift to God." Mk 7:11.
Kor·**chi**, -**chim** (Korathite, -s; Korhite, -s)
Ko·re (Core)
Ko·resh (Cyrus)
Ko·sam (Cosam)—in Messianic genealogy. Lk 3:28.
Kotz (Coz)
Koz·**bi** (Cozbi)
Ko·ze·**va** (Cozeba)
K'·**ran** (Cheran)
K'ri·**ot** (Kerioth)—town about twenty miles south of Yerushalayim. Home of Judas Iscariot (Y'hudah from K'riot; see glossary entry). Mt 10:4+.
k'ru·vim (cherubim, cherubims)—Heavenly creatures (angels) who guarded the way to the Tree of Life in Gan-'Eden (Genesis 3:24), were described by Ezekiel as having four faces and four wings (Ezekiel 10:20–21), and

were ridden by God (Psalm 18:11(10)); compare the "living beings" of Rv 4:6ff. The term also refers to the gold-overlaid wooden images of same, constructed in obedience to God's command, which overshadowed the ark of the covenant in the tabernacle and in the temple. MJ 9:5.
K'·sa·**lon** (Chesalon)
K'·**sil** (Chesil)
K'su·**lot** (Chesulloth)
K'tu·**rah** (Keturah)
K'tu·vim—Writings, the third of the three parts of the *Tanakh* (see glossary entry), consisting of the books of Psalms, Proverbs, Job, the Five Scrolls (Song of Songs, Ruth, Esther, Lamentations, Ecclesiastes), Daniel, Ezra-Nehemiah and Chronicles.
K'tzi·**'ah** (Kezia)
Kuf (Qoph)—19th letter of Hebrew alphabet
Kun (Chun)
Kush (Cun)
Ku·**shan** (Cushan)
Ku·**shan**-Rish·**'a·ta**·yim (Cushan-rishathaim)
Ku·sha·**ya**·hu (Kushaiah)
Ku·**shi** (Cushi, Cushite)
Ku·**tah** (Cuthah)
Kuv (Chub)
Ku·za (Chuza) [A]—Herod's finance minister. The name means "little jug." Lk 8:3.
K'·**var** (Chebar)
kvetch·ing [Y]—complaining, fretting, whining. Pp 2:14.
K'·**ziv** (Chezib)
La·**'a·dah**
Lab·**ben**
Lach·**mas** (Lahmam)
Lach·**mi** (Lahmi)
La·**'dan** (Laadan)
La·**'el**
La·had
La·**khish** (Lachish)
La·**kum**

La·med (Lamedh)—12th letter of Hebrew alphabet

La·pi·**dot** (Lapidoth)

La·**van** (Laban)

La·yish (Laish)

Le·**'ah**

Le·chi (Lehi)

Lekh L'·kha—Parashah 3; Genesis 12:1–17:27

Le·mekh (Lamech)—father of Noach; in Messianic genealogy. Lk 3:36.

Le·sha (Lasha)

Le·shem

Lev-Ka·**mai**

Le·vi (Levite), pl. *L'vi'im*—Temple worker. The *Torah* prescribes that the descendents of Levi would be priests and Levites. Lk 10:32+.

Le·**vi**—(1) Third son of the Patriarch Ya'akov. MJ 7:5+. (2) The tribe of Israel descended from him. Rv 7:7. (3–4) Two ancestors of Yeshua. Lk 3:24, 29. (5) A disciple of Yeshua also known as Mattityahu. Mk 2:14+.

Le·vi ben-Chal·**fai**—Levi, the son of Alpheus; same as Levi #5 above. Mk 2:14+.

Le·vo·**nah** (Lebonah)

L'·ha·**vim** (Lehabim)

Lid·**vir** (Debir)

Lik'·**chi** (Likhi)

Li·**lit** (Lilith)

Liv·**nah** (Libnah)

Liv·**ni** (Libni)

Liv·ya·**tan** (Leviathan)

L'mu·**'el** (Lemuel)

Lo-'Am·**mi**

Lod

Lo-D'·**var** (Lo-debar)

Lo-Ru·cha·**mah** (Lo-ruhamah)

Lot—Avraham's nephew, saved from God's destruction of S'dom. Lk 17:28+.

Lo·**tan**

L'·tu·**shim** (Letushim)

Lu·**chit** (Luhith)

Lud (Lod, Lydda)—town in the plain northwest of Yerushalayim and east of what is now Tel Aviv and Yafo, near Ben-Gurion International Airport. Ac 9:32ff.

Lu·**dim**

L·'u·**mim** (Leummim)

Lu·**vim** (Lubim)

Luz

L'·va·**nah** (Lebanah)

L'·va·**non** (Lebanon)

L'·va·**'ot** (Lebaoth)

L'vi·'im (Levites)—see *Levi* glossary entry.

Ma·'a·**dai**

Ma·'a·di·**yah** (Maadiah)

Ma·**'ai**

Ma·'a·**khah** (Maachah, Maacah)

Ma·'a·**khat** (Maacat)

Ma·'a·kha·**ti** (Maachathite)

Ma·'a·**lei**-A·du·**mim** (the ascent to Adummim)

Ma·'a·**rat** (Maarath)

Ma·'a·**reh**-Ge·va (Maareh-geba)

Ma·'a·**sai** (Maasiai)

Ma·'a·sei·**yah** , -**ya**·hu (Maaseiah)

Ma·**'atz** (Maaz)

Ma·'az·**yah**, -**ya**·hu (Maaziah)

Ma·cha·**lat** (Mahalath)

ma·cha·lat—a musical instruction

Ma·cha·**na**·yim (Mahanaim)

Ma·cha·**neh**-Dan (Mahaneh-dan)

Ma·chat (Maath)—in Messianic genealogy. Lk 3:26.

Ma·cha·**vim** (Mahavites)

Ma·ch·be·**nah**

ma·cher [Y]—literally, "doer, maker." Someone zealous and active in a group, a "big wheel," but often with overtones of self-importance, hence a person who "throws his weight around," has "connections," is an "operator" or "fixer." 1K 5:3.

Ma·**chir**

Mach·**lah** (Mahlah)

Mach·**li** (Mahli)

Mach·**lon** (Mahlon)

Ma·**chol** (Mahol)

Mach·se·**yah** (Mahseiah)

Mach·zi·'ot (Mahazioth)
Ma·dai
Mad·ma·nah (Madmannah)
Mad·mein (Madmen)
Mad·me·nah
Ma·don
Maf·tir—last few verses of *Torah* portion, read by *Haftarah*-reader before reading the *Haftarah* in the synagogue.
Ma·ga·dan—town on Lake Kinneret, perhaps same as Magdala. Mt 15:39.
Mag·bish
Mag·da·la—town on Lake Kinneret, home of Mary Magdalene (see Miryam of Magdala). Mt 27:56+.
Mag·di·'el
Ma·gog—Place from which Gog arises to make war against God's people (Ezekiel 38–39). Rv 20:8.
Ma·gor-Mis·sa·viv (Magor-missabib)
Mag·pi·'ash
Ma·ha·lal·'el (Mahalaleel, Maleleel)—between Adam and Noach in Messianic genealogy. Lk 3:37.
Ma·her Sha·lal Hash Baz
Mah·rai (Mahari)
Ma·katz (Makaz)
Makh·ba·nai (Machbanai)
Mak'·he·lot (Makheloth)
Ma·khi (Machi)
Ma·khir (Machir)
Ma·khi·ri (Machirite)
Makh·nad·bai (Machnadebai)
Makh·pe·lah (Machpelah)
Mak·ke·dah
Mal·'ah (Melea)—in Messianic genealogy. Lk 3:31.
Mal·'a·khi (Malachi)
Mal·kam (Malcham)
Mal·ki (Melchi)—two figures in Messianic genealogy. Lk 3:24, 28.
Mal·ki·'el (Malchiel)
Mal·ki·'e·li (Malchielite)
Mal·ki·ram (Malchiram)
Mal·ki·shu·a (Malchishua)
Mal·ki-Tze·dek (Melchizedek, Melchisedec)–priest of *El 'Elyon* ("the Most High God"), to whom *Avraham avinu* gave a tenth of the battle spoil (Genesis 14:18–20). In Psalm 110:4 he becomes the model for a new priesthood. The literal meaning of the name is, "My king is righteousness." MJ 5:6+.

Mal·ki·yah, -ya·hu (Malchiah)
Ma·lo·ti (Mallothi)
Ma·lukh (Malluch)
Mam·re
mam·zer—technically, the offspring of a sexual relationship between persons forbidden by the *Torah* to marry each other (*e.g.*, uncle and niece), but usually translated "bastard." Like that word, it can be used as a strong insult. Yn 9:34; MJ 12:8.
man (manna)—bread God gave the people of Israel as they wandered forty years in the desert, named from the question they asked, "*Man hu*? [What is it?]"
Ma·na·chat (Manahath)
Ma·na·cha·ti (Manahathite)
Ma·nah (Menna, Menan)—in Messianic genealogy. Lk 3:31.
ma·neh, pl. *ma·nim*—sum of money, 100 denarii (see glossary entry), about three months' wages for an average worker. Usually rendered "pound." Lk 19:12 ff.
Ma·no·ach (Manoah)
Ma·'okh (Maoch)
Ma·'on
Ma·rah
Mar·'a·lah
Ma·ra·na, ta! (Maranatha!) [A]—"Our Lord, come!"—1C 16:22.
Ma·re·shah
ma·ror—bitter herbs, prescribed for the *seder* at *Pesach* (see glossary entries).
Ma·rot (Maroth)
Mars·na (Marsena)
Mar·ta (Martha) [A]—sister of Miryam #6 and El'azar. The name means "lady." The masculine equivalent, *mar* ("lord"—see above, *Marana, ta!*) is

used in modern Hebrew as the equivalent of English "Mr." Lk 10:38+.

Ma·sa (Massa)

Ma·sa· **'ei**—Parashah 43; Numbers 33:1–36:13

Mash

Ma·shal

Ma·shi·ach (Messiah, Christ)—literally, "anointed," "an anointed one." Transliterated into English as "Messiah." Equivalent to Greek *christos*, which also means "anointed" and comes into English as "Christ." In the *Tanakh*, kings and *cohanim* were ordained by being anointed with olive oil (Exodus 30:30; 1 Samuel 15:1; Psalm 133). The *CJB* uses "*Mashiach*" to render Greek *messias*, which appears only twice (Yn 1:41; 4:25), and in four dramatic passages to render *christos*: Mt 16:16; Mk 8:29; 14:61; Lk 9:20.

mas·kil — an instructional poem.

Mas·re·kah

Mas·sa

Mas·sah

Ma·tan·yah, **-ya·hu** (Mattaniah)

Ma·ta·tah (Mattatha)

Mat·nai (Mattenai)

Mat·red

Mat·ri

Mat·tan (Matthan)—in Messianic genealogy. Mt 1:15.

Mat·ta·nah

Mat·tan·yah, **-ya·hu** (Mattaniah)

Mat·tat (Matthat)—two figures in Messianic genealogy. Lk 3:24, 29.

Mat·ta·tah (Mattatha)—in Messianic genealogy. Lk 3:31.

Mat·tit·yah, **-ya·hu** (Matthew, Matthias, Mattathias)—(1) One of Yeshua's twelve *talmidim*, author of one of the Gospels, also known as Levi (Mt 9:9+); usually rendered in English as "Matthew." (2) The twelfth emissary of Yeshua, replacing Y'hudah from K'riot (Ac 1:23, 26); usually rendered in English as "Matthias." (3–4) Two figures in Messianic genealogy (Lk 3:25, 26); usually rendered in English as "Mattathias."

Mat·tot—Parashah 42; Numbers 30:2(1)–32:42

ma·tzah—unleavened bread. Plural *ma·tzot*. The "first day for *matzah*" would be the day on which, when evening comes, the *Seder* is held.

M'·chi·da (Mehida)

M'·chir (Mehir)

m'chi·tzah—divider which separates people into two groups, *e.g.*, the partition separating men from women in an Orthodox synagogue. At Ep 2:14 it refers at least metaphorically to the fence which separates the inner parts of the Temple, where only Jews could enter, from the Court of the Gentiles. This *m'chitzah*, also called a *soreg*, was a stone partition about five feet high.

Me·cho·la·ti (Meholathite)

Me·chu·ya·'el (Mehujael)

Me·dad

Me·dan

Me·'a·rah

Me·fa·'at (Mephaath)

Me·gid·do*—see glossary entry at Har Megiddo.

Me·hu·man

Mei-Za·hav (Mezahab)

Meid·va (Medeba)

Mei·shakh (Meshach)

Me·'u·nim

Me·lekh (Malchus, Melech)—slave of Kayafa the *cohen gadol*, the Hebrew word means "king." Yn 18:10.

Mem—13th letter of Hebrew alphabet

Me·mu·khan (Memucan)

Me·na·chem* (Manaen)—"who had been brought up with Herod the governor." The name means "comforter." Ac 13:1.

Me·ni

me·no·rah*—lamp; the menorah in the Temple had seven branches. MJ 9:2; Rv 1:12+.

mentsh [Y]—a good, reliable person; a real human being, energetic, moral and compassionate. 1C 16:13.

Me·ra·ta·yim (Merathaim)

Me·rav (Merab)

Me·red

Me·res

Me·rom

Me·ro·no·ti (Meronothite)

Me·roz

Me·sha

Me·shei·zav·'el (Meshezabeel)

Me·shekh (Meshech)

Me·she·lem·yah, -ya·hu (Meshelemiah)

Me·shil·le·mot (Meshillemoth)

Me·shil·mit (Meshillemith)

Me·sho·vav (Meshobab)

me·shug·ga*—crazy. Yn 10:20.

me·shug·ga·'im—crazy people

Me·shu·lam (Meshullam)

Me·shu·le·met (Meshullemeth)

Me·teg-A·mah (Metheg-ammah)

Me·tu·sha·'el (Methusael)

Me·tu·she·lach (Methuselah, Mathusala)—grandfather of Noach, in Messianic genealogy. Lk 3:37.

Me·'u·nim

M'·fi·vo·shet (Mephibosheth)

M'·hei·tav·'el (Mehetabel)

Mid·din

mid·rash—allegorical interpretation or homiletical application of a text. The hearer is expected to understand that the maker of the midrash is not expounding the plain meaning of the text but introducing his own ideas. Ga 4:24.

Mid·yan (Midian, Madian)—desert region including parts of the Sinai Peninsula and what is now southern Jordan. Ac 7:29.

Mid·ya·ni, -nim (Midianite, -s)

Mig·dal-'E·der (tower of Edar)

Mig·dal-El

Mig·dal-Gad

Mig·dol

Mig·ron

Mi·kha (Micha)

Mi·kha·'el (Michael)—a ruling angel ("archangel") described at Daniel 10:21 and 12:1 as watching out for the interests of the nation of Israel, and in the New Testament as the commander of the angels contending with the Adversary, Satan. Yd 9; Rv 12:7.

Mi·khah (Micah)

Mi·khal (Michal)

Mi·kha·yah, -ya·hu (Michaiah)

Mi·khay'·hu (Micaiah)

Mikh·mas (Michmas)

Mikh·m'·tat (Michmethath)

Mikh·ri (Michri)

mikh·tam—poem

Mik·ketz—Parashah 10; Genesis 41:1–44:17

Mik·lot (Mikloth)

Mik·ne·ya·hu (Mikneiah)

mik·veh—bath or pool with a flow of fresh water; used in Orthodox Judaism to this day for ritual purification. Ti 3:5.

Mi·la·lai

Mil·kah (Milcah)

Mil·kom (Milcom)

Mil·lo

min·chah—the afternoon Temple sacrifice, which was accompanied by prayers. In today's Judaism the afternoon synagogue service is called minchah by way of commemoration. Ac 3:1; 10:30.

Min·ni

Min·nit (Minnith)

Min·ya·min (Miniamin)

min·yan—quorum needed for certain public prayers; Orthodox Judaism sets it at ten men, while Conservative Judaism includes women. Ac 16:13.

Mir·mah (Mirma)

Mir·yam (Mary, Miriam)—(1) The original Miryam was the sister of Moshe, but she does not appear in the New Testament. (2) Mother of Yeshua the Messiah. Mt 1:16+. (3) Miryam from Magdala (see below). (4) Mother of Ya'akov #7 and Yosef #8 (Yosi #2). Mt 27:56+. (5) Wife of Klofah. Yn 19:25. (6) Sister of Marta and El'azar in Beit-Anyah. Lk 10:39+. (7) Mother of Yochanan Mark. Ac 12:12. (8) A believer in Rome. Ro 16:6.

Mir·yam from Mag·da·la; Mir·yam, called Mag·da·lit (Mary Magdalene)—*talmidah* of Yeshua from the town of Magdala (see glossary entry). Mt 27:56+.

Mis·gav (Misgab)

Mi·sha·'el

Mi·shal

Mish·'am

Mish·ma

Mish·ma·nah (Mishmannah)

Mish·pa·tim—Parashah 18; Exodus 21:1–24:18

Mish·ra·'i (Mishraite)

Mis·par

Mis·pe·ret (Mispereth)

Mis·re·fot-Ma·yim (Misrephoth-maim)

Mit·kah (Mithcah)

Mit·ni (Mithnite)

Mit·r'·dat (Mithredath)

Mitz·pah (Mizpah)

Mitz·peh (Mizpeh)

Mitz·ra·yim (Mizraim)—Egypt.

mitz·vah*, pl. *mitz·vot*—literally: "command," "commandment"; more broadly: general principle for living, good deed. Mt 5:19+.

Miv·char (Mibhar)

Miv·sam (Mibsam)

Miv·tzar (Mibsar

Mi·ya·min (Mijamin)

Mi·zah

Mi·zar

M'·khe·ra·ti (Mecherathite)

M'·kho·nah (Mekonah)

M'·lat·yah (Melatiah)

M'·li·khu (Melicu)

M'na·sheh (Manasseh, Manasses)—(1) Son of Yosef #1 and grandson of Ya'akov #1. He does not appear in the New Testament, but the half-tribe of Israel named for him does. Rv 7:6. (2) A king of Y'hudah; in Messianic genealogy. Mt 1:10.

M'·na·shi (Manassite)

M'·ne! *M'·ne*! *T'·kel u·far·sin*—see Dani'el 5:25–28 and footnote.

M'·nu·chot (Menuhoth)

Mo·'ad·yah (Moadiah)

Mo·'av (Moab)

Mo·'a·vi, -vim (Moabite, -s)

Mo·'a·vit (Moabite woman)

Mo·la·dah

Mo·lekh (Moloch)—false god worshipped in the ancient Near East. Ac 7:43.

Mo·lid

M·'o·no·tai (Meonothai)

Mo·rash·ti (Morasthite)

Mor·de·khai (Mordecai)

Mo·reh

Mo·re·shet (Moresheth)

Mo·re·shet-Gat (Moresheth-gath)

Mo·ri·yah (Moriah)

Mo·se·rah (Mosera)

Mo·se·rot (Moseroth)

Mo·she* (Moses)—(1) Deliverer of Israel from Egypt, agent through whom Israel received the *Torah*. Mt 8:4+. (2) In the time of Yeshua and after, the "seat of Moshe" was not only a metaphor for the authority of the *Torah*-teachers, but an actual chair on which they sat when they taught. An example, from the third century C.E., discovered in the ruins of Korazin (see glossary entry), is on display at the Israel Museum in Yerushalayim. Mt 23:2.

Mo·tza (Moza)

Mo·tza·'ei-Shab·bat—literally, the "going-out of the Sabbath," i.e., Saturday night. By biblical and Jewish reckoning days begin at sunset; so where the text tells us that the believers met on "the first day of the week." it means Saturday night, not Sunday. Ac 20:7; 1C 16:2.

Mo·**tzah** (Mozah)

M'·ra·**ri** (Merari)

M'·ra·**yah** (Meraiah)

M'·ra·**yot** (Meraioth)

M'·re·**mot** (Meremoth)

M'·ri·**vat**-Ka·**desh** (Meribah in Kadesh)

M'·riv-**Ba**·'al (Merib-baal)

M'·ri·**vot**-Ka·**desh** (Meriboth-kadesh)

M'·ro·**dakh**-Bal·'a·**dan** (Merodach-baladan)

M'·tzo·ra—Parashah 28; Leviticus 14:1–15:33

M'·tzo·va·**yah** (Mesobaite)

Mu·**pim** (Muppim)

Mu·**shi**

M'·vu·**nai** (Mebunnai)

Na·'am

Na·'a·**mah**

Na·'a·**man** (Naaman)—Syrian general healed of serious skin disease by God through the prophet Elisha (2 Kings 5). Lk 4:27.

Na·'a·ma·**ti** (Naamathite)

Na·'a·**mi** (Naamite)

Na·'a·**rah**

Na·'a·**rai**

Na·'a·**ran**

Na·cha·li·**'el** (Nahaliel)

Na·**cham** (Naham)

Na·**chash** (Nahash)

Na·chat (Nahath)

Nach·**bi** (Nahbi)

Nach·ma·**ni** (Nahamani)

Na·**chor** (Nahor)—grandfather of Avraham; in Messianic genealogy. Lk 3:34.

Nach·**rai** (Nahari)

Nach·**shon** (Nahshon, Naasson)—ancestor of King David; in Messianic genealogy. Mt 1:4; Lk 3:32.

Na·**chum** (Nahum, Naum)—in Messianic genealogy. Lk 3:25.

Na·**dav** (Nadab)

Na·**fish** (Naphish)

Naf·ta·**li** (Naphtali, Nephthalim)—(1) Tribe of Israel descended from a son of the Patriarch Ya'akov. Rv 7:6. (2) The territory in *Eretz-Yisra'el* assigned to that tribe (Joshua 19–21). Mt 4:13ff.

Naf·tu·**chim** (Naphtuhim)

Nag·**gai** (Nagge)—in Messianic genealogy. Lk 3:25.

Na·ha·**lal**

Na·ha·**lol**

Na·**'im** (Nain)—town in the Galil where Yeshua raised a widow's son from the dead. The name means "pleasant." Lk 7:11.

Nak·di·**mon** (Nicodemus)—*Parush*, member of the Sanhedrin and "teacher in Israel." Though the name Nicodemus is Greek, it was hebraized to Nakdimon, and a well-known 1st-century Jerusalemite was named Nakdimon Ben-Gurion (*Ta'anit* 19b, *Genesis Rabbah* 42, etc.) Yn 3:1+.

Na·**khon** (Nachon)

Na·**'o·mi**

Na·so—Parashah 35; Numbers 4:21–7:89

Na·**tan** (Nathan)—son of King David; in Messianic genealogy. Lk 3:31.

Na·tan·**'el** (Nathanael)—*talmid* of Yeshua. Yn 1:45+.

Na·**tze·ret** (Nazareth)—town in the Galil where Yeshua grew up and lived most of his life. Mt 2:23+.

Natz·ra·ti (Nazarene), pl. *Natz·ra·tim*—In regard to Mattityahu, the *Tanakh* nowhere says that the Messiah is to be called a *Natzrati*, but Isaiah 11:1 refers to him as a *netzer* ("branch, shoot"). Since *Natzrati* means "resident of Natzeret," the name *Natzratim* (followers of the man from Natzeret) is given to the Jewish followers of Yeshua. Thus Mattityahu's "fulfillment" apparently involves a word play, although other explanations have been offered. The modern Hebrew word for "Christian" is *Notzri*, a variant of *Natzrati*. Mt 2:23; Ac 24:5.

Na·val (Nabal)
Na·vot (Naboth)
na·zir, n'zi·rim (nazirite, -s)
N'·chum (Nehum)
N'·chush·ta (Nehushta)
N'·chush·tan (Nehushtan)
N'·dav·yah (Nedabiah)
Ne·'ah
Ne·'ar·yah (Neariah)
Ne·che·la·mi (Nehelamite)
Ne·chem·yah (Nehemiah)
Ne·feg (Nepheg)
Nef·to·ach (Nephtoah)
Ne·gev— the south, the southern desert of Isra'el.
Ne·'i·'el
Nei·vai (Nebai)
Ner
Ner·gal
Ner·gal-Sar·'e·tzer (Nergal-sharezer)
Ne·ri—in Messianic genealogy. Lk 3:27.
Ne·ri·yah (Neriah)
Ne·vi·'im—Prophets, the second of the three parts of the *Tanakh* (see glossary entry), including the Early Prophets (the historical books), namely, Joshua, Judges, Samuel and Kings; and the Later Prophets, namely, Isaiah, Jeremiah, Ezekiel, and the Twelve "minor prophets."
N'·fi·lim (Nephilim)
N'·fish'·sim (Nephushesim)
N'·fu·sim (Nephusim)
nid·dah*—(1) menstrual uncleanness, (2) the time of same.
Nim·rah
Nim·rim
Nim·rod
Nim·shi
Nin·veh (Nineveh, Nineve)—capital of ancient Assyria where the prophet Yonah preached. Mt 12:41+.
Ni·san—1st month of the biblical year, 7th month of the modern Jewish year (in March-April)

Nis·rokh (Nisroch)
Ni·tza·vim—Parashah 51; Deuteronomy 29:9(10)–30:20
Niv·chaz (Nibhaz)
Niv·shan (Nibshan)
N'·kho (Necho)
N'·ko·da (Nekoda)
N'·mu·'el (Nemuel)
N'·mu·'e·li (Nemuelite)
No
No·ach (Noah)—builder of the ark, survivor of the Flood and ancestor of all mankind since then (Genesis 5–11); in Messianic genealogy. Mt 24:37+.
No·ach—Parashah 2; Genesis 6:9–11:32
No·'ad·yah (Noadiah)
No·'ah
No·'am
No-A·mon
No·chah (Nohah)
Nod
No·dav (Nodab)
Nof (Noph)
No·fach (Nophah)
No·gah
Nov (Nob)
No·vach (Nobah)
N'·ta·'im (Netaim)
N'·tan·'el (Nethaneel)
N'·tan-Me·lekh
N'·tan·yah, ·ya·hu
n'ti·lat-ya·da·yim—ceremonial handwashing prescribed by the Oral *Torah* to be done before meals and at other times in order to be ritually pure; it continues to be a norm in Orthodox Judaism. Mt 15:2+.
N'·ti·nim (Nethinim)—Temple servants
N'·to·fah (Netophah)
N'·to·fa·ti (Netophathite)
N'·tzi·ach (Neziah)
N'·tziv (Nezib)
nu [Y]—a general-purpose word meaning variously, "Well?" "So?" "Indeed!" "I challenge you," or "If not that, then what?"—with many possible inflections and overtones. Mt 11:9+.

nud·nik [Y]—(1) a bore, (2) a pest, (3) both.
Lk 18:5.

Nun—14th letter of Hebrew alphabet

N'·va·**lat** (Neballat)

N'·**vat** (Nebat)

N'·va·**yot** (Nebaioth)

N'·**vo** (Nebo)

N'·vu·khad·ne·**tzar** (Nebuchadnezzar)

N'·vu·khad·re·**tzar** (Nebuchadrezzar)

N'·vu·shaz·**ban** (Nebushasban)

N'·vu·zar·'a·**dan** (Nebuzaradan)

n'zi·rim (nazirites)

'O·**ded**

'**O**·fel (Ophel)

O·**fir** (Ophir)

'Of·**ni** (Ophni)

'Of·**rah** (Ophrah)

'**Og**

O·**had**

O·hel

O·ho·**lah** (Oholah)

O·ho·li·'**av** (Oholiab)

O·ho·li·**vah** (Oholibah)

O·ho·li·va·**mah** (Oholibamah)

Okh·**ran** (Ochran)

'o·lah—burnt offering, that which goes up

'o·lam ha·ba—the world to come, the age
to come. Mt 12:32+.

'o·lam ha·zeh—this world, this age. Mt
12:32+.

O·**mar**

'o·mer—two-quart dry measure

'Om·**ri**

On

O·**nam**

O·**nan**

O·**no**

O·ren

'O·**rev**

Or·**nan**

'Or·**pah**

Os·**nat**

'Ot·ni·'**el** (Othniel)

O·tzem (Ozem)

'o·tzev—pain

'O·vad·**yah**, -**ya**·hu (Obadiah)

'O·**val** (Obal)

'O·**ved** (Obed)—grandfather of King
David; in Messianic genealogy. Mt
1:5; Lk 3:32.

'O·**ved**-E·**dom** (Obed-edom)

O·**vil** (Obil)

O·**vot** (Oboth)

Oz·**ni**

Pa·'a·**rai**

Pa·chat-Mo·'**av** (Pahath-moab)

Pad·**dan** (Padan)

Pad·**dan**-A·**ram** (Padan-aram)

Pa·**don**

Pag·'i·'**el**

Pa·'**i**

Pa·**lal**

Pal·**lu**

Pal·lu·'**i** (Palluite)

Pal·**ti**

Pal·ti·'**el**

Pa·**rah**

Pa'·**ran**

Pa·**ras** (Persia)

pa·ra·shah—*Torah* "portion" read in the
synagogue on *Shabbat* or on a festival
or fast day.

Par·**mash**·ta

Par·**nakh** (Parnach)

pa·ro·khet—curtain, specifically the one
dividing the Especially Holy Place
from the rest of the temple or tabernacle. There were actually two
such *p'rokhot* (see MJ 9:3). The
first separated the Holy Place from
the outer court (Exodus 26:36–37;
36:37–38), whereas the second
separated the Especially Holy Place
from the Holy Place (Exodus
26:31–33; 36:35–36). The curtain
covering the ark of the *Torah* in a
modern synagogue is also called a
parokhet. Mt 27:51+.

Par·'**osh**

Par·**par** (Pharpar)

Par·shan·**da**·ta (Parshandatha)

Par·**tzi** (Pharzite)

Pa·ru·**ach** (Paruah)

Pa·rush (Pharisee)—*see P'rushim*, below.

Par·va·yim (Parvaim)
pa·sach—he passed over; see *Pesach* glossary entry.
Pa·sakh (Pasach)
Pas-Da·mim (Pas-dammim)
Pa·se·ach (Paseah)
Pash'·chur (Pashur)
Pat·ros (Pathros)
Pat·ru·sim (Pathrusim)
Pa·'u
P'·dah·'el (Pedahel)
P'·dah·tzur (Pedahzur)
P'·da·yah (Pedaiah)
Peh (Pe)—17th letter of Hebrew alphabet
Pe·kach (Pekah)
Pe·leg (Phalec)—ancestor of Avraham; in Messianic genealogy. Lk 3:35.
Pe·let (Pelet, Peleth)
Pe·le-Yo·'etz (wonderful counselor)—wonder of a counselor
Pe·resh
Pe·retz (Perez, Phares)—grandson of the Patriarch Ya'akov; in Messianic genealogy. Mt 1:3.
Pe·retz-'U·za, -zah (Perez-uzza)
Pe·sach (Passover)—the feast which celebrates the Exodus of the Jewish nation from Egypt under the leadership of Moshe. It is, along with *Shavu'ot and Sukkot*, one of the three pilgrim festivals when Jews were to come to Yerushalayim. Mt 26:2+.
Pe·'ul·tai (Peulthai)
Pi-Ha·chi·rot (Pi-hahiroth)
Pi·khol (Pichol)
Pil·cha (Pileha)
Pil·dash
Pil·tai
Pin·chas (Phinehas)
Pin·chas—Parashah 41; Numbers 25:10–30:1(29:40)
Pi·non
Pir·'am
Pir·'a·ton (Pirathon)
Pis·gah
Pi·shon (Pison)
Pis·pah

Pi·tom (Pithom)
Pi·ton (Pithon)
Pi-Ve·set (Pibeseth)
P'·kach·yah (Pekahiah)
P'·kod (Pekod)
P'·ku·dei—Parashah 23; Exodus 38:21–40:38
P'·lal·yah (Pelaliah)
P'·lat·yah, -ya·hu (Pelatiah)
P'·la·yah (Pelaiah)
P'·le·shet (Palestina, Palestine)
P'·lish·ti, -tim (Philistines)
P'lo·ni (Pelonite)
P'nei-Ha·chi·rot (Pi-hahiroth)
P'ni-El (Peniel)
P'ni·nah (Peninnah)
P'nu·el (Phanuel)—father of Hannah, the aged widow who blessed Yeshua in the Temple. Lk 2:36.
Po·khe·ret-Ha·tzva·yim (Pochereth-hazzebaim)
P·'or (Peor)
Po·ra·ta (Poratha)
Po·ti-Fe·ra (Potipherah)
Po·ti·far (Potiphar)
P'·res (Peres)
P'ri·da (Perida)
P'ru·da (Peruda)
P'ru·shim (Pharisees), sing. *Parush*—The *P'rushim* and *Tz'dukim* were the two main components of the religious establishment in Yeshua's time. The *P'rushim* focussed on the *Torah* and what it requires of ordinary people, rather than on the temple ritual. When the temple was destroyed in 70 C.E., the *P'rushim* were in a position to develop their tradition into the basis for Jewish life everywhere; this tradition is the core of the *Talmud* and of modern religious Judaism. Mt 3:7+.
P'tach·yah (Petahiah)
P'·tor (Pethor)
P'tu·'el (Pethuel)
Pu·'ah (Puah)
Pu·'ah (Puah)

Pul

Pu·ni (Punite)

Pu·non

Pu·rah

pur—lot

Pu·rim—festival decreed by Mordekhai in the book of Ester to celebrate the victory of the Jews of Shushan over Haman's evil plot.

Pu·ti (Puthites)

Pu·ti·'el

Pu·vah (Pua)

Ra·'am·ses

Ra·'am·yah (Raamiah)

Rab·bah

Rab·ba·ni—literally, "my great one," hence, "teacher." In the *Mishna* the title *Rabban* is given to Gamli'el (see glossary entry). Yn 20:16.

rab·bi—literally, "my great one," hence, a teacher. In modern Judaism a rabbi is someone ordained to determine *halakhah* (Jewish law), to judge, and to teach *Torah*. Still more recently, the term "rabbi" has come to mean a Jewish clergyman, i.e., a leader with congregational or community responsibilities. Mt 8:19+.

Ra·bit (Rabbith)

Ra·cham (Raham)

Ra·chav (Rahab, Rachab)—the prostitute in Yericho who hid the Israelite spies in the days of Y'hoshua; in Messianic genealogy (Joshua 2; 6). Mt 1:5+.

Ra·chel—wife of the Patriarch Ya'akov, one of the four Mothers of Israel. Mt 2:18.

Ra·dai (Raddai)

Ra·fa (Rapha)

Ra·fah (Raphah)

Ra·fu (Raphu)

Ra·hav (Rahab)

Ra·kat (Rakkath)

Ra·khal (Rachal)

Ra·kon (Rakkon)

Ram (Aram)—ancestor of King David; in Messianic genealogy. Mt 1:3–4.

Ra·'·ma

Ra·mah—town in the vicinity of Yerushalayim, in the tribal portion allotted to Binyamin. Mt 2:18.

Ra·'·mah

Ra·'·mat (Ramath)

Ra·ma·ta·yim (Arimathea, Arimathaea)— town in the foothills (*sh'felah*) northeast of Lud and northwest of Yerushalayim. Home of Yosef #9, who took Yeshua's body and had it buried in his own tomb. Mt 27:57+.

Ra·ma·ta·yim-Tzo·fim (Ramathaim-zophim)

Ra·ma·ti (Ramathite)

Ra·mat-Le·chi (Ramath-lehi)

Ra·mot (Ramoth)

Ra·mot-Gil·'ad (Ramoth-gilead)

Ra·mot-Mitz·peh (Ramoth-mizpeh)

Ram'·ses (Rameses)

Ram·yah (Ramiah)

Rav-Mag (Rab-mag)

Rav-Sa·ris (Rab-saris)

Rav-Sha·keh (Rab-shakeh)

Re·'a·yah (Reaiah)

Re·chav·'am (Rehoboam, Roboam)— son of King Shlomo; in Messianic genealogy. Mt 1:7.

Re·chav·yah, ·ya·hu (Rehabiah)

Re·chov (Rehob)

Re·cho·vot (Rehoboth)

Re·chum (Rehum)

Re·'eh—Parashah 47; Deuteronomy 11:26–16:17

Re·fach (Rephah)

Re·fa·'el (Rephael)

Re·fa·'im (Rephaim)

Re·fa·yah (Rephaiah)

Re·fi·dim (Rephidim)

Re·gem

Re·gem-Me·lekh (Regem-melech)

Re·'i

Rei·fan (Rephan, Remphan)—Babylonian god called Keivan in the *Tanakh* and corresponding to Saturn. Ac 7:43.

Rei·sha (Rhesa)—son of Z'rubavel; in Messianic genealogy. Lk 3:27.

Re·kem

Re·**khah** (Rechah)
Re·**khav** (Rechab)
Re·kha·**vim** (Rechabites)
Re·mal·**yah**, -**ya**·hu
Re·met (Remeth)
Re·sen
Resh—20th letter of Hebrew alphabet
Re·shef (Resheph)
Re·tzef (Rezeph)
Re·**tzin** (Rezin)
Re·**'u** (Reu, Ragau)—ancestor of Avraham; in Messianic genealogy. Lk 3:35.
Re·'u·**'el**
Re·'u·**mah**
Re·'u·**ven** (Reuben)—tribe of Israel named after the first son of the Patriarch Ya'akov. Rv 7:5.
Re·'u·ve·**ni** (Reubenite)
Re·va (Reba)
Re·**zon** (Rezon)
Ri·**fat** (Riphath)
Rim·**mon**
Rim·**mon**-Pe·retz (Rimmon-perez)
Ri·**nah** (Rinnah)
Ris·**sah**
Rit·**mah** (Rithmah)
Ritz·**pah** (Rizpah)
Ritz·**ya** (Rizia)
Ri·**vai** (Ribai)
Riv·**kah** (Rebecca)—wife of the Patriarch Yitz'chak, one of the four Mothers of Israel. Ro 9:10.
Riv·**lah** (Riblah)
Ro·da·**nim**
Rog·**lim** (Rogelim)
Ro·mam·ti-**'E**·zer
Rosh
Rosh-Ho·desh—the festival, observed to this day in Judaism, celebrating the beginning of each Jewish lunar month. Co 2:16.
Ru·ach Ha·Ko·desh—the Holy Spirit, referred to four times in the *Tanakh* as such, and many times as the Spirit of God. Mt 1:18+.
Ru·cha·**mah** (Ruhamah)
Ru·**mah**

Rut (Ruth)—Moabite woman who joined the Jewish people, became the wife of Bo'az and was the great-grandmother of King David; in Messianic genealogy. Mt 1:5.
Saf (Saph)
Sa·**khar** (Sacar)
Sa·**lai** (Sallai)
Sal·**khah** (Salchah)
Sal·**ma**
Sal·**mai**
Sal·**mon**—ancestor of King David; in Messianic genealogy. Mt 1:4–5; Lk 3:32.
Sa·**lu**
Sa·mekh—15th letter of Hebrew alphabet
Sam·**gar**-N'·vo (Samgar-nebo)
Sam·**lah**
San·che·**riv** (Sennacherib)
san·hed·rin—Jewish religious court. Lower *sanhedrins* had 3 or 23 judges; the high *Sanhedrin* in Yerushalayim had 70. Mt 5:22+.
San·sa·**nah** (Sansannah)
San·va·**lat** (Sanballat)
Sa·**raf** (Saraph)
Sa·**rah** (Sara)—wife of Avraham, first of the four Mothers of Israel. Ro 4:19+.
Sa·**rai**
Sar·**di** (Sardite)
Sar·**'e**·tzer (Sharezer)
Sar·**gon**
Sa·**rid**
Sar·s'·**khim** (Sarsechim)
Sa·**tan**—literally, "the Adversary," i.e., Satan, the Devil. In the *Tanakh* he is described specifically at Job 1–2 and by implication in Isaiah 14:11–15 and Ezekiel 28. Mt 4:10+.
Sav·**ta** (Sabta)
Sav·t'·**kha** (Sabtechah)
S'**dom** (Sodom, Sodoma)—city near the Dead Sea destroyed by God (Genesis 19). Mt 10:15+.
Se·der—the ceremonial evening meal with which *Pesach* begins in Jewish homes. Mt 26:17+.

se·khel—intelligence, common sense, "smarts." Lk 16:8.

S'·**guv** (Segub)

Se·**'ir**

Se·**'i·rah** (Seirath)

Se·**khu** (Sechu)

Se·la

se·lah—pause in the music accompanying a psalm or prayer

Se·la-Ha·mach·le·**kot** (Sela-hammahlekoth)

Se·led

Se·**neh**

Se·rach (Serah)

Se·red

S'·**far** (Sephar)

S'·fa·**rad** (Sepharad)

S'·far·**va**·yim (Sepharvayim)

S'·far·**vim** (Sepharvite)

Sha·'af (Shaaph)

Sha·'a·la·**bin** (Shaalabbin)

Sha·'al·**bim**

Sha·'a·**lim**

Sha·'al·**vim** (Shaalbim)

Sha·'al·vo·**ni** (Shaalbonite)

Sha·'a·ra·yim (Shaaraim)

Sha·'ash·**gaz**

Shab·bat, pl. *Shab·ba·tot*—Sabbath. Mt 12:1+.

Shab·**tai** (Shabbethai)

Sha·cha·ra·yim (Shaharaim)

Sha·cha·**tzimah** (Shahazimah)

Shad·dai—the Almighty, a name of God

Shad·**rakh** (Shadrach)

Sha·**fam** (Shapham)

Sha·**fan** (Shaphan)

Sha·**fat** (Shaphat)

Sha·**geh** (Shage)

sha·ked—almond tree

Sh'·**al** (Sheal)

Sha·**lem** (Salem, Salim)—(1) Place near Einayim. Yn 3:23. (2) Yerushalayim; see Psalm 76:3(2). MJ 7:1–2.

Sha·li·**shah** (Shalisha)

Shal·le·khet (Shallecheth)

Shal·**man**

Shal·man·**'e**·ser

sha·lom—peace, tranquillity, safety, well-being, welfare, health, contentment, success, comfort, wholeness and integrity. "*Shalom!*" is a common greeting. Mt 10:12+.

Sha·lom a·lei·khem!—"Peace be upon you (plural)!" A common greeting. Mt 10:12+.

Sha·lom rav!—Abundant peace! (a greeting)

Sh'·al·ti·**el** (Shealtiel, Salathiel)—father of Z'rubavel; in Messianic genealogy. Mt 1:12; Lk 3:27.

Sha·**lum** (Shallum)

Sha·**lun** (Shallun)

sham—there

Sha·**ma** (Shamma)

Sha·mah (there)

Sha·**mai** (Shammai)

Sham·**gar**

Sham·**hut** (Shamhuth)

Sha·**mir**

Sham·**mah**

sham·mash, pl. *sham·ma·shim*—attendant, servant, caretaker, deacon. Lk 4:20+.

Sham·sh'·**rai** (Shamsherai)

Sha·mu·a (Shammua)

Shap·pi·**rah** (Sapphira)—person who conspired to lie to the Holy Spirit. Ac 5:1+.

Sha·**rai**

Sha·**rar**

sha·rav—hot dry wind which blows over the Land of Israel from the deserts to the east in the spring and fall. In modern Israel it is also known by its Arabic name, *hamsin* ("fifty"), which refers to the fifty days between *Pesach* and *Shavu'ot*, the most common season for such weather. Ya 1:11.

Shar·**'e**·tzer (Sharezer)

Sh'·a·**rim** (Shaarim)

Sha·**ron**, the—one of the four major geographical regions of Israel, namely, the low-lying plain near the Mediterranean Sea. The other three, which also parallel the coast, are, from west to east, the Sh'felah (foothills), the hill country of

Y'hudah and Shomron, and the Yarden Valley-Dead Sea rift. Ac 9:35.

Sha·ru·chen (Sharuhen)

Sh·'ar·yah (Sheariah

Sh·'ar Ya·shuv (Shear-jashub)

Sha·shai

Sha·shak

Sha·'ul (Saul)—"also known as Paul" (Ac 13:9). Yeshua the Messiah's emissary to the Gentile world, who presented Israel's New Covenant faith in God and his Messiah in a way that does not require Gentiles to convert to Judaism. Ac 7:58+ Named for Sha·'ul Ben-Kish (Saul the son of Kish), Israel's first king. Ac 13:21.

Sha·'u·li (Shaulite)

Sha·veh

Sha·veh-Kir·ya·ta·yim (Shaveh-kiriathaim)

Shav·sha

Sha·vu·'ot—the Feast of Weeks, since it comes seven weeks after Passover; also called Pentecost (from Greek *pentekostos*, "fifty"), since one counts 50 days after Passover. One of the three *regalim* ("pilgrim festivals") when Jews were expected to celebrate before God in Yerushalayim; the other two are *Pesach* and *Sukkot*. Ac 2:1+.

Sh'·char·yah (Shehariah)

Sh'·de·'ur (Shedeur)

She·'e·rah

Shee·tim (Shittim)

sh·'ei·lah, pl. *sh·'ei·lot*—question. In Judaism *"sh'eilah"* can be a technical term meaning a question about *halakhah* (Jewish law) or some other aspect of the Bible or Jewish tradition. Mt 22:23+.

she·kel—a weight, variously from three to six tenths of an ounce. In Yeshua's day the half-*shekel* was rarely coined, so that two people could pay the Temple tax (see Exodus 30:11ff.) with a silver *shekel* coin. Mt 17:24.

She·lach (Shelah)

She·lah (Sala)—ancestor of Avraham; in Messianic genealogy. Lk 3:35.

She·la·ni (Shelanite)

She·lef (Sheleph)

She·lem·yah, -ya·hu (Shelemiah)

She·lesh

Shem (Sem)—son of Noach; in Messianic genealogy. Lk 3:36.

She·ma

She·med

She·mer

Shem·'e·ver (Shemeber)

Shen

Shen·'a·tzar (Shenazar)

She·resh

She·rev·yah (Sherebiah)

She·shai

She·shakh (Sheshach)

She·shan

Shesh·ba·tzar (Sheshbazzar)

Shet (Seth)—son of Adam; in Messianic genealogy. Lk 3:38.

She·tar (Shethar)

She·va (Sheba)

She·ver (Sheber)

Shev·na (Shebna)

Shev·nah (Shebnah)

Sh'·fam (Shepham)

Sh'fat·yah, -ya·hu (Shephatiah)

Sh'fe·lah—foothill region of *Eretz-Yisra'el*; see Sharon glossary entry.

Sh'·fi (Shephi)

Sh'·fo (Shepho)

Sh'fu·fam (Shephupham)

Sh'fu·fan (Shephuphan)

Shib·bo·let (Shibboleth)

Shi·chor (Shihor)

Shi·chor-Liv·nat (Shihor-libnath)

Shif·'i (Shiphi)

Shif·mi (Shiphmi)

Shif·rah (Shiphrah)

Shif·tan (Shiphtan)

shig·ga·yon, pl. *shig·yo·no*—(1) a meditative poem, (2) a musical instrument

Shikh·mi (Shechemites)

Shik·ron (Shicron)

Shil·chi (Shilhi)

Shil·**chim** (Shilhim)
Shil·**lem** (Shillem)
Shil·le·**mi** (Shillemite)
Shi·lo·ach (Siloam)—(1) A tower. Lk 13:4.
(2) A pool near the city walls of
Yerushalayim. The word *shiloach* means
"aqueduct" (from the root *sh-l-ch*,
"send"); the aqueduct, dug when
Hizkiyahu was king of Y'hudah in the
eighth century B.C.E., sent water from the
Gichon Spring to the pool at Shiloach.
One can still walk through a tunnel which
formed part of the aqueduct. Yn 9:7ff.
Shi·**loh**—to whom it belongs; also a
place-name.
Shi·lo·**ni** (Shilonite)
Shil·**shah**
Shim·**'a** (Shimea)
Shim·**'ah** (Shimeah)
Shim·**'ah** (Shimeah)
Shim·**'am** (Shimeam)
Shim·**'at** (Shimeath)
Shim·'a·**tim** (Shimeathites)
Shim·**'i** (Shimei, Semein)—in Messianic
genealogy. Lk 3:26.
Shi·**mon**
Shim·**'on** (Simon, Simeon)—(1) Tribe of
Israel descended from the second son
of Ya'akov. Rv 7:7. (2) Old man who
blessed Yeshua in the Temple. Lk
2:25ff. (3) Ancestor of Yeshua the
Messiah. Lk 3:30. (4) Shim'on Bar-
Yochanan (Simon, son of John; Simon
Barjona)—Shim'on Kefa (see below).
(5) Another of Yeshua's *talmidim*,
known as Shim'on the Zealot, i.e., a
member of the party set on revolt
against the Roman conquerors. Mt
10:4+. (6) Brother of Yeshua. Mt
13:55; Mk 6:3. (7) Person in Beit-
Anyah who had had a skin disease. Mt
26:6+. (8) Cyrenian compelled to carry
Yeshua's execution-stake. Mt 27:32+.
(9) *Parush* in whose house Yeshua ate.
Lk 7:40ff. (10) Father of Y'hudah from
K'riot. Yn 6:71+. (11) Sorcerer in
Shomron. Ac 8:9ff. (12) Tanner in Yafo

with whom Kefa lodged. Ac 9:43+.
(13) Follower of Yeshua and prophet
in Antioch, called "the Black." Ac 13:1.
Shim·**'o·ni** (Simeonites)
Shim·**'on Ke·fa** (Simon Peter)—one of
the twelve emissaries of Yeshua
(see Kefa). Mt 4:18+.
Shim·**rat** (Shimrath)
Shim·**ri**
Shim·**rit** (Shimrith)
Shim·**ron**
Shim·**ron-M'·ron** (Shimron-meron)
Shim·ro·**ni** (Shimronite)
Shim·**shai**
Shim·**shon** (Samson)—a judge of Israel
(Judges 13–16). MJ 11:32.
Shin—21st letter of Hebrew alphabet
Shin·**'ar**
Shin·**'av** (Shinab)
Shir·**tai** (Shitrai)
Shi·**sha**
Shi·**shak**
Shiv·**'ah** (Shibah)
shiv·'ah*—literally, "seven." After the
burial of a father, mother, brother, sis-
ter, son, daughter or spouse a Jewish
mourner remains at home for seven
days; this custom is called "sitting
shiv'ah." Yn 11:20.
Shi·**za**
Sh'·khan·**yah**, **-ya·hu** (Shechaniah)
Sh·**'khem** (Shechem, Sychem, Sychar)—
city in the mountains of Shomron, on
the southeast edge of modern Nablus
(Neapolis). Yn 4:5+.
Sh'khi·nah—Divine Presence, the mani-
fest glory of God present with men.
Lk 2:9+.
Shlach L'·kha—Parashah 37; Numbers
13:1–15:41
Shlo·**mi** (Shelomi)
Shlo·**mit** (Shelomith, Salome)—
talmidah of Yeshua. Mk 15:40+.
Shlo·mo* (Solomon)—king of Israel; in
Messianic genealogy. Mt 1:6+.
Shlo·**mot** (Shelomoth)
Shlu·mi·**'el** (Shelumiel)

Sh'ma Yis·ra·'el, A·do·nai E·lo·hei·nu, A·do·nai e·chad—"Hear, O Isra'el, the LORD *(Yud-Heh-Vav-Heh)* your God, the LORD is one" (Deuteronomy 6:4), the central affirmation of Judaism both then and now. Together with the next verse of Deuteronomy, which enjoins loving God with everything one is and has, Yeshua called this the most important *mitzvah* in the *Torah*. Mk 12:29.

Sh'ma·mah, —Desolate

Sh'ma'·yah, -ya·hu (Shemariah)

Sh'mi·da (Shemidah)

Sh'·mi·ni—Parashah 26; Leviticus 9:1–11:47

sh'mi·nit—low-pitched music?

sh'mit·tah—release. Debtors are released from their debts every seven years (Deuteronomy 15).

shmoose [Y]—engage in friendly gossipy chit-chat. The word is derived from Hebrew *shmu'ot*, "things heard, rumors." Lk 10:4.

Sh'·mot—Parashah 13; Exodus 1:1–6:1

Sh'mu·'el (Samuel)—prophet in the days of Kings Sha'ul and David. Ac 3:24+.

Sho·a

Sho·fakh (Shophach)

sho·far*—ram's horn; often rendered as "trumpet." Mt 24:31+.

Shof'·tim—Parashah 48; Deuteronomy 16:18–21:9

Sho·ham

sho·ked—watching

Sh'·ol (Sheol, Hades, hell)—the place of the dead, according to the *Tanakh*. Mt 11:23+.

Sho·mer

Shom·ron (Samaria)—region of *Eretz-Yisra'el* in the hill country north of Yerushalayim and south of the Galil. The Samaritans, a mixed ethnic group descended from Jews deported by the Assyrians in the 8th century B.C.E. and other peoples ruled by the Assyrians, followed a religion combining pagan and Jewish elements. According to the book of Nehemiah in the *Tanakh*,

they arrayed themselves against those rebuilding Yerushalayim. By the first century most Jews regarded them as pariahs. Mt 10:5+.

Shom·ro·nim (Samaritans)

Sho·sha·nah (Susanna)—a follower of Yeshua. The name means "lily" or "rose." Lk 8:3.

Sho·vai (Shobai)

Sho·vakh (Shobach)

Sho·val (Shobal)

Sho·vav (Shobab)

Sho·vek (Shobek)

Sho·vi (Shobi)

Shu·a

Shu·ach (Shuah)

Shu·'al

Shu·chah (Shuhah)

Shu·cham (Shuham)

Shu·cha·mi (Shuhamite)

Shu·chi (Shuhite)

Shu·fa·mi (Shuphamite)

girl from **Shu·lam** (Shulammite)

Shu·ma·ti (Shumathite)

Shu·na·mit (Shunammite)

Shu·nem

Shu·ni

Shu·pim (Shuppim)

Shur

Shu·shan

Shu·shan'·ka·yim (Shushanchites)

Shu·tal·chi (Shutalhite)

Shu·te·lach (Shutelah)

Sh'·va (Sheba)

Sh'van·yah, -ya·hu (Shebaniah)

Sh'va·rim (Shebarim)

Sh'·vat (Shebat)— 11th month of the biblical year, 5th month of the modern Jewish year (in January–February).

Si·'a

Si·a'·ha

Sib·bo·let

Sib·khai (Sibbecai)

Sib·mah

Sib·ra·yim (Sibraim)

Si·chon (Sihon)

Sid·dim

Sif·mot (Siphmoth)

Sik·kut

Si·la (Silas)—co-worker with Sha'ul. Ac 15:22+.

Si·nai (Sina)—mountain in the desert between Egypt and *Eretz-Yisra'el* where Israel received the *Torah* from God through Moshe. Ac 7:30+.

Si·ni, -nim (Sinite, -s)

Si·pai (Sippai)

Si·rah

Sir·yon (Sirion)

Sis·mai (Sisamai)

Sis·ra (Sisera)

Sit·nah

Sit·ri (Sithri)

Si·van—3rd month of the biblical year, 9th month of the modern Jewish year (in May–June).

Siv·mah (Sibmah)

S'kha·khah (Secacah)

S'makh·ya·hu (Semachiah)

s'mi·khah—laying on of hands, hence ordination, grant of authority. Mt 21:23+.

S'na·'ah (Senaah)

S'·nir (Senir)

So·di

So·fe·ret (Sopheret)

So·kho, -khoh (Socoh)

Sokh·ya (Shachia)

So·rek

S·'o·rim (Seorim)

So·tai

s'ra·fim (seraphim)—a class of angelic beings, like the *k'ruvim* (see glossary entry)

S'ra·yah, -ya·hu (Seraiah)

S'·rug (Serug, Saruch)—ancestor of Avraham; in Messianic genealogy. Lk 3:35.

S'·tur (Sethur)

Su·ach (Suah)

Suf (Suph)

Su·fah (Suphah)

Su·kha·tim (Suchathites)

Su·ki·'im (Sukiims)

Suk·kot (Succoth)—the feast of Booths (Tabernacles), celebrating the forty years when the people of Israel lived in *suk·kot* (booths, tents, shacks; singular *suk·kah*) in the desert between Egypt and *Eretz-Yisra'el*. It is one of three pilgrim festivals when Jews were expected to go up to Yerushalayim in Y'hudah. Yn 7:2.

Suk·kot-B'·not (Succoth-benoth)

Sur

Su·si

S'·va (Seba)

S'·vam (Sebam)

S'·ve·nah (Seveneh)

Ta·'a·nakh (Taanach)

Ta·'a·nat-Shi·loh (Taanath-shiloh)

Ta·ba·'ot (Tabbaoth)

Ta·bat (Tabbath)

Ta·chan (Tahan)

Ta·cha·ni (Tahanite)

Ta·chash (Tahash)

Ta·chat (Tahat)

Tach'·k'·mo·ni (Tachmonite)

Tach·pan·ches (Tahapanes)

Tach·p'·neis (Tahpenes)

Tach·tim-Hod·shi (Tahtim-hodshi)

Tad·dai (Thaddeus, Thaddaeus)—one of the twelve emissaries of Yeshua. Mt 10:3+.

Tad·mor

Ta·fat (Taphath)

talent [O]—a weight variously between 60 and 100 pounds. A talent of gold would be worth around $300,000 at the current price of $300/ounce. Mt 25:15+.

ta·li·ta, ku·mi! [A]—Little girl, get up! The word *talita*, being the feminine form of the word for "lamb," is therefore an affectionate diminutive (compare English "lambikin"). Mk 5:41.

Tal·mai—Hebrew form of Egyptian *ptolemy*, the name given to Egyptian kings during the centuries before Yeshua. In the New Testament the name is found in the form *Bar-Talmai* (Bartholomew), "son of ptolemy." Mt 10:3+.

tal·**mid**, fem. *tal·mi·dah*, pl. *tal·mi·dim*— disciple, student. The relationship between a *talmid* and his rabbi was very close: not only did the *talmid* learn facts, reasoning processes and how to perform religious practices from his rabbi, but he regarded him as an example to be imitated in conduct and character (see Mt 10:24–25; Lk 6:40; Yn 13:13–15; 1C 11:1). The rabbi, in turn, was considered responsible for his *talmidim* (Mt 12:2; Lk 19:39; Yn 17:12). Mt 5:1+.

Tal·**mon**

Ta·**mar** (Thamar)—mother of Peretz and Zerach; in Messianic genealogy. Mt 1:3.

Tam·**muz**

Ta'·**nakh** (Tanach)

Ta·nakh—acronym formed from the first letters of the three parts of the Hebrew Bible: *Torah*, *Nevi'im* and *K'tuvim* (see glossary entries). Hence, the Old Testament. Rendered "scripture" or "it is written" in most translations of the New Testament. The reason the New Testament writers cite the *Tanakh* so frequently is that they understand it as God's authoritative Word to mankind. Mt 4:4+.

Tan·chu·**met** (Tanhumeth)

Ta·**pu**·ach (Tappuah)

Tar·'a·**lah** (Taralah)

Ta'·**re**·a

Tar·p'·**lim** (Tarpelites)

Tar·**shish**

"Tar·**shish**" ships—ships seaworthy enough to sail to Tarshish, usually identified with Spain

Tar·**shi**·shah (Tarshish)

Tar·**tak**

Tar·**tan**

Tat·**nai**

Tav—last (22nd) letter of Hebrew alphabet

Tav·'**el** (Tabeel)

Tav·'e·**rah** (Taberah)

Ta·vi·**ta** (Tabitha)—woman in Yafo whom Kefa raised from the dead. Ac 9:36.

Ta·**vor** (Tabor)

Tav·rim·**mon** (Tabrimon)

Taz·ri·a—Parashah 27; Leviticus 12:1–13:59

T'chi·**nah** (Tehinnah)

Tei·**ma** (Tema)

Tei·**man** (Teman)

Tei·ma·**ni** (Temanite)

Teim·**ni** (Temeni)

Te·**lach** (Telah)

tel—mound of remains which accumulates under a city over the centuries

Tel·'a·**sar** (Telassar)

Tel-A·**viv** (Tel-abib)

Te·**lem**

Tel-Har·**sha** (Tel-haresha)

Tel-Me·**lach** (Tel-melah)

Te·**mach** (Temah)

Te·**rach** (Terah, Thara)—father of *Avraham avinu*; in Messianic genealogy. Lk 3:34.

Te·**resh**

Tet (Teth)—9th letter of Hebrew alphabet

Te·tza·veh—Parashah 20; Exodus 27:20–30:10

Te·**vach** (Tebah)

Te·**vet** (Tebeth)—4th month of the biblical year, 10th month of the modern Jewish year (in December–January).

Te·**vetz** (Thebez)

*t'·fil·lin** [A]—two black leather boxes containing scrolls with Bible passages on them (Exodus 13:1–16; Deuteronomy 6:4–9; 11:13–21). During synagogue prayers men affix one to their hand and arm and the other to their forehead, in obedience to Deuteronomy 6:8. *T'fillin* are called phylacteries in most translations. To "lay" *t'fillin* is to use them, to put them in place. Mt 23:5.

Tid·'al

Tif·sach (Tiphsah)

Tig·lat-Pil·'e·ser (Tiglath-pileser)

Tik·vah

Til·gat-Pil·n'·e·ser (Tilgath-pilneser)

Ti·lon

Ti·mai (Timaeus)—Hebrew name based on Greek *timê*, "value." Mk 10:46.

Tim·na

Tim·nah

Tim·nat-He·res (Timnath-heres)

Tim·nat-Se·rach (Timnath-serah)

Ti·ras

Tir·'a·tim (Tirathites)

Tir·cha·nah (Tirhanah)

Tir·ha·kah

Tir·sha·ta (Tirshatha)—governor

Tir·tzah (Tirzah)

Tir·ya (Tiria)

Tish·be, from (Tishbite)

Ti·tzi (Tizite)

Tiv·ni (Tibni)

T'·*kel*—see entry at *M'ne.*

T'·ko·a (Tekoa)

T'·la·'im (Telaim)

To·ach (Toah)

To·chu (Tohu)

To·dah (Theudas)—There was a false Messiah with this name who promised to divide the waters of the Yarden River and lead his followers across, c. 44 C.E.; but the Todah of Ac 5:36 was the leader of a rebellion against Rome around 6 C.E.

To·fel (Tophel)

To·fet (Tophet)

To·gar·mah

To·'i

To·k'·hat (Tokhath)

To·khen (Tochen)

To·la

To·lad

To·la·'i (Tolaite)

Tol'dot—Parashah 6; Genesis 25:19–28:9

T'·'o·ma (Thomas) [A]—one of the twelve emissaries of Yeshua. Mt 10:3+.

To·rah*—literally, "teaching," but usu-ally translated "Law" because Greek uses *nomos* ("law") to render Hebrew *Torah.* (1) The Five Books of Moses, the Pentateuch (Genesis, Exodus, Leviticus, Numbers, Deuteronomy), called the Written *Torah.* Mt 5:17. (2) That plus the *Nevi'im* (Prophets) and *K'tuvim* (Writings), i.e., the whole *Tanakh.* Yn 10:34. (3) That plus additional material (the Oral *Torah*) considered in varying degree authoritative in Judaism, Ga 5:3. (4) Uncapitalized, *Torah* can be understood generically as "law" or "principle." Ro 7:21ff.

To·rah*-teacher—this term translates Hebrew *sofer* (pl. *sofrim*), corresponding to Greek *grammateus*, and usually rendered "scribe." The first-century scribes were apparently non-ordained teachers of *Torah.* Mt 2:4+.

Tor·mah

To·'u

Tov (Tob)

Tov-A·do·ni·yah (Tob-adonijah)

To·vi·yah (Tobiah)

treif—literally "torn." Since meat torn by wild animals is forbidden under the Jewish dietary laws, *treif* means, by extension, "non-kosher" ("not fit" to be eaten by Jews). Ac 10:14+.

T'ru·mah—Parashah 19; Exodus 25:1–27:19

t'shu·vah—literally, "turning." In the context of behavior it means repentance, since the sinner who "does *t'shuvah*" is turning from sin to God. Mt 13:15+.

tsu·ris [Y]—troubles (from Hebrew *tzarot*). Mt 6:34+.

tu·mim (thummim)—together with the *urim*, the means used by the *cohanim* to determine God's will in certain situations.

Tu·val (Tubal)

Tu·val-Ka·yin (Tubal-cain)

Tu·vi·ya·hu (Tobijah)

T'·val·ya·hu (Tebaliah)

Tza·'a·nan (Zaanan)

Tza·'a·na·**nim** (Zaanannim)
tzad·dik, pl. *tzad·di·kim*—righteous person. At Ac 7:52 and elsewhere "the *Tzaddik*" with the definite article, means the Messiah. Mt 10:41+.
Tza·deh (Tsadhe)—18th letter of Hebrew alphabet
Tza·**dok** (Zadok, Sadoc)—in Messianic genealogy (see also below; *Tz'dukim*). Mt 1:14.
Tzaf·**nat**-Pa'·**ne**·ach (Zaphenath-Paneah)
Tza·**fon** (Zaphon)
Tza·**'ir** (Zair)
Tza·**laf** (Zalaph)
Tzal·**mon** (Zalmon)
Tzal·mo·**nah** (Zalmonah)
Tzal·mu·**na** (Zalmunna)
tza·ra·'at (leprosy)—a contagious disease and source of ritual uncleanness evidenced by skin lesions; dealt with in Leviticus 13–14. Generally believed not to be Hansen's Disease, which is the modern meaning of "leprosy."
Tzar·**fat** (Zarephath, Sarepta)—town near Tzidon. Lk 4:26.
Tzar·**tan** (Zartan)
Tzav—Parashah 25; Leviticus 6:1(8)–8:36
tzav la·tzav—precept by precept
Tz'·**dad** (Zedad)
Tz'du·kim (Sadducees), sing. *Tza·dok*—One of the two main components of the religious establishment in Yeshua's time, the other being the *P'rushim*. The *Tz'dukim* tended to be richer, more skeptical, more worldly, and more willing to cooperate with the Roman conquerors than the *P'rushim*. The *Tz'dukim* emphasized Temple rituals; when it was destroyed (70 C.E.), so was their viability. Mt 3:7+.
tze·da·kah—literally, "righteousness," but since ancient times also used to mean "charity." Mt 6:1+.
Tze·dek·**yah** (Zedekiah)
Tze·**fi** (Zephi)
Tze·**fo** (Zepho)
Tze·**la** (Zelah)

Tze·**lek** (Zelek)
Tzel·**tzah** (Zelzah)
Tze·mach—Branch or Shoot (a name of the Messiah). Isaiah 11:1, Jeremiah 23:5.
Tzer (Zer)
Tze·**ret** (Zereth)
Tze·ret-**Sha**·char (Zereth-shahar)
Tze·**ri** (Zeri)
Tz'·fan·**yah**, -**ya**·hu (Zephaniah)
Tz'·**fat** (Zephat)
Tz'·**fon** (Zephon)
Tz'·fo·**ni** (Zephonite)
Tzi·**cha** (Ziha)
Tzi·**dim** (Ziddim)
Tzid·ki·**yah**, -**ya**·hu (Zedekiah)
Tzi·**don** (Sidon)—town on the coast north of Tzor, in what is today Lebanon. Mt 11:21+.
Tzi·do·**ni**, -**nim** (Sidonians)
Tzif·**yon** (Ziphion)
Tzi·**lah** (Zillah)
Tzil·**tai** (Zilthai)
Tzin (Zin)
Tzi·**'or** (Zior)
Tzip·**por** (Zippor)
Tzip·po·**rah*** (Zipporah)
Tzitz (Ziz)
tzi·tzit, pl. *tzi·tzi·yot*—specially made fringes worn on the four corners of a man's *tallit*, fulfilling the *mitzvah* in Numbers 15:37–41. In ancient times, including the first century, the *tallit* was a cloak or robe included in normal male attire. After clothes stopped being made with "corners," Judaism created the modern *tallit* (prayer shawl) so that the *mitzvah* could be performed. Mt 9:20+.
Tzi·**va** (Ziba)
Tziv·**'on** (Zibeon)
Tziv·**ya** (Zibia)
Tziv·**yah** (Zibiah)
Tzi·**yon** (Zion, Sion)—Mount Tziyon was originally the City of David, south of the modern Old City of Yerushalayim. Later the name Tziyon

came to refer metaphorically to the Temple Mount, Yerushalayim, the people of Yerushalayim, or the people of Israel. (The hill now called Mount Tziyon was given its name in the fourth century C.E.) Mt 21:5+.

Tz'lo·f'·**chad** (Zelophehad)

Tz'ma·**ra**·yim (Zemaraim)

Tz'ma·**ri** (Zemarite)

Tz'·**nan** (Zenan)

Tzo·**'an** (Zoan)

Tzo·**'ar** (Zoar)

Tzo·char (Zohar)

Tzo·**fai** (Zophai)

Tzo·**far** (Zophar)

Tzo·**fim** (Zophim)

Tzor (Tyre)—town on the Mediterranean coast of what is now southern Lebanon. Mt 11:21+.

Tzor·**'ah** (Zorah)

Tzor·**'a·ti** (Zorathite)

Tzor·**'i** (Zorite)

Tzo·**vah** (Zobah)

Tzo·ve·**vah** (Zobebah)

Tz're·**dah** (Zereda)

Tz're·**rah** (Zererath)

Tz'·**ror** (Zeror)

Tz'ru·**'ah** (Zeruah)

Tz'ru·**yah** (Zeruiah)

Tzu·**'ar** (Zuar)

Tzuf (Zuph)

Tzur (Zur)

Tzu·ri·**'el** (Zuriel)

Tzu·ri·shad·**dai** (Zurishaddai)

Tzva·**'ot**—armies, hosts

Tz'vo·**yim** (Zeboiim)

U·**'el**

U·**faz** (Uphaz)

U·**khal** (Ucal)

'U·**la** (Ulla)

U·**lai**

U·**lam** (Ullam)

'U·**mah** (Ummah)

U·**ni** (Unni)

'U·**ni** (Unni)

Ur

U·ri*

U·ri·**'el**

u·**rim**—together with the *tumim*, the means used by the *cohanim* to determine God's will in certain situations.

U·ri·**yah**, -**ya**·hu, (Uriah, Urias)—husband of *Bat*-Sheva (Bathsheba) the mother of King Shlomo. Mt 1:6.

Ur-Kas·**dim** (Ur of the Chaldees)

'U·**za** (Uzza)

'U·**zah** (Uzzah)

U·**zai**

U·**zal**

U·zen-She·**'e·rah** (Uzzen-sherah)

'U·zi* (Uzzi)

'U·zi·**'el** (Uzziel)

'U·zi·**'e·**li (Uzzielite)

'U·zi·**yah**, -**ya**·hu (Uzziah, Ozias)—king of Y'hudah; in Messianic genealogy. Mt 1:8–9.

Va·di [Arabic *wadi*]—valley or ravine with stream that usually dries up in summer.

Va'·et·cha·nan—Parashah 45; Deuteronomy 3:23–7:11

Va·**hev** (Vaheb)

Vai·za·ta (Vajezatha)

Van·**yah** (Vaniah)

Vash·**ni**

Vash·ti*

Vav—6th letter of Hebrew alphabet

Va·yak'·hel—Parashah 22; Exodus 35:1–38:20

Va·ye·chi—Parashah 12; Genesis 47:28–50:26

Va·ye·lekh—Parashah 52; Deuteronomy 31:1–30

Va·ye·ra—Parashah 4; Genesis 18:1–22:24

Va·ye·shev—Parashah 9; Genesis 37:1–40:23

Va·ye·tze—Parashah 7; Genesis 28:10–32:3(2)

Va·yi·gash—Parashah 11; Genesis 44:18–47:27

Va·yik·ra—Parashah 24; Leviticus 1:1–5:26(6:7)

Va·yish·lach—Parashah 8; Genesis 32:4–36:43

V'·zot Ha-Bra·chah—Parashah 54; Deuteronomy 33:1–34:12

V'·dan (Vedan)

V'·e·ra—Parashah 14; Exodus 6:2–9:35

Vof·si (Vophsi)
Ya·'a·kan (Jaakan)
Ya·'a·kov (Jacob, James)—The English
name "James" comes from Hebrew
Ya'akov through Greek *Iakôbos* and
Late Latin *Jacomus.* (1) *Ya'akov
avinu* (Jacob, our father), i.e., the
Patriarch Jacob. Mt 1:2+. (2) His
descendants, the House of Ya'akov,
meaning the Jewish people. Lk 1:33;
Ro 11:26. (3) The father of Yosef #3.
Mt 1:15–16. (4) A *talmid* of Yeshua
called Ya'akov Ben-Zavdai (James,
son of Zebedee), brother of Yochanan
#2. Mt 4:21+. (5) A *talmid* of Yeshua
called Ya'akov Ben-Halfai (James,
son of Alpheus). Mt 10:3+. (6) A
brother of Yeshua the Messiah who
became leader of the Messianic com-
munity in Yerushalayim and is under-
stood to be the author of the book of
Ya'akov. Mt 13:55+. (7) A son of Miryam
#4, called "the younger Ya'akov." Mt
27:56; Mk 15:40. (8) Father of Yeshua's
talmid Y'hudah ben-Ya'akov (Judas,
son of James). Lk 6:16+.
Ya·'a·ko·vah (Jaakobah)
Ya·'a·lah (Jaalah)
Ya·'a·rei-Or·gim (Jaare-oregim)
Ya·'a· resh·yah (Jaareshiah)
Ya·'a·sai (Jaasu)
Ya·'a·si·'el (Jaasiel)
Ya·'a·zan·yah, -ya·hu (Jaazaniah)
Ya·'a·zi·'el (Jaaziel)
Ya·'a·zi·ya·hu (Jaaziah)
Ya'·betz (Jabez)
Ya·bok (Jabbok)
Ya·chat (Jahath)
Ya·chatz (Jahaz)
Ya·cha·zi·'el (Jahaziah)
Yach·di·'el (Jahdiel)
Yach·do (Jahdo)
Yach·le·'el (Jahleel)
Yach·le·'e·li (Jahleelite)
Yach·mai (Jahmai)
Yach·tzah (Jahzah)
Yach·tze·'el (Jahzeel)

Yach·tze·'e·li (Jahzeelite)
Yach·tzi·'el (Jahziel)
Yach·ze·rah (Jahzerah)
Yach·zi·'el (Jahaziel)
Yach·z'·yah (Jahzeiah)
Ya·da (Jada)
Ya·dai (Iddo)
Ya·don (Jadon)
Ya·du·a (Jaddua)
Ya·'el (Jael)
Ya·fi·a (Japhia)
Yaf·let (Japhlet)
Yaf·le·ti (Japhleti)
Ya·fo* (Jaffa, Joppa, Japho)—port city on the
Mediterranean Sea adjoining modern
Tel Aviv to the south. Ac 9:35+.
Ya·gur (Jagur)
Yah (Jah)—a name of God.
Ya·hatz (Jahaz)
Yah·dai (Jahdai)
Ya·'ir (Jairus)—synagogue president
whose daughter Yeshua raised from
the dead. The name means, "He will
enlighten." Mk 5:22; Lk 8:41.
Ya·'i·ri (Jairite)
Ya·'·kan (Jakan)
Ya·keh (Jakeh)
Ya·khin (Achim)—in Messianic geneal-
ogy. Mt 1:14.
Ya·khi·ni (Jachinites)
Ya·kim (Jakim)
Ya'·lah (Jalah)
Ya'·lam (Jalam)
Ya·lon (Jalon)
Ya·min (Jamin)
Ya·mi·ni (Jaminites)
Yam·lekh (Jamlech)
Yan·nai (Janai, Janna)—in Messianic
genealogy. Mt 1:14.
Ya·no·ach (Janoah)
Ya·no·chah (Janohah)
Ya·num (Janum)
Ya'·ra (Jarah)
Yar·cha (Jarja)
Yar·den (Jordan)—river flowing from
Mount Hermon in the north to Lake
Kinneret and in to the Dead Sea. Mt 3:5+.

Ya·riv (Jarib)
Yar·kon Springs (Me-jarkon)
Yar·mut (Jarmuth)
Ya·ro·ach (Jaroah)
Ya·rov·'am (Jeroboam)
Ya·shar (Jashar)
Ya·shen (Jashen)
Ya·shov·'am (Jashobeam)
Ya·shuv (Jashub)
Ya·shu·vi (Jashubite)
Ya·shu·vi-**Le·**chem (Jashubi-lehem)
Ya·tir (Jattir)
Yat·ni·'el (Jathniel)
Ya·val (Jabal)
Ya·van (Javan
Ya·vesh (Jabesh)
Ya·vesh-Gil·'ad (Jabesh-gilead)
Ya·vin (Jabin)
Yav·neh (Jabneh)
Yav·ne·'el (Jabneel)
Ya'·zer (Jazer)
Ya·ziz (Jaziz)
Y'·chiz·ki·**yah**, -**ya·**hu (Hezekiah)
Y'·da·**yah** (Jedaiah)
Y'·da'·**yah** (Jedaiah)
Y'·di·a·**'el** (Jediael)
Y'·di·**dah** (Jedidah)
Y'·did·**yah** (Jedidiah)
Y'·du·**tun** (Jeduthun)
Ye·'a·**trai** (Jeatherai)
Yech·d'·yah, -**ya·**hu (Jehdeiah)
Ye·chez·**k'el** (Ezekiel)
Ye·chi·**'el** (Jehiel)
Ye·chi·'e·**li** (Jehieli)
Ye·chi·**yah** (Jehiah)
Ye'·do (Iddo)
Ye·fet (Japheth)
Ye·hal·lel·**'el** (Jehaleleel)
Ye·hu (Jehu)
Ye·'i·'el (Jeiel)
Ye·rach (Jerah)
Ye·rach·me·**'el** (Jerahmeel)
Ye·rach·me·'e·**li** (Jerahmeelite)
Ye·red (Jared)—ancestor of Noach; in
　　Messianic genealogy. Lk 3:37.
Ye·re·**mai** (Jermai)
Ye·re·**mot** (Jeremoth)

Ye·ri·cho (Jericho)—one of the world's
　　oldest cities (one tower dates from
　　7,000 B.C.E.), located in the Yarden
　　River Valley east of Yerushalayim. Mt
　　20:29+.
Ye·ri·'el (Jeriel)
Ye·ri·mot (Jerimoth)
Ye·ri·'ot (Jerioth)
Ye·ri·vai (Jeribai)
Ye·ri·yah, -**ya·**hu (Jerijah)
Ye·ro·cham (Jeroham)
Ye·ru·ba·'al (Jerubbaal)
Ye·ru·be·shet (Jerubbesheth)
Ye·ru·'el (Jeruel)
Ye·ru·sha (Jerusha)
Ye·ru·shah (Jerushah)
Ye·ru·sha·la·yim (Jerusalem)—capital of
　　Eretz-Yisra'el since the days of King
　　David. Psalm 48 calls it "the city of
　　our God, . . . beautiful for situation,
　　the joy of the whole earth." Mt 2:1+.
Ye·sha'·yah, -**ya·**hu (Isaiah, Esaias)—
　　Tanakh prophet. Mt 3:3+.
Ye·sher (Jesher)
Ye·shev·**'av** (Jeshebeab)
Ye·shi·mon (Jeshimon)
Ye·shi·shai (Jeshishai)
ye·shi·vah—Jewish religious school.
　　Ac 19:9.
Ye·shu·a (Jesus)—Variant of "Y'hoshua"
　　(Joshua; see below). In the *Tanakh*
　　nine persons and a city have the name
　　Yeshua, usually transliterated as
　　"Jeshua" or "Jeshuah." In the Septuagint
　　and the New Testament the name was
　　brought over into Greek as *Iêsous* and
　　thence into English as "Jesus." It means
　　"*Y-H-V-H* saves" (Mt 1:21) and is
　　also the masculine form of *yeshu'ah*
　　("salvation"). (1) The Messiah of Israel,
　　Yeshua from Natzeret. In modern
　　Hebrew Yeshua's name is pronounced
　　and written "*Yeshu*," which may have
　　been the ancient pronunciation in the
　　Galil. However, reflecting two thou-
　　sand years of conflict between the
　　Church and the Synagogue, it is also

an acronym for *Yimach sh'mo v'zikhrono* ("May his name and memory be blotted out"). However, the late Yosef Vaktor, a Messianic Jewish Holocaust survivor, took it as an acronym for *Yigdal sh'mo umalkhuto* ("May his name and kingdom grow"). Mt 1:1+. (2) A Messianic Jew in Rome, "Yeshua, the one called Justus." Co 4:11.

ye·shu·'ah—salvation; used in a word play on Yeshua's name at Lk 2:30.

Ye·shu·run (Jeshurun)—The upright one.

Ye·ter (Jether)

Ye·tzer (Jezer)

Ye·'u·'el (Jeuel)

Ye·'ush (Jeush)

Ye·'utz (Jeuz)

Y'·fu·neh (Jephunneh)

Y'·gar-Sa·ha·du·ta [A] (Jegar-sahadutha)

Y'ho·'a·chaz (Jehoahaz)

Y'ho·'a·dah (Jehoadah)

Y'ho·'a·dan (Jehoaddan)

Y'ho·'ash (Jehoash)

Y'ho·cha·nan (Jehohanan)

Y'ho·na·dav (Jehonadab)

Y'ho·na·tan (Jehonathan)

Y'ho·ram (Jehoram)

Y'ho·sef (Joseph)

Y'ho·sha·fat (Jehoshaphat, Josaphat)— king of Y'hudah; in Messianic genealogy. Mt 1:8.

Y'ho·shu·a (Joshua)—leader of the people of Israel who led the conquest of *Eretz-Yisra'el* after Moshe's death. The name means, "*Y-H-V-H* saves, *Y-H-V-H* delivers." See also Yeshua, above. Ac 7:45; MJ 4:8.

Y'ho·tza·dak (Jehozadak)

Y'ho·ya·da (Jehoiada)

Y'ho·ya·khin (Jehoiachin)

Y'ho·ya·kim (Jehoiakim)

Y'ho·ya·riv (Jehoiarib)

Y'ho·za·vad (Jehozabad)

Y'hu·dah (Judah, Judas, Juda, Jude)— (1) The fourth son of *Ya'akov avinu*. Mt 1:2+. (2) The tribe of Israel named after him. Rv 5:5+. (3) The southern kingdom over which various kings reigned, c. 926–586 B.C.E.; contrasted with the northern kingdom, Israel. MJ 8:8. (4) Y'hudah from K'riot, Yeshua's betrayer (see below). (5) Another emissary of Yeshua, perhaps identical with Taddai. Yn 14:22. (6) A brother of Yeshua, traditionally the author of the book of Y'hudah (Jude). Mt 13:55; Mk 6:3. (7) *Talmid* of Yeshua and son of Ya'akov #5. Lk 6:16+. (8) Y'hudah HaG'lili (see below). (9) Prophet surnamed Bar-Sabba. Ac 15:22ff. (10) Messianic Jew in Dammesek. Ac 9:11.

Y'hu·dah (Judea, Judah, Juda)—the portion of *Eretz-Yisra'el* allotted to the tribe of Y'hudah. Yerushalayim was at its northern border, and it extended southward past Hevron (Hebron). Mt 2:1+.

Y'hu·dah of K'ri·ot (Judas Iscariot)— Yeshua's betrayer's full name in Hebrew is *Y'hudah Ben-Shim'on Ish-K'riot* (Yn 6:71), which means "Judah, son of Simon, a man of K'riot," a town some twenty miles south of Yerushalayim. Mt 10:4+.

Y'hu·dah Ha·G'li·li (Judah the Galilean, Judas of Galilee)—popular Jewish leader who led a rebellion against Rome in 6–7 C.E. and founded the party of the Zealots (Sicarii). Ac 5:37.

Y'hu·di, pl. Y'hu·dim (Jew, Judean)— This term, which means "one who praises," does not appear in the *CJB*. When it or the equivalent Greek word *Ioudaios* is used by a non-Jew, or by a Jew outside *Eretz-Yisra'el*, it is generally rendered "Jew." When used by a Jew within *Eretz-Yisra'el*, it is rendered "Judean," i.e., a resident or citizen of Y'hudah.

Y'hu·dit (Judith)

Y'hu·khal (Jucal)

Yid·'a·lah (Idalah)

Yid·bash (Idbash)

Yid·do (Iddo)
Yid·laf (Jidlaph)
Yif·de·yah (Iphedeiah)
Yif·tach (Jepthah, Jephthae)—a judge of Israel. MJ 11:32.
Yif·tach·'el (Iphtahel)
Yig·'al (Igal)
Yig·dal·ya·hu (Igdaliah)
Yim·lah (Imlah)
Yim·nah (Imnah)
Yim·rah (Imrah)
Yin·non
Yir·'i·yah (Irijah)
Yir·me·yah, -ya·hu (Jeremiah, Jeremias, Jeremy)—*Tanakh* prophet. Mt 2:17+.
Yir·'on (Iron)
Yir·pe·'el (Irpeel)
Yis'·chak (Isaac)
Yi·shai (Jesse)—father of King David; in Messianic genealogy. Mt 1:5+.
Yish·bach (Ishbah)
Yish·bak (Ishbak)
Yish·bi-B'·nov (Ishbibenob)
Yish·'i (Ishi)
Yish·i·yah, -ya·hu (Ishiah, Ishijah)
Yish·ma (Ishma)
Yish·ma'·el (Ishmael)
Yish·ma'·e·li, -lim (Ishmaelite, -s)
Yish·ma'·yah, -ya·hu (Ishmaiah)
Yish·m'·rai (Ishmerai)
Yish·pah (Ishpah)
Yish·pan (Ishpan)
Yish·vah (Ishuah)
Yish·vi (Ishui, Ishvite)
Yis·kah (Iscah)
Yis·mach·yah (Ismachiah)
Yis·ra·'el (Israel)—see glossary entry on Isra'el.
Yis·sa·khar (Issachar)—one of the twelve tribes of Israel, named after a son of *Ya'akov avinu*. Rv 7:7.
Yit·lah (Ithlah)
Yit·mah (Ithmah)
Yit·nan (Ithnan)
Yit·ra (Ithra)
Yit·ran (Ithran)
Yit·re·'am (Ithream)

Yit·ri (Ithrite)
Yit·ro (Jethro)
Yit·ro—Parashah 17; Exodus 18:1–20:23(26)
Yitz'·chak (Isaac)—Second of the three Patriarchs of the Jewish people. Mt 1:2+.
Yitz'·har (Izhar)
Yitz'·hari (Izharite)
Yitz·ri (Izri)
Yiv·char (Ibhar)
Yiv·le·'am (Ibleam)
Yiv·ne·yah (Ibneiah)
Yiv·sam (Jibsam)
Yiz·li·'ah (Izliah)
Yiz·rach, from (Izrahite)
Yiz·rach·yah (Izrahiah)
Yiz·re·'el (Jezreel)
Yiz·re·'e·li (Jezreelite)
Yiz·zi·yah (Izziah)
Y'·kab·ze·'el (Jekabzeel)
Y'·kam·'am (Jekameam)
Y'·kam·yah (Jekamiah)
Y'khan·yah, -ya·hu (Jeconiah, Jeconias)— king of Y'hudah, also called Y'hoyakhin (Jehoiachin); in Messianic genealogy. Mt 1:11–12.
Y'·khol·ya·hu (Jecholiah)
Y'·khon·yah (Jeconiah)
Y'·ku·ti·'el (Jekuthiel)
Yo·'ach (Joah)
Yo·'a·chaz (Jehoahaz)
Yo·'ash (Joash)
Yo·'av (Joab)
Yo·cha (Joha)
Yo·cha·nah (Joanna)—wife of Herod's finance minister. Lk 8:3+.
Yo·cha·nan (John, Jona, Jonas)—The English name "John" is derived from Hebrew *Yochanan*, which means, "God gives grace." (1) Yochanan the Immerser (see entry below). (2) *Talmid* of Yeshua, son of Zavdai, brother of Ya'akov #4 and author of several New Testament books. Mt 4:21+. (3) Father of Kefa. Mt 16:17; Yn 21:15, 17. (4) Surnamed Mark, nephew of Bar-Nabba, co-worker with him and

Sha'ul. Ac 12:25+. (5) Ancestor of Yeshua. Lk 3:27. (6) Relative of 'Anan the *cohen hagadol*. Ac 4:6. (7) The author of the book of Revelation (if different from #2). Rv 1:9; 22:8.

Yo·cha·nan Ben-Z'khar·yah—See Yocha-nan the Immerser, below. Lk 3:2.

Yo·cha·nan the Immerser (John the Baptist, John the Baptizer)—His full name is given at Lk 3:2 as Yochanan Ben-Z'kharyah (John, son of Zechariah). The Greek words *baptô* and *baptizô* mean "to immerse, to dip," so that what is dipped absorbs the character of what it is immersed in, *e.g.*, leather in tanning solution. Mt 3:1+.

Yo·dah (Joda, Juda)—in Messianic genealogy. Lk 3:26.

Yo·'ed (Joed)

Yo·'el (Joel)—*Tanakh* prophet. Ac 2:16.

Yo·'e·lah (Joelah)

Yo·'e·zer (Joezer)

Yog·be·hah (Jogbehah)

Yog·li (Jogli)

Yok·de·'am (Jokdeam)

Yo·khe·ved (Jochebed)

Yo·kim (Jokim)

Yok·me·'am (Jokmeam)

Yok·ne·'am (Jokneam)

Yok·shan (Jokshan)

Yok·tan (Joktan)

Yok·te·'el (Joktheel)

Yom-Kip·pur—the Day of Atonement. The Greek says, literally, "the fast," but a Jewish fast-day in the fall spoken of with the definite article can refer only to *Yom-Kippur*. Ac 27:9.

Yo·na·dav (Jonadab)

Yo·nah (Jonah)—*Tanakh* prophet. Mt 12:39+.

Yo·nam (Jonan)—in Messianic genealogy. Lk 3:30.

Yo·na·tan (Jonathan)

Yo·rah (Jorah)

Yo·rai (Jorai)

Yo·ram (Jehoram, Joram, Jorim)—(1) King of Y'hudah; in Messianic genealogy.

Mt 1:8. (2) A second figure in the Messianic genealogy. Lk 3:29.

Yor·ke·'am (Jorkoam)

Yo·sef (Joseph, Josech)—(1) Son of *Ya'akov avinu*. Yn 4:5+. (2) The tribe of Israel called by his name. Rv 7:8. (3) Husband of Miryam the mother of Yeshua. Mt 1:16+. (4–6) Three different ancestors of Yeshua. Lk 3:24, 26, 30. (7) Brother of Yeshua. Mt 13:55. (8) Son of Miryam #4, same as Yosi #2. Mt 27:56. (9) Messianic Jewish member of the Sanhedrin in whose tomb Yeshua was buried; known as Yosef of Ramatayim (Joseph of Arimathea). Mt 27:57+. (10) Messianic Jew, surnamed Bar-Nabba, who worked with Sha'ul to establish the Gospel among the Gentiles. Ac 4:36.

Yo·sha·fat (Joshaphat)

Yo·shah (Joshah)

Yo·shav·yah (Joshaviah)

Yosh·b'·ka·shah (Joshbekashah)

Yo·shev-Ba·she·vet (Josheb-basshebeth)

Yo·shiv·yah (Josibiah)

Yo·shi·yah, -ya·hu (Josiah, Josias)—king of Y'hudah; in Messianic genealogy. Mt 1:10–11.

Yo·si (Joseph, Joses, Jose)—(1) Brother of Yeshua. Mk 6:3. (2) Son of Miryam #4. Mk 15:40. "Yosi" is sometimes a diminutive of "Yosef," as "Joe" is of "Joseph."

Yo·sif·yah (Josiphiah)

Yo·tam (Jotham)—king of Y'hudah; in Messianic genealogy. Mt 1:9.

Yot·vah (Jotbah)

Yot·va·tah (Jotbathah)

Yo·tza·dak (Jozadak)

Yov (Job)

Yo·vav (Jobab)

yo·vel (jubilee)—the English word comes directly from the Hebrew

Yo·ya·da (Jehoiada)

Yo·ya·kim (Joiakim)

Yo·ya·riv (Joiarib)

Yo·za·khar (Jozachar)

Yo·za·**vad** (Jozabad)
Y'·sar·'e·**lah** (Jesharelah)
Y'·sha·**nah** (Jeshanah)
Y'·sho·cha·**yah** (Jeshohaiah)
Y'·si·mi·**'el** (Jesimiel)
Y'·**tur** (Jetur)
Yud (Yodh, jot)—the 10th and smallest letter in the Hebrew alphabet. Mt 5:18.
Yud-Heh-Vav-Heh—the four-letter Hebrew name of God. See glossary entry at *Adonai*.
Yu·**khal** (Jucal)
Yu·**shav-He**·sed (Jushab-hesed)
Yu·**tah** (Jutah, Juttah)
Yu·**val** (Jubal)
*Y'·va·**rekh**'·kha A·DO·NAI v'·yish·me·re·kha. Ya·'er A·DO·NAI pa·**nav** e·lei·kha vi·chu·**nek**·ka. Yis·sa A·DO·NAI pa·**nav** e·lei·kha v'·ya·sem l'·**kha** sha·**lom***—the Aaronic benediction (see Numbers 6:24–26).
Y'·ve·rekh·**ya**·hu (Jeberechiah)
Y'·vu·**si** (Jebusite)
Y'·zan·**yah**, -**ya**·hu (Jezaniah)
Za·'a·**van** (Zaavan)
Za·**bai** (Zabbai)
Za·**ham**
Zak·**kai** (Zacchaeus)—tax collector who got saved. The name means "innocent." Lk 19:2ff.
Za·**kur** (Zaccur)
Zam·zu·**mim** (Zamzummim)
Za·**no**·ach (Zanoah)
Zar·**chi** (Zarhite)
Za·**tu** (Zattu)
Za·**vad** (Zabad)
Zav·**dai** (Zebedee)—father of Yochanan #2 and Ya'akov #4. Mt 4:21+.
Zav·**di** (Zabdi)
Zav·di·**'el** (Zabdiel)
Za·**vud** (Zabud)
Za·yin—7th letter of Hebrew alphabet
Za·**za**
Ze·**'ev** (Zeeb)

Zei·**tan** (Zethan)
Ze·kher (Zecher)
Ze·rach (Zerah, Zara, Zarah)—son of Y'hudah; in Messianic genealogy. Mt 1:3.
Ze·resh
Ze·**tam** (Zetham)
Ze·**tar** (Zethar)
Ze·**vach** (Zebah)
Zi·a
Zif (Ziph)
Zi·**fah** (Ziphah)
Zi·**fim** (Ziphites)
Zif·**ron** (Ziphron)
Zikh·**ri** (Zichri)
Zik·**lag**
Zil·**pah**
Zi·**mah** (Zimmah)
Zim·**ran**
Zim·**ri**
Zi·**na**
Ziv
Zi·**za**
Z'khar·**yah**, -**ya**·hu (Zechariah, Zacharias)—(1) *Tanakh* prophet. Mt 23:35; Lk 11:51. (2) Father of Yochanan the Immerser. Lk 1:5+.
Z'mi·**rah** (Zemira)
Zo·chet (Zoheth)
Zo·**fach** (Zophah)
Z'rach·**yah** (Zerahiah)
Zru·ba·**vel** (Zerubbabel, Zorobabel)—builder of the Second Temple, c. 520–516 B.C.E.; in Messianic genealogy. Mt 1:12–13; Lk 3:27.
Zu·**zim** (Zuzims)
Z'vad·**yah**, -**ya**·hu (Zebadiah)
Z'vi·**na** (Zebina)
Z'vu·**dah** (Zebudah)
Z'vul (Zebul)
Z'vu·lo·**ni** (Zebulonite)
Z'vu·**lun** (Zebulun, Zabulon)—(1) Tribe of Israel descended from a son of the Patriarch Ya'akov. Rv 7:8. (2) The territory in *Eretz-Yisra'el* assigned to that tribe (Joshua 19). Mt 4:13, 15.

"Reverse" Pronouncing Glossary

Many names and terms familiar to readers of other versions of the Bible do not appear in the *Complete Jewish Bible*. The following alphabetical list of the more common ones enables you to learn what the *CJB* uses in their place. For pronunciation guidance see the first page of the Pronouncing Explanatory Glossary.

Aaron— A·ha·**ron**
Abel—**He**·vel
Abiathar—Ev·ya·**tar**
Abigail—A·vi·ga·**yil**
Abraham—Av·ra·**ham**
Absalom—Av·sha·**lom**
Aceldama, Akeldama—Ha·**kal**·D'ma
age to come—*'o·lam ha·ba*
Ahab—Ach·**'av**
Ahasuerus—A·chash·ve·**rosh**
Almighty, the—*Shad·dai*
Alpheus—Ha·nan·**yah**
Ananias—Hal·**fai**
apostle—emissary
Arimathea—Ra·ma·**ta**·yim
Armageddon—Har-Me·gid·**do**
Assyria—A·**shur**
Balaam—Bil·**'am**
Babel—Ba·**vel**
Babylon—Ba·**vel**
Babylonians—Bav·**lim**
baptize—immerse
Barabbas—Bar-**Ab**·ba
Barnabas—Bar-**Nab**·ba
Bartholomew—Bar-Tal·**mai**
Bartimaeus—Bar-Ti·**mai**
Bath-sheba—Bat-**She**·va
Beer-sheba—Be·'er-**She**·va
Belial—B'li·**ya**·'al
Benjamin—Bin·ya·**min**
Bethany—Beit-An·**yah**
Beth-el—Beit-**El**
Bethlehem—Beit-**Le**·chem
Bethphage—Beit-Pa·**gei**
Bethsaida—Beit-Tzai·**dah**
Bezalel—B'·tzal·**'el**
blessing—*b'ra·khah*, pl. -*khot*

burnt offering—*'o·lah*
Caiaphas—Ka·ya·**fa**
Cain—**Ka**·yin
Caleb—Ka·**lev**
Calvary—Gul·**gol**·ta
Cana—Ka·**nah**
Canaan—Ke·**na**·'an
Canaanite—Ke·na·**'a·ni**, pl. -**nim**
Capernaum—K'far-Na·**chum**
Carchemish—Kar·**k'**·**mish**
Carmel—Kar·**mel**
Carmi—Kar·**mi**
Cephas—Ke·**fa**
Chaldean—Kas·**di**, pl. -**dim**
Chebar—K'·**var**
Chedorlaomer—K'dor·la·**'o**·mer
Chemosh—K'·**mosh**
cherub, -im, -ims—*ke·ruv*, pl. *k'ru·vim*
Christ—Messiah, *Ma·shi·ach*
church—Messianic Community,
   community, congregation
circumcision—*b'rit-mi·lah*
Cleophas—K'lo·**fah**
Clopas—K'lo·**fah**
coastal plain— the Sha·**ron**
commandment—*mitz·vah*, pl. *mitz·vot*
crazy—*me·shug·ga*
crazy people—*me·shug·ga·'im*
cross—execution stake
crucify—execute on a stake (as a criminal)
curtain—*pa·ro·khet*
Cyrus—**Ko**·resh
Damascus—Dam·**me**·sek
Darius—Dar·**ya**·vesh
daughter—*bat*
Day of Atonement—*Yom-Kip·pur*
deacon—*sham·mash*, pl. *sham·ma·shim*

1605

Deborah—D'·vo·**rah**
Delilah—D'li·**lah**
disciple—*tal·mid*, pl. *tal·mi·dim*
Dispersion—Di·**a**·spo·ra
dividing wall of partition—*m'chi·tzah*
Elias, Elijah—E·li·**yah**, -**ya**·hu
Elizabeth—E·li·**she**·va
Emmanuel—'Im·**ma**·nu **El**
En-dor—'Ein-**Dor**
En-gedi— 'Ein-**Ge**·di
Enoch—Ha·**nokh**
Ephraim—E·**fra**·yim
Esau—E·**sav**
Esther—Es·**ter**
Eve—Ha·**vah**
Ezekiel—Ye·chez·k'**el**
fast, the—*Yom Kip·pur*
Feast of Booths—*Suk·kot*
Feast of Dedication—*Ha·nuk·kah*
Feast of Passover—***Pe·sach***
Feast of Tabernacles—*Suk·kot*
Feast of Weeks—*Sha·vu·'ot*
first day of the week—*Mo·tza·'ei-Shab·bat*
foothills near coastal plain—the Sh'fe·**lah**
fringe of garment—*tzi·tzit*, pl. *tzi·tzi·yot*
Gabriel—Gav·ri·**'el**
Galilee— the Ga·**lil**
Gamaliel—Gam·li·**'el**
Garden of Eden—Gan-'**E**·den
Gath—Gat
Gaza—'A·**zah**
Gehazi—Gei·**cha**·zi
Gehenna—Gei·Hin·**nom**
Gennesaret—Gi·no·**sar**
Gentile—*Goy*, pl. *Go·yim*
Gethsemane—**Gat**-Sh'ma·**nim**
Gibeah—Giv·**'ah**
Gibeon—Giv·**'on**
Gideon—Gid·**'on**
Gilead—Gil·**'ad**
Gileadite—Gil·**'a**·di
glory of God—*Sh'khi·nah*
God, gods—*E·lo·him*
God Almighty—*El Shad·dai*
God Most High—*El 'El·yon*
Golgotha—Gul·**gol**·ta

Goliath—Gol·**yat**
Gomorrah— 'A·mo·**ra**
great day (of the feast)—*Ho·sha·na Rab·bah*
Greatness on High—*Ha·G'du·lah Ba·M'ro·mim*
Hades—Sh'·**ol**
Hebron—Hev·**ron**
Hell— Gei-Hin·**nom**, Sh'·**ol**
hem of garment—*tzi·tzit*, pl. *tzi·tzi·yot*
Hepzibah—Hef·tzi·**bah**
Hezekiah—Hiz·ki·**yah**, -**ya**·hu;
  Y'·chiz·ki·**yah**, -**ya**·hu
high priest—*co·hen ga·dol*, pl. *co·ha·nim g'do·lim*
Highest, the—*Ha·'El·yon*
Hittite, -s—Hit·**ti**, pl. Hit·**tim**
Hivite, -s—Hi·**vi**
Holy One, the—*Ha·Ka·dosh*
Holy Spirit, the—***Ru·ach Ha·Ko·desh***
Horeb—Ho·**rev**
horn—*sho·far**
Hosea—Ho·**she**·a
hymn of praise—*Hal·lel*
Ichabod—I-Kha·**vod**
Immanuel—'Im·**ma**·nu El
Isaac—Yitz'·**chak**
Isaiah—Ye·sha'·**yah**, -**ya**·hu
Ishmael—Yish·ma'·**el**
Ishmaelite—Yish·ma'·e·**li**, pl. -**lim**
Issachar—Yis·sa·**khar**
Jabbok—Ya·**bok**
Jacob—Ya·'a·**kov**
Jaffa—Ya·**fo**
Jah—*Yah*
Jairus—Ya·**'ir**
James—Ya·'a·**kov**
Japheth—**Ye**·fet
Jared—**Ye**·red
Jashar—Ya·**shar**
Jebusite—Y'·vu·**si**
Jeconiah—Y'khan·**yah**, -**ya**·hu
Jedidiah—Y'·did·**yah**
Jehoiachin—Y'ho·ya·**khin**
Jehoiada—Y'ho·ya·**da**
Jehoiakim—Y'ho·ya·**kim**
Jehoram—Yo·**ram**

Jehoshaphat—Y'ho·sha·**fat**
Jehozadak—Y'ho·tza·**dak**
Jehu—Ye·**hu**
Jephthah—Yif·**tach**
Jephunneh—Y'·fu·**neh**
Jeremiah—Yir·me·**yah**, -**ya**·hu
Jericho—Ye·ri·**cho**
Jeroboam—Ya·rov·**'am**
Jerubbaal—Ye·ru·**ba**·'al
Jerusalem—Ye·ru·sha·**la**·yim
Jeshurun—Ye·shu·**run**
Jesse—Yi·**shai**
Jesus—Ye·**shu**·a
Jethro—Yit·**ro**
Jezebel—I·**ze**·vel
Jezreel—Yiz·re·**'el**
Joab—Yo·**'av**
Joanna—Yo·cha·**nah**
Joash—Yo·**'ash**
Job—I·**yov**
Jochebed—Yo·**khe**·ved
John the Baptist—Yo·cha·**nan** the
  Immerser
John—Yo·cha·**nan**
Jonah—Yo·**nah**
Jonathan—Y'ho·na·**tan**
Joppa—Ya·**fo***
Jordan—Yar·**den**
Joseph—Yo·**sef**
Joshua—Y'ho·**shu**·a
Josiah—Yo·shi·**yah**, -**ya**·hu
Jotham—Yo·**tam**
Judah—Y'hu·**dah**
Judas Iscariot—Y'hu·**dah** from K'ri·ot
Judas of Galilee—Y'hu·**dah** Ha·G'li·**li**
Judas—Y'hu·**dah**
Jude—Y'hu·**dah**
Judea—Y'hu·**dah**
Kenite, -s—Ke·**ni**
Kirjath-arba—Kir·yat-Ar·**ba**
Kirjath-jearim—Kir·yat-Ye·'a·**rim**
Kohath—K'·**hat**
Kohathite—K'ha·**ti**
Korah—**Ko**·rach
lamp—*me*·*no*·*rah**
Land of Israel—*E*·*retz*-*Yis*·*ra*·*'el*
Law—*To*·*rah**

Lazarus—El·'a·**zar**
leavened dough—*ha*·*metz*
Lebanon—the L'·va·**non**
leprosy—*tza*·*ra*·'at
Leviathan—Liv·ya·**tan**
Levite—*Le*·*vi*, pl. *L'vi'im*
Lilith—Li·**lit**
loaf—*hal*·*lah*
LORD God of Hosts—*A*·*DO*·*NAI* *E*·*lo*·*hei*-
  Tzva·'ot
Lord GOD—*A*·*do*·*nai* *E*·*LO*·*HIM*
LORD of Hosts—*A*·*DO*·*NAI*-*Tzva*·'ot
LORD of Sabaoth—*A*·*DO*·*NAI*-*Tzva*·'ot
Lydda—Lud
Majesty on High, the—*Ha*·*G'du*·*lah*
  Ba·*M'ro*·*mim*
Malachi—Mal·'a·**khi**
Malchus—**Me**·lekh
Manasseh—M'na·**sheh**
manna—*man*
Manoah—Ma·**no**·ach
Martha—Mar·**ta**
Mary—Mir·**yam**
Mary Magdalene—Mir·**yam** from
  Mag·**da**·la; Mir·**yam**, called
  Mag·da·**lit**
Matthew—Mat·tit· **ya**·hu
Matthias—Mat·tit·**ya**·hu
Mehetabel—M'·hei·tav·**'el**
Melchizedek—**Mal**·ki-Tze·dek
Mephibosheth—M'·fi·**vo**·shet
Merari—M'·ra·**ri**
Methuselah—Me·tu·**she**·lach
Micah—Mi·**khah**
Micaiah—Mi·khay·**hu**
Michael—Mi·kha·**'el**
Michal—Mi·**khal**
Miriam—Mir·**yam**
Moab—Mo·**'av**
Moabite—Mo·'a·**vi**, pl. -**vim**
Moloch—**Mo**·lekh
Mordecai—Mor·de·**khai**
Moses—**Mo**·she*
Most High, the—*Ha*·'El·*yon*
Most High—'El·**yon**
Nabal—Na·**val**
Nadab—Na·**dav**

Nahshon—Nach·**shon**
Nahum—Na·**chum**
Nain—Na·**'im**
Naphtali—Naf·ta·li
Nathan—Na·**tan**
Nathanael—Na·tan·**'el**
Nazarene, Nazorean—*Natz·ra·ti*,
   pl. *-tim*
Nazareth—Na·**tze**·ret
nazirite—*na·zir*, pl. *n'zi·rim*
Nebo—N'·**vo**
Nebuchadnezzar—N'·vu·khad·ne·**tzar**
Nebuchadrezzar—N'·vu·khad·re·**tzar**
Necho—N'·**kho**
Nehemiah—Ne·chem·**yah**
new moon—*Rosh-Ho·desh*
Nicodemus—Nak·di·**mon**
Nineveh—Nin·**veh**
Noah—**No**·ach
Obadiah—'O·vad·**yah**, -**ya**·hu
Obed—'O·**ved**
Ophir—O·**fir**
Othniel—'Ot·ni·**'el**
pagan—*Goy,* pl. *Go·yim*
Palestine—P'·**le**·shet
Paradise—Gan-'**E**·den
Passover—*Pe·sach*
Paul—Sha·**'ul**
Peniel—P'ni-**El**
Pentecost —*Sha·vu·'ot*
Perez—**Pe**·retz
Persia—Pa·**ras**
Peter—Ke·**fa**
Phanuel—P'nu·'el
Pharisee—*Pa·rush,* pl. *P'ru·shim*
Philistine—P'·lish·ti, pl. -**tim**
Phinehas—Pin·**chas**
phylacteries—*t'·fil·lin**
Power, the—*Ha·G'vu·rah*
praying—*dav·ven·ing*
priest —*co·hen,* pl. *co·ha·nim*
Rahab—Ra·**chav**
Rameses—Ram'·ses
Rebecca—Riv·**kah**
Rechabites—Re·kha·**vim**
Rehoboam—Re·chav·**'am**
Rehoboth—Re·cho·**vot**

repent—turn from sin to God, do
   t'shu·vah
Rephaim—Re·fa·**'im**
Reuben—Re·'u·**ven**
Ruth—Rut
Sabbath—*Shab·bat*
Sadducee—*Tza·dok,* pl. *Tz'du·kim*
Salem—Sha·**lem**
Salome—Shlo·**mit**
Samaria—Shom·**ron**
Samaritans—Shom·ro·**nim**
Samson—Shim·**shon**
Samuel—Sh'mu·**'el**
Sanballat—San·va·**lat**
Sapphira—Shap·pi·**rah**
Satan—the Adversary
Saul—Sha·**'ul**
scribe—*To·rah**-teacher
Scripture—the *Ta·nakh*
Sea of Galilee—Lake Kin·**ne**·ret
Sennacherib—San·che·**riv**
seraphim—*s'ra·fim*
Seth—Shet
Shear-jashub—Sh·**'ar**-Ya·**shuv**
Sheba—Sh'·**va**
Shechem—Sh·**'khem**
Sheol—Sh'·**ol**
Sidon—Tzi·**don**
Sidonian—Tzi·do·**ni**, pl. -**nim**
Sihon—Si·**chon**
Silas—Sila
Siloam—Shi·**lo**·ach
Simeon—Shim·**'on**
Simon—Shim·**'on**
Sisera—Sis·**ra**
Sodom—S'**dom**
Solomon—**Shlo**·mo*
son—*bar, ben*
Son of the Blessed—*Ben-HaM'vo·rakh*
Succoth—*Suk·kot*
south part of Israel—**Ne**·gev
Susanna—Sho·sha·**nah**
Tabor—Ta·**vor**
Thaddeus—Tad·**dai**
Theudas—To·**dah**
this world/age—*'o·lam ha·zeh*
Tobiah—To·vi·**yah**

Tyre—Tzor
trumpet—*sho·far**
unleavened bread—*ma·tzah*, pl. *ma·tzot*
Ur of the Chaldees—Ur-Kas·**dim**
Uriah—U·ri·**yah**, -**ya**·hu
Uzziah—U·zi·**yah**, -**ya**·hu
veil of the temple—*pa·ro·khet*
voice from heaven—*bat-kol*
wash hands (ritually, before meal)—
 do *n'ti·lat-ya·da·yim*
world to come—*'o·lam ha·ba*
writing of divorcement—*get*
Zaccheus—Zak·**kai**

Zacharias—Z'khar·**yah**, -**ya**·hu
Zarephath—Tzar·**fat**
Zebedee—Zav·**dai**
Zebulun—Z'vu·**lun**
Zechariah—Z'khar·**yah**, -**ya**·hu
Zedekiah—Tzid·ki·**yah**, -**ya**·hu
Zelophehad—Tz'lo·f'·**chad**
Zephaniah—Tz'·fan·**yah**, -**ya**·hu
Zerubbabel—Z'ru·ba·**vel**
Zeruiah—Tz'ru·**yah**
Zion—Tzi·**yon**
Zipporah—Tzip·**po**·rah*

Index of *Tanakh* Passages
Cited in the *B'rit Hadashah*

There are 484 passages from the *Tanakh* cited a total of 695 times in the *Complete Jewish Bible*'s *B'rit Hadashah*. This index shows the verses in the *B'rit Hadashah* which cite each of these passages. The books of the *Tanakh* are listed in the same order as in the *CJB*, and the system for citing verses is the same—that is, the *Tanakh* passages are listed by their Hebrew Bible chapter-and-verse numbers, with Christian Bible chapter-and-verse numbers shown in parentheses, if different. The English names of the books of the *Tanakh* are used. The abbreviations for books of the *B'rit Hadashah* are shown at the beginning of the Pronouncing Explanatory Glossary. Inclusive passages are listed first, as with these seven successive entries: Deuteronomy 5:16-20, 5:16, 5:17-20, 5:17-18, 5:17, 5:18, 5:19.

GENESIS		GENESIS (Continued)	
1:26-27	Ya 3:9	22:16	MJ 6:13
1:27	Mt 19:4, Mk 10:6	22:17	MJ 6:14, 11:12
1:28	Co 1:6	22:18	Ac 3:25
2:2	MJ 4:4	23:4	1K 2:11
2:7	1C 15:45	24:7	Ac 7:5, Ga 3:16
2:24	Mt 19:5, Mk 10:8,	25:23	Ro 9:12
	1C 6:16, Ep 5:31	26:4	Ac 3:25
3:17-18	MJ 6:8	28:12	Yn 1:51
5:2	Mt 19:4, Mk 10:6	32:13	MJ 11:12
5:24	MJ 11:5	37:11	Ac 7:9
8:21	Pp 4:18	37:28	Ac 7:9
12:1	Ac 7:3, MJ 11:8	39:1-3	Ac 7:9
12:3	Ga 3:8	39:21	Ac 7:9
12:7	Ac 7:5, Ga 3:16	39:23	Ac 7:9
13:15	Ac 7:5, Ga 3:16	41:37-44	Ac 7:10
14:17-20	MJ 7:1-2	41:54	Ac 7:11
15:3	Ro 4:13	42:5	Ac 7:11
15:4	Ac 7:5	45:1	Ac 7:13
15:5-6	MJ 11:12	47:4	1K 2:11
15:5	Ro 4:13, 18	47:31	MJ 11:21
15:6	Ro 4:3, 22; Ga 3:6; Ya 2:23	48:4	Ac 7:5
15:7	Ac 7:5		
15:13-14	Ac 7:7	EXODUS	
15:16	Ac 7:7	1:7-8	Ac 7:18
15:18-21	Ac 7:5	2:2	MJ 11:23
17:5	Ro 4:17	2:11	MJ 11:24
17:7	Ga 3:16	2:14	Ac 7:27-28
17:8	Ac 7:5	3:1-2	Ac 7:30
18:14	Ro 9:9	3:6-10	Ac 7:32-34
21:10	Ga 4:30	3:6	Mt 22:32, Mk 12:26,
21:12	Ro 9:7, MJ 11:18		Lk 20:37, Ac 3:13

ISAIAH (Continued)

40:13	Ro 11:34, 1C 2:16
41:8-9	MJ 2:16
41:8	Ya 2:23
42:1-4	Mt 12:18-21
43:6	2C 6:18
43:20	1K 2:9
43:21	1K 2:9
45:9	Ro 9;20
45:23	Ro 14:11, Pp 2:10-11
49:6	Ac 13:47
49:8	2C 6:2
49:10	Rv 7:16-17
50:6	Mk 10:34
52:5	Ro 2:24
52:7	Ro 10:15, Ep 6:15
52:11	2C 6:17
52:15	Ro 15:21, 1C 2:9
53:1	Yn 12:38, Ro 2:16
53:4	Mt 8:17, 2K 2:24
53:5	2K 2:24
53:6	2K 2:25
53:7-8	Ac 8:32-33
53:9	2K 2:22
53:12	Mk 15:28, Lk 22:37, MJ 9:28, 1K 2:24
54:1	Ga 4:27
54:13	Yn 6:45
55:3	Ac 13:34
56:7	Mt 21:13, Mk 11:17, Lk 19:46
56:12	1C 15:32
57:19	Ep 2:17
58:6	Lk 4:18-19
59:7-8	Ro 3:15-17
59:17	Ep 6:14, 17; 1Th 5:8
59:20-21	Ro 11:26-27
61:1-2	Lk 4:18-19
61:1	Mt 11:5, Lk 7:22
61:6	2K 2:9
63:10	Ac 7:51
64:3(4)	1C 2:9
65:1	Ro 10:20
65:2	Ro 10:21
65:17	2K 3:13, Rv 21:1
66:1-2	Ac 7:49-50
66:1	Mt 5:35
66:15	2Th 1:8
66:22	2K 3:13, Rv 21:1
66:24	Mk 10:44, 46, 48

JEREMIAH

2:13	Rv 7:17
5:24	Ya 5:7
6:10	Ac 7:51
6:16	Mt 11:29
7:11	Mt 21:13, Mk 11:17, Lk 19:46
9:23(24)	1C 1:31, 2C 10:17
9:25(26)	Ac 7:51
10:25	2Th 1:8
15:2	Rv 13:10
19:13	Ac 7:42
22:5	Mt 23:38
31:14(15)	Mt 2:18
31:30(31)-33(34)	MJ 8:8-12
31:30(31)	MJ 9:15
31:32(33)	Ro 2:15, 2C 6:16, MJ 10:16
31:33(34)	MJ 10:17, Rv 21:3
32:38	2C 6:16
43:11	Rv 13:10

EZEKIEL

1:5-10	Rv 4:7
1:24	Rv 1:13-15
20:34	2C 6:17
20:41	2C 6:17
28:2	2Th 2:4
32:7	Mt 24:29, Mk 13:24-25
34:23	Rv 7:17
36:20	Ro 2:24
36:25	MJ 10:22
37:27	2C 6:16, Rv 21:3
38:2	Rv 20:8
43:2	Rv 1:13-15

HOSEA

2:1(1:10)	Ro 9:25-26
2:25(23)	Ro 9:25-26, 1K 2:10
6:2	Mk 10:34
6:6	Mt 9:13, 12:17
10:8	Lk 23:30, Rv 6:16
11:1	Mt 2:15
12:9(8)	Rv 3:17
13:14	1C 15:55

JOEL

2:2	Mt 24:21, Mk 13:19
2:10	Mt 24:29, Mk 13:24-25
2:23	Ya 5:7
3:1-5(2:28-32)	Ac 2:17-21
3:4(2:31)	Mt 24:29, Mk 13:24-25

Scripture Readings
for *Shabbat* and Holidays

This appendix, which relates to Section XV of the Introduction, lists the *parashot-hashavua* (the Scripture readings from the *Torah* and the Prophets read each week in the synagogue on *Shabbat*) and the Scripture readings for the Jewish holidays. In the tables that follow, "A" and "S" refer to Ashkenazic and Sefardic customary readings, respectively, where these differ. "M" means "suggested Messianic adaptation." The *B'rit Hadashah* readings are suggestions only and often include more material than most congregations will wish to use on any particular occasion. The abbreviations for *B'rit Hadashah* books are given at the bottom of page 1556.

There are 54 *parashot-hashavua* to allow for readings on 54 *Shabbat*s – which can happen during a Jewish leap year, since a leap year adds a thirteenth lunar month to the calendar. Regular years, those with twelve months, have fewer *Shabbat*s, so that in some weeks two *parashot* are read. The table below indicates these with "RY." On the holiday called *Simchat Torah*, which usually falls in October, there is a reading from the end of Deuteronomy (*parashah* #54); then the *Torah* scroll is rewound, and the reading continues from Genesis 1:1 (*parashah* #1). In other words, the cycle takes a year, ending and beginning on *Simchat Torah* (which means, literally, "joy of the *Torah*"), and continuing *parashah* by *parashah* each week until the next year's *Simchat Torah*.

The special readings from the *Torah* and the Prophets for the Jewish holidays are arranged chronologically according to the Jewish calendar, which begins with *Rosh HaShanah* (the Jewish New Year) in September or early October. The readings are those used in the Diaspora, where some Jewish holidays are celebrated for an extra day beyond what is specified in the Bible (and observed in Israel), because of uncertainty about the calendar in earlier times. (Determination of the new month required that the crescent moon actually be seen in the west from Jerusalem, and whether it had been seen yet could not be quickly communicated to distant points.) Therefore Israelis using the *Complete Jewish Bible* should consult local calendars.

PG	PARASHAH	TORAH	PROPHETS	B'RIT HADASHAH
1	1. *B'resheet*	Genesis 1:1-6:8	Isaiah 42:5-43:10 (A); 42:5-21 (S)	Mt. 1:1-17, 19:3-9; Mk 10:1-12; Lk 3:23-38; Yn 1:1-18; 1C 6:15-20, 15:35-58; Ro 5:12-21; Ep 5:21-32; Co 1:14-17; 1Ti 2:11-15; MJ 1:1-3, 3:7-4:11, 11:1-7; 2K 3:3-14; Rv 21:1-5, 22:1-5
6	2. *Noach*	Genesis 6:9-11:32	Isaiah 54:1-55:5 (A); 54:1-10 (S) [M: start at 52:13]	Mt 24:36-44; Lk 17:26-37; Ac 2:1-16; 1K 3:18-22; 2K 2:5
11	3. *Lekh L'kha*	Genesis 12:1-17:27	Isaiah 40:27-41:16	Ac 7:1-8; Ro 3:19-5:6; Ga 3:15-18, 5:1-6; Co 2:11-15; MJ 7:1-19, 11:8-12
16	4. *Vayera*	Genesis 18:1-22:24	2 Kings 4:1-37 (A); 4:1-23 (S)	Lk 17:26-37; Ro 9:6-9; Ga 4:21-31; MJ 6:13-20, 11:13-19; Ya 2:14-24; 2K 2:4-10
22	5. *Hayyei-Sarah*	Genesis 23:1-25:18	1 Kings 1:1-31	Mt 8:19-22, 27:3-10; Lk 9:57-62
25	6. *Tol'dot*	Genesis 25:19-28:9	Malachi 1:1-2:7	Ro 9:6-16; MJ 11:20, 12:14-17
29	7. *Vayetze*	Genesis 28:10-32:3(2)	Hosea 12:13(12)-14:10(9) (A); 11:7-12:12(11) (S)	Yn 1:43-51
35	8. *Vayishlach*	Genesis 32:4(3)-36:43	Hosea 11:7-12:12(11) (A); Obadiah 1-21 (S)	1C 5:1-13; Rv 7:1-12
41	9. *Vayeshev*	Genesis 37:1-40:23	Amos 2:6-3:8	Ac 7:9-16 [specifically vv. 9-10]
45	10. *Mikketz*	Genesis 41:1-44:17	1 Kings 3:15-4:1	Ac 7:9-16 specifically vv. 11-12]
50	11. *Vayigash*	Genesis 44:18-47:27	Ezekiel 37:15-28	Ac 7:9-16 [specifically vv. 13-15]
55	12. *Vayechi*	Genesis 47:28-50:26	1 Kings 2:1-12	Ac 7:9-16 [specifically vv. 15-16]; MJ 11:21-22; 1K 1:3-9, 2:11-17

WEEKLY SCRIPTURE READINGS (*PARASHOT*) FOR *SHABBATS*

PG	PARASHAH	TORAH	PROPHETS	B'RIT HADASHAH
60	13. *Sh'mot*	Exodus 1:1-6:1	Isaiah 27:6-28:13, 29:22-23 (A); Jeremiah 1:1-2:3 (S)	Mt 22:23-33, 41-46; Mk 12:18-27, 35-37; Lk 20:27-44; Ac 3:12-15, 5:27-32, 7:17-36, 22:12-16, 24:14-16; MJ 11:23-26
65	14. *Va'era*	Exodus 6:2-9:35	Ezekiel 28:25-29:21	Ro 9:14-17, 2C 6:14-7:1
70	15. *Bo*	Exodus 10:1-13:16	Jeremiah 46:13-28	Lk 2:22-24; Yn 19:31-37; Ac 13:16-17; Rv 8:6-9:12, 16:1-21
74	16. *B'shallach*	Exodus 13:17-17:16	Judges 4:4-5:31 (A); 5:1-31 (S)	Lk 2:22-24; Yn 6:25-35, 19:31-37; 1C 10:1-13; 2C 8:1-15; Rv 15:1-4
80	17. *Yitro*	Exodus 18:1-20:23(26)	Isaiah 6:1-7:6, 9:5(6)-6(7) (A); 6:1-13 (S)	Mt 5:21-30, 15:1-11, 19:16-30; Mk 7:5-15, 10:17-31; Lk 18:18-30; Ac 6:1-7; Ro 2:17-29, 7:7-12, 13:8-10; Ep 6:1-3; 1Ti 3:1-14; 2Ti 2:2; Ti 1:5-9; MJ 12:18-29; Ya 2:8-13; 1K 2:9-10
83	18. *Mishpatim*	Exodus 21:1-24:18	Jeremiah 34:8-22, 33:25-26	Mt 5:38-42, 15:1-20; Mk 7:1-23; Ac 23:1-11; MJ 9:15-22, 10:28-29
88	19. *T'rumah*	Exodus 25:1-27:19	1 Kings 5:26(12)-6:13	MJ 8:1-6, 9:23-24, 10:1
91	20. *Tetzaveh*	Exodus 27:20-30:10	Ezekiel 43:10-27	Pp 4:10-20
95	21. *Ki Tissa*	Exodus 30:11-34:35	1 Kings 18:1-39 (A); 18:20-39 (S)	Lk 11:14-20; Ac 7:35-8:1; 1C 10:1-13; 2C 3:1-18
101	22. *Vayak'hel* [RY: with 23]	Exodus 35:1-38;20	1 Kings 7:40-50 (A); 7:13-26 (S)	2C 9:1-15; MJ 9:1-14; Rv 11:1-13
105	23. *P'kudei* [RY: with 22]	Exodus 38:21-40:38	1 Kings 7:51-8:21 (A); 7:40-50 (S)	Rv 15:5-8
109	24. *Vayikra*	Leviticus 1:1-5:26 (6:7)	Isaiah 43:21-44:23	Ro 8:1-13; MJ 10:1-14, 13:10-16
114	25. *Tzav*	Leviticus 6:1(8)-8:36	Jeremiah 7:21-8:3, 9:22(23)-23(24)	Mk 12:28-34; Ro 12:1-2; 1C 10:14-23

PG	PARASHAH	TORAH	PROPHETS	B'RIT HADASHAH
117	26. *Sh'mini*	Leviticus 9:1-11:47	2 Samuel 6:1-7:17 (A); 6:1-19 (S)	Mk 7:1-23; Ac 5:1-11, 10:1-35; 2C 6:14-7:1; Ga 2:11-16; 1K 1:14-16
121	27. *Tazria* [RY: with 28]	Leviticus 12:1-13:59	2 Kings 4:42-5:19	Mt 8:1-4, 11:2-6; Mk 1:40-45; Lk 2:22-24, 5:12-16, 7:18-23
124	28. *M'tzora* [RY: with 27]	Leviticus 14:1-15:33	2 Kings 7:3-20	Mt 9:20-26; Mk 5:24b-34; Lk 8:42b-48; MJ 13:4
128	29. *Acharei Mot* [RY: with 30]	Leviticus 16:1-18:30	Ezekiel 22:1-19 (A) 22:1-16 (S)	Ro 3:19-28, 9:30-10:13; 1C 5:1-13 with 2C 2:1-11; Ga 3:10-14; MJ 7:23-10:25
131	30. *K'doshim* [RY: with 29]	Leviticus 19:1-20:27	Amos 9:7-15 (A) Ezekiel 20:2-20 (S)	Mt 5:33-37, 43-48; 15:1-11; 19:16-30; 22:33-40; Mk 7:1-23; 12:28-34; Lk 10:25-37; Ro 13:8-10; Ga 5:13-26; Ya 2:1-9; 1K 1:13-21
134	31. *Emor*	Leviticus 21:1-24:23	Ezekiel 44:15-31	Mt 5:38-42; Ga 3:26-29 [in connection with the feasts, see readings for Parashah 41]
139	32. *B'har* [RY: with 33]	Leviticus 25:1-26:2	Jeremiah 32:6-27	Lk 4:16-21; 1C 7:21-24; Ga 6:7-10
141	33. *B'chukkotai* [RY: with 32]	Leviticus 26:3-27:34	Jeremiah 16:19-17:14	Yn 14:15-21, 15:10-12; 1Y
145	34. *B'midbar*	Numbers 1:1-4:20	Hosea 2:1(1:10)-2:22(20)	Lk 2:1-7; 1C 12:12-31
150	35. *Naso*	Numbers 4:21-7:89	Judges 13:2-25	Yn 7:53-8:11; Ac 21:17-32
157	36. *B'ha'alotkha*	Numbers 8:1-12:16	Zechariah 2:14-4:7	Yn 19:31-37; MJ 3:1-6
162	37. *Shlach L'kha*	Numbers 13:1-15:41	Joshua 2:1-24	MJ 3:7-19
167	38. *Korach*	Numbers 16:1-18:32	1 Samuel 11:14-12:22	2Ti 2:8-21; Yd 1-25
171	39. *Hukkat* [RY: with 40]	Numbers 19:1-22:1	Judges 11:1-33	Yn 3:9-21, 4:3-30, 12:27-50
175	40. *Balak* [RY: with 39]	Numbers 22:2-25:9	Micah 5:6(7)-6:8	2K 2:1-22; Yd 11; Rv 2:14-15

PG	PARASHAH	TORAH	PROPHETS	B'RIT HADASHAH
181	41. *Pinchas*	Numbers 25:10-30:1 (29:40)	1 Kings 18:46-19:21	Mt 26:1-30; Mk 14:1-26; Lk22:1-20; Yn 2:13-22; 7:1-13, 37-39; 11:55-12:1; 13:1; 18:28, 39; 19:14; Ac 2:1-21; 12:3-4; 20:5-6, 16; 27:9-11; 1C 5:6-8; 16:8; MJ 11:28
187	42. *Mattot* [RY: with 43]	Numbers 30:2(1)-32:42	Jeremiah 1:1-2:3	Mt 5:33-37
191	43. *Masa'ei* [RY: with 42]	Numbers 33:1-36:13	Jeremiah 2:4-28, 3:4 (A); 2:4-28, 4:1-2 (S)	Ya 4:1-12
196	44. *D'varim*	Deuteronomy 1:1-3:22	Isaiah 1:1-27	Yn 15:1-11; MJ 3:7-4:11
200	45. *Va'etchanan*	Deuteronomy 3:23-7:11	Isaiah 40:1-26	Mt 4:1-11, 22:33-40; Mk 12:28-34; Lk 4:1-13; 10:25-37; Ac 13:13-43; Ro 3:27-31; 1Ti 2:4-6; Ya 2:14-26; and all the readings for Parashah 17
206	46. *Ekev*	Deuteronomy 7:12-11:25	Isaiah 49:14-51:3	Mt 4:1-11; Lk 4:1-13; Ya 5:7-11
210	47. *Re'eh*	Deuteronomy 11:26-16:17	Isaiah 54:11-55:5	1C 5:9-13; 1Y 4:1-6
216	48. *Shof'tim*	Deuteronomy 16:18-21:9	Isaiah 51:12-52:12 [M: continue through 53:12]	Mt 5:38-42, 18:15-20; Ac 3:13-26; 7:35-53; 1C 5:9-13; 1Ti 5:17-22; MJ 10:28-31
220	49. *Ki Tetze*	Deuteronomy 21:10-25:19	Isaiah 54:1-10 [M: start at 52:13]	Mt 5:31-32, 19:3-12, 22:23-32; Mk 10:2-12, 12:18-27; Lk 20:27-38; 1C 9:4-18; Ga 3:9-14; 1Ti 5:17-18
225	50. *Ki Tavo*	Deuteronomy 26:1-29:8(9)	Isaiah 60:1-22	Mt 13:1-23; Lk 21:1-4; Ac 28:17-31; Ro 11:1-15
230	51. *Nitzavim* [RY: with 52]	Deuteronomy 29:9(10)-30:20	Isaiah 61:10-63:9	Ro 9:30-10:13; MJ 12:14-15
232	52. *Vayelekh* [RY: with 51]	Deuteronomy 31:1-30	Hosea 14:2(1)-10(9), Micah 7:18-20, Joel 2:15-27	MJ 13:5-8
234	53. *Ha'azinu*	Deuteronomy 32:1-52	2 Samuel 22:1-51	Ro 10:14-21, 12:14-21; MJ 12:28-29
238	54. *V'Zot HaBrachah*	Deuteronomy 33:1-34:12	Joshua 1:1-18 (A); 1:1-9 (S)	Mt 17:1-9; Mk 9:2-10; Lk 9:28-36; Yd 3-4, 8-10

SCRIPTURE READINGS FOR THE FESTIVALS AND FASTS

EVENT	TORAH	PROPHETS	B'RIT HADASHAH

Rosh HaShanah (New Year; the biblical feast of *shofar*s)

1st day	Genesis 21, Numbers 29:1-6	1 Samuel 1:1-2:10	Any time during the festival: Mt 24, Mk 13, Lk 21
2nd day	Genesis 22, Numbers 29:1-6	Jeremiah 31:1-19(2-20)	1Th 4:13-18, Rv 8-9 Second day: MJ 11:17-19

Shabbat Shuvah (*Shabbat* of Repentance, just before *Yom Kippur*)

	Weekly portion	A: Hosea 14:2-10, Joel 2:15-17, Micah 7:18-20; S: Hosea 14:2-10, Micah 7:18-20	Ro 5-6

Yom Kippur (Day of Atonement)

Morning	Leviticus 16, Numbers 29:7-11	Isaiah 57:14-58:14 [M: add Isaiah 52:13-53:12]	Ro 3:21-26, MJ 7-8
Afternoon	Leviticus 18 [M: add Leviticus 17]	Jonah 1-4, Micah 7:18-20	MJ 9-10

Sukkot (Tabernacles, Booths)

1st day	Leviticus 22:26-23:44, Numbers 29:12-16	Zechariah 14:1-21	Any time during the festival: Yn 7
2nd day	Leviticus 22:26-23:44, Numbers 29:12-16	1 Kings 8:2-21	
Shabbat during middle days	Daily portion from Numbers 29	Ezekiel 38:18-39:16	
7th day (*Hoshana Rabbah*)	Numbers 29:32-34	(None)	Yn 7:37-39

Sh'mini Atzeret (Solemn assembly on the 8th day of *Sukkot*)

	Deuteronomy 14:22-16:17, Numbers 29:35-30:1	1 Kings 8:54-66	Mk 12:28-34

Simchat Torah (Rejoicing of the Torah)

	Deuteronomy 33:1-34:12, Genesis 1:1-2:3, Numbers 29:35-30:1	A: Joshua 1:1-18 S: Joshua 1:1-9	Mt 5-7 (especially 5:17-20), Mk 12:28-34 Ro 7-8, Rv 21:1-22:5

SCRIPTURE READINGS FOR THE FESTIVALS AND FASTS

EVENT	TORAH	PROPHETS	B'RIT HADASHAH
Hanukkah (Dedication, 8 Days)			
1st *Shabbat*	Weekly & Hanukkah portions	Zechariah 2:14-4:7	Any time during the festival: Yn 10:22-39
2nd *Shabbat*	Weekly & Hanukkah portions	1 Kings 7:40-50	
Shabbat Sh'kalim (Shekels)			
	Weekly portion, Exodus 30:11-16	A: 2 Kings 12:1-17 S: 2 Kings 11:17-12:17	Mt 17:24-27, Mk 12:13-17
Shabbat Zakor (Remember)			
	Weekly portion, Deuteronomy 25:17-19	A: 1 Samuel 15:2-34 S: 1 Samuel 15:1-34	Ep 6:10-18, Rv 18:1-24
Purim			
	Exodus 17:8-16	(None)	Mt 10:16-42, Ac 16:11-40
Shabbat Parah (Heifer)			
	Weekly portion, Numbers 19:1-22	A: Ezekiel 36:16-38 S: Ezekiel 36:16-36	MJ 9:13-14
HaHodesh (start of the month of *Nisan*)			
	Weekly portion, Exodus 12:1-20	A: Ezekiel 45:16-46:18 S: Ezekiel 45:18-46:15	Co 2:16-17, Rv 21:1-22:5
Shabbat HaGadol (the Great *Shabbat*, just before *Pesach*)			
	Weekly portion	Malachi 3:4-24(3:4-4:6)	Mt 16:13-28, 20:17-19
Pesach (Passover)			
1st day	Exodus 12:21-51, Numbers 28:16-25	A: Joshua 3:5-7, 5:2-6:1, 6:27; S: Joshua 5:2-6:1 [M: add Isaiah 52:13-53:12]	Any time during the festival: Mt 26-28, Mk 14-16, Lk 22-24, Yn 13-21,
2nd day	Leviticus 22:26-23:44, Numbers 28:16-25	2 Kings 23:1-9, 21-25	1C 5:6-8
Shabbat during middle days	Exodus 33:12-34:26 Numbers 28:19-25	A: Ezekiel 36:37-37:14 S: Ezekiel 37:1-14	
7th day	Exodus 13:17-15:26, Numbers 28:19-25	2 Samuel 22:1-51	
8th day	Deuteronomy 15:19-16:17, Numbers 28:19-25	Isaiah 10:32-12:6	

EVENT	TORAH	PROPHETS	B'RIT HADASHAH

Shavu'ot (Weeks, Pentecost)

1st day	Exodus 19-20, Numbers 28:26-31	Ezekiel 1:1–28, 3:12	Any time during the festival: Ac 1-2 (especially 2:1-13)
2nd day	Deuteronomy 15:19-16:17, Numbers 28:26-31	Habakkuk 3:1-19	

Tish'ah B'av (9th of *Av*, a fast day)

Morning	Deuteronomy 4:25-40	Jeremiah 8:13-9:23	Mk 13, Lk 5:33-39
Afternoon	Exodus 32:11-14, 34:1-10	A: Isaiah 55:6-56:8 S: Hosea 14:2-10, Micah 7:18-20 [M: add Zechariah 12]	

Other fast days

	Exodus 32:11-14, 34:1-10	A: Isaiah 55:6-56:8 S: (None)	Mt 17:14-21, Lk 5:33-39

Shabbat on *Rosh Hodesh* (start of month, new moon)

	Weekly portion, Numbers 28:9-15	Isaiah 66:1-24	Co 2:16-17, Rv 21:1-22:5

Shabbat just before *Rosh Hodesh*

	Weekly portion	1 Samuel 20:18-42	Co 2:16-17, Rv 21:1-22:5

TANAKH MAPS
Index and Key

The following map index is for the first three maps, which relate to the *Tanakh*. The usual English names are in parentheses. The key letters and numbers refer to both the names and the places.

Key letters A–D refer to Map 1, The Exodus (c.15th–13th Centuries B.C.E.)

Key letters E–H refer to Map 2, *Eretz-Yisra'el* (The Land of Isra'el) in the Times of Y'hoshua, the Judges, Sh'mu'el and Sha'ul (c.1400–1000 B.C.E.)

Key letters J–M refer to Map 3, *Eretz-Yisra'el* (The Land of Isra'el) in the Times of Kings David and Shlomo and the Divided Kingdom (Isra'el and Y'hudah) (c.1000–586 B.C.E.)

Achlav (Achlab)—G2
Achziv (Achzib)—G2
'Ad'adah—G5
Adam—G4
'Adulam (Adullam)—G4-5
'Ai—G4
Akhshaf (Achshaph)—G3
Akko—G2-3
'Amon (land of the Ammonites)—H4, KL3
Arabia—M4-6
'Arad—D1-2, G5
'Aravah (Arabah), the (the Jordan-rift desert)—G3-6
Aram (Syria), land of—L2-3
Arnon River—GH5
'Aro'er—H5
Arvad—K2
Ashdod—D1, F4
Asher, tribal territory—G2
Ashkelon—F4
Asia Minor—JK1
'Atzmon (Azmon)—C2
Ayalon (Aijalon)—FG4
'Azah (Gaza)—C1, F5, K3
'Azekah—D1
Ba'al-Gad—GH2
Bavel (Babylon)—M2
Be'er-Sheva (Beersheba)—CD1, F5
Beit-'Anah (Beth-anath)—G2-3
Beit-Dagon (Beth-dagon)—FG4
Beit-El (Beth-el)—G4, K3

Beit-Sh'an (Beth-shean)—G3
Beit-Shemesh (Beth-shemesh)—FG4
Betzer (Bezer)—H4
Binyamin (Benjamin), tribal territory—G4
B'nei-Ya'akan (Bene-jaakan)—CD2
Botzrah (Bozrah)—D2
Cyprus—J2
Dammesek (Damascus)—H1, L3
Dan, tribal territory—F4, H2
Dead Sea—D1, G4-5,
Divon (Dibon)—D1
Dofkah (Dophkah)?—BC4
Dor—F3
D'vir (Debir)—D1
Edom, land of—D2-3, GH6, K4
Efrayim (Ephraim), tribal territory—G4
'Efron (Ephron)—G4
'Eglon—F4-5
Egypt—A1-4, J4
Eilat—D3, K4-5
'Ein-Gedi (En-gedi)—G5
'Eival (Ebal), Mount—G3
'Etzyon-Gever (Ezion-geber)—D3, K4-5
Euphrates River—M1
Gad, tribal territory—H4
Gat (Gath)—F4
Gezer—FG4
Gilboa, Mount—G3
Giv'ah (Gibeah)—G4

Giv'on (Gibeon)—G4
Golan—H3
Goshen—A2
G'rar (Gerar)—CD1
Great Sea—ABC1, EFG1-5, JK1-3
G'rizim (Gerizim), Mount—G3-4
G'shur (Geshur), land of—KL3
Gulf of Eilat—CD4
Gulf of Suez—B4
Hamat—L2
Haran—M1
Hatzar-Adar (Hazar-addar)—CD2
Hatzor (Hazor)—G2
Heliopolis—A3
Hermon, Mount—H1-2
Heshbon—H4
Hevron (Hebron)—D1, G5, K4
Hormah—D2, G5
Isra'el (Northern Kingdom)—KL3
Kadesh-Barnea—CD2, F6
Kamon—H3
Kark'mish (Carchemish)—L1
Karmel (Carmel), Mount—FG3
Kedesh—G2
Kena'an (Canaan), land of—D1
King's Highway—D1-2-3
Kinneret, Lake—GH3
Kir-Hareset (Kir-hareseth)—D1
Kir-Mo'av (Kir-moab)—KL4
Kiryat-Ye'arim (Kiriath-jearim)—FG4
Lakhish (Lachish)—D1

B'RIT HADASHAH MAPS
Index and Key

The following map index of 173 locations includes all the place-names in the *B'rit Hadashah* and relate to the last two maps. The English names found in some versions of the New Testament are in parentheses. The key letters and numbers refer to both the names and the places. An asterisk (*) indicates a place in or very near Yerushalayim not shown on either map.

Key letters N–Q refer to Map 4, *Eretz-Israel* (The Land of Isra'el) in the Time of Yeshua (1st Century C.E.)

Key letters R–U refer to Map 5, The Eastern Mediterranean and Near East in the Second Temple Period (1st Century C.E.)

MAP INDEX

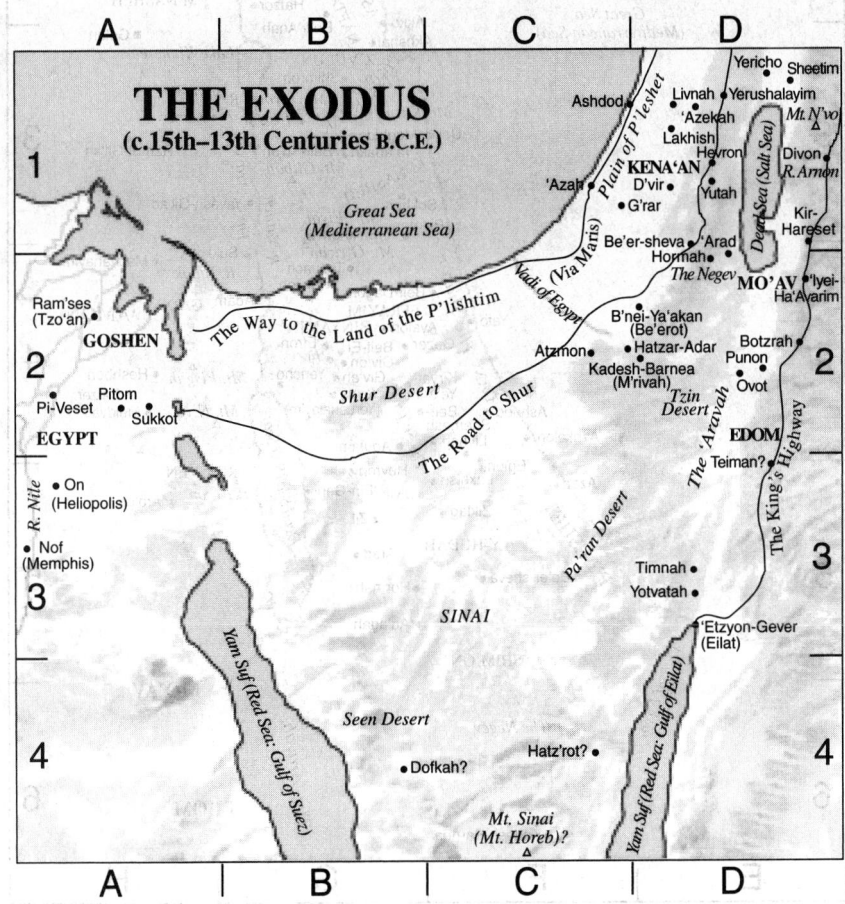

THE EXODUS
(c.15th–13th Centuries B.C.E.)

MAP 2

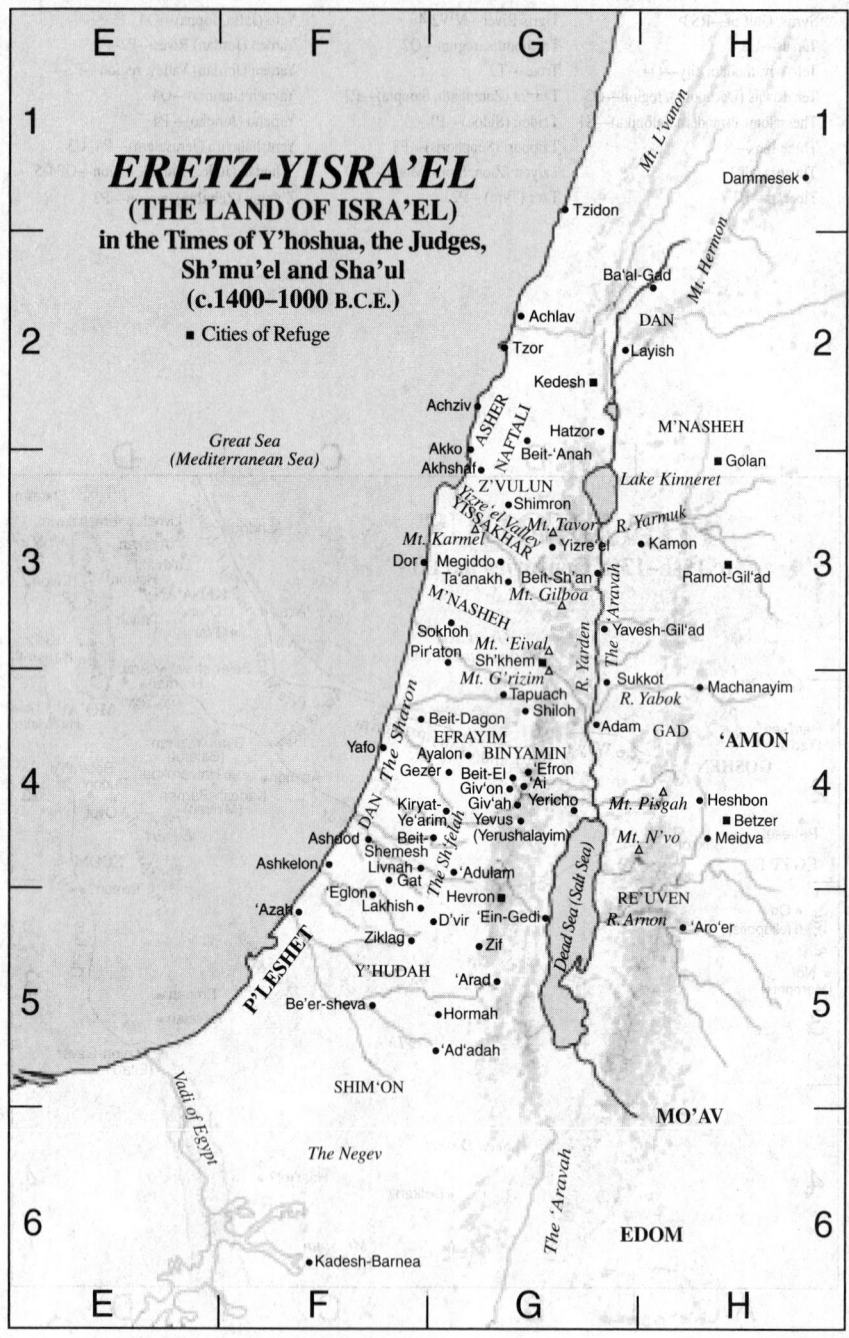

ERETZ-YISRA'EL
(THE LAND OF ISRA'EL)
**in the Times of Y'hoshua, the Judges,
Sh'mu'el and Sha'ul
(c.1400–1000 B.C.E.)**

■ Cities of Refuge

*Great Sea
(Mediterranean Sea)*

Tzidon

Dammesek ●

Mt. Livanon

Mt. Hermon

Ba'al-Gad ●

Achlav ●

Tzor ●

DAN

● Layish

Kedesh ■

Achziv ●

ASHER

NAFTALI

Hatzor ●

M'NASHEH

Akko ●

Beit-'Anah ●

● Golan

Akhshaf ●

Lake Kinneret

Z'VULUN

Yizre'el Valley

● Shimron

YISASKHAR

Mt. Tavor

R. Yarmuk

Mt. Karmel

Yizre'el ●

● Kamon

Dor ●

Megiddo ●

Beit-Sh'an ●

Ramot-Gil'ad ■

Ta'anakh ●

Mt. Gilboa

M'NASHEH

The 'Aravah

● Yavesh-Gil'ad

Sokhoh ●

Pir'aton ●

Mt. 'Eival

Sh'khem ●

Sukkot ●

R. Yabok

● Machanayim

Mt. G'rizim

● Tapuach

R. Yarden

Shiloh ●

● Adam

GAD

'AMON

● Beit-Dagon

EFRAYIM

Yafo ●

Ayalon ●

DAN

BINYAMIN

● Efron

Gezer ●

Beit-El ●

● 'Ai

Mt. Pisgah

● Heshbon

Giv'on ●

Giv'ah ●

Yericho ●

■ Betzer

Kiryat-

The Sharon

Yevus

Mt. N'vo

● Meidva

Ye'arim ●

Beit- ●

(Yerushalayim)

Ashdod ●

Shemesh

RE'UVEN

Ashkelon ●

Livnah ●

'Adulam ●

Gat ●

Hevron ■

R. Arnon

● 'Aro'er

'Eglon ●

Lakhish ●

'Ein-Gedi ●

Dead Sea (Salt Sea)

'Azah ●

D'vir ●

Zif ●

P'LESHET

Ziklag ●

Y'HUDAH

'Arad ●

Be'er-sheva ●

Hormah ●

MO'AV

●'Ad'adah

SHIM'ON

The Negev

Wadi of Egypt

The 'Aravah

● Kadesh-Barnea

EDOM

1628

MAP 3

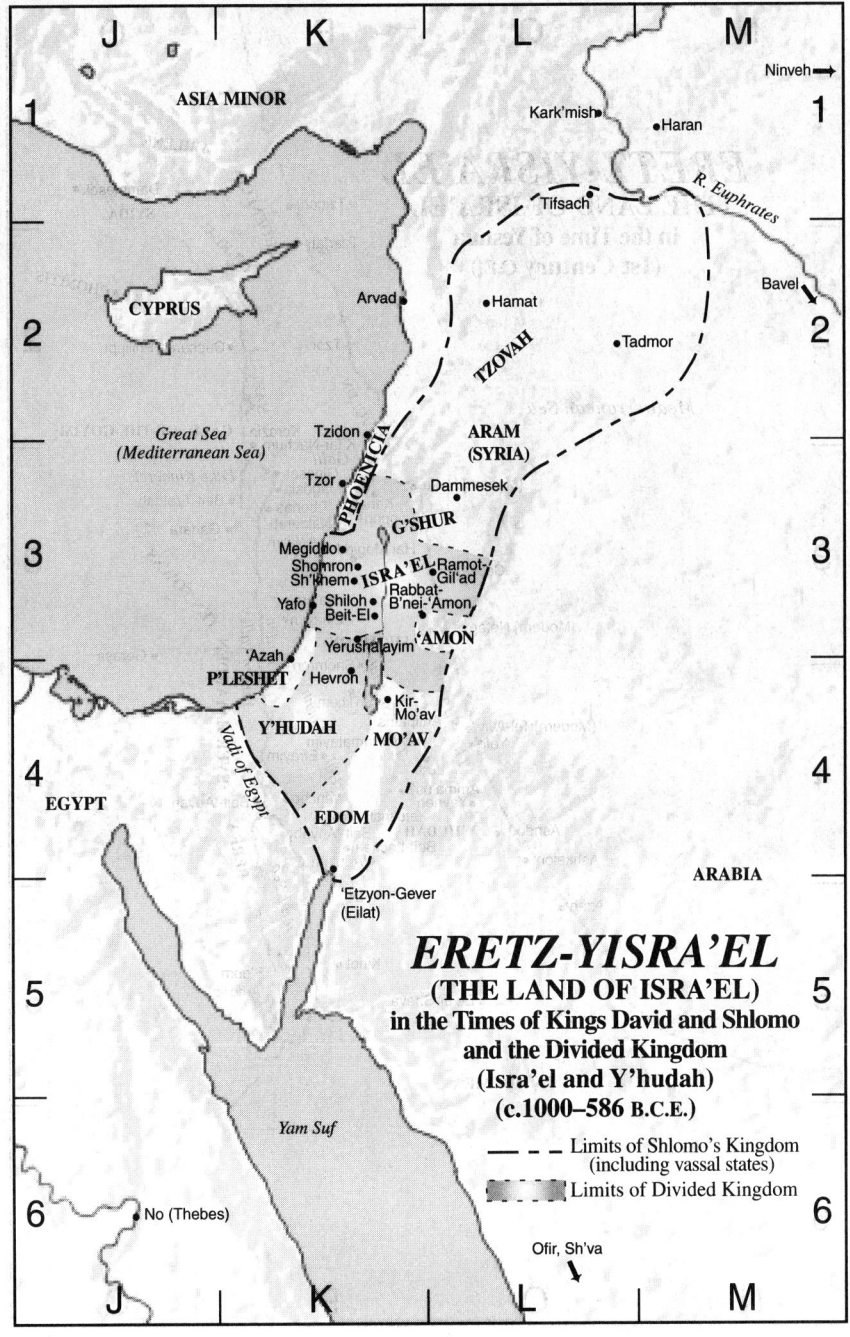

J   K   L   M

ASIA MINOR

Ninveh →

Kark'mish

Haran

1

R. Euphrates

Tifsach

CYPRUS

Arvad

Hamat

Bavel

2

TZOVAH

Tadmor

*Great Sea
(Mediterranean Sea)*

Tzidon

**ARAM
(SYRIA)**

Tzor

PHOENICIA

Dammesek

G'SHUR

Megiddo
Shomron
Sh'khem

ISRA'EL

Ramot-
Gil'ad

Yafo
Shiloh
Beit-El

Rabbat-
B'nei-'Amon

'Azah

Yerushalayim

'AMON

P'LESHET

Hevron

Kir-
Mo'av

Y'HUDAH

MO'AV

4

EGYPT

Vadi of Egypt

EDOM

ARABIA

'Etzyon-Gever
(Eilat)

ERETZ-YISRA'EL
(THE LAND OF ISRA'EL)
in the Times of Kings David and Shlomo
and the Divided Kingdom
(Isra'el and Y'hudah)
(c.1000–586 B.C.E.)

5

Yam Suf

— — — Limits of Shlomo's Kingdom
(including vassal states)

Limits of Divided Kingdom

6

No (Thebes)

Ofir, Sh'va

J   K   L   M

MAP 4

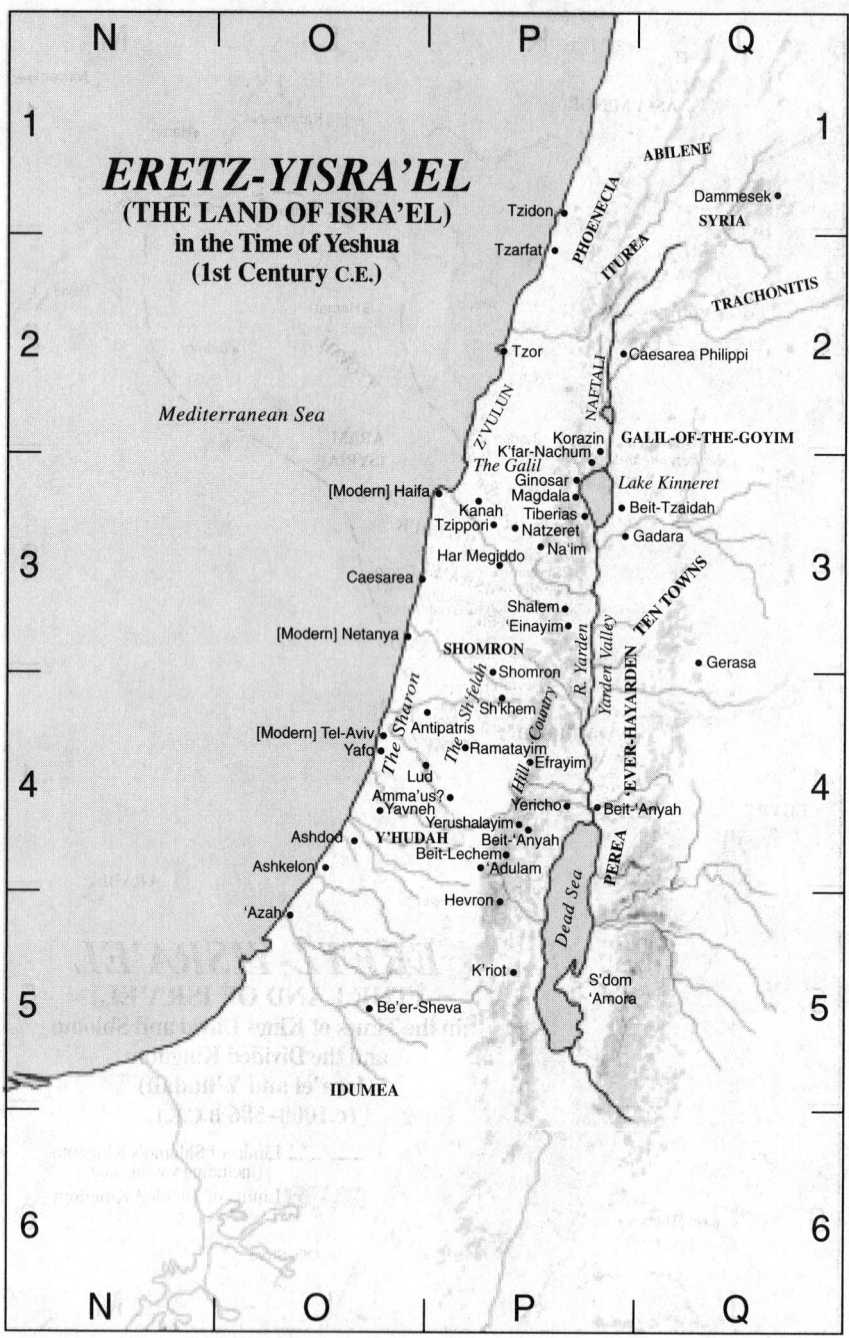

ERETZ-YISRA'EL
(THE LAND OF ISRA'EL)
in the Time of Yeshua
(1st Century C.E.)

Mediterranean Sea

ABILENE

Tzidon •

PHOENECIA

Dammesek •

SYRIA

Tzarfat •

ITUREA

TRACHONITIS

Tzor •

Z'VULUN

NAFTALI

• Caesarea Philippi

Korazin •

GALIL-OF-THE-GOYIM

K'far-Nachum •

The Galil

Lake Kinneret

[Modern] Haifa •

Ginosar •

Magdala •

• Beit-Tzaidah

Kanah •

Tiberias •

Tzippori •

Natzeret •

• Gadara

• Na'im

Har Megiddo •

Caesarea •

Shalem •

'Einayim •

[Modern] Netanya •

R. Yarden

Yarden Valley

TEN TOWNS

SHOMRON

• Gerasa

The Sharon

Sh'felah •

• Shomron

'EVER-HAYARDEN

• Sh'khem

[Modern] Tel-Aviv •

Antipatris •

The Hill Country

Yafo •

• Ramatayim

Lud •

• Efrayim

Amma'us? •

Yericho •

• Yavneh

Yerushalayim •

• Beit-'Anyah

PEREA

Ashdod •

Y'HUDAH

Beit-'Anyah

Beit-Lechem •

Ashkelon •

• 'Adulam

Dead Sea

Hevron •

'Azah •

K'riot •

S'dom
'Amora

• Be'er-Sheva

IDUMEA

MAP 5

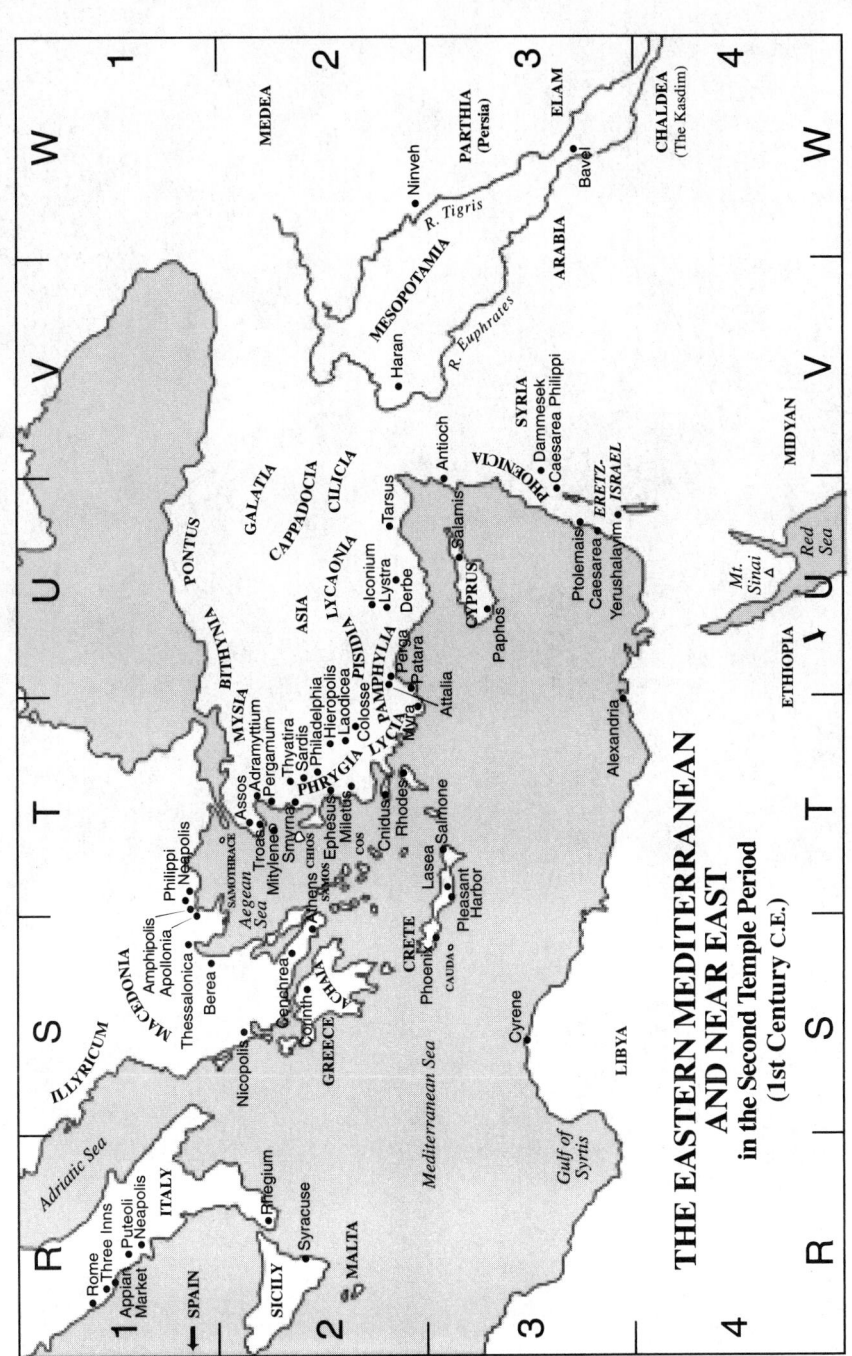

THE EASTERN MEDITERRANEAN
AND NEAR EAST
in the Second Temple Period
(1st Century C.E.)

ABOUT THE TRANSLATOR

DAVID H. STERN was born in Los Angeles in 1935, the great-grandson of two of the city's first twenty Jews. He earned a Ph.D. in economics at Princeton University and was a professor at UCLA, mountain-climber, co-author of a book on surfing and owner of health-food stores.

In 1972 he came to believe in Yeshua as the Messiah, after which he received a Master of Divinity degree at Fuller Theological Seminary and did graduate work at the University of Judaism.

He was married in 1976 to Martha Frankel, also a Messianic Jew, and together they served one year on the staff of Jews for Jesus. Dr. Stern taught Fuller Theological Seminary's first course in "Judaism and Christianity," organized Messianic Jewish conferences and leaders' meetings, and was an officer of the Messianic Jewish Alliance of America.

In 1979 the Stern family made *aliyah* (immigrated to Israel). They now live in Jerusalem with their two children and are active in Israel's Messianic Jewish community.

Dr. Stern is the author of *Messianic Jewish Manifesto*, which outlines the destiny, identity, history, theology and program of today's Messianic Jewish movement. He also wrote *Restoring the Jewishness of the Gospel: A Message for Christians*. It consists of excerpts from the former book selected for Christians to whom the Jewishness of the Gospel is an unfamiliar idea.

His *Jewish New Testament*, which has been incorporated into the *Complete Jewish Bible*, is the basis for its companion volume, the *Jewish New Testament Commentary*. This book discusses Jewish issues raised in the New Testament — questions Jews have about Yeshua, the New Testament and Christianity; questions Christians have about Judaism and the Jewish roots of their faith; and questions Messianic Jews have about their own identity and role.

The *Jewish New Testament* and the *Jewish New Testament Commentary* are available together as a boxed set and on CD-ROM for Windows 98+. The *Jewish New Testament* has also been produced on sixteen audio cassettes. Several of his books are available in other languages.